The Wadsworth Anthology of
Drama

The Wadsworth Anthology of
Drama

BRIEF SIXTH EDITION

W. B. WORTHEN

Barnard College, Columbia University

WADSWORTH
CENGAGE Learning™

Australia • Brazil • Japan • Korea • Mexico • Singapore • Spain • United Kingdom • United States

WADSWORTH
CENGAGE Learning

**The Wadsworth Anthology of Drama,
Brief Sixth Edition**
W.B. Worthen

Senior Publisher: Lyn Uhl

Publisher: Michael Rosenberg

Development Editor: Mary Beth Walden

Assistant Editor: Jillian D'Urso

Editorial Assistant: Erin Pass

Media Editor: Amy Gibbons

Marketing Manager: Christina Shea

Marketing Coordinator: Ryan Ahern

Marketing Communications Manager:
Laura Localio

Content Project Manager: Georgia Young

Senior Art Director: Cate Rickard Barr

Print Buyer: Marcia Locke

Permissions Editor: Timothy Sisler

Text Researcher: Ashley Liening

Production Service: Lindsay Burt,
MPS Limited, A Macmillan Company

Text Designer: Glenna Collett

Photo Manager: Robyn Young

Photo Researcher: Bill Studio Group

Cover Designer: Anne S. Katzeff, ASK Design

Cover Image Researcher: Stephen Forsling

Cover Image: *Death and the King's
Horseman*, the National Theatre,
London © Robbie Jack

Compositor: MPS Limited,
A Macmillan Company

For product information and technology assistance, contact us at
Cengage Learning Customer & Sales Support, 1-800-354-9706

For permission to use material from this text or product,
submit all requests online at **www.cengage.com/permissions.**
Further permissions questions can be emailed to
permissionrequest@cengage.com.

Library of Congress Control Number: 2009941920

ISBN-13: 978-1-4282-8815-7

ISBN-10: 1-4282-8815-5

Wadsworth Cengage Learning
20 Channel Center Street
Boston, MA 02210
USA

Cengage Learning is a leading provider of customized learning solutions with office locations around the globe, including Singapore, the United Kingdom, Australia, Mexico, Brazil and Japan. Locate your local office at **international.cengage.com/region**

Cengage Learning products are represented in Canada by Nelson Education, Ltd.

For your course and learning solutions, visit **www.cengage.com.**

Purchase any of our products at your local college store or at our preferred online store **www.ichapters.com.**

Printed in Canada
1 2 3 4 5 6 7 13 12 11 10 09

Contents

V Modern Europe 393

VI   The United States

647

VII   World Stages

873

Preface

Studying drama is more than reading plays. It requires us to study the theaters where the plays were produced, the cultures that framed those theaters, and the critical and performance history that has framed the meanings of drama over time. *The Wadsworth Anthology of Drama, Brief Edition* presents drama in these two important contexts: in the play's original theater and the society that sustained it, and in **our** culture, where the play continues to live both as literature and as theatrical performance.

The Wadsworth Anthology of Drama, Brief Edition offers a comprehensive collection of classic and contemporary plays from Europe, the Americas, Africa, and Asia. Designed to be used in a variety of drama and theater courses, in general surveys of drama and theater, in courses on tragedy and/or comedy, or in classes on modern theater, *The Wadsworth Anthology of Drama, Brief Edition* offers an unusually comprehensive collection of classic theater and an unrivaled selection of contemporary drama drawn from around the world.

The Wadsworth Anthology of Drama, Brief Edition builds on the strengths and success of previous editions of the full-length *Wadsworth Anthology of Drama*, now in its sixth edition. It is divided into seven units, each focused on a significant period in the history of drama and theater: Classical Athens and Rome in the fifth century BCE (three plays); feudal Japan (two plays); England in the late Middle Ages and Renaissance (three plays); England, France, Spain, and colonial Mexico in the seventeenth and eighteenth centuries (four plays); Europe from 1850 through the twentieth century (eight plays); the United States (nine plays); and contemporary stages around the world (six plays). Each unit begins with an extensive introduction, placing drama in the context of a specific historical era and using illustrations of theater design to develop a precise sense of stage practice. The Unit introductions also include a section, "Reading the Material Theater," which presents original documents from the history of the theater for students' consideration. Each play is accompanied by a brief biography of the playwright and a short introduction to the play. Each unit concludes with a selection of critical essays drawn from the period. *The Wadsworth Anthology of Drama, Brief Edition* emphasizes the diversity of drama and theater throughout history, both in its selection of plays and essays and in the issues and ideas raised for discussion as well.

Although *The Wadsworth Anthology of Drama, Brief Sixth Edition* is not as comprehensive as the full-scale *Wadsworth Anthology of Drama*, it does incorporate many of the innovative features of that edition.

- inclusion of Roman theater in the Classical European theater unit, and the text of Plautus' **The Brothers Menaechmus**
  – inclusion of Horace's **On the Art of Poetry**
- a greater emphasis on the history of theatrical production and contemporary production practices
- a large selection of plays by women (eight)
- a large selection of comedies (six)
- a contemporary restaging of the **Medea** narrative by Ireland's Marina Carr, **By the Bog of Cats . . .**
- a significant expansion of the unit on American drama, which now includes Arthur Miller's **Death of a Salesman**

- inclusion of Luis Valdez's brilliant acto, **Los vendidos** to accompany plays from Latin America (Gambaro's **Information for Foreigners**), a Spanish Golden Age classic (Calderón's **Life is a Dream**) and a brilliant play from colonial Mexico, Sor Juana's **loa** to **The Divine Narcissus**
- a significant focus on "race" in American theater, including plays by Luis Valdez, Amiri Baraka/LeRoi Jones (**Dutchman**), David Henry Hwang (**M. Butterfly**), and Anna Deavere Smith's **Fires in the Mirror**
- Chinese playwright and Nobel Prize winner Gao Xingjian's **The Other Shore**
- "Aside" sections in each unit-opening essay devoted to topics of special importance: Roman acting, Sanskrit drama and theater, the masque, the new Shakespeare's Globe Theatre in London, **commedia dell' arte**, melodrama, the Federal Theater Project, performance art, and intercultural performance
  – an extensive glossary
- two student essays in the "Writing about Drama and Theater" section, focusing on different approaches to Caryl Churchill's **Cloud Nine**, available online
  – a bibliography, also available online

The Wadsworth Anthology of Drama, Brief Sixth Edition is designed for both beginning and advanced students. An introduction to writing about drama and theater (available online) furnishes beginning students with an outline of the formal and rhetorical practices used in writing about plays; this essay complements the documentary essays on "Reading the Material Theater" in each unit. The book also includes a useful glossary of dramatic, theatrical, and literary terms as well as an extensive bibliography of drama and theater history and theory and of works about plays and playwrights (available online). *The Wadsworth Anthology of Drama, Brief Edition* provides a wide-ranging survey of drama and theater, one that presents both traditional issues and the materials to interrogate those traditions.

Acknowledgments

The Wadsworth Anthology of Drama provides a wide-ranging survey of drama and theater, one that presents both traditional issues and the materials to interrogate those traditions.

This Brief edition of *The Wadsworth Anthology of Drama* has faced many unique challenges, and I am grateful to the editorial staff of Cengage Wadsworth for bringing it to fruition. I'm especially grateful to Michael Rosenberg, and Mary Beth Walden for their involvement in the project, and to Lindsay Burt and Georgia Young, for their keen attention to bringing the book into its final shape.

I would also like to thank the many instructors and scholars who commented on earlier editions of *The Wadsworth Anthology of Drama*, suggesting directions for improvement:

Dr. Anne Beck, *Eastern New Mexico University*
Sandra L. Dahlberg, *University of Houston–Downtown*
Peter Greenfield, *University of Puget Sound*
Wendy C. Nielsen, *Montclair State University*

I would also like to thank the many instructors and scholars who commented on the fourth edition, suggesting ways we might improve this edition:

Gwendolyn Alker, *New York University*
Joe Allen, *Dutchess Community College*
Lisa Bernd, *Case Western Reserve University*
Cynthia Bowers, *Kennesaw State University*
Barry Brunetti, *DePaul University*
Paul Buczkowski, *Eastern Michigan University*
Lon Bumgarner, *University of North Carolina–Charlotte*
Steven Burch, *University of Alabama*

Sydney Chalfa, *Macon State College*
David Charles, *Rollins College*
Una Chaudhuri, *New York University*
Greg A. Chavez, *DePaul University*
Teresa Choate, *Kean University*
Gail Ciociola, *Villanova University*
Linda Nell Cooper, *Liberty University*
Michael Cooper, *Texarkana College*
Mark Cosdon, *Allegheny College*
Sergio Costola, *Southwestern University*
Thomas DeFrantz, *Massachusetts Institute of Technology*
Kathleen Dimmick, *Bennington College*
Bill Dynes, *University of Indianapolis*
Jay Edelnant, *University of Northern Iowa*
D. Layne Ehlers, *Bacone College*
Brenda Eppley, *Harrisburg Area Community College*
David S. Escoffery, *Southwest Missouri State University*
Anne Megan Evans, *Reed College*
Patsy Fowler, *Gonzaga University*
Jeffrey Frame, *Trevecca Nazarene University*
Dave Hartley, *Central Florida Community College*
Anne-Charlotte Harvey, *San Diego State University*
Ann Haugo, *Illinois State University*
Charles L. Hayes, *Radford University*
Graley Herren, *Xavier University*
Robin Huber, *Cerritos College*
Amy Hughes, *Baruch College*
Melissa Hurt, *Dodge City Community College*
David Jortner, *Allegheny College*
Hilary Justice, *Illinois State University*
Jonathan Kalb, *Hunter College, City University of New York*
Douglas Lanier, *University of New Hampshire*
Dawn Larsen, *Volunteer State College*
Ralph Leary, *Clarion University*
David E. Majewski, *Richard Bland College*
Joan McAfee, *Southern Connecticut State University*
Janet E. McLean, *Viterbo University*
Lee E. Neibert, *St. Gregory's University*
Wendy C. Nielsen, *Montclair State University*
Karen O'Brien, *University of California, Irvine*
Keith O'Neill, *Dutchess Community College*
Elinor L. Parker, *Westfield State College*
Jennifer Parker, *Florida State University*
Leslie Pasternack, *Northeastern University*
Katricia G. Pierson, *William Woods University*
Mark Pizzato, *University of North Carolina–Charlotte*
Marthe Reed, *University of Louisiana at Lafayette*
Joan E. Robbins, *Ohio Northern University*
R. Gary Rogers, *Lake-Sumter Community College*
Jeff Skillings, *Dean College*
James Symons, *University of Colorado, Boulder*
C. Patrick Tyndall, *University of Arkansas–Fayetteville*

Jef Vowell, *University of California, Irvine*
Chris Wixson, *Eastern Illinois University*
Boyd H. Wolz, *University of Louisiana at Monroe*
Leigh Woods, *University of Michigan*
Robert L. Yowell, *Northern Arizona University*

I would also like to thank the instructors and scholars who commented on the third edition, suggesting ways we might improve the fourth edition: Sherri Dienstfrey (Idaho State University), Oliver Gerland (University of Colorado at Boulder), Sue Hagedorn (Virginia Tech), Michael Harrawood (Florida Atlantic University), Gregory Kable (University of North Carolina at Chapel Hill), Margaret Knapp (Arizona State University), Kim Marra (University of Iowa), Jenna Moskowitz (New York University), Scott Phillips (Auburn University), Gary Rogers (Lake Sumter Community College), Susan Speers (University of Akron), Wanda Strukus (Boston College), Stephani Etheridge Woodson (Arizona State University).

I would also like to thank those who responded to our survey on the second edition, suggesting ways we might improve the third edition: David Adamson (University of North Carolina, Chapel Hill), Gilbert L. Bloom (Ball State University), Brian Boney (University of Texas), Cynthia Bowers (Loyola University), Karen Buckley (University of Wisconsin, Whitewater), Susan Carlson (Iowa State University), Allen Chesler (Northern Illinois University), Barbara Clayton (University of Wisconsin, Madison), Kathleen Colligan Cleary (Clark State Community College), Jill Dolan (City University of New York), David S. Escoffery (University of Pittsburgh), Anthony Graham-White (University of Illinois at Chicago), John E. Hallwas (Western Illinois University), L.W. Harrison (Santa Rosa Junior College), Anne-Charlotte Harvey (San Diego State University), Gregory Kable (University of North Carolina, Chapel Hill), Lawrence Kinsman (New Hampshire College), Ann Klautsch (Boise State University), Margaret Knapp (Arizona State University), Josephine Lee (University of Minnesota), Michael J. Longrie (University of Wisconsin, Whitewater), Kim Marra (University of Iowa), Carla McDonough (Eastern Illinois University), John F. O'Malley (DePaul University), Michael Peterson (Millikin University), Carol Rocamora (NYU Tisch School of the Arts), Hans Rudnick (Southern Illinois University), Terry Donovan Smith (University of Washington), Tramble Turner (Penn State University), Jon W. Tuttle (Francis Marion University), Timothy Wiles (Indiana University), Barry Yzereef (University of Calgary).

I am also indebted to Stanton Garner, Jr. (University of Tennessee), Josephine Lee (University of Minnesota), Sarah Bryant-Bertail (University of Washington), Jorge Huerta (University of California, San Diego), Kristin Pauka (Univerrsity of Hawai'i), and Barbara Sellars-Young (University of California, Davis) for their help and advice on the third edition.

My special thanks to Lurana Donnels O'Malley, of the University of Hawai'i, for her assistance with Units 2 and 7; to James Brandon, again of the University of Hawai'i, for graciously providing photographs and other materials related to the University's productions of *Matsukaze* and *Chuwshingura;* and to Octavio Rivera, of la Universidad de las Américas, for his help in providing photographs of his excellent production of Sor Juana's *loa* to *The Divine Narcissus.*

I would also like to thank reviewers for the second edition: George R. Adams (University of Wisconsin, Whitewater), Bonnie M. Anderson (San Diego State University), Karen Buckley (University of Wisconsin, Whitewater), Kathleen Colligan Cleary (Clark State Community College), Mary Ann Emery (University of Wisconsin, Whitewater), Lawrence E. Fink (Ohio State University), Melissa Gibson (University of Pittsburgh), Kiki Gounaridou (University of Pittsburgh), Anne-Charlotte Harvey (San Diego State University), Dennis Kennedy (Trinity College, Dublin), Chris Mullen (University of North Carolina, Chapel

Hill), Lurana O'Malley (University of Hawai'i), Gwen Orel (University of Pittsburgh), Angela Peckenpaugh (University of Wisconsin, Whitewater), Ruth Schauer (University of Wisconsin, Whitewater). In addition, I am grateful to the following reviewers of the manuscript of the second edition for their valuable revision suggestions: Bradley Boney (University of Texas, Austin), Anne Brannen (Duquesne University), Susan Carlson (Iowa State University), S. Alan Chesler (Northern Illinois University), Cyndia Susan Clegg (Pepperdine University), Jill Dolan (City University of New York), Anthony J. Fichera (University of North Carolina, Chapel Hill), L.W. Harrison (Santa Rosa Junior College), Margaret Knapp (Arizona State University), Josephine Lee (University of Minnesota), Michael Longrie (University of Wisconsin, Whitewater), Michael Peterson (University of Wisconsin, Madison), Eula Thompson (Jefferson State Community College), Jon Tuttle (Francis Marion University).

My thanks to the people who read and commented on the manuscript of the first edition, making it more accurate and useful for instructors: Stanton B. Garner, Jr. (University of Tennessee), Josephine Lee (University of Minnesota), Don Moore (Louisiana State University).

I remain grateful to Sharon Mazer, of the University of Canterbury (New Zealand) and Kathleen Gough, of the University of Glasgow, for their superb work on the Instructor's Manual to previous editions. And my sincere thanks to the late Stephen T. Jordan for originally proposing this project, to Oscar G. Brockett of the University of Texas at Austin for allowing me to think out loud about what a book like this one might accomplish, and long overdue thanks to Hana Worthen for her insight, guidance, and rigor on many matters here.

Finally, I would like to encourage anyone using this book to feel free to drop me a line with ideas and suggestions for later editions. To the many students and colleagues who have called, sent me a note to correct my oversights and omissions, or have graciously spoken to me about the book at professional meetings and conferences, my sincere thanks for your attention and kindness. The flaws and faults that remain are, of course, entirely my own doing.

—W. B. W.

About the Author

W. B. Worthen is Alice Brady Pels Professor in the Arts, and Chair of the Department of Theatre at Barnard College, Columbia University. He is the author of *Print and the Poetics of Modern Drama* (Cambridge University Press, 2005), *Shakespeare and the Force of Modern Performance* (Cambridge University Press, 2003) *Shakespeare and the Authority of Performance* (Cambridge University Press, 1997), *Modern Drama and the rhetoric of Theater* (University of California Press, 1992), *The Idea of the Actor: Drama and the Ethics of Performance* (Princeton University Press, 1984), *Modern Drama: Plays, Criticism, Theory* (Wadsworth, 1995), and of many articles on modern drama, Shakespeare,

by Patricia Kantzos

and theories of performance; his most recent book, *Drama: Between Poetry and Performance,* appeared in 2010 (Wiley-Blackwell, 2010).

He is the past editor of *Theatre Journal* and of *Modern Drama,* and is the editor of several widely used critical collections, including the Blackwell *A Companion to Shakespeare and Performance,* with Barbara Hodgdon (Blackwell, 2005), *Modern Drama: Defining the Field,* with Ric Knowles and Joanne Tompkins (University of Toronto Press, 2003), *Theorizing Practice: Redefining Theatre History,* with Peter Holland (Palgrave, 2003), *Theatre History and National Identities,* with Helka Mäkinen and S.E. Wilmer (University of Helsinki Press, 2001); his anthology *Modern Drama: Plays / Criticism / Theory* (Harcourt Brace, 1995) won the Association for Theatre in Higher Education Research Award in 1995. Professor Worthen received his B.A. in English from the University of Massachusetts at Amherst, his Ph. D. in English from Princeton University, and has held research fellowships for the Guggenheim Foundation, the National Endowment for the Humanities, and the "Interweaving Performance Cultures" International Research Institute of the Freie Universität, Berlin. He has taught widely in the United States and Europe, and has been appointed at the University of Texas-Austin, Northwestern University, the University of California-Davis, the University of California-Berkeley, and the University of Michigan. He is a founding faculty member of the International Centre for Advanced Theatre Studies, University of Helsinki.

Introduction: Drama, Theater, and Culture

Of the many kinds of literature, drama is perhaps the most immediately involved in the life of its community. Drama shares with such other literary modes as lyric poetry, the novel, the epic, and romance the ability to represent and challenge social, political, philosophical, and esthetic attitudes. But unlike most literature, drama has generally been composed for performance, confronting the audience in the public, sociable confines of a theater.

To understand **DRAMA**, we need to understand **THEATER**, because the theater forges the active interplay between drama and its community.[1] On a practical level, for instance, the community must determine where drama will take place, and it is in the theater that a space is carved out for dramatic performance. Not surprisingly, the place of the theater in a city's social and physical geography often symbolizes drama's place in the culture at large. In classical Athens, the theater adjoined a sacred precinct, and plays were part of an extensive religious and civic festival.

Greek drama accordingly engages questions of moral, political, and religious authority. In seventeenth-century Paris, the close affiliation between the theater and the court of Louis XIV is embodied in drama's concern with power, authority, and the regulation of rebellious passions. In the United States today, most live theater takes place either in the privileged setting of colleges and universities or in the "theater districts" of major cities, competing for an audience alongside movie theaters, nightclubs, and other entertainments. Drama also seems to be struggling to define itself as part of an established cultural tradition reaching back to Aeschylus and as part of the lively diversity of contemporary popular culture. Social attitudes are reflected in the theater in other ways, too; during performance, the theater constructs its own "society" of performers and spectators. Staging a play puts it immediately into a dynamic social exchange: the interaction between dramatic characters, between characters and the actors who play them, between the performers and the audience, between the drama onstage and the drama of life outside the theater.

Reading Drama and Seeing Theater

The Greek word for theater, *THEATRON,* means "seeing place," and plays performed in the theater engage their audiences largely through visual means. Less than a century ago, live plays could be seen only on the stage; today, most of us see drama in a variety of media: on film and television as well as in the theater. Yet for the past 500 years or so we have also had access to plays in another, nontheatrical venue: by reading them in books. To see a play performed and to read it in a book are two very different activities, but these distinct experiences of drama can be made to enrich one another in a number of ways.

In the theater, a dramatic text is fashioned into an event, something existing in space and time. The space of the stage, with whatever setting is devised, becomes the place of the drama. The characters are embodied by specific individuals. How a given actor interprets a role tends to shape the audience's sense of that dramatic character; for the duration of the play, it is difficult to imagine another kind of performance—a different Oedipus, Lear, or Nora Helmer than the one standing before us in the flesh. The drama onstage is also bound by the temporal exigencies of performance. The process of performance is irreversible; for the duration of the performance, each moment becomes significant and yet

---

[1]Terms in boldface small capital letters are defined in the Glossary; italicized terms are non-English terms.

unrecoverable—we can't flip back a few pages to an earlier scene, or rewind the videotape. When a company puts a play into stage production, it inevitably confronts these material facts of the theater: a specific cast of actors, a given theatrical space, a certain amount of money to spend, and the necessity of transforming the rich possibilities offered by the play into a clear and meaningful performance. To make the drama active and concrete, theatrical production puts a specific interpretation of the play on the stage. Whether or not to play Caliban in Shakespeare's *The Tempest* as a native of the West Indies; whether to play Torvald Helmer in Ibsen's *A Doll House* as a patriarchal autocrat or as someone bewildered by a changing world; whether to set *Phaedra* in a classical, neoclassical, or a modern setting; whether to use cross-gender or intercultural casting in *The Homecoming*—these are some of the kinds of questions that a production must face, and how the production decides such issues inevitably leads the audience toward a particular sense of the play. Everything that happens onstage becomes meaningful for an audience, something to interpret. Even apparently irrelevant facts—a short actor cast to play Hamlet in Shakespeare's play, or a beautiful actress playing Brecht's Mother Courage—become part of the audience's experience of the play, particularizing the play, lending it a definite flavor and meaning.

Reading a play presents us with a different experience of the drama. Reading plays is, first of all, a relatively recent phenomenon. In early theaters, such as those of classical Athens and Rome, medieval Europe, and even Renaissance Europe of the sixteenth century, drama was almost entirely a theatrical mode, rather than a mode of literature. Although the texts of plays were written down, by and large, audiences came into contact with drama primarily through theatrical performance. By the late sixteenth century, though, the status of drama began to change. The recovery and prestige of Greek and Latin literature led to pervasive familiarity with classical texts, including plays. Throughout Europe, schooling was conducted mainly in Latin, and the plays of Roman playwrights such as Plautus, Terence, and Seneca were frequently used to teach Latin grammar and rhetoric. These plays were widely imitated by playwrights writing drama in vernacular languages for emerging secular, commercial theaters. Printing made it possible to disseminate texts more widely, and plays slowly came to be regarded as worthy of publication and preservation in book form. By the late nineteenth century, widespread literacy created a large reading public and a great demand for books; continued improvements in printing technology provided the means to meet the demand. Playwrights often published their plays as books before they could be produced onstage, with some profound effects. The detailed narrative stage directions in plays by Bernard Shaw, Eugene O'Neill, or Henrik Ibsen, for instance, are useful to a stage director and set designer, but they principally fill in a kind of novelistic background for the reading audience who will experience the play only on the page.

Theater audiences are bound to the temporality and specificity of the stage, but readers have the freedom to compose the play in much more varied ways. A reader can pause over a line, teasing out possible meanings, in effect stopping the progress of the play. Readers are not bound by the linear progress of the play's action, in that they can flip back and forth in the play, looking for clues, confirmations, or connections. Nor are readers bound by the stringent physical economy of the stage, the need to embody the characters with individual actors, to specify the dramatic locale as a three-dimensional space. While actors and directors must decide on a specific interpretation of each moment and every character in the play, readers can keep several competing interpretations alive in the imagination at the same time.

Both ways of thinking about drama are demanding, and students of drama should try to develop a sensitivity to both approaches. Treating the play like a novel or poem, decomposing and recomposing it critically, leads to a much fuller sense of the play's potential meanings, its gaps and inconsistencies; it allows us to question the text without the need to come to definite conclusions. Treating the play as a design for the stage forces us to make commitments, to articulate and defend a particular version of the play, and to find ways of making those meanings active onstage, visible in performance. As readers, one way to develop a sense of the reciprocity between stage and page is to think of the play as constructed mainly of actions, not of words.

Think of seeing a play in an unknown language: the *action* of the play would still emerge in its larger outlines, carried by the deeds of the characters. Not knowing the words would not prevent the audience from understanding what a character is doing onstage—threatening, lying, persuading, boasting. When reading a play, it is easy to be seduced by the text, to think of the play's language as mainly narrative, describing the attitudes of the character. For performers onstage, however, speech—language in action—is always a way of doing something. One way for readers to attune themselves to this active quality of dramatic writing is to ask questions of the text from the point of view of performers or characters. What do I—Lysistrata, Everyman, Miranda, Winston—want in this speech? How can I use this speech to help me get it? What am I trying to do by speaking in this way? Although questions like these are still removed from the actual practice of performance, they can help readers unfamiliar with drama begin to read plays in theatrical terms. Another way to enrich the reading experience of drama is to imagine staging the play: how could the design of the set, the movements of the actors, the pacing of the scenes affect the play's meaning, make the play mean something in particular?

Questions of this kind can help to make the play seem more concrete, but they have one important limitation. When asking questions like these, it is tempting to imagine the play being performed in today's theaters, according to our conventions of acting and stagecraft, and within the social and cultural context that frames the theater now. To imagine the play on our stage is, of course, to produce it in our contemporary idiom, informed by our notions both of theater and of the world our theater represents. However, while envisioning performance, we should also imagine the play in the circumstances of its original theater, a theater located in a different culture and possibly sharing few practices of stagecraft with the modern theater. How would Hamlet's advice to the players have appeared on the Globe theater's empty platform stage in 1601? Are there ways in which the text capitalizes on this likeness between Shakespeare's company of actors and those Hamlet addresses fictively in the play? In a theater where a complete, "realistic" illusion was not possible (and perhaps not even desirable), how does Shakespeare's play turn the conditions of theatrical performance to dramatic advantage? Both reading drama and staging drama involve a complex double-consciousness, inviting us to see the plays with contemporary questions in mind, while at the same time imagining them on their original stages. In this doubleness lies an important dramatic principle: plays can speak to us in our theater but perhaps always retain something of their original accents.

Drama and Theater in History

Throughout its development, dramatic art has changed as the theater's place in the surrounding society has changed. The categories that we apply to drama and theater today—art versus entertainment, popular versus classic, literary versus theatrical—are of relatively recent vintage. They imply ways of thinking about drama and theater that are foreign to the function of theater in many other cultures. Much as drama and theater today emerge in relation to other media of dramatic performance like film and television, so in earlier eras the theater defined itself in relation to other artistic, social, and religious institutions. Placed in a different sphere of culture, drama and theater gained a different kind of significance than they have in the United States today.

Drama and theater often arise in relation to religious observance. In ancient Egypt, for instance, religious rituals involved the imitation of events in a god's or goddess's life. In Greece, drama may have had similar origins; by the sixth century BCE, the performance of plays had become part of a massive religious festival celebrating the god Dionysus. The plays performed in this theater—including those of Aeschylus, Sophocles, Euripides, and Aristophanes gathered here—were highly wrought and intellectually, morally, and esthetically complex and demanding works. Aristotle classes drama among other forms of poetry, but in classical Athens these plays occupied a very different position in the spectrum of culture than do drama or "art" today, precisely because of their central role in the City Dionysia. The Roman theater set drama in the context of a much greater variety of performance—chariot racing, juggling, gladiatorial shows—and while plays were performed on religious holidays, drama was more clearly related to secular entertainments than it had been in Athens.

Institutional theater waned in Europe with the decline of the Roman Empire and the systematic efforts of the Catholic church to prevent theatrical performance. Yet when theater was revived in the late Middle Ages, it emerged with the support of the church itself. By the year 1000, brief dramatizations illustrated the liturgy of the Catholic Mass; by the fourteenth century, a full range of dramatic forms—plays dramatizing the lives of saints, morality plays, narrative plays on Christian history—was used to illustrate Christian doctrine and to celebrate important days in the Christian year. Like plays in classical Athens, these plays were produced through community effort rather than by specialized "theaters" in the modern sense. Although we now regard medieval drama as extraordinarily rich and complex "literature," in its own era it was part of a different strand of culture, sharing space with other forms of pageantry and religious celebration, rather than being read with the poetry of Chaucer or Dante.

Similarly, in feudal Japan, the Buddhists developed a form of theater to illustrate the central concepts of their faith. Throughout the twelfth and thirteenth centuries, an increasing number of professional players came to imitate these dramatic performances on secular occasions, and for secular audiences. By the fourteenth century, it became conventional for the great samurai lords, or *SHOGUNS,* to patronize a theatrical company, giving rise to the classical era of the Noh theater. The social history of theater in Japan was complicated by other factors as well. The aristocratic NOH theater was rivaled by the popular, often quite contemporary, KABUKI theater. Government restrictions on the professions (which tended to make acting a family business, passed on through generations), and Japan's militant isolationism (coming to an end only in the mid-nineteenth century), have contributed to making Japan's classical theater survive in many ways unchanged. Moreover, in many parts of Asia, including China and India, theater was understood as a mixed medium, more centrally emphasizing song and dance as a way of developing the narrative, and many forms of performance—the wide variety of Indian folk theater forms, and of Chinese traditional forms, including BEIJING OPERA—developed extremely disciplined and highly stylized performance conventions. These traditional theaters, sometimes tied to aristocratic privilege, sometimes to religious ritual, sometimes to civic celebration, were sharply challenged by the influence of Western dramatic and theatrical practices—spoken drama, dramatic realism, and the notion of a secular, profit-making entertainment-theater—beginning in the eighteenth and nineteenth centuries. The rise of *SHINGEKI* or modern theater in the early twentieth century in Japan, of "spoken drama" at the same time in China, and of Western theatrical methods in India are closely tied to the characteristic forms of globalization of that period, economic imperialism and political colonialism; anticolonial, nationalist, and independence movements throughout Asia have tended both to revive classical forms of traditional theater, and to force a rapprochement with the imported forms of Western theater.

Secular performance did, of course, also take place in classical and medieval Europe, including improvised farces on contemporary life, fairground shows, puppetry, mimes, and other quasidramatic events. Many plays were performed only on religious occasions, though, and their performers were usually itinerant, lacking the social and institutional support that would provide them with lasting and continuous existence. Only in the Renaissance of the fifteenth and sixteenth centuries did the Western theater begin to assume the function it has today: a fully secular, profit-making, commercial enterprise. Although Renaissance theaters continually vied with religious and state officials for the freedom to practice their trade, by the sixteenth century, the European theater was part of a secular entertainment market, competing with bear-baiting, animal shows, athletic contests, public executions, royal and civic pageants, public preaching, and many other attractions to draw a paying public. The theater emerged in this period as a distinct institution, supported by its own income; the theater became a trade, a profession, a business, rather than a necessary function of the state or of religious worship. Indeed, if drama in classical Athens was conceived more as religious ritual than as "art" in a modern sense, drama in Renaissance London was classed mainly as popular "entertainment." The theater only gradually became recognized as an arena for "literary" accomplishment, for literary status in this period was reserved mainly for skill demonstrated in forms like the sonnet, the prose romance, or the epic—forms that could win the authors a measure of aristocratic prestige and patronage. As part of the motley, vulgar world of the public theater, plays were not considered serious, permanent literature.

However, the desire to transform drama from ephemeral theatrical "entertainment" into permanent literary "art" begins to be registered in the Renaissance. The poet and playwright Ben Jonson included plays in the 1616 edition of his *Works,* insisting on the literary importance of the volume by publishing it in the large, **FOLIO** format generally reserved for classical authors. In 1623, seven years after his death, William Shakespeare's friends and colleagues published a similar, folio-sized collection of his plays, a book that was reprinted several times throughout the seventeenth century. By the 1660s and 1670s, writers at the court of Louis XIV in Paris could achieve both literary and social distinction as dramatists; Jean Racine's reputation as a playwright, in part at least, helped to win his appointment as Louis's royal historiographer. Yet, despite many notable exceptions, the theatrical origins of drama prevented contemporary plays from being regarded as "literature"—although plays from earlier eras were increasingly republished and gradually seen to have "literary" merit. Indeed, by the nineteenth century, contemporary plays often achieved "literary" recognition by avoiding the theater altogether. English poets like Lord Byron and Percy Bysshe Shelley, for instance, wrote plays that were in many ways unstageable, and so preserved them from degrading contact with the tawdry stage. The English critic Charles Lamb remarked in a famous essay that he preferred reading Shakespeare's plays to seeing them in the theater; for Lamb, the practical mechanics of acting and the stage intruded on the experience of the drama's poetic dimension. In fact, the great playwrights of the late nineteenth century— Henrik Ibsen, Anton Chekhov, August Strindberg, and even the young Bernard Shaw—carved a space for themselves as dramatists by writing plays *in opposition* to the values of their contemporary audiences and to the practice of their contemporary theater—a strategy that would have seemed unimaginable to Aeschylus, Shakespeare, or even Molière. To bring their plays successfully to the stage, new theaters and new theater practices had to be devised, and a new audience had to be found, or made.

This split between the "literary drama" and the "popular theater" has become the condition of twentieth-century drama and theater: plays of the artistic **AVANT-GARDE** are more readily absorbed into the **CANON** of literature, while more conventional entertainments—television screenplays, for instance—remain outside it. The major modern playwrights from Ibsen to Luigi Pirandello to Samuel Beckett first wrote for small theaters and were produced by experimental companies playing to coterie audiences on the fringes of the theatrical "mainstream." This sense of modernist "art" as opposed to the values of bourgeois culture was not confined to drama and theater. Modernist fiction and poetry, cubist and abstract painting and sculpture, modern dance, and modern music all developed a new formal complexity, thematic abstraction, and critical self-consciousness in opposition to the sentimental superficiality they found in conventional art forms. This modernist tendency has itself produced a kind of reaction, a desire to bring the devices of popular culture and mass culture into drama, as a way of altering the place of the theater in society and changing the relationship between the spectators and the stage. Bertolt Brecht's **ALIENATION EFFECT,** Samuel Beckett's importation of circus and film clowns to absurdist theater, Heiner Müller's PASTICHE of *Hamlet* in his POSTMODERN *Hamletmachine,* or Wole Soyinka's interweaving of African ritual and fourth-wall realism in *Death and the King's Horseman* are all examples of this reaction. For the theater has been challenged by film and television to define its space in contemporary culture, and, given the pervasive availability of other media, theater has increasingly seemed to occupy a place akin to that of opera, among the privileged, elite forms of "high culture." As a result, innovation in today's theater often takes place on the margins or fringes of mainstream theater and mainstream culture: in smaller companies experimenting with new performance forms, in subversive theaters confronting political oppression in many parts of the world, and in theaters working to form a new audience and a new sense of theater by conceiving new forms of drama. And yet, as David Hare's *Stuff Happens* suggests, it's still possible, even for a major institutional theater like London's Royal National Theatre, to use the space of the stage to interrogate the sphere of contemporary politics.

Dramatic Genres

Perhaps because its meaning must emerge rapidly and clearly in performance, drama tends to be compressed and condensed; its characters tend toward types, and its action tends toward certain general patterns as well. It is conventional to speak of these kinds of drama as GENRES, each with its own identifying formal structure and typical themes. In the Western theater, following Aristotle's *The Poetics,* TRAGEDY is usually considered to concern the fate of an individual hero, singled out from the community through circumstances and through his or her own actions. In the course of the drama, the hero's course of action entwines with events and circumstances beyond his or her control. As a result, the hero's final downfall—usually, but not always, involving death—seems at once both chosen and inevitable. COMEDY on the other hand, focuses on the fortunes of the community itself. While the hero of tragedy is usually unique, the heroes of comedy often come in pairs—the lovers who triumph over their parents in romantic comedies, the dupe and the trickster at the center of more ironic or satirical comic modes. While tragedy points toward the hero's downfall or death, comedy generally points toward some kind of broader reform or remaking of society, usually signaled by a wedding or other celebration at the end of the play.

To speak of genre in this way, though, is to suggest that these ideal critical abstractions actually exist in some form, exemplified more or less adequately by particular plays. Yet, as the very different genres of Japanese or Indian theater suggest, terms like *tragedy* and *comedy,* or MELODRAMA, TRAGICOMEDY, FARCE, and others, arise from our efforts to find continuities between extraordinarily different kinds of drama: between plays written in different theaters, for different purposes, to please different audiences, under different historical pressures. When we impose these terms in a prescriptive way, we usually find that the drama eludes them or even calls them into question. Aristotle's brilliant sense of Greek tragedy in *The Poetics,* for instance, hardly "applies" with equal force to Greek plays as different as *Agamemnon, Oedipus the King,* and *Medea,* or Kan'ami's elegant Noh drama, *Matsukaze,* let alone later plays like *Hamlet* or *Endgame.* In his essay, "Tragedy and the Common Man," Arthur Miller tries to preserve "tragedy" for modern drama by redefining Aristotle's description of the hero of tragedy. Instead of Aristotle's hero, a man (not a woman) of an elevated social station, Miller argues that the modern hero should be an average, "common" man (not a woman), precisely because the "best families" do not seem normative to us or representative of our basic values, a goal he pursued in his classic American tragedy, *Death of a Salesman.* Our exemplary characters are taken from the middle classes. Yet to redefine the hero in this way calls Aristotle's other qualifications—the idea of the hero's character and actions, the meaning of the tragic "fall"—into question as well, forcing us to redefine Aristotelian tragedy in ways that make it something entirely new, something evocative in modern terms.

In approaching the question of genre, then, it is often useful to avoid asking how a play exemplifies the universal and unchanging features of tragedy or comedy. Instead, one could ask how a play or a theater *invents* tragedy or comedy for its contemporary audience. What terms does the drama present, what formal features does it use, to represent human experience? How do historically "local" genres—Renaissance REVENGE TRAGEDY, French NEOCLASSICAL DRAMA, modern THEATER OF THE ABSURD, KABUKI, or even the KATHAKALI of southern India—challenge, preserve, or redefine broader notions of genre?

In about 335 BCE, Aristotle's *The Poetics* set down the formal elements of drama, and the influence of Aristotle's description has been massive: today we still speak of dramatic form in terms of its PLOT, CHARACTERS, LANGUAGE, THEME, and its performative elements, what Aristotle called MUSIC and SPECTACLE. Any student of drama can profit by thinking about how these formal elements function in a given play. How are the incidents of the play—its plot—arranged? What effects are achieved by *this* ordering, rather than by another? How does the plot relate to the play's narrative story, which includes events dating from before the play begins? How does the plot, the structure of the events—for instance, Nora Helmer's first act in *A Doll House* is to enter the house, and her last act is to leave it—develop the play's themes? We might then ask how the play defines its characters. What elements of human experience—family history, psychological motivation, public action—seem to be most prominent in a play's conception of "character"? How do the formal conventions of characterization, such as blank verse in Shakespeare's plays and the densely poetic language of Noh theater, affect our reading of the characters and our understanding of them as representations of human beings?

Although Aristotle presents these elements of drama as distinct, in practice they are mutually defining, making it very difficult to speak of them separately. A play's language, for example, can be analyzed purely for its verbal and rhetorical features, but it is more interesting to ask how the language affects our understanding of the characters or invests the play with certain thematic possibilities. Similarly, while we may regard a play's themes as inside the play, they actually arise only in our interpretation of the play. The themes are something we create by asking certain questions about the play's plotting, its characterization, its use of language. The artificiality of separating these features becomes especially clear when we turn to a play's theatrical dimension. Although Aristotle suggests that a play's literary and theatrical dimensions are independent, to get a real sense of drama we must see the play both as literature and as theater. We must assess how an audience's sense of the play's plot, characters, and themes are shaped by the kinds of spectacle demanded by the play and provided by the theater. The "meaning" of Greek drama cannot be separated from its conditions of performance: the religious festival, the huge amphitheater, the masked actors, the singing, dancing chorus. The barren "sterile promontory" of *Hamlet,* Phaedra's claustral chamber, cross-dressed performance in Churchill's *Cloud Nine,* the elements of Yoruba ritual in *Death and the King's Horseman*: these elements of the theatrical spectacle are not outside the meaning of the drama; they are its means, the vehicle for achieving that meaning on the stage.

Dramatic Form

In a book like this one—indeed, in any book—it is difficult to convey a real sense of the power of theater. It is possible, though, to imagine this experience and to discuss it through the materials collected here: dramatic texts, descriptions of stage practice, illustrations of theaters, photographs, essays. However, an obstacle to understanding arises from a split between the disciplines we use to understand drama and theater. At many colleges and universities, this split is represented in the geography of the campus itself, where the English or Literature departments, which teach dramatic literature, are housed in one building, and the Theater or Drama department, which teaches acting, directing, design, and which actually stages the plays, is housed in another. "Literary" approaches to drama focus our attention initially, sometimes exclusively, on the text of a play and train the complex strategies of poetics and poetic interpretation on it. Such interpretation regards the dramatic text as

The Stage in Critical Practice

incomplete and specifies the text's range of possible meanings by placing it in various textual and cultural contexts; in a sense, the negotiation between the text and these contexts determines what we can say the play *means*. "Theatrical" approaches to drama tend to see a play in terms of stage practice, both in the terms of the play's original production and in the light of performance practice today. This approach interrogates the play's staging: how it can be set, what obstacles it presents to acting and casting, what the dramatic effects of costume and design will be. "Theatrical" interpretation regards the dramatic text as an incomplete design for performance and trains the complex machinery of stage representation—directing, acting, design, costuming—on the task of fleshing the script out as performed action. The meaning of the play in this regard emerges from what we can make the play *do*.

The literary and theatrical approaches to drama and theater share the assumption that plays are not fully meaningful in themselves; they share the sense that the meaning of drama emerges from the kinds of questions we ask of it, the contexts—literary, historical, theoretical, theatrical—in which we can make it perform, and make it mean something in particular. Although each approach can seem needlessly mysterious, involving its own specialized language and critical practice, its own set of "right" questions and "right" answers, this book has been assembled with the belief that the literary and the theatrical approaches are necessary complements to each other.

Interpreting the Material Past

In the units that follow, each introductory essay attempts to provide an overview of the dense implication of drama and theater in its culture, and, often, how dramatic literature and theatrical practices have been revived, engaged, or transformed by succeeding generations. Each essay, in other words, introduces the social, political, and cultural milieu of the theater; the theater's physical and symbolic position in the landscape of its culture; the theater's representation of gendered, sexual, and racial identities; the physical design of theaters, and the practices of acting and staging; and the dynamic impact of dramatic—literary—innovation on the work of performance.

Although these issues are treated differently, given different prominence in each essay, this constellation of questions stems from a single conviction: that thinking about drama requires that we think about how plays perform as literature, in culture and history, and on the stage.

One of the greatest challenges, for professional scholars and students alike, to understanding the history of drama and theater has to do with the nature of evidence. As any detective drama illustrates—think of Sherlock Holmes—"facts" only become "evidence" when they are subjected to a coherent interpretation, an explanatory narrative. So, too, understanding the "facts" of the theatrical past means transforming them into "evidence," evidence that materializes a certain understanding, interpretation, or explanation of the meaning of drama and theater in history. The difficulties of historiography—the writing of history—with regard to early drama and theater are self-evident. Most of the plays of classical Athens, for example, have been lost; those that survive represent only a small percentage of the "evidence" for the practice of Greek playwrights. Much of the evidence for theatrical practice—how actors worked, the movements of the chorus, the function of music, the behavior of audiences, even the composition of audiences—has had to be adduced from written documents and visual images often far-removed from the theater itself, for these practices (much like the teaching of acting today) were part of an ongoing tradition that was handed directly from performer to performer, or citizen to citizen.

Many theatrical traditions around the world originated in nonliterate oral cultures, which successfully preserved the developing forms and practices of performance over centuries, as long as the communities who sustained them continued to flourish. Often regarded as "primitive," "uncivilized," or simply subversive by invading colonial powers, even traditional practices that survived well into the historical period have sometimes been eradicated (Wole Soyinka's *Death and the King's Horseman* provides a striking image of the ways the English governors of Nigeria regarded several centuries-old traditional performance practices). Nonetheless, some of these traditions survive: though they date from about the sixteenth century, *kathakali* performances in southern India seem to preserve some of the dramatic and performance traditions of ancient Sanskrit performance, as it was described in Bharatamuni's *Natyasastra*. Of course, the rise of print not only forged a fissure between literary drama and theatrical performance: it also provided the means to document a wide variety of theatrical practice and—since the purpose of print is to multiply texts in great numbers—to provide a greater chance that such documents would survive. For this reason, beginning in the sixteenth century, the print-record provides a massive archive of information about the practices of performance: in the publication of plays; in the efflorescence of diaries and memoirs containing information about the stage; in the rise of theatrical journalism in the eighteenth century; in playbills, posters, programs; and in a wide variety of theatrical illustrations—pictures of actors, plays, theaters. In combination with the increasing likelihood that theatrical buildings, sets, costumes, and the records of theater companies have survived, the history of the modern theater is, comparatively speaking, an embarrassment of riches. Needless to say, it has recently become possible even to record performance, on still photographs and film, videotape, and digital media. While it is important to recognize that such recordings are themselves only partial "evidence" for the work of a given production—What is the camera leaving out of the picture? How is close-up distorting what an audience might see? How did the production change in order to be filmed? How did the live production change after it was filmed?—they do provide an invaluable resource for future generations of students.

In each unit, this edition of *The Wadsworth Anthology of Drama* provides a range of material to help contextualize drama in the theater: Reading the Material Theater, Critical Contexts, and Critical Perspectives. Reading the Material Theater, offers a piece of the material past of the stage, a document or an image that provides some insight into theatrical practice. Some of these records are visual, and indeed may have had no direct relation to performance in their day: scholars now use them to attempt to reconstruct elements of lost theaters. Several of these records are written documents, often chestnuts in the history of drama and theater. The purpose of including these records here is experimental: how can you use such records to interrogate some aspect of a past performance? What kind of story does the document tell, and what stories does it conceal? What kind of interpretation of theater history does the document enable? What kinds of evidentiary problems does it pose? Reading the documents of the theater's material past is one way to engage in the challenging work of imagining the power of dramatic performance.

Beyond that, each unit offers three kinds of critical material. The Critical Contexts gather classic texts—essays, commentaries, or practical writing on the training of actors and directors—contemporary with the plays of the unit itself. These essays were often conceived in dialogue with the plays that shared the cultural horizon with them. The Critical Perspectives suggest more recent perspectives on the work of theater and drama, often in essays written by major scholars and theorists writing today. We hope these materials will help to promote the ongoing discussion of how drama shapes the dialogue between the page and the stage.

The Theater of Classical Europe: Athens and Rome

Greek amphitheater at the site of the ancient city of Morgantina, Sicily.

I

Great drama arises where the theater occupies an important place in the life of the community. In many respects, Western understanding of drama originated in fifth-century (500–400) BCE classical Athens, where the theater played a central role in politics, religion, and society. The Athenians invented forms of **TRAGEDY** and **COMEDY** that persist to the present day. In tragedy, the Greeks dramatized climactic events in the lives of legendary heroes from prehistory and myth, bringing ethical problems of motive and action to the stage. In comedy, the theater staged satiric portraits of the life of the **POLIS** (the city-state), vividly depicting the energetic conflicts of contemporary Athens in matters of politics, war, education—even the arts of drama. Playwrights through the long history of the theater have continued to find in Greek drama both a model and a point of resistance against which to practice their own craft (see, for example, Bernard Shaw's *Major Barbara* in this book). And we need only recall Sigmund Freud's understanding of the "Oedipus complex" to sense the influence of models of action derived from the Greek theater on later Western culture.

Athens and Sparta were dominant rival powers in fifth-century Greece, which comprised many small independent city-states, each with its own political and cultural institutions, form of government, and alliances. Dramatic performances took place under a variety of circumstances in all Greek cities, but drama as we know it developed in Athens. Dramatic performance in Athens was part of citywide religious festivals honoring the god Dionysus, the most important being the **CITY DIONYSIA**. Plays were produced for contests in which playwrights, actors, and choruses competed for prizes and for distinction among their fellow citizens. These contests, held in an outdoor amphitheater adjoining the sacred temple of the god, followed several days of religious parades and sacrifices. This connection between early drama and religion suggests that the essential nature of Greek drama lies in its supposed "origins" in religious ritual. But the City Dionysia was also a massive civic spectacle that went far beyond religious worship, emphasizing the theater's implication in other areas of public life. Dramatic performance contributed to this celebration of Athens' economic power, cultural accomplishment, and military might. The City Dionysia united religion and politics, enabling Athenians to celebrate both Dionysus and the achievements of their *polis*.

The City Dionysia

The City Dionysia was the most prominent of four religious festivals held in Athens and the surrounding province of Attica between December and April; it took place in the month of Elaphebolion (March–April), one month after the previous festival. Although its purpose was primarily a religious one, the City Dionysia was structured around a series of contests between individual citizens and between major Athenian social groups—the ten (later twelve to fifteen) "tribes" that formed the city's basic political and military units. Dramatic performance was introduced to the City Dionysia during the sixth century BCE and became the centerpiece of the elaborate festival. Each year a city magistrate, or **ARCHON,** honored selected wealthy citizens by choosing them to finance one of the three principal tragic dramatists competing for a prize at the festival. Each sponsor, called a **CHOREGOS,** was responsible for hiring the **CHORUS** of young men who sang and danced in the plays. The *choregos* hired musicians and provided costumes and other support for the playwright to whom he was assigned. Later in the period, the state assigned the leading actor to the *choregos* as well, and this actor also competed for a prize. The playwright was responsible for training the chorus and the actors, and for some of the acting himself, and he shared his prize with the *choregos*. Serving as a *choregos* was both a civic duty and an important honor, equivalent to other tasks imposed on the wealthy—maintaining a battleship for a year or training athletes for the Olympic games.

Taking place over several days, the City Dionysia opened with a display of actors and choruses to the city; on the next day there was a lavish parade of religious officials through the city, followed by religious observances and sacrifices held in the theater. Athens also received its annual tribute of goods, money, and slaves from subject and allied states at this time, and war orphans raised at state expense were displayed to the audience. After this display of religious worship and civic pride, two days were devoted to contests of **DITHYRAMBS**, hymns sung and danced by a large chorus. Each of Athens' tribes sponsored two choruses: one consisting of fifty men, another consisting of fifty boys. The city's politics revolved around the tribes, and their contribution to the festival was prominent in this contest. The dithyrambic contest involved a thousand Athenian citizens directly in the performance, a significant portion of the adult male citizens. (It is estimated that Athens in the fifth century had a total population of about 300,000: 100,000 slaves, 30,000 noncitizen foreigners, and 30,000 to 40,000 adult male citizens; women and children were not citizens.) Following the dithyrambs, the main dramatic contest began. The competing playwrights each produced a **TRILOGY** of tragedies, staged over three days. A trilogy could take a single theme or series of events as its subject (like the three plays of Aeschylus' *Oresteia*, 458 BCE), or present three distinct, unrelated dramas. A rugged farce called a **SATYR PLAY** followed the performance of each complete trilogy and was considered part of it; these plays parodied a god's activities, with actors dressed as satyrs—half-man, half-goat. After 486 BCE, comedies were also awarded prizes, but it is unclear whether the comedies were performed on a single day or spread over several days. Prominent citizens representing each of the tribes served as judges and awarded prizes to the playwrights, their *choregoi*, and the actors.

The Theater of Dionysus

The Greek theater was a public spectacle, a kind of combination of Inauguration Day, the Super Bowl, the Academy Awards, Memorial Day, and a major religious holiday. Plays were first produced in the **AGORA** (marketplace), which often served as a performance place for festivals in Athens and in the surrounding **DEMES** of Attica, which also staged dramatic performances. However, the size and importance of the City Dionysia required a separate site, and a theater was built on the slope of the Acropolis, near the precinct of Dionysus. The original theater, a ring of wooden seats facing a circular floor, was later refined, enlarged, and constructed of stone. By the time of Aeschylus, Euripides, Sophocles, and Aristophanes, the Athenian theater had achieved its basic design: a circular floor for dancing and acting, ringed by a hillside **AMPHITHEATER** and backed by a low, rectangular building.

The focus of the classical amphitheater, which seated about 14,000 people, was the round **ORCHESTRA** ("dancing place") containing the central altar of Dionysus, at which the festival sacrifices were performed. The dithyrambic choruses performed their ecstatic dances in the orchestra, and most of the action of the plays took place there as well. Facing the orchestra, the hillside was divided into wedge-shaped seating areas. The citizens sat on wooden benches with their tribes: leaders and priests in the front of the sections, women perhaps toward the rear or possibly in a separate section. *Metics* (resident aliens) and visitors were probably seated in a separate area. Special front and center seats, called *prohedria*, were reserved for the judges and the priests of Dionysus.

Behind the *orchestra*, a low building called the **SKENE** faced the audience. Although the *skene* became a permanent stone structure in the fourth century BCE, in the fifth century it was a temporary wooden building, used for changing masks and possibly also for changing costumes. Playwrights quickly found the theatrical potential latent in the *skene*'s facade and set of doors; through these doors the audience heard Agamemnon being murdered in his bath, or saw eyeless Oedipus return to confront the Chorus and his future in exile. In Aeschylus' *Agamemnon*, the Watchman awaits the signal fires on the palace roof, and in performance he may have waited on the roof of the *skene*. The theater also used some machinery for scenic effects: a rolling platform (the **EKKYKLEMA**) used to bring objects or bodies from the *skene* into the orchestra; a crane (**MACHINA**) to raise or lower characters— the gods, for instance—from the orchestra over the roof of the *skene;* later, in the fourth century, painted panels were used to indicate the play's setting or location.

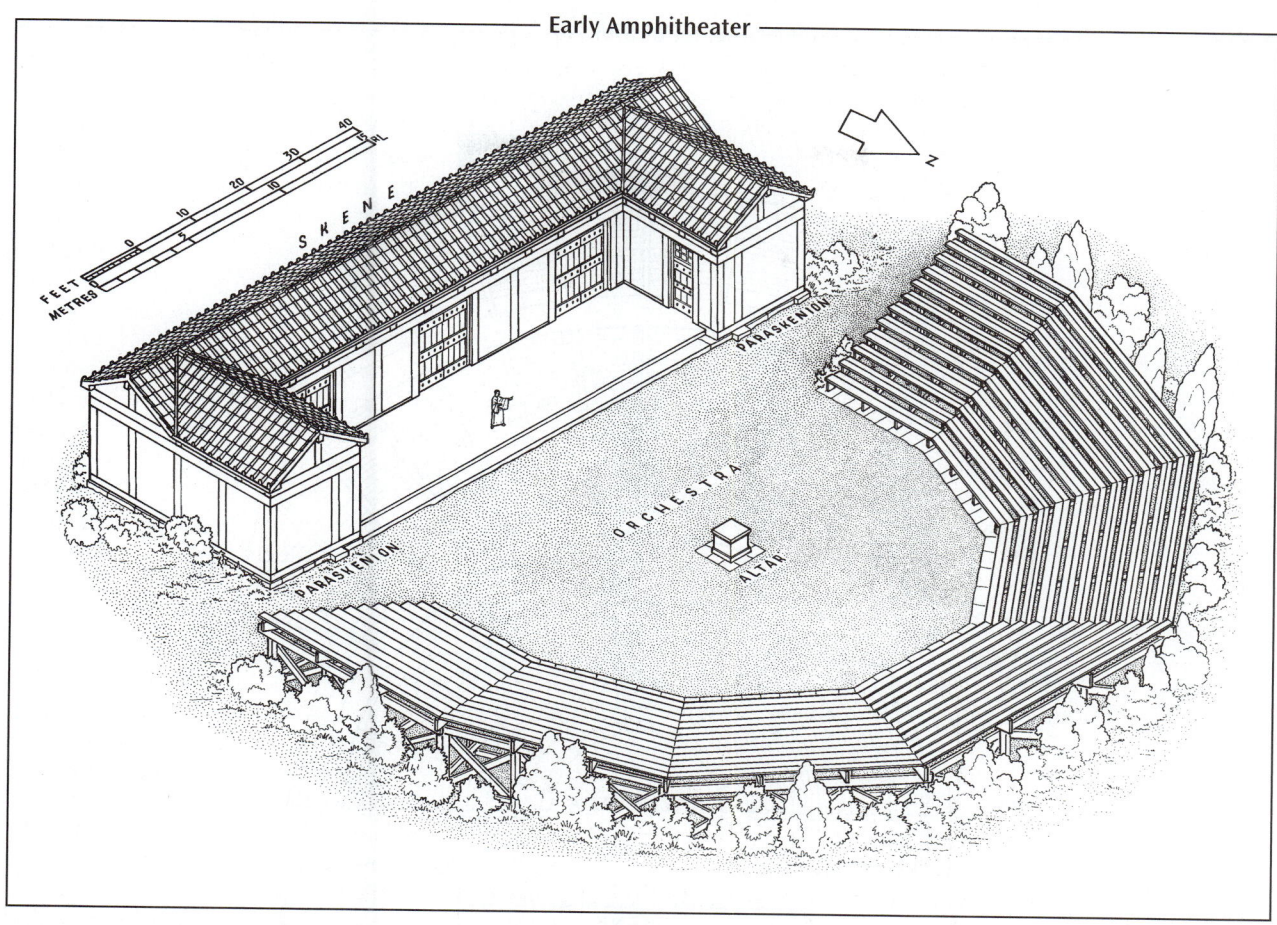

Early Amphitheater

This is an artist's reconstruction of an early theater in Eretria, Greece. Notice that the seating is constructed of wooden benches and the *skene* is a temporary structure.

The Theater and Social Life

The experience of theater in classical Athens was in some ways akin to participation in other institutions of civic life. Athens was a participatory democracy for its citizens, although citizenship was restricted to adult male Athenians: women, foreigners, slaves, freed slaves, and children were not citizens. Citizens sat in the assembly to discuss and vote on matters of state policy, and they were eligible to serve in all public and military offices as well. Attendance at the City Dionysia was, then, like other aspects of Athenian public life, a privilege and an obligation mainly reserved for citizens. Citizens received tickets to the festival from officials in their neighborhood, or *DEME;* tickets may have been awarded on the basis of participation in other civic obligations—serving in the courts, the assembly, the army. At the theater, citizens sat together with members of their tribe. In a sense, the theater offered a visual map of the organization of Athenian society, for the tribes formed the basis of political participation outside the theater: The Athenian Assembly and the army were similarly arranged by tribe. Organized by tribes, with precedence given to religious officials and with inferior status or nonparticipation accorded to noncitizens such as women, slaves, and foreigners, the theater of Dionysus mirrored the structure of Athenian society.

The fifth century BCE was the era of Athens' greatest political power and cultural vitality and an era of intense reciprocity between Athenian theater and society. Yet the tension manifest in Greek drama perhaps points to the precarious stability of the Athenian

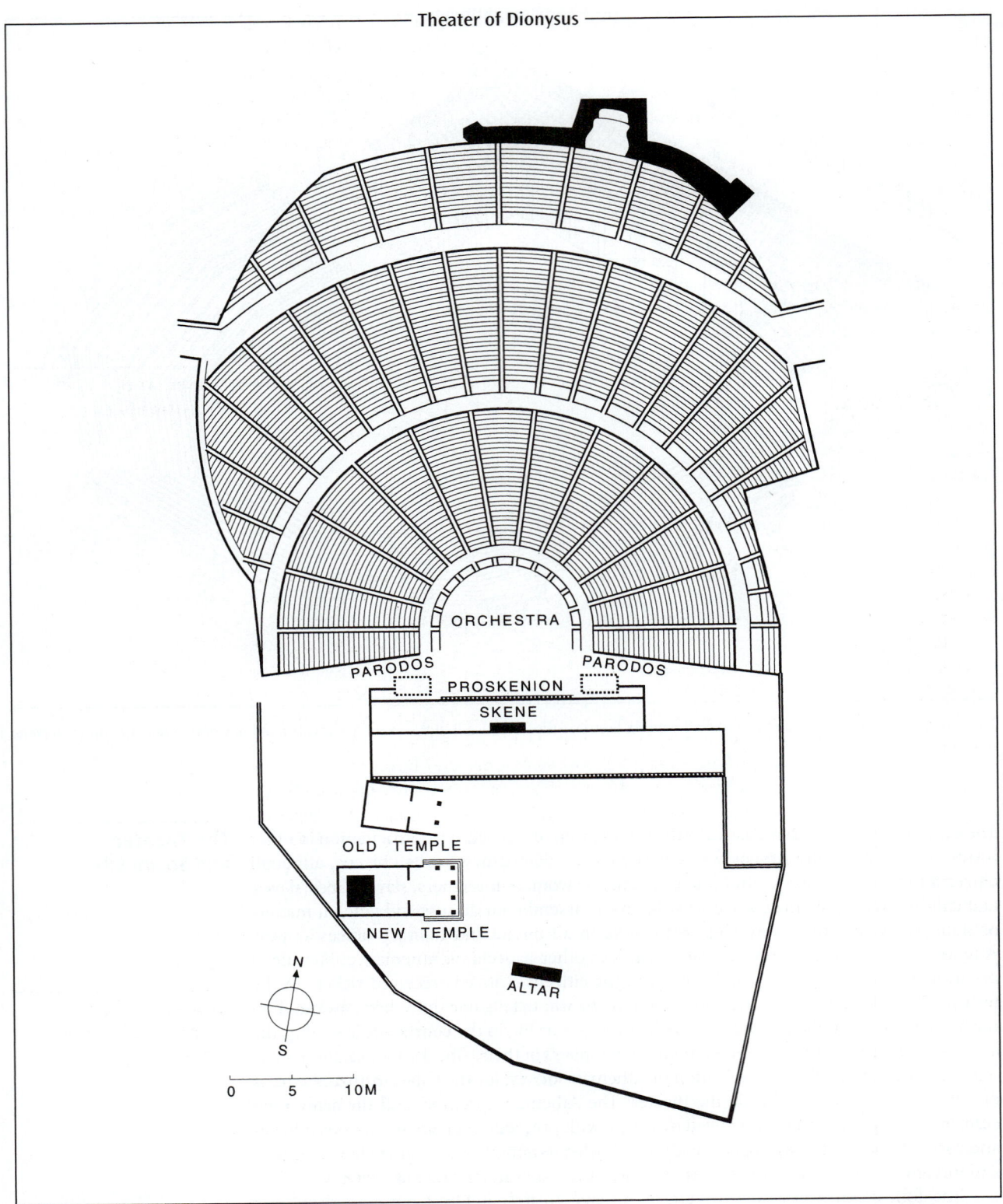

Theater of Dionysus

ORCHESTRA

PARODOS   PARODOS

PROSKENION

SKENE

OLD TEMPLE

NEW TEMPLE

ALTAR

N

S

0   5   10M

This ground plan is of the sacred precinct of Dionysus in Athens, fourth century BCE. Notice that the theater is much larger than the earlier theater at provincial Eretria. The large and permanent *skene* was constructed after the fifth century BCE.

polis. The Athenian maritime empire, forged after the defeat of massive Persian forces in 479, was resisted by the smaller Greek states and opposed by Athens' chief rival, the military state of Sparta. Following a long period of hostility and skirmishing, Athens and Sparta declared war against each other in 431 BCE, resulting in Athens' utter defeat in 404. Athenian democracy was replaced by an oppressive oligarchy, the Thirty Tyrants. Although the tyrants were rapidly overthrown and democracy restored, Athens never regained the dynamic cultural life and political power it enjoyed during the fifth century. And although dramatic performance continued after the restoration of democracy, the theater's central role in the *polis* seems to have declined after the Spartan victory. Yet, the theater became one of Greece's most widely disseminated cultural products. When Alexander the Great conquered Greece, the Near East, and northern Africa, he took Greek culture—including theater and drama—with him throughout his empire. And when the Roman Empire later absorbed Alexander's former dominions, it also appropriated Greek dramatic traditions, the design of Greek theaters, and the arts and religion of Greece, as well.

Drama and Performance

In his *Poetics,* Aristotle suggests that drama originated in the singing of the dithyrambic choruses; a masked actor was first used to respond to the chorus as an individualized "character" in the mid–sixth century BCE, an innovation attributed to the playwright Thespis, about whom little else is known. Aeschylus was the first to use two actors, probably taking one of the parts himself; in the 460s, Sophocles introduced a third actor and was successfully imitated by Aeschylus in his *Oresteia* in 458 BCE. In general, classical tragedy can be performed with three actors and comedy with four, although each actor may play several parts. All of the performers in the Greek theater—the dramatists, actors, musicians, and chorus members—were male citizens of Athens, as was most of the audience. The dramatic choruses were perhaps composed of young men between the ages of seventeen, when military training began, and twenty-one, when Athenian men entered into adulthood.

The chorus of tragedy both sang and danced, and it was expected to perform with grace and precision. Actors and choruses wore full-head masks made of painted linen or lightweight wood. The main characters' masks were individualized, but the members of the chorus all wore identical masks, giving a special force to the conflict between the unique claims of the protagonist and the more diffuse claims of his society. Costuming in comedy was somewhat more complex. Aristophanes' plays suggest that the chorus at times wore animal masks. The comic protagonists' masks, though, were again individualized; since Aristophanes often put his contemporaries in his plays—Socrates in *Clouds,* for instance, or Euripides in *Frogs*—the masks probably resembled these citizens quite closely. Comic actors often sported a leather PHALLUS, clearly visible in statues depicting comic actors and of much dramatic use in plays like *Lysistrata.* In reading Greek drama, we should remember that its leading parts—both the leading character and the chorus—were designed for competition, as instruments for the actor and chorus to win prizes. The literary brilliance of the plays is, in this sense, a means to enable a particular virtuosity in performance.

Women in the Athenian Theater

In Athenian tragedy and comedy, female characters were played by men. Not only did men sponsor and write the plays, but the "women" onstage were literally men in disguise. Yet, many plays throw the theatrical convention of men playing women into relief. In Euripides' play *The Bacchae,* Pentheus is possessed by Dionysus when he dresses up as a woman and Dionysus admires his good looks; in *Lysistrata,* the Spartan woman Lampito is closely and physically examined by Lysistrata and the other women in ways that focus the audience's attention precisely on the fact that the woman is being played by a man. Drama, then, participated fully in Athens' denial of equality to women. Athena says as much in Aeschylus' *The Eumenides* when she judges Orestes' murder of his mother as a lesser crime than Clytaemnestra's murder of her husband. Looking closely at both the drama and its performance can help us to see how justice, power, and gender came to be arranged in Athenian society.

Although the theater—like Athenian society—was a male-dominated institution, Greek drama repeatedly inquires into the nature of gendered behavior and uses female characters to focus some of its most challenging questions. Given the absence of women from the stage and their marginal status in the theater and in the state, it is fascinating to note how many plays turn on the action of female characters. Women were not themselves citizens of Athens, and their prerogatives, which were considerable, in the *polis* were defined only through marriage to a citizen. Yet many of the plays raise critical moral, ethical, and political problems through the actions of women: Clytaemnestra and Cassandra in Aeschylus' *Agamemnon*, Medea in Euripides' *Medea,* and the women of Aristophanes' *Lysistrata* and *Assembly of Women*. Although Aristotle probably voices his contemporaries' views when he remarks in his *Poetics* that "a woman can be good, or a slave, although one of these classes [women] is inferior and the other, as a class, worthless," the theater stages women in ways that implicitly challenge the authority of this "natural" connection between the good, the legitimate, and the masculine. As a category that troubles the "natural" linkage between masculinity and humanity itself, women in Greek drama often appear to stage a crisis in how the state imagines and justifies itself.

Forms of Greek Drama

Formally, the organization of Greek tragedy is somewhat different from that of modern plays, because Greek drama is based on the singing and dancing of the chorus, for whom many of the plays were named. Most plays begin with a **PROLOGUE**, such as the Watchman's speech at the opening of *Agamemnon,* followed by the **PARODOS** (entrance) of the singing and dancing chorus. Several **EPISODES** follow, in which the central characters engage one another and the chorus; the chorus itself often sings (and dances) several **ODES**, which are used to enunciate and enlarge on the play's pivotal issues, and the chorus often becomes a decisive character in the play, as it does in Aeschylus' *Agamemnon* or Euripides' *The Bacchae.* The choral odes are written in lyric meters different from the meters used for the characters' speeches. The play's **CATASTROPHE**, literally its "down turn," marks some change in the hero's status and is followed by the departure of the characters from the stage and the **EXODOS**, or final song, dance, and departure of the chorus. Comedy—at least for Aristophanes, whose plays are the only surviving comedies from the period—is structured similarly, although Aristophanes' plays usually include a long **PARABASIS**, a choral ode delivered to the audience discussing political issues, and a final **KOMOS**, a scene of choral dancing and revelry.

This formal description, however, hardly accounts for the real and continued power of Greek drama, which arises from an intense and economical relationship between (1) a situation, usually at the point of climax as the play opens, (2) a complex of characters, each with distinctive goals and motives, (3) a chorus used both as a character and as a commentator on the action, and (4) a series of incidents that precipitates a crisis and brings the meaning of the **PROTAGONIST**'s actions into focus. Aristotle called this crisis the **PERIPETEIA**, or "reversal," in the external situation or fortunes of the main character, and he argued that it should be accompanied by an act of **ANAGNORISIS**, or "recognition," in which the character responds to this change. Indeed, Aristotle argued that when the pressure of the tragic action produces a close relationship between reversal and recognition, it instills in the audience intense feelings of fear and pity and then effects **CATHARSIS**, a purgation of these emotions.

Because the plays were written for a contest, it is not surprising that their language and construction provide opportunity for powerful acting, particularly since the plays were judged only in performance. Yet the stage action of Greek drama is hardly spectacular in the modern sense. Although the visual dimension of Agamemnon's descent from the chariot onto the blood-red tapestry, or Medea's appearance in the dragon-drawn chariot, or even the aching gait of the men in *Lysistrata* is critical to any understanding of these plays, scenes of murder, suicide, or battle usually take place offstage, to be vividly reported by messengers—as in the reports of Jocasta's death and Oedipus' blinding, or of the death of Jason's young bride in *Medea.* Cassandra's graphic prophecy of Agamemnon's murder likewise provides a brutal counterpoint to the slaughter taking place offstage.

The scenic simplicity of the Greek theater enabled playwrights to achieve a special kind of concentration, one that capitalized on the special circumstances of the open-air, festival theater. Greek comedy has come down to us in the work of only two playwrights, Aristophanes and Menander (c. 342–c. 291 BCE). While Aristophanes' plays—usually called **OLD COMEDY**—are energetic and sometimes ribald comedies lampooning the Athenian *polis* and its leading citizens, Menander's comedies—called **NEW COMEDY**—are more generally concerned with mores and manners. Menander wrote more than 100 plays, but only one of his comedies—*The Grouch*—survives in its entirety. Menander's plays—and those of his contemporaries, Philemon, Diphilus, and Apollodorus—were often focused on a comic conflict between parents and children, devising situations and characters that forged an important link between the Greek and Roman theaters, and helped to establish the enduring traditions of stage comedy.

While the comedies center on the life of the community, the stage action of Greek tragedy focuses on the relation between the hero's intention, action, and consequence in ways that typically pit the hero's greatest talents against his unavoidable destiny, his society, his family, and himself. This recipe has provided—in plays from the era of Aeschylus, Sophocles, and Euripides to our own—the substance of tragic drama. The characteristic concerns of Greek drama speak undeniably of classical Athens, but the plays also represent trials of decision, suffering, and desperation with a power and purpose that continue to speak to us in accents very much our own.

Greek Drama in Performance History

The forms of Greek drama and theater remained in use after the fall of Athens to Sparta; indeed, they were both exported to Rome, Egypt, and the Middle East by Alexander. Yet while tragedy and comedy continued to be written and performed throughout the Greek Mediterranean throughout the Hellenistic period (fourth and third centuries BCE) and beyond, and theater design continued to develop and refine the classical amphitheater, in an important sense the tradition of dramatic writing and performance inaugurated in fifth-century Athens was confined to the Greek provinces. The modes of Greek drama and (to a lesser extent) performance survived somewhat longer in the eastern reaches of the Roman Empire, but in the west they gradually disappeared under the influence of Roman culture. Moreover, although the manuscripts of Greek drama—and of important collateral texts, such as Aristotle's *Poetics*—continued to be copied for students and readers, they fell out of public circulation. The few texts that have survived of the plays of Aeschylus, Sophocles, Euripides, and Aristophanes are based on copies made for teachers and scholars in Byzantium, dating from the third and fourth centuries CE. Not only have most of their plays been lost (Sophocles is said to have written 123 plays, of which we have seven; Aeschylus is thought to have written more than seventy, of which seven remain; Euripides' nineteen plays are all that remain of more than ninety), but the entire dramatic output of 700 years of theater was lost as well—the names of Agathon, Thespis, Chairemon, Theodektes, Philokles, Ariastas, and others are all that remain of their work. Moreover, since these manuscripts were collected in scholarly or monastic libraries, they have been subject to the destructive forces of history. Many Greek plays were lost in the burning of the library at Alexandria during Caesar's invasion of Egypt; the crusaders sacked Constantinople (previously known as Byzantium) in 1204, and in the process destroyed a city that had joined eastern and western cultures for centuries.

However, for all their violence, the Crusades also reopened cultural contact with the Islamic Middle East; many of the texts of Greek and Roman culture had been translated into Arabic or had been preserved by Islamic scholars and libraries. With the reopening of European trading and military contacts in the fourteenth, fifteenth, and sixteenth centuries, Europe was able to rediscover the literature of classical Greece, sometimes in Latin translations, sometimes only through commentaries on still-lost texts (such as Aristotle's *Poetics*). In many respects, though, this recovery was principally of Roman theater and drama.

The prestige and availability of texts by Latin authors like Plautus, Terence, and Seneca meant that these playwrights were widely taught in schools, convents (such as Gandersheim, where the canoness Hrosvitha [953–973 CE] wrote six comedies modeled on Terence's plays), and universities, where their plays were often performed; the influence of these playwrights can be felt everywhere in European drama of the sixteenth century, most familiarly in Shakespeare's early comedies (like *A Comedy of Errors,* based on Plautus' *The Menaechmus Twins*) and in the vogue for violent tragedies reminiscent of Seneca's unstaged dramas, plays like Shakespeare's *Titus Andronicus* (see Unit III). The rediscovery of Vitruvius' first-century book on Roman architecture, *De Architectura,* in 1414 (it was printed—a new technology—in 1486) also led a generation of fifteenth- and sixteenth-century architects to design and build theaters on what they took to be a Roman model.

In many respects, though, Greek drama only became widely known in Europe in the later seventeenth and eighteenth centuries, where Greek plays often provided the models for contemporary playwrights, such as Jean Racine, as well as for the first operas. And it was only in the nineteenth and twentieth centuries that the restoration of classical amphitheaters and the historical and archaeological recovery of the theatrical practices of classical Athens began to make possible experiments in staging classical Greek drama in ways that attempted to approximate the circumstances of classical theater or that attempted to translate those circumstances into a more effective modern idiom. Since the late nineteenth century, for example, the amphitheater at Epidaurus has often been used to stage classical Greek plays in ways that attempt to approximate the traditions of fifth-century Athenian performance.

Clearly, of course, much has changed in the last 2,500 years, and performing classical drama poses a series of challenges to modern performers. First, the chorus—both its singing and dancing performance style and its function in the drama—has posed a critical problem for modern companies and audiences: German director Max Reinhardt staged a production of *The Oresteia* in 1919 that was among the first of his productions to experiment with large crowds onstage; later productions have tended to make the chorus smaller and more energetic in an attempt to recapture the exciting movement of the classical chorus. Beyond that, the use of masks in classical theater is no longer conventional on the modern stage, although many modern playwrights—Eugene O'Neill, for example, in *Strange Interlude* (1928)—have experimented with masks in an attempt to render psychological complexity with what they take to be "classical" decorum. The 1981 National Theatre (London) production of *The Oresteia,* directed by Sir Peter Hall, used an entirely male cast and performed the play in masks; this production was the first English-language production of a Greek tragedy to be performed in the classical theater at Epidaurus. Although this effort to "recover" the initial circumstances and flavor of Greek performance has driven many performances, Greek drama has also provided the framework for a number of important AVANT-GARDE theatrical experiments in the modern era. Of course, Racine's adaptation of Euripides in *Phaedra* might be considered an "updating" of this kind, but in the modern era, stage practices have often been used not so much to recover the classical past as to restage the plays in a modern idiom. Josef Svoboda's brilliant 1963 production of *Oedipus the King* in Prague, for example, took place on a thirty-foot-wide staircase that rose from the bottom of the orchestra pit to beyond the top of the proscenium. The French director Ariane Mnouchkine staged a production of Euripides' *Iphigeneia at Aulis* as an introduction to her staging of *The Oresteia* in 1990 (under the overall title *Les Atrides*); this brilliant production used makeup, costume, movement, and dance idioms from classical Indian and Indonesian theater, implying that a contemporary staging of the Greek classics might well turn to another tradition of "classical" performance to find a still-living stage language. Both for directors—Peter Sellars' 1993 staging of Aeschylus' *The Persians* framed the play with allusions to the Gulf War—and for writers, such as Heiner Müller (*Medeamaterial*), Charles Mee, Jr. (*Orestes*), Caryl Churchill (*A Mouthful of Birds,* based on Euripides' *The Bacchae,* and written with David Lan), Timberlake Wertenbaker (who has translated several

Photographer: John Vickers. Courtesy of University of Bristol Theatre Collection

Framed by a masked member of the Chorus and Jocasta, Oedipus—played here by Laurence Olivier in the landmark 1945 production of *Oedipus the King*—seems finally to recognize the "truth" that he has been seeking.

© Joan Marcus

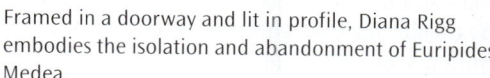

Framed in a doorway and lit in profile, Diana Rigg embodies the isolation and abandonment of Euripides' Medea.

Greek plays), Wole Soyinka (*The Bacchae of Euripides*), and others, the theater and drama of classical Athens continue to provide a way to see and understand ourselves.

Classical Rome

Although many of their traditions originated in Greek culture, the Romans developed a distinctive theater, quite different from the Athenian stage. From its beginnings, Roman entertainment was more varied than the Greek, including various forms of dramatic, quasi-dramatic and improvised performance, as well as acrobatics, juggling, athletic events, gladiatorial combats, and public spectacles. In the sixth and seventh centuries BCE, Rome was a relatively unimportant town, ruled by the Etruscan kingdoms of northern Italy. In 509 the Romans drove out the Etruscans and founded a republic; the republic expanded its influence throughout the fourth century BCE and by 265 BCE—well after the Peloponnesian War that marked the decline of Athens's political and cultural predominance in the region—controlled the Italian peninsula, including territories once governed by the Greeks and by Alexander. Much as the Romans absorbed other Greek institutions, they also absorbed Greek theater and drama, which were first performed in Rome in the mid–third century, in 240 BCE. As Rome's political influence expanded, particularly under the successor to the Republic, the Roman Empire (27 BCE–476 CE), the Romans disseminated their characteristic cultural institutions—including theater and drama—throughout Europe, North Africa, and the Middle East.

Roman Festivals and Drama

Like the Greeks, the Romans associated drama with festivals. The Romans not only produced plays on festival occasions throughout the year, however; they also developed a much wider variety of theatrical entertainments, of which drama was only a small part. Some of the Roman entertainments descended from the sixth-century BCE *LUDI ROMANI*, and eventually included a variety of entertainments: chariot racing at the *circus*, gladiatorial combats, beast hunts, rope-dancing, boxing and wrestling, and other athletic contests; dramatic performances were included beginning in 364. Greek drama was performed in the former Greek cities of southern Italy; Latin adaptations of tragedy and comedy were first produced at the *ludi Romani* in 240 BCE, during the First Punic War with Carthage (soldiers are common characters in Roman comedies), a year that also saw the importation of the first mortal gladiatorial combats from Etruria. Theater in Rome expanded during the Punic Wars, even as—during the Second Punic War, when Hannibal crossed the Alps with elephants—the war was fought in Italy itself. Dramatic performances were introduced to several other festivals, and by 179 BCE, drama was being performed at major religious festivals throughout the year: at the *ludi Romani* honoring Jupiter in September, at the *ludi Plebei* also honoring to Jupiter in November, at the *ludi Megalensia* (the Great Mother) in early April and the *ludi Florales* honoring Flora in late April, and at a festival honoring Apollo, the *ludi Apollinares*, in July. Dramatic performances, though still associated with festivals, were much more common in late republican and imperial Rome than in fifth-century Athens, not only because special celebrations sometimes also included theatrical performance, but also because any disruption or inconsistency in the performance of the religious rituals connected with a festival required that the entire festival be repeated, a not-uncommon occurrence. Throughout the Roman period, as the Republic gave way to the Empire, the number of festival days regularly increased: by 354 CE, seventy-five days were given to gladiatorial combats and chariot races, and one hundred to theatrical performances. Audiences attended the theater for free, and plays drew—as the sometimes-disdainful, sometimes-placating comments of playwrights suggest—an energetic, if not always sophisticated audience. Indeed, plays could also be performed on other occasions—such as a wedding or a funeral—and so playwrights and performers had to work hard to attract and hold their audience's attention.

As in Greece, the organization of a festival usually fell to a prominent citizen or magistrate, who was granted a fee to fund the games; the magistrate typically contracted a manager (**DOMINUS**) of an acting company (**GREX**). Actors, however, were considerably lower in status in Roman than Greek culture. Companies producing scripted drama consisted of several male actors (or **HISTRIONES**, adapting the Etruscan term) and slave musicians, and they maintained stock costumes and properties; they typically purchased the script directly from a playwright for a fee. Although actors in the earlier Republic often had been freed, actors in the Empire were frequently slaves, suggesting something of the relationship between actors and their audiences. Tragedies and comedies were performed with masks. Made of linen and attached to a wig, the mask covered the entire head of the actor; like the masks, costumes tended to be conventional. Given the reliance of Roman comedy on music, actors had to be good singers.

Roman Theater Architecture

Given the variety of entertainments offered in Rome—including the chariot races, wild animal hunts (*venationes*), full-scale sea battles (*naumachiae*), and gladiatorial combats that became increasingly popular in the later Empire, especially after 300 CE—it is not surprising that the Romans built several different kinds of entertainment buildings, stadiums (such as the Flavian Amphitheatre, or Colosseum, begun by the emperor Vespasian and dedicated by Titus in 80 CE), and racecourses (such as the *Circus Maximus*, built 600 BCE) as well as theaters. Having settled southern Italy and Sicily, the Greeks built several permanent theaters, and performances of Aeschylus and Euripides are recorded there in the mid-fifth century BCE. Although many Roman cities had enjoyed the permanent theaters built by their Greek predecessors for centuries, all theaters in Rome were temporary, built and taken down for each festival; indeed, in 159 BCE, when officials attempted to erect a stone theater in Rome they were successfully challenged by Publius Scipio Nasica, whose concern for the corrupting influence of the stage led the Roman Senate to ban seating at any public entertainment. Only in 55 BCE, was Pompey the Great (Gnaeus Pompeius

Magnus) able to persuade the Romans to build a large theater in the Campus Martius as part of a new architectural complex—including a colonnaded forecourt behind the auditorium where audiences could get out of the sun and rain, and a temple to Venus—perhaps a sign of Pompey's political skill in maneuvering the building through moral opposition.

The Romans built theaters of stone throughout the Empire; many of the Greek theaters that remain today were refurbished and redesigned by the Romans. Like their Greek predecessors, the Roman theaters were outdoor amphitheaters, but the Romans built their theaters on level ground rather than into an existing hillside, and their superior engineering—particularly the Romans' use of arches in construction—enabled them to build much more massive buildings. Roman theaters were generally three stories in height. A stage house, or *SCAENA,* stood like the Greek *skene* behind the semicircular orchestra and faced a steeply tiered semicircular auditorium. The facade (or *FRONS*) of the *scaena* was elaborately ornamented with columns and porticos, and—extending the structure of earlier temporary theaters—typically had two or three stage doors facing the audience, enabling the stage readily to resemble the street setting of most Roman comedy. The auditorium, or *CAVEA,* of Pompey's theatre was divided into thirty-two sections, separated by aisles and ascending stairs, and audiences sat according to class; different sections of the auditorium could be reached by separate entryways (*VOMITORIA*); *vomitoria* also led into the orchestra as well. Permanent Roman theaters varied in capacity, but the largest could hold nearly 17,000 spectators; actors played on a large rectangular stage (*PULPITUM*) raised about five feet above the orchestra. In Pompey's theater on the Campus Martius, the stage was 300 feet long (the length of a football field), and 20–40 feet deep; most theaters had an apparatus to lower a curtain through the front of the stage. A short staircase led from the stage to the orchestra, and playwrights frequently complained about townspeople occupying the stage during performances. The Roman theater used little scenery, much along the lines of the *periaktoi* and *ekkyklema* of the Greek theatre.

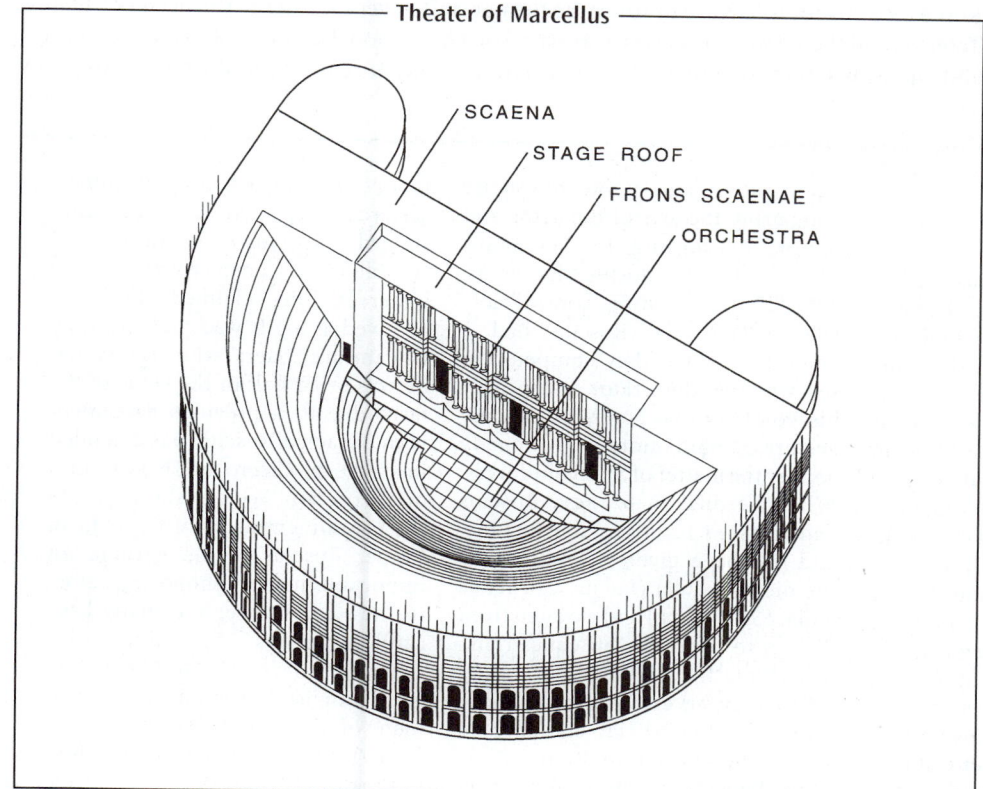

— Theater of Marcellus —

SCAENA

STAGE ROOF

FRONS SCAENAE

ORCHESTRA

The Theater of Marcellus was built in Rome, 13–11 BCE.

Roman Drama   Although the Romans continued to perform plays from the Greek theater, they also developed a native strain of drama—represented in the plays of Plautus, Terence, and Seneca—that flourished during the middle and later years of the Republic. In Italy, comedy first derived from farcical parodies of tragedy, called *PHYLAKES*—the word is also used to mean "gossips"—whose performances resembled those of itinerant MIME companies. Roman drama is often said to originate from Livius Andronicus (240–204 BCE), possibly a freed slave, who adapted Greek drama into Latin, wrote original plays, and became a fine actor; the titles of eight of his tragedies and three of his comedies remain. It's notable, though, that some of this history derives from the Roman historian Titus Livius (59 BCE–17 CE), allegedly the descendant of the man who first freed Livius Andronicus. Gnaeus Naevius (270–201 BCE) wrote comedies (which have not survived), and possibly collaborated with Titus Maccius Plautus (c. 254–c. 184 BCE), the most influential Roman comic playwright. Roman comedy embodies the generic indeterminacy of Roman entertainments: heavily dependent on music and singing, comedy provided actors with signal opportunities to interact with the theater's lively audiences, and Plautus' plays are definitive in this regard. Plautus' earliest surviving plays date from 205 BCE, or about thirty-five years after Greek drama was first introduced to Rome. Plautus based many of his comedies on Greek New Comedy, yet since none of these prototypes survive it is difficult to gauge the extent of his originality, though in action and characterization Plautus's plays are fully Romanized. Plautus is thought to have written more than 100 comedies, many of which—*Amphitryon, The Braggart Warrior, The Rope,* and *The Brothers Menaechmus,* for example—established the formal conventions of later comedy. Publius Terentius Afer (c. 195–159 BCE), usually called Terence, was probably born in Carthage and brought to Rome as a slave. Unlike the prolific Plautus, Terence wrote only six comedies, all of which survive; he, too, strove throughout his career to adapt Greek originals to the Roman stage: *The Woman of Andros, Mother-in-Law, Self-Tormentor, Eunuch, Phormio,* and *The Brothers.* Terence died mysteriously, leaving Rome on a voyage to Greece to study the theater, and never returning. The plays of Plautus, Terence, and their contemporaries were based on Greek models, and involved Greek settings and characters; they are often called *FABULAE PALLIATA,* referring to the Greek costumes

---

(*Aside*)
ROSCIUS

Roscius—Quintus Roscius Gallus, 126–62 BCE—is the most celebrated of classical actors; born near Lanuvium, he became a distinguished comic actor in the first century, notably the friend of Cicero (Marcus Tullius Cicero, 106–43 BCE), the great Roman orator. Cicero, who is said to have studied with Roscius to improve his skill as a public speaker, speaks frequently of him, notably praising Roscius' care and attention to the preparation of his parts, and more generally noting that the actor should have the physical training of both an athlete and a dancer; he was praised by Horace (Quintus Horatius Flaccus, 65–8 BCE) and by the poet Catullus as well (Gaius Valerius Catullus,

84–54 BCE), and wrote a treatise comparing the arts of the actor and orator. Acccording to Macrobius (Ambrosius Theodosius Macrobius, 395–423 CE), writing considerably later, Cicero and Roscius had a contest in which they competed to see whether the orator, using only his voice, or the actor, using only gestures, could more convincingly convey the matter of a public address. When he died in 62 BCE, Roscius had amassed a considerable fortune, and had been given a gold ring by the dictator Sulla (Lucius Cornelius Sulla, 138–78 BCE) and elevated from *plebian* to the status of "equestrian," just below the *patricians* or ruling aristocracy, an extraordinary honor given the low social standing of actors and theater in Rome. Pliny (Gaius Plinus Secundus, 23 BCE–79 CE)

reports Roscius earning 50 million sesterces per year, a huge sum. Indeed, Roscius fell into legal trouble when a farm (worth 100,000 sesterces) he claimed to have received as a gift was challenged by C. Fannius Chaera, who argued that he was owed half of the value of the farm due to a previous agreement with the actor. Roscius was defended in court by Cicero in 76 BCE, in a brief oration which survives. As the preeminent actor of Republican Rome, Roscius' name became an important means of honoring actors in the Renaissance, and many later actors—perhaps beginning with Edward Alleyn (1566–1626), the great English actor and creator of many of Marlowe's roles (see Unit III below)—were called the "Roscius" of the day. ■

worn by the actors, the Greek cloak or *pallium* for men and *palla* for women. Earlier comedies written in the first century were set in Rome and involved Roman characters, and were called **FABULAE TOGATA,** for the togas worn by the actors.

Roman comedy used music extensively, especially in the ironic or satirical song that usually opened the principal scenes of the plays; Roman tragedy, like Roman comedy, also eliminated the chorus. While tragedy was, like comedy, performed at festivals, the depictions of tragic performance on Roman tombs witnesses the fact that tragedies were often performed at funerals as well. The influence of Euripides in the Hellenistic period was massive, and played a role in the development of the first generation of Roman tragic writers, notably in the plays of Accius (b. 170 BCE) and Ennius (234–169 BCE). The rise of Gaius Julius Caesar Octavianus (63 BCE–14 CE) to power—he was crowned as the first Emperor, taking the title Augustus in 27 BCE—marked the end of an era of civil war (dramatized in Shakespeare's *Julius Caesar* and *Antony and Cleopatra*) and the beginning of the two-hundred-year *Pax Romana*; it also initiated a brilliant age of Roman literary writing, including the careers of Ovid (Publius Ovidius Naso, 43–17 BCE) and Virgil (Publius Vergilius Maro, 70–19 BCE), whose *Aeneid* celebrated Augustus' reign by creating the heroic epic of the founding of Rome by Aeneas. Ovid and Varius (Lucius Varius Rufus, 74–14 BCE) each wrote a tragedy this period (Ovid's *Medea*, and Varius' *Thyestes*, both now lost), but the only surviving Roman tragedies were written by Lucius Annaeus Seneca (5 BCE–65 CE). Seneca was an influential philosopher, and the tutor of the young emperor Nero (Claudius Caesar Augustus Germanicus, 37–68 CE), the last of the imperial line descended from Julius Caesar; Nero's mother Agrippina played a crucial role in his rise to the throne, but when she objected to his divorce from his step-sister Octavia, Nero had her murdered (Octavia was subsequently banished, and executed upon her return to Rome). Seneca had a long and difficult relationship with the Emperor, serving as his advisor from 54 to 62: as part of his struggle with Agrippina, Nero accused Seneca of sexual relations with her, but Seneca was acquitted in 55 CE. He was also accused of taking part in a conspiracy to murder Nero; the historian Tacitus (Publius Cornelius Tacitus, 56–117 CE) described Seneca's subsequent suicide, indicating that he slit his wrists, then took poison, and when neither worked quickly enough he jumped into a pool to help the blood drain more quickly—Tacitus reports that he only died from choking on the steam. Though Nero's name today is usually synonymous with lascivious spectacle and personal immorality, he frequently performed plays in a private theater in the palace, commanding masks to be made resembling members of the Roman elite; Nero also had the Athenian Theater of Dionysus rebuilt and dedicated to him, and appeared there in the costume of Dionysus. Seneca's tragedies were adapted from Greek plays but tend to be more sensational and violent; indeed, it is doubtful that they were performed in the theater. The only drama based on contemporary Roman history, *Octavia*, is sometimes attributed to Seneca; although only nine of Seneca's plays survive—*The Trojan Women, Medea, Oedipus, Phaedra, Thyestes, Hercules on Oeta, Hercules Mad, The Phoenecian Women, Agamemnon*—Senecan tragedy exerted an important influence on later drama, providing a crucial prototype for the nascent drama of sixteenth-century England.

Literature and architecture flourished in the Augustan age, but the social standing of the theater continued to decline, which may explain why the great writers of the period were by and large not attracted to dramatic writing; indeed, Livy regarded the contemporary theater—not least the actual execution of criminals as "characters" in plays, and the display of sexual acts onstage—as essentially degrading to public morality. By the first century BCE, the formal genres of comedy and tragedy seem to have lost much of their appeal for writers and audiences, displaced in part by the more spectacular gladiatorial contests, and by more home-grown dramatic genres, the **ATELLAN FARCE, MIME** and **PANTOMIME.**

Atellan farce originated in the city of Atella, near modern Naples, and was originally improvised, built around stock scenes—usually of low-life cheating and skullduggery—and coarse character types, similar to the manner of later **COMMEDIA DELL' ARTE:** *Pappus*, the

READING THE MATERIAL THEATER

This illustration, taken from an Attic red-figure volute *krater* painted by the "Pronomos painter" c. 450 BCE, is an important document in the history of Greek theater. While it doesn't directly represent the performance of a satyr play onstage, there is much to learn from this vase painting. Look closely at the illustration: What distinctions can you make among the various figures? First, of course, many of the figures seem to be holding their theatrical masks, and several seem to be gazing at them. But among the male figures, several are bearded adult men, while a larger number are beardless, suggesting that they are younger, adolescents. What role do you think they play in the performance? One hint here may be the figure dancing in the bottom row

The Pronomos Krater

These actors, apparently in a satyr play, appear on a vase painting by the Pronomos painter. Notice that the central seated figure of Dionysus (holding the polelike *thyrsus*) is surrounded by actors holding their masks. The older, bearded actor to the right of Dionysus, wearing the lionskin over his shoulder, is

comic old man; *Maccus,* the gluttonous fool; *Bucco,* the braggart; and *Dossenus,* the hunchback. In the first century BCE, Atellan farce was scripted as well, though only 42 titles and about 140 lines remain. The Roman mime descends from a form of Greek performance as well; "mime" was the generic term for the short entertainments undertaken by itinerant troupes of men, women, and children who set up a platform stage in the market and performed various acts: singing and dancing, acrobatic and juggling skills, and dramatic skits. These companies were known by their **RICINIUM,** a square hood that could be thrown over the shaved head as a disguise, and they generally wore a patchwork jacket, tights, and the phallus. Like other forms of comedy, it seems to have had a number of stock character types; mimes were performed by both men and women, though a Roman *mima* would be recognized as little better than a prostitute, perhaps given the generally salacious character of the performances. Mimes were certainly performed earlier, but are first recorded at the *ludi Florales* in 212 BCE, where Pompilius is said to have danced during the Romans' victorious battle with the Carthaginians; the festival's fertility theme is often said to have prompted the mimes' focus on adultery and sexual adventure. Many of the dramatic mimes were on contemporary subjects and scandals, and one Roman emperor ordered mimes to include live sex acts; the intimacy and satirical element of the mimes was perhaps underlined by the fact that they were performed without masks. Their salacious reputation contributed to their stigmatization by the early Christians; for their part, the mimes often ridiculed the bizarre religious practices of this still-new and of figures: He has put on his mask, is wearing the *phallos,* and seems to have a satyr's tail. The central figure seated on the throne, with the *thyrsus* in his hand and vines growing just to the left, is labeled "Dionysus," as though the god were seated among the players (he shares the seat with his wife, Ariadne), but there are several other characters who seem to be in costume; the most identifiable is looking at his mask, wearing a full-body costume and carrying the lion-skin of Hercules. Although the illustration seems to provide some fascinating clues to the nature of theatrical performance, it is also misleading in some obvious ways: Just to the right of Ariadne is a seated female figure holding a mask. ∎

apparently playing Hercules, the protagonist of the play. The other, younger and beardless figures may compose the chorus. While Hercules holds an individualized mask, the chorus members all hold masks similar to each other, and they wear costumes suggestive of satyrs.

unfamiliar religious sect. Roman pantomime was, perhaps, closer to modern narrative ballet, usually taking a serious, mythological theme of the kind approached by tragedy; performed with masks, it gradually superseded the performance of spoken tragic drama.

As Polonius puts it in *Hamlet,* announcing the arrival and praising the versatility of the players, "Seneca cannot be too heavy, nor Plautus too light." Roman comedy and tragedy were particularly influential on the form and structure of later European drama. In the late Middle Ages and Renaissance, Roman drama was often used to teach Latin in schools and universities, giving rise to generations of playwrights (including William Shakespeare, Christopher Marlowe and others) who found in Roman drama the plot and character types—the confusion of identities, the young lovers, the bitter old man, the tricky servant, the braggart soldier in comedy; the passionate tirade and bloody climax in tragedy—for their own contemporary plays. Shakespeare's *The Comedy of Errors* baldly rewrites Plautus' *Brothers Menaechmus,* and the gruesome events of his *Titus Andronicus*—the hero's daughter is raped, has her hands amputated and tongue cut out; other characters are variously dismembered, and the rapist sons are served up to their mother baked in a pie—are usually attributed to Seneca's example. Since the sixteenth century, Seneca's tragedies have continued to have a literary descent, producing adaptations by some of the twentieth century's greatest writers, notably the poet Ted Hughes and the playwright Caryl Churchill.

Roman Drama in Performance History

Sophocles

Like Aeschylus, Sophocles (c. 496–406 BCE) had an important career in the civic life of Athens as well as in the theater. He was treasurer for the Athenian imperial league, and served as one of ten generals who led a campaign against Samos, an island threatening to secede from the Athenian alliance. In 411 BCE, he was appointed to a committee called to examine Athens' disastrous military campaign in Sicily. Sophocles' greatest achievements, though, were in the theater. Sophocles was responsible for introducing a third actor into dramatic performance, an innovation rapidly imitated by other playwrights, including Aeschylus and Euripides. He also enlarged the size of the chorus from twelve to fifteen. Sophocles won his first victory, against Aeschylus, in 468 BCE; he was victorious twenty-four times in his career and never finished lower than second in the dramatic competition. Of the 120 plays attributed to Sophocles, only seven survive: *Ajax, Trachiniae, Antigone, Oedipus the King, Electra, Philoctetes,* and *Oedipus at Colonus.* Fragments of a satyr play, *The Trackers,* also remain.

The three "Theban" plays—*Antigone, Oedipus the King,* and *Oedipus at Colonus*—are thematically related, but, unlike *The Oresteia* of Aeschylus, were not composed as a trilogy. *Antigone,* a play about Oedipus' daughters after his banishment from Thebes, was composed about 441 BCE; *Oedipus the King* was first produced sometime shortly after the declaration of war with Sparta in 431 BCE; and *Oedipus at Colonus* was first produced after Sophocles' death and Athens' defeat.

Oedipus the King

Oedipus the King is framed by two acts of identification, recognition, and acknowledgment. The action of the play is about the deepening and horrible understanding of what it means for the hero to recognize who he is—what it means to *be* Oedipus.

In *The Poetics,* written nearly a century later (about 335 BCE), Aristotle frequently refers to *Oedipus the King* as a definitive example of the form and purpose of tragedy. Modern audiences, though, sometimes find the play baffling, in part because the prophecy delivered to Oedipus' parents, Laius and Jocasta—that their son will murder his father and marry his mother—seems to rob Oedipus of the ability to act, to decide his fate through his own deeds. The tension between destiny and discovery is central to the play; to understand it, we should pay attention to the function of the oracle at Delphi both in the Greek world and in Oedipus the King. The Greeks consulted the oracle at Delphi on a variety of matters, ranging from personal decisions to problems of state. For example, in the play, Laius and Jocasta have consulted the oracle to learn the future of their child, and Oedipus turns to Delphi to find out whether Polybus is actually his father. At the same time, the oracle also speaks on important public issues—about the cause of the plague afflicting Thebes and about what should be done with Oedipus after his blinding. Sophocles lived in an era of increasing skepticism, when political conflict and the rise of rhetorical training raised questions about the nature and significance of truth—even the truth of oracular revelation. It is not surprising that characters in *Oedipus the King* frequently question such prophecy or have difficulty learning how to accept and interpret it, as when Oedipus flees Corinth to avoid murdering his father.

Critical as the prophecy is to Oedipus' life, Oedipus' deeds are really at issue in *Oedipus the King.* Sophocles chose to begin and end his drama on the day of Oedipus' discovery of his own identity. The play focuses less on the prophecy than on the course and meaning of Oedipus' actions, on *how* he comes to recognize himself as the criminal he seeks. Oedipus arrives at this recognition only through an extraordinary effort of action and decision: Oedipus calls for the exile of Laius' murderer; he insults Tiresias when the prophet tries to evade his questions; he accuses Creon; he threatens the old shepherd with torture in order to learn the truth of his birth. The oracle says that Oedipus will commit his terrible crimes of murder and incest, but Oedipus *chooses* the relentless, brutal pursuit of the truth himself, even to the point of his own incrimination and destruction. The tragedy of *Oedipus the King* lies in the fearsome turn of events caused by Oedipus' inflexible compulsion to discover the truth.

Aristotle considers the hero of tragedy at some length, in terms that are at once compelling and confusing, particularly in the case of Oedipus. Aristotle suggests in *The Poetics* that the hero of tragedy should be "a man who is neither a paragon of virtue and justice nor undergoes the change to misfortune through any real badness or wickedness but because of some mistake," a description that leads some to look for the cause of this error within Oedipus' character, in a so-called tragic flaw. But, in fact, when he says that the character's "mistake"—or **HAMARTIA**—is not the result of "any real badness or wickedness," Aristotle seems to deny that the hero's downfall is the effect of any moral "flaw" at all. It might help us to remember that to his audience, Oedipus may have seemed to share some typically "Athenian" characteristics. Oedipus' passion for inquiry, his abrupt decisiveness, and his impulsive desire to act were seen as the stereotypical traits of Athenian citizens and of Athens as a city. Far from being "flaws," these are just the qualities that made Oedipus (and Athens) successful. What is "tragic" about Oedipus' fate in *Oedipus the King* is the way that his own surest strengths—the aggressive, pragmatic qualities that enabled him to outwit the Sphinx—lead, on this one occasion, to his destruction. Oedipus' "mistake" is neither a moral failing nor a deed that he might have avoided; it is simply that he is Oedipus and acts like Oedipus—intelligent, masterful, assertive, impatient, impulsive. The tragedy lies in the way that acting like Oedipus leads him, as it has always led him in the past, to the discovery of the truth he seeks, this time with ruinous consequences.

© T. Charles Erickson

This production of Sophocles' *Oedipus the King* adapts the ritualized elements of Greek theater to a modern African setting.

Oedipus The King

Sophocles

TRANSLATED BY ROBERT FAGLES

CHARACTERS

OEDIPUS, *king of Thebes*
A PRIEST *of Zeus*
CREON, *brother of Jocasta*
A CHORUS *of Theban citizens
and their* LEADER
TIRESIAS, *a blind prophet*
JOCASTA, *the queen, wife of
Oedipus*

A MESSENGER *from Corinth*
A SHEPHERD
A MESSENGER *from inside the
palace*
ANTIGONE, ISMENE, *daughters
of Oedipus and Jocasta*
GUARDS *and* ATTENDANTS
PRIESTS *of Thebes*

TIME AND SCENE: *The royal house of Thebes. Double doors
dominate the façade; a stone altar stands at the center of the stage.*

Many years have passed since OEDIPUS *solved the riddle of the
Sphinx and ascended the throne of Thebes, and now a plague has
struck the city. A procession of* PRIESTS *enters; suppliants, broken
and despondent, they carry branches wound in wool and lay them
on the altar.*

The doors open. GUARDS *assemble.* OEDIPUS *comes forward,
majestic but for a telltale limp, and slowly views the condition of
his people.*

OEDIPUS: Oh my children, the new blood of ancient Thebes,
    why are you here? Huddling at my altar,
    praying before me, your branches wound in wool.
    Our city reeks with the smoke of burning incense,
5   rings with cries for the Healer and wailing for the dead.
    I thought it wrong, my children, to hear the truth
    from others, messengers. Here I am myself—
    you all know me, the world knows my fame:
    I am Oedipus.

(*Helping a* PRIEST *to his feet.*)

                        Speak up, old man. Your years,
10   your dignity—you should speak for the others.
    Why here and kneeling, what preys upon you so?
    Some sudden fear? some strong desire?
    You can trust me. I am ready to help,
    I'll do anything. I would be blind to misery
15   not to pity my people kneeling at my feet.
PRIEST: O Oedipus, king of the land, our greatest power!
    You see us before you now, men of all ages
    clinging to your altars. Here are boys,
    still too weak to fly from the nest,
20   and here the old, bowed down with the years,
    the holy ones—a priest of Zeus myself—and here
    the picked, unmarried men, the young hope of Thebes.
    And all the rest, your great family gathers now,
    branches wreathed, massing in the squares,
25   kneeling before the two temples of queen Athena
    or the river-shrine where the embers glow and die
    and Apollo sees the future in the ashes.
                        Our city—
    look around you, see with your own eyes
    our ship pitches wildly, cannot lift her head
30   from the depths, the red waves of death . . .
    Thebes is dying. A blight on the fresh crops
    and the rich pastures, cattle sicken and die,
    and the women die in labor, children stillborn,
    and the plague, the fiery god of fever hurls down
    on the city, his lightning slashing through us—   35
    raging plague in all its vengeance, devastating
    the house of Cadmus! And black Death luxuriates
    in the raw, wailing miseries of Thebes.

    Now we pray to you. You cannot equal the gods,
    your children know that, bending at your altar.   40
    But we do rate you first of men,
    both in the common crises of our lives
    and face-to-face encounters with the gods.
    You freed us from the Sphinx, you came to Thebes
    and cut us loose from the bloody tribute we had paid   45
    that harsh, brutal singer. We taught you nothing,
    no skill, no extra knowledge, still you triumphed.
    A god was with you, so they say, and we believe it—
    you lifted up our lives.
                        So now again,
    Oedipus, king, we bend to you, your power—   50
    we implore you, all of us on our knees:
    find us strength, rescue! Perhaps you've heard
    the voice of a god or something from other men,
    Oedipus . . . what do you know?
    The man of experience—you see it every day—   55
    his plans will work in a crisis, his first of all.

    Act now—we beg you, best of men, raise up our city!
    Act, defend yourself, your former glory!
    Your country calls you savior now
    for your zeal, your action years ago.   60
    Never let us remember of your reign:
    you helped us stand, only to fall once more.
    Oh raise up our city, set us on our feet.
    The omens were good that day you brought us joy—
    be the same man today!   65
    Rule our land, you know you have the power,
    but rule a land of the living, not a wasteland.
    Ship and towered city are nothing, stripped of men
    alive within it, living all as one.
OEDIPUS: My children,
    I pity you. I see—how could I fail to see   70
    what longings bring you here? Well I know
    you are sick to death, all of you,
    but sick as you are, not one is sick as I.

75   Your pain strikes each of you alone, each
      in the confines of himself, no other. But my spirit
      grieves for the city, for myself and all of you.
      I wasn't asleep, dreaming. You haven't wakened me—
      I have wept through the nights, you must know that,
      groping, laboring over many paths of thought.
80   After a painful search I found one cure:
      I acted at once. I sent Creon,
      my wife's own brother, to Delphi—
      Apollo the Prophet's oracle—to learn
      what I might do or say to save our city.

85   Today's the day. When I count the days gone by
      it torments me . . . what is he doing?
      Strange, he's late, he's gone too long.
      But once he returns, then, then I'll be a traitor
      if I do not do all the god makes clear.
90 PRIEST: Timely words. The men over there
      are signaling—Creon's just arriving.
      OEDIPUS: (*Sighting* CREON, *then turning to the altar.*) Lord Apollo,
      let him come with a lucky word of rescue,
      shining like his eyes!
      PRIEST: Welcome news, I think—he's crowned, look,
95   and the laurel wreath is bright with berries.
      OEDIPUS: We'll soon see. He's close enough to hear

(*Enter* CREON *from the side; his face is shaded with a wreath.*)

      Creon, prince, my kinsman, what do you bring us?
      What message from the god?
      CREON: Good news.
      I tell you even the hardest things to bear,
100   if they should turn out well, all would be well.
      OEDIPUS: Of course, but what were the god's *words*? There's
      no hope
      and nothing to fear in what you've said so far.
      CREON: If you want my report in the presence of these
      people . . .

(*Pointing to the* PRIESTS *while drawing* OEDIPUS *toward the palace.*)

      I'm ready now, or we might go inside.
      OEDIPUS: Speak out,
105   speak to us all. I grieve for these, my people,
      far more than I fear for my own life.
      CREON: Very well,
      I will tell you what I heard from the god.
      Apollo commands us—he was quite clear—
      "Drive the corruption from the land,
110   don't harbor it any longer, past all cure,
      don't nurse it in your soil—root it out!"
      OEDIPUS: How can we cleanse ourselves—what rites?
      What's the source of the trouble?
      CREON: Banish the man, or pay back blood with blood.
115   Murder sets the plague-storm on the city.
      OEDIPUS: Whose murder?
      Whose fate does Apollo bring to light?
      CREON: Our leader,
      my lord, was once a man named Laius,
      before you came and put us straight on course.
      OEDIPUS: I know—
      or so I've heard. I never saw the man myself.

CREON: Well, he was killed, and Apollo commands us now—   120
      he could not be more clear,
      "Pay the killers back—whoever is responsible."
OEDIPUS: Where on earth are they? Where to find it now,
      the trail of the ancient guilt so hard to trace?
CREON: "Here in Thebes," he said.   125
      Whatever is sought for can be caught, you know,
      whatever is neglected slips away.
OEDIPUS: But where,
      in the palace, the fields or foreign soil,
      where did Laius meet his bloody death?
CREON: He went to consult an oracle, Apollo said,   130
      and he set out and never came home again.
OEDIPUS: No messenger, no fellow-traveler saw what happened?
      Someone to cross-examine?
CREON: No,
      they were all killed but one. He escaped,
      terrified, he could tell us nothing clearly,   135
      nothing of what he saw—just one thing.
OEDIPUS: What's that?
      One thing could hold the key to it all,
      a small beginning give us grounds for hope.
CREON: He said thieves attacked them—a whole band,
      not single-handed, cut King Laius down.   140
OEDIPUS: A thief,
      so daring, so wild, he'd kill a king? Impossible,
      unless conspirators paid him off in Thebes.
CREON: We suspected as much. But with Laius dead
      no leader appeared to help us in our troubles.
OEDIPUS: Trouble? Your *king* was murdered—royal blood!   145
      What stopped you from tracking down the killer
      then and there?
CREON: The singing, riddling Sphinx.
      She . . . persuaded us to let the mystery go
      and concentrate on what lay at our feet.
OEDIPUS: No,
      I'll start again—I'll bring it all to light myself!   150
      Apollo is right, and so are you, Creon,
      to turn our attention back to the murdered man.
      Now you have *me* to fight for you, you'll see:
      I am the land's avenger by all rights,
      and Apollo's champion too.   155
      But not to assist some distant kinsman, no,
      for my own sake I'll rid us of this corruption.
      Whoever killed the king may decide to kill me too,
      with the same violent hand—by avenging Laius
      I defend myself.   160

(*To the* PRIESTS.)

                  Quickly, my children.
Up from the steps, take up your branches now.

(*To the* GUARDS.)

      One of you summon the city here before us,
      tell them I'll do everything. God help us,
      we will see our triumph—or our fall.

(OEDIPUS *and* CREON *enter the palace, followed by the* GUARDS.)

165   PRIEST: Rise, my sons. The kindness we came for
    Oedipus volunteers himself.
    Apollo has sent his word, his oracle—
    Come down, Apollo, save us, stop the plague.

(*The* PRIESTS *rise, remove their branches, and exit to the side. Enter a* CHORUS, *the citizens of Thebes, who have not heard the news that* CREON *brings. They march around the altar, chanting.*)

CHORUS: Zeus!
    Great welcome voice of Zeus, what do you bring?
170   What word from the gold vaults of Delphi
    comes to brilliant Thebes? Racked with terror—
               terror shakes my heart
    and I cry your wild cries, Apollo, Healer of Delos
    I worship you in dread . . . what now, what is your price?
175   some new sacrifice? some ancient rite from the past
    come round again each spring?—
          what will you bring to birth?
    Tell me, child of golden Hope
        warm voice that never dies!

180   You are the first I call, daughter of Zeus
    deathless Athena—I call your sister Artemis,
    heart of the market place enthroned in glory,
               guardian of our earth—
    I call Apollo, Archer astride the thunderheads of heaven—
185   O triple shield against death, shine before me now!
    If ever, once in the past, you stopped some ruin
    launched against our walls
        you hurled the flame of pain
    far, far from Thebes—you gods
190   come now, come down once more!
                No, no
    the miseries numberless, grief on grief, no end—
    too much to bear, we are all dying
    O my people . . .
        Thebes like a great army dying
195   and there is no sword of thought to save us, no
    and the fruits of our famous earth, they will not ripen
    no and the women cannot scream their pangs to birth—
    screams for the Healer, children dead in the womb
        and life on life goes down
200   you can watch them go
    like seabirds winging west, outracing the day's fire
    down the horizon, irresistibly
        streaking on to the shores of Evening
                Death
    so many deaths, numberless deaths on deaths, no end—
205   Thebes is dying, look, her children
    stripped of pity . . .
        generations strewn on the ground
    unburied, unwept, the dead spreading death
    and the young wives and gray-haired mothers with them
210   cling to the altars, trailing in from all over the city—
    Thebes, city of death, one long cortege
        and the suffering rises
           wails for mercy rise
    and the wild hymn for the Healer blazes out
215   clashing with our sobs our cries of mourning—
        O golden daughter of god, send rescue
    radiant as the kindness in your eyes!

Drive him back!—the fever, the god of death
            that raging god of war
not armored in bronze, not shielded now, he burns me,   220
battle cries in the onslaught burning on—
O rout him from our borders!
Sail him, blast him out to the Sea-queen's chamber
          the black Atlantic gulfs
    or the northern harbor, death to all   225
where the Thracian surf comes crashing.
Now what the night spares he comes by day and kills—
the god of death.
        O lord of the stormcloud,
you who twirl the lightning, Zeus, Father,
thunder Death to nothing!   230

Apollo, lord of the light, I beg you—
    whip your longbow's golden cord
showering arrows on our enemies—shafts of power
champions strong before us rushing on!

Artemis, Huntress,   235
torches flaring over the eastern ridges—
        ride Death down in pain!

God of the headdress gleaming gold, I cry to you—
your name and ours are one, Dionysus—
    come with your face aflame with wine
          your raving women's cries   240
    your army on the march! Come with the lightning
come with torches blazing, eyes ablaze with glory!
Burn that god of death that all gods hate!

(OEDIPUS *enters from the palace to address the* CHORUS, *as if addressing the entire city of Thebes.*)

OEDIPUS: You pray to the gods? Let me grant your prayers.
    Come, listen to me—do what the plague demands: 245
    you'll find relief and lift your head from the depths.

I will speak out now as a stranger to the story,
a stranger to the crime. If I'd been present then,
there would have been no mystery, no long hunt   250
without a clue in hand. So now, counted
a native Theban years after the murder,
to all of Thebes I make this proclamation:
if any one of you knows who murdered Laius,
the son of Labdacus, I order him to reveal   255
the whole truth to me. Nothing to fear,
even if he must denounce himself,
let him speak up
and so escape the brunt of the charge—
he will suffer no unbearable punishment,   260
nothing worse than exile, totally unharmed.

(OEDIPUS *pauses, waiting for a reply.*)

               Next,
if anyone knows the murderer is a stranger,
a man from alien soil, come, speak up.
I will give him a handsome reward, and lay up   265
gratitude in my heart for him besides.

(*Silence again, no reply.*)

But if you keep silent, if anyone panicking,
trying to shield himself or friend or kin,
rejects my offer, then hear what I will do.
I order you, every citizen of the state
270 where I hold throne and power: banish this man—
whoever he may be—never shelter him, never
speak a word to him, never make him partner
to your prayers, your victims burned to the gods.
Never let the holy water touch his hands.
275 Drive him out, each of you, from every home.
He is the plague, the heart of our corruption,
as Apollo's oracle has just revealed to me.
So I honor my obligations:
I fight for the god and for the murdered man.

280 Now my curse on the murderer. Whoever he is,
a lone man unknown in his crime
or one among many, let that man drag out
his life in agony, step by painful step—
I curse myself as well . . . if by any chance
285 he proves to be an intimate of our house,
here at my hearth, with my full knowledge,
may the curse I just called down on him strike me!

These are your orders: perform them to the last.
I command you, for my sake, for Apollo's, for this country
290 blasted root and branch by the angry heavens.
Even if god had never urged you on to act,
how could you leave the crime uncleansed so long?
A man so noble—your king, brought down in blood—
you should have searched. But I am the king now,
295 I hold the throne that he held then, possess his bed
and a wife who shares our seed . . . why, our seed
might be the same, children born of the same mother
might have created blood-bonds between us
if his hope of offspring had not met disaster—
300 but fate swooped at his head and cut him short.
So I will fight for him as if he were my father,
stop at nothing, search the world
to lay my hands on the man who shed his blood,
the son of Labdacus descended of Polydorus,
305 Cadmus of old and Agenor, founder of the line:
their power and mine are one.

                        Oh dear gods,
my curse on those who disobey these orders!
Let no crops grow out of the earth for them—
shrivel their women, kill their sons,
310 burn them to nothing in this plague
that hits us now, or something even worse.
But you, loyal men of Thebes who approve my actions,
may our champion, Justice, may all the gods
be with us, fight beside us to the end!
315 LEADER: In the grip of your curse, my king, I swear
I'm not the murderer, I cannot point him out.
As for the search, Apollo pressed it on us—
he should name the killer.

OEDIPUS: Quite right,
but to force the gods to act against their will
320 no man has the power.

LEADER: Then if I might mention
the next best thing . . .

OEDIPUS: The third best too—
don't hold back, say it.

LEADER: I still believe . . .
Lord Tiresias sees with the eyes of Lord Apollo.
Anyone searching for the truth, my king,
might learn it from the prophet, clear as day.   325

OEDIPUS: I've not been slow with that. On Creon's cue
I sent the escorts, twice, within the hour.
I'm surprised he isn't here.

LEADER: We need him—
without him we have nothing but old, useless rumors.

OEDIPUS: Which rumors? I'll search out every word.   330

LEADER: Laius was killed, they say, by certain travelers.

OEDIPUS: I know—but no one can find the murderer.

LEADER: If the man has a trace of fear in him
he won't stay silent long,
not with your curses ringing in his ears.   335

OEDIPUS: He didn't flinch at murder,
he'll never flinch at words.

(*Enter* TIRESIAS, *the blind prophet, led by a boy with escorts in attendance. He remains at a distance.*)

LEADER: Here is the one who will convict him, look,
they bring him on at last, the seer, the man of god.
The truth lives inside him, him alone.   340

OEDIPUS: O Tiresias,
master of all the mysteries of our life,
all you teach and all you dare not tell,
signs in the heavens, signs that walk the earth!
Blind as you are, you can feel all the more
what sickness haunts our city. You, my lord,   345
are the one shield, the one savior we can find.

We asked Apollo—perhaps the messengers
haven't told you—he sent his answer back:
"Relief from the plague can only come one way.
Uncover the murderers of Laius,   350
put them to death or drive them into exile."
So I beg you, grudge us nothing now, no voice,
no message plucked from the birds, the embers
or the other mantic ways within your grasp.
Rescue yourself, your city, rescue me—   355
rescue everything infected by the dead.
We are in your hands. For a man to help others
with all his gifts and native strength:
that is the noblest work.

TIRESIAS: How terrible—to see the truth
when the truth is only pain to him who sees!   360
I knew it well, but I put it from my mind,
else I never would have come.

OEDIPUS: What's this? Why so grim, so dire?

TIRESIAS: Just send me home. You bear your burdens,
I'll bear mine. It's better that way,   365
please believe me.

OEDIPUS: Strange response . . . unlawful,
unfriendly too to the state that bred and reared you—
you withhold the word of god.

TIRESIAS: I fail to see
that your own words are so well-timed.
I'd rather not have the same thing said of me . . .   370

OEDIPUS: For the love of god, don't turn away,
   not if you know something. We beg you,
   all of us on our knees.
TIRESIAS: None of you knows—
   and I will never reveal my dreadful secrets,
375   not to say your own.
   OEDIPUS: What? You know and you won't tell?
   You're bent on betraying us, destroying Thebes?
   TIRESIAS: I'd rather not cause pain for you or me.
   So why this . . . useless interrogation?
380   You'll get nothing from me.
   OEDIPUS: Nothing! You,
   you scum of the earth, you'd enrage a heart of stone!
   You won't talk? Nothing moves you?
   Out with it, once and for all!
   TIRESIAS: You criticize my temper . . . unaware
385   of the one *you* live with, you revile me.
   OEDIPUS: Who could restrain his anger hearing you?
   What outrage—you spurn the city!
   TIRESIAS: What will come will come.
   Even if I shroud it all in silence.
390   OEDIPUS: What will come? You're bound to *tell* me that.
   TIRESIAS: I will say no more. Do as you like, build your anger
   to whatever pitch you please, rage your worst—
   OEDIPUS: Oh I'll let loose, I have such fury in me—
   now I see it all. You helped hatch the plot,
395   you did the work, yes, short of killing him
   with your own hands—and given eyes I'd say
   you did the killing single-handed!
   TIRESIAS: Is that so!
   I charge you, then, submit to that decree
   you just laid down: from this day onward
400   speak to no one, not these citizens, not myself.
   You are the curse, the corruption of the land!
   OEDIPUS: You, shameless—
   aren't you appalled to start up such a story?
   You think you can get away with this?
   TIRESIAS: I have already.
405   The truth with all its power lives inside me.
   OEDIPUS: Who primed you for this? Not your prophet's trade.
   TIRESIAS: You did, you forced me, twisted it out of me.
   OEDIPUS: What? Say it again—I'll understand it better.
   TIRESIAS: Didn't you understand, just now?
410   Or are you tempting me to talk?
   OEDIPUS: No, I can't say I grasped your meaning.
   Out with it, again!
   TIRESIAS: I say you are the murderer you hunt.
   OEDIPUS: That obscenity, twice—by god, you'll pay.
415   TIRESIAS: Shall I say more, so you can really rage?
   OEDIPUS: Much as you want. Your words are nothing—
   futile.
   TIRESIAS: You cannot imagine . . . I tell you,
   you and your loved ones live together in infamy,
   you cannot see how far you've gone in guilt.
420   OEDIPUS: You think you can keep this up and never suffer?
   TIRESIAS: Indeed, if the truth has any power.
   OEDIPUS: It does
   but not for you, old man. You've lost your power,
   stone-blind, stone-deaf—senses, eyes blind as stone!
   TIRESIAS: I pity you, flinging at me the very insults
425   each man here will fling at you so soon.

OEDIPUS: Blind,
   lost in the night, endless night that nursed you!
   You can't hurt me or anyone else who sees the light—
   you can never touch me.
TIRESIAS: True, it is not your fate
   to fall at my hands. Apollo is quite enough,
   and he will take some pains to work this out.   430
OEDIPUS: Creon! Is this conspiracy his or yours?
TIRESIAS: Creon is not your downfall, no, you are your own.
OEDIPUS: O power—
   wealth and empire, skill outstripping skill
   in the heady rivalries of life,
   what envy lurks inside you! Just for this,   435
   the crown the city gave me—I never sought it,
   they laid it in my hands—for this alone, Creon,
   the soul of trust, my loyal friend from the start
   steals against me . . . so hungry to overthrow me
   he sets this wizard on me, this scheming quack,   440
   this fortune-teller peddling lies, eyes peeled
   for his own profit—seer blind in his craft!

Come here, you pious fraud. Tell me,
   when did you ever prove yourself a prophet?
   When the Sphinx, that chanting Fury kept her   445
   deathwatch here,
   why silent then, not a word to set our people free?
   There was a riddle, not for some passer-by to solve—
   it cried out for a prophet. Where were you?
   Did you rise to the crisis? Not a word,
   you and your birds, your gods—nothing.   450
   No, but I came by, Oedipus the ignorant,
   I stopped the Sphinx! With no help from the birds,
   the flight of my own intelligence hit the mark.

And this is the man you'd try to overthrow?
   You think you'll stand by Creon when he's king?   455
   You and the great mastermind—
   you'll pay in tears, I promise you, for this,
   this witch-hunt. If you didn't look so senile
   the lash would teach you what your scheming means!
LEADER: I would suggest his words were spoken in anger,   460
   Oedipus . . . yours too, and it isn't what we need.
   The best solution to the oracle, the riddle
   posed by god—we should look for that.
TIRESIAS: You are the king no doubt, but in one respect,
   at least, I am your equal: the right to reply.   465
   I claim that privilege too.
   I am not your slave. I serve Apollo.
   I don't need Creon to speak for me in public.
                    So,
   you mock my blindness? Let me tell you this.
   You with your precious eyes,   470
   you're blind to the corruption of your life,
   to the house you live in, those you live with—
   who *are* your parents? Do you know? All unknowing
   you are the scourge of your own flesh and blood,
   the dead below the earth and the living here above,   475
   and the double lash of your mother and your father's
   curse
   will whip you from this land one day, their footfall
   treading you down in terror, darkness shrouding
   your eyes that now can see the light!

Soon, soon
480   you'll scream aloud—what haven won't reverberate?
What rock of Cithaeron won't scream back in echo?
That day you learn the truth about your marriage,
the wedding-march that sang you into your halls,
the lusty voyage home to the fatal harbor!
485   And a crowd of other horrors you'd never dream
will level you with yourself and all your children.

There. Now smear us with insults—Creon, myself
and every word I've said. No man will ever
be rooted from the earth as brutally as you.
490   OEDIPUS: Enough! Such filth from him? Insufferable—
what, still alive? Get out—
faster, back where you came from—vanish!
TIRESIAS: I would never have come if you hadn't called me here.
OEDIPUS: If I thought you would blurt out such absurdities,
495   you'd have died waiting before I'd had you summoned.
TIRESIAS: Absurd, am I! To you, not to your parents:
the ones who bore you found me sane enough.
OEDIPUS: Parents—who? Wait . . . who is my father?
TIRESIAS: This day will bring your birth and your destruction.
500   OEDIPUS: Riddles—all you can say are riddles, murk and
darkness.
TIRESIAS: Ah, but aren't you the best man alive at solving riddles?
OEDIPUS: Mock me for that, go on, and you'll reveal my greatness.
TIRESIAS: Your great good fortune, true, it was your ruin.
OEDIPUS: Not if I saved the city—what do I care?
505   TIRESIAS: Well then, I'll be going.

(*To his* ATTENDANT.)

Take me home, boy.
OEDIPUS: Yes, take him away. You're a nuisance here.
Out of the way, the irritation's gone.

(*Turning his back on* TIRESIAS, *moving toward the palace.*)

TIRESIAS: I will go,
once I have said what I came here to say.
I will never shrink from the anger in your eyes—
510   you can't destroy me. Listen to me closely:
the man you've sought so long, proclaiming,
cursing up and down, the murderer of Laius—
he is here. A stranger,
you may think, who lives among you,
515   he soon will be revealed a native Theban
but he will take no joy in the revelation.
Blind who now has eyes, beggar who now is rich,
he will grope his way toward a foreign soil,
a stick tapping before him step by step.

(OEDIPUS *enters the palace.*)

520   Revealed at last, brother and father both
to the children he embraces, to his mother
son and husband both—he sowed the loins
his father sowed, he spilled his father's blood!

Go in and reflect on that, solve that.
525   And if you find I've lied
from this day onward call the prophet blind.

(TIRESIAS *and the boy exit to the side.*)

CHORUS: Who—
who is the man the voice of god denounces
resounding out of the rocky gorge of Delphi?
The horror too dark to tell,
whose ruthless bloody hands have done the work?   530
His time has come to fly
to outrace the stallions of the storm
his feet a streak of speed—
Cased in armor, Apollo son of the Father
lunges on him, lightning-bolts afire!   535
And the grim unerring Furies
closing for the kill.
Look,
the word of god has just come blazing
flashing off Parnassus' snowy heights!
That man who left no trace—   540
after him, hunt him down with all our strength!
Now under bristling timber
up through rocks and caves he stalks
like the wild mountain bull—
cut off from men, each step an agony, frenzied, racing blind   545
but he cannot outrace the dread voices of Delphi
ringing out of the heart of Earth,
the dark wings beating around him shrieking doom
the doom that never dies, the terror—
The skilled prophet scans the birds and shatters me with   550
terror!
I can't accept him, can't deny him, don't know what to say,
I'm lost, and the wings of dark foreboding beating—
I cannot see what's come, what's still to come . . .
and what could breed a blood feud between
Laius' house and the son of Polybus?   555
I know of nothing, not in the past and not now,
no charge to bring against our king, no cause
to attack his fame that rings throughout Thebes—
not without proof—not for the ghost of Laius,
not to avenge a murder gone without a trace.   560

Zeus and Apollo know, they know, the great masters
of all the dark and depth of human life.
But whether a mere man can know the truth,
whether a seer can fathom more than I—
there is no test, no certain proof   565
though matching skill for skill
a man can outstrip a rival. No, not till I see
these charges proved will I side with his accusers.
We saw him then, when the she-hawk swept against him,
saw with our own eyes his skill, his brilliant triumph—   570
there was the test—he was the joy of Thebes!
Never will I convict my king, never in my heart.

(Enter CREON *from the side.*)

CREON: My fellow-citizens, I hear King Oedipus
levels terrible charges at me. I had to come.
I resent it deeply. If, in the present crisis,   575
he thinks he suffers any abuse from me,
anything I've done or said that offers him
the slightest injury, why, I've no desire
to linger out this life, my reputation in ruins.

580 The damage I'd face from such an accusation
is nothing simple. No, there's nothing worse:
branded a traitor in the city, a traitor
to all of you and my good friends.
LEADER: True,
but a slur might have been forced out of him,
585 by anger perhaps, not any firm conviction.
CREON: The charge was made in public, wasn't it?
I put the prophet up to spreading lies?
LEADER: Such things were said . . .
I don't know with what intent, if any.
590 CREON: Was his glance steady, his mind right
when the charge was brought against me?
LEADER: I really couldn't say, I never look
to judge the ones in power.

(*The doors open.* OEDIPUS *enters.*)

                              Wait,
here's Oedipus now.
OEDIPUS: You—here? You have the gall
595 to show your face before the palace gates?
You, plotting to kill me, kill the king—
I see it all, the marauding thief himself
scheming to steal my crown and power!
                              Tell me,
in god's name, what did you take me for,
600 coward or fool, when you spun out your plot?
Your treachery—you think I'd never detect it
creeping against me in the dark? Or sensing it,
not defend myself? Aren't you the fool,
you and your high adventure. Lacking numbers,
605 powerful friends, out for the big game of empire—
you need riches, armies to bring that quarry down!
CREON: Are you quite finished? It's your turn to listen
for just as long as you've . . . instructed me.
Hear me out, then judge me on the facts.
610 OEDIPUS: You've a wicked way with words, Creon,
but I'll be slow to learn—from you.
I find you a menace, a great burden to me.
CREON: Just one thing, hear me out in this.
OEDIPUS: Just one thing,
don't tell *me* you're not the enemy, the traitor.
615 CREON: Look, if you think crude, mindless stubbornness
such a gift, you've lost your sense of balance.
OEDIPUS: If you think you can abuse a kinsman,
then escape the penalty, you're insane.
CREON: Fair enough, I grant you. But this injury
620 you say I've done you, what is it?
OEDIPUS: Did you induce me, yes or no,
to send for that sanctimonious prophet?
CREON: I did. And I'd do the same again.
OEDIPUS: All right then, tell me, how long is it now
625 since Laius . . .
CREON: Laius—what did *he* do?
OEDIPUS: Vanished,
swept from sight, murdered in his tracks.
CREON: The count of the years would run you far back . . .
OEDIPUS: And that far back, was the prophet at his trade?
CREON: Skilled as he is today, and just as honored.

OEDIPUS: Did he ever refer to me then, at that time?   630
CREON: No,
never, at least, when I was in his presence.
OEDIPUS: But you did investigate the murder, didn't you?
CREON: We did our best, of course, discovered nothing.
OEDIPUS: But the great seer never accused me then—why not?
CREON: I don't know. And when I don't, *I* keep quiet.   635
OEDIPUS: You do know this, you'd tell it too—
if you had a shred of decency.
CREON: What?
If I know, I won't hold back.
OEDIPUS: Simply this:
if the two of you had never put heads together,
we would never have heard about *my* killing Laius.   640
CREON: If that's what he says . . . well, you know best.
But now I have a right to learn from you
as you just learned from me.
OEDIPUS: Learn your fill,
you never will convict me of the murder.
CREON: Tell me, you're married to my sister, aren't you?   645
OEDIPUS: A genuine discovery—there's no denying that.
CREON: And you rule the land with her, with equal power?
OEDIPUS: She receives from me whatever she desires.
CREON: And I am the third, all of us are equals?
OEDIPUS: Yes, and it's there you show your stripes—   650
you betray a kinsman.
CREON: Not at all.
Not if you see things calmly, rationally,
as I do. Look at it this way first:
who in his right mind would rather rule
and live in anxiety than sleep in peace?   655
Particularly if he enjoys the same authority.
Not I, I'm not the man to yearn for kingship,
not with a king's power in my hands. Who would?
No one with any sense of self-control.
Now, as it is, you offer me all I need,   660
not a fear in the world. But if I wore the crown . . .
there'd be many painful duties to perform,
hardly to my taste.
                    How could kingship
please me more than influence, power
without a qualm? I'm not that deluded yet,   665
to reach for anything but privilege outright,
profit free and clear.
Now all men sing my praises, all salute me,
now all who request your favors curry mine.
I am their best hope: success rests in me.   670
Why give up that, I ask you, and borrow trouble?
A man of sense, someone who sees things clearly
would never resort to treason.
No, I have no lust for conspiracy in me,
nor could I ever suffer one who does.   675

Do you want proof? Go to Delphi yourself,
examine the oracle and see if I've reported
the message word-for-word. This too:
if you detect that I and the clairvoyant
have plotted anything in common, arrest me,   680
execute me. Not on the strength of one vote,
two in this case, mine as well as yours.

But don't convict me on sheer unverified surmise.
How wrong it is to take the good for bad,
685   purely at random, or take the bad for good.
But reject a friend, a kinsman? I would as soon
tear out the life within us, priceless life itself.
You'll learn this well, without fail, in time.
Time alone can bring the just man to light—
690   the criminal you can spot in one short day.
LEADER: Good advice,
   my lord, for anyone who wants to avoid disaster.
   Those who jump to conclusions may go wrong.
OEDIPUS: When my enemy moves against me quickly,
   plots in secret, I move quickly too, I must,
695   I plot and pay him back. Relax my guard a moment,
   waiting his next move—he wins his objective,
   I lose mine.
CREON: What do you want?
   You want me banished?
OEDIPUS: No, I want you dead.
CREON: Just to show how ugly a grudge can . . .
OEDIPUS: So,
700   still stubborn? you don't think I'm serious?
CREON: I think you're insane.
OEDIPUS: Quite sane—in my behalf.
CREON: Not just as much in mine?
OEDIPUS: You—my mortal enemy?
CREON: What if you're wholly wrong?
OEDIPUS: No matter—I must rule.
CREON: Not if you rule unjustly.
OEDIPUS: Hear him, Thebes, my city!
705 CREON: My city too, not yours alone!
LEADER: Please, my lords.

(*Enter* JOCASTA *from the palace.*)

              Look, Jocasta's coming,
   and just in time too. With her help
   you must put this fighting of yours to rest.
JOCASTA: Have you no sense? Poor misguided men,
710   such shouting—why this public outburst?
   Aren't you ashamed, with the land so sick,
   to stir up private quarrels?

(*To* OEDIPUS.)

   Into the palace now. And Creon, you go home.
   Why make such a furor over nothing?
715 CREON: My sister, it's dreadful . . . Oedipus, your husband,
   he's bent on a choice of punishments for me,
   banishment from the fatherland or death.
OEDIPUS: Precisely. I caught him in the act, Jocasta,
   plotting, about to stab me in the back.
720 CREON: Never—curse me, let me die and be damned
   if I've done you any wrong you charge me with.
JOCASTA: Oh god, believe it, Oedipus,
   honor the solemn oath he swears to heaven.
   Do it for me, for the sake of all your people.

(*The* CHORUS *begins to chant.*)

725 CHORUS: Believe it, be sensible
     give way, my king, I beg you!

OEDIPUS: What do you want from me, concessions?
CHORUS: Respect him—he's been no fool in the past
   and now he's strong with the oath he swears to god.
OEDIPUS: You know what you're asking?   730
CHORUS: I do.
OEDIPUS: Then out with it!
CHORUS: The man's your friend, your kin, he's under oath—
   don't cast him out, disgraced,
   branded with guilt on the strength of hearsay only.
OEDIPUS: Know full well, if that is what you want
   you want me dead or banished from the land.   735
CHORUS: Never—
   no, by the blazing Sun, first god of the heavens!
     Stripped of the gods, stripped of loved ones,
   let me die by inches if that ever crossed my mind.
   But the heart inside me sickens, dies as the land dies
   and now on top of the old griefs you pile this,   740
   your fury—both of you!
OEDIPUS: Then let him go,
   even if it does lead to my ruin, my death
   or my disgrace, driven from Thebes for life.
   It's you, not him I pity—your words move me.
   He, wherever he goes, my hate goes with him.   745
CREON: Look at you, sullen in yielding, brutal in your rage—
   you will go too far. It's perfect justice:
   natures like yours are hardest on themselves.
OEDIPUS: Then leave me alone—get out!
CREON: I'm going.
   You're wrong, so wrong. These men know I'm right.   750

(*Exit to the side. The* CHORUS *turns to* JOCASTA.)

CHORUS: Why do you hesitate, my lady
    why not help him in?
JOCASTA: Tell me what's happened first.
CHORUS: Loose, ignorant talk started dark suspicions
   and a sense of injustice cut deeply too.   755
JOCASTA: On both sides?
CHORUS: Oh yes.
JOCASTA: What did they say?
CHORUS: Enough, please, enough! The land's so racked already
   or so it seems to me . . .
   End the trouble here, just where they left it.
OEDIPUS: You see what comes of your good intentions now?   760
   And all because you tried to blunt my anger.
CHORUS: My king,
   I've said it once, I'll say it time and again—
    I'd be insane, you know it,
   senseless, ever to turn my back on you.
   You who set our beloved land—storm-tossed, shattered—   765
   straight on course. Now again, good helmsman,
   steer us through the storm!

(*The* CHORUS *draws away, leaving* OEDIPUS *and* JOCASTA *side by side.*)

JOCASTA: For the love of god,
   Oedipus, tell me too, what is it?
   Why this rage? You're so unbending.
OEDIPUS: I will tell you. I respect you, Jocasta,   770
   much more than these men here . . .

(*Glancing at the* CHORUS.)

Creon's to blame, Creon schemes against me.
JOCASTA: Tell me clearly, how did the quarrel start?
OEDIPUS: He says I murdered Laius—I am guilty.
775 JOCASTA: How does he know? Some secret knowledge
or simple hearsay?
OEDIPUS: Oh, he sent his prophet in
to do his dirty work. You know Creon,
Creon keeps his own lips clean.
JOCASTA: A prophet?
Well then, free yourself of every charge!
780 Listen to me and learn some peace of mind:
no skill in the world,
nothing human can penetrate the future.
Here is proof, quick and to the point.

An oracle came to Laius one fine day
785 (I won't say from Apollo himself
but his underlings, his priests) and it declared
that doom would strike him down at the hands of a son,
our son, to be born of our own flesh and blood. But Laius,
so the report goes at least, was killed by strangers,
790 thieves, at a place where three roads meet . . . my son—
he wasn't three days old and the boy's father
fastened his ankles, had a henchman fling him away
on a barren, trackless mountain.
                           There, you see?
Apollo brought neither thing to pass. My baby
795 no more murdered his father than Laius suffered—
his wildest fear—death at his own son's hands.
That's how the seers and all their revelations
mapped out the future. Brush them from your mind.
Whatever the god needs and seeks
800 he'll bring to light himself, with ease.
OEDIPUS: Strange,
hearing you just now . . . my mind wandered,
my thoughts racing back and forth.
JOCASTA: What do you mean? Why so anxious, startled?
OEDIPUS: I thought I heard you say that Laius
805 was cut down at a place where three roads meet.
JOCASTA: That was the story. It hasn't died out yet.
OEDIPUS: Where did this thing happen? Be precise.
JOCASTA: A place called Phocis, where two branching roads,
one from Daulia, one from Delphi,
810 come together—a crossroads.
OEDIPUS: When? How long ago?
JOCASTA: The heralds no sooner reported Laius dead
than you appeared and they hailed you king of Thebes.
OEDIPUS: My god, my god—what have you planned to do to me?
815 JOCASTA: What, Oedipus? What haunts you so?
OEDIPUS: Not yet.
Laius—how did he look? Describe him.
Had he reached his prime?
JOCASTA: He was swarthy,
and the gray had just begun to streak his temples,
and his build . . . wasn't far from yours.
OEDIPUS: Oh no no,
820 I think I've just called down a dreadful curse
upon myself—I simply didn't know!

JOCASTA: What are you saying? I shudder to look at you.
OEDIPUS: I have a terrible fear the blind seer can see.
I'll know in a moment. One thing more—
JOCASTA: Anything,
afraid as I am—ask, I'll answer, all I can.   825
OEDIPUS: Did he go with a light or heavy escort,
several men-at-arms, like a lord, a king?
JOCASTA: There were five in the party, a herald among them,
and a single wagon carrying Laius.
OEDIPUS: Ai—
now I can see it all, clear as day.   830
Who told you all this at the time, Jocasta?
JOCASTA: A servant who reached home, the lone survivor.
OEDIPUS: So, could he still be in the palace—even now?
JOCASTA: No indeed. Soon as he returned from the scene
and saw you on the throne with Laius dead and gone,   835
he knelt and clutched my hand, pleading with me
to send him into the hinterlands, to pasture,
far as possible, out of sight of Thebes.
I sent him away. Slave though he was,
he'd earned that favor—and much more.   840
OEDIPUS: Can we bring him back, quickly?
JOCASTA: Easily. Why do you want him so?
OEDIPUS: I am afraid,
Jocasta, I have said too much already.
That man—I've got to see him.
JOCASTA: Then he'll come.
But even I have a right, I'd like to think,   845
to know what's torturing you, my lord.
OEDIPUS: And so you shall—I can hold nothing back from you,
now I've reached this pitch of dark foreboding.
Who means more to me than you? Tell me,   850
whom would I turn toward but you
as I go through all this?

My father was Polybus, king of Corinth.
My mother, a Dorian, Merope. And I was held
the prince of the realm among the people there,   855
till something struck me out of nowhere,
something strange . . . worth remarking perhaps,
hardly worth the anxiety I gave it.
Some man at a banquet who had drunk too much
shouted out—he was far gone, mind you—
that I am not my father's son. Fighting words!   860
I barely restrained myself that day
but early the next I went to mother and father,
questioned them closely, and they were enraged
at the accusation and the fool who let it fly.
So as for my parents I was satisfied,   865
but still this thing kept gnawing at me,
the slander spread—I had to make my move.
                           And so,
unknown to mother and father I set out for Delphi,
and the god Apollo spurned me, sent me away
denied the facts I came for,   870
but first he flashed before my eyes a future
great with pain, terror, disaster—I can hear him cry,
"You are fated to couple with your mother, you will bring
a breed of children into the light no man can bear to see—
you will kill your father, the one who gave you life!" 875

I heard all that and ran. I abandoned Corinth,
from that day on I gauged its landfall only
by the stars, running, always running
toward some place where I would never see
880 the shame of all those oracles come true.
And as I fled I reached that very spot
where the great king, you say, met his death.

Now, Jocasta, I will tell you all.
Making my way toward this triple crossroad
885 I began to see a herald, then a brace of colts
drawing a wagon, and mounted on the bench . . . a man,
just as you've described him, coming face-to-face,
and the one in the lead and the old man himself
were about to thrust me off the road—brute force—
890 and the one shouldering me aside, the driver,
I strike him in anger!—and the old man, watching me
coming up along his wheels—he brings down
his prod, two prongs straight at my head!
I paid him back with interest!
895 Short work, by god—with one blow of the staff
in this right hand I knock him out of his high seat,
roll him out of the wagon, sprawling headlong—
I killed them all—every mother's son!

Oh, but if there is any blood-tie
900 between Laius and this stranger . . .
what man alive more miserable than I?
More hated by the gods? *I* am the man
no alien, no citizen welcomes to his house,
law forbids it—not a word to me in public,
905 driven out of every hearth and home.
And all these curses I—no one but I
brought down these piling curses on myself!
And you, his wife, I've touched your body with these,
the hands that killed your husband cover you with blood.

910 Wasn't I born for torment? Look me in the eyes!
I am abomination—heart and soul!
I must be exiled, and even in exile
never see my parents, never set foot
on native ground again. Else I am doomed
915 to couple with my mother and cut my father down . . .
Polybus who reared me, gave me life.

                              But why, why?
Wouldn't a man of judgment say—and wouldn't he be right—
some savage power has brought this down upon my head?

Oh no, not that, you pure and awesome gods,
920 never let me see that day! Let me slip
from the world of men, vanish without a trace
before I see myself stained with such corruption,
stained to the heart.
  LEADER: My lord, you fill our hearts with fear.
925 But at least until you question the witness,
  do take hope.
  OEDIPUS: Exactly. He is my last hope—
I am waiting for the shepherd. He is crucial.
  JOCASTA: And once he appears, what then? Why so urgent?
  OEDIPUS: I will tell you. If it turns out that his story
930 matches yours, I've escaped the worst.
  JOCASTA: What did I say? What struck you so?

OEDIPUS: You said
  thieves—
he told you a whole band of them murdered Laius.
So, if he still holds to the same number,
I cannot be the killer. One can't equal many.
But if he refers to one man, one alone,   935
clearly the scales come down on me:
I am guilty.
  JOCASTA: Impossible. Trust me,
I told you precisely what he said,
and he can't retract it now;
the whole city heard it, not just I.   940
And even if he should vary his first report
by one man more or less, still, my lord,
he could never make the murder of Laius
truly fit the prophecy. Apollo was explicit:
my son was doomed to kill my husband . . . my son,   945
poor defenseless thing, he never had a chance
to kill his father. They destroyed him first.

So much for prophecy. It's neither here nor there.
From this day on, I wouldn't look right or left.
  OEDIPUS: True, true. Still, that shepherd,   950
  someone fetch him—now!
  JOCASTA: I'll send at once. But do let's go inside.
  I'd never displease you, least of all in this.

(OEDIPUS *and* JOCASTA *enter the palace.*)

CHORUS: Destiny guide me always
  Destiny find me filled with reverence   955
      pure in word and deed.
  Great laws tower above us, reared on high
  born for the brilliant vault of heaven—
      Olympian Sky their only father,
  nothing mortal, no man gave them birth,   960
  their memory deathless, never lost in sleep:
  within them lives a mighty god, the god does not
      grow old.

  Pride breeds the tyrant
  violent pride, gorging, crammed to bursting
      with all that is overripe and rich with ruin—   965
  clawing up to the heights, headlong pride
  crashes down the abyss—sheer doom!
      No footing helps, all foothold lost and gone.
  But the healthy strife that makes the city strong—
  I pray that god will never end that wrestling: 970
  god, my champion, I will never let you go.

  But if any man comes striding, high and mighty
      in all he says and does,
  no fear of justice, no reverence
  for the temples of the gods—   975
      let a rough doom tear him down,
  repay his pride, breakneck, ruinous pride!
  If he cannot reap his profits fairly
      cannot restrain himself from outrage—
  mad, laying hands on the holy things untouchable!   980

      Can such a man, so desperate, still boast
  he can save his life from the flashing bolts of god?

If all such violence goes with honor now
    why join the sacred dance?

985   Never again will I go reverent to Delphi,
      the inviolate heart of Earth
    or Apollo's ancient oracle at Abae
    or Olympia of the fires—
990   unless these prophecies all come true
    for all mankind to point toward in wonder.
    King of kings, if you deserve your titles
      Zeus, remember, never forget!
    You and your deathless, everlasting reign.

    They are dying, the old oracles sent to Laius,
995   now our masters strike them off the rolls.
      Nowhere Apollo's golden glory now—
        the gods, the gods go down.

(*Enter* JOCASTA *from the palace, carrying a suppliant's branch wound in wool.*)

JOCASTA: Lords of the realm, it occurred to me,
    just now, to visit the temples of the gods,
1000   so I have my branch in hand and incense too.

    Oedipus is beside himself. Racked with anguish,
    no longer a man of sense, he won't admit
    the latest prophecies are hollow as the old—
    he's at the mercy of every passing voice
1005   if the voice tells of terror.
    I urge him gently, nothing seems to help,
    so I turn to you, Apollo, you are nearest.

(*Placing her branch on the altar, while an old herdsman enters from the side, not the one just summoned by the King but an unexpected* MESSENGER *from Corinth.*)

    I come with prayers and offerings . . . I beg you,
    cleanse us, set us free of defilement!
1010   Look at us, passengers in the grip of fear,
    watching the pilot of the vessel go to pieces.
MESSENGER: (*Approaching* JOCASTA *and the* CHORUS.) Strangers,
    please, I wonder if you could lead us
    to the palace of the king . . . I think it's Oedipus.
    Better, the man himself—you know where he is?
1015 LEADER: This is his palace, stranger. He's inside.
    But here is his queen, his wife and mother
    of his children.
MESSENGER: Blessings on you, noble queen,
    queen of Oedipus crowned with all your family—
    blessings on you always!
1020 JOCASTA: And the same to you, stranger, you deserve it . . .
    such a greeting. But what have you come for?
    Have you brought us news?
MESSENGER: Wonderful news—
    for the house, my lady, for your husband too.
JOCASTA: Really, what? Who sent you?
MESSENGER: Corinth.
1025   I'll give you the message in a moment.
    You'll be glad of it—how could you help it?—
    though it costs a little sorrow in the bargain.
JOCASTA: What can it be, with such a double edge?

MESSENGER: The people there, they want to make your Oedipus
    king of Corinth, so they're saying now.   1030
JOCASTA: Why? Isn't old Polybus still in power?
MESSENGER: No more. Death has got him in the tomb.
JOCASTA: What are you saying? Polybus, dead?—dead?
MESSENGER: If not,
    if I'm not telling the truth, strike me dead too.
JOCASTA: (*To a* SERVANT.) Quickly, go to your master, tell him
    this!   1035

    You prophecies of the gods, where are you now?
    This is the man that Oedipus feared for years,
    he fled him, not to kill him—and now he's dead,
    quite by chance, a normal, natural death,
    not murdered by his son.   1040
OEDIPUS: (*Emerging from the palace.*)
      Dearest,
    what now? Why call me from the palace?
JOCASTA: (*Bringing the* MESSENGER *closer.*) Listen to *him,* see for
    yourself what all
    those awful prophecies of god have come to.
OEDIPUS: And who is he? What can he have for me?
JOCASTA: He's from Corinth, he's come to tell you   1045
    your father is no more—Polybus—he's dead!
OEDIPUS: (*Wheeling on the* MESSENGER.) What? Let me have it
    from your lips.
MESSENGER: Well,
    if that's what you want first, then here it is:
    make no mistake, Polybus is dead and gone.
OEDIPUS: How—murder? sickness?—what? what killed him?   1050
MESSENGER: A light tip of the scales can put old bones to rest.
OEDIPUS: Sickness then—poor man, it wore him down.
MESSENGER: That,
    and the long count of years he'd measured out.
OEDIPUS: So!
    Jocasta, why, why look to the Prophet's hearth,
    the fires of the future? Why scan the birds   1055
    that scream above our heads? They winged me on
    to the murder of my father, did they? That was my doom?
    Well look, he's dead and buried, hidden under the earth,
    and here I am in Thebes, I never put hand to sword—
    unless some longing for me wasted him away,   1060
    then in a sense you'd say I caused his death.
    But now, all those prophecies I feared—Polybus
    packs them off to sleep with him in hell!
    They're nothing, worthless.
JOCASTA: There.
    Didn't I tell you from the start?   1065
OEDIPUS: So you did. I was lost in fear.
JOCASTA: No more, sweep it from your mind forever.
OEDIPUS: But my mother's bed, surely I must fear—
JOCASTA: Fear?
    What should a man fear? It's all chance,
    chance rules our lives. Not a man on earth   1070
    can see a day ahead, groping through the dark.
    Better to live at random, best we can.
    And as for this marriage with your mother—
    have no fear. Many a man before you,
    in his dreams, has shared his mother's bed.   1075
    Take such things for shadows, nothing at all—
    Live, Oedipus,
    as if there's no tomorrow!

OEDIPUS: Brave words,
and you'd persuade me if mother weren't alive.
1080   But mother lives, so for all your reassurances
I live in fear, I must.
JOCASTA: But your father's death,
that, at least, is a great blessing, joy to the eyes!
OEDIPUS: Great, I know . . . but I fear *her*—she's still alive.
MESSENGER: Wait, who is this woman, makes you so afraid?
1085   OEDIPUS: Merope, old man. The wife of Polybus.
MESSENGER: The queen? What's there to fear in her?
OEDIPUS: A dreadful prophecy, stranger, sent by the gods.
MESSENGER: Tell me, could you? Unless it's forbidden
other ears to hear.
OEDIPUS: Not at all.
1090   Apollo told me once—it is my fate—
I must make love with my own mother,
shed my father's blood with my own hands.
So for years I've given Corinth a wide berth,
and it's been my good fortune too. But still,
1095   to see one's parents and look into their eyes
is the greatest joy I know.
MESSENGER: You're afraid of that?
That kept you out of Corinth?
OEDIPUS: My *father,* old man—
so I wouldn't kill my father.
MESSENGER: So that's it.
Well then, seeing I came with such good will, my king,
1100   why don't I rid you of that old worry now?
OEDIPUS: What a rich reward you'd have for that!
MESSENGER: What do you think I came for, majesty?
So you'd come home and I'd be better off.
OEDIPUS: Never, I will never go near my parents.
1105   MESSENGER: My boy, it's clear, you don't know what you're
doing.
OEDIPUS: What do you mean, old man? For god's sake, explain.
MESSENGER: If you ran from *them,* always dodging home . . .
OEDIPUS: Always, terrified Apollo's oracle might come true—
MESSENGER: And you'd be covered with guilt, from both your
parents.
1110   OEDIPUS: That's right, old man, that fear is always
with me.
MESSENGER: Don't you know? You've really nothing to fear.
OEDIPUS: But why? If I'm their son—Merope, Polybus?
MESSENGER: Polybus was nothing to you, that's why, not in blood.
OEDIPUS: What are you saying—Polybus was not my father?
1115   MESSENGER: No more than I am. He and I are equals.
OEDIPUS: My father—
how can my father equal nothing? You're nothing to me!
MESSENGER: Neither was he, no more your father than I am.
OEDIPUS: Then why did he call me his son?
MESSENGER: You were a gift,
years ago—know for a fact he took you
1120   from my hands.
OEDIPUS: No, from another's hands?
Then how could he love me so? He loved me, deeply . . .
MESSENGER: True, and his early years without a child
made him love you all the more.
OEDIPUS: And you, did you . . .
buy me? find me by accident?
MESSENGER: I stumbled on you,
1125   down the woody flanks of Mount Cithaeron.

OEDIPUS: So close,
what were you doing here, just passing through?
MESSENGER: Watching over my flocks, grazing them on the
slopes.
OEDIPUS: A herdsman, were you? A vagabond, scraping for
wages?
MESSENGER: Your savior too, my son, in your worst hour.
OEDIPUS: Oh—
when you picked me up, was I in pain? What exactly?   1130
MESSENGER: Your ankles . . . they tell the story. Look at them.
OEDIPUS: Why remind me of that, that old affliction?
MESSENGER: Your ankles were pinned together. I set you free.
OEDIPUS: That dreadful mark—I've had it from the cradle.
MESSENGER: And you got your name from that misfortune too,   1135
the name's still with you.
OEDIPUS: Dear god, who did it?—
mother? father? Tell me.
MESSENGER: I don't know.
The one who gave you to me, he'd know more.
OEDIPUS: What? You took me from someone else?
You didn't find me yourself?   1140
MESSENGER: No sir,
another shepherd passed you on to me.
OEDIPUS: Who? Do you know? Describe him.
MESSENGER: He called himself a servant of . . .
if I remember rightly—Laius.

(JOCASTA *turns sharply.*)

OEDIPUS: The king of the land who ruled here long ago?   1145
MESSENGER: That's the one. That herdsman was *his* man.
OEDIPUS: Is he still alive? Can I see him?
MESSENGER: They'd know best, the people of these parts.

(OEDIPUS *and the* MESSENGER *turn to the* CHORUS.)

OEDIPUS: Does anyone know that herdsman,
the one he mentioned? Anyone seen him   1150
in the fields, here in the city? Out with it!
The time has come to reveal this once for all.
LEADER: I think he's the very shepherd you wanted to see,
a moment ago. But the queen, Jocasta,
she's the one to say.   1155
OEDIPUS: Jocasta,
you remember the man we just sent for?
Is *that* the one he means?
JOCASTA: That man . . .
why ask? Old shepherd, talk, empty nonsense,
don't give it another thought, don't even think—
OEDIPUS: What—give up now, with a clue like this?   1160
Fail to solve the mystery of my birth?
Not for all the world!
JOCASTA: Stop—in the name of god,
if you love your own life, call off this search!
My suffering is enough.
OEDIPUS: Courage!
Even if my mother turns out to be a slave,   1165
and I a slave, three generations back,
you would not seem common.
JOCASTA: Oh no,
listen to me, I beg you, don't do this.

OEDIPUS: Listen to you? No more. I must know it all,
1170   must see the truth at last.
JOCASTA: No, please—
   for your sake—I want the best for you!
OEDIPUS: Your best is more than I can bear.
JOCASTA: You're doomed—
   may you never fathom who you are!
OEDIPUS: (*To a servant.*) Hurry, fetch me the herdsman, now!
1175   Leave her to glory in her royal birth.
JOCASTA: Aieeeeee—
                    man of agony—
   that is the only name I have for you,
   that, no other—ever, ever, ever!

(*Flinging through the palace doors. A long, tense silence follows.*)

LEADER: Where's she gone, Oedipus?
1180   Rushing off, such wild grief . . .
   I'm afraid that from this silence
   something monstrous may come bursting forth.
OEDIPUS: Let it burst! Whatever will, whatever must!
   I must know my birth, no matter how common
1185   it may be—I must see my origins face-to-face.
   She perhaps, she with her woman's pride
   may well be mortified by my birth,
   but I, I count myself the son of Chance,
   the great goddess, giver of all good things—
1190   I'll never see myself disgraced. She is my mother!
   And the moons have marked me out, my blood-brothers,
   one moon on the wane, the next moon great with power.
   That is my blood, my nature—I will never betray it,
   never fail to search and learn my birth!
1195   CHORUS: Yes—if I am a true prophet
                    if I can grasp the truth,
          by the boundless skies of Olympus,
       at the full moon of tomorrow, Mount Cithaeron
   you will know how Oedipus glories in you—
1200   you, his birthplace, nurse, his mountain-mother!
   And we will sing you, dancing out your praise—
   you lift our monarch's heart!
             Apollo, Apollo, god of the wild cry
                    may our dancing please you!
                              Oedipus—
1205   son, dear child, who bore you?
   Who of the nymphs who seem to live forever
   mated with Pan, the mountain-striding Father?
   Who was your mother? who, some bride of Apollo
   the god who loves the pastures spreading toward the sun?
1210   Or was it Hermes, king of the lightning ridges?
   Or Dionysus, lord of frenzy, lord of the barren peaks—
   did he seize you in his hands, dearest of all his lucky
             finds?—
             found by the nymphs, their warm eyes dancing, gift
   to the lord who loves them dancing out his joy!

(OEDIPUS *strains to see a figure coming from the distance. Attended by palace* GUARDS, *an old* SHEPHERD *enters slowly, reluctant to approach the king.*)

1215   OEDIPUS: I never met the man, my friends . . . still,
       if I had to guess, I'd say that's the shepherd,
       the very one we've looked for all along.

Brothers in old age, two of a kind,
   he and our guest here. At any rate
   the ones who bring him in are my own men,   1220
   I recognize them.

(*Turning to the* LEADER.)

                    But you know more than I,
   you should, you've seen the man before.
LEADER: I know him, definitely. One of Laius' men,
   a trusty shepherd, if there ever was one.
OEDIPUS: You, I ask you first, stranger,   1225
   you from Corinth—is this the one you mean?
MESSENGER: You're looking at him. He's your man.
OEDIPUS: (*To the* SHEPHERD.) You, old man, come over here—
   look at me. Answer all my questions.
   Did you ever serve King Laius?   1230
SHEPHERD: So I did . . .
   a slave, not bought on the block though,
   born and reared in the palace.
OEDIPUS: Your duties, your kind of work?
SHEPHERD: Herding the flocks, the better part of my life.
OEDIPUS: Where, mostly? Where did you do your grazing?   1235
SHEPHERD: Well,
   Cithaeron sometimes, or the foothills round about.
OEDIPUS: This man—you know him? ever see him there?
SHEPHERD: (*Confused, glancing from the* MESSENGER *to the king.*)
   Doing what? What man do you mean?
OEDIPUS: (*Pointing to the* MESSENGER.) This one here—ever have
   dealings with him?
SHEPHERD: Not so I could say, but give me a chance,   1240
   my memory's bad . . .
MESSENGER: No wonder he doesn't know me, master.
   But let me refresh his memory for him.
   I'm sure he recalls old times we had
   on the slopes of Mount Cithaeron;   1245
   he and I, grazing our flocks, he with two
   and I with one—we both struck up together,
   three whole seasons, six months at a stretch
   from spring to the rising of Arcturus in the fall,
   then with winter coming on I'd drive my herds   1250
   to my own pens, and back he'd go with his
   to Laius' folds.

(*To the* SHEPHERD.)

                    Now that's how it was,
   wasn't it—yes or no?
SHEPHERD: Yes, I suppose . . .
   it's all so long ago.
MESSENGER: Come, tell me,
   you gave me a child back then, a boy, remember?   1255
   A little fellow to rear, my very own.
SHEPHERD: What? Why rake up that again?
MESSENGER: Look, here he is, my fine old friend—
   the same man who was just a baby then.
SHEPHERD: Damn you, shut your mouth—quiet!   1260
OEDIPUS: Don't lash out at him, old man—
   you need lashing more than he does.
SHEPHERD: Why,
   master, majesty—what have I done wrong?
OEDIPUS: You won't answer his question about the boy.

1265 SHEPHERD: He's talking nonsense, wasting his breath.
OEDIPUS: So, you won't talk willingly—
      then you'll talk with pain.

(*The* GUARDS *seize the* SHEPHERD.)

SHEPHERD: No, dear god, don't torture an old man!
OEDIPUS: Twist his arms back, quickly!
SHEPHERD: God help us, why?—
1270   what more do you need to know?
OEDIPUS: Did you give him that child? He's asking.
SHEPHERD: I did . . . I wish to god I'd died that day.
OEDIPUS: You've got your wish if you don't tell the truth.
SHEPHERD: The more I tell, the worse the death I'll die.
1275 OEDIPUS: Our friend here wants to stretch things out,
      does he?

(*Motioning to his men for torture.*)

SHEPHERD: No, no, I gave it to him—I just said so.
OEDIPUS: Where did you get it? Your house? Someone else's?
SHEPHERD: It wasn't mine, no, I got it from . . . someone.
OEDIPUS: Which one of them?

(*Looking at the citizens.*)

                              Whose house?
SHEPHERD: No—
1280   god's sake, master, no more questions!
OEDIPUS: You're a dead man if I have to ask again.
SHEPHERD: Then—the child came from the house . . .
      of Laius.
OEDIPUS: A slave? or born of his own blood?
SHEPHERD: Oh no,
1285   I'm right at the edge, the horrible truth—I've got to say it!
OEDIPUS: And I'm at the edge of hearing horrors, yes, but I
      must hear!
SHEPHERD: All right! His son, they said it was—his son!
      But the one inside, your wife,
      she'd tell it best.
OEDIPUS: My wife—
1290   *she* gave it to you?
SHEPHERD: Yes, yes, my king.
OEDIPUS: Why, what for?
SHEPHERD: To kill it.
OEDIPUS: Her own child,
1295   how could she?
SHEPHERD: She was afraid—
      frightening prophecies.
OEDIPUS: What?
SHEPHERD: They said—
      he'd kill his parents.
1300 OEDIPUS: But you gave him to this old man—why?
SHEPHERD: I pitied the little baby, master,
      hoped he'd take him off to his own country,
      far away, but he saved him for this, this fate.
      If you are the man he says you are, believe me,
1305   you were born for pain.
OEDIPUS: O god—
      all come true, all burst to light!
      O light—now let me look my last on you!
      I stand revealed at last—

cursed in my birth, cursed in marriage,
cursed in the lives I cut down with these hands!   1310

(*Rushing through the doors with a great cry. The Corinthian*
MESSENGER, *the* SHEPHERD, *and* ATTENDANTS *exit slowly to*
the side.)

CHORUS: O the generations of men
      the dying generations—adding the total
      of all your lives I find they come to nothing . . .
            does there exist, is there a man on earth
      who seizes more joy than just a dream, a vision?   1315
      And the vision no sooner dawns than dies
      blazing into oblivion.

      You are my great example, you, your life
      your destiny, Oedipus, man of misery—
      I count no man blest.   1320

                  You outranged all men!
            Bending your bow to the breaking-point
      you captured priceless glory, O dear god,
      and the Sphinx came crashing down,
                  the virgin, claws hooked
      like a bird of omen singing, shrieking death—   1325
      like a fortress reared in the face of death
      you rose and saved our land.

      From that day on we called you king
      we crowned you with honors, Oedipus, towering over all—
      mighty king of the seven gates of Thebes.   1330
      But now to hear your story—is there a man more agonized?
      More wed to pain and frenzy? Not a man on earth,
      the joy of your life ground down to nothing
      O Oedipus, name for the ages—
            one and the same wide harbor served you   1335
                  son and father both
      son and father came to rest in the same bridal chamber.
      How, how could the furrows your father plowed
      bear you, your agony, harrowing on
      in silence O so long?   1340

                        But now for all your power
      Time, all-seeing Time has dragged you to the light,
      judged your marriage monstrous from the start—
      the son and the father tangling, both one—
      O child of Laius, would to god
            I'd never seen you, never never!   1345
            Now I weep like a man who wails the dead
      and the dirge comes pouring forth with all my heart!
      I tell you the truth, you gave me life
      my breath leapt up in you
      and now you bring down night upon my eyes.   1350

(*Enter a* MESSENGER *from the palace.*)

MESSENGER: Men of Thebes, always first in honor,
      what horrors you will hear, what you will see,
      what a heavy weight of sorrow you will shoulder . . .
      if you are true to your birth, if you still have
      some feeling for the royal house of Thebes.   1355
      I tell you neither the waters of the Danube

nor the Nile can wash this palace clean.
Such things it hides, it soon will bring to light—
terrible things, and none done blindly now,
1360   all done with a will. The pains
we inflict upon ourselves hurt most of all.
LEADER: God knows we have pains enough already.
What can you add to them?
MESSENGER: The queen is dead.
LEADER: Poor lady—how?
1365 MESSENGER: By her own hand. But you are spared the worst,
you never had to watch . . . I saw it all,
and with all the memory that's in me
you will learn what that poor woman suffered.

Once she'd broken in through the gates,
1370   dashing past us, frantic, whipped to fury,
ripping her hair out with both hands—
straight to her rooms she rushed, flinging herself
across the bridal-bed, doors slamming behind her—
once inside, she wailed for Laius, dead so long,
1375   remembering how she bore his child long ago,
the life that rose up to destroy him, leaving
its mother to mother living creatures
with the very son she'd borne.
Oh how she wept, mourning the marriage-bed
1380   where she let loose that double brood—monsters—
husband by her husband, children by her child.
                              And then—
but how she died is more than I can say. Suddenly
Oedipus burst in, screaming, he stunned us so
we couldn't watch her agony to the end,
1385   our eyes were fixed on him. Circling
like a maddened beast, stalking, here, there,
crying out to us—
                    Give him a sword! His wife,
no wife, his mother, where can he find the mother earth
that cropped two crops at once, himself and all his children?
1390   He was raging—one of the dark powers pointing the way,
none of us mortals crowding around him, no,
with a great shattering cry—someone, something leading
    him on—
he hurled at the twin doors and bending the bolts back
out of their sockets, crashed through the chamber.
1395   And there we saw the woman hanging by the neck,
cradled high in a woven noose, spinning,
swinging back and forth. And when he saw her,
giving a low, wrenching sob that broke our hearts,
slipping the halter from her throat, he eased her down,
1400   in a slow embrace he laid her down, poor thing . . .
then, what came next, what horror we beheld!

He rips off her brooches, the long gold pins
holding her robes—and lifting them high,
looking straight up into the points,
1405   he digs them down the sockets of his eyes, crying, "You,
you'll see no more the pain I suffered, all the pain I caused!
Too long you looked on the ones you never should have seen,
blind to the ones you longed to see, to know! Blind
from this hour on! Blind in the darkness—blind!"
1410   His voice like a dirge, rising, over and over
raising the pins, raking them down his eyes.

And at each stroke blood spurts from the roots,
splashing his beard, a swirl of it, nerves and clots—
black hail of blood pulsing, gushing down.

These are the griefs that burst upon them both,   1415
coupling man and woman. The joy they had so lately,
the fortune of their old ancestral house
was deep joy indeed. Now, in this one day,
wailing, madness and doom, death, disgrace,
all the griefs in the world that you can name,   1420
all are theirs forever.
LEADER: Oh poor man, the misery—
has he any rest from pain now?

(A voice within, in torment.)

MESSENGER: He's shouting,
"Loose the bolts, someone, show me to all of Thebes!
My father's murderer, my mother's—"
No, I can't repeat it, it's unholy.   1425
Now he'll tear himself from his native earth,
not linger, curse the house with his own curse.
But he needs strength, and a guide to lead him on.
This is sickness more than he can bear.

(The palace doors open.)

                              Look,
he'll show you himself. The great doors are opening—   1430
you are about to see a sight, a horror
even his mortal enemy would pity.

(Enter OEDIPUS, blinded, led by a boy. He stands at the palace
steps, as if surveying his people once again.)

CHORUS: Oh, the terror—
the suffering, for all the world to see,
the worst terror that ever met my eyes.
What madness swept over you? What god,   1435
what dark power leapt beyond all bounds,
beyond belief, to crush your wretched life?—
godforsaken, cursed by the gods!
I pity you but I can't bear to look.
I've much to ask, so much to learn,   1440
so much fascinates my eyes,
but you . . . I shudder at the sight.
OEDIPUS: Oh, Ohh—
the agony! I am agony—
where am I going? where on earth?
    where does all this agony hurl me?   1445
where's my voice?—
    winging, swept away on a dark tide—
My destiny, my dark power, what a leap you made!
CHORUS: To the depths of terror, too dark to hear, to see.
OEDIPUS: Dark, horror of darkness   1450
    my darkness, drowning, swirling around me
crashing wave on wave—unspeakable, irresistible
    headwind, fatal harbor! Oh again,
the misery, all at once, over and over
the stabbing daggers, stab of memory   1455
raking me insane.

CHORUS: No wonder you suffer
twice over, the pain of your wounds,
the lasting grief of pain.
OEDIPUS: Dear friend, still here?
Standing by me, still with a care for me,
1460   the blind man? Such compassion,
                    loyal to the last. Oh it's you,
I know you're here, dark as it is
I'd know you anywhere, your voice—
it's yours, clearly yours.
CHORUS: Dreadful, what you've done . . .
1465   how could you bear it, gouging out your eyes?
What superhuman power drove you on?
OEDIPUS: Apollo, friends, Apollo—
he ordained my agonies—these, my pains on pains!
But the hand that struck my eyes was mine,
1470   mine alone—no one else—
                    I did it all myself!
What good were eyes to me?
Nothing I could see could bring me joy.
CHORUS: No, no, exactly as you say.
OEDIPUS: What can I ever see?
1475   What love, what call of the heart
can touch my ears with joy? Nothing, friends.
Take me away, far, far from Thebes,
quickly, cast me away, my friends—
this great murderous ruin, this man cursed to heaven,
1480   the man the deathless gods hate most of all!
CHORUS: Pitiful, you suffer so, you understand so much . . .
I wish you had never known.
OEDIPUS: Die, die—
whoever he was that day in the wilds
who cut my ankles free of the ruthless pins,
1485   he pulled me clear of death, he saved my life
for this, this kindness—
                    Curse him, kill him!
If I'd died then, I'd never have dragged myself,
my loved ones through such hell.
CHORUS: Oh if only . . . would to god.
1490   OEDIPUS: I'd never have come to this,
my father's murderer—never been branded
mother's husband, all men see me now! Now,
loathed by the gods, son of the mother I defiled
coupling in my father's bed, spawning lives in the loins
1495   that spawned my wretched life. What grief can crown this
grief?
                    It's mine alone, my destiny—I am Oedipus!
CHORUS: How can I say you've chosen for the best?
Better to die than be alive and blind.
OEDIPUS: What I did was best—don't lecture me,
1500   no more advice. I, with *my* eyes,
how could I look my father in the eyes
when I go down to death? Or mother, so abused . . .
I have done such things to the two of them,
crimes too huge for hanging.
                    Worse yet,
1505   the sight of my children, born as they were born,
how could I long to look into their eyes?
No, not with these eyes of mine, never.
Not this city either, her high towers,
the sacred glittering images of her gods—
1510   I am misery! I, her best son, reared

as no other son of Thebes was ever reared,
I've stripped myself, I gave the command myself.
All men must cast away the great blasphemer,
the curse now brought to light by the gods,
the son of Laius—I, my father's son!   1515

Now I've exposed my guilt, horrendous guilt,
could I train a level glance on you, my countrymen?
Impossible! No, if I could just block off my ears,
the springs of hearing, I would stop at nothing—
I'd wall up my loathsome body like a prison,   1520
blind to the sound of life, not just the sight.
Oblivion—what a blessing . . .
for the mind to dwell a world away from pain.

O Cithaeron, why did you give me shelter?
Why didn't you take me, crush my life out on the spot?   1525
I'd never have revealed my birth to all mankind.

O Polybus, Corinth, the old house of my fathers,
so I believed—what a handsome prince you raised—
under the skin, what sickness to the core.
Look at me! Born of outrage, outrage to the core.   1530
O triple roads—it all comes back, the secret,
dark ravine, and the oaks closing in
where the three roads join . . .
You drank my father's blood, my own blood
spilled by my own hands—you still remember me?   1535
What things you saw me do? Then I came here
and did them all once more!
                    Marriages! O marriage,
you gave me birth, and once you brought me into
     the world
you brought my sperm rising back, springing to light,
fathers, brothers, sons—one murderous breed—   1540
brides, wives, mothers. The blackest things
a man can do, I have done them all!
                    No more—
it's wrong to name what's wrong to do. Quickly,
for the love of god, hide me somewhere,
kill me, hurl me into the sea   1545
where you can never look on me again.

(*Beckoning to the* CHORUS *as they shrink away.*)

                    Closer,
it's all right. Touch the man of grief.
Do. Don't be afraid. My troubles are mine
and I am the only man alive who can sustain them.

(*Enter* CREON *from the palace, attended by palace* GUARDS.)

LEADER: Put your requests to Creon. Here he is,   1550
just when we need him. He'll have a plan, he'll act.
Now that he's the sole defense of the country
in your place.
OEDIPUS: Oh no, what can I say to him?
How can I ever hope to win his trust?
I wronged him so, just now, in every way.   1555
You must see that—I was so wrong, so wrong.
CREON: I haven't come to mock you, Oedipus,
or to criticize your former failings.

(*Turning to the* GUARDS.)

You there,
have you lost all respect for human feelings?
1560   At least revere the Sun, the holy fire
that keeps us all alive. Never expose a thing
of guilt and holy dread so great it appalls
the earth, the rain from heaven, the light of day!
Get him into the halls—quickly as you can.
1565   Piety demands no less. Kindred alone
should see a kinsman's shame. This is obscene.
OEDIPUS: Please, in god's name . . . you wipe my fears away,
coming so generously to me, the worst of men.
Do one thing more, for your sake, not mine.
1570   CREON: What do you want? Why so insistent?
OEDIPUS: Drive me out of the land at once, far from sight,
where I can never hear a human voice.
CREON: I'd have done that already, I promise you.
First I wanted the god to clarify my duties.
1575   OEDIPUS: The god? His command was clear, every word:
death for the father-killer, the curse—
he said destroy me!
CREON: So he did. Still. In such a crisis
it's better to ask precisely what to do.
OEDIPUS: So miserable—
1580   you would consult the god about a man like me?
CREON: By all means. And this time, I assume,
even you will obey the god's decrees.
OEDIPUS: I will,
I will. And you, I command you—I beg you . . .
the woman inside, bury her as you see fit.
1585   It's the only decent thing,
to give your own the last rites. As for me,
never condemn the city of my fathers
to house my body, not while I'm alive, no,
let me live on the mountains, on Cithaeron,
1590   my favorite haunt, I have made it famous.
Mother and father marked out that rock
to be my everlasting tomb—buried alive.
Let me die there, where they tried to kill me.

Oh but this I know: no sickness can destroy me,
1595   nothing can. I would never have been saved
from death—I have been saved
for something great and terrible, something strange.
Well let my destiny come and take me on its way!
About my children, Creon, the boys at least,
1600   don't burden yourself. They're men,
wherever they go, they'll find the means to live.
But my two daughters, my poor helpless girls,
clustering at our table, never without me
hovering near them . . . whatever I touched,
1605   they always had their share. Take care of them,
I beg you. Wait, better—permit me, would you?
Just to touch them with my hands and take
our fill of tears. Please . . . my king.
Grant it, with all your noble heart.
1610   If I could hold them, just once, I'd think
I had them with me, like the early days
when I could see their eyes.

(ANTIGONE *and* ISMENE, *two small children, are led in from the palace by a nurse.*)

What's that?
O god! Do I really hear you sobbing?—
my two children. Creon, you've pitied me?
Sent me my darling girls, my own flesh and blood!   1615
Am I right?
CREON: Yes, it's my doing.
I know the joy they gave you all these years,
the joy you must feel now.
OEDIPUS: Bless you, Creon!
May god watch over you for this kindness,
better than he ever guarded me.   1620
                    Children, where are you?
Here, come quickly—

(*Groping for* ANTIGONE *and* ISMENE, *who approach their father cautiously, then embrace him.*)

Come to these hands of mine,
your brother's hands, your own father's hands
that served his once bright eyes so well—
that made them blind. Seeing nothing, children,
knowing nothing, I became your father,   1625
I fathered you in the soil that gave me life.

How I weep for you—I cannot see you now . . .
just thinking of all your days to come, the bitterness,
the life that rough mankind will thrust upon you.
Where are the public gatherings you can join,   1630
the banquets of the clans? Home you'll come,
in tears, cut off from the sight of it all,
the brilliant rites unfinished.
And when you reach perfection, ripe for marriage,
who will he be, my dear ones? Risking all   1635
to shoulder the curse that weighs down my parents,
yes and you too—that wounds us all together.
What more misery could you want?
Your father killed his father, sowed his mother,
one, one and the selfsame womb sprang you—   1640
he cropped the very roots of his existence.

Such disgrace, and you must bear it all!
Who will marry you then? Not a man on earth.
Your doom is clear: you'll wither away to nothing,
single, without a child.   1645

(*Turning to* CREON.)

Oh Creon,
you are the only father they have now . . .
we who brought them into the world
are gone, both gone at a stroke—
Don't let them go begging, abandoned,
women without men. Your own flesh and blood!   1650
Never bring them down to the level of my pains.
Pity them. Look at them, so young, so vulnerable,
shorn of everything—you're their only hope.
Promise me, noble Creon, touch my hand!

(*Reaching toward* CREON, *who draws back.*)

1655 You, little ones, if you were old enough
to understand, there is much I'd tell you.
Now, as it is, I'd have you say a prayer.
Pray for life, my children,
live where you are free to grow and season.
1660 Pray god you find a better life than mine,
the father who begot you.
CREON: Enough.
You've wept enough. Into the palace now.
OEDIPUS: I must, but I find it very hard.
CREON: Time is the great healer, you will see.
1665 OEDIPUS: I am going—you know on what condition?
CREON: Tell me. I'm listening.
OEDIPUS: Drive me out of Thebes, in exile.
CREON: Not I. Only the gods can give you that.
OEDIPUS: Surely the gods hate me so much—
1670 CREON: You'll get your wish at once.
OEDIPUS: You consent?
CREON: I try to say what I mean; it's my habit.
OEDIPUS: Then take me away. It's time.
CREON: Come along, let go of the children.

OEDIPUS: No—
don't take them away from me, not now! No no no!

(*Clutching his daughters as the* GUARDS *wrench them loose and
take them through the palace doors.*)

CREON: Still the king, the master of all things?   1675
No more: here your power ends.
None of your power follows you through life.

(*Exit* OEDIPUS *and* CREON *to the palace. The* CHORUS *comes forward to address the audience directly.*)

CHORUS: People of Thebes, my countrymen, look on Oedipus.
He solved the famous riddle with his brilliance,
he rose to power, a man beyond all power.   1680
Who could behold his greatness without envy?
Now what a black sea of terror has overwhelmed him.
Now as we keep our watch and wait the final day,
count no man happy till he dies, free of pain at last.

(*Exit in procession.*)

Euripides

Euripides (c. 484–406 BCE) was the youngest of the three tragic playwrights whose plays remain today. Although he first competed in the City Dionysia in 455 BCE and won his first victory in 441 BCE, Euripides won only four victories in his lifetime and left Athens about 408 BCE for the court of King Archileus of Macedon, where he died. We do not know why Euripides won so infrequently, but his tragedies are much more bitter and ironic than those of Aeschylus or Sophocles, brilliantly unfolding the selfish capriciousness of gods and heroes alike. Of the roughly ninety plays Euripides is thought to have written, eighteen survive, and most of these were written and produced during the war with Sparta: *Alcestis, Medea, Heracleidae, Hippolytus, Cyclops* (a satyr play), *Heracles, Iphigeneia in Tauris, Helen, Hecuba, Andromache, The Trojan Women, Ion, The Suppliant Women, Orestes, Electra, The Phoenician Women.* Three additional plays—*Iphigeneia at Aulis, The Bacchae,* and *Alcmaeon at Corinth* (now lost)—were written in Macedon and brought to Athens by the playwright's son, Euripides the Younger. This trilogy, produced after Euripides' death, won him his final prize at the City Dionysia.

Medea Although many Greek tragedies center on female characters—think of Clytaemnestra in Aeschylus' *Agamemnon,* for example, or Sophocles' *Antigone*—Euripides was famous in Athens for centering his tragedies so frequently on women. Euripides was hardly a feminist in any modern sense, yet more than his contemporaries, he used his tragic heroines to explore the relationship between gender and the other conceptual, political, social, and esthetic categories organizing Athenian life.

As in all roles in the Athenian theater, the role of Medea was played by a male actor; nonetheless, in many ways *Medea* illustrates Euripides' skeptical and ironic regard for conventional attitudes and his tendency toward a more sensational form of tragic action. Like Shakespeare's *Hamlet, Medea* is a tragedy of revenge, in which Medea poisons her husband Jason's newly married wife and her father, Creon, and in the play's climactic moment executes her own children from her marriage with Jason. What sometimes seems most

In this modernized production of Euripides' *Medea* by the Abbey Theatre of Dublin, Fiona Shaw's Medea enacts the slaughter of the children behind an illuminated Plexiglas screen.

monstrous to modern readers and audiences is that Medea herself—in one of Euripides' most striking uses of the *machina*—flees Corinth alive at the end of the play, rising above the *skene* in a dragon-drawn chariot, draped in the bodies of her dead children, taunting and reviling the impotent Jason. That is, modern audiences sometimes feel that Medea herself should die at the play's close if *Medea* is to be a truly tragic drama, as though by dying Medea would be "punished" for her revenge in some appalling vision of tragic "justice." But Euripides seems uninterested in such a moralized version of tragedy. Indeed, as Aristotle implies in *The Poetics,* tragedy is a deeply dialectical, contradictory way of representing human experience: tragedy arises from the unresolvable tension between pity and fear, from the relationship between the hero's actions (remembering that the tragic hero is neither a paragon of virtue nor inherently wicked) and their terrible, somehow fitting consequences. Although Aristotle praises Sophocles' *Oedipus the King* as the best-constructed tragedy, he also remarks that Euripides "is felt by the audience to be the most tragic, at least, of the poets." To grasp Euripides' sense of tragedy means placing Medea's execution of the children within the context of the action as a whole—an act that brings her history to bear in one exacting deed; an act like Agamemnon's treading on the carpet or Oedipus' blistering interrogation of the ancient shepherd.

At the play's opening, Medea is an outcast, a foreign exile in Corinth, and the play repeatedly stresses Medea's otherness—she is an Eastern exotic, she has little respect for Greek culture and its institutions, and she is a sorceress as well. Medea is consistently shown to be a figure of willful passion, brought into exile through her love for Jason. Falling in love with Jason when he went to Colchis in search of the Golden Fleece, Medea used her sorcery to help Jason gain the Fleece, betraying her father and killing her brother in the bargain. When the play opens, Jason has returned to Greece with Medea and their children; in Corinth, however, Jason decides to marry the daughter of King Creon. Creon, no doubt recognizing that Medea and her children will pose a constant threat to his own line of succession, has ruled that Medea and her children must again be sent into exile.

Yet as Medea suggests to the Chorus, the indignity that Jason has thrust upon her—being doubly exiled, from her country and from her marriage—is in an important sense merely an extension of the state of all women in Greek culture. For once women "Buy a husband and take for our bodies / A master," they are exiled from their own homes, and from the mastery of their own lives. Inasmuch as women are represented as creatures of passion, they are "exiled" as well from the organizing principles of the Greek state: Reason, the law, and legitimate society are identified in the play as the preserve of men. Euripides makes Jason the spokesman for these values. When Jason first confronts Medea, he takes pride in his talents as a speaker, listing his arguments in support of taking a new wife almost as though he were arguing in the courtroom or conducting a philosophical demonstration. But while Oedipus, for instance, uses the strategies of philosophic inquiry to discover the truth, Jason's arguments seem to conceal the truth—he is betraying Medea and their children, after all—behind a smokescreen of sophistic rhetoric. Having brought Medea into exile, Jason argues that she is fortunate merely to "inhabit a Greek land and understand our ways / How to live by law instead of the sweet will of force." Yet the law that Jason praises seems designed to enable him to act out his own "sweet will"—taking a second wife—while it prevents Medea from acting on hers. The more Jason insists that he is acting reasonably, the more unreasonable his arguments become; he grows increasingly irritable, and finally insulting: "You women have got into such a state of mind / That, if your life at night is good, you think you have / Everything." Euripides' treatment of Jason is typical of his tendency to present an ironic view of the heroes of Greek mythology. Here, in making Jason the representative of Greek values—reason, law, justice—Euripides suggests the limits of those values. For the Chorus clearly sees Jason's "reason" as a self-indulgent pretense: "Though you have made this speech of yours look well, / . . . / You have betrayed your wife and are acting badly."

As Medea comes to recognize, both Jason and the masculine laws of Corinth are willing to betray her, to call her fidelity and love merely irrational, to force her again into exile. Having poisoned Creon and his daughter, Medea first claims to kill the children in order that they not be slain "by another hand less kindly to them." But it is also clear that in killing the children, Medea revenges herself on Jason in the only way open to her; he has little regard for her love for him, but the children are his property, an extension of himself, of his identity. What is more important, the children are his successors, representing his continued presence in the world. For as Jason laments, Medea has contrived a punishment for him that no Greek woman would have dared: In leaving him childless, Medea transforms Jason into an exile like herself, prophesying that he will die "without distinction."

Medea's acts epitomize the ethical ambiguity that drives Greek tragedy. Agamemnon strides on the blood-red carpet, magisterially desecrating the honor of his family as he had once done in sacrificing Iphigeneia; Oedipus sentences the hidden criminal to exile, only to discover that he is the criminal he seeks. To force Jason into a childless exile, Medea commits the kind of crime that Jason has repeatedly drawn her to enact: She murders what she loves in order to insist on the priority and power of her love for him. As in other classical tragedies, the hero chooses to act in a way that is not only consistent with her past, but a self-conscious reenactment of it. The *peripeteia,* the reversal that defines the tragic action, seems in many ways to be a kind of restoration as well, revealing destructive consequences that have been latent in the action from the beginning.

It should be clear that while Euripides interrogates the relationship between reason and passion, culture and nature, the rational and the irrational, science and magic, *Medea* does not finally disrupt or overturn this relationship. Nor does the play finally question the way that Greek culture gendered these categories as masculine and feminine, expressing the conceptual and political hierarchies of its own making as the "natural" outgrowth of some essential gender difference. Euripides exposes the destructive tension lurking in Greek conceptions of gender, power, and identity, but the language of tragedy is not the language of revolution, because although tragedy frequently exposes the values of its world as contradictory and destructive, it also accepts those values as somehow inevitable, unavoidable. Medea flees Corinth and the abusive Jason, but only by destroying herself in the same way she destroys Jason; Medea triumphs over Jason, but only by destroying her family and becoming an exile yet again. The only alternative that *Medea* offers to the way that Medea— and, she argues, all women—is positioned as an outsider, an "exile" to the governing categories of Greek life, is a deeper, more permanent isolation.

Medea

Euripides

TRANSLATED BY REX WARNER

CHARACTERS

MEDEA, *princess of Colchis and wife of*
JASON, *son of Aeson, king of Iolcus*
TWO CHILDREN *of Medea and Jason*
CREON, *king of Corinth*

AEGEUS, *king of Athens*
NURSE *to Medea*
TUTOR *to Medea's children*
MESSENGER
CHORUS *of Corinthian women*
ATTENDANTS

SCENE: *In front of* MEDEA's *house in Corinth.*

Enter from the house Medea's NURSE.

NURSE: How I wish the Argo never had reached the land
    Of Colchis, skimming through the blue Symplegades,
    Nor ever had fallen in the glades of Pelion
    The smitten fir-tree to furnish oars for the hands
5   Of heroes who in Pelias' name attempted
    The Golden Fleece! For then my mistress Medea
    Would not have sailed for the towers of the land of Iolcus,
    Her heart on fire with passionate love for Jason;
    Nor would she have persuaded the daughters of Pelias
10   To kill their father, and now be living here
    In Corinth with her husband and children. She gave
    Pleasure to the people of her land of exile,
    And she herself helped Jason in every way.
    This is indeed the greatest salvation of all—
15   For the wife not to stand apart from the husband.
    But now there's hatred everywhere, Love is diseased.
    For, deserting his own children and my mistress,
    Jason has taken a royal wife to his bed,
    The daughter of the ruler of this land, Creon.
20   And poor Medea is slighted, and cries aloud on the
    Vows they made to each other, the right hands clasped
    In eternal promise. She calls upon the gods to witness
    What sort of return Jason has made to her love.
    She lies without food and gives herself up to suffering,
25   Wasting away every moment of the day in tears.
    So it has gone since she knew herself slighted by him.
    Not stirring an eye, not moving her face from the ground,
    No more than either a rock or surging sea water
    She listens when she is given friendly advice.
30   Except that sometimes she twists back her white neck and
    Moans to herself, calling out on her father's name,
    And her land, and her home betrayed when she came away with
    A man who now is determined to dishonor her.
    Poor creature, she has discovered by her sufferings
35   What it means to one not to have lost one's own country.

---

1 **Argo** Jason's ship on the expedition of the Argonauts, sent by Pelias, king of Iolcus in Thessaly (Jason's uncle, who had usurped the throne), to Colchis on the Black Sea. The Symplegades were clashing rocks, one of the obstacles along the way. Pelion is a mountain in Thessaly. Medea was a princess of Colchis who fell in love with Jason and followed him back to Greece

    She has turned from the children and does not like to see them.
    I am afraid she may think of some dreadful thing,
    For her heart is violent. She will never put up with
    The treatment she is getting. I know and fear her
40   Lest she may sharpen a sword and thrust to the heart,
    Stealing into the palace where the bed is made,
    Or even kill the king and the new-wedded groom,
    And thus bring a greater misfortune on herself.
    She's a strange woman. I know it won't be easy
45   To make an enemy of her and come off best.
    But here the children come. They have finished playing.
    They have no thought at all of their mother's trouble.
    Indeed it is not usual for the young to grieve.

(Enter from the right the slave who is the TUTOR *to Medea's two small children. The* CHILDREN *follow him.)*

TUTOR: You old retainer of my mistress' household,
50   Why are you standing here all alone in front of the
    Gates and moaning to yourself over your misfortune?
    Medea could not wish you to leave her alone.
NURSE: Old man, and guardian of the children of Jason,
    If one is a good servant, it's a terrible thing
55   When one's master's luck is out; it goes to one's heart.
    So I myself have got into such a state of grief
    That a longing stole over me to come outside here
    And tell the earth and air of my mistress' sorrows.
TUTOR: Has the poor lady not yet given up her crying?
NURSE: Given up? She's at the start, not halfway through her
60   tears.
TUTOR: Poor fool—if I may call my mistress such a name—
    How ignorant she is of trouble more to come.
NURSE: What do you mean, old man? You needn't fear to
    speak.
TUTOR: Nothing. I take back the words which I used just now.
NURSE: Don't, by your beard, hide this from me, your
65   fellow-servant.
    If need be, I'll keep quiet about what you tell me.
TUTOR: I heard a person saying, while I myself seemed
    Not to be paying attention, when I was at the place
    Where the old draught-players sit, by the holy fountain,
70   That Creon, ruler of the land, intends to drive
    These children and their mother in exile from Corinth.
    But whether what he said is really true or not
    I do not know. I pray that it may not be true.

NURSE: And will Jason put up with it that his children
75   Should suffer so, though he's no friend to their mother?
TUTOR: Old ties give place to new ones. As for Jason, he
     No longer has a feeling for this house of ours.
NURSE: It's black indeed for us, when we add new to old
     Sorrows before even the present sky has cleared.
80 TUTOR: But you be silent, and keep all this to yourself.
     It is not the right time to tell our mistress of it.
NURSE: Do you hear, children, what a father he is to you?
     I wish he were dead—but no, he is still my master.
     Yet certainly he has proved unkind to his dear ones.
85 TUTOR: What's strange in that? Have you only just discovered
     That everyone loves himself more than his neighbor?
     Some have good reason, others get something out of it.
     So Jason neglects his children for the new bride.
NURSE: Go indoors, children. That will be the best thing.
90   And you, keep them to themselves as much as possible.
     Don't bring them near their mother in her angry mood.
     For I've seen her already blazing her eyes at them
     As though she meant some mischief and I am sure that
     She'll not stop raging until she has struck at someone.
95   May it be an enemy and not a friend she hurts!

(MEDEA *is heard inside the house.*)

MEDIA: Ah, wretch! Ah, lost in my sufferings,
     I wish, I wish I might die.
NURSE: What did I say, dear children? Your mother
     Frets her heart and frets it to anger.
100   Run away quickly into the house.
     And keep well out of her sight.
     Don't go anywhere near, but be careful
     Of the wildness and bitter nature
     Of that proud mind.
105   Go now! Run quickly indoors.
     It is clear that she soon will put lightning
     In that cloud of her cries that is rising
     With a passion increasing. O, what will she do,
     Proud-hearted and not to be checked on her course,
110   A soul bitten into with wrong?

(*The* TUTOR *takes the* CHILDREN *into the house.*)

MEDEA: Ah, I have suffered
     What should be wept for bitterly. I hate you,
     Children of a hateful mother. I curse you
     And your father. Let the whole house crash.
115 NURSE: Ah, I pity you, you poor creature.
     How can your children share in their father's
     Wickedness? Why do you hate them? Oh children,
     How much I fear that something may happen!
     Great people's tempers are terrible, always
120   Having their own way, seldom checked.
     Dangerous they shift from mood to mood.
     How much better to have been accustomed
     To live on equal terms with one's neighbors.
     I would like to be safe and grow old in a
125   Humble way. What is moderate sounds best,
     Also in practice is best for everyone.
     Greatness brings no profit to people.
     God indeed, when in anger, brings
     Greater ruin to great men's houses.

(*Enter, on the right, a* CHORUS *of Corinthian women. They have come to inquire about* MEDEA *and to attempt to console her.*)

CHORUS: I heard the voice, I heard the cry   130
     Of Colchis' wretched daughter.
     Tell me, mother, is she not yet
     At rest? Within the double gates
     Of the court I heard her cry. I am sorry
     For the sorrow of this home. O, say, what has happened?   135
NURSE: There is no home. It's over and done with.
     Her husband holds fast to his royal wedding,
     While she, my mistress, cries out her eyes
     There in her room, and takes no warmth from
     Any word of any friend.   140
MEDEA: O, I wish
     That lightning from heaven would split my head open.
     Oh, what use have I now for life?
     I would find my release in death
     And leave hateful existence behind me.   145
CHORUS: O God and Earth and Heaven!
     Did you hear what a cry was that
     Which the sad wife sings?
     Poor foolish one, why should you long.
     For that appalling rest?   150
     The final end of death comes fast.
     No need to pray for that.
     Suppose your man gives honor
     To another woman's bed.
     It often happens. Don't be hurt.   155
     God will be your friend in this.
     You must not waste away
     Grieving too much for him who shared your bed.
MEDEA: Great Themis, lady Artemis, behold
     The things I suffer, though I made him promise, 160
     My hateful husband. I pray that I may see him,
     Him and his bride and all their palace shattered
     For the wrong they dare to do me without cause.
     Oh, my father! Oh, my country! In what dishonor
     I left you, killing my own brother for it.   165
NURSE: Do you hear what she says, and how she cries
     On Themis, the goddess of Promises, and on Zeus,
     Whom we believe to be the Keeper of Oaths?
     Of this I am sure, that no small thing
     Will appease my mistress' anger.   170
CHORUS: Will she come into our presence?
     Will she listen when we are speaking
     To the words we say?
     I wish she might relax her rage
     And temper of her heart.   175
     My willingness to help will never
     Be wanting to my friends.
     But go inside and bring her
     Out of the house to us,
     And speak kindly to her: hurry,   180
     Before she wrongs her own.
     This passion of hers moves to something great.

---

159 **Themis . . . Artemis** goddesses: Themis was the goddess of justice; the virgin Artemis would be sensitive to the plight of women
165 **brother** during the escape from Colchis, to delay her father's pursuit

NURSE: I will, but I doubt if I'll manage
    To win my mistress over.
185   But still I'll attempt it to please you.
    Such a look she will flash on her servants
    If any comes near with a message.
    Like a lioness guarding her cubs,
    It is right, I think, to consider
190   Both stupid and lacking in foresight
    Those poets of old who wrote songs
    For revels and dinners and banquets.
    Pleasant sounds for men living at ease;
    But none of them all has discovered
195   How to put to an end with their singing
    Or musical instruments grief,
    Bitter grief, from which death and disaster
    Cheat the hopes of a house. Yet how good
    If music could cure men of this! But why raise
200   To no purpose the voice at a banquet? For *there* is
    Already abundance of pleasure for men
    With a joy of its own.

(*The* NURSE *goes into the house.*)

CHORUS: I heard a shriek that is laden with sorrow,
    Shrilling out her hard grief she cries out
205   Upon him who betrayed both her bed and her marriage.
    Wronged, she calls on the gods,
    On the justice of Zeus, the oath sworn,
    Which brought her away
    To the opposite shore of the Greeks
210   Through the gloomy salt straits to the gateway
    Of the salty unlimited sea.

(MEDEA, *attended by servants, comes out of the house.*)

MEDEA: Women of Corinth, I have come outside to you
    Lest you should be indignant with me; for I know
    That many people are overproud, some when alone,
215   And others when in company. And those who live
    Quietly, as I do, get a bad reputation.
    For a just judgment is not evident in the eyes
    When a man at first sight hates another, before
    Learning his character, being in no way injured;
220   And a foreigner especially must adapt himself.
    I'd not approve of even a fellow-countryman
    Who by pride and want of manners offends his neighbors.
    But on me this thing has fallen so unexpectedly,
    It has broken my heart. I am finished. I let go
225   All my life's joy. My friends, I only want to die.
    It was everything to me to think well of one man,
    And he, my own husband, has turned out wholly vile.
    Of all things which are living and can form a judgment
    We women are the most unfortunate creatures.
230   Firstly, with an excess of wealth it is required
    For us to buy a husband and take for our bodies
    A master; for not to take one is even worse.
    And now the question is serious whether we take
    A good or bad one; for there is no easy escape
235   For a woman, nor can she say no to her marriage.
    She arrives among new modes of behavior and manners,
    And needs prophetic power, unless she has learned at home,
    How best to manage him who shares the bed with her.

    And if we work out all this well and carefully,
    And the husband lives with us and lightly bears his yoke, 240
    Then life is enviable. If not, I'd rather die.
    A man, when he's tired of the company in his home,
    Goes out of the house and puts an end to his boredom
    And turns to a friend or companion of his own age.
    But we are forced to keep our eyes on one alone. 245
    What they say of us is that we have a peaceful time
    Living at home, while they do the fighting in war.
    How wrong they are! I would very much rather stand
    Three times in the front of battle than bear one child.
    Yet what applies to me does not apply to you. 250
    You have a country. Your family home is here.
    You enjoy life and the company of your friends.
    But I am deserted, a refugee, thought nothing of
    By my husband—something he won in a foreign land.
    I have no mother or brother, nor any relation 255
    With whom I can take refuge in this sea of woe.
    This much then is the service I would beg from you:
    If I can find the means or devise any scheme
    To pay my husband back for what he has done to me—
    Him and his father-in-law and the girl who married him— 260
    Just to keep silent. For in other ways a woman
    Is full of fear, defenseless, dreads the sight of cold
    Steel; but, when once she is wronged in the matter of love,
    No other soul can hold so many thoughts of blood.
CHORUS: This I will promise. You are in the right, Medea, 265
    In paying your husband back. I am not surprised at you
    For being sad.
            But look! I see our King Creon
    Approaching. He will tell us of some new plan.

(*Enter, from the right,* CREON, *with attendants.*)

CREON: You, with that angry look, so set against your husband.
    Medea, I order you to leave my territories 270
    An exile, and take along with you your two children,
    And not to waste time doing it. It is my decree,
    And I will see it done. I will not return home
    Until you are cast from the boundaries of my land.
MEDEA: Oh, this is the end for me. I am utterly lost. 275
    Now I am in the full force of the storm of hate
    And have no harbor from ruin to reach easily.
    Yet still, in spite of it all, I'll ask the question:
    What is your reason, Creon, for banishing me?
CREON: I am afraid of you—why should I dissemble it?— 280
    Afraid that you may injure my daughter mortally.
    Many things accumulate to support my feeling.
    You are a clever woman, versed in evil arts,
    And are angry at having lost your husband's love.
    I hear that you are threatening, so they tell me, 285
    To do something against my daughter and Jason
    And me, too. I shall take my precautions first.
    I tell you, I prefer to earn your hatred now
    Than to be soft-hearted and afterward regret it.
MEDEA: This is not the first time, Creon. Often previously 290
    Through being considered clever I have suffered much.
    A person of sense ought never to have his children
    Brought up to be more clever than the average.
    For, apart from cleverness bringing them no profit,
    It will make them objects of envy and ill-will. 295
    If you put new ideas before the eyes of fools

They'll think you foolish and worthless into the bargain;
And if you are thought superior to those who have
Some reputation for learning, you will become hated.
300   I have some knowledge myself of how this happens;
For being clever, I find that some will envy me,
Others object to me. Yet all my cleverness
Is not so much.
                        Well, then, are you frightened, Creon,
That I should harm you? There is no need. It is not
305   My way to transgress the authority of a king.
How have you injured me? You gave your daughter away
To the man you wanted. Oh, certainly I hate
My husband, but you, I think, have acted wisely;
Nor do I grudge it you that your affairs go well.
310   May the marriage be a lucky one! Only let me
Live in this land. For even though I have been wronged,
I will not raise my voice, but submit to my betters.

CREON: What you say sounds gentle enough. Still in my heart
I greatly dread that you are plotting some evil,
315   And therefore I trust you even less than before.
A sharp-tempered woman, or, for that matter, a man,
Is easier to deal with than the clever type
Who holds her tongue. No. You must go. No need for more
Speeches. The thing is fixed. By no manner of means
320   Shall you, an enemy of mine, stay in my country.

MEDEA: I beg you. By your knees, by your new-wedded girl.

CREON: Your words are wasted. You will never persuade me.

MEDEA: Will you drive me out, and give no heed to my prayers?

CREON: I will, for I love my family more than you.

325   MEDEA: O my country! How bitterly now I remember you!

CREON: I love my country too—next after my children.

MEDEA: O what an evil to men is passionate love!

CREON: That would depend on the luck that goes along with it.

MEDEA: O God, do not forget who is the cause of this!

330   CREON: Go. It is no use. Spare me the pain of forcing you.

MEDEA: I'm spared no pain. I lack no pain to be spared me.

CREON: Then you'll be removed by force by one of my men.

MEDEA: No. Creon, not that! But do listen, I beg you.

CREON: Woman, you seem to want to create a disturbance.

335   MEDEA: I *will* go into exile. *This* is not what I beg for.

CREON: Why then this violence and clinging to my hand?

MEDEA: Allow me to remain here just for this one day,
So I may consider where to live in my exile.
And look for support for my children, since their father
340   Chooses to make no kind of provision for them.
Have pity on them! You have children of your own.
It is natural for you to look kindly on them.
For myself I do not mind if I go into exile.
It is the children being in trouble that I mind.

345   CREON: There is nothing tyrannical about my nature,
And by showing mercy I have often been the loser.
Even now I know that I am making a mistake.
All the same you shall have your will. But this I tell you,
That if the light of heaven tomorrow shall see you,
350   You and your children in the confines of my land,
You die. This word I have spoken is firmly fixed.
But now, if you must stay, stay for this day alone.
For in it you can do none of the things I fear.

(*Exit* CREON, *with his attendants*.)

CHORUS: Oh, unfortunate one! Oh, cruel!
Where will you turn? Who will help you?   355
What house or what land to preserve you
From ill can you find?
Medea, a god has thrown suffering
Upon you in waves of despair.

MEDEA: Things have gone badly every way. No doubt of that   360
But not these things this far, and don't imagine so.
There are still trials to come for the new-wedded pair,
And for their relations pain that will mean something.
Do you think that I would ever have fawned on that man
Unless I had some end to gain or profit in it?   365
I would not even have spoken or touched him with my hands.
But he has got to such a pitch of foolishness
That, though he could have made nothing of all my plans
By exiling me, he has given me this one day
To stay here, and in this I will make dead bodies   370
Of three of my enemies—father, the girl, and my husband.
I have many ways of death which I might suit to them,
And do not know, friends, which one to take in hand;
Whether to set fire underneath their bridal mansion,
Or sharpen a sword and thrust it to the heart.   375
Stealing into the palace where the bed is made.
There is just one obstacle to this. If I am caught
Breaking into the house and scheming against it,
I shall die, and give my enemies cause for laughter.
It is best to go by the straight road, the one in which   380
I am most skilled, and make away with them by poison.
So be it then.
And now suppose them dead. What town will receive me?
What friend will offer me a refuge in his land,
Or the guaranty of his house and save my own life?   385
There is none. So I must wait a little time yet,
And if some sure defense should then appear for me,
In craft and silence I will set about this murder.
But if my fate should drive me on without help,
Even though death is certain, I will take the sword   390
Myself and kill, and steadfastly advance to crime.
It shall not be—I swear it by her, my mistress,
Whom most I honor and have chosen as partner,
Hecate, who dwells in the recesses of my hearth—
That any man shall be glad to have injured me.   395
Bitter I will make their marriage for them and mournful,
Bitter the alliance and the driving me out of the land.
Ah, come, Medea, in your plotting and scheming
Leave nothing untried of all those things which you know.
Go forward to the dreadful act. The test has come   400
For resolution. You see how you are treated. Never
Shall you be mocked by Jason's Corinthian wedding,
Whose father was noble, whose grandfather Helius.
You have the skill. What is more, you were born a woman,
And women, though most helpless in doing good deeds,   405
Are of every evil the cleverest of contrivers.

CHORUS: Flow backward to your sources, sacred rivers,
And let the world's great order be reversed.
It is the thoughts of *men* that are deceitful,
Their pledges that are loose.   410

---

394 **Hecate** a goddess of the night   403 **Helius** sun god

Story shall now turn my condition to a fair one,
Women are paid their due.
No more shall evil-sounding fame be theirs.

Cease now, you muses of the ancient singers,
415 To tell the tale of my unfaithfulness;
For not on us did Phoebus, lord of music,
Bestow the lyre's divine
Power, for otherwise I should have sung an answer
To the other sex. Long time
420 Has much to tell of us, and much of them.

You sailed away from your father's home,
With a heart on fire you passed
The double rocks of the sea.
And now in a foreign country
425 You have lost your rest in a widowed bed,
And are driven forth, a refugee
In dishonor from the land.

Good faith has gone, and no more remains
In great Greece a sense of shame.
430 It has flown away to the sky.
No father's house for a haven
Is at hand for you now, and another queen
Of your bed has dispossessed you and
Is mistress of your home.

(Enter JASON, *with attendants.*)

435 JASON: This is not the first occasion that I have noticed
How hopeless it is to deal with a stubborn temper.
For, with reasonable submission to our ruler's will,
You might have lived in this land and kept your home.
As it is you are going to be exiled for your loose speaking.
440 Not that I mind myself. You are free to continue
Telling everyone that Jason is a worthless man.
But as to your talk about the king, consider
Yourself most lucky that exile is your punishment.
I, for my part, have always tried to calm down
445 The anger of the king, and wished you to remain.
But you will not give up your folly, continually
Speaking ill of him, and so you are going to be banished.
All the same, and in spite of your conduct, I'll not desert
My friends, but have come to make some provision for you,
450 So that you and the children may not be penniless
Or in need of anything in exile. Certainly
Exile brings many troubles with it. And even
If you hate me, I cannot think badly of you.
MEDEA: O coward in every way—that is what I call you,
455 With bitterest reproach for your lack of manliness,
You have come, you, my worst enemy, have come to me!
It is not an example of overconfidence
Or of boldness thus to look your friends in the face,
Friends you have injured—no, it is the worst of all
460 Human diseases, shamelessness. But you did well
To come, for I can speak ill of you and lighten
My heart, and you will suffer while you are listening.
And first I will begin from what happened first.

I saved your life, and every Greek knows I saved it.
Who was a shipmate of yours aboard the Argo. 465
When you were sent to control the bulls that breathed fire
And yoke them, and when you would sow that deadly field.
Also that snake, who encircled with his many folds
The Golden Fleece and guarded it and never slept,
I killed, and so gave you the safety of the light. 470
And I myself betrayed my father and my home,
And came with you to Pelias' land of Iolcus.
And then, showing more willingness to help than wisdom,
I killed him, Pelias, with a most dreadful death
At his own daughters' hands, and took away your fear. 475
This is how I behaved to you, you wretched man,
And you forsook me, took another bride to bed,
Though you had children; for, if that had not been,
You would have had an excuse for another wedding.
Faith in your word has gone. Indeed, I cannot tell 480
Whether you think the gods whose names you swore by then
Have ceased to rule and that new standards are set up,
Since you must know you have broken your word to me.
O my right hand, and the knees which you often clasped
In supplication, how senselessly I am treated 485
By this bad man, and how my hopes have missed their mark!
Come, I will share my thoughts as though you were a
    friend—
You! Can I think that you would ever treat me well?
But I will do it, and these questions will make you
Appear the baser. Where am I to go? To my father's? 490
Him I betrayed and his land when I came with you.
To Pelias' wretched daughters? What a fine welcome
They would prepare for me who murdered their father!
For this is my position—hated by my friends
At home, I have, in kindness to you, made enemies 495
Of others whom there was no need to have injured.
And how happy among Greek women you have made me
On your side for all this! A distinguished husband
I have—for breaking promises. When in misery
I am cast out of the land and go into exile, 500
Quite without friends and all alone with my children,
That will be a fine shame for the new-wedded groom,
For his children to wander as beggars and she who saved
    him.
O God, you have given to mortals a sure method
Of telling the gold that is pure from the counterfeit; 505
Why is there no mark engraved upon men's bodies,
By which we could know the true ones from the false ones?
CHORUS: It is a strange form of anger, difficult to cure,
When two friends turn upon each other in hatred.
JASON: As for me, it seems I must be no bad speaker. 510
But, like a man who has a good grip of the tiller,
Reef up his sail, and so run away from under
This mouthing tempest, woman, of your bitter tongue.
Since you insist on building up your kindness to me.
My view is that Cypris was alone responsible 515
Of men and gods for the preserving of my life.
You are clever enough—but really I need not enter
Into the story of how it was love's inescapable
Power that compelled you to keep my person safe.
On this I will not go into too much detail. 520

---

416 **Phoebus** Apollo

515 **Cypris** Aphrodite, goddess of love

In so far as you helped me, you did well enough.
But on this question of saving me, I can prove
You have certainly got from me more than you gave.
Firstly, instead of living among barbarians,
525 You inhabit a Greek land and understand our ways,
How to live by law instead of the sweet will of force.
And all the Greeks considered you a clever woman.
You were honored for it; while, if you were living at
The ends of the earth, nobody would have heard of you.
530 For my part, rather than stores of gold in my house
Or power to sing even sweeter songs than Orpheus,
I'd choose the fate that made me a distinguished man.
There is my reply to your story of my labors.
Remember it was you who started the argument.
535 Next for your attack on my wedding with the princess:
Here I will prove that, first, it was a clever move,
Secondly, a wise one, and, finally, that I made it
In your best interests and the children's. Please keep calm.
When I arrived here from the land of Iolcus,
540 Involved, as I was, in every kind of difficulty,
What luckier chance could I have come across than this,
An exile to marry the daughter of the king?
It was not—the point that seems to upset you—that I
Grew tired of your bed and felt the need of a new bride;
545 Nor with any wish to outdo your number of children.
We have enough already. I am quite content.
But—this was the main reason—that we might live well,
And not be short of anything. I know that all
A man's friends leave him stone-cold if he becomes poor.
550 Also that I might bring my children up worthily
Of my position, and, by producing more of them
To be brothers of yours, we would draw the families
Together and all be happy. You need no children.
And it pays me to do good to those I have now
555 By having others. Do you think this a bad plan?
You wouldn't if the love question hadn't upset you.
But you women have got into such a state of mind
That, if your life at night is good, you think you have
Everything; but, if in that quarter things go wrong,
560 You will consider your best and truest interests
Most hateful. It would have been better far for men
To have got their children in some other way, and women
Not to have existed. Then life would have been good.
CHORUS: Jason, though you have made this speech of yours
       look well,
565 Still I think, even though others do not agree,
You have betrayed your wife and are acting badly.
MEDEA: Surely in many ways I hold different views
       From others, for I think that the plausible speaker
       Who is a villain deserves the greatest punishment.
570 Confident in his tongue's power to adorn evil,
He stops at nothing. Yet he is not really wise.
As in your case. There is no need to put on the airs
Of a clever speaker, for one word will lay you flat.
If you were not a coward, you would not have married
575 Behind my back, but discussed it with me first.
JASON: And you, no doubt, would have furthered the proposal,
       If I had told you of it, you who even now
       Are incapable of controlling your bitter temper.
MEDEA: It was not that. No, you thought it was not respectable
580 As you got on in years to have a foreign wife.

JASON: Make sure of this: it was not because of a woman
       I made the royal alliance in which I now live.
       But, as I said before, I wished to preserve you
       And breed a royal progeny to be brothers
       To the children I have now, a sure defense to us.   585
MEDEA: Let me have no happy fortune that brings pain with it,
       Or prosperity which is upsetting to the mind!
JASON: Change your ideas of what you want, and show more sense.
       Do not consider painful what is good for you.
       Nor, when you are lucky, think yourself unfortunate.   590
MEDEA: You can insult me. You have somewhere to turn to.
       But I shall go from this land into exile, friendless.
JASON: It was what you chose yourself. Don't blame others for it.
MEDEA: And how did I choose it? Did I betray my husband?
JASON: You called down wicked curses on the king's family.   595
MEDEA: A curse, that is what I am become to your house too.
JASON: I do not propose to go into all the rest of it;
       But, if you wish for the children or for yourself
       In exile to have some of my money to help you,
       Say so, for I am prepared to give with open hand,   600
       Or to provide you with introductions to my friends
       Who will treat you well. You are a fool if you do not
       Accept this. Cease your anger and you will profit.
MEDEA: I shall never accept the favors of friends of yours,
       Nor take a thing from you, so you need not offer it.   605
       There is no benefit in the gifts of a bad man.
JASON: Then, in any case, I call the gods to witness that
       I wish to help you and the children in every way,
       But you refuse what is good for you. Obstinately
       You push away your friends. You are sure to suffer for it. 610
MEDEA: Go! No doubt you hanker for your virginal bride,
       And are guilty of lingering too long out of her house.
       Enjoy your wedding. But perhaps—with the help of God—
       You will make the kind of marriage that you will regret.

(JASON *goes out with his attendants.*)

CHORUS: When love is in excess
        It brings a man no honor   615
        Nor any worthiness.
        But if in moderation Cypris comes,
        There is no other power at all so gracious.
        O goddess, never on me let loose the unerring
        Shaft of your bow in the poison of desire.   620

        Let my heart be wise.
        It is the gods' best gift.
        On me let mighty Cypris
        Inflict no wordy wars or restless anger
        To urge my passion to a different love.   625
        But with discernment may she guide women's weddings,
        Honoring most what is peaceful in the bed.

        O country and home,
        Never, never may I be without you,   630
        Living the hopeless life,
        Hard to pass through and painful,
        Most pitiable of all.
        Let death first lay me low and death
        Free me from this daylight,   635
        There is no sorrow above
        The loss of a native land.

I have seen it myself,
Do not tell of a secondhand story.
640　Neither city nor friend
Pitied you when you suffered
The worst of sufferings.
O let him die ungraced whose heart
Will not reward his friends,
645　Who cannot open an honest mind
No friend will he be of mine.

(Enter AEGEUS, *king of Athens, an old friend of* MEDEA.)

AEGEUS: Medea, greeting! This is the best introduction
　　Of which men know for conversation between friends.
MEDEA: Greeting to you too, Aegeus, son of King Pandion.
650　　Where have you come from to visit this country's soil?
AEGEUS: I have just left the ancient oracle of Phoebus.
MEDEA: And why did you go to earth's prophetic center?
AEGEUS: I went to inquire how children might be born to me.
MEDEA: Is it so? Your life still up to this point is childless?
655　AEGEUS: Yes. By the fate of some power we have no children.
MEDEA: Have you a wife, or is there none to share your bed?
AEGEUS: There is. Yes, I am joined to my wife in marriage.
MEDEA: And what did Phoebus say to you about children?
AEGEUS: Words too wise for a mere man to guess their meaning.
660　MEDEA: It is proper for me to be told the god's reply?
AEGEUS: It is. For sure what is needed is cleverness.
MEDEA: Then what was his message? Tell me, if I may hear.
AEGEUS: I am not to loosen the hanging foot of the wineskin . . .
MEDEA: Until you have done something, or reached some
　　country?
665　AEGEUS: Until I return again to my hearth and house.
MEDEA: And for what purpose have you journeyed to this land?
AEGEUS: There is a man called Pittheus, king of Troezen.
MEDEA: A son of Pelops, they say, a most righteous man.
AEGEUS: With him I wish to discuss the reply of the god.
670　MEDEA: Yes. He is wise and experienced in such matters.
AEGEUS: And to me also the dearest of all my spear-friends.
MEDEA: Well, I hope you have good luck, and achieve your will.
AEGEUS: But why this downcast eye of yours, and this pale cheek?
MEDEA: O Aegeus, my husband has been the worst of all to me.
675　AEGEUS: What do you mean? Say clearly what has caused this grief.
MEDEA: Jason wrongs me, though I have never injured him.
AEGEUS: What has he done? Tell me about it in clearer words.
MEDEA: He has taken a wife to his house, supplanting me.
AEGEUS: Surely he would not dare to do a thing like that.
680　MEDEA: Be sure he has. Once dear, I now am slighted by him.
AEGEUS: Did he fall in love? Or is he tired of your love?
MEDEA: He was greatly in love, this traitor to his friends.
AEGEUS: Then let him go, if, as you say, he is so bad.
MEDEA: A passionate love—for an alliance with the king.
685　AEGEUS: And who gave him his wife? Tell me the rest of it.
MEDEA: It was Creon, he who rules this land of Corinth.
AEGEUS: Indeed, Medea, your grief was understandable.
MEDEA: I am ruined. And there is more to come: I am banished.
AEGEUS: Banished? By whom? Here you tell me of a new wrong.
690　MEDEA: Creon drives me an exile from the land of Corinth.
AEGEUS: Does Jason consent? I cannot approve of this.
MEDEA: He pretends not to, but he will put up with it.
　　Ah, Aegeus, I beg and beseech you, by your beard
　　And by your knees I am making myself your suppliant,
695　　Have pity on me, have pity on your poor friend,

And do not let me go into exile desolate,
But receive me in your land and at your very hearth.
So may your love, with God's help, lead to the bearing
Of children, and so may you yourself die happy.
You do not know what a chance you have come on here.　　700
I will end your childlessness, and I will make you able
To beget children. The drugs I know can do this.
AEGEUS: For many reasons, woman, I am anxious to do
　　This favor for you. First, for the sake of the gods,
　　And then for the birth of children which you promise,　　705
　　For in that respect I am entirely at my wits' end.
　　But this is my position: if you reach my land,
　　I, being in my rights, will try to befriend you.
　　But this much I must warn you of beforehand:
　　I shall not agree to take you out of this country;　　710
　　But if you by yourself can reach my house, then you
　　Shall stay there safely. To none will I give you up
　　But from this land you must make your escape yourself,
　　For I do not wish to incur blame from my friends.
MEDEA: It shall be so. But, if I might have a pledge from you　　715
　　For this, then I would have from you all I desire.
AEGEUS: Do you not trust me? What is it rankles with you?
MEDEA: I trust you, yes. But the house of Pelias hates me,
　　And so does Creon. If you are bound by this oath,
　　When they try to drag me from your land, you will not　　720
　　Abandon me; but if our pact is only words,
　　With no oath to the gods, you will be lightly armed,
　　Unable to resist their summons. I am weak,
　　While they have wealth to help them and a royal house.
AEGEUS: You show much foresight for such negotiations.　　725
　　Well, if you will have it so, I will not refuse.
　　For, both on my side this will be the safest way
　　To have some excuse to put forward to your enemies,
　　And for you it is more certain. You may name the gods.
MEDEA: Swear by the plain of Earth, and Helius, father　　730
　　Of my father, and name together all the gods . . .
AEGEUS: That I will act or not act in what way? Speak.
MEDEA: That you yourself will never cast me from your land,
　　Nor, if any of my enemies should demand me,
　　Will you, in your life, willingly hand me over.　　735
AEGEUS: I swear by the Earth, by the holy light of Helius,
　　By all the gods, I will abide by this you say.
MEDEA: Enough. And, if you fail, what shall happen to you?
AEGEUS: What comes to those who have no regard for heaven.
MEDEA: Go on your way. Farewell. For I am satisfied.　　740
　　And I will reach your city as soon as I can,
　　Having done the deed I have to do and gained my end.

(AEGEUS *goes out*.)

CHORUS: May Hermes, god of travelers,
　　Escort you, Aegeus, to your home!
　　And may you have the things you wish　　745
　　So eagerly; for you
　　Appear to me to be a generous man.
MEDEA: God, and God's daughter, justice, and light of Helius!
　　Now, friends, has come the time of my triumph over
　　My enemies, and now my foot is on the road.　　750
　　Now I am confident they will pay the penalty.
　　For this man, Aegeus, has been like a harbor to me
　　In all my plans just where I was most distressed.
　　To him I can fasten the cable of my safety

755 When I have reached the town and fortress of Pallas.
And now I shall tell to you the whole of my plan.
Listen to these words that are not spoken idly.
I shall send one of my servants to find Jason
And request him to come once more into my sight.
760 And when he comes, the words I'll say will be soft ones.
I'll say that I agree with him, that I approve
The royal wedding he has made, betraying me.
I'll say it was profitable, an excellent idea.
But I shall beg that my children may remain here:
765 Not that I would live in a country that hates me
Children of mine to feel their enemies' insults,
But that by a trick I may kill the king's daughter.
For I will send the children with gifts in their hands
To carry to the bride, so as not to be banished—
770 A finely woven dress and a golden diadem.
And if she takes them and wears them upon her skin
She and all who touch the girl will die in agony;
Such poison will I lay upon the gifts I send.
But there, however, I must leave that account paid.
775 I weep to think of what a deed I have to do
Next after that; for I shall kill my own children.
My children, there is none who can give them safety.
And when I have ruined the whole of Jason's house,
I shall leave the land and flee from the murder of my
780 Dear children, and I shall have done a dreadful deed.
For it is not bearable to be mocked by enemies.
So it must happen. What profit have I in life?
I have no land, no home, no refuge from my pain.
My mistake was made the time I left behind me
785 My father's house, and trusted the words of a Greek,
Who, with heaven's help, will pay me the price for that.
For those children he had from me he will never
See alive again, nor will he on his new bride
Beget another child, for she is to be forced
790 To die a most terrible death by these my poisons.
Let no one think me a weak one, feeble-spirited,
A stay-at-home, but rather just the opposite,
One who can hurt my enemies and help my friends;
For the lives of such persons are most remembered.
795 CHORUS: Since you have shared the knowledge of your plan
        with us,
I both wish to help you and support the normal
Ways of mankind, and tell you not to do this thing.
MEDEA: I can do no other thing. It is understandable
For you to speak thus. You have not suffered as I have.
800 CHORUS: But can you have the heart to kill your flesh and blood?
MEDEA: Yes, for this is the best way to wound my husband.
CHORUS: And you, too. Of women you will be most unhappy.
MEDEA: So it must be. No compromise is possible.

(*She turns to the* NURSE.)

Go, you, at once, and tell Jason to come to me.
805 You I employ on all affairs of greatest trust.
Say nothing of these decisions which I have made.
If you love your mistress, if you were born a woman.
CHORUS: From of old the children of Erechtheus are
        Splendid, the sons of blessed gods. They dwell

In Athens' holy and unconquered land, 810
Where famous Wisdom feeds them and they pass gaily
Always through that most brilliant air where once, they say,
That golden Harmony gave birth to the nine
Pure Muses of Pieria.

And beside the sweet flow of Cephisus' stream, 815
Where Cypris sailed, they say, to draw the water,
And mild soft breezes breathed along her path,
And on her hair were flung the sweet-smelling garlands
Of flowers of roses by the Lovers, the companions
Of Wisdom, her escort, the helpers of men 820
In every kind of excellence.

How then can these holy rivers
Or this holy land love you,
Or the city find you a home,
You, who will kill your children, 825
You, not pure with the rest?
O think of the blow at your children
And think of the blood that you shed.
O, over and over I beg you,
By your knees I beg you do not 830
Be the murderess of your babes!

O where will you find the courage
Or the skill of hand and heart,
When you set yourself to attempt
A deed so dreadful to do? 835
How, when you look upon them,
Can you tearlessly hold the decision
For murder? You will not be able,
When your children fall down and implore you,
You will not be able to dip 840
Steadfast your hand in their blood.

(*Enter* JASON, *with attendants.*)

JASON: I have come at your request. Indeed, although you are
        Bitter against me, this you shall have: I will listen
        To what new thing you want, woman, to get from me.
MEDEA: Jason, I beg you to be forgiving toward me 845
For what I said. It is natural for you to bear with
My temper, since we have had much love together.
I have talked with myself about this and I have
Reproached myself. "Fool" I said, "why am I so mad?
Why am I set against those who have planned wisely? 850
Why make myself an enemy of the authorities
And of my husband, who does the best thing for me
By marrying royalty and having children who
Will be as brothers to my own? What is wrong with me?
Let me give up anger, for the gods are kind to me. 855
Have I not children, and do I not know that we
In exile from our country must be short of friends?"
When I considered this I saw that I had shown
Great lack of sense, and that my anger was foolish.
Now I agree with you. I think that you are wise 860
In having this other wife as well as me, and I
Was mad. I should have helped you in these plans of yours,

---

755 **fortress of Pallas** Athens, the town of Athena   808 **children of
Erechtheus** the Athenians

815 **beside . . . stream** at Athens

Have joined in the wedding, stood by the marriage bed,
Have taken pleasure in attendance on your bride.
865 But we women are what we are—perhaps a little
Worthless; and you men must not be like us in this,
Nor be foolish in return when we are foolish.
Now, I give in, and admit that then I was wrong.
I have come to a better understanding now.

(She turns toward the house.)

870 Children, come here, my children, come outdoors to us!
Welcome your father with me, and say goodbye to him,
And with your mother, who just now was his enemy,
Join again in making friends with him who loves us.

(Enter the CHILDREN, *attended by the* TUTOR.)

We have made peace, and all our anger is over.
875 Take hold of his right hand—O God, I am thinking
Of something which may happen in the secret future.
O children, will you just so, after a long life,
Hold out your loving arms at the grave? O children,
How ready to cry I am, how full of foreboding!
880 I am ending at last this quarrel with your father,
And, look my soft eyes have suddenly filled with tears.
CHORUS: And the pale tears have started also in my eyes.
O may the trouble not grow worse than now it is!
JASON: I approve of what you say. And I cannot blame you
Even for what you said before. It is natural
885 For a woman to be wild with her husband when he
Goes in for secret love. But now your mind has turned
To better reasoning. In the end you have come to
The right decision, like the clever woman you are.
And of you, children, your father is taking care.
890 He has made, with God's help, ample provision for you.
For I think that a time will come when you will be
The leading people in Corinth with your brothers.
You must grow up. As to the future, your father
And those of the gods who love him will deal with that.
895 I want to see you, when you have become young men,
Healthy and strong, better men than my enemies.
Medea, why are your eyes all wet with pale tears?
Why is your cheek so white and turned away from me?
Are not these words of mine pleasing for you to hear?
900 MEDEA: It is nothing. I was thinking about these children.
JASON: You must be cheerful. I shall look after them well.
MEDEA: I will be. It is not that I distrust your words,
But a woman is a frail thing, prone to crying.
JASON: But why then should you grieve so much for these
children?
905 MEDEA: I am their mother. When you prayed that they
might live
I felt unhappy to think that these things will be.
But come, I have said something of the things I meant
To say to you, and now I will tell you the rest.
910 Since it is the king's will to banish me from here—
And for me, too, I know that this is the best thing,
Not to be in your way by living here or in
The king's way, since they think me ill-disposed to them—
I then am going into exile from this land;
915 But do you, so that you may have the care of them,
Beg Creon that the children may not be banished.

JASON: I doubt if I'll succeed, but still I'll attempt it.
MEDEA: Then you must tell your wife to beg from her father
That the children may be reprieved from banishment.
JASON: I will, and with her I shall certainly succeed. 920
MEDEA: If she is like the rest of us women, you will.
And I, too, will take a hand with you in this business,
For I will send her some gifts which are far fairer,
I am sure of it, than those which now are in fashion,
A finely woven dress and a golden diadem, 925
And the children shall present them. Quick, let one of you
Servants bring here to me that beautiful dress.

(One of her attendants goes into the house.)

She will be happy not in one way, but in a hundred,
Having so fine a man as you to share her bed,
And with this beautiful dress which Helius of old, 930
My father's father, bestowed on his descendants.

(Enter attendant carrying the poisoned dress and diadem.)

There, children, take these wedding presents in your hands.
Take them to the royal princess, the happy bride,
And give them to her. She will not think little of them.
JASON: No, don't be foolish, and empty your hands of these. 935
Do you think the palace is short of dresses to wear?
Do you think there is no gold there? Keep them, don't
give them
Away. If my wife considers me of any value,
She will think more of me than money, I am sure of it.
MEDEA: No, let me have my way. They say the gods themselves 940
Are moved by gifts, and gold does more with men than words.
Hers is the luck, her fortune that which god blesses;
She is young and a princess; but for my children's reprieve
I would give my very life, and not gold only.
Go children, go together to that rich palace, 945
Be suppliants to the new wife of your father,
My lady, beg her not to let you be banished.
And give her the dress—for this is of great importance,
That she should take the gift into her hand from yours.
Go, quick as you can. And bring your mother good news 950
By your success of those things which she longs to gain.

*(*JASON *goes out with his attendants, followed by the* TUTOR *and
the* CHILDREN *carrying the poisoned gifts.)*

CHORUS: Now there is no hope left for the children's lives.
Now there is none. They are walking already to murder.
The bride, poor bride, will accept the curse of the gold,
Will accept the bright diadem. 955
Around her yellow hair she will set that dress
Of death with her own hands.

The grace and the perfume and glow of the golden robe
Will charm her to put them upon her and wear the wreath,
And now her wedding will be with the dead below, 960
Into such a trap she will fall,
Poor thing, into such a fate of death and never
Escape from under that curse.

You, too, O wretched bridegroom, making your match
with kings,

965   You do not see that you bring
    Destruction on your children and on her,
    Your wife, a fearful death.
    Poor soul, what a fall is yours!

    In your grief, too, I weep, mother of little children,
970   You who will murder your own,
    In vengeance for the loss of married love
    Which Jason has betrayed
    As he lives with another wife.

(*Enter the* TUTOR *with the* CHILDREN.)

    TUTOR: Mistress, I tell you that these children are reprieved,
975   And the royal bride has been pleased to take in her hands
    Your gifts. In that quarter the children are secure.
    But come,
    Why do you stand confused when you are fortunate?
    Why have you turned round with your cheek away from me?
980   Are not these words of mine pleasing for you to hear?
    MEDEA: Oh! I am lost!
    TUTOR: That word is not in harmony with my tidings.
    MEDEA: I am lost, I am lost!
    TUTOR: Am I in ignorance telling you
    Of some disaster, and not the good news I thought?
985   MEDEA: You have told what you have told. I do not blame you.
    TUTOR: Why then this downcast eye, and this weeping of tears?
    MEDEA: Oh, I am forced to weep, old man. The gods and I,
    I in a kind of madness, have contrived all this.
    TUTOR: Courage! You, too, will be brought home by your
    children.
990   MEDEA: Ah, before that happens I shall bring others home.
    TUTOR: Others before you have been parted from their children.
    Mortals must bear in resignation their ill luck.
    MEDEA: That is what I shall do. But go inside the house,
    And do for the children your usual daily work.

(*The* TUTOR *goes into the house.* MEDEA *turns to her* CHILDREN.)

995   O children, O my children, you have a city,
    You have a home, and you can leave me behind you,
    And without your mother you may live there forever.
    But I am going in exile to another land
    Before I have seen you happy and taken pleasure in you,
1000   Before I have dressed your brides and made your marriage beds
    And held up the torch at the ceremony of wedding.
    Oh, what a wretch I am in this my self-willed thought!
    What was the purpose, children, for which I reared you?
    For all my travail and wearing myself away?
1005   They were sterile, those pains I had in the bearing of you.
    Oh surely once the hopes in you I had, poor me,
    Were high ones: you would look after me in old age,
    And when I died would deck me well with your own hands;
    A thing which all would have done. Oh but now it is gone,
1010   That lovely thought. For, once I am left without you,
    Sad will be the life I'll lead and sorrowful for me.
    And you will never see your mother again with
    Your dear eyes, gone to another mode of living.
    Why, children, do you look upon me with your eyes?
1015   Why do you smile so sweetly that last smile of all?
    Oh, Oh, what can I do? My spirit has gone from me,
    Friends, when I saw that bright look in the children's eyes.

    I cannot bear to do it. I renounce my plans
    I had before. I'll take my children away from
    This land. Why should I hurt their father with the pain   1020
    They feel, and suffer twice as much of pain myself?
    No, no, I will not do it. I renounce my plans.
    Ah, what is wrong with me? Do I want to let go
    My enemies unhurt and be laughed at for it?
    I must face this thing. Oh, but what a weak woman   1025
    Even to admit to my mind these soft arguments.
    Children, go into the house. And he whom law forbids
    To stand in attendance at my sacrifices,
    Let him see to it. I shall not mar my handiwork.
    Oh! Oh!   1030
    Do not, O my heart, you must not do these things!
    Poor heart, let them go, have pity upon the children.
    If they live with you in Athens they will cheer you.
    No! By Hell's avenging furies it shall not be—
    This shall never be, that I should suffer my children   1035
    To be the prey of my enemies' insolence.
    Every way is it fixed. The bride will not escape.
    No, the diadem is now upon her head, and she,
    The royal princess, is dying in the dress, I know it.
    But—for it is the most dreadful of roads for me   1040
    To tread, and them I shall send on a more dreadful still—
    I wish to speak to the children.

(*She calls the* CHILDREN *to her.*)

                        Come, children, give
    Me your hands, give your mother your hands to kiss them.
    Oh the dear hands, and O how dear are these lips to me,
    And the generous eyes and the bearing of my children!   1045
    I wish you happiness, but not here in this world.
    What is here your father took. Oh how good to hold you!
    How delicate the skin, how sweet the breath of children!
    Go, go! I am no longer able, no longer
    To look upon you. I am overcome by sorrow.   1050

(*The* CHILDREN *go into the house.*)

    I know indeed what evil I intend to do,
    But stronger than all my afterthoughts is my fury,
    Fury that brings upon mortals the greatest evils.

(*She goes out to the right, toward the royal palace.*)

    CHORUS: Often before
    I have gone through more subtle reasons,   1055
    And have come upon questionings greater
    Than a woman should strive to search out.
    But we too have a goddess to help us
    And accompany us into wisdom.
    Not all of us. Still you will find   1060
    Among many women a few,
    And our sex is not without learning.
    This I say, that those who have never
    Had children, who know nothing of it,
    In happiness have the advantage   1065
    Over those who are parents.
    The childless, who never discover
    Whether children turn out as a good thing
    Or as something to cause pain, are spared

1070 Many troubles in lacking this knowledge.
And those who have in their homes
The sweet presence of children, I see that their lives
Are all wasted away by their worries.
First they must think how to bring them up well and
1075 How to leave them something to live on.
And then after this whether all their toil
Is for those who will turn out good or bad,
Is still an unanswered question.
And of one more trouble, the last of all,
1080 That is common to mortals I tell.
For suppose you have found them enough for their living,
Suppose that the children have grown into youth
And have turned out good, still, if God so wills it,
Death will away with your children's bodies,
1085 And carry them off into Hades.
What is our profit, then, that for the sake of
Children the gods should pile upon mortals
After all else
This most terrible grief of all?

(Enter MEDEA, *from the spectators' right*.)

1090 MEDEA: Friends, I can tell you that for long I have waited
For the event. I stare toward the place from where
The news will come. And now, see one of Jason's servants
Is on his way here, and that labored breath of his
Shows he has tidings for us, and evil tidings.

(Enter, *also from the right, the* MESSENGER.)

1095 MESSENGER: Medea, you who have done such a dreadful thing,
So outrageous, run for your life, take what you can,
A ship to bear you hence or chariot on land.
MEDEA: And what is the reason deserves such flight as this?
MESSENGER: She is dead, only just now, the royal princess,
1100 And Creon dead, too, her father, by your poisons.
MEDEA: The finest words you have spoken. Now and hereafter
I shall count you among my benefactors and friends.
MESSENGER: What! Are you right in the mind? Are you not mad,
Woman? The house of the king is outraged by you.
1105 Do you enjoy it? Not afraid of such doings?
MEDEA: To what you say I on my side have something too
To say in answer. Do not be in a hurry, friend,
But speak. How did they die? You will delight me twice
As much again if you say they died in agony.
1110 MESSENGER: When those two children, born of you, had
entered in,
Their father with them, and passed into the bride's house,
We were pleased, we slaves who were distressed by your
wrongs.
All through the house we were talking of but one thing,
How you and your husband had made up your quarrel.
1115 Some kissed the children's hands and some their yellow hair,
And I myself was so full of my joy that I
Followed the children into the women's quarters.
Our mistress, whom we honor now instead of you,
Before she noticed that your two children were there,
1120 Was keeping her eye fixed eagerly on Jason.
Afterwards, however, she covered up her eyes,
Her cheek paled, and she turned herself away from him,
So disgusted was she at the children's coming there.

But your husband tried to end the girl's bad temper,
And said "You must not look unkindly on your friends. 1125
Cease to be angry. Turn your head to me again.
Have as your friends the same ones as your husband has.
And take these gifts, and beg your father to reprieve
These children from their exile. Do it for my sake."
She, when she saw the dress, could not restrain herself. 1130
She agreed with all her husband said, and before
He and the children had gone far from the palace,
She took the gorgeous robe and dressed herself in it,
And put the golden crown around her curly locks,
And arranged the set of the hair in a shining mirror, 1135
And smiled at the lifeless image of herself in it.
Then she rose from her chair and walked about the room,
With her gleaming feet stepping most soft and delicate,
All overjoyed with the present. Often and often
She would stretch her foot out straight and look along it. 1140
But after that it was a fearful thing to see.
The color of her face changed, and she staggered back,
She ran, and her legs trembled, and she only just
Managed to reach a chair without falling flat down.
An aged woman servant who, I take it, thought 1145
This was some seizure of Pan or another god,
Cried out "God bless us," but that was before she saw
The white foam breaking through her lips and her rolling
The pupils of her eyes and her face all bloodless.
Then she raised a different cry from that "God bless us," 1150
A huge shriek, and the women ran, one to the king,
One to the newly wedded husband to tell him
What had happened to his bride; and with frequent sound
The whole of the palace rang as they went running.
One walking quickly round the course of a race-track 1155
Would now have turned the bend and be close to the goal,
When she, poor girl, opened her shut and speechless eye,
And with a terrible groan she came to herself.
For a twofold pain was moving up against her.
The wreath of gold that was resting around her head 1160
Let forth a fearful stream of all-devouring fire,
And the finely woven dress your children gave to her,
Was fastening on the unhappy girl's fine flesh.
She leapt up from the chair, and all on fire she ran,
Shaking her hair now this way and now that, trying 1165
To hurl the diadem away; but fixedly
The gold preserved its grip, and, when she shook her hair,
Then more and twice as fiercely the fire blazed out.
Till, beaten by her fate, she fell down to the ground,
Hard to be recognized except by a parent. 1170
Neither the setting of her eyes was plain to see,
Nor the shapeliness of her face. From the top of
Her head there oozed out blood and fire mixed together.
Like the drops on pine-bark, so the flesh from her bones
Dropped away, torn by the hidden fang of the poison. 1175
It was a fearful sight; and terror held us all
From touching the corpse. We had learned from what had
happened.
But her wretched father, knowing nothing of the event,
Came suddenly to the house, and fell upon the corpse,
And at once cried out and folded his arms about her, 1180
And kissed her and spoke to her, saying, "O my poor child,
What heavenly power has so shamefully destroyed you?
And who has set me here like an ancient sepulcher,
Deprived of you? O let me die with you, my child!"

1185 And when he had made an end of his wailing and crying,
Then the old man wished to raise himself to his feet;
But, as the ivy clings to the twigs of the laurel,
So he stuck to the fine dress, and he struggled fearfully.
For he was trying to lift himself to his knee,
1190 And she was pulling him down, and when he tugged hard
He would be ripping his aged flesh from his bones.
At last his life was quenched, and the unhappy man
Gave up the ghost, no longer could hold up his head.
There they lie close, the daughter and the old father,
1195 Dead bodies, an event he prayed for in his tears.
As for your interests, I will say nothing of them,
For you will find your own escape from punishment.
Our human life I think and have thought a shadow,
And I do not fear to say that those who are held
1200 Wise among men and who search the reasons of things
Are those who bring the most sorrow on themselves.
For of mortals there is no one who is happy.
If wealth flows in upon one, one may be perhaps
Luckier than one's neighbor, but still not happy.

(*Exit.*)

1205 CHORUS: Heaven, it seems, on this day has fastened many
Evils on Jason, and Jason has deserved them.
Poor girl, the daughter of Creon, how I pity you
And your misfortunes, you who have gone quite away
To the house of Hades because of marrying Jason.
1210 MEDEA: Women, my task is fixed: as quickly as I may
To kill my children, and start away from this land,
And not, by wasting time, to suffer my children
To be slain by another hand less kindly to them.
Force every way will have it they must die, and since
1215 This must be so, then I, their mother, shall kill them.
Oh, arm yourself in steel, my heart! Do not hang back
From doing this fearful and necessary wrong.
Oh, come, my hand, poor wretched hand, and take the sword.
Take it, step forward to this bitter starting point,
1220 And do not be a coward, do not think of them,
How sweet they are, and how you are their mother. Just for
This one short day be forgetful of your children,
Afterward weep; for even though you will kill them,
They were very dear—Oh, I am an unhappy woman!

(*With a cry she rushes into the house.*)

1225 CHORUS: O Earth, and the far shining
Ray of the Sun, look down, look down upon
This poor lost woman, look, before she raises
The hand of murder against her flesh and blood.
Yours was the golden birth from which
1230 She sprang, and now I fear divine
Blood may be shed by men.
O heavenly light, hold back her hand,
Check her, and drive from out the house
The bloody Fury raised by fiends of Hell.
1235 Vain waste, your care of children;
Was it in vain you bore the babes you loved,
After you passed the inhospitable strait
Between the dark blue rocks, Symplegades?
O wretched one, how has it come,
1240 This heavy anger on your heart,

This cruel bloody mind?
For God from mortals asks a stern
Price for the stain of kindred blood
In like disaster falling on their homes.

(*A cry from* ONE OF THE CHILDREN *is heard.*)

CHORUS: Do you hear the cry, do you hear the children's cry?   1245
O you hard heart, O woman fated for evil!
ONE OF THE CHILDREN: (*From within.*) What can I do and how
escape my mother's hands?
ANOTHER CHILD: (*From within.*) O my dear brother, I cannot tell.
We are lost.
CHORUS: Shall I enter the house? Oh, surely I should
Defend the children from murder.   1250
A CHILD: (*From within.*) O help us, in God's name, for now we
need your help.
Now, now we are close to it. We are trapped by the sword.
CHORUS: O your heart must have been made of rock or steel,
You who can kill
With your own hand the fruit of your own womb.   1255
Of one alone I have heard, one woman alone
Of those of old who laid her hands on her children,
Ino, sent mad by heaven when the wife of Zeus
Drove her out from her home and made her wander;
And because of the wicked shedding of blood   1260
Of her own children she threw
Herself, poor wretch, into the sea and stepped away
Over the sea-cliff to die with her two children.
What horror more can be? O women's love,
So full of trouble,   1265
How many evils have you caused already!

(*Enter* JASON, *with attendants.*)

JASON: You women, standing close in front of this dwelling,
Is she, Medea, she who did this dreadful deed,
Still in the house, or has she run away in flight?
For she will have to hide herself beneath the earth,   1270
Or raise herself on wings into the height of air,
If she wishes to escape the royal vengeance.
Does she imagine that, having killed our rulers,
She will herself escape uninjured from this house?
But I am thinking not so much of her as for   1275
The children—her the king's friends will make to suffer
For what she did. So I have come to save the lives
Of my boys, in case the royal house should harm them
While taking vengeance for their mother's wicked deed.
CHORUS: O Jason, if you but knew how deeply you are   1280
Involved in sorrow, you would not have spoken so.
JASON: What is it? That she is planning to kill me also?
CHORUS: Your children are dead, and by their own mother's
hand.
JASON: What! That is it? O woman, you have destroyed me!
CHORUS: You must make up your mind your children are no   1285
more.
JASON: Where did she kill them? Was it here or in the house?
CHORUS: Open the gates and there you will see them
murdered.
JASON: Quick as you can unlock the doors, men, and undo
The fastenings and let me see this double evil,
My children dead and her—Oh her I will repay.   1290

(*His attendants rush to the door.* MEDEA *appears above the house in a chariot drawn by dragons. She has the dead bodies of the* CHILDREN *with her.*)

MEDEA: Why do you batter these gates and try to unbar them,
    Seeking the corpses and for me who did the deed?
    You may cease your trouble, and, if you have need of me,
    Speak, if you wish. You will never touch me with your hand,
1295   Such a chariot has Helius, my father's father,
    Given me to defend me from my enemies.
JASON: You hateful thing, you woman most utterly loathed
    By the gods and me and by all the race of mankind,
    You who have had the heart to raise a sword against
1300   Your children, you, their mother, and left me childless—
    You have done this, and do you still look at the sun
    And at the earth, after these most fearful doings?
    I wish you dead. Now I see it plain, though at that time
    I did not, when I took you from your foreign home
1305   And brought you to a Greek house, you, an evil thing,
    A traitress to your father and your native land.
    The gods hurled the avenging curse of yours on me.
    For your own brother you slew at your own hearthside,
    And then came aboard that beautiful ship, the Argo.
1310   And that was your beginning. When you were married
    To me, your husband, and had borne children to me,
    For the sake of pleasure in the bed you killed them.
    There is no Greek woman who would have dared such deeds,
    Out of all those whom I passed over and chose you
1315   To marry instead, a bitter destructive match,
    A monster, not a woman, having a nature
    Wilder than that of Scylla in the Tuscan sea.
    Ah! no, not if I had ten thousand words of shame
    Could I sting you. You are naturally so brazen.
1320   Go, worker in evil, stained with your children's blood.
    For me remains to cry aloud upon my fate,
    Who will get no pleasure from my newly wedded love,
    And the boys whom I begot and brought up, never
    Shall I speak to them alive. Oh, my life is over!
1325 MEDEA: Long would be the answer which I might have made to
    These words of yours, if Zeus the father did not know
    How I have treated you and what you did to me.
    No, it was not to be that you should scorn my love,
    And pleasantly live your life through, laughing at me;
1330   Nor would the princess, nor he who offered the match,
    Creon, drive me away without paying for it.
    So now you may call me a monster, if you wish,
    A Scylla housed in the caves of the Tuscan sea.
    I too, as I had to, have taken hold of your heart.
1335 JASON: You feel the pain yourself. You share in my sorrow.
MEDEA: Yes, and my grief is gain when you cannot mock it.
JASON: O children, what a wicked mother she was to you!
MEDEA: They died from a disease they caught from their father.
JASON: I tell you it was not my hand that destroyed them.
1340 MEDEA: But it was your insolence, and your virgin wedding.

1317 **Scylla** a monster in the *Odyssey*

JASON: And just for the sake of that you chose to kill them.
MEDEA: Is love so small a pain, do you think, for a woman?
JASON: For a wise one, certainly. But you are wholly evil.
MEDEA: The children are dead. I say this to make you suffer.
JASON: The children, I think, will bring down curses on you. 1345
MEDEA: The gods know who was the author of this sorrow.
JASON: Yes, the gods know indeed, they know your loathsome
    heart.
MEDEA: Hate me. But I tire of your barking bitterness.
JASON: And I of yours. It is easier to leave you.
MEDEA: How then? What shall I do? I long to leave you too. 1350
JASON: Give me the bodies to bury and to mourn them.
MEDEA: No, that I will not. I will bury them myself,
    Bearing them to Hera's temple on the promontory;
    So that no enemy may evilly treat them
    By tearing up their grave. In this land of Corinth 1355
    I shall establish a holy feast and sacrifice
    Each year for ever to atone for the blood guilt.
    And I myself go to the land of Erechtheus
    To dwell in Aegeus' house, the son of Pandion.
    While you, as is right, will die without distinction, 1360
    Struck on the head by a piece of the Argo's timber,
    And you will have seen the bitter end of my love.
JASON: May a Fury for the children's sake destroy you,
    And justice, Requitor of blood.
MEDEA: What heavenly power lends an ear 1365
    To a breaker of oaths, a deceiver?
JASON: Oh, I hate you, murderess of children.
MEDEA: Go to your palace. Bury your bride.
JASON: I go, with two children to mourn for.
MEDEA: Not yet do you feel it. Wait for the future. 1370
JASON: Oh, children I loved!
MEDEA: I loved them, you did not.
JASON: You loved them, and killed them.
MEDEA: To make you feel pain.
JASON: Oh, wretch that I am, how I long
    To kiss the dear lips of my children!
MEDEA: Now you would speak to them, now you would kiss them. 1375
    Then you rejected them.
JASON: Let me, I beg you,
    Touch my boys delicate flesh.
MEDEA: I will not. Your words are all wasted.
JASON: O God, do you hear it, this persecution,
    These my sufferings from this hateful 1380
    Woman, this monster, murderess of children?
    Still what I can do that I will do:
    I will lament and cry upon heaven,
    Calling the gods to bear me witness
    How you have killed my boys and prevent me from 1385
    Touching their bodies or giving them burial.
    I wish I had never begot them to see them
    Afterward slaughtered by you.
CHORUS: Zeus in Olympus is the overseer
    Of many doings. Many things the gods 1390
    Achieve beyond our judgment. What we thought
    Is not confirmed and what we thought not god
    Contrives. And so it happens in this story.

Plautus

Titus Maccius Plautus (254–184 BCE) is thought to have been born in Sardinia; because the name *Maccius* recalls the stock glutton of Atellan farce, Plautus may have acted as an itinerant actor, and he served in the Roman army as well, returning to Rome more or less penniless. He began adapting Greek comedies for the Roman theatre sometime before 215 BCE and quickly became the standard against which other comic playwrights were compared. Indeed, at the height of his career, Plautus was hugely popular, and other playwrights and companies vied for success by producing plays under his name; Marcus Terentius Varro (116–27 BCE), writing roughly a century later, attempted to sort the authentic Plautine plays from impostors, and the twenty-one plays he attributed to Plautus are generally accepted today. Plautus' plays represent the largest canon of any classical playwright, and are the earliest remaining Roman literature; at the same time, his plays openly—and brilliantly—appeal to the taste for broad humor of a perhaps drunken, certainly festive audience, and have relatively recently gained deserved appreciation for their mastery of the stage. Indeed, Plautus' rambunctious comedies were written during a period of strict morality in the Roman republic, exemplified by the *Lex Oppia*, or sumptuary laws enacted in 215 BCE, and perhaps typified by the rise of Marcius Porcius Cato (234–149 BCE), known as "Cato the Elder," or "Cato the Censor" to power. When Plautus died in 184 BCE, he had acquired, lost, and regained a large fortune from the stage, but was renowned as Rome's preeminent playwright. Of his many plays, the best known today are *Ampnitrui, Bacchides, Menaechmi, Miles Gloriosus,* and *Pseudolus*; the 1962 Broadway musical *A Funny Thing Happened on the Way to the Forum* (music by Stephen Sondheim, book by Burte Shevelove and Larry Gelbart) adapts Plutarch's *Pseudolus* and elements of other plays.

The Brothers Menaechmus

Plautus' *Brothers Menaechmus* is, today, the most familiar of his comedies, not least due to Shakespeare's amplified revision in *The Comedy of Errors*, itself the source for Richard Rodgers's and Lorenz Hart's 1938 Broadway musical, *The Boys from Syracuse*. As it stands, though, the play reveals Plautus' secure grasp of the conditions of his theater. Set in Greece, *The Brothers Menaechmus* develops a fully Roman ethos and sense of festivity, from the Prologue's opening song advertising Plautus' authorship, to the series of opportunities the script offers for comic byplay with the spectators, beginning with Penicululus' first hungry speech. The play's basic scene—two doorways on a street—provides the conventional backdrop for Plautus' mastery of quick characterization: the hen-pecked husband Menaechmus, his neighbor the beautiful prostitute Erotium (Desirée in this translation), and the ever-hungry slave Peniculus. Developed in part from the conventions of New Comedy, Plautus' character types continue to populate the comic world: we can see types like the clever servant or the *Miles Gloriosus* (braggart soldiier) populating Shakespeare's plays (Puck and Bottom are versions; and Falstaff defined the *Miles Gloriosus* for English audiences) and beyond.

The premise of the play is simple, and directly presented by the prologue: what would happen if a man, coming to a strange town, were taken for his unknown twin brother, by the brother's slave, mistress, and wife? The mainspring of the action is "mistaken identity," though Plautus' whirligig raises the question of "identity" itself: is it something one possesses, or a consequence of social life? Menaechmus I flees his wife, wearing her dress to give to his mistress; for Menaechmus II, Epidamnus is a surprisingly welcoming city, at least until he's assaulted by Peniculus' rage at having been left out of the promised feast, and attacked by "his" wife and father in law—a scrape he eludes by feigning madness. While Plautus is associated with the most morally-upright, even censorious period of the Roman republic, his comedy theatricalizes the extraordinary vitality of our appetites: for food, for sex, and for the festive release from the limits of the self.

Palmer Bovie's English translation attempts to preserve some of the richness of Plautus' Latin, using a relatively flexible iambic pentameter, and striving for rhyme, assonance, and alliteration.

The Brothers Menaechmus

Texas Wesleyan University, Directed by Connie Whitt-Lambert. Pictured: Joy Millard as Sponge and Rene Fuller as the Wife.

This scene from a contemporary college production of Plautus' *The Brothers Menaechmus* dramatizes the play's emphasis on oversight and intrigue.

The Brothers Menaechmus

Plautus

TRANSLATED BY PALMER BOVIE

CHARACTERS

PENICULUS [Brush], *a parasite*
MENAECHMUS I, *a young gentleman living in Epidamnus*
MENAECHMUS II [Sosicles], *a young gentleman of Syracuse*
DÉSIRÉE [Erotium], *a courtesan*
MIXMASTER [Cylindrus], *her cook*
MESSENIO, *slave of Menaechmus II*

MAID, *in the service of Désirée*
WIFE, *wife of Menaechmus I*
OLD MAN, *father-in-law of Menaechmus I*
A DOCTOR
WHIPSTER I
WHIPSTER II

PROLOGUE

Ladies and gentlemen, and everybody else, I announce
In the first fine foremost and friendly words I pronounce,
Myself! How are you all out there? Do let me greet you.
It's a particular pride and personal privilege to meet you,
5 And present to you Plautus in person, that is, as he looks
When he speaks in his very own words; I don't mean in books
Where you read what he says, but here on the stage where
    he *is*.
Won't you lend us your ears and put yourselves quite at ease,
Tune in on our logic, and turn your minds to the plot
10 I now go over in a very few words, not a lot?
    Oh yes . . . poets often insist, more often than not
In their comedies, "It's an action in Athens," it takes place
Where you're expected to find it most charming, in Greece
    (*Irish pronunciation*).
      But I'm not the underhanded sort who is willing to say
15 It takes place somewhere it doesn't, or . . . anyway
Nowhere except *when* it does occur there. And today
While I grant that our play bubbles up through Greek grounds,
It's distilled in Sicilian, not acted in Attic towns.
So your Prologue expounds the preface to his foreword. He
    pounds
20 In the plot now, not a little, but a lot; it's scoops of synopsis
To ladle out. I'll shovel on now, and bury my worries,
In view of the generous way you hear out our stories.
      A certain old man was a merchant in Syracuse.
To him twin sons were born, identical youths
25 So alike in appearance the wet nurse could never get used
To telling them apart when she popped up to offer her breasts;
Their own mother didn't know which was which, she just
    guessed.
Well . . . at least, that's what someone who saw these boys
    once told me:
I don't want you thinking *I* went there and saw them, you see.
Now one day when both boys were seven, their father
30   loaded up
A huge cargo ship full of goods to be sold, and toted up
One of the boys on the boat. Then off they went
To the market together being held in the town of Tarentum;
The other son, of course, he left back home with the mother.
35 And when they got to Tarentum, the father and the other,
There was some sort of fair going on, with hundreds of games,
And hundreds of people to watch them, which quickly explains

How the boy wandered off in the crowd, away from his dad.
A merchant from Epidamnus latched on to the lad
And snatched him off home. And then when the father
    discovered   40
He'd lost his son, sick at heart, he never recovered
From the fatal depression that carried him right to his grave
In Tarentum a few days later on. When the messenger arrived
At Syracuse with this grisly news of how the father lay dead
At Tarentum, and twin number one was completely mislaid,   45
The affectionate grandfather promptly took it in his head
To rename the Syracuse son in honor of the other,
And call him Menaechmus from now on, after his brother—
So dear to the grandfather's heart was that boy and his name:
The grandfather's own, as a matter of fact, was the same.   50
I remember that name *Menaechmus* all right, all the better
Because I'm sure I've seen it stuck up somewhere in *Big
    Letters.*
Isn't that just like us? "Hmmm, *Menaechmus* . . . ," we say,
Funny how it strikes us . . . "Haven't I seen that somewhere
    today?"
But, not to lead you astray,   55
I hereby officially announce, pronounce, and relay
The fact that both twins henceforth have identical names.
      Now, my feet must head Epidamnuswards, for the claims
Of this complicated plot I must measure by the foot; this
    explains,
I hope, how metricalloused my rhythmic diet may be.   60
To survey this plot I must personally run on and see
Where it happens to be ambling along itself, iambically.
And if any of you out there have something you'd like me to do
At Epidamnus for you, speak up and let me know.
Don't forget what things cost, though; I'll need some dough.   65
If you don't tip you're bound to be rooked, even though
When you do tip you'll also be had, for the money will flow
Even farther; the less you hold on to, the more you let go.
      Anyway, here I am back where I started. I stand as
I originally did when I came out and ran on. Epidamnus   70
Is the name of the place, you remember, the merchant of which
Kidnapped the other twin brother. Being very rich,
But childless, he adopted the boy to add interest to his life,
And invested as well for his son in a suitable wife
With a juicy dowry, to marry, and arranged his whole life   75
By making Menaechmus his heir, when he passed away.
Not bad for a lad whose dad was a thief, wouldn't you say?

And curiously enough, that end came around rather soon;
For the merchant was out in the country, not far from town
80   On a day it had rained very hard, and started across a river.
Darned if that body-snatching sliver of a river didn't deliver
The kidnapper himself into the hands of his jailer forever,
And clap the chap off the scene in death's unseen trap.
Menaechmus promptly inherited a fortune; although kidnapped,
85   He is very well off in Epidamnus. He feels quite at ease
And at home with his funds. And guess now, just who would breeze
Into town just today with his slave on the run right behind him?
Menaechmus (you like this?) to search for his brother, and find him,
Perhaps . . . we'll see about that. *Twins Billed to Appear*
90   At Epidamnus today. Of course, they wouldn't be here
Not a bit of it, if our plot didn't admit of it, but *there*
Wherever the story demanded, and in that case I'd steer
You to the right destination and make the situation clear.
    In the acting profession things tend to change: the town
95   The play's in, the actor's part, the lines handed down
He has to say. That house front behind me, for instance,
Depends for its very existence on the playwright's insistence
In installing inside it the characters he would provide it
With, and let live a moment; not even reside, it
100   Appears, but multiply or divide there. Shifty as the truth,
It houses an oldster, kings, beggars, gangsters, a youth;
A sharp-witted bellyaching sponger, any kind of quack
You can think of, the real one, the fake. Our profession is kind,
And makes room for all. Like me, the actors will remind
105   You of the double dealings dwelling anon in our comedy.
I'm off and away now, just going down on one knee
To hope you'll applaud us: smile on poor Plautus
    And not frown on me!

ACT I

SCENE 1

PENICULUS: The boys all call me Peniculus, which may sound ridiculous
But just means *Table Duster* and shows *How Able an Adjuster*
110   I am to dinner and meticulous in clearing off the table:
You can call me Soft Hairbrush: It seems to be my fate
To be famous as a famished feaster and wear such a tail plate.
You know, some men chain down their captives, and they shackle
The legs of runaway slaves. I think *that's* ridiculous,
115   To load still worse weight on a badly enough burdened crate.
If you put pressure on him, the underdog *wants* to get up
And take off, and never do another stroke of work.
Somehow, they'll always wriggle loose, file off the link
Or knock the lock to bits with a rock. Are chains worth the pains?
120   If you'd like to rope someone in, so he doesn't feel
Like escaping, snare him with wine and a meal!
You're putting a ring through his nose when you take him to dinner.
And as long as you keep him well stocked with food and liquor,
Regularly and the way he likes it, he'll stick with you,

Even though he's under heavy sentence. He'll want to serve you; 125
As long as you're bound to give him food, he's bound to eat it.
The nets and meshes of food are remarkably strong
And elastic, and squeeze even tighter when they get long.
I'm off to Menaechmus's at the moment, where I've signed on
To appear for dinner. I volunteer gaily for a jail 130
Like his, especially at meals. He doesn't feed; he deals
With his guests, increasing their status; like a good restauranteur
He doesn't diagnose, he offers a cure. This sharp epicure
Puts out a very fine spread; he doesn't spare the courses;
He builds up skyscrapers of dishes—you see something delicious 135
And have to stand up on the couch and stretch out to reach it
Over all the other things that look nearly as luscious.
I've been out of commission for quite a long intermission,
Not in the preferred position at Menaechmus's house, but at home,
Domiciled and dominated by my own little sweetmeats.
    Those treats 140
I provide for myself and my near ones have proved dear ones'
Thanks to my expensive tastes—and they all go to waist.
So I'm drumming myself out of those ranks, not burning up money
Trooping in with food for the group. Instead, I'm turning tummy
To Menaechmus's place. He may just embrace my company.
    Here he comes now 145
Flouncing out of the house—looks like they've had a row.

SCENE 2

MENAECHMUS I: If you weren't such a mean, prying snoop,
You stoop, you'd see that when I blow up
It's *your* fault. You'd better stop, or
I'll pack you right back to your papa, 150
Drooping out-of-doors, divorced, good and proper.
Every time I go for a walk, you let go a squawk
And assault me with questions. Where am I going?
What's doing? Where? What's *that* I've got there?
I didn't bring home a wife; I brought home a hawk- 155
Eyed customs inspector, an unconscientious objector
To everything I do. One who makes me *declare*
Everything I've got in mind. O woemankind!
Personal effects, you defect detective. Oh, the heck with it!
I guess I've spoiled you with too much attention 160
And turned this into a house of detention.
From now on, things will be different. I'm here to mention
What I expect or else from your lie detector: shelves full of silence;
No more prying, my high-powered Highness; absolute, utter compliance.
I gave you money and clothes, 165
Robes and dresses, domestics;
I've been pretty good and elastic
In meeting your demands.
You keep your hands, and your nose,
Out of my business. That's the best trick 170
To play if you want to stay on good terms with me.
Why look over, inspect, and go right on shaking
The man who's made you a major in his own homemaking?
To prove that you can't fence me in, I've promised today
To take a girl out to dinner and reward you that way. 175

PENICULUS: Taking it out on his wife? Taking that line
   Won't ruin his wife, but will leave me out on a limb.
MENAECHMUS I: Ah now, by God, and good show! I've finally told
      my wife where to go:
   Inside, and to leave me alone. Now where are you uxorious
      types, all of you
   Out there, you who ought to be oozing up front to shower your
      thanks
180   On me for fighting the good fight? And look what I've done,
      each and every one
   Of you, my fellow sufferers. I've taken this delicate mantilladress
   Out of my wife's most favorite chest, to present to my girl.
   An excellent trick, don't you think, to reward the warden
185   By stealing something right from under her nose? I propose
   A subject for congratulations: this beautifully planned,
   Charming little crime, dutifully and well carried out:
   Converting a legalized loss to a preferable self-ruination.
   Diverting the loot from the foe's hands to those of our allies.
PENICULUS: I say there, young fellow, what share in the prize
190   can I
   Hope to realize?
MENAECHMUS I: God! I've dropped into a trap!
PENICULUS: Not at all, a fortified position.
MENAECHMUS I: Who in perdition
   Are you?
PENICULUS: Fine, thanks, who are you? I'm me, as a matter of fact.
MENAECHMUS I: Oh, you. My most modern convenience, you
         beautifully timed supergadget!
PENICULUS: Greetings.
MENAECHMUS I: What are you doing at the moment?
195 PENICULUS: Fervently latching
   Onto the hand of my right-hand man.
MENAECHMUS I: You couldn't be stringing
      along
   At a better time than this that's bringing you on into my orbit.
PENICULUS: That's how I usually time my launching forth in
      search of a luncheon.
   I've studied, got the thing down pat, I don't just play my
      hunches.
MENAECHMUS I: Want to feast your eyes on a sparkling treat I've
200   completed
   The arrangements for?
PENICULUS: It'll look less crooked to me when I see
   Who's cooked it up. If there's been any slip-up in preparing
      this fête
   I'll know when I see what's left untouched on the plate.
MENAECHMUS I: Say, you've seen the famous painting plastered
      against a wall,
   Showing the eagle ferrying off that handsome sort of fancy-bred
205   boyfriend
   To his handler in the sky? Or the one that shows Venus's and
      Adonis's
   Bare . . . ?
PENICULUS: Kneeness? Sure, lots of times, but what do I care
      about art?
MENAECHMUS I: Just look at me? Don't I do that part to
      perfection?
PENICULUS: Cahn't sigh I'm accustomed to a costume . . . what the
      hell is that you're wearing?
MENAECHMUS I: Aren't I the apple of your eye, your Prince
210   Charming? Come on, say it.

PENICULUS: Not until I know what time dinner is and whether
   I'm invited.
MENAECHMUS I: Why not be so disarming as to admit what I ask
   you to?
PENICULUS: All right, all right, prince, you're charming.
MENAECHMUS I: Anything else
   You'd like to add voluntarily?
PENICULUS: Well, that's a fairly airily merrily
   Wingspread you've got there.
MENAECHMUS I: More, more! Makes me *soar!*   215
PENICULUS: Damned if I'll say any more, by God in heaven, until
      I get some whiff
   Of what my reward will be if. You've had a row with your wife.
   I'd better look out warily, carefully; my life is in danger.
MENAECHMUS I: Incidentally, my wife hasn't a clue about where
      we're going, to do
   The town today. We're going to set the hot spots on fire.   220
PENICULUS: Well, thank heavens, now you make sense. How soon
   do I light the pyre?
   The day's half used up already, dead down to the navel.
MENAECHMUS I: You're slowing up the show, interrupting with
      that drivel.
PENICULUS: Knock out my eye, Menaechmus, dig it into the
      ground, bash it
   Back and below til it comes out my ankle, if I ever make a
      sound   225
   From now on, except to say what you order me to.
MENAECHMUS I: Just step over here, away from my door.
PENICULUS: How's this for size?
MENAECHMUS I: A little farther, please.
PENICULUS: It's a breeze. How's this?
      Far enough?
MENAECHMUS I: Now, step out, like a man safe out of reach of the
      lion's den.
PENICULUS: By God in heaven, if you wouldn't make the best
      jockey.   230
MENAECHMUS I: How come?
PENICULUS: You keep looking back over your
      shoulder to see
   If your wife isn't thudding up behind you.
MENAECHMUS I: You're telling me?
PENICULUS: I'm telling you? Well, fellow, I'm not telling you
      anything,
   Let's get that clear; just what you want to hear, or you don't.
   That much I'll say, or I won't. I'm your best yes man yet.   235
MENAECHMUS I: All right, let's have a guess, then, at what you
      can make of
   This garment I'm exposing to your nose. What sort of scent
   Does it put you on the trail of . . . ? Why get pale and shove it
      out of range?
PENICULUS: Strange, it doesn't put me on the trail of; it pins me to
      the tail of . . .
   Look here, old boy, you know as well as I do, men shouldn't
      try to   240
   Imbibe the fragrance of feminine apparel except from up near
      the top
   Of same dainty. Down lower the unwashed part makes you
      feel fainty.
MENAECHMUS I: All right, Peniculus, try this part over here;
      tickle your nose
   With this wholesome whiff. Aha! Now you make like truffles.

PENICULUS: Sure, it suits my snuffles.

MENAECHMUS I: Oh, puffle, come on and say,

245   Say what it tells you. What sort of smells you deduce.

PENICULUS: Phew, what a naral escape! I'm glad to produce my solution.

This is my diagnosis: You steal a *jeune fille* for a meal;

You purloin a *fräulein* for some sirloin; you flirt with a skirt

250   And alert your tastebuds to a smorgasbord; a distress

And theft, and this dress is left for your mistress to drape round

Her; gleaming napery; conjugal japery, all very vapory. The whole deal,

From my point of view, leads straight toward an excellent meal, and I'm joining you.

MENAECHMUS I: Don't! I'm not coming apart. But you've hit

The female suggestion on the head, no question, and orated

255   convincingly.

For I've pretty winsomely sneaked this dress from my wife

And am spiriting it off to the niftiest mistress of mine,

Désirée. I'm ordering a banquet, this very day

For you and me, a treat at her place.

PENICULUS: Oh, I say!

MENAECHMUS I: We'll drink from now til tomorrow's morning

260   star puts out

This night so bibulous.

PENICULUS: I say, you *are* fabulous. Shall I knock

At Désirée's door?

MENAECHMUS I: Sure, go ahead. No, better knock off.

Hold it! I said.

PENICULUS: You're the one that's holding it: my head

Wants to get at that bottle, not back off a mile in the distance.

MENAECHMUS I: Knock very gently.

265   PENICULUS: The door, evidently, 's the

consistency

Of papyrus.

MENAECHMUS I: Knock off, I insist, do desist! God in heaven!

Lay off or I'll knock your block off! And besides, rub your eyes:

Can't you see? Here she comes out, herself, free and easy. Her body

270   Eclipses the sun. An excellent exit, dancing

Into view like this; she wins more acclaim than the flame

Of the sun. He goes quite blind, when I find her so entrancing.

SCENE 3

DÉSIRÉE: Oh, my dear, *dear* Menaechmus, how *are* you today?

PENICULUS: Hey, say!

What about me? Don't I rate a greeting?

DÉSIRÉE: Zero, you cipher.

PENICULUS: Well, a soldier has to get used to being a serial

275   number, I guess.

MENAECHMUS I: Now darling, look here, I would love to have you

go and fix up . . .

PENICULUS: Ohhh, fray can you see? Let's have us a mix-up: you

be the smorgas

And I'll come aboard you. We'll fight it out all day; ohhh, I

say . . .

Til the dawn's early light, which of us battlers is the heavier

weight

When it comes to hitting the bottle. Daisy, you can be the

general,   280

And feel free to choose which company you'll spend the duration

Of this dark operation with. Let's hope your proper ration

is . . . me.

MENAECHMUS I: Sweet and lovely! How loathly my wife appears

in my eyes

When they light on you.

PENICULUS: Meanwhile you put on her things

And wifey still clings to you.

DÉSIRÉE: What in the world . . . ?

MENAECHMUS I: I'm unfurled. 285

My dear girl. Here's the dress I deprive my wife of and provide

You with. You look better in her clothes than she does without

them,

My rose.

DÉSIRÉE: Touché or not touché, I must say I must give way

To so supersartorial an assault on my virtue. You win the day.

PENICULUS: Listen to the mistress whisper sweet somethings, as

long as   290

She sees he's bringing her that gay thing for nothing. Now is

The time, if you love her, to have what you want of her

In the form of some toothsome kisses.

MENAECHMUS I: Oh, hang up, Brush Face.

I've only done just what I swore I would with this garment:

placed

It on the altar of her grace.

PENICULUS: By God in heaven, I give in! 295

Listen, *twist* in it, won't you? I can see you in the ballet, like

a fine

Boy, a dear for the dance, with the veil trailing behind your

tight pants.

MENAECHMUS I: Dance? Me? By God in heaven, you're crazy.

PENICULUS: Me, crazy?

I'd say, easy does it, you may be *that* way instead, in your

head.

DÉSIRÉE: If you're not going to wear it, take it off then. And stop

saying   300

"By God in heaven!"

MENAECHMUS I: After all I won this today by playing a

A pretty dangerous game; I stole it.

PENICULUS: On the whole, it's even

more fraying

To the nerves than Hercules (or "heavenly God," if you please)

Swerving round those curves to steal Hippolyta's girdle and

sneak off swaying.

I'd say you were in more mortal danger than that thievish

stranger   305

Ever ran into, even though he was stronger.

MENAECHMUS I: I can no longer

Hold back this offer I proffer to you, Désirée. So do have it,

You wonderful girl, sole creature alive sympathetic to my

wants.

DÉSIRÉE: This is the true-hearted sort of fervor nature should

always transplant

In the souls of romancers whose desires are their favorite

haunts.   310

PENICULUS: Or at least sharp sparks going broke at full speed

chasing spooks.

MENAECHMUS I: I bought it for my wife last year, $85.00.

PENICULUS: We can close the books on that sum and kiss it good-bye.

MENAECHMUS I: And now can you guess what I want to do?

DÉSIRÉE: Yes, I know.
And what's more I'll do what you want.

315 MENAECHMUS I: Dinner for three,
Chez Daisy. Order this done and I'll be pleased.

PENICULUS: And say, see
While you're at it that whoever goes to buy the food at the forum
Picks out something specially tasty; a perfect little pork filet
Or savory thin-sliced prosciutto, ham recherché,
Like a succulent half-section head of a pig—let's do it the
320   big way,
And have that ham so well cooked that I can pounce on the table like a hawk
Who knows what he likes, and then strikes. And let's make it quick.

DÉSIRÉE: By Jiminy, yes! You're on!

MENAECHMUS I: That's very nice, the way you didn't
Say "By God in heaven." Me and old slothful here, we're heading down-
Town to hang around the forum and see what's up. We'll be
325   right back.
While dinner's cooking, we'll start with the drinking.

DÉSIRÉE: Come on
Along whenever you want. Things will be ready.

MENAECHMUS I: But do get a
steady move on.
Now let's go, and let's you keep up.

PENICULUS: By God in heaven, how true!
I'll follow you all right and I'll slave for you too. If I lost you
Today and got all the wealth in heaven, I wouldn't break
330   even.

(MENAECHMUS I and PENICULUS exit)

DÉSIRÉE: (Alone) I wonder why they always say "God in heaven"?
Where else could he be?
You, girls in there! Call out Mixmaster, the head cook,
And tell him to come outside here. I need him this minute.

(MIXMASTER enters)

DÉSIRÉE: Take this shopping basket, my man, and, yes, here's
335   some money;
Let's see . . . $9.63.

MIXMASTER: Right you are, miss.

DÉSIRÉE: Now scoot, sonny-boy,
And get on with your catering. Buy enough for three people only,
No more, no less.

MIXMASTER: Who's coming?

DÉSIRÉE: Menaechmus, and that lonely
Crowd of his, Soft Hair, the never-to-be-brushed off, plus me.

MIXMASTER: Well, miss, that's three times three plus one,
340   actually:
Peniculus eats enough for eight, and you both make two.

DÉSIRÉE: I've given out the guest list. The rest of this is up to you.

MIXMASTER: Right you are, miss. The dinner is as good as all done.
You can all take your places. Won't you all please sit down?

DÉSIRÉE: Get going now, you fix-faster, and hurry right back from
345   town.

MIXMASTER: I'll be back here so soon you won't even know I've been gone.

ACT II

SCENE 1

(Enter MENAECHMUS II and MESSENIO, accompanied by several crew members)

MENAECHMUS II: Messenio, I tell you, there's no greater source of delight
For sailors than to look out across the deep water and sight
The land they're heading for.

MESSENIO: I couldn't be more   350
In agreement, provided the land you refer to is home. Therefore,
Why in hell, I implore you, are we in Epidamnus?
Do you plan to act like the ocean and noisily slam us
Against every damned piece of land we can touch?

MENAECHMUS II: As much
As I need to cover to locate my own twin, my brother.   355

MESSENIO: But how much longer do we have to keep looking for him?
It's six years now since we started. When we departed
You didn't say we'd try everywhere, moseying to Marseilles,
Skirting around Spain, bounding back to menace Venice,
And do the whole coastal bit from Trieste to Dubrovnik to
360   Split,
Or skim the whole rim of Italy, littorally. As the sea
Goes, that's where we rows. My point is—a haystack
With the well-known needle in it . . . you'd have found it. But we lack
The object to bring our search to a head. He's quite dead,
The man you're after, while you ransack the land of the living   365
If he were anywhere around you'd have found him.

MENAECHMUS II: I won't give in
Until I've found out for sure from someone I have to believe in
Who'll say that he knows that my brother is dead. And when that day
Arrives, our travels are over. But I won't stop pursuing
My other half, and I know what I'm doing: he means   370
Everything to me.

MESSENIO: You're looking for a knot in a marshmallow reed.
We won't go home until we've gone round the world, then, as fellow
Travelers, and written a book about what it looks like?

MENAECHMUS II: I doubt it.
But see here, my boy, you just do as you're told; don't be too bold;
Eat your food; be good; don't be a bother. It's not your good   375
That matters in this expedition.

MESSENIO: Take that definition
Of a typical slave's condition. I know who I am now, all right.
He couldn't have put a bigger proposition in many fewer words,
Or in so clear a light. Still and all, I just can't keep stalling
Around; I can't just stop talking. You listening, Menaechmus?   380

My purse, I mean, our purse, now that I look at it,
  Has too much vacation space; our wardrobe there looks quite
    scanty,
  Are we going in for summer sports? By God in heaven, you'll
    groan,
  Exhausted by the search for your twin, unless you turn back
    home.
385 They'll *wham* us in Epidamnus, positive; Dubrovnik us to
    clinkers.
  The town's chock full of nuts, fast-living long-range drinkers,
  Go-betweens wheedlers, middlemen who take you, the
    stinkers,
  In to be cleaned and doused by the masters of the house,
  I mean mistresses, who whisper sweet slopniks to you,
390 And profit from your losses in the process. That's what
    they do,
  Damn us strangers in this town. No wonder it's called, up and
    down,
  Epidamnus; every damn one of us innocents in Greece
  Gets introduced here to the golden fleece, before he's released,
  Enormously decreased in value.
MENAECHMUS II: Take it easy. Hand me that greasy
  Wallet.
MESSENIO: What do you want with it?
MENAECHMUS II: Your speech has haunted
395 Me. I'm panicked by your frantic appeal to the facts of life.
MESSENIO: Afraid, why afraid for me . . . ?
MENAECHMUS II: You'll whammy us both
    in Epidamnus.
  You're a great lady's man, Messenio: I know you. And I?
  I'm a man of many moods, all of which prompt me to fly
  Off the handle in a hurry. And since I'm the furious sort,
400 And you the luxurious sport, always in pursuit of a skirt,
  I'll manage both crises nicely, and simply divert
  The money into my control. Then you won't waste the whole
  Thing on women; and I won't get mad when you do; or even
    peeved.
MESSENIO: Take it and keep it then, do. I'm somewhat relieved.

SCENE 2

MIXMASTER: I've shopped very shrewdly and well, if I say so
405   myself:
  I'll spread a fine feast in front of these dauntless diners.
  Oh, oh, Menaechmus, already! I'll bet I'm in for a beating:
  The guests have arrived and here I've just gotten back
  From the market. They're walking around in front of the house;
410 I'll go up and greet them. Menaechmus, good afternoon!
MENAECHMUS II: Best wishes, old chap, whoever you happen
    to be.
MIXMASTER: Whoever I'm . . . ? You don't say, Menaechmus, you
    don't know?
MENAECHMUS II: Oh God in heaven, you know I don't.
MIXMASTER: But where
  Are the rest of our guests?
MENAECHMUS II: What guests?
MIXMASTER: Your parasite, for one.
MENAECHMUS II: My parasite? Obviously this fellow is quite off
415   his nut.
MESSENIO: Didn't I tell you this town was lousy with scroungers?

MENAECHMUS II: Which parasite of mine did you mean, young
    man?
MIXMASTER: Why that peachy little Peniculus, the fuzzy table
    duster.
MESSENIO: Oh *him*, peenie brush? He's safe all right, here in
    our bag.
MIXMASTER: Menaechmus, you've come along a bit soon for
    dinner: 420
  I'm just getting back from buying the food.
MENAECHMUS II: Listen here,
  How much does a good box of sure-fire tranquilizers cost
  In this town?
MIXMASTER: $1.98 for the economy size.
MENAECHMUS II: Here's $3.96. Get yourself a double prescription.
  I can see you're quite out of control, making trouble like this 425
  For someone like me you don't even know, whoever *you* are.
MIXMASTER: I'm Mixmaster: that's not complicated, and don't say
  you don't know it.
MENAECHMUS II: You can be Mixmaster, or Sizzling Ham Steak
    with Cloves en Brochette,
  I couldn't care less. I've never seen you before today
  And now that I have, I'm not at all very pleased to meet you. 430
MIXMASTER: Your name's Menaechmus.
MENAECHMUS II: You seem to be talking sense
  At the moment, since you call me by name, but where did you
    learn
  Who I am?
MIXMASTER: Who you are? When I work for your mistress right
    in this house?
  Désirée?
MENAECHMUS II: By God, she's *not* my mistress and I *do not*
  Know you.
MIXMASTER: Don't know *me*, who pours you out drink after drink
    when you come here   435
  For dinner?
MESSENIO: I wish I could lay hands on something to bat this nut
    with.
MENAECHMUS II: *You* mix drinks and pour them for *me*, for *me*,
  Who never even came this way, much less saw Epidamnus
  Before today?
MIXMASTER: Never even saw it, you say?
MENAECHMUS II: Yes; I mean *no*, dear God in heaven, so help
  me, *no!*   440
MIXMASTER: I suppose you don't really live in that house over there?
MENAECHMUS II: May the gods cave the roof in hard on whoever
    does!
MIXMASTER: Stark, raving loony. Wishing himself such bad luck.
  Can you hear me, Menaechmus?
MENAECHMUS II: Depends on what you're
    saying.
MIXMASTER: Now look, take my advice. Remember that $3.96   445
  You offered to give me a minute ago for the pills?
  Go spend it on yourself; you're the one who needs it the most,
  And the soonest, calling down curses, by God in heaven,
  On your very own head. You're just not *all there*, Menaechmus.
  If you've any brains left you'll send out at once for the
    medicine;   450
  There's a new triple dose thing out, The Three Little Big
    Tranquilizers,
  Frightens off all kinds of weird wolves.

MENAECHMUS II: He sure talks a lot.
MIXMASTER: Of course, Menaechmus always teases me, like this;
        he's a joker
    When his wife's not around. What's that you're saying,
        Menaechmus?
MENAECHMUS II: I beg your pardon, Mixmaster, did you say
455   something?
MIXMASTER: How does this stuff look? Like enough for dinner for
        three?
    Or shall I go out and buy more for the girlfriend and you
    And your parasite pal?
MENAECHMUS II: Women? Parasite? Pals? What women,
        what parasites, pal?
MESSENIO: Look here, old boy, what terrible crime is weighing on
        your mind
    And making you pester him so?
460 MIXMASTER: Stranger boy, you stay out
    Of my business; I'll conduct that with the person I know
    And am talking to.
MESSENIO: Oh God in . . . I give up; except for the fact
    That I'm sure as can be that this cook is completely cracked.
MIXMASTER: Well, now, I'll just get busy with these things. I can
        promise you
465   Some succulent results, very soon. You'll stay around the house,
    Menaechmus, I hope. Anything else you can think of?
MENAECHMUS II: I can think of you as one real upside-down cake.
        You're baked.
MIXMASTER: Oh by God in . . . somewhere or other, I could
        swear it's you
    Who are the mixed-up master. I wish you would go . . . lie
        down
470   Somewhere until you feel better, while I take this stuff
    And commit it to the fire-breathing forces of Vulcan. I'll tell
    Désirée you're out here. She'll want to ask you in, I feel sure.

(*He goes into the house*)

MENAECHMUS II: Gone, has he? God, how right I see your words
        were
    When you talked about this place.
MESSENIO: Mark my words further.
    One of those fast-working, loose-jointed women lives here, you
475   can bet,
    As sure as that crackpot cook who went in there said she did.
MENAECHMUS II: I do wonder, though, how he came by my name?
MESSENIO: That's easy.
    Why, that's a cinch. The women have it all worked out.
    They send their slave boys or housemaids–down to the docks.
480   When a strange ship comes in, they ask the passenger's name,
    And find out where he's from. Later on, they pick him up
        casually
    And stick close to him. If their charms have the right effect
    They ship him back home plucked quite clean of his money.
    (*Pointing to* DÉSIRÉE's *house*)
    And right over there rocks a fast little pirate sloop at anchor:
485   We'd better look out for her, and look sharp, commander.
MENAECHMUS II: Damned if I don't think you're right.
MESSENIO: I'll know what
        you think
    For sure when I see what preeeeecautions you're taking.
MENAECHMUS II: Just a moment.
    I hear the door swinging open; let's see who comes out.

MESSENIO: I'll drop our seabag right here. Heave ho, my
        bellboys!
    You fleet runners, shift this gear into neutral for a while.   490

SCENE 3

DÉSIRÉE: (*Singing gaily*) Open the doors, open wide: I don't want
        them shut.
    You in there, look to it, come here and do it,
    What has to be done:
    Couches to be hung with fine drapes;
    Tables adorned; some incense burned;   495
    Lights set blazing; the place made amazing.
    To dazzle and delight your bright lover's heart
    Is to play with skill your gay charming part,
    And importune at his expense while you make your fortune.
    Where is he though? A moment ago, my cook said I'd find him
        standing   500
    Around by the door . . . oh there he is, the one I adore when
        he's handing
    His money over freely. I'll ask him in now for the meal he
        wanted made ready
    And get him started on the drinks, to keep him from staying
        too steady.
    I'll just slip over and speak to him first.
    O my favorite fellow, my poor heart will burst   505
    If you keep standing here outside
    When the doors to our house are open wide
    To take you in. It's much more your place,
    This house, than your own home is, an embrace,
    A bright smile on its face just for you, and a kiss   510
    On that most generous of mouths. This really is your house.
    And now all is prepared just the way you wanted
    And shortly we'll serve you your dinner and pour out the wine.
    (*Pause*)
    I said, the meal's all in order, just as you commanded;
    Whenever you're ready, come on in now, honey, any time.   515
MENAECHMUS II: Who in the world does this woman think she's
        talking to?
DÉSIRÉE: To you, that's who.
MENAECHMUS II: But what business have I with you
    At present, or what have I ever had to do with you up to now?
DÉSIRÉE: Heavens! It's you that Venus has inspired me to prize
    Over all the others, and you've certainly turned out to be
        worth it.   520
    Heavens above! You've set me up high enough with your
        generous gifts!
MENAECHMUS II: This woman is surely quite crazy or definitely
        drunk,
    Messenio, talking such intimate stuff to me,
    A man she doesn't even know.
MESSENIO: I told you so!
    And now, it's only the leaves that are falling. Just wait;   525
    Spend three more days in this town and the trees themselves
    Will be crashing down down on your head. The women are
        biased,
    Buy us this, buy us that, and buzzing around for your money.
    But let me talk to her. Hey, sweetie, I'm speaking to you.
DÉSIRÉE: You're what?
MESSENIO: No, I'm not, I'm who. And while I'm at it,
        just *where*   530
    Did you get to know the man here who's with me so well?

DÉSIRÉE: Why, right here in Epidamnus, where I've been for
    so long.

MESSENIO: Epidamnus? A place he never set foot in before today?

DÉSIRÉE: A *delicious* joke, you rascal. Now, Menaechmus, darling,

535   Won't you come in? You'll feel much cozier and settled.

MENAECHMUS II: By God, the woman's quite right to call me by
    my own name.
    Still I can't help wondering what's up.

MESSENIO: She's got wind of your
    money-bag,
    The one you relieved me of.

MENAECHMUS II: And damned if you didn't alert me
    To that very thing. Here, you'd better take it. That way,

540   I can find out for sure whether she's after me, or my money.

DÉSIRÉE: *Andiam', O caro bene!* And we'll tuck right into that meal;
    Mangiamo, igitur, et cetera.

MENAECHMUS II: Music to my ears,
    And you're very nice to sing it, my dear. I only regret
    I cannot accept.

DÉSIRÉE: But why in the world did you tell me, a short
    while ago,
    To have dinner ready for you?

545 MENAECHMUS II: *I* told *you* to have dinner ready?

DÉSIRÉE: Of course, dinner for three, you, your parasite, and me.

MENAECHMUS II: Oh hell, lady, what the hell is all this parasite stuff?
    God, what a woman! She's crazy as can be once again.

DÉSIRÉE: Cookie duster Peniculus, C. D. Peniculus, the crumb
    devourer.

MENAECHMUS II: But I mean what kind of a peniculus? We all

550   know that's a soft hair
    Brush, but I don't know anyone *named* that. You mean my
    ridiculous
    Little thing, the traveling shoebrush I carry for my suede
    sandals,
    The better to buff them with? What peniculus hangs so close
    to me?

DÉSIRÉE: You know I mean that local leech who just now came by
    with you
    When you brought me that sweet silk dress you stole from your

555   wife.

MENAECHMUS II: I gave you a dress, did I? One I stole from my
    wife?
    You're sure? I'd swear you were asleep, like a horse standing up.

DÉSIRÉE: Oh gosh, what's the fun of making fun of me and
    denying
    Everything you've done?

MENAECHMUS II: Just tell me what I'm denying.

DÉSIRÉE: That you gave me today your wife's most expensive silk

560   dress.

MENAECHMUS II: All right, I deny that. I'm not married. And I've
    never been married.
    And I've never come near this port since the day I was born,
    Much less set foot in it. I dined on board ship, disembarked,
    And ran into you.

DÉSIRÉE: Some situation! I'm nearly a wreck. What's
    that ship
    You're talking about?

565 MENAECHMUS II: Oh, an old prewar propeller job,
    Wood and canvas, patched in a million places; transportation,
    I guess, runs on force of habit. She's got so many pegs
    Pounded in now, one right up against the next, she looks like
    the rack

You see in a fur-seller's store, where the strips are hung all in
    a row.

DÉSIRÉE: Oh, do stop now, please, making fun, and come on in
    with me.   570

MENAECHMUS II: My dear woman, you're looking for some other
    man, not me.

DÉSIRÉE: I don't know you, Menaechmus? The son of Moschus,
    Born at Syracuse in Sicily, when Agathocles ruled,
    And after him, Phintia; then Leporello passed on the power
    After his death to Hiero, so that Hiero is now the man in
    control?   575

MENAECHMUS II: Well, that information seems certainly accurate,
    miss.

MESSENIO: By God Himself! Is the woman *from* Syracuse to have
    This all down so pat?

MENAECHMUS II: By the various gods, I don't see
    How I can now really decline that offer she's making.

MESSENIO: Please do, I mean *don't* step over that doorstep!
    You're gone if you do.

MENAECHMUS II: Pipe down. This is working out well.   580
    I'll admit to anything she says, if I can just take advantage
    Of the good time in store. Mademoiselle, a moment ago
    I was holding back on purpose, afraid that my wife might hear
    About the silk dress and our dinner date. I'm all set
    Now, anytime you are.

DÉSIRÉE: You won't wait for Soft Hair?   585

MENAECHMUS II: No, let's brush *him* off; I don't care a whisker if
    he never, ...
    And besides, when he does, I don't want him let in.

DÉSIRÉE: Heavens to Castor!
    I'm more than happy to comply with that one. But now,
    Just one thing, darling, you know what I'd like you to do?

MENAECHMUS II: All you need do is name it.

DÉSIRÉE: That sweet silk dress:
    send it over   590
    To the Persian's place, the embroiderer's shop. I want
    It taken in, and a pattern I've specially designed added to it.

MENAECHMUS II: What a good idea! It won't look at all like
    the dress
    I stole, if my wife should happen to meet you in town.

DÉSIRÉE: Good. Take it with you, then, when you go.

MENAECHMUS II: Yes, of course. 595

DÉSIRÉE: And now let's go on in.

MENAECHMUS II: Right away. I've just got to speak
    To him for a minute. Hey, Messenio, hop over here!

MESSENIO: What's cooking?

MENAECHMUS II: Jump, boy.

MESSENIO: What's all the hurry?

MENAECHMUS II: We're all the hurry, that's what. I know what
    you'll say.

MESSENIO: You're a dope.

MENAECHMUS II: Nope, I'm a fiend. I've already stolen
    some loot.   600
    Real loot. This is a big deal: Operation Mix-up.
    And I'm one up already without even throwing up
    earthworks.
    Race off, fast as you can, and drape all those sea troops
    (*Points to the sailors*)
    In the local bar, on the double. Stay where you are then,
    Until just before sunset, when it's time to come pick me up. 605

MESSENIO: Really, commander, you're not *on* to those call girls.

MENAECHMUS II: You manage your affairs, I'll handle mine,
    and you
    Can hang up and stay there. If I get into trouble, it's me
    Who'll suffer for it, not you. That girl isn't crazy; she's dumb
610   And doesn't know what's up, at least as far as I can see,
    Or where could this high-priced, pretty little dress have come
      from?

(He exits)

MESSENIO: I give up. You've gone, have you? In there? You're
    gone,
    And done for. The pirate ship's got the rowboat on the run,
    And you'll end up in the drink, *Menaechmus on the rocks.*
615   But who am I, a dumb slave, to try to outfox
    That woman, with my hopes of showing Menaechmus the
      ropes?
    He bought me to listen to him: I'm not in command.
    Come on, kids, let's do what he says. But I'll be on hand
    Later on, as he wanted, and drag him out to dry land.

ACT III

SCENE 1

PENICULUS: In all my born days—and it's more than thirty years'
620   worth—I've never
    Pulled a boner like this. I'm a treacherous fiend, and this time
    I guess I've really transgressed. Imagine my missing a meal!
    And why? I got involved in listening to a public speech
    And while I stood around gawking, all open mouth and ears,
625   Menaechmus made his getaway and got back to his girl,
    And didn't want *me* along, I suppose. May the heavenly gods
    Crack down on whoever it was that thought up public
      speeches,
    That invented this out-of-doors way to use up people's good
      time
    Who haven't any. Shouldn't the audience consist only of those
630   With time on their hands? And shouldn't they perhaps be fined
    If they fail to attend those meetings where someone gets up
    In public and starts sounding off? There are people enough
    With nothing much to do, who eat only one meal a day,
    Never dine out, or have guests in, and it's to them the duty
    To show up at meetings or official functions should be
635   assigned.
    If I hadn't stuck around today to listen, I wouldn't
    Have lost out on the dinner Menaechmus invited
    Me to come to—and I do think he meant it, as sure as I can see
    I'm alive. I'll show up, anyway, on the off-chance
640   There's still something left; the mere hope makes my mouth
      water.
    What's this I see? Menaechmus *leaving*, well looped?
    That means *dinner's over*: by God, my timing is perfect.
    I'll hide over here and watch a bit to see what he does
    Before I go up to my host and give him a buzz.

SCENE 2

MENAECHMUS II: Calm down in there, woman! I'll bring the dress
645   back soon enough,
    Expertly, so charmingly changed you won't even know it.
PENICULUS: Dinner's done, the wine's all gone, the parasite's lost,

And *he's* off to the couturier, with that dress in tow.
    Is *that* so? I'm not who I am if I take this last bit
    In my stride, lying down. Watch how I handle that garment
      worker.   650
MENAECHMUS II: I thank you, immortal gods, each and all
    of you.
    On whom have you ever showered so many good gifts
    As you have on me today? And who could have hoped for them
      less?
    I've dined, I've wined, I've reclined, and at very close quarters,
    With one of the most delicious daughters . . . well, I've had it
      in the best sense   655
    Of that past tense. And here I am at present, still gifted
    With a precious piece of silk. No one else will inherit
    These convertible goods, much less wear it. How high am I, its
    Heir—Oh!
PENICULUS: Hell, I can't hear from over here—did he say "hair,"
    though?
    That's my cue to brush in, isn't it, and sweep up my share?   660
    Hair today and bald tomorrow . . . Drink to me only with
      mayonnaise . . .
    I'll demand redressing . . . I'll scrape something out of this
      mess yet.
MENAECHMUS II: She said I stole it from my wife and gave it to her.
    When I realized how wrong she was, of course I began
    To agree with everything she said, as if we agreed   665
    On whatever it was we were doing. Need I say more?
    I never had so good a time for so little money.
PENICULUS: Here I go; I'm raring to get in my licks.
MENAECHMUS II: Well, well, who's this comes to see me?
PENICULUS: What's that you say,
    You featherhead, you worst of all possible, good-for-nothing
      . . . man?   670
    Man? You're not even a mistake, you're a premeditated crime,
    That's what you are, you shifty little good-for-nothing . . . I just
      said that . . .
    So-and-so. And so you spirited yourself away
    From me at the forum a while ago, and celebrated my funeral
    At this cheerful dinner your friend just couldn't attend?   675
    Some nerve, when you said I was invited to share it with you.
MENAECHMUS II: Look, kiddo, what's with it, with you and me,
    that can make
    You curse out a man you don't even know? Would you like
    A nice hole in the head in return for turning loose your lip?
PENICULUS: God damn it to God damn. That hole's already in my
    stomach;   680
    You gave my mouth the slip.
MENAECHMUS II: What's your name, kid,
    Anyway? Spit that much out.
PENICULUS: Still being funny,
    As if you didn't know?
MENAECHMUS II: As far as I know, no.
    God knows I never saw you before today, never knew you,
    Whoever you are. I do know, though, if you don't   685
    Get funny with me, I won't make it hard for you.
PENICULUS: For heck's sake, Menaechmus, wake up!
MENAECHMUS II: For Hercules' sake,
    I'm up and walking around. I'm completely convinced of it.
PENICULUS: But you don't recognize me?
MENAECHMUS II: If I did, I wouldn't say I
    didn't.

PENICULUS: You don't know your old parasite pal?

MENAECHMUS II: It's your old
690   paralyzed dome
      That's slipped, or cracked. You'd better have it patched up and
         fixed.

PENICULUS: All right. Here's a question for you. Did you, or did
      you not,
      Sneak a dress out from under your own wife's nose today,
      And give it to dear Désirée?

MENAECHMUS II: For Hercle's sake, no.
695   I don't happen to be married, and I didn't happen to
      Give it to Désirée, and I didn't happen to fasten onto
      A dress. Are you quite sure you've got it in the head, enough?

PENICULUS: Well, that's that, I guess. *Caput! E pluribus* be none.
      Of course I didn't meet you coming out of your house and
         wearing
      The dress, just a while ago?

700 MENAECHMUS II: Ohhhhh for *sex'* sake!
      (*Very effeminate sibilants*)
      You think we're all fairy fine fellows just because you're such
      A *native* dancer, in a perfect fright at what's under our tights?
      You say I put on a dress, and I wore it?

PENICULUS: Could of swore it, on Hercules' head.

MENAECHMUS II: Don't bring him up,
705   He was a he-man, but you aren't even a me-man:
      You don't even know who you are or I am, you absolute nut.
      You'd better take the cure; you're asking for trouble from the
         gods.

PENICULUS: Yeee gods, that's it! Now nobody's going to stop me
      from going
      Straight to your wife to spill the beans about you and your
         schemes
      You've creamed me, and I'm whipped. But banquet boy, just
710   you wait
      Until this stuff starts coming back at you. That dinner you ate
      And I never got to, is going to give you bad dreams.

MENAECHMUS II: What's going on around here? Is everyone I see
      Planted here on purpose to make fun of me? And what for?
715 And here comes another, whoever it is, out that door.

SCENE 3

MAID: Menaechmus, Désirée would like you to take
      This bracelet to the jeweler's, as long as you're going downtown
      With the dress, and have this piece of gold worked into it.

MENAECHMUS II: Oh, glad to take care of both things, of course,
      and anything
      Else you want done along those lines; you only need
720   mention it.

MAID: You remember the bracelet, don't you?

MENAECHMUS II: It's just a gold
      bracelet.

MAID: But this is the one you sneaked out of your wife's jewel box
      And stole from her.

MENAECHMUS II: I don't do things like that, I'm damned
      sure.

MAID: Well, if you don't recognize it . . . look, you'd better give it
      back to me.

MENAECHMUS II: Hold on . . . I think I do remember it now. . . .
725   Yes, that's the one I gave her, that's it all right.
      But where are the armlets I gave Désirée when I gave her
      The bracelet?

MAID: You never gave her no armlets at all.

MENAECHMUS II: Oh yes, that's right, it was just the bracelet,
      come to think of it.

MAID: Can I tell her you'll have this fixed up?

MENAECHMUS II: Yes, I'll take care of it.

MAID: And look, be a dear, and have him design me some earrings, 730
      Won't you, teardrop-style, six dollars of gold work in each?
      If you do, you'll be *persona* terribly *grata* to me, your
      Obedient, cooperative servant, the next time you visit.

MENAECHMUS II: Why of course. Just give me the gold, and I'll
      stand the cost
      Of having it set.

MAID: Oh, you furnish the gold, why don't you? 735
      And I'll pay you back later.

MENAECHMUS II: No, no, after you, my fair lady.
      You let me pay you back later, and I'll pay twice as much.

MAID: I don't have the gold at the moment.

MENAECHMUS II: When you get it, I'll
      take it.

MAID: Is there anything else, kind sir?

MENAECHMUS II: No, just say I'll handle this.
      (MAID *exits*)
      And make a quick turnover on the market value of the stuff. 740
      She's gone in? Yes, I see she's closed the door.
      The gods must be on my side the way they're helping me out,
      Enriching me, and doing me favors. But why hang around
      When now is my chance to get away and out of reach
      Of these foxy, and I must say, sexy, confidence women? 745
      Come on, Menaechmus, my boy, my own likeness, enjoy
      Your rapture; and pick up your feet, old chap, let those sandals
         slap.
      Here goes the laurel lei for today.
      (*Throws it right*)
      But I think I'll go this way,
      In case they come looking for me; they can follow this lead 750
      In the wrong direction. I'll dash off and make enough speed
      To head off my slave, I hope, and tell that good lad
      The good news about the goods we've acquired. Won't he be
         glad?

ACT IV

SCENE 1

WIFE: I suppose I'm supposed to submit to total frustration
      Because I married a man who steals everything in the house 755
      He can lay hands on and carts it off to his mistress?

PENICULUS: Not so loud, please. You'll catch him with the goods,
      I promise.
      Come over here. Now look over there. He was taking
      Your dress to the couturier; he was well looped and weaving
      Downtown with the same dress he snuck from your closet
         today. 760
      And look, there's the laurel loop he had on, lying on the
         ground.
      Now do you believe me? He must have gone in that direction.
      If you'd like to follow up his tracks. Hey, we're in luck:
      Here he comes back, just this moment; but not with the dress.

WIFE: What should I do?

PENICULUS: Oh, what you always do, start nagging, 765
      Nag him to pieces; don't take it, let him have it, I say.
      Meanwhile, let's duck over here on the sly and not let him
      See us. He'll tangle himself in the birdcatchers' net.

SCENE 2

MENAECHMUS I: This is some social system we've got going here,

770 The troublesome custom of patrons and clients:
Bothersome clients, and jittery patrons, who fear
They may not have a big enough following. Compliance
And conformity to habit require even the best of us
To just make the most of it; and as for the rest of those

775 Trapped in place in the status race, let's face it,
They're coming at us, pushing forward from the ends
To swell out the middle. And it isn't *fides*, it's *res*
That matters in the clientele deal, which depends,
Not on the client's value as man and as friend,

780 But simply on his assets. Money is what he's worth
And you must amass it to show off less dearth
Of a deficit than the next aristocrat. You give a wide berth
To the poor man who needs you, however fine he may seem,
But if some rich bastard shows up and wants you to use

785 Your influence, you're ready to go to any extreme
To hang onto him. That's the scheme, and does it confuse
Us poor patrons with a gang of fast-breaking scofflaws
To stand up for in court? Thereby hang the loss
And the profits for us poor patricians. The client's position

790 Is: pressure on the middle. He's got the money,
We've got the rank; we need his dough, he needs our thanks.
It's only lucky the prolies don't rate either of any;
Thank heavens, they're not powerful, just many.
　　　　I'm from a good family and entitled to go into court

795 And represent as I wish some client who's short
Of the necessary social credentials. And, confidentially,
I say a lot that I wish I didn't have to. A lawyer can manage
To do this pretty well if he concentrates on it; and damages
Are his principal concern: to collect for, to sue for, to affirm

800 What is said to be false, and to deny what is said to be true for.
On behalf of some client whose character makes him squirm
He will bribe the witnesses or rehearse them in what to do.
When the client's case comes up on the calendar, of course
That's a day we have to be on hand too, and be resourceful

805 In speaking up professionally in defense of his actions, awful
And impossible to defend though they are.
It's either a private hearing at the bar;
Or a public proceeding before a jury with people in the
　　　congregation;
Or a third form it takes is what you would call arbitration,

810 When a mediator is appointed to decide this special situation.
　　　　Well, today a client of mine had me right on the ropes;
His case came up as a private hearing, and my hopes
Of doing what I'd planned to today, and doing
It with the person I wanted to, have drooped and dropped near
　　　to ruin;

815 He kept me and kept me; there was angle after angle.
He was obviously at fault, with his wrong, tangled,
Illegal action, and I knew it when I went in.
So in arguing the case I laid it on pretty thin,
And pleaded *extenuating circumstances;* that's a logical maze

820 And a judge's jungle, but a lawyer's paradise.
I summed up the case in the most complicated terms
I could summon up, overstating, sliding words like worms
Off the track, leaving a lot out when the need
Of the argument indicated, and the magistrate agreed

825 To drop the proceedings; he granted permission
For a settlement by *sponsio.*

There's a legal ounce for you, of the words we pronounce in due
　　　process,
Full of awful, responsible-sounding phrases like: I promise
You this *sponsio* I owe you, et cetera. What it comes down to
Is that a civil hearing can be brought to an end by payment　830
Of a fixed fee known as a forfeit or *sponsio,* a defrayment
Of the expenses plus a sum added on: call it "costs
And considerations" if you will, in consideration for the lost
Time and money involved. What happened today was that I
Had worked hard and fast to convince the judge that my　835
Client should be allowed to settle for costs and considerations.
The judge came around; and I was set to leave for the
　　　celebration
Of a good time at Désirée's party, when what did my other
　　　smarty party
Of a client pull but an "Oh, well . . . I don't know about that
　　　sponsio . . .
I don't think I ought to flounce in with a lot of money all at
　　　once　　　　　　　　　　　　　　　　　　　　　　　　840
You know . . . I'm not so sure I've even got it. Are you sure
That's the way we want it to go, the case, et cetera?" The totally
　　　pure
Imbecile, caught redhanded, absolutely without a legal leg to
　　　stand on
And three unimpeachable witnesses were waiting just to get
　　　their hands on
Him and wring his neck! He nearly let it come up for trial.　845
And that's where I've been all this while.
　　　　May the gods, all the gods, blast that fool
Who wrecked my beautiful day
And they might as well, while they're at it, lay
Into me for thinking I could steal　　　　　　　　　　　　850
Off to town and look the forum over that way
Without being spotted and tapped for something dutiful.
No doubt, I've messed up a day
That promised to be quite alluring
From the moment I told Désirée　　　　　　　　　　　　855
To set things up nicely for dinner. All during
The time I've been detained, she's been waiting for me
And here I am at last, the first instant I could break free.
If she's angry, I suppose she has some reason to be.
But perhaps the dress I purloined from my wife won't
　　　annoy her　　　　　　　　　　　　　　　　　　　　860
In the least, and I'll win this one too, as my own lawyer.

PENICULUS: What do you say to that?

WIFE:　　　　　　　　　　　　　　That I've made a bad
　　　marriage
With an unworthy husband.

PENICULUS:　　　　　　　　　　Can you hear well enough where
　　　you are?

WIFE: All too well.

MENAECHMUS I: The smart thing for me is to go on in there
　　　Where I can count on a pretty good time.　　　　　　865

PENICULUS:　　　　　　　　　　　　　　　Just you wait,
　　　Bad times are just around the corner.

WIFE: (*Confronting him*)　　　　　　　You think you got away
　　　With it, do you? This time you'll pay up, with interest.

PENICULUS: That's it, let him have it.

WIFE:　　　　　　　　　　　Pulled a fast one on the sly,
　　　didn't you?

MENAECHMUS I: What fast one are you referring to, dear?

WIFE: You're asking me?

MENAECHMUS I: Should I ask him, instead?

870 WIFE: Take your paws off me.

PENICULUS: That's the way!

MENAECHMUS I: Why so cross?

WIFE: You ought to know.

PENICULUS: He knows, all right, he's just faking.

MENAECHMUS I: With reference
       to what?

WIFE: To that dress, that's what.

MENAECHMUS I: That dress that's what what?

WIFE: A certain silk dress.

PENICULUS: Why is your face turning pale?

MENAECHMUS I: It isn't.

PENICULUS: Not much paler than a thin silk dress,
875   it isn't.
       And don't think you can go off and eat dinner behind my back.
       Keep pitching into him.

MENAECHMUS I: Won't you hang up for a moment?

PENICULUS: God damn it, no, I won't. He's shaking his head
       To warn me not to say anything.

MENAECHMUS I: God damn it, yourself,
880   If I'm shaking my head, or winking or blinking or nodding.

PENICULUS: Cool! Shakes his head to deny he was shaking his
       head.

MENAECHMUS I: I swear to you, wife, by Jupiter, and all the other
       gods—
       I hope that's reinforced strong enough to satisfy you—
       I did *not* nod at that nut.

PENICULUS: Oh, she'll accept that
885   On good faith. Now let's return to the first case.

MENAECHMUS I: What first case?

PENICULUS: The case of the costly couturier's
       place.
       The dress-fixer's.

MENAECHMUS I: Dress? What dress?

PENICULUS: Perhaps I'd better bow out.
       After all, it's my client who's suing for redress of grievance
       And now she can't seem to remember a thing she wanted to
       ask you.

WIFE: Oh dear, I'm just a poor woman in trouble.

MENAECHMUS I: Come on, tell me,
       What is it? One of the servants has upset you by answering
890   back?
       You can tell me about it; I'll see that he's punished.

WIFE: Don't be silly.

MENAECHMUS I: Really, you're *so* cross. I don't like you that way.

WIFE: Don't be silly.

MENAECHMUS I: Obviously, it's one of the servants you're mad at?

WIFE: Don't be silly.

MENAECHMUS I: You're not mad at me, are you?

WIFE: Now you're not
       being so silly.

895 MENAECHMUS I: But, for God's sake, I haven't done anything.

WIFE: Don't start being silly all over again.

MENAECHMUS I: Come on, dear, what is it that's wrong
       And upsets you so?

PENICULUS: Smooth husband, smooths everything over.

MENAECHMUS I: Oh, hang up, I didn't call you.

WIFE: *Please* take your
       paw off me.

PENICULUS: That's the way, lady, stick up for your rights. We'll
       teach him   900
       To run off to dinner and not wait for me, and then stagger out
       Afterwards and lurch around in front of the house still wearing
       His wreath and having a good laugh on me.

MENAECHMUS I: Dear God in heaven,
       If I've even eaten yet, much less gone into that house.

PENICULUS: You don't say?

MENAECHMUS I: That's right, I don't say, you're damned right I
       don't.

PENICULUS: God, that's some nerve. Didn't I see you over there
       just now,   905
       In front of the house, standing there with a wreath on your
       head?
       Didn't I hear you telling me I was way off my nut, and insisting
       You didn't know who I was, and were a stranger here yourself?

MENAECHMUS I: But I left you some time ago, and I'm just
       getting back.

PENICULUS: That's what you say. You didn't think I'd fight back,
       did you?   910
       Well, by God, I've spined the whole thing to your wife.

MENAECHMUS I: Saying what?

PENICULUS: How should I know? Ask her.

MENAECHMUS I: How about it, dear?
       What all has this type told you? Come on, don't repress it;
       Won't you tell me what it is?

WIFE: As if you didn't know.
       You ask me?

MENAECHMUS I: If I knew, for God's sake, I wouldn't be asking.   915

PENICULUS: This is really some man the way he fakes out. Look,
       you can't
       Keep it from her, she knows all about it. By God in wherever
       he is,
       I practically dictated it.

MENAECHMUS I: Dictated what?

WIFE: All right. Since you seem not to have an ounce of shame
       left,
       And you won't own up, give me your undivided attention.   920
       This is why I'm upset and this is what he told me. I repeat,
       I'm not really "cross"; I'm double-crossed, and doubly upset.
       Someone sneaked one of my very best dresses right out of my
       house.

MENAECHMUS I: A dress? Right out of my house?

PENICULUS: *Listen* to that
       louse,
       Trying to scratch his way into your affections. Look,
       Menaechmus,   925
       We're not playing matched towels in the doctor's bathroom
       Marked "Hisia" and "Hernia"; we're discussing a valuable
       dress,
       And its *hers* not yours, and she's lost it, at least for the time
       being.
       If *yours* were missing, it would really be missing for good.

MENAECHMUS I: Will you please disappear? Now dear, what's
       your point of view?   930

WIFE: The way I see it, one of my best silk dresses is not at home.

MENAECHMUS I: I wonder who might have taken it?

WIFE: I'm pretty sure
       I know a man who knows who took it, because he did.

MENAECHMUS I: Who dat?

WIFE: Welllll . . . I'd like us to think of a certain Menaechmus.

MENAECHMUS I: Some man, just like us! Isn't that the fancy one,
935   that man?
        But he's a mean man. And who the hell are all the men you
          mean
        Named Menaechmus?
WIFE: You, that's what I say, you.
MENAECHMUS I: Who accuses me to you?
WIFE: I do, for one.
PENICULUS: I do too. And I say you gave it to a dear little Daisy.
MENAECHMUS I: I? Me? I'm that mean aechmus who . . .
WIFE: Yes, you,
940   that's who,
        You brute, *et tu*.
PENICULUS: You who too too too . . .
        What is this, the Owl Movement from the Bird Symphony?
        My ears are feeling the strain of that to-who refrain.
MENAECHMUS I: I swear, Wife, by Jupiter, and all other gods
          within hearing distance—
        And I hope that's a strongly enough reinforced religious
945   insistence—
        That I did not *give* . . .
PENICULUS: But *we* can appeal to Hercules and he's
        Even stronger, that we're not exactly not telling the truth.
MENAECHMUS I: That technically I did not *give* it, I only
          conveyed it
        To Daisy today; you see, she doesn't have it, she's just using it.
950 WIFE: I don't go around lending out your jacket or cloak.
        A woman ought to lend out women's clothes, a man men's.
        You'll bring back the dress?
MENAECHMUS I: I'll see that that's done.
WIFE: If you know what's good for you, you will, I'm here to
          assure you.
        You won't get back in this house unless you're carrying that
          dress.
        I'm going in.
955 PENICULUS: What about me and my work?
WIFE: I'll pay you back when something is stolen from your house.
PENICULUS: Oh God, that means never. There's nothing in my
          place worth stealing.
        Well, Husband and Wife, may the gods do their very worst for
          you both!
        I'll run along now, to the forum. It's quite plain to see
960   I've lost out, and lost my touch, with this family.

(*He exits; never returns*)

MENAECHMUS I: My wife thinks she's making life hard for me,
          shutting me out
        Of the house. As if I didn't have a much more pleasant place
        To go into. Fallen from your favor, have I? I imagine
        I'll bear up under that and prove pleasing to an even more
          desirable
965   Favorite. Désirée won't lock me out; she'll lock me in.
        I guess I'll go in there and ask her to *lend* back the dress
        I *conveyed* to her this morning, and buy her something much
          better.
        Hey, where's the doorman? Open up, somebody, and tell
        Désirée to come out; there's someone to see her.

SCENE 3

DÉSIRÉE: Who's calling me?
970 MENAECHMUS I: A man who'd be his own enemy

Before he'd be yours.
DÉSIRÉE: Menaechmus, *dahling*, come in!
        Why stand out there?
MENAECHMUS I: I bet you can't guess why I'm here.
DÉSIRÉE: Oh, yes I can. You want something sweet from your
          honey,
        And what's more you'll get it, you naughty little tumblebee.
MENAECHMUS I: As a matter of fact, or thank heavens, or
          something . . .   975
        What I have to have is that silly dress back I gave you
        This morning. My wife's found out all about it.
        But I'll buy you one worth twice as much, whatever kind you
          want,
        So be a good girl and romp in there and get it, won't you?
DÉSIRÉE: But I just handed it over to you to take to the Persian's,   980
        Just a while ago, and gave you that bracelet to take to the jeweler
        And have the gold added to it.
MENAECHMUS I: The dress and a bracelet?
        I think you may find you did no such thing. I gave
        The dress to you and then went to the forum, and here
        I am looking at you for the first time again since I left you.   985
DÉSIRÉE: Don't look at me, I'll look at you. I see
        Just what you're up to, and what I'm down to, for that matter.
        You take the stuff off my two trusting hands and then
        Do me out of it and pocket the cash for yourself.
MENAECHMUS I: I'm not asking for it to cheat you out of it, I swear.   990
        I tell you, my wife's cracked the case.
DÉSIRÉE: Well, I didn't ask
        For it in the first place. You brought it of your own free will,
        And you gave it to me as a gift; you didn't *convey* it, you shyster.
        Now you want it back. I give up. You can have the stuff;
        Take it away, wear it yourself if you want,   995
        Or let your wife wear it, or lock the loot in your safe.
        You're not setting foot in my house from this moment on,
        Don't kid yourself about that. I deserve better treatment
        From you than being jerked around and laughed at like a clown.
        I've been your friend, lover boy—but that's at an end.   1000
        From now on, it's strictly for cash, if and when.
        Find some other doll to play with and then let her down.
MENAECHMUS I: God damn it, don't get so God damn mad. Hey,
          don't go
        Off like that. Wait a minute! Come back here. You won't?
        Oh, come on, Dee. Not even for me? You won't? So I see.   1005
        She's gone in and locked the door too. And I guess that
          makes me
        Just about the most locked-out fellow in this town today,
        Most unwanted man, most unlikely to get in, much less to say
        Anything that a wife, or a mistress, might take to be true.
        I'll go ask my friends what they think I ought to do.   1010

ACT V

SCENE 1

MENAECHMUS II: It was really pretty dumb of me to put that
          purseful of money
        In Messenio's hands, the way I did. He's probably holed up
        In some dive, drinking it down, and looking them over.
WIFE: I think I'll just take a look and see how soon Husband
        Wends his way home. There he is now. And all's well for me: 1015
        He's got the dress with him.
MENAECHMUS II: Where in hell has Messenio
        wandered off to?

WIFE: I'll go up and welcome him now in the terms he deserves.
Aren't you ashamed to show up in my sight, you mistake
Of a man . . . I mean, you deliberate premeditated crime,
Tricked out with that fancy gown?

1020 MENAECHMUS II: I don't get it, do I?
What's on your mind, my good woman?

WIFE: How dare you address me?
How dare you utter a single slimy syllable, you snake?

MENAECHMUS II: What have I done that's so bad I don't dare
address you?

WIFE: You must have cast-iron nerves to inquire about that.

1025 MENAECHMUS II: I don't know if you read much, lady, but Hecuba,
The Greeks always called her a bitch. I suppose you know why?

WIFE: As a matter of fact, no. I don't.

MENAECHMUS II: Because she acted the way
You're acting right now. She kept dumping insults and curses
On everyone she met, and snarling at, pitching into everyone
1030 Her eyes lighted on. No wonder they called her a prime bitch.

WIFE: I really can't take this kind of abuse any longer.
I'd much rather never have been married, than submit to
The kind of dirt you shovel on me the way you do now.

MENAECHMUS II: What's it to me whether you like being married
or not,
1035 Or want to leave your husband? Do all the people around here
Tell their stories to every new man that blows into town?

WIFE: What stories? I simply won't take it any longer, I tell you.
I'd rather live all alone than put up with you.

MENAECHMUS II: For God's sake, then, live alone, as far as I care,
1040 Or as long as Jupiter may decide to grant you the option.

WIFE: A few moments ago you were insisting you hadn't sneaked off
That mantilla-dress of mine, but now you're waving it
In front of my eyes. Aren't you a tiny bit conscience-stricken?

MENAECHMUS II: God only knows what kind of a squeeze play
you're pulling,
1045 You whack, you brazen. . . . How dare you say I took this,
When another woman gave it to me to take and have altered?

WIFE: By God (my God, this time), a statement like that
Makes me want to . . . and I'm going to send for my father,
And tell him every single horrible thing you've done,
1050 That's what I'll do. Hey, Decio, in there, come out,
And go find my father and ask him to come here with you,
Tell him please to come quickly, I simply have to see him.
I'll show him every single horrible thing you've done to me.

MENAECHMUS II: Are you feeling all right? What single horrible
thing?

1055 WIFE: You housebreaker-into! You steal my dress and my jewels
From my house and rob your wife of her goods to throw at
The feet of or load in the arms of your girlfriend as loot.
Have I rehearsed the story accurately enough for your ears to
take in?

MENAECHMUS II: Lady, you ought to watch your prepositions; and
while you're at it
1060 Could you mix me a sedative of half hemlock, half lime juice?
You must have some hemlock around here. I must be kept *quiet*
If I'm meant to sustain your attacks. I'm not sure I know
Exactly who you think I am. I may have known you
Long ago in the days of Hercules' father-in-law's father.

1065 WIFE: Laugh at me all you want, but your father-in-law
Won't stand for that. Here he comes now. Take a good look,
Won't you? Recognize somebody?

MENAECHMUS II: Oh, him? I may have known
him . . .

Yes, I did . . . oh sure, I remember old George from the Trojan
War:
He was our chaplain, bless his old heart. No. I guess not.
I've never seen him before, just as I've never seen
You before either, either of you, before today. 1070

WIFE: You say you don't know me, and you don't know my father?

MENAECHMUS II: You're right. And actually, if you produced your
grandfather,
I'd say the same.

WIFE: One joke after another. What a bother!

SCENE 2

OLD MAN: Here I come, pushing one foot after the other,
As fast and as far as my age allows, and to meet 1075
This crisis at my own pace, pushing these pedals, progressing
As best I can. Papa isn't planning to pretend,
Though, to anybody, that it's easy. He's not so spry anymore.
I'm pretty darned pregnant with years, that's a fact; planted 1080
With a crop of them, if you conceive of me carrying the
burden
Of this body. And there's precious little power left. Oh, it's a
bad deal,
This business of being old. We're stuck with the bulk
Of our unwanted goods. Maybe we get more than we
bargained for
Out of life. Old age brings the most of the worst when it
comes, 1085
To the ones who want it the least. If I named every pain
It bestows on us oldsters, I'd be drawing up a long, long list,
And you'd have too much to listen to.
I wonder why my
daughter
Sent for me all of a sudden? It weighs on my mind
And tugs at my heart to know what's afoot that can bring me 1090
Running over here to see her. She didn't say why she sent
for me,
Or tell me what's up. I can figure it out pretty well,
Of course. A quarrel with her husband has sprung up, I bet.
That's the way wives behave who bring a big dowry,
Coming loaded into the marriage and expecting their
husbands 1095
To love, honor, and slave away for them. They can be rough.
Of course, the husbands are at fault themselves, every now
and then.
But there's a point at which it's no longer dignified
For the husband to take it any longer. That dear daughter of
mine,
Darn her, never sends for me unless they've both of them been
doing 1100
Something wrong and a quarrel has started or is definitely
brewing.
Whatever it is, I'll find out. *Yup!* I'll get brought up on the news.
Here she is now in front of the house. I see how aroused
They both are. She must have lashed into him; he looks
Pretty dashed. *Yup!* Just as I thought. I'll go call to her. 1105

WIFE: I'll go greet Father. Good afternoon, Dad. How are you?

OLD MAN: Fine, thank you dear, and you? I hope everything's all
right.
You didn't send for me because you're in trouble? But you look
Pretty peaked. And why's he standing over there looking mad?

1110 You both look as if you've been trading punches, exchanged a
few blows
Just for size, to see how it goes. Fill me in on the facts.
Tell me who's to blame, and explain the whole situation.
But briefly, I implore you. Let's not have even one oration,
Much less two.

WIFE: I didn't do anything, Father,
1115 Don't worry. But I can't live here any longer, I can't
Stick it out. Please take me back.

OLD MAN: How did this happen?

WIFE: I've become someone just to be laughed at.

OLD MAN: By whom?

WIFE: By him,
The man, the husband you conferred me on.

OLD MAN: A fight, eh?
That's it, eh? How many times have I told you both of you
To watch out you don't come whining to me with your
1120   troubles?

WIFE: How could I watch out, Father dear?

OLD MAN: You really ask that?

WIFE: Only if you don't mind my asking.

OLD MAN: How often have I told you
To put up with your husband? Don't watch where he goes;
Don't see what he does; don't pry into what he's engaged in.

WIFE: But he's crazy about this daisy of a flower girl; and she lives
1125   right next door.

OLD MAN: That's perfectly natural, and in view of the way you're
so busy
Keeping an eye on his business, he'll get even dizzier about
Daisy,
I just bet you.

WIFE: But he goes over there for drinks all the time.

OLD MAN: What's it to you whether he drinks over there? If he
drinks,
He'll have to do it somewhere. And what's so terrible about
1130   that?
You might as well ask him to stop having dinner in town,
Or never bring anyone home for a meal. Are husbands
Supposed to take orders from you? Let them run the house
then,
And order the maids around, hand out wool to be carded
And get on with their spinning and weaving.

1135 WIFE: But Father, I ask you
To represent *me*, not to be *his* lawyer in this case.
You're standing here on my side, but you're taking his.

OLD MAN: Of course, if he's misbehaved, I'll get after him as
much
As I've lit into you—in fact, more so. But he seems to be taking
1140 Pretty good care of you, giving you jewels, clothes,
Your servants, furnishing the food. You ought to take a
practical,
More sensible view of the thing.

WIFE: But he's rooked me by stealing
Jewels and dresses from my closet at home to sneak off with,
My clothes, my jewels, to dress up that girl he calls on on the
sly with.

OLD MAN: That's some prep . . . I mean proposition, I mean some
1145   imposition.
I mean, that's terrible if that's going on—if it isn't
Your supposition's as bad, putting an innocent man under
suspicion.

WIFE: But Dad, he's got them there with him, the dress and that
sweet
Gold flexible bracelet. He took them to her
And now, since I've found out about it, he's bringing them
back.   1150

OLD MAN: Well, now, we'll see about that. I'm going to find out
About that. I'm going right over there and ask him, I am.
Oh say, Menaechmus, would you mind telling me, if you don't
Mind, about the matter you've been . . . discussing with her?
I'm curious to know. And why are you looking so down   1155
In the mouth, old fellow? Why's my girl standing over there
By herself, all alone and so cross?

MENAECHMUS II: I summon all the gods,
And Jupiter Himself Supreme, as they are my witnesses. . . .
Old boy, whoever you are, whatever your name
May happen to be.

OLD MAN: As they are your witnesses to what?
Why do you need such a cloud of high-ranking witnesses?   1160

MENAECHMUS II: That I have not done anything wrong to this
woman
Who claims that I surreptitiously deprived her
Of this dress and carried it off under suspicious
circumstances.

WIFE: Well, that's a clear enough lie. He's perjured himself for
sure.

MENAECHMUS II: If I have ever even set foot inside her house   1165
May I be of all men the most terribly tremendously miserable.

OLD MAN: That's not a very bright thing to wish for, is it? You
don't say
You've never set foot in the house there you live in, do you,
You stupid goop?

MENAECHMUS II: What's that you're saying about me
Living in that house, you goofy duffer? *I live there?*   1170

OLD MAN: You deny it?

MENAECHMUS II: Oh for Hercle's sake, of course I deny it.

OLD MAN: Oh, for Hercle's sake right back, you lie if you do
Say you don't, I mean deny it. Unless you moved out last
night.
Come here, Daughter, listen: You two haven't moved
Recently, have you?

WIFE: Heavens! Where to? Or why should we
have?   1175

OLD MAN: Well, of course, I couldn't know about that.

WIFE: Don't you
get it?
He's joking around with you.

OLD MAN: All right, Menaechmus, I've taken
Enough of your joking now. Come on, boy, let's get down to
business.

MENAECHMUS II: *Je vous en prie!* What the hell business have you
got with me?
In the first place, who the hell are you? And, in the second
place,   1180
I don't owe you any money. Nor her, in the third place.
Who's giving me all this trouble, in the next few places?

WIFE: Look, do you notice how his eyes seem to be going all green
All of a sudden? And there's a green tinge developing on the
skin
Around his temples and forehead. Look at his eyes glowing
red,   1185
Or is it green?

MENAECHMUS II: I wonder if I'd better not pretend I *am* crazy
    And scare them away by throwing a fit? They're the ones
    Who seem to be insisting on it.
WIFE: His arms twitch, his jaw drops.
    Oh, Father, what shall I do?
OLD MAN: Come here to your father,
1190   My girl, stay as far away as you can from him.
MENAECHMUS II: *Ho yo to yo! Tobacco Boy! Take me back to ya!*
    I hear ya callin' me out to that happy hunting ground
    Deep down in desegregated Damnasia (that's in the Near East),
    Callin' your boy to come on out huntin' with his hound dogs!
1195   *I hear ya, Bromie Boy, but I jes' cain come near ya.*
    They won't let me loose from this toothpickin' witch-huntin'
        northland.
    They's an old foam-covered bitch and she's keeping watch
    On my left. And right behind me here they's a goat,
    An ole toothpickin' garlic-stinking but I mean old goat,
1200   *Who's been buttin' down innocent citizens all of his life*
    By bringing up things that ain't true against them
    And then rounding up people to come listen to them refute them.
OLD MAN: I'm afraid your mind's been affected.
MENAECHMUS II: I've just swallowed an oracle
    Of Apollo that orders me instantly to start setting about
1205   Finding two red hot searchlights to put her eyes out with.
WIFE: Goodness, what a prepositionous preposterous proposition,
    Father. He's threatening to burn out my eyes in.
MENAECHMUS II: Touché, for me. They say I'm raving, but they
    Are rather wild at the moment. The straitjacket's on the other
        foot.
OLD MAN: Oh, my poor girl.
WIFE: Yes, Father?
1210 OLD MAN: What shall we do?
    Suppose I send for the slaves in a hurry; I'll go
    And bring them myself, to take him away and chain him
    Safely at home before he starts getting more destructive.
MENAECHMUS II: Trapped! Strung up by my own guitar! If I don't
1215   Improvise something soon they'll come on and cart me away.
    Yes I hear you, sugar Radiant Apollo! I'll follow through
    With my fists (you insist?) and spare not the laying on of hands.
    Punch that woman in the jaw, you say, according to your law,
    Unless she disappears from my view and gets herself gone
1220   *The holy hell and crucified crutch of a cross*
    Out of my way? Apollo, I'll do what you say!
OLD MAN: Scoot into the house, fast as poss, or he'll slug you.
WIFE: Scoot I go,
    Father, *ergo*, soon I'll be out of the way. But please, Father,
    Keep stalling him, don't let him slip out of reach. Don't you
        agree,
1225   I'm a most put-upon specimen of woman to put up with that?
MENAECHMUS II: I've got rid of her: not bad. Now for Dad. You
        slob,
    Listen, you baggy bearded, quavering long-since-past father,
    You shriveled old, dried-up grasshopper—and besides your
        voice's changed,
    Singing your Glorias Swansong soprano in your second
        childhood
1230   *What's that, Apollo? Thou sayest I should smashest his frame,*
    His bones, and the joints that hook them to same? I'm game.
    Smashomin, you say, with his owncluboff? Use his cane?
OLD MAN: There'll be trouble for you if you lay a finger on me,
    Or move any closer.
MENAECHMUS II: *Oh sir, Apollo? The following*
1235   *Changes in wording? Take one each two-headed ax*

And split right down through the frame, through the guts to the
    bones,
And hack his back to bits and make slivers of his liver and his
Whole intestinal tract, don't just cudgel the codger?
Roger to tower. Look at that geezer cower and run for cover.
OLD MAN: I suppose I'd better look to my laurels, what's left of
    them, withered   1240
    As an old man's may be. I'll look after me. He's a menace,
    That's clear enough. He just may decide to take it out on my
    hide.
MENAECHMUS II: For God's sake, Apollo, what's this? Another
    message? The traffic's
    Getting heavy. Take four wild bucking broncos and hitch
    Them up to a buckboard, and climb aboard and drive them over 1245
    This lion, this bearded biped, this antique toothless
    Gumclicking biped with bad breath? Roger, I'm mounted, oh joy
    To Yoy, King Roy Apolloy. I'm holding that wagon's reins
    And flicking the whip already. Up there, you double pair
    Of quadruplets. Drum it out on the ground when you trample
    him down.   1250
    Bend your knees, noble steeds, be nimble as the breeze.
    Pound you there, pound.
OLD MAN: He's coming at me with two pairs
    Of horses?
MENAECHMUS II: Whoa there! *Yes, Apollo, of course I hear you*
    Telling me to launch my attack against him, yes, him
    Over there, and murder him. Whoa there! *Who's hauling me*
    back   1255
    By the hair, and pulling me out of the chariot? Who does this
    Reverses the very command and eeeeeeedict of Apollo.
OLD MAN: It's really this poor fellow who's having the attack, I
    would say.
    And he's really having one, the full-scale deluxe one with nuts
    in it,
    God save us all. Well, that's how it is, by God. Here's a fellow   1260
    Completely crackers, and a minute ago he was perfectly
    rational.
    When that mad stuff hits you it lands hard all of a sudden.

(He exits)

MENAECHMUS II:
    (Alone, faces audience and addresses them across the
    stagefront)
    Now I ask you, have those two at last gotten out of my sight,
    Who forced me to play this mad role, when, as *you* know,
    I'm perfectly well? This is my chance to pick up and go   1265
    Winging back to my ship, don't you think, quick as a wink,
    While I'm still safe and sound? Listen, if you're still around
    When the old man comes back, you won't tell—he'll be in a
    rage—
    Where I went when I left the stage? You won't say where I can
    be found?

(He exits)

SCENE 3

OLD MAN: My back's stiff with sitting, my eyes nearly worn out
    with looking,   1270
    Hanging around waiting for God darn that darn medicine
    man
    To finish with his patients and meet this emergency.

Well *finally* he's pulled himself away—not much urgency
Either, from his victims. He's his own worst pain in the neck!
1275 Such a specialist, in name-dropping at least, of who's on his list
Of big shots with big troubles only he can fix. When I insisted
He hike over here, he said, "Right away," but first he must set
This broken leg, to the Greater Glory of Aesculapius,
And then put an arm back in place, On Behalf of Apollo.
1280 Which half of Apollo beats the Belvedere out of me: but I see
Him racing over now, weaving down the track like an ant
With lumbago. It's just his ego slows him down, the hot
    airman.
Putting those pieces together! What is he, a repairman,
A tinker, a joiner at heart? Are his patients all coming apart?
DOCTOR: Now let us see, my man. . . . You described the case of
1285   the diseased
As *larvated, id est,* he sees actual, live, dead ghost spooks?
Or *cerebrated, id est,* perturbated footzled left lobar cavity?
Which is of course only a false hallucination and would show
Some degree of mental inquietude. Would you be so good
1290 As to describe the condition again, so I can decide
What to prescribe or proscribe, indeed just how to proceed?
Did you mention a species of *Hibernating* coma, a kind of
Tendency to feel sleepy all the time? Or did you more
    plainly see
A subaqueous subcutaneous *slurpation,* like say, water on the
    knee?
1295 OLD MAN: The reason I've brought you in on the case is to find out
From you just what's wrong and ask you to cure it.
DOCTOR: How true,
And I'll do it to perfection, never fear; upon my profession
I assure you he'll be quite well again.
OLD MAN: You'll give him
The most careful attention?
DOCTOR: First-class care, rest assured.
1300 My word, Deluxe! Private room; personal visits from me.
I'll see him daily and ponder him most thoughtfully,
Heave hundreds of luxury sighs. He'll rate a thrill
Being ill; and so will you when you see the bill.
OLD MAN: Shh. Here's our man. Let's watch and see what he does.

SCENE 4

1305 MENAECHMUS I: By God in heaven, if this hasn't been the worst
Of all possible days for me! Everything's gone blooey.
What I planned to do on the sly, that particular parasite,
Peniculus, brought to light, and flooded me with shame and
    remorse
In the process. Some Ulysses type, doping out this dirty deal
For his own best protector and patron. Why that . . . sure as I
1310   live,
I'll do him right out of his ensuing existence, I'll unroll
His scroll for him. *His* existence? I'm a fool
To call *his* what's actually mine. I'm the one who brought him up
By wining and dining him. It was my subsistence he lived on:
1315 All he ever managed was coexistence. I'll snuff out
That half of his light by cutting off the supplies.
As for that mercenary Daisy, all I can say is she
Acted quite in keeping with the character of a kept woman,
And I suppose that's human, if meretricious. A very
    meretricious

And a happy new year to her. When in doubt, just give money. 1320
All I did was ask her for the dress to return to my wife
And she claimed she'd already handed it over. Turned it over,
I bet, to some dealer for cash. Crash! Oh God in heaven,
Did any man ever let himself in for this big a cave-in?
OLD MAN: You hear that?
DOCTOR: He says he's unhappy.
OLD MAN: Go on up to him. 1325
DOCTOR: Meeeeenaechmus, *ciao!* How are you? Why expose
    your arm
That way? Exposure can aggravate your serious condition.
MENAECHMUS I: Why don't you go hang up, yourself, on the
    nearest branch?
OLD MAN: Notice anything peculiar?
DOCTOR: Anything? The whole thing,
That's what I notice. This case couldn't be kept under control 1330
By a peck of Prozac. Menaechmus, just a word with
    you, please.
MENAECHMUS I: What's up, doc?
DOCTOR: You are. Answer a few questions, please,
And take them in order. First, what color wine do you drink?
White wine, or red?
MENAECHMUS I: Oh, my crucified crotch!
    What's that to you?
DOCTOR: I seem to detect a slight tendency 1335
To rave here.
MENAECHMUS I: Why not color-quiz me on bread?
Do I take purple, cerise, or golden red? As a rule,
Do I eat fish with their feathers or birds with their scales
    and all?
OLD MAN: I win! Ill, eh? Pu! Can't you hear he's delirious?
    Hurry up
With that sedative, can't you? Why wait for the fit to come on? 1340
DOCTOR: Just hold on a bit. I've a few more questions to ask.
OLD MAN: You'll finish him off with the questions you keep
    inventing.
DOCTOR: Do your eyes ever feel like they're starting out of your
    head?
MENAECHMUS I: What do you take me for, you seahorse doctor, a
    lobster?
DOCTOR: Do your bowels rumble powerfully, as far as you can
    tell?   1345
MENAECHMUS I: They're perfectly still when I'm full; when
    hungry, they grumble.
DOCTOR: Well now, that's a perfectly straightforward, digestible
    answer,
Not the word of a nut. You sleep until dawn, and sleep well?
MENAECHMUS I: I sleep right through, if I've paid all my bills.
    Listen, you
Special investigator, I wish to heaven the gods would crack
    down on you.   1350
DOCTOR: Ah, now, to judge from that statement, he's being
    irrational.
OLD MAN: Oh no, that's a wise saying, worthy of Nestor,
    compared
To what he was saying a while back, when he called his own
    wife
A stark raving bitch.
MENAECHMUS I: What's that you say I said?
OLD MAN: You're out of your head, that's what I say.

MENAECHMUS I: Who's out of
1355   what? Me?
OLD MAN: Yes, you, that's who. Boo! Threatening to flatten me out
     With a four-horsepower chariot. I can swear to it.
     I saw you with my own eyes. I charge you with it.
MENAECHMUS I: Ah, but here's what I know about you. You
          purloined the crown
1360   Of Jupiter, his sacred crown, and were locked up in jail.
     That's what I know about you. And when they let you out,
     It was to put you under the yoke and whip you in public,
     With birch rods. That's what I know about you. And then, too,
     You killed your own father and sold off your mother as a slave,
1365   That's what I know about you. Don't you think that might
          possibly do
     As a reasonably sound reply to the charges you're letting fly?
OLD MAN: Oh hurry up, doctor, for Hercle's sake, and do what
          you ought to.
     Can't you see, the man's *off*?
DOCTOR: You know what I think is best?
     Have him brought over to my place.
OLD MAN: You're sure?
DOCTOR: Sure, why not?
1370   I'll be able to treat him there by the very latest methods.
OLD MAN: Good. You know best.
DOCTOR: I assure you, Menaechmus,
          you'll lap up
     Super tranquilizers for twenty days.
MENAECHMUS I: Is that medicine,
     Your madness? I'll gore you, hanging there, for thirty days.
DOCTOR: (*Aside*) Go call the help, to carry him over to my house.
OLD MAN: (*Aside*) How many men do we need?
1375 DOCTOR: (*Aside*)   At least four, to judge
     From the way he's raving at present.
OLD MAN: (*Aside*)   They're practically here.
     I'll go run and get them. You stay right here, doctor, do,
     And keep a close eye on him.
DOCTOR: (*Aside*)   No. As a matter of fact,
     I think I'll be off for home, and make the preparations
1380   To receive him. There's quite a lot to do. You go get the help;
     Have them bring him to me.
OLD MAN: (*Aside*)   He's as good as carried there
          already.
DOCTOR: I'm off.
OLD MAN: So am I.
MENAECHMUS I: Now I'm alone. That father-in-law
     And that doctor have gone, somewhere or other. But what in
          God's name
     Makes these men insist I'm insane? I've never been sick
1385   A day in my life, and I'm not ailing now. I don't start fights,
     Or dispute everything that comes up. I wish others well
     When I meet them, quite calmly, I recognize people I know,
     And speak to them civilly enough. I wonder if they,
     Who absurdly declare that I'm mad, since they're in the wrong,
1390   Aren't in fact crazy themselves? I wish I knew what to do.
     I'd like to go home, but my wife won't allow it—as for that
          place,
     (*Points to* DÉSIRÉE's *house*)
     No one will let me in there. Well, it's all worked out
     All right; worked me out of house and home. So I guess
     I'll stick around here. I imagine, by the time night comes,
1395   I'll be welcome to enter the right one of these two homes.

SCENE 5

MESSENIO: God slave the king!
     And of me I sing.
     Or rather, the slave's the thing
     I present and I represent.
     The good slave, intent   1400
     On making his master content,
     Looks after his master's affairs.
     Arranging and planning, he never spares
     Any effort in lavishing cares
     On everything that needs being done.   1405
     When the master's away, he handles all alone
     Problems that keep coming up, and he solves them
     As well as the boss could, himself, all of them;
     And sometimes manages the whole business better than
          Master.
     You need a good sense of balance, to fend off disaster   1410
     From your legs and your back. And you've got to remember
     That your throat and your stomach are not the most vital
          members.
     If you go off guzzling and eating, instead of performing,
     When you come back you're in for a beating and a good body-
          warming.
     May I remind all the shiftless delinquents who keep hanging
          back   1415
     From doing their work, of the price all masters exact
     From good-for-nothings, men they can't count on, in fact?
     Lashes and chains;
     Turning those wheels at the mill
     Until you begin to feel   1420
     Your brains churning loose and writhing like eels.
     You'll be starved and left out to sleep in the cold open fields.
     That's the wages of laziness.
     Not to fear earning—that would be the worst sort of craziness.
     Therefore, I've decided, for once and for all, to be good 1425
     And not bad. I'd rather be lashed by the tongue than the wood.
     As for meal, I find it more pleasant to eat than to grind it.
     Therefore, I always comply with the will of my lord
     Calmly, and well I preserve it; and I can afford
     To deserve whatever I get by way of reward.   1430
     Let others look after their interests; they'll find a good way.
     But this is how to serve your man best. That's what I say.
     Let me always be careful, and pretty darn prayerful
     Not to get in any trouble, so that I'll always be there, full
     Of energy, coming in on the double where he needs me most, 1435
     His assistant host. Slaves who keep themselves good and scared
     When they're not in the wrong usually find that they are
          declared
     Highly usable by their owners. The fearless ones are the goners;
     When it comes time to face the music, these singsongers
     Will be cheeping like jailbirds and wishing they weren't such
          gone-wrongers.   1440
     But I don't have to worry much longer, not me.
     The time's almost here now when he promised to set me free.
     That's how I slave and work well, and how I decide
     To do the best thing and take the best care of my hide.
     Soooooo . . . now that I've seen all the baggage and the porters
          in their bedding   1445
     In the tavern downtown, as Menaechmus instructed, I'm
          heading

Back to meet him. Guess I'll knock on the door
So he'll know I'm out here and get up off the floor
Or at least let me pull him outside
1450 From this den of iniquity, now that he's tried
To have a good time, and probably found out the cost.
I hope I'm not too late and that the battle's not already lost.

SCENE 6

OLD MAN: Now I tell you, by all that's human or holy, make sure
You carry out my orders just right as I ordered you to
1455 And order you now. You're to heft that man on your shoulders
And hustle him off to the clinic, if you don't want your legs
And your back pounded in. And don't pay the least attention,
Any one of you, to anything he says. Well, don't just stand
there.
What are you waiting for? You ought to be after him, lifting
him.
1460 I'll trot on over to the doctor's and be there when you pull in.
MENAECHMUS I: Well I'll be *God* damned! What's on the schedule
now?
Why are these men rushing at me, what in the name of . . . ?
What do you guys want? What's all the racket about?
Why are you closing in on me all of a sudden? What's the hurry?
Where we going? Some rumble. Creepers! They're giving me
1465 the tumble
God *damn* us! Citizens all, of Epidamnus! To the rescue!
Save me, my fellow men! Help! Let go me, you whipster bastards.
MESSENIO: Holy smoke! Creepers! What's this bunch of gypsters
think
They're gonna get away with? My master? Why those hijacking
lifters,
They've got him on their shoulders. Let's see who gets the
1470 most blisters.
MENAECHMUS I: Won't *anyone* lend me a hand?
MESSENIO: I will sir, at your command;
You brave captain. Boy, this is gonna give Epidamnus a
black eye,
A mugging like this, right out in the open. *Epidam-nee-ee-ee-I!*
My master's being towed away in broad daylight, a free man
1475 Who came to your city in peace, attacked on the street. *Can*
Anybody help us? Stay off, you lugs. Lay off.
MENAECHMUS I: Hey, for God's sake, whoever you are, help
me out,
Won't you? Don't let them get away with murder. You can see
I'm in the right.
MESSENIO: Quite. Of course I'll pitch in
1480 And come to your defense and stand by you with all might.
I'd never let you go under, commander, I'd sink first.
Now you sink your fist in that guy's eye . . . No, not that one,
The one who's got you by the shoulder. That's it. Now a bolder
Swipe at the ball, gouge it out for him. I'll start distributing
1485 A crack in the puss here, a sock in the jaw there. I'm at liberty
To do so? By the heavyweight Hercules, you thugs are
gonna lug
Him away like a carload of lead, today. You'll pay by the ounce
When you feel my fists bounce all over your faces. Let go his
grace.
MENAECHMUS I: I've got this guy's eye.
MESSENIO: Make like it's just a hole in his head.
You're a bunch of bums, you body-snatching, loot-latching
1490 whipsters.

WHIPSTER I: Hey, this wasn't what the doctor ordered, was it, or
the old mister?
WHIPSTER II: They didn't say we'd be on the receiving end, did
they . . . ouch!
Gee Hercules, Jerkules, that hurt!
MESSENIO: Well, let him loose, then.
MENAECHMUS I: How dare this ape lay hands on me? Bongo him,
jungle boy.
MESSENIO: Here we go, kids, you too; take off, fade out, monkey
face;   1495
Get the crucified cross of a holy hell and gone out of here.
You too, take that, you vandal. Get a lift from my sandal.
You're the last one, might as well get what's left behind.
Well . . . Phew . . . ! Say, I made it, didn't I? Just about in time.
MENAECHMUS I: Young man, whoever you are, may the gods
always shine   1500
On your face. If it hadn't been for you I wouldn't have lasted
Through sunset today.
MESSENIO: By all that's holy, if you wanted
To reward me, O Master, you could free me.
MENAECHMUS I: Me liberate you?
I'm afraid I don't follow, young fellow. Aren't you making
some mistake.
MESSENIO: Me make a mistake?
MENAECHMUS I: By our father Jupiter, I swear
I am not your master.
MESSENIO: Don't talk that way.
MENAECHMUS I: I'm not lying.   1505
No slave of mine ever helped me as you did today.
MESSENIO: Well, then, let me go free, even if you say you don't
know me.
Then I won't be yours.
MENAECHMUS I: But of course! Far as I'm concerned,
Thou art henceforth free—and thou mayest go wherever thou
wantest to.
MESSENIO: You say that officially?
MENAECHMUS I: By Hercules, yes. In my official
capacity,
Insofar as that governs you.   1510
MESSENIO: Thanks very much.
And greetings, dear patron! Now that I'm free to be your
client
And depend on you on equal terms.

(Turns to audience)

Gaudete! He's free today!
Good show for Messenio!   1515
Aren't you all glad he's let go?

(Audience cheers and applauds—and that is some stage direction)

(Still to audience)

Well, I guess I'll accept it from you; thanks for the
congratulations.
You've all given me quite a hand. I feel *man you mitted.*
But, Menaechmus, my patron, I'm just as much at your service
As I was when I used to be your slave. I want to stay by you.   1520
And when you go home I want to go with you too.
MENAECHMUS I: *(Aside)* God, no! Not another client.

MESSENIO: I'll ankle downtown
    To the tavern and bring back the baggage and cash. That purse
    I hid away and locked in the trunk with the traveler's checks.
1525   I'll go get it now and deliver it all back to you.
MENAECHMUS I: Oh yes, do bring that.
MESSENIO: I'll bring it all back intact
    Just as you handed it over. You wait here for me.

(He exits)

MENAECHMUS I: There's a bumper crop of miracles manifesting
        marvels by the millions
    Around here today: some people saying I'm not who I am
1530   And keeping me out from where I belong; then comes along
    This slave who says he belongs to me, whom I've just set free.
    Now he says he'll go bring me back a purseful of cash;
    And if he does that I'll insist he feel perfectly free
    To take leave of me and go where he wants, just in case
    When he comes to his senses he begins asking back for the
1535   dough.
    The doctor and my father-in-law, though, claim I'm out of my
        head.
    At least, that's what they said. It's all very hard to get hold of,
    Like a dream you dream you're having or are just being told of.
    Oh well, I'll go on in here to visit my mistress, even though
1540   She's provoked at me, and do my best to prevail
    On her to give back the dress. I can certainly use it as bail
    To get off the street and into my house, *id est,* my jail.

SCENE 7

MENAECHMUS II: You have the nerve to be telling me you
        reported back to me
    Since the time I sent you away and told you to meet me?
MESSENIO: Exactly. Only a moment ago I saved you from
1545   destruction
    At the hands of those four whipsters hoisting you on their
        shoulders
    And carting you off, right in front of this house. You were
        letting out
    Loud shouts, calling on all the gods and on men,
    When I roared in and pulled you loose by sheer brute
        strength
1550   And knocked the block off them all, much to their surprise.
    And for the service I rendered in saving you, you set me free.
    Then I told you I'd go get the baggage and our cash—and
        then *you*
    Doubled round the corner as fast as you could, to meet me
    And deny the whole thing.
MENAECHMUS II: I told you you could be free?
MESSENIO: Positive.
1555 MENAECHMUS II: I'm more positive still that before I'd see
    You turned free man I'd turn into a slave, yes me, man.

SCENE 8

MENAECHMUS I: *(Coming out of* DÉSIRÉE'S *house)* You can swear
        by your two jaundiced eyes if you want, that won't
    Make it any more true that I took away the dress and bracelet
        today,
    You whole bunch of blue-eyed, organized man-eaters for pay.

MESSENIO: Heavens to . . . let's see . . . What's this I see?
MENAECHMUS II: So, what   1560
    Do you see?
MESSENIO: Your looking glass, boss.
MENAECHMUS II: You mean to say what?
MESSENIO: I say I see your reflection over there. I could swear
    It's your face exactly.
MENAECHMUS II: God, if it isn't like me,
    When I stop to consider how I look.
MENAECHMUS I: Oh boy, there, whoever you are,
    You saved my life. Glad to see you.
MESSENIO: Young man, I wonder   1565
    If you'd mind telling me what your name is, by God in heaven?
MENAECHMUS I: Heavenly God, no, of course I don't mind. The
    favor
    You did me rates in return my nonreluctant behavior:
    After all, you're my savior. I go by the name of Menaechmus.
MENAECHMUS II: So do I, for God's sake.
MENAECHMUS I: I'm Sicilian, from Syracuse.   1570
MENAECHMUS II: And my native city is the same.
MENAECHMUS I: What's that you claim?
MENAECHMUS II: Only what's the truth.
MESSENIO: I can tell you which is
    which easily.
    I'm his slave,
    (Points to MENAECHMUS I*)*
               but I thought all along I was his.
    And I thought you were him. That's why I talked back that way.
    Please excuse me if I've spoken too stupidly for words to you.   1575
MENAECHMUS II: You're raving right now. Think back. Remember
    how
    You got off the ship with me today?
MESSENIO: A fair enough question.
    I'll change my mind. You're my master and I am your slave.
    So long, you. Good afternoon, again, to you. And I mean you.
    I say, this one's Menaechmus.
MENAECHMUS I: I say that's me.   1580
MENAECHMUS II: What's the story, you? Menaechmus?
MENAECHMUS I: Yep. Menaechmus.
    Son of Moschus.
MENAECHMUS II: You're my father's son?
MENAECHMUS I: No, fellow, *my* father's.
    I'm not
    After yours. I don't want to hop on yours and take him
    from you.
MESSENIO: By all the gods, all over heaven, can my mind
    Be sure of what it hopes for so desperately? *I've got' em*
    untwined!   1585
    These men are the two twins who separately now are combined
    To recall the same father and fatherland they shared in their
    likeness.
    I'll speak to my master. Ahoy there, Menaechmus.
MENAECHMUS I and MENAECHMUS II: *(Together)* What is it?
MESSENIO: No, no, not both. I only want my shipmate.
MENAECHMUS I: Not me.
MENAECHMUS II: But me.
MESSENIO: You're the one I must talk to.
    Come here.
MENAECHMUS II: Here I am. What's up?
MESSENIO: That man's either your
    absolute brother   1590

Or an absolute fake. I never saw one man look more like
    another.
Water's no more like water, or milk more like milk
Than you two drops of the same identical ilk.
Besides, he cites the same fatherland and father.
Don't you think investigating further might be worth the
1595   bother?
MENAECHMUS II: Say, that's very good advice you're giving me.
    Thanks very much.
Keep boring in, I implore you, by Hercules' knee.
If you come up with my brother, I fully intend to see
That *thou shalt go free.*
1600 MESSENIO: I hope I come out right in the end.
MENAECHMUS II: I hope the same thing for you.
MESSENIO: (*To* MENAECHMUS I) Now, fellow, what do you say?
    Menaechmus, I believe that is what you said you were called.
MENAECHMUS I: Right you are.
1605 MESSENIO: Now this fellow here has the name of Menaechmus,
    Just like you, and you said you were born at Syracuse.
    So was he. Now both of you pay close attention to me,
    And see if what I work out doesn't prove well worth it.
MENAECHMUS I: You've already earned the right to whatever you
    want
1610   From me. You've only to ask and you'll gain it. If it's money
    You want, I'm ready to supply it. Just ask. I won't deny it.
MESSENIO: I am hopeful at the moment of setting about to discover
    The fact that you two are twins, born for each other
    And on the same day to the very same father and mother.
MENAECHMUS I: That sounds miraculous. I wish you could keep
1615   that promise.
MESSENIO: I'll come through all right. Now listen here, each one
    of you
    To just what I say. And answer my questions in turn.
MENAECHMUS I: Ask what you will. I'll answer and never keep
    back
    Anything I know.
MESSENIO: Is your name Menaechmus?
MENAECHMUS I: I admit it.
MESSENIO: Is that your name too?
MENAECHMUS II: So it is.
1620 MESSENIO: You say that your father
    Was Moschus?
MENAECHMUS I: So I do.
MENAECHMUS II: Me too.
MESSENIO: You're from Syracuse?
MENAECHMUS I: That I am.
MESSENIO: How about you?
MENAECHMUS II: Naturally, me too.
MESSENIO: So far, it all checks perfectly. Now let's forge ahead.
    Tell me, how far back do you remember having been in your
    country?
MENAECHMUS I: Well, I remember the day I went to Tarentum,
1625   to the fair
    And wandered off away from my father among some men who
    took me
    And brought me here.
MENAECHMUS II: Jupiter One and Supreme, that can only
    mean . . . !
MESSENIO: What's all the racket? Can't you pipe down? Now,
    how old
    Were you when your father took you with him from Sicily?

MENAECHMUS I: Seven. I was just beginning to lose my first teeth, 1630
    And I never saw my father again.
MESSENIO: Here's another question:
    How many sons did your father have?
MENAECHMUS I: Two, to my knowledge.
MESSENIO: Were you the older, or was the other?
MENAECHMUS I: Both the same age.
MESSENIO: That's impossible.
MENAECHMUS I: I mean, we were twins.
MENAECHMUS II: The gods are
    on my side.
MESSENIO: If you keep interrupting, I'll stop.
MENAECHMUS I: No, no. I'll be quiet. 1635
MESSENIO: Tell me, did you both have the same name?
MENAECHMUS I: Not at all. I had
    The name I have now, Menaechmus. They called him Sosicles.
MENAECHMUS II: The lid's off! I just can't keep from hugging him
    hard.
    My own twin brother, *ciao!* It's me: Sosicles!
MENAECHMUS I: How come you changed your name to
    Menaechmus? 1640
MENAECHMUS II: After they told us how you had been taken away
    From our father, and carried off by strangers, and Father died,
    Our grandfather gave me your name. He made the changes.
MENAECHMUS I: I bet that's just how it happened. But tell me
    something.
MENAECHMUS II: Ask me something.
MENAECHMUS I: What was our dear mother's name? 1645
MENAECHMUS II: Henrietta Battleship.
MENAECHMUS I: That's it, all right. Never
    on a diet.
    Oh, *Brother,* this is a riot. I just *can't* keep quiet.
    Imagine meeting you here after all these years, I mean,
    I never thought I'd ever lay eyes on you again, much less
    Wring your neck, you old numero *uno,* I mean *duo.* 1650
MENAECHMUS II: Oh, you big beautiful brute, you. *Et ego et tu.*
    You know
    How long I've been hunting for you, and how much trouble
    I've gone to to locate my double! I'm glad to be here, lad.
MESSENIO: You see, Boss, that's why that mercenary much of a
    wench in there
    Called you by his name. She thought he was you when she
    hauled 1655
    You in to dinner.
MENAECHMUS I: As a matter of heavenly fact, I did order dinner
    set up
    Behind my wife's back, right here today, and sneaked out
    a dress,
     And gave it to Désirée.
MENAECHMUS II: Wouldn't be this dress, Brother,
    Would it?
MENAECHMUS I: That's it, Brother. But how did you happen to
    come by it?
MENAECHMUS II: I just happened to come by and the girlfriend
    pulled me in to dinner 1660
    And said I'd given her the dress. I dined very well,
    I wined like a lord, I reclined with my refined escort.
    Then I took away the dress, and this gold bracelet too.
MENAECHMUS I: Good for you.
    Old boy, Because of me, you've at least enjoyed
    Your day in Epidamnus. I'm glad of that. Now, when she

1665 Called you in, she of course thought sure you were me.

MESSENIO: Ahem! Need I wait much longer to be free as you
commanded?

MENAECHMUS I: Brother, he's asking for only what is his just due.
Just do it

For my sake, won't you?

MENAECHMUS II: *Thou art henceforth free.*

MENAECHMUS I:

1670 *Gaudete! He's free today!*
Good show for Messenio!
Aren't you all glad he's let go?

MESSENIO: Congratulations are all very fine, but perhaps
something more *exchangeable*

Like, say, money, will make a free future not only assured but

1675 *manageable.*

MENAECHMUS II: Now, brother, everything's finally worked out so
well,

Let's both go back to our homeland.

MENAECHMUS I: I'll do anything you wish,

Brother. I'll have a big auction here and sell all I own.
Meanwhile, temporarily, here we go home rejoicing.

MENAECHMUS II: I'm with you.

MESSENIO: I've a favor to ask.

MENAECHMUS I: Don't hesitate. 1680

MESSENIO: Appoint me auctioneer.

MENAECHMUS I: Sold! To the former slave!

MESSENIO: Well, shall I announce the sale then?

MENAECHMUS I: Sure, for a week
from today.

MESSENIO: (*To audience*) Big auction at Menaechmus's house a
week from today!

Must sell slaves, furniture, town house, country estate!
Everything's going, everything, for whatever you can pay! 1685
He'll even sell the wife to any buyer willing to try her.
We'll make a million dollars and we may even go higher
If you count my commission. All invited! It ought to be great!
—But, oh, wait, spectators! Don't forget the theater's laws.
We'll leave you first, on a burst of good loud applause! 1690

CRITICAL CONTEXTS

ARISTOTLE (384–322 BCE)

from *The Poetics* (c. 335 BCE)

Translated by GERALD F. ELSE

Born near Macedonia, Aristotle entered the Academy in Athens at the age of seventeen to study with Plato. After Plato's death, Aristotle conducted research in natural history, mainly botany and zoology, throughout the Aegean region and served as the tutor of the young Alexander the Great in Macedon before returning to Athens to found the Lyceum in 355 BCE.

Aristotle wrote extensively on topics ranging from ethics, rhetoric, and metaphysics to physics and natural history. In *The Poetics,* he analyzes the field of poetry into different "species" or genres (epic, tragedy, comedy, dithyramb) and attempts to discover the basic features of each. *The Poetics* demonstrates Aristotle's extensive knowledge of drama, which he uses to refine a keen sense of the form and purpose of tragedy. We should remember that *The Poetics* was written sometime after 335 BCE, roughly a century after the height of the Athenian theater. And although *The Poetics* is the cornerstone of Western dramatic criticism, the meaning of several of Aristotle's key terms—*MIMESIS* (imitation), *CATHARSIS* (purgation), and *HAMARTIA* (error)—remain controversial.

Students approaching *The Poetics* for the first time often have difficulty with the compressed logic of Aristotle's text, which may have formed something akin to notes for a lecture—a basis for expansion and discussion. Given Aristotle's representation of poetry according to natural "species," one way into his thinking may be to attempt to relate the functions of the various parts of tragedy: What is the relationship between Aristotle's conception of plot and of character? What is the logic that sustains his claim that plot is the principal element of tragedy, more important than character, language, or spectacle? What is the nature of "imitation," as Aristotle expresses it here? Given Aristotle's sense of just and unjust imitation, should we take imitation as a straightforward synonym for realism?

Basic Considerations

The art of poetic composition in general and its various species, the function and effect of each of them; how the plots should be constructed if the composition is to be an artistic success; how many other component elements are involved in the process, and of what kind; and similarly all the other questions that fall under this same branch of inquiry—these are the problems we shall discuss; let us begin in the right and natural way, with basic principles.

Epic composition, then; the writing of tragedy, and of comedy also; the composing of dithyrambs; and the greater part of the making of music with flute and lyre: these are all in point of fact, taken collectively, imitative processes. They differ from each other, however, in three ways, namely by virtue of having (1) different means, (2) different objects, and (3) different methods of imitation.

The Differentiation According to Medium

First, in the same way that certain people imitate a variety of things by means of shapes and colors, making visible replicas of them (some doing this on the basis of art, others out of habit), while another group produces its mimicry with the voice, so in the case of the arts we just mentioned: they all carry on their imitation through the media of rhythm, speech, and melody, but with the latter two used separately or together. Thus the arts of flute and lyre music, and any others of similar nature and effect, such as the art of the panpipe, produce their imitation using melody and rhythm alone, while there is another which does so using speeches or verses alone, bare of music, and either mixing the verses with one another or employing just one certain kind—an art which is, as it happens, nameless up to the present time. In fact, we could not even assign a common name to the mimes of Sophron and Xenarchus and the Socratic discourses: nor again if somebody should compose his imitation in trimeters or elegiac couplets or certain other verses of that kind. (Except people do link up poetic composition with verse and speak of "elegiac poets," "epic poets," not treating them as poets by virtue of their imitation, but employing the term as a common appellation going along with the use of verse. And in fact the name is also applied to anyone who treats a medical or scientific topic in verses, yet Homer and Empedocles actually have nothing in common except their verse; hence the proper term for the one is "poet," for the other, "science-writer" rather than "poet.") and likewise if someone should mix all the kinds of verse together in composing his imitation, as Chaeremon composed a *Centaur* using all the verses.

Such is the disjunction we feel is called for in these cases. There are on the other hand certain arts which use all the aforesaid media, I mean such as rhythm, song, and verse. The composition of dithyrambs and of nomes does so, and both tragedy and comedy. But there is a difference in that some of these arts use all the media at once while others use them in different parts of the work.

These then are the differentiations of the poetic arts with respect to the media in which the poets carry on their imitation.

The Objects of Imitation

Since those who imitate men in action, and these must necessarily be either worthwhile or worthless people (for definite characters tend pretty much to develop in men of action), it follows that they imitate men either better or worse than the average, as the painters do—for Polygnotus used to portray superior and Pauson inferior men; and it is evident that each of the forms of imitation afore-mentioned will include these differentiations, that is, will differ by virtue of imitating objects which are different in this sense. Indeed, it is possible for these dissimilari-ties to turn up in flute and lyre playing, and also in prose dialogues and bare verses: Thus Homer imitated superior men and Hegemon of Thasos, the inventor of parody, and Nicochares, the author of the *Deiliad,* inferior ones, like-wise in connection with dithyrambs and nomes, for one can make the imitation the way Timotheus and Philoxenus did their *Cyclopes.* Finally, the difference between tragedy and comedy coincides exactly with the master-difference: Namely the one tends to imitate people better, the other one people worse, than the average.

The Modes of Imitation

The third way of differentiating these arts is by the mode of imitation. For it is possible to imitate the same objects, and in the same media, (1) by narrating part of the time and dramatizing the rest of the time, which is the way Homer composes (mixed mode), or (2) with the same person continuing without change (straight narrative), or (3) with all the persons who are performing the imitation acting, that is, carrying on for themselves (straight dra-matic mode).

Jottings, Chiefly on Comedy

Poetic imitation, then, shows these three *differentiae,* as we said at the beginning: in the media, objects, and modes of imitation. So in one way Sophocles would be the same (kind of) imitator as Homer, since they both imi-tate worthwhile people, and in another way the same as Aristophanes, for they both imitate people engaged in ac-tion, doing things. In fact some authorities maintain that that is why plays are called dramas, because the imitation is of men acting (*drôntas,* from *drân,* "do, act"). It is also the reason why both tragedy and comedy are claimed by the Dorians: comedy by the Megarians, both those from hereabouts, who say that it came into being during the period of their democracy, and those in Sicily, and tragedy by some of those in the Peloponnese. They use the names "comedy" and "drama" as evidence; for *they* say that they call their outlying villages *kômai* while the Athenians call theirs "demes" (*dêmoi*)—the assumption being that the participants in comedy were called *kômôidoi* not from their being revelers but because they wandered from one village to another, being degraded and excluded from the city—and that they call "doing" or "acting" *drân* while the Athenians designate it by *prattein.*

The Origin and Development of Poetry

So much, then, for the *differentiae* of imitation, their number and identity. As to the origin of the poetic art as a whole, it stands to reason that two operative causes brought it into being, both of them rooted in human nature. Namely (1) the habit of imitating is congenital to human beings from childhood (actually man differs from the other animals in that he is the most imitative and learns his first lessons through imitation), and so is (2) the pleasure that all men take in works of imitation. A proof of this is what happens in our experience. There are things which we see with pain so far as they themselves are concerned but whose images, even when executed in very great detail, we view with pleasure. Such is the case for example with renderings of the least favored animals, or of cadavers. The cause of this also is that learning is eminently pleasurable not only to philosophers but to the rest of mankind in the same way, although their share in the pleasure is restricted. For the reason they take plea-sure in seeing the images is that in the process of view-ing they find themselves learning, that is, reckoning what kind a given thing belongs to: "This individual is a So-and-so." Because if the viewer happens not to have seen such a thing before, the reproduction will not produce the pleasure *qua* reproduction but through its workmanship or color or something else of that sort.

Since, then, imitation comes naturally to us, and mel-ody and rhythm too (it is obvious that verses are segments of the respective rhythms), in the beginning it was those who were most gifted in these respects who, developing them little by little, brought the making of poetry into being out of improvisations. And the poetic enterprise split into two branches, in accordance with the two kinds of character. Namely, the soberer spirits were imitating noble actions and the actions of noble persons, while the cheaper ones were imitating those of the worthless, pro-ducing lampoons and invectives at first just as the other sort were producing hymns and encomia. . . . In them (that is, the invectives), in accordance with what is suitable and fitting, iambic verse also put in its appearance; indeed that is why it is called "iambic" now, because it is the verse in which they used to "iambize," that is, lampoon each other. And so some of the early poets became composers of epic, the others of iambic, verses.

Now it happens that we cannot name anyone before Homer as the author of that kind of poem (that is, an iambic poem), though it stands to reason that there were many who were; but from Homer on we can do so: thus his *Margites* and other poems of that sort. However, just as on the serious side Homer was most truly a poet, since he was the only one who not only composed well but constructed dramatic imitations, so too he was the first to adumbrate the forms of comedy by producing a (1) dramatic presentation, and not of invective but of (2) the ludicrous. For as the *Iliad* stands in relation to our tragedies, so the *Margites* stands in relation to our comedies.

Once tragedy and comedy had been partially brought to light, those who were out in pursuit of the two kinds of poetic activity, in accordance with their own respective natures, became in the one case comic poets instead of iambic poets, in the other case producers of tragedies instead of epics, because these genres were higher and more esteemed than the others. Now to review the question whether even tragedy is adequate to the basic forms or not—a question which is (can be) judged both by itself, in the abstract, and in relationship to our theater audiences—that is another story. However that may be, it did spring from an improvisational beginning (both it and comedy: the one from those who led off the dithyramb, the other from those who did so for the phallic performances [?] which still remain on the program in many of our cities); it did expand gradually, each feature being further developed as it appeared; and after it had gone through a number of phases it stopped upon attaining its full natural growth. Thus Aeschylus was the first to expand the troupe of assisting actors from one to two, shorten the choral parts, and see to it that the dialogue takes first place; (. . .) at the same time the verse became iambic trimeter instead of trochaic tetrameter. For in the beginning they used the tetrameter because the form of composition was "satyr-like," that is, more given over to dancing, but when speech came along the very nature of the case turned up the appropriate verse. For iambic is the most speech-like of verses. An indication of this is that we speak more iambics than any other kind of verse in our conversation with each other, whereas we utter hexameters rarely, and when we do we abandon the characteristic tone-pattern of ordinary speech.

Further, as to plurality of episodes and the other additions which are recorded as having been made to tragedy, let our account stop here; for no doubt it would be burdensome to record them in detail.

Comedy

Comedy is as we said it was, an imitation of persons who are inferior; not, however, going all the way to full villainy, but imitating the ugly, of which the ludicrous is one part. The ludicrous, that is, is a failing or a piece of ugliness which causes no pain or destruction; thus, to go no farther, the comic mask is something ugly and distorted but painless.

Now the stages of development of tragedy, and the men who were responsible for them, have not escaped notice, but comedy did escape notice in the beginning because it was not taken seriously. (In fact it was late in its history that the presiding magistrate officially "granted a chorus" to the comic poets; until then they were volunteers.) Thus comedy already possessed certain defining characteristics when the first "comic poets," so-called, appear in the record. Who gave it masks, or prologues, or troupes of actors and all that sort of thing, is not known. The composing of plots came originally from Sicily; of the Athenian poets, Crates was the first to abandon the lampooning mode and compose arguments, that is, plots, of a general nature.

Epic and Tragedy

Well then, epic poetry followed in the wake of tragedy up to the point of being a (1) good-sized (2) imitation (3) in verse (4) of people who are to be taken seriously; but in its having its verse unmixed with any other and being narrative in character, there they differ. Further, so far as its length is concerned tragedy tries as hard as it can to exist during a single daylight period, or to vary but little, while the epic is not limited in its time and so differs in that respect. Yet originally they used to do this in tragedies just as much as they did in epic poems.

The constituent elements are partly identical and partly limited to tragedy. Hence anybody who knows about good and bad tragedy knows about epic also; for the elements that the epic possesses appertain to tragedy as well, but those of tragedy are not all found in the epic.

Tragedy and Its Six Constituent Elements

Our discussions of imitative poetry in hexameters, and of comedy, will come later; at present let us deal with tragedy, recovering from what has been said so far the definition of its essential nature, as it was in development. Tragedy, then, is a process of imitating an action which has serious implications, is complete, and possesses magnitude; by means of language which has been made sensuously attractive, with each of its varieties found separately in the parts; enacted by the persons themselves and not presented through narrative; through a course of pity and fear completing the purification of tragic acts which have those emotional characteristics. By "language made sensuously attractive" I mean language that has rhythm and melody, and by "its varieties found separately" I mean the fact that certain parts of the play are carried on through spoken verses alone and others the other way round, through song.

Now first of all, since they perform the imitation through action (by acting it), the adornment of their visual appearance will perforce constitute some part of the making of tragedy; and song-composition and verbal expression also, for those are the media in which they perform the imitation. By "verbal expression" I mean the actual composition of the verses, and by "song-composition" something whose meaning is entirely clear.

Next, since it is an imitation of an action and is enacted by certain people who are performing the action, and since those people must necessarily have certain traits both of character and thought (for it is thanks to these two factors that we speak of people's actions also as having a defined character, and it is in accordance with their actions that all either succeed or fail); and since the imitation of the action is the plot, for by "plot" I mean here the structuring of the events, and by the "characters" that in accordance with which we say that the persons who are acting have a defined moral character, and by "thought" all the passages in which they attempt to prove some thesis or set forth an opinion—it follows of necessity, then, that tragedy as a whole has just six constituent elements, in relation to the essence that makes it a distinct species; and they are plot, characters, verbal expression, thought, visual adornment, and song-composition. For the elements by which they imitate are two (i.e., verbal expression and song-composition), the manner in which they imitate is one (visual adornment), the things they imitate are three (plot, characters, thought), and there is nothing more beyond these. These then are the constituent forms they use.

The Relative Importance of the Six Elements

The greatest of these elements is the structuring of the incidents. For tragedy is an imitation not of men but of a life, an action, and they have moral quality in accordance with their characters but are happy or unhappy in accordance with their actions; hence they are not active in order to imitate their characters, but they include the characters along with the actions for the sake of the latter. Thus the structure of events, the plot, is the goal of tragedy, and the goal is the greatest thing of all.

Again: a tragedy cannot exist without a plot, but it can without characters: thus the tragedies of most of our modern poets are devoid of character, and in general many poets are like that; so also with the relationship between Zeuxis and Polygnotus, among the painters: Polygnotus is a good portrayer of character, while Zeuxis' painting has no dimension of character at all.

Again: if one strings end to end speeches that are expressive of character and carefully worked in thought and expression, he still will not achieve the result which we said was the aim of tragedy; the job will be done much better by a tragedy that is more deficient in these other respects but has a plot, a structure of events. It is much the same case as with painting: the most beautiful pigments smeared on at random will not give as much pleasure as a black-and-white outline picture. Besides, the most powerful means tragedy has for swaying our feelings, namely the peripeties and recognitions, are elements of the plot.

Again: an indicative sign is that those who are beginning a poetic career manage to hit the mark in verbal expression and character portrayal sooner than they do in plot construction; and the same is true of practically all the earliest poets.

So plot is the basic principle, the heart and soul, as it were, of tragedy, and the characters come second: . . . it is the imitation of an action and imitates the persons primarily for the sake of their action.

Third in rank is thought. This is the ability to state the issues and appropriate points pertaining to a given topic, an ability which springs from the arts of politics and rhetoric; in fact the earlier poets made their characters talk "politically," the present-day poets rhetorically. But "character" is that kind of utterance which clearly reveals the bent of a man's moral choice (hence there is no character in that class of utterances in which there is nothing at all that the speaker is choosing or rejecting), while "thought" is the passages in which they try to prove that something is so or not so, or state some general principle.

Fourth is the verbal expression of the speeches. I mean by this the same thing that was said earlier, that the "verbal expression" is the conveyance of thought through language: a statement which has the same meaning whether one says "verses" or "speeches."

The song-composition of the remaining parts is the greatest of the sensuous attractions, and the visual adornment of the dramatic persons can have a strong emotional effect but is the least artistic element, the least connected with the poetic art; in fact the force of tragedy can be felt even without benefit of public performance and actors, while for the production of the visual effect the property man's art is even more decisive than that of the poets.

General Principles of the Tragic Plot

With these distinctions out of the way, let us next discuss what the structuring of the events should be like, since this is both the basic and the most important element in the tragic art. We have established, then, that tragedy is an imitation of an action which is complete and whole and has some magnitude (for there is also such a thing as a whole that has no magnitude). "Whole" is that which has beginning, middle, and end. "Beginning" is that which does not necessarily follow on something else, but after it something else naturally is or happens; "end," the other way round, is that which naturally follows on something else, either necessarily or for the most part, but nothing else after it; and "middle" that which naturally follows on something else and something else on it. So, then, well-constructed plots should neither begin nor end at any chance point but follow the guidelines just laid down.

Furthermore, since the beautiful, whether a living creature or anything that is composed of parts, should not only have these in a fixed order to one another but also possess a definite size which does not depend on chance—for beauty depends on size and order; hence neither can a very tiny creature turn out to be beautiful (since our perception of it grows blurred as it approaches the period of imperceptibility) nor an excessively huge one (for then it cannot all be perceived at once and so its unity and wholeness are lost), if for example there were a creature a thousand miles long—so, just as in the case of living creatures they must have some size, but one that can be taken in in a single view, so with plots: they should have length, but such that they are easy to remember. As to a limit of the length, the one is determined by the tragic competitions and the ordinary span of attention. (If they had to compete with a hundred tragedies they would compete by the water clock, as they say used to be done [?].) But the limit fixed by the very nature of the case is: the longer the plot, up to the point of still being perspicuous as a whole, the finer it is so far as size is concerned; or to put it in general terms, the length in which, with things happening in unbroken sequence, a shift takes place either probably or necessarily from bad to good fortune or from good to bad—that is an acceptable norm of length.

But a plot is not unified, as some people think, simply because it has to do with a single person. A large, indeed an indefinite number of things can happen to a given individual, some of which go to constitute no unified event; and in the same way there can be many acts of a given individual from which no single action emerges. Hence it seems clear that those poets are wrong who have composed *Heracleïds, Theseïds,* and the like. They think that since Heracles was a single person it follows that the plot will be single too. But Homer, superior as he is in all other respects, appears to have grasped this point well also, thanks either to art or nature, for in composing an *Odyssey* he did not incorporate into it everything that happened to the hero, for example how he was wounded on Mt. Parnassus or how he feigned madness at the muster, neither of which events, by happening, made it at all necessary or probable that the other should happen. Instead, he composed the *Odyssey*—and the *Iliad* similarly—around a unified action of the kind we have been talking about.

A poetic imitation, then, ought to be unified in the same way as a single imitation in any other mimetic field, by having a single object: since the plot is an imitation of an action, the latter ought to be both unified and complete, and the component events ought to be so firmly compacted that if any one of them is shifted to another place, or removed, the whole is loosened up and dislocated; for an element whose addition or subtraction makes no perceptible extra difference is not really a part of the whole.

From what has been said it is also clear that the poet's job is not to report what has happened but what is likely to happen: that is, what is capable of happening according to the rule of probability or necessity. Thus the difference between the historian and the poet is not in their utterances being in verse or prose (it would be quite possible for Herodotus' work to be translated into verse, and it would not be any the less a history with verse than it is without it); the difference lies in the fact that the historian speaks of what has happened, the poet of the kind of thing that *can* happen. Hence also poetry is a more philosophical and serious business than history; for poetry speaks more of universals, history of particulars. "Universal" in this case is what kind of person is likely to do or say certain kinds of things, according to probability or necessity; that is what poetry aims at, although it gives its persons particular names afterward; while the "particular" is what Alcibiades did or what happened to him.

In the field of comedy this point has been grasped: our comic poets construct their plots on the basis of general probabilities and then assign names to the persons quite arbitrarily, instead of dealing with individuals as the old iambic poets did. But in tragedy they still cling to the historically given names. The reason is that what is possible is persuasive; so what has not happened we are not yet ready to believe is possible, while what has happened is, we feel, obviously possible: for it would not have happened if it were impossible. Nevertheless, it is a fact that even in our tragedies, in some cases only one or two of the names are traditional, the rest being invented, and in some others none at all. It is so, for example, in Agathon's *Antheus*—the names in it are as fictional as the events—and it gives no less pleasure because of that. Hence the poets ought not to cling at all costs to the traditional plots, around which our tragedies are constructed. And in fact it is absurd to go searching for this kind of authentication, since even the familiar names are familiar to only a few in the audience and yet give the same kind of pleasure to all.

So from these considerations it is evident that the poet should be a maker of his plots more than of his verses, insofar as he is a poet by virtue of his imitations and what he imitates is actions. Hence even if it happens that he puts something that has actually taken place into poetry, he is none the less a poet; for there is nothing to prevent some of the things that have happened from being the kind of things that can happen, and that is the sense in which he is their maker.

Simple and Complex Plots

Among simple plots and actions the episodic are the worst. By "episodic" plot I mean one in which there is no probability or necessity for the order in which the episodes follow one another. Such structures are composed by the bad poets because they are bad poets, but by the good poets because of the actors: in composing contest pieces for them, and stretching out the plot beyond its capacity, they are forced frequently to dislocate the sequence.

Furthermore, since the tragic imitation is not only of a complete action but also of events that are fearful and pathetic, and these come about best when they come about contrary to one's expectation yet logically, one following from the other; that way they will be more productive of wonder than if they happen merely at random, by chance—because even among chance occurrences the ones people consider most marvelous are those that seem to have come about as if on purpose: for example the way the statue of Mitys at Argos killed the man who had been the cause of Mitys' death, by falling on him while he was attending the festival; it stands to reason, people think, that such things don't happen by chance—so plots of that sort cannot fail to be artistically superior.

Some plots are simple, others are complex; indeed the actions of which the plots are imitations already fall into these two categories. By "simple" action I mean one the development of which being continuous and unified in the manner stated above, the reversal comes without peripety or recognition, and by "complex" action one in which the reversal is continuous but with recognition or peripety or both. And these developments must grow out of the very structure of the plot itself, in such a way that on the basis of what has happened previously this particular outcome follows either by necessity or in accordance with probability; for there is a great difference in whether these events happen because of those or merely after them.

"Peripety" is a shift of what is being undertaken to the opposite in the way previously stated, and that in accordance with probability or necessity as we have just been saying; as for example in the *Oedipus* the man who has come, thinking that he will reassure Oedipus, that is, relieve him of his fear with respect to his mother, by revealing who he once was, brings about the opposite; and in the *Lynceus,* as he (Lynceus) is being led away with every prospect of being executed, and Danaus pursuing

him with every prospect of doing the executing, it comes about as a result of the other things that have happened in the play that he is executed and Lynceus is saved. And "recognition" is, as indeed the name indicates, a shift from ignorance to awareness, pointing in the direction either of close blood ties or of hostility, of people who have previously been in a clearly marked state of happiness or unhappiness.

The finest recognition is one that happens at the same time as a peripety, as is the case with the one in the *Oedipus.* Naturally, there are also other kinds of recognition: it is possible for one to take place in the prescribed manner in relation to inanimate objects and chance occurrences, and it is possible to recognize whether a person has acted or not acted. But the form that is most integrally a part of the plot, the action, is the one aforesaid; for that kind of recognition combined with peripety will excite either pity or fear (and these are the kinds of action of which tragedy is an imitation according to our definition), because both good and bad fortune will also be most likely to follow that kind of event. Since, further, the recognition is a recognition of persons, some are of one person by the other one only (when it is already known who the "other one" is), but sometimes it is necessary for both persons to go through a recognition, as for example Iphigenia is recognized by her brother through the sending of the letter, but of him by Iphigenia another recognition is required.

These then are two elements of plot: peripety and recognition; third is the *pathos.* Of these, peripety and recognition have been discussed; a *pathos* is a destructive or painful act, such as deaths on stage, paroxysms of pain, woundings, and all that sort of thing.

The Tragic Side of Tragedy: Pity and Fear and the Patterns of the Complex Plot

The "parts" of tragedy which should be used as constituent elements were mentioned earlier; . . . but what one should aim at and what one should avoid in composing one's plots, and whence the effect of tragedy is to come, remains to be discussed now, following immediately upon what has just been said.

Since, then, the construction of the finest tragedy should be not simple but complex, and at the same time imitative of fearful and pitiable happenings (that being the special character of this kind of poetry), it is clear first of all that (1) neither should virtuous men appear undergoing a change from good to bad fortune, for that is not fearful, nor pitiable either, but morally repugnant; nor (2) the wicked from bad fortune to good—that is the most untragic form of all, it has none of the qualities that one wants: it is productive neither of ordinary sympathy nor of pity nor of fear—nor again (3) the really wicked man changing from good fortune to bad, for that kind of structure will excite sympathy but neither pity nor fear, since the one (pity) is directed towards the man who does not deserve his misfortune and the other (fear) towards the one who is like the rest of mankind—what is left is the man who falls between these extremes. Such is a man who is neither a paragon of virtue and justice nor undergoes the change to misfortune through any real badness or wickedness but because of some mistake; one of those who stand in great repute and prosperity, like Oedipus and Thyestes: conspicuous men from families of that kind.

So, then, the artistically made plot must necessarily be single rather than double, as some maintain, and involve a change not from bad fortune to good fortune but the other way round, from good fortune to bad, and not thanks to wickedness but because of some mistake of great weight and consequence, by a man such as we have described or else on the good rather than the bad side. An indication comes from what has been happening in tragedy: at the beginning the poets used to "tick off" whatever plots came their way, but nowadays the finest tragedies are composed about a few houses: they deal with Alcmeon, Oedipus, Orestes, Meleager, Thyestes, Telephus, and whichever others have had the misfortune to do or undergo fearful things.

Thus the technically finest tragedy is based on this structure. Hence those who bring charges against Euripides for doing this in his tragedies are making the same mistake. His practice is correct in the way that has been shown. There is a very significant indication: on our stages and in the competitions, plays of this structure are accepted as the most tragic, *if* they are handled successfully, and Euripides, though he may not make his other arrangements effectively, still is felt by the audience to be the most tragic, at least, of the poets.

Second comes the kind which is rated first by certain people, having its structure double like the *Odyssey* and with opposite endings for the good and bad. Its being put first is due to the weakness of the audiences; for the poets follow along, catering to their wishes. But this particular pleasure is not the one that springs from tragedy but is more characteristic of comedy.

Pity and Fear and the Tragic Act

Now it is possible for the fearful or pathetic effect to come from the actors' appearance, but it is also possible for it to arise from the very structure of the events, and this is closer to the mark and characteristic of a better poet. Namely, the plot must be so structured, even without benefit of any visual effect, that the one who is hearing the events unroll shudders with fear and feels pity at what happens: which is what one would experience on hearing the plot

of the *Oedipus*. To set out to achieve this by means of the masks and costumes is less artistic, and requires technical support in the staging. As for those who do not set out to achieve the fearful through the masks and costumes, but only the monstrous, they have nothing to do with tragedy at all; for one should not seek any and every pleasure from tragedy, but the one that is appropriate to it.

Since it is the pleasure derived from pity and fear by means of imitation that the poet should seek to produce, it is clear that these qualities must be built into the constituent events. Let us determine, then, which kinds of happening are felt by the spectator to be fearful, and which pitiable. Now such acts are necessarily the work of persons who are near and dear (close blood kin) to one another, or enemies, or neither. But when an enemy attacks an enemy there is nothing pathetic about either the intention or the deed, except in the actual pain suffered by the victim; nor when the act is done by "neutrals"; but when the tragic acts come within the limits of close blood relationship, as when brother kills or intends to kill brother or do something else of that kind to him, or son to father or mother to son or son to mother—those are the situations one should look for.

Now although it is not admissible to break up the transmitted stories—I mean for instance that Clytemestra was killed by Orestes, or Eriphyle by Alcmeon—one should be artistic both in inventing stories and in managing the ones that have been handed down. But what we mean by "artistic" requires some explanation.

It is possible, then, (1) for the act to be performed as the older poets presented it, knowingly and wittingly; Euripides did it that way also, in Medea's murder of her children. It is possible (2) to refrain from performing the deed, with knowledge. Or it is possible (3) to perform the fearful act, but unwittingly, then recognize the blood relationship later, as Sophocles' Oedipus does; in that case the act is outside the play, but it can be in the tragedy itself, as with Astydamas' Alcmeon, or Telegonus in the *Wounding of Odysseus*. A further mode, in addition to these, is (4) while intending because of ignorance to perform some black crime, to discover the relationship before one does it. And there is no other mode besides these; for one must necessarily either do the deed or not, and with or without knowledge of what it is.

Of these modes, to know what one is doing but hold off and not perform the act (No. 2) is worst: it has the morally repulsive character and at the same time is not tragic; for there is no tragic act. Hence nobody composes that way, or only rarely, as, for example, Haemon threatens Creon in the *Antigone*. Performing the act (with knowledge) (No. 1) is second (poorest). Better is to perform it in ignorance and recognize what one has done afterward

(No. 3); for the repulsive quality does not attach to the act, and the recognition has a shattering emotional effect. But the best is the last (No. 4): I mean a case like the one in the *Cresphontes* where Merope is about to kill her son but does not do so because she recognizes him first; or in *Iphigenia in Tauris* the same happens with sister and brother; or in the *Helle* the son recognizes his mother just as he is about to hand her over to the enemy.

The reason for what was mentioned a while ago, namely that our tragedies have to do with only a few families, is this: It was because the poets, when they discovered how to produce this kind of effect in their plots, were conducting their search on the basis of chance, not art; hence they have been forced to focus upon those families which happen to have suffered tragic happenings of this kind.

The Tragic Characters

Enough, then, concerning the structure of events and what traits the tragic plots should have. As for the characters, there are four things to be aimed at. First and foremost, that they be good. The persons will have character if in the way previously stated their speech or their action reveals the moral quality of some choice, and good character if a good choice. Good character exists, moreover, in each category of persons; a woman can be good, or a slave, although one of these classes (to wit, women) is inferior and the other, as a class, worthless. Second, that they be appropriate; for it is possible for a character to be brave, but inappropriately to a woman. Third is likeness to human nature in general; for this is different from making the character good and appropriate according to the criteria previously mentioned. And fourth is consistency. For even if the person being imitated is inconsistent, and that kind of character has been taken as the theme, he should be inconsistent in a consistent fashion.

An example of moral depravity that accomplishes no necessary purpose is the Menelaus in Euripides' *Orestes;* of an unsuitable and inappropriate character, the lamentation of Odysseus in the *Scylla* and the speech of Melanippe; and of the inconsistent, *Iphigenia at Aulis,* for the girl who pleads for her life is in no way like the later one.

In character portrayal also, as in plot construction, one should always strive for either the necessary or the probable, so that it is either necessary or probable for that kind of person to do or say that kind of thing, just as it is for one event to follow the other. It is evident, then, that the dénouements of plots also should come out of the character itself, and not from the "machine" as in the *Medea* or with the sailing of the fleet in the *Aulis.* Rather the machine should be used for things that lie outside the drama proper, either previous events that a human being cannot know, or subsequent events which require advance

prophecy and exposition; for we grant the gods the ability to foresee everything. But let there be no illogicality in the web of events, or if there is, let it be outside the play like the one in Sophocles' *Oedipus.*

Since tragedy is an imitation of persons who are better than average, one should imitate the good portrait painters, for in fact, while rendering likenesses of their sitters by reproducing their individual appearance, they also make them better-looking; so the poet, in imitating men who are irascible or easygoing or have other traits of that kind, should make them, while still plausibly drawn, morally good, as Homer portrayed Achilles as good yet like other men.

Techniques of Recognition

What recognition is generically, was stated earlier; now as to its varieties: First comes the one that is least artistic and is most used, merely out of lack of imagination, that by means of tokens. Of these some are inherited, like "the lance that all the Earth-born wear," or "stars" such as Carcinus employs in his *Thyestes;* some are acquired, and of those some are on the body, such as scars, others are external, like the well-known amulets or the recognition in the *Tyro* by means of the little ark. There are better and poorer ways of using these; for example, Odysseus was recognized in different ways by means of his scar, once by the nurse and again by the swineherds. Those that are deliberately cited for the sake of establishing an identity, and all that kind, are less artistic, while those that develop naturally but unexpectedly, like the one in the foot-washing scene, are better.

Second poorest are those that are contrived by the poet and hence are inartistic; for example the way, in the *Iphigenia,* she recognizes that it is Orestes: *she* was recognized by means of the letter, but *he* goes out of his way to say what the poet, rather than the plot, wants him to say. Thus this mode is close kin to the error mentioned above: he might as well have actually worn some tokens. Similarly, in Sophocles' *Tereus,* the "voice of the shuttle."

Third poorest is that through recollection, by means of a certain awareness that follows on seeing or hearing something, like the one in the *Cypriotes* of Dicaeogenes where the hero bursts into tears on seeing the picture, and the one in Book 8 of the *Odyssey:* Odysseus weeps when he hears the lyre-player and is reminded of the War; in both cases the recognition follows.

Fourth in ascending order is the recognition based on reasoning; for example in the *Libation-Bearers:* "Somebody like me has come; nobody is like me but Orestes; therefore he has come." And the one suggested by the sophist Polyidus in speaking of the *Iphigenia:* it would have been natural, he said, for Orestes to draw the conclusion (aloud): "My sister was executed as a sacrifice, and now it is my turn." Also in the *Tydeus* of Theodectes: "I came expecting to find my son, and instead I am being destroyed myself." Or the one in the *Daughters of Phineus:* when they see the spot they reflect that it was indeed their fate to die here; for they had been exposed here as babies also. There is also one based on mistaken inference on the part of the audience, as in *Odysseus the False Messenger.* In that play, that he and no one else can string the bow is an assumption, a premise invented by the poet, and also his saying that he would recognize the bow when in fact he had not seen it; whereas the notion that he (the poet) has made his invention for the sake of the other person who would make the recognition, that is a mistaken inference.

The best recognition of all is the one that arises from the events themselves; the emotional shock of surprise is then based on probabilities, as in Sophocles' *Oedipus* and in the *Iphigenia;* for it was only natural that she should wish to send a letter. Such recognitions are the only ones that dispense with artificial inventions and visible tokens. And second-best are those based on reasoning. . . .

HORACE (QUINTUS HORATIUS FLACCUS) (65 BCE–8 BCE)

from *On the Art of Poetry* (18 BCE)

Translated, complete, by C. SMART, from *The Works of Horace literally translated into English prose* (New York. n. d.). Unsigned footnotes are by the translator. The brackets enclose words or phrases by the translator intended to complete the sense of the original.

Born in rural Venusia, Horace moved to Rome when his father took up business there, and was later sent to Athens to study. A supporter of Brutus' faction, after the assassination of Julius Caesar, Horace fought for the losing cause at the Battle of Philippi, returning to Rome after the defeat to find his property and land confiscated. Nonetheless, Octavius— Emperor Augustus—gave amnesty to Brutus' army, and Horace was eventually appointed to a post in the Roman Treasury, where he worked to support his career as a poet. A friend of Virgil, Horace became one of the most celebrated of Roman poets, known especially for his Odes and Satires; he was late in life patronized by the wealthy Maecenas, who gave Horace an estate outside Rome which passed to the state upon the poet's death.

Horace's *Letter to the Pisones*—usually called *Ars Poetica,* or *On the Art of Poetry*—was written in 18 BCE. Unlike Aristotle's *Poetics,* which was known in Europe only through commentaries on an Arabic translation until the eighteenth century, Horace's *Ars Poetica* was the predominant document of Latin literary criticism throughout the Middle Ages and well into the early modern period; it clearly stands behind Sir Philip Sidney's *Apology for Poetry* (see Unit III), and was translated into English by Queen Elizabeth I. In *Ars Poetica,* Horace develops a famous analogy between poetry and painting—*ut pictura poesis,* "as is painting, so is poetry"—suggesting that the purpose of poetry was to frame a significant image, what Sidney called a "speaking picture," of the world, and that it was similarly subject to the principal "law" of the arts, namely "to delight and instruct."

Thespis[1] is said to have invented a new kind of tragedy, and to have carried his pieces about in carts, which [certain strollers] who had their faces besmeared with lees of wine, sang and acted. After him Æschylus, the inventor of the vizard mask and decent robe, laid the stage over with boards of a tolerable size, and taught to speak in lofty tone, and strut in the buskin. To these succeeded the old comedy, not without considerable praise: but its personal freedom degenerated into excess and violence, worthy to be regarded by law; a law was made accordingly, and the chorus, the right of abusing being taken away, disgracefully became silent.

Our poets have left no species of the art unattempted; nor have those of them merited the least honor, who dared to forsake the footsteps of the Greeks, and celebrate domestic facts; whether they have instructed us in tragedy, or in comedy. Nor would Italy be raised higher by valor and feats of arms, than by its language, did not the fatigue and tediousness of using the file disgust every one of our poets. Do you, the descendants of Pompilius, reject that poem, which many days and many a blot have not ten times subdued to the most perfect accuracy. Because Democritus believes that genius is more successful than wretched

---

[1] *Thespis.* A native of Icarius, a village in Attica, to whom the invention of the drama has been ascribed. Before his time there were no performers except the chorus. He led the way to the formation of a dramatic plot and language, by directing a pause in the performance of the chorus, during which he came forward and recited with gesticulation a very theological story [Wheeler].

art, and excludes from Helicon all poets who are in their senses, a great number do not care to part with their nails or beard, frequent places of solitude, shun the baths. For he will acquire, [he thinks,] the esteem and title of a poet, if he neither submits his head, which is not to be cured by even three Anticyras, to Licinius the barber. What an unlucky fellow am I, who am purged for the bile in spring-time! Else nobody would compose better poems; but the purchase is not worth the expense. Therefore I will serve instead of a whetstone, which though not able of itself to cut, can make steel sharp: so I, who can write no poetry myself, will teach the duty and business [of an author]; whence he may be stocked with rich materials; what nour-ishes and forms the poet; what gives grace, what not; what is the tendency of excellence, what that of error.

To have good sense, is the first principle and fountain of writing well. The Socratic papers will direct you in the choice of your subjects; and words will spontaneously ac-company the subject, when it is well conceived. He who has learned what he owes to his country, and what to his friends; with what affection a parent, a brother, and a stranger, are to be loved; what is the duty of a senator, what of a judge; what the duties of a general sent out to war; he, [I say,] certainly knows how to give suitable attri-butes to every character. I should direct the learned imita-tor to have a regard to the mode of nature and manners, and thence draw his expressions to the life.[2] Sometimes a play, that is showy with common-places, and where the manners are well marked, though of no elegance, with-out force or art, gives the people much higher delight and more effectually commands their attention, than verse void of matter, and tuneful trifles.

To the Greeks, covetous of nothing but praise, the muse gave genius; to the Greeks the power of expressing themselves in round periods. The Roman youth learn by long computation to subdivide a pound into an hundred parts. Let the son of Albinus tell me, if from five ounces one be subtracted, what remains? He would have said the third of a pound.— Bravely done! you will be able to take care of your own affairs. An ounce is added: what will that be? Half a pound. When this sordid rust and hankering after wealth has once tainted their minds, can we expect that such verses should be made as are worthy of being anointed with the oil of cedar, and kept in the well-polished cypress?[3]

Poets wish either to profit or to delight; or to deliver at once both the pleasures and the necessaries of life. What-ever precepts you give, be concise, that docile minds may soon comprehend what is said, and faithfully retain it. All superfluous instructions flow from the too full memory. Let whatever is imagined for the sake of entertainment, have as much likeness to truth as possible; let not your play demand belief for whatever [absurdities] it is inclinable [to exhibit]: nor take out of a witch's belly a living child, that she had dined upon. The tribes of the seniors rail against everything that is void of edification: the exalted knights disregard poems which are austere. He who joins the in-structive with the agreeable, carries off every vote,[4] by de-lighting and at the same time admonishing the reader. This book gains money for the Sosii; this crosses the sea, and continues to its renowned author a lasting duration.

Yet there are faults, which we should be ready to par-don: for neither does the string [always] form the sound which the hand and conception [of the performer] in-tends, but very often returns a sharp note when he de-mands a flat; nor will the bow always hit whatever mark it threatens. But when there is a great majority of beauties in a poem, I will not be offended with a few blemishes, which either inattention has dropped, or human nature has not sufficiently provided against. What therefore [is to be determined in this matter]? As a transcriber, if he still commits the same fault though he has been reproved, is without excuse; and the harper who always blunders on the same string, is sure to be laughed at; so he who is excessively deficient becomes another Chœrilus; whom, when I find him tolerable in two or three places, I wonder at with laughter; and at the same time am I grieved when-ever honest Homer grows drowsy? But it is allowable, that sleep should steal upon [the progress of] a long work.

As is painting, so is poetry: some pieces will strike you more if you stand near, and some if you are at a greater distance: one loves the dark; another, which is not afraid of the critic's subtile judgment, chooses to be seen in the light; the one has pleased once; the other will give plea-sure if ten times repeated.

O you elder of the youths, though you are framed to a right judgment by your father's instructions, and are wise in yourself, yet take this truth along with you, [and] re-member it; that in certain things a medium and tolerable degree of eminence may be admitted: a counselor and pleader at the bar of the middle rate is far removed from the merit of eloquent Messala, nor has so much knowl-edge of the law as Cassellius Aulus, but yet he is in re-quest; [but] a mediocrity in poets neither gods, nor men,

---

[2] Truth, in poetry, means such an expression, as conforms to the gen-eral nature of things; falsehood, that which, however suitable to the particular instance in view, doth yet not correspond to such general nature [Tr].

[3] To preserve their books, the ancients rubbed them with oil of cedar, and kept them in cases of cypress, because these kinds of wood were not liable to corruption.

---

[4] *Omne tulit punctum.* Alluding to the manner of voting at the comitia by putting a point over the name of a candidate [Tr].

nor [even] the booksellers' shops have endured. As at an agreeable entertainment discordant music, and muddy perfume, and poppies mixed with Sardinian[5] honey give offense, because the supper might have passed without them; so poetry, created and invented for the delight of our souls, if it comes short ever so little of the summit, sinks to the bottom.

He who does not understand the game, abstains from the weapons of the Campus Martius: and the unskillful in the tennis ball, the quoit, and the troques, keeps himself quiet; lest the crowded ring should raise a laugh at his expense: notwithstanding this, he who knows nothing of verses presumes to compose. Why not! He is free-born, of a good family; above all, he is registered at an equestrian sum of monies, and clear from every vice. You, [I am persuaded,] will neither say nor do anything in opposition to Minerva: such is your judgment, such your disposition. But if ever you shall write anything, let it be submitted to the ears of Metius [Tarpa], who is a judge, and your father's, and mine; and let it be suppressed till the ninth year, your papers being laid up within your own custody. You will have it in your power to blot out what you have not made public: a word once sent abroad can never return.

Orpheus, the priest and interpreter of the gods, deterred the savage race of men from slaughters and inhuman diet; hence said to tame tigers and furious lions. Amphion, too, the builder of the Theban wall, was said to give the stones motion with the sound of his lyre, and to lead them whithersoever he would, by engaging persuasion. This was deemed wisdom of yore, to distinguish the public from private weal; things sacred from things profane; to prohibit a promiscuous commerce between the sexes; to give laws to married people; to plan out cities; to engrave laws on [tables of] wood. This honor accrued to divine poets, and their songs. After these, excellent Homer and Tyrtæus animated the manly mind to martial achievements with their verses. Oracles were delivered in poetry, and the economy of life pointed out, and the favor of sovereign princes was solicited by Pierian strains, games were instituted, and a [cheerful] period put to the tedious labors of the day; [this I remind you of,] lest haply you should be ashamed of the lyric muse, and Apollo the god of song.

It has been made a question, whether good poetry be derived from nature or from art. For my part, I can neither conceive what study can do without a rich natural vein, nor what rude genius can avail of itself: so much does the one require the assistance of the other, and so

amicably do they conspire [to produce the same effect]. He who is industrious to reach the wished-for goal, has done and suffered much when a boy; he has sweated, and shivered with cold; he has abstained from love and wine; he who sings the Pythian strains, was first a learner, and in awe of a master. But [in poetry] it is now enough for a man to say to himself: "I make admirable verses: a murrain seize the hindmost: it is scandalous for me to be outstripped, and fairly to acknowledge that I am ignorant of that which I never learned."

As a crier who collects the crowd together to buy his goods, so a poet rich in land, rich in money put out at interest, invites flatterers to come [and praise his works] for a reward. But if he be one who is well able to set out an elegant table, and give security for a poor man, and relieve him when entangled in gloomy lawsuits; I shall wonder if with his wealth he can distinguish a true friend from a false one. You, whether you have made, or intend to make, a present to any one, do not bring him full of joy directly to your finished verses: for then he will cry out: "Charming, excellent, judicious"; he will turn pale; at some parts he will even distill the dew from his friendly eyes; he will jump about; he will beat the ground [with ecstasy]. As those who mourn friends at funerals for pay, do and say more than those that are afflicted from their hearts; so the sham admirer is more moved than he that praises with sincerity. Certain kings are said to ply with frequent bumpers, and by wine make trial of a man whom they are sedulous to know, whether he be worthy of their friendship or not. Thus, if you compose verses, let not the fox's concealed intentions impose upon you.

If you had recited anything to Quintilius, he would say, "Alter, I pray, this and this": if you replied, you could do it no better, having made the experiment twice or thrice in vain; he would order you to blot out, and once more apply to the anvil your ill-formed verses: if you choose rather to defend than correct a fault, he spent not a word more nor fruitless labor, but you alone might be fond of yourself and your own works, without a rival. A good and sensible man will censure spiritless verses, he will condemn the rugged, on the incorrect he will draw across a black stroke with his pen; he will lop off ambitious [and redundant] ornaments; he will make him throw light on the parts that are not perspicuous; he will arraign what is expressed ambiguously; he will mark what should be altered; [in short,] he will be an Aristarchus:[6] he will not say, "Why should I give my friend offense about mere

---

[5] Sardinia was full of bitter herbs, from whence the honey was bitter. White poppy seed, roasted, was mingled with honey by the ancients.

[6] Aristarchus was a critic, who wrote above four score volumes of comments on the Greek poets. His criticisms on Homer were so much esteemed that no line was thought genuine until he had acknowledged it. He was surnamed the prophet or diviner, for his sagacity [Francis].

trifles?" These trifles will lead into mischiefs of serious consequence, when once made an object of ridicule, and used in a sinister manner.

Like one whom an odious plague or jaundice, fanatic phrensy or lunacy, distresses; those who are wise avoid a mad poet, and are afraid to touch him: the boys jostle him, and the incautious pursue him. If, like a fowler intent upon his game, he should fall into a well or a ditch while he belches out his fustian verses and roams about, though he should cry out for a long time, "Come to my assistance, O my country-men"; not one would give himself the trouble of taking him up. Were any one to take pains to give him aid, and let down a rope; "How do you know, but he threw himself in hither on purpose?" I shall say: and will relate the death of the Sicilian poet. Empedocles, while he was ambitious of being esteemed an immortal god, in cold blood leaped into burning Etna. Let poets have the privilege and license to die [as they please]. He who saves a man against his will, does the same with him who kills him [against his will]. Neither is it the first time that he has behaved in this manner; nor, were he to be forced from his purposes, would he now become a man, and lay aside his desire of such a famous death. Neither does it appear sufficiently, why he makes verses: whether he has defiled his father's ashes, or sacrilegiously removed the sad enclosure of the vindictive thunder: it is evident that he is mad, and like a bear that has burst through the gates closing his den, this unmerciful rehearser chases the learned and unlearned. And whomsoever he seizes, he fastens on and assassinates with recitation: a leech that will not quit the skin, till satiated with blood.

The Theater of Classical Japan

II

Acting in the Noh theater.

The drama and theater of the Asian world has a history as complex and multi-faceted as the histories of the many civilizations, peoples, and nations that have been said—by the West—to compose the "Asian world." India, for example, has a literature—in SANSKRIT—more than 3,000 years old. Although the golden age of Sanskrit theater took place in the fourth and fifth centuries, theater of various kinds—folk, classical, and modern—thrives in India today. The conventions of Indian theater have pervasively influenced the theater of southeast Asia; the Sanskrit epic poems *Mahabharata* and *Ramayana* provide the characters and settings, for example, for the beautiful shadow-puppet theater of Java in Indonesia—the *WAYANG KULIT*—and related forms of performance using dolls or live actors.

The masked dance drama of Korea—called *KAMYONGUK*—is related both to Chinese and Japanese theater, and Korea, like other Asian countries, has developed an important modern theater as well.

European knowledge of China's theater probably dates from Marco Polo's visits (1254–1324); we know of more than 550 playwrights who wrote after the Mongol invasion during China's Yüan dynasty (1279–1368), part of a theatrical tradition that is recorded as early as 1000 BCE and that developed throughout the Han (206 BCE–221 CE), Hui (589–614), T'ang (618–904), and Sung (960–1279) periods. Several plays from the Yüan theater have been adapted by European playwrights; Voltaire's *The Orphan of China* (1755), an adaptation of Chi Chunhsiang's *The House of Chao,* was the first Chinese play to become widely known in Europe, and Li Hsing's *The Story of the Chalk Circle* has been adapted several times, notably by Bertolt Brecht in *The Caucasian Chalk Circle* (1944). After the Mongols were expelled during the Ming dynasty (1368–1644), the center of theatrical activity shifted from northern China toward southern cities such as Hangchow. It was only during the eighteenth and nineteenth centuries, under the Ch'ing dynasty (1644–1912), that the most characteristic form of modern Chinese theater, the *BEIJING OPERA,* began to take the shape that it has today, sharing the stage with both Western and Western-style plays, and with a vigorous experimental theater working in a more distinctly Chinese dramatic idiom.

Although no one theater can be said to represent these rich and diverse theatrical traditions, the classical theater of Japan shares many features common to other Asian theaters: it blends aristocratic and popular affiliations; it descends from social and religious ritual traditions; it coordinates acting, dance, music, and spectacle; many of its plots and characters are derived from familiar literary and historical narratives and legends; its performance conventions are elaborately stylized and refined; and its performers are often trained with a level of formality not found in Western theater. This is hardly surprising, in that the introduction of Buddhism into Japan during the sixth century coincided with an important period of Japanese cultural and political expansion; for the next two centuries, Japan was actively in contact with the vital cultures of India, China, and Korea. Although the period of "classical" Japanese theater—roughly the twelfth through the eighteenth centuries—coincides with an extended period of cultural isolation, the expansion of Japan's military, political, and economic power in the nineteenth and twentieth centuries has again brought Japanese culture into dialogue with Asia and the West. Indeed, while Japan's imperial ambitions—the invasion of China and much of the Pacific Rim before and during World War II—were extinguished with the atomic bombing of Hiroshima and Nagasaki, Japanese theater and drama have continued to develop both in response to Western culture and through the experimental innovation of its own traditions.

The classical Japanese theater is a product of a distinctive period in the history of Japan, extending from 1192, when the emperor gave all civil and secular power to a *SHOGUN,* a hereditary military leader, to 1868, when the emperor regained state as well as religious authority. For better than 750 years the Japanese emperors lived in Kyoto, engaged in largely ceremonial duties, while the *shoguns,* based in Edo, exercised all political and judicial authority. The Genroku period (1680–1730) saw an extraordinary flowering of Japanese art and culture supported by the shogunate; this was the period of Basho, the famous *haiku* poet; of Ihara Saikaku, the novelist; and of Chikamatsu Monzaemon, Japan's greatest playwright. Although the Noh theater was in decline by the Genroku period, the three principal modes of Japanese classical theater—NOH, DOLL THEATER, and KABUKI—are in different ways the product of the elaborately hierarchical culture of feudal Japan, and of the increasing tension between the class of warriors who ruled Japan and a class of artisans and merchants—sometimes called simply CHONIN, or townsmen—whose economic power was centered in Japan's cities. With the rise of the shogunate, Japanese society assumed a feudal character that represented the interests and values of its ruling class of SAMURAI warriors. Owing their allegiance to the *shogun,* the ranks of the *samurai* comprised various warrior lords, or DAIMYO, and their attendant warriors. As in other feudal societies, in Japan it was both a right and an obligation to display the signs and behavior of one's caste. The *samurai,* for example, were expected to obey a stringent honor code, one that required their absolute loyalty to the *shogun,* to the *samurai* caste, and to its military ethos. If a *samurai* betrayed his lord, he and his followers risked becoming outcasts, called RŌNIN or "men adrift." The most famous Kabuki drama, *Chūshingura* (1748), takes the fortunes of such a *samurai* lord and his forty-seven followers as its subject, and *rōnin* are common figures in the Japanese theater. This organization extended throughout Japanese society; not only was Japanese society divided into major castes, but its professions—including theater and prostitution, often closely associated in the popular imagination—were strictly controlled through an elaborate guild system. In the major cities, theaters were built in specifically licensed quarters, and actors were generally required to live in or near those districts. Much as tradespeople had to make their trade known through conventions of dress (a practice common in Europe at this time as well), so actors were required in 1709 to shave their forelocks as a public sign of their profession.

Under the Ashikaga shogunate, which began in 1338 and ended in a civil war in the late sixteenth century, not only were the values of the *samurai* dominant, but the privileges of the *samurai* relative to other castes—such as the many ranks of merchants, artisans, farmers, and peasants—were rigidly observed. The principal forms of theatrical entertainment, especially Noh (or Nō) theater, were both sponsored by and largely reserved for the elite *samurai* castes and represented the literary and cultural values of their patrons. In 1603, Tokugawa Ieyasu (1542–1616) became the Emperor's *shogun,* and in the Tokugawa period (1603–1867; sometimes called the Edo period, after the city that was his seat, present-day Tokyo), Japan entered a period of extended peace and increasing cultural isolation. In the seventeenth century, the *shoguns* began to expel all foreigners from Japan, reserving specific enclaves in port cities like Nagasaki as protected zones where foreign trade might be undertaken. As cities such as Osaka, Tokyo, and Kyoto became significant urban centers, the merchant classes became wealthier and more powerful. Although their status was lower than that of the *samurai,* many of the merchants amassed huge fortunes that far exceeded the wealth of many *samurai.* The *samurai* still exerted political authority—in 1705 the *samurai* confiscated the fortune of a merchant to whom many of them were indebted—but the merchant classes came to dominate the cultural sphere as they became the principal audience for poetry, fiction, and theater. Although all three forms of classical Japanese theater are preserved and performed today, they first became popular in different eras of Japan's history: The Noh, as it is now known, was developed largely between the fourteenth and early seventeenth centuries; the doll theater's greatest popularity was in the late seventeenth century; Kabuki, which is said to have originated when Okuni, a dancer from the Izumo Shrine in Kyoto, began to perform satirical skits in Kyoto in 1603, developed largely between the late seventeenth and mid-eighteenth centuries.

Although Noh theater achieved its highly literary and ceremonial form in the fourteenth century, it is usually said to have developed from performance modes popular throughout the tenth and eleventh centuries, the *SARUGAKU-NO,* and a related form, *DENGAKU-NO.* "Noh" means "accomplishment" or "performance," and both forms of entertainment contributed elements to the development of Noh theater and drama. *Dengaku-no* may have had more explicit ritual elements, and was initially associated with the native Japanese religion of Shinto, but both forms involved acrobatics, comic role-playing, and dance. *Sarugaku* means "monkey music," which may give some idea of the exuberance of these performances. In the twelfth century, however, *sarugaku-no* was adapted by Buddhist priests to illustrate tenets of Buddhist thought and belief, and performances were given to large audiences at major temples, acted by lower-ranking priests. In time, professional players both imitated these performances outside the temples and were hired to replace the priests in temple performances; by the mid-twelfth century, guilds of performers were attached to major temples. In return for free performances during religious ceremonies and festivals, the professional guilds were given a monopoly on performing in the region of the temple.

Although the *sarugaku-no* and *dengaku-no* seem to have been energetic and spirited forms of entertainment, it was the association with the contemplative and literary elements of Buddhism that were to have the greatest effect on the formation of Noh theater. In 1374, Kan'ami Kiyotsugu (1333–1384)—a leader of one of the four main *sarugaku-no* troupes— performed before the *shogun* Yoshimitsu Ashikaga (1358–1408). Kan'ami was one of the great innovators of his era and is thought to have contributed to giving the Noh its current form. He emphasized the rhythmic nature of the musical accompaniment, developed a greater use of mime in acting, and correlated dance and musical elements more closely with a dramatic plot. These innovations might well have been lost, however, had the *shogun* not been so impressed that he took Kan'ami and his son, Zeami Motokiyo (1363–1444), under his patronage. Kan'ami's troupe became the most influential in Japan, and after his father's death Zeami assumed control of the company, until he was exiled from the court in 1434 by one of Yoshimitsu's sons. Together, Kan'ami and Zeami gave the Noh drama its now-traditional ethos and shape. Kan'ami's innovations were explored and formalized by Zeami, who wrote or revised more than 100 of the 241 plays that make up the Noh repertoire and described the philosophical, esthetic, and practical goals of Noh performance in several theoretical essays. In time, the *daimyo,* emulating the *shogun,* came to sponsor their own Noh performers. Because the performers and performances were so closely bound to the status of the *samurai* caste, however, Noh never became a popular or even very public form of theater. Although *samurai* occasionally sponsored "subscription" performances of Noh for the "townsmen," these highly refined, intensely literary dramas were definitively the entertainment of the elite.

The esthetics of Noh derive from the Buddhist emphasis on ZEN, or contemplation, an attitude of repose and withdrawal from worldly desire and distraction. Noh performance aims to induce a similar kind of attentive repose in its audience, to evoke what is called *YUGEN* (often translated as "grace," although for Western readers this may have irrelevant Christian connotations), a mood or state of mind responsive to the mysterious, graceful, and impermanent beauty of the performance. For this reason, perhaps, Noh drama is not really driven by the cause-and-effect narrative logic of Western drama. Noh plays are typically centered on scenes of revelation that climax in the main actor's principal dance. Rather than imitating life, a Noh play should evoke the "flower," as Zeami termed the fusion of esthetic, spiritual, and moral beauty arising from the performance.

A "typical" Noh play might begin with the *WAKI,* or secondary actor, meeting the *SHITE,* or principal actor, at a site of historical, legendary, or mythological importance. The *waki* enters first, and in his opening song—sometimes called the TRAVELING SONG, because

The Development of Noh Theater

Noh Dramatic Form

he sings it while making his entrance—announces who he is (often a priest) and where he is going. The *shite* then enters, taking the role of an ordinary person. They discuss the significance of the place, perhaps where a legendary warrior was killed in battle. The characters speak a densely literary language, for part of the Noh dramatist's skill is shown in his cunning ability to borrow allusions and quotations from Japanese literature; the actors repeat and emphasize a network of phrases and images that convey the play's central theme. The chorus—kneeling stage left—also contributes to this "literary" texture, narrating some of the action and singing or reciting some of the dialogue. The *shite* then leaves the stage, and in some Noh productions a **KYŌGEN** (a brief farce also descended from *sarugaku*) is performed. When the *shite* returns, however, he reveals who he really is, usually a god, hero, or demon connected with the place whose destiny is troubled; he might, for example, be the ghost of the legendary warrior. In a manner of speaking, the character continues to haunt this place because he or she is unable to let go of the world, of the "character" and its investment in the world that are the essence of his or her being. The ghost is haunted by the tortuous attitude or emotion that keeps him or her connected to the world. Unlike a Greek or Shakespearean tragedy, a Noh play does not conclude with a speech of recognition or response; instead, Noh drama concludes with an intricate dance, a beautiful interplay of dialogue, dance, narration, and music for the audience's contemplation.

Since the active repertoire of Noh drama has remained more or less the same for over 400 years, it is perhaps not surprising that other elements of Noh theater and performance have become highly systematic and conventionalized. There are five types of Noh drama—plays praising the gods, plays about warriors, plays about women, plays about madness or spirits, and plays about demons—and in classical Japan, a program of Noh performance included one play from each of these categories, performed in this order, with a *kyōgen* between each Noh play. In modern Japan it has become more common to perform only two or three plays followed by a *kyōgen,* in part because the pace of performance is much slower today. Although women at one time performed in Noh theater, in 1629 women

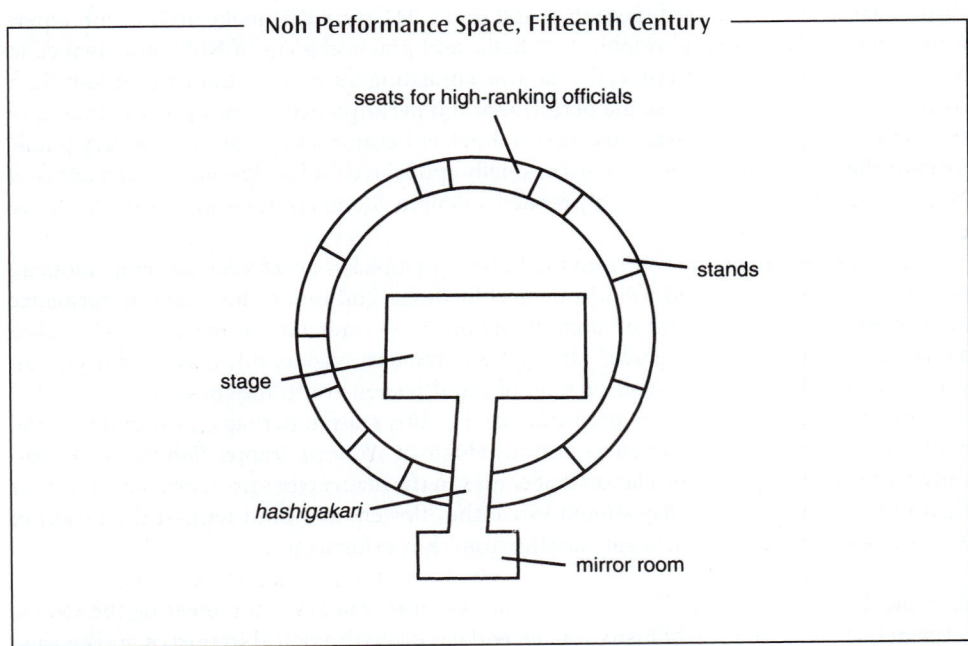

This is the ground plan of the performance space in the time of Zeami.

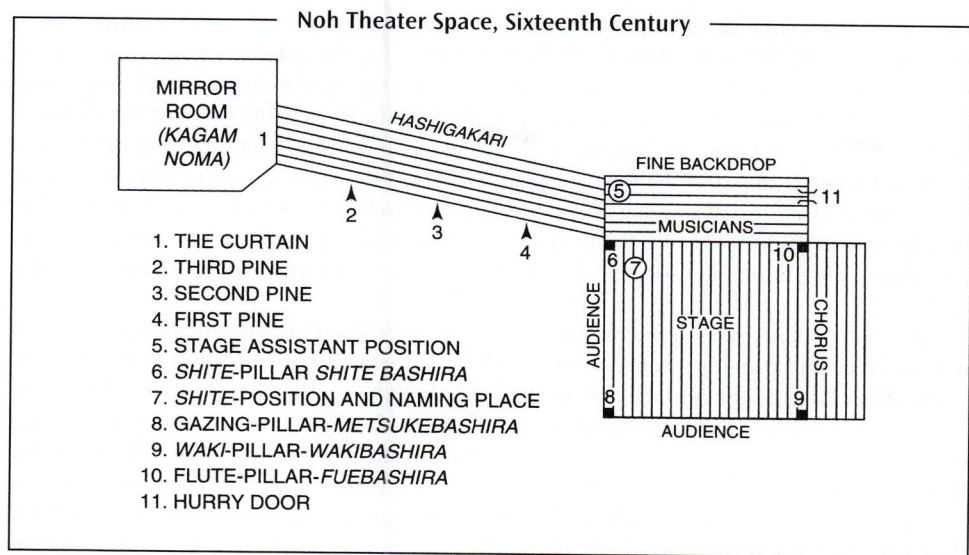

Noh Theater Space, Sixteenth Century

MIRROR ROOM (KAGAM NOMA)

HASHIGAKARI

FINE BACKDROP

MUSICIANS

AUDIENCE

STAGE

CHORUS

AUDIENCE

1. THE CURTAIN
2. THIRD PINE
3. SECOND PINE
4. FIRST PINE
5. STAGE ASSISTANT POSITION
6. *SHITE*-PILLAR *SHITE BASHIRA*
7. *SHITE*-POSITION AND NAMING PLACE
8. GAZING-PILLAR-*METSUKEBASHIRA*
9. *WAKI*-PILLAR-*WAKIBASHIRA*
10. FLUTE-PILLAR-*FUEBASHIRA*
11. HURRY DOOR

This ground plan shows the stage with the mirror room, the *hashigakari*, the *shitebashira*, the *wakibashira*, the *metsukebashira*, and the *fuebashira*, as well as the locations for the musicians and the chorus.

were banned from the Japanese stage; while women do perform in the modern Japanese theater, Noh companies are now traditionally all male. Plays are performed by the *shite* who is masked, an unmasked *waki,* and actors who play the *shite*'s companions (TSURE). A chorus of six to ten men both sings and narrates from a position to the side of the stage, and musicians—a flute and two or three drums—are positioned at the rear of the stage. The drums beat rhythmically, punctuating and accentuating the actors' delivery, while the flute plays in a kind of counterpoint to their speech. The *shite*'s mask is drawn from one of five categories—old person, male, female, gods, monsters—and the clothing of the performers is similarly stylized: The actors sometimes wear elaborate headdresses, and sumptuous silk clothing, arranged and layered in particular ways for certain roles. The members of the chorus wear the traditional dress of the *samurai.* Attendants clothed in black are present onstage throughout the performance, helping the actors with costumes and masks and placing and removing properties when needed; they are always senior actors of the company, because they may also need to step in to finish a performance if an actor is unable to continue. The stage is bare of sets, and hand properties are few and conventional; a bundle of firewood might be represented by a few sticks bound with flowers. Similarly, many of the properties are purely symbolic: A twig carried by a grieving woman is the sign of her madness. Throughout the performance, the actors move slowly and ceremonially; indeed, many of their actions must take place at a prescribed area of the stage.

The Noh Stage

Although the Noh stage was shaped somewhat differently in Kan'ami's and Zeami's era, by 1615 it had assumed the shape it retains to this day. A stage (BUTAI), roughly eighteen feet square, extends into the audience area; the stage is roofed like the early shrines from which it derives, and the audience is seated in front and on the stage-right side. A painted backdrop behind the stage always pictures the Yogo Pine at the Kasuga Shrine in Nara. The stage is always of highly polished wood, with sounding jars concealed beneath it to resonate with the emphatic stamping that is part of the actors' performance. The musicians are seated directly behind the main stage area on a second, narrow stage (ATOZA); they are in full view of the audience and are able to see the actors and adjust their playing to the actors' performance throughout the play. A small entrance, called the HURRY DOOR, leads off the stage left side of the *atoza*, which is used by the stage assistants, the chorus, and for the exit of dead characters. A second narrow stage runs along the stage-left side of the stage, the WAKIZA, where the chorus is seated, again in view of the audience and able to adjust their narration and singing to the pace of the actors. Finally, a long bridge, the HASHIGAKARI, leads from the upstage right corner of the stage out to the MIRROR ROOM, where the costumed actors have been studying themselves to get into the character. The *hashigakari* is six feet wide by thirty-three to fifty-two feet long; it is bordered by a narrow strip of white pebbles, on which stand three pine trees, representing heaven, earth, and man.

The four pillars that support the roof over the stage also have specific functions in the performance and provide a sense of the ceremonial formality of Noh theater. The upstage right pillar closest to the *hashigakari* is called the SHITEBASHIRA, or *shite*'s pillar. When the *shite* enters the *hashigakari*, he slides his feet (which are bound in cotton cloth) slowly along the floor; reaching the *shitebashira*, he pauses to announce who he is, where he is coming from, and where he is going (sometimes the *waki* will make this announcement when the *shite* reaches the *shitebashira*). The pillar downstage right is called the METSUKEBASHIRA, the gazing or eye-fixing pillar. It is the place where the *shite* looks while delivering his speech and which he watches through the slits in his mask to help orient his performance; given the tiny eye-openings in Noh masks, the *metsukebashira* is nearly all the *shite* can see. Downstage left, diagonally across from the *shitebashira*, is the WAKIBASHIRA, where the *waki* is often stationed when the *shite* enters. Upstage left is the FUEBASHIRA, the flute-player's pillar, where the flute-player is positioned.

As Zeami suggests in "Teachings on Style and the Flower", the training of a Noh actor in the fourteenth century was presumed to be lifelong, more a vocation than an occupation. Under the shogunate, Noh performers were given the privileges of the *samurai* caste, and five schools for training Noh actors were founded. These schools were run by hereditary masters, and certain families of Noh performers have influenced the theater over several generations; indeed, we owe the preservation of many documents (including Zeami's treatises), properties, and masks to the unusually closed and traditional ways in which Noh training has been passed from generation to generation. Four of the five current Noh companies were founded in Zeami's lifetime. Although Japan is no longer a caste society, acting in a Noh company today still requires years of dedication and intense training, something between the priesthood and the military. Moreover, because the relatively small number of classical Noh plays was stabilized in the early seventeenth century, Noh actors have generally mastered all the roles of the repertoire and perform without rehearsal. Their intensive training in movement, song, and dance prepares the actors, chorus, musicians, and stage assistants to be closely responsive to the many subtleties of their collective performance. And given the stability of the repertoire, of training, and of performance conventions, Noh theater has been performed in an unbroken tradition from Zeami's era to the present day.

The Development of Doll Theater

Like the Noh theater, the doll theater owes something to the desire of Buddhist priests to educate a wider Japanese audience in their teachings. Unlike the Noh, however, the doll theater was not supported or protected directly by the shogunate, and it came to enjoy a more popular audience. The doll theater arose from the confluence of two kinds of performance: puppet shows and storytelling to music. Much like the itinerant performers of *sarugaku-no*, wandering puppeteers became associated with shrines and temples in the twelfth century. At the same time, a form of live storytelling also became popular, the singing and recitation of legends and stories to the accompaniment of the BIWA, a four-stringed, plucked instrument. One of the most popular of these narratives was *The Tale of Jōruri*, a love story about a wealthy girl named Jōruri; although the story dates from the fifteenth century, it became popular when it was performed to a musical instrument imported from the Ryukyu Islands between 1558 and 1569, the **SAMISEN**. The *samisen,* a three-stringed instrument that is both plucked and struck, has a much wider tonal and dynamic range than the *biwa.* Samisen-accompanied dialogue and narrative became so popular that this kind of performance was termed simply **JŌRURI**. In effect, the doll theater is a form of *jōruri* in which the song and spoken narrative are accompanied by puppet performance.

Although puppets had been used in Japan for several centuries, puppets were first used in conjunction with *jōruri* performances in the sixteenth century; puppet-*jōruri* performances have been recorded in Kyoto as early as 1596, and by the late seventeenth century there were important doll theaters in both Tokyo and Osaka. As in the Noh, the plays performed in the doll theaters used narrative, dialogue, music, and acting to convey the dramatic action, and in the seventeenth century playwrights writing for the doll theaters adapted plots and characters directly from Noh models. In part, however, because of their derivation from the romantic *jōruri* narratives, in part because their audiences were well-to-do merchants and citizens rather than the aristocratic *samurai,* and in part because they were competing with the more salacious Kabuki theaters for that audience, the doll theaters came to dramatize events more closely approaching contemporary life. Although the earliest doll theater plays were on historical and legendary subjects (like the Noh plays), by the late seventeenth and early eighteenth centuries, doll drama concerned stagings of current events, and romanticized portrayals of contemporary life, called "domestic plays" or **SEWAMONO**. Although the shogunate forbade the staging of current events in 1703, the shoguns were more concerned about the satirical portrayals of *samurai* common in Kabuki; playwrights continued to write about contemporary events.

The doll theater played a major role in the development of Japanese theater generally. When Gidayu Takemoto (1651–1714), a famous performer of *jōruri,* opened the Takemoto Theater in Osaka in 1684, he began a collaboration with Chikamatsu Monzaemon (1653–1725), now generally recognized as Japan's greatest dramatist. Chikamatsu wrote an important body of plays for the doll theater, on historical subjects as well as on contemporary life. His play *Love Suicides at Sonezaki* (1703) concerns the double suicide of a young merchant and a prostitute in 1703 and was renowned for the beauty of its language and the power of its performance. The genre became so popular that in 1722 the shogunate banned plays about double suicide, which were common in both the doll theater and the Kabuki theater, perhaps fearing that Chikamatsu's play would be imitated by romantic young Japanese. Not only did Chikamatsu and other playwrights—notably Chikamatsu Hanji (1725–1783) and Uemura Bunrakuken (1737–1810), for whom the current puppet theater of Japan, **BUNRAKU**, is named—produce an extraordinarily rich body of plays, but also these plays were immediately mined by the Kabuki theaters, providing a source of material for living actors as well as the doll theater's elaborate puppets.

The Doll Theater Stage

The stage of the doll theater is thirty-six feet wide by twenty-six feet deep and is divided into three sections, each separated by a low screen. The three puppeteers who operate each puppet are visible throughout the performance. They are costumed in elegant traditional clothes and are seated behind the screens. The puppeteers and their dolls share the stage with several other performers: the stage assistants, dressed in black as in the Noh theater; the announcer; the narrator; and the *samisen* player. The announcer begins the performance by announcing the title of the play and introducing the narrator and the *samisen* player. The narrator is responsible for the verbal art of the play in a direct development of his role in the *jōruri:* he narrates the story of the play, speaks the dialogue of the characters and expresses their emotions as well, smiling, laughing, weeping, and so on. Later in the eighteenth century several narrators were used, one for each of the major characters in the drama. The *samisen* is played to augment, clarify, and deepen the narrator's performance, lending it a special plangency.

As in the Noh theater, performance in the doll theater is extremely ceremonial and precise, and performers undergo years of training to achieve their craft. Although marionettes were used in the seventeenth century, hand-operated puppets became increasingly popular and by 1736 had supplanted earlier forms. The typical doll is three or four feet tall and is operated by three puppeteers. The most senior operator, dressed in a formal nineteenth-century costume, stands behind the doll and holds it up; he works a system of strings and pulleys within the head that control the doll's head, eyebrows, and eyelids, and he also operates the doll's right arm and right hand by means of hidden strings. His two assistants are clothed in black like the stage assistants, and their faces are covered; one assistant operates the left arm and hand, and the other assistant operates the legs and feet. Much as training in the Noh theater resembles that of a traditional art, so learning to operate the puppets of the doll theater entails a lifetime of commitment. Puppeteers take an apprenticeship of ten years to learn to operate the legs and feet of the dolls with sufficient grace; they then take another ten years to learn the correct operation of the left arm and hand before spending the final ten years on mastering the subtleties of the right arm, right hand, and head.

Doll theater contributed extensively to the dramatic repertoire of the Kabuki theater, and the fixed poses of the puppets are sometimes thought to contribute to the exaggerated expressive stance of the Kabuki actors, the MIE. But the doll theater contributed other innovations to Japanese theater and to world theater generally. Much as the dolls increased in complexity throughout the late seventeenth century and early eighteenth century—gaining eye movement in 1730, finger joints and movements in 1733, and so on—so the stage itself became increasingly mechanized. By 1715 the doll theaters were using movable settings, and by 1727 elevator traps were used to raise and lower scenery visibly through the floor of the stage. This machinery not only was put to use in the more spectacular Kabuki theater, but also was adapted and imitated by theaters around the world. Although the doll theater was surpassed in popularity by the Kabuki in the nineteenth century, it continues to be sponsored by the Japanese government and performed regularly in Osaka and Tokyo.

The Development of Kabuki Theater

Kabuki is in many ways the most energetic and spectacular mode of classical Japanese theater, using live actors to stage intense and passionate dramas whose effect is heightened by a range of powerful performance conventions and by an elaborately mechanized stage. As in the doll theater, Kabuki arose as a popular form of entertainment, supported by audiences outside the aristocratic sphere of Noh performance. Although Kabuki drama, as in the drama of the doll theaters, was initially derived from the plays of the Noh theater, Kabuki theater rapidly developed its own dramatic style and performance esthetics.

Unlike Noh and doll theater, Kabuki did not originate in medieval performance forms like the *sarugaku-no* and the *biwa*-accompanied narratives that became *jōruri*. Instead, Kabuki began in 1603, when Okuni, who claimed to be a priestess from the Izumo Grand Shrine, set up an impromptu stage in the Kyoto riverbed, where she performed dances and satirical skits. Okuni's company was largely composed of women, and within a short time a number of companies—some involving prostitutes, who offered performances as entertainment—were established in Kyoto and elsewhere. Although comic roles—called SARUWAKA—were always performed by men, the earliest troupes were composed mainly of women, called either ONNA KABUKI (women's Kabuki) or YŪGO KABUKI (prostitutes' Kabuki). At the same time, however, other Kabuki companies, composed mainly of adolescent boys, became popular.

Throughout the early period of Kabuki, its performers—both women and boys—were frequently associated with prostitution, which extended in various ways to a variety of leisure activities: to bathhouses, dances, and to the practice of GEISHA, which has its origins at this time. All of these activities, however, were distinct from the work of the *YŪGO*, or professional prostitute. As in other respects, the shogunate treated Kabuki like prostitution, beginning in 1624 to license companies and theater districts.

The boundary between theater and prostitution—by men, women, and boys—was difficult to police, though, and in 1652 authorities finally banned the boys' Kabuki—*WAKASHU KABUKI*—outright. Thereafter, the only Kabuki companies that were licensed to perform were the *YARO KABUKI,* or adult male Kabuki companies, which are now traditional.

The repertoire of Kabuki theater contains two kinds of plays, one based on historical or legendary incidents, and *sewamono* or "domestic plays," based on contemporary events. Okuni had once acted the role of a young *samurai* soliciting a prostitute, and plays based on the visit of a wealthy and powerful young man to the "licensed quarter" became a popular Kabuki genre, particularly in Kyoto and Osaka. Many of these plays, including *Love Letter from the Licensed Quarter* (1780), concern the fortunes of Yūgiri, a well-known courtesan of the Osaka Shinmachi quarter who died in 1678. Chikamatsu—whose *Love Suicides at Sonezaki* (1703) adapted the conventions of Kabuki to the doll stage—played a central role in this regard as well: he worked as the house playwright to a famous Kabuki company for more than twenty years. Although plays that dramatize love suicides and plays staging the scandals of the *samurai* caste were banned after 1722, playwrights continued to write about contemporary life under the guise of one of the other major genres of Kabuki theater, the history play. It quickly became apparent that by changing names and setting the drama in the past, playwrights were able to write domestic plays thinly veiled as history. For example, in 1703 the forty-seven retainers of Lord Asano took revenge on their master's disgrace at the hands of a shogunate official by killing the official and then committing *seppuku,* or ritual disembowelment. Within two weeks, a Kabuki play alluding to the incident was staged, and then was rapidly closed by the government. When Chikamatsu turned to these events in 1710, he set the play in the fourteenth century to sidestep the ban, and one of the most famous Kabuki plays—*Chūshingura* (1748)—concerns these events as well.

The Kabuki Stage

Kabuki is very much a performance genre, and its plays were organized around the abilities of its actors rather than around a literary script. For this reason, even the plays written by the most influential Kabuki playwrights—Chikamatsu Monzaemon, Takedo Izumo (1691–1756), and Kawatake Mokuami (1816–1893)—began as outlines of scenes to be elaborated by a cadre of assistant playwrights. A Kabuki company contained forty to sixty actors, each of whom specialized in a certain kind of role and expected the playwright to devise scenes that would allow him to display his talents. Companies generally included a leading-man actor, or *TACHIYAKU,* and specialists in villainous men (*KATAKIYAKU*), in young men and boys (*WAKASHUGATA*), in comic roles (*DOKEKATA*), and in women's roles (*ONNAGATA*), which were also divided according to age and type.

Finally, the unusual duration of a Kabuki performance also demanded the talents of the playwright's staff of assistants. Kabuki performances originally began about three o'clock in the morning and did not conclude until dusk; the fourteen- to fifteen-hour production was composed of a series of scenes arranged around a common theme or mood. The production usually began with a dance play, followed by a familiar play from the company's repertoire. Because the play was familiar to the company, it required little preparation. Then the company would perform one or two short practice plays, written by apprentice playwrights and performed by actors-in-training as part of their education. The main play—the *HON KYŌGEN*—would be performed at about seven o'clock in the morning and lasted until dusk. This play was outlined by the house playwright in collaboration with the company's leading actor and manager, and he would write the most important sections himself; the company's second and third rank playwrights would elaborate dialogue for the rest of the play. The play

Kabuki Stage, Nineteenth Century

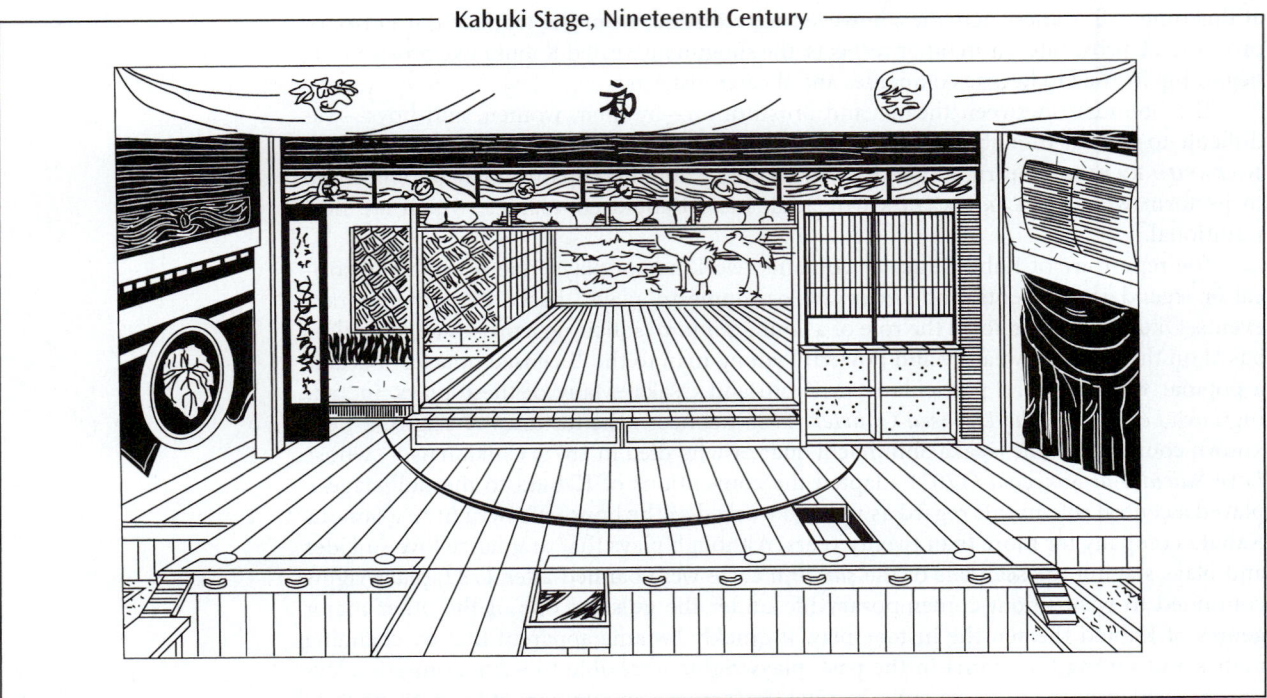

Notice the screens to the side of the stage, the *hanamichi* (which attaches to the front of the stage in the lower left-center of the picture), and a revolving platform in the center of the stage. (From Brockett, Oscar G. *History of the Theatre,* 7th Edition. Published by Allyn and Bacon, Boston, MA. Copyright © 1995 by Pearson Education. Reprinted by permission of the publisher.)

was customarily divided into four sections: a history section in four to six acts (**JIDAIMONO**) concerning the exploits of the *samurai;* a dance; a *sewamono* (contemporary) section in one to three acts, set in the milieu of artisans, traders, and merchants; and a concluding dance drama. Kabuki performances today are generally given in two programs, lasting from eleven to four o'clock and from four-thirty until nine-thirty in the evening. Although it is rare to see a full-length Kabuki play performed today, the four-part sequence is still followed.

Kabuki is very much an actor's theater. The actors undergo a long period of training, and as in Noh theater, certain families of actors have dominated the history of Kabuki. Indeed, Kabuki actors often wear their family crest in performance, and audiences frequently compare an actor's performance in a given role with his father's or his uncle's. Originating as a form of dance, Kabuki places a premium on choreography, which accompanies gesture and speech as a means of realizing the character's essential tone or feeling in a precise and elegant image. Yet the actors play directly to the audience, and the most striking moments in the performance—the *mie,* a highly conventionalized posed performance of passion—are underscored as performance when the stage assistants clap two pieces of wood loudly and rhythmically together. The actors play conventional roles, and each role in the Kabuki repertoire has a conventional costume associated with it. The costumes are extremely cumbersome, so the actors are often helped by stage assistants clothed in black who position properties and move pieces of the set. The actors are not masked, but wear an elaborate and conventionalized makeup, usually of red and black lines and patterns ranged over a white base; *onnagata* actors generally add only eyebrow lines and rouged cheeks and lips to an otherwise white face. Given its close relationship to *jōruri* and doll theater, it is not surprising that Kabuki usually requires a narrator onstage as well who not only sets the scene, but comments on the action throughout; he also occasionally speaks dialogue. Kabuki actors never sing, so their songs are sung by the narrator and by an onstage chorus. Moreover, each play is accompanied by traditional music, played by musicians wearing the traditional *samurai* costume. The orchestra for Kabuki is considerably larger than that for Noh and makes use of flutes, bells, drums, cymbals, and gongs, as well as the *samisen*.

Although the first Kabuki companies played on impromptu stages, they soon were allowed to use Noh theaters; given their raffish character, however, Kabuki companies were not allowed to have roofed theaters until 1724. Like the doll theater, Kabuki theater quickly made use of scenic technology; the elevator stage was in use by 1736, and by the late eighteenth century it was common for Kabuki theaters to have a revolving stage, sometimes two independent turntables with one turning inside the other. Kabuki makes extensive use of scenery, though much of it is of a symbolic or ornamental nature. Like properties in this theater, which tend to be suggestive of the objects they represent, the scenery of a Kabuki performance is openly theatrical in character: the scenery is changed in view of the audience by visible assistants (who help the actors as well) and aims to suggest the locale of the scene rather than put it on the stage in a realistic way. It is a measure, though, of the relationship between the extroverted Kabuki performance and its audience that its most distinguishing feature involves the audience more directly in the production. In the early eighteenth century, Kabuki theaters added a *HANAMICHI*, or elevated bridge, extending from the rear of the auditorium to the stage. Actors made their exits and entrances here, and scenes could be played on the *hanamichi* as well. By the 1770s, a second *hanamichi* was added, and the area between the two *hanamichi* was divided into floor boxes, while other rows of seating ran along the sides of the auditorium. Although the second *hanamichi* is still required for some plays, it is generally no longer in use.

The restoration of the emperor in 1868 not only brought about the collapse of the shogunate, but also ended Japan's isolation. It also dramatized the economic weakness of the *samurai* relative to the merchant class. In many respects, Japan's theater was vulnerable to extinction, especially the Noh and doll theaters, which had no truly popular audience; Kabuki was the only theater continuing to attract new plays, playwrights, and audiences in the nineteenth and twentieth centuries. But the Japanese worked to preserve their classical theater, and it is still possible today to see plays from the Noh, doll theater, and Kabuki repertoire in excellent, traditional productions.

Classical Japanese Drama in Performance History

After 1868, Japan became open to cultural influence from the West, and a variety of dramatic and theatrical forms came to rival the traditional genres of Noh, *jōruri*, and Kabuki. *SHIMPA*, a theatrical movement originating in Osaka in the 1880s, responded to the Western theater's use of more colloquial language and contemporary dramatic settings. However, because many of the *shimpa* actors were drawn from Kabuki, *shimpa* gradually came to resemble Kabuki in performance, even though its dramas were more evidently based on recent news events, crimes, and political controversies. Although *shimpa* and its successor, *SHINGEKI*—a "realistic" dramatic movement that both imported and imitated the plays of Ibsen, Chekhov, Shaw, and others—marked an important move away from the classical genres, they continued to be performed in the twentieth century.

Indeed, the Japanese classical theater was perhaps most keenly threatened by Japan's defeat in World War II and the subsequent occupation. As part of the postwar occupation of Japan, the United States established a Civil Information and Education Section, which had as part of its duties both the protection of traditional Japanese culture and the importation of "progressive," democratic culture, including American literature and drama. This office often came into conflict with the occupation's censorship office, concerned as it was to prevent the spread of imperial Japanese political ideas. Although neither Noh nor *jōruri* seemed to pose much of a political threat, the popular Kabuki theater had long been associated with the feudal ideology of Japanese nationalism, and the censors were much more careful in their approval of Kabuki theater. The first Kabuki play to be produced after the end of occupation censorship in 1948 was, in fact, the great *samurai* revenge play, *Chūshingura,* often known in English as *The Loyal Forty-Seven Samurai.*

(Aside)

SANSKRIT DRAMA AND THEATER

The cultures, languages, and theater of the Indian subcontinent have been transformed by three massive invasions: by the Aryans sometime between 3000 and 2000 BCE; by the Moslems, who brought both the Persian language and the Koran, in the tenth and eleventh centuries; and by the British, beginning in the seventeenth century. The Aryan language—Sanskrit (literally, "the perfected tongue")—became the foundation of ancient Indian culture. Sanskrit was a spoken language until early in the first millennium, when Prakit became the vernacular. Something like Latin in medieval Europe, Sanskrit was reserved for ritual, religious, and academic uses, and for India's rich literature and theater. Sanskrit is the language of the *Rgveda,* a collection of prayers and hymns composed between 1500 and 1000 BCE that is the oldest work in any Indo-European language.

The two major epics of Indian culture—the *Mahabharata* and the *Ramayana*—date from around 1000 BCE, but took their current form during India's golden age, which lasted from the second century CE into the ninth century. Although it had long been thought in the West that Sanskrit theater gradually disappeared after the Moslem invasions of the tenth and eleventh centuries, Sanskrit plays were still performed in Kerala—a state in the southwest of India—by performers who were part of a hereditary caste connected to religious temples.

Hindu belief and the caste structure of ancient Indian society inform the esthetics of Sanskrit theater and drama. Ancient India was a rigidly stratified society composed of four hereditary castes, each of which was subdivided: the *Brahmins* (priests and intellectuals), *Kshatriyas* (aristocrats, warriors), *Vaisyas* (craftsmen, farmers), and *Sudras* (unskilled workers, peasants). Although these castes were devised and perpetuated along racial and economic lines, they also translated Hindu religious beliefs into the organizing structure of society. Hindu is based on a belief in Brahman, or "world-soul." Although different aspects of Brahman are often represented as distinct gods—Brahma the creator, Siva the destroyer, Vishnu the preserver, for example—these gods are really aspects of Brahman, the only whole, perfect, and unchanging being. The created universe is arrayed hierarchically, according to the degree that each being is able to contemplate or participate in this sense of wholeness or perfection.

In performance, Sanskrit drama emblematizes this dichotomy between the distracting diversity of lived experience and the contemplation of wholeness and perfection; Sanskrit theater offers its audience a richly varied performance while inducing the audience to adopt a unifying and impersonal, even contemplative mood. Most of our understanding of Sanskrit drama derives from the second-century *Natyasastra,* or *Art of the Theater,* usually attributed to the playwright Bharata, from several other treatises, and from the twenty-five plays that remain. Much as ancient Greek plays were based on myth and legend mainly drawn from the *Iliad* and the *Odyssey,* Sanskrit plays were generally based on heroic stories taken from the *Mahabharata* and the *Ramayana* and were divided into two groups: **RUPAKA** (major drama) and **UPA-RUPAKA** (minor drama). *Rupaka* are of various lengths and include the plays of Bharata; Bhasa's second-century plays *The Vision of Vasavadatta* and *Carudatta;* King Sudraka's *The Clay Cart* (written sometime between the fourth and eighth centuries); Kalidasa's fifth-century *Sakuntala;* and the seventh-century plays of King Harsa and Bhavabhuti. As in the Japanese Noh, the narrative of the play is less critical than the attitude it produces: the impersonal and contemplative mood of wholeness called **RASA.** According to the *Natyasastra,* there are eight basic *rasas* or moods that a play should strive to produce—erotic, comic, pathetic, furious, heroic, terrible, odious, and marvelous—and while a given play may include several *rasas,* it should be designed so that one mood dominates. Moreover, these *rasas* are related to the **BHAVA,** the emotions or feelings displayed in the play by the characters. The eight *bhavas*—desire, comic or sympathetic laughter, sadness, anger, vigor or power, fear, loathing, and wonder—are the organizing, "stable" emotions staged in the play, and are complicated by thirty-three "unstable"

Since the war, the traditional modes of Japanese theater have become popular not only in Japan, but throughout the world. Several modern playwrights—notably Mishima Yukio—have either written new Noh or Kabuki plays or have adapted earlier dramas to modern settings. Moreover, the revival of Japanese classical theater has been part of an important resurgence of interest in traditional modes of artistic expression in Japan, which has taken place alongside Japan's emergence as a leading political, economic, and cultural power in the late twentieth century.

---

emotions. The subtle balance and interplay of the *bhavas* should evoke a sense of harmony and perfection, the dominant *rasa* of the play.

As in Hindu philosophy, Sanskrit drama aims to produce a sense of oneness from the diversity of experience; *rasa* arises from each play's cunning interplay of the range of *bhavas,* of dialogue written in both verse and prose, of Sanskrit and Prakit, and of character types ranging from gods, kings, and heroes to servants, peasants, and children. Yet despite this diversity, Sanskrit plays have several common characteristics. Each play not only produces its main mood or *rasa,* it also illustrates the workings of *karma* or cosmic justice. For this reason, Sanskrit drama falls outside the Western understanding of tragedy, and Sanskrit playwrights are urged by the *Natyasastra* not to represent death onstage. Sanskrit is spoken by all the male Brahmin and Kshatriya characters in the play, whereas women, peasants, and children speak Prakit, as does the jester character who appears in most plays, often as the hero's sidekick. Although plays vary in length from one act to ten acts, each act generally takes place within a single day; the action usually takes place in several earthly and heavenly locations.

Plays were performed on a variety of occasions in ancient India—at festivals, weddings, coronations, and at other public events—and the play's *rasa* was appropriate to the occasion. The *Natyasastra* describes three kinds of theater structure—square, rectangular, and triangular—each

Classical Sanskrit Performance

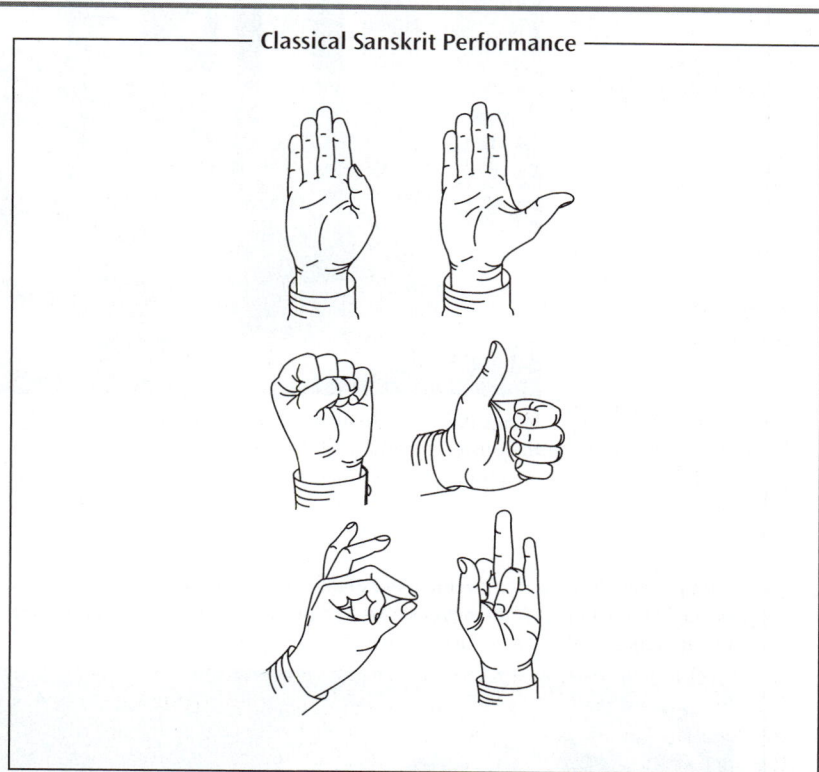

These six hand positions are used in a classical Sanskrit performance.

in three different sizes. The rectangular theaters were divided into two equal areas. The audience area was supported by four pillars, representing both the four compass points and the four principal castes. The stage area was divided into two parts—a relatively shallow performing space divided from a backstage area by a wall.

Performances were accompanied by a variety of musical instruments and were elaborately ceremonial in character; actors used an elaborate system of movement, gesture, and speech. Because the performers were to represent codified *bhavas,* the *Natyasastra* describes the gestures appropriate to them: for instance, thirty-two different eye movements, thirty-two positions for the feet, twenty-four gestures for one hand. Both the Sanskrit drama and texts like the *Natyasastra* document the extraordinary theatrical vitality of the golden age of classical Indian culture. ∎

In this 1989 English-language production at the University of Hawai'i, *Matsukaze* is played on a traditional Noh stage.

Exemplifying the elegant movement of Kabuki theater, this scene from the University of Hawai'i production of *Chūshingura* shows Kampei protecting Okaru from attackers, who threaten them with cherry-blossom weapons.

This view of the *Matsukaze* shows the musicians and chorus, as well as the *hashigakari*.

Directed by James R. Brandon, Department of Theater and Dance, University of Hawaii at Manoa

In the University of Hawai'i production of *Chūshingura* (1979), Lord Enya Hangan commits *seppuku*, watched by the shogun's messengers.

Chushingura produced by Kennedy Theatre, University of Hawaii at Manoa, March 1979. Directed by James R. Brandon; Photograph by Diane Chong.

READING THE MATERIAL THEATER

One of the great traditions of Japan is the art of portraiture, and many of Japan's greatest artists made portraits of celebrated actors. As historical records, however, these portraits are somewhat difficult to use: like the Japanese theater, Japanese painting was itself a highly conventionalized activity. Nonetheless, these illustrations provide a striking insight into the power of performance on Japan's classical stage. Here is a portrait of Soki Sanjuro in the role of Kudo Yoritsura, by the artist Toyokuni (1769–1825). Toyokuni was born in Edo; his father not only carved dolls and puppets, but also portrait figures of famous Kabuki actors. In his early adolescence, Toyokuni was apprenticed to study art with Utagawa Toyoharu; like other pupils, he took his master's name (Utagawa Toyokuni, the "u" that both share as a common second syllable is part of this identification as well), and developed a readily-visible style in his chosen field: portraits of Kabuki actors. His series of pictures from the mid 1790s established the conventions of portraiture for a generation, notably making use of the actor's entire figure in full-length portraits. Utagawa Toyokuni was also the instructor of several generations of artists, notably the great artist Utagawa Kunisada (1786–1865), who also took the Utagawa name, and adopted Toyokuni's name as his own, first adding the KUNI syllable to his own same (Sumida Shozo) to form Kunisada. After 1844, he merely signed his prints "Toyokuni."

The cartouches—the small bars with engraved Japanese characters—list the actor's name and the role he is playing in the illustration, as well as the artist's signature. In many respects these portraits seem heavily conventionalized, even idealized, and we know that they were often based on earlier portraits, sometimes on portraits executed by other artists. Nonetheless the portraits capture a number of significant features of Kabuki theatre—even when, as in this image, the portrait captures a scene from the represented action of the drama, rather than from a live theatrical performance. What features of the portrait seem prominent? What is the apparent relationship between the figures? Given the conventionality of the portrait, how do you interpret the strong and energetic sense of line in the image? How would you characterize the style of the portrait as a representation of theater? ■

The actor Soki Sanjuro in the role of Kudo Yoritsura.

Kan'ami Kiyotsugu

Kan'ami Kiyotsugu (1333–1384) was one of the principal performers of *sarugaku-no* and the leader of a prominent company. When he appeared before the *shogun* Yoshimitsu Ashikaga in 1374, the *shogun* was so impressed with the company that he retained them as his players. Kan'ami is generally credited with refining and systematizing the Noh for his aristocratic audience and with writing many of the plays that became part of the standard Noh repertoire. Kan'ami's son, Zeami Motokiyo (1363–1444), succeeded his father as the leader of the company and had a massive influence on the development of the Noh. Zeami both reworked older plays and wrote many new plays of his own; of the 241 plays in the Noh repertoire, more than 100 are connected to Zeami. Zeami influenced the development of Noh in other respects as well, mainly in writing sixteen essays on Noh esthetics. These essays cover a range of topics, including the training of actors, the proper style of dramatic writing, and the goals of performance. Although Zeami enjoyed the favor of Yoshimitsu until the *shogun's* death in 1408, he fared less well under the rule of Yoshimitsu's son, Yoshimochi (1386–1428) and was banished to the remote island of Sado in 1434 when Yoshimochi's younger brother Yoshinori (1394–1441) became *shogun*. The reasons for Yoshinori's hostility to Zeami are not clear but may involve Yoshinori's preference for another playwright, On'ami. Zeami did succeed in passing his essays on to his son-in-law, Komparu Zenchiku (1405–1468), who became an important Noh playwright and theoretician. Not much is known about the end of Zeami's life; legend has it that he was able to return to the mainland after Yoshinori was assassinated in 1441.

Matsukaze

Matsukaze was originally written by Kan'ami and extensively reworked by Zeami; it has remained in the Noh repertoire since the fifteenth century and is performed by all Noh companies.

This elegant drama, like most Noh plays, takes place in a setting familiar from the classic literature of Japan, the Bay of Suma. Suma is principally associated with the famous poet, courtier, and scholar Ariwaka no Yukihira (818–893), whose exile at Suma was recounted in his own poetry and formed the basis for many stories and legends. It also inspired the narrative of Genji's exile at Suma in the Japanese epic *Tale of Genji*. The narrative of the play, though, seems to have been invented by Kan'ami. The play opens when the *waki*—playing a priest—enters the stage, singing a traveling song about his arrival at Suma. He asks the *kyōgen* (playing a villager) about the significance of the pine tree, and he is informed that it memorializes two fisher girls, Murasame and Matsukaze, who have long since died. Shortly thereafter, Murasame—played by the *tsure*—enters, followed by the *shite*, Matsukaze. The two girls elaborately mime dipping brine into their cart with their fans, and in speeches that quote from Yukihira and from other poets, they describe their desolation. Their language here is rich with imagery, particularly of the changing sea, the hard lives of the fishermen, and of the moon, a Buddhist symbol of enlightenment. As is typical of the Noh, many of their lines are spoken by the Chorus.

Although the *shite* and his *tsure* do not leave the stage, they retire to the *shitebashira*, where they mime sitting in their small hut. The *waki*—who has observed them throughout the first scene—approaches the hut and asks for shelter, quoting one of Yukihira's poems in passing. The girls then reveal that they are the ghosts of Matsukaze and Murasame, still "steeped in longing" for the exiled poet, even in death. They had fallen in love with Yukihira during his exile at Suma, and he had given them their names, "Wind in the Pines" (*matsukaze*) and "Autumn Rain" (*murasame*), names redolent of the imagery of classical Japanese poetry. The girls were not able to follow Yukihira when he returned to court after

The classic Noh Play Matsukaze (The Pining Wind), was performed by UH students in English, directed by Noh Master Artist Nomura Shiro, and produced by Kennedy Theatre. Department of Theatre and Dance, University of Hawaii at Manoa in 1989. Photographer: James Giles.

This production of Kan'ami's *Matsukaze* emphasizes the traditional spatial, costume, and performance elements of Noh theater.

his exile; all they have in his memory is his hunting cloak and court hat. Driven nearly to madness with her eternal grief, Matsukaze puts on Yukihira's cloak and hat for her final dance.

Matsukaze is an evocative example of the way Noh theater attempts to capture a particular mood through the collaborative interplay between each of its highly wrought arts. The beauty of the language, the delicacy of characterization, the succinct action, the music of the flute and drums, the chanting of the Chorus, and the refinement of the acting combine to capture the subtle intensity of feeling for which Noh theater is famous.

Matsukaze

Kan'ami Kiyotsugu
TRANSLATED BY ROYALL TYLER

CHARACTERS

AN ITINERANT PRIEST (*waki*)   MATSUKAZE (*shite*)   PLACE: *Suma Bay in Settsu Province*
A VILLAGER (*kyōgen*)   MURASAME (*tsure*)   TIME: *Autumn, the Ninth Month*

(*The stage assistant places a stand with a pine sapling set into it at the front of the stage. The* PRIEST *enters and stands at the naming-place. He carries a rosary.*)

PRIEST: I am a priest who travels from province to province. Lately I have been in the Capital. I visited the famous sites and ancient ruins, not missing a one. Now I intend to make a pilgrimage to the western provinces. (*He faces forward.*)
5   I have hurried, and here I am already at the Bay of Suma in Settsu Province. (*His attention is caught by the pine tree.*) How strange! That pine on the beach has a curious look. There must be a story connected with it. I'll ask someone in the neighborhood. (*He faces the bridgeway.*) Do
10   you live in Suma?

(*The* VILLAGER *comes down the bridgeway to the first pine. He wears a short sword.*)

VILLAGER: Perhaps I am from Suma; but first tell me what you want.
PRIEST: I am a priest and I travel through the provinces. Here on the beach I see a solitary pine tree with a wooden
15   tablet fixed to it, and a poem slip hanging from the tablet. Is there a story connected with the tree? Please tell me what you know.
VILLAGER: The pine is linked with the memory of two fisher girls, Matsukaze and Murasame. Please say a prayer for them as
20   you pass.
PRIEST: Thank you. I know nothing about them, but I will stop at the tree and say a prayer for them before I move on.
VILLAGER: If I can be of further service, don't hesitate to ask.
PRIEST: Thank you for your kindness.
25 VILLAGER: At your command, sir.

(*The* VILLAGER *exits. The* PRIEST *goes to stage center and turns toward the pine tree.*)

PRIEST: So, this pine tree is linked with the memory of two fisher girls, Matsukaze and Murasame. It is sad! Though their bodies are buried in the ground, their names linger on. This lonely pine tree lingers on also, ever green and
30   untouched by autumn, their only memorial. Ah! While I have been chanting sutras and invoking Amida Buddha for their repose, the sun, as always on autumn days, has quickly set. That village at the foot of the mountain is a long way. Perhaps I can spend the night in this fisherman's
35   salt shed.

(*He kneels at the waki-position. The stage assistant brings out the prop, a cart for carrying pails of brine, and sets it by the gazing-pillar. He places a pail on the cart.*)

(MURASAME *enters and comes down the bridgeway as far as the first pine. She wears the tsure mask.* MATSUKAZE *follows her and stops at the third pine. She wears the wakaonna mask. Each carries a water pail. They face each other.*)

MATSUKAZE AND MURASAME: A brine cart wheeled along
the beach
Provides a meager livelihood:
The sad world rolls
Life by quickly and in misery!
MURASAME: Here at Suma Bay   40
The waves shatter at our feet,
And even the moonlight wets our sleeves
With its tears of loneliness.

(MURASAME *goes to stage center while* MATSUKAZE *moves to the* shite *position.*)

MATSUKAZE: The autumn winds are sad.
When the Middle Counselor Yukihira   45
Lived here back a little from the sea,
They inspired his poem,
"Salt winds blowing from the mountain pass. . . ."
On the beach, night after night,
Waves thunder at our door;   50
And on our long walks to the village
We've no companion but the moon.
Our toil, like all of life, is dreary,
But none could be more bleak than ours.
A skiff cannot cross the sea,   55
Nor we this dream world.
Do we exist, even?
Like foam on the salt sea,
We draw a cart, friendless and alone,

---

48 **"Salt . . . pass"** from the poem by Yukihira, No. 876 in the *Shinkokinshū*: "The sleeves of the traveler have turned cold; the wind from Suma Bay blows through the pass."   52 **We've . . . moon** a modified quotation from the poem by Hōkyō Chūmei, No. 187 in the *Kin'yōshū*: "Pillow of grass—as I sleep on my journey I realize I have no companion but the moon." 58–59 **salt sea** the words "salt sea," which can also be translated "brine," lead to mention of the brine cart even though the cart does not logically belong in the context

60   Poor fisher girls whose sleeves are wet
        With endless spray, and tears
        From our hearts' unanswered longing.
CHORUS: Our life is so hard to bear
        That we envy the pure moon
65   Now rising with the tide.
        But come, let us dip brine,
        Dip brine from the rising tide!
        Our reflections seem to shame us!

(*They look down as if catching a glimpse of their reflections in the water. The movement of their heads "clouds" the expression on their masks, making it seem sad.*)

        Yes, they shame us!
70   Here, where we shrink from men's eyes,
        Drawing our timorous cart;
        The withdrawing tide
        Leaves stranded pools behind.
        How long do they remain?
75   If we were the dew on grassy fields,
        We would vanish with the sun.
        But we are sea tangle,
        Washed up on the shore,
        Raked into heaps by the fishermen,
80   Fated to be discarded, useless,
        Withered and rotting,
        Like our trailing sleeves,
        Like our trailing sleeves.

(*They look down again.*)

        Endlessly familiar, still how lovely
85   The twilight at Suma!
        The fishermen call out in muffled voices;
        At sea, the small boats loom dimly.
        Across the faintly glowing face of the moon
        Flights of wild geese streak,
90   And plovers flock below along the shore.
        Fall gales and stiff sea winds:
        These are things, in such a place,
        That truly belong to autumn.
        But oh, the terrible, lonely nights!

(*They hide their faces.*)

95 MATSUKAZE: Come, dip the brine.
    MURASAME: Where the seas flood and fall,
        Let us tie our sleeves back to our shoulders.
    MATSUKAZE: Think only, "Dip the brine."
    MURUSAME: We ready ourselves for the task,
100 MATSUKAZE: But for women, this cart is too hard.
    CHORUS: While the rough breakers surge and fall,

(MURASAME *moves upstage to stand beside* MATSUKAZE.)

        While the rough breakers surge and fall,
        And cranes among the reeds
        Fly up with sharp cries.
        The four winds add their wailing.   105
        How shall we pass the cold night?

(*They look up.*)

        The late moon is so brilliant—
        What we dip is its reflection!
        Smoke from the salt fires
        May cloud the moon—take care!   110
        Are we always to spend only
        The sad autumns of fishermen?
        At Ojima in Matsushima

(MATSUKAZE *half-kneels by the brine cart and mimes dipping with her fan.*)

        The fisherfolk, like us,
        Delight less in the moon   115
        Than in the dipping of its reflection;
        There they take delight in dipping
        Reflections of the moon.

(MATSUKAZE *returns to the* shite *position.*)

        We haul our brine from afar,
        As in far-famed Michinoku   120
        And at the salt kilns of Chika—
        Chika, whose name means "close by."
    MATSUKAZE: Humble folk hauled wood for salt fires
        At the ebb tide on Akogi Shore.
    CHORUS: On Ise Bay there's Twice-See Beach—   125
        Oh, could I live my life again!

(MATSUKAZE *looks off into the distance.*)

    MATSUKAZE: On days when pine groves stand hazy,
        And the sea lanes draw back
        From the coast at Narumi—
    CHORUS: You speak of Narumi; this is Naruo,   130
        Where pines cut off the moonlight
        From the reed-thatched roofs of Ashinoya.

---

113 **Ojima** is one of the islands at Matsushima, a place renowned for its scenic beauty. Both names are conventionally associated in poetry with *ama*, fisherwomen   120 **As in far-famed** the following passage is a *tsukushi*, or "exhaustive enumeration," of place-names associated with the sea, including allusions and plays on words. This passage was apparently borrowed from an older work, a play called *Tōei* that was set by Ashinoya Bay. Michinoku is a general name for the northern end of the island of Honshu. Chika was another name for Shiogama ("Salt Kiln"), and sounds like the word meaning "near"   124 **Akogi** the name of a stretch of shore on Ise Bay. The pulling in of the nets and the hauling of the wood for the salt kilns at Akogi were frequently mentioned in poetry   125 **Twice-See Beach** (*Futami-ga-ura*) is a word evocative of Ise and often used in poetry for the meaning of its name   129 **Narumi** often mentioned in poetry because of its dry flats that appeared at low tide   132 **Ashinoya** (modern Ashiya) and Naruo are two places near Suma. Ashinoya means literally "reed house"

---

64 **That . . . moon** from the poem by Fujiwara Takamitsu, No. 435 in the *Shūishū*: "In this world which seems difficult to pass through, how I envy the pure moon!"   85 **The twilight** the following description is generally inspired by the "Exile at Suma" chapter of *The Tale of Genji*

MATSUKAZE: Who is to tell of our unhappiness
Dipping brine at Nada?
135   With boxwood combs set in our hair,
From rushing seas we draw the brine,
Oh look! I have the moon in my pail!

(MURASAME *kneels before the brine cart and places her pail on it.*
MATSUKAZE, *still standing, looks into her pail.*)

MATSUKAZE: In my pail too I hold the moon!
CHORUS: How lovely! A moon here too!

(MURASAME *picks up the rope tied to the cart and gives it to* MAT-
SUKAZE, *then moves to the* shite *position.* MATSUKAZE *looks up.*)

140   MATSUKAZE: The moon above is one;
Below it has two, no, three reflections

(*She looks into both pails.*)

Which shine in the flood tide tonight,

(*She pulls the cart to a spot before the musicians.*)

And on our cart we load the moon!
No, life is not all misery
145   Here by the sea lanes.

(*She drops the rope. The stage assistant removes the cart.*
MATSUKAZE *sits on a low stool and* MURASAME *kneels beside her,
a sign that the two women are resting inside their hut. The* PRIEST
rises.)

PRIEST: The owner of the salt shed has returned. I shall ask for
a night's lodging. (*To* MATSUKAZE *and* MURASAME.) I beg
your pardon. Might I come inside?
MURASAME: (*Standing and coming forward a little.*) Who might
150   you be?
PRIEST: A traveler, overtaken by night on my journey. I should
like to ask lodging for the night.
MURASAME: Wait here. I must ask the owner. (*She kneels before*
MATSUKAZE.) A traveler outside asks to come in and spend
155   the night.
MATSUKAZE: That is little enough, but our hut is so wretched we
cannot ask him in. Please tell him so.
MURASAME: (*Standing, to the* PRIEST.) I have spoken to the owner.
She says the house is too wretched to put anyone up.
160 PRIEST: I understand those feelings
Perfectly, but poverty makes
No difference at all to me.
I am only a priest. Please
Say I beg her to let
165   Me spend the night.

---

134 **Dipping . . . Nada** derived from the poem in the eighty-seventh
episode of the *Ise Monogatari:* "At Nada by Ashinoya, I have no respite
from boiling brine for salt; I have come without even putting a boxwood
comb in my hair."   135 **With boxwood** the line recalls the poem quoted
in the previous note, but it is used because of the pivot-word *tsuge no,* "of
boxwood," and *tsuge,* "to inform." Similarly, *kushi sashi,* "Setting a comb
(in the hair)," leads into *sashi-kuru nami,* "in-rushing waves"

MURASAME: No, we really cannot put you up.
MATSUKAZE: (*To* MURASAME.) Wait!
I see in the moonlight
One who has renounced the world.
He will not mind a fisherman's hut,   170
With its rough pine pillars and bamboo fence;
I believe it is very cold tonight,
So let him come in and warm himself
At our sad fire of rushes.
You may tell him that.   175
MURASAME: Please come in.
PRIEST: Thank you very much. Forgive me for intruding.

(*He takes a few steps forward and kneels.* MURASAME *goes back
beside* MATSUKAZE.)

MATSUKAZE: I wished from the beginning to invite you in,
but this place is so poor I felt I must refuse.
PRIEST: You are very kind. I am a priest and a traveler, and   180
never stay anywhere very long. Why prefer one lodging to
another? In any case, what sensitive person would not
prefer to live here at Suma, in the quiet solitude. Yukihira
wrote,
"If ever anyone   185
Chances to ask for me,
Say I live alone,
Soaked by the dripping seaweed
On the shore of Suma Bay."
(*He looks at the pine tree.*) A while ago I asked someone   190
the meaning of that solitary pine on the beach. I was told it
grows there in memory of two fisher girls, Matsukaze and
Murasame. There is no connection between them and me,
but I went to the pine anyway and said a prayer for them.
(MATSUKAZE *and* MURASAME *weep. The* PRIEST *stares at*   195
them.) This is strange! They seem distressed at the mention
of Matsukaze and Murasame. Why?
MATSUKAZE AND MURASAME: Truly, when a grief is hidden,
Still, signs of it will show.
His poem, "If ever anyone   200
Chances to ask for me,"
Filled us with memories which are far too fond.
Tears of attachment to the world
Wet our sleeves once again.
PRIEST: Tears of attachment to the world? You speak as though   205
you are no longer of the world. Yukihira's poem overcame you
with memories. More and more bewildering! Please, both of
you, tell me who you are.
MATSUKAZE AND MURASAME: We would tell you our names,
But we are too ashamed!   210
No one, ever,
Has chanced to ask for us,
Long dead as we are,
And so steeped in longing
For the world by Suma Bay   215
That pain has taught us nothing.
Ah, the sting of regret!
But having said this,
Why should we hide our names any longer?
At twilight you said a prayer   220
By a mossy grave under the pine

185–189 **"If ever . . . Bay"** poem No. 962 in the *Kokinshū*

For two fisher girls,
Matsukaze and Murasame.
We are their ghosts, come to you.
225 When Yukihira was here he whiled away
Three years of weary exile
Aboard his pleasure boat,
His heart refreshed
By the moon of Suma Bay.
230 There were, among the fisher girls
Who hauled brine each evening,
Two sisters whom he chose for his favors.
"Names to fit the season!"
He said, calling us
235 Pine Wind and Autumn Rain.
We had been Suma fisher girls,
Accustomed to the moon,
But he changed our salt makers' clothing
To damask robes,
240 Burnt with the scent of faint perfumes.
MATSUKAZE: Then, three years later, Yukihira
Returned to the Capital.
MURASAME: Soon, we heard he had died, oh so young!
MATSUKAZE: How we both loved him!
245 Now the message we pined for
Would never, never come.
CHORUS: Pine Wind and Autumn Rain
Both drenched their sleeves with the tears
Of hopeless love beyond their station,
250 Fisher girls of Suma.
Our sin is deep, O priest.
Pray for us, we beg of you!

(*They press their palms together in supplication.*)

Our love grew rank as wild grasses;
Tears and love ran wild.
255 It was madness that touched us.
Despite spring purification,
Performed in our old robes,
Despite prayers inscribed on paper streamers,
The gods refused us their help.
260 We were left to melt away
Like foam on the waves,
And, in misery, we died.

(MATSUKAZE *looks down, shading her mask.*)

Alas! How the past evokes our longing!
Yukihira, the Middle Counselor,

(*The stage assistant puts a man's cloak and court hat in*
MATSUKAZE's *left hand.*)

Lived three years here by Suma Bay.   265
Before he returned to the Capital,
He left us these keepsakes of his stay:
A court hat and a hunting cloak.
Each time we see them,

(*She looks at the cloak.*)

Our love grows again,   270
And gathers like dew
On the tip of a leaf
So that there's no forgetting,
Not for an instant.
Oh endless misery!   275

(*She places the cloak in her lap.*)

"This keepsake
Is my enemy now;
For without it

(*She lifts the cloak.*)

I might forget."

(*She stares at the cloak.*)

The poem says that   280
And it's true:
My anguish only deepens.

(*She weeps.*)

MATSUKAZE: "Each night before I go to sleep,
I take off the hunting cloak
CHORUS: And hang it up . . ."   285

(*The keepsakes in her hand, she stands and, as in a trance, takes a
few steps toward the gazing-pillar.*)

I hung all my hopes
On living in the same world with him,
But being here makes no sense at all
And these keepsakes are nothing.

(*She starts to drop the cloak, only to cradle it in her arms and press
it to her.*)

I drop it, but I cannot let it lie;   290
So I take it up again
To see his face before me yet once more.

(*She turns to her right and goes toward the naming-place, then
stares down the bridgeway as though something were coming
after her.*)

---

240 **Burnt . . .** derived from a poem by Fujiwara Tameuji, No. 361 in
the *Shingo-senshū:* "The fishermen of Suma are accustomed to the
moon, spending the autumn in clothes wet with waves blown by the salt
wind."   258 **Despite prayers . . .** literally, "purification on the day of the
serpent." The ceremony was performed on the first day of the serpent
in the third month. Genji had the ceremony performed while he was at
Suma. The streamers were conventional Shinto offerings

276–279 "**This keepsake . . . forget**" a slightly modified quotation of
the anonymous poem, No. 746 in the *Kokinshū*. It is also quoted in *Lady
Han*   283–285 "**Each night . . . up**" the first part of a poem by Ki no
Tomomori, No. 593 in the *Kokinshū*. The last two lines run: "When I
wear it there is no instant when I do not long for him."

"Awake or asleep,
From my pillow, from the foot of my bed,
295   Love rushes in upon me."
Helplessly I sink down,
Weeping in agony.

(*She sits at the* shite *position, weeping. The stage assistant helps her take off her outer robe and replace it with the cloak. He also helps tie on the court hat.*)

MATSUKAZE: The River of Three Fords
Has gloomy shallows
300   Of never-ending tears;
I found, even there,
An abyss of wildest love.
Oh joy! Look! Over there!
Yukihira has returned!

(*She rises, staring at the pine tree.*)

305   He calls me by my name, Pine Wind!
I am coming!

(*She goes to the tree.* MURASAME *hurriedly rises and follows. She catches* MATSUKAZE's *sleeve.*)

MURASAME: For shame! For such thoughts as these
You are lost in the sin of passion.
All the delusions that held you in life—
310   None forgotten!

(*Both step back from the tree.*)

That is a pine tree.
And Yukihira is not here.
MATSUKAZE: You are talking nonsense!

(*She looks at the pine tree.*)

This pine is Yukihira!
315   "Though we may part for a time,
If I hear you are pining for me,
I'll hurry back."
Have you forgotten those words he wrote?
MURASAME: Yes, I had forgotten!
320   He said, "Though we may part for a time,
If you pine, I will return to you."
MATSUKAZE: I have not forgotten.
And I wait for the pine wind
To whisper word of his coming.
325 MURASAME: If that word should ever come,
My sleeves for a while
Would be wet with autumn rain.

MATSUKAZE: So we await him. He will come,
Constant ever, green as a pine.
MURASAME: Yes, we can trust   330
MATSUKAZE: his poem:
CHORUS: "I have gone away

(MURASAME, *weeping, kneels before the flute player.* MATSUKAZE *goes to the first pine on the bridgeway, then returns to the stage and dances.*)

MATSUKAZE: Into the mountains of Inaba,
Covered with pines,
But if I hear you pine,   335
I shall come back at once."
Those are the mountain pines
Of distant Inaba,

(*She looks up the bridgeway.*)

And these are the pines
On the curving Suma shore.   340
Here our dear prince once lived.
If Yukihira comes again,
I shall go stand under the tree

(*She approaches the tree.*)

Bent by the sea-wind,
And, tenderly, tell him   345

(*She stands next to the tree.*)

I love him still!

(*She steps back a little and weeps. Then she circles the tree, her dancing suggesting madness.*)

CHORUS: Madly the gale howls through the pines,
And breakers crash in Suma Bay;
Through the frenzied night
We have come to you   350
In a dream of deluded passion.
Pray for us! Pray for our rest!

(*At stage center,* MATSUKAZE *presses her palms together in supplication.*)

Now we take our leave. The retreating waves
Hiss far away, and a wind sweeps down
From the mountain to Suma Bay.   355
The cocks are crowing on the barrier road.
Your dream is over. Day has come.
Last night you heard the autumn rain;
This morning all that is left
Is the wind in the pines,   360
The wind in the pines.

293–295 "**Awake . . . me**" the first part of an anonymous poem, No. 1023 in the *Kokinshū*. The last part runs: "Helpless, I stay in the middle of the bed." 298 **River of Three Fords** the river of the afterworld 315–317 "**Though . . . back**" paraphrase of the poem by Yukihira, No. 365 in the *Kokinshū*. Another paraphrase is given in the following speech by Murasame, and the poem is given in its correct form below. In Japanese *matsu* means both "pine tree" and "to wait."

---

336 "**I . . . once**" the poem by Yukihira mentioned in the previous note

Chūshingura: The Forty-Seven Samurai

In 1701, at the court of the *shogun* in Edo, the *daimyo* of Akō, Lord Asano, drew his sword and slightly wounded Lord Kira, one of the *shogun's* officials; as a consequence of drawing his sword at the court—a capital crime—Lord Asano was sentenced to *seppuku,* or ritual suicide. In the following months, Asano's *rōnin,* or retainers, felt themselves to have been dishonored and humiliated by the ruling against their lord, and plotted to take revenge. In January of 1703 they made a bold nighttime raid on Lord Kira's mansion. When they found Kira, they beheaded him, and ceremoniously marched with his head to Lord Asano's tomb. The raid on Lord Kira was, not surprisingly, a major scandal, and posed the shogunate with a difficult legal and political problem: on the one hand, Lord Asano's *rōnin* had acted with superb loyalty, risking their lives to avenge the honor of their feudal lord, upholding the values of the *samurai;* on the other hand, they had formed an illegal secret conspiracy and had carried out murder. Two months after taking revenge on Lord Kira, the *rōnin* were ordered by the *shogun* to commit *seppuku* themselves.

These are the historical events standing behind one of the *jōruri* and Kabuki theaters' most famous and enduring narratives, the tale of *The Forty-Seven Samurai.* Within weeks of the verdict, a host of plays were written and performed, mainly in the *jōruri* theaters; in most cases, however, the Tokagawa edict against staging contemporary events forced playwrights to alter the characters' names, and to set the story in an earlier historical period. In 1710, the great playwright Chikamatsu Monzaemon (1623–1725) wrote a play for the puppet theater entitled *Goban Taiheiki,* which relocated the events of contemporary Edo to

Chushingura, produced by Kennedy Theatre, University of Hawaii at Manoa, March 1979. Directed by James R. Brandon; Photograph by Diane Chong.

This scene from the University of Hawai'i production of *Chūshingura* emphasizes the formal energy of Kabuki theater.

the fourteenth century. Probably the first professional playwright in Japanese history, Chikamatsu (born Sugimori Nobumori) was the second son of the Sugimori *samurai* family. He moved with his family to Kyoto in his teens, and took the stage name Chikamatsu in his thirties, becoming a celebrated playwright for the *jōruri* theater, and collaborating with the most famous Kabuki actor of his era, Tojuro Sakata (1647–1709). A member of the *rōnin* himself, Chikamatsu was sympathetic with the dishonor done to Asano's retainers, and in his staging of their dramatic revenge established many of the dramatic conventions that would become standard in later versions of the story. In the next thirty years, Chikamatsu's play was one of hundreds of plays on the subject performed before the opening of the classic version of the story—*Kanadehon Chūshingura*—at the Takemoto puppet theater in 1748. Within the year, four Kabuki theaters (three in Edo and one in Kyoto) staged versions of *Chūshingura* which rapidly became part of the standard Kabuki repertory. The story of the forty-seven samurai has been one of the most enduring and popular of all Kabuki plays.

Although the Kabuki versions of *Chūshingura* are based on *jōruri* narratives, the genesis of plays in the Kabuki theater was quite different from that in the puppet theater. While the *jōruri* theaters closely followed the elaborately crafted dramatic text supplied by the playwright, in the Kabuki theater, the performers tended to take existing stories and refashion them in order to showcase their talents. While *Chūshingura* is one of the few plays still occasionally performed in the all-day form of *jōruri*, Kabuki performance tends to concentrate on several scenes from the narrative that have now become standard, which enables the play to be performed within the shorter duration of contemporary Kabuki theater. In this sense, the version of *Chūshingura: The Forty-Seven Samurai* printed here follows traditional Kabuki practice: it is a version of *Kanadehon Chūshingura* prepared by the professional Kabuki actor Nakamura Matagorō II, for a three-hour, English-language production at the University of Hawai'i in 1979. Readers who wish to consult the entire *jōruri* text should consult Donald Keene's *Chūshingura: The Treasury of Loyal Retainers*.

Chūshingura: The Forty-Seven Samurai

Adaptation by Nakamura Matagorō II and James R. Brandon

TRANSLATED BY JAMES R. BRANDON, JUNKO BERBERICH, AND MICHAEL FELDMAN

CHARACTERS

TADAYOSHI, *younger brother of the shogun*

KŌNO MORONAO, *chief councilor of the shogun and governor of Kamakura*

MOMONOI WAKASANOSUKE, *a young samurai*

ENYA HANGAN, *a young provincial lord*

KAOYO, *wife of Enya Hangan*

KAKOGAWA HONZŌ, *chief retainer of Wakasanosuke*

SAGISAKA BANNAI, *retainer of Moronao*

OKARU, *in love with Kampei, and later his wife*

KAMPEI, *retainer of Enya Hangan*

ISHIDŌ, *the shogun's representative at Hangan's death*

YAKUSHIJI, *envoy from the shogun*

GOEMON, *elderly retainer of Enya Hangan*

RIKIYA, *son of Yuranosuke*

ŌBOSHI YURANOSUKE, *chief retainer of Enya Hangan*

KUDAYŪ, *former retainer of Enya Hangan, now Moronao's spy*

HEIEMON, *older brother of Okaru*

SHIMIZU ICHIGAKU, *Moronao's bodyguard*

TAKEMORI KITAHACHI, *retainer to Enya Hangan*

PROVINCIAL LORDS

FOOTMEN

RETAINERS

LADIES-IN-WAITING

MAIDS

MALE GEISHA

FIGHTING CHORUS

SOLDIERS

STAGE ASSISTANTS

SAMISEN PLAYER

NARRATOR

STAGE MANAGER

SECOND STAGE MANAGER

KIYOMOTO SINGER

JESTER

TIME AND PLACE OF ACTION

Act I SCENE 1: Hachiman Shrine in Kamakura, 1338.
　　　SCENE 2: Outside the gate of the shogunal mansion in Kamakura, the next evening.
　　　SCENE 3: The Pine Room of the shogunal mansion in Kamakura, a few minutes later.

Act II SCENE 1: Along the road, near Mt. Fuji, the following morning.
　　　SCENE 2: A reception room in Enya Hangan's mansion, the same day.
　　　SCENE 3: The rear gate of Enya Hangan's mansion, immediately following.

Act III SCENE 1: The Ichiriki Brothel in Kyoto, eighteen months later.
　　　SCENE 2: The garden of Moronao's mansion in Kamakura, several days later.

ACT ONE

SCENE I

Hachiman Shrine

Two sharp clacks of the hardwood ki signal offstage musicians to begin slow and regular drum and flute music, "Kata Shagiri" ("Half-Shagiri"). The deliberate pace of the music gradually accelerates. The lights in the auditorium dim slightly; the audience watches the kabuki curtain of broad rust, black, and green stripes. Very slowly, the curtain is pushed open by a STAGE ASSISTANT walking from stage right to left. Ki clacks intersperse every eighth, every fourth, then every second drum beat. Drumming and ki intermingle as the tempo rapidly increases during the last few feet of the curtain opening. The scene is a ceremonial audience before Hachiman Shrine in Kamakura. The shogun's brother, TADAYOSHI, is seated on the center of a broad stone platform running across the back of the stage. He wears a subdued Chinese-style court robe with bloused trousers and a gold lacquered hat. On his left sits the highest local official of the government, KŌNO MORONAO. A voluminous black robe with large sleeves and trailing trousers encase his body and a high black hat increases his height. Six PROVINCIAL LORDS kneel behind them on the platform. Kneeling on the ground before them are two samurai officials, MOMONOI WAKASANOSUKE and ENYA HANGAN dressed, respectively, in powder blue and yellow robes of the same exaggerated cut as MORONAO's, and HANGAN's wife, KAOYO. She wears a silk embroidered kimono and outer robe of deep blue. Two FOOTMEN sit on the ground cross-legged to the right. The heads of all the characters are dropped forward limply on their chests, in imitation of puppets before they have been brought to life. Two ki clacks signal the music to stop and the action of the scene to begin.

STAGE MANAGER: (*Rhythmic, prolonged calls from offstage right.*) Hear ye, hear ye, hear ye, hear ye, hear ye, hear ye . . . hear ye!

(*Deep, thick chords of a jōruri, or puppet-style, samisen are heard from the small room above the set stage left. The team of jōruri SAMISEN PLAYER and NARRATOR are not seen, but they can see the action on stage through the thin bamboo blind that hangs in front of them. The NARRATOR constantly shifts his vocal style between a kind of half-spoken chanting and singing. His tones are rich and full and unabashedly project the extremes of human emotion. Each syllable is precisely uttered. Sharp samisen chords punctuate the end of a chanted phrase; they become melodic under sung passages. A syllable can be clipped or staccato, or it can be prolonged into a lengthy obligato, spread over many samisen chords, so that the narrative line compresses or expands in time in order to best project the theatrical needs of the moment.*)

NARRATOR: (*Chants.*) "A banquet laid out before your eyes! Without eating of its food, never will you be able to know its taste!" Likewise, a country in peace . . . its able retainers will hide their gallantry and chivalry. (*Sings.*) Take our story as an example . . . witness here and now . . . 　　5

SECOND STAGE MANAGER: (*Calling from offstage left.*) Hear ye, hear ye, hear ye, hear ye . . . hear ye!

STAGE MANAGER: (*Calling from offstage center.*) Hear ye, hear ye . . . hear ye! 　　10

NARRATOR: (*Chants.*) Ashikaga government chief Takauji has Kyoto as the headquarters of his reign, his power expanding far. The time is the closing of February, thirteen thirty-eight. The place is Kamakura in the east, at Hachiman Shrine, now completed in its awesome grandeur. (*Sings.*) Gathered here to celebrate a battle fought and won are lords of distinction, in 　　15

their solemn moments. (*Chants.*) Acting as government proxy, Ashikaga Tadayoshi has just arrived from the
20   capital . . . of Kyoto!

(*At the mention of his name,* TADAYOSHI *raises his head, opens his eyes, and elegantly flicks open his sleeves: puppetlike, he has been "brought to life."*)

Here in Kamakura, he is received by the shogun's official, Kōno Moronao! The officers of the reception are: Momonoi Wakasanosuke Yasuchika, Moronao's target of displeasure for his rough manners, and Hakushu's castle lord, Enya Hangan
25   Takasada. (*Sings.*) Among these men, a single flower, Lady Kaoyo, wife of Hangan.

(*Each character, as named, comes to life, showing his or her personality through the simple actions of lifting the head, opening the eyes, and adjusting the trailing kimono sleeves:* MORONAO's *evil nature—seven abrupt head jerks ending in a fierce mie pose with eyes crossed, arms extending aggressively forward as two loud beats of the wooden tsuke call attention to the pose;* WAKASANOSUKE's *impetuosity—five strong movements of the head, sudden opening of the eyes, each arm flicked out independently;* HANGAN's *composure—three smooth head movements, gentle eye opening, and both sleeves elegantly adjusted;* KAOYO's *modesty—no movement at all except for the slow raising of the head. Narrative shifts to song.*)

Moronao casts amorous eyes at this rare beauty. Loyal men, bowing low. . .

(MORONAO *leers openly at* KAOYO. *Then everyone places their hands on the floor and they make a ceremonious, deep bow to* TADAYOSHI. *Narrative returns to chanting.*)

As Tadayoshi speaks, all listen in reverence!

(*All lift their heads and listen respectfully.*)

30   TADAYOSHI: (*Clear, unaffected voice, looking straight ahead.*)
Attend, Lady Kaoyo!
KAOYO: (*Bowing.*) My lord.
TADAYOSHI: It is the shogun, not I, who has summoned you here.
You served the emperor Godaigo when he bestowed upon
35   the warrior Yoshisada the imperial battle crown. Now, with prayers commemorating our victory in battle, my brother the shogun wills that this battle crown be dedicated to the shrine of Hachiman, god of war. If you can, confirm that this, and no other, is the one! Come, come! Answer me,
40   answer me!
KAOYO: (*Bowing.*) My lord.
NARRATOR: (*Chants.*) Attendants carry forth the precious battle crown, bending down to open up the heavy wooden chest. Lifting up the battle crown . . . is it the one of fame?
45   (*Sings.*) Though gazing closely at the battle crown held high, she will only speak when she is certain . . . and then, floating famous fragrance of the crown well known . . .

(*The two* FOOTMEN *place a large wooden chest center and remove its lid. They bring out a samurai helmet. Its golden fittings gleam in the light.* KAOYO *moves forward the better to observe it, kneels, and noticing its special perfume, nods decisively.*)

KAOYO: This is the very crown Yoshisada wore in battle, I can say with certainty.
NARRATOR: (*Chants.*) Saying these words, Kaoyo bows deep in   50
reverence.

(*She bows. A* FOOTMAN *places the helmet at* TADAYOSHI's *feet. With the second* FOOTMAN, *he carries off the chest.*)

TADAYOSHI: Enya Hangan! Momonoi Wakasanosuke! In conjunction with the dedication, all ceremonies are placed in your care. Consult Lord Moronao. Kaoyo, you may go!
KAOYO: (*Bowing.*) My lord.   55
NARRATOR: (*Chants.*) Kaoyo has now been freed of her demanding task, waiting as his lordship . . . into the palace goes!

(TADAYOSHI *rises; a* STAGE ASSISTANT *takes off the stool he has been sitting on. Without looking to the right or left, he walks with a dignified gait down the steps. He stops and poses. Drum and flute play stately exit music.* TADAYOSHI *flicks open his sleeves, turns, and moves slowly off left.* PROVINCIAL LORDS *rise and follow, their formal court trousers trailing behind them.* FOOTMEN *bring up the rear. They exit. The music continues in the background as* HANGAN, WAKASANOSUKE, *and* KAOYO *play out in silence their petitions to* MORONAO *for permission to depart. To* HANGAN's *polite bow of request* MORONAO *nods condescendingly.* HANGAN *rises, and with unruffled composure, goes off left, carrying the helmet with him, to be deposited in the shrine.* WAKASANOSUKE *bows brusquely, scarcely bothering to conceal his contempt for* MORONAO. *In response,* MORONAO *deliberately and disdainfully averts his gaze. Moving to where he is in* MORONAO's *line of sight again,* WAKASANOSUKE *bows a second time, more brusquely still. Again* MORONAO *ignores him and looks away. Trembling with fury,* WAKASANOSUKE *moves directly in front of* MORONAO *and bows a third time.* MORONAO *looks over his head as if the young samurai were not there.* WAKASANOSUKE *leaps up in rage, strikes back his sleeve, and rushes off left. Music stops.* MORONAO *laughs soundlessly, then looks expectantly to* KAOYO, *who bows politely, rises, and starts to move away.* MORONAO *rises, a* STAGE ASSISTANT *removing the stool on which he has been sitting. He stops* KAOYO *with an unctuous, but clearly threatening, command.*)

MORONAO: One moment, Lady Kaoyo! I wish to have a word with you. I believe that you and I share in common an unspoken passion, for the art of writing poetry. Will you accept from me   60
this poem, composed with loving care, your reply to which I will not be displeased to receive from your own lips, Kaoyo, my lady.
NARRATOR: (*Chants.*) From his sleeve to her sleeve, a love letter from Moronao! (*Sings.*) Saying not a single word, she throws   65
it aside.

(*Crossing to her,* MORONAO *looks around to see that no one is watching. He passes a love letter into* KAOYO's *sleeve. She takes it out, and looking at the salutation, knows immediately what it is. Coldly she drops it to the ground.* MORONAO *scoops it up and tucks it away in the breast of his kimono.*)

MORONAO: (*Insinuatingly.*) Casually you cast my letter to the ground, but you will not cast down my intentions that easily. Until you accept my love, I will track you, chase you, wear you down. In the palace your husband is my puppet, to rise or to   70 fall in his duties, solely on Moronao's will. Kaoyo, my lady . . . well? Do you not agree?

(*He glances about again, then moves behind her and enfolds her in a rough embrace. She discreetly tries to free herself: their bodies sway back and forth.*)

NARRATOR: (*Sings.*) In her heart are angry words but Kaoyo refrains. Dear Lady Kaoyo, tears in her eyes.

(*Without warning* WAKASANOSUKE *strides on. Taking in the situation at a glance, he turns his back.*)

75 WAKASANOSUKE: Ahem! Ahem! (*Furious,* MORONAO *breaks away.* WAKASANOSUKE *moves beside* KAOYO.) Lady Kaoyo, Lord Tadayoshi dismissed you long ago. If you linger, you are risking his displeasure. Go! Do not stay a moment longer!

80 KAOYO: Yes, good Lord Wakasanosuke, with your permission, I shall take my leave.

NARRATOR: (*Sings.*) Burdened with care, to her mansion . . . Kaoyo returns.

(KAOYO *bows and moves quickly onto the* hanamichi, *the rampway which extends from the stage, through the audience, to the rear of the auditorium. She stops at the "seven-three" position, that is, the position seven-tenths of the distance from the back of the auditorium and three-tenths from the stage. She poses, puts her hands inside her kimono sleeves, then regally moves down the* hanamichi. *She passes out of sight as the narration ends.*)

MORONAO: (*Snarling.*) No one summoned you! You are insolent,
85 Wakasanosuke! Kaoyo was entreating me, in private audience, to guide Hangan in his palace duties. That is how even the mighty must grovel before the shogun's chief councilor. And who are you? A country rustic, a nobody. So low a single word from Moronao would send you tumbling
90 into the streets to beg for your food! And you call yourself a samurai? A samurai? (MORONAO *strikes* WAKASANOSUKE's *chest with his heavy fan.*) You . . . a sa-mu-rai? (*On the last three syllables,* MORONAO *strikes* WAKASANOSUKE's *chest, sword hilt, and chest again.* WAKASANOSUKE *falls back.*)
95 B-b-blockhead country bumpkin!

NARRATOR: (*Chants.*) You dare to meddle, little man? Moronao's revenge! Bursting in hot anger, Wakasanosuke . . . here in the sacred shrine before his Majesty, a moment of patience is all I need! One more word decides my life, death may be my fate!
100 Wakasanosuke now holds himself in!

(*To the narration:* WAKASANOSUKE *poses with hand on the hilt of his sword; he notices he is in a sacred shrine and falls back; his hand trembles; he nods with determination, throws his fan into the air, and lunges forward as if to draw his sword.* MORONAO *slaps his fan against* WAKASANOSUKE's *sword arm and glares at his young opponent in alarm and rage. At that moment a cry is heard from offstage announcing the return of* TADAYOSHI.)

VOICES OFF: (*In unison.*) Bow down!
MORONAO: (*Snarling.*) Bow down, I say!

(MORONAO *strikes* WAKASANOSUKE's *sword arm viciously with his closed fan.* WAKASANOSUKE *drops to one knee, glares at* MORONAO, *and poses with his hand on his sword.* MORONAO *rushes up the platform steps, suddenly pivots back to face* WAKASANOSUKE, *flips*

open his sleeves, and poses in a fierce mie. MORONAO *crosses his eyes and glares to two loud beats of the* tsuke. WAKASANOSUKE *restrains himself; his chest heaves. The curtain is run closed to accelerating* ki *clacks. A single* ki *clack marks the end of the scene and signals the offstage drum and flute to play "Sagariha" ["Departure"] as the scene is changed.*)

SCENE II

Bribery and Rendezvous

Two ki *clacks: the curtain is run open. Ki clacks accelerate, then fade away. The scene is the rear gate of the shogunal mansion in Kamakura where the state ceremonies are to be held. It is night. Pale blue light floods the stage. One* ki *clack signals action to begin.*

NARRATOR: (*Chants.*) Chief retainer of Wakasanosuke, (*Sings.*) Kakogawa Honzō comes in with a tray full of gifts, a self-assigned task.

(HONZŌ, *carrying a tray of silks as a bribe for* MORONAO, *comes onto the* hanamichi. *He stops at the seven-three position, looks toward the gate, and poses.*)

HONZŌ: Bannai. Master Bannai.

(BANNAI, *a comic villain, enters from inside the gate.* HONZŌ *moves quickly onto the stage, places the gifts on the ground, and kneels respectfully before* BANNAI.)

BANNAI: (*Officiously.*) Someone calls me. Who is it, who is it? 5
(*Notices* HONZŌ. *Starts.*) State your business, I am a busy man!
HONZŌ: (*Bowing obsequiously.*) I am Kakogawa Honzō, chief retainer of Momonoi Wakasanosuke.
BANNAI: (*Chuckles delightedly.*) The bluebird Wakasanosuke 10
and his friend, the yellow canary Enya Hangan, are country chickens. What a cackling they will make in the palace. Oh, my master, Lord Moronao, will pluck them clean!
HONZŌ: (*Carefully watching* BANNAI's *expression.*) That is the matter on which I have come, good Bannai. My master is 15
young and untutored in the intricacies of palace etiquette. Only with Lord Moronao's generous guidance will he be able to carry out his important duties. Taking this opportunity, I express my gratitude for your master's favor.

(HONZŌ *bows low.* BANNAI *turns front with a self-satisfied smirk on his face.*)

BANNAI: Everyone needs a chief councilor's favors. But your 20
Wakasanosuke was rude to my master. Go back where you came from, go back, go away! (BANNAI *strikes a pose: feet together, head up, right fist extended toward* HONZŌ.)
HONZŌ: What you say is true, still please accept these gifts on behalf of Wakasanosuke and his grateful followers. 25

(HONZŌ *bows toward the gifts of silk. He looks about, to be sure they are unseen, then takes out a wrapped package of gold coins. Moving forward on his knees to* BANNAI's *side, he drops the package into the open kimono sleeve.*)

Carry my message to Lord Moronao. Do what is necessary, good Bannai. Will you do so, Bannai? Bannai?

(HONZŌ *tugs lightly on* BANNAI's *sleeve.*)

NARRATOR: (*Chants.*) Wondering, Bannai takes it in his hand!

(BANNAI *flicks* HONZŌ's *hand away and in doing so strikes the heavy coins. He clutches his fingers in pain, then wonders what his hand hit. He sneaks a look at the coins. He reacts with delighted surprise.*)

NARRATOR: (*Sings.*) Money talks words of power!
30 BANNAI: (*Effusive, his attitude completely changed.*) Well, well, Kakogawa Honzō, how nice of you to come. (*He squats and bows to* HONZŌ.) You have come at the right moment: the ceremonial rooms are being prepared. Come, come!

(BANNAI *picks up the tray of gifts, rises, and gestures for* HONZŌ *to follow him.*)

HONZŌ: (*Bowing carefully.*) I am a person of no importance, I do
35   not dare enter the palace.
BANNAI: (*Proudly.*) If Lord Moronao is with you, who would dare object? Come, I will show you the rooms.
HONZŌ: I will enter then, most gratefully.
BANNAI: Then come along. Come along!

(BANNAI *poses.* Honzō *bows. They cross toward the gate: three times* BANNAI *turns back, chuckling and bowing, to beckon* HONZŌ *forward. At the gate* BANNAI *stops short.*)

40   Master Honzō, the threshold is high.
NARRATOR: (*Sings.*) Moronao is happy. Honzō bought the life of Wakasanosuke. His scheme now is accomplished. Together they go.

(BANNAI *steps carefully over the foot-high threshold of the gate and goes inside, followed by* HONZŌ.)

NARRATOR: (*A nō song, as if part of the entertainment inside the mansion.*)
      "At the end of the journey we have reached Takasago Bay;
45   At the end of the journey we have reached Takasago Bay."

(OKARU, *a beautiful young girl in her late teens, enters on the* hanamichi. *She wears a maiden's trailing kimono with long sleeves, in a purple arrow pattern. She holds a lacquered letter box in her right hand. She stops at the seven-three position, looks toward the gate, and poses.*)

OKARU: My Lady Kaoyo urgently sends this letter to her husband, Lord Enya Hangan. How fortunate that I, her favorite, was allowed to bring it. Dearest Kampei, I cannot bear to be apart from you a single moment.

(*Offstage musicians play nō-style drum and flute music in the background.* KAMPEI, *a young samurai, enters from the gate followed by a* RETAINER. *They wear black kimono under stiff vests; their divided skirts are folded up to their knees, showing that they are on guard duty.* KAMPEI *is in the service of* HANGAN *and is* OKARU's *lover.* OKARU *sees him and runs to meet him.*)

50 KAMPEI: Okaru, is it you?
OKARU: (*Coquettishly.*) Dearest Kampei, I missed you so.

KAMPEI: (*Flustered and worried about meeting her while he is on duty.*) But why are you here at the palace gate, at night, and all alone?
OKARU: I've come for Lady Kaoyo. "Meet Kampei and tell him he   55
is to ask my husband to deliver this letter to Lord Moronao"—those were her very words.

(OKARU *passes him the letter box.*)

KAMPEI: (*Unsure.*) I am to deliver this directly to Lord Hangan?
HOKARU: Yes, dearest Kampei.

(*She smiles invitingly at him.*)

KAMPEI: Wait for me, Okaru.   60

(*He turns to go.*)

OKARU: (*She holds his sleeve.*) Kampei!
KAMPEI: I should take it to our master myself. I should be with him. It is my duty not to leave his side in the palace. I . . .

(*He is irresolute. He tries to leave; she tugs gently, persuasively at his sleeve. He looks into her pleading eyes. He decides. He turns to the* RETAINER.)

      Take this immediately to Lord Hangan.   65
RETAINER: I will.

(*The* RETAINER *takes the letter box, bows, and crosses into the gate.*)

OKARU: I want to be with you so. Now that we are here, together . . .
KAMPEI: You are flushed with excitement, Okaru!
OKARU: (*Taking his hand in hers.*) Please come. I don't care!   70
NARRATOR: (*Sings.*) Seizing fast her lover's hand . . . she leads him away!

(*She presses against him boldly, folding her arm over his. They pose: a sharp ki clack emphasizes the moment. Offstage drum and samisen resume in the background. They look excitedly into each other's eyes and then hurriedly cross into the darkness of the trees beyond the gate. The curtain is run quickly closed to accelerating ki clacks. Music ends. Soft, intermittent ki clacks mark time while the scene is changed.*)

SCENE III

Pine Room

Two ki clacks: the curtain opens. The scene is a large reception room of the shogunal mansion called the Pine Room because of the designs painted on the gold sliding doors extending across the full stage. A single ki clack: action begins.

NARRATOR: (*Chants.*) Utter indignation, for Moronao is late! Impatiently waiting in the palace . . . Wakasanosuke!

(WAKASANOSUKE *rushes onto the* hanamichi. *He drops to one knee at the seven-three position, resolutely slaps his thigh, and poses, waiting for the arrival of* MORONAO. *A sliding door left opens. Rapid drum and flute music.* BANNAI *ushers* MORONAO *on stage, bowing obsequiously. He carries a small paper lantern to light the room. Without a word,* WAKASANOSUKE *leaps to his feet, slips his sword arm free of the restricting formal vest, and rushes to attack* MORONAO. BANNAI *momentarily is able to block* WAKASANOSUKE's *path, but then is hurled to the floor as* WAKASANOSUKE *pushes past.* MORONAO *falls to his knees. He clasps his hands together pleadingly.* BANNAI *throws his arms around* WAKASANOSUKE's *lower leg, holding him fast. Music stops.*)

MORONAO: There you are, there you are, Lord Wakasanosuke, good Wakasanosuke. Your early arrival makes me ashamed,
5   ashamed, so very ashamed. I was rude to you at Hachiman Shrine. I was. (WAKASANOSUKE *edges forward as if to draw.*) Now, now, now, you have every right to be angry. But have pity on a foolish old samurai. I throw my sword at your feet. I clasp my hands and apologize. Bannai, Bannai, you too, bow,
10   apologize to Lord Wakasanosuke.
NARRATOR: (*Sings.*) Flattering, and what is more, detestable words so sweet. Taken aback completely, Wakasanosuke wonders what has happened. There is nothing he can do . . .

(MORONAO *bows his head low to the floor.* WAKASANOSUKE *cannot believe his eyes, seeing the proud councilor abasing himself. He kicks* BANNAI *away, slips his sword arm inside his vest, and strides past* MORONAO. MORONAO *circles to avoid him, crawling on his hands and knees indecorously.* WAKASANOSUKE *turns back, spitting out his words.*)

WAKASANOSUKE: Contemptible samurai!

(*He strides off stage left.*)

15   MORONAO: I was wrong, I was wrong, I apologize, I apologize, I . . .

(*Eyes fearfully on the ground,* MORONAO *continues.* BANNAI *registers comic shock, seeing his master bowing and speaking to no one. He scurries forward on his hands and knees. He pulls* MORONAO's *sleeve. Music stops. Their eyes meet.* BANNAI *nods in the direction of* WAKASANOSUKE's *exit.* MORONAO *sees that he is alone and sighs with relief. Recovering his dignity, he sits up.*)

MORONAO: Bannai, that stupid young puppy meant, I think, to kill me. "A sword in a fool's hand makes the wise man cautious."
20   BANNAI: (*Bowing.*) Oh yes, my lord, how true.
NARRATOR: (*Chants "Jo no Mai" ["Slow Dance"] drum and flute music.*) Who has planned this mischievous fate? (*Sings.*) Enya Hangan . . . innocent of this all, proceeds to Moronao. (*Chants.*) Moronao . . . seeing his victim!

(*Simultaneously,* BANNAI *arranges his master's sword and the lantern and exits stage left while* HANGAN *appears on the* hanamichi, *carrying in his left hand the letter box given by* KAMPEI's *retainer. Noh-style "Jo no Mai" drum and flute music continues in the background.*)

MORONAO: (*Ominously.*) Late, late, late! You're late, Hangan!

(HANGAN *bows slightly and hurries on stage. He kneels, bowing again.*)

HANGAN: I humbly beg your pardon for being a few moments late.   25
I come ready for your instructions. First, however, I have been asked by my wife to place this letter in your hands.

(*He moves forward on his knees, places the letter box on the floor beside* MORONAO, *moves back, and bows respectfully.*)

MORONAO: (*Feigning ignorance.*) Hmm, hmm. A letter from Lady Kaoyo? To me? (*Opens the box and removes the letter card.*) Ah, I understand. My poetic skill is renowned. No   30
doubt she wishes me to place the touch of my pen upon her heartfelt words, to correct any blemishes. There is time before the ceremonies. Sit and be at ease. (*He reads.*) "A woman's love does, not lie in the hopeful eye, of her beholder; not beholden to lie I, aver never to lie with you."   35
(*Music stops.* MORONAO *again.*) "Not beholden to lie, I, aver never to lie . . . with you."
NARRATOR: (*Chanting rapidly.*) After weighing the words . . . Kaoyo has rejected my love and this is the proof! This must mean that Hangan has found out my intention! (*Sings.*) Anger   40
and humiliation . . . but pretending ignorance.

(MORONAO *looks straight forward, his face frozen in humiliated rage, his right hand slowly closing into a rigid fist that crushes his brocade silk robe. Masking his emotions he turns toward* HANGAN. *Drum and flute music resume.*)

MORONAO: Hangan, was this poem shown to you?
HANGAN: (*Bows politely.*) I have not seen it until this moment, your Excellency.

(*Reassured that* HANGAN *is not party to* KAOYO's *insult,* MORONAO *proceeds to deliberately humiliate him.*)

MORONAO: Is that so? Well, the lord of little Hakushu castle   45
has a clever wife. She can dash off a subtle poem like this. A woman so talented and famous for her beauty must be a source of great husbandly pride. Such a superlative creature in fact, that her infatuated husband, not bearing to be separated from her, finds his sacred duties at the palace . . .   50
wearisome!

(MORONAO *casually turns his back to* HANGAN, *idly playing with his fan.*)

NARRATOR: (*Chants.*) Moronao is filled with spiteful words of insinuation. Riding on his frustration . . . any may be his prey. Hangan is perplexed at the burst of displeasure. (*Sings.*) Gushing anger, he holds it down, holds it in!   55

(HANGAN *starts. He almost turns to confront* MORONAO, *but then suppresses his anger. He pretends to smile, as if sharing* MORONAO's *joke. Ominous drum beats continue in the background.*)

HANGAN: Ha, ha, ha, ha. I see my lordship is in a playful mood. He has, perhaps, been drinking and is feeling in good humor. Yes, surely my lord has been drinking. Ha, ha, ha, ha.
MORONAO: (*Dangerously, facing* HANGAN.) What is that? When   60
have you seen me drinking? You, who have never offered me as much as a cup of wine? Whether I, Moronao, choose to drink or not, nothing keeps me from *my* duty! The one who's been drinking is you, Hangan. You've

65 come from a drinking party with your charming wife,
she pouring for you, and you pouring for her! Isn't that why
you come to the palace late?

(HANGAN's *face tightens.* MORONAO *notices and turns away with a malicious look in his eye.*)

Isn't there a story about a stay-at-home like you, helpless
beyond his front door? I seem to recall . . . ah, yes, the
70 "Tadpole in the Puddle." There once was a young tadpole
that lived in a tiny puddle. He knew no other place between
heaven and earth, and so he thought his puddle the
most wonderful home in the world. One day a compassionate
person passed by, just like Moronao, who, taking pity,
75 lifted him from his stagnant pool and released him in the
waters of a broad river. (*Arms out,* MORONAO *deliberately
strikes* HANGAN's *chest with his heavy fan.*) Well, the tadpole
was out of his depth, dropped suddenly into the great
world from his shallow one. Completely at a loss, willy-nilly
80 he went this way, and willy-nilly he went that way. (*Pointing
with fan.*) And in the end he ran headfirst smack into a
bridgepost. (*Strikes* HANGAN *full in the chest with his fan.*)
And shivering and quivering, and shivering and quivering,
the little tadpole expired. (*Twirling his fan in limp fingers.*)
85 The tadpole is . . . you! (*Looks full into* HANGAN's *straining
face.*) Oh? I do believe the young tadpole has lost his tail and
is turning into a toad. (HANGAN *turns and glares furiously
at* MORONAO.) Yes, with your eyes bulging out, Hangan,
you look exactly like a toad. Ha, ha, ha, ha! This Moronao
90 has lived many years, but this is the first time I've seen in
the palace a toad wearing clothes. Oh, come here, come
here, Bannai, Hangan's turning into a toad. Hangan *is* a
toad, a sa-mu-rai toad! (*Drum beats stop. Silence.* MORONAO
deliberately strikes HANGAN's *chest, sword hilt, and chest with
95 his fan.*) Ha, ha, ha, ha, ha!
NARRATOR: (*Chants.*) Toad! Devil talk! Demon words!

(MORONAO *rears back, points contemptuously at* HANGAN *with his
fan, rotates his head, and poses in a* mie *to two loud* tsuke *beats.
Music stops.*)

Hangan can no more take the vile old man!
HANGAN: (*Slowly, with dangerous, suppressed fury.*) Do you dare
compare Enya Hangan Takasada, castle lord of Hakushu . . .
100 to a toad? You cannot possibly mean the words you have
said! Have you gone out of your mind . . . Councilor
Moronao!

(HANGAN *pivots to face* MORONAO, *slapping his thigh for emphasis.*)

MORONAO: (*Darkly.*) Watch yourself, Hangan! Remember I am
councilor of the shogun. No one calls me insane. You are
105 ludicrous!
HANGAN: You have been deliberately insulting me? Do you dare
tell me that!
MORONAO: (*Insinuating.*) Indeed, I dare. And if I dare, who are
you to complain?
110 HANGAN: (*Drawn out.*) If you dare . . .
MORONAO: (*Leaning in insolently.*) If I dare . . . ?
HANGAN: Hmm!

(HANGAN's *patience snaps. He rises on one knee, his hand on his sword.*
MORONAO *instantly parries* HANGAN's *sword arm with his closed fan.*)

MORONAO: (*Commandingly.*) The palace! (MORONAO *slaps*
HANGAN's *sword arm away and the two men pull back:*
MORONAO *fearfully,* HANGAN *furious.*) The palace! The palace! 115
It is the palace! Don't you know the law? Draw your sword
in the palace and your house will be destroyed! Don't you
know that! (*Drum beats resume.* MORONAO *slaps his fan
commandingly on the floor.* HANGAN, *anguished that he must
restrain his rage, folds his arms tightly over the hilts of his* 120
swords and slowly sinks back onto his haunches. MORONAO
notes this and is emboldened to continue his provocation.) Hm,
since you know . . . then go ahead, kill me. Well . . . draw . . .
draw . . . draw your sword. Come, kill me! Kill me . . . Hangan!

(MORONAO *forces himself bodily against* HANGAN *and leans
against* HANGAN's *swords. They pose. Burning with humiliation,*
HANGAN *abases himself in order to fulfill his ceremonial duties.
He backs away and bows low.*)

HANGAN: A moment, a moment, Lord Moronao, I beg your 125
indulgence. Without thinking I spoke out of turn. I implore
you, instruct me in my duties for the ceremony. I will do as
you say. Humbly, I beseech you, your Excellency.

(*Music stops.* HANGAN *looks up from his bow.* MORONAO *smugly
turns away, avoiding his gaze.* HANGAN's *patience snaps a second
time: his hand leaps for his sword. Instantly* MORONAO *reacts.*)

MORONAO: Your hand!
HANGAN: My hand?
MORONAO: (*With all his authority.*) Yes, your hand! 130
HANGAN: This hand . . .

(*He hesitates, looks at his trembling hand, then drops his hands to
the floor and bows in defeat.*)

. . . humbly begs your forgiveness.
MORONAO: (*Savoring his victory.*) So, you apologize, do you? Very
well, very well. Soon instructions in great detail for today's 135
ceremony . . .
HANGAN: (*Looks up hopefully.*) . . . will be given to me?
MORONAO: (*Viciously.*) No, not to you! To Wakasanosuke!
(HANGAN *is stunned, motionless. In silence* MORONAO *casually
rises, tears* KAOYO's *letter card in two, and throws the pieces in* 140
HANGAN's *face.*) There is no educating a provincial barbarian.

(MORONAO *deliberately turns his back and kicks his left and right
trailing trouser legs in* HANGAN's *face.* HANGAN *rears back. Chuckling,* MORONAO *starts to leave.*)

HANGAN: Moronao! Wait!

(HANGAN *steps on* MORONAO's *trailing trouser leg.* MORONAO *is
brought up short. He tugs at the trouser; it is held fast.*)

MORONAO: (*Deadly calm.*) Be careful. You'll soil my trousers.
Hop. Hop, hop, hop. (MORONAO *turns to leave, but cannot* 145
move.) So, you won't hop away, little toad? Can there be
something else you want?
HANGAN: What I want is . . .
MORONAO: What you want is . . . ?

(HANGAN *quietly slips his sword arm free of the stiff vest.*
MORONAO *turns and thrusts his sneering face toward* HANGAN.)

150 HANGAN: (*A scream.*) You!

(HANGAN's *short sword flashes out of its sheath and gashes* MORONAO's *forehead. Drum and flute play furious "Haya Mai" ("Fast Dance").* MORONAO *staggers and falls.* BANNAI *rushes on to help his master flee.* HANGAN *leaps to his feet and is about to finish* MORONAO *with a second blow when* HONZŌ, *who has been hiding behind a decorative screen stage right, rushes out and seizes* HANGAN *from behind.*)

NARRATOR: "Hold me not! My foe is there!"

(*Six* PROVINCIAL LORDS *run on from right.* HANGAN *struggles to get free, but he is encircled and held fast. In desperation he hurls his sword after the disappearing enemy. A single sharp clack of the* ki. *The sword falls short. He reaches out with both hands after* MORONAO *and poses: his fingers curl into fists and his chest heaves with sobs of mortification. But* HONZŌ *and the* PROVINCIAL LORDS *hold him fast. To gradually accelerating* ki *clacks the curtain is run closed. Offstage musicians play "Shagiri." A single* ki *clack concludes the act.*)

ACT TWO

SCENE I

Fugitive Travel

The large drum beats melancholy "Yama Oto" ("Mountain Pattern"). To accelerating ki *clacks the curtain is slowly pushed open. A sky-blue curtain fills the stage. A single* ki *clack: the blue curtain drops and is whisked away by black-robed* STAGE ASSISTANTS *to reveal a colorful springtime scene in the country. Snow-covered Mt. Fuji is seen in the background, pink cherry blossoms bloom everywhere.* OKARU *and* KAMPEI *stand center, their faces hidden behind a straw hat. A temple bell tolls in the distance. Kiyomoto music begins from offstage.* KAMPEI *lowers the hat and we see the lovers dressed for traveling: kimono skirts raised and a bundle over* KAMPEI's *shoulder. They mime in slow dance movements to the kiyomoto lyrics the story of their disgrace and flight.*

KIYOMOTO SINGER: Oh, you who flee, do you not see yon green field, a veil of new green?

(*They look at the flowers at their feet, to the left and the right. They look into each other's eyes, then pose gazing into the distance. Singing ends;* samisen *continues in the background. Facing upstage, they pass their sandals and* KAMPEI's *hat and bundle to two* STAGE ASSISTANTS. *They turn front and kneel center stage.* KAMPEI *places his long sword on the ground beside him.*)

KAMPEI: (*Melancholy.*) Giving myself over in love to you, I failed
5   our master when he needed me, and now we are fugitives fleeing in the dead of night I know not where. When I think of it, I no longer have the heart to live. Say prayers over the grave of this dishonored samurai. Okaru . . . farewell.

(KAMPEI *takes his short sword from his sash and is about to draw the blade. Gently she seizes it and prevents him.*)

OKARU: No, I won't have you saying that again. I am to blame that
10   you were not beside Lord Hangan. I cannot live without you.

If you die then so must I. But rather than praising your spirit, people will say we died as lovers frequently do. Please, live, dearest Kampei. Live . . . in love . . . for me.

(KAMPEI *tries to draw the sword again. She pulls one way, he the other.* KAMPEI, *irresolute, allows her to take the short sword. She places it beside her, away from his reach.*)

KIYOMOTO SINGER: " 'Twas then my heart went astray. It was
    when you, yes, you made me love, oh, so imprudently. Blame   15
    my imprudent heart that spoke to me thus: 'So easy it is to die,
    but you must live, live on.' "

(KAMPEI *takes up the long sword to kill himself. Again, she gently holds the scabbard so that he cannot draw. They rise and move left, then right, in a delicate struggle for the sword. Allowing himself to be persuaded, they pose with the sword held firmly in her hands. He looks away, wiping his falling tears. She takes the sword and places it out of his reach. They kneel side-by-side.*)

KAMPEI: Your tenderness overwhelms me. (*Nods with resolution.*)
    We will flee across the mountains to your father's home.
OKARU: (*Smiling, relieved.*) You make me so happy.   20
KAMPEI: In time I know I can find a way to atone for deserting
    my master. Come, let us go.
OKARU: (*Meekly.*) Yes, Kampei.
KIYOMOTO SINGER: Now for travel they prepare, but who should
    confront them!   25

(KAMPEI *rises and poses facing front.*)

BANNAI: (*Off, at the rear of the* hanamichi.) Hey, hey! Here we go!
FIGHTING CHORUS: (*Also off.*) Haaa!

(*Loud beats of the big drum. Strong accelerating* tsuke *pattern as* BANNAI *runs onto the* hanamichi *followed by eight of his men, the* FIGHTING CHORUS. BANNAI *has his kimono tucked up to his knees, and a cord holds back his sleeves. His makeup has become ludicrous: bat-shaped eyebrows, drooping eyes, and a tiny blue-gray mustache. The* FIGHTING CHORUS *is dressed identically in red leggings and arm coverings and red and white patterned kimono that stop at their knees. Each carries a branch of cherry blossoms as a weapon.* BANNAI *stops at the seven-three position.* KAMPEI *escorts* OKARU *to the left, out of harm's way, and stands calmly.*)

BANNAI: (*A comic challenge.*) Hey, hey! Kampei!

(*He stamps forward with two steps, each accented by two* tsuke *beats. He and his men march on stage. The men, alert for their master's call, kneel upstage in two rows.* BANNAI *faces front, with a supercilious look. He speaks in a special rhythmical pattern,* nori, *in which each dialogue phrase fits into an eight-beat* samisen *musical phrase. He accompanies the tale with comic gestures.*)

Your stupid master, Enya Hangan, Takasada and my
    honored master, Councilor Moronao, met in the palace   30
    while, chittering chattering, chittering chattering, your
    master Hangan, flew into a snit. Taking a teensy sword, he
    whipped it out, he made a slash. He is a traitor, locked up
    in his residence, boxed up like a criminal. Ha ha ha . . . ha
    ha ha . . . haha haha hahaha! Hangan has been hauled away!   35
    I'll catch you like a chick! I'll pluck you like a duck! I am

claiming Okaru! Well? Well? Well, well? (*Accelerating.*) Well, well, well, well, well! Kampei! Your goose is cooked! Give her . . . to me!

(BANNAI *stands on tiptoe, holds his sword hilts threateningly, and cocks his head in comic* mie *to two beats of the* tsuke.)

40 KIYOMOTO SINGER: "Give her to me," yells Sagisaka Bannai. Kampei bursts out with mocking laughter.
KAMPEI: (*Laughs, then speaks in rhythmic* nori *phrases.*) You are a funny bird, Sagisaka Bannai, a little chirping sparrow, I could swallow in a bite. (*Rapidly.*) Kampei's fiery gaze could
45 fry you to a crisp! But instead of eating you, I will make you eat crow!

(KAMPEI *slips his fists out of the breast of his kimono, allowing the black outer kimono to drop. An inner kimono of brilliant crimson color is revealed. He stamps aggressively forward, then poses with arms outstretched, head cocked in a* mie *to two* tsuke *beats.* BANNAI *tumbles to the ground terrified.*)

KIYOMOTO SINGER: Glaring and with arms outstretched, Kampei stands before him!
BANNAI: (*Weakly.*) Help!

(KIYOMOTO *samisen and drums play instrumental music as the eight members of the* FIGHTING CHORUS *attack* KAMPEI. KAMPEI *waves half of them past him until he stands center in a* mie *position. Four men face him from either side, holding their cherry branches as if they were swords. They strike at him right, left, right. He forces them back. They fall away. They pose in a* mie *to two* tsuke *beats.* KAMPEI *now fights his opponents in a series of group combats that are executed in delicate, controlled dance patterns. Rhythmic drums and* samisen *support the action.*)

50 KIYOMOTO SINGER: Cherry, cherry blossoms! A name, oh, so beloved.

(*One man on each side strikes at* KAMPEI *with the cherry branch. Three times* KAMPEI *avoids, then seizing the tips of the branches, he whirls them in a circle and presses them to their knees. He poses in a* mie. *Flicking the branches away, the men are hit on the forehead; they retreat.* KAMPEI *nonchalantly dusts off his hands.*)

"No, no, you can't have her," and why should that be?

(*One man on each side seizes* KAMPEI's *arms. They struggle right, left, right.* KAMPEI *flicks them forward onto their knees. They try to seize his feet, he backs up. They rush in to encircle him. He avoids, then casually taps them on the back. They do a cartwheel and fall prostrate on the ground.* KAMPEI *poses in a* mie.)

So tender, so fine, so frail, never to be won by you!

(*Four men form a square around* KAMPEI. *Two-by-two they attack, but he pivots to avoid them. Six men strike with their cherry branches.* KAMPEI *drops to his knees, deftly knocks the wind out of them with an open-hand blow, and, with a sweeping gesture, knocks them off their feet. They fall on their bottoms in unison.*)

Delightful, though she's only to be seen. How can you ever
55 feel true love, if she won't play with you!

(*The* FIGHTING CHORUS *retires upstage.* BANNAI *pulls* OKARU *by the sleeve. Foolishly flirting, he touches his cheek to her hand.* KAMPEI *pushes him away, and when* BANNAI *tries to get past to* OKARU, *blocks his way.* BANNAI *slips under* KAMPEI's *sleeve, but is caught and held by the nape of the neck.* BANNAI *struggles free, strikes at* KAMPEI, *is kicked to his knees, and finally is grasped by the ear, lifted, and spun around.* BANNAI *is near tears in frustration and humiliation. Trying once again, he raises his fist, but* KAMPEI *turns and casually pushes* BANNAI *to the ground.* KAMPEI *stamps forward and poses in a strong* mie *to two* tsuke *beats.*)

BANNAI: (*Plaintively.*) Take him!

(*Large drum and* tsuke *beats. The* FIGHTING CHORUS *attacks in unison:* KAMPEI *passes them off right and left as he strides from stage left to right; he turns and passes unharmed between them as they strike at him with their cherry branches. One man, coming from hiding, strikes at* KAMPEI *from behind.* KAMPEI *kicks him to the ground, places his foot on his back, and poses in a strong* mie *to two beats of the* tsuke. KAMPEI *kicks the man away and attacks. Booming drum accelerates. The* FIGHTING CHORUS *retreats. They run pell-mell down the* hanamichi *and out of sight.* KAMPEI *poses in a powerful "stone-throwing"* mie *to two beats of the* tsuke. BANNAI *sneaks up.*)

BANNAI: Kampei, here I come!

(BANNAI *raises his sword to strike.* KAMPEI *catches his wrist, spins him around, forces him to his knees, and raises the sword.*)

KAMPEI: (*Bantering.*) Shall I cut your ears off? (*Terrified,* BANNAI *covers his ears with wildly trembling hands.*) Shall I cut off your nose? (BANNAI *covers his nose.*) Or shall I simply kill you? 60
OKARU: Killing him would bring more trouble. So, please, just let him go.
BANNAI: (*Foolishly, imitating* OKARU's *inflections.*) So, please, just let him go!

(BANNAI *clasps his trembling hands together in prayer.*)

KIYOMOTO SINGER: Oh, how he prattles on, that bird, Sagisaka! 65
Smoothing his ruffled feathers, slowly, then faster, flirts with death, and yet to live, away he flies!

(KAMPEI *nods agreement. He casually rolls* BANNAI *across the stage away from* OKARU. *He poses facing front.* BANNAI *rubs his throat, then noticing* KAMPEI *is holding his sword, meekly gestures a request that it be returned. Contemptuously,* KAMPEI *tosses the sword on the ground.* BANNAI *leaps back in terror. Gathering his courage, he snares the sword with his foot, then suddenly turns and raises the sword as if to strike. A fierce glance from* KAMPEI *deflates him completely. He turns and escapes off right, lifting his legs high in the air in a "stork walk."*)

KAMPEI: He deserved to die. But his death would be a crime to add to my disloyalty.

(*A cock crows in the distance. They both look up into the sky. They speak in melancholy, poetic tones.*)

Already it is dawning . . . 70
OKARU: . . . on the peaks of the mountains . . .

KAMPEI: . . . the eastern light glows . . .
OKARU and KAMPEI: (*In unison.*) . . . lighting trailing clouds.

(*They pose together center stage, absorbed in their own melancholy.*)

KIYOMOTO SINGER: They fly away at daybreak, like the crows that
75   cry, "caw, caw." So dear to each other, in love, in love.

(*A* STAGE ASSISTANT *passes to* OKARU *the hat, bundle, and swords. Dutifully,* OKARU *helps* KAMPEI *adjust the bundle and slide the swords into his sash. They put on their sandals. A temple bell tolls. They move apart, pose, then move back-to-back.*)

Though they must hasten to depart, their minds are filled
with woe. Who would doubt their loyalty if they proved the
guilt they feel? Away they go.

(*They look into each other's eyes. Restraining tears,* KAMPEI *puts on a manly bearing, takes* OKARU *by the hand, and turns to begin their long journey.* BANNAI *sneaks up behind them. He holds* OKARU *by the waist.*)

BANNAI: Okaru is mine, all mine!

(KAMPEI *moves to block* BANNAI, *passing* OKARU *to safety on the* hanamichi. *He pushes* BANNAI *away and turns to join* OKARU.)

80   BANNAI: Kampei, wait!
KAMPEI: (*Turning back at the seven-three position.*) Bannai, you
want. . . . ?
BANNAI: (*Posing.*) Kampei, I want . . .
KAMPEI: Hmm?
85   BANNAI: (*Deflated.*) Nothing.
KAMPEI: Simpleton!

(*A loud* ki *clack:* BANNAI *collapses to the ground. Drum booms loudly.* KAMPEI *takes* OKARU'*s hand and slowly they exit down the* hanamichi. *Kiyomoto samisen plays plaintive chords and* ki *clacks accelerate as the curtain begins to close.* BANNAI *is in the path of the curtain. He retreats before it, then, realizing it is hopeless, seizes the curtain with both hands and, grinning happily, prances across the stage, closing the curtain and disappearing from sight. A single* ki *clack: drum and flute play lively "Shagiri" to close the scene.*)

SCENE II

Hangan's Suicide

Two ki *clacks: the curtain is slowly opened to the rachetlike sound of an old-fashioned clock. The scene is a large, formal room in* HANGAN'*s mansion. Sliding doors that make up the rear wall are painted powder blue and covered with silver crests of* HANGAN'*s clan. Tatami matting covers the floor.* HANGAN, *dressed in a simple kimono and vest so pale a blue-gray that it verges on white, kneels center. He faces two envoys from the shogun,* ISHIDŌ *and* YAKUSHIJI, *who are sitting stage left on high stools. They wear dark kimono, vests, and trousers.* ISHIDŌ'*s sympathetic manner contrasts sharply with* YAKUSHIJI'*s derisive attitude.* GOEMON, *a senior retainer of* HANGAN, *kneels upstage. Silence.* ISHIDŌ *rises and faces* HANGAN. *He takes from the breast of his kimono a large folded letter. He holds it reverently to his forehead.*

ISHIDŌ: Hear the shogun's command. (*Removing the letter from its envelope, he reads.*) "Whereas, Enya Hangan Takasada, you have willfully committed an act of bloodshed against our chief councilor, Moronao, and thereby have defiled the palace, know that your estates, large and small, are   5
hereby confiscated and you are ordered to end your life by *seppuku.*"

(ISHIDŌ *gravely holds the open letter in front of him, so* HANGAN *can read the order with his own eyes. After glancing at it,* HANGAN *bows respectfully.*)

HANGAN: (*With perfect control.*) In all respects I accept the shogun's command.
NARRATOR: (*Chants.*) From the adjoining room, knocking on the   10
door . . .

(*A* RETAINER *knocks on the sliding door. He speaks in a faint, muffled voice, suggesting tears.*)

RETAINER: (*Off.*) Goemon, Goemon. We, Lord Hangan's retainers, beg permission to see our master . . .
RETAINERS: (*Off, quietly in unison.*) . . . one last time.
GOEMON: (*Bowing to* HANGAN.) My lord, your retainers wish to   15
see you.
HANGAN: Tell them not until Chief Retainer Yuranosuke has arrived from our province.
GOEMON: (*Facing the door.*) You heard our lord. You may enter when Yuranosuke arrives, not before.   20
RETAINERS: (*Scarcely audible.*) Ahhh.
NARRATOR: (*Sings.*) Their plea, not granted . . . no one dares utter a single word. In the room, silence prevails.

(HANGAN *rises and retires upstage, where he kneels with his back to the audience.*)

GOEMON: (*Quietly, facing offstage right.*) Proceed.
RETAINER: (*Faintly, off.*) Yes.   25

(*In complete silence arrangements are made for* HANGAN'*s death by ritual disembowelment.* RETAINERS, *dressed in somber blue and gray kimono, vests, and split trousers, swiftly and unobtrusively enter. They place two tatami mats center to make a six-foot square platform. They cover it with a pure white cloth. Sprigs of green, in small bamboo holders, are placed at the four corners. With downcast eyes, the* RETAINERS *slip quietly away.* GOEMON *bows to* HANGAN *indicating that the place of suicide is ready.* HANGAN *rises, slowly pivots front, and crosses down to the cloth seat. Unconsciously his gaze drifts to the* hanamichi: *he is waiting for the arrival of his chief retainer,* YURANOSUKE, *and does not want to die before passing to him his last instructions. His right foot touches the cloth. He remembers it is obligatory to step into the place of suicide with the left foot. He glances at the envoys to see if they have noticed: they are gazing straight ahead. He deliberately steps onto the cloth and slowly kneels.*)

NARRATOR: (*Chants.*) Rikiya proceeds with the saddest order.
(*Sings.*) The master's suicide blade weighing heavy on his heart . . .

(YURANOSUKE'*s son,* RIKIYA, *enters from up left. He carries a plain wooden tray bearing the short dagger with which* HANGAN *will kill himself. The long sleeves of his black kimono and a delicate forelock of hair indicate he is a youth, not yet grown to manhood. He places the tray on the floor before the envoys for their verification. He bows.* ISHIDŌ *and* YAKUSHIJI *look at the blade, then nod to each other that it is satisfactory.* ISHIDŌ *nods gravely to* RIKIYA.)

NARRATOR: Before Lord Hangan he lays the blade.

(RIKIYA *places the tray on the cloth before* HANGAN, *bows low, and then looks up for instructions.* HANGAN *looks gently into* RIKIYA's *eyes and with a single head movement indicates that* RIKIYA *is to leave: a boy so young should not have to witness* seppuku. RIKIYA *politely shakes his head: until his father arrives, he must fulfill his father's duties.* HANGAN *repeats the order to leave; again* RIKIYA *shakes his head. Impressed by the boy's loyalty,* HANGAN *nods that he may stay.* RIKIYA *bows gratefully, rises, backs away, and takes a place beside* GOEMON.)

30 NARRATOR: (*Sings.*) Taking off, in hushed silence, his outer clothes to expose his death robe . . . securing the seat of death.

(HANGAN *prepares himself for death with calm deliberation. He slips off the vest, letting it drop to his waist. He tucks the ends under his legs so as to hold his body in place after he has died. He drops the outer kimono to his waist and tucks it in as well. Beneath he is wearing a pure white kimono appropriate for death, an indication to the envoys that he was prepared to die even before they brought the shogun's command. He places his hands firmly on his thighs and looks intently down the* hanamichi.)

HANGAN: (*Softly but urgently.*) Rikiya.
RIKIYA: (*Bowing.*) Yes.
35 HANGAN: Yuranosuke . . . ?
RIKIYA: Yuranosuke . . . (*He looks down the* hanamichi *for a sign that his father has arrived.*) . . . has not as yet arrived.
NARRATOR: (*Sings.*) Proper steps for suicide, he lifts the tray and bows. (*Chants.*) Waiting no longer, the blade in his
40 hand.

(HANGAN *prepares the dagger. He lifts the tray to his forehead respectfully. He ceremoniously takes the dagger in his right hand and a sheet of white paper in his left. He wraps the paper around the blade until only its tip is bare. He is now able to grasp the blade low for extra leverage. He holds the blade at ready on his thigh. The tip points to his stomach. Outwardly calm, his voice betrays his anxiety.*)

HANGAN: Rikiya, Rikiya!
RIKIYA: (*Bowing.*) Yes.
HANGAN: Yuranosuke . . . ?
45 RIKIYA: Yes! (RIKIYA *bows and rushes to the end of the* hanamichi. *He falls to his knees, looks to the right, the left, then straight ahead, searching for sight of his father. His lip trembles, he is close to tears.*) Yuranosuke . . . (*He rushes back and throws himself on the floor before* HANGAN.) . . . has not as yet arrived!
HANGAN: (*Calmly.*) Tell him that I regret . . . not seeing him one
50 last time. (HANGAN *nods that* RIKIYA *may retire and pivots slightly toward* ISHIDŌ.) Lord Ishidō, I ask that you witness and report my death.
NARRATOR: (*Sings.*) Here at last the time has come, the blade is aimed. Hangan . . . thrusts it in . . . thrusts it deep!

(HANGAN *places the tray behind him. He rises slightly on his knees, looking one last time down the* hanamichi *for* YURANOSUKE. *He holds the dagger under the ribs on his left side. With a sudden jerk he thrusts the blade into his stomach. Involuntarily his body drops forward and his head falls. Rapid narrative shifts to chanting.*)

Running at a desperate speed, the awaited person comes! 55
Here at last is Ōboshi Yuranosuke! A frantic gaze at his master: "Is he still alive?" Overcome by the sight, he falls on his knees!

(YURANOSUKE *bursts onto the* hanamichi, *running frantically, all decorum cast aside. He wears a formal gray kimono, vest, and trousers pulled up for travel. Reaching the seven-three position, he sees his master in the midst of suicide. He reels, falls back, then slowly sinks to his knees.*)

ISHIDŌ: (*Rising.*) Is it Ōboshi Yuranosuke?
YURANOSUKE: It is. 60
ISHIDŌ: (*Urgently.*) Approach, approach quickly!

(YURANOSUKE *attempts to rise, but his legs will not function. He weeps unashamedly. To gain control of himself, he reaches inside the breast of his kimono to pull tight the inner cloth binding his waist. With great effort he pushes himself up from the floor and moves unsteadily to* HANGAN's *side. He falls to his knees and bows deeply.*)

NARRATOR: (*Chants.*) The men of Hangan, all, till now forbidden . . . but no longer! They come rushing in!

(Ten RETAINERS *enter swiftly from up right. They are barefooted and carry no swords. They fall to their knees in a row upstage and, following* YURANOSUKE's *lead, bow deeply to their master* HANGAN. YURANOSUKE's *eyes remain downcast and* HANGAN, *in pain, does not yet look up.*)

YURANOSUKE: Ōboshi Yuranosuke kneels before my lord.
HANGAN: (*Weakly.*) Yuranosuke? 65
YURANOSUKE: I am here.
HANGAN: At last you've come.
YURANOSUKE: All that I could ever ask is to be at your side in these last moments . . .
HANGAN: Ah, it makes me content as well. (*Slowly their gazes* 70
meet.) You have heard, have you not . . . everything . . . everything . . . ?

(*His voice trails off in pain.* YURANOSUKE *edges closer, looking meaningfully at* HANGAN.)

YURANOSUKE: Yes!
HANGAN: (*Rousing himself.*) I am humiliated . . . !
YURANOSUKE: (*Interrupting.*) No words can express such feelings 75
as I hold. Nothing remains now but for me to assure you a just end.
HANGAN: (*Meaningfully.*) One thing remains.
NARRATOR: (*Chants.*) Gripping tight the blade, cutting straight across in disembowelment. (*Sings.*) Such moments of 80
agony . . . exhaling his breath . . .

(HANGAN *cuts his stomach across from left to right. Although the pain is excruciating and his lips tremble and his breathing grows labored,* HANGAN *maintains the stoic decorum expected of a samurai until the blade reaches its final point just under the right ribs. Then breath seems to leave him. His body sags. He braces his left hand on his thigh.*)

HANGAN: (*Faintly.*) Yuranosuke . . . Yuranosuke . . . come
close . . .
YURANOSUKE: Yes.

(HANGAN *is near death.* YURANOSUKE *slides forward urgently.
Knowing* HANGAN *cannot speak openly because the shogun's envoys are present, he searches his master's face for some command.*)

85 HANGAN: Take this blade . . . to remind you . . . do not forget.
Re-ve-n . . . (YURANOSUKE *starts.* HANGAN *must not say
"revenge" out loud.* HANGAN *catches himself.*) . . . remember me.

(*Weakly* HANGAN *looks into* YURANOSUKE's *face, then down the*
hanamichi. YURANOSUKE *follows* HANGAN's *gaze. Master and
retainer look deeply into each other's eyes.* YURANOSUKE *understands that in spite of his master's seeming calm acceptance of the
death sentence,* HANGAN *passionately desires vengeance against
the enemy outside the mansion, that is,* MORONAO.)

YURANOSUKE: (*Passionately.*) I swear!

(YURANOSUKE *slaps his chest for emphasis and bows deeply.*
HANGAN *knows that* YURANOSUKE *understands. He is now free to
die. He smiles.*)

HANGAN: Ha ha. Ha ha. Ha, ha, ha, ha . . .

(*The laugh fades. With ebbing strength,* HANGAN *pulls the blade
from his stomach. He gasps.*)

90 NARRATOR: (*Chants.*) Aiming the blade at his throat . . . one slash
across. Breathing his last breath, lifeless he crumples.

(*Weakened hands, trembling violently, lift the blade upward. He
tilts his head. His neck is exposed. A quick slash and the jugular
vein is cut. His body rises upward in three spasms of breath. His
eyes flutter closed. He falls limply forward, dead. Silently* ISHIDŌ
rises. A STAGE ASSISTANT *whisks his stool offstage.* ISHIDŌ *places
the shogun's letter on his open fan and places them on* HANGAN's
body. He moves stage right and kneels beside YURANOSUKE.)

ISHIDŌ: (*Quietly.*) Yuranosuke, Yakushiji now assumes authority
over Hangan's estates. Hangan's retainers are hereby denied
the rank of samurai and are disbanded. I will report to the
95   shogun that the death of Hangan is accomplished. You have
my deepest sympathy, Yuranosuke.
NARRATOR: (*Sings.*) Ishidō, the envoy, expresses sympathy. His
sad assignment is over.

(ISHIDŌ *rises facing the line of* RETAINERS. *He raises his arms in a
gesture of condolence. The* RETAINERS *look up, then bow respectfully. Slowly* ISHIDŌ *walks to the seven-three position on the*
hanamichi. *At a signal from* YURANOSUKE, RIKIYA *moves forward
to see him out.* ISHIDŌ *turns back.*)

ISHIDŌ: There is no need. There is no need.
100 NARRATOR: He prays silently.

(ISHIDŌ *folds his hands and, with downcast eyes, walks slowly
down the* hanamichi *and out of sight.*)

NARRATOR: (*Chants.*) Yakushiji holds them in contempt!

(YAKUSHIJI *rises brusquely. The* STAGE ASSISTANT *takes away his stool.*)

YAKUSHIJI: Now that he's dead, I'm master here! Cart the corpse
away, while I settle in. Show me the way! (*He starts to go, then
turns back.*) It's a sad time, isn't it! Ha, ha, ha, ha!

(YAKUSHIJI *strides off left, shown out by a* RETAINER. *Complete
silence.* YURANOSUKE *moves in to attend to his master's body. He
straightens the legs and brings kimono and vest up over the torso.
He moves closer and tries to take the dagger from* HANGAN's *hand.
In death* HANGAN's *fingers hold it tightly.* YURANOSUKE *falls back
weeping. He gently massages his master's hand until the fingers are
warmed, softened, and the dagger slips from their grasp.* YURANO-
SUKE *places the dagger carefully into the breast of his kimono. He
backs away. He and the* RETAINERS *bow expectantly.*)

NARRATOR: (*Singing plaintively.*) Lady Kaoyo enters from another   105
room. Her hair so long and black, oh, so beautiful, now
pitiful, it is no more. She will pray as a nun, till her end.

(KAOYO *and four* LADIES-IN-WAITING *enter from the left, walking
with downcast eyes. They are dressed in pure white kimono and
hold Buddhist rosaries. The last* LADY-IN-WAITING *carries a small
tray on which rests the cloth-wrapped remains of* KAOYO's *long
hair. They kneel left. The* MAIDS *bow deeply.*)

KAOYO: (*Quietly.*) Yuranosuke. When I think of why my husband
had to die, and that I was the cause . . .
YURANOSUKE: (*Firmly.*) My lady, please understand our   110
heartfelt feelings. All of us, each retainer offers his deepest
condolence.

(YURANOSUKE *bows to* KAOYO, *then nods to* GOEMON. GOEMON
and the RETAINERS *rise and move in a circle around their master.
Silently, they take up the white cloth, the tatami mats, tray, and
sprigs of green. They exit upstage right.* HANGAN *moves off behind
the cloth. In an instant all sign of the suicide is removed.*)

KAOYO: Yuranosuke.
YURANOSUKE: Yes, my lady.
KAOYO: I offer my lock of hair.

(*The* LADY-IN-WAITING *places the tray with the hair center stage.*
YURANOSUKE *sees it and weeps.* KAOYO *turns to show her close-
cropped head.*)

NARRATOR: (*Prolonged, melancholy singing.*) Kaoyo is left behind,   115
her grief is so . . . o . . . o . . . She yearns to go to the temple . . .

(*She rises, as if to follow her husband, but* YURANOSUKE *stops her
with a commanding gesture.*)

YURANOSUKE: My lady!

(*She falls back weakly. A single* ki *clack. They move into a pose:*
YURANOSUKE *picks up the tray with one hand and forces her back
with the other;* KAOYO *faces front, lifts the rosary to her eyes, and sobs
silently.* Ki *clacks accelerate as the curtain is slowly walked closed.*)

SCENE III

Outer Gate

Two ki *clacks signal drum and flute to play "Toki no Taiko" ("Time Drum"). The curtain is pushed quickly open. The scene is outside the massive outer gate of* HANGAN's *mansion. No one is on stage.*

NARRATOR: (*Chanting rapidly.*) Farewell to Hangan. Now his body lies alone. The young retainers run back from the temple! They no longer can hold the shame inside!

(*To loud, accelerating* tsuke *beats,* RIKIYA *leads a band of* RETAINERS *onto the* hanamichi. *They urge each other on with shouts of "Kill them!" "They won't have our lord's mansion!" "We'll fight them!" "Lord Hangan was unjustly killed!" At the same time* YURANOSUKE *and* GOEMON *come out of a small door in the gate.* GOEMON *rushes up to the* RETAINERS *with outstretched arms, shouting, "Stop, stop!"* YURANOSUKE *roughly pushes* RIKIYA *to the ground.*)

YURANOSUKE: (*Furious.*) What, you too, Rikiya? What are you
5 thinking of, trying to attack the mansion? We are no longer samurai. We cannot fight Yakushiji's men. (*Drops to one knee, hand on the hilt of his short sword.*) If you do not stop, I shall commit seppuku on this very spot! Do you want to be my seconds, all of you?
10 RETAINERS: No, but master . . .
YURANOSUKE: (*Implacably.*) Then will you stop when I tell you?
RETAINERS: Yes, but . . .
YURANOSUKE: It will achieve nothing to die now!

(*The* RETAINERS *cannot disobey. Grumbling and rebellious, they begin to fall back.*)

NARRATOR: (*Chants.*) Behind the gate is heard . . . Yakushiji's
15 voice!
YAKUSHIJI: (*Off.*) Hey, men, there's a sight. Newly hatched ex-samurai, milling around like chickens with their heads cut off! It's enough to make you laugh!
YAKUSHIJI'S MEN: (*Off.*) Ha, ha, ha, ha, ha!
20 FIRST RETAINER: Do you . . .
RETAINERS: . . . hear that?

(*Furious, they turn to storm the gate, hands on the hilts of their swords.* YURANOSUKE *springs into their path and blocks the way.*)

YURANOSUKE: Have you forgotten our late lord?
RETAINERS: No, but . . .
YURANOSUKE: Not now! Go back, go back! Go back I tell you!

(YURANOSUKE *draws himself up commandingly. He runs his hand up the edge of his vest and poses in a furious* mie. *Two* tsuke *beats.*)

25 NARRATOR: (*Sings.*) "Go back," he commands!
YURANOSUKE: (*Almost in a scolding tone now.*) Back, back, back.

(YURANOSUKE *waves them away. They fall back grudgingly, then turn and stride off down the* hanamichi. YURANOSUKE *watches them leave. He is alone. Silence. He sighs with relief. The hand at his breast slides down until it accidentally touches the dagger. He slowly drops to his knees and takes it out. He unwraps the covering purple cloth. The blade tip is red with* HANGAN's *blood.*)

NARRATOR: (*Sings.*) The suicide blade, red with blood, cries out for revenge . . . cries out for revenge! Burning tears rake his heart, tears . . . falling . . . falling . . . falling . . . falling . . .

(*Gazing at the blade,* YURANOSUKE's *chest heaves. He covers his eyes to hide the tears.*)

Hangan's last words of vengeance imbedded deep in   30
Yuranosuke. (*Chanting.*) We know indeed the motive of Yuranosuke, his revenge to be noted for many ages . . . forty-seven loyal men immortalized!

(*He wipes blood from the blade onto his palm and then deliberately brings his hand up to his mouth. He licks the blood as an oath of vengeance. Music stops. Silence.* YURANOSUKE *begins his long pantomime of departure. He carefully wraps the dagger in the purple cloth. He holds it to his forehead respectfully. He places it in the breast of his kimono. He rises and stands. He slaps the dust from his knees. He adjusts his trousers. He folds both hands inside his kimono sleeves. He rests his hands on the hilts of his swords. He half-closes his eyes, regretting deeply that he must abandon his master's mansion. A temple bell tolls in the distance. Pensively, he begins to walk away from the gate. The gate recedes, indicating* YURANOSUKE *has covered a long distance. He turns back. A crow caws in the distance. He resumes the painful separation. A crow caws a second time. A second bell tolls. He stops, stricken with the finality of parting. Then, he moves onto the* hanamichi. *Once more he turns back and, as if he has no heart to continue, slides to his knees. A temple bell tolls. Plaintive, tentative chords of the* samisen *begin. He rises, begins to walk away, looks sadly over his shoulder for one last glimpse, then resolutely turns and strides down the* hanamichi *and out of sight. Music crescendoes and* ki *clacks accelerate: the curtain is run closed. Drum and flute play rapid "Shagiri" to end the scene.*)

ACT THREE

SCENE I

Ichiriki Brothel

Two ki *clacks: the curtain is pushed open to offstage singing of "Hana ni Asobaba" ("If You Play in the Flowers"). The scene is the Ichiriki Brothel in the Gion licensed quarter in Kyoto. Two pavilions are set in a garden. Lying on his side in the larger room, stage center, is* YURANOSUKE. *He is feigning sleep, his face covered with a half-open fan. He wears an elegant purple kimono and matching cloak. Curtains are at the back and a stone water basin is left. Three steps lead down into the garden. Paper-covered sliding doors conceal the interior of the smaller pavilion, stage left. It is several feet higher off the ground than the center pavilion.*

NARRATOR: (*Singing briskly.*) The mountains and the moon. From the eastern mountains, just a few miles, breathless from running fast, the young man . . . Rikiya.

(RIKIYA *enters on the* hanamichi. *A purple scarf covers his head and serves as a partial disguise. His black kimono is hiked up at the sides, to free his legs for running. He stops at a garden gate set on the* hanamichi *at the seven-three position. He looks back to see if he is being observed, then swiftly passes through the gate, closing it.*)

Entering the brothel garden . . . there lies Yuranosuke,
5   pretending to be drunk. Taking caution to wake his father in
secrecy, he walks softly in, stepping close to him. The sword
guard speaks!

(RIKIYA *sees his father. He mounts the steps, kneels, and makes a
ringing sound by striking sword guard against sheath.* YURANO-
SUKE *gestures* RIKIYA *away with a sleepy movement of the fan.*
RIKIYA *crosses swiftly back through the gate, closes it, looks around
to be certain they are not being observed, and kneels to wait for
his father. Offstage samisen play tentative chords.* YURANOSUKE
*rises. He staggers as if drunk, ad-libbing, "That was heady wine. I
need some air. Don't go away, girls. I'll be in the garden." He looks
through the curtains to see if anyone is watching. He crosses to the
gate, stumbling several times in order to have the chance to look
carefully in all directions. He stands swaying, fan before his face.
He speaks guardedly.*)

YURANOSUKE: Rikiya, do I hear the sound of urgency in the echo
   of your sword?
10 RIKIYA: Yes, Father. I bring a secret message from Lady Kaoyo.
   (RIKIYA *brings out a letter from his right sleeve and passes it
to* YURANOSUKE, *who puts it immediately into the breast of his
kimono without examining it.*)
YURANOSUKE: (*Carefully.*) Did she say anything to you?
15 RIKIYA: (*Rising on his knees urgently.*) Soon, soon our enemy . . .
YURANOSUKE: Rikiya! "Soon at night our enemy, flees like plovers
   o'er the sea. . . ."

(*Music swells. To cover the slip of his son's tongue,* YURANOSUKE
*sings a well-known passage from a now play. He staggers in a circle
looking to see if anyone has heard* RIKIYA's *remark. Simultaneously,*
RIKIYA *pivots in the opposite direction, looking for eavesdroppers.*
YURANOSUKE *gestures for* RIKIYA *to come closer;* RIKIYA *whispers*
KAOYO's *message in his father's ear. The curtains in the room center
part.* KUDAYŪ *peeks out. He is a gray-haired former retainer of*
HANGAN, *now secretly working for* MORONAO. *He wears a plain
brown kimono and cloak. He watches for a moment, then slips
away.*)

YURANOSUKE: Send a palanquin for me tonight. Tell the others to
   be ready. Go, go!
20 NARRATOR: (*Sings.*) No time left for hesitation . . . to the eastern
   hills, homeward now . . .

(YURANOSUKE *sharply gestures with the fan.* RIKIYA *bows, rises,
and holding firmly onto the hilts of his swords, begins to leave.*)

YURANOSUKE: Rikiya!
RIKIYA: (*Returning and bowing.*) Yes.
YURANOSUKE: Be careful while passing through the quarter.
25   Then hurry! Go now!
RIKIYA: Yes!
NARRATOR: Rikiya returns home.

(RIKIYA *realizes his mistake; he is holding his swords ready to
draw, thus calling attention to himself. He hides the hilts with his
sleeves. Swiftly, carefully, he hurries down the hanamichi out of
sight. Offstage samisen play "Odoriji Aikata" ("Dance Melody").
Four* MAIDS *and a male* JESTER *enter through the curtain, ad-
libbing, "Yura, where are you?" "Come drink with us." "Don't leave
us, Yura."* YURANOSUKE *pretends drunkenness again.*)

FIRST MAID: Yura, Yura, are you here?
YURANOSUKE: Hmm. You've come to get me? I'm a lucky man.
   Come close all of you, let's amuse ourselves. Come, sing and   30
   dance for me.

(YURANOSUKE *sits on the steps. The* MAIDS *and the* JESTER *kneel in
the garden in a semicircle around him.*)

SECOND MAID: Very well . . .
ALL: . . . let's begin, let's begin!

(*Lilting music of offstage* samisen, *drum, and bell accompanies
various dances and songs. These are extemporized by the performers from production to production.* MAIDS *and* JESTER *ad-lib comic
banter throughout.*)

MAIDS: (*Clapping as they sing.*) "What will it be like, what will it
   be like? If you don't be careful, we will make you drink. Ah,   35
   what will it be like, what will it be like?"

(JESTER *and* THIRD MAID *rise and move center. They do a game of
jan-ken-po, "scissors-paper-stone." He loses. She laughingly pushes
him. He falls in a heap on the ground. The* MAIDS *rise and form pairs.*)

FOURTH MAID: Come, let's dance!
ALL: "First your left foot, then your right, tap, tap, tap;
   Around we go, back again;
   Are you ready, one, two, three!"   40

(*They circle left, then right, touching palms of their outstretched
hands. They turn their backs to each other and bump bottoms on
the count of three. With peals of laughter they recover their balance. The* JESTER *and* YURANOSUKE *laugh and applaud.*)

YURANOSUKE: Very good, very good!
FIRST MAID: How about a game, Yura dear?
JESTER: Blind man's bluff!
SECOND MAID: You be It!
ALL: Yes, yes!   45

(YURANOSUKE *tries to wave them away, but they playfully surround him and put a cloth over his eyes. They twirl him around in
the center of the garden, and move left, laughing and clapping in
time to their song.*)

ALL: "Yura, Yura, over here;
   Listen to our clapping hands."
YURANOSUKE: (*Sings.*) "I'll catch you all, soon enough you'll see."

(*He stumbles in their direction. They easily avoid his outstretched
arms and flee to the other side of the garden.*)

ALL: "Yura, Yura over here;
   Come and catch us if you can."   50
YURANOSUKE: "I'll catch you all, and make you drink with me."

(*They duck under his arms. When he turns back to continue
pursuit, they take him by the hands and, still singing and clapping,
lead him off to the inner room with his blindfold still in place. They
are no sooner off than* KUDAYŪ's *head pops through the curtain
on the other side of the stage. Samisen music stops.* KUDAYŪ *peers
about intently. He slips into the room.*)

KUDAYŪ: That letter Rikiya gave to Yuranosuke . . . the rumor of a vendetta must be true! He has not forgotten; they are plotting, just as I thought. When I tell Moronao, what will be my great
55 reward? If, of course, it's true. I'll spy him out! Here's a perfect place to hide.

(*He sees a hiding place. He removes a board under the veranda, opening a space for him to crawl in. He hides behind the steps.* YURANOSUKE *enters alone from upstage, pretending to be drunk.*)

YURANOSUKE: I'll be back . . . don't wait, girls . . . in a minute, I'll be back.

(Samisen *music resumes. He looks around. Seeing he is alone, he drops his pretense. He rinses his mouth with water from the stone basin. He spits it out. It falls on the unsuspecting* KUDAYŪ. *He takes out the letter from* KAOYO *and holds it respectfully to his forehead. He begins to read, slowly unrolling the letter until it reaches the ground. At the same time the paper doors slide open to reveal* OKARU *in the small room left. She wears the elaborate hairstyle and clinging kimono of a courtesan.*)

NARRATOR: (*Sings.*) Evening breeze, brings a courtesan, Kampei's
60 wife Okaru, away from her love. Someone has sent a love letter, "I wish it were for me." Okaru from a room above, tries to see the words. Too far in the evening dusk, the letters are not clear to read. Thinking of a way out, a mirror in her hand, she leans back . . . mirror held up high, reflection of the letter.
65 Under the floor a spy, Kudayū waits . . . the trailing letter glows in the moonlight. (*Chants.*) Who could know someone is reading words of confidence?

(*The three form a tableau:* YURANOSUKE *is engrossed in reading the secret letter;* OKARU *views the letter backwards in a mirror; and* KUDAYŪ, *spectacles on his nose, reads the bottom portion, line-by-line, as it comes down to him. Narrative shifts to singing.*)

Okaru, unaware that her hairpin has loosened! (*Chants.*) It drops to the floor! Surprised by the sound above, he
70 quickly hides the letter . . . Yuranosuke! Underneath Kudayū smirking at his game. (*Sings.*) Okaru pretends nothing has happened here.

(YURANOSUKE *quickly resumes his drunken role. He begins to roll up the letter, but not before* KUDAYŪ *rips off the part he has been reading.* OKARU *puts down the mirror, picks up a fan, and turns to* YURANOSUKE.)

OKARU: (*Languidly.*) Yura dear, is it you?
75 YURANOSUKE: Hmm, Okaru? So close at hand, what are you doing?
OKARU: (*In poetic form of seven and five syllables.*) Yura dear, it's all your fault, I drank too much wine; my head is whirling round and I can scarcely see; I have come to sober up, wafted by the evening breeze.

(YURANOSUKE *reaches the end of the letter. He feels the ragged edge. Startled, he looks quickly at the letter, then puts it away in the breast of his kimono. He takes out a piece of tissue paper and wads it up, covering his action by improvising conversation with* OKARU.)

80 YURANOSUKE: Hmm. Wafted by the evening breeze, you say? Wafted by the evening breeze? Ah!

(*He drops the wad of paper to the ground.* KUDAYŪ, *thinking it is part of the letter, snatches it and stuffs it into his kimono breast.* YURANOSUKE *falls back, supposedly in a drunken stupor, but actually wanting to ponder what to do next. He decides. Soft* samisen *plays "Odoriji Aikata" in the background.*)

Hm. Okaru, there is something I want to talk to you about. Come over here.
OKARU: (*Rises as if to leave her room.*) Very well, I'll come around
and visit you. 85
YURANOSUKE: (*Coming down into the garden.*) No, Okaru, if you go that way the maids will catch you. They will force on you more wine. Ah, a ladder. Fortune smiles. Climb down this way and you won't be seen. (*Places a ladder against* OKARU's *pavilion. Bantering.*) Descend for me, Okaru! 90
OKARU: (*Coquettishly on the ladder.*) I've never climbed a ladder before.
YURANOSUKE: You've climbed other things.
OKARU: I'm not used to this strange position. It frightens me.
YURANOSUKE: You're past the age to be afraid of a new position. 95 Straddle it, open your legs, it'll all go smoothly.
OKARU: Don't be naughty, Yura. I tell you it frightens me. It's swaying like a boat.
YURANOSUKE: Never mind, I'll throw in my anchor. That will hold you down. Where shall I put it? (*He tries to lift her skirt* 100 *with his fan. She brushes his hand away.*)
OKARU: You mustn't peek, Yura.
YURANOSUKE: (*Singing.*) "I adore your crescent moon, glistening in its secret grotto." Ha, ha, ha.
OKARU: (*Pouting.*) If you talk that way, I won't come down. 105
YURANOSUKE: Don't prattle like a virgin. You're a courtesan in the Gion brothel. I'll take you from behind. (YURANOSUKE *embraces her from behind.*)
OKARU: Oh, stop it.
YURANOSUKE: Then come, come. 110
OKARU: I am, I am!

(*Laughing, she slips off the final rung of the ladder and moves away from* YURANOSUKE. *She kneels right, fanning herself.* YURANOSUKE *glances at her sharply, then resumes the drunken pose. He stoops to retrieve the dropped hairpin and crosses to give it to her.*)

YURANOSUKE: (*Casually.*) Just now, Okaru, did something catch your eye?
OKARU: I . . . nothing.
YURANOSUKE: (*Coaxing.*) Come now, didn't you see, didn't you 115 see . . .
OKARU: . . . your interesting letter . . .
YURANOSUKE: . . . from up above?
OKARU: (*Lightly.*) Hmm, yes.
YURANOSUKE: And you read it all? 120
OKARU: Oh, you do go on.

(*Covering his concern, he pretends to stumble. He recovers his balance, singing a nou song which both hides and expresses his feelings.*)

YURANOSUKE: "Fate conspires to bring, my life to this crisis. . . ." (*Mimes striking a* nō *drum.*) Ya, tum, tum, tum! Ha, ha, ha!
OKARU: (*Turns to him, laughing.*) What in the world do you mean? 125
YURANOSUKE: It means that of all the women in the world, I have become enamored of you. Come live with me, Okaru.
OKARU: Stop it. You're such a tease!

YURANOSUKE: (*Grandiloquently.*) I will redeem your contract
130   with the master of the brothel and take you away.
OKARU: I don't believe it. You're making fun of me.
YURANOSUKE: I'll prove it's not a lie. Be my mistress for just three
       days, and after that, Okaru, your spirit will be free to go where
       it will.
135 OKARU: (*Taking him seriously for the first time.*) For three days?
YURANOSUKE: On my sacred oath as a samurai. Live with me for
       three days. I'll find the master and buy your contract now.
       Well, is it agreed?

(OKARU *looks carefully at him to see if it possibly can be true. They
pose. She bows low.*)

OKARU: I am grateful, Yuranosuke.
140 YURANOSUKE: Can it make you happy to be redeemed . . . by this
       Yuranosuke?
OKARU: Oh, yes!
YURANOSUKE: Such radiance shines in that happy face.

(*They pose: she looks at him with gratitude; flicking open his fan,
he covers his face to hide his stricken expression.*)

YURANOSUKE: Don't go away now. I'll be right back.
145 OKARU: Three days? Yes, Yuranosuke. I'll be here.

(*Offstage, sad "Yo ni mo Inga" ["Nighttime Fate"] is sung quietly.
They lightly ad-lib to cover his exit. Still pretending to be drunk,
he staggers up the steps. He turns back several times. He passes
through the curtains in search of the master of the house. When he
is gone she kneels center stage, trembling with excitement.*)

OKARU: How happy I am! I must write to dearest Kampei that
       I am coming home! And to Mother and Father, to tell the
       wonderful news!

(*She hurries up the steps into the center room, brings out a writing
box and roll of letter paper, kneels, and begins to write a letter
home. Song ends.*)

NARRATOR: (*Chants.*) Now appears . . . Heiemon!

(*Offstage* samisen *briskly play "Odoriji Aikata." A young samurai
strides on from the right into the garden. His hair is severely
drawn back and his plain kimono suggests poverty. It is* HEIEMON,
OKARU's *older brother, in search of both* YURANOSUKE *and* OKARU.
*He looks around, then seeing a woman in the room, enters and sits
behind her. He speaks brusquely, almost rudely.*)

150 HEIEMON: Sorry to trouble you, Miss, but I am looking for a
       young woman, from my hometown of Yamazaki, by the
       name of Okaru, brought here a year ago . . .

(*Hearing her name* OKARU *turns. They recognize each other.*)

       Sister!
OKARU: Heiemon! Oh! I feel ashamed for you to see me here!

(OKARU's *demeanor completely changes: in the presence of a male
family member who is her elder, she becomes submissive, gentle,
a little girl seeking approbation. She hides her face. She rushes
down the steps, and falls to her knees.* HEIEMON, *though stern, acts
protectively toward her. He rises and poses on the steps.*)

HEIEMON: What is there to feel ashamed of? When I returned   155
       home Mother told me you had sold yourself to this brothel,
       hoping that with your contract price Kampei could
       contribute to the vendetta against Lord Hangan's enemy.
       You have willingly sacrificed yourself for your husband
       and for Lord Hangan. I am proud of you, Okaru!   160

(*He poses at the top of the steps: right foot forward, right
arm extended protectively in her direction.*)

OKARU: (*Hesitantly, looks up at him.*) Then you're not going to
       scold me?
HEIEMON: Scold you? I am filled with admiration, filled with   165
       admiration!

(*He crosses down the steps and kneels. He sits proudly, sword
placed on the ground beside him.*)

OKARU: I'm happy that you think kindly of me. (*Becoming
       excited.*) Oh, there are so many things I want to ask my dear
       big brother. I don't know where to begin . . . how is Kam . . .
HEIEMON: (*Uneasy.*) Kam . . . ?   170

(OKARU *is embarrassed to have asked about her husband first. She
changes the subject.*)

OKARU: Come . . . tell me, how is Mother?
HEIEMON: Set your mind at ease. Mother is well.
OKARU: And Father? Nothing troubles him, I hope?
HEIEMON: (*Uncomfortably.*) Hm . . . Father . . . he is at rest . . .   175
       he is at rest.
OKARU: (*Modestly.*) And what of Kampei?
HEIEMON: Kampei? Ah . . . well . . . he is as well as can be.
OKARU: You set my heart at ease. (*Bubbling.*) Oh, I forgot. . .
       be happy for me, Brother. Tonight, without warning,
       Yuranosuke offered to buy out my contract.   180
HEIEMON: Yuranosuke did that? (*Trying to understand how such a
       thing could be.*) Ah, then he's become your patron?
OKARU: Nonsense. We have only drunk together two or three
       times. And Heiemon, it's almost too good to be true. After
       three days he will let me come home.   185
HEIEMON: Hm? Then you told him you are Kampei's wife?
OKARU: How could I, a prostitute, tell him that and bring disgrace
       to Kampei and to my parents?
HEIEMON: (*Facing front.*) Hm! Then he is no more than a
       whoremaster! (*He slaps his thigh in anger.*) He has no intention   190
       of avenging Hangan, our lord and master!
OKARU: Oh, no, Brother, he has. He has. Listen . . .
NARRATOR: (*Sings.*) In whispers, the content of the letter is
       revealed.

(OKARU *and* HEIEMON *rise. He leans forward. She whispers in his
ear. They pose for a moment, then break apart and kneel.*)

OKARU: . . . so you see?   195
HEIEMON: (*Shocked.*) Then you read it all?
OKARU: Yes, and after reading it, his eye met mine, and flirting,
       he looked me up and down, up and down, and then began to
       talk of taking me away.

(OKARU *mimes his flirting by pressing the backs of her index fingers
together, right on top of left, then left on top of right.* HEIEMON *is
puzzled. He tries to understand her words, miming as she did.*)

200 HEIEMON: What? After reading it, flirting, he looked you up and
      down, up and down . . . (*He slaps his thigh for emphasis.*) Ah!
      Now I understand!
   OKARU: (*Laughing.*) You startled me.
   HEIEMON: (*Facing the inner room, he bows low.*) Forgive me, Mas-
205   ter Yuranosuke, I misjudged you! I was wrong, forgive me!
   OKARU: Dearest Brother, what in the world are you doing?
   HEIEMON: (*Turns and looks into* OKARU's *eyes.*) Dear Sister.
      There is something I must ask of you. Okaru, do now exactly
      as I say.
210 OKARU: You sound so very stiff and formal. What must you ask
      of me?
   HEIEMON: What I must ask of you is . . .
   OKARU: What you must ask of me is . . . ?
   HEIEMON: Okaru, let your brother take your life!

(*He springs to his feet and whips out his long sword. She falls back.
Rapid "Odoriji Aikata." To double beats of the* tsuke, *he slashes at
her right, left, right. She avoids. She rises and pushes him away.
He turns to strike; she distracts him with a shower of tissue paper
drawn from her breast and thrown in the air. She runs to the
hanamichi; he follows. She closes the gate between them. They pose
in a mie to two loud tsuke beats: on the ground, she holds up her
hands imploringly; he stands with legs together, the sword directly
overhead as if to strike. Music stops.*)

215 OKARU: (*Appealing to him.*) What am I supposed to have done
      wrong? You have no right to just do as you please. I have my
      husband and both my parents to care for. Forgive me if I have
      spoken out of turn. I clasp my hands and beg you to spare me!
220 NARRATOR: (*Sings.*) Seeing his sister's clasped hands . . . a
      brother's love overwhelms the dutiful heart. He can only cry.

(*He tries to but cannot strike his sister. He falls back distraught,
turns upstage to face away from her, holds the sword behind his
back, and weeps unashamedly. When the narration is finished, he
turns to face* OKARU. *He is contrite. Slow offstage "Odoriji Aikata"
resumes in the background.*)

HEIEMON: I was wrong, Okaru, not to explain. Come, come over
      here.

(*He waves her to him. She flounces.*)

OKARU: No, I will not come near you.
225 HEIEMON: (*Sternly.*) When your elder brother calls, why don't
      you come?
   OKARU: (*Sweetly.*) If you want to know, I'll tell you why: I think
      you still intend to kill me, and I don't like that at all!

(HEIEMON *notices the long sword in his hand. He puts it on the
ground and pushes it toward her.*)

HEIEMON: Ah, this. There is nothing to stop you now. So come,
230   come!
   OKARU: Yes, there is. Something else.

(*She points at the short sword in his sash. Annoyed, he pushes it
toward her.*)

HEIEMON: There, now. Come over here!

(*She rises and is about to cross through the gate. She looks at him
and stops.*)

OKARU: Your face is so frightening.
HEIEMON: I can't help that. This is the face I was born with.
OKARU: Well then, please turn around.   235
HEIEMON: What a nuisance. Like this? Like this?

(*Grumbling, he turns his back. He poses with arms stretched out to
either side.*)

OKARU: Now, don't look. Keep your face turned away. (*She
      cautiously goes through the gate, picks up the swords, and
      puts them out of his reach. She kneels behind him, placing her
      hands on his sash. Music stops. She poses.*) All right, here I am. 240
      Brother dear, what is it you want? (*He turns to face her. He
      places his hands protectively on her shoulders. They pose.*)
   HEIEMON: (*Voice filled with emotion, he speaks in poetic form
      of seven and five syllables.*) Once you were a samurai, now a
      courtesan; combing out your silken hair, while the world has   245
      changed; precious Sister how pitiful, totally unaware of the
      life you left behind!

(HEIEMON *breaks away and kneels left.* OKARU *moves close.*)

OKARU: Totally unaware . . . of what, Heiemon?
HEIEMON: Soon after you left home last year, one rainy night,
      Father was . . .   250
   OKARU: (*Frightened.*) Father was . . . ?
   HEIEMON: (*Choked scream.*) . . . struck down by a robber and slain
      by his sword!
   OKARU: (*Falls back slackly.*) That cannot be true.
   HEIEMON: You must be strong, Okaru. You look forward to   255
      leaving here and being with your husband . . .
   OKARU: Yes . . . Kampei . . . what about Kampei?
   HEIEMON: Kampei . . .
   OKARU: Kampei . . . ?
   HEIEMON: (*A terrible scream.*) Cut open his stomach and is dead! 260

(*He mimes the suicide and collapses, weeping.* OKARU *falls back,
shocked, hardly able to breathe.*)

OKARU: Kampei . . . oh . . . no. What shall I do? What shall
      I do?
   HEIEMON: I know, I know, I know . . .

(*They speak alternately, then faster and faster, until they are speaking at the same time. Then their grief-stricken voices fade away.
OKARU crawls to her older brother and puts her head on his lap.
She weeps pitiably. At last* HEIEMON *gains control of himself. He
gently disengages himself.*)

HEIEMON: Don't you see? Yuranosuke is not a man to be
      infatuated, and he did not know you were Kampei's wife.   265
      Okaru, you were wrong to have read that secret letter.
      Yuranosuke's loyalty is clear. He cannot risk letting you
      live and he intends to buy your contract . . . just to kill you!
      Rather than dying at someone else's hand, let me be the
      one to take your life. Let me prove to Yuranosuke and his   270
      followers that though I am a mere foot soldier, my spirit is
      as loyal as theirs. Let me serve our late master. Give me your
      life, dear Sister!

NARRATOR: (*Sings.*) The tragedy is disclosed! Okaru is prepared!

(HEIEMON *is agonized by the conflict between his duty to* HANGAN *and his love for* OKARU. *He beseeches her with clasped hands.* OKARU *willingly prepares to sacrifice herself. Gently she opens his hands.*)

275 OKARU: It is my karma not to meet my beloved husband and father again. There is no reason for me to live.

(*She crosses to get the swords, returns, and places them before him.*)

Brother dear, please end my life now.

(*She turns her back, clasps her hands in prayer, and drops her head forward, exposing her neck to his sword.*)

HEIEMON: Admirable resolve. Namu Amida Butsu. Praise Buddha the Merciful.

(*He stands. He unsheaths the sword. He raises it to strike.* YURA-NOSUKE'*s voice is heard from behind the curtain.*)

280 YURANOSUKE: (*Off.*) Wait, wait! Stop at once! (*He enters.*) Your behavior is admirable, both of you. I acknowledge your loyalty. Heiemon, I hereby permit you to accompany us on our journey to the east.

(HEIEMON *and* OKARU *move right and kneel respectfully.* HEIEMON *is excited by* YURANOSUKE'*s acceptance of him into the vendetta group.*)

HEIEMON: Then you are ready? And I may go with you?
285 Okaru, Sister, do you hear? I am forever grateful.

(HEIEMON *bows to* YURANOSUKE. YURANOSUKE *comes down the steps.*)

YURANOSUKE: Okaru, for your loyalty, your husband, Kampei, will be admitted to our league. And since he was unable during his life to kill even a single enemy, let your action, Okaru, serve as his apology to Lord Hangan in the
290 afterlife . . . here and now . . .

(YURANOSUKE *takes* HEIEMON'*s long sword and places it in* OKARU'*s hands. He guides her to the veranda. They pose.*)

NARRATOR: (*Chants.*) Thrusting deep through the dark of the hiding place. The hateful spy, Kudayū, a fatal blow in his shoulder, rolls and turns in deadly pain!

(*They thrust the sword under the veranda. Double* tsuke *beats.* KUDAYŪ *cries out.* HEIEMON *drags the mortally wounded* KUDAYŪ *into the garden and throws him to the ground.* YURANOSUKE *kneels, and holding* KUDAYŪ *by the scruff of the neck, strikes furiously with closed fan.*)

YURANOSUKE: Kudayū, you wretch! Traitor! More than forty of
295 us day and night have shed tears of agony. We have parted from our children, deserted our parents, and sold our wives into prostitution all in order to avenge our Lord Hangan's

death. And you, who enjoyed wealth and honor in his service, have betrayed your master and become Moronao's spy! Fiend! Demon! You are a monster! 300

NARRATOR: (*Sings.*) As if to grind him into the ground, Yuranosuke . . . his burst of anger cannot be gratified!

(*He strikes him five times to sharp* tsuke *beats. Then contemptuously he pushes him away. Bringing his hand to his eyes,* YURA-NOSUKE *openly weeps. Just then the* MAIDS *cry out offstage. Rapid "Odoriji Aikata." Instantly* YURANOSUKE *reverts to his pose as a drunken brothel patron. He rises, staggering. The* MAIDS *enter and kneel in a semicircle in the center room.*)

FIRST MAID: Master Yuranosuke, Master Yuranosuke . . .
SECOND MAID: . . . your palanquin has arrived.
YURANOSUKE: You've come for me? 305
ALL: We will see you out.

(YURANOSUKE *crosses up the steps and stands at the top. He gestures for* OKARU *to join him there and for* HEIEMON *to pick up the nearly dead* KUDAYŪ. *Music stops.*)

YURANOSUKE: Heiemon. Take our drunken friend to the Kamo River. Let him drown his sorrows . . . in the waters there!

(YURANOSUKE *flicks open his fan and raises it overhead.* OKARU *kneels beside* YURANOSUKE, *placing her hands on his sash.* HEIEMON *drapes* KUDAYŪ'*s limp body over his shoulder. A single sharp clack of the* ki. *They freeze in a group* mie *pose. Ki clacks accelerate, drum beats speed up, and offstage "Odoriji Aikata" crescendoes as the curtain is slowly pushed closed.*)

SCENE II

Vendetta

Two sharp ki clacks: large drum softly beats "Yuki Oto" ("Snow Sound"). The ki clacks accelerate to accompany the opening of the curtain. The scene is the garden of MORONAO'*s mansion in Edo. It is night. Snow is falling. Rocks, trees, ground, and small bridge across a pond are covered with a mantle of white. Soft, rapid* tsuke *beats. Several* WOMEN *from* MORONAO'*s household rush on from the left. They are wearing nightclothes. Frightened and confused they urge each other to flee. They disappear. Drum and* tsuke *beats crescendo. Two* RETAINERS *with drawn swords rush on from the right. They pose.*

MORONAO'S RETAINER: I am Riku Handayū, retainer of Moronao. Name yourself!
HANGAN'S RETAINER: Akagaki Genzō, loyal to Enya Hangan. Let me pass!

(*They pose. Another two* RETAINERS *run on from the left.*)

MORONAO'S RETAINER: You will burn in hell before you touch 5
Lord Moronao!
HANGAN'S RETAINER: I, Katayama Genta, will take his head for Lord Hangan! Stand aside!

(*Large drum pattern of triple beats, "Mitsudaiko," and loud continuous* tsuke *beats. The paired opponents fight: they slash and parry with their long swords. In the end* HANGAN'*s men gain the upper hand;* MORONAO'*s men turn and are pursued off stage. Drumming changes to quiet "Snow Sound."* SHIMIZU *enters on the hanamichi. He is a famous swordsman hired by* MORONAO *as a bodyguard. A woman's kimono is draped over his head as a disguise, to allow him to reach the side of his master without being detained by* HANGAN'S *men. He stops at the seven-three position.)*

SHIMIZU: The war drum. Yuranosuke has come at last. But he will not succeed. The moon shall see the severed heads of forty-seven rōnin before it witnesses the death of Lord Moronao!

*(*SHIMIZU *rushes on stage. He meets* TAKEMORI, *one of* HANGAN'S *men. They circle each other warily.* SHIMIZU'S *swords are seen.)*

TAKEMORI: Stop! Who are you?

SHIMIZU: *(Dropping the kimono to his waist.)* I am Shimizu Ichigaku, protector of Lord Moronao.

TAKEMORI: And I am Takemori Kitahachi! I've come for Moronao's head!

SHIMIZU: Then you must take mine first.

TAKEMORI: Come, fight! Fight!

("Mitsudaiko" drumming, loud tsuke *beats, and "Chuwya Aikata"* samisen *music accompany the battle.* TAKEMORI *attacks, rushing past* SHIMIZU. SHIMIZU *throws tiny daggers at* TAKEMORI, *who falls to the ground to evade. One of* HANGAN'S *spearmen rushes on from the right, forcing* SHIMIZU *away from* TAKEMORI. SHIMIZU *is attacked from both sides. He slips free and runs onto the bridge over the pond. He is attacked by spear and sword simultaneously.* TAKEMORI *reaches under his guard and stabs* SHIMIZU *in the chest. A second slash, down his back, sends* SHIMIZU *toppling into the water of the pond and out of sight. Drum crescendoes. A loud whistle is heard off left. It signals* MORONAO'S *capture.* MORONAO *is dragged on by several of* HANGAN'S *men. He is thrown to the ground. He wears nothing except a white sleeping kimono. He is unarmed.* YURANOSUKE, RIKIYA, GOEMON, HEIEMON, *and other* RETAINERS *enter. They surround* MORONAO, *watching him carefully.* YURANOSUKE *kneels beside* MORONAO *politely.)*

YURANOSUKE: We allow you to die, Moronao, by your own hand . . . with this blade.

(He unwraps HANGAN'S *suicide dagger and respectfully places it before* MORONAO, *offering him the opportunity to die with honor,* *instead of being killed.* MORONAO *is shaking with fright. He picks up the dagger as if to kill himself, then lunges at* YURANOSUKE. *Seizing* MORONAO'S *wrist,* YURANOSUKE *turns the dagger against* MORONAO *and plunges it into his breast.* MORONAO *cries out once, then falls back dead. The* RETAINERS *form a ring around* MORONAO, *hiding him from view.* TAKEMORI *raises his sword and with a single stroke cuts off* MORONAO'S *head. Two loud* tsuke *beats. It is wrapped in a white cloth and held high at the end of a spear.* MORONAO *moves offstage unseen behind a black cloth held by a* STAGE ASSISTANT. *The* RETAINERS *rise triumphantly.)*

YURANOSUKE: You have fought bravely, all of you. Your years of hardship, endured without thought of self, have brought success to our cherished plan. What joy Lord Hangan's spirit must feel for your deeds. On his behalf I thank you.

GOEMON: And now, let us bring Moronao's head to our master!

(Spoken lightly, the lines are in poetic phrases of seven and five syllables.)

YURANOSUKE: Deep concerns like drifted snow, melt in the clear of day . . .

RIKIYA: . . . at last our long awaited, vengeance is achieved . . .

GOEMON: . . . together with the clearing, of the morning clouds . . .

AGAKI: . . . at the cock's crow announcing, dawn of a new day . . .

TAKEMORI: . . . our hearts filled to overflowing, rise with the rising sun . . .

GOEMON: . . . as we go together to . . .

ALL: . . . our Lord Hangan's grave.

YURANOSUKE: Shout victory together! Victory!

(Single ki *clack: offstage drum and samisen play "Taka no Hara" ("Hawk Plain") slowly, gradually accelerating until the scene is over. Each person turns to those next to him, nods, wipes tears of gratitude, grips an elbow, or places a hand on a shoulder. Then their thoughts return to their master,* HANGAN, *and all of them stand silent, posed in mingled happiness and grief. The curtain closes to rapidly accelerating* ki *clacks. The offstage musicians play "Shagiri" indicating the play is over.)*

CRITICAL CONTEXTS

ZEAMI MOTOKIYO (1363–1444)

from "A Mirror Held to the Flower" (1424)

Translated by J. THOMAS RIMER and YAMAZAKI MASAKAZU

Although Zeami's treatises describe the practical and esthetic foundations of the Noh (Nō) theater, they were not well known until the twentieth century. Since the Noh was organized around prominent families of actors, Zeami's texts were passed on in private and shown only to those who had been properly initiated. The first definitive edition of the treatises was published in 1940.

In "A Mirror Held to the Flower," Zeami discusses the training of Noh performers, emphasizing the interplay between physical training, spiritual development, and acting style in the production of the "flower"—beauty—in Noh performance. In this translation, the central term yugen has been translated as "Grace." Although Zeami's language can seem remote to modern students, it is important to pay attention to the ways his understanding of acting relates to the process of Noh drama. How would you relate the kind of skills and attention that Zeami describes here to the demands of Noh drama?

An actor must not only rehearse thoroughly with his teachers but he must learn through practice to imitate their peerless performances. Indeed, it is precisely because the art of these great performers has been brought to the highest levels of training that they can present in their acting an appearance of total mastery and ease, thus fascinating their audiences. If a beginner wishes merely to imitate this level of accomplishment, he may seem to achieve its semblance, yet there will be nothing moving in his performance. A truly great artist has for many years succeeded in training both his body and his spirit; he can hold back much of his potential in reserve and perform in an easy fashion, so that only seven-tenths of his art is visible. If a beginner tries to perform in this fashion, without the proper practice, he will only imitate what he can observe, and so his spirit and his performance can not reach beyond that seven-tenths he can grasp. What is more, his own progress will be blocked.

Therefore, when a student is learning his craft, the teacher should show not his own high level of ability [in which there is a reserve of artistry], but, as he did when he too was a beginner, indicate to his pupils how to use fully both their minds and bodies. After such lessons have been absorbed the students will gradually reach a level of mastery and attain a level of ease in their own performances, understand how to hold in reserve a certain amount of their own physical energy, and grasp of themselves the principle that "what is felt by the heart is ten, what appears in movement seven."

Understanding the Proper Meaning of Learning Our Art

In general, a performance of Perfect Fluency cannot be imitated. And if an actor makes an attempt to imitate it, the very effort involved in the attempt will produce a tension that cannot be a part of Perfect Fluency. Only something that is meant to appear difficult can actually be imitated. "The truth and what looks like it are two different things,"[1] it is said. Thus, could there be any way to imitate the truth of the master actor's easy performance? Indeed, ease and difficulty are two aspects of the same thing. There is a separate teaching on this matter. The means by which a student learns from a teacher are well known, and so no special comment is needed here. However, the teacher's official certification of the student must be based on a thorough examination of his capacities and devotion; otherwise, certification should not be given. If the student's basic abilities are insufficient, no certification is possible. Should certification be given when talent is lacking, a level of accomplishment is suggested that cannot actually be matched. The certification will be fraudulent and the results meaningless; therefore, it should not be given. In the *Book of Changes* it is written that "if suitable teachings are given to those who are not suitable, the hatred of Heaven will be aroused."[2] In order that such a suitable person can be created, three conditions must be present. First, he must possess himself the requisite talent. Secondly, he must adore his art and show a total dedication to the path of *Nō*. Thirdly, he must have a teacher capable of showing him the proper way. If these three conditions cannot be met, the candidate will not be suitable. A suitable person is one who has the capacity to achieve the highest reaches of his art, to be recognized himself as a teacher.

---

[1] A popular saying found in many texts circulated in this period.

[2] The quotation as recorded here does not appear in the *Book of Changes* (*I ching*).

When I observe the artistic abilities of young performers now, it appears that "skipping"[3] has become commonplace. This situation comes about because they imitate without study. An actor must begin by studying the Two Basic Arts and the Three Role Types, continue to practice all that is appropriate for his age, and carry on his studies in the proper sequence, so that he will reach a stage of mastery in all the arts of the Nō that can permit him to perform in any artistic style. To learn only by imitation and so only manage a temporary resolution seems indeed to represent a kind of "skipping." For example, when studying the Two Basic Arts, one must not study the Three Role Types. When the time comes to study the Three Role Types, one must put off for a certain time the study of military roles [as they demand intense physical effort]. When an actor does come to study the military roles, then the demon roles in both the Delicacy within Strength and Rough styles of movement should be put off for a certain time, since there is an appropriate moment to learn them as well. To attempt to learn all these roles at once—what a terribly difficult thing it would be. And the degree of difficulty would be unexpectedly high. Therefore, even if by "skipping" a young performer manages to fool the public into thinking that he is a master, he will achieve a momentary Flower. And as such an artist grows older, his art will decline. And even should his art not decline, it would be impossible for him to achieve true renown. This point must be firmly kept in mind.

Concerning "skipping," there is another matter to consider. If an actor is inordinately fond of new plays, and should he come step by step to abandon the older repertory he performed in the past, he can never master the art of Nō and will only be "skipping." Rather, the actor must fix a repertory of standard plays at which he excels and then mix new plays in with them. If he plays only fresh pieces and neglects the plays to which he is accustomed, the results, in terms of the art of the Nō, will be a disgraceful "skipping" indeed. Besides, if only unusual pieces are performed, then that procedure of itself loses its novelty. If a mixture of old and new is achieved, then both the old and the new alike will seem novel. Such becomes the undying flower. As Confucius said, "He who by reanimating the Old can gain knowledge of the New is fit to be a teacher."[4]

Having a Real Understanding of Skill

If an actor has become fully proficient at music and dance, he may be called skillful. If he has not become fully accomplished, there will be no denying his shortcomings. On the other hand, there is a kind of real skill based on still different considerations. For example, there are actors whose abilities in dance and chant show no shortcomings, yet who have not achieved a high reputation. Then again, there are actors whose voices are not attractive and whose mastery of dancing and singing show defects, yet who are widely thought of as accomplished performers. The reason for this is that both dancing and gesture are external skills. The essentials of our art lie in the spirit. They represent a true enlightenment established through art. Thus, if an actor knows how to create interest and can perform from an understanding of this spirit, he will gain a reputation as a fine actor even if he has not mastered every aspect of his craft. Such being the case, if an actor really wants to become a master, he cannot simply depend on his skill in dance and gesture. Rather, mastery seems to depend on the actor's own state of self-understanding and the sense of style with which he has been blessed. Real discernment of the nature of the differences between external skill and interior understanding forms the basis of true mastery. Thus it is that an actor who has merely perfected his technique will have little of interest to show. Other actors, from the beginning of their careers, can fascinate their audiences. So it is that an actor, from the time he is young until he masters seven-tenths, eight-tenths, even all of his technique and reaches the level of a master, will continue to interest others for quite separate considerations.

Still higher than the level of interest, there is a level of skill that will simply make the audience gasp, without reflection, in surprise and pleasure. This level will be termed one of a pure Feeling that Transcends Cognition. The response to such a performance is such that there is no occasion for reflection, no time for a spectator to realize how well the performance is contrived. Such a state might be referred to as "purity unmixed."[5] In the *Book of Changes,* when the Chinese character for "feeling" (kan) is written, the element that stands for "mind" (kokoro) is eliminated [and the character is written as] in order to illustrate the fact that when true feeling is involved, there is no room in the concept for reflection as a function of the mind.[6]

Thus it is that the actor comes to possess various levels of artistic skill. If a beginning actor continues on through all the various stages of his training, he will be called a good actor, but not necessarily anything more. Yet there is still a higher level where real mastery is possible. If

---

[3]"Skipping" (tendoku) was a term originally used to mean "turning the sutras," chanting the first few lines and then skipping the rest to save time, as a kind of devotional exercise. Zeami of course uses the term ironically.

[4]See Arthur Waley, *The Analects of Confucius,* Book II, No. 11, page 90.

[5]A term sometimes used to indicate the high level of excellence in *waka* poetry. The term is probably of Zen origin.

[6]For a translation into English of this section of the *I ching,* see Richard Wilhelm, tr., *The I Ching or Book of Changes,* pages 122–125. The interpretation of the passage is evidently Zeami's.

the spectators are truly fascinated with an actor's performance, he can be said to have reached the level of a master. If, in addition, he possesses the ability to create for his audience an intensity of pure feeling that goes beyond the workings of the mind, he will have achieved the level of greatest reputation. Thus an actor should pursue his study of Nō through these various levels, develop his skills, and through his own spiritual understanding, bring his art to the highest possible level of fulfillment.

Shallow and Deep

Concerning Nō performance, there is one matter that must be given particularly serious consideration. If a performance is given without sufficient attention to detail, it will be without interest. On the other hand, if too much attention is given by the performer to details, the whole performance risks to shrink in scale. Then again, if the actor thinks to play his part as liberally as possible, the opportunities for the audience to witness his skill will be fewer, and there will be a tendency for his performance to become slow and monotonous. An understanding of this distinction is of the greatest importance. An actor might, on first reflection, think that the parts of the play requiring intricate skills should be played in as complex a fashion as possible, while those moments requiring a more general approach should be played as broadly as possible. Yet in fact this kind of distinction cannot be made unless an actor knows the art of Nō very well indeed. A student must question his teacher closely on such matters, so that these distinctions become clear. There is, however, one general principle that can be kept in mind. For the chant, the dance, and the various sorts of gestures that will be employed, the actor's spirit should be as delicately attuned as possible, but, at the same time, his physical stance should be as relaxed and broad as possible. An actor must comprehend these principles and stick to them.

In general, it can be said that, in the case of the Nō, an art that is based on general and flexible principles can be made subtle and detailed. But a Nō that is merely meticulous in conception cannot easily develop on a large and relaxed scale. After all, the small can be contained in the large, but not the large in the small. A great deal of skill needs to be given over to this matter. A Nō that possesses both these qualities will truly be full and rich. Indeed, when ice formed during the deep cold melts, the ice formed during a brief chilly spell will melt as well.

Entering the Realm of Grace

The aesthetic quality of Grace is considered the highest ideal of perfection in many arts. Particularly in the Nō, Grace can be regarded as the highest principle. However, although the quality of Grace is manifested in performance and audiences give it high appreciation, there are very few actors who in fact possess that quality. This is because they have never had a taste of the real Grace themselves. So it is that few actors have entered this world.

What kind of realm is represented by what is termed Grace? For example, if we take the general appearance of the world and observe the various sorts of people who live there, it might be said that Grace is best represented in the character of the nobility, whose deportment is of such a high quality and who receive the affection and respect not given to others in society. If such is the case, then their dignified and mild appearance represents the essence of Grace. Therefore, the stage appearance of Grace is best indicated by their refined and elegant carriage. If an actor examines closely the nobility's beautiful way of speaking and studies the words and habitual means of expression that such elevated persons use, even to observing their tasteful choice of language when saying the smallest things, such can be taken to represent the Grace of speech. In the case of the chant, when the melody flows smoothly and naturally on the ear and sounds suitably mild and calm, this quality can be said to represent the Grace of music. In the case of the dance, if the actor studies until he is truly fluent, so that his appearance on stage will be sympathetic and his carriage both unostentatious and moving to those who observe him, he will surely manifest the Grace of the dance. When he is acting a part, if he makes his appearance beautiful in the Three Role Types, he will have achieved Grace in his performance. Again, when presenting a role of fearsome appearance, a demon's role for example, even should the actor use a rough manner to a certain extent, he must not forget to preserve a graceful appearance, and he must remember the principles of "what is felt in the heart is ten," and "violent body movements, gentle foot movements," so that his stage appearance will remain elegant. Thus he may manifest the Grace of a demon's role.

An actor must come to grasp those various types of Grace and absorb them within himself; for no matter what kind of role he may assume, he must never separate himself from the virtue of Grace. No matter what the role—whether the character be of high or low rank, a man, a woman, a priest or lay person, a farmer or country person, even a beggar or an outcast—it should seem as though each were holding a branch of flowers in his hand. In this one respect they exhibit the same appeal, despite whatever differences they may show in their social positions. This Flower represents the beauty of their stance in the nō, and the ability to reveal this kind of stance in performance represents, of course, its spirit. In order to study the Grace of words, the actor must study the art of composing poetry; and to study the Grace of physical appearance, he must study the aesthetic qualities of elegant costume, so that, in every aspect of his art, no matter how the role may change that the actor is playing, he will always maintain one aspect in his performance that shows Grace. Such it is to know the seed of Grace.

However, it may well happen that an actor will put such an importance on his impersonation of the particulars of his role, regarding this aspect of his performance as the highest of his art, that he will neglect to maintain the beauty of the stance he has properly assumed. Thus he will fail to enter the world of Grace. And if he does not enter into the world of Grace, he cannot approach the level of Highest Fruition. And unless he reaches this highest level of accomplishment, he will never be recognized as a great actor. There are indeed few masters who have attained those heights. Thus an actor must rehearse with the utmost diligence on this critical point of the representation of Grace.

This Highest Fruition of an actor represents precisely the appearance of this deeply beautiful posture. I cannot repeat too often that an actor must rehearse with the need for the proper preparation of his body always in mind. Thus it is of crucial importance that, beginning with the Two Basic Arts down to the specifics of any role that may be played, the stance of the actor be attractive so as to represent this Highest Fruition in every circumstance. If the actor's posture is unattractive, his art will invariably appear vulgar. In any case, whatever gestures may be seen or music may be heard, however great the variety, the fact that the actor's stance is beautifully assumed represents the true attainment of Grace. An actor may be said to have entered the world of Grace when he has of his own accord studied these principles and made himself master of them. If an actor does not work to fulfill them and thinks that, without mastering every aspect of his art, he can still try to attain this Grace, he will, in fact, never know it during his entire lifetime.

Paying Heed to the Accumulation of Skills

Studying the art of the *Nō*, having the reputation of a superior actor, and rising in merit as the years pass by depends on a proper accumulation of skills. Yet the nature of such an accumulation will differ depending on where the actor lives and performs. Even if he earns a reputation as a fine actor, if the praise he earns is not from those who live in the capital, it can have little significance for him. Even an actor who has earned genuine praise in the capital, should he return to his native place and continue to perform in the countryside, will merely expend his energies in attempting not to forget those means of expression that he learned in the capital, and because of his false sense that he still remembers how to perform properly, he

will little by little slacken in his persistence in maintaining his beauty of performance. The result will be an accumulation of bad experiences. Such a stagnation of experience must be shunned.

In the capital, on the other hand, the actor will be performing before discerning spectators so that, should he become careless concerning any element in his art and so fail to progress, he will soon notice a response from his audience; then too, as criticism and comment come to him, he will eventually disregard the unsatisfactory elements in his art, accumulate only positive artistic experiences, and discover that his art has become polished. Of its own accord his skill will become as burnished as a jewel. There is a saying that "sagebrush, which has the ability to bend, even should it grow up among flax plants, will come out straight, without correction, while white sand, when mixed with earth, will become black like the rest."[7] Thus by living in the capital, an actor is in the proper environment, and the insufficiencies in his art will naturally disappear. This gradual lessening of error is in itself the accumulation of good experience. There is no way that an artist can simply set out to pile up these experiences of his own accord. Rather, let me repeat again and again a warning that, if an actor does not take cognizance of his good experiences, they will stagnate and turn into an accumulation of bad experiences.

So it is that even a skilled performer as he grows older will come to depend on his increasingly old-fashioned art, which has become so through an accumulation caused by his own stagnation. Although audiences may dislike his performances, he thinks only that he has been recognized as an artist of great merit for a long time. Thus he does not recognize the real feelings of his audiences. He therefore loses the chance to make his final appearances on the stage successful—such an important opportunity in an actor's career.

All of this is the result of piling up of such bad experiences. The greatest caution must be taken against this.

Connecting All the Arts Through One Intensity of Mind

It is often commented on by audiences that "many times a performance is effective when the actor does nothing." Such an accomplishment results from the actor's greatest, most secret skill. From the techniques involved in the Two Basic Arts down to all the gestures and the various kinds of Role Playing, all such skills are based on the abilities found in the actor's body. Thus to speak of an actor "doing

---

[7]An expression widely circulated during the medieval period in various forms, probably originating in the writings of Tseng Ts'an, one of the most important disciples of Confucius.

nothing" actually signifies that interval which exists between two physical actions. When one examines why this interval "when nothing happens" may seem so fascinating, it is surely because of the fact that, at the bottom, the artist never relaxes his inner tension. At the moment when the dance has stopped, or the chant has ceased, or indeed at any of those intervals that can occur during the performance of a role, or, indeed, during any pause or interval, the actor must never abandon his concentration but must keep his consciousness of that inner tension. It is this sense of inner concentration that manifests itself to the audience and makes the moment enjoyable.

However, it is wrong to allow an audience to observe the actor's inner state of control directly. If the spectators manage to witness this, such concentration will merely become another ordinary skill or action, and the feeling in the audience that "nothing is happening" will disappear.

The actor must rise to a selfless level of art, imbued with a concentration that transcends his own consciousness, so that he can bind together the moments before and after that instant when "nothing happens." Such a process constitutes that inner force that can be termed "connecting all the arts through one intensity of mind."

"Indeed, when we come to face death, our life might be likened to a puppet on a cart (decorated for a great festival). As soon as one string is cut, the creature crumbles and fades."[8] Such is the image given of the existence of man, caught in the perpetual flow of life and death. This constructed puppet, on a cart, shows various aspects of himself but cannot come to life of itself. It represents a deed performed by moving strings. At the moment when the strings are cut, the figure falls and crumbles. *Sarugaku* too is an art that makes use of just such artifice. What supports these illusions and gives them life is the intensity of mind of the actor. Yet the existence of this intensity must not be shown directly to the audience. Should they see it, it would be as though they could see the strings of a puppet. Let me repeat again: the actor must make his spirit the strings, and without letting his audience become aware of them, he will draw together the forces of his art. In that way, true life will reside in his *Nō*.

In general, such attitudes need not be limited to the moments involved in actual performance. Morning and night alike, and in all the activities of daily life, an actor must never abandon his concentration, and he must retain his resolve. Thus, if without ever slackening, he manages to increase his skills, his art of the *Nō* will grow ever greater. This particular point represents one of the most secret of all the teachings concerning our art. However, in actual rehearsal, there must be within this concentration some variations of tension and relaxation.

The Moment of Peerless Charm

The character *myō* in the term *myōsho* [Peerless Charm] means "exquisite" or "delicate." But it also has the meaning of an appearance that transcends any specific form. Such a transcendence of form represents an expression of this Peerless Charm.

When one speaks of such moments in terms of the *Nō*, this Charm should exist in every aspect of our art, from the Two Basic Arts to gesture. Yet precisely where can it be located? It seems to be found nowhere. If an actor can possess this arresting power, he must be a performer of surpassing skill. However, if an actor is truly blessed with great talent, he will show from his beginnings some shadow of this Charm. The actor will not himself be conscious of it, but spectators of discernment will always find this quality within him. Ordinary spectators, on the other hand, will merely find that his performances are enjoyable in some mysterious fashion. And indeed even in the case of an actor of the highest skill, he will at best have come only to the realization that he somehow does possess this skill. Still, he will have no consciousness that he is practicing it at any given moment. An actor will possess this quality precisely because he does not recognize it; if such a moment could in any way be put into words, this Charm could no longer exist.

When one ponders carefully the substance of this Peerless Charm, can it not be said that an artist may approach it when he has truly learned his craft and attained Perfect Fluency, when he has transcended all stages of his art to the point where he performs everything with ease and exhibits every skill without care, thus achieving a selfless art that rises above any artifice? When an actor manages to ascend to the aesthetic level of Grace, will he indeed not be somewhat closer to this power of beauty? These matters must be pondered deeply.

Judging the *Nō*

When it comes to making crucial judgments concerning the *Nō*, people invariably have different ideas. It is difficult indeed for any particular *Nō* to match the tastes of everyone. Thus the basis of judgment should be made on the strength of the performances of accomplished actors who enjoy a wide reputation.

First of all, one should look and listen with great care during actual performances so as to understand why some plays succeed and why others do not. Plays that succeed possess three qualities: Sight, Sound, and Heart.

As for the *Nō* that succeeds through Sight, the stage atmosphere will be colorful from the beginning, the

---

[8]A saying attributed to a priest of the Rinzai sect of Zen Buddhism in Japan, Gettan Sowkow (1316?–1389).

dancing and music will have an attractive air, the spectators, noblemen and commoners alike, will be spontaneous in their praise, the atmosphere brilliant. Such is the *Nō* that is effective to the eye. It goes without saying that such a performance will please the discriminating; even those who know nothing of the *Nō* will find such a performance enjoyable. However, concerning such performances, there is one point that an actor must keep in mind. If the performance passes by altogether too well and with too much appeal, and if every aspect seems enjoyable, then the feelings of the audience will tend to become over-stimulated, and their sensibilities in appreciating the details of the acting will be coarsened. For this part, an actor may be impetuous and, since he wants to exhaust every aspect of his art, will make no allowance for a slackening of pace, either for himself or for the audience. In an attempt to make every aspect of the performance successful, a surface brilliance is achieved, but the end results may be unsatisfactory. This kind of abuse arises when the play goes too well. On such an occasion, the play should be performed in a more restrained manner, all the artistic appearances made more moderate, and the eyes and ears of the spectators given some surcease, so that they can have an occasion to rest and breathe easily and the audience can be given the quiet necessary to observe the really skillful elements in the performance. Then, if the results are successful, the plays that follow will seem stronger, so that, whatever the number of plays that may be staged, their fascination for the audience will never be exhausted. So it is that an effective *Nō* performance can be said to succeed through the art of Sight.

Nō that can be said to succeed through Sound shows from the very beginning a serious atmosphere. The music and text are chosen in accord with the season [and the time of day], thus creating a gentle, relaxed, and enjoyable effect. Above all, it is the chant that should create the main impression. Only a peerless artist of highest experience can achieve this effect during a performance. However, the kind of sober flavor engendered by such a performance cannot be understood by country audiences and the like.

This kind of *Nō*, when performed by a peerless actor, can give rise through his spiritual resources to various aesthetic qualities that make the play become more and more enjoyable as it goes along. In the case of an artist of the second rank, however, whose art has not fully matured, he will cause the day's performance to lag if he decides to follow such a presentation by a famous actor with one of his own in a *Nō* that is also of this particular variety. When such a player follows the kind of performance that has successfully created a cool and quiet atmosphere, as he continues on he will only create a gloomy mood in the succeeding plays. An actor must be aware of this difficulty and put his energies into his performance in order to begin to increase the number of stimulating moments in the play, so as to bring an element of surprise to his audience. Of course, as a truly peerless player has naturally a wide repertory and is highly trained in body and mind, his art will be effectively manifested in his dance and chant, so that his performance will naturally progress in an enjoyable manner. A player of the second rank, however, must take great care so that, as the performance continues, the atmosphere does not go dead. Concerning this point, when thinking to keep up the atmosphere of his performance, the actor must not reveal his methods to the audience. The spectators must merely feel that the performance is enjoyable. Such is the actor's secret, based on long-mastered precedents as to how to perform successfully. All I have written above can explain how a *Nō* can succeed through Sound.

When it comes to the *Nō* that succeeds through the Heart, a truly gifted actor of *sarugaku*, after he has mastered the whole repertory, will have the ability even when performing a play of no particular distinction in terms of chant, dance, gesture, or plot, to create even in the midst of a certain dullness a particular poetic quality that can move the hearts of his audience. This level of attainment is not usually grasped even by connoisseurs; how much more beyond any imaginings of a country audience must be such an art. Indeed, such a quality must seem to represent the propitious manifestation of an actor of the highest abilities. Such a performance can be termed a *Nō* that succeeds through the Heart, a *Nō* that surpasses technique, a *Nō* that transcends outward manifestation.

An actor must learn to discriminate between the kinds of artistic qualities that display those various differences. There are spectators of discernment who do not really understand the art of the *Nō*. On the other hand, there are those spectators who possess a true grasp of the essential nature of the *Nō* but who cannot observe subtle differences. Those who have both a practical and a theoretical understanding of *Nō* represent the highest level of spectator. For example, there are occasions when a fine performance does not meet with success, and times when an unskilled performance pleases, but no one must use these exceptions as a basis for one's general judgments. For example, truly gifted players customarily have success with outdoor and other large-scale performances, while lesser actors perform profitably at smaller playing areas at country fairs or on other such occasions.

An actor who understands how to make his performance attractive to his audience brings good fortune to the *Nō*. Then too, a spectator who understands the heart of the actor as he watches a performance is a gifted spectator. The following might be said concerning making judgments: forget the specifics of a performance and examine the whole. Then forget the performance and examine the actor. Then forget the actor and examine his inner spirit. Then, forget that spirit, and you will grasp the nature of the Nō.

The Matter of Mastering the Chant

There are two aspects to the study of the chant. The person who composes the text should know the principles of music and how to make the words flow together in a euphonious fashion. For his part, the performer who sings must know how to fit the melody to the words and to chant the syllables and words in a clear and correct manner. Since the beauty of the chant derives from the syllables and the words performed, the melodies must be composed in such a way that the pronunciation is always correctly represented, and the linking between the phrases smooth and flexible. When the chant is performed, if the singer has mastered these principles and really knows them well, both the composition and the performance will reinforce each other and produce an enjoyable effect. As this is true, a standard should be established by which the melody is attached to the chant. The flow of the phrases must be attractive, and the sound characteristics of the text must be in harmony with the melody, so that the results will of themselves be musical. That is, the melody provides the basic frame for the musical composition, and the artistic effect derives from the spirit of the performer, who shades the melody in terms of the flow of the phrases. Thus an actor has various elements of music that he must master—the physical problems of using the breath, the development of his own emotional concentration in order to direct it properly, and the understanding of the melody, as well as the music that lies behind the melody. In terms of practicing the musical aspects of Nō, the following should be taken to heart: forget the voice and understand the shading of the melody. Forget the melody and understand the pitch. Forget the pitch and understand the rhythm.

In learning the art of musical performance, there is a proper order to be followed: first, the words of the text must be learned thoroughly; then the melody must be mastered; then the actor must learn how to color the melody; finally, he must learn how to apply the proper pitch accent. After all these steps are taken, the actor must concentrate on how to bring his performances to flower. At every stage, an emphasis must be placed on the rhythm. When practicing the voice, miss no occasion to obtain this kind of training, so beneficial to personal development.

Then there is the matter of accent in musical performance. In the case of auxiliary words or particles, the problem is not a serious one. However, mistaken accents on such substantive words as nouns, verbs, and adjectives[9] are harmful. Understanding the importance of this distinction is crucial. Serious study must be given to this point. When speaking of mistaken accents on these substantive words, I refer to pronunciations with improper pitch accent, which affect the meaning of the words. In the case of particles and auxiliary words, the problem has to do with the voicing of such sounds as te, ni, ha, and the like. Concerning correct pronunciation for these sounds, when the flow of words in the course of the singing moves effectively, even if the pronunciation becomes altered to some extent, so long as the rhythm is correct, the problem is not a serious one. It is said that words that make a heavy or a light effect, that are clear or complex in sound, depend on the forward flow of the text. In addition, there are various customs and rules concerning sound changes when words are juxtaposed together. Study the transmitted teachings carefully on this matter. As concerns particles that come at the end of phrases, such as ha, ni, no, o, ka, te, mo, shi, and so forth, even if there should be some deviation in their pronunciation, there will be nothing disagreeable in the sound as long as the melody is tasteful. In other words, the movement of the melody should be supported by these various particles. In the chanting, every syllable must not simply be pronounced in a flat manner, with an equal length and emphasis given to all of them. Those sounds which represent substantive words should be pronounced briskly, so that their meaning remains clear, while the sound of the auxiliary syllables can be rather freely regulated—slow or fast—in order to make the melody more colorful.

[Remember that] the principle of using four basic tones is used [in Chinese].[10]

In The History of the Former Han by Pan Ku,[11] it is written [concerning the legendary origin of the melody] that "as for the origins of the twelve-pitch gamut, a man [named Ling Lun] climbed Mount Kun-lun and, hearing the voice of the male and female phoenix, created the six ryo pitches and six ritsu pitches of the twelve-pitch

---

[9]That is, independent, uninflected words usually written with Chinese characters.

[10]Zeami doubtless wished to stress the importance of proper pitch accent for substantive words in Japanese, usually written in Chinese characters, by this reference to the Chinese language. For a concise description of the function of tones in classical Chinese, see James J.Y. Liu, The Art of Chinese Poetry, pages 21–22.

[11]Pan Ku's history was the first of the so-called dynastic histories of China. For a general description of the text and its subject matter, see Burton Watson, Early Chinese Literature, pages 103–109. Zeami's quotation contains minor errors. For an explanation of the significance of the passage in the history of Chinese music, see Kenneth J. DeWoskin, A Song for One or Two, pages 59–61.

gamut." *Ritsu*, since it is derived from the voice of the male phoenix, represents the principle of *yang*. *Ryo*, which imitates the voice of the female phoenix, represents *yin*. *Ritsu* represents the kind of sound that goes from high to low, and the breath is inhaled. *Ryo* represents a sound that goes from low to high, and the breath is exhaled. Breathing appropriate to *ritsu* is produced through a state of tension; *ryo* is produced in a state of ease. Then too, *ritsu* can be considered as appropriate to Non-Being, *ryo* appropriate to Being. Thus, a thin, high voice [a "vertical" voice] is appropriate for *ritsu*, while a thick, low voice [a "horizontal" voice] is appropriate for *ryo*.

In the *Analects*,[12] it is written that "the hides of the bear, the tiger, and the panther are used as targets [for the hunter's] arrow. The tiger is the prince's target, the panther the nobleman's target, and the bear the target of the officers of state." If this sequence is followed, it would doubtless be correct to write "tiger, panther, bear." But for the sake of euphony, the order is changed to "bear, tiger, and panther."

The Ultimate Keys of Our Art

The contents of this work have now all been set forth. There is nothing to learn in addition to what has been set down here. Indeed, there is nothing else involved but to "understand the *Nō*" with one's very being. If this fundamental principle is not observed, the various matters discussed here will serve no purpose. If an actor really wishes to master the *Nō*, he must set aside all other pursuits and truly give his whole soul to our art; then, as his learning increases and his experience grows, he will gradually of himself reach a level of awareness and so come to understand the *Nō*.

First of all, an actor must deeply believe what his teacher tells him and take those instructions to heart. The numerous teachings involved are contained in the various points discussed in this book, but the actor must truly master them and engrave them on his heart, so that, when he is actually in a performance, he can try out in practice the various things that he has learned. Then, as a result, he will value those principles, and, as he comes to revere the art of *Nō*, he will as time passes come to understand the real secret of success in our art. In whatever artistic pursuit, one studies and then understands, so that he will know how to carry out his art in actual practice. In *sarugaku* as well, one must study and learn, so that these various principles can be put into practice.

All these secret teachings can be summed up by saying that an actor must continually earn mastery through constant practice, from his apprenticeship through his old age. When I speak of studying through old age, I refer to the fact that from the time of an actor's apprenticeship until the peak of his maturity there are various arts that must be mastered. It is only from the time that an actor passes forty that he can slowly begin to make use of restraint in his physical performance. In other words, he must learn the means of artistic expression appropriate for an actor of his age. When the actor passes fifty, then he can begin to use the technique of "doing nothing." This represents a crucial stage in an actor's career. The first thing to learn at this point is the necessity to limit the kinds of plays in the actor's repertory. His musical performance now becomes the center of his style of performance, his acting style becomes simpler, and his dancing and gestures grow more restrained. He should only give a hint of his former colorful appearance. In fact, the art of music remains the one area in which an actor at this age can excel. This is true because an older voice will have exhausted its natural and untrained qualities, and the voice that remains will be highly polished, in whatever style of vocal production the actor may wish to use; thus whatever music is chanted, the results will always be enjoyable. This is a sure means to achieve a successful performance. Thus an older actor should learn carefully to make his age serve his own artistic purposes and work all the harder to train himself appropriately.

Concerning roles that can be played by older actors, old men and women are doubtless the most appropriate. However, depending on the strong points of a particular actor, he may not necessarily be limited to these two. Still, an actor who wishes to create an atmosphere of serenity in his performance will find the roles of older characters best suited to him. If his special strength lies in roles demanding energetic movement, however, those will not be suitable for the aesthetic qualities appropriate to the art of older actors. In any case, within these limits, he should perform his dances and gestures while limiting himself to six-tenths or seven-tenths of "what is felt by the heart is ten," so as to perform in a manner appropriate to his age. Such is the means to master the art suitable for the older actor.

In our Kanze school, there is one phrase that is of infinite value concerning the fundamentals of any artistic accomplishment: an actor must never forget the experiences he has undergone as a beginning artist. In the transmitted teaching, there are three explanations provided for this. Accordingly:

—He must never forget the fresh experiences he first went through as a young performer.

---

[12]No such passage appears in the *Analects*, but a somewhat similar one does appear in the *Chou li* or *Rites of Chou*. Both this passage and the preceding section on *The History of the Former Han* were added to Zeami's text in the form of notes, and may not be by his hand.

—At each level of accomplishment, there are new levels of fresh experience that the actor must encounter for the first time, as though he were a beginner, and then never forget.

—After the actor becomes older, there are still new stages of fresh experience that must never be forgotten.

Here are the teachings contained in these maxims in more detail.

Concerning the maxim that "he must never forget the fresh experiences he first went through as a young performer," it can be said that, if the actor retains the feelings he had at that time, he will profit from them in many ways as he grows older. As the expression has it, "an understanding of errors in the past will turn them into advantages in the future." Or, "seeing the cart in front turn over serves as a warning to the cart that follows." Forgetting the arts one has learned as a beginner amounts in fact to forgetting the skills an actor may possess at a later point in his career. The fact that his art has been perfected and his reputation has been made can only be the result of the development of his own skill. But if he does not take cognizance of how his skills have improved, he will unknowingly revert to the level he possessed as a beginner. Such a reversal means that his art is actually degenerating. His ability to maintain a sense of his present level of accomplishment shows that he has not forgotten the skills learned as a young performer. I cannot stress this principle too strongly: if an actor loses his memory of his unmatured skills, he will be forced to revert to them. On the other hand, if he does not forget them, his later accomplishments will be genuine. And, if they are genuine, his abilities, as they increase, will insure that his art can never retrogress. Thus, this truth can serve as a distinction between truth and error.

Young actors must therefore take cognizance of the current level of their accomplishment, realize that they are still only beginners, and understand that they must not lose sight of their own skills that still remain to be developed. In this way, they can truly work to lift the level of their art. To lose consciousness of the level of one's ability is to forget how to advance in the art; under such circumstances, an artist's skill will not increase. Therefore, young artists must never lose their perceptions of their actual level of ability.

Secondly, there is the principle that "at each level of accomplishment, there are new levels of fresh experience that the actor must encounter for the first time, as though he were a beginner, and then never forget." This means that, for the actor, from his beginnings through the height of his career and into his old age, there are always various suitable means of expression he must practice and learn. On all these occasions he can be seen as a beginner. Therefore, if at each stage he abandons and forgets what

has come before, he will only possess the artistic ability that matches what he is doing at that particular moment in his career. If, on the other hand, he has managed to maintain in himself all the skills that he has previously mastered, so that he can still make use of them, then he can perform in an ever-increasing variety of styles. These "new skills" refer to those he has learned for the first time at every successive stage in his career. Maintaining them all and combining them together at one time means that he has forgotten none of them. It is just through such efforts that a *shite* becomes an artist of wide-ranging abilities. Thus one must never forget what he has learned at each stage of his career.

Finally, "after the actor becomes older, there are still new stages of fresh experience that must never be forgotten." Truly, although there are limits on a human life, the *Nō* never comes to an end. If an actor has mastered every technique appropriate to each stage in his career, then when it comes time to learn what is correct for an older actor, he will still be able to enjoy a new experience even at this late stage in his career. If an actor still possesses this attitude when he reaches this high level, his art will still contain everything about the *Nō* that he has managed to learn before. When he passes the age of fifty, as I have said, an actor need have no other plan than to "do nothing special." To face the challenge of having no other technique than to "do nothing special"—is the art of an older actor really so different than that of a beginner?

So it is that if an actor manages to live his whole life without forgetting how and what he has learned at any one time in his career, the level of his art will steadily increase during his last years, and his abilities will never degenerate. To live one's life without ever exhausting the depths of the *Nō* represents the most profound principle of our school, a principle that must be passed on from child to grandchild, generation to generation as a secret teaching of our house. Passing on the importance of these attitudes I have described above will serve as a means to develop the artistry of all generations to come. On the other hand, if an actor forgets this "experience of a beginner," he will surely not be able to pass the conception along to others in later generations. An artist must not forget this "experience of a beginner," but must convey it to those who follow, for countless generations.

In addition to what I have written here, another who studies the *Nō* may, depending on his own abilities and discernment, be able to discover still other truths.

All of the *Teachings on Style and the Flower* (Zeami's treatise on Noh theater), beginning with the chapter called "The Practice of the *Nō* in Relation to the Age of the Actor" down to the "Separate Secret Teaching," is a secret document that makes clear the *Nō* by using the metaphor of the flower. That text represents an account of various elements in the art of my father Kan'ami, set down twenty years after his death, and serves as a record of what I learned from him. The present treatise, on the other hand, represents discoveries that have occurred to me from time to time concerning the *Nō* over a period of forty years, down to the time of my own advanced age. Summing them up, I have written out my observations in six sections and twenty parts,[13] which I leave behind as a memento of my art.

Ōe 31 [1424], 1st day of the 6th month

Zeami

This teaching was passed on by Zeami himself for the succeeding generations of his house and should not be shown to actors from other troupes. Luckily, thanks to the Will of Heaven, which knows that my heart reveres the art of the *Nō,* this manuscript has come into my hands. This secret teaching forms the very core of the art of our school, and it has been written down to guide the art of our family. It is a text of fearsome power. Thus it must not be shown carelessly to others.

Eikyō 9 [1437], 8th month, 8th day

Komparu Zenchiku[14]

---

[13]The indication of twenty parts suggests that the manuscript was originally arranged in some different fashion.

[14]Komparu's signature is an attribution; the identity of the writer is not altogether certain.

III

The Theater of Medieval and Renaissance England

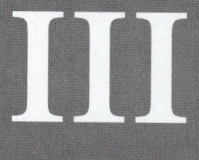

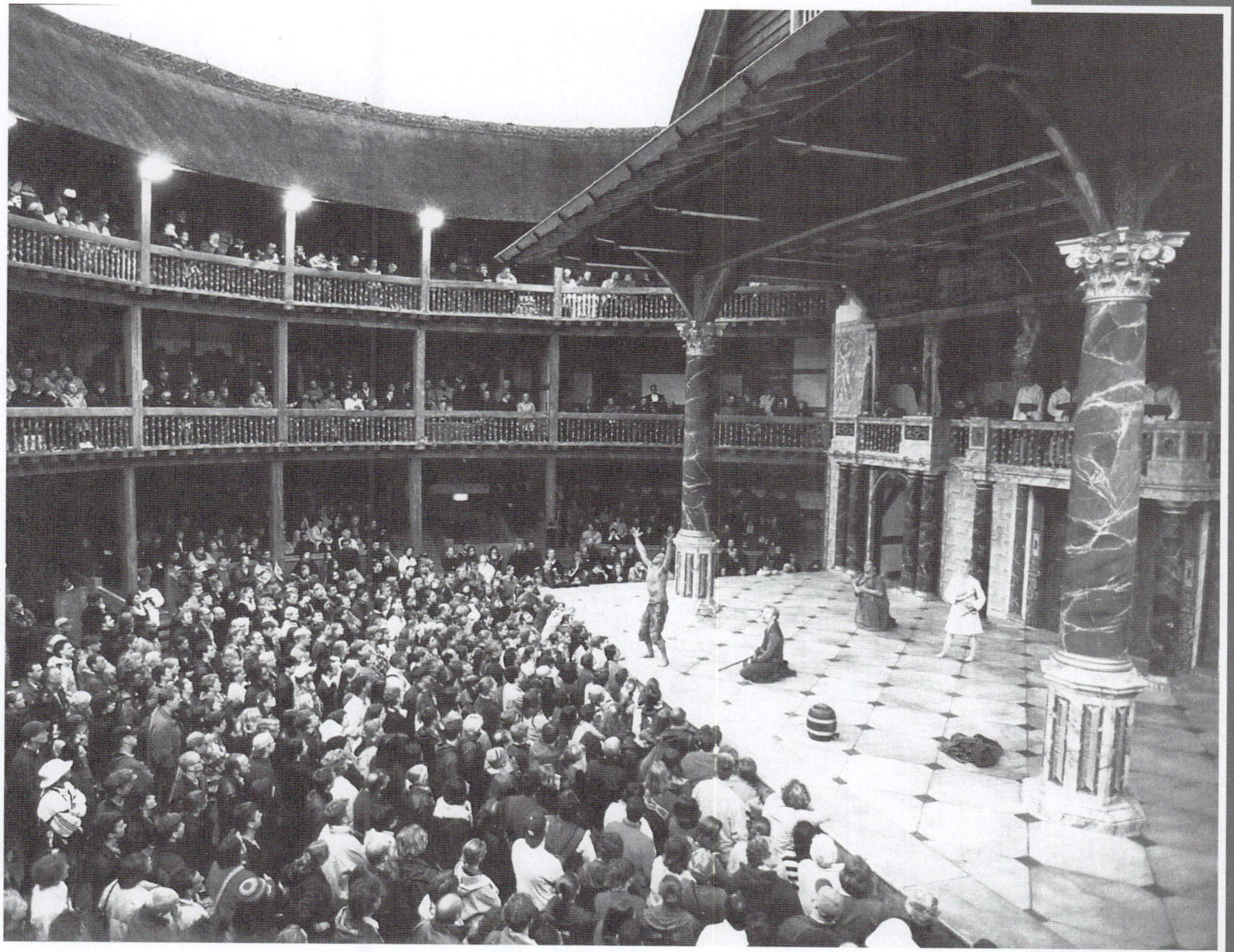

Courtesy of the Globe Theatre; Photograph by Donald Cooper

A performance of *The Tempest* at the new Shakespeare's Globe Theatre, on the Bankside in London. The theater is a meticulous reconstruction of the Globe Theatre of 1613.

III

The Theater of Medieval and Renaissance England

The fifteenth, sixteenth, and seventeenth centuries saw Europe transformed by the extraordinary cultural revolution we now call the European Renaissance. Fueled by new technology such as printing and by new scientific, political, and religious ideas, explosive change transformed European culture. The known world expanded beyond the sea to embrace the New World; the recovery of Greek and Latin literature spurred a sweeping intellectual revolution; strong centralized monarchies in Spain, Portugal, France, and England created new empires abroad and fought to control an increasingly restive populace at home; the Protestant Reformation undermined the religious and political authority of the Catholic church, beginning a period of violent religious conflict; and the "new philosophy"—modern science—of Copernicus, Bacon, and Galileo seemed to put even the physical world of heaven and earth in doubt. "'Tis all in pieces, all coherence gone," the poet John Donne wrote in 1611, voicing the profound anxiety and exhilaration of many of his contemporaries: "Prince, subject, father, son are things forgot. / For every man alone thinks that he hath got / To be a Phoenix." The changing tides of thought swept away the crumbling edifice of the medieval world—the feudal state, the universal church, scholastic philosophy, an ordered heaven, and revealed truth—and opened the way for the modern world.

This revolution also infused the theater; the Renaissance, especially in Italy, France, Spain, and England, is one of the great ages of theatrical and dramatic achievement. In England, the professional theater as we know it originated at this time: the history of the secular, profit-making, commercial theater is conventionally dated from the opening of The Theatre in London in 1576. Licensed and protected as an aristocratic entertainment, the theater was also a popular institution in which commoners such as William Shakespeare, Richard Burbage, Edward Alleyn, Inigo Jones, and others, could indeed rise like the phoenix. However, to understand the revolutionary impact of theater and drama in Shakespeare's era, we need to understand their conservative inheritance, their deep indebtedness to the medieval stage that preceded them.

Dramatic performance in medieval Europe was thoroughly conditioned by the Catholic church's central role in the life of the community. Having closed the Roman theaters in the sixth century, the church maintained a vigilant opposition to the secular theater and the vices associated with it. Yet the revival of theater in Europe, beginning in the tenth century, was inspired and sponsored by the church itself. The four major dramatic forms in the late Middle Ages were connected with the church, its rituals, and its calendar of religious observances: LITURGICAL DRAMA enacted as part of the liturgy of the Catholic Mass; CYCLE PLAYS, illustrating scriptural history and performed by craft guilds on the feast of Corpus Christi; MORALITY DRAMA, enacting the symbolic structure of Christian life; and plays written and performed in schools and universities, sometimes imitating classical plays. In England, cycle and morality plays particularly influenced the later, secular drama of the sixteenth century.

Drama and Theater in Medieval England

Morality Drama

Like the cycle plays, morality plays dramatized elements of Christian life. Instead of staging events from scriptural history, morality drama stages a symbolic ALLEGORY of the Christian's spiritual journey through life. Increasingly popular throughout the fourteenth and fifteenth centuries, plays like *The Castle of Perseverance* (c. 1425), *Mankind* (c. 1470), and *Everyman* (c. 1500) emphasized the individual's struggle with sin, while the cycle plays emphasized the larger patterns of Christian history. Later playwrights, including Shakespeare, found both models useful. The cycles provided a pattern for staging the epic sweep of secular English history, and morality drama provided a supple device for representing psychological and moral conflict. Morality plays often provided the structure for the secular plays written at schools and universities as well, and for the INTERLUDES performed at court as a break from holiday feasting. They also provided a staple technique for characterization in the later secular drama. Christopher Marlowe's *Doctor Faustus* (1590) uses the Good and Evil

Angels to externalize Faustus's moral conflict, and other playwrights frequently used the devices of morality drama to dramatize the difficulties of political choice. In John Skelton's interlude, *Magnificence* (1516), written for Henry VIII or Thomas Sackville, and Thomas Norton's *Gorboduc* (1561), the monarch is shown to make his decisions framed by a host of allegorized counselors, good and bad advisers who approximate the role played in morality drama by angels and demons.

Staging Medieval Drama

Medieval plays were often acted on or near **PAGEANT WAGONS**. In some towns the audience seems to have remained stationary at various locations while the wagons and their plays proceeded past them; in other towns, the wagons were drawn in a procession of **TABLEAUX VIVANTS** (posed scenes) through the town and then arranged in an open area for the performance, allowing the audience to move from play to play. In Chester, for example, a list survives of the stations where the plays were performed, and for York it is possible to trace the route of the pageant wagons through the city; citizens—sometimes those with businesses—could pay to have a station located adjacent to their houses. In York a city official was posted with a copy of the entire cycle as a kind of censor, noting whether the plays were performed according to the script. Given the size and complexity of these performances, it's not surprising to find that they were not easily performed on one day: the procession took three days at Chester, and began at 4:30 A.M. in York, lasting until past midnight. The plays combined historical and contemporary elements; in performance, the staging produced a close and powerful relationship between the dramatic characters and the audience. In the Coventry play of the Magi, for example, Herod raves when he discovers that the three kings have escaped him:

> I Stamp! I Stare! I look all about!
>
> Might I them take, I should them burn at a glede [fire]!
>
> I rant! I run! and now run I wode [mad] A! That these villain traitors hath marred this my mood!
>
> They shall be hanged, if I may come them to!
>
> (*Here Herod rages in the pagond* [pageant wagon] *and in the street also.*)[1]

Herod's rage was certainly one of the highlights of the medieval cycles. Shakespeare, at least, seems to refer to it in *Hamlet* (1600), when he has Hamlet remind his actors that they should be restrained and natural in their performance, because overacting "out-Herods Herod." The stage direction also suggests that Herod's frenzy carried him from the wagon and into the street, into a closer and more effective relationship to his audience. This interaction between actor and audience is characteristic of popular theater and is a feature of medieval performance carried into Renaissance acting. It also suggests that the "place" of medieval drama, the fictitious locale of the play, was not firmly localized onstage; the actors/characters could move easily back and forth between Herod's Jerusalem and the medieval audience, and even onstage places could be rapidly and easily transformed. This flexibility also allowed medieval playwrights to treat stage space symbolically. The ground plot for *The Castle of Perseverance,* for instance—with its scaffolds for various evils, its moat, and its central castle—clearly offers us a symbolic locale rather than an actual geography. The various demons on their scaffolds stand at a symbolic distance, not an actual distance, from the central castle.

The English cycle plays are among the highest achievements of Middle English literature, and we are fortunate that these immense popular spectacles remain in written form: the York, N-Town, and Towneley cycles each exist today in a single manuscript; the Chester

---

[1]The Coventry *Magi, Herod, and the Slaughter of the Innocents,* in *Chief Pre-Shakespearean Dramas,* ed. Joseph Quincy Adams (Boston: Houghton Mifflin, 1924), 163.

Medieval Pageant Wagon

One actor is playing in the street in front of the wagon.

cycle survives in five different copies. What these texts show is that the complex of dramatic conventions, staging practices, and audience attitudes is a legacy of the medieval theater passed on to later theater. Although the medieval stage was only one of many influences on it, the drama of the sixteenth and seventeenth centuries is reminiscent of medieval drama in many ways. Renaissance drama frequently treats secular history according to a providential design similar to that of the cycles; it often treats its characters in the symbolic terms of the medieval morality dramas; and it uses both acting and stage space to create a sense of immediacy between the fictive play and its audience. These habits take on very different meanings in Renaissance London, in a city and in a state in which the Anglican Protestant church is the state religion and where signs of Catholicism—or, in fact, of any religious subject matter—in the theater could be read as an act of sedition. The medieval

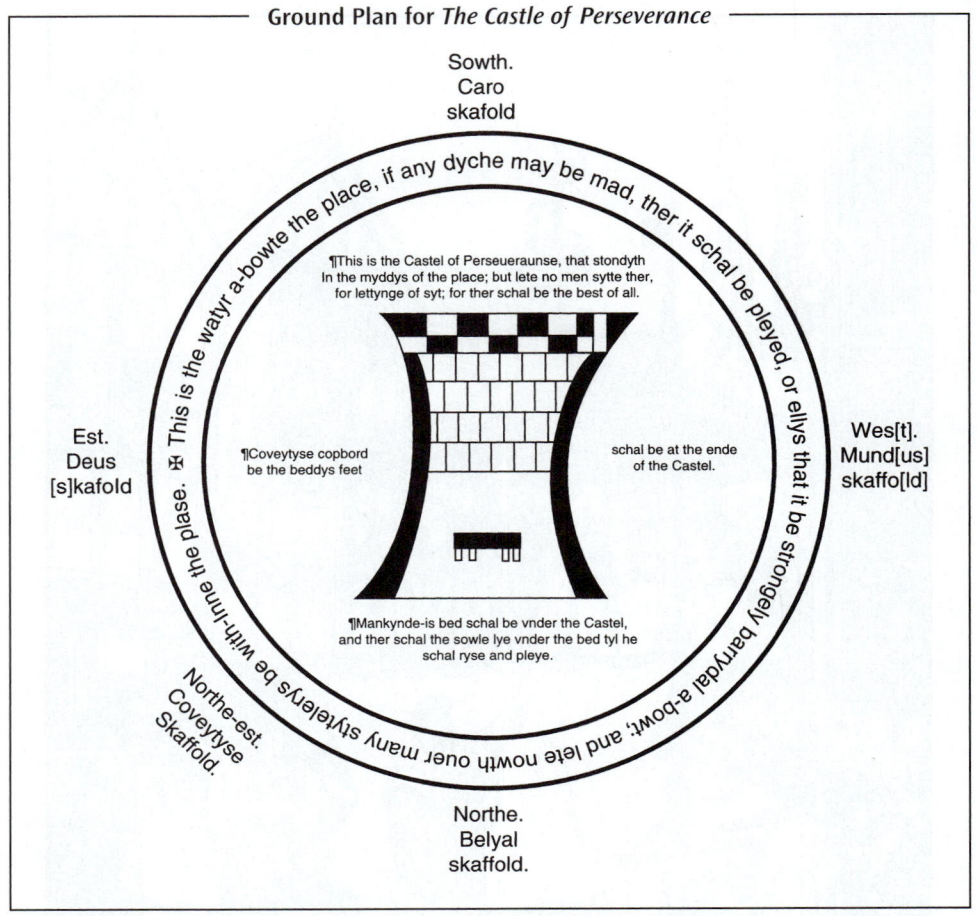

Ground Plan for *The Castle of Perseverance*

The ground-plot for the medieval morality play shows five scaffolds (North, Northeast, South, East, and West) arranged around a playing area, with a castle in the center. A ditch enclosed the castle to keep spectators at a distance. In the manuscript, a note beneath the drawing describes the costumes and special effects: "He that shall play Belial (a devil), look that he have gunpowder burning in pipes in his hands and in his ears, and in his arse, when he goes to battle. The four daughters should be clad in mantles; Mercy in white, Ruthwiseness in red, all together, Truth in sad green, and Peace all in black; and they shall play in the place all together until they bring up the soul."

theater provided the forms of drama and the practices of theater that were refashioned by the political, social, and theatrical pressures of the new era.

Drama and Theater in Renaissance London

The explosion of theatrical and dramatic activity in London can be marked by two dates: 1567, when John Brayne built the Red Lion, London's first purpose-built theater (his brother-in-law, James Burbage, built The Theatre in 1576); and 1642, when plays were suspended and theaters were closed at the outbreak of the Civil War. The theater underwent profound changes from the reign of Elizabeth I (ruled 1558–1603) to the reigns of her successors James I (1603–1625) and Charles I (1625–1642, executed 1649), yet at the same time it endured the intense social and cultural upheavals of the period with remarkable consistency.

As an institution, the new professional theater witnessed the emergence of England as a modern state; the rise of England as an important mercantile and naval power, aided by the defeat of the Spanish Armada in 1588; the expansion of English interests in the New

World; the growth of the city of London to roughly 250,000 inhabitants; and the ascendance of the Puritan faction that closed the theaters and deposed and executed the king. The professional theater—a new institution in England, though already established on the continent—necessarily reflected the political and social strains of the time. These strains are most readily visible in the many laws regulating theatrical performance. The location of theater buildings, the structure and organization of theater companies, and the entire scene of theatrical activity in Renaissance London epitomized the fundamental tensions of English society as it moved from the medieval to the modern world.

The Professional Theater and Its Society

The sixteenth century witnessed intense religious and civil controversy, dating in part from Henry VIII's divorce from Catherine of Aragon in 1532 and his consequent excommunication from the Catholic church in 1533. Once Henry established the Protestant Church of England as the religion of the realm in 1535, English politics were often dictated by England's vulnerability to the massive, hostile powers of the Catholic church in Rome and Catholic states such as France and Spain. Within England, a variety of Protestant sects competed with each other, with the government, and with the Church of England for power. This was also a period of profound changes in the ordering of society, a period of growing mercantile power, of aristocratic discontent with the power of the monarchy, and of the rise of new merchants and other social groups into prominence and power. As a result, the Crown was eternally on guard to suppress civil unrest or religious nonconformity.

Given this volatile political climate, it is not surprising that the Crown sought to limit and control public assembly, including theatrical performances. Laws were frequently directed against the theater, particularly against productions identified with England's Catholic past. In 1548, for example, the English church cancelled the Feast of Corpus Christi, and the production of the cycle plays was systematically suppressed. In 1569, the York cycle was performed for the last time, and in 1575, the mayor of Chester was arrested for allowing cycle plays to be performed. The last cycle performance took place in Coventry in 1576, and the last record of any Corpus Christi play being performed in England (before the modern era) dates from 1605, in Kendal. Morality plays may have seemed less sectarian in the kind of instruction they offered; features of morality drama were more readily absorbed by the secular theater.

Yet while the Crown limited and censored the stage, it also maintained its traditional patronage of the theater. The population of London nearly tripled in Shakespeare's lifetime, from roughly 80,000 in 1564 to more than 200,000 at his death in 1616. The Elizabethan era was characterized by several large crop failures, a deflation in the value of currency, repeated bouts of the plague, and persistent threats of invasion from without and sedition from within. Not surprisingly, both the queen and her Privy Council, and the local city magistrates throughout England, were fearful both of itinerant travelers and of large—potentially riotous—assemblies. The famous "Act for the punishment of Vagabonds" of 1572 is a case in point. The law prohibited itinerant players and entertainers from wandering throughout the realm, but its ultimate effect was to establish permanent theatrical companies under the protection of noble patrons. The law ordered that "all Fencers, Bearwards, Common Players in Interludes, and Minstrels, not belonging to any Baron of this Realm, or towards any other honorable Personage of greater Degree . . . [who] wander abroad and have not License of two Justices of the Peace at the least . . . shall be taken adjudged and deemed Rogues Vagabonds and Sturdy Beggars." Unless they belonged to the retinue of a nobleman, players were classed with common vagrants and could be arrested and fined. Protected as servants, a company of players could receive a license to perform in public.

The statute points to the strong bond between the theater and the aristocracy, and patents granted by Elizabeth entitled noblemen to retain companies of actors as servants. These patents—granted for the Lord Chamberlain's Men (Shakespeare's company), the Lord Admiral's Men (who produced Marlowe's plays), and others—shaped the professional theater of Renaissance London. Elizabeth authorized such companies to perform "Comedies,

Tragedies, Interludes, and stage plays" in public, in London and elsewhere. Yet, in granting these privileges, the Crown made significant qualifications. Elizabeth expanded the powers of her Master of Revels, Edmund Tilney, requiring "all and every plaier or plaiers with their playmakers, either belonging to any noble man or otherwise" to "appear before him with all such plaies, Tragedies, Comedies or showes as they shall in readiness or meane to sett forth," and to receive his approval before their performance. Censorship in the period was extensive, and Elizabeth also stipulated that plays "be not published or shown in the time of common prayer, or in the time of great and common plague in our said City of London." Religious and civic officials exerted considerable authority over when and where plays could actually be performed and where theaters could legally be built, and they often closed theaters for months at a time because of plague or civil strife.

Professional Companies   The City of London, as in many towns, had its own ordinances prohibiting plays within the city limits, and for this reason James Burbage—a member of the Earl of Leicester's company—built The Theatre to the north of the city. Within a decade theaters had been built to the north of the city and to the south, across the Thames River.

Although they were technically liveried "servants" (wearing their patron's insignia when at court), the major acting companies—the most famous being the Lord Chamberlain's Men, patented in 1593 and then given royal sponsorship as the King's Men when King James I succeeded Elizabeth in 1603—were organized as stockholding, profit-making corporations; that is, as business enterprises in the modern sense. Their economic survival depended on their public performances, because their patron might command and finance only a few productions per year. Several investors, or SHARERS, put up the capital to finance the company and took a percentage of its profits. The sharers were not just investors; they were involved in all aspects of the theater. In 1603, for instance, the sharers of the King's Men included Shakespeare (playwright and actor), Richard Burbage (James Burbage's son and the company's principal actor, who was the first to play Shakespeare's King Lear, Hamlet, and Macbeth), the actors John Heminges and Henry Condell (who later published Shakespeare's plays), and the comic actors William Kempe (likely played Bottom in *A Midsummer Night's Dream*) and Robert Armin (who played the Fool in *King Lear*), among others. The sharers were responsible for building or leasing a theater, for purchasing plays, for taking on boy actors as apprentices, and for hiring other actors for each production. They also were liable when legal proceedings were brought against the company.

Although several companies flourished during the theater's heyday, life for actors and playwrights was hard. Until 1594, all professional playing companies were forced to perform in a variety of places, in London's various theaters and on tour. Although the scene with the players in *Hamlet* implies that touring was an occasional hardship of the London companies, recent research demonstrates that touring had been commonplace before the building of London's theaters and remained an important aspect of a theater company's vitality throughout the period. Playwrights, who were paid a flat fee by the company for the script of a play, hustled to scrape together a living: Thomas Dekker spent time in debtors' prison, and Ben Jonson died in penury. On the other hand, the theater also provided an opportunity for advancement as well. Several actors, including Richard Burbage and Edward Alleyn, were able to amass considerable fortunes. Shakespeare used the money he received as sharer to invest in property both in London and in his home, Stratford-upon-Avon, where he purchased a large house and land. Such careers were the exception rather than the rule, however, in an era when the theater was widely regarded as illicit and was frequently declared illegal.

The Theaters   English companies performed on three kinds of stage—large, open, outdoor buildings called PUBLIC THEATERS or AMPHITHEATERS that held as many as 3,000 people; smaller, indoor, more elite PRIVATE THEATERS or HALL THEATERS holding perhaps 700; and private performances at court or at the home of the patron. Public theaters, inspired both by

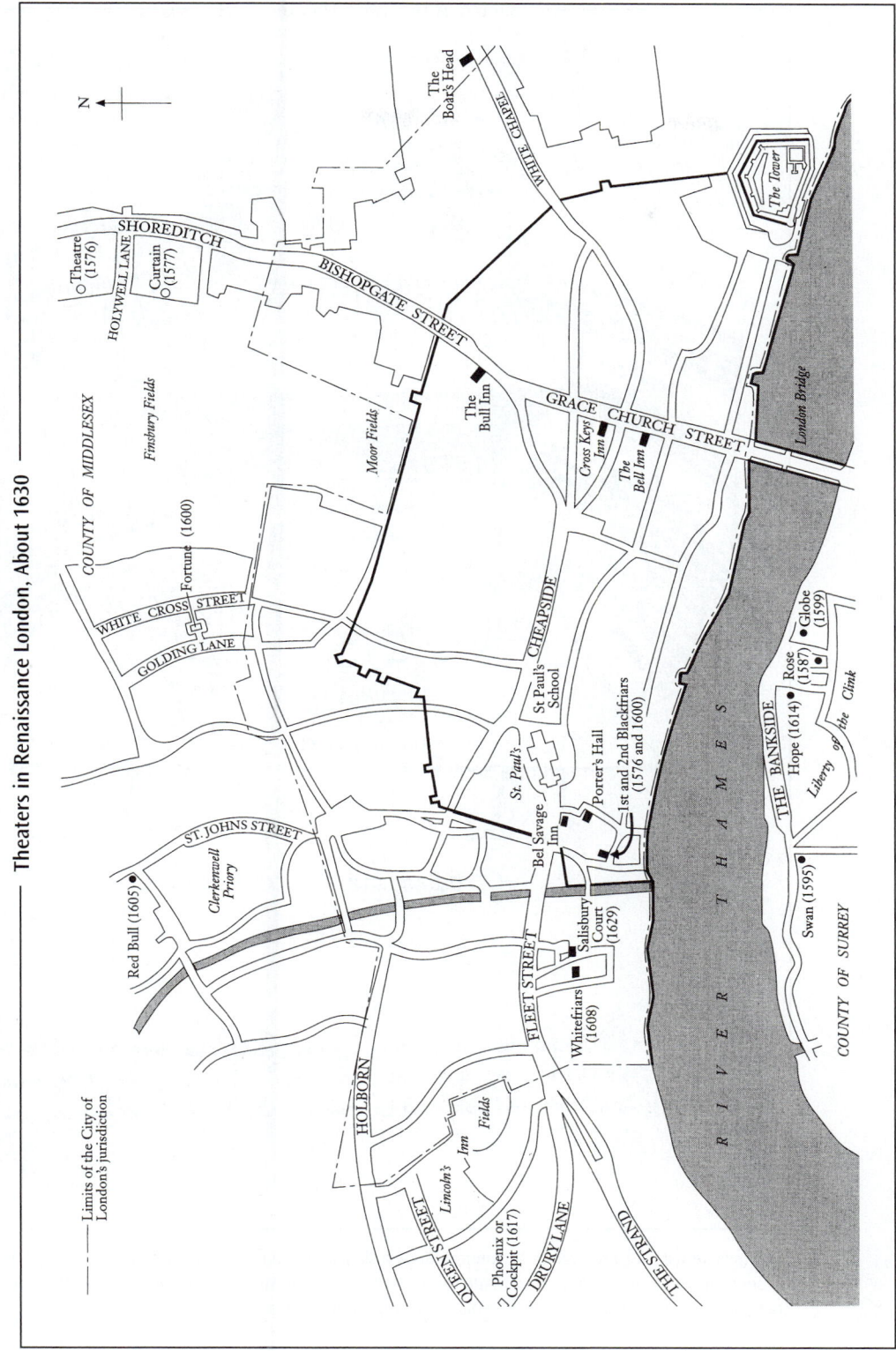

Theaters in Renaissance London, About 1630

N

COUNTY OF MIDDLESEX

SHOREDITCH

Theatre (1576)
HOLYWELL LANE
Curtain (1577)

BISHOPGATE STREET

Finsbury Fields

Moor Fields

The Boat's Head

WHITE CHAPEL

The Bull Inn

GRACE CHURCH STREET

Cross Keys Inn

The Bell Inn

WHITE CROSS STREET
Fortune (1600)
GOLDING LANE

CHEAPSIDE

St. Paul's School

St. Paul's

Porter's Hall
1st and 2nd Blackfriars (1576 and 1600)

Bel Savage Inn

ST. JOHNS STREET

Red Bull (1605)

Clerkenwell Priory

Salisbury Court (1629)

FLEET STREET

Whitefriars (1608)

HOLBORN

Lincoln's Inn Fields

QUEEN STREET

Phoenix or Cockpit (1617)
DRURY LANE

THE STRAND

The Tower

London Bridge

THE BANKSIDE
Hope (1614)
Rose (1587)
Globe (1599)
Libery of the Clink

Swan (1595)

R I V E R   T H A M E S

COUNTY OF SURREY

- - - - Limits of the City of London's jurisdiction

A number of theaters were constructed in London after 1574. The dark line extending from The Tower (lower right) to Blackfriars in the west is the old city wall. Note that, with the exception of the first and second Blackfriars theaters, the theaters are either north of the city (the Fortune, The Theatre, the Curtain, the Red Bull) or south of the Thames River (the Swan, the Hope, the Rose, the Globe). For a sense of scale, the city of London was smaller in area than today's Hyde Park in London, or Central Park in New York.

Sketch of the Swan Theater, 1596

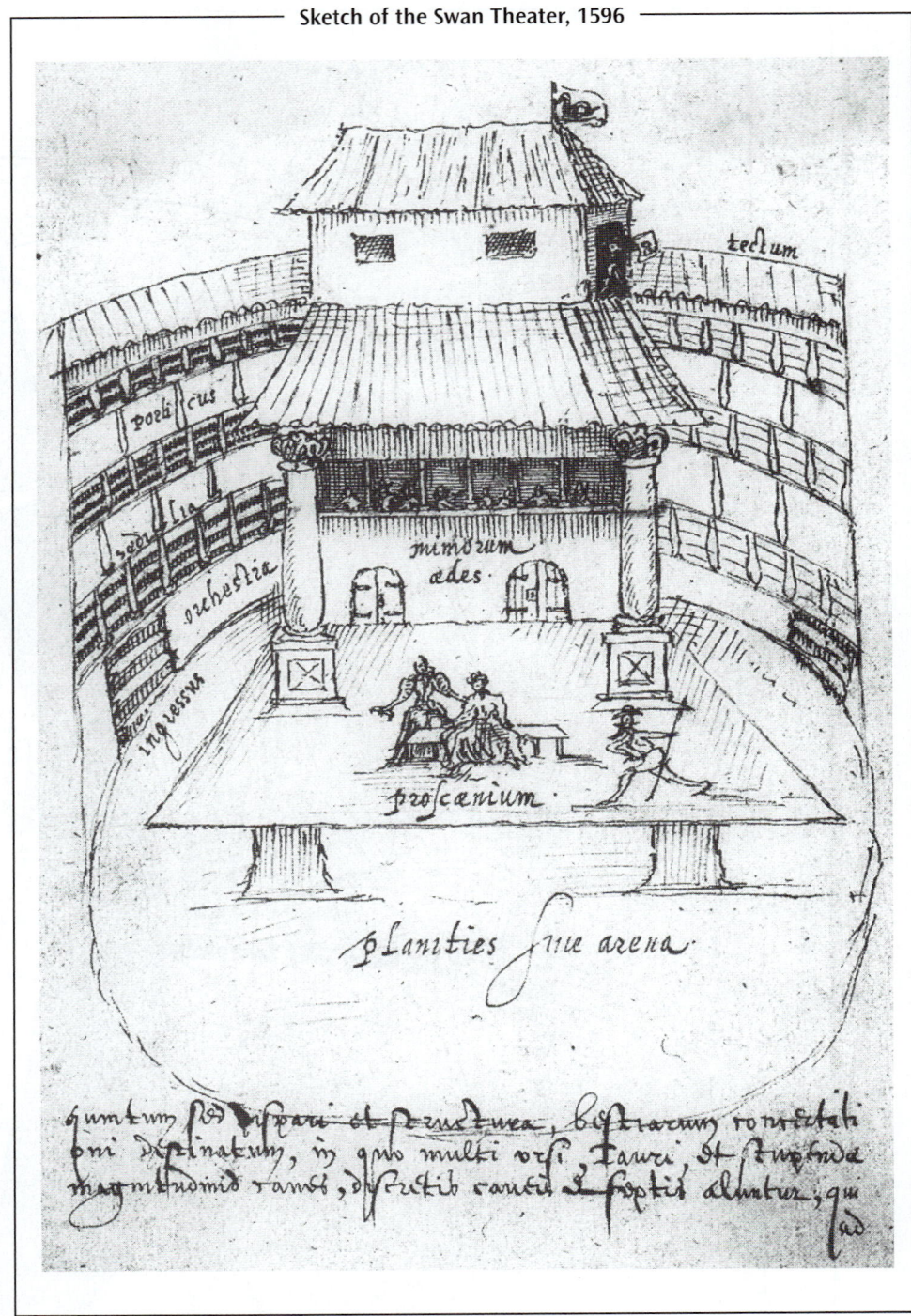

Johannes de Witt, a Dutch visitor to London, drew a sketch of a play in progress at the Swan in 1596. He sent the sketch to a friend, who made this copy. The drawing shows the tiring house with its two stage doors, a three-tiered gallery, the platform stage, and the standing pit.

Modern Reconstruction of the Swan Theater

C. Walter Hodges based this reconstruction on the de Witt sketch.

the innyard booths where companies performed on tour and by the circular arenas used for animal baiting, were outdoor buildings accommodating a large and diverse audience for afternoon performances. Although one theater, the Fortune, was rectangular, most public theaters were polygonal structures. The roughly circular, three-story gallery surrounded an open pit for standing audiences, into which a stage extended at a height of about five feet. The stage was partly roofed, and two doors used for entrances were set into the rear wall, or **TIRING HOUSE**. On the gallery level above the stage, small rooms were used for aristocratic seating, for music, and for scenes requiring action above the stage—as in the balcony scene in *Romeo and Juliet,* or when Prospero appears "aloft" in *The Tempest.* The stage had a central trapdoor (or **GRAVE TRAP**), and its roofed area held a pulley for raising or lowering actors (as in the masque scene in *The Tempest*) or properties. The public theaters catered to a paying audience, charging one penny to enter the pit and an additional penny to enter each of the galleries, where seating was provided on benches. Estimates on the size of the theaters vary, but the largest, such as the Globe or the Fortune, were about 100 feet in external diameter, with a standing yard about 70 feet across, and a stage 45 feet wide and 27 feet deep; they could hold tightly-packed audiences of 2,000 to 3,000 people. Some theaters were considerably smaller. The Rose Theater (whose foundation was discovered in 1989) was a twelve-sided building about 70 feet across, with a pit 50 feet in diameter and a stage roughly 25 by 15 feet. Most of the plays we associate with the Renaissance theater—those of Marlowe, Shakespeare, Jonson, John Webster, John Fletcher, and others—were produced in public theaters such as the Globe, the Rose, the Hope, the Swan, and the Fortune.

(Aside)

SHAKESPEARE'S GLOBE

One of the most fascinating constellations of scholarly, architectural, and theatrical ambition in recent years has been the building of a replica of the 1613 Globe theater on the banks of the Thames River, a few hundred yards from the site of Shakespeare's original theater. Although a variety of efforts have been made throughout the world to build models of the Globe or other English Renaissance theaters, the Bankside project has been notable for the scrupulousness of its research into the location, size, and materials of the Globe and for the care with which it has been constructed. Within the limits of modern legal requirements (fire laws) and social conventions (accessible bathrooms), "Shakespeare's Globe" has been built both as an experiment in Tudor and Stuart building practices and to foster an experiential experiment in the performance of Renaissance plays.

The American actor Sam Wanamaker instigated the project and remained its guiding force until his death in 1993. Part of Wanamaker's vision was that the theater should be both a theatrical and a scholarly endeavor, and much of the success of the final project is due to the team he assembled, including the scholar Andrew Gurr, architect Theo Crosby (who died in 1994), and artistic director Mark Rylance. The accuracy of the building was immeasurably helped by the discovery in 1989 of a section of the Globe's foundation beneath a nineteenth-century building adjacent to the Southwark bridge; although Anchor Terrace is protected as a landmark (preventing much excavation of the Globe's foundation), the section of foundation that has been unearthed has enabled scholars,

using the familiar seventeenth-century engraving of the London skyline by Wenceslaus Hollar, to deduce that the Globe was a polygon constructed of twenty bays, with an exterior diameter of 100 feet. However, building the theater as part of the Bankside Globe Centre—which will also include a replica of a theater designed by Inigo Jones and has exhibition and other facilities—was not an easy task, and much of what has been learned about the Globe has been the result of scholarly investigation into Tudor building practices and the efforts to reconstruct them.

Shakespeare's Globe is an impressively handmade building, using traditional building practices: the bays are made of oak timbers and are held together by more than 6,000 wooden pegs. Once the bays were erected, the walls were filled in with oak staves, lath, and then plastered: rather than using modern plaster, research showed that Tudor builders used a plaster made of lime and cow's hair. Because the hair of modern English cows is too short, the new Globe's builders used a lime plaster mixed with goat hair. A fire sheet was put between each wall, and tests on the resulting lath-and-plaster showed that it could resist 1,000 degrees Fahrenheit for three hours—long enough to empty the theater in an emergency (when the Globe burned in 1613, no injuries were reported, either). The building is also the first wood-framed building to be built in London since the great fire of 1666: its thatched roof is applied in the traditional manner and has been treated with a fire-retardant chemical, and a sprinkler system is installed just under the roofline.

By far the most controversial aspect of the building has been the location of the two pillars that hold up the "heavens," and the design of

the back wall of the stage, the tiring house wall. Between the Prologue Season (1996) and the Globe's opening in 1997, a variety of changes in both were made, resulting in a sumptuously painted backdrop with additional tapestries, and faux-marble columns. Audiences going to the Globe today find themselves in a theater somewhat less crowded than a full house in Shakespeare's day might have been. Although the original Globe held 3,000, the current Globe seats just over 1,000 and can hold about 500 standing "groundlings" in the pit (today, the average audience member is about 10% larger than his or her Elizabethan predecessor; beyond that, modern audiences are not willing—nor are they allowed by fire regulations—to be jammed together as tightly as Elizabethan patrons probably were). But what they will also find—as the production of *Henry V* in 1997 showed—is a theater operating as a kind of experimental venue, using the instrument of Shakespeare's drama to explore how the plays might have worked in their original conditions. At the present time, the company does some productions in period dress (the costumes often themselves made with Tudor clothmaking and dye techniques), and also sometimes experiments with period accents as well; other productions are not held to this "historical" program. The result of a massive and energetic combination of talents, Shakespeare's Globe is finally meant to work as a living theater.[1] ▪

---

[1] The building of the Globe was recorded in a variety of newspaper and scholarly accounts throughout the early 1990s; students interested in learning more about Shakespeare's Globe should consult Shakespeare's Globe Education Centre, Bankside, London SE1 9DT, United Kingdom.

The Globe Theater Foundation

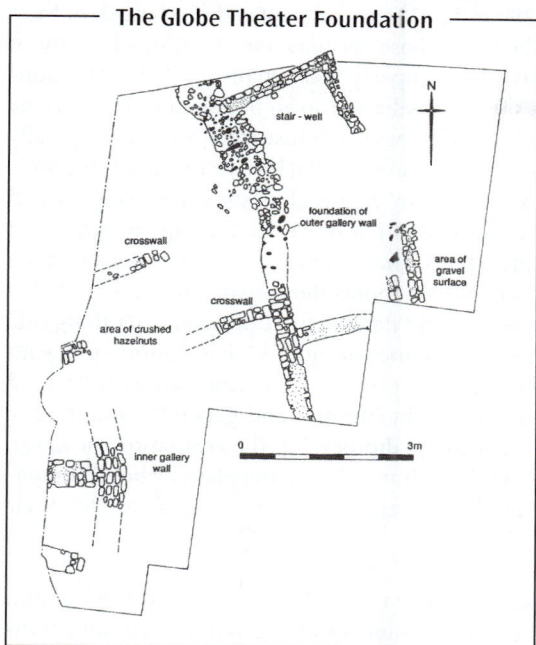

In 1989, part of the foundation of the Globe theater was discovered. This portion of the Globe foundation extends from beneath a landmark nineteenth-century building; the remainder of the Globe foundation is beneath the building and therefore cannot be excavated. Nonetheless, this section of the inner and outer wall of the theater, and of the exterior stairwell which led to the galleries, has enabled scholars to gauge with much greater accuracy both the size and configuration of Shakespeare's theater.

Designing Shakespeare's Globe

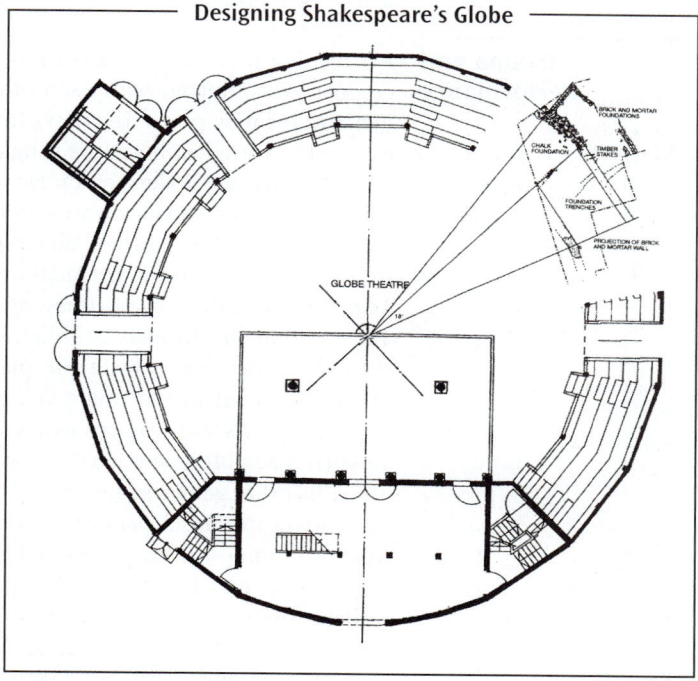

This illustration shows how the archaeological evidence of the Globe theater foundations has been used, along with other evidence, to develop a new understanding of the theater's size and shape. The foundations, which comprise two "bays" or sections of the Globe's exterior structure, enabled Theo Crosby, the architect of the reconstructed Shakespeare's Globe in London, to estimate the overall dimensions of the building (about ninety-nine feet in diameter) and also to determine that the Globe was a twenty-sided polygon.

Although a number of theaters were built in this period, the prestige of the public theaters seems to have declined in the 1620s and 1630s as companies shifted much of their attention to the more lucrative private theaters. These theaters stood within the City of London, on lands called "liberties"; a liberty was a property that had once belonged to monasteries and had remained outside the city's legal jurisdiction, even though it was within the city limit. Best known of these theaters is the Blackfriars playhouse (the property originally belonged to the Dominican friars, who wore black gowns). Blackfriars was used intermittently in the 1590s by boys' companies, troupes of boy chapel choristers who were formed into companies for acting plays. Blackfriars was acquired by James Burbage in 1596, and used by the King's Men for performances after 1608. These theaters were modeled along the lines of a great-house banqueting room: long indoor rooms illuminated by candles, with a low stage at one end, faced by benches for seating and flanked by additional seats along side galleries. The private theaters generally charged sixpence or more for basic admission, with additional charges for special seating in the galleries or on the stage. Companies performed at private theaters in winter and at public theaters in summer and generally brought the same repertoire to both venues. The private theaters did develop the reputation, however, for originating a more satirical and erudite body of drama, including plays by boys' companies like those Rosencrantz describes to Hamlet, explaining why the players have left their usual—and profitable—home in the city.

Drama and Performance

Performing plays in **REPERTORY** over perhaps as many as 200 days a year, the London companies competed with each other for their audiences and generated an enormous demand for new plays. The plays that they bought and performed are among the greatest works of English literature. English drama in this period comprises plays on English history (such as Shakespeare's *Henry V* and *Richard III,* or Marlowe's *Edward II*); on classical history (Shakespeare's *Julius Caesar* and *Coriolanus,* Ben Jonson's *Sejanus*); romantic comedies (such as Shakespeare's *A Midsummer Night's Dream*); city comedies (Shakespeare's *Measure for Measure*); heroic tragedies (Shakespeare's *Hamlet* and *King Lear,* John Webster's *The Duchess of Malfi*); and plays of intrigue or satire (John Marston's *The Malcontent,* Thomas Middleton's *The Changeling*). Later in the period, audiences seemed to develop a taste for plays they called **TRAGICOMEDIES,** usually romantic plays that begin in the tragic vein but proceed to a happy resolution. Several of John Fletcher's plays are tragicomedies of this kind, and Shakespeare's *Cymbeline* and *The Tempest* resemble tragicomedy as well.

This list of genres suggests both the fertile range of innovation in the Renaissance theater and the drama's dependence on models drawn from the classical and medieval theaters. Roman drama—the comedies of Plautus and Terence and the tragedies of Seneca—was widely used in schools and universities as part of the teaching of Latin, and university students often staged these plays in Latin. It is not surprising, then, that some features of classical drama made their way into the Renaissance theater. The model of Shakespearean romantic comedy—mistaken identities, separated lovers, an irascible old man or father, a wily servant—derives directly from Plautus's plays; indeed, Shakespeare's *Comedy of Errors* directly adapts Plautus's *The Brothers Menaechmus* (see Unit 1). In a similar fashion, the violence of Seneca's tragedies makes its way directly into the action of Elizabethan drama. Formally and thematically, however, Renaissance drama also differs sharply from its classical ancestors. Renaissance plays tend to be more diffuse, involving a greater variety of characters and multiple plots; in tragedy, the action is often not quite as closely focused on the fortunes of a single hero as it is in classical tragedy. In these and other ways—in the Christian providence that seems to stand behind the action of many plays, in its variety of contemporary characters, in its use of symbolic anachronism, and in the complex relationship between the dramatic world and the world of the audience—Renaissance drama bears the signs of its medieval inheritance.

Playwrights generally wrote in BLANK VERSE, an unrhymed IAMBIC PENTAMETER line (ten syllables with alternating stress), and occasionally used other verse forms as well. They often used prose, sometimes for emphasis, sometimes to develop the qualities of a particular character. Although modern editors divided the plays into five acts, in most cases Renaissance playwrights probably did not compose their plays in this form. Performance on the public theater stage was rapid and continuous. The theaters used an open stage, few large properties, and had little or no scenery onstage, so that scenes could follow one another without interruption.

Despite the absence of elaborate stage sets, performance in the Renaissance theater was nonetheless spectacular. Actors used costumes, properties, and language to transform the midafternoon stage into a dramatic locale—Prospero's desert island, Lear's heath, Faustus's study. Some larger properties could be wheeled out from the rear doors, or perhaps raised from the trap: a throne, for instance, or a bed for Desdemona in *Othello,* or the hell-mouth used at the end of *Doctor Faustus.* A cannon fired during a production of Shakespeare's *Henry VIII* in 1613 unfortunately set fire to the Globe and burned it to the ground. The unlocalized stage of medieval drama can be seen as the forerunner of the Renaissance theater's fluid use of stage space. The open stage made for an almost cinematic flexibility in performance, as the play could range rapidly from scene to scene, place to place. Costuming was eclectic and anachronistic: the actors wore mainly Elizabethan clothing, adding armor, royal finery, motley, or some "classical" style of gowns when needed. The actors—Burbage, Alleyn, Will Kemp, among many others—were widely praised for their power and effectiveness. Their acting style was oratorical in tragedy and extemporaneous in comedy, but there is no doubt that many were consummate performers, in command of dozens of roles that could be put into play at short notice.

Women in Drama and Performance

Boy actors played a significant part in the experience of English theater, for boy actors played the parts of women and girls onstage, including major roles like Lady Macbeth, Ophelia, and Cleopatra. Much as they did in classical Athens, "women" emerged onstage in Renaissance London only as a side-effect of masculine attitudes and performances. In the English theater, this CROSS-DRESSING came into special prominence, though, because the romantic, sexual, and political intrigue so popular in Renaissance plays was often focused on female characters and therefore on the performance of the boy actors. Indeed, the drama frequently uses cross-dressing as a way of interrogating the power and perquisites of gender, in ways that sometimes confirm and sometimes question the role of gender in English society. English society was an overtly hierarchical one, and despite the power of the "Virgin Queen," women had little access to education, most could not hold property, and they were generally subject to discrimination of many kinds. In this social economy and in a theater in which Puritan opposition to the stage frequently criticized the theater's "effeminacy," the absence of women from the stage became a powerful sign of their absence from other scenes of power. Much as sumptuary laws prevented individuals from wearing jewels and clothing above their social station, so too was cross-dressing a legal offense in sixteenth-century England, punishable by whipping and a prison sentence. The license of the theater, the freedom to create magical new worlds on the stage, was, like other forms of power in the period, the prerogative of men, and the images that men created for the stage are in important ways imprinted with the signs of a specifically masculine imagination. As with all stage conventions, cross-dressing was deeply implicated in the values of the culture outside the theater, so much so that when women did perform onstage in England—a French company used actresses at Blackfriars in 1629—they met with hostility, ridicule, and rejection.

Nonetheless, women not only attended the theater, but a few—aristocratic women, who often patronized poets and other artists—also wrote plays, and sometimes performed in them at court. Queen Elizabeth is thought to have translated a passage from Seneca's *Hercules on Mount Oeta,* and other women similarly adapted or wrote plays. Mary Sidney,

Costumes for Shakespeare's *Titus Andronicus*

Dating from about 1595, this drawing appears to show a scene from *Titus Andronicus,* by William Shakespeare. Two of the actors wear pseudoclassical Roman costumes; the others are dressed in Elizabethan clothing.

Countess of Pembroke and sister of Sir Philip Sidney, translated Robert Garnier's play *The Tragedy of Antonie* in the 1590s. Her niece, Lady Mary Wroth (daughter of Mary Sidney's brother, Robert, and a frequent participant in Jacobean court masques), wrote a mythological play, *Love's Victory,* probably in the early 1620s. Perhaps the best-known plays today are Elizabeth Cary, Viscountess of Falkland's *Tragedy of Miriam* (published in 1613) and the plays published by Margaret Cavendish, Marchioness of Newcastle, in 1662 and 1668. Although these plays were not staged—aristocratic women did not traffic in theater business—they have since become a critical part of our understanding of English Renaissance drama.

The theater had an extraordinary hold on the English imagination. In their many progresses, pageants, and allegorical entertainments, the English monarchs revealed a keen sense of the power of fictive images to represent reality, or a version of it, and so to shape their subjects' understanding of royal power. Playwrights and audiences also found in the theater a magical image of human possibility. Think of Prospero summoning the storm, Ariel, and other spirits with his stagey magic; or of the playwright John Webster's description of "an excellent actor": "All men have been of his occupation, and indeed what he doth feignedly, that do others essentially: this day one plays a Monarch, the next a private person. Here one acts a Tyrant, on the morrow an Exile; a Parasite [sponger] this man tonight, tomorrow a Precisian [Puritan], and so of divers others." Acting and the theater provided a liberating image of human—or, at least, masculine—power: the power to transform oneself and the world. However, the rich, strange, transforming freedom of the theater could also seem empty and terrifying, even demonic. Rather than an image of human potential, the theater could seem to offer an image of the poverty of human action, the sterile and deceptive emptiness of the world we make and inhabit. As King Lear preaches to blinded Gloucester, "When we are born, we cry that we are come / To this great stage of fools." Puritan critics of the theater insistently reminded audiences that the stage's methods—to seduce with the vain and showy image of a false reality—were also Satan's, and that the theater subversively invited audiences to "unman, unChristian, uncreate themselves." Yet it is precisely this transforming power that lies at the heart of the Renaissance theater's fascination for its audience. Although the theater sometimes seemed to depict a world threatened with constant change and loss, it also presented the power of illusion to recreate the real.

Although the banning of the cycle dramas in England in the sixteenth century marked an ending of the traditions of medieval drama and theater there, the same was not true on the continent, where both cycle dramas and morality dramas continued to be performed. In Spain, for example, the AUTOS SACRAMENTALES—morality plays on Christian themes—were produced in major cities such as Madrid, and had an important influence on dramatic writing as well (see Unit IV). Similarly, staging short pageants—like the shepherd plays or *pastorelas* performed today throughout Latin America, and in many Latino communities in the United States, before Christmas—has remained a part of religious festivities in many places; perhaps the most striking of these is the processional staging of the Passion held in Oberammergau, Germany.

In many respects, though, the vivid and popular style of the cycle plays had to wait until the late nineteenth and early twentieth centuries to find an audience; when the manuscripts of the four English cycles first began to be studied seriously in the nineteenth century, their plays were seen merely as primitive precursors to the more finished, literary achievement of English Renaissance dramatists. However, this model of the "evolution" of dramatic forms, from "simple" to "complex," is not really borne out by a close examination of the plays themselves, which use a popular literary and theatrical medium to undertake a drama of enormous subtlety, scope, and power. Beginning in the twentieth century, a number of efforts were made to stage medieval drama—both the cycle plays and morality plays, such as *Everyman*—and the force and theatrical vitality of the plays became immediately apparent. In recent years, the cycle plays have been staged frequently, both in their traditional locations (at York, for instance), and elsewhere: the University of Toronto and the Court Theater at the University of Chicago have mounted very well received versions.

Although the English theaters were closed in 1642, interrupting the practices both of playwriting and of theatrical performance, the secular drama of Renaissance England has had in many respects a more sustained tradition. When the theaters reopened in 1660, they reopened in a very different form—indoor theaters, using lights and stage machinery, replaced the outdoor public theaters of the Jacobean and Caroline periods—and to a much more narrowly circumscribed audience (see Unit IV). And while there was considerable demand for new plays, for many years some plays of the Renaissance period held the stage, and indeed provided the dramatic conventions on which new plays were mapped. While today we tend to think of Shakespeare as the preeminent writer of his era, in the Restoration period, Shakespeare's plays were revived less frequently than those of other playwrights, notably Ben Jonson, James Shirley, and Francis Beaumont and John Fletcher; it was only in the eighteenth century that Shakespeare's plays began to have something approaching their current popularity.

The history of Shakespeare in the theater, however, is a history of adaptation: the concept that Shakespeare's plays have an inner logic and should be performed "as they were written" is a purely modern idea. Shakespeare's plays were, of course, altered in the practice of his own company, and playwrights in the later seventeenth and eighteenth centuries adapted the plays to the taste of their era. John Dryden, for example, transformed Shakespeare's erotically supercharged Antony and Cleopatra into an honorable Roman and his staid matron in his version of *Antony and Cleopatra,* called *All for Love* (1677). Nahum Tate's version of Shakespeare's *King Lear* (1681) concludes with Edgar marrying Cordelia (yes, she lives) and retiring happily offstage with Lear (he lives, too) and Kent; this version

Medieval and Renaissance Drama in Performance and History

of *Lear* held the stage well into the nineteenth century. Rather than regarding these revisions as quaintly misguided, we should recognize that theatrical production always rewrites the drama in the idiom of the day; to their audiences, these productions were fully "Shakespearean," just as films—Kenneth Branagh's setting of *Hamlet* in the nineteenth century, Baz Luhrmann's framing *Romeo and Juliet* as a gang war in a Latin American Verona, or Michael Almereyda's use of Ethan Hawke as an alienated, technologically adept modern New Yorker in his *Hamlet*—are efforts to make Shakespeare speak in ways that will be powerful to audiences today.

Indeed, today we tend to think of Shakespeare across a variety of media: in film and television and advertising as well as in a range of theatrical venues. But for the seventeenth, eighteenth, and nineteenth centuries, Shakespeare was the property of the theater, and many actors and actresses became famous for their portrayals of Shakespearean roles: Thomas Betterton (1635–1710), Charles Macklin (1700–1797), Sarah Siddons (1755–1831), Edmund Kean (1789–1833), Sir Henry Irving (1838–1905), the first English actor to be knighted, and Ellen Terry (1847–1928) are just a few. In many respects, though, David Garrick (1717–1779) had the greatest impact as a Shakespearean actor. In part through his celebrated performances—he was renowned as Hamlet, Macbeth, and Richard III—Garrick helped to create a new interest in Shakespeare in the theater: he had his portrait painted frequently in Shakespearean roles (Hogarth's painting of Garrick as Richard III is a famous example), and he used his popularity to advance Shakespeare's reputation, not least by staging a Shakespeare Jubilee in Stratford. Garrick was a friend of the great literary critic Samuel Johnson, and Garrick's efforts in the theater coincided with a series of attempts to produce better, more accurate editions of Shakespeare's plays. But although Garrick had the reputation of restoring "Shakespeare's" original texts to the stage, he could hardly hope to succeed in the face of a century of popular stage adaptations. Although Garrick did introduce some Shakespearean material that had previously been cut from performances, his King Lear survived the play just as Nahum Tate's did, and his Richard III bawled out—as he had ever since Colley Cibber revised the play in 1700—"Off with his head!" (Indeed, Cibber's version of *Richard III* cuts several characters and persisted onstage well into the twentieth century; it also partly informs Laurence Olivier's film of the play.)

The stage production of Shakespearean drama has always responded to the beliefs and values of its contemporary audiences. Tate's adaptation of *King Lear* was praised by Johnson, for example, for its happy ending seemed to restore justice in the theater; Johnson thought Shakespeare's original ending fine for readers, but too bleak and destructive for the stage. Shakespeare's plays were adapted to the more melodramatic and sentimental tastes of the eighteenth century; in the nineteenth century, a vogue for historical accuracy and stage realism led to a series of splendid efforts to reconstruct the historical setting of the plays: medieval Scotland in Charles Kean's 1853 *Macbeth* or Christian-era England in Henry Irving's *Cymbeline* (1896). These changes in taste are reflected in acting style as well: Betterton's portrayal of Hamlet was renowned in the late seventeenth century for its gravity and grace; Betterton is said never to have raised his arms above his waist, an illustration of neoclassical decorum in performance. By the early decades of the nineteenth century, Samuel Taylor Coleridge remarked that watching Edmund Kean in performance was akin to reading Shakespeare "by flashes of lightning"; Kean's performance impressed his audiences precisely through his well-crafted *lack* of decorum, in accord with Romantic beliefs about emotional expressivity. Irving is in many ways the first modern actor in what we would recognize as a psychological tradition of acting; although his career preceded the Russian director Constantin Stanislavski's pioneering work on the style of realistic performance (see Unit V), Irving's penchant for subtle physical details of characterization—his enemies called them mannerisms—gave his work a psychological concreteness and complexity that was powerful to an audience whose understanding of dramatic character was trained on the novels of Charles Dickens and George Eliot.

The theater also registers its culture's changing social attitudes in its portrayal of Shakespearean roles. Charles Macklin, for example, was probably the first actor to take a more sympathetic portrayal of the Jewish moneylender Shylock in *The Merchant of Venice;* the role had traditionally been performed as a satiric stereotype. Yet even Macklin retained the comic red wig and beard with which Shylock had always been performed; Edmund Kean was the first actor to get rid of them. Henry Irving's production of the play ended after the Act IV trial scene: in his version, *The Merchant of Venice* becomes something more like "The Tragedy of Shylock." In 1994, Peter Sellars set the play in a version of Los Angeles and drew explicit parallels to the police beating of Rodney King and the uprising that followed the acquittal of the officers involved. In Sellars's production the play's Jews were all played as African Americans; the Venetians were all played as Latinos and Latinas; and Portia and her retinue were all played as Asian Americans. Although Sellars's production was deservedly controversial, it illustrates a sense that Shakespeare's drama is capable of entering into new situations unimagined by Shakespeare, and of saying new things as well.

In the twentieth century, the pictorial style favored by Victorian theaters has largely been replaced in an effort to stage the plays in the simpler style of Shakespeare's theater. The first experiments of this kind were undertaken by William Poel (1852–1934), who used his Elizabethan Stage Society to produce versions of *Twelfth Night* and other plays on an open stage, and using a text more closely approximating Shakespeare's. Poel made it possible to see Shakespeare's plays as lively and fast-moving (all those scene changes in Victorian productions had made a Shakespeare play a very long evening, requiring many cuts to compensate for all the time it took to raise and lower sets), and regardless of whether directors (a new role in the theater also dating to this period) have chosen to stage the plays in Elizabethan or other settings, the sense of a rapidly changing series of scenes, localized not by extensive sets onstage but by the language and action, informs most twentieth-century Shakespeare. Indeed, one way to measure the distance between the early twentieth and mid-twentieth centuries would be to compare Beerbohm Tree's 1900 London production of *A Midsummer Night's Dream*—which featured live rabbits onstage in a meticulously constructed "forest"—with Peter Brook's landmark 1970 version, which set the play in a white box onstage, casting the fairies as acrobats on trapezes.

It is now possible to see a range of Shakespeares on the contemporary stage—not only Shakespeare performed in languages other than English, but through the eclectic range of theatrical styles characteristic of the modern stage. Some productions—the "restored" versions, such as the 1997 *Henry V,* at Shakespeare's Globe in London—work hard to use Elizabethan costumes to produce the flavor of Shakespeare's theater. Other productions set the plays in a different historical era (there have been several recent *Henry V* productions set in the American Civil War, for example) to make the workings of the play's society visible to us in more familiar circumstances. Still others use eclectic staging, combining set and costume elements from a variety of periods to take Shakespeare out of history—in the Royal Shakespeare Company's 1991 *Troilus and Cressida,* for example, Agamemnon appeared in a breastplate and a ratty old cardigan sweater: a kind of timeless image of the doddering old general; the RSC's 2005 *Tempest* relocated the play in time and space, to an arctic shipwreck sometime in the early twentieth century. Shakespeare has also been a prominent site of INTERCULTURAL PERFORMANCE investigation, an effort to bring about a dialogue between what is often a "colonial" text and "indigenous" performance traditions: this is the dialectic animating several superb recent performances, notably the *Kathakali King Lear,* performed at Shakespeare's Globe Theater in 1999, and the work of Ong Keng Sen's

READING THE MATERIAL THEATER

One of the most chastening facts concerning the early modern theater is that most of the drama performed on its stages has been lost: plays were given to the theater companies in handwritten manuscript; they were copied out by hand into parts—scrolls containing each actor's part, with cues for each of his speeches—and the copy of the play maintained by the company was, likewise, a handwritten copy. Needless to say, nearly all such manuscripts have been lost.

Although by the later sixteenth century typesetting was a familiar technology in Renaissance England, the proliferation of printed documents—volumes of classical Latin texts, broadsides, ballads, religious pamphlets, guides to domestic work, conduct books for courtiers—presented Shakespeare's audiences with an information explosion much akin to the one we face in the digital age. At the same time, print was not understood to be an appropriate vehicle for all forms of writing. Poets, for example, saw print—associated with the declassé mercantile world of commerce—as an inferior mode for circulating their poems: to gain the kind of aristocratic prestige (and patronage) they most desired, poets typically circulated their poems in manuscript among the aristocrats at court.

Nonetheless, plays were published, increasingly with elaborate prefatory material laying claim to the play's literary merit, even sometimes claiming—as is the case with the version of Shakespeare's *Troilus and Cressida* published in 1609—that the play was never actually performed. Plays were generally published in a small, inexpensive format; because the sheet of paper on which the text is printed is folded twice (into four) before the book is bound, these small books are known bibliographically as **QUARTOS**. It's not entirely clear what incentive either printers or theatre companies might have had to publish plays; it remains controversial whether a printer could have made any money from a quarto play, though quarto editions of plays were published with increasing regularity after 1594, sometimes going into several editions. Although there was no copyright protection, theatre companies had little to fear from the publication of one of their plays: plays were licensed by the Master of Revels to an individual company, so staging a printed play approved for another company would have been a very big risk. What seems to be the case is that the emerging industry of print was, in a sense, conceptually independent of the stage: plays seem to have had a rather different identity in each location, and while some playwrights (Jonson, George Chapman, John Webster) seem to have taken considerable care with even the quarto publication of their plays,

others—notably Shakespeare—seem to have given little attention to the accuracy and quality of these books. Because of their size, the sometimes slipshod character of their presswork, and their association with the theater, quarto volumes of plays were also stigmatized; Sir Thomas Bodley—whose library, the Bodleian, remains the Oxford University library—famously refused to purchase such "idle rifferaffes" for his collection. Since quarto-sized volumes of individual plays were usually published in very small quantities, they are today quite rare. While over 300 copies of the folio-size collection of Shakespeare's plays remain, only two (slightly different) copies of the 1603 quarto of *Hamlet* are known to exist, and only five copies of the much-superior 1604 second quarto.

Many of Shakespeare's plays were published in quarto form during his lifetime (*Hamlet,* for example), but nearly half of his plays—including *Macbeth, Antony and Cleopatra, The Tempest,* and others—would be unknown to us without the efforts of two of his fellow-sharers, John Heminges and Henry Condell, who published a nearly complete collection of Shakespeare's plays (in the large-size **FOLIO** format) in 1623, seven years after the playwright's death. This was a signal event in the history of dramatic publishing—in 1623, only one other English dramatist, Ben Jonson, had published a collected *Works* on this scale.

Theatreworks Company of Singapore, notably *King Lear* (1997) and *Desdemona* (2000), productions that mix a range of Asian languages and performance styles.

Of course, the ability of the modern stage to bring a great technological flexibility to Shakespeare is matched by the possibilities of film. Shakespeare plays were among the first subjects of silent filmmakers, and many of the most distinguished films of the twentieth century are versions of Shakespearean drama. Indeed, contemporary students of Shakespeare are often much more likely to see a Shakespeare film than a

READING THE MATERIAL THEATER

We can learn a lot about the condition of the theater and about the relationship between theater practice and the emerging norms of print culture by closely examining the printed texts of Shakespeare's plays in both quarto and folio versions. Here, for example, is the title page of *Titus Andronicus,* one of Shakespeare's earliest successes, a play that has been adapted for film by the director and designer Julie Taymor, and a play that testifies to the fascination that Senecan drama held for playwrights and audiences in the 1580s and 1590s. It is a violent, rhetorically rich play. What can we learn about the theater, and about Renaissance attitudes toward theater, drama, and literature, from this title page? Some aspects to consider: How is the page designed? What are its most prominent visual features? How are different typefaces used to highlight different kinds of information? How is the book designed to appeal to a potential purchaser? What elements are visually prominent and which are less prominent? Is there information missing that might seem necessary to a modern purchaser? How can we read the information presented here as an index of the relation between two newly emerging industries—professional theater and literary publishing—in the period? ■

Title page of Titus Andronicus.

live Shakespeare performance, especially with the number of exciting Shakespeare films produced in the 1990s: Kenneth Branagh in *Henry V, Much Ado About Nothing,* and *Hamlet;* Ian McKellan in *Richard III;* Mel Gibson in *Hamlet;* Leonardo Di Caprio and Claire Danes in *Romeo + Juliet.* As a part of the common cultural inheritance of the West—and indeed, frequently challenged as such by resistant, postcolonial productions in India, Canada, Africa, and elsewhere—Shakespeare is produced today across the spectrum of performance.

Michael Pennington appears as Hamlet in the Royal Shakespeare Company production, 1980.

In this scene from an American Shakespeare Theater production of *The Tempest,* Ariel describes how he has performed Prospero's commands.

As the "cavalier" costumes suggest, John Gielgud's acclaimed 1934 production of *Hamlet* was set in the later seventeenth century, rather than in the Elizabethan era; here, Hamlet and Laertes duel in the play's final scene.

The York Crucifixion

The cycle of Corpus Christi pageants produced in the city of York is the oldest and best-recorded of any of the English Corpus Christi cycles. The cycle was devised as part of the celebration of the Feast of Corpus Christi and was first produced during the late fourteenth century. In the late Middle Ages, York was a flourishing and important city, with the wealth necessary to stage a great cycle of more than fifty plays; the York cycle continued to be performed as late as the 1560s. As in other towns, craft guilds—sometimes called "mysteries"—were given the responsibility for staging individual pageants, and the pageants were occasionally assigned to "appropriate" guilds; while each guild paid for its pageant wagon and the costs of the production, it's not clear to what extent guild-members may have had additional involvement. In the York cycle, for example, the shipwrights produced the *Building of the Ark* pageant, the fishers and mariners produced *Noah and the Flood,* the masons and the goldsmiths guilds produced *Herod* and *The Adoration of the Magi,* and the bakers produced *The Last Supper.* The pinners—makers of wooden pegs—produced the play on the Crucifixion. Each guild elected an officer called a **PAGEANT MASTER,** who was responsible for gathering money from the guild's members to finance the pageant and for hiring an individual to supervise the play's production—hiring, rehearsing, and paying the actors.

In York, each play in the Corpus Christi cycle was performed on a separate pageant wagon; the wagons were arranged in the order of the plays—from the first play, *The Fall of the Angels,* to the last, *The Last Judgment*—and proceeded through the city, stopping at each of twelve stations. The first station was opposite the gates to the Holy Trinity priory, and the city's Common Clerk was stationed there with the Registry of the pageants, presumably to supervise. Audiences could choose one station and watch while each of the pageants was performed in order. The procession began at 4:30 in the morning, and the last play was probably performed at the twelfth station sometime after midnight. Although little is known about the pageant wagons themselves, records suggest that the wagons were elaborately decorated and often included impressive scenery and special effects. The York mercers guild, which produced *The Last Judgment,* had a wagon that held a complicated set, including a "heaven," a winch to raise and lower God, and a "hell-mouth." Some device operated the nine mechanical angels who sat with God, among the brightly colored clouds (made of cloth) in the "heaven." Because the pageant wagons were expensive to build and decorate and were owned by the guild, they were stored between annual performances of the cycle; when a pageant wagon became dilapidated or the guild became wealthier, a new wagon would be devised for the pageant.

Each guild was responsible for maintaining the text of its pageant; the city of York, however, began keeping an official record of the Corpus Christi plays sometime between 1463 and 1477. This volume, called the *Register,* is the sole manuscript of the York cycle of plays, and

This photograph shows a contemporary production of the York cycle Crucifixion play at the University of Toronto. One element of the play's original performance is reenacted here: the hard work the Roman soldiers have to do as part of the act of crucifixion.

contains forty-seven of the more than fifty pageants. The *Register* at once preserved the plays and functioned as a document of civic control: it enabled city clerks to assess how faithfully the guilds were upholding their chartered performances. Only one copy of an original play survives, the scriveners' guild's *Incredulity of Thomas.* Comparison with other surviving documents from the period reveals that the cycle underwent several changes during the two centuries of its performance. Some pageants were reassigned to different guilds and several were revised. The most notable of these revisions took place in the fifteenth century and are attributed to an unknown playwright now called the "York Realist:" *The Crucifixion* is a particularly fine example of this work. As in other cycle plays, the York Realist uses recognizably contemporary characters as part of the setting of Biblical events. Like the author of the Wakefield/Towneley *Second Shepherds' Pageant,* who makes the Bethlehem shepherds appear to be much like fifteenth-century English peasants, the York Realist makes the four Roman soldiers seem like familiar members of the medieval community: they are medieval laborers, and share many of the audience's attitudes and prejudices, notably its deep antisemitism. But the York playwright's skill goes well beyond an eye for realistic characterization. With a sure sense of drama, he gives Christ only two speeches in the play, one as the soldiers bring him to the cross, and another after the cross has been raised and jarringly dropped into its mortise. Christ's silence stands out against the soldiers' cruel joking as they nail him to the cross, and the playwright clearly contrasts Christ's effort to redeem mankind with the selfish and earthbound imagination of the soldiers, who ridicule his final words and fall to gambling for his cloak. Like many of the cycle plays, the York *Crucifixion* asked its audience to contemplate the relationship between the eternal and the temporal by staging the Christian narrative in the everyday terms of medieval life.

The York Crucifixion

Anonymous

EDITED BY A. C. CAWLEY

CHARACTERS

JESUS
FOUR SOLDIERS

SCENE: *Calvary.*

1 SOLDIER: Sir knights, take heed hither in hie:
    This deed undree we may not draw;
    Ye wot yourselves as well as I
    How lords and leaders of our law
5   Have given doom that this dote shall die.
2 SOLDIER: Sir, all their counsel well we know.
    Since we are come to Calvary,
    Let ilk man help now as him owe.
3 SOLDIER: We are all ready, lo,
10   That forward to fulfil.
4 SOLDIER: Let hear how we shall do,
    And go we tite theretill.

1 SOLDIER: It may not help here for to hone,
    If we shall any worship win.
15 2 SOLDIER: He must be dead needlings by noon.
3 SOLDIER: Then it is good time that we begin.
4 SOLDIER: Let ding him down! Then is he done.
    He shall not dere us with his din.
1 SOLDIER: He shall be set and learned soon,
20   With care to him and all his kin.
2 SOLDIER: The foulest death of all
    Shall he die for his deeds.
3 SOLDIER: That means cross him we shall.
4 SOLDIER: Behold, so right he redes.

25 1 SOLDIER: Then to this work as must take heed,
    So that our working be not wrong.
2 SOLDIER: None other note to neven is need,
    But let us haste him for to hang.
3 SOLDIER: And I have gone for gear, good speed,
30   Both hammers and nails large and long.
4 SOLDIER: Then may we boldly do this deed;
    Come on, let kill this traitor strong.
1 SOLDIER: Fair might ye fall in fere,
    That have wrought on this wise.
35 2 SOLDIER: Us needs not for to lere
    Such faitours to chastise.

3 SOLDIER: Since ilka thing is right arrayed,
    The wiselier now work may we.

4 SOLDIER: The cross on ground is goodly graid,
    And bored even as it ought to be.   40
1 SOLDIER: Look that the lad on length be laid,
    And made be ta'en unto this tree.
2 SOLDIER: For all his fare he shall be flayed:
    That on essay soon shall ye see.
3 SOLDIER: Come forth, thou cursed knave,   45
    Thy comfort soon shall keel.
4 SOLDIER: Thine hire here shalt thou have.
1 SOLDIER: Walk on! Now work we well.

JESUS: Almighty God, my Father free,
    Let these matters be marked in mind: 50
    Thou bade that I should buxom be,
    For Adam's plight to be pined.
    Here to death I oblige me,
    From that sin for to save mankind,
    And sovereignly beseech I thee   55
    That they for me may favour find;
    And from the fiend them fend,
    So that their souls be safe
    In wealth withouten end;
    I keep not else to crave.   60

1 SOLDIER: We! hark, sir knights, for Mahound's blood!
    Of Adam's kind is all his thought.
2 SOLDIER: The warlock waxes worse than wood;
    This doleful death ne dreadeth he nought.
3 SOLDIER: Thou shouldst have mind, with main and mood,   65
    Of wicked works that thou has wrought.
4 SOLDIER: I hope that he had been as good
    Have ceased of saws that he up sought.
1 SOLDIER: Those saws shall rue him sore,
    For all his sauntering, soon.   70
2 SOLDIER: Ill speed them that him spare
    Till he to death be done!

3 SOLDIER: Have done belive, boy, and make thee boun,
    And bend thy back unto this tree.

1–2 **Sir knights . . . draw** Quickly pay attention to me: we cannot do this deed negligently 5 **dote** fool 8 **ilk** each; **owe** ought 10 **forward** agreement 12 **tite theretill** quickly to it 13 **to hone** delay 15 **needlings** of necessity 17 **ding** knock 18 **dere** harm 19 **He shall . . . soon** He shall be beaten and soon taught a lesson 20 **care** sorrow 23–24 **That means . . . redes** That means we shall crucify him. . . . See, he advises rightly 27 **None . . . need** There is no need to mention any other sort of work (i.e., other than hanging) 29 **good speed** quickly 33 **Fair might . . . fere** Good luck to you all 34 **wrought . . . wise** in this way 35 **Us needs** we need; **lere** learn 36 **faitours** impostors 37 **ilka** every; **arrayed** arranged 39 **goodly graid** made ready

40 **bored even** bored with holes 41–42 **Look that . . . tree** See that the fellow is laid lengthwise and fastened to this cross 43 **fare** boasting; **flayed** terrified 44 **That on . . . see** That you shall soon see when we try 46 **keel** grow cold 47 **hire** payment 49 **free** noble 51 **buxom** ready 52 **pined** tortured 53 **oblige me** pledge myself 55 **sovereignly** above all 57 **fend** defend 59 **withouten** happiness 60 **I keep . . . crave** I have no wish to ask for anything else 61 **We!** an exclamation of surprise; **for . . . blood** by Mahomet's blood 62 **kind** race 63 **The warlock . . . wood** The sorcerer waxes worse than mad (i.e., behaves worse than a madman) 64 **doleful** painful 65 **Thou . . . main and mood** You should try hard to remember 67–70 **I hope . . . soon** I think he would have done well to stop telling those tales he made up. . . . Soon he shall bitterly regret all his babbling 71 **Ill speed** bad luck to 73 **Have done . . . boun** Be quick, knave, and get ready

(JESUS *lies down.*)

75 4 SOLDIER: Behold, himself has laid him down,
　　　In length and breadth as he should be.
1 SOLDIER: This traitor here tainted of treason,
　　　Go fast and fetter him then, ye three;
　　　And since he claimeth kingdom with crown,
80　　Even as a king here hang shall he.
2 SOLDIER: Now, certes, I shall not fine
　　　Ere his right hand be fast.
3 SOLDIER: The left hand then is mine;
　　　Let see who bears him best.

85 4 SOLDIER: His limbs on length then shall I lead,
　　　And even unto the bore them bring.
1 SOLDIER: Unto his head I shall take heed,
　　　And with my hand help him to hang.
2 SOLDIER: Now since we four shall do this deed,
90　　And meddle with this unthrifty thing,
　　　Let no man spare for special speed,
　　　Till that we have made ending.
2 SOLDIER: This forward may not fail;
　　　Now we are right arrayed.
95 4 SOLDIER: This boy here in our bail
　　　Shall bide full bitter braid.

1 SOLDIER: Sir knights, say now, work we ought?
2 SOLDIER: Yes, certes, I hope I hold this hand.
3 SOLDIER: And to the bore I have it brought
100　Full buxomly withouten band.
1 SOLDIER: Strike on then hard, for him thee bought.
2 SOLDIER: Yes, here is a stub will stiffly stand;
　　　Through bones and sinews it should be sought.
　　　This work is well, I will warrant.
105 1 SOLDIER: Say, sir, how do we there?
　　　This bargain may not blin.
3 SOLDIER: It fails a foot and more;
　　　The sinews are so gone in.

4 SOLDIER: I hope that mark amiss be bored.
110 2 SOLDIER: Then must he bide in bitter bale.
3 SOLDIER: In faith, it was over-scantily scored;
　　　That makes it foully for to fail.

1 SOLDIER: Why carp ye so? Fast on a cord,
　　　And tug him to, by top and tail.
3 SOLDIER: Yea, thou commandest lightly as a lord; 115
　　　Come help to hale him, will ill hail!
1 SOLDIER: Now certes that shall I do—
　　　Full snelly as a snail.
3 SOLDIER: And I shall tache him to,
　　　Full nimbly with a nail. 120

　　This work will hold, that dare I heet,
　　　For now are fest fast both his hend.
4 SOLDIER: Go we all four then to his feet,
　　　So shall our space be speedily spent.
2 SOLDIER: Let see what bourd his bale might beet; 125
　　　Thereto my back now would I bend.
4 SOLDIER: Oh! this work is all unmeet:
　　　This boring must all be amend.
1 SOLDIER: Ah, peace, man, for Mahoun!
　　　Let no man wot that wonder; 130
　　　A rope shall rug him down,
　　　If all his sinews go asunder.

2 SOLDIER: That cord full kindly can I knit,
　　　The comfort of this carl to keel.
1 SOLDIER: Fest on then fast that all be fit; 135
　　　It is no force how fell he feel.
2 SOLDIER: Lug on, ye both, a little yet.
3 SOLDIER: I shall not cease, as I have sele.
4 SOLDIER: And I shall fond him for to hit.
2 SOLDIER: Oh, hale! 140
4 SOLDIER:　　　　Ho now! I hold it well.
1 SOLDIER: Have done, drive in that nail,
　　　So that no fault be found.
4 SOLDIER: This working would not fail,
　　　If four bulls here were bound.

1 SOLDIER: These cords have evil increased his pains, 145
　　　Ere he were till the borings brought.
2 SOLDIER: Yea, asunder are both sinews and veins
　　　On ilka side, so have we sought.
3 SOLDIER: Now all his gauds nothing him gains;
　　　His sauntering shall with bale be bought. 150
4 SOLDIER: I will go say to our sovereigns
　　　Of all these works how we have wrought.

---

77 **tainted** convicted　81 **certes** certainly; **fine** stop　84 **Let see . . . best** Let's see who acquits himself best　85 **His limbs . . . lead** Then I shall draw his limbs to their full length　86 **bore** hole　90 **unthrifty** unprofitable　91 **Let no . . . speed** Let no one use less than his best possible speed　93 **This forward . . . fail** i.e., we must not fail to carry out our agreement　94 **right arrayed** properly prepared　95 **boy** knave; **bail** charge　96 **Shall bide . . . braid** Shall suffer a most bitter onslaught　97 **Sir knights . . . ought** Are we doing anything? (The First Soldier is evidently in charge)　98 **hope** think　100 **Full buxomly . . . band** Quite obediently without [having to use a] rope　101 **for him . . . bought** by Him who redeemed you　102–103 **here . . . be sought** Here is a nail that will stand fast; [in order to find it] we shall have to look for it through bones and sinews　106–108 **This bargain . . . in** This business may not cease (i.e., must go on). . . . It [the hole] is out by a foot or more; his sinews are so shrunken　109 **I hope . . . bored** I think that mark is bored wrongly (i.e., the hole has not been bored in the place marked for it)　110 **bittle bale** grievous torment　111–112 **It was . . . fail** i.e., the mark was put in the wrong place; that is why the hole is badly out

113 **carp** prate; **Fast** fasten　114 **And tug . . . tail** And tug him to [the holes] by his head and feet　115 **lightly** readily　116 **Come help . . . hail** Come and help pull him, confound you!　118 **snelly** quickly (A sarcastic aside by the First Soldier, who considers himself a foreman, not a workman)　119 **tache him to** fasten him to [the cross]　121 **heet** promise　122 **For now . . . hend** For now both his hands are firmly fastened　124–125 **So shall . . . beet** So shall our time be well spent. . . . Let's see what jest can lighten his misery　127 **unmeet** unfit　128 **amend** improved　130 **Let no . . . wonder** Let no one know about this extraordinary thing. (The First Soldier seems to believe that their work has been undone by magic)　131 **rug** pull　133 **kindly** thoroughly　134 **carl** churl　135–136 **Fest on . . . feel** Get hold of it firmly then so that all shall be ready; it doesn't matter how cruelly he feels it　138 **I shall . . . sele** As I hope for happiness　139 **fond** try　140 **hale** pull　145 **evil** severely　146 **borings** boreholes　148 **On ilka . . . sought** Everywhere, so fare as we have looked　149 **gauds** tricks　150 **His sauntering . . . bought** His babbling shall be paid for with suffering　152 **Of all . . . wrought** How well we have done our work

1 SOLDIER: Nay, sirs, another thing
    Falls first to you and me:
155   They bade we should him hang
    On high that men might see.

2 SOLDIER: We wot well so their words were;
    But, sir, that deed will do us dere.
1 SOLDIER: It may not mend for to moot more;
160   This harlot must be hanged here.
2 SOLDIER: The mortice is made fit therefor.
3 SOLDIER: Fest on your fingers then, in fere.
4 SOLDIER: I ween it will never come there;
    We four raise it not right to-year.
165 1 SOLDIER: Say, man, why carp'st thou so?
    Thy lifting was but light.
2 SOLDIER: He means there must be mo
    To heave him up on height.

3 SOLDIER: Now certes, I hope it shall not need
170   To call to us more company.
    Methink we four should do this deed,
    And bear him to yon hill on high.
1 SOLDIER: It must be done, without dread.
    No more, but look ye be ready,
175   And this part shall I lift and lead;
    On length he shall no longer lie.
    Therefore now make ye boun:
    Let bear him to yon hill.
4 SOLDIER: Then will I bear here down,
180   And tent his toes until.

2 SOLDIER: We two shall see till either side,
    For else this work will wry all wrong.
3 SOLDIER: We are ready, good sirs. Abide,
    And let me first his feet up fong.
185 2 SOLDIER: Why tent ye so to tales this tide?
1 SOLDIER: Lift up!

(*They lift the cross.*)

4 SOLDIER: Let see!
2 SOLDIER: Oh, lift along!
3 SOLDIER: From all this harm he should him hide,
    And he were God.
4 SOLDIER: The devil him hang!
1 SOLDIER: For-great harm have I hent:
190   My shoulder is asunder.

2 SOLDIER: And certes I am near shent,
    So long have I borne under.

3 SOLDIER: This cross and I in two must twin,
    Else breaks my back asunder soon.
4 SOLDIER: Lay down again and leave your din;   195
    This deed for us will never be done.

(*They lay it down.*)

1 SOLDIER: Essay, sirs, let see if any gin
    May help him up withouten hone;
    For here should wight men worship win,
    And not with gauds all day to gone.   200
2 SOLDIER: More wighter men than we
    Full few I hope ye find.
3 SOLDIER: This bargain will not be,
    For certes me wants wind.

4 SOLDIER: So will of work never we were;   205
    I hope this carl some cautels cast.
2 SOLDIER: My burden sat me wondrous sore;
    Unto the hill I might not last.
1 SOLDIER: Lift up, and soon he shall be there;
    Therefore fest on your fingers fast.   210
3 SOLDIER: Oh, lift!

(*They lift up the cross again.*)

1 SOLDIER: We lo!
4 SOLDIER: A little more.
2 SOLDIER: Hold then!
1 SOLDIER: How now!
2 SOLDIER: The worst is past.
3 SOLDIER: He weighs a wicked weight.
2 SOLDIER: So may we all four say,
    Ere he was heaved on height,   215
    And raised in this array.

4 SOLDIER: He made us stand as any stones,
    So boistous was he for to bear.
1 SOLDIER: Now raise him nimbly for the nonce,
    And set him by this mortice here;   220
    And let him fall in all at once,
    For certes that pain shall have no peer.
3 SOLDIER: Heave up!
4 SOLDIER: Let down, so all his bones
    Are asunder now on sides sere.

(*They drop the cross into its mortice.*)

---

157 **We wot . . . were** We know well that their words were so (i.e., that they said so) 158 **dere** harm 159 **It may . . . more** It won't help to argue any more 160 **harlot** rascal 161 **fit therefor** ready for it 162 **Fest on . . . fere** Fasten your fingers on to it then, all together 163 **ween** think 164 **We four . . . to-year** We four won't lift it up-right this year 166 **light** feeble 167 **mo** more 168 **height** high 173 **dread** doubt 174 **No more** No more [talking] 175 **this part** i.e., the head of the cross; **lead** carry 176 **length** prone 179–180 **Then will . . . until** Then I will carry him down here (i.e., at the foot of the cross), and attend to his toes 181 **We two . . . side** i.e., to each arm of the cross 182 **wry** go 184 **fong** take 185 **Why tent . . . tide** Why do you now listen to such talk [when there's work to be done]? 186 **along** lengthwise 187 **hide** protect 188 **And** if 189 **For-great** very great; **hent** suffered

191 **shent** exhausted 192 **borne under** held it up 193 **twin** part 197 **gin** contrivance 198 **hone** delay 199 **wight** valiant 200 **And not . . . gone** And not spend all day playing pranks 203–204 **This bargain . . . wind** This business won't get finished, for certainly I am short of breath 205–206 **So will . . . cast** We were never at such a loss in our work; I think this fellow has played some tricks [magic] 207 **sore** grieved 211 **We lo!** Ah well! 216 **array** fashion 217–218 **He made . . . bear** He brought us to a standstill; he was so bulky to carry 219 **for the nonce** [a metrical tag] 223–224 **so all . . . sere** so that all his bones break asunder everywhere

225 1 SOLDIER: This falling was more fell
Than all the harms he had;
Now may a man well tell
The least lith of this lad.

3 SOLDIER: Methinketh this cross will not abide,
230 Ne stand still in this mortice yet.
4 SOLDIER: At the first time was it made over-wide:
That makes it wave, thou mayst well wit.
1 SOLDIER: It shall be set on ilka side,
So that it shall not further flit;
235 Good wedges shall we take this tide,
And fest the foot, then all is fit.
2 SOLDIER: Here are wedges arrayed
For that, both great and small.
3 SOLDIER: Where are our hammers laid,
240 That we should work withal?

4 SOLDIER: We have them here even at our hand.
2 SOLDIER: Give me this wedge; I shall it in drive.
4 SOLDIER: Here is another yet ordand.
3 SOLDIER: Do take it me hither belive.
245 1 SOLDIER: Lay on then fast.
3 SOLDIER: Yes, I warrant
I thring them sam, so mote I thrive.
Now will this cross full stably stand;
All if he rave, they will not rive.
1 SOLDIER: (*To Christ.*) Say, sir, how likes you now
250 This work that we have wrought?
4 SOLDIER: We pray you say us how
Ye feel, or faint ye aught.

JESUS: All men that walk by way or street,
Take tent ye shall no travail tine;
255 Behold my head, my hands, my feet,
And fully feel now, ere ye fine,
If any mourning may be meet,
Or mischief measured unto mine.
My Father, that all bales may beet,
260 Forgive these men that do me pine.
What they work wot they nought;
Therefore, my Father, I crave,

Let never their sins be sought,
But see their souls to save.

1 SOLDIER: We! hark! he jangles like a jay.   265
2 SOLDIER: Methink he patters like a pie.
3 SOLDIER: He has been doing so all day,
And made great moving of mercy.
4 SOLDIER: Is this the same that gan us say
That he was God's Son almighty?   270
1 SOLDIER: Therefore he feels full fell affray,
And deemed this day for to die.
2 SOLDIER: Vah! qui destruis templum. . .
3 SOLDIER: His saws were so, certain.
4 SOLDIER: And, sirs, he said to some   275
He might raise it again.

1 SOLDIER: To muster that he had no might,
For all the cautels that he could cast;
All if he were in word so wight,
For all his force now he is fast.   280
As Pilate deemed, is done and dight;
Therefore I rede that we go rest.
2 SOLDIER: This race mun be rehearsed right,
Through the world both east and west.
3 SOLDIER: Yea, let him hang there still,   285
And make mows on the moon.
4 SOLDIER: Then may we wend at will.
1 SOLDIER: Nay, good sirs, not so soon.

For certes us needs another note:
This kirtle would I of you crave.   290
2 SOLDIER: Nay, nay, sir, we will look by lot
Which of us four falls it to have.
3 SOLDIER: I rede we draw cut for this coat—
Lo, see how soon—all sides to save.
4 SOLDIER: The short cut shall win, that well ye wot,   295
Whether it fall to knight or knave.
1 SOLDIER: Fellows, ye thar not flite,
For this mantle is mine.
4 SOLDIER: Go we then hence tite;
This travail here we tine.   300

---

225 **fell** painful   227 **tell** count   228 **lith** limb; **lad** fellow   229 **not abide** not stand firm   230 **Ne** nor   231 **it** i.e., the mortice   232 **it** i.e., the cross; **wave** move; **wit** know   233 **set on. . . side** fixed on each side   234 **flit** move   237 **arrayed** prepared   240 **withal** with   243–244 **Here is . . . believe** Here is yet another made ready. . . . Bright it here to me quickly   246 **I thring . . . thrive** I shall press them (i.e., wedge and cross) together, as I hope to prosper   247 **stably** firmly   248 **All if . . . rive** All if he rave, they will not rive   249 **how likes you** do you like   252 **or faint . . . aught** or whether you are faint at all   254 **Take tent . . . tine** Take care that you waste none of my suffering   256 **fine** stop   257 **meet** fitting   258 **mischief** misfortune   259 **that all . . . beet** who may remedy all ills   260–261 **do me . . . nought** that inflict suffering on me. They know not what they do

263 **sought** examined   264 **But see . . . save** But see that their souls are saved   265 **jangles** clatters   266 **pie** magpie   268 **made great . . . mercy** made a great show of moving God to mercy   269 **gan** did   271 **Therefore he . . . affray** That is why he suffers this deadly assault   272 **deemed** was judged   273 **Vah! . . . templum** Ah, thou that destroyest the temple (Mark xiv. 58; John ii.19)   274 **saws** words   277 **muster** show   278 **cautels** tricks; **cast** play   279 **All if . . . wight** Even if he was so valiant in work   281 **As Pilate . . . dight** It is done and performed as Pilate decreed   283 **This race . . . right** This action must be rightly reported   286 **mows on** grimaces at   287 **wend** go   289 **For certes . . . note** For, to be sure, there's another thing we need to do   291–292 **we will . . . have** we shall draw lots to see which of us four is to have it   293 **rede** advise; **cut** lots   294 **all sides . . . save** to protect all our interests   297 **thar** need; **flite** wrangle   299 **tite** quickly   300 **This travail . . . tine** We are wasting our efforts here

William Shakespeare

Given the fact that William Shakespeare (1564–1616) was a commoner and that he worked in the ephemeral trades of the theater, what we know about his life is extraordinarily rich and revealing, especially in comparison to the lives of other playwrights of the period, such as Christopher Marlowe or John Webster. William Shakespeare was born in Stratford-upon-Avon, a town to the northwest of London in Warwickshire. He was baptized on April 26, 1564, and was probably born a few days earlier—his birth date is conventionally given as April 23, the feast day of St. George, the patron saint of England, and the day on which Shakespeare died fifty-two years later in 1616, again at his home in Stratford. One of eight children, Shakespeare was the son of a glover—a tradesman who worked with a variety of leather goods. It is not known whether Shakespeare attended the local school, the King's New School, but like other schools of the period, it would have provided him with an extensive grounding in Latin grammar, rhetoric, and literature. Later in his career, Shakespeare often drew on works he could have read at such a school: plays by Terence and Plautus, the poetry of Virgil and Ovid, the writings of Caesar.

He married Anne Hathaway in November 1582; she was twenty-six and he was eighteen. In May 1583 they had their first daughter, Susannah, followed by twins, Hamnet and Judith, born in 1585. Although his wife and children remained in Stratford throughout his career, Shakespeare went to London sometime in the late 1580s, possibly joining one of the theater companies that passed through Stratford.

By the 1590s, Shakespeare was established in London as an up-and-coming playwright; he was associated with the Lord Chamberlain's Men in 1594; he had written several plays on English history; and he was at work on several comedies and tragedies. When plague closed the theaters in London from the summer of 1592 through the spring of 1594, Shakespeare wrote two narrative poems, *Venus and Adonis* and *The Rape of Lucrece,* which he dedicated to Henry Wriothesley, the third Earl of Southampton, in a bid for patronage. He later wrote *The Phoenix and the Turtle* and circulated a brilliant and ambitious sequence of sonnets in manuscript before publishing it in 1609. As a shareholder of the Lord Chamberlain's Men, Shakespeare would have had many duties; no doubt he acted many parts, and we know he appeared in two plays by his contemporary, Ben Jonson—*Every Man in His Humour* and *Sejanus.* In 1598, the Lord Chamberlain's men tore down The Theatre, brought the timbers south of the city, and used them to build a new theater, the Globe. The Globe would remain the principal public-theater venue for the rest of Shakespeare's career, complemented by court and private-theater performances.

Shakespeare became the most popular playwright in London. He profited handsomely from his efforts at the Globe and from the patronage of the court, particularly after James I came to the throne in 1603 and took on the Lord Chamberlain's company as his own King's Men. Shakespeare used his income to buy a large house, called New Place, in Stratford, and throughout his career added to his property there; he retired and returned to Stratford in 1613. He drew up a will shortly before he died in 1616, leaving property to his family and mentioning gifts for several of his friends, including members of the King's Men: Richard Burbage, John Heminges, and Henry Condell. Heminges and Condell proved true to Shakespeare, for in 1623 they took Shakespeare's plays and published them in a single large volume, an astonishingly important event in an era in which plays were not widely regarded as "literature." Although many of Shakespeare's plays had been published individually during his lifetime, roughly half of Shakespeare's plays (*Macbeth, Antony and Cleopatra,* and *The Tempest,* for instance) existed only in manuscript form at Shakespeare's death and certainly would not have survived without the efforts of Heminges and Condell. This complete volume is now usually called the "First Folio," because it is printed in a large, **FOLIO**-sized format (about twice the dimensions of this book). The First Folio contains thirty-six of

Shakespeare's plays; two more plays all or partly by Shakespeare and published in his life-time (*Pericles* and *The Two Noble Kinsmen*) were left out of the Folio, and it is generally thought that Shakespeare contributed to a thirty-ninth play, *Sir Thomas More,* of which only a short manuscript section survives. More recently, several scholars have argued that early in his career Shakespeare collaborated on a history play, *Edward III.* Finally, although many people have advanced the thesis that someone else actually wrote the "Shakespeare" plays—Sir Francis Bacon, Francis Walsingham, the Earl of Oxford, among others—these claims belong to the realm of myth, not to the realm of history.

The range of Shakespeare's accomplishment as a playwright is astonishing. Early in his career, Shakespeare wrote two cycles of plays on English history—*Henry VI* (Parts 1, 2, and 3) and *Richard III;* and *Richard II, Henry IV* (Parts 1 and 2), and *Henry V*—that not only established a vogue for history plays but gave the English audience an epic version of the struggles that founded the Tudor and Stuart dynasties. Shakespeare's early comedies—*The Comedy of Errors, Two Gentlemen of Verona*—are very much in the vein of Plautus. Later comedies—*A Midsummer Night's Dream, As You Like It, Twelfth Night, The Merchant of Venice*—explore a variety of complex relations between love, sexuality, adulthood, ethnic discrimination, power, politics, and money. To many audiences today, Shakespeare is most remembered for *Hamlet* and the magisterial series of tragedies that followed, including *Othello, King Lear,* and *Macbeth.* Shakespeare's achievements often began with experimentation. The major tragedies benefitted from his earlier efforts in the mode of the Roman playwright Seneca in *Titus Andronicus,* in morality drama in *Richard III,* in romantic tragedy in *Romeo and Juliet,* and political intrigue-drama in *Julius Caesar.* In his final years as a playwright, Shakespeare seems to have collaborated with John Fletcher on a few occasions and to have turned his hand to plays in the vein of "tragicomedy," now generally called ROMANCE: *Pericles, Cymbeline, The Winter's Tale,* and *The Tempest.*

A Midsummer Night's Dream

Although the diarist Samuel Pepys described a 1662 revival of *A Midsummer Night's Dream* as "the most insipid ridiculous play that ever I saw in my life," the play has been successful in the theater from its first production in the 1590s to the present day. Shakespeare's contemporary Francis Meres mentions the play in his commonplace collection *Palladis Tamia* (1598), and when it was published in a 1600 quarto it was advertised as "it hath been sundry times publicly acted by the right honorable Lord Chamberlain's servants." It is one of several of Shakespeare's plays to be published with his name on the title page around the turn of the century.

Although *A Midsummer Night's Dream* draws on a variety of mythological narratives for the background of Theseus and Hippolyta, the play has no narrative "source" like *Julius Caesar* or *Hamlet.* Yet while it springs authentically from Shakespeare's imagination, the play does have a number of conventional and cultural precedents. The characterization of manifestly English artisans, "hard-handed men" whose names betoken their professions—Bottom the weaver, Starveling the tailor, Flute the bellows-maker—roots the play firmly in Shakespeare's contemporary culture, as does the folkloric background embodied in the fairies (Cobweb, Mustardseed), and in the characterization of the sprightly Puck/Robin Goodfellow (he's given both names in Shakespeare's text, and different modern editions sometimes use alternate speech prefixes), a familiar figure of English folklore. At the same time, the play gracefully deploys the formal structures and character conventions of classical comedy. Shakespeare had already undertaken his adaptation of Plautus' *The Brothers Menaechmus* (see Unit 1) in *A Comedy of Errors,* and *A Midsummer Night's Dream* witnesses an energetic confrontation with and reinvention of the paradigms of romantic comedy: the generational theme, in which the young lovers overcome the apparently irrational law of an older generation (embodied by the old man or *senex* figure, here Egeus, invoking Theseus' harsh law on his daughter) to win through to adulthood, sexuality, and marriage, symbolically rejuvenating rather than revolutionizing the social order of the play. Shakespeare complicates this paradigm by parceling out Athenian society into three distinct groups, each with its own challenging conflict: the Athenian aristocrats, whose adolescent lovers— for all that they seem really indistinguishable—refuse to follow their love-assignments; the "rude mechanicals" struggling with the challenging assignment to stage a play; and the fairies, whose king and queen enter the play squabbling about who is assigned the right to an abducted changeling boy.

The action of the play, described by C. L. Barber in *Shakespeare's Festive Comedy* as working "through release to comprehension," takes place in three symbolic phases. The first three scenes stage conflict among the three separate casts; once they all enter the moonlit forest, the juice of Puck's "little western flower" not only reorganizes their romantic relationships, it jumbles the groups all together. But when they return to Athens, something "of great constancy" nonetheless emerges, allowing Peter Quince and his band—hilariously, if ineptly—to stage their comic lovers' tragedy, the aristocrats to be satisfactorily paired off, and the fairies to restore the natural order, giving their blessing to the marriages. Of course, while the moonlit forest is the scene of magic, it also tends to locate an ironic perspective on romantic "love," literalizing attraction as the doting madness of sexual desire. Helena

follows Demetrius into the forest, saying that she'd be happy simply to be his spaniel; he nearly threatens her with rape. That is, Helena's "doting" affection is given literal expression by Puck's magic juice, which simply transfers and intensifies it. The final image of the aristocrats' "love" in the forest is a wild chase to exhaustion, in which "my legs can keep no pace with my desires." In Homer's *Odyssey,* Circe transforms Odysseus' men into swine, literalizing their gluttony. Here, Shakespeare offers a gentler, but fundamentally similar image of the brutishness of desire, its ability to make asses of us all: the fairy queen Titania in love with "translated" Bottom.

While the play offers a searching critique of the work of desire, it also offers Shakespeare's first thorough self-reflexive examination of the arts of theatre. Bottom and his fellows are surely ridiculed as incompetent: after all, we don't need a man with a lantern representing Moonshine to "see" the moonlit forest on a sunny English afternoon. But we should be wary of identifying too closely with Theseus' perspective on these theatrically challenged actors, that "The best in this kind are but shadows, and the worst are no worse if imagination amend them." In the final scene of *A Midsummer Night's Dream,* any theatrical audience wants more of Bottom— probably played in the first productions by Will Kemp, the famous clown of Shakespeare's company—and less of the intrusive, interrupting, irritatingly pedantic onstage audience. And, of course, the play's performance, in which Bottom's comic incompetence is created and conveyed by the actor's palpable skill, witnesses exactly the opposite of Theseus' truth: it takes a

Private Collection/Lebrecht Music & Arts

This photo of John Gielgud as Oberon and Peggy Ashcroft as Titania in the 1945 production of *A Midsummer Night's Dream* at the Haymarket Theatre, London, is a testament to the emphasis on realistic illusion that was one hallmark of mid-century Shakespeare.

good actor to make bad acting a theatrical success. Theseus' great set-piece at the opening of the play's final act—"The lunatic, the lover, and the poet / Are of imagination all compact"— tends to dismiss the works of the imagination for giving to "airy nothing / A local habitation and a name." And yet the play's final scene seems to invite an alternative perspective on the evanescent magic of theatrical performance, one that makes it difficult to decide the limits of art. After all, while Puck speaks the play's final lines, only an actor can invite our applause.

Pyramus and Thisby makes plain the fact that Shakespeare's theater could move from the court to the forest with Puck's facility (he puts "a girdle round about the earth / In forty minutes"), without the need for a loam and roughcast Wall or Moonshine's lantern. But the possibilities of visualizing Shakespeare's brilliant fantasy have continually fascinated the theater, particularly so in the materialist theater of nineteenth-century London. Driven by a fascination with historical detail, and powerful new technologies (lighting, electrification), the play increasingly seemed to demand a large corps of fairies, a meticulously classical Athens, and a verdant, living forest, all to the accompaniment of Mendelssohn. The climax of this tendency is surely Sir Herbert Beerbohm Tree's 1900 production of the play at Her Majesty's Theatre, featuring real trees and bunny rabbits hopping about the stage. The landmark production of the twentieth century was not Tree's, but Peter Brook's 1970 Royal Shakespeare Company production, which set the play in a white box, lowered the fairies—all dressed in clownlike jumpsuits—on trapezes, and created its world through the resolutely visible, physical, stagey magic of acrobatics.

A Midsummer Night's Dream

William Shakespeare

EDITED BY G. BLAKEMORE EVANS

THESEUS, *Duke of Athens*
EGEUS, *father to Hermia*
LYSANDER }
DEMETRIUS } *in love with Hermia*
PHILOSTRATE, *Master of the Revels to Theseus*

QUINCE, *a carpenter* }
BOTTOM, *a weaver* }
FLUTE, *a bellows-mender* } *presenting* {
SNOUT, *a tinker* }
SNUG, *a joiner* }
STARVELING, *a tailor* }

{ PROLOGUE
{ PYRAMUS
{ THISBY
{ WALL
{ LION
{ MOONSHINE

HIPPOLYTA, *Queen of the Amazons, betrothed to Theseus*
HERMIA, *daughter to Egeus, in love with Lysander*
HELENA, *in love with Demetrius*

OBERON, *King of the Fairies*
TITANIA, *Queen of the Fairies*
PUCK, *or* ROBIN GOODFELLOW
PEASEBLOSSOM }
COBWEB }
MOTH } *fairies*
MUSTARDSEED }

Other FAIRIES *attending their King and Queen;* ATTENDANTS *on Theseus and Hippolyta*

SCENE: *Athens, and a wood near it*

ACT I

SCENE I

Enter THESEUS, HIPPOLYTA, [PHILOSTRATE,] *with others.*

THESEUS: Now, fair Hippolyta, our nuptial hour
    Draws on apace. Four happy days bring in
    Another moon; but O, methinks, how slow
    This old moon [wanes]! She lingers my desires,
5   Like to a step-dame, or a dowager,
    Long withering out a young man's revenue.
HIPPOLYTA: Four days will quickly steep themselves in night;
    Four nights will quickly dream away the time;
    And then the moon, like to a silver bow
10   [New] bent in heaven, shall behold the night
    Of our solemnities.
THESEUS: Go, Philostrate,
    Stir up the Athenian youth to merriments,
    Awake the pert and nimble spirit of mirth,
    Turn melancholy forth to funerals:
15   The pale companion is not for our pomp.
                    [*Exit Philostrate.*]
    Hippolyta, I woo'd thee with my sword,
    And won thy love doing thee injuries;
    But I will wed thee in another key,
    With pomp, with triumph, and with revelling.

Enter EGEUS *and his daughter* HERMIA *and* LYSANDER *and* DEMETRIUS.

Words and passages enclosed in square brackets in the text above are either emendations of the copy-text or additions to it. The Textual Notes immediately following the play cite the earliest authority for every such change or insertion and supply the reading of the copy-text wherever it is emended in this edition.

I.i. Location: Athens. The palace of Theseus   **4 lingers** delays the fulfillment of   5 **step-dame** stepmother; **dowager** widow with property rights charged upon an estate during her lifetime   6 **withering out** diminishing   11 **solemnities** i.e. marriage rites   13 **pert** lively, brisk   15 **companion** fellow (contemptuous); **pomp** ceremonial splendor   16–17 **I . . . injuries** Theseus had made war against the Amazons and taken their queen captive   19 **triumph** public spectacle

EGEUS: Happy be Theseus, our renowned Duke!   20
THESEUS: Thanks, good Egeus. What's the news with thee?
EGEUS: Full of vexation come I, with complaint
    Against my child, my daughter Hermia.
    Stand forth, Demetrius. My noble lord,
    This man hath my consent to marry her.   25
    Stand forth, Lysander. And, my gracious Duke,
    This man hath bewitch'd the bosom of my child.
    Thou, thou, Lysander, thou hast given her rhymes,
    And interchang'd love-tokens with my child;
    Thou hast by moonlight at her window sung   30
    With faining voice verses of faining love,
    And stol'n the impression of her fantasy
    With bracelets of thy hair, rings, gawds, conceits,
    Knacks, trifles, nosegays, sweetmeats—messengers
    Of strong prevailment in unhardened youth.   35
    With cunning hast thou filch'd my daughter's heart,
    Turn'd her obedience (which is due to me)
    To stubborn harshness. And, my gracious Duke,
    Be it so she will not here before your Grace
    Consent to marry with Demetrius,   40
    I beg the ancient privilege of Athens:
    As she is mine, I may dispose of her;
    Which shall be either to this gentleman,
    Or to her death, according to our law
    Immediately provided in that case.   45
THESEUS: What say you, Hermia? Be advis'd, fair maid.
    To you your father should be as a god;
    One that compos'd your beauties; yea, and one
    To whom you are but as a form in wax,
    By him imprinted, and within his power,   50
    To leave the figure, or disfigure it.
    Demetrius is a worthy gentleman.

---

31 **faining . . . faining** (1) loving . . . longing; (2) feigning . . . feigned   32 **stol'n . . . fantasy** stealthily stamped your image on her imagination, i.e. made her fall in love with you   33 **bracelets . . . hair** Hair bracelets were a common love token; **gawds** toys, trinkets; **conceits** ingenious trifles   34 **Knacks** knickknacks   38 **harshness** discordance, i.e. disobedience   39 **Be it** so if   45 **Immediately** expressly   46 **Be advis'd** consider well   49 **a form** i.e. the impression of a seal   51 **leave** i.e. leave unchanged   **disfigure** obliterate

HERMIA: So is Lysander.

THESEUS: In himself he is;
But in this kind, wanting your father's voice,
55   The other must be held the worthier.

HERMIA: I would my father look'd but with my eyes.

THESEUS: Rather your eyes must with his judgment look.

HERMIA: I do entreat your Grace to pardon me.
I know not by what power I am made bold,
60   Nor how it may concern my modesty,
In such a presence here to plead my thoughts;
But I beseech your Grace that I may know
The worst that may befall me in this case,
If I refuse to wed Demetrius.

65   THESEUS: Either to die the death, or to abjure
For ever the society of men.
Therefore, fair Hermia, question your desires,
Know of your youth, examine well your blood,
Whether (if you yield not to your father's choice)
70   You can endure the livery of a nun,
For aye to be in shady cloister mew'd,
To live a barren sister all your life,
Chaunting faint hymns to the cold fruitless moon.
Thrice blessed they that master so their blood
75   To undergo such maiden pilgrimage;
But earthlier happy is the rose distill'd,
Than that which withering on the virgin thorn
Grows, lives, and dies in single blessedness.

HERMIA: So will I grow, so live, so die, my lord,
80   Ere I will yield my virgin patent up
Unto his lordship, whose unwished yoke
My soul consents not to give sovereignty.

THESEUS: Take time to pause, and by the next new moon—
The sealing-day betwixt my love and me
85   For everlasting bond of fellowship—
Upon that day either prepare to die
For disobedience to your father's will,
Or else to wed Demetrius, as he would,
Or on Diana's altar to protest
90   For aye austerity and single life.

DEMETRIUS: Relent, sweet Hermia, and, Lysander, yield
Thy crazed title to my certain right.

LYSANDER: You have her father's love, Demetrius,
Let me have Hermia's; do you marry him.

95   EGEUS: Scornful Lysander, true, he hath my love;
And what is mine, my love shall render him.
And she is mine, and all my right of her
I do estate unto Demetrius.

LYSANDER: I am, my lord, as well deriv'd as he,
As well possess'd; my love is more than his;   100
My fortunes every way as fairly rank'd
(If not with vantage) as Demetrius';
And (which is more than all these boasts can be)
I am belov'd of beauteous Hermia.
Why should not I then prosecute my right?   105
Demetrius, I'll avouch it to his head,
Made love to Nedar's daughter, Helena,
And won her soul; and she, sweet lady, dotes,
Devoutly dotes, dotes in idolatry,
Upon this spotted and inconstant man.   110

THESEUS: I must confess that I have heard so much,
And with Demetrius thought to have spoke thereof;
But, being over-full of self-affairs,
My mind did lose it. But, Demetrius, come,
And come, Egeus, you shall go with me;   115
I have some private schooling for you both.
For you, fair Hermia, look you arm yourself
To fit your fancies to your father's will;
Or else the law of Athens yields you up
(Which by no means we may extenuate)   120
To death, or to a vow of single life.
Come, my Hippolyta; what cheer, my love?
Demetrius and Egeus, go along;
I must employ you in some business
Against our nuptial, and confer with you   125
Of something nearly that concerns yourselves.

EGEUS: With duty and desire we follow you.
            Exeunt. [Manent Lysander and Hermia.]

LYSANDER: How now, my love? why is your cheek so pale?
How chance the roses there do fade so fast?

HERMIA: Belike for want of rain; which I could well
Beteem them from the tempest of my eyes.   131

LYSANDER: Ay me! for aught that I could ever read,
Could ever hear by tale or history,
The course of true love never did run smooth;
But either it was different in blood—   135

HERMIA: O cross! too high to be enthrall'd to [low].

LYSANDER: Or else misgraffed in respect of years—

HERMIA: O spite! too old to be engag'd to young.

LYSANDER: Or else it stood upon the choice of friends—

HERMIA: O hell, to choose love by another's eyes!   140

LYSANDER: Or if there were a sympathy in choice,
War, death, or sickness did lay siege to it,
Making it momentany as a sound,
Swift as a shadow, short as any dream,
Brief as the lightning in the collied night,   145
That, in a spleen, unfolds both heaven and earth;

---

54 **in this kind** in this respect, i.e. as your wooer; **wanting** lacking; **voice** authorization, consent   60 **how . . . concern** whether it befit   65 **die the death** be put to death by judicial sentence   68 **Know . . . youth** inquire of your youthful feelings; **blood** passions   70 **livery** dress, distinctive garb   71 **mew'd** shut up, confined   73 **moon** i.e. Diana, the virgin goddess, whose votary Hermia would become   75 **maiden pilgrimage** i.e. journey through life as a virgin.   Lines 74–75 are a saving compliment to the Virgin Queen, Elizabeth, though lines 76–78 rather diminish its effect   76 **distill'd** made into perfume. With the image in this passage cf. Sonnet 5   77 **thorn** brier rose bush   78 **single blessedness** "divine blessing accorded to a life of celibacy" (*O.E.D.*)   80 **virgin patent** privilege of virginity   89 **protest** vow   92 **crazed** cracked, flawed; **title** claim to possession   98 **estate unto** settle or bestow upon   99 **well deriv'd** well born

100 **possess'd** endowed with wealth   101 **fairly** handsomely   102 **with vantage** better   106 **head** face   110 **spotted and inconstant** stained with inconstancy   113 **self-affairs** my own affairs   116 **schooling** admonition   117 **For** as for; **look you arm** see that you prepare   118 **fancies** affections   120 **extenuate** mitigate   123 **go along** come with us   125 **Against** in preparation for   126 **nearly that** that closely   127 **duty and desire** eagerness to serve   s.d. **Manent** remain   130 **Belike** very likely   131 **Beteem** afford   135 **blood** birth, hereditary station   136 **cross** vexation, thwarting   137 **misgraffed** ill grafted, i.e. badly matched   139 **friends** i.e. relatives   143 **momentany** momentary   145 **collied** dark (literally, blackened with coal)   146 **in a spleen** i.e. as if in a sudden fit of passion (?) or in a flash (?). The spleen was thought to be the seat of sudden impulsive feelings and actions   **unfolds** reveals

And ere a man hath power to say "Behold!"
The jaws of darkness do devour it up:
So quick bright things come to confusion.
HERMIA: If then true lovers have been ever cross'd,
151   It stands as an edict in destiny.
Then let us teach our trial patience,
Because it is a customary cross,
As due to love as thoughts and dreams and sighs,
155   Wishes and tears, poor fancy's followers.
LYSANDER: A good persuasion; therefore hear me, Hermia:
I have a widow aunt, a dowager,
Of great revenue, and she hath no child.
From Athens is her house remote seven leagues;
160   And she respects me as her only son.
There, gentle Hermia, may I marry thee;
And to that place the sharp Athenian law
Cannot pursue us. If thou lovest me, then
Steal forth thy father's house to-morrow night;
165   And in the wood, a league without the town
(Where I did meet thee once with Helena
To do observance to a morn of May),
There will I stay for thee.
HERMIA: My good Lysander,
I swear to thee, by Cupid's strongest bow,
170   By his best arrow with the golden head,
By the simplicity of Venus' doves,
By that which knitteth souls and prospers loves,
And by that fire which burn'd the Carthage queen
When the false Troyan under sail was seen,
175   By all the vows that ever men have broke
(In number more than ever women spoke),
In that same place thou hast appointed me
To-morrow truly will I meet with thee.
LYSANDER: Keep promise, love. Look, here comes Helena.

Enter HELENA.

180 HERMIA: God speed fair Helena! whither away?
HELENA: Call you me fair? That fair again unsay.
Demetrius loves your fair, O happy fair!
Your eyes are lodestars, and your tongue's sweet air
More tuneable than lark to shepherd's ear
When wheat is green, when hawthorn buds appear.
186 Sickness is catching; O, were favor so,
[Yours would] I catch, fair Hermia, ere I go;
My ear should catch your voice, my eye your eye,

My tongue should catch your tongue's sweet melody.
Were the world mine, Demetrius being bated,   190
The rest I'll give to be to you translated.
O, teach me how you look, and with what art
You sway the motion of Demetrius' heart.
HERMIA: I frown upon him; yet he loves me still.
HELENA: O that your frowns would teach my smiles such skill! 195
HERMIA: I give him curses; yet he gives me love.
HELENA: O that my prayers could such affection move!
HERMIA: The more I hate, the more he follows me.
HELENA: The more I love, the more he hateth me.
HERMIA: His folly, Helena, is no fault of mine.   200
HELENA: None but your beauty; would that fault were mine!
HERMIA: Take comfort; he no more shall see my face;
Lysander and myself will fly this place.
Before the time I did Lysander see,
Seem'd Athens as a paradise to me;   205
O then, what graces in my love do dwell,
That he hath turn'd a heaven unto a hell!
LYSANDER: Helen, to you our minds we will unfold:
To-morrow night, when Phoebe doth behold
Her silver visage in the wat'ry glass,   210
Decking with liquid pearl the bladed grass
(A time that lovers' flights doth still conceal),
Through Athens gates have we devis'd to steal.
HERMIA: And in the wood, where often you and I
Upon faint primrose beds were wont to lie,   215
Emptying our bosoms of their counsel [sweet],
There my Lysander and myself shall meet;
And thence from Athens turn away our eyes,
To seek new friends and [stranger companies].
Farewell, sweet playfellow, pray thou for us;   220
And good luck grant thee thy Demetrius!
Keep word, Lysander; we must starve our sight
From lovers' food till morrow deep midnight.
LYSANDER: I will, my Hermia.   *Exit Hermia.*
         Helena, adieu:
As you on him, Demetrius dote on you!   225
            Exit Lysander.
HELENA: How happy some o'er other some can be!
Through Athens I am thought as fair as she.
But what of that? Demetrius thinks not so;
He will not know what all but he do know;
And as he errs, doting on Hermia's eyes,   230
So I, admiring of his qualities.
Things base and vile, holding no quantity,
Love can transpose to form and dignity.
Love looks not with the eyes but with the mind;
And therefore is wing'd Cupid painted blind.   235
Nor hath Love's mind of any judgment taste;
Wings, and no eyes, figure unheedy haste;

---

149 **quick** quickly, suddenly (perhaps with additional sense of "living" or "lively," modifying *things*) **confusion** ruin   150 **ever** always   152 **teach . . . patience** i.e. discipline ourselves to meet this trial patiently   154 **As . . . love** as much love's due; **thoughts** melancholy moods   155 **fancy's** love's   156 **persuasion** opinion, doctrine   160 **respects** regards   167 **do . . . May** perform the ceremonies of May-day   168 **stay** wait   170 **arrow . . . head** According to Ovid's *Metamorphoses*, Cupid's sharp, gold-tipped arrow produced love, his blunt, lead-tipped arrow aversion   171 **simplicity** harmlessness, innocence   173 **Carthage queen** Dido, who immolated herself on a funeral pyre after the Trojan hero Aeneas, her lover, secretly sailed away from Carthage   182 **fair . . . fair** beauty . . . fair one (with special reference to her blonde coloring)   **happy** lucky   183 **lodestars** guiding stars; **air** melody, music   184 **tuneable** tuneful   186 **favor** attributes, features (with play on "being favored")

190 **bated** excepted   191 **translated** transformed   192 **art** skill (i.e. in magic)   193 **motion** impulse, desire   197 **affection** passion; **move** arouse   209 **Phoebe** Diana, the moon   210 **glass** mirror   212 **still** always   213 **Athens** Adjectival; cf. "Verona streets," *Romeo and Juliet*

III.i.89 **devis'd** decided   215 **faint** pale (?) or faintly scented (?)   216 **counsel** inmost thought   219 **stranger companies** the company of strangers   222–23 **starve . . . food** i.e. refrain from seeing each other   231 **admiring of** wondering at   232 **holding no quantity** lacking proportion, unshapely   233 **transpose** change, transform; **dignity** worth   236 **taste** any trace   237 **figure** symbolize

And therefore is Love said to be a child,
Because in choice he is so oft beguil'd.
240 As waggish boys in game themselves forswear,
So the boy Love is perjur'd every where;
For ere Demetrius look'd on Hermia's eyne,
He hail'd down oaths that he was only mine;
And when this hail some heat from Hermia felt,
245 So he dissolv'd, and show'rs of oaths did melt,
I will go tell him of fair Hermia's flight;
Then to the wood will he to-morrow night
Pursue her; and for this intelligence
If I have thanks, it is a dear expense.
250 But herein mean I to enrich my pain,
To have his sight thither and back again.   *Exit.*

SCENE II

Enter QUINCE *the carpenter and* SNUG *the joiner and* BOTTOM *the
weaver and* FLUTE *the bellows-mender and* SNOUT *the tinker and*
STARVELING *the tailor.*

QUINCE: Is all our company here?
BOTTOM: You were best to call them generally, man by man,
    according to the scrip.
QUINCE: Here is the scroll of every man's name,
5   which is thought fit, through all Athens, to play in
    our enterlude before the Duke and the Duchess, on
    his wedding-day at night.
BOTTOM: First, good Peter Quince, say what the play
    treats on; then read the names of the actors; and so
10   grow to a point.
QUINCE: Marry, our play is *The most lamentable
    comedy and most cruel death of Pyramus and Thisby.*
BOTTOM: A very good piece of work, I assure you, and
    a merry. Now, good Peter Quince, call forth your
15   actors by the scroll. Masters, spread yourselves.
QUINCE: Answer as I call you. Nick Bottom the
    weaver.
BOTTOM: Ready. Name what part I am for, and
    proceed.
QUINCE: You, Nick Bottom, are set down for
21   Pyramus.

---

240 **game** fun, sport   242 **eyne** eyes (archaic even in Elizabethan
English; used for the sake of rhyme)   248 **intelligence** information
249 **dear expense** painful purchase, costly gain   251 **his sight** the
sight of him

I.ii. Location: Athens. Quince's house   o.s.d. The names of the craftsmen are derived in one way or another from their work. Quince's name
is probably a form of *quoins* or *quines,* wedge-shaped pieces of wood
used in carpentry. Snug's name suggests the expert joining of pieces of
wood by a maker of fine furniture. Bottom is named for the *bottom* or
core on which thread is wound. Flute would repair fluted church organs
as well as domestic bellows. Snout's name suggests the spout of a kettle,
an article very familiar to tinkers. Starveling takes his name from the
proverbial leanness of tailors ("Nine tailors make a man")   2 **You were
best** it would be best for you; **generally** The first of Bottom's characteristic verbal blunders; Here he obviously means "individually"—just
the opposite of what he says   3 **scrip** script, written list   6 **enterlude**
interlude, brief play   10 **grow . . . point** come systematically to a conclusion   11 **Marry** why, indeed (originally the name of the Virgin Mary
used as an oath); **lamentable** mournful

BOTTOM: What is Pyramus? a lover, or a tyrant?
QUINCE: A lover, that kills himself most gallant
    for love.   24
BOTTOM: That will ask some tears in the true performing
    of it. If I do it, let the audience look to their eyes.
    I will move storms; I will condole in some measure.
    To the rest—yet my chief humor is for a tyrant.
    I could play Ercles rarely, or a part to tear a
    cat in, to make all split.   30
                "The raging rocks
                And shivering shocks
                Shall break the locks
                    Of prison gates;
                And Phibbus' car   35
                Shall shine from far,
                And make and mar
                    The foolish Fates."
    This was lofty! Now name the rest of the players.
    This is Ercles' vein, a tyrant's vein; a lover is more
    condoling.   41
QUINCE: Francis Flute the bellows-mender.
FLUTE: Here, Peter Quince.
QUINCE: Flute, you must take Thisby on you.
FLUTE: What is Thisby? a wand'ring knight?   45
QUINCE: It is the lady that Pyramus must love.
FLUTE: Nay, faith; let not me play a woman; I have
    a beard coming.
QUINCE: That's all one; you shall play it in a mask,
    and you may speak as small as you will.   50
BOTTOM: And I may hide my face, let me play Thisby
    too. I'll speak in a monstrous little voice, "Thisne!
    Thisne! Ah, Pyramus, my lover dear! thy Thisby
    dear, and lady dear!"
QUINCE: No, no, you must play Pyramus; and,
    Flute, you Thisby.   56
BOTTOM: Well, proceed.
QUINCE: Robin Starveling the tailor.
STARVELING: Here, Peter Quince.
QUINCE: Robin Starveling, you must play Thisby's
    mother. Tom Snout the tinker.   61
SNOUT: Here, Peter Quince.
QUINCE: You, Pyramus' father; myself, Thisby's
    father; Snug the joiner, you the lion's part. And I
    hope here is a play fitted.   65
SNUG: Have you the lion's part written? Pray
    you, if it be, give it me, for I am slow of study.
QUINCE: You may do it extempore, for it is nothing
    but roaring.   69
BOTTOM: Let me play the lion too. I will roar, that I
    will do any man's heart good to hear me. I will roar,

---

26 **look . . . eyes** take care not to injure their eyes with weeping
27 **condole** speak pathetically, arouse pity   28 **humor** temperamental
bent   29 **Ercles** Hercules; The tradition for ranting in this part grew
from Seneca's *Hercules Furens*   29–30 **tear a cat** i.e. rant   30 **make
all split** cause great commotion   35 **Phibbus' car** the chariot of
Phoebus, the sun-god   41 **condoling** pathetic   45 **What** what sort
of man; **wand'ring knight** knight-errant   47–48 **I . . . coming** On
the Elizabethan stage, female parts were played by boys   49 **That's all
one** that makes no difference   50 **small** high-pitched   51 **And** if
65 **fitted** cast

that I will make the Duke say, "Let him roar again;
let him roar again."

QUINCE: And you should do it too terribly, you
75 would fright the Duchess and the ladies, that
they would shrike; and that were enough to hang
us all.

ALL: That would hang us, every mother's son.

BOTTOM: I grant you, friends, if you should fright the
80 ladies out of their wits, they would have no more
discretion but to hang us; but I will aggravate my
voice so that I will roar you as gently as any sucking
dove; I will roar you and 'twere any
84 nightingale.

QUINCE: You can play no part but Pyramus; for
Pyramus is a sweet-fac'd man; a proper man as one
shall see in a summer's day; a most lovely gentleman-like
man: therefore you must needs play
Pyramus.

BOTTOM: Well; I will undertake it. What beard were
91 I best to play it in?

QUINCE: Why, what you will.

BOTTOM: I will discharge it in either your straw-
color beard, your orange-tawny beard, your
95 purple-in-grain beard, or your French-crown-color
beard, your perfit yellow.

QUINCE: Some of your French crowns have no hair
at all; and then you will play barefac'd. But, masters,
here are your parts, and I am to entreat you,
100 request you, and desire you, to con them by
tomorrow night; and meet me in the palace wood, a
mile without the town, by moonlight; there will
we rehearse; for if we meet in the city, we shall be
dogg'd with company, and our devices known. In
105 the mean time I will draw a bill of properties, such
as our play wants. I pray you fail me not.

BOTTOM: We will meet, and there we may rehearse
most obscenely and courageously. Take pains, be
perfit; adieu.

110 QUINCE: At the Duke's oak we meet.

BOTTOM: Enough; hold, or cut bow-strings.   *Exeunt.*

ACT II

SCENE I

Enter a FAIRY *at one door and* ROBIN GOODFELLOW [PUCK] *at
another.*

PUCK: How now, spirit, whither wander you?

FAIRY: Over hill, over dale,
Thorough bush, thorough brier,
Over park, over pale,
Thorough flood, thorough fire,   5
I do wander every where,
Swifter than the moon's sphere;
And I serve the Fairy Queen,
To dew her orbs upon the green.
The cowslips tall her pensioners be,   10
In their gold coats spots you see:
Those be rubies, fairy favors,
In those freckles live their savors.
I must go seek some dewdrops here,
And hang a pearl in every cowslip's ear.   15
Farewell, thou lob of spirits; I'll be gone.
Our Queen and all her elves come here anon.

PUCK: The King doth keep his revels here to-night;
Take heed the Queen come not within his sight;
For Oberon is passing fell and wrath,   20
Because that she as her attendant hath
A lovely boy stolen from an Indian king;
She never had so sweet a changeling.
And jealous Oberon would have the child
Knight of his train, to trace the forests wild;   25
But she, perforce, withholds the loved boy,
Crowns him with flowers, and makes him all her joy.
And now they never meet in grove or green,
By fountain clear, or spangled starlight sheen,
But they do square, that all their elves for fear 30
Creep into acorn-cups, and hide them there.

FAIRY: Either I mistake your shape and making quite,
Or else you are that shrewd and knavish sprite
Call'd Robin Goodfellow. Are not you he
That frights the maidens of the villagery,   35
Skim milk, and sometimes labor in the quern,
And bootless make the breathless huswife churn,
And sometime make the drink to bear no barm,
Mislead night-wanderers, laughing at their harm?
Those that Hobgoblin call you, and sweet Puck,   40
You do their work, and they shall have good luck.
Are not you he?

PUCK: Thou speakest aright;
I am that merry wanderer of the night.
I jest to Oberon and make him smile
When I a fat and bean-fed horse beguile,   45
Neighing in likeness of a filly foal;
And sometime lurk I in a gossip's bowl,

---

70 **that** so that   74 **terribly** terrifyingly   76 **shrike** shriek   81 **aggravate**
He means just the opposite   83 **and** as if   86 **proper** handsome   90 **Well**
very well   93 **discharge** perform; **your** The indefinite use, meaning
vaguely "that you know of"; a colloquialism   94–95 **purple-in-grain**
dyed a fast purple or deep red   95 **French-crown-color** yellowish color
of a gold coin   96 **perfit** perfect   97–98 **Some...all** Alluding to loss of
hair from the "French disease," syphilis   99 **am to** must   100 **con** learn
by heart   105 **bill** list   108 **obscenely** Bottom may connect this word
with *seen* and mean "without being observed," or with *scene* and mean
"dramatically"   109 **perfit** i.e. letter-perfect in your parts   111 **hold...
bow-strings** an expression of uncertain meaning, from archery; perhaps
equivalent to "hold to our agreement or the project is done for"

II.i. Location: A wood near Athens

3 **Thorough** through   4 **pale** enclosure   7 **sphere** In the Ptolemaic
system of astronomy, the moon and the other heavenly bodies were
thought to revolve about the earth fixed in transparent spheres   9 **orbs**
circles, i.e. fairy rings   10 **pensioners** Members of the royal bodyguard
were called gentlemen pensioners   12 **favors** love tokens   13 **savors**
perfumes   16 **lob** country bumpkin   17 **anon** at once   20 **passing...
wrath** exceedingly fierce and angry   23 **changeling** child exchanged
for another by fairies   25 **trace** traverse   26 **perforce** forcibly
29 **fountain** spring   30 **square** quarrel; **that** so that   32 **making**
form   33 **shrewd** mischievous   35 **villagery** village folk, peasantry
36 **quern** handmill for grinding grain   37 **bootless** unavailingly
huswife housewife, woman who manages a household   38 **sometime**
at times; **bear no barm** fail to ferment (?) or go flat (?). *Barm* yeast
47 **gossip's** garrulous old woman's

In very likeness of a roasted crab,
And when she drinks, against her lips I bob,
50 And on her withered develop pour the ale.
The wisest aunt, telling the saddest tale,
Sometime for three-foot stool mistaketh me;
Then slip I from her bum, down topples she,
And "tailor" cries, and falls into a cough;
55 And then the whole quire hold their hips and loff,
And waxen in their mirth, and neeze, and swear
A merrier hour was never wasted there.
But room, fairy! here comes Oberon.
FAIRY: And here my mistress. Would that he were gone!

Enter the King of Fairies [OBERON] at one door with his.
TRAIN, and the Queen [TITANIA] at another with hers.

60 OBERON: Ill met by moonlight, proud Titania.
TITANIA: What, jealous Oberon? [Fairies,] skip hence—
I have forsworn his bed and company.
OBERON: Tarry, rash wanton! Am not I thy lord?
TITANIA: Then I must be thy lady; but I know
65 When thou hast stolen away from fairy land,
And in the shape of Corin sat all day,
Playing on pipes of corn, and versing love,
To amorous Phillida. Why art thou here
Come from the farthest steep of India?
70 But that, forsooth, the bouncing Amazon,
Your buskin'd mistress, and your warrior love,
To Theseus must be wedded, and you come
To give their bed joy and prosperity.
OBERON: How canst thou thus for shame, Titania,
75 Glance at my credit with Hippolyta,
Knowing I know thy love to Theseus?
Didst not thou lead him through the glimmering night
From Perigenia, whom he ravished?
And make him with fair [Aegles] break his faith,
80 With Ariadne, and Antiopa?
TITANIA: These are the forgeries of jealousy;
And never, since the middle summer's spring,

Met we on hill, in dale, forest, or mead,
By paved fountain or by rushy brook,
Or in the beached margent of the sea, 85
To dance our ringlets to the whistling wind,
But with thy brawls thou hast disturb'd our sport.
Therefore the winds, piping to us in vain,
As in revenge, have suck'd up from the sea
Contagious fogs; which, falling in the land, 90
Hath every pelting river made so proud
That they have overborne their continents.
The ox hath therefore stretch'd his yoke in vain,
The ploughman lost his sweat, and the green corn
Hath rotted ere his youth attain'd a beard. 95
The fold stands empty in the drowned field,
And crows are fatted with the murrion flock;
The nine men's morris is fill'd up with mud,
And the quaint mazes in the wanton green,
For lack of tread, are undistinguishable. 100
The human mortals want their winter here;
No night is now with hymn or carol blest.
Therefore the moon (the governess of floods),
Pale in her anger, washes all the air,
That rheumatic diseases do abound. 105
And thorough this distemperature, we see
The seasons alter: hoary-headed frosts
Fall in the fresh lap of the crimson rose,
And on old Hiems' [thin] and icy crown
An odorous chaplet of sweet summer buds 110
Is, as in mockery, set; the spring, the summer,
The childing autumn, angry winter, change
Their wonted liveries; and the mazed world,
By their increase, now knows not which is which.
And this same progeny of evils comes 115
From our debate, from our dissension;
We are their parents and original.
OBERON: Do you amend it then; it lies in you.
Why should Titania cross her Oberon?

---

48 **crab** crab apple   50 **dewlop** dewlap, loose skin on the neck   51 **aunt** old woman, gossip; **saddest** soberest   54 **tailor** Probably referring to the fact that she finds herself sitting cross-legged on the floor as tailors did to sew; **cough** Probably with a suggestion of breaking wind   55 **quire** choir, i.e. company; **loff** laugh   56 **waxen** increase (with archaic plural ending in *-en*); **neeze** sneeze   57 **wasted** spent   63 **rash wanton** impetuous and willful creature   66, 68 **Corin, Phillida** Conventional names in pastoral poetry   67 **corn** oat stalks; **versing love** making love verses   69 **steep** mountain range   71 **buskin'd** wearing buskins or half-boots   75 **Glance . . . Hippolyta** cast aspersion on my good name by accusing me with Hippolyta   78 **Perigenia** Perigouna, daughter of the brigand Sinis, whom the youthful Theseus slew on his first journey to Athens. Shakespeare took this and the following names of Theseus' mistresses from the "Life of Theseus" in North's translation of Plutarch (which, however, reads *Perigouna*)   79 **Aegles** Aegle, a nymph for whose love Theseus, in some accounts, deserted Ariadne   80 **Ariadne** daughter of Minos, king of Crete. Having slain the Minotaur with her aid, Theseus fled Crete with her, but abandoned her on the voyage back to Athens; **Antiopa** another name for the Amazon queen captured by Theseus; here obviously taken to be distinct from Hippolyta   82 **middle summer's spring** beginning of midsummer

---

84 **paved fountain** spring with pebbled bottom; **rushy** edged with rushes   85 **in** on; **margent** margin, edge   86 **ringlets** circular dances   87 **brawls** noisy quarrels (with probably play on *brawl* as the name of a dance [French *branle*] described as "base" by contemporary writers)   90 **Contagious** noxious   91 **pelting** paltry   92 **overborne their continents** overflowed their banks   94 **corn** grain   95 **his** its   97 **murrion** dead of the murrain, a disease of cattle and sheep   98 **nine men's morris** i.e. the turf marked with squares on which the rustic game of this name was played   99 **quaint mazes** complicated pattern of paths to be traced rapidly by a line of boys as a sport; **wanton** luxuriant   101 **want their winter here** A controversial passage. Perhaps it means "lack under these circumstances their proper winter season" (with an allusion in *hymn or carol* in line 102 to Christmas observances). Most editors, following Theobald, emend *here* to *cheer*   103 **Therefore** As in lines 88 and 93, this means "in consequence of the breach between us"   105 **That** so that; **rheumatic diseases** colds, catarrh, and other such disorders characterized by a flow of watery "rheum"   106 **distemperature** disturbance in the natural order, i.e. bad weather (perhaps with play on the sense "ill humor," harking back to the moon's "anger" in line 104)   109 **Hiems** the god of winter   112 **childing** fruitful (literally, pregnant)   113 **wonted liveries** customary apparel; **mazed** bewildered, confused   114 **their increase** what they produce   116 **debate** disagreement, quarrelling   117 **original** origin   119 **cross** thwart

120 I do but beg a little changeling boy,
To be my henchman.

TITANIA: Set your heart at rest;
The fairy land buys not the child of me.
His mother was a vot'ress of my order,
And in the spiced Indian air, by night,
125 Full often hath she gossip'd by my side,
And sat with me on Neptune's yellow sands,
Marking th' embarked traders on the flood;
When we have laugh'd to see the sails conceive
And grow big-bellied with the wanton wind;
130 Which she, with pretty and with swimming gait,
Following (her womb then rich with my young squire)
Would imitate, and sail upon the land
To fetch me trifles, and return again,
As from a voyage, rich with merchandise.
135 But she, being mortal, of that boy did die,
And for her sake do I rear up her boy;
And for her sake I will not part with him.

OBERON: How long within this wood intend you stay?

TITANIA: Perchance till after Theseus' wedding-day.
140 If you will patiently dance in our round,
And see our moonlight revels, go with us;
If not, shun me, and I will spare your haunts.

OBERON: Give me that boy, and I will go with thee.

TITANIA: Not for thy fairy kingdom. Fairies, away!
145 We shall chide downright, if I longer stay.

Exeunt [Titania and her Train].

OBERON: Well; go thy way. Thou shalt not from this grove
Till I torment thee for this injury.
My gentle Puck, come hither. Thou rememb'rest
Since once I sat upon a promontory,
150 And heard a mermaid on a dolphin's back
Uttering such dulcet and harmonious breath
That the rude sea grew civil at her song,
And certain stars shot madly from their spheres,
To hear the sea-maid's music?

PUCK: I remember.

OBERON: That very time I saw (but thou couldst not),
156 Flying between the cold moon and the earth,
Cupid all arm'd. A certain aim he took
At a fair vestal throned by [the] west,
And loos'd his love-shaft smartly from his bow,
160 As it should pierce a hundred thousand hearts;
But I might see young Cupid's fiery shaft
Quench'd in the chaste beams of the wat'ry moon,
And the imperial vot'ress passed on,
In maiden meditation, fancy-free.

Yet mark'd I where the bolt of Cupid fell. 165
It fell upon a little western flower,
Before milk-white, now purple with love's wound,
And maidens call it love-in-idleness.
Fetch me that flow'r; the herb I showed thee once.
The juice of it on sleeping eyelids laid 170
Will make or man or woman madly dote
Upon the next live creature that it sees.
Fetch me this herb, and be thou here again
Ere the leviathan can swim a league.

PUCK: I'll put a girdle round about the earth 175
In forty minutes. [*Exit.*]

OBERON: Having once this juice,
I'll watch Titania when she is asleep,
And drop the liquor of it in her eyes;
The next thing then she waking looks upon
(Be it on lion, bear, or wolf, or bull, 180
On meddling monkey, or on busy ape),
She shall pursue it with the soul of love.
And ere I take this charm from off her sight
(As I can take it with another herb),
I'll make her render up her page to me. 185
But who comes here? I am invisible,
And I will overhear their conference.

Enter DEMETRIUS, HELENA *following him.*

DEMETRIUS: I love thee not; therefore pursue me not.
Where is Lysander and fair Hermia?
The one I'll [slay]; the other [slayeth] me. 190
Thou toldst me they were stol'n unto this wood;
And here am I, and wode within this wood,
Because I cannot meet my Hermia.
Hence, get thee gone, and follow me no more.

HELENA: You draw me, you hard-hearted adamant;
But yet you draw not iron, for my heart 196
Is true as steel. Leave you your power to draw,
And I shall have no power to follow you.

DEMETRIUS: Do I entice you? Do I speak you fair?
Or rather do I not in plainest truth 200
Tell you I do not [nor] I cannot love you?

HELENA: And even for that do I love you the more:
I am your spaniel; and, Demetrius,
The more you beat me, I will fawn on you.
Use me but as your spaniel; spurn me, strike me, 205
Neglect me, lose me; only give me leave,
Unworthy as I am, to follow you.
What worser place can I beg in your love
(And yet a place of high respect with me)
Than to be used as you use your dog? 210

---

121 **henchman** page of honor; **Set . . . rest** i.e. give up that notion
127 **traders** trading vessels; **flood** flood tide 129 **wanton** amorous 140 **round** circular dance 142 **spare** stay away from
145 **chide** quarrel 146 **from** go from 147 **injury** affront 149 **Since** when 151 **breath** voice, music 152 **rude** rough, boisterous; **civil** well-behaved, gentle 157 **all** fully, completely 158 **vestal** i.e. vestal virgin. The passage is a compliment to Queen Elizabeth, and may allude to some actual entertainment in her honor, such as the water pageant with which the Earl of Hertford amused her when she visited him at Elvetham in 1591 160 **As** as if 162 **moon** i.e. Diana, the virgin goddess, whose votaress the "fair vestal" is 164 **fancy-free** free of love-thoughts

---

168 **love-in-idleness** a name for the pansy 171 **or . . . or** either . . . or 174 **leviathan** gigantic sea-beast (see Job 41), usually identified with the whale 176 **forty** Used frequently as an indefinite number 177 **watch . . . asleep** i.e. watch for a time when I can catch her sleeping 186 **I am invisible** Spoken for the benefit of the audience, to explain how he can eavesdrop unseen 192 **wode** mad (pronounced *wood*) 195 **adamant** (1) lodestone, magnet; (2) the hardest substance 196 **you . . . iron** i.e. what you draw (my heart) is not iron, but steel of the finest temper 197 **Leave** give up 199 **fair** courteously 206 **Neglect** ignore

DEMETRIUS: Tempt not too much the hatred of my spirit,
  For I am sick when I do look on thee.
HELENA: And I am sick when I look not on you.
DEMETRIUS: You do impeach your modesty too much,
215   To leave the city and commit yourself
  Into the hands of one that loves you not;
  To trust the opportunity of night,
  And the ill counsel of a desert place,
  With the rich worth of your virginity.
220 HELENA: Your virtue is my privilege. For that
  It is not night when I do see your face,
  Therefore I think I am not in the night,
  Nor doth this wood lack worlds of company,
  For you in my respect are all the world.
225 Then how can it be said I am alone,
  When all the world is here to look on me?
DEMETRIUS: I'll run from thee, and hide me in the brakes,
  And leave thee to the mercy of wild beasts.
HELENA: The wildest hath not such a heart as you.
230 Run when you will; the story shall be chang'd:
  Apollo flies, and Daphne holds the chase;
  The dove pursues the griffin; the mild hind
  Makes speed to catch the tiger—bootless speed,
  When cowardice pursues and valor flies.
DEMETRIUS: I will not stay thy questions. Let me go;
236 Or if thou follow me, do not believe
  But I shall do thee mischief in the wood.
HELENA: Ay, in the temple, in the town, the field,
  You do me mischief. Fie, Demetrius!
240 Your wrongs do set a scandal on my sex.
  We cannot fight for love, as men may do.
  We should be woo'd, and were not made to woo.
                   [Exit Demetrius.]
  I'll follow thee and make a heaven of hell,
  To die upon the hand I love so well.   *[Exit.]*
OBERON: Fare thee well, nymph. Ere he do leave this
245 grove,
  Thou shalt fly him, and he shall seek thy love.

Enter PUCK.

  Hast thou the flower there? Welcome, wanderer.
PUCK: Ay, there it is.
OBERON: I pray thee give it me.
  I know a bank where the wild thyme blows,
250 Where oxlips and the nodding violet grows,
  Quite over-canopied with luscious woodbine,
  With sweet musk-roses and with eglantine;

There sleeps Titania sometime of the night,
Lull'd in these flowers with dances and delight;
And there the snake throws her enamell'd skin,   255
Weed wide enough to wrap a fairy in;
And with the juice of this I'll streak her eyes,
And make her full of hateful fantasies.
Take thou some of it, and seek through this grove:
A sweet Athenian lady is in love   260
With a disdainful youth; anoint his eyes,
But do it when the next thing he espies
May be the lady. Thou shalt know the man
By the Athenian garments he hath on.
Effect it with some care, that he may prove   265
More fond on her than she upon her love;
And look thou meet me ere the first cock crow.
PUCK: Fear not, my lord! your servant shall do so.

                            Exeunt.

SCENE II

Enter TITANIA, *queen of fairies, with her* TRAIN.

TITANIA: Come, now a roundel and a fairy song;
  Then, for the third part of a minute, hence,
  Some to kill cankers in the musk-rose buds,
  Some war with rere-mice for their leathren wings   4
  To make my small elves coats, and some keep back
  The clamorous owl, that nightly hoots and wonders
  At our quaint spirits. Sing me now asleep;
  Then to your offices, and let me rest.

FAIRIES *sing.*

[1. FAIRY.]   You spotted snakes with double tongue,
  Thorny hedgehogs, be not seen,   10
  Newts and blind-worms, do no wrong,
  Come not near our fairy queen.
CHORUS: Philomele, with melody,
  Sing in our sweet lullaby,
  Lulla, lulla, lullaby, lulla, lulla, lullaby.   15
    Never harm,
      Nor spell, nor charm,
  Come our lovely lady nigh.
  So good night, with lullaby.
1. FAIRY: Weaving spiders, come not here;   20
  Hence, you long-legg'd spinners, hence!
  Beetles black, approach not near;
  Worm nor snail, do no offense.
CHORUS: Philomele, with melody, etc.

---

211 **Tempt** try, put to the test   214 **impeach** discredit, call into question   218 **desert** deserted, unpeopled   220 **Your . . . privilege** your excellence in my eyes is my warrant for doing so; **For that** because   224 **in my respect** as far as I am concerned   227 **brakes** thickets   231 **Apollo . . . chase** According to the myth, Daphne, pursued by Apollo, was saved from rape by being transformed into a laurel tree   232 **griffin** fabulous monster with the body of a lion and the head of an eagle; **hind** female of the red deer   235 **stay thy questions** delay to listen to your talk   240 **Your . . . sex** Because he forces her to be the wooer instead of the wooed   244 **upon** by   249 **blows** blooms   250 **oxlips** flowering plant resembling the cowslip   251 **woodbine** honeysuckle   252 **musk-roses** variety of large, fragrant rose; **eglantine** sweet-brier, another variety of rose

---

253 **sometime of** at some time during   255 **throws** sheds   256 **Weed** garment   257 **streak** anoint   266 **fond on** infatuated with

II.ii. Location: The wood. 1 **roundel** dance in a circle   3 **cankers** cankerworms   4 **rere-mice** bats   **leathren** leathern   7 **quaint** pretty, dainty   8 **offices** duties   9 **double** forked   11 **Newts** water lizards. Newts, blind-worms, and spiders (line 20) were all thought to be poisonous   13 **Philomele** the nightingale. Philomela, daughter of King Pandion of Athens, was transformed into a nightingale, according to Ovid, after her rape by her brother-in-law Tereus   21 **spinners** spiders or (Cairncross) daddy-longlegs

25 2. FAIRY: Hence, away! now all is well.
　　　　One aloof stand sentinel.
　　　　　　　　[*Exeunt Fairies. Titania sleeps.*]

Enter OBERON [*and squeezes the flower on Titania's eyelids*].

　　OBERON: What thou seest when thou dost wake,
　　　　Do it for thy true-love take;
　　　　Love and languish for his sake.
30　　Be it ounce, or cat, or bear,
　　　　Pard, or boar with bristled hair,
　　　　In thy eye that shall appear
　　　　When thou wak'st, it is thy dear:
　　　　Wake when some vile thing is near.　　[*Exit.*]

Enter LYSANDER *and* HERMIA.

35 LYSANDER: Fair love, you faint with wand'ring in the wood;
　　　　And to speak troth I have forgot our way.
　　　　We'll rest us, Hermia, if you think it good,
　　　　And tarry for the comfort of the day.
　　HERMIA: Be't so, Lysander. Find you out a bed;
40　　For I upon this bank will rest my head.
　　LYSANDER: One turf shall serve as pillow for us both,
　　　　One heart, one bed, two bosoms, and one troth.
　　HERMIA: Nay, [good] Lysander; for my sake, my dear,
　　　　Lie further off yet; do not lie so near.
　　LYSANDER: O, take the sense, sweet, of my innocence!
46　　Love takes the meaning in love's conference:
　　　　I mean, that my heart unto yours [is] knit,
　　　　So that but one heart we can make of it;
　　　　Two bosoms interchained with an oath,
50　　So then two bosoms and a single troth.
　　　　Then by your side no bed-room me deny;
　　　　For lying so, Hermia, I do not lie.
　　HERMIA: Lysander riddles very prettily.
　　　　Now much beshrew my manners and my pride,
55　　If Hermia meant to say Lysander lied.
　　　　But, gentle friend, for love and courtesy,
　　　　Lie further off, in humane modesty;
　　　　Such separation as may well be said
　　　　Becomes a virtuous bachelor and a maid,
60　　So far be distant; and good night, sweet friend.
　　　　Thy love ne'er alter till thy sweet life end!
　　LYSANDER: Amen, amen, to that fair prayer, say I,
　　　　And then end life when I end loyalty!
　　　　Here is my bed; sleep give thee all his rest!
　　HERMIA: With half that wish the wisher's eyes be press'd!
65　　　　　　　　　　　　　　[*They sleep.*]

Enter PUCK.

　　PUCK: Through the forest have I gone,
　　　　But Athenian found I none,

　　　　On whose eyes I might approve
　　　　This flower's force in stirring love.
　　　　Night and silence—Who is here?　　　　　　70
　　　　Weeds of Athens he doth wear:
　　　　This is he, my master said,
　　　　Despised the Athenian maid;
　　　　And here the maiden, sleeping sound,
　　　　On the dank and dirty ground.　　　　　　75
　　　　Pretty soul, she durst not lie
　　　　Near this lack-love, this kill-courtesy.
　　　　Churl, upon thy eyes I throw
　　　　All the power this charm doth owe.
　　　　When thou wak'st, let love forbid　　　　80
　　　　Sleep his seat on thy eyelid.
　　　　So awake when I am gone,
　　　　For I must now to Oberon.　　　　　　*Exit.*

Enter DEMETRIUS *and* HELENA, *running.*

　　HELENA: Stay—though thou kill me, sweet Demetrius.
　　DEMETRIUS: I charge thee hence, and do not haunt me thus.　85
　　HELENA: O, wilt thou darkling leave me? do not so.
　　DEMETRIUS: Stay, on thy peril; I alone will go.　　[*Exit.*]
　　HELENA: O, I am out of breath in this fond chase!
　　　　The more my prayer, the lesser is my grace.
　　　　Happy is Hermia, wheresoe'er she lies,　　　90
　　　　For she hath blessed and attractive eyes.
　　　　How came her eyes so bright? Not with salt tears;
　　　　If so, my eyes are oft'ner wash'd than hers.
　　　　No, no; I am as ugly as a bear;
　　　　For beasts that meet me run away for fear.　　95
　　　　Therefore no marvel though Demetrius
　　　　Do, as a monster, fly my presence thus.
　　　　What wicked and dissembling glass of mine
　　　　Made me compare with Hermia's sphery eyne!
　　　　But who is here? Lysander! on the ground?　　100
　　　　Dead, or asleep? I see no blood, no wound.
　　　　Lysander, if you live, good sir, awake.
　　LYSANDER: [*Awaking.*] And run through fire I will for thy
　　　　　　sweet sake.
　　　　Transparent Helena, nature shows art,
　　　　That through thy bosom makes me see thy heart.　105
　　　　Where is Demetrius? O, how fit a word
　　　　Is that vile name to perish on my sword!
　　HELENA: Do not say so, Lysander, say not so.
　　　　What though he love your Hermia? Lord, what though?
　　　　Yet Hermia still loves you; then be content.　　110
　　LYSANDER: Content with Hermia? No; I do repent
　　　　The tedious minutes I with her have spent.
　　　　Not Hermia, but Helena I love.
　　　　Who will not change a raven for a dove?
　　　　The will of man is by his reason sway'd;　　　115

---

30 **ounce** lynx; **cat** wildcat　31 **Pard** leopard　36 **troth** truth　42 **troth** pledged faith　45 **take . . . innocence** interpret my meaning as entirely innocent　46 **Love . . . conference** i.e. a lover should be able to understand what is meant when he and his beloved talk together　52 **I . . . lie** i.e. I am not false　53 **prettily** ingeniously, skillfully　54 **beshrew** mischief take　57 **humane** courteous, decorous　65 **With . . . press'd** i.e. may half of all sleep's rest (which "all" you have wished for me) be yours

---

68 **approve** test　73 **Despised** who despised　79 **owe** possess　85 **haunt** follow persistently　86 **darkling** in the dark　87 **Stay . . . peril** i.e. it will be dangerous for you if you don't remain here　88 **fond** doting, foolishly loving　89 **my grace** the favor I am granted　90 **lies** dwells　91 **attractive** magnetic　97 **as a monster** i.e. as he would fly from a monster　99 **Made me compare** induced me to compare my eyes; **sphery eyne** eyes as bright as stars in their spheres　104 **Transparent** (1) bright, radiant; (2) capable of being seen through　109 **What though** what does it matter if　115 **will** desire

And reason says you are the worthier maid.
Things growing are not ripe until their season,
So I, being young, till now ripe not to reason;
And touching now the point of human skill,
120   Reason becomes the marshal to my will,
And leads me to your eyes, where I o'erlook
Love's stories written in Love's richest book.
HELENA: Wherefore was I to this keen mockery born?
When at your hands did I deserve this scorn?
125   Is't not enough, is't not enough, young man,
That I did never, no, nor never can,
Deserve a sweet look from Demetrius' eye,
But you must flout my insufficiency?
Good troth, you do me wrong (good sooth, you do)
130   In such disdainful manner me to woo.
But fare you well; perforce I must confess
I thought you lord of more true gentleness.
O that a lady, of one man refus'd,
Should of another therefore be abus'd!   *Exit.*
135   LYSANDER: She sees not Hermia. Hermia, sleep thou there,
And never mayst thou come Lysander near!
For as a surfeit of the sweetest things
The deepest loathing to the stomach brings,
Or as the heresies that men do leave
140   Are hated most of those they did deceive,
So thou, my surfeit and my heresy,
Of all be hated, but the most of me!
And, all my powers, address your love and might
To honor Helen and to be her knight.   *Exit.*
HERMIA: [*Starting up.*] Help me, Lysander, help me!
145   do thy best
To pluck this crawling serpent from my breast!
Ay me, for pity! what a dream was here!
Lysander, look how I do quake with fear.
Methought a serpent eat my heart away,
150   And you sate smiling at his cruel prey.
Lysander! what, remov'd? Lysander! lord!
What, out of hearing gone? No sound, no word?
Alack, where are you? Speak, and if you hear;
Speak, of all loves! I swoon almost with fear.
155   No? then I well perceive you are not nigh:
Either death, or you, I'll find immediately.   *Exit.*

ACT III

SCENE I

Enter the Clowns [QUINCE, SNUG, BOTTOM, FLUTE, SNOUT, *and* STARVELING].

BOTTOM: Are we all met?

QUINCE: Pat, pat; and here's a marvail's convenient
place for our rehearsal. This green plot shall
be our stage, this hawthorn brake our tiring-house,
and we will do it in action as we will do it before
the Duke.   6
BOTTOM: Peter Quince!
QUINCE: What sayest thou, bully Bottom?
BOTTOM: There are things in this comedy of Pyramus
and Thisby that will never please. First, Pyramus   10
must draw a sword to kill himself; which the ladies
cannot abide. How answer you that?
SNOUT: By'r lakin, a parlous fear.
STARVELING: I believe we must leave the killing out, when
all is done.   15
BOTTOM: Not a whit! I have a device to make all well.
Write me a prologue, and let the prologue seem to
say we will do no harm with our swords, and that
Pyramus is not kill'd indeed; and for the more
better assurance, tell them that I Pyramus am not   20
Pyramus, but Bottom the weaver. This will put
them out of fear.
QUINCE: Well; we will have such a prologue, and it
shall be written in eight and six.
BOTTOM: No; make it two more; let it be written in
eight and eight.   26
SNOUT: Will not the ladies be afeard of the lion?
STARVELING: I fear it, I promise you.
BOTTOM: Masters, you ought to consider with your-
[selves], to bring in (God shield us!) a lion among   30
ladies, is a most dreadful thing; for there is
not a more fearful wild-fowl than your lion living;
and we ought to look to't.
SNOUT: Therefore another prologue must tell he is
not a lion.   35
BOTTOM: Nay; you must name his name, and half his
face must be seen through the lion's neck, and he
himself must speak through, saying thus, or to
the same defect: "Ladies," or "Fair ladies, I would
wish you," or "I would request you," or "I would   40
entreat you, not to fear, not to tremble: my life
for yours. If you think I come hither as a lion, it
were pity of my life. No! I am no such thing; I am
a man as other men are"; and there indeed let him
name his name, and tell them plainly he is Snug the
joiner.   46
QUINCE: Well; it shall be so. But there is two hard
things: that is, to bring the moonlight into a chamber;
for you know, Pyramus and Thisby meet by
moonlight.   50

---

119 **point** summit; **skill** discernment, judgment   121 **o'erlook** survey, read   123 **keen** bitter   127 **Deserve** earn   129 **Good troth, good sooth** Both phrases mean "in very truth"   132 **gentleness** courtesy   133 **of** by (so also in lines 134, 140, 142)   134 **abus'd** ill used   149 **eat** ate (common preterite form, pronounced *et*)   150 **sate** sat; **prey** preying   153 **and if** if   154 **of all loves** for the sake of all true love

III.i. Location: Scene continues. (Although F1 marks an act break here, III.i is obviously a continuation of II.ii, since Titania remains asleep on stage, to wake at line 129.)

---

2 **marvail's** marvellous   4 **tiring-house** dressing room   13 **By'r lakin** by our ladykin, i.e. the Virgin Mary; **parlous** perilous   14–15 **when . . . done** after all   24 **eight and six** the common ballad measure of alternating eight- and six-syllable lines   30–31 **lion among ladies** It has been suggested that Shakespeare here alludes to an episode at a court entertainment in Scotland in 1594, when a tame lion which was to have drawn a chariot was replaced by a black African so as not to frighten the spectators   32 **fearful** (1) dreadful (as referring to a lion); (2) full of fear (as referring to a bird); **your** See note on I.ii.93   39 **defect** blunder for *effect*   41–42 **ray . . . yours** I pledge my life in defense of yours   43 **were . . . life** would endanger my life

SNOUT: Doth the moon shine that night we play
  our play?
BOTTOM: A calendar, a calendar! Look in the almanac.
  Find out moonshine, find out moonshine.
55 QUINCE: Yes; it doth shine that night.
  [BOTTOM:] Why then may you leave a casement of the
    great chamber window (where we play) open; and the
    moon may shine in at the casement.
  QUINCE: Ay; or else one must come in with a bush
60 of thorns and a lantern, and say he comes to disfigure,
    or to present, the person of Moonshine. Then,
    there is another thing: we must have a wall in the
    great chamber; for Pyramus and Thisby (says the
    story) did talk through the chink of a wall.
  SNOUT: You can never bring in a wall. What say
66 you, Bottom?
  BOTTOM: Some man or other must present Wall; and
    let him have some plaster, or some loam, or some
    rough-cast about him, to signify wall; or let him hold
    his fingers thus, and through that cranny shall Pyramus
71 and Thisby whisper.
  QUINCE: If that may be, then all is well. Come, sit
    down' every mother's son, and rehearse your parts.
    Pyramus, you begin. When you have spoken your
    speech, enter into that brake; and so every one according
76 to his cue.

Enter ROBIN [PUCK, behind].

PUCK: What hempen home-spuns have we swagg'ring here,
  So near the cradle of the Fairy Queen?
  What, a play toward? I'll be an auditor,
80 An actor too perhaps, if I see cause.
QUINCE: Speak, Pyramus. Thisby, stand forth.
BOTTOM: "Thisby, the flowers of odious savors sweet"—
QUINCE: [Odorous], odorous.
BOTTOM: —"odors savors sweet;
85 So hath thy breath, my dearest Thisby dear.
  But hark; a voice! Stay thou but here a while,
  And by and by I will to thee appear." Exit.
[PUCK:] A stranger Pyramus than e'er played here. [Exit.]
89 FLUTE: Must I speak now?
QUINCE: Ay, marry, must you; for you must understand
  he goes but to see a noise that he heard, and is
  to come again.
FLUTE: "Most radiant Pyramus, most lily-white of hue,
  Of color like the red rose on triumphant brier,
95 Most brisky juvenal, and eke most lovely jew,
  As true as truest horse, that yet would never tire,
  I'll meet thee, Pyramus, at Ninny's tomb."

QUINCE: "Ninus' tomb," man. Why, you must not
  speak that yet. That you answer to Pyramus. You
  speak all your part at once, cues and all. Pyramus,
  enter. Your cue is past; it is "never tire." 101
FLUTE: O—"As true as truest horse, that yet would never tire."

[Enter PUCK, and BOTTOM with an ass's head.]

BOTTOM: "If I were fair, Thisby, I were only thine."
QUINCE: O monstrous! O strange! We are haunted.
  Pray, masters, fly, masters! Help! 105
    [Exeunt Quince, Snug, Flute, Snout, and Starveling.]
PUCK: I'll follow you, I'll lead you about a round,
  Through bog, through bush, through brake, through brier:
  Sometime a horse I'll be, sometime a hound,
  A hog, a headless bear, sometime a fire,
  And neigh, and bark, and grunt, and roar, and burn,
  Like horse, hound, hog, bear, fire, at every turn. 111
    Exit.
BOTTOM: Why do they run away? This is a knavery of
  them to make me afeard.

Enter SNOUT.

SNOUT: O Bottom, thou art chang'd! What do I
  see on thee? 115
BOTTOM: What do you see? You see an ass-head of
  your own, do you? [Exit Snout.]

Enter QUINCE.

QUINCE: Bless thee, Bottom, bless thee! Thou art
  translated. Exit.
BOTTOM: I see their knavery. This is to make an ass of
  me, to fright me, if they could; but I will not stir 121
  from this place, do what they can. I will walk up and
  down here, and I will sing, that they shall hear I am
  not afraid. [Sings.]
    The woosel cock so black of hue, 125
      With orange-tawny bill,
    The throstle with his note so true,
      The wren with little quill—
TITANIA: [Awaking.] What angel wakes me from my flow'ry bed?
BOTTOM: [Sings.]
    The finch, the sparrow, and the lark, 130
      The plain-song cuckoo grey,
    Whose note full many a man doth mark,
      And dares not answer nay—
    for indeed, who would set his wit to so foolish a bird?

59–60 **bush of thorns** English peasants saw "the man in the moon" as bearing a bundle of sticks on his back 60–61 **disfigure** blunder for *prefigure* 61 **present** represent 69 **rough-cast** plaster mixed with pebbles for coating the outside of buildings 77 **hempen home-spuns** uncouth rustics (literally, persons wearing home-spun cloth made of hemp); **swagg'ring** blustering about 79 **toward** about to take place 82 **odious** blunder for *odorous*. Dogberry makes the reverse error in *Much Ado* III.v. 16: "Comparisons are odorous" 95 **brisky juvenal** lively youth; **eke** also; **Jew** Probably suggested by the first syllable *of juvenal* and used to provide a rhyme

98 **Ninus** mythical founder of Nineveh; his wife, Semiramis, reputedly erected Babylon, the scene of the story of Pyramus and Thisbe 103 **fair** handsome; **were** would be 106 **about a round** roundabout 109 **fire** will-o'-the-wisp 116–17 **an ass-head . . . own** i.e. something dreamed up inside your own asinine head 119 **translated** transformed 125 **woosel cock** male ousel or blackbird 127 **throstle** song thrush 128 **quill** piping voice (literally, pipe made of a hollow stalk) 131 **plain-song** melody without variations 132–33 **Whose . . . may** The similarity between *cuckoo* and *cuckold* gave rise to a common jest

Who would give a bird the lie, though he cry "cuckoo"
136   never so?
TITANIA: I pray thee, gentle mortal, sing again.
    Mine ear is much enamored of thy note;
    So is mine eye enthralled to thy shape;
    And thy fair virtue's force (perforce) doth move me
141   On the first view to say, to swear, I love thee.
BOTTOM: Methinks, mistress, you should have little
    reason for that. And yet, to say the truth, reason
    and love keep little company together now-a-days.
145   The more the pity that some honest neighbors
    will not make them friends. Nay, I can gleek upon
    occasion.
TITANIA: Thou art as wise as thou art beautiful.
BOTTOM: Not so, neither; but if I had wit enough to
    get out of this wood, I have enough to serve mine
151   owe turn.
TITANIA: Out of this wood do not desire to go;
    Thou shalt remain here, whether thou wilt or no.
    I am a spirit of no common rate;
155   The summer still doth tend upon my state;
    And I do love thee; therefore go with me.
    I'll give thee fairies to attend on thee;
    And they shall fetch thee jewels from the deep,
    And sing while thou on pressed flowers dost sleep.
160   And I will purge thy mortal grossness so,
    That thou shalt like an aery spirit go.
    Peaseblossom! Cobweb! Moth! and Mustardseed!

Enter four Fairies [PEASEBLOSSOM, COBWEB, MOTH, *and* MUSTARDSEED].

[PEASEBLOSSOM:]   Ready.
[COBWEB:]   And I.
[MOTH:]   And I.
[MUSTARDSEED:]   And I.
[ALL:]   Where shall we go?
TITANIA: Be kind and courteous to this gentleman,
165   Hop in his walks and gambol in his eyes;
    Feed him with apricocks and dewberries,
    With purple grapes, green figs, and mulberries;
    The honey-bags steal from the humble-bees,
    And for night-tapers crop their waxen thighs,
170   And light them at the fiery glow-worm's eyes,
    To have my love to bed and to arise;
    And pluck the wings from painted butterflies,
    To fan the moonbeams from his sleeping eyes.
    Nod to him, elves, and do him courtesies.
175 [PEASEBLOSSOM:] Hail, mortal!
[COBWEB:] Hail!
[MOTH:] Hail!
[MUSTARDSEED:] Hail!

BOTTOM: I cry your worships mercy, heartily. I be-
    seech your worship's name.   180
COBWEB: Cobweb.
BOTTOM: I shall desire you of more acquaintance, good
    Master Cobweb. If I cut my finger, I shall make
    bold with you. Your name, honest gentleman?
PEASEBLOSSOM: Peaseblossom.   185
BOTTOM: I pray you commend me to Mistress Squash,
    your mother, and to Master Peascod, your father.
    Good Master Peaseblossom, I shall desire you of more
    acquaintance too. Your name, I beseech you, sir?
MUSTARDSEED: Mustardseed.   190
BOTTOM: Good Master Mustardseed, I know your
    patience well. That same cowardly, giant-like
    ox-beef hath devour'd many a gentleman of your house.
    I promise you your kindred hath made my eyes water
    ere now. I desire you [of] more acquaintance, good
    Master Mustardseed.   196
TITANIA: Come wait upon him; lead him to my bower.
    The moon methinks looks with a wat'ry eye;
    And when she weeps, weeps every little flower,
    Lamenting some enforced chastity.   200
    Tie up my lover's tongue, bring him silently.   *Exeunt.*

SCENE II

Enter King of Fairies [OBERON].

OBERON: I wonder if Titania be awak'd;
    Then what it was that next came in her eye,
    Which she must dote on in extremity.

[*Enter* PUCK.]

    Here comes my messenger. How now, mad spirit?
    What night-rule now about this haunted grove?   5
PUCK: My mistress with a monster is in love.
    Near to her close and consecrated bower,
    While she was in her dull and sleeping hour,
    A crew of patches, rude mechanicals,
    That work for bread upon Athenian stalls,   10
    Were met together to rehearse a play
    Intended for great Theseus' nuptial day.
    The shallowest thick-skin of that barren sort,
    Who Pyramus presented, in their sport,
    Forsook his scene, and ent'red in a brake;   15
    When I did him at this advantage take,
    An ass's nole I fixed on his head.
    Anon his Thisby must be answered,

---

179 **cry . . . mercy** beg pardon of your honors   182 **of more acquaintance** to be better acquainted with me   183–84 **If . . . you** Cobwebs were applied to cuts to inhibit bleeding   186 **commend me** give my regards; **Squash** unripe pea pod   187 **Peascod** mature pea pod   192 **patience** calmness in suffering   199 **she weeps** i.e. causes dew   200 **enforced** violated

III.ii. Location: The wood   2 **next** nearest, i.e. first   3 **in extremity** to the utmost degree   5 **night-rule** night activity, night sport, **haunted** much frequented   7 **close** secret   8 **dull** drowsy   9 **patches** clowns, fools **rude mechanicals** ignorant workingmen   10 **stalls** street or market booths where wares were sold   13 **thick-skin** blockhead **barren sort** stupid crew   15 **scene** playing place   17 **nole** noddle, head

---

135 **give . . . lie** call a bird a liar   136 **never so** i.e. ever so much, continually   140 **thy . . . force** the power of your beauty   146 **gleek** gibe, jest   151 **owe** own   154 **rate** value, worth   155 **still** ever, always; **doth . . . state** attends upon me as one of my retinue   160 **grossness** corporeal nature   162 **Moth** Pronounced *mote* or *mot* by the Elizabethans, and probably intended by Shakespeare to represent here the word now written *mote*, which he seems regularly to have spelled *moth*   166 **apricocks** apricots   171 **have** i.e. attend (with lights)

And forth my mimic comes. When they him spy,
20 As wild geese that the creeping fowler eye,
Or russet-pated choughs, many in sort
(Rising and cawing at the gun's report),
Sever themselves and madly sweep the sky,
So, at his sight, away his fellows fly;
25 And at our stamp, here o'er and o'er one falls;
He murther cries, and help from Athens calls.
Their sense thus weak, lost with their fears thus strong,
Made senseless things begin to do them wrong,
For briers and thorns at their apparel snatch;
30 Some sleeves, some hats, from yielders all things catch.
I led them on in this distracted fear,
And left sweet Pyramus translated there;
When in that moment (so it came to pass)
Titania wak'd, and straightway lov'd an ass.
35 OBERON: This falls out better than I could devise.
But hast thou yet latch'd the Athenian's eyes
With the love-juice, as I did bid thee do?
PUCK: I took him sleeping (that is finish'd too)
And the Athenian woman by his side;
40 That when he wak'd, of force she must be ey'd.

Enter DEMETRIUS *and* HERMIA.

OBERON: Stand close; this is the same Athenian.
PUCK: This is the woman; but not this the man.
DEMETRIUS: O, why rebuke you him that loves you so?
Lay breath so bitter on your bitter foe.
45 HERMIA: Now I but chide; but I should use thee worse,
For thou (I fear) hast given me cause to curse.
If thou hast slain Lysander in his sleep,
Being o'er shoes in blood, plunge in the deep,
And kill me too.
50 The sun was not so true unto the day
As he to me. Would he have stolen away
From sleeping Hermia? I'll believe as soon
This whole earth may be bor'd, and that the moon
May through the centre creep, and so displease
55 Her brother's noontide with th' Antipodes.
It cannot be but thou hast murd'red him;
So should a murtherer look—so dead, so grim.
DEMETRIUS: So should the murthered look, and so should I,
Pierc'd through the heart with your stern cruelty.
60 Yet you, the murtherer, look as bright, as clear,
As yonder Venus in her glimmering sphere.
HERMIA: What's this to my Lysander? Where is he?
Ah, good Demetrius, wilt thou give him me?
DEMETRIUS: I had rather give his carcass to my hounds.
65 HERMIA: Out, dog, out, cur! thou driv'st me past the bounds
Of maiden's patience. Hast thou slain him then?

Henceforth be never numb'red among men!
O, once tell true; tell true, even for my sake!
Durst thou have look'd upon him being awake?
And hast thou kill'd him sleeping? O brave touch!
Could not a worm, an adder, do so much?   71
An adder did it! for with doubler tongue
Than thine, thou serpent, never adder stung.
DEMETRIUS: You spend your passion on a mispris'd mood.
I am not guilty of Lysander's blood;   75
Nor is he dead, for aught that I can tell.
HERMIA: I pray thee, tell me then that he is well.
DEMETRIUS: And if I could, what should I get therefore?
HERMIA: A privilege never to see me more.
And from thy hated presence part I [so]:   80
See me no more, whether he be dead or no.   *Exit.*
DEMETRIUS: There is no following her in this fierce vein.
Here therefore for a while I will remain.
So sorrow's heaviness doth heavier grow
For debt that bankrout [sleep] doth sorrow owe;   85
Which now in some slight measure it will pay,
If for his tender here I make some stay.

Lie down [and sleep].

OBERON: What hast thou done? Thou hast mistaken quite,
And laid the love-juice on some true-love's sight.
Of thy misprision must perforce ensue   90
Some true love turn'd, and not a false turn'd true.
PUCK: Then fate o'errules, that one man holding troth,
A million fail, confounding oath on oath.
OBERON: About the wood go swifter than the wind,
And Helena of Athens look thou find.   95
All fancy-sick she is and pale of cheer
With sighs of love, that costs the fresh blood dear.
By some illusion see thou bring her here.
I'll charm his eyes against she do appear.
PUCK: I go, I go, look how I go,   100
Swifter than arrow from the Tartar's bow.   [*Exit.*]
OBERON: Flower of this purple dye,
Hit with Cupid's archery,
Sink in apple of his eye.
When his love he doth espy,   105
Let her shine as gloriously
As the Venus of the sky.
When thou wak'st, if she be by,
Beg of her for remedy.

Enter PUCK.

PUCK: Captain of our fairy band,   110
Helena is here at hand,
And the youth, mistook by me,
Pleading for a lover's fee.

---

19 **mimic** actor 21 **russet-pated choughs** grey-headed jackdaws **in sort** in company, together 25 **at our stamp** Puck's use of *our* instead of *my* has puzzled editors, as has the notion that a fairy's stamp would be frightening. (This is the first occurrence of the word in that sense recorded in the *O.E.D.*). Many editors adopt Theobald's conjecture *at a stump* 26 **calls** calls for 36 **latch'd** anointed 40 **of force** perforce, necessarily 53 **whole** solid; **be bor'd** have a hole bored through it 55 **her brother's** i.e. the sun's; **with th' Antipodes** among the people on the other side of the earth 57 **dead** deadly (?) or deathly pale (?) 60 **clear** shining 62 **What's this to** what has all this to do with

70 **brave touch** noble exploit 71 **worm** snake, serpent 74 **passion** passionate outburst; **on . . . mood** in mistaken anger 84 **heavier** With play on the sense "drowsier." 85 **bankrupt** bankrupt 87 **for his tender** until sleep offers itself (in payment of the deficit) 90 **misprision** mistake 92 **troth** faith 93 **confounding . . . oath** invalidating one oath with another 96 **fancy-sick** lovesick; **cheer** face 97 **costs . . . dear** Each sigh was thought to draw a drop of blood from the heart 99 **against . . . appear** in preparation for her coming 101 **arrow . . . bow** Proverbial for swiftness 113 **fee** right, privilege

Shall we their fond pageant see?
115   Lord, what fools these mortals be!
OBERON: Stand aside. The noise they make
    Will cause Demetrius to awake.
PUCK: Then will two at once woo one;
    That must needs be sport alone.
120 And those things do best please me
    That befall prepost'rously.

Enter LYSANDER *and* HELENA.

LYSANDER: Why should you think that I should woo in scorn?
    Scorn and derision never come in tears.
    Look when I vow, I weep; and vows so born,
125   In their nativity all truth appears.
    How can these things in me seem scorn to you,
    Bearing the badge of faith to prove them true?
HELENA: You do advance your cunning more and more;
    When truth kills truth, O devilish-holy fray!
130 These vows are Hermia's. Will you give her o'er?
    Weigh oath with oath, and you will nothing weigh.
    Your vows to her and me, put in two scales,
    Will even weigh; and both as light as tales.
LYSANDER: I had no judgment when to her I swore.
135 HELENA: Nor none, in my mind, now you give her o'er.
LYSANDER: Demetrius loves her; and he loves not you.
DEMETRIUS: [*Awaking.*] O Helen, goddess, nymph,
      perfect, divine!
    To what, my love, shall I compare thine eyne?
    Crystal is muddy. O, how ripe in show
140 Thy lips, those kissing cherries, tempting grow!
    That pure congealed white, high Taurus' snow,
    Fann'd with the eastern wind, turns to a crow
    When thou hold'st up thy hand. O, let me kiss
    This princess of pure white, this seal of bliss!
145 HELENA: O spite! O hell! I see you all are bent
    To set against me for your merriment.
    If you were civil and knew courtesy,
    You would not do me thus much injury.
    Can you not hate me, as I know you do,
150 But you must join in souls to mock me too?
    If you were men, as men you are in show,
    You would not use a gentle lady so;
    To vow, and swear, and superpraise my parts,
    When I am sure you hate me with your hearts.
155 You both are rivals, and love Hermia;
    And now both rivals, to mock Helena.
    A trim exploit, a manly enterprise,
    To conjure tears up in a poor maid's eyes
    With your derision! None of noble sort
160 Would so offend a virgin, and extort
    A poor soul's patience, all to make you sport.

LYSANDER: You are unkind, Demetrius; be not so;
    For you love Hermia; this you know I know.
    And here, with all good will, with all my heart,
    In Hermia's love I yield you up my part; 165
    And yours of Helena to me bequeath,
    Whom I do love, and will do till my death.
HELENA: Never did mockers waste more idle breath.
DEMETRIUS: Lysander, keep thy Hermia; I will none.
    If e'er I lov'd her, all that love is gone. 170
    My heart to her but as guest-wise sojourn'd,
    And now to Helen is it home return'd,
    There to remain.
LYSANDER: Helen, it is not so.
DEMETRIUS: Disparage not the faith thou dost not know,
    Lest, to thy peril, thou aby it dear. 175
    Look where thy love comes; yonder is thy dear.

Enter HERMIA.

HERMIA: Dark night, that from the eye his function takes,
    The ear more quick of apprehension makes;
    Wherein it doth impair the seeing sense,
    It pays the hearing double recompense. 180
    Thou art not by mine eye, Lysander, found;
    Mine ear, I thank it, brought me to thy sound.
    But why unkindly didst thou leave me so?
LYSANDER: Why should he stay, whom love doth press to go?
HERMIA: What love could press Lysander from my side? 185
LYSANDER: Lysander's love, that would not let him bide—
    Fair Helena! who more engilds the night
    Than all yon fiery oes and eyes of light.
    Why seek'st thou me? Could not this make thee know,
    The hate I bare thee made me leave thee so? 190
HERMIA: You speak not as you think. It cannot be.
HELENA: Lo! she is one of this confederacy.
    Now I perceive, they have conjoin'd all three
    To fashion this false sport, in spite of me.
    Injurious Hermia, most ungrateful maid! 195
    Have you conspir'd, have you with these contriv'd
    To bait me with this foul derision?
    Is all the counsel that we two have shar'd,
    The sisters' vows, the hours that we have spent,
    When we have chid the hasty-footed time 200
    For parting us—O, is all forgot?
    All school-days friendship, childhood innocence?
    We, Hermia, like two artificial gods,
    Have with our needles created both one flower,
    Both on one sampler, sitting on one cushion, 205
    Both warbling of one song, both in one key,
    As if our hands, our sides, voices, and minds
    Had been incorporate. So we grew together,
    Like to a double cherry, seeming parted,
    But yet an union in partition, 210
    Two lovely berries moulded on one stem;

---

114 **fond pageant** foolish show 119 **alone** unparalleled
121 **prepost'rously** out of the natural order 124–25 **vows . . . appears**
i.e. when vows are so born, the nature of their birth makes their sincerity
manifest 127 **badge** identifying mark (like the family crest or other
device worn on livery to identify a gentleman's retainers) 128 **advance**
hold high, i.e. display 133 **tales** lies 141 **Taurus** a mountain range
in Asiatic Turkey 142 **turns . . . crow** i.e. seems black in comparison
144 **seal** pledge 151 **show** appearance 153 **superpraise** overpraise;
parts qualities 157 **trim** fine 160 **extort** wring, torture

---

169 **none** i.e. of her 175 **aby** pay for, atone for 177 **his** its 188 **oes**
circles, i.e. stars 194 **in . . . me** to vex me 195 **Injurious** insulting
196 **contriv'd** plotted 197 **bait** torment 198 **counsel** private
thoughts, confidences 203 **artificial** skilled in art, able to create
208 **incorporate** united in one body 209 **seeming** apparently
211 **lovely** loving

So with two seeming bodies, but one heart,
Two of the first, [like] coats in heraldry,
Due but to one, and crowned with one crest.
215 And will you rent our ancient love asunder,
To join with men in scorning your poor friend?
It is not friendly, 'tis not maidenly.
Our sex, as well as I, may chide you for it,
Though I alone do feel the injury.
220 HERMIA: I am amazed at your [passionate] words.
I scorn you not; it seems that you scorn me.
HELENA: Have you not set Lysander, as in scorn,
To follow me and praise my eyes and face?
And made your other love, Demetrius
225 (Who even but now did spurn me with his foot),
To call me goddess, nymph, divine and rare,
Precious, celestial? Wherefore speaks he this
To her he hates? And wherefore doth Lysander
Deny your love (so rich within his soul)
230 And tender me (forsooth) affection,
But by your setting on, by your consent?
What though I be not so in grace as you,
So hung upon with love, so fortunate
(But miserable most, to love unlov'd)?
235 This you should pity rather than despise.
HERMIA: I understand not what you mean by this.
HELENA: Ay, do! persever, counterfeit sad looks,
Make mouths upon me when I turn my back,
Wink each at other, hold the sweet jest up;
240 This sport, well carried, shall be chronicled.
If you have any pity, grace, or manners,
You would not make me such an argument.
But fare ye well; 'tis partly my own fault,
Which death, or absence, soon shall remedy.
245 LYSANDER: Stay, gentle Helena; hear my excuse,
My love, my life, my soul, fair Helena!
HELENA: O excellent!
HERMIA: Sweet, do not scorn her so.
DEMETRIUS: If she cannot entreat, I can compel.
LYSANDER: Thou canst compel no more than she entreat.
250 Thy threats have no more strength than her weak [prays].
Helen, I love thee, by my life I do!
I swear by that which I will lose for thee,
To prove him false that says I love thee not.
254 DEMETRIUS: I say I love thee more than he can do.
LYSANDER: If thou say so, withdraw, and prove it too.
DEMETRIUS: Quick, come!
HERMIA: Lysander, whereto tends all this?
LYSANDER: Away, you Ethiop!
DEMETRIUS: No, no; he'll
Seem to break loose—take on as you would follow,
But yet come not. You are a tame man, go!

LYSANDER: Hang off, thou cat, thou bur! Vile thing, let loose; 260
Or I will shake thee from me like a serpent!
HERMIA: Why are you grown so rude? What change is this,
Sweet love?
LYSANDER: Thy love? Out, tawny Tartar, out!
Out, loathed med'cine! O hated potion, hence!
HERMIA: Do you not jest?
HELENA: Yes, sooth; and so do you. 265
LYSANDER: Demetrius, I will keep my word with thee.
DEMETRIUS: I would I had your bond, for I perceive
A weak bond holds you. I'll not trust your word.
LYSANDER: What? should I hurt her, strike her, kill her dead?
Although I hate her, I'll not harm her so. 270
HERMIA: What? can you do me greater harm than hate?
Hate me, wherefore? O me, what news, my love!
Am not I Hermia? Are not you Lysander?
I am as fair now as I was erewhile.
Since night you lov'd me; yet since night you left me: 275
Why then, you left me (O, the gods forbid!)
In earnest, shall I say?
LYSANDER: Ay, by my life:
And never did desire to see thee more.
Therefore be out of hope, of question, of doubt;
Be certain! nothing truer; 'tis no jest 280
That I do hate thee, and love Helena.
HERMIA: O me, you juggler, you canker-blossom,
You thief of love! What, have you come by night
And stol'n my love's heart from him?
HELENA: Fine, i' faith!
Have you no modesty, no maiden shame, 285
No touch of bashfulness? What, will you tear
Impatient answers from my gentle tongue?
Fie, fie, you counterfeit, you puppet, you!
HERMIA: "Puppet"? Why so? Ay, that way goes
the game.
Now I perceive that she hath made compare 290
Between our statures: she hath urg'd her height,
And with her personage, her tall personage,
Her height, forsooth, she hath prevail'd with him.
And are you grown so high in his esteem,
Because I am so dwarfish and so low? 295
How low am I, thou painted maypole? Speak!
How low am I? I am not yet so low
But that my nails can reach unto thine eyes.
HELENA: I pray you, though you mock me, [gentlemen],
Let her not hurt me. I was never curst; 300
I have no gift at all in shrewishness;
I am a right maid for my cowardice.
Let her not strike me. You perhaps may think,
Because she is something lower than myself,
That I can match her.
HERMIA: "Lower"? hark again. 305

213–14 **Two . . . crest** "we had *two of the first*, i.e. bodies, like double coats in heraldry that belong to a man and wife as *one person,* but which, like our *single heart,* have but *one crest*" (Douce)   215 **rent** rend   220 **amazed** utterly bewildered   225 **even but now** just now   229 **your love** his love of you   232 **grace** favor   237 **sad** serious, grave   238 **mouths** a common corruption of *mows,* "grimaces." **upon** at   239 **hold . . . up** carry . . . on   240 **carried** managed   242 **argument** subject matter (for jesting)   248 **If . . . compel** i.e. if Hermia cannot influence you by pleas, I can do so by force   250 **prays** prayings, prayers   257 **Ethiop** blackamoor. Hermia is a brunette

260 **Hang off** let go   268 **weak bond** i.e. Hermia's arms. Demetrius implies that Lysander is not trying very hard to break away from her   272 **what news** what is the matter   275 **Since night** i.e. last night   282 **canker-blossom** worm that destroys the bud   288 **puppet** i.e. a mere doll rather than a woman (cf. the preceding *counterfeit*), but Hermia takes it as a reference to her small stature   292 **personage** figure   295 **low** short   300 **curst** shrewish, sharp-tongued   302 **right** real, true; **for** with respect to   304 **something** somewhat   305 **match** be a match for

HELENA: Good Hermia, do not be so bitter with me.
　　　I evermore did love you, Hermia,
　　　Did ever keep your counsels, never wrong'd you;
　　　Save that, in love unto Demetrius,
310　　I told him of your stealth unto this wood.
　　　He followed you; for love I followed him.
　　　But he hath chid me hence, and threat'ned me
　　　To strike me, spurn me, nay, to kill me too.
　　　And now, so you will let me quiet go,
315　　To Athens will I bear my folly back,
　　　And follow you no further. Let me go.
　　　You see how simple and how fond I am.
HERMIA: Why, get you gone. Who is't that hinders you?
HELENA: A foolish heart, that I leave here behind.
HERMIA: What, with Lysander?
320 HELENA:　　　　　　　　With Demetrius.
LYSANDER: Be not afraid; she shall not harm thee, Helena.
DEMETRIUS: No, sir; she shall not, though you take her part.
HELENA: O, when she is angry, she is keen and shrewd!
　　　She was a vixen when she went to school;
325　　And though she be but little, she is fierce.
HERMIA: "Little" again? Nothing but "low" and "little"?
　　　Why will you suffer her to flout me thus?
　　　Let me come to her.
LYSANDER:　　　　　Get you gone, you dwarf;
　　　You minimus, of hind'ring knot-grass made;
　　　You bead, you acorn.
330 DEMETRIUS:　　　　　You are too officious
　　　In her behalf that scorns your services.
　　　Let her alone; speak not of Helena,
　　　Take not her part. For if thou dost intend
　　　Never so little show of love to her,
　　　Thou shalt aby it.
335 LYSANDER:　　　Now she holds me not;
　　　Now follow, if thou dar'st, to try whose right,
　　　Of thine or mine, is most in Helena.
DEMETRIUS: Follow? Nay; I'll go with thee, cheek by
　　　jowl.　　　　[Exeunt Lysander and Demetrius.]
HERMIA: You, mistress, all this coil is long of you.
　　　Nay, go not back.
340 HELENA:　　　　I will not trust you, I,
　　　Nor longer stay in your curst company.
　　　Your hands than mine are quicker for a fray;
　　　My legs are longer though, to run away.　　[Exit.]
HERMIA: I am amaz'd, and know not what to say. Exit.
OBERON: This is thy negligence. Still thou mistak'st,
346　　Or else commit'st thy knaveries willfully.
PUCK: Believe me, king of shadows, I mistook.
　　　Did not you tell me I should know the man
　　　By the Athenian garments he had on?
350　　And so far blameless proves my enterprise,
　　　That I have 'nointed an Athenian's eyes;
　　　And so far am I glad it so did sort,
　　　As this their jangling I esteem a sport.

OBERON: Thou seest these lovers seek a place to fight;
　　　Hie therefore, Robin, overcast the night;　　355
　　　The starry welkin cover thou anon
　　　With drooping fog as black as Acheron,
　　　And lead these testy rivals so astray
　　　As one come not within another's way.
　　　Like to Lysander sometime frame thy tongue;　　360
　　　Then stir Demetrius up with bitter wrong;
　　　And sometime rail thou like Demetrius;
　　　And from each other look thou lead them thus,
　　　Till o'er their brows death-counterfeiting sleep
　　　With leaden legs and batty wings doth creep.　　365
　　　Then crush this herb into Lysander's eye;
　　　Whose liquor hath this virtuous property,
　　　To take from thence all error with his might,
　　　And make his eyeballs roll with wonted sight.
　　　When they next wake, all this derision　　370
　　　Shall seem a dream and fruitless vision,
　　　And back to Athens shall the lovers wend
　　　With league whose date till death shall never end.
　　　Whiles I in this affair do thee employ,
　　　I'll to my queen and beg her Indian boy;　　375
　　　And then I will her charmed eye release
　　　From monster's view, and all things shall be peace.
PUCK: My fairy lord, this must be done with haste,
　　　For Night's swift dragons cut the clouds full fast,
　　　And yonder shines Aurora's harbinger,　　380
　　　At whose approach, ghosts, wand'ring here and there,
　　　Troop home to churchyards. Damned spirits all,
　　　That in crossways and floods have burial,
　　　Already to their wormy beds are gone.
　　　For fear lest day should look their shames upon,　　385
　　　They willfully themselves exile from light,
　　　And must for aye consort with black-brow'd Night.
OBERON: But we are spirits of another sort.
　　　I with the Morning's love have oft made sport,
　　　And like a forester, the groves may tread　　390
　　　Even till the eastern gate; all fiery red,
　　　Opening on Neptune with fair blessed beams,
　　　Turns into yellow gold his salt green streams.
　　　But notwithstanding, haste, make no delay;
　　　We may effect this business yet ere day.　　[Exit.]
PUCK: Up and down, up and down,　　396
　　　I will lead them up and down;

---

355 **Hie** hasten   356 **welkin** sky   357 **Acheron** a river of Hades; here, Hades itself   361 **wrong** insults   365 **batty** batlike   366 **this herb** i.e. the herb that Oberon has mentioned (II.i.184) as the antidote to love-in-idleness   367 **virtuous** powerful   368 **with his might** by its efficacy   370 **derision** laughable mockery   371 **fruitless** having no effect, inconsequential   373 **date** duration   379 **dragons** i.e. those that were supposed to draw the chariot of the goddess of night; **full** very   380 **Aurora's harbinger** the precursor of dawn, i.e. the morning star   382–83 **Damned . . . burial** Suicides were commonly buried at cross-roads; to these Puck adds those who have drowned themselves and whose bodies have not been recovered   389 **the Morning's love** Cephalus, a mighty hunter, and lover of Aurora; or perhaps Aurora herself. If the first, Oberon means that he has often hunted in early morning with Cephalus; if the second, he means that he has often enjoyed the pleasures of the dawn, instead of being driven off by it   390 **like** in the guise of; **forester** keeper of a royal forest or hunting preserve

---

310 **stealth** stealing away   323 **shrewd** sharp-tongued (synonymous with *curst* in line 300)   324 **vixen** shrew (literally, she-fox)   329 **minimus** diminutive creature; **knot-grass** a weed that was thought to stunt the growth of animals or children   333 **intend** offer; or, possibly, pretend   335 **aby** pay for   338 **cheek by jowl** side by side   339 **coil** uproar; **long of** because of   345 **Still** continually   350 **so far** to this extent   352 **sort** turn out   353 **As** that; **jangling** disputing, wrangling

I am fear'd in field and town.
Goblin, lead them up and down.
400 Here comes one.

Enter LYSANDER.

LYSANDER: Where art thou, proud Demetrius? Speak thou now.
PUCK: Here, villain, drawn and ready. Where art thou?
LYSANDER: I will be with thee straight.
PUCK.   Follow me then
To plainer ground.

[Exit Lysander, as following the voice.]

Enter DEMETRIUS.

DEMETRIUS: Lysander, speak again!
405 Thou runaway, thou coward, art thou fled?
Speak! In some bush? Where dost thou hide thy head?
PUCK: Thou coward, art thou bragging to the stars,
Telling the bushes that thou look'st for wars,
And wilt not come? Come, recreant, come, thou child,
410 I'll whip thee with a rod. He is defil'd
That draws a sword on thee.
DEMETRIUS: Yea, art thou there?
PUCK: Follow my voice; we'll try no manhood here.
                                    Exeunt.

[Enter LYSANDER.]*

LYSANDER: He goes before me, and still dares me on.
When I come where he calls, then he is gone.
415 The villain is much lighter-hee'd than I;
I followed fast, but faster he did fly,
That fallen am I in dark uneven way,
And here will rest me. [*Lie down.*] Come, thou gentle day!
419 For if but once thou show me thy grey light,
I'll find Demetrius and revenge this spite.   [*Sleeps.*]

[Enter] ROBIN [PUCK] *and* DEMETRIUS.

PUCK: Ho, ho, ho! Coward, why com'st thou not?
DEMETRIUS: Abide me, if thou dar'st; for well I wot
Thourun'st before me, shifting every place,
And dar'st not stand, nor look me in the face.
Where art thou now?
425 PUCK: Come hither; I am here.
DEMETRIUS: Nay then thou mock'st me. Thou shalt buy this dear,
If ever I thy face by daylight see.
Now, go thy way. Faintness constraineth me
To measure out my length on this cold bed.
430 By day's approach look to be visited.
                            [Lies down and sleeps.]

Enter HELENA.

HELENA: O weary night, O long and tedious night,

Abate thy hours! Shine, comforts, from the east,
That I may back to Athens by daylight,
From these that my poor company detest.
And sleep, that sometimes shuts up sorrow's eye,   435
Steal me a while from mine own company.   *Sleep.*
PUCK: Yet but three? Come one more;
Two of both kinds makes up four.

[Enter HERMIA.]*

Here she comes, curst and sad.
Cupid is a knavish lad,   440
Thus to make poor females mad.
HERMIA: Never so weary, never so in woe,
Bedabbled with the dew and torn with briers,
I can no further crawl, no further go;
My legs can keep no pace with my desires.   445
Here will I rest me till the break of day.
Heavens shield Lysander, if they mean a fray!
                            [Lies down and sleeps.]

PUCK: On the ground,
Sleep sound;
I'll apply,   450
[To] your eye,
Gentle lover, remedy.
        [Squeezing the juice on LySander's eyes.]
When thou wak'st,
Thou tak'st
True delight   455
In the sight
Of thy former lady's eye;
And the country proverb known,
That every man should take his own,
In your waking shall be shown.   460
    Jack shall have Jill;
    Nought shall go ill:
The man shall have his mare again, and all shall be
well.   *[Exit.]*

ACT IV

SCENE I

Enter Queen of Fairies [TITANIA] *and Clown* [BOTTOM], *and
Fairies* [PEASEBLOSSOM, COBWEB, MOTH, MUSTARDSEED,
and others, attending]; *and the King* [OBERON] *behind them
[unseen].*
TITANIA: Come sit thee down upon this flow'ry bed,
While I thy amiable cheeks do coy,
And stick musk-roses in thy sleek smooth head,
And kiss thy fair large ears, my gentle joy.

---

402 **drawn** with drawn sword   403 **straight** straightway   404 **plainer**
more level   409 **recreant** coward   412 **try** test   417 **uneven** rough
422 **Abide me** face me in fight; **wot** know   429 **measure . . . length**
i.e. stretch out

---

432 **Abate** shorten   439 **curst** ill-tempered   444 **go** walk

IV.i. Location: Scene continues. (Again F1 marks an act break where the
action is clearly continuous, the lovers remaining asleep on the stage.
The F1 act division is preceded by the notation "They sleepe all the Act.";
this may mean that they sleep during some kind of inter-act music, as
well as into the next scene, but it need be nothing more than an inexact
reference to the fact that they sleep during the first 138 lines of the next
scene.)   2 **amiable** lovely; **coy** caress

5   BOTTOM: Where's Peaseblossom?

PEASEBLOSSOM: Ready.

BOTTOM: Scratch my head, Peaseblossom. Where's
        Mounsieur Cobweb?

9   COBWEB: Ready.

BOTTOM: Mounsieur Cobweb, good mounsieur, get you
        your weapons in your hand, and kill me a red-hipp'd
        humble-bee on the top of a thistle; and, good mounsieur,
        bring me the honey-bag. Do not fret yourself too much
        in the action, mounsieur; and, good mounsieur, have

15   a care the honey-bag break not, I would be loath
        to have you overflowen with a honey-bag, signior.
        Where's Mounsieur Mustardseed?

MUSTARDSEED: Ready.

BOTTOM: Give me your neaf, Mounsieur Mustardseed.

20   Pray you, leave your curtsy, good mounsieur.

MUSTARDSEED: What's your will?

BOTTOM: Nothing, good mounsieur, but to help
        Cavalery Cobweb to scratch. I must to the barber's,
        mounsieur; for methinks I am marvail's hairy
        about the face; and I am such a tender ass, if my hair
        do but tickle me, I must scratch.

TITANIA: What, wilt thou hear some music, my sweet love?

BOTTOM: I have a reasonable good ear in music. Let's

29   have the tongs and the bones.

                           [*Music. Tongs. Rural music.*]

TITANIA: Or say, sweet love, what thou desirest to eat.

BOTTOM: Truly, a peck of provender; I could munch
        your good dry oats. Methinks I have a great desire
        to a bottle of hay. Good hay, sweet hay, hath no fellow.

35 TITANIA: I have a venturous fairy that shall seek
        The squirrel's hoard, and fetch thee new nuts.

BOTTOM: I had rather have a handful or two of dried
        peas. But, I pray you, let none of your people stir

39   me; I have an exposition of sleep come upon me.

TITANIA: Sleep thou, and I will wind thee in my arms.
        Fairies, be gone, and be [all ways] away.

                                   [*Exeunt Fairies.*]

        So doth the woodbine the sweet honeysuckle
        Gently entwist; the female ivy so

44   Enrings the barky fingers of the elm.
        O, how I love thee! how I dote on thee! [*They sleep.*]

Enter ROBIN GOODFELLOW [PUCK.]

OBERON: [*Advancing.*] Welcome, good Robin. Seest thou this
        sweet sight?
        Her dotage now I do begin to pity.
        For meeting her of late behind the wood,
        Seeking sweet favors for this hateful fool,

50   I did upbraid her, and fall out with her.

For she his hairy temples then had rounded
With coronet of fresh and fragrant flowers;
And that same dew which sometime on the buds
Was wont to swell like round and orient pearls,
Stood now within the pretty flouriets' eyes,   55
Like tears that did their own disgrace bewail.
When I had at my pleasure taunted her,
And she in mild terms begg'd my patience,
I then did ask of her her changeling child;
Which straight she gave me, and her fairy sent   60
To bear him to my bower in fairy land.
And now I have the boy, I will undo
This hateful imperfection of her eyes.
And, gentle Puck, take this transformed scalp
From off the head of this Athenian swain,   65
That he, awaking when the other do,
May all to Athens back again repair,
And think no more of this night's accidents
But as the fierce vexation of a dream.
But first I will release the Fairy Queen.   70
                           [*Touching her eyes.*]
        Be as thou wast wont to be;
        See as thou wast wont to see.
        Dian's bud [o'er] Cupid's flower
        Hath such force and blessed power.
Now, my Titania, wake you, my sweet queen.   75

TITANIA: My Oberon, what visions have I seen!
        Methought I was enamor'd of an ass.

OBERON: There lies your love.

TITANIA: How came these things to pass?
        O, how mine eyes do loathe his visage now!

OBERON: Silence a while. Robin, take off this head.
        Titania, music call, and strike more dead   81
        Than common sleep of all these [five] the sense.

TITANIA: Music, ho, music, such as charmeth sleep!
                                   [*Music, still.*]

PUCK: Now, when thou wak'st, with thine own fool's eyes peep.

OBERON: Sound, music! [*Louder music.*] Come, my
        queen, take hands with me,   85
        And rock the ground whereon these sleepers be.
        Now thou and I are new in amity,
        And will to-morrow midnight solemnly
        Dance in Duke Theseus' house triumphantly,
        And bless it to all fair prosperity.   90
        There shall the pairs of faithful lovers be
        Wedded, with Theseus, all in jollity.

PUCK: Fairy King, attend and mark;
        I do hear the morning lark.

OBERON: Then, my queen, in silence sad,   95
        Trip we after night's shade.
        We the globe can compass soon,
        Swifter than the wand'ring moon.

---

16 **overflowen with** submerged by   19 **neaf** fist   20 **leave your curtsy**
i.e. put on your hat   23 **Cavalery** cavalier (form of address for a fashionable gentleman); **Cobweb** Peaseblossom has been asked to do the
scratching. This may be Shakespeare's slip or Bottom's   29 **tongs, bones**
rustic musical instruments; the tongs were struck with a key (as a triangle),
and the bones were rattled between the fingers (as clappers)   33 **bottle**
bundle   34 **fellow** equal   39 **exposition** blunder for *disposition,* i.e.
desire, inclination   41 **all ways away** off in all directions   42 **woodbine**
Obviously not the honeysuckle here (as at II.i.251). Various vines were
known by this name   49 **favors** i.e. flowers as love gifts

---

51 **rounded** encircled   53 **sometime** formerly   54 **orient pearls**
i.e. the most beautiful of pearls   55 **flouriets'** flowerets'   64 **scalp**
skull   66 **other** others   68 **accidents** events, incidents   69 **fierce**
excessive, wild   73 **Dian's bud** i.e. the herb of II.i.184, III.ii.366, perhaps the flower of the *agnus castus* or chaste tree, thought to preserve
chastity   82 **these five** i.e. the four lovers and Bottom   83 **s.d. Music,
still** i.e. soft music   88 **solemnly** ceremoniously   89 **triumphantly**
festively   95 **sad** sober

TITANIA: Come, my lord, and in our flight,
100   Tell me how it came this night
  That I sleeping here was found,
  With these mortals on the ground.
              Exeunt. Wind horn [within].

   Enter THESEUS, [HIPPOLYTA, EGEUS,] *and all his* TRAIN.

THESEUS: Go, one of you, find out the forester,
  For now our observation is perform'd,
105   And since we have the vaward of the day,
  My love shall hear the music of my hounds.
  Uncouple in the western valley, let them go.
  Dispatch, I say, and find the forester.
          [Exit an Attendant.]
  We will, fair queen, up to the mountain's top,
110   And mark the musical confusion
  Of hounds and echo in conjunction.
HIPPOLYTA: I was with Hercules and Cadmus once,
  When in a wood of Crete they bay'd the bear
  With hounds of Sparta. Never did I hear
115   Such gallant chiding; for besides the groves,
  The skies, the fountains, every region near
  Seem all one mutual cry. I never heard
  So musical a discord, such sweet thunder.
THESEUS: My hounds are bred out of the Spartan kind;
120   So flew'd, so sanded; and their heads are hung
  With ears that sweep away the morning dew;
  Crook-knee'd, and dewlapp'd like Thessalian bulls;
  Slow in pursuit; but match'd in mouth like bells,
  Each under each. A cry more tuneable
125   Was never hollow'd to, nor cheer'd with horn,
  In Crete, in Sparta, nor in Thessaly.
  Judge when you hear. But soft! What nymphs are
  these?
EGEUS: My lord, this' my daughter here asleep,
  And this Lysander, this Demetrius is,
130   This Helena, old Nedar's Helena.
  I wonder of their being here together.
THESEUS: No doubt they rose up early to observe
  The rite of May; and hearing our intent,
  Came here in grace of our solemnity.
135   But speak, Egeus, is not this the day
  That Hermia should give answer of her choice?
EGEUS: It is, my lord.
THESEUS: Go, bid the huntsmen wake them with their horns.
    [Exit an Attendant.] Shout within. Wind horns.
     They all start up.
  Good morrow, friends. Saint Valentine is past;
140   Begin these wood-birds but to couple now?
LYSANDER: Pardon, my lord.   *[They kneel.]*

THESEUS: I pray you all, stand up.
  I know you two are rival enemies.
  How comes this gentle concord in the world,
  That hatred is so far from jealousy
  To sleep by hate and fear no enmity?   145
LYSANDER: My lord, I shall reply amazedly,
  Half sleep, half waking; but, as yet, I swear,
  I cannot truly say how I came here.
  But, as I think—for truly would I speak,
  And now I do bethink me, so it is—   150
  I came with Hermia hither. Our intent
  Was to be gone from Athens, where we might,
  Without the peril of the Athenian law—
EGEUS: Enough, enough, my lord; you have enough.
  I beg the law, the law, upon his head.   155
  They would have stol'n away, they would, Demetrius,
  Thereby to have defeated you and me:
  You of your wife, and me of my consent,
  Of my consent that she should be your wife.
DEMETRIUS: My lord, fair Helen told me of their stealth,
  Of this their purpose hither to this wood,   161
  And I in fury hither followed them,
  Fair Helena in fancy following me.
  But, my good lord, I wot not by what power
  (But by some power it is), my love to Hermia   165
  (Melted as the snow) seems to me now
  As the remembrance of an idle gaud,
  Which in my childhood I did dote upon;
  And all the faith, the virtue of my heart,
  The object and the pleasure of mine eye,   170
  Is only Helena. To her, my lord,
  Was I betrothed ere I [saw] Hermia;
  But like a sickness did I loathe this food;
  But, as in health, come to my natural taste,
  Now I do wish it, love it, long for it,   175
  And will for evermore be true to it.
THESEUS: Fair lovers, you are fortunately met;
  Of this discourse we more will hear anon.
  Egeus, I will overbear your will;
  For in the temple, by and by, with us   180
  These couples shall eternally be knit.
  And, for the morning now is something worn,
  Our purpos'd hunting shall be set aside.
  Away with us to Athens. Three and three,
  We'll hold a feast in great solemnity.   185
  Come, Hippolyta.
    [Exeunt Theseus, Hippolyta, Egeus, and Train.]
DEMETRIUS: These things seem small and undistinguishable,
  Like far-off mountains turned into clouds.
HERMIA: Methinks I see these things with parted eye,
  When every thing seems double.
HELENA: So methinks;   190
  And I have found Demetrius like a jewel,
  Mine own, and not mine own.

---

102 **s.d. Wind** blow   104 **observation** observance, May-day rites (cf. I.i.167)   105 **vaward** early part   107 **Uncouple** unleash them   108 **Dispatch** make haste   113 **bay'd** brought to bay   114 **hounds of Sparta** Famous for hunting ability   115 **chiding** baying   117 **Seem** Usually emended to *Seem'd*   120 **flew'd** having large chaps; **sanded** of a sandy color   122 **dewlapp'd** having a pendulous flap of skin at the throat   123–24 **match'd . . . each** with voices of varying but harmonious pitch, like a peal of bells   124 **cry** pack of hounds; **tuneable** melodious   127 **soft** stop   128 **this'** this is   134 **in . . . solemnity** to honor our observance of the same rites   139 **Saint Valentine** It was supposed that birds chose their mates on St. Valentine's Day

---

144 **jealousy** suspicion, apprehension of evil   145 **To . . . hate** as to sleep side by side with a foe   146 **amazedly** perplexedly   152 **where we might** wherever we could   153 **Without the peril** beyond the dangerous reach   157 **defeated** defrauded   163 **fancy** love   167 **idle gaud** worthless trinket   182 **for** since   189 **parted** out of focus   191–92 **like . . . mine own** like some precious thing found by accident, and hence not certainly belonging to me, though in my possession

DEMETRIUS: Are you sure
   That we are awake? It seems to me
   That yet we sleep, we dream. Do not you think
195   The Duke was here, and bid us follow him?
HERMIA: Yea, and my father.
HELENA: And Hippolyta.
LYSANDER: And he did bid us follow to the temple.
DEMETRIUS: Why then, we are awake. Let's follow him,
   And by the way let's recount our dreams.

                             [*Exeunt Lovers.*]

200 BOTTOM: [*Awaking.*] When my cue comes, call
   me, and I will answer. My next is, "Most fair Pyramus."
   Heigh-ho! Peter Quince! Flute the bellows-
   mender! Snout the tinker! Starveling! God's my life,
   stol'n hence, and left me asleep! I have had a most
205   rare vision. I have had a dream, past the wit of
   man to say what dream it was. Man is but an ass,
   if he go about [t'] expound this dream. Methought
   I was—there is no man can tell what. Methought I
   was, and methought I had—but man is but [a patch'd]
210   fool, if he will offer to say what methought I
   had. The eye of man hath not heard, the ear of man
   hath not seen, man's hand is not able to taste, his
   tongue to conceive, nor his heart to report, what
   my dream was. I will get Peter Quince to write a
215   ballet of this dream. It shall be call'd "Bottom's
   Dream," because it hath no bottom; and I will
   sing it in the latter end of a play, before the Duke.
   Peradventure, to make it the more gracious, I shall
   sing it at her death.   [*Exit.*]

SCENE II

Enter QUINCE, *Thisby* [FLUTE], *and the rabble* [SNOUT,
STARVELING].

QUINCE: Have you sent to Bottom's house? Is he
   come home yet?
[STARVELING:] He cannot be heard of. Out of doubt he is
   transported.
FLUTE: If he come not, then the play is marr'd. It goes not
6   forward, doth it?
QUINCE: It is not possible. You have not a man in all Athens able
   to discharge Pyramus but he.
FLUTE: No, he hath simply the best wit of any handicraft man in
10   Athens.
QUINCE: Yea, and the best person too; and he is a very paramour
   for a sweet voice.
FLUTE: You must say "paragon." A paramour is
14   (God bless us!) a thing of naught.

Enter SNUG *the joiner.*

SNUG: Masters, the Duke is coming from the temple,
   and there is two or three lords and ladies more
   married. If our sport had gone forward, we had all
   been made men.
FLUTE: O sweet bully Bottom! Thus hath he lost
   sixpence a day during his life; he could not
   have scap'd sixpence a day. And the Duke had not   20
   given him sixpence a day for playing Pyramus, I'll be
   hang'd. He would have deserv'd it. Sixpence a day in
   Pyramus, or nothing.

                                           24

Enter BOTTOM.

BOTTOM: Where are these lads? Where are these
   hearts?
QUINCE: Bottom! O most courageous day! O most
   happy hour!
BOTTOM: Masters, I am to discourse wonders; but
   ask me not what; for if I tell you, I am [no] true   30
   Athenian. I will tell you every thing, right as it
   fell out.
QUINCE: Let us hear, sweet Bottom.
BOTTOM: Not a word of me. All that I will tell you
   is, that the Duke hath din'd. Get your apparel   35
   together, good strings to your beards, new ribands
   to your pumps; meet presently at the palace; every
   man look o'er his part; for the short and the long
   is, our play is preferr'd. In any case, let Thisby
   have clean linen; and let not him that plays the   40
   lion pare his nails, for they shall hang out for the
   lion's claws. And, most dear actors, eat no onions
   nor garlic, for we are to utter sweet breath; and I do
   not doubt but to hear them say, it is a sweet comedy.
   No more words. Away, go, away!   [*Exeunt.*]   45

ACT V

SCENE I

Enter THESEUS, HIPPOLYTA, *and* PHILOSTRATE, [LORDS, *and*
ATTENDANTS].

HIPPOLYTA: 'Tis strange, my Theseus, that these lovers speak of.
THESEUS: More strange than true. I never may believe
   These antic fables, nor these fairy toys.
   Lovers and madmen have such seething brains,
   Such shaping fantasies, that apprehend   5
   More than cool reason ever comprehends.

---

202 **Heigh-ho** A yawn   203 **God's** God save   207 **go about** attempt
209 **patch'd** wearing motley   210 **offer** venture   211–14 **The eye . . .
was** A parody of 1 Corinthians 2:9: "The eye hath not seen, and the ear hath
not heard, neither have entered into the heart of man . . ." (Bishops')
215 **ballet** ballad   216 **hath no bottom** i.e. is all tangled up because
it lacks a core (*bottom*)   218 **gracious** attractive, elegant   219 **her** i.e.
Thisbe's

IV.ii. Location: Athens. Quince's house   4 **transported** carried away by
the fairies   8 **discharge** successfully perform the role of   14 **a thing of
naught** something wicked

---

20 **sixpence a day** i.e. as a royal pension   20–21 **he . . . scap'd** his reward
would certainly not have been less than   21 **And if**   26 **hearts** good
fellows   29 **am . . . wonders** have wonders to recount   31 **right** exactly,
just   34 **of** from   36 **strings** To attach their false beards (?) **ribands**
ribbons   37 **presently** immediately   39 **preferr'd** recommended, put
forward

V.i. Location: Athens. The palace of Theseus   1 **that** what   2 **may**
can   3 **antic** grotesque; **fairy toys** trifling tales about fairy doings
5 **shaping fantasies** fertile imaginations; **apprehend** perceive, imagine
6 **comprehends** takes in, includes

The lunatic, the lover, and the poet
Are of imagination all compact.
One sees more devils than vast hell can hold;
10   That is the madman. The lover, all as frantic,
Sees Helen's beauty in a brow of Egypt.
The poet's eye, in a fine frenzy rolling,
Doth glance from heaven to earth, from earth to heaven;
And as imagination bodies forth
15   The forms of things unknown, the poet's pen
Turns them to shapes, and gives to aery nothing
A local habitation and a name.
Such tricks hath strong imagination,
That if it would but apprehend some joy,
20   It comprehends some bringer of that joy;
Or in the night, imagining some fear,
How easy is a bush suppos'd a bear!
HIPPOLYTA: But all the story of the night told over,
And all their minds transfigur'd so together,
25   More witnesseth than fancy's images,
And grows to something of great constancy;
But howsoever, strange and admirable.

Enter lovers, LYSANDER, DEMETRIUS, HERMIA, *and* HELENA.

THESEUS: Here come the lovers, full of joy and mirth.
Joy, gentle friends, joy and fresh days of love
Accompany your hearts!
30   LYSANDER: More than to us
Wait in your royal walks, your board, your bed!
THESEUS: Come now; what masques, what dances shall we have,
To wear away this long age of three hours
Between [our] after-supper and bed-time?
35   Where is our usual manager of mirth?
What revels are in hand? Is there no play
To ease the anguish of a torturing hour?
Call Philostrate.
PHILOSTRATE: Here, mighty Theseus.
PHILOSTRATE: Say, what abridgment have you for this evening?
40   What masque? what music? How shall we beguile
The lazy time, if not with some delight?
PHILOSTRATE: There is a brief how many sports are ripe.
Make choice of which your Highness will see first.
                                    [*Giving a paper.*]
THESEUS: [*Reads.*] "The battle with the Centaurs, to be sung
45   By an Athenian eunuch to the harp."
We'll none of that: that have I told my love,

In glory of my kinsman Hercules.
"The riot of the tipsy Bacchanals,
Tearing the Thracian singer in their rage."
That is an old device; and it was play'd   50
When I from Thebes came last a conqueror.
"The thrice three Muses mourning for the death
Of Learning, late deceas'd in beggary."
That is some satire, keen and critical,
Not sorting with a nuptial ceremony.   55
"A tedious brief scene of young Pyramus
And his love Thisby; very tragical mirth."
Merry and tragical? Tedious and brief?
That is hot ice and wondrous strange snow.
How shall we find the concord of this discord?   60
PHILOSTRATE: A play there is, my lord, some ten words long,
Which is as brief as I have known a play;
But by ten words, my lord, it is too long,
Which makes it tedious; for in all the play
There is not one word apt, one player fitted.   65
And tragical, my noble lord, it is;
For Pyramus therein doth kill himself;
Which when I saw rehears'd, I must confess,
Made mine eyes water; but more merry tears
The passion of loud laughter never shed.   70
THESEUS: What are they that do play it?
PHILOSTRATE: Hard-handed men that work in Athens here,
Which never labor'd in their minds till now;
And now have toiled their unbreathed memories
With this same play, against your nuptial.   75
THESEUS: And we will hear it.
PHILOSTRATE: No, my noble lord,
It is not for you. I have heard it over,
And it is nothings nothing, in the world;
Unless you can find sport in their intents,   80
Extremely stretch'd, and conn'd with cruel pain,
To do you service.
THESEUS: I will hear that play;
For never any thing can be amiss,
When simpleness and duty tender it.
Go bring them in; and take your places, ladies.
                                    [*Exit Philostrate.*]
HIPPOLYTA: I love not to see wretchedness o'ercharged,
And duty in his service perishing.   86
THESEUS: Why, gentle sweet, you shall see no such thing.

---

8 **compact** formed, composed   11 **Helen** Helen of Troy, a paragon of beauty; **brow of Egypt** gipsy's face   19 **would but** merely wishes to   20 **comprehends . . . joy** has no trouble including or creating in his fantasy some source of the joy   21 **some fear** something to be feared   25 **More witnesseth** gives evidence of more; **fancy's images** ideas created by imagination   26 **grows to** arrives at; **constancy** consistency, hence certainty   27 **howsoever** in any event; **admirable** to be wondered at   34 **after-supper** light repast following supper (?)   39 **abridgment** pastime (to abridge or shorten the time)   42 **brief** list, abstract; **ripe** ready for presentation   44 **battle . . . Centaurs** battle between the Centaurs and the Lapithae at the wedding feast of Theseus' friend Pirithous, where the Centaurs attempted to carry off the bride, Hippodamia

47 **glory . . . kinsman** One version of the tradition placed Hercules at the battle against the Centaurs. He and Theseus, according to Plutarch's life of the latter, were kinsmen   48–49 **The riot . . . rage** Orpheus, the Thracian musician, was torn to pieces by Bacchantes at the height of their orgiastic frenzy   50 **device** i.e. something devised for dramatic representation   52–53 **The thrice . . . beggary** Perhaps a topical allusion, though laments on the low estate of learning were commonplace   54 **critical** censorious   55 **sorting with** befitting   59 **strange** Perhaps an error, replacing some word which with *snow* would produce a "discord" similar to *hot ice*   65 **fitted** well cast   74 **toiled** taxed **unbreathed** unexercised   75 **against** in preparation for   80 **Extremely stretch'd** strained to the uttermost; **conn'd** learned by heart   83 **simpleness** sincerity   85 **wretchedness o'ercharged** feebleness overburdened   86 **his service** its attempt to perform due service

HIPPOLYTA: He says they can do nothing in this kind.
THESEUS: The kinder we, to give them thanks for nothing.
90   Our sport shall be to take what they mistake;
And what poor duty cannot do, noble respect
Takes it in might, not merit.
Where I have come, great clerks have purposed
To greet me with premeditated welcomes;
95   Where I have seen them shiver and look pale,
Make periods in the midst of sentences,
Throttle their practic'd accent in their fears,
And in conclusion dumbly have broke off,
Not paying me a welcome. Trust me, sweet,
100   Out of this silence yet I pick'd a welcome;
And in the modesty of fearful duty
I read as much as from the rattling tongue
Of saucy and audacious eloquence.
Love, therefore, and tongue-tied simplicity
105   In least speak most, to my capacity.

[*Enter* PHILOSTRATE.]

PHILOSTRATE: So please your Grace, the Prologue is address'd.
THESEUS: Let him approach.   [*Flourish trumpet.*]

Enter [QUINCE *for*] *the Prologue.*

PROLOGUE: If we offend, it is with our good will.
That you should think, we come not to offend,
110   But with good will. To show our simple skill,
That is the true beginning of our end.
Consider then, we come but in despite.
We do not come, as minding to content you,
Our true intent is. All for your delight
We are not here. That you should here repent you,
116   The actors are at hand; and, by their show,
You shall know all, that you are like to know.
THESEUS: This fellow doth not stand upon points.
LYSANDER: He hath rid his prologue like a rough colt;
he knows not the stop. A good moral, my lord: it is
121   not enough to speak, but to speak true.
HIPPOLYTA: Indeed he hath play'd on this prologue like
a child on a recorder—a sound, but not in
government.
125   THESEUS: His speech was like a tangled chain;
nothing impair'd, but all disorder'd. Who is next?

---

88 **in this kind** of this sort   91 **noble respect** generous consideration   92 **Takes . . . merit** judges it in relation to the abilities of the performers, not the merit of the performance   93 **clerks** scholars   101 **fearful** timorous, frightened   105 **least** i.e. saying least; **to my capacity** in my opinion   In the kindly speech of Theseus, a tribute was very likely intended to the graciousness of Queen Elizabeth. Attempts have been made to identify the passage with some particular occasion   106 **Prologue** speaker of the prologue; **address'd** ready   107 s.d. **Flourish** sound a fanfare   108–17 **If . . . know** The humor of the passage is in the blunders of its punctuation   112 **despite** ill will, defiance of your wishes   113 **minding** intending   118 **stand upon points** (1) bother about trifles; (2) heed his punctuation   119 **rough** unbroken   120 **stop** (1) reining in a horse to a quick halt; (2) period   121 **true** (1) the truth; (2) correctly   123 **recorder** wind instrument resembling a flute or flageolet   123–24 **government** control, management

---

Enter [*with a Trumpet before them*] PYRAMUS *and* THISBY *and* WALL *and* MOONSHINE *and* LION.

PROLOGUE: Gentles, perchance you wonder at this show;
But wonder on till truth make all things plain.
This man is Pyramus, if you would know;
This beauteous lady Thisby is certain.   130
This man, with lime and rough-cast, doth present
Wall, that vile Wall, which did these lovers sunder;
And through Wall's chink, poor souls, they are content
To whisper. At the which let no man wonder.
This man, with lantern, dog, and bush of thorn,   135
Presenteth Moonshine; for if you will know,
By moonshine did these lovers think no scorn
To meet at Ninus' tomb, there, there to woo.
This grisly beast, which Lion hight by name,
The trusty Thisby, coming first by night,   140
Did scare away, or rather did affright;
And as she fled, her mantle she did fall,
Which Lion vile with bloody mouth did stain.
Anon comes Pyramus, sweet youth and tall,
And finds his trusty Thisby's mantle slain;   145
Whereat, with blade, with bloody blameful blade,
He bravely broach'd his boiling bloody breast;
And Thisby, tarrying in mulberry shade,
His dagger drew, and died. For all the rest,
Let Lion, Moonshine, Wall, and lovers twain   150
At large discourse, while here they do remain.
Exit [*with Pyramus,*] *Thisby, Lion, and Moonshine.*
THESEUS: I wonder if the lion be to speak.
DEMETRIUS: No wonder, my lord; one lion may, when
many asses do.
WALL: In this same enterlude it doth befall   155
That I, one [Snout] by name, present a wall;
And such a wall, as I would have you think,
That had in it a crannied hole or chink,
Through which the lovers, Pyramus and Thisby,
Did whisper often, very secretly.   160
This loam, this rough-cast, and this stone doth show
That I am that same wall; the truth is so;
And this the cranny is, right and sinister,
Through which the fearful lovers are to whisper.   164
THESEUS: Would you desire lime and hair to speak better?
DEMETRIUS: It is the wittiest partition that ever I heard discourse,
my lord.

[*Enter* PYRAMUS.]

THESEUS: Pyramus draws near the wall. Silence!
PYRAMUS: O grim-look'd night! O night with hue so
black!   170
O night, which ever art when day is not!
O night, O night! alack, alack, alack,
I fear my Thisby's promise is forgot!

---

126 **nothing impair'd** i.e. still unbroken (*nothing* is here, as often, adverbial, meaning "in no respect, not at all")   137 **think no scorn** regard it as no disgrace   139 **hight** is called   142 **fall** let fall   144 **tall** brave   147 **broach'd** stabbed   151 **At large** at length   154 **No wonder** it will be no wonder if he does   163 **right and sinister** running right and left, i.e. horizontal   167 **wittiest** cleverest   170 **grim-look'd** grim-looking

174 And thou, O wall, O sweet, O lovely wall,
That stand'st between her father's ground and mine!
Thou wall, O wall, O sweet and lovely wall,
Show me thy chink, to blink through with mine eyne!
                               [*Wall holds up his fingers.*]
Thanks, courteous wall; Jove shield thee well for this!
But what see I? No Thisby do I see.
180 O wicked wall, through whom I see no bliss!
Curs'd be thy stones for thus deceiving me!
THESEUS: The wall methinks, being sensible, should
   curse again:
PYRAMUS: No, in truth, sir, he should not. "Deceiving me"
185 is Thisby's cue. She is to enter now, and
I am to spy her through the wall. You shall see it
will fall pat as I told you. Yonder she comes.

Enter THISBY.

THISBY: O wall, full often hast thou heard my moans,
   For parting my fair Pyramus and me!
190 My cherry lips have often kiss'd thy stones,
   Thy stones with lime and hair knit [up in thee].
PYRAMUS: I see a voice! Now will I to the chink,
   To spy and I can hear my Thisby's face.
   Thisby!
194 THISBY: My love thou art, my love I think.
PYRAMUS: Think what thou wilt, I am thy lover's grace;
   And, like Limander, am I trusty still.
THISBY: And I, like Helen, till the Fates me kill.
PYRAMUS: Not Shafalus to Procrus was so true.
199 THISBY: As Shafalus to Procrus, I to you.
PYRAMUS: O, kiss me through the hole of this vild wall!
THISBY: I kiss the wall's hole, not your lips at all.
PYRAMUS: Wilt thou at Ninny's tomb meet me straightway?
THISBY: 'Tide life, 'tide death, I come without delay.
                  [*Exeunt Pyramus and Thisby.*]
WALL: Thus have I, Wall, my part discharged so;
205 And being done, thus Wall away doth go.   [*Exit.*]
THESEUS: Now is the moon used between the two
   neighbors.
DEMETRIUS: No remedy, my lord, when walls are so willful to
   hear without warning.
210 HIPPOLYTA: This is the silliest stuff that ever I heard.
THESEUS: The best in this kind are but shadows; and
   the worst are no worse, if imagination amend them.
HIPPOLYTA: It must be your imagination then, and not
214 theirs.

---

182 **sensible** capable of feeling 183 **again** in return 187 **fall pat**
happen exactly 193 **and** if 194 **My . . . think** The Q1 punctuation
is here retained, although it "doth not stand upon points." 195 **lover's
grace** i.e. lover 196, 197 **Limander, Helen** blunders for *Leander*
and *Hero* 198 **Shafalus, Procrus** blunders for *Cephalus* and
Procris 200 **vild** vile 203 **'Tide** betide, come 206 **Now . . . used**
i.e. Moonshine, Wall being down, will now come into play. Most
editors follow Pope in emending *moon used* to *mural* [i.e. wall] *down*
(which is close to the F1 reading, *morall downe*) 208–9 **so . . . hear**
so willing to hear (?) or so perverse as to hear (?)—in either case, with
humorous allusion to the proverb "Walls have ears" (certainly true of
Snout!) 209 **without warning** surreptitiously (?) or without warning
the parents (?) 211 **in this kind** of this profession, i.e. actors. **shadows**
likenesses, representations

THESEUS: If we imagine no worse of them than they
   of themselves, they may pass for excellent men.
   Here come two noble beasts in, a man and a
   lion.   218

Enter LION *and* MOONSHINE.

LION: You, ladies, you, whose gentle hearts do fear
   The smallest monstrous mouse that creeps on floor,
   May now, perchance, both quake and tremble here,
   When lion rough in wildest rage doth roar.   222
   Then know that I as Snug the joiner am
   A lion fell, nor else no lion's dam,
   For, if I should, as lion, come in strife   225
   Into this place, 'twere pity on my life.
THESEUS: A very gentle beast, and of a good conscience.
DEMETRIUS: The very best at a beast, my lord, that e'er
   I saw.   230
LYSANDER: This lion is a very fox for his valor.
THESEUS: True; and a goose for his discretion.
DEMETRIUS: Not so, my lord; for his valor cannot carry
   his discretion, and the fox carries the goose.   234
THESEUS: His discretion, I am sure, cannot carry his
   valor; for the goose carries not the fox. It is well;
   leave it to his discretion, and let us listen to the
   Moon.
MOONSHINE: This lanthorn doth the horned moon present—
DEMETRIUS: He should have worn the horns on his head.   241
THESEUS: He is no crescent, and his horns are invisible within the
   circumference.
MOONSHINE: This lanthorn doth the horned moon present;
   Myself the man i' th' moon do seem to be.   245
THESEUS: This is the greatest error of all the rest.
   The man should be put into the lanthorn.
   How is it else the man i' th' moon?
DEMETRIUS: He dares not come there for the candle; for,
   you see, it is already in snuff.   250
HIPPOLYTA: I am a-weary of this moon. Would he would change!
THESEUS: It appears, by his small light of discretion,
   that he is in the wane; but yet in courtesy, in all
   reason, we must stay the time.   255
LYSANDER: Proceed, Moon.
MOONSHINE: All that I have to say is to tell you that the
   lanthorn is the moon, I the man i' th' moon, this
   thorn-bush my thorn-bush, and this dog my dog.   259
DEMETRIUS: Why, all these should be in the lanthorn; for
   all these are in the moon. But silence! here comes
   Thisby.

223–24 **I . . . dam** i.e. only as Snug the joiner am I a lion, or even a
lioness 224 **lion fell** cruel lion (but with additional sense "lionskin"—an
unintentionally humorous reference to Snug's costume) 227 **gentle**
polite 231 **very . . . valor** i.e. more crafty (diplomatic) than
courageous 232 **goose . . . discretion** i.e. more foolish than
crafty 239 **lanthorn** a variant of *lantern,* influenced by the fact that
lanterns usually had sides of transparent horn rather than glass; hence
there is wordplay in the reference to the "horned" (i.e. crescent) moon, as
well as in the jest about the cuckold's horns in the next speech 249 **for
the candle** on account of the candle 250 **in snuff** (1) offended; (2) in
need of snuffing 255 **stay** wait for

Enter THISBY.

THISBY: This is old Ninny's tomb. Where is my love?
LION. O!   [*The Lion roars. Thisby runs off.*]
265   DEMETRIUS: Well roar'd, Lion.
THESEUS: Well run, Thisby.
HIPPOLYTA: Well shone, Moon. Truly, the moon shines
    with a good grace. [*The Lion shakes Thisby's mantle.*]
THESEUS: Well mous'd, Lion.

Enter PYRAMUS.

270   DEMETRIUS: And then came Pyramus. [*Exit Lion.*]
LYSANDER: And so the lion vanish'd.
PPYRAMUS: Sweet Moon, I thank thee for thy sunny beams;
    I thank thee, Moon, for shining now so bright;
    For by thy gracious, golden, glittering [gleams],
275   I trust to take of truest Thisby sight.
        But stay! O spite!
        But mark, poor knight,
    What dreadful dole is here!
        Eyes, do you see?
280   How can it be?
    O dainty duck! O dear!
        Thy mantle good,
        What, stain'd with blood?
    Approach, ye Furies fell!
285   O Fates, come, come,
        Cut thread and thrum,
    Quail, crush, conclude, and quell!
THESEUS: This passion, and the death of a dear friend,
    would go near to make a man look sad.
290   HIPPOLYTA: Beshrew my heart, but I pity the man.
PYRAMUS: O, wherefore, Nature, didst thou lions frame?
    Since lion vild hath here deflow'r'd my dear;
    Which is—no, no—which was the fairest dame
    That liv'd, that lov'd, that lik'd, that look'd with cheer.
295   Come, tears, confound,
        Out, sword, and wound
    The pap of Pyramus;
        Ay, that left pap,
        Where heart doth hop. [*Stabs himself.*]
300   Thus die I, thus, thus, thus.
            Now am I dead,
            Now am I fled;
        My soul is in the sky.
304   Tongue, lose thy light,
            Moon, take thy flight,   [*Exit Moonshine.*]
        Now die, die, die, die, die.   [*Dies.*]

DEMETRIUS: No die, but an ace, for him; for he is but one.
LYSANDER: Less than an ace, man; for he is dead, he is
    nothing.
THESEUS: With the help of a surgeon he might yet
    recover, and yet prove an ass.   311
HIPPOLYTA: How chance Moonshine is gone before
    Thisby comes back and finds her lover?

[*Enter* THISBY.]

THESEUS: She will find him by starlight. Here she
    comes, and her passion ends the play.   315
HIPPOLYTA: Methinks she should not use a long one for
    such a Pyramus. I hope she will be brief.
DEMETRIUS: A mote will turn the balance, which
    Pyramus, which Thisby, is the better: he for a man, God
    warr'nt us; she for a woman, God bless us.   320
LYSANDER: She hath spied him already with those sweet
    eyes.
DEMETRIUS: And thus she means, *videlicet*—
THISBY: Asleep, my love?
        What, dead, my dove?   325
    O Pyramus, arise!
        Speak, speak! Quite dumb?
        Dead, dead? A tomb
    Must cover thy sweet eyes.
        These lily lips,   330
        This cherry nose,
    These yellow cowslip cheeks,
        Are gone, are gone!
        Lovers, make moan;
    His eyes were green as leeks.   335
        O Sisters Three,
        Come, come to me,
    With hands as pale as milk;
        Lay them in gore,
        Since you have shore   340
    With shears his thread of silk.
        Tongue, not a word!
        Come, trusty sword,
    Come, blade, my breast imbrue!
                        [*Stabs herself.*]
        And farewell, friends;   345
        Thus Thisby ends;
    Adieu, adieu, adieu.   [*Dies.*]
THESEUS: Moonshine and Lion are left to bury the
    dead.
DEMETRIUS: Ay, and Wall too.   350

---

269 **mous'd** shaken, torn (like a mouse in the jaws of a cat)   276 **spite** malicious stroke of fortune   278 **dole** grievous sight   286 **thread and thrum** warp and the loose ends of the warp; here, the complete thread (of life)   287 **Quail** overpower **conclude** bring to an end **quell** kill   288 **passion** violent expression of sorrow   289 **go . . . make** almost succeed in making   294 **cheer** Almost certainly the meaning here is "countenance"   295 **confound** destroy (me)   304–5 **Tongue . . . flight** Pyramus reverses the order of *Tongue* and *Moon,* with the result that Moonshine receives his walking orders. "Tongue, take your flight" would mean "be made dumb (by death)"

---

307 **No . . . ace** not a whole die but a single face—the one-spot; **one** (1) a single person; (2) in a class by himself   311 **ass** With pun on *ace*   315 **passion** passionate speech   318–19 **which . . . which** whether . . . or   320 **warr'nt** defend "God warrant us" and "God bless us" were both used conventionally to ward off an evil omen, and hence here imply Demetrius' opinion of the performances   323 **means** laments; *videlicet* as follows   336 **Sisters Three** the Fates   340 **shore** shorn   344 **imbrue** stain with blood

[BOTTOM:] [*Starting up.*] No, I assure you, the wall is
    down that parted their fathers. Will it please you to
    see the epilogue, or to hear a Bergomask dance between
354   two of our company?
  THESEUS: No epilogue, I pray you; for your play needs
    no excuse. Never excuse; for when the players are
    all dead, there need none to be blam'd. Marry, if
    he that writ it had play'd Pyramus, and hang'd him-
    self in Thisby's garter, it would have been a fine
360   tragedy; and so it is, truly, and very notably
    discharg'd. But come, your Bergomask; let your
    epilogue alone.   [*A dance.*]
    The iron tongue of midnight hath told twelve.
    Lovers, to bed, 'tis almost fairy time.
365   I fear we shall outsleep the coming morn
    As much as we this night have overwatch'd.
    This palpable-gross play hath well beguil'd
    The heavy gait of night. Sweet friends, to bed.
    A fortnight hold we this solemnity,
370   In nightly revels and new jollity.   *Exeunt.*

Enter PUCK.

PUCK: Now the hungry [lion] roars,
    And the wolf [behowls] the moon;
    Whilst the heavy ploughman snores,
    All with weary task foredone.
375   Now the wasted brands do glow,
    Whilst the screech-owl, screeching loud,
    Puts the wretch that lies in woe
    In remembrance of a shroud.
    Now it is the time of night
380   That the graves, all gaping wide,
    Every one lets forth his sprite,
    In the church-way paths to glide.
    And we fairies, that do run
    By the triple Hecat's team
385   From the presence of the sun,
    Following darkness like a dream,
    Now are frolic. Not a mouse
    Shall disturb this hallowed house.
    I am sent with broom before,
390   To sweep the dust behind the door.

Enter King and Queen of Fairies [OBERON *and* TITANIA] *with all
their* TRAIN.

OBERON: Through the house give glimmering light
    By the dead and drowsy fire,
    Every elf and fairy sprite
    Hop as light as bird from brier,
    And this ditty, after me,   395
    Sing, and dance it trippingly.
TITANIA: First, rehearse your song by rote,
    To each word a warbling note.
    Hand in hand, with fairy grace,
    Will we sing, and bless this place.   400
                        [*Song and dance.*]
OBERON: Now, until the break of day,
    Through this house each fairy stray.
    To the best bride-bed will we,
    Which by us shall blessed be;
    And the issue, there create,   405
    Ever shall be fortunate.
    So shall all the couples three
    Ever true in loving be;
    And the blots of Nature's hand
    Shall not in their issue stand;   410
    Never mole, hare-lip, nor scar,
    Nor mark prodigious, such as are
    Despised in nativity,
    Shall upon their children be.
    With this field-dew consecrate,   415
    Every fairy take his gait,
    And each several chamber bless,
    Through this palace, with sweet peace,
    And the owner of it blest
    Ever shall in safety rest.   420
    Trip away; make no stay;
    Meet me all by break of day.
          Exeunt [*Oberon, Titania, and Train*].
PUCK: If we shadows have offended,
    Think but this, and all is mended,
    That you have but slumb'red here   425
    While these visions did appear.
    And this weak and idle theme,
    No more yielding but a dream,
    Gentles, do not reprehend.
    If you pardon, we will mend.   430
    And, as I am an honest Puck,
    If we have unearned luck
    Now to scape the serpent's tongue,
    We will make amends ere long;
    Else the Puck a liar call.   435
    So, good night unto you all.
    Give me your hands, if we be friends,
    And Robin shall restore amends.   [*Exit.*]

---

353 **see, hear** Order reversed by Bottom; **Bergomask dance** a rustic dance taking its name from Bergamo in Italy 356 **no excuse** no extenuation of faults 363 **told** struck 366 **overwatch'd** stayed up too late 367 **palpable-gross** obviously dull 368 **heavy** torpid, dull 374 **foredone** exhausted 375 **wasted . . . glow** logs have burned down into glowing embers 381 **his sprite** its ghost 384 **triple Hecat's team** Hecate ruled in three capacities: as Luna (or Cynthia) in heaven, as Diana on earth, and as Proserpina in hell. Here she is the queen of night, drawn by her team of dragons (cf. III.ii.379) 387 **frolic** merry 390 **behind** i.e. from behind. Robin Goodfellow was a household spirit, and was thus sent to clean the house in preparation for the coming of his king and queen

---

405 **create** created 412 **prodigious** abnormal 416 **take his gait** go his way 417 **several** separate 425 **That . . . here** i.e. that it is but a "midsummer night's dream" 428 **No . . . but** yielding nothing more than 430 **mend** do better the next time 433 **serpent's tongue** hissing 437 **Give . . . hands** applaud 438 **restore amends** make amends in the future

NOTE ON THE TEXT

A Midsummer Night's Dream was first published in quarto (Q1) in 1600 by Thomas Fisher; this edition is here used as copy-text. A second quarto (Q2), set from a copy of Q1, was printed by James Roberts in 1619 with the fraudulent date 1600; it is essentially a reprint of Q1, with a few added stage directions and an occasional correction of obvious errors. The text of the First Folio (1623) was based on a copy of Q2 which had either itself served as a prompt-book or, more probably, been corrected against an official prompt-book.

Q1 displays a number of what are thought of as Shakespearean spellings and the kinds of stage directions which are generally associated with Shakespeare's "foul papers," though the text is unusually clean and may possibly have been printed from some sort of "fair copy" of the "foul papers." It has been suggested that Q1 also shows evidence of a book-keeper's hand in a few stage directions, but nothing in these directions makes it impossible to accept them as authorial notations.

The theatrical provenience behind certain aspects of the printer's copy for F1 is unquestionable (see, for example, the Textual Notes, III.ii.416, 463, IV.i.101, IV.ii o.s.d., V.i.126, 264; the omission of the double reference to God in V.i.319–20 probably points in the "same direction"). The two most substantial changes are both found in V.i: the substitution of Egeus for Philostrate, except in 76–81, throughout the scene, and the alternating distribution of Theseus' speech at ll. 44–60 between Lysander and Theseus. The more significant F1 variants are recorded in the Textual Notes. In the present text the excessively heavy use of phrasal commas in Q1 has been considerably lightened.

For further information, see: J. D. Wilson, ed., New Shakespeare *A Midsummer Night's Dream* (Cambridge, 1924); W. W. Greg, *The Shakespeare First Folio* (Oxford, 1955); R. K Turner, "Printing Methods and Textual Problems in *A Midsummer Night's Dream Q1*," *SB*, XV (1962), 34–8; Madeleine Doran, ed., Pelican *A Midsummer Night's Dream* (Baltimore, Maryland, 1969); J. K. Walton, *The Quarto Copy for the First Folio of Shakespeare* (Dublin, 1971); H. F. Brooks, ed., New Arden *A Midsummer Night's Dream* (London, 1979); R. A. Foakes, ed., New Cambridge *A Midsummer Night's Dream* (Cambridge, 1984); Barbara Hodgdon, "Gaining a Father: The Role of Egeus in the Quarto and the Folio," *RES*, n.s. XVII (1986), 534–42; Stanley Wells, Gary Taylor, John Jowett, and William Montgomery, *William Shakespeare: A Textual Companion* (Oxford, 1987); Peter Holland, ed., New Oxford *A Midsummer Night's Dream* (Oxford, 1994).

TEXTUAL NOTES

Title: **A . . . Dream]** *F1*; A Midsommer nights dreame. As it hath been sundry times publickely acted, by the Right honourable, the Lord Chamberlaine his seruants. Written by William Shakespeare. *Q1 (title-page)*

Dramatis personae: *subs. as first given by Rowe*

Act-scene division: *none in Q1–2; F1 marks acts only; scene divisions from Rowe and later editors (see first note to each scene); present act-scene arrangement as a whole first established by Capell.*

I.i

I.i] *Rowe*; Actus primus. *F1*
Location: *Theobald*
o.s.d. **Philostrate]** *Theobald*
4 **wanes]** *Q2, F1*; waues *Q1*
10 **New]** *Rowe*; Now *Q1–2, F1*
15 s.d. **Exit Philostrate.]** *Theobald*
19 s.d. **Lysander and Demetrius]** *F1*; Lysander and Helena, and Demetrius *Q1–2 (Helena does not enter until I. 179)*
24 **Stand forth, Demetrius.]** *Rowe; in italics as s.d., Q1–2, F1*
26 **Stand forth, Lysander.]** *Rowe; in italics as s.d., Q1–2, F1*
29 **love-tokens]** *hyphen, F1*
84 **sealing-day]** *hyphen, Capell*
113 **over-full]** *hyphen, F1*
113 **self-affairs]** *hyphen, Q2, F1*

127 s.d. **Manent . . . Hermia,]** *F1 (Manet)*
132 **Ay me!]** *Dyce*; Eigh me: *Q1*; Eigh me; *Q2*; *om. F1*; Hermia *F2*
136 **low]** *Theobald*; loue *Q1–2, F1*
139 **friends]** merit *F1*
143 **momentany]** momentarie *F1*
159 **remote]** remou'd *F1*
187 **Yours would]** *Hanmer*; Your words *Q1–2, F1*
200 **no fault]** none *Q2, F1*
216 **sweet]** *Theobald*; sweld *Q1–2, F1 (a barely possible reading)*
219 **stranger companies]** *Theobald*; strange companions *Q1–2, F1*
224 s.d. **Exit Hermia.]** *placed as in Dyce; after I. 223, Q1–2, F1*
226 **other some]** *Hanmer*; othersome *Q1–2, F1*
237 **figure]** *Rowe*; figure, *Q1–2, F1*
247 **wood]** *Q2, F1*; wodde *Q1*

I.ii

I.ii] *Capell*
Location: *Capell*
10 **grow]** grow on *F1*
11 **Marry]** *Q2, F1*; Mary *Q1*
11–2 **The . . . Thisby.]** *distinguished as a title, Capell*
23 **gallant]** gallantly *F1*

28 **rest—yet]** *Theobald (subs.)*; rest yet, *Q1–2, F1*
30–1 **split. "The]** *Theobald (subs.)*; split the *Q1–2, F1*
31–8 **"The . . . Fates."]** *as verse, Johnson; as prose, Q1–2, F1*
42 **bellows-mender]** *hyphen, F1*
86 **sweet-fac'd]** *hyphen, F1*
92 **Why,]** *Q2, F1*; Why? *Q1*

93 **straw-color**] *hyphen, F1*
94 **orange-tawny**] *hyphen, F4*
94–5 **purple-in-grain**] *hyphens, Rowe*

II.i] *Rowe; Actus Secundus, F1*
Location: *Theobald*
o.s.d. **Puck**] *Rowe*
1 s.p. **Puck.**] *Rowe;* Robin. *Q1–2,* **F1** (*until I. 154*)
2–9 **Over . . . green.**] *arranged as in Pope;* **as four verse lines,**
Q1–2, F1
22 **stolen**] *Q2;* stollen, *Q1;* stolne *F1*
52 **three-foot**] *hyphen, F1*
61 s.p. **Tita.**] *Capell;* Qu. *Q1–2, F1* (*throughout scene*)
61 **Fairies**] *Theobald;* Fairy *Q1–2, F1*
69 **steep**] *Q2, F1;* steppe *Q1*
79 **Aegles**] *Chambers* (*after North's Plutarch*); Eagles
Q1–2, F1
91 **pelting**] petty *F1*
107 **hoary-headed**] *hyphen, Rowe;* hoared headed *Q2, F1*
109 **thin**] *Tyrwhitt conj.;* chinne *Q1–2, F1*

II.ii] *Capell*
Location: *Pelican* (*after Capell*)
1 s.p. **Tita.**] *Capell;* Quee. *Q1–2, F1*
4 **leathren**] *Wilson;* lethten *Q1;* leathern *Q2, F1*
9 s.p. **1. Fairy.**] *Capell*
13, 24 s.pp. **Cho.**] *Capell*
14 **our**] your *F1*
20 s.p. **1. Fairy.**] 2. Fairy. *F1*
25 s.p. **2. Fairy.**] 1. Fairy. *F1*
26 s.d. **Exeunt Fairies.**] *Rowe*
26 s.d. **Titania sleeps.**] *F1* (Shee sleepes.)
26 s.d. **and . . . eyelids**] *Capell*
27 **dost**] *Q2, F1;* **doest** *Q1*
28 **true-love**] *hyphen. Harness*

III.i] *Rowe; Actus Tertius. F1*
Location: *ed.* (*after Wilson*)
2 **marvail's**] *Kittredge;* maruailes *QI;* maruailous *Q2, F1*
13 **By'r lakin**] *Pope* (*subs.*); Berlakin *Q1;* Berlaken *Q2, F1*
16 **device**] *Q2, F1;* deuise *Q1*
29 **yourselves**] *F1;* your selfe *Q1–2*
32 **wild-fowl**] *hyphen, Pope*
51 s.p. **Snout.**] *Cambridge;* Sn. *Q1–2, F1;* Snug. *F2*
56 s.p. **Bot.**] *Q2, F1;* Cet. *Q1*
76 s.d. **behind**] *Theobald; F1 gives an earlier duplicate s.d.* Enter
Pucke. *after I. 54*
82, 84, 89, 93, 102, 103 s.pp. **Bot., Flu.**] *Q1–2, F1 give as s.pp. the*
character names in the play-within-the-play: Pyra., This.
83 **Odorous, odorous**] *Collier conj.;* Odours,
odorous *Q1–2;* Odours, odours *F1*
88 s.p. **Puck.**] *F1;* Quin. *Q1–2*
88 s.d. **Exit.**] *Capell*
90, 98, 104 s.pp. **Quin.**] **Pet.** *Q2, F1*
102 s.d. **Enter . . . head.**] *Capell* (*after Rowe*);
Enter Piramus with the Asse head. *F1* (*after I. 111*)

95 **French-crown-color**] *first hyphen, F1;*
second hyphen, Rowe
104 **devices**] *F3;* deuises *Q1–2, F1*

II.i

115 **evils comes**] *F2;* euils, / Comes *Q1–2, F1*
145 s.d. **Titania . . . Train**] *Theobald*
158 **the**] *F1*
164 **fancy-free**] *hyphen, F2*
168 **love-in-idleness**] *hyphens, Capell*
176 s.d. **Exit.**] *F2*
183 **from off**] off from *Q2, F1*
183 **off**] *Q2, F1* (*see preceding note*); of *Q1*
190 **slay . . . slayeth**] *Thirlby conj.;* stay . . .
stayeth *Q1–2, F1* (*cf. Romeo and Juliet, IV.i.72*)
194 **thee**] *Q2, F1;* the *Q1*
201 **nor**] *F1;* not *Q1–2*
210 **use**] doe *F1*
242 s.d. **Exit Demetrius.**] *Capell*
244 s.d. **Exit.**] *Q2, F1*
246 s.d. **Enter Puck.**] *placed as in Capell; after I. 247, Q1–2, F1*

II.ii

34 s.d. **Exit.**] *Rowe*
38 **comfort**] *Q2, F1;* comfor *Q1*
39 **Be't**] *Pope;* Bet it *Q1;* Be it *Q2, F1*
43 **good**] *Q2, F1;* god *Q1*
47 **is**] *Q2, F1;* it *Q1*
48 **we can**] can you *F1*
49 **interchained**] interchanged *F1*
65 s.d. **They sleep.**] *F1*
87 s.d. **Exit.**] *F1* (Exit Demetrius.)
103 s.d. **Awaking.**] *Rowe*
119 **human**] *F4;* humane *Q1–2, F1*
145 s.d. **Starting up.**] *Capell*
152 **hearing**] *Theobald;* hearing, *Q1–2, F1*

III.i

105 s.d. **Exeunt . . . Starveling.**] *Dyce;* The Clownes all
Exit. *F1*
117 s.d. **Exit Snout.**] *Dyce*
124, 129 s.dd. **Sings.**] *Pope*
126 **orange-tawny**] *hyphen, F1*
129 s.d. **Awaking.**] *Rowe* (*subs.*)
139–41] *Ordered as 141, 139, 140, Q2, F1*
162 s.d. **Peaseblossom . . . Mustardseed**] *Dyce; F1 om. I. 162*
and has as s.d.: Enter Pease-blossom, Cobweb, Moth,
Mustardseede, and foure Fairies.
163 **Peas. Ready . . . go?**] *Dyce* (*after Capell*);
Fairies. [Fai. *Q2, F1*] Readie: and I, and I, and I. Where shall
we goe? *Q1–2, F1*
175 s.p. **Peas.**] *Dyce;* 1. Fai. *Q1–2, F1*
176 s.p. **Cob.**] *Dyce* (*after Capell* 2. Fairy);
continued to 1. Fai., *Q1–2, F1*
177 s.p. **Moth.**] *Dyce;* 2. Fai. *Q1–2, F1*
178 s.p. **Mus.**] *Dyce;* 3. Fai. *Q1–2, F1*
195 **of**] *Collier*
201 s.d. **Exeunt.**] *Rowe;* Exit. *Q1–2, F1*

III.ii

III.ii] *Capell*
Location: *Pelican (after Capell)*
o.s.d. **Enter . . . Oberon.]** Enter King of Fairies, and Robin
goodfellow. *Q1–2;* Enter King of Pharies, solus. *F1*
3 s.d. **Enter Puck.]** *F1 (see preceding note)*
6–7 **love . . . . bower,]** *Rowe;* loue, . . . bower.
Q1; love, . . . bower, *Q2, F1*
14 **sport]** *Rowe;* sport, *Q1–2, F1*
15–6 **brake; . . . take,]** *Pope;* brake, . . . take:
Q1; brake, . . . take, *Q2, F1*
19 **mimic]** *F1;* Minnick *Q1;* Minnock *Q2*
37, 89 **love-juice]** *hyphen, Theobald*
38 s.p. **Puck.]** Rob. *Q1–2, F1 (until I. 110)*
52 **From]** *Q2, F1;* Frow *Q1*
80 **so]** *Pope*
84 **grow]** *Pope;* grow. *Q1–2;* grow: *F1*
85 **sleep]** *Rowe;* slippe *Q1;* slip *Q2, F1*
87 s.d. **and sleep]** *ed. (after Collier)*
89 **true-love's]** *hyphen, Capell*
96 **fancy-sick]** *hyphen, F2*
101 s.d. **Exit.]** *Q2, F1*
104 **eye.]** *Rowe (subs.);* eye, *Q1–2, F1*
109 **her]** *Q2, F1;* her, *Q1*
129 **devilish-holy]** *hyphen, Capell*
137 s.d. **Awaking.]** *Rowe:* Awa. *F1 (after I. 136)*
137 **perfect,]** *Q2, F1;* perfect *Q1*
159 **derision! None]** *F1 (subs.);* derision None, *Q1;*
derision, none *Q2*
164 **here]** *Q2, F1;* heare *Q1*
175 **aby]** abide *F1 (again at I. 335)*
199 **sisters']** *Steevens;* sisters *Q1–2, F1*
213 **first, like]** *Theobald (Folkes conj.);* first life *Q1–2, F1*
220 **passionate]** *F1*
227 **Precious,]** *Q2, F1;* Pretious *Q1*
237 **Ay, do!]** *Rowe (subs.);* I doe. *Q1;* I, do, *Q2, F1*
250 **prays]** *Capell (Theobald conj.);* praise *Q1–2, F1*
252 **thee,]** *Q2, F1;* thee; *Q1*
257 **no; he'll]** no, hee'l *Q2;* no, Sir, *F1*
260 **off]** *Q2, F1;* of *Q1*

279 **Therefore]** *Q2, F1;* Thefore *Q1*
282 **canker-blossom]** *hyphen, F3*
299 **gentlemen]** *Q2, F1;* gentleman *Q1*
338 s.d. **Exeunt . . . Demetrius.]** *F1 (Exit);* Exit. *Q2*
343 s.d. **Exit.]** *Capell*
344 **Her. I . . . say.]** *om. F1 (following I. 343 F1 reads:* Enter
Oberon and Pucke.)
344 s.d. **Exit.]** *Capell;* Exeunt. *Q1–2*
346 **willfully]** willingly *F1*
364 **death-counterfeiting]** *Q2, F1;* **death-counterfaiting,** *Q1*
383 **all,]** *Q2, F1;* all; *Q1*
385 **lest]** *F4;* least *Q1–2, F1 (a possible reading, meaning* smallest
amount of)
387 **black-brow'd]** *Q2, F1 (hyphen, F3);* black browed *Q1*
394 **notwithstanding]** *Q2, F1;* notwistanding *Q1*
395 s.d. **Exit.]** *Rowe*
402 s.p. **Puck.]** Rob. *Q1–2, F1 (throughout rest of scene)*
404 s.d. **Exit . . . voice.]** *Cambridge (after Capell)*
406 **Speak! . . . bush?]** *Capell;* Speake in some bush. *Q1–2, F1*
(bush:)
406 **dost]** *Q2, F1,* doest *Q1*
412 s.d. **Enter Lysander.]** *Theobald (subs.)*
416 *Opposite this line F1 reads:* shifting places. (*presumably a
prompter's note*)
418 s.d. **Lie down.]** *F1 (after 1. 418); placed as in Capell*
420 s.d. **Sleeps.]** *Capell*
420 s.d. **Enter]** *F1*
426 **shalt]** *Q2, F1;* shat *Q1*
430 s.d. **Lies . . . sleeps.]** *Malone (after Rowe and Capell)*
432 **Shine, comforts,]** *Theobald;* shine comforts, *Q1;* shine
comforts *Q2, F1*
438 s.d. **Enter Hermia.]** *Q2, F1 (after I. 440); placed as
in Neilson*
447 s.d. **Lies . . . sleeps.]** *Dyce (after Rowe and Capell)*
451 **To]** *Rowe*
452 s.d. **Squeezing . . . eyes.]** *Rowe*
463 s.d. **Exit.]** *Rowe (following I. 463 F1 reads:* They sleepe
all the Act.)

IV.i

IV.i] *Rowe;* Actus Quartus. *F1*
Location: *ed.*
o.s.d. **Peaseblossom . . . attending]** *Dyce (after Rowe)*
o.s.d. **unseen]** *Capell*
24 **marvail's]** *Kittredge;* Maruailes *Q1;* maruailous *Q2;*
maruellous *F1*
29 s.d. **Music. . . . music]** *F1 (no period after* Music)
41 **all ways]** *Theobald;* alwaies *Q1–2, F1*
41 s.d. **Exeunt Fairies.]** *Capell*
42 **woodbine . . . honeysuckle]** *Rowe;* woodbine, . . . Honisuckle,
Q1–2, F1
45 s.d. **They sleep.]** *Capell*
45 s.d. **Enter . . . Puck.]** Enter Robin goodfellow and
Oberon. *F1*
46 s.d. **Advancing.]** *Collier*
70 s.d. **Touching her eyes.]** *Capell*
71 **Be]** Be thou *F1*

73 **bud . . . Bower]** *Thirlby conj.;* budde, or *Cupids* flower,
Q1–2, F1
82 **sleep . . . five]** *Theobald;* sleepe: of all these, fine *Q1,*
(sleepe;) *Q2, F1*
83 **ho]** *Q2, F1;* howe *Q1*
83 s.d. **Music, still.]** *F1*
84, 93 s.pp. **Puck.]** *Rowe;* Rob. *Q1–2, F1*
85 s.d. **Louder music.]** *ed. (after Wilson)*
96 **night's]** the nights *Q2, F1*
101 *After this line F1 adds s.d.:* Sleepers Lye still, (*i.e. remain
lying down*)
102 s.d. **horn]** homes *Q2, F1*
102 s.d. **within]** *Capell*
102 s.d. **Hippolyta, Egeus,]** *F1 (in reverse order)*
107 **Uncouple]** *Q2, F1;* Vncouple, *Q1*
108 s.d. **Exit an Attendant.]** *Dyce*
113 **bay'd]** *Rowe;* bayed *Q1–2, F1*

122 **Crook-knee'd**] *hyphen, F2*
128 **this'**] *ed.;* this *Q1;* this is *Q2, F1*
133 **rite**] *Pope;* right *Q1–2, F1*
138 s.d. **Exit an Attendant.**] *Dyce*
138 s.d. **Shout . . . up.**] *arranged as in Kittredge;* Shoute within: they all start vp. Winde hornes. *Q1–2;* Hornes and they wake. Shout within, they all start vp. *F1*
141 s.d. **They kneel.**] *Capell (subs.)*
149–50 **—for . . . is—**] *Capell;* (for . . . speake) / And . . . is; *Q1–2, F1*
152 **might,**] *Dyce;* might *Q1;* might be *Q2, F1*
153 **law—**] *Dyce;* lawe, *Q1;* Law. *Q2, F1*
172 **saw**] *Steevens (after Rowe);* see *Q1–2, F1*

IV.ii] *Capell*
Location: *Capell*
o.s.d. **and the rabble**] *om. F1*
o.s.d. **Snout, Starveling**] *F1 (Snout and Starueling)*
3 s.p. **Star.**] *F1;* F1ut. *Q1–2*
5 s.p. **F1u.**] *Rowe;* Thys. *Q1–2, F1 (throughout scene)*

V.i] *Rowe;* Actus Quintus. *F1*
Location: *Theobald*
o.s.d. **Philostrate**] Egeus *F1 (see I. 38)*
o.s.d. **Lords**] *F1 (and his Lords)*
o.s.d. **and Attendants**] *Capell*
3 **antic**] *Q2, F1;* antique *Q1*
4 **madmen**] *Rowe;* mad men *Q1–2, F1*
5–8, 12–7] *As Wilson suggests, the mislining in Q1 (followed in Q2, F1) probably shows that Shakespeare at some stage added these lines on the poet to the original speech; on similar evidence other insertions can also be traced in the first 84 lines of the scene*
10 **madman**] *F3 (mad-man);* mad man *Q1–2, F1*
30–1 **More . . . bed!**] *as verse, F2; as prose, Q1–2, F1*
34 **our**] *F1;* Or *Q1;* or *Q2*
34 **after-supper**] *hyphen, F4*
38 **Philostrate**] Egeus *F1 (all Philostrate's lines, except 76–81, are given to Egeus in F1)*
43 s.d. **Giving a paper.**] *Theobald*
44–5, 48–9, 52–3, 56–7] *These lines are assigned to Lis. (i.e. Lysander) in F1*
44 s.d. **Reads.**] *Theobald*
50 **device**] *Q2, F1;* deuise *Q1*
58–60 **Merry . . . discord?**] *as regular verse. Pope (om. l. 59); as irregular verse, Q1, as mixed irregular verse and prose, Q2; as prose, F1*
84 s.d. **Exit Philostrate.**] *Pope*
105 s.d. **Enter Philostrate.**] *Capell*
107 s.d. **F1ourish trumpet.**] *ed.;* F1or. Trum. *F1*
107 s.d. **Quince for**] *Rowe (F1 places Quince. opposite Enter the Prologue.)*
122 **this**] his *F1*
126 s.d. **with . . . them**] *from F1* Tawyer with a Trumpet before them. *(Tawyer was a servant in Shakespeare's company who died in 1625)*
141 **scare**] *F3;* scarre *Q1–2, F1*

186 s.d. **Exeunt . . . Train.**] *Capell;* Exit. *Q2;* Exit Duke and Lords. *F1*
192–3 **Are . . . awake?**] *om. F1*
198–9 **Why . . . dreams.**] *as verse, Rowe; as prose, Q1–2, F1*
199 **let's**] let vs *Q2, F1*
199 s.d. **Exeunt Lovers.**] *F1 (Exit);* Exit *Q2*
200 s.p., s.d. **Bot. Awaking.**] *from F1:* Bottome wakes. / Clo.; Clo. *Q1–2*
205 **have**] *om. F1*
207 **t' expound**] *ed.;* expound *Q1;* to expound *Q2, F1*
209 **a patch'd**] *F1;* patcht a *Q1–2*
219 s.d. **Exit.**] *Q2, F10*

IV.ii
6 **forward,**] *Q2, F1;* forward. *Q1*
14 **naught**] *F2;* nought *Q1–2, F1*
30 **no**] *F1;* not *Q1–2*
45 **go,**] *Theobald;* go *Q1–2, F1*
45 s.d. **Exeunt.**] *F1*

V.i
145 **trusty**] *om. F1;* gentle *F2*
151 s.d. **with Pyramus**] *Cambridge (subs.);* Q1–2 *s.d. after 1. 154 (here placed as in F1);* F1 *s.d.:* Exit all but Wall.
156 **Snout**] *F1;* F1ute *Q1–2*
168 s.d. **Enter Pyramus.**] *F1 (after 1. 169); placed as in Neilson*
170 **grim-look'd**] *hyphen, Theobald*
177 s.d. **Wall . . . fingers.**] *Capell*
184–7 **No . . . comes.**] *as prose, Pope; as verse, Q1–2, F1*
187 s.d. **Enter Thisby.**] *after fall 1. 187. F1*
191 **hair**] *Q2, F1;* hayire *Q1*
191 **up in thee**] *F1;* now againe *Q1–2*
203 s.d. **Exeunt. . . Thisby.**] *Dyce*
205 s.d. **Exit.**] *Dyce;* Exit Clow. *F1 (i.e. the Clowns: Pyramus, Thisby, and Wall)*
206 s.p. **The.**] *Rowe;* Duk. (or Duke.) *Q1–2, F1 (throughout rest of scene)*
206 **moon used**] morall downe *F1 (both readings are corrupt; some eds. read* mural down *[Pope], others* wall down *[Collier MS])*
210 s.p. **Hip.**] *Rowe;* Dutch. *Q1–2, F1 (throughout rest of scene)*
217 **beasts in,**] *Rowe;* beasts, in *Q1–2, F1*
223 **as**] one *F1*
263, 328 **tomb**] *Q2 (subs.), F1;* tumbe *Q1*
264 s.d. **The . . . off.**] *F1*
268 s.d. **The . . . mantle.**] *Capell*
269 s.d **Enter Pyramus.**] *placed as in Alexander; after 1.271, Q1–2 F1*
270 s.d. **Exit Loin.**] *ed. (after Wilson)*
274 **gleams**] *Knight conj.;* beames *Q1–2, F1*
275 **take**] taste *F1*
299 s.d. **Stabs himself.**] *Dyce (after Collier MS)*
305 s.d. **Exit Moonshine.**] *Capell*
306 s.d. **Dies.**] *Capell*
311 **yet**] *om. F1*
312–3 **before**] *Rowe;* before? *Q1–2, F1*
313 s.d. **Enter Thisby.**] *F1*

318 **mote**] *Heath conj.*; moth *Q1–2, F1*

319–20 **he . . . us.**] com. *F1*

320 **warr'nt**] *Wilson;* warnd *Q1–2*

335 **leeks.**] *Q2, F1;* leekes, *Q1*

344 s.d. **Stabs herself.**] *Dyce*

347 s.d. **Dies.**] *Warburton*

351 s.p. **Bot.**] *F1;* Lyon. *Q1–2*

351 s.d. **Starting up.**] *Capell*

357 **Marry**] *Q2, F1;* Mary *Q1*

362 s.d. **A dance.**] *Rowe*

367 **palpable-gross**] *hyphen, Capell*

371 **lion**] *Rowe;* Lyons *Q1–2, F1*

372 **behowls**] *Theobald;* beholds *Q1–2, F1*

384 **Hecat's**] *Johnson;* Hecates *Q1–2, F1*

400 s.d. **Song and dance.**] *Capell*

401–22] *Called* The Song. *and not assigned to Oberon, F1*

419–20 **And . . . rest.**] *arranged as in Staunton; lines reversed in Q1–2, F1*

422 s.d. **Oberon . . . Train**] *Capell*

423 s.p. **Puck.**] *Rowe;* Robin. *Q1–2, F1*

438 s.d. **Exit.**] *Capell;* FINIS. *Q1–2, F1*

Hamlet

In his landmark study, *The Idea of a Theater,* actor/scholar Francis Fergusson characterized *Hamlet* as one of the "sphinxes of literature," a play that has repeatedly drawn actors, audiences, and scholars into its labyrinthine mystery. Yet while *Hamlet,* like the brooding young prince of Denmark, may now seem like a difficult and philosophical problem, to its original audiences the play was a version of a popular genre on the Elizabethan stage, the revenge tragedy. As in many of his other plays, Shakespeare adapted his tragedy from a variety of known materials. The story of Amlethus, a disinherited Danish prince who uses feigned madness and cunning to avenge his father's murder and regain the throne from his villainous uncle, dates from the twelfth-century *Historia Danica* of the Danish historian Saxo Grammaticus; it was later adapted as a tragic narrative by François de Belleforest and included in his *Histoires tragiques* in 1576. Although Shakespeare may have known these versions, it is more certain that he knew a now-lost play on the subject of Hamlet's revenge that was staged in the 1580s. This play—usually called the *Ur-Hamlet* by scholars—was possibly written by Thomas Kyd, the author of another popular revenge tragedy, *The Spanish Tragedy.* While little is known about this play, we do know that it had at least one element of Shakespeare's play; in 1596, the playwright and novelist Thomas Lodge remarked on a play in which a pale ghost "cried so miserably at the Theater, like an oyster-wife, 'Hamlet, revenge!'"

A ghost, a sinister and deceptive family, a court full of busybodies and spies, a broken romance, an elaborate play-within-the-play, a command, sometimes from beyond the grave, to take revenge, an elaborate finale in which the stage is littered with corpses—these devices were common in revenge tragedies preceding Shakespeare's play, such as *The Spanish Tragedy,* and common also in those which capitalized on *Hamlet's* success in 1601, plays like John Marston's *The Malcontent* and Cyril Tourneur's *The Revenger's Tragedy* (which opens with a man speaking to a skull) and John Webster's *The White Devil. Hamlet* avails itself of all these devices, but it also reflects and refracts them; the play seems to question what it means to take action, simply to act, let alone take revenge, in a world of such complete duplicity that any behavior might seem the treacherous "actions that a man might play." In his famous essay, "The World of *Hamlet,*" Maynard Mack suggests that the play is in the "interrogative mood": not only does Hamlet repeatedly ask questions of himself and others ("To be or not to be . . . ," "Is it not monstrous . . . ," and so on), but much of the action of the play involves, as Polonius suggests, using theatrical "indirections" to "find directions out": Polonius sends Reynaldo to spread dishonorable rumors about Laertes, to see whether Laertes is being virtuous in Paris; Claudius and Polonius "stage" Ophelia for Hamlet, hoping to discover whether he's mad for revenge or madly in love; Hamlet hopes that the players' *The Murder of Gonzago* will reveal Claudius's guilt; Polonius hides fatally behind the arras while Hamlet interrogates Gertrude; Claudius stages a "duel" between Hamlet and Laertes that is really a design for murder.

In the celebrated 1954 production of Shakespeare's *Hamlet,* Richard Burton takes leave of Claire Bloom as Ophelia.

The world of *Hamlet* is a world in which appearances sometimes deceive and sometimes speak the truth: not being able to read the signs—as Ophelia, Rosencrantz and Guildenstern, and Polonius all discover—can be fatal. Indeed, the play's obsession with seeming ("Seems, madam? Nay, it is. I know not 'seems,'" Hamlet declares in his first scene in the play) perhaps explains its obsession with the arts of seeming, with acting, performance, theater. In *Hamlet,* Shakespeare undertakes an extended meditation on the purpose and limits of theater. Hamlet, of course, is quite familiar with the theater, and Shakespeare clearly characterizes the troupe of players as his audience's contemporaries; not only is the company all male, but they seem to have left the city—as many professional companies may have done, since they toured frequently—as a result of the "war of the theaters," the contemporary vogue for companies of boy-actors performing satirical plays. Moreover, Hamlet's famous advice to the players (3.2) suggests that he has a keen eye for performance. He chastens the actors not to "mouth it, as many of our players do," not to "saw the air too much with your hand," but to "Suit the action to the word, the word to the action." Yet in *Hamlet,* words and actions are more often than not suited to deception, to the extent that to Hamlet "this goodly frame, the earth, seems . . . a sterile promontory." Hamlet's blatant reference to the Globe itself—an actor, surrounded by the circular frame of the Globe, standing on the bare platform of the stage—suggests a skeptical regard for the theater's creation. While plays like *A Midsummer Night's Dream* or perhaps *The Tempest* suggest the theater's ability to present healing fictions, the theater in *Hamlet* is presented from a more ironic, even disaffected perspective: to be trapped in a theatrical world, a world where performance outruns truth, is to be trapped in a world of empty and sterile pretending.

Shakespeare was clearly captivated by the character of Hamlet, which is often described as the richest acting role in the theatrical repertoire. But the theatricality that besets Hamlet in the shady world of Elsinore also poses problems for Hamlet's many interpreters, not only for Polonius and Claudius—who spend much of the play trying to "read" Hamlet, figure him out—but for the generations of actors, audiences, and scholars who have attempted to "pluck out the heart of [his] mystery." The difficulties of sounding Hamlet, however, are also part of the play's elaborate design. From his opening scene in the play, in which Hamlet both wears the conventional black of mourning and chides his mother for presuming that he is seeming to be in mourning, Hamlet's performance challenges his audiences (both onstage and off) to "read" him, to interpret his character through the signs and signals of his behavior. That is, Hamlet presents the audience with the same challenges that any actor does, inviting us to interpret "that within" from the various behaviors that pass "show." And, contrary to Laurence Olivier—whose brilliant film of the play opens with a voice intoning that *Hamlet* is the story "of a man who could not make up his mind"—Hamlet seems to act decisively throughout the play; what's difficult about reading Hamlet is that it's hard to tell when he's *acting* and when he's "acting in earnest." Hamlet feigns madness in some scenes, but seems madly out of control in others, such as the "nunnery" scene with Ophelia or the scene in Gertrude's closet. He asks the player to act the part of vengeful Pyrrhus, then seems to adopt the murderous swagger of the stage revenger, and then to question his performance ("Why, what an ass am I"). He directs the players to insert a scene into *The Murder of Gonzago* to trick Claudius into revealing his guilt, and then can't seem to keep himself off the stage, interrupting and interpreting the play as they play it. He's so offended when Laertes stagily leaps into Ophelia's grave that he outperforms Laertes's overacting: "Nay, an thou'lt mouth, / I'll rant as well as thou." Even Hamlet's famous soliloquies are problematic in this regard. For although we might think that we hear the "true" Hamlet when he speaks alone onstage, how can we know that Hamlet isn't trying on another role, either for his own benefit or ours—as he seems to do when he plays the revenger in the "O what a rogue and peasant slave am I" speech? And as the play proceeds, Hamlet's soliloquies become less frequent, and less revealing: when he returns from England in Act 5—having sent his friends

Rosencrantz and Guildenstern to their death—the play provides him with no more solo speeches; like the court, we have only Hamlet's abrupt and irritable actions to go on.

Hamlet was evidently a success when it was first performed in 1600 or 1601; a version of the play was published in quarto format in 1603 (now called the first quarto, or Q1), and followed almost immediately by a version nearly twice as long, also in quarto in 1604–5, the second quarto. The title page of Q2 says that this version is "Newly imprinted and enlarged to almost as much again as it was, according to the true and perfect Copy." Although the Q1 version contains many lines in common with the Q2 text, it is generally much different: more quickly (some would say more logically) paced, from the perspective of the *Hamlet* we know, Q1 seems garbled at best, and scholarship remains deeply divided about this text (is it a pirated version? a version reported to a printer by an unscrupulous actor, possibly the actor playing Marcellus, whose lines are mostly the same as in Q2? a version adapted for touring?). Yet this version remains tantalizing; despite what seem like lapses—Hamlet's most famous soliloquy begins, "To be, or not to be; ay, there's the point. / To die, to sleep: is that all? Ay, all."—it has intriguing stage directions, that may point to the theatrical practice of Shakespeare's company. In the closet scene, for example, the Ghost appears to Hamlet "*in his night-gown*," and Ophelia enters in Act IV "*playing on a lute, and her hair down, singing.*" This situation is complicated by the version of *Hamlet* published in the First Folio of 1623. This version is much more like Q2, though it contains some lines not found in Q2, and omits others found there; that is, we cannot read either Q2 or F as merely an expedient, "cut" version of the other text. What's most surprising, though, is that this version also resembles some aspects of Q1 more than it does Q2. The version of *Hamlet* printed here follows the modern practice of attempting to collate the two "good" versions of the play, Q2 and F; students should be aware, though, that this practice is no longer standard, and other versions of *Hamlet* might look somewhat different on the page, representing either the Q2 or F version of the play.

From its inception, *Hamlet* has been a popular play with actors and audiences, and from Richard Burbage's creation of the role, Hamlet has been a mark of distinction in the history of English acting: the Restoration actor Thomas Betterton and the great eighteenth-century actor David Garrick were both admired in the part (Henry Fielding's novel *Tom Jones* contains a memorable parody of Garrick's performance). In the late nineteenth century Sir Henry Irving, the first actor to be knighted in England, gave a celebrated performance in which Hamlet never left the stage, but several other characters (Rosencrantz and Guildenstern, for instance) were cut entirely. In the twentieth century, the play has, if anything, confirmed its reputation as an obligatory test for great actors, who have given a host of brilliant performances: Sir John Gielgud and Sir Laurence Olivier both produced fine stage versions of the play, and Olivier later won a Best Picture Oscar for his film version (which, like its nineteenth-century stage predecessors, cut Rosencrantz, Guildenstern, Fortinbras and about half the play's lines). Since World War II, Richard Burton, Jonathan Pryce, Derek Jacobi, and Michael Pennington are among the many actors to have given distinguished performances of this demanding play. Olivier's film is only one of several distinguished film performances, accompanied by Nicoll Williamson in the 1960s, and more recently by Mel Gibson, Ethan Hawke, and Adrian Lester. The complexity of the play is something that faces actors even more immediately than readers of the play, because they will have to find a way to suit their acting to Hamlet's wild and whirling character. As Michael Pennington remarks in an essay on playing Hamlet, "To pull it off will take the actor further down into his psyche, memory and imagination, and further outwards to the limits of his technical knowledge and equipment, than he has probably been before."[1]

---

[1]Philip Brockbank, ed., *Players of Shakespeare: Essays in Shakespearean Performance by Twelve Players with the Royal Shakespeare Company* (Cambridge: Cambridge University Press, 1985), 117.

Hamlet

William Shakespeare
EDITED BY CYRUS HOY

CHARACTERS

CLAUDIUS, *King of Denmark*
HAMLET, *son to the late, and nephew to the present king*
POLONIUS, *Lord Chamberlain*
HORATIO, *friend to Hamlet*
LAERTES, *son to Polonius*
VOLTEMAND
CORNELIUS
ROSENCRANTZ } *courtiers*
GUILDENSTERN
OSRIC
A GENTLEMAN
A PRIEST
MARCELLUS } *officers*
BERNARDO

FRANCISCO, *a soldier*
REYNALDO, *servant to Polonius*
PLAYERS
TWO CLOWNS, *grave-diggers*
FORTINBRAS, *Prince of Norway*
A NORWEGIAN CAPTAIN
ENGLISH AMBASSADORS
GERTRUDE, *Queen of Denmark, and mother of Hamlet*
OPHELIA, *daughter to Polonius*
GHOST OF HAMLET'S FATHER
LORDS, LADIES, OFFICERS, SOLDIERS, SAILORS, MESSENGERS,
    and ATTENDANTS

SCENE: *Denmark.*

ACT ONE

SCENE I

Enter BERNARDO *and* FRANCISCO, *two sentinels.*

BERNARDO: Who's there?
FRANCISCO: Nay, answer me. Stand, and unfold yourself.
BERNARDO: Long live the king!
FRANCISCO: Bernardo?
5   BERNARDO: He.
FRANCISCO: You come most carefully upon your hour.
BERNARDO: 'Tis now struck twelve. Get thee to bed, Francisco.
FRANCISCO: For this relief much thanks. 'Tis bitter cold,
    And I am sick at heart.
10 BERNARDO: Have you had quiet guard?
FRANCISCO: Not a mouse stirring.
BERNARDO: Well, good night.
    If you do meet Horatio and Marcellus,
    The rivals of my watch, bid them make haste.

(Enter HORATIO *and* MARCELLUS.)

FRANCISCO: I think I hear them. Stand, ho! Who is there?
15 HORATIO: Friends to this ground.
MARCELLUS: And liegemen to the Dane.
FRANCISCO: Give you good night.
MARCELLUS: O, farewell, honest soldier!
    Who hath relieved you?
FRANCISCO: Bernardo hath my place.
    Give you good night.

(Exit FRANCISCO.)

MARCELLUS: Holla, Bernardo!
BERNARDO: Say—
    What, is Horatio there?
HORATIO: A piece of him.

BERNARDO: Welcome, Horatio. Welcome, good Marcellus.   20
HORATIO: What, has this thing appeared again to-night?
BERNARDO: I have seen nothing.
MARCELLUS: Horatio says 'tis but our fantasy,
    And will not let belief take hold of him
    Touching this dreaded sight twice seen of us.   25
    Therefore I have entreated him along
    With us to watch the minutes of this night,
    That if again this apparition come,
    He may approve our eyes and speak to it.
HORATIO: Tush, tush, 'twill not appear.   30
BERNARDO: Sit down awhile,
    And let us once again assail your ears,
    That are so fortified against our story,
    What we have two nights seen.
HORATIO: Well, sit we down,
    And let us hear Bernardo speak of this.
BERNARDO: Last night of all,   35
    When yond same star that's westward from the pole
    Had made his course t' illume that part of heaven
    Where now it burns, Marcellus and myself,
    The bell then beating one—

(Enter GHOST.)

MARCELLUS: Peace, break thee off. Look where it comes again.   40
BERNARDO: In the same figure like the king that's dead.
MARCELLUS: Thou art a scholar; speak to it, Horatio.
BERNARDO: Looks 'a not like the king? Mark it, Horatio.
HORATIO: Most like. It harrows me with fear and wonder.
BERNARDO: It would be spoke to.   45
MARCELLUS: Question it, Horatio.
HORATIO: What art thou that usurp'st this time of night
    Together with that fair and warlike form
    In which the majesty of buried Denmark
    Did sometimes march? By heaven I charge thee, speak.

---

29 **approve** confirm   36 **pole** polestar   44 **harrows** afflicts, distresses
48 **buried Denmark** the buried King of Denmark   49 **sometimes**
formerly

I.i.   13 **rivals** partners   15 **Dane** King of Denmark

50 MARCELLUS: It is offended.
BERNARDO: See, it stalks away.
HORATIO: Stay. Speak, speak. I charge thee, speak.

(*Exit* GHOST.)

MARCELLUS: 'Tis gone and will not answer.
BERNARDO: How now, Horatio! You tremble and look pale.
    Is not this something more than fantasy?
55   What think you on't?
HORATIO: Before my God, I might not this believe
    Without the sensible and true avouch
    Of mine own eyes.
MARCELLUS: Is it not like the king?
HORATIO: As thou art to thyself.
60   Such was the very armour he had on
    When he the ambitious Norway combated.
    So frowned he once when, in an angry parle,
    He smote the sledded Polacks on the ice.
    'Tis strange.
65 MARCELLUS: Thus twice before, and jump at this dead hour,
    With martial stalk hath he gone by our watch.
HORATIO: In what particular thought to work I know not,
    But in the gross and scope of mine opinion,
    This bodes some strange eruption to our state.
70 MARCELLUS: Good now, sit down, and tell me he that knows,
    Why this same strict and most observant watch
    So nightly toils the subject of the land,
    And why such daily cast of brazen cannon
    And foreign mart for implements of war;
75   Why such impress of shipwrights, whose sore task
    Does not divide the Sunday from the week.
    What might be toward that this sweaty haste
    Doth make the night joint-laborer with the day?
    Who is't that can inform me?
HORATIO: That can I.
80   At least, the whisper goes so. Our last king,
    Whose image even but now appeared to us,
    Was as you know by Fortinbras of Norway,
    Thereto pricked on by a most emulate pride,
    Dared to the combat; in which our valiant Hamlet
85   (For so this side of our known world esteemed him)
    Did slay this Fortinbras; who by a sealed compact
    Well ratified by law and heraldry,
    Did forfeit, with his life, all those his lands
    Which he stood seized of, to the conqueror;
90   Against the which a moiety competent
    Was gagèd by our king; which had returned
    To the inheritance of Fortinbras,
    Had he been vanquisher; as, by the same comart
    And carriage of the article designed,

His fell to Hamlet. Now, sir, young Fortinbras, 95
Of unimprovèd mettle hot and full,
Hath in the skirts of Norway here and there
Sharked up a list of lawless resolutes
For food and diet to some enterprise
That hath a stomach in't; which is no other, 100
As it doth well appear unto our state,
But to recover of us by strong hand
And terms compulsatory, those foresaid lands
So by his father lost; and this, I take it,
Is the main motive of our preparations, 105
The source of this our watch, and the chief head
Of this post-haste and romage in the land.
BERNARDO: I think it be no other but e'en so.
    Well may it sort that this portentous figure
    Comes armèd through our watch; so like the king 110
    That was and is the question of these wars.
HORATIO: A mote it is to trouble the mind's eye.
    In the most high and palmy state of Rome,
    A little ere the mightiest Julius fell,
    The graves stood tenantless and the sheeted dead 115
    Did squeak and gibber in the Roman streets;
    As stars with trains of fire, and dews of blood,
    Disasters in the sun; and the moist star,
    Upon whose influence Neptune's empire stands,
    Was sick almost to doomsday with eclipse. 120
    And even the like precurse of feared events,
    As harbingers preceding still the fates
    And prologue to the omen coming on,
    Have heaven and earth together demonstrated
    Unto our climatures and countrymen. 125

(*Enter* GHOST.)

But soft, behold, lo where it comes again!
I'll cross it though it blast me.—Stay, illusion.

([GHOST] *spreads his arms.*)

If thou hast any sound or use of voice,
Speak to me.
If there be any good thing to be done,
That may to thee do ease, and grace to me, 130
Speak to me.
If thou art privy to thy country's fate,
Which happily foreknowing may avoid,
O, speak! 135
Or if thou hast uphoarded in thy life
Extorted treasure in the womb of earth,
For which, they say, you spirits oft walk in death,

(*The cock crows.*)

---

57 **sensible** confirmed by one of the senses 61 **Norway** King of Norway 62 **parle** parley 63 **sledded Polacks** the Poles mounted on sleds or sledges 65 **jump** just, exactly 68 **gross and scope** general drift 72 **toils** causes to toil; **subject** people 74 **mart** traffic, bargaining 75 **impress** conscription 77 **toward** imminent, impending 83 **emulate** ambitious 87 **heraldry** the law of arms, regulating tournaments and state combats 89 **seized** possessed 90 **moiety competent** sufficient portion 91 **gagèd** pledged 93 **comart** joint bargain 94 **carriage** import

96 **unimprovèd** unrestrained 98 **Sharked up** picked up indiscriminately 100 **stomach** spice of adventure 106 **head** fountainhead 107 **romage** turmoil 109 **sort suit,** be in accordance 112 **mote** particle of dust 113 **palmy** flourishing 115 **sheeted** in shrouds 118 **Disasters** ominous signs; **moist star** the moon 121 **precurse** heralding, foreshadowing 122 **harbingers** forerunners; **still** ever 123 **omen** ominous event 125 **climatures** regions 127 **cross it** cross its path 134 **happily** haply, perchance

Speak of it. Stay, and speak. Stop it, Marcellus.

140 MARCELLUS: Shall I strike at it with my partisan?

HORATIO: Do, if it will not stand.

BERNARDO: 'Tis here.

HORATIO: 'Tis here!

(*Exit* GHOST.)

MARCELLUS: 'Tis gone!
    We do it wrong, being so majestical,
    To offer it the show of violence;

145 For it is as the air, invulnerable,
    And our vain blows malicious mockery.

BERNARDO: It was about to speak when the cock crew.

HORATIO: And then it started like a guilty thing
    Upon a fearful summons. I have heard

150 The cock, that is the trumpet to the morn,
    Doth with his lofty and shrill-sounding throat
    Awake the god of day and at his warning,
    Whether in sea or fire, in earth or air,
    Th' extravagant and erring spirit hies

155 To his confine; and of the truth herein
    This present object made probation.

MARCELLUS: It faded on the crowing of the cock.
    Some say that ever 'gainst that season comes
    Wherein our Saviour's birth is celebrated,

160 The bird of dawning singeth all night long,
    And then, they say, no spirit dare stir abroad.
    The nights are wholesome, then no planets strike,
    No fairy takes, nor witch hath power to charm,
    So hallowed and so gracious is that time.

165 HORATIO: So have I heard and do in part believe it.
    But look, the morn in russet mantle clad
    Walks o'er the dew of yon high eastward hill.
    Break we our watch up, and by my advice
    Let us impart what we have seen to-night

170 Unto young Hamlet, for, upon my life
    This spirit, dumb to us, will speak to him.
    Do you consent we shall acquaint him with it,
    As needful in our loves, fitting our duty?

MARCELLUS: Let's do't, I pray, and I this morning know

175 Where we shall find him most convenient.

(*Exeunt.*)

SCENE II

Flourish. Enter CLAUDIUS, KING OF DENMARK, GERTRUDE THE
QUEEN, COUNCILLORS, [*including*] POLONIUS *and his son* LAERTES,
HAMLET, *cum aliis* [*including* VOLTEMAND *and* CORNELIUS.]

KING: Though yet of Hamlet our dear brother's death
    The memory be green, and that it us befitted
    To bear our hearts in grief, and our whole kingdom
    To be contracted in one brow of woe,

5   Yet so far hath discretion fought with nature
    That we with wisest sorrow think on him,

Together with remembrance of ourselves.
Therefore our sometime sister, now our queen,
Th' imperial jointress to this warlike state,
Have we, as 'twere with a defeated joy,   10
With an auspicious and a dropping eye,
With mirth in funeral and with dirge in marriage,
In equal scale weighing delight and dole,
Taken to wife; nor have we herein barred
Your better wisdoms, which have freely gone   15
With this affair along. For all, our thanks.
Now follows that you know young Fortinbras,
Holding a weak supposal of our worth,
Or thinking by our late dear brother's death
Our state to be disjoint and out of frame,   20
Colleaguèd with this dream of his advantage,
He hath not failed to pester us with message
Importing the surrender of those lands
Lost by his father, with all bands of law,
To our most valiant brother. So much for him.   25
Now for ourself, and for this time of meeting,
Thus much the business is: we have here writ
To Norway, uncle of young Fortinbras—
Who, impotent and bedrid, scarcely hears
Of this his nephew's purpose—to suppress   30
His further gait herein, in that the levies,
The lists, and full proportions are all made
Out of his subject; and we here dispatch
You, good Cornelius, and you, Voltemand,
For bearers of this greeting to old Norway,   35
Giving to you no further personal power
To business with the king, more than the scope
Of these delated articles allow.
Farewell, and let your haste commend your duty.

CORNELIUS: ⎫
VOLTEMAND: ⎬ In that and all things will we show our duty. 40

KING: We doubt it nothing, heartily farewell.

(*Exeunt* VOLTEMAND *and* CORNELIUS.)

And now, Laertes, what's the news with you?
You told us of some suit. What is't, Laertes?
You cannot speak of reason to the Dane
And lose your voice. What wouldst thou beg, Laertes,   45
That shall not be my offer, not thy asking?
The head is not more native to the heart,
The hand more instrumental to the mouth,
Than is the throne of Denmark to thy father.
What wouldst thou have, Laertes?   50

LAERTES: My dread lord,
Your leave and favour to return to France,
From whence, though willingly, I came to Denmark
To show my duty in your coronation,
Yet now I must confess, that duty done,
My thoughts and wishes bend again toward France,   55
And bow them to your gracious leave and pardon.

---

140 **partisan** pike   154 **extravagant** straying, vagrant; **erring** wandering   156 **probation** proof   158 **'gainst** just before   162 **strike** blast,
destroy by malign influence   163 **takes** bewitches

I.ii. s.d. **cum aliis** with others

---

9 **jointress** a widow who holds a jointure or life interest in an estate
14 **barred** excluded   21 **Colleaguèd** united   31 **gait** proceeding
32 **proportions** forces or supplies for war   38 **delated** expressly
stated   44 **Dane** King of Denmark   45 **lose your voice** speak in
vain   47 **native** joined by nature   48 **instrumental** serviceable
56 **pardon** indulgence

KING: Have you your father's leave? What says Polonius?

POLONIUS: He hath, my lord, wrung from me my slow leave
By laborsome petition, and at last
60 Upon his will I sealed my hard consent.
I do beseech you give him leave to go.

KING: Take thy fair hour, Laertes. Time be thine,
And thy best graces spend it at thy will.
But now, my cousin Hamlet, and my son—

65 HAMLET: (*Aside.*) A little more than kin, and less than kind.

KING: How is it that the clouds still hang on you?

HAMLET: Not so, my lord. I am too much in the sun.

QUEEN: Good Hamlet, cast thy nighted color off,
And let thine eye look like a friend on Denmark.
70 Do not for ever with thy vailèd lids
Seek for thy noble father in the dust.
Thou know'st 'tis common—all that lives must die,
Passing through nature to eternity.

HAMLET: Ay, madam, it is common.

QUEEN: If it be,
75 Why seems it so particular with thee?

HAMLET: Seems, madam? Nay, it is. I know not 'seems.'
'Tis not alone my inky cloak, good mother,
Nor customary suits of solemn black,
Nor windy suspiration of forced breath,
80 No, nor the fruitful river in the eye,
Nor the dejected haviour of the visage,
Together with all forms, moods, shapes of grief,
That can denote me truly. These indeed seem,
For they are actions that a man might play,
85 But I have that within which passeth show—
These but the trappings and the suits of woe.

KING: 'Tis sweet and commendable in your nature, Hamlet,
To give these mourning duties to your father,
But you must know your father lost a father,
90 That father lost, lost his, and the survivor bound
In filial obligation for some term
To do obsequious sorrow. But to persever
In obstinate condolement is a course
Of impious stubbornness. 'Tis unmanly grief.
95 It shows a will most incorrect to heaven,
A heart unfortified, a mind impatient,
An understanding simple and unschooled.
For what we know must be, and is as common
As any the most vulgar thing to sense,
100 Why should we in our peevish opposition
Take it to heart? Fie, 'tis a fault to heaven,
A fault against the dead, a fault to nature,
To reason most absurd, whose common theme
Is death of fathers, and who still hath cried,
105 From the first corse till he that died to-day,
'This must be so.' We pray you throw to earth
This unprevailing woe, and think of us
As of a father, for let the world take note
You are the most immediate to our throne,
110 And with no less nobility of love

Than that which dearest father bears his son
Do I impart toward you. For your intent
In going back to school in Wittenberg,
It is most retrograde to our desire,
115 And we beseech you, bend you to remain
Here in the cheer and comfort of our eye,
Our chiefest courtier, cousin, and our son.

QUEEN: Let not thy mother lose her prayers, Hamlet.
I pray thee stay with us, go not to Wittenberg.

HAMLET: I shall in all my best obey you, madam. 120

KING: Why, 'tis a loving and a fair reply.
Be as ourself in Denmark. Madam, come.
This gentle and unforced accord of Hamlet
Sits smiling to my heart, in grace whereof,
125 No jocund health that Denmark drinks to-day
But the great cannon to the clouds shall tell,
And the king's rouse the heaven shall bruit again,
Respeaking earthly thunder. Come away.

(*Flourish. Exeunt all but* HAMLET.)

HAMLET: O, that this too too sallied flesh would melt,
130 Thaw and resolve itself into a dew,
Or that the Everlasting had not fixed
His canon 'gainst self-slaughter. O God, God,
How weary, stale, flat, and unprofitable
Seem to me all the uses of this world!
135 Fie on't, ah, fie, 'tis an unweeded garden
That grows to seed. Things rank and gross in nature
Possess it merely. That it should come to this,
But two months dead, nay, not so much, not two.
So excellent a king, that was to this
140 Hyperion to a satyr, so loving to my mother,
That he might not beteem the winds of heaven
Visit her face too roughly. Heaven and earth,
Must I remember? Why, she would hang on him
As if increase of appetite had grown
145 By what it fed on, and yet, within a month—
Let me not think on't. Frailty, thy name is woman—
A little month, or ere those shoes were old
With which she followed my poor father's body
Like Niobe, all tears, why she—
150 O God, a beast that wants discourse of reason
Would have mourned longer—married with my uncle,
My father's brother, but no more like my father

---

114 **retrograde** contrary   127 **rouse** full draught of liquor; **bruit** echo   129 **sallied** sullied. "Sallied" is the reading of *Quarto 2* (*Q2*, also *Q1*). *Folio* (*F*) reads "solid." Since Hamlet's primary concern is with the fact of the flesh's impurity, not with its corporeality, the choice as between *Q* and *F* clearly lies with *Q*. "Sally" is a legitimate sixteenth-century form of "sully"; it occurs in Dekker's *Patient Grissil* (1.1.12), printed in 1603, as F.T. Bowers has pointed out (in "Hamlet's 'Sullied' or 'Solid' Flesh. A Bibliographical Case-History," *Shakespeare Survey* 9 [1956]: p. 44); and it occurs as a noun at 2.1.39 of *Hamlet*   132 **canon** law   137 **merely** entirely   140 **Hyperion** the sun god   141 **beteem** allowed   149 **Niobe** wife of Amphion, King of Thebes, she boasted of having more children than Leto and was punished when her seven sons and seven daughters were slain by Apollo and Artemis, children of Leto; in her grief she was changed by Zeus into a stone, which continually dropped tears   150 **wants** lacks; **discourse of reason** the reasoning faculty

---

60 **hard** reluctant   64 **cousin** kinsman of any kind except parent, child, brother, or sister   65 **kin** related as nephew; **kind** (1) affectionate (2) natural, lawful   70 **vailèd** lowered   75 **particular** personal, individual   92 **obsequious** dutiful in performing funeral obsequies or manifesting regard for the dead; **persever** persevere   105 **corse** corpse

Than I to Hercules. Within a month,
Ere yet the salt of most unrighteous tears
155   Had left the flushing in her gallèd eyes,
She married. O, most wicked speed, to post
With such dexterity to incestuous sheets!
It is not, nor it cannot come to good.
But break my heart, for I must hold my tongue.

(*Enter* HORATIO, MARCELLUS, *and* BERNARDO.)

160   HORATIO: Hail to your lordship!
    HAMLET: I am glad to see you well.
      Horatio—or I do forget myself.
    HORATIO: The same, my lord, and your poor servant ever.
    HAMLET: Sir, my good friend, I'll change that name with you.
      And what make you from Wittenberg, Horatio?
165   Marcellus?
    MARCELLUS: My good lord!
    HAMLET: I am very glad to see you. (*To* BERNARDO.) Good
      even, sir.—
      But what, in faith, make you from Wittenberg?
    HORATIO: A truant disposition, good my lord.
170   HAMLET: I would not hear your enemy say so,
      Nor shall you do my ear that violence
      To make it truster of your own report
      Against yourself. I know you are no truant.
      But what is your affair in Elsinore?
175   We'll teach you to drink deep ere you depart.
    HORATIO: My lord, I came to see your father's funeral.
    HAMLET: I prithee, do not mock me, fellow-student,
      I think it was to see my mother's wedding.
    HORATIO: Indeed, my lord, it followed hard upon.
180   HAMLET: Thrift, thrift, Horatio. The funeral baked meats
      Did coldly furnish forth the marriage tables.
      Would I had met my dearest foe in heaven
      Or ever I had seen that day, Horatio!
      My father—methinks I see my father.
185   HORATIO: Where, my lord?
    HAMLET: In my mind's eye, Horatio.
    HORATIO: I saw him once, 'a was a goodly king.
    HAMLET: 'A was a man, take him for all in all,
      I shall not look upon his like again.
    HORATIO: My lord, I think I saw him yesternight.
190   HAMLET: Saw who?
    HORATIO: My lord, the king your father.
    HAMLET: The king my father?
    HORATIO: Season your admiration for a while
      With an attent ear, till I may deliver
      Upon the witness of these gentlemen
195   This marvel to you.
    HAMLET: For God's love, let me hear!
    HORATIO: Two nights together had these gentlemen,
      Marcellus and Bernardo, on their watch
      In the dead waste and middle of the night
      Been thus encountered. A figure like your father,
200   Armed at point exactly, cap-a-pe,

Appears before them, and with solemn march
Goes slow and stately by them. Thrice he walked
By their oppressed and fear-surprisèd eyes
Within his truncheon's length, whilst they, distilled
Almost to jelly with the act of fear,   205
Stand dumb and speak not to him. This to me
In dreadful secrecy impart they did,
And I with them the third night kept the watch,
Where, as they had delivered, both in time,
Form of the thing, each word made true and good, 210
The apparition comes. I knew your father.
These hands are not more like.
HAMLET: But where was this?
MARCELLUS: My lord, upon the platform where we watch.
HAMLET: Did you not speak to it?
HORATIO: My lord, I did,
  But answer made it none. Yet once methought   215
  It lifted up it head and did address
  Itself to motion, like as it would speak;
  But even then the morning cock crew loud,
  And at the sound it shrunk in haste away
  And vanished from our sight.   220
HAMLET: 'Tis very strange.
HORATIO: As I do live, my honoured lord, 'tis true,
  And we did think it writ down in our duty
  To let you know of it.
HAMLET: Indeed, sirs, but
  This troubles me. Hold you the watch to-night?
ALL: We do, my lord.   225
HAMLET: Armed, say you?
ALL: Armed, my lord.
HAMLET: From top to toe?
ALL: My lord, from head to foot.
HAMLET: Then saw you not his face.
HORATIO: O yes, my lord, he wore his beaver up.
HAMLET: What, looked he frowningly?
HORATIO: A countenance more in sorrow than in anger. 230
HAMLET: Pale or red?
HORATIO: Nay, very pale.
HAMLET: And fixed his eyes upon you?
HORATIO: Most constantly.
HAMLET: I would I had been there.
HORATIO: It would have much amazed you.
HAMLET: Very like.
  Stayed it long?   235
HORATIO: While one with moderate haste might tell a
  hundred.
BOTH: Longer, longer.
HORATIO: Not when I saw't.
HAMLET: His beard was grizzled, no?
HORATIO: It was as I have seen it in his life,
  A sable silvered.
HAMLET: I will watch to-night.
  Perchance 'twill walk again.   240
HORATIO: I warr'nt it will.
HAMLET: If it assume my noble father's person,
  I'll speak to it though hell itself should gape

---

155 **gallèd** sore from rubbing or chafing 163 **change** exchange
164 **make** do 182 **dearest** direst 192 **Season** temper, moderate;
admiration wonder, astonishment 200 **at point** exactly in every particular; **cap-a-pe** from head to foot

---

204 **truncheon** military leader's baton 216 **it** its 228 **beaver** the part
of the helmet that was drawn down to cover the face 235 **tell** count
237 **grizzled** grayish 239 **sable silvered** black mixed with white

And bid me hold my peace. I pray you all,
If you have hitherto concealed this sight,
245 Let it be tenable in your silence still,
And whatsomever else shall hap to-night,
Give it an understanding but no tongue.
I will requite your loves. So fare you well.
Upon the platform 'twixt eleven and twelve
250 I'll visit you.
ALL: Our duty to your honor.
HAMLET: Your loves, as mine to you. Farewell.

(*Exeunt* [*all but* HAMLET].)

My father's spirit in arms? All is not well.
I doubt some foul play. Would the night were come!
Till then sit still, my soul. Foul deeds will rise,
255 Though all the earth o'erwhelm them, to men's eyes.

(*Exit.*)

SCENE III

Enter LAERTES *and* OPHELIA *his sister.*

LAERTES: My necessaries are embarked. Farewell.
And, sister, as the winds give benefit
And convoy is assistant, do not sleep,
But let me hear from you.
OPHELIA: Do you doubt that?
5 LAERTES: For Hamlet, and the trifling of his favor,
Hold it a fashion and a toy in blood,
A violet in the youth of primy nature,
Forward, not permanent, sweet, not lasting,
The perfume and suppliance of a minute,
10 No more.
OPHELIA: No more but so?
LAERTES: Think it no more.
For nature crescent does not grow alone
In thews and bulk, but as this temple waxes
The inward service of the mind and soul
Grows wide withal. Perhaps he loves you now,
15 And now no soil nor cautel doth besmirch
The virtue of his will, but you must fear,
His greatness weighed, his will is not his own,
For he himself is subject to his birth.
He may not, as unvalued persons do,
20 Carve for himself, for on his choice depends
The safety and health of this whole state,
And therefore must his choice be circumscribed
Unto the voice and yielding of that body
Whereof he is the head. Then if he says he loves you,
25 It fits your wisdom so far to believe it

---

245 **tenable** retained   246 **whatsomever** whatsover   253 **doubt**
suspect

I.iii. 6 **fashion** the creation of a season only; **toy in blood** passing
fancy   7 **primy** of the springtime   11 **crescent** growing   12 **thews**
sinews, strength; **this temple** the body   15 **cautel** deceit   16 **will**
desire   17 **greatness weighed** high position considered   19 **unvalued**
persons persons of no social importance   20 **Carve for himself** act
according to his own inclination   23 **yielding** assent

As he in his particular act and place
May give his saying deed, which is no further
Than the main voice of Denmark goes withal.
Then weigh what loss your honor may sustain
If with too credent ear you list his songs,   30
Or lose your heart, or your chaste treasure open
To his unmastered importunity.
Fear it, Ophelia, fear it, my dear sister,
And keep you in the rear of your affection,
Out of the shot and danger of desire.   35
The chariest maid is prodigal enough
If she unmask her beauty to the moon.
Virtue itself scapes not calumnious strokes.
The canker galls the infants of the spring
Too oft before their buttons be disclosed,   40
And in the morn and liquid dew of youth
Contagious blastments are most imminent.
Be wary then; best safety lies in fear.
Youth to itself rebels, though none else near.
OPHELIA: I shall the effect of this good lesson keep   45
As watchman to my heart. But, good my brother,
Do not as some ungracious pastors do,
Show me the steep and thorny way to heaven,
Whiles like a puffed and reckless libertine
Himself the primrose path of dalliance treads   50
And recks not his own rede.
LAERTES: O, fear me not.

(*Enter* POLONIUS.)

I stay too long. But here my father comes.
A double blessing is a double grace;
Occasion smiles upon a second leave.
POLONIUS: Yet here, Laertes? Aboard, aboard, for shame!   55
The wind sits in the shoulder of your sail,
And you are stayed for. There, my blessing with thee,
And these few precepts in thy memory
Look thou character. Give thy thoughts no tongue,
Nor any unproportioned thought his act.   60
Be thou familiar, but by no means vulgar.
Those friends thou hast, and their adoption tried,
Grapple them to thy soul with hoops of steel,
But do not dull thy palm with entertainment
Of each new-hatched, unfledged courage. Beware   65
Of entrance to a quarrel, but being in,
Bear't that th' opposèd may beware of thee.
Give every man thy ear, but few thy voice;
Take each man's censure, but reserve thy judgement.
Costly thy habit as thy purse can buy,   70
But not expressed in fancy; rich not gaudy,
For the apparel oft proclaims the man,
And they in France of the best rank and station
Are of a most select and generous chief in that.
Neither a borrower nor a lender be,   75
For loan oft loses both itself and friend,
And borrowing dulls th' edge of husbandry.

---

30 **credent** trusting   34 **affection** feeling   39 **canker** canker-worm
(which feeds on roses); **galls** injures   40 **buttons** buds   42 **blastments**
blights   51 **recks** regards; **rede** counsel   59 **character** engrave
60 **unproportioned** inordinate   61 **vulgar** common   65 **courage** young
blood, man of spirit   74 **chief** eminence   77 **husbandry** thriftiness

This above all, to thine own self be true,
And it must follow as the night the day
80 Thou canst not then be false to any man.
Farewell. My blessing season this in thee!
LAERTES: Most humbly do I take my leave, my lord.
POLONIUS: The time invites you. Go, your servants tend.
LAERTES: Farewell, Ophelia, and remember well
85   What I have said to you.
OPHELIA: 'Tis in my memory locked,
And you yourself shall keep the key of it.
LAERTES: Farewell.

(*Exit* LAERTES.)

POLONIUS: What is 't, Ophelia, he hath said to you?
OPHELIA: So please you, something touching the Lord Hamlet.
90 POLONIUS: Marry, well bethought.
'Tis told me he hath very oft of late
Given private time to you, and you yourself
Have of your audience been most free and bounteous.
If it be so—as so 'tis put on me,
95   And that in way of caution—I must tell you,
You do not understand yourself so clearly
As it behooves my daughter and your honor.
What is between you? Give me up the truth.
OPHELIA: He hath, my lord, of late made many tenders
100   Of his affection to me.
POLONIUS: Affection? Pooh! You speak like a green girl,
Unsifted in such perilous circumstance.
Do you believe his tenders, as you call them?
OPHELIA: I do not know, my lord, what I should think.
105 POLONIUS: Marry, I will teach you. Think yourself a baby
That you have ta'en these tenders for true pay
Which are not sterling. Tender yourself more dearly,
Or (not to crack the wind of the poor phrase,
Running it thus) you'll tender me a fool.
110 OPHELIA: My lord, he hath importuned me with love
In honorable fashion.
POLONIUS: Ay, fashion you may call it. Go to, go to.
OPHELIA: And hath given countenance to his speech, my lord,
With almost all the holy vows of heaven.
115 POLONIUS: Ay, springes to catch woodcocks. I do know,
When the blood burns, how prodigal the soul
Lends the tongue vows. These blazes, daughter,
Giving more light than heat, extinct in both
Even in their promise, as it is a-making,
120   You must not take for fire. From this time
Be something scanter of your maiden presence.
Set your entreatments at a higher rate
Than a command to parle. For Lord Hamlet,
Believe so much in him that he is young,
125   And with a larger tether may he walk
Than may be given you. In few, Ophelia,
Do not believe his vows, for they are brokers,
Not of that dye which their investments show,
But mere implorators of unholy suits,

Breathing like sanctified and pious bawds,   130
The better to beguile. This is for all:
I would not, in plain terms, from this time forth
Have you so slander any moment leisure
As to give words or talk with the Lord Hamlet.
Look to 't, I charge you. Come your ways.   135
OPHELIA: I shall obey, my lord.

(*Exeunt.*)

SCENE IV

Enter HAMLET, HORATIO, *and* MARCELLUS.

HAMLET: The air bites shrewdly; it is very cold.
HORATIO: It is a nipping and an eager air.
HAMLET: What hour now?
HORATIO: I think it lacks of twelve.
MARCELLUS: No, it is struck.
HORATIO: Indeed? I heard it not. It then draws near the season   5
Wherein the spirit held his wont to walk.

(*A flourish of trumpets, and two pieces go off.*)

What does this mean, my lord?
HAMLET: The king doth wake to-night and takes his rouse,
Keeps wassail, and the swagg'ring up-spring reels,
And as he drains his draughts of Rhenish down,   10
The kettledrum and trumpet thus bray out
The triumph of his pledge.
HORATIO: Is it a custom?
HAMLET: Ay, marry, is 't,
But to my mind, though I am native here
And to the manner born, it is a custom   15
More honored in the breach than the observance.
This heavy-headed revel east and west
Makes us traduced and taxed of other nations.
They clepe us drunkards, and with swinish phrase
Soil our addition, and indeed it takes   20
From our achievements, though performed at height,
The pith and marrow of our attribute.
So oft it chances in particular men,
That for some vicious mole of nature in them,
As, in their birth, wherein they are not guilty   25
(Since nature cannot choose his origin),
By the o'ergrowth of some complexion,
Oft breaking down the pales and forts of reason,
Or by some habit that too much o'er-leavens
The form of plausive manners—that these men,   30
Carrying, I say, the stamp of one defect,
Being nature's livery or fortune's star,
His virtues else, be they as pure as grace,
As infinite as man may undergo,
Shall in the general censure take corruption   35

---

81 **season** ripen 83 **tend** attend, wait 90 **Marry** by Mary
99 **tenders** offers 102 **Unsifted** untried 115 **springes** snares
122 **entreatments** military negotiations for surrender 127 **brokers**
go-betweens 128 **investments** clothes 129 **implorators** solicitors

---

I.iv. 2 **eager** sharp 9 **wassail** carousal; **up-spring** a German dance
18 **taxed of** censured by 19 **clepe** call 20 **addition** title added to a
man's name to denote his rank 22 **attribute** reputation 26 **his** its
27 **complexion** one of the four temperaments (sanguine, melancholy,
choleric, and phlegmatic) 29 **o'er-leavens** works change throughout
30 **plausive** pleasing 32 **livery** badge; **star** a person's fortune, rank,
or destiny, viewed as determined by the stars

From that particular fault. The dram of evil
Doth all the noble substance often doubt
To his own scandal.

(*Enter* GHOST.)

HORATIO: Look, my lord, it comes.
HAMLET: Angels and ministers of grace defend us!
40   Be thou a spirit of health or goblin damned,
Bring with thee airs from heaven or blasts from hell,
Be thy intents wicked or charitable,
Thou com'st in such a questionable shape
That I will speak to thee. I'll call thee Hamlet,
45   King, father, royal Dane. O, answer me!
Let me not burst in ignorance, but tell
Why thy canonized bones, hearsèd in death,
Have burst their cerements; why the sepulchre
Wherein we saw thee quietly interred,
50   Hath oped his ponderous and marble jaws
To cast thee up again. What may this mean
That thou, dead corse, again in complete steel
Revisits thus the glimpses of the moon,
Making night hideous, and we fools of nature
55   So horridly to shake our disposition
With thoughts beyond the reaches of our souls?
Say, why is this? wherefore? What should we do?

([GHOST] *beckons.*)

HORATIO: It beckons you to go away with it,
As if it some impartment did desire
60   To you alone.
MARCELLUS: Look, with what courteous action
It waves you to a more removèd ground.
But do not go with it.
HORATIO: No, by no means.
HAMLET: It will not speak; then I will follow it.
HORATIO: Do not, my lord.
HAMLET: Why, what should be the fear?
65   I do not set my life at a pin's fee,
And for my soul, what can it do to that,
Being a thing immortal as itself?
It waves me forth again. I'll follow it.
HORATIO: What if it tempt you toward the flood, my lord,
70   Or to the dreadful summit of the cliff
That beetles o'er his base into the sea,
And there assume some other horrible form,
Which might deprive your sovereignty of reason
And draw you into madness? Think of it.
75   The very place puts toys of desperation,
Without more motive, into every brain
That looks so many fathoms to the sea
And hears it roar beneath.
HAMLET: It waves me still.
Go on. I'll follow thee.
80 MARCELLUS: You shall not go, my lord.

HAMLET: Hold off your hands.
HORATIO: Be ruled; You shall not go.
HAMLET: My fate cries out,
And makes each petty artere in this body
As hardy as the Nemean lion's nerve.
Still am I called. Unhand me, gentlemen.
By heaven, I'll make a ghost of him that lets me.   85
I say, away—Go on. I'll follow thee.

([*Exeunt*] GHOST *and* HAMLET.)

HORATIO: He waxes desperate with imagination.
MARCELLUS: Let's follow. 'Tis not fit thus to obey him.
HORATIO: Have after. To what issue will this come?
MARCELLUS: Something is rotten in the state of Denmark.   90
HORATIO: Heaven will direct it.
MARCELLUS: Nay, let's follow him.

(*Exeunt.*)

SCENE V

Enter GHOST *and* HAMLET.

HAMLET: Whither wilt thou lead me? Speak. I'll go no further.
GHOST: Mark me.
HAMLET: I will.
GHOST: My hour is almost come
When I to sulph'rous and tormenting flames
Must render up myself.
HAMLET: Alas, poor ghost!
GHOST: Pity me not, but lend thy serious hearing   5
To what I shall unfold.
HAMLET: Speak. I am bound to hear.
GHOST: So art thou to revenge, when thou shalt hear.
HAMLET: What?
GHOST: I am thy father's spirit,
Doomed for a certain term to walk the night,   10
And for the day confined to fast in fires,
Till the foul crimes done in my days of nature
Are burnt and purged away. But that I am forbid
To tell the secrets of my prison house,
I could a tale unfold whose lightest word   15
Would harrow up thy soul, freeze thy young blood,
Make thy two eyes like stars start from their spheres,
Thy knotted and combinèd locks to part,
And each particular hair to stand an end,
Like quills upon the fretful porpentine.   20
But this eternal blazon must not be
To ears of flesh and blood. List, list, O, list!
If thou didst ever thy dear father love—
HAMLET: O God!
GHOST: Revenge his foul and most unnatural murder.   25
HAMLET: Murder!
GHOST: Murder most foul, as in the best it is,
But this most foul, strange, and unnatural.

---

37 **doubt** put out, obliterate   38 **his** its   47 **canonized** buried according
to the church's rule; **hearsèd** coffined, buried   59 **impartment** communication   71 **beetles** juts out   73 **sovereignty of reason** state of being
ruled by reason   75 **toys** fancies, impules

82 **artere** artery   83 **Nemean lion** slain by Hercules in the performance
of one of his twelve labors   85 **lets** hinders

I.v. 19 **an** on   20 **porpentine** porcupine   21 **eternal blazon** proclamation of the secrets of eternity

HAMLET: Haste me to know't, that I, with wings as swift
30   As meditation or the thoughts of love,
        May sweep to my revenge.
    GHOST: I find thee apt,
        And duller shouldst thou be than the fat weed
        That roots itself in ease on Lethe wharf,
        Wouldst thou not stir in this. Now, Hamlet, hear.
35   'Tis given out that, sleeping in my orchard,
        A serpent stung me. So the whole ear of Denmark
        Is by a forgèd process of my death
        Rankly abused. But know, thou noble youth,
        The serpent that did sting thy father's life
40   Now wears his crown.
    HAMLET: O my prophetic soul!
        My uncle!
    GHOST: Ay, that incestuous, that adulterate beast,
        With witchcraft of his wits, with traitorous gifts—
        O wicked wit and gifts that have the power
45   So to seduce!—won to his shameful lust
        The will of my most seeming virtuous queen.
        O Hamlet, what a falling off was there,
        From me, whose love was of that dignity
        That it went hand in hand even with the vow
50   I made to her in marriage, and to decline
        Upon a wretch whose natural gifts were poor
        To those of mine!
        But virtue, as it never will be moved,
        Though lewdness court it in a shape of heaven,
55   So lust, though to a radiant angel linked,
        Will sate itself in a celestial bed
        And prey on garbage.
        But soft, methinks I scent the morning air.
        Brief let me be. Sleeping within my orchard,
60   My custom always of the afternoon,
        Upon my secure hour thy uncle stole,
        With juice of cursed hebona in a vial,
        And in the porches of my ears did pour
        The leperous distilment, whose effect
65   Holds such an enmity with blood of man
        That swift as quicksilver it courses through
        The natural gates and alleys of the body,
        And with a sudden vigor it doth posset
        And curd, like eager droppings into milk,
70   The thin and wholesome blood. So did it mine,
        And a most instant tetter barked about
        Most lazar-like with vile and loathsome crust
        All my smooth body.
        Thus was I sleeping by a brother's hand
75   Of life, of crown, of queen, at once dispatched,
        Cut off even in the blossoms of my sin,
        Unhouseled, disappointed, unaneled,
        No reck'ning made, but sent to my account
        With all my imperfections on my head.
80   O, horrible! O, horrible! most horrible!
        If thou hast nature in thee, bear it not,

        Let not the royal bed of Denmark be
        A couch for luxury and damnèd incest.
        But howsomever thou pursues this act,
        Taint not thy mind, nor let thy soul contrive   85
        Against thy mother aught. Leave her to heaven,
        And to those thorns that in her bosom lodge
        To prick and sting her. Fare thee well at once.
        The glowworm shows the matin to be near,
        And gins to pale his uneffectual fire.   90
        Adieu, adieu, adieu. Remember me.

(*Exit.*)

HAMLET: O all you host of heaven! O earth! What else?
        And shall I couple hell? O, fie! Hold, hold, my heart,
        And you, my sinews, grow not instant old,
        But bear me stiffly up. Remember thee?   95
        Ay, thou poor ghost, whiles memory holds a seat
        In this distracted globe. Remember thee?
        Yea, from the table of my memory
        I'll wipe away all trivial fond records,
        All saws of books, all forms, all pressures past   100
        That youth and observation copied there,
        And thy commandment all alone shall live
        Within the book and volume of my brain,
        Unmixed with baser matter. Yes, by heaven!
        O most pernicious woman!   105
        O villain, villain, smiling, damnèd villain!
        My tables—meet it is I set it down
        That one may smile, and smile, and be a villain
        At least I am sure it may be so in Denmark.   (*Writing.*)
        So, uncle, there you are. Now to my word: 110
        It is 'Adieu, adieu! Remember me,'
        I have sworn't.

(*Enter* HORATIO *and* MARCELLUS.)

HORATIO: My lord, my lord!
MARCELLUS: Lord Hamlet!
HORATIO: Heavens secure him!
HAMLET: So be it!
MARCELLUS: Illo, ho, ho, my lord!   115
HAMLET: Hillo, ho, ho, boy! Come, bird, come.
MARCELLUS: How is't, my noble lord?
HORATIO: What news, my lord?
HAMLET: O, wonderful!
HORATIO: Good my lord, tell it.
HAMLET: No, you will reveal it.
HORATIO: Not I, my lord, by heaven.   120
MARCELLUS: Nor I, my lord.
HAMLET: How say you then, would heart of man once think it?
        But you'll be secret?
BOTH: Ay, by heaven, my lord.
HAMLET: There's never a villain dwelling in all Denmark
        But he's an arrant knave.

---

33 **Lethe** the river in Hades that brings forgetfulness 37 **process** account 61 **secure** free from suspicion 62 **hebona** an imaginary poison, associated with henbane 68 **posset** curdle 69 **eager** acid 71 **tetter** a skin eruption; **barked** covered as with bark 77 **Unhouseled** without having received the sacrament; **disappointed** unprepared; **unaneled** without extreme unction

---

83 **luxury** lust 89 **matin** morning 97 **globe** head 98 **table** writing tablet, memorandum book (as at line 107, below; here metaphorically of the mind) 99 **fond** foolish 100 **saws** sayings; **forms** concepts; **pressures** impressions 115 **Illo, ho, ho** cry of the falconer to summon his hawk

125 HORATIO: There needs no ghost, my lord, come from the grave
    To tell us this.
  HAMLET: Why, right, you are in the right,
    And so without more circumstance at all
    I hold it fit that we shake hands and part,
    You, as your business and desire shall point you,
130   For every man has business and desire
    Such as it is, and for my own poor part,
    I will go pray.
  HORATIO: These are but wild and whirling words, my lord.
  HAMLET: I am sorry they offend you, heartily;
135   Yes, faith, heartily.
  HORATIO: There's no offence, my lord.
  HAMLET: Yes, by Saint Patrick, but there is, Horatio,
    And much offence too. Touching this vision here,
    It is an honest ghost, that let me tell you
    For your desire to know what is between us,
140   O'ermaster't as you may. And now, good friends,
    As you are friends, scholars, and soldiers,
    Give me one poor request.
  HORATIO: What is't, my lord? We will.
  HAMLET: Never make known what you have seen to-night.
145 BOTH: My lord, we will not.
  HAMLET: Nay, but swear't.
  HORATIO: In faith,
    My lord, not I.
  MARCELLUS: Nor I, my lord, in faith.
  HAMLET: Upon my sword.
  MARCELLUS: We have sworn, my lord, already.
  HAMLET: Indeed, upon my sword, indeed.

(GHOST *cries under the stage.*)

  GHOST: Swear.
  HAMLET: Ha, ha, boy, say'st thou so? Art thou there, truepenny?
150   Come on. You hear this fellow in the cellarage.
    Consent to swear.
  HORATIO: Propose the oath, my lord.
  HAMLET: Never to speak of this that you have seen,
    Swear by my sword.
  GHOST: (*Beneath.*) Swear.
155 HAMLET: Hic et ubique? Then we'll shift our ground.
    Come hither, gentlemen,
    And lay your hands again upon my sword.
    Swear by my sword
    Never to speak of this that you have heard.
160 GHOST: (*Beneath.*) Swear by his sword.
  HAMLET: Well said, old mole! Canst work i' th' earth so fast?
    A worthy pioneer! Once more remove, good friends.
  HORATIO: O day and night, but this is wondrous strange!
  HAMLET: And therefore as a stranger give it welcome.
165   There are more things in heaven and earth, Horatio,
    Than are dreamt of in your philosophy.
    But come.
    Here as before, never, so help you mercy,
    How strange or odd some'er I bear myself
170   (As I perchance hereafter shall think meet

    To put an antic disposition on),
    That you, at such times, seeing me, never shall,
    With arms encumbered thus, or this head-shake,
    Or by pronouncing of some doubtful phrase,
    As 'Well, well, we know,' or 'We could, and if we would'   175
    Or 'If we list to speak,' or 'There be, and if they might'
    Or such ambiguous giving out, to note
    That you know aught of me—this do swear,
    So grace and mercy at your most need help you.
  GHOST: (*Beneath.*) Swear.   180
  HAMLET: Rest, rest, perturbèd spirit! So, gentlemen,
    With all my love I do commend me to you,
    And what so poor a man as Hamlet is
    May do t' express his love and friending to you,
    God willing, shall not lack. Let us go in together,   185
    And still your fingers on your lips, I pray.
    The time is out of joint. O cursèd spite
    That ever I was born to set it right!
    Nay, come, let's go together.

(*Exeunt.*)

ACT TWO

SCENE I

Enter old POLONIUS *with his man* [REYNALDO].

POLONIUS: Give him this money and these notes. Reynaldo.
REYNALDO: I will, my lord.
POLONIUS: You shall do marvellous wisely, good Reynaldo,
    Before you visit him, to make inquire
    Of his behavior.   5
REYNALDO: My lord, I did intend it.
POLONIUS: Marry, well said, very well said. Look you, sir,
    Enquire me first what Danskers are in Paris,
    And how, and who, what means, and where they keep,
    What company, at what expense; and finding
    By this encompassment and drift of question   10
    That they do know my son, come you more nearer
    Than your particular demands will touch it.
    Take you as 'twere some distant knowledge of him,
    As thus, 'I know his father and his friends,
    And in part him,' do you mark this, Reynaldo?   15
REYNALDO: Ay, very well, my lord.
POLONIUS: 'And in part him, but,' you may say, 'not well,
    But if't be he I mean, he's very wild,
    Addicted so and so.' And there put on him
    What forgeries you please; marry, none so rank   20
    As may dishonour him. Take heed of that.
    But, sir, such wanton, wild, and usual slips
    As are companions noted and most known
    To youth and liberty.
REYNALDO: As gaming, my lord?
POLONIUS: Ay, or drinking, fencing, swearing, quarrelling,   25
    Drabbing—you may go so far.
REYNALDO: My lord, that would dishonour him.

---

136 **Saint Patrick** associated, in the late middle ages, with purgatory, whence the ghost has presumably come   **149 truepenny** honest fellow   **155 Hic et ubique** here and everywhere   **162 pioneer** miner

171 **antic** mad   173 **encumbered** folded

II.i. 7 **Danskers** Danes   8 **means** wealth   10 **encompassment** talking round the matter   20 **forgeries** invented wrongdoings   24 **liberty** license   26 **Drabbing** whoring

POLONIUS: Faith, no, as you may season it in the charge.
　　You must not put another scandal on him,
30　That he is open to incontinency.
　　That's not my meaning. But breathe his faults so quaintly
　　That they may seem the taints of liberty,
　　The flash and outbreak of a fiery mind,
　　A savageness in unreclaimèd blood,
35　Of general assault.
REYNALDO:　　　　　But, my good lord—
POLONIUS: Wherefore should you do this?
REYNALDO:　　　　　　　　Ay, my lord,
　　I would know that.
POLONIUS:　　　　　Marry, sir, here's my drift,
　　And I believe it is a fetch of warrant.
　　You laying these slight sullies on my son,
40　As 'twere a thing a little soiled i' th' working,
　　Mark you,
　　Your party in converse, him you would sound,
　　Having ever seen in the prenominate crimes
　　The youth you breathe of guilty, be assured
45　He closes with you in this consequence,
　　'Good sir', or so, or 'friend', or 'gentleman',
　　According to the phrase or the addition
　　Of man and country.
REYNALDO:　　　　　Very good, my lord.
POLONIUS: And then, sir, does 'a this—'a does—What was I about
　　　to say?
50　By the mass, I was about to say something.
　　Where did I leave?
REYNALDO: At 'closes in the consequence.'
POLONIUS: At 'closes in the consequence'—ay, marry,
　　He closes thus: 'I know the gentleman.
55　I saw him yesterday, or th' other day,
　　Or then, or then, with such, or such, and as you say,
　　There was 'a gaming, there o'ertook in 's rouse;
　　There falling out at tennis', or perchance
　　'I saw him enter such a house of sale',
60　Videlicet, a brothel, or so forth.
　　See you, now—
　　Your bait of falsehood takes this carp of truth,
　　And thus do we of wisdom and of reach,
　　With windlasses and with assays of bias,
65　By indirections find directions out;
　　So by my former lecture and advice
　　Shall you my son. You have me, have you not?
REYNALDO: My lord, I have.
POLONIUS:　　　　　God bye ye; fare ye well.
REYNALDO: Good my lord.
70　POLONIUS: Observe his inclination in yourself.
REYNALDO: I shall, my lord.
POLONIUS: And let him ply his music.
REYNALDO:　　　　　Well, my lord.
POLONIUS: Farewell.

(*Exit* REYNALDO.)

(*Enter* OPHELIA.)

　　　　　　　How now, Ophelia! what's the matter?
OPHELIA: O my lord, my lord, I have been so affrighted!
POLONIUS: With what, i' th' name of God?　　　　　75
OPHELIA: My lord, as I was sewing in my closet,
　　Lord Hamlet, with his doublet all unbraced,
　　No hat upon his head, his stockings fouled,
　　Ungartered, and down-gyvèd to his ankle,
　　Pale as his shirt, his knees knocking each other,　　80
　　And with a look so piteous in purport
　　As if he had been loosèd out of hell
　　To speak of horrors—he comes before me.
POLONIUS: Mad for thy love?
OPHELIA:　　　　　My lord, I do not know,
　　But truly I do fear it.　　　　　85
POLONIUS:　　　　　What said he?
OPHELIA: He took me by the wrist, and held me hard,
　　Then goes he to the length of all his arm,
　　And with his other hand thus o'er his brow,
　　He falls to such perusal of my face
　　As 'a would draw it. Long stayed he so.　　　　90
　　At last, a little shaking of mine arm
　　And thrice his head thus waving up and down,
　　He raised a sigh so piteous and profound
　　As it did seem to shatter all his bulk
　　And end his being. That done, he lets me go,　　95
　　And with his head over his shoulder turned,
　　He seemed to find his way without his eyes,
　　For out adoors he went without their helps,
　　And to the last bended their light on me.
POLONIUS: Come, go with me. I will go seek the king.　　100
　　This is the very ecstasy of love,
　　Whose violent property fordoes itself,
　　And leads the will to desperate undertakings
　　As oft as any passion under heaven
　　That does afflict our natures. I am sorry.　　　　105
　　What, have you given him any hard words of late?
OPHELIA: No, my good lord, but as you did command
　　I did repel his letters, and denied
　　His access to me.
POLONIUS:　　　　　That hath made him mad.　　110
　　I am sorry that with better heed and judgement
　　I had not quoted him. I feared he did but trifle,
　　And meant to wrack thee; but beshrew my jealousy.
　　By heaven, it is as proper to our age
　　To cast beyond ourselves in our opinions
　　As it is common for the younger sort　　　　115
　　To lack discretion. Come, go we to the king.
　　This must be known, which being kept close,
　　　　might move
　　More grief to hide than hate to utter love.
　　Come.

(*Exeunt.*)

---

28 **season** moderate　31 **quaintly** delicately　34 **unreclaimèd** untamed　35 **Of general assault** assailing all　38 **fetch of warrant**
allowable device　43 **prenominate** before-named　45 **closes** agrees; **in
this consequence** as follows　47 **addition** title　60 **Videlicet** namely
63 **reach** ability　64 **windlasses** roundabout approaches; **assays of bias**
indirect attempts　68 **God buy ye** God be with you

76 **closet** private room　77 **unbraced** unlaced　79 **down-gyvèd** hanging down, like gyves or fetters on a prisoner's ankles　101 **ecstasy**
madness　102 **fordoes** destroys　111 **quoted** observed　112 **wrack**
ruin　113 **proper to** characteristic of　117 **close** secret; **move** cause

SCENE II

Flourish. Enter KING *and* QUEEN, ROSENCRANTZ, *and* GUILDENSTERN [*and* ATTENDANTS].

KING: Welcome, dear Rosencrantz and Guildenstern.
    Moreover that we much did long to see you,
    The need we have to use you did provoke
    Our hasty sending. Something have you heard
5   Of Hamlet's transformation—so call it,
    Sith nor th' exterior nor the inward man
    Resembles that it was. What it should be,
    More than his father's death, that thus hath put him
    So much from th' understanding of himself,
10 I cannot dream of. I entreat you both
    That, being of so young days brought up with him,
    And sith so neighboured to his youth and havior,
    That you vouchsafe your rest here in our court
    Some little time, so by your companies
15 To draw him on to pleasures, and to gather
    So much as from occasion you may glean,
    Whether aught to us unknown afflicts him thus,
    That opened, lies within our remedy.
QUEEN: Good gentlemen, he hath much talked of you,
20 And sure I am two men there is not living
    To whom he more adheres. If it will please you
    To show us so much gentry and good will
    As to expend your time with us awhile
    For the supply and profit of our hope,
25 Your visitation shall receive such thanks
    As fits a king's remembrance.
ROSENCRANTZ: Both your majesties
    Might, by the sovereign power you have of us,
    Put your dread pleasures more into command
    Than to entreaty.
GUILDENSTERN: But we both obey,
30 And here give up ourselves in the full bent
    To lay our service freely at your feet,
    To be commanded.
KING: Thanks, Rosencrantz and gentle Guildenstern.
QUEEN: Thanks, Guildenstern and gentle Rosencrantz.
35 And I beseech you instantly to visit
    My too much changed son. Go, some of you,
    And bring these gentlemen where Hamlet is.
GUILDENSTERN: Heavens make our presence and our practices
    Pleasant and helpful to him!
QUEEN: Ay, amen!

(*Exeunt* ROSENCRANTZ *and* GUILDENSTERN [*with some* ATTENDANTS].)

(*Enter* POLONIUS.)

40 POLONIUS: Th' ambassadors from Norway, my good lord,
    Are joyfully returned.
KING: Thou still hast been the father of good news.
POLONIUS: Have I, my lord? I assure my good liege,
    I hold my duty as I hold my soul,

Both to my God and to my gracious king;   45
    And I do think—or else this brain of mine
    Hunts not the trail of policy so sure
    As it hath used to do—that I have found
    The very cause of Hamlet's lunacy.
KING: O, speak of that, that do I long to hear.   50
POLONIUS: Give first admittance to th' ambassadors.
    My news shall be the fruit to that great feast.
KING: Thyself do grace to them, and bring them in.

(*Exit* POLONIUS.)

He tells me, my dear Gertrude, he hath found
    The head and source of all your son's distemper.   55
QUEEN: I doubt it is no other but the main,
    His father's death and our o'erhasty marriage.
KING: Well, we shall sift him.

(*Enter* AMBASSADORS [VOLTEMAND *and* CORNELIUS], *with* POLONIUS.)

                        Welcome, my good friends,
    Say, Voltemand, what from our brother Norway?
VOLTEMAND: Most fair return of greetings and desires.   60
    Upon our first, he sent out to suppress
    His nephew's levies, which to him appeared
    To be a preparation 'gainst the Polack,
    But better looked into, he truly found
    It was against your highness, whereat grieved,   65
    That so his sickness, age, and impotence
    Was falsely borne in hand, sends out arrests
    On Fortinbras, which he in brief obeys,
    Receives rebuke from Norway, and in fine,
    Makes vow before his uncle never more   70
    To give th' assay of arms against your majesty.
    Whereon old Norway, overcome with joy,
    Gives him three score thousand crowns in annual fee,
    And his commission to employ those soldiers,
    So levied as before, against the Polack,   75
    With an entreaty, herein further shown,   (*Gives a paper.*)
    That it might please you to give quiet pass
    Through your dominions for this enterprise,
    On such regards of safety and allowance
    As therein are set down.   80
KING: It likes us well,
    And at our more considered time we'll read,
    Answer, and think upon this business.
    Meantime we thank you for your well-took labor.
    Go to your rest; at night we'll feast together.
    Most welcome home!   85

(*Exeunt* AMBASSADORS.)

POLONIUS: This business is well ended.
    My liege and madam, to expostulate
    What majesty should be, what duty is,
    Why day is day, night night, and time is time,

II.ii. 6 **Sith** since   18 **opened** disclosed   22 **gentry** courtesy   42 **still** ever

56 **doubt** suspect   63 **the Polack** the Polish nation   67 **borne in hand** deceived   69 **in fine** in the end   71 **assay** trial   79 **regards** considerations

Were nothing but to waste night, day and time.
90 Therefore, since brevity is the soul of wit,
And tediousness the limbs and outward flourishes,
I will be brief. Your noble son is mad.
Mad call I it, for to define true madness,
What is't but to be nothing else but mad?
95 But let that go.
QUEEN: More matter with less art.
POLONIUS: Madam, I swear I use no art at all.
That he is mad, 'tis true: 'tis true 'tis pity.
And pity 'tis 'tis true. A foolish figure,
But farewell it, for I will use no art.
100 Mad let us grant him, then, and now remains
That we find out the cause of this effect,
Or rather say the cause of this defect,
For this effect defective comes by cause.
Thus it remains, and the remainder thus.
105 Perpend.
I have a daughter—have while she is mine—
Who in her duty and obedience, mark,
Hath given me this. Now gather, and surmise.   (*Reads.*)
'To the celestial, and my soul's idol, the most beautified
110 Ophelia'—That's an ill phrase, a vile phrase, 'beautified' is a
vile phrase. But you shall hear. Thus: (*Reads.*)
'In her excellent white bosom, these, etc.'
QUEEN: Came this from Hamlet to her?
POLONIUS: Good madam, stay awhile. I will be faithful.
(*Reads letter.*)

115   'Doubt thou the stars are fire,
Doubt that the sun doth move;
Doubt truth to be a liar;
But never doubt I love.

'O dear Ophelia, I am ill at these numbers. I have not
120 art to reckon my groans, but that I love thee best, O most
best, believe it. Adieu.
'Thine evermore, most dear lady, whilst
this machine is to him, Hamlet.'
This in obedience hath my daughter shown me,
125 And more above, hath his solicitings,
As they fell out by time, by means and place,
All given to mine ear.
KING: But how hath she
Received his love?
POLONIUS: What do you think of me?
KING: As of a man faithful and honourable.
130 POLONIUS: I would fain prove so. But what might you think,
When I had seen this hot love on the wing,
(As I perceived it, I must tell you that,
Before my daughter told me), what might you,
Or my dear majesty your queen here, think,
135 If I had played the desk or table-book,
Or given my heart a winking, mute and dumb,
Or looked upon this love with idle sight,
What might you think? No, I went round to work,
And my young mistress thus I did bespeak:
140 'Lord Hamlet is a prince out of thy star.

This must not be'. and then I prescripts gave her,
That she should lock herself from his resort,
Admit no messengers, receive no tokens.
Which done, she took the fruits of my advice;
And he repelled, a short tale to make,   145
Fell into a sadness, then into a fast,
Thence to a watch, thence into a weakness,
Thence to a lightness, and, by this declension,
Into the madness wherein now he raves,
And all we mourn for.   150
KING: Do you think 'tis this?
QUEEN: It may be, very like.
POLONIUS: Hath there been such a time—I would fain
know that—
That I have positively said ''Tis so,'
When it proved otherwise?
KING: Not that I know.
POLONIUS: (*Pointing to his head and shoulder.*) Take this from   155
this, if this be otherwise:
If circumstances lead me, I will find
Where truth is hid, though it were hid indeed
Within the centre.
KING: How may we try it further?
POLONIUS: You know, sometimes he walks four hours together
Here in the lobby.   160
QUEEN: So he does, indeed.
POLONIUS: At such a time I'll loose my daughter to him.
Be you and I behind an arras then.
Mark the encounter. If he love her not,
And be not from his reason fall'n thereon,
Let me be no assistant for a state,   165
But keep a farm and carters.
KING: We will try it.

(*Enter* HAMLET [*reading on a book*].)

QUEEN: But look where sadly the poor wretch comes reading.
POLONIUS: Away, I do beseech you both away,
I'll board him presently.

([*Exeunt*] KING *and* QUEEN [*with attendants*].)

O, give me leave.
How does my good Lord Hamlet?   170
HAMLET: Well, God-a-mercy.
POLONIUS: Do you know me, my lord?
HAMLET: Excellent well, you are a fishmonger.
POLONIUS: Not I, my lord.
HAMLET: Then I would you were so honest a man.   175
POLONIUS: Honest, my lord?
HAMLET: Ay, sir, to be honest as this world goes, is to be one man
picked out of ten thousand.
POLONIUS: That's very true, my lord.
HAMLET: For if the sun breed maggots in a dead dog, being a   180
good kissing carrion—Have you a daughter?
POLONIUS: I have, my lord.
HAMLET: Let her not walk i' th' sun. Conception is a blessing, but
as your daughter may conceive—friend, look to 't.

---

90 **wit** understanding 95 **matter** meaning, sense 105 **Perpend** consider 119 **numbers** verses 123 **machine** body 135 **played . . . table-book** acted as silent go-between 138 **round** directly

147 **watch** sleeplessness 148 **lightness** lightheadedness 158 **centre** centre of the earth and of the Ptolemaic universe 169 **board** accost; **presently** immediately

185 POLONIUS: (*Aside.*) How say you by that? Still harping on
my daughter. Yet he knew me not at first. 'A said I was a
fishmonger. 'A is far gone. And truly in my youth I suffered
much extremity for love, very near this. I'll speak to him
again.—What do you read, my lord?

190 HAMLET: Words, words, words.

POLONIUS: What is the matter, my lord?

HAMLET: Between who?

POLONIUS: I mean the matter that you read, my lord.

HAMLET: Slanders, sir; for the satirical rogue says here that old
195 men have grey beards, that their faces are wrinkled, their
eyes purging thick amber and plum-tree gum, and that
they have a plentiful lack of wit, together with most weak
hams—all which, sir, though I most powerfully and potently
believe, yet I hold it not honesty to have it thus set down,
200 for yourself, sir, shall grow old as I am, if like a crab you
could go backward.

POLONIUS: (*Aside.*) Though this be madness, yet there is method
in 't.—Will you walk out of the air, my lord?

HAMLET: Into my grave?

205 POLONIUS: (*Aside.*) Indeed, that's out of the air. How pregnant
sometimes his replies are! a happiness that often madness
hits on, which reason and sanity could not so prosperously
be delivered of. I will leave him, and suddenly contrive the
means of meeting between him and my daughter.—My lord,
210 I will take my leave of you.

HAMLET: You cannot take from me anything that I will not more
willingly part withal—except my life, except my life, except
my life.

(*Enter* GUILDENSTERN *and* ROSENCRANTZ.)

POLONIUS: Fare you well, my lord.

215 HAMLET: These tedious old fools!

POLONIUS: You go to seek the Lord Hamlet. There he is.

ROSENCRANTZ: (*To* POLONIUS.) *God save you, sir!*

(*Exit* POLONIUS.)

GUILDENSTERN: My honored lord!

ROSENCRANTZ: My most dear lord!

220 HAMLET: My excellent good friends! How dost thou,
Guildenstern?
Ah, Rosencrantz! Good lads, how do ye both?

ROSENCRANTZ: As the indifferent children of the earth.

GUILDENSTERN: Happy in that we are not over-happy;
225 On Fortune's cap we are not the very button.

HAMLET: Nor the soles of her shoe?

ROSENCRANTZ: Neither, my lord.

HAMLET: Then you live about her waist, or in the middle of her
favors?

230 GUILDENSTERN: Faith, her privates we.

HAMLET: In the secret parts of Fortune? O, most true, she is a
strumpet. What news?

ROSENCRANTZ: None, my lord, but that the world's grown
honest.

235 HAMLET: Then is doomsday near. But your news is not true. Let
me question more in particular. What have you, my good
friends, deserved at the hands of Fortune, that she sends you
to prison hither?

GUILDENSTERN: Prison, my lord! 240

HAMLET: Denmark's a prison.

ROSENCRANTZ: Then is the world one.

HAMLET: A goodly one, in which there are many confines, wards,
and dungeons, Denmark being one o' th' worst.

ROSENCRANTZ: We think not so, my lord.

HAMLET: Why then 'tis none to you; for there is nothing either 245
good or bad, but thinking makes it so. To me it is a prison.

ROSENCRANTZ: Why then your ambition makes it one. 'Tis too
narrow for your mind.

HAMLET: O God, I could be bounded in a nutshell and count
myself a king of infinite space, were it not that I have bad 250
dreams.

GUILDENSTERN: Which dreams indeed are ambition; for the
very substance of the ambitious is merely the shadow of a
dream.

HAMLET: A dream itself is but a shadow. 255

ROSENCRANTZ: Truly, and I hold ambition of so airy and light a
quality that it is but a shadow's shadow.

HAMLET: Then are our beggars bodies, and, our monarchs and
outstretched heroes the beggars' shadows. Shall we to th'
court? for, by my fay, I cannot reason. 260

BOTH: We'll wait upon you.

HAMLET: No such matter. I will not sort you with the rest of my
servants; for to speak to you like an honest man, I am most
dreadfully attended. But in the beaten way of friendship, what
make you at Elsinore? 265

ROSENCRANTZ: To visit you, my lord; no other occasion.

HAMLET: Beggar that I am, I am ever poor in thanks, but I
thank you; and sure, dear friends, my thanks are too dear a
halfpenny. Were you not sent for? Is it your own inclining? Is
it a free visitation? Come, come, deal justly with me. Come, 270
come, nay speak.

GUILDENSTERN: What should we say, my lord?

HAMLET: Anything but to the purpose. You were sent for, and
there is a kind of confession in your looks, which your
modesties have not craft enough to color. I know the good 275
king and queen have sent for you.

ROSENCRANTZ: To what end, my lord?

HAMLET: That you must teach me. But let me conjure you by the
rights of our fellowship, by the consonancy of our youth, by
the obligation of our ever-preserved love, and by what more 280
dear a better proposer can charge you withal be even and
direct with me whether you were sent for or no.

ROSENCRANTZ: (*Aside to* GUILDENSTERN.) What say you?

HAMLET: (*Aside.*) Nay, then, I have an eye of you.—If you love me,
hold not off. 285

GUILDENSTERN: My lord, we were sent for.

HAMLET: I will tell you why; so shall my anticipation prevent
your discovery, and your secrecy to the king and queen moult
no feather. I have of late—but wherefore I know not—lost all
my mirth, forgone all custom of exercises; and indeed it goes 290
so heavily with my disposition, that this goodly frame the
earth seems to me a sterile promontory, this most excellent
canopy the air, look you, this brave o'er-hanging firmament,
this majestical roof fretted with golden fire, why it appeareth 295

---

205 **pregnant** full of meaning 206 **happiness** aptness 223 **indifferent** average 225 **button** knob on the top of the cap

260 **fay** faith 262 **sort you with** put you in the same class with 287 **prevent** forestall 288 **discovery** disclosure 294 **fretted** decorated with fretwork

nothing to me but a foul and pestilent congregation of vapors. What a piece of work is a man, how noble in reason, how infinite in faculties, in form and moving, how express and admirable in action, how like an angel in apprehension, how like a god:
300   the beauty of the world, the paragon of animals. And yet to me, what is this quintessence of dust? Man delights not me, nor woman neither, though by your smiling you seem to say so.

ROSENCRANTZ: My lord, there was no such stuff in my thoughts.

305   HAMLET: Why did ye laugh, then, when I said 'Man delights not me'?

ROSENCRANTZ: To think, my lord, if you delight not in man, what lenten entertainment the players shall receive from you. We coted them on the way, and hither are they coming to offer
310   you service.

HAMLET: He that plays the king shall be welcome—his majesty shall have tribute on me; the adventurous knight shall use his foil and target; the lover shall not sigh gratis; the humorous man shall end his part in peace; the clown shall make those
315   laugh whose lungs are tickle o' th' sere; and the lady shall say her mind freely, or the blank verse shall halt for 't. What players are they?

ROSENCRANTZ: Even those you were wont to take such delight in, the tragedians of the city.

320   HAMLET: How chances it they travel? Their residence, both in reputation and profit, was better both ways.

ROSENCRANTZ: I think their inhibition comes by the means of the late innovation.

HAMLET: Do they hold the same estimation they did when I was
325   in the city? Are they so followed?

ROSENCRANTZ: No, indeed, are they not.

HAMLET: How comes it? Do they grow rusty?

ROSENCRANTZ: Nay, their endeavour keeps in the wonted pace; but there is, sir, an eyrie of children, little eyases, that cry out
330   on the top of question, and are most tyrannically clapped for't. These are now the fashion, and so berattle the common stages (so they call them) that many wearing rapiers are afraid of goose quills and dare scarce come thither.

HAMLET: What, are they children? Who maintains 'em? How
335   are they escoted? Will they pursue the quality no longer than they can sing? Will they not say afterwards, if they should

grow themselves to common players (as it is most like, if their means are no better), their writers do them wrong to make them exclaim against their own succession?

ROSENCRANTZ: 'Faith, there has been much to do on both sides;   340
and the nation holds it no sin to tarre them to controversy. There was for a while no money bid for argument, unless the poet and the player went to cuffs in the question.

HAMLET: Is't possible?

GUILDENSTERN: O, there has been much throwing about of   345
brains.

HAMLET: Do the boys carry it away?

ROSENCRANTZ: Ay, that they do, my lord, Hercules and his load too.

HAMLET: It is not very strange, for my uncle is King of Denmark,   350
and those that would make mouths at him while my father lived give twenty, forty, fifty, a hundred ducats apiece for his picture in little. 'Sblood, there is something in this more than natural, if philosophy could find it out.

(*A flourish.*)

GUILDENSTERN: There are the players.   355

HAMLET: Gentlemen, you are welcome to Elsinore. Your hands. Come then th' appurtenance of welcome is fashion and ceremony. Let me comply with you in this garb, lest my ex-tent to the players, which I tell you must show fairly outwards, should more appear like entertainment than yours.   360
You are welcome. But my uncle-father and aunt-mother are deceived.

GUILDENSTERN: In what, my dear lord?

HAMLET: I am but mad north-north-west; when the wind is southerly I know a hawk from a handsaw.   365

(*Enter* POLONIUS.)

POLONIUS: Well be with you, gentlemen.

HAMLET: Hark you, Guildenstern—and you too—at each ear a hearer. That great baby you see there is not yet out of his swaddling clouts.

ROSENCRANTZ: Happily he is the second time come to   370
them, for they say an old man is twice a child.

HAMLET: I will prophesy he comes to tell me of the players. Mark it.—You say right, sir, a Monday morning, 'twas then indeed.

POLONIUS: My lord, I have news to tell you.   375

HAMLET: My lord, I have news to tell you. When Roscius was an actor in Rome—

POLONIUS: The actors are come hither, my lord.

HAMLET: Buzz, buzz.

POLONIUS: Upon my honor—   380

HAMLET: Then came each actor on his ass—

---

308 **lenten** scanty   309 **coted** passed   313 **foil and target** spear and shield   313–314 **humorous man** the actor who plays the eccentric character dominated by one of the four humors   315 **tickle o' th' sere** easily set off (**sere** is that part of a gunlock which keeps the hammer at full or half cock)   316 **halt** limp   322 **inhibition** prohibition of plays by authority (possibly with reference to decree of the Privy Council of 22 June 1600, limiting the number of London theater companies to two, and stipulating that the two were to perform only twice a week)   323 **innovation** meaning uncertain (sometimes taken to refer to the reintroduction, ca. 1600, on the London theatrical scene of companies of boy actors performing in private theaters; sometimes interpreted as "political upheaval," with special reference to Essex's rebellion, February, 1601)   329 **eyrie** nest; **eyases** nestling hawks (here, the boys in the children's companies training as actors)   330 **on the top of question** louder than all others on matter of dispute   331–332 **common stages** public theaters of the **common players** (below, line 337), organized in companies composed mainly of adult actors   333 **goose quills** pens (of the satiric dramatists writing for the private theaters)   335 **escoted** maintained; **pursue the quality** continue in the profession of acting   336 **sing** i.e., until their voices change

---

341 **tarre** incite   342 **argument** plot of a play   349 **load** i.e., the world (the sign of the Globe theater represented Hercules bearing the world on his shoulders)   351 **mouths** grimaces   353 **in little** in miniature   357 **appurtenance** adjuncts   358–359 **extent** welcome   365 **hawk** mattock or pickaxe (also called "hack," here used with a play on *hawk* as a bird); **handsaw** a saw managed with one hand (here used with a play on some corrupt form of *hernshaw,* "heron")   370 **Happily** perhaps   376 **Roscius** the greatest of Roman comic actors, though regarded by the Elizabethans as a tragic one

POLONIUS: The best actors in the world, either for tragedy,
comedy, history, pastoral, pastoral-comical, historical-
pastoral, tragical-historical, tragical-comical-historical-
385 pastoral, scene individable, or poem unlimited. Seneca cannot
be too heavy nor Plautus too light. For the law of writ and the
liberty, these are the only men.
HAMLET: O Jephthah, judge of Israel, what a treasure hadst
thou!
390 POLONIUS: What a treasure had he, my lord?
HAMLET: Why—

> 'One fair daughter, and no more,
> The which he loved passing well.'

POLONIUS: (*Aside.*) Still on my daughter.
395 HAMLET: Am I not i' th' right, old Jephthah?
POLONIUS: If you call me Jephthah, my lord, I have a daughter
that I love passing well.
HAMLET: Nay, that follows not.
POLONIUS: What follows then, my lord?
400 HAMLET: Why—

> 'As by lot, God wot,'

and then, you know,

> 'It came to pass, as most like it was.'

The first row of the pious chanson will show you more, for
405 look where my abridgement comes.

(*Enter the* PLAYERS.)

You are welcome, masters; welcome, all.—I am glad to see
thee well.—Welcome, good friends. O, old friend! Why thy
face is valanced since I saw thee last. Come'st thou to beard
me in Denmark?—What, my young lady and mistress? By'r
410 lady, your ladyship is nearer to heaven than when I saw
you last by the altitude of a chopine. Pray God, your voice,
like a piece of uncurrent gold, be not cracked within the
ring.—Masters, you are all welcome. We'll e'en to't like French
falconers, fly at any thing we see. We'll have a speech
415 straight. Come give us a taste of your quality, come a
passionate speech.
1 PLAYER: What speech, my good lord?
HAMLET: I heard thee speak me a speech once, but it was never
acted, or if it was, not above once, for the play, I remember,
420 pleased not the million; 'twas caviary to the general. But it
was—as I received it, and others whose judgements in such
matters cried in the top of mine—an excellent play, well

digested in the scenes, set down with as much modesty as
cunning. I remember one said there were no sallets in the
lines to make the matter savory, nor no matter in the phrase   425
that might indict the author of affectation, but called it an
honest method, as wholesome as sweet, and by very much
more handsome than fine. One speech in't I chiefly loved.
'Twas Æneas' tale to Dido and thereabout of it especially
when he speaks of Priam's slaughter. If it live in your memory, 430
begin at this line—let me see, let me see:

> 'The rugged Pyrrhus, like th' Hyrcanian beast'—

'tis not so;—it begins with Pyrrhus—

> 'The rugged Pyrrhus, he whose sable arms,
> Black as his purpose, did the night resemble
> When he lay couchèd in the ominous horse,   435
> Hath now this dread and black complexion smeared
> With heraldry more dismal; head to foot
> Now is he total gules, horridly tricked
> With blood of fathers, mothers, daughters, sons,   440
> Baked and impasted with the parching streets,
> That lend a tyrannous and a damnèd light
> To their lord's murder. Roasted in wrath and fire,
> And thus o'er-sizèd with coagulate gore,
> With eyes like carbuncles, the hellish Pyrrhus   445
> Old grandsire Priam seeks.'

So, proceed you.
POLONIUS: Fore God, my lord, well spoken, with good accent and
good discretion.
1 PLAYER: 'Anon he finds him   450
> Striking too short at Greeks. His antique sword,
> Rebellious to his arm, lies where it falls,
> Repugnant to command. Unequal matched,
> Pyrrhus at Priam drives, in rage strikes wide.
> But with the whiff and wind of his fell sword   455
> Th' unnervèd father falls. Then senseless Ilium,
> Seeming to feel this blow, with flaming top
> Stoops to his base, and with a hideous crash
> Takes prisoner Pyrrhus' ear. For, lo! his sword,
> Which was declining on the milky head   460
> Of reverend Priam, seemed i' th' air to stick.
> So as a painted tyrant Pyrrhus stood,
> And like a neutral to his will and matter,
> Did nothing.
> But as we often see, against some storm,   465
> A silence in the heavens, the rack stand still,
> The bold winds speechless, and the orb below
> As hush as death, anon the dreadful thunder
> Doth rend the region; so, after Pyrrhus' pause,
> A rousèd vengeance sets him new awork,   470

384–385 **scene individable** i.e., a play that observes the unities of
time and place   385 **poem unlimited** a play that does not observe
the unities; **Seneca** Roman writer of tragedies   386 **Plautus** Roman
comic dramatist; **law of writ and the liberty** i.e., plays according
to strict classical rules, and those that ignored the unities of time
and place   388 **Jephthah** was compelled to sacrifice a beloved
daughter (Judges 2). Hamlet quotes from a contemporary ballad titled *Jephthah, Judge of Israel* at lines 392–393, 401, and 403
404 **row** stanza   408 **valanced** bearded   409 **young lady** i.e., the boy
who plays female roles   411 **chopine** a shoe with high cork heel and
sole   412–413 **cracked within the ring** a coin cracked within the circle surrounding the head of the sovereign was no longer legal tender
and so *uncurrent*   415 **straight** immediately   420 **caviary** caviare;
general multitude

422–423 **digested** arranged   424 **sallets** salads, highly seasoned passages   428 **more handsome than fine** admirable rather than appealing by mere cleverness   432 **Hyrcanian beast** tiger   436 **horse** i.e.,
the Trojan horse   439 **gules** heraldic term for red; tricked delineated
444 **o'er-sizèd** covered as with size; **coagulate** clotted   453 **Repugnant**
refractory   455 **fell** fierce, cruel   465 **against** just before   466 **rack**
mass of cloud   469 **region** air

And never did the Cyclops' hammers fall
On Mars's armor, forged for proof eterne
With less remorse than Pyrrhus' bleeding sword
Now falls on Priam.

475 Out, out, thou strumpet, Fortune! All you gods,
In general synod take away her power,
Break all the spokes and fellies from her wheel,
And bowl the round nave down the hill of heaven
As low as to the fiends.'

480 POLONIUS: This is too long.
HAMLET: It shall to the barber's with your beard.—Prithee, say
on. He's for a jig, or a tale of bawdry, or he sleeps. Say on,
come to Hecuba.
1 PLAYER: 'But who, ah woe! had seen the mobled queen—'

485 HAMLET: 'The mobled queen'?
POLONIUS: That's good.
1 PLAYER: 'Run barefoot up and down, threat'ning the flames
With bisson rheum; a clout upon that head
Where late the diadem stood, and for a robe,

490 About her lank and all o'er-teemèd loins,
A blanket, in the alarm of fear caught up—
Who this had seen, with tongue in venom steeped,
'Gainst Fortune's state would treason have pronounced.
But if the gods themselves did see her then,

495 When she saw Pyrrhus make malicious sport
In mincing with his sword her husband's limbs,
The instant burst of clamor that she made,
Unless things mortal move them not at all,
Would have made milch the burning eyes of heaven,

500 And passion in the gods.'
POLONIUS: Look whe'r he has not turned his color, and has tears
in's eyes. Prithee no more.
HAMLET: 'Tis well. I'll have thee speak out the rest of this
soon.—Good my lord, will you see the players well

505 bestowed? Do you hear, let them be well used, for they are
the abstract and brief chronicles of the time; after your
death you were better have a bad epitaph than their
ill report while you live.
POLONIUS: My lord, I will use them according to their desert.

510 HAMLET: God's bodkin, man, much better. Use every man
after his desert, and who shall 'scape whipping? Use them
after your own honor and dignity. The less they deserve, the
more merit is in your bounty. Take them in.
POLONIUS: Come, sirs.

515 HAMLET: Follow him, friends. We'll hear a play tomorrow. (Aside
to 1 PLAYER.) Dost thou hear me, old friend, can you play the
'Murder of Gonzago'?
1 PLAYER: Ay, my lord.
HAMLET: We'll ha't tomorrow night. You could for a need

520 study a speech of some dozen or sixteen lines which
I would set down and insert in't, could you not?
1 PLAYER: Ay, my lord.
HAMLET: Very well. Follow that lord, and look you mock him not.

(Exeunt POLONIUS and PLAYERS.)

My good friends, I'll leave you till night. You are welcome   525
to Elsinore.
ROSENCRANTZ: Good my lord!

(Exeunt [ROSENCRANTZ and GUILDENSTERN].)

HAMLET: Ay, so God by to you. Now I am alone.
O, what a rogue and peasant slave am I!
Is it not monstrous that this player here,   530
But in a fiction, in a dream of passion,
Could force his soul so to his own conceit
That from her working all his visage wanned;
Tears in his eyes, distraction in his aspect,
A broken voice, and his whole function suiting   535
With forms to his conceit? And all for nothing,
For Hecuba!
What's Hecuba to him or he to Hecuba,
That he should weep for her? What would he do
Had he the motive and the cue for passion   540
That I have? He would drown the stage with tears,
And cleave the general ear with horrid speech,
Make mad the guilty, and appal the free,
Confound the ignorant, and amaze indeed
The very faculties of eyes and ears.   545
Yet I,
A dull and muddy-mettled rascal, peak
Like John-a-dreams, unpregnant of my cause,
And can say nothing; no, not for a king
Upon whose property and most dear life   550
A damned defeat was made. Am I a coward?
Who calls me villain, breaks my pate across,
Plucks off my beard and blows it in my face,
Tweaks me by the nose, gives me the lie i' th' throat
As deep as to the lungs? Who does me this?   555
Ha, 'swounds, I should take it; for it cannot be
But I am pigeon-livered and lack gall
To make oppression bitter, or ere this
I should 'a fatted all the region kites
With this slave's offal. Bloody, bawdy villain!   560
Remorseless, treacherous, lecherous, kindless villain!
Why, what an ass am I! This is most brave,
That I, the son of a dear father murdered,
Prompted to my revenge by heaven and hell,
Must like a whore unpack my heart with words,   565
And fall a-cursing like a very drab,
A scullion! Fie upon 't! foh!
About, my brains! Hum—I have heard

---

532 **conceit** imagination   542 **general** public   547 **muddy-mettled**
dull-spirited; **peak** mope   548 **unpregnant** not quickened to action
559 **region kites** kites of the air   561 **kindless** unnatural. Following this
line, *F* adds the words "Oh Vengeance!" Their inappropriateness to the
occasion is noted by Professor Harold Jenkins (in his "Playhouse Inter-
polations in the Folio Text of Hamlet," *Studies in Bibliography* 13 [1960]:
37). Professor Jenkins remarks that the folio text, by introducing
Hamlet's "call for vengeance while he is still absorbed in self-reproaches,
both anticipates and misconstrues" the crisis of his passion and of the
speech, which comes in fact at line 568 ("**About, my brains**"),
when "he abandons his self-reproaches and plans action"   567 **scullion**
kitchen wench

---

471 **Cyclops** giant workmen who made armor in the smithy of
Vulcan   472 **proof eterne** to be forever impenetrable   477 **fellies** the
curved pieces forming the rim of a wheel   478 **nave** hub of a wheel
484 **mobled** muffled   488 **bisson rheum** blinding tears   490 **o'er-
teemed** exhausted by many births   493 **state** government   499 **milch**
moist, tearful (lit., milk, giving)   506 **abstract** summary account
510 **God's bodkin** by God's dear body

570 That guilty creatures sitting at a play,
Have by the very cunning of the scene
Been struck so to the soul that presently
They have proclaimed their malefactions:
For murder, though it have no tongue, will speak
With most miraculous organ. I'll have these players
575 Play something like the murder of my father
Before mine uncle. I'll observe his looks.
I'll tent him to the quick. If 'a do blench,
I know my course. The spirit that I have seen
May be the devil, and the devil hath power
580 T' assume a pleasing shape, yea, and perhaps
Out of my weakness and my melancholy,
As he is very potent with such spirits,
Abuses me to damn me. I'll have grounds
More relative than this. The play's the thing
585 Wherein I'll catch the conscience of the king.

(*Exit.*)

ACT THREE

SCENE I

Enter KING, QUEEN, POLONIUS, OPHELIA, ROSENCRANTZ, GUILDENSTERN, LORDS.

KING: And can you by no drift of conference
Get from him why he puts on this confusion,
Grating so harshly all his days of quiet
With turbulent and dangerous lunacy?
5 ROSENCRANTZ: He does confess he feels himself distracted,
But from what cause 'a will by no means speak.
GUILDENSTERN: Nor do we find him forward to be sounded,
But with a crafty madness keeps aloof
When we would bring him on to some confession
10 Of his true state.
QUEEN: Did he receive you well?
ROSENCRANTZ: Most like a gentleman.
GUILDENSTERN: But with much forcing of his disposition.
ROSENCRANTZ: Niggard of question, but of our demands
Most free in his reply.
QUEEN: Did you assay him
15 To any pastime?
ROSENCRANTZ: Madam, it so fell out that certain players
We o'er-raught on the way. Of these we told him,
And there did seem in him a kind of joy
To hear of it. They are here about the court,
20 And as I think, they have already order
This night to play before him.
POLONIUS: 'Tis most true,
And he beseeched me to entreat your majesties
To hear and see the matter.
KING: With all my heart, and it doth much content me
25 To hear him so inclined.

Good gentlemen, give him a further edge,
And drive his purpose into these delights.
ROSENCRANTZ: We shall, my lord.

(*Exeunt* ROSENCRANTZ *and* GUILDENSTERN.)

KING: Sweet Gertrude, leave us too;
For we have closely sent for Hamlet hither,
That he, as 'twere by accident, may here   30
Affront Ophelia.
Her father and myself (lawful espials)
We'll so bestow ourselves that, seeing unseen,
We may of their encounter frankly judge,
And gather by him, as he is behaved,   35
If 't be th' affliction of his love or no
That thus he suffers for.
QUEEN: I shall obey you.—
And for your part, Ophelia, I do wish
That your good beauties be the happy cause
Of Hamlet's wildness. So shall I hope your virtues 40
Will bring him to his wonted way again,
To both your honors.
OPHELIA: Madam, I wish it may.

(*Exit* QUEEN *with* LORDS.)

POLONIUS: Ophelia, walk you here.—Gracious, so please you,
We will bestow ourselves.—(*To* OPHELIA.) Read on this book,
That show of such an exercise may color   45
Your loneliness.—We are oft to blame in this,
'Tis too much proved, that with devotion's visage
And pious action we do sugar o'er
The devil himself.
KING: (*Aside.*)   O, 'tis too true.
How smart a lash that speech doth give my conscience! 50
The harlot's cheek, beautied with plast'ring art,
Is not more ugly to the thing that helps it
Then is my deed to my most painted word.
O heavy burden!
POLONIUS: I hear him coming. Let's withdraw, my lord. 55

(*Exeunt* KING *and* POLONIUS.)

(*Enter* HAMLET.)

HAMLET: To be, or not to be, that is the question:
Whether 'tis nobler in the mind to suffer
The slings and arrows of outrageous fortune,
Or to take arms against a sea of troubles,
And by opposing end them. To die, to sleep—   60
No more; and by a sleep to say we end
The heartache, and the thousand natural shocks
That flesh is heir to: 'tis a consummation
Devoutly to be wished. To die, to sleep—
To sleep, perchance to dream, ay there's the rub; 65
For in that sleep of death what dreams may come

---

571 **presently** immediately   577 **tent** probe; **blench** flinch   583 **Abuses**
deludes   584 **relative** relevant

III.i.   7 **forward** willing   14 **assay** try to win   17 **o'er-raught** overtook

---

26 **give him a further edge** sharpen his inclination   29 **closely** privately   31 **Affront** meet face to face   32 **espials** spies   45 **exercise** act of devotion; **color** give an appearance of naturalness to   52 **to** compared to   65 **rub** obstacle (lit., obstruction encountered by bowler's ball)

When we have shuffled off this mortal coil
Must give us pause. There's the respect
That makes calamity of so long life:
70 For who would bear the whips and scorns of time,
Th' oppressor's wrong, the proud man's contumely,
The pangs of despised love, the law's delay,
The insolence of office, and the spurns
That patient merit of th' unworthy takes,
75 When he himself might his quietus make
With a bare bodkin? Who would fardels bear,
To grunt and sweat under a weary life,
But that the dread of something after death,
The undiscovered country, from whose bourn
80 No traveller returns, puzzles the will,
And makes us rather bear those ills we have
Than fly to others that we know not of?
Thus conscience does make cowards of us all,
And thus the native hue of resolution
85 Is sicklied o'er with the pale cast of thought,
And enterprises of great pitch and moment
With this regard their currents turn awry
And lose the name of action. Soft you now,
The fair Ophelia.—Nymph, in thy orisons
90 Be all my sins remembered.
OPHELIA: Good my lord,
How does your honor for this many a day?
HAMLET: I humbly thank you, well.
OPHELIA: My lord, I have remembrances of yours
That I have longed long to re-deliver.
95 I pray you now receive them.
HAMLET: No, not I,
I never gave you aught.
OPHELIA: My honored lord, you know right well you did,
And with them words of so sweet breath composed
As made the things more rich. Their perfume lost,
100 Take these again, for to the noble mind
Rich gifts wax poor when givers prove unkind.
There, my lord.
HAMLET: Ha, ha! are you honest?
OPHELIA: My lord?
105 HAMLET: Are you fair?
OPHELIA: What means your lordship?
HAMLET: That if you be honest and fair, your honesty should
admit no discourse to your beauty.
OPHELIA: Could beauty, my lord, have better commerce than
110 with honesty?
HAMLET: Ay, truly, for the power of beauty will sooner transform
honesty from what it is to a bawd than the force of honesty
can translate beauty into his likeness. This was sometime a
paradox, but now the time gives it proof. I did
115 love you once.
OPHELIA: Indeed, my lord, you made me believe so.
HAMLET: You should not have believed me, for virtue cannot so
inoculate our old stock but we shall relish of it. I loved
you not.
120 OPHELIA: I was the more deceived.
HAMLET: Get thee to a nunnery. Why wouldst thou be a

breeder of sinners? I am myself indifferent honest, but yet I
could accuse me of such things that it were better my
mother had not borne me: I am very proud, revengeful, ambitious, with more offences at my beck than I have thoughts 125
to put them in, imagination to give them shape, or time to act
them in. What should such fellows as I do crawling between
earth and heaven? We are arrant knaves all; believe none of
us. Go thy ways to a nunnery. Where's your father?
OPHELIA: At home, my lord. 130
HAMLET: Let the doors be shut upon him, that he may play
the fool nowhere but in's own house. Farewell.
OPHELIA: O, help him, you sweet heavens!
HAMLET: If thou dost marry, I'll give thee this plague for thy
dowry: be thou as chaste as ice, as pure as snow, thou shalt 135
not escape calumny. Get thee to a nunnery, farewell. Or if
thou wilt needs marry, marry a fool, for wise men know well
enough what monsters you make of them. To a nunnery, go,
and quickly too. Farewell.
OPHELIA: Heavenly powers, restore him! 140
HAMLET: I have heard of your paintings well enough. God hath
given you one face, and you make yourselves another. You
jig and amble, and you lisp; you nickname God's creatures,
and make your wantonness your ignorance. Go to, I'll no
more on't, it hath made me mad. I say we will have no moe 145
marriage. Those that are married already, all but one, shall
live. The rest shall keep as they are. To a nunnery, go.

(*Exit.*)

OPHELIA: O, what a noble mind is here o'erthrown!
The courtier's, soldier's, scholar's, eye, tongue, sword,
Th' expectancy and rose of the fair state, 150
The glass of fashion and the mould of form,
Th' observed of all observers, quite quite down!
And I of ladies most deject and wretched,
That sucked the honey of his musiced vows,
Now see that noble and most sovereign reason 155
Like sweet bells jangled, out of time and harsh;
That unmatched form and feature of blown youth
Blasted with ecstasy. O, woe is me
T' have seen what I have seen, see what I see!

(*Enter* KING *and* POLONIUS.)

KING: Love? His affections do not that way tend, 160
Nor what he spake, though it lacked form a little,
Was not like madness. There's something in his soul,
O'er which his melancholy sits on brood,
And I do doubt the hatch and the disclose
Will be some danger; which for to prevent, 165
I have in quick determination
Thus set it down: he shall with speed to England
For the demand of our neglected tribute,
Haply the seas and countries different,
With variable objects, shall expel 170
This something-settled matter in his heart

---

67 **coil** bustle, turmoil   75 **quietus** settlement   76 **bodkin** dagger;
fardels burdens   79 **bourn** realm   86 **pitch** height   87 **regard** consideration   89 **orisons** prayers   103 **honest** chaste   118 **inoculate** graft

122 **indifferent** honest moderately respectable   144 **make your
wantonness your ignorance** excuse your wanton behavior with the
plea that you don't know any better   145 **moe** more   150 **expectancy**
hope   151 **glass** mirror   157 **blown** blooming   158 **ecstasy** madness
160 **affections** emotions   164 **doubt** fear

Whereon his brains still beating puts him thus
From fashion of himself. What think you on't?
POLONIUS: It shall do well. But yet do I believe
175 The origin and commencement of his grief
Sprung from neglected love.—How now, Ophelia?
You need not tell us what Lord Hamlet said;
We heard it all.—My lord, do as you please,
But if you hold it fit, after the play
180 Let his queen-mother all alone entreat him
To show his grief. Let her be round with him,
And I'll be placed, so please you, in the ear
Of all their conference. If she find him not,
To England send him; or confine him where
185 Your wisdom best shall think.
KING: It shall be so.
Madness in great ones must not unwatched go.

(*Exeunt.*)

SCENE II

Enter HAMLET *and three of the* PLAYERS.

HAMLET: Speak the speech, I pray you, as I pronounced it to
you, trippingly on the tongue; but if you mouth it as many
of our players do, I had as lief the town-crier spoke my
lines. Nor do not saw the air too much with your hand
5 thus, but use all gently, for in the very torrent, tempest, and as
I may say, whirlwind of your passion, you must acquire and
beget a temperance that may give it smoothness. O, it offends
me to the soul to hear a robustious periwig-pated fellow tear
a passion to tatters, to very rags, to split the ears of the
10 groundlings, who for the most part are capable of nothing
but inexplicable dumb shows and noise. I would have such
a fellow whipped for o'erdoing Termagant. It out-Herods
Herod. Pray you avoid it.
1 PLAYER: I warrant your honour.
15 HAMLET: Be not too tame neither, but let your own discretion
be your tutor. Suit the action to the word, the word to the
action, with this special observance, that you o'erstep not
the modesty of nature; for any thing so o'erdone is from
the purpose of playing, whose end both at the first,
20 and now, was and is, to hold as 'twere the mirror up to
nature, to show virtue her own feature, scorn her own
image, and the very age and body of the time his form and
pressure. Now this overdone, or come tardy off, though it
make the unskilful laugh, cannot but make the judicious
25 grieve, the censure of the which one must in your allowance
o'erweigh a whole theatre of others. O, there be players that
I have seen play—and heard others praise, and that highly—
not to speak it profanely, that neither having th' accent of
Christians, nor the gait of Christian, pagan, nor man, have
30 so strutted and bellowed that I have thought some of nature's
journeymen had made men, and not made them well, they
imitated humanity so abominably.

---

181 **round** plain-spoken

III.ii. 10 **groundlings** spectators who paid least and stood on the
ground 12 **Termagant** thought to be a Mohammedan deity, and
represented in medieval mystery plays as a violent and ranting personage; **Herod** represented in the mystery plays as a blustering tyrant
25 **censure** judgment, opinion

1 PLAYER: I hope we have reformed that indifferently with us.
HAMLET: O, reform it altogether. And let those that play your
clowns speak no more than is set down for them, for there be 35
of them that will themselves laugh, to set on some quantity of
barren spectators to laugh too, though in the meantime some
necessary question of the play be then to be considered. That's
villanous, and shows a most pitiful ambition in the fool that
uses it. Go, make you ready. 40

(*Exeunt* PLAYERS.)

(*Enter* POLONIUS, GUILDENSTERN, *and* ROSENCRANTZ.)

How now, my lord? Will the king hear this piece of work?
POLONIUS: And the queen too, and that presently.
HAMLET: Bid the players make haste. (*Exit* POLONIUS.)
Will you two help to hasten them?
ROSENCRANTZ: Ay, my lord. 45

(*Exeunt they two.*)

HAMLET: What, ho! Horatio!

(*Enter* HORATIO.)

HORATIO: Here, sweet lord, at your service.
HAMLET: Horatio, thou art e'en as just a man
As e'er my conversation coped withal.
HORATIO: O my dear lord! 50
HAMLET: Nay, do not think I flatter,
For what advancement may I hope from thee,
That no revenue hast but thy good spirits
To feed and clothe thee? Why should the poor be flattered?
No, let the candied tongue lick absurd pomp,
And crook the pregnant hinges of the knee 55
Where thrift may follow fawning. Dost thou hear?
Since my dear soul was mistress of her choice
And could of men distinguish her election,
S'hath sealed thee for herself, for thou hast been
As one in suff'ring all that suffers nothing, 60
A man that Fortune's buffets and rewards
Hast ta'en with equal thanks; and blest are those
Whose blood and judgment are so well comeddled
That they are not a pipe for Fortune's finger
To sound what stop she please. Give me that man 65
That is not passion's slave, and I will wear him
In my heart's core, ay, in my heart of heart,
As I do thee. Something too much of this.
There is a play to-night before the king.
One scene of it comes near the circumstance 70
Which I have told thee of my father's death.
I prithee, when thou seest that act afoot,
Even with the very comment of thy soul
Observe my uncle. If his occulted guilt
Do not itself unkennel in one speech, 75

---

33 **indifferently** fairly well 49 **coped** encountered 55 **pregnant**
ready 56 **thrift** profit 58 **election** choice 63 **co-meddled** mingled 73 **the very comment of thy soul** with a keenness of observation
that penetrates to the very being 74 **occulted** hidden 75 **unkennel**
reveal

It is a damnèd ghost that we have seen,
And my imaginations are as foul
As Vulcan's stithy. Give him heedful note,
For I mine eyes will rivet to his face,

80 And after we will both our judgements join
In censure of his seeming.
HORATIO: Well, my lord.
If 'a steal aught the whilst this play is playing,
And 'scape detecting, I will pay the theft.

(*Enter Trumpets and Kettledrums,* KING, QUEEN, POLONIUS,
OPHELIA, [ROSENCRANTZ, GUILDENSTERN, *and other* LORDS
attendant].)

HAMLET: They are coming to the play. I must be idle.
85   Get you a place.
KING: How fares our cousin Hamlet?
HAMLET: Excellent, i' faith, of the chameleon's dish. I eat the air,
      promise-crammed. You cannot feed capons so.
KING: I have nothing with this answer, Hamlet. These words
90   are not mine.
HAMLET: No, nor mine now. (*To* POLONIUS.) My lord, you played
      once i' th' university, you say?
POLONIUS: That did I, my lord; and was accounted a good
      actor.
95 HAMLET: What did you enact?
POLONIUS: I did enact Julius Caesar. I was killed i' th' Capitol;
      Brutus killed me.
HAMLET: It was a brute part of him to kill so capital a calf there.
      Be the players ready?
100 ROSENCRANTZ: Ay, my lord, they stay upon your patience.
QUEEN: Come hither, my dear Hamlet, sit by me.
HAMLET: No, good mother, here's metal more attractive.
POLONIUS: (*To the* KING.) O, ho! do you mark that?
HAMLET: Lady, shall I lie in your lap?

(*Lying down at* OPHELIA's *feet*.)

105 OPHELIA: No, my lord.
HAMLET: I mean, my head upon your lap?
OPHELIA: Ay, my lord.
HAMLET: Do you think I meant country matters?
OPHELIA: I think nothing, my lord.
110 HAMLET: That's a fair thought to lie between maids' legs.
OPHELIA: What is, my lord?
HAMLET: Nothing.
OPHELIA: You are merry, my lord.
HAMLET: Who, I?
115 OPHELIA: Ay, my lord.
HAMLET: O God, your only jig-maker! What should a man do but
      be merry? For look you how cheerfully my mother looks, and
      my father died within's two hours.
OPHELIA: Nay, 'tis twice two months, my lord.
120 HAMLET: So long? Nay then, let the devil wear black, for I'll
      have a suit of sables. O heavens! die two months ago, and
      not forgotten yet? Then there's hope a great man's memory

may outlive his life half a year, but, by'r lady 'a must build
churches then, or else shall 'a suffer not thinking on, with the   125
hobby-horse, whose epitaph is

      'For O, for O, the hobby-horse is forgot!'

(*The trumpets sound. Dumb Show follows.*)

(*Enter a* KING *and a* QUEEN [*very lovingly*]; *the* QUEEN *embracing him and he her.* [*She kneels, and makes show of protestation
unto him.*] *He takes her up, and declines his head upon her neck.
He lies him down upon a bank of flowers; she, seeing him asleep,
leaves him. Anon comes in another man, takes off his crown,
kisses it, pours poison in the sleeper's ears, and leaves him. The*
QUEEN *returns, finds the* KING *dead, makes passionate action.
The* POISONER *with some three or four come in again, seem to
condole with her. The dead body is carried away. The* POISONER
woos the QUEEN *with gifts; she seems harsh awhile, but in the end
accepts love.*)

(*Exeunt.*)

OPHELIA: What means this, my lord?
HAMLET: Marry, this is miching mallecho; it means mischief.
OPHELIA: Belike this show imports the argument of the play.

(*Enter* PROLOGUE.)

HAMLET: We shall know by this fellow. The players cannot   130
      keep counsel; they'll tell all.
OPHELIA: Will 'a tell us what this show meant?
HAMLET: Ay, or any show that you will show him. Be not you
      ashamed to show, he'll not shame to tell you what it means.
OPHELIA: You are naught, you are naught. I'll mark the play.   135
PROLOGUE:
            For us, and for our tragedy,
            Here stooping to your clemency,
            We beg your hearing patiently.

(*Exit.*)

HAMLET: Is this a prologue, or the posy of a ring?
OPHELIA: 'Tis brief, my lord.   140
HAMLET: As woman's love.

(*Enter* [*the* PLAYER] KING *and* QUEEN.)

PLAYER KING: Full thirty times hath Phoebus' cart gone round
      Neptune's salt wash and Tellus' orbèd ground,
      And thirty dozen moons with borrowed sheen
      About the world have times twelve thirties been,   145

---

78 **stithy** forge   81 **censure** opinion   84 **idle** crazy   87 **chameleon's dish**
the air, on which the chameleon was supposed to feed

---

126 **hobby-horse** the figure of a horse fastened round the waist of a
morris dancer. Puritan efforts to suppress the country sports in which
the hobby-horse figured led to a popular ballad lamenting the fact that
"the hobby-horse is forgot"   128 **miching mallecho** skulking or crafty
crime   135 **naught** naughty, lewd   139 **posy** brief motto engraved on
a fingerring   142 **Phoebus' cart** the sun's chariot   143 **Tellus' orbed
ground** the earth (Tellus was the Roman goddess of the earth)

Since love our hearts and Hymen did our hands
Unite comutual in most sacred bands.
PLAYER QUEEN: So many journeys may the sun and moon
Make us again count o'er ere love be done!
150 But woe is me, you are so sick of late,
So far from cheer and from your former state,
That I distrust you. Yet though I distrust,
Discomfort you, my lord, it nothing must.
For women's fear and love hold quantity,
155 In neither aught, or in extremity.
Now what my love is proof hath made you know,
And as my love is sized, my fear is so.
Where love is great, the littlest doubts are fear;
Where little fears grow great, great love grows there.
160 PLAYER KING: Faith, I must leave thee, love, and shortly too;
My operant powers their functions leave to do.
And thou shalt live in this fair world behind,
Honored, beloved; and haply one as kind
For husband shalt thou—
PLAYER QUEEN: O, confound the rest!
165 Such love must needs be treason in my breast.
In second husband let me be accurst!
None wed the second but who killed the first.
HAMLET: That's wormwood.
PLAYER QUEEN: The instances that second marriage move
170 Are base respects of thrift, but none of love.
A second time I kill my husband dead,
When second husband kisses me in bed.
PLAYER KING: I do believe you think what now you speak,
But what we do determine oft we break.
175 Purpose is but the slave to memory,
Of violent birth, but poor validity;
Which now, like fruit unripe, sticks on the tree,
But fall unshaken when they mellow be.
Most necessary 'tis that we forget
180 To pay ourselves what to ourselves is debt.
What to ourselves in passion we propose,
The passion ending, doth the purpose lose.
The violence of either grief or joy
Their own enactures with themselves destroy.
185 Where joy most revels, grief doth most lament;
Grief joys, joy grieves, on slender accident.
This world is not for aye, nor 'tis not strange
That even our loves should with our fortunes change;
For 'tis a question left us yet to prove,
190 Whether love lead fortune, or else fortune love.
The great man down, you mark his favorite flies;
The poor advanced makes friends of enemies;
And hitherto doth love on fortune tend,
For who not needs shall never lack a friend,
195 And who in want a hollow friend doth try,
Directly seasons him his enemy.
But orderly to end where I begun,
Our wills and fates do so contrary run
That our devices still are overthrown;

Our thoughts are ours, their ends none of our own. 200
So think thou wilt no second husband wed,
But die thy thoughts when thy first lord is dead.
PLAYER QUEEN: Nor earth to me give food, nor heaven light,
Sport and repose lock from me day and night.
To desperation turn my trust and hope, 205
An anchor's cheer in prison be my scope,
Each opposite that blanks the face of joy
Meet what I would have well, and it destroy,
Both here and hence pursue me lasting strife,
If once a widow, ever I be wife! 210
HAMLET: If she should break it now!
PLAYER KING: 'Tis deeply sworn. Sweet, leave me here awhile.
My spirits grow dull, and fain I would beguile
The tedious day with sleep.

(Sleeps.)

PLAYER QUEEN: Sleep rock thy brain.
And never come mischance between us twain! 215

(Exit.)

HAMLET: Madam, how like you this play?
QUEEN: The lady doth protest too much, methinks.
HAMLET: O, but she'll keep her word.
KING: Have you heard the argument? Is there no offence in't?
HAMLET: No, no, they do but jest, poison in jest; no offence 220
i' th' world.
KING: What do you call the play?
HAMLET: 'The Mouse-trap.' Marry, how? Tropically. This play is
the image of a murder done in Vienna. Gonzago is the duke's
name; his wife, Baptista. You shall see anon. 'Tis a 225
knavish piece of work, but what of that? Your majesty, and
we that have free souls, it touches us not. Let the galled jade
winch, our withers are unwrung.

(Enter LUCIANUS.)

This is one Lucianus, nephew to the king.
OPHELIA: You are as good as a chorus, my lord. 230
HAMLET: I could interpret between you and your love, if I could
see the puppets dallying.
OPHELIA: You are keen, my lord, you are keen.
HAMLET: It would cost you a groaning to take off mine edge.
OPHELIA: Still better, and worse. 235
HAMLET: So you mis-take your husbands.—Begin, murderer.
Leave thy damnable faces and begin. Come, the croaking
raven doth bellow for revenge.
LUCIANUS: Thoughts black, hands apt, drugs fit, and time
agreeing, 240
Confederate season, else no creature seeing.
Thou mixture rank, of midnight weeds collected,
With Hecate's ban thrice blasted, thrice infected,
Thy natural magic and dire property
On wholesome life usurp immediately.

(Pours the poison in his ears.)

---

146 **Hymen** god of marriage   152 **distrust** fear for   154 **hold quantity** are proportional, weigh alike   157 **as my love is sized** according to the greatness of my love   161 **operant** vital   169 **instances** motives   176 **validity** endurance   184 **enactures** enactments   187 **aye** ever   196 **seasons him** ripens him into

---

206 **anchor's** anchorite's   227 **galled jade** sorebacked horse   242 **Hecate** goddess of witchcraft; **blasted** fallen under a blight

245 HAMLET: 'A poisons him i' th' garden for his estate. His
name's Gonzago. The story is extant, and written in very
choice Italian. You shall see anon how the murderer gets
the love of Gonzago's wife.
OPHELIA: The king rises.
250 HAMLET: What, frighted with false fire?
QUEEN: How fares my lord?
POLONIUS: Give o'er the play.
KING: Give me some light. Away!
POLONIUS: Lights, lights, lights!

(*Exeunt all but* HAMLET *and* HORATIO.)

255 HAMLET: Why, let the strucken deer go weep,
The hart ungallèd play.
For some must watch, while some must sleep;
Thus runs the world away.

Would not this, sir, and a forest of feathers—if the rest of
260 my fortunes turn Turk with me—with two Provincial roses
on my razed shoes, get me a fellowship in a cry of players?
HORATIO: Half a share.
HAMLET: A whole one, I.

For thou dost know, O Damon dear,
265 This realm dismantled was
Of Jove himself, and now reigns here
A very, very—pajock.

HORATIO: You might have rhymed.
HAMLET: O good Horatio, I'll take the ghost's word for a
270 thousand pound. Didst perceive?
HORATIO: Very well, my lord.
HAMLET: Upon the talk of the poisoning.
HORATIO: I did very well note him.
HAMLET: Ah, ha! Come, some music. Come, the recorders.

275 For if the king like not the comedy,
Why then, belike, he likes it not, perdy.

Come, some music.

(*Enter* ROSENCRANTZ *and* GUILDENSTERN.)

GUILDENSTERN: Good my lord, vouchsafe me a word with you.
HAMLET: Sir, a whole history.
280 GUILDENSTERN: The king, sir—
HAMLET: Ay, sir what of him?
GUILDENSTERN: Is in his retirement marvellous distempered.
HAMLET: With drink, sir?
GUILDENSTERN: No, my lord, with choler.
285 HAMLET: Your wisdom should show itself more richer to signify
this to the doctor, for for me to put him to his purgation

would perhaps plunge him into more choler.
GUILDENSTERN: Good my lord, put your discourse into some
frame, and start not so wildly from my affair.
HAMLET: I am tame, sir. Pronounce. 290
GUILDENSTERN: The queen, your mother, in most great affliction
of spirit, hath sent me to you.
HAMLET: You are welcome.
GUILDENSTERN: Nay, good my lord, this courtesy is not of the
right breed. If it shall please you to make me a wholesome 295
answer, I will do your mother's commandment. If not, your
pardon and my return shall be the end of my business.
HAMLET: Sir, I cannot.
GUILDENSTERN: What, my lord?
HAMLET: Make you a wholesome answer; my wit's diseased. 300
But, sir, such answer as I can make, you shall command, or
rather, as you say, my mother. Therefore no more, but to the
matter. My mother, you say—
ROSENCRANTZ: Then thus she says: your behaviour hath
struck her into amazement and admiration. 305
HAMLET: O wonderful son, that can so stonish a mother! But
is there no sequel at the heels of this mother's admiration?
Impart.
ROSENCRANTZ: She desires to speak with you in her closet
ere you go to bed. 310
HAMLET: We shall obey, were she ten times our mother. Have
you any further trade with us?
ROSENCRANTZ: My lord, you once did love me.
HAMLET: And do still, by these pickers and stealers.
ROSENCRANTZ: Good my lord, what is your cause of distemper? 315
You do surely bar the door upon your own liberty, if you deny
your griefs to your friend.
HAMLET: Sir, I lack advancement.
ROSENCRANTZ: How can that be, when you have the voice
of the king himself for your succession in Denmark? 320
HAMLET: Ay, sir, but 'While the grass grows'—the proverb is
something musty.

(*Enter the* PLAYERS *with recorders.*)

O, the recorders! Let me see one. To withdraw with
you—why do you go about to recover the wind of me, as
if you would drive me into a toil? 325
GUILDENSTERN: O, my lord, if my duty be too bold, my love is too
unmannerly.
HAMLET: I do not well understand that. Will you play upon
this pipe?
GUILDENSTERN: My lord, I cannot. 330
HAMLET: I pray you.
GUILDENSTERN: Believe me, I cannot.
HAMLET: I beseech you.
GUILDENSTERN: I know no touch of it, my lord.
HAMLET: It is easy as lying. Govern these ventages with your 335
fingers and thumb, give it breath with your mouth, and it
will discourse most eloquent music. Look you, these are
the stops.

---

259 **feathers** plumes for actors' costumes   260 **Provincial roses** i.e.,
Provençal roses. Ribbon rosettes resembling these French roses were
used to decorate shoes   261 **razed** with ornamental slashing; **cry** company   267 **pajock** presumably a variant form of "patch-cock," a despicable person. Cf. 3.4.104   275 **For if . . . comedy** a seeming parody of
The Spanish Tragedy, 4.1.197–98 ("And if the world like not this tragedy, /
Hard is the hap of old Hieronimo"), where another revenger's dramatic
entertainment is referred to

---

287 **choler** one of the four bodily humors, an excess of which gave
rise to anger   295 **wholesome** reasonable   307 **admiration** wonder
314 **pickers and stealers** hands   321 **'while the grass grows'** a proverb ending 'the horse starves'   323 **withdraw** step aside for private
conversation   325 **toil** net, snare   335 **ventages** holes or stops in the
recorder

GUILDENSTERN: But these cannot I command to any utt'rance of
340   harmony. I have not the skill.
HAMLET: Why look you now, how unworthy a thing you make
    of me! You would play upon me, you would seem to know
    my stops, you would pluck out the heart of my mystery, you
    would sound me from my lowest note to the top of my
345   compass; and there is music, excellent voice, in this little
    organ, yet cannot you make it speak. 'Sblood, do you think
    I am easier to be played on than a pipe? Call me what
    instrument you will, though you can fret me, you cannot play
    upon me.

(*Enter* POLONIUS.)

350   God bless you, sir!
POLONIUS: My lord, the queen would speak with you, and
    presently.
HAMLET: Do you see yonder cloud that's almost in shape of a
    camel?
355 POLONIUS: By th' mass and 'tis, like a camel indeed.
HAMLET: Methinks it is like a weasel.
POLONIUS: It is backed like a weasel.
HAMLET: Or like a whale.
POLONIUS: Very like a whale.
360 HAMLET: Then I will come to my mother by and by. (*Aside.*) They
    fool me to the top of my bent.—I will come by and by.
POLONIUS: I will say so.

(*Exit* POLONIUS.)

HAMLET: 'By and by' is easily said. Leave me, friends.

(*Exeunt all but* HAMLET.)

    'Tis now the very witching time of night,
365   When churchyards yawn and hell itself breathes out
    Contagion to this world. Now could I drink hot blood,
    And do such bitter business as the day
    Would quake to look on. Soft, now to my mother.
    O heart, lose not thy nature; let not ever
370   The soul of Nero enter this firm bosom.
    Let me be cruel, not unnatural;
    I will speak daggers to her, but use none.
    My tongue and soul in this be hypocrites:
    How in my words somever she be shent,
375   To give them seals never my soul consent!

(*Exit.*)

SCENE III

Enter KING, ROSENCRANTZ, *and* GUILDENSTERN.

KING: I like him not, nor stands it safe with us
    To let his madness range. Therefore prepare you,
    I your commission will forthwith dispatch,
    And he to England shall along with you.

The terms of our estate may not endure   5
Hazard so near's as doth hourly grow
Out of his brows.
GUILDENSTERN: We will ourselves provide,
    Most holy and religious fear it is
    To keep those many many bodies safe
    That live and feed upon your majesty.   10
ROSENCRANTZ: The single and peculiar life is bound
    With all the strength and armor of the mind
    To keep itself from noyance, but much more
    That spirit upon whose weal depends and rests
    The lives of many. The cess of majesty   15
    Dies not alone, but like a gulf doth draw
    What's near it with it. It is a massy wheel
    Fixed on the summit of the highest mount,
    To whose huge spokes ten thousand lesser things
    Are mortised and adjoined, which when it falls,   20
    Each small annexment, petty consequence,
    Attends the boist'rous ruin. Never alone
    Did the king sigh, but with a general groan.
KING: Arm you, I pray you, to this speedy voyage,
    For we will fetters put about this fear,   25
    Which now goes too free-footed.
ROSENCRANTZ: We will haste us.

(*Exeunt Gentlemen* [ROSENCRANTZ *and* GUILDENSTERN].)

(*Enter* POLONIUS.)

POLONIUS: My lord, he's going to his mother's closet.
    Behind the arras I'll convey myself
    To hear the process. I'll warrant she'll tax him home,
    And as you said, and wisely was it said,   30
    'Tis meet that some more audience than a mother,
    Since nature makes them partial, should o'erhear
    The speech of vantage. Fare you well, my liege.
    I'll call upon you ere you go to bed,
    And tell you what I know.   35
KING: Thanks, dear my lord. (*Exit* POLONIUS.)
    O, my offence is rank, it smells to heaven;
    It hath the primal eldest curse upon't,
    A brother's murder. Pray can I not,
    Though inclination be as sharp as will.
    My stronger guilt defeats my strong intent,   40
    And like a man to double business bound,
    I stand in pause where I shall first begin,
    And both neglect. What if this cursèd hand
    Were thicker than itself with brother's blood,
    Is there not rain enough in the sweet heavens   45
    To wash it white as snow? Whereto serves mercy
    But to confront the visage of offence?
    And what's in prayer but this twofold force,
    To be forestallèd ere we come to fall,
    Or pardoned being down? Then I'll look up.   50
    My fault is past. But, O, what form of prayer

III.iii. 5 **terms of our estate** conditions required for our rule as king
7 **brows** threatening looks that suggest the dangerous plots Hamlet's
brain is hatching   11 **peculiar** private   13 **noyance** harm   15 **cess**
cessation, extinction   20 **mortised** jointed (as with mortise and
tenon)   33 **of vantage** (1) in addition; (2) from a convenient place for
listening   39 **will** carnal desire

---

348 **fret** (1) a stop on the fingerboard of a guitar (2) annoy   370 **Nero**
Roman emperor who murdered his mother   374 **somever,** soever;
shent reproved, abused

Can serve my turn? 'Forgive me my foul murder'?
That cannot be, since I am still possessed
Of those effects for which I did the murder—
55   My crown, mine own ambition, and my queen.
May one be pardoned and retain th' offence?
In the corrupted currents of this world
Offence's gilded hand may shove by justice,
And oft 'tis seen the wicked prize itself
60   Buys out the law. But 'tis not so above
There is no shuffling: there the action lies
In his true nature, and we ourselves compelled,
Even to the teeth and forehead of our faults,
To give in evidence. What then? What rests?
65   Try what repentance can. What can it not?
Yet what can it when one can not repent?
O wretched state! O bosom black as death!
O limèd soul, that struggling to be free
Art more engaged! Help, angels! Make assay.
70   Bow, stubborn knees, and heart with strings of steel,
Be soft as sinews of the new-born babe.
All may be well.

(*He kneels.*)

(*Enter* HAMLET.)

HAMLET: Now might I do it pat, now 'a is a-praying,
And now I'll do't—and so 'a goes to heaven,
75   And so am I revenged. That would be scanned.
A villain kills my father, and for that,
I, his sole son, do this same villain send
To heaven.
Why, this is hire and salary, not revenge.
80   'A took my father grossly, full of bread,
With all his crimes broad blown, as flush as May;
And how his audit stands who knows save heaven?
But in our circumstance and course of thought
'Tis heavy with him; and am I then revenged
85   To take him in the purging of his soul,
When he is fit and seasoned for his passage?
No.
Up, sword, and know thou a more horrid hent.
When he is drunk asleep, or in his rage,
90   Or in th' incestuous pleasure of his bed,
At game a-swearing, or about some act
That has no relish of salvation in't—
Then trip him, that his heels may kick at heaven,
And that his soul may be as damned and black
95   As hell, whereto it goes. My mother stays.
This physic but prolongs thy sickly days.

(*Exit.*)

KING: (*Rising.*) My words fly up, my thoughts remain below.
Words without thoughts never to heaven go.

(*Exit.*)

─────────────

61 **shuffling** doubledealing; **action** legal action   68 **limèd** soul caught
by sin as the bird by lime   69 **assay** an effort   80 **grossly** unprepared
spiritually   81 **as flush as May** in full flower   83 **in our circumstance**
considering all evidence; **course** beaten way, habit   88 **hent** occasion,
opportunity

SCENE IV

Enter [QUEEN] GERTRUDE *and* POLONIUS.

POLONIUS: 'A will come straight. Look you lay home to him.
Tell him his pranks have been too broad to bear with,
And that your grace hath screened and stood between
Much heat and him. I'll silence me even here.
Pray you be round.   5
QUEEN: I'll warrant you. Fear me not.
Withdraw, I hear him coming.

(POLONIUS *goes behind the arras.*)

(*Enter* HAMLET.)

HAMLET: Now, mother, what's the matter?
QUEEN: Hamlet, thou hast thy father much offended.
HAMLET: Mother, you have my father much offended.
QUEEN: Come, come, you answer with an idle tongue.   10
HAMLET: Go, go, you question with a wicked tongue.
QUEEN: Why, how, now, Hamlet?
HAMLET: What's the matter now?
QUEEN: Have you forgot me?
HAMLET: No, by the rood, not so:
You are the queen, your husband's brother's wife,
And would it were not so, you are my mother.   15
QUEEN: Nay, then I'll set those to you that can speak.
HAMLET: Come, come, and sit you down. You shall not budge.
You go not till I set you up a glass
Where you may see the inmost part of you.
QUEEN: What will thou do? Thou wilt not murder me?   20
Help, ho!
POLONIUS: (*Behind.*) What, ho! help!
HAMLET: (*Draws.*) How now! a rat?
Dead for a ducat, dead!

(*Thrusts his sword through the arras and kills* POLONIUS.)

POLONIUS: (*Behind.*) O, I am slain!   25
QUEEN: O me, what hast thou done?
HAMLET: Nay, I know not.
Is it the king?
QUEEN: O, what a rash and bloody deed is this!
HAMLET: A bloody deed? Almost as bad, good mother,
As kill a king and marry with his brother.   30
QUEEN: As kill a king?
HAMLET: Ay, lady, it was my word.

(*Lifts up the arras and sees the body of* POLONIUS.)

Thou wretched, rash, intruding fool, farewell!
I took thee for thy better. Take thy fortune.
Thou find'st to be too busy is some danger.—
Leave wringing of your hands. Peace, sit you down   35
And let me wring your heart, for so I shall
If it be made of penetrable stuff,

─────────────

III.iv. 5 Following Polonius's "Pray you be round" (which in *F* reads
"Pray you be round with him"), *F* adds the line: "*Hamlet within.* Mother,
mother, mother"   13 **rood** cross

If damnèd custom have not brazed it so
That it be proof and bulwark against sense.

40 QUEEN: What have I done that thou dar'st wag thy tongue
In noise so rude against me?

HAMLET: Such an act
That blurs the grace and blush of modesty,
Calls virtue hypocrite, takes off the rose
From the fair forehead of an innocent love,
45 And sets a blister there, makes marriage-vows
As false as dicers' oaths. O, such a deed
As from the body of contraction plucks
The very soul, and sweet religion makes
A rhapsody of words. Heaven's face does glow
50 O'er this solidity and compound mass
With heated visage, as against the doom—
Is thought-sick at the act.

QUEEN: Ay me, what act,
That roars so loud, and thunders in the index?

HAMLET: Look here, upon this picture and on this.
55 The counterfeit presentment of two brothers.
See what a grace was seated on this brow:
Hyperion's curls, the front of Jove himself,
An eye like Mars, to threaten and command,
A station like the herald Mercury
60 New lighted on a heaven-kissing hill—
A combination and a form indeed
Where every god did seem to set his seal
To give the world assurance of a man.
This was your husband. Look you now what follows.
65 Here is your husband, like a mildewed ear
Blasting his wholesome brother. Have you eyes?
Could you on this fair mountain leave to feed,
And batten on this moor? Ha! have you eyes?
You cannot call it love, for at your age
70 The heyday in the blood is tame, it's humble,
And waits upon the judgement, and what judgement
Would step from this to this? Sense sure you have,
Else could you not have motion, but sure that sense
Is apoplexed, for madness would not err
75 Nor sense to ecstasy was ne'er so thralled
But it reserved some quantity of choice
To serve in such a difference. What devil was't
That thus hath cozened you at hoodman-blind?
Eyes without feeling, feeling without sight,
80 Ears without hands or eyes, smelling sans all,
Or but a sickly part of one true sense
Could not so mope. O shame! where is thy blush?
Rebellious hell,
If thou canst mutine in a matron's bones,
85 To flaming youth let virtue be as wax

And melt in her own fire. Proclaim no shame
When the compulsive ardor gives the charge,
Since frost itself as actively doth burn,
And reason pandars will.

QUEEN: O Hamlet, speak no more!
Thou turn'st mine eyes into my very soul,   90
And there I see such black and grainèd spots
As will not leave their tinct.

HAMLET: Nay, but to live
In the rank sweat of an enseamèd bed,
Stewed in corruption, honeying and making love
Over the nasty sty—   95

QUEEN: O, speak to me no more!
These words like daggers enter in mine ears.
No more, sweet Hamlet.

HAMLET: A murderer and a villain,
A slave that is not twentieth part the tithe
Of your precedent lord, a vice of kings,
A cutpurse of the empire and the rule,   100
That from a shelf the precious diadem stole
And put it in his pocket—

QUEEN: No more.

(*Enter* GHOST.)

HAMLET: A king of shreds and patches—
Save me and hover o'er me with your wings,   105
You heavenly guards! What would your gracious figure?

QUEEN: Alas, he's mad.

HAMLET: Do you not come your tardy son to chide,
That lapsed in time and passion lets go by
Th' important acting of your dread command?   110
O, say!

GHOST: Do not forget. This visitation
Is but to whet thy almost blunted purpose.
But look, amazement on thy mother sits.
O, step between her and her fighting soul!   115
Conceit in weakest bodies strongest works.
Speak to her, Hamlet.

HAMLET: How is it with you, lady?

QUEEN: Alas, how is't with you,
That you do bend your eye on vacancy,
And with th' incorporal air do hold discourse?   120
Forth at your eyes your spirits wildly peep,
And as the sleeping soldiers in th' alarm,
Your bedded hair like life in excrements
Start up and stand an end. O gentle son,
Upon the heat and flame of thy distemper   125
Sprinkle cool patience. Whereon do you look?

HAMLET: On him, on him! Look you how pale he glares.
His form and cause conjoined, preaching to stones,
Would make them capable.—Do not look upon me,
Lest with this piteous action you convert   130
My stern effects. Then what I have to do
Will want true color—tears perchance for blood.

---

38 **brazed** plated it as with brass   39 **proof** impenetrable, as of armor   47 **contraction** the contract of marriage   50 **this solidity and compound mass** the earth, as compounded of the four elements   51 **doom** Judgment Day   53 **index** table of contents; thus, indication of what is to follow   55 **counterfeit presentment** portrait   57 **front** forehead   59 **station** bearing figure   68 **batten** feed like an animal   70 **heyday** ardor   72 **Sense** the senses collectively, which according to Aristotelian tradition are found in all creatures that have the power of locomotion   75 **ecstasy** madness   78 **hoodman-blind** blindman's bluff   80 **sans** without   82 **mope** act without full use of one's wits

---

89 **will** desire   91 **grainèd spots** indelible stains   92 **tinct** color   93 **enseamèd** greasy   99 **vice** a character in the morality plays, presented often as a buffoon (here, a caricature)   116 **Conceit** imagination   123 **excrements** nails, hair (whatever grows out of the body)   124 **an** on   129 **capable** able to respond   132 **want** lack

QUEEN: To whom do you speak this?

HAMLET: Do you see nothing there?

135 QUEEN: Nothing at all, yet all that is I see.

HAMLET: Nor did you nothing hear?

QUEEN: No, nothing but ourselves.

HAMLET: Why, look you there. Look, how it steals away.
    My father, in his habit as he lived!

140   Look where he goes even now out at the portal.

(*Exit* GHOST.)

QUEEN: This is the very coinage of your brain.
    This bodiless creation ecstasy
    Is very cunning in.

HAMLET: My pulse as yours doth temperately keep time,

145   And makes us healthful music. It is not madness
    That I have uttered. Bring me to the test,
    And I the matter will re-word, which madness
    Would gambol from. Mother, for love of grace,
    Lay not that flattering unction to your soul,

150   That not your trespass but my madness speaks.
    It will but skin and film the ulcerous place
    Whiles rank corruption, mining all within,
    Infects unseen. Confess yourself to heaven,
    Repent what's past, avoid what is to come,

155   And do not spread the compost on the weeds,
    To make them ranker. Forgive me this my virtue,
    For in the fatness of these pursy times
    Virtue itself of vice must pardon beg,
    Yea, curb and woo for leave to do him good.

160 QUEEN: O Hamlet, thou hast cleft my heart in twain.

HAMLET: O, throw away the worser part of it,
    And live the purer with the other half.
    Good night—but go not to my uncle's bed.
    Assume a virtue, if you have it not.

165   That monster custom, who all sense doth eat,
    Of habits devil, is angel yet in this,
    That to the use of actions fair and good
    He likewise gives a frock or livery
    That aptly is put on. Refrain to-night,

170   And that shall lend a kind of easiness
    To the next abstinence; the next more easy;
    For use almost can change the stamp of nature,
    And either curb the devil, or throw him out
    With wondrous potency. Once more, good night,

175   And when you are desirous to be blest,
    I'll blessing beg of you. For this same lord,
    I do repent; but heaven hath pleased it so,

To punish me with this, and this with me,
    That I must be their scourge and minister.
    I will bestow him and will answer well   180
    The death I gave him. So, again, good night.
    I must be cruel only to be kind.
    This bad begins and worse remains behind.
    One word more, good lady.

QUEEN: What shall I do?

HAMLET: Not this, by no means, that I bid you do: 185
    Let the bloat king tempt you again to bed,
    Pinch wanton on your cheek, call you his mouse,
    And let him, for a pair of reechy kisses,
    Or paddling in your neck with his damned fingers,
    Make you to ravel all this matter out,   190
    That I essentially am not in madness,
    But mad in craft. 'Twere good you let him know,
    For who that's but a queen, fair, sober, wise,
    Would from a paddock, from a bat, a gib,
    Such dear concernings hide? Who would so do?   195
    No, in despite of sense and secrecy,
    Unpeg the basket on the house's top,
    Let the birds fly, and like the famous ape,
    To try conclusions, in the basket creep
    And break your own neck down.   200

QUEEN: Be thou assured, if words be made of breath
    And breath of life, I have no life to breathe
    What thou hast said to me.

HAMLET: I must to England; you know that?

QUEEN: Alack,
    I had forgot. 'Tis so concluded on.   205

HAMLET: There's letters sealed, and my two school-fellows,
    Whom I will trust as I will adders fanged,
    They bear the mandate; they must sweep my way
    And marshal me to knavery. Let it work,
    For 'tis the sport to have the engineer   210
    Hoist with his own petar; and 't shall go hard
    But I will delve one yard below their mines
    And blow them at the moon. O, 'tis most sweet
    When in one line two crafts directly meet.
    This man shall set me packing.   215
    I'll lug the guts into the neighbour room.
    Mother, good night indeed. This counsellor
    Is now most still, most secret and most grave,
    Who was in life a foolish prating knave.
    Come sir, to draw toward an end with you.   220
    Good night, mother.

(*Exit* [HAMLET *tugging in* POLONIUS].)

---

148 **gambol** leap or start, as a shying horse   149 **unction** ointment; hence, soothing notion   152 **mining** undermining   157 **fatness** grossness, slackness; **pursy** corpulent   165 **who all sense doth eat** who consumes all human sense, both bodily and spiritual   166 **Of habits devil** being a devil in, or in respect of, habits (with a play on "habits," as meaning both settled practices and garments, whereby devilish practices contrast with "actions fair and good," line 167, and devilish garments contrast with the "frock or livery" of line 168, which custom in its angelic aspect provides)

183 **This** i.e., the death of Polonius (cf. line 178); **remains behind** is yet to come   188 **reechy** dirty   191 **essentially** in fact   194 **paddock** toad; **gib** tom-cat   197–200 **Unpeg the basket . . . neck down** the story is lost (in it, apparently, the ape carries a cage of birds to the top of a house, releases them by accident, and, surprised at their flight, imagines he can imitate it by first creeping into the basket and then leaping out. The moral of the story, for the queen, is not to expose herself to destruction by making public what good sense decrees should be kept secret.)   211 **petar** a bomb or charge for blowing in gates   217 **indeed** in earnest (cf. lines 163, 174, 181)

ACT FOUR

SCENE I

Enter KING [*to the*] QUEEN, *with* ROSENCRANTZ *and* GUILDENSTERN.

KING: There's matter in these sighs, these profound heaves,
  You must translate, 'tis fit we understand them.
  Where is your son?
QUEEN: Bestow this place on us a little while.

(*Exeunt* ROSENCRANTZ *and* GUILDENSTERN.)

5   Ah, mine own lord, what have I seen to-night!
KING: What, Gertrude, how does Hamlet?
QUEEN: Mad as the sea and wind when both contend
  Which is the mightier. In his lawless fit,
  Behind the arras hearing something stir,
10 Whips out his rapier, cries 'A rat, a rat!'
  And in this brainish apprehension kills
  The unseen good old man.
KING: O heavy deed!
  It had been so with us had we been there.
  His liberty is full of threats to all—
15 To you yourself, to us, to every one.
  Alas, how shall this bloody deed be answered?
  It will be laid to us, whose providence
  Should have kept short, restrained, and out of haunt,
  This mad young man. But so much was our love,
20 We would not understand what was most fit,
  But like the owner of a foul disease,
  To keep it from divulging, let it feed
  Even on the pith of life. Where is he gone?
QUEEN: To draw apart the body he hath killed,
25 O'er whom his very madness, like some ore
  Among a mineral of metals base,
  Shows itself pure: 'a weeps for what is done.
KING: O Gertrude, come away!
  The sun no sooner shall the mountains touch
30 But we will ship him hence, and this vile deed
  We must with all our majesty and skill,
  Both countenance and excuse. Ho, Guildenstern!

(*Enter* ROSENCRANTZ *and* GUILDENSTERN.)

  Friends both, go join you with some further aid.
  Hamlet in madness hath Polonius slain,
35 And from his mother's closet hath he dragged him.
  Go seek him out; speak fair, and bring the body
  Into the chapel. I pray you haste in this.

(*Exeunt* ROSENCRANTZ *and* GUILDENSTERN.)

  Come, Gertrude, we'll call up our wisest friends
  And let them know both what we mean to do
40 And what's untimely done; so haply slander—
  Whose whisper o'er the world's diameter,

As level as the cannon to his blank,
  Transports his poisoned shot—may miss our name,
  And hit the woundless air. O, come away!
  My soul is full of discord and dismay.   45

(*Exeunt.*)

SCENE II

Enter HAMLET.

HAMLET: Safely stowed.—But soft, what noise? who calls on
  Hamlet? O, here they come.

([*Enter*] ROSENCRANTZ, [GUILDENSTERN,] *and* OTHERS.)

ROSENCRANTZ: What have you done, my lord, with the dead
  body?
HAMLET: Compounded it with dust, whereto 'tis kin.   5
ROSENCRANTZ: Tell us where 'tis, that we may take it thence
  And bear it to the chapel.
HAMLET: Do not believe it.
ROSENCRANTZ: Believe what?
HAMLET: That I can keep your counsel and not mine own.   10
  Besides, to be demanded of a sponge—what replication should
  be made by the son of a king?
ROSENCRANTZ: Take you me for a sponge, my lord?
HAMLET: Ay, sir, that soaks up the king's countenance, his
  rewards, his authorities. But such officers do the king best   15
  service in the end. He keeps them, like an apple in the corner
  of his jaw, first mouthed to be last swallowed. When he needs
  what you have gleaned, it is but squeezing you and, sponge,
  you shall be dry again.
ROSENCRANTZ: I understand you not, my lord.   20
HAMLET: I am glad of it. A knavish speech sleeps in a foolish
  ear.
ROSENCRANTZ: My lord, you must tell us where the body is, and
  go with us to the king.
HAMLET: The body is with the king, but the king is not with the   25
  body.
    The king is a thing—
GUILDENSTERN: A thing, my lord!
HAMLET: Of nothing. Bring me to him. Hide fox, and all after.

(*Exeunt.*)

SCENE III

Enter KING, *and two or three.*

KING: I have sent to seek him, and to find the body.
  How dangerous is it that this man goes loose!
  Yet must not we put the strong law on him.

---

42 **As level as** sure of aim; **blank** target

IV.ii. 1 After the words "Safely stowed," *F* adds the line: "*Gentlemen within. Hamlet, Lord Hamlet.*" Here, as at 3.4.5 "when a character speaks of hearing someone coming, *F* provides, though *Q* does not, for the audience to hear it too" (Jenkins, *SB*, 13.35) 11 **replication** reply 29 **Hide fox, and all after** presumably a cry in some game such as hide-and-seek. The words, which do not occur in *Q2,* may be an actor's addition

---

IV.i. The action is continuous with that of the preceding scene. The Queen does not leave the stage. 2 **translate** explain 11 **brainish apprehension** frenzied delusion 18 **out of haunt** away from society 26 **mineral** mine

He's loved of the distracted multitude,
5   Who like not in their judgement but their eyes,
     And where 'tis so, th' offender's scourge is weighed,
     But never the offence. To bear all smooth and even,
     This sudden sending him away must seem
     Deliberate pause. Diseases desperate grown
10   By desperate appliance are relieved,
     Or not at all.

(*Enter* ROSENCRANTZ, [GUILDENSTERN,] *and all the rest.*)

                    How now! what hath befall'n?
ROSENCRANTZ: Where the dead body is bestowed, my lord,
     We cannot get from him.
KING: But where is he?
ROSENCRANTZ: Without, my lord; guarded, to know your
     pleasure.
15   KING: Bring him before us.
ROSENCRANTZ: Ho! bring in the lord.

(*They enter* [*with* HAMLET].)

KING: Now, Hamlet, where's Polonius?
HAMLET: At supper.
KING: At supper? Where?
HAMLET: Not where he eats, but where 'a is eaten. A certain
20   convocation of politic worms are e'en at him. Your worm is
     your only emperor for diet. We fat all creatures else to fat us,
     and we fat ourselves for maggots. Your fat king and your lean
     beggar is but variable service—two dishes, but to one table.
     That's the end.
25   KING: Alas, alas!
HAMLET: A man may fish with the worm that hath eat of a king,
     and eat of the fish that hath fed of that worm.
KING: What dost thou mean by this?
HAMLET: Nothing but to show you how a king may go a
30   progress through the guts of a beggar.
KING: Where is Polonius?
HAMLET: In heaven. Send thither to see. If your messenger find
     him not there, seek him i' th' other place yourself. But if,
     indeed, you find him not within this month, you shall nose
35   him as you go up the stairs into the lobby.
KING: (*To* ATTENDANTS.) Go seek him there.
HAMLET: 'A will stay till you come.

(*Exeunt* ATTENDANTS.)

KING: Hamlet, this deed, for thine especial safety—
     Which we do tender, as we dearly grieve
40   For that which thou hast done—must send thee hence
     With fiery quickness. Therefore prepare thyself.
     The bark is ready, and the wind at help,
     Th' associates tend, and everything is bent
     For England.
HAMLET: For England?
KING: Ay, Hamlet.
HAMLET: Good.
45   KING: So is it, if thou knew'st our purposes.

HAMLET: I see a cherub that sees them. But come, for England!
     Farewell, dear mother.
KING: Thy loving father, Hamlet.
HAMLET: My mother. Father and mother is man and wife, man
     and wife is one flesh. So, my mother. Come, for England.   50

(*Exit.*)

KING: Follow him at foot: tempt him with speed aboard.
     Delay it not: I'll have him hence to-night.
     Away! for every thing is sealed and done
     That else leans on th' affair. Pray you make haste.

(*Exeunt all but the* KING.)

     And, England, if my love thou hold'st at aught—   55
     As my great power thereof may give thee sense,
     Since yet thy cicatrice looks raw and red
     After the Danish sword, and thy free awe
     Pays homage to us—thou mayst not coldly set
     Our sovereign process, which imports at full   60
     By letters congruing to that effect
     The present death of Hamlet. Do it, England.
     For like the hectic in my blood he rages,
     And thou must cure me. Till I know 'tis done,
     Howe'er my haps, my joys were ne'er begun.   65

(*Exit.*)

SCENE IV

Enter FORTINBRAS *with his* ARMY *over the stage.*

FORTINBRAS: Go, captain, from me greet the Danish king.
     Tell him that by his license Fortinbras
     Craves the conveyance of a promised march
     Over his kingdom. You know the rendezvous.
     If that his majesty would aught with us,   5
     We shall express our duty in his eye,
     And let him know so.
CAPTAIN: I will do't, my lord.
FORTINBRAS: Go softly on.

(*Exeunt all but the* CAPTAIN.)

(*Enter* HAMLET, ROSENCRANTZ, [GUILDENSTERN,] *and* OTHERS.)

HAMLET: Good sir, whose powers are these?
CAPTAIN: They are of Norway, sir.   10
HAMLET: How purposed, sir, I pray you?
CAPTAIN: Against some part of Poland.
HAMLET: Who commands them, sir?
CAPTAIN: The nephew to old Norway, Fortinbras.

---

46 **cherub** one of the cherubim, the watchmen or sentinels of heaven,
and thus endowed with the keenest vision   57 **cicatrice** scar, used here
of memory of a defeat   59 **coldly set** regard with indifference   60 **process** mandate   61 **congruing to** in accordance with   63 **hectic** con-
sumptive fever   65 **haps** fortunes

IV.iv. 3 **conveyance** conduct   6 **eye** presence

IV.iii. 9 **Deliberate pause** carefully considered   30 **progress** the state
journey of a ruler   39 **tender** value

15 HAMLET: Goes it against the main of Poland, sir,
　　Or for some frontier?
CAPTAIN: Truly to speak, and with no addition,
　　We go to gain a little patch of ground
　　That hath in it no profit but the name.
20 　　To pay five ducats, five, I would not farm it;
　　Nor will it yield to Norway or the Pole
　　A ranker rate should it be sold in fee.
HAMLET: Why, then the Polack never will defend it.
CAPTAIN: Yes, it is already garrisoned.
25 HAMLET: Two thousand souls and twenty thousand ducats
　　Will not debate the question of this straw.
　　This is th' imposthume of much wealth and peace,
　　That inward breaks, and shows no cause without
　　Why the man dies. I humbly thank you, sir.
30 CAPTAIN: God buy you, sir.

(*Exit.*)

ROSENCRANTZ: 　　　　　Will 't please you go, my lord?
HAMLET: I'll be with you straight. Go a little before.

(*Exeunt all but* HAMLET.)

　　How all occasions do inform against me,
　　And spur my dull revenge! What is a man,
　　If his chief good and market of his time
35 　　Be but to sleep and feed? A beast, no more.
　　Sure he that made us with such large discourse,
　　Looking before and after, gave us not
　　That capability and godlike reason
　　To fust in us unused. Now, whether it be
40 　　Bestial oblivion, or some craven scruple
　　Of thinking too precisely on th' event—
　　A thought which, quartered, hath but one part wisdom
　　And ever three parts coward—I do not know
　　Why yet I live to say 'This thing's to do',
45 　　Sith I have cause, and will, and strength, and means,
　　To do 't. Examples gross as earth exhort me:
　　Witness this army of such mass and charge,
　　Led by a delicate and tender prince,
　　Whose spirit, with divine ambition puffed,
50 　　Makes mouths at the invisible event,
　　Exposing what is mortal and unsure
　　To all that fortune, death, and danger dare,
　　Even for an eggshell. Rightly to be great
　　Is not to stir without great argument,
55 　　But greatly to find quarrel in a straw
　　When honor's at the stake. How stand I then,
　　That have a father killed, a mother stained,
　　Excitements of my reason and my blood,
　　And let all sleep, while to my shame I see

The imminent death of twenty thousand men 60
That for a fantasy and trick of fame
Go to their graves like beds, fight for a plot
Whereon the numbers cannot try the cause,
Which is not tomb enough and continent
To hide the slain? O, from this time forth, 65
My thoughts be bloody, or be nothing worth!

(*Exit.*)

SCENE V

Enter HORATIO, [QUEEN] GERTRUDE, *and a* GENTLEMAN.

QUEEN: I will not speak with her.
GENTLEMAN: She is importunate, indeed distract.
　　Her mood will needs be pitied.
QUEEN: 　　　　　　　What would she have?
GENTLEMAN: She speaks much of her father, says she hears
　　There's tricks i' th' world, and hems, and beats her heart, 5
　　Spurns enviously at straws, speaks things in doubt
　　That carry but half sense. Her speech is nothing,
　　Yet the unshaped use of it doth move
　　The hearers to collection; they aim at it,
　　And botch the words up fit to their own thoughts, 10
　　Which, as her winks and nods and gestures yield them,
　　Indeed would make one think there might be thought,
　　Though nothing sure, yet much unhappily.
HORATIO: 'Twere good she were spoken with, for she may strew
　　Dangerous conjectures in ill-breeding minds. 15
QUEEN: Let her come in. (*Exit* GENTLEMAN.)
　　(*Aside.*) To my sick soul, as sin's true nature is,
　　Each toy seems prologue to some great amiss.
　　So full of artless jealousy is guilt,
　　It spills itself in fearing to be spilt. 20

(*Enter* OPHELIA [*distracted*].)

OPHELIA: Where is the beauteous majesty of Denmark?
QUEEN: How now, Ophelia!
OPHELIA: (*She sings.*)

　　　　How should I your true love know
　　　　From another one?
　　　　By his cockle hat and staff, 25
　　　　And his sandal shoon.

QUEEN: Alas, sweet lady, what imports this song?
OPHELIA: Say you? Nay, pray you mark. (*Song.*)

　　　　He is dead and gone, lady,
　　　　He is dead and gone; 30

---

15 **main** chief part　17 **addition** exaggeration　20 **To pay** i.e., for a yearly rental　22 **a ranker rate** a greater price; sold in fee sold with absolute and perpetual possession　27 **imposthume** abscess　32 **inform** take shape　34 **market** profit　36 **discourse** power of reasoning 39 **fust** grow musty　50 **Makes mouths at** makes scornful faces at, derides　53–56 **Rightly to be great . . . honor's at the stake** i.e., to be rightly great is *not* to refuse to act ("stir") in a dispute ("argument") because the grounds are insufficient, but to be moved to action even in trivial circumstances where a question of honor is involved

---

63 **try the cause** settle by combat　64 **continent** receptacle

IV.v. 6 **Spurns enviously at straws** takes exception, spitefully, to trifles　7 **nothing** nonsense　8 **unshaped use** disordered manner 9 **collection** attempts at shaping meaning; **aim** guess　13 **sure** certain 18 **toy** trifle　19 **artless jealousy** ill-concealed suspicion　20 **spills** destroys　25 **cockle hat** hat bearing a cockle shell, worn by a pilgrim who had been to the shrine of St. James of Compostella, in Spain　26 **shoon** shoes

At his head a grass-green turf,
At his heels a stone.

O, ho!
QUEEN: Nay, but Ophelia—
OPHELIA: Pray you mark.

(*Sings.*)

35   White his shroud as the mountain snow—

(*Enter* KING.)

QUEEN: Alas, look here, my lord.
OPHELIA: (*Song.*)

           Larded all with sweet flowers;
           Which bewept to the grave did not go
           With true-love showers.

40 KING: How do you, pretty lady?
OPHELIA: Well, good dild you! They say the owl was a baker's
     daughter. Lord, we know what we are, but know not what we
     may be. God be at your table!
KING: Conceit upon her father.
45 OPHELIA: Pray let's have no words of this, but when they ask you
     what it means, say you this:

(*Song.*)

           To-morrow is Saint Valentine's day,
           All in the morning betime,
           And I a maid at your window,
50   To be your Valentine.
           Then up he rose, and donned his clo'es,
           And dupped the chamber-door,
           Let in the maid, that out a maid
           Never departed more.

55 KING: Pretty Ophelia—
OPHELIA: Indeed, without an oath, I'll make an end on't:

(*Sings.*)

           By Gis and by Saint Charity,
           Alack, and fie for shame!
           Young men will do't, if they come to't;
60   By cock, they are to blame.
           Quoth she 'Before you tumbled me,
           You promised me to wed.'

He answers:

           'So would I a' done, by yonder sun,

           An thou hadst not come to my bed.'   65

KING: How long hath she been thus?
OPHELIA: I hope all will be well. We must be patient, but I cannot
     choose but weep, to think they would lay him i' th' cold
     ground. My brother shall know of it, and so I thank you for
     your good counsel. Come, my coach! Good night, ladies, good   70
     night. Sweet ladies, good night, good night.

(*Exit.*)

KING: Follow her close; give her good watch, I pray you.

(*Exeunt* HORATIO *and* GENTLEMEN.)

           O, this is the poison of deep grief; it springs
           All from her father's death, and now behold!
           O Gertrude, Gertrude,   75
           When sorrows come, they come not single spies,
           But in battalions: first, her father slain;
           Next, your son gone, and he most violent author
           Of his own just remove; the people muddied,
           Thick and unwholesome in their thoughts and whispers   80
           For good Polonius' death; and we have done but greenly
           In hugger-mugger to inter him; poor Ophelia
           Divided from herself and her fair judgement,
           Without the which we are pictures, or mere beasts;
           Last, and as much containing as all these,   85
           Her brother is in secret come from France,
           Feeds on his wonder, keeps himself in clouds,
           And wants not buzzers to infect his ear
           With pestilent speeches of his father's death.
           Wherein necessity, of matter beggared,   90
           Will nothing stick our person to arraign
           In ear and ear, O my dear Gertrude, this,
           Like to a murd'ring piece, in many places
           Gives me superfluous death. Attend,   (*A noise within.*)

(*Enter a* MESSENGER.)

           Where are my Switzers? Let them guard the door.   95
           What is the matter?
MESSENGER: Save yourself, my lord.
           The ocean, overpeering of his list,
           Eats not the flats with more impiteous haste
           Then young Laertes, in a riotous head,
           O'erbears your officers. The rabble call him lord,   100
           And as the world were now but to begin,
           Antiquity forgot, custom not known,
           The ratifiers and props of every word,
           They cry 'Choose we, Laertes shall be king'.
           Caps, hands, and tongues, applaud it to the clouds,   105
           'Laertes shall be king, Laertes king!'

---

37 **Larded** garnished, strewn 41 **good dild you** God yield (requite)
you 41–42 **They say the owl was a baker's daughter** allusion to a folk-
tale in which a baker's daughter was transformed into an owl because of
her ungenerous behavior (giving short measure) when Christ asked for
bread in the baker's shop 44 **Conceit upon her father** i.e., obsessed
with her father's death 48 **betime** early 52 **dupped** opened 57 **Gis**
Jesus 60 **cock** corruption of God

79 **remove** banishment, departure; **muddied** stirred up and confused 81 **greenly** without judgment 82 **hugger-mugger** secrecy
and disorder 87 **in clouds** i.e., of suspicion and rumor 88 **wants**
lacks 90 **of matter beggared** lacking facts 91 **nothing stick** in no way
hesitate 93 **murd'ring piece** cannon loaded with shot meant to scatter 94 *F* omits the King's 'Attend,' but substitutes, by way of drawing
attention to the "noise within" 95 **Switzers** Swiss bodyguard 97 **list**
boundary 99 **riotous head** turbulent mob

QUEEN: How cheerfully on the false trail they cry!

(*A noise within.*)

O, this is counter, you false Danish dogs!
KING: The doors are broke.

(*Enter* LAERTES *with* OTHERS.)

110 LAERTES: Where is this king?—Sirs, stand you all without.
ALL: No, let's come in.
LAERTES: I pray you give me leave.
ALL: We will, we will.

(*Exeunt his followers.*)

LAERTES: I thank you. Keep the door.—O thou vile king,
    Give me my father!
QUEEN: Calmly, good Laertes,
115 LAERTES: That drop of blood that's calm proclaims me bastard,
    Cries cuckold to my father, brands the harlot
    Even here between the chaste unsmirchèd brow
    Of my true mother.
KING: What is the cause, Laertes,
    That thy rebellion looks so giant-like?
120   Let him go, Gertrude. Do not fear our person.
    There's such divinity doth hedge a king
    That treason can but peep to what it would,
    Acts little of his will. Tell me, Laertes,
    Why thou art thus incensed. Let him go, Gertrude.
125   Speak, man.
LAERTES: Where is my father?
KING: Dead.
QUEEN: But not by him.
KING: Let him demand his fill.
LAERTES: How came he dead? I'll not be juggled with.
    To hell allegiance, vows to the blackest devil,
130   Conscience and grace to the profoundest pit!
    I dare damnation. To this point I stand,
    That both the worlds I give to negligence,
    Let come what comes, only I'll be revenged
    Most throughly for my father.
135 KING: Who shall stay you?
LAERTES: My will, not all the world's.
    And for my means, I'll husband them so well
    They shall go far with little.
KING: Good Laertes,
    If you desire to know the certainty
    Of your dear father, is 't writ in your revenge
140   That, swoopstake, you will draw both friend and foe,
    Winner and loser?
LAERTES: None but his enemies.
KING: Will you know them, then?
LAERTES: To his good friends thus wide I'll ope my arms,
    And like the kind life-rend'ring pelican,
145   Repast them with my blood.

---

108 **counter** hunting backward on the trail 120 **fear** fear for
134 **throughly** thoroughly 140 **swoopstake** sweepstake, taking all the
stakes on the gambling table 144 **pelican** supposed to feed her young
with her own blood

KING: Why, now you speak
    Like a good child and a true gentleman.
    That I am guiltless of your father's death,
    And am most sensibly in grief for it,
    It shall as level to your judgement 'pear   150
    As day does to your eye.

(*A noise within:* 'Let her come in.')

LAERTES: How now! what noise is that?

(*Enter* OPHELIA.)

O heat, dry up my brains! tears seven times salt
Burn out the sense and virtue of mine eye!
By heaven, thy madness shall be paid with weight
Till our scale turn the beam. O rose of May,   155
Dear maid, kind sister, sweet Ophelia!
O heavens! is 't possible a young maid's wits
Should be as mortal as an old man's life?
Nature is fine in love, and where 'tis fine
It sends some precious instance of itself   160
After the thing it loves.
OPHELIA: (*Song.*)

    They bore him barefac'd on the bier;
    Hey non nonny, nonny, hey nonny;
    And in his grave rain'd many a tear—

Fare you well, my dove!   165
LAERTES: Hadst thou thy wits, and didst persuade revenge,
    It could not move thus.
OPHELIA: You must sing 'A-down, a-down,' and you 'Call him
    a-down-a.' O, how the wheel becomes it! It is the false stew
    ard, that stole his master's daughter.   170
LAERTES: This nothing's more than matter.
OPHELIA: There's rosemary, that's for remembrance. Pray you,
    love, remember. And there is pansies, that's for thoughts.
LAERTES: A document in madness, thoughts and remembrance
    fitted.   175
OPHELIA: There's fennel for you, and columbines. There's rue for
    you, and here's some for me. We may call it herb of grace a
    Sundays. O, you must wear your rue with a difference. There's
    a daisy. I would give you some violets, but they with ered
    all when my father died. They say 'a made a good end,   180

(*Sings.*)   For bonny sweet Robin is all my joy.

---

149 **level** plain   153 **virtue** power   159 **fine** refined to purity   169 **wheel**
burden, refrain   172–180 Harold Jenkins, in his Arden edition of *Hamlet*
(London and New York, 1982) 536–542, suggests that Ophelia gives rosemary (emblematic of remembrance) and pansies (of thoughts) to Laertes;
that she gives fennel and columbines (both signifying marital infidelity) to
the queen; she gives rue (for repentance) to the king (keeping some for herself as a sign of her sorrow, but noting that the king is to wear his rue with
a **difference,** an heraldic term designating a mark for distinguishing one
branch of a family from another in a coat-of-arms). The daisy, an emblem
of love's victims, is given to the king as substitute for the absent Hamlet,
whose absence he has caused. The king would also be given the violets
(emblems of faithfulness, associated both with Ophelia's love for Hamlet,
and Polonius's service to the state, both now lost) were these still available.
Each gift of flowers represents a symbolic reproach to the recipient

LAERTES: Thought and affliction, passion, hell itself,
    She turns to favor and to prettiness.
OPHELIA: (*Song.*)

                And will 'a not come again?
185   And will 'a not come again?
                No, no, he is dead:
                Go to thy death-bed:
                He never will come again.

                His beard was as white as snow,
190   All flaxen was his poll:
                He is gone, he is gone,
                And we cast away moan:
                God ha' mercy on his soul!

    And of all Christian souls, I pray God. God buy you. (*Exit.*)
195 LAERTES: Do you see this, O God?
    KING: Laertes, I must commune with your grief,
      Or you deny me right. Go but apart,
      Make choice of whom your wisest friends you will,
      And they shall hear and judge 'twixt you and me.
200   If by direct or by collateral hand
      They find us touched, we will our kingdom give,
      Our crown, our life, and all that we call ours,
      To you in satisfaction; but if not,
      Be you content to lend your patience to us,
205   And we shall jointly labour with your soul
      To give it due content.
    LAERTES: Let this be so.
      His means of death, his obscure funeral—
      No trophy, sword, nor hatchment, o'er his bones,
      No noble rite nor formal ostentation—
210   Cry to be heard, as 'twere from heaven to earth,
      That I must call't in question.
    KING: So you shall;
      And where th' offence is let the great axe fall.
      I pray you go with me.

(*Exeunt.*)

SCENE VI

Enter HORATIO *and* OTHERS.

HORATIO: What are they that would speak with me?
GENTLEMAN: Sea-faring men, sir. They say they have letters
    for you.
HORATIO: Let them come in. (*Exit* GENTLEMAN.)
    I do not know from what part of the world
5   I should be greeted, if not from Lord Hamlet.

(*Enter* SAILORS.)

SAILOR: God bless you, sir.
HORATIO: Let him bless thee too.
SAILOR: 'A shall sir, an't please him. There's a letter for you, sir—it
    comes from th' ambassador that was bound for England—if
10   your name be Horatio, as I am let to know it is.

HORATIO: (*Reads.*) 'Horatio, when thou shalt have overlooked
this, give these fellows some means to the king. They have
letters for him. Ere we were two days old at sea, a pirate of
very warlike appointment gave us chase. Finding ourselves
too slow of sail, we put on a compelled valor, and in the 15
grapple I boarded them. On the instant they got clear of our
ship, so I alone became their prisoner. They have dealt with
me like thieves of mercy, but they knew what they did; I
am to do a good turn for them. Let the king have the letters
I have sent, and repair thou to me with as much speed as 20
thou wouldest fly death. I have words to speak in thine ear
will make thee dumb; yet are they much too light for the
bore of the matter. These good fellows will bring thee where
I am. Rosencrantz and Guildenstern hold their course for
England. Of them I have much to tell thee, Farewell. 25
                'He that thou knowest thine, Hamlet.'
Come, I will give you way for these your letters,
And do't the speedier that you may direct me
To him from whom you brought them.

(*Exeunt.*)

SCENE VII

Enter KING *and* LAERTES.

KING: Now must your conscience my acquittance seal,
    And you must put me in your heart for friend,
    Sith you have heard, and with a knowing ear,
    That he which hath your noble father slain
    Pursued my life. 5
LAERTES: It well appears. But tell me
    Why you proceeded not against these feats,
    So criminal and so capital in nature,
    As by your safety, wisdom, all things else,
    You mainly were stirred up.
KING: O, for two special reasons,
    Which may to you, perhaps, seem much unsinewed, 10
    But yet to me th' are strong. The queen his mother
    Lives almost by his looks, and for myself—
    My virtue or my plague, be it either which—
    She's so conjunctive to my life and soul
    That, as the star moves not but in his sphere, 15
    I could not but by her. The other motive,
    Why to a public count I might not go,
    Is the great love the general gender bear him,
    Who, dipping all his faults in their affection,
    Work, like the spring that turneth wood to stone, 20
    Convert his gyves to graces; so that my arrows,
    Too slightly timbered for so loud a wind,
    Would have reverted to my bow again,
    And not where I had aimed them.
LAERTES: And so have I a noble father lost, 25
    A sister driven into desp'rate terms,
    Whose worth, if praises may go back again,
    Stood challenger on mount of all the age
    For her perfections. But my revenge will come.

IV.vi. 23 **bore** literally, caliber of a gun; hence, size, importance

IV.vii. 7 **capital** punishable by death 10 **unsinewed** weak 14 **conjunctive** closely joined 17 **count** reckoning 18 **general gender** common people 21 **gyves** fetters

---

190 **poll** head 208 **hatchment** coat of arms

30 KING: Break not your sleeps for that. You must not think
   That we are made of stuff so flat and dull
   That we can let our beard be shook with danger,
   And think it pastime. You shortly shall hear more.
   I loved your father, and we love our self,
35 And that, I hope, will teach you to imagine—

(Enter a MESSENGER *with letters.)*

MESSENGER: These to your majesty; this to the queen.
KING: From Hamlet! Who brought them?
MESSENGER: Sailors, my lord, they say. I saw them not.
   They were given me by Claudio; he received them
40 Of him that brought them.
   KING: Laertes, you shall hear them.—
   Leave us. *(Exit* MESSENGER.*)*
   (Reads.) 'High and mighty, you shall know I am set naked
   on your kingdom. To-morrow shall I beg leave to see
   your kingly eyes, when I shall, first asking your pardon,
45 thereunto recount the occasion of my sudden and more
   strange return.   Hamlet.'
   What should this mean? Are all the rest come back?
   Or is it some abuse, and no such thing?
LAERTES: Know you the hand?
50 KING: 'Tis Hamlet's character. 'Naked!'
   And in a postscript here, he says 'alone.'
   Can you devise me?
LAERTES: I am lost in it, my lord. But let him come.
   It warms the very sickness in my heart
55 That I shall live and tell him to his teeth
   'Thus didst thou.'
   KING: If it be so, Laertes—
   As how should it be so, how otherwise?—
   Will you be ruled by me?
LAERTES: Ay, my lord,
   So you will not o'errule me to a peace.
60 KING: To thine own peace. If he be now returned,
   As checking at his voyage, and that he means
   No more to undertake it, I will work him
   To an exploit now ripe in my device,
   Under the which he shall not choose but fall;
65 And for his death no wind of blame shall breathe
   But even his mother shall uncharge the practice
   And call it accident.
LAERTES: My lord, I will be ruled;
   The rather if you could devise it so
   That I might be the organ.

---

35 Following the entrance of the Messenger, the King says in *F* "How
now? What Newes?" and the Messenger replies, "Letters my Lord from
Hamlet." Jenkins comments (*SB* 13.36): "In *Q* the King is not told the
letters come from Hamlet; he is left to find this out as he reads, and
his cry 'From *Hamlet*' betokens his astonishment on doing so. I think
Hamlet would not have approved of the *F* messenger who robs his bomb
of the full force of its explosion. Shakespeare's messenger did not even
know he carried such a bomb, for the letters had reached him via sailors
who were ignorant of their sender. They took him for 'th' Embassador
that was bound for *England*' (4.4.9). *F*, with its too knowledgeable
messenger, by seeking to enhance the effect, destroys it" 52 **devise**
explain to 61 **checking at** turning aside from (like a falcon turning
from its quarry for other prey) 66 **uncharge the practice** regard the
deed as free from villainy 69 **organ** instrument

KING: It falls right.
   You have been talked of since your travel much,   70
   And that in Hamlet's hearing, for a quality
   Wherein they say you shine. Your sum of parts
   Did not together pluck such envy from him
   As did that one, and that, in my regard,
   Of the unworthiest siege.   75
LAERTES: What part is that, my lord?
KING: A very riband in the cap of youth,
   Yet needful too, for youth no less becomes
   The light and careless livery that it wears
   Than settled age his sables and his weeds,
   Importing health and graveness. Two months since   80
   Here was a gentleman of Normandy.
   I have seen myself, and served against, the French,
   And they can well on horseback, but this gallant
   Had witchcraft in't. He grew unto his seat,
   And to such wondrous doing brought his horse,   85
   As had he been incorpsed and demi-natured
   With the brave beast. So far he topped my thought
   That I, in forgery of shapes and tricks,
   Come short of what he did.
LAERTES: A Norman was't?
KING: A Norman.   90
LAERTES: Upon my life, Lamord.
KING: The very same.
LAERTES: I know him well. He is the brooch indeed
   And gem of all the nation.
KING: He made confession of you,
   And gave you such a masterly report   95
   For art and exercise in your defence,
   And for your rapier most especial,
   That he cried out 'twould be a sight indeed
   If one could match you. The scrimers of their nation,
   He swore had neither motion, guard, nor eye,   100
   If you opposed them. Sir, this report of his
   Did Hamlet so envenom with his envy
   That he could nothing do but wish and beg
   Your sudden coming o'er, to play with you.
   Now out of this—   105
LAERTES: What out of this, my lord?
KING: Laertes, was your father dear to you?
   Or are you like the painting of a sorrow,
   A face without a heart?
LAERTES: Why ask you this?
KING: Not that I think you did not love your father,
   But that I know love is begun by time,   110
   And that I see, in passages of proof,
   Time qualifies the spark and fire of it.
   There lives within the very flame of love
   A kind of wick or snuff that will abate it,
   And nothing is at a like goodness still,   115
   For goodness, growing to a plurisy,
   Dies in his own too much. That we would do,
   We should do when we would; for this 'would' changes,

---

75 **siege** rank 79 **weeds** garments 86 **incorpsed** made one body;
demi-natured like a centaur, half man half horse 87 **topped** excelled
88 **forgery** invention 99 **scrimers** fencers (French *escrimeurs*) 111 **passages of proof** incidents of experience 112 **qualifies** weakens 116 **plurisy**
excess

And hath abatements and delays as many
120 As there are tongues, are hands, are accidents,
And then this 'should' is like a spendthrift's sigh,
That hurts by easing. But to the quick of th' ulcer—
Hamlet comes back; what would you undertake
To show yourself in deed your father's son
125 More than in words?
LAERTES: To cut his throat i' th' church.
KING: No place, indeed, should murder sanctuarize;
Revenge should have no bounds. But good Laertes,
Will you do this, keep close within your chamber;
Hamlet returned shall know you are come home;
130 We'll put on those shall praise your excellence,
And set a double varnish on the fame
The Frenchman gave you, bring you in fine together,
And wager on your heads. He, being remiss,
Most generous, and free from all contriving,
135 Will not peruse the foils, so that with ease,
Or with a little shuffling, you may choose
A sword unbated, and in a pass of practice
Requite him for your father.
LAERTES: I will do't,
And for that purpose I'll anoint my sword.
140 I bought an unction of a mountebank
So mortal that but dip a knife in it,
Where it draws blood no cataplasm so rare,
Collected from all simples that have virtue
Under the moon, can save the thing from death
145 That is but scratched withal. I'll touch my point
With this contagion, that if I gall him slightly,
It may be death.
KING: Let's further think of this,
Weigh what convenience both of time and means
May fit us to our shape. If this should fail,
150 And that our drift look through our bad performance,
'Twere better not assayed. Therefore this project
Should have a back or second that might hold
If this should blast in proof. Soft! let me see.
We'll make a solemn wager on your cunnings—
155 I ha't.
When in your motion you are hot and dry—
As make your bouts more violent to that end—
And that he calls for drink, I'll have preferred him
A chalice for the nonce, whereon but sipping,
160 If he by chance escape your venomed stuck,
Our purpose may hold there.—But stay, what noise?

(*Enter* QUEEN.)

QUEEN: One woe doth tread upon another's heel,
So fast they follow. Your sister's drowned, Laertes.
LAERTES: Drowned! O, where?
165 QUEEN: There is a willow grows askant the brook

That shows his hoar leaves in the glassy stream.
Therewith fantastic garlands did she make
Of crowflowers, nettles, daisies, and long purples
That liberal shepherds give a grosser name,
But our cold maids do dead men's fingers call them.   170
There on the pendent boughs her crownet weeds
Clamb'ring to hang, an envious sliver broke,
When down her weedy trophies and herself
Fell in the weeping brook. Her clothes spread wide,
And mermaid-like awhile they bore her up,   175
Which time she chanted snatches of old lauds,
As one incapable of her own distress,
Or like a creature native and indued
Unto that element. But long it could not be
Till that her garments, heavy with their drink,   180
Pulled the poor wretch from her melodious lay
To muddy death.
LAERTES: Alas, then, she is drowned?
QUEEN: Drowned, drowned.
LAERTES: Too much of water hast thou, poor Ophelia,
And therefore I forbid my tears; but yet   185
It is our trick; nature her custom holds,
Let shame say what it will. When these are gone,
The woman will be out. Adieu, my lord.
I have a speech o' fire that fain would blaze
But that this folly drowns it.   190

(*Exit.*)

KING: Let's follow, Gertrude.
How much I had to do to calm his rage!
Now fear I this will give it start again;
Therefore let's follow.

(*Exeunt.*)

ACT FIVE

SCENE I

Enter two CLOWNS.

CLOWN: Is she to be buried in Christian burial when she wilfully
seeks her own salvation?
OTHER: I tell thee she is, therefore make her grave straight.
The crowner hath sat on her, and finds it Christian burial.
CLOWN: How can that be, unless she drowned herself in her own   5
defence?
OTHER: Why, 'tis found so.
CLOWN: It must be 'se offendendo', it cannot be else. For here
lies the point: if I drown myself wittingly, it argues an act,
and an act hath three branches—it is to act, to do, and to   10
perform; argal, she drowned herself wittingly.

---

122 **quick** sensitive flesh   126 **sanctuarize** give sanctuary to
133 **remiss** careless   135 **peruse** inspect   137 **unbated** not blunted;
pass of practice treacherous thrust   142 **cataplasm** poultice
143 **simples** medicinal herbs   149 **shape** plan   150 **drift** scheme
152 **back or second** something in support   153 **blast in proof** burst
during trial (like a faulty cannon)   156 **motion** exertion   158 **preferred**
offered to   159 **nonce** occasion   160 **stuck** thrust   165 **askant**
alongside

---

166 **hoar** gray   169 **liberal** free-spoken, licentious   170 **cold** chaste
171 **crownet** coronet   172 **envious** malicious   176 **lauds** hymns
177 **incapable of** insensible to   178 **indued** endowed   188 **woman**
unmanly part of nature

V.i. s.d. **clowns** rustics   4 **crowner** coroner   8 **se offendendo** the
Clown's blunder for **se defendendo** ("in self-defense")   11 **argal** therefore (corrupt form of *ergo*)

OTHER: Nay, but hear you, Goodman Delver.

CLOWN: Give me leave. Here lies the water; good. Here
stands the man; good. If the man go to this water and
15 drown himself, it is, will he, nill he, he goes—mark you
that. But if the water come to him and drown him, he
drowns not himself. Argal, he that is not guilty of his own
death shortens not his own life.

OTHER: But is this law?

20 CLOWN: Ay, marry, is't; crowner's quest law.

OTHER: Will you ha' the truth on 't? If this had not been a
gentlewoman, she should have been buried out o' Christian
burial.

CLOWN: Why, there thou say'st. And the more pity that great
25 folk should have count'nance in this world to drown or
hang themselves more than their even-Christen. Come, my
spade. There is no ancient gentlemen but gard'ners, ditchers,
and grave-makers. They hold up Adam's profession.

OTHER: Was he a gentleman?

30 CLOWN: 'A was the first that ever bore arms.

OTHER: Why, he had none.

CLOWN: What, art a heathen? How dost thou understand the
Scripture? The Scripture says Adam digged. Could he dig
without arms? I'll put another question to thee. If thou
35 answerest me not to the purpose, confess thyself—

OTHER: Go to.

CLOWN: What is he that builds stronger than either the mason,
the shipwright, or the carpenter?

OTHER: The gallows-maker for that frame outlives a thousand
40 tenants.

CLOWN: I like thy wit well, in good faith. The gallows does
well. But how does it well? It does well to those that do
ill. Now thou dost ill to say the gallows is built stronger
than the church. Argal, the gallows may do well to thee.
45 To't again, come.

OTHER: 'Who builds stronger than a mason, a shipwright, or
a carpenter?'

CLOWN: Ay tell me that, and unyoke.

OTHER: Marry, now I can tell.

50 CLOWN: To't.

OTHER: Mass, I cannot tell.

(*Enter* HAMLET *and* HORATIO *afar off.*)

CLOWN: Cudgel thy brains no more about it, for your dull ass
will not mend his pace with beating. And when you are
asked this question next, say 'a grave-maker.' The houses
55 he makes lasts till doomsday. Go, get thee in, and fetch me
a stoup of liquor. (*Exit* OTHER CLOWN.)

(HAMLET *and* HORATIO *come forward as* CLOWN *digs and sings.*)

(*Song.*)

> In youth, when I did love, did love,
>   Methought it was very sweet,
> To contract-O-the time, for-a-my behove,
60   O, methought, there-a-was nothing-a-meet.

HAMLET: Has this fellow no feeling of his business, that 'a sings at
gravemaking?

HORATIO: Custom hath made it in him a property of easiness.

HAMLET: 'Tis e'en so. The hand of little employment hath the
daintier sense.   65

CLOWN: (*Song.*)

> But age, with his stealing steps,
>   Hath clawed me in his clutch,
> And hath shipped me into the land,
>   As if I had never been such.

(*Throws up a skull.*)

HAMLET: That skull had a tongue in it, and could sing once.   70
How the knave jowls it to the ground, as if 'twere Cain's
jawbone, that did the first murder! This might be the pate
of a politician, which this ass now o'erreaches; one that
would circumvent God, might it not?

HORATIO: It might, my lord.   75

HAMLET: Or of a courtier, which could say 'Good morrow,
sweet lord! How dost thou, sweet lord?' This might be my
Lord Such-a-one, that praised my Lord Such-a-one's
horse, when 'a went to beg it, might it not?

HORANTIO: Ay, my lord.   80

HAMLET: Why, e'en so, and now my Lady Worm's, chopless,
and knock'd about the mazzard with a sexton's spade.
Here's fine revolution, an we had the trick to see't. Did
these bones cost no more the breeding but to play at
loggats with them? Mine ache to think on't.   85

CLOWN: (*Song.*)

> A pick-axe and a spade, a spade,
>   For and a shrouding sheet:
> O, a pit of clay for to be made
>   For such a guest is meet.

(*Throws up another skull.*)

HAMLET: There's another. Why may not that be the skull of   90
a lawyer? Where be his quiddities now, his quillets, his
cases, his tenures, and his tricks? Why does he suffer this
mad knave now to knock him about the sconce with a
dirty shovel, and will not tell him of his action of battery?
Hum! This fellow might be in's time a great buyer of land,   95
with his statutes, his recognizances, his fines, his double
vouchers, his recoveries. Is this the fine of his fines, and the
recovery of his recoveries, to have his fine pate full of fine
dirt? Will his vouchers vouch him no more of his
purchases, and double ones too, than the length and   100
breadth of a pair of indentures? The very conveyances
of his lands will scarcely lie in this box, and must th'
inheritor himself have no more, ha?

---

20 **quest** inquest   26 **even-Christen** fellow Christian   48 **tell me that,
and unyoke** answer the question and then you can relax   56 **stoup** tan-
kard   59 **behove** benefit   59–60 The repeated *a* and *o* may represent
the Clown's vocal embellishments, but more probably they represent his
grunting as he takes breath in the course of his digging

63 **a property of easiness** a habit that comes easily to him   71 **jowls**
hurls   74 **circumvent** cheat   81 **chopless** with lower jaw missing   82 **mazzard** head   84–85 **loggats** small logs of wood for
throwing at a mark   91 **quiddities** subtle distinctions; **quillets** quib-
bles   96 **recognizances** legal bonds, defining debts; **vouchers** persons
vouched or called on to warrant a title   97 **recoveries** legal processes to
break an entail   100–101 **pair of indentures** deed or legal agreement in
duplicate   101 **conveyances** deeds by which property is transferred

HORATIO: Not a jot more, my lord.

105 HAMLET: Is not parchment made of sheepskins?

HORANTIO: Ay, my lord, and of calves' skins too.

HAMLET: They are sheep and calves which seek out assurance in that. I will speak to this fellow. Whose grave's this, sirrah?

CLOWN: Mine, sir. (*Sings.*)

110   O, a pit of clay for to be made—

HAMLET: I think it be thine indeed, for thou liest in't.

CLOWN: You lie out on't, sir, and therefore 'tis not yours. For my part, I do not lie in't, yet it is mine.

HAMLET: Thou dost lie in't, to be in't and say it is thine. 'Tis for
115 the dead, not for the quick; therefore thou liest.

CLOWN: 'Tis a quick lie, sir; 'twill away again from me to you.

HAMLET: What man dost thou dig it for?

CLOWN: For no man, sir.

HAMLET: What woman, then?

120 CLOWN: For none neither.

HAMLET: Who is to be buried in't?

CLOWN: One that was a woman, sir; but, rest her soul, she's dead.

HAMLET: How absolute the knave is! We must speak by the
125 card, or equivocation will undo us. By the Lord, Horatio, this three years I have took note of it, the age is grown so picked that the toe of the peasant comes so near the heel of the courtier, he galls his kibe. How long hast thou been a grave-maker?

130 CLOWN: Of all the day i' th' year, I came to't that day that our last King Hamlet overcame Fortinbras.

HAMLET: How long is that since?

CLOWN: Cannot you tell that? Every fool can tell that. It was that very day that young Hamlet was born—he that is mad,
135 and sent into England.

HAMLET: Ay, marry, why was he sent into England?

CLOWN: Why, because 'a was mad. 'A shall recover his wits there; or, if a do not, 'tis no great matter there.

HAMLET: Why?

140 CLOWN: 'Twill not be seen in him there. There the men are as mad as he.

HAMLET: How came he mad?

CLOWN: Very strangely, they say.

HAMLET: How strangely?

145 CLOWN: Faith, e'en with losing his wits.

HAMLET: Upon what ground?

CLOWN: Why, here in Denmark. I have been sexton here, man and boy, thirty years.

HAMLET: How long will a man lie i' th' earth ere he rot?

150 CLOWN: Faith, if 'a be not rotten before 'a die—as we have many pocky corses now-a-days that will scarce hold the laying in—'a will last you some eight year or nine year. A tanner will last you nine year.

HAMLET: Why he more than another?

155 CLOWN: Why, sir, his hide is so tanned with his trade that 'a will keep out water a great while and your water is a sore decayer of your whoreson dead body. Here's a skull now hath lain you i' th' earth three and twenty years.

HAMLET: Whose was it?

CLOWN: A whoreson mad fellow's it was. Whose do you think 160
it was?

HAMLET: Nay, I know not.

CLOWN: A pestilence on him for a mad rogue! 'a poured a flagon of Rhenish on my head once. This same skull, sir, was, sir, Yorick's skull, the king's jester. 165

HAMLET: (*Takes the skull.*) This?

CLOWN: E'en That.

HAMLET: Alas, poor Yorick! I knew him, Horatio—a fellow of infinite jest, of most excellent fancy. He hath bore me on his back a thousand times, and now how abhorred in my 170
imagination it is! My gorge rises at it. Here hung those lips that I have kissed I know not how oft. Where be your gibes now, your gambols, your songs, your flashes of merriment that were wont to set the table on a roar? Not one now to mock your own grinning? Quite chop-fall'n? 175
Now get you to my lady's chamber, and tell her, let her paint an inch thick, to this favour she must come. Make her laugh at that. Prithee, Horatio, tell me one thing.

HORATIO: What's that, my lord?

HAMLET: Dost thou think Alexander looked o' this fashion i' 180
th' earth?

HORATIO: E'en so.

HAMLET: And smelt so? Pah!

(*Throws down the skull.*)

HORATIO: E'en so, my lord.

HAMLET: To what base uses we may return, Horatio! Why 185
may not imagination trace the noble dust of Alexander till
'a find it stopping a bung-hole?

HORATIO: 'Twere to consider too curiously to consider so.

HAMLET: No, faith, not a jot, but to follow him thither with modesty enough, and likelihood to lead it. Alexander died, 190
Alexander was buried, Alexander returneth to dust; the dust is earth; of earth we make loam; and why of that loam whereto he was converted might they not stop a beer-barrel?

    Imperious Caesar, dead and turned to clay,
    Might stop a hole to keep the wind away. 195
    O, that that earth which kept the world in awe
    Should patch a wall t'expel the winter's flaw!

But soft, but soft awhile! Here comes the king,
The queen, the courtiers.

(*Enter* KING, QUEEN, LAERTES, *and the Corse* [*with a Doctor of Divinity as* PRIEST *and* LORDS *attendant*].)

                 Who is this they follow?
And with such maimèd rites? This doth betoken 200
The corse they follow did with desperate hand
Fordo it own life. 'Twas of some estate.
Couch we awhile and mark.

(*Retires with* HORATIO.)

---

124 **absolute** positive   125 **card** card on which the points of the mariner's compass are marked (i.e., absolutely to the point)   127 **picked** fastidious   128 **kibe** chilblain   151 **pocky** infected with pox (syphilis)

---

164 **Rhenish** Rhine wine   188 **too curiously** over ingeniously   197 **flaw** gust   202 **Fordo** destroy; **it** its

LAERTES: What ceremony else?
205 HAMLET: That is Laertes, a very noble youth. Mark.
LAERTES: What ceremony else?
DOCTOR: Her obsequies have been as far enlarged
  As we have warranty. Her death was doubtful,
  And but that great command o'ersways the order,
210 She should in ground unsanctified been lodged
  Till the last trumpet. For charitable prayers,
  Shards, flints and pebbles should be thrown on her.
  Yet here she is allowed her virgin crants,
  Her maiden strewments and the bringing home
215 Of bell and burial.
LAERTES: Must there no more be done?
DOCTOR: No more be done.
  We should profane the service of the dead
  To sing a requiem and such rest to her
  As to peace-parted souls.
LAERTES: Lay her i' th' earth,
220 And from her fair and unpolluted flesh
  May violets spring! I tell thee, churlish priest,
  A minist'ring angel shall my sister be
  When thou liest howling.
HAMLET: What, the fair Ophelia!
QUEEN: Sweets to the sweet. Farewell!

(Scatters flowers.)

225 I hoped thou shouldst have been my Hamlet's wife.
  I thought thy bride-bed to have decked, sweet maid,
  And not have strewed thy grave.
LAERTES: O treble woe
  Fall ten times treble on that cursèd head,
  Whose wicked deed thy most ingenious sense
230 Deprived thee of! Hold off the earth awhile,
  Till I have caught her once more in mine arms.

(Leaps into the grave.)

  Now pile your dust upon the quick and dead,
  Till of this flat a mountain you have made
  T' o'er-top old Pelion or the skyish head
235 Of blue Olympus.
HAMLET: (Coming forward.) What is he whose grief
  Bears such an emphasis, whose phrase of sorrow
  Conjures the wand'ring stars, and makes them stand
  Like wonder-wounded hearers? This is I,
  Hamlet the Dane.

(LAERTES climbs out of the grave.)

240 LAERTES: The devil take thy soul!

---

212 **Shards** bits of broken pottery 213 **crants** garland 229 **most ingenious** of quickest apprehension 234 **Pelion** a mountain in Thessaly, like Olympus, line 235, and Ossa, line 266 (the allusion is to the war in which the Titans fought the gods and, in their attempt to scale heaven, heaped Ossa and Olympus on Pelion, or Pelion and Ossa on Olympus) 237 **such an emphasis** so vehement an expression or display

(Grappling with him.)

HAMLET: Thou pray'st not well.
  I prithee take thy fingers from my throat,
  For though I am not splenitive and rash,
  Yet have I in me something dangerous,
  Which let thy wisdom fear. Hold off thy hand.
KING: Pluck them asunder.   245
QUEEN: Hamlet! Hamlet!
ALL: Gentlemen!
HORATIO: Good my lord, be quiet.

(The ATTENDANTS part them.)

HAMLET: Why, I will fight with him upon this theme
  Until my eyelids will no longer wag.   250
QUEEN: O my son, what theme?
HAMLET: I loved Ophelia. Forty thousand brothers
  Could not with all their quantity of love
  Make up my sum. What wilt thou do for her?
KING: O, he is mad, Laertes.   255
QUEEN: For love of God, forbear him.
HAMLET: 'Swounds, show me what thou't do.
  Woo't weep, woo't fight, woo't fast, woo't tear thyself,
  Woo't drink up eisel, eat a crocodile?
  I'll do't. Dost come here to whine?   260
  To outface me with leaping in her grave?
  Be buried quick with her, and so will I,
  And if thou prate of mountains, let them throw
  Millions of acres on us, till our ground,
  Singeing his pate against the burning zone,   265
  Make Ossa like a wart! Nay, an thou'lt mouth,
  I'll rant as well as thou.
QUEEN: This is mere madness;
  And thus awhile the fit will work on him.
  Anon, as patient as the female dove
  When that her golden couplets are disclosed,   270
  His silence will sit drooping.
HAMLET: Hear you, sir.
  What is the reason that you use me thus?
  I loved you ever. But it is no matter.
  Let Hercules himself do what he may,
  The cat will mew, and dog will have his day.   275
KING: I pray thee, good Horatio, wait upon him.

(Exit HAMLET and HORATIO.)

  (To LAERTES.) Strengthen your patience in our last night's
    speech.
  We'll put the matter to the present push.—
  Good Gertrude, set some watch over your son.—
  This grave shall have a living monument.   280
  An hour of quiet shortly shall we see;
  Till then in patience our proceeding be.

(Exeunt.)

---

242 **splenitive** fiery-tempered (from the spleen, seat of anger) 258 **Woo't** wilt (thou) 259 **eisel** vinegar 270 **couplets** newly hatched pair

SCENE II

Enter HAMLET *and* HORATIO.

HAMLET: So much for this, sir; now shall you see the other.
　　You do remember all the circumstance?
HORATIO: Remember it, my lord!
HAMLET: Sir, in my heart there was a kind of fighting
5　　That would not let me sleep. Methought I lay
　　Worse than the mutines in the bilboes. Rashly,
　　And praised be rashness for it—let us know,
　　Our indiscretion sometime serves us well,
　　When our deep plots do pall; and that should learn us
10　　There's a divinity that shapes our ends,
　　Rough-hew them how we will—
HORATIO:　　　　　　　　　　That is most certain.
HAMLET: Up from my cabin,
　　My sea-gown scarfed about me, in the dark
　　Groped I to find out them, had my desire,
15　　Fingered their packet, and in fine withdrew
　　To mine own room again, making so bold,
　　My fears forgetting manners, to unseal
　　Their grand commission; where I found, Horatio—
　　Ah, royal knavery!—an exact command,
20　　Larded with many several sorts of reasons
　　Importing Denmark's health and England's too,
　　With, ho! such bugs and goblins in my life,
　　That on the supervise, no leisure bated,
　　No, not to stay the grinding of the axe,
25　　My head should be struck off.
HORATIO:　　　　　　　　　　Is't possible?
HAMLET: Here's the commission; read it at more leisure.
　　But will thou hear me how I did proceed?
HORATIO: I beseech you.
HAMLET: Being thus benetted round with villainies,
30　　Or I could make a prologue to my brains,
　　They had begun the play. I sat me down,
　　Devised a new commission, wrote it fair.
　　I once did hold it, as our statists do,
　　A baseness to write fair, and laboured much
35　　How to forget that learning; but sir, now
　　It did me yeoman's service. Wilt thou know
　　Th' effect of what I wrote?
HORATIO:　　　　　　　　　　Ay, good my lord.
HAMLET: An earnest conjuration from the king,
　　As England was his faithful tributary,
40　　As love between them like the palm might flourish,
　　As peace should still her wheaten garland wear
　　And stand a comma 'tween their amities,
　　And many such like as's of great charge,
　　That on the view and knowing of these contents,
45　　Without debatement further more or less,

He should the bearers put to sudden death,
　　Not shriving-time allowed.
HORATIO:　　　　　　　　　　How was this sealed?
HAMLET: Why, even in that was heaven ordinant,
　　I had my father's signet in my purse,
　　Which was the model of that Danish seal,　　50
　　Folded the writ up in the form of th' other,
　　Subscribed it, gave't th' impression, placed it safely,
　　The changeling never known. Now the next day
　　Was our sea-fight, and what to this was sequent
　　Thou knowest already.　　55
HORATIO: So Guildenstern and Rosencrantz go to't.
HAMLET: Why, man, they did make love to this employment.
　　They are not near my conscience; their defeat
　　Does by their own insinuation grow.
　　'Tis dangerous when the baser nature comes　　60
　　Between the pass and fell incensèd points
　　Of mighty opposites.
HORATIO:　　　　　　　　　Why, what a king is this!
HAMLET: Does it not, think thee, stand me now upon—
　　He that hath killed my king and whored my mother,
　　Popped in between th' election and my hopes,　　65
　　Thrown out his angle for my proper life,
　　And with such coz'nage—is't not perfect conscience,
　　To quit him with this arm? And is't not to be damned
　　To let this canker of our nature come
　　In further evil?　　70
HORATIO: It must be shortly known to him from England
　　What is the issue of the business there.
HAMLET: It will be short; the interim is mine.
　　And a man's life's no more than to say 'one.'
　　But I am very sorry, good Horatio,　　75
　　That to Laertes I forgot myself;
　　For by the image of my cause I see
　　The portraiture of his. I'll court his favours.
　　But sure the bravery of his grief did put me
　　Into a tow'ring passion.　　80
HORATIO:　　　　　　　　　Peace; who comes here?

(*Enter* [OSRIC] *a courtier.*)

OSRIC: Your lordship is right welcome back to Denmark.
HAMLET: I humbly thank you, sir. (*Aside to* HORATIO.) Dost know
　　this water-fly?
HORATIO: (*Aside to* HAMLET.) No, my good lord.
HAMLET: (*Aside to* HORATIO.) Thy state is the more gracious,　　85
　　for 'tis a vice to know him. He hath much land, and fertile.
　　Let a beast be lord of beasts, and his crib shall stand at the
　　king's mess. 'Tis a chough, but as I say, spacious in the
　　possession of dirt.
OSRIC: Sweet lord, if your lordship were at leisure, I should impart　90
　　a thing to you from his majesty.
HAMLET: I will receive it, sir, with all diligence of spirit. Put your
　　bonnet to his right use. 'Tis for the head.

V.ii. 6 mutines mutineers; **bilboes** fetters   **9 pall** fail   **15 Fingered**
filched   **20 Larded** garnished   **22 bugs and goblins** imaginary
horrors (here, horrendous crimes attributed to Hamlet, and represented
as dangers should he be allowed to live)   **23 supervise** perusal; **bated**
deducted, allowed   **24 stay** await   **30 Or** ere   **33 statists** statesmen   **42 comma** a connective that also acknowledges separateness
43 charge (1) importance (2) burden (the double meaning fits the play
that makes "as's" into "asses")

---

48 ordinant guiding   **52 Subscribed** signed   **59 insinuation** intrusion   **61 pass** thrust; **fell** fierce   **63 Does it not . . . stand me now
upon** is it not incumbent upon me   **65 election** i.e., to the kingship.
Denmark being an elective monarchy   **66 angle** fishing line; **proper**
own   **68 quit** repay   **79 bravery** ostentatious display   **88 mess** table;
chough jackdaw; thus, a chatterer

OSRIC: I thank you lordship, it is very hot.

95 HAMLET: No, believe me, 'tis very cold; the wind is northerly.

OSRIC: It is indifferent cold, my lord, indeed.

HAMLET: But yet methinks it is very sultry and hot for my complexion.

OSRIC: Exceedingly, my lord; it is very sultry, as 'twere—I can
100   not tell how. My lord, his majesty bade me signify to you
that 'a has laid a great wager on your head. Sir, this is the
matter—

HAMLET: I beseech you, remember.

(HAMLET *moves him to put on his hat.*)

OSRIC: Nay, good my lord; for my ease, in good faith. Sir, here
105   is newly come to court Laertes; believe me, an absolute
gentleman, full of most excellent differences, of very soft
society and great showing. Indeed, to speak feelingly of
him, he is the card or calendar of gentry, for you shall find
in him the continent of what part a gentleman would see.

110 HAMLET: Sir, his definement suffers, no perdition in you,
though I know to divide him inventorially would dozy th'
arithmetic of memory, and yet but yaw neither in respect
of his quick sail. But in the verity of extolment, I take him
to be a soul of great article, and his infusion of such dearth
115   and rareness as, to make true diction of him, his semblable
is his mirror, and who else would trace him, his umbrage,
nothing more.

OSRIC: Your lordship speaks most infallibly of him.

HAMLET: The concernancy, sir? Why do we wrap the gentleman
120   in our more rawer breath?

OSRIC: Sir?

HORATIO: It's not possible to understand in another tongue?
You will to't, sir, really.

HAMLET: What imports the nomination of this gentleman?

125 OSRIC: Of Laertes?

HORATIO: (*Aside.*) His purse is empty already. All's golden words
are spent.

HAMLET: Of him, sir.

OSRIC: I know you are not ignorant—

130 HAMLET: I would you did, sir; yet, in faith, if you did, it would
not much approve me. Well, sir.

OSRIC: You are not ignorant of what excellence Laertes is—

HAMLET: I dare not confess that, lest I should compare with
him in excellence; but to know a man well were to know
135   himself.

OSRIC: I mean, sir, for his weapon; but in the imputation laid
on him by them in his meed, he's unfellowed.

HAMLET: What's his weapon?

OSRIC: Rapier and dagger.

140 HAMLET: That's two of his weapons—but well.

OSRIC: The king, sir, hath wagered with him six Barbary
horses, against the which he has impawned, as I take it, six
French rapiers and poniards, with their assigns, as girdle,
hangers, and so. Three of the carriages, in faith, are very
dear to fancy, very responsive to the hilts, most delicate   145
carriages, and of very liberal conceit.

HAMLET: What call you the carriages?

HORATIO: (*Aside to* HAMLET.) I knew you must be edified by the
margent ere you had done.

OSRIC: The carriages, sir, are the hangers.   150

HAMLET: The phrase would be more germane to the matter if we
could carry cannon by our sides. I would it might be hangers
till then. But on! Six Barbary horses against six French
swords, their assigns, and three liberal conceited carriages;
that's the French bet against the Danish. Why is this all   155
impawned, as you call it?

OSRIC: The king, sir, hath laid, sir, that in a dozen passes between
yourself and him he shall not exceed you three hits;
he hath laid on twelve for nine, and it would come to
immediate trial if your lordship would vouchsafe the answer.   160

HAMLET: How if I answer no?

OSRIC: I mean, my lord, the opposition of your person in trial.

HAMLET: Sir, I will walk here in the hall. If it please his
majesty, it is the breathing time of day with me. Let the
foils be brought, the gentleman willing, and the king hold   165
his purpose; I will win for him an I can. If not, I will gain
nothing but my shame and the odd hits.

OSRIC: Shall I deliver you so?

HAMLET: To this effect, sir, after what flourish your nature will.

OSRIC: I commend my duty to your lordship.   170

HAMLET: Yours. (*Exit* OSRIC.) He does well to commend it
himself; there are no tongues else for's turn.

HORATIO: This lapwing runs away with the shell on his head.

HAMLET: 'A did comply, sir, with his dug, before 'a sucked it.
Thus has he, and many more of the same bevy that I know   175
the drossy age dotes on, only got the tune of the time; and
out of an habit of encounter, a kind of yesty collection which
carries them through and through the most fanned and
winnowed opinions; and do but blow them to their trial,
the bubbles are out.   180

(*Enter a* LORD.)

---

142 **impawned** staked 143 **assigns** appendages 144 **carriages**
an affected word for hangers, i.e., straps from which the weapon was
hung 146 **liberal conceit** elaborate design 149 **margent** margin
(where explanatory notes were printed) 157–158 **in a dozen passes . . .
he shall not exceed you three hits** the odds the King proposes seem to be
that in a match of twelve bouts, Hamlet will win at least five. Laertes would
need to win by at least eight to four 159 **he hath laid on twelve for nine**
"he" apparently is Laertes, who has seemingly raised the odds against himself by wagering that out of twelve bouts he will win nine 164 **breathing
time** time for taking exercise 166 **an** if 173 **lapwing** a bird reputedly so precocious as to run as soon as hatched 174 **comply** observe
the formalities of courtesy; **dug** mother's nipple 175 **bevy** a covey of
quails or lapwings 176 **drossy** frivolous 177 **encounter** manner of
address or accosting; **yesty collection** a frothy and superficial patchwork
of terms from the conversation of others 179 **winnowed** tested, freed
from inferior elements

---

96 **indifferent** somewhat 98 **complexion** temperament 106 **differences** distinguishing qualities 107 **great showing** distinguished
appearance 108 **card** map 109 **continent** all-containing embodiment 110 **definement** definition 111 **divide him inventorially** clas-
sify him in detail; **dozy** dizzy 112 **yaw** hold to a course unsteadily, like
a ship that steers wild 114 **article** scope, importance; **infusion** essence;
dearth scarcity 115 **semblable** likeness 116 **trace** (1) draw, (2) follow; **umbrage** shadow 119 **concernancy** import, relevance 123 **to't**
i.e., to get an understanding 124 **nomination** mention 131 **approve**
commend 133 **compare** compete 137 **meed** pay; **unfellowed**
unequaled

LORD: My lord, his majesty commended him to you by young
    Osric, who brings back to him that you attend him in the hall.
    He sends to know if your pleasure hold to play with Laertes,
    or that you will take longer time.
185 HAMLET: I am constant to my purposes: they follow the
    king's pleasure. If his fitness speaks, mine is ready; now or
    whensoever, provided I be so able as now.
  LORD: The king and queen and all are coming down.
  HAMLET: In happy time.
190 LORD: The queen desires you to use some gentle entertainment to
    Laertes before you fall to play.
  HAMLET: She well instructs me.

(*Exit* LORD.)

HORATIO: You will lose, my lord.
  HAMLET: I do not think so. Since he went into France, I have
195   been in continual practice. I shall win at the odds. But thou
    wouldst not think how ill all's here about my heart. But it is
    no matter.
  HORATIO: Nay, good my lord—
  HAMLET: It is but foolery, but it is such a kind of gaingiving as
200   would perhaps trouble a woman.
  HORATIO: If your mind dislike any thing, obey it. I will forestall
    their repair hither, and say you are not fit.
  HAMLET: Not a whit, we defy augury. There is a special
    providence in the fall of a sparrow. If it be now, 'tis not to
205   come; if it be not to come, it will be now; if it be not now, yet
    it will come. The readiness is all. Since no man of aught he
    leaves knows, what is't to leave betimes? Let be.

(*A table prepared.* [*Enter*] *trumpets, drums, and* OFFICERS *with
cushions;* KING, QUEEN, [OSRIC,] *and all the* STATE, [*with*] *foils,
daggers, and* LAERTES.)

KING: Come, Hamlet, come, and take this hand from me.

(*The* KING *puts* LAERTES' *hand into* HAMLET'*s.*)
210

HAMLET: Give me your pardon, sir. I have done you wrong,
    But pardon 't as you are a gentleman.
    This presence knows, and you must needs have heard,
    How I am punished with a sore distraction.
215   What I have done
    That might your nature, honour, and exception,
    Roughly awake, I here proclaim was madness.
    Was 't Hamlet wronged Laertes? Never Hamlet.
    If Hamlet from himself be ta'en away,
220   And when he's not himself does wrong Laertes,
    Then Hamlet does it not. Hamlet denies it.
    Who does it then? His madness. If't be so,
    Hamlet is of the faction that is wronged;
    His madness is poor Hamlet's enemy.
225   Sir, in this audience,
    Let my disclaiming from a purposed evil
    Free me so far in your most generous thoughts
    That I have shot mine arrow o'er the house,
    And hurt my brother.

LAERTES: I am satisfied in nature,
    Whose motive in this case should stir me most   230
    To my revenge. But in my terms of honor
    I stand aloof, and will no reconcilement
    Till by some elder masters of known honor,
    I have a voice and precedent of peace
    To keep my name ungored. But till that time   235
    I do receive your offered love like love,
    And will not wrong it.
  HAMLET: I embrace if freely,
    And will this brother's wager frankly play.
    Give us the foils.
  LAERTES: Come, one for me.
  HAMLET: I'll be your foil, Laertes. In mine ignorance   240
    Your skill shall, like a star i' th' darkest night,
    Stick fiery off indeed.
  LAERTES: You mock me, sir.
  HAMLET: No, by this hand.
  KING: Give them the foils, young Osric. Cousin Hamlet,
    You know the wager?
  HAMLET: Very well, my lord;   245
    Your Grace has laid the odds o'th' weaker side.
  KING: I do not fear it, I have seen you both;
    But since he is bettered, we have therefore odds.
  LAERTES: This is too heavy; let me see another.
  HAMLET: This likes me well. These foils have all a length?

(*They prepare to play.*)
              250
OSRIC: Ay, my good lord.
  KING: Set me the stoups of wine upon that table.
    If Hamlet give the first or second hit,
    Or quit in answer of the third exchange,
    Let all the battlements their ordnance fire.   255
    The king shall drink to Hamlet's better breath,
    And in the cup an union shall he throw,
    Richer than that which four successive kings
    In Denmark's crown have worn. Give me the cups,
    And let the kettle to the trumpet speak,   260
    The trumpet to the cannoneer without,
    The cannons to the heavens, the heaven to earth,
    'Now the king drinks to Hamlet.' Come begin—

(*Trumpets the while.*)

    And you, the judges, bear a wary eye.
  HAMLET: Come on, sir.
  LAERTES: Come, my lord.

(*They play.*)

  HAMLET: One.
  LAERTES: No.
  HAMLET: Judgment.
  OSRIC: A hit, a very palpable hit.

---

232 **voice and precedent** authoritative statement justified by precedent 238 **foil** (1) setting for gem (2) weapon 246 **bettered** perfected through training 248 **have all a length** are all of the same
length 252 **quit in answer** literally, give as good as he gets (i.e., if the
third bout is a draw) 255 **union** pearl

---

186 **fitness** convenience, inclination   199 **gaingiving** misgiving

265 (*Drums, trumpets, and shot. Flourish; a piece goes off.*)

LAERTES: Well, again.
KING: Stay, give me drink. Hamlet, this pearl is thine.
    Here's to thy health. Give him the cup.
HAMLET: I'll play this bout first; set it by awhile.
    Come.

270 (*They play.*)

    Another hit; what say you?
LAERTES: I do confess't.
KING: Our son shall win.
QUEEN: He's fat, and scant of breath.
275   Here, Hamlet, take my napkin, rub thy brows.
    The queen carouses to thy fortune, Hamlet.
HAMLET: Good madam!
KING: Gertrude, do not drink.
QUEEN: I will, my lord; I pray you pardon me.
280 KING: (*Aside.*) It is the poisoned cup; it is too late.
HAMLET: I dare not drink yet, madam; by and by.
QUEEN: Come, let me wipe thy face.
LAERTES: My lord, I'll hit him now.
KING: I do not think't.
LAERTES: (*Aside.*) And yet it is almost against my conscience.
285 HAMLET: Come, for the third, Laertes. You but dally.
    I pray you pass with your best violence;
    I am afeard you make a wanton of me.
LAERTES: Say you so? come on.

(*They play.*)

OSRIC: Nothing, neither way.
LAERTES: Have at you now!

(LAERTES *wounds* HAMLET; *then, in scuffling, they change rapiers.*)
290

KING: Part them. They are incensed.
HAMLET: Nay, come again.

(HAMLET *wounds* LAERTES. *The* QUEEN *falls.*)

OSRIC: Look to the queen there, ho!
HORATIO: They bleed on both sides. How is it, my lord?
295 OSRIC: How is't Laertes?
LAERTES: Why, as a woodcock to mine own springe, Osric.
    I am justly killed with mine own treachery.
HAMLET: How does the queen?
KING: She swoons to see them bleed.
QUEEN: No, no, the drink, the drink! O my dear Hamlet!
    The drink, the drink! I am poisoned.

(*Dies.*)
300

HAMLET: O villany! Ho! let the door be locked.
    Treachery! Seek it out.

(LAERTES *falls. Exit* OSRIC.)

LAERTES: It is here, Hamlet. Hamlet, thou art slain;
    No med'cine in the world can do thee good.
    In thee there is not half an hour's life.   305
    The treacherous instrument is in thy hand,
    Unbated and envenomed. The foul practice
    Hath turned itself on me. Lo, here I lie,
    Never to rise again. Thy mother's poisoned.
    I can no more. The king, the king's to blame.   310
HAMLET: The point envenomed too!
    Then, venom, to thy work.

(*Wounds the* KING.)

ALL: Treason! treason!
KING: O, yet defend me, friends. I am but hurt.
HAMLET: Here, thou incestuous, murd'rous, damnèd Dane,   315
    Drink off this potion. Is thy union here?
    Follow my mother.

(KING *dies.*)

LAERTES: He is justly served.
    It is a poison tempered by himself.
    Exchange forgiveness with me, noble Hamlet.
    Mine and my father's death come not upon thee,
    Nor thine on me!

(*Dies.*)   320

HAMLET: Heaven make thee free of it! I follow thee.
    I am dead, Horatio. Wretched queen, adieu!
    You that look pale and tremble at this chance,
    That are but mutes or audience to this act,   325
    Had I but time, as this fell sergeant Death
    Is strict in his arrest, O, I could tell you—
    But let it be. Horatio, I am dead:
    Thou livest; report me and my cause aright
    To the unsatisfied.
HORATIO: Never believe it: 330
    I am more an antique Roman than a Dane.
    Here's yet some liquor left.
HAMLET: As th'art a man,
    Give me the cup. Let go. By heaven, I'll ha't.
    O God, Horatio, what a wounded name,
    Things standing thus unknown, shall live behind me!   335
    If thou didst ever hold me in thy heart,
    Absent thee from felicity awhile,
    And in this harsh world draw thy breath in pain,
    To tell my story.

(*A march afar off.*)

        What warlike noise is this?

(*Enter* OSRIC.)

OSRIC: Young Fortinbras, with conquest come from Poland,   340
    To th' ambassadors of England gives
    This warlike volley.

---

272 **fat** out of training   285 **make a wanton of me** trifle with me
294 **springe** trap

305 **Unbated** unblunted; **practice** plot   324 **fell** cruel; **sergeant** an
officer whose duty is to summon persons to appear before a court

HAMLET: O, I die, Horatio!
The potent poison quite o'er-crows my spirit.
I cannot live to hear the news from England,
345   But I do prophesy th' election lights
On Fortinbras. He has my dying voice.
So tell him, with th' occurrents, more and less,
Which have solicited—the rest is silence.

(*Dies.*)

HORATIO: Now cracks a noble heart. Good night, sweet prince,
    And flights of angels sing thee to thy rest!

(*March within.*)

    Why does the drum come hither?

(*Enter* FORTINBRAS, *with the* AMBASSADORS [*and with drum,*
350   *colors, and* ATTENDANTS].)

FORTINBRAS: Where is this sight?
HORATIO: What is it you would see?
    If aught of woe or wonder, cease your search.
FORTINBRAS: This quarry cries on havoc. O proud Death,
355   What feast is toward in thine eternal cell
That thou so many princes at a shot
So bloodily hast struck?
AMBASSADORS: The sight is dismal;
    And our affairs from England come too late.
The ears are senseless that should give us hearing
360   To tell him his commandment is fulfilled,
That Rosencrantz and Guildenstern are dead.
Where should we have our thanks?

---

341 **o'er-crows** triumphs over   344 **voice** vote   345 **more and less**
great and small   346 **solicited** incited, prompted   352 **quarry** pile of
dead   353 **toward** impending

HORATIO: Not from his mouth,
Had it th' ability of life to thank you.
He never gave commandment for their death.
But since, so jump upon this bloody question,   365
You from the Polack wars, and you from England,
Are here arrived, give order that these bodies
High on a stage be placèd to the view,
And let me speak to th' yet unknowing world
How these things came about. So shall you hear   370
Of carnal, bloody, and unnatural acts;
Of accidental judgements, casual slaughters;
Of deaths put on by cunning and forced cause;
And, in this upshot, purposes mistook
Fall'n on th' inventors' heads. All this can I
Truly deliver.   375
FORTINBRAS: Let us haste to hear it.
And call the noblest to the audience.
For me, with sorrow I embrace my fortune.
I have some rights of memory in this kingdom,
Which now to claim my vantage doth invite me.   380
HORATIO: Of that I shall have also cause to speak,
And from his mouth whose voice will draw on more.
But let this same be presently performed,
Even while men's minds are wild, lest more mischance
On plots and errors happen.
FORTINBRAS: Let four captains   385
Bear Hamlet like a soldier to the stage,
For he was likely, had he been put on,
To have proved most royal; and for his passage
The soldier's music and the rite of war
Speak loudly for him.   390
Take up the bodies. Such a sight as this
Becomes the field, but here shows much amiss.
Go, bid the soldiers shoot.

---

363 **jump** exactly   371 **put on** instigated; **forced cause** by reason of
compulsion   385 **put on** set to perform in office   386 **passage** death

CRITICAL CONTEXTS

SIR PHILIP SIDNEY (1554–1586)
from *Apology for Poetry* (1598)
Edited by FORREST G. ROBINSON

Philip Sidney was one of the preeminent courtiers of his day. He was a familiar figure at the court of Queen Elizabeth I, led an ill-fated military expedition to the Netherlands (where he was fatally wounded), wrote an important sonnet sequence, *Astrophil and Stella,* and a prose romance, *Arcadia.* His *Apology for Poetry* develops a defense of poets and poetry based on their ability to offer a fictive "golden world," an idealized image of reality that can edify, entertain, and instruct. Reading Sidney's *Apology,* it is useful to bear several questions in mind: What is the problem that Sidney is attempting to address here? Is there a moral or ethical problem posed by poetry, particularly by the fact that poetry is a form of fiction, of lying? Why is it important to Sidney to compare the poet with the historian and the philosopher? What are the underlying problems that Sidney is attempting to address in his assessment of contemporary dramatic genres? How can you read Sidney's essay against Aristotle's or Horace's?

. . . There is no art delivered to mankind that hath not the works of nature for his principal object, without which they could not consist, and on which they so depend, as they become actors and players, as it were, of what nature will have set forth. So doth the astronomer look upon the stars, and by that he seeth, setteth down what order nature hath taken therein. So do the geometrician and arithmetician in their diverse sorts of quantities. So doth the musician in times tell you which by nature agree, which not. The natural philosopher thereon hath his name, and the moral philosopher standeth upon the natural virtues, vices, and passions of man; and follow nature (saith he) therein, and thou shalt not err. The lawyer saith what men have determined; the historian what men have done. The grammarian speaketh only of the rules of speech, and the rhetorician and logician, considering what in nature will soonest prove and persuade, thereon give artificial[1] rules, which still are compassed within the circle of a question, according to the proposed matter. The physician weigheth the nature of a man's body, and the nature of things helpful or hurtful unto it. And the metaphysic, though it be in the second and abstract notions, and therefore be counted supernatural, yet doth he indeed build upon the depth of nature. Only the poet, disdaining to be tied to any such subjection, lifted up with the vigor of his own invention, doth grow in effect another nature, in making things either better than nature bringeth forth, or quite anew, forms such as never were in nature, as the Heroes, Demigods, Cyclops, Chimeras, Furies, and such like; so as he goeth hand in hand with nature, not enclosed within the narrow warrant of her gifts, but freely ranging only within the zodiac of his own wit.

Nature never set forth the earth in so rich tapestry as divers poets have done, neither with pleasant rivers, fruitful trees, sweet smelling flowers, nor whatsoever else may make the too much loved earth more lovely. Her world is brazen, the poets only deliver a golden. . . . Our tragedies and comedies (not without cause cried out against), observing rules neither of honest civility nor of skillful poetry, excepting *Gorboduc*[2] (again I say, of those that I have seen), which notwithstanding, as it is full of stately speeches and well sounding phrases, climbing to the height of Seneca his[3] style, and as full of notable morality, which it doth most delightfully teach, and so obtain the very end of poesy; yet in troth it is very defectious in the circumstances, which grieveth me, because it might not remain as an exact model of all tragedies. For it is faulty both in place and time, the two necessary companions of all corporal actions. For where the stage should always represent but one place, and the uttermost time presupposed in it should be, both by Aristotle's precept and common reason, but one day, there is both many days and many places inartificially[4] imagined.

But if it be so in *Gorboduc,* how much more in all the rest? where you shall have Asia of the one side, and Afric of the other, and so many other under-kingdoms, that the player, when he cometh in, must ever begin with telling where he is, or else the tale will not be conceived. Now ye shall have three ladies walk to gather flowers, and then we must believe the stage to be a garden. By and by we hear news of shipwreck in the same place, and then we are to blame if we accept it not for a rock. Upon the back of that comes out a hideous monster with fire and smoke, and then the miserable beholders are bound to take it for a cave. While in the meantime two armies fly in, represented with four swords and bucklers, and then what hard heart will not receive it for a pitched field?

---

[1]**artificial** humanly contrived, rather than natural

[2]**Gorboduc** an early English play (first performed in 1562), modeled on the tragedies of Seneca
[3]**Seneca his** Seneca's
[4]**inartificially** artlessly

Now of time they are much more liberal, for ordinary it is that two young princes fall in love. After many traverses, she is got with child, delivered of a fair boy, he is lost, groweth a man, falls in love, and is ready to get another child, and all this in two hours' space: which, how absurd it is in sense, even sense may imagine, and art hath taught, and all ancient examples justified, and at this day, the ordinary players in Italy will not err in. Yet will some bring in an example of Eunuchus in Terence, that containeth matter of two days, yet far short of twenty years. True it is, and so was it to be played in two days, and so fitted to the time it set forth. And though Plautus hath in one place done amiss, let us hit with him, and not miss with him. But they will say, how then shall we set forth a story which containeth both many places and many times? And do they not know that a tragedy is tied to the laws of poesy, and not of history, not bound to follow the story, but having liberty, either to feign a quite new matter, or to frame the history to the most tragical conveniency? Again, many things may be told which cannot be showed, if they know the difference betwixt reporting and representing. . . .

Early Modern Europe IV

The 1993 Willamette College production of Aphra Behn's *The Rover*.

In London, Paris, and Madrid, theater and drama experienced a second "renaissance" in the later seventeenth century. In these cities, the theater came under the influence and protection of the king and his court, and the theaters of both London and Paris adapted Italian staging practices, as did the theaters of the Spanish court. As scenic technology became increasingly complex and spectacular, theater buildings achieved the form they would hold well into the nineteenth century, and the work of new playwrights and new dramatic designs invigorated the dramatic repertoire.

Yet for all their similarities, the theaters of Restoration England, of Louis XIV's France, and of the Spanish "Golden Age" were sustained by very different social and political climates. In France, Louis XIV declared *"L'état, c'est moi"*—"I am the state"—in 1660, confidently drawing all state authority into the person of the king and his magnificent court. The later seventeenth century in France was a period of royal absolutism, as the throne worked to consolidate its power. In England, conditions were very different, for 1660 brought the restoration of the monarchy, which had to negotiate its authority with a still-powerful Parliament, which gradually gained control of many royal prerogatives; the religious issues surrounding the succession of the English monarch remained a divisive problem throughout the period as well. In both countries, the theater became associated with the throne and reflected the tensions animating social and political life.

The Political Climate

In France, a character in Molière's play *Tartuffe* drew the official portrait of the absolute monarch: "A Prince who sees into our inmost hearts, / And can't be fooled by any trickster's arts." Yet the authoritarian policies of the French government, the internecine competition among members of the court, and even the fortunes of the theater suggest that the king's claim of absolute power was challenged in a variety of ways. Under Louis XIII (reigned 1610–1643) and Louis XIV (reigned 1643–1715), the Crown strove to centralize its power by crushing the claims of the landed nobility and by expanding French rule in a series of costly wars. Since Louis XIII came to the throne at the age of nine, when his father—Henry IV—was assassinated, much of this expansion was carried on by his chief minister, Cardinal Richelieu (1585–1642), and Richelieu's successor, Cardinal Mazarin (1602–1661). The suppression of the traditional nobility was achieved largely through Richelieu's formation of a new bureaucracy loyal to the Crown, partly composed of politically active clergy and partly of commoners promoted over the heads of the nobility to critical positions in the government. Allowing these "new men" to buy aristocratic titles, the Crown raised money and further diluted the power of the nobility. The Crown's ravenous appetite for cash to pay for the lavish life of the court and for expensive building projects, such as the palace of Versailles (built by Louis XIV in 1673), further weakened the nobility and alienated the peasantry. Using tax-farmers, who paid a fixed sum to the government in exchange for the authority to collect taxes and pocket the excess as profit, the Crown squeezed the nobles' wealth directly into the royal coffers, impoverishing their lands and making the peasantry increasingly rebellious.

A poor and disaffected peasantry, a jealous aristocracy, an upstart bourgeoisie, and an increasingly authoritarian and isolated monarchy: this became the recipe for revolution. Although the French Revolution did not erupt until 1789, France suffered civil convulsions throughout the seventeenth century that dramatize the tension between Louis' absolutist rhetoric and the political realities of his reign. The nobles led a series of rebellions called the Fronde throughout the 1640s and 1650s, in an effort to unseat Louis and his powerful ministers. Louis defeated these uprisings and finally sealed the fate of his enemies when he required the nobility to attend him at Versailles, so he could keep his eye on their activities. However, the Fronde was part of a more pervasive unrest. Relentless taxation, economic stagnation, and repeated famines throughout the seventeenth century made the peasants angry as well, and peasant riots and rebellions took place in nearly every province of France in nearly every decade of the century. Finally, Louis XIV also had difficulty with the most volatile issue of seventeenth-century Europe—religious dissent. The close ties between the

Crown and the church often resulted in the suppression of Protestant sects, particularly the Calvinist French Huguenots. Protestant rebellion had forced the enactment of the Edict of Nantes in 1598, granting the Huguenots considerable religious freedom. Louis XIV revoked the Edict in 1685, giving the government wider latitude to suppress increasingly energetic religious protest. Louis XIV carefully crafted the image of the "Le Roi Soleil"—the Sun King—whose absolute authority seemed almost a force of nature, not a fact of politics. Throughout his reign, though, Louis had to contend with recalcitrant factions who refused to accept completely his characterization of the king's power.

In England, resistance to royal authority had been much more successful. Between 1603 and 1642, the Stuart kings James I (reigned 1603–1625) and his son, Charles I (reigned 1625–1649), worked to limit the power of Parliament and to enforce increasingly strict religious laws that suppressed the Protestant Puritan sects and demanded conformity with the Church of England. In 1642, Parliament passed legislation limiting the powers of the throne, and Civil War between Parliamentary and Royalist forces erupted. Charles I was executed in 1649; his wife and children (including the future king, Charles II) escaped to France. From 1653 to 1658, Oliver Cromwell served as Lord Protector of the realm, but Royalist sentiments eventually prevailed and established Charles II (reigned 1660–1685) on the throne.

Although the monarchy was restored—the term *Restoration* refers generally to the period beginning with the reign of Charles II and extending to the end of the seventeenth century—Charles II was in no position to command the nation, and English politics in the later seventeenth century mainly concerned the negotiation of power between the Crown and Parliament. Charles' death in 1685 spurred a crisis in that his son James II (reigned 1685–1688) was Catholic and threatened to compromise English religious and civil autonomy from the Catholic church and the Catholic states of Europe. In 1689, Parliament effectively deposed James, inviting his Protestant daughter Mary (reigned as Mary II, 1689–1694) and her husband, William of Orange (reigned as William III, 1689–1702), to return to England and assume the throne. While Louis XIV increasingly insisted on the autonomous power of the throne in France, the Parliament in England finally achieved a lasting compromise with the Crown in the form of a constitutional monarchy. In bringing William and Mary into power, Parliament gained the authority of consent over royal succession, a power it confirmed in 1702 in naming the daughter of James II, Anne, as successor (reigned as Queen Anne, 1702–1714).

While in an important sense the gulf separating French and English culture has always been narrow and deep, like the English Channel, Spanish culture in the Renaissance arises from a very different history. Spain was occupied by Muslim and Arab invaders from North Africa, then known as the "Moors," in 711 and is still marked by its five centuries of Islamic culture. In 1479, Ferdinand of Aragon and Isabella of Castile were married, forming the alliance that gave rise to modern Spain. In 1480 they joined forces with the Catholic Inquisition, expelling Jews from the country. At the Conquest of Granada in 1492, the "Moors" were finally driven out of Spain.

Having formed a single state, the Spanish monarchy successfully expanded its reach into the global empire of the sixteenth and seventeenth centuries. Under Charles V, Spain's territory included its many New World colonies as well as the Netherlands and the Holy Roman Empire of central Europe, and the culture of the Spanish court was unrivaled in Europe; this was the era of Cervantes and Calderón, Velásquez and El Greco. During the reign of Philip II (1556–1598), however, Spain's domination of Europe began to wane. Spain became involved in a brutal and expensive effort to retain control of the Netherlands, a hotbed of Protestant resistance. English soldiers—Sir Philip Sidney and Ben Jonson, among others—fought the Spanish in the Netherlands, and Philip tried in several ways to outmaneuver the English. He proposed marriage to Queen Elizabeth, but as with other suitors, she strung him along for political purposes and finally refused him. He also mounted a massive naval invasion of England, the Spanish Armada of 1588, which was surprisingly defeated. Spain continued to wane in the seventeenth century, eventually losing the Netherlands and losing Portugal in 1657. By 1665, Spain was ruled by the last of the Hapsburg kings, the deformed imbecile Charles II (1665–1700). The death of Charles II drew all of Europe into the Wars of the Spanish Succession.

Theater in France, 1660–1700

Louis XIV's familiar sobriquet, "Le Roi Soleil," derives from a role he played in a court ballet devised for him in 1653. A fine dancer, Louis sponsored and took part in a wide variety of entertainments. Moreover, the centralization of power in the king and the court paralleled the increasing institutionalization of the arts under Louis XIV, as a means of advancing his own prestige and of keeping control over potentially seditious activities. The most famous of these institutions—the ACADÉMIE FRANÇAISE—was chartered in 1637 and used by Cardinal Richelieu to evaluate a critical controversy surrounding Pierre Corneille's play *The Cid*. Corneille's detractors had sharply attacked the play, and Richelieu urged the Académie to resolve whether *The Cid* could legitimately be described as effective tragedy in neoclassical terms (on *neoclassicism*, see p. 460). In return, Richelieu promoted the Académie and its aims, the purification of French language and literature, and the advancement of official French culture. Louis XIV assumed the role of official protector of the Académie Française in 1672 and sponsored other institutions as ornaments to his reign: the Académie Royale de Musique (1672), the Académie Royale de Peinture et de Sculpture (1648), the Académie des Inscriptions (1663), the Académie des Sciences (1666), and the Académie de l'Architecture (1671). The institution of the stage was no exception. Theatrical companies had always needed the king's license to play in Paris, and Louis licensed several companies and named Molière's company as the *Troupe du roi*. After Molière's death in 1673, the leading tragic actress in Paris, Mademoiselle Champmeslé, joined with Molière's troupe and gained the king's patronage. The new company—the COMÉDIE FRANÇAISE—opened in August of 1680. It held a MONOPOLY on the production of all spoken drama in French, and although this monopoly has long since vanished, the Comédie Française remains the principal company performing the French classical repertoire.

In Louis XIV's Paris, the institutions of art—including the theater—were identified with the prerogatives of the king and his court, though the structure of the theater had its roots in practices dating back to the Middle Ages. Throughout the later Middle Ages and into the sixteenth century, stage production in Paris was controlled by the Confrérie de la Passion, a guildlike corporation initially formed to stage religious drama. In 1545 the Confrérie purchased land in Paris from the Duke of Burgundy and erected the Hôtel de Bourgogne, at the time probably the only permanent theater building in Europe (*hôtel* in this case means "hall" or "large building"). Extensively remodeled in 1647, the Hôtel de Bourgogne served as the model for other theaters built in the seventeenth century: the Théâtre du Marais (built in a tennis court in 1629, rebuilt in 1644); the Palais-Cardinal (built by Richelieu in 1640; later renamed the Palais-Royal); the Salle des Machines (1642), and the Comédie Française (1689).

The shape of these theaters owes something to the Hôtel de Bourgogne, and something to tennis courts as well, for tennis courts were often used as theaters. (In the sixteenth and seventeenth centuries, tennis courts were long indoor rooms with side galleries.) These theaters generally had deep, RAKED STAGES (40 feet deep, 45 feet wide at the Hôtel de Bourgogne) that faced an open PIT called the PARTERRE (literally, "on the ground") which was used for standing spectators. The auditorium had BOXES on three sides; GALLERY seating rose above the boxes opposite the stage; some patrons were also seated on the stage itself. The theaters were large—the Hôtel de Bourgogne initially held 1,600 spectators, the Comédie Française held 2,000—and many theaters made extensive use of stage scenery, sometimes concocting extraordinary spectacles. In a fantasy celebrating Louis XIV's wedding in 1662, the entire royal family and its entourage were "flown" by machines in the Salle

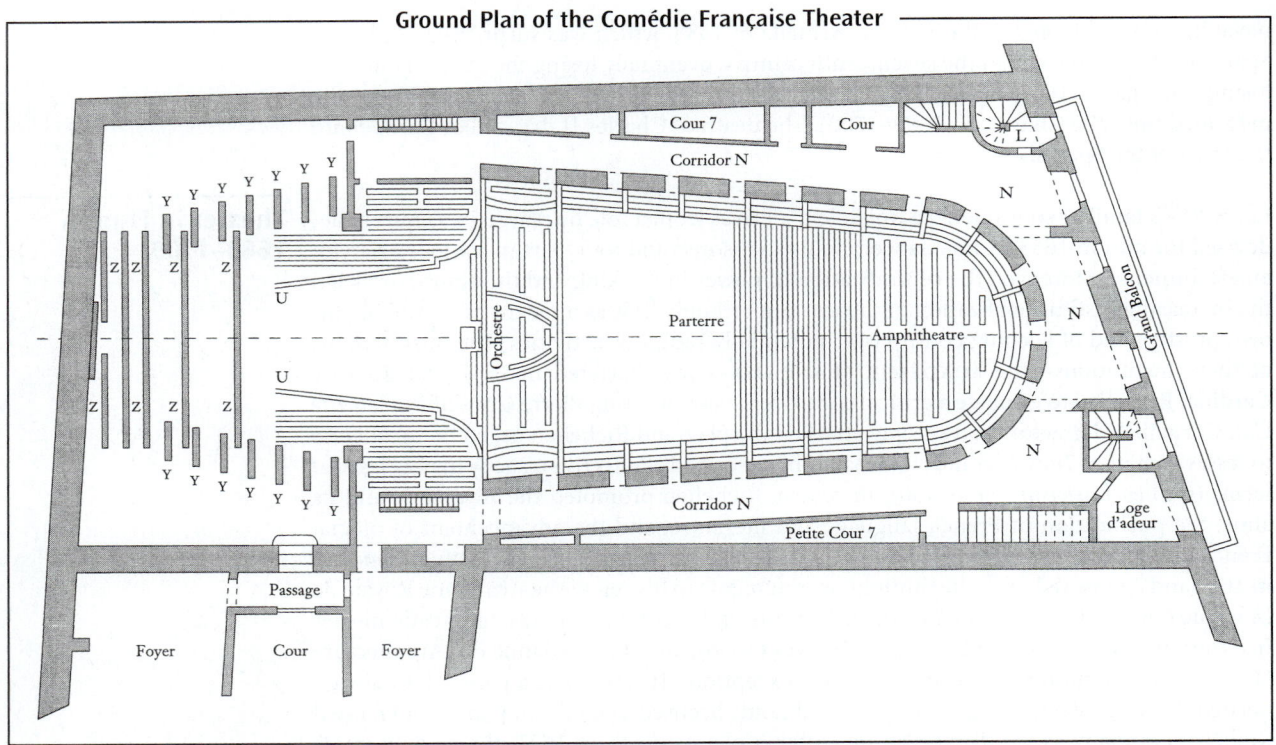

Ground Plan of the Comédie Française Theater

The Comédie Française had this basic design from 1689 to 1770. Note the open *parterre*, the wings (marked Y), and the backdrops (Z). The benches on the stage were added during the eighteenth century.

des Machines; in a production in 1671, 300 deities were lifted aloft. The dramatic theaters—the Hôtel de Bourgogne, the Palais-Royal, the Comédie Française—tended to avoid such effects, using instead a single setting for each play, depending on the genre of the play. The theaters generally used a series of staggered **WINGS AND BACKDROP** to create the effect of perspective, adapting both scenic practices and scene-changing technology from Italian theaters.

Acting companies in Paris were organized as investment corporations requiring the patronage of the Crown and had long included women in their ranks. Louis XIV's reign saw a series of great actresses take the stage, Mademoiselle DuParc and Mademoiselle Champmeslé among them. Companies were comprised of twelve members (eight men, four women), who shared the company's profits. The company hired additional actors when necessary. The Comédie Française standardized this practice: its twelve main actors—called **SOCIÉTAIRES**—ran the company for twenty years, and new *sociétaires* could be recruited only after the retirement of current members. Actors in the Comédie Française received an annual subsidy from the Crown and a retirement pension if they completed their twenty years with the company. The company purchased plays, which were cast by the author. Throughout the 1650s and 1660s the major companies kept about 70 plays in repertoire and generally played three or four times per week. After the 1680s, the Comédie Française began daily performances, beginning at 5 P.M.

We should recall that life at court was itself a kind of performance, and that attending the theater provided ample opportunity for aristocrats, courtiers, and aspiring courtiers to display and preen themselves. In a milieu so dependent on the king's preference, we can easily imagine how stage seating and side boxes emphasized that the evening's entertainment included the audience's performances as well as the actors'. This sense of the reciprocity between court and stage is signaled more concretely by the fortunes of the Parisian theaters after Louis XIV moved the court to Versailles. Although five companies flourished in Paris while Louis kept court in the city, by 1700 only two remained.

Theater in England, 1660–1737

At the outbreak of the English Civil War in 1642, Parliament closed the London theaters, putting a stop to dramatic performance. Some companies managed to mount secret productions between 1642 and 1660, but Parliament and city officials moved quickly to suppress them, sometimes by destroying the theater buildings. In the 1650s, however, William Davenant (1606–1668), a Royalist supporter of Charles I and successor to Ben Jonson as writer of court masques, attempted to mount operas. In 1656 he succeeded in staging a production of *The Siege of Rhodes* at Rutland House, performing it again in 1658 and 1659 at the Cockpit theater and elsewhere in London.

The restoration of Charles II to the throne in 1660 inaugurated a period of renewed theatrical vitality. As in France—where Charles developed a taste for theater during his exile—the theater was closely associated with royal prerogatives. Upon his return, Charles rewarded **PATENTS** to William Davenant and Thomas Killegrew (1612–1683) to open theaters under royal authority. These **PATENT THEATERS** (also called "theaters royal")—Davenant's Duke's company, and Killigrew's King's company—thus held a royal monopoly on the production of spoken English drama. Although they underwent huge modifications, the patent theaters dominated the legitimate theater until the mid-nineteenth century, when legislation was passed that finally broke their monopoly. Yet monopoly could not guarantee support. The two companies, unable to turn a profit, were united into a single company from 1682 to 1695.

When the theaters reopened in 1660, theatrical taste had changed significantly. Although a few of the older, pre-1642 theater buildings were still standing, they could not handle the new theater technology. For, as in the French theater, the English theater rapidly encouraged the development of scenic practices already well-known in Italy—a **PROSCENIUM** stage and moveable painted wings and backdrop used to create a visual setting for the play. Onstage, theaters used stock sets—one for classical tragedy, one for romantic comedy, and so on—that conformed to the dramatic genre of the play. In 1661, Davenant converted Lisle's Tennis Court to the Lincoln's Inn Fields Theater, which measured 30 by 70 feet; he replaced this theater with the Dorset Garden Theater in 1671. Killegrew erected his Theatre Royal in Bridges Street in 1663. When it burned in 1672, he built a new Theatre Royal in Drury Lane, which opened in 1674; a theater has occupied this site down to the present time.

The new English theaters were much smaller than the French theaters. The Drury Lane theater, for example, held 650 to 700 people, though it was expanded throughout the late seventeenth and eighteenth centuries and eventually held more than 2,000. Nonetheless, like the French theaters, the English houses also introduced new design and staging practices: a proscenium stage flanked by a large **APRON**, footlights to illuminate the stage, a raked pit with benches (the French *parterre* was flat and had no seats), side and rear box seats, and a rear gallery. This division of the house accorded with social and class distinctions in the audience, which was in any event a narrow selection of the English public, in part because the theater was recognized as the ornament of the privileged, and—not incidentally—because plays were produced in the afternoon, when working people could not easily attend. The entire auditorium was lighted by chandeliers, making the audience itself very much a part of the show: in an important sense the performance did not stop at the edge of the stage. Although the theaters were not at the court itself, they were frequently patronized by courtiers and the nobility, who preened and displayed themselves to the audience—sometimes from seats onstage. Charles II—who numbered the well-known actress Nell Gwynn (1650–1687) among his many mistresses—was also frequently in the audience.

Companies were generally managed by one of the actors, and they avoided the need for lengthy casting and rehearsal by developing LINES OF BUSINESS, in which each actor would specialize in a particular type of character: heroic lead, comic lead, male heavy, female heavy, utility player, and so on. Acting style was relatively formal, and actors often played downstage on the apron directly to the audience; a famous speech—one of Hamlet's soliloquies, for example—would be delivered directly to the audience, something like an operatic aria today, a practice called POINTING. As the theater developed in the later seventeenth century, sharing companies were replaced by companies financed by outside investors, who paid the actors salaries and took a percentage of the profits. Companies were large and salaries low; actors were compensated by BENEFIT performances, in which the actor (on his or her benefit night) received the entire profit from a given evening's performance, minus the operating expenses of the house. The practice of supplementing salaries with benefit performances continued well into the nineteenth century, and although most benefit nights—after the house expenses were deducted—left the actors with little additional pay, benefits provided an excuse to keep actors' salaries low.

By far the greatest innovation in the English theater, though, was the introduction of actresses onstage. English comedies in this period were often frankly concerned with sexual intrigue, and the actresses who played in them—and in the new heroic tragedies, and in

Christopher Wren's Theatre Royal, Drury Lane

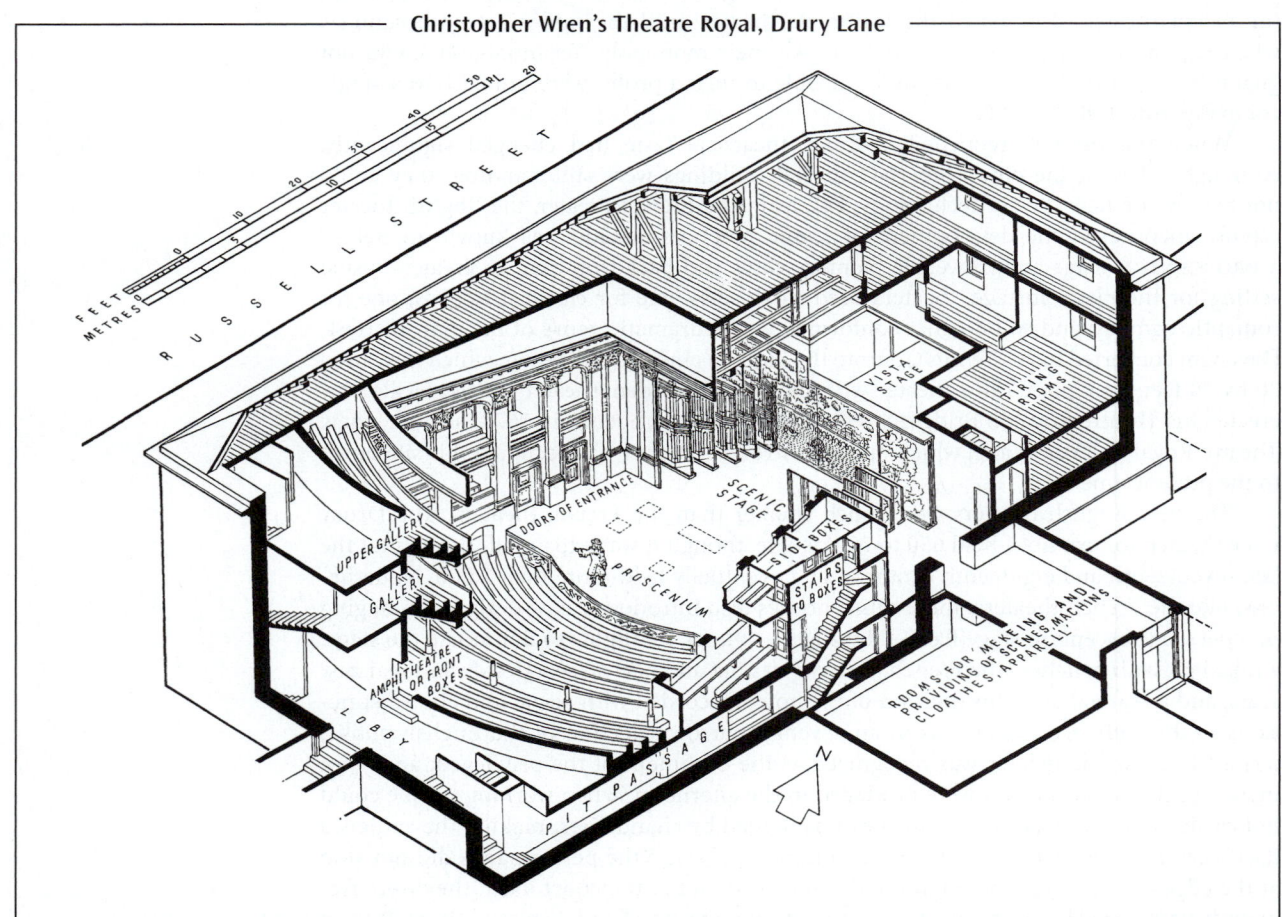

In 1674, Christopher Wren designed a new Theatre Royal, Drury Lane. Note that the acting area extends to the apron, in front of the wing and backdrop stage scenery. Pit seating, side boxes, and two galleries also are visible.

the plays by Shakespeare, Jonson, Fletcher, and other Renaissance playwrights who continued to hold the stage—also had a reputation for sexual licentiousness. Yet, while several actresses, like Nell Gwynne, were mistresses of the famous and powerful, the phenomenon of regarding actresses as sexual objects, of classing them with prostitutes, has more to do with the status and vulnerability of working women in a highly stratified and patriarchal society than it does with the immorality of the stage or its performers. Indeed, actresses' ongoing struggle to assert themselves as legitimate performers was born at this time as well, epitomized in the careers of Elizabeth Barry (1658–1713), Anne Bracegirdle (1663–1748), and many others.

Theater in Spain's Golden Age, 1580–1680

As in medieval England and France, medieval Spanish theater was strongly influenced by the church, which saw in the drama a source of instruction and inspiration. Although there is some evidence for liturgical drama as early as the twelfth century, the principal form of medieval theater was the *AUTO SACRAMENTALE,* a form of allegorical religious drama initially devised to celebrate the feast of Corpus Christi. But while the mystery cycles were suppressed in Protestant England, the Spanish *autos* continued to be performed alongside the secular theater until they were banned in 1765. Like the English cycles, the *autos* were in civic hands, and by the late sixteenth century major cities would perform *autos* as many as three times per year, usually in the central city plaza before a gathering of citizens and civic officials. Professional actors were hired for the *autos* and were drawn through the city on wagons (*CARROS*); the *carros* were heavily decorated, and a prize was given for the most spectacular *carro*. Despite their abstract themes, the *autos* remained extremely popular and drew on the talents of the best playwrights of the era— between 1647 and 1681, for instance, all the *autos* performed in Madrid were written by Pedro Calderón de la Barca.

Philip II, Philip III, and Philip IV were all interested in theater and commissioned playwrights to devise entertainments; during the reign of Philip III, Spain developed an impressive court theater. Early in the seventeenth century, this court theater merely occupied a hall at the Alcázar palace, as Ben Jonson and Inigo Jones had done at Whitehall palace in England, and it produced a similar kind of entertainment: mythological dramas that required spectacular scenery, effects, and costumes. But by the 1630s, the center of court theater shifted to the new palace of Buen Retiro. Here, in 1640 Cosme Lotti (d. 1643) was retained to build a permanent theater that could perform the scenic effects of the Italian theater. This theater was roofed, but in its basic design resembled the most influential of Spanish theaters in the Golden Age, the public theater or *CORRAL.*

Although the Spanish public theater resembled the public theaters of Elizabethan London, it stood in a much different relationship to city life. While the English theaters were banned from the city proper and were erected across the Thames in Southwark, the Spanish theaters were public institutions. Since the medieval church held the rights to theatrical production, the public theaters were licensed by religious confraternities in the sixteenth century, which used the funds for various charitable purposes, including maintaining the general hospital of Madrid. By the early seventeenth century, these funds were paid directly to the city, and theaters continued to subsidize charities well into the nineteenth century. Companies of actors were licensed to play in the city, and took a lease on a *corral* for a stated period of time. In general, Spanish companies toured major cities and towns, and only Seville and Madrid allowed two companies to perform at the same time. While playwrights were initially associated with individual companies, by the seventeenth century playwrights would sell their plays to the company: they were paid very well for an *auto,* and adequately for a regular play—about 500 reales, or about 10 times the daily wage of a laborer. Companies were composed of men and boys until 1587, when women were allowed to appear onstage. The church issued a decree banning women from performing onstage in 1596, but by 1599, a royal council ruled that actresses could be permitted, providing they were

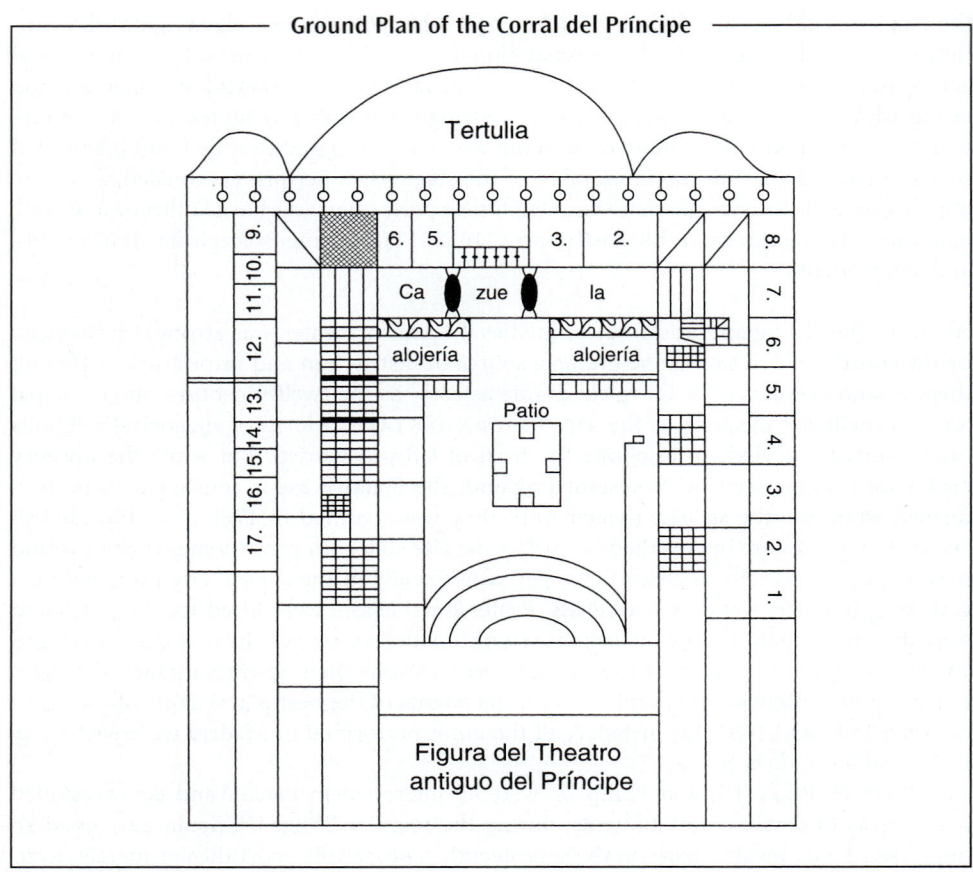

Made in 1730, this drawing of the Corral del Príncipe shows the important features of the theater: the *patio,* the *alojería,* the *gradas* (unmarked), and the *cazuela.*

married to a member of the company; it also ruled against cross-dressing, so that when Rosaura appeared dressed as a man in Calderón's *Life Is a Dream,* the actress wore a man's costume only down to the waist with a skirt below.

The reciprocity between the city and the theater is also revealed in the design of public theaters of the golden age, particularly the two principal theaters of Madrid, the Corral de la Cruz, opened in 1579 as Spain's first theater, and the Corral del Príncipe, opened in 1583. The theaters were originally merely stages placed in a courtyard enclosed on three or four sides by four-story buildings; over time the theaters gradually acquired possession of these structures, but in the meantime the buildings' galleries and windows could be sold to spectators separately. The central courtyard or **PATIO** was unroofed, and like the pit of English theaters was occupied by standing spectators. In the seventeenth century, a few rows of benches (called **TABURETES**) were erected near the stage, on a raised and fenced dais. Along the sides of the *patio* rose the **GRADAS,** steeply raked rows of seats that rose to the second floor. The **ALOJERÍA,** a tavern, served refreshments, and was located at the rear of the *patio;* above the *alojería* were several stories of galleries: the **CAZUELA,** or women's gallery, on the second floor; above it galleries for the City of Madrid and Council of Castile officials; and a gallery for intellectual and church officials, the **TERTULIA.** Above the *gradas,* the grated windows of the houses served as box seats. The third and fourth floors of the buildings were converted to **DESVANES** or "attics," small open galleries.

View of the Corral del Príncipe

This illustration provides a view of the Corral del Príncipe from the rear of the *patio,* perhaps from the *cazuela.*

Although theatrical production extended into a number of other forms—ballet, opera, royal pageants, and the special-effects extravaganzas called **MACHINE PLAYS**—prevailing attitudes, particularly in France, prohibited the mixing of dramatic genres: Tragedy and comedy were firmly discriminated from one another and from others kinds of entertainment. In France, comedy—and, indeed, the organization of theatrical companies—was particularly influenced by the techniques of the Italian **COMMEDIA DELL' ARTE.** French tragic drama inherited a taste for classical subject matter from the schools and universities, which had led Europe in translating Greek and Roman playwrights into French. Throughout the sixteenth century, the court sponsored a variety of efforts to classicize the theater, supporting several important playwrights, including Robert Garnier and Étienne Jodelle, who created highly wrought and refined tragedies based on the model of classical drama. The heroic tragedies of Pierre Corneille (1606–1684) and Jean Racine (1639–1699) epitomize this tradition while also turning it in a new direction, refracting contemporary moral, political, and philosophical issues through the lens of a classical style.

English drama in the Restoration also was affected by the **HEROIC TRAGEDIES** of France and Spain, by the comedies of Ben Jonson and James Shirley, and by the tragedies

Dramatic Innovation in France, England, and Spain

of Shakespeare and of Francis Beaumont and John Fletcher, which continued to be performed, though often in revised or adapted form. John Dryden (1631–1700), for example, not only adapted versions of *The Tempest* and *Antony and Cleopatra* (the latter as *All for Love,* 1677), but also wrote plays in the mode of heroic tragedy, such as *Aureng-Zebe* (1675) and *The Conquest of Granada* (1669). Heroic tragedy generally represents the idealized passions of characters forced to choose between love and personal honor. Comic drama took its inspiration both from European models—Molière's plays, for example—and from the earlier plays of Ben Jonson, but in the plays of William Wycherly (1640–1716), Sir George Etherege (1635–1692), and William Congreve (1670–1729), English comedy rapidly developed its own original style. Restoration comedies are most often in the vein of **COMEDY OF MANNERS,** contemporary dramas in which witty aristocrats, city dupes and dandies, and dull country gentlemen are engaged in an elaborate adventure of sexual intrigue. Restoration comedy is often elegant and verbally polished, and obsessed with issues of class, privilege, manners, and sex. In addition, much as the Restoration theater witnessed the rise of actresses onstage, it also saw the first women to achieve success as playwrights: Aphra Behn (1640–1689), Catharine Trotter (1679–1749), and Susanna Centlivre (1670–1723).

After the turn of the century, the risqué character of many plays spurred one of the perennial movements to restrain the theater as an immoral institution. Partly as a result of Jeremy Collier's diatribe *A Short View of the Immorality and Profaneness of the English Stage* (1698), and partly as a result of changing attitudes and social mores, English comedy after 1700—the plays of Sir Richard Steele (1672–1729), Colley Cibber (1671–1757), George Farquhar (1678–1707), Oliver Goldsmith (1728–1774), and Richard Brinsley Sheridan (1751–1816), for instance—became more romantic and sentimental. Moreover, political satire in English theater was also sharply limited with the passing of the Stage Licensing Act of 1737. After 1737, all plays produced for public entertainment had to be submitted for censorship prior to production. The censor could require changes, delete words, passages, or scenes, or refuse to grant permission entirely. Confronting the Act by producing a nonlicensed play was to risk the fining and imprisonment of everyone involved in the production. While theaters found a variety of ways to subvert or sidestep the law, the censorship remained in effect—with some modifications—until 1968, inhibiting the possibility of dramatic innovation.

In the early sixteenth century, a Spanish theatrical manager may well have written his own plays and acted in them himself. Lope de Rueda (1510–1565), for example, was a touring performer and the author of both *autos* and secular plays. But by the late sixteenth century, companies would pay a playwright for the play, and the theaters had made several genres popular: the **CAPA Y ESPADA** or heroic/romantic "cape and sword" play was very popular, as was the **RUIDO** or "noise" play. But the forms of Golden Age drama were in many ways determined by the extraordinary and prolific career of Lope Félix de Vega Carpio (1562–1635). Lope de Vega is frequently said to have written more than 1,500 plays—which points to the immense popularity of the theater and its constant need for new material—and more than 450 of his plays have survived. He is particularly associated with **COMEDIA NUEVA,** a genre mixing the tragic and the comic, high and low characters (including the **GRACIOSO,** a comic fool), and usually having a romantic plot. In the intervals between the acts of his plays, short interludes (**ENTREMESES**) were performed, which were coherent plays in themselves. Like other playwrights in this period, Lope de Vega also wrote *autos,* but his best-known work is *Fuente Ovejuna* (1614), a play about a vicious tyrant that critics have seen as an allegory on Portuguese independence.

Lope shared the stage with several equally brilliant playwrights, principally with Pedro Calderón de la Barca (1600–1681), who succeeded Lope deVega as Spain's most influential dramatist. Miguel de Cervantes (1547–1616), the author of *Don Quixote,* wrote about thirty

COMMEDIA DELL' ARTE

The term *commedia dell' arte* means the "comedy of the professional players," and *commedia* became popular throughout Europe in the sixteenth century. *Commedia* companies were itinerant (though one was established in Paris for part of Louis XIV's reign), organized around ten or twelve actors, men and women, each of whom played a stock character who could be easily recognized by typical and routine behavior. Although the characters were fixed, the plots that *commedia* companies played were generally improvised; the actor relied on the traits of his or her character and a core of stage business from which to invent action and dialogue. The cast usually included one or two pairs of young lovers (the INNAMORATO and INNAMORATA), good-looking, aristocratic, or fashionable characters played without masks. The rest of the cast was masked and played more stereotypical roles: the CAPITANO, a military braggart and coward, played with sword and cape; the PANTALONE, an elderly dupe, often in love, played in stockings, breeches, and slippers; the DOTTORE, sometimes actually a doctor, but otherwise a pedantic friend of the Pantalone; and a variety of comic parts called ZANNI, usually sly servants. The most familiar of these parts is *Arlecchino*, or HARLEQUIN, a cunning character who is usually an acrobat, wearing a patched costume (later refined to a diamondshaped pattern), a black cap, and carrying his slapstick—the origin of our term "slapstick," which gives some idea of what *commedia* humor was like. *Commedia* was also popular in England, but it had fewer long-term effects on the comic drama than on the rise of English PANTOMIME. In England, plays were often followed by a short AFTERPIECE, which frequently led Harlequin into adventures with mythological characters. John Rich (1692–1761), taking the name Lun, was the most famous Harlequin of the early eighteenth century English stage. ■

Pantalone and Harlequin

Note the mask and breeches of the Pantalone (left), and the mask, slapstick, and diamond-shaped patches of the Harlequin (right).

plays, of which sixteen remain. Tirso de Molina (1584–1648) was a friar who had written more than 400 plays—eighty survive—before he was reprimanded by the Council of Castile; his best-known play, *El Burlador de Seville* (*The Trickster of Seville*) is the earliest play on the subject of Don Juan. The playwright Guillén de Castro (1569–1631) was a friend of Lope deVega; his influence on the French theater is perhaps as marked as it was in Spain. Guillén de Castro wrote *Las Mocedades del Cid* (*TheYouthful Adventures of the Cid*), which was adapted by Corneille as *Le Cid* and ignited a furious controversy about neoclassical esthetics.

Neoclassicism, Drama, and Theater

In both France and England, the arts in general and drama in particular were closely regulated by the state, a state of affairs sustained by the rise of NEOCLASSICISM. Neoclassicism is, in the simplest sense, the revival of what was taken to be a "classical" ordering of the arts. The literature of classical Greece and Rome began to be recovered in the fourteenth and fifteenth centuries, first through the dissemination of texts preserved in monasteries and later through expanded contact with the Islamic world in the sixteenth and seventeenth centuries. Translating, imitating, and adapting classical texts, European writers in the later seventeenth century appeared to "revive" the principles of classical art. In practice, however, neoclassicism offered an *interpretation* of the classics, emphasizing order, control, decorum, reason, and harmony.

In many respects, neoclassicism relied on the authority of Aristotle's *Poetics,* published first in Latin translation in 1498 and then in Italian in 1549, and on the series of critical commentaries written on Aristotle throughout the sixteenth century. Aristotle's *Poetics* is something of a naturalist's description of the several species of poetry and their characteristics, but readers in the sixteenth and seventeenth centuries fell under the influence of Aristotle's enormous authority (see *Doctor Faustus,* Act 1) and quickly transformed the *Poetics* into a prescription, a series of rules, for producing the most perfect and effective tragedies. Two central precepts of the *Poetics* regard the tragic hero's actions: Those acts must seem both necessary and probable, and they should not entirely violate moral expectations. Neoclassical critics and playwrights schematized Aristotle's descriptions as necessary features of dramatic composition, arguing that a tragedy should be rigorously and causally plotted and should reveal the workings of providential justice through the actions of universalized or typical characters. These goals were transformed into the famous "unities" of neoclassicism: A play should take place within a single day (unity of time), in one location (unity of place), and consist of a single line of action, a single plot (unity of action). The action of neoclassical tragedy, therefore, is concentrated, maintaining a uniformity of tone and style called DECORUM. Plays in this mode maintain a single, narrow range of language and behavior; the action is either idealized (rather than realistic) in tragedy, or commonplace in comedy: tragic characters are classic and heroic, while comic characters are contemporary, even bourgeois; tragedy undertakes the conflict between the ideal passions of love and honor, while comedy takes its cue from more earthly desires—lust, greed, hypocrisy, and so on. Following the recovery of Vitruvius' *De Architectura* (15 BCE) in 1414, this neoclassical sensibility urged the modern stage to imitate Vitruvius' distinction between the proper stage settings of tragedy and comedy: classical architecture for tragedy, urban architecture for comedy. Especially in seventeenth-century Paris, theaters adjusted their stagecraft to these ideals of regularity and decorum, assigning a generalized palace setting to the elevated world of tragedy, and the *chambre à quatre portes*—the room with four doors—to the lower, contemporary world of comedy.

Writing later in the eighteenth century, the Englishman Thomas Davies characterized the differences between French and English audiences and suggests that neoclassical ideals did not take root as deeply in the English theater as they did in France:

> The Frenchman, when he goes to a play, seems to make his entertainment a matter of importance. The long speeches in the plays of Corneille, Racine, Crébillon, and Voltaire, which would disgust an English ear, are extremely pleasing to our light neighbours: they sit in silence, and enjoy the beauty of sentiment, and energy of language; and are taught habitually

to cry at scenes of distress. The Englishman looks upon the theatre as a place of amusement; he does not expect to be alarmed with terror, or wrought upon by scenes of commiseration; but he is surprised into the feeling of those passions, and sheds tears because he cannot avoid it. The theatre, to most Englishmen, becomes a place of instruction by chance.

Davies, of course, betrays a common chauvinism of the English toward the French: while the French are pedantic and calculating, the English are spontaneous. But this distinction between English and French theaters—one for "art," one for "entertainment"; one tragic, one comic—conceals the fundamental likenesses between the two institutions and the plays they put on the stage. As the plays of Corneille, Racine, and Dryden suggest, neoclassical tragedy imposes severe and artificial forms on the irrepressible forces of the passions, which inevitably break through the formal speech and decorous behavior of the characters to destroy them and sometimes the state as well. Comedy of the period in England and in France reveals a cognate tension, as the formal acting styles and stereotyped characters common in Restoration comedy seem barely able to contain the bottomless appetites of the plays' heroes. To this extent, neoclassical decorum embodies a barely contained anxiety about the power of forms—forms of conduct, forms of art, forms of state—to prevent a revolution of unreason and disorder.

Early Modern Drama in Performance and History

In many respects, the theater of seventeenth-century Europe is continuous with our own. Given the fact that the European monarchies were rapidly expanding their political and mercantile influence around the globe, it's not surprising to find that their culture became exported as well, often to the cultivated elites of their new colonies. In Mexico, for example, the seventeenth-century nun Sor Juana Inés de la Cruz (1651–1695) composed both *autos* and full-length dramas that echo—and, indeed, rival—the plays of the Spanish playwrights Calderón and Lope de Vega. The English drama of this period was exported as well; Farquhar's *The Recruiting Officer* was the first play to be performed in the penal colony of Australia. Moreover, the seventeenth century saw the institutionalization of theater as a commercial activity: in its architecture (indoor theaters, proscenium stages), in its greater appeal to a bourgeois audience, even in institutions like the Comédie Française (which, of course, continues to produce the plays of Molière and Racine), this theater is the direct forebear of the modern European theater, and in many ways the progenitor of its colonial theaters as well.

While the plays in this unit are all still in the classical repertory of modern theaters, these plays tend to pose particular problems to modern directors and actors. Although many plays of this period—*Tartuffe* or *The Rover*—are given a contemporary setting, and concern themselves with relatively familiar characters, their language and characterization tends to be quite formal. Molière, for example, writes in a rich and fluid verse, even for the part of Tartuffe; Behn's cavaliers speak in prose, but their language is nonetheless dynamic and rhetorically complex. For modern actors, the elegance of this language often provides a point of entry to these characters, a way of seizing on the carefully discriminated social hierarchies at work in the cultures of these plays. Indeed, this verbal formality often becomes a kind of keynote to other aspects of performance as well, leading to a certain stateliness of physical movement and gesture, and an elegant balance of design elements as well. And yet in part because they are part of a classical repertoire, these plays have also inspired experiment and adaptation, a challenge to directors, designers, and actors to make it new.

READING THE MATERIAL THEATER

One of the most challenging elements of theater history is the interpretation of the documentary record. Indeed, with the rise of print, the theater spawned its own information explosion, as newspaper descriptions, reviews, memoirs, and even published letters provide accounts of the practices of the stage. Yet these documents themselves often require a skeptical eye.

Anthony Aston's *A Brief Supplement to Colley Cibber, Exq: His Lives of the Late Famous Actors and Actresses* (published in London in 1748) provides what seems to be an eyewitness account of the acting style of Thomas Betterton (1635–1710). What features of Betterton's physique and style emerge most strongly to Aston? Are there class or cultural implications in the various terms Aston uses to praise Betterton? How does Aston distinguish between Betterton's success in comic and tragic roles? How does he distinguish between Betterton's style in comedy and that of Estcourt and Harper?

Mr. Betterton (although a superlative good Actor) labour'd under ill Figure, being clumsily made, having a great Head, a short thick Neck, stoop'd in the Shoulders, and had fat short Arms, which he rarely lifted higher than his Stomach. –His Left Hand frequently lodg'd in his Breast, between his Coat and Waistcoat, while, with his Right, he prepar'd his Speech. –His Actions were few, but just. –He had little Eyes, and a broad Face, a little Pockfretten, a corpulent Body, and thick Legs, with large Feet. –He was better to meet, than to follow; for his Aspect was serious, venerable, and majestic; in his latter Time a little Paralytic. –His Voice was low and grumbling; yet he could Time it by an artificial *Climax*, which enforc'd universal Attention, even from the *Fops* and *Orange-girls*. –He was incapable of dancing, even in a Country-Dance; as was MRS. BARRY: But their good Qualities were more than equal to their Deficiencies. –While MRS. BRACEGIRDLE sung very agreeably in the LOVES of *Mars and Venus,* and danced in a Country-Dance, as well as MR. WILKS, though not with so much Art and Foppery, but like a well-bred Gentleman. –MR. BETTERTON was the most extensive Actor, from *Alexander* to *Sir John Falstaff;* but in that last Character, he wanted the Waggery of ESTCOURT, the Drollery of HARPER, and Sallaciousness of JACK EVANS. –But, then *Estcourt* was too trifling; *Harper* had too much of the *Bartholomew-Fair*; and *Evans* misplac'd his Humour. –Thus, you see what *Flaws* are in *bright Diamonds*; –And I have often wish'd that Mr. *Betterton* would have resign'd the Part of HAMLET to some young Actor, (who might have Personated, though not have Acted, it better) for, when he threw himself at *Ophelia's* Feet, he appear'd a little too grave for a young Student, lately come from the University of *Wirtemberg;* and his *Repartees* seem'd rather as *Apophthegms* from a *sage Philosopher,* than the *sporting Flashes* of a young HAMLET; and no one else could have pleas'd the Town, he was so rooted in their Opinion. His younger Contemporary (*Betterton* 63, *Powell* 40 Years old), POWELL attempted several of *Betterton's* Parts, as *Alexander, Jaffeir, &c,* but lost his Credit; as, in *Alexander,* he maintain'd not the Dignity of a King, but Out-Heroded HEROD; and in his poison'd mad Scene, *outrav'd all Probability;* while *Betterton* kept his Passion under, and shew'd it most (as Fame smoaks most, when stifled). *Betterton,* from the Time he was dress'd to the End of the Play, kept his Mind in the same Temperament and Adaptness, as the present Character required. ■

Pedro Calderón de la Barca

Like many of his contemporaries, Pedro Calderón de la Barca (1600–1681) was a prolific playwright; he is thought to have written more than 200 plays, of which about 100 survive. Calderón was born in Madrid on January 17, 1600, the son of a minor court official. He was educated at a Jesuit "college," or preparatory school, before attending the University of Alcalá de Henares and the University of Salamanca. In 1620 he entered and won a poetry competition in honor of St. Isidore, which brought his writing to the attention of Lope de Vega, one of the judges of the contest. His first play, *Love, Honor, and Power,* was performed at court in 1623, but Calderón—who served intermittently in the military in the early 1620s—did not become established as a playwright until some time after 1626, when his plays were popular both at court and in the public theaters. With the death of Lope in 1635, Calderón became the most important playwright in Spain; he was knighted by Philip IV and became the principal court playwright in 1636.

Many of Calderón's plays in this period are either *capa y espada* plays, like *The Phantom Lady* (1629), or "love and honor" plays. *El alcalde de Zalamea* (*The Mayor of Zalamea,* 1642) is typical of the "love and honor" genre. In the play, a peasant's daughter is raped by a soldier; through a series of coincidences, the peasant becomes the mayor just as the soldier is apprehended, and he is torn between his desire for revenge, his obligation to enforce the process of law, and Christian charity. Calderón's most important play, *La vida es sueño* (*Life Is a Dream*) was produced in 1636. Throughout his career, Calderón also wrote *autos sacramentales,* but these became more significant later in his life. Calderón's mistress died in 1648, and Calderón entered the priesthood in 1651, possibly in grief over her loss; he also adopted and raised her child, who may have been his natural son. He was appointed priest of a Toledo parish, but the bishop objected to his playwriting, and Calderón devoted himself to *autos* thereafter; his *autos* were so popular that between 1647 and 1681 the only *autos* performed in Madrid were by Calderón. Calderón was made chaplain to the king in 1663 and died in retirement in 1681.

Life Is a Dream

Life Is a Dream typifies the concerns of Calderón's mature drama: It is a play that tests the relationship between love and honor and conducts a searching meditation on human nature itself. The play is set in a mythological Poland, ruled by King Basil. Several years before the current action, it was predicted that if Basil's son, Segismund, were to succeed to the throne, he "would be the most outrageous / Of all men, the most cruel of all princes, / And impious of all monarchs, by whose acts / The kingdom would be torn up and divided." Basil, not willing to murder his son to save his country, has had Segismund removed from court and imprisoned in a cave, where he is attended only by the old courtier Clotaldo. This is where Rosaura—a well-born woman, also forsaken by her father—finds Segismund at the opening of the play.

Calderón begins his interrogation of human nature in the characterization of Segismund. Raised like a beast, Segismund is impulsive and untamed; though he opens the play complaining about his life of constant punishment, when he sees Rosaura (disguised as a man) watching him, he seizes and threatens to kill her. Yet when Rosaura kneels to him and begs for mercy, Segismund feels a strange sensation:

> "Your voice has softened me, your presence halted me,
> And now, confusingly, I feel respect
> For you."

Living in captivity and isolation, Segismund is a "human monster": his behavior is ruled neither by reason nor by the conventions of polite society. Yet Segismund responds to Rosaura's plea for mercy as though some element of human sympathy were native to

© T. Charles Erickson

In the opening of Pedro Calderon de la Barca's *Life Is a Dream,* Rosaura defends herself against Segismund, who is clothed in animal hides.

him. At the outset of the play, Calderón presents two contrasting views of human nature. In one perspective, human beings—like other animals—are ruled by their passions, which can only be governed by the civilizing force of law and reason; since Segismund has been raised without benefit of culture, he represents humanity in this unadorned state. Yet at the same time, Segismund's innate response to Rosaura suggests a second view of human nature, one in which sympathy, kindness, and morality are not imposed on human nature by education and society, but are somehow innate to humanity itself.

Just as Segismund relents toward Rosaura, Clotaldo suddenly bursts in and arrests her; Basil has decreed that even the existence of his son must remain a secret. But in arresting Rosaura, Clotaldo takes her sword, which he immediately recognizes as the sword he had left "fair Violante" years before: Rosaura—who has traveled to Poland disguised as a man for protection—must be Clotaldo's "son." Clotaldo is now caught in the classic "love-and-honor" bind. His duty to his king requires him to arrest and eventually execute anyone who spies Basil's secret son; yet to honor his bond to the king, he must betray the natural love he should show to his own child.

As the play proceeds, Clotaldo's effort to reclaim his son is paralleled by Basil's guilty desire to restore his own son to society. Basil hits on an experiment: He will put Segismund to sleep and awaken him at court; when he awakens, Segismund will be told that he is now the king. If his behavior is civilized and restrained, then Basil will know that the prophecy was wrong and will acknowledge Segismund as his heir; if his behavior is threatening, he will be sent back to prison. But Basil's plan has one flaw: Having been raised in solitude, Segismund has no understanding of the elaborate conventions of courtly behavior. When he awakens as "king," he is rude to Prince Astolfo, offensively forward to Stella, and murderously impulsive to the servants who try to restrain and control his behavior. His behavior is so outrageous that he is again knocked unconscious and sent back to his prison.

Returned to captivity, Segismund can only understand his sojourn at court as a beautiful dream, a dream that becomes an image for the fleeting and illusory joys of life itself. But this recognition reforms Segismund, enables him to recognize that he can only assume his full humanity by governing his passions. In the play's final moments, Segismund is released from prison by a rebellious mob, who have come to release Segismund in order to overthrow Basil. When Segismund and his army confront Basil, the old king not only assumes that he has lost his kingdom, but that Segismund will kill him, in part to repay Basil for stealing the better part of his life. But Segismund now understands that although Basil's treatment has made him "savage" in his passions—an "inhuman monster"—the only way to regain his humanity is to govern his desire for revenge. So Segismund submits himself to Basil, who recognizes that his son has been reformed and gives him the kingdom: in conquering himself, Segismund wins the throne as well.

Calderón's drama is a deeply philosophical play, and the characters meditate extensively on the nature and meaning of their behavior. But *Life Is a Dream* is in some sense also a political play; its rich examination of "human nature" is conducted from a deeply aristocratic perspective. The only way that Segismund can demonstrate his humanity, after all, is to recognize and accept the conventions of courtly behavior as "natural." It is a sign of Segismund's acceptance of those values that his first act as king is to sentence the soldier who liberated him from prison to a life imprisonment of his own.

One element of Calderón's drama that does not emerge in English translation is his mastery of a wide range of verse forms. Lope de Vega's treatise *Arte Nuevo de hacer comedias* (1609) required playwrights to assign different verse forms for different dramatic situations: the *decima* (an octosyllabic form of 10 lines) for complaints, the sonnet (fourteen lines) for those waiting in expectation, the *tercet* (various meters and rhyme schemes, but in three line stanzas) for serious matters, and *redondillas* for love scenes (four rhyming octosyllabic stanzas). In *Life is a Dream,* as in other plays, Calderón will have a given character move through a range of verse forms as demanded by the situation of the moment.

Life Is a Dream

Pedro Calderón de la Barca

TRANSLATED BY ROY CAMPBELL

CHARACTERS

BASIL, *King of Poland*
SEGISMUND, *Prince*
ASTOLFO, *Duke of Muscovy*
CLOTALDO, *old man*
CLARION, *a comical servant*
ROSAURA, *a lady*

STELLA, *a princess*
SOLDIERS, GUARDS, MUSICIANS, SERVANTS, RETINUES, WOMEN

The scene is laid in the court of Poland, a nearby fortress, and the open country

---

ACT ONE

On one side a craggy mountain: on the other a rude tower whose base serves as a prison for SEGISMUND. *The door facing the spectators is open. The action begins at nightfall.*

ROSAURA, *dressed as a man, appears on the rocks climbing down to the plain: behind her comes* CLARION.

ROSAURA: You headlong hippogriff who match the gale
  In rushing to and fro, you lightning-flicker
  Who give no light, you scaleless fish, you bird
  Who have no coloured plumes, you animal
5 Who have no natural instinct, tell me whither
  You lead me stumbling through this labyrinth
  Of naked crags! Stay here upon this peak
  And be a Phaëthon to the brute-creation!
  For I, pathless save only for the track
10 The laws of destiny dictate for me,
  Shall, blind and desperate, descend this height
  Whose furrowed brows are frowning at the sun.
  How rudely, Poland, you receive a stranger
  (Hardly arrived, but to be treated hardly)
15 And write her entry down in blood with thorns.
  My plight attests this well, but after all,
  Where did the wretchèd ever pity find?
CLARION: Say *two* so wretchèd. Don't you leave me out
  When you complain! If we two sallied out
20 From our own country, questing high adventure,
  And after so much madness and misfortune
  Are still two here, and were two when we fell
  Down those rough crags—shall I not be offended
  To share the trouble yet forego the credit?
25 ROSAURA: I did not give you shares in my complaint
  So as not to rob you of the right to sorrow
  Upon your own account. There's such relief
  In venting grief that a philosopher
  Once said that sorrows should not be bemoaned
30 But sought for pleasure.
CLARION: Philosopher?
  I call him a long-bearded, drunken sot
  And would they'd cudgelled him a thousand blows
  To give him something worth his while lamenting!
  But, madam, what should we do, by ourselves,
35 On foot and lost at this late hour of day,
  Here on this desert mountain far away—
  The sun departing after fresh horizons?

ROSAURA: Clarion, how can I answer, being both
  The partner of your plight and your dilemma?
CLARION: Would anyone believe such strange events?   40
ROSAURA: If there my sight is not deceived by fancy,
  In the last timid light that yet remains
  I seem to see a building.
CLARION: Either my hopes
  Are lying or I see the signs myself.
ROSAURA: Between the towering crags, there stands so small   45
  A royal palace that the lynx-eyed sun
  Could scarce perceive it at midday, so rude
  In architecture that it seems but one
  Rock more down-toppled from the sun-kissed crags
50 That form the jaggèd crest.
CLARION: Let's go closer,
  For we have stared enough: it would be better
  To let the inmates makes us welcome.
ROSAURA: See:
  The door, or, rather, that funereal gap,
  Is yawning wide—whence night itself seems born,
55 Flowing out from its black, rugged centre.

(A sound of chains is heard.)

CLARION: Heavens! What's that I hear?
ROSAURA: I have become
  A block immovable of ice and fire.
CLARION: Was that a little chain? Why, I'll be hanged
  If that is not the clanking ghost of some
60 Past galley-slave—my terror proves it is!
SEGISMUND: Oh, miserable me! Unhappy me!
ROSAURA: How sad a cry that is! I fear new trials
  And torments.
CLARION: It's a fearful sound.
ROSAURA: Oh, come,
  My Clarion, let us fly from suffering!
CLARION: I'm in such sorry trim, I've not the spirit   65
  Even to run away.
ROSAURA: And if you had,
  You'd not have seen that door, not known of it.
  When one's in doubt, the common saying goes
  One walks between two lights.
CLARION: I'm the reverse.
  It's not that way with me.   70
ROSAURA: What then disturbs you?
CLARION: I walk in doubt between two darknesses.

ROSAURA: Is not that feeble exhalation there
    A light? That pallid star whose fainting tremors,
    Pulsing a doubtful warmth of glimmering rays,
75   Make even darker with its spectral glow
    That gloomy habitation? Yes! because
    By its reflection (though so far away)
    I recognise a prison, grim and sombre,
    The sepulchre of some poor living carcase.
80   And, more to wonder at, a man lies there
    Clothed in the hides of savage beasts, with limbs
    Loaded with fetters, and a single lamp
    For company. So, since we cannot flee,
    Let us stay here and listen to his plaint
85   And what his sorrows are.
SEGISMUND: Unhappy me!
    Oh, miserable me! You heavens above,
    I try to think what crime I've done against you
    By being born. Although to have been born,
    I know, is an offence, and with just cause
90   I bear the rigours of your punishment:
    Since to be born is man's worst crime. But yet
    I long to know (to clarify my doubts)
    What greater crime, apart from being born,
    Can thus have earned my greater chastisement.
95   Aren't others born like me? And yet they seem
    To boast a freedom that I've never known.
    The bird is born, and in the hues of beauty
    Clothed with its plumes, yet scarce has it become
    A feathered posy—or a flower with wings—
100   When through ethereal halls it cuts its way,
    Refusing the kind shelter of its nest.
    And I, who have more soul than any bird,
    Must have less liberty?
    The beast is born, and with its hide bright-painted,
105   In lovely tints, has scarce become a spangled
    And starry constellation (thanks to the skilful
    Brush of the Painter) than its earthly needs
    Teach it the cruelty to prowl and kill,
    The monster of its labyrinth of flowers.
110   Yet I, with better instincts than a beast,
    Must have less liberty?
    The fish is born, the birth of spawn and slime,
    That does not even live by breathing air.
    No sooner does it feel itself a skiff
115   Of silver scales upon the wave than swiftly
    It roves about in all directions taking
    The measure of immensity as far
    As its cold blood's capacity allows.
    Yet I, with greater freedom of the will,
120   Must have less liberty?
    The brook is born, and like a snake unwinds
    Among the flowers. No sooner, silver serpent,
    Does it break through the blooms than it regales
    And thanks them with its music for their kindness,
125   Which opens to its course the majesty
    Of the wide plain. Yet I, with far more life,
    Must have less liberty?
    This fills me with such passion, I become
    Like the volcano Etna, and could tear
130   Pieces of my own heart out of my breast!
    What law, justice, or reason can decree

    That man alone should never know the joys
    And be alone excepted from the rights
    God grants a fish, a bird, a beast, a brook?
ROSAURA: His words have filled me full of fear and pity.   135
SEGISMUND: Who is it overheard my speech? Clotaldo?
CLARION: Say "yes!"
ROSAURA: It's only a poor wretch, alas,
    Who in these cold ravines has overheard
    Your sorrows.
SEGISMUND: Then I'll kill you

(Seizes her.)

    So as to leave no witness of my frailty.   140
    I'll tear you into bits with these strong arms!
CLARION: I'm deaf. I wasn't able to hear that.
ROSAURA: If you were human born, it is enough
    That I should kneel to you for you to spare me.
SEGISMUND: Your voice has softened me, your presence   145
       halted me,
    And now, confusingly, I feel respect
    For you. Who are you? Though here I have learned
    So little of the world, since this grim tower
    Has been my cradle and my sepulchre;
    And though since I was born (if you can say   150
    I really have been born) I've only seen
    This rustic desert where in misery
    I dwell alone, a living skeleton,
    An animated corpse; and though till now,
    I never spoke, save to one man who hears   155
    My griefs and through whose converse I have heard
    News of the earth and of the sky; and though,
    To astound you more, and make you call me
    A human monster, I dwell here, and am
    A man of the wild animals, a beast   160
    Among the race of men; and though in such
    Misfortune, I have studied human laws,
    Instructed by the birds, and learned to measure
    The circles of the gentle stars, you only
    Have curbed my furious rage, amazed my vision,   165
    And filled with wonderment my sense of hearing.
    Each time I look at you, I feel new wonder!
    The more I see of you, the more I long
    To go on seeing more of you. I think
    My eyes are dropsical, to go on drinking   170
    What it is death for them to drink, because
    They go on drinking that which I am dying
    To see and that which, seen, will deal me death.
    Yet let me gaze on you and die, since I
    Am so bewitched I can no longer think   175
    What not seeing you would do to me—the sight
    Itself being fatal! that would be more hard
    Than dying, madness, rage, and fiercest grief:
    It would be life—worst fate of all because
    The gift of life to such a wretchèd man   180
    Would be the gift of death to happiness!
ROSAURA: Astonished as I look, amazed to hear,
    I know not what to say nor what to ask.
    All I can say is that heaven guided me
    Here to be comforted, if it is comfort   185
    To see another sadder than oneself.

They say a sage philosopher of old,
Being so poor and miserable that he
Lived on the few plain herbs he could collect,
190   One day exclaimed: "Could any man be poorer
Or sadder than myself?"—when, turning round,
He saw the very answer to his words.
For there another sage philosopher
Was picking up the scraps he'd thrown away.
195   I lived cursing my fortune in this world
And asked within me: "Is there any other
Suffers so hard a fate?" Now out of pity
You've given me the answer. For within me
I find upon reflection that my griefs
200   Would be as joys to you and you'd receive them
To give you pleasure. So if they perchance
In any measure may afford relief,
Listen attentively to my misfortune
And take what is left over for yourself.
205   I am . . .
CLOTALDO: (*Within.*) Guards of the tower! You sluggards
      Or cowards, you have let two people pass
      Into the prison bounds . . .
   ROSAURA: Here's more confusion!
SEGISMUND: That is Clotaldo, keeper of my prison.
      Are my misfortunes still not at an end?
210 CLOTALDO: Come. Be alert, and either seize or slay them
      Before they can resist!
VOICES: (*Within.*)   Treason! Betrayal!
CLARION: Guards of the tower who let us pass unhindered,
      Since there's a choice, to seize us would be simpler.

(*Enter* CLOTALDO *with* SOLDIERS. *He holds a pistol and they all
wear masks.*)

CLOTALDO: (*Aside to the* SOLDIERS.) Cover your faces, all! It's
      a precaution
215   Imperative that nobody should know us
      While we are here.
   CLARION: What's this? A masquerade?
CLOTALDO: O you, who ignorantly passed the bounds
      And limits of this region, banned to all—
      Against the king's decree which has forbidden
220   That any should find out the prodigy
      Hidden in these ravines—yield up your weapons
      Or else this pistol, like a snake of metal,
      Will spit the piercing venom of two shots
      With scandalous assault upon the air.
225 SEGISMUND: Tyrannic master, ere you harm these people
      Let my life be the spoil of these sad bonds
      In which (I swear it by Almighty God)
      I'll sooner rend myself with hands and teeth
      Amid these rocks than see them harmed and mourn
230   Their suffering.
   CLOTALDO: Since you know, Segismund,
      That your misfortunes are so huge that, even
      Before your birth, you died by heaven's decree,
      And since you know these walls and binding chains
      Are but the brakes and curbs to your proud frenzies,
235   What use is it to bluster?

(*To the* GUARDS.)

                              Shut the door
      Of this close prison! Hide him in its depths!
SEGISMUND: Ah, heavens, how justly you denied me freedom!
      For like a Titan I would rise against you,
      Pile jasper mountains high on stone foundations
      And climb to burst the windows of the sun!   240
CLOTALDO: Perhaps you suffer so much pain today
      Just to forestall that feat.
   ROSAURA: Now that I see
      How angry pride offends you, I'd be foolish
      Not to plead humbly at your feet for life.
      Be moved by me to pity. It would be   245
      Notoriously harsh that neither pride
      Nor humbleness found favour in your eyes!
CLARION: And if neither Humility nor Pride
      Impress you (characters of note who act
      And motivate a thousand mystery plays)   250
      Let me, here, who am neither proud nor humble,
      But merely something halfway in between,
      Plead to you both for shelter and for aid.
CLOTALDO: Ho, there!
SOLDIER: Sir?
CLOTALDO: Take their weapons. Bind their eyes
      So that they cannot see the way they're led.   255
ROSAURA: This is my sword. To nobody but you
      I yield it, since you're, after all, the chief.
      I cannot yield to one of meaner rank.
CLARION: My sword is such that I will freely give it
      To the most mean and wretched.   260

(*To one* SOLDIER.)

                              Take it, you!
ROSAURA: And if I have to die, I'll leave it to you
      In witness of your mercy. It's a pledge
      Of great worth and may justly be esteemed
      For someone's sake who wore it long ago.
CLOTALDO: (*Apart.*) Each moment seems to bring me new   265
      misfortune!
ROSAURA: Because of that, I ask you to preserve
      This sword with care. Since if inconstant Fate
      Consents to the remission of my sentence,
      It has to win me honour. Though I know not
      The secret that it carries, I do know   270
      It has got one—unless I trick myself—
      And prize it just as the sole legacy
      My father left me.
CLOTALDO: Who then was your father?
ROSAURA: I never knew.
CLOTALDO: And why have you come here?
ROSAURA: I came to Poland to avenge a wrong.   275
CLOTALDO: (*Apart.*) Sacred heavens!

(*On taking the sword he becomes very perturbed.*)

                              What's this? Still worse and worse.
      I am perplexed and troubled with more fears.

(*Aloud.*)

Tell me: who gave that sword to you?

ROSAURA: A woman.
CLOTALDO: Her name?
ROSAURA: A secret I am forced to keep.
280 CLOTALDO: What makes you think this sword contains a
        secret?
   ROSAURA: That she who gave it to me said: "Depart
     To Poland. There with subtlety and art
     Display it so that all the leading people
     And noblemen can see you wearing it,
285   And I know well that there's a lord among them
     Who will both shelter you and grant you favour."
     But, lest he should be dead, she did not name him.
   CLOTALDO: (*Aside.*) Protect me, heavens! What is this I hear?
     I cannot say if real or imagined
290   But here's the sword I gave fair Violante
     In token that, whoever in the future
     Should come from her to me wearing this sword,
     Would find in me a tender father's love.
     Alas, what can I do in such a pass,
295   When he who brings the sword to win my favour
     Brings it to find his own red death instead
     Arriving at my feet condemned already?
     What strange perplexity! How hard a fate!
     What an inconstant fortune to be plagued with!
300   This is my son not only by all signs
     But also by the promptings of my heart,
     Since, seeing him, my heart seems to cry out
     To him, and beat its wings, and, though unable
     To break the locks, behaves as one shut in,
305   Who, hearing noises in the street outside,
     Cranes from the window-ledge. Just so, not knowing
     What's really happening, but hearing sounds,
     My heart runs to my eyes which are its windows
     And out of them flows into bitter tears.
310   Protect me, heaven! What am I to do?
     To take him to the king is certain death.
     To hide him is to break my sacred oath
     And the strong law of homage. From one side
     Love of one's own, and from the other loyalty—
315   Call me to yield. Loyalty to my king
     (Why do I doubt?) comes before life and honour.
     Then live my loyalty, and let him die!
     When I remember, furthermore, he came
     To avenge an injury—a man insulted
320   And unavenged is in disgrace. My son
     Therefore he is not, nor of noble blood.
     But if some danger has mischanced, from which
     No one escapes, since honour is so fragile
     That any act can smash it, and it takes
325   A stain from any breath of air, what more
     Could any nobleman have done than he,
     Who, at the cost of so much risk and danger,
     Comes to avenge his honour? Since he's so brave
     He is my son, and my blood's in his veins.
330   And so betwixt the one doubt and the other,
     The most important mean between extremes
     Is to go to the king and tell the truth—
     That he's my son, to kill, if so he wishes.
     Perhaps my loyalty thus will move his mercy
335   And if I thus can merit a live son
     I'll help him to avenge his injury.

     But if the king prove constant in his rigour
     And deal him death, he'll die in ignorance
     That I'm his father.

(*Aloud to* ROSAURA *and* CLARION.)

                Come then, strangers, come!
     And do not fear that you have no companions   340
     In your misfortunes, since, in equal doubt,
     Tossed between life and death, I cannot guess
     Which is the greater evil or the less.

A hall at the royal palace, in court

Enter ASTOLFO *and* SOLDIERS *at one side: from the other side*
PRINCESS STELLA *and* WOMEN. *Military music and salvos.*

ASTOLFO: To greet your excellent bright beams
     As brilliant as a comet's rays,   345
     The drums and brasses mix their praise
     With those of fountains, birds, and streams.
     With sounds alike, in like amaze,
     Your heavenly face each voice salutes,
     Which puts them in such lively fettle,   350
     The trumpets sound like birds of metal,
     The songbirds play like feathered flutes.
     And thus they greet you, fair señora—
     The salvos, as their queen, the brasses,
     As to Minerva when she passes,   355
     The songbirds to the bright Aurora,
     And all the flowers and leaves and grasses
     As doing homage unto Flora,
     Because you come to cheat the day
     Which now the night has covered o'er—   360
     Aurora in your spruce array,
     Flora in peace, Pallas in war,
     But in my heart the queen of May.
STELLA: If human voice could match with acts
     You would have been unwise to say   365
     Hyperboles that a few facts
     May well refute some other day
     Confounding all this martial fuss
     With which I struggle daringly,
     Since flatteries you proffer thus   370
     Do not accord with what I see.
     Take heed that it's an evil thing
     And worthy of a brute accursed,
     Loud praises with your mouth to sing
     When in your heart you wish the worst.   375
ASTOLFO: Stella, you have been badly misinformed
     If you doubt my good faith. Here let me beg you
     To listen to my plea and hear me out.
     The third Eugtorgius died, the King of Poland.
     Basil, his heir, had two fair sisters who   380
     Bore you, my cousin, and myself. I would not
     Tire you with all that happened here. You know
     Clorilene was your mother who enjoys,
     Under a better reign, her starry throne.
     She was the elder. Lovely Recisunda   385
     (Whom may God cherish for a thousand years!)
     The younger one, my mother and your aunt,

Was wed in Muscovy. Now to return:
Basil has yielded to the feebleness
390 Of age, loves learnèd study more than women,
Has lost his wife, is childless, will not marry.
And so it comes that you and I both claim
The heirdom of the realm. You claim that you
Were daughter to the elder daughter. I
395 Say that my being born a man, although
Son of the younger daughter, gives me title
To be preferred. We've told the king, our uncle,
Of both of our intentions. And he answered
That he would judge between our rival claims,
400 For which the time and place appointed was
Today and here. For the same reason I
Have left my native Muscovy. With that
Intent I come—not seeking to wage war
But so that you might thus wage war on me!
405 May Love, wise god, make true what people say
(Your "people" is a wise astrologer)
By settling this through your being chosen queen—
Queen and my consort, sovereign of my will;
My uncle crowning you, for greater honour;
410 Your courage conquering, as it deserves;
My love applauding you, its emperor!
STELLA: To such chivalrous gallantry, my breast
Cannot hold out. The imperial monarchy
I wish were mine only to make it yours—
415 Although my love is not quite satisfied
That you are to be trusted since your speech
Is somewhat contradicted by that portrait
You carry in the locket round your neck.
ASTOLFO: I'll give you satisfaction as to that.

(*Drums.*)

420 But these loud instruments will not permit it
That sound the arrival of the king and council.

(*Enter* KING BASIL *with his following.*)

STELLA: Wise Thales . . .
ASTOLFO: Learned Euclid . . .
STELLA: Among the signs . . .
ASTOLFO: Among the stars . . .
STELLA: Where you preside in power . . .
ASTOLFO: Where you reside . . .
STELLA: And plot their paths . . .
425 ASTOLFO: And trace their fiery trails . . .
STELLA: Describing . . .
ASTOLFO: . . . Measuring and judging them . . .
STELLA: Please read my stars that I, in humble bonds . . .
ASTOLFO: Please read them, so that I in soft embraces . . .
STELLA: May twine as ivy to this tree!
ASTOLFO: May find
430 Myself upon my knees before these feet!
BASIL: Come and embrace me, niece and nephew. Trust me,
Since you're both loyal to my loving precepts,
And come here so affectionately both—
In nothing shall I leave you cause to cavil,
435 And both of you as equals will be treated.
The gravity of what I have to tell

Oppresses me, and all I ask of you
Is silence: the event itself will claim
Your wonderment. So be attentive now,
440 Belovèd niece and nephew, illustrious courtiers,
Relatives, friends, and subjects! You all know
That for my learning I have merited
The surname of The Learnèd, since the brush
Of great Timanthes, and Lisippus' marbles—
445 Stemming oblivion (consequence of time)—
Proclaimed me to mankind Basil the Great.
You know the science that I most affect
And most esteem is subtle mathematics
(By which I forestall time, cheat fame itself)
450 Whose office is to show things gradually.
For when I look my tables up and see,
Present before me, all the news and actions
Of centuries to come, I gain on Time—
Since Time recounts whatever I have said
455 After I say it. Those snowflaking haloes,
Those canopies of crystal spread on high,
Lit by the sun, cut by the circling moon,
Those diamond orbs, those globes of radiant crystal
Which the bright stars adorn, on which the signs
460 Parade in blazing excellence, have been
My chiefest study all through my long years.
They are the volumes on whose adamantine
Pages, bound up in sapphire, heaven writes,
In lines of burnished gold and vivid letters,
465 All that is due to happen, whether adverse
Or else benign. I read them in a flash,
So quickly that my spirit tracks their movements—
Whatever road they take, whatever goal
They aim at. Would to heaven that before
470 My genius had been the commentary
Writ in their margins, or the index to
Their pages, that my life had been the rubble,
The ruin, and destruction of their wrath,
And that my tragedy in them had ended,
475 Because, to the unlucky, even their merit
Is like a hostile knife, and he whom knowledge
Injures is but a murderer to himself.
And this I say myself, though my misfortunes
Say it far better, which, to marvel at,
480 I beg once more for silence from you all.
With my late wife, the queen, I had a son,
Unhappy son, to greet whose birth the heavens
Wore themselves out in prodigies and portents.
Ere the sun's light brought him live burial
485 Out of the womb (for birth resembles death)
His mother many times, in the delirium
And fancies of her sleep, saw a fierce monster
Bursting her entrails in a human form,
Born spattered with her lifeblood, dealing death,
490 The human viper of this century!
The day came for his birth, and every presage
Was then fulfilled, for tardily or never
Do the more cruel ones prove false. At birth
His horoscope was such that the bright sun,
495 Stained in its blood, entered ferociously
Into a duel with the moon above.
The whole earth seemed a rampart for the strife

Of heaven's two lights, who—though not hand-to-hand—
Fought light-to-light to gain the mastery!
500 The worst eclipse the sun has ever suffered
Since Christ's own death horrified earth and sky.
The whole earth overflowed with conflagrations
So that it seemed the final paroxysm
Of existence. The skies grew dark. Buildings shook.
505 The clouds rained stones. The rivers ran with blood.
In this delirious frenzy of the sun,
Thus, Segismund was born into the world,
Giving a foretaste of his character
By killing his own mother, seeming to speak thus
510 By his ferocity: "I am a man,
Because I have begun now to repay
All kindnesses with evil." To my studies
I went forthwith, and saw in all I studied
That Segismund would be the most outrageous
515 Of all men, the most cruel of all princes,
And impious of all monarchs, by whose acts
The kingdom would be torn up and divided
So as to be a school of treachery
And an academy of vices. He,
520 Risen in fury, amidst crimes and horrors,
Was born to trample me (with shame I say it)
And make of my grey hairs his very carpet.
Who is there but believes an evil Fate?
And more if he discovers it himself,
525 For self-love lends its credit to our studies.
So I, believing in the Fates, and in
The havoc that their prophecies predestined,
Determined to cage up this newborn tiger
To see if on the stars we sages have
530 Some power. I gave out that the prince had died
Stillborn, and, well-forewarned, I built a tower
Amidst the cliffs and boulders of yon mountains
Over whose tops the light scarce finds its way,
So stubbornly their obelisks and crags
535 Defend the entry to them. The strict laws
And edicts that I published then (declaring
That nobody might enter the forbidden
Part of the range) were passed on that account.
There Segismund lives to this day, a captive,
540 Poor and in misery, where, save Clotaldo,
His guardian, none have seen or talked to him.
The latter has instructed him in all
Branches of knowledge and in the Catholic faith,
Alone the witness of his misery.
545 There are three things to be considered now:
Firstly, Poland, that I love you greatly,
So much that I would free you from the oppression
And servitude of such a tyrant king.
He would not be a kindly ruler who
550 Would put his realm and homeland in such danger.
The second fact that I must bear in mind
Is this: that to deny my flesh and blood
The rights which law, both human and divine,
Concedes, would not accord with Christian charity,
555 For no law says that, to prevent another
Being a tyrant, I may be one myself,
And if my son's a tyrant, to prevent him
From doing outrage, I myself should do it.

Now here's the third and last point I would speak of,
Namely, how great an error it has been   560
To give too much belief to things predicted,
Because, even if his inclination should
Dictate some headlong, rash precipitancies,
They may perhaps not conquer him entirely,
For the most accursèd destiny, the most   565
Violent inclination, the most impious
Planet—all can but influence, not force,
The free will which man holds direct from God.
And so, between one motive and another
Vacillating discursively, I hit   570
On a solution that will stun you all.
I shall tomorrow, but without his knowing
He is my son—your king—place Segismund
(For that's the name with which he was baptised)
Here on my throne, beneath my canopy,   575
Yes, in my very place, that he may govern you
And take command. And you must all be here
To swear him fealty as his loyal subjects.
Three things may follow from this test, and these
I'll set against the three which I proposed.   580
The first is that should the prince prove prudent,
Stable, and benign—thus giving the lie
To all that prophecy reports of him—
Then you'll enjoy in him your rightful ruler
Who was so long a courtier of the mountains   585
And neighbour to the beasts. Here is the second:
If he prove proud, rash, cruel, and outrageous,
And with a loosened rein gallop unheeding
Across the plains of vice, I shall have done
My duty, and fulfilled my obligation   590
Of mercy. If I then re-imprison him,
That's incontestably a kingly deed—
Not cruelty but merited chastisement.
The third thing's this: that if the prince should be
As I've described him, then—by the love I feel   595
For you, my vassals—I shall give you worthier
Rulers to wear the sceptre and the crown;
Because your king and queen will be my nephew
And niece, each with an equal right to rule,
Each gaining the inheritance he merits,   600
And joined in faith of holy matrimony.
This I command you as a king, I ask you
As a kind father, as a sage I pray you,
As an experienced old man I tell you,
And (if it's true, as Spanish Seneca   605
Says, that the king is slave unto his nation)
This, as a humble slave, I beg of you.
ASTOLFO: If it behoves me to reply (being
The person most involved in this affair)
Then, in the name of all, let Segismund   610
Appear! It is enough that he's your son!
ALL: Give us our prince: we want him for our king!
BASIL: Subjects, I thank you for your kindly favour.
Accompany these, my two Atlases,
Back to their rooms. Tomorrow you shall see him.   615
ALL: Long live the great King Basil! Long live Basil!

(*Exeunt all, accompanying* STELLA *and* ASTOLFO. *The king remains.*)

(*Enter* CLOTALDO *with* ROSAURA *and* CLARION.)

CLOTALDO: May I have leave to speak, sire?
BASIL: Oh, Clotaldo!
 You're very welcome.
CLOTALDO: Thus to kneel before you
 Is always welcome, sire—yet not today
620 When sad and evil Fate destroys the joy
 Your presence normally concedes.
BASIL: What's wrong?
CLOTALDO: A great misfortune, sire, has come upon me
 Just when I should have met it with rejoicing.
BASIL: Continue.
CLOTALDO: Sire, this beautiful young man
625 Who inadvertently and daringly
 Came to the tower, wherein he saw the prince,
 Is my . . .
BASIL: Do not afflict yourself, Clotaldo.
 Had it not been just now, I should have minded,
 I must confess. But I've revealed the secret,
630 And now it does not matter if he knows it.
 Attend me afterwards. I've many things
 To tell you. You in turn have many things
 To do for me. You'll be my minister,
 I warn you, in the most momentous action
635 The world has ever seen. These prisoners, lest you
 Should think I blame your oversight, I'll pardon.

(*Exit.*)

CLOTALDO: Long may you live, great sire! A thousand years!

(*Aside.*)

 Heaven improves our fates. I shall not tell him
 Now that he is my son, since it's not needed
640 Till he's avenged.

(*Aloud.*)

 Strangers, you may go free.
ROSAURA: Humbly I kiss your feet.
CLARION: Whilst I'll just *miss* them—
 Old friends will hardly quibble at one letter.
ROSAURA: You've granted me my life, sir. I remain
645 Your servant and eternally your debtor.
CLOTALDO: No! It was not your life I gave you. No!
 Since any wellborn man who, unavenged,
 Nurses an insult does not live at all.
 And seeing you have told me that you came
650 For that sole reason, it was not life I spared—
 Life in disgrace is not a life at all.

(*Aside.*)

 I see this spurs him.
ROSAURA: Freely I confess it—
 Although you spared my life, it was no life.
 But I will wipe my honour's stain so spotless
655 That after I have vanquished all my dangers
 Life well may seem a shining gift from you.

CLOTALDO: Take here your burnished steel: 'twill be enough,
 Bathed in your enemies' red blood, to right you.
 For steel that once was mine (I mean of course
 Just for the time I've had it in my keeping)   660
 Should know how to avenge you.
ROSAURA: Now, in your name I gird it on once more
 And on it I will swear to take revenge
 Although my foe were even mightier.
CLOTALDO: Is he so powerful?   665
ROSAURA: So much so that . . .
 Although I have no doubt in your discretion . . .
 I say no more because I'd not estrange
 Your clemency.
CLOTALDO: You would have won me had you told me, since
 That would prevent me helping him.   670

(*Aside.*)

 If only I could discover who he is!
ROSAURA: So that you'll not think that I value lightly
 Such confidence, know that my adversary
 Is no less than Astolfo, Duke of Muscovy.
CLOTALDO: (*Aside.*) (I hardly can withstand the grief it gives me 675
 For it is worse than aught I could imagine!
 Let us inquire of him some further facts.)

(*Aloud.*)

 If you were born a Muscovite, your ruler
 Could never have affronted you. Go back
 Home to your country. Leave this headstrong valour. 680
 It will destroy you.
ROSAURA: Though he's been my prince,
 I know that he has done me an affront.
CLOTALDO: Even though he slapped your face, that's no
 affront.

(*Aside.*)

 O heavens!
ROSAURA: My insult was far deeper!
CLOTALDO: Tell it:
 Since nothing I imagine could be deeper.   685
ROSAURA: Yes. I will tell it, yet, I know not why,
 With such respect I look upon your face,
 I venerate you with such true affection,
 With such high estimation do I weigh you,
 That I scarce dare to tell you—these men's clothes 690
 Are an enigma, not what they appear.
 So now you know. Judge if it's no affront
 That here Astolfo comes to wed with Stella   695
 Although betrothed to me. I've said enough.

(*Exeunt* ROSAURA *and* CLARION.)

CLOTALDO: Here! Listen! Wait! What mazed confusion!
 It is a labyrinth wherein the reason
 Can find no clue. My family honour's injured.
 The enemy's all powerful. I'm a vassal
 And she's a woman. Heavens! Show a path
 Although I don't believe there is a way!   700

There's nought but evil bodings in the sky.
The whole world is a prodigy, say I.

ACT TWO

A hall in the royal palace.

Enter BASIL *and* CLOTALDO.

CLOTALDO: All has been done according to your orders.
BASIL: Tell me, Clotaldo, how it went?
CLOTALDO: Why, thus:
    I took to Segismund a calming drug
    Wherein are mixed herbs of especial virtue,
5   Tyrannous in their overpowering strength
    Which seize and steal and alienate man's gift
    Of reasoning, thus making a live corpse
    Of him. His violence evaporated
    With all his faculties and senses too.
10   There is no need to prove it's possible
    Because experience teaches us that medicine
    Is full of natural secrets, that there is no
    Animal, plant, or stone that has not got
    Appointed properties. If human malice
15   Explores a thousand poisons which deal death,
    Who then can doubt, that being so, that other
    Poisons, less violent, cause only sleep?
    But (leaving that doubt aside, as proven false
    By every evidence) hear then the sequel:
20   I went down into Segismund's close prison
    Bearing the drink wherein, with opium,
    Henbane and poppies had been mixed. With him
    I talked a little while of the humanities,
    In which dumb Nature has instructed him,
25   The mountains and the heavens and the stars,
    In whose divine academies he learned
    Rhetoric from the birds and the wild creatures.
    To lift his spirit to the enterprise
    Which you require of him, I chose for subject
30   The swiftness of a stalwart eagle, who,
    Deriding the base region of the wind,
    Rises into the sphere reserved for fire,
    A feathered lightning, an untethered comet.
    Then I extolled such lofty flight and said:
35   "After all, he's the king of birds, and so
    Takes precedence, by right, over the rest."
    No more was needful for, in taking up
    Majesty for his subject, he discoursed
    With pride and high ambition, as his blood
40   Naturally moves, incites, and spurs him on
    To grand and lofty things, and so he said
    That in the restless kingdom of the birds
    There should be those who swear obedience, too!
    "In this, my miseries console me greatly,
45   Because if I'm a vassal here, it's only
    By force, and not by choice. Of my own will
    I would not yield in rank to any man."
    Seeing that he grew furious—since this touched
    The theme of his own griefs—I gave the potion
50   And scarcely had it passed from cup to breast
    Before he yielded all his strength to slumber.
    A chill sweat ran through all his limbs and veins.

    Had I not known that this was mere feigned death
    I would have thought him dead. Then came the men
55   To whom you've trusted this experiment,
    Who placed him in a coach and brought him here
    To your own rooms, where all things were prepared
    In royalty and grandeur as befitting
    His person. In your own bed they have laid him
60   Where, when the torpor wanes, they'll do him service
    As if he were Your Majesty himself.
    All has been done as you have ordered it,
    And if I have obeyed you well, my lord,
    I'd beg a favour (pardon me this freedom)—
65   To know what your intention is in thus
    Transporting Segismund here to the palace.
BASIL: Your curiosity is just, Clotaldo,
    And yours alone I'll satisfy. The star
    Which governs Segismund, my son, in life,
70   Threatens a thousand tragedies and woes.
    And now I wish to see whether the stars
    (Which never lie—and having shown to us
    So many cruel signs seem yet more certain)
    May yet be brought to moderate their sentence,
75   Whether by prudence charmed or valour won,
    For man does have the power to rule his stars.
    I would examine this, bringing him here
    Where he may know he is my son, and make
    Trial of his talent. If magnanimously
80   He conquers and controls himself, he'll reign,
    But if he proves a tyrant and is cruel,
    Back to his chains he'll go. Now, you will ask,
    Why did we bring him sleeping in this manner
    For the experiment? I'll satisfy you,
85   Down to the smallest detail, with my answer.
    If he knows that he is my son today,
    And if tomorrow he should find himself
    Once more reduced to prison, to misery,
    He would despair entirely, knowing truly
90   Who, and whose son, he is. What consolation
    Could he derive, then, from his lot? So I
    Contrive to leave an exit for such grief,
    By making him believe it was a dream.
    By these means we may learn two things at once:
95   First, his character—for he will really be
    Awake in all he thinks and all his actions;
    Second, his consolation—which would be
    (If he should wake in prison on the morrow,
    Although he saw himself obeyed today)
100   That he might understand he had been dreaming,
    And he will not be wrong, for in this world,
    Clotaldo, all who live are only dreaming.
CLOTALDO: I've proofs enough to doubt of your success,
    But now it is too late to remedy it.
105   From what I can make out, I think he's awakened
    And that he's coming this way, by the sound.
BASIL: I shall withdraw. You, as his tutor, go
    And guide him through his new bewilderments
    By answering his queries with the truth.
CLOTALDO: You give me leave to tell the truth of it?
110 BASIL: Yes, because knowing all things, he may find
    Known perils are the easiest to conquer.

(Exit BASIL. *Enter* CLARION.)

CLARION: It cost me four whacks to get here so quickly.
    I caught them from a red-haired halberdier
115   Sprouting a ginger beard over his livery,
    And I've come to see what's going on.
    No windows give a better view than those
    A man brings with him in his head, not asking
    For tickets of admission or paid seats,
120   Since at all functions, festivals, or feasts
    He looks out with the same nice self-composure.
CLOTALDO: (*Aside.*) Here's Clarion who's the servant of that
        person—
    That trader in woes, importer from Poland
    Of my disgrace.

(*Aloud.*)

                    Come, Clarion, what news?
125 CLARION: Item the first: encouraged by the fact
    Your clemency's disposed to venge her insult,
    Rosaura has resumed her proper clothing.
CLOTALDO: That's right: it's less indecorous and bold.
CLARION: Item: she's changed her name, and given out
130   That she's your niece. And now they've made so much
    Of her that she's been raised to maid of honour
    To the unique and only princess, Stella.
CLOTALDO: That's right: her honour stands to my account.
CLARION: Indeed she merely bides the time till you
135   Will settle all accounts about her honour.
CLOTALDO: Biding the time is wise, for in the end
    It's Time that's going to settle all accounts!
CLARION: Item: that she's attended like a queen,
    Because they take her for your niece. Item:
140   That I, who trudged along with her, am dying
    Of hunger. Nobody remembers me,
    Nor yet remembers that I'm like my name
    And (should I sound my Clarion) could tell
    All to the king and Stella and Astolfo.
145   For I am both a Clarion and a servant—
    Two things which ill-accord with secrecy.
    If silence should, by chance, let slip my hand,
    Then there's a chorus which would fit me well:
    "Dawn-breaking Clarion plays no better tune!"
150 CLOTALDO: You've reason for complaint. I'll satisfy it
    If you'll but serve me . . .
    CLARION: Hush, here's Segismund!

(*Enter* MUSICIANS, *singing, and* SERVANTS *arraying* SEGISMUND,
who seems amazed.)

SEGISMUND: Heavens above! What's this that I am seeing?
    I wonder at it all, with naught of fear!
    But with a mighty doubt, I disbelieve it!
155   I?—in a sumptuous palace? I—encircled
    With rich brocades and silks? I—overwhelmed
    With servants in such brilliant liveries?
    I—to awake in such a gorgeous bed?
    I—in the middle of so many footmen?
160   Who clothe me in rich garments? I'm awake:
    It would be false to take this for a dream.
    Am I not Segismund? Heavens! disabuse me
    If I'm mistaken. Say, what could have happened
    In my imagination while I slept—

That I should find myself in such a place?   165
    But why should I worry, whatever it was?
    I'll let myself be served and entertained—
    Befall what may.
FIRST SERVANT: (*Aside to* SECOND SERVANT *and* CLARION.)
            He's very melancholy!
SECOND SERVANT: Who would not be, considering all that's
        happened
    To him?   170
CLARION: I would not be!
SECOND SERVANT: You, speak to him.
FIRST SERVANT: Shall they begin to sing again?
SEGISMUND: Why, no,
    I would not have them sing.
SECOND SERVANT: You're so distraught,
    I wish you entertained.
SEGISMUND: My griefs are such
    That no mere voices can amuse me now—
    Only the martial music pleased my mind.   175
CLOTALDO: Your Highness, mighty prince, give me your hand
    To kiss. I'm glad to be the first to offer
    Obedience at your feet.
SEGISMUND: (*Aside.*)   This is Clotaldo.
    How is it he, that tyrannised my thralldom,
    Should now be treating me with such respect?   180

(*Aloud.*)

    Tell me what's happening all round me here.
CLOTALDO: With the perplexities of your new state,
    Your reason will encounter many doubts,
    But I shall try to free you from them all
    (If that may be) because you now must know   185
    You are hereditary Prince of Poland.
    If you have been withdrawn from public sight
    Under restraint, it was in strict obedience
    To Fate's inclemency, which will permit
    A thousand woes to fall upon this empire   190
    The moment that you wear the sovereign's crown.
    But trusting that you'll prudently defeat
    Your own malignant stars (since they can be
    Controlled by magnanimity) you've been
    Brought to this palace from the tower you knew   195
    Even while your soul was yielded up to sleep.
    My lord the king, your father, will be coming
    To see you, and from him you'll learn the rest.
SEGISMUND: Then, vile, infamous traitor, what have I
    To know more than this fact of who I am,   200
    To show my pride and power from this day onward?
    How have you played your country such a treason
    As to deny me, against law and right,
    The rank which is my own?
CLOTALDO: Unhappy me!
SEGISMUND: You were a traitor to the law, a flattering liar   205
    To your own king, and cruel to myself.
    And so the king, the law, and I condemn you,
    After such fierce misfortunes as I've borne,
    To die here by my hands.
SECOND SERVANT: My lord!
SEGISMUND: Let none
    Get in the way. It is in vain. By God!   210
    If you intrude, I'll throw you through the window.

SECOND SERVANT: Clotaldo, fly!
CLOTALDO: Alas, poor Segismund!
 That you should show such pride, all unaware
 That you are dreaming this.

(*Exit.*)

SECOND SERVANT: Take care! Take care!
215 SEGISMUND: Get out!
 SECOND SERVANT: He was obeying the king's orders.
 SEGISMUND: In an injustice, no one should obey
  The king, and I'm his prince.
 SECOND SERVANT: He had no right
  To look into the rights and wrongs of it.
 SEGISMUND: You must be mad to answer back at me.
220 CLARION: The prince is right. It's you who're in the
   wrong!
 SECOND SERVANT: Who gave you right to speak?
 CLARION: I simply took it.
 SEGISMUND: And who are you?
 CLARION: I am the go-between,
  And in this art I think I am a master—
  Since I'm the greatest jackanapes alive.
225 SEGISMUND: (*To* CLARION.) In all this new world, you're the
   only one
  Of the whole crowd who pleases me.
 CLARION: Why, my lord,
  I am the best pleaser of Segismunds
  That ever was: ask anybody here!

(*Enter* ASTOLFO.)

ASTOLFO: Blessèd the day, a thousand times, my prince,
230 On which you landed here on Polish soil
  To fill with so much splendour and delight
  Our wide horizons, like the break of day!
  For you arise as does the rising sun
  Out of the rugged mountains, far away.
235 Shine forth then! And although so tardily
  You bind the glittering laurels on your brows,
  The longer may they last you still unwithered.
 SEGISMUND: God save you.
 ASTOLFO: That you do not know me, sir,
  Is some excuse for greeting me without
240 The honour due to me. I am Astolfo
  The Duke of Muscovy. You are my cousin.
  We are of equal rank.
 SEGISMUND: Then if I say,
  "God save you," do I not display good feeling?
  But since you take such note of who you are,
245 The next time that I see you, I shall say
  "God save you *not*," if you would like that better.
 SECOND SERVANT: (*To* ASTOLFO.) Your Highness, make
   allowance for his breeding
  Amongst the mountains. So he deals with all.

(*To* SEGISMUND.)

 Astolfo does take precedence, Your Highness—
250 SEGISMUND: I have no patience with the way he came
  To make his solemn speech, then put his hat on!
 SECOND SERVANT: He's a grandee!
 SEGISMUND: I'm grander than grandees!

SECOND SERVANT: For all that, there should be respect
  between you,
 More than among the rest.
 SEGISMUND: And who told you
  To mix in my affairs?   255

(*Enter* STELLA.)

STELLA: Many times welcome to Your Royal Highness,
 Now come to grace the dais that receives him
 With gratitude and love. Long may you live
 August and eminent, despite all snares,
 And count your life by centuries, not years! 260
SEGISMUND: (*Aside to* CLARION.) Now tell me, who's this
  sovereign deity
 At whose divinest feet Heaven lays down
 The fleece of its aurora in the east?
CLARION: Sir, it's your cousin Stella.
SEGISMUND: She were better
 Named "sun" than "star"!   265

(*To* STELLA.)

       Though your speech was fair,
 Just to have seen you and been conquered by you
 Suffices for a welcome in itself.
 To find myself so blessed beyond my merit
 What can I do but thank you, lovely Stella,
 For you could add more brilliance and delight 270
 To the most blazing star? When you get up
 What work is left the sun to do? O give me
 Your hand to kiss, from out whose cup of snow
 The solar horses drink the fires of day!
STELLA: Be a more gentle courtier.   275
ASTOLFO: I am lost.
SECOND SERVANT: I know Astolfo's hurt. I must divert him.

(*To* SEGISMUND.)

 Sir, you should know that thus to woo so boldly
 Is most improper. And, besides, Astolfo . . .
SEGISMUND: Did I not tell you not to meddle with me?
SECOND SERVANT: I only say what's just.   280
SEGISMUND: All this annoys me.
 Nothing seems just to me but what I want.
SECOND SERVANT: Why, sir, I heard you say that no obedience
 Or service should be lent to what's unjust.
SEGISMUND: You also heard me say that I would throw
 Anyone who annoys me from that balcony. 285
SECOND SERVANT: With men like me you cannot do such
  things.
SEGISMUND: No? Well, by God, I'll have to prove it then!

(*He takes him in his arms and rushes out, followed by many, to
return soon after.*)

ASTOLFO: What on earth have I seen? Can it be true?
STELLA: Go, all, and stop him!
SEGISMUND: (*Returning.*) From the balcony
 He's fallen in the sea. How strange it seems! 290
ASTOLFO: Measure your acts of violence, my lord:
 From crags to palaces, the distance is
 As great as that between man and the beasts.

SEGISMUND: Well, since you are for speaking out so boldly,
295   Perhaps one day you'll find that on your shoulders
You have no head to place your hat upon.

(*Exit* ASTOLFO. *Enter* BASIL.)

BASIL: What's happened here?
SEGISMUND: Nothing at all. A man
Wearied me, so I threw him in the sea.
CLARION: (*To* SEGISMUND.) Be warned. That is the king.
BASIL: On the first day,
300   So soon, your coming here has cost a life?
SEGISMUND: He said I couldn't: so I won the bet.
BASIL: It grieves me, Prince, that, when I hoped to see you
Forewarned, and overriding Fate, in triumph
Over your stars, the first thing I should see
305   Should be such rigour—that your first deed here
Should be a grievous homicide. Alas!
With what love, now, can I offer my arms,
Knowing your own have learned to kill already?
Who sees a dirk, red from a mortal wound,
310   But does not fear it? Who can see the place
Soaking in blood, where late a man was murdered,
But even the strongest must respond to nature?
So in your arms seeing the instrument
Of death, and looking on a blood-soaked place,
315   I must withdraw myself from your embrace,
And though I thought in loving bonds to bind
Your neck, yet fear withholds me from your arms.
SEGISMUND: Without your loving arms I can sustain
Myself as usual. That such a loving father
320   Could treat me with such cruelty, could thrust me
From his side ungratefully, could rear me
As a wild beast, could hold me for a monster,
And pray that I were dead, that such a father
Withholds his arms from winding round my neck,
325   Seems unimportant, seeing that he deprives
Me of my very being as a man.
BASIL: Would to heaven I had never granted it,
For then I never would have heard your voice,
Nor seen your outrages.
SEGISMUND: Had you denied
330   Me being, then I would not have complained,
But that you took it from me when you gave it—
That is my quarrel with you. Though to give
Is the most singular and noble action,
It is the basest action if one gives
335   Only to take away.
BASIL: How well you thank me
For being raised from pauper to a prince!
SEGISMUND: In this what is there I should thank you for?
You tyrant of my will! If you are old
And feeble, and you die, what can you give me
340   More than what is my own by right of birth?
You are my father and my king, therefore
This grandeur comes to me by natural law.
Therefore, despite my present state, I'm not
Indebted to you, rather can I claim
345   Account of all those years in which you robbed me
Of life and being, liberty, and honour.
You ought to thank me that I press no claim
Since you're my debtor, even to bankruptcy.

BASIL: Barbarous and outrageous brute! The heavens
Have now fulfilled their prophecy: I call   350
Them to bear witness to your pride. Although
You know now, disillusioned, who you are,
And see yourself where you take precedence,
Take heed of this I say: be kind and humble
Since it may be that you are only dreaming,   355
Although it seems to you you're wide-awake.

(*Exit* BASIL.)

SEGISMUND: Can I perhaps be dreaming, though I seem
So wide-awake? No: I am not asleep,
Since I can touch, and realise what I
Have been before, and what I am today.   360
And if you even now relented, Father,
There'd be no cure since I know who I am
And you cannot, for all your sighs and groans,
Cheat me of my hereditary crown.
And if I was submissive in my chains   365
Before, then I was ignorant of what I am,
Which I now know (and likewise know that I
Am partly man but partly beast as well).

(*Enter* ROSAURA *in woman's clothing.*)

ROSAURA: (*Aside.*) I came in Stella's train. I am afraid
Of meeting with Astolfo, since Clotaldo   370
Says he must not know who I am, not see me,
Because (he says) it touches on my honour.
And well I trust Clotaldo since I owe him
The safety of my life and honour both.
CLARION: What pleases you, and what do you admire   375
Most, of the things you've seen here in the world?
SEGISMUND: Why, nothing that I could not have foreseen—
Except the loveliness of women! Once,
I read among the books I had out there
That who owes God most grateful contemplation   380
Is Man: who is himself a tiny world.
But I think who owes God more grateful study
Is Woman—since she is a tiny heaven,
Having as much more beauty than a man
As heaven than earth. And even more, I say,   385
If she's the one that I am looking at.
ROSAURA: (*Aside.*) That is the prince. I'll go.
SEGISMUND: Stop! Woman! Wait!
Don't join the sunset with the breaking day
By fading out so fast. If east and west
Should clash like that, the day would surely suffer   390
A syncope. But what is this I see?
ROSAURA: What I am looking at I doubt, and yet
Believe.
SEGISMUND: (*Aside.*) This beauty I have seen before.
ROSAURA: (*Aside.*) This pomp and grandeur I have seen before
Cooped in a narrow dungeon.   395
SEGISMUND: (*Aside.*)   I have found
My life at last.

(*Aloud.*)

                Woman (for that sole word
Outsoars all wooing flattery of speech

From one that is a man), woman, who are you?
If even long before I ever saw you
400 You owed me adoration as your prince,
How much the more should you be conquered by me
Now I recall I've seen you once before!
Who are you, beauteous woman?
ROSAURA: (*Aside.*)   I'll pretend.

(*Aloud.*)

In Stella's train, I am a luckless lady.
405 SEGISMUND: Say no such thing. You are the sun from which
The minor star that's Stella draws its life,
Since she receives the splendour of your rays.
I've seen how in the kingdom of sweet odours,
Commander of the squadrons of the flowers,
410 The rose's deity presides, and is
Their empress by divine right of her beauty.
Among the precious stones which can be listed
In the academy of mines, I've seen
The diamond much preferred above the rest,
415 And crowned their emperor, for shining brightest.
In the revolving empire of the stars
The morning star takes pride among the others.
In their perfected spheres, when the sun calls
The planets to his council, he presides
420 And is the very oracle of day.
Then if among stars, gems, planet, and flowers
The fairest are exalted, why do you
Wait on a lesser beauty than yourself
Who are, in greater excellence and beauty,
425 The sun, the morning star, the diamond, and the rose!

(*Enter* CLOTALDO, *who remains by the stage-curtain.*)

CLOTALDO: (*Aside.*) I wish to curb him, since I brought him up.
But, what is this?
ROSAURA: I reverence your favour,
And yet reply, rhetorical, with silence,
For when one's mind is clumsy and untaught,
430 He answers best who does not speak at all.
SEGISMUND: Stay! Do not go! How can you wish to go
And leave me darkened by my doubts?
ROSAURA: Your Highness,
I beg your leave to go.
SEGISMUND: To go so rudely
Is not to beg my leave but just to take it.
435 ROSAURA: But if you will not grant it, I must take it.
SEGISMUND: That were to change my courtesy to rudeness.
Resistance is like venom to my patience.
ROSAURA: But even if this deadly, raging venom
Should overcome your patience, yet you dare not
440 And could not treat me with dishonour, sir.
SEGISMUND: Why, just to see then if I can, and dare to—
You'll make me lose the fear I bear your beauty,
Since the impossible is always tempting
To me. Why, only now I threw a man
445 Over this balcony who said I couldn't:
And so to find out if I can or not
I'll throw your honour through the window too.
CLOTALDO: (*Aside.*) He seems determined in this course.
Oh, heavens!

What's to be done that for a second time
My honour's threatened by a mad desire?   450
ROSAURA: Then with good reason it was prophesied
Your tyranny would wreak this kingdom
Outrageous scandals, treasons, crimes, and deaths.
But what can such a creature do as you
Who are not even a man, save in the name—   455
Inhuman, barbarous, cruel, and unbending
As the wild beasts amongst whom you were nursed?
SEGISMUND: That you should not insult me in this way
I spoke to you most courteously, and thought
I'd thereby get my way; but if you curse me thus   460
Even when I am speaking gently, why,
By the living God, I'll really give you cause.
Ho there! Clear out, the lot of you, at once!
Leave her to me! Close all the doors upon us.
Let no one enter!   465

(*Exeunt* CLARION *and other* ATTENDANTS.)

ROSAURA: I am lost . . . I warn you . . .
SEGISMUND: I am a tyrant and you plead in vain.
CLOTALDO: (*Aside.*) Oh, what a monstrous thing! I must
restrain him
Even if I die for it.

(*Aloud.*)

           Sir! Wait! Look here!
SEGISMUND: A second time you have provoked my anger,
You feeble, mad old man! Do you prize lightly   470
My wrath and rigour that you've gone so far?
CLOTALDO: Brought by the accents of her voice, I came
To tell you you must be more peaceful
If still you hope to reign, and warn you that
You should not be so cruel, though you rule—   475
Since this, perhaps, is nothing but a dream.
SEGISMUND: When you refer to disillusionment
You rouse me near to madness. Now you'll see,
Here as I kill you, if it's truth or dreaming!

(*As he tries to pull out his dagger,* CLOTALDO *restrains him and throws himself on his knees before him.*)

CLOTALDO: It's thus I'd save my life: and hope to do so—   480
SEGISMUND: Take your presumptuous hand from off this steel.
CLOTALDO: Till people come to hold your rage and fury
I shall not let you go.
ROSAURA: O heavens!
SEGISMUND: Loose it,

(*They struggle.*)

I say, or else—you interfering fool—
I'll crush you to your death in my strong arms!   485
ROSAURA: Come quickly! Here's Clotaldo being killed!

(*Exit.*)

(ASTOLFO *appears as* CLOTALDO *falls on the floor, and the former stands between* SEGISMUND *and* CLOTALDO.)

ASTOLFO: Why, what is this, most valiant prince? What? Staining
    Your doughty steel in such old, frozen blood?
    For shame! For shame! Sheathe your illustrious weapon!
490 SEGISMUND: When it is stained in his infamous blood!
ASTOLFO: At my feet here he has found sanctuary
    And there he's safe, for it will serve him well.
SEGISMUND: Then serve me well by dying, for like this
    I will avenge myself for your behaviour
495   In trying to annoy me first of all.
ASTOLFO: To draw in self-defence offends no king,
    Though in his palace.

(ASTOLFO *draws his sword and they fight.*)

CLOTALDO: (*To* ASTOLFO.) Do not anger him!

(*Enter* BASIL, STELLA, *and* ATTENDANTS.)

BASIL: Hold! Hold! What's this? Fighting with naked swords?
STELLA: (*Aside.*) It is Astolfo! How my heart misgives me!
500 BASIL: Why, what has happened here?
ASTOLFO: Nothing, my Lord,
    Since you've arrived.

(*Both sheathe their swords.*)

SEGISMUND: Much, though you have arrived.
    I tried to kill the old man.
BASIL: Had you no
    Respect for those white hairs?
CLOTALDO: Sire, since they're only
    Mine, as you well can see, it does not matter!
505 SEGISMUND: It is in vain you'd have me hold white hairs
    In such respect, since one day you may find
    Your own white locks prostrated at my feet
    For still I have not taken vengeance on you
    For the foul way in which you had me reared.

(*Exit.*)

510 BASIL: Before that happens you will sleep once more
    Where you were reared, and where what's happened may
    Seem just a dream (being mere earthly glory).

(*All save* ASTOLFO *and* STELLA *leave.*)

ASTOLFO: How seldom does prediction fail, when evil!
    How oft, foretelling good! Exact in harm,
515   Doubtful in benefit! Oh, what a great
    Astrologer would be one who foretold
    Nothing but harms, since there's no doubt at all
    That they are always due! In Segismund
    And me the case is illustrated clearly.
520   In him, crimes, cruelties, deaths, and disasters
    Were well predicted, since they all came true.
    But in my own case, to predict for me
    (As I foresaw beholding rays which cast
    The sun into the shade and outface heaven)
525   Triumphs and trophies, happiness and praise,
    Was false—and yet was true: it's only just
    That when predictions start with promised favours
    They should end in disdain.

STELLA: I do not doubt
    Your protestations are most heartfelt; only
    They're not for me, but for another lady   530
    Whose portrait you were wearing round your neck
    Slung in a locket when you first arrived.
    Since it is so, she only can deserve
    These wooing flatteries. Let her repay you
    For in affairs of love, flatteries and vows   535
    Made for another are mere forged credentials.

(ROSAURA *enters but waits by the curtain.*)

ROSAURA: (*Aside.*) Thanks be to God, my troubles are near ended!
    To judge from what I see, I've naught to fear.
ASTOLFO: I will expel that portrait from my breast
    To make room for the image of your beauty   540
    And keep it there. For there where Stella is
    Can be no room for shade, and where the sun is
    No place for any star. I'll fetch the portrait.

(*Aside.*)

    Forgive me, beautiful Rosaura, that,
    When absent, men and women seldom keep   545
    More faith than this.

(*Exit.*)

(ROSAURA *comes forward.*)

ROSAURA: (*Aside.*)   I could not hear a word. I was afraid
    That they would see me.
STELLA: Oh, Astrea!
ROSAURA: My lady!
STELLA: I am delighted that you came. Because
    To you alone would I confide a secret.
ROSAURA: Thereby you greatly honour me, your servant.   550
STELLA: Astrea, in the brief time I have known you
    I've given you the latchkey of my will.
    For that, and being who you are, I'll tell you
    A secret which I've very often hidden
    Even from myself.   555
ROSAURA: I am your slave.
STELLA: Then, briefly:
    Astolfo, who's my cousin (the word cousin
    Suffices, since some things are plainly said
    Even by thinking them), is to wed me
    If Fortune thus can wipe so many cares
    Away with one great joy. But I am troubled   560
    In that, the day he first came here, he carried
    A portrait of a lady round his neck.
    I spoke to him about it courteously.
    He was most amiable, he loves me well,
    And now he's gone for it. I am embarrassed   565
    That he should give it me himself. Wait here,
    And tell him to deliver it to you.
    Do not say more. Since you're discreet and fair:
    You'll surely know just what love is.

(*Exit.*)

ROSAURA: Great heavens!
    How I wish that I did not! For who could be   570

So prudent or so skilful as would know
What to advise herself in such a case?
Lives there a person on this earth today
Who's more beset by the inclement stars,
575 Who has more cares besieging him, or fights
So many dire calamities at once?
What can I do in such bewilderment
Wherein it seems impossible to find
Relief or comfort? Since my first misfortune
580 No other thing has chanced or happened to me
But was a new misfortune. In succession
Inheritors and heirs of their own selves
(Just like the Phoenix, his own son and father)
Misfortunes reproduce themselves, are born,
585 And live by dying. In their sepulchre
The ashes they consume are hot forever.
A sage once said misfortunes must be cowards
Because they never dare to walk alone
But come in crowds. I say they are most valiant
590 Because they always charge so bravely on
And never turn their backs. Who charges with them
May dare all things because there is no fear
That they'll ever desert him; and I say it
Because in all my life I never once
595 Knew them to leave me, nor will they grow tired
Of me till, wounded and shot through and through
By Fate, I fall into the arms of death.
Alas, what can I do in this dilemma?
If I reveal myself, then old Clotaldo,
600 To whom I owe my life, may take offence,
Because he told me to await the cure
And mending of my honour in concealment.
If I don't tell Astolfo who I am
And he detects me, how can I dissimulate?
605 Since even if I say I am not I,
The voice, the language, and the eyes will falter,
Because the soul will tell them that they lie.
What shall I do? It is in vain to study
What I should do, when I know very well
610 That, whatsoever way I choose to act,
When the time comes I'll do as sorrow bids,
For no one has control over his sorrows.
Then since my soul dares not decide its actions
Let sorrow fill my cup and let my grief
615 Reach its extremity and, out of doubts
And vain appearances, once and for all
Come out into the light—and Heaven shield me!

(*Enter* ASTOLFO.)

ASTOLFO: Here, lady, is the portrait . . . but . . . great God!
ROSAURA: Why does Your Highness halt, and stare astonished?
620 ASTOLFO: Rosaura! Why, to see you here!
ROSAURA: Rosaura?
Sir, you mistake me for some other lady.
I am Astrea, and my humble station
Deserves no perturbation such as yours.
ASTOLFO: Enough of this pretence, Rosaura, since
625 The soul can never lie. Though as Astrea
I see you now, I love you as Rosaura.
ROSAURA: Not having understood Your Highness' meaning

I can make no reply except to say
That Stella (who might be the star of Venus)
Told me to wait here and to tell you from her   630
To give to me the portrait you were fetching
(Which seems a very logical request)
And I myself will take it to my lady.
Thus Stella bids: even the slightest things
Which do me harm are governed by some star.   635
ASTOLFO: Even if you could make a greater effort
How poorly you dissimulate, Rosaura!
Tell your poor eyes they do not harmonise
With your own voice, because they needs must jangle
When the whole instrument is out of time.   640
You cannot match the falsehood of your words
With the sincerity of what you're feeling.
ROSAURA: All I can say is—that I want the portrait.
ASTOLFO: As you require a fiction, with a fiction
I shall reply. Go and tell Stella this: 645
That I esteem her so, it seems unworthy
Only to send the counterfeit to her
And that I'm sending her the original.
And you, take the original along with you,
Taking yourself to her.   650
ROSAURA: When a man starts
Forth on a definite task, resolved and valiant,
Though he be offered a far greater prize
Than what he seeks, yet he returns with failure
If he returns without his task performed.
I came to get that portrait. Though I bear   655
The original with me, of greater value,
I would return in failure and contempt
Without the copy. Give it me, Your Highness,
Since I cannot return without it.
ASTOLFO: But
If I don't give it you, how can you do so?   660
ROSAURA: Like this, ungrateful man! I'll take it from you.

(*She tries to wrest it from him.*)

ASTOLFO: It is in vain.
ROSAURA: By God, it shall not come
Into another woman's hands!
ASTOLFO: You're terrifying!
ROSAURA: And you're perfidious!
ASTOLFO: Enough, my dear
Rosaura!   665
ROSAURA: I, your dear? You lie, you villain!

(*They are both clutching the portrait.*)

(*Enter* STELLA.)

STELLA: Astrea and Astolfo, what does this mean?
ASTOLFO: (*Aside.*) Here's Stella.
ROSAURA: (*Aside.*)   Love, grant me the strength to win
My portrait.

(*To* STELLA.)

                         If you want to know, my lady,
What this is all about, I will explain.

670 ASTOLFO: (*To* ROSAURA, *aside.*) What do you mean?

ROSAURA: You told me to await
Astolfo here and ask him for a portrait
On your behalf. I waited here alone
And as one thought suggests another thought,
Thinking of portraits, I recalled my own

675 Was here inside my sleeve. When one's alone,
One is diverted by a foolish trifle
And so I took it out to look at it.
It slipped and fell, just as Astolfo here,
Bringing the portrait of the other lady,

680 Came to deliver it to you as promised.
He picked my portrait up, and so unwilling
Is he to give away the one you asked for,
Instead of doing so, he seized upon
The other portrait which is mine alone

685 And will not give it back though I entreated
And begged him to return it. I was angry
And tried to snatch it back. That's it he's holding,
And you can see yourself if it's not mine.

STELLA: Let go the portrait.

(*She snatches it from him.*)

ASTOLFO: Madam!

STELLA: The draughtsman

690 Was not unkind to truth.

ROSAURA: Is it not mine?

STELLA: Why, who could doubt it?

ROSAURA: Ask him for the other.

STELLA: Here, take your own, Astrea. You may leave us.

ROSAURA: (*Aside.*) Now I have got my portrait, come what will.

(*Exit.*)

STELLA: Now give me up the portrait that I asked for

695 Although I'll see and speak to you no more.
I do not wish to leave it in your power
Having been once so foolish as to beg it.

ASTOLFO: (*Aside.*) Now how can I get out of this foul trap?

(*To* STELLA.)

Beautiful Stella, though I would obey you,

700 And serve you in all ways, I cannot give you
The portrait, since . . .

STELLA: You are a crude, coarse villain
And ruffian of a wooer. For the portrait—
I do not want it now, since, if I had it,
It would remind me I had asked you for it.

(*Exit.*)

705 ASTOLFO: Listen! Look! Wait! Let me explain!

(*Aside.*)

Oh, damn
Rosaura! How the devil did she get
To Poland for my ruin and her own?

The prison of SEGISMUND *in the tower.*

SEGISMUND *lying on the ground loaded with fetters and clothed in skins as before.* CLOTALDO, *two* ATTENDANTS, *and* CLARION.

CLOTALDO: Here you must leave him—since his reckless pride
Ends here today where it began.

ATTENDANT: His chain

710 I'll rivet as it used to be before.

CLARION: O Prince, you'd better not awake too soon
To find how lost you are, how changed your fate,
And that your fancied glory of an hour
Was but a shade of life, a flame of death!

715 CLOTALDO: For one who knows so well to wield his tongue
It's fit a worthy place should be provided
With lots of room and lots of time to argue.
This is the fellow that you have to seize

(*To the* ATTENDANTS.)

And that's the room in which you are to lock him.

(*Points to the nearest cell.*)

720 CLARION: Why me?

CLOTALDO: Because a Clarion who knows
Too many secrets must be kept in gaol—
A place where even clarions are silent.

CLARION: Have I, by chance, wanted to kill my father
Or thrown an Icarus from a balcony?

725 Am I asleep or dreaming? To what end
Do you imprison me?

CLOTALDO: You're Clarion.

CLARION: Well, say I swear to be a cornet now,
A silent one, a wretched instrument . . . ?

(*They hustle him off.* CLOTALDO *remains.*)

(*Enter* BASIL, *wearing a mask.*)

BASIL: Clotaldo.

CLOTALDO: Sire . . . and is it thus alone

730 Your Majesty has come?

BASIL: Vain curiosity
To see what happens here to Segismund.

CLOTALDO: See where he lies, reduced to misery!

BASIL: Unhappy prince! Born at a fatal moment!
Come waken him, now he has lost his strength

735 With all the opium he's drunk.

CLOTALDO: He's stirring
And talking to himself.

BASIL: What is he dreaming?
Let's listen now.

SEGISMUND: He who chastises tyrants
Is a most pious prince . . . Now let Clotaldo
Die by my hand . . . my father kiss my feet . . .

740 CLOTALDO: He threatens me with death!

BASIL: And me with insult
And cruelty.

CLOTALDO: He'd take my life away.

BASIL: And he'd humiliate me at his feet.

SEGISMUND: (*Still in a dream.*) Throughout the expanse of this
world's theatre

745 I'll show my peerless valour, let my vengeance
Be wreaked, and the Prince Segismund be seen
To triumph—over his father . . . but, alas!

(*Awakening.*)

Where am I?
BASIL: (*To* CLOTALDO.) Since he must not see me here,
I'll listen further off. You know your cue.

(*Retires to one side.*)

SEGISMUND: Can this be I? Am I the same who, chained
750 And long imprisoned, rose to such a state?
Are you not still my sepulchre and grave,
You dismal tower? God! What things I have dreamed!
CLOTALDO: (*Aside.*) Now I must go to him to disenchant him.

(*Aloud.*)

Awake already?
SEGISMUND: Yes: it was high time.
755 CLOTALDO: What? Do you have to spend all day asleep?
Since I was following the eagle's flight
With tardy discourse, have you still lain here
Without awaking?
SEGISMUND: No. Nor even now
Am I awake. It seems I've always slept,
760 Since, if I've dreamed what I've just seen and heard
Palpably and for certain, then I am dreaming
What I see now—nor is it strange I'm tired,
Since what I, sleeping, see, tells me that I
Was dreaming when I thought I was awake.
765 CLOTALDO: Tell me your dream.
SEGISMUND: That's if it *was* a dream!
No, I'll not tell you what I dreamed; but what
I lived and saw, Clotaldo, I *will* tell you.
I woke up in a bed that might have been
The cradle of the flowers, woven by Spring.
770 A thousand nobles, bowing, called me Prince,
Attiring me in jewels, pomp, and splendour.
My equanimity you turned to rapture
Telling me that I was the Prince of Poland.
CLOTALDO: I must have got a fine reward!
SEGISMUND: Not so:
775 For as a traitor, twice, with rage and fury,
I tried to kill you.
CLOTALDO: Such cruelty to me?
SEGISMUND: I was the lord of all, on all I took revenge,
Except I loved one woman . . . I believe
That *that* was true, though all the rest has faded.

(*Exit* BASIL.)

780 CLOTALDO: (*Aside.*) I see the king was moved, to hear him
speak.

(*Aloud.*)

Talking of eagles made you dream of empires,
But even in your dreams it's good to honour
Those who have cared for you and brought you up.

For Segismund, even in dreams, I warn you
Nothing is lost by trying to do good.   785

(*Exit.*)

SEGISMUND: That's true, and therefore let us subjugate
The bestial side, this fury and ambition,
Against the time when we may dream once more,
As certainly we shall, for this strange world
Is such that but to live here is to dream.   790
And now experience shows me that each man
Dreams what he is until he is awakened.
The king dreams he's a king and in this fiction
Lives, rules, administers with royal pomp.
Yet all the borrowed praises that he earns   795
Are written in the wind, and he is changed
(How sad a fate!) by death to dust and ashes.
What man is there alive who'd seek to reign
Since he must wake into the dream that's death.
The rich man dreams his wealth which is his care   800
And woe. The poor man dreams his sufferings.
He dreams who thrives and prospers in this life.
He dreams who toils and strives. He dreams who injures,
Offends, and insults. So that in this world
Everyone dreams the thing he is, though no one   805
Can understand it. I dream I am here,
Chained in these fetters. Yet I dreamed just now
I was in a more flattering, lofty station.
What is this life? A frenzy, an illusion,
A shadow, a delirium, a fiction.   810
The greatest good's but little, and this life
Is but a dream, and dreams are only dreams.

ACT THREE

The tower.

Enter CLARION.

CLARION: I'm held in an enchanted tower, because
Of all I know. What would they do to me
For all I don't know, since—for all I know—
They're killing me by starving me to death.
O that a man so hungry as myself   5
Should live to die of hunger while alive!
I am so sorry for myself that others
May well say "I can well believe it," since
This silence ill accords with my name "Clarion,"
And I just can't shut up. My fellows here?   10
Spiders and rats—fine feathered songsters those!
My head's still ringing with a dream of fifes
And trumpets and a lot of noisy humbug
And long processions as of penitents
With crosses, winding up and down, while some   15
Faint at the sight of blood besmirching others.
But now to tell the truth, I am in prison.
For knowing secrets, I am kept shut in,
Strictly observed as if I were a Sunday,
And feeling sadder than a Tuesday, where   20
I neither eat nor drink. They say a secret
Is sacred and should be as strictly kept
As any saint's day on the calendar.

Saint Secret's Day for me's a working day
25   Because I'm never idle then. The penance
I suffer here is merited, I say:
Because being a lackey, I was silent,
Which, in a servant, is a sacrilege.

(*A noise of drums and trumpets.*)

FIRST SOLDIER: (*Within.*) Here is the tower in which he is
        imprisoned.
30   Smash in the door and enter, everybody!
CLARION: Great God! They've come to seek me. That is certain
        Because they say I'm here. What can they want?

(*Enter several soldiers.*)

FIRST SOLDIER: Go in.
SECOND SOLDIER: He's here!
CLARION: No, he's not here!
ALL THE SOLDIERS: Our lord!
CLARION: What, are they drunk?
FIRST SOLDIER: You are our rightful prince.
35   We do not want and never shall allow
A stranger to supplant our trueborn prince.
Give us your feet to kiss!
ALL THE SOLDIERS: Long live the prince!
CLARION: Bless me, if it's not real! In this strange kingdom
        It seems the custom, everyday, to take
40   Some fellow and to make him prince and then
Shut him back in this tower. That *must* be it!
So I must play my role.
ALL THE SOLDIERS: Give us your feet.
CLARION: I can't. They're necessary. After all
        What sort of use would be a footless prince?
45   SECOND SOLDIER: All of us told your father, as one man,
        We want no prince of Muscovy but you!
CLARION: You weren't respectful to my father? Shame!
FIRST SOLDIER: It was our loyalty that made us tell him.
CLARION: If it was loyalty, you have my pardon.
50   SECOND SOLDIER: Restore your empire. Long live Segismund!
CLARION: (*Aside.*) That is the name they seem to give to all
        These counterfeited princes.

(*Enter* SEGISMUND.)

SEGISMUND: Who called Segismund?
CLARION: (*Aside.*) I seem to be a hollow sort of prince.
FIRST SOLDIER: Which of you's Segismund?
SEGISMUND: I am.
SECOND SOLDIER: (*To* CLARION.)   Then why,
55   Rash fool, did you impersonate the prince
Segismund?
CLARION: What? I, Segismund? Yourselves
        Be-Segismunded me without request.
        All yours was both the rashness and the folly.
FIRST SOLDIER: Prince Segismund, whom we acclaim our lord,
60   Your father, great King Basil, in his fear
That heaven would fulfil a prophecy
That one day he would kneel before your feet
Wishes now to deprive you of the throne
And give it to the Duke of Muscovy.
65   For this he called a council, but the people

Discovered his design and knowing, now,
They have a native king, will have no stranger.
So scorning the fierce threats of destiny,
We've come to seek you in your very prison,
That aided by the arms of the whole people,   70
We may restore you to the crown and sceptre,
Taking them from the tyrant's grasp. Come, then:
Assembling here, in this wide desert region,
Hosts of plebeians, bandits, and freebooters,
Acclaim you king. Your liberty awaits you!   75
Hark to its voice!

(*Shouts within.*)

                    Long life to Segismund!
SEGISMUND: Once more, you heavens will that I should dream
Of grandeur, once again, 'twixt doubts and shades,
Behold the majesty of pomp and power
Vanish into the wind, once more you wish   80
That I should taste the disillusion and
The risk by which all human power is humbled,
Of which all human power should live aware.
It must not be. I'll not be once again
Put through my paces by my fortune's stars.   85
And since I know this life is all a dream,
Depart, vain shades, who feign, to my dead senses,
That you have voice and body, having neither!
I want no more feigned majesty, fantastic
Display, nor void illusions, that one gust   90
Can scatter like the almond tree in flower,
Whose rosy buds, without advice or warning,
Dawn in the air too soon and then, as one,
Are all extinguished, fade, and fall, and wither
In the first gust of wind that comes along!   95
I know you well. I know you well by now.
I know that all that happens in yourselves
Happens as in a sleeping man. For me
There are no more delusions and deceptions
Since I well know this life is all a dream.   100
SECOND SOLDIER: If you think we are cheating, just sweep
Your gaze along these towering peaks, and see
The hosts that wait to welcome and obey you.
SEGISMUND: Already once before I've seen such crowds
Distinctly, quite as vividly as these: 105
And yet it was a dream.
SECOND SOLDIER: No great event
Can come without forerunners to announce it
And this is the real meaning of your dream.
SEGISMUND: Yes, you say well. It was the fore-announcement
And just in case it was correct, my soul,   110
(Since life's so short) let's dream the dream anew!
But it must be attentively, aware
That we'll awake from pleasure in the end.
Forewarned of that, the shock's not so abrupt,
The disillusion's less. Evils anticipated   115
Lose half their sting. And armed with this precaution—
That power, even when we're sure of it, is borrowed
And must be given back to its true owner—
We can risk anything and dare the worst.
Subjects, I thank you for your loyalty.   120
In me you have a leader who will free you,
Bravely and skilfully, from foreign rule.

Sound now to arms, you'll soon behold my valour.
Against my father I must march and bring
125 Truth from the stars. Yes: he must kneel to me.

(*Aside.*)

But yet, since I may wake before he kneels,
Perhaps I'd better not proclaim what may not happen.
ALL: Long live Segismund!

(*Enter* CLOTALDO.)

CLOTALDO: Gracious heavens! What is
This riot here?
SEGISMUND: Clotaldo!
CLOTALDO: Sir!

(*Aside.*)

                                        He'll prove
130 His cruelty on me.
CLARION: I bet he throws him
Over the mountain.
CLOTALDO: At your royal feet
I kneel, knowing my penalty is death.
SEGISMUND: Rise, rise, my foster father, from the ground,
For you must be the compass and the guide
135 In which I trust. You brought me up, and I
Know what I owe your loyalty. Embrace me!
CLOTALDO: What's that you say?
SEGISMUND: I know I'm in a dream,
But I would like to act well, since good actions,
Even in a dream, are not entirely lost.
140 CLOTALDO: Since doing good is now to be your glory,
You will not be offended that I too
Should do what's right. You march against your father!
I cannot give you help against my king.
Here at your feet, my lord, I plead for death.
145 SEGISMUND: (*Aloud.*) Villain!

(*Aside.*)

                                        But let us suffer this annoyance.
Though my rage would slay him, yet he's loyal.
A man does not deserve to die for that.
How many angry passions does this leash
Restrain in me, this curb of knowing well
150 That I must wake and find myself alone!
SECOND SOLDIER: All this fine talk, Clotaldo, is a cruel
Spurn of the public welfare. We are loyal
Who wish our own prince to reign over us.
CLOTALDO: Such loyalty, after the king were dead,
155 Would honour you. But while the king is living
He is our absolute, unquestioned lord.
There's no excuse for subjects who oppose
His sovereignty in arms.
FIRST SOLDIER: We'll soon see well
Enough, Clotaldo, what this loyalty
160 Is worth.
CLOTALDO: You would be better if you had some.
It is the greatest prize.
SEGISMUND: Peace, peace, I pray you.
CLOTALDO: My lord!

SEGISMUND: Clotaldo, if your feelings
Are truly thus, go you, and serve the king;
That's prudence, loyalty, and common sense.
But do not argue here with anyone   165
Whether it's right or wrong, for every man
Has his own honour.
CLOTALDO: Humbly I take my leave.

(*Exit.*)

SEGISMUND: Now sound the drums and march in rank and order
Straight to the palace.
ALL: Long live Segismund!
SEGISMUND: Fortune, we go to reign! Do not awake me   170
If I am dreaming! Do not let me fall
Asleep if it is true! To act with virtue
Is what matters, since if this proves true,
That truth's sufficient reason in itself;
If not, we win us friends against the time   175
When we at last awake.

A room in the royal palace.

Enter BASIL *and* ASTOLFO.

BASIL: Whose prudence can rein in a bolting horse?
Who can restrain a river's pride, in spate?
Whose valour can withstand a crag dislodged
And hurtling downwards from a mountain peak?   180
All these are easier by far than to hold back
A crowd's proud fury, once it has been roused.
It has two voices, both proclaiming war,
And you can hear them echoing through the mountains,
Some shouting "Segismund," others "Astolfo."   185
The scene I set for swearing of allegiance
Lends but an added horror to this strife:
It has become the back cloth to a stage
Where Fortune plays out tragedies in blood.
ASTOLFO: My lord, forget the happiness and wealth   190
You promised me from your most blessèd hand.
If Poland, which I hope to rule, refuses
Obedience to my right, grudging me honour,
It is because I've got to earn it first.
Give me a horse, that I with angry pride   195
May match the thunder in my voice and ride
To strike, like lightning, terror far and wide.

(*Exit* ASTOLFO.)

BASIL: No remedy for what's infallible!
What is foreseen is perilous indeed!
If something has to be, there's no way out;   200
In trying to evade it, you but court it.
This law is pitiless and horrible.
Thinking one can evade the risk, one meets it:
My own precautions have been my undoing,
And I myself have quite destroyed my kingdom.   205

(*Enter* STELLA.)

STELLA: If you, my lord, in person do not try
To curb the vast commotion that has started

In all the streets between the rival factions,
You'll see your kingdom, swamped in waves of crimson,
210 Swimming in its own blood, with nothing left
But havoc, dire calamity, and woe.
So frightful is the damage to your empire
That, seen, it strikes amazement; heard, despair.
The sun's obscured, the very winds are hindered.
215 Each stone is a memorial to the dead.
Each flower springs from a grave while every building
Appears a mausoleum, and each soldier
A premature and walking skeleton.

(*Enter* CLOTALDO.)

CLOTALDO: Praise be to God, I reach your feet alive!
220 BASIL: Clotaldo! What's the news of Segismund?
CLOTALDO: The crowd, a headstrong monster blind with rage,
Entered his dungeon tower and set him free.
He, now exalted for the second time,
Conducts himself with valour, boasting how
225 He will bring down the truth out of the stars.
BASIL: Give me a horse, that I myself, in person,
May vanquish such a base, ungrateful son!
For I, in the defence of my own crown,
Shall do by steel what science failed to do.

(*Exit.*)

230 STELLA: I'll be Bellona to your Sun, and try
To write my name next yours in history.
I'll ride as though I flew on outstretched wings
That I may vie with Pallas.

(*Exit.*)

(*Enter* ROSAURA, *holding back* CLOTALDO.)

ROSAURA: I know that all is war, Clotaldo, yet
235 Although your valour calls you to the front,
First hear me out. You know quite well that I
Arrived in Poland poor and miserable,
Where, shielded by your valour, I found mercy.
You told me to conceal myself, and stay
240 Here in the palace, hiding from Astolfo.
He saw me in the end, and so insulted
My honour that (although he saw me clearly)
He nightly speaks with Stella in the garden.
I have the key to it and I will show you
245 How you can enter there and end my cares.
Thus bold, resolved, and strong, you can recover
My honour, since you're ready to avenge me
By killing him.
CLOTALDO: It's true that I intended,
Since first I saw you (having heard your tale)
250 With my own life to rectify your wrongs.
The first step that I took was bid you dress
According to your sex, for fear Astolfo
Might see you as you were, and deem you wanton.
I was devising how we could recover
255 Your honour (so much did it weigh on me)
Even though we had to kill him. (A wild plan—

Though since he's not my king, I would not flinch
From killing him.) But then, when suddenly
Segismund tried to kill me, it was he
260 Who saved my life with his surpassing valour.
Consider: how can I requite Astolfo
With death for giving me my life so bravely,
And when my soul is full of gratitude?
So torn between the two of you I stand—
265 Rosaura, whose life I saved, and Astolfo,
Who saved my life. What's to be done? Which side
To take, and whom to help, I cannot judge.
What I owe you in that I gave you life
I owe to him in that he gave me life.
270 And so there is no course that I can take
To satisfy my love. I am a person
Who has to act, yet suffer either way.
ROSAURA: I should not have to tell so brave a man
That if it is nobility to give,
275 It's baseness to receive. That being so
You owe no gratitude to him, admitting
That it was he who gave you life, and you
Who gave me life, since he forced you to take
A meaner role, and through me you assumed
280 A generous role. So you should side with me:
My cause is so far worthier than his own
As giving is than taking.
CLOTALDO: Though nobility
Is with the giver, it is gratitude
That dwells with the receiver. As a giver
285 I have the name of being generous:
Then grant me that of being grateful too
And let me earn the title and be grateful,
As I am liberal, giving or receiving.
ROSAURA: You granted me my life, at the same time
290 Telling me it was worthless, since dishonoured,
And therefore was no life. Therefore from you
I have received no life at all. And since
You should be liberal first and grateful after
(Since so you said yourself) I now entreat you
295 Give me the life, the life you never gave me!
As giving magnifies the most, give first
And then be grateful after, if you will!
CLOTALDO: Won by your argument, I will be liberal.
Rosaura, I shall give you my estate
300 And you shall seek a convent, there to live.
This measure is a happy thought, for, see,
Fleeing a crime, you find a sanctuary.
For when the empire's threatened with disasters
And is divided thus, I, born a noble,
305 Am not the man who would augment its woes.
So with this remedy which I have chosen
I remain loyal to the kingdom, generous
To you, and also grateful to Astolfo.
And thus I choose the course that suits you best.
310 Were I your father, what could I do more?
ROSAURA: Were you my father, then I would accept
The insult. Since you are not, I refuse.
CLOTALDO: What do you hope to do then?
ROSAURA: Kill the duke!
CLOTALDO: A girl who never even knew her father
315 Armed with such courage?

ROSAURA: Yes.
CLOTALDO: What spurs you on?
ROSAURA: My good name.
CLOTALDO: In Astolfo you will find . . .
ROSAURA: My honour rides on him and strikes him down!
CLOTALDO: Your king, too, Stella's husband!
ROSAURA: Never, never
    Shall that be, by almighty God, I swear!
320 CLOTALDO: Why, this is madness!
ROSAURA: Yes it is!
CLOTALDO: Restrain it.
ROSAURA: That I cannot.
CLOTALDO: Then you are lost forever!
ROSAURA: I know it!
CLOTALDO: Life and honour both together!
ROSAURA: I well believe it!
CLOTALDO: What do you intend?
ROSAURA: My death.
CLOTALDO: This is despair and desperation.
325 ROSAURA: It's honour.
CLOTALDO: It is nonsense.
ROSAURA: It is valour.
CLOTALDO: It's frenzy.
ROSAURA: Yes, it's anger! Yes, it's fury!
CLOTALDO: In short you cannot moderate your passion?
ROSAURA: No.
CLOTALDO: Who is there to help you?
ROSAURA: I, myself.
CLOTALDO: There is no cure?
ROSAURA: There is no cure!
CLOTALDO: Think well
330   If there's not some way out . . .
ROSAURA: Some other way
    To do away with me . . .

(*Exit.*)

CLOTALDO: If you are lost,
    My daughter, let us both be lost together!

In the country.

Enter SEGISMUND *clothed in skins.* SOLDIERS *marching.* CLARION.
Drums beating.

SEGISMUND: If Rome, today, could see me here, renewing
    Her olden triumphs, she might laugh to see
335   A wild beast in command of mighty armies,
    A wild beast, to whose fiery aspirations
    The firmament were all too slight a conquest!
    But stoop your flight, my spirit. Do not thus
    Be puffed to pride by these uncertain plaudits
340   Which, when I wake, will turn to bitterness
    In that I won them only to be lost.
    The less I value them, the less I'll miss them.

(*A trumpet sounds.*)

CLARION: Upon a rapid courser (pray excuse me,
    Since if it comes to mind I must describe it)
345   In which it seems an atlas was designed
    Since if its body is earth, its soul is fire

Within its breast, its foam appears the sea,
The wind its breath, and chaos its condition,
Since in its soul, its foam, its breath and flesh,
It seems a monster of fire, earth, sea, and wind,   350
Upon the horse, all of a patchwork colour,
Dappled, and rushing forward at the will
Of one who plies the spur, so that it flies
Rather than runs—see how a woman rides
Boldly into your presence.   355
SEGISMUND: Her light blinds me.
CLARION: Good God! Why, here's Rosaura!
SEGISMUND: It is heaven
    That has restored her to my sight once more.

(*Enter* ROSAURA *with sword and dagger in riding costume.*)

ROSAURA: Generous Segismund, whose majesty
    Heroically rises in the lustre
    Of his great deeds out of his night of shadows,   360
    And as the greatest planet, in the arms
    Of his aurora, lustrously returns
    To plants and roses, over hills and seas,
    When, crowned with gold, he looks abroad, dispersing
    Radiance, flashing his rays, bathing the summits,   365
    And broidering the fringes of the foam,
    So may you dawn upon the world, bright sun
    Of Poland, that a poor unhappy woman
    May fall before your feet and beg protection
    Both as a woman and unfortunate—   370
    Two things that must oblige you, sire, as one
    Who prizes yourself as valiant, each of them
    More than suffices for your chivalry.
    Three times you have beheld me now, three times
    Been ignorant of who I am, because   375
    Three times you saw me in a different clothing.
    The first time you mistook me for a man,
    Within that rigorous prison, where your hardships
    Made mine seem pleasure. Next time, as a woman,
    You saw me, when your pomp and majesty   380
    Were as a dream, a phantasm, a shade.
    The third time is today when, as a monster
    Of both the sexes, in a woman's costume
    I bear a soldier's arms. But to dispose you
    The better to compassion, hear my story.   385
    My mother was a noble in the court
    Of Moscow, who, since most unfortunate,
    Must have been beautiful. Then came a traitor
    And cast his eyes on her (I do not name him,
    Not knowing who he is). Yet I deduce   390
    That he was valiant too from my own valour,
    Since he gave form to me—and I could wish
    I had been born in pagan times, that I might
    Persuade myself he was some god of those
    Who rain in showers of gold, turn into swans   395
    Or bulls, for Danaës, Ledas, or Europas.
    That's strange: I thought I was just rambling on
    By telling old perfidious myths, yet find
    I've told you how my mother was cajoled.

343–355 **Upon a . . . presence** Clarion's speech is a parody of exaggerated style including Calderón's [R.C.]

400   Oh, she was beautiful as no one else
      Has been, but was unfortunate like all.
      He swore to wed her (that's an old excuse)
      And this trick reached so nearly to her heart
      That thought must weep, recalling it today.
405   The tyrant left her only with his sword
      As Aeneas left Troy. I sheathed its blade here
      Upon my thigh, and I will bare it too
      Before the ending of this history.
      Out of this union, this poor link which neither
410   Could bind the marriage nor handcuff the crime,
      Myself was born, her image and her portrait,
      Not in her beauty, but in her misfortune,
      For mine's the same. That's all I need to say.
      The most that I can tell you of myself
415   Is that the man who robbed me of the spoils
      And trophies of my honour is Astolfo.
      Alas! to name him my heart rages so
      (As hearts will do when men name enemies).
      Astolfo was my faithless and ungrateful
420   Lord, who (quite forgetful of our happiness,
      Since of a past love even the memory fades)
      Came here to claim the throne and marry Stella
      For she's the star who rises as I set.
      It's hard to credit that a star should sunder
425   Lovers the stars had made conformable!
      So hurt was I, so villainously cheated,
      That I became mad, brokenhearted, sick,
      Half wild with grief, and like to die, with all
      Hell's own confusion ciphered on my mind
430   Like Babel's incoherence. Mutely I told
      My griefs (since woes and griefs declare themselves
      Better than can the mouth, by their effects),
      When, with my mother (we were by ourselves),
      She broke the prison of my pent-up sorrows
435   And from my breast they all rushed forth in troops.
      I felt no shyness, for in knowing surely
      That one to whom one's errors are recounted
      Has also been an ally in her own,
      One finds relief and rest, since bad example
440   Can sometimes serve for a good purpose too.
      She heard my plaint with pity, and she tried
      To palliate my sorrows with her own.
      How easily do judges pardon error
      When they've offended too! An example,
445   A warning, in herself, she did not trust
      To idleness, or the slow cure of time,
      Nor try to find a remedy for her honour
      In my misfortunes, but, with better counsel,
      She bade me follow him to Poland here
450   And with prodigious gallantry persuade him
      To pay the debt to honour that he owes me.
      So that it would be easier to travel,
      She bade me don male clothing, and took down
      This ancient sword which I am wearing now.
455   Now it is time that I unsheathe the blade
      As I was bid, for, trusting in its sign,
      She said: "Depart to Poland, show this sword
      That all the nobles may behold it well,
      And it may be that one of them will take
460   Pity on you, and counsel you, and shield you."
      I came to Poland and, you will remember,

      Entered your cave. You looked at me in wonder.
      Clotaldo passionately took my part
      To plead for mercy to the king, who spared me,
      Then, when he heard my story, bade me change   465
      Into my own clothes and attend on Stella,
      There to disturb Astolfo's love and stop
      Their marriage. Again you saw me in woman's dress
      And were confused by the discrepancy.
      But let's pass to what's new: Clotaldo, now   470
      Persuaded that Astolfo must, with Stella,
      Come to the throne, dissuades me from my purpose,
      Against the interests of my name and honour.
      But seeing you, O valiant Segismund,
      Are claiming your revenge, now that the heavens   475
      Have burst the prison of your rustic tower,
      (Wherein you were the tiger of your sorrows,
      The rock of sufferings and direful pains)
      And sent you forth against your sire and country,
      I come to aid you, mingling Dian's silks   480
      With the hard steel of Pallas. Now, strong Captain,
      It well behoves us both to stop this marriage—
      Me, lest my promised husband should be wed,
      You, lest, when their estates are joined, they weigh
      More powerfully against your victory.   485
      I come, as a mere woman, to persuade you
      To right my shame; but, as a man, I come
      To help you battle for your crown. As woman,
      To melt your heart, here at your feet I fall;
      But, as a man, I come to serve you bravely   490
      Both with my person and my steel, and thus,
      If you today should woo me as a woman,
      Then I should have to kill you as a man would
      In honourable service of my honour;
      Since I must be three things today at once—   495
      Passionate, to persuade you: womanly,
      To ply you with my woes: manly, to gain
      Honour in battle.

SEGISMUND: Heavens! If it is true I'm dreaming,
      Suspend my memory, for in a dream
      So many things could not occur. Great heavens!   500
      If I could only come free of them all!
      Or never think of any! Who ever felt
      Such grievous doubts? If I but dreamed that triumph
      In which I found myself, how can this woman
      Refer me to such sure and certain facts?   505
      Then all of it was true and not a dream.
      But if it be the truth, why does my past life
      Call it a dream? This breeds the same confusion.
      Are dreams and glories so alike, that fictions
      Are held for truths, realities for lies?   510
      Is there so little difference in them both
      That one should question whether what one sees
      And tastes is true or false? What? Is the copy
      So near to the original that doubt
      Exists between them? Then if that is so,   515
      And grandeur, power, majesty, and pomp,
      Must all evaporate like shades at morning,
      Let's profit by it, this time, to enjoy
      That which we only can enjoy in dreams.
      Rosaura's in my power: my soul adores her beauty.   520
      Let's take the chance. Let love break every law
      On which she has relied in coming here

And kneeling, trustful, prostrate at my feet.
This is a dream. If so, dream pleasures now
525 Since they must turn to sorrows in the end!
But with my own opinions, I begin
Once again to convince myself. Let's think.
If it is but vainglory and a dream,
Who for mere human vainglory would lose
530 True glory? What past blessing is not merely
A dream? Who has known heroic glories,
That deep within himself, as he recalls them
Has never doubted that they might be dreams?
But if this all should end in disenchantment,
535 Seeing that pleasure is a lovely flame
That's soon converted into dust and ashes
By any wind that blows, then let us seek
That which endures in thrifty, lasting fame
In which no pleasures sleep, nor grandeurs dream.
540 Rosaura's without honour. In a prince
It's worthier to restore it than to steal it.
I shall restore it, by the living God,
Before I win my throne! Let's shun the danger
And fly from the temptation which is strong!
545 Then sound to arms!

(*To a* SOLDIER.)

Today I must give battle before darkness
Buries the rays of gold in green-black waves!
ROSAURA: My lord! Alas, you stand apart, and offer
No word of pity for my plight. How is it
550 You neither hear nor see me nor even yet
Have turned your face on me?
SEGISMUND: Rosaura, for your honour's sake
I must be cruel to you, to be kind.
My voice must not reply to you because
My honour must reply to you. I am silent
555 Because my deeds must speak to you alone.
I do not look at you since, in such straits,
Having to see your honour is requited,
I must not see your beauty.

(*Exit with* SOLDIERS.)

ROSAURA: What strange enigma's this? After such trouble
560 Still to be treated with more doubtful riddles!

(*Enter* CLARION.)

CLARION: Madam, may you be visited just now?
ROSAURA: Why, Clarion, where have you been all this time?
CLARION: Shut in the tower, consulting cards
About my death: "to be or not to be."
565 And it was a near thing.
ROSAURA: Why?
CLARION: Because I know
The secret who you are: in fact, Clotaldo . . .

(*Drums.*)

But hush what noise is that?
ROSAURA: What can it be?

CLARION: From the beleaguered palace a whole squadron
Is charging forth to harry and defeat
That of fierce Segismund.   570
ROSAURA: Why, what a coward
Am I, not to be at his side, the terror
And scandal of the world, while such fierce strife
Presses all round in lawless anarchy.

(*Exit.*)

VOICES OF SOME: Long live our king!
VOICES OF OTHERS: Long live our liberty!
CLARION: Long live both king and liberty. Yes, live!   575
And welcome to them both! I do not worry.
In all this pother, I behave like Nero
Who never grieved at what was going on.
If I had anything to grieve about
It would be me, myself. Well hidden here   580
Now, I can watch the sport that's going on.
This place is safe and hidden between crags,
And since death cannot find me here, two figs for death!

(*He hides. Drums and the clash of arms are heard.*)

(*Enter* BASIL, CLOTALDO, *and* ASTOLFO, *fleeing.*)

BASIL: Was ever king so hapless as myself
Or father more ill used?   585
CLOTALDO: Your beaten army
Rush down, in all directions, in disorder.
ASTOLFO: The traitors win!
BASIL: In battles such as these
Those on the winning side are ever "loyal,"
And traitors the defeated. Come, Clotaldo,
Let's flee from the inhuman cruelty   590
Of my fierce son!

(*Shots are fired within.* CLARION *falls wounded.*)

CLARION: Heavens, save me!
ASTOLFO: Who is this
Unhappy soldier bleeding at our feet?
CLARION: I am a most unlucky man who, wishing
To guard myself from death, have sought it out
By fleeing from it. Shunning it, I found it,   595
Because, to death, no hiding-place is secret.
So you can argue that whoever shuns it
Most carefully runs into it the quickest.
Turn, then, once more into the thick of battle:
There is more safety there amidst the fire   600
And clash of arms than here on this secluded
Mountain, because no hidden path is safe
From the inclemency of Fate; and so,
Although you flee from death, yet you may find it
Quicker than you expect, if God so wills.   605

(*He falls dead.*)

BASIL: "If God so wills" . . . With what strange eloquence
This corpse persuades our ignorance and error
To better knowledge, speaking from the mouth

Of its fell wound, where the red liquid flowing
610   Seems like a bloody tongue which teaches us
That the activities of man are vain
When they are pitted against higher powers.
For I, who wished to liberate my country
From murder and sedition, gave it up
615   To the same ills from which I would have saved it.
CLOTALDO: Though Fate, my lord, knows every path, and finds
Him whom it seeks even in the midst of crags
And thickets, it is not a Christian judgment
To say there is no refuge from its fury.
620   A prudent man can conquer Fate itself.
Though you are not exempted from misfortune,
Take action to escape it while you can!
ASTOLFO: Clotaldo speaks as one mature in prudence,
And I as one in valour's youthful prime.
625   Among the thickets of this mount is hidden
A horse, the very birth of the swift wind.
Flee on him, and I'll guard you in the rear.
BASIL: If it is God's will I should die, or if
Death waits here for my coming, I will seek
630   Him out today, and meet him face to face.

(*Enter* SEGISMUND, STELLA, ROSAURA, SOLDIERS, *and their* TRAIN.)

A SOLDIER: Amongst the thickets of this mountain
635   The king is hiding.
SEGISMUND: Seek him out at once!
Leave no foot of the summit unexplored
But search from stem to stem and branch to branch!
CLOTALDO: Fly, sir!
BASIL: What for?
ASTOLFO: What do you mean to do?
BASIL: Astolfo, stand aside!
CLOTALDO: What is your wish?
BASIL: To take a cure I've needed for sometime.

(*To* SEGISMUND.)

If you have come to seek me, here I am.

(*Kneeling.*)

Your father, prince, kneels humbly at your feet.
640   The white snow of my hair is now your carpet.
Tread on my neck and trample on my crown!
Lay low and drag my dignity in dust!
Take vengeance on my honour! Make a slave
Of me and, after all I've done to thwart them,
645   Let Fate fulfil its edict and claim homage
And Heaven fulfil its oracles at last!
SEGISMUND: Illustrious court of Poland, who have been
The witnesses of such unwonted wonders,
Attend to me, and hear your prince speak out.
650   What Heaven decrees and God writes with his finger
(Whose prints and ciphers are the azure leaves
Adorned with golden lettering of the stars)
Never deceives nor lies. They only lie
Who seek to penetrate the mystery
655   And, having reached it, use it to ill purpose.
My father, who is here to evade the fury
Of my proud nature, made me a wild beast:

So, when I, by my birth of gallant stock,
My generous blood, and inbred grace and valour,
Might well have proved both gentle and forbearing,   660
The very mode of life to which he forced me,
The sort of bringing up I had to bear
Sufficed to make me savage in my passions.
What a strange method of restraining them!
If one were to tell any man: "One day   665
You will be killed by an inhuman monster,"
Would it be the best method he could choose
To wake that monster when it was asleep?
Or if they told him: "That sword which you're wearing
Will be your death," what sort of cure were it   670
To draw it forth and aim it at his breast?
Or if they told him: "Deep blue gulfs of water
Will one day be your sepulchre and grave
Beneath a silver monument of foam,"
He would be mad to hurl himself in headlong   675
When the sea highest heaved its showy mountains
And crystalline sierras plumed with spray.
The same has happened to the king as to him
Who wakes a beast which threatens death, to him
Who draws a naked sword because he fears it,   680
To him who dives into the stormy breakers.
Though my ferocious nature (hear me now)
Was like a sleeping beast, my inborn rage
A sheathèd sword, my wrath a quiet ripple,
Fate should not be coerced by man's injustice—   685
This rouses more resentment. So it is
That he who seeks to tame his fortune must
Resort to moderation and to measure.
He who foresees an evil cannot conquer it
Thus in advance, for though humility   690
Can overcome it, this it can do only
When the occasion's there, for there's no way
To dodge one's fate and thus evade the issue.
Let this strange spectacle serve as example—
This prodigy, this horror, and this wonder,   695
Because it is no less than one, to see,
After such measures and precautions taken
To thwart it, that a father thus should kneel
At his son's feet, a kingdom thus be shattered.
This was the sentence of the heavens above,   700
Which he could not evade, much though he tried.
Can I, younger in age, less brave, and less
In science than the king, conquer that fate?

(*To the* KING.)

Sire, rise, give me your hand, now that the heavens
Have shown you that you erred as to the method   705
To vanquish them. Humbly I kneel before you
And offer you my neck to tread upon.
BASIL: Son, such a great and noble act restores you
Straight to my heart. Oh, true and worthy prince!
You have won both the laurel and the palm.   710
Crown yourself with your deeds! For you *have* conquered!
ALL: Long live Segismund! Long live Segismund!
SEGISMUND: Since I have other victories to win,
The greatest of them all awaits me now:
To conquer my own self. Astolfo, give   715
Your hand here to Rosaura, for you know

It is a debt of honour and must be paid.
ASTOLFO: Although, it's true, I owe some obligations—
  She does not know her name or who she is,
720 It would be base to wed a woman who . . .
CLOTALDO: Hold! Wait! Rosaura's of as noble stock
  As yours, Astolfo. In the open field
  I'll prove it with my sword. She is my daughter
  And that should be enough.
ASTOLFO: What do you say?
725 CLOTALDO: Until I saw her married, righted, honoured,
  I did not wish for it to be discovered.
  It's a long story but she is my daughter.
ASTOLFO: That being so, I'm glad to keep my word.
SEGISMUND: And now, so that the princess Stella here
730 Will not remain disconsolate to lose
  A prince of so much valour, here I offer
  My hand to her, no less in birth and rank.
  Give me your hand.
STELLA: I gain by meriting
  So great a happiness.
SEGISMUND: And now, Clotaldo,
735 So long so loyal to my father, come
  To my arms. Ask me anything you wish.

FIRST SOLDIER: If thus you treat a man who never served you,
  What about me who led the revolution
  And brought you from your dungeon in the tower?
  What will you give me?   740
SEGISMUND: That same tower and dungeon
  From which you never shall emerge till death.
  No traitor is of use after his treason.
BASIL: All wonder at your wisdom!
ASTOLFO: What a change
  Of character!
ROSAURA: How wise and prudent!
SEGISMUND: Why
  Do you wonder? Why do you marvel, since   745
  It was a dream that taught me and I still
  Fear to wake up once more in my close dungeon?
  Though that may never happen, it's enough
  To dream it might, for thus I came to learn
  That all our human happiness must pass   750
  Away like any dream, and I would here
  Enjoy it fully ere it glide away,
  Asking (for noble hearts are prone to pardon)
  Pardon for faults in the actors or the play.

Molière

Jean-Baptiste Poquelin (1622–1673) was born into a prosperous mercantile family with connections at court; his father, Jean Poquelin, secured the honor of *tapissier ordinaire du roi,* the upholsterer to the court, which carried an annual pension. Jean Poquelin also educated his son in the traditional disciplines of the humanities, philosophy, and the classics and must have intended a life at court for him. In 1643, Jean-Baptiste joined with the Illustre Théâtre, a theatrical company run by the Béjart family, took the stage name Molière, and after a brief period performing in Parisian tennis courts, left with the company to play in the provinces. In 1658, after several hard and impoverished years of touring, when Molière is thought to have mastered the techniques of *commedia dell' arte,* the company was invited to perform in Paris.

Molière's career was closely tied to the court. When his brother died in 1660, he received the position of court upholsterer and the income it provided. More important, Molière became a significant playwright and both wrote and acted in a splendid series of plays that satirized the manners and morals of elegant society: *Les Précieuses Ridicules* (1659), *Sganarelle* (1660), *School for Husbands* (1661), *School for Wives* (1662), *Dom Juan* (1665), *The Misanthrope* (1666), *The Doctor in Spite of Himself* (1666), *The Miser* (1668), *The Learned Ladies* (1672), and *The Imaginary Invalid* (1673). Molière also prepared other entertainments at court, including many royal pageants, ballets, and machine plays devised by and for Louis XIV. In addition to being a great dramatist, Molière was a fine comic actor as well and performed in his own plays; he died shortly after playing the title role in the fourth performance of *The Imaginary Invalid.*

The fortunes of his play *Tartuffe* suggest Molière's importance at court. When Molière initially produced the first three acts of the play in 1664, the clergy protested and banned the play from production in Paris. Many of Molière's plays had excited controversy, and in this case Molière appealed to the king and proceeded to revise the play. Louis's attitude is perhaps revealed by the fact that he made Molière's company the *Troupe du roi* ("King's Company") in 1665, but even the throne could not prevent the clergy from censoring Molière's second version of the play in 1667, newly titled *The Impostor.* Molière finally produced the play to acclaim in 1669, and the record of his efforts is preserved in the series of letters and prefaces included here.

Molière's theatrical company was the most influential of its day. After his death, his young wife Amanda Béjart and the actress Mademoiselle Champmeslé—newly defected from the rival company at the Hôtel de Bourgogne—established a new company, the Comédie Française. Yet although Molière achieved extraordinary status at court, because he was an actor he remained stigmatized in ways that playwrights like Racine and Corneille were not. Following its standard practice, and perhaps because of *Tartuffe's* notoriety, the church refused to bury Molière in sacred ground. Louis XIV intervened, but was only able to persuade the Archbishop of Paris to bury Molière in a parish cemetery. The burial was conducted at night, by two priests, with no funeral ceremony.

Tartuffe   The Catholic church criticized *Tartuffe* for its portrait of hypocritical piety, but the fact that Molière played the part of Orgon may suggest that the play is as much about Tartuffe's effect on that benighted householder as it is about the title character. For if Tartuffe is hypocritical, Orgon is obsessed, less with piety than with his own desire to achieve a kind of total power and authority in his household, a kind of domestic absolutism; he is, in a sense, a comic, bourgeois Louis XIV in miniature. Moreover, Tartuffe dupes Orgon not by tricking him, but by inviting Orgon to fulfill his own fantasy of autonomy and authority. As he brags to the sensible Cléante, under Tartuffe's teaching, "my soul's been freed / From earthly loves, and every human tie: / My mother, children, brother, and wife could die, / And I'd not feel a single moment's pain." Helping Orgon to realize this fantasy, Tartuffe transforms him into a

Tartuffe seduces Elmire while Orgon hides beneath the table in Molière's *Tartuffe*.

© T. Charles Erickson

kind of monster: Orgon comes near to selling his daughter, disinheriting his son, allowing his wife to be raped, and losing his family's property and fortune.

Tartuffe is very much a play of the world, a satiric comedy. Set in an urban landscape, the play insistently translates the idealized passions of tragedy and romantic comedy—love, honor, loyalty—into their ironic counterparts—lust, hypocrisy, betrayal. Molière peoples the play with individualized versions of the unchanging types of *commedia dell' arte* and the Roman comedy that inspired it: the reasonable and attractive heroes; an old, pedantic, self-absorbed dupe; a wily and conniving villain; a clever and witty servant. Yet Molière reinvents this range of stock characters, brilliantly turning his play toward an exploration of the folly of self-deception. For while we might take the neoclassical conflict between reason and the passions to be the hallmark of tragedy, it surges through this play as well. Orgon's passionate solipsism is, for all its ridiculousness, no less profound, troubling, or destructive than the obsessed affections of Racine's Phaedra and Hippolytus. Also, Orgon's redemption, by fiat of the king, seems no less arbitrary than the vengeful caprice of Venus or Neptune in Racine's tragedy.

Since the characters cannot change in Molière's comedy, change must happen to them. Molière's most brilliant device here arises in the person of the king's officer, who appears to apprehend Tartuffe and to restore Orgon and his family to their property: property is what establishes the position, the place, the social and individual identity of these characters. Although Molière's DEUS EX MACHINA might be regarded as an elegant (though somewhat clumsy) compliment to the king—and, perhaps, as a sly jab at the clerical critics who attacked *Tartuffe*—this device plays a subtle role in dramatizing the nature of royal authority. For in *Tartuffe*, the king has the power to assign every person to his or her proper place, to see into our inmost hearts, to structure the moral and social order of the world as the reflection of his own will and judgment: "*L'état, c'est moi.*" In this sense, even though *Tartuffe* unleashes the uncontrollable power of self-delusion and the power and destructive fantasies of absolute authority, the play concludes by asserting the legitimacy of that absolute power. Molière's *deus ex machina* testifies both to the power and to the arbitrariness of the king's authority.

Preface[1]

TRANSLATED BY RICHARD WILBUR

Here is a comedy that has excited a good deal of discussion and that has been under attack for a long time; and the persons who are mocked by it have made it plain that they are more powerful in France than all whom my plays have satirized up to this time. Noblemen, ladies of fashion, cuckolds, and doctors all kindly consented to their presentation, which they themselves seemed to enjoy along with everyone else; but hypocrites do not understand banter: they became angry at once, and found it strange that I was bold enough to represent their actions and to care to describe a profession shared by so many good men. This is a crime for which they cannot forgive me, and they have taken up arms against my comedy in a terrible rage. They were careful not to attack it at the point that had wounded them: they are too crafty for that and too clever to reveal their true character. In keeping with their lofty custom, they have used the cause of God to mask their private interests; and *Tartuffe*, they say, is a play that offends piety: It is filled with abominations from beginning to end, and nowhere is there a line that does not deserve to be burned. Every syllable is wicked, the very gestures are criminal, and the slightest glance, turn of the head, or step from right to left conceals mysteries that they are able to explain to my disadvantage. In vain did I submit the play to the criticism of my friends and the scrutiny of the public: all the corrections I could make, the judgment of the king and queen who saw the play,[2] the approval of great princes and ministers of state who honored it with their presence, the opinion of good men who found it worthwhile; all this did not help. They will not let go of their prey, and every day of the week they have pious zealots abusing me in public and damning me out of charity.

I would care very little about all they might say except that their devices make enemies of men whom I respect and gain the support of genuinely good men, whose faith they know and who, because of the warmth of their piety, readily accept the impressions that others present to them. And it is this which forces me to defend myself. Especially to the truly devout do I wish to vindicate my play, and I beg of them with all my heart not to condemn it before seeing it, to rid themselves of preconceptions, and not aid the cause of men dishonored by their actions.

If one takes the trouble to examine my comedy in good faith, he will surely see that my intentions are innocent throughout, and tend in no way to make fun of what men revere; that I have presented the subject with all the precautions that its delicacy imposes; and that I have used all the art and skill that I could to distinguish clearly the character of the hypocrite from that of the truly devout man. For that purpose I used two whole acts to prepare the appearance of my scoundrel. Never is there a moment's doubt about his character; he is known at once from the qualities I have given him; and from one end of the play to the other, he does not say a word, he does not perform an action which does not depict to the audience the character of a wicked man, and which does not bring out in sharp relief the character of the truly good man which I oppose to it.

I know full well that by way of reply, these gentlemen try to insinuate that it is not the role of the theater to speak of these matters; but with their permission, I ask them on what do they base this fine doctrine. It is a proposition they advance as no more than a supposition, for which they offer not a shred of proof; and surely it would not be difficult to show them that comedy, for the ancients, had its origin in religion and constituted a part of its ceremonies; that our neighbors, the Spaniards, have hardly a single holiday celebration in which a comedy is not a part; and that even here in France, it owes its birth to the efforts of a religious brotherhood who still own the Hôtel de Bourgogne, where the most important

---

[1]Molière added his three petitions to Louis XIV; they follow the preface.

[2]Louis XIV was married to Marie Thérèse of Austria.

mystery plays of our faith were presented[3]; that you can still find comedies printed in gothic letters under the name of a learned doctor of the Sorbonne[4]; and without going so far, in our own day the religious dramas of Pierre Corneille[5] have been performed to the admiration of all France.

If the function of comedy is to correct men's vices, I do not see why any should be exempt. Such a condition in our society would be much more dangerous than the thing itself; and we have seen that the theater is admirably suited to provide correction. The most forceful lines of a serious moral statement are usually less powerful than those of satire; and nothing will reform most men better than the depiction of their faults. It is a vigorous blow to vices to expose them to public laughter. Criticism is taken lightly, but men will not tolerate satire. They are quite willing to be mean, but they never like to be ridiculed.

I have been attacked for having placed words of piety in the mouth of my impostor. Could I avoid doing so in order to represent properly the character of a hypocrite? It seemed to me sufficient to reveal the criminal motives which make him speak as he does, and I have eliminated all ceremonial phrases, which nonetheless he would not have been found using incorrectly. Yet some say that in the fourth act he sets forth a vicious morality; but is not this a morality which everyone has heard again and again? Does my comedy say anything new here? And is there any fear that ideas so thoroughly detested by everyone can make an impression on men's minds; that I make them dangerous by presenting them in the theater; that they acquire authority from the lips of a scoundrel? There is not the slightest suggestion of any of this; and one must either approve the comedy of *Tartuffe* or condemn all comedies in general.

This has indeed been done in a furious way for some time now, and never was the theater so much abused.[6] I cannot deny that there were Church Fathers who condemned comedy; but neither will it be denied me that there were some who looked on it somewhat more favorably. Thus authority, on which censure is supposed to depend, is destroyed by this disagreement; and the only conclusion that can be drawn from this difference of opinion among men enlightened by the same wisdom is that they viewed comedy in different ways, and that some considered it in its purity, while others regarded it in its corruption and confused it with all those wretched performances which have been rightly called performances of filth.

And in fact, since we should talk about things rather than words, and since most misunderstanding comes from including contrary notions in the same word, we need only to remove the veil of ambiguity and look at comedy in itself to see if it warrants condemnation. It will surely be recognized that as it is nothing more than a clever poem which corrects men's faults by means of agreeable lessons, it cannot be condemned without injustice. And if we listened to the voice of ancient times on this matter, it would tell us that its most famous philosophers have praised comedy—they who professed so austere a wisdom and who ceaselessly denounced the vices of their times. It would tell us that Aristotle spent his evenings at the theater[7] and took the trouble to reduce the art of making comedies to rules. It would tell us that some of its greatest and most honored men took pride in writing

---

[3]A reference to the *Confrérie de la Passion et Résurrection de Notre-Seigneur* (the Fraternity of the Passion and Resurrection of Our Saviour), founded in 1402. The Hôtel de Bourgogne was a rival theater of Molière.

[4]Probably Maitre Jehán Michel, a medical doctor who wrote mystery plays.

[5]Pierre Corneille (1606–1684) and Racine were France's two greatest writers of classic tragedy. The two dramas Molière doubtlessly had in mind were *Polyeucte* (1643) and *Théodore, vierge et martyre* (1645).

[6]Molière had in mind Nicole's two attacks on the theater: *Visionnaries* (1666) and *Traité de Comédie,* and the Prince de Condé's *Traité de Comédie* (1666).

[7]A reference to Aristotle's *The Poetics* (composed between 335 and 322 BCE, the year of his death).

comedies themselves,[8] and that others did not disdain to recite them in public; that Greece expressed its admiration for this art by means of handsome prizes and magnificent theaters to honor it; and finally, that in Rome this same art also received extraordinary honors; I do not speak of Rome run riot under the license of the emperors, but of disciplined Rome, governed by the wisdom of the consuls, and in the age of the full vigor of Roman dignity.

I admit that there have been times when comedy became corrupt. And what do men not corrupt every day? There is nothing so innocent that men cannot turn it to crime; nothing so beneficial that its values cannot be reversed; nothing so good in itself that it cannot be put to bad uses. Medical knowledge benefits mankind and is revered as one of our most wonderful possessions; and yet there was a time when it fell into discredit, and was often used to poison men. Philosophy is a gift of Heaven; it has been given to us to bring us to the knowledge of a God by contemplating the wonders of nature; and yet we know that often it has been turned away from its function and has been used openly in support of impiety. Even the holiest of things are not immune from human corruption, and every day we see scoundrels who use and abuse piety, and wickedly make it serve the greatest of crimes. But this does not prevent one from making the necessary distinctions. We do not confuse in the same false inference the goodness of things that are corrupted with the wickedness of the corrupt. The function of an art is always distinguished from its misuse; and as medicine is not forbidden because it was banned in Rome,[9] nor philosophy because it was publicly condemned in Athens,[10] we should not suppress comedy simply because it has been condemned at certain times. This censure was justified then for reasons which no longer apply today; it was limited to what was then seen; and we should not seize on these limits, apply them more rigidly than is necessary, and include in our condemnation the innocent along with the guilty. The comedy that this censure attacked is in no way the comedy that we want to defend. We must be careful not to confuse the one with the other. There may be two persons whose morals may be completely different. They may have no resemblance to one another except in their names, and it would be a terrible injustice to want to condemn Olympia, who is a good woman, because there is also an Olympia who is lewd. Such procedures would make for great confusion everywhere. Everything under the sun would be condemned; now since this rigor is not applied to the countless instances of abuse we see every day, the same should hold for comedy, and those plays should be approved in which instruction and virtue reign supreme.

I know there are some so delicate that they cannot tolerate a comedy, who say that the most decent are the most dangerous, that the passions they present are all the more moving because they are virtuous, and that men's feelings are stirred by these presentations. I do not see what great crime it is to be affected by the sight of a generous passion; and this utter insensitivity to which they would lead us is indeed a high degree of virtue! I wonder if so great a perfection resides within the strength of human nature, and I wonder if it is not better to try to correct and moderate men's passions than to try to suppress them altogether. I grant that there are places better to visit than the theater; and if we want to condemn every single thing that does not bear directly on God and our salvation, it is right that comedy be included, and I should willingly grant that it be condemned along with everything else. But if we admit, as is in fact true, that the exercise of piety will permit interruptions, and that men need amusement, I maintain that there is none more innocent than comedy. I have

---

[8]The Roman consul and general responsible for the final destruction of Carthage in 146 BCE, Scipio Africanus Minor (c. 185–129 BCE), collaborated with the writer of comedies, Terence (Publius Terentius Afer, c. 195 or 185–c. 159 BCE).

[9]Pliny the Elder says that the Romans expelled their doctors at the same time that the Greeks did theirs.

[10]An allusion to Socrates' condemnation to death.

dwelled too long on this matter. Let me finish with the words of a great prince on the comedy, *Tartuffe*.[11]

Eight days after it had been banned, a play called *Scaramouche the Hermit*[12] was performed before the court; and the king, on his way out, said to this great prince: "I should really like to know why the persons who make so much noise about Molière's comedy do not say a word about *Scaramouche*." To which the prince replied, "It is because the comedy of *Scaramouche* makes fun of Heaven and religion, which these gentlemen do not care about at all, but that of Molière makes fun of *them,* and that is what they cannot bear."

Molière

First Petition[13]
(PRESENTED TO THE KING ON THE COMEDY OF TARTUFFE)

Sire,

As the duty of comedy is to correct men by amusing them, I believed that in my occupation I could do nothing better than attack the vices of my age by making them ridiculous; and as hypocrisy is undoubtedly one of the most common, most improper, and most dangerous, I thought, Sire, that I would perform a service for all good men of your kingdom if I wrote a comedy which denounced hypocrites and placed in proper view all of the contrived poses of these incredibly virtuous men, all of the concealed villainies of these counterfeit believers who would trap others with a fraudulent piety and a pretended virtue.

I have written this comedy, Sire, with all the care and caution that the delicacy of the subject demands; and so as to maintain all the more properly the admiration and respect due to truly devout men, I have delineated my character as sharply as I could; I have left no room for doubt; I have removed all that might confuse good with evil, and have used for this painting only the specific colors and essential lines that make one instantly recognize a true and brazen hypocrite.

Nevertheless, all my precautions have been to no avail. Others have taken advantage of the delicacy of your feelings on religious matters, and they have been able to deceive you on the only side of your character which lies open to deception: your respect for holy things. By underhanded means, the Tartuffes have skillfully gained Your Majesty's favor, and the models have succeeded in eliminating the copy, no matter how innocent it may have been and no matter what resemblance was found between them.

Although the suppression of this work was a serious blow for me, my misfortune was nonetheless softened by the way in which Your Majesty explained his attitude on the matter; and I believed, Sire, that Your Majesty removed any cause I had for complaint, as you were kind enough to declare that you found nothing in this comedy that you would forbid me to present in public.

Yet, despite this glorious declaration of the greatest and most enlightened king in the world, despite the approval of the Papal Legate[14] and of most of our churchmen, all of whom, at private readings of my work, agreed with the views of Your Majesty, despite all

---

[11]One of Molière's benefactors who liked the play was the Prince de Condé; the Prince had *Tartuffe* read to him and also privately performed for him.

[12]A troupe of Italian comedians had just performed the licentious farce, where a hermit dressed as a monk makes love to a married woman, announcing that *questo e per mortificar la carne* ("this is to mortify the flesh").

[13]The first of the three *petitions* or *placets* to Louis XIV concerning the play. On May 12, 1664, *Tartuffe*—or at least the first three acts roughly as they now stand—was performed at Versailles. A cabal unfavorable to Molière, including the Archbishop of Paris, Hardouin de Péréfixe, Queen-Mother Anne of Austria, certain influential courtiers, and the Brotherhood or Company of the Holy Sacrament (formed in 1627 to enforce morality), arranged that the play be banned and Molière censured.

[14]Cardinal Legate Chigi, nephew to Pope Alexander VII, heard a reading of *Tartuffe* at Fontainebleau on August 4, 1664.

this, a book has appeared by a certain priest[15] which boldly contradicts all of these noble judgments. Your Majesty expressed himself in vain, and the Papal Legate and churchmen gave their opinion to no avail: Sight unseen, my comedy is diabolical, and so is my brain; I am a devil garbed in flesh and disguised as a man,[16] a libertine, a disbeliever who deserves a punishment that will set an example. It is not enough that fire expiate my crime in public, for that would be letting me off too easily: The generous piety of this good man will not stop there; he will not allow me to find any mercy in the sight of God; he demands that I be damned, and that will settle the matter.

This book, Sire, was presented to Your Majesty; and I am sure that you see for yourself how unpleasant it is for me to be exposed daily to the insults of these gentlemen, what harm these abuses will do my reputation if they must be tolerated, and finally, how important it is for me to clear myself of these false charges and let the public know that my comedy is nothing more than what they want it to be. I will not ask, Sire, for what I need for the sake of my reputation and the innocence of my work: enlightened kings such as you do not need to be told what is wished of them; like God, they see what we need and know better than we what they should give us. It is enough for me to place my interests in Your Majesty's hands, and I respectfully await whatever you may care to command.

(August, 1664)

Second Petition[17]
(PRESENTED TO THE KING IN HIS CAMP BEFORE THE CITY OF LILLE, IN FLANDERS)

Sire,

It is bold indeed for me to ask a favor of a great monarch in the midst of his glorious victories; but in my present situation, Sire, where will I find protection anywhere but where I seek it, and to whom can I appeal against the authority of the power that crushes me,[18] if not to the source of power and authority, the just dispenser of absolute law, the sovereign judge and master of all?

My comedy, Sire, has not enjoyed the kindnesses of Your Majesty. All to no avail, I produced it under the title of *The Hypocrite* and disguised the principal character as a man of the world; in vain I gave him a little hat, long hair, a wide collar, a sword, and lace clothing,[19] softened the action and carefully eliminated all that I thought might provide even the shadow of grounds for discontent on the part of the famous models of the portrait I wished to present; nothing did any good. The conspiracy of opposition revived even at mere conjecture of what the play would be like. They found a way of persuading those who in all other matters plainly insist that they are not to be deceived. No sooner did my comedy appear than it was struck down by the very power which should impose respect; and all that I could do to save myself from the fury of this tempest was to say that Your Majesty had given me permission to present the play and I did not think it was necessary to ask this permission of others, since only Your Majesty could have refused it.

I have no doubt, Sire, that the men whom I depict in my comedy will employ every means possible to influence Your Majesty, and will use, as they have used already, those truly

---

[15]Pierre Roullé, the curate of St. Barthélémy, who wrote a scathing attack on the play and sent his book to the king.

[16]Molière took some of these phrases from Roullé.

[17]On August 5, 1667, *Tartuffe* was performed at the Palais-Royal. The opposition—headed by the First President of Parliament—brought in the police, and the play was stopped. Since Louis was campaigning in Flanders, friends of Molière brought the second *placet* to Lille. Louis had always been favorable toward the playwright; in August 1665, Molière's company, the *Troupe de Monsieur* (nominally sponsored by Louis's brother Philippe, Duc d'Orléans) had become the *Troupe du Roi*.

[18]President de Lanvignon, in charge of the Paris police.

[19]There is evidence that in 1664 Tartuffe played his role dressed in a cassock, thus allying him more directly to the clergy.

good men who are all the more easily deceived because they judge of others by themselves.[20] They know how to display all of their aims in the most favorable light; yet, no matter how pious they may seem, it is surely not the interests of God which stir them; they have proven this often enough in the comedies they have allowed to be performed hundreds of times without making the least objection. Those plays attacked only piety and religion, for which they care very little; but this play attacks and makes fun of them, and that is what they cannot bear. They will never forgive me for unmasking their hypocrisy in the eyes of everyone. And I am sure that they will not neglect to tell Your Majesty that people are shocked by my comedy. But the simple truth, Sire, is that all Paris is shocked only by its ban, that the most scrupulous persons have found its presentation worthwhile, and men are astounded that individuals of such known integrity should show so great a deference to people whom everyone should abominate and who are so clearly opposed to the true piety which they profess.

I respectfully await the judgment that Your Majesty will deign to pronounce: But it's certain, Sire, that I need not think of writing comedies if the Tartuffes are triumphant, if they thereby seize the right to persecute me more than ever, and find fault with even the most innocent lines that flow from my pen.

Let your goodness, Sire, give me protection against their envenomed rage, and allow me, at your return from so glorious a campaign, to relieve Your Majesty from the fatigue of his conquests, give him innocent pleasures after such noble accomplishments, and make the monarch laugh who makes all Europe tremble!

(August, 1667)

Third Petition
(PRESENTED TO THE KING)

Sire,

A very honest doctor[21] whose patient I have the honor to be, promises and will legally contract to make me live another thirty years if I can obtain a favor for him from Your Majesty. I told him of his promise that I do not deserve so much, and that I should be glad to help him if he will merely agree not to kill me. This favor, Sire, is a post of canon at your royal chapel of Vincennes, made vacant by death.

May I dare to ask for this favor from Your Majesty on the very day of the glorious resurrection of *Tartuffe*, brought back to life by your goodness? By this first favor I have been reconciled with the devout, and the second will reconcile me with the doctors.[22] Undoubtedly this would be too much grace for me at one time, but perhaps it would not be too much for Your Majesty, and I await your answer to my petition with respectful hope.

(February, 1669)

---

[20]Molière apparently did not know that de Lanvignon had been affiliated with the Company of the Holy Sacrament for the previous ten years.

[21]A physician friend, M. de Mauvillain, who helped Molière with some of the medical details of *Le Malade imaginaire*.

[22]Doctors are ridiculed to varying degrees in earlier plays of Molière: *Dom Juan, L'Amour médecin*, and *Le Médecin malgré lui*.

Tartuffe

Molière

TRANSLATED BY RICHARD WILBUR

CHARACTERS

MADAME PERNELLE, *Orgon's mother*
ORGON, *Elmire's husband*
ELMIRE, *Orgon's wife*
DAMIS, *Orgon's son, Elmire's stepson*
MARIANE, *Orgon's daughter, Elmire's stepdaughter, in love with Valère*
VALÈRE, *in love with Mariane*
CLÉANTE, *Orgon's brother-in-law*

TARTUFFE, *a hypocrite*
DORINE, *Mariane's lady's-maid*
M. LOYAL, *a bailiff*
A POLICE OFFICER
FLIPOTE, *Madame Pernelle's maid*

The scene throughout: Orgon's house in Paris

ACT ONE

SCENE I

MADAME PERNELLE *and* FLIPOTE, *her maid,* ELMIRE, MARIANE, DORINE, DAMIS, CLÉANTE

MADAME PERNELLE: Come, come, Flipote; it's time I left this place.
ELMIRE: I can't keep up, you walk at such a pace.
MADAME PERNELLE: Don't trouble, child; no need to show me out.
    It's not your manners I'm concerned about.
5 ELMIRE: We merely pay you the respect we owe.
    But, Mother, why this hurry? Must you go?
MADAME PERNELLE: I must. This house appals me. No one in it
    Will pay attention for a single minute.
    Children, I take my leave much vexed in spirit.
10 I offer good advice, but you won't hear it.
    You all break in and chatter on and on.
    It's like a madhouse with the keeper gone.
DORINE: If . . .
MADAME PERNELLE: Girl, you talk too much, and I'm afraid
    You're far too saucy for a lady's-maid.
15 You push in everywhere and have your say.
DAMIS: But . . .
MADAME PERNELLE: You, boy, grow more foolish every day.
    To think my grandson should be such a dunce!
    I've said a hundred times, if I've said it once,
    That if you keep the course on which you've started,
20 You'll leave your worthy father broken-hearted.
MARIANE: I think . . .
MADAME PERNELLE: And you, his sister, seem so pure,
    So shy, so innocent, and so demure.
    But you know what they say about still waters.
    I pity parents with secretive daughters.
25 ELMIRE: Now, Mother . . .
MADAME PERNELLE: And as for you, child, let me add
    That your behavior is extremely bad,
    And a poor example for these children, too.
    Their dear, dead mother did far better than you.
    You're much too free with money, and I'm distressed
30 To see you so elaborately dressed.
    When it's one's husband that one aims to please,
    One has no need of costly fripperies.
CLÉANTE: Oh, Madam, really . . .

MADAME PERNELLE: You are her brother, Sir,
    And I respect and love you; yet if I were
35 My son, this lady's good and pious spouse,
    I wouldn't make you welcome in my house.
    You're full of worldly counsels which, I fear,
    Aren't suitable for decent folk to hear.
    I've spoken bluntly, Sir; but it behooves us
40 Not to mince words when righteous fervor moves us.
DAMIS: Your man Tartuffe is full of holy speeches . . .
MADAME PERNELLE: And practises precisely what he preaches.
    He's a fine man, and should be listened to.
    I will not hear him mocked by fools like you.
45 DAMIS: Good God! Do you expect me to submit
    To the tyranny of that carping hypocrite?
    Must we forgo all joys and satisfactions
    Because that bigot censures all our actions?
DORINE: To hear him talk—and he talks all the time—
50 There's nothing one can do that's not a crime.
    He rails at everything, your dear Tartuffe.
MADAME PERNELLE: Whatever he reproves deserves reproof.
    He's out to save your souls, and all of you
    Must love him, as my son would have you do.
55 DAMIS: Ah no, Grandmother, I could never take
    To such a rascal, even for my father's sake.
    That's how I feel, and I shall not dissemble.
    His every action makes me seethe and tremble
    With helpless anger, and I have no doubt
60 That he and I will shortly have it out.
DORINE: Surely it is a shame and a disgrace
    To see this man usurp the master's place—
    To see this beggar who, when first he came,
    Had not a shoe or shoestring to his name
65 So far forget himself that he behaves
    As if the house were his, and we his slaves.
MADAME PERNELLE: Well, mark my words, your souls would fare far better
    If you obeyed his precepts to the letter.
DORINE: You see him as a saint. I'm far less awed;
70 In fact, I see right through him. He's a fraud.
MADAME PERNELLE: Nonsense!
DORINE: His man Laurent's the same, or worse;
    I'd not trust either with a penny purse.
MADAME PERNELLE: I can't say what his servant's morals may be;
    His own great goodness I can guarantee.
    You all regard him with distaste and fear
75

Because he tells you what you're loath to hear,
Condemns your sins, points out your moral flaws,
And humbly strives to further Heaven's cause.
DORINE: If sin is all that bothers him, why is it
80   He's so upset when folk drop in to visit?
Is Heaven so outraged by a social call
That he must prophesy against us all?
I'll tell you what I think: if you ask me,
He's jealous of my mistress' company.
85   MADAME PERNELLE: Rubbish! (*To* ELMIRE.) He's not alone,
        child, in complaining
Of all of your promiscuous entertaining.
Why, the whole neighborhood's upset, I know,
By all these carriages that come and go,
With crowds of guests parading in and out
90   And noisy servants loitering about.
In all of this, I'm sure there's nothing vicious;
But why give people cause to be suspicious?
CLÉANTE: They need no cause; they'll talk in any case.
Madam, this world would be a joyless place
95   If, fearing what malicious tongues might say,
We locked our doors and turned our friends away.
And even if one did so dreary a thing,
D'you think those tongues would cease their chattering?
One can't fight slander; it's a losing battle;
100   Let us instead ignore their tittle-tattle.
Let's strive to live by conscience' clear decrees,
And let the gossips gossip as they please.
DORINE: If there is talk against us, I know the source:
It's Daphne and her little husband, of course.
105   Those who have greatest cause for guilt and shame
Are quickest to besmirch a neighbor's name.
When there's a chance for libel, they never miss it;
When something can be made to seem illicit
They're off at once to spread the joyous news,
110   Adding to fact what fantasies they choose.
By talking up their neighbor's indiscretions
They seek to camouflage their own transgressions,
Hoping that others' innocent affairs
Will lend a hue of innocence to theirs,
115   Or that their own black guilt will come to seem
Part of a general shady color-scheme.
MADAME PERNELLE: All that is quite irrelevant. I doubt
That anyone's more virtuous and devout
Than dear Orante; and I'm informed that she
120   Condemns your mode of life most vehemently.
DORINE: Oh, yes, she's strict, devout, and has no taint
Of worldliness; in short, she seems a saint.
But it was time which taught her that disguise;
She's thus because she can't be otherwise.
125   So long as her attractions could enthrall,
She flounced and flirted and enjoyed it all,
But now that they're no longer what they were
She quits a world which fast is quitting her,
And wears a veil of virtue to conceal
130   Her bankrupt beauty and her lost appeal.
That's what becomes of old coquettes today:
Distressed when all their lovers fall away,
They see no recourse but to play the prude,
And so confer a style on solitude.
135   Thereafter, they're severe with everyone,
Condemning all our actions, pardoning none,

And claiming to be pure, austere, and zealous
When, if the truth were known, they're merely jealous,
And cannot bear to see another know
The pleasures time has forced them to forgo.   140
MADAME PERNELLE: (*Initially to* ELMIRE.) That sort of talk is
        what you like to hear;
Therefore you'd have us all keep still, my dear,
While Madam rattles on the livelong day.
Nevertheless, I mean to have my say.
I tell you that you're blest to have Tartuffe   145
Dwelling, as my son's guest, beneath this roof;
That Heaven has sent him to forestall its wrath
By leading you, once more, to the true path;
That all he reprehends is reprehensible,
And that you'd better heed him, and be sensible.   150
These visits, balls, and parties in which you revel
Are nothing but inventions of the Devil.
One never hears a word that's edifying:
Nothing but chaff and foolishness and lying,
As well as vicious gossip in which one's neighbor   155
Is cut to bits with épée, foil, and saber.
People of sense are driven half-insane
At such affairs, where noise and folly reign
And reputations perish thick and fast.
As a wise preacher said on Sunday last,   160
Parties are Towers of Babylon, because
The guests all babble on with never a pause;
And then he told a story which, I think . . .

(*To* CLÉANTE.)

I heard that laugh, Sir, and I saw that wink!
Go find your silly friends and laugh some more!   165
Enough; I'm going; don't show me to the door.
I leave this household much dismayed and vexed;
I cannot say when I shall see you next.

(*Slapping* FLIPOTE.)

Wake up, don't stand there gaping into space!
I'll slap some sense into that stupid face.
Move, move, you slut.   170

SCENE II

CLÉANTE, DORINE

CLÉANTE: I think I'll stay behind;
I want no further pieces of her mind.
How that old lady . . .
DORINE: Oh, what wouldn't she say
If she could hear you speak of her that way!
She'd thank you for the *lady*, but I'm sure
She'd find the *old* a little premature.   5
CLÉANTE: My, what a scene she made, and what a din!
And how this man Tartuffe has taken her in!
DORINE: Yes, but her son is even worse deceived;
His folly must be seen to be believed.
In the late troubles, he played an able part   10
And served his king with wise and loyal heart,
But he's quite lost his senses since he fell
Beneath Tartuffe's infatuating spell.
He calls him brother, and loves him as his life,   15

Preferring him to mother, child, or wife.
In him and him alone will he confide;
He's made him his confessor and his guide;
He pets and pampers him with love more tender
20 Than any pretty mistress could engender,
Gives him the place of honor when they dine,
Delights to see him gorging like a swine,
Stuffs him with dainties till his guts distend,
And when he belches, cries "God bless you, friend!"
25 In short, he's mad; he worships him; he dotes;
His deeds he marvels at, his words he quotes,
Thinking each act a miracle, each word
Oracular as those that Moses heard.
Tartuffe, much pleased to find so easy a victim,
30 Has in a hundred ways beguiled and tricked him,
Milked him of money, and with his permission
Established here a sort of Inquisition.
Even Laurent, his lackey, dares to give
Us arrogant advice on how to live;
35 He sermonizes us in thundering tones
And confiscates our ribbons and colognes.
Last week he tore a kerchief into pieces
Because he found it pressed in a *Life of Jesus*:
He said it was a sin to juxtapose
40 Unholy vanities and holy prose.

SCENE III

ELMIRE, MARIANE, DAMIS, CLÉANTE, DORINE

ELMIRE: (*To* CLÉANTE.) You did well not to follow; she stood
    in the door
    And said *verbatim* all she'd said before.
    I saw my husband coming. I think I'd best
    Go upstairs now, and take a little rest.
5 CLÉANTE: I'll wait and greet him here; then I must go.
    I've really only time to say hello.
DAMIS: Sound him about my sister's wedding, please.
    I think Tartuffe's against it, and that he's
    Been urging Father to withdraw his blessing.
10 As you well know, I'd find that most distressing.
    Unless my sister and Valère can marry,
    My hopes to wed *his* sister will miscarry,
    And I'm determined . . .
DORINE: He's coming.

SCENE IV

ORGON, CLÉANTE, DORINE

ORGON: Ah, Brother, good-day.
CLÉANTE: Well, welcome back. I'm sorry I can't stay.
    How was the country? Blooming, I trust, and green?
ORGON: Excuse me, Brother; just one moment.

(*To* DORINE.)

                                    Dorine . . .

(*To* CLÉANTE.)

5   To put my mind at rest, I always learn
    The household news the moment I return.

(*To* DORINE.)

    Has all been well, these two days I've been gone?
    How are the family? What's been going on?
DORINE: Your wife, two days ago, had a bad fever,
    And a fierce headache which refused to leave her.   10
ORGON: Ah. And Tartuffe?
DORINE: Tartuffe? Why, he's round and red,
    Bursting with health, and excellently fed.
ORGON: Poor fellow!
DORINE: That night, the mistress was unable
    To take a single bite at the dinner-table.
    Her headache-pains, she said, were simply hellish.   15
ORGON: Ah. And Tartuffe?
DORINE: He ate his meal with relish,
    And zealously devoured in her presence
    A leg of mutton and a brace of pheasants.
ORGON: Poor fellow!
DORINE: Well, the pains continued strong,
    And so she tossed and tossed the whole night long,   20
    Now icy-cold, now burning like a flame.
    We sat beside her bed till morning came.
ORGON: Ah. And Tartuffe?
DORINE: Why, having eaten, he rose
    And sought his room, already in a doze,
    Got into his warm bed, and snored away   25
    In perfect peace until the break of day.
ORGON: Poor fellow!
DORINE: After much ado, we talked her
    Into dispatching someone for the doctor.
    He bled her, and the fever quickly fell.
ORGON: Ah. And Tartuffe?   30
DORINE: He bore it very well.
    To keep his cheerfulness at any cost,
    And make up for the blood *Madame* had lost,
    He drank, at lunch, four beakers full of port.
ORGON: Poor fellow!
DORINE: Both are doing well, in short.
    I'll go and tell *Madame* that you've expressed   35
    Keen sympathy and anxious interest.

SCENE V

ORGON, CLÉANTE

CLÉANTE: That girl was laughing in your face, and though
    I've no wish to offend you, even so
    I'm bound to say that she had some excuse.
    How can you possibly be such a goose?
    Are you so dazed by this man's hocus-pocus   5
    That all the world, save him, is out of focus?
    You've given him clothing, shelter, food, and care;
    Why must you also . . .
ORGON: Brother, stop right there.
    You do not know the man of whom you speak.
CLÉANTE: I grant you that. But my judgment's not so weak   10
    That I can't tell, by his effect on others . . .
ORGON: Ah, when you meet him, you two will be like brothers!
    There's been no loftier soul since time began.
    He is a man who . . . a man who . . . an excellent man.
    To keep his precepts is to be reborn,   15
    And view this dunghill of a world with scorn.

Yes, thanks to him I'm a changed man indeed.
Under his tutelage my soul's been freed
From earthly loves, and every human tie:
20   My mother, children, brother, and wife could die,
And I'd not feel a single moment's pain.
  CLÉANTE: That's a fine sentiment, Brother; most humane.
  ORGON: Oh, had you seen Tartuffe as I first knew him,
Your heart, like mine, would have surrendered to him.
25   He used to come into our church each day
And humbly kneel nearby, and start to pray.
He'd draw the eyes of everybody there
By the deep fervor of his heartfelt prayer;
He'd sigh and weep, and sometimes with a sound
30   Of rapture he would bend and kiss the ground;
And when I rose to go, he'd run before
To offer me holy-water at the door.
His serving-man, no less devout than he,
Informed me of his master's poverty.
35   I gave him gifts, but in his humbleness
He'd beg me every time to give him less.
"Oh, that's too much," he'd cry, "too much by twice!
I don't deserve it. The half, Sir, would suffice."
And when I wouldn't take it back, he'd share
40   Half of it with the poor, right then and there.
At length, Heaven prompted me to take him in
To dwell with us, and free our souls from sin.
He guides our lives, and to protect my honor
Stays by my wife, and keeps an eye upon her;
45   He tells me whom she sees, and all she does,
And seems more jealous than I ever was!
And how austere he is! Why, he can detect
A mortal sin where you would least suspect;
In smallest trifles, he's extremely strict.
50   Last week, his conscience was severely pricked
Because, while praying, he had caught a flea
And killed it, so he felt, too wrathfully.
  CLÉANTE: Good God, man! Have you lost your common sense—
Or is this all some joke at my expense?
55   How can you stand there and in all sobriety . . .
  ORGON: Brother, your language savors of impiety.
Too much free-thinking's made your faith unsteady,
And as I've warned you many times already,
'Twill get you into trouble before you're through.
60   CLÉANTE: So I've been told before by dupes like you:
Being blind, you'd have all others blind as well;
The clear-eyed man you call an infidel,
And he who sees through humbug and pretense
Is charged, by you, with want of reverence.
65   Spare me your warnings, Brother; I have no fear
Of speaking out, for you and Heaven to hear,
Against affected zeal and pious knavery.
There's true and false in piety, as in bravery,
And just as those whose courage shines the most
70   In battle, are the least inclined to boast,
So those whose hearts are truly pure and lowly
Don't make a flashy show of being holy.
There's a vast difference, so it seems to me,
Between true piety and hypocrisy:
75   How do you fail to see it, may I ask?
Is not a face quite different from a mask?
Cannot sincerity and cunning art,
Reality and semblance, be told apart?

Are scarecrows just like men, and do you hold
That a false coin is just as good as gold?   80
Ah, Brother, man's a strangely fashioned creature
Who seldom is content to follow Nature,
But recklessly pursues his inclination
Beyond the narrow bounds of moderation,
And often, by transgressing Reason's laws,   85
Perverts a lofty aim or noble cause.
A passing observation, but it applies.
  ORGON: I see, dear Brother, that you're profoundly wise;
You harbor all the insight of the age.
You are our one clear mind, our only sage,   90
The era's oracle, its Cato too,
And all mankind are fools compared to you.
  CLÉANTE: Brother, I don't pretend to be a sage,
Nor have I all the wisdom of the age.
There's just one insight I would dare to claim: 95
I know that true and false are not the same;
And just as there is nothing I more revere
Than a soul whose faith is steadfast and sincere,
Nothing that I more cherish and admire
Than honest zeal and true religious fire,   100
So there is nothing that I find more base
Than specious piety's dishonest face—
Than these bold mountebanks, these histrios
Whose impious mummeries and hollow shows
Exploit our love of Heaven, and make a jest   105
Of all that men think holiest and best;
These calculating souls who offer prayers
Not to their Maker, but as public wares,
And seek to buy respect and reputation
With lifted eyes and sighs of exaltation;   110
These charlatans, I say, whose pilgrim souls
Proceed, by way of Heaven, toward earthly goals,
Who weep and pray and swindle and extort,
Who preach the monkish life, but haunt the court,
Who make their zeal the partner of their vice—   115
Such men are vengeful, sly, and cold as ice,
And when there is an enemy to defame
They cloak their spite in fair religion's name,
Their private spleen and malice being made
To seem a high and virtuous crusade,   120
Until, to mankind's reverent applause,
They crucify their foe in Heaven's cause.
Such knaves are all too common; yet, for the wise,
True piety isn't hard to recognize,
And, happily, these present times provide us   125
With bright examples to instruct and guide us.
Consider Ariston and Périandre;
Look at Oronte, Alcidamas, Clitandre;
Their virtue is acknowledged; who could doubt it?
But you won't hear them beat the drum about it.   130
They're never ostentatious, never vain,
And their religion's moderate and humane;
It's not their way to criticize and chide:
They think censoriousness a mark of pride,
And therefore, letting others preach and rave,   135
They show, by deeds, how Christians should behave.
They think no evil of their fellow man,
But judge of him as kindly as they can.
They don't intrigue and wangle and conspire;
To lead a good life is their one desire;   140

The sinner wakes no rancorous hate in them;
It is the sin alone which they condemn;
Nor do they try to show a fiercer zeal
For Heaven's cause than Heaven itself could feel.
145   These men I honor, these men I advocate
As models for us all to emulate.
Your man is not their sort at all, I fear:
And, while your praise of him is quite sincere,
I think that you've been dreadfully deluded.
150   ORGON: Now then, dear Brother, is your speech concluded?
CLÉANTE: Why, yes.
ORGON: Your servant, Sir.

(*He turns to go.*)

CLÉANTE: No, Brother; wait.
There's one more matter. You agreed of late
That young Valère might have your daughter's hand.
ORGON: I did.
CLÉANTE: And set the date, I understand.
155   ORGON: Quite so.
CLÉANTE: You've now postponed it; is that true?
ORGON: No doubt.
CLÉANTE: The match no longer pleases you?
ORGON: Who knows?
CLÉANTE: D'you mean to go back on your word?
ORGON: I won't say that.
CLÉANTE: Has anything occurred
Which might entitle you to break your pledge?
160   ORGON: Perhaps.
CLÉANTE: Why must you hem, and haw, and hedge?
The boy asked me to sound you in this affair . . .
ORGON: It's been a pleasure.
CLÉANTE: But what shall I tell Valère?
ORGON: Whatever you like.
CLÉANTE: But what have you decided?
What are your plans?
ORGON: I plan, Sir, to be guided
165   By Heaven's will.
CLÉANTE: Come, Brother, don't talk rot.
You've given Valère your word; will you keep it, or not?
ORGON: Good day.
CLÉANTE: This looks like poor Valère's undoing;
I'll go and warn him that there's trouble brewing.

ACT TWO

SCENE I

ORGON, MARIANE

ORGON: Mariane.
MARIANE: Yes, Father?
ORGON: A word with you; come here.
MARIANE: What are you looking for?
ORGON: (*Peering into a small closet.*)
                    Eavesdroppers, dear.
I'm making sure we shan't be overheard.
Someone in there could catch our every word.
5   Ah, good, we're safe. Now, Mariane, my child,
You're a sweet girl who's tractable and mild,
Whom I hold dear, and think most highly of.

MARIANE: I'm deeply grateful, Father, for your love.
ORGON: That's well said, Daughter; and you can repay me
If, in all things, you'll cheerfully obey me.   10
MARIANE: To please you, Sir, is what delights me best.
ORGON: Good, good. Now, what d'you think of Tartuffe, our
        guest?
MARIANE: I, Sir?
ORGON: Yes. Weigh your answer; think it through.
MARIANE: Oh, dear. I'll say whatever you wish me to.
ORGON: That's wisely said, my Daughter. Say of him, then,   15
That he's the very worthiest of men,
And that you're fond of him, and would rejoice
In being his wife, if that should be my choice.
Well?
MARIANE: What?
ORGON: What's that?
MARIANE: I . . .
ORGON: Well?
MARIANE: Forgive me, pray.
ORGON: Did you not hear me?   20
MARIANE: Of *whom,* Sir, must I say
That I am fond of him, and would rejoice
In being his wife, if that should be your choice?
ORGON: Why, of Tartuffe.
MARIANE: But, Father, that's false, you know.
Why would you have me say what isn't so?
ORGON: Because I am resolved it shall be true.   25
That it's my wish should be enough for you.
MARIANE: You can't mean, Father . . .
ORGON: Yes, Tartuffe shall be
Allied by marriage to this family,
And he's to be your husband, is that clear?
It's a father's privilege . . .   30

SCENE II

DORINE, ORGON, MARIANE

ORGON: (*To* DORINE.)   What are you doing in here?
Is curiosity so fierce a passion
With you, that you must eavesdrop in this fashion?
DORINE: There's lately been a rumor going about—
Based on some hunch or chance remark, no doubt—   5
That you mean Mariane to wed Tartuffe.
I've laughed it off, of course, as just a spoof.
ORGON: You find it so incredible?
DORINE: Yes, I do.
I won't accept that story, even from you.
ORGON: Well, you'll believe it when the thing is done.   10
DORINE: Yes, yes, of course. Go on and have your fun.
ORGON: I've never been more serious in my life.
DORINE: Ha!
ORGON: Daughter, I mean it; you're to be his wife.
DORINE: No, don't believe your father; it's all a hoax.
ORGON: See here, young woman . . .   15
DORINE: Come, Sir, no more jokes;
You can't fool us.
ORGON: How dare you talk that way?
DORINE: All right, then: we believe you, sad to say.
But how a man like you, who looks so wise
And wears a moustache of such splendid size,   20
Can be so foolish as to . . .

ORGON: Silence, please!
    My girl, you take too many liberties.
    I'm master here, as you must not forget.
DORINE: Do let's discuss this calmly; don't be upset.
    You can't be serious, Sir, about this plan.
25 What should that bigot want with Mariane?
    Praying and fasting ought to keep him busy.
    And then, in terms of wealth and rank, what is he?
    Why should a man of property like you
    Pick out a beggar son-in-law?
    ORGON: That will do.
30 Speak of his poverty with reverence.
    His is a pure and saintly indigence
    Which far transcends all worldly pride and pelf.
    He lost his fortune, as he says himself,
    Because he cared for Heaven alone, and so
35 Was careless of his interests here below.
    I mean to get him out of his present straits
    And help him to recover his estates—
    Which, in his part of the world, have no small fame.
    Poor though he is, he's a gentleman just the same.
40 DORINE: Yes, so he tells us; and, Sir, it seems to me
    Such pride goes very ill with piety.
    A man whose spirit spurns this dungy earth
    Ought not to brag of lands and noble birth;
    Such worldly arrogance will hardly square
45 With meek devotion and the life of prayer.
    . . . But this approach, I see, has drawn a blank;
    Let's speak, then, of his person, not his rank.
    Doesn't it seem to you a trifle grim
    To give a girl like her to a man like him?
50 When two are so ill-suited, can't you see
    What the sad consequences is bound to be?
    A young girl's virtue is imperilled, Sir,
    When such a marriage is imposed on her;
    For if one's bridegroom isn't to one's taste,
55 It's hardly an inducement to be chaste,
    And many a man with horns upon his brow
    Has made his wife the thing that she is now.
    It's hard to be a faithful wife, in short,
    To certain husbands of a certain sort,
60 And he who gives his daughter to a man she hates
    Must answer for her sins at Heaven's gates.
    Think, Sir, before you play so risky a role.
    ORGON: This servant-girl presumes to save my soul!
    DORINE: You would do well to ponder what I've said.
65 ORGON: Daughter, we'll disregard this dunderhead.
    Just trust your father's judgment. Oh, I'm aware
    That I once promised you to young Valère;
    But now I hear he gambles, which greatly shocks me;
    What's more, I've doubts about his orthodoxy.
70 His visits to church, I note, are very few.
    DORINE: Would you have him go at the same hours as you,
    And kneel nearby, to be sure of being seen?
    ORGON: I can dispense with such remarks, Dorine.

(*To* MARIANE.)

    Tartuffe, however, is sure of Heaven's blessing,
75 And that's the only treasure worth possessing.
    This match will bring you joys beyond all measure;
    Your cup will overflow with every pleasure;

    You two will interchange your faithful loves
    Like two sweet cherubs, or two turtle-doves.
    No harsh word shall be heard, no frown be seen,   80
    And he shall make you happy as a queen.
DORINE: And she'll make him a cuckold, just wait and see.
ORGON: What language!
DORINE: Oh, he's a man of destiny;
    He's *made* for horns, and what the stars demand
    Your daughter's virtue surely can't withstand.   85
ORGON: Don't interrupt me further. Why can't you learn
    That certain things are none of your concern?
DORINE: It's for your own sake that I interfere.

(*She repeatedly interrupts* ORGON *just as he is turning to speak to his daughter.*)

ORGON: Most kind of you. Now, hold your tongue, d'you hear?
DORINE: If I didn't love you . . .   90
ORGON: Spare me your affection.
DORINE: I'll love you, Sir, in spite of your objection.
ORGON: Blast!
DORINE: I can't bear, Sir, for your honor's sake,
    To let you make this ludicrous mistake.
ORGON: You mean to go on talking?
DORINE: If I didn't protest
    This sinful marriage, my conscience couldn't rest.   95
ORGON: If you don't hold your tongue, you little shrew . . .
DORINE: What, lost your temper? A pious man like you?
ORGON: Yes! Yes! You talk and talk. I'm maddened by it.
    Once and for all, I tell you to be quiet.
DORINE: Well, I'll be quiet. But I'll be thinking hard.   100
ORGON: Think all you like, but you had better guard
    That saucy tongue of yours, or I'll . . .

(*Turning back to* MARIANE.)

                                    Now, child,
    I've weighed this matter fully.
DORINE: (*Aside.*)   It drives me wild
    That I can't speak.

(ORGON *turns his head, and she is silent.*)

ORGON: Tartuffe is no young dandy,
    But, still, his person . . .   105
DORINE: (*Aside.*)   Is as sweet as candy.
ORGON: Is such that, even if you shouldn't care
    For his other merits . . .

(*He turns and stands facing* DORINE, *arms crossed.*)

DORINE: (*Aside.*)   They'll make a lovely pair.
    If I were she, no man would marry me
    Against my inclination, and go scot-free.
    He'd learn, before the wedding-day was over,   110
    How readily a wife can find a lover.
ORGON: (*To* DORINE.) It seems you treat my orders as a joke.
DORINE: Why, what's the matter? 'Twas not to you I spoke.
ORGON: What *were* you doing?
DORINE: Talking to myself, that's all.
ORGON: Ah! (*Aside.*) One more bit of impudence and gall,   115
    And I shall give her a good slap in the face.

(He puts himself in position to slap her; DORINE, *whenever he glances at her, stands immobile and silent.)*

Daughter, you shall accept, and with good grace,
The husband I've selected . . . Your wedding-day . . .

(To DORINE.)

Why don't you talk to yourself?
DORINE: I've nothing to say.
120 ORGON: Come, just one word.
DORINE: No thank you, Sir. I pass.
ORGON: Come, speak; I'm waiting.
DORINE: I'd not be such an ass.
ORGON: *(Turning to* MARIANE.) In short, dear Daughter, I
      mean to be obeyed,
And you must bow to the sound choice I've made.
DORINE: *(Moving away.)* I'd not wed such a monster, even in jest.

*(*ORGON *attempts to slap her, but misses.)*

125 ORGON: Daughter, that maid of yours is a thorough pest;
She makes me sinfully annoyed and nettled.
I can't speak further; my nerves are too unsettled.
She's so upset me by her insolent talk,
I'll calm myself by going for a walk.

SCENE III

DORINE, MARIANE

DORINE: *(Returning.)* Well, have you lost your tongue, girl?
      Must I play
Your part, and say the lines you ought to say?
Faced with a fate so hideous and absurd,
Can you not utter one dissenting word?
5 MARIANE: What good would it do? A father's power is great.
DORINE: Resist him now, or it will be too late.
MARIANE: But . . .
DORINE: Tell him one cannot love at a father's whim;
That you shall marry for yourself, not him;
That since it's you who are to be the bride,
10 It's you, not he, who must be satisfied;
And that if his Tartuffe is so sublime,
He's free to marry him at any time.
MARIANE: I've bowed so long to Father's strict control,
I couldn't oppose him now, to save my soul.
15 DORINE: Come, come, Mariane. Do listen to reason, won't you?
Valère has asked your hand. Do you love him, or don't you?
MARIANE: Oh, how unjust of you! What can you mean
By asking such a question, dear Dorine?
You know the depth of my affection for him;
20 I've told you a hundred times how I adore him.
DORINE: I don't believe in everything I hear;
Who knows if your professions were sincere?
MARIANE: They were, Dorine, and you do me wrong to doubt it;
Heaven knows that I've been all too frank about it.
25 DORINE: You love him, then?
MARIANE: Oh, more than I can express.
DORINE: And he, I take it, cares for you no less?
MARIANE: I think so.

DORINE: And you both, with equal fire,
Burn to be married?
MARIANE: That is our one desire.
DORINE: What of Tartuffe, then? What of your father's plan?
MARIANE: I'll kill myself, if I'm forced to wed that man.   30
DORINE: I hadn't thought of that recourse. How splendid!
Just die, and all your troubles will be ended!
A fine solution. Oh, it maddens me
To hear you talk in that self-pitying key.
MARIANE: Dorine, how harsh you are! It's most unfair.   35
You have no sympathy for my despair.
DORINE: I've none at all for people who talk drivel
And, faced with difficulties, whine and snivel.
MARIANE: No doubt I'm timid, but it would be wrong . . .
DORINE: True love requires a heart that's firm and strong.   40
MARIANE: I'm strong in my affection for Valère,
But coping with my father is his affair.
DORINE: But if your father's brain has grown so cracked
Over his dear Tartuffe that he can retract
His blessing, though your wedding-day was named,   45
It's surely not Valère who's to be blamed.
MARIANE: If I defied my father, as you suggest,
Would it not seem unmaidenly, at best?
Shall I defend my love at the expense
Of brazenness and disobedience?   50
Shall I parade my heart's desires, and flaunt . . .
DORINE: No, I ask nothing of you. Clearly you want
To be Madame Tartuffe, and I feel bound
Not to oppose a wish so very sound.
What right have I to criticize the match?   55
Indeed, my dear, the man's a brilliant catch.
Monsieur Tartuffe! Now, there's a man of weight!
Yes, yes, Monsieur Tartuffe, I'm bound to state,
Is quite a person; that's not to be denied;
'Twill be no little thing to be his bride.   60
The world already rings with his renown;
He's a great noble—in his native town;
His ears are red, he has a pink complexion,
And all in all, he'll suit you to perfection.
MARIANE: Dear God!   65
DORINE: Oh, how triumphant you will feel
At having caught a husband so ideal!
MARIANE: Oh, do stop teasing, and use your cleverness
To get me out of this appalling mess.
Advise me, and I'll do whatever you say.
DORINE: Ah no, a dutiful daughter must obey   70
Her father, even if he weds her to an ape.
You've a bright future; why struggle to escape?
Tartuffe will take you back where his family lives,
To a small town aswarm with relatives—
Uncles and cousins whom you'll be charmed to meet.   75
You'll be received at once by the elite,
Calling upon the bailiff's wife, no less—
Even, perhaps, upon the mayoress,
Who'll sit you down in the *best* kitchen chair.
Then, once a year, you'll dance at the village fair   80
To the drone of bagpipes—two of them, in fact—
And see a puppet-show, or an animal act.
Your husband . . .
MARIANE: Oh, you turn my blood to ice!
Stop torturing me, and give me your advice.

DORINE: (*Threatening to go.*)
85   Your servant, Madam.
MARIANE: Dorine, I beg of you . . .
DORINE: No, you deserve it; this marriage must go through.
MARIANE: Dorine!
DORINE: No.
MARIANE: Not Tartuffe! You know I think him . . .
DORINE: Tartuffe's your cup of tea, and you shall drink him.
MARIANE: I've always told you everything, and relied . . .
90 DORINE: No. You deserve to be tartuffified.
MARIANE: Well, since you mock me and refuse to care,
    I'll henceforth seek my solace in despair:
    Despair shall be my counsellor and friend,
    And help me bring my sorrows to an end.

(*She starts to leave.*)

95 DORINE: There now, come back; my anger has subsided.
    You do deserve some pity, I've decided.
MARIANE: Dorine, if Father makes me undergo
    This dreadful martyrdom, I'll die, I know.
DORINE: Don't fret; it won't be difficult to discover
100   Some plan of action . . . But here's Valère, your lover.

SCENE IV

VALÈRE, MARIANE, DORINE

VALÈRE: Madam, I've just received some wondrous news
    Regarding which I'd like to hear your views.
MARIANE: What news?
VALÈRE: You're marrying Tartuffe.
MARIANE: I find
    That Father does have such a match in mind.
5 VALÈRE: Your father, Madam . . .
MARIANE: . . . has just this minute said
    That it's Tartuffe he wishes me to wed.
VALÈRE: Can he be serious?
MARIANE: Oh, indeed he can;
    He's clearly set his heart upon the plan.
VALÈRE: And what position do you propose to take,
10   Madam?
MARIANE: Why—I don't know.
VALÈRE: For heaven's sake—
    You don't know?
MARIANE: No.
VALÈRE: Well, well!
MARIANE: Advise me, do.
VALÈRE: Marry the man. That's my advice to you.
MARIANE: That's your advice?
VALÈRE: Yes.
MARIANE: Truly?
VALÈRE: Oh, absolutely.
    You couldn't choose more wisely, more astutely.
15 MARIANE: Thanks for this counsel; I'll follow it, of course.
VALÈRE: Do, do; I'm sure 'twill cost you no remorse.
MARIANE: To give it didn't cause your heart to break.
VALÈRE: I gave it, Madam, only for your sake.
MARIANE: And it's for your sake that I take it, Sir.
20 DORINE: (*Withdrawing to the rear of the stage.*) Let's see which
    fool will prove the stubborner.
VALÈRE: So! I am nothing to you, and it was flat

Deception when you . . .
MARIANE: Please, enough of that.
    You've told me plainly that I should agree
    To wed the man my father's chosen for me,
    And since you've deigned to counsel me so wisely,   25
    I promise, Sir, to do as you advise me.
VALÈRE: Ah, no, 'twas not by me that you were swayed.
    No, your decision was already made;
    Though now, to save appearances, you protest
    That you're betraying me at my behest.   30
MARIANE: Just as you say.
VALÈRE: Quite so. And I now see
    That you were never truly in love with me.
MARIANE: Alas, you're free to think so if you choose.
VALÈRE: I choose to think so, and here's a bit of news:
    You've spurned my hand, but I know where to turn   35
    For kinder treatment, as you shall quickly learn.
MARIANE: I'm sure you do. Your noble qualities
    Inspire affection . . .
VALÈRE: Forget my qualities, please.
    They don't inspire you overmuch, I find.
    But there's another lady I have in mind   40
    Whose sweet and generous nature will not scorn
    To compensate me for the loss I've borne.
MARIANE: I'm no great loss, and I'm sure that you'll transfer
    Your heart quite painlessly from me to her.
VALÈRE: I'll do my best to take it in my stride.   45
    The pain I feel at being cast aside.
    Time and forgetfulness may put an end to.
    Or if I can't forget, I shall pretend to.
    No self-respecting person is expected
    To go on loving once he's been rejected.   50
MARIANE: Now, that's a fine, high-minded sentiment.
VALÈRE: One to which any sane man would assent.
    Would you prefer it if I pined away
    In hopeless passion till my dying day?
    Am I to yield you to a rival's arms   55
    And not console myself with other charms?
MARIANE: Go then: console yourself; don't hesitate.
    I wish you to; indeed, I cannot wait.
VALÈRE: You wish me to?
MARIANE: Yes.
VALÈRE: That's the final straw.
    Madam, farewell. Your wish shall be my law.   60

(*He starts to leave, and then returns: this repeatedly.*)

MARIANE: Splendid.
VALÈRE: (*Coming back again.*)
          This breach, remember, is of your making;
    It's you who've driven me to the step I'm taking.
MARIANE: Of course.
VALÈRE: (*Coming back again.*)
          Remember, too, that I am merely
    Following your example.
MARIANE: I see that clearly.
VALÈRE: Enough. I'll go and do your bidding, then.   65
MARIANE: Good.
VALÈRE: (*Coming back again.*)
          You shall never see my face again.
MARIANE: Excellent.
VALÈRE: (*Walking to the door, then turning about.*)
         Yes?

MARIANE: What?
VALÈRE: What's that? What did you say?
MARIANE: Nothing. You're dreaming.
VALÈRE: Ah. Well, I'm on my way.
    Farewell, *Madame.*

(*He moves slowly away.*)

MARIANE: Farewell.
DORINE: (*To* MARIANE.)   If you ask me,
70   Both of you are as mad as mad can be.
    Do stop this nonsense, now. I've only let you
    Squabble so long to see where it would get you.
    Whoa there, Monsieure Valère!

(*She goes and seizes* VALÈRE *by the arm; he makes a great show of resistance.*)

VALÈRE: What's this, Dorine?
DORINE: Come here.
VALÈRE: No, no, my heart's too full of spleen.
75   Don't hold me back; her wish must be obeyed.
DORINE: Stop!
VALÈRE: It's too late now; my decision's made.
DORINE: Oh, pooh!
MARIANE: (*Aside.*)
              He hates the sight of me, that's plain.
    I'll go, and so deliver him from pain.
DORINE: (*Leaving* VALÈRE, *running after* MARIANE.) And now
    you run away! Come back.
MARIANE: No, no.
80   Nothing you say will keep me here. Let go!
VALÈRE: (*Aside.*) She cannot bear my presence, I perceive.
    To spare her further torment, I shall leave.
DORINE: (*Leaving* MARIANE, *running after* VALÈRE.) Again!
    You'll not escape, Sir; don't you try it.
    Come here, you two. Stop fussing, and be quiet.

(*She takes* VALÈRE *by the hand, then* MARIANE, *and draws them together.*)

VALÈRE: (*To* DORINE.)
85   What do you want of me?
MARIANE: (*To* DORINE.)
                What is the point of this?
DORINE: We're going to have a little armistice.

(*To* VALÈRE.)

    Now, weren't you silly to get so overheated?
VALÈRE: Didn't you see how badly I was treated?
DORINE: (*To* MARIANE.) Aren't you a simpleton, to have lost
    your head?
90 MARIANE: Didn't you hear the hateful things he said?
DORINE: (*To* VALÈRE.) You're both great fools. Her sole
    desire, Valère,
    Is to be yours in marriage. To that I'll swear.

(*To* MARIANE.)

    He loves you only, and he wants no wife
    But you, Mariane. On that I'll stake my life.

MARIANE: (*To* VALÈRE.) Then why you advised me so,
    I cannot see.   95
VALÈRE: (*To* MARIANE.) On such a question, why ask advice
    of *me?*
DORINE: Oh, you're impossible. Give me your hands, you two.

(*To* VALÈRE.)

    Yours first.
VALÈRE: (*Giving* DORINE *his hand.*)
           But why?
DORINE: (*To* MARIANE.)
               And now a hand from you.
MARIANE: (*Also giving* DORINE *her hand.*)
    What are you doing?
DORINE: There: a perfect fit.
    You suit each other better than you'll admit.   100

(VALÈRE *and* MARIANE *hold hands for some time without looking at each other.*)

VALÈRE: (*Turning toward* MARIANE.) Ah, come, don't be so
    haughty. Give a man
    A look of kindness, won't you, Mariane?

(MARIANE *turns toward* VALÈRE *and smiles.*)

DORINE: I tell you, lovers are completely mad!
VALÈRE: (*To* MARIANE.) Now come, confess that you were very bad
    To hurt my feelings as you did just now.   105
    I have a just complaint, you must allow.
MARIANE: *You* must allow that you were most unpleasant . . .
DORINE: Let's table that discussion for the present;
    Your father has a plan which must be stopped.
MARIANE: Advise us, then; what means must we adopt?   110
DORINE: We'll use all manner of means, and all at once.

(*To* MARIANE.)

    Your father's addled; he's acting like a dunce.
    Therefore you'd better humor the old fossil.
    Pretend to yield to him, be sweet and docile,
    And then postpone, as often as necessary,   115
    The day on which you have agreed to marry.
    You'll thus gain time, and time will turn the trick.
    Sometimes, for instance, you'll be taken sick,
    And that will seem good reason for delay;
    Or some bad omen will make you change the day—   120
    You'll dream of muddy water, or you'll pass
    A dead man's hearse, or break a looking-glass.
    If all else fails, no man can marry you
    Unless you take his ring and say "I do."
    But now, let's separate. If they should find   125
    Us talking here, our plot might be divined.

(*To* VALÈRE.)

    Go to your friends, and tell them what's occurred,
    And have them urge her father to keep his word.
    Meanwhile, we'll stir her brother into action,
    And get Elmire, as well, to join our faction.   130
    Good-bye.

VALÈRE: (*To* MARIANE.)
        Though each of us will do his best,
        It's your true heart on which my hopes shall rest.
MARIANE: (*To* VALÈRE.) Regardless of what Father may decide,
        None but Valère shall claim me as his bride.
135 VALÈRE: Oh, how those words content me! Come what will . . .
DORINE: Oh, lover, lovers! Their tongues are never still.
        Be off, now.
VALÈRE: (*Turning to go, then turning back.*)
                One last word . . .
DORINE: No time to chat:
        You leave by this door; and *you* leave by that.

(DORINE *pushes them, by the shoulders, toward opposing doors.*)

ACT THREE

SCENE I

DAMIS, DORINE

DAMIS: May lightning strike me even as I speak,
        May all men call me cowardly and weak,
        If any fear or scruple holds me back
        From settling things, at once, with that great quack!
5 DORINE: Now, don't give way to violent emotion.
        Your father's merely talked about this notion,
        And words and deeds are far from being one.
        Much that is talked about is left undone.
DAMIS: No, I must stop that scoundrel's machinations;
10   I'll go and tell him off; I'm out of patience.
DORINE: Do calm down and be practical. I had rather
        My mistress dealt with him—and with your father.
        She has some influence with Tartuffe, I've noted.
        He hangs upon her words, seems most devoted,
15   And may, indeed, be smitten by her charm.
        Pray Heaven it's true! 'Twould do our cause no harm.
        She sent for him, just now, to sound him out
        On this affair you're so incensed about;
        She'll find out where he stands, and tell him, too,
20   What dreadful strife and trouble will ensue
        If he lends countenance to your father's plan.
        I couldn't get in to see him, but his man
        Says that he's almost finished with his prayers.
        Go, now. I'll catch him when he comes downstairs.
25 DAMIS: I want to hear this conference, and I will.
DORINE: No, they must be alone.
DAMIS: Oh, I'll keep still.
DORINE: Not you. I know your temper. You'd start a brawl,
        And shout and stamp your foot and spoil it all.
        Go on.
DAMIS: I won't; I have a perfect right . . .
30 DORINE: Lord, you're a nuisance! He's coming; get out of sight.

(DAMIS *conceals himself in a closet at the rear of the stage.*)

SCENE II

TARTUFFE, DORINE

TARTUFFE: (*Observing* DORINE, *and calling to his manservant offstage.*)

Hang up my hair-shirt, put my scourge in place,
        And pray, Laurent, for Heaven's perpetual grace.
        I'm going to the prison now, to share
        My last few coins with the poor wretches there.
DORINE: (*Aside.*) Dear God, what affectation! What a fake!   5
TARTUFFE: You wished to see me?
DORINE: Yes . . .
TARTUFFE: (*Taking a handkerchief from his pocket.*)
                        For mercy's sake,
        Please take this handkerchief, before you speak.
DORINE: What?
TARTUFFE: Cover that bosom, girl. The flesh is weak,
        And unclean thoughts are difficult to control.
        Such sights as that can undermine the soul.   10
DORINE: Your soul, it seems, has very poor defenses,
        And flesh makes quite an impact on your senses.
        It's strange that you're so easily excited;
        My own desires are not so soon ignited,
        And if I saw you naked as a beast,   15
        Not all your hide would tempt me in the least.
TARTUFFE: Girl, speak more modestly; unless you do,
        I shall be forced to take my leave of you.
DORINE: Oh, no, it's I who must be on my way;
        I've just one little message to convey.   20
        Madame is coming down, and begs you, Sir,
        To wait and have a word or two with her.
TARTUFFE: Gladly.
DORINE: (*Aside.*) *That* had a softening effect!
        I think my guess about him was correct.
TARTUFFE: Will she be long?   25
DORINE: No: that's her step I hear.
        Ah, here she is, and I shall disappear.

SCENE III

ELMIRE, TARTUFFE

TARTUFFE: May Heaven, whose infinite goodness we adore,
        Preserve your body and soul forevermore,
        And bless your days, and answer thus the plea
        Of one who is its humblest votary.
ELMIRE: I thank you for that pious wish. But please,   5
        Do take a chair and let's be more at ease.

(*They sit down.*)

TARTUFFE: I trust that you are once more well and strong?
ELMIRE: Oh, yes: the fever didn't last for long.
TARTUFFE: My prayers are too unworthy, I am sure,
        To have gained from Heaven this most gracious cure;   10
        But lately, Madam, my every supplication
        Has had for object your recuperation.
ELMIRE: You shouldn't have troubled so. I don't deserve it.
TARTUFFE: Your health is priceless, Madam, and to preserve it
        I'd gladly give my own, in all sincerity.   15
ELMIRE: Sir, you outdo us all in Christian charity.
        You've been most kind. I count myself your debtor.
TARTUFFE: 'Twas nothing, Madam. I long to serve you better.
ELMIRE: There's a private matter I'm anxious to discuss.
        I'm glad there's no one here to hinder us.   20
TARTUFFE: I too am glad; it floods my heart with bliss
        To find myself alone with you like this.

For just this chance I've prayed with all my power—
But prayed in vain, until this happy hour.

25 ELMIRE: This won't take long, Sir, and I hope you'll be
Entirely frank and unconstrained with me.

TARTUFFE: Indeed, there's nothing I had rather do
Than bare my inmost heart and soul to you.
First, let me say that what remarks I've made
30 About the constant visits you are paid
Were prompted not by any mean emotion,
But rather by a pure and deep devotion,
A fervent zeal . . .

ELMIRE: No need for explanation.
Your sole concern, I'm sure, was my salvation.

TARTUFFE: (*Taking* ELMIRE's *hand and pressing her fingertips.*)
35 Quite so; and such great fervor do I feel . . .

ELMIRE: Ooh! Please! You're pinching!

TARTUFFE: 'Twas from excess of zeal.
I never meant to cause you pain, I swear.
I'd rather . . .

(*He places his hand on* ELMIRE's *knee.*)

ELMIRE: What can your hand be doing there?

TARTUFFE: Feeling your gown; what soft, fine-woven stuff!

40 ELMIRE: Please, I'm extremely ticklish. That's enough.

(*She draws her chair away;* TARTUFFE *pulls his after her.*)

TARTUFFE: (*Fondling the lace collar of her gown.*) My, my, what
lovely lacework on your dress!
The workmanship's miraculous, no less.
I've not seen anything to equal it.

ELMIRE: Yes, quite. But let's talk business for a bit.
45 They say my husband means to break his word
And give his daughter to you, Sir. Had you heard?

TARTUFFE: He did once mention it. But I confess
I dream of quite a different happiness.
It's elsewhere, Madam, that my eyes discern
50 The promise of that bliss for which I yearn.

ELMIRE: I see: you care for nothing here below.

TARTUFFE: Ah, well—my heart's not made of stone, you know.

ELMIRE: All your desires mount heavenward, I'm sure,
In scorn of all that's earthly and impure.

55 TARTUFFE: A love of heavenly beauty does not preclude
A proper love for earthly pulchritude;
Our senses are quite rightly captivated
By perfect works our Maker has created.
Some glory clings to all that Heaven has made;
60 In you, all Heaven's marvels are displayed.
On that fair face, such beauties have been lavished,
The eyes are dazzled and the heart is ravished;
How could I look on you, O flawless creature,
And not adore the Author of all Nature,
65 Feeling a love both passionate and pure
For you, his triumph of self-portraiture?
At first, I trembled lest that love should be
A subtle snare that Hell had laid for me;
I vowed to flee the sight of you, eschewing
70 A rapture that might prove my soul's undoing;
But soon, fair being, I became aware
That my deep passion could be made to square
With rectitude, and with my bounden duty.

I thereupon surrendered to your beauty.
It is, I know, presumptuous on my part   75
To bring you this poor offering of my heart,
And it is not my merit, Heaven knows,
But your compassion on which my hopes repose.
You are my peace, my solace, my salvation;
On you depends my bliss—or desolation;   80
I bide your judgment and, as you think best,
I shall be either miserable or blest.

ELMIRE: Your declaration is most gallant, Sir,
But don't you think it's out of character?
You'd have done better to restrain your passion   85
And think before you spoke in such a fashion.
It ill becomes a pious man like you . . .

TARTUFFE: I may be pious, but I'm human too:
With your celestial charms before his eyes,
A man has not the power to be wise.   90
I know such words sound strangely, coming from me,
But I'm no angel, nor was meant to be,
And if you blame my passion, you must needs
Reproach as well the charms on which it feeds.
Your loveliness I had no sooner seen   95
Than you became my soul's unrivalled queen;
Before your seraph glance, divinely sweet,
My heart's defenses crumbled in defeat,
And nothing fasting, prayer, or tears might do
Could stay my spirit from adoring you.   100
My eyes, my sighs have told you in the past
What now my lips make bold to say at last,
And if, in your great goodness, you will deign
To look upon your slave, and ease his pain,—
If, in compassion for my soul's distress,   105
You'll stoop to comfort my unworthiness,
I'll raise to you, in thanks for that sweet manna,
An endless hymn, an infinite hosanna.
With me, of course, there need be no anxiety.
No fear of scandal or of notoriety.   110
These young court gallants, whom all the ladies fancy,
Are vain in speech, in action rash and chancy;
When they succeed in love, the world soon knows it;
No favor's granted them but they disclose it
And by the looseness of their tongues profane   115
The very altar where their hearts have lain.
Men of my sort, however, love discreetly,
And one may trust our reticence completely.
My keen concern for my good name insures
The absolute security of yours;   120
In short, I offer you, my dear Elmire,
Love without scandal, pleasure without fear.

ELMIRE: I've heard your well-turned speeches to the end,
And what you urge I clearly apprehend.
Aren't you afraid that I may take a notion   125
To tell my husband of your warm devotion,
And that, supposing he were duly told,
His feelings toward you might grow rather cold?

TARTUFFE: I know, dear lady, that your exceeding charity
Will lead your heart to pardon my temerity;   130
That you'll excuse my violent affection
As human weakness, human imperfection;
And that—O fairest!—you will bear in mind
That I'm but flesh and blood, and am not blind.

ELMIRE: Some women might do otherwise, perhaps,   135

But I shall be discreet about your lapse;
I'll tell my husband nothing of what's occurred
If, in return, you'll give your solemn word
To advocate as forcefully as you can
140   The marriage of Valère and Mariane,
Renouncing all desire to dispossess
Another of his rightful happiness,
And . . .

SCENE IV

DAMIS, ELMIRE, TARTUFFE

DAMIS: (*Emerging from the closet where he has been hiding.*)
            No! We'll not hush up this vile affair;
I heard it all inside that closet there,
Where Heaven, in order to confound the pride
Of this great rascal, prompted me to hide.
5   Ah, now I have my long-awaited chance
To punish his deceit and arrogance,
And give my father clear and shocking proof
Of the black character of his dear Tartuffe.
ELMIRE: Ah no, Damis; I'll be content if he
10   Will study to deserve my leniency.
I've promised silence—don't make me break my word;
To make a scandal would be too absurd.
Good wives laugh off such trifles, and forget them;
Why should they tell their husbands, and upset them?
15 DAMIS: You have your reasons for taking such a course,
And I have reasons, too, of equal force.
To spare him now would be insanely wrong.
I've swallowed my just wrath for far too long
And watched this insolent bigot bringing strife
20   And bitterness into our family life.
Too long he's meddled in my father's affairs,
Thwarting my marriage-hopes, and poor Valère's.
It's high time that my father was undeceived,
And now I've proof that can't be disbelieved—
25   Proof that was furnished me by Heaven above.
It's too good not to take advantage of.
This is my chance, and I deserve to lose it
If, for one moment, I hesitate to use it.
ELMIRE: Damis . . .
DAMIS: No, I must do what I think right.
30   Madam, my heart is bursting with delight,
And, say whatever you will, I'll not consent
To lose the sweet revenge on which I'm bent.
I'll settle matters without more ado;
And here, most opportunely, is my cue.

SCENE V

ORGON, DAMIS, TARTUFFE, ELMIRE

DAMIS: Father, I'm glad you've joined us. Let us advise you
Of some fresh news which doubtless will surprise you.
You've just now been repaid with interest
For all your loving-kindness to our guest.
5   He's proved his warm and grateful feelings toward you;
It's with a pair of horns he would reward you.
Yes, I surprised him with your wife, and heard
His whole adulterous offer, every word.

She, with her all too gentle disposition,
Would not have told you of his proposition;   10
But I shall not make terms with brazen lechery,
And feel that not to tell you would be treachery.
ELMIRE: And I hold that one's husband's peace of mind
Should not be spoilt by tattle of this kind.
One's honor doesn't require it: to be proficient   15
In keeping men at bay is quite sufficient.
These are my sentiments, and I wish, Damis,
That you had heeded me and held your peace.

SCENE VI

ORGON, DAMIS, TARTUFFE

ORGON: Can it be true, this dreadful thing I hear?
TARTUFFE: Yes, Brother, I'm a wicked man, I fear:
A wretched sinner, all depraved and twisted,
The greatest villain that has ever existed.
My life's one heap of crimes, which grows each minute;   5
There's naught but foulness and corruption in it;
And I perceive that Heaven, outraged by me,
Has chosen this occasion to mortify me.
Charge me with any deed you wish to name;
I'll not defend myself, but take the blame.   10
Believe what you are told, and drive Tartuffe
Like some base criminal from beneath your roof;
Yes, drive me hence, and with a parting curse:
I shan't protest, for I deserve far worse.
ORGON: (*To* DAMIS.) Ah, you deceitful boy, how dare you try   15
To stain his purity with so foul a lie?
DAMIS: What! Are you taken in by such a bluff?
Did you not hear . . . ?
ORGON: Enough, you rogue, enough!
TARTUFFE: Ah, Brother, let him speak: you're being unjust.
Believe his story; the boy deserves your trust.   20
Why, after all, should you have faith in me?
How can you know what I might do, or be?
Is it on my good actions that you base
Your favor? Do you trust my pious face?
Ah, no, don't be deceived by hollow shows;   25
I'm far, alas, from being what men suppose;
Though the world takes me for a man of worth,
I'm truly the most worthless man on earth.

(*To* DAMIS.)

Yes, my dear son, speak out now: call me the chief
Of sinners, a wretch, a murderer, a thief;   30
Load me with all the names men most abhor;
I'll not complain; I've earned them all, and more;
I'll kneel here while you pour them on my head
As a just punishment for the life I've led.
ORGON: (*To* TARTUFFE.)
This is too much, dear Brother.   35

(*To* DAMIS.)

                    Have you no heart?
DAMIS: Are you so hoodwinked by this rascal's art. . . ?
ORGON: Be still, you monster.

(*To* TARTUFFE.)

                   Brother, I pray you, rise.

(*To* DAMIS.)

    Villain!
DAMIS: But . . .
ORGON: Silence!
DAMIS: Can't you realize. . . ?
ORGON: Just one word more, and I'll tear you limb from limb.
40   TARTUFFE: In God's name, Brother, don't be harsh with him.
    I'd rather far be tortured at the stake
    Than see him bear one scratch for my poor sake.
   ORGON: (*To* DAMIS.)
    Ingrate!
   TARTUFFE: If I must beg you, on bended knee,
    To pardon him . . .
   ORGON: (*Falling to his knees, addressing* TARTUFFE.)
            Such goodness cannot be!

(*To* DAMIS.)

45   Now, *there's* true charity!
   DAMIS: What, you. . . ?
   ORGON: Villain, be still!
    I know your motives; I know you wish him ill:
    Yes, all of you—wife, children, servants, all—
    Conspire against him and desire his fall,
    Employing every shameful trick you can
50   To alienate me from this saintly man.
    Ah, but the more you seek to drive him away,
    The more I'll do to keep him. Without delay,
    I'll spite this household and confound its pride
    By giving him my daughter as his bride.
55   DAMIS: You're going to force her to accept his hand?
   ORGON: Yes, and this very night, d'you understand?
    I shall defy you all, and make it clear
    That I'm the one who gives the orders here.
    Come, wretch, kneel down and clasp his blessed feet,
60   And ask his pardon for your black deceit.
   DAMIS: I ask that swindler's pardon? Why, I'd rather . . .
   ORGON: So! You insult him, and defy your father!
    A stick! A stick! (*To* TARTUFFE.) No, no—release me, do.

(*To* DAMIS.)

    Out of my house this minute! Be off with you,
65   And never dare set foot in it again.
   DAMIS: Well, I shall go, but . . .
   ORGON: Well, go quickly, then.
    I disinherit you; an empty purse
    Is all you'll get from me—except my curse!

SCENE VII

ORGON, TARTUFFE

ORGON: How he blasphemed your goodness! What a son!
TARTUFFE: Forgive him, Lord, as I've already done.

(*To* ORGON.)

You can't know how it hurts when someone tries
To blacken me in my dear Brother's eyes.
ORGON: Ahh!   5
TARTUFFE: The mere thought of such ingratitude
    Plunges my soul into so dark a mood . . .
    Such horror grips my heart . . . I gasp for breath,
    And cannot speak, and feel myself near death.
ORGON:

(*He runs, in tears, to the door through which he has just driven
his son.*)

    You blackguard! Why did I spare you? Why did I not
    Break you in little pieces on the spot?   10
    Compose yourself, and don't be hurt, dear friend.
TARTUFFE: These scenes, these dreadful quarrels, have got to end.
    I've much upset your household, and I perceive
    That the best thing will be for me to leave.
ORGON: What are you saying!   15
TARTUFFE: They're all against me here;
    They'd have you think me false and insincere.
ORGON: Ah, what of that? Have I ceased believing in you?
TARTUFFE: Their adverse talk will certainly continue,
    And charges which you now repudiate
    You may find credible at a later date.   20
ORGON: No, Brother, never.
TARTUFFE: Brother, a wife can sway
    Her husband's mind in many a subtle way.
ORGON: No, no.
TARTUFFE: To leave at once is the solution;
    Thus only can I end their persecution.
ORGON: No, no, I'll not allow it; you shall remain.   25
TARTUFFE: Ah, well; 'twill mean much martyrdom and pain,
    But if you wish it . . .
ORGON: Ah!
TARTUFFE: Enough; so be it.
    But one thing must be settled, as I see it.
    For your dear honor, and for our friendship's sake,
    There's one precaution I feel bound to take.   30
    I shall avoid your wife, and keep away . . .
ORGON: No, you shall not, whatever they may say.
    It pleases me to vex them, and for spite
    I'd have them see you with her day and night.
    What's more, I'm going to drive them to despair   35
    By making you my only son and heir;
    This very day, I'll give to you alone
    Clear deed and title to everything I own.
    A dear, good friend and son-in-law-to-be
    Is more than wife, or child, or kin to me.   40
    Will you accept my offer, dearest son?
TARTUFFE: In all things, let the will of Heaven be done.
ORGON: Poor fellow! Come, we'll go draw up the deed.
    Then let them burst with disappointed greed!

ACT FOUR

SCENE I

CLÉANTE, TARTUFFE

CLÉANTE: Yes, all the town's discussing it, and truly,
    Their comments do not flatter you unduly.

I'm glad we've met, Sir, and I'll give my view
Of this sad matter in a word or two.
5 As for who's guilty, that I shan't discuss;
Let's say it was Damis who caused the fuss;
Assuming, then, that you have been ill-used
By young Damis, and groundlessly accused,
Ought not a Christian to forgive, and ought
10 He not to stifle every vengeful thought?
Should you stand by and watch a father make
His only son an exile for your sake?
Again I tell you frankly, be advised:
The whole town, high and low, is scandalized;
15 This quarrel must be mended, and my advice is
Not to push matters to a further crisis.
No, sacrifice your wrath to God above,
And help Damis regain his father's love.
TARTUFFE: Alas, for my part I should take great joy
20 In doing so. I've nothing against the boy.
I pardon all, I harbor no resentment;
To serve him would afford me much contentment.
But Heaven's interest will not have it so:
If he comes back, then I shall have to go.
25 After his conduct—so extreme, so vicious—
Our further intercourse would look suspicious.
God knows what people would think! Why, they'd describe
My goodness to him as a sort of bribe;
They'd say that out of guilt I made pretense
30 Of loving-kindness and benevolence—
That, fearing my accuser's tongue, I strove
To buy his silence with a show of love.
CLÉANTE: Your reasoning is badly warped and stretched,
And these excuses, Sir, are most far-fetched.
35 Why put yourself in charge of Heaven's cause?
Does Heaven need our help to enforce its laws?
Leave vengeance to the Lord, Sir; while we live,
Our duty's not to punish, but forgive;
And what the Lord commands, we should obey
40 Without regard to what the world may say.
What! Shall the fear of being misunderstood
Prevent our doing what is right and good?
No, no; let's simply do what Heaven ordains,
And let no other thoughts perplex our brains.
45 TARTUFFE: Again, Sir, let me say that I've forgiven
DAMIS, and thus obeyed the laws of Heaven;
But I am not commanded by the Bible
To live with one who smears my name with libel.
CLÉANTE: Were you commanded, Sir, to indulge the whim
50 Of poor Orgon, and to encourage him
In suddenly transferring to your name
A large estate to which you have no claim?
TARTUFFE: 'Twould never occur to those who know me best
To think I acted from self-interest.
55 The treasures of this world I quite despise;
Their specious glitter does not charm my eyes;
And if I have resigned myself to taking
The gift which my dear Brother insists on making,
I do so only, as he well understands,
60 Lest so much wealth fall into wicked hands,
Lest those to whom it might descend in time
Turn it to purposes of sin and crime,
And not, as I shall do, make use of it.
For Heaven's glory and mankind's benefit.

CLÉANTE: Forget these trumped-up fears. Your argument 65
Is one the rightful heir might well resent;
It is a moral burden to inherit
Such wealth, but give Damis a chance to bear it.
And would it not be worse to be accused
Of swindling, than to see that wealth misused? 70
I'm shocked that you allowed Orgon to broach
This matter, and that you feel no self-reproach;
Does true religion teach that lawful heirs
May freely be deprived of what is theirs?
And if the Lord has told you in your heart 75
That you and young Damis must dwell apart,
Would it not be the decent thing to beat
A generous and honorable retreat,
Rather than let the son of the house be sent,
For your convenience, into banishment? 80
Sir, if you wish to prove the honesty
Of your intentions . . .
TARTUFFE: Sir, it is half-past three.
I've certain pious duties to attend to,
And hope my prompt departure won't offend you.
CLÉANTE: (*Alone.*) Damn. 85

SCENE II

ELMIRE, MARIANE, CLÉANTE, DORINE

DORINE: Stay, Sir, and help Mariane, for Heaven's sake!
She's suffering so, I fear her heart will break.
Her father's plan to marry her off tonight
Has put the poor child in a desperate plight.
I hear him coming. Let's stand together, now, 5
And see if we can't change his mind, somehow,
About this match we all deplore and fear.

SCENE III

ORGON, ELMIRE, MARIANE, CLÉANTE, DORINE

ORGON: Hah! Glad to find you all assembled here.

(*To* MARIANE.)

This contract, child, contains your happiness,
And what it says I think your heart can guess.
MARIANE: (*Falling to her knees.*) Sir, by that Heaven which sees
me here distressed,
And by whatever else can move your breast, 5
Do not employ a father's power, I pray you,
To crush my heart and force it to obey you,
Nor by your harsh commands oppress me so
That I'll begrudge the duty which I owe—
And do not so embitter and enslave me 10
That I shall hate the very life you gave me.
If my sweet hopes must perish, if you refuse
To give me to the one I've dared to choose,
Spare me at least—I beg you, I implore—
The pain of wedding one whom I abhor; 15
And do not, by a heartless use of force,
Drive me to contemplate some desperate course.
ORGON: (*Feeling himself touched by her.*) Be firm, my soul.
No human weakness, now.

MARIANE: I don't resent your love for him. Allow
20   Your heart free rein, Sir; give him your property,
        And if that's not enough, take mine from me;
        He's welcome to my money; take it, do,
        But don't, I pray, include my person too.
        Spare me, I beg you; and let me end the tale
25   Of my sad days behind a convent veil.
    ORGON: A convent! Hah! When crossed in their amours,
        All lovesick girls have the same thought as yours.
        Get up! The more you loathe the man, and dread him,
        The more ennobling it will be to wed him.
30   Marry Tartuffe, and mortify your flesh!
        Enough; don't start that whimpering afresh.
    DORINE: But why. . . ?
    ORGON: Be still, there. Speak when you're
            spoken to.
        Not one more bit of impudence out of you.
    CLÉANTE: If I may offer a word of counsel here . . .
35 ORGON: Brother, in counseling you have no peer;
        All your advice is forceful, sound, and clever;
        I don't propose to follow it, however.
    ELMIRE: (To ORGON.) I am amazed, and don't know what to say;
        Your blindness simply takes my breath away.
40   You are indeed bewitched, to take no warning
        From our account of what occurred this morning.
    ORGON: Madam, I know a few plain facts, and one
        Is that you're partial to my rascal son;
        Hence, when he sought to make Tartuffe the victim
45   Of a base lie, you dared not contradict him.
        Ah, but you underplayed your part, my pet;
        You should have looked more angry, more upset.
    ELMIRE: When men make overtures, must we reply
        With righteous anger and a battle-cry?
50   Must we turn back their amorous advances
        With sharp reproaches and with fiery glances?
        Myself, I find such offers merely amusing,
        And make no scenes and fusses in refusing;
        My taste is for good-natured rectitude,
55   And I dislike the savage sort of prude
        Who guards her virtue with her teeth and claws,
        And tears men's eyes out for the slightest cause;
        The Lord preserve me from such honor as that,
        Which bites and scratches like an alley-cat!
60   I've found that a polite and cool rebuff
        Discourages a lover quite enough.
    ORGON: I know the facts, and I shall not be shaken.
    ELMIRE: I marvel at your power to be mistaken.
        Would it, I wonder, carry weight with you
65   If I could *show* you that our tale was true?
    ORGON: Show me?
    ELMIRE: Yes.
    ORGON: Rot.
    ELMIRE: Come, what if I found a way
        To make you see the facts as plain as day?
    ORGON: Nonsense.
    ELMIRE: Do answer me; don't be absurd.
        I'm not now asking you to trust our word.
70   Suppose that from some hiding-place in here
        You learned the whole sad truth by eye and ear—
        What would you say of your good friend, after that?
    ORGON: Why, I'd say . . . nothing, by Jehoshaphat!
        It can't be true.

ELMIRE: You've been too long deceived,
        And I'm quite tired of being disbelieved.   75
        Come now: let's put my statements to the test,
        And you shall see the truth made manifest.
    ORGON: I'll take that challenge. Now do your uttermost.
        We'll see how you make good your empty boast.
    ELMIRE: (To DORINE.)
        Send him to me.   80
    DORINE: He's crafty; it may be hard
        To catch the cunning scoundrel off his guard.
    ELMIRE: No, amorous men are gullible. Their conceit
        So blinds them that they're never hard to cheat.
        Have him come down. (To CLÉANTE and MARIANE.)
            Please leave us, for a bit.

SCENE IV

ELMIRE, ORGON

ELMIRE: Pull up this table, and get under it.
    ORGON: What?
    ELMIRE: It's essential that you be well-hidden.
    ORGON: Why there?
    ELMIRE: Oh, Heavens! Just do as you are bidden
        I have my plans; we'll soon see how they fare.
        Under the table, now; and once you're there,   5
        Take care that you are neither seen nor heard.
    ORGON: Well, I'll indulge you, since I gave my word
        To see you through this infantile charade.
    ELMIRE: Once it is over, you'll be glad we played.

(*To her husband, who is now under the table.*)

        I'm going to act quite strangely, now, and you   10
        Must not be shocked at anything I do.
        Whatever I may say, you must excuse
        As part of that deceit I'm forced to use.
        I shall employ sweet speeches in the task
        Of making that impostor drop his mask;   15
        I'll give encouragement to his bold desires,
        And furnish fuel to his amorous fires.
        Since it's for your sake, and for his destruction,
        That I shall seem to yield to his seduction,
        I'll gladly stop whenever you decide   20
        That all your doubts are fully satisfied.
        I'll count on you, as soon as you have seen
        What sort of man he is, to intervene,
        And not expose me to his odious lust
        One moment longer than you feel you must.   25
        Remember: you're to save me from my plight
        Whenever . . . He's coming! Hush! Keep out of sight!

SCENE V

TARTUFFE, ELMIRE, ORGON

TARTUFFE: You wish to have a word with me, I'm told.
    ELMIRE: Yes. I've a little secret to unfold.
        Before I speak, however, it would be wise
        To close that door, and look about for spies.

(TARTUFFE *goes to the door, closes it, and returns.*)

5   The very last thing that must happen now
       Is a repetition of this morning's row.
       I've never been so badly caught off guard.
       Oh, how I feared for you! You saw how hard
       I tried to make that troublesome Damis
10   Control his dreadful temper, and hold his peace.
       In my confusion, I didn't have the sense
       Simply to contradict his evidence;
       But as it happened, that was for the best,
       And all has worked out in our interest.
15   This storm has only bettered your position;
       My husband doesn't have the least suspicion,
       And now, in mockery of those who do,
       He bids me be continually with you.
       And that is why, quite fearless of reproof,
20   I now can be alone with my Tartuffe,
       And why my heart—perhaps too quick to yield—
       Feels free to let its passion be revealed.
     TARTUFFE: Madam, your words confuse me. Not long ago,
       You spoke in quite a different style, you know.
25 ELMIRE: Ah, Sir, if that refusal made you smart,
       It's little that you know of woman's heart,
       Or what that heart is trying to convey
       When it resists in such a feeble way!
       Always, at first, our modesty prevents
30   The frank avowal of tender sentiments;
       However high the passion which inflames us,
       Still, to confess its power somehow shames us.
       Thus we reluct, at first, yet in a tone
       Which tells you that our heart is overthrown,
35   That what our lips deny, our pulse confesses,
       And that, in time, all noes will turn to yesses.
       I fear my words are all too frank and free,
       And a poor proof of woman's modesty;
       But since I'm started, tell me, if you will—
40   Would I have tried to make Damis be still,
       Would I have listened, calm and unoffended,
       Until your lengthy offer of love was ended,
       And been so very mild in my reaction,
       Had your sweet words not given me satisfaction?
45   And when I tried to force you to undo
       The marriage-plans my husband has in view,
       What did my urgent pleading signify
       If not that I admired you, and that I
       Deplored the thought that someone else might own
50   Part of a heart I wished for mine alone?
     TARTUFFE: Madam, no happiness is so complete
       As when, from lips we love, come words so sweet;
       Their nectar floods my every sense, and drains
       In honeyed rivulets through all my veins.
55   To please you is my joy, my only goal;
       Your love is the restorer of my soul;
       And yet I must beg leave, now, to confess
       Some lingering doubts as to my happiness
       Might this not be a trick? Might not the catch
60   Be that you wish me to break off the match
       With Mariane, and so have feigned to love me?
       I shan't quite trust your fond opinion of me
       Until the feelings you've expressed so sweetly
       Are demonstrated somewhat more concretely,
65   And you have shown, by certain kind concessions,
       That I may put my faith in your professions.

ELMIRE:

(She coughs, to warn her husband.)

       Why be in such a hurry? Must my heart
       Exhaust its bounty at the very start?
       To make that sweet admission cost me dear,
       But you'll not be content, it would appear,   70
       Unless my store of favors is disbursed
       To the last farthing, and at the very first.
     TARTUFFE: The less we merit, the less we dare to hope,
       And with our doubts, mere words can never cope.
       We trust no promised bliss till we receive it;   75
       Not till a joy is ours can we believe it.
       I, who so little merit your esteem,
       Can't credit this fulfillment of my dream,
       And shan't believe it, Madam, until I savor
       Some palpable assurance of your favor.   80
     ELMIRE: My, how tyrannical your love can be,
       And how it flusters and perplexes me!
       How furiously you take one's heart in hand,
       And make your every wish a fierce command!
       Come, must you hound and harry me to death?   85
       Will you not give me time to catch my breath?
       Can it be right to press me with such force,
       Give me no quarter, show me no remorse,
       And take advantage, by your stern insistence,
       Of the fond feelings which weaken my resistance?   90
     TARTUFFE: Well, if you look with favor upon my love,
       Why, then, begrudge me some clear proof thereof?
     ELMIRE: But how can I consent without offense
       To Heaven, toward which you feel such reverence?
     TARTUFFE: If Heaven is all that holds you back, don't worry.   95
       I can remove that hindrance in a hurry.
       Nothing of that sort need obstruct our path.
     ELMIRE: Must one not be afraid of Heaven's wrath?
     TARTUFFE: Madam, forget such fears, and be my pupil,
       And I shall teach you how to conquer scruple.   100
       Some joys, it's true, are wrong in Heaven's eyes;
       Yet Heaven is not averse to compromise;
       There is a science, lately formulated,
       Whereby one's conscience may be liberated,
       And any wrongful act you care to mention   105
       May be redeemed by purity of intention.
       I'll teach you, Madam, the secrets of that science;
       Meanwhile, just place on me your full reliance.
       Assuage my keen desires, and feel no dread:
       The sin, if any, shall be on my head.   110

(ELMIRE coughs, this time more loudly.)

       You've a bad cough.
     ELMIRE: Yes, yes. It's bad indeed.
     TARTUFFE: *(Producing a little paper bag.)* A bit of licorice may be
       what you need.
     ELMIRE: No, I've a stubborn cold, it seems. I'm sure it
       Will take much more than licorice to cure it.
     TARTUFFE: How aggravating.   115
     ELMIRE: Oh, more than I can say.
     TARTUFFE: If you're still troubled, think of things this way:
       No one shall know our joys, save us alone,
       And there's no evil till the act is known;

It's scandal, Madam, which makes it an offense,
120   And it's no sin to sin in confidence.
ELMIRE: (*Having coughed once more.*) Well, clearly I must do as
          you require,
      And yield to your importunate desire.
      It is apparent, now, that nothing less
      Will satisfy you, and so I acquiesce.
125   To go so far is much against my will;
      I'm vexed that it should come to this; but still,
      Since you are so determined on it, since you
      Will not allow mere language to convince you,
      And since you ask for concrete evidence, I
130   See nothing for it, now, but to comply.
      If this is sinful, if I'm wrong to do it,
      So much the worse for him who drove me to it.
      The fault can surely not be charged to me.
TARTUFFE: Madam, the fault is mine, if fault there be,
135   And . . .
ELMIRE: Open the door a little, and peek out;
      I wouldn't want my husband poking about.
TARTUFFE: Why worry about the man? Each day he grows
      More gullible; one can lead him by the nose.
      To find us here would fill him with delight,
140   And if he saw the worst, he'd doubt his sight.
ELMIRE: Nevertheless, do step out for a minute
      Into the hall, and see that no one's in it.

SCENE VI

ORGON, ELMIRE

ORGON: (*Coming out from under the table.*) That man's a perfect
          monster, I must admit!
      I'm simply stunned. I can't get over it.
ELMIRE: What, coming out so soon? How premature!
      Get back in hiding, and wait until you're sure.
5   Stay till the end, and be convinced completely;
      We mustn't stop till things are proved concretely.
ORGON: Hell never harbored anything so vicious!
ELMIRE: Tut, don't be hasty. Try to be judicious.
      Wait, and be certain that there's no mistake.
10   No jumping to conclusions, for Heaven's sake!

(*She places* ORGON *behind her, as* TARTUFFE *re-enters.*)

SCENE VII

TARTUFFE, ELMIRE, ORGON

TARTUFFE: (*Not seeing* ORGON.) Madam, all things have
          worked out to perfection;
      I've given the neighboring rooms a full inspection;
      No one's about; and now I may at last . . .
ORGON: (*Intercepting him.*) Hold on, my passionate fellow,
          not so fast!
5   I should advise a little more restraint.
      Well, so you thought you'd fool me, my dear saint!
      How soon you wearied of the saintly life—
      Wedding my daughter, and coveting my wife!
      I've long suspected you, and had a feeling
10   That soon I'd catch you at your double-dealing.
      Just now, you've given me evidence galore;

It's quite enough; I have no wish for more.
ELMIRE: (*To* TARTUFFE.) I'm sorry to have treated you so slyly.
      But circumstances forced me to be wily.
TARTUFFE: Brother, you can't think . . .   15
ORGON: No more talk from you;
      Just leave this household, without more ado.
TARTUFFE: What I intended . . .
ORGON: That seems fairly clear.
      Spare me your falsehoods and get out of here.
TARTUFFE: No, I'm the master, and you're the one to go!
      This house belongs to me, I'll have you know,   20
      And I shall show you that you can't hurt *me*
      By this contemptible conspiracy,
      That those who cross me know not what they do,
      And that I've means to expose and punish you,
      Avenge offended Heaven, and make you grieve   25
      That ever you dared order me to leave.

SCENE VIII

ELMIRE, ORGON

ELMIRE: What was the point of all that angry chatter?
ORGON: Dear God, I'm worried. This is no laughing matter.
ELMIRE: How so?
ORGON: I fear I understood his drift.
      I'm much disturbed about that deed of gift.
ELMIRE: You gave him . . . ?   5
ORGON: Yes, it's all been drawn and signed.
      But one thing more is weighing on my mind.
ELMIRE: What's that?
ORGON: I'll tell you; but first let's see if there's
      A certain strong-box in his room upstairs.

ACT FIVE

SCENE I

ORGON, CLÉANTE

CLÉANTE: Where are you going so fast?
ORGON: God knows!
CLÉANTE: Then wait;
      Let's have a conference, and deliberate
      On how this situation's to be met.
ORGON: That strong-box has me utterly upset;
      This is the worst of many, many shocks.   5
CLÉANTE: Is there some fearful mystery in that box?
ORGON: My poor friend Argas brought that box to me
      With his own hands, in utmost secrecy;
      'Twas on the very morning of his flight.
      It's full of papers which, if they came to light,   10
      Would ruin him—or such is my impression.
CLÉANTE: Then why did you let it out of your possession?
ORGON: Those papers vexed my conscience, and it seemed best
      To ask the counsel of my pious guest.
      The cunning scoundrel got me to agree   15
      To leave the strong-box in his custody,
      So that, in case of an investigation,
      I could employ a slight equivocation
      And swear I didn't have it, and thereby,
      At no expense to conscience, tell a lie.   20

CLÉANTE: It looks to me as if you're out on a limb.
    Trusting him with that box, and offering him
    That deed of gift, were actions of a kind
    Which scarcely indicate a prudent mind.
25   With two such weapons, he has the upper hand,
    And since you're vulnerable, as matters stand,
    You erred once more in bringing him to bay.
    You should have acted in some subtler way.
ORGON: Just think of it: behind that fervent face,
30   A heart so wicked, and a soul so base!
    I took him in, a hungry beggar, and then . . .
    Enough, by God! I'm through with pious men:
    Henceforth I'll hate the whole false brotherhood.
    And persecute them worse than Satan could.
35 CLÉANTE: Ah, there you go—extravagant as ever.
    Why can you not be rational? You never
    Manage to take the middle course, it seems,
    But jump, instead, between absurd extremes
    You've recognized your recent grave mistake
40   In falling victim to a pious fake;
    Now, to correct that error, must you embrace
    An even greater error in its place,
    And judge our worthy neighbors as a whole
    By what you've learned of one corrupted soul?
45   Come, just because one rascal made you swallow
    A show of zeal which turned out to be hollow,
    Shall you conclude that all men are deceivers,
    And that, today, there are no true believers?
    Let atheists make that foolish inference;
50   Learn to distinguish virtue from pretense,
    Be cautious in bestowing admiration,
    And cultivate a sober moderation.
    Don't humor fraud, but also don't asperse
    True piety; the latter fault is worse,
55   And it is best to err, if err one must,
    As you have done, upon the side of trust.

SCENE II

DAMIS, ORGON, CLÉANTE

DAMIS: Father, I hear that scoundrel's uttered threats
    Against you; that he pridefully forgets
    How, in his need, he was befriended by you,
    And means to use your gifts to crucify you.
5 ORGON: It's true, my boy. I'm too distressed for tears.
DAMIS: Leave it to me, Sir; let me trim his ears.
    Faced with such insolence, we must not waver.
    I shall rejoice in doing you the favor
    Of cutting short his life, and your distress.
10 CLÉANTE: What a display of young hotheadedness!
    Do learn to moderate your fits of rage.
    In this just kingdom, this enlightened age,
    One does not settle things by violence.

SCENE III

MADAME PERNELLE, MARIANE, ELMIRE, DORINE, DAMIS, ORGON,
CLÉANTE

MADAME PERNELLE: I hear strange tales of very strange events.
ORGON: Yes, strange events which these two eyes beheld.

The man's ingratitude is unparalleled.
I save a wretched pauper from starvation.
House him, and treat him like a blood relation,   5
Shower him every day with my largesse,
Give him my daughter, and all that I possess;
And meanwhile the unconscionable knave
Tries to induce my wife to misbehave;
And not content with such extreme rascality,   10
Now threatens me with my own liberality,
And aims, by taking base advantage of
The gifts I gave him out of Christian love,
To drive me from my house, a ruined man,
And make me end a pauper, as he began.   15
DORINE: Poor fellow!
MADAME PERNELLE: No, my son, I'll never bring
    Myself to think him guilty of such a thing.
ORGON: How's that?
MADAME PERNELLE: The righteous always were maligned.
ORGON: Speak clearly, Mother. Say what's on your mind.
MADAME PERNELLE: I mean that I can smell a rat, my dear.   20
    You know how everybody hates him, here.
ORGON: That has no bearing on the case at all.
MADAME PERNELLE: I told you a hundred times, when you
      were small,
    That virtue in this world is hated ever;
    Malicious men may die, but malice never.   25
ORGON: No doubt that's true, but how does it apply?
MADAME PERNELLE: They've turned you against him by a
      clever lie.
ORGON: I've told you, I was there and saw it done.
MADAME PERNELLE: Ah, slanderers will stop at nothing, Son.
ORGON: Mother, I'll lose my temper . . . For the last time,   30
    I tell you I was witness to the crime.
MADAME PERNELLE: The tongues of spite are busy night and noon
    And to their venom no man is immune.
ORGON: You're talking nonsense. Can't you realize
    I saw it; saw it; saw it with my eyes?   35
    Saw, do you understand me? Must I shout it
    Into your ears before you'll cease to doubt it?
MADAME PERNELLE: Appearances can deceive, my son.
      Dear me,
    We cannot always judge by what we see.
ORGON: Drat! Drat!   40
MADAME PERNELLE: One often interprets things awry;
    Good can seem evil to a suspicious eye.
ORGON: Was I to see his pawing at Elmire
    As an act of charity?
MADAME PERNELLE: Till his guilt is clear,
    A man deserves the benefit of the doubt.
    You should have waited, to see how things turned out.   45
ORGON: Great God in Heaven, what more proof did I need?
    Was I to sit there, watching, until he'd . . .
    You drive me to the brink of impropriety.
MADAME PERNELLE: No, no, a man of such surpassing piety
    Could not do such a thing. You cannot shake me.   50
    I don't believe it, and you shall not make me.
ORGON: You vex me so that, if you weren't my mother,
    I'd say to you . . . some dreadful thing or other.
DORINE: It's your turn now, Sir, not to be listened to;
    You'd not trust us, and now she won't trust you.   55
CLÉANTE: My friends, we're wasting time which should be spent
    In facing up to our predicament.

I fear that scoundrel's threats weren't made in sport.
DAMIS: Do you think he'd have the nerve to go to court?
60 ELMIRE: I'm sure he won't: they'd find it all too crude
A case of swindling and ingratitude.
CLÉANTE: Don't be too sure. He won't be at a loss
To give his claims a high and righteous gloss;
And clever rogues with far less valid cause
65 Have trapped their victims in a web of laws.
I say again that to antagonize
A man so strongly armed was most unwise.
ORGON: I know it; but the man's appalling cheek
Outraged me so, I couldn't control my pique.
70 CLÉANTE: I wish to Heaven that we could devise
Some truce between you, or some compromise.
ELMIRE: If I had known what cards he held, I'd not
Have roused his anger by my little plot.
ORGON: (*To* DORINE, *as* M. LOYAL *enters.*) What is that fellow
looking for? Who is he?
75 Go talk to him—and tell him that I'm busy.

SCENE IV

MONSIEUR LOYAL, MADAME PERNELLE, ORGON, DAMIS, MARIANE,
DORINE, ELMIRE, CLÉANTE

MONSIEUR LOYAL: Good day, dear sister. Kindly let me see
Your master.
DORINE: He's involved with company,
And cannot be disturbed just now, I fear.
MONSIEUR LOYAL: I hate to intrude; but what has brought me here
5   Will not disturb your master, in any event.
Indeed, my news will make him most content.
DORINE: Your name?
MONSIEUR LOYAL: Just say that I bring greetings from
Monsieur Tartuffe, on whose behalf I've come.
DORINE: (*To* ORGON.) Sir, he's a very gracious man, and bears
10   A message from Tartuffe, which, he declares,
Will make you most content.
CLÉANTE: Upon my word,
I think this man had best be seen, and heard.
ORGON: Perhaps he has some settlement to suggest.
How shall I treat him? What manner would be best?
15 CLÉANTE: Control your anger, and if he should mention
Some fair adjustment, give him your full attention.
MONSIEUR LOYAL: Good health to you, good Sir. May
Heaven confound
Your enemies, and may your joys abound.
ORGON: (*Aside, to* CLÉANTE.) A gentle salutation: it confirms
20   My guess that he is here to offer terms.
MONSIEUR LOYAL: I've always held your family most dear;
I served your father, Sir, for many a year.
ORGON: Sir, I must ask your pardon; to my shame,
I cannot now recall your face or name.
25 MONSIEUR LOYAL: Loyal's my name; I come from Normandy,
And I'm a bailiff, in all modesty.
For forty years, praise God, it's been my boast
To serve with honor in that vital post,
And I am here, Sir, if you will permit
30   The liberty, to serve you with this writ . . .
ORGON: To—*what?*
MONSIEUR LOYAL: Now, please, Sir, let us have no friction:
It's nothing but an order of eviction.

You are to move your goods and family out
And make way for new occupants, without
Deferment or delay, and give the keys . . .   35
ORGON: I? Leave this house?
MONSIEUR LOYAL: Why yes, Sir, if you please.
This house, Sir, from the cellar to the roof,
Belongs now to the good Monsieur Tartuffe,
And he is lord and master of your estate
By virtue of a deed of present date,   40
Drawn in due form, with clearest legal phrasing . . .
DAMIS: Your insolence is utterly amazing!
MONSIEUR LOYAL: Young man, my business here is not with you,
But with your wise and temperate father, who,
Like every worthy citizen, stands in awe   45
Of justice, and would never obstruct the law.
ORGON: But . . .
MONSIEUR LOYAL: Not for a million, Sir, would you rebel
Against authority; I know that well.
You'll not make trouble, Sir, or interfere
With the execution of my duties here.   50
DAMIS: Someone may execute a smart tattoo
On that black jacket of yours, before you're through.
MONSIEUR LOYAL: Sir, bid your son be silent. I'd much regret
Having to mention such a nasty threat
Of violence, in writing my report.   55
DORINE: (*Aside.*) This man Loyal's a most disloyal sort!
MONSIEUR LOYAL: I love all men of upright character,
And when I agreed to serve these papers, Sir,
It was your feelings that I had in mind.
I couldn't bear to see the case assigned   60
To someone else, who might esteem you less
And so subject you to unpleasantness.
ORGON: What's more unpleasant than telling a man to leave
His house and home?
MONSIEUR LOYAL: You'd like a short reprieve?
If you desire, Sir, I shall not press you,   65
But wait until tomorrow to dispossess you.
Splendid. I'll come and spend the night here, then,
Most quietly, with half a score of men.
For form's sake, you might bring me, just before
You go to bed, the keys to the front door.   70
My men, I promise, will be on their best
Behavior, and will not disturb your rest.
But bright and early, Sir, you must be quick
And move out all your furniture, every stick;
The men I've chosen are both young and strong,   75
And with their help it shouldn't take you long.
In short, I'll make things pleasant and convenient,
And since I'm being so extremely lenient,
Please show me, Sir, a like consideration,
And give me your entire cooperation.   80
ORGON: (*Aside.*) I may be all but bankrupt, but I vow
I'd give a hundred louis, here and now,
Just for the pleasure of landing one good clout
Right on the end of that complacent snout.
CLÉANTE: Careful; don't make things worse.   85
DAMIS: My bootsole itches
To give that beggar a good kick in the breeches.
DORINE: Monsieur Loyal, I'd love to hear the whack
Of a stout stick across your fine broad back.
MONSIEUR LOYAL: Take care: a woman too may go to jail if
She uses threatening language to a bailiff.   90

CLÉANTE: Enough, enough, Sir. This must not go on.
    Give me that paper, please, and then begone.
MONSIEUR LOYAL: Well, *au revoir*. God give you all good cheer!
ORGON: May God confound you, and him who sent you here!

SCENE V

ORGON, CLÉANTE, MARIANE, ELMIRE, MADAME PERNELLE, DORINE, DAMIS

ORGON: Now, Mother, was I right or not? This writ
    Should change your notion of Tartuffe a bit.
    Do you perceive his villainy at last?
MADAME PERNELLE: I'm thunderstruck. I'm utterly aghast.
5 DORINE: Oh, come, be fair. You mustn't take offense
    At this new proof of his benevolence.
    He's acting out of selfless love, I know.
    Material things enslave the soul, and so
    He kindly has arranged your liberation
10   From all that might endanger your salvation.
ORGON: Will you not ever hold your tongue, you dunce?
CLÉANTE: Come, you must take some action, and at once.
ELMIRE: Go tell the world of the low trick he's tried.
    The deed of gift is surely nullified
15   By such behavior, and public rage will not
    Permit the wretch to carry out his plot.

SCENE VI

VALÈRE, ORGON, CLÉANTE, ELMIRE, MARIANE, MADAME PERNELLE, DAMIS, DORINE

VALÈRE: Sir, though I hate to bring you more bad news,
    Such is the danger that I cannot choose.
    A friend who is extremely close to me
    And knows my interest in your family
5   Has, for my sake, presumed to violate
    The secrecy that's due to things of state,
    And sends me word that you are in a plight
    From which your one salvation lies in flight.
    That scoundrel who's imposed upon you so
10   Denounced you to the King an hour ago
    And, as supporting evidence, displayed
    The strong-box of a certain renegade
    Whose secret papers, so he testified,
    You had disloyally agreed to hide.
15   I don't know just what charges may be pressed,
    But there's a warrant out for your arrest;
    Tartuffe has been instructed, furthermore,
    To guide the arresting officer to your door.
CLÉANTE: He's clearly done this to facilitate
20   His seizure of your house and your estate.
ORGON: That man, I must say, is a vicious beast!
VALÈRE: Quick, Sir; you mustn't tarry in the least.
    My carriage is outside, to take you hence;
    This thousand louis should cover all expense.
25   Let's lose no time, or you shall be undone;
    The sole defense, in this case, is to run.
    I shall go with you all the way, and place you
    In a safe refuge to which they'll never trace you.
ORGON: Alas, dear boy, I wish that I could show you
30   My gratitude for everything I owe you.

    But now is not the time; I pray the Lord
    That I may live to give you your reward.
    Farewell, my dears; be careful . . .
CLÉANTE: Brother, hurry.
    We shall take care of things; you needn't worry.

SCENE VII

The OFFICER, TARTUFFE, VALÈRE, ORGON, ELMIRE, MARIANE, MADAME PERNELLE, DORINE, CLÉANTE, DAMIS

TARTUFFE: Gently, Sir, gently; stay right where you are.
    No need for haste; your lodging isn't far.
    You're off to prison, by order of the Prince.
ORGON: This is the crowning blow, you wretch; and since
    It means my total ruin and defeat,   5
    Your villainy is now at last complete.
TARTUFFE: You needn't try to provoke me; it's no use.
    Those who serve Heaven must expect abuse.
CLÉANTE: You are indeed most patient, sweet, and blameless.
DORINE: How he exploits the name of Heaven! It's shameless.   10
TARTUFFE: Your taunts and mockeries are all for naught;
    To do my duty is my only thought.
MARIANE: Your love of duty is more meritorious,
    And what you've done is little short of glorious.
TARTUFFE: All deeds are glorious, Madam, which obey   15
    The sovereign prince who sent me here today.
ORGON: I rescued you when you were destitute,
    Have you forgotten that, you thankless brute?
TARTUFFE: No, no, I well remember everything;
    But my first duty is to serve my King.   20
    That obligation is so paramount
    That other claims, beside it, do not count;
    And for it I would sacrifice my wife,
    My family, my friend, or my own life.
ELMIRE: Hypocrite!   25
DORINE: All that we most revere, he uses
    To cloak his plots and camouflage his ruses.
CLÉANTE: If it is true that you are animated
    By pure and loyal zeal, as you have stated,
    Why was this zeal not roused until you'd sought
    To make Orgon a cuckold, and been caught?   30
    Why weren't you moved to give your evidence
    Until your outraged host had driven you hence?
    I shan't say that the gift of all his treasure
    Ought to have damped your zeal in any measure;
    But if he is a traitor, as you declare,   35
    How could you condescend to be his heir?
TARTUFFE: (*To the* OFFICER.) Sir, spare me all this clamor; it's
        growing shrill.
    Please carry out your orders, if you will.
OFFICER: Yes, I've delayed too long, Sir. Thank you kindly.
    You're just the proper person to remind me.   40
    Come, you are off to join the other boarders
    In the King's prison, according to his orders.
TARTUFFE: Who? I, Sir?
OFFICER: Yes.
TARTUFFE: To prison? This can't be true!
OFFICER: I owe an explanation, but not to you.

(*To* ORGON.)

45 Sir, all is well; rest easy, and be grateful.
    We serve a Prince to whom all sham is hateful,
    A Prince who sees into our inmost hearts,
    And can't be fooled by any trickster's arts.
    His royal soul, though generous and human,
50 Views all things with discernment and acumen;
    His sovereign reason is not lightly swayed,
    And all his judgments are discreetly weighed.
    He honors righteous men of every kind,
    And yet his zeal for virtue is not blind,
55 Nor does his love of piety numb his wits
    And make him tolerant of hypocrites.
    'Twas hardly likely that this man could cozen
    A King who's foiled such liars by the dozen.
    With one keen glance, the King perceived the whole
60 Perverseness and corruption of his soul,
    And thus high Heaven's justice was displayed:
    Betraying you, the rogue stood self-betrayed.
    The King soon recognized Tartuffe as one
    Notorious by another name, who'd done
65 So many vicious crimes that one could fill
    Ten volumes with them, and be writing still.
    But to be brief: our sovereign was appalled
    By this man's treachery toward you, which he called
    The last, worst villainy of a vile career,
70 And bade me follow the impostor here
    To see how gross his impudence could be,
    And force him to restore your property.
    Your private papers, by the King's command,
    I hereby seize and give into your hand.
75 The King, by royal order, invalidates

The deed which gave this rascal your estates,
And pardons, furthermore, your grave offense
In harboring an exile's documents.
By these decrees, our Prince rewards you for
Your loyal deeds in the late civil war,   80
And shows how heartfelt is his satisfaction
In recompensing any worthy action,
How much he prizes merit, and how he makes
More of men's virtues than of their mistakes.

DORINE: Heaven be praised!   85

MADAME PERNELLE: I breathe again, at last.

ELMIRE: We're safe.

MARIANE: I can't believe the danger's past.

ORGON: (*To* TARTUFFE.)
    Well, traitor, now you see . . .

CLÉANTE: Ah, Brother, please,
    Let's not descend to such indignities.
    Leave the poor wretch to his unhappy fate,
    And don't say anything to aggravate   90
    His present woes; but rather hope that he
    Will soon embrace an honest piety,
    And mend his ways, and by a true repentance
    Move our just King to moderate his sentence.
    Meanwhile, go kneel before your sovereign's throne   95
    And thank him for the mercies he has shown.

ORGON: Well said: let's go at once and, gladly kneeling,
    Express the gratitude which all are feeling.
    Then, when that first great duty has been done,
    We'll turn with pleasure to a second one,   100
    And give Valère, whose love has proven so true,
    The wedded happiness which is his due.

Aphra Behn

L ittle is known about the early life of England's first female professional playwright, Aphra Behn (1640–1689), who may have been born Eaffrey Johnson in Kent. She left England just after the restoration of Charles II for the South American colony of Surinam, where she lived from 1663 to 1664. Again, many of the details about her life there are unknown, though Surinam provided the setting for her great novel, *Oronooko: or, The Royal Slave,* published in 1688. Returning to England, she appears to have married someone named Behn; in *The Passionate Shepherdess: Aphra Behn 1640–89* (London: Jonathan Cape, 1977; p. 48), Maureen Duffy accounts for several possible candidates, but also suggests that Aphra Behn's marriage may have been a legitimating fiction: "Mr. Behn, her putative husband, has less substance than any character she invented." By the mid-1660s, however, Aphra Behn was serving Charles II as a spy in Antwerp and seems to have been caught up in the politics surrounding the Dutch invasion of Surinam. When she returned to England penniless in 1667, she was sent to debtors' prison and appealed to the government for her wages. Between 1670 and her death in 1689, however, Behn emerged as a famous and influential writer; in addition to her novel *Orinooko,* Behn had a successful career as a poet and celebrated playwright. She wrote fifteen plays, beginning with *The Forced Marriage: or, The Jealous Bridegroom* (1668), a tragicomedy produced by Thomas Betterton at Lincoln's Inn Fields. Behn's major plays are mainly in the mode of Restoration comedy and were successful both in their day and well into the eighteenth century: her best-known plays today are *The Rover* (1677), *The Feigned Courtesans* (1679), which was dedicated to her friend and supporter (and the King's mistress), the actress Nell Gwynn, *The Second Part of The Rover* (1681), and *The City Heiress* (1682). Her novel *Oronooko* was dramatized by Thomas Southerne in 1695 and was popular on stage throughout the eighteenth century. Aphra Behn was part of the elite milieu of intellectual culture of her day, the friend of courtiers such as Buckingham and Rochester, and of writers like Otway and Dryden. Although her work was, in a sense, recovered for modern readers by Virginia Woolf's famous essay *A Room of One's Own,* Behn's plays have been increasingly popular and successful in the theater. Aphra Behn is buried in Westminster Abbey.

The Rover

The Rover is a comedy of intrigue, set in Naples during the Carnival. The play concerns the sexual adventures of a band of Englishmen—Belvile, Willmore (the Rover), and Blunt—and their efforts to seduce the heroine Florinda and her sister Hellena. As in many Restoration comedies, *The Rover* takes a frank attitude toward sexual and financial negotiations, which are often paired in the play. The play opens with Hellena's rejection of a life in the convent and her decision to "provide my self this Carnival, if there be e'er a handsome proper fellow." In the course of the play, Hellena flirts with Willmore; Willmore wins the services (and, unfortunately, the love) of the courtesan Angelica, who eventually tries to murder him; Willmore and Blunt nearly rape Florinda on several occasions; and Blunt is tricked by a prostitute and turned out into the street in his shirt and underwear, "before consummation."

Yet despite the licentiousness of its action, the play clearly depends on a deeply ingrained sense of propriety, much of which operates through class distinctions. While it "would anger us vilely to be trussed up for a rape upon a maid of quality," one of the gentlemen declares, it seems otherwise acceptable to "ruffle a harlot." Morality, in *The Rover,* is in many ways determined by class and wealth. These distinctions are both troubled and confirmed by the important function of disguise and masking in the play. Since the action of *The Rover* takes place during Carnival, the main characters meet only in disguise. Masking enables the characters both to flirt without dishonoring themselves and to discover the truth about one another. In fact, masking in the play empowers the women, in that the temporary masking of the Carnival allows the women to escape their enforced lives at home and to meet men

© Williamstown Festival production featuring Edward Herman, Harry Groener, Christopher Reeve, and Stephen Collins (Photo: Nina Krieger)

The Williamstown Theatre Festival production of *The Rover,* featuring Edward Hermann, Harry Groener, Christopher Reeve, and Stephen Collins.

in public. Florinda and Hellena, for instance, can marry only with their brother Pedro's permission. He wants to marry his sisters to the wealthiest— and oldest—suitors, who will be able to settle large fortunes on them. However, the young Englishmen who attract the two sisters are Royalist supporters of Charles II, currently exiled from Cromwell's Protectorate because they support the Crown. As a result, although they are well-born, they are currently without funds and so are a poor match for Florinda and Hellena, at least in Pedro's eyes.

Masking also enables the women to escape Pedro's control, to act on their own behalf. Indeed, although the women are more modest than the Rover, they are equally devious in their pursuit of a lover—though the women insist on marriage as the price of their virginity. In Behn's brilliant comedy, the women emerge as the agents—as well as the objects—of the play's erotic intrigue.

In recent years, *The Rover* has received a number of excellent stage productions—at Minneapolis's Guthrie Theater, the Royal Shakespeare Company, and on many university campuses.

The Rover

OR THE BANISH'D CAVALIERS

Aphra Behn

EDITED BY MONTAGUE SUMMERS

CHARACTERS

Don ANTONIO, *the Vice-
Roy's Son*
Don PEDRO, *a Noble
Spaniard, his Friend*
BELVILE, *an English Colonel
in love with Florinda*
WILLMORE, *the Rover*
FREDERICK, *an English
Gentleman, and Friend
to Belvile and Blunt*
BLUNT, *an English Country
Gentleman*

STEPHANO, *Servant to Don Pedro*
PHILIPPO, *Lucetta's Gallant*
SANCHO, *Pimp to Lucetta*
BISKEY *and* SEBASTIAN, *two
Bravoes to Angelica*
DIEGO, *Page to Don Antonio*
PAGE *to Hellena*
BOY, *Page to Belvile*
Blunt's MAN
OFFICERS *and* SOLDIERS
FLORINDA, *Sister to Don Pedro*

HELLENA, *a gay young Woman design'd for a Nun,
and Sister to Florinda*
VALERIA, *a Kinswoman to Florinda*
ANGELICA BIANCA, *a famous Curtezan*
MORETTA, *her Woman*
CALLIS, *Governess to Florinda and Hellena*
LUCETTA, *a jilting Wench*
SERVANTS, *other* MASQUERADERS, MEN *and* WOMEN

SCENE: *Naples, in Carnival-time.*

PROLOGUE

WRITTEN BY A PERSON OF QUALITY

WITS, like Physicians, never can agree,
When of a different Society;
And Rabel's Drops were never more cry'd down
By all the Learned Doctors of the Town,
5   Than a new Play, whose Author is unknown:
Nor can those Doctors with more Malice sue
(And powerful Purses) the dissenting Few,
Than those with an insulting Pride do rail
At all who are not of their own Cabal.
10   If a Young Poet hit your Humour right,
You judge him then out of Revenge and Spite;
So amongst Men there are ridiculous Elves,
Who Monkeys hate for being too like themselves:
So that the Reason of the Grand Debate,
15   Why Wit so oft is damn'd, when good Plays take,
Is, that you censure as you love or hate.
Thus, like a learned Conclave, Poets sit
Catholick Judges both of Sense and Wit,
And damn or save, as they themselves think fit.
20   Yet those who to others Faults are so severe,
Are not so perfect, but themselves may err.
Some write correct indeed, but then the whole
(Bating their own dull Stuff i'th' Play) is stole:
As Bees do suck from Flowers their Honey-dew,
25   So they rob others, striving to please you.
        Some write their Characters genteel and fine,
But then they do so toil for every Line,
That what to you does easy seem, and plain,
Is the hard issue of their labouring Brain.
30   And some th' Effects of all their Pains we see,
Is but to mimick good Extempore.
Others by long Converse about the Town,
Have Wit enough to write a leud Lampoon,
But their chief Skill lies in a Baudy Song.
35   In short, the only Wit that's now in Fashion
Is but the Gleanings of good Conversation.
As for the Author of this coming Play,

I ask'd him what he thought fit I should say,
In thanks for your good Company to day:
He call'd me Fool, and said it was well known,   40
You came not here for our sakes, but your own.
New Plays are stuff'd with Wits, and with Debauches,
That croud and sweat like Cits in *May*-day Coaches.

ACT ONE

SCENE I

A Chamber.

Enter FLORINDA *and* HELLENA.

FLORINDA: What an impertient thing is a young Girl bred in a
    Nunnery! How full of Questions! Prithee no more, Hellena;
    I have told thee more than thou understand'st already.
HELLENA: The more's my Grief; I wou'd fain know as much as
    you, which makes me so inquisitive; nor is't enough to know   5
    you're a Lover, unless you tell me too, who 'tis you sigh for.
FLORINDA: When you are a Lover, I'll think you fit for a Secret
    of that nature.
HELLENA: 'Tis true, I was never a Lover yet—but I begin to
    have a shreud Guess, what 'tis to be so, and fancy it very   10
    pretty to sigh, and sing, and blush and wish, and dream and
    wish, and long and wish to see the Man; and when I do,
    look pale and tremble; just as you did when my Brother
    brought home the fine *English* Colonel to see you—what
    do you call him? Don *Belvile*.   15
FLORINDA: Fie, *Hellena*.
HELLENA: That Blush betrays you—I am sure 'tis so—or is it Don
    Antonio the Vice-Roy's Son?—or perhaps the rich old Don
    Vincentio, whom my father designs for your Husband?—Why
    do you blush again?   20
FLORINDA: With Indignation; and how near soever my Father
    thinks I am to marrying that hated Object, I shall let him
    see I understand better what's due to my Beauty, Birth and
    Fortune, and more to my Soul, than to obey those unjust
    Commands.   25

HELLENA: Now hang me, if I don't love thee for that dear
Disobedience. I love Mischief strangely, as most of our Sex
do, who are come to love nothing else—But tell me, dear
Florinda, don't you love that fine *Anglese*?—for I vow next
30　　to loving him my self, 'twill please me most that you do
so, for he is so gay and so handsom.

FLORINDA: *Hellena*, a Maid design'd for a Nun ought not to be so
curious in a Discourse of Love.

HELLENA: And dost thou think that ever I'll be a Nun? Or at least
35　　till I'm so old, I'm fit for nothing else. Faith no, Sister; and
that which makes me long to know whether you love *Belvile*,
is because I hope he has some mad Companion or other,
that will spoil my Devotion; nay I'm resolv'd to provide my
self this Carnival, if there be e'er a handsom Fellow of my
40　　Humour above Ground, tho I ask first.

FLORINDA: Prithee be not so wild.

HELLENA: Now you have provided your self with a Man, you take
no Care for poor me—Prithee tell me, what dost thou see
about me that is unfit for Love—have not I a world of Youth?
45　　a Humour gay? a Beauty passable? a Vigour desirable? well
shap'd? clean limb'd? sweet breath'd? and Sense enough
to know how all these ought to be employ'd to the best
Advantage: yes, I do and will. Therefore lay aside your Hopes
of my Fortune, by my being a Devotee, and tell me how you
50　　came acquainted with this *Belvile*; for I perceive you knew
him before he came to *Naples*.

FLORINDA: Yes, I knew him at the Siege of *Pampelona*, he was
then a Colonel of *French* Horse, who when the Town was
ransack'd, nobly treated my Brother and my self, preserving
55　　us from all Insolencies; and I must own, (besides great
Obligations) I have I know not what, that pleads kindly for
him about my Heart, and will suffer no other to enter—But
see my Brother.

(*Enter Don* PEDRO, STEPHANO, *with a Masquing Habit, and*
CALLIS.)

PEDRO: Good morrow, Sister. Pray, when saw you your Lover
60　　Don *Vincentio*?

FLORINDA: I know not, Sir—*Callis*, when was he here? for I
consider it so little, I know not when it was.

PEDRO: I have a Command from my Father here to tell you, you
ought not to despise him, a Man of so vast a Fortune, and
65　　such a Passion for you—*Stephano*, my things—

(*Puts on his Masquing Habit.*)

FLORINDA: A Passion for me! 'tis more than e'er I saw, or had
a desire should be known—I hate *Vincentio*, and I would
not have a Man so dear to me as my Brother follow the ill
Customs of our Country, and make a Slave of his Sister—And
70　　Sir, my Father's Will, I'm sure, you may divert.

PEDRO: I know not how dear I am to you, but I wish only to
be rank'd in your Esteem, equal with the *English* Colonel
Belvile—Why do you frown and blush? Is there any Guilt
belongs to the Name of that Cavalier?

75　FLORINDA: I'll not deny I value *Belvile*: when I was expos'd
to such Dangers as the licens'd Lust of common Soldiers

threatened, when Rage and Conquest flew thro the City—then
Belvile, this Criminal for my sake, threw himself into all
Dangers to save my Honour, and will you not allow him my
Esteem?

PEDRO: Yes, pay him what you will in Honour—but you must　80
consider Don *Vincentio*'s Fortune, and the Jointure he'll
make you.

FLORINDA: Let him consider my Youth, Beauty and Fortune;
which ought not to be thrown away on his Age and Jointure.

PEDRO: 'Tis true, he's not so young and fine a Gentleman as that　85
Belvile—but what Jewels will that Cavalier present you with?
those of his Eyes and Heart?

HELLENA: And are not those better than any Don *Vincentio* has
brought from the *Indies*?

PEDRO: Why how now! Has your Nunnery-breeding taught you to　90
understand the Value of Hearts and Eyes?

HELLENA: Better than to believe *Vincentio* deserves Value from
any woman—He may perhaps encrease her Bags, but not her
Family.

PEDRO: This is fine—Go up to your Devotion, you are not　95
design'd for the Conversation of Lovers.

HELLENA: (*Aside.*) Nor Saints yet a while I hope.
Is't not enough you make a Nun of me, but you must cast my
Sister away too, exposing her to a worse confinement than a
religious Life?　100

PEDRO: The Girl's mad—Is it a Confinement to be carry'd into
the Country, to an antient Villa belonging to the Family of
the *Vincentio*'s these five hundred Years, and have no other
Prospect than that pleasing one of seeing all her own that
meets her Eyes—a fine Air, large Fields and Gardens, where　105
she may walk and gather Flowers?

HELLENA: When? By Moon-Light? For I'm sure she dares not
encounter with the heat of the Sun; that were a Task only for
Don *Vincentio* and his *Indian* Breeding, who loves it in the
Dog-days—And if these be her daily Divertisements, what　110
are those of the Night? to lie in a wide Moth-eaten Bed-
Chamber with Furniture in Fashion in the Reign of King
Sancho the First; the Bed that which his Forefathers liv'd and
dy'd in.

PEDRO: Very well.　115

HELLENA: This Apartment (new furbisht and fitted out for the
young Wife) he (out of Freedom) makes his Dressing-room;
and being a frugal and a jealous Coxcomb, instead of a
Valet to uncase his feeble Carcase, he desires you to do that
Office—Signs of Favour, I'll assure you, and such as you must　120
not hope for, unless your Woman be out of the way.

PEDRO: Have you done yet?

HELLENA: That Honour being past, the Giant stretches it self,
yawns and sighs a Belch or two as loud as a Musket, throws
himself into Bed, and expects you in his foul Sheets, and　125
e'er you can get your self undrest, calls you with a Snore or
two—And are not these fine Blessings to a young Lady?

PEDRO: Have you done yet?

HELLENA: And this man you must kiss, nay, you must kiss
none but him too—and nuzle thro his Beard to find　130
his Lips—and this you must submit to for threescore
Years, and all for a Jointure.

---

52 **Siege of *Pampelona*** Pampluna, the strongly fortified capital of Navarra
and very frequently a center of military operations

---

113 **King *Sancho* the First** Sancho I, 'the Fat,' of Castile and Leon,
reigned 955–967: Sancho I of Aragon 1067–1094. But the phrase is here
only in a vague general sense to denote some musty and immemorial
antiquity without any exact reference

PEDRO: For all your Character of Don *Vincentio,* she is as like
to marry him as she was before.

135 HELLENA: Marry Don *Vincentio!* hang me, such a Wedlock would
be worse than Adultery with another Man: I had rather see
her in the *Hostel de Dieu,* to waste her Youth there in Vows,
and be a Handmaid to Lazers and Cripples, than to lose it in
such a Marriage.

140 PEDRO: You have consider'd, Sister, that *Belvile* has no Fortune
to bring you to, is banisht his Country, despis'd at home,
and pity'd abroad.

HELLENA: What then? the Vice-Roy's Son is better than that
Old Sir Fisty. Don *Vincentio!* Don *Indian!* he thinks he's

145 trading to *Gambo* still, and wou'd barter himself (that Bell
and Bawble) for your Youth and Fortune.

PEDRO: *Callis,* take her hence, and lock her up all this Carnival,
and at Lent she shall begin her everlasting Penance in a
Monastery.

150 HELLENA: I care not, I had rather be a Nun, than be oblig'd to
marry as you wou'd have me, if I were design'd for't.

PEDRO: Do not fear the Blessing of that Choice—you shall be a
Nun.

HELLENA: Shall I so? you may chance to be mistaken in my way of

155 Devotion—(*Aside.*) A Nun! yes I am like to make a fine Nun!
I have an excellent Humour for a Grate: No, I'll have a Saint
of my own to pray to shortly, if I like any that dares venture
on me.

PEDRO: *Callis,* make it your Business to watch this wild Cat. As

160 for you, *Florinda,* I've only try'd you all this while, and urg'd
my Father's Will; but mine is, that you would love *Antonio,* he
is brave and young, and all that can compleat the Happiness
of a gallant Maid—This Absence of my Father will give us
opportunity to free you from *Vincentio,* by marrying here,

165 which you must do to morrow.

FLORINDA: To morrow!

PEDRO: To morrow, or 'twill be too late—'tis not my Friendship
to *Antonio,* which makes me urge this, but Love to thee, and
Hatred to *Vincentio*—therefore resolve upon't to morrow.

170 FLORINDA: Sir, I shall strive to do, as shall become your Sister.

PEDRO: I'll both believe and trust you—Adieu.

(*Exeunt* PEDRO *and* STEPHANO.)

HELLENA: As become his Sister!—That is, to be as resolved your
way, as he is his—

(HELLENA *goes to* CALLIS.)

FLORINDA: I ne'er till now perceiv'd my Ruin near,

175 I've no Defence against *Antonio's* Love,
For he has all the Advantages of Nature,
The moving Arguments of Youth and Fortune.

HELLENA: But hark you, *Callis,* you will not be so cruel to
lock me up indeed: will you?

180 CALLIS: I must obey the Commands I hate—besides, do you
consider what a Life you are going to lead?

HELLENA: Yes, *Callis,* that of a Nun: and till then I'll be indebted
a World of Prayers to you, if you let me now see, what I never
did, the Divertisements of a Carnival.

CALLIS: What, go in Masquerade? 'twill be a fine farewell to the 185
World I take it—pray what wou'd you do there?

HELLENA: That which all the World does, as I am told, be as
mad as the rest, and take all innocent Freedom—Sister,
you'll go too, will you not? come prithee be not sad—
We'll out-wit twenty Brothers, if you'll be ruled by me— 190
Come put off this dull Humour with your Clothes, and
assume one as gay, and as fantastick as the Dress my
Cousin *Valeria* and I have provided, and let's ramble.

FLORINDA: *Callis,* will you give us leave to go?

CALLIS: (*Aside.*) I have a youthful Itch of going my self. 195
—Madam, if I thought your Brother might not know it, and
I might wait on you, for by my troth I'll not trust young Girls
alone.

FLORINDA: Thou see'st my Brother's gone already, and thou shalt
attend and watch us. 200

(*Enter* STEPHANO.)

STEPHANO: Madam, the Habits are come, and your Cousin
Valeria is drest, and stays for you.

FLORINDA: 'Tis well—I'll write a Note, and if I chance to see
Belvile, and want an opportunity to speak to him, that shall
let him know what I've resolv'd in favour of him. 205

HELLENA: Come, let's in and dress us.

(*Exeunt.*)

SCENE II

A Long Street.

Enter BELVILE, MELANCHOLY, BLUNT, *and* FREDERICK.

FREDERICK: Why, what the Devil ails the Colonel, in a time when
all the World is gay, to look like mere Lent thus? Hadst thou
been long enough in *Naples* to have been in love, I should have
sworn some such Judgment had befall'n thee.

BELVILE: No, I have made no new Amours since I came to 5
Naples.

FREDERICK: You have left none behind you in *Paris.*

BELVILE: Neither.

FREDERICK: I can't divine the Cause then; unless the old Cause,
the want of Mony. 10

BLUNT: And another old Cause, the want of a Wench—Wou'd not
that revive you?

BELVILE: You're mistaken, *Ned.*

BLUNT: Nay, 'Sheartlikins, then thou art past Cure.

FREDERICK: I have found it out; thou hast renew'd thy 15
Acquaintance with the Lady that cost thee so many Sighs at
the Siege of *Pampelona*—pox on't, what d'ye call her—her
Brother's a noble *Spaniard*—Nephew to the dead General—
Florinda—ay, *Florinda*—And will nothing serve thy turn but
that damn'd virtuous Woman, whom on my Consience thou 20
lov'st in spite too, because thou seest little or no possibility of
gaining her?

---

137 **Hostel de Dieu** the first Spanish hospital was erected at Granada by
St. Juan de Dios before 1550   145 **Gambo** the Gambia in West Africa
has been a British Colony since 1664, when a fort, now Fort James, was
founded at the mouth of the river

14 **'Sheartlikins** by God's heart

BELVILE: Thou art mistaken, I have Interest enough in that lovely Virgin's Heart, to make me proud and vain, were
25 it not abated by the Severity of a Brother, who perceiving my Happiness—

FREDERICK: Has civilly forbid thee the House?

BELVILE: 'Tis so, to make way for a powerful Rival, the Vice-Roy's Son, who has the advantage of me, in being a Man of Fortune,
30 a *Spaniard,* and her Brother's Friend; which gives him liberty to make his Court, whilst I have recourse only to Letters, and distant Looks from her Window, which are as soft and kind as those which Heav'n sends down on Penitents.

BLUNT: Hey day! 'Sheartlikins, Simile! by this Light the Man is
35 quite spoil'd—*Frederick,* what the Devil are we made of, that we cannot be thus concern'd for a Wench?—'Sheartlikins, our *Cupids* are like the Cooks of the Camp, they can roast or boil a Woman, but they have none of the fine Tricks to set 'em off, no Hogoes to make the Sauce pleasant, and the
40 Stomach sharp.

FREDERICK: I dare swear I have had a hundred as young, kind and handsom as this *Florinda;* and Dogs eat me, if they were not as troublesom to me i'th' Morning as they were welcome o'er night.

45 BLUNT: And yet, I warrant, he wou'd not touch another Woman, if he might have her for nothing.

BELVILE: That's thy Joy, a cheap Whore.

BLUNT: Why, 'dsheartlikins, I Love a frank Soul—When did you ever hear of an honest Woman that took a Man's Mony?
50 I warrant 'em good ones—But, Gentlemen, you may be free, you have been kept so poor with Parliaments and Protectors, that the little Stock you have is not worth preserving—but I thank my Stars, I have more Grace than to forfeit my Estate by Cavaliering.

55 BELVILE: Methinks only following the Court should be sufficient to entitle 'em to that.

BLUNT: 'Sheartlikins, they know I follow it to do it no good, unless they pick a hole in my Coat for lending you Mony now and then; which is a greater Crime to my Conscience,
60 Gentlemen, than to the Common-wealth.

(*Enter* WILLMORE.)

WILLMORE: Ha! dear *Belvile!* noble Colonel!

BELVILE: *Willmore!* welcome ashore, my dear Rover!—what happy Wind blew us this good Fortune?

WILLMORE: Let me salute you my dear *Fred,* and then com-
65 mand me—How is't honest Lad?

FREDERICK: Faith, Sir, the old Complement, infinitely the better to see my dear mad *Willmore* again—Prithee why camest thou ashore? and where's the Prince?

WILLMORE: He's well, and reigns still Lord of the watery
70 Element—I must aboard again within a Day or two, and my Business ashore was only to enjoy my self a little this Carnival.

BELVILE: Pray know our new Friend, Sir, he's but bashful, a raw Traveller, but honest, stout, and one of us.

(*Embraces* BLUNT.)

WILLMORE: That you esteem him, gives him an Interest here.

---

39 **Hogoes** Haut-goût, a relish

BLUNT: Your Servant, Sir. 75

WILLMORE: But well—Faith I'm glad to meet you again in a warm Climate, where the kind Sun has its god-like Power still over the Wine and Woman.—Love and Mirth are my Business in *Naples*; and if I mistake not the Place, here's an excellent Market for Chapmen of my Humour. 80

BELVILE: See here be those kind Merchants of Love you look for.

(*Enter several* MEN *in masquing Habits, some playing on Musick, others dancing after;* WOMEN *drest like Curtezans, with Papers pinn'd to their Breasts, and Baskets of Flowers in their Hands.*)

BLUNT: 'Sheartlikins, what have we here!

FREDERICK: Now the Game begins.

WILLMORE: Fine pretty Creatures! may a stranger have leave to 85 look and love?—What's here—(*Reads the Paper.*): *Roses for every Month!*

BLUNT: Roses for every Month! what means that?

BELVILE: They are, or wou'd have you think they're Curtezans, who here in *Naples* are to be hir'd by the Month. 90

WILLMORE: Kind and obliging to inform us—Pray where do these Roses grow? I would fain plant some of 'em in a Bed of mine.

WOMAN: Beware such Roses, Sir.

WILLMORE: A Pox of fear: I'll be bak'd with thee between a 95 pair of Sheets, and that's thy proper Still, so I might but strow such Roses over me and under me—Fair one, wou'd you wou'd give me leave to gather at your Bush this idle Month, I wou'd go near to make some Body smell of it all the Year after. 100

BELVILE: And thou hast need of such a Remedy, for thou stinkest of Tar and Rope-ends, like a Dock or Pesthouse.

(*The* WOMAN *puts her self into the Hands of a* MAN, *and Exit.*)

WILLMORE: Nay, nay, you shall not leave me so.

BELVILE: By all means use no Violence here.

WILLMORE: Death! just as I was going to be damnably in love, to 105 have her led off! I could pluck that Rose out of his Hand, and even kiss the Bed, the Bush it grew in.

FREDERICK: No Friend to Love like a long Voyage at Sea.

BLUNT: Except a Nunnery, *Frederick.*

WILLMORE: Death! but will they not be kind, quickly be kind? 110 Thou know'st I'm no tame Sigher, but a rampant Lion of the Forest.

(*Two* MEN *drest all over with Horns of several sorts, making Grimaces at one another, with Papers pinn'd on their Backs, advance from the farther end of the Scene.*)

BELVILE: Oh the fantastical Rogues, how they are dress'd! 'tis a Satir against the whole Sex.

WILLMORE: Is this a Fruit that grows in this warm Country? 115

BELVILE: Yes: 'Tis pretty to see these *Italian* start, swell, and stab at the Word *Cuckold,* and yet stumble at Horns on every Threshold.

WILLMORE: See what's on their Back—(*Reads.*) *Flowers for every Night.*—Ah Rogue! And more sweet than Roses of ev'ry 120 Month! This is a Gardiner of *Adam's* own breeding.

(*They dance.*)

BELVILE: What think you of those grave People?—is a Wake in
 Essex half so mad or extravagant?

WILLMORE: I like their sober grave way, 'tis a kind of legal
125 authoriz'd Fornication, where the Men are not chid for 't, nor
 the Women despis'd, as amongst our dull *English;* even the
 Monsieurs want that part of good Manners.

BELVILE: But here in *Italy* a Monsieur is the humblest best-bred
130 Gentleman—Duels are so baffled by Bravos that an age
 shews not one, but between a *Frenchman* and a Hangman,
 who is as much too hard for him on the Piazza, as
 they are for a *Dutchman* on the new Bridge—But see
 another Crew.

(Enter FLORINDA, HELLENA, *and* VALERIA, *drest like Gipsies;* CALLIS
and STEPHANO, LUCETTA, PHILIPPO, *and* SANCHO *in Masquerade.)*

HELLENA: Sister, there's your *Englishman,* and with him a
135 handsome proper Fellow—I'll to him, and instead of telling
 him his Fortune, try my own.

WILLMORE: Gipsies, on my Life—Sure these will prattle if a Man
 cross their Hands. *(Goes to* HELLENA.)—Dear pretty (and I
 hope) young Devil, will you tell an amorous Stranger what
140 Luck he's like to have?

HELLENA: Have a care how you venture with me, Sir, lest I pick
 your Pocket, which will more vex your *English* Humour, than
 an *Italian* Fortune will please you.

WILLMORE: How the Devil cam'st thou to know my Country and
145 Humour?

HELLENA: The first I guess by a certain forward Impudence,
 which does not displease me at this time; and the Loss of
 your Money will vex you, because I hope you have but very
 little to lose.

150 WILLMORE: Egad Child, thou'rt i'th' right; it is so little, I dare
 not offer it thee for a Kindness—But cannot you divine what
 other things of more value I have about me, that I would more
 willingly part with?

HELLENA: Indeed no, that's the Business of a Witch, and I am
155 but a Gipsy yet—Yet, without looking in your Hand, I
 have a parlous Guess, 'tis some foolish Heart you mean, an
 inconstant *English* Heart, as little worth stealing as your
 Purse.

WILLMORE: Nay, then thou dost deal with the Devil, that's
160 certain—Thou hast guess'd as right as if thou hadst been one
 of that Number it has languisht for—I find you'll be better
 acquainted with it; nor can you take it in a better time, for
 I am come from Sea, Child; and *Venus* not being propitious
 to me in her own Element, I have a world of Love in store—
165 Wou'd you would be good-natur'd, and take some on't off
 my Hands.

HELLENA: Why—I could be inclin'd that way—but for a foolish
 Vow I am going to make—to die a Maid.

WILLMORE: Then thou art damn'd without Redemption; and as
170 I am a good Christian, I ought to charity to divert so wicked
 a Design—therefore prithee, dear Creature, let me know
 quickly when and where I shall begin to set a helping hand to
 so good a Work.

HELLENA: If you should prevail with my tender Heart (as I
175 begin to fear you will, for you have horrible loving Eyes)
 there will be difficulty in't that you'll hardly undergo for
 my sake.

WILLMORE: Faith, Child, I have been bred in Dangers, and wear
 a Sword that has been employ'd in a worse Cause, than for
 a handsom kind Woman—Name the Danger—let it be any
 thing but a long Siege, and I'll undertake it. 180

HELLENA: Can you storm?

WILLMORE: Oh, most furiously.

HELLENA: What think you of a Nunnery-wall? for he that
 wins me, must gain that first.

WILLMORE: A Nun! Oh how I love thee for't! there's no Sin- 185
 ner like a young Saint—Nay, now there's no denying me:
 the old Law had no Curse (to a Woman) like dying a
 Maid; witness *Jephtha's* Daughter.

HELLENA: A very good Text this, if well handled; and I perceive,
 Father Captain, you would impose no severe Penance on her 190
 who was inclin'd to console her self before she took Orders.

WILLMORE: If she be young and handsom.

HELLENA: Ay, there's it—but if she be not—

WILLMORE: By this Hand, Child, I have an implicit Faith, and
 dare venture on thee with all Faults—besides, 'tis more 195
 meritorious to leave the World when thou hast tasted and
 prov'd the Pleasure on't; then 'twill be a Virtue in thee,
 which now will be pure Ignorance.

HELLENA: I perceive, good Father Captain, you design only to
 make me fit for Heaven—but if on the contrary you should 200
 quite divert me from it, and bring me back to the World again,
 I should have a new Man to seek I find; and what a grief that
 will be—for when I begin, I fancy I shall love like any thing:
 I never try'd yet.

WILLMORE: Egad, and that's kind—Prithee, dear Creature, give 205
 me Credit for a Heart, for faith, I'm a very honest Fellow—Oh,
 I long to come first to the Banquet of Love; and such a
 swinging Appetite I bring—Oh, I'm impatient. Thy Lodging,
 Sweetheart, thy Lodging, or I'm a dead man.

HELLENA: Why must we be either guilty of Fornication or 210
 Murder, if we converse with you Men?—And is there no
 difference between leave to love me, and leave to lie with me?

WILLMORE: Faith, Child, they were made to go together.

LUCETTA: *(Pointing to* BLUNT.) Are you sure this is the Man?

SANCHO: When did I mistake your Game? 215

LUCETTA: This is a stranger, I know by his gazing; if he be brisk
 he'll venture to follow me; and then, if I understand my Trade,
 he's mine: he's *English* too, and they say that's a sort of good
 natur'd loving People, and have generally so kind an opinion
 of themselves, that a Woman with any Wit may flatter 'em 220
 into any sort of Fool she pleases.

BLUNT: 'Tis so—she is taken—I have Beauties which my false
 Glass at home did not discover.

(She often passes by BLUNT *and gazes on him; he struts, and cocks,
and walks, and gazes on her.)*

FLORINDA: This Woman watches me so, I shall get no
 Opportunity to discover my self to him, and so miss the 225
 intent of my coming—But as I was saying, Sir—*(Looking in his
 Hand.)* by this Line you should be a Lover.

BELVILE: I thought how right you guess'd, all Men are in love,
 or pretend to be so—Come, let me go, I'm weary of this
 fooling. 230

(Walks away.)

FLORINDA: I will not, till you have confess'd whether the Passion that you have vow'd *Florinda* be true or false.

(*She holds him, he strives to get from her.*)

BELVILE: *Florinda!*

(*Turns quick towards her.*)

235   FLORINDA: Softly.
BELVILE: Thou hast nam'd one will fix me here for ever.
FLORINDA: She'll be disappointed then, who expects you this Night at the Garden-gate, and if you'll fail not—as let me see the other Hand—you will go near to do—she vows to die or
240   make you happy.

(*Looks on* CALLIS, *who observes 'em.*)

BELVILE: What canst thou mean?
FLORINDA: That which I say—Farewell.

(*Offers to go.*)

BELVILE: Oh charming Sybil, stay, complete that Joy, which, as it is, will turn into Distraction!—Where must I be? at the
245   Garden-gate? I know it—at night you say—I'll sooner forfeit Heaven than disobey.

(*Enter* DON PEDRO *and other Masquers, and pass over the Stage.*)

CALLIS: Madam, your Brother's here.
FLORINDA: Take this to instruct you farther.

(*Gives him a Letter, and goes off.*)

FREDERICK: Have a care, Sir, what you promise; this may be a
250   Trap laid by her Brother to ruin you.
BELVILE: Do not disturb my Happiness with Doubts.

(*Opens the Letter.*)

WILLMORE: My dear pretty Creature, a Thousand Blessings on thee; still in this Habit, you say, and after Dinner at this Place.
255   HELLENA: Yes, if you will swear to keep your Heart, and after bestow it between this time and that.
WILLMORE: By all the little Gods of Love I swear, I'll leave it with you; and if you run away with it, those Deities of Justice will revenge me.

(*Exeunt all the* WOMEN *except* LUCETTA.)

FREDERICK: Do you know the Hand?
260   BELVILE: 'Tis *Florinda's.*
All Blessings fall upon the virtuous Maid.
FREDERICK: Nay, no Idolatry, a sober Sacrifice I'll allow you.
BELVILE: Oh Friends! the welcom'st News, the softest Letter!— nay, you shall see it; and could you now be serious, I might be
265   made the happiest Man the Sun shines on.
WILLMORE: The Reason of this mighty Joy.
BELVILE: See how kindly she invites me to deliver her from the threaten'd Violence of her Brother—will you not assist me?
WILLMORE: I know not what thou mean'st, but I'll make one

at any Mischief where a Woman's concern'd—but she'll   270
begrateful to us for the Favour, will she not?
BELVILE: How mean you?
WILLMORE: How should I mean? Thou know'st there's but one way for a Woman to oblige me.
BELVILE: Don't prophane—the Maid is nicely virtuous.   275
WILLMORE: Who pox, then she's fit for nothing but a Husband; let her e'en go, Colonel.
FREDERICK: Peace, she's the Colonel's Mistress, Sir.
WILLMORE: Let her be the Devil; if she be thy Mistress, I'll serve her—name the way.   280
BELVILE: Read here this Postcript.

(*Gives him a Letter.*)

WILLMORE: (*Reads.*) *At Ten at night—at the Garden-Gate—of which, if I cannot get the Key, I will contrive a way over the Wall—come attended with a Friend or two.—Kind heart, if we three cannot weave a String to let her down a Garden-Wall,   285
'twere pity but the Hangman wove one for us all.*
FREDERICK: Let her alone for that: your Woman's Wit, your fair kind Woman, will not out-trick a Brother or a Jew, and contrive like a Jesuit in Chains—but see, *Ned Blunt* is stoln out after the Lure of a Damsel.   290

(*Exit* BLUNT *and* LUCETTA.)

BELVILE: So he'll scarce find his way home again, unless we get him cry'd by the Bell-man in the Market-place, and 'twou'd sound prettily—a lost *English* Boy of Thirty.
FREDERICK: I hope 'tis some common crafty Sinner, one that will fit him; it may be she'll sell him for *Peru*, the Rogue's sturdy   295
and would work well in a Mine; at least I hope she'll dress him for our Mirth; cheat him of all, then have him well-favour'dly bang'd, and turn'd out naked at Midnight.
WILLMORE: Prithee what Humour is he of, that you wish him so well?   300
BELVILE: Why, of an *English* Elder Brother's Humour, educated in a Nursery, with a Maid to tend him till Fifteen, and lies with his Grand-mother till he's of Age; one that knows no Pleasure beyond riding to the next Fair, or going up to *London* with his right Worshipful Father in Parliament-time; wearing gay   305
Clothes, or making honourable Love to his Lady Mother's Landry-Maid; gets drunk at a Hunting-Match, and ten to one then gives some Proofs of his Prowess—A pox upon him, he's our Banker, and has all our Cash about him, and if he fail we are all broke.   310
FREDERICK: Oh let him alone for that matter, he's of a damn'd stingy Quality, that will secure our Stock. I know not in what Danger it were indeed, if the Jilt should pretend she's in love with him, for 'tis a kind believing Coxcomb; otherwise if he part with more than a Piece of Eight—geld   315
him: for which offer he may chance to be beaten, if she be a Whore of the first Rank.
BELVILE: Nay the Rogue will not be easily beaten, he's stout enough; perhaps if they talk beyond his Capacity, he may chance to exercise his Courage upon some of them; else   320
I'm sure they'll find it as difficult to beat as to please him.

---

315 **a Piece of Eight** a piastre, a coin of varying values in different countries

WILLMORE: 'Tis a lucky Devil to light upon so kind a Wench!

FREDERICK: Thou hadst a great deal of talk with thy little Gipsy,
325 coud'st thou do no good upon her? for mine was hard-
hearted.

WILLMORE: Hang her, she was some damn'd honest Person of
Quality, I'm sure, she was so very free and witty. If her Face
be but answerable to her Wit and Humour, I would be bound
330 to Constancy this Month to gain her. In the mean time, have
you made no kind Acquaintance since you came to Town?—
You do not use to be honest so long, Gentlemen.

FREDERICK: Faith Love has kept us honest, we have been all fir'd
with a Beauty newly come to Town, the famous *Paduana
Angelica Bianca.*

335 WILLMORE: What, the Mistress of the dead *Spanish* General?

BELVILE: Yes, she's now the only ador'd Beauty of all the Youth
in *Naples,* who put on all their charms to appear lovely in
her sight, their Coaches, Liveries, and themselves, all gay,
as on a Monarch's Birth-Day, to attract the Eyes of this fair
340 Charmer, while she has the Pleasure to behold all languish
for her that see her.

FREDERICK: 'Tis pretty to see with how much Love the Men
regard her, and how much Envy the Women.

WILLMORE: What Gallant has she?

345 BELVILE: None, she's exposed to Sale, and four Days in the Week
she's yours—for so much a Month.

WILLMORE: The very Thought of it quenches all manner of Fire
in me—yet prithee let's see her.

BELVILE: Let's first to Dinner, and after that we'll pass the Day as
350 you please—but at Night ye must all be at my Devotion.

WILLMORE: I will not fail you.

(*Exeunt.*)

ACT TWO

SCENE I

The Long Street.

Enter BELVILE and FREDERICK *in Masquing-Habits, and* WILLMORE
in his own Clothes, with a Vizard in his Hand.

WILLMORE: But why thus disguis'd and muzzl'd?

BELVILE: Because whatever Extravagances we commit in these
Faces, our own may not be oblig'd to answer 'em.

WILLMORE: I should have chang'd my Eternal Buff too: but no
5 matter, my little Gipsy wou'd not have found me out then: for
if she should change hers, it is impossible I should know her,
unless I should hear her prattle—A Pox on't, I cannot get her
out of my Head: Pray Heaven, if ever I do see her again, she
prove damnable ugly, that I may fortify my self against her
10 Tongue.

BELVILE: Have a care of Love, for o' my conscience she was not
of a Quality to give thee any hopes.

WILLMORE: Pox on 'em, why do they draw a Man in then? She has
play'd with my Heart so, that 'twill never lie still till I have
15 met with some kind Wench, that will play the Game out with
me—Oh for my Arms full of soft, white, kind—Woman! such
as I fancy *Angelica.*

BELVILE: This is her House, if you were but in stock to get
admittance; they have not din'd yet; I perceive the Picture is
20 not out.

(*Enter* BLUNT.)

WILLMORE: I long to see the Shadow of the fair Substance, a Man
may gaze on that for nothing.

BLUNT: Colonel, thy Hand—and thine, *Frederick.* I have been an
Ass, a deluded Fool, a very Coxcomb from my Birth till this
Hour, and heartily repent my little Faith. 25

BELVILE: What the Devil's the matter with thee *Ned?*

BLUNT: Oh such a Mistress, *Frederick,* such a Girl!

WILLMORE: Ha! where? *Frederick.* Ay where!

BLUNT: So fond, so amorous, so toying and fine! and all for
sheer Love, ye Rogue! Oh how she lookt and kiss'd! and 30
sooth'd my Heart from my Bosom. I cannot think I was
awake, and yet methinks I see and feel her Charms still—
Frederick.—Try if she have not left the Taste of her balmy
Kisses upon my Lips—

(*Kisses him.*)

BELVILE: Ha, ha, ha! *Willmore.* Death Man, where is she? 35

BLUNT: What a Dog was I to stay in dull *England* so long—
How have I laught at the Colonel when he sigh'd for
Love! but now the little Archer has reveng'd him, and by
his own Dart, I can guess at all his Joys, which then I took
for Fancies, mere Dreams and Fables—Well, I'm resolved to 40
sell all in Essex, and plant here for ever.

BELVILE: What a Blessing 'tis, thou hast a Mistress thou dar'st
boast of; for I know thy Humour is rather to have a proclaim'd
Clap, than a secret Amour.

WILLMORE: Dost know her Name? 45

BLUNT: Her Name? No, 'sheartlikins: what care I for Names?—
She's fair, young, brisk and kind, even to ravishment: and
what a Pox care I for knowing her by another Title?

WILLMORE: Didst give her anything?

BLUNT: Give her!—Ha, ha, ha! why, she's a Person of Quality 50
—That's a good one, give her! 'sheartlikins dost think such
Creatures are to be bought? Or are we provided for such a
Purchase? Give her, quoth ye? Why she presented me with
this Bracelet, for the Toy of a Diamond I us'd to wear: No,
Gentlemen, *Ned Blunt* is not every Body—She expects me 55
again to night.

WILLMORE: Egad that's well; we'll all go.

BLUNT: Not a Soul: No, Gentlemen, you are Wits; I am a dull
Country Rogue, I.

FREDERICK: Well, Sir, for all your Person of Quality, I shall be 60
very glad to understand your Purse be secure; 'tis our whole
Estate at present, which we are loth to hazard in one Bottom:
come, Sir, unload.

BLUNT: Take the necessary Trifle, useless now to me, that am
belov'd by such a Gentlewoman—'sheartlikins Money! 65
Here take mine too.

FREDERICK: No, keep that to be cozen'd, that we may laugh.

WILLMORE: Cozen'd!—Death! wou'd I cou'd meet with one,
that wou'd cozen me of all the Love I cou'd spare to night.

FREDERICK: Pox 'tis some common Whore upon my Life. 70

BLUNT: A Whore! yes with such Clothes! such Jewels! such a
House! such Furniture, and so attended! a Whore!

BELVILE: Why yes, Sir, they are Whores, tho they'll neither
entertain you with Drinking, Swearing, or Baudy; are
Whores in all those gay Clothes, and right Jewels; are 75
Whores with great Houses richly furnisht with Velvet Beds,
Store of Plate, handsome Attendance, and fine Coaches, are
Whores and errant ones.

WILLMORE: Pox on't, where do these fine Whores live?

80 BELVILE: Where no Rogue in Office yclep'd Constables dare give 'em laws, nor the Wine-inspired Bullies of the Town break their Windows; yet they are Whores, tho this *Essex* Calf believe them Persons of Quality.

85 BLUNT: 'Sheartlikins, y'are all Fools, there are things about this *Essex* Calf, that shall take with the Ladies, beyond all your Wits and Parts—This Shape and Size, Gentlemen, are not to be despis'd; my Waste tolerably long, with other inviting Signs, that shall be nameless.

90 WILLMORE: Egad I believe he may have met with some Person of Quality that may be kind to him.

BELVILE: Dost thou perceive any such tempting things about him, should make a fine Woman, and of Quality, pick him out from all Mankind, to throw away her Youth and Beauty upon, nay, and her dear Heart too?—no, no, *Angelica* has rais'd the Price

95 too high.

WILLMORE: May she languish for Mankind till she die, and be damn'd for that one Sin alone.

(*Enter two* BRAVOES, *and hang up a great Picture of* ANGELICA's *against the Balcony, and two little ones at each side of the Door.*)

BELVILE: See there the fair Sign to the Inn, where a Man may lodge that's Fool enough to give her Price.

(WILLMORE *gazes on the Picture.*)

100 BLUNT: 'Sheartlikins, Gentlemen, what's this?

BELVILE: A famous Curtezan that's to be sold.

BLUNT: How! to be sold! nay then I have nothing to say to her—sold! what Impudence is practis'd in this Country?—With Order and Decency Whoring's established here by virtue

105 of the Inquisition—Come let's be gone, I'm sure we're no Chapmen for this Commodity.

FREDERICK: Thou art none, I'm sure, unless thou could'st have her in thy Bed at the Price of a Coach in the Street.

WILLMORE: How wondrous fair she is—a Thousand Crowns a

110 Month—by Heaven as many Kingdoms were too little. A plague of this Poverty—of which I ne'er complain, but when it hinders my Approach to Beauty, which Virtue ne'er could purchase.

(*Turns from the Picture.*)

BLUNT: What's this?—(*Reads.*) *A Thousand Crowns a Month!*—

115 'Sheartlikins, here's a Sum! sure 'tis a mistake.—Hark you, Friend, does she take or give so much by the Month!

FREDERICK: A Thousand Crowns! Why, 'tis a Portion for the *Infanta.*

BLUNT: Hark ye, Friends, won't she trust?

120 BRAVO: This is a Trade, Sir, that cannot live by Credit.

(*Enter* DON PEDRO *in Masquerade, follow'd by* STEPHANO.)

BELVILE: See, here's more Company, let's walk off a while.

(PEDRO *reads. Exeunt* ENGLISH. *Enter* ANGELICA *and* MORETTA *in the Balcony, and draw a Silk Curtain.*)

PEDRO: Fetch me a Thousand Crowns, I never wish to buy this Beauty at an easier Rate.

(*Passes off.*)

ANGELICA: Prithee what said those Fellows to thee?

BRAVO: Madam, the first were Admirers of Beauty only, but no 125 purchasers; they were merry with your Price and Picture, laught at the Sum, and so past off.

ANGELICA: No matter, I'm not displeas'd with their rallying; their Wonder feeds my Vanity, and he that wishes to buy, gives me more Pride, than he that gives my Price can 130 make me Pleasure.

BRAVO: Madam, the last I knew thro all his disguises to be Don *Pedro,* Nephew to the General, and who was with him in *Pampelona.*

ANGELICA: Don *Pedro*! my old Gallant's Nephew! When his 135 Uncle dy'd, he left him a vast Sum of Money; it is he who was so in love with me at *Padua,* and who us'd to make the General so jealous.

MORETTA: Is this he that us'd to prance before our Window and take such care to shew himself an amorous Ass? if I am not 140 mistaken, he is the likeliest Man to give your Price.

ANGELICA: The Man is brave and generous, but of an Humour so uneasy and inconstant, that the victory over his Heart is as soon lost as won; a Slave that can add little to the Triumph of the Conqueror; but inconstancy's the Sin of all Mankind, 145 therefore I'm resolv'd that nothing but Gold shall charm my Heart.

MORETTA: I'm glad on't; 'tis only interest that Women of our Profession ought to consider: tho I wonder what has kept you from that general Disease of our Sex so long, I mean that of 150 being in love.

ANGELICA: A kind, but sullen Star, under which I had the Happiness to be born; yet I have had no time for Love; the bravest and noblest of Mankind have purchas'd my Favours at so dear a Rate, as if no Coin but Gold were current with our 155 Trade—But here's Don *Pedro* again, fetch me my Lute—for 'tis for him or Don *Antonio* the Vice-Roy's Son, that I have spread my Nets.

(*Enter at one Door Don* PEDRO, *and* STEPHANO; *Don* ANTONIO *and* DIEGO [*his page*], *at the other Door, with people following him in Masquerade, antickly attir'd, some with Musick: they both go up to the Picture.*)

ANTONIO: A thousand Crowns! had not the Painter flatter'd her, 160 I should not think it dear.

PEDRO: Flatter'd her! by Heaven he cannot. I have seen the Original, nor is there one Charm here more than adorns her Face and Eyes; all this soft and sweet, with a certain languishing Air, that no Artist can represent.

ANTONIO: What I heard of her Beauty before had fir'd my Soul, 165 but this confirmation of it has blown it into a flame.

PEDRO: Ha!

PAGE: Sir, I have known you throw away a Thousand Crowns on a worse Face, and tho y' are near your Marriage, you may venture a little Love here; *Florinda*—will not miss it. 170

PEDRO: (*Aside.*) Ha! *Florinda*! Sure 'tis *Antonio.*

ANTONIO: *Florinda*! name not those distant Joys, there's not one thought of her will check my Passion here.

PEDRO: Florinda scorn'd! and all my Hopes defeated of the Possession of Angelica! (*A noise of a Lute above. Antonio gazes* 175 *up.*) Her Injuries by Heaven he shall not boast of.

(*Song to a Lute above.*)

Song

When *Damon* first began to love,
He languisht in a soft Desire,
And knew not how the Gods to move,
180   To lessen or increase his Fire,
For *Caelia* in her charming Eyes
    Wore all Love's Sweet, and all his Cruelties.

II

But as beneath a Shade he lay,
Weaving of Flow'rs for *Caelia*'s Hair,
185   She chanc'd to lead her Flock that way,
And saw the am'rous Shepherd there.
She gaz'd around upon the Place,
And saw the Grove (resembling Night)
190   To all the Joys of Love invite,
    Whilst guilty Smiles and Blushes drest her Face.
At this the bashful Youth all Transport grew,
And with kind Force he taught the Virgin how
To yield what all his Sighs cou'd never do.

ANTONIO: By Heav'n she's charming fair!

(ANGELICA *throws open the Curtains, and bows to* ANTONIO, *who pulls off his Vizard, and bows and blows up Kisses.* PEDRO *unseen looks in his Face.*)

195 PEDRO: 'Tis he, the false *Antonio!*
ANTONIO: Friend, where must I pay my offering of Love?

(*To the bravo.*)

My Thousand Crowns I mean.
PEDRO: That offering I have design'd to make,
    And yours will come too late.
200 ANTONIO: Prithee be gone, I shall grow angry else,
    And then thou art not safe.
PEDRO: My Anger may be fatal, Sir, as yours;
    And he that enters here may prove this Truth.
ANTONIO: I know not who thou art, but I am sure thou'rt worth
205   my killing, and aiming at *Angelica.*

(*They draw and fight.*)

(*Enter* WILLMORE *and* BLUNT, *who draw and part 'em.*)

BLUNT: 'Sheartlikins, here's fine doings.
WILLMORE: Tilting for the Wench I'm sure—nay gad, if that
    wou'd win her, I have as good a Sword as the best of ye—Put
    up—put up, and take another time and place, for this is
210   design'd for Lovers only.

(*They all put up.*)

PEDRO: We are prevented; dare you meet me to morrow
    on the *Molo?*
    For I've a Title to a better quarrel,
    That of *Florinda,* in whose credulous Heart
215   Thou'st made an Int'rest, and destroy'd my Hopes.
ANTONIO: Dare?
    I'll meet thee there as early as the Day.

PEDRO: We will come thus disguis'd, that whosoever chance to
    get the better, he may escape unknown.
ANTONIO: It shall be so.

(*Exit* PEDRO *and* STEPHANO.)

Who shou'd this Rival be? unless the *English* Colonel, of   220
whom I've often heard Don Pedro speak; it must be he, and
time he were removed, who lays a Claim to all my Happiness.

(WILLMORE *having gaz'd all this while on the Picture, pulls down a little one.*)

WILLMORE: This posture's loose and negligent,
    The sight on't wou'd beget a warm desire
    In Souls, whom Impotence and Age had chill'd.   225
    —This must along with me.
BRAVO: What means this rudeness, Sir?—restore the Picture.
ANTONIO: Ha! Rudeness committed to the fair *Angelica!*—
    Restore the Picture, Sir.
WILLMORE: Indeed I will not, Sir.   230
ANTONIO: By Heav'n but you shall.
WILLMORE: Nay, do not shew your Sword; if you do, by this dear
    Beauty—I will shew mine too.
ANTONIO: What right can you pretend to't?
WILLMORE: That of Possession which I will maintain—you   235
    perhaps have 1000 Crowns to give for the Original.
ANTONIO: No matter, Sir, you shall restore the Picture.
ANGELICA: Oh, *Moretta!* what's the matter?

(ANGELICA *and* MORETTA *above.*)

ANTONIO: Or leave your Life behind.
WILLMORE: Death! you lye—I will do neither.   240
ANGELICA: Hold, I command you, if for me you fight.

(*They fight, the Spaniards join with* ANTONIO, BLUNT *laying on like mad. They leave off and bow.*)

WILLMORE: How heavenly fair she is!—ah Plague of her Price.
ANGELICA: You Sir in Buff, you that appear a Soldier, that first
    began this Insolence.
WILLMORE: 'Tis true, I did so, if you call it Insolence for a Man   245
    to preserve himself; I saw your charming Picture, and was
    wounded: quite thro my Soul each pointed Beauty ran; and
    wanting a Thousand Crowns to procure my Remedy, I laid
    this little Picture to my Bosom—which if you cannot allow
    me, I'll resign.   250
ANGELICA: No, you may keep the Trifle.
ANTONIO: You shall first ask my leave, and this.

(*Fight again as before.*)

(*Enter* BELVILE *and* FREDERICK *who join with the English.*)

ANGELICA: Hold; will you ruin me?—*Biskey, Sebastian,* part
    them.

(*The* SPANIARDS *are beaten off.*)

MORETTA: Oh Madam, we're undone, a pox upon that rude
    Fellow, he's set on to ruin us: we shall never see good days, till   255
    all these fighting poor Rogues are sent to the Gallies.

(*Enter* BELVILE, BLUNT *and* WILLMORE, *with his shirt bloody.*)

BLUNT: 'Sheartlikins, beat me at this Sport, and I'll ne'er wear Sword more.

BELVILE: The Devil's in thee for a mad Fellow, thou art always one
260   at an unlucky Adventure.—Come, let's be gone whilst we're safe, and remember these are *Spaniards,* a sort of People that know how to revenge an Affront.

FREDERICK: (*To* WILLMORE.) You bleed; I hope you are not wounded.

265 WILLMORE: Not much:—a plague upon your Dons, if they fight no better they'll ne'er recover *Flanders.*—What the Devil was't to them that I took down the Picture?

BLUNT: Took it! 'Sheartlikins, we'll have the great one too; 'tis ours by Conquest.—Prithee, help me up, and I'll pull it
270   down.—

ANGELICA: Stay, Sir, and e'er you affront me further, let me know how you durst commit this Outrage—To you I speak, Sir, for you appear like a Gentleman.

WILLMORE: To me, Madam?—Gentlemen, your Servant.

(BELVILE *stays him.*)

275 BELVILE: Is the Devil in thee? Do'st know the danger of entring the house of an incens'd Curtezan?

WILLMORE: I thank you for your care—but there are other matters in hand, there are, tho we have no great Temptation.—Death! let me go.

280 FREDERICK: Yes, to your Lodging, if you will, but not in here.—Damn these gay Harlots—by this Hand I'll have as sound and hansome a Whore for a Patacoone.—Death, Man, she'll murder thee.

WILLMORE: Oh! fear me not, shall I not venture where a Beauty
285   calls? a lovely charming Beauty? for fear of danger! when by Heaven there's none so great as to long for her, whilst I want Money to purchase her.

FREDERICK: Therefore 'tis loss of time, unless you had the thousand Crowns to pay.

290 WILLMORE: It may be she may give a Favour, at least I shall have the pleasure of saluting her when I enter, and when I depart.

BELVILE: Pox, she'll as soon lie with thee, as kiss thee, and sooner stab than do either—you shall not go.

ANGELICA: Fear not, Sir, all I have to wound with, is my Eyes.

295 BLUNT: Let him go, 'Sheartlikins, I believe the Gentlewoman means well.

BELVILE: Well, take thy Fortune, we'll expect you in the next Street.—Farewell Fool,—farewell—

WILLMORE: B'ye Colonel—

(*Goes in.*)

300 FREDERICK: The Rogue's stark mad for a Wench.

(*Exeunt.*)

SCENE II

A Fine Chamber.

Enter WILLMORE, ANGELICA, *and* MORETTA.

ANGELICA: Insolent, Sir, how durst you pull down my Picture?

WILLMORE: Rather, how durst you set it up, to tempt poor amorous Mortals with so much Excellence? which I find you have but too well consulted by the unmerciful price you set upon't.—Is all this Heaven of Beauty shewn to 5 move Despair in those that cannot buy? and can you think the effects of that Despair shou'd be less extravagant than I have shewn?

ANGELICA: I sent for you to ask my Pardon, Sir, not to aggravate your Crime.—I thought I shou'd have seen you at my Feet 10 imploring it.

WILLMORE: You are deceived, I came to rail at you, and talk such Truths, too, as shall let you see the Vanity of that Pride, which taught you how to set such a Price on Sin. For such it is, whilst that which is Love's due is meanly barter'd for. 15

ANGELICA: Ha, ha, ha, alas, good Captain, what pity 'tis your edifying Doctrine will do no good upon me—*Moretta,* fetch the Gentleman a Glass, and let him survey himself, to see what Charms he has,—(*Aside in a soft tone.*) and guess my Business. 20

MORETTA: He knows himself of old, I believe those Breeches and he have been acquainted ever since he was beaten at *Worcester.*

ANGELICA: Nay, do not abuse the poor Creature.—

MORETTA: Good Weather-beaten Corporal, will you march 25 off? we have no need of your Doctrine, tho you have of our Charity; but at present we have no Scraps, we can afford no kindness for God's sake; in fine, Sirrah, the Price is too high i'th' Mouth for you, therefore troop, I say.

WILLMORE: Here, good Fore-Woman of the Shop, serve me, and 30 I'll be gone.

MORETTA: Keep it to pay your Landress, your Linen stinks of the Gun-Room; for here's no selling by Retail.

WILLMORE: Thou hast sold plenty of thy stale Ware at a cheap Rate. 35

MORETTA: Ay, the more silly kind Heart I, but this is an Age wherein Beauty is at higher Rates.—In fine, you know the price of this.

WILLMORE: I grant you 'tis here set down a thousand Crowns a Month—Baud, take your black Lead and sum it up, that I may 40 have a Pistole-worth of these vain gay things, and I'll trouble you no more.

MORETTA: Pox on him, he'll fret me to Death:—abominable Fellow, I tell thee, we only sell by the whole Piece.

WILLMORE: 'Tis very hard, the whole Cargo or nothing—Faith, 45 Madam, my Stock will not reach it, I cannot be your Chapman.—Yet I have Countrymen in Town, Merchants of Love, like me; I'll see if they'll put for a share, we cannot lose much by it, and what we have no use for, we'll sell upon the *Friday's* Mart, at—*Who gives more?* I am studying, Madam, 50 how to purchase you, tho at present I am unprovided of Money.

ANGELICA: Sure, this from any other Man would anger me—nor shall he know the Conquest he has made—Poor angry Man, how I despise this railing. 55

WILLMORE: Yes, I am poor—but I'm a Gentleman,
    And one that scorns this Baseness which you practise.
    Poor as I am, I would not sell my self,
    No, not to gain your charming high-priz'd Person.
    Tho I admire you strangely for your Beauty, 60

---

282 **Patacoone** a Spanish coin

41 **Pistole** a gold coin

Yet I contemn your Mind.
—And yet I wou'd at any rate enjoy you;
At your own rate—but cannot—See here
The only Sum I can command on Earth;
65 I know not where to eat when this is gone:
Yet such a Slave I am to Love and Beauty,
This last reserve I'll sacrifice to enjoy you.
—Nay, do not frown, I know you are to be bought,
And wou'd be bought by me, by me,
70 For a mean trifling Sum, if I could pay it down.
Which happy knowledge I will still repeat,
And lay it to my Heart, it has a Virtue in't,
And soon will cure those Wounds your Eyes have made.
—And yet—there's something so divinely powerful there—
75 Nay, I will gaze—to let you see my Strength.

(*Holds her, looks on her, and pauses and sighs.*)

By Heaven, bright Creature—I would not for the World
Thy Fame were half so fair as thy Face.

(*Turns her away from him.*)

ANGELICA: (*Aside.*) His words go thro me to the very Soul.
—If you have nothing else to say to me.
80 WILLMORE: Yes, you shall hear how infamous you are—
For which I do not hate thee:
But that secures my Heart, and all the Flames it feels
Are but so many Lusts,
I know it by their sudden bold intrusion.
85 The Fire's impatient and betrays, 'tis false—
For had it been the purer Flame of Love,
I should have pin'd and languish'd at your Feet,
E'er found the Impudence to have discover'd it.
I now dare stand your Scorn, and your Denial.
90 MORETTA: Sure she's bewitcht, that you can stand thus tamely,
and hear his saucy railing.—Sirrah, will you be gone?
ANGELICA: How dare you take this liberty?—(*To* MORETTA.)
Withdraw.—Pray, tell me, Sir, are not you guilty of the same
mercenary Crime? When a Lady is proposed to you for a
95 Wife, you never ask, how fair, discreet, or virtuous she is; but
what's her Fortune—which if but small, you cry—She will not
do my business—and basely leave her, tho she languish for
you.—Say, is not this as poor?
WILLMORE: It is a barbarous Custom, which I will scorn to defend
100 in our Sex, and do despise in yours.
ANGELICA: Thou art a brave Fellow! put up thy Gold, and know
That were thy Fortune large, as is thy Soul,
Thou shouldst not buy my Love,
Couldst thou forget those mean Effects of Vanity,
105 Which set me out to sale; and as a Lover, prize
My yielding Joys.
Canst thou believe they'l be entirely thine,
Without considering they were mercenary?
WILLMORE: (*Aside.*) I cannot tell, I must bethink me first—
110 ha, Death, I'm going to believe her.
ANGELICA: Prithee, confirm that Faith—or if thou canst not—
flatter me a little, 'twill please me from thy Mouth.
WILLMORE: Curse on thy charming Tongue! dost thou return
My feign'd Contempt with so much subtilty?

(*Aside.*)

Thou'st found the easiest way into my Heart, 115
Tho I yet know that all thou say'st is false.

(*Turning from her in a Rage.*)

ANGELICA: By all that's good 'tis real,
I never lov'd before, tho oft a Mistress.
—Shall my first Vows be slighted?
WILLMORE: (*Aside.*) What can she mean? 120
ANGELICA: (*In an angry tone.*) I find you cannot credit me.
WILLMORE: I know you take me for an errant Ass,
An Ass that may be sooth'd into Belief,
And then be us'd at pleasure.
—But, Madam, I have been so often cheated 125
By perjur'd, soft, deluding Hypocrites,
That I've no Faith left for the cozening Sex,
Especially for Women of your Trade.
ANGELICA: The low esteem you have of me, perhaps
May bring my Heart again: 130
For I have Pride that yet surmounts my Love.

(*She turns with Pride, he holds her.*)

WILLMORE: Throw off this Pride, this Enemy to Bliss,
And shew the Power of Love: 'tis with those Arms
I can be only vanquisht, made a Slave.
ANGELICA: Is all my mighty Expectation vanisht? 135
—No, I will not hear thee talk,—thou hast a Charm
In every word, that draws my Heart away.
And all the thousand Trophies I design'd,
Thou hast undone—Why art thou soft?
Thy Looks are bravely rough, and meant for War. 140
Could thou not storm on still?
I then perhaps had been as free as thou.
WILLMORE: (*Aside.*) Death! how she throws her Fire about
my Soul!
—Take heed, fair Creature, how you raise my Hopes,
Which once assum'd pretend to all Dominion. 145
There's not a Joy thou hast in store
I shall not then command:
For which I'll pay thee back my Soul, my Life.
Come, let's begin th' account this happy minute.
ANGELICA: And will you pay me then the Price I ask? 150
WILLMORE: Oh, why dost thou draw me from an awful Worship,
By shewing thou art no Divinity?
Conceal the Fiend, and shew me all the Angel;
Keep me but ignorant, and I'll be devout,
And pay my Vows for ever at this Shrine. 155

(*Kneels, and kisses her Hand.*)

ANGELICA: The Pay I mean is but thy Love for mine.—Can you
give that?
WILLMORE: Intirely—come, let's withdraw: where I'll renew my
vows,—and breathe 'em with such Ardour, thou shalt not
doubt my Zeal. 160
ANGELICA: Thou hast a Power too strong to be resisted.

(*Exit* WILLMORE *and* ANGELICA.)

MORETTA: Now my Curse go with you—Is all our Project fallen
to this? to love the only Enemy to our Trade? Nay, to love

165   such a Shameroon, a very Beggar; nay, a Pirate-Beggar, whose
Business is to rifle and be gone, a No-Purchase, No-Pay
Tatterdemalion, an English Piccaroon; a Rogue that fights
for daily Drink, and takes a Pride in being loyally lousy—
Oh, I could curse now, if I durst—This is the Fate of most
Whores.

170   *Trophies, which from believing Fops we win,*
Are Spoils to those who cozen us again.

ACT THREE

SCENE I

A Street.

Enter FLORINDA, VALERIA, HELLENA, *in Antick different Dresses*
from what they were in before, CALLIS *attending.*

FLORINDA: I wonder what should make my Brother in so ill
a Humour: I hope he has not found out our Ramble this
Morning.
HELLENA: No, if he had, we should have heard on't at both Ears,
5   and have been mew'd up this Afternoon; which I would not
for the World should have happen'd—Hey ho! I'm sad as a
Lover's Lute.
VALERIA: Well, methinks we have learnt this Trade of Gipsies as
readily as if we had been bred upon the Road to *Loretto:* and
10   yes I did so fumble, when I told the Stranger his Fortune,
that I was afraid I should have told my own and yours by
mistake—But methinks *Hellena* has been very serious ever
since.
FLORINDA: I would give my Garters she were in love, to be
15   reveng'd upon her, for abusing me—How is't, *Hellena?*
HELLENA: Ah!—would I had never seen my mad Monsieur—and
yet for all your laughing I am not in love—and yet this small
Acquaintance, o'my Conscience, will never out of my Head.
VALERIA: Ha, ha, ha—I laugh to think how thou art fitted with a
20   Lover, a Fellow that, I warrant, loves every new Face he sees.
HELLENA: Hum—he has not kept his Word with me here—and
may be taken up—that thought is not very pleasant to
me—what the Duce should this be now that I feel?
VALERIA: What is't like?
25   HELLENA: Nay, the Lord knows—but if I should be hanged, I
cannot chuse but be angry and afraid, when I think that mad
Fellow should be in love with any Body but me—What to
think of my self I know not—Would I could meet with some
true damn'd Gipsy, that I might know my Fortune.
30   VALERIA: Know it! why there's nothing so easy; thou wilt love this
wandering Inconstant till thou find'st thy self hanged about
his Neck, and then be as mad to get free again.
FLORINDA: Yes, *Valeria;* we shall see her bestride his Baggage-
horse, and follow him to the Campaign.
35   HELLENA: So, so; now you are provided for, there's no care
taken of poor me—But since you have set my Heart a wishing,
I am resolv'd to know for what. I will not die of the Pip, so I
will not.
FLORINDA: Art thou mad to talk so? Who will like thee well

---

164 **shameroon** a trickster, a cozening rascal

enough to have thee, that hears what a mad Wench thou art?   40
HELLENA: Like me! I don't intend every he that likes me
shall have me, but he that I like: I shou'd have staid in the
Nunnery still, if I had lik'd my Lady Abbess as well as
she lik'd me. No, I came thence, not (as my wise Brother
imagines) to take an eternal Farewel of the World, but   45
to love and to be belov'd; and I will be belov'd, or I'll get one
of your Men, so I will.
VALERIA: Am I put into the Number of Lovers?
HELLENA: You! my Couz, I know thou art too good natur'd
to leave us in any Design: Thou wou't venture a Cast, tho   50
thou comest off a Loser, especially with such a Gamester—I
observ'd your Man, and your willing ears incline that way;
and if you are not a Lover, 'tis an Art soon learnt—that I find.

(Sighs.)

FLORINDA: I wonder how you learnt to love so easily, I had a
thousand Charms to meet my Eyes and Ears, e'er I cou'd yield;   55
and 'twas the knowledge of *Belvile's* Merit, not the surprising
Person, took my Soul—Thou art too rash to give a Heart at
first sight.
HELLENA: Hang your considering Lover; I ne'er thought beyond
the Fancy, that 'twas a very pretty, idle, silly kind of Pleasure   60
to pass ones time with, to write little, soft, nonsensical Billets,
and with great difficulty and danger receive Answers; in
which I shall have my Beauty prais'd, my Wit admir'd (tho
little or none) and have the Vanity and Power to know I am
desirable; then I have the more Inclination that way, because   65
I am to be a Nun, and so shall not be suspected to have any
such earthly Thoughts about me—But when I walk thus—
and sigh thus—they'll think my Mind's upon my Monastery,
and cry, how happy 'tis she's so resolv'd!—But not a Word
of Man.   70
FLORINDA: What a mad Creature's this!
HELLENA: I'll warrant, if my Brother hears either of you sigh, he
cries (gravely)—I fear you have the Indiscretion to be in love,
but take heed of the Honour of our House, and your own
unspotted Fame; and so he conjures on till he has laid the soft-   75
wing'd God in your Hearts, or broke the Birdsnest—But see
here comes your Lover: but where's my inconstant? let's stop
aside, and we may learn something.

(Go aside.)

(Enter BELVILE, FREDERICK, *and* BLUNT.)

BELVILE: What means this? the Picture's taken in.
BLUNT: It may be the Wench is good-natur'd, and will be kind   80
gratis. Your Friend's a proper handsom Fellow.
BELVILE: I rather think she has cut his Throat and is fled: I am
mad he should throw himself into Dangers—Pox on't, I shall
want him to night—let's knock and ask for him.
HELLENA: My heart goes a-pit a-pat, for fear 'tis my Man they   85
talk of.

(Knock, MORETTA *above.)*

MORETTA: What would you have?
BELVILE: Tell the Stranger that enter'd here about two Hours ago,
that his Friends stay here for him.

90 MORETTA: A Curse upon him for *Moretta,* would he were at the
Devil—but he's coming to you.

(*Enter* WILLMORE.)

HELLENA: I, I, 'tis he. Oh how this vexes me.

BELVILE: And how, and how, dear Lad, has Fortune smil'd? Are
we to break her Windows, or raise up Altars to her! hah!

95 WILLMORE: Does not my Fortune sit triumphant on my Brow?
dost not see the little wanton God there all gay and smiling?
have I not an Air about my Face and Eyes, that distinguish
me from the Croud of common Lovers! By Heav'n, *Cupid's*
Quiver has not half so many Darts as her Eyes—Oh such

100 a Bona Roba, to sleep in her Arms is lying in Fresco, all
perfum'd Air about me.

HELLENA: (*Aside.*) Here's fine encouragement for me to fool on.

WILLMORE: Hark ye, where didst thou purchase that rich Canary
we drank to-day? Tell me, that I may adore the Spigot, and

105 sacrifice to the Butt: the Juice was divine, into which I must
dip my Rosary, and then bless all things that I would have
bold or fortunate.

BELVILE: Well, Sir, let's go take a Bottle, and hear the Story of
your Success.

110 FREDERICK: Would not *French* Wine do better?

WILLMORE: Damn the hungry Balderdash; cheerful Sack has a
generous Virtue in't, inspiring a successful Confidence, gives
Eloquence to the Tongue, and Vigour to the Soul; and has in
a few Hours compleated all my Hopes and Wishes. There's

115 nothing left to raise a new Desire in me—Come let's be gay
and wanton—and, Gentlemen, study, study what you want,
for here are Friends,—that will supply, Gentlemen,—hark!
what a charming sound they make—'tis he and she Gold
whilst here, shall beget new Pleasures every moment.

120 BLUNT: But hark ye, Sir, you are not married, are you?

WILLMORE: All the Honey of Matrimony, but none of the Sting,
Friend.

BLUNT: 'Sheartlikins, thou'rt a fortunate Rogue.

WILLMORE: I am so, Sir, let these inform you.—Ha, how sweetly they

125 chime! Pox of Poverty, it makes a Man a Slave, makes Wit
and Honour sneak, my Soul grew lean and rusty for want of
Credit.

BLUNT: 'Sheartlikins, this I like well, it looks like my lucky
Bargain! Oh how I long for the Approach of my Squire,

130 that is to conduct me to her House again. Why! here's two
provided for.

FREDERICK: By this light y're happy Men.

BLUNT: Fortune is pleased to smile on us, Gentlemen,—to smile
on us.

(*Enter* SANCHO, *and pulls* BLUNT *by the Sleeve. They go aside.*)

135 SANCHO: Sir, my Lady expects you—she has remov'd all that
might oppose your Will and Pleasure—and is impatient till
you come.

BLUNT: Sir, I'll attend you—Oh the happiest Rogue! I'll take no
leave, lest they either dog me, or stay me.

(*Exit with* SANCHO.)

140 BELVILE: But then the little Gipsy is forgot?

WILLMORE: A Mischief on thee for putting her into my thoughts;
I had quite forgot her else, and this Night's Debauch had
drunk her quite down.

HELLENA: Had it so, good Captain?

(*Claps him on the Back.*)

WILLMORE: Ha! I hope she did not hear.   145

HELLENA: What, afraid of such a Champion!

WILLMORE: Oh! you're a fine Lady of your word, are you not? to
make a Man languish a whole day—

HELLENA: In tedious search of me.

WILLMORE: Egad, Child, thou'rt in the right, hadst thou seen   150
what a melancholy Dog I have been ever since I was a Lover,
how I have walkt the Streets like a *Capuchin,* with my Hands
in my Sleeves—Faith, Sweetheart, thou wouldst pity me.

HELLENA: Now, if I should be hang'd, I can't be angry with him,
he dissembles so heartily—Alas, good Captain, what pains   155
you have taken—Now were I ungrateful not to reward so true
a Servant.

WILLMORE: Poor Soul! that's kindly said, I see thou bearest a
Conscience—come then for a beginning shew me thy dear
Face.   160

HELLENA: I'm afraid, my small Acquaintance, you have been
staying that swinging stomach you boasted of this morning;
I remember then my little Collation would have gone down
with you, without the Sauce of a handsom Face—Is your
Stomach so quesy now?   165

WILLMORE: Faith long fasting, Child, spoils a Man's Appetite—
yet if you durst treat, I could so lay about me still.

HELLENA: And would you fall to, before a Priest says Grace?

WILLMORE: Oh fie, fie, what an old out-of-fashion'd thing
hast thou nam'd? Thou could'st not dash me more out of   170
Countenance, shouldst thou shew me an ugly Face.

(*Whilst he is seemingly courting* HELLENA, *enter* ANGELICA,
MORETTA, BISKEY, *and* SEBASTIAN, *all in Masquerade:* ANGELICA
sees WILLMORE *and starts.*)

ANGELICA: Heavens, is't he? and passionately fond to see another
Woman?

MORETTA: What cou'd you expect less from such a Swaggerer?

ANGELICA: Expect! as much as I paid him, a Heart intire,   175
Which I had pride enough to think when e'er I gave
It would have rais'd the Man above the Vulgar,
Made him all Soul, and that all soft and constant.

HELLENA: You see, Captain, how willing I am to be Friends with
you, till Time and Ill-luck make us Lovers; and ask you the   180
Question first, rather than put your Modesty to the blush, by
asking me: for alas, I know you Captains are such strict Men,
severe Observers of your Vows to Chastity, that 'twill be hard
to prevail with your tender Conscience to marry a young
willing Maid.   185

WILLMORE: Do not abuse me, for fear I should take thee at thy
word, and marry thee indeed, which I'm sure will be Revenge
sufficient.

HELLENA: O' my Conscience, that will be our Destiny, because we
are both of one humour; I am as inconstant as you, for I have   190
considered, Captain, that a handsom Woman has a great deal
to do whilst her Face is good, for then is our Harvest-time
to gather Friends; and should I in these days of my Youth,
catch a fit of foolish Constancy, I were undone; 'tis loitering by
day-light in our great Journey: therefore declare, I'll allow but   195
one year for Love, one year for Indifference, and one year for
Hate—and then—go hang your self—for I profess myself the

gay, the kind, and the inconstant—the Devil's in't if this won't please you.

200 WILLMORE: Oh most damnably!—I have a Heart with a hole quite thro it too, no Prison like mine to keep a Mistress in.

ANGELICA: (*Aside.*) Purjur'd Man! how I believe thee now!

HELLENA: Well, I see our Business as well as Humours are alike, yours to cozen as many Maids as will trust you, and I as many

205 Men as have Faith—See if I have not as desperate a lying look, as you can have for the heart of you.

(*Pulls off her Vizard; he starts.*)

—How do you like it, Captain?

WILLMORE: Like it! by Heav'n, I never saw so much Beauty. Oh the Charms of those sprightly black Eyes, that strangely fair

210 Face, full of Smiles and Dimples! those soft round melting cherry Lips! and small even white Teeth! not to be exprest, but silently adored!—Oh one Look more, and strike me dumb, or I shall repeat nothing else till I am mad.

(*He seems to court her to pull off her Vizard: she refuses.*)

ANGELICA: I can endure no more—nor is it fit to interrupt him;

215 for if I do, my Jealousy has so destroy'd my Reason,—I shall undo him—Therefore I'll retire. And you *Sebastian* (*To one of her bravoes.*) follow that Woman, and learn who 'tis; (*To the other bravo.*) while you tell the Fugitive, I would speak to him instantly.

(*Exit.*)

(*This while* FLORINDA *is talking to* BELVILE, *who stands sullenly.* FREDERICK *courting* VALERIA.)

220 VALERIA: Prithee, dear Stranger, be not so sullen; for tho you have lost your Love, you see my Friend frankly offers you hers, to play with in the mean time.

BELVILE: Faith, Madam, I am sorry I can't play at her Game.

FREDERICK: Pray leave your Intercession, and mind your own

225 Affair, they'll better agree apart; he's a model Sigher in Company, but alone no Woman escapes him.

FLORINDA: Sure he does but rally—yet if it should be true—I'll tempt him farther—Believe me, noble Stranger, I'm no common Mistress—and for a little proof on't—wear this

230 Jewel—nay, take it, Sir, 'tis right, and Bills of Exchange may sometimes miscarry.

BELVILE: Madam, why am I chose out of all Mankind to be the Object of your Bounty?

VALERIA: There's another civil Question askt.

235 FREDERICK: Pox of's Modesty, it spoils his own Markets, and hinders mine.

FLORINDA: Sir, from my Window I have often seen you; and Women of Quality have so few opportunities for Love, that we ought to lose none.

240 FREDERICK: Ay, this is something! here's a Woman!—When shall I be blest with so much kindness from your fair Mouth? (*Aside to* BELVILE.) Take the Jewel, Fool.

BELVILE: You tempt me strangely, Madam, every way.

FLORINDA: (*Aside.*) So, if I find him false, my whole Repose

245 is gone.

BELVILE: And but for a Vow I've made to a very fine Lady, this Goodness had subdu'd me.

FREDERICK: Pox on't be kind, in pity to me be kind, for I am to thrive here but as you treat her Friend.

HELLENA: Tell me what did you in yonder House, and I'll 250 unmasque.

WILLMORE: Yonder House—oh—I went to—a—to—why, there's a Friend of mine lives there.

HELLENA: What a she, or a he Friend?

WILLMORE: A Man upon my Honour! a Man—A she Friend! no, 255 no, Madam, you have done my Business, I thank you.

HELLENA: And was't your Man Friend, that had more Darts in's Eyes than *Cupid* carries in a whole Budget of Arrows?

WILLMORE: So—

HELLENA: Ah such a *Bona Roba*: to be in her Arms is lying in 260 *Fresco,* all perfumed Air about me—Was this your Man Friend too?

WILLMORE: So—

HELLENA: That gave you the He, and the She—Gold, that begets young Pleasures. 265

WILLMORE: Well, well, Madam, then you see there are Ladies in the World, that will not be cruel—there are, Madam, there are—

HELLENA: And there be Men too as fine, wild, inconstant Fellows as your self, there be, Captain, there be, if you go to that 270 now—therefore I'm resolv'd—

WILLMORE: Oh!

HELLENA: To see your Face no more—

WILLMORE: Oh!

HELLENA: Till to morrow. 275

WILLMORE: Egad you frighted me.

HELLENA: Nor then neither, unless you'l swear never to see that Lady more.

WILLMORE: See her!—why! never to think of Womankind again? 280

HELLENA: Kneel, and swear.

(*Kneels, she gives him her Hand.*)

WILLMORE: I do, never to think—to see—to love—nor lie with any but thy self.

HELLENA: Kiss the Book.

WILLMORE: Oh, most religiously. 285

(*Kisses her Hand.*)

HELLENA: Now what a wicked Creature am I, to damn a proper Fellow.

CALLIS: (*To* FLORINDA.) Madam, I'll stay no longer, 'tis e'en dark.

FLORINDA: However, Sir, I'll leave this with you—that when I'm gone, you may repent the opportunity you have lost by your 290 modesty.

(*Gives him the Jewel, which is her Picture, and Exits. He gazes after her.*)

WILLMORE: 'Twill be an Age till to morrow,—and till then I will most impatiently expect you—Adieu, my dear pretty Angel.

(*Exeunt all the* WOMEN.)

BELVILE: Ha! *Florinda*'s Picture! 'twas she her self—what a dull 295 Dog was I? I would have given the World for one minute's discourse with her.—

FREDERICK: This comes of your Modesty,—ah pox on your Vow, 'twas ten to one but we had lost the Jewel by't.

300 BELVILE: *Willmore!* the blessed'st Opportunity lost!—*Florinda,* Friends, *Florinda!*

WILLMORE: Ah Rogue! such black Eyes, such a Face, such a Mouth, such Teeth,—and so much Wit!

BELVILE: All, all, and a thousand Charms besides.

305 WILLMORE: Why, dost thou know her?

BELVILE: Know her! ay, ay, and a Pox take me with all my Heart for being modest.

WILLMORE: But hark ye, Friend of mine, are you my Rival? and have I been only beating the Bush all this while?

310 BELVILE: I understand thee not—I'm mad—see here—

(*Shews the Picture.*)

WILLMORE: Ha! whose Picture is this?—'tis a fine Wench.

FREDERICK: The Colonel's Mistress, Sir.

WILLMORE: Oh, oh, here—I thought it had been another Prize— come, come, a Bottle will set thee right again.

(*Gives the Picture back.*)

315 BELVILE: I am content to try, and by that time 'twill be late enough for our Design.

WILLMORE: Agreed.
　　Love does all day the Soul's great Empire keep,
　　But Wine at night lulls the soft God asleep.

(*Exeunt.*)

SCENE II

LUCETTA's *House.*

Enter BLUNT *and* LUCETTA *with a Light.*

LUCETTA: Now we are safe and free, no fears of the coming home of my old jealous Husband, which made me a little thoughtful when you came in first—but now Love is all the business of my Soul.

5 BLUNT: (*Aside.*) I am transported—Pox on't, that I had but some fine things to say to her, such as Lovers use—I was a Fool not to learn of *Frederick* a little by Heart before I came— something I must say.—'Sheartlikins, sweet Soul, I am not us'd to complement, but I'm an honest Gentleman, and thy
10 humble Servant.

LUCETTA: I have nothing to pay for so great a Favour, but such a Love as cannot but be great, since at first sight of that sweet Face and Shape it made me your absolute Captive.

BLUNT: (*Aside.*) Kind heart, how prettily she talks! Egad I'll show
15 her Husband a *Spanish* Trick; send him out of the World, and marry her: she's damnably in love with me, and will ne'er mind Settlements, and so there's that sav'd.

LUCETTA: Well, Sir, I'll go and undress me, and be with you instantly.

20 BLUNT: Make haste then, for 'dsheartlikins, dear Soul, thou canst not guess at the pain of a longing Lover, when his Joys are drawn within the compass of a few minutes.

LUCETTA: You speak my Sense, and I'll make haste to provide it.

(*Exit.*)

BLUNT: 'Tis a rare Girl, and this one night's enjoyment with her 25 will be worth all the days I ever past in Essex.—Would she'd go with me into *England,* tho to say truth, there's plenty of Whores there already.—But a pox on 'em they are such mercenary prodigal Whores, that they want such a one as this, that's free and generous, to give 'em good Examples:—Why, 30 what a House she has! how rich and fine!

(*Enter* SANCHO.)

SANCHO: Sir, my Lady has sent me to conduct you to her Chamber.

BLUNT: Sir, I shall be proud to follow—Here's one of her Servants too: 'dsheartlikins, by his Garb and Gravity he might be a 35 Justice of Peace in *Essex,* and is but a Pimp here.

(*Exeunt.*)

(*The Scene changes to a Chamber with an Alcove-Bed in it, a Table, &c.* LUCETTA *in Bed. Enter* SANCHO *and* BLUNT, *who takes the Candle of* SANCHO *at the Door.*)

SANCHO: Sir, my Commission reaches no farther.

BLUNT: Sir, I'll excuse your Complement:—what, in Bed, my sweet Mistress?

LUCETTA: You see, I still out-do you in kindness. 40

BLUNT: And thou shalt see what haste I'll make to quit scores—oh the luckiest Rogue!

(*Undresses himself.*)

LUCETTA: Shou'd you be false or cruel now!

BLUNT: False, 'Sheartlikins, what dost thou take me for a *Jew?* an insensible Heathen,—A Pox of thy old jealous Husband: and 45 he were dead, egad, sweet Soul, it shou'd be none of my fault, if I did not marry thee.

LUCETTA: It never shou'd be mine.

BLUNT: Good Soul, I'm the fortunatest Dog!

LUCETTA: Are you not undrest yet? 50

BLUNT: As much as my Impatience will permit.

(*Goes towards the Bed in his Shirt and Drawers.*)

LUCETTA: Hold, Sir, put out the Light, it may betray us else.

BLUNT: Any thing, I need no other Light but that of thine Eyes!—(*Aside.*) 'sheartlikins, there I think I had it.

(*Puts out the Candle, the Bed descends, he gropes about to find it.*)

—Why—why—where am I got? what, not yet?—where are 55 your sweetest?—ah, the Rogue's silent now—a pretty Love-trick this—how she'll laugh at me anon!—you need not, my dear Rogue! you need not! I'm all on a fire already— come, come, now call me in for pity—Sure I'm enchanted! I have been round the Chamber, and can find neither 60 Woman, nor Bed—I lockt the Door, I'm sure she cannot go that way; or if she cou'd, the Bed cou'd not—Enough, enough, my pretty Wanton, do not carry the Jest too far—Ha, betray'd! Dogs! Rogues! Pimps! help! help!

(*Lights on a Trap, and is let down. Enter* LUCETTA, PHILIPPO, *and* SANCHO *with a Light.*)

65 PHILIPPO: Ha, ha, ha, he's dispatcht finely.

LUCETTA: Now, Sir, had I been coy, we had mist of this Booty.

PHILIPPO: Nay when I saw 'twas a substantial Fool, I was mollified; but when you doat upon a Serenading Coxcomb, upon a Face, fine Clothes, and a Lute, it makes me rage.

70 LUCETTA: You know I never was guilty of that Folly, my dear *Philippo*, but with your self—But come let's see what we have got by this.

PHILIPPO: A rich Coat!—Sword and Hat!—these Breeches too—are well lin'd!—see here a Gold Watch!—a Purse—

75 ha! Gold!—at least two hundred Pistoles! a bunch of Diamond Rings; and one with the Family Arms!—a Gold Box!—with a Medal of his King! and his Lady Mother's Picture!—these were sacred Reliques, believe me!—see, the Wasteband of his Breeches have a Mine of Gold!—

80 Old Queen *Bess's*. We have a Quarrel to her ever since Eighty Eight, and may therefore justify the Theft, the Inquisition might have committed it.

LUCETTA: See, a Bracelet of bow'd Gold, these his Sister ty'd about his Arm at parting—but well—for all this, I fear his being a

85 Stranger may make a noise, and hinder our Trade with them hereafter.

PHILIPPO: That's our security; he is not only a Stranger to us, but to the Country too—the Common-Shore into which he is descended, thou know'st, conducts him into another Street,

90 which this Light will hinder him from ever finding again—he knows neither your Name, nor the Street where your House is, nay, nor the way to his own Lodgings.

LUCETTA: And art not thou an unmerciful Rogue, not to afford him one Night for all this?—I should not have been

95 such a *Jew*.

PHILIPPO: Blame me not, *Lucetta*, to keep as much of thee as I can to my self—come, that thought makes me wanton,—let's to Bed,—*Sancho*, lock up these.

This is the Fleece which Fools do bear,
100 *Design'd for witty Men to sheer.*

(*Exeunt.*)

(*The Scene changes, and discovers* BLUNT, *creeping out of a Common-Shore, his Face, &c., all dirty.*)

BLUNT: Oh Lord!

(*Climbing up.*)

I am got out at last, and (which is a Miracle) without a Clue—and now to Damning and Cursing—but if that would ease me, where shall I begin? with my Fortune, my
105 self, or the Quean that cozen'd me—What a dog was I to believe in Women! Oh Coxcomb—ignorant conceited Coxcomb! to fancy she cou'd be enamour'd with my Person at the first sight enamour'd—Oh, I'm a cursed Puppy, 'tis plain, Fool was writ upon my Forehead, she perceiv'd it,—saw
110 the *Essex* Calf there—for what Allurements could there

---

83 **bow'd Gold** bowed is still used in the North of England for bent: 'a bowed pin'

be in this Countenance? which I can indure, because I'm acquainted with it—Oh, dull silly Dog! to be thus sooth'd into a Cozening! Had I been drunk, I might fondly have credited the young Quean! but as I was in my right Wits, to be thus
115 cheated, confirms I am a dull believing *English* Country Fop.—But my Comrades! Death and the Devil, there's the worst of all—then a Ballad will be sung to Morrow on the *Prado*, to a lousy Tune of the enchanted Squire, and the annihilated Damsel—But *Frederick* that Rogue, and the
120 Colonel, will abuse me beyond all Christian patience—had she left me my Clothes, I have a Bill of Exchange at home wou'd have sav'd my Credit—but now all hope is taken from me—Well, I'll home (if I can find the way) with this Consolation, that I am not the first kind believing Coxcomb;
125 but there are, Gallants, many such good Natures amongst ye.

And tho you've better Arts to hide your Follies,
Adsheartlikins y'are all as errant Cullies.

SCENE III

The Garden, in the Night.

Enter FLORINDA, *undress'd, with a Key, and a little Box.*

FLORINDA: Well, thus far I'm in my way to Happiness; I have got my self free from *Callis*; my Brother too, I find by yonder light, is gone into his Cabinet, and thinks not of me: I have by good Fortune got the Key of the Garden Back-door,—
5 I'll open it, to prevent *Belvile's* knocking,—a little noise will now alarm my Brother. Now am I as fearful as a young Thief. (*Unlocks the Door.*)—Hark,—what noise is that?—Oh, 'twas the Wind that plaid amongst the Boughs.—*Belvile* stays long, methinks—it's time—stay—for fear of a surprize, I'll hide
10 these Jewels in yonder Jessamin.

(*She goes to lay down the Box.*)

(*Enter* WILLMORE *drunk.*)

WILLMORE: What the Devil is become of these Fellows, *Belvile* and *Frederick*? They promis'd to stay at the next corner for me, but who the Devil knows the corner of a full Moon?— Now—whereabouts am I?—hah—what have we here? a
15 Garden!—a very convenient place to sleep in—hah—what has God sent us here?—a Female—by this light, a Woman; I'm a Dog if it be not a very Wench.

FLORINDA: He's come!—hah—who's there?

WILLMORE: Sweet Soul, let me salute thy Shoe-string.

FLORINDA: 'Tis not my *Belvile*—good Heavens, I know him
20 not.—Who are you, and from whence come you!

WILLMORE: Prithee—prithee, Child—not so many hard Questions—let it suffice I am here, Child—Come, come kiss me.

FLORINDA: Good Gods! what luck is mine?

WILLMORE: Only good luck, Child, parlous good luck.—Come
25 hither,—'tis a delicate shining Wench,—by this Hand she's perfum'd, and smells like any Nosegay.—Prithee, dear Soul, let's not play the Fool, and lose time,—precious time—for as Gad shall save me, I'm as honest a Fellow as breathes, tho I am a little disguis'd at present.—Come, I say,—why, thou may'st
30

---

30 **disguis'd** a common phrase for drunk

be free with me, I'll be very secret. I'll not boast who 'twas
oblig'd me, not I—for hang me if I know thy Name.
FLORINDA: Heavens! what a filthy beast is this!
WILLMORE: I am so, and thou oughtst the sooner to lie with
35 me for that reason,—for look you, Child, there will be no
Sin in't, because 'twas neither design'd nor premeditated;
'tis pure Accident on both sides—that's a certain thing
now—Indeed should I make love to you, and you vow
Fidelity—and swear and lye till you believ'd and yielded—
40 Thou art therefore (as thou art a good Christian) oblig'd
in Conscience to deny me nothing. Now—come, be kind,
without any more idle prating.
FLORINDA: Oh, I am ruin'd—wicked Man, unhand me.
WILLMORE: Wicked! Egad, Child, a Judge, were he young and
45 vigorous, and saw those Eyes of thine, would know 'twas
they gave the first blow—the first provocation.—Come,
prithee let's lose no time, I say—this is a fine convenient
place.
FLORINDA: Sir, let me go, I conjure you, or I'll call out.
50 WILLMORE: Ay, ay, you were best to call Witness to see how finely
you treat me—do.—
FLORINDA: I'll cry Murder, Rape, or any thing, if you do not
instantly let me go.
WILLMORE: A Rape! Come, come, you lye, you Baggage, you lye:
55 What, I'll warrant you would fain have the World believe now
that you are not so forward as I. No, not you,—why at this
time of Night was your Cobweb-door set open, dear Spider—
but to catch Flies?—Hah come—or I shall be damnably
angry.—Why what a Coil is here.—
60 FLORINDA: Sir, can you think—
WILLMORE: That you'd do it for nothing? oh, oh, I find what
you'd be at—look here, here's a Pistole for you—here's a work
indeed—here—take it, I say.—
FLORINDA: For Heaven's sake, Sir, as you're a Gentleman—
65 WILLMORE: So—now—she would be wheedling me for more—
what, you will not take it then—you're resolv'd you will
not.—Come, come, take it, or I'll put it up again; for, look
ye, I never give more.—Why, how now, Mistress, are you so
high i'th' Mouth, a Pistole won't down with you?—hah—why,
70 what a work's here—in good time—come, no struggling, be
gone—But an y'are good at a dumb Wrestle, I'm for ye,—look
ye,—I'm for ye.—

(*She struggles with him.*)

(*Enter* BELVILE *and* FREDERICK.)

BELVILE: The Door is open, a Pox of this mad Fellow, I'm angry
75 that we've lost him, I durst have sworn he had follow'd us.
FREDERICK: But you were so hasty, Colonel, to be gone.
FLORINDA: Help, help,—Murder!—help—oh, I'm ruin'd.
BELVILE: Ha, sure that's *Florinda*'s Voice.

(*Comes up to them.*)

—A Man! Villain, let go that Lady.

(*A noise.*)

(WILLMORE *turns and draws,* FREDERICK *interposes.*)

FLORINDA: *Belvile!* Heavens! my Brother too is coming, and
80 'twill be impossible to escape.—*Belvile,* I conjure you to
walk under my Chamber-window, from whence I'll give

you some instructions what to do—This rude Man has
undone us.

(*Exit.*)

WILLMORE: *Belvile!*

(*Enter* PEDRO, STEPHANO, *and other Servants with Lights.*)

PEDRO: I'm betray'd; run, *Stephano,* and see if *Florinda* be safe. 85

(*Exit* STEPHANO.)

So who'er they be, all is not well, I'll to *Florinda*'s Chamber.

(*They fight, and* PEDRO's *Party beats 'em out; going out, meets*
STEPHANO.)

STEPHANO: You need not, Sir, the poor Lady's fast asleep,
and thinks no harm: I wou'd not wake her, Sir, for fear of
frightning her with your danger.
PEDRO: I'm glad she's there—Rascals, how came the Garden-Door 90
open?
STEPHANO: That Question comes too late, Sir: some of my
Fellow-Servants Masquerading I'll warrant.
PEDRO: Masquerading! a leud Custom to debauch our
Youth—there's something more in this than I imagine. 95

(*Exeunt.*)

SCENE IV

Changes to the Street.

Enter BELVILE *in Rage,* FREDERICK *holding him, and* WILLMORE
melancholy.

WILLMORE: Why, how the Devil shou'd I know *Florinda?*
BELVILE: Ah plague of your ignorance! if it had not been
Florinda, must you be a Beast?—a Brute, a senseless
Swine?
WILLMORE: Well, Sir, you see I am endu'd with Patience—I can 5
bear—tho egad y're very free with me methinks,—I was in
good hopes the Quarrel wou'd have been on my side, for so
uncivilly interrupting me.
BELVILE: Peace, Brute, whilst thou'rt safe—oh, I'm distracted.
WILLMORE: Nay, nay, I'm an unlucky Dog, that's certain. 10
BELVILE: Ah curse upon the Star that rul'd my Birth! or what-
soever other Influence that makes me still so wretched.
WILLMORE: Thou break'st my Heart with these Complaints;
there is no Star in fault, no Influence but Sack, the cursed
Sack I drank. 15
FREDERICK: Why, how the Devil came you so drunk?
WILLMORE: Why, how the Devil came you so sober?
BELVILE: A curse upon his thin Skull, he was always before-hand
that way.
FREDERICK: Prithee, dear Colonel, forgive him, he's sorry for his 20
fault.
BELVILE: He's always so after he has done a mischief—a plague on
all such Brutes.
WILLMORE: By this Light I took her for an errant Harlot.
BELVILE: Damn your debaucht Opinion: tell me, Sot, hadst thou 25
so much sense and light about thee to distinguish her to be a

Woman, and could'st not see something about her Face and
Person, to strike an awful Reverence into thy Soul?

30 WILLMORE: Faith no, I consider'd her as mere a Woman as I
could wish.

BELVILE: 'Sdeath I have no patience—draw, or I'll kill you.

WILLMORE: Let that alone till to morrow, and if I set not all right
again, use your Pleasure.

BELVILE: To morrow, damn it.

35 The spiteful Light will lead me to no happiness.
To morrow is *Antonio*'s, and perhaps
Guides him to my undoing;—oh that I could meet
This Rival, this powerful Fortunate.

WILLMORE: What then?

40 BELVILE: Let thy own Reason, or my Rage instruct thee.

WILLMORE: I shall be finely inform'd then, no doubt; hear
me, Colonel—hear me—shew me the Man and I'll do his
Business.

BELVILE: I know him no more than thou, or if I did, I should not
45 need thy aid.

WILLMORE: This you say is *Angelica*'s House, I promis'd the kind
Baggage to lie with her to Night.

(*Offers to go in.*)

(*Enter* ANTONIO *and his Page.* ANTONIO *knocks on the Hilt of his
Sword.*)

ANTONIO: You paid the thousand Crowns I directed?

PAGE: To the Lady's old Woman, Sir, I did.

50 WILLMORE: Who the Devil have we here?

BELVILE: I'll now plant my self under *Florinda*'s Window, and if I
find no comfort there, I'll die.

(*Exit* BELVILE *and* FREDERICK. *Enter* MORETTA.)

MORETTA: Page!

PAGE: Here's my Lord.

55 WILLMORE: How is this, a Piccaroon going to board my Frigate!
here's one Chase-Gun for you.

(*Drawing his Sword, justles* ANTONIO *who turns and draws. They
fight,* ANTONIO *falls.*)

MORETTA: Oh, bless us, we are all undone!

(*Runs in, and shuts the Door.*)

PAGE: Help, Murder!

(BELVILE *returns at the noise of fighting.*)

BELVILE: Ha, the mad Rogue's engag'd in some unlucky
60 Adventure again.

(*Enter two or three* MASQUERADERS.)

MASQUERADER: Ha, a Man kill'd!

WILLMORE: How! a Man kill'd! then I'll go home to sleep.

(*Puts up, and reels out. Exeunt* MASQUERADERS *another way.*)

BELVILE: Who shou'd it be! pray Heaven the Rogue is safe, for all
my Quarrel to him.

(*As* BELVILE *is groping about, enter an* OFFICER *and six* SOLDIERS.)

SOLDIER: Who's there? 65

OFFICER: So, here's one dispatcht—secure the Murderer.

BELVILE: Do not mistake my Charity for Murder: I came to his
Assistance.

(SOLDIERS *sieze on* BELVILE.)

OFFICER: That shall be tried, Sir.—St. *Jago,* Swords drawn in the
Carnival time! 70

(*Goes to* ANTONIO.)

ANTONIO: Thy Hand prithee.

OFFICER: Ha, Don *Antonio!* look well to the Villain there.—How
is't, Sir?

ANTONIO: I'm hurt.

BELVILE: Has my Humanity made me a Criminal? 75

OFFICER: Away with him.

BELVILE: What a curst Chance is this!

(*Exeunt* SOLDIERS *with* BELVILE.)

ANTONIO: (*To the* OFFICER.) This is the Man that has set upon
me twice—carry him to my Apartment till you have further
Orders from me. 80

(*Exit.* ANTONIO *led.*)

ACT FOUR

SCENE I

A fine Room.

Discovers BELVILE, *as by Dark alone.*

BELVILE: When shall I be weary of railing on Fortune, who is
resolv'd never to turn with Smiles upon me?—Two such
Defeats in one Night—none but the Devil and that mad
Rogue could have contriv'd to have plagued me with—I am
here a Prisoner—but where?—Heaven knows—and if there 5
be Murder done, I can soon decide the Fate of a Stranger in
a Nation without Mercy—Yet this is nothing to the Torture
my Soul bows with, when I think of losing my fair, my dear
Florinda.—Hark—my Door opens—a Light—a Man—and
seems of Quality—arm'd too.—Now shall I die like a Dog 10
without defence.

(*Enter* ANTONIO *in a Night-Gown, with a Light; his Arm in a Scarf,
and a Sword under his Arm: He sets the Candle on the Table.*)

ANTONIO: Sir, I come to know what Injuries I have done you,
that could provoke you to so mean an Action, as to attack me
basely, without allowing time for my Defence.

BELVILE: Sir, for a Man in my Circumstances to plead Innocence, 15
would look like Fear—but view me well, and you will find
no marks of a Coward on me, nor any thing that betrays that
Brutality you accuse me of.

ANTONIO: In vain, Sir, you impose upon my Sense,
You are not only he who drew on me last Night, 20
But yesterday before the same House, that of *Angelica.*
Yet there is something in your Face and Mein—

BELVILE: I own I fought to day in the defence of a Friend of mine,
  with whom you (if you're the same) and your
25 Party were first engag'd.
  Perhaps you think this Crime enough to kill me,
  But if you do, I cannot fear you'll do it basely.
ANTONIO: No, Sir, I'll make you fit for a Defence with this.

(*Gives him the Sword.*)

BELVILE: This Gallantry surprises me—nor know I how to use
30 this Present, Sir, against a Man so brave.
ANTONIO: You shall not need;
  For know, I come to snatch you from a Danger
  That is decreed against you;
  Perhaps your Life, or long Imprisonment:
35 And 'twas with so much Courage you offended,
  I cannot see you punisht.
BELVILE: How shall I pay this Generosity?
ANTONIO: It had been safer to have kill'd another,
  Than have attempted me:
40 To shew your Danger, Sir, I'll let you know my Quality;
  And 'tis the Vice-Roy's Son whom you have wounded.
BELVILE: (*Aside.*) The Vice-Roy's Son!
  Death and Confusion! was this Plague reserved
  To compleat all the rest?—oblig'd by him!
45 The Man of all the World I would destroy.
ANTONIO: You seem disorder'd, Sir.
BELVILE: Yes, trust me, Sir, I am, and 'tis with pain
  That Man receives such Bounties,
  Who wants the pow'r to pay 'em back again.
50 ANTONIO: To gallant Spirits 'tis indeed uneasy;
  —But you may quickly over-pay me, Sir.
BELVILE: Then I am well—(*Aside.*) kind Heaven! but set us even,
  That I may fight with him, and keep my Honour safe.
  —Oh, I'm impatient, Sir, to be discounting
55 The mighty Debt I owe you; command me quickly—
ANTONIO: I have a Quarrel with a Rival, Sir,
  About the Maid we love.
BELVILE: (*Aside.*) Death, 'tis *Florinda* he means—
  That Thought destroys my Reason, and I shall kill him—
60 ANTONIO: My Rival, Sir.
  Is one has all the Virtues Man can boast of.
BELVILE: Death! who shou'd this be?
ANTONIO: He challeng'd me to meet him on the *Molo*,
  As soon as Day appear'd; but last Night's quarrel
65 Has made my Arm unfit to guide a Sword.
BELVILE: I apprehend you, Sir, you'd have me kill the Man
  That lays a claim to the Maid you speak of.
  —I'll do't—I'll fly to do it.
ANTONIO: Sir, do you know her?
70 BELVILE: —No, Sir, but 'tis enough she is admired by you.
ANTONIO: Sir, I shall rob you of the Glory on't,
  For you must fight under my Name and Dress.
BELVILE: That Opinion must be strangely obliging that makes
  You think I can personate the brave *Antonio*,
75 Whom I can but strive to imitate.
ANTONIO: You say too much to my Advantage.
  Come, Sir, the Day appears that calls you forth.
  Within, Sir, is the Habit.

(*Exit ANTONIO.*)

BELVILE: Fantastick Fortune, thou deceitful Light,
  That cheats the wearied Traveller by Night,   80
  Tho on a Precipice each step you tread,
  I am resolv'd to follow where you lead.

(*Exit.*)

SCENE II

The Molo.

Enter FLORINDA and CALLIS in Masques, with STEPHANO.

FLORINDA: (*Aside.*) I'm dying with my fears; *Belvile's* not coming,
  As I expected, underneath my Window,
  Makes me believe that all those Fears are true.
  —Canst thou not tell with whom my Brother fights?
STEPHANO: No, Madam, they were both in Masquerade, I was by   5
  when they challeng'd one another, and they had decided the
  Quarrel then, but were prevented by some Cavaliers; which
  made 'em put it off till now—but I am sure 'tis about you
  they fight.
FLORINDA: (*Aside.*) Nay then 'tis with *Belvile*, for what other   10
  Lover have I that dares fight for me, except *Antonio?* and he
  is too much in favour with my Brother—If it be he, for whom
  shall I direct my Prayers to Heaven?
STEPHANO: Madam, I must leave you; for if my Master see me,
  I shall be hang'd for being your Conductor.—I escap'd   15
  narrowly for the Excuse I made for you last night i'th' Garden.
FLORINDA: And I'll reward thee for't—prithee no more.

(*Exit STEPHANO.*)

(*Enter Don PEDRO in his Masquing Habit.*)

PEDRO: *Antonio's* late to day, the place will fill, and we may be
  prevented.

(*Walks about.*)

FLORINDA: (*Aside.*) Antonio! sure I heard amiss.   20
PEDRO: But who would not excuse a happy Lover.
  When soft fair Arms comfine the yielding Neck;
  And the kind Whisper languishingly breathes,
  Must you be gone so soon?
  Sure I had dwelt for ever on her Bosom.   25
  —But stay, he's here.

(*Enter BELVILE drest in ANTONIO's Clothes.*)

FLORINDA: 'Tis not *Belvile*, half my Fears are vanisht.
PEDRO: *Antonio!*—
BELVILE: (*Aside.*) This must be he.
  You're early, Sir,—I do not use to be out-done this way.   30
PEDRO: The wretched, Sir, are watchful, and 'tis enough
  You have the advantage of me in *Angelica*.
BELVILE: (*Aside.*) Angelica!
  Or I've mistook my Man! Or else *Antonio*,
  Can he forget his Interest in *Florinda*,   35
  And fight for common Prize?
PEDRO: Come, Sir, you know our terms—
BELVILE: (*Aside.*) Be Heaven, not I.
  —No talking, I am ready, Sir.

(*Offers to fight.* FLORINDA *runs in.*)

40 FLORINDA: (*To* BELVILE.) Oh, hold! who'er you be, I do conjure
  you hold. If you strike here—I die—
  PEDRO: *Florinda!*
  BELVILE: *Florinda* imploring for my Rival!
  PEDRO: Away, this Kindness is unseasonable.

(*Puts her by, they fight; she runs in just as* BELVILE *disarms* PEDRO.)

45 FLORINDA: Who are you, Sir, that dare deny my Prayers?
  BELVILE: Thy Prayers destroy him; if thou wouldst preserve him.
    Do that thou'rt unacquainted with, and curse him.

(*She holds him.*)

  FLORINDA: By all you hold most dear, by her you love,
    I do conjure you, touch him not.
50 BELVILE: By her I love!
    See—I obey—and at your Feet resign
    The useless Trophy of my Victory.

(*Lays his sword at her Feet.*)

  PEDRO: *Antonio,* you've done enough to prove you love *Florinda.*
  BELVILE: Love *Florinda!*
55   Does Heaven love Adoration, Pray'r, or Penitence?
    Love her! here Sir,—your Sword again.

(*Snatches up the Sword, and gives it him.*)

    Upon this Truth I'll fight my Life away.
  PEDRO: No, you've redeem'd my Sister, and my Friendship.
  BELVILE: Don *Pedro!*

(*He gives him* FLORINDA *and pulls off his Vizard to shew his Face,
and puts it on again.*)

60 PEDRO: Can you resign your Claims to other Women,
    And give your Heart intirely to *Florinda?*
  BELVILE: Intire, as dying Saints Confessions are.
    I can delay my happiness no longer.
    This minute let me make *Florinda* mine:
65 PEDRO: This minute let it be—no time so proper,
    This Night my Father will arrive from *Rome,*
    And possibly may hinder what we propose.
  FLORINDA: Oh Heavens! this Minute!

(*Enter* MASQUERADERS, *and pass over.*)

  BELVILE: Oh, do not ruin me!
70 PEDRO: The place begins to fill; and that we may not be observ'd,
    do you walk off to St. *Peter's* Church, where I will meet you,
    and conclude your Happiness.
  BELVILE: I'll meet you there—(*Aside.*) if there be no more Saints
    Churches in *Naples.*
75 FLORINDA: Oh stay, Sir, and recall your hasty Doom:
    Alas I have not yet prepar'd my Heart
    To entertain so strange a Guest.
  PEDRO: Away, this silly Modesty is assum'd too late.
  BELVILE: Heaven, Madam! what do you do?
80 FLORINDA: Do! despise the Man that lays a Tyrant's Claim
    To what he ought to conquer by Submission.
  BELVILE: You do not know me—move a little this way.

(*Draws her aside.*)

  FLORINDA: Yes, you may even force me to the Altar,
    But not the holy Man that offers there
    Shall force me to be thine.   85

(PEDRO *talks to* CALLIS *this while.*)

  BELVILE: Oh do not lose so blest an opportunity!
    See—'tis your *Belvile*—not *Antonio,*
    Whom your mistaken Scorn and Anger ruins.

(*Pulls off his Vizard.*)

  FLORINDA: *Belvile!*
    Where was my Soul it cou'd not meet thy Voice,   90
    And take this knowledge in?

(*As they are talking, enter* WILLMORE *finely* DREST, *and* FREDERICK.)

  WILLMORE: No Intelligence! no News of *Belvile* yet—well I am the
    most unlucky Rascal in Nature—ha!—am I deceiv'd—or is it
    he—look, *Frederick*—'tis he—my dear *Belvile.*

(*Runs and embraces him.* BELVILE's *Vizard falls out on's Hand.*)

  BELVILE: Hell and Confusion seize thee!   95
  PEDRO: Ha! *Belvile!* I beg your Pardon, Sir.

(*Takes* FLORINDA *from him.*)

  BELVILE: Nay, touch her not, she's mine by Conquest, Sir.
    I won her by my Sword.
  WILLMORE: Did'st thou so—and egad, Child, we'll keep her
    by the Sword.   100

(*Draws on* PEDRO, BELVILE *goes between.*)

  BELVILE: Stand off.
    Thou'rt so profanely leud, so curst by Heaven,
    All Quarrels thou espousest must be fatal.
  WILLMORE: Nay, an you be so hot, my Valour's coy,
    And shall be courted when you want it next.   105

(*Puts up his Sword.*)

  BELVILE: You know I ought to claim a Victor's Right,

(*To* PEDRO.)

    But you're the Brother to divine *Florinda,*
    To whom I'm such a Slave—to purchase her,
    I durst not hurt the Man she holds so dear.
  PEDRO: 'Twas by *Antonio's,* not by *Belvile's* Sword,   110
    This Question should have been decided, Sir:
    I must confess much to your Bravery's due,
    Both now, and when I met you last in Arms.
    But I am nicely punctual in my word,
    As Men of Honour ought, and beg your Pardon.   115

(*Aside to* FLORINDA *as they are going out.*)

—For this Mistake another Time shall clear.
—This was some Plot between you and *Belvile*:
But I'll prevent you.

(BELVILE *looks after her, and begins to walk up and down in a Rage.*)

WILLMORE: Do not be modest now, and lose the Woman: but if we
120   shall fetch her back, so—
BELVILE: Do not speak to me.
WILLMORE: Not speak to you!—Egad, I'll speak to you, and will
       be answered too.
BELVILE: Will you, Sir?
125 WILLMORE: I know I've done some mischief, but I'm so dull
       a Puppy, that I am the Son of a Whore, if I know how, or
       where—prithee inform my Understanding.—
BELVILE: Leave me I say, and leave me instantly.
WILLMORE: I will not leave you in this humour, nor till I know
130   my Crime.
BELVILE: Death, I'll tell you, Sir—

(*Draws and runs at* WILLMORE; *he runs out;* BELVILE *after him,* FREDERICK *interposes.*)

(*Enter* ANGELICA, MORETTA, *and* SEBASTIAN.)

ANGELICA: Ha—*Sebastian*—Is not that *Willmore?* haste, haste,
       and bring him back.
FREDERICK: The Colonel's mad—I never saw him thus before; I'll
135   after 'em, lest he do some mischief, for I am sure *Willmore* will
       not draw on him.

(*Exit.*)

ANGELICA: I am all Rage! my first desires defeated
       For one, for ought he knows, that has no
       Other Merit than her Quality,—
140   Her being Don *Pedro's* Sister—He loves her:
       I know 'tis so—dull, dull, insensible—
       He will not see me now tho oft invited;
       And broke his Word last night—false perjur'd Man!
       —He that but yesterday fought for my Favours,
145   And would have made his Life a Sacrifice
       To've gain'd one Night with me,
       Must now be hired and courted to my Arms.
MORETTA: I told you what wou'd come on't, but *Moretta's* an
       old doating Fool—Why did you give him five hundred
150   Crowns, but to set himself out for other Lovers? You
       shou'd have kept him poor, if you had meant to have had
       any good from him.
ANGELICA: Oh, name not such mean Trifles.—Had I given him all
       My Youth has earn'd from Sin,
155   I had not lost a Thought nor Sigh upon't.
       But I have given him my eternal Rest,
       My whole Repose, my future Joys, my Heart;
       My Virgin Heart. *Moretta!* oh 'tis gone!
MORETTA: Curse on him, here he comes;
160   How fine she has made him too!

(*Enter* WILLMORE *and* SEBASTIAN. ANGELICA *turns and walks away.*)

WILLMORE: How now, turn'd Shadow?
       Fly when I pursue, and follow when I fly!

(*Sings.*)

> Stay gentle Shadow of my Dove,
>   And tell me e'er I go,
> Whether the Substance may not prove   165
>   A fleeting Thing like you.

There's a soft kind Look remaining yet.

(*As she turns she looks on him.*)

ANGELICA: Well, Sir, you may be gay; all Happiness, all Joys
       pursue you still, Fortune's your Slave, and gives you every
       hour choice of new Hearts and Beauties, till you are cloy'd   170
       with the repeated Bliss, which others vainly languish for—But
       know, false Man, that I shall be reveng'd.

(*Turns away in a Rage.*)

WILLMORE: So, 'gad, there are of those faint-hearted Lovers,
       whom such a sharp Lesson next their Hearts would make as
       impotent as Fourscore—pox o' this whining—my Bus'ness is   175
       to laugh and love—a pox on't; I hate your sullen Lover, a Man
       shall lose as much time to put you in Humour now, as would
       serve to gain a new Woman.
ANGELICA: I scorn to cool that Fire I cannot raise,
       Or do the Drudgery of your virtuous Mistress.   180
WILLMORE: A virtuous Mistress! Death, what a thing thou
       hast found out for me! why what the Devil should I do
       with a virtuous Woman?—a fort of ill'natur'd Creatures,
       that take a Pride to torment a Lover. Virtue is but an
       Infirmity in Women, a Disease that renders even the   185
       handsom ungrateful; whilst the ill-favour'd, for want of
       Sollicitations and Address, only fancy themselves so.—I have
       lain with a Woman of Quality, who has all the while been
       railing at Whores.
ANGELICA: I will not answer for your Mistress's Virtue,   190
       Tho she be young enough to know no Guilt:
       And I could wish you would persuade my Heart,
       'Twas the two hundred thousand Crowns you courted.
WILLMORE: Two hundred thousand Crowns! what Story's
       this?—what Trick?—what Woman?—ha.   195
ANGELICA: How strange you make it! have you forgot the
       Creature you entertain'd on the Piazza last night?
WILLMORE: Ha, my Gipsy worth two hundred thousand
       Crowns!—oh how I long to be with her—pox, I knew she was
       of Quality.   200
ANGELICA: False Man, I see my Ruin in thy Face.
       How many vows you breath'd upon my Bosom,
       Never to be unjust—have you forgot so soon?
WILLMORE: Faith no, I was just coming to repeat 'em—but here's a
       Humour indeed—would make a Man a Saint—(*Aside.*) Wou'd   205
       she'd be angry enough to leave me, and command me not to
       wait on her.

(*Enter* HELLENA, *drest in Man's Clothes.*)

HELLENA: This must be *Angelica,* I know it by her mumping
       Matron here—Ay, ay, 'tis she: my mad Captain's with her too,
       for all his swearing—how this unconstant Humour makes   210
       me love him:—pray, good grave Gentlewoman, is not this
       Angelica?

MORETTA: My too young Sir, it is—I hope 'tis one from Don
Antonio.

(Goes to ANGELICA.)

215 HELLENA: (Aside.) Well, something I'll do to vex him for this.
ANGELICA: I will not speak with him; am I in humour to receive
a Lover?
WILLMORE: Not speak with him! why I'll be gone—and wait your
idler minutes—Can I shew less Obedience to the thing I love
220 so fondly?

(Offers to go.)

ANGELICA: A fine Excuse this—stay—
WILLMORE: And hinder your Advantage: should I repay your
Bounties so ungratefully?
ANGELICA: Come, hither, Boy,—that I may let you see
225 How much above the Advantages you name
I prize one Minute's Joy with you.
WILLMORE: Oh, you destroy me with this Endearment.

(Impatient to be gone.)

—Death, how shall I get away!—Madam, 'twill not be
fit I should be seen with you—besides, it will not be
230 convenient—and I've a Friend—that's dangerously sick.
ANGELICA: I see you're impatient—yet you shall stay.
WILLMORE: And miss my Assignation with my Gipsy.

(Aside, and walks about impatiently. MORETTA brings HELLENA,
who addresses her self to ANGELICA.)

HELLENA: Madam, You'l hardly pardon my Intrusion,
When you shall know my Business;
235 And I'm too young to tell my Tale with Art:
But there must be a wondrous store of Goodness
Where so much Beauty dwells.
ANGELICA: A pretty Advocate, whoever sent thee,
—Prithee proceed—Nay, Sir, you shall not go.

(To WILLMORE, who is stealing off.)

240 WILLMORE: Then shall I lose my dear Gipsy for ever.
(Aside.)—Pox on't, she stays me out of spite.
HELLENA: I am related to a Lady, Madam,
Young, rich, and nobly born, but has the fate
To be in love with a young English Gentleman.
245 Strangely she loves him, at first sight she lov'd him,
But did adore him when she heard him speak;
For he, she said, had Charms in every word,
That fail'd not to surprize, to wound, and conquer—
WILLMORE: (Aside.) Ha, Egad I hope this concerns me.
250 ANGELICA: 'Tis my false Man, he means—wou'd he were gone.
This Praise will raise his Pride and ruin me—(To WILLMORE.)
Well,
Since you are so impatient to be gone.
I will release you, Sir.
WILLMORE: (Aside.) Nay, then I'm sure 'twas me he spoke of, this
255 cannot be the Effects of Kindness in her.
—No, Madam, I've consider'd better on't,
And will not give you cause of Jealousy.
ANGELICA: But, Sir, I've—business, that—
WILLMORE: This shall not do, I know 'tis but to try me.

ANGELICA: (Aside.) Well, to your Story, Boy,—tho 'twill undo me. 260
HELLENA: With this Addition to his other Beauties,
He won her unresisting tender Heart,
He vow'd and sigh'd, and swore he lov'd her dearly;
And she believ'd the cunning Flatterer,
And thought her self the happiest Maid alive: 265
To day was the appointed time by both,
To consummate their Bliss;
The Virgin, Altar, and the Priest were drest,
And whilst she languisht for the expected Bridegroom,
She heard, he paid his broken Vows to you. 270
WILLMORE: (Aside.) So, this is some dear Rogue that's in love with
me, and this way lets me know it; or if it be not me, she means
some one whose place I may supply.
ANGELICA: Now I perceive
The cause of thy Impatience to be gone, 275
And all the business of this glorious Dress.
WILLMORE: Damn the young Prater, I know not what he means.
HELLENA: Madam,
In your fair Eyes I read too much concern
To tell my farther Business. 280
ANGELICA: Prithee, sweet Youth, talk on, thou may'st perhaps
Raise here a Storm that may undo my Passion,
And then I'll grant thee any thing.
HELLENA: Madam, 'tis to intreat you, (oh unreasonable!)
You wou'd not see this Stranger; 285
For if you do, she vows you are undone,
Tho Nature never made a Man so excellent;
And sure he'ad been a God, but for Inconstancy.
WILLMORE: (Aside.) Ah, Rogue, how finely he's instructed!
—'Tis plain some Woman that has seen me en passant. 290
ANGELICA: Oh, I shall burst with Jealousy! do you know the Man
you speak of?—
HELLENA: Yes, Madam, he us'd to be in Buff and Scarlet.
ANGELICA: (To WILLMORE.) Thou, false as Hell, what canst thou
say to this? 295
WILLMORE: By Heaven—
ANGELICA: Hold, do not damn thy self—
HELLENA: Nor hope to be believ'd.

(He walks about, they follow.)

ANGELICA: Oh, perjur'd Man!
Is't thus you pay my generous Passion back? 300
HELLENA: Why wou'd you, Sir, abuse my Lady's Faith?
ANGELICA: And use me so unhumanly?
HELLENA: A Maid so young, so innocent—
WILLMORE: Ah, young Devil!
ANGELICA: Dost thou not know thy Life is in my Power? 305
HELLENA: Or think my Lady cannot be reveng'd?
WILLMORE: (Aside.) So, so, the Storm comes finely on.
ANGELICA: Now thou art silent, Guilt has struck thee dumb.
Oh, hadst thou still been so, I'd liv'd in safety.

(She turns away and weeps.)

WILLMORE: (Aside to HELLENA, looks towards ANGELICA to 310
watch her turning; and as she comes towards them, he meets
her.) Sweetheart, the Lady's Name and House—quickly: I'm
impatient to be with her.
HELLENA: (Aside.) So now is he for another Woman.
WILLMORE: The impudent'st young thing in Nature! 315
I cannot persuade him out of his Error, Madam.

ANGELICA: I know he's in the right,—yet thou'st a Tongue
That wou'd persuade him to deny his Faith.

(*In Rage walks away.*)

WILLMORE: (*Said softly to* HELLENA.) Her Name, her Name,
dear Boy—

320 HELLENA: Have you forgot it, Sir?

WILLMORE: (*Aside.*) Oh, I perceive he's not to know I am a
Stranger to his Lady.
—Yes, yes, I do know—but—I have forgot the—

(ANGELICA *turns.*)

—By Heaven, such early confidence I never saw.

ANGELICA: Did I not charge you with this Mistress, Sir?
325 Which you denied, tho I beheld your Perjury.
This little Generosity of thine has render'd back my Heart.

(*Walks away.*)

WILLMORE: So, you have made sweet work here, my little
mischief;
Look your Lady be kind and good-natur'd now, or
I shall have but a cursed Bargain on't.

(ANGELICA *turns towards them.*)

330 —The Rogue's bred up to Mischief,
Art thou so great a Fool to credit him?

ANGELICA: Yes, I do; and you in vain impose upon me.
—Come hither, Boy—Is not this he you speak of?

HELLENA: (HELLENA *looks in his Face, he gazes on her.*) I think—it
335 is; I cannot swear, but I vow he has just such another lying
Lover's look.

WILLMORE: (*Aside.*) Hah! do not I know that Face?—
By Heaven, my little Gipsy! what a dull Dog was I?
Had I but lookt that way, I'd known her.
340 Are all my hopes of a new Woman banisht?
—Egad, if I don't fit thee for this, hang me.
—Madam, I have found out the Plot.

HELLENA: Oh Lord, what does he say? am I discover'd now?

WILLMORE: Do you see this young Spark here?

345 HELLENA: He'll tell her who I am.

WILLMORE: Who do you think this is?

HELLENA: Ay, ay, he does know me.—Nay, dear Captain, I'm
undone if you discover me.

WILLMORE: Nay, nay, no cogging; she shall know what a precious
350 Mistress I have.

HELLENA: Will you be such a Devil?

WILLMORE: Nay, nay, I'll teach you to spoil sport you will not
make.—This small Ambassador comes not from a Person of
Quality, as you imagine, and he says; but from a very errant
355 Gipsy, the talkingst, pratingst, cantingst little Animal thou
ever saw'st.

ANGELICA: What news you tell me! that's the thing I mean.

HELLENA: (*Aside.*) Wou'd I were well off the place.—If ever I go a
Captain-hunting again.—

WILLMORE: Mean that thing? that Gipsy thing? thou may'st as   360
well be jealous of thy Monkey, or Parrot as her: a *German*
Motion were worth a dozen of her, and a Dream were a
better Enjoyment, a Creature of Constitution fitter for
Heaven than Man.

HELLENA: (*Aside.*) Tho I'm sure he lyes, yet this vexes me.   365

ANGELICA: You are mistaken, she's a *Spanish* Woman
Made up of no such dull Materials.

WILLMORE: Materials! Egad, and she be made of any that will
either dispense, or admit of Love, I'll be bound to
continence.   370

HELLENA: (*Aside to him.*) Unreasonable Man, do you think so?

WILLMORE: You may Return, my little Brazen Head, and tell your
Lady, that till she be handsom enough to be belov'd, or I dull
enough to be religious, there will be small hopes of me.

ANGELICA: Did you not promise then to marry her?   375

WILLMORE: Not I, by Heaven.

ANGELICA: You cannot undeceive my fears and torments, till you
have vow'd you will not marry her.

HELLENA: If he swears that, he'll be reveng'd on me indeed for all
my Rogueries.   380

ANGELICA: I know what Arguments you'll bring against me,
Fortune and Honour.

WILLMORE: Honour! I tell you, I hate it in your Sex; and those
that fancy themselves possest of that Foppery, are the most
impertinently troublesom of all Woman-kind, and will   385
transgress nine Commandments to keep one: and to satisfy
your Jealousy I swear—

HELLENA: (*Aside to him.*) Oh, no swearing, dear Captain—

WILLMORE: If it were possible I should ever be inclin'd to marry,
it should be some kind young Sinner, one that has Generosity   390
enough to give a favour handsomely to one that can ask it
discreetly, one that has Wit enough to manage an Intrigue of
Love—oh, how civil such a Wench is, to a Man than does her
the Honour to marry her.

ANGELICA: By Heaven, there's no Faith in any thing he says.   395

(*Enter* SEBASTIAN.)

SEBASTIAN: Madam, *Don Antonio*—

ANGELICA: Come hither.

HELLENA: Ha, *Antonio!* he may be coming hither, and he'll
certainly discover me, I'll therefore retire without a
Ceremony.

(*Exit* HELLENA.)

ANGELICA: I'll see him, get my Coach ready.   400

SEBASTIAN: It waits you, Madam.

WILLMORE: This is lucky: what, Madam, now I may be gone and
leave you to the enjoyment of my Rival?

ANGELICA: Dull Man, that canst not see how ill, how poor
That false dissimulation looks—Be gone,   405
And never let me see thy cozening Face again,
Lest I relapse and kill thee.

WILLMORE: Yes, you can spare me now,—farewell till you are in a
better Humour—I'm glad of this release—
Now for my Gipsy: 410
For tho to worse we change, yet still we find
New Joys, New Charms, in a new Miss that's kind.

(*Exit* WILLMORE.)

---

349 **cogging** to cog = to trick, wheedle, or cajole

ANGELICA: He's gone, and in this Ague of My Soul
    The shivering Fit returns;
415   Oh with what willing haste he took his leave,
    As if the long'd for Minute were arriv'd,
    Of some blest Assignation.
    In vain I have consulted all my Charms,
    In vain this Beauty priz'd, in vain believ'd
420   My eyes cou'd kindle any lasting Fires.
    I had forgot my Name, my Infamy,
    And the Reproach that Honour lays on those
    That dare pretend a sober passion here.
    Nice Reputation, tho it leave behind
425   More Virtues than inhabit where that dwells,
    Yet that once gone, those virtues shine no more.
    —Then since I am not fit to belov'd,
    I am resolv'd to think on a Revenge
    On him that sooth'd me thus to my undoing.

(*Exeunt.*)

SCENE III

A Street.

Enter FLORINDA *and* VALERIA *in Habits different from what they have been seen in.*

FLORINDA: We're happily escap'd, yet I tremble still.
VALERIA: A Lover and fear! why, I am but half a one, and yet
    I have Courage for any Attempt. Would *Hellena* were here.
    I wou'd fain have had her as deep in this Mischief as we,
5   she'll fare but ill else I doubt.
FLORINDA: She pretended a Visit to the *Augustine* Nuns, but
    I believe some other design carried her out, pray Heavens
    we light on her.
VALERIA: When I saw no reason wou'd go good on her, I follow'd
10   her into the Wardrobe, and as she was looking for something
    in a great Chest, I tumbled her in by the Heels, snatcht the
    Key of the Apartment where you were confin'd, lockt her in,
    and left her bauling for help.
FLORINDA: 'Tis well you resolve to follow my Fortunes, for thou
15   darest never appear at home again after such an Action.
VALERIA: That's according as the young Stranger and I shall
    agree—But to our business—I deliver'd your Letter, your Note
    to *Belvile,* when I got out under pretence of going to Mass, I
    found him at his Lodging, and believe me it came seasonably;
20   for never was Man in so desperate a Condition. I told him of
    your Resolution of making your escape to day, if your Brother
    would be absent long enough to permit you; if not, die rather
    than be *Antonio's.*
FLORINDA: Thou shou'dst have told him I was confin'd to my
25   Chamber upon my Brother's suspicion, that the Business on
    the *Molo* was a Plot laid between him and I.
VALERIA: I said all this, and told him your Brother was now gone
    to his Devotion, and he resolves to visit every Church till he
    find him; and not only undeceive him in that, but caress him
30   so as shall delay his return home.
FLORINDA: Oh Heavens! he's here, and *Belvile* with him too.

(*They put on their Vizards.*)

(*Enter Don* PEDRO, BELVILE, WILLMORE; BELVILE, *and Don* PEDRO *seeming in serious Discourse.*)

VALERIA: Walk boldly by them, I'll come at a distance, lest he
    suspect us.

(*She walks by them, and looks back on them.*)

WILLMORE: Ha! A Woman! and of an excellent Mien!
PEDRO: She throws a kind look back on you.   35
WILLMORE: Death, tis a likely Wench, and that kind look shall not
    be cast away—I'll follow her.
BELVILE: Prithee do not.
WILLMORE: Do not! By Heavens to the Antipodes, with such an
    Invitation.   40

(*She goes out, and* WILLMORE *follows her.*)

BELVILE: 'Tis a mad Fellow for a Wench.

(*Enter* FREDERICK.)

FREDERICK: Oh Colonel, such News.
BELVILE: Prithee what?
FREDERICK: News that will make you laugh in spite of Fortune.
BELVILE: What, *Blunt* has had some damn'd Trick put upon him,   45
    cheated, bang'd, or clapt?
FREDERICK: Cheated, Sir, rarely cheated of all but his Shirt
    and Drawers; the unconscionable Whore too turn'd him
    out before Consummation, so that traversing the Streets
    at Midnight, the Watch found him in this *Fresco,* and   50
    conducted him home: By Heaven 'tis such a slight, and yet
    I durst as well have been hang'd as laugh at him, or pity
    him; he beats all that do but ask him a Question, and is in
    such an Humour—
PEDRO: Who is't has met with this ill usage, Sir?   55
BELVILE: (*Aside.*) A Friend of ours, whom you must see for
    Mirth's sake. I'll imploy him to give *Florinda* time for an
    escape.
PEDRO: Who is he?
BELVILE: A young Countryman of ours, one that has been   60
    educated at so plentiful a rate, he yet ne'er knew the want of
    Money, and 'twill be a great Jest to see how simply he'll look
    without it. For my part I'll lend him none, and the Rogue
    knows not how to put on a borrowing Face, and ask first.
    I'll let him see how good 'tis to play our parts whilst I play   65
    his—Prithee, *Frederick* do go home and keep him in that
    posture till we come.

(*Exeunt.*)

(*Enter* FLORINDA *from the farther end of the Scene, looking behind her.*)

FLORINDA: I am follow'd still—hah—my Brother too
    advancing this way, good Heavens defend me from being
    seen by him.   70

(*She goes off.*)

(*Enter* WILLMORE, *and after him* VALERIA, *at a little distance.*)

WILLMORE: Ah! There she sails, she looks back as she were willing
    to be boarded, I'll warrant her Prize.

(*He goes out,* VALERIA *following.*)

(*Enter* HELLENA, *just as he goes out, with a* PAGE.)

HELLENA: Hah, is not that my Captain that has a Woman in
chase?—'tis not *Angelica*. Boy, follow those People at a
75 distance, and bring me an Account where they go in.—I'll
find his Haunts, and plague him every where.—ha—my
Brother!

(*Exit* PAGE. BELVILE, WILLMORE, *and* PEDRO *cross the Stage:*
HELLENA *runs off.*)

(*Scene changes to another Street. Enter* FLORINDA.)

FLORINDA: What shall I do, my Brother now pursues me. Will
no kind Power protect me from his Tyranny?—Hah, here's a
80 Door open, I'll venture in, since nothing can be worse than to
fall into his Hands, my Life and Honour are at stake, and my
Necessity has no choice.

(*She goes in. Enter* VALERIA, *and* HELLENA's PAGE *peeping after*
FLORINDA.)

PAGE: Here she went in, I shall remember this House.

(*Exit* PAGE.)

VALERIA: This is *Belvile*'s Lodgings; she's gone in as readily as if
85 she knew it—hah—here's that mad Fellow again, I dare not
venture in—I'll watch my Opportunity.

(*Goes aside. Enter* WILLMORE, *gazing about him.*)

WILLMORE: I have lost her hereabouts—Pox on't she must not
scape me so.

(*Goes out.*)

(*Scene changes to* BLUNT's *chamber, discovers him sitting on a
couch in his shirt and drawers, reading.*)

BLUNT: So, now my Mind's a little at Peace, since I have
90 resolv'd Revenge—A Pox on this Taylor tho, for not
bringing home the Clothes I bespoke; and a Pox of all
poor Cavaliers, a Man can never keep a spare Suit for 'em;
and I shall have these Rogues come in and find me naked;
and then I'm undone; but I'm resolv'd to arm my self—the
95 Rascals shall not insult over me too much.

(*Puts on an old rusty Sword and Buff-Belt.*)

—Now, how like a Morrice-Dancer I am equipt—a fine
Lady-like Whore to cheat me thus, without affording me a
Kindness for my Money, a Pox light on her, I shall never be
reconciled to the Sex more, she has made me as faithless as
100 a Physician, as uncharitable as a Churchman, and as ill-
natur'd as a Poet. O how I'll use all Womenkind hereafter!
what wou'd I give to have one of 'em within my reach now!
any Mortal thing in Petticoats, kind Fortune, send me; and
I'll forgive thy last Night's Malice—Here's a cursed Book
105 too, (a Warning to all young Travellers) that can instruct me
how to prevent such Mischiefs now 'tis too late. Well 'tis a
rare convenient thing to read a little now and then, as well
as hawk and hunt.

(*Sits down again and reads.*)

(*Enter to him* FLORINDA.)

FLORINDA: This House is haunted sure, 'tis well furnisht and
no living thing inhabits it—hah—a Man! Heavens how he's 110
attir'd! sure 'tis some Rope-dancer, or Fencing-Master; I
tremble now for fear, and yet I must venture now to speak to
him—Sir, if I may not interrupt your Meditations—

(*He starts up and gazes.*)

BLUNT: Hah—what's here? Are my wishes granted? and is not
that a she Creature? Adsheartlikins 'tis! what wretched 115
thing art thou—hah!
FLORINDA: Charitable Sir, you've told your self already what
I am; a very wretched Maid, forc'd by a strange unlucky
Accident, to seek a safety here, and must be ruin'd, if you
do not grant it. 120
BLUNT: Ruin'd? Is there any Ruin so inevitable as that which
now threatens thee? Dost thou know, miserable Woman,
into what Den of Mischiefs thou art fall'n? what a Bliss of
Confusion?—hah—dost not see something in my looks
that frights thy guilty Soul, and makes thee wish to change 125
that Shape of Woman for any humble Animal, or Devil? for
those were safer for thee, and less mischievous.
FLORINDA: Alas, what mean you, Sir? I must confess your Looks
have something in 'em makes me fear; but I beseech you, as
you seem a Gentleman, pity a harmless Virgin, that takes your 130
House for Sanctuary.
BLUNT: Talk on, talk on, and weep too, till my faith return. Do,
flatter me out of my Senses again—a harmless Virgin with
a Pox, as much one as t'other, adsheartlikins. Why, what
the Devil can I not be safe in my House for you? not in my 135
Chamber? nay, even being naked too cannot secure me. This
is an Impudence greater than has invaded me yet.—Come, no
Resistance.

(*Pulls her rudely.*)

FLORINDA: Dare you be so cruel?
BLUNT: Cruel, adsheartlikins as a Gally-slave, or a *Spanish* 140
Whore: Cruel, yes, I will kiss and beat thee all over; kiss,
and see thee all over; thou shalt lie with me too, not that
I care for the Injoyment, but to let you see I have ta'en
deliberated Malice to thee, and will be revenged on one
Whore for the Sins of another; I will smile and deceive 145
thee, flatter thee, and beat thee, kiss and swear, and lye to
thee, imbrace thee and rob thee, as she did me, fawn
on thee, and strip thee stark naked, then hang thee out at my
Window by the Heels, with a Paper of scurvey Verses
fasten'd to thy Breast, in praise of damnable Women—Come, 150
come along.
FLORINDA: Alas, Sir, must I be sacrific'd for the Crimes of the most
infamous of my Sex? I never understood the Sins you name.
BLUNT: Do, persuade the Fool you love him, or that one of you
can be just or honest; tell me I was not an easy Coxcomb, 155
or any strange impossible Tale: it will be believ'd sooner
than thy false Showers or Protestations. A Generation of
damn'd Hypocrites, to flatter my very Clothes from my back!
dissembling Witches! are these the Returns you make an
honest Gentleman that trusts, believes, and loves you?—But if 160
I be not even with you—Come along, or I shall—

(Pulls her again.)

(Enter FREDERICK.*)*

FREDERICK: Hah, what's here to do?

BLUNT: Adsheartlikins, *Frederick* I am glad thou art come, to be a Witness of my dire Revenge.

165 FREDERICK: What's this, a Person of Quality too, who is upon the Ramble to supply the Defects of some grave impotent Husband?

BLUNT: No, this has another Pretence, some very unfortunate Accident brought her hither, to save a Life pursued by I

170 know not who, or why, and forc'd to take Sanctuary here at Fools Haven. Adsheartlikins to me of all Mankind for Protection? Is the Ass to be cajol'd again, think ye? No, young one, no Prayers or Tears shall mitigate my Rage; therefore prepare for both my Pleasure of Enjoyment and

175 Revenge, for I am resolved to make up my Loss here on thy Body, I'll take it out in kindness and in beating.

FREDERICK: Now, Mistress of mine, what do you think of this?

FLORINDA: I think he will not—dares not be so barbarous.

FREDERICK: Have a care, *Blunt,* she fetch'd a deep Sigh, she

180 is inamour'd with thy Shirt and Drawers, she'll strip thee even of that. There are of her Calling such unconscionable Baggages, and such dexterous Thieves, they'll flea a Man, and he shall ne'er miss his Skin, till he feels the Cold. There was a Country-man of ours robb'd of a Row of

185 Teeth whilst he was sleeping, which the Jilt made him buy again when he wak'd—You see, Lady, how little Reason we have to trust you.

BLUNT: 'Dsheartlikins, why, this is most abominable.

FLORINDA: Some such Devils there may be, but by all that's holy I

190 am none such, I entered here to save a Life in danger.

BLUNT: For no goodness I'll warrant her.

FREDERICK: Faith, Damsel, you had e'en confess the plain Truth, for we are Fellows not to be caught twice in the same Trap: Look on that Wreck, a tight Vessel when he set out of Haven,

195 well trim'd and laden, and see how a Female Piccaroon of this Island of Rogues has shatter'd him, and canst thou hope for any Mercy?

BLUNT: No, no, Gentlewoman, come along, adsheartlikins we must be better acquainted—we'll both lie with her, and then

200 let me alone to bang her.

FREDERICK: I am ready to serve you in matters of Revenge, that has a double Pleasure in't.

BLUNT: Well said. You hear, little one, how you are condemn'd by publick Vote to the Bed within, there's no resisting your

205 Destiny, Sweetheart.

(Pulls her.)

FLORINDA: Stay, Sir, I have seen you with *Belvile,* an *English* Cavalier, for his sake use me kindly; you know how, Sir.

BLUNT: *Belvile!* why, yes, Sweeting, we do know *Belvile,* and wish

210 he were with us now, he's a Cormorant at Whore and Bacon, he'd have a Limb or two of thee, my Virgin Pullet: but 'tis no matter, we'll leave him the Bones to pick.

FLORINDA: Sir, if you have any Esteem for that *Belvile,* I conjure you to treat me with more Gentleness; he'll thank you for the Justice.

215 FREDERICK: Hark ye, *Blunt,* I doubt we are mistaken in this matter.

FLORINDA: Sir, If you find me not worth *Belvile's* Care, use me as you please; and that you may think I merit better treatment than you threaten—pray take this Present—

(Gives him a Ring: He looks on it.)

BLUNT: Hum—A Diamond! why, 'tis a wonderful Virtue now that lies in this Ring, a mollifying Virtue; adsheartlikins 220 there's more persuasive Rhetorick in't, than all her Sex can utter.

FREDERICK: I begin to suspect something; and 'twou'd anger us vilely to be truss'd up for a Rape upon a Maid of Quality, 225 when we only believe we ruffle a Harlot.

BLUNT: Thou art a credulous Fellow, but adsheartlikins I have no Faith yet; why, my Saint prattled as parlously as this does, she gave me a Bracelet too, a Devil on her: but I sent my Man to sell it to day for Necessaries, and it prov'd as counterfeit as her 230 Vows of Love.

FREDERICK: However let it reprieve her till we see *Belvile.*

BLUNT: That's hard, yet I will grant it.

(Enter a SERVANT.*)*

SERVANT: Oh, Sir, the Colonel is just come with his new Friend and a *Spaniard* of Quality, and talks of having you to Dinner 235 with 'em.

BLUNT: 'Dsheartlikins, I'm undone—I would not see 'em for the World: Harkye, *Frederick* lock up the Wench in your Chamber.

FREDERICK: Fear nothing, Madam, whate'er he threatens, you're 240 safe whilst in my Hands.

(Exit FREDERICK *and* FLORINDA.*)*

BLUNT: And, Sirrah—upon your Life, say—I am not at home—or that I am asleep—or—or any thing—away—I'll prevent them coming this way.

(Locks the Door and Exeunt.)

ACT FIVE

SCENE I

BLUNT's *Chamber.*

After a great knocking as at his Chamber-door, enter BLUNT *softly, crossing the Stage in his Shirt and Drawers, as before.*

(Call within.) Ned, Ned Blunt, Ned Blunt.

BLUNT: The Rogues are up in Arms, 'dsheartlikins, this villainous *Frederick* has betray'd me, they have heard of my blessed Fortune.

(And knocking within.) Ned Blunt, Ned, Ned— 5

BELVILE: Why, he's dead, sir, without dispute dead, he has not been seen to day; let's break open the Door—here—Boy—

BLUNT: Ha, break open the Door! 'dsheartlikins that mad Fellow will be as good as his word.

BELVILE: Boy, bring something to force the Door. 10

(*A great noise within at the Door again.*)

BLUNT: So, now must I speak in my own Defence, I'll try
what Rhetorick will do—hold—hold, what do you mean,
Gentlemen, what do you mean?

BELVILE: Oh Rogue, art alive? prithee open the Door, and
15   convince us.

BLUNT: Yes, I am alive, Gentlemen—but at present a little busy.

BELVILE: (*Within.*) How! *Blunt* grown a man of Business! come,
come, open, and let's see this Miracle.

BLUNT: No, no, no, no, Gentlemen, 'tis no great Business—but—I
20   am—at—my Devotion,—'dsheartlikins, will you not allow a
man time to pray?

BELVILE: (*Within.*) Turn'd religious! a greater Wonder than the
first, therefore open quickly, or we shall unhinge, we shall.

BLUNT: This won't do—Why, hark ye, Colonel; to tell you the
25   plain Truth, I am about a necessary Affair of Life.—I have a
Wench with me—you apprehend me? the Devil's in't if they be
so uncivil as to disturb me now.

WILLMORE: How, a Wench! Nay, then we must enter and partake;
no Resistance,—unless it be your Lady of Quality, and then
30   we'll keep our distance.

BLUNT: So, the Business is out.

WILLMORE: Come, come, lend more hands to the Door,—now
heave altogether—so, well done, my Boys—

(*Breaks open the Door. Enter* BELVILE, WILLMORE, FREDERICK,
PEDRO, *and* BELVILE's *page:* BLUNT *looks simply, they all laugh at
him, he lays his hand on his Sword, and comes up to* WILLMORE.)

BLUNT: Hark ye, Sir, laugh out your laugh quickly, d'ye hear,
35   and be gone, I shall spoil your sport else; 'dsheartlikins, Sir,
I shall—the Jest has been carried on too long,—(*Aside.*) a
Plague upon my Taylor—

WILLMORE: 'Sdeath, how the Whore has drest him! Faith, Sir, I'm
sorry.

40 BLUNT: Are you so, Sir? keep't to your self then, Sir, I advise you,
d'ye hear? for I can as little endure your Pity as his Mirth.

(*Lays his Hand on's Sword.*)

BELVILE: Indeed, *Willmore*, thou wert a little too rough with *Ned
Blunt's* Mistress; call a Person of Quality Whore, and one so
young, so handsome, and so eloquent!—ha, ha, ha.

45 BLUNT: Hark ye, Sir, you know me, and know I can be angry; have
a care—for 'dsheartlikins I can fight too—I can, Sir,—do you
mark me—no more.

BELVILE: Why so peevish, good *Ned?* some Disappointments, I'll
warrant—What! did the jealous Count her Husband return
50   just in the nick?

(*They laugh.*)

BLUNT: Or the Devil, Sir,—d'ye laugh?
Look ye, settle me a good sober Countenance, and that
quickly too, or you shall know *Ned Blunt* is not—

BELVILE: Not every Body, we know that.

55 BLUNT: Not an Ass, to be laught at, Sir.

WILLMORE: Unconscionable Sinner, to bring a Lover so near his
Happiness, a vigorous passionate Lover, and then not only
cheat him of his Moveables, but his Desires too.

BELVILE: Ah, Sir, a Mistress is a Trifle with *Blunt,* he'll have a
dozen the next time he looks abroad; his Eyes have Charms 60
not to be resisted: There needs no more than to expose that
taking Person to the view of the Fair, and he leads 'em all in
Triumph.

PEDRO: Sir, tho I'm a stranger to you, I'm ashamed at the rudeness
of my Nation; and could you learn who did it, would assist 65
you to make an Example of 'em.

BLUNT: Why, ay, there's one speaks sense now, and handsomly;
and let me tell you Gentlemen, I should not have shew'd my
self like a Jack-Pudding, thus to have made you Mirth, but
that I have revenge within my power; for know, I have got into 70
my possession a Female, who had better have fallen under
any Curse, than the Ruin I design her: 'dsheartlikins, she
assaulted me here in my own Lodgings, and had doubtless
committed a Rape upon me, had not this Sword defended me.

FREDERICK: I knew not that, but o' my Conscience thou hadst 75
ravisht her, had she not redeem'd her self with a Ring—let's
see't, *Blunt.*

(BLUNT *shews the Ring.*)

BELVILE: (*Goes to whisper to him.*) Hah!—the Ring I gave *Florinda*
when we exchang'd our Vows!—hark ye, *Blunt*—

WILLMORE: No whispering, good Colonel, there's a Woman in the 80
case, no whispering.

BELVILE: Hark ye, Fool, be advis'd, and conceal both the Ring and
the Story, for your Reputation's sake; don't let People know
what despis'd Cullies we *English* are: to be cheated and abus'd
by one Whore, and another rather bribe thee than be kind to 85
thee, is an Infamy to our Nation.

WILLMORE: Come, come, where's the Wench! we'll see her, let her
be what she will, we'll see her.

PEDRO: Ay, ay, let us see her, I can soon discover whether she be of
Quality, or for your Diversion. 90

BLUNT: She's in *Frederick's* Custody.

WILLMORE: Come, come, the Key.

(*To* FREDERICK *who gives him the Key, they are going.*)

BELVILE: Death! what shall I do?—stay, Gentlemen—yet if I
hinder 'em, I shall discover all—hold, let's go one at once—
give me the Key. 95

WILLMORE: Nay, hold there, Colonel, I'll go first.

FREDERICK: Nay, no Dispute, *Ned* and I have the property of her.

WILLMORE: Damn Property—then we'll draw Cuts.

(BELVILE *goes to whisper* WILLMORE.)

Nay, no Corruption, good Colonel: come, the longest Sword
carries her.— 100

(*They all draw, forgetting Don* PEDRO, *being a Spaniard, had the
longest.*)

BLUNT: I yield up my Interest to you Gentlemen, and that will be
Revenge sufficient.

WILLMORE: The Wench is yours—(*To* PEDRO.) Pox of his *Toledo,* I
had forgot that.

FREDERICK: Come, Sir, I'll conduct you to the Lady. 105

(*Exit* FREDERICK *and* PEDRO.)

BELVILE: (*Aside.*) To hinder him will certainly discover—
Dost know, dull Beast, what Mischief thou hast done?

(WILLMORE *walking up and down out of Humour.*)

WILLMORE: Ay, ay, to trust our Fortune to Lots, a Devil on't, 'twas
madness, that's the Truth on't.
110 BELVILE: Oh intolerable Sot!

(*Enter* FLORINDA, *running masqu'd,* PEDRO *after her,* WILLMORE
gazing round her.)

FLORINDA: (*Aside.*) Good Heaven, defend me from discovery.
PEDRO: 'Tis but in vain to fly me, you are fallen to my Lot.
BELVILE: Sure she is undiscover'd yet, but now I fear there is no
way to bring her off.
115 WILLMORE: Why, what a Pox is not this my Woman, the same I
follow'd but now?

(PEDRO *talking to* FLORINDA, *who walks up and down.*)

PEDRO: As if I did not know ye, and your Business here.
FLORINDA: (*Aside.*) Good Heaven! I fear he does indeed—
PEDRO: Come, pray be kind, I know you meant to be so when you
120 enter'd here, for these are proper Gentlemen.
WILLMORE: But, Sir—perhaps the Lady will not be impos'd upon,
she'll chuse her Man.
PEDRO: I am better bred, than not to leave her Choice free.

(*Enter* VALERIA, *and is surpriz'd at the Sight of Don* PEDRO.)

VALERIA: (*Aside.*) Don *Pedro* here! there's no avoiding him.
125 FLORINDA: (*Aside.*) *Valeria!* then I'm undone—
VALERIA: (*To* PEDRO, *running to him.*) Oh! have I found you,
Sir—
—The strangest Accident—if I had breath—to tell it.
PEDRO: Speak—is *Florinda* safe? *Hellena* well?
130 VALERIA: Ay, ay, Sir—*Florinda*—is safe—from any fears of you.
PEDRO: Why, where's *Florinda?*—speak.
VALERIA: Ay, where indeed, Sir? I wish I could inform you,—
But to hold you no longer in doubt—
FLORINDA: (*Aside.*) Oh, what will she say!
135 VALERIA: She's fled away in the Habit of one of her Pages,
Sir—but *Callis* thinks you may retrieve her yet,
if you make haste away; she'll tell you, Sir, the rest—(*Aside.*)
if you can find her out.
PEDRO: Dishonourable Girl, she has undone my Aim—Sir—you
140 see my necessity of leaving you, and I hope you'll pardon it:
my Sister, I know, will make her flight to you; and if she do, I
shall expect she should be render'd back.
BELVILE: I shall consult my Love and Honour, Sir.

(*Exit* PEDRO.)

FLORINDA: (*To* VALERIA.) My dear Preserver, let me imbrace
145 thee.
WILLMORE: What the Devil's all this?
BLUNT: Mystery by this Light.
VALERIA: Come, come, make haste and get your selves married
quickly, for your Brother will return again.
150 BELVILE: I am so surpriz'd with Fears and Joys, so amaz'd to find
you here in safety, I can scarce persuade my Heart into a Faith
of what I see—

WILLMORE: Harkye, Colonel, is this that Mistress who has cost
you so many Sighs, and me so many Quarrels with you?
BELVILE: It is—(*To* FLORINDA.) Pray give him the Honour of your 155
Hand.
WILLMORE: Thus it must be receiv'd then.

(*Kneels and kisses her Hand.*)

And with it give your Pardon too.
FLORINDA: The Friend to *Belvile* may command me anything.
WILLMORE: (*Aside.*) Death, wou'd I might, 'tis a surprizing 160
Beauty.
BELVILE: Boy, run and fetch a Father instantly.

(*Exit* PAGE.)

FREDERICK: So, now do I stand like a Dog, and have not a
Syllable to plead my own Cause with: by this Hand,
Madam, I was never thorowly confounded before, nor 165
shall I ever more dare look up with Confidence, till you
are pleased to pardon me.
FLORINDA: Sir, I'll be reconcil'd to you on one Condition, that
you'll follow the Example of your Friend, in marrying a Maid
that does not hate you, and whose Fortune (I believe) will not 170
be unwelcome to you.
FREDERICK: Madam, had I no Inclinations that way, I shou'd obey
your kind Commands.
BELVILE: Who, *Frederick* marry; he has so few Inclinations for
Womankind, that had he been possest of Paradise, he might 175
have continu'd there to this Day, if no Crime but Love cou'd
have disinherited him.
FREDERICK: Oh, I do not use to boast of my Intrigues.
BELVILE: Boast! why thou do'st nothing but boast; and I dare
swear, wer't thou as innocent from the Sin of the Grape, as 180
thou art from the Apple, thou might'st yet claim that right in
Eden which our first Parents lost by too much loving.
FREDERICK: I wish this Lady would think me so modest a Man.
VALERIA: She shou'd be sorry then, and not like you half so well,
and I shou'd be loth to break my Word with you; which was, 185
That if your Friend and mine are agreed, it shou'd be a Match
between you and I.

(*She gives him her Hand.*)

FREDERICK: Bear witness, Colonel, 'tis a Bargain.

(*Kisses her Hand.*)

BLUNT: (*To* FLORINDA.) I have a Pardon to beg too; but adsheartlikins I am so out of Countenance, that I am a Dog 190
if I can say any thing to purpose.
FLORINDA: Sir, I heartily forgive you all.
BLUNT: That's nobly said, sweet Lady—*Belvile*, prithee present her
her Ring again, for I find I have not Courage to approach her
my self. 195

(*Gives him the Ring, he gives it to* FLORINDA. *Enter* BOY.)

BOY: Sir, I have brought the Father that you sent for.
BELVILE: 'Tis well, and now my dear *Florinda*, let's fly to compleat
that mighty Joy we have so long wish'd and sigh'd for. Come,
Frederick you'll follow?

200 FREDERICK: Your Example, Sir, 'twas ever my Ambition in War,
  and must be so in Love.
  WILLMORE: And must not I see this juggling Knot ty'd?
  BELVILE: No, thou shalt do us better Service, and be our Guard,
  lest Don *Pedro's* sudden Return interrupt the Ceremony.
205 WILLMORE: Content; I'll secure this Pass.

(*Exit* BELVILE, FLORINDA, FREDERICK, *and* VALERIA. *Enter page.*)

  BOY: (*To* WILLMORE.) Sir, there's a Lady without wou'd speak
  to you.
  WILLMORE: Conduct her in, I dare not quit my Post.
  BOY: And, Sir, your Taylor waits you in your Chamber.
210 BLUNT: Some comfort yet, I shall not dance naked at the
  Wedding.

(*Exit* BLUNT *and* BOY.)

(*Enter again the* BOY, *conducting in* ANGELICA *in a masquing
Habit and a Vizard,* WILLMORE *runs to her.*)

  WILLMORE: This can be none but my pretty Gipsy—Oh, I see
  you can follow as well as fly—Come, confess thy self the
  most malicious Devil in Nature, you think you have done my
215 Bus'ness with *Angelica*—
  ANGELICA: Stand off, base Villain—

(*She draws a Pistol and holds to his Breast.*)

  WILLMORE: Hah, 'tis not she: who art thou? and what's thy
  Business?
  ANGELICA: One thou hast injur'd, and who comes to kill thee
220 for't.
  WILLMORE: What the Devil canst thou mean?
  ANGELICA: By all my Hopes to kill thee—

(*Holds still the Pistol to his Breast, he going back, she following still.*)

  WILLMORE: Prithee on what Acquaintance? for I know thee not.
  ANGELICA: Behold this Face!—so lost to thy Remembrance!
225 And then call all thy Sins about thy Soul,

(*Pulls off her Vizard.*)

  And let them die with thee.
  WILLMORE: *Angelica!*
  ANGELICA: Yes, Traitor.
  Does not thy guilty Blood run shivering thro thy Veins?
230 Hast thou no Horrour at this Sight, that tells thee,
  Thou hast not long to boast thy shameful Conquest?
  WILLMORE: Faith, no Child, my Blood keeps its old Ebbs and
  Flows still, and that usual Heat too, that cou'd oblige thee
  with a Kindness, had I but opportunity.
235 ANGELICA: Devil! dost wanton with my Pain—have at thy
  Heart.
  WILLMORE: Hold, dear Virago! hold thy Hand a little,
  I am not now at leisure to be kill'd—hold and hear me—
  (*Aside.*) Death, I think she's in earnest.
  ANGELICA: (*Aside, turning from him.*) Oh if I take not heed,
240 My coward Heart will leave me to his Mercy.
  —What have you, Sir, to say?—but should I hear thee,
  Thou'd'st talk away all that is brave about me:

(*Follows him with the Pistol to his Breast.*)

  And I have vow'd thy Death, by all that's sacred.
  WILLMORE: Why, then, there's an end of a proper handsom
  Fellow, that might have liv'd to have done good Service   245
  yet:—That's all I can say to't.
  ANGELICA: (*Pausingly.*) Yet—I wou'd give thee—time for
  Penitence.
  WILLMORE: Faith, Child, I thank God, I have ever took care to
  lead a good, sober, hopeful Life, and am of a Religion that
  teaches me to believe, I shall depart in Peace.   250
  ANGELICA: So will the Devil: tell me
  How many poor believing Fools thou hast undone;
  How many Hearts thou hast betray'd to ruin!
  —Yet, these are little Mischiefs to the Ills
  Thou'st taught mine to commit: thou'st taught it Love.   255
  WILLMORE: Egad, 'twas shreudly hurt the while.
  ANGELICA: —Love, that has robb'd it of its Unconcern,
  Of all that Pride that taught me how to value it,
  And in its room a mean submissive Passion was convey'd,
  That made me humbly bow, which I ne'er did   260
  To any thing but Heaven.
  —Thou, perjur'd Man, didst this, and with thy Oaths,
  Which on thy Knees thou didst devoutly make,
  Soften'd my yielding Heart—And then, I was a Slave—
  Yet still had been content to've worn my Chains,   265
  Worn 'em with Vanity and Joy for ever,
  Hadst thou not broke those Vows that put them on.
  —'Twas then I was undone.

(*All this while follows him with a Pistol to his Breast.*)

  WILLMORE: Broke my Vows! why, where hast thou lived?
  Amongst the Gods! For I never heard of mortal Man,   270
  That has not broke a thousand Vows.
  ANGELICA: Oh, Impudence!
  WILLMORE: *Angelica!* that Beauty has been too long tempting,
  Not to have made a thousand Lovers languish,
  Who in the amorous Favour, no doubt have sworn   275
  Like me; did they all die in that Faith? still adoring?
  I do not think they did.
  ANGELICA: No, faithless Man: had I repaid their Vows, as
  I did thine, I wou'd have kill'd the ungrateful that had
  abandon'd me.   280
  WILLMORE: This old General has quite spoil'd thee, nothing
  makes a Woman so vain, as being flatter'd; your old Lover
  ever supplies the Defects of Age, with intolerable Dotage,
  vast Charge, and that which you call Constancy; and
  attributing all this to your own Merits, you domineer, and   285
  throw your Favours i'n Teeth, upbraiding him still with the
  Defects of Age, and cuckold him as often as he deceives your
  Expectations. But the gay, young, brisk Lover, that brings his
  equal Fires, and can give you Dart for Dart, he'll be as nice as
  you sometimes.   290
  ANGELICA: All this thou'st made me know, for which I hate thee.
  Had I remain'd in innocent Security,
  I shou'd have thought all Men were born my Slaves;
  And worn my Pow'r like Lightning in my Eyes,
  To have destroy'd at Pleasure when offended.   295
  —But when Love held the Mirror, the undeceiving Glass
  Reflected all the Weakness of my Soul, and made me know,
  My richest Treasure being lost, my Honour,

All the remaining Spoil cou'd not be worth
300 The Conqueror's Care or Value.
—Oh how I fell like a long worship'd Idol,
Discovering all the Cheat!
Wou'd not the Incense and rich Sacrifice,
Which blind Devotion offer'd at my Altars,
305 Have fall'n to thee?
Why woud'st thou then destroy my fancy'd Power?
WILLMORE: By Heaven thou art brave, and I admire thee
strangely.
I wish I were that dull, that constant thing,
Which thou woud'st have, and Nature never meant me:
310 I must, like chearful Birds, sing in all Groves,
And perch on every Bough,
Billing the next kind She that flies to meet me;
Yet after all cou'd build my Nest with thee,
Thither repairing when I'd lov'd my round,
315 And still reserve a tributary Flame.

(*Offers her a Purse of Gold.*)

—To gain your Credit, I'll pay you back your Charity,
And be oblig'd for nothing but for Love.
ANGELICA: Oh that thou wert in earnest!
So mean a Thought of me,
320 Wou'd turn my Rage to Scorn, and I shou'd pity thee,
And give thee leave to live;
Which for the publick Safety of our Sex,
And my own private Injuries, I dare not do.
Prepare—

(*Follows still, as before.*)

325 —I will no more be tempted with Replies.
WILLMORE: Sure—
ANGELICA: Another Word will damn thee! I've heard thee talk
too long.

(*She follows him with a Pistol ready to shoot: he retires still amaz'd.*)

(*Enter Don* ANTONIO, *his Arm in a Scarf, and lays hold on the Pistol.*)

ANTONIO: Hah! *Angelica!*
ANGELICA: *Antonio!* What Devil brought thee hither?
330 ANTONIO: Love and Curiosity, seeing your Coach at Door.
Let me disarm you of this unbecoming Instrument of
Death.—

(*Takes away the Pistol.*)

Amongst the Number of your Slaves, was there not one
worthy the Honour to have fought your Quarrel?
335 —Who are you, Sir, that are so very wretched
To merit Death from her?
WILLMORE: One, sir, that cou'd have made a better End of an
amorous Quarrel without you, than with you.
ANTONIO: Sure 'tis some Rival—hah—the very Man took down
340 her Picture yesterday—the very same that set on me last
night—Blest opportunity—

(*Offers to shoot him.*)

ANGELICA: Hold, you're mistaken, Sir.
ANTONIO: By Heaven the very same!
—Sir, what pretensions have you to this Lady? 345
WILLMORE: Sir, I don't use to be examin'd, and am ill at all
Disputes but this—

(*Draws,* ANTONIO *offers to shoot.*)

ANGELICA: (*To* WILLMORE.) Oh, hold! you see he's arm'd with
certain Death:
—And you, *Antonio,* I command you hold,
By all the Passion you've so lately vow'd me.

(*Enter Don* PEDRO, *sees* ANTONIO, *and stays.*)

PEDRO: (*Aside.*) Hah, *Antonio!* and *Angelica!* 350
ANTONIO: When I refuse Obedience to your Will,
May you destroy me with your mortal Hate.
By all that's Holy I adore you so,
That even my Rival, who has Charms enough
To make him fall a Victim to my Jealousy, 355
Shall live, nay, and have leave to love on still.
PEDRO: (*Aside.*) What's this I hear?
ANGELICA: (*Pointing to* WILLMORE.) Ah thus, 'twas thus he talk'd,
and I believ'd.
—*Antonio,* yesterday,
I'd not have sold my Interest in his Heart, 360
For all the Sword has won and lost in Battle.
—But now to show my utmost of Contempt,
I give thee Life—which if thou would'st preserve,
Live where my Eyes may never see thee more,
Live to undo some one, whose Soul may prove 365
So bravely constant to revenge my Love.

(*Goes out,* ANTONIO *follows, but* PEDRO *pulls him back.*)

PEDRO: *Antonio*—stay.
ANTONIO: Don *Pedro*—
PEDRO: What Coward Fear was that prevented thee
From meeting me this Morning on the *Molo?* 370
ANTONIO: Meet thee?
PEDRO: Yes me; I was the Man that dar'd thee to't.
ANTONIO: Hast thou so often seen me fight in War,
To find no better Cause to excuse my Absence?
—I sent my Sword and one to do thee Right, 375
Finding my self uncapable to use a Sword.
PEDRO: But 'twas *Florinda's* Quarrel that we fought,
And you to shew how little you esteem'd her,
Sent me your Rival, giving him your Interest.
—But I have found the Cause of this Affront, 380
But when I meet you fit for the Dispute,
—I'll tell you my Resentment.
ANTONIO: I shall be ready, Sir, e'er long to do your Reason.

(*Exit* ANTONIO.)

PEDRO: If I cou'd find *Florinda,* now whilst my Anger's high, I
think I shou'd be kind, and give her to *Belvile* in Revenge. 385
WILLMORE: Faith, Sir, I know not what you wou'd do, but I
believe the Priest within has been so kind.

PEDRO: How! my Sister married?

WILLMORE: I hope by this time she is, and bedded too, or he has
390   not my longings about him.

PEDRO: Dares he do thus? Does he not fear my Pow'r?

WILLMORE: Faith not at all. If you will go in, and thank him
for the Favour he has done your Sister, so; if not, Sir, my Power's
greater in this House than yours; I have a damn'd surly Crew
395   here, that will keep you till the next Tide, and then clap you
an board my Prize; my Ship lies but a League off the *Molo*,
and we shall show your Donship a damn'd *Tramontana*
Rover's Trick.

(*Enter* BELVILE.)

BELVILE: This Rogue's in some new Mischief—hah, *Pedro*
400   return'd!

PEDRO: Colonel *Belvile*, I hear you have married my Sister.

BELVILE: You have heard truth then, Sir.

PEDRO: Have I so? then, Sir, I wish you Joy.

BELVILE: How!

405 PEDRO: By this Embrace I do, and I glad on't.

BELVILE: Are you in earnest?

PEDRO: By our long Friendship and my Obligations to thee, I am.
The sudden Change I'll give you Reasons for anon. Come
lead me into my Sister, that she may know I now approve
410   her Choice.

(*Exit* BELVILE *with* PEDRO. WILLMORE *goes to follow them. Enter*
HELLENA *as before in Boy's Clothes, and pulls him back.*)

WILLMORE: Ha! my Gipsy—Now a thousand Blessings on thee for
this Kindness. Egad, Child, I was e'en in despair of ever seeing
thee again; my Friends are all provided for within, each Man
his kind Woman.

415 HELLENA: Hah! I thought they had serv'd me some such Trick.

WILLMORE: And I was e'en resolv'd to go aboard, condemn my
self to my lone Cabin, and the Thoughts of thee.

HELLENA: And cou'd you have left me behind? wou'd you have
been so ill-natur'd?

420 WILLMORE: Why, 'twou'd have broke my Heart, Child—but since
we are met again, I defy foul Weather to part us.

HELLENA: And wou'd you be a faithful Friend now, if a Maid
shou'd trust you?

WILLMORE: For a Friend I cannot promise, thou art of a Form
425   so excellent, a Face and Humour too good for cold dull
Friendship; I am parlously afraid of being in love, Child, and
you have not forgot how severely you have us'd me.

HELLENA: That's all one, such Usage you must still look for, to
find out all your Haunts, to rail at you to all that love you, till I
430   have made you love only me in your own Defence, because no
body else will love.

WILLMORE: But hast thou no better Quality to recommend thy
self by?

HELLENA: Faith none, Captain—Why, 'twill be the greater
435   Charity to take me for thy Mistress, I am a lone Child, a
kind of Orphan Lover; and why I shou'd die a Maid, and in a
Captain's Hands too, I do not understand.

WILLMORE: Egad, I was never claw'd away with Broad-Sides
from any Female before, thou hast one Virtue I adore,

good-Nature; I hate a coy demure Mistress, she's as
440   troublesom as a Colt, I'll break none; no, give me a mad
Mistress when mew'd, and in flying on[e] I dare trust upon
the Wing, that whilst she's kind will come to the Lure.

HELLENA: Nay, as kind as you will, good Captain, whilst it lasts,
but let's lose no time.

445 WILLMORE: My time's as precious to me, as thine can be;
therefore, dear Creature, since we are so well agreed, let's
retire to my Chamber, and if ever thou were treated with such
savory Love—Come—My Bed's prepar'd for such a Guest,
all clean and sweet as thy fair self; I love to steal a Dish and a
450   Bottle with a Friend, and hate long Graces—Come, let's retire
and fall to.

HELLENA: 'Tis but getting my Consent, and the Business is
soon done; let but old Gaffer *Hymen* and his Priest say Amen
to't, and I dare lay my Mother's Daughter by as proper a
455   Fellow as your Father's Son, without fear or blushing.

WILLMORE: Hold, hold, no Bugg Words, Child, Priest and
Hymen: prithee add Hangman to 'em to make up the
Consort—No, no, we'll have no Vows but Love, Child, nor
Witness but the Lover; the kind Diety injoins naught but
460   love and enjoy. *Hymen* and Priest wait still upon Portion,
and Joynture; Love and Beauty have their own Ceremonies.
Marriage is as certain a Bane to Love, as lending
Money is to Friendship: I'll neither ask nor give a Vow, tho
I could be content to turn Gipsy, and become a Left-hand
465   Bridegroom, to have the Pleasure of working that great
Miracle of making a Maid a Mother, if you durst venture;
'tis upse Gipsy that, and if I miss, I'll lose my Labour.

HELLENA: And if you do not lose, what shall I get? A Cradle full
of Noise and Mischief, with a Pack of Repentance at my Back?
470   Can you teach me to weave Incle to pass my time with? 'Tis
upse Gipsy that too.

WILLMORE: I can teach thee to weave a true Love's Knot better.

HELLENA: So can my Dog.

WILLMORE: Well, I see we are both upon our Guard, and I see
475   there's no way to conquer good Nature, but by yielding—
here—give me thy Hand—one Kiss and I am thine—

HELLENA: One Kiss! How like my Page he speaks; I am resolv'd
you shall have none, for asking such a sneaking Sum—He that
will be satisfied with one Kiss, will never die of that Longing;
480   good Friend single-Kiss, is all your talking come to this?
A Kiss, a Caudle! farewel, Captain single-Kiss.

(*Going out he stays her.*)

WILLMORE: Nay, if we part so, let me die like a Bird upon a Bough,
at the Sheriff's Charge. By Heaven, both the *Indies* shall not
buy thee from me. I adore thy Humour and will marry thee,
485   and we are so of one Humour, it must be a Bargain—give me
thy Hand—

(*Kisses her hand.*)

And now let the blind ones (Love and Fortune) do their worst.

HELLENA: Why, God-a-mercy, Captain!

WILLMORE: But harkye—The Bargain is now made; but is it not
490   fit we should know each other's Names? That when we have

---

398 **Tramontana** Italian and Spanish *tramontano* = from beyond the
mountains

468 **upse** *Op zijn* (Dutch) = in the fashion or manner of, *Upse Gipsy* =
like a gipsy   471 **Incle** linen thread or yarn which was woven into a tape
once very much in use

Reason to curse one another hereafter, and People ask me who 'tis I give to the Devil, I may at least be able to tell what Family you came of.

495 HELLENA: Good reason, Captain; and where I have cause, (as I doubt not but I shall have plentiful) that I may know at whom to throw my—Blessings—I beseech ye your Name.

WILLMORE: I am call'd *Robert the Constant.*

HELLENA: A very fine Name! pray was it your Faulkner or
500   Butler that christen'd you? Do they not use to whistle when then call you?

WILLMORE: I hope you have a better, that a Man may name without crossing himself, you are so merry with mine.

HELLENA: I am call'd *Hellena the Inconstant.*

(*Enter* PEDRO, BELVILE, FLORINDA, FREDERICK, *and* VALERIA.)

505 PEDRO: Hah! *Hellena!*

FLORINDA: *Hellena!*

HELLENA: The very same—hah my Brother! now, Captain, shew your Love and Courage; stand to your Arms, and defend me bravely, or I am lost for ever.

510 PEDRO: What's this I hear? false Girl, how came you hither, and what's your Business? Speak.

(*Goes roughly to her.*)

WILLMORE: Hold off, Sir, you have leave to parly only.

(*Puts himself between.*)

HELLENA: I had e'en as good tell it, as you guess it. Faith, Brother, my Business is the same with all living Creatures
515   of my Age, to love, and be loved, and here's the Man.

PEDRO: Perfidious Maid, hast thou deceiv'd me too, deceiv'd thy self and Heaven?

HELLENA: 'Tis time enough to make my Peace with that: Be you but kind, let me alone with Heaven.

520 PEDRO: *Belvile,* I did not expect this false Play from you; was't not enough you'd gain *Florinda* (which I pardon'd) but your leud Friends too must be inrich'd with the Spoils of a noble Family?

BELVILE: Faith, Sir, I am as much surpriz'd at this as you can be:
525   Yet, Sir, my Friends are Gentlemen, and ought to be esteem'd for their Misfortunes, since they have the Glory to suffer with the best of Men and Kings; 'tis true, he's a Rover of Fortune, yet a Prince aboard his little wooden World.

PEDRO: What's this to the maintenance of a Woman or her Birth
530   and Quality?

WILLMORE: Faith, Sir, I can boast of nothing but a Sword which does me Right where-e'er I come, and has defended a worse Cause than a Woman's: and since I lov'd her before I either knew her Birth or Name, I must pursue my Resolution, and
535   marry her.

PEDRO: And is all your holy Intent of becoming a Nun debauch'd into a Desire of Man?

HELLENA: Why—I have consider'd the matter, Brother, and find the Three hundred thousand Crowns my Uncle left me (and
540   you cannot keep from me) will be better laid out in Love than in Religion, and turn to as good an Account—let most Voices carry it, for Heaven or the Captain?

ALL CRY: Captain, a Captain.

HELLENA: Look ye, Sir, 'tis a clear Case.

545 PEDRO: (*Aside.*) Oh I am mad—if I refuse, my Life's in Danger— Come—There's one motive induces me—take her—I shall now be free from the fear of her Honour; guard it you now, if you can, I have been a Slave to't long enough.

(*Gives her to him.*)

WILLMORE: Faith, Sir, I am of a Nation, that are of opinion a Woman's Honour is not worth guarding when she has a mind
550   to part with it.

HELLENA: Well said, Captain.

PEDRO: (*To* VALERIA.) This was your Plot, Mistress, but I hope you have married one that will revenge my Quarrel to
555   you—

VALERIA: There's no altering Destiny, Sir.

PEDRO: Sooner than a Woman's Will, therefore I forgive you all—and wish you may get my Father's Pardon as easily; which I fear.

(*Enter* BLUNT *drest in a Spanish Habit, looking very ridiculously; his* MAN *adjusting his Band.*)

560 MAN: 'Tis very well, Sir.

BLUNT: Well, Sir, 'dsheartlikins I tell you 'tis damnable ill, Sir—a Spanish Habit, good Lord! cou'd the Devil and my Taylor devise no other Punishment for me, but the Mode of a Nation I abominate?

565 BELVILE: What's the matter, *Ned?*

BLUNT: Pray view me round, and judge—

(*Turns round.*)

BELVILE: I must confess thou art a kind of an odd Figure.

BLUNT: In a Spanish Habit with a Vengeance! I had rather be in the Inquisition for Judaism, than in this Doublet
570   and Breeches; a Pillory were an easy Collar to this, three Hand-fuls high; and these Shoes too are worse than the Stocks, with the Sole an Inch shorter than my Foot: In fine, Gentlemen, methinks I look altogether like a Bag of Bays stuff'd full of Fools Flesh.

575 BELVILE: Methinks 'tis well, and makes the look *en Cavalier:* Come, Sir, settle your Face, and salute our Friends, Lady—

BLUNT: Hah! Say'st thou so, my little Rover?

(*To* HELLENA.)

Lady—(if you be one) give me leave to kiss your Hand, and tell you, adsheartlikins, for all I look so, I am your humble
580   Servant—A Pox of my *Spanish* Habit.

WILLMORE: Hark—what's this?

(*Musick is heard to Play. Enter* BOY.)

BOY: Sir, as the Custom is, the gay People in Masquerade, who make every Man's House their own, are coming up.

(*Enter several* MEN *and* WOMEN *in masquing Habits, with Musick, they put themselves in order and dance.*)

BLUNT: Adsheartlikins, wou'd 'twere lawful to pull off their false Faces, that I might see if my Doxy were not amongst
585   'em.

BELVILE: Ladies and Gentlemen, since you are come so *a propos,* you must take a small Collation with us.

(*To the* MASQUERADERS.)

590 WILLMORE: Whilst we'll to the Good Man within, who stays to give us a Cast of his Office.

(*To* HELLENA.)

—Have you no trembling at the near approach?
HELLENA: No more than you have in an Engagement or a Tempest.
595 WILLMORE: Egad, thou'rt a brave Girl, and I admire thy Love and Courage.
Lead on, no other Dangers they can dread,
Who venture in the Storms o'th' Marriage-Bed.

(*Exeunt.*)

EPILOGUE

THE banisht Cavaliers! a Roving Blade!
A popish Carnival! a Masquerade!
The Devil's in't if this will please the Nation,
In these our blessed Times of Reformation,
5   When Conventicling is so much in Fashion.
And yet—
That mutinous Tribe less Factions do beget,
Than your continual differing in Wit;
Your Judgment's (as your Passions) a Disease:
10 Nor Muse nor Miss your Appetite can please;
You're grown as nice as queasy Consciences,
Whose each Convulsion, when the Spirit moves,
Damns every thing that Maggot disapproves.
    With canting Rule you wou'd the Stage refine,
And to dull Method all our Sense confine.   15
With th' Insolence of Common-wealths you rule,
Where each gay Fop, and politick brave Fool
On Monarch Wit impose without controul.
As for the last who seldom sees a Play,
Unless it be the old Black-Fryers way,   20
Shaking his empty Noodle o'er *Bamboo,*
He crys—Good Faith, these Plays will never do.
—Ah, Sir, in my young days, what lofty Wit,
What high-strain'd Scenes of Fighting there were writ:
These are slight airy Toys. But tell me, pray,   25
What has the *House of Commons* done to day?
Then shews his Politicks, to let you see
Of State Affairs he'll judge as notably,
As he can do of Wit and Poetry.
The younger Sparks, who hither do resort,   30
Cry—
Pox o' your gentle things, give us more Sport;
—Damn me, I'm sure 'twill never please the Court.
    Such Fops are never pleas'd, unless the Play
Be stuff'd with Fools, as brisk and dull as they: 35
Such might the Half-Crown spare, and in a Glass
At home behold a more accomplist Ass,
Where they may set their Cravats, Wigs and Faces,
And practice all their Buffoonry Grimaces;
See how this—Huff becomes—this Dammy—flare—   40
Which they at home may act, because they dare,
But—must with prudent Caution do elsewhere.
Oh that our *Nokes,* or *Tony Lee* could show
A Fop but half so much to th' Life as you.

---

43 ***Nokes,* or *Tony Lee*** James Nokes and Antony Leigh, the two famous actors, were the leading low comedians of the day

Sor Juana Inés de la Cruz

Juana Inés de Asbaje y Ramírez de Santillana (1648/1651–1695) was probably born in late November or early December of 1648 to the daughter of a wealthy landowner (Isabel Ramírez de Santillana) and an army officer (Pedro Manuel de Asbaje y Vargas Manchucha) serving in the Spanish New World colony of New Spain—present-day Mexico. Although her parents had two other children (Isabel Ramírez had three additional children with another officer), they were not married, and Juana Inés was born an illegitimate "daughter of the church." Raised in the provincial town of Panoyan, Juana had access to her grandfather's library and, by her own account, was a voracious reader, as she later wrote in her *Answer to Sor Filotea* (written 1691):

> When I was six or seven years old and already knew how to read and write, along with all the other skills like embroidery and sewing that women learn, I heard that in Mexico City there were a University and Schools where they studied sciences. As soon as I heard this I began to slay my poor mother with insistent and annoying pleas, begging her to dress me in men's clothes and send me to the capital, to the home of some relatives she had there, so that I could enter the University and study. She refused, and was right in doing so; but I quenched my desire by reading a great variety of books that belonged to my grandfather, and neither punishments nor scoldings could prevent me. And so when I did go to Mexico City, people marveled not so much at my intelligence as at my memory and the facts I knew at an age when it seemed I had scarcely had time to speak.[1]

Juana was sent to live with her mother's relatives in Mexico City in 1659. She lived with them for five years until she moved into the home of the viceroy, where she served in the court of the vicereine, Doña Leonor Carreto, Marquisa de Mancera.

Although she began to write on both religious and secular subjects while at court, Juana's career was closely tied to the church. In 1666, she joined the Carmelite convent of San José, but the penitential strictness of the order seems to have caused her health to suffer, and she left the convent after three months. Still eager to join a convent, she agreed to sit for an examination by the viceroy and forty scholars assembled to test the range of her knowledge, as a means to confirm her suitability for religious life. According to Diego Callega, a priest who wrote the first biography of Sor Juana, she performed like a "royal galleon attacked by canoes," and was admitted to the convent of Santa Paula in 1669, where she took the name Sor Juana Inés de la Cruz. (Illegitimate children were not admissible to convent life; at this time, Juana claimed that her parents had been married, and that her birth date was November 12, 1651; a baptismal record for 1648—listing Juana's aunt and uncle as godparents of an infant "Inés"—is now usually taken as evidence for her birth in that year.)

Although the convent was cloistered, Sor Juana received money to support her servants and was able to receive guests, to study, and to write; she was also closely connected to the social life of New Spain's capital city. The Aztec city of Tenochtitlán had supported some 250,000 inhabitants before the conquest in 1520, but Mexico City was a much smaller city in the seventeenth century. While war, disease, and enslavement drastically reduced the native population, the general population was augmented not only by the annual arrival of *peninsulares* (new inhabitants from Spain), but by an increasing population of *criollos* (people of European descent born in Mexico, like Sor Juana) and *mestizos,* as well as by a growing number of African slaves and immigrants from other Spanish colonies. In the 1800 census, for example, the population of Mexico City was 137,000, making it the largest city in the Americas. The church wielded extensive political power in Mexico (there were sixteen convents in Mexico City alone), and—as in Europe—the leaders of the church and of the state

---

[1] See *The Answer/La Respuesta, Including a Selection of Poems,* ed. and trans. Electa Arenal and Amanda Powell (New York: Feminist Press, 1994).

Religion, costumed as a Spanish nobleman, surveys the fallen Aztec men and women after the battle between Zeal and Occident, in the 1997 Universidad de las Americas production of the *loa* to *The Divine Narcissus* by Sor Juana Inés de la Cruz.

were often drawn from the same aristocratic families. In this sense, it's not surprising that throughout her life, Sor Juana was an intimate acquaintance of aristocratic circles in Mexico City, particularly of the viceroys and vicereines. One vicereine, Maria Luisa Manrique de Lara y Gonzaga (whose husband was viceroy 1680–1686), was the inspiration of several of Sor Juana's poems and had her first volume, *Inundación Castálida,* published in Madrid in 1689 (the title refers to the nymph Castálida, who drowned herself rather than be seduced by Apollo); the title-page described Sor Juana as "the Tenth Muse." By 1690, Sor Juana was arguably the most accomplished secular and philosophical writer in the Americas: She mastered the baroque forms of secular Spanish poetry, writing not only sixty-five sonnets and many ballads and occasional poems, but two well-known comedies (including *Los empeños de una casa*) that were staged. She also wrote sixteen sets of **VILLANCICOS,** carols performed at the Mass; these often incorporate her understanding both of African dialects and of the indigenous Nahua language and were performed at cathedrals throughout Mexico during her lifetime. She wrote three *auto sacramentales,* two of which were performed; thirty-two **LOAS;** a brilliant philosophical treatise *The First Dream* (1685); and a defense of women's claim to an intellectual and spiritual life, *Answer to Sor Filotea.*

Yet despite her fame, Sor Juana was under continual pressure from the church to conform to the more "feminine" role of quiet devotion and service. Early in her career she struggled with her confessor, Antonio Núñez de Miranda, who regarded writing as improper for women, especially for women of the church. Although Sor Juana succeeded in dismissing him as her confessor, he continued to agitate for her silence with higher church officials, including the misogynist archbishop Francisco Aguian y Seijas. In 1690—shortly after her second volume of poetry had been published in Madrid, and her brilliant *auto The Divine Narcissus,* had been published in Mexico—the church's opposition came to a head. During that year, Sor Juana wrote a theological critique of a sermon written forty years earlier, an essay clearly not intended for publication; her friend, the bishop of Puebla, Manuel Fernández de Santa Cruz, asked her to send it to him. Without her permission, he published Sor Juana's essay under the title *Carta atenagórica*—"Letter Worthy of Athena." Despite the praise implied in the title, the bishop was in fact eager to expose Sor Juana to censure and appended his own corrective letter to her treatise—from "Sor Filotea," "lover of God." This public rebuke spurred Sor Juana's brilliant *Answer to Sor Filotea de la Cruz,* a passionate defense of both her intellectual life and its contribution to her faith, written in 1691 but published only after her death in 1700. Despite her defense, however, Sor Juana acceded to the will of the church in 1692. Her last set of *villancicos* was performed at the cathedral in Oaxaca; she sold both her musical instruments and her extensive library (among the largest private libraries in the Americas at the time), and in 1694 she signed—in blood—a new declaration of faith, vowing to give up secular studies as well. She died during an epidemic that swept Mexico City in April 1695.

Sor Juana's poetry, plays, and philosophical writings are well known in Spanish, and many have been published in English translations; the Mexican poet Octavio Paz has written a celebrated biography of Sor Juana: *Sor Juana, or, The Traps of Faith,* trans. Margaret Sayers Peden (Cambridge: Harvard University Press, 1988).

Loa to the Divine Narcissus

The Divine Narcissus is a full-length *auto sacramental,* an allegorical drama on the subject of the Eucharist that Sor Juana wrote in 1687. She intended to submit it to be performed in Madrid as part of a competition for new *autos* following the death of Calderón, who had been the sole author of *autos* performed in the Spanish capital before his death in 1681. Although the death of the queen in 1689 forced the cancellation of the festival, Sor Juana's *The Divine Narcissus* and its introductory *loa* remain among the most accomplished examples of this important genre of Spanish-language drama.

Although the *loa* can be used for either secular or sacred purposes, Sor Juana uses it here specifically to introduce the themes of the *auto,* which uses the Greek story of Echo and Narcissus to allegorize the theological doctrine of the Eucharist. However, to modern readers and audiences, the *loa* is perhaps more interesting for its staging of colonial conflict; through an allegorical conversation between Zeal (a *conquistador*), Religion (a Spanish lady), and the Aztec rulers (Occident and America), the short play also stages an allegory of the conquest of Mexico and its consequences. Although there is no record of the play being performed in Sor Juana's lifetime, it clearly records aspects of Aztec life—the opening dance and ritual worship of the God of the Seeds—that were legally prohibited in seventeenth-century New Spain, while staging a debate between the Aztec leaders and the Spanish invaders who insist on replacing the native religion with the practice of Christianity. While the bullheaded *conquistador,* Zeal, is on the point of murdering the defeated Aztecs, they are spared by Religion, who hears in their account of their religious rituals a profane version of the miracle of the Eucharist:

> What images,
> what dark designs, what shadowings
> of truths most sacred to our Faith
> do these lies seek to imitate?"

Religion works to bring Christian salvation to Occident and America by pointing out the similarities between their religion and the mysteries of the Eucharist:

> a God composed
> of human blood, an offering
> of sacrifice, and in himself
> does He combine with bloody death
> the life-sustaining seeds of earth?"

To instruct Occident and America, Religion decides to

> make for you a metaphor
> a concept clothed in rhetoric
> so colorful that what I show
> to you, your eyes will clearly see.

The *auto* that follows, *The Divine Narcissus,* is Religion's illustrative "metaphor," her way of explaining the Eucharist to the inhabitants of the New World.

Written by a *criolla,* as part of a competition to take place in Madrid, Sor Juana's play is in many ways a barometer of the situation of colonial writing; the final dialogue between Zeal and Religion considers whether such a play, written in the colony about colonial subjects, will be received in "the crown city of Madrid, / which is the center of the Faith, / the seat of Catholic majesty" as an act of "impropriety." Although written at the height of Spain's imperial expansion, and indeed in many ways written to celebrate that expansion, Sor Juana's *loa* to *The Divine Narcissus* deftly registers many of the tensions that typically inform colonial writing: between the colony and the capital, between the native population and their invaders, for instance. But particularly in the brittle relationship between Zeal and Religion and the more charitable relationship between Religion and America, Sor Juana seems to open another kind of critique as well; Religion refuses, for example, to sanction the extermination, or even the subjugation, of Occident and America. While the *loa* testifies unambigiously to Sor Juana's confidence in the universality of her faith, it also seems to question some of the ways religion is used to advance Spain's political and economic mission in this new and distinct society.

Loa to The Divine Narcissus

Sor Juana Inés de la Cruz

TRANSLATED BY PATRICIA A. PETERS AND RENÉE DOMEIER, O.S.B.

CHARACTERS

OCCIDENT	RELIGION	AZTECS
AMERICA	MUSIC	DANCERS
ZEAL	SOLDIERS	

SCENE ONE

Enter OCCIDENT, *a gallant-looking Aztec, wearing a crown. By his side is* AMERICA, *an Aztec woman of poised self-possession. They are dressed in the mantas and huipiles worn for singing a tocotín. They seat themselves on two chairs. On each side, Aztec men and women dance with feathers and rattles in their hands, as is customary for those doing this dance. While they dance,* MUSIC *sings.*

MUSIC: O, Noble Mexicans,
  whose ancient ancestry
  comes forth from the clear light
  and brilliance of the Sun,
5 since this, of all the year,
  is your most happy feast
  in which you venerate
  your greatest deity,
  come and adorn yourselves
10 with vestments of your rank;
  let your holy fervor be
  made one with jubilation;
  and celebrate in festive pomp
  the great God of the Seeds!

15 MUSIC: Since the abundance of
  our native fields and farms
  is owed to him alone
  who gives fertility,
  then offer him your thanks,
20 for it is right and just
  to give from what has grown,
  the first of the new fruits.
  From your own veins, draw out
  and give, without reserve,
25 the best blood, mixed with seed,
  so that his cult be served,
  and celebrate in festive pomp,
  the great God of the Seeds!

(OCCIDENT *and* AMERICA *sit, and* MUSIC *ceases.*)

OCCIDENT: Of all the deities to whom
30 our rites demand I bend my knee—
  among two thousand gods or more
  who dwell within this royal city
  and who require the sacrifice
  of human victims still entreating
35 for life until their blood is drawn
  and gushes forth from hearts still beating
  and bowels still pulsing—I declare,
  among all these, (it bears repeating),
  whose ceremonies we observe,

the greatest is, surpassing all   40
  this pantheon's immensity
  the great God of the Seeds.
AMERICA: And you are right, since he alone
  daily sustains our monarchy
  because our lives depend on his   45
  providing crops abundantly;
  and since he gives us graciously
  the gift from which all gifts proceed,
  our fields rich with golden maize,
  the source of life through daily bread,   50
  we render him our highest praise.
  Then how will it improve our lives
  if rich America abounds
  in gold from mines whose smoke deprives
  the fields of their fertility   55
  and with their clouds of filthy soot
  will not allow the crops to grow
  which blossom now so fruitfully
  from seeded earth? Moreover, his
  protection of our people far   60
  exceeds our daily food and drink,
  the body's sustenance. Indeed,
  he feeds us with his very flesh
  (first purified of every stain).
  We eat his body, drink his blood,   65
  and by this sacred meal are freed
  and cleansed from all that is profane,
  and thus, he purifies our soul.
  And now, attentive to his rites,
  together let us all proclaim: 70
OCCIDENT, AMERICA, DANCERS *and* MUSIC: We celebrate in
    festive pomp,
  the great God of the Seeds!

SCENE TWO

They exit dancing. Enter Christian RELIGION *as a Spanish lady,* ZEAL *as a Captain General in armor, and Spanish* SOLDIERS.

RELIGION: How, being Zeal, can you suppress
  the flames of righteous Christian wrath
  when here before your very eyes
  idolatry, so blind with pride,
  adores, with superstitious rites   5
  an idol, leaving your own bride,
  the holy faith of Christ disgraced?
ZEAL: Religion, trouble not your mind
  or grieve my failure to attack,
  complaining that my love is slack,   10
  for now the sword I wear is bared,

its hilt in hand, clasped ready and
my arm raised high to take revenge.
Please stand aside and deign to wait
15   till I requite your grievances.

(*Enter* OCCIDENT *and* AMERICA *dancing, and accompanied by*
MUSIC, *who enters from the other side.*)

MUSIC: And celebrate in festive pomp,
the great God of the Seeds!
ZEAL: Here they come! I will confront them.
RELIGION: And I, in peace, will also go
20   (before your fury lays them low)
for justice must with mercy kiss;
I shall invite them to arise
from superstitious depths to faith.
ZEAL: Let us approach while they are still
25   absorbed in their lewd rituals.
MUSIC: And celebrate in festive pomp,
the great God of the Seeds!

(ZEAL *and* RELIGION *cross the stage.*)

RELIGION: Great Occident, most powerful;
America, so beautiful
30   and rich; you live in poverty
amid the treasures of your land.
Abandon this irreverent cult
with which the demon has waylaid you.
Open your eyes! Follow the path
35   that leads straightforwardly to truth,
to which my love yearns to persuade you.
OCCIDENT: Who are these unknown people, so
intrusive in my sight, who dare
to stop us in our ecstasy?
40   Heaven forbid such infamy!
AMERICA: Who are these nations, never seen,
that wish, by force, to pit themselves
against my ancient power supreme?
OCCIDENT: Oh, you alien beauty fair;
45   oh, pilgrim woman from afar,
who comes to interrupt my prayer,
please speak and tell me who you are.
RELIGION: Christian Religion is my name,
and I intend that all this realm
50   will make obeisance unto me.
OCCIDENT: An impossible concession!
AMERICA: Yours is but a mad obsession!
OCCIDENT: You will meet with swift repression.
AMERICA: Pay no attention; she is mad!
55   Let us go on with our procession.
MUSIC and AZTECS: And celebrate in festive pomp,
the great God of the Seeds!
ZEAL: How is this, barbarous Occident?
Can it be, sightless Idolatry,
60   that you insult Religion,
the spouse I cherish tenderly?
Abomination fills your cup
and overruns the brim, but see
that God will not permit you to
65   continue drinking down delight,
and I am sent to deal your doom.

OCCIDENT: And who are you who frightens all
who only look upon your face?
ZEAL: I am Zeal. Does that surprise you?
70   Take heed! for when your excesses
bring disgrace to fair Religion,
then will Zeal arise to vengeance;
for insolence I will chastise you.
I am the minister of God,
75   Who growing weary with the sight
of overreaching tyrannies
so sinful that they reach the height
of error, practiced many years,
has sent me forth to penalize you.
80   And thus, these military hosts
with flashing thunderbolts of steel,
the ministers of His great wrath
are sent, His anger to reveal.
OCCIDENT: What god? What sin? What tyranny?
85   What punishment do you foresee?
Your reasons make no sense to me,
nor can I make the slightest guess
who you might be with your insistence
on tolerating no resistance,
90   impeding us with rash persistence
from lawful worship as we sing.
MUSIC: And celebrate with festive pomp,
the great God of the Seeds!
AMERICA: Madman, blind, and barbarous,
95   with mystifying messages
you try to mar our calm and peace,
destroying the tranquility
that we enjoy. Your plots must cease,
unless, of course, you wish to be
100   reduced to ashes, whose existence
even the winds will never sense.
(*To* OCCIDENT.) And you, my spouse, and your cohort,
close off your hearing and your sight
to all their words; refuse to heed
105   their fantasies of zealous might;
proceed to carry out your rite.
Do not concede to insolence
from foreigners intent to dull
our ritual's magnificence.
110   MUSIC: And celebrate with festive pomp,
the great God of the Seeds!
ZEAL: Since our initial offering
of peaceful terms, you held so cheap,
the dire alternative of war,
115   I guarantee you'll count more dear.
Take up your arms! To war! To war!

(*Drums and trumpets sound.*)

OCCIDENT: What miscarriages of justice
has heaven sent against me?
What are these weapons, blazing fire,
120   before my unbelieving eyes?
Get ready, guards! Aim well, my troops,
Your arrows at this enemy!
AMERICA: What lightening bolts does heaven send
to lay me low? What molten balls
of burning lead so fiercely rain?   125

What centaurs crush with monstrous force
and cause my people such great pain?
(*Within.*) *To arms! To arms! War! War!*

([*Drums and trumpets*] *sound.*)

(*Within.*) *Long life to Spain! Long live her king!*

(*The battle begins. Indians enter through one door and flee through another with the Spanish pursuing at their heels. From back stage,* OCCIDENT *backs away from* RELIGION *and* AMERICA *retreats before* ZEAL'S *onslaught.*)

SCENE THREE

RELIGION: Give up, arrogant Occident!
OCCIDENT: I must bow to your aggression,
    but not before your arguments.
ZEAL: Die, impudent America!
5 RELIGION: Desist! Do not give her to Death;
    her life is of some worth to us.
ZEAL: How can you now defend this maid
    who has so much offended you?
RELIGION: America has been subdued
10   because your valor won the strife,
    but now my mercy intervenes
    in order to preserve her life.
    It was your part to conquer her
    by force with military might;
15   mine is to gently make her yield,
    persuading her by reason's light.
ZEAL: But you have seen the stubbornness
    with which these blind ones still abhor
    your creed; is it not better far
20   that they all die?
RELIGION: Good Zeal, restrain
    your justice, and do not kill them.
    My gentle disposition deigns
    to forbear vengeance and forgive.
    I want them to convert and live.
25 AMERICA: If your petition for my life
    and show of Christian charity
    are motivated by the hope
    that you, at last, will conquer me,
    defeating my integrity
30   with verbal steel where bullets failed,
    then you are sadly self-deceived.
    A weeping captive, I may mourn
    for liberty, yet my will grows
    beyond these bonds; my heart is free,
35   and I will worship my own gods!
OCCIDENT: Forced to surrender to your power,
    I have admitted my defeat,
    but still it must be clearly said
    that violence cannot devour
40   my will, nor force constrain its right.
    Although in grief, I now lament,
    a prisoner, your cruel might
    has limits. You cannot prevent
    my saying here within my heart
45   I worship the great God of Seeds!

SCENE FOUR

RELIGION: Wait! What you perceive as force
    is not coercion, but affection.
    What god is this that you adore?
OCCIDENT: The great God of the Seeds
    who causes fields to bring forth fruit.   5
    To him the lofty heavens bow;
    to him the rains obedience give;
    and when, at last, he cleanses us
    from stains of sin, then he invites
    us to the meal that he prepares.   10
    Consider whether you could find
    a god more generous and good
    who blesses more abundantly
    than he whom I describe to you.
RELIGION: (*Aside.*) O God, help me! What images,   15
    what dark designs, what shadowings
    of truths most sacred to our Faith
    do these lies seek to imitate?
    O false, sly, and deceitful snake!
    O asp, with sting so venomous!   20
    O hydra, that from seven mouths
    pours noxious poisons, every one
    a passage to oblivion!
    To what extent, with this facade
    do you intend maliciously   25
    to mock the mysteries of God?
    Mock on! for with your own deceit,
    if God empowers my mind and tongue,
    I'll argue and impose defeat.
AMERICA: Why do you find yourself perplexed?   30
    Do you not see there is no god
    other than ours who verifies
    with countless blessings his great works?
RELIGION: In doctrinal disputes, I hold
    with the apostle Paul, for when   35
    he preached to the Athenians
    and found they had a harsh decree
    imposing death on anyone
    who tried to introduce new gods,
    since he had noticed they were free   40
    to worship at a certain shrine,
    an altar to "the Unknown God,"
    he said to them, "This Lord of mine
    is no new god, but one unknown
    that you have worshipped in this place,   45
    and it is He, my voice proclaims."
    And thus I—

(OCCIDENT *and* AMERICA *whisper to each other.*)

        Listen, Occident!
    and hear me, blind Idolatry!
    for all your happiness depends
    on listening attentively.   50
    These miracles that you recount,
    these prodigies that you suggest,
    these apparitions and these rays
    of light in superstition dressed
    are glimpsed but darkly through a veil.   55
    These portents you exaggerate,

attributing to your false gods
effects that you insinuate,
but wrongly so, for all these works
60 proceed from our true God alone,
and of His Wisdom come to birth.
Then if the soil richly yields,
and if the fields bud and bloom,
if fruits increase and multiply,
65 if seeds mature in earth's dark womb,
if rains pour forth from leaden sky,
all is the work of His right hand;
for neither the arm that tills the soil
nor rains that fertilize the land
70 nor warmth that calls life from the tomb
of winter's death can make plants grow;
for they lack reproductive power
if Providence does not concur,
by breathing into each of them
75 a vegetative soul.
AMERICA: That might be so;
then tell me, is this God so kind—
this deity whom you describe—
that I might touch Him with my hands,
these very hands that carefully
80 create the idol, here before you,
an image made from seeds of earth
and innocent, pure human blood
shed only for this sacred rite?
RELIGION: Although the Essence of Divinity
85 is boundless and invisible,
because already It has been
eternally united with
our nature, He resembles us
so much in our humanity
90 that He permits unworthy priests
to take Him in their humble hands.
AMERICA: In this, at least, we are agreed,
for to my god no human hands
are so unstained that they deserve
95 to touch him; nonetheless, he gives
this honor graciously to those
who serve him with their priestly lives.
No others dare to touch the god,
nor in the sanctuary stand.
100 ZEAL: A reverence most worthily
directed to the one true God!
OCCIDENT: Whatever else you claim, now tell
me this: Is yours a God composed
of human blood, an offering
105 of sacrifice, and in Himself
does He combine with bloody death
the life-sustaining seeds of earth?
RELIGION: As I have said, His boundless
Majesty is insubstantial,
110 but in the Holy Sacrifice
of Mass, His blessed humanity
is placed unbloody under the
appearances of bread, which comes
from seeds of wheat and is transformed
115 into His Body and His Blood;
and this most holy Blood of Christ,
contained within a sacred cup,

is verily the offering
most innocent, unstained, and pure
that on the altar of the cross   120
was the redemption of the world.
AMERICA: Such miracles, unknown to us,
make me desire to believe;
but would the God that you reveal
offer Himself so lovingly   125
transformed for me into a meal
as does the god that I adore?
RELIGION: In truth, He does. For this alone
His Wisdom came upon the earth
to dwell among all humankind.   130
AMERICA: And so that I can be convinced,
may I not see this Deity?
OCCIDENT: And so that I can be made free
of old beliefs that shackle me?
RELIGION: Yes, you will see when you are bathed   135
in crystal waters from the font
of baptism.
OCCIDENT: And well I know,
in preparation to attend
a banquet, I must bathe, or else
our ancient custom I offend.   140
ZEAL: Your vain ablutions will not do
the cleansing that your stains require.
OCCIDENT: Then what?
RELIGION: There is a sacrament
of living waters, which can cleanse
and purify you of your sins.   145
AMERICA: Because you deluge my poor mind
with concepts of theology,
I've just begun to understand;
there is much more I want to see,
and my desire to know is now   150
by holy inspiration led.
OCCIDENT: And I desire more keenly still
to know about the life and death
of the God you say is in the bread.
RELIGION: Then come along with me, and I   155
shall make for you a metaphor,
a concept clothed in rhetoric
so colorful that what I show
to you, your eyes will clearly see;
for now I know that you require   160
objects of sight instead of words,
by which faith whispers in your ears
too deaf to hear; I understand,
for you necessity demands
that through the eyes, faith find her way   165
to her reception in your hearts.
OCCIDENT: Exactly so. I do prefer
to see the things you would impart.

SCENE FIVE

RELIGION: Then come.
ZEAL: Religion, answer me:
what metaphor will you employ
to represent these mysteries?
RELIGION: An *auto* will make visible
through allegory images   5

of what America must learn
and Occident implores to know
about the questions that now burn
within him so.

ZEAL: What will you call
10   this play in allegory cast?

RELIGION: *Divine Narcissus*, let it be,
because if that unhappy maid
adored an idol which disguised
in such strange symbols the attempt
15   the demon made to counterfeit
the great and lofty mystery
of the most Blessed Eucharist,
then there were also, I surmise,
among more ancient pagans hints
20   of such high marvels symbolized.

ZEAL: Where will your drama be performed?

RELIGION: In the crown city of Madrid,
which is the center of the Faith,
the seat of Catholic majesty,
25   to whom the Indies owe their best
beneficence, the blessed gift
of Holy Writ, the Gospel light
illuminating all the West.

ZEAL: That you should write in Mexico
30   for royal patrons don't you see
to be an impropriety?

RELIGION: Is it beyond imagination
that something made in one location
can in another be of use?
35   Furthermore, my writing it
comes, not of whimsical caprice,
but from my vowed obedience
to do what seems beyond my reach.
Well, then, this work, however rough
40   and little polished it might be,
results from my obedience,
and not from any arrogance.

ZEAL: Then answer me, Religion, how
(before you leave the matter now),
45   will you respond when you are chid
for loading the whole Indies on
a stage to transport to Madrid?

RELIGION: The purpose of my play can be

none other than to glorify
the Eucharistic Mystery;   50
and since the cast of characters
are no more than abstractions which
depict the theme with clarity,
then surely no one should object
if they are taken to Madrid;   55
distance can never hinder thought
with persons of intelligence,
nor seas impede exchange of sense.

ZEAL: Then, prostrate at his royal feet,
beneath whose strength two worlds are joined   60
we beg for pardon of the King;

RELIGION: and from her eminence, the Queen;

AMERICA: whose sovereign and anointed feet
the humble Indies bow to kiss;

ZEAL: and from the Royal High Council;   65

RELIGION: and from the ladies, who bring light
into their hemisphere;

AMERICA: and from
their poets, I most humbly beg
forgiveness for my crude attempt,
desiring with these awkward lines   70
to represent the Mystery.

OCCIDENT: Let's go, for anxiously I long to see
exactly how this God of yours
will give Himself as food to me.

(AMERICA, OCCIDENT, *and* ZEAL *sing:*)

The Indies know   75
and do concede
who is the true
God of the Seeds.
In loving tears
which joy prolongs   80
we gladly sing
our happy songs.

ALL: Blest be the day
when I could see
and worship the
great God of Seeds.   85

(*They all exit, dancing and singing.*)

CRITICAL CONTEXTS

JOHN DRYDEN (1631–1700)

"Preface to *Troilus and Cressida,* Containing the Grounds of Criticism in Tragedy" (1679)

Edited by ARTHUR C. KIRSCH

John Dryden is the most important English critic and poet of the late seventeenth century; he was appointed poet laureate and royal historiographer in 1668 and was also the author of many plays, both comedies and heroic tragedies. In 1679, he wrote an adaptation of Shakespeare's *Troilus and Cressida,* and in his "Preface" to the play Dryden argues for neoclassical principles of unity and decorum.

In the "Preface," Dryden frames a specifically neoclassical sense of the purpose and function of tragedy. One way into this essay is through a comparison with Aristotle, and indeed, with Greek tragedy. How do Dryden's criteria at once invoke and revise the sense of tragic construction in Aristotle's *The Poetics?* Beyond that, what are the features of Shakespearean drama that seem to require Dryden's attention as a reviser? What is the sense of decorum that Dryden wishes to urge and that Shakespeare's original play seems to violate?

The poet Aeschylus was held in the same veneration by the Athenians of after ages as Shakespeare is by us; and Longinus has judged, in favor of him, that he had a noble boldness of expression, and that his imaginations were lofty and heroic; but, on the other side, Quintilian affirms that he was daring to extravagance. 'Tis certain that he affected pompous words, and that his sense too often was obscured by figures. Notwithstanding these imperfections, the value of his writings after his decease was such that his countrymen ordained an equal reward to those poets who could alter his plays to be acted on the theater, with those whose productions were wholly new, and of their own. The case is not the same in England; though the difficulties of altering are greater, and our reverence for Shakespeare much more just, than that of the Grecians for Aeschylus. In the age of that poet, the Greek tongue was arrived to its full perfection; they had then amongst them an exact standard of writing and of speaking. The English language is not capable of such a certainty; and we are at present so far from it that we are wanting in the very foundation of it, a perfect grammar. Yet it must be allowed to the present age that the tongue in general is so much refined since Shakespeare's time that many of his words, and more of his phrases, are scarce intelligible. And of those which we understand, some are ungrammatical, others coarse; and his whole style is so pestered with figurative expressions, that it is as affected as it is obscure. 'Tis true, that in his later plays he had worn off somewhat of the rust; but the tragedy which I have undertaken to correct was, in all probability, one of his first endeavors on the stage.[1]

The original story was written by one Lollius, a Lombard, in Latin verse, and translated by Chaucer into English; intended, I suppose, a satire on the inconstancy of women: I find nothing of it among the Ancients; not so much as the name Cressida once mentioned. Shakespeare (as I hinted), in the apprenticeship of his writing, modeled it into that play which is now called by the name of *Troilus and Cressida;* but so lamely is it left to us, that it is not divided into acts; which fault I ascribe to the actors who printed it after Shakespeare's death; and that too so carelessly, that a more uncorrect copy I never saw. For the play itself, the author seems to have begun it with some fire; the characters of Pandarus and Thersites are promising enough; but as if he grew weary of his task, after an entrance or two, he lets 'em fall: and the later part of the tragedy is nothing but a confusion of drums and trumpets, excursions and alarms. The chief persons, who give name to the tragedy, are left alive; Cressida is false, and is not punished. Yet after all, because the play was Shakespeare's, and that there appeared in some places of it the admirable genius of the author, I undertook to remove that heap of rubbish under which many excellent thoughts lay wholly buried. Accordingly, I new modeled the plot; threw out many unnecessary persons; improved those characters which were begun and left unfinished: as Hector, Troilus, Pandarus, and Thersites; and added that of Andromache. After this I made, with no small trouble, an order and connection of all the scenes; removing them from the places where they were inartificially set; and though it was impossible to keep 'em all unbroken, because the scene must be sometimes in the city and sometimes in the camp, yet I have so ordered them that there is a coherence of 'em with one another, and a

---

[1] Actually, *Troilus and Cressida,* which was probably written around 1602, came at the midpoint of Shakespeare's career.

dependence on the main design: no leaping from Troy to the Grecian tents, and thence back again in the same act; but a due proportion of time allowed for every motion. I need not say that I have refined his language, which before was obsolete; but I am willing to acknowledge that as I have often drawn his English nearer to our times, so I have sometimes conformed my own to his; and consequently, the language is not altogether so pure as it is significant. The scenes of Pandarus and Cressida, of Troilus and Pandarus, of Andromache with Hector and the Trojans, in the second act, are wholly new; together with that of Nestor and Ulysses with Thersites, and that of Thersites with Ajax and Achilles. I will not weary my reader with the scenes which are added of Pandarus and the lovers, in the third; and those of Thersites, which are wholly altered; but I cannot omit the last scene in it, which is almost half the act, betwixt Troilus and Hector. The occasion of raising it was hinted to me by Mr. Betterton: the contrivance and working of it was my own. They who think to do me an injury by saying that it is an imitation of the scene betwixt Brutus and Cassius, do me an honor by supposing I could imitate the incomparable Shakespeare; but let me add that if Shakespeare's scene, or that faulty copy of it in *Amintor and Melantius*, had never been, yet Euripides had furnished me with an excellent example in his *Iphigenia*, between Agamemnon and Menelaus; and from thence, indeed, the last turn of it is borrowed.[2] The occasion which Shakespeare, Euripides, and Fletcher have all taken is the same; grounded upon friendship: and the quarrel of two virtuous men, raised by natural degrees to the extremity of passion, is conducted in all three to the declination of the same passion, and concludes with a warm renewing of their friendship. But the particular groundwork which Shakespeare has taken is incomparably the best; because he has not only chosen two of the greatest heroes of their age, but has likewise interested the liberty of Rome, and their own honors who were the redeemers of it, in this debate. And if he has made Brutus, who was naturally a patient man, to fly into excess at first, let it be remembered in his defense that, just before, he has received the news of Portia's death; whom the poet, on purpose neglecting a little chronology, supposes to have died before Brutus, only to give him an occasion of being more easily exasperated. Add to this that the injury he had received from Cassius had long been brooding in his mind; and that a melancholy man, upon consideration of

an affront, especially from a friend, would be more eager in his passion than he who had given it, though naturally more choleric.

Euripides, whom I have followed, has raised the quarrel betwixt two brothers who were friends. The foundation of the scene was this: the Grecians were windbound at the port of Aulis, and the oracle had said that they could not sail, unless Agamemnon delivered up his daughter to be sacrificed: he refuses; his brother Menelaus urges the public safety; the father defends himself by arguments of natural affection, and hereupon they quarrel. Agamemnon is at last convinced, and promises to deliver up Iphigenia, but so passionately laments his loss that Menelaus is grieved to have been the occasion of it and, by a return of kindness, offers to intercede for him with the Grecians, that his daughter might not be sacrificed. But my friend Mr. Rymer has so largely, and with so much judgment, described this scene, in comparing it with that of Melantius and Amintor, that it is superfluous to say more of it; I only named the heads of it, that any reasonable man might judge it was from thence I modeled my scene betwixt Troilus and Hector. I will conclude my reflections on it with a passage of Longinus, concerning Plato's imitation of Homer: "We ought not to regard a good imitation as a theft, but as a beautiful idea of him who undertakes to imitate, by forming himself on the invention and the work of another man; for he enters into the lists like a new wrestler, to dispute the prize with the former champion. This sort of emulation, says Hesiod, is honorable, 'this strife is wholesome to man,'[3] when we combat for victory with a hero, and are not without glory even in our overthrow. Those great men whom we propose to ourselves as patterns of our imitation serve us as a torch, which is lifted up before us to enlighten our passage; and often elevate our thoughts as high as the conception we have of our author's genius."[4]

I have been so tedious in three acts that I shall contract myself in the two last. The beginning scenes of the fourth act are either added or changed wholly by me; the middle of it is Shakespeare altered, and mingled with my own; three or four of the last scenes are altogether new. And the whole fifth act, both the plot and the writing, are my own additions.

But having written so much for imitation of what is excellent, in that part of the preface which related only to myself, methinks it would neither be unprofitable nor unpleasant to inquire how far we ought to imitate our own poets, Shakespeare and Fletcher, in their tragedies: and

---

[2]The comparison of the quarrels between Amintor and Melantius in Beaumont and Fletcher's *Maid's Tragedy* and Agamemnon and Menelaus in Euripides's *Iphigenia in Aulis* had already been made by Rymer in his *Tragedies of the Last Age* (1678), as Dryden acknowledges in the following paragraph.

[3]ἀγαθὴ δ᾽ ἔρις ἐστὶ βροτοῖσιν (*Works and Days,* 1.24).

[4]*On the Sublime,* 13.4.

this will occasion another inquiry, how those two writers differ between themselves. But since neither of these questions can be solved unless some measures be first taken by which we may be enabled to judge truly of their writings, I shall endeavor, as briefly as I can, to discover the grounds and reason of all criticism, applying them in this place only to tragedy. Aristotle with his interpreters, and Horace, and Longinus, are the authors to whom I owe my lights; and what part soever of my own plans, or of this, which no mending could make regular, shall fall under the condemnation of such judges, it would be impudence in me to defend. . . .

The Grounds of Criticism in Tragedy

Tragedy is thus defined by Aristotle (omitting what I thought unnecessary in his definition). 'Tis an imitation of one entire, great, and probable action; not told, but represented; which, by moving in us fear and pity, is conducive to the purging of those two passions in our minds. More largely thus, tragedy describes or paints an action, which action must have all the proprieties above named. First, it must be one or single, that is, it must not be a history of one man's life; suppose of Alexander the Great, or Julius Caesar, but one single action of theirs. This condemns all Shakespeare's historical plays, which are rather chronicles represented than tragedies, and all double action of plays. As to avoid a satire upon others, I will make bold with my own *Marriage à-la-Mode,* where there are manifestly two actions, not depending on one another: but in *Oedipus* there cannot properly be said to be two actions, because the love of Adrastus and Eurydice has a necessary dependence on the principal design, into which it is woven. The natural reason of rule is plain; for two different independent actions distract the attention and concernment of the audience, and consequently destroy the intention of the poet: if his business be to move terror and pity, and one of his actions be comical, the other tragical, the former will divert the people, and utterly make void his greater purpose. Therefore, as in perspective, so in tragedy, there must be a point of sight in which all the lines terminate; otherwise the eye wanders, and the work is false. This was the practice of the Grecian stage. But Terence made an innovation in the Roman: all his plays have double actions; for it was his custom to translate two Greek comedies, and to weave them into one of his, yet so that both the actions were comical, and one was principal, the other but secondary or subservient. And this has obtained on the English stage, to give us the pleasure of variety.

As the action ought to be one, it ought, as such, to have order in it, that is, to have a natural beginning, a middle, and an end. A natural beginning, says Aristotle, is that which could not necessarily have been placed after

another thing, and so of the rest. This consideration will arraign all plays after the new model of Spanish plots, where accident is heaped upon accident, and that which is first might as reasonably be last: an inconvenience not to be remedied but by making one accident naturally produce another, otherwise 'tis a farce and not a play. Of this nature is the *Slighted Maid,*[5] where there is no scene in the first act which might not by as good reason be in the fifth. And if the action ought to be one, the tragedy ought likewise to conclude with the action of it. Thus in *Mustapha,*[6] the play should naturally have ended with the death of Zanger, and not have given us the grace cup after dinner of Solyman's divorce from Roxolana.

The following properties of the action are so easy that they need not my explaining. It ought to be great, and to consist of great persons, to distinguish it from comedy, where the action is trivial, and the persons of inferior rank. The last quality of the action is that it ought to be *probable,* as well as admirable and great. 'Tis not necessary that there should be historical truth in it; but always necessary that there should be a likeness of truth, something that is more than barely possible, *probable* being that which succeeds or happens oftener than it misses. To invent therefore a probability, and to make it wonderful, is the most difficult undertaking in the art of poetry; for that which is not wonderful is not great; and that which is not probable will not delight a reasonable audience. This action, thus described, must be represented and not told, to distinguish dramatic poetry from epic: but I hasten to the end or scope of tragedy, which is to rectify or purge our passions, fear and pity.

To instruct delightfully is the general end of all poetry. Philosophy instructs, but it performs its work by precept: which is not delightful, or not so delightful as example. To purge the passions by example is therefore the particular instruction which belongs to tragedy. Rapin, a judicious critic, has observed from Aristotle that pride and want of commiseration are the most predominant vices in mankind: therefore, to cure us of these two, the inventors of tragedy have chosen to work upon two other passions, which are fear and pity. We are wrought to fear by their setting before our eyes some terrible example of misfortune, which happened to persons of the highest quality; for such an action demonstrates to us that no condition is privileged from the turns of fortune; this must of necessity cause terror in us, and consequently abate our pride. But when we see that the most virtuous, as well as the greatest, are not exempt from such misfortunes, that consideration moves pity in us, and insensibly works us to be helpful to,

---

[5]By Sir Robert Stapylton (1663).

[6]By Roger Boyle, Earl of Orrery (first performed in 1665).

and tender over, the distressed, which is the noblest and most god-like of moral virtues. Here 'tis observable that it is absolutely necessary to make a man virtuous, if we desire he should be pitied: we lament not, but detest, a wicked man; we are glad when we behold his crimes are punished, and that poetical justice[7] is done upon him. Euripides was censured by the critics of his time for making his chief characters too wicked: for example, Phaedra, though she loved her son-in-law with reluctancy, and that it was a curse upon her family for offending Venus, yet was thought too ill a pattern for the stage. Shall we therefore banish all characters of villainy? I confess I am not of that opinion; but it is necessary that the hero of the play be not a villain; that is, the characters which should move our pity ought to have virtuous inclinations, and degrees of moral goodness in them. As for a perfect character of virtue, it never was in nature, and therefore there can be no imitation of it; but there are allays of frailty to be allowed for the chief persons, yet so that the good which is in them shall outweigh the bad, and consequently leave room for punishment on the one side, and pity on the other.

After all, if anyone will ask me whether a tragedy cannot be made upon any other grounds than those of exciting pity and terror in us, Bossu,[8] the best of modern critics, answers thus in general: that all excellent arts, and particularly that of poetry, have been invented and brought to perfection by men of a transcendent genius; and that therefore they who practice afterwards the same arts are obliged to tread in their footsteps, and to search in their writings the foundation of them; for it is not just that new rules should destroy the authority of the old. But Rapin writes more particularly thus[9]: that no passions in a story are so proper to move our concernment as fear and pity; and that it is from our concernment we receive our pleasure, is undoubted; when the soul becomes agitated with fear for one character, or hope for another, then it is that we are pleased in tragedy by the interest which we take in their adventures.

Here, therefore, the general answer may be given to the first question, how far we ought to imitate Shakespeare and Fletcher in their plots: namely, that we ought to follow them so far only as they have copied the excellencies of those who invented and brought to perfection dramatic poetry: those things only excepted which religion, customs of countries, idioms of languages, etc., have altered in the superstructures, but not in the foundation of the design.

How defective Shakespeare and Fletcher have been in all their plots, Mr. Rymer has discovered in his criticisms: neither can we who follow them be excused from the same or greater errors; which are the more unpardonable in us, because we want their beauties to countervail our faults. The best of their designs, the most approaching to antiquity, and the most conducing to move pity, is the *King and No King;* which, if the farce of Bessus were thrown away, is of that inferior sort of tragedies which end with a prosperous event. 'Tis probably derived from the story of Oedipus, with the character of Alexander the Great, in his extravagancies, given to Arbaces. The taking of this play, amongst many others, I cannot wholly ascribe to the excellency of the action; for I find it moving when it is read: 'tis true, the faults of the plot are so evidently proved that they can no longer be denied. The beauties of it must therefore lie either in the lively touches of the passion: or we must conclude, as I think we may, that even in imperfect plots there are less degrees of nature, by which some faint emotions of pity and terror are raised in us: as a less engine will raise a less proportion of weight, though not so much as one of Archimedes' making; for nothing can move our nature, but by some natural reason, which works upon passions. And since we acknowledge the effect, there must be something in the cause.

The difference between Shakespeare and Fletcher in their plotting seems to be this: that Shakespeare generally moves more terror, and Fletcher more compassion. For the first had a more masculine, a bolder and more fiery genius; the second, a more soft and womanish. In the mechanic beauties of the plot, which are the observation of the three unities, time, place, and action, they are both deficient; but Shakespeare most. Ben Jonson reformed those errors in his comedies, yet one of Shakespeare's was regular before him; which is, *The Merry Wives of Windsor.* For what remains concerning the design, you are to be referred to our English critic. That method which he has prescribed to raise it from mistake, or ignorance of the crime, is certainly the best, though 'tis not the only: for amongst all the tragedies of Sophocles, there is but one, *Oedipus,* which is wholly built after that model.

After the plot, which is the foundation of the play, the next thing to which we ought to apply our judgment is the manners, for now the poet comes to work above ground: the ground-work indeed is that which is most necessary, as that upon which depends the firmness of the whole fabric; yet it strikes not the eye so much as the beauties or imperfections of the manners, the thoughts, and the expressions.

The first rule which Bossu prescribes to the writer of an heroic poem, and which holds too by the same reason in all dramatic poetry, is to make the moral of the work,

---

[7]A phrase first coined by Rymer in *The Tragedies of the Last Age.*

[8]Le Bossu, author of *Traité du poème épique* (1675).

[9]In *Réflexions sur la poétique d'Aristote* (1674).

that is, to lay down to yourself what that precept of morality shall be, which you would insinuate into the people; as namely, Homer's (which I have copied in my *Conquest of Granada*) was, that union preserves a commonwealth, and discord destroys it; Sophocles, in his *Oedipus*, that no man is to be accounted happy before his death. 'Tis the moral that directs the whole action of the play to one center; and that action or fable is the example built upon the moral, which confirms the truth of it to our experience: when the fable is designed, then and not before, the persons are to be introduced with their manners, characters, and passions.

The manners in a poem are understood to be those inclinations, whether natural or acquired, which move and carry us to actions, good, bad, or indifferent, in a play; or which incline the persons to such or such actions. I have anticipated part of this discourse already, in declaring that a poet ought not to make the manners perfectly good in his best persons; but neither are they to be more wicked in any of his characters than necessity requires. To produce a villain, without other reason than a natural inclination to villainy is, in poetry, to produce an effect without a cause; and to make him more a villain than he has just reason to be, is to make an effect which is stronger than the cause.

The manners arise from many causes; and are either distinguished by complexion, as choleric and phlegmatic, or by the differences of age or sex, of climates, or quality of the persons, or their present condition. They are likewise to be gathered from the several virtues, vices, or passions, and many other commonplaces which a poet must be supposed to have learned from natural philosophy, ethics, and history; of all which whosoever is ignorant, does not deserve the name of poet.

But as the manners are useful in this art, they may be all comprised under these general heads: first, they must be apparent; that is, in every character of the play, some inclinations of the person must appear: and these are shown in the actions and discourse. Secondly, the manners must be suitable, or agreeing to the persons; that is, to the age, sex, dignity, and the other general heads of manners: thus, when a poet has given the dignity of a king to one of his persons, in all his actions and speeches, that person must discover majesty, magnanimity, and jealousy of power, because these are suitable to the general manners of a king. The third property of manners is resemblance; and this is founded upon the particular characters of men, as we have them delivered to us by relation or history; that is, when a poet has the known character of this or that man before him, he is bound to represent him such, at least not contrary to that which fame has reported him to have been. Thus, it is not a poet's choice to make Ulysses choleric, or Achilles patient, because Homer has described

'em quite otherwise. Yet this is a rock on which ignorant writers daily split; and the absurdity is as monstrous as if a painter should draw a coward running from a battle, and tell us it was the picture of Alexander the Great.

The last property of manners is that they be constant and equal, that is, maintained the same through the whole design: thus, when Virgil had once given the name of *pious* to Aeneas, he was bound to show him such, in all his words and actions through the whole poem. All these properties Horace has hinted to a judicious observer: "1. you must mark the manners of each age; 2. or follow tradition; 3. or create your own convention; 4. let each character remain constant and consistent with itself."[10]

From the manners, the characters of persons are derived; for indeed the characters are no other than the inclinations, as they appear in the several persons of the poem; a character being thus defined, that which distinguishes one man from another. Not to repeat the same things over again which have been said of the manners, I will only add what is necessary here. A character, or that which distinguishes one man from all others, cannot be supposed to consist of one particular virtue, or vice, or passion only; but 'tis a composition of qualities which are not contrary to one another in the same person; thus the same man may be liberal and valiant, but not liberal and covetous; so in a comical character, or humour (which is an inclination to this or that particular folly), Falstaff is a liar, and a coward, a glutton, and a buffoon, because all these qualities may agree in the same man; yet it is still to be observed that one virtue, vice, and passion ought to be shown in every man, as predominant over all the rest; as covetousness in Crassus, love of his country in Brutus; and the same in characters which are feigned.

The chief character or hero in a tragedy, as I have already shown, ought in prudence to be such a man who has so much more in him of virtue than of vice, that he may be left amiable to the audience, which otherwise cannot have any concernment for his sufferings; and 'tis on this one character that the pity and terror must be principally, if not wholly, founded—a rule which is extremely necessary, and which none of the critics that I know have fully enough discovered to us. For terror and compassion work but weakly when they are divided into many persons. If Creon had been the chief character in *Oedipus*, there had neither been terror nor compassion moved; but only detestation of the man and joy for his punishment; if Adrastus and Eurydice had been made more appealing characters, then the pity had been divided, and lessened

---

[10] 1. *notandi sunt tibi mores*; 2. *aut famam sequere*; 3. *aut sibi convenientia finge*; 4. *servetur ad imum, qualis ab incepto processerit, et sibi constet* (*Ars poetica*, 11.156, 119, 126–127).

on the part of Oedipus: but making Oedipus the best and bravest person, and even Jocasta but an underpart to him, his virtues and the punishment of his fatal crime drew both the pity and the terror to himself.

By what had been said of the manners, it will be easy for a reasonable man to judge whether the characters be truly or falsely drawn in a tragedy; for if there be no manners appearing in the characters, no concernment for the persons can be raised; no pity or horror can be moved, but by vice or virtue; therefore, without them, no person can have any business in the play. If the inclinations be obscure, 'tis a sign the poet is in the dark, and knows not what manner of man he presents to you; and consequently you can have no idea, or very imperfect, of that man; nor can judge what resolutions he ought to take; or what words or actions are proper for him. Most comedies made up of accidents or adventures are liable to fall into this error; and tragedies with many turns are subject to it; for the manners never can be evident where the surprises of fortune take up all the business of the stage; and where the poet is more in pain to tell you what happened to such a man than what he was. 'Tis one of the excellencies of Shakespeare that the manners of his persons are generally apparent, and you see their bent and inclinations. Fletcher comes far short of him in this, as indeed he does almost in everything: there are but glimmerings of manners in most of his comedies, which run upon adventures: and in his tragedies, *Rollo, Otto, A King and No King,* Melantius,[11] and many others of his best, are but pictures shown you in the twilight; you know not whether they resemble vice or virtue, and they are either good, bad, or indifferent, as the present scene requires it. But of all poets, this commendation is to be given to Ben Jonson, that the manners even of the most inconsiderable persons in his plays are everywhere apparent.

By considering the second quality of manners, which is that they be suitable to the age, quality, country, dignity, etc., of the character, we may likewise judge whether a poet has followed nature. In this kind, Sophocles and Euripides have more excelled among the Greeks than Aeschylus; and Terence more than Plautus among the Romans. Thus Sophocles gives to Oedipus the true qualities of a king, in both those plays which bear his name; but in the latter, which is the *Oedipus Colonœus,* he lets fall on purpose his tragic style; his hero speaks not in the arbitrary tone, but remembers, in the softness of his complaints, that he is an unfortunate blind old man, that he is banished from his country, and persecuted by his next relations. The present French poets are generally accused that wheresoever they lay the scene, or in whatsoever age, the manners of

their heroes are wholly French. Racine's Bajazet is bred at Constantinople, but his civilities are conveyed to him, by some secret passage, from Versailles into the Seraglio. But our Shakespeare, having ascribed to Henry the Fourth the character of a king and of a father, gives him the perfect manners of each relation, when either he transacts with his son or with his subjects. Fletcher, on the other side, gives neither to Arbaces, nor to his King in the *Maid's Tragedy,* the qualities which are suitable to a monarch; though he may be excused a little in the latter, for the King there is not uppermost in the character; 'tis the lover of Evadne, who is King only in a second consideration; and though he be unjust, and has other faults which shall be nameless, yet he is not the hero of the play. 'Tis true, we find him a lawful prince (though I never heard of any King that was in Rhodes), and therefore Mr. Rymer's criticism stands good; that he should not be shown in so vicious a character. Sophocles has been more judicious in his *Antigone;* for though he represents in Creon a bloody prince, yet he makes him not a lawful king, but an usurper, and Antigona herself is the heroine of the tragedy. But when Philaster wounds Arethusa and the boy; and Perigot his mistress, in the *Faithful Shepherdess,* both these are contrary to the character of manhood. Nor is Valentinian managed much better, for though Fletcher has taken his picture truly, and shown him as he was, an effeminate, voluptuous man, yet he has forgotten that he was an Emperor, and has given him none of those royal marks which ought to appear in a lawful successor of the throne. If it be inquired what Fletcher should have done on this occasion: ought he not to have represented Valentinian as he was? Bossu shall answer this question for me, by an instance of the like nature: Mauritius, the Greek Emperor, was a prince far surpassing Valentinian, for he was endued with many kingly virtues; he was religious, merciful, and valiant, but withal he was noted of extreme covetousness, a vice which is contrary to the character of a hero, or a prince: therefore, says the critic, that emperor was no fit person to be represented in a tragedy, unless his good qualities were only to be shown, and his covetousness (which sullied them all) were slurred over by the artifice of the poet.[12] To return once more to Shakespeare: no man ever drew so many characters, or generally distinguished 'em better from one another, excepting only Jonson. I will instance but in one, to show the copiousness of his invention: 'tis that of Caliban, or the Monster in the *Tempest.* He seems there to have created a person which was not in nature, a boldness which at first sight would appear intolerable; for he makes him a species of himself, begotten by an incubus on a witch; but this, as I have elsewhere

---

[11] Otto is Rollo's brother; Melantius is a character in *The Maid's Tragedy.*

[12] *Traité du poème épique,* 4.7

proved, is not wholly beyond the bounds of credibility, at least the vulgar still believe it. We have the separated notions of a spirit, and of a witch (and spirits, according to Plato, are vested with a subtle body; according to some of his followers, have different sexes); therefore, as from the distinct apprehensions of a horse, and of a man, imagination has formed a centaur; so from those of an incubus and a sorceress, Shakespeare has produced his monster. Whether or no his generation can be defended, I leave to philosophy; but of this I am certain, that the poet has most judiciously furnished him with a person, a language, and a character, which will suit him, both by father's and mother's side: he has all the discontents and malice of a witch, and of a devil, besides a convenient proportion of the deadly sins; gluttony, sloth, and lust are manifest; the dejectedness of a slave is likewise given him, and the ignorance of one bred up in a desert island. His person is monstrous, as he is the product of unnatural lust; and his language is as hobgoblin as his person; in all things he is distinguished from other mortals. The characters of Fletcher are poor and narrow, in comparison of Shakespeare's; I remember not one which is not borrowed from him; unless you will except that strange mixture of a man in the *King and No King;* so that in this part Shakespeare is generally worth our imitation; and to imitate Fletcher is but to copy after him who was a copier.

Under this general head of manners, the passions are naturally included, as belonging to the characters. I speak not of pity and of terror, which are to be moved in the audience by the plot; but of anger, hatred, love, ambition, jealousy, revenge, etc., as they are shown in this or that person of the play. To describe these naturally, and to move them artfully, is one of the greatest commendations which can be given to a poet: to write pathetically, says Longinus, cannot proceed but from a lofty genius. A poet must be born with this quality; yet, unless he help himself by an acquired knowledge of the passions, what they are in their own nature, and by what springs they are to be moved, he will be subject either to raise them where they ought not to be raised, or not to raise them by the just degrees of nature, or to amplify them beyond the natural bounds, or not to observe the crisis and turns of them, in their cooling and decay: all which errors proceed from want of judgment in the poet, and from being unskilled in the principles of moral philosophy. Nothing is more frequent in a fanciful writer than to foil himself by not managing his strength; therefore, as in a wrestler, there is first required some measure of force, a well-knit body, and active limbs, without which all instruction would be vain; yet, these being granted, if he want the skill which is necessary to a wrestler, he shall make but small advantage of his natural robustuousness: so, in a poet, his inborn

vehemence and force of spirit will only run him out of breath the sooner, if it be not supported by the help of art. The roar of passion indeed may please an audience, three parts of which are ignorant enough to think all is moving which is noise, and it may stretch the lungs of an ambitious actor, who will die upon the spot for a thundering clap; but it will move no other passion than indignation and contempt from judicious men. Longinus, whom I have hitherto followed, continues thus: *If the passions be artfully employed, the discourse becomes vehement and lofty: if otherwise, there is nothing more ridiculous than a great passion out of season:* and to this purpose he animadverts severely upon Aeschylus, who writ nothing in cold blood, but was always in a rapture, and in fury with his audience:[13] the inspiration was still upon him, he was ever tearing it upon the tripos[14]; or (to run off as madly as he does, from one similitude to another) he was always at high flood of passion, even in the dead ebb and lowest water-mark of the scene. He who would raise the passion of a judicious audience, says a learned critic, must be sure to take his hearers along with him; if they be in a calm, 'tis in vain for him to be in a huff: he must move them by degrees, and kindle with 'em; otherwise he will be in danger of setting his own heap of stubble on a fire, and of burning out by himself without warming the company that stand about him. They who would justify the madness of poetry from the authority of Aristotle have mistaken the text, and consequently the interpretation: I imagine it to be false read, where he says of poetry that it is εὐφυοῦς ἤ μανικοῦ, that it had always somewhat in it either of a genius, or of a madman. 'Tis more probable that the original ran thus, that poetry was εὐφυοῦς οὐ μανικοῦ, that it belongs to a witty man, but not to a madman.[15] Thus then the passions, as they are considered simply and in themselves, suffer violence when they are perpetually maintained at the same height; for what melody can be made on that instrument, all whose strings are screwed up at first to their utmost stretch, and to the same sound? But this is not the worst: for the characters likewise bear a part in the general calamity, if you consider the passions embodied in them; for it follows of necessity that no man can be distinguished from another by his discourse, when every man is ranting, swaggering, and exclaiming with the same excess: as if it were the only business of all the characters to contend with each other for the prize at Billingsgate; or that the scene of the tragedy lay in Bet'lem.[16]

---

[13]*On the Sublime,* 3.

[14]A reference to the tripod at Delphi on which the priestess of Apollo delivered her raving oracles.

[15]Aristotle, *The Poetics,* 17.

[16]Bedlam, a London hospital for the insane.

Suppose the poet should intend this man to be choleric, and that man to be patient; yet when they are confounded in the writing, you cannot distinguish them from one another: for the man who was called patient and tame is only so before he speaks; but let his clack be set a-going, and he shall tongue it as impetuously, and as loudly, as the errantest hero in the play. By this means, the characters are only distinct in name; but, in reality, all the men and women in the play are the same person. No man should pretend to write who cannot temper his fancy with his judgment: nothing is more dangerous to a raw horseman than a hot-mouthed jade without a curb.

'Tis necessary therefore for a poet who would concern an audience by describing of a passion, first to prepare it, and not to rush upon it all at once. Ovid has judiciously shown the difference of these two ways, in the speeches of Ajax and Ulysses: Ajax, from the very beginning, breaks out into his exclamations, and is swearing by his Maker, "'By Jupiter,' he cried."[17] Ulysses, on the contrary, prepares his audience with all the submissiveness he can practice, and all the calmness of a reasonable man; he found his judges in a tranquillity of spirit, and therefore set out leisurely and softly with 'em, till he had warmed 'em by degrees; and then he began to mend his pace, and to draw them along with his own impetuousness: yet so managing his breath, that it might not fail him at his need, and reserving his utmost proofs of ability even to the last. The success, you see, was answerable; for the crowd only applauded the speech of Ajax:

> and the applause of the crowd followed his closing words.[18]

But the judges awarded the prize for which they contended to Ulysses:

> the assembly was very moved; and the power of eloquence was revealed, and the skillful orator carried off the hero's arms.[19]

The next necessary rule is to put nothing into the discourse which may hinder your moving of the passions. Too many accidents, as I have said, encumber the poet, as much as the arms of Saul did David; for the variety of passions which they produce are ever crossing and jostling each other out of the way. He who treats of joy and grief together is in a fair way of causing neither of those effects. There is yet another obstacle to be removed, which is pointed wit, and sentences affected out of season; these

are nothing of kin to the violence of passion: no man is at leisure to make sentences and similes when his soul is in an agony. I the rather name this fault that it may serve to mind me of my former errors; neither will I spare myself, but give an example of this kind from my *Indian Emperor*. Montezuma, pursued by his enemies, and seeking sanctuary, stands parleying without the fort, and describing his danger to Cydaria, in a simile of six lines:

> As on the sands the frighted traveller
> Sees the high seas come rolling from afar, etc.[20]

My Indian potentate was well skilled in the sea for an inland prince, and well improved since the first act, when he sent his son to discover it. The image had not been amiss from another man, at another time: "but not now, in this place"[21]; he destroyed the concernment which the audience might otherwise have had for him; for they could not think the danger near when he had the leisure to invent a simile.

If Shakespeare be allowed, as I think he must, to have made his characters distinct, it will easily be inferred that he understood the nature of the passions: because it has been proved already that confused passions make undistinguishable characters. Yet I cannot deny that he has his failings; but they are not so much in the passions themselves as in his manner of expression: he often obscures his meaning by his words, and sometimes makes it unintelligible. I will not say of so great a poet that he distinguished not the blown puffy style from true sublimity; but I may venture to maintain that the fury of his fancy often transported him beyond the bounds of judgment, either in coining of new words and phrases or racking words which were in use into the violence of a catachresis.[22] 'Tis not that I would explode[23] the use of metaphors from passions, for Longinus thinks 'em necessary to raise it: but to use 'em at every word, to say nothing without a metaphor, a simile, an image, or description, is I doubt to smell a little too strongly of the buskin. I must be forced to give an example of expressing passion figuratively; but that I may do it with respect to Shakespeare, it shall not be taken from anything of his: 'tis an exclamation against Fortune, quoted in his *Hamlet*, but written by some other poet:

> Out, out, thou strumpet Fortune! all you gods,
> In general synod, take away her power;
> Break all the spokes and felleys from her wheel,
> And bowl the round nave down the hill of Heav'n,
> As low as to the fiends.

---

[17]*agimus, pro Jupiter, inquit* (*Metamorphoses*, 13.5).

[18] *vulgique secutum ultima mumur erat.* Ibid., 123.

[19]*mota manus procerum est; et quid facundia posset tum patuit, fortisque viri tulit arma disertus.* Ibid., 282–83.

---

[20]Act 5.

[21]*sed nunc non erat hisce locus* (*Ars poetica*, 1.19).

[22]A misuse of terms.

[23]Banish, reject.

And immediately after, speaking of Hecuba, when Priam was killed before her eyes:

> The mobled queen ran up and down,
> Threatening the flame with bisson rheum; a clout about that head
> Where late the diadem stood; and for a robe,
> About her lank and all o'er-teemed loins,
> A blanket in th' alarm of fear caught up.
> Who this had seen, with tongue in venom steep'd
> 'Gainst Fortune's state would treason have pronounced;
> But if the gods themselves did see her then,
> When she saw Pyrrhus make malicious sport
> In mincing with his sword her husband's limbs,
> The instant burst of clamour that she made
> (Unless things mortal move them not at all)
> Would have made milch the burning eyes of Heaven,
> And passion in the gods.[24]

What a pudder is here kept in raising the expression of trifling thoughts! Would not a man have thought that the poet had been bound prentice to a wheelwright, for his first rant? and had followed a ragman for the clout and blanket, in the second? Fortune is painted on a wheel, and therefore the writer, in a rage, will have poetical justice down upon every member of that engine: after this execution, he bowls the nave down hill, from Heaven to the fiends (an unreasonable long mark, a man would think); 'tis well there are no solid orbs to stop it in the way, or no element of fire to consume it: but when it came to the earth, it must be monstrous heavy, to break ground as low as to the center. His making milch the burning eyes of Heaven was a pretty tolerable flight too: and I think no man ever drew milk out of eyes before him: yet to make the wonder greater, these eyes were burning. Such a sight indeed were enough to have raised passion in the gods; but to excuse the effects of it, he tells you perhaps they did not see it. Wise men would be glad to find a little sense couched under all those pompous words; for bombast is commonly the delight of that audience which loves poetry, but understands it not: and as commonly has been the practice of those writers who, not being able to infuse a natural passion into the mind, have made it their business to ply the ears and to stun their judges by the noise. But Shakespeare does not often thus; for the passions in his scene between Brutus and Cassius are extremely natural, the thoughts are such as arise from the matter, and the expression of 'em not viciously figurative. I cannot leave

this subject before I do justice to that divine poet by giving you one of his passionate descriptions: 'tis of Richard the Second when he was deposed, and led in triumph through the streets of London by Henry of Bolingbroke: the painting of it is so lively, and the words so moving, that I have scarce read anything comparable to it in any other language. Suppose you have seen already the fortunate usurper passing through the crowd, and followed by the shouts and acclamations of the people; and now behold King Richard entering upon the scene: consider the wretchedness of his condition, and his carriage in it; and refrain from pity if you can:

> As in a theater, the eyes of men,
> After a well-graced actor leaves the stage,
> Are idly bent on him that enters next,
> Thinking his prattle to be tedious:
> Even so, or with much more contempt, men's eyes
> Did scowl on Richard: no man cried, God save him:
> No joyful tongue gave him his welcome home,
> But dust was thrown upon his sacred head,
> Which with such gentle sorrow he shook off,
> His face still combating with tears and smiles
> (The badges of his grief and patience),
> That had not God (for some strong purpose) steel'd
> The hearts of men, they must perforce have melted,
> And barbarism itself have pitied him.[25]

To speak justly of this whole matter: 'tis neither height of thought that is discommended, nor pathetic vehemence, nor any nobleness of expression in its proper place; but 'tis a false measure of all these, something which is like 'em, and is not them; 'tis the Bristol-stone,[26] which appears like a diamond; 'tis an extravagant thought, instead of a sublime one; 'tis roaring madness, instead of vehemence; and a sound of words, instead of sense. If Shakespeare were stripped of all the bombast in his passions, and dressed in the most vulgar words, we should find the beauties of his thoughts remaining; if his embroideries were burnt down, there would still be silver at the bottom of the melting-pot: but I fear (at least let me fear it for myself) that we who ape his sounding words have nothing of his thought, but are all outside; there is not so much as a dwarf within our giant's clothes. Therefore, let not Shakespeare suffer for our sakes; 'tis our fault, who succeed him in an age which is more refined, if we imitate him so ill that we copy his failings only, and make a virtue of that in our writings which in his was an imperfection.

For what remains, the excellency of that poet was, as I have said, in the more manly passions; Fletcher's in the

---

[24]*Hamlet*, 2.2.475–79, 487–500. [Line numbers cited here are those in this anthology; the lines that Dryden quotes differ slightly from this anthology because of his use of another version of Shakespeare's play.—Editor]

[25]*Richard II*, 5.2.23–36.

[26]A rock crystal.

softer: Shakespeare writ better betwixt man and man; Fletcher, betwixt man and woman: consequently, the one described friendship better; the other love: yet Shakespeare taught Fletcher to write love: and Juliet, and Desdemona, are originals. 'Tis true, the scholar had the softer soul; but the master had the kinder. Friendship is both a virtue and a passion essentially; love is a passion only in its nature, and is not a virtue but by accident: good nature makes friendship, but effeminacy love. Shakespeare had an universal mind, which comprehended all characters and passions; Fletcher a more confined and limited: for though he treated love in perfection, yet honor, ambition, revenge, and generally all the stronger passions, he either touched not, or not masterly. To conclude all, he was a limb of Shakespeare.

I had intended to have proceeded to the last property of manners, which is that they must be constant, and the characters maintained the same from the beginning to the end; and from thence to have proceeded to the thoughts and expressions suitable to a tragedy: but I will first see how this will relish with the age. 'Tis, I confess, but cursorily written; yet the judgment which is given here is generally founded upon experience: but because many men are shocked at the name of rules, as if they were a kind of magisterial prescription upon poets, I will conclude with the words of Rapin, in his reflections on Aristotle's work of poetry: "If the rules be well considered, we shall find them to be made only to reduce nature into method, to trace her step by step, and not to suffer the least mark of her to escape us: 'tis only by these that probability in fiction is maintained, which is the soul of poetry. They are founded upon good sense, and sound reason, rather than on authority; for though Aristotle and Horace are produced, yet no man must argue that what they write is true because they writ it; but 'tis evident, by the ridiculous mistakes and gross absurdities which have been made by those poets who have taken their fancy only for their guide, that if this fancy be not regulated, 'tis a mere caprice, and utterly incapable to produce a reasonable and judicious poem."[27]

---

[27] *Réflexions*, 12.

Modern Europe

© Dixie Sheridan

Hamm in one of the definitive spaces of modern drama, the empty room of Samuel Beckett's *Endgame,* in the 2000 Rude Mechanicals Theater Company production.

In some ways the world we live in today was forged between 1850 and 1950. Since the mid-nineteenth century, enormous political changes have redrawn the map of the planet: two world wars; the rise of the United States and the rise and fall of the Union of Soviet Socialist Republics as world superpowers; revolutions in Russia and China; worldwide liberation from European colonial rule in Mexico, the Philippines, Latin America, Africa, India, and Southeast Asia. Political change was spurred by a series of industrial and technological revolutions. This century saw the introduction of the telephone, radio, film, and television; of the automobile and the highway; of the airplane and the rocket; of penicillin, anesthetics, vaccinations, and artificial organs; of the assembly line and mass production; of multinational corporations extending their markets and influence around the globe. The acceleration of technological change altered the fabric of daily life, creating new forms of living, working, and relating to one another, and new ways of measuring our lives: suburbs and housing developments, trade unions and public corporations, the time clock and the wristwatch, public education and compulsory retirement. It witnessed huge changes in the landscape of life: the growth of the modern cityscape, of modern slums, skyscrapers, subways, and even city streets; of massive public projects like the Panama and Suez canals, the Empire State Building, the Eiffel Tower, and their grim cousins—the gas chambers of Auschwitz and the nuclear bombing of Hiroshima and Nagasaki.

Political and social changes were rivaled by the intellectual and cultural revolutions that gave—or attempted to give—meaning to modern experience. This was the century of Darwin and the theory of evolution; of Marx and Lenin; of Gandhi's nonviolent resistance; of Einstein, Oppenheimer, and Teller, and a revolution in our understanding of the physical cosmos; of Freud's discovery of the unconscious; of Proust, Joyce, Stein, Eliot, and Woolf; of the Impressionist painters, and of Picasso, and Pollock; of Diaghilev and Nijinsky, of Fred Astaire and Ginger Rogers, of Isadora Duncan and Martha Graham; of Wagner, of Stravinsky and Schoenberg, of ragtime and jazz.

This complex of revolutions extends to the modern theater. Technological innovation, political developments, and two major wars encouraged an increasing internationalism across the arts of Europe, evident in the "international" style of architecture popularized by Le Corbusier, the Bauhaus, and their followers; in Cubist painting and sculpture; and in modernist writing and music. This internationalism, however, hardly fostered a single, monolithic sense of "modernism" in the arts. Instead, it gave rise to a series of fragmentary AVANT-GARDE movements—imagism, cubism, vorticism, futurism, symbolism, surrealism, Dada, and so on—each with its own ideals, esthetics, and audience, and usually with its own resistant posture toward society as well. The fragment—the poetic image, Joyce's "epiphanies," Schoenberg's twelve-tone row, montage in film—came to be valued as a means of expression in itself. Since the 1950s, a variety of social, political, and esthetic challenges have been made to modernism—usually under the general rubric of POSTMODERNISM—and will be discussed later in this essay.

Modernist art also developed a distinction between "high art" and the esthetics of mass culture that parallels the modern division of labor and implies a division between highbrow and lowbrow, the elite and the popular. In many respects, the modernist theater became definitive of "high art" as it was edged from the center of cultural life by other performance media—film, radio, and later, television—which claimed greater immediacy and wider distribution. After the turn of the twentieth century, the modern theater and drama were increasingly pressed to define what is germane, special, and essential to live dramatic performance.

Units V, VI, and VII survey the theater more widely than previous units, focusing not on a single city or site of performance, but instead on the broader developments of national and international movements. For although the theaters of Chekhov's Moscow, Shaw's London, Brecht's Berlin, or Beckett's Paris reflected very different social dynamics, they were engaged in a common, distinctly modernist project: bringing the stage into a critical relation to the forms of modern life by taking an experimental attitude toward theatrical production. And many of these projects have a visible legacy in the work of their successors: in Müller's assault on the dynamics of temporality and identity, in Churchill's parallel between sexual and colonial politics, in the critical HYBRIDIZATION of Soyinka's drama.

The Modern Theater

Theatrical innovation always takes place on three fronts: as technology, as esthetics, and as ideology. The history of the modern theater is in one sense a history of new strategies and techniques for stage production: electric lighting, revolving stages, increasingly spectacular and illusionistic stage machinery, and new techniques of stage design, acting, and direction. What makes these changes meaningful is how they are used to represent and explain the world around us.

Reviewing the history of nineteenth-century drama, Brander Matthews, the first professor of dramatic literature in the United States, remarked in 1910 that modern drama owed its innovation more to Edison than to Ibsen, that the new drama was "the inevitable consequence of the incandescent bulb." The technological revolutions that brought engines and electricity to the public transformed theater throughout Europe and America: the replacement of candle lighting and gas lighting with more flexible electric lighting; the installation of the PROSCENIUM frame, emphasizing the pictorial coherence of the stage; the gradual disappearance of galleries and boxes in favor of seating the audience in darkened, fan-shaped theaters, emphasizing a perspective view of the proscenium; elevators to raise and lower sets; revolving stages on which several settings could be placed at one time. This technology could be put to a variety of uses, and the nineteenth-century theaters of Europe and America had an extraordinarily spectacular dimension, fostering a taste for EXTRAVAGANZAS, MELODRAMAS, NAUTICAL SHOWS, PANTOMIMES, and TABLEAUX. However, the apparatus of the modern theater came increasingly to be dominated by the notion of SCENIC UNITY, the idea that the stage set, the costumes, the behavior of the actors, and the dramatic action all should correspond to a single historical era and social milieu. Shakespeare's actors had mixed contemporary Elizabethan dress with "antique" costumes in the production of plays with classical settings. Throughout the eighteenth century, actors wore contemporary clothing regardless of the historical era of the play. By the late nineteenth century, however—following the example of Charles Kean and Henry Irving in England, the company of George II, the Duke of Saxe-Meiningen in Germany, and others—productions increasingly strove to establish a unified style on the stage, in which the dialogue, acting style, costumes, setting, and dramatic action all conformed to a single point of view.

The use of a unified theatrical style to assert a thorough VERISIMILITUDE, a photographic "slice of life" onstage, became the cornerstone of modern REALISM in drama and theater and of the movement called NATURALISM in which it began. In a series of essays calling for a "naturalism in the theater," published in the 1870s, the French novelist and playwright Émile Zola argued that the technology of the late nineteenth-century theater could be used to represent a more clinical or scientific attitude toward the world. He urged the stage to adopt a more lifelike and "naturalistic" style by adopting the "objective" methods and perspective of the natural sciences. By filling the stage with objects—real doors, real walls, pictures, furniture, fireplaces—the theater could place men and women in their "environment" rather than in the idealized "setting" of the classical theater, and the characters could then be seen as influenced by that material environment. In contrast to the ideal heroes of earlier drama, the characters of modern plays would become part of that stage milieu, influenced by the forces of history, society, economy, and psychology. Naturalism uses the technology of the stage to claim a "scientific" attitude toward social problems, usually emphasizing the determining role that the social environment plays in the characters' actions. It organized the theater's new technology and the idea of scenic unity it made possible, and provided modern theater with a characteristic kind of meaning: the achievement of verisimilitude.

──── **A Proscenium Stage: Shakespeare Memorial Theatre** ────

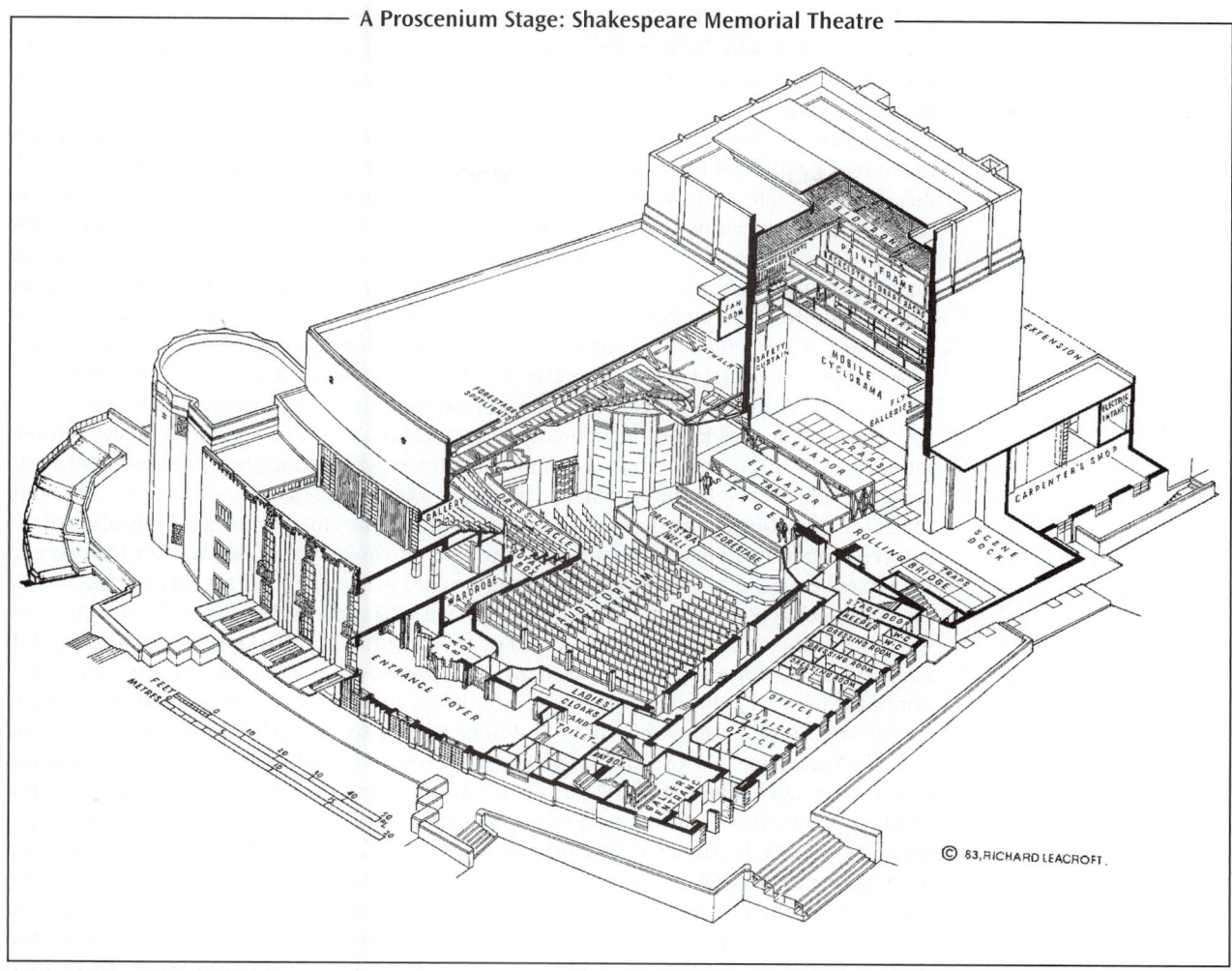

The Shakespeare Memorial Theatre, Stratford-upon-Avon, 1932, displays an extensive backstage area used for scenic machinery.

Naturalism and realism are notoriously difficult to distinguish; here we can describe them as two phases in the history of modern theater and drama. In this sense, naturalism provides the thematic inspiration and many of the dramatic techniques we now associate with modern realistic drama. Realism in the theater is also committed to verisimilitude, but usually develops a wider range of style and a more problematic sense of the relationship of character and environment. While naturalistic plays tend to be preoccupied with the duplication of material reality onstage, realistic plays sometimes distort the verisimilitude of the stage picture in order to dramatize an inner, psychological truth. The domestic space of Sam Shepard's *True West*, for example, at first seems to frame a reunion between two brothers but rapidly transforms itself into the landscape of fantasy. Realism extends and refines the techniques first explored by Zola's generation of playwrights, directors, and actors: a simple and direct speaking style that usually masks a **SUBTEXT** of subtle, unspoken motives; middle- or lower-class characters; action that revolves around the discovery of some past crime or indiscretion; a three-dimensional stage set, usually a domestic interior. Rather than using the play as a vehicle for a single "star" actor, realistic performance emphasizes the ensemble playing of the cast, so that each character becomes important in the overall action. Onstage, realism often treats the boundary of the proscenium as an invisible fourth wall dividing the environment onstage from the audience. The FOURTH WALL prevents the actors from playing to the audience and so from destroying the unity of illusion onstage.

Realism has become the dominant mode of dramatic performance today, so pervasive that it may be difficult for us to recapture its special excitement and danger when first introduced in the 1880s and 1890s. In the first blush of the modern era, the ability to picture an untheatrical, apparently "real" world on the stage was in itself a kind of spectacle, akin to the magic of the new, competing art of photography. Moreover, the first generation of realistic playwrights often adopted a critical posture toward the pieties of the middle-class audience whose attitudes were embodied in the "realistic" vision of the world. Plays such as Ibsen's *Ghosts* and *A Doll House,* Strindberg's *Miss Julie,* and even Glaspell's *Trifles* raised the scandalous topics of sexual betrayal, marital discord, class conflict, sexual freedom, and gender politics in ways that challenged the conventional morality of the bourgeois audience.

The realistic theater developed many of the practices we are familiar with today: new sets for each production, rather than the same furniture recycled from show to show, in order to create the play's specific environment; the fourth wall; the darkened auditorium. Although realistic drama became pervasive, it first flourished in the small avant-garde theaters of the INDEPENDENT THEATER MOVEMENT at the turn of the century. Throughout Europe and the United States, playwrights and directors worked to carve a place for themselves outside the commercial mainstream, which often resisted and sometimes censored the controversial plays of the new realism. André Antoine founded the Théâtre Libre ("Free Theater") in Paris as a subscription theater in 1887; since the shows were open only to subscribers and not to the general public, he was able to avoid censorship and to produce plays like Ibsen's *Ghosts* and Strindberg's *The Father*. Antoine's work was paralleled by the German Freie Bühne ("Free Stage") in 1889. In England, the actress Janet Achurch mounted a production of Ibsen's *A Doll House* in 1889; J.T. Grein's Independent Theater opened in 1891 with a production of *Ghosts* and went on to produce plays by Ibsen, Shaw, and other contemporary playwrights. In Russia, Constantin Stanislavski and Vladimir Nemirovich-Danchenko founded the Moscow Art Theater in 1898, launching one of the most influential of modern theaters with their production of Chekhov's *The Seagull*. Independent theaters were often part of nationalist movements as well, especially in Norway, Sweden, Finland, Italy, and Ireland. In Ireland, W. B. Yeats, Lady Augusta Gregory, John Millington Synge, and a solid cast of amateur actors established a nationalist theater company in 1902 and opened The Abbey Theater in 1904. Here, the artistic resistance of the independent theater was allied to political resistance and national self-definition. The influence of these theaters was felt in the United States throughout the first decades of the twentieth century. David Belasco's minute fidelity to detail had firmly established a realistic idiom in the American theater, but it took the LITTLE THEATER MOVEMENT, inaugurated by Eugene O'Neill, Susan Glaspell, and the Provincetown Playhouse in 1915, to establish a repertoire of modern drama in the United States, and they were soon followed by other companies.

Forms of Modern Drama   The rise of the independent theaters also points to the theater's fragmentation and its marginalization in modern society. The theater no longer commands the cultural centrality that it had in classical Athens or in London and Paris in the sixteenth and seventeenth centuries. Instead, it has become the site for a diverse, sometimes confusing array of artistic experiments. Naturalism and realism were the first dramatic modes to consider themselves not as expressing the dominant political and ideological order, but as criticizing the values and institutions of middle-class society. The major plays of the realistic canon often tend to criticize modern life, particularly its dehumanizing, exploitative routine. The major heroes of the realistic mode—Nora Helmer, Major Barbara, Laura Wingfield—are all characters whose desire for freedom, vitality, and life is threatened by the deadening, deceptive world

Shakespeare Memorial Theatre, Interior View

Although the Shakespeare Memorial Theatre had a forestage apron extending toward the audience, it was in many respects typical of the proscenium theaters of the early twentieth century. The audience was seated in a fan-shaped auditorium, in fixed seats, facing the illuminated stage. This theatre was built in 1932; it has recently been replaced by a new structure.

in which they live. Because realistic drama usually sees that world as an all-embracing "environment," though, its social themes don't finally lead to a call for social change. Modern society may be a prison, but the liberation urged by realistic drama is imagined on the individual level; the characters' search for freedom, value, and meaning leaves the world unchanged. Despite its critical stance toward modern society, realistic drama tacitly accepts the world and its values as an unchanging, and unchangeable, environment in which the characters live out their lives.

For this reason, realistic drama has often seemed an inadequate vehicle for a sustained critique of the forces of modern life, and almost from the moment of its inception in the 1880s and 1890s, realism inspired antagonistic forms of drama and theater. The history of modern drama is a series of reactions against bourgeois society and its values, and against the realistic drama that seemed to represent it and its vision of the world.

Although it was finally concerned with many of the same issues, the **EXPRESSIONIST THEATER** popular from the turn of the century through the 1930s marked an exciting stylistic departure from the realistic mode. Expressionist plays like Strindberg's *A Dream Play,* or American plays like Elmer Rice's *The Adding Machine,* Sophie Treadwell's *Machinal,* or Eugene O'Neill's *The Hairy Ape,* transformed the terms of realistic theater and drama. Rather than showing a character whose inner vitality is crushed by the bourgeois environment, expressionist plays try to show the mind and heart of the character visually, to express it directly in the objects and actions of the stage. The stage set becomes distorted, nearly dreamlike, and it is often peopled by characters who are exaggerated, mechanized, or fantastic, as a way of conveying the emotional coloring of the central character's experience. In O'Neill's *The Emperor Jones,* for instance, Jones is haunted by his "Little Formless Fears" when he flees into the forest; his flight is accompanied by the sound of a drum, which beats faster and louder as the play proceeds. More often, characters in expressionist drama are unnamed, like the Young Woman of *Machinal* or Mr. Zero of *The Adding Machine,* emphasizing that they have become cogs in the modern social and industrial machine. The action of expressionist drama is episodic and much like morality drama. Ernst Toller even named the scenes of his play *Transfiguration* "stations" to stress the play's likeness to a Christian passion play.

Thematically, expressionist theater resembles realism in its attention to character psychology and in its portrayal—however distorted or exaggerated—of the dehumanizing process of modern life. However, the style of expressionism also subverts realism in important ways, challenging both the logical, causal ordering of realistic dramatic action and the visual verisimilitude of the realistic theater. The SYMBOLIST THEATER also developed antirealistic attitudes toward drama and staging and extended the expressionist theater's repudiation of the drama of modern life. Written in prose or in verse, symbolic drama created a dim and mysterious other world, sometimes drawn from mythology or simply from the poet's imagination. The Belgian playwright Maurice Maeterlinck created a vogue for this kind of drama at the turn of the century, a drama which finds analogies in the work of Stéphane Mallarmé, August Strindberg, T. S. Eliot, W. B. Yeats, and Samuel Beckett. Yeats's mythological plays—such as *On Baile's Strand*—are typical of this special and influential mode. Relatively static in action, the plays rely on a densely figurative language to enlarge and energize the "poetic" meaning of events onstage.

Finally, an explicitly Marxist theory of the ideologically coercive dimension of realism—the sense that realism claims that its special perspective of the world is *natural;* that is, unavoidable and *real*—stands at the center of modern EPIC THEATER. Though usually associated with Bertolt Brecht, many of the techniques of epic theater were developed by Erwin Piscator in Berlin during the 1920s and early 1930s and by Vsevolod Meyerhold in his brilliant experiments with CONSTRUCTIVIST THEATER after the Russian Revolution of 1917. Brecht assimilated these techniques to a political purpose that he called epic theater. Rather than claiming to represent reality directly onstage by concealing the workings of the theater, epic theater alerts the audience to the ideological dimension of theater practice by constantly keeping the stage's "means of production" in view. Brecht developed the ALIENATION EFFECT as a way of alerting the audience to the constructed nature of stage events. While the realistic theater claims that the theater and drama, actor and character, stage and dramatic locale are the same, epic theater shows how they are different. In so doing, Brecht argued, the epic theater enables the audience to ask how—with what purpose, to what effect—stage practice is making this dramatic effect come about, and so leads the audience to take a more critical view of the process of the theater. Epic acting, then, comments on itself as "acting." The stage is not unified as a single dramatic locale, but always remains visibly a stage. Brecht also argued that epic drama should be structured differently than realistic plays. Instead of the apparently organic, "causal" action of realistic drama, Brecht's plays are written in a series of episodes. This technique, Brecht argued, allows the actors and the audience to reconsider the character's possibilities for action and change afresh in each scene. By calling the audience's attention to how the play comes into being onstage, epic theater encourages the audience to develop a dialectical sense of how social reality—in the theater and in the world at large—comes into being, how it is made through the interaction of individual and social forces and the interaction of material reality and IDEOLOGY. Epic theater has had an enormous influence on drama and theater around the world.

Stage practice has developed its own rich history, too—again often in reaction to realistic verisimilitude. Throughout the twentieth century, for instance, designers and architects have experimented with different ways of orienting the audience to the stage, in **THEATER IN THE ROUND** and in **ENVIRONMENTAL THEATER,** for instance. To see the dramatic action surrounded by spectators or to have the play take place among the audience members alters the audience's relationship to both the drama and its performance and changes how they can read the production. The Constructivist experiments of Vsevolod Meyerhold following the Russian Revolution placed a nonrepresentational "construction" onstage, a structure that the actors used as a "machine for acting" rather than as a realistic set. Similarly, experimental performance altered notions of what dramatic and theatrical representation could be like. Following World War I, writers such as Tristan Tzara called for an art that was formless and irrational, a process rather than a product; such "Dada"—a nonsense term— poems, plays, and monologues were often given **CABARET PERFORMANCE** in Zurich, Berlin, and Paris. **DADA** and **SURREALIST THEATER** developed a kind of hallucinatory intimacy between stage and audience, laying the foundations for Artaud's **THEATER OF CRUELTY.** In all of these experiments, the theater worked to disperse the visual unity characteristic of the realistic stage in ways that led to new configurations of the relationship between the audience and the performers and to new interpretive perspectives on drama and the possibilities of theater.

Realism, expressionism, symbolist theater, and *epic theater*—these useful labels necessarily limit and categorize the rich variety of the stage in ways that are artificial and untrue to the dynamics of change in the modern theater because new innovations tend to draw their techniques from several of these modes. Modern plays, for instance, often blend representational techniques as a way of challenging the audience's understanding of the drama and its implication in the world. Despite their "realistic" anchoring in a material, lifelike setting, for example, Chekhov's plays sometimes disturb the stability of that illusion with odd, almost "symbolic" effects—the breaking string in *The Cherry Orchard,* for instance. The action of Strindberg's *A Dream Play,* for all its expressionistic fantasy and symbol, nonetheless also focuses on the suffocating moral and domestic environment. In Pirandello's *Six Characters in Search of an Author*—a play indebted in many ways to the "symbolist" theater—the Characters want the Actors to produce a play much in the manner of Ibsen's drama, a realistic drama of hidden crime and its discovery. These labels are useful in helping us to describe some of the outlines of a given play, but we should remember that many modern playwrights wrote in a variety of modes, and that each play is itself a kind of experiment.

Acting and Performance

The modern theater's radical redefinitions of the style and purpose of drama required similar redefinitions of acting and performance. At the turn of the century, a theatrical company would have been organized according to each actor's typical **LINE OF BUSINESS.** Something like the company in Pirandello's *Six Characters,* companies had a leading comic actor, a villain or "heavy," a leading man, a leading lady, a comic old man, a comic woman, and a variety of other parts. Unlike *commedia dell' arte,* actors each played a variety of different characters; nonetheless, each actor would have elaborated some relatively conventional "business" for acting the kind of character he or she usually played. The unity of illusion demanded by the realistic theater, however, required each character to be more finely individualized. Much as the stage designer provided a new set for each production and the costume designer provided clothing appropriate to the character and his or her setting, so the actors were forced to particularize their performances in new ways.

A second stimulus for this innovation was the drama itself. Playwrights like Ibsen and Chekhov typically created characters against the grain of theatrical stereotypes. Nora Helmer, for example, seems like a typical **SOUBRETTE** at the opening of *A Doll House,* the pert and clever young woman of light comedy. However, as the play develops, Ibsen challenges this convention and forces the actress to discover new ways of producing the

MELODRAMA

Although most of the plays included in *The Wadsworth Anthology of Drama* have been popular in the theater, they are all to some extent plays that have been canonized for their qualities as dramatic "literature": rich language and characterization, complex engagement with social and moral issues, deft and original use of dramatic convention, and so on. However, theater and drama pose special problems to the idea of a single literary canon. As popular entertainments, plays have not always been regarded as having "literary" merit. Plays were published only irregularly in Shakespeare's era, and even today few publishers have much commitment to keeping contemporary plays in print—which makes it particularly difficult for contemporary drama to become part of *any* literary canon. More important, plays are produced under very different conditions than novels and poems. Plays are made to be meaningful in a specific theater; their "literary" impact on readers is often secondary to their original purpose, which is to make a theatrical impact on a given body of spectators.

In late-eighteenth and nineteenth-century Europe—in part as a result of the relaxing of restrictions on theatrical performance, and in part as a reflection of a sense of "literature" as part of a circumscribed sphere of "high culture"—a variety of new dramatic genres became popular, of which the most important is MELODRAMA. The term was initially used to indicate plays in which music was used to accentuate the emotional coloring of the action; the term became more generally applied to plays with a conventionalized set of characters, a clear narrative structure, and a distinct moral cosmos. In the nineteenth-century theater, melodrama was an extremely popular genre, fusing the theater's increasing capacity for visual spectacle with a strongly colored and direct dramatic action. The world of melodrama is a world of clear-cut moral absolutes: the hero and heroine are thoroughly virtuous and are threatened by villains who are proportionately unscrupulous. The action is organized in a series of episodes, in each of which the hero/heroine's happiness, virtue, fortune, or life is threatened with destruction; each act of a melodrama usually ends with some striking crisis, often calling for an elaborate stage effect—an explosion, train wreck, or storm. The action of melodrama is often highly involved and coincidental, yet usually works eventually toward a happy—or at least sentimental—ending. If the hero must die, he usually dies in the heroine's arms; more often, the couple are restored to one another and live happily ever after.

Melodrama is usually dated from the popularity of plays like Johann Christoph Friedrich von Schiller's (1759–1805) *The Robbers* (1782), August Friedrich Ferdinand von Kotzebue's (1761–1819) *Menschenhass und Reue* (1789), and René Charles Guilbert de Pixérécourt's (1773–1844) *Coelina* (1800); although Kotzebue and Pixérécourt are now rarely read, their plays were widely adapted throughout Europe. Thirty-six of Kotzebue's plays were translated into English, and several remained popular throughout the nineteenth century. Richard Brinsley Sheridan (1751–1816) adapted Kotzebue's *Der Spanier in Peru* as *Pizarro* in 1799, which became a brilliant success for the actor John Philip Kembel; Thomas Holcroft (1744–1809) adapted Pixérécourt's *Coelina* as *A Tale of Mystery* in 1802. While early nineteenth-century melodrama tended toward Gothic settings—mysterious castles, ghostly visitors, and the like—by later in the century melodrama's typical formal and moral patterns were applied to plays with local and contemporary settings. Pierce Egan's novel *Life in London* was adapted as *Tom and Jerry; or, Life in London* in 1821; Edward George Bulwer-Lytton's (1803–1873)

character. Realistic plays frequently ask actors to work against the apparent "type" of the role, to discover the psychological subtext of will and desire beneath the spoken words that motivates the character's actions. Actors and actresses at the turn of the century frequently had difficulty reading the new realistic plays, precisely because they could not see how to represent the more indirect action and individualized characters through the kinds of stage behavior they had been trained to use.

A new kind of drama requires a new kind of acting, and companies throughout Europe developed ways of acting more behavioristically onstage. The most systematic approach to acting was undertaken by the actor and director Constantin Stanislavski at the Moscow Art Theater around the turn of the twentieth century. Although Stanislavski thought that his techniques could be applied to any play, he discovered the need for such acting largely in his work on Chekhov's plays. Chekhov's plays were frustrating to actors of the old school, because the characters did not conform to traditional types and the action seemed so indirect and inconsequential, lacking familiar dramatic rhythms

Money (1840) was one of several plays that held the stage through the end of the century.

Since melodrama drew a wide audience, and often centered on poor-but-virtuous heroes and heroines, it has sometimes been thought to articulate social resistance. For while early versions like Douglas Jerrold's (1803–1857) hugely popular nautical melodrama *Black Ey'd Susan* (1829) emphasized the undying loyalty and patriotism of British navy sailors (or "tars"), the polarized moral ethos of melodrama could be turned into a vehicle for social critique. In the United States, melodrama became one vehicle for dramatizing ethnic and racial conflict. John Augustus Stone's (1800–1834) *Metamora; or, The Last of the Wampanoags* (1829), dramatized a heroic Indian chief's losing battle to save the land of his ancestors from his rapacious white enemies. In *The Octoroon* (1859), Dion Boucicault (1820–1890) staged the fatal love story between the octoroon Zoe, the virtuous plantation owner who loves her, and the wicked Yankee overseer, McCloskey, who threatens to buy her when it emerges that Zoe was never actually freed from slavery. Although these plays end with "tragic" consequences for their heroes and heroines, melodrama tends to locate its evils in the character of its villains, rather than in the structure of society

Melodrama: The Bells

Sir Henry Irving's (1838–1905) performance in Leopold Lewis's melodrama *The Bells* was one of his greatest roles. The illustration presents both the emotionally exaggerated quality of melodramatic acting and melodrama's use of special effects. In the play, Mathias (Irving's role) has murdered and concealed the body of a Polish Jew. Although many years have passed since the murder, Mathias is haunted by the sound of his victim's sleigh bells. In this scene, he staggers before a vision of the crime itself.

itself: for this reason, melodrama is usually unable to develop a deeper analysis of the social institutions—racism, for example—that afflict its characters' lives. When Bernard Shaw turned to melodrama as a vehicle for his own drama of social critique, he strategically inverted its patterns of characterization as a way of opening its social order to criticism: one way *Major Barbara,* for example, attempts to jolt the audience into examining its attitudes about society at large is by casting Andrew Undershaft—so similar to the scheming and all-powerful industrialist villain of countless popular melodramas—as the moral "hero" of the play. ■

and climaxes. Stanislavski developed techniques for approaching each character as an individual, techniques that were later systematized as a "method" of actor-training. Stanislavski trained the actor to associate his or her personal history with the invented actions of the dramatic character so that the actor could tap that emotional spontaneity, a "life in art," as part of the performance. By using the MAGIC IF—imagining themselves *as* the character, rather than applying a stock line of business—and using their own EMOTION MEMORY to vivify the character's inner life, Stanislavski's actors were taught to bring authentic emotional experience into their performances. Of course, Stanislavski also emphasized the many other abilities that an actor must develop—physical training, vocal control, grace, concentration—but his real contribution to the modern stage is the emphasis on the actor's emotional reality in performance. The realistic theater uses real objects to create a persuasive material environment, and its characters come alive through the actor's real feeling. Stanislavski's work has been extremely influential, particularly in the United States, where it was adapted as the school of METHOD ACTING in the 1930s, and it remains—in very different and modified forms—at the center of much actor-training today.

Antirealistic drama also called for the development of new styles of performance. Meyerhold developed BIOMECHANICS as a way to make the actor's performance more physical, less directly concerned with the behavioral and psychological verisimilitude typical of Stanislavskian realistic acting. His work has analogies in the use of dance and ritualized performance in symbolist theater and in the nonrepresentational physicality of Antonin Artaud's Theater of Cruelty. Symbolist theater also repudiated the lifelike quality of realistic acting. It required a highly artificial and statuesque stillness from performers, allowing the actors to strike powerful but ethereal poses in order to deliver the densely poetic language of the play without interference. Yeats—whose antipathy to realism was profound—thought of training his actors in barrels, to keep them from moving and gesturing as they would do in everyday life: the art of the symbolist theater should be emphatically artificial, thoroughly apart from the conduct of life beyond the stage.

Brecht, again, voiced the most thorough critique of realistic acting. To Brecht, the problem of realistic acting was that it showed the "character" as a finished product, a commodity, rather than revealing *how* the character had come into being, both through the social forces described in the drama and through the decisions taken by the actor as part of the performance. Brecht argued that the actor should acknowledge that he or she both empathizes with the character and demonstrates the character to the audience, that acting is both feeling and showing at the same time. This dialectical approach invites the audience to see how the actor is making the "character" and allows the public to interpret both the process and the product of theater art, the dramatic "character" and the actor's labor.

Women in Modern Drama and Theater

Most readers of modern drama immediately note the prominence of women characters in the plays—Nora Helmer in *A Doll House,* the Daughter in *A Dream Play,* Barbara in *Major Barbara,* Courage in *Mother Courage.* Playwrights frequently associated the political and social limitations of middle-class life with male characters and used female characters to pose subversive questions about that social order. However, in the drama, as in society, this subversive freedom sometimes emerges as illusory or problematic. Ibsen, for instance, enables Nora to recognize how she has been defined by the men in her life, but the world outside her home hardly seems inviting; is there really anywhere for her to go? Many of the women—the Stepdaughter of Pirandello's *Six Characters,* Major Barbara—are also assigned an erotic power opposed to the "reason" of their male antagonists. While this power, too, can be disruptive, it sometimes also reinforces traditional gender stereotypes. Feminine erotic power in the drama carries with it other ascribed values, defining women as more emotional, as more subject to the influence of the body, as closer to "nature." Men retain a pragmatic, "rational" authority that places them at the center of society, and that defines the arena of culture and civilization as an implicitly male domain. The apparent freedom of these stage women, that is, often signals their deeper captivity to the gendered economy of modern society, a captivity shared by actresses in the period as well. Although this is also a period in which actresses—Sarah Bernhardt, Eleonora Duse, Elizabeth Robins, or Ellen Terry, for example—could earn an international reputation, they worked in a theater in which men greatly outnumbered women in the audience and in which nearly all of the managers and producers were men. Women were also important playwrights throughout Europe in the first decades of the twentieth century: Elizabeth Robins's *Votes for Women!* brought the "woman question" to the English stage in 1907; Minna Canth was the leading playwright of the Finnish Theater (her portrait graces the proscenium of the National Theater today); Marieluise Fleisser's *Pioneers in Ingolstadt* (1924) in many ways rivaled Brecht's early vision of epic theater. In a male-dominated industry like the modern theater, it is not surprising that women onstage—both dramatic characters and performers—should reflect fundamentally masculine attitudes about the place of women in society.

To think of the history of theater and drama since Ibsen is to think of an increasingly large and problematic array of dramatic styles, modes of theatrical production, and conceptions of the audience and its world. Many of these innovations were local at first, responding to the social and theatrical conditions of a specific time and place: Brecht's Marxist theater arose in the cabaret culture of Berlin in the late 1920s; Pirandello's METATHEATER was part of the lively Italian avant-garde following World War I; Shaw's drama was informed by the progressive politics of the British Fabian Society and by dramatic conventions drawn from the popular plays of the late Victorian stage. The drama of modern Europe develops a posture of resistant inquiry toward the pieties of contemporary social life. It works both to represent that world and to change it, to affect our ideas about character and personality, about the political realities of our world, and even about the metaphysical certainties we have come to believe. But it is the impact of global political and cultural change that marks the theater of the second half of the twentieth century.

The impact of film and television has forced the theater to work to define what kinds of performance are specific to the stage, how live dramatic performances can offer something unique, something not already available in other performance media. For this reason, perhaps, theater and drama since 1950 have necessarily been "experimental," working to develop new kinds of plays, new practices of stage production, and new kinds of theatrical experience for their audiences. Much as the proscenium theaters of the early twentieth century have given way to other, more flexible kinds of theater spaces, so dramatic writing has become much more varied and experimental. Even stage realism—the mode of Ibsen and Chekhov, Miller and Williams—has undergone an important reworking in the plays of Sam Shepard, Harold Pinter, Heiner Müller, and others.

Here, we can identify three patterns of innovation as a way of organizing our thinking about the diversity of the contemporary stage. One strategy—inspired most directly by Antonin Artaud's THEATER OF CRUELTY—attacks the notion that the theater is essentially a *representational* medium, emphasizing instead the *experiential* aspect of theater. Rather than staging images of some fictive world to an audience of passive spectators, this kind of theater works to structure the *present experience* of the audience in new ways, as in the participatory and ritualistic theater experiments of the 1960s and 1970s. The influence of Artaud's assault on representation is evident in the contemporary theater in several ways: in absurdist drama, in the focus on the body in Griselda Gambaro's *Information for Foreigners,* in the dreamlike density of Müller's *Hamletmachine,* or in the poetic realism of Marina Carr's *By the Bog of Cats. . . .*

The second mode of innovation, THEATER OF THE ABSURD, originated as a new form of playwriting rather than as theatrical experimentation. The plays of Samuel Beckett, Slawomir Mrozek, Eugène Ionesco, Boris Vian, Edward Albee, Harold Pinter, Václav Havel, and others create a strangely dislocated dramatic world, in which arbitrary or "absurd" events both confront and mystify the characters.

While Artaud inspired an existential or experiential theater, Bertolt Brecht—whose work became widely known and imitated only after World War II—inspired a different kind of assault on the conventions of realistic theater. Contemporary POLITICAL THEATER also criticizes the notion of "representation," but in different terms than Artaud or theater of the absurd, *representation* is a word with two senses: in "representing" a picture of the world, the arts necessarily claim that their images are "representative" in some way. Political theater frequently shows how a social or political order uses its power to "represent" others coercively—for example, by depicting those others through demeaning or limiting stereotypes. For this reason, political theater today is intent on using live performance to change the prejudicial attitudes concealed in conventional ideas of representation.

Of course, no plays fit easily or fully into these three categories, but to think of the drama of the postwar period as raising questions of our existential or our political relation to the theater—and so to the world—provides a useful and powerful way of opening that

Theater and Culture Since 1950

Theater in the Round

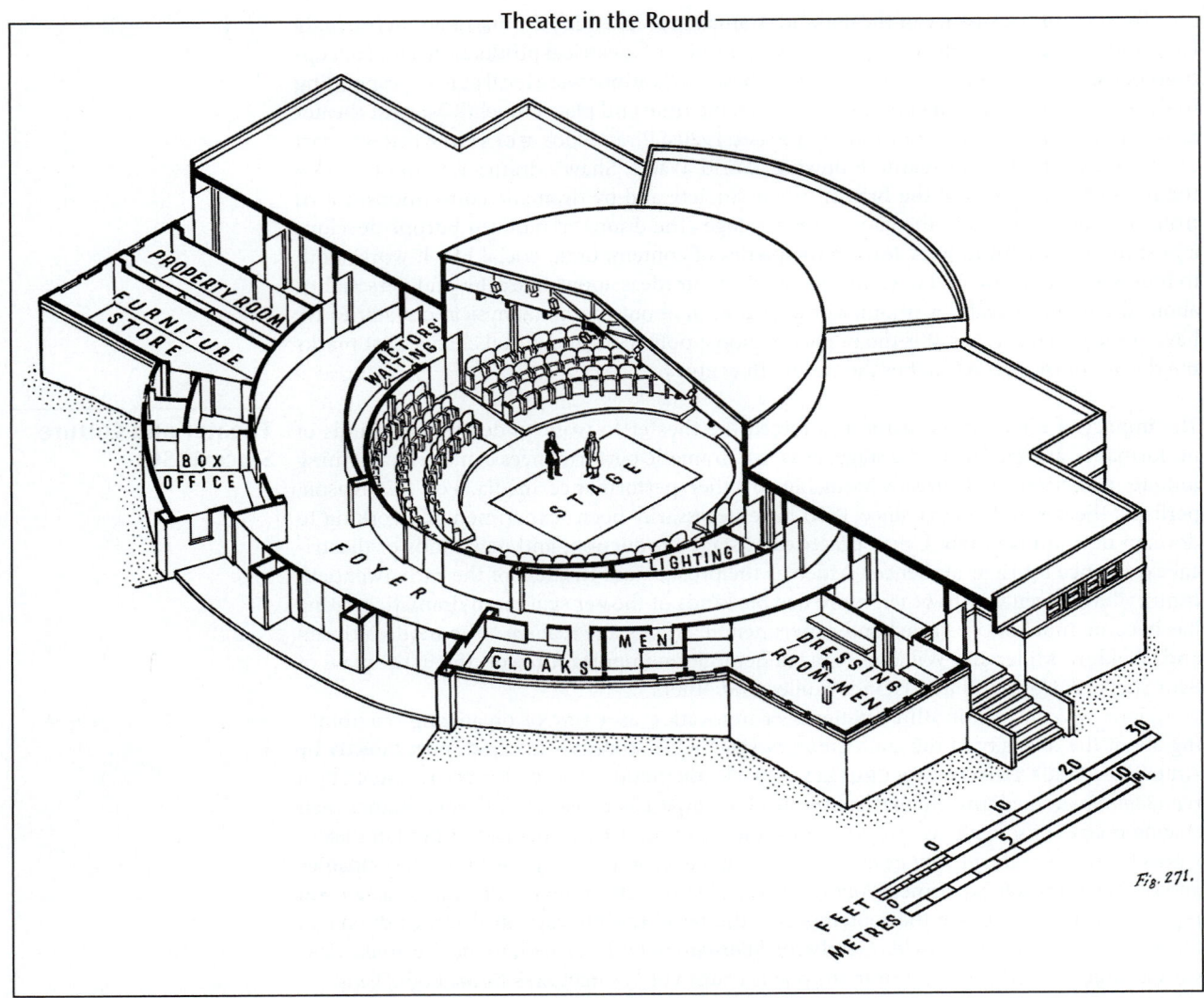

In a theater in the round, the audience surrounds the action, rather than facing the stage as in a proscenium theater. Theater space of this kind lends itself to greater immediacy and contact between the performers and the audience.

drama to our understanding. Each of these modes of theater creates a different relationship between the stage and its audience, and we should examine each of them in some detail.

Artaud and the Theater of Cruelty The writings of Antonin Artaud, particularly the essays collected in the volume *The Theater and Its Double* (written in the late 1920s and 1930s, published in France in 1938, translated to English in 1958), have had an extraordinary impact on our sense of theater. Like many innovators of his generation—think of Brecht or Pirandello—Artaud worked to undermine the notion that the theater can only show its audiences realistic vignettes of daily life. Instead, Artaud argued that the theater should alter the balance between presentation—the actual, immediate activities of actors and audiences, their *presence* in the theater—and representation, the fictive "drama" that had seemed to define the purpose and scope of theater. Artaud—who used the term *theater of cruelty* for this project—advocated transforming the theater into an all-consuming spectacle, akin both to rituals like the Catholic Mass and to public festivals, in which the boundaries between acting and observing, actor and spectator, fiction and reality, conscious and unconscious would be broken or transgressed. The idea that the theater would "communicate," but not through rational means, is captured in one of Artaud's most powerful metaphors for this nearly unimaginable theater: the plague. Artaud envisioned a theater that would transmit its experiences corporeally, through the body, like disease, like mystical wisdom, alchemically transforming all of its participants. To avoid staging conventional dramas, Artaud called for a theater of "no more masterpieces," one that would use the dramatic text to transform the relations between stage and spectator by making the production a total experience—visual, auditory, gustatory, olfactory, tactile, physical—for the audience.

Stage director Peter Brook once remarked, "Artaud applied is Artaud betrayed," and it is true that Artaud's sense of theater is deeply metaphorical, a kind of theater experience that is almost unimaginable to us, and certainly not imaginable to us as theater. Artaud rarely offers a practical description of how this theater could come into being. Instead, the value and influence of Artaud's writing has been indirect and inspirational, bearing in a variety of tangential ways on kinds of theater that are not in any literal sense "Artaudian." In that Artaud imagines a theater of *presence*—not of representation—involving the audience in an experience rather than showing them a picture, his theater comes into contact with several very different kinds of innovation. Although the American experimental theater of the 1960s and 1970s is the most direct application—and betrayal—of Artaud, Artaud's conception of theater stands distantly behind a variety of more formally constructed plays: the dislocating imagery of Beckett and Müller; the ritualized, hallucinatory violence of Pinter's plays; the elaborate physical rituals of Gao Xingjian's *The Other Shore*. Of course, as *written* plays, "masterpieces," these plays are specifically opposed to the ideals of Artaud's unrealizable theater, while at the same time they explore part of the terrain opened by Artaud's vision.

Theater of the Absurd

Coined by the theater critic Martin Esslin in 1961, the phrase *theater of the absurd* tries to capture the special irrationality and unpredictability of a certain wave of dramatic writing of the late 1950s and 1960s, including the plays of Samuel Beckett and Harold Pinter, for example. Taking as his keynote Beckett's famous play *Waiting for Godot* (1953)—a play in which two Chaplinesque tramps wait for a mysterious man named Godot, who never arrives—Esslin finds the theater of the absurd to have certain stylistic and thematic characteristics. It rejects the sense of causality found in realistic plays, the sense that it is possible to find the causes for events either in the environment or in the psychological motives of the characters themselves. Instead, theater of the absurd tends to be about a world in which inexplicable, arbitrary, or irrational events happen. Although the events usually seem to be part of some kind of order or scheme, it is an order that the characters and their audience cannot quite grasp. As Hamm says in Beckett's play *Endgame*, "Something is taking its course," but neither the characters nor the audience are ever sure what that "something" is. In Eugène Ionesco's play *Rhinoceros* (1960), the inhabitants of a small French village begin to turn inexplicably into rhinoceroses. In each act of Boris Vian's *The Empire Builders* (1959), a family moves to a smaller room in an apartment building, always accompanied by a mysterious, bandaged figure. In Slawomir Mrozek's *Striptease* (1961), two men are commanded by a huge, silent finger to remove their clothes and don huge conical hats that conceal and blind them. As Esslin suggests, this drama insists that the fictions we use to make sense of our world—ideas of order, causality, rationality—are just that: fictions imposed on an arbitrary and mysterious reality, whose meanings remain fugitive and elusive.

Absurdist drama treats its audience somewhat differently than realistic plays do, rejecting the "dramatic irony" of the traditional theater, in which the audience understands more than the characters onstage. Instead, the theater of the absurd refuses to provide this privilege to its spectators. We are as baffled and frustrated by our attempts to make the events mean something as the characters are; "Mean something!" a character remarks in *Endgame*, "You and I, mean something! (*Brief laugh*)." Our *present* experience as an audience is structured and made significant by absurdist theatrical production. In the theater, we don't just observe the "absurd" drama onstage, we are forced to undergo it, to live it through. For this reason, both the drama onstage and the audience's experience in the theater are sometimes described as *existential*. We have to *decide* the meaning of our being in the theater, without the comfort, solace, or guidance of some transcendent, predetermined world view.

Political Theater

Much as theater of the absurd works to make the spectators' situation in the theater an extension of the characters' situation on the stage, political theater since Brecht has worked to make the audience's performance in the theater a recognizably political one. By fragmenting the stage space, by showing how the illusion is made rather than concealing its means of production, and by involving the audience more overtly in deciding the meaning of the play's events, the theater is shown to be a political instrument. Like television, newspapers, universities, the courts, and so on, the theater is an institution that produces the ideas and images with which we govern our lives. Both the example of Brecht's plays and his challenging theory of performance have been absorbed and redefined by the world theater. In common with theater of the absurd, political theater works to resist and complicate realistic representation, the "slice of life" of Ibsen, Chekhov, and Miller. Instead of staging an arbitrarily unreal and absurd world, political theater examines "representative" images of reality. Who makes those images? Who benefits from them? Who is injured, governed, or oppressed by them? How do they help to maintain the social *status quo*?

For this reason, much political theater connects representation onstage with representation in society, showing how various social groups—women, gay men, lesbians, ethnic and racial groups, the poor—have been staged in society and in the theater. A fundamental assumption of political theater is that these stereotypes are part of the larger system of discrimination that operates in society, and that they reveal the dominant attitudes of those who govern, control, or influence society from positions of power. In plays like Amiri Baraka's *Dutchman*, Caryl Churchill's *Cloud Nine*, and Wole Soyinka's *Death and the King's Horseman*, the racial conflicts informing contemporary society and culture are explored in very different ways: in relation to colonialism, to the mythologies of imperial history, to women's experience. These plays are very different in style, ranging from a kind of realism in *Death and the King's Horseman* to the testifying monologues of Anna Deavere Smith. It is not a single point of view or a single dramatic style that defines political theater, but the use of theatrical representation itself as a way to analyze representation in society at large.

A similar approach to theater informs many of the modern plays gathered in this anthology, for many of them explore the issue of representation: how Asia is represented in the minds of the West in David Henry Hwang's *M. Butterfly*, how the English remapped and so represented the Irish in their own language and political system in Brian Friel's *Translations*, how African tribal traditions are tragically misunderstood by British imperialists in Wole Soyinka's *Death and the King's Horseman*, how the Chicano and Anglo cultures interact in Luis Valdez's *Los vendidos*, how torture and tourism are connected in Griselda Gambaro's *Information for Foreigners*, or the literal consumption of the Third World by the First in Manjula Padmanabhan's *Harvest*. Political theater sometimes seems highly message oriented, overtly didactic to readers and audiences used to the more subtle instruction offered by realistic plays. Yet the messages of contemporary political theater tend to be fused into the process of theater, so that the politics of the play come into being not in the prepared script of the play but in our experience as an audience. All of these plays disrupt the expectations, attitudes, and preconceptions of the empowered audience and invite the audience to develop different ways of reading their society as part of their involvement in the play.

Drama, Theater, and the "Postmodern"

On the contemporary stage, though, these modes of theater do not work in isolation from one another, but interact with one another, as part of the dynamic means the theater uses to engage its audiences in an understanding of the world. Indeed, to describe the contemporary theater in terms of its historical inheritance from the modernist theater of Brecht,

Artaud, and the absurdists is in an important sense to overlook what is most significant about the stage today: its break from the traditions of modernism. If we look at the range of contemporary performance activity, much of it has little to do with traditional drama. Think of the performance-art monologues of Spalding Gray (one of his best-known, *Swimming to Cambodia,* was made into a film by Jonathan Demme) or Karen Finley (whose work was at the center of the 1990 censorship controversy at the National Endowment for the Arts); of the use of live-feed video in works like The Wooster Group's *Hamlet* or The Builders Association's *Continuous City*; of video art and film; of music television and advertising; of the disorienting stage spectacles of Robert Wilson; of pervasive gaming and flash mobs; even of "plays" like Peter Handke's *Offending the Audience* and *The Ride Across Lake Constance,* or Heiner Müller's *Hamletmachine,* or Samuel Beckett's later work for the theater, *Not I, Footfalls,* and *Ohio Impromptu.*

Theorists of culture and the arts have related these developments to innovations in the visual arts, in architecture, and in writing, characterizing their common features as **POSTMODERN.** The term itself is a difficult one, suggesting that these works often share some of the features of earlier, "modernist" art; the literary and cultural theorist Fredric Jameson suggests that the distinguishing feature of postmodern art is its attitude toward history. Jameson points out that postmodern works frequently invoke or appropriate the style of earlier historical periods, as in the use of neoclassical ornamentation in recent architecture, or the recollection of earlier film styles in more recent movies (**FILM NOIR** in *Chinatown* or *L.A. Confidential*). Jameson labels this technique **PASTICHE.** What is striking about these postmodern quotations of style, though, is not any systematic reinterpretation of tradition or any statement of value, but their tonelessness, their neutrality, the absence of the kind of moral and historical sense we might expect from the act of confronting history. In postmodern pastiche, the recollection of an earlier style does not provide a new understanding of the past, nor does it illuminate our contemporary historical situation. Instead, pastiche denatures that style by removing it from history, and history from it. Style becomes exactly that: simply another option. Hamm's many quotations from English literature in *Endgame* or the pastiche of Gilbert and Sullivan operetta in Churchill's *Cloud Nine* are perhaps part of this complex problem, for in each case the "past" is presented to the audience in terms of an artistic style that is largely emptied of its force as history.

Moreover, Jameson's discussion of pastiche also emphasizes the importance of the esthetic *surface* in postmodern art. Music video and advertising are sometimes taken as the paradigmatic postmodern forms, forms whose "message" lies almost exclusively in a rapidly changing, brilliantly seductive, series of images. Although this technique relates to the modernist use of **MONTAGE** in film and theater, it is different in several important ways. Modernist montage uses a series of images narratively, to tell a story. As the camera cuts quickly from image to image, the audience assembles the images in a single complete narrative. Both the narrative and the interpreting spectator achieve a sense of wholeness. In contrast, postmodern images are juxtaposed in striking, sometimes contradictory combinations that resist our ability to impose a single narrative explanation, a single story line. Postmodern performance—on film or video or in the theater—is insistently fragmentary; it asserts the incompletion of the artistic object and the incomplete quality of the spectator's experience as well. Postmodern arts resist imposing a single explanatory interpretation that would both complete the narrative and confirm the audience's sense of wholeness, of self-integration. In this sense, postmodern arts are sometimes described as concerned with the "death of the subject." They question the possibility both of a comprehensible world and of a comprehending individual. By disorienting language, fragmenting narrative, and dispensing with such organizing principles as "plot" and "character," postmodern art claims that we have entered a new age in which the complex disconnections of modern culture have made obsolete many of our beliefs about the world and our ways of representing the world and ourselves.

Modern European Drama in Performance and History

The understanding of theater that was inaugurated in the mid-nineteenth century is in many respects continuous with our own today: although various experiments—environmental theater, theater of cruelty, performance art—have contributed to a rich sense of the diversity of theatrical performance forms today, to many people "going to the theater" means going to a specially designated building, sitting in a darkened auditorium, and watching the events that take place on the stage. Of course, this activity is shaped today by social and economic forces still just emerging in the early-modern period: whereas earlier audiences usually had a small number of theaters to turn to for performance, performances are available today in a wide range of spaces—subsidized state and municipal theaters throughout Europe, commercial theaters like those in London's West End and New York's Broadway, college and university playhouses, festival theaters like the annual festival at Grahamstown in South Africa or the Shaw Festival in Stratford, Ontario, and many more. Theater in the twentieth century is characterized by its "optional" character: we choose theater from among a range of other forms of dramatic performance, like film and television; the theaters we attend are positioned in their ambient cultures in a much wider variety of ways; and the performances we see tend to value their "uniqueness" rather than their conventionality in typically modern ways.

Moreover, while the performance practices of earlier European theaters were highly conventionalized—masks and *cothurni* for tragedy in Athens, the phallus for comedy; a standard comic or tragic stage set in the neoclassical theaters of France and Italy—in the modern period, the style of dramatic production has become much more varied, not only as a sign of the director's and designer's artistic signature in the production, but also as part of what the play has to sell to its audiences. Indeed, the invention of the stage director in the late nineteenth century is symptomatic of a trend in modernist esthetics more generally, a trend from the polished deployment of convention to an emphasis on the artwork's originality—an originality that signals the individual creative presence of an author or *auteur*. In earlier theaters, of course, someone usually had the responsibility of organizing and rehearsing the actors: this was sometimes the playwright in classical Athenian theater, or the company's leading actor, like David Garrick, in the later eighteenth century. But in these theaters, performance practice was extremely conventionalized: actors, like Shakespeare's, who have a solid line of business, don't really need much rehearsal—an actor whose typical line of business is comic old men will more or less have an approach ready for characters like Polonius. In the modern theater, however, the director has the responsibility for shaping the diverse talents of the company—set, costume, and lighting designs; acting; music—into a single whole, one that seems to deploy the performance in a unique way. Much as we think of a film as embodying the director's vision, so too in the theater the performance is often understood as an expression of the director's ability to shape the play, the players, and the physical milieu of the stage into a uniquely expressive whole.

For this reason, the modern theater is often called the "director's theater," and in many respects the history of modern stage practice is the history of the innovations of brilliant directors. Although naturalistic or realistic drama—the plays of Ibsen and Chekhov and O'Neill—are duly appreciated for their striking departures from the standard practices of nineteenth-century playwriting, transforming these innovations from the page to the stage required a generation of brilliant directors: Antoine, Stanislavski, Meyerhold, Max Reinhardt. Indeed, throughout the history of the modern theater, actors and directors have sometimes been baffled by the new demands of these scripts; Stanislavski, for example, can be understood to have devised his famous Method in response to the obliquity of Chekhov's plays. Similarly, when one thinks of the landmark theatrical productions of the twentieth-century European theater, they are always associated with the director: Stanislavski's productions of Chekhov at the turn of the century; Meyerhold's brilliant *Hedda Gabler,* with its white set and Hedda's snakelike green dress; Piscator's work with Brecht in the 1920s, and Brecht's direction of the Berliner Ensemble in his own and others' plays after World War II; Peter Brook's use of the circus to realize the "magic" of Shakespeare's *A Midsummer Night's Dream* in 1970; Robert Wilson's visualization of Heiner Müller's *Hamletmachine* in the 1980s. As a consequence, one of the most energetic kinds of experiment in the later part of the century has been in the area of a more collaborative theater practice. Like Complicite, many contemporary theater companies are organized as collectives, in which responsibility for the "artistic" decisions is shared, rather than given over to a single person. But even in more conventional circumstances, companies often work to make the playwright's, actors', and designers' work have a more direct impact on the final stage of theater work. Caryl Churchill's play *Cloud Nine,* for example, arose from a series of workshops undertaken by members of the Joint Stock Company, in which the actors experimented by playing different gender, sexual, or racial roles in a variety of situations: Churchill wrote the text of the play out of the workshops, and director Max Stafford-Clark used the results of the workshops as a foundation for the play's theatrical performance. Given the increasing complexity of theatrical production—the use not only of complex technology backstage, but the inclusion of multimedia production as part of the performance itself—we can expect that this struggle to shape the authority of the stage will continue well into the future.

READING THE MATERIAL THEATER

Compared with the documentary record of earlier theaters, the modern theater offers an embarrassment of riches: not only is the print tradition rich in reviews, memoirs, and other accounts of the production and reception of plays in the theater, but also playwrights themselves have often left working drafts of their plays. Henrik Ibsen is particularly notable in this regard: an extremely disciplined and methodical writer, Ibsen not only began most of his plays with a detailed scenario; he retained many of the successive drafts of his plays. These materials provide a unique insight into the process of Ibsen's imagination, and indeed into his practice as a writer as well.

What follows beginning at the bottom of this page are Ibsen's "Notes for the Modern Tragedy," dated 19 October 1878, and his original scenario for *A Doll House.* Not surprisingly, perhaps, many of the elements of the finished play remain in this outline. At the same time, this document differs from the final drama in a number of respects (including some of the characters' names). Granted that a scenario necessarily tends to streamline the action and emphasize the plot of the play, do you find this scenario surprising in any way? Does it seem to present the same kinds of moral or ethical emphases you find in the play? Are there elements of the finished play that seem larger or more powerful than you might have expected from this scenario alone? Are there elements of the scenario that are less prominent in the final draft? The final lines of the scenario are particularly chilling: "Five:— seven hours till midnight. Twenty-four hours till the next midnight. Twenty-four and seven—thirty-one. Thirty-one hours to live. . . ." How do these lines figure in Ibsen's final imagining of the action of the finale of *A Doll House?*

NOTES FOR THE MODERN TRAGEDY
Rome, 19. 10, 78.

There are two kinds of spiritual law, two kinds of conscience, one in man and another, altogether different, in woman. They do not understand each other; but in practical life the woman is judged by man's law, as though she were not a woman but a man.

The wife in the play ends by having no idea of what is right or wrong; natural feeling on the one hand and belief in authority on the other have altogether bewildered her.

A woman cannot be herself in the society of the present day, which is an exclusively masculine society, with laws framed by men and with a judicial system that judges feminine conduct from a masculine point of view.

She has committed forgery, and she is proud of it; for she did it out of love for her husband, to save his life. But this husband with his commonplace principles of honour is on the side of the law and regards the question with masculine eyes.

READING THE MATERIAL THEATER (cont'd)

Spiritual conflicts. Oppressed and bewildered by the belief in authority, she loses faith in her moral right and ability to bring up her children. Bitterness. A mother in modern society, like certain insects who go away and die when she has done her duty in the propagation of the race.[1] Love of life, of home, of husband and children and family. Here and there a womanly shaking-off of her thoughts. Sudden return of anxiety and terror. She must bear it all alone. The catastrophe approaches, inexorably, inevitably. Despair, conflict and destruction.

(Krogstad has acted dishonourably and thereby become well-to-do; now his prosperity does not help him, he cannot recover his honour.)

PERSONS

STENBORG, a Government clerk.

NORA, his wife.

MISS (MRS.) LIND, (a widow).

ATTORNEY KROGSTAD.

KAREN, nurse at the Stenborgs'.

A PARLOUR-MAID at the Stenborgs'.

A PORTER.

THE STENBORGS' THREE LITTLE CHILDREN.

DOCTOR HANK.

SCENARIO
FIRST ACT

A room comfortably, but not show-ily, furnished. In the back, on the right, a door leads to the hall; on the left another door leads to the room or office of the master of the house, which can be seen when the door is opened. A fire in the stove. Winter day.

She enters from the back, humming gaily; she is in outdoor dress and carries several parcels, has been shopping. As she opens the door, a Porter is seen in the hall, carrying a Christmas-tree. She: Put it down there for the present. (Taking out her purse) How much? Porter: Fifty öre. She: Here is a crown. No, keep the change. The Porter thanks her and goes. She continues humming and smiling with quiet glee as she opens several of the parcels she has brought. Calls off, is he at home? Yes! At first, conversation through the closed door; then he opens it and goes on talking to her while continuing to work most of the time, standing at his desk. There is a ring at the hall-door; he does not want to be disturbed; shuts himself in. The maid opens the door to her mistress's friend, just arrived in town. Happy surprise. Mutual explanation of the position of affairs. He has received the post of manager in the new joint-stock bank and is to enter on his duties at the New Year; all financial worries are at an end. The friend has come to town to look for some small employment in an office or whatever may present itself. Mrs. Stenborg gives her good hopes, is certain that all will turn out well. The maid opens the front-door to the debt collector. Mrs. Stenborg terrified; they exchange a few words; he is shown into the office. Mrs. Stenborg and her friend; the circumstances of the debt-collector are touched upon. Stenborg enters in his overcoat; has sent the collector out the other way. Conversation about the friend's affairs; hesitation on his part. He and the friend go out; his wife follows them into the hall; the Nurse enters with the children. Mother and children play. The collector enters. Mrs. Stenborg sends the children out to the left. Great scene between her and him. He goes. Stenborg enters; has met him on the stairs; displeased; wants to know what he came back for? Her support? No intrigues. His wife cautiously tries to pump him. Strict legal answers. Exit to his room. She (repeating her words when the collector went out) But that's impossible. Why, I did it from love!

SECOND ACT

The last day of the year. Midday. Nora and the old Nurse. Nora, impelled by uneasiness, is putting on her things to go out. Anxious random questions of one kind and another give a hint that thoughts of death are in her mind. Tries to banish these thoughts, to turn it off, hopes that something or other may intervene. But what? The Nurse goes off to the left.—Stenborg enters from his room. Short dialogue between him and Nora.—The Nurse re-enters, looking for Nora; the youngest child is crying. Annoyance and questioning on Stenborg's part; exit the Nurse; Stenborg is going in to the children.—Doctor Hank enters. Scene between him and Stenborg.—Nora soon re-enters; she has turned back; anxiety has driven her home again. Scene between her, the Doctor and Stenborg. Stenborg goes into his room.—Scene between Nora and the Doctor. The Doctor goes out.—Nora alone.—Mrs.

---

[1] The sentence is elliptical in the original.

Linde enters. Scene between her and Nora.—Krogstad enters. Short scene between him, Mrs. Linde and Nora. Mrs. Linde goes in to the children.—Scene between Krogstad and Nora.—she entreats and implores him for the sake of her little children; in vain. Krogstad goes out. The letter is seen to fall from outside into the letterbox.—Mrs. Linde re-enters after a short pause. Scene between her and Nora. Half confession. Mrs. Linde goes out.— Nora alone.—Stenborg enters. Scene between him and Nora. He wants to empty the letter-box. Entreaties, jests, half playful persuasion. He promises to let business wait till after New Year's Day; but at 12 o'clock midnight—! Exit. Nora alone. Nora (looking at the clock:) It is five o'clock. Five;—seven hours till midnight. Twenty-four hours till the next midnight.

Twenty-four and seven—thirty-one. Thirty-one hours to live.—

THIRD ACT

A muffled sound of dance music is heard from the floor above. A lighted lamp on the table. Mrs. Linde sits in an armchair and absently turns the pages of a book, tries to read, but seems unable to fix her attention; once or twice she looks at her watch. Nora comes down from the dance; uneasiness has driven her; surprise at finding Mrs. Linde, who pretends that she wanted to see Nora in her costume. Helmer, displeased at her going away, comes to fetch her back. The Doctor also enters, but to say good-bye. Meanwhile Mrs. Linde has gone into the side room on the right. Scene between the Doctor, Helmer and Nora. He is going to bed, he says, never to get up again; they are not to come and see him; there is ugliness about a death-bed. He goes out. Helmer goes upstairs again with Nora, after the latter has exchanged a few words of farewell with Mrs. Linde. Mrs. Linde alone. Then Krogstad. Scene and explanation between them. Both go out. Nora and the children. Then she alone. Then Helmer. He takes the letters out of the letter-box. Short scene; good-night; he goes into his room. Nora in despair prepares for the final step; is ready at the door when Helmer enters with the open letter in his hand. Great scene. A ring. Letter to Nora from Krogstad. Final scene. Divorce. Nora leaves the house. ∎

In this production of Luigi Pirandello's *Six Characters in Search of an Author,* the statuesque "characters" arrive at the stage door, clothed in black and bathed in an eerie light.

© Richard Feldman

In this scene from Henrik Ibsen's *A Doll House,* Doctor Rank, Helmer, and Nora have just returned from the party; Nora wears her tarantella costume, and Helmer has been given a "mask" of middle-class respectability.

© T. Charles Erickson

The photograph of the Moscow Art Theater's original production of Anton Chekhov's *The Cherry Orchard* shows the naturalistic detail for which Constantin Stanislavski's company was famous; Stanislavski is at the left in the role of Gaev, gesturing to the bookcase.

Bill Rose Theater Collection, The New York Public Library for the Performing Arts. Astor, Lenox and Tilden Foundation.

Henrik Ibsen

At the turn of the century, Henrik Ibsen's name was synonymous with modernity in the European theater; much of the territory of modern drama was first explored in Ibsen's work. Born into a mercantile family in provincial Norway, Ibsen (1828–1906) had planned to study medicine; however, after failing to matriculate at the university, he turned to a career as a writer. From 1850 through 1864, Ibsen worked for the nationalist Norwegian Theater in Bergen and then for the Mollergate Theater in Christiania (now Oslo). As literary manager, stage manager, and assistant to the director, Ibsen learned the craft of practical theater firsthand. He also wrote a series of romantic history plays, some in prose and some in verse. Although his fame now rests on the realistic plays he wrote later in his career, in his own lifetime these history plays—such as *The Vikings at Helgeland* (1858)—were quite popular, especially in Norway.

In 1864, Ibsen left Norway and settled in Rome, where he wrote two pivotal plays, *Brand* (1866) and *Peer Gynt* (1867). The story of an idealistic minister, *Brand* established Ibsen as an important European writer and announced one of his central themes: the cost of moral idealism in the modern world. *Peer Gynt* is often taken as a companion-piece to *Brand,* for Peer's picaresque journey throughout Europe is undertaken simply for the purpose of his own self-satisfaction: while Brand's motto is "Be wholly what you are," Peer Gynt's is "To thine own self be . . . enough." In 1877, after extensive work on the Hegelian history drama *Emperor and Galilean,* Ibsen wrote *Pillars of Society,* a prose drama of modern life, inaugurating the stunning series of plays that made him famous and established the contours of modern realistic drama. In *A Doll House* (1879), *Ghosts* (1881), and *An Enemy of the People* (1882), Ibsen explored the conflict between the social and moral restrictions of bourgeois society and the psychological, often unconscious, demands of individual freedom. Ibsen adapted the suspenseful, rigorously plotted form of the WELL-MADE PLAY (or *pièce bien faite*) popularized throughout Europe by French playwrights Eugène Scribe and Victorien Sardou and used it in plays of modern life critical of bourgeois morality and society. The well-made play is notoriously difficult to define, even though its features are familiar: a rigorously "causal" plot, a secret gradually revealed to the audience, a "necessary scene" (the *scène-à-faire*) in which the secret is revealed to the characters, a character (the *raisonneur*) who explains and moralizes the action to the others, and a predominance of coincidental events. In his earlier plays, Ibsen takes these formal conventions and makes them function as forces in the dramatic world. The world of the play comes to seem mechanistic, determined by a secret that will out, full of busybodies explaining and interpreting the action. The mechanics of the well-made play, that is, are identified with the deadening force of social convention, which painfully threatens to extinguish the vitality of the central characters. This conflict between deadening social convention and a mysterious inner vitality pervades Ibsen's mature plays as well, which increasingly moved away from the "well-made" form: *The Wild Duck* (1885), *Rosmersholm* (1887), *The Lady from the Sea* (1888), and *Hedda Gabler* (1890). Ibsen's last plays seem more poetic or symbolic, though they take place in the familiar milieu of the realistic stage: *The Master Builder* (1892), *Little Eyolf* (1894), *John Gabriel Borkman* (1896), and the unfinished *When We Dead Awaken* (1900). Ibsen suffered a paralyzing series of strokes in 1900 that left him unable to write. He died in 1906.

Ibsen's effect on his contemporaries and his influence on the course of modern drama were immediate and profound. His plays were rapidly translated into the major European languages, and stage productions—which often inaugurated the new "independent" theaters—frequently became the subject of sensation and controversy. Indeed, "Ibsenism" came to be a catchword for a variety of social causes, though Ibsen himself generally avoided politics. Although Ibsen's plays brought new issues to the stage, it was his practice as a playwright that proved truly revolutionary. Many playwrights had adopted the realistic theater's use of a material stage environment, its emphasis on the burden of the past, and its sense of a mechanized and constricting society. Ibsen not only used this material with powerful subtlety and resonance, he gave the stage its first distinctively modern characters: complex, contradictory individuals driven by a desire for something—the "joy of life," a sense of themselves—that they can barely recognize or name.

A Doll House

A Doll House was inspired by a series of incidents that came to Ibsen's attention in 1878 when a woman named Laura Kieler contacted him. Kieler had signed a secret—and illegal— loan to raise money for a cure for her tubercular husband. She wrote to Ibsen asking him to recommend the novel she had written to his publisher, in hopes that the profits from its sale would allow her to repay the loan. Ibsen refused. Kieler forged a check and was caught. Her husband committed her to an asylum, had her charged as an unfit mother, and demanded a legal separation. When she was released from the asylum, however, the family remained together.

We can see the shaping power of Ibsen's imagination in his transformation of Laura Kieler's tragedy into the ironic masterpiece, *A Doll House.* The play, which by the turn of the century was a rallying point for international feminist demands for the vote and for other legal rights and protections for women, organizes the conflict between Nora and Helmer around a subtle set of contrasts: the childlike and protected Nora and the world weary Mrs. Linde; the upright and protective Helmer and the shady—yet finally generous— Krogstad; the privations of the past and the financial freedom Nora sees on the horizon. However, as the play proceeds, the stable, bourgeois world that Helmer represents is revealed as a tissue of deception; the institutions of marriage, respectability, and social justice turn out to be fictions that the privileged use to manipulate their world. Nora comes to seem effective, efficient, worldly wise, and finally independent, while Helmer readily compromises his principles to save his reputation. The world of financial freedom Nora glimpses at the play's outset turns out to be a kind of prison and is replaced by another kind of freedom at the end of the play: the frightening freedom to cut herself loose from the bonds of marriage, family, and society.

Helmer had more authority with audiences in the 1880s and 1890s than he does today, and Nora was conventionally criticized as an "unwomanly woman" for taking the loan, deceiving her husband, and leaving her family. Indeed, the first English actress to be offered the part turned it down, because she didn't want audiences to think of her as the kind of woman who would desert her children. Yet the play tends to validate Nora's personal growth and her final decision to leave her family and cannily uses the material environment of the stage setting to convey the suffocating situation in which Nora finds herself.

Owen Teale and Janet McTeer in Henrik Ibsen's *A Doll House,* in the 1997 production using a new translation by Frank McGuinness.

© Joan Marcus

The play takes place in one room: the drawing room where the upwardly mobile Helmers (deluxe books on the shelf, piano against the wall, framed art prints) receive their guests and conduct their lives. The room itself represents the Helmers' concern for social status and assumes a symbolic importance as well: it stands between the unseen privacy of the kitchen and bedroom—the domestic world of marriage and children—and the threatening public world beyond the front door, the world of Krogstad, of the dark and icy river, of Nora's final escape. The room becomes a kind of prison, a room in which Rank's declaration of love for Nora seems inappropriate, in which Helmer criticizes her dizzying tarantella—a Sicilian dance thought to imitate the death throes of someone bitten by a tarantula—as too abandoned, and in which Nora's final discussion with Helmer makes her submission to him impossible. That is, the room makes concrete the play's concern for the social constraints on a woman's life, becoming a visual image of how Helmer's masculine, bourgeois moral authority imprisons Nora. It is not entirely clear that Nora can survive in the harsh social and economic climate outside the comfortable parlor, but it is clear that escape from the parlor is her final alternative.

A Doll House was a successful—and a scandalous—play throughout Europe in the last decades of the nineteenth century, and it has remained in the repertoire ever since. Nora has always been associated with feminist politics, and several productions in the 1960s and 1970s saw in *A Doll House* an anticipatory allegory of the women's movement. Indeed, whereas Helmer appeared to 1880s audiences as a romantic leading man, the challenge for contemporary productions is to make him appear sympathetic, someone worth Nora's years of sacrifice, and someone she will have to struggle to leave.

A Doll House

Henrik Ibsen

TRANSLATED BY ROLF FJELDE

CHARACTERS

TORVALD HELMER, *a lawyer*
NORA, *his wife*
DR. RANK
MRS. LINDE
NILS KROGSTAD, *a bank clerk*
THE HELMERS' THREE SMALL CHILDREN

ANNE-MARIE, *their nurse*
A MAID, *Helene*
A DELIVERY BOY

The action takes place in Helmer's residence.

ACT ONE

A comfortable room, tastefully but not expensively furnished. A door to the right in the back wall leads to the entryway; another to the left leads to HELMER's *study. Between these doors, a piano. Midway in the left-hand wall a door, and further back a window. Near the window a round table with an armchair and a small sofa. In the right-hand wall, toward the rear, a door, and nearer the foreground a porcelain stove with two armchairs and a rocking chair beside it. Between the stove and the side door, a small table. Engravings on the walls. An etagère with china figures and other small art objects; a small bookcase with richly bound books; the floor carpeted; a fire burning in the stove. It is a winter day.*

A bell rings in the entryway; shortly after we hear the door being unlocked. NORA *comes into the room, humming happily to herself; she is wearing street clothes and carries an armload of packages, which she puts down on the table to the right. She has left the hall door open; and through it a* DELIVERY BOY *is seen, holding a Christmas tree and a basket, which he gives to the* MAID *who let them in.*

NORA: Hide the tree well, Helene. The children mustn't get a glimpse of it till this evening, after it's trimmed. (*To the* DELIVERY BOY, *taking out her purse.*) How much?

DELIVERY BOY: Fifty, ma'am.

5 NORA: There's a crown. No, keep the change. (*The* BOY *thanks her and leaves.* NORA *shuts the door. She laughs softly to herself while taking off her street things. Drawing a bag of macaroons from her pocket, she eats a couple, then steals over and listens at her husband's study door.*) Yes, he's home. (*Hums again as*

10 *she moves to the table right.*)

HELMER: (*From the study.*) Is that my little lark twittering out there?

NORA: (*Busy opening some packages.*) Yes, it is.

HELMER: Is that my squirrel rummaging around?

15 NORA: Yes!

HELMER: When did my squirrel get in?

NORA: Just now. (*Putting the macaroon bag in her pocket and wiping her mouth.*) Do come in, Torvald, and see what I've bought.

20 HELMER: Can't be disturbed. (*After a moment he opens the door and peers in, pen in hand.*) Bought, you say? All that there? Has the little spendthrift been out throwing money around again?

NORA: Oh, but Torvald, this year we really should let ourselves

25 go a bit. It's the first Christmas we haven't had to economize.

HELMER: But you know we can't go squandering.

NORA: Oh yes, Torvald, we can squander a little now. Can't

we? Just a tiny, wee bit. Now that you've got a big salary and are going to make piles and piles of money.

HELMER: Yes—starting New Year's. But then it's a full three 30 months till the raise comes through.

NORA: Pooh! We can borrow that long.

HELMER: Nora! (*Goes over and playfully takes her by the ear.*) Are your scatterbrains off again? What if today I borrowed a thousand crowns, and you squandered them over Christmas 35 week, and then on New Year's Eve a roof tile fell on my head, and I lay there—

NORA: (*Putting her hand on his mouth.*) Oh! Don't say such things!

HELMER: Yes, but what if it happened—then what? 40

NORA: If anything so awful happened, then it just wouldn't matter if I had debts or not.

HELMER: Well, but the people I'd borrowed from?

NORA: Them? Who cares about them! They're strangers.

HELMER: Nora, Nora, how like a woman! No, but seriously, 45 Nora, you know what I think about that. No debts! Never borrow! Something of freedom's lost—and something of beauty, too—from a home that's founded on borrowing and debt. We've made a brave stand up to now, the two of us; and we'll go right on like that the little while we have to. 50

NORA: (*Going toward the stove.*) Yes, whatever you say, Torvald.

HELMER: (*Following her.*) Now, now, the little lark's wings mustn't droop. Come on, don't be a sulky squirrel. (*Taking out his wallet.*) Nora, guess what I have here.

NORA: (*Turning quickly.*) Money! 55

HELMER: There, see. (*Hands her some notes.*) Good grief, I know how costs go up in a house at Christmastime.

NORA: Ten—twenty—thirty—forty. Oh, thank you, Torvald; I can manage no end on this.

HELMER: You really will have to. 60

NORA: Oh yes, I promise I will! But come here so I can show you everything I bought. And so cheap! Look, new clothes for Ivar here—and a sword. Here a horse and a trumpet for Bob. And a doll and a doll's bed here for Emmy; they're nothing much, but she'll tear them to bits in no time any- 65 way. And here I have dress material and handkerchiefs for the maids. Old Anne-Marie really deserves something more.

HELMER: And what's in that package there?

NORA: (*With a cry.*) Torvald, no! You can't see that till tonight!

HELMER: I see. But tell me now, you little prodigal, what have you 70 thought of for yourself?

NORA: For myself? Oh, I don't want anything at all.

HELMER: Of course you do. Tell me just what—within reason— you'd most like to have.

NORA: I honestly don't know. Oh, listen, Torvald— 75

HELMER: Well?

NORA: (*Fumbling at his coat buttons, without looking at him.*) If you want to give me something, then maybe you could—you could—

80 HELMER: Come on, out with it.

NORA: (*Hurriedly.*) You could give me money, Torvald. No more than you think you can spare; then one of these days I'll buy something with it.

HELMER: But Nora—

85 NORA: Oh, please, Torvald darling, do that! I beg you, please. Then I could hang the bills in pretty gilt paper on the Christmas tree. Wouldn't that be fun?

HELMER: What are those little birds called that always fly through their fortunes?

90 NORA: Oh yes, spendthrifts; I know all that. But let's do as I say, Torvald; then I'll have time to decide what I really need most. That's very sensible, isn't it?

HELMER: (*Smiling.*) Yes, very—that is, if you actually hung onto the money I give you, and you actually used it to buy yourself

95 something. But it goes for the house and for all sorts of foolish things, and then I only have to lay out some more.

NORA: Oh, but Torvald—

HELMER: Don't deny it, my dear little Nora. (*Putting his arm around her waist.*) Spendthrifts are sweet, but they use up a

100 frightful amount of money. It's incredible what it costs a man to feed such birds.

NORA: Oh, how can you say that! Really, I save everything I can.

HELMER: (*Laughing.*) Yes, that's the truth. Everything you can.

105 But that's nothing at all.

NORA: (*Humming, with a smile of quiet satisfaction.*) Hm, if you only knew what expenses we larks and squirrels have, Torvald.

HELMER: You're an odd little one. Exactly the way your father

110 was. You're never at a loss for scaring up money; but the moment you have it, it runs right out through your fingers; you never know what you've done with it. Well, one takes you as you are. It's deep in your blood. Yes, these things are hereditary, Nora.

115 NORA: Ah, I could wish I'd inherited many of Papa's qualities.

HELMER: And I couldn't wish you anything but just what you are, my sweet little lark. But wait; it seems to me you have a very—what should I call it?—a very suspicious look today—

120 NORA: I do?

HELMER: You certainly do. Look me straight in the eye.

NORA: (*Looking at him.*) Well?

HELMER: (*Shaking an admonitory finger.*) Surely my sweet tooth hasn't been running riot in town today, has she?

125 NORA: No. Why do you imagine that?

HELMER: My sweet tooth really didn't make a little detour through the confectioner's?

NORA: No, I assure you, Torvald—

HELMER: Hasn't nibbled some pastry?

130 NORA: No, not at all.

HELMER: Not even munched a macaroon or two?

NORA: No, Torvald, I assure you, really—

HELMER: There, there now. Of course I'm only joking.

NORA: (*Going to the table, right.*) You know I could never think of

135 going against you.

HELMER: No, I understand that; and you *have* given me your word. (*Going over to her.*) Well, you keep your little Christmas

secrets to yourself, Nora darling. I expect they'll come to light this evening, when the tree is lit.

140 NORA: Did you remember to ask Dr. Rank?

HELMER: No. But there's no need for that; it's assumed he'll be dining with us. All the same, I'll ask him when he stops by here this morning. I've ordered some fine wine. Nora, you can't imagine how I'm looking forward to this evening.

145 NORA: So am I. And what fun for the children, Torvald!

HELMER: Ah, it's so gratifying to know that one's gotten a safe, secure job, and with a comfortable salary. It's a great satisfaction, isn't it?

NORA: Oh, it's wonderful!

150 HELMER: Remember last Christmas? Three whole weeks before, you shut yourself in every evening till long after mid-night, making flowers for the Christmas tree, and all the other decorations to surprise us. Ugh, that was the dullest time I've ever lived through.

155 NORA: It wasn't at all dull for me.

HELMER: (*Smiling.*) But the outcome *was* pretty sorry, Nora.

NORA: Oh, don't tease me with that again. How could I help it that the cat came in and tore everything to shreds.

HELMER: No, poor thing, you certainly couldn't. You wanted so

160 much to please us all, and that's what counts. But it's just as well that the hard times are past.

NORA: Yes, it's really wonderful.

HELMER: Now I don't have to sit here alone, boring myself, and you don't have to tire your precious eyes and your fair little

165 delicate hands—

NORA: (*Clapping her hands.*) No, is it really true, Torvald, I don't have to? Oh, how wonderfully lovely to hear! (*Taking his arm.*) Now I'll tell you just how I've thought we should plan things. Right after Christmas—(*The doorbell rings.*)

170 Oh, the bell. (*Straightening the room up a bit.*) Somebody would have to come. What a bore!

HELMER: I'm not at home to visitors, don't forget.

MAID: (*From the hall doorway.*) Ma'am, a lady to see you—

NORA: All right, let her come in.

175 MAID: (*To* HELMER.) And the doctor's just come too.

HELMER: Did he go right to my study?

MAID: Yes, he did.

(HELMER *goes into his room. The* MAID *shows in* MRS. LINDE, *dressed in traveling clothes, and shuts the door after her.*)

MRS. LINDE: (*In a dispirited and somewhat hesitant voice.*) Hello, Nora.

180 NORA: (*Uncertain.*) Hello—

MRS. LINDE: You don't recognize me.

NORA: No, I don't know—but wait, I think—(*Exclaiming.*) What! Kristine! Is it really you?

MRS. LINDE: Yes, it's me.

185 NORA: Kristine! To think I didn't recognize you. But then, how could I? (*More quietly.*) How you've changed, Kristine!

MRS. LINDE: Yes, no doubt I have. In nine—ten long years.

NORA: Is it so long since we met! Yes, it's all of that. Oh, these last eight years have been a happy time, believe me. And so now

190 you've come in to town, too. Made the long trip in the winter. That took courage.

MRS. LINDE: I just got here by ship this morning.

NORA: To enjoy yourself over Christmas, of course. Oh, how lovely! Yes, enjoy ourselves, we'll do that. But take your coat

195 off. You're not still cold? (*Helping her.*) There now, let's get

cozy here by the stove. No, the easy chair there! I'll take the rocker here. (*Seizing her hands.*) Yes, now you have your old look again; it was only in that first moment. You're a bit more pale, Kristine—and maybe a bit thinner.

200 MRS. LINDE: And much, much older, Nora.

NORA: Yes, perhaps a bit older; a tiny, tiny bit; not much at all. (*Stopping short; suddenly serious.*) Oh, but thoughtless me, to sit here, chattering away. Sweet, good Kristine, can you forgive me?

205 MRS. LINDE: What do you mean, Nora?

NORA: (*Softly.*) Poor Kristine, you've become a widow.

MRS. LINDE: Yes, three years ago.

NORA: Oh, I knew it, of course; I read it in the papers. Oh, Kristine, you must believe me; I often thought of writing

210 you then, but I kept postponing it, and something always interfered.

MRS. LINDE: Nora dear, I understand completely.

NORA: No, it was awful of me, Kristine. You poor thing, how much you must have gone through. And he left you

215 nothing?

MRS. LINDE: No.

NORA: And no children?

MRS. LINDE: No.

NORA: Nothing at all, then?

220 MRS. LINDE: Not even a sense of loss to feed on.

NORA: (*Looking incredulously at her.*) But Kristine, how could that be?

MRS. LINDE: (*Smiling wearily and smoothing her hair.*) Oh, sometimes it happens, Nora.

225 NORA: So completely alone. How terribly hard that must be for you. I have three lovely children. You can't see them now; they're out with the maid. But now you must tell me everything—

MRS. LINDE: No, no, no, tell me about yourself.

230 NORA: No, you begin. Today I don't want to be selfish. I want to think only of you today. But there *is* something I must tell you. Did you hear of the wonderful luck we had recently?

MRS. LINDE: No, what's that?

235 NORA: My husband's been made manager in the bank, just think!

MRS. LINDE: Your husband? How marvelous!

NORA: Isn't it? Being a lawyer is such an uncertain living, you know, especially if one won't touch any cases that aren't

240 clean and decent. And of course Torvald would never do that, and I'm with him completely there. Oh, we're simply delighted, believe me! He'll join the bank right after New Year's and start getting a huge salary and lots of commissions. From now on we can live quite differently—just

245 as we want. Oh, Kristine, I feel so light and happy! Won't it be lovely to have stacks of money and not a care in the world?

MRS. LINDE: Well, anyway, it would be lovely to have enough for necessities.

250 NORA: No, not just for necessities, but stacks and stacks of money!

MRS. LINDE: (*Smiling.*) Nora, Nora, aren't you sensible yet? Back in school you were such a free spender.

NORA: (*With a quiet laugh.*) Yes, that's what Torvald still says.

255 (*Shaking her finger.*) But "Nora, Nora" isn't as silly as you all think. Really, we've been in no position for me to go squandering. We've had to work, both of us.

MRS. LINDE: You too?

NORA: Yes, at odd jobs—needlework, crocheting, embroidery, and such—(*Casually.*) and other things too. You remember 260 that Torvald left the department when we were married? There was no chance of promotion in his office, and of course he needed to earn more money. But that first year he drove himself terribly. He took on all kinds of extra work that kept him going morning and night. It wore him down, and then 265 he fell deathly ill. The doctors said it was essential for him to travel south.

MRS. LINDE: Yes, didn't you spend a whole year in Italy?

NORA: That's right. It wasn't easy to get away, you know. Ivar had just been born. But of course we had to go. Oh, that was a 270 beautiful trip, and it saved Torvald's life. But it cost a frightful sum, Kristine.

MRS. LINDE: I can well imagine.

NORA: Four thousand, eight hundred crowns it cost. That's really a lot of money. 275

MRS. LINDE: But it's lucky you had it when you needed it.

NORA: Well, as it was, we got it from Papa.

MRS. LINDE: I see. It was just about the time your father died.

NORA: Yes, just about then. And, you know, I couldn't make that trip out to nurse him. I had to stay here, expecting Ivar any 280 moment, and with my poor sick Torvald to care for. Dearest Papa, I never saw him again, Kristine. Oh, that was the worst time I've known in all my marriage.

MRS. LINDE: I know how you loved him. And then you went off to Italy? 285

NORA: Yes. We had the means now, and the doctors urged us. So we left a month after.

MRS. LINDE: And your husband came back completely cured?

NORA: Sound as a drum!

MRS. LINDE: But—the doctor? 290

NORA: Who?

MRS. LINDE: I thought the maid said he was a doctor, the man who came in with me.

NORA: Yes, that was Dr. Rank—but he's not making a sick call. He's our closest friend, and he stops by at least once a day. 295 No, Torvald hasn't had a sick moment since, and the children are fit and strong, and I am, too. (*Jumping up and clapping her hands.*) Oh, dear God, Kristine, what a lovely thing to live and be happy! But how disgusting of me—I'm talking of nothing but my own affairs. (*Sits on a stool close by* 300 KRISTINE, *arms resting across her knees.*) Oh, don't be angry with me! Tell me, is it really true that you weren't in love with your husband? Why did you marry him, then?

MRS. LINDE: My mother was still alive, but bedridden and helpless—and I had my two younger brothers to look after. 305 In all conscience, I didn't think I could turn him down.

NORA: No, you were right there. But was he rich at the time?

MRS. LINDE: He was very well off, I'd say. But the business was shaky, Nora. When he died, it all fell apart, and nothing was left. 310

NORA: And then—?

MRS. LINDE: Yes, so I had to scrape up a living with a little shop and a little teaching and whatever else I could find. The last three years have been like one endless workday without a rest for me. Now it's over, Nora. My poor mother doesn't 315 need me, for she's passed on. Nor the boys, either; they're working now and can take care of themselves.

NORA: How free you must feel—

320 MRS. LINDE: No—only unspeakably empty. Nothing to live for now. (*Standing up anxiously.*) That's why I couldn't take it any longer out in that desolate hole. Maybe here it'll be easier to find something to do and keep my mind occupied. If I could only be lucky enough to get a steady job, some office work—

325 NORA: Oh, but Kristine, that's so dreadfully tiring, and you already look so tired. It would be much better for you if you could go off to a bathing resort.

MRS. LINDE: (*Going toward the window.*) I have no father to give me travel money, Nora.

330 NORA: (*Rising.*) Oh, don't be angry with me.

MRS. LINDE: (*Going to her.*) Nora dear, don't you be angry with me. The worst of my kind of situation is all the bitterness that's stored away. No one to work for, and yet you're always having to snap up your opportunities. You have to live; and

335 so you grow selfish. When you told me the happy change in your lot, do you know I was delighted less for your sakes than for mine?

NORA: How so? Oh, I see. You think maybe Torvald could do something for you.

340 MRS. LINDE: Yes, that's what I thought.

NORA: And he will, Kristine! Just leave it to me; I'll bring it up so delicately—find something attractive to humor him with. Oh, I'm so eager to help you.

MRS. LINDE: How very kind of you, Nora, to be so concerned over

345 me—doubly kind, considering you really know so little of life's burdens yourself.

NORA: I—? I know so little—?

MRS. LINDE: (*Smiling.*) Well, my heavens—a little needlework and such—Nora, you're just a child.

350 NORA: (*Tossing her head and pacing the floor.*) You don't have to act so superior.

MRS. LINDE: Oh?

NORA: You're just like the others. You all think I'm incapable of anything serious—

355 MRS. LINDE: Come now—

NORA: That I've never had to face the raw world.

MRS. LINDE: Nora dear, you've just been telling me all your troubles.

NORA: Hm! Trivia! (*Quietly.*) I haven't told you the big thing.

360 MRS. LINDE: Big thing? What do you mean?

NORA: You look down on me so, Kristine, but you shouldn't. You're proud that you worked so long and hard for your mother.

MRS. LINDE: I don't look down on a soul. But it is true: I'm

365 proud—and happy, too—to think it was given to me to make my mother's last days almost free of care.

NORA: And you're also proud thinking of what you've done for your brothers.

MRS. LINDE: I feel I've a right to be.

370 NORA: I agree. But listen to this, Kristine—I've also got something to be proud and happy for.

MRS. LINDE: I don't doubt it. But whatever do you mean?

NORA: Not so loud. What if Torvald heard! He mustn't, not for anything in the world. Nobody must know, Kristine. No one

375 but you.

MRS. LINDE: But what is it, then?

NORA: Come here. (*Drawing her down beside her on the sofa.*) It's true—I've also got something to be proud and happy for. I'm the one who saved Torvald's life.

380 MRS. LINDE: Saved—? Saved how?

NORA: I told you about the trip to Italy. Torvald never would have lived if he hadn't gone south—

MRS. LINDE: Of course; your father gave you the means—

NORA: (*Smiling.*) That's what Torvald and all the rest think,

385 but—

MRS. LINDE: But—?

NORA: Papa didn't give us a pin. I was the one who raised the money.

MRS. LINDE: You? That whole amount?

390 NORA: Four thousand, eight hundred crowns. What do you say to that?

MRS. LINDE: But Nora, how was it possible? Did you win the lottery?

NORA: (*Disdainfully.*) The lottery? Pooh! No art to that.

395 MRS. LINDE: But where did you get it from then?

NORA: (*Humming, with a mysterious smile.*) Hmm, tra-la-la-la.

MRS. LINDE: Because you couldn't have borrowed it.

NORA: No? Why not?

MRS. LINDE: A wife can't borrow without her husband's consent.

400 NORA: (*Tossing her head.*) Oh, but a wife with a little business sense, a wife who knows how to manage—

MRS. LINDE: Nora, I simply don't understand—

NORA: You don't have to. Whoever said I borrowed the money? I could have gotten it other ways. (*Throwing herself

405 back on the sofa.*) I could have gotten it from some admirer or other. After all, a girl with my ravishing appeal—

MRS. LINDE: You lunatic.

NORA: I'll bet you're eaten up with curiosity, Kristine.

MRS. LINDE: Now listen here, Nora—you haven't done something

410 indiscreet?

NORA: (*Sitting up again.*) Is it indiscreet to save your husband's life?

MRS. LINDE: I think it's indiscreet that without his knowledge you—

415 NORA: But that's the point: he mustn't know! My Lord, can't you understand? He mustn't ever know the close call he had. It was to *me* the doctors came to say his life was in danger—that nothing could save him but a stay in the south. Didn't I try strategy then! I began talking about

420 how lovely it would be for me to travel abroad like other young wives; I begged and I cried; I told him please to remember my condition, to be kind and indulge me; and then I dropped a hint that he could easily take out a loan. But at that, Kristine, he nearly exploded. He said I was

425 frivolous, and it was his duty as man of the house not to indulge me in whims and fancies—as I think he called them. Aha, I thought, now you'll just have to be saved—and that's when I saw my chance.

MRS. LINDE: And your father never told Torvald the money

430 wasn't from him?

NORA: No, never. Papa died right about then. I'd considered bringing him into my secret and begging him never to tell. But he was too sick at the time—and then, sadly, it didn't matter.

435 MRS. LINDE: And you've never confided in your husband since?

NORA: For heaven's sake, no! Are you serious? He's so strict on that subject. Besides—Torvald, with all his masculine pride—how painfully humiliating for him if he ever found out he was in debt to me. That would just ruin our relationship. Our beautiful, happy home would never be the same.

440 MRS. LINDE: Won't you ever tell him?

NORA: (*Thoughtfully, half smiling.*) Yes—maybe sometime,

years from now, when I'm no longer so attractive. Don't laugh! I only mean when Torvald loves me less than now, when he stops enjoying my dancing and dressing up and reciting for him. Then it might be wise to have something in reserve—(*Breaking off.*) How ridiculous! That'll never happen—Well, Kristine, what do you think of my big secret? I'm capable of something too, hm? You can imagine, of course, how this thing hangs over me. It really hasn't been easy meeting the payments on time. In the business world there's what they call quarterly interest and what they call amortization, and these are always so terribly hard to manage. I've had to skimp a little here and there, wherever I could, you know. I could hardly spare anything from my house allowance, because Torvald has to live well. I couldn't let the children go poorly dressed; whatever I got for them, I felt I had to use up completely—the darlings!

MRS. LINDE: Poor Nora, so it had to come out of your own budget, then?

NORA: Yes, of course. But I was the one most responsible, too. Every time Torvald gave me money for new clothes and such, I never used more than half; always bought the simplest, cheapest outfits. It was a godsend that everything looks so well on me that Torvald never noticed. But it did weigh me down at times, Kristine. It *is* such a joy to wear fine things. You understand.

MRS. LINDE: Oh, of course.

NORA: And then I found other ways of making money. Last winter I was lucky enough to get a lot of copying to do. I locked myself in and sat writing every evening till late in the night. Ah, I was tired so often, dead tired. But still it was wonderful fun, sitting and working like that, earning money. It was almost like being a man.

MRS. LINDE: But how much have you paid off this way so far?

NORA: That's hard to say, exactly. These accounts, you know, aren't easy to figure. I only know that I've paid out all I could scrape together. Time and again I haven't known where to turn. (*Smiling.*) Then I'd sit here dreaming of a rich old gentleman who had fallen in love with me—

MRS. LINDE: What! Who is he?

NORA: Oh, really! And that he'd died, and when his will was opened, there in big letters it said, "All my fortune shall be paid over in cash, immediately, to that enchanting Mrs. Nora Helmer."

MRS. LINDE: But Nora dear—who was this gentleman?

NORA: Good grief, can't you understand? The old man never existed; that was only something I'd dream up time and again whenever I was at my wits' end for money. But it makes no difference now; the old fossil can go where he pleases for all I care; I don't need him or his will—because now I'm free. (*Jumping up.*) Oh, how lovely to think of that, Kristine! To know you're carefree, utterly carefree; to be able to romp and play with the children, and to keep up a beautiful, charming home—everything just the way Torvald likes it! And think, spring is coming, with big blue skies. Maybe we can travel a little then. Maybe I'll see the ocean again. Oh yes, it is so marvelous to live and be happy!

(*The front doorbell rings.*)

MRS. LINDE: (*Rising.*) There's the bell. It's probably best that I go.

NORA: No, stay. No one's expected. It must be for Torvald.

MAID: (*From the hall doorway.*) Excuse me, ma'am—there's a gentleman here to see Mr. Helmer, but I didn't know—since the doctor's with him—

NORA: Who is the gentleman?

KROGSTAD: (*From the doorway.*) It's me, Mrs. Helmer.

(MRS. LINDE *starts and turns away toward the window.*)

NORA: (*Stepping toward him, tense, her voice a whisper.*) You? What is it? Why do you want to speak to my husband?

KROGSTAD: Bank business—after a fashion. I have a small job in the investment bank, and I hear now your husband is going to be our chief—

NORA: In other words, it's—

KROGSTAD: Just dry business, Mrs. Helmer. Nothing but that.

NORA: Yes, then please be good enough to step into the study. (*She nods indifferently as she sees him out by the hall door, then returns and begins stirring up the stove.*)

MRS. LINDE: Nora—who was that man?

NORA: That was a Mr. Krogstad—a lawyer.

MRS. LINDE: Then it really was him.

NORA: Do you know that person?

MRS. LINDE: I did once—many years ago. For a time he was a law clerk in our town.

NORA: Yes, he's been that.

MRS. LINDE: How he's changed.

NORA: I understand he had a very unhappy marriage.

MRS. LINDE: He's a widower now.

NORA: With a number of children. There now, it's burning. (*She closes the stove door and moves the rocker a bit to one side.*)

MRS. LINDE: They say he has a hand in all kinds of business.

NORA: Oh? That may be true; I wouldn't know. But let's not think about business. It's so dull.

(DR. RANK *enters from* HELMER'S *study.*)

RANK: (*Still in the doorway.*) No, no, really—I don't want to intrude, I'd just as soon talk a little while with your wife. (*Shuts the door, then notices* MRS. LINDE.) Oh, beg pardon. I'm intruding here too.

NORA: No, not at all. (*Introducing him.*) Dr. Rank, Mrs. Linde.

RANK: Well now, that's a name much heard in this house. I believe I passed the lady on the stairs as I came.

MRS. LINDE: Yes, I take the stairs very slowly. They're rather hard on me.

RANK: Uh-hm, some touch of internal weakness?

MRS. LINDE: More overexertion, I'd say.

RANK: Nothing else? Then you're probably here in town to rest up in a round of parties?

MRS. LINDE: I'm here to look for work.

RANK: Is that the best cure for overexertion?

MRS. LINDE: One has to live, Doctor.

RANK: Yes, there's a common prejudice to that effect.

NORA: Oh, come on, Dr. Rank—you really do want to live yourself.

RANK: Yes, I really do. Wretched as I am, I'll gladly prolong my torment indefinitely. All my patients feel like that. And it's quite the same, too, with the morally sick. Right at this moment there's one of those moral invalids in there with Helmer—

MRS. LINDE: (*Softly.*) Ah!

NORA: Who do you mean?

560 RANK: Oh, it's a lawyer, Krogstad, a type you wouldn't know. His character is rotten to the root—but even he began chattering all-importantly about how he had to *live*.

NORA: Oh? What did he want to talk to Torvald about?

RANK: I really don't know. I only heard something about the 565 bank.

NORA: I didn't know that Krog—that this man Krogstad had anything to do with the bank.

RANK: Yes, he's gotten some kind of berth down there. (*To* 570 MRS. LINDE.) I don't know if you also have, in your neck of the woods, a type of person who scuttles about breathlessly, sniffing out hints of moral corruption, and then maneuvers his victim into some sort of key position where he can keep an eye on him. It's the healthy these days that are out in the cold.

575 MRS. LINDE: All the same, it's the sick who most need to be taken in.

RANK: (*With a shrug.*) Yes, there we have it. That's the concept that's turning society into a sanatorium.

(NORA, *lost in her thoughts, breaks out into quiet laughter and claps her hands.*)

RANK: Why do you laugh at that? Do you have any real idea of 580 what society is?

NORA: What do I care about dreary old society? I was laughing at something quite different—something terribly funny. Tell me, Doctor—is everyone who works in the bank dependent now on Torvald?

585 RANK: Is that what you find so terribly funny?

NORA: (*Smiling and humming.*) Never mind, never mind! (*Pacing the floor.*) Yes, that's really immensely amusing: that we—that Torvald has so much power now over all those people. (*Taking the bag out of her pocket.*) Dr. Rank, a little 590 macaroon on that?

RANK: See here, macaroons! I thought they were contraband here.

NORA: Yes, but these are some that Kristine gave me.

MRS. LINDE: What? I—?

595 NORA: Now, now, don't be afraid. You couldn't possibly know that Torvald had forbidden them. You see, he's worried they'll ruin my teeth. But hmp! Just this once! Isn't that so, Dr. Rank? Help yourself! (*Puts a macaroon in his mouth.*) And you too, Kristine. And I'll also have one, only a little 600 one—or two, at the most. (*Walking about again.*) Now I'm really tremendously happy. Now there's just one last thing in the world that I have an enormous desire to do.

RANK: Well! And what's that?

NORA: It's something I have such a consuming desire to say so 605 Torvald could hear.

RANK: And why can't you say it?

NORA: I don't dare. It's quite shocking.

MRS. LINDE: Shocking?

RANK: Well, then it isn't advisable. But in front of us you certainly 610 can. What do you have such a desire to say so Torvald could hear?

NORA: I have such a huge desire to say—to hell and be damned!

RANK: Are you crazy?

MRS. LINDE: My goodness, Nora!

615 RANK: Go on, say it. Here he is.

NORA: (*Hiding the macaroon bag.*) Shh, shh, shh!

(HELMER *comes in from his study, hat in hand, overcoat over his arm.*)

NORA: (*Going toward him.*) Well, Torvald dear, are you through with him?

HELMER: Yes, he just left.

NORA: Let me introduce you—this is Kristine, who's arrived here 620 in town.

HELMER: Kristine—? I'm sorry, but I don't know—

NORA: Mrs. Linde, Torvald dear. Mrs. Kristine Linde.

HELMER: Of course. A childhood friend of my wife's, no doubt?

MRS. LINDE: Yes, we knew each other in those days. 625

NORA: And just think, she made the long trip down here in order to talk with you.

HELMER: What's this?

MRS. LINDE: Well, not exactly—

NORA: You see, Kristine is remarkably clever in office work, 630 and so she's terribly eager to come under a capable man's supervision and add more to what she already knows—

HELMER: Very wise, Mrs. Linde.

NORA: And then when she heard that you'd become a bank manager—the story was wired out to the papers—then she 635 came in as fast as she could and—Really, Torvald, for my sake you can do a little something for Kristine, can't you?

HELMER: Yes, it's not at all impossible. Mrs. Linde, I suppose you're a widow?

MRS. LINDE: Yes. 640

HELMER: Any experience in office work?

MRS. LINDE: Yes, a good deal.

HELMER: Well, it's quite likely that I can make an opening for you—

NORA: (*Clapping her hands.*) You see, you see! 645

HELMER: You've come at a lucky moment, Mrs. Linde.

MRS. LINDE: Oh, how can I thank you?

HELMER: Not necessary. (*Putting his overcoat on.*) But today you'll have to excuse me—

RANK: Wait, I'll go with you. (*He fetches his coat from the hall and* 650 *warms it at the stove.*)

NORA: Don't stay out long, dear.

HELMER: An hour; no more.

NORA: Are you going too, Kristine?

MRS. LINDE: (*Putting on her winter garments.*) Yes, I have to see 655 about a room now.

HELMER: Then perhaps we can all walk together.

NORA: (*Helping her.*) What a shame we're so cramped here, but it's quite impossible for us to—

MRS. LINDE: Oh, don't even think of it! Good-bye, Nora dear, and 660 thanks for everything.

NORA: Good-bye for now. Of course you'll be back this evening. And you too, Dr. Rank. What? If you're well enough? Oh, you've got to be! Wrap up tight now.

(*In a ripple of small talk the company moves out into the hall; children's voices are heard outside on the steps.*)

NORA: There they are! There they are! (*She runs to open the* 665 *door. The* CHILDREN *come in with their nurse,* ANNE-MARIE.) Come in, come in! (*Bends down and kisses them.*) Oh, you darlings—! Look at them, Kristine. Aren't they lovely!

RANK: No loitering in the draft here.

670 HELMER: Come, Mrs. Linde—this place is unbearable now for anyone but mothers.

(DR. RANK, HELMER, *and* MRS. LINDE *go down the stairs.* ANNE-MARIE *goes into the living room with the* CHILDREN. NORA *follows, after closing the hall door.*)

NORA: How fresh and strong you look. Oh, such red cheeks you have! Like apples and roses. (*The* CHILDREN *interrupt her throughout the following.*) And it was so much fun? That's
675 wonderful. Really? You pulled both Emmy and Bob on the sled? Imagine, all together! Yes, you're a clever boy, Ivar. Oh, let me hold her a bit, Anne-Marie. My sweet little doll baby! (*Takes the smallest from* ANNE-MARIE *and dances with her.*) Yes, yes, Mama will dance with Bob as well. What? Did you
680 throw snowballs? Oh, if I'd only been there! No, don't bother, Anne-Marie—I'll undress them myself. Oh yes, let me. It's such fun. Go in and rest; you look half frozen. There's hot coffee waiting for you on the stove. (ANNE-MARIE *goes into the room to the left.* NORA *takes the* CHILDREN'S *winter things off,*
685 *throwing them about, while the children talk to her all at once.*) Is that so? A big dog chased you? But it didn't bite? No, dogs never bite little, lovely doll babies. Don't peek in the packages, Ivar! What is it? Yes, wouldn't you like to know. No, no, it's an ugly something. Well? Shall we play? What shall we play?
690 Hide-and-seek? Yes, let's play hide-and-seek. Bob must hide first. I must? Yes, let me hide first. (*Laughing and shouting, she and the* CHILDREN *play in and out of the living room and the adjoining room to the right. At last* NORA *hides under the table. The* CHILDREN *come storming in, search, but cannot find her,*
695 *then hear her muffled laughter, dash over to the table, lift the cloth up and find her. Wild shouting. She creeps forward as if to scare them. More shouts. Meanwhile, a knock at the hall door; no one has noticed it. Now the door half opens, and* KROGSTAD *appears. He waits a moment; the game goes on.*)
700 KROGSTAD: Beg pardon, Mrs. Helmer—
NORA: (*With a strangled cry, turning and scrambling to her knees.*) Oh! What do you want?
KROGSTAD: Excuse me. The outer door was ajar; it must be someone forgot to shut it—
705 NORA: (*Rising.*) My husband isn't home, Mr. Krogstad.
KROGSTAD: I know that.
NORA: Yes—then what do you want here?
KROGSTAD: A word with you.
NORA: With—? (*To the* CHILDREN, *quietly.*) Go in to Anne-Marie.
710 What? No, the strange man won't hurt Mama. When he's gone, we'll play some more. (*She leads the* CHILDREN *into the room to the left and shuts the door after them. Then, tense and nervous:*) You want to speak to me?
KROGSTAD: Yes, I want to.
715 NORA: Today? But it's not yet the first of the month—
KROGSTAD: No, it's Christmas Eve. It's going to be up to you how merry a Christmas you have.
NORA: What is it you want? Today I absolutely can't—
KROGSTAD: We won't talk about that till later. This is something
720 else. You do have a moment to spare, I suppose?
NORA: Oh yes, of course—I do, except—
KROGSTAD: Good. I was sitting over at Olsen's Restaurant when I saw your husband go down the street—
NORA: Yes?
725 KROGSTAD: With a lady.

NORA: Yes. So?
KROGSTAD: If you'll pardon my asking: wasn't that lady a Mrs. Linde?
NORA: Yes.
KROGSTAD: Just now come into town? 730
NORA: Yes, today.
KROGSTAD: She's a good friend of yours?
NORA: Yes, she is. But I don't see—
KROGSTAD: I also knew her once.
NORA: I'm aware of that. 735
KROGSTAD: Oh? You know all about it. I thought so. Well, then let me ask you short and sweet: is Mrs. Linde getting a job in the bank?
NORA: What makes you think you can cross-examine me, Mr. Krogstad—you, one of my husband's employees? But 740 since you ask, you might as well know—yes, Mrs. Linde's going to be taken on at the bank. And I'm the one who spoke for her, Mr. Krogstad. Now you know.
KROGSTAD: So I guessed right.
NORA: (*Pacing up and down.*) Oh, one does have a tiny bit of 745 influence, I should hope. Just because I am a woman, don't think it means that—When one has a subordinate position, Mr. Krogstad, one really ought to be careful about pushing somebody who—hm—
KROGSTAD: Who has influence? 750
NORA: That's right.
KROGSTAD: (*In a different tone.*) Mrs. Helmer, would you be good enough to use your influence on my behalf?
NORA: What? What do you mean?
KROGSTAD: Would you please make sure that I keep my sub- 755 ordinate position in the bank?
NORA: What does that mean? Who's thinking of taking away your position?
KROGSTAD: Oh, don't play the innocent with me. I'm quite aware that your friend would hardly relish the chance of running 760 into me again; and I'm also aware now whom I can thank for being turned out.
NORA: But I promise you—
KROGSTAD: Yes, yes, yes, to the point: there's still time, and I'm advising you to use your influence to prevent it. 765
NORA: But Mr. Krogstad, I have absolutely no influence.
KROGSTAD: You haven't? I thought you were just saying—
NORA: You shouldn't take me so literally. I! How can you believe that I have any such influence over my husband?
KROGSTAD: Oh, I've known your husband from our student days. 770 I don't think the great bank manager's more steadfast than any other married man.
NORA: You speak insolently about my husband, and I'll show you the door.
KROGSTAD: The lady has spirit. 775
NORA: I'm not afraid of you any longer. After New Year's, I'll soon be done with the whole business.
KROGSTAD: (*Restraining himself.*) Now listen to me, Mrs. Helmer. If necessary, I'll fight for my little job in the bank as if it were life itself. 780
NORA: Yes, so it seems.
KROGSTAD: It's not just a matter of income; that's the least of it. It's something else—All right, out with it! Look, this is the thing. You know, just like all the others, of course, that once, a good many years ago, I did something rather rash. 785
NORA: I've heard rumors to that effect.

KROGSTAD: The case never got into court; but all the same, every door was closed in my face from then on. So I took up those various activities you know about. I had to grab
790 hold somewhere; and I dare say I haven't been among the worst. But now I want to drop all that. My boys are growing up. For their sakes, I'll have to win back as much respect as possible here in town. That job in the bank was like the first
795 rung in my ladder. And now your husband wants to kick me right back down in the mud again.

NORA: But for heaven's sake, Mr. Krogstad, it's simply not in my power to help you.

KROGSTAD: That's because you haven't the will to—but I have the means to make you.

800 NORA: You certainly won't tell my husband that I owe you money?

KROGSTAD: Hm—what if I told him that?

NORA: That would be shameful of you. (*Nearly in tears.*) This secret—my joy and my pride—that he should learn it in
805 such a crude and disgusting way—learn it from you. You'd expose me to the most horrible unpleasantness—

KROGSTAD: Only unpleasantness?

NORA: (*Vehemently.*) But go on and try. It'll turn out the worse for you, because then my husband will really see what a
810 crook you are, and then you'll *never* be able to hold your job.

KROGSTAD: I asked if it was just domestic unpleasantness you were afraid of?

NORA: If my husband finds out, then of course he'll pay what I owe at once, and then we'd be through with you for good.

815 KROGSTAD: (*A step closer.*) Listen, Mrs. Helmer—you've either got a very bad memory, or else no head at all for business. I'd better put you a little more in touch with the facts.

NORA: What do you mean?

KROGSTAD: When your husband was sick, you came to me for a
820 loan of four thousand, eight hundred crowns.

NORA: Where else could I go?

KROGSTAD: I promised to get you that sum—

NORA: And you got it.

KROGSTAD: I promised to get you that sum, on certain conditions.
825 You were so involved in your husband's illness, and so eager to finance your trip, that I guess you didn't think out all the details. It might just be a good idea to remind you. I promised you the money on the strength of a note I drew up.

NORA: Yes, and that I signed.

830 KROGSTAD: Right. But at the bottom I added some lines for your father to guarantee the loan. He was supposed to sign down there.

NORA: Supposed to? He did sign.

KROGSTAD: I left the date blank. In other words, your father
835 would have dated his signature himself. Do you remember that?

NORA: Yes, I think—

KROGSTAD: Then I gave you the note for you to mail to your father. Isn't that so?

840 NORA: Yes.

KROGSTAD: And naturally you sent it at once—because only some five, six days later you brought me the note, properly signed. And with that, the money was yours.

NORA: Well, then; I've made my payments regularly, haven't I?

845 KROGSTAD: More or less. But—getting back to the point—those were hard times for you then, Mrs. Helmer.

NORA: Yes, they were.

KROGSTAD: Your father was very ill, I believe.

NORA: He was near the end.

KROGSTAD: He died soon after? 850

NORA: Yes.

KROGSTAD: Tell me, Mrs. Helmer, do you happen to recall the date of your father's death? The day of the month, I mean.

NORA: Papa died the twenty-ninth of September.

KROGSTAD: That's quite correct; I've already looked into that. And 855
now we come to a curious thing—(*Taking out a paper.*) which I simply cannot comprehend.

NORA: Curious thing? I don't know—

KROGSTAD: This is the curious thing: that your father co-signed the note for your loan three days after his death. 860

NORA: How—? I don't understand.

KROGSTAD: Your father died the twenty-ninth of September. But look. Here your father dated his signature October second. Isn't that curious, Mrs. Helmer? (NORA *is silent.*) Can you explain it to me? (NORA *remains silent.*) It's also 865
remarkable that the words "October second" and the year aren't written in your father's hand, but rather in one that I think I know. Well, it's easy to understand. Your father forgot perhaps to date his signature, and then someone or other added it, a bit sloppily, before anyone knew of his death. 870
There's nothing wrong in that. It all comes down to the signature. And there's no question about *that,* Mrs. Helmer. It really *was* your father who signed his own name here, wasn't it?

NORA: (*After a short silence, throwing her head back and looking* 875
squarely at him.) No, it wasn't. I signed Papa's name.

KROGSTAD: Wait, now—are you fully aware that this is a dangerous confession?

NORA: Why? You'll soon get your money.

KROGSTAD: Let me ask you a question—why didn't you send the 880
paper to your father?

NORA: That was impossible. Papa was so sick. If I'd asked him for his signature, I also would have had to tell him what the money was for. But I couldn't tell him, sick as he was, that my husband's life was in danger. That was just impossible. 885

KROGSTAD: Then it would have been better if you'd given up the trip abroad.

NORA: I couldn't possibly. The trip was to save my husband's life. I couldn't give that up.

KROGSTAD: But didn't you ever consider that this was a fraud 890
against me?

NORA: I couldn't let myself be bothered by that. You weren't any concern of mine. I couldn't stand you, with all those cold complications you made, even though you knew how badly off my husband was. 895

KROGSTAD: Mrs. Helmer, obviously you haven't the vaguest idea of what you've involved yourself in. But I can tell you this: it was nothing more and nothing worse that I once did—and it wrecked my whole reputation.

NORA: You? Do you expect me to believe that you ever acted 900
bravely to save your wife's life?

KROGSTAD: Laws don't inquire into motives.

NORA: Then they must be very poor laws.

KROGSTAD: Poor or not—if I introduce this paper in court, you'll be judged according to law. 905

NORA: This I refuse to believe. A daughter hasn't a right to protect her dying father from anxiety and care? A wife hasn't a right to save her husband's life? I don't know much about laws, but I'm sure that somewhere in the books these things are allowed. And you don't know 910 anything about it—you who practice the law? You must be an awful lawyer, Mr. Krogstad.

KROGSTAD: Could be. But business—the kind of business we two are mixed up in—don't you think I know about that?

915 All right. Do what you want now. But I'm telling you *this:* if I get shoved down a second time, you're going to keep me company. (*He bows and goes out through the hall.*)

NORA: (*Pensive for a moment, then tossing her head.*) Oh, really! Trying to frighten me! I'm not so silly as all that. (*Begins*

920 *gathering up the* CHILDREN's *clothes, but soon stops.*) But—? No, but that's impossible! I did it out of love.

THE CHILDREN: (*In the doorway, left.*) Mama, that strange man's gone out the door.

NORA: Yes, yes, I know it. But don't tell anyone about the strange

925 man. Do you hear? Not even Papa!

THE CHILDREN: No, Mama. But now will you play again?

NORA: No, not now.

THE CHILDREN: Oh, but Mama, you promised.

NORA: Yes, but I can't now. Go inside; I have too much to do. Go

930 in, go in, my sweet darlings. (*She herds them gently back in the room and shuts the door after them. Settling on the sofa, she takes up a piece of embroidery and makes some stitches, but soon stops abruptly.*) No! (*Throws the work aside, rises, goes to the hall door and calls out.*) Helene! Let me have the tree in

935 here. (*Goes to the table, left, opens the table drawer, and stops again.*) No, but that's utterly impossible!

MAID: (*With the Christmas tree.*) Where should I put it, ma'am?

NORA: There. The middle of the floor.

MAID: Should I bring anything else?

940 NORA: No, thanks. I have what I need.

(*The* MAID, *who has set the tree down, goes out.*)

NORA: (*Absorbed in trimming the tree.*) Candles here—and flowers here. That terrible creature! Talk, talk, talk! There's nothing to it at all. The tree's going to be lovely. I'll do anything to please you, Torvald. I'll sing for you, dance

945 for you—

(HELMER *comes in from the hall, with a sheaf of papers under his arm.*)

NORA: Oh! You're back so soon?

HELMER: Yes. Has anyone been here?

NORA: Here? No.

HELMER: That's odd. I saw Krogstad leaving the front door.

950 NORA: So? Oh yes, that's true. Krogstad was here a moment.

HELMER: Nora, I can see by your face that he's been here, begging you to put in a good word for him.

NORA: Yes.

HELMER: And it was supposed to seem like your own idea? You

955 were to hide it from me that he'd been here. He asked you that, too, didn't he?

NORA: Yes, Torvald, but—

HELMER: Nora, Nora, and you could fall for that? Talk with that sort of person and promise him anything? And then in the

960 bargain, tell me an untruth.

NORA: An untruth—?

HELMER: Didn't you say that no one had been here? (*Wagging his finger.*) My little songbird must never do that again. A songbird needs a clean beak to warble with. No false

965 notes. (*Putting his arm about her waist.*) That's the way it

should be, isn't it? Yes, I'm sure of it. (*Releasing her.*) And so, enough of that. (*Sitting by the stove.*) Ah, how snug and cozy it is here. (*Leafing among his papers.*)

NORA: (*Busy with the tree, after a short pause.*) Torvald!

HELMER: Yes. 970

NORA: I'm so much looking forward to the Stenborgs' costume party, day after tomorrow.

HELMER: And I can't wait to see what you'll surprise me with.

NORA: Oh, that stupid business!

HELMER: What? 975

NORA: I can't find anything that's right. Everything seems so ridiculous, so inane.

HELMER: So my little Nora's come to *that* recognition?

NORA: (*Going behind his chair, her arms resting on its back.*) Are you very busy, Torvald? 980

HELMER: Oh—

NORA: What papers are those?

HELMER: Bank matters.

NORA: Already?

HELMER: I've gotten full authority from the retiring management 985 to make all necessary changes in personnel and procedure. I'll need Christmas week for that. I want to have everything in order by New Year's.

NORA: So that was the reason this poor Krogstad—

HELMER: Hm. 990

NORA: (*Still leaning on the chair and slowly stroking the nape of his neck.*) If you weren't so very busy, I would have asked you an enormous favor, Torvald.

HELMER: Let's hear. What is it?

NORA: You know, there isn't anyone who has your good taste— 995 and I want so much to look well at the costume party. Torvald, couldn't you take over and decide what I should be and plan my costume?

HELMER: Ah, is my stubborn little creature calling for a life-guard? 1000

NORA: Yes, Torvald, I can't get anywhere without your help.

HELMER: All right—I'll think it over. We'll hit on something.

NORA: Oh, how sweet of you. (*Goes to the tree again. Pause.*) Aren't the red flowers pretty—? But tell me, was it really such a crime that this Krogstad committed? 1005

HELMER: Forgery. Do you have any idea what that means?

NORA: Couldn't he have done it out of need?

HELMER: Yes, or thoughtlessness, like so many others. I'm not so heartless that I'd condemn a man categorically for just one mistake. 1010

NORA: No, of course not, Torvald!

HELMER: Plenty of men have redeemed themselves by openly confessing their crimes and taking their punishment.

NORA: Punishment—?

HELMER: But now Krogstad didn't go that way. He got himself 1015 out by sharp practices, and that's the real cause of his moral breakdown.

NORA: Do you really think that would—?

HELMER: Just imagine how a man with that sort of guilt in him has to lie and cheat and deceive on all sides, has to wear a 1020 mask even with the nearest and dearest he has, even with his own wife and children. And with the children, Nora—that's where it's most horrible.

NORA: Why?

HELMER: Because that kind of atmosphere of lies infects the 1025 whole life of a home. Every breath the children take in is filled with the germs of something degenerate.

NORA: (*Coming closer behind him.*) Are you sure of that?

HELMER: Oh, I've seen it often enough as a lawyer. Almost
1030 everyone who goes bad early in life has a mother who's a
chronic liar.

NORA: Why just—the mother?

HELMER: It's usually the mother's influence that's dominant,
but the father's works in the same way, of course. Every
1035 lawyer is quite familiar with it. And still this Krogstad's
been going home year in, year out, poisoning his own children with lies and pretense; that's why I call him morally
lost. (*Reaching his hands out toward her.*) So my sweet little
Nora must promise me never to plead his cause. Your hand
1040 on it. Come, come, what's this? Give me your hand. There,
now. All settled. I can tell you it'd be impossible for me to
work alongside of him. I literally feel physically revolted when
I'm anywhere near such a person.

NORA: (*Withdraws her hand and goes to the other side of the
1045 Christmas tree.*) How hot it is here! And I've got so much to do.

HELMER: (*Getting up and gathering his papers.*) Yes, and I have to
think about getting some of these read through before dinner.
I'll think about your costume, too. And something to hang
on the tree in gilt paper, I may even see about that. (*Putting
1050 his hand on her head.*) Oh you, my darling little songbird. (*He
goes into his study and closes the door after him.*)

NORA: (*Softly, after a silence.*) Oh, really! it isn't so. It's impossible.
It must be impossible.

ANNE-MARIE: (*In the doorway, left.*) The children are begging so
1055 hard to come in to Mama.

NORA: No, no, no, don't let them in to me! You stay with them,
Anne-Marie.

ANNE-MARIE: Of course, ma'am. (*Closes the door.*)

NORA: (*Pale with terror.*) Hurt my children—! Poison my home?
1060 (*A moment's pause; then she tosses her head.*) That's not true.
Never. Never in all the world.

ACT TWO

*Same room. Beside the piano the Christmas tree now stands
stripped of ornament, burned-down candle stubs on its ragged
branches.* NORA's *street clothes lie on the sofa.* NORA, *alone in the
room, moves restlessly about; at last she stops at the sofa and picks
up her coat.*

NORA: (*Dropping the coat again.*) Someone's coming! (*Goes
toward the door, listens.*) No—there's no one. Of course—
nobody's coming today, Christmas Day—or tomorrow, either.
But maybe—(*Opens the door and looks out.*) No, nothing in
5 the mailbox. Quite empty. (*Coming forward.*) What nonsense!
He won't do anything serious. Nothing terrible could happen.
It's impossible. Why, I have three small children.

(ANNE-MARIE, *with a large carton, comes in from the room to the
left.*)

ANNE-MARIE: Well, at last I found the box with the masquerade
clothes.

10 NORA: Thanks. Put it on the table.

ANNE-MARIE: (*Does so.*) But they're all pretty much of a mess.

NORA: Ahh! I'd love to rip them in a million pieces!

ANNE-MARIE: Oh, mercy, they can be fixed right up. Just a little
patience.

NORA: Yes, I'll go get Mrs. Linde to help me.

ANNE-MARIE: Out again now? In this nasty weather? Miss Nora
will catch cold—get sick.

NORA: Oh, worse things could happen—How are the children?

ANNE-MARIE: The poor mites are playing with their Christmas
presents, but—

NORA: Do they ask for me much?

ANNE-MARIE: They're so used to having Mama around, you
know.

NORA: Yes, but Anne-Marie, I *can't* be together with them as
much as I was.

ANNE-MARIE: Well, small children get used to anything.

NORA: You think so? Do you think they'd forget their mother if
she was gone for good?

ANNE-MARIE: Oh, mercy—gone for good!

NORA: Wait, tell me, Anne-Marie—I've wondered so often—
how could you ever have the heart to give your child over to
strangers?

ANNE-MARIE: But I had to, you know, to become little Nora's
nurse.

NORA: Yes, but how could you *do* it?

ANNE-MARIE: When I could get such a good place? A girl who's
poor and who's gotten in trouble is glad enough for that.
Because that slippery fish, he didn't do a thing for me, you
know.

NORA: But your daughter's surely forgotten you.

ANNE-MARIE: Oh, she certainly has not. She's written to me,
both when she was confirmed and when she was married.

NORA: (*Clasping her about the neck.*) You old Anne-Marie, you
were a good mother for me when I was little.

ANNE-MARIE: Poor little Nora, with no other mother but me.

NORA: And if the babies didn't have one, then I know that
you'd—What silly talk! (*Opening the carton.*) Go in to
them. Now I'll have to—Tomorrow you can see how
lovely I'll look.

ANNE-MARIE: Oh, there won't be anyone at the party as lovely as
Miss Nora. (*She goes off into the room, left.*)

NORA: (*Begins unpacking the box, but soon throws it aside.*) Oh,
if I dared to go out. If only nobody would come. If only
nothing would happen here while I'm out. What craziness—
nobody's coming. Just don't think. This muff—needs a
brushing. Beautiful gloves, beautiful gloves. Let it go. Let
it go! One, two, three, four, five, six—(*With a cry.*) Oh,
there they are! (*Poises to move toward the door, but remains
irresolutely standing.* MRS. LINDE *enters from the hall, where
she has removed her street clothes.*)

NORA: Oh, it's you, Kristine. There's no one else out there? How
good that you've come.

MRS. LINDE: I hear you were up asking for me.

NORA: Yes, I just stopped by. There's something you really can
help me with. Let's get settled on the sofa. Look, there's going
to be a costume party tomorrow evening at the Stenborgs'
right above us, and now Torvald wants me to go as a
Neapolitan peasant girl and dance the tarantella that I
learned in Capri.

MRS. LINDE: Really, are you giving a whole performance?

NORA: Torvald says yes, I should. See, here's the dress. Torvald
had it made for me down there; but now it's all so tattered that
I just don't know—

MRS. LINDE: Oh, we'll fix that up in no time. It's nothing more
than the trimmings—they're a bit loose here and there.
Needle and thread? Good, now we have what we need.

(line numbers:) 15, 20, 25, 30, 35, 40, 45, 50, 55, 60, 65, 70, 75

NORA: Oh, how sweet of you!

MRS. LINDE: (*Sewing.*) So you'll be in disguise tomorrow, Nora. You know what? I'll stop by then for a moment and have a look at you all dressed up. But listen, I've absolutely forgotten to thank you for that pleasant evening yesterday.

80

NORA: (*Getting up and walking about.*) I don't think it was as pleasant as usual yesterday. You should have come to town a bit sooner, Kristine—Yes, Torvald really knows how to give a home elegance and charm.

85

MRS. LINDE: And you do, too, if you ask me. You're not your father's daughter for nothing. But tell me, is Dr. Rank always so down in the mouth as yesterday?

NORA: No, that was quite an exception. But he goes around critically ill all the time—tuberculosis of the spine, poor man. You know, his father was a disgusting thing who kept mistresses and so on—and that's why the son's been sickly from birth.

90

MRS. LINDE: (*Lets her sewing fall to her lap.*) But my dearest Nora, how do you know about such things?

95

NORA: (*Walking more jauntily.*) Hmp! When you've had three children, then you've had a few visits from—from women who know something of medicine, and they tell you this and that.

MRS. LINDE: (*Resumes sewing; a short pause.*) Does Dr. Rank come here every day?

100

NORA: Every blessed day. He's Torvald's best friend from childhood, and *my* good friend, too. Dr. Rank almost belongs to this house.

MRS. LINDE: But tell me—is he quite sincere? I mean, doesn't he rather enjoy flattering people?

105

NORA: Just the opposite. Why do you think that?

MRS. LINDE: When you introduced us yesterday, he was proclaiming that he'd often heard my name in this house; but later I noticed that your husband hadn't the slightest idea who I really was. So how could Dr. Rank—?

110

NORA: But it's all true, Kristine. You see, Torvald loves me beyond words, and, as he puts it, he'd like to keep me all to himself. For a long time he'd almost be jealous if I even mentioned any of my old friends back home. So of course I dropped that. But with Dr. Rank I talk a lot about such things, because he likes hearing about them.

115

MRS. LINDE: Now listen, Nora; in many ways you're still like a child. I'm a good deal older than you, with a little more experience. I'll tell you something: you ought to put an end to all this with Dr. Rank.

120

NORA: What should I put an end to?

MRS. LINDE: Both parts of it, I think. Yesterday you said something about a rich admirer who'd provide you with money—

125

NORA: Yes, one who doesn't exist—worse luck. So?

MRS. LINDE: Is Dr. Rank well off?

NORA: Yes, he is.

MRS. LINDE: With no dependents?

130

NORA: No, no one. But—

MRS. LINDE: And he's over here every day?

NORA: Yes, I told you that.

MRS. LINDE: How can a man of such refinement be so grasping?

NORA: I don't follow you at all.

135

MRS. LINDE: Now don't try to hide it, Nora. You think I can't guess who loaned you the forty-eight hundred crowns?

NORA: Are you out of your mind? How could you think such a thing! A friend of ours, who comes here every single

day. What an intolerable situation that would have been!

MRS. LINDE: Then it really wasn't him.   140

NORA: No, absolutely not. It never even crossed my mind for a moment—And he had nothing to lend in those days; his inheritance came later.

MRS. LINDE: Well, I think that was a stroke of luck for you, Nora dear.   145

NORA: No, it never would have occurred to me to ask Dr. Rank—Still, I'm quite sure that if I had asked him—

MRS. LINDE: Which you won't, of course.

NORA: No, of course not. I can't see that I'd ever need to. But I'm quite positive that if I talked to Dr. Rank—   150

MRS. LINDE: Behind your husband's back?

NORA: I've got to clear up this other thing; *that's* also behind his back. I've *got* to clear it all up.

MRS. LINDE: Yes, I was saying that yesterday, but—

NORA: (*Pacing up and down.*) A man handles these problems so much better than a woman.   155

MRS. LINDE: One's husband does, yes.

NORA: Nonsense. (*Stopping.*) When you pay everything you owe, then you get your note back, right?

MRS. LINDE: Yes, naturally.   160

NORA: And can rip it into a million pieces and burn it up—that filthy scrap of paper!

MRS. LINDE: (*Looking hard at her, laying her sewing aside, and rising slowly.*) Nora, you're hiding something from me.

NORA: You can see it in my face?   165

MRS. LINDE: Something's happened to you since yesterday morning. Nora, what is it?

NORA: (*Hurrying toward her.*) Kristine! (*Listening.*) Shh! Torvald's home. Look, go in with the children a while. Torvald can't bear all this snipping and stitching. Let   170
Anne-Marie help you.

MRS. LINDE: (*Gathering up some of the things.*) All right, but I'm not leaving here until we've talked this out. (*She disappears into the room, left, as* TORVALD [HELMER] *enters from the hall.*)

NORA: Oh, how I've been waiting for you, Torvald dear.   175

HELMER: Was that the dressmaker?

NORA: No, that was Kristine. She's helping me fix up my costume. You know, it's going to be quite attractive.

HELMER: Yes, wasn't that a bright idea I had?

NORA: Brilliant! But then wasn't I good as well to give in to you?   180

HELMER: Good—because you give in to your husband's judgment? All right, you little goose, I know you didn't mean it like that. But I won't disturb you. You'll want to have a fitting, I suppose.   185

NORA: And you'll be working?

HELMER: Yes. (*Indicating a bundle of papers.*) See, I've been down to the bank. (*Starts toward his study.*)

NORA: Torvald.

HELMER: (*Stops.*) Yes.   190

NORA: If your little squirrel begged you, with all her heart and soul, for something—?

HELMER: What's that?

NORA: Then would you do it?

HELMER: First, naturally, I'd have to know what it was.   195

NORA: Your squirrel would scamper about and do tricks, if you'd only be sweet and give in.

HELMER: Out with it.

NORA: Your lark would be singing high and low in every room—   200

HELMER: Come on, she does that anyway.

NORA: I'd be a wood nymph and dance for you in the moonlight.

HELMER: Nora—don't tell me it's that same business from this
205 morning?

NORA: (*Coming closer.*) Yes, Torvald, I beg you, please!

HELMER: And you actually have the nerve to drag that up
again?

NORA: Yes, yes, you've got to give in to me; you *have* to let
210 Krogstad keep his job in the bank.

HELMER: My dear Nora, I've slated his job for Mrs. Linde.

NORA: That's awfully kind of you. But you could just fire another
clerk instead of Krogstad.

HELMER: This is the most incredible stubbornness! Because you
215 go and give an impulsive promise to speak up for him, I'm
expected to—

NORA: That's not the reason, Torvald. It's for your own sake. That
man does writing for the worst papers; you said it yourself.
He could do you any amount of harm. I'm scared to death of
220 him—

HELMER: Ah, I understand. It's the old memories haunting you.

NORA: What do you mean by that?

HELMER: Of course, you're thinking about your father.

NORA: Yes, all right. Just remember how those nasty gossips wrote
225 in the papers about Papa and slandered him so cruelly. I think
they'd have had him dismissed if the department hadn't sent
you up to investigate, and if you hadn't been so kind and
open-minded toward him.

HELMER: My dear Nora, there's a notable difference between your
230 father and me. Your father's official career was hardly above
reproach. But mine is; and I hope it'll stay that way as long as I
hold my position.

NORA: Oh, who can ever tell what vicious minds can invent?
We could be so snug and happy now in our quiet, carefree
235 home—you and I and the children, Torvald! That's why I'm
pleading with you so—

HELMER: And just by pleading for him you make it impossible for
me to keep him on. It's already known at the bank that I'm
firing Krogstad. What if it's rumored around now that the
240 new bank manager was vetoed by his wife—

NORA: Yes, what then—?

HELMER: Oh yes—as long as our little bundle of stubbornness
gets her way—! I should go and make myself ridiculous in
front of the whole office—give people the idea I can be swayed
245 by all kinds of outside pressure. Oh, you can bet I'd feel the
effects of that soon enough! Besides—there's something
that rules Krogstad right out at the bank as long as I'm the
manager.

NORA: What's that?

250 HELMER: His moral failings I could maybe overlook if I
had to—

NORA: Yes, Torvald, why not?

HELMER: And I hear he's quite efficient on the job. But he was a
crony of mine back in my teens—one of those rash friend-
255 ships that crop up again and again to embarrass you later
in life. Well, I might as well say it straight out: we're on a
firstname basis. And that tactless fool makes no effort
at all to hide it in front of others. Quite the contrary—he
thinks that entitles him to take a familiar air around me, and
260 so every other second he comes booming out with
his "Yes, Torvald!" and "Sure thing, Torvald!" I tell you, it's
been excruciating for me. He's out to make my place in the
bank unbearable.

NORA: Torvald, you can't be serious about all this.

HELMER: Oh no? Why not? 265

NORA: Because these are such petty considerations.

HELMER: What are you saying? Petty? You think I'm petty!

NORA: No, just the opposite, Torvald dear. That's exactly
why—

HELMER: Never mind. You call my motives petty; then I might as 270
well be just that. Petty! All right! We'll put a stop to this for
good. (*Goes to the hall door and calls.*) Helene!

NORA: What do you want?

HELMER: (*Searching among his papers.*) A decision. (*The* MAID
comes in.) Look here; take this letter; go out with it at once. 275
Get hold of a messenger and have him deliver it. Quick
now. It's already addressed. Wait, here's some money.

MAID: Yes, sir. (*She leaves with the letter.*)

HELMER: (*Straightening his papers.*) There, now, little Miss
Willful. 280

NORA: (*Breathlessly.*) Torvald, what was that letter?

HELMER: Krogstad's notice.

NORA: Call it back, Torvald! There's still time. Oh, Torvald, call
it back! Do it for my sake—for your sake, for the children's
sake! Do you hear, Torvald; do it! You don't know how this 285
can harm us.

HELMER: Too late.

NORA: Yes, too late.

HELMER: Nora dear, I can forgive you this panic, even though
basically you're insulting me. Yes, you are! Or isn't it an 290
insult to think that I should be afraid of a courtroom
hack's revenge? But I forgive you anyway, because this
shows so beautifully how much you love me. (*Takes her in
his arms.*) This is the way it should be, my darling Nora.
Whatever comes, you'll see: when it really counts, I have 295
strength and courage enough as a man to take on the
whole weight myself.

NORA: (*Terrified.*) What do you mean by that?

HELMER: The whole weight, I said.

NORA: (*Resolutely.*) No, never in all the world. 300

HELMER: Good. So we'll share it, Nora, as man and wife.
That's as it should be. (*Fondling her.*) Are you happy now?
There, there, there—not these frightened dove's eyes. It's
nothing at all but empty fantasies—Now you should run
through your tarantella and practice your tambourine. I'll 305
go to the inner office and shut both doors, so I won't hear a
thing; you can make all the noise you like. (*Turning in the
doorway.*) And when Rank comes, just tell him where he can
find me. (*He nods to her and goes with his papers into the
study, closing the door.*) 310

NORA: (*Standing as though rooted, dazed with fright, in a whisper.*)
He really could do it. He will do it. He'll do it in spite of
everything. No, not that, never, never! Anything but that!
Escape! A way out—(*The doorbell rings.*) Dr. Rank! Anything
but that! Anything, whatever it is! (*Her hands pass over her 315
face, smoothing it; she pulls herself together, goes over and
opens the hall doo.* DR. RANK *stands outside, hanging his fur
coat up. During the following scene, it begins getting dark.*)
Hello, Dr. Rank. I recognized your ring. But you mustn't
go in to Torvald yet; I believe he's working. 320

RANK: And you?

NORA: For you, I always have an hour to spare—you know that.
(*He has entered, and she shuts the door after him.*)

RANK: Many thanks. I'll make use of these hours while I can.

NORA: What do you mean by that? While you can? 325

RANK: Does that disturb you?

NORA: Well, it's such an odd phrase. Is anything going to happen?

RANK: What's going to happen is what I've been expecting so
330 long—but I honestly didn't think it would come so soon.

NORA: (*Gripping his arm.*) What is it you've found out? Dr. Rank, you have to tell me!

RANK: (*Sitting by the stove.*) It's all over with me. There's nothing to be done about it.

335 NORA: (*Breathing easier.*) Is it you—then—?

RANK: Who else? There's no point in lying to one's self. I'm the most miserable of all my patients, Mrs. Helmer. These past few days I've been auditing my internal accounts. Bankrupt! Within a month I'll probably be laid out and rotting in the
340 churchyard.

NORA: Oh, what a horrible thing to say.

RANK: The thing itself is horrible. But the worst of it is all the other horror before it's over. There's only one final examination left; when I'm finished with that, I'll know about
345 when my disintegration will begin. There's something I want to say. Helmer with his sensitivity has such a sharp distaste for anything ugly. I don't want him near my sickroom.

NORA: Oh, but Dr. Rank—

RANK: I won't have him in there. Under no condition. I'll
350 lock my door to him—As soon as I'm completely sure of the worst, I'll send you my calling card marked with a black cross, and you'll know then the wreck has started to come apart.

NORA: No, today you're completely unreasonable. And I wanted
355 you so much to be in a really good humor.

RANK: With death up my sleeve? And then to suffer this way for somebody else's sins. Is there any justice in that? And in every single family, in some way or another, this inevitable retribution of nature goes on—

360 NORA: (*Her hands pressed over her ears.*) Oh, stuff! Cheer up! Please—be gay!

RANK: Yes, I'd just as soon laugh at it all. My poor, innocent spine, serving time for my father's gay army days.

NORA: (*By the table, left.*) He was so infatuated with asparagus
365 tips and *pâté de foie gras,* wasn't that it?

RANK: Yes—and with truffles.

NORA: Truffles, yes. And then with oysters, I suppose?

RANK: Yes, tons of oysters, naturally.

NORA: And then the port and champagne to go with it. It's so sad
370 that all these delectable things have to strike at our bones.

RANK: Especially when they strike at the unhappy bones that never shared in the fun.

NORA: Ah, that's the saddest of all.

RANK: (*Looks searchingly at her.*) Hm.

375 NORA: (*After a moment.*) Why did you smile?

RANK: No, it was you who laughed.

NORA: No, it was you who smiled, Dr. Rank!

RANK: (*Getting up.*) You're even a bigger tease than I'd thought.

NORA: I'm full of wild ideas today.

380 RANK: That's obvious.

NORA: (*Putting both hands on his shoulders.*) Dear, dear Dr. Rank, you'll never die for Torvald and me.

RANK: Oh, that loss you'll easily get over. Those who go away are soon forgotten.

385 NORA: (*Looks fearfully at him.*) You believe that?

RANK: One makes new connections, and then—

NORA: Who makes new connections?

RANK: Both you and Torvald will when I'm gone. I'd say you're
well under way already. What was that Mrs. Linde doing here
390 last evening?

NORA: Oh, come—you can't be jealous of poor Kristine?

RANK: Oh yes, I am. She'll be my successor here in the house. When I'm down under, that woman will probably—

NORA: Shh! Not so loud. She's right in there.

395 RANK: Today as well. So you see.

NORA: Only to sew on my dress. Good gracious, how unreasonable you are. (*Sitting on the sofa.*) Be nice now, Dr. Rank. Tomorrow you'll see how beautifully I'll dance; and you can imagine then that I'm dancing only for you—yes, and
400 of course for Torvald, too—that's understood. (*Takes various items out of the carton.*) Dr. Rank, sit over here and I'll show you something.

RANK: (*Sitting.*) What's that?

NORA: Look here. Look.

405 RANK: Silk stockings.

NORA: Flesh-colored. Aren't they lovely? Now it's so dark here, but tomorrow—No, no, no, just look at the feet. Oh well, you might as well look at the rest.

RANK: Hm—

410 NORA: Why do you look so critical? Don't you believe they'll fit?

RANK: I've never had any chance to form an opinion on that.

NORA: (*Glancing at him a moment.*) Shame on you. (*Hits him lightly on the ear with the stockings.*) That's for you. (*Puts them
415 away again.*)

RANK: And what other splendors am I going to see now?

NORA: Not the least bit more, because you've been naughty. (*She hums a little and rummages among her things.*)

RANK: (*After a short silence.*) When I sit here together with you
420 like this, completely easy and open, then I don't know—I simply can't imagine—whatever would have become of me if I'd never come into this house.

NORA: (*Smiling.*) Yes, I really think you feel completely at ease with us.

425 RANK: (*More quietly, staring straight ahead.*) And then to have to go away from it all—

NORA: Nonsense, you're not going away.

RANK: (*His voice unchanged.*)—and not even be able to leave some poor show of gratitude behind, scarcely a fleeting regret—no
430 more than a vacant place that anyone can fill.

NORA: And if I asked you now for—? No—

RANK: For what?

NORA: For a great proof of your friendship—

RANK: Yes, yes?

435 NORA: No, I mean—for an exceptionally big favor—

RANK: Would you really, for once, make me so happy?

NORA: Oh, you haven't the vaguest idea what it is.

RANK: All right, then tell me.

NORA: No, but I can't, Dr. Rank—it's all out of reason. It's advice
440 and help, too—and a favor—

RANK: So much the better. I can't fathom what you're hinting at. Just speak out. Don't you trust me?

NORA: Of course. More than anyone else. You're my best and truest friend, I'm sure. That's why I want to talk to you. All
445 right, then, Dr. Rank: there's something you can help me prevent. You know how deeply, how inexpressibly dearly Torvald loves me; he'd never hesitate a second to give up his life for me.

RANK: (*Leaning close to her.*) Nora—do you think he's the only
450   one—
NORA: (*With a slight start.*) Who—?
RANK: Who'd gladly give up his life for you.
NORA: (*Heavily.*) I see.
RANK: I swore to myself you should know this before I'm
455   gone. I'll never find a better chance. Yes, Nora, now you
    know. And also you know now that you can trust me beyond
    anyone else.
NORA: (*Rising, natural and calm.*) Let me by.
RANK: (*Making room for her, but still sitting.*) Nora—
460 NORA: (*In the hall doorway.*) Helene, bring the lamp in. (*Goes over
    to the stove.*) Ah, dear Dr. Rank, that was really mean of you.
RANK: (*Getting up.*) That I've loved you just as deeply as somebody
    else? Was *that* mean?
NORA: No, but that you came out and told me. That was quite
465   unnecessary—
RANK: What do you mean? Have you known—?

(*The* MAID *comes in with the lamp, sets it on the table, and goes out
again.*)

RANK: Nora—Mrs. Helmer—I'm asking you: have you known
    about it?
NORA: Oh, how can I tell what I know or don't know?
470   Really, I don't know what to say—Why did you have to be so
    clumsy, Dr. Rank! Everything was so good.
RANK: Well, in any case, you now have the knowledge that
    my body and soul are at your command. So won't you
    speak out?
475 NORA: (*Looking at him.*) After that?
RANK: Please, just let me know what it is.
NORA: You can't know anything now.
RANK: I have to. You mustn't punish me like this. Give me the
    chance to do whatever is humanly possible for you.
480 NORA: Now there's nothing you can do for me. Besides, actually,
    I don't need any help. You'll see—it's only my fantasies. That's
    what it is. Of course! (*Sits in the rocker, looks at him, and
    smiles.*) What a nice one you are, Dr. Rank. Aren't you a little
    bit ashamed, now that the lamp is here?
485 RANK: No, not exactly. But perhaps I'd better go—for good?
NORA: No, you certainly can't do that. You must come here just as
    you always have. You know Torvald can't do without you.
RANK: Yes, but *you?*
NORA: You know how much I enjoy it when you're here.
490 RANK: That's precisely what threw me off. You're a mystery to me.
    So many times I've felt you'd almost rather be with me than
    with Helmer.
NORA: Yes—you see, there are some people that one loves most
    and other people that one would almost prefer being with.
495 RANK: Yes, there's something to that.
NORA: When I was back home, of course I loved Papa most. But I
    always thought it was so much fun when I could sneak down
    to the maids' quarters, because they never tried to improve
    me, and it was always so amusing, the way they talked to each
500   other.
RANK: Aha, so it's *their* place that I've filled.
NORA: (*Jumping up and going to him.*) Oh, dear, sweet Dr. Rank,
    that's not what I meant at all. But you can understand that
    with Torvald it's just the same as with Papa—

(*The* MAID *enters from the hall.*)

MAID: Ma'am—please! (*She whispers to* NORA *and hands her a* 505
    calling card.)
NORA: (*Glancing at the card.*) Ah! (*Slips it into her pocket.*)
RANK: Anything wrong?
NORA: No, no, not at all. It's only some—it's my new dress—
RANK: Really? But—there's your dress. 510
NORA: Oh, that. But this is another one—I ordered it—
    Torvald mustn't know—
RANK: Ah, now we have the big secret.
NORA: That's right. Just go in with him—he's back in the inner
    study. Keep him there as long as— 515
RANK: Don't worry. He won't get away. (*Goes into the study.*)
NORA: (*To the* MAID.) And he's standing waiting in the kitchen?
MAID: Yes, he came up by the back stairs.
NORA: But didn't you tell him somebody was here?
MAID: Yes, but that didn't do any good. 520
NORA: He won't leave?
MAID: No, he won't go till he's talked with you, ma'am.
NORA: Let him come in, then—but quietly. Helene, don't breathe
    a word about this. It's a surprise for my husband.
MAID: Yes, yes, I understand—(*Goes out.*) 525
NORA: This horror—it's going to happen. No, no, no, it can't
    happen, it mustn't. (*She goes and bolts* HELMER's *door. The*
    MAID *opens the hall door for* KROGSTAD *and shuts it behind*
    him. He is dressed for travel in a fur coat, boots, and a fur cap.)
NORA: (*Going toward him.*) Talk softly. My husband's home. 530
KROGSTAD: Well, good for him.
NORA: What do you want?
KROGSTAD: Some information.
NORA: Hurry up, then. What is it?
KROGSTAD: You know, of course, that I got my notice. 535
NORA: I couldn't prevent it, Mr. Krogstad. I fought for you to the
    bitter end, but nothing worked.
KROGSTAD: Does your husband's love for you run so thin? He
    knows everything I can expose you to, and all the same he
    dares to— 540
NORA: How can you imagine he knows anything about this?
KROGSTAD: Ah, no—I can't imagine it either, now. It's not at all
    like my fine Torvald Helmer to have so much guts—
NORA: Mr. Krogstad, I demand respect for my husband!
KROGSTAD: Why, of course—all due respect. But since the lady's 545
    keeping it so carefully hidden, may I presume to ask if you're
    also a bit better informed than yesterday about what you've
    actually done?
NORA: More than you ever could teach me.
KROGSTAD: Yes, I *am* such an awful lawyer. 550
NORA: What is it you want from me?
KROGSTAD: Just a glimpse of how you are, Mrs. Helmer. I've been
    thinking about you all day long. A cashier, a night—court
    scribbler, a—well, a type like me also has a little of what they
    call a heart, you know. 555
NORA: Then show it. Think of my children.
KROGSTAD: Did you or your husband ever think of mine? But
    never mind. I simply wanted to tell you that you don't need
    to take this thing too seriously. For the present, I'm not
    proceeding with any action. 560
NORA: Oh no, really! Well—I knew that.
KROGSTAD: Everything can be settled in a friendly spirit. It
    doesn't have to get around town at all; it can stay just among
    us three.
NORA: My husband must never know anything of this. 565

KROGSTAD: How can you manage that? Perhaps you can pay me the balance?

NORA: No, not right now.

KROGSTAD: Or you know some way of raising the money in a day or two?

NORA: No way that I'm willing to use.

KROGSTAD: Well, it wouldn't have done you any good, anyway. If you stood in front of me with a fistful of bills, you still couldn't buy your signature back.

575 NORA: Then tell me what you're going to do with it.

KROGSTAD: I'll just hold onto it—keep it on file. There's no outsider who'll even get wind of it. So if you've been thinking of taking some desperate step—

NORA: I have.

580 KROGSTAD: Been thinking of running away from home—

NORA: I have!

KROGSTAD: Or even of something worse—

NORA: How could you guess that?

KROGSTAD: You can drop those thoughts.

585 NORA: How could you guess I was thinking of *that?*

KROGSTAD: Most of us think about *that* at first. I thought about it too, but I discovered I hadn't the courage—

NORA: (*Lifelessly.*) I don't either.

KROGSTAD: (*Relieved.*) That's true, you haven't the courage?

590 You too?

NORA: I don't have it—I don't have it.

KROGSTAD: It would be terribly stupid, anyway. After that first storm at home blows out, why, then—I have here in my pocket a letter for your husband—

595 NORA: Telling everything?

KROGSTAD: As charitably as possible.

NORA: (*Quickly.*) He mustn't ever get that letter. Tear it up. I'll find some way to get money.

KROGSTAD: Beg pardon, Mrs. Helmer, but I think I just told

600 you—

NORA: Oh, I don't mean the money I owe you. Let me know how much you want from my husband, and I'll manage it.

KROGSTAD: I don't want any money from your husband.

605 NORA: What do you want, then?

KROGSTAD: I'll tell you what. I want to recoup, Mrs. Helmer; I want to get on in the world—and there's where your husband can help me. For a year and a half I've kept myself clean of anything disreputable—all that time strug-

610 gling with the worst conditions; but I was satisfied, working my way up step by step. Now I've been written right off, and I'm just not in the mood to come crawling back. I tell you, I want to move on. I want to get back in the bank—in a better position. Your husband can set up a

615 job for me—

NORA: He'll never do that!

KROGSTAD: He'll do it. I know him. He won't dare breathe a word of protest. And once I'm in there together with him, you just wait and see! Inside of a year, I'll be the manager's

620 righthand man. It'll be Nils Krogstad, not Torvald Helmer, who runs the bank.

NORA: You'll never see the day!

KROGSTAD: Maybe you think you can—

NORA: I have the courage now—for *that.*

625 KROGSTAD: Oh, you don't scare me. A smart, spoiled lady like you—

NORA: You'll see; you'll see!

KROGSTAD: Under the ice, maybe? Down in the freezing, coal-black water? There, till you float up in the spring, ugly, unrecognizable, with your hair falling out— 630

NORA: You don't frighten me.

KROGSTAD: Nor do you frighten me. One doesn't do these things, Mrs. Helmer. Besides, what good would it be? I'd still have him safe in my pocket.

NORA: Afterwards? When I'm no longer—? 635

KROGSTAD: Are you forgetting that *I'll* be in control then over your final reputation? (NORA *stands speechless, staring at him.*) Good; now I've warned you. Don't do anything stupid. When Helmer's read my letter, I'll be waiting for his reply. And bear in mind that it's your husband himself who's 640 forced me back to my old ways. I'll never forgive him for that. Good-bye, Mrs. Helmer. (*He goes out through the hall.*)

NORA: (*Goes to the hall door, opens it a crack, and listens.*) He's gone. Didn't leave the letter. Oh no, no, that's impossible too! (*Opening the door more and more.*) What's that? He's 645 standing outside—not going downstairs. He's thinking it over? Maybe he'll—? (*A letter falls in the mailbox; then* KROGSTAD's *footsteps are heard, dying away down a flight of stairs.* NORA *gives a muffled cry and runs over toward the sofa table. A short pause.*) In the mailbox. (*Slips warily over to the* 650 *hall door.*) It's lying there. Torvald, Torvald—now we're lost!

MRS. LINDE: (*Entering with the costume from the room, left.*) There now, I can't see anything else to mend. Perhaps you'd like to try—

NORA: (*In a hoarse whisper.*) Kristine, come here. 655

MRS. LINDE: (*Tossing the dress on the sofa.*) What's wrong? You look upset.

NORA: Come here. See that letter? *There!* Look—through the glass in the mailbox.

MRS. LINDE: Yes, yes, I see it. 660

NORA: That letter's from Krogstad—

MRS. LINDE: Nora—it's Krogstad who loaned you the money!

NORA: Yes, and now Torvald will find out everything.

MRS. LINDE: Believe me, Nora, it's best for both of you.

NORA: There's more you don't know. I forged a name. 665

MRS. LINDE: But for heaven's sake—?

NORA: I only want to tell you that, Kristine, so that you can be my witness.

MRS. LINDE: Witness? Why should I—?

NORA: If I should go out of my mind—it could easily happen— 670

MRS. LINDE: Nora!

NORA: Or anything else occurred—so I couldn't be present here—

MRS. LINDE: Nora, Nora, you aren't yourself at all!

NORA: And someone should try to take on the whole weight, 675 all of the guilt, you follow me—

MRS. LINDE: Yes, of course, but why do you think—?

NORA: Then you're the witness that it isn't true, Kristine. I'm very much myself; my mind right now is perfectly clear; and I'm telling you: nobody else has known about this; I alone did 680 everything. Remember that.

MRS. LINDE: I will. But I don't understand all this.

NORA: Oh, how could you ever understand it? It's the miracle now that's going to take place.

MRS. LINDE: The miracle? 685

NORA: Yes, the miracle. But it's so awful, Kristine. It mustn't take place, not for anything in the world.

MRS. LINDE: I'm going right over and talk with Krogstad.

NORA: Don't go near him; he'll do you some terrible harm!

690 MRS. LINDE: There was a time once when he'd gladly have done anything for me.

NORA: He?

MRS. LINDE: Where does he live?

NORA: Oh, how do I know? Yes. (*Searches in her pocket.*) Here's

695 his card. But the letter, the letter—!

HELMER: (*From the study, knocking on the door.*) Nora!

NORA: (*With a cry of fear.*) Oh! What is it? What do you want?

HELMER: Now, now, don't be so frightened. We're not coming in. You locked the door—are you trying on the dress?

700 NORA: Yes, I'm trying it. I'll look just beautiful, Torvald.

MRS. LINDE: (*Who has read the card.*) He's living right around the corner.

NORA: Yes, but what's the use? We're lost. The letter's in the box.

705 MRS. LINDE: And your husband has the key?

NORA: Yes, always.

MRS. LINDE: Krogstad can ask for his letter back unread; he can find some excuse—

NORA: But it's just this time that Torvald usually—

710 MRS. LINDE: Stall him. Keep him in there. I'll be back as quick as I can. (*She hurries out through the hall entrance.*)

NORA: (*Goes to* HELMER's *door, opens it, and peers in.*) Torvald!

HELMER: (*From the inner study.*) Well—does one dare set foot in one's own living room at last? Come on, Rank, now we'll get a

715 look—(*In the doorway.*) But what's this?

NORA: What, Torvald dear?

HELMER: Rank had me expecting some grand masquerade.

RANK: (*In the doorway.*) That was my impression, but I must have been wrong.

720 NORA: No one can admire me in my splendor—not till tomorrow.

HELMER: But Nora dear, you look so exhausted. Have you practiced too hard?

NORA: No, I haven't practiced at all yet.

725 HELMER: You know, it's necessary—

NORA: Oh, it's absolutely necessary, Torvald. But I can't get anywhere without your help. I've forgotten the whole thing completely.

HELMER: Ah, we'll soon take care of that.

730 NORA: Yes, take care of me, Torvald, please! Promise me that? Oh, I'm so nervous. That big party—You must give up everything this evening for me. No business—don't even touch your pen. Yes? Dear Torvald, promise?

HELMER: It's a promise. Tonight I'm totally at your service—you

735 little helpless thing. Hm—but first there's one thing I want to—(*Goes toward the hall door.*)

NORA: What are you looking for?

HELMER: Just to see if there's any mail.

NORA: No, no, don't do that, Torvald!

740 HELMER: Now what?

NORA: Torvald, please. There isn't any.

HELMER: Let me look, though. (*Starts out.* NORA, *at the piano, strikes the first notes of the tarantella.* HELMER, *at the door, stops.*) Aha!

745 NORA: I can't dance tomorrow if I don't practice with you.

HELMER: (*Going over to her.*) Nora dear, are you really so frightened?

NORA: Yes, so terribly frightened. Let me practice right now; there's still time before dinner. Oh, sit down and play for

750 me, Torvald. Direct me. Teach me, the way you always have.

HELMER: Gladly, if it's what you want. (*Sits at the piano.*)

NORA: (*Snatches the tambourine up from the box, then a long, varicolored shawl, which she throws around herself, whereupon she springs forward and cries out:*) Play for me now! Now I'll 755 dance!

(HELMER *plays and* NORA *dances.* RANK *stands behind* HELMER *at the piano and looks on.*)

HELMER: (*As he plays.*) Slower. Slow down.

NORA: Can't change it.

HELMER: Not so violent, Nora!

NORA: Has to be just like this. 760

HELMER: (*Stopping.*) No, no, that won't do at all.

NORA: (*Laughing and swinging her tambourine.*) Isn't that what I told you?

RANK: Let me play for her.

HELMER: (*Getting up.*) Yes, go on. I can teach her more easily 765 then.

(RANK *sits at the piano and plays;* NORA *dances more and more wildly.* HELMER *has stationed himself by the stove and repeatedly gives her directions; she seems not to hear them; her hair loosens and falls over her shoulders; she does not notice, but goes on danc-ing.* MRS. LINDE *enters.*)

MRS. LINDE: (*Standing dumbfounded at the door.*) Ah—!

NORA: (*Still dancing.*) See what fun, Kristine!

HELMER: But Nora darling, you dance as if your life were at stake. 770

NORA: And it is.

HELMER: Rank, stop! This is pure madness. Stop it, I say!

(RANK *breaks off playing, and* NORA *halts abruptly*).

HELMER: (*Going over to her.*) I never would have believed it. You've forgotten everything I taught you.

NORA: (*Throwing away the tambourine.*) You see for yourself. 775

HELMER: Well, there's certainly room for instruction here.

NORA: Yes, you see how important it is. You've got to teach me to the very last minute. Promise me that, Torvald?

HELMER: You can bet on it.

NORA: You mustn't, either today or tomorrow, think about 780 anything else but me; you mustn't open any letters—or the mailbox—

HELMER: Ah, it's still the fear of that man—

NORA: Oh yes, yes, that too.

HELMER: Nora, it's written all over you—there's already a letter 785 from him out there.

NORA: I don't know. I guess so. But you mustn't read such things now; there mustn't be anything ugly between us before it's all over.

RANK: (*Quietly to* HELMER.) You shouldn't deny her. 790

HELMER: (*Putting his arm around her.*) The child can have her way. But tomorrow night, after you've danced—

NORA: Then you'll be free.

MAID: (*In the doorway, right.*) Ma'am, dinner is served.

NORA: We'll be wanting champagne, Helene. 795

MAID: Very good, ma'am. (*Goes out.*)

HELMER: So—a regular banquet, hm?

NORA: Yes, a banquet—champagne till daybreak! (*Calling out.*) And some macaroons, Helene. Heaps of them—just this once. 800

HELMER: (*Taking her hands.*) Now, now, now—no hysterics. Be my own little lark again.

NORA: Oh, I will soon enough. But go on in—and you, Dr. Rank. Kristine, help me put up my hair.

805 RANK: (*Whispering, as they go.*) There's nothing wrong—really wrong, is there?

HELMER: Oh, of course not. It's nothing more than this childish anxiety I was telling you about. (*They go out, right.*)

NORA: Well?

810 MRS. LINDE: Left town.

NORA: I could see by your face.

MRS. LINDE: He'll be home tomorrow evening. I wrote him a note.

NORA: You shouldn't have. Don't try to stop anything now. After 815 all, it's a wonderful joy, this waiting here for the miracle.

MRS. LINDE: What is it you're waiting for?

NORA: Oh, you can't understand that. Go in to them; I'll be along in a moment.

(MRS. LINDE *goes into the dining room.* NORA *stands a short while as if composing herself; then she looks at her watch.*)

NORA: Five. Seven hours to midnight. Twenty-four hours to the 820 midnight after, and then the tarantella's done. Seven and twenty-four? Thirty-one hours to live.

HELMER: (*In the doorway, right.*) What's become of the little lark?

NORA: (*Going toward him with open arms.*) Here's your lark!

ACT THREE

Same scene. The table, with chairs around it, has been moved to the center of the room. A lamp on the table is lit. The hall door stands open. Dance music drifts down from the floor above. MRS. LINDE *sits at the table, absently paging through a book, trying to read, but apparently unable to focus her thoughts. Once or twice she pauses, tensely listening for a sound at the outer entrance.*

MRS. LINDE: (*Glancing at her watch.*) Not yet—and there's hardly any time left. If only he's not—(*Listening again.*) Ah, there he is. (*She goes out in the hall and cautiously opens the outer door. Quiet footsteps are heard on the stairs. She whispers:*) Come in.
5 Nobody's here.

KROGSTAD: (*In the doorway.*) I found a note from you at home. What's back of all this?

MRS. LINDE: I just *had* to talk to you.

KROGSTAD: Oh? And it just *had* to be here in this house?

10 MRS. LINDE: At my place it was impossible; my room hasn't a private entrance. Come in; we're all alone. The maid's asleep, and the Helmers are at the dance upstairs.

KROGSTAD: (*Entering the room.*) Well, well, the Helmers are dancing tonight? Really?

15 MRS. LINDE: Yes, why not?

KROGSTAD: How true—why not?

MRS. LINDE: All right, Krogstad, let's talk.

KROGSTAD: Do we two have anything more to talk about?

MRS. LINDE: We have a great deal to talk about.

20 KROGSTAD: I wouldn't have thought so.

MRS. LINDE: No, because you've never understood me, really.

KROGSTAD: Was there anything more to understand—except what's all too common in life? A calculating woman throws over a man the moment a better catch comes by.

MRS. LINDE: You think I'm so thoroughly calculating? You think 25 I broke it off lightly?

KROGSTAD: Didn't you?

MRS. LINDE: Nils—is that what you really thought?

KROGSTAD: If you cared, then why did you write me the way you did? 30

MRS. LINDE: What else could I do? If I had to break off with you, then it was my job as well to root out everything you felt for me.

KROGSTAD: (*Wringing his hands.*) So that was it. And this—all this, simply for money! 35

MRS. LINDE: Don't forget I had a helpless mother and two small brothers. We couldn't wait for you, Nils; you had such a long road ahead of you then.

KROGSTAD: That may be; but you still hadn't the right to abandon me for somebody else's sake. 40

MRS. LINDE: Yes—I don't know. So many, many times I've asked myself if I did have that right.

KROGSTAD: (*More softly.*) When I lost you, it was as if all the solid ground dissolved from under my feet. Look at me; I'm a half-drowned man now, hanging onto a wreck. 45

MRS. LINDE: Help may be near.

KROGSTAD: It was near—but then you came and blocked it off.

MRS. LINDE: Without my knowing it, Nils. Today for the first time I learned that it's you I'm replacing at the bank.

KROGSTAD: All right—I believe you. But now that you know, will 50 you step aside?

MRS. LINDE: No, because that wouldn't benefit you in the slightest.

KROGSTAD: Not "benefit" me, hm! I'd step aside anyway.

MRS. LINDE: I've learned to be realistic. Life and hard, bitter 55 necessity have taught me that.

KROGSTAD: And life's taught me never to trust fine phrases.

MRS. LINDE: Then life's taught you a very sound thing. But you do have to trust in actions, don't you?

KROGSTAD: What does that mean? 60

MRS. LINDE: You said you were hanging on like a half-drowned man to a wreck.

KROGSTAD: I've good reason to say that.

MRS. LINDE: I'm also like a half-drowned woman on a wreck. No one to suffer with; no one to care for. 65

KROGSTAD: You made your choice.

MRS. LINDE: There wasn't any choice then.

KROGSTAD: So—what of it?

MRS. LINDE: Nils, if only we two shipwrecked people could reach across to each other. 70

KROGSTAD: What are you saying?

MRS. LINDE: Two on one wreck are at least better off than each on his own.

KROGSTAD: Kristine!

MRS. LINDE: Why do you think I came into town? 75

KROGSTAD: Did you really have some thought of me?

MRS. LINDE: I have to work to go on living. All my born days, as long as I can remember, I've worked, and it's been my best and my only joy. But now I'm completely alone in the world; it frightens me to be so empty and lost. To work for 80 yourself—there's no joy in that. Nils, give me something—someone to work for.

KROGSTAD: I don't believe all this. It's just some hysterical feminine urge to go out and make a noble sacrifice.

MRS. LINDE: Have you ever found me to be hysterical? 85

KROGSTAD: Can you honestly mean this? Tell me—do you know everything about my past?

MRS. LINDE: Yes.

KROGSTAD: And you know what they think I'm worth around here.

90

MRS. LINDE: From what you were saying before, it would seem that with me you could have been another person.

KROGSTAD: I'm positive of that.

MRS. LINDE: Couldn't it happen still?

95 KROGSTAD: Kristine—you're saying this in all seriousness? Yes, you are! I can see it in you. And do you really have the courage, then—?

MRS. LINDE: I need to have someone to care for; and your children need a mother. We both need each other. Nils, I

100 have faith that you're good at heart—I'll risk everything together with you.

KROGSTAD: (*Gripping her hands.*) Kristine, thank you, thank you—Now I know I can win back a place in their eyes. Yes—but I forgot—

105 MRS. LINDE: (*Listening.*) Shh! The tarantella. Go now! Go on!

KROGSTAD: Why? What is it?

MRS. LINDE: Hear the dance up there? When that's over, they'll be coming down.

KROGSTAD: Oh, then I'll go. But—it's all pointless. Of course, you

110 don't know the move I made against the Helmers.

MRS. LINDE: Yes, Nils, I know.

KROGSTAD: And all the same, you have the courage to—?

MRS. LINDE: I know how far despair can drive a man like you.

KROGSTAD: Oh, if I only could take it all back.

115 MRS. LINDE: You easily could—your letter's still lying in the mailbox.

KROGSTAD: Are you sure of that?

MRS. LINDE: Positive. But—

KROGSTAD: (*Looks at her searchingly.*) Is that the meaning of it,

120 then? You'll save your friend at any price. Tell me straight out. Is that it?

MRS. LINDE: Nils—anyone who's sold herself for somebody else once isn't going to do it again.

KROGSTAD: I'll demand my letter back.

125 MRS. LINDE: No, no.

KROGSTAD: Yes, of course. I'll stay here till Helmer comes down; I'll tell him to give me my letter again—that it only involves my dismissal—that he shouldn't read it—

MRS. LINDE: No, Nils, don't call the letter back.

130 KROGSTAD: But wasn't that exactly why you wrote me to come here?

MRS. LINDE: Yes, in that first panic. But it's been a whole day and night since then, and in that time I've seen such incredible things in this house. Helmer's got to learn everything; this

135 dreadful secret has to be aired; those two have to come to a full understanding; all these lies and evasions can't go on.

KROGSTAD: Well, then, if you want to chance it. But at least there's one thing I can do, and do right away—

MRS. LINDE: (*Listening.*) Go now, go, quick! The dance is over.

140 We're not safe another second.

KROGSTAD: I'll wait for you downstairs.

MRS. LINDE: Yes, please do; take me home.

KROGSTAD: I can't believe it; I've never been so happy. (*He leaves by way of the outer door; the door between the room and the*

145 *hall stays open.*)

MRS. LINDE: (*Straightening up a bit and getting together her street clothes.*) How different now! How different! Someone to

work for, to live for—a home to build. Well, it is worth the try! Oh, if they'd only come! (*Listening.*) Ah, there

150 they are. Bundle up. (*She picks up her hat and coat.* NORA's and HELMER's *voices can be heard outside; a key turns in the lock, and* HELMER *brings* NORA *into the hall almost by force. She is wearing the Italian costume with a large black shawl about her; he has on evening dress, with a black domino open over it.*)

155 NORA: (*Struggling in the doorway.*) No, no, no, not inside! I'm going up again. I don't want to leave so soon.

HELMER: But Nora dear—

NORA: Oh, I beg you, please, Torvald. From the bottom of my heart, *please*—only an hour more!

160 HELMER: Not a single minute, Nora darling. You know our agreement. Come on, in we go; you'll catch cold out here. (*In spite of her resistance, he gently draws her into the room.*)

MRS. LINDE: Good evening.

NORA: Kristine!

165 HELMER: Why, Mrs. Linde—are you here so late?

MRS. LINDE: Yes, I'm sorry, but I did want to see Nora in costume.

NORA: Have you been sitting here, waiting for me?

MRS. LINDE: Yes. I didn't come early enough; you were all

170 upstairs; and then I thought I really couldn't leave without seeing you.

HELMER: (*Removing* NORA's *shawl.*) Yes, take a good look. She's worth looking at, I can tell you that, Mrs. Linde. Isn't she lovely?

175 MRS. LINDE: Yes, I should say—

HELMER: A dream of loveliness, isn't she? That's what everyone thought at the party, too. But she's horribly stubborn—this sweet little thing. What's to be done with her? Can you imagine, I almost had to use force to pry her away.

180 NORA: Oh, Torvald, you're going to regret you didn't indulge me, even for just a half hour more.

HELMER: There, you see. She danced her tarantella and got a tumultuous hand—which was well earned, although the performance may have been a bit too naturalistic—I mean

185 it rather overstepped the proprieties of art. But never mind—what's important is, she made a success, an overwhelming success. You think I could let her stay on after that and spoil the effect? Oh no; I took my lovely little Capri girl—my capricious little Capri girl, I should say—

190 took her under my arm; one quick tour of the ballroom, a curtsy to every side, and then—as they say in novels—the beautiful vision disappeared. An exit should always be effective, Mrs. Linde, but that's what I can't get Nora to grasp. Phew, it's hot in here. (*Flings the domino on a chair and opens the door to his room.*) Why's it dark in here? Oh yes, of course.

195 Excuse me. (*He goes in and lights a couple of candles.*)

NORA: (*In a sharp, breathless whisper.*) So?

MRS. LINDE: (*Quietly.*) I talked with him.

NORA: And—?

MRS. LINDE: Nora—you must tell your husband everything.

200

NORA: (*Dully.*) I knew it.

MRS. LINDE: You've got nothing to fear from Krogstad, but you have to speak out.

NORA: I won't tell.

MRS. LINDE: Then the letter will.

205

NORA: Thanks, Kristine. I know now what's to be done. Shh!

HELMER: (*Reentering.*) Well, then, Mrs. Linde—have you admired her?

MRS. LINDE: Yes, and now I'll say good night.

210 HELMER: Oh, come, so soon? Is this yours, this knitting?

MRS. LINDE: Yes, thanks. I nearly forgot it.

HELMER: Do you knit, then?

MRS. LINDE: Oh yes.

HELMER: You know what? You should embroider instead.

215 MRS. LINDE: Really? Why?

HELMER: Yes, because it's a lot prettier. See here, one holds the embroidery so, in the left hand, and then one guides the needle with the right—so—in an easy, sweeping curve—right?

MRS. LINDE: Yes, I guess that's—

220 HELMER: But, on the other hand, knitting—it can never be anything but ugly. Look, see here, the arms tucked in, the knitting needles going up and down—there's something Chinese about it. Ah, that was really a glorious champagne they served.

225 MRS. LINDE: Yes, good night, Nora, and don't be stubborn anymore.

HELMER: Well put, Mrs. Linde!

MRS. LINDE: Good night, Mr. Helmer.

HELMER: (*Accompanying her to the door.*) Good night, good

230 night. I hope you get home all right. I'd be very happy to—but you don't have far to go. Good night, good night. (*She leaves. He shuts the door after her and returns.*) There, now, at last we got her out the door. She's a deadly bore, that creature.

235 NORA: Aren't you pretty tired, Torvald?

HELMER: No, not a bit.

NORA: You're not sleepy?

HELMER: Not at all. On the contrary, I'm feeling quite exhilarated. But you? Yes, you really look tired and sleepy.

240 NORA: Yes, I'm very tired. Soon now I'll sleep.

HELMER: See! You see! I was right all along that we shouldn't stay longer.

NORA: Whatever you do is always right.

HELMER: (*Kissing her brow.*) Now my little lark talks sense. Say,

245 did you notice what a time Rank was having tonight?

NORA: Oh, was he? I didn't get to speak with him.

HELMER: I scarcely did either, but it's a long time since I've seen him in such high spirits. (*Gazes at her a moment, then comes nearer her.*) Hm—it's marvelous, though, to be back home

250 again—to be completely alone with you. Oh, you bewitchingly lovely young woman!

NORA: Torvald, don't look at me like that!

HELMER: Can't I look at my richest treasure? At all that beauty that's mine, mine alone—completely and utterly.

255 NORA: (*Moving around to the other side of the table.*) You mustn't talk to me that way tonight.

HELMER: (*Following her.*) The tarantella is still in your blood, I can see—and it makes you even more enticing. Listen. The guests are beginning to go. (*Dropping his voice.*) Nora—it'll

260 soon be quiet through this whole house.

NORA: Yes, I hope so.

HELMER: You do, don't you, my love? Do you realize—when I'm out at a party like this with you—do you know why I talk to you so little, and keep such a distance away; just

265 send you a stolen look now and then—you know why I do it? It's because I'm imagining then that you're my secret darling, my secret young bride-to-be, and that no one suspects there's anything between us.

NORA: Yes, yes; oh, yes, I know you're always thinking of me.

270 HELMER: And then when we leave and I place the shawl over those fine young rounded shoulders—over that wonderful curving neck—then I pretend that you're my young bride, that we're just coming from the wedding, that for the first time I'm bringing you into my house—that for the first time I'm alone with you—completely alone with you, your 275 trembling young beauty! All this evening I've longed for nothing but you. When I saw you turn and sway in the tarantella—my blood was pounding till I couldn't stand it—that's why I brought you down here so early—

NORA: Go away, Torvald! Leave me alone. I don't want all this. 280

HELMER: What do you mean? Nora, you're teasing me. You will, won't you? Aren't I your husband—?

(*A knock at the outside door.*)

NORA: (*Startled.*) What's that?

HELMER: (*Going toward the hall.*) Who is it?

RANK: (*Outside.*) It's me. May I come in a moment? 285

HELMER: (*With quiet irritation.*) Oh, what does he want now? (*Aloud.*) Hold on. (*Goes and opens the door.*) Oh, how nice that you didn't just pass us by!

RANK: I thought I heard your voice, and then I wanted so badly to have a look in. (*Lightly glancing about.*) Ah, me, these old 290 familiar haunts. You have it snug and cozy in here, you two.

HELMER: You seemed to be having it pretty cozy upstairs, too.

RANK: Absolutely. Why shouldn't I? Why not take in everything in life? As much as you can, anyway, and as long as you can. The wine was superb— 295

HELMER: The champagne especially.

RANK: You noticed that too? It's amazing how much I could guzzle down.

NORA: Torvald also drank a lot of champagne this evening.

RANK: Oh? 300

NORA: Yes, and that always makes him so entertaining.

RANK: Well, why shouldn't one have a pleasant evening after a well-spent day?

HELMER: Well spent? I'm afraid I can't claim that.

RANK: (*Slapping him on the back.*) But I can, you see! 305

NORA: Dr. Rank, you must have done some scientific research today.

RANK: Quite so.

HELMER: Come now—little Nora talking about scientific research! 310

RANK: Indeed you may.

NORA: Then they were good?

RANK: The best possible for both doctor and patient— certainty.

NORA: (*Quickly and searchingly.*) Certainty? 315

RANK: Complete certainty. So don't I owe myself a gay evening afterwards?

NORA: Yes, you're right, Dr. Rank.

HELMER: I'm with you—just so long as you don't have to suffer for it in the morning. 320

RANK: Well, one never gets something for nothing in life.

NORA: Dr. Rank—are you very fond of masquerade parties?

RANK: Yes, if there's a good array of odd disguises—

NORA: Tell me, what should we two go as at the next masquerade? 325

HELMER: You little featherhead—already thinking of the next!

RANK: We two? I'll tell you what: you must go as Charmed Life—

HELMER: Yes, but find a costume for *that*!

RANK: Your wife can appear just as she looks every day. 330

HELMER: That was nicely put. But don't you know what
you're going to be?

RANK: Yes, Helmer, I've made up my mind.

HELMER: Well?

335 RANK: At the next masquerade I'm going to be invisible.

HELMER: That's a funny idea.

RANK: They say there's a hat—black, huge—have you never heard
of the hat that makes you invisible? You put it on, and then no
one on earth can see you.

340 HELMER: (*Suppressing a smile.*) Ah, of course.

RANK: But I'm quite forgetting what I came for. Helmer, give me a
cigar, one of the dark Havanas.

HELMER: With the greatest pleasure. (*Holds out his case.*)

RANK: Thanks. (*Takes one and cuts off the tip.*)

345 NORA: (*Striking a match.*) Let me give you a light.

RANK: Thank you. (*She holds the match for him; he lights the
cigar.*) And now good-bye.

HELMER: Good-bye, good-bye, old friend.

NORA: Sleep well, Doctor.

350 RANK: Thanks for that wish.

NORA: Wish me the same.

RANK: You? All right, if you like—Sleep well. And thanks for the
light. (*He nods to them both and leaves.*)

HELMER: (*His voice subdued.*) He's been drinking heavily.

355 NORA: (*Absently.*) Could be. (HELMER *takes his keys from his
pocket and goes out in the hall.*) Torvald—what are you after?

HELMER: Got to empty the mailbox; it's nearly full. There won't be
room for the morning papers.

NORA: Are you working tonight?

360 HELMER: You know I'm not. Why—what's this? Someone's been
at the lock.

NORA: At the lock—?

HELMER: Yes, I'm positive. What do you suppose—? I can't
imagine one of the maids—? Here's a broken hairpin. Nora,

365 it's yours—

NORA: (*Quickly.*) Then it must be the children—

HELMER: You'd better break them of that. Hm, hm—well,
opened it after all. (*Takes the contents out and calls into the
kitchen.*) Helene! Helene, would you put out the lamp in

370 the hall. (*He returns to the room, shutting the hall door, then
displays the handful of mail.*) Look how it's piled up. (*Sorting
through them.*) Now what's this?

NORA: (*At the window.*) The letter! Oh, Torvald, no!

HELMER: Two calling cards—from Rank.

375 NORA: From Dr. Rank?

HELMER: (*Examining them.*) "Dr. Rank, Consulting Physician."
They were on top. He must have dropped them in as he left.

NORA: Is there anything on them?

HELMER: There's a black cross over the name. See? That's a

380 gruesome notion. He could almost be announcing his
own death.

NORA: That's just what he's doing.

HELMER: What! You've heard something? Something he's told
you?

385 NORA: Yes. That when those cards came, he'd be taking his leave
of us. He'll shut himself in now and die.

HELMER: Ah, my poor friend! Of course I knew he wouldn't be
here much longer. But so soon—And then to hide himself
away like a wounded animal.

390 NORA: If it has to happen, then it's best it happens in silence—
don't you think so, Torvald?

HELMER: (*Pacing up and down.*) He'd grown right into our

lives. I simply can't imagine him gone. He with his suffering
and loneliness—like a dark cloud setting off our sun-
lit happiness. Well, maybe it's best this way. For him, at 395
least. (*Standing still.*) And maybe for us too, Nora. Now
we're thrown back on each other, completely. (*Embracing
her.*) Oh you, my darling wife, how can I hold you close
enough? You know what, Nora—time and again I've
wished you were in some terrible danger, just so I could 400
stake my life and soul and everything, for your sake.

NORA: (*Tearing herself away, her voice firm and decisive.*) Now
you must read your mail, Torvald.

HELMER: No, no, not tonight. I want to stay with you, dearest.

NORA: With a dying friend on your mind? 405

HELMER: You're right. We've both had a shock. There's ugliness
between us—these thoughts of death and corruption. We'll
have to get free of them first. Until then—we'll stay apart.

NORA: (*Clinging about his neck.*) Torvald—good night! Good
night! 410

HELMER: (*Kissing her on the cheek.*) Good night, little songbird.
Sleep well, Nora. I'll be reading my mail now. (*He takes the
letters into his room and shuts the door after him.*)

NORA: (*With bewildered glances, groping about, seizing* HELMER's
domino, throwing it around her, and speaking in short, hoarse, 415
broken whispers.) Never see him again. Never, never.
(*Putting her shawl over her head.*) Never see the children
either—them, too. Never, never. Oh, the freezing black
water! The depths—down—Oh, I wish it were over—He
has it now; he's reading it—now. Oh no, no, not yet. 420
Torvald, good-bye, you and the children—(*She starts for
the hall; as she does,* HELMER *throws open his door and
stands with an open letter in his hand.*)

HELMER: Nora!

NORA: (*Screams.*) Oh—! 425

HELMER: What is this? You know what's in this letter?

NORA: Yes, I know. Let me go! Let me out!

HELMER: (*Holding her back.*) Where are you going?

NORA: (*Struggling to break loose.*) You can't save me, Torvald!

HELMER: (*Slumping back.*) True! Then it's true what he writes? 430
How horrible! No, no, it's impossible—it can't be true.

NORA: It is true. I've loved you more than all this world.

HELMER: Ah, none of your slippery tricks.

NORA: (*Taking one step toward him.*) Torvald—!

HELMER: What *is* this you've blundered into! 435

NORA: Just let me loose. You're not going to suffer for my sake.
You're not going to take on my guilt.

HELMER: No more playacting. (*Locks the hall door.*) You stay right
here and give me a reckoning. You understand what you've
done? Answer! You understand? 440

NORA: (*Looking squarely at him, her face hardening.*) Yes. I'm
beginning to understand everything now.

HELMER: (*Striding about.*) Oh, what an awful awakening! In
all these eight years—she who was my pride and joy—a
hypocrite, a liar—worse, worse—a criminal! How infinitely 445
disgusting it all is! The shame! (NORA *says nothing and goes on
looking straight at him. He stops in front of her.*) I should have
suspected something of the kind. I should have known. All
your father's flimsy values—Be still! All your father's flimsy
values have come out in you. No religion, no morals, no 450
sense of duty—Oh, how I'm punished for letting him off! I
did it for your sake, and you repay me like this.

NORA: Yes, like this.

HELMER: Now you've wrecked all my happiness—ruined my

455 whole future. Oh, it's awful to think of. I'm in a cheap little
grafter's hands; he can do anything he wants with me, ask for
anything, play with me like a puppet—and I can't breathe a
word. I'll be swept down miserably into the depths on account
of a featherbrained woman.

460 NORA: When I'm gone from this world, you'll be free.
HELMER: Oh, quit posing. Your father had a mess of those
speeches too. What good would that ever do me if you were
gone from this world, as you say? Not the slightest. He can
still make the whole thing known; and if he does, I could be

465 falsely suspected as your accomplice. They might even think
that I was behind it—that I put you up to it. And all that I
can thank you for—you that I've coddled the whole of our
marriage. Can you see now what you've done to me?
NORA: (*Icily calm.*) Yes.

470 HELMER: It's so incredible, I just can't grasp it. But we'll have
to patch up whatever we can. Take off the shawl. I said,
take it off! I've got to appease him somehow or other.
The thing has to be hushed up at any cost. And as for you
and me, it's got to seem like everything between us is just

475 as it was—to the outside world, that is. You'll go right on
living in this house, of course. But you can't be allowed to
bring up the children; I don't dare trust you with them—
Oh, to have to say this to someone I've loved so much,
and that I still—! Well, that's done with. From now on

480 happiness doesn't matter; all that matters is saving the bits
and pieces, the appearance—(*The doorbell rings.* HELMER
starts.) What's that? And so late. Maybe the worst—? You
think he'd—? Hide, Nora! Say you're sick. (NORA *remains
standing motionless.* HELMER *goes and opens the door.*)

485 MAID: (*Half dressed, in the hall.*) A letter for Mrs. Helmer.
HELMER: I'll take it. (*Snatches the letter and shuts the door.*) Yes,
it's from him. You don't get it; I'm reading it myself.
NORA: Then read it.
HELMER: (*By the lamp.*) I hardly dare. We may be ruined, you

490 and I. But—I've got to know. (*Rips open the letter, skims
through a few lines, glances at an enclosure, then cries out joyfully.*) Nora! (NORA *looks inquiringly at him.*) Nora! Wait—
better check it again—Yes, yes, it's true. I'm saved. Nora, I'm
saved!

495 NORA: And I?
HELMER: You too, of course. We're both saved, both of us.
Look. He's sent back your note. He says he's sorry and
ashamed—that a happy development in his life—oh, who
cares what he says! Nora, we're saved! No one can hurt

500 you. Oh, Nora, Nora—but first, this ugliness all has to go.
Let me see—(*Takes a look at the note.*) No, I don't want to
see it; I want the whole thing to fade like a dream. (*Tears
the note and both letters to pieces, throws them into the stove
and watches them burn.*) There—now there's nothing left—He

505 wrote that since Christmas Eve you—Oh, they must have been
three terrible days for you, Nora.
NORA: I fought a hard fight.
HELMER: And suffered pain and saw no escape but—No,
we're not going to dwell on anything unpleasant. We'll

510 just be grateful and keep on repeating: it's over now, it's
over! You hear me, Nora? You don't seem to realize—it's over.
What's it mean—that frozen look? Oh, poor little Nora,
I understand. You can't believe I've forgiven you. But I have,
Nora; I swear I have. I know that what you did, you did out of

515 love for me.
NORA: That's true.

HELMER: You loved me the way a wife ought to love her husband. It's simply the means that you couldn't judge. But
you think I love you any the less for not knowing how to
handle your affairs? No, no—just lean on me; I'll guide 520
you and teach you. I wouldn't be a man if this feminine
helplessness didn't make you twice as attractive to me.
You mustn't mind those sharp words I said—that was all
in the first confusion of thinking my world had collapsed.
I've forgiven you, Nora; I swear I've forgiven you. 525
NORA: My thanks for your forgiveness. (*She goes out through the
door, right.*)
HELMER: No, wait—(*Peers in.*) What are you doing in there?
NORA: (*Inside.*) Getting out of my costume.
HELMER: (*By the open door.*) Yes, do that. Try to calm yourself 530
and collect your thoughts again, my frightened little songbird. You can rest easy now; I've got wide wings to shelter you
with. (*Walking about close by the door.*) How snug
and nice our home is, Nora. You're safe here; I'll keep you
like a hunted dove I've rescued out of a hawk's claws. I'll 535
bring peace to your poor, shuddering heart. Gradually it'll
happen, Nora; you'll see. Tomorrow all this will look different to you; then everything will be as it was. I won't
have to go on repeating I forgive you; you'll feel it for
yourself. How can you imagine I'd ever conceivably want 540
to disown you—or even blame you in any way? Ah, you
don't know a man's heart, Nora. For a man there's something indescribably sweet and satisfying in knowing he's
forgiven his wife—and forgiven her out of a full and open
heart. It's as if she belongs to him in two ways now: in a 545
sense he's given her fresh into the world again, and she's
become his wife and his child as well. From now on that's
what you'll be to me—you little, bewildered, helpless
thing. Don't be afraid of anything, Nora; just open your
heart to me, and I'll be conscience and will to you both— 550
(NORA *enters in her regular clothes.*) What's this? Not in bed?
You've changed your dress?
NORA: Yes, Torvald, I've changed my dress.
HELMER: But why now, so late?
NORA: Tonight I'm not sleeping. 555
HELMER: But Nora dear—
NORA: (*Looking at her watch.*) It's still not so very late. Sit down,
Torvald; we have a lot to talk over. (*She sits at one side of the
table.*)
HELMER: Nora—what is this? That hard expression— 560
NORA: Sit down. This'll take some time. I have a lot to say.
HELMER: (*Sitting at the table directly opposite her.*) You worry me,
Nora. And I don't understand you.
NORA: No, that's exactly it. You don't understand me. And
I've never understood you either—until tonight. No, don't 565
interrupt. You can just listen to what I say. We're closing out
accounts, Torvald.
HELMER: How do you mean that?
NORA: (*After a short pause.*) Doesn't anything strike you about
our sitting here like this? 570
HELMER: What's that?
NORA: We've been married now eight years. Doesn't it occur to
you that this is the first time we two, you and I, man and wife,
have ever talked seriously together?
HELMER: What do you mean—seriously? 575
NORA: In eight whole years—longer even—right from our first
acquaintance, we've never exchanged a serious word on any
serious thing.

HELMER: You mean I should constantly go and involve you in
580   problems you couldn't possibly help me with?
NORA: I'm not talking of problems. I'm saying that we've never
     sat down seriously together and tried to get to the bottom of
     anything.
HELMER: But dearest, what good would that ever do you?
585 NORA: That's the point right there: you've never understood me.
     I've been wronged greatly, Torvald—first by Papa, and then
     by you.
HELMER: What! By us—the two people who've loved you more
     than anyone else?
590 NORA: (*Shaking her head.*) You never loved me. You've thought it
     fun to be in love with me, that's all.
HELMER: Nora, what a thing to say!
NORA: Yes, it's true now, Torvald. When I lived at home with
     Papa, he told me all his opinions, so I had the same ones too;
595   or if they were different I hid them, since he wouldn't have
     cared for that. He used to call me his doll-child, and he played
     with me the way I played with my dolls. Then I came into your
     house—
HELMER: How can you speak of our marriage like that?
600 NORA: (*Unperturbed.*) I mean, then I went from Papa's hands
     into yours. You arranged everything to your own taste,
     and so I got the same taste as you—or I pretended to; I
     can't remember. I guess a little of both, first one, then the
     other. Now when I look back, it seems as if I'd lived here
605   like a beggar—just from hand to mouth. I've lived by doing
     tricks for you, Torvald. But that's the way you wanted it. It's
     a great sin what you and Papa did to me. You're to blame that
     nothing's become of me.
HELMER: Nora, how unfair and ungrateful you are! Haven't you
610   been happy here?
NORA: No, never. I thought so—but I never have.
HELMER: Not—not happy!
NORA: No, only lighthearted. And you've always been so
     kind to me. But our home's been nothing but a playpen.
615   I've been your doll-wife here, just as at home I was Papa's
     doll-child. And in turn the children have been my dolls.
     I thought it was fun when you played with me, just as they
     thought it fun when I played with them. That's been our
     marriage, Torvald.
620 HELMER: There's some truth in what you're saying—under all
     the raving exaggeration. But it'll all be different after this.
     Playtime's over; now for the schooling.
NORA: Whose schooling—mine or the children's?
HELMER: Both yours and the children's, dearest.
625 NORA: Oh, Torvald, you're not the man to teach me to be a good
     wife to you.
HELMER: And you can say that?
NORA: And I—how am I equipped to bring up children?
HELMER: Nora!
630 NORA: Didn't you say a moment ago that that was no job to trust
     me with?
HELMER: In a flare of temper! Why fasten on that?
NORA: Yes, but you were so very right. I'm not up to the job.
     There's another job I have to do first. I have to try to educate
635   myself. You can't help me with that. I've got to do it alone.
     And that's why I'm leaving you now.
HELMER: (*Jumping up.*) What's that?
NORA: I have to stand completely alone, if I'm ever going to
     discover myself and the world out there. So I can't go on
640   living with you.

HELMER: Nora, Nora!
NORA: I want to leave right away. Kristine should put me up for
     the night—
HELMER: You're insane! You've no right! I forbid you!
NORA: From here on, there's no use forbidding me anything. I'll 645
     take with me whatever is mine. I don't want a thing from you,
     either now or later.
HELMER: What kind of madness is this!
NORA: Tomorrow I'm going home—I mean, home where I came
     from. It'll be easier up there to find something to do. 650
HELMER: Oh, you blind, incompetent child!
NORA: I must learn to be competent, Torvald.
HELMER: Abandon your home, your husband, your children! And
     you're not even thinking what people will say.
NORA: I can't be concerned about that. I only know how essential 655
     this is.
HELMER: Oh, it's outrageous. So you'll run out like this on your
     most sacred vows.
NORA: What do you think are my most sacred vows?
HELMER: And I have to tell you that! Aren't they your duties to 660
     your husband and children?
NORA: I have other duties equally sacred.
HELMER: That isn't true. What duties are they?
NORA: Duties to myself.
HELMER: Before all else, you're a wife and a mother. 665
NORA: I don't believe in that anymore. I believe that, before all
     else, I'm a human being, no less than you—or anyway, I ought
     to try to become one. I know the majority thinks you're right,
     Torvald, and plenty of books agree with you, too. But I can't
     go on believing what the majority says, or what's written in 670
     books. I have to think over these things myself and try to
     understand them.
HELMER: Why can't you understand your place in your own
     home? On a point like that, isn't there one everlasting guide
     you can turn to? Where's your religion? 675
NORA: Oh, Torvald, I'm really not sure what religion is.
HELMER: What—?
NORA: I only know what the minister said when I was confirmed.
     He told me religion was this thing and that. When I get clear
     and away by myself, I'll go into that problem too. I'll see if 680
     what the minister said was right, or, in any case, if it's right
     for me.
HELMER: A young woman your age shouldn't talk like that. If
     religion can't move you, I can try to rouse your conscience.
     You do have some moral feeling? Or, tell me—has that 685
     gone too?
NORA: It's not easy to answer that, Torvald. I simply don't know.
     I'm all confused about these things. I just know I see them so
     differently from you. I find out, for one thing, that the law's
     not at all what I'd thought—but I can't get it through my 690
     head that the law is fair. A woman hasn't a right to protect
     her dying father or save her husband's life! I can't believe
     that.
HELMER: You talk like a child. You don't know anything of the
     world you live in. 695
NORA: No, I don't. But now I'll begin to learn for myself. I'll try to
     discover who's right, the world or I.
HELMER: Nora, you're sick; you've got a fever. I almost think
     you're out of your head.
NORA: I've never felt more clearheaded and sure in my life. 700
HELMER: And—clearheaded and sure—you're leaving your
     husband and children?

NORA: Yes.

HELMER: Then there's only one possible reason.

705 NORA: What?

HELMER: You no longer love me.

NORA: No. That's exactly it.

HELMER: Nora! You can't be serious!

NORA: Oh, this is so hard, Torvald—you've been so kind to me

710   always. But I can't help it. I don't love you anymore.

HELMER: (*Struggling for composure.*) Are you also clearheaded
   and sure about that?

NORA: Yes, completely. That's why I can't go on staying here.

HELMER: Can you tell me what I did to lose your love?

715 NORA: Yes, I can tell you. It was this evening when the miraculous
   thing didn't come—then I knew you weren't the man I'd
   imagined.

HELMER: Be more explicit; I don't follow you.

NORA: I've waited now so patiently eight long years—for, my

720   Lord, I know miracles don't come every day. Then this
   crisis broke over me, and such a certainty filled me: *now* the
   miraculous event would occur. While Krogstad's letter was
   lying out there, I never for an instant dreamed that you could
   give in to his terms. I was so utterly sure you'd say to him:

725   go on, tell your tale to the whole wide world. And when he'd
   done that—

HELMER: Yes, what then? When I'd delivered my own wife into
   shame and disgrace—!

NORA: When he'd done that, I was so utterly sure that you'd

730   step forward, take the blame on yourself and say: I am the
   guilty one.

HELMER: Nora—!

NORA: You're thinking I'd never accept such a sacrifice from
   you? No, of course not. But what good would my protests

735   be against you? That was the miracle I was waiting for, in
   terror and hope. And to stave that off, I would have taken
   my life.

HELMER: I'd gladly work for you day and night, Nora—and take
   on pain and deprivation. But there's no one who gives up

740   honor for love.

NORA: Millions of women have done just that.

HELMER: Oh, you think and talk like a silly child.

NORA: Perhaps. But you neither think nor talk like the man I
   could join myself to. When your big fright was over—and

745   it wasn't from any threat against me, only for what might
   damage you—when all the danger was past, for you it was
   just as if nothing had happened. I was exactly the same, your
   little lark, your doll, that you'd have to handle with double
   care now that I'd turned out so brittle and frail. (*Gets up.*)

750   Torvald—in that instant it dawned on me that for eight
   years I've been living here with a stranger, and that I'd even
   conceived three children—oh, I can't stand the thought of it! I
   could tear myself to bits.

HELMER: (*Heavily.*) I see. There's a gulf that's opened between

755   us—that's clear. Oh, but Nora, can't we bridge it somehow?

NORA: The way I am now, I'm no wife for you.

HELMER: I have the strength to make myself over.

NORA: Maybe—if your doll gets taken away.

HELMER: But to part! To part from you! No, Nora, no—I can't
   imagine it.   760

NORA: (*Going out, right.*) All the more reason why it has to be.
   (*She reenters with her coat and a small overnight bag, which
   she puts on a chair by the table.*)

HELMER: Nora, Nora, not now! Wait till tomorrow.

NORA: I can't spend the night in a strange man's room.   765

HELMER: But couldn't we live here like brother and sister—

NORA: You know very well how long that would last. (*Throws her
   shawl about her.*) Good-bye, Torvald. I won't look in on the
   children. I know they're in better hands than mine. The way
   I am now, I'm no use to them.   770

HELMER: But someday, Nora—someday—?

NORA: How can I tell? I haven't the least idea what'll become
   of me.

HELMER: But you're my wife, now and wherever you go.

NORA: Listen, Torvald—I've heard that when a wife deserts her   775
   husband's house just as I'm doing, then the law frees him
   from all responsibility. In any case, I'm freeing you from
   being responsible. Don't feel yourself bound, any more than I
   will. There has to be absolute freedom for us both. Here, take
   your ring back. Give me mine.   780

HELMER: That too?

NORA: That too.

HELMER: There it is.

NORA: Good. Well, now it's all over. I'm putting the keys here.
   The maids know all about keeping up the house—better than   785
   I do. Tomorrow, after I've left town, Kristine will stop by to
   pack up everything that's mine from home. I'd like those
   things shipped up to me.

HELMER: Over! All over! Nora, won't you ever think about me?

NORA: I'm sure I'll think of you often, and about the children and   790
   the house here.

HELMER: May I write you?

NORA: No—never. You're not to do that.

HELMER: Oh, but let me send you—

NORA: Nothing. Nothing.   795

HELMER: Or help you if you need it.

NORA: No. I accept nothing from strangers.

HELMER: Nora—can I never be more than a stranger to you?

NORA: (*Picking up the overnight bag.*) Ah, Torvald—it would take
   the greatest miracle of all—   800

HELMER: Tell me the greatest miracle!

NORA: You and I both would have to transform ourselves to the
   point that—Oh, Torvald, I've stopped believing in miracles.

HELMER: But I'll believe. Tell me! Transform ourselves to the
   point that—?   805

NORA: That our living together could be a true marriage. (*She goes
   out down the hall.*)

HELMER: (*Sinks down on a chair by the door, face buried in his
   hands.*) Nora! Nora! (*Looking about and rising.*) Empty. She's
   gone. (*A sudden hope leaps in him.*) The greatest miracle—?   810

(*From below, the sound of a door slamming shut.*)

Alfred Jarry

Inventive and iconoclastic, Alfred Jarry (1873–1907) mesmerized the Parisian avant-garde of the 1890s. Born in Laval, near Brittany, Jarry was a small, homely, sickly child; at the same time, he seems to have been intellectually ferocious, direct, and charming. Jarry's precocious career occupied a single decade, roughly from his fifteenth to his twenty-fifth year, beginning with the merciless satire he wrote and continued to elaborate during his studies at the *lycée* in Rennes. The school's apparently benighted physics teacher, Professor Hébert, had long been a butt of juvenile joking, both for his apparent stupefaction by the demands of teaching, and by his infirm grasp of physics. Jarry not only baited Hébert in class, but collaborated with two other students—Henri and Charles Morin—on a series of satires on the hopelessly dull teacher. Renaming Hébert as Père Heb, Jarry both circulated the satires and eventually performed the play, under the title *Les Polonais*, using his beloved marionettes.

Père Heb was the foundation of Jarry's most enduring creation, Père Ubu of *Ubu Roi*. Competing the *lycée*, Jarry was accepted at L'Ecole Normale in Paris in 1891. For the next decade, Jarry would be a Paris sensation, flaunting a cape and stovepipe hat that seemed to double his height; living in a flat with a ceiling so low that only he could stand erect in it; making lifelong friendships with literary figures like Alfred Vallette (the editor of the literary journal *Mercure de France*); publishing fiction, poetry, and essays on his faux-philosophy, *pataphysics*; meeting artists like the painter Henri Rousseau. In 1894, Jarry was called for military service, but his comic appearance in uniform and clowning with his rifle were apparently so demoralizing that he was relieved of parade duty; he drank acid in order to get a medical discharge, and eventually received one for his gallstones.

Despite this interruption, and the debilitation he suffered from heavy drinking, Jarry continued to elaborate the figure of Père Heb, writing several texts on this figure before completing the play *Ubu Roi* in 1896, which he published in the journal *Le Livre d'Art*. Almost immediately, Jarry approached Aurelien Lugné-Poe, the director of the independent Théâtre de l'Oeuvre, to produce the play. Hoping to persuade Lugné-Poe that the play could be done within his relatively small budget, Jarry advised using only one actor to play the Polish army, and to eliminate anything resembling a realistic set. When the play opened in December, with the distinguished actor Firmin Gémier in the title role, it was an immediate *succès de scandale*. In the following years, Jarry wrote the novels *Days and Nights* (1897), and *The Exploits and Opinions of Doctor Faustroll* (1898), and other works on his timeless creation, Ubu: an *Almanac of Père Ubu*, and the plays *Ubu Cuckolded* and *Ubu Bound*. Jarry died in penury only a decade after his greatest success.

Ubu Roi

From its opening word, an expansion of the French *merde*—*Merdre! Shittt!*—Jarry's masterwork attacked the conventions and proprieties of the stage and Parisian bourgeois culture. As Jarry declared when he delivered a prologue/lecture to the opening night audience, "The acting, which is about to begin, takes place in Poland, that is to say, Nowhere." Although it centers on the rise of a Macbeth-like murderer to the throne, *Ubu Roi* is animated by a childish, profoundly comic delight in the uncontrollable body. The curtain rose on a set painted by Jarry to resemble a child's view of the landscape, a fit setting for the irrepressible Ubu, a great id of a man. Gemier delivered the play's first word—which could be reported only euphemistically in the press—and the theatre exploded: outraged spectators were then attacked by Jarry's supporters, outraged by their outrage. Although the initial burst lasted only fifteen minutes, as the crapulous Ubu mounts his assault on the throne, waving his toilet-brush scepter, he has frequent recourse to "*merde*," and each reignited the Parisian audience. But although the play traces the rise of Ubu to power, it's hardly a political drama:

This recent production of Jarry's *Ubu Roi* emphasizes the dreamlike, surrealist dimension of the play.

Richard Melloul

instead, Ubu is a grotesque figure of bodily and intellectual rebellion, and to many in the audience the play seemed to herald the opening of a new era in the theatre and in European culture more generally. As the Irish poet W. B. Yeats noted, reflecting on the play's unremitting, rather brutal irony, "After us the Savage God."

Jarry's satire marked a different role for art, not merely contesting the attitudes of contemporary society, but directly, indeed savagely attacking them. In its thoroughgoing rejection of the proprieties of polite society, and in its childish, perhaps nightmarish quality, Jarry's drama has remained an ongoing inspiration: Antonin Artaud named his theatre after Jarry, and more recently the South African team of playwright Jane Taylor, artist William Kentridge, and the Handspring Puppet Company used Jarry's play to explore the consequences of the work of the Truth Commission in post-apartheid South Africa, in *Ubu and the Truth Commission* (1997) (See Unit VII).

Ubu Roi

Alfred Jarry

TRANSLATED BY CYRIL CONNOLLY AND SIMON WATSON TAYLOR

CHARACTERS

PA UBU	STANISLAS LESZCZYNSKI	PEOPLE	THE ENTIRE POLISH ARMY
MA UBU	JOHN SOBIESKI III	MICHAEL FEDOROVITCH	MA UBU'S GUARDS
CAPTAIN MACNURE	NICOLAS RENSKI	NOBLES	A CAPTAIN
KING WENCESLAS	THE TSAR ALEXIS	JUDGES	THE BEAR
QUEEN ROSAMUND	GYRON	COUNSELLORS	THE PHYNANCE CHARGER
BOLESLAS	HEADS	FINANCIERS	THE DEBRAINING MACHINE
LADISLAS } their sons	TAILS } Palcontents	LACKEYS OF THE PHYNANCES	THE CREW
BOGGERLAS	CONSPIRATORS AND	PEASANTS	THE SEA-CAPTAIN
GENERAL LASKI	SOLDIERS	THE ENTIRE RUSSIAN ARMY	

The play was originally presented by Lugné-Poe and the Théâtre de l'Œuvre at the Salle du Nouveau Théâtre on December 10th, 1896. The direction was by Lugné-Poe with décor by Paul Sérusier, masks by Alfred Jarry and music by Claude Terrasse.

The cast included Firmin Gémier as Père Ubu and Louise France as Mère Ubu.

ACT ONE

SCENE ONE

PA UBU, MA UBU.

PA UBU: Pschitt!

MA UBU: Ooh! what a nasty word. Pa Ubu, you're a dirty old old man.

PA UBU: Watch out I don't bash yer nut in, Ma Ubu!

MA UBU: It's not me you should want to do in, Old Ubu. Oh, no!
5   There's someone else for the high jump.

PA UBU: By my green candle, I'm not with you.

MA UBU: How come, Old Ubu, you mean you're content with your lot?

PA UBU: By my green candle, pschitt, Madam. Yes, by God,
10   I'm perfectly satisfied. Who wouldn't be? Captain of the Dragoons, aide de camp to King Wenceslas, decorated with the order of the Red Eagle of Poland, and ex-King of Aragon. You can't go higher than that!

MA UBU: SO what! After having been King of Aragon, you're
15   content to ride in reviews at the head of fifty bumpkins armed with billhooks when you could get your loaf measured for the crown of Poland?

PA UBU: Huh? I don't understand a word you're saying, Mother.

MA UBU: How stupid can you get!

20   PA UBU: By my green candle, King Wenceslas is still alive, isn't he? And even if he does kick the bucket, hasn't he masses of children?

MA UBU: Why shouldn't you finish off the whole bunch and put yourself in their place?

25   PA UBU: Ha! Madam, now you have gone too far, and you shall very shortly be beaten up good and proper.

MA UBU: You poor slob, if I get beaten up who'll patch the seat of your pants?

PA UBU: So what! Haven't I a bum like everyone else?

MA UBU: If I were you, I'd try to get that bum sitting on a throne.   30
You could become enormously rich, eat as many bangers as you liked, and roll through the streets in a fine carriage.

PA UBU: If I were king, I'd get them to make me a great bonnet like the one I used to wear in Aragon, which those lousy Spaniards had the nerve to pinch off me.   35

MA UBU: And you could get yourself an umbrella and a guards officer's greatcoat that would come down to your feet.

PA UBU: It is more than I can resist! Pschittabugger and buggerapschitt, if ever I come across him alone on a dark night, he's for it.   40

MA UBU: Well done, Pa Ubu, now you're talking like a man.

PA UBU: Oh no! Me—a captain of dragoons—brutally murder the King of Poland! I would rather die!

MA UBU (*aside*): Oh, pschitt! (*Aloud.*) So you want to stay poor as a church mouse, Mister Ubu?   45

PA UBU: God's bones, yes, by my green candle, I'd rather be poor as the skinniest mouse than rich as the cruellest cat.

MA UBU: And your bonnet? And your umbrella? And your greatcoat?

PA UBU: And then what, you old cow?

He leaves, banging the door behind him.

MA UBU (*alone*): Pfartt, pschitt, what a stingy bastard, but pfartt,   50
pschitt, I think I've got him shifting all the same. Thanks be to God and myself, in a week, perhaps, I may be Queen of Poland.

SCENE TWO

A room in Pa Ubu's house, where a magnificent collation is set out.

PA UBU, MA UBU.

MA UBU: Well, our guests are pretty late.

PA UBU: Yes, by my green candle, I'm dying of hunger. You're looking exceptionally ugly tonight, Madam, is it because we have company?

MA UBU (*shrugging her shoulders*): Pschitt.   5

PA UBU (*seizing a roast chicken*): I'm quite hungry. I think I'll get my teeth into this bird. Hmm, a chicken, I reckon, and not bad at all.

MA UBU: Stop it, you wretch! What are our guests going to eat?

443

10 PA UBU: There'll still be plenty for them. I shan't touch another thing. Go and look out of the window, Ma Ubu, and see if our guests are arriving.

MA UBU (*going over*): I don't see a soul.

Meanwhile, PA UBU *gets his hands on a fillet of veal.*

MA UBU: Ah, here comes Captain M'Nure and his merry men.
15 Hey, Old Ubu, what are you eating?

PA UBU: Nothing, nothing. Just a spot of veal.

MA UBU: Oh, my veal, my veal! The lout! He's eaten the veal! Help! Help!

PA UBU: By my green candle, I'll gouge your eyes out.

The door opens.

SCENE THREE

PA UBU, MA UBU, CAPTAIN MACNURE *and his* MERRY MEN.

MA UBU: Good day, gentlemen, we have been awaiting your arrival with impatience. Pray be seated.

CAPTAIN MACNURE: Good day, Madam. But where is Mister Ubu?

PA UBU: Here I am, here I am! By my green candle, dammit,
5 I shouldn't have thought I was so easy to miss.

CAPTAIN MACNURE: Good day, Mister Ubu. Sit ye down, my merry men.

They all sit down.

PA UBU: Ouch! A little more and I'd have had stove in my chair.

CAPTAIN MACNURE: Well, Mistress Ubu, what succulent dishes
10 have you prepared for us today?

MA UBU: Here's the menu.

PA UBU: That's right up my street.

MA UBU: Polish broth, spare ribs of Polish bison, veal, chicken and hound pie, parsons' noses from the royal Polish turkeys,
15 charlotte russe . . .

PA UBU: That's enough, I should think. Is there any more?

MA UBU: Ice-pudding, salad, fruit, cheese, boiled beef, Jerusalem fartichokes, cauliflower à la pschitt.

PA UBU: Hey, do you think I'm an oriental potentate, shelling out
20 all that money?

MA UBU: Pay no attention to him. He's off his rocker.

PA UBU: You wait. I shall sharpen my teeth on your shanks.

MA UBU: Just eat up and shut up, Old Ubu! Here, try the Polish broth.

25 PA UBU: Urghh, what muck!

CAPTAIN MACNURE: You're right. It hasn't quite come off.

MA UBU: Ill-mannered louts, what do you want then?

PA UBU (*clapping his brow*): Ah! I've got an idea. Back in a jiffy.

He goes out.

MA UBU: Gentlemen, let's try the veal.
30 CAPTAIN MACNURE: Excellent. What there was of it.

MA UBU: Now for the parsons' noses.

CAPTAIN MACNURE: Absolutely delicious. Hurrah for Ma Ubu!

ALL: Hurrah for Ma Ubu.

PA UBU (*returning*): And soon you'll be yelling hurrah for Old Ubu.

He holds an unmentionable brush in his hand and hurls it at the gathering.

PA UBU: Try a taste of that. (*Several taste and collapse poisoned.*) 35
Now pass me the spare ribs of Polish bison, Mother, and I'll dish them out.

MA UBU: Here they are.

PA UBU: Get out everybody! I have something to say to you, Captain M'Nure. 40

THE REST: But we haven't had our dinner!

PA UBU: Not had dinner? Get out, I tell you. Not you, M'Nure. (*Nobody budges.*) You're still here? By my green candle, I'll do you all in with bison ribs.

He begins to throw them.

ALL: Ooh! Ow! Help, rescue! Let's stick up for ourselves! Curses! 45
He's done for me!

PA UBU: Pschitt, pschitt and pschitt again. Get out, all of you. Do I make myself plain?

ALL: Every man for himself! Rotten old Ubu! Mean, double-crossing skunk! 50

PA UBU: Ah, they've gone. Now I can relax again, but I've had a lousy meal. Come, M'Nure.

They leave with MA UBU.

SCENE FOUR

PA UBU, MA UBU, CAPTAIN MACNURE.

PA UBU: Well, captain, how did you enjoy your dinner?

CAPTAIN MACNURE: Very much, Sir, except for the pschitt.

PA UBU: Oh, I didn't think the pschitt was too bad.

MA UBU: A little of what you fancy, they say.

PA UBU: Captain M'Nure, I've decided to create you Duke of 5
Lithuania.

CAPTAIN MACNURE: But I thought you were completely broke, Mister Ubu?

PA UBU: In a day or two, with your help, I shall be King of Poland.

CAPTAIN MACNURE: You will assassinate Wenceslas? 10

PA UBU: The bugger's no fool. He's guessed it.

CAPTAIN MACNURE: If it's a question of killing Wenceslas, I'm with you. I am his deadly enemy, and I can answer for my men.

PA UBU (*throwing himself upon him to embrace him*): Oh, M'Nure, 15
I love you dearly for that.

CAPTAIN MACNURE: Pooh, how you stink, man! Don't you ever wash?

PA UBU: Occasionally.

MA UBU: Never! 20

PA UBU: I'm going to tread on your toes.

MA UBU: Fat lump of pschitt!

PA UBU: Right, M'Nure, that's all for now. But by my green candle, I swear on the head of Madam Ubu to make you Duke of Lithuania. 25

MA UBU: But . . .

PA UBU: Silence, my angel . . .

They all go out.

SCENE FIVE

PA UBU, MA UBU, A MESSENGER.

PA UBU: What do you want, Sir? Piss off. You make me sick and tired.

MESSENGER: Sir, you are summoned immediately to the royal presence.

He goes out.

5 PA UBU: Oh pschitt! God's whiskers! By my green candle, all is discovered. I'll be beheaded. Woe is me!

MA UBU: What a feeble creature! And time's getting short.

PA UBU: Ah! I've got an idea. I'll say it was Ma Ubu and M'Nure.

MA UBU: You big P.U., you just try . . .

10 PA UBU: I'd better get out while the going's good.

He goes out.

MA UBU (*running after him*): Oh! Pa Ubu, Pa Ubu, I'll give you some fine fat sausages.

She goes out.

PA UBU (*offstage*): Oh pschitt! You're a fine fat sausage yourself.

SCENE SIX

The King's Palace.

KING WENCESLAS, *surrounded by his* OFFICERS, MACNURE, *the king's* SONS, BOLESLAS, LADISLAS *and* BOGGERLAS.

PA UBU (*entering*): Oh! you know, it wasn't me, it was the old woman and M'Nure.

THE KING: What's up with you, Old Ubu?

CAPTAIN MACNURE: He's tight.

5 THE KING: Like me this morning. I was tight as two Poles.

PA UBU: Yes, I'm tight. It's because I've drunk too much champagne.

THE KING: Master Ubu, I have resolved to reward you for your many services as Captain of Dragoons, and I therefore

10 proclaim you Count of Sandomir.

PA UBU: O, Sire! I am speechless with gratitude.

THE KING: Tut, think nothing of it, Master Ubu. But be sure to be present tomorrow morning at our Grand Review.

PA UBU: I shall be there, Sire. Meanwhile, pray deign to accept

15 this magnificently decorated kazoo.

He presents THE KING *with a kazoo.*

THE KING: You don't expect me to start playing a kazoo at my age, surely? Well, I'll give it to young Boggerlas.

BOGGERLAS: What an old fool he is, this Ubu creature.

PA UBU: And now I shall fuck off. (*He falls, as he turns round.*)

20 Oh! ow! Help, rescue! By my green candle, I've ruptured my gut and smashed my rattle-trap.

THE KING (*helping him up*): Old Ubu, are you hurt?

PA UBU: Yes, badly, and I'm certainly going to croak. What will happen to Madam Ubu?

25 THE KING: We shall provide for her upkeep.

PA UBU: You are most kind and gracious, Sire, (*Aside, as he leaves.*) But you'll be liquidated just the same, King Wenceslas.

SCENE SEVEN

Ubu's House.

GYRON, HEADS, TAILS, PA UBU, MA UBU, CONSPIRATORS *and* SOLDIERS, CAPTAIN MACNURE.

PA UBU: Well, my good friends, it's high time we planned our little conspiracy. Let each give his counsel. With your permission, we will begin with mine.

CAPTAIN MACNURE: Speak, Mister Ubu.

5 PA UBU: Very good, my friends. I'm of the opinion that we should simply poison the King by stuffing his lunch with arsenic. When he starts the browsing and scoffing, he'll drop dead, and I shall be king.

ALL: Oo, you wicked old thing, you!

10 PA UBU: What, you don't like that idea? All right then, let's hear from M'Nure.

CAPTAIN MACNURE: My suggestion is that I fetch him a good wallop with my sword and cleave him from top to toe.

ALL: Ah yes! that's noble and gallant.

15 PA UBU: But supposing he gives you a few kicks? I've just remembered: for his Grand Reviews, he wears iron boots that are jolly painful. If I had half a chance, I'd snitch on the lot of you. That way, I'd be rid of this whole beastly business, and probably pick up a reward into the bargain.

20 MA UBU: Oh, the traitor, the coward, the rotten, mean skunk!

ALL: Down with Old Ubu!

PA UBU: Hey, gentlemen, shut your traps unless you want me to turn you all in. Well, all right, then, I'll take all the risks on your behalf. So, M'Nure, it's agreed that your job is to split the

25 king down the middle.

CAPTAIN MACNURE: Wouldn't it be better for us all to jump on him at once, shouting and yelling? That way, we'd have a better chance of winning over the troops.

PA UBU: Look, I'll tell you what. I shall try to step on his toe, he'll

30 kick out at me, I'll say 'PSCHITT' to him, and that will be the signal for you all to hurl yourselves on him.

MA UBU: Yes, and the moment he's dead, you'll take his crown and sceptre.

CAPTAIN MACNURE: And I and my men will go in pursuit of the

35 royal family.

PA UBU: Yes, and keep a special look-out for young Boggerlas.

They go out.

PA UBU *runs after them and makes them come back.*

Gentlemen, we have forgotten an indispensable ceremony. We must take an oath to quit ourselves like men.

CAPTAIN MACNURE: How can we? We haven't got a priest.

PA UBU: My old woman will act as priest.

40 ALL: All right, so be it.

PA UBU: And so you all swear to kill the King good and proper?

ALL: We swear it. Long live Old Ubu!

ACT TWO

SCENE ONE

The King's Palace.

WENCESLAS, QUEEN ROSAMUND, BOLESLAS, LADISLAS *and* BOGGERLAS.

THE KING: Prince Boggerlas, you were extremely cheeky this morning to Master Ubu, Knight of my Orders and Count of Sandomir. Therefore I forbid you to appear at our Grand Review.

THE QUEEN: But, Wenceslas, you will need every single member 5 of your family around you to protect you vigilantly today.

THE KING: Madam, I never take back what I've said. You bore me with your idle chatter.

BOGGERLAS: My royal father, I submit.

10 THE QUEEN: Really, Sire, are you quite determined to attend this Parade?

THE KING: Pray, Madam, why not?

THE QUEEN: I'll tell you once more. I saw him in a dream, smiting you with massed weapons and throwing you into the Vistula,

15 and an eagle like that which figures in the Arms of Poland placing the crown on his head.

THE KING: Whose head?

THE QUEEN: Old Ubu's.

THE KING: Ridiculous! The Lord Ubu is a most worthy gentleman

20 who would let himself be dragged apart by wild horses rather than betray my interests.

THE QUEEN *and* BOGGERLAS (*together*): How wrong you are!

THE KING: Silence, young rascal. And as for you, Madam, to show you what complete confidence I have in Master Ubu,

25 I shall attend the Grand Review as I am, without sword and breastplate.

THE QUEEN: What fatal rashness! I shall never see you again alive.

THE KING: Come, Ladislas. Come, Boleslas.

They go out. THE QUEEN *and* BOGGERLAS *go to the window.*

THE QUEEN *and* BOGGERLAS (*together*): May God and the great

30 Saint Nicholas protect you!

THE QUEEN: Boggerlas, accompany me to the chapel to pray for your father and your brothers.

SCENE TWO

The Parade Ground.

THE POLISH ARMY, THE KING, BOLESLAS, LADISLAS, PA UBU, CAPTAIN MACNURE *and his* MERRY MEN, GYRON, HEADS, TAILS.

THE KING: Noble Master Ubu, enter the royal enclosure with your followers, and we will review the march past together.

PA UBU (*to his* HEN CHMEN): Look sharp, you clots. (*To* THE KING.) Coming, Sire, coming.

UBU'S MEN *surround* THE KING.

5 THE KING: Ah, there's my regiment of Danziger Horseguards. What a magnificent spectacle!

PA UBU: You think so? They look to me like something the cat brought in. Look at that one! (*Pointing to a soldier.*) How many days since you last had a shave, you lousy scum?

10 THE KING: But this soldier is very well turned out. What on earth is the matter with you, Old Ubu?

PA UBU: This! (*He stamps on* THE KING's *foot.*)

THE KING: Treason!

PA UBU: PSCHITT. Rally round me, my fine fellows.

15 CAPTAIN MACNURE: Up guards and at him! Hurrah!

All strike THE KING. *A* PALCONTENT *explodes.*

THE KING: Help, help! Holy Virgin, I'm dying.

BOLESLAS (*to* LADISLAS): What's going on? Have at them!

PA UBU: Ha! I have the crown. Now for the others.

CAPTAIN MACNURE: Death to the traitors!

The King's SONS *flee. All pursue them.*

SCENE THREE

THE QUEEN *and* BOGGERLAS.

THE QUEEN: At last I begin to feel reassured.

BOGGERLAS: You have nothing to be afraid of. (*A fearful din is heard outside.*) Oh no! What do I see? My two brothers pursued by Old Ubu and his men.

THE QUEEN: Oh God! Holy Virgin, they are losing ground. 5

BOGGERLAS: The whole army is following Ubu. The King is no longer there. It's horrible. Help, help!

THE QUEEN: Now Boleslas is dead! Struck by a fatal bullet.

BOGGERLAS: Ho there! (LADISLAS *turns round.*) Defend yourself. Bravo, Ladislas! 10

THE QUEEN: Oh! he's surrounded.

BOGGERLAS: He's done for. M'Nure has just split him in two like a sausage.

THE QUEEN: Help, help! Those maniacs have forced their way into the palace. They're coming up the stairs. 15

The din grows louder.

THE QUEEN
BOGGERLAS } (*on their knees*): May God protect us!

BOGGERLAS: Oh, that vile Ubu, wretch, rascal, I'd just like to get hold of him . . .

SCENE FOUR

The same. The door is broken in. PA UBU *enters, followed by his mob of* LUNATICS.

PA UBU: Oh, you would, would you, Boggerlas? And what, pray, would you do to me?

BOGGERLAS: By God's will, I shall defend my mother to the death. The first man to take a step forward is as good as dead.

PA UBU: M'Nure, I'm scared, Get me out of here. 5

A SOLDIER (*advances*): Boggerlas, surrender.

BOGGERLAS: Here's one for you, you dog! (*He splits his skull*).

THE QUEEN: That's the spirit, Boggerlas, keep it up!

SEVERAL (*advancing*): Boggerlas, we promise to save your life.

BOGGERLAS: Blackguards, wine-bladders, mercenary scum. 10

He flourishes his sword and massacres the lot of them.

PA UBU: Bother! But I'll still win in the end.

BOGGERLAS: Mother, escape by the secret staircase.

THE QUEEN: And you, my son, what about you?

BOGGERLAS: I'll follow you.

PA UBU: Quick. Capture the Queen. Drat, she's got away. As for 15
you, you little worm! . . . (*He advances on* BOGGERLAS.)

BOGGERLAS: Ah! by God's will, here's my vengeance!

He rips open PA UBU's *boodle with a terrible sword-thrust.*

Mother, I follow you!

He disappears by the secret staircase.

SCENE FIVE

A cavern in the mountains.

BOGGERLAS *enters, followed by* QUEEN ROSAMUND.

BOGGERLAS: Here we shall be safe.

THE QUEEN: Oh, I do hope so. Boggerlas, support me!

She falls on the snow.

BOGGERLAS: What ails you, mother dear?

THE QUEEN: I am sick unto death, Boggerlas, and fear I have only
5 a few hours to live.

BOGGERLAS: What! have you caught a chill?

THE QUEEN: How do you think I can stand up to so many
misfortunes? The King murdered, our family destroyed, and
you, a scion of the noblest race that ever carried a sword,
10 forced to flee to the mountains like a common smuggler?

BOGGERLAS: And by whom, great God, by whom? A vulgar
wretch like Ubu, a common little adventurer, a mister nobody
from nowhere, fat toad, stinking tramp! And when I think
that my father decorated him and made him a count,
15 and the very next day that villain shamelessly laid violent
hands on him.

THE QUEEN: O Boggerlas! When I think how happy we all were
before that wicked Old Ubu arrived on the scene. But now,
alas, everything is changed.

20 BOGGERLAS: What can we do, but wait in hope and never
renounce our rights?

THE QUEEN: I long for your just restitution, my dear child, but I
fear that I myself shall never see that happy day.

BOGGERLAS: Here, what's come over you? She grows pale, she
25 swoons! Help, help! But we are alone in the wilderness! My
God, her heart has stopped beating. She is dead. Can it be
possible? Yet another victim of the fiendish Ubu!

He buries his face in his hands and weeps.

Ah God, how tragic to find oneself all alone at the age of fourteen with a terrible vengeance to pursue!

He falls prey to the most violent despair.
Meanwhile, the SOULS *of* WENCESLAS, BOLESLAS, LADISLAS *and*
ROSAMUND *enter the cavern. The oldest of them approaches*
BOGGERLAS *and rouses him gently from his stupor.*

30 BOGGERLAS: Ah! What do I see? My whole family, my
ancestors . . . What miracle is this?

THE SHADE: Learn, Boggerlas, that during my lifetime I was Lord
Mathias of Königsberg, the first king—and founder—of our
House. I leave our vengeance in your hands. (*He presents*
35 *him with an enormous sword.*) And may this sword which I
present to you know no rest until it shall have dealt death to
the usurper.

All vanish, and BOGGERLAS *remains alone in an attitude of*
ecstasy.

SCENE SIX

The King's Palace.

PA UBU, MA UBU, CAPTAIN MACNURE.

PA UBU: No! nothing doing, I say! Do you want to ruin me just for
these buffoons?

CAPTAIN MACNURE: But look here, Old Ubu, don't you see that
your people are expecting gifts to celebrate your glorious
5 coronation?

MA UBU: If you don't give them a great feast and plenty of gold,
you'll be overthrown in a couple of hours.

PA UBU: A feast, yes, but money, never! Slaughter three old nags,
that's quite good enough for such scum.

MA UBU: Scum yourself! How did such a crummy creature as you   10
ever get slapped together?

PA UBU: Do I have to repeat myself? I intend to get rich, I won't
fork out a penny.

MA UBU: Don't forget you hold in your hands all the treasure of
Poland!   15

CAPTAIN MACNURE: Yes, I know where there's a vast hoard
hidden in the chapel; let's distribute that.

PA UBU: Just you try that on, you wretch.

CAPTAIN MACNURE: Listen, Old Ubu, if you don't distribute some
money, no one will want to pay their taxes.   20

PA UBU: Is that really true?

MA UBU: Yes, yes!

PA UBU: Oh, in that case, I agree to everything. Bring up two or
three million gold pieces, roast a hundred and fifty oxen and
the same number of sheep, and see that there's plenty left over   25
for me.

They go out.

SCENE SEVEN

The Courtyard of the Palace, full of People.

PA UBU, *crowned,* MA UBU, CAPTAIN MACNURE, LACKEYS *loaded*
with dishes of roast meat.

PEOPLE: There's the King! Long live the King! Hurrah!

PA UBU (*throwing gold*): Here, you, catch. Don't thank me. All
this throwing gold away is no pleasure to me at all, but my old
woman insisted. At least, promise you'll pay your taxes now.

ALL: Yes, yes!   5

CAPTAIN MACNURE: Just look, Madam Ubu, how they are fighting
over the gold. What a battle!

MA UBU: Perfectly dreadful! Ugh! there's one who's had his skull
bashed in.

PA UBU: What a beautiful sight! Bring up more chests of gold.   10

CAPTAIN MACNURE: How about organizing a race?

PA UBU: Yes, that's an idea. (*To the* PEOPLE.) My friends, you see
this chest full of gold? It contains three hundred thousand
rose-nobles in gold, all genuine Polish coin of the realm.
Those who want to run in the race go to the end of the   15
courtyard. You start running when I wave my handkerchief,
and the winner gets the chest. And for the losers, there's this
second chest of gold to share out as a booby prize.

ALL: Yes! Long live Old Ubu! What a decent King! We never had
fun like this during the reign of Wenceslas.   20

PA UBU (*to* MA UBU, *joyfully*): Just listen to them!

All the PEOPLE *line up at the far end of the courtyard.*

PA UBU: One, two, three! Are you ready?

ALL: Yes! Yes!

PA UBU: Go!

They start running. Tripping, tumbling and falling over each other.
Cries and tumult.

CAPTAIN MACNURE: They're coming! They're coming!   25

PA UBU: Ha! The one in front is losing ground.

MA UBU: No, he's ahead again.

CAPTAIN MACNURE: Oh! he's losing, he's losing! All over! It's the other one.

The one who had been second finishes first.

30 ALL: Long live Michael Federovitch! Long live Michael Federovitch!

MICHAEL FEDEROVITCH: Sire, I really don't know how to thank Your Majesty . . .

PA UBU: Oh, my dear friend, it's nothing. Take that chest home
35 with you, Michael. And the rest of you share the other chest: each take a gold piece until there are none left.

ALL: Long live Michael Federovitch! Long live Old Ubu!

PA UBU: All of you, my friends, come and dine with me. The gates of my palace are open to you today, please honour me with
40 your presence at table.

PEOPLE: In we go! In we go! Long live Old Ubu! The noblest of all monarchs!

They enter the Palace. The noise of the orgy, which lasts till the following day, can be heard. The curtain falls.

ACT THREE

SCENE ONE

The Palace.

PA UBU, MA UBU.

PA UBU: By my green candle, behold me, monarch of this fair land. I've already got the gut-ache from overeating, and soon they are going to bring in my great bonnet.

MA UBU: What's it made of, my beloved lord and master? Because,
5 even though we are now King and Queen, we've still got to be economical.

PA UBU: Madam my female, it's of sheepskin, with a clasp and tie-strings of doghide.

MA UBU: That sounds pretty good, but royalty's even better.
10 PA UBU: Yes, you were right as usual, Ma Ubu.

MA UBU: We owe a great debt of gratitude to the Duke of Lithuania.

PA UBU: Who's that?

MA UBU: Why, Captain M'Nure.
15 PA UBU: For heaven's sake, woman, don't even mention that slob to me. Now that I don't need him any more, he can whistle for his dukedom, because he certainly won't get it.

MA UBU: You're making a big mistake, Old Ubu. He'll turn against you.
20 PA UBU: I should worry! As far as I'm concerned, he and Boggerlas can go jump in a lake.

MA UBU: And do you think you've heard the last of Boggerlas?

PA UBU: Sword of phynance, obviously! What harm do you think he can do me, that little fourteen-year-old squirt?
25 MA UBU: Just you mark my words, Pa Ubu. You should try to win over Boggerlas to you by your generosity.

PA UBU: More money to dish out? Not on your life! You've already made me pour at least two millions down the drain.

MA UBU: Have it your own way, Old Ubu. But I warn you, he'll
30 settle your hash.

PA UBU: Then you'll find yourself in the same stewpot with me.

MA UBU: For the last time, I warn you. Young Boggerlas may very well carry the day. After all, he has justice on his side.

PA UBU: Oh, tripe! Isn't injustice just as good as justice? Ah! you're taking the piss out of me, Madam, I'm going to chop you into 35 tiny pieces.

MA UBU *flees for her life, pursued by* PA UBU.

SCENE TWO

The Great Hall of the Palace.

PA UBU, MA UBU, OFFICERS *and* SOLDIERS; GYRON, HEADS, TAILS, NOBLES *in chains,* FINANCIERS, JUDGES, REGISTRARS.

PA UBU: Bring out the chest for Nobles, and the boat-hook for Nobles, and the slasher for Nobles and the account book for Nobles, and then—bring in the Nobles.

The NOBLES *are brutally shoved in.*

MA UBU: For pity's sake restrain yourself, Old Ubu.

PA UBU: My lords, I have the honour to inform you that as a 5 gesture to the economic welfare of my kingdom, I have resolved to liquidate the entire nobility and confiscate their goods.

NOBLES: Horror of horrors! Soldiers and citizens, defend us.

PA UBU: Bring up the first Noble and pass me the boat-hook. 10 Those who are condemned to death, I shall push through this trap door. They wil fall down into the bleed-pig chambers, and will then proceed to the cash-room where they will be debrained. (*To the* NOBLE.) What's your name, you slob?

NOBLE: Count of Vitebsk. 15

PA UBU: What's your income?

NOBLE: Three million rix-dollars.

PA UBU: Guilty. (*He grabs him with the hook and pushes him down the hole.*)

MA UBU: What base brutality! 20

PA UBU: You, there, what's your name? (*The* NOBLE *doesn't answer.*) Go on—answer, you slob.

NOBLE: Grand Duke of Posen.

PA UBU: Excellent! Excellent! I couldn't ask for a better. Down the hatch. Next one. What's your name, ugly mug? 25

NOBLE: Duke of Courland, and of the cities of Riga, Revel and Mitau.

PA UBU: Very good indeed. Sure that's the lot?

NOBLE: That's all.

PA UBU: Down the hatch, then. Number four, what's your name? 30

NOBLE: Prince of Podolia.

PA UBU: Income?

NOBLE: I'm bankrupt.

PA UBU: Take that for disrespect. (*Hits him with the hook.*) Now get down that hatch. Your name, number five? 35

NOBLE: Margrave of Thorn, Count Palatine of Polock.

PA UBU: That's not much. Is that all you are?

NOBLE: It's been good enough for me.

PA UBU: Well, it's better than nothing. Down the hatch. What's eating you, Ma Ubu? 40

MA UBU: You're too bloodthirsty, Pa Ubu.

PA UBU: Bah! I'm getting rich. Now I'll have them read the list of what *I've* got. Registrar, read *my* list of *my* titles and possessions.

REGISTRAR: Count of Sandomir. 45

PA UBU: Begin with the princedoms, stupid bugger!

REGISTRAR: Princedom of Podolia, Grand Duchy of Posen,
Duchy of Courland, County of Sandomir, County of Vitebsk,
Palatinate of Polock, Margravate of Thorn
50 PA UBU: Well, go on.
REGISTRAR: That's the lot.
PA UBU: What do you mean, that's the lot! Oh well, then, forward
all the Nobles and, since I don't propose to stop getting richer,
I shall execute them all and confiscate their revenues. Come
55 on, down the hatch with the whole lot. (*They are stuffed down
the hatch.*) Hurry up, faster, faster, I'm going to make some
laws next.
SEVERAL: That'll be worth watching.
PA UBU: First of all, I shall reform the code of justice, then we will
60 proceed to financial matters.
SEVERAL JUDGES: We are strongly opposed to any change.
PA UBU: Pschitt! Firstly, judges will no longer receive a salary.
JUDGES: And what shall we live on? We're all poor men.
PA UBU: You can keep the fines you impose and the possessions
65 of those you condemn to death.
FIRST JUDGE: It's unthinkable.
SECOND JUDGE: Infamous.
THIRD JUDGE: Scandalous.
FOURTH JUDGE: Contemptible.
70 ALL: We refuse to judge under such conditions.
PA UBU: Down the hatch with the judges. (*They struggle in vain.*)
MA UBU: Oh, what have you done, Pa Ubu? Who will administer
justice now?
PA UBU: Why, I will. You'll see how well things will go.
75 MA UBU: Yes, it will be a right old mess.
PA UBU: Aw, shut your gob, clownish female. Gentlemen, we will
proceed to financial matters.
FINANCIERS: There's no need to change anything.
PA UBU: How come? I wish to change everything, I do. To begin
80 with, I intend to pocket half the tax receipts.
FINANCIERS: What cheek!
PA UBU: Gentlemen, we shall establish a tax of ten percent on all
property, another on industry, and a third of fifteen francs a
head on all marriages and funerals.
85 FIRST FINANCIER: But that's ridiculous, Pa Ubu.
SECOND FINANCIER: Quite absurd.
THIRD FINANCIER: Doesn't make sense.
PA UBU: You're making fun of me? Down the hatch, all of you.
(*The* FINANCIERS *are shoved in.*)
90 MA UBU: Come, come, Lord Ubu, kings aren't supposed to behave
like that. You're butchering the whole world.
PA UBU: So pschitt!
MA UBU: No more justice, no financial system!
PA UBU: Fear nothing, my sweet child, I'll go from village to
95 village myself and collect the taxes.

SCENE THREE

A Peasant's House in the Environs of Warsaw.

Several PEASANTS *are assembled.*

A PEASANT (*entering*): Hey! did you hear the news? The King is
dead, and all the nobles as well; young Boggerlas has fled to
the mountains with his mother. What's more, Pa Ubu has
seized the throne.
5 ANOTHER: Yes, and here's something else. I've just come from
Cracow, where I saw them carting off the bodies of more than
three hundred nobles and five hundred magistrates that he's

had slaughtered, and it seems they're going to double the taxes
and that Pa Ubu is going to make the rounds in person to
collect them. 10
ALL: Great God! What will become of us? Pa Ubu is a foul beast
and they say that his whole family is equally repulsive.
A PEASANT: Hark! It sounds like someone's knocking at the door.
A VOICE (*off*): Hornstrumpot! Open up, pschitt, in the names of
St John, St Peter and St Nicolas! Open up, by my cash-sword 15
and my cash-horn, I've come to collect the taxes!

The door is smashed in. UBU *enters, followed by an army of money-grubbers.*

SCENE FOUR

PA UBU: Which of you is the oldest? (*A* PEASANT *steps forward.*)
What's your name?
PEASANT: Stanislas Leczinski.
PA UBU: Well then, hornstrumpot, listen carefully, or these
gentlemen will extrude your nearoles. Hey, listen, will you! 5
STANISLAS: But Your Excellency hasn't said anything yet.
PA UBU: What! I've been talking for an hour. Do you think I came
here simply to amuse myself with the echo of my own voice?
STANISLAS: No thought could be farther from my mind, Sire.
PA UBU: All right, then. I've come to tell you, order you, and 10
inform you that you are to produce and display your ready
cash immediately, or you'll be massacred. Come on in,
my lords of phynance, you sons of whores, wheel in the
phynancial wheelbarrow.

The wheelbarrow is wheeled in.

STANISLAS: Sire, we are down on the register for only one 15
hundred and fifty-two rix-dollars, which we've already paid
over six weeks ago come Michaelmas.
PA UBU: That may well be so, but I've changed the government
and I've had it announced in the official gazette that all the
present taxes have to be paid twice over, and all those I may 20
think up later on will have to be paid three times over. With
this system, I'll soon make a fortune: then I'll kill everyone in
the world, and go away.
PEASANTS: Mercy, Lord Ubu, have pity on us. We are poor, simple
people. 25
PA UBU: I couldn't care less. Pay up.
PEASANTS: But we can't, we've already paid.
PA UBU: Fork out! Or I'll give you the works good and
proper: torture, twisting of the neck, and decapitation.
Hornstrumpot, am I or am I not your King? 30
ALL: Ho, in that case, to arms, fellows! Long live Boggerlas, by the
grace of God King of Poland and Lithuania!
PA UBU: Advance, gentlemen of the Phynances, do your duty.

*A fight takes place. The house is razed to the ground, and only
old* STANISLAS *escapes and flees alone across the plain.* UBU *stays
behind to scoop up the cash.*

SCENE FIVE

A casemate in the fortifications of Thorn. MACNURE *in chains,* PA UBU.

PA UBU: Well, citizen, you're in a fine pickle, aren't you? You
wanted me to pay you what I owed you, and when I refused to
you rebelled and plotted against me, and where did that land

5 you? In jug! Hornboodle, the clever trick I played on you was
so mean it should be right up your street.
MACNURE: Take care, treacherous Old Ubu. In the five days
you've been King you've committed more crimes and murders
than it would take to damn all the saints in Paradise. The
blood of the King and the Nobles cries for vengeance, and
10 those cries will be heard.
PA UBU: Ha, my fine friend, you've got a glib tongue, all right,
and I don't doubt that if you should escape you might make
things difficult for me. But, to the best of my knowledge, the
casemates of Thorn have never released from their clutches
15 any of the fine fellows entrusted to their tender care. So, good
night to you, and sleep tight if you can, though I should warn
you that the rats here go through a very pretty routine at night.

He goes out. The TURNKEYS *arrive and lock and bolt all the doors.*

SCENE SIX

The Palace in Moscow.

THE TSAR ALEXIS *and his court,* MACNURE.

ALEXIS: So it was you, base soldier of fortune, who took part in
the assassination of our cousin Wenceslas?
MACNURE: Sire, grant me your royal pardon. I was dragged into
the plot by Old Ubu, despite myself.
5 ALEXIS: Oh, what a bare-faced liar! Well, what do you want?
MACNURE: Old Ubu accused me falsely of conspiracy and had me
thrown in gaol. I managed to escape and have been spurring
my horse for five days and nights across the steppes to come
and plead for your gracious mercy.
10 ALEXIS: What can you show me as practical proof of your loyalty?
MACNURE: The sword I wielded as a soldier of fortune, and a
detailed map of the fortified city of Thorn.
ALEXIS: I accept the sword as a symbol of your submission, but by
St George, burn the map. I don't intend to achieve my victory
through treachery.
15 MACNURE: One of the sons of Wenceslas, young Boggerlas, is still
alive. I would do anything in my power to help restore him to
the throne.
ALEXIS: What was your rank in the Polish army?
20 MACNURE: I commanded the fifth regiment of Vilna dragoons
and a company of mercenaries in the service of Captain Ubu.
ALEXIS: Good. I appoint you second lieutenant in the tenth
Cossack regiment, and woe betide you if you betray me. If you
fight well, you shall be rewarded.
25 MACNURE: Courage I have in plenty, Sire.
ALEXIS: Good. Remove yourself from my presence.

He leaves.

SCENE SEVEN

Ubu's council chamber.

PA UBU, MA UBU, PHYNANCIAL COUNSELLORS.

PA UBU: Gentlemen, I declare this meeting open. Try to keep your
ears open and your mouths shut. First, we shall deal with
finance, and then we shall discuss a little system I've thought
up for bringing fine weather and keeping rain away.
5 A COUNSELLOR: Splendid, Mister Ubu, Sir.
MA UBU: What a numbskull.

PA UBU: Madam of my pschitt, look out, I'm not going to
stand any more of your nonsense. As I was about to say to
you, gentlemen, our finances are in a fairly good state. A
considerable number of our hirelings clutching well-filled 10
stockings prowl the streets every morning and the sons of
whores are doing fine. In all directions there is a vista of
burning houses and the sight of our peoples groaning under
the weight of our phynance.
SAME COUNSELLOR: And how are the new taxes going, Mister 15
Ubu, sir?
MA UBU: Not at all well. The tax on marriages has only produced
eleven pence so far, even though Mister Ubu's been chasing
people all over the place to force them to marry.
PA UBU: Sword of phynance, horn of my strumpot, madam 20
financieress, I have nearoles to speak with and you have a
mouth to listen to me with. (*Bursts of laughter.*) No, no, that's
not what I meant to say! You're always getting me mixed up,
yes, it's your fault I'm so stupid! But, by the horn of Ubu! ...
(*A* MESSENGER *enters.*) Now what does this fellow want? Get 25
out, oaf, before I black both your eyes, cut your head off and
make corkscrews out of your legs.
MA UBU: He's gone already, but he's left a letter.
PA UBU: Read it. I don't know, I'm either going out of my mind
or I've forgotten how to read. Hurry up, clownish female, it's 30
probably from M'Nure.
MA UBU: Exactly. He says that the Tsar has welcomed him most
graciously, that he's going to invade your Territories to restore
Boggerlas to the throne and that you'll certainly end up
swinging at the end of a rope. 35
PA UBU: Hooh! Hah! I'm scared! Ooh, I'm frightened. I'm at
death's door. Poor wretch that I am. Ye gods, what's to
become of me? This nasty man is going to kill me. St Anthony
and all the Saints, protect me. I'll shell out bags of phynance
and even burn candles to you. Lord God, what's to become of 40
me? (*He weeps and sobs.*)
MA UBU: There's only one course to adopt, Pa Ubu.
PA UBU: What's that, my love?
MA UBU: War!!
ALL: May God defend the right! Well and nobly spoken! 45
PA UBU: Oh yes, and I'll get knocked about all over again.
FIRST COUNSELLOR: Let us get the army to battle stations with all
speed.
SECOND: And requisition the supplies.
THIRD: Mobilise the artillery, man the fortresses. 50
FOURTH: And set aside enough money to pay the troops.
PA UBU: Ah, not likely! I'm going to do you in, you. I'm not giving
any money away. What an idea! I used to be paid to make war
and now I have to do it at my own expense. No, by my green
candle, let's have a war since you're all so steamed up about it, 55
but let's not spend a single sou.
ALL: Long live war, three cheers for the war.

SCENE EIGHT

The Camp outside Warsaw.

[*On the right, a mill with a practicable window. On the left, rocks.
Backdrop showing the ocean.
Enter the* POLISH ARMY, *with* GENERAL LASKI *at their head, sing-
ing a marching song:*

My uniform has buttons one, thunder a gun,
My uniform has buttons two, first of the few,

Buttons one, two, three four,
Gone to the War!
5 Five, six, seven, eight,
Buttons are great,
Nine, ten and eleven,
Buttons are heaven,
Twelve, thirteen, fourteen
10 Buttons to clean,
Fifteen, sixteen, seventeen, eighteen,
Buttons awaiting,
Nineteen, twenty,
Buttons aplenty.
15 My tunic has thirty buttons,
Boozers and gluttons,
Forty, fifty, sixty more,
Buttons galore,
Seventy, eighty, ninety-six
20 Buttons for kicks!
A hundred buttons on my chest
To shine with the rest.
My tunic has fifty thousand buttons!

GENERAL LASKI: Division, halt! Left turn, about face! Right
25 turn, dress your ranks! Eyes front! Stand at ease. Soldiers,
I am pleased with you. Never forget that you are military
men and that military men make the best soldiers. To march
in the paths of glory and victory, you should first put the
whole weight of your body on your right leg, and then step
30 out smartly, left leg foremost . . . Attention! File off: by the
right . . . to the right! Division, forward! eyes right, quick
march! Left right, left right . . .

The SOLDIERS, *with* LASKI *at their head, march off, shouting.*]*

SOLDIERS: Long live Poland! God save Old Ubu!
PA UBU: Come on, Ma, hand me my breastplate and my little
35 wooden pick. I'll soon be so cluttered up that I won't be able
to run if they chase me.
MA UBU: Pooh! What a coward!
PA UBU: Drat, there's my pschittasword slipping off, and my
phynance-hook won't stay put either! I'll never be ready, and
40 the Russians are advancing and will certainly kill me.
A PALCONTENT: Hey, Lord Ubu, your nearole-incisors are falling
down.
PA UBU: Urghh! Me I kill you with my pschittahook and my face-
chopper. Now you dead.
45 MA UBU: How handsome he looks in his breastplate and helmet,
just like an armour-plated pumpkin.
PA UBU: Ah! now I shall mount my horse. Gentlemen, lead in the
phynance charger.
MA UBU: Pa Ubu, your horse will never be able to carry you, it
50 hasn't been fed for five days and is half dead.
PA UBU: That's a good one! They rook me a dollar a day for that
old nag and it can't even carry me. Are you making fun of
me, horn of Ubu, or are you pocketing the cash, perhaps, eh?
(MA UBU *blushes and lowers her eyes.*) All right, bring me out
55 another beast, but I refuse to go on foot, hornstrumpot! (*An
enormous horse is led in.*) I'm going to get up on it. Oh, I'd
better sit down, otherwise I'll fall off! (*The horse ambles off.*)

From Ubu sur la Butte, *II*, I.

Hi, stop this runaway brute! God almighty, I shall fall off and
suddenly find I'm dead!!
MA UBU: Oh, what an idiot. Ah, he's back in his saddle again. No, 60
he's fallen off.
PA UBU: Horn of physics, I'm half dead, but no matter, I'm off to
the war and I'll kill everyone. Woe betide any of you who step
out of line, because I'll give him the full treatment, including
a session of nose and tooth twisting and tongue pulling. 65
MA UBU: Good luck, Ubu, my lord and master.
PA UBU: I forgot to tell you, I'm making you regent. But I'm taking
the account-books with me, so if you try to cheat me you'll
be in for a hot time. I'm leaving the Palcontent Gyron as your
assistant. Farewell, Madam. 70
MA UBU: Farewell, great commander, and mind you kill the Tsar
good and proper.
PA UBU: Don't you worry about that. Nose and tooth twisting,
tongue pulling and perforation of the nearoles by my little
wooden pick. 75

He clatters off, to the sound of fanfares.

MA UBU (*alone*): Now that that overstuffed dummy is out of the
way, let's get down to business, assassinate Boggerlas and get
our hands on the treasures of Poland.

ACT FOUR

SCENE ONE

The crypt of the former Kings of Poland in Warsaw Cathedral.

MA UBU: Now, where can that treasure be? None of these
flagstones sound hollow. Well, I've certainly counted thirteen
stones from the tomb of Ladislas the Great, keeping to the
wall, but there's nothing. Someone's made a fool of me. Ah!
wait a minute, this flagstone sounds hollow. To work, Ma 5
Ubu. Let's get down to it, and we'll soon have it prised up.
It won't budge. Let's try inserting the end of this phynance-
hook and hope that it will be working for once. Ah, there it is!
There's the gold all mixed up with the bones of the kings. Into
our sack with the whole lot. Oh, what's that noise? Can there 10
still be anyone alive in these ancient vaults? No, it's nothing,
let's take the lot and get out quick. These gold pieces will look
far better in the light of day than buried in the graves of these
old princes. Now we'll put the stone back. What's that? That
noise again. This place is beginning to give me the creeps. I'll 15
come back tomorrow for the rest of the gold.
A VOICE (*rising from the tomb of John Sigismund*): Never, Ma Ubu!

MA UBU *escapes in a panic by way of a secret door, taking the stolen
gold with her.*

[*Act Four, Scene One of* Ubu Rex *may be replaced by Act Two,
Scene Two, of* Ubu sur la Butte, *which commences with Ma Ubu's
closing speech in* Ubu Rex, *Act Three, Scene Eight, as follows:*

MA UBU: Now that that overstuffed dummy is out of the way, let's
get down to business, assassinate Boggerlas and get our hands
on the treasures of Poland. First, the treasures. Hey, Gyron, 20
come and help me.
GYRON: Help you do what, mistress?
MA UBU: Everything! My dear husband desires you to take over
from him completely while he's off at the wars. So tonight . . .

25 GYRON: Oh! mistress!
  MA UBU: Don't blush, darling! In any case, with your complexion
      it's invisible.* But to work, give me a hand carting these
      treasures away.

  Sung very fast, while carrying off the objects described in the song.

  MA UBU: Can I believe my eyes or not?
30   I see a pot . . . a Polish pot!
  GYRON: A bed-side rug of reindeer skin,
      Once trod on by the poor dead queen!
  MA UBU: A faithful portrait, I am sure,
      Of my lord and spouse whom I adore.
35 GYRON: Bottles whose contents made Poles sing
      In the good old days of the Drunken King.
  MA UBU (*brandishing a pschittapump*):
      And here's the special Turkish hookah
      Made for Queen Leczinska.
40 GYRON: These rolls of paper in their crate
      Are secret documents of state.
  MA UBU (*brandishing a lavatory brush*):
      And the little sceptre made of straw
      Which kept the peace in old Warsaw.
45 MA UBU: Hey! I can hear a noise! It must be Pa Ubu coming back.
      So soon?! Quick, run for it!

  They run off, dropping their treasures on the way.]

SCENE TWO

The Main Square in Warsaw.

BOGGERLAS *and his men,* PEOPLE *and* SOLDIERS.

  BOGGERLAS: Forward, my friends! Long live Poland and King
      Wenceslas! That old scoundrel Ubu has fled, which only leaves
      Old Mother Ubu and her Palcontent to deal with. I ask only
      to march at your head and restore the royal succession of my
5   ancestors.
  ALL: Long live Boggerlas!
  BOGGERLAS: And we shall abolish all the taxes imposed by that
      horrible Old Ubu.
  ALL: Hurrah! Forward! Onward to the palace! Let's wipe out the
10   whole vile breed!
  BOGGERLAS: Aha! There's the old hag coming out on to the palace
      steps, surrounded by her guards.
  MA UBU: What can I do for you, gentlemen? Ah! It's Boggerlas.

  The crowd throw stones.

  FIRST GUARD: All the windows are broken.
15 SECOND GUARD: By St George, they've got me.
  THIRD GUARD: I die, by God's holy horn!
  BOGGERLAS: Keep throwing stones, my friends.
  PALCONTENT GYRON: Ho! So that's the way it is!

  *He draws his sword and plunges into the crowd, wreaking terrible
  carnage.*

  ———————————

  *Jarry specifies, in *Ubu sur la Butte*, that the Palcontent Gyron is to be
  played by a Negro. (*Editor's note.*)

BOGGERLAS: Defend yourself, cowardly bumpkin! I challenge you
      to single combat!   20
  GYRON: I'm done for!
  BOGGERLAS: Victory, my friends! Now for Ma Ubu! (*Trumpets
      sound.*) Ah, here come the Nobles. Quick, let's seize the
      wicked harpy.
  ALL: Yes, she'll do, until we can string up the old bandit himself. 25

MA UBU *escapes, pursued by all the* POLES. *Rifle shots and hails of
stones.*

SCENE THREE

The POLISH ARMY *marching through the Ukraine.*

  PA UBU: By God's holy horn, by God's third leg, we shall
      certainly perish, for we are dying of thirst and are quite
      exhausted. Honourable soldier, have the kindness to carry our
      phynancial helmet, and you, honourable lancer, take charge
      of our pschitt-scissors and our physick-stick to relieve our   5
      burden for, I repeat, we are fatigued.

  The SOLDIERS *obey.*

  HEADS: Ho there, Sire! Ain't it odd that there's no sign of the
      Russians yet.
  PA UBU: It is most regrettable that the state of our finances does
      not permit us to own a carriage commensurate with our   10
      dimensions, for, since we were afraid of our mount collapsing
      under us, we have completed the whole journey on foot,
      leading the animal on the rein. But as soon as we get back to
      Poland we shall, by making use of our knowledge of physics
      and in consultation with our learned advisers, invent a wind-   15
      driven carriage capable of transporting the entire army.
  TAILS: Here comes Nicolas Renski at full speed.
  PA UBU: What's he in such a flap about?
  RENSKI: All is lost, Sire. The Poles have rebelled, Gyron has been
      killed, and Madam Ubu has fled to the mountains.   20
  PA UBU: Night-bird, creature of ill omen, shiftless mongrel!
      Where did you snuffle up that rubbish? Here's a fine kettle of
      fish. Well, who's responsible, eh? Boggerlas, I'll bet. Where
      have you just come from?
  RENSKI: Warsaw, noble Lord.   25
  PA UBU: Pschitt upon you, young fellow, if I believed you I'd order
      the whole army to about turn and march back in the direction
      it's just come from. But, honourable infant, you are feather-
      brained and therefore light-headed, and have been dreaming
      foolish dreams. Go to the forward posts, my lad, and you'll   30
      see that the Russians aren't far away. In fact we'll soon have
      to strike out with all our arms, including the pschittical,
      phynancial and physical varieties.
  GENERAL LASKI: Master Ubu, do you see? That's the Russian army
      down there in the plain.   35
  PA UBU: You're right, it's the Russians! Here's a fine state of affairs.
      If only there was some way of escape—but no, we're on a
      hilltop and exposed to attack on every side.
  THE ARMY: The Russians! The enemy!
  PA UBU: Come, gentlemen, let us take up our battle positions.   40
      We'll stay on top of this hill and we'll not be so silly as to
      venture down. I shall remain in your midst like an animated
      citadel, and the rest of you will gravitate around me. I
      recommend you to load your rifles with as many bullets as
      they will hold, since eight bullets can kill eight Russians and 45

that's just so many more I won't have on my back. We shall station the light infantry around the bottom of the hill to take the brunt of the Russian attack and slay a few of them, with the cavalry behind to charge around and add to the confusion, and the artillery set up around this windmill here to fire into the general mêlée. As for ourselves, we shall assume our command position inside the windmill, fire through the window with our phynancial pistol, bar the door with our physick-stick, and if anyone tries to break in he'd better look out for our pschittahook!!!

OFFICERS: Your orders shall be carried out, Lord Ubu.

PA UBU: Ah, well that's all right, then. We shall be victorious. What time is it?

[*The sound 'cuckoo!' is heard three times.**]

GENERAL LASKI: Eleven o'clock in the morning.

PA UBU: Let's have lunch, then. The Russians never attack before noon. Tell the soldiers my Lord General, to fall out for a quick piss and then strike up our anthem, the Financial Song.

LASKI *goes out.*

SOLDIERS *and* PALCONTENTS: Long live Old Ubu, our great Financier! Ting, ting, ting; ting, ting, ting; ting, ting, taring!

PA UBU: Oh, the fine fellows, I adore them. (*A cannon-ball whizzes past and breaks the sail of the windmill.*) Hooh! Hah! I'm frightened. Great God, I'm dead! No, I'm all right after all.

[*Or substitute the following ending to Scene Three, from* Ubu sur la Butte, *Act Two, Scene Three:*

PA UBU: Let's have lunch, then. The Russians never attack before noon. Tell the soldiers, my Lord General, to fall out for a quick piss and then strike up our anthem, the Song of Poland.

GENERAL LASKI: 'Ten-shun! By the right! By the left! Form a circle! Two steps backward . . . march! Dismiss!

THE ARMY *marches out, accompanied by flourishes of trumpets.*

PA UBU *starts to sing, and* THE ARMY *marches back in time to join in the chorus at the end of the first verse.*

Song of Poland

PA UBU: Let's drain it dry,
Every drop from this jug!
Here's mud in your eye,
As it goes down glug-glug,

CHORUS: Glug-glug, glug-glug, glug-glug.

PA UBU: When thirst grips my throat
And makes me feel grumpy,
I push out the boat
And get drunk as an M.P.

CHORUS: Pee-pee, pee-pee, pee-pee.

PA UBU: By my beard in full bloom,
I dare any mocker
To sneer at the plume
Of my great Lancer's chapka.

CHORUS: Ca-ca, ca-ca, ca-ca.

PA UBU: Bloated face, trembling hand
Are the drunkard's just due:

Stage direction from Ubu sur la Butte.

So hurrah for Poland
And good old Ubu!

CHORUS: Poo-poo, poo-poo, poo-poo.

PA UBU: Oh the fine fellows, I adore them. (*A cannon-ball whizzes past and breaks the sail of the windmill.*) Hooh! Hah! I'm frightened. Great God, I'm dead! No, I'm all right after all.]

SCENE FOUR

The same. A CAPTAIN, *then* THE RUSSIAN ARMY.

A CAPTAIN (*coming in*): Lord Ubu, Sire, the Russians are attacking.

PA UBU: Well, what do you expect me to do about it? I didn't tell them to. Nevertheless, Gentlemen of the Phynances, let us prepare ourselves for battle.

GENERAL LASKI: Another cannon-ball!

PA UBU: Oh, I've had enough of this. It's raining lead and steel around here, and our precious person might even suffer some damage. Let's get out of here.

They all descend the slope at the double. The battle opens. They disappear in clouds of smoke at the foot of the hill.

A RUSSIAN (*striking out*): For God and the Tsar!

RENSKI: Oh, I'm done for.

PA UBU: Forward! Hey you, take that, sir, for scaring me, you drunken clot, by waving that rusty old musket at me.

THE RUSSIAN: Try this then! (*He fires his revolver at him.*)

PA UBU: Ooh! ah! ouch! I'm hit, I'm holed, I'm perforated, I've received extreme unction, I'm buried. Oh well, not quite. Ah, I've got him. (*He tears him into little bits.*) There, now start something up again!

GENERAL LASKI: Forward, one last effort, men. Once across the trench and victory is ours.

PA UBU: Are you quite sure? So far, my brow is wreathed with lumps rather than laurels.

RUSSIAN CAVALRY: Hurrah! Make way for the Tsar!

THE TSAR *arrives, accompanied by* MACNURE *in disguise.*

A POLE: Oh, Christ! Every man for himself, here comes the Tsar.

ANOTHER: My God, he's over the trench!

ANOTHER: Bing! Bang! There's four of our men annihilated by that big bugger of a lieutenant.

MACNURE: What, the rest of you haven't had enough yet? All right then, here's one for you, Jan Sobieski! (*He slays him.*) I'll settle your hash, the lot of you!

He makes a bloodbath of Poles.

PA UBU: Forward, my friends. Get hold of that lousy sod! Make mincemeat of the Russians! Victory is ours. Three cheers for the Red Eagle!

ALL: Forward! Hurrah! By God's third leg, let's get that big bugger.

MACNURE: By St George, I've come a cropper.

PA UBU (*recognising him*): Ah! so it's you, M'Nure. Well, well, well, my dear old friend! We are delighted to see you again, and so is the rest of the company. I shall roast you over a slow fire. Gentlemen of the Phynances, pray light a fire. Oh! Ah! Oh!

I'm a dead man. That must have been a cannon-ball that just hit me. Dear God, I beseech you, forgive me my sins. Ouch! It was a cannon-ball, all right.

MACNURE: Ha ha! It was a cap-pistol.

45 PA UBU: Ah, so you're making fun of me, are you? Well, that's the last time! You've had it now. (*He throws himself on* MACNURE *and tears him to pieces.*)

GENERAL LASKI: Master Ubu, we are advancing on all fronts.

PA UBU: So I see. But I'm all in, I'm dented all over with kicks, and 50   I think I'll sit down and take it easy. Ooh, my poor gutbag!

GENERAL LASKI: Go and puncture the Tsar's gutbag, Pa Ubu.

PA UBU: Ha yes, that's the ticket. Let's get at him. Now then, pschittasword, to your duty; and you, phynance-hook, don't lag behind. Physick-stick, go to work in eager emulation 55   of them and share with the little wooden pick the honour of slaughtering, scooping out and stuffing the Muscovite Emperor. Forward, my noble phynance charger. (*He hurls himself upon* THE TSAR.)

A RUSSIAN OFFICER: Look out, Your Majesty!

60 PA UBU: Take that, you! Oo! Ow! I say, do you mind! I mean, please excuse me, Sir, leave me alone. Ouch! I didn't do it on purpose. (*He runs away, pursued by* THE TSAR.) Holy Virgin, this lunatic's chasing me! Dear God, what did I do? Oh, goodness, there's still the trench to get across: I can feel his 65   breath down my neck and the trench is looming up in front of me! Courage—eyes shut!

He jumps the trench. THE TSAR *falls in.*

THE TSAR: Now I'm in the soup!

THE POLES: Hurrah! The Tsar's fallen in!

PA UBU: Oof! I hardly dare look back! Ha, he's stuck in the trench, 70   and they're bopping him on the top. That's it, gallant Poles, bash him hard, there's room for plenty of whacks on his surface, the wretch. I don't dare look at him, myself! And yet it's all turned out as we foretold, the physick-stick has worked miracles and there's no doubt that we would certainly 75   have made mincemeat of him if an inexplicable terror had not suddenly arisen within us to combat and annihilate the mechanism of our bravery. But we were obliged suddenly to turn tail, and we owe our safety entirely to our skill in horsemanship and to the solid hocks of our phynance charger 80   who is as swift as he is strong and whose agility is proverbial, and likewise to the depth of the trench which happened to lie so opportunely beneath the feet of the enemy of ourselves the aforementioned and here-present Master of Phynances. Hmm! what a pretty speech, a pity no one was listening. 85   Right, back to business!

The RUSSIAN DRAGOONS *charge and rescue* THE TSAR.

GENERAL LASKI: It looks like they're routing us.

PA UBU: Aha! Then I'd better get out while the going's good. Now then, my brave Poles, forward! I mean, backward!

THE POLES: Every man for himself!

90 PA UBU: Come on, let's go! What a mob, what a rout, what a stampede! How shall I ever get out of this mess? (*He is jostled.*) Hey, you there, mind where you're going, or you will certainly sample the fiery valour of the Master of Phynances. Ah, he's gone. Now let's beat a hasty retreat while Laski isn't watching.

(*He runs off.* THE TSAR *and* THE RUSSIAN ARMY *cross the stage in pursuit of the* POLES.)

SCENE FIVE

A cave in Lithuania, It is snowing.

PA UBU, *the* PALCONTENTS, HEADS *and* TAILS.

PA UBU: What vile weather! It's freezing hard enough to split a rock, and the person of the Master of Phynances finds itself excessively inconvenienced thereby.

HEADS: Hoy there! Mister Ubu, Sir, have you recovered from your terror and your running away?   5

PA UBU: Yes, I'm not frightened any more, but my guts are still running.

TAILS: Pooh! What a crappy creature!

PA UBU: You there, Mister Tails, how's your nearole?

TAILS: As well as can be expected, Sire, considering the fact that 10   it is not well at all. In consequench of whish, the lead inside it makes it tilt earthwards since I haven't been able to extract the bullet.

PA UBU: How splendid! You're like me, boy, always spoiling for a fight. As for me, I displayed the greatest valour, and without 15   endangering myself in the least I massacred four of the enemy with my bare hands, not counting all those who were already dead when I dispatched them.

TAILS: Hey, Heads, do you have any idea what happened to little Renski ?   20

HEADS: He got a bullet through the head.

PA UBU: Just as the poppy and the dandelion are scythed down in the flower of their youth by the pitiless scythe of the pitiless scyther who pitilessly scythes their pitiful pans, so poor Renski has played the pretty poppy's pitiful part—he fought 25   gallantly, but there were just too many Russians around.

HEADS *and* TAILS (*together*): Hoy there! Mister!

AN ECHO: Hhrumph!

HEADS: What's that noise? On guard with our pea-shooters and catapults.   30

PA UBU: Oh, no, damn it, not the Russians again! I've had enough of them! Any more nonsense from them and I'll fuggem up good and proper.

SCENE SIX

The same. Enter a BEAR.

TAILS: Hoy there, Mister Phynance!

PA UBU: Oh, my! Look at that little bow-wow. Isn't it cute?

HEADS: Look out! Oh, what an enormous bear. Where's my ammunition?

PA UBU: A bear! Arghh! what a monstrous beast. Oh, poor little 5   me, I'm a gonner. God save me! And it's coming for me. No, it's got hold of Tails. Whew! that was a close shave.

The BEAR *throws itself on* TAILS. HEADS *attacks it with a knife.* UBU *takes refuge on a rock.*

TAILS: Help, Heads! Help! Come to my aid, Mister Ubu, Sir!

PA UBU: Nothing doing! Look after yourself, my friend. Just at the moment we are reciting our Pater Noster. Everyone will have 10   his turn to get eaten.

HEADS: I've got it. I've got a half-nelson on it.

TAILS: Keep it up, pal, it's beginning to let go of me.

PA UBU: *Sanctificetur notnen tuum.*

TAILS: Cowardly sod!   15

HEADS: Ow! it's biting me! Oh, Lord save us, I'm as good as dead.

PA UBU: *Fiat voluntas tua!*

TAILS: Ah! I've managed to wound the brute.

HEADS: Hurrah! it's bleeding.

While the PALCONTENTS *yell and shout, the* BEAR *bellows in pain and* UBU *continues to mumble.*

20 TAILS: Hold it tight while I go get my explosive knuckle-duster.

PA UBU: *Panem nostrum quotidianum da nobis hodie.*

HEADS: Hurry up, I can't hold out much longer.

PA UBU: *Sicut et nos dimittimus debitoribus nostris.*

TAILS: Ah, here it is.

A tremendous explosion. The BEAR *drops dead.*

25 HEADS *and* TAILS: Victory.

PA UBU: *Sed libera nos a malo.* Amen. Well, is he really dead? Can I come down off my rock?

HEADS (*contemptuously*): Do whatever you like.

PA UBU (*climbing down*): You may pride yourselves that if you
30   be still alive and still trampling underfoot the snows of
        Lithuania, you owe the fact entirely to the generous virtue of
        the Master of Phynances, who has strained his integument,
        acquired a slipped disc and ruptured his larynx in reciting
        paternosters for your salvation, and who has wielded the
35   spiritual weapon of prayer with a courage equal to the
        dexterity you have shown in wielding the temporal weapon
        of the here-present Palcontent Tails' explosive knuckleduster.
        We carried our own devotion even further, in that we did not
        hesitate to climb to the top of a very high rock so that our
40   prayers should have less far to travel to mount to heaven.

HEADS: Lousy swine!

PA UBU: My, what a fat animal. Thanks to me, you've got
        something to eat. What a belly, gentlemen! The Greeks would
        have found it more comfortable in there than in their wooden
45   horse, and we were very near, dear friends, to being able to
        verify with our own eyes its interior capacity.

HEADS: I'm dying of hunger. What's there to eat?

TAILS: The bear!

PA UBU: My poor friends, are you going to eat it raw? We don't
50   have anything to start a fire with.

HEADS: We've got our gun-flints, haven't we?

PA UBU: Ah yes, that's true. And besides, I think I can see just
        over there a small copse where we should be able to find some
        dry branches. Go and fetch some, Mister Tails, Sire.

55 TAILS *trudges off across the snow.*

HEADS: And now, Mister Ubu, Sire, go ahead and carve up the
        bear.

PA UBU: Oh, no! The creature may not be quite dead yet. In any
        case, since you're already half eaten yourself and bitten all
60   over, you're just the man for that job. I shall light a fire while
        waiting for the other knave to bring the wood.

HEADS *starts carving up the* BEAR.

PA UBU: Oo, look out! I distinctly saw it move.

HEADS: But, Mister Ubu, Sire, it's already cold.

PA UBU: Oh, that's a pity, it would have been nicer to eat it while
65   still warm. This is bound to give the Master of Phynances an
        attack of indigestion.

HEADS (*aside*): He really is repulsive. (*Aloud.*) Give us a hand,
        Mister Ubu, I can't do the whole job myself.

PA UBU: No, I have no intention of lifting a finger. I happen to be
        very tired.   70

TAILS (*coming back*): What snow, my friends, anyone would think
        we were in cold Castille or the North Pole. Night is beginning
        to fall. In an hour it will be dark. Let's hurry up while there's
        still some light.

PA UBU: Yes, do you hear that, Heads? Hurry up. Hurry up, both   75
        of you! Put the beast on a spit and roast it quick. I'm hungry,
        you know.

HEADS: Ah! that's the last straw! You either share the work or you
        get nothing to eat; understand, you fat pig?

PA UBU: Oh well, it's all the same to me. I'd just as soon eat it raw,   80
        as a matter of fact; it's your stomachs that will suffer. In any
        case, I'm sleepy.

TAILS: He's hopeless, Heads! Let's get dinner ready by ourselves.
        He won't have any, that's all. If we feel generous we might
        throw him a few bones.   85

HEADS: Agreed. Ah, the fire's catching!

PA UBU: Oh, that's nice, it's getting warm now. But I see Russians
        everywhere. God Almighty, what a rout! Aah!

He falls asleep.

TAILS: I wonder if Renski was telling the truth when he said that
        Ma Ubu really was dethroned. It wouldn't surprise me at all.   90

HEADS: Let's finish cooking the meal.

TAILS: No, we have more important things to do. I think we
        should find out whether these rumours are true or not.

HEADS: You're right. Should we desert Pa Ubu or stay with him?

TAILS: Let's sleep on it. We can decide what to do tomorrow   95
        morning.

HEADS: No, let's slip away now, under cover of darkness.

TAILS: Let's go, then.

They leave.

SCENE SEVEN

PA UBU (*talking in his sleep*): Hey, mister Russian dragoon, Sir,
        don't shoot in this direction, there's someone here. Ah! there's
        M'Nure, he's got a nasty look about him, just like a bear. And
        there's Boggerlas coming after me! The bear, the bear! Ah, it's
        down! What a tough monster, great God! No, I won't lend a   5
        hand. Go away, Boggerlas! Do you hear me, you lout? Here's
        Renski now, and the Tsar! Oh! they're going to hit me. Ugh,
        there's madam my female! Where did you get all that gold ?
        You've stolen my gold, you slut, you've been scrabbling around
        in my tomb which is in Warsaw Cathedral, not far from the   10
        Moon. I've been dead a long time, yes, it's Boggerlas who
        killed me and I'm buried at Warsaw by the side of Ladislas the
        Great, and also at Cracow by the side of Jan Sigismund, and
        also at Thorn in the casemate with M'Nure! There it is again.
        Be off with you, accursed bear. You look just like M'Nure.   15
        And you smell just like M'Nure. Do you hear me, beast of
        Satan? No, he can't hear me, the Phynance-extortioners have
        perforated his nearoles. Debraining, killing off, perforation
        of nearoles, money grabbing and drinking oneself to death,
        that's the life for a Phynance-extortioner, and the Master of   20
        Phynances revels in such joys.

He falls silent and sleeps.

ACT FIVE

SCENE ONE

It is night. PA UBU *is asleep.* MA UBU *enters without seeing him. It is pitch dark.*

MA UBU: Shelter at last! I'm alone here, which is fine as far as I'm concerned, but what a dreadful journey: crossing the whole of Poland in four days! Every possible misfortune struck me at the same moment. As soon as that great, fat oaf had clattered
5 off on his nag I crept into the crypt to grab the treasure, but then everything went wrong. I just escaped being stoned to death by Boggerlas and his madmen. I lost my gallant Palcontent Gyron who was so enamoured of my charms that he swooned with delight every time he saw me and even, I've
10 been told, every time he didn't see me—and there can be no higher love than that. Poor boy, he would have let himself be cut in half for my sake, and the proof is that Boggerlas cut him in quarters. Biff, bam, boom! Ooh, I thought it was all up with me. Then I fled for my life with the bloodthirsty
15 mob hard on my heels. I managed to get out of the palace and reach the Vistula, but all the bridges were guarded. I swam across the river, hoping to shake off my pursuers. The entire nobility rallied and joined in the chase. I nearly breathed my last a thousand times, half smothered by the surrounding
20 Poles all screaming for my blood. Finally, I escaped their clutches, and after four days of trudging through the snows of what was once my kingdom have at last reached refuge here. I've had nothing to eat or drink these past four days, and Boggerlas breathing down my neck the whole time. Now here
25 I am, safe at last. Ah! I'm dead with exhaustion and hunger. But I'd give a lot to know what became of my big fat buffoon, I mean to say my esteemed spouse. Lord, how I've skinned him, and relieved him of his rix-dollars! I've certainly rolled him plenty! And his phynance charger that was dying of
30 hunger—it didn't get oats to munch very often, poor beast! It was fun while it lasted, but alas, I had to leave my treasure behind in Warsaw, where it's up for grabs.

PA UBU (*beginning to wake up*): Catch Ma Ubu, chop off her nears!
MA UBU: My God, where am I? I'm losing my mind. But, no,
35 heavens above, for—

Thanks be to God, by my side I behold
The sleeping form of Sir Ubu the Bold.

Let's play it cool. Well, you fat oaf, have you slept well?
PA UBU: No, very badly! Oof, that bear was tough! Battle to the
40 death between the voracious and the coriaceous, but the voracious completely ate up and devoured the coriaceous, as you will see when it gets light. Do you hear me, brave Palcontents ?
MA UBU: What's he babbling about? He's even stupider than when
45 he left. Who's he having a go at?
PA UBU: Tails, Heads, answer me, pschittbag! Where are you? Oh, I'm scared. But somebody spoke, who was it? Not the bear, I hope. Pschitt! Where are my matches? I must have lost them during the battle.
50 MA UBU: Let's take advantage of the situation and the darkness. Let's pretend to be a supernatural apparition and make him promise to forgive our peculations.
PA UBU: But by St Anthony, someone's speaking! By God's third leg, I'll be hanged if someone isn't speaking.

MA UBU (*in a great hollow voice*): Yes, Mister Ubu, someone is 55 indeed speaking, and with the tongue of the archangel's trumpet that shall summon the dead from their graves to meet their judgement! Listen to that terrible voice. It is the voice of the archangel Gabriel who is incapable of giving anything but good advice. 60
PA UBU: He can stuff his advice.
MA UBU: Don't interrupt or I shall fall silent and you'll find your bumboozle's on the hot seat!
PA UBU: Ah! by my strumpot! I'll keep quiet, I won't breathe a word. Pray continue, Mrs Apparition. 65
MA UBU: We were saying, Mister Ubu, that you were a fat oaf.
PA UBU: Hmm! Fat, yes, I grant you that.
MA UBU: Shut up, goddammit!
PA UBU: Hey! Angels aren't supposed to swear!
MA UBU (*aside*): Pschitt! (*Continuing.*) You are married, Mister 70 Ubu?
PA UBU: Too true. To a vile hag.
MA UBU: You mean, to a charming lady.
PA UBU: An old horror. She sprouts claws all over, it's impossible to get one's hand up her anywhere. 75
MA UBU: You should give her a hand up kindly and gently, honest Mister Ubu, and were you to do so you would see that she was just as appealing as Aphrodite.
PA UBU: Who did you say wears an appalling frayed nightie?
MA UBU: You are not listening, Mister Ubu. Lend us a more 80 attentive ear. (*Aside.*) But we must hurry, for dawn is breaking. Mister Ubu, your wife is a delightful and adorable person, who hasn't a single defect.
PA UBU: On the contrary, she's got the lot.
MA UBU: Silence, Sir! Your wife has never been unfaithful to you! 85
PA UBU: Only because the old hag's so ugly that no man in his right mind would ever give her a chance of being unfaithful!
MA UBU: She doesn't drink!
PA UBU: Not since I kept the cellar door locked. Before that, she was plastered by seven in the morning and perfumed with the 90 scent of brandy. Now that she can afford to perfume herself with heliotrope she doesn't smell any worse. One stink's as good as another, as far as I'm concerned. But now I have to get plastered all on my own.
MA UBU: Silly idiot! Your wife doesn't steal your bags of gold. 95
PA UBU: Come off it!
MA UBU: She doesn't pocket a single penny!
PA UBU: As witness our noble and unfortunate phynance charger who, having been starved for three months, had to go through the entire campaign being led by the reins across the Ukraine, 100 until the poor beast finally died in harness.
MA UBU: All this is false. Your wife is an absolute saint, and you are a great monster.
PA UBU: All this is true. My wife's a lazy slut and you're a great booby! 105
MA UBU: Have a care, Mister Ubu.
PA UBU: You're right—I was forgetting to whom I was speaking. I take it all back.
MA UBU: You killed King Wenceslas.
PA UBU: That wasn't *my* fault, oh no, it was Ma Ubu who egged 110 me on.
MA UBU: You had Boleslas and Ladislas assassinated.
PA UBU: Serve them right! They tried to hit me!
MA UBU: You not only broke your promise to M'Nure, you killed him as well. 115

PA UBU: I'd rather it was me than him that reigned in Lithuania. For the moment it's neither of us. At least you can see it's not me.

MA UBU: There's only one way for you to gain redemption of
120   your sins.

PA UBU: What's that? I wouldn't at all mind becoming a holy man, in fact I'd like to be a bishop and see my name in the calendar.

MA URU: You must forgive Madam Ubu for having pocketed a little bit of your spare cash.

125 PA UBU: All right, I'll tell you what! I'll forgive her when she's handed over all the loot, when she's been soundly walloped, and when she's brought my phynance charger back to life.

MA UBU: He's got that damn horse on the brain. Oh, it's beginning to get light. I'm lost!

130 PA UBU: Still, I'm glad to learn definitely that my dear wife has been swindling me. I have it now on the best authority. *Omnis a Deo scientia,* which means: *Omnis,* all; *a Deo,* wisdom; *scientia,* comes from God. Which explains the whole miraculous revelation. But Madam Apparition has fallen
135   silent. What healing draught can I offer her to bring back her voice? For her conversation was most amusing. Why, it's daybreak already. Ha, by heavens and by my phynance charger, it's Ma Ubu!

MA UBU (*brazening it out*): That's not true. I shall excommunicate
140   you.

PA UBU: Carrion!

MA UBU: Oh, what blasphemy.

PA UBU: This is too much. I can see perfectly well that it's you, you silly old bag. What the devil are you doing here?

145 MA UBU: Gyron is dead and the Poles were after me, so I thought I'd better get out while the going was good.

PA UBU: The Russians were after *me,* so I thought I'd better get out while the going was good. Ah well, they say that great minds think alike.

150 MA UBU: They can say that if they want, but my great mind thinks it's just met a pea-brained idiot.

PA UBU: Oh, very well, and in a moment it's going to meet a palmiped.

He hurls the BEAR *at her.*

MA UBU (*falling prostrate under the weight of the* BEAR): Great
155   God! How horrible! I'm dying! I'm suffocating! It's biting me! It's swallowing me! It's digesting me!

PA UBU: It's dead, you freak! Oh, but maybe it isn't after all. Lord, no, it's not dead, let's escape. (*Climbing up onto his rock again.*) *Pater noster qui es* . . .

160 MA UBU (*emerging from beneath the* BEAR): Now where's he got to?

PA UBU: Oh Lord, there she is again! Am I going to be saddled with this stupid bitch for ever? Is that bear dead?

MA UBU: Saddle yourself, you donkey. Yes, it's stiff already. How
165   did it get here?

PA UBU (*confused*): I don't know. Oh yes, I remember. It wanted to eat Heads and Tails and I killed it single-handed with one blow of my paternoster.

MA UBU: Heads, Tails, paterooster—what's he going un about?
170 He's off his rocker, the silly chump.

PA UBU: It's the gospel truth, I'm telling you, you bumboozle-faced idiot.

MA UBU: Tell me all about your campaign, Captain Ubu.

PA UBU: No, no, it would take too long. All I know is that despite my incontestable valour, everyone defeated me. 175

MA UBU: What, even the Poles?

PA UBU: They were all shouting 'Long live Wenceslas and Boggerlas!' I thought they were going to tear me to pieces. What madmen! And then they lynched Renski.

MA UBU: I couldn't care less! You know that Boggerlas slaughtered 180 the Palcontent Gyron?

PA UBU: I couldn't care less! And then they lynched poor Laski.

MA UBU: I couldn't care less!

PA UBU: Oh, that's quite enough from you. Come here, carrion, and kneel before your master. (*He seizes her and forces her to* 185 *her knees.*) You are about to undergo the extreme penalty.

MA UBU: Ow, ow, ow, Mister Ubu!

PA UBU: Have you quite finished with your ow, ow, ows? Because now *I'm* going to begin: twisting of the nose, tearing out of the hair, penetration of the nearoles by the little wooden pick, 190 extraction of the brain-matter by way of the heels, laceration of the posterior, partial or even total suppression of the spinal marrow (thus confirming the fact that the victim is a spineless creature), not to mention the puncturing of the swimming-bladder, and finally the grand new version of the decollation 195 of St John the Baptist as specified in the most Holy Scriptures of both the Old and New Testaments, as edited, corrected and perfectioned by yours truly the here-present Master of Phynances! How does that suit you, puddinghead?

He starts tearing her to pieces.

MA UBU: Mercy, mercy, Mister Ubu, Sir! 200

Loud noise at the entrance to the cave.

SCENE TWO

The same. BOGGERLAS, *storming the cave with his* SOLDIERS.

BOGGERLAS: Forward, my friends! Long live Poland!

PA UBU: Hey there, just a minute, Mister Polack. Wait till I'm through with madam my worse half.

BOGGERLAS (*striking him*): Take that, coward, scavenger, scoundrel, infidel, Mussulman! 5

PA UBU (*countering*): Take that, great clot, pisspot, son of a harlot, nose-snot, bigot, faggot, gut-rot, squawking parrot, Huguenot!

MA UBU (*hitting him too*): Take that, pork-snout, layabout, whore's tout, pox-riddled spout, idle lout, boy scout, Polish Kraut. 10

The SOLDIERS *hurl themselves on the* UBUS *who defend themselves as best they can.*

PA UBU: Ye gods, we're getting a drubbing!

MA UBU: Let's tread on the Polacks' toes.

PA UBU: By my green candle, this is going on too long. There's another of them! Oh, if only I had my phynance charger with me here! 15

BOGGERLAS: Hit them, go on hitting them!

VOICES (*offstage*): Long live Pa Ubu, our great Phynancier!

PA UBU: Ah, here they are! Hurrah! Here come the Ubuists. Come on, quick march, to the rescue, phynancial gentlemen!

The PALCONTENTS *enter and throw themselves into the fight.*

20 TAILS: Get out, you Poles!

HEADS: Hoy, Mister Phynance, we meet once again! Come on, men, fight your way through to the entrance, and once we're outside let's run for it.

PA UBU: Oh yes, I'm very good at that. Look how Heads is hitting

25   out around him.

BOGGERLAS: God, I'm wounded.

STANISLAS LECZINSKI: It's nothing, Sire.

BOGGERLAS: Yes, I'm all right. I just came over all peculiar suddenly.

30 JAN SOBIESKI: Hit them, go on hitting them, the scoundrels are getting away.

TAILS: We're almost there, follow me everybody. By consequench of whish I see daylight.

HEADS: Courage, Lord Ubu!

35 PA UBU: Ooh, I've done it in my pants. Forward, hornstrumpot! Killemoff, bleedemoff, skinnemoff, shaggemoff, by Ubu's horn. Ah, they're falling back.

TAILS: There's only two left guarding the door.

PA UBU (*swinging the* BEAR *round his head, and knocking them*

40   *down with it*): That's for you! And for you! Ha, I'm outside! Let's get the hell out of here! Come on, the rest of you, follow me, and look sharp about it!

SCENE THREE

The scene represents the Province of Livonia covered with snow. The UBUS *and their followers in flight.*

PA UBU: At last, I think they've abandoned the chase.

MA UBU: Yes, Boggerlas has gone off to get himself crowned.

PA UBU: He knows what he can do with his crown!

MA UBU: Oh how right you are, Old Ubu.

They vanish into the distance.

SCENE FOUR

The bridge of a ship sailing close to the wind on the Baltic. On the bridge, PA UBU *and his whole* GANG.

THE CAPTAIN: What a lovely breeze!

PA UBU: It's a fact that we are moving at an almost miraculous speed, which I estimate at, give or take a bit, about a million knots an hour, and the remarkable thing about these knots is

5   that once they've been tied they can't come untied again. And of course we have the wind in the poop.

HEADS: He's a nincompoop full of wind.

A squall comes up, the ship heels over, the sea foams.

PA UBU: Oh my God, we're capsizing. Hey, it's going all which ways, your boat, it's going to fall over.

10 THE CAPTAIN: All hands to leeward. Close-haul the mizzen!

PA UBU: Ah, no! What an idea! Don't all stand on the same side, it's dangerous. Just supposing the wind changed suddenly! We'd all go to the bottom and the fishes would eat us up.

THE CAPTAIN: Don't bear away. Hug the wind full and by!

PA UBU: Yes, yes, tear away. I'm in a tearing hurry, do you hear! 15 It's your fault, you fool of a skipper, if we don't get there. We should have arrived by now. There's only one solution: I'll take over command myself. Ready about. 'Bout ship. Let go the anchor. Go about in stays, wear ship, hoist more sail, haul down sail, put the tiller hard over, up with the helm, down 20 with the helm, full speed astern, give her more lee, splice the top gallant. How am I doing? Tight as a rivet! Meet the wave crosswise and everything will be shipshape. Avast there.

All are convulsed with laughter, the wind freshens.

THE CAPTAIN: Haul down the main jib, take a reef in the topsails.

PA UBU: That's a good one. That's not bad at all. Did you get that, 25 Mister Grew? Boil down the main rib; roast beef and oxtails!

Several die of laughter. A wave breaks over everyone.

PA UBU: Oh, what a ducking! That is the logical result of the manoeuvres we have just ordered.

MA UBU *and* HEADS: Isn't navigation wonderful?

A second wave breaks over them.

HEADS (*drenched*): Beware of Satan and all pomps and vanities. 30

PA UBU: That's right, beware of sitting under pumps, it's insanitary. Hey, steward, sirrah, bring us something to drink.

They all sit down to drink.

MA UBU: Oh what bliss it will be to see our sweet France once more, and all our old friends, and our Castle of Mondragon.

PA UBU: Yes, we'll soon be there. See, we are tacking past the 35 Castle of Elsinore at this very moment.

HEADS: The prospect of seeing my beloved Spain again has put new heart into me.

TAILS: Yes, and we'll amaze our countrymen with tales of our marvellous adventures. 40

PA UBU: Oh yes, there's no doubt about that. As for me, I'll be off to Paris to get myself appointed Master of Phynances.

MA UBU: That's nice. Oo, what a bump that was.

TAILS: It's nothing. We've just doubled Cape Elsinore.

HEADS: And now our gallant bark speeds like a bird over the 45 wine-dark waves of the North Sea.

PA UBU: Wild and inhospitable ocean which laps the shores of the land called Germany, so named because it's exactly half way to Jermyn Street as the blow flies.

MA UBU: Now that's what I call erudition. It's a beautiful country, 50 I'm told.

PA UBU: Beautiful though it may be, it's not a patch on Poland. Ah gentlemen, there'll always be a Poland. Otherwise there wouldn't be any Poles!

August Strindberg

The Swedish playwright August Strindberg (1849–1912) was a modern Renaissance man: he wrote some fifty plays, several autobiographical novels, and a variety of scientific and occult works as well. A series of tempestuous marriages marked Strindberg's life and are reflected in his corrosively misogynistic attitudes and in his hostility toward Ibsen, who seemed to Strindberg to advocate a new order of feminine domination. Calling *A Doll House* "sick like its father," Strindberg wrote *The Father* (1887) in reply to Ibsen, a play in which a calculating woman drives her husband into madness. Although Strindberg considered the play to be an experiment in the new "naturalism," it is really a kind of psychological thriller: the characters are so consumed by their sexual combat with one another that the worldly environment hardly seems important. Strindberg sent the play to Émile Zola, who found it absorbing and curious, but lacking in the material social reality he demanded of the new drama. Strindberg then wrote *Miss Julie* (1888) and considered the play's use of naturalism in his famous preface to the play. The battle of the sexes is one of Strindberg's preoccupations, examined in a series of plays including *Creditors* (1888) and *The Dance of Death, Parts 1 and 2* (1901). The battle of the sexes was also the battle that occupied Strindberg's life outside the theater. His three marriages all involved periods of psychological breakdown and creative fertility. His breakdown of the mid-1890s after marrying his second wife is documented in *The Inferno* (1897) and is symptomatic of Strindberg's volatile and unstable frame of mind. Much of Strindberg's manic energy was focused on women—he believed that his wife was attempting to drive him mad by sending rays through the walls. Strindberg also developed a passion for the occult and for alchemy, and in addition to his plays, poems, and novels, he wrote a number of scientific and pseudoscientific treatises. Unlike Ibsen, Strindberg experimented in a variety of dramatic genres throughout his career. Calling himself the "Zola of the occult," Strindberg wrote an influential series of expressionist and symbolic plays; the best known today are *To Damascus* (in three parts, 1898–1901) and *A Dream Play* (1901). He also wrote several important plays on Swedish history, including *Erik XIV* (1899), *Gustav Adolph* (1900), and *Gustav III* (1902). In 1907 he founded a small theater—the Intimate Theater—which brought the independent theater movement to Sweden and produced his intense and often symbolic series of "chamber plays," including *The Ghost Sonata* (1907) and *The Pelican* (1907). When Strindberg died in 1912, he had become not only the most significant literary and theatrical figure in Swedish history, but also a major influence on the course of modern drama.

A Dream Play

Written in 1901—a year after Sigmund Freud published *The Interpretation of Dreams*—and first staged in Stockholm in 1907, *A Dream Play* often seems to readers a nearly unstageable work, requiring the cutting and montage techniques of film, a medium still in its infancy when Strindberg wrote the play. Yet *A Dream Play* has been staged many times in Sweden (where it is one of Strindberg's most-produced plays), in Europe, and in the United States, sometimes produced lavishly, sometimes simply. For although the play's many settings—the "clouds resembling shattered slate cliffs with ruins of castles and fortresses" framing Indra's Daughter in the Prologue, the chrysanthemum-topped castle rising from the manure of the first and last scenes, the Stage Door, the claustral Lawyer's office, Fingal's Cave, Foul Strand and Fair Haven—have an important symbolic function, the vitality of the play on the stage is really not dependent on the densely particularized environment of realism. Instead, as Strindberg suggests in his "Note" to the play, *A Dream Play* is held together by its "musical treatment," in which themes are sounded, amplified, modulated, and counterpointed in the play's rich harmony.

For this reason, too, the play's structure seems more cyclic than linear, as Indra's Daughter progresses from eternity through various scenes of human suffering, loss, and disappointment. *A Dream Play*, that is, maintains a consistent dichotomy between the sorrows of human life and the Daughter's elevated sympathy. As a form of expressionist theater,

This 2005 production of Strindberg's *A Dream Play* at the Royal National Theatre in London featured men dressed as ballerinas.

Tristram Kenton/Lebrecht Music & Arts

A Dream Play also has a vaguely "morality-play" dimension, as the Daughter proceeds through representative scenes of human life and sorrow to the visionary center of the play in Fingal's Cave, and then returns back to her point of origin in the world, the castle. And Strindberg is also true to his hope that "the characters split, double, multiply, dissolve, condense, float apart, coalesce" in the play. In a sense, the men who accompany the Daughter on her journey—the Officer, the Lawyer, the Poet—all blend into one another, emanations, perhaps, of the mind of the dreamer. To respond closely to the play is to try to feel into its peculiar, repetitive, metaphorical logic, to avoid the kind of materialist narrative logic of realistic theater in order to seek the thematic parallels and symmetries more typically found in poetry. For *A Dream Play* is imagined in the densely analogical register of poetry, a poetry that is for Strindberg at once visual, verbal, narrative, and symbolic, an imagistic poetry perhaps best captured in the play's final vision: *Music. The rear of the stage is lit up by the burning castle and reveals a wall of human faces, questioning, sorrowful, despairing. As the castle burns, the flower bud at the top bursts and blossoms into a huge chrysanthemum.*

Preface
TRANSLATED BY EVERT SPRINCHORN

In this preface to his play, Strindberg describes the relationship between characters, dramatic form, and the "dreamer" that he hoped to achieve in the play—Trans.

Following the example of my previous dream play *To Damascus,* I have in this present dream play sought to imitate the incoherent but ostensibly logical form of our dreams. Anything can happen; everything is possible and probable. Time and space do not exist. Working with some insignificant real events as a background, the imagination spins out its threads of thoughts and weaves them into new patterns—a mixture of memories, experiences, spontaneous ideas, impossibilities, and improvisations.

The characters split, double, multiply, dissolve, condense, float apart, coalesce. But one mind stands over and above them all, the mind of the dreamer; and for him there are no secrets, no inconsistencies, no scruples, no laws. He does not condemn, does not acquit; he only narrates the story. And since the dream is more often painful than cheerful, a tone of melancholy and of sympathy with all living creatures runs through the pitching and swaying narrative. Sleep, which should free the dreamer, often plagues and tortures him instead. But when the pain is most excruciating, the moment of waking comes and reconciles the dreamer to reality, which, however agonizing it may be, is a joy and a pleasure at that moment compared with the painful dream.

The idea that life is a dream* seemed to us in the past to be no more than a poetic dream of Calderon's. But when Shakespeare in *The Tempest* has Prospero say that "we are such stuff as dreams are made on," and when elsewhere this wise Briton, speaking through Macbeth, talks about life as "a tale told by an idiot," we should probably give the matter some more thought.

Whoever during these brief hours follows the sleepwalking author on his wanderings may find a certain similarity between the apparent jumble of a dream and the disordered and mottled cloth of life, woven by the great World Weaver, who winds the warp of human destinies and then fills the woof using our conflicting aims and changeable passions. Anyone who notes the similarity is surely entitled to think that there may be some substance to it.

As far as the loose, disconnected shape of the play is concerned, that too is only apparent. On closer examination, the composition is seen to be quite firm and solid—a symphony, polyphonic, now and then like a fugue with a constantly recurring main theme, which is repeated in all registers and varied by the more than thirty voices. There are no solos with accompaniments, that is, no big parts, no characters—or rather, no caricatures; no intrigue; no strong curtains demanding applause. The voice parts are subjected to strict musical treatment; and in the sacrificial scene of the finale, all that has happened passes in review, with the themes once again repeated, just as a man's life with all its incidents is said to do at the moment of death. Yet another similarity!

Now it is time to see the play itself—and to hear it. With a little goodwill on your part, the battle is half-won. That is all we ask of you.

Curtain going up!

---

*This paragraph and the ones following were written in 1907 in connection with the first staging of the play. They were inserted in the director's copy of the play but not printed at that time.—Trans.

A Dream Play

August Strindberg

TRANSLATED BY EVERT SPRINCHORN

PROLOGUE*

The backdrop represents banks of clouds resembling shattered slate cliffs with ruins of castles and fortresses.

*The constellations Leo, Virgo, and Libra can be seen; in their midst the planet Jupiter is shining brightly.***

Indra's Daughter is standing on the highest cloud.

THE VOICE OF INDRA:
> (*from above*) Where are you, my daughter? Where?

INDRA'S DAUGHTER:
> Here, Father! Here!

THE VOICE OF INDRA:
> You've gone astray, my child. Be careful;
> you're drifting down.
> How did you get there?

INDRA'S DAUGHTER:
> I followed a flash of lightning from the empyrean,
> riding on a cloud. But the cloud
> sank beneath me, and now I'm drifting down.
> Tell me, Indra, my father, what place is this
> that I have come to? Why is it so stifling,
> so hard to breathe?

THE VOICE OF INDRA:
> You've left the second world and gone into the third.
> You've left Sukra,*** the morning star, far behind,
> And now you've entered the atmosphere of earth.
> Regard, my child, the seventh house of the zodiac,
> Libra, the Scales, in which the daystar stands
> as the year tips toward autumn
> and day balances night.

INDRA'S DAUGHTER:
> The earth, you said? This dark and heavy world
> that is lit by the light of the moon?

THE VOICE OF INDRA:
> Earth is the heaviest, the most leaden
> of all the orbs that roam the void.

INDRA'S DAUGHTER:
> Tell me doesn't the sun shine there?

THE VOICE OF INDRA:
> Of course the sun shines there; only not all the time.

INDRA'S DAUGHTER:
> There's a rift in the cloud. I can see all that's below.

THE VOICE OF INDRA:
> And what do you see, my child?

INDRA'S DAUGHTER:
> I see . . . how beautiful it is . . . Green woods,

10

20

30

blue waters, white peaks, golden fields.

THE VOICE OF INDRA:
> Yes, beautiful like all Brahma's creations.
> But it was still more beautiful once
> at the dawning of time. Something happened,
> a warping of its orbit—or was it something else?
> A revolt, and in its wake
> crimes that had to be quelled.

INDRA'S DAUGHTER:
> Now I can hear sounds from there . . .
> What sort of beings are they who dwell below?

THE VOICE OF INDRA:
> Go down and see for yourself.
> Far be it from me to malign
> the Creator's creatures, but that sound you hear
> is the language they speak.

INDRA'S DAUGHTER:
> It sounds like—. Well, to my ears
> it doesn't ring with joy.

THE VOICE OF INDRA:
> I can well imagine. All their tongues can speak
> is the language of complaint. Indeed
> those earthly beings are a bickering, badgering,
> ungrateful race.

INDRA'S DAUGHTER:
> Don't say that. I can hear cries of joy,
> and shots and roars; see flares bursting.
> Bells are ringing, fires blazing,
> and voices, thousands upon thousands,
> singing the praises of heaven.
> (*Pause.*)
> You judge them too harshly, Father.

THE VOICE OF INDRA:
> Go down and see. Listen to them.
> Then come back up here and tell me
> if there is any reason, any grounds
> for all their wailing and complaining.

INDRA'S DAUGHTER:
> Very well. I will go down there.
> But you come with me, Father.

THE VOICE OF INDRA:
> No, I cannot breathe in those depths.

INDRA'S DAUGHTER:
> The cloud is sinking. The air's so heavy,
> I'm suffocating. It isn't air, it's smoke and water.
> So heavy, heavy, it's dragging me down, down.
> Now I can see it clearly, wobbling and careening. . . .
> No, the third world is not the best of worlds.

THE VOICE OF INDRA:
> The best? Of course not. Neither is it the worst.
> Dust they call it, and it rolls round like the others.
> That's why those creatures of dust are always dizzy,
> lurching between folly and madness.
> Don't be afraid, my child. It's only a test.

INDRA'S DAUGHTER:
> (*on her knees, as the cloud descends*) I'm sinking.

40

50

60

70

80

90

---

* This prologue is a later addition to the play. It was written in 1906, in anticipation of the first production of the work, which took place in Stockholm on 17 April 1907.
** Leo, the Lion, is associated with Hercules and stands for man; Virgo, the Virgin, represents woman; Libra is the balance; and Jupiter is God.
*** Venus, in Sanskrit.

SCENE I

The backdrop represents a forest of giant hollyhocks in full bloom—white, pink, purple, violet, sulphur-yellow—and over the top of them can be seen the top of a castle crowned with a dome that resembles a flower bud. Beneath the footings of the castle are scattered stacks of straw covering the manure and litter from the stables. The wings and tormentors, which remain unchanged throughout the play, are stylized wall paintings suggesting rooms, buildings, and landscapes simultaneously.

The Glazier, an elderly man, and Indra's Daughter enter.

DAUGHTER: The castle is still growing up out of the earth—you see how much it's grown since last year.
GLAZIER: (*to himself*) I've never seen that castle before in my life—never heard of a castle growing. Oh, well—. (*To the*
100   *Daughter, with complete conviction.*) Yes, indeed, it's grown two yards. That's because they've manured it good. And if you'll notice, another wing is beginning to sprout over there on the sunny side.
DAUGHTER: It's going to bloom soon, isn't it? It's past mid-summer.
GLAZIER: Don't you see that flower bud up there?
DAUGHTER: Oh, yes, yes, I do! (*Claps her hands in joy.*) I wonder, why do flowers grow up from dirt?
GLAZIER: (*gently, piously*) They don't like to be in the dirt, so
110   they hurry up into the light as fast as they can—to bloom and die.
DAUGHTER: Who lives in that castle? Do you know?
GLAZIER: I used to know. Can't seem to remember now.
DAUGHTER: I think there's a man imprisoned there. . . . And I'm sure he's waiting for me to come and rescue him.
GLAZIER: Careful. You both might get more than you bargain for.
DAUGHTER: One doesn't haggle over what has to be done! Come on, let's go in!
120   GLAZIER: All right, all right, let's go.

SCENE II

They approach the backdrop, which slowly opens up toward the sides.

The stage is now a simple, bare room with a table and a few chairs. An Officer in a very unusual modern uniform is sitting in a chair. He is rocking back and forth and striking the table with his saber.

The Daughter goes over to the Officer and carefully and gently takes the saber from his hands.

DAUGHTER: (*as if to a child*) Mustn't do, mustn't do!
OFFICER: Oh, please be nice to me, Agnes; let me keep my saber.
DAUGHTER: No, no! You're chopping the table to pieces! (*To the Glazier.*) You can go down to the harness room and put in the windowpane. I'll meet you later.

(*The Glazier leaves.*)

DAUGHTER: You are a prisoner in your own rooms. I have come to rescue you!

OFFICER: I think I've been expecting this, but I couldn't be sure
130   you'd want to help.
DAUGHTER: It's a strong castle—it's got seven walls—but— well, we'll think of something. . . . Well, do you want to or don't you?
OFFICER: To be perfectly frank, I really don't know. Either way I'll be in trouble. You have to pay for every joy in life with twice its price in sorrow. I hate to sit imprisoned here, but if I bought myself some joy and freedom, I'd pay for it three times over in pain and suffering.—Agnes, I'd just as soon put up with it, as long as I can look at you.
DAUGHTER: What do you see in me?   140
OFFICER: Beauty personified, the harmony of the universe. There are curves and lines in your form and features that can't be found anywhere else except in the orbits of the planets, in the strings that vibrate with music, in the trembling pulsations of the light. . . . You've come from heaven.
DAUGHTER: So have you.
OFFICER: Then why do I have to take care of horses? Be a stableboy and carry out manure?
DAUGHTER: So that you'll want to get away from it.
OFFICER: I do want to, I do! I want to rise above it. But it's so   150
difficult, so hard.
DAUGHTER: But, don't you see, it's your duty to find your way to the light.
OFFICER: Duty? Doesn't life owe me something?
DAUGHTER: You think life's been unfair to you? Is that what you think?
OFFICER: Yes! Unfair, unjust. . . .

(*One can now hear voices from behind a partition, which is promptly drawn aside. The Officer and the Daughter look in that direction and then freeze in position, their gestures and expressions frozen, too.*)

(*The Mother, looking very ill, is sitting at a table. In front of her is a lighted tallow candle, which she trims and crops now and again with candle snuffers. On the table are piles of new-made shirts and linen, which she is marking with ink and a quill pen. To the left stands a brown wardrobe or clothespress.*)

(*The Father hands her a silk shawl.*)

FATHER: (*gently*) You mean you don't want it?
MOTHER: A silk shawl—for me? Oh, dearest, what use can I have for a silk shawl? I'm not long for this world.   160
FATHER: Do you believe what the doctor says?
MOTHER: Not only what he says. Most of all I believe the voice I hear inside me.
FATHER: (*gloomily*) Then it's really serious? . . . And here you are thinking only of the children—first, last, and always.
MOTHER: They were my whole life, my reason for living . . . my joy . . . and my sorrow.
FATHER: Forgive me, Christine. . . . For everything.
MOTHER: For what? You must forgive me, my darling. We've been hard on each other. And why? We don't know. We   170
couldn't help ourselves. . . . Anyway, here are new shirts and linen for the children. You must see to it that they change twice a week. Wednesdays and Sundays. And be sure Louisa gives them their baths, and washes them—all over, you understand . . . Are you going out?
FATHER: I have to be up at the school—eleven o'clock.

MOTHER: Would you ask Alfred to come in before you leave?

FATHER: (*pointing at the Officer*) But, dearest, he's standing right here.

180 MOTHER: Can you imagine, I'm beginning to lose my sight, too. . . . Yes, yes, it's getting dark. (*She trims the candlewick.*) Alfred, come here.

. . . .

(*The Father goes out straight through the wall, nodding good-bye.*)

. . . .

(*The Officer goes over to his Mother.*)

MOTHER: Who is that girl?

OFFICER: (*whispering*) Why, that's Agnes.

MOTHER: Oh, really, is that Agnes? Do you know what they're saying? That she's the daughter of the god Indra, and that she asked to come down here on earth to find out what life is really like.—Shh! Not a word!

OFFICER: Yes, indeed, she is a child of the gods.

190 MOTHER: (*aloud*) My dearest Alfred, soon I'll have to leave you and the rest of my children. There's something I want to tell you, something I want you to remember all through life.

OFFICER: (*dark and gloomy*) Yes, Mother.

MOTHER: Just one word of advice: don't ever quarrel with God.

OFFICER: I don't understand you, Mother.

MOTHER: You mustn't go around thinking that life has treated you unfairly.

OFFICER: Not even when it has, when I know I've been unjustly accused?

200 MOTHER: I know, I know. You're thinking of the time you were punished because they said you stole a coin and later it turned up.

OFFICER: That's right. It was unjust. It got me started through life on the wrong foot. Things were never the same.

MOTHER: I see. Now just go over to that wardrobe and—

OFFICER: (*blushing in the shame*) You mean you know? You know? That's where—

MOTHER: *The Swiss Family Robinson.* . . . And your—

OFFICER: Please! Don't say any more!

210 MOTHER: —your brother got punished for having torn it up. But it was *you* who tore it up and hid it.

OFFICER: It's strange. That wardrobe is still standing there after twenty years. We've moved so many times since then, and Mother died ten years ago.

MOTHER: Now, what's that got to do with it? There you go— always asking questions. That's how you destroy the best things in life for yourself. . . . Oh, here's Lina!

. . . .

LINA: (*entering*) Oh, missis, it's awfully kind of you, and I want to thank you, but I can't go to the christening.

220 MOTHER: But why not, my child?

LINA: I haven't a thing to wear.

MOTHER: Why, I'll lend you my shawl!—This one.

LINA: Oh, dearest me, I can't take *that!* It wouldn't be right.

MOTHER: I don't understand you. Don't you see, I'll never be going to parties again.

. . . .

OFFICER: What will Papa say? He gave it to you. It was a gift.

MOTHER: Oh, what small minds!

. . . .

FATHER: (*sticking his head in*) Don't tell me you're going to lend my present to a scrubwoman?

MOTHER: Don't say that. . . . I was once a maid, too— remember? . . . Why do you have to hurt the feelings of an innocent girl? 230

FATHER: Why hurt *my* feelings? I'm your husband.

MOTHER: Oh, I give up! If you're nice to somebody, you're mean to someone else. Help one, hurt another. What a life!

(*She trims and crops the candle until it dies. The stage grows dark, and the partition is drawn back in and conceals the scene.*)

. . . .

DAUGHTER: Yes, what a life. Poor souls, I feel sorry for them.

OFFICER: Do you really?

DAUGHTER: Yes, life is hard. But love—love conquers everything. You'll see! Come.

(*They move toward the rear of the stage.*)

SCENE III

The backdrop is drawn up, and a new backdrop is seen, representing a dirty, brick or stone, peeling party wall. In the middle of the wall is a gate opening onto an alleyway that leads out to a bright green area, in the center of which stands a colossal plant—a blue monkshood (Aconitum). The gate functions as a stage door entrance and to the left of it sits the Stage-Door Keeper—a woman wearing a shawl over her head and shoulders. She is working on a huge bedspread with a pattern of stars. To the right is a billboard, and the Billposter is washing it. Leaning against the wall next to him is a dip net with a green handle. Farther to the right is a door with an air hole in the shape of a cloverleaf. Left of the gate stands a small linden tree with a pitch-black trunk and a few pale green leaves. Next to it is a small, round, cellar window.

DAUGHTER: (*approaching the Stage-Door Keeper*) Haven't you 240 finished that star quilt yet?

STAGE-DOOR KEEPER: Of course not, deary! Twenty-six years is no time at all for a job as big as this.

DAUGHTER: Your fiancé never came back?

STAGE-DOOR KEEPER: No. Wasn't his fault, my dear girl. He *had* to leave, *had* to . . . the poor man. Thirty years it's been.

DAUGHTER: (*to the Billposter*) She was with the ballet, wasn't she? Here in the opera house?

BILLPOSTER: She was prima ballerina. But when *he* up and left *her,* he took all her dances with him, you might say. . . . She 250 never got any parts after that . . .

DAUGHTER: All they do is complain. At least with their eyes— and their tone of voice . . .

BILLPOSTER: Oh, I don't. Not like I used to—not since I got my dip net and my green fish pot.

DAUGHTER: That makes you happy?

BILLPOSTER: Yes. So happy, I—I—. It was what I dreamed of when I was a boy, and now it's come true. Of course, I'm fifty years old, but—

DAUGHTER: Fifty years for a dip net and a fish pot . . . 260

BILLPOSTER: Not any fish pot! A *green* one. Green! . . .

. . . .

DAUGHTER: (*to the Stage-Door Keeper*) Let me have the shawl. I'll sit here for a while and watch the passing parade. You stand behind me and let me know what's going on. (*She puts on the shawl and sits down at the gate.*)

STAGE-DOOR KEEPER: This is the last day of the opera before it's closed for the season. This is when they find out if they got renewed for next year.

DAUGHTER: And those who don't get a place—what about
270 them?

STAGE-DOOR KEEPER: God, I can't bear to see them! I have to
cover my face with the shawl, I really do.

DAUGHTER: Those poor people. How awful.

STAGE-DOOR KEEPER: Look, there's one of the girls coming
now! . . . She's not one of the lucky ones. Look at her cry.

. . . .

(*A Singer enters from the right and hurries through the gate. She
is holding her handkerchief to her eyes. She stands for a moment
in the passageway outside the gate, and leans her head against the
wall. Then rushes out.*)

DAUGHTER: Poor souls, I feel so sorry for them.

. . . .

STAGE-DOOR KEEPER: Ah, but look at him! Want to see a really
happy man? There he is!

. . . .

(*The Officer comes down the alleyway and through the gate.
He is wearing a high hat and tails and carrying a bouquet of
roses. He is beaming with happiness.*)

STAGE-DOOR KEEPER: He's going to marry Miss Victoria!
280 OFFICER: (*coming downstage, looks upward, and sings out*)
Victoria!

STAGE-DOOR KEEPER: Miss Victoria will be down in just a
moment.

OFFICER: Good, good! The carriage is waiting, the table is
spread, the champagne's on ice—oh, let me kiss you, ladies!
(*He embraces the Daughter and the Stage-Door Keeper.
Sings out.*) Victoria!

A WOMAN'S VOICE: (*from above, singing out liltingly*) Here
I am!

290 OFFICER: (*beginning to wander up and down*) All right, I'll be
waiting!

. . . .

DAUGHTER: Don't you recognize me?

OFFICER: No, for me there's only one woman in the whole
world—Victoria!—For seven years I've walked up and
down here, waiting for her. In the morning when the sun
reached the chimney tops, and in the evening as night began
to fall. . . . Look here in the asphalt; you can see the path
worn by true love. Hurrah, hurrah! She's mine, she's all
mine! (*Calls out.*) Victoria!

(*No answer.*)

300 Hm, I guess she must be getting dressed. . . . (*To the
Billposter.*) I see you've got a dip net. Everybody at the opera
is crazy about dip nets—or should I say, about fish. You know
why? No voices, that's why. No competition.—How much
does a thing like that cost?

BILLPOSTER: Pretty expensive.

OFFICER: (*singing out*) Victoria! . . . (*Shakes the linden tree.*)
It's blooming again! Look! For the eighth time. . . . (*Singing
out.*) Victoria! . . . Now she's combing her bangs. . . . (*To the
Daughter.*) Oh, come on now, my good woman, let me go up
310 and fetch my bride!

STAGE-DOOR KEEPER: Sorry, no one's allowed backstage.

OFFICER: Seven years I've been walking and waiting! Seven
years! Seven times three hundred and sixty-five makes two

thousand five hundred and fifty-five. (*Stops and pokes with
his cane at the door with the cloverleaf air hole.*) And I've
looked at this door two thousand five hundred and fifty-five
times without ever finding out where it leads to. And that
cloverleaf hole to let in light—who's in there who needs to
have light? Is there anyone in there? Someone live there?

STAGE-DOOR KEEPER: I don't know. I've never seen anyone   320
open that door.

OFFICER: It looks like a door to a pantry I saw when I was four
years old and nanny took me out one Sunday afternoon to
visit her friends. Out—other families, other maids—but
I never got farther than the kitchen—had to sit there and
wait between the water barrel and the salt tub—I've seen so
many kitchens in my time—and the pantry was always out
next to the porch—with round holes bored through it and a
cloverleaf. . . . But an opera house can't have a pantry—   330
there's no kitchen! (*Singing out.*) Victoria! . . . Say, she
couldn't possibly leave the theater by some other door,
could she?

STAGE-DOOR KEEPER: Oh, no, dearie, there's no other way out.

OFFICER: Good, then I can't miss her!

(*The Actors and Dancers come pouring out. The Officer looks
them all over.*)

. . . .

OFFICER: She's got to come along pretty soon. . . . Madame—
that blue flower out there—that monkshood. I remember it
from the time I was a child. Can't be the same one, can
it? . . . It was at the parsonage, I remember, the minister
house—the garden. I was seven years old. . . . Fold back the
top petals—the pistil and stamen look like two doves we   340
used to do that as children. . . . But this time a bee came—
went into the flower. "Got you!" I said. And I pinched the
flower together. And the bee stung me . . . And I cried . . .
Then the minister's wife came and put mud on my
finger. . . . Later we had strawberries and cream for dessert
at supper. . . . I do believe it's getting dark already.—Where
are you off to?

BILLPOSTER: Home. Time for my supper.

OFFICER: (*rubbing his eyes*) Supper?! At this time of day?—
Say, wait a minute! Do you mind if I make a phone call to   350
"the growing castle"? Take just a minute.

DAUGHTER: Why, what do you have to do?

OFFICER: I have to tell the glazier to put in the storm windows.
Winter's almost here, and I'm freezing to death. (*He goes
into the Stage-Door Keeper's office.*)

. . . .

DAUGHTER: Who is this Victoria he keeps calling for?

STAGE-DOOR KEEPER: His sweetheart. The dearest person in
the world to him.

DAUGHTER: I understand. What she may be to us or to anyone
else doesn't concern him at all. Whatever he sees in her,   360
that's what she really is.

(*It grows dark very suddenly.*)

STAGE-DOOR KEEPER: (*lights a lamp.*) It's getting dark so early
today.

DAUGHTER: For the gods in heaven a year is only a minute.

STAGE-DOOR KEEPER: And for us here on earth a minute can
seem like a year . . .

....

(*The Officer returns. He looks rather dusty and dirty. The roses have withered.*)

OFFICER: Hasn't she come down yet?

STAGE-DOOR KEEPER: No.

OFFICER: She will, she will. I know *she'll* come! (*Walks up and* 370   *down.*) But it's true, the sensible thing for me to do, I suppose, is to cancel the dinner reservation anyway—since it's already nighttime. . . . Yes—yes, that's what I'll do. (*Goes in to telephone.*)

....

STAGE-DOOR KEEPER: (*to the Daughter*) I guess I'd better take my shawl back now.

DAUGHTER: No, no this is your time off. I'll do your work for you . . . I want to learn all about people and this life on earth—I want to find out if it is as hard as they say it is.

STAGE-DOOR KEEPER: You know you can't sleep at this post, 380   don't you? Can't ever sleep—neither day nor night.

DAUGHTER: Not sleep night?

STAGE-DOOR KEEPER: Well, you can try—with a string from the doorbell tied to your arm. You see, they've got watchmen on duty backstage, and they spell each other every three hours.

DAUGHTER: Forced to stay awake—sounds like torture!

STAGE-DOOR KEEPER: You think so? I know a lot of people who would be glad to have my job. You don't know how they envy me.

DAUGHTER: Envy you! Envy someone who's being tortured?

390   STAGE-DOOR KEEPER: Well, they do. . . . Darling, I haven't told you the worst part. The worst part isn't slaving all day and staying awake all night, or sitting in the draft, getting cold and damp—it's to have to listen, like I have to, to all their sad stories. All the actors, all the dancers, they all come to me and pour their hearts out. Why do they come to me? I guess it's these wrinkles. What I've suffered is scrawled all over my face, and that's what makes them confide in me. . . . In this shawl, dearie, there's thirty years of suffering, my own and others', all tucked away.

400   DAUGHTER: It's so heavy—and it stings like nettles . . .

STAGE-DOOR KEEPER: Wear it if you want to, dearie. If it gets too heavy, give a call, and I'll come and relieve you.

DAUGHTER: You run along. If you can bear it, I certainly should be able to.

STAGE-DOOR KEEPER: You be kind to my friends now. Don't let their complaining get you down. (*She disappears down the passageway.*)

(*Complete blackout while the scene changes. The linden tree is stripped bare of all its leaves. The monkshood is virtually dead and withered. And when it grows light again, the green patch seen through the perspective of the alleyway has turned autumn-brown.*)

(*The Officer enters when the lights come up. Now his hair and beard are gray. His clothes are shabby and threadbare. His detachable shirt collar is badly soiled and limp as a rag. The roses have fallen from his bouquet so that nothing is left but a bunch of twigs. He wanders up and down.*)

OFFICER: No doubt about it. Everything points to the fact that summer is over and autumn is on its way. I can tell from the 410   linden tree—and the monkshood. (*Wanders up and down.*) So what! Autumn is spring for me! That's when the theater

opens again. And then she's got to come!—My dear lady, would you mind if I sat down on that chair a few minutes?

DAUGHTER: No, of course not. I can stand for a while.

OFFICER: (*sitting down*) If I could grab forty winks, I'd feel better. . . . (*He falls asleep for a moment, then wakes up with a start and begins to pace up and down. Stops in front of the cloverleaf door and pokes at it.*) That door . . . can't get it out of my mind. . . . What's behind it? There's got to be something behind it.   420

(*From above one can hear the soft strains of ballet music.*)

Ah ha! The rehearsals have begun!

(*The stage is lit up in flashes as if by the revolving lamp in a lighthouse.*)

What's going on? (*In time with the flashes.*) Light and dark—light and dark!

DAUGHTER: Day and night—day and night! . . . A merciful providence wants to shorten the time you have to wait. The days are flying by, chasing the nights.

(*The flashes die away, and the light becomes constant. The Billposter enters with his dip net and his paste bucket, paste brush, and the rest of his equipment.*)

OFFICER: The billposter, with his net.—Make a good catch?

BILLPOSTER: Sure did! It was a hot summer and it dragged on a bit. . . . The net was all right, I guess, but it wasn't exactly what I'd imagined.   430

OFFICER: (*stressing the words*) "Not exactly what I'd imagined." Perfectly put! Nothing is as I imagined it to be. You see, the thought is greater than the deed, finer than the thing itself . . . (*Paces up and down and slaps the rose bouquet against the wall so that the last few petals fall off.*)

BILLPOSTER: You mean to say she hasn't come down yet?

OFFICER: No, not yet. She's on her way, on her way. . . . Say, you don't happen to know what's behind that door, do you?

BILLPOSTER: No, can't say as I do. Never saw that door open.

OFFICER: Well, I think it's about time. I'm going to phone for 440   a locksmith to come and open it. (*Goes in to telephone.*)

(*The Billposter pastes up a poster and moves out to the right.*)

DAUGHTER: What was the matter with the dip net?

BILLPOSTER: Matter? Nothing. There wasn't anything really the matter—it just wasn't exactly like I imagined it would be. So the pleasure wasn't all *that* great.

DAUGHTER: How had you imagined it would be?

BILLPOSTER: How had I—? Well, it's hard to say . . .

DAUGHTER: Let me say it. You had imagined it *different* from what it was. It was supposed to be green, but not *that* green!

BILLPOSTER: That's right. It just wasn't the same. You know 450   what it's like, don't you? You really do—and that's why everybody comes to you with their troubles. . . . Maybe you'd listen to me too . . . sometime?

DAUGHTER: Of course I will. . . . Come in here and pour out your heart . . . (*She goes into the Stage-Door Keeper's cage.*)

(*The Billposter stands outside and talks to her through the window.*)

(*Complete blackout again. When the lights come up, the linden tree is leafy, the monkshood is in full bloom, and the sun is shining on the green place at the end of the alleyway.*)

(*The Officer comes in. He is old and completely gray-haired. Clothes ragged and torn, shoes full of holes. Carries the bare twigs of what was once the bouquet of roses. Walks up and down—slowly, like an old man. He studies the poster.*)
. . . .
(*A Ballet Girl enters from the right.*)

OFFICER: Has Victoria left?
BALLET GIRL: No, she's still here.
OFFICER: Good, I'll wait. You think she'll be leaving soon?
BALLET GIRL: (*earnestly*) I'm sure she will.
460 OFFICER: Don't run off now or you won't get to see what's behind this door. I've sent for a locksmith.
BALLET GIRL: How exciting! I'd love to see that door opened. That door gets me—and that growing castle.—Do you know the growing castle?
OFFICER: Do I? Who do you think was imprisoned there?
BALLET GIRL: No! Was that you?!—Tell me, why did they have so many horses there?
OFFICER: Because they had all those stalls—why do you think?
BALLET GIRL: (*hurt; almost crying*) Oh, I'm so dumb! Why
470 didn't I think of that?
. . . .
(*A Singer from the Chorus enters from the right.*)

OFFICER: Has Miss Victoria left?
SINGER: (*earnestly*) Of course she hasn't left. She never leaves.
OFFICER: That's because she loves me!—Don't go away before the locksmith gets here. He's going to open this door.
SINGER: Really? The door's going to be opened? Hey, that's great!—Excuse me, I want to ask the doorkeeper something.
. . . .
(*The Prompter enters from the right.*)

OFFICER: Has Miss Victoria left?
PROMPTER: Not as far as I know.
480 OFFICER: You see! What did I tell you, didn't I say she was waiting for me?—Don't go, don't go, the door's going to be opened.
PROMPTER: What door?
OFFICER: What door? Is there more than one door?
PROMPTER: Oh, that one! The door with the cloverleaf! Don't worry, of course I'll stay for that.—Just have to say a few words to the doorkeeper.
. . . .
(*The Ballet Girl, the Chorus Singer, and the Prompter group themselves beside the Billposter outside the window to the Stage-Door Keeper's cage, and they all take turns talking to the Daughter.*)

(*The Glazier enters through the gate.*)

OFFICER: Are you the locksmith?
GLAZIER: No, he couldn't come; he had company. I'm a glazier
490 and I can handle it just as well.
OFFICER: Of course . . . of course. . . . But do you have your diamond with you?

GLAZIER: Naturally! A glazier without his diamond! What do you take me for?
OFFICER: Never mind, never mind.—All right, let us proceed! (*Claps his hands.*)

(*Everyone gathers in a circle around the door. Singers from the Chorus in "Die Meistersinger" and Ballet Dancers and Extras from "Aida," both groups in costume, pour onstage from the right.*)
. . . .
OFFICER: Locksmith—or glazier, or whatever you are: do your duty!

(*The Glazier comes forward with his diamond.*)

OFFICER: Moments like this recur very seldom in one's life, my good friends, and therefore I urge you strongly to—to— 500 consider carefully what—
. . . .
(*Policemen come forward.*)

POLICEMAN: In the name of the law I forbid the opening of this door!
OFFICER: Oh, my God, what a lot of fuss and feathers whenever you want to do something new and great! . . . All right, we'll take it to court! We'll get a lawyer. We'll see what the law has to say! They can't stop us! To the lawyer!

SCENE IV

In full view of the audience, the set is changed to the Lawyer's office in the following way. The gate remains standing but now functions as the gate in the office railing, which runs straight across the stage. The Stage-Door Keeper's office or cage remains as the Lawyer's small inner office with his desk, but the opening of the office now faces downstage. The linden tree, stripped of its leaves, serves as a hat tree. The billboard is now a bulletin board covered with government decrees and court decisions. The cloverleaf door now belongs to a filing cabinet.

The Lawyer, dressed in white tie and tails, is sitting at a high desk, completely covered with papers and documents, just to the left inside the gate. His appearance suggests he has experienced indescribable suffering in his life. His face is white as chalk and scarred with deep wrinkles, and the hollows of his face are filled with purple shadows.

He looks hideous, his face reflecting all the crimes and sins his profession has brought him in contact with.

He has two Clerks, one of whom has only one eye, the other only one arm.

The crowd that had gathered for the opening of the door remain in their places, but now they seem to be clients waiting to see the Lawyer, and they appear to have been standing there always.

The Daughter, wearing the shawl, and the Officer are far downstage.

LAWYER: (*goes down to the Daughter*) Excuse me, Sister Agnes, but may I have that shawl? I'll hang it in my office

510 until I get a fire going in the stove. Then I'll burn it, and
send all the sorrows it contains up in smoke.

DAUGHTER: Not just yet, Brother Axel. First I want to fill it to
bursting. Above all, I want to gather up all your pains, all the
confessions you've had to take to your heart, of crimes and
vices, false arrests, libels, slanders . . .

LAWYER: My dear friend, your shawl wouldn't be nearly large
enough. Look at these walls—black with the soot of sin. Look
at these legal briefs: one miscarriage of justice after another.
Look at *me!* No one comes to me with a smile on his face.

520 They glare at me, bare their teeth, shake their fists. They
spew their venom at me, their malice, their envy, their
suspicions. Look at my hands—black, and I can never wash
them clean. Cracked and bleeding. My clothes have to be
cleaned almost everyday they smell so of crime. Sometimes
I fumigate the office with sulphur, but it doesn't help. I
sleep on a couch in the next room, and all I dream about is
crime. Right now I've got a murder case on my hands. That's
all right. I can get through that. What's much worse—the
worst of all—is divorce. A divorce case is like a cry from the

530 center of the earth, a shriek heard in heaven. Because it
goes against nature itself, against the source of all good,
against love. And what's the cause of it all? When both
parties have filled reams of paper with mutual accusations
and finally some dear soul grabs one of them, looks him—or
her—straight in the eye, and gently asks, "Come now, what
have you really got against your husband—or wife?"—that
person will stand there tongue-tied, unable to offer one good
explanation. One time—yes, one time all the trouble started
over a vegetable salad. Another time, a single wrong word.

540 Most times, nothing at all. But the anguish, the pain! It all
falls on me. Look at my face! Look at me. No woman could
love me; I look like the worst sort of criminal. Do you think
anyone wants me as a friend? No; I'm the man who makes
them pay up—either for their debts or their sins.
I tell you it's a wretched business. Living, I mean.

DAUGHTER: Poor souls. I feel so sorry for them.

LAWYER: Well you might! What do they live on? They get married on an income of ten thousand a year when they know
they need twenty thousand. They borrow, of course, every-

550 body borrows. They scrimp and scrape—live on credit—
until the day they die. Who finally pays? Can you tell me
that?

DAUGHTER: What of the birds of the air and the lilies of the
field? Someone has his eye on them.

LAWYER: Yes. Perhaps He should take His eye off them, come
down to earth and take a look at human beings. Then He
might have pity for them.

DAUGHTER: Poor souls. I do feel sorry for them.

LAWYER: Who wouldn't? (*To the Officer.*) What can I do for

560 you?

. . . .

OFFICER: I just wanted to find out if Miss Victoria has left.

LAWYER: No, she hasn't, I assure you. You can put your mind
at ease about that.—Why are you poking at my filing
cabinet?

OFFICER: This cloverleaf—it's just like—

LAWYER: Oh, no, no. Oh no.

(*Church bells begin to ring.*)

. . . .

OFFICER: Is there a funeral today?

LAWYER: No, commencement exercises at the university! I'm
just about to receive my degree: Doctor of Laws.—Say,

maybe you might like to come along, get a degree and wear 570
a mortarboard.

OFFICER: Yes, why not? Might help to break up the day a bit.

LAWYER: Excellent! Time to get ready to march in the
procession.— Hurry and change your clothes!

SCENE V

*The Officer exits. Blackout onstage while the following changes
are made. The office railing remains standing, but it now
serves as the railing to the choir in a cathedral. The bulletin
board becomes a hymn board with numbers of the psalms to be
sung. The linden tree/hat tree becomes a candelabrum. The
Lawyer's high desk in its niche becomes the dais and lectern
for the Dean conferring the degrees. The cloverleaf door now
leads to the sacristy of the cathedral.*

*The Singers from "Die Meistersinger" become Heralds with staffs,
and the Extras in "Aida" carry the laurel crowns that are to be given
to the degree candidates. The rest of the company are spectators.*

*The backdrop is pulled up, and the new drop represents im-
mensely high organ pipes; at bottom, the console and the organist's mirror.*

*Music is heard. The faculties of philosophy, theology,
medicine, and law are grouped at the sides of the stage. The
rest of the stage is empty for a moment.*

*The Heralds enter from the right. Following them come the
Extras from "Aida," carrying the laurel crowns on their outstretched arms.*

*Three Doctoral Candidates enter one after the other from the left,
are invested, crowned with laurel wreaths, and go out to the right.*

*The Lawyer comes forward to receive his laurel crown. The
Extras turn their backs on him, refusing to give him one. They
leave. The Lawyer, shattered, leans against a pillar. Everyone
leaves. The Lawyer is left alone.*

. . . .

(*The Daughter enters. She is wearing a white veil over her
head and shoulders.*)

DAUGHTER: Do you see? I've washed the shawl.—Why are you
standing here? Didn't you get the laurel crown?

LAWYER: No, I wasn't worthy of it.

DAUGHTER: Why on earth not? Because you spoke up for the
poor, put in a good word for the criminal, lightened the
burden of the guilty, sought to pardon the condemned? . . . 580
What wretched people! They're not angels, are they? Still, I
feel sorry for them.

LAWYER: Don't say anything bad about human beings. I'm
going to take their case.

DAUGHTER: (*leaning against the organ*) Why do they spit in the
face of anyone who tries to help them?

LAWYER: Because they don't know any better.

DAUGHTER: Can't we teach them? Will you help? You and I
together!

LAWYER: They don't want to be taught. . . . Oh, if only our 590
grievances could be heard by the gods in heaven—!

DAUGHTER: They shall be heard, they shall reach the highest
throne! (*Standing before the organ.*) Do you know what I

see in that mirror?—The world—right way round. Because in reality it's backwards.

LAWYER: How did it get turned around?

DAUGHTER: When the copy was made—

LAWYER: How right you are! A copy . . . I'd always suspected it was a bad copy. And when I began to recollect the original image, everything was a disappointment to me. People said I did nothing but complain and that I had bits of the devil's mirror in my eyes*—and so on . . .

DAUGHTER: It's a mad world. Just look at the four faculties of the university. The conservative government pays the salaries of all four of them. Theology, the study of God, which is always being attacked and ridiculed by philosophy, which sets itself up to be the essence of wisdom. And medicine, which is always challenging philosophy and dismissing religion from the learned disciplines and calling it superstition. And yet they all sit together on the University Council which is supposed to teach the youth of the land respect—for the university. It's a madhouse. Heaven help him who first comes to his senses.

LAWYER: The first ones to do so are the theologians. As undergraduates they study philosophy, which teaches them that theology is nonsense. Then they go on to study theology, where they learn that philosophy is nonsense. Fools, aren't they?

DAUGHTER: And the law! Serving everyone—everyone who can afford to have servants!

LAWYER: And the poor judges!—when they try to execute justice, they end up executing people. Justice—so often unjust.

DAUGHTER: What a mess you children of God have made of your earthly lives. Children, little children! . . . Come here. I shall give you a crown—one that becomes you better. (*She places a crown of thorns on his head.*) And I shall play for you! (*She seats herself at the organ and plays a Kyrie. But instead of organ notes human voices well up.*)

VOICES OF CHILDREN: Lord Almighty! Lord Almighty! (*The last note is held.*)

VOICES OF WOMEN: Have mercy on us! (*The last note is held.*)

VOICES OF MEN: Show us thy mercy and deliver us! (*The last note is held.*)

VOICES OF MEN: (*basses*) Spare us, oh Lord! Be not angry with your children.

. . . .

EVERYONE: Have mercy on us! Listen to our voices! Pity us mortals! . . . Oh, Almighty One, why art thou so far away? . . . From the depths we call to you: mercy, oh Almighty One! Lay not too heavy a burden on thy children! Hear our voices! Hear!

SCENE VI

The stage grows dark. The Daughter rises and approaches the Lawyer. By means of lighting, the organ is transformed into Fingal's Cave. The waves of the sea wash in under the basalt pillars, producing a choir of wind and waves.

LAWYER: Where are we, Agnes?

DAUGHTER: Don't you hear—?

LAWYER: I hear . . . drops . . . falling.

———————

*See H. C. Andersen's fairy tale *The Snow Queen.*

DAUGHTER: Those are tears. . . . People are crying. What else do you hear?

LAWYER: Sighing . . . wailing . . . moaning . . .

DAUGHTER: The complaints of mortals. They reach this far and no farther. Why are they always complaining? Are there no joys in life at all?

LAWYER: Yes, yes! The sweetest thing in life. And the most bitter! Love. A wife and a home. The best of life and the worst.

DAUGHTER: I want to know it. I want to know everything, try everything.

LAWYER: With me?

DAUGHTER: With you. You know where the dangerous corners are, the stumbling blocks. We can avoid them.

LAWYER: I'm a poor man. Haven't a penny.

DAUGHTER: What does that matter, as long as we have each other? A little joy and beauty doesn't cost anything.

LAWYER: What if we don't like the same things? You like what I dislike?

DAUGHTER: We'll have to learn to get along with each other.

LAWYER: Suppose we get bored with each other?

DAUGHTER: A baby will come. We'll be too busy to be bored.

LAWYER: You really want to marry me? Me—a poor and ugly man, cast out, despised by all?

DAUGHTER: Yes. Let us unite our destinies.

LAWYER: If you wish. So be it.

SCENE VII

A very plain and simple room adjacent to the Lawyer's office. To the right, a large four-poster double bed with tester and hangings. A window near it. To the left, a kitchen stove with pots and pans on it. Christine is busy sealing up the inner window of the double window, using strips of paper as weather stripping. In the rear the door to the office stands open; through it can be seen a group of poor clients waiting to see the Lawyer.

CHRISTINE: I'm pasting and sealing. I'm pasting and sealing!

DAUGHTER: (*pale and haggard, is sitting at the stove*) You're shutting out all the air. I'm suffocating.

CHRISTINE: Just one little crack left.

DAUGHTER: I've got to have air! Air! I can't breathe.

CHRISTINE: I'm pasting and sealing. I'm pasting and sealing!

LAWYER: That's right, Christine. You're doing fine. Heat's expensive.

DAUGHTER: Oh, I feel as if you were sealing up my mouth.

LAWYER: (*standing in the doorway to his office with papers in his hand*) Is the baby asleep?

DAUGHTER: Yes—finally!

LAWYER: (*gently*) I'm sorry. It's just that his bawling frightens away my clients.

DAUGHTER: (*without harshness*) I don't know what we can do about it, do you?

LAWYER: Nothing.

DAUGHTER: We'll have to get a larger apartment.

LAWYER: With what?

DAUGHTER: Do you mind if I open the window? This stale air is suffocating me.

LAWYER: You'll let all the heat out. You want to sit here and freeze to death?

DAUGHTER: I don't know. It's awful. . . . Maybe at least we could scrub the floor out there?

LAWYER: You're not up to scrubbing any floors now. I'm not either. And Christine's got to go on pasting. She's got to seal up the whole house—every crack—in the ceiling, in the floor, in the walls.

DAUGHTER: I expected to be poor, but I didn't expect to be dirty.

700 LAWYER: The poor are always relatively dirty.

DAUGHTER: It's worse than I ever dreamed it could be.

LAWYER: We don't have it the worst. There's still food in the pot.

DAUGHTER: Do you call that food?

LAWYER: What's wrong with cabbage? It's cheap—nourishing—tastes good—

DAUGHTER:—If you happen to like cabbage! It makes me sick.

LAWYER: Well, why didn't you say so?

DAUGHTER: Because I want you to be happy. I don't mind giving up something I like for you.

710 LAWYER: All right, then I have to give up something I like: cabbage. The sacrifices have to be mutual.

DAUGHTER: Then what will we eat? Fish? You hate fish.

LAWYER: It is also expensive.

DAUGHTER: I never imagined it would be like this.

LAWYER: (making a joke of it) You don't have to imagine any longer—you can see for yourself. . . . What about the baby? It was supposed to be a blessing. It's going to be the death of us.

720 DAUGHTER: Darling . . . dearest. . . . I'll die in this air, in this room, with nothing to look at but a backyard—with the baby crying for hours on end and never a moment's sleep—with all those people out there, always complaining, quarreling, accusing one another. I can't stand it any longer. I'll die in here.

LAWYER: My poor beautiful flower—without sun, without air . . .

DAUGHTER: And you say some people have got it even worse!

LAWYER: In this part of town I'm envied.

730 DAUGHTER: I think I could stand anything, if only I could have some beauty in my home.

LAWYER: I know, I know. A flower—a heliotrope—that's what you want! But it costs as much as six quarts of milk or half a bushel of potatoes.

DAUGHTER: I wouldn't mind starving if I could have flowers to look at.

LAWYER: Well, now that you mention it, there is one kind of beauty that doesn't cost anything. And a man with a sense of beauty misses it more than anything else when he can't find it in his home.

740 DAUGHTER: What's that?

LAWYER: No, you'll get mad.

DAUGHTER: No, I won't! We've agreed not to get mad.

LAWYER: So we have. We can say whatever's on our minds—as long as we don't snap at each other. So far we haven't.

DAUGHTER: And never will.

LAWYER: Never, as far as I'm concerned.

DAUGHTER: All right, now tell me what you were going to say.

LAWYER: All right. When I come into somebody's house, the

750 first thing I look at is the curtains, to see if they're hanging straight. (He goes over to the window and straightens the curtain.) If they hang like strings or old rags, I leave—right away. The next thing I look at is the chairs. If they're grouped properly, I stay. (He adjusts the position of a chair against the wall.) And then I look at the candles in the

candlesticks. If they're crooked, it's a sign the whole house needs straightening. (He straightens a candle on the chest of drawers.) There, you see! Now that, my friend, is the kind of beauty that doesn't cost a cent!

DAUGHTER: (lowering her head to her bosom) You're being 760 snappish!

LAWYER: I am not being snappish!

DAUGHTER: Yes, you are!

LAWYER: Oh, for Christ's sake—!!

DAUGHTER: You see?! Listen to you!

LAWYER: I'm sorry, Agnes . . . but I've suffered just as much from your untidiness as you have from the dirt. And I haven't dared to tidy up things myself, because then you'd think I was reproaching you and you'd get mad.—Oh, what's the use! We'll stop right now. Not a word more. All 770 right?

DAUGHTER: It's awfully hard to be married. It's the hardest thing of all. I guess you have to be an angel.

LAWYER: I guess so.

DAUGHTER: I think I'll begin to hate you after this.

LAWYER: Heaven help us! . . . I tell you what: let's forestall the hate before it comes! I promise I'll never make any more remarks about your housekeeping . . . although it is sheer torture to me.

DAUGHTER: And I'll eat cabbage—although it makes me sick. 780

LAWYER: Fine! We'll live together and make each other sick. Your pleasure—my pain; and vice versa.

DAUGHTER: We poor souls. I feel sorry for us.

LAWYER: You've come to realize that, have you?

DAUGHTER: Yes. But in the name of God, let's avoid the dangerous corners, since we know exactly where they are.

LAWYER: Let's! After all, we're humane, reasonable, enlightened people. We should be able to make allowances, forget and forgive—

DAUGHTER:—Laugh at the small things— 790

LAWYER: That's right. If anyone can, we can! . . . You know, I read in *The Times* this morning that—by the way, where is the paper?

DAUGHTER: (abashed) Which paper?

LAWYER: (snappishly) Do I get more than one?

DAUGHTER: Smile! And don't bark at me.—I used the paper to start the fire.

LAWYER: (sharply) Oh, for Christ's sake!

DAUGHTER: Come on now, smile.—I hate that paper. It makes fun of everything that I love and respect. 800

LAWYER: And that I hate and detest!—Ohhh! (Throws up his arms, unable to contain himself.) All right, I'll smile. Grin and bear it. I'll be humane, reasonable, and keep my opinions to myself, and say yes to everything, and be sneaky and hypocritical! . . . So you burned up my paper. . . . How about that! . . . (He adjusts the bed hangings.) Look at me! Here I am tidying up again and making you mad. . . . Agnes, the whole thing's impossible.

DAUGHTER: It certainly is.

LAWYER: But we still have to go on with it. Not because of the 810 promises we swore to each other, but because of the child.

DAUGHTER: That's true. For the sake of the child. (Sighing deeply.) We have to go on with it . . .

LAWYER: And I've got to go to work. My clients are waiting for me. Listen to them. Growling with impatience to get at one another's throats, tear each other to pieces, force each other to pay penalties and go to jail. . . . Cursed creatures . . .

DAUGHTER: Poor, wretched people. . . . And this pasting, pasting . . . (*She bows her head in silent despair.*)
820 CHRISTINE: I'm pasting and sealing. I'm pasting and sealing!

(*The Lawyer stands at the door, nervously twisting the doorknob.*)

DAUGHTER: Oh, how that doorknob squeals. It's as if you were squeezing my heart . . .
LAWYER: I squeeze, I squeeze . . .
DAUGHTER: Don't! Don't!
LAWYER: I squee-ee-ze . . .
DAUGHTER: No, no!
LAWYER: I—.

. . . .

OFFICER: (*from inside the office, grabbing the doorknob from the other side*) May I come in?
830 LAWYER: (*letting go of the doorknob*) Help yourself! You're a big shot! You've got your doctor's degree!
OFFICER: That's right. The world is at my feet. I can go where I want, do what I want. I've climbed Parnassus, won the laurel crown. Honor, fame, immortality, it's all mine!
LAWYER: And what are you going to live on?
OFFICER: Live on?
LAWYER: Yes. Clothing, housing, food?
OFFICER: Oh, you can always make out, as long as there is someone who loves you and wants you to be happy.
840 LAWYER: Oh, sure! Sure! . . . Paste away, Christine! Paste until they suffocate! (*He is moving out backward, nodding his head.*)
CHRISTINE: I'm pasting and sealing. I'm pasting and sealing! Until they suffocate!

. . . .

OFFICER: Well, are you coming along?
DAUGHTER: Right away! Where are we going?
OFFICER: To Fair Haven! It's summer there, the sun is shining. There's youth and happiness, children and flowers, singing and dancing, picnics and parties!
850 DAUGHTER: That's where I want to go!
OFFICER: Well, come on!

. . . .

LAWYER: (*reenters*) Now I shall go back to my first hell. This here was the second hell—and the greatest. The most beautiful was the greatest hell of all. . . . Look, she's been dropping hairpins on the floor again . . . (*He is picking them off the floor.*)
OFFICER: Good Lord! He's found out about the hairpins too.
LAWYER: Too? Of course! There are two prongs, but one hairpin. Two making one: If I straighten it out, it's one
860 single piece. If I bend it, it's two, without ceasing to be one. This means the two are one. But if I break one off—like this—then the two are two. (*He breaks the hairpin and throws away the pieces.*)
OFFICER: Marvelous! He's understood the whole thing!—But before you can break it, the prongs must diverge. If they converge, they stay together.
LAWYER: And if they're parallel, they never meet. It neither breaks nor holds.
OFFICER: The hairpin is absolutely the most nearly perfect of
870 all created things. A straight line that is the same as two parallel lines!
LAWYER: A lock that holds when it's open.

OFFICER: Holds a free band of hair that remains free when it closes.
LAWYER: Like this door! When I close it, I open the way—for you, Agnes! (*He withdraws and closes the door.*)

. . . .

DAUGHTER: And now what?

SCENE VIII

Scene change. The four-poster with its tester and hangings is transformed into a tent. The stove remains where it was. The backdrop is drawn up. In the foreground to the right are charred hills covered with the red brush and black and white tree stumps remaining after a forest fire; also red pigsties and privies. At the foot of this is an open-air gymnasium for invalids and convalescents where the patients exercise on mechanical contraptions and machines that resemble instruments of torture. To the left in the foreground are some of the open sheds of the quarantine station, housing the boilers, piping systems, and furnaces used in the disinfecting processes. Beyond the foreground is a strait of water. The backdrop represents a beautiful wooded shore lined with docks decorated with flags. White boats, some with sails hoisted, others not, are moored alongside. Between the trees one can catch glimpses of small Italian-style villas, with pavilions, belvederes, and marble statues.

Dressed up like a Moor, the Medical Inspector of the quarantine station is walking along the shore. The Officer goes over and shakes his hand.

OFFICER: Well, I'll be darned, if it isn't old Gabby himself! So this is where you disappeared to!
MEDICAL INSPECTOR: That's right. Here I am! 880
OFFICER: Is this Fair Haven or isn't it?
MEDICAL INSPECTOR: No, Fair Haven is on the opposite shore. You're in Foul Strand.
OFFICER: Oops! We've come the wrong way.
MEDICAL INSPECTOR: We?—Ah, yes! Aren't you going to introduce me?
OFFICER: Can't. Just wouldn't do. (*Sotto voce.*) She's the daughter of Indra himself!
MEDICAL INSPECTOR: Indra? Don't you mean Varuna himself? —Well, what do you say? Aren't you surprised my face is 890 black?
OFFICER: Dear boy, I'm fifty years old. At that age nothing surprises you. I guessed right away that you were going to a masquerade tonight.
MEDICAL INSPECTOR: Right on the head! Why don't you come along? How about it?
OFFICER: Great idea! This place isn't—. Can't say it attracts me . . . . What sort of people live here, anyway?
MEDICAL INSPECTOR: The sick ones here, the healthy ones over on the other side 900
OFFICER: You mean these are all poor people here?
MEDICAL INSPECTOR: Don't be ridiculous! The rich ones here. Look at the fellow on the rack. He's eaten too much *pâté de foie gras,* and drunk so much Burgundy he's got knotted feet.
OFFICER: Knotted?
MEDICAL INSPECTOR: That's right; feet like knotted wood. . . . And that fellow over there lying on the guillotine—he's drunk so much cognac, we've got to straighten out his spine by putting him through the mangle. 910

OFFICER: Don't like the sound of that!

MEDICAL INSPECTOR: Fact is, on this side everyone's got some sort of problem he wants to hide. Look at the one who's coming now. A real dilly!

(*An elderly Dandy enters in a wheelchair, pushed by an Attendant. Accompanying him is a scrawny, ugly, sixty-year-old Coquette, dressed in the height of fashion. She in turn is accompanied by the "Friend," a man in his early forties.*)

OFFICER: Why, there's the Major himself! Went to school with us, didn't he?

MEDICAL INSPECTOR: Yes, that's him: Don Juan! Look at him— he's still in love with that skinny spook at his side. He can't see that she's grown old—that she's ugly, faithless, cruel!

920   OFFICER: That's real love for you. I never thought that old playboy could ever be so deeply in love, so seriously in love.

MEDICAL INSPECTOR: You do see the bright side of things, I must say.

OFFICER: Well, you see, I've been in love myself. Victoria. . . . Yes, yes, I'm still walking up and down in that corridor waiting for her.

MEDICAL INSPECTOR: Don't tell me. you're the stage-door Johnny waiting in the corridor!

OFFICER: That's me.

930   MEDICAL INSPECTOR: Well, well. Have you got the door open yet?

OFFICER: No, the case is still pending in the courts. The lawyers are fighting it out. . . . Trouble is that the billposter is out fishing with his net, as you might have known, so he's not available to give evidence . . . And in the meantime, the glazier has put the windowpanes in the castle, which has grown half a story. . . . It's really been a very good year this year. . . . Very warm and humid.

MEDICAL INSPECTOR: You don't know what heat is. I've got heat

940   like nobody else!

OFFICER: How hot does it get in those ovens anyway?

MEDICAL INSPECTOR: When we're disinfecting cholera carriers, we get it up to one hundred forty degrees.

OFFICER: Not another cholera epidemic?

MEDICAL INSPECTOR: Yes, didn't you know?

OFFICER: Of course I knew. My trouble is I keep forgetting what I know.

MEDICAL INSPECTOR: I wish I could forget—at least forget myself. That's why I dress up, go to masquerades, Halloween parties,

950   play charades.

OFFICER: What have you been up to anyway?

MEDICAL INSPECTOR: If I tell you, you'll say I'm bragging. If I don't, you'll call me a hypocrite.

OFFICER: I get it. That's why you painted your face black!

MEDICAL INSPECTOR: That's right. A little blacker than I really am!

OFFICER: Who's that coming this way?

MEDICAL INSPECTOR: That, my friend, is a real live poet. On his way to his mud bath.

(*The Poet comes in. He is walking with his eyes fixed on the heavens, and he is carrying a bucket of mud.*)

960   OFFICER: Mud? Damnation! He should be bathing himself in light and air!

MEDICAL INSPECTOR: Oh, no. He's got his head in the clouds so much of the time, he gets homesick for the mud. Wallowing in the mud makes his skin tough—same as with pigs. After that he doesn't feel the gadflies stinging.

OFFICER: What a strange world! All contradictions!

. . . .

POET: (*ecstatically*) Out of clay the god Ptah created man on a potter's wheel, a turning lathe—(*Skeptically.*) or what the hell was it? (*Ecstatically.*) Out of clay the sculptor creates his more or less imperishable masterpieces—(*Skeptically.*)   970 or are they only junk? (*Ecstatically.*) Out of clay are created for the world's kitchens and pantries those indispensable vessels known under the generic name of pots, plates, and— (*Skeptically.*) actually, I really don't care what they're called. (*Ecstatically.*) I say to you: lo, here is clay! In its liquid state, it's called mud.—And that's where I come in. (*Calls out.*) Lina!

. . . .

(*Lina enters with a bucket.*)

POET: Lina, come here and let Agnes have a look at you. She knew you ten years ago, when you were young, happy, and—let's say—pretty. . . . Look at her now! Five kids—and a husband   980 who beats her! Scrimping, slaving, starving! All her beauty faded, all her joy withered, while she was being a good mother and wife—which should have given her an inner satisfaction, a sense of fulfillment that should have found expression in a radiant smile on her face and the glow of contentment in her eyes—.

MEDICAL INSPECTOR: (*puts his hand over the Poet's mouth*) Shut up, you fool! Shut up!

POET: That's what they all say! And if you shut up, they say, "Speak out, man, speak out!" Crazy people. No rhyme or   990 reason.

. . . .

DAUGHTER: (*moves over to Lina*) What's the matter? I want to know.

LINA: No, I don't dare. They'll punish me. Make things worse for me.

DAUGHTER: Who would be that cruel?

LINA: I don't dare tell you. They'll beat me!

POET: That's the truth! But I can talk—even if this big Moor here knocks my teeth out.—Let me tell you, Agnes, daughter of the gods, about injustice. Do you hear music and dancing up   1000 there on the hill? You know who that's for? That's for Lina's sister. She's just come home from the big city. When she was in the big city, she wasn't exactly a good girl, if you know what I mean. But now they've slaughtered the fatted calf for her. And Lina, who stayed at home, has to carry the buckets to feed the pigs!

DAUGHTER: Don't you see? They're happy because the girl was going astray and she found her way back, not because she's come home. What's wrong with that?

POET: Then why not give a party every night for the blameless   1010 working girl who never went dancing down the primrose path? Why not? Where's Lina's party? When she quits work, she has to go to a prayer meeting and be preached at for not being perfect. Is that fair?

DAUGHTER: I don't know. It's hard to say because—because there are always unforeseen circumstances.

POET: That's what the famous caliph realized, too: Harun al-Rashid, Harun the Just sat quietly on his throne, and from up there he could never see how the others had to live way 1020 down here. But finally some complaints floated up to his sublime ear. Then one fine day he climbed down from his throne, disguised himself, and took his place with the crowds in the street to learn all about justice in this world.

DAUGHTER: You surely don't take me for Harun the Just, do you?

OFFICER: Let's change the subject.—Look at the new arrivals.

(*Gliding into the strait from the left comes a white boat shaped like a dragon, with a pale blue, silken sail hoist on a golden arm and a rose-colored pennant flying from a golden masthead. Sitting at the helm with their arms around each other are He and She.*)

OFFICER: Now just look at that, will you? Look at that! There's real happiness, boundless bliss, the ecstasy of young love!

(*The stage grows bright.*)

. . . .

HE: (stands up in the boat and sings)

1030
> Hail to thee, my beautiful bay,
> Where in my green seasons
> I dreamed my golden dreams.
> I've come back to you,
> Not alone as I was then.
> Blue water, blue skies,
> Sparkling bays, shady bowers,
> Greet the girl of my dreams—
> My love, my bride,
> My sunshine, my life!

(*The flags on the docks at Fair Haven dip in salute. White handkerchiefs can be seen waving from the villas and from the shore. An arpeggio of harps and violins ripples across the water.*)

1040 POET: See how the world is lit up by love. Listen to the music ringing across the water!—Eros!

OFFICER: Why, that's Victoria!

MEDICAL INSPECTOR: Now you've had it!

OFFICER: That's *his* Victoria. I've got my own all to myself. And my Victoria—nobody can see her! She's mine! . . . All right, time to hoist the quarantine flag, and I'll haul in our catch.

(*The Medical Inspector waves a yellow flag. The Officer tugs on a line that makes the boat head in toward Foul Strand.*)

OFFICER: Put in! Put in! Come ashore! Come ashore!

(*He and She suddenly notice the hideous landscape and utter cries of fear and loathing.*)

MEDICAL INSPECTOR: Yes, I know, it's pretty tough on you, but everyone who comes from infected places has got to 1050 go through this station. You've got to be inspected and fumigated.

POET: How can you talk that way, how can you act this way?! They're two people deeply in love. Leave them alone. Let the lovers be. Meddling with true love is a capital crime . . . Why does everything beautiful have to be dragged down, dragged through the mud?

(*Ashamed and downcast, He and She come ashore.*)

HE: What do you want with us? What have we done?

MEDICAL INSPECTOR: Who says you've done anything? You needn't have done anything to have to suffer the little vexations of life. 1060

SHE: Happiness never lasts.

HE: How long do we have to stay here?

MEDICAL INSPECTOR: Forty days and nights.

SHE: I'd rather end it all!

HE: Yes. Live here among charred hills and pigsties? Not a chance!

POET: Wait! Love conquers everything—including sulphur fumes and carbolic acid!

. . . .

MEDICAL INSPECTOR: (*lights the stove. Blue sulphur fumes rise up*) I'm getting the sulphur going. Now, if you don't mind, please 1070 step in.

SHE: But this blue dress will lose its color!

MEDICAL INSPECTOR: And turn white! And those red roses will turn white!

HE: And your cheeks, too. Forty days! Forty nights!

SHE: (*to the Officer*) I hope you're satisfied! This is just what you wanted!

OFFICER: No, not at all!—It's true that your happiness was the source of my unhappiness, but—well, it doesn't matter anymore. I've got my degree from the university, and I've got 1080 a very good position right across there. . . . Ho, ho, yes, yes, I'm doing all right! . . . And this fall I'll be teaching in a school. . . . Teaching class to the little boys, the same lessons I read all the time I was a child . . . all my youth . . . And now I'll have to read the same old assignments, the same old lessons over and over again while I pass through middle age. . . . And then through old age . . . the same old assignments. How much is two times two? How many times does two go into four? . . . Until they retire me. . . . Nothing to do but wait for the next meal and the morning paper and the evening paper. . . . Until 1090 by and by I'm hauled out to the crematory and burned to ashes. . . . Don't you have any retired people out here? That's the worst thing, you know—after two times two is four—to start in grade school again after you've been through the university—to ask the same questions over and over again until you die . . .

(*A Middle-aged Man walks by with his hands clasped behind his back.*)

There goes a retired man, living on his pension, and waiting for his life to trickle out. Probably an army captain who never got to be major. Or a CPA who never quite made it to office manager. Many are called but few are chosen. . . . Walking and waiting for his breakfast— 1100

MIDDLE-AGED MAN: No! For my paper. My morning paper!

OFFICER: And he's only fifty-four. He can go on for another twenty years like that, waiting for his meals and his papers. . . . It's enough to make you sick.

MIDDLE-AGED MAN: What is there in life that doesn't make you sick? Tell me that, will you? Tell me that.

OFFICER: I wish someone could. . . . Now I've got to go and study
with little boys—two times two is four—how many times does
1110 two go into four? (*He grabs his head in desperation.*)—Oh,
Victoria, Victoria! I loved her and wanted her to be the
happiest girl in the world. Now she is happy, as happy as she
can be. And that makes my heart ache—ache—ache!

. . . .

SHE: Do you really think I can be happy when I see how you
suffer? How can you think that? Maybe your heart won't ache
so much when you see me sitting here like a prisoner for forty
days and nights? Maybe you won't suffer so much?

OFFICER: Maybe yes, maybe no. It can't make me happy to see you
suffer. Ohhh . . .

1120 HE: How do you think I feel? How can I build a happy life out of
your agony?

OFFICER: We are poor lost souls—all of us!

EVERYONE: (*stretching their arms toward heaven and giving out a
cry or shriek like a dissonant chord*) Ohhhh—!

DAUGHTER: Almighty One, listen to them! Life is cruel! Poor lost
souls! Take pity on them!

EVERYONE: (*as before*) Ohh—!

SCENE IX

*Blackout for a moment while all those onstage either leave or
change places. When the lights come up again the shoreline of Foul
Strand is in the back and lying in shadow. The strait lies between
it and Fair Haven, which is now in the foreground. Both Fair
Haven and the strait are brightly lit. To the right, one corner of a
ballroom, its windows wide open, can be seen. Couples are dancing
within. Standing on an empty box outside the ballroom are three
Young Girls, holding one another around the waist and looking in
at the dance. On the terrace steps to the casino is a bench on which
Ugly Edith is sitting, bareheaded, melancholy-looking, with her
hair like a wild mop. In front of her is a grand piano with its lid
raised. To the left, a yellow frame house. Outside it two Children,
in summer clothes, are playing catch.*

*Back of the foreground is a pier with white boats tied up and with
flags flying from flagpoles. Lying at anchor out in the strait is a
white ship of war, square-rigged, gunports open.*

*But the landscape as a whole suggests winter, with snow on the
ground and on the bare trees.*

The Daughter and the Officer enter.

DAUGHTER: How wonderful! This is vacation land! Everybody's
resting and happy! No work for anybody—parties every
1130 day—everybody's dressed in their finest clothes—music and
dancing even before lunch! (*To the three Young Girls.*) Why
aren't you girls in there dancing?

YOUNG GIRLS: Us?

OFFICER: Don't you see they're chambermaids?

DAUGHTER: Oh, of course! . . . But why is Edith sitting out here?
Why isn't she dancing?

(*Edith hides her face in her hands.*)

OFFICER: Don't embarrass her! She's been sitting there for three
hours and nobody's asked her to dance. (*He goes into the
yellow house at the left.*)

1140 DAUGHTER: What a cruel game!

. . . .

MOTHER: (*in a low-cut dress, comes out and goes over to Edith*)
What are you doing out here? Why don't you go in and dance
like I told you?

EDITH: Please, Mother! . . . I can't be forward like the other girls,
I can't. I know I'm ugly, I know that no one wants to dance with
me. Why do you have to remind me of it all the time? (*She
begins to play on the piano Johann Sebastian Bach's "Toccata
con Fuga," in D Minor, BWV 913.*)

Adagio

(*From within the ballroom the waltz can be heard softly at first,
then growing louder, as if it were competing with Bach's Toccata.
But Edith outplays it, and reduces the waltz to silence. The guests
at the ball can be seen in the doorway listening to her play.
Everyone on the stage stands entranced by her playing.*)

(*Then a Navy Lieutenant grabs Alice, one of the guests at the ball,
around the waist, and rushes off with her down to the pier.*)

NAVY LIEUTENANT: Come on, let's get out of here!

(*Edith breaks off playing, rises and follows them with her eyes, her
face registering her heartache. She remains standing as if turned
to stone.*)

. . . .

(*Now a wall of the yellow frame house is lifted away and we see the
interior of a small schoolhouse and three benches with small boys
sitting on them. Among them is the Officer, looking troubled and ill
at ease. Standing in front of them is the Teacher, wearing glasses, a
piece of chalk in one hand and a ruler in the other. He handles the
ruler as if threatening punishment.*)

TEACHER: (*to the Officer*) Now, boy, tell me: how much is two 1150
times two?

(*The Officer remains sitting. Searches desperately for the answer.*)

TEACHER: Stand up when I ask you a question!

OFFICER: (*in torment, gets to his feet*) Two . . . times two . . . is—let
me see now, it's . . . it's two—two!

TEACHER: I see. I see. You haven't learned your lesson.

OFFICER: (*ashamed*) Yes, I have, it's just that . . . well, I know
how to do it, but I—I just can't tell you.

TEACHER: Don't try to wiggle out of it!—So you know what it
is, but you just can't say it. Well, now, maybe I can help you.
(*He grabs the Officer by the hair and shakes him.*) Maybe 1160
that will shake it out of you!

OFFICER: My God, this is disgraceful! Disgraceful!

TEACHER: It's disgraceful to see a big boy like you turning into
a lazy—

OFFICER: (*hurt and stung*) A *big* boy?! Yes, I am big, much bigger
than these boys. I've finished school—(*As if waking up.*) I've
got my doctor's degree. What am I doing sitting here?
Don't I have my doctorate?

TEACHER: Certainly you do. But you've got to sit here and mature. You've got to mature.—Don't you think that's right?

1170 OFFICER: (*his hand on his forehead*) Yes, of course. That's right; you've got to mature. . . . Yes. . . . Two times two—. Two times two—is two! Yes! I shall prove it by means of analogy, the highest form of proof. Follow carefully. One times one is one; therefore two times two is two. What applies to one applies to the other.

TEACHER: Your proof is completely in accord with the laws of logic. But the answer is wrong!

OFFICER: Whatever is in accord with the laws of logic can't be wrong. Let's test it. One goes into one once; therefore two

1180 goes into two twice!

TEACHER: Absolutely right according to analogy. But now tell me how much is one times three?

OFFICER: Three!

TEACHER: It therefore follows that two times three is also three!

OFFICER: (*pondering*) No, that can't be right. . . . It can't be. . . . Or maybe . . . (*Sits down, looking lost and hopeless.*) I guess I'm not mature yet.

TEACHER: You're not nearly mature enough! Not nearly!

1190 OFFICER: How long will I have to sit here?

TEACHER: How long here? Do you think time and space exist? Suppose time exists. Then you should be able to tell me what time is. All right, what is time?

OFFICER: Time. . . . (*Thinking.*) I can't exactly tell you, but I know what it is. Ergo, I can know how much two times two is without being able to tell you! Can Teacher tell us what time it is?

TEACHER: Of course I can!

ALL THE BOYS: Tell us! Tell us!

1200 TEACHER: Time . . . ? Let me think. (*Stands motionless with his finger alongside his nose.*) While we're talking, time is flying. Therefore time is something that flies while I'm talking!

ONE OF THE BOYS: (*stands up*) Teacher, how you're talking, and while Teacher is talking, I'm going to fly from here. Therefore I am time! (*He flees from the classroom.*)

TEACHER: Absolutely correct according to the laws of logic!

OFFICER: Then the laws of logic are crazy. Johnny who flew away can't be time!

1210 TEACHER: That, too, is absolutely correct according to the laws of logic, even though it's crazy.

OFFICER: Then logic is crazy!

TEACHER: It does seem so, doesn't it? But if logic is crazy, then the whole world's crazy. And I'll be damned if I'll sit here and teach these boys how to act crazy! What do you say? If someone will treat me to a drink, we'll go for a swim!

OFFICER: That's a *posterus prius* or the world upside down! You're supposed to take a swim first and a drink after. Stupid old fool!

TEACHER: Don't get arrogant with me, Doctor!

1220 OFFICER: Colonel, if you don't mind! I'm an army officer. And I don't understand why I have to sit here and be scolded and insulted and treated like a schoolboy.

TEACHER: (*raising his finger*) We have to mature!

. . . .

MEDICAL INSPECTOR: (*enters*) We're all under quarantine as of now!

OFFICER: Ah, there you are! Where have you been? Do you realize this fellow here has been making me sit on this bench with the other boys—and I've got a Ph.D.

MEDICAL INSPECTOR: Really? Why don't you just get up and leave? 1230

OFFICER: Leave! That's a good one! . . . Easier said than done!

TEACHER: You know it, boy! Just you try to leave!

OFFICER: (*to the Medical Inspector*) Save me! Hide me from his eyes!

MEDICAL INSPECTOR: Well, come on, never mind! Come and help us dance and make merry. Dance before the plague breaks out! We've got to dance!

OFFICER: Will the warship sail then?

MEDICAL INSPECTOR: That's the first thing! The ship will sail away. What a lot of sobbing and crying there'll be. 1240

OFFICER: Always crying. When the ship comes in and when it puts to sea. . . . Well, let's go!

(*They leave the schoolhouse. The Teacher continues teaching silently.*)

. . . .

(*The three Young Girls, who were watching the dance through the window, move sadly down to the pier. Edith, who has been standing as if turned to stone at the piano, follows them slowly.*)

DAUGHTER: (*to the Officer*) You mean there isn't a single happy person in this paradise?

OFFICER: Yes, there is. Two of them. A newlywed couple. Listen to them.

(*The Newlywed Couple enters.*)

HUSBAND: (*to his Wife*) I'm so happy I want to die.

WIFE: Die because you're happy?

HUSBAND: Yes. "There lives within the very flame of love a kind 1250 of wick or snuff that will abate it."* And knowing what's to come turns my love to ashes when it burns most brightly.

WIFE: Then let's die together. Now, before it's too late.

HUSBAND: Die? Why not? I'm afraid of happiness. A mirage, made to lure us on.

(*They go down toward the sea.*)

. . . .

DAUGHTER: (*to the Officer*) What a cruel world! And the poor souls who live in it!

OFFICER: You think so? Look at this man who's coming now. Of all the mortals in this place he's the most envied.

(*A Blind Mind is led in.*)

He owns every one of these hundred villas. The bays and 1260 harbors, the beaches and woods are all his, including the fish in the water, the birds in the air, and the beasts in the woods. All these thousands of people are nothing more than his tenants. The sun rises on his waters and sets on his lands—

DAUGHTER: So? Does he have something to complain about, too?

OFFICER: Yes, and with good reason: he can't see.

MEDICAL INSPECTOR: He's totally blind.

DAUGHTER: The most envied of them all!

OFFICER: He's come to see the warship sail. His son is on 1270 board.

---

*Strindberg does not quote this passage from *Hamlet* (IV. vii) but seems to echo it.

....

BLIND MAN: I can't see it, but I can hear it. I can hear the claws of the anchor tearing at the mud at the bottom of the sea. Sounds like the hook when it's pulled out of the fish and the heart is ripped out through the throat. . . . My son, my one and only child, is leaving me to travel far from home, to sail the seven seas; and all I can do is follow him in my thoughts. . . . I can hear the anchor chain clanking and scraping. . . . And there's something flapping and snapping like wet sheets on the line whipped by the wind . . . handkerchiefs wet

1280 with tears, hm? . . . And I can hear sighing and sobbing and sniffling, like people crying . . . maybe little waves lapping against the hull, maybe the girls on the shore . . . the girls that get left behind . . . with nothing to console them. . . . I once asked a little boy why the sea was salt, and the boy, whose father was away on a long journey, said right away, "The sea is salt because the sailors cry so much." "But why do the sailors cry so much?" I asked. "Because," he said, "they always have to go away from home—and that's why

1290 they're always drying their handkerchiefs up on the mast-head!" And then I asked him, "But why do people cry when they're sad?" And he said, "That's because they have to wash the glasses of their eyes so they can see better."

(*The warship has gotten under sail and glides away. The Girls on the shore are alternately waving goodbye with their handkerchiefs and drying their tears with them. Suddenly, a signal flag with red, white, and blue stripes** signifying "Yes" is hoisted on a halyard to the yardarm of the foremast. Alice jubilantly waves her answer back with her handkerchief.*)

DAUGHTER: (*to the Officer*) What does the flag mean?
OFFICER: It means "Yes." It's the lieutenant's way of writing "yes" with the red blood of his heart on the blue cloth of heaven.
DAUGHTER: What does "No" look like?
OFFICER: A blue and white checkerboard—tainted blood and

1300 anemia.*** —Look at Alice! Have you ever seen anyone look so happy?
DAUGHTER: Look at Edith! Have you ever seen anyone look so sad?
BLIND MAN: Coming and going—meeting each other and leaving each other—that's life. I met his mother one day— and then she left me. But at least I had my son with me. Now he's gone!
DAUGHTER: But he'll surely come again!
BLIND MAN: Who are you? I've heard your voice before . . . in

1310 my dreams . . . in my youth . . . when summer vacation began . . . when I was a newlywed . . . when my child was born. . . . Every time life smiled on me, I heard that voice, like a softly stirring south wind, like harps from heaven, like the songs I imagine the angels sang the first Christmas . . .

....

(*The Lawyer enters, goes over to the Blind Man, and whispers in his ear.*)

BLIND MAN: Is that so!
LAWYER: The honest truth! (*He approaches the Daughter.*) You've seen just about everything there is to see, but you

_____

**In the original, a red ball on a white field, which most people today would take for the Japanese flag.
***A blue flag in the original. The translator has followed the modern International Code of Signals.

haven't experienced the worst thing we've got to live through.
DAUGHTER: The worst! What can that be?   1320
LAWYER: Repeating everything . . . going through it again! Going back to the beginning! . . . Having to learn your lesson all over again!—Come on!
DAUGHTER: Where?
LAWYER: Back to your duties!
DAUGHTER: Duties? What are my duties?
LAWYER: Everything you shy away from. Everything you hate to do and have to do! It means doing without, giving up, denying yourself. It means everything unpleasant, disgusting, and painful.   1330
DAUGHTER: You mean there aren't any pleasant duties?
LAWYER: Yes. After you've done them, they're pleasant.
DAUGHTER: You mean when they don't exist. If duty is everything that's unpleasant, then what's pleasure?
LAWYER: What's pleasant is sin.
DAUGHTER: Sin?
LAWYER: That's right. And sin is something to be punished for. If I have a good time, the next day I have a bad conscience and suffer the torments of hell.
DAUGHTER: Strange!   1340
LAWYER: But true. I wake up in the morning with a headache, and then I have to go through the whole thing again, repeat everything, but in a perverted way. So that all the beauty, fun, and wit of the night before appears, in the light of the morning after, to be ugly, disgusting, and stupid. The good times turn sour; the laughter rings hollow. It's the same with success. Success just sets you up to be knocked down. All the successes I had were the death of me. Because people instinctively hate to see someone get lucky. They think it's unfair that fate should favor any one person, so they try to   1350
make things even by switching the dice or changing the rules. Take talent, for instance. A real handicap. If you've got a real gift, you can easily starve to death.—Why are we talking? You've got to go back to your duties! Or else I'll take you to court—county, state, federal, and Supreme Court, if necessary.
DAUGHTER: Go back! To the kitchen stove, with the cabbage stinking up the place, the diapers in the sink—
LAWYER: That's right, my dear! We've got a big wash today— all the handkerchiefs!   1360
DAUGHTER: Oh, no, I can't go through it again!
LAWYER: That's what life is—going through it again and again. —Look at the teacher in there. He got his doctor's degree yesterday, was crowned with the laurel, honored with a ten-gun salute, climbed Parnassus, and got a medal from the king. And today he begins school all over again, asking how much two times two is, and he'll keep on asking until the day he dies. . . . That's how it is. Now come back with me, back to your chores.
DAUGHTER: I'd rather die!   1370
LAWYER: You mean kill yourself? You can't. The game isn't played that way. Suicide is a disgrace—in the first place—so much so that one's corpse is defiled. And in the second place—you'll send yourself to perdition; it's a mortal sin.
DAUGHTER: It isn't easy to be a human being, is it?

....

EVERYONE: Bravo! Hear, hear!

....

DAUGHTER: I won't go back with you. I won't sink back and be treated like dirt. I want to rise. I want to rise to the place I

first came from. . . . But before I go, I want the door to be
1380 opened so that I shall know the secret. I want the door to be
opened!

LAWYER: Then you'll have to double back on your tracks, go
back the same way you came, and suffer through all the
horrors of a trial and lawsuit, the hearings and rehearings,
the repetitions and transcriptions, the recapitulations and
summations!

DAUGHTER: If that's the way it has to be, very well. But first I want
to be alone. I want to go out into the wilderness where I can
find myself. We'll see each other soon. (*To the Poet.*) Come
1390 along with me.

(*Distant cries, wails, and moans are heard from the rear.*)

DAUGHTER: What is that?
LAWYER: The lost souls of Foul Strand.
DAUGHTER: Why are they complaining more than ever now?
LAWYER: Because the sun is shining *here*, because there's music
here, and dancing *here,* and youth and life *here.* That's why
they feel their misery so much more deeply.
DAUGHTER: We must set them free!
LAWYER: Go ahead. Try! Someone once came to set them free.
They hanged him on a cross.
1400 DAUGHTER: Who did?
LAWYER: *They* did. All the right-minded, well-meaning people.
DAUGHTER: Who are *they*?
LAWYER: You mean you don't know the right-minded, well-
meaning people? You soon will!
DAUGHTER: Were they the ones who turned against you at the
university?
LAWYER: Yes.
DAUGHTER: I know them!

SCENE X

The Riviera. In the foreground to the left stands a white wall, over
the top of which the fruit-laden branches of an orange tree can be
seen. In the rear are villas and a casino. On the terrace of the
casino are tables with parasols. To the right is a huge pile of coal,
and near it two wheelbarrows. In the rear to the right one can
catch a glimpse of the blue ocean.*

*Two Coal Haulers, naked to the waist, their faces, hands, and
bodies blackened with coal soot, are sitting, hunched in tired
despair, on the wheelbarrows.*

The Daughter and the Lawyer enter at the rear.

DAUGHTER: Oh! This is paradise!
1410 FIRST COAL HAULER: This is hell.
SECOND COAL HAULER: Hundred twenty in the shade.
FIRST COAL HAULER: Let's go for a swim.
SECOND COAL HAULER: Can't. Police will stop you. No swimming
allowed.
FIRST COAL HAULER: What about picking an orange?
SECOND COAL HAULER: Can't Police will come.
FIRST COAL HAULER: But I can't work in this heat. I've had it!
I'm getting out of here.

---

*In Strindberg's manuscript the Riviera scene has been added as an
afterthought.

SECOND COAL HAULER: Can't. Police will stop you. (*Pause.*)
Besides, you'd starve to death. 1420
FIRST COAL HAULER: Starve to death? We do most of the work
and we get the least to eat. And the rich who don't do nothing
get the most. . . . Wouldn't it be fair to say—without being too
blunt about it—something's wrong somewhere? Daughter of
the gods, what do you say?

. . . .

DAUGHTER: I have no answer. . . . But tell me, what have you
done? Why are you so black? Why do you have to work so
hard?
FIRST COAL HAULER: What have we done? We picked the
wrong parents—poor and disreputable. . . . And maybe 1430
we got arrested and sentenced a couple of times.
DAUGHTER: Sentenced?
FIRST COAL HAULER: Sure. Some get away with it and some don't.
Those who get away with it are sitting up there in the casino
eating eight-course dinners—with wine.
DAUGHTER: (*to the Lawyer*) Can that be true?
LAWYER: Generally speaking, yes.
DAUGHTER: You mean that everybody at one time or another
broke some law and could have been sent to prison?
LAWYER: Yes. 1440
DAUGHTER: Even you?
LAWYER: Even I.

. . . .

DAUGHTER: Is it true that the poor folks can't go swimming
here?
LAWYER: That's right—not even with their clothes on. Only those
who try to drown themselves get away without paying. But
don't worry, they have to settle up in court.
DAUGHTER: Why can't they go outside the town, out in the
country for a swim?
LAWYER: There isn't any open country; it's all fenced in. 1450
DAUGHTER: I mean way out, where there aren't any fences, where
the land is free.
LAWYER: There isn't any free land. It's all owned and occupied.
DAUGHTER: The ocean, the wide-open sea—
LAWYER: Everything! You can't even take a boat out or come
ashore without signing a piece of paper and paying money.
Neat, isn't it?
DAUGHTER: This is no paradise.
LAWYER: I can promise you that!
DAUGHTER: Why don't the people do something to change 1460
things?
LAWYER: They do. But all who want to make the world better end
up in prison or in the madhouse.
DAUGHTER: Who puts them in prison?
LAWYER: All the right-thinking, fair-minded—
DAUGHTER: But not the madhouse?
LAWYER: Their own despair puts them there when they realize
how hopeless it all is.
DAUGHTER: Hasn't it occurred to anyone that there might be a
good reason why things are the way they are? 1470
LAWYER: Yes, as a matter of fact. Everyone who is well-off believes
that.
DAUGHTER: Believes that things are best as they are?

. . . .

FIRST COAL HAULER: You see in us the foundation of society. If
we didn't carry the coal, the kitchen stoves would go out, the
rooms you live in would grow cold, the factories would close
down. The lights in your streets, your stores, your homes

would die. Darkness and cold would fall upon you. Yet we sweat like the damned in hell to carry the black coal. . . . What
1480   wilt thou do for us?

LAWYER: (*to the Daughter*) Do something for them. . . .
   (*Pause.*) I realize that complete equality is impossible, but why, why must there be such great inequality?

. . . .

(*A Man and his Wife cross the stage.*)

WIFE: Are you going to join us for a game of cards?
MAN: No, I've got to take my constitutional. Got to work up an appetite.

. . . .

FIRST COAL HAULER: Work up an appetite!
SECOND COAL HAULER: Work up—!

. . . .

(*Some Children come running in. When they see the coal-blackened workers, they cry and scream in terror.*)

FIRST COAL HAULER: One look at us and they scream! They
1490   scream . . . !
SECOND COAL HAULER: God damn it! It's a sick society. I say it's time to operate on it—with the guillotine!
FIRST COAL HAULER: Damn right! (*He spits in disgust.*)

. . . .

LAWYER: (*to the Daughter*) Something's wrong. Anyone can see that. People aren't so bad. It's just that—
DAUGHTER: Just what?
LAWYER: The system. The organization.
DAUGHTER: (*hides her face and leaves*) It's no paradise!
BOTH COAL HAULERS: No. It's hell.

SCENE XI

Fingal's Cave. Long green waves roll gently into the cavern. In the foreground a red whistling buoy rocks on the waves, but the bell does not sound except when indicated.

The music of the winds. The music of the waves.

The Daughter and the Poet onstage.

1500   POET: Where have you brought me?
DAUGHTER: Far from the murmuring and moaning of human beings—to the outermost edge of the world and the sea—to this grotto we call Indra's Ear. For it is said that here the god of the skies and sovereign of the heavens listens to the pleas and petitions of mortals.
POET: Listens? How?
DAUGHTER: Don't you see that this grotto is built like a seashell? You see it is. Don't you know that your ear is shaped like a seashell? You know it is, but you never thought
1510   about it before. (*She picks up a shell from the shore.*) When you were a child, did you never hold a shell to your ear and listen? Listen to the singing of your blood, to the swirling of the thoughts in your brain, to the thousands of tiny little explosions as the wornout threads in the fabric of your body snap and break? . . . If you can hear all that in such a little shell, imagine what you can hear in this great big one!
POET: (*listening*) I don't hear anything, except the sighing of the wind . . .

DAUGHTER: Let me help you. I'll be the interpreter. Listen.
   . . . The lament of the winds. (*Recitative to the accompaniment*   1520
of soft music.)

Born in the clouds,
chased by Indra's lightning,
we fled to clayey earth.
The mulch in the fields
sullied our feet.
The dust of the road,
the smoke of the city
we had to endure—
foul smell of crowds,   1530
stale beer, sour wine.
Out to the open sea we swept
to breathe clean air,
to flutter our wings,
to bathe our feet.
Indra, ruler of heaven,
listen to us.
Hear our sighs.
The earth is not clean,
life is not kind.   1540
Man is not evil,
nor is he good.
People live as best they can,
one day at a time.
Living in ashes and dust,
they breed and die:
ashes to ashes, dust to dust.
Feet for plodding
were they given,
not wings for flying.   1550
So the dust covers them
Is the fault theirs
or yours?

. . . .

POET: Once long ago I heard the same—
DAUGHTER: Shhh! The winds are still singing. (*Recitative to the accompaniment of soft music.*)

We are the winds.
It is we who carry
man's complaints.
On autumn nights you heard us   1560
whistling in chimneys,
howling in the stove,
as the autumn rain
cried, on the roof.
On winter nights you heard us
whisper in the snow-laden trees.
Out on the storm-swept sea
you heard our whining
in the ropes and sails.
You heard us,   1570
creatures of air,
who learned our songs
in passing through
the lungs of men.
The hospital, the battlefield
taught us what to sing.

Most we learned in the nursery
where the newborn cry,
mewl, and scream
1580   *with the pain of coming alive.*
We are the winds,
howling, whining,
whistling, wailing.

. . . .

POET: I believe that once before—
DAUGHTER: Shh! Now the waves are singing. (*Recitative to the accompaniment of soft music.*)

We are the waves.
We cradle the winds
and lull the winds
1590   *to sleep.*
Green cradles, wet and salt,
shaped like flames,
flames of water,
slaking, burning,
cleansing, bathing,
spuming, spawning.
We are the waves.
We cradle the winds
and lull the winds
1600   *to sleep.*

. . . .

DAUGHTER: False and faithless waves! Everything on earth that doesn't get burned up gets drowned—in the waves.—Do you see what I mean? Look. (*She points to a scrap heap.*) Look at what the sea has pillaged and plundered and destroyed. . . . All that's left of the sunken ships are these figureheads—and their names. The good ships *Justice, Friendship, The Golden Peace, Hope*—here's all that's left of *Hope*—deceptive *Hope* . . . leeboards, oarlocks, bailing buckets . . . ! And there's the life buoy. It saved itself and let
1610   the souls in distress go down.
POET: (*poking around in the scrap heap*) Here's the nameplate of the *Justice.* It must be the same one that sailed from Fair Haven with the Blind Man's son. It must have gone down. And on board was Alice's fiancé, too, the lieutenant Edith loves so hopelessly.
DAUGHTER: Blind Man? Fair Haven? I must have dreamed all that. And Alice's lieutenant, ugly Edith, Foul Strand and the quarantine, sulphur and phenol. Graduation exercises in the cathedral, the lawyer's office, the corridor and
1620   Victoria, the growing castle and the officer—it's all a dream I've dreamed.
POET: It's all in a poem I once wrote.
DAUGHTER: Then you know what poetry is.
POET: I know what dreams are. What is poetry?
DAUGHTER: Not reality. Something more than reality. Not dreams, but wide-awake dreams.
POET: And people, innocent earthlings, believe that we poets merely play and pretend and make it all up.
DAUGHTER: And a good thing, too, my friend. Else no one
1630   would believe there was any point to living and working, and the world would go to rack and ruin. Everyone would lie on his back and look at the sky. No one would lift a hand to use a plow or rake, pick or shovel.
POET: You admit that, do you? You the daughter of Indra, whose home is the heavens?

DAUGHTER: You're right to reproach me. I've been down here on earth too long and taken too many of your mud baths. My thoughts refuse to take wing. My wings are laden with clay, my feet are heavy with dirt and earth. . . . And, as for my-self—(*She lifts her arms up high.*) I'm sinking, sinking. . . . 1640 Help me, Father. God of heaven, help me! (*Silence.*) I can no longer hear him. The ether cannot carry the sound of his voice from his lips to the sounding shell of my ear. The silver cord is broken. . . . I am earthbound . . . earthbound.
POET: Do you intend to rise from earth soon?
DAUGHTER: As soon as I have burned away the ashes and dust that cling to me for not all the water in the world can wash me clean. Why do you ask?
POET: Because I—I have a prayer and a plea—
DAUGHTER: What sort of plea? 1650
POET: A petition on behalf of humanity addressed to the ruler of the world and drawn up by a dreamer.
DAUGHTER: And to be conveyed and presented by—?
POET: By Indra's daughter.
DAUGHTER: Can you say the words of your poem?
POET: I can.
DAUGHTER: Then say them.
POET: Better if you did.
DAUGHTER: Where are they?
POET: In my thoughts. And here. (*He hands her a scroll.*) 1660
DAUGHTER: Very well, I shall say them. (*She takes the scroll but recites without looking at it.*)

. . . .

DAUGHTER: "Why are we born in pain,
we human beings? Why
do we hurt our mothers
when we should be giving them
the greatest of joys?
Why do we come crying hither,
why do we greet the light,
wailing in pain and wrath? 1670
Why do we not laugh and smile?
The gift of life should be full of joy.
Why are we, the progeny of angels,
the image of God, born like beasts?
Our souls would have a vesture
other than this of blood and filth.
Must the paragon of created beings
cut his eyeteeth and descend into the flesh?"

You presume too much! The work should praise its creator."*
No one has yet solved the riddle of life and being. 1680

"Now the passage through life begins,
over thorns, thistles, sharp stones.
If you find a smooth, well-worn path,
there will soon be detours through the rough.
If flowers will make your journey lighter,
they will cost you more than you can pay.
To make your way you'll have to fight
the crowd and step on someone's toes.

---

*The Daughter alludes to a saying. "The work praises the master," not uncommon in Swedish, from Ecclesiasticus, an apocryphal book of the Bible. The standard version in English is ineffective: "For the hand of the artificer the work shall be commended."

No matter: soon the others will step
1690   on yours to keep the race a close one.
Every joy that comes to you will leave
some poor soul depressed and sadder.
But sorrow breeds no happiness;
all goes one way: from joy to pain,
and the world's cup fills up with sorrow.
So shall it be even when you're dead:
your grave will be the digger's bread."

Is this how you hope to approach the throne of the
    Almighty?
1700 POET: How can a man of earth like me
find words bright enough, pure enough,
light enough to fly from earth?
Child of the gods, will you
render our lament in the tongue
the immortals best comprehend?
DAUGHTER: I will.
POET: (*indicating the whistling buoy*) What is that floating there?
    A buoy?
DAUGHTER: Yes.
1710 POET: It looks like a human lung with the larynx attached.
DAUGHTER: It's the watchman of the sea. When danger lurks,
    it sings.
POET: I think the sea is rising now. The waves are turning
    white.
DAUGHTER: I believe you are right!
POET: There's trouble ahead. Do you see what I see? A ship—
    out beyond the reef.
DAUGHTER: What ship can that be?
POET: It looks to me like the ghost ship.
1720 DAUGHTER: The ghost ship?
POET: *The Flying Dutchman.*
DAUGHTER: Is that the *Dutchman?* . . . Why was he punished
    so harshly? And why does he never put in to land?
POET: Because he had seven unfaithful wives.
DAUGHTER: Why should he be punished for that?
POET: All the right-thinking people condemned him.
DAUGHTER: Strange world! . . . How can he be freed from his
    curse?
POET: Freed? Best beware setting anyone free—
1730 DAUGHTER: Why?
POET: Because that—. No, it isn't the *Dutchman,* after all. It's
    an ordinary ship in distress!—Why doesn't the buoy sound
    off and warn them? Before it's too late!—Look, the sea is
    rising, the waves are mounting higher. In a minute we'll be
    trapped in this cave!—The ship's bells are ringing! Abandon
    ship!—Won't be long before we can add another figurehead to
    the pile!—Cry out, buoy! Come on! Do your duty, sentinel of
    the sea!

(*The whistling buoy sings out with a four-tone chord of a fifth and
sixth, the sound resembling foghorns.*)

POET: The crew is waving for us to help—but we ourselves are
1740   drowning!
DAUGHTER: I thought you wanted to be set free!
POET: Yes, of course I do. But not now! And not in water!

    . . . .

THE CREW: (*singing in four-part harmony*) Christ Kyrie!

Christ Ky - ri - e!

POET: Now they're calling. And the sea is calling. But no one
    hears.
THE CREW: (*as before*) Christ Kyrie!
DAUGHTER: Who is that out there coming toward us?
POET: Walking on water? There's only one who walks on water—
    certainly not Peter "the rock"; he sank like a stone.

(*A white glow appears out on the water.*)

THE CREW: *Christ Kyrie!*   1750
DAUGHTER: Is that he?
POET: Yes, that is He, the Crucified One . . .
DAUGHTER: Why—tell me now, why was he crucified?
POET: Because He wanted to set all men free . . .
DAUGHTER: And who—I have forgotten—who wanted to
    crucify Him?
POET: All the right-thinking ones.
DAUGHTER: It is a strange world!
POET: The sea is rising. Darkness is falling. The storm rages.

(*The Crew screams.*)

POET: The sailors scream in terror when they see their Saviour.   1760
    . . . And now . . . they're jumping overboard—afraid of their
    Redeemer!

(*The Crew screams again.*)

POET: Now they're screaming because they're about to die.
    They scream when they're born and they scream when they
    die!

(*The rising waves threaten to drown them in the cave.*)

DAUGHTER: If I could only be certain that it is a ship—
POET: I see what you mean—I don't think it is. It's a two-
    story house, with trees around it—and—a telephone
    communication tower—a tower reaching up to the skies. It's
    a modern Tower of Babel, sending its wires upward—to let   1770
    those up there know—
DAUGHTER: You know better than that. Thoughts do not need
    metal threads to move from place to place. Devout prayers
    can force their way through all the world. I say it's definitely
    not a Tower of Babel. If you want to storm the walls of heaven,
    besiege it with your prayers.
POET: No, it's not a house . . . not a telephone tower. . . . You
    see what it is?
DAUGHTER: No, what do you see?
POET: I see a plain covered with snow—a drill field. . . . The   1780
    winter sun is shining behind a church on a hill, and the
    church tower casts a long shadow on the snow . . . a platoon
    of soldiers is marching across the field—marching across
    the tower—up the spire—now they're on the cross—I have
    a feeling that the first one who steps on the weathercock

1790 at the top must die—they're getting closer—the corporal's leading the way.—Ha! a cloud is sweeping over the plain, blotting out the sun, naturally—it's all disappeared—the wet cloud put out the sun's fire. The light of the sun created the dark tower, but the cloud's dark shadow smothered the tower's dark shadow . . .

SCENE XII

While the Poet has been speaking, the set has changed back to the theater corridor.

DAUGHTER: (*to the Stage-Door Keeper*) Has the president of the university arrived yet?
STAGE-DOOR KEEPER: No, he hasn't.
DAUGHTER: The deans of the colleges and faculties?
STAGE-DOOR KEEPER: No.
DAUGHTER: Well then, you'd better call them. Right away! Because the door is going to be opened.
1800 STAGE-DOOR KEEPER: Is it really so urgent?
DAUGHTER: Yes, very urgent. A lot of people have come to suspect that the key to the mystery of the universe is kept there. So if you don't mind, call the president and the deans at once.

(*The Stage-Door Keeper pulls out a whistle and blows on it.*)

DAUGHTER: And don't forget the glazier and his diamond. Without him there can be no opening of the door.
. . . .
(*The Actors and Dancers come in from the left, as at the beginning of the play.*)
. . . .
OFFICER: (*enters from the rear, wearing top hat and tails, carrying a bouquet of roses, radiantly happy*) Victoria!
STAGE-DOOR KEEPER: Miss Victoria will be down in just a
1810 moment.
OFFICER: Good, good! The carriage is waiting, the table is spread, the champagne's on ice. Oh, let me kiss you, madame! (*He embraces the Stage-Door Keeper.*) Victoria!
. . . .
A WOMAN'S VOICE: (*from above, singing out liltingly*) Here I am!
OFFICER: (*beginning to pace back and forth*) Very good. I'll be waiting!
. . . .
POET: I have a strange feeling I've been through this before.
DAUGHTER: Me too.
1820 POET: Maybe I dreamed it . . . ?
DAUGHTER: Or wrote it in a poem, maybe?
POET: Or wrote it in a poem.
DAUGHTER: Then you know what poetry is.
POET: Then I know what dreams are.
DAUGHTER: And I have the strange feeling that we once stood somewhere else and said these same words.
POET: Then it shouldn't take you long to figure out what reality is.
DAUGHTER: Or dreams!
POET: Or poetry!
. . . .
1830 (*Enter the President of the University, the Dean of the Theological Seminary, the Dean of the Faculty of Philosophy, the Dean of the School of Medicine, and the Dean of the School of Law.*)

PRESIDENT: You all know what brings us here: the opening of the door. Let me call first upon the Dean of the Theological Seminary. What is your view of the matter?
DEAN OF THEOLOGY: I don't have any views; I believe! — *Credo*—
DEAN OF PHILOSOPHY: I postulate—
DEAN OF MEDICINE: I know—
DEAN OF LAW: I object—until I've seen the evidence and heard the witness.
1840 PRESIDENT: Here we go! Quarreling already! . . . Let me begin again. What does the Dean of Theology *believe*?
DEAN OF THEOLOGY: I believe that this door should not be opened. It obviously conceals dangerous truths.
DEAN OF PHILOSOPHY: The truth is never dangerous!
DEAN OF MEDICINE: What is truth?
DEAN OF LAW: Whatever two witnesses testify to.
DEAN OF THEOLOGY: With two false witnesses anything can be proved—by a shyster!
1850 DEAN OF PHILOSOPHY: Truth is wisdom; and wisdom and knowledge constitute philosophy itself. Philosophy is the science of sciences, the knowledge of knowledge; and all other branches of learning are its servants.
DEAN OF MEDICINE: The only science is natural science. Philosophy is not science; it's only empty speculation.
DEAN OF THEOLOGY: Bravo!
DEAN OF PHILOSOPHY: (*to Dean of Theology*) Bravo, you say! What do you think you are? You're the archenemy of all knowledge. You're the very antithesis of science. You're ignorance and obscurantism itself—!
1860 DEAN OF MEDICINE: Bravo!
DEAN OF THEOLOGY: (*to Dean of Medicine*) Bravo, you say! You of all people! Who can't see farther than the end of your nose in a magnifying glass—you, who don't believe in anything but what your deceptive senses tell you—what your eyes tell you, for example, even though you may be far-sighted or near-sighted; cross-eyed, wall-eyed, or one-eyed; color blind, red-blind, green-blind.
DEAN OF MEDICINE: You blithering idiot!
DEAN OF THEOLOGY: Jackass!

(*They start fighting.*)

1870 PRESIDENT: Stop that! Let's not have you birds pecking each other's eyes out.
DEAN OF PHILOSOPHY: Well, if I had to choose between those two—theology and medicine—I would choose—neither!
DEAN OF LAW: And if I sat on the bench and you three were brought before me, I'd sentence—all three of you! You can't agree on a single point, and you never could. . . . Let's get back to business. Mr. President, what is your own view on the opening of this door?
1880 PRESIDENT: My view? I don't have any views. I have simply been appointed by the state to see to it that during our executive meetings you don't tear one another to pieces— while you're educating our youth. Views? Ah, no, indeed, I'm very careful not to have any views. There was a time when I had a few, but they were quickly refuted. Views are always quickly refuted—by those with the opposite views, you understand. . . . And now, perhaps we might proceed to the opening of the door, even at the risk of revealing some dangerous truths?
DEAN OF LAW: What is truth? What is *the* truth?

1890 DEAN OF THEOLOGY: I am the truth, the way, and the life—
DEAN OF PHILOSOPHY: I am knowledge of knowledge—
DEAN OF MEDICINE: I am exact knowledge—
DEAN OF LAW: I object!

(*They all start to fight.*)

....

DAUGHTER: Aren't you ashamed? You, the teacher of our youth!
DEAN OF LAW: Mr. President! As the representative of the government and as the head of the faculty, you must bring charges against this woman for her remarks. She said we ought to be ashamed. Now that's an insult. And when she
1900 referred to us as the teacher of the young, her ironic tone of voice implied that we were incapable. Now that's slander!
DAUGHTER: Heaven help the students!
DEAN OF LAW: Do you hear? She's excusing the students!— That's the same as accusing us. Mr. President, I insist that you prosecute her!
DAUGHTER: Yes, that's right. I accuse you, you as a group, of sowing doubt and breeding skepticism in the minds of our youth.
DEAN OF LAW: Listen to her! There she stands telling the
1910 students to have no respect for our authority, and yet she has the gall to accuse us of breeding skepticism! If that isn't a criminal act, what is? I put it to you, all you good, right-thinking people.

....

ALL THE RIGHT-THINKING PEOPLE: Yes, yes, absolutely criminal!
DEAN OF LAW: There! All the right-thinking people have condemned you!—Now go in peace and be content with thy gain. Otherwise—!
DAUGHTER: My gain?—Otherwise! Otherwise what??
1920 DEAN OF LAW: Otherwise thou shall be stoned.
POET: Or crucified.
DAUGHTER: Very well, I'll go.—Come with me and I'll give you the answer to the riddle.
POET: What riddle?
DAUGHTER: What did he mean by "my gain"?*
POET: Probably nothing. Just a lot of hot air, as we say. Talking through his hat.
DAUGHTER: But nothing could have hurt me more.
POET: I suppose that's why he said it. That's how people are.

....

1930 ALL THE RIGHT-THINKING PEOPLE: Hooray! The door is open!

....

PRESIDENT: What lay hidden behind the door?
GLAZIER: I can't see anything.
PRESIDENT: You can't see anything? Well, I can't say I'm surprised—. Learned deans, what lay hidden behind the door?
DEAN OF THEOLOGY: Nothing. That is the key to the riddle of the world. In the beginning God created heaven and earth out of nothing.
DEAN OF PHILOSOPHY: Nothing comes of nothing.
DEAN OF MEDICINE: Bosh! Nothing. Period.
1940 DEAN OF LAW: I object to the whole thing. It's a clear case of

---

*The exchange between the Dean of Law and the Daughter evidently reflects the words of Paul, I Timothy 6:1–6, with the Dean turning Paul's admonition against the Daughter.

fraud. I appeal to all the right-thinking people!
DAUGHTER: (*to the Poet*) What are the right-thinking people?
POET: I wish I knew. They usually turn out to be a party of one. Today it's me and my side—tomorrow it's you and your side. . . . You get appointed—or rather, you're self-appointed.

....

ALL THE RIGHT-THINKING PEOPLE: We've been swindled! Tricked!
PRESIDENT: And who has swindled you?
ALL THE RIGHT-THINKING PEOPLE: She did! The Daughter!
PRESIDENT: (*to the Daughter*) Would you be so good as to tell   1950
us what you had in mind with this door-opening?
DAUGHTER: No, good people, I won't. "If I tell you, ye will not believe."
DEAN OF MEDICINE: But there's nothing—nothing at all.
DAUGHTER: You say right. But you understand not.
DEAN OF MEDICINE: She's talking nonsense!
EVERYONE: Nonsense! Boo!
DAUGHTER: (*to the Poet*) Poor lost souls. I feel sorry for them.
POET: You serious?
DAUGHTER: Always serious.   1960
POET: Do you also feel sorry for the right-thinking people?
DAUGHTER: Perhaps most of all for them.
POET: And what about the four learned faculties?
DAUGHTER: Them too, no less than the others. Four heads on one body, four minds! Who created the monster?
EVERYONE: She's not answering us!
PRESIDENT: Down with her!
DAUGHTER: But I have answered you!
PRESIDENT: Don't you talk back to me!
EVERYONE: Listen to her! She's talking back!   1970
DAUGHTER: Answer or not answer, I can't win. . . . Come with me, you poet and seer, and I shall tell you—somewhere far from here—the answer to the riddle. Somewhere, out in the desert, where no one can hear us, no one see us. Because—

....

LAWYER: (*coming forward and grabbing the Daughter by the arm*) Have you forgotten your responsibilities?
DAUGHTER: God knows I haven't. But I have more important responsibilities.
LAWYER: What about your child?
DAUGHTER: My child—oh yes! What about her?   1980
LAWYER: Your child is crying for you.
DAUGHTER: My child! How that child ties me down! I feel chained to the earth. . . . And I have this pain in my breast, this feeling of anguish. What is it?
LAWYER: Don't you know?
DAUGHTER: No.
LAWYER: The pangs of conscience.
DAUGHTER: Is that what it is? The pangs of conscience?
LAWYER: That's right. They show up after every duty you neglect, after every pleasure you enjoy, however innocent—if there are   1990
any innocent pleasures (which I doubt), and after every harm you do your friends and neighbors.
DAUGHTER: And there's no cure for these pangs, I suppose?
LAWYER: Oh, yes; but only one. You must discharge your duty without a moment's hesitation.
DAUGHTER: You know, you look just like a demon when you say that word "duty."—But what am I supposed to do if I have two duties to discharge?
LAWYER: Simple! First you discharge one, and then the other.
DAUGHTER: The most important one first.—So I leave my child in   2000
your care, while I go to discharge my first duty.

LAWYER: But the child needs you; you'll break its heart. Can you bear to know that someone is suffering on account of you?

DAUGHTER: You're turning me against myself. You've broken my heart in two and it's pulling me both ways.

LAWYER: Life is full of little conflicts like that.

DAUGHTER: Oh, how my heart is torn. I don't know which way to turn.

. . . .

2010 POET: If you knew how much sorrow and misery I caused by discharging the obligations I owed to my calling in life— notice: my calling, the most important duty of all—you would shun me.

DAUGHTER: Why? What did you do?

POET: My father placed all his hopes in me. I was his only son and he dreamed about how I would carry on the business he had built up. I ran away from business school and my father never got over it. My mother wanted me to study religion, but I didn't have the heart for it. So she disowned me. I had
2020 a friend who gave me a helping hand when I was down and out. But my friend had different political views, fought against the causes I spoke for and fought for. I had to cut down my best friend and benefactor in order to be true to myself. Since then I've never known any peace. They call me disloyal, a stinker. And a fat lot of good it does me to hear my conscience tell me, "You did right," because the next moment it's telling me how wrong I was. And that's life for you.

. . . .

DAUGHTER: Come with me out into the desert.

2030 LAWYER: Your child! Your child!

DAUGHTER: (*indicating all those present*) Here are my children! Taken one by one, they're good and gentle. But put them together and they fight with one another and turn into demons. . . . Goodbye . . .

SCENE XIII

Outside the castle. Same set as in the first scene of the first act. Only now the ground below the footings is covered with flowers (blue monkshood or aconite). At the very top of the castle, surmounting its tower and lantern, is a chrysanthemum bud ready to burst into bloom. The windows have candles burning in them.

The Daughter and the Poet are onstage.

DAUGHTER: The time has nearly come when with the help of the fire. I shall rise and return to the empyrean. This is what you call death, what you approach with fear in your hearts.

POET: Fear of the unknown.

DAUGHTER: Which you really know.

2040 POET: Who knows?

DAUGHTER: Everyone! Why do you not believe your prophets?

POET: Prophets have never been believed. I wonder why?—"If God has spoken, why will men not believe?" His power to persuade must surely be irresistible!

DAUGHTER: Have you always been a skeptic?

POET: No. Many a time I've had absolute faith and certitude, but it always faded away after a while, like a dream upon awakening.

---

*In place of the funeral wreaths, the original has "white sheets in the windows, pine cuttings on the walk"—once customary features at Swedish funerals.

DAUGHTER: It isn't easy to be a human being. I know that.

POET: You have come to realize that, have you, and admit it?

DAUGHTER: Yes.   2050

POET: Tell me something. Was it not Indra who once sent his son here to earth to hear the complaints of mankind?

DAUGHTER: Yes, it was. And how did the people receive him?

POET: What did he do to accomplish his mission?—to answer with a question.

DAUGHTER: To answer with another question: was not the condition of mankind improved as a result of his visit to earth? Tell me truly.

POET: Improved? Yes, a little. Very little! —Now, instead of asking questions, will you solve the riddle?   2060

DAUGHTER: I could. But what good would it do? You wouldn't believe the answer.

POET: You, I will believe. I know who you are.

DAUGHTER: Very well, I shall tell you. . . . At the dawn of time before the sun shone, Brahma, the divine primal potency, went forth and let himself be seduced by Maya, the creative mother of the world, so that he might propagate himself. The divine element thus joined with earthly matter. This was the fall of heaven. Consequently, the world and its inhabitants and life itself are nothing more than phantoms, mirages, images in a dream—   2070

POET: My dream!

DAUGHTER: A dream come true. Now, to free themselves from earthly matter the progeny of Brahma seek deprivation and suffering. There you have suffering as the redeemer. But this yearning for suffering comes into conflict with the craving for pleasure. Which is love. Now do you understand what love is, offering the most sublime joys along with the most profound suffering, sweetest when it is most bitter? Do you understand what woman is? Woman, through whom sin and death entered into life?   2080

POET: I do understand. And the upshot?

DAUGHTER: I don't have to tell you. Constant strife between the anguish of joy and, the pleasure of suffering, the torments of remorse and the delights of sensuality.

POET: Strife—is that all we can hope for?

DAUGHTER: The conflict between opposites produces energy, just as fire and water generate steam power.

POET: And peace? And rest?

DAUGHTER: I've said enough. You mustn't ask any more, and I   2090
mustn't answer. . . . The altar is decked for the sacrifice. . . . The flowers keep watch, the lights are lit. . . . The funeral wreaths hang in the windows and doors.

POET: You say that as calmly and coolly as if you didn't know what it means to suffer.

DAUGHTER: Not know? I have suffered all that mortal man suffers but felt it a hundred times more, because my senses are keener.

POET: Tell me what you suffered.

DAUGHTER: You're a poet, but could even you tell me your   2100
troubles in words that said it all? Was there ever a time when your words and your thoughts were in perfect harmony? A time when your words soared to the level of your thoughts?

POET: No, you're right. Before my own thoughts I stood deaf and dumb. And when the crowd listened in admiration to my song, it sounded like bawling to me. I guess that's why I always blushed when I heard my praises sung.

DAUGHTER: And yet you expect me to—? Look me in the eye!

POET: I can't. Your gaze is too intense.   2110

DAUGHTER: And so would my words be if I spoke in my own tongue.

POET: At least tell me—before you go—what was the hardest thing to endure—down here?

DAUGHTER: Being, just being. Feeling my sight clouded by these eyes, my hearing muffled by these ears, and my thoughts, my bright, airy thoughts trapped in the labyrinth of coiled fat. You know what a brain looks like—what crooked ways, what secret passages!

2120 POET: I know. I suppose that's why all the right-thinking people think crooked.

DAUGHTER: Always ready with sarcasm. That's how you all are.

POET: What do you expect?

DAUGHTER: Now I'm going to shake the dust off my feet first— the earth, the clay. (*She takes off her shoes and lays them on the fire.*)

. . . .

STAGE-DOOR KEEPER: (*enters and lays her shawl on the fire*) Maybe you wouldn't mind if I added my shawl to the fire, would you, deary? (*Exits.*)

2130 OFFICER: (*enters*) And I my roses? Nothing left but thorns. (*Exits.*)

BILLPOSTER: (*enters*) The posters can go. But my dip net, never! (*Exits.*)

GLAZIER: (*enters*) The diamond glass cutter that opened the door! Goodbye! (*Exits.*)

LAWYER: (*enters*) The minutes of the great lawsuit concerning the pope's beard or the diminishing water supply in the sources of the Ganges River. (*Exits.*)

MEDICAL INSPECTOR: (*enters*) Only a small contribution: the black
2140 mask that made me black against my will. (*Exits.*)

VICTORIA: (*enters*) My beauty—my sorrow! (*Exits.*)

EDITH: (*enters*) My ugliness—my sorrow! (*Exits.*)

BLIND MAN: (*enters, sticks his hand into the fire*) I give my hand in place of my eye! (*Exits.*)

(*The old Don Juan enters in his wheelchair, accompanied by the Coquette and the "Friend."*)

DON JUAN: Hurry up! Hurry up! Life is short! (*Exits with the others.*)

. . . .

POET: I once read that when life nears its end, everything in it comes rushing past in single file. Is this the end?

DAUGHTER: It is for me. Goodbye.

2150 POET: Not even a few parting words?

DAUGHTER: There's nothing I can say. Do you still believe that your words can express our thoughts?

. . . .

DEAN OF THEOLOGY: (*enters, raging mad*) I've been repudiated by my God, I'm persecuted by the people, disowned by the administration, ridiculed by my colleagues! How can I have

faith, how can I believe, when no one else does? How can I fight for a God who does not fight for his own? Junk! That's what it is—junk! (*He throws a book on the fire and leaves.*)

. . . .

POET: (*snatching the book from the fire*) You know what it is? A martyrology. It lists a martyr for each day of the year.   2160

DAUGHTER: Martyr?

POET: Yes—someone who was tortured and put to death for his beliefs. And why?—Do you think that everyone who is tortured suffers, and that everyone who is put to death feels pain? Doesn't suffering melt our chains and doesn't death set us free?

. . . .

CHRISTINE: (*enters with her strips of paper and weatherstripping*) I'm going to paste and seal and paste and seal until there's nothing more to paste and seal!

POET: And if heaven itself split wide open, you'd try to paste and   2170
seal that too! Go away!

CHRISTINE: Aren't there any inner windows in the castle for me to seal up?

POET: No, there certainly aren't! Not there!

CHRISTINE: (*leaving*) Well, then I'm leaving.

. . . .

DAUGHTER: It's time! Give me your hand, my friend,
Farewell, you human being, you dreamer,
you poet, who knows best how to live,
soaring on wings above the earth,
swooping down when you feel like it,   2180
to graze the dust, not to drown in it.
Now when I must leave, how hard it is
to say goodbye, to bid farewell.
One longs for all that one has loved,
regrets all that one has offended.
Now, now I know what it means to live;
I feel the pain of being human.
You miss what you never wanted;
regret even misdeeds never done.
You want to leave, you want to stay;   2190
your heart's drawn and quartered, torn apart
by conflicting wishes, indecision, doubt.
Goodbye, my friend! Tell your fellow men
that where I'm going I shall think of them
and that in your name I shall convey
their plaints and protests to the throne on high.
Farewell!

(*She enters the castle. Music. The rear of the stage is lit up by the burning castle and reveals a wall of human faces, questioning, sorrowful, despairing.*)

(*As the castle burns, the flower bud at the top bursts and blossoms into a huge chrysanthemum.*)

Bernard Shaw

George Bernard Shaw (1856–1950) was a man of wide-ranging passions and huge abilities (Shaw disliked the name "George" and never used it, preferring "Bernard" or simply "G.B.S."). By his fortieth birthday he had written five novels, three volumes of classic music criticism, and three volumes of incendiary theater reviews; he had become visible in the influential socialist political organization, the **FABIAN SOCIETY**; he had written the first books in English on Wagner's operas and on Ibsen's plays; and he had just started his career as a dramatist, a career that would eventually include more than fifty plays.

Shaw was born in Dublin. Like Jonathan Swift and Richard Brinsley Sheridan before him, Shaw retained the satiric perspective of the Irish outsider in England. His mother was a music teacher and his sister was a promising singer when they left for London while Shaw was in his teens. He followed them to London in 1876. A shy and self-effacing young man, Shaw took a variety of jobs that brought him into contact with the public, and he used the opportunity of lecturing for the Fabian Society to develop the brilliantly articulate persona we recognize today as "G.B.S." Throughout the 1880s, Shaw worked with the Fabians, adopting their plan of gradual social reform in place of a more rigorously Marxist call for social revolution. The Fabians strove to change society through a strategy of permeation, working to get their members elected into prominent offices, where their educational and social reforms might be put into effect. Shaw was deeply influenced by the Fabians' gradualist scheme for social improvement—scheme that underlies the utopian project of his greatest plays—for Fabian gradualism synchronized with Shaw's other passion, Creative Evolution. Appalled by what he regarded as the mindless mechanism of Darwinian natural selection, Shaw resisted the notion that human evolution followed a random and inevitable process. He urged instead that humanity take command of its future by willing itself to evolve in certain humane directions, and he advocated eugenics, capital punishment, and other ideas in the interest of the development of the species. Shaw attempted an uneasy synthesis of the Fabian socialist project of gradual social evolution with the individualist metaphysics of Creative Evolution: the improvement of society through the improvement of each of its members.

Shaw's friend William Archer once described seeing Shaw in the British Museum reading room simultaneously reading Marx's *Das Kapital* and the score of Wagner's *Ring of the Niebelung* cycle. The blending of political substance with a rich and deeply harmonized verbal music became a constant feature of Shaw's drama. Writing as a theater critic in the 1890s, Shaw became the champion of Ibsen in England. Vowing to lay siege to the conventions of the nineteenth-century theater, he touted Ibsen's plays and lambasted the corny tearjerkers, simplistic melodramas, and overstuffed Shakespearean productions that were the theater's common fare. Not incidentally, he worked to create a taste for his own plays, an operatic drama of the intellectual passions.

Shaw's career as a playwright falls into three main phases. Shaw's earliest plays—*Widowers' Houses* (1892) and *Mrs. Warren's Profession* (1893)—attacked specific social problems, like slum landlords and international prostitution. But Shaw more often linked social ills to the smug pieties of conventional morality. His plays generally work to disillusion his main characters—and his audience—from the ready acceptance of bourgeois ideology as a natural "reality." This process of disillusionment informs Shaw's lighter comedies of the 1890s, plays like *Arms and the Man* (1894), *Candida* (1894), and *Caesar and Cleopatra* (1898). After the turn of the century, however, Shaw entered on his maturity as a playwright, undertaking a series of major comedies that place this process of disillusionment directly in conflict with society's most important institutions: marriage and sexuality in *Man and Superman* (1903); British imperialism in Ireland in *John Bull's Other Island* (1904); salvation, damnation, and raw power in *Major Barbara* (1905); medicine in *The Doctor's Dilemma*

(1906); language and class in *Pygmalion* (1912). Several of these plays were first produced at the Court Theater, under the management of Shaw's close friend Harley Granville Barker, who originated the part of Cusins in *Major Barbara* and other Shavian roles. Under Barker and his partner J.E. Vedrenne, the Court Theater in 1904–1907 became the most influential theater in London before World War I. Through its efforts, and Shaw's own energy as playwright, director, and advisor, the Court made Shaw's reputation as a major dramatist. With the coming of World War I, and the violent waste of civilization it brought with it, Shaw's confidence in the eventual perfection of humanity was deeply shaken, and the plays of his final half-century are much bleaker, more uncertain in tone: his magnificent "fantasia in the Russian manner on English themes," *Heartbreak House* (1919), modeled on Chekhov's *The Cherry Orchard*; *Saint Joan* (1923), perhaps his best-loved play; his five-play quintet on the origin and future of the species, *Back to Methuselah* (1921); and many others. In contrast to the confidence of Shaw's earlier plays, the later dramas generally seem to ask the question that Shaw gave to his Saint Joan: "O God that madest this beautiful earth, when will it be ready to receive Thy saints? How long, O Lord, how long?"

Major Barbara Shaw was born before the publication of Darwin's *Origin of Species* in 1859, and he died after the dropping of the atomic bomb on Hiroshima. His major plays, like *Major Barbara,* treat the problems of the twentieth century in the dramatic vocabulary of Edwardian **COMEDY OF MANNERS.** *Major Barbara* is typical of the dialectical process of Shaw's plays. From the outset—when Stephen learns that his income is derived from his father's munitions empire—Shaw forces the audience and his characters to question the nature of their

Adolphus Cusins beats the big drum in the finale of Act 2 of Bernard Shaw's *Major Barbara.*

© Joan Marcus

values, particularly the sense that good and evil, morality and economics, the power to save and the power to destroy can be easily or conveniently distinguished from one another. As a result, the play forces a deeply ironic experience on its characters and on the audience. For Shaw is interested in salvation, not simply the moralizing salvation promised by the Salvation Army, but a Nietzschean transvaluation of values, a salvation beyond the conventional abstractions of good and evil that he regards as necessary to the transformation of English society.

The play is structured dialectically, progressing from thesis, to antithesis, to a problematic synthesis. The "thesis" of act 1 concerns the values of Wilton Crescent: the comfortable morality of the English upper classes. As the scene proceeds, though, Shaw suggests that conventional morality, the innate knowledge of right and wrong, is in fact supported by Undershaft's money and gunpowder. The "antithesis" of act 2 offers the unconventional morality of the Salvation Army; Barbara's shelter in West Ham claims to provide true salvation by requiring a more sincere form of religious conviction. However, as it turns out, both Wilton Crescent and West Ham are equally in the grip of Bodger and Undershaft. The distiller and the munitions-maker determine the material realities on which society erects its illusory social "ideals" and calls them "reality." The Dionysian sacrifice of Barbara at the end of act 2—with its echoes of Christ's crucifixion as well—prepares us for her resurrection in the "synthesis" offered by act 3; in Perivale St Andrews, the spiritual Barbara and the intellectual Cusins are married with the blessing of the explosive Undershaft. We might be troubled, though, by the "synthesis" offered by the utopian factory town, for Undershaft's utopia hardly seems revolutionary. In many ways, Perivale St Andrews largely duplicates turn-of-the-century English class society and industrial capitalism, with the poverty and dirt cleaned up. The play's last act is often said to be unconvincing, and we might wonder whether that is in fact part of Shaw's purpose in *Major Barbara*. Once Shaw instructs us in the process of dialectical criticism, perhaps he invites us to scrutinize even Undershaft's bourgeois utopia, to see Perivale St Andrews as itself in need of further (r)evolution.

Shaw made Andrew Undershaft a magnificently melodramatic, attractive, amoral munitions-maker, whose creative ability is harnessed to the power to destroy. Moreover, Shaw drew a parallel between Undershaft and a crucial dramatic precursor, the Dionysus of Euripides' *The Bacchae.* The character of Cusins was modeled on Shaw's friend, the well-known classical scholar Gilbert Murray, and in the original production, Cusins was even played to resemble Murray. In act 2, Cusins quotes a brief passage adapted from Murray's translation of *The Bacchae,* part of the choral speech delivered just before Pentheus is led out to spy on the Bacchae and be killed. We might take this invocation of Dionysus as a final clue to the play's attitude. Much like Euripides, Shaw prevents his audience from sympathizing entirely with his hero, from readily accepting the terrible power necessary to change the world. Although the play ends with a ceremonial marriage characteristic of ROMANTIC COMEDY—symbolizing the union of intellect, spirit, and power—the fact that Dionysus Undershaft presides over this union should give us pause. Can the power he wields really be harnessed for our salvation? Shaw, not surprisingly, had a systematic but unconventional approach to English spelling and punctuation, and insisted that publisher's observe it when printing his plays; this edition of *Major Barbara* accordingly preserves Shaw's style.

Major Barbara

Bernard Shaw

CHARACTERS

STEPHEN UNDERSHAFT	CHARLES LOMAX
LADY BRITOMART	RUMMY MITCHENS
BARBARA UNDERSHAFT	SNOBBY PRICE
SARAH UNDERSHAFT	PETER SHIRLEY
ANDREW UNDERSHAFT	BILTON
JENNY HILL	MRS BAINES
BILL WALKER	ADOLPHUS CUSINS
MORRISON	

ACT ONE

It is after dinner in January 1906, in the library in LADY BRITO-MART UNDERSHAFT'S *house in Wilton Crescent. A large and comfortable settee is in the middle of the room, upholstered in dark leather. A person sitting on it (it is vacant at present) would have, on his right,* LADY BRITOMART'S *writing table, with the lady herself busy at it; a smaller writing table behind him on his left; the door behind him on* LADY BRITOMART'S *side; and a window with a window seat directly on his left. Near the window is an armchair.*

LADY BRITOMART *is a woman of fifty or thereabouts, well dressed and yet careless of her dress, well bred and quite reckless of her breeding, well mannered and yet appallingly outspoken and indifferent to the opinion of her interlocutors, amiable and yet peremptory, arbitrary, and high-tempered to the last bearable degree, and withal a very typical managing matron of the upper class, treated as a naughty child until she grew into a scolding mother, and finally settling down with plenty of practical ability and worldly experience, limited in the oddest way with domestic and class limitations, conceiving the universe exactly as if it were a large house in Wilton Crescent, though handling her corner of it very effectively on that assumption, and being quite enlightened and liberal as to the books in the library, the pictures on the walls, the music in the portfolios, and the articles in the papers.*

Her son, STEPHEN, *comes in. He is a gravely correct young man under 25, taking himself very seriously, but still in some awe of his mother, from childish habit and bachelor shyness rather than from any weakness of character.*

STEPHEN: Whats the matter?
LADY BRITOMART: Presently, Stephen.

(STEPHEN *submissively walks to the settee and sits down. He takes up a Liberal weekly called* The Speaker.)

LADY BRITOMART: Dont begin to read, Stephen. I shall require all your attention.
5 STEPHEN: It was only while I was waiting—
LADY BRITOMART: Dont make excuses, Stephen. (*He puts down* The Speaker.) Now! (*She finishes her writing; rises; and comes to the settee.*) I have not kept you waiting very long, I think.
STEPHEN: Not at all, mother.
10 LADY BRITOMART: Bring me my cushion. (*He takes the cushion from the chair at the desk and arranges it for her as she sits down on the settee.*) Sit down. (*He sits down and fingers his tie nervously.*) Dont fiddle with your tie, Stephen: there is nothing the matter with it.

STEPHEN: I beg your pardon. (*He fiddles with his watch chain instead.*) 15
LADY BRITOMART: Now are you attending to me, Stephen?
STEPHEN: Of course, mother.
LADY BRITOMART: No: it's not of course. I want something much more than your everyday matter-of-course attention. I am going to speak to you very seriously, Stephen. I wish you 20 would let that chain alone.
STEPHEN: (*Hastily relinquishing the chain.*) Have I done anything to annoy you, mother? If so, it was quite unintentional.
LADY BRITOMART: (*Astonished.*) Nonsense! (*With some remorse.*) 25 My poor boy, did you think I was angry with you?
STEPHEN: What is it, then, mother? You are making me very uneasy.
LADY BRITOMART: (*Squaring herself at him rather aggressively.*) Stephen: may I ask how soon you intend to realize that you 30 are a grown-up man, and that I am only a woman?
STEPHEN: (*Amazed.*) Only a—
LADY BRITOMART: Dont repeat my words, please: it is a most aggravating habit. You must learn to face life seriously, Stephen. I really cannot bear the whole burden of our family 35 affairs any longer. You must advise me: you must assume the responsibility.
STEPHEN: I!
LADY BRITOMART: Yes, you, of course. You were 24 last June. Youve been at Harrow and Cambridge. Youve been to India 40 and Japan. You must know a lot of things, now; unless you have wasted your time most scandalously. Well, advise me.
STEPHEN: (*Much perplexed.*) You know I have never interfered in the household—
LADY BRITOMART: No: I should think not. I dont want you to 45 order the dinner.
STEPHEN: I mean in our family affairs.
LADY BRITOMART: Well, you must interfere now; for they are getting quite beyond me.
STEPHEN: (*Troubled.*) I have thought sometimes that perhaps I 50 ought; but really, mother, I know so little about them; and what I do know is so painful! it is so impossible to mention some things to you—(*He stops, ashamed.*)
LADY BRITOMART: I suppose you mean your father.
STEPHEN: (*Almost inaudibly.*) Yes. 55
LADY BRITOMART: My dear: we cant go on all our lives not mentioning him. Of course you were quite right not to open the subject until I asked you to; but you are old enough now to be taken into my confidence, and to help me to deal with him about the girls. 60
STEPHEN: But the girls are all right. They are engaged.

LADY BRITOMART: (*Complacently.*) Yes: I have made a very good match for Sarah. Charles Lomax will be a millionaire at 35. But that is ten years ahead; and in the meantime his trustees cannot under the terms of his father's will allow him more than £800 a year.

STEPHEN: But the will says also that if he increases his income by his own exertions, they may double the increase.

LADY BRITOMART: Charles Lomax's exertions are much more likely to decrease his income than to increase it. Sarah will have to find at least another £800 a year for the next ten years; and even then they will be as poor as church mice. And what about Barbara? I thought Barbara was going to make the most brilliant career of all of you. And what does she do? Joins the Salvation Army; discharges her maid; lives on a pound a week and walks in one evening with a professor of Greek whom she has picked up in the street, and who pretends to be a Salvationist, and actually plays the big drum for her in public because he has fallen head over ears in love with her.

STEPHEN: I was certainly rather taken aback when I heard they were engaged. Cusins is a very nice fellow, certainly: nobody would ever guess that he was born in Australia; but—

LADY BRITOMART: Oh, Adolphus Cusins will make a very good husband. After all, nobody can say a word against Greek: it stamps a man at once as an educated gentleman. And my family, thank Heaven, is not a pig-headed Tory one. We are Whigs, and believe in liberty. Let snobbish people say what they please: Barbara shall marry, not the man they like, but the man *I* like.

STEPHEN: Of course I was thinking only of his income. However, he is not likely to be extravagant.

LADY BRITOMART: Dont be too sure of that, Stephen. I know your quiet, simple, refined, poetic people like Adolphus: quite content with the best of everything! They cost more than your extravagant people, who are always as mean as they are second rate. No: Barbara will need at least £2000 a year. You see it means two additional households. Besides, my dear, you must marry soon. I dont approve of the present fashion of philandering bachelors and late marriages; and I am trying to arrange something for you.

STEPHEN: It's very good of you, mother; but perhaps I had better arrange that for myself.

LADY BRITOMART: Nonsense! you are much too young to begin matchmaking: you would be taken in by some pretty little nobody. Of course I dont mean that you are not to be consulted: you know that as well as I do. (STEPHEN *closes his lips and is silent.*) Now dont sulk, Stephen.

STEPHEN: I am not sulking, mother. What has all this got to do with—with—with my father?

LADY BRITOMART: My dear Stephen: where is the money to come from? It is easy enough for you and the other children to live on my income as long as we are in the same house; but I cant keep four families in four separate houses. You know how poor my father is: he has barely seven thousand a year now; and really, if he were not the Earl of Stevenage, he would have to give up society. He can do nothing for us. He says, naturally enough, that it is absurd that he should be asked to provide for the children of a man who is rolling in money. You see, Stephen, your father must be fabulously wealthy, because there is always a war going on somewhere.

STEPHEN: You need not remind me of that, mother. I have hardly ever opened a newspaper in my life without seeing our name in it. The Undershaft torpedo! The Undershaft quick firers! The Undershaft ten inch! the Undershaft disappearing rampart gun! the Undershaft submarine! and now the Undershaft aerial battleship! At Harrow they called me the Woolwich Infant. At Cambridge it was the same. A little brute at King's who was always trying to get up revivals, spoilt my Bible—your first birthday present to me—by writing under my name, "Son and heir to Undershaft and Lazarus, Death and Destruction Dealers: address Christendom and Judea." But that was not so bad as the way I was kowtowed to everywhere because my father was making millions by selling cannons.

LADY BRITOMART: It is not only the cannons, but the war loans that Lazarus arranges under cover of giving credit for the cannons. You know, Stephen, it's perfectly scandalous. Those two men, Andrew Undershaft and Lazarus, positively have Europe under their thumbs. That is why your father is able to behave as he does. He is above the law. Do you think Bismarck or Gladstone or Disraeli could have openly defied every social and moral obligation all their lives as your father has? They simply wouldnt have dared. I asked Gladstone to take it up. I asked The Times to take it up. I asked the Lord Chamberlain to take it up. But it was just like asking them to declare war on the Sultan. They wouldnt. They said they couldnt touch him. I believe they were afraid.

STEPHEN: What could they do? He does not actually break the law.

LADY BRITOMART: Not break the law! He is always breaking the law. He broke the law when he was born: his parents were not married.

STEPHEN: Mother! Is that true?

LADY BRITOMART: Of course it's true: that was why we separated.

STEPHEN: He married without letting you know that!

LADY BRITOMART: (*Rather taken aback by this inference.*) Oh no. To do Andrew justice, that was not the sort of thing he did. Besides, you know the Undershaft motto: Unashamed. Everybody knew.

STEPHEN: But you said that was why you separated.

LADY BRITOMART: Yes, because he was not content with being a foundling himself: he wanted to disinherit you for another foundling. That was what I couldnt stand.

STEPHEN: (*Ashamed.*) Do you mean for—for—for—

LADY BRITOMART: Dont stammer, Stephen. Speak distinctly.

STEPHEN: But this is so frightful to me, mother. To have to speak to you about such things!

LADY BRITOMART: It's not pleasant for me, either, especially if you are still so childish that you must make it worse by a display of embarrassment. It is only in the middle classes, Stephen, that people get into a state of dumb helpless horror when they find that there are wicked people in the world. In our class, we have to decide what is to be done with wicked people; and nothing should disturb our self-possession. Now ask your question properly.

STEPHEN: Mother: have you no consideration for me? For Heaven's sake either treat me as a child, as you always do, and tell me nothing at all or tell me everything and let me take it as best I can.

LADY BRITOMART: Treat you as a child! What do you mean? It is most unkind and ungrateful of you to say such a thing.

185 You know I have never treated any of you as children. I have always made you my companions and friends, and allowed you perfect freedom to do and say whatever you like, so long as you liked what I could approve of.

STEPHEN: (*Desperately.*) I daresay we have been the very imperfect children of a very perfect mother; but I do beg you to
190 let me alone for once, and tell me about this horrible business of my father wanting to set me aside for another son.

LADY BRITOMART: (*Amazed.*) Another son! I never said anything of the kind. I never dreamt of such a thing. This is what comes of interrupting me.

195 STEPHEN: But you said—

LADY BRITOMART: (*Cutting him short.*) Now be a good boy, Stephen, and listen to me patiently. The Undershafts are descended from a foundling in the parish of St Andrew Undershaft in the city. That was long ago, in the reign of
200 James the First. Well, this foundling was adopted by an armorer and gun-maker. In the course of time the foundling succeeded to the business; and from some notion of gratitude, or some vow or something, he adopted another foundling, and left the business to him. And that foundling
205 did the same. Ever since that, the cannon business has always been left to an adopted foundling named Andrew Undershaft.

STEPHEN: But did they never marry? Were there no legitimate sons?

210 LADY BRITOMART: Oh yes: they married just as your father did; and they were rich enough to buy land for their own children and leave them well provided for. But they always adopted and trained some foundling to succeed them in the business; and of course they always quarrelled with
215 their wives furiously over it. Your father was adopted in that way; and he pretends to consider himself bound to keep up the tradition and adopt somebody to leave the business to. Of course I was not going to stand that. There may have been some reason for it when the Undershafts
220 could only marry women in their own class, whose sons were not fit to govern great estates. But there could be no excuse for passing over my son.

STEPHEN: (*Dubiously.*) I am afraid I should make a poor hand of managing a cannon foundry.

225 LADY BRITOMART: Nonsense! you could easily get a manager and pay him a salary.

STEPHEN: My father evidently had no great opinion of my capacity.

LADY BRITOMART: Stuff, child! you were only a baby: it had
230 nothing to do with your capacity. Andrew did it on principle, just as he did every perverse and wicked thing on principle. When my father remonstrated, Andrew actually told him to his face that history tells us of only two successful institutions: one the Undershaft firm, and the other the
235 Roman Empire under the Antonines. That was because the Antonine emperors all adopted their successors. Such rubbish! The Stevenages are as good as the Antonines, I hope; and you are a Stevenage. But that was Andrew all over. There you have the man! Always clever and unanswerable when he
240 was defending nonsense and wickedness: always awkward and sullen when he had to behave sensibly and decently!

STEPHEN: Then it was on my account that your home life was broken up, mother. I am sorry.

LADY BRITOMART: Well, dear, there were other differences. I
245 really cannot bear an immoral man. I am not a Pharisee, I hope; and I should not have minded his merely doing

wrong things: we are none of us perfect. But your father didnt exactly do wrong things: he said them and thought them: that was what was so dreadful. He really had a sort
250 of religion of wrongness. Just as one doesnt mind men practising immorality so long as they own that they are in the wrong by preaching morality; so I couldnt forgive Andrew for preaching immorality while he practised morality. You would all have grown up without principles,
255 without any knowledge of right and wrong, if he had been in the house. You know, my dear, your father was a very attractive man in some ways. Children did not dislike him; and he took advantage of it to put the wickedest ideas into their heads, and make them quite unmanageable. I did
260 not dislike him myself: very far from it; but nothing can bridge over moral disagreement.

STEPHEN: All this simply bewilders me, mother. People may differ about matters of opinion, or even about religion; but how can they differ about right and wrong? Right is right;
265 and wrong is wrong; and if a man cannot distinguish them properly, he is either a fool or a rascal: thats all.

LADY BRITOMART: (*Touched.*) Thats my own boy! (*She pats his cheek.*) Your father never could answer that: he used to laugh and get out of it under cover of some affectionate nonsense.
270 And now that you understand the situation, what do you advise me to do?

STEPHEN: Well, what can you do?

LADY BRITOMART: I must get the money somehow.

STEPHEN: We cannot take money from him. I had rather go
275 and live in some cheap place like Bedford Square or even Hampstead than take a farthing of his money.

LADY BRITOMART: But after all, Stephen, our present income comes from Andrew.

STEPHEN: (*Shocked.*) I never knew that.

280 LADY BRITOMART: Well, you surely didnt suppose your grandfather had anything to give me. The Stevenages could not do everything for you. We gave you social position. Andrew had to contribute something. He had a very good bargain, I think.

285 STEPHEN: (*Bitterly.*) We are utterly dependent on him and his cannons, then?

LADY BRITOMART: Certainly not: the money is settled. But he provided it. So you see it is not a question of taking money from him or not: it is simply a question of how
290 much. I dont want any more for myself.

STEPHEN: Nor do I.

LADY BRITOMART: But Sarah does; and Barbara does. That is, Charles Lomax and Adolphus Cusins will cost them more. So I must put my pride in my pocket and ask for it, I suppose.
295 That is your advice, Stephen, is it not?

STEPHEN: No.

LADY BRITOMART: (*Sharply.*) Stephen!

STEPHEN: Of course if you are determined—

LADY BRITOMART: I am not determined: I ask your advice; and I am waiting for it. I will not have all the responsibility
300 thrown on my shoulders.

STEPHEN: (*Obstinately.*) I would die sooner than ask him for another penny.

LADY BRITOMART: (*Resignedly.*) You mean that I must ask him. Very well, Stephen: it shall be as you wish. You will be glad
305 to know that your grandfather concurs. But he thinks I ought to ask Andrew to come here and see the girls. After all, he must have some natural affection for them.

STEPHEN: Ask him here!!!

310 LADY BRITOMART: Do not repeat my words, Stephen. Where else can I ask him?

STEPHEN: I never expected you to ask him at all.

LADY BRITOMART: Now dont tease, Stephen. Come! you see that it is necessary that he should pay us a visit, dont you?

315 STEPHEN: (*Reluctantly.*) I suppose so, if the girls cannot do without his money.

LADY BRITOMART: Thank you, Stephen: I knew you would give me the right advice when it was properly explained to you. I have asked your father to come this evening. (STEPHEN

320 *bounds from his seat.*) Dont jump, Stephen: it fidgets me.

STEPHEN: (*In utter consternation.*) Do you mean to say that my father is coming here tonight—that he may be here at any moment?

LADY BRITOMART: (*Looking at her watch.*) I said nine. (*He gasps.*

325 *She rises.*) Ring the bell, please. (STEPHEN *goes to the smaller writing table; presses a button on it; and sits at it with his elbows on the table and his head in his hands, outwitted and overwhelmed.*) It is ten minutes to nine yet; and I have to prepare the girls. I asked Charles Lomax and Adolphus to

330 dinner on purpose that they might be here. Andrew had better see them in case he should cherish any delusions as to their being capable of supporting their wives. (*The butler enters:* LADY BRITOMART *goes behind the settee to speak to him.*) Morrison: go up to the drawing room and tell everybody

335 to come down here at once. (MORRISON *withdraws.* LADY BRITOMART *turns to* STEPHEN.) Now remember, Stephen: I shall need all your countenance and authority. (*He rises and tries to recover some vestige of these attributes.*) Give me a chair, dear. (*He pushes a chair forward from the wall to where

340 she stands, near the smaller writing table. She sits down; and he goes to the armchair, into which he throws himself.*) I dont know how Barbara will take it. Ever since they made her a major in the Salvation Army she has developed a propensity to have her own way and order people about which quite cows

345 me sometimes. It's not ladylike: I'm sure I dont know where she picked it up. Anyhow, Barbara shant bully me; but still it's just as well that your father should be here before she has time to refuse to meet him or make a fuss. Dont look nervous, Stephen: it will only encourage Barbara to make difficulties. I

350 am nervous enough, goodness knows; but I dont shew it.

(SARAH *and* BARBARA *come in with their respective young men,* CHARLES LOMAX *and* ADOLPHUS CUSINS. SARAH *is slender, bored, and mundane.* BARBARA *is robuster, jollier, much more energetic.* SARAH *is fashionably dressed:* BARBARA *is in Salvation Army uniform.* LOMAX, *a young man about town, is like many other young men about town. He is afflicted with a frivolous sense of humor which plunges him at the most inopportune moments into paroxysms of imperfectly suppressed laughter.* CUSINS *is a spectacled student, slight, thin haired, and sweet voiced, with a more complex form of* LOMAX's *complaint. His sense of humor is intellectual and subtle, and is complicated by an appalling temper. The lifelong struggle of a benevolent temperament and a high conscience against impulses of inhuman ridicule and fierce impatience has set up a chronic strain which has visibly wrecked his constitution. He is a most implacable, determined, tenacious, intolerant person who by mere force of character presents himself as—and indeed actually is—considerate, gentle, explanatory, even mild and apologetic, capable possibly of murder, but not of cruelty or coarseness. By the operation of some instinct which is not*

merciful enough to blind him with the illusions of love, he is obstinately bent on marrying BARBARA. LOMAX *likes* SARAH *and thinks it will be rather a lark to marry her. Consequently he has not attempted to resist* LADY BRITOMART's *arrangements to that end.*)

(*All four look as if they had been having a good deal of fun in the drawing room. The girls enter first, leaving the swains outside.* SARAH *comes to the settee.* BARBARA *comes in after her and stops at the door.*)

BARBARA: Are Cholly and Dolly to come in?

LADY BRITOMART: (*Forcibly.*) Barbara: I will not have Charles called Cholly: the vulgarity of it positively makes me ill.

BARBARA: It's all right, mother: Cholly is quite correct nowadays. Are they to come in? 355

LADY BRITOMART: Yes, if they will behave themselves.

BARBARA: (*Through the door.*) Come in, Dolly; and behave yourself.

(BARBARA *comes to her mother's writing table.* CUSINS *enters smiling, and wanders towards* LADY BRITOMART.)

SARAH: (*Calling.*) Come in, Cholly. (LOMAX *enters, controlling his features very imperfectly, and places himself vaguely between* 360 SARAH *and* BARBARA.)

LADY BRITOMART: (*Peremptorily.*) Sit down, all of you. (*They sit.* CUSINS *crosses to the window and seats himself there.* LOMAX *takes a chair.* BARBARA *sits at the writing table and* SARAH *on the settee.*) I dont in the least know what you are laughing at, 365 Adolphus. I am surprised at you, though I expected nothing better from Charles Lomax.

CUSINS: (*In a remarkably gentle voice.*) Barbara has been trying to teach me the West Ham Salvation March.

LADY BRITOMART: I see nothing to laugh at in that; nor should 370 you if you are really converted.

CUSINS: (*Sweetly.*) You were not present. It was really funny, I believe.

LOMAX: Ripping.

LADY BRITOMART: Be quiet, Charles. Now listen to me, children. 375 Your father is coming here this evening.

(*General stupefaction.* LOMAX, SARAH, *and* BARBARA *rise:* SARAH *scared, and* BARBARA *amused and expectant.*)

LOMAX: (*Remonstrating.*) Oh I say!

LADY BRITOMART: You are not called on to say anything, Charles.

SARAH: Are you serious, mother? 380

LADY BRITOMART: Of course I am serious. It is on your account, Sarah, and also on Charles's. (*Silence.* SARAH *sits, with a shrug.* CHARLES *looks painfully unworthy.*) I hope you are not going to object, Barbara.

BARBARA: I! why should I? My father has a soul to be saved 385 like anybody else. He's quite welcome as far as I am concerned. (*She sits on the table, and softly whistles 'Onward, Christian Soldiers.'*)

LOMAX: (*Still remonstrant.*) But really, dont you know! Oh I say!

LADY BRITOMART: (*Frigidly.*) What do you wish to convey, 390 Charles?

LOMAX: Well, you must admit that this is a bit thick.

LADY BRITOMART: (*Turning with ominous suavity to* CUSINS.) Adolphus: you are a professor of Greek. Can you translate
395   Charles Lomax's remarks into reputable English for us?

CUSINS: (*Cautiously.*) If I may say so, Lady Brit, I think Charles has rather happily expressed what we all feel. Homer, speaking of Autolycus, uses the same phrase. πυκινὸν δόμον ἐλθεῖν means a bit thick.

400 LOMAX: (*Handsomely.*) Not that I mind, you know, if Sarah dont. (*He sits.*)

LADY BRITOMART: (*Crushingly.*) Thank you. Have I your permission, Adolphus, to invite my own husband to my own house?

405 CUSINS: (*Gallantly.*) You have my unhesitating support in everything you do.

LADY BRITOMART: Tush! Sarah: have you nothing to say?

SARAH: Do you mean that he is coming regularly to live here?

LADY BRITOMART: Certainly not. The spare room is ready for
410   him if he likes to stay for a day or two and see a little more of you; but there are limits.

SARAH: Well, he cant eat us, I suppose. *I* dont mind.

LOMAX: (*Chuckling.*) I wonder how the old man will take it.

LADY BRITOMART: Much as the old woman will, no doubt,
415   Charles.

LOMAX: (*Abashed.*) I didnt mean—at least—

LADY BRITOMART: You didnt think, Charles. You never do; and the result is, you never mean anything. And now please attend to me, children. Your father will be quite a
420   stranger to us.

LOMAX: I suppose he hasnt seen Sarah since she was a little kid.

LADY BRITOMART: Not since she was a little kid, Charles, as you express it with that elegance of diction and refinement of thought that seem never to desert you. Accordingly—
425   er—(*Impatiently.*) Now I have forgotten what I was going to say. That comes of your provoking me to be sarcastic, Charles. Adolphus: will you kindly tell me where I was.

CUSINS: (*Sweetly.*) You were saying that as Mr Undershaft has not seen his children since they were babies, he will form
430   his opinion of the way you have brought them up from their behavior tonight, and that therefore you wish us all to be particularly careful to conduct ourselves well, especially Charles.

LADY BRITOMART: (*With emphatic approval.*) Precisely.

435 LOMAX: Look here, Dolly: Lady Brit didnt say that.

LADY BRITOMART: (*Vehemently.*) I did, Charles. Adolphus's recollection is perfectly correct. It is most important that you should be good; and I do beg you for once not to pair off into opposite corners and giggle and whisper while I
440   am speaking to your father.

BARBARA: All right, mother. We'll do you credit. (*She comes off the table, and sits in her chair with ladylike elegance.*)

LADY BRITOMART: Remember, Charles, that Sarah will want to feel proud of you instead of ashamed of you.

445 LOMAX: Oh I say! theres nothing to be exactly proud of, dont you know.

LADY BRITOMART: Well, try and look as if there was.

(MORRISON, *pale and dismayed, breaks into the room in unconcealed disorder.*)

MORRISON: Might I speak a word to you, my lady?

LADY BRITOMART: Nonsense! Shew him up.

MORRISON: Yes, my lady. (*He goes.*)

LOMAX: Does Morrison know who it is?   450

LADY BRITOMART: Of course. Morrison has always been with us.

LOMAX: It must be a regular corker for him, dont you know.

LADY BRITOMART: Is this a moment to get on my nerves, Charles, with your outrageous expressions?

LOMAX: But this is something out of the ordinary, really—   455

MORRISON: (*At the door.*) The—er—Mr Undershaft. (*He retreats in confusion.*)

(ANDREW UNDERSHAFT *comes in. All rise.* LADY BRITOMART *meets him in the middle of the room behind the settee.*)

(ANDREW *is, on the surface, a stoutish, easygoing elderly man, with kindly patient manners, and an engaging simplicity of character. But he has a watchful, deliberate, waiting, listening face, and formidable reserves of power, both bodily and mental, in his capacious chest and long head. His gentleness is partly that of a strong man who has learnt by experience that his natural grip hurts ordinary people unless he handles them very carefully, and partly the mellowness of age and success. He is also a little shy in his present very delicate situation.*)

LADY BRITOMART: Good evening, Andrew.

UNDERSHAFT: How d'ye do, my dear.   460

LADY BRITOMART: You look a good deal older.

UNDERSHAFT: (*Apologetically.*) I am somewhat older. (*Taking her hand with a touch of courtship.*) Time has stood still with you.

LADY BRITOMART: (*Throwing away his hand.*) Rubbish! This is your family.   465

UNDERSHAFT: (*Surprised.*) Is it so large? I am sorry to say my memory is failing very badly in some things. (*He offers his hand with paternal kindness to* LOMAX.)

LOMAX: (*Jerkily shaking his hand.*) Ahdedoo.

UNDERSHAFT: I can see you are my eldest. I am very glad to meet   470
you again, my boy.

LOMAX: (*Remonstrating.*) No, but look here dont you know— (*Overcome.*) Oh I say!

LADY BRITOMART: (*Recovering from momentary speechlessness.*) Andrew: do you mean to say that you dont remember how   475
many children you have?

UNDERSHAFT: Well, I am afraid I—. They have grown so much—er. Am I making any ridiculous mistake? I may as well confess: I recollect only one son. But so many things have happened since, of course—er—   480

LADY BRITOMART: (*Decisively.*) Andrew: you are talking nonsense. Of course you have only one son.

UNDERSHAFT: Perhaps you will be good enough to introduce me, my dear.

LADY BRITOMART: That is Charles Lomax, who is engaged to   485
Sarah.

UNDERSHAFT: My dear sir, I beg your pardon.

LOMAX: Notatall. Delighted, I assure you.

LADY BRITOMART: This is Stephen.

UNDERSHAFT: (*Bowing.*) Happy to make your acquaintance,   490
Mr Stephen. Then (*Going to* CUSINS.) you must be my son. (*Taking* CUSINS' *hands in his.*) How are you, my young friend? (*To* LADY BRITOMART.) He is very like you, my love.

CUSINS: You flatter me, Mr Undershaft. My name is Cusins: engaged to Barbara. (*Very explicitly.*) That is Major Barbara   495
Undershaft, of the Salvation Army. That is Sarah, your second daughter. This is Stephen Undershaft, your son.

UNDERSHAFT: My dear Stephen, I beg your pardon.

STEPHEN: Not at all.

500 UNDERSHAFT: Mr Cusins: I am much indebted to you for explaining so precisely. (*Turning to* SARAH.) Barbara, my dear—

SARAH: (*Prompting him.*) Sarah.

UNDERSHAFT: Sarah, of course. (*They shake hands. He goes over*
505 *to* BARBARA.) Barbara—I am right this time, I hope?

BARBARA: Quite right. (*They shake hands.*)

LADY BRITOMART: (*Resuming command.*) Sit down, all of you. Sit down, Andrew. (*She comes forward and sits on the settee.* CUSINS *also brings his chair forward on her left.* BARBARA *and*
510 STEPHEN *resume their seats.* LOMAX *gives his chair to* SARAH *and goes for another.*)

UNDERSHAFT: Thank you, my love.

LOMAX: (*Conversationally, as he brings a chair forward between the writing table and the settee, and offers it to* UNDERSHAFT.)
515 Takes you some time to find out exactly where you are, dont it?

UNDERSHAFT: (*Accepting the chair, but remaining standing.*) That is not what embarrasses me, Mr Lomax. My difficulty is that if I play the part of a father, I shall produce the effect of an intrusive stranger; and if I play the part of a discreet stranger,
520 I may appear a callous father.

LADY BRITOMART: There is no need for you to play any part at all, Andrew. You had much better be sincere and natural.

UNDERSHAFT: (*Submissively.*) Yes, my dear: I daresay that will be best. (*He sits down comfortably.*) Well, here I am. Now
525 what can I do for you all?

LADY BRITOMART: You need not do anything, Andrew. You are one of the family. You can sit with us and enjoy yourself.

(*A painfully conscious pause.* BARBARA *makes a face at* LOMAX, *whose too long suppressed mirth immediately explodes in agonized neighings.*)

LADY BRITOMART: (*Outraged.*) Charles Lomax: if you can behave yourself, behave yourself. If not, leave the room.
530 LOMAX: I'm awfully sorry, Lady Brit; but really you know, upon my soul! (*He sits on the settee between* LADY BRITOMART *and* UNDERSHAFT, *quite overcome.*)

BARBARA: Why dont you laugh if you want to, Cholly? It's good for your inside.

535 LADY BRITOMART: Barbara: you have had the education of a lady. Please let your father see that; and dont talk like a street girl.

UNDERSHAFT: Never mind me, my dear. As you know, I am not a gentleman; and I was never educated.

540 LOMAX: (*Encouragingly.*) Nobody'd know it, I assure you. You look all right, you know.

CUSINS: Let me advise you to study Greek, Mr Undershaft. Greek scholars are privileged men. Few of them know Greek; and none of them know anything else; but their
545 position is unchallengeable. Other languages are the qual- ifications of waiters and commercial travellers: Greek is to a man of position what the hallmark is to silver.

BARBARA: Dolly: dont be insincere. Cholly: fetch your con- certina and play something for us.
550 LOMAX: (*Jumps up eagerly, but checks himself to remark doubtfully to* UNDERSHAFT.) Perhaps that sort of thing isnt in your line, eh?

UNDERSHAFT: I am particularly fond of music.

LOMAX: (*Delighted.*) Are you? Then I'll get it. (*He goes upstairs for the instrument.*)

555 UNDERSHAFT: Do you play, Barbara?

BARBARA: Only the tambourine. But Cholly's teaching me the concertina.

UNDERSHAFT: Is Cholly also a member of the Salvation Army?

BARBARA: No: he says it's bad form to be a dissenter. But I dont
560 despair of Cholly. I made him come yesterday to a meeting at the dock gates, and take the collection in his hat.

UNDERSHAFT: (*Looks whimsically at his wife.*)!!

LADY BRITOMART: It is not my doing, Andrew. Barbara is old enough to take her own way. She has no father to advise her.

565 BARBARA: Oh yes she has. There are no orphans in the Salvation Army.

UNDERSHAFT: Your father there has a great many children and plenty of experience, eh?

BARBARA: (*Looking at him with quick interest and nodding.*) Just
570 so. How did you come to understand that? (LOMAX *is heard at the door trying the concertina.*)

LADY BRITOMART: Come in, Charles. Play us something at once.

LOMAX: Righto! (*He sits down in his former place, and preludes.*)

UNDERSHAFT: One moment, Mr Lomax. I am rather interested in the Salvation Army. Its motto might be my own: Blood
575 and Fire.

LOMAX: (*Shocked.*) But not your sort of blood and fire, you know.

UNDERSHAFT: My sort of blood cleanses: my sort of fire purifies.

BARBARA: So do ours. Come down tomorrow to my shelter—the
580 West Ham shelter—and see what we're doing. We're going to march to a great meeting in the Assembly Hall at Mile End. Come and see the shelter and then march with us: it will do you a lot of good. Can you play anything?

UNDERSHAFT: In my youth I earned pennies, and even shillings
585 occasionally, in the streets and in public house parlors by my natural talent for stepdancing. Later on, I became a member of the Undershaft orchestral society, and performed passably on the tenor trombone.

LOMAX: (*Scandalized—putting down the concertina.*) Oh I say!
590 BARBARA: Many a sinner has played himself into heaven on the trombone, thanks to the Army.

LOMAX: (*To* BARBARA, *still rather shocked.*) Yes; but what about the cannon business, dont you know? (*To* UNDERSHAFT.) Getting into heaven is not exactly in your line, is it?
595 LADY BRITOMART: Charles!!!

LOMAX: Well; but it stands to reason, dont it? The cannon business may be necessary and all that: we cant get on without cannons; but it isnt right, you know. On the other hand, there may be a certain amount of tosh about the
600 Salvation Army—I belong to the Established Church myself— but still you cant deny that it's religion; and you cant go against religion, can you? At least unless youre downright immoral, dont you know.

UNDERSHAFT: You hardly appreciate my position, Mr Lomax—
605 LOMAX: (*Hastily.*) I'm not saying anything against you personally—

UNDERSHAFT: Quite so, quite so. But consider for a moment. Here I am, a profiteer in mutilation and murder. I find myself in a specially amiable humor just now because, this
610 morning, down at the foundry, we blew twenty-seven dummy soldiers into fragments with a gun which formerly destroyed only thirteen.

LOMAX: (*Leniently.*) Well, the more destructive war becomes, the sooner it will be abolished, eh?
615

UNDERSHAFT: Not at all. The more destructive war becomes the more fascinating we find it. No, Mr Lomax: I am obliged to you for making the usual excuse for my trade; but I am not ashamed of it. I am not one of those men who keep their
620 morals and their business in watertight compartments. All the spare money my trade rivals spend on hospitals, cathedrals, and other receptacles for conscience money, I devote to experiments and researches in improved methods of destroying life and property. I have always done so; and
625 I always shall. Therefore your Christmas card moralities of peace on earth and goodwill among men are of no use to me. Your Christianity, which enjoins you to resist not evil, and to turn the other cheek, would make me a bankrupt. My morality—my religion—must have a place for cannons and
630 torpedoes in it.

STEPHEN: (*Coldly—almost sullenly.*) You speak as if there were half a dozen moralities and religions to choose from, instead of one true morality and one true religion.

UNDERSHAFT: For me there is only one true morality; but it might
635 not fit you, as you do not manufacture aerial battleships. There is only one true morality for every man; but every man has not the same true morality.

LOMAX: (*Overtaxed.*) Would you mind saying that again? I didnt quite follow it.

640 CUSINS: It's quite simple. As Euripides says, one man's meat is another man's poison morally as well as physically.

UNDERSHAFT: Precisely.

LOMAX: Oh, that! Yes, yes, yes. True. True.

STEPHEN: In other words, some men are honest and some are
645 scoundrels.

BARBARA: Bosh! There are no scoundrels.

UNDERSHAFT: Indeed? Are there any good men?

BARBARA: No. Not one. There are neither good men nor scoundrels: there are just children of one Father; and the
650 sooner they stop calling one another names the better. You neednt talk to me: I know them. I've had scores of them through my hands: scoundrels, criminals, infidels, philanthropists, missionaries, county councillors, all sorts. Theyre all just the same sort of sinner; and theres the same
655 salvation ready for them all.

UNDERSHAFT: May I ask have you ever saved a maker of cannons?

BARBARA: No. Will you let me try?

UNDERSHAFT: Well, I will make a bargain with you. If I go to see you tomorrow in your Salvation Shelter, will you come
660 the day after to see me in my cannon works?

BARBARA: Take care. It may end in your giving up the cannons for the sake of the Salvation Army.

UNDERSHAFT: Are you sure it will not end in your giving up the Salvation Army for the sake of the cannons?

665 BARBARA: I will take my chance of that.

UNDERSHAFT: And I will take my chance of the other. (*They shake hands on it.*) Where is your shelter?

BARBARA: In West Ham. At the sign of the cross. Ask anybody in Canning Town. Where are your works?

670 UNDERSHAFT: In Perivale St Andrews. At the sign of the sword. Ask anybody in Europe.

LOMAX: Hadnt I better play something?

BARBARA: Yes. Give us 'Onward, Christian Soldiers.'

LOMAX: Well, thats rather a strong order to begin with, dont
675 you know. Suppose I sing 'Thou'rt passing hence, my brother.' It's much the same tune.

BARBARA: It's too melancholy. You get saved, Cholly; and youll pass hence, my brother, without making such a fuss about it.

LADY BRITOMART: Really, Barbara, you go on as if religion were a pleasant subject. Do have some sense of propriety. 680

UNDERSHAFT: I do not find it an unpleasant subject, my dear. It is the only one that capable people really care for.

LADY BRITOMART: (*Looking at her watch.*) Well, if you are determined to have it, I insist on having it in a proper and respectable way. Charles: ring for prayers. 685

(*General amazement.* STEPHEN *rises in dismay.*)

LOMAX: (*Rising.*) Oh I say!

UNDERSHAFT: (*Rising.*) I am afraid I must be going.

LADY BRITOMART: You cannot go now, Andrew: it would be most improper. Sit down. What will the servants think?

UNDERSHAFT: My dear: I have conscientious scruples. May I 690 suggest a compromise? If Barbara will conduct a little service in the drawing room, with Mr Lomax as organist, I will attend it willingly. I will even take part, if a trombone can be procured.

LADY BRITOMART: Dont mock, Andrew. 695

UNDERSHAFT: (*Shocked—to* BARBARA.) You dont think I am mocking, my love, I hope.

BARBARA: No, of course not; and it wouldnt matter if you were: half the Army came to their first meeting for a lark. (*Rising.*) Come along. (*She throws her arm round her father* 700 *and sweeps him out, calling to the others from the threshold.*) Come, Dolly. Come, Cholly.

(CUSINS *rises.*)

LADY BRITOMART: I will not be disobeyed by everybody. Adolphus: sit down. (*He does not.*) Charles: you may go. You are not fit for prayers: you cannot keep your countenance. 705

LOMAX: Oh I say! (*He goes out.*)

LADY BRITOMART: (*Continuing.*) But you, Adolphus, can behave yourself if you choose to. I insist on your staying.

CUSINS: My dear Lady Brit: there are things in the family prayer book that I couldnt bear to hear you say. 710

LADY BRITOMART: What things, pray?

CUSINS: Well, you would have to say before all the servants that we have done things we ought not to have done, and left undone things we ought to have done, and that there is no health in us. I cannot bear to hear you doing yourself 715 such an injustice, and Barbara such an injustice. As for myself, I flatly deny it: I have done my best. I shouldnt dare to marry Barbara—I couldnt look you in the face—if it were true. So I must go to the drawing room.

LADY BRITOMART: (*Offended.*) Well, go. (*He starts for the door.*) 720 And remember this, Adolphus (*He turns to listen.*): I have a very strong suspicion that you went to the Salvation Army to worship Barbara and nothing else. And I quite appreciate the very clever way in which you systematically humbug me. I have found you out. Take care Barbara 725 doesnt. Thats all.

CUSINS: (*With unruffled sweetness.*) Dont tell on me. (*He steals out.*)

LADY BRITOMART: Sarah: if you want to go, go. Anything's better than to sit there as if you wished you were a thousand miles away. 730

SARAH: (*Languidly.*) Very well, mamma. (*She goes.*)

(LADY BRITOMART, *with a sudden flounce, gives way to a little gust of tears.*)

STEPHEN: (*Going to her.*) Mother: whats the matter?

LADY BRITOMART: (*Swishing away her tears with her handkerchief.*) Nothing. Foolishness. You can go with him, too, if
735 you like, and leave me with the servants.

STEPHEN: Oh, you mustnt think that, mother. I—I dont like him.

LADY BRITOMART: The others do. That is the injustice of a
740 woman's lot. A woman has to bring up her children; and
that means to restrain them, to deny them things they want,
to set them tasks, to punish them when they do wrong, to
do all the unpleasant things. And then the father, who has
nothing to do but pet them and spoil them, comes in when
all her work is done and steals their affection from her.

745 STEPHEN: He has not stolen our affection from you. It is only
curiosity.

LADY BRITOMART: (*Violently.*) I wont be consoled, Stephen.
There is nothing the matter with me. (*She rises and goes
towards the door.*)

750 STEPHEN: Where are you going, mother?

LADY BRITOMART: To the drawing room, of course. (*She goes
out. 'Onward, Christian Soldiers,' on the concertina, with
tambourine accompaniment, is heard when the door opens.*)
Are you coming, Stephen?

755 STEPHEN: No. Certainly not. (*She goes. He sits down on the settee,
with compressed lips and an expression of strong dislike.*)

ACT TWO

*The yard of the West Ham shelter of the Salvation Army is a cold
place on a January morning. The building itself, an old warehouse,
is newly whitewashed. Its gabled end projects into the yard in the
middle, with a door on the ground floor, and another in the loft
above it without any balcony or ladder, but with a pulley rigged
over it for hoisting sacks. Those who come from this central gable
end into the yard have the gateway leading to the street on their
left, with a stone horse-trough just beyond it, and, on the right, a
penthouse shielding a table from the weather. There are forms at
the table; and on them are seated a man and a woman, both much
down on their luck, finishing a meal of bread (one thick slice each,
with margarine and golden syrup) and diluted milk.*

*The man, a workman out of employment, is young, agile, a talker, a
poser, sharp enough to be capable of anything in reason except honesty or altruistic considerations of any kind. The woman is a commonplace old bundle of poverty and hard-worn humanity. She looks
sixty and probably is forty-five. If they were rich people, gloved and
muffed and well wrapped up in furs and overcoats, they would be
numbed and miserable; for it is a grindingly cold raw January day;
and a glance at the background of grimy warehouses and leaden sky
visible over the whitewashed walls of the yard would drive any idle
rich person straight to the Mediterranean. But these two, being no
more troubled with visions of the Mediterranean than of the moon,
and being compelled to keep more of their clothes in the pawn-
shop, and less on their persons, in winter than in summer, are not
depressed by the cold: rather are they stung into vivacity, to which
their meal has just now given an almost jolly turn. The man takes a
pull at his mug, and then gets up and moves about the yard with his
hands deep in his pockets, occasionally breaking into a stepdance.*

THE WOMAN: Feel better arter your meal, sir?

THE MAN: No. Call that a meal! Good enough for you, praps;
but wot is it to me, an intelligent workin man.

THE WOMAN: Workin man! Wot are you?

THE MAN: Painter. 5

THE WOMAN: (*Sceptically.*) Yus, I dessay.

THE MAN: Yus, you dessay! I know. Every loafer that cant do
nothink calls isself a painter. Well, I'm a real painter:
grainer, finisher, thirty-eight bob a week when I can get it.

THE WOMAN: Then why dont you go and get it? 10

THE MAN: I'll tell you why. Fust: I'm intelligent—fffff! it's rotten
cold here (*He dances a step or two.*)—yes: intelligent beyond
the station o life into which it has pleased the capitalists to
call me; and they dont like a man that sees through em.
Second, an intelligent bein needs a doo share of appiness; 15
so I drink somethink cruel when I get the chawnce. Third,
I stand by my class and do as little as I can so's to leave
arf the job for me fellow workers. Fourth, I'm fly enough to
know wots inside the law and wots outside it; and inside it
I do as the capitalists do: pinch wot I can lay me ands on. 20
In a proper state of society I am sober, industrious and
honest: in Rome, so to speak, I do as the Romans do. Wots
the consequence? When trade is bad—and it's rotten bad
just now—and the employers az to sack arf their men, they
generally start on me. 25

THE WOMAN: Whats your name?

THE MAN: Price. Bronterre O'Brien Price. Usually called Snobby
Price, for short.

THE WOMAN: Snobby's a carpenter, aint it? You said you was
a painter. 30

PRICE: Not that kind of snob, but the genteel sort. I'm too uppish,
owing to my intelligence, and my father being a Chartist and
a reading, thinking man: a stationer, too. I'm none of your
common hewers of wood and drawers of water; and dont you
forget it. (*He returns to his seat at the table, and takes up his 35
mug.*) Wots your name?

THE WOMAN: Rummy Mitchens, sir.

PRICE: (*Quaffing the remains of his milk to her.*) Your elth, Miss
Mitchens.

RUMMY: (*Correcting him.*) Missis Mitchens. 40

PRICE: Wot! Oh Rummy, Rummy! Respectable married woman,
Rummy, gittin rescued by the Salvation Army by pretendin to
be a bad un. Same old game!

RUMMY: What am I to do? I cant starve. Them Salvation lasses
is dear good girls; but the better you are, the worse they likes 45
to think you were before they rescued you. Why shouldnt
they av a bit o credit, poor loves? theyre worn to rags by their
work. And where would they get the money to rescue us if
we was to let on we're no worse than other people? You know
what ladies and gentlemen are. 50

PRICE: Thievin swine! Wish I ad their job, Rummy, all the same.
Wot does Rummy stand for? Pet name praps?

RUMMY: Short for Romola.

PRICE: For wot!?

RUMMY: Romola. It was out of a new book. Somebody me mother 55
wanted me to grow up like.

PRICE: We're companions in misfortune, Rummy. Both on us
got names that nobody cawnt pronounce. Consequently I'm
Snobby and youre Rummy because Bill and Sally wasnt good
enough for our parents. Such is life! 60

RUMMY: Who saved you, Mr Price? Was it Major Barbara?

PRICE: No: I come here on my own. I'm going to be Bronterre
O'Brien Price, the converted painter. I know wot they like.
I'll tell em how I blasphemed and gambled and wopped my

65 poor old mother—

RUMMY: (*Shocked.*) Used you to beat your mother?

PRICE: Not likely. She used to beat me. No matter: you come and
listen to the converted painter, and youll hear how she was a
pious woman that taught me me prayers at er knee, an how I

70 used to come home drunk and drag her out o bed be er snow
white airs, an lam into er with the poker.

RUMMY: Thats whats so unfair to us women. Your confessions
is just as big lies as ours: you dont tell what you really done
no more than us; but you men can tell your lies right out

75 at the meetins and be made much of for it; while the sort o
confessions we az to make az to be wispered to one lady at a
time. It aint right, spite of all their piety.

PRICE: Right! Do you spose the Army'd be allowed if it went
and did right? Not much. It combs our air and makes us

80 good little blokes to be robbed and put upon. But I'll play
the game as good as any of em. I'll see somebody struck by
lightnin, or hear a voice sayin 'Snobby Price: where will
you spend eternity?' I'll av a time of it, I tell you.

RUMMY: You wont be let drink, though.

85 PRICE: I'll take it out in gorspellin, then. I dont want to drink if I
can get fun enough any other way.

(JENNY HILL, *a pale, overwrought, pretty Salvation lass of 18,
comes in through the yard gate, leading* PETER SHIRLEY, *a half
hardened, half worn-out elderly man, weak with hunger.*)

JENNY: (*Supporting him.*) Come! pluck up. I'll get you something
to eat. Youll be all right then.

PRICE: (*Rising and hurrying officiously to take the old man off*

90 JENNY's *hands.*) Poor old man! Cheer up, brother: youll find
rest and peace and appiness ere. Hurry up with the food, miss:
e's fair done. (JENNY *hurries into the shelter.*) Ere, buck up,
daddy! she's fetchin y'a thick slice o breadn treacle, an a mug o
skyblue. (*He seats him at the corner of the table.*)

95 RUMMY: (*Gaily.*) Keep up your old art! Never say die!

SHIRLEY: I'm not an old man. I'm only 46. I'm as good as ever I
was. The grey patch come in my hair before I was thirty. All it
wants is three pennorth o hair dye: am I to be turned on the
streets to starve for it? Holy God! I've worked ten to twelve

100 hours a day since I was thirteen, and paid my way all through;
and now am I to be thrown into the gutter and my job given
to a young man that can do it no better than me because Ive
black hair that goes white at the first change?

PRICE: (*Cheerfully.*) No good jawrin about it. Youre only a

105 jumped-up, jerked-off, orspittle-turned-out incurable of
an ole workin man: who cares about you? Eh? Make the
thievin swine give you a meal: theyve stole many a one
from you. Get a bit o your own back. (JENNY *returns with
the usual meal.*) There you are, brother. Awsk a blessin an

110 tuck that into you.

SHIRLEY: (*Looking at it ravenously but not touching it, and crying
like a child.*) I never took anything before.

JENNY: (*Petting him.*) Come, come! the Lord sends it to you: he
wasnt above taking bread from his friends; and why should

115 you be? Besides, when we find you a job you can pay us for it
if you like.

SHIRLEY: (*Eagerly.*) Yes, yes: thats true. I can pay you back: it's
only a loan. (*Shivering.*) O Lord! oh Lord! (*He turns to the
table and attacks the meal ravenously.*)

JENNY: Well, Rummy, are you more comfortable now? 120

RUMMY: God bless you, lovey! youve fed my body and saved
my soul, havnt you? (JENNY, *touched, kisses her.*) Sit down
and rest a bit: you must be ready to drop.

JENNY: Ive been going hard since morning. But theres more
work than we can do. I mustnt stop. 125

RUMMY: Try a prayer for just two minutes. Youll work all the
better after.

JENNY: (*Her eyes lighting up.*) Oh isnt it wonderful how a few
minutes prayer revives you! I was quite lightheaded at
twelve o'clock, I was so tired; but Major Barbara just sent 130
me to pray for five minutes; and I was able to go on as if
I had only just begun. (*To* PRICE.) Did you have a piece of
bread?

PRICE: (*With unction.*) Yes, miss; but Ive got the piece that I
value more; and thats the peace that passeth hall hanner- 135
stennin.

RUMMY: (*Fervently.*) Glory Hallelujah!

(BILL WALKER, *a rough customer of about 25, appears at the yard
gate and looks malevolently at* JENNY.)

JENNY: That makes me so happy. When you say that, I feel wicked
for loitering here. I must get to work again.

(*She is hurrying to the shelter, when the new-comer moves quickly up
to the door and intercepts her. His manner is so threatening that she
retreats as he comes at her truculently, driving her down the yard.*)

BILL: Aw knaow you. Youre the one that took awy maw girl. 140
Youre the one that set er agen me. Well, I'm gowin to ev
er aht. Not that Aw care a carse for er or you: see? Bat Aw'll
let er knaow; and Aw'll let you knaow. Aw'm gowing to give
her a doin thatll teach er to cat awy from me. Nah in wiv
you and tell er to cam aht afore Aw cam in and kick er aht. 145
Tell er Bill Walker wants er. She'll knaow wot thet means;
and if she keeps me witin itll be worse. You stop to jawr beck
at me; and Aw'll stawt on you: d'ye eah? Theres your wy. In
you gow. (*He takes her by the arm and slings her towards the
door of the shelter. She falls on her hand and knee.* RUMMY 150
helps her up again.)

PRICE: (*Rising, and venturing irresolutely towards* BILL.) Easy
there, mate. She aint doin you no arm.

BILL: Oo are you callin mite? (*Standing over him threateningly.*)
Youre gowin to stend ap for er, aw yer? Put ap your ends. 155

RUMMY: (*Running indignantly to him to scold him.*) Oh, you great
brute—(*He instantly swings his left hand back against her face.
She screams and reels back to the trough, where she sits down,
covering her bruised face with her hands and rocking herself
and moaning with pain.*) 160

JENNY: (*Going to her.*) Oh, God forgive you! How could you strike
an old woman like that?

BILL: (*Seizing her by the hair so violently that she also screams, and
tearing her away from the old woman.*) You Gawd forgimme
again an Aw'll Gawd forgive you one on the jawr thetll stop 165
you pryin for a week. (*Holding her and turning fiercely on*
PRICE.) Ev you ennything to sy agen it?

PRICE: (*Intimidated.*) No, matey: she aint anything to do with me.

170 BILL: Good job for you! Aw'd pat two meals into you and fawt you with one finger arter, you stawved cur. (*To* JENNY.) Nah are you gowin to fetch Mog Ebbijem; or em Aw to knock your fice off you and fetch her meself?

JENNY: (*Writhing in his grasp.*) Oh please someone go in and
175 tell Major Barbara—(*She screams again as he wrenches her head down; and* PRICE *and* RUMMY *flee into the shelter.*)

BILL: You want to gow in and tell your Mijor of me, do you?

JENNY: Oh please dont drag my hair. Let me go.

BILL: Do you or downt you? (*She stifles a scream.*) Yus or nao?

180 JENNY: God give me strength—

BILL: (*Striking her with his fist in the face.*) Gow an shaow her thet, and tell her if she wants one lawk it to cam and interfere with me. (JENNY, *crying with pain, goes into the shed. He goes to the form and addresses the old man.*) Eah: finish your mess;
185 an git aht o maw wy.

SHIRLEY: (*Springing up and facing him fiercely, with the mug in his hand.*) You take a liberty with me, and I'll smash you over the face with the mug and cut your eye out. Aint you satisfied—young whelps like you—with takin the bread out
190 o the mouths of your elders that have brought you up and slaved for you, but you must come shovin and cheekin and bullyin in here, where the bread o charity is sickenin in our stummicks?

BILL: (*Contemptuously, but backing a little.*) Wot good are you,
195 you aold palsy mag? Wot good are you?

SHIRLEY: As good as you and better. I'll do a day's work agen "you or any fat young soaker of your age. Go and take my job at Horrockses, where I worked for ten year. They want young men there: they cant afford to keep men over
200 forty-five. Theyre very sorry—give you a character and happy to help you to get anything suited to your years—sure a steady man wont be long out of a job. Well, let em try you. Theyll find the differ. What do you know? Not as much as how to beeyave yourself—layin your dirty fist across the
205 mouth of a respectable woman!

BILL: Downt provowk me to ly it across yours: d'ye eah?

SHIRLEY: (*With blighting contempt.*) Yes: you like an old man to hit, dont you, when youve finished with the women. I aint seen you hit a young one yet.

210 BILL: (*Stung.*) You loy, you aold soupkitchener, you. There was a yang menn eah. Did Aw offer to itt him or did Aw not?

SHIRLEY: Was he starvin or was he not? Was he a man or only a crosseyed thief an a loafer? Would you hit my son-in-law's brother?

215 BILL: Oo's ee?

SHIRLEY: Todger Fairmile o Balls Pond. Him that won £20 off the Japanese wrastler at the music hall by standin out 17 minutes 4 seconds agen him.

BILL: (*Sullenly.*) Aw'm nao music awl wrastler. Ken he box?
220 SHIRLEY: Yes: an you cant.

BILL: Wot! Aw cawnt, cawnt Aw? Wots thet you sy (*Threatening him.*)?

SHIRLEY: (*Not budging an inch.*) Will you box Todger Fairmile if I put him on to you? Say the word.

225 BILL: (*Subsiding with a slouch.*) Aw'll stend ap to enny menn alawv, if he was ten Todger Fairmawls. But Aw dont set ap to be a perfeshnal.

SHIRLEY: (*Looking down on him with unfathomable disdain.*) You box! Slap an old woman with the back o your hand! You hadnt
230 even the sense to hit her where a magistrate couldnt see the

mark of it, you silly young lump of conceit and ignorance. Hit a girl in the jaw and ony make her cry! If Todger Fairmile'd done it, she wouldnt a got up inside o ten minutes, no more than you would if he got on to you. Yah! I'd set about you
235 myself if I had a week's feedin in me instead o two months' starvation. (*He turns his back on him and sits down moodily at the table.*)

BILL: (*Following him and stooping over him to drive the taunt in.*) You loy! youve the bread and treacle in you that you cam
240 eah to beg.

SHIRLEY: (*Bursting into tears.*) Oh God! it's true: I'm only an old pauper on the scrap heap. (*Furiously.*) But youll come to it yourself; and then youll know. Youll come to it sooner than a teetotaller like me, fillin yourself with gin at this
245 hour o the mornin!

BILL: Aw'm nao gin drinker, you oald lawr; bat wen Aw want to give my girl a bloomin good awdin Aw lawk to ev a bit o devil in me: see? An eah Aw emm, talkin to a rotten aold blawter like you sted o givin her wot for. (*Working himself
250 into a rage.*) Aw'm gowin in there to fetch her aht. (*He makes vengefully for the shelter door.*)

SHIRLEY: Youre going to the station on a stretcher, more likely; and theyll take the gin and the devil out of you there when they get you inside. You mind what youre about: the major
255 here is the Earl o Stevenage's granddaughter.

BILL: (*Checked.*) Garn!

SHIRLEY: Youll see.

BILL: (*His resolution oozing.*) Well, Aw aint dan nathin to er.

SHIRLEY: Spose she said you did! who'd believe you?

260 BILL: (*Very uneasy, skulking back to the corner of the penthouse.*) Gawd! theres no jastice in this cantry. To think wot them people can do! Aw'm as good as er.

SHIRLEY: Tell her so. It's just what a fool like you would do.

(BARBARA, *brisk and businesslike, comes from the shelter with a note book, and addresses herself to* SHIRLEY. BILL, *cowed, sits down in the corner on a form, and turns his back on them.*)

BARBARA: Good morning.

SHIRLEY: (*Standing up and taking off his hat.*) Good morning,
265 miss.

BARBARA: Sit down: make yourself at home. (*He hesitates; but she puts a friendly hand on his shoulder and makes him obey.*) Now then! since youve made friends with us, we want to know all about you. Names and addresses and trades.
270
SHIRLEY: Peter Shirley. Fitter. Chucked out two months ago because I was too old.

BARBARA: (*Not at all surprised.*) Youd pass still. Why didnt you dye your hair?

SHIRLEY: I did. Me age come out at a coroner's inquest on me
275 daughter.

BARBARA: Steady?

SHIRLEY: Teetotaller. Never out of a job before. Good worker. And sent to the knackers like an old horse!

BARBARA: No matter: if you did your part God will do his.
280
SHIRLEY: (*Suddenly stubborn.*) My religion's no concern of anybody but myself.

BARBARA: (*Guessing.*) I know. Secularist?

SHIRLEY: (*Hotly.*) Did I offer to deny it?

BARBARA: Why should you? My own father's a Secularist, I
285 think. Our Father—yours and mine—fulfils himself in many ways; and I daresay he knew what he was about when he made a Secularist of you. So buck up, Peter! we

can always find a job for a steady man like you. (SHIRLEY, *disarmed and a little bewildered, touches his hat. She turns from him to* BILL.) Whats your name?

BILL: (*Insolently.*) Wots thet to you?

BARBARA: (*Calmly making a note.*) Afraid to give his name. Any trade?

295 BILL: Oo's afride to give is nime? (*Doggedly, with a sense of heroically defying the House of Lords in the person of Lord Stevenage.*) If you want to bring a chawge agen me, bring it. (*She waits, unruffled.*) Moy nime's Bill Walker.

BARBARA: (*As if the name were familiar: trying to remember how.*) Bill Walker? (*Recollecting.*) Oh, I know: you're the man that Jenny Hill was praying for inside just now. (*She enters his name in her note book.*)

BILL: Oo's Jenny Ill? And wot call as she to pry for me?

BARBARA: I dont know. Perhaps it was you that cut her lip.

305 BILL: (*Defiantly.*) Yus, it was me that cat her lip. Aw aint afride o you.

BARBARA: How could you be, since youre not afraid of God? Youre a brave man, Mr Walker. It takes some pluck to do our work here; but none of us dare lift our hand against a girl like that, for fear of her father in heaven.

BILL: (*Sullenly.*) I want nan o your kentin jawr. I spowse you think Aw cam eah to beg from you, like this demmiged lot eah. Not me. Aw downt want your bread and scripe and ketlep. Aw dont blieve in your Gawd, no more than you do yourself.

315 BARBARA: (*Sunnily apologetic and ladylike, as on a new footing with him.*) Oh, I beg your pardon for putting your name down, Mr Walker. I didnt understand. I'll strike it out.

BILL: (*Taking this as a slight, and deeply wounded by it.*) Eah! you let maw nime alown. Aint it good enaff to be in your book?

320 BARBARA: (*Considering.*) Well, you see, theres no use putting down your name unless I can do something for you, is there? Whats your trade?

BILL: (*Still smarting.*) Thets nao concern o yours.

BARBARA: Just so. (*Very businesslike.*) I'll put you down as (*Writing.*) the man who—struck—poor little Jenny Hill—in the mouth.

BILL: (*Rising threateningly.*) See eah. Awve ed enaff o this.

BARBARA: (*Quite sunny and fearless.*) What did you come to us for?

330 BILL: Aw cam for maw gel, see? Aw cam to tike her aht o this and to brike er jawr for er.

BARBARA: (*Complacently.*) You see I was right about your trade. (BILL, *on the point of retorting furiously, finds himself, to his great shame and terror, in danger of crying instead. He sits down again suddenly.*) Whats her name?

BILL: (*Dogged.*) Er nime's Mog Ebbijem: thets wot her nime is.

BARBARA: Mog Habbijam! Oh, she's gone to Canning Town, to our barracks there.

BILL: (*Fortified by his resentment of Mog's perfidy.*) Is she? (*Vindictively.*) Then Aw'm gowin to Kennintahn arter her. (*He crosses to the gate; hesitates; finally comes back at* BARBARA.) Are you loyin to me to git shat o me?

BARBARA: I dont want to get shut of you. I want to keep you here and save your soul. Youd better stay: youre going to have a bad time today, Bill.

BILL: Oo's gowin to give it to me? You, preps?

BARBARA: Someone you dont believe in. But youll be glad afterwards.

BILL: (*Slinking off.*) Aw'll gow to Kennintahn to be aht o reach o your tangue. (*Suddenly turning on her with intense malice.*)

And if Aw downt fawnd Mog there, Aw'll cam beck and do two years for you, selp me Gawd if Aw downt!

BARBARA: (*A shade kindlier, if possible.*) It's no use, Bill. She's got another bloke.

BILL: Wot!

BARBARA: One of her own converts. He fell in love with her when he saw her with her soul saved, and her face clean, and her hair washed.

BILL: (*Surprised.*) Wottud she wash it for, the carroty slat? It's red.

BARBARA: It's quite lovely now, because she wears a new look in her eyes with it. It's a pity youre too late. The new bloke has put your nose out of joint, Bill.

BILL: Aw'll put his nowse aht o joint for him. Not that Aw care a carse for er, mawnd thet. But Aw'll teach her to drop me as if Aw was dirt. And Aw'll teach him to meddle with maw judy. Wots iz bleedin nime?

BARBARA: Sergeant Todger Fairmile.

SHIRLEY: (*Rising with grim joy.*) I'll go with him, miss. I want to see them two meet. I'll take him to the infirmary when it's over.

BILL: (*To* SHIRLEY, *with undissembled misgiving.*) Is thet im you was speakin on?

SHIRLEY: Thats him.

BILL: Im that wrastled in the music awl?

SHIRLEY: The competitions at the National Sportin Club was worth nigh a hundred a year to him. He's gev em up now for religion; so he's a bit fresh for want of the exercise he was accustomed to. He'll be glad to see you. Come along.

BILL: Wots is wight?

SHIRLEY: Thirteen four. (BILL'*s last hope expires.*)

BARBARA: Go and talk to him, Bill. He'll convert you.

SHIRLEY: He'll convert your head into a mashed potato.

BILL: (*Sullenly.*) Aw aint afride of im. Aw aint afride of ennybody. Bat e can lick me. She's dan me. (*He sits down moodily on the edge of the horse trough.*)

SHIRLEY: You aint going. I thought not. (*He resumes his seat.*)

BARBARA: (*Calling.*) Jenny!

JENNY: (*Appearing at the shelter door with a plaster on the corner of her mouth.*) Yes, Major.

BARBARA: Send Rummy Mitchens out to clear away here.

JENNY: I think she's afraid.

BARBARA: (*Her resemblance to her mother flashing out for a moment.*) Nonsense! she must do as she's told.

JENNY: (*Calling into the shelter.*) Rummy: the Major says you must come.

(JENNY *comes to* BARBARA, *purposely keeping on the side next to* BILL, *lest he should suppose that she shrank from him or bore malice.*)

BARBARA: Poor little Jenny! Are you tired? (*Looking at the wounded cheek.*) Does it hurt?

JENNY: No: it's all right now. It was nothing.

BARBARA: (*Critically.*) It was as hard as he could hit, I expect. Poor Bill! You dont feel angry with him, do you?

JENNY: Oh no, no, no: indeed I dont, Major, bless his poor heart! (BARBARA *kisses her; and she runs away merrily into the shelter.* BILL *writhes with an agonizing return of his new and alarming symptoms, but says nothing.* RUMMY MITCHENS *comes from the shelter.*)

BARBARA: (*Going to meet* RUMMY.) Now Rummy, bustle. Take in those mugs and plates to be washed; and throw the crumbs about for the birds.

(RUMMY *takes the three plates and mugs; but* SHIRLEY *takes back his mug from her, as there is still some milk left in it.*)

410 RUMMY: There aint any crumbs. This aint a time to waste good
bread on birds.

PRICE: (*Appearing at the shelter door.*) Gentleman come to see
the shelter, Major. Says he's your father.

BARBARA: All right. Coming. (SNOBBY [PRICE] *goes back into*
415 *the shelter, followed by* BARBARA.)

RUMMY: (*Stealing across to* BILL *and addressing him in a subdued
voice, but with intense conviction.*) I'd av the lor of you, you
flat eared pignosed potwalloper, if she'd let me. Youre no
gentleman, to hit a lady in the face. (BILL, *with greater things*
420 *moving in him, takes no notice.*)

SHIRLEY: (*Following her.*) Here! in with you and dont get yourself
into more trouble by talking.

RUMMY: (*With hauteur.*) I aint ad the pleasure o being hintro-
duced to you, as I can remember. (*She goes into the shelter*
425 *with the plates.*)

SHIRLEY: Thats the—

BILL: (*Savagely.*) Downt you talk to me, d'ye eah? You lea me
alown, or Aw'll do you a mischief. Aw'm not dirt under
your feet, ennywy.

430 SHIRLEY: (*Calmly.*) Dont you be afeerd. You aint such prime
company that you need expect to be sought after. (*He is
about to go into the shelter when* BARBARA *comes out, with*
UNDERSHAFT *on her right.*)

BARBARA: Oh, there you are, Mr Shirley! (*Between them.*) This
435 is my father: I told you he was a Secularist, didnt I? Perhaps
youll be able to comfort one another.

UNDERSHAFT: (*Startled.*) A Secularist! Not the least in the world:
on the contrary, a confirmed mystic.

BARBARA: Sorry, I'm sure. By the way, papa, what is your religion?
440 in case I have to introduce you again.

UNDERSHAFT: My religion? Well, my dear, I am a Millionaire.
That is my religion.

BARBARA: Then I'm afraid you and Mr Shirley wont be able
to comfort one another after all. Youre not a Millionaire,
445 are you, Peter?

SHIRLEY: No; and proud of it.

UNDERSHAFT: (*Gravely.*) Poverty, my friend, is not a thing to
be proud of.

SHIRLEY: (*Angrily.*) Who made your millions for you? Me and
450 my like. Whats kep us poor? Keepin you rich. I wouldnt
have your conscience, not for all your income.

UNDERSHAFT: I wouldnt have your income, not for all your
conscience, Mr Shirley. (*He goes to the penthouse and sits
down on a form.*)

455 BARBARA: (*Stopping* SHIRLEY *adroitly as he is about to retort.*)
You wouldnt think he was my father, would you, Peter?
Will you go into the shelter and lend the lasses a hand for
a while: we're worked off our feet.

SHIRLEY: (*Bitterly.*) Yes: I'm in their debt for a meal, aint I?

460 BARBARA: Oh, not because youre in their debt, but for love of
them, Peter, for love of them. (*He cannot understand, and
is rather scandalized.*) There! dont stare at me. In with you;
and give that conscience of yours a holiday (*Bustling him
into the shelter.*)

465 SHIRLEY: (*As he goes in.*) Ah! it's a pity you never was trained to
use your reason, miss. Youd have been a very taking lecturer
on Secularism.

(BARBARA *turns to her father.*)

UNDERSHAFT: Never mind me, my dear. Go about your work;
and let me watch it for a while.

BARBARA: All right.   470

UNDERSHAFT: For instance, whats the matter with that outpatient
over there?

BARBARA: (*Looking at* BILL, *whose attitude has never changed,
and whose expression of brooding wrath has deepened.*) Oh, we
shall cure him in no time. Just watch. (*She goes over to* BILL   475
*and waits. He glances up at her and casts his eyes down again,
uneasy, but grimmer than ever.*) It would be nice to just stamp
on Mog Habbijam's face, wouldnt it, Bill?

BILL: (*Starting up from the trough in consternation.*) It's a loy: Aw
never said so. (*She shakes her head.*) Oo taold you wot was in   480
moy mawnd?

BARBARA: Only your new friend.

BILL: Wot new friend?

BARBARA: The devil, Bill. When he gets round people they get
miserable, just like you.   485

BILL: (*With a heartbreaking attempt at devil-may-care cheerfulness.*)
Aw aint miserable. (*He sits down again, and stretches his legs
in an attempt to seem indifferent.*)

BARBARA: Well, if youre happy, why dont you look happy, as
we do?   490

BILL: (*His legs curling back in spite of him.*) Aw'm eppy enaff, Aw
tell you. Woy cawnt you lea me alown? Wot ev I dan to you?
Aw aint smashed your fice, ev Aw?

BARBARA: (*Softly: wooing his soul.*) It's not me thats getting at
you, Bill.   495

BILL: Oo else is it?

BARBARA: Somebody that doesnt intend you to smash women's
faces, I suppose. Somebody or something that wants to make
a man of you.

BILL: (*Blustering.*) Mike a menn o me! Aint Aw a menn? eh?   500
Oo sez Aw'm not a menn?

BARBARA: Theres a man in you somewhere, I suppose. But why
did he let you hit poor little Jenny Hill? That wasnt very
manly of him, was it?

BILL: (*Tormented.*) Ev dan wiv it, Aw tell you. Chack it. Aw'm   505
sick o your Jenny Ill and er silly little fice.

BARBARA: Then why do you keep thinking about it? Why
does it keep coming up against you in your mind? Youre
not getting converted, are you?

BILL: (*With conviction.*) Not ME. Not lawkly.   510

BARBARA: Thats right, Bill. Hold out against it. Put out your
strength. Dont lets get you cheap. Todger Fairmile said he
wrestled for three nights against his salvation harder than
he ever wrestled with the Jap at the music hall. He gave in to
the Jap when his arm was going to break. But he didnt give   515
in to his salvation until his heart was going to break. Perhaps
youll escape that. You havnt any heart, have you?

BILL: Wot d'ye mean? Woy aint Aw got a awt the sime as
ennybody else?

BARBARA: A man with a heart wouldnt have bashed poor little   520
Jenny's face, would he?

BILL: (*Almost crying.*) Ow, will you lea me alown? Ev Aw ever
offered to meddle with you, that you cam neggin and
provowkin me lawk this? (*He writhes convulsively from his
eyes to his toes.*)   525

BARBARA: (*With a steady soothing hand on his arm and a gentle
voice that never lets him go.*) It's your soul thats hurting you,
Bill, and not me. Weve been through it all ourselves. Come
with us, Bill. (*He looks wildly round.*) To brave manhood

530 on earth and eternal glory in heaven. (*He is on the point of breaking down.*) Come. (*A drum is heard in the shelter; and* BILL, *with a gasp, escapes from the spell as* BARBARA *turns quickly.* ADOLPHUS [CUSINS] *enters from the shelter with a big drum.*) Oh! there you are, Dolly. Let me introduce a

535 new friend of mine, Mr Bill Walker. This is my bloke, Bill: Mr Cusins. (CUSINS *salutes with his drumstick.*)

BILL: Gowin to merry im?

BARBARA: Yes.

BILL: (*Fervently.*) Gawd elp im! Gaw-aw-aw-awd elp im!

540 BARBARA: Why? Do you think he wont be happy with me?

BILL: Awve aony ed to stend it for a mawnin: e'll ev to stend it for a lawftawm.

CUSINS: That is a frightful reflection, Mr Walker. But I cant tear myself away from her.

545 BILL: Well, Aw ken. (*To* BARBARA.) Eah! do you knaow where Aw'm gowin to, and wot Aw'm gowin to do?

BARBARA: Yes: youre going to heaven; and youre coming back here before the week's out to tell me so.

BILL: You loy. Aw'm gowin to Kennintahn, to spit in Todger

550 Fairmawl's eye. Aw beshed Jenny Ill's fice; an nar Aw'll git me aown fice beshed and cam beck and shaow it to er. Ee'll itt me ardern Aw itt her. Thatll mike us square. (*To* ADOLPHUS [CUSINS].) Is thet fair or is it not? Youre a genlmn: you oughter knaow.

555 BARBARA: Two black eyes wont make one white one, Bill.

BILL: Aw didnt awst you. Cawnt you never keep your mahth shat? Oy awst the genlmn.

CUSINS: (*Reflectively.*) Yes: I think youre right, Mr Walker. Yes: I should do it. It's curious: it's exactly what an ancient Greek

560 would have done.

BARBARA: But what good will it do?

CUSINS: Well, it will give Mr Fairmile some exercise; and it will satisfy Mr Walker's soul.

BILL: Rot! there aint nao such a thing as a saoul. Ah kin you

565 tell wevver Awve a saoul or not? You never seen it.

BARBARA: Ive seen it hurting you when you went against it.

BILL: (*With compressed aggravation.*) If you was maw gel and took the word aht o me mahth lawk thet, Aw'd give you sathink youd feel urtin, Aw would. (*To* CUSINS.) You tike

570 maw tip, mite. Stop er jawr; or youll doy afoah your tawm (*With intense expression.*) Wore aht: thets wot youll be: wore aht. (*He goes away through the gate.*)

CUSINS: (*Looking after him.*) I wonder!

BARBARA: Dolly! (*Indignant, in her mother's manner.*)

575 CUSINS: Yes, my dear, it's very wearing to be in love with you. If it lasts, I quite think I shall die young.

BARBARA: Should you mind?

CUSINS: Not at all. (*He is suddenly softened, and kisses her over the drum, evidently not for the first time, as people cannot kiss

580 over a big drum without practice.* UNDERSHAFT *coughs.*)

BARBARA: It's all right, papa, weve not forgotten you. Dolly: explain the place to papa: I havnt time. (*She goes busily into the shelter.*)

(UNDERSHAFT *and* ADOLPHUS [CUSINS] *now have the yard to themselves.* UNDERSHAFT, *seated on a form, and still keenly attentive, looks hard at* ADOLPHUS [CUSINS]. ADOLPHUS [CUSINS] *looks hard at him.*)

UNDERSHAFT: I fancy you guess something of what is in my

585 mind, Mr Cusins. (CUSINS *flourishes his drumsticks as if in the*

act of beating a lively rataplan, but makes no sound.) Exactly so. But suppose Barbara finds you out!

CUSINS: You know, I do not admit that I am imposing on Barbara. I am quite genuinely interested in the views of the Salvation Army. The fact is, I am a sort of collector of religions; and the 590 curious thing is that I find I can believe them all. By the way, have you any religion?

UNDERSHAFT: Yes.

CUSINS: Anything out of the common?

UNDERSHAFT: Only that there are two things necessary to 595 Salvation.

CUSINS: (*Disappointed, but polite.*) Ah, the Church Catechism. Charles Lomax also belongs to the Established Church.

UNDERSHAFT: The two things are—

CUSINS: Baptism and— 600

UNDERSHAFT: No. Money and gunpowder.

CUSINS: (*Surprised, but interested.*) That is the general opinion of our governing classes. The novelty is in hearing any man confess it.

UNDERSHAFT: Just so. 605

CUSINS: Excuse me: is there any place in your religion for honor, justice, truth, love, mercy and so forth?

UNDERSHAFT: Yes: they are the graces and luxuries of a rich, strong, and safe life.

CUSINS: Suppose one is forced to choose between them and 610 money or gunpowder?

UNDERSHAFT: Choose money and gunpowder; for without enough of both you cannot afford the others.

CUSINS: That is your religion?

UNDERSHAFT: Yes. 615

(*The cadence of this reply makes a full close in the conversation,* CUSINS *twists his face dubiously and contemplates* UNDERSHAFT. UNDERSHAFT *contemplates him.*)

CUSINS: Barbara wont stand that. You will have to choose between your religion and Barbara.

UNDERSHAFT: So will you, my friend. She will find out that that drum of yours is hollow.

CUSINS: Father Undershaft: you are mistaken: I am a sincere 620 Salvationist. You do not understand the Salvation Army. It is the army of joy, of love, of courage: it has banished the fear and remorse and despair of the old hell-ridden evangelical sects: it marches to fight the devil with trumpet and drum, with music and dancing, with banner and palm, as 625 becomes a sally from heaven by its happy garrison. It picks the waster out of the public house and makes a man of him: it finds a worm wriggling in a back kitchen, and lo! a woman! Men and women of rank too, sons and daughters of the Highest. It takes the poor professor of Greek, 630 the most artificial and self-suppressed of human creatures, from his meal of roots, and lets loose the rhapsodist in him; reveals the true worship of Dionysos to him; sends him down the public street drumming dithyrambs (*He plays a thundering flourish on the drum.*) 635

UNDERSHAFT: You will alarm the shelter.

CUSINS: Oh, they are accustomed to these sudden ecstasies. However, if the drum worries you—(*He pockets the drumsticks; unhooks the drum; and stands it on the ground opposite the gateway.*) 640

UNDERSHAFT: Thank you.

CUSINS: You remember what Euripides says about your money and gunpowder?

UNDERSHAFT: No.

645 CUSINS: (*Declaiming.*)

> One and another
> In money and guns may outpass his brother;
> And men in their millions float and flow
> And seethe with a million hopes as leaven;
650 And they win their will; or they miss their will;
> And their hopes are dead or are pined for still;
> But who'er can know
> As the long days go
> That to live is happy, has found his heaven.

655 My translation: what do you think of it?

UNDERSHAFT: I think, my friend, that if you wish to know, as the long days go, that to live is happy, you must first acquire money enough for a decent life, and power enough to be your own master.

660 CUSINS: You are damnably discouraging. (*He resumes his declamation.*)

> Is it so hard a thing to see
> That the spirit of God—whate'er it be—
> The law that abides and changes not, ages long,
665 The Eternal and Nature-born: these things be strong?
> What else is Wisdom? What of Man's endeavor,
> Or God's high grace so lovely and so great?
> To stand from fear set free? to breathe and wait?
> To hold a hand uplifted over Fate?
670 And shall not Barbara be loved for ever?

UNDERSHAFT: Euripides mentions Barbara, does he?

CUSINS: It is a fair translation. The word means Loveliness.

UNDERSHAFT: May I ask—as Barbara's father—how much a year she is to be loved for ever on?

675 CUSINS: As for Barbara's father, that is more your affair than mine. I can feed her by teaching Greek: that is about all.

UNDERSHAFT: Do you consider it a good match for her?

CUSINS: (*With polite obstinacy.*) Mr Undershaft: I am in many ways a weak, timid, ineffectual person; and my health is
680 far from satisfactory. But whenever I feel that I must have anything, I get it, sooner or later. I feel that way about Barbara. I dont like marriage: I feel intensely afraid of it; and I dont know what I shall do with Barbara or what she will do with me. But I feel that I and nobody else must marry
685 her. Please regard that as settled.—Not that I wish to be arbitrary; but why should I waste your time in discussing what is inevitable?

UNDERSHAFT: You mean that you will stick at nothing: not even the conversion of the Salvation Army to the worship
690 of Dionysos.

CUSINS: The business of the Salvation Army is to save, not to wrangle about the name of the pathfinder. Dionysos or another: what does it matter?

UNDERSHAFT: (*Rising and approaching him.*) Professor Cusins:
695 you are a young man after my own heart.

CUSINS: Mr Undershaft: you are, as far as I am able to gather, a most infernal old rascal; but you appeal very strongly to my sense of ironic humor.

(UNDERSHAFT *mutely offers his hand. They shake.*)

UNDERSHAFT: (*Suddenly concentrating himself.*) And now to business. 700

CUSINS: Pardon me. We are discussing religion. Why go back to such an uninteresting and unimportant subject as business?

UNDERSHAFT: Religion is our business at present, because it is through religion alone that we can win Barbara.

CUSINS: Have you, too, fallen in love with Barbara? 705

UNDERSHAFT: Yes, with a father's love.

CUSINS: A father's love for a grown-up daughter is the most dangerous of all infatuations. I apologize for mentioning my own pale, coy, mistrustful fancy in the same breath with it.

UNDERSHAFT: Keep to the point. We have to win her; and we are 710 neither of us Methodists.

CUSINS: That doesnt matter. The power Barbara wields here—the power that wields Barbara herself—is not Calvinism, not Presbyterianism, not Methodism—

UNDERSHAFT: Not Greek Paganism either, eh? 715

CUSINS: I admit that. Barbara is quite original in her religion.

UNDERSHAFT: (*Triumphantly.*) Aha! Barbara Undershaft would be. Her inspiration comes from within herself.

CUSINS: How do you suppose it got there?

UNDERSHAFT: (*In towering excitement.*) It is the Undershaft 720 inheritance. I shall hand on my torch to my daughter. She shall make my converts and preach my gospel—

CUSINS: What! Money and gunpowder!

UNDERSHAFT: Yes, money and gunpowder. Freedom and power. Command of life and command of death. 725

CUSINS: (*Urbanely: trying to bring him down to earth.*) This is extremely interesting, Mr Undershaft. Of course you know that you are mad.

UNDERSHAFT: (*With redoubled force.*) And you?

CUSINS: Oh, mad as a hatter. You are welcome to my secret since 730 I have discovered yours. But I am astonished. Can a madman make cannons?

UNDERSHAFT: Would anyone else than a madman make them? And now (*With surging energy.*) question for question. Can a sane man translate Euripides? 735

CUSINS: No.

UNDERSHAFT: (*Seizing him by the shoulder.*) Can a sane woman make a man of a waster or a woman of a worm?

CUSINS: (*Reeling before the storm.*) Father Colossus—Mammoth Millionaire— 740

UNDERSHAFT: (*Pressing him.*) Are there two mad people or three in this Salvation shelter today?

CUSINS: You mean Barbara is as mad as we are?

UNDERSHAFT: (*Pushing him lightly off and resuming his equanimity suddenly and completely.*) Pooh, Professor! let us call 745 things by their proper names. I am a millionaire; you are a poet; Barbara is a savior of souls. What have we three to do with the common mob of slaves and idolators? (*He sits down again with a shrug of contempt for the mob.*)

CUSINS: Take care! Barbara is in love with the common people. 750 So am I. Have you never felt the romance of that love?

UNDERSHAFT: (*Cold and sardonic.*) Have you ever been in love with Poverty, like St Francis? Have you ever been in love with Dirt, like St Simeon? Have you ever been in love with disease and suffering, like our nurses and philanthropists? 755 Such passions are not virtues, but the most unnatural of all the vices. This love of the common people may please an earl's granddaughter and a university professor; but I have been a common man and a poor man; and it has no romance

760 for me. Leave it to the poor to pretend that poverty is a blessing: leave it to the coward to make a religion of his cowardice by preaching humility: we know better than that. We three must stand together above the common people: how else can 765 we help their children to climb up beside us? Barbara must belong to us, not to the Salvation Army.

CUSINS: Well, I can only say that if you think you will get her away from the Salvation Army by talking to her as you have been talking to me, you dont know Barbara.

UNDERSHAFT: My friend: I never ask for what I can buy.

770 CUSINS: (*In a white fury.*) Do I understand you to imply that you can buy Barbara?

UNDERSHAFT: No; but I can buy the Salvation Army.

CUSINS: Quite impossible.

UNDERSHAFT: You shall see. All religious organizations exist by 775 selling themselves to the rich.

CUSINS: Not the Army. That is the Church of the poor.

UNDERSHAFT: All the more reason for buying it.

CUSINS: I dont think you quite know what the Army does for the poor.

780 UNDERSHAFT: Oh yes I do. It draws their teeth: that is enough for me as a man of business.

CUSINS: Nonsense! It makes them sober—

UNDERSHAFT: I prefer sober workmen. The profits are larger.

CUSINS: —honest—

785 UNDERSHAFT: Honest workmen are the most economical.

CUSINS: —attached to their homes—

UNDERSHAFT: So much the better: they will put up with anything sooner than change their shop.

CUSINS: —happy—

790 UNDERSHAFT: An invaluable safeguard against revolution.

CUSINS: —unselfish—

UNDERSHAFT: Indifferent to their own interests, which suits me exactly.

CUSINS: —with their thoughts on heavenly things—

795 UNDERSHAFT: (*Rising.*) And not on Trade Unionism nor Socialism. Excellent.

CUSINS: (*Revolted.*) You really are an infernal old rascal.

UNDERSHAFT: (*Indicating* PETER SHIRLEY, *who has just come from the shelter and strolled dejectedly down the yard between* 800 *them.*) And this is an honest man!

SHIRLEY: Yes; and what av I got by it? (*He passes on bitterly and sits on the form, in the corner of the penthouse.*)

(SNOBBY PRICE, *beaming sanctimoniously, and* JENNY HILL, *with a tambourine full of coppers, come from the shelter and go to the drum, on which* JENNY *begins to count the money.*)

UNDERSHAFT: (*Replying to* SHIRLEY.) Oh, your employers must have got a good deal by it from first to last. (*He sits on the* 805 *table, with one foot on the side form,* CUSINS, *overwhelmed, sits down on the same form nearer the shelter.* BARBARA *comes from the shelter to the middle of the yard. She is excited and a little overwrought.*)

BARBARA: Weve just had a splendid experience meeting at the 810 other gate in Cripps's lane. Ive hardly ever seen them so much moved as they were by your confession, Mr Price.

PRICE: I could almost be glad of my past wickedness if I could believe that it would elp to keep hathers stright.

BARBARA: So it will, Snobby. How much, Jenny?

JENNY: Four and tenpence, Major. 815

BARBARA: Oh Snobby, if you had given your poor mother just one more kick, we should have got the whole five shillings!

PRICE: If she heard you say that, miss, she'd be sorry I didnt. But I'm glad. Oh what a joy it will be to her when she hears I'm saved! 820

UNDERSHAFT: Shall I contribute the odd twopence, Barbara? The millionaire's mite, eh? (*He takes a couple of pennies from his pocket.*)

BARBARA: How did you make that twopence?

UNDERSHAFT: As usual. By selling cannons, torpedoes, 825 submarines, and my new patent Grand Duke hand grenade.

BARBARA: Put it back in your pocket. You cant buy your salvation here for twopence: you must work it out.

UNDERSHAFT: Is twopence not enough? I can afford a little more, if you press me. 830

BARBARA: Two million millions would not be enough. There is bad blood on your hands; and nothing but good blood can cleanse them. Money is no use. Take it away. (*She turns to* CUSINS.) Dolly: you must write another letter for me to the papers. (*He makes a wry face.*) Yes: I know you dont 835 like it; but it must be done. The starvation this winter is beating us: everybody is unemployed. The General says we must close this shelter if we cant get more money. I force the collections at the meetings until I am ashamed: dont I, Snobby? 840

PRICE: It's a fair treat to see you work it, miss. The way you got them up from three-and-six to four-and-ten with that hymn, penny by penny and verse by verse, was a caution. Not a Cheap Jack on Mile End Waste could touch you at it.

BARBARA: Yes; but I wish we could do without it. I am getting 845 at last to think more of the collection than of the people's souls. And what are those hatfuls of pence and halfpence? We want thousands! tens of thousands! hundreds of thousands! I want to convert people, not to be always begging for the Army in a way I'd die sooner than beg for myself. 850

UNDERSHAFT: (*In profound irony.*) Genuine unselfishness is capable of anything, my dear.

BARBARA: (*Unsuspectingly, as she turns away to take the money from the drum and put it in a cash bag she carries.*) Yes, isnt it? (UNDERSHAFT *looks sardonically at* CUSINS.) 855

CUSINS: (*Aside to* UNDERSHAFT.) Mephistopheles! Machiavelli!

BARBARA: (*Tears coming into her eyes as she ties the bag and pockets it.*) How are we to feed them? I cant talk religion to a man with bodily hunger in his eyes. (*Almost breaking down.*) It's frightful. 860

JENNY: (*Running to her.*) Major, dear—

BARBARA: (*Rebounding.*) No: dont comfort me. It will be all right. We shall get the money.

UNDERSHAFT: How?

JENNY: By praying for it, of course. Mrs Baines says she prayed 865 for it last night; and she has never prayed for it in vain: never once. (*She goes to the gate and looks out into the street.*)

BARBARA: (*Who has dried her eyes and regained her composure.*) By the way, dad, Mrs Baines has come to march with us to our big meeting this afternoon; and she is very anxious to meet 870 you, for some reason or other. Perhaps she'll convert you.

UNDERSHAFT: I shall be delighted, my dear.

JENNY: (*At the gate: excitedly.*) Major! Major! heres that man back again.

BARBARA: What man? 875

JENNY: The man that hit me. Oh, I hope he's coming back to join us.

(BILL WALKER, *with frost on his jacket, comes through the gate, his hands deep in his pockets and his chin sunk between his shoulders, like a cleaned-out gambler. He halts between* BARBARA *and the drum.*)

BARBARA: Hullo, Bill! Back already!

BILL: (*Nagging at her.*) Bin talkin ever sence, ev you?

880 BARBARA: Pretty nearly. Well, has Todger paid you out for poor Jenny's jaw?

BILL: Nao e aint.

BARBARA: I thought your jacket looked a bit snowy.

BILL: Sao it is snaowy. You want to knaow where the snaow 885 cam from, downt you?

BARBARA: Yes.

BILL: Well, it cam from orf the grahnd in Pawkinses Corner in Kennintahn. It got rabbed orf be maw shaoulders: see?

BARBARA: Pity you didnt rub some off with your knees, Bill! 890 That would have done you a lot of good.

BILL: (*With sour mirthless humor.*) Aw was sivin another menn's knees at the tawm. E was kneelin on moy ed, e was.

JENNY: Who was kneeling on your head?

BILL: Todger was. E was pryin for me: pryin camfortable wiv 895 me as a cawpet. Sow was Mog. Sao was the aol bloomin meetin. Mog she sez 'Ow Lawd brike is stabborn sperrit; bat downt urt is dear art.' Thet was wot she said. 'Downt urt is dear art'! An er blowk—thirteen stun four!—kneelin wiv all is wight on me. Fanny, aint it?

900 JENNY: Oh no. We're so sorry, Mr Walker.

BARBARA: (*Enjoying it frankly.*) Nonsense! of course it's funny. Served you right, Bill! You must have done something to him first.

BILL: (*Doggedly.*) Aw did wot Aw said Aw'd do. Aw spit in is eye. 905 E looks ap at the skoy and sez, 'Ow that Aw should be fahnd worthy to be spit upon for the gospel's sike!' e sez; an Mog sez 'Glaory Allelloolier!'; an then e called me Braddher, an dahned me as if Aw was a kid and e was me mather worshin me a Setterda nawt. Aw ednt jast nao shaow wiv im at all. 910 Arf the street pryed; an the tather arf larfed fit to split thereselves. (*To* BARBARA.) There! are you settisfawd nah?

BARBARA: (*Her eyes dancing.*) Wish I'd been there, Bill.

BILL: Yus: youd a got in a hextra bit o talk on me, wouldnt you?

JENNY: I'm so sorry, Mr Walker.

915 BILL: (*Fiercely.*) Downt you gow being sorry for me: youve no call. Listen eah. Aw browk your jawr.

JENNY: No, it didn't hurt me: indeed it didnt, except for a moment. It was only that I was frightened.

BILL: Aw downt want to be forgive be you, or be ennybody. 920 Wot Aw did Aw'll py for. Aw trawd to gat me aown jawr browk to settisfaw you—

JENNY: (*Distressed.*) Oh no—

BILL: (*Impatiently.*) Tell y' Aw did: cawnt you listen to wots bein taold you? All Aw got be it was bein mide a sawt of 925 in the pablic street for me pines. Well, if Aw cawnt settisfaw you one wy, Aw ken anather. Listen eah! Aw ed two quid sived agen the frost; an Awve a pahnd of it left. A mite o mawn last week ed words with the judy e's gowing to merry. E give er wot-for; an e's bin fawnd fifteen bob. 930 E ed a rawt to itt er cause they was gowin to be merrid;

but Aw ednt nao rawt to itt you; sao put anather fawv bob on an call it a pahnd's worth. (*He produces a sovereign.*) Eahs the manney. Tike it; and lets ev no more o your forgivin an prying and your Mijor jawrin me. Let wot Aw dan be dan an pide for; and let there be a end of it. 935

JENNY: Oh, I couldnt take it, Mr Walker. But if you would give a shilling or two to poor Rummy Mitchens! you really did hurt her; and she's old.

BILL: (*Contemptuously.*) Not lawkly. Aw'd give her anather as soon as look at er. Let her ev the lawr o me as she threatened! 940 She aint forgiven me: not mach. Wot Aw dan to er is not on me mawnd—wot she (*Indicating* BARBARA.) mawt call on me conscience—no more than stickin a pig. It's this Christian gime o yours that Aw wownt ev plyed agen me: this bloomin forgivin an neggin an jawrin that mikes a menn 945 thet sore that iz lawf's a burdn to im. Aw wownt ev it, Aw tell you; sao tike your manney and stop thraowin your silly beshed fice hap agen me.

JENNY: Major: may I take a little of it for the Army?

BARBARA: No: the Army is not to be bought. We want your soul, 950 Bill; and we'll take nothing less.

BILL: (*Bitterly.*) Aw knaow. Me an maw few shillins is not good enaff for you. Youre a earl's grendorter, you are. Nathink less than a andered pahnd for you.

UNDERSHAFT: Come, Barbara! you could do a great deal of 955 good with a hundred pounds. If you will set this gentleman's mind at ease by taking his pound, I will give the other ninety-nine.

(BILL, *dazed by such opulence, instinctively touches his cap.*)

BARBARA: Oh, youre too extravagant, papa. Bill offers twenty pieces of silver. All you need offer is the other ten. That will 960 make the standard price to buy anybody who's for sale. I'm not; and the Army's not. (*To* BILL.) Youll never have another quiet moment, Bill, until you come round to us. You cant stand out against your salvation.

BILL: (*Sullenly.*) Aw cawnt stend aht agen music awl wrastlers and 965 awtful tangued women. Awve offered to py. Aw can do no more. Tike it or leave it. There it is. (*He throws the sovereign on the drum, and sits down on the horse-trough. The coin fascinates* SNOBBY PRICE, *who takes an early opportunity of dropping his cap on it.*) 970

(MRS BAINES *comes from the shelter. She is dressed as a Salvation Army Commissioner. She is an earnest looking woman of about 40, with a caressing, urgent voice, and an appealing manner.*)

BARBARA: This is my father, Mrs Baines. (UNDERSHAFT *comes from the table, taking his hat off with marked civility.*) Try what you can do with him. He wont listen to me, because he remembers what a fool I was when I was a baby. (*She leaves them together and chats with* JENNY.) 975

MRS BAINES: Have you been shewn over the shelter, Mr Undershaft? You know the work we're doing, of course.

UNDERSHAFT: (*Very civilly.*) The whole nation knows it, Mrs Baines.

MRS BAINES: No, sir: the whole nation does not know it, or we 980 should not be crippled as we are for want of money to carry our work through the length and breadth of the land. Let me tell you that there would have been rioting this winter in London but for us.

985   UNDERSHAFT: You really think so?

MRS BAINES: I know it. I remember 1886, when you rich gentlemen hardened your hearts against the cry of the poor. They broke the windows of your clubs in Pall Mall.

UNDERSHAFT: (*Gleaming with approval of their method.*) And

990   the Mansion House Fund went up next day from thirty thousand pounds to seventy-nine thousand! I remember quite well.

MRS BAINES: Well, wont you help me to get at the people? They wont break windows then. Come here, Price. Let me shew you

995   to this gentleman (PRICE *comes to be inspected.*) Do you remember the window breaking?

PRICE: My ole father thought it was the revolution, maam.

MRS BAINES: Would you break windows now?

PRICE: Oh no, maam. The windows of eaven av bin opened to

1000   me. I know now that the rich man is a sinner like myself.

RUMMY: (*Appearing above at the loft door.*) Snobby Price!

SNOBBY: Wot is it?

RUMMY: Your mother's askin for you at the other gate in Cripps's Lane. She's heard about your confession (PRICE *turns pale.*)

1005   MRS BAINES: Go, Mr Price; and pray with her.

JENNY: You can go through the shelter, Snobby.

PRICE: (*To* MRS BAINES.) I couldnt face her now, maam, with all the weight of my sins fresh on me. Tell her she'll find her son at ome, waitin for her in prayer. (*He skulks off through*

1010   *the gate, incidentally stealing the sovereign on his way out by picking up his cap from the drum.*)

MRS BAINES: (*With swimming eyes.*) You see how we take the anger and the bitterness against you out of their hearts, Mr Undershaft.

1015   UNDERSHAFT: It is certainly most convenient and gratifying to all large employers of labor, Mrs Baines.

MRS BAINES: Barbara: Jenny: I have good news: most wonderful news. (JENNY *runs to her.*) My prayers have been answered. I told you they would, Jenny, didnt I?

1020   JENNY: Yes, yes.

BARBARA: (*Moving nearer to the drum.*) Have we got money enough to keep the shelter open?

MRS BAINES: I hope we shall have enough to keep all the shelters open. Lord Saxmundham has promised us five

1025   thousand pounds—

BARBARA: Hooray!

JENNY: Glory!

MRS BAINES: —if—

BARBARA: 'If!' If what?

1030   MRS BAINES: —if five other gentlemen will give a thousand each to make it up to ten thousand.

BARBARA: Who is Lord Saxmundham? I never heard of him.

UNDERSHAFT: (*Who has pricked up his ears at the peer's name, and is now watching* BARBARA *curiously.*) A new creation, my

1035   dear. You have heard of Sir Horace Bodger?

BARBARA: Bodger! Do you mean the distiller? Bodger's whisky!

UNDERSHAFT: That is the man. He is one of the greatest of our public benefactors. He restored the cathedral at Hakington. They made him a baronet for that. He gave half a million to

1040   the funds of his party: they made him a baron for that.

SHIRLEY: What will they give him for the five thousand?

UNDERSHAFT: There is nothing left to give him. So the five thousand, I should think, is to save his soul.

MRS BAINES: Heaven grant it may! Oh Mr Undershaft, you

1045   have some very rich friends. Cant you help us towards the other five thousand? We are going to hold a great meeting this afternoon at the Assembly Hall in the Mile End Road. If I could only announce that one gentleman had come forward to support Lord Saxmundham, others would follow. Dont you know somebody? couldnt you? wouldnt you? 1050 (*Her eyes fill with tears.*) oh, think of those poor people, Mr Undershaft: think of how much it means to them, and how little to a great man like you.

UNDERSHAFT: (*Sardonically gallant.*) Mrs Baines: you are irresistible. I cant disappoint you; and I cant deny myself the 1055 satisfaction of making Bodger pay up. You shall have your five thousand pounds.

MRS BAINES: Thank God!

UNDERSHAFT: You dont thank me?

MRS BAINES: Oh sir, dont try to be cynical: dont be ashamed 1060 of being a good man. The Lord will bless you abundantly; and our prayers will be like a strong fortification round you all the days of your life. (*With a touch of caution.*) You will let me have the cheque to shew at the meeting, wont you? Jenny: go in and fetch a pen and ink. (JENNY *runs to* 1065 *the shelter door.*)

UNDERSHAFT: Do not disturb Miss Hill: I have a fountain pen. (JENNY *halts. He sits at the table and writes the cheque.* CUSINS *rises to make room for him. They all watch him silently.*)

BILL: (*Cynically, aside to* BARBARA, *his voice and accent horribly* 1070 *debased.*) Wot prawce selvytion nah?

BARBARA: Stop. (UNDERSHAFT *stops writing: they all turn to her in surprise.*) Mrs Baines: are you really going to take this money?

MRS BAINES: (*Astonished.*) Why not, dear? 1075

BARBARA: Why not! Do you know what my father is? Have you forgotten that Lord Saxmundham is Bodger the whisky man? Do you remember how we implored the County Council to stop him from writing Bodger's Whisky in letters of fire against the sky; so that the poor drink-ruined creatures on 1080 the Embankment could not wake up from their snatches of sleep without being reminded of their deadly thirst by that wicked sky sign? Do you know that the worst thing I have had to fight here is not the devil, but Bodger, Bodger, Bodger, with his whisky, his distilleries, and his tied houses? Are 1085 you going to make our shelter another tied house for him, and ask me to keep it?

BILL: Rotten dranken whisky it is too.

MRS BAINES: Dear Barbara: Lord Saxmundham has a soul to be saved like any of us. If heaven has found the way to make 1090 a good use of his money, are we to set ourselves up against the answer to our prayers?

BARBARA: I know he has a soul to be saved. Let him come down here; and I'll do my best to help him to his salvation. But he wants to send his cheque down to buy us, and go on being as 1095 wicked as ever.

UNDERSHAFT: (*With a reasonableness which* CUSINS *alone perceives to be ironical.*) My dear Barbara: alcohol is a very necessary article. It heals the sick—

BARBARA: It does nothing of the sort. 1100

UNDERSHAFT: Well, it assists the doctor: that is perhaps a less questionable way of putting it. It makes life bearable to millions of people who could not endure their existence if they were quite sober. It enables Parliament to do things at eleven at night that no sane person would do at eleven in 1105 the morning. Is it Bodger's fault that this inestimable gift is deplorably abused by less than one per cent of the poor? (*He turns again to the table; signs the cheque; and crosses it.*)

1110 MRS BAINES: Barbara: will there be less drinking or more if all those poor souls we are saving come tomorrow and find the doors of our shelters shut in their faces? Lord Saxmundham gives the money to stop drinking—to take his own business from him.

CUSINS: (*Impishly.*) Pure self-sacrifice on Bodger's part, clearly!
1115 Bless dear Bodger! (BARBARA *almost breaks down as* ADOLPHUS, *too, fails her.*)

UNDERSHAFT: (*Tearing out the cheque and pocketing the book as he rises and goes past* CUSINS *to* MRS BAINES.) I also, Mrs Baines, may claim a little disinterestedness. Think of my
1120 business! think of the widows and orphans! the men and lads torn to pieces with shrapnel and poisoned with lyddite! (MRS BAINES *shrinks; but he goes on remorselessly.*) the oceans of blood, not one drop of which is shed in a really just cause! the ravaged crops! the peaceful peasants forced, women and
1125 men, to till their fields under the fire of opposing armies on pain of starvation! the bad blood of the fierce little cowards at home who egg on others to fight for the gratification of their national vanity! All this makes money for me: I am never richer, never busier than when the papers are full of it. Well,
1130 it is your work to preach peace on earth and good will to men. (MRS BAINES's *face lights up again.*) Every convert you make is a vote against war. (*Her lips move in prayer.*) Yet I give you this money to help you to hasten my own commercial ruin. (*He gives her the cheque.*)
1135 CUSINS: (*Mounting the form in an ecstasy of mischief.*) The millennium will be inaugurated by the unselfishness of Undershaft and Bodger. Oh be joyful! (*He takes the drumsticks from his pocket and flourishes them.*)

MRS BAINES: (*Taking the cheque.*) The longer I live the more
1140 proof I see that there is an Infinite Goodness that turns everything to the work of salvation sooner or later. Who would have thought that any good could have come out of war and drink? And yet their profits are brought today to the feet of salvation to do its blessed work. (*She is affected*
1145 *to tears.*)

JENNY: (*Running to* MRS BAINES *and throwing her arms round her.*) Oh dear! how blessed, how glorious it all is!

CUSINS: (*In a convulsion of irony.*) Let us seize this unspeakable moment. Let us march to the great meeting at once. Excuse
1150 me just an instant. (*He rushes into the shelter.* JENNY *takes her tambourine from the drum head.*)

MRS BAINES: Mr Undershaft: have you ever seen a thousand people fall on their knees with one impulse and pray? Come with us to the meeting. Barbara shall tell them that
1155 the Army is saved, and saved through you.

CUSINS: (*Returning impetuously from the shelter with a flag and a trombone, and coming between* MRS BAINES *and* UNDERSHAFT.) You shall carry the flag down the first street, Mrs Baines. (*He gives her the flag.*) Mr Undershaft is a gifted
1160 trombonist: he shall intone an Olympian diapason to the West Ham Salvation March. (*Aside to* UNDERSHAFT, *as he forces the trombone on him.*) Blow, Machiavelli, blow.

UNDERSHAFT: (*Aside to him, as he takes the trombone.*) The trumpet in Zion! (CUSINS *rushes to the drum, which he takes*
1165 *up and puts on.* UNDERSHAFT *continues, aloud.*) I will do my best. I could vamp a bass if I knew the tune.

CUSINS: It is a wedding chorus from one of Donizetti's operas; but we have converted it. We convert everything to good here, including Bodger. You remember the chorus. 'For thee immense rejoicing—immenso giubilo—immenso
1170 giubilo.' (*With drum obbligato.*) Rum tum ti tum tum, tum tum ti ta—

BARBARA: Dolly: you are breaking my heart.

CUSINS: What is a broken heart more or less here? Dionysos Undershaft has descended. I am possessed.
1175 MRS BAINES: Come, Barbara: I must have my dear Major to carry the flag with me.

JENNY: Yes, yes, Major darling.

(CUSINS *snatches the tambourine out of* JENNY's *hand and mutely offers it to* BARBARA.)

BARBARA: (*Coming forward a little as she puts the offer behind her with a shudder, whilst* CUSINS *recklessly tosses the tambourine*
1180 *back to* JENNY *and goes to the gate.*) I cant come.

JENNY: Not come!

MRS BAINES: (*With tears in her eyes.*) Barbara: do you think I am wrong to take the money?

BARBARA: (*Impulsively going to her and kissing her.*) No, no: God
1185 help you, dear, you must: you are saving the Army. Go; and may you have a great meeting!

JENNY: But arnt you coming?

BARBARA: No. (*She begins taking off the silver S brooch from her collar.*)
1190 MRS BAINES: Barbara: what are you doing?

JENNY: Why are you taking your badge off? You cant be going to leave us, Major.

BARBARA: (*Quietly.*) Father: come here.

UNDERSHAFT: (*Coming to her.*) My dear! (*Seeing that she is going*
1195 *to pin the badge on his collar, he retreats to the penthouse in some alarm.*)

BARBARA: (*Following him.*) Dont be frightened. (*She pins the badge on and steps back towards the table, shewing him to the others.*) There! It's not much for £5000, is it?
1200 MRS BAINES: Barbara: if you wont come and pray with us, promise me you will pray for us.

BARBARA: I cant pray now. Perhaps I shall never pray again.

MRS BAINES: Barbara!

JENNY: Major!
1205 BARBARA: (*Almost delirious.*) I cant bear any more. Quick march!

CUSINS: (*Calling to the procession in the street outside.*) Off we go. Play up, there! Immenso giubilo. (*He gives the time with his drum; and the band strikes up the march, which rapidly*
1210 *becomes more distant as the procession moves briskly away.*)

MRS BAINES: I must go, dear. Youre overworked: you will be all right tomorrow. We'll never lose you. Now Jenny: step out with the old flag. Blood and Fire! (*She marches out through the gate with her flag.*)
1215 JENNY: Glory Hallelujah! (*Flourishing her tambourine and marching.*)

UNDERSHAFT: (*To* CUSINS, *as he marches out past him easing the slide of his trombone.*) 'My ducats and my daughter'!

CUSINS: (*Following him out.*) Money and gunpowder!
1220 BARBARA: Drunkenness and Murder! My God: why hast thou forsaken me?

(*She sinks on the form with her face buried in her hands. The march passes away into silence.* BILL WALKER *steals across to her.*)

BILL: (*Taunting.*) Wot prawce selvytion nah?

SHIRLEY: Dont you hit her when she's down.

1225 BILL: She itt me wen aw wiz dahn. Waw shouldnt Aw git a bit o me aown beck?

BARBARA: (*Raising her head.*) I didnt take your money, Bill. (*She crosses the yard to the gate and turns her back on the two men to hide her face from them.*)

1230 BILL: (*Sneering after her.*) Naow, it warnt enaff for you. (*Turning to the drum, he misses the money.*) Ellow! If you aint took it sammun else ez. Weres it gorn? Bly me if Jenny Ill didnt tike it after all!

1235 RUMMY: (*Screaming at him from the loft.*) You lie, you dirty blackguard! Snobby Price pinched it off the drum when he took up his cap. I was up here all the time an see im do it.

BILL: Wot! Stowl maw manney! Waw didnt you call thief on him, you silly aold macker you?

RUMMY: To serve you aht for ittin me across the fice. It's cost 1240 y'pahnd, that az. (*Raising a pæan of squalid triumph.*) I done you. I'm even with you. Uve ad it aht o y—(BILL *snatches up* SHIRLEY's *mug and hurls it at her. She slams the loft door and vanishes. The mug smashes against the door and falls in fragments.*)

1245 BILL: (*Beginning to chuckle.*) Tell us, aol menn, wot o'clock this mawnin was it wen im as they call Snobby Prawce was sived?

BARBARA: (*Turning to him more composedly, and with unspoiled sweetness.*) About half past twelve, Bill. And he pinched your 1250 pound at a quarter to two. *I* know. Well, you cant afford to lose it. I'll send it to you.

BILL: (*His voice and accent suddenly improving.*) Not if Aw wiz to stawve for it. Aw aint to be bought.

SHIRLEY: Aint you? Youd sell yourself to the devil for a pint 1255 o beer; only there aint no devil to make the offer.

BILL: (*Unashamed.*) Sao Aw would, mite, and often ev, cheerful. But she cawnt baw me. (*Approaching* BARBARA.) You wanted maw saoul, did you? Well, you aint got it.

BARBARA: I nearly got it, Bill. But weve sold it back to you for 1260 ten thousand pounds.

SHIRLEY: And dear at the money!

BARBARA: No, Peter: it was worth more than money.

BILL: (*Salvationproof.*) It's nao good: you cawnt get rahnd me nah. Aw downt blieve in it; and Awve seen tody that Aw was 1265 rawt. (*Going.*) Sao long, aol soupkitchener! Ta, ta, Mijor Earl's Grendorter! (*Turning at the gate.*) Wot prawce selvytion nah? Snobby Prawce! Ha! ha!

BARBARA: (*Offering her hand.*) Goodbye, Bill.

BILL: (*Taken aback, half plucks his cap off; then shoves it on again* 1270 *defiantly.*) Git aht. (BARBARA *drops her hand, discouraged. He has a twinge of remorse.*) But thets aw rawt, you knaow. Nathink pasnl. Naow mellice. Sao long, Judy. (*He goes.*)

BARBARA: No malice. So long, Bill.

SHIRLEY: (*Shaking his head.*) You make too much of him, miss, 1275 in your innocence.

BARBARA: (*Going to him.*) Peter: I'm like you now. Cleaned out, and lost my job.

SHIRLEY: Youve youth an hope. Thats two better than me.

BARBARA: I'll get you a job, Peter. Thats hope for you: the youth 1280 will have to be enough for me. (*She counts her money.*) I have just enough left for two teas at Lockharts, a Rowton doss for you, and my tram and bus home. (*He frowns and rises with offended pride. She takes his arm.*) Dont be proud, Peter: it's sharing between friends. And promise me youll talk to me 1285 and not let me cry. (*She draws him towards the gate.*)

SHIRLEY: Well, I'm not accustomed to talk to the like of you—

BARBARA: (*Urgently.*) Yes, yes: you must talk to me. Tell me about Tom Paine's books and Bradlaugh's lectures. Come along.

SHIRLEY: Ah, if you would only read Tom Paine in the proper 1290 spirit, miss! (*They go out through the gate together.*)

ACT THREE

Next day after lunch LADY BRITOMART *is writing in the library in Wilton Crescent.* SARAH *is reading in the armchair near the window.* BARBARA, *in ordinary fashionable dress, pale and brooding, is on the settee.* CHARLES LOMAX *enters. He starts on seeing* BARBARA *fashionably attired and in low spirits.*

LOMAX: Youve left off your uniform!

(BARBARA *says nothing; but an expression of pain passes over her face.*)

LADY BRITOMART: (*Warning him in low tones to be careful.*) Charles!

LOMAX: (*Much concerned, coming behind the settee and bending sympathetically over* BARBARA.) I'm awfully sorry, Barbara. 5 You know I helped you all I could with the concertina and so forth. (*Momentously.*) Still, I have never shut my eyes to the fact that there is a certain amount of tosh about the Salvation Army. Now the claims of the Church of England—

LADY BRITOMART: Thats enough, Charles. Speak of something 10 suited to your mental capacity.

LOMAX: But surely the Church of England is suited to all our capacities.

BARBARA: (*Pressing his hand.*) Thank you for your sympathy, Cholly. Now go and spoon with Sarah. 15

LOMAX: (*Dragging a chair from the writing table and seating himself affectionately by* SARAH's *side.*) How is my ownest today?

SARAH: I wish you wouldnt tell Cholly to do things, Barbara. He always comes straight and does them. Cholly: we're going to the works this afternoon. 20

LOMAX: What works?

SARAH: The cannon works.

LOMAX: What? your governor's shop!

SARAH: Yes.

LOMAX: Oh I say! 25

(CUSINS *enters in poor condition. He also starts visibly when he sees* BARBARA *without her uniform.*)

BARBARA: I expected you this morning, Dolly. Didnt you guess that?

CUSINS: (*Sitting down beside her.*) I'm sorry. I have only just breakfasted.

SARAH: But weve just finished lunch. 30

BARBARA: Have you had one of your bad nights?

CUSINS: No: I had rather a good night: in fact, one of the most remarkable nights I have ever passed.

BARBARA: The meeting?

35 CUSINS: No: after the meeting.

LADY BRITOMART: You should have gone to bed after the meeting. What were you doing?

CUSINS: Drinking.

LADY BRITOMART:) (Adolphus!
40 SARAH:) (Dolly!
BARBARA:) (Dolly!
LOMAX:) (Oh I say!

LADY BRITOMART: What were you drinking, may I ask?

CUSINS: A most devilish kind of Spanish burgundy, warranted
45 free from added alcohol: a Temperance burgundy in fact. Its richness in natural alcohol made any addition superfluous.

BARBARA: Are you joking, Dolly?

CUSINS: (*Patiently.*) No. I have been making a night of it with the nominal head of this household: that is all.

50 LADY BRITOMART: Andrew made you drunk!

CUSINS: No: he only provided the wine. I think it was Dionysos who made me drunk. (*To* BARBARA.) I told you I was possessed.

LADY BRITOMART: Youre not sober yet. Go home to bed at
55 once.

CUSINS: I have never before ventured to reproach you, Lady Brit; but how could you marry the Prince of Darkness?

LADY BRITOMART: It was much more excusable to marry him than to get drunk with him. That is a new accomplishment
60 of Andrew's, by the way. He usent to drink.

CUSINS: He doesnt now. He only sat there and completed the wreck of my moral basis, the rout of my convictions, the purchase of my soul. He cares for you, Barbara. That is what makes him so dangerous to me.

65 BARBARA: That has nothing to do with it, Dolly. There are larger loves and diviner dreams than the fireside ones. You know that, dont you?

CUSINS: Yes: that is our understanding. I know it. I hold to it. Unless he can win me on that holier ground he may amuse me
70 for a while; but he can get no deeper hold, strong as he is.

BARBARA: Keep to that; and the end will be right. Now tell me what happened at the meeting?

CUSINS: It was an amazing meeting. Mrs Baines almost died of emotion. Jenny Hill simply gibbered with hysteria. The
75 Prince of Darkness played his trombone like a madman: its brazen roarings were like the laughter of the damned. 117 conversions took place then and there. They prayed with the most touching sincerity and gratitude for Bodger, and for the anonymous donor of the £5000. Your father
80 would not let his name be given.

LOMAX: That was rather fine of the old man, you know. Most chaps would have wanted the advertisement.

CUSINS: He said all the charitable institutions would be down on him like kites on a battle-field if he gave his name.

85 LADY BRITOMART: Thats Andrew all over. He never does a proper thing without giving an improper reason for it.

CUSINS: He convinced me that I have all my life been doing improper things for proper reasons.

LADY BRITOMART: Adolphus: now that Barbara has left the
90 Salvation Army, you had better leave it too. I will not have you playing that drum in the streets.

CUSINS: Your orders are already obeyed, Lady Brit.

BARBARA: Dolly: were you ever really in earnest about it? Would you have joined if you had never seen me?

CUSINS: (*Disingenuously.*) Well—er—well, possibly, as a collector 95 of religions—

LOMAX: (*Cunningly.*) Not as a drummer, though, you know. You are a very clearheaded brainy chap, Dolly; and it must have been apparent to you that there is a certain amount of tosh about— 100

LADY BRITOMART: Charles: if you must drivel, drivel like a grown-up man and not like a schoolboy.

LOMAX: (*Out of countenance.*) Well, drivel is drivel, dont you know, whatever a man's age.

LADY BRITOMART: In good society in England, Charles, men 105 drivel at all ages by repeating silly formulas with an air of wisdom. Schoolboys make their own formulas out of slang, like you. When they reach your age, and get political private secretaryships and things of that sort, they drop slang and get their formulas out of the *Spectator* or *The Times*. You had 110 better confine yourself to *The Times*. You will find that there is a certain amount of tosh about *The Times*; but at least its language is reputable.

LOMAX: (*Overwhelmed.*) You are so awfully strong-minded, Lady Brit— 115

LADY BRITOMART: Rubbish! (MORRISON *comes in.*) What is it?

MORRISON: If you please, my lady, Mr Undershaft has just drove up to the door.

LADY BRITOMART: Well, let him in. (MORRISON *hesitates.*) Whats the matter with you? 120

MORRISON: Shall I announce him, my lady; or is he at home here, so to speak, my lady?

LADY BRITOMART: Announce him.

MORRISON: Thank you, my lady. You wont mind my asking, I hope. The occasion is in a manner of speaking new to me. 125

LADY BRITOMART: Quite right. Go and let him in.

MORRISON: Thank you, my lady. (*He withdraws.*)

LADY BRITOMART: Children: go and get ready. (SARAH *and* BARBARA *go upstairs for their out-of-door wraps.*) Charles: go and tell Stephen to come down here in five minutes: you will 130 find him in the drawing room. (CHARLES *goes.*) Adolphus: tell them to send round the carriage in about fifteen minutes. (ADOLPHUS [CUSINS] *goes.*)

MORRISON: (*At the door.*) Mr Undershaft.

(UNDERSHAFT *comes in.* MORRISON *goes out.*)

UNDERSHAFT: Alone! How fortunate! 135

LADY BRITOMART: (*Rising.*) Dont be sentimental, Andrew. Sit down. (*She sits on the settee: he sits beside her, on her left. She comes to the point before he has time to breathe.*) Sarah must have £800 a year until Charles Lomax comes into his property. Barbara will need more, and need it permanently, 140 because Adolphus hasnt any property.

UNDERSHAFT: (*Resignedly.*) Yes, my dear: I will see to it. Anything else? for yourself, for instance?

LADY BRITOMART: I want to talk to you about Stephen.

UNDERSHAFT: (*Rather wearily.*) Dont, my dear. Stephen doesnt 145 interest me.

LADY BRITOMART: He does interest me. He is our son.

UNDERSHAFT: Do you really think so? He has induced us to bring him into the world; but he chose his parents very incongruously, I think. I see nothing of myself in him, and 150 less of you.

LADY BRITOMART: Andrew: Stephen is an excellent son, and a
most steady, capable, highminded young man. You are simply
trying to find an excuse for disinheriting him.

155 UNDERSHAFT: My dear Biddy: the Undershaft tradition
disinherits him. It would be dishonest of me to leave the
cannon foundry to my son.

LADY BRITOMART: It would be most unnatural and improper
of you to leave it to anyone else, Andrew. Do you suppose

160 this wicked and immoral tradition can be kept up for
ever? Do you pretend that Stephen could not carry on the
foundry just as well as all the other sons of the big business houses?

UNDERSHAFT: Yes: he could learn the office routine without

165 understanding the business, like all the other sons; and
the firm would go on by its own momentum until the real
Undershaft—probably an Italian or a German—would
invent a new method and cut him out.

LADY BRITOMART: There is nothing that any Italian or German

170 could do that Stephen could not do. And Stephen at least
has breeding.

UNDERSHAFT: The son of a foundling! Nonsense!

LADY BRITOMART: My son, Andrew! And even you may have
good blood in your veins for all you know.

175 UNDERSHAFT: True. Probably I have. That is another argument
in favour of a foundling.

LADY BRITOMART: Andrew: dont be aggravating. And dont be
wicked. At present you are both.

UNDERSHAFT: This conversation is part of the Undershaft

180 tradition, Biddy. Every Undershaft's wife has treated him
to it ever since the house was founded. It is mere waste
of breath. If the tradition be ever broken it will be for
an abler man than Stephen.

LADY BRITOMART: (*Pouting.*) Then go away.

185 UNDERSHAFT: (*Deprecatory.*) Go away!

LADY BRITOMART: Yes: go away. If you will do nothing for
Stephen, you are not wanted here. Go to your foundling,
whoever he is; and look after him.

UNDERSHAFT: The fact is, Biddy—

190 LADY BRITOMART: Dont call me Biddy. I dont call you Andy.

UNDERSHAFT: I will not call my wife Britomart: it is not good
sense. Seriously, my love, the Undershaft tradition has
landed me in a difficulty. I am getting on in years; and my
partner Lazarus has at last made a stand and insisted that the

195 succession must be settled one way or the other; and of course
he is quite right. You see, I havent found a fit successor yet.

LADY BRITOMART: (*Obstinately.*) There is Stephen.

UNDERSHAFT: Thats just it: all the foundlings I can find are
exactly like Stephen.

200 LADY BRITOMART: Andrew!!

UNDERSHAFT: I want a man with no relations and no schooling:
that is, a man who would be out of the running altogether if
he were not a strong man. And I cant find him. Every blessed
foundling nowadays is snapped up in his infancy by Barnardo

205 homes, or School Board officers, or Boards of Guardians; and
if he shews the least ability he is fastened on by schoolmasters;
trained to win scholarships like a racehorse; crammed with
secondhand ideas; drilled and disciplined in docility and
what they call good taste; and lamed for life so that he is fit for

210 nothing but teaching. If you want to keep the foundry in the
family, you had better find an eligible foundling and marry
him to Barbara.

LADY BRITOMART: Ah! Barbara! Your pet! You would sacrifice
Stephen to Barbara.

215 UNDERSHAFT: Cheerfully. And you, my dear, would boil Barbara
to make soup for Stephen.

LADY BRITOMART: Andrew: this is not a question of our likings
and dislikings: it is a question of duty. It is your duty to make
Stephen your successor.

220 UNDERSHAFT: Just as much as it is your duty to submit to your
husband. Come, Biddy! these tricks of the governing class
are of no use with me. I am one of the governing class myself;
and it is waste of time giving tracts to a missionary. I have the
power in this matter; and I am not to be hum-bugged into

225 using it for your purposes.

LADY BRITOMART: Andrew: you can talk my head off; but you
cant change wrong into right. And your tie is all on one side.
Put it straight.

UNDERSHAFT: (*Disconcerted.*) It wont stay unless it's pinned

230 (*He fumbles at it with childish grimaces.*)—

(STEPHEN *comes in.*)

STEPHEN: (*At the door.*) I beg your pardon. (*About to retire.*)

LADY BRITOMART: No: come in, Stephen. (STEPHEN *comes forward to his mother's writing table.*)

UNDERSHAFT: (*Not very cordially.*) Good afternoon.

235 STEPHEN: (*Coldly.*) Good afternoon.

UNDERSHAFT: (*To* LADY BRITOMART.) He knows all about the
tradition, I suppose?

LADY BRITOMART: Yes. (*To* STEPHEN.) It is what I told you last
night, Stephen.

240 UNDERSHAFT: (*Sulkily.*) I understand you want to come into the
cannon business.

STEPHEN: *I* go into trade! Certainly not.

UNDERSHAFT: (*Opening his eyes, greatly eased in mind and
manner.*) Oh! in that case—

245 LADY BRITOMART: Cannons are not trade, Stephen. They are
enterprise.

STEPHEN: I have no intention of becoming a man of business in
any sense. I have no capacity for business and no taste for it. I
intend to devote myself to politics.

250 UNDERSHAFT: (*Rising.*) My dear boy: this is an immense relief
to me. And I trust it may prove an equally good thing
for the country. I was afraid you would consider yourself
disparaged and slighted. (*He moves towards* STEPHEN *as if to
shake hands with him.*)

255 LADY BRITOMART: (*Rising and interposing.*) Stephen: I cannot
allow you to throw away an enormous property like this.

STEPHEN: (*Stiffly.*) Mother: there must be an end of treating me
as a child, if you please. (LADY BRITOMART *recoils, deeply
wounded by his tone.*) Until last night I did not take your

260 attitude seriously, because I did not think you meant it
seriously. But I find now that you left me in the dark as to
matters which you should have explained to me years ago.
I am extremely hurt and offended. Any further discussion
of my intentions had better take place with my father, as

265 between one man and another.

LADY BRITOMART: Stephen! (*She sits down again, her eyes filling
with tears.*)

UNDERSHAFT: (*With grave compassion.*) You see, my dear, it is
only the big men who can be treated as children.

270 STEPHEN: I am sorry, mother, that you have forced me—

UNDERSHAFT: (*Stopping him.*) Yes, yes, yes, yes: thats all right, Stephen. She wont interfere with you any more: your independence is achieved: you have won your latchkey. Dont rub it in; and above all, dont apologize. (*He resumes his seat.*) Now what about your future, as between one man and another—I beg your pardon, Biddy: as between two men and a woman.

LADY BRITOMART: (*Who has pulled herself together strongly.*) I quite understand, Stephen. By all means go your own way if you feel strong enough. (STEPHEN *sits down magisterially in the chair at the writing table with an air of affirming his majority.*)

UNDERSHAFT: It is settled that you do not ask for the succession to the cannon business.

STEPHEN: I hope it is settled that I repudiate the cannon business.

UNDERSHAFT: Come, come! dont be so devilishly sulky: it's boyish. Freedom should be generous. Besides, I owe you a fair start in life in exchange for disinheriting you. You cant become prime minister all at once. Havnt you a turn for something? What about literature, art, and so forth?

STEPHEN: I have nothing of the artist about me, either in faculty or character, thank Heaven!

UNDERSHAFT: A philosopher, perhaps? Eh?

STEPHEN: I make no such ridiculous pretension.

UNDERSHAFT: Just so. Well, there is the army, the navy, the Church, the Bar. The Bar requires some ability. What about the Bar?

STEPHEN: I have not studied law. And I am afraid I have not the necessary push—I believe that is the name barristers give to their vulgarity—for success in pleading.

UNDERSHAFT: Rather a difficult case, Stephen. Hardly anything left but the stage, is there? (STEPHEN *makes an impatient movement.*) Well, come! is there anything you know or care for?

STEPHEN: (*Rising and looking at him steadily.*) I know the difference between right and wrong.

UNDERSHAFT: (*Hugely tickled.*) You dont say so! What! no capacity for business, no knowledge of law, no sympathy with art, no pretension to philosophy; only a simple knowledge of the secret that has puzzled all the philosophers, baffled all the lawyers, muddled all the men of business, and ruined most of the artists: the secret of right and wrong. Why, man, youre a genius, a master of masters, a god! At twentyfour, too!

STEPHEN: (*Keeping his temper with difficulty.*) You are pleased to be facetious. I pretend to nothing more than any honorable English gentleman claims as his birthright (*He sits down angrily.*)

UNDERSHAFT: Oh, thats everybody's birthright. Look at poor little Jenny Hill, the Salvation lassie! she would think you were laughing at her if you asked her to stand up in the street and teach grammar or geography or mathematics or even drawing room dancing; but it never occurs to her to doubt that she can teach morals and religion. You are all alike, you respectable people. You cant tell me the bursting strain of a ten-inch gun, which is a very simple matter; but you all think you can tell me the bursting strain of a man under temptation. You darent handle high explosives; but youre all ready to handle honesty and truth and justice and the whole duty of man, and kill one another at that game. What a country! What a world!

LADY BRITOMART: (*Uneasily.*) What do you think he had better do, Andrew?

UNDERSHAFT: Oh, just what he wants to do. He knows nothing and he thinks he knows everything. That points clearly to a political career. Get him a private secretaryship to someone who can get him an Under Secretaryship; and then leave him alone. He will find his natural and proper place in the end on the Treasury Bench.

STEPHEN: (*Springing up again.*) I am sorry, sir, that you force me to forget the respect due to you as my father. I am an Englishman and I will not hear the Government of my country insulted. (*He thrusts his hands in his pockets, and walks angrily across to the window.*)

UNDERSHAFT: (*With a touch of brutality.*) The government of your country! I am the government of your country: I, and Lazarus. Do you suppose that you and half a dozen amateurs like you, sitting in a row in that foolish gabble shop, can govern Undershaft and Lazarus? No, my friend: you will do what pays us. You will make war when it suits us, and keep peace when it doesnt. You will find out that trade requires certain measures when we have decided on those measures. When I want anything to keep my dividends up, you will discover that my want is a national need. When other people want something to keep my dividends down, you will call out the police and military. And in return you shall have the support and applause of my newspapers, and the delight of imagining that you are a great statesman. Government of your country! Be off with you, my boy, and play with your caucuses and leading articles and historic parties and great leaders and burning questions and the rest of your toys. *I* am going back to my counting-house to pay the piper and call the tune.

STEPHEN: (*Actually smiling, and putting his hand on his father's shoulder with indulgent patronage.*) Really, my dear father, it is impossible to be angry with you. You dont know how absurd all this sounds to me. You are very properly proud of having been industrious enough to make money; and it is greatly to your credit that you have made so much of it. But it has kept you in circles where you are valued for your money and deferred to for it, instead of in the doubtless very old-fashioned and behind-the-times public school and university where I formed my habits of mind. It is natural for you to think that money governs England; but you must allow me to think I know better.

UNDERSHAFT: And what does govern England, pray?

STEPHEN: Character, father, character.

UNDERSHAFT: Whose character? Yours or mine?

STEPHEN: Neither yours nor mine, father, but the best elements in the English national character.

UNDERSHAFT: Stephen: Ive found your profession for you. Youre a born journalist. I'll start you with a high-toned weekly review. There!

(*Before* STEPHEN *can reply,* SARAH, BARBARA, LOMAX, *and* CUSINS *come in ready for walking.* BARBARA *crosses the room to the window and looks out.* CUSINS *drifts amiably to the armchair.* LOMAX *remains near the door, whilst* SARAH *comes to her mother.*)

(STEPHEN *goes to the smaller writing table and busies himself with his letters.*)

SARAH: Go and get ready, mamma: the carriage is waiting. (LADY BRITOMART *leaves the room.*)

UNDERSHAFT: (*To* SARAH.) Good day, my dear. Good afternoon,
385   Mr Lomax.

LOMAX: (*Vaguely.*) Ahdedoo.

UNDERSHAFT: (*To* CUSINS.) Quite well after last night,
    Euripides, eh?

CUSINS: As well as can be expected.

390 UNDERSHAFT: Thats right. (*To* BARBARA.) So you are coming to
    see my death and devastation factory, Barbara?

BARBARA: (*At the window.*) You came yesterday to see my
    salvation factory. I promised you a return visit.

LOMAX: (*Coming forward between* SARAH *and* UNDERSHAFT.)
395   Youll find it awfully interesting. Ive been through the
    Woolwich Arsenal; and it gives you a ripping feeling of
    security, you know, to think of the lot of beggars we could
    kill if it came to fighting. (*To* UNDERSHAFT, *with sudden
    solemnity.*) Still, it must be rather an awful reflection for you,
400   from the religious point of view as it were. Youre getting on,
    you know, and all that.

SARAH: You dont mind Cholly's imbecility, papa, do you?

LOMAX: (*Much taken aback.*) Oh I say!

UNDERSHAFT: Mr Lomax looks at the matter in a very proper
405   spirit, my dear.

LOMAX: Just so. Thats all I meant, I assure you.

SARAH: Are you coming, Stephen?

STEPHEN: Well, I am rather busy—er—(*Magnanimously.*) Oh
    well, yes: I'll come. That is, if there is room for me.

410 UNDERSHAFT: I can take two with me in a little motor I am
    experimenting with for field use. You wont mind its being
    rather unfashionable. It's not painted yet; but it's bullet
    proof.

LOMAX: (*Appalled at the prospect of confronting Wilton Crescent
415   in an unpainted motor.*) Oh I say!

SARAH: The carriage for me, thank you. Barbara doesnt mind
    what she's seen in.

LOMAX: I say, Dolly, old chap: do you really mind the car being a
    guy? Because of course if you do I'll go in it. Still—

420 CUSINS: I prefer it.

LOMAX: Thanks awfully, old man. Come, my ownest. (*He hurries
    out to secure his seat in the carriage.* SARAH *follows him.*)

CUSINS: (*Moodily walking across to* LADY BRITOMART'S *writing
    table.*) Why are we two coming to this Works Department of
425   Hell? that is what I ask myself.

BARBARA: I have always thought of it as a sort of pit where lost
    creatures with blackened faces stirred up smoky fires and
    were driven and tormented by my father? Is it like that, dad?

UNDERSHAFT: (*Scandalized.*) My dear! It is a spotlessly clean and
430   beautiful hillside town.

CUSINS: With a Methodist chapel? Oh do say theres a Methodist
    chapel.

UNDERSHAFT: There are two: a Primitive one and a sophisti-
    cated one. There is even an Ethical Society; but it is not
435   much patronized, as my men are all strongly religious. In
    the High Explosives Sheds they object to the presence of
    Agnostics as unsafe.

CUSINS: And yet they dont object to you!

BARBARA: Do they obey all your orders?

440 UNDERSHAFT: I never give them any orders. When I speak to one
    of them it is 'Well, Jones, is the baby doing well? and has Mrs
    Jones made a good recovery?' 'Nicely, thank you, sir.' And
    thats all.

CUSINS: But Jones has to be kept in order. How do you maintain
445   discipline among your men?

UNDERSHAFT: I dont. They do. You see, the one thing Jones
    wont stand is any rebellion from the man under him, or
    any assertion of social equality between the wife of the man
    with 4 shillings a week less than himself, and Mrs Jones! Of
    course they all rebel against me, theoretically. Practically, 450
    every man of them keeps the man just below him in his place.
    I never meddle with them. I never bully them. I dont even
    bully Lazarus. I say that certain things are to be done; but I
    dont order anybody to do them. I dont say, mind you, that
    there is no ordering about and snubbing and even bullying. 455
    The men snub the boys and order them about; the carmen
    snub the sweepers; the artisans snub the unskilled laborers;
    the foremen drive and bully both the laborers and artisans;
    the assistant engineers find fault with the foremen; the chief
    engineers drop on the assistants; the departmental managers 460
    worry the chiefs; and the clerks have tall hats and hymnbooks
    and keep up the social tone by refusing to associate on equal
    terms with anybody. The result is a colossal profit, which
    comes to me.

CUSINS: (*Revolted.*) You really are a—well, what I was saying 465
    yesterday.

BARBARA: What was he saying yesterday?

UNDERSHAFT: Never mind, my dear. He thinks I have made you
    unhappy. Have I?

BARBARA: Do you think I can be happy in this vulgar silly 470
    dress? I! who have worn the uniform. Do you understand
    what you have done to me? Yesterday I had a man's soul
    in my hand. I set him in the way of life with his face to
    salvation. But when we took your money he turned back
    to drunkenness and derision. (*With intense conviction.*) I 475
    will never forgive you that. If I had a child, and you destroyed
    its body with your explosives—if you murdered Dolly with
    your horrible guns—I could forgive you if my forgiveness
    would open the gates of heaven to you. But to take a human
    soul from me, and turn it into the soul of a wolf! that is worse 480
    than any murder.

UNDERSHAFT: Does my daughter despair so easily? Can you
    strike a man to the heart and leave no mark on him?

BARBARA: (*Her face lighting up.*) Oh, you are right: he can never
    be lost now: where was my faith? 485

CUSINS: Oh, clever clever devil!

BARBARA: You may be a devil; but God speaks through you
    sometimes. (*She takes her father's hands and kisses them.*) You
    have given me back my happiness: I feel it deep down now,
    though my spirit is troubled. 490

UNDERSHAFT: You have learnt something. That always feels at
    first as if you had lost something.

BARBARA: Well, take me to the factory of death; and let me learn
    something more. There must be some truth or other behind
    all this frightful irony. Come, Dolly. (*She goes out.*) 495

CUSINS: My guardian angel! (*To* UNDERSHAFT.) Avaunt! (*He
    follows* BARBARA.)

STEPHEN: (*Quietly, at the writing table.*) You must not mind
    Cusins, father. He is a very amiable good fellow; but he is a
    Greek scholar and naturally a little eccentric. 500

UNDERSHAFT: Ah, quite so. Thank you, Stephen. Thank you.
    (*He goes out.*)

(STEPHEN *smiles patronizingly; buttons his coat responsibly; and
crosses the room to the door.* LADY BRITOMART, *dressed for out-
of-doors, opens it before he reaches it. She looks round for others;
looks at* STEPHEN; *and turns to go without a word.*)

STEPHEN: (*Embarrassed.*) Mother—

LADY BRITOMART: Dont be apologetic, Stephen. And dont forget
505 that you have outgrown your mother. (*She goes out.*)

(*Perivale St Andrews lies between two Middlesex hills, half climbing the northern one. It is an almost smokeless town of white
walls, roofs of narrow green slates or red tiles, tall trees, domes,
campaniles, and slender chimney shafts, beautifully situated and
beautiful in itself. The best view of it is obtained from the crest of
a slope about half a mile to the east, where the high explosives are
dealt with. The foundry lies hidden in the depths between, the tops
of its chimneys sprouting like huge skittles into the middle distance.
Across the crest runs an emplacement of concrete, with a firestep,
and a parapet which suggests a fortification, because there is a huge
cannon of the obsolete Woolwich Infant pattern peering across it at
the town. The cannon is mounted on an experimental gun carriage:
possibly the original model of the Undershaft disappearing rampart
gun alluded to by* STEPHEN. *The firestep, being a convenient place
to sit, is furnished here and there with straw disc cushions; and at
one place there is the additional luxury of a fur rug.*)

(*BARBARA is standing on the firestep, looking over the parapet
towards the town. On her right is the cannon; on her left the end of
a shed raised on piles, with a ladder of three or four steps up to the
door, which opens outwards and has a little wooden landing at the
threshold, with a fire bucket in the corner of the landing. Several
dummy soldiers more or less mutilated, with straw protruding from
their gashes, have been shoved out of the way under the landing. A
few others are nearly upright against the shed; and one has fallen
forward and lies, like a grotesque corpse, on the emplacement. The
parapet stops short of the shed, leaving a gap which is the beginning
of the path down the hill through the foundry to the town. The rug
is on the firestep near this gap. Down on the emplacement behind
the cannon is a trolley carrying a huge conical bombshell with a
red band painted on it. Further to the right is the door of an office,
which, like the sheds, is of the lightest possible construction.*)

(*CUSINS arrives by the path from the town.*)

BARBARA: Well?

CUSINS: Not a ray of hope. Everything perfect! wonderful! real!
It only needs a cathedral to be a heavenly city instead of a
hellish one.

510 BARBARA: Have you found out whether they have done anything
for old Peter Shirley?

CUSINS: They have found him a job as gatekeeper and time-
keeper. He's frightfully miserable. He calls the time-keeping
brainwork, and says he isnt used to it; and his gate lodge is
515 so splendid that he's ashamed to use the rooms, and skulks
in the scullery.

BARBARA: Poor Peter!

(*STEPHEN arrives from the town. He carries a fieldglass.*)

STEPHEN: (*Enthusiastically.*) Have you two seen the place? Why
did you leave us?

520 CUSINS: I wanted to see everything I was not intended to see; and
Barbara wanted to make the men talk.

STEPHEN: Have you found anything discreditable?

CUSINS: No. They call him Dandy Andy and are proud of his
being a cunning old rascal; but it's all horribly, frightfully,
525 immorally, unanswerably perfect.

(*SARAH arrives.*)

SARAH: Heavens! what a place! (*She crosses to the trolley.*) Did you
see the nursing home!? (*She sits down on the shell.*)

STEPHEN: Did you see the libraries and schools!?

SARAH: Did you see the ball room and the banqueting chamber in
the Town Hall!? 530

STEPHEN: Have you gone into the insurance fund, the pension
fund, the building society, the various applications of
cooperation!?

(*UNDERSHAFT comes from the office, with a sheaf of telegrams in
his hand.*)

UNDERSHAFT: Well, have you seen everything? I'm sorry I was
called away. (*Indicating the telegrams.*) Good news from 535
Manchuria.

STEPHEN: Another Japanese victory?

UNDERSHAFT: Oh, I dont know. Which side wins does not
concern us here. No: the good news is that the aerial
battleship is a tremendous success. At the first trial it has 540
wiped out a fort with three hundred soldiers in it.

CUSINS: (*From the platform.*) Dummy soldiers?

UNDERSHAFT: (*Striding across to* STEPHEN *and kicking the
prostrate dummy brutally out of his way.*) No: the real thing.

(*CUSINS and BARBARA exchange glances. Then CUSINS sits on
the step and buries his face in his hands. BARBARA gravely
lays her hand on his shoulder. He looks up at her in whimsical
desperation.*)

UNDERSHAFT: Well, Stephen, what do you think of the place? 545

STEPHEN: Oh, magnificent. A perfect triumph of modern
industry. Frankly, my dear father, I have been a fool: I had
no idea of what it all meant: of the wonderful forethought,
the power of organization, the administrative capacity, the
financial genius, the colossal capital it represents. I have been 550
repeating to myself as I came through your streets 'Peace hath
her victories no less renowned than War.' I have only one
misgiving about it all.

UNDERSHAFT: Out with it.

STEPHEN: Well, I cannot help thinking that all this provision for 555
every want of your workmen may sap their independence
and weaken their sense of responsibility. And greatly as we
enjoyed our tea at that splendid restaurant—how they gave us
all that luxury and cake and jam and cream for threepence
I really cannot imagine!—still you must remember that 560
restaurants break up home life. Look at the continent, for
instance! Are you sure so much pampering is really good for
the men's characters?

UNDERSHAFT: Well you see, my dear boy, when you are
organizing civilization you have to make up your mind 565
whether trouble and anxiety are good things or not. If you
decide that they are, then, I take it, you simply dont organize
civilization; and there you are, with trouble and anxiety
enough to make us all angels! But if you decide the other way,
you may as well go through with it. However, Stephen, our 570
characters are safe here. A sufficient dose of anxiety is always
provided by the fact that we may be blown to smithereens at
any moment.

SARAH: By the way, papa, where do you make the explosives?

575   UNDERSHAFT: In separate little sheds, like that one. When one of them blows up, it costs very little; and only the people quite close to it are killed.

(STEPHEN, *who is quite close to it, looks at it rather scaredly, and moves away quickly to the cannon. At the same moment the door of the shed is thrown abruptly open; and a foreman in overalls and list slippers comes out on the little landing and holds the door for* LOMAX, *who appears in the doorway.*)

LOMAX: (*With studied coolness.*) My good fellow: you neednt get into a state of nerves. Nothing's going to happen to you; and
580   I suppose it wouldnt be the end of the world if anything did. A little bit of British pluck is what you want, old chap. (*He descends and strolls across to* SARAH.)

UNDERSHAFT: (*To the foreman.*) Anything wrong, Bilton?

BILTON: (*With ironic calm.*) Gentleman walked into the high
585   explosives shed and lit a cigaret, sir: thats all.

UNDERSHAFT: Ah, quite so. (*Going over to* LOMAX.) Do you happen to remember what you did with the match?

LOMAX: Oh come! I'm not a fool. I took jolly good care to blow it out before I chucked it away.

590   BILTON: The top of it was red hot inside, sir.

LOMAX: Well, suppose it was! I didnt chuck it into any of your messes.

UNDERSHAFT: Think no more of it, Mr Lomax. By the way, would you mind lending me your matches.

595   LOMAX: (*Offering his box.*) Certainly.

UNDERSHAFT: Thanks. (*He pockets the matches.*)

LOMAX: (*Lecturing to the company generally.*) You know, these high explosives dont go off like gunpowder, except when theyre in a gun. When theyre spread loose, you can put a
600   match to them without the least risk: they just burn quietly like a bit of paper. (*Warming to the scientific interest of the subject.*) Did you know that, Undershaft? Have you ever tried?

UNDERSHAFT: Not on a large scale, Mr Lomax. Bilton will
605   give you a sample of gun cotton when you are leaving if you ask him. You can experiment with it at home. (BILTON *looks puzzled.*)

SARAH: Bilton will do nothing of the sort, papa. I suppose it's your business to blow up the Russians and Japs; but you
610   might really stop short of blowing up poor Cholly. (BILTON *gives it up and retires into the shed.*)

LOMAX: My ownest, there is no danger. (*He sits beside her on the shell.*)

(LADY BRITOMART *arrives from the town with a bouquet.*)

LADY BRITOMART: (*Impetuously.*) Andrew: you shouldnt have let
615   me see this place.

UNDERSHAFT: Why, my dear?

LADY BRITOMART: Never mind why: you shouldnt have: thats all. To think of all that (*Indicating the town.*) being yours! and that you have kept it to yourself all these years!

620   UNDERSHAFT: It does not belong to me. I belong to it. It is the Undershaft inheritance.

LADY BRITOMART: It is not. Your ridiculous cannons and that noisy banging foundry may be the Undershaft inheritance; but all that plate and linen, all that furniture and those houses
625   and orchards and gardens belong to us. They belong to me:

they are not a man's business. I wont give them up. You must be out of your senses to throw them all away; and if you persist in such folly, I will call in a doctor.

UNDERSHAFT: (*Stooping to smell the bouquet.*) Where did you get
630   the flowers, my dear?

LADY BRITOMART: Your men presented them to me in your William Morris Labor Church.

CUSINS: Oh! It needed only that. A Labor Church! (*He mounts the firestep distractedly, and leans with his elbows on the parapet,
635   turning his back to them.*)

LADY BRITOMART: Yes, with Morris's words in mosaic letters ten feet high round the dome. NO MAN IS GOOD ENOUGH TO BE ANOTHER MAN'S MASTER. The cynicism of it!

UNDERSHAFT: It shocked the men at first, I am afraid. But now
640   they take no more notice of it than of the ten commandments in church.

LADY BRITOMART: Andrew: you are trying to put me off the subject of the inheritance by profane jokes. Well, you shant. I dont ask it any longer for Stephen: he has inherited far too
645   much of your perversity to be fit for it. But Barbara has rights as well as Stephen. Why should not Adolphus succeed to the inheritance? I could manage the town for him; and he can look after the cannons, if they are really necessary.

UNDERSHAFT: I should ask nothing better if Adolphus were a
650   foundling. He is exactly the sort of new blood that is wanted in English business. But he's not a foundling; and theres an end of it. (*He makes for the office door.*)

CUSINS: (*Turning to them.*) Not quite. (*They all turn and stare at him.*) I think—Mind! I am not committing myself in any way
655   as to my future course—but I think the foundling difficulty can be got over. (*He jumps down to the emplacement.*)

UNDERSHAFT: (*Coming back to him.*) What do you mean?

CUSINS: Well, I have something to say which is in the nature of a confession.

660   SARAH: ⎫
LADY BRITOMART: ⎪
BARBARA: ⎬   Confession!
STEPHEN: ⎭

LOMAX: Oh I say!

CUSINS: Yes, a confession. Listen, all. Until I met Barbara I
665   thought myself in the main an honorable, truthful man, because I wanted the approval of my conscience more than I wanted anything else. But the moment I saw Barbara, I wanted her far more than the approval of my
670   conscience.

LADY BRITOMART: Adolphus!

CUSINS: It is true. You accused me yourself, Lady Brit, of joining the Army to worship Barbara; and so I did. She bought my soul like a flower at a street corner; but she bought it for
675   herself.

UNDERSHAFT: What! Not for Dionysos or another?

CUSINS: Dionysos and all the others are in herself. I adored what was divine in her, and was therefore a true worshipper. But I was romantic about her too. I thought she was a woman of the people, and that a marriage with a professor of Greek would
680   be far beyond the wildest social ambitions of her rank.

LADY BRITOMART: Adolphus!!

LOMAX: Oh I say!!!

CUSINS: When I learnt the horrible truth—

LADY BRITOMART: What do you mean by the horrible truth,
685   pray?

CUSINS: That she was enormously rich; that her grandfather was an earl; that her father was the Prince of Darkness—

UNDERSHAFT: Chut!

690 CUSINS: —and that I was only an adventurer trying to catch a rich wife, then I stooped to deceive her about my birth.

BARBARA: (*Rising.*) Dolly!

LADY BRITOMART: Your birth! Now Adolphus, dont dare to make up a wicked story for the sake of these wretched cannons.

695 Remember: I have seen photographs of your parents; and the Agent General for South Western Australia knows them personally and has assured me that they are most respectable married people.

CUSINS: So they are in Australia; but here they are outcasts. Their

700 marriage is legal in Australia, but not in England. My mother is my father's deceased wife's sister; and in this island I am consequently a foundling. (*Sensation.*)

BARBARA: Silly! (*She climbs to the cannon, and leans, listening, in the angle it makes with the parapet.*)

705 CUSINS: Is the subterfuge good enough, Machiavelli?

UNDERSHAFT: (*Thoughtfully.*) Biddy: this may be a way out of the difficulty.

LADY BRITOMART: Stuff! A man cant make cannons any the better for being his own cousin instead of his proper self

710 (*She sits down on the rug with a bounce that expresses her downright contempt for their casuistry.*)

UNDERSHAFT: (*To* CUSINS.) You are an educated man. That is against the tradition.

CUSINS: Once in ten thousand times it happens that the schoolboy

715 is a born master of what they try to teach him. Greek has not destroyed my mind: it has nourished it. Besides, I did not learn it at an English public school.

UNDERSHAFT: Hm! Well, I cannot afford to be too particular: you have cornered the foundling market. Let it pass. You are

720 eligible, Euripides: you are eligible.

BARBARA: Dolly: yesterday morning, when Stephen told us all about the tradition, you became very silent; and you have been strange and excited ever since. Were you thinking of your birth then?

725 CUSINS: When the finger of Destiny suddenly points at a man in the middle of his breakfast, it makes him thoughtful.

UNDERSHAFT: Aha! You have had your eye on the business, my young friend, have you?

CUSINS: Take care! There is an abyss of moral horror between me

730 and your accursed aerial battleships.

UNDERSHAFT: Never mind the abyss for the present. Let us settle the practical details and leave your final decision open. You know that you will have to change your name. Do you object to that?

735 CUSINS: Would any man named Adolphus—any man called Dolly!—object to be called something else?

UNDERSHAFT: Good. Now, as to money! I propose to treat you handsomely from the beginning. You shall start at a thousand a year.

740 CUSINS: (*With sudden heat, his spectacles twinkling with mischief.*) A thousand! You dare offer a miserable thousand to the son-in-law of a millionaire! No, by Heavens, Machiavelli! you shall not cheat me. You cannot do without me; and I can do without you. I must have two thousand five hundred a year for

745 two years. At the end of that time, if I am a failure, I go. But if I am a success, and stay on, you must give me the other five thousand.

UNDERSHAFT: What other five thousand?

CUSINS: To make the two years up to five thousand a year. The

750 two thousand five hundred is only half pay in case I should turn out a failure. The third year I must have ten per cent on the profits.

UNDERSHAFT: (*Taken aback.*) Ten per cent! Why, man, do you know what my profits are?

755 CUSINS: Enormous, I hope: otherwise I shall require twenty-five per cent.

UNDERSHAFT: But, Mr Cusins, this is a serious matter of business. You are not bringing any capital into the concern.

CUSINS: What! no capital! Is my mastery of Greek no capital?

760 Is my access to the subtlest thought, the loftiest poetry yet attained by humanity, no capital? My character! my intellect! my life! my career! what Barbara calls my soul! are these no capital? Say another word; and I double my salary.

UNDERSHAFT: Be reasonable—

765 CUSINS: (*Peremptorily.*) Mr Undershaft: you have my terms. Take them or leave them.

UNDERSHAFT: (*Recovering himself.*) Very well. I note your terms; and I offer you half.

CUSINS: (*Disgusted.*) Half!

770 UNDERSHAFT: (*Firmly.*) Half.

CUSINS: You call yourself a gentleman; and you offer me half!!

UNDERSHAFT: I do not call myself a gentleman; but I offer you half.

CUSINS: This to your future partner! your successor! your

775 son-in-law!

BARBARA: You are selling your own soul, Dolly, not mine. Leave me out of the bargain, please.

UNDERSHAFT: Come! I will go a step further for Barbara's sake. I will give you three fifths; but that is my last word.

780 CUSINS: Done!

LOMAX: Done in the eye! Why, *I* get only eight hundred, you know.

CUSINS: By the way, Mac, I am a classical scholar, not an arithmetical one. Is three fifths more than half or less?

785 UNDERSHAFT: More, of course.

CUSINS: I would have taken two hundred and fifty. How you can succeed in business when you are willing to pay all that money to a University don who is obviously not worth a junior clerk's wages!—well! What will Lazarus say?

790 UNDERSHAFT: Lazarus is a gentle romantic Jew who cares for nothing but string quartets and stalls at fashionable theatres. He will be blamed for your rapacity in money matters, poor fellow! as he has hitherto been blamed for mine. You are a shark of the first order, Euripides. So much the better for the

795 firm!

BARBARA: Is the bargain closed, Dolly? Does your soul belong to him now?

CUSINS: No: the price is settled: that is all. The real tug of war is still to come. What about the moral question?

800 LADY BRITOMART: There is no moral question in the matter at all, Adolphus. You must simply sell cannons and weapons to people whose cause is right and just, and refuse them to foreigners and criminals.

UNDERSHAFT: (*Determinedly.*) No: none of that. You must keep

805 the true faith of an Armorer, or you dont come in here.

CUSINS: What on earth is the true faith of an Armorer?

UNDERSHAFT: To give arms to all men who offer an honest price for them, without respect of persons or principles: to

810 aristocrat and republican, to Nihilist and Tsar, to Capitalist and Socialist, to Protestant and Catholic, to burglar and policeman, to black man, white man and yellow man, to all sorts and conditions, all nationalities, all faiths, all follies, all causes and all crimes. The first Undershaft wrote up in his shop IF GOD GAVE THE HAND, LET NOT MAN WITHHOLD THE

815 SWORD. The second wrote up ALL HAVE THE RIGHT TO FIGHT: NONE HAVE THE RIGHT TO JUDGE. The third wrote up TO MAN THE WEAPON: TO HEAVEN THE VICTORY. The fourth had no literary turn; so he did not write up anything; but he sold cannons to Napoleon under the nose of George the Third.

820 The fifth wrote up PEACE SHALL NOT PREVAIL SAVE WITH A SWORD IN HER HAND. The sixth, my master, was the best of all. He wrote up NOTHING IS EVER DONE IN THIS WORLD UNTIL MEN ARE PREPARED TO KILL ONE ANOTHER IF IT IS NOT DONE. After that, there was nothing left for the seventh to say. So he

825 wrote up, simply, UNASHAMED.
CUSINS: My good Machiavelli, I shall certainly write something up on the wall; only, as I shall write it in Greek, you wont be able to read it. But as to your Armorer's faith, if I take my neck out of the noose of my own morality I am not going to put it

830 into the noose of yours. I shall sell cannons to whom I please and refuse them to whom I please. So there!
UNDERSHAFT: From the moment when you become Andrew Undershaft, you will never do as you please again. Dont come here lusting for power, young man.

835 CUSINS: If power were my aim I should not come here for it. You have no power.
UNDERSHAFT: None of my own, certainly.
CUSINS: I have more power than you, more will. You do not drive this place: it drives you. And what drives the place?

840 UNDERSHAFT: (Enigmatically.) A will of which I am a part.
BARBARA: (Startled.) Father! Do you know what you are saying; or are you laying a snare for my soul?
CUSINS: Dont listen to his metaphysics, Barbara. The place is driven by the most rascally part of society, the money hunters,

845 the pleasure hunters, the military promotion hunters; and he is their slave.
UNDERSHAFT: Not necessarily. Remember the Armorer's Faith. I will take an order from a good man as cheerfully as from a bad one. If you good people prefer preaching and shirking to

850 buying my weapons and fighting the rascals, dont blame me. I can make cannons: I cannot make courage and conviction. Bah! you tire me, Euripides, with your morality mongering. Ask Barbara: she understands. (He suddenly reaches up and takes BARBARA's hands, looking powerfully into her eyes.) Tell

855 him, my love, what power really means.
BARBARA: (Hypnotized.) Before I joined the Salvation Army, I was in my own power; and the consequence was that I never knew what to do with myself. When I joined it, I had not time enough for all the things I had to do.

860 UNDERSHAFT: (Approvingly.) Just so. And why was that, do you suppose?
BARBARA: Yesterday I should have said, because I was in the power of God. (She resumes her self-possession, withdrawing her hands from his with a power equal to his own.) But you

865 came and shewed me that I was in the power of Bodger and Undershaft. Today I feel—oh! how can I put it into words? Sarah: do you remember the earthquake at Cannes, when we were little children?—how little the surprise of the first shock mattered compared to the dread

870 and horror of waiting for the second? That is how I feel in this place today. I stood on the rock I thought eternal; and without a word of warning it reeled and crumbled under me. I was safe with an infinite wisdom watching me, an army marching to Salvation with me; and in a

875 moment, at a stroke of your pen in a cheque book, I stood alone; and the heavens were empty. That was the first shock of the earthquake: I am waiting for the second.
UNDERSHAFT: Come, come, my daughter! dont make too much of your little tinpot tragedy. What do we do here when we

880 spend years of work and thought and thousands of pounds of solid cash on a new gun or an aerial battleship that turns out just a hairsbreadth wrong after all? Scrap it. Scrap it without wasting another hour or another pound on it. Well, you have made for yourself something that you call

885 a morality or a religion or what not. It doesnt fit the facts. Well, scrap it. Scrap it and get one that does fit. That is what is wrong with the world at present. It scraps its obsolete steam engines and dynamos; but it wont scrap its old prejudices and its old moralities and its old religions and its old political

890 constitutions. Whats the result? In machinery it does very well; but in morals and religion and politics it is working at a loss that brings it nearer bankruptcy every year. Dont persist in that folly. If your old religion broke down yesterday, get a newer and a better one for tomorrow.

895 BARBARA: Oh how gladly I would take a better one to my soul! But you offer me a worse one. (Turning on him with sudden vehemence.) Justify yourself: shew me some light through the darkness of this dreadful place, with its beautifully clean workshops, and respectable workmen, and model homes.

900 UNDERSHAFT: Cleanliness and respectability do not need justification, Barbara: they justify themselves. I see no darkness here, no dreadfulness. In your Salvation shelter I saw poverty, misery, cold and hunger. You gave them bread and treacle and dreams of heaven. I give from thirty shillings

905 a week to twelve thousand a year. They find their own dreams; but I look after the drainage.
BARBARA: And their souls?
UNDERSHAFT: I save their souls just as I saved yours.
BARBARA: (Revolted.) You saved my soul! What do you mean?

910 UNDERSHAFT: I fed you and clothed you and housed you. I took care that you should have money enough to live handsomely—more than enough; so that you could be wasteful, careless, generous. That saved your soul from the seven deadly sins.

915 BARBARA: (Bewildered.) The seven deadly sins!
UNDERSHAFT: Yes, the deadly seven. (Counting on his fingers.) Food, clothing, firing, rent, taxes, respectability and children. Nothing can lift those seven millstones from Man's neck but money; and the spirit cannot soar until the millstones

920 are lifted. I lifted them from your spirit. I enabled Barbara to become Major Barbara; and I saved her from the crime of poverty.
CUSINS: Do you call poverty a crime?
UNDERSHAFT: The worst of crimes. All the other crimes are

925 virtues beside it: all the other dishonors are chivalry itself by comparison. Poverty blights whole cities; spreads horrible pestilences; strikes dead the very souls of all who come within sight, sound, or smell of it. What you call crime is nothing: a murder here and a theft there, a blow now and a

930 curse then: what do they matter? they are only the accidents

and illnesses of life: there are not fifty genuine professional criminals in London. But there are millions of poor people, abject people, dirty people, ill fed, ill clothed people. They poison us morally and physically: they kill the happiness of society: they force us to do away with our own liberties and to organize unnatural cruelties for fear they should rise against us and drag us down into their abyss. Only fools fear crime: we all fear poverty. Pah! (*Turning on* BARBARA.) you talk of your halfsaved ruffian in West Ham: you accuse me of dragging his soul back to perdition. Well, bring him to me here; and I will drag his soul back again to salvation for you. Not by words and dreams; but by thirty-eight shillings a week, a sound house in a handsome street, and a permanent job. In three weeks he will have a fancy waistcoat; in three months a tall hat and a chapel sitting; before the end of the year he will shake hands with a duchess at a Primrose League meeting, and join the Conservative Party.

BARBARA: And will he be the better for that?

UNDERSHAFT: You know he will. Dont be a hypocrite, Barbara. He will be better fed, better housed, better clothed, better behaved; and his children will be pounds heavier and bigger. That will be better than an American cloth mattress in a shelter, chopping firewood, eating bread and treacle, and being forced to kneel down from time to time to thank heaven for it: knee drill, I think you call it. It is cheap work converting starving men with a Bible in one hand and a slice of bread in the other. I will undertake to convert West Ham to Mahometanism on the same terms. Try your hand on my men: their souls are hungry because their bodies are full.

BARBARA: And leave the east end to starve?

UNDERSHAFT: (*His energetic tone dropping into one of bitter and brooding remembrance.*) I was an east ender. I moralized and starved until one day I swore that I would be a full-fed free man at all costs; that nothing should stop me except a bullet, neither reason nor morals nor the lives of other men. I said 'Thou shalt starve ere I starve'; and with that word I became free and great. I was a dangerous man until I had my will: now I am a useful, beneficent, kindly person. That is the history of most self-made millionaires, I fancy. When it is the history of every Englishman we shall have an England worth living in.

LADY BRITOMART: Stop making speeches, Andrew. This is not the place for them.

UNDERSHAFT: (*Punctured.*) My dear: I have no other means of conveying my ideas.

LADY BRITOMART: Your ideas are nonsense. You got on because you were selfish and unscrupulous.

UNDERSHAFT: Not at all. I had the strongest scruples about poverty and starvation. Your moralists are quite unscrupulous about both: they make virtues of them. I had rather be a thief than a pauper. I had rather be a murderer than a slave. I dont want to be either; but if you force the alternative on me, then, by Heaven, I'll choose the braver and more moral one. I hate poverty and slavery worse than any other crimes whatsoever. And let me tell you this. Poverty and slavery have stood up for centuries to your sermons and leading articles: they will not stand up to my machine guns. Dont preach at them: dont reason with them. Kill them.

BARBARA: Killing. Is that your remedy for everything?

UNDERSHAFT: It is the final test of conviction, the only lever strong enough to overturn a social system, the only way of saying Must. Let six hundred and seventy fools loose in the streets; and three policemen can scatter them. But huddle them together in a certain house in Westminster; and let them go through certain ceremonies and call themselves certain names until at last they get the courage to kill; and your six hundred and seventy fools become a government. Your pious mob fills up ballot papers and imagines it is governing its masters; but the ballot paper that really governs is the paper that has a bullet wrapped up in it.

CUSINS: That is perhaps why, like most intelligent people, I never vote.

UNDERSHAFT: Vote! Bah! When you vote, you only change the names of the cabinet. When you shoot, you pull down governments, inaugurate new epochs, abolish old orders and set up new. Is that historically true, Mr Learned Man, or is it not?

CUSINS: It is historically true. I loathe having to admit it. I repudiate your sentiments. I abhor your nature. I defy you in every possible way. Still, it is true. But it ought not to be true.

UNDERSHAFT: Ought! ought! ought! ought! ought! Are you going to spend your life saying ought, like the rest of our moralists? Turn your oughts into shalls, man. Come and make explosives with me. Whatever can blow men up can blow society up. The history of the world is the history of those who had courage enough to embrace this truth. Have you the courage to embrace it, Barbara?

LADY BRITOMART: Barbara: I positively forbid you to listen to your father's abominable wickedness. And you, Adolphus, ought to know better than to go about saying that wrong things are true. What does it matter whether they are true if they are wrong?

UNDERSHAFT: What does it matter whether they are wrong if they are true?

LADY BRITOMART: (*Rising.*) Children: come home instantly. Andrew: I am exceedingly sorry I allowed you to call on us. You are wickeder than ever. Come at once.

BARBARA: (*Shaking her head.*) It's no use running away from wicked people, mamma.

LADY BRITOMART: It is every use. It shews your disapprobation of them.

BARBARA: It does not save them.

LADY BRITOMART: I can see that you are going to disobey me. Sarah: are you coming home or are you not?

SARAH: I daresay it's very wicked of papa to make cannons; but I dont think I shall cut him on that account.

LOMAX: (*Pouring oil on the troubled waters.*) The fact is, you know, there is a certain amount of tosh about this notion of wickedness. It doesnt work. You must look at facts. Not that I would say a word in favor of anything wrong; but then, you see, all sorts of chaps are always doing all sorts of things; and we have to fit them in somehow, dont you know. What I mean is that you cant go cutting everybody; and thats about what it comes to. (*Their rapt attention to his eloquence makes him nervous.*) Perhaps I dont make myself clear.

LADY BRITOMART: You are lucidity itself, Charles. Because Andrew is successful and has plenty of money to give to Sarah, you will flatter him and encourage him in his wickedness.

LOMAX: (*Unruffled.*) Well, where the carcase is, there will the eagles be gathered, dont you know. (*To* UNDERSHAFT.) Eh? What?

UNDERSHAFT: Precisely. By the way, may I call you Charles?

LOMAX: Delighted. Cholly is the usual ticket.

1055 UNDERSHAFT: (*To* LADY BRITOMART.) Biddy—

LADY BRITOMART: (*Violently.*) Dont dare call me Biddy. Charles Lomax: you are a fool. Adolphus Cusins: you are a Jesuit. Stephen: you are a prig. Barbara: you are a lunatic. Andrew: you are a vulgar tradesman. Now you all know my opinion;

1060 and my conscience is clear, at all events. (*She sits down with a vehemence that the rug fortunately softens.*)

UNDERSHAFT: My dear: you are the incarnation of morality. (*She snorts.*) Your conscience is clear and your duty done when you have called everybody names. Come, Euripides! it is getting

1065 late; and we all want to go home. Make up your mind.

CUSINS: Understand this, you old demon—

LADY BRITOMART: Adolphus!

UNDERSHAFT: Let him alone, Biddy. Proceed, Euripides.

CUSINS: You have me in a horrible dilemma. I want Barbara.

1070 UNDERSHAFT: Like all young men, you greatly exaggerate the difference between one young woman and another.

BARBARA: Quite true, Dolly.

CUSINS: I also want to avoid being a rascal.

UNDERSHAFT: (*With biting contempt.*) You lust for personal

1075 righteousness, for self-approval, for what you call a good conscience, for what Barbara calls salvation, for what I call patronizing people who are not so lucky as yourself.

CUSINS: I do not: all the poet in me recoils from being a good man. But there are things in me that I must reckon with. Pity—

1080 UNDERSHAFT: Pity! The scavenger of misery.

CUSINS: Well, love.

UNDERSHAFT: I know. You love the needy and the outcast: you love the oppressed races, the negro, the Indian ryot, the underdog everywhere. Do you love the Japanese? Do you love

1085 the French? Do you love the English?

CUSINS: No. Every true Englishman detests the English. We are the wickedest nation on earth; and our success is a moral horror.

UNDERSHAFT: That is what comes of your gospel of love, is it?

1090 CUSINS: May I not love even my father-in-law?

UNDERSHAFT: Who wants your love, man? By what right do you take the liberty of offering it to me? I will have your due heed and respect, or I will kill you. But your love! Damn your impertinence!

1095 CUSINS: (*Grinning.*) I may not be able to control my affections, Mac.

UNDERSHAFT: You are fencing, Euripides. You are weakening: your grip is slipping. Come! try your last weapon. Pity and love have broken in your hand: forgiveness is still left.

1100 CUSINS: No: forgiveness is a beggar's refuge. I am with you there: we must pay our debts.

UNDERSHAFT: Well said. Come! you will suit me. Remember the words of Plato.

CUSINS: (*Starting.*) Plato! You dare quote Plato to me!

1105 UNDERSHAFT: Plato says, my friend, that society cannot be saved until either the Professors of Greek take to making gunpowder, or else the makers of gunpowder become Professors of Greek.

CUSINS: Oh, tempter, cunning tempter!

1110 UNDERSHAFT: Come! choose, man, choose.

CUSINS: But perhaps Barbara will not marry me if I make the wrong choice.

BARBARA: Perhaps not.

CUSINS: (*Desperately perplexed.*) You hear!

BARBARA: Father: do you love nobody? 1115

UNDERSHAFT: I love my best friend.

LADY BRITOMART: And who is that, pray?

UNDERSHAFT: My bravest enemy. That is the man who keeps me up to the mark.

CUSINS: You know, the creature is really a sort of poet in his way. 1120
Suppose he is a great man, after all!

UNDERSHAFT: Suppose you stop talking and make up your mind, my young friend.

CUSINS: But you are driving me against my nature. I hate war.

UNDERSHAFT: Hatred is the coward's revenge for being 1125
intimidated. Dare you make war on war? Here are the means: my friend Mr Lomax is sitting on them.

LOMAX: (*Springing up.*) Oh I say! You dont mean that this thing is loaded, do you? My ownest: come off it.

SARAH: (*Sitting placidly on the shell.*) If I am to be blown up, the 1130
more thoroughly it is done the better. Dont fuss, Cholly.

LOMAX: (*To* UNDERSHAFT, *strongly remonstrant.*) Your own daughter, you know!

UNDERSHAFT: So I see! (*To* CUSINS.) Well, my friend, may we expect you here at six tomorrow morning? 1135

CUSINS: (*Firmly.*) Not on any account. I will see the whole establishment blown up with its own dynamite before I will get up at five. My hours are healthy, rational hours: eleven to five.

UNDERSHAFT: Come when you please: before a week you will 1140
come at six and stay until I turn you out for the sake of your health. (*Calling.*) Bilton! (*He turns to* LADY BRITO-MART, *who rises.*) My dear: let us leave these two young people to themselves for a moment. (BILTON *comes from the shed.*) I am going to take you through the gun cotton shed. 1145

BILTON: (*Barring the way.*) You cant take anything explosive in here, sir.

LADY BRITOMART: What do you mean? Are you alluding to me?

BILTON: (*Unmoved.*) No, maam. Mr Undershaft has the other 1150
gentleman's matches in his pocket.

LADY BRITOMART: (*Abruptly.*) Oh! I beg your pardon. (*She goes into the shed.*)

UNDERSHAFT: Quite right, Bilton, quite right: here you are. (*He gives* BILTON *the box of matches.*) Come, Stephen. Come, Charles. Bring Sarah. (*He passes into the shed.*) 1155

(BILTON *opens the box and deliberately drops the matches into the fire-bucket.*)

LOMAX: Oh! I say (BILTON *stolidly hands him the empty box.*) Infernal nonsense! Pure scientific ignorance! (*He goes in.*)

SARAH: Am I all right, Bilton?

BILTON: Youll have to put on list slippers, miss: thats all. Weve got em inside. (*She goes in.*) 1160

STEPHEN: (*Very seriously to* CUSINS.) Dolly, old fellow, think. Think before you decide. Do you feel that you are a sufficiently practical man? It is a huge undertaking, an enormous responsibility. All this mass of business will be Greek to you. 1165

CUSINS: Oh, I think it will be much less difficult than Greek.

STEPHEN: Well, I just want to say this before I leave you to yourselves. Dont let anything I have said about right and wrong prejudice you against this great chance in life. I have satisfied myself that the business is one of the highest character and a 1170 credit to our country. (*Emotionally.*) I am very proud of my father. I—(*Unable to proceed, he presses* CUSINS' *hand and goes hastily into the shed, followed by* BILTON.)

(BARBARA *and* CUSINS, *left alone together, look at one another silently.*)

CUSINS: Barbara: I am going to accept this offer.

1175 BARBARA: I thought you would.

CUSINS: You understand, dont you, that I had to decide without consulting you. If I had thrown the burden of the choice on you, you would sooner or later have despised me for it.

BARBARA: Yes: I did not want you to sell your soul for me any

1180 more than for this inheritance.

CUSINS: It is not the sale of my soul that troubles me: I have sold it too often to care about that. I have sold it for a professorship. I have sold it for an income. I have sold it to escape being imprisoned for refusing to pay taxes for

1185 hangmen's ropes and unjust wars and things that I abhor. What is all human conduct but the daily and hourly sale of our souls for trifles? What I am now selling it for is nei-ther money nor position nor comfort, but for reality and for power.

1190 BARBARA: You know that you will have no power, and that he has none.

CUSINS: I know. It is not for myself alone. I want to make power for the world.

BARBARA: I want to make power for the world too; but it must be

1195 spiritual power.

CUSINS: I think all power is spiritual: these cannons will not go off by themselves. I have tried to make spiritual power by teaching Greek. But the world can never be really touched by a dead language and a dead civilization. The people must have

1200 power; and the people cannot have Greek. Now the power that is made here can be wielded by all men.

BARBARA: Power to burn women's houses down and kill their sons and tear their husbands to pieces.

CUSINS: You cannot have power for good without having

1205 power for evil too. Even mother's milk nourishes murder-ers as well as heroes. This power which only tears men's bodies to pieces has never been so horribly abused as the intellectual power, the imaginative power, the poetic, reli-gious power that can enslave men's souls. As a teacher of

1210 Greek I gave the intellectual man weapons against the common man. I now want to give the common man weapons against the intellectual man. I love the common people. I want to arm them against the lawyers, the doc-tors, the priests, the literary men, the professors, the artists,

1215 and the politicians, who, once in authority, are more disastrous and tyrannical than all the fools, rascals, and impostors. I want a power simple enough for common men to use, yet strong enough to force the intellectual oligarchy to use its genius for the general good.

1220 BARBARA: Is there no higher power than that? (*Pointing to the shell.*)

CUSINS: Yes; but that power can destroy the higher powers just as a tiger can destroy a man: therefore Man must mas-ter that power first. I admitted this when the Turks and

1225 Greeks were last at war. My best pupil went out to fight for Hellas. My parting gift to him was not a copy of Plato's *Republic,* but a revolver and a hundred Undershaft car-tridges. The blood of every Turk he shot—if he shot any—is

on my head as well as on Undershaft's. That act committed me to this place for ever. Your father's challenge has beaten me. 1230 Dare I make war on war? I must. I will. And now, is it all over between us?

BARBARA: (*Touched by his evident dread of her answer.*) Silly baby Dolly! How could it be!

CUSINS: (*Overjoyed.*) Then you—you—you—Oh for my drum! (*He* 1235 *flourishes imaginary drumsticks.*)

BARBARA: (*Angered by his levity.*) Take care, Dolly, take care. Oh, if only I could get away from you and from father and from it all! if I could have the wings of a dove and fly away to heaven! 1240

CUSINS: And leave me!

BARBARA: Yes, you, and all the other naughty mischievous children of men. But I cant. I was happy in the Salvation Army for a moment. I escaped from the world into a paradise of enthusiasm and prayer and soul saving; but the moment 1245 our money ran short, it all came back to Bodger: it was he who saved our people: he, and the Prince of Darkness, my papa. Undershaft and Bodger: their hands stretch everywhere: when we feed a starving fellow creature, it is with their bread, because there is no other bread; when we 1250 tend the sick, it is in the hospitals they endow; if we turn from the churches they build, we must kneel on the stones of the streets they pave. As long as that lasts, there is no getting away from them. Turning our backs on Bodger and Undershaft is turning our backs on life. 1255

CUSINS: I thought you were determined to turn your back on the wicked side of life.

BARBARA: There is no wicked side: life is all one. And I never wanted to shirk my share in whatever evil must be endured, whether it be sin or suffering. I wish I could cure you of 1260 middle-class ideas, Dolly.

CUSINS: (*Gasping.*) Middle cl———! A snub! A social snub to me! from the daughter of a foundling!

BARBARA: That is why I have no class, Dolly: I come straight out of the heart of the whole people. If I were middle- 1265 class I should turn my back on my father's business; and we should both live in an artistic drawing room, with you reading the reviews in one corner, and I in the other at the piano, playing Schumann: both very superior persons, and neither of us a bit of use. Sooner than that, I would sweep 1270 out the guncotton shed, or be one of Bodger's barmaids. Do you know what would have happened if you had refused papa's offer?

CUSINS: I wonder!

BARBARA: I should have given you up and married the man 1275 who accepted it. After all, my dear old mother has more sense than any of you. I felt like her when I saw this place— felt that I must have it—that never, never, never could I let it go; only she thought it was the houses and the kitchen ranges and the linen and china, when it was really all the 1280 human souls to be saved: not weak souls in starved bodies, sobbing with gratitude for a scrap of bread and treacle, but fullfed, quarrelsome, snobbish, uppish creatures, all standing on their little rights and dignities, and thinking that my father ought to be greatly obliged to them for making so 1285 much money for him—and so he ought. That is where sal-vation is really wanted. My father shall never throw it in my teeth again that my converts were bribed with bread. (*She is transfigured.*) I have got rid of the bribe of bread. I have got rid of the bribe of heaven. Let God's work be done for its own 1290 sake: the work he had to create us to do because it cannot be done except by living men and women. When I die, let him be in my debt, not I in his; and let me forgive him as becomes a woman of my rank.

1295 CUSINS: Then the way of life lies through the factory of death?

BARBARA: Yes, through the raising of hell to heaven and of man to God, through the unveiling of an eternal light in the Valley of The Shadow. (*Seizing him with both hands.*) Oh!
1300 did you think my courage would never come back? did you believe that I was a deserter? that I, who have stood in the streets, and taken my people to my heart, and talked of the holiest and greatest things with them, could ever turn back and chatter foolishly to fashionable people about nothing in a drawing room? Never, never, never, never: Major Barbara
1305 will die with the colors. Oh! and I have my dear little Dolly boy still; and he has found me my place and my work. Glory Hallelujah! (*She kisses him.*)

CUSINS: My dearest: consider my delicate health. I cannot stand as much happiness as you can.

1310 BARBARA: Yes: it is not easy work being in love with me, is it? But it's good for you. (*She runs to the shed, and calls, childlike.*)

Mamma! Mamma! (BILTON *comes out of the shed, followed by* UNDERSHAFT.) I want Mamma.

UNDERSHAFT: She is taking off her list slippers, dear. (*He passes on to* CUSINS.) Well? What does she say? 1315

CUSINS: She has gone right up into the skies.

LADY BRITOMART: (*Coming from the shed and stopping on the steps, obstructing* SARAH, *who follows with* LOMAX. BARBARA *clutches like a baby at her mother's skirt.*) Barbara: when will you learn to be independent and to act and think 1320 for yourself? I know as well as possible what that cry of 'Mamma, Mamma,' means. Always running to me!

SARAH: (*Touching* LADY BRITOMART's *ribs with her finger tips and imitating a bicycle horn.*) Pip! pip!

LADY BRITOMART: (*Highly indignant.*) How dare you say Pip! 1325 pip! to me, Sarah? You are both very naughty children. What do you want, Barbara?

BARBARA: I want a house in the village to live in with Dolly. (*Dragging at the skirt.*) Come and tell me which one to take.

UNDERSHAFT: (*To* CUSINS.) Six o'clock tomorrow morning, 1330 Euripides.

Bertolt Brecht

Bertolt Brecht (1898–1956) changed the course of the modern European theater—and theater around the world—more than any playwright since Ibsen. However, Brecht's sphere of influence extends beyond his career as a playwright. As a dramatist, he wrote an unsurpassed body of plays; as a theoretician, Brecht's conception of "alienation" in the epic theater opened the way for sweeping innovation in our understanding of the possibilities of the stage; as a director, Brecht's work with his company, the Berliner Ensemble, made it the most influential and important theater in postwar Europe. The challenge of understanding Brecht is to understand the dialectical interplay between theory and practice that informs his assault on stage realism, and on the bourgeois theater itself.

Eugen Berthold Brecht (he later changed his name to Bertolt) was born in Augsburg, Bavaria, in 1898 to a prosperous family. In 1917, he enrolled at Munich University in the natural sciences and worked as a drama critic on the side. He also began work on several plays, including *Baal* (1917). In 1918 he was conscripted into military service for the remainder of World War I and worked in a military hospital. He returned briefly to the university after the war, but soon turned his attention full time to the theater. He moved to Berlin—Germany's theatrical capital at the time—and had the good fortune to work with two influential directors, Max Reinhardt and Erwin Piscator. Piscator advocated the use of new technologies in the theater, as a way of developing a kind of performance more responsive to the mechanized and accelerated routines of modern life. Brecht acknowledged that many of his own staging techniques were derived from his work with Piscator in the 1920s. Throughout the 1920s and early 1930s, Brecht wrote a series of plays that brought him notoriety, largely for their satire of the bourgeois establishment: *Drums in the Night* (1919), *In the Jungle of Cities* (1921), *Man Is Man* (1926), and the musical plays he wrote in collaboration with the composer Kurt Weill, *The Threepenny Opera* (1928) and *The Rise and Fall of the City of Mahagonny* (1930). In the 1920s, Brecht also began to collaborate with Margarete Steffin, one of several women—including Marieluise Fleißer, Elisabeth Hauptmann, Hella Wuolijoki, and Ruth Berlau—with whom he collaborated as director and playwright.

Brecht also began his serious reading of Marx in the 1920s, and it was his application of Marxist dialectic to the process of theater that gave rise to his most powerful and original ideas for the stage. From Marx, Brecht adopted a revolutionary posture, not only toward the class struggle, but toward the stage of bourgeois "realism." To Brecht, the realistic theater was not an unbiased window on social reality. Instead, Brecht argued that realistic theater presented a particular political vision, a view of society as inevitably determined by history and evolution, and therefore not susceptible to change. In order to displace "realism," and to demonstrate these hidden politics, Brecht redefined Marx's conception of "alienation" as a theatrical practice. In *Das Kapital*, Marx argues that the division of labor in modern industrial production has altered the relationship between mankind and the world. In modern industry, workers sell their labor in order to produce commodities. These commodities, Marx contends, then seem "alien" in that they appear to have arisen magically, as though the means of industrial production—with its history of enriching the owners at the expense of the exploited workers—were themselves a kind of "nature." In this sense, capitalist production conceals the social structure of the means of production, so that commodities come to have a "natural" life of their own: Marx aligned this spurious, magical "life" with that of religious objects in traditional cultures, as a kind of "fetishism." Yet, even as commodities seem to come alive, the workers become dehumanized, incorporated into the machinery of production. In the world of capital, where everything is for sale, all human relations, lives, and desires become commodified. The prevailing view of the world—in which commodities confront workers as something natural and entirely separate from their makers—is, to Marx, a *false* view, perpetuated within the bourgeois social order to the political advantage of the ruling classes.

Brecht's theater works to provide its audience with ways of regarding bourgeois reality—including realistic theater and drama—as "unnatural," as a political vision, as an ideological view of the world produced in the interest of profit. Brecht's theater, that is, works to "alienate" or "estrange" the audience from the commonplace "realities" of daily life—which we have unreflectively come to regard as "natural" and "inevitable"—in order to train us to question the world made by modern capitalism and the society it sustains. As he wrote in "The Modern Theater Is the Epic Theater," his theater is based on a "radical separation of the elements" of production, rather than on the scenic unity typical of realism. The seamless illusion of the realistic stage is that theater's most seductive commodity: it constantly and subliminally urges the audience to accept its "picture" of reality as a natural, apolitical image of the world as it is. Brecht's theater, in contrast, always shows both the dramatic illusion (the character, the setting, the action) and the process of its making (the work of the actor, the machinery of the theater, the activities of the stage). Brecht works to show the "means of production" in his theater, as a way of suggesting that stage realism, like social reality outside the theater, is *made*, not given.

Brecht called this theater by a variety of names, including **EPIC THEATER,** the term now generally used for Brecht's body of theory and technique. Brecht's plays tend to be episodic, a disconnected, open-ended **MONTAGE** of scenes: The audience must arrive at its own understanding of how the events are linked together, rather than being given an apparently inevitable narrative. Brecht generally left the stage bare in his productions, as a way of preventing the audience from seeing a complete illusion of some fictional dramatic locale. He exposed the lights above the stage, so the audience could see how lights influence the mood of the scene and so influence the audience's judgment. Brecht fragmented the "realistic" unity of the setting in other ways, too. Films could be projected on screens above the stage, forcing the audience to hold the drama in counterpoint to more recent events; placards onstage described the action to take place before the scene began. Finally, Brecht also urged his actors not to empathize entirely with the characters they played, but to strike a balance between a Stanislavskian identification with the character (being "in character," acting the character entirely from his or her point of view) and a more demonstrative attitude, one that enables the actor to represent the character from a variety of perspectives. Through these means, Brecht worked to involve the audience in the process of the play's production. Rather than being seduced by a commodified illusion of reality, the audience of epic theater is invited to consider, and enjoy, how the theater makes its fictions—as a way of teaching the audience to adopt a more critical, "alienated" way of seeing life outside the theater.

Brecht used many of these devices in *The Threepenny Opera* and in the series of plays he wrote in exile. Forced to flee Germany by Nazi purges of left-wing writers in 1933, Brecht spent the greater part of his creative life on the run, living briefly in Sweden, in Finland, and finally in Santa Monica, California, from 1941 to 1947. Although he had drafted *Life of Galileo* in 1938, Brecht continued to work on the play in California, collaborating on an English version with the actor Charles Laughton. He was also questioned by the House Un-American Activities Committee in 1947, as part of its infamous investigation of communism in the entertainment industry. Brecht was not charged and left the United States the following day to return to Europe and Germany. Living in exile, with no theater and little support, Brecht wrote his major plays: *Life of Galileo* (1938), *The Good Person of Szechwan* (1939), *Mother Courage and Her Children* (1939), and *The Caucasian Chalk Circle* (1944). He also wrote his most important theoretical essays, including *A Short Organum for the Theater,* written in Zurich, Switzerland in 1947, but published in 1948 after Brecht returned to Germany.

Brecht returned to East Berlin in 1947 and established his company, the Berliner Ensemble. Brecht's antirealist plays had long been the source of conflict with the **SOCIAL REALISM** advocated by the Communist Party, and even after the war Brecht had to work with a wary eye on the East German authorities. Nonetheless, the Berliner Ensemble—under Brecht's guidance and with the talents of his wife, Helene Weigel—became the leading European production company of the 1950s, sowing the seeds of innovation in every country they visited. Brecht died in August of 1956, just before the Berliner Ensemble's stunning visit to London, but the influence of his conception of theater has become worldwide, visible in plays from Luis Valdez's *Los vendidos* to Caryl Churchill's *Cloud Nine* to Tony Kushner's *Angels in America* to Griselda Gambaro's *Information for Foreigners*.

Mother Courage and Her Children

Mother Courage and Her Children is typical of Brecht's innovative approach to theater and to "political theater" as well. Rather than presenting a thesis, the play works to question the audience's attitudes about a variety of social institutions: warfare, business, motherhood, morality. In a parable-like series of scenes reminiscent both of expressionist theater and of morality drama, *Mother Courage and Her Children* invites the audience to estrange, and so reconsider, its ways of mapping the world.

In his model-book of the play, Brecht wrote that he wanted to show that "war, which is a continuation of business by other means, makes the human virtues fatal to their possessors." The play considers this problem in a variety of challenging ways. Although it is perhaps tempting to see Courage—Why is she called Courage? Was she courageous?—as a tragic heroine, the play relentlessly questions her "heroic" survival, and our own attitudes about the distinctions between war, business, and morality. As Scene I demonstrates, war and business create an all-embracing market in which everything is commodified, everything is for sale. Mother Courage sells a belt buckle and loses a son as part of the same transaction.

Much of the play's power onstage arises through its use of physical space and a few significant properties. The wagon—Courage's home, her means of survival, her mode of production—becomes in a sense the play's central "character." Placing it on a turntable, most productions convey the sense that the wagon is almost always in motion, yet never actually getting anywhere, much as Courage herself enters the play and leaves it singing the same song. Courage's fortunes are emblematized by the wagon as well. Loaded with goods and pulled by her two strong sons in the first scene, it is battered, barren, and empty in the

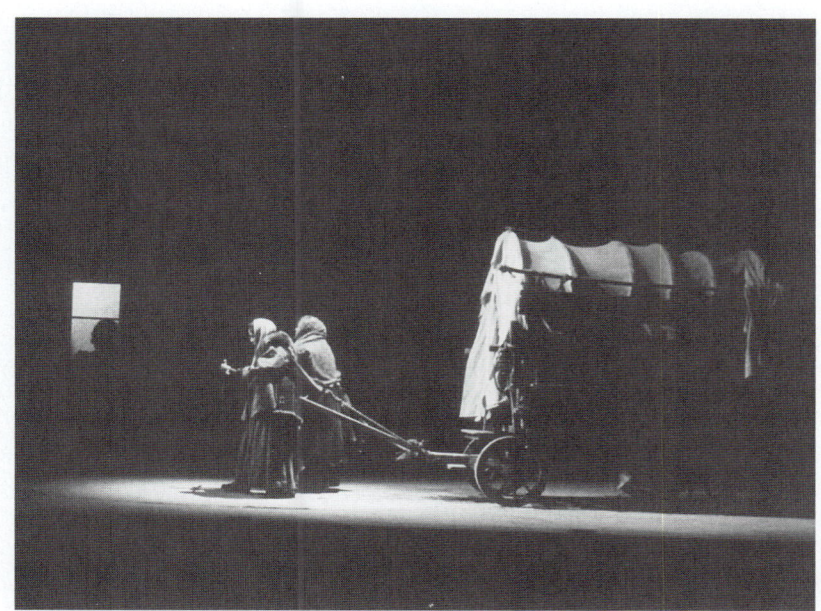

© Joan Marcus

Mother Courage and Kattrin harness themselves to the wagon in Bertolt Brecht's *Mother Courage and Her Children*.

last, pulled by Mother Courage herself as she struggles to catch up with the army. Brecht was attracted to the idea of using the wagon, the play's economic and material "base," so to speak, to elucidate some of the play's symbolic or moral themes. He used Courage's washline to link the wagon to the cannon at the opening of scene 3, tying warfare, the economy, and the domestic sphere together. He raised the harness-poles to form a kind of crucifix after the death of her son Swiss Cheese. Many of the most ironic moments of the Berliner Ensemble production of the play were Weigel's invention: as Mother Courage, she bit the coin in Scene I and slowly measured her pennies out of her purse when she paid the peasants to bury Kattrin at the end of the play. This is the kind of moment that Brecht worked—in theory, as a playwright, in directing productions—to make happen in the theater, a moment when a single gesture forces the audience to consider the scene in a new light, to question the relationship between its ideas of identity and morality and the society that gives them shape and meaning. Incidentally, one of the most revealing elements of the production was—and is—invisible: the original turntable supporting Weigel's wagon revolved on metal wheels, making a distracting noise during the production. Weigel scavenged the rubber-rimmed wheels used to guide tank tracks from the abandoned Russian tanks littering East Berlin, and they support the now-quiet Berliner Ensemble turntable to this day. Mother Courage's wagon continues to ride on the resourceful reuse of wartime goods.

Mother Courage and Her Children

A CHRONICLE OF THE THIRTY YEARS' WAR

Bertolt Brecht

TRANSLATED BY JOHN WILLETT

CHARACTERS

MOTHER COURAGE	A CLERK
KATTRIN, *her dumb daughter*	A YOUNG SOLDIER
EILIF, *the elder son*	AN OLDER SOLDIER
SWISS CHEESE, *the younger son*	A PEASANT
THE RECRUITER	THE PEASANT'S WIFE
THE SERGEANT	THE YOUNG MAN
THE COOK	THE OLD WOMAN
THE GENERAL	ANOTHER PEASANT
THE CHAPLAIN	HIS WIFE
THE ARMOURER	THE YOUNG PEASANT
YVETTE POTTIER	THE ENSIGN
THE MAN WITH THE PATCH	SOLDIERS
ANOTHER SERGEANT	A VOICE
THE ANCIENT COLONEL	

SCENE ONE

Spring 1624. The Swedish Commander-in-Chief Count Oxenstierna is raising troops in Dalecarlia for the Polish campaign. The canteen woman Anna Fierling, known under the name of Mother Courage, loses one son.

Country road near a town.

A SERGEANT *and a* RECRUITER *stand shivering.*

RECRUITER: How can you muster a unit in a place like this? I've been thinking about suicide, sergeant. Here am I, got to find our commander four companies before the twelfth of the month, and people round here are so nasty I can't sleep
5 nights. S'pose I get hold of some bloke and shut my eye to his pigeon chest and varicose veins, I get him proper drunk, he signs on the line, I'm just settling up, he goes for a piss, I follow him to the door because I smell a rat; bob's your uncle, he's off like a flea with the itch. No notion of word of honour,
10 loyalty, faith, sense of duty. This place has shattered my confidence in the human race, sergeant.
SERGEANT: It's too long since they had a war here; stands to reason. Where's their sense of morality to come from? Peace—that's just a mess; takes a war to restore order.
15 Peacetime, the human race runs wild. People and cattle get buggered about, who cares? Everyone eats just as he feels inclined, a hunk of cheese on top of his nice white bread, and a slice of fat on top of the cheese. How many young blokes and good horses in that town there, nobody knows; they never
20 thought of counting. I been in places ain't seen a war for nigh seventy years: folks hadn't got names to them, couldn't tell one another apart. Takes a war to get proper nominal rolls and inventories—shoes in bundles and corn in bags, and man and beast properly numbered and carted off, cause it stands to
25 reason: no order, no war.
RECRUITER: Too true.

SERGEANT: Same with all good things, it's a job to get a war going. But once it's blossomed out there's no holding it; folk start fighting shy of peace like punters what can't stop for fear of having to tot up what they lost. Before that it's 30 war they're fighting shy of. It's something new to them.
RECRUITER: Hey, here's a cart coming. Two tarts with two young fellows. Stop her, sergeant. If this one's a flop I'm not standing around in your spring winds any longer, I can tell you. 35

(*Sound of a jew's-harp. Drawn by two young fellows, a covered cart rolls in. On it sit* MOTHER COURAGE *and her dumb daughter* KATTRIN.)

MOTHER COURAGE: Morning, sergeant.
SERGEANT: (*Blocking the way.*) Morning, all. And who are you?
MOTHER COURAGE: Business folk. (*Sings.*)

> You captains, tell the drums to slacken
> And give your infanteers a break: 40
> It's Mother Courage with her waggon
> Full of the finest boots they make.
> With crawling lice and looted cattle
> With lumbering guns and straggling kit—
> How can you flog them into battle 45
> Unless you get them boots that fit?
> > The new year's come. The watchmen shout.
> > The thaw sets in. The dead remain.
> > Whatever life has not died out
> > It staggers to its feet again. 50
>
> Captains, how can you make them face it—
> Marching to death without a brew?
> Courage has rum with which to lace it
> And boil their souls and bodies through.
> Their musket primed, their stomach hollow— 55
> Captains, your men don't look so well.
> So feed them up and let them follow

While you command them into hell.
The new year's come. The watchmen shout.
60   The thaw sets in. The dead remain.
Wherever life has not died out
It staggers to its feet again.

SERGEANT: Halt! Who are you with, you trash?

THE ELDER SON: Second Finnish Regiment.

65   SERGEANT: Where's your papers?

MOTHER COURAGE: Papers?

THE YOUNGER SON: What, mean to say you don't know Mother
Courage?

SERGEANT: Never heard of her. What's she called Courage for?

70   MOTHER COURAGE: Courage is the name they gave me because
I was scared of going broke, sergeant, so I drove me cart
right through the bombardment of Riga with fifty loaves of
bread aboard. They were going mouldy, it was high time,
hadn't any choice really.

75   SERGEANT: Don't be funny with me. Your papers.

MOTHER COURAGE: (Pulling a bundle of papers from a tin box and
climbing down off the cart.) That's all my papers, sergeant.
You'll find a whole big missal from Altötting in Bavaria for
wrapping gherkins in, and a road map of Moravia, the Lord
80   knows when I'll ever get there, might as well chuck it away,
and here's a stamped certificate that my horse hasn't got
foot-and-mouth, only he's dead worse luck, cost fifteen
florins he did—not me luckily. That enough paper for you?

SERGEANT: You pulling my leg? I'll knock that sauce out of
85   you. S'pose you know you got to have a licence.

MOTHER COURAGE: Talk proper to me, do you mind, and don't
you dare say I'm pulling your leg in front of my unsullied
children, 'tain't decent, I got no time for you. My honest
face, that's me licence with the Second Regiment, and if it's
90   too difficult for you to read there's nowt I can do about it.
Nobody's putting a stamp on that.

RECRUITER: Sergeant, methinks I smell insubordination in this
individual. What's needed in our camp is obedience.

MOTHER COURAGE: Sausage, if you ask me.

95   SERGEANT: Name.

MOTHER COURAGE: Anna Fierling.

SERGEANT: You all called Fierling then?

MOTHER COURAGE: What d'you mean? It's me's called Fierling,
not them.

100 SERGEANT: Aren't all this lot your children?

MOTHER COURAGE: You bet they are, but why should they all
have to be called the same, eh? (Pointing to her elder son.)
For instance, that one's called Eilif Nojocki—Why? his
father always claimed he was called Kojocki or Mojocki or
105   something. The boy remembers him clearly, except that the
one he remembers was someone else, a Frenchie with a little
beard. Aside from that he's got his father's wits; that man
knew how to snitch a peasant's pants off his bum without
him noticing. This way each of us has his own name, see.

110 SERGEANT: What, each one different?

MOTHER COURAGE: Don't tell me you ain't never come
across that.

SERGEANT: So I s'pose he's a Chinaman? (Pointing to the
younger son.)

115 MOTHER COURAGE: Wrong. Swiss.

SERGEANT: After the Frenchman?

MOTHER COURAGE: What Frenchman? I never heard tell of
no Frenchman. You keep muddling things up, we'll be
hanging around here till dark. A Swiss, but called Fejos,
and the name has nowt to do with his father. He was called   120
something quite different and was a fortifications engineer,
only drunk all the time.

(SWISS CHEESE beams and nods; dumb KATTRIN too is amused.)

SERGEANT: How in hell can he be called Fejos?

MOTHER COURAGE: I don't like to be rude, sergeant, but you
ain't got much imagination, have you? Course he's called   125
Fejos, because when he arrived I was with a Hungarian,
very decent fellow, had terrible kidney trouble though he
never touched a drop. The boy takes after him.

SERGEANT: But he wasn't his father . . .

MOTHER COURAGE: Took after him just the same. I call him   130
Swiss Cheese. (Pointing to her daughter.) And that's Kattrin
Haupt, she's half German.

SERGEANT: Nice family, I must say.

MOTHER COURAGE: Aye, me cart and me have seen the world.

SERGEANT: I'm writing all this down. (He writes.) And you're   135
from Bamberg in Bavaria; how d'you come to be here?

MOTHER COURAGE: Can't wait till war chooses to visit Bamberg,
can I?

RECRUITER: (To EILIF.) You two should be called Jacob Ox and
Esau Ox, pulling the cart like that. I s'pose you never get out   140
of harness?

EILIF: Ma, can I clobber him one? I wouldn't half like to.

MOTHER COURAGE: And I says you can't; just you stop where
you are. And now two fine officers like you, I bet you
could use a good pistol, or a belt buckle, yours is on its last   145
legs, sergeant.

SERGEANT: I could use something else. Those boys are healthy
as young birch trees, I observe: chests like barrels, solid leg
muscles. So why are they dodging their military service,
may I ask?   150

MOTHER COURAGE: (Quickly.) Nowt doing, sergeant. Yours is no
trade for my kids.

RECRUITER: But why not? There's good money in it, glory too.
Flogging boots is women's work. (To EILIF.) Come here,
let's see if you've muscles in you or if you're a chicken.   155

MOTHER COURAGE: He's a chicken. Give him a fierce look, he'll
fall over.

RECRUITER: Killing a young bull that happens to be in his way.
(Wants to lead him off.)

MOTHER COURAGE: Let him alone, will you? He's nowt for   160
you folk.

RECRUITER: He was crudely offensive and talked about clob-
bering me. The two of us are going to step into that field
and settle it man to man.

EILIF: Don't you worry, mum, I'll fix him.   165

MOTHER COURAGE: Stop there! You varmint! I know you, nowt
but fights. There's a knife down his boot. A slasher, that's
what he is.

RECRUITER: I'll draw it out of him like a milk-tooth. Come
along, sonny.   170

MOTHER COURAGE: Sergeant, I'll tell the colonel. He'll have
you both in irons. The lieutenant's going out with my
daughter.

SERGEANT: No rough stuff, chum. (*To* MOTHER COURAGE.)
175   What you got against military service? Wasn't his own father
    a soldier? Died a soldier's death, too? Said it yourself.
MOTHER COURAGE: He's nowt but a child. You want to take him
    off to slaughterhouse, I know you lot. They'll give you five
    florins for him.
180 RECRUITER: First he's going to get a smart cap and boots, eh?
EILIF: Not from you.
MOTHER COURAGE: Let's both go fishing, said angler to worm.
    (*To* SWISS CHEESE.) Run off, call out they're trying to kidnap
    your brother. (*She pulls a knife.*) Go on, you kidnap him, just
185   try. I'll slit you open, trash. I'll teach you to make war with
    him. We're doing an honest trade in ham and linen, and we're
    peaceable folk.
SERGEANT: Peaceable I don't think; look at your knife. You
    should be ashamed of yourself; put that knife away, you old
190   harridan. A minute back you were admitting you live off the
    war, how else should you live, what from? But how's anyone to
    have war without soldiers?
MOTHER COURAGE: No need for it to be my kids.
SERGEANT: Oh, you'd like war to eat the pips but spit out the
195   apple? It's to fatten up your kids, but you won't invest in it.
    Got to look after itself, eh? And you called Courage, fancy
    that. Scared of the war that keeps you going? Your sons aren't
    scared of it, I can see that.
EILIF: Take more than a war to scare me.
200 SERGEANT: And why? Look at me: has army life done all that
    badly by me? Joined up at seventeen.
MOTHER COURAGE: Still got to reach seventy.
SERGEANT: I don't mind waiting.
MOTHER COURAGE: Under the sod, eh?
205 SERGEANT: You trying to insult me, saying I'll die?
MOTHER COURAGE: S'pose it's true? S'pose I can see the mark's
    on you? S'pose you look like a corpse on leave to me? Eh?
SWISS CHEESE: She's got second sight, Mother has.
RECRUITER: Go ahead, tell the sergeant's fortune, might
210   amuse him.
MOTHER COURAGE: Gimme helmet. (*He gives it to her.*)
SERGEANT: It don't mean a bloody sausage. Anything for a
    laugh though.
MOTHER COURAGE: (*Taking out a sheet of parchment and tearing
215   it up.*) Eilif, Swiss Cheese and Kattrin, may all of us be torn
    apart like this if we lets ourselves get too mixed up in the war.
    (*To the* SERGEANT.) Just for you I'm doing it for free. Black's
    for death. I'm putting a big black cross on this slip of paper.
SWISS CHEESE: Leaving the other one blank, see?
220 MOTHER COURAGE: Then I fold them across and shake them.
    All of us is jumbled together like this from our mother's
    womb, and now draw a slip and you'll know. (*The* SERGEANT
    hesitates.*)
RECRUITER: (*To* EILIF.) I don't take just anybody, they all know
225   I'm choosey, but you got the kind of fire I like to see.
SERGEANT: (*Fishing in the helmet.*) Too silly. Load of eyewash.
SWISS CHEESE: Drawn a black cross, he has. Write him off.
RECRUITER: They're having you on; not everybody's name's
    on a bullet.
230 SERGEANT: (*Hoarsely.*) You've put me in the shit.
MOTHER COURAGE: Did that yourself the day you became a
    soldier. Come along, let's move on now. 'Tain't every day we
    have a war, I got to get stirring.

SERGEANT: God damn it, you can't kid me. We're taking that
    bastard of yours for a soldier.   235
EILIF: Swiss Cheese'd like to be a soldier too.
MOTHER COURAGE: First I've heard of that. You'll have to draw
    too, all three of you. (*She goes to the rear to mark crosses on
    further slips.*)
RECRUITER: (*To* EILIF.) One of the things they say against us is that   240
    it's all holy-holy in the Swedish camp; but that's a malicious
    rumour to do us down. There's no hymn-singing but Sundays,
    just a single verse, and then only for those got voices.
MOTHER COURAGE: (*Coming back with the slips, which she drops
    into the* SERGEANT's *helmet.*) Trying to get away from their ma,   245
    the devils, off to war like calves to salt-lick. But I'm making
    you draw lots, and that'll show you the world is no vale of
    joys with 'Come along, son, we need a few more generals'.
    Sergeant, I'm so scared they won't get through the war. Such
    dreadful characters, all three of them. (*She hands the helmet*   250
    to EILIF.) Hey, come on, fish out your slip. (*He fishes one out,
    unfolds it. She snatches it from him.*) There you are, it's a cross.
    Oh, wretched mother that I am, o pain-racked giver of birth!
    Shall he die? Aye, in the springtime of life he is doomed. If he
    becomes a soldier he shall bite the dust, it's plain to see. He is   255
    too foolhardy, like his dad was. And if he ain't sensible he'll
    go the way of all flesh, his slip proves it. (*Shouts at him.*) You
    going to be sensible?
EILIF: Why not?
MOTHER COURAGE: Sensible thing is stay with your mother,   260
    never mind if they poke fun at you and call you chicken,
    just you laugh.
RECRUITER: If you're pissing in your pants I'll make do with
    your brother.
MOTHER COURAGE: I told you laugh. Go on, laugh. Now you   265
    draw, Swiss Cheese. I'm not so scared on your account,
    you're honest. (*He fishes in the helmet.*) Oh, why look at your
    slip in that strange way? It's got to be a blank. There can't be
    any cross on it. Surely I'm not going to lose *you*. (*She takes
    the slip.*) A cross? What, you too? Is that because you're so   270
    simple, perhaps? O Swiss Cheese, you too will be sunk if
    you don't stay utterly honest all the while, like I taught you
    from childhood when you brought the change back from the
    baker's. Else you can't save yourself. Look, sergeant, that's a
    black cross, ain't it?   275
SERGEANT: A cross, that's right. Can't think how I come to get
    one. I always stay in the rear. (*To the* RECRUITER.) There's no
    catch. Her own family get it too.
SWISS CHEESE: I get it too. But I listen to what I'm told.
MOTHER COURAGE: (*To* KATTRIN.) And now you're the only one I   280
    know's all right, you're a cross yourself; got a kind heart you
    have. (*Holds the helmet up to her on the cart, but takes the slip
    out herself.*) No, that's too much. That can't be right; must have
    made a mistake shuffling. Don't be too kindhearted, Kattrin,
    you'll have to give it up, there's a cross above your path too.   285
    Lie doggo, girl, it can't be that hard once you're born dumb.
    Right, all of you know now. Look out for yourselves, you'll
    need to. And now up we get and on we go. (*She climbs on to
    the cart.*)
RECRUITER: (*To the* SERGEANT.) Do something.   290
SERGEANT: I don't feel very well.
RECRUITER: Must of caught a chill taking your helmet off in that
    wind. Involve her in a deal. (*Aloud.*) Might as well have a look

295 at that belt-buckle, sergeant. After all, our friends here have to live by their business. Hey, you people, the sergeant wants to buy that belt-buckle.

MOTHER COURAGE: Half a florin. Two florins is what a belt like that's worth. (*Climbs down again.*)

SERGEANT: 'Tain't new. Let me get out of this damned wind and

300 have a proper look at it. (*Goes behind the cart with the buckle.*)

MOTHER COURAGE: Ain't what I call windy.

SERGEANT: I s'pose it might be worth half a florin, it's silver.

MOTHER COURAGE: (*Joining him behind the cart.*) It's six solid ounces.

305 RECRUITER: (*To* EILIF.) And then we men'll have one together. Got your bounty money here, come along. (EILIF *stands undecided.*)

MOTHER COURAGE: Half a florin it is.

SERGEANT: It beats me. I'm always at the rear. Sergeant's the

310 safest job there is. You can send the others up front, cover themselves with glory. Me dinner hour's properly spoiled. Shan't be able to hold nowt down, I know.

MOTHER COURAGE: Mustn't let it prey on you so's you can't eat. Just stay at the rear. Here, take a swig of brandy, man. (*Gives*

315 *him a drink.*)

RECRUITER: (*Has taken* EILIF *by the arm and is leading him away up stage.*) Ten florins bounty money, then you're a gallant fellow fighting for the king and women'll be after you like flies. And you can clobber me for free for insulting you.

(*Exeunt both.*)

(*Dumb* KATTRIN *leans down from the cart and makes hoarse noises.*)

320 MOTHER COURAGE: All right, Kattrin, all right. Sergeant's just paying. (*Bites the half-florin.*) I got no faith in any kind of money. Burnt child, that's me, sergeant. This coin's good, though. And now let's get moving. Where's Eilif?

SWISS CHEESE: Went off with the recruiter.

325 MOTHER COURAGE: (*Stands quite still, then.*) You simpleton. (*To* KATTRIN.) 'Tain't your fault, you can't speak, I know.

SERGEANT: Could do with a swig yourself, ma. That's life. Plenty worse things than being a soldier. Want to live off war, but keep yourself and family out of it, eh?

330 MOTHER COURAGE: You'll have to help your brother pull now, Kattrin.

(*Brother and sister hitch themselves to the cart and start pulling.* MOTHER COURAGE *walks alongside. The cart rolls on.*)

SERGEANT: (*Looking after them.*)
Like the war to nourish you?
Have to feed it something too.

SCENE TWO

In the years 1625 and 1626 Mother Courage crosses Poland in the train of the Swedish armies. Before the fortress of Wallhof she meets her son again. Successful sale of a capon and heyday of her dashing son.

The GENERAL'S *tent.*

Beside it, his kitchen. Thunder of cannon. The COOK *is arguing with* MOTHER COURAGE, *who wants to sell him a capon.*

THE COOK: Sixty hellers for a miserable bird like that?

MOTHER COURAGE: Miserable bird? This fat brute? Mean to say some greedy old general—and watch your step if you got nowt for his dinner—can't afford sixty hellers for him?

THE COOK: I can get a dozen like that for ten hellers just down 5 the road.

MOTHER COURAGE: What, a capon like this you can get just down the road? In time of siege, which means hunger that tears your guts. A rat you might get: 'might' I say because they're all being gobbled up, five men spending best part of 10 day chasing one hungry rat. Fifty hellers for a giant capon in time of siege!

THE COOK: But it ain't us having the siege, it's t'other side. We're conducting the siege, can't you get that in your head?

MOTHER COURAGE: But we got nowt to eat too, even worse than 15 them in the town. Took it with them, didn't they? They're having a high old time, everyone says. And look at us! I been to the peasants, there's nowt there.

THE COOK: There's plenty. They're sitting on it.

MOTHER COURAGE: (*Triumphantly.*) They ain't. They're bust, 20 that's what they are. Just about starving. I saw some, were grubbing up roots from sheer hunger, licking their fingers after they boiled some old leather strap. That's way it is. And me got a capon here and supposed to take forty hellers for it. 25

THE COOK: Thirty, not forty. I said thirty.

MOTHER COURAGE: Here, this ain't just any old capon. It was such a gifted beast, I been told, it could only eat to music, had a military march of its own. It could count, it was that intelligent. And you say forty hellers is too much? General 30 will make mincemeat of you if there's nowt on his table.

THE COOK: See what I'm doing? (*He takes a piece of beef and puts his knife to it.*) Here I got a bit of beef, I'm going to roast it. Make up your mind quick.

MOTHER COURAGE: Go on, roast it. It's last year's. 35

THE COOK: Last night's. That animal was still alive and kicking, I saw him myself.

MOTHER COURAGE: Alive and stinking, you mean.

THE COOK: I'll cook him five hours if need be. I'll just see if he's still tough. (*He cuts into it.*) 40

MOTHER COURAGE: Put plenty of pepper on it so his lordship the general don't smell the pong.

(*The* GENERAL, *a* CHAPLAIN *and* EILIF *enter the tent.*)

THE GENERAL: (*Slapping* EILIF *on the shoulder.*) Now then, Eilif my son, into your general's tent with you and sit thou at my right hand. For you accomplished a deed of heroism, 45 like a pious cavalier; and doing what you did for God, and in a war of religion at that, is something I commend in you most highly, you shall have a gold bracelet as soon as we've taken this town. Here we are, come to save their souls for them, and what do those insolent dung-encrusted yokels 50 go and do? Drive their beef away from us. They stuff it into those priests of theirs all right, back and front, but you taught 'em manners, ha! So here's a pot of red wine for you, the two of us'll knock it back at one gulp. (*They do so.*) Piss all for the chaplain, the old bigot. And now, what would you like 55 for dinner, my darling?

EILIF: A bit of meat, why not?

THE GENERAL: Cook! Meat!

THE COOK: And then he goes and brings guests when there's
60   nowt there.

(MOTHER COURAGE *silences him so she can listen.*)

EILIF: Hungry job cutting down peasants.

MOTHER COURAGE: Jesus Christ, it's my Eilif.

THE COOK: Your what?

MOTHER COURAGE: My eldest boy. It's two years since I lost sight
65   of him, they pinched him from me on the road, must think
    well of him if the general's asking him to dinner, and what
    kind of a dinner can you offer? Nowt. You heard what the
    visitor wishes to eat: meat. Take my tip, you settle for the
    capon, it'll be a florin.

70 THE GENERAL: (*Has sat down with* EILIF, *and bellows.*) Food,
    Lamb, you foul cook, or I'll have your hide.

THE COOK: Give it over, dammit, this is blackmail.

MOTHER COURAGE: Didn't someone say it was a miserable bird?

THE COOK: Miserable; give it over, and a criminal price, fifty
75   hellers.

MOTHER COURAGE: A florin, I said. For my eldest boy, the
    general's guest, no expense is too great for me.

THE COOK: (*Gives her the money.*) You might at least pluck it while
    I see to the fire.

80 MOTHER COURAGE: (*Sits down to pluck the fowl.*) He won't half be
    surprised to see me. He's my dashing clever son. Then I got a
    stupid one too, he's honest though. The girl's nowt. One good
    thing, she don't talk.

THE GENERAL: Drink up, my son, this is my best Falernian; only
85   got a barrel or two left, but that's nothing to pay for a sign
    that's there's still true faith to be found in my army. As for
    that shepherd of souls he can just look on, because all he does
    is preach, without the least idea how it's to be carried out.
    And now, my son Eilif, tell us more about the neat way you
90   smashed those yokels and captured the twenty oxen. Let's
    hope they get here soon.

EILIF: A day or two at most.

MOTHER COURAGE: Thoughtful of our Eilif not to bring the
    oxen in till tomorrow, else you lot wouldn't have looked
95   twice at my capon.

EILIF: Well, it was like this, see. I'd heard peasants had been
    driving the oxen they'd hidden, out of the forest into one
    particular wood, on the sly and mostly by night. That's where
    people from the town were s'posed to come and pick them
100   up. So I holds off and lets them drive their oxen together,
    reckoning they'd be better than me at finding 'em. I had my
    blokes slavering after the meat, cut their emergency rations
    even further for a couple of days till their mouths was
    watering at the least sound of any word beginning with 'me-',
105   like 'measles' say.

THE GENERAL: Very clever of you.

EILIF: Possibly. The rest was a piece of cake. Except that the
    peasants had cudgels and outnumbered us three to one and
    made a murderous attack on us. Four of 'em shoved me into
110   a thicket, knocked my sword from my hand and bawled out
    'Surrender!' What's the answer, I wondered; they're going to
    make mincemeat of me.

THE GENERAL: What did you do?

EILIF: I laughed.

115 THE GENERAL: You did what?

EILIF: Laughed. So we got talking. I put it on a business footing
    from the start, told them 'Twenty florins a head's too much.

I'll give you fifteen'. As if I was meaning to pay. That threw
them, and they began scratching their heads. In a flash
I'd picked up my sword and was hacking 'em to pieces. 120
Necessity's the mother of invention, eh, sir?

THE GENERAL: What is your view, pastor of souls?

THE CHAPLAIN: That phrase is not strictly speaking in the
Bible, but when Our Lord turned the five loaves into five
hundred there was no war on and he could tell people to 125
love their neighbours as they'd had enough to eat. Today
it's another story.

THE GENERAL: (*Laughs.*) Quite another story. You can have a swig
after all for that, you old Pharisee. (*To* EILIF.) Hacked 'em to
pieces, did you, so my gallant lads can get a proper bite to eat? 130
What do the Scriptures say? 'Whatsoever thou doest for the
least of my brethren, thou doest for me'. And what did you
do for them? Got them a good square meal of beef, because
they're not accustomed to mouldy bread, the old way was to
fix a cold meal of rolls and wine in your helmet before you 135
went out to fight for God.

EILIF: Aye, in a flash I'd picked up my sword and was hacking
them to pieces.

THE GENERAL: You've the makings of a young Caesar. You ought
to see the King. 140

EILIF: I have from a distance. He kind of glows. I'd like to model
myself on him.

THE GENERAL: You've got something in common already. I
appreciate soldiers like you, Eilif, men of courage. Somebody
like that I treat as I would my own son. (*He leads him over to* 145
the map.) Have a look at the situation, Eilif; it's a long haul
still.

MOTHER COURAGE: (*Who has been listening and now angrily*
plucks the fowl.) That must be a rotten general.

THE COOK: He's ravenous all right, but why rotten? 150

MOTHER COURAGE: Because he's got to have men of courage,
that's why. If he knew how to plan a proper campaign what
would he be needing men of courage for? Ordinary ones
would do. It's always the same; whenever there's a load of
special virtues around it means something stinks. 155

THE COOK: I thought it meant things is all right.

MOTHER COURAGE: No, that they stink. Look, s'pose some general
or king is bone stupid and leads his men up shit creek, then
those men've got to be fearless, there's another virtue for you.
S'pose he's stingy and hires too few soldiers, then they got to 160
be a crowd of Hercules's. And s'pose he's slapdash and don't
give a bugger, then they got to be clever as monkeys else their
number's up. Same way they got to show exceptional loyalty
each time he gives them impossible jobs. Nowt but virtues
no proper country and no decent king or general would ever 165
need. In decent countries folk don't have to have virtues, the
whole lot can be perfectly ordinary, average intelligence, and
for all I know cowards.

THE GENERAL: I'll wager your father was a soldier.

EILIF: A great soldier, I been told. My mother warned me about 170
it. There's a song I know.

THE GENERAL: Sing it to us. (*Roars.*) When's that dinner coming?

EILIF: It's called The Song of the Girl and the Soldier. (*He sings it,*
dancing a war dance with his sabre.)

The guns blaze away, and the bay'nit'll slay 175
And the water can't hardly be colder.
What's the answer to ice? Keep off's my advice!

That's what the girl told the soldier.
Next thing the soldier, wiv' a round up the spout
180 Hears the band playing and gives a great shout:
Why, it's marching what makes you a soldier!
So it's down to the south and then northwards once more:
See him catching that bay'nit in his naked paw!
That's what his comrades done told her.

185 Oh, do not despise the advice of the wise
Learn wisdom from those that are older
And don't try for things that are out of your reach—
That's what the girl told the soldier.
Next thing the soldier, his bay'nit in place
190 Wades into the river and laughs in her face
Though the water comes up to his shoulder.
When the shingle roof glints in the light o' the moon
We'll be wiv' you again, not a moment too soon!
That's what his comrades done told her.

195 MOTHER COURAGE: (*Takes up the song in the kitchen, beating on a pot with her spoon.*)

You'll go out like a light! And the sun'll take flight
For your courage just makes us feel colder.
Oh, that vanishing light! May God see that it's right!—
200 That's what the girl told the soldier.

EILIF: What's that?
MOTHER COURAGE: (*Continues singing.*)

Next thing the soldier, his bay'nit in place
Was caught by the current and went down without trace
205 And the water couldn't hardly be colder.
Then the shingle roof froze in the light o' the moon
As both soldier and ice drifted down to their doom—
And d'you know what his comrades done told her?

He went out like a light. And the sunshine took flight
210 For his courage just made 'em feel colder.
Oh, do not despise the advice of the wise!
That's what the girl told the soldier.

THE GENERAL: The things they get up to in my kitchen these days.
215 EILIF: (*Has gone into the kitchen. He flings his arms round his mother.*) Fancy seeing you again, ma! Where's the others?
MOTHER COURAGE: (*In his arms.*) Snug as a bug in a rug. They made Swiss Cheese paymaster of the Second Finnish; any road he'll stay out of fighting that way, I couldn't keep him
220 out altogether.
EILIF: How's the old feet?
MOTHER COURAGE: Bit tricky getting me shoes on of a morning.
THE GENERAL: (*Has joined them.*) So you're his mother, I hope you've got plenty more sons for me like this one.
225 EILIF: Ain't it my lucky day? You sitting out there in the kitchen, ma, hearing your son commended . . .
MOTHER COURAGE: You bet I heard. (*Slaps his face.*)
EILIF: (*Holding his cheek.*) What's that for? Taking the oxen?
MOTHER COURAGE: No. Not surrendering when those four went
230 for you and wanted to make mincemeat of you. Didn't I say you should look after yourself? You Finnish devil!

(*The* GENERAL *and the* CHAPLAIN *stand in the doorway laughing.*)

SCENE THREE

Three years later Mother Courage is taken prisoner along with elements of a Finnish regiment. She manages to save her daughter, likewise her covered cart, but her honest son is killed.

Military camp.

Afternoon. A flagpole with the regimental flag. From her cart, festooned now with all kinds of goods, MOTHER COURAGE *has stretched a washing line to a large cannon, across which she and* KATTRIN *are folding the washing. She is bargaining at the same time with an* ARMOURER *over a sack of shot.* SWISS CHEESE, *now wearing a paymaster's uniform, is looking on.*

A comely person, YVETTE POTTIER, *is sewing a gaily coloured hat, a glass of brandy before her. She is in her stockinged feet, having laid aside her red high-heeled boots.*

THE ARMOURER: I'll let you have that shot for a couple of florins. It's cheap at the price, I got to have the money because the colonel's been boozing with his officers since two days back, and the drink's run out.
MOTHER COURAGE: That's troops' munitions. They catch me with 5
that, I'm for court-martial. You crooks flog the shot, and troops got nowt to fire at enemy.
THE ARMOURER: Have a heart, can't you; you scratch my back and I'll scratch yours.
MOTHER COURAGE: I'm not taking army property. Not at that 10
price.
THE ARMOURER: You can sell it on the q.t. tonight to the Fourth Regiment's armourer for five florins, eight even, if you let him have a receipt for twelve. He's right out of ammunition. 15
MOTHER COURAGE: Why not you do it?
THE ARMOURER: I don't trust him, he's a pal of mine.
MOTHER COURAGE: (*Takes the sack.*) Gimme. (*To* KATTRIN.) Take it away and pay him a florin and a half. (*The* ARMOURER *protests.*) I said a florin and a half. (KATTRIN *drags the sack* 20
upstage, the ARMOURER *following her* MOTHER COURAGE *addresses* SWISS CHEESE.) Here's your woollies, now look after them, it's October and autumn may set in any time. I ain't saying it's got to, cause I've learned nowt's got to come when you think it will, not even seasons of the year. But your 25
regimental accounts got to add up right, come what may. Do they add up right?
SWISS CHEESE: Yes, mother.
MOTHER COURAGE: Don't you forget they made you paymaster cause you was honest, not dashing like your brother, and 30
above all so stupid I bet you ain't even thought of clearing off with it, no not you. That's a big consolation to me. And don't lose those woollies.
SWISS CHEESE: No, mother, I'll put them under my mattress. (*Begins to go.*) 35
THE ARMOURER: I'll go along with you, paymaster.
MOTHER COURAGE: And don't you start learning him none of your tricks.

(*The* ARMOURER *leaves with* SWISS CHEESE *without any farewell gesture.*)

YVETTE: (*Waving to him.*) No reason not to say goodbye,
40   armourer.
MOTHER COURAGE: (*To* YVETTE.) I don't like to see them together.
He's wrong company for our Swiss Cheese. Oh well, war's off
to a good start. Easily take four, five years before all countries
are in. A bit of foresight, don't do nothing silly, and business'll
45   flourish. Don't you know you ain't s'posed to drink before
midday with your complaint?
YVETTE: Complaint, who says so, it's a libel.
MOTHER COURAGE: They all say so.
YVETTE: Because they're all telling lies, Mother Courage, and me
50   at my wits' end cause they're all avoiding me like something
the cat brought in thanks to those lies, what the hell am I
remodelling my hat for? (*She throws it away.*) That's why I
drink before midday. Never used to, gives you crows' feet, but
now what the hell? All the Second Finnish know me. Ought to
55   have stayed at home when my first fellow did me wrong. No
good our sort being proud. Eat shit, that's what you got to do,
or down you go.
MOTHER COURAGE: Now don't you start up again about that
Pieter of yours and how it all happened, in front of my
60   innocent daughter too.
YVETTE: She's the one should hear it, put her off love.
MOTHER COURAGE: Nobody can put 'em off that.
YVETTE: Then I'll go on, get it off my chest. It all starts with
yours truly growing up in lovely Flanders, else I'd never of
65   seen him and wouldn't be stuck here now in Poland, cause
he was an army cook, fair-haired, a Dutchman but thin for
once. Kattrin, watch out for the thin ones, only in those days I
didn't know that, or that he'd got a girl already, or that they all
called him Puffing Piet cause he never took his pipe out of his
70   mouth when he was on the job, it meant that little to him. (*She
sings the Song of Fraternisation.*)

    When I was only sixteen
    The foe came into our land.
    He laid aside his sabre
75   And with a smile he took my hand.
    After the May parade
    The May light starts to fade.
    The regiment dressed by the right
    The drums were beaten, that's the drill.
80   The foe took us behind the hill
    And fraternised all night.

    There were so many foes then
    But mine worked in the mess.
    I loathed him in the daytime.
85   At night I loved him none the less.
    After the May parade
    The May light starts to fade.
    The regiment dressed by the right
    The drums were beaten, that's the drill.
90   The foe took us behind the hill
    And fraternised all night.

    The love which came upon me
    Was wished on me by fate.
    My friends could never grasp why
95   I found it hard to share their hate.
    The fields were wet with dew

    When sorrow first I knew.
    The regiment dressed by the right
    The drums were beaten, that's the drill.
    And then the foe, my lover still   100
    Went marching out of sight.

I followed him, fool that I was, but I never found him, and that
was five years back. (*She walks unsteadily behind the cart.*)
MOTHER COURAGE: You left your hat here.
YVETTE: Anyone wants it can have it.   105
MOTHER COURAGE: Let that be a lesson, Kattrin. Don't you
start anything with them soldiers. Love makes the world
go round, I'm warning you. Even with fellows not in the
army it's no bed of roses. He says he'd like to kiss the
ground your feet walk on—reminds me, did you wash   110
them yesterday?—and after that you're his skivvy. Be
thankful you're dumb, then you can't contradict yourself
and won't be wanting to bite your tongue off for speaking
the truth; it's a godsend, being dumb is. And here comes
the general's cook, now what's he after?   115

(*Enter the* COOK *and the* CHAPLAIN.)

THE CHAPLAIN: I have a message for you from your son Eilif,
and the cook has come along because you made such a
profound impression on him.
THE COOK: I just came along to get a bit of air.
MOTHER COURAGE: That you can always do here if you behave   120
yourself, and if you don't I can deal with you. What does he
want? I got no spare cash.
THE CHAPLAIN: Actually I had a message for his brother the
paymaster.
MOTHER COURAGE: He ain't here now nor anywhere else   125
neither. He ain't his brother's paymaster. He's not to lead
him into temptation nor be clever at his expense. (*Giving
him money from the purse slung round her.*) Give him this,
it's a sin, he's banking on mother's love and ought to be
ashamed of himself.   130
THE COOK: Not for long, he'll have to be moving off with the
regiment, might be to his death. Give him a bit extra, you'll
be sorry later. You women are tough, then later on you're
sorry. A little glass of brandy wouldn't have been a problem,
but it wasn't offered and, who knows, a bloke may lie beneath   135
the green sod and none of you people will ever be able to dig
him up again.
THE CHAPLAIN: Don't give way to your feelings, cook. To fall in
battle is a blessing, not an inconvenience, and why? It is a war
of faith. None of your common wars but a special one, fought   140
for the faith and therefore pleasing to God.
THE COOK: Very true. It's a war all right in one sense, what with
requisitioning, murder and looting and the odd bit of rape
thrown in, but different from all the other wars because it's a
war of faith; stands to reason. But it's thirsty work at that, you   145
must admit.
THE CHAPLAIN: (*To* MOTHER COURAGE, *indicating the* COOK.) I
tried to stop him, but he says he's taken a shine to you, you
figure in his dreams.
THE COOK: (*Lighting a stumpy pipe.*) Just want a glass of brandy   150
from a fair hand, what harm in that? Only I'm groggy already
cause the chaplain here's been telling such jokes all the way
along you bet I'm still blushing.

MOTHER COURAGE: Him a clergyman too. I'd best give the pair
155   of you a drink or you'll start making me immoral suggestions
         cause you've nowt else to do.

THE CHAPLAIN: Behold a temptation, said the court preacher, and
         fell. (*Turning back to look at* KATTRIN *as he leaves.*) And who
         is this entrancing young person?

160 MOTHER COURAGE: That ain't an entrancing but a decent young
         person. (*The* CHAPLAIN *and the* COOK *go behind the cart with*
         MOTHER COURAGE. KATTRIN *looks after them, then walks
         away from her washing towards the hat. She picks it up and sits
         down, pulling the red boots towards her.* MOTHER COURAGE
165   *can be heard in the background talking politics with the*
         CHAPLAIN *and the* COOK.)

MOTHER COURAGE: Those Poles here in Poland had no business
         sticking their noses in. Right, our king moved in on them,
         horse and foot, but did they keep the peace? no, went and
170   stuck their noses into their own affairs, they did, and fell on
         king just as he was quietly clearing off. They committed a
         breach of peace, that's what, so blood's on their own head.

THE CHAPLAIN: All our king minded about was freedom. The
         emperor had made slaves of them all, Poles and Germans
175   alike, and the king had to liberate them.

THE COOK: Just what I say, your brandy's first rate, I weren't
         mistaken in your face, but talk of the king, it cost the king
         dear trying to give freedom to Germany, what with giv-
         ing Sweden the salt tax, what cost the poor folk a bit, so
180   I've heard, on top of which he had to have the Germans
         locked up and drawn and quartered cause they wanted to
         carry on slaving for the emperor. Course the king took a
         serious view when anybody didn't want to be free. He set
         out by just trying to protect Poland against bad people,
185   particularly the emperor, then it started to become a habit
         till he ended up protecting the whole of Germany. They
         didn't half kick. So the poor old king's had nowt but trou-
         ble for all his kindness and expenses, and that's something
         he had to make up for by taxes of course, which caused
190   bad blood, not that he'd let a little matter like that depress
         him. One thing he had on his side, God's word, that was a
         help. Because otherwise folk would of been saying he
         done it all for himself and to make a bit on the side. So
         he's always had a good conscience, which was the main
195   point.

MOTHER COURAGE: Anyone can see you're no Swede or you
         wouldn't be talking that way about the Hero King.

THE CHAPLAIN: After all he provides the bread you eat.

THE COOK: I don't eat it, I bake it.

200 MOTHER COURAGE: They'll never beat him, and why, his men
         got faith in him. (*Seriously.*) To go by what the big shots say,
         they're waging war for almighty God and in the name of
         everything that's good and lovely. But look closer, they ain't so
         silly, they're waging it for what they can get. Else little folk like
205   me wouldn't be in it at all.

THE COOK: That's the way it is.

THE CHAPLAIN: As a Dutchman you'd do better to glance at the
         flag above your head before venting your opinions here in
         Poland.

210 MOTHER COURAGE: All good Lutherans here. Prosit!

(KATTRIN *has put on* YVETTE's *hat and begun strutting around in
imitation of her way of walking.*)

(*Suddenly there is a noise of cannon fire and shooting. Drums.*
MOTHER COURAGE, *the* COOK *and the* CHAPLAIN *rush out from
behind the cart, the two last-named still carrying their glasses. The*
ARMOURER *and another* SOLDIER *run up to the cannon and try to
push it away.*)

MOTHER COURAGE: What's happening? Wait till I've taken my
         washing down, you louts! (*She tries to rescue her washing.*)

THE ARMOURER: The Catholics! Broken through. Don't know if
         we'll get out of here. (*To the* SOLDIER.) Get that gun shifted!   215
         (*Runs on.*)

THE COOK: God, I must find the general. Courage, I'll drop by
         in a day or two for another talk.

MOTHER COURAGE: Wait, you forgot your pipe.

THE COOK: (*In the distance.*) Keep it for me. I'll be needing it.

MOTHER COURAGE: Would happen just as we're making a bit   220
         of money.

THE CHAPLAIN: Ah well, I'll be going too. Indeed, if the enemy
         is so close as that it might be dangerous. Blessèd are the
         peacemakers is the motto in wartime. If only I had a cloak
         to cover me.   225

MOTHER COURAGE: I ain't lending no cloaks, not on your life.
         I been had too often.

THE CHAPLAIN: But my faith makes it particularly dangerous
         for me.

MOTHER COURAGE: (*Gets him a cloak.*) Goes against my   230
         conscience, this does. Now you run along.

THE CHAPLAIN: Thank you, dear lady, that's very generous of
         you, but I think it might be wiser for me to remain seated here;
         it could arouse suspicion and bring the enemy down on me
         if I were seen to run.   235

MOTHER COURAGE: (*To the* SOLDIER.) Leave it, you fool, who's
         going to pay you for that? I'll look after it for you, you're
         risking your neck.

THE SOLDIER: (*Running away.*) You can tell 'em I tried.

MOTHER COURAGE: Cross my heart. (*Sees her daughter with*   240
         the hat.) What you doing with that strumpet's hat? Take
         that lid off, you gone crazy? And the enemy arriving any
         minute! (*Pulls the hat off* KATTRIN's *head.*) Want 'em to
         pick you up and make a prostitute of you? And she's gone
         and put those boots on, whore of Babylon! Off with those   245
         boots! (*Tries to tug them off her.*) Jesus Christ, chaplain,
         gimme a hand, get those boots off her, I'll be right back.
         (*Runs to the cart.*)

YVETTE: (*Arrives, powdering her face.*) Fancy that, the Catholics
         are coming. Where's my hat? Who's been kicking it around?   250
         I can't go about looking like this if the Catholics are
         coming. What'll they think of me? No mirror either. (*To the*
         CHAPLAIN.) How do I look? Too much powder?

THE CHAPLAIN: Exactly right.

YVETTE: And where are them red boots? (*Fails to find them*   255
         as KATTRIN *hides her feet under her skirt.*) I left them here
         all right. Now I'll have to get to me tent barefoot. It's an
         outrage.

(*Exit.*)

(SWISS CHEESE *runs in carrying in a small box.*)

MOTHER COURAGE: (*Arrives with her hands full of ashes. To*
         KATTRIN.) Here some ashes. (*To* SWISS CHEESE.) What's   260
         that you're carrying?

SWISS CHEESE: Regimental cash box.

MOTHER COURAGE: Chuck it away. No more paymastering for you.

265 SWISS CHEESE: I'm responsible. (*He goes to the rear.*)

MOTHER COURAGE: (*To the* CHAPLAIN.) Take your clerical togs off, padre, or they'll spot you under that cloak. (*She rubs* KATTRIN*'s face with ash.*) Keep still, will you? There you are, a bit of muck and you'll be safe. What a disaster. Sentries were
270 drunk. Hide your light under a bushel, it says. Take a soldier, specially a Catholic one, add a clean face, and there's your instant whore. For weeks they get nowt to eat, then soon as they manage to get it by looting they're falling on anything in skirts. That ought to do. Let's have a look. Not bad. Looks like
275 you been grubbing in muckheap. Stop trembling. Nothing'll happen to you like that. (*To* SWISS CHEESE.) Where d'you leave cash box?

SWISS CHEESE: Thought I'd put it in cart.

MOTHER COURAGE: (*Horrified.*) What, my cart? Sheer criminal
280 idiocy. Only take me eyes off you one instant. Hang us all three, they will.

SWISS CHEESE: I'll put it somewhere else then, or clear out with it.

MOTHER COURAGE: You sit on it, it's too late now.

285 THE CHAPLAIN: (*Who is changing his clothes downstage.*) For heaven's sake, the flag!

MOTHER COURAGE: (*Hauls down the regimental flag.*) Bozhe moi! I'd given up noticing it were there. Twenty-five years I've had it.

(*The thunder of cannon intensifies.*)

(*A morning three days later. The cannon has gone.* MOTHER COURAGE, KATTRIN, *the* CHAPLAIN *and* SWISS CHEESE *are sitting gloomily over a meal.*)

290 SWISS CHEESE: That's three days I been sitting around with nowt to do, and sergeant's always been kind to me but any moment now he'll start asking where's Swiss Cheese with the pay box?

MOTHER COURAGE: You thank your stars they ain't after you.

295 THE CHAPLAIN: What can I say? I can't even hold a service here, it might make trouble for me. Whosoever hath a full heart, his tongue runneth over, it says, but heaven help me if mine starts running over.

MOTHER COURAGE: That's how it goes. Here they sit, one with
300 his faith and the other with his cash box. Dunno which is more dangerous.

THE CHAPLAIN: We are all of us in God's hands.

MOTHER COURAGE: Oh, I don't think it's as bad as that yet, though I must say I can't sleep nights. If it weren't for you,
305 Swiss Cheese, things'd be easier. I think I got meself cleared. I told 'em I didn't hold with Antichrist, the Swedish one with horns on, and I'd observed left horn was a bit unserviceable. Half way through their interrogation I asked where I could get church candles not too dear. I knows the lingo cause
310 Swiss Cheese's dad were Catholic, often used to make jokes about it, he did. They didn't believe me all that much, but they ain't got no regimental canteen lady. So they're winking an eye. Could turn out for the best, you know. We're prisoners, but same like fleas on dog.

THE CHAPLAIN: That's good milk. But we'll need to cut down
315 our Swedish appetites a bit. After all, we've been defeated.

MOTHER COURAGE: Who's been defeated? Look, victory and defeat ain't bound to be same for the big shots up top as for them below, not by no means. Can be times the bottom lot find a defeat really pays them. Honour's lost, nowt else. I remember
320 once up in Livonia our general took such a beating from enemy I got a horse off our baggage train in the confusion, pulled me cart seven months, he did, before we won and they checked up. As a rule you can say victory and defeat both come expensive to us ordinary folk. Best thing for us is when
325 politics get bogged down solid. (*To* SWISS CHEESE.) Eat up.

SWISS CHEESE: Got no appetite for it. What's sergeant to do when pay day comes round?

MOTHER COURAGE: They don't have pay days on a retreat.

SWISS CHEESE: It's their right, though. They needn't retreat if
330 they don't get paid. Needn't stir a foot.

MOTHER COURAGE: Swiss Cheese, you're that conscientious it makes me quite nervous. I brought you up to be honest, you not being clever, but you got to know where to stop. Chaplain and me, we're off now to buy Catholic flag and
335 some meat. Dunno anyone so good at sniffing meat, like sleepwalking it is, straight to target. I'd say he can pick out a good piece by the way his mouth starts watering. Well, thank goodness they're letting me go on trading. You don't ask tradespeople their faith but their prices. And Lutheran
340 trousers keep cold out too.

THE CHAPLAIN: What did the mendicant say when he heard the Lutherans were going to turn everything in town and country topsy-turvy? 'They'll always need beggars'. (MOTHER COURAGE *disappears into the cart.*) So she's still
345 worried about the cash box. So far they've taken us all for granted as part of the cart, but how long for?

SWISS CHEESE: I can get rid of it.

THE CHAPLAIN: That's almost more dangerous. Suppose you're seen. They have spies. Yesterday a fellow popped up out of
350 the ditch in front of me just as I was relieving myself first thing. I was so scared I only just suppressed an ejaculatory prayer. That would have given me away all right. I think what they'd like best is to go sniffing people's excrement to see if they're Protestants. The spy was a little runt with a patch over
355 one eye.

MOTHER COURAGE: (*Clambering out of the cart with a basket.*) What have I found, you shameless creature? (*She holds up the red boots in triumph.*) Yvette's red high-heeled boots! Coolly went and pinched them, she did. Cause you put it in her head
360 she was an enchanting young person. (*She lays them in the basket.*) I'm giving them back. Stealing Yvette's boots! She's wrecking herself for money. That's understandable. But you'd do it for nothing, for pleasure. What did I tell you: you're to wait till it's peace. No soldiers for you. You're not to start
365 exhibiting yourself till it's peacetime.

THE CHAPLAIN: I don't find she exhibits herself.

MOTHER COURAGE: Too much for my liking. Let her be like a stone in Dalecarlia, where there's nowt else, so folk say 'Can't see that cripple', that's how I'd lief have her. Then nowt'll
370 happen to her. (*To* SWISS CHEESE.) You leave that box where it is, d'you hear? And keep an eye on your sister, she needs it. The pair of you'll have me in grave yet. Sooner be minding a bagful of fleas.

(She leaves with the CHAPLAIN. KATTRIN *clears away the dishes.)*

375 SWISS CHEESE: Won't be able to sit out in the sun in shirt-sleeves much longer. (KATTRIN *points at a tree.*) Aye, leaves turning yellow. (KATTRIN *asks by gestures if he wants a drink.*) Don't want no drink. I'm thinking. *(Pause.)* Said she can't sleep.
380 Best if I got rid of that box, found a good place for it. All right, let's have a glass. (KATTRIN *goes behind the cart.*) I'll stuff it down the rat-hole by the river for the time being. Probably pick it up tonight before first light and take it to Regiment. How far can they have retreated in three days? Bet sergeant's surprised. I'm agreeably disappointed in you, Swiss Cheese,
385 he'll say. I make you responsible for the cash, and you go and bring it back.

(As KATTRIN *emerges from behind the cart with a full glass in her hand, two men confront her. One is a* SERGEANT, *the other doffs his hat to her. He has a patch over one eye.)*

THE MAN WITH THE PATCH: God be with you, mistress. Have you seen anyone round here from Second Finnish Regimental Headquarters?

*(*KATTRIN, *badly frightened, runs downstage, spilling the brandy. The two men look at one another, then withdraw on seeing* SWISS CHEESE *sitting there.)*

390 SWISS CHEESE: *(Interrupted in his thoughts.)* You spilt half of it. What are those faces for? Jabbed yourself in eye? I don't get it. And I'll have to be off, I've thought it over, it's the only way. *(He gets up. She does everything possible to make him realise the danger. He only shrugs her off.)* Wish I knew what you're
395 trying to say. Sure you mean well, poor creature, just can't get words out. What's it matter your spilling my brandy, I'll drink plenty more glasses yet, what's one more or less? *(He gets the box from the cart and takes it under his tunic.)* Be back in a moment. Don't hold me up now, or I'll be angry. I know you
400 mean well. Too bad you can't speak.

(As she tries to hold him back he kisses her and tears himself away. Exit. She is desperate, running hither and thither uttering little noises. The CHAPLAIN *and* MOTHER COURAGE *return.* KATTRIN *rushes to her mother.)*

MOTHER COURAGE: What's all this? Pull yourself together, love. They done something to you? Where's Swiss Cheese? Tell it me step by step, Kattrin. Mother understands you. What, so that bastard did take the box? I'll wrap it round his ears, the
405 little hypocrite. Take your time and don't gabble, use your hands, I don't like it when you howl like a dog, what'll his reverence say? Makes him uncomfortable. What, a one-eyed man came along?
THE CHAPLAIN: That one-eyed man is a spy. Have they arrested
410 Swiss Cheese? (KATTRIN *shakes her head, shrugs her shoulders.*) We're done for.
MOTHER COURAGE: *(Fishes in her basket and brings out a Catholic flag, which the* CHAPLAIN *fixes to the mast.)* Better hoist new flag.
415 THE CHAPLAIN: *(Bitterly.)* All good Catholics here.

(Voices are heard from the rear. The two men bring in SWISS CHEESE.)*

SWISS CHEESE: Let me go, I got nowt. Don't twist my shoulder, I'm innocent.
SERGEANT: Here's where he came from. You know each other.
MOTHER COURAGE: Us? How?
SWISS CHEESE: I don't know her. Got no idea who she is, had 420 nowt to do with them. I bought me dinner here, ten hellers it cost. You might have seen me sitting here, it was too salty.
SERGEANT: Who are you people, eh?
MOTHER COURAGE: We're law-abiding folk. That's right, he 425 bought a dinner. Said it was too salty.
SERGEANT: Trying to pretend you don't know each other, that it?
MOTHER COURAGE: Why should I know him? Can't know everyone. I don't go asking 'em what they're called and are 430 they a heretic; if he pays he ain't a heretic. You a heretic?
SWISS CHEESE: Go on.
THE CHAPLAIN: He sat there very properly, never opening his mouth except when eating. Then he had to.
SERGEANT: And who are you? 435
MOTHER COURAGE: He's just my potboy. Now I expect you gentlemen are thirsty, I'll get you a glass of brandy, you must be hot and tired with running.
SERGEANT: No brandy on duty. *(To* SWISS CHEESE.*)* You were carrying something. Must have hidden it by the river. Was a 440 bulge in your tunic when you left here.
MOTHER COURAGE: You sure it was him?
SWISS CHEESE: You must be thinking of someone else. I saw someone bounding off with a bulge in his tunic. I'm the wrong man. 445
MOTHER COURAGE: I'd say it was a misunderstanding too, such things happen. I'm a good judge of people, I'm Courage, you heard of me, everyone knows me, and I tell you that's an honest face he has.
SERGEANT: We're on the track of the Second Finnish Regiment's 450 cash box. We got the description of the fellow responsible for it. Been trailing him two days. It's you.
SWISS CHEESE: It's not me.
SERGEANT: And you better cough it up, or you're a goner, you know. Where is it? 455
MOTHER COURAGE: *(Urgently.)* Of course he'd give it over rather than be a goner. Right out he'd say: I got it, here it is, you're too strong. He ain't all that stupid. Speak up, stupid idiot, here's the sergeant giving you a chance.
SWISS CHEESE: S'pose I ain't got it. 460
SERGEANT: Then come along. We'll get it out of you. *(They lead him off.)*
MOTHER COURAGE: *(Calls after them.)* He'd tell you. He's not that stupid. And don't you twist his shoulder! *(Runs after them.)* 465

(Evening of the same day. The CHAPLAIN *and dumb* KATTRIN *are cleaning glasses and polishing knives.)*

THE CHAPLAIN: Cases like that, where somebody gets caught, are not unknown in religious history. It reminds me of the Passion of Our Lord and Saviour. There's an old song about that. *(He sings the Song of the Hours.)*

---

469 **Song of the Hours** translated by Ralph Manheim

470 In the first hour Jesus mild
   Who had prayed since even
   Was betrayed and led before
   Pontius the heathen.

   Pilate found him innocent
475 Free from fault and error
   Therefore, having washed his hands
   Sent him to King Herod.

   In the third hour he was scourged
   Stripped and clad in scarlet
480 And a plaited crown of thorns
   Set upon his forehead.

   On the Son of Man they spat
   Mocked him and made merry.
   Then the cross of death was brought
485 Given him to carry.

   At the sixth hour with two thieves
   To the cross they nailed him
   And the people and the thieves
   Mocked him and reviled him.

490 This is Jesus King of Jews
   Cried they in derision
   Till the sun withdrew its light
   From that awful vision.

   At the ninth hour Jesus wailed
495 Why hast thou me forsaken?
   Soldiers brought him vinegar
   Which he left untaken.

   Then he yielded up the ghost
   And the earth was shaken.
500 Rended was the temple's veil
   And the saints were wakened.

   Soldiers broke the two thieves' legs
   As the night descended.
   Thrust a spear in Jesus' side
505 When his life had ended.

   Still they mocked, as from his wound
   Flowed the blood and water
   And blasphemed the Son of Man
   With their cruel laughter.

510 MOTHER COURAGE: (*Entering excitedly.*) It's touch and go. They say sergeant's open to reason though. Only we mustn't let on it's Swiss Cheese else they'll say we helped him. It's a matter of money, that's all. But where's money to come from? Hasn't Yvette been round? I ran into her, she's got her hooks on some 515 colonel, maybe he'd buy her a canteen business.
  THE CHAPLAIN: Do you really wish to sell?
  MOTHER COURAGE: Where's money for sergeant to come from?
  THE CHAPLAIN: What'll you live on, then?
  MOTHER COURAGE: That's just it.

(YVETTE POTTIER *arrives with an extremely ancient* COLONEL.)

520 YVETTE: (*Embracing* MOTHER COURAGE.) My dear Courage, fancy seeing you so soon. (*Whispers.*) He's not unwilling. (*Aloud.*) This is my good friend who advises me in business

matters. I happened to hear you wanted to sell your cart on account of circumstances. I'll think it over.
 MOTHER COURAGE: Pledge it, not sell, just not too much hurry, 525 'tain't every day you find a cart like this in wartime.
 YVETTE: (*Disappointed.*) Oh, pledge. I thought it was for sale. I'm not so sure I'm interested. (*To the* COLONEL.) How do you feel about it?
 THE COLONEL: Just as you feel, pet. 530
 MOTHER COURAGE: I'm only pledging it.
 YVETTE: I thought you'd got to have the money.
 MOTHER COURAGE: (*Firmly.*) I got to have it, but sooner run myself ragged looking for a bidder than sell outright. And why? The cart's our livelihood. It's a chance for you, Yvette; 535 who knows when you'll get another like it and have a special friend to advise you, am I right?
 YVETTE: Yes, my friend thinks I should clinch it, but I'm not sure. If it's only a pledge . . . so you agree we ought to buy outright? 540
 THE COLONEL: I agree, pet.
 MOTHER COURAGE: Best look and see if you can find anything for sale then; maybe you will if you don't rush it, take your friend along with you, say a week or fortnight, might find something suits you. 545
 YVETTE: Then let's go looking. I adore going around looking for things, I adore going around with you, Poldi, it's such fun, isn't it? No matter if it takes a fortnight. How soon would you pay the money back if you got it?
 MOTHER COURAGE: I'd pay back in two weeks, maybe one. 550
 YVETTE: I can't make up my mind, Poldi chéri, you advise me. (*Takes the* COLONEL *aside.*) She's got to sell, I know, no problem there. And there's that ensign, you know, the fair-haired one, he'd be glad to lend me the money. He's crazy about me, says there's someone I remind him of. What do 555 you advise?
 THE COLONEL: You steer clear of him. He's no good. He's only making use of you. I said I'd buy you something, didn't I, pussykins?
 YVETTE: I oughtn't to let you. Of course if you think the ensign 560 might try to take advantage . . . Poldi, I'll accept it from you.
 THE COLONEL: That's how I feel too.
 YVETTE: Is that your advice?
 THE COLONEL: That is my advice.
 YVETTE: (*To* COURAGE *once more.*) My friend's advice would 565 be to accept. Make me out a receipt saying the cart's mine once two weeks are up, with all its contents, we'll check it now, I'll bring the two hundred florins later. (*To the* COLONEL.) You go back to the camp, I'll follow, I got to check it all and see there's nothing missing from my cart. 570 (*She kisses him. He leaves. She climbs up on the cart.*) Not all that many boots, are there?
 MOTHER COURAGE: Yvette, it's no time for checking your cart, s'posing it is yours. You promised you'd talk to sergeant about Swiss Cheese, there ain't a minute to lose, they say in an hour 575 he'll be courtmartialled.
 YVETTE: Just let me count the shirts.
 MOTHER COURAGE: (*Pulling her down by the skirt.*) You bloody vampire. Swiss Cheese's life's at stake. And not a word about who's making the offer, for God's sake, pretend it's your 580 friend, else we're all done for cause we looked after him.
 YVETTE: I fixed to meet that one-eyed fellow in the copse, he should be there by now.

585 THE CHAPLAIN: It doesn't have to be the whole two hundred either, I'd go up to a hundred and fifty, that may be enough.

MOTHER COURAGE: Since when has it been your money? You kindly keep out of this. You'll get your hotpot all right, don't worry. Hurry up and don't haggle, it's life or death. (*Pushes* YVETTE *off.*)

590 THE CHAPLAIN: Far be it from me to interfere, but what are we going to live on? You're saddled with a daughter who can't earn her keep.

MOTHER COURAGE: I'm counting on regimental cash box, Mr. Clever. They'll allow it as his expenses.

595 THE CHAPLAIN: But will she get the message right?

MOTHER COURAGE: It's her interest I should spend her two hundred so she gets the cart. She's set on that, God knows how long that colonel of hers'll last. Kattrin, polish the knives, there's the pumice. And you, stop hanging round like Jesus 600 on Mount of Olives, get moving, wash them glasses, we'll have fifty or more of cavalry in tonight and I don't want to hear a lot of 'I'm not accustomed to having to run about, oh my poor feet, we never ran in church'. Thank the Lord they're corruptible. After all, they ain't wolves, just humans out for 605 money. Corruption in humans is same as compassion in God. Corruption's our only hope. Long as we have it there'll be lenient sentences and even an innocent man'll have a chance of being let off.

YVETTE: (*Comes in panting.*) They'll do it for two hundred. But 610 it's got to be quick. Soon be out of their hands. Best thing is I go right away to my colonel with the one-eyed man. He's admitted he had the box, they put the thumb-screws on him. But he chucked it in the river soon as he saw they were on his track. The box is a write-off. I'll go and get the money from 615 my colonel, shall I?

MOTHER COURAGE: Box is a write-off? How'm I to pay back two hundred then?

YVETTE: Oh, you thought you'd get it from the box, did you? And I was to be Joe Soap I suppose? Better not count on 620 that. You'll have to pay up if you want Swiss Cheese back, or would you sooner I dropped the whole thing so's you can keep your cart?

MOTHER COURAGE: That's something I didn't allow for. Don't worry, you'll get your cart, I've said goodbye to it, had it 625 seventeen years, I have. I just need a moment to think, it's bit sudden, what'm I to do, two hundred's too much for me, pity you didn't beat 'em down. Must keep a bit back, else any Tom, Dick and Harry'll be able to shove me in ditch. Go and tell them I'll pay hundred and twenty florins, else it's all off, either 630 way I'm losing me cart.

YVETTE: They won't do it. That one-eyed man's impatient already, keeps looking over his shoulder, he's so worked up. Hadn't I best pay them the whole two hundred?

MOTHER COURAGE: (*In despair.*) I can't pay that. Thirty years I 635 been working. She's twenty-five already, and no husband. I got her to think of too. Don't push me, I know what I'm doing. Say a hundred and twenty, or it's off.

YVETTE: It's up to you. (*Rushes off.*)

(*Without looking at either the* CHAPLAIN *or her daughter,* MOTHER COURAGE *sits down to help* KATTRIN *polish knives.*)

MOTHER COURAGE: Don't smash them glasses, they ain't ours 640 now. Watch what you're doing, you'll cut yourself. Swiss Cheese'll be back, I'll pay two hundred if it comes to the

pinch. You'll get your brother, love. For eighty florins we could fill a pack with goods and start again. Plenty of folk has to make do.

THE CHAPLAIN: The Lord will provide, it says. 645

MOTHER COURAGE: See they're properly dry. (*She cleans knives in silence.* KATTRIN *suddenly runs behind the cart, sobbing.*)

YVETTE: (*Comes running in.*) They won't do it. I told you so. The one-eyed man wanted to leave right away, said there was no point. He says he's just waiting for the drum-roll; that means 650 sentence has been pronounced. I offered a hundred and fifty. He didn't even blink. I had to convince him to stay there so's I could have another word with you.

MOTHER COURAGE: Tell him I'll pay the two hundred. Hurry! (YVETTE *runs off. They sit in silence. The* CHAPLAIN *has* 655 *stopped polishing the glasses.*) I reckon I bargained too long.

(*In the distance drumming is heard. The* CHAPLAIN *gets up and goes to the rear.* MOTHER COURAGE *remains seated. It grows dark. The drumming stops. It grows light once more.* MOTHER COURAGE *is sitting exactly as before.*)

YVETTE: (*Arrives, very pale.*) Well, you got what you asked for, with your haggling and trying to keep your cart. Eleven bullets they gave him, that's all. You don't deserve I should bother any more about you. But I did hear they don't believe 660 the box really is in the river. They've an idea it's here and anyhow that you're connected with him. They're going to bring him here, see if you gives yourself away when you sees him. Thought I'd better warn you so's you don't recognise him, else you'll all be for it. They're right on my heels, best 665 tell you quick. Shall I keep Kattrin away? (MOTHER COURAGE *shakes her head.*) Does she know? She mayn't have heard the drumming or know what it meant.

MOTHER COURAGE: She knows. Get her.

(YVETTE *fetches* KATTRIN, *who goes to her mother and stands beside her.* MOTHER COURAGE *takes her hand. Two lansequenets come carrying a stretcher with something lying on it covered by a sheet. The* SERGEANT *marches beside them. They set down the stretcher.*)

SERGEANT: Here's somebody we dunno the name of. It's got to 670 be listed, though, so everything's shipshape. He had a meal here. Have a look, see if you know him. (*He removes the sheet.*) Know him? (MOTHER COURAGE *shakes her head.*) What, never see him before he had that meal here? (MOTHER COURAGE *shakes her head.*) Pick him up. Chuck him in the pit. He's 675 got nobody knows him. (*They carry him away.*)

SCENE FOUR

| Mother Courage sings the Song of the Grand Capitulation. |

Outside an officer's tent.

MOTHER COURAGE *is waiting. A* CLERK *looks out of the tent.*

THE CLERK: I know you. You had a paymaster from the Lutherans with you, what was in hiding. I'd not complain if I were you.

MOTHER COURAGE: But I got a complaint to make. I'm innocent, would look as how I'd a bad conscience if I let this pass. 5

Slashed everything in me cart to pieces with their sabres, they did, then wanted I should pay five taler fine for nowt, I tell you, nowt.

THE CLERK: Take my tip, better shut up. We're short of canteens,
10 so we let you go on trading, specially if you got a bad conscience and pay a fine now and then.

MOTHER COURAGE: I got a complaint.

THE CLERK: Have it your own way. Then you must wait till the captain's free. (*Withdraws inside the tent.*)

15 YOUNG SOLDIER: (*Enters aggressively.*) Bouque la Madonne! Where's that bleeding pig of a captain what's took my reward money to swig with his tarts? I'll do him.

OLDER SOLDIER: (*Running after him.*) Shut up. They'll put you in irons.

20 YOUNG SOLDIER: Out of there, you thief! I'll slice you into pork chops, I will. Pocketing my prize money after I'd swum the river, only one in the whole squadron, and now I can't even buy meself a beer. I'm not standing for that. Come on out there so I can cut you up!

25 OLDER SOLDIER: Blessed Mother of God, he's asking for trouble.

MOTHER COURAGE: Is it some reward he weren't paid?

YOUNG SOLDIER: Lemme go, I'll slash you too while I'm at it.

OLDER SOLDIER: He rescued the colonel's horse and got no reward
30 for it. He's young yet, still wet behind the ears.

MOTHER COURAGE: Let him go, he ain't a dog you got to chain up. Wanting your reward is good sound sense. Why be a hero otherwise?

YOUNG SOLDIER: So's he can sit in there and booze. You're shit-
35 scared, the lot of you. I done something special and I want my reward.

MOTHER COURAGE: Don't you shout at me, young fellow. Got me own worries, I have; any road you should spare your voice, be needing it when captain comes, else there he'll be and you too
40 hoarse to make a sound, which'll make it hard for him to clap you in irons till you turn blue. People what shouts like that can't keep it up ever; half an hour, and they have to be rocked to sleep, they're so tired.

YOUNG SOLDIER: I ain't tired and to hell with sleep. I'm hungry.
45 They make our bread from acorns and hemp-seed, and they even skimp on that. He's whoring away my reward and I'm hungry. I'll do him.

MOTHER COURAGE: Oh I see, you're hungry. Last year that general of yours ordered you all off roads and across fields so corn
50 should be trampled flat; I could've got ten florins for a pair of boots s'pose I'd had boots and s'pose anyone'd been able to pay ten florins. Thought he'd be well away from that area this year, he did, but here he is, still there, and hunger is great. I see what you're angry about.

55 YOUNG SOLDIER: I won't have it, don't talk to me, it ain't fair and I'm not standing for that.

MOTHER COURAGE: And you're right; but how long? How long you not standing for unfairness? One hour, two hours? Didn't ask yourself that, did you, but it's the whole point, and why, once
60 you're in irons it's too bad if you suddenly finds you can put up with unfairness after all.

YOUNG SOLDIER: What am I listening to you for, I'd like to know? Bouque la Madonne, where's that captain?

MOTHER COURAGE: You been listening to me because you knows
65 it's like what I say, your anger has gone up in smoke already, it was just a short one and you needed a long one, but where you going to get it from?

YOUNG SOLDIER: Are you trying to tell me asking for my reward is wrong?

MOTHER COURAGE: Not a bit. I'm just telling you your anger 70
ain't long enough, it's good for nowt, pity. If you'd a long one I'd be trying to prod you on. Cut him up, the swine, would be my advice to you in that case; but how about if you don't cut him up cause you feels your tail going between your legs? Then I'd look silly and captain'd take 75
it out on me.

OLDER SOLDIER: You're perfectly right, he's just a bit crazy.

YOUNG SOLDIER: Very well, let's see if I don't cut him up. (*Draws his sword.*) When he arrives I'm going to cut him up.

THE CLERK: (*Looks out.*) The captain'll be here in one minute. 80
Sit down.

(*The* YOUNG SOLDIER *sits down.*)

MOTHER COURAGE: He's sitting now. See, what did I say? You're sitting now. Ah, how well they know us, no one need tell 'em how to go about it. Sit down! and, bingo, we're sitting. And sitting and sedition don't mix. Don't try to stand up, you 85
won't stand the way you was standing before. I shouldn't worry about what I think; I'm no better, not one moment. Bought up all our fighting spirit, they have. Eh? S'pose I kick back, might be bad for business. Let me tell you a thing or two about the Grand Capitulation. (*She sings the Song of the* 90
Grand Capitulation.)

Back when I was young, I was brought to realise
What a very special person I must be
(Not just any old cottager's daughter, what with my looks and
my talents and my urge towards Higher Things)
And insisted that my soup should have no hairs in it. 95
No one makes a sucker out of me!
(All or nothing, only the best is good enough, each man for
himself, nobody's telling *me* what to do.)
Then I heard a tit
Chirp: Wait a bit!
And you'll be marching with the band 100
In step, responding to command
And striking up your little dance:
Now we advance.
And now: parade, form square!
Then men swear God's there— 105
Not the faintest chance!

In no time at all anyone who looked could see
That I'd learned to take my medicine with good grace.
(Two kids on my hands and look at the price of bread,
and things they expect of you!)
When they finally came to feel that they were through 110
with me
They'd got me grovelling on my face.
(Takes all sorts to make a world, you scratch my back and
I'll scratch yours, no good banging your head against
a brick wall.)
Then I heard that tit
Chirp: Wait a bit!
And you'll be marching with the band 115
In step, responding to command
And striking up your little dance:
Now they advance.
And now: parade, form square!

120   Then men swear God's there—
        Not the faintest chance!

        I've known people tried to storm the summits:
        There's no star too bright or seems too far away.
        (Dogged does it, where there's a will there's a way, by
            hook or by crook.)
125   As each peak disclosed fresh peaks to come, it's
        Strange how much a plain straw hat could weigh.
        (You have to cut your coat according to your cloth.)
        Then I hear the tit
        Chirp: Wait a bit!
130   And they'll be marching with the band
            In step, responding to command
            And striking up their little dance:
            Now they advance
            And now: parade, form square!
135   Then men swear God's there—
        Not the faintest chance!

MOTHER COURAGE: (*To the* YOUNG SOLDIER.) That's why I reckon
    you should stay there with your sword drawn if you're
    truly set on it and your anger's big enough, because you got
140   grounds, I agree, but if your anger's a short one best leave
    right away.
YOUNG SOLDIER: Oh stuff it. (*He staggers off with the* OLDER
    SOLDIER *following.*)
THE CLERK: (*Sticks his head out.*) Captain's here now. You can
145   make your complaint.
MOTHER COURAGE: I changed me mind. I ain't complaining.
    (*Exit.*)

SCENE FIVE

Two years have gone by. The war is spreading to new areas.
Ceaselessly on the move, Courage's little cart crosses
Poland, Moravia, Bavaria, Italy, then Bavaria again. 1631.
Tilly's victory at Magdeburg costs Mother Courage four
officers' shirts.

MOTHER COURAGE's *cart has stopped in a badly shot-up village.
Thin military music in the distance. Two* SOLDIERS *at the bar being
served by* KATTRIN *and* MOTHER COURAGE. *One of them has a
lady's fur coat over his shoulders.*

MOTHER COURAGE: Can't pay, that it? No money, no schnapps.
    They give us victory parades, but catch them giving men
    their pay.
FIRST SOLDIER: I want my schnapps. I missed the looting. That
5   double-crossing general only allowed an hour's looting in
    the town. He ain't an inhuman monster, he said. Town must
    of paid him.
THE CHAPLAIN: (*Stumbles in.*) There are people still lying in
    that yard. The peasant's family. Somebody give me a hand.
10   I need linen.

(*The* SECOND SOLDIER *goes off with him.* KATTRIN *becomes very
excited and tries to make her mother produce linen.*)

MOTHER COURAGE: I got none. All my bandages was sold to
    regiment. I ain't tearing up my officer's shirts for that lot.
THE CHAPLAIN: (*Calling back.*) I need linen, I tell you.
MOTHER COURAGE: (*Blocking* KATTRIN's *way into the cart by
    sitting on the step.*) I'm giving nowt. They'll never pay, and   15
    why, nowt to pay with.
THE CHAPLAIN: (*Bending over a woman he has carried in.*) Why
    d'you stay around during the gunfire?
PEASANT WOMAN: (*Feebly.*) Farm.
MOTHER COURAGE: Catch them abandoning anything. But now   20
    I'm s'posed to foot the bill. I won't do it.
FIRST SOLDIER: Those are Protestants. What they have to be
    Protestants for?
MOTHER COURAGE: They ain't bothering about faith. They lost
    their farm.   25
SECOND SOLDIER: They're no Protestants. They're Catholics
    like us.
FIRST SOLDIER: No way of sorting 'em out in a bombardment.
A PEASANT: (*Brought in by the* CHAPLAIN.) My arm's gone.
THE CHAPLAIN: Where's that linen?   30
MOTHER COURAGE: I can't give nowt. What with expenses, taxes,
    loan interest and bribes. (*Making guttural noises,* KATTRIN
    raises a plank and threatens her mother with it.) You gone
    plain crazy? Put that plank away or I'll paste you one, you
    cow. I'm giving nowt, don't want to, got to think of meself.   35
    (*The* CHAPLAIN *lifts her off the steps and sets her on the ground,
    then starts pulling out shirts and tearing them into strips.*) My
    officers' shirts! Half a florin apiece! I'm ruined. (*From the
    house comes the cry of a child in pain.*)
THE PEASANT: The baby's in there still. (KATTRIN *dashes in.*)   40
THE CHAPLAIN: (*To the woman.*) Don't move. They'll get it out.
MOTHER COURAGE: Stop her, roof may fall in.
THE CHAPLAIN: I'm not going back in there.
MOTHER COURAGE: (*Torn both ways.*) Don't waste my pre-
    cious linen.   45

(KATTRIN *brings a baby out of the ruins.*)

MOTHER COURAGE: How nice, found another baby to cart
    around? Give it to its ma this instant, unless you'd have
    me fighting for hours to get it off you, like last time, d'you
    hear? (*To the* SECOND SOLDIER.) Don't stand there gawping,
    you go back and tell them cut out that music, we can see   50
    it's a victory with our own eyes. All your victories mean
    to me is losses.
THE CHAPLAIN: (*Tying a bandage.*) Blood's coming through.

(KATTRIN *is rocking the baby and making lullaby noises.*)

MOTHER COURAGE: Look at her, happy as a queen in all this
    misery; give it back at once, its mother's coming round. (*She   55
    catches the* FIRST SOLDIER, *who has been attacking the drinks
    and is trying to make off with one of the bottles.*) Psia krew!
    Thought you'd score another victory, you animal? Now pay.
FIRST SOLDIER: I got nowt.
MOTHER COURAGE: (*Pulling the fur coat off his back.*) Then leave   60
    that coat, it's stolen any road.
THE CHAPLAIN: There's still someone under there.

SCENE SIX

Outside the Bavarian town of Ingolstadt Courage participates in the funeral of the late Imperial commander Tilly. Discussions are held about war heroes and the war's duration. The Chaplain complains that his talents are lying fallow, and dumb Kattrin gets the red boots. The year is 1632.

Inside a canteen tent.

It has a bar towards the rear. Rain. Sound of drums and Funeral music. The CHAPLAIN *and the regimental* CLERK *are playing a board game.* MOTHER COURAGE *and her daughter are stocktaking.*

THE CHAPLAIN: Now the funeral procession will be moving off.

MOTHER COURAGE: Too bad about commander in chief—
twenty-two pairs those socks—he fell by accident, they say. Mist over fields, that was the trouble. General had just

5   been haranguing a regiment saying they must fight to last man and last round, he was riding back when mist made him lose direction so he was up front and a bullet got him in midst of battle—only four hurricane lamps left. (*A whistle from the rear. She goes to the bar.*) You scrimshankers,

10   dodging your commander in chief's funeral, scandal I call it. (*Pours drinks.*)

THE CLERK: They should never of paid troops out before the funeral. Instead of going now they're all getting pissed.

THE CHAPLAIN: (*To the* CLERK.) Aren't you supposed to go to

15   the funeral?

THE CLERK: Dodged it cause of the rain.

MOTHER COURAGE: It's different with you, your uniform might get wet. I heard they wanted to toll bells for funeral as usual, except it turned out all churches had been blown

20   to smithereens by his orders, so poor old commander in chief won't be hearing no bells as they let the coffin down. They're going to let off three salvoes instead to cheer things up—seventeen belts.

SHOUTS: (*From the bar.*) Hey, Missis, a brandy!

25 MOTHER COURAGE: Let's see your money. No, I ain't having you in my tent with your disgusting boots. You can drink outside, rain or no rain. (*To the* CLERK.) I'm only letting in sergeants and up. Commander in chief had been having his worries, they say. S'posed to have been trouble with Second

30   Regiment cause he stopped their pay, said it was a war of faith and they should do it for free. (*Funeral march. All look to the rear.*)

THE CHAPLAIN: Now they'll be filing past the noble corpse.

MOTHER COURAGE: Can't help feeling sorry for those generals

35   and emperors, there they are maybe thinking they're doing something extra special what folk'll talk about in years to come, and earning a public monument, like conquering the world for instance, that's a fine ambition for a general, how's he to know any better? I mean, he plagues hisself to death,

40   then it all breaks down on account of ordinary folk what just wants their beer and bit of a chat, nowt higher. Finest plans get bolloxed up by the pettiness of them as should be carrying them out, because emperors can't do nowt themselves, they just counts on soldiers and people to back 'em up whatever

45   happens, am I right?

THE CHAPLAIN: (*Laughs.*) Courage, you're right, aside from the soldiers. They do their best. Give me that lot outside there, for

instance, drinking their brandy in the rain, and I'd guarantee to make you one war after another for a hundred years if need be, and I'm no trained general.   50

MOTHER COURAGE: You don't think war might end, then?

THE CHAPLAIN: What, because the commander in chief's gone? Don't be childish. They're two a penny, no shortage of heroes.

MOTHER COURAGE: Ee, I'm not asking for fun of it, but because I'm thinking whether to stock up, prices are low now, but if   55 war's going to end it's money down the drain.

THE CHAPLAIN: I realise it's a serious question. There've always been people going round saying 'the war can't go on for ever'. I tell you there's nothing to stop it going on for ever. Of course there can be a bit of a breathing space. The war may   60 need to get its second wind, it may even have an accident so to speak. There's no guarantee against that; nothing's perfect on this earth of ours. A perfect war, the sort you might say couldn't be improved on, that's something we shall probably never see. It can suddenly come to a standstill for some quite   65 unforeseen reason, you can't allow for everything. A slight case of negligence, and it's bogged down up to the axles. And then it's a matter of hauling the war out of the mud again. But emperor and kings and popes will come to its rescue. So on the whole it has nothing serious to worry about, and will live   70 to a ripe old age.

A SOLDIER: (*Sings at the bar.*)

        A schnapps, landlord, you're late!
        A soldier cannot wait
        To do his emperor's orders.   75

Make it a double, this is a holiday.

MOTHER COURAGE: S'pose I went by what you say . . .

THE CHAPLAIN: Think it out for yourself. What's to compete with the war?

THE SOLDIER: (*At the rear.*)   80

        Your breast, my girl, you're late!
        A soldier cannot wait
        To ride across the borders.

THE CLERK: (*Unexpectedly.*) And what about peace? I'm from Bohemia and I'd like to go home some day.   85

THE CHAPLAIN: Would you indeed? Ah, peace. Where is the hole once the cheese has been eaten?

THE SOLDIER: (*At the rear.*)

        Lead trumps, my friend, you're late!
        A soldier cannot wait.   90
        His emperor needs him badly.

        Your blessing, priest, you're late!
        A soldier cannot wait.
        Must lay his life down gladly.

THE CLERK: In the long run life's impossible if there's no peace.   95

THE CHAPLAIN: I'd say there's peace in war too; it has its peaceful moments. Because war satisfies all requirements, peaceable ones included, they're catered for, and it would simply fizzle out if they weren't. In war you can do a crap like in the depths of peacetime, then between one battle and the next you   100 can have a beer, then even when you're moving up you can lay your head on your arms and have a bit of shuteye in the ditch, it's entirely possible. During a charge you can't play cards maybe, but nor can you in the depths of peacetime

105 when you're ploughing, and after a victory there are various openings. You may get a leg blown off, then you start by making a lot of fuss as though it were serious, but afterwards you calm down or get given a schnapps, and you end up hopping around and the war's no worse off than before.

110 And what's to stop you being fruitful and multiplying in the middle of all the butchery, behind a barn or something, in the long run you can't be held back from it, and then the war will have your progeny and can use them to carry on with. No, the war will always find an outlet, mark my words. Why

115 should it ever stop?

(KATTRIN *has ceased working and is staring at the* CHAPLAIN.)

MOTHER COURAGE: I'll buy fresh stock then. If you say so. (KATTRIN *suddenly flings a basket full of bottles to the ground and runs off.*) Kattrin! (*Laughs.*) Damn me if she weren't waiting for peace. I promised her she'd get a husband soon

120 as peace came. (*Hurries after her.*)

THE CLERK: (*Standing up.*) I won. You been talking too much. Pay up.

MOTHER COURAGE: (*Returning with* KATTRIN.) Don't be silly, war'll go on a bit longer, and we'll make a bit more money,

125 and peacetime'll be all the nicer for it. Now you go into town, that's ten minutes' walk at most, fetch things from Golden Lion, the expensive ones, we can fetch rest in cart later, it's all arranged, regimental clerk here will go with you. Nearly everybody's attending commander in chief's funeral, nowt

130 can happen to you. Careful now, don't let them steal nowt, think of your dowry.

(KATTRIN *puts a cloth over her head and leaves with the* CLERK.)

THE CHAPLAIN: Is that all right to let her go with the clerk?

MOTHER COURAGE: She's not that pretty they'd want to ruin her.

THE CHAPLAIN: I admire the way you run your business and

135 always win through. I see why they called you Courage.

MOTHER COURAGE: Poor folk got to have courage. Why, they're lost. Simply getting up in morning takes some doing in their situation. Or ploughing a field, and in a war at that. Mere fact they bring kids into world shows they got courage, cause

140 there's no hope for them. They have to hang one another and slaughter one another, so just looking each other in face must call for courage. Being able to put up with emperor and pope shows supernatural courage, cause those two cost 'em their lives. (*She sits down, takes a little pipe from her purse and*

145 *smokes.*) You might chop us a bit of kindling.

THE CHAPLAIN: (*Reluctantly removing his coat and preparing to chop up sticks.*) I happen to be a pastor of souls, not a woodcutter.

MOTHER COURAGE: I got no soul, you see. Need firewood, though.

150 THE CHAPLAIN: Where's that stumpy pipe from?

MOTHER COURAGE: Just a pipe.

THE CHAPLAIN: What d'you mean, 'just', it's a quite particular pipe, that.

MOTHER COURAGE: Aha?

155 THE CHAPLAIN: That stumpy pipe belongs to the Oxenstierna Regiment's cook.

MOTHER COURAGE: If you know that already why ask, Mr Clever?

THE CHAPLAIN: Because I didn't know if you were aware what

160 you're smoking. You might just have been rummaging around

in your things, come across some old pipe or other, and used it out of sheer absence of mind.

MOTHER COURAGE: And why not?

THE CHAPLAIN: Because you didn't. You're smoking that

165 deliberately.

MOTHER COURAGE: And why shouldn't I?

THE CHAPLAIN: Courage, I'm warning you. It's my duty. Probably you'll never clap eyes on the gentleman again, and that's no loss but your good fortune. He didn't make at all a reliable

170 impression on me. Quite the opposite.

MOTHER COURAGE: Really? Nice fellow that.

THE CHAPLAIN: So he's what you would call a nice fellow? I wouldn't. Far be it from me to bear him the least ill-will, but nice is not what I would call him. More like one of those Don

175 Juans, a slippery one. Have a look at that pipe if you don't believe me. You must admit it tells you a good deal about his character.

MOTHER COURAGE: Nowt that I can see. Worn out, I'd call it.

THE CHAPLAIN: Practically bitten through, you mean. A man of

180 wrath. That is the pipe of an unscrupulous man of wrath; you must see that if you have any discrimination left.

MOTHER COURAGE: Don't chop my chopping block in two.

THE CHAPLAIN: I told you I'm not a woodcutter by trade. I studied to be a pastor of souls. My talent and abilities are

185 being abused in this place, by manual labour. My God-given endowments are denied expression. It's a sin. You have never heard me preach. One sermon of mine can put a regiment in such a frame of mind it'll treat the enemy like a flock of sheep. Life to them is a smelly old foot-cloth

190 which they fling away in a vision of final victory. God has given me the gift of speech. I can preach so you'll lose all sense of sight and hearing.

MOTHER COURAGE: I don't wish to lose my sense of sight and hearing. Where'd that leave me?

195 THE CHAPLAIN: Courage, I have often thought that your dry way of talking conceals more than just a warm heart. You too are human and need warmth.

MOTHER COURAGE: Best way for us to get this tent warm is have plenty of firewood.

200 THE CHAPLAIN: Don't change the subject. Seriously, Courage, I sometimes ask myself what it would be like if our relationship were to become somewhat closer. I mean, given that the whirlwind of war has so strangely whirled us together.

MOTHER COURAGE: I'd say it was close enough. I cook meals for

205 you and you run around and chop firewood for instance.

THE CHAPLAIN: (*Coming closer.*) You know what I mean by closer; it's not a relationship founded on meals and woodchopping and other such base necessities. Let your head speak, harden thyself not.

210 MOTHER COURAGE: Don't you come at me with that axe. That'd be too close a relationship.

THE CHAPLAIN: You shouldn't make a joke of it. I'm a serious person and I've thought about what I'm saying.

MOTHER COURAGE: Be sensible, padre. I like you. I don't want

215 to row you. All I'm after is get myself and children through all this with my cart. I don't see it as mine, and I ain't in the mood for private affairs. Right now I'm taking a gamble, buying stores just when commander in chief's fallen and all the talk's of peace. Where d'you reckon you'd turn if I'm

220 ruined? Don't know, do you? You chop us some kindling wood, then we can keep warm at night, that's quite something

these times. What's this? (*She gets up. Enter* KATTRIN, *out of breath, with a wound above her eye. She is carrying a variety of stuff: parcels, leather goods, a drum and so on.*)

225 MOTHER COURAGE: What happened, someone assault you? On way back? She was assaulted on her way back. Bet it was that trooper was getting drunk here. I shouldn't have let you go, love. Drop that stuff. Not too bad, just a flesh wound you got. I'll bandage it and in a week it'll be all right. Worse than wild
230 beasts, they are. (*She ties up the wound.*)

THE CHAPLAIN: It's not them I blame. They never went raping back home. The fault lies with those that start wars, it brings humanity's lowest instincts to the surface.

MOTHER COURAGE: Calm down. Didn't clerk come back
235 with you? That's because you're respectable, they don't bother. Wound ain't a deep one, won't leave no mark. There you are, all bandaged up. You'll get something, love, keep calm. Something I put aside for you, wait till you see. (*She delves into a sack and brings out* YVETTE's *red high-*
240 *heeled boots.*) Made you open your eyes, eh? Something you always wanted. They're yours. Put 'em on quick, before I change me mind. Won't leave no mark, and what if it does? Ones I'm really sorry for's the ones they fancy. Drag them around till they're worn out, they do. Those they don't
245 care for they leaves alive. I seen girls before now had pretty faces, then in no time looking fit to frighten a hyaena. Can't even go behind a bush without risking trouble, horrible life they lead. Same like with trees, straight well-shaped ones get chopped down to make beams for houses and crooked ones
250 live happily ever after. So it's a stroke of luck for you really. Them boots'll be all right, I greased them before putting them away.

(KATTRIN *leaves the boots where they are and crawls into the cart.*)

THE CHAPLAIN: Let's hope she's not disfigured.
MOTHER COURAGE: She'll have a scar. No use her waiting for
255 peacetime now.
THE CHAPLAIN: She didn't let them steal the things.
MOTHER COURAGE: Maybe I shouldn't have dinned that into her so. Wish I knew what went on in that head of hers. Just once she stayed out all night, once in all those years.
260 Afterwards she went around like before, except she worked harder. Couldn't get her to tell what had happened. Worried me quite a while, that did. (*She collects the articles brought by* KATTRIN, *and sorts them angrily.*) That's war for you. Nice way to get a living!

(*Sound of cannon fire.*)

265 THE CHAPLAIN: Now they'll be burying the commander in chief. This is a historic moment.
MOTHER COURAGE: What I call a historic moment is them bashing my daughter over the eye. She's half wrecked already, won't get no husband now, and her so crazy about kids; any
270 road she's only dumb from war, soldier stuffed something in her mouth when she was little. As for Swiss Cheese I'll never see him again, and where Eilif is God alone knows. War be damned.

SCENE SEVEN

| Mother Courage at the peak of her business career. |

High road.

The CHAPLAIN, MOTHER COURAGE *and* KATTRIN *are pulling the cart, which is hung with new wares.* MOTHER COURAGE *is wearing a necklace of silver coins.*

MOTHER COURAGE: I won't have you folk spoiling my war for me. I'm told it kills off the weak, but they're write-off in peacetime too. And war gives its people a better deal. (*She sings.*)

> And if you feel your forces fading   5
> You won't be there to share the fruits.
> But what is war but private trading
> That deals in blood instead of boots?

And what's the use of settling down? Them as does are first to go. (*Sings.*)   10

> Some people think to live by looting
> The goods some others haven't got.
> You think it's just a line they're shooting
> Until you hear they have been shot.

> And some I saw dig six feet under   15
> In haste to lie down and pass out.
> Now they're at rest perhaps they wonder
> Just what was all their haste about.

(*They pull it further.*)

SCENE EIGHT

| The same year sees the death of the Swedish king Gustavus Adolphus at the battle of Lützen. Peace threatens to ruin Mother Courage's business. Courage's dashing son performs one heroic deed too many and comes to a sticky end. |

Camp.

A summer morning. In front of the cart stand an OLD WOMAN *and her son. The son* [YOUNG MAN] *carries a large sack of bedding.*

MOTHER COURAGE'S VOICE: (*From inside the cart.*) Does it need to be this ungodly hour?
THE YOUNG MAN: We walked twenty miles in the night and got to be back today.
MOTHER COURAGE'S VOICE: What am I to do with bedding?   5
Folk've got no houses.
THE YOUNG MAN: Best have a look first.
THE OLD WOMAN: This place is no good either. Come on.
THE YOUNG MAN: What, and have them sell the roof over our head for taxes? She might pay three florins if you throw in   10
the bracelet. (*Bells start ringing.*) Listen, mother.
VOICES: (*From the rear.*) Peace! Swedish king's been killed.
MOTHER COURAGE: (*Sticks her head out of the cart. She has not yet done her hair.*) What's that bell-ringing about in mid-week?
THE CHAPLAIN: (*Crawling out from under the cart.*) What are they   15
shouting? Peace?

MOTHER COURAGE: Don't tell me peace has broken out just after I laid in new stock.

THE CHAPLAIN: (*Calling to the rear.*) That true? Peace?

20 VOICES: Three weeks ago, they say, only no one told us.

THE CHAPLAIN: (*To* COURAGE.) What else would they be ringing the bells for?

VOICES: A whole lot of Lutherans have driven into town, they brought the news.

25 THE YOUNG MAN: Mother, it's peace. What's the matter?

(*The* OLD WOMAN *has collapsed.*)

MOTHER COURAGE: (*Speaking into the cart.*) Holy cow! Kattrin, peace! Put your black dress on, we're going to church. Least we can do for Swiss Cheese. Is it true, though?

THE YOUNG MAN: The people here say so. They've made peace.

30 Can you get up? (*The* OLD WOMAN *stands up dumbfounded.*) I'll get the saddlery going again, I promise. It'll all work out. Father will get his bedding back. Can you walk? (*To the* CHAPLAIN.) She came over queer. It's the news. She never thought there'd be peace again. Father always said so. We're

35 going straight home. (*They go off.*)

MOTHER COURAGE'S VOICE: Give her a schnapps.

THE CHAPLAIN: They've already gone.

MOTHER COURAGE'S VOICE: What's up in camp?

THE CHAPLAIN: They're assembling. I'll go on over. Shouldn't

40 I put on my clerical garb?

MOTHER COURAGE'S VOICE: Best check up before parading yourself as heretic. I'm glad about peace, never mind if I'm ruined. Any road I'll have got two of me children through the war. Be seeing Eilif again now.

45 THE CHAPLAIN: And who's that walking down the lines? Bless me, the army commander's cook.

THE COOK: (*Somewhat bedraggled and carrying a bundle.*) What do I behold? The padre!

THE CHAPLAIN: Courage, we've got company.

(MOTHER COURAGE *clambers out.*)

50 THE COOK: I promised I'd drop over for a little talk soon as I had the time. I've not forgotten your brandy, Mrs Fierling.

MOTHER COURAGE: Good grief, the general's cook! After all these years! Where's my eldest boy Eilif?

THE COOK: Hasn't he got here? He left before me, he was on his

55 way to see you too.

THE CHAPLAIN: I shall don my clerical garb, just a moment.

(*Goes off behind the cart.*)

MOTHER COURAGE: Then he may be here any minute. (*Calls into the cart.*) Kattrin, Eilif's on his way. Get cook a glass of brandy, Kattrin! (KATTRIN *does not appear.*) Drag your hair

60 down over it, that's all right. Mr Lamb's no stranger. (*Fetches the brandy herself.*) She don't like to come out, peace means nowt to her. Took too long coming, it did. They gave her a crack over one eye, you barely notice it now but she thinks folks are staring at her.

65 THE COOK: Ah yes. War. (*He and* MOTHER COURAGE *sit down.*)

MOTHER COURAGE: Cooky, you caught me at bad moment. I'm ruined.

THE COOK: What? That's hard.

MOTHER COURAGE: Peace'll wring my neck. I went and took Chaplain's advice, laid in fresh stocks only t'other day.

70 And now they're going to demobilise and I'll be left sitting on me wares.

THE COOK: What d'you want to go and listen to padre for? If I hadn't been in such a hurry that time, the Catholics arriving so quickly and all, I'd warned you against that man. All piss

75 and wind, he is. So he's the authority around here, eh?

MOTHER COURAGE: He's been doing washing-up for me and helping pull.

THE COOK: Him pull! I bet he told you some of those jokes of his too, I know him, got a very unhealthy view of

80 women, he has, all my good influence on him went for nowt. He ain't steady.

MOTHER COURAGE: You steady then?

THE COOK: Whatever else I ain't, I'm steady. Mud in your eye!

MOTHER COURAGE: Steady, that's nowt. I only had one steady

85 fellow, thank God. Hardest I ever had to work in me life; he flogged the kids' blankets soon as autumn came, and he called me mouth-organ an unchristian instrument. Ask me, you ain't saying much for yourself admitting you're steady.

THE COOK: Still tough as nails, I see; but that's what I like about

90 you.

MOTHER COURAGE: Now don't tell me you been dreaming of me nails.

THE COOK: Well, well, here we are, along with armistice bells and your brandy like what nobody else ever serves, it's famous,

95 that is.

MOTHER COURAGE: I don't give two pins for your armistice bells just now. Can't see 'em handing out all the back pay what's owing, so where does that leave me with my famous brandy? Had your pay yet?

100 THE COOK: (*Hesitantly.*) Not exactly. That's why we all shoved off. If that's how it is, I thought, I'll go and visit friends. So here I am sitting with you.

MOTHER COURAGE: Other words you got nowt.

THE COOK: High time they stopped that bloody clanging.

105 Wouldn't mind getting into some sort of trade. I'm fed up being cook to that lot. I'm s'posed to rustle them up meals out of tree roots and old bootsoles, then they fling the hot soup in my face. Cook these days is a dog's life. Sooner do war service, only of course it's peacetime now. (*He sees the*

110 CHAPLAIN *reappearing in his old garments.*) More about that later.

THE CHAPLAIN: It's still all right, only had a few moths in it.

THE COOK: Can't see why you bother. You won't get your old job back, who are you to inspire now to earn his pay honourably

115 and lay down his life? What's more I got a bone to pick with you, cause you advised this lady to buy a lot of unnecessary goods saying war would go on for ever.

THE CHAPLAIN: (*Heatedly.*) I'd like to know what concern that is of yours.

120 THE COOK: Because it's unscrupulous, that sort of thing is. How dare you meddle in other folks' business arrangements with your unwanted advice?

THE CHAPLAIN: Who's meddling? (*To* COURAGE.) I never knew this gentleman was such an intimate you had to account to

125 him for everything.

MOTHER COURAGE: Keep your hair on, cook's only giving his personal opinion and you can't deny your war was a flop.

THE CHAPLAIN: You should not blaspheme against peace,
130   Courage. You are a hyaena of the battlefield.
MOTHER COURAGE: I'm what?
THE COOK: If you're going to insult this lady you'll have to settle
        with me.
THE CHAPLAIN: It's not you I'm talking to. Your intentions
135   are only too transparent. (*To* COURAGE.) But when I see
        you picking up peace betwixt your finger and your thumb
        like some dirty old snot-rag, then my humanity feels out-
        raged; for then I see that you don't want peace but war,
        because you profit from it; in which case you shouldn't
140   forget the ancient saying that whosoever sups with the devil
        needs a long spoon.
MOTHER COURAGE: I got no use for war, and war ain't got much
        use for me. But I'm not being called no hyaena, you and me's
        through.
145 THE CHAPLAIN: Then why grumble about peace when every-
        body's breathing sighs of relief? Because of some old junk
        in your cart?
MOTHER COURAGE: My goods ain't old junk but what I lives by,
        and you too up to now.
150 THE CHAPLAIN: Off war, in other words. Aha.
THE COOK: (*To the* CHAPLAIN.) You're old enough to know it's
        always a mistake offering advice. (*To* COURAGE.) Way things
        are, your best bet's to get rid of certain goods quick as you can
        before prices hit rock-bottom. Dress yourself and get moving,
155   not a moment to lose.
MOTHER COURAGE: That ain't bad advice. I'll do that, I guess.
THE CHAPLAIN: Because cooky says it.
MOTHER COURAGE: Why couldn't you say it? He's right, I'd best
        go off to market. (*Goes inside the cart.*)
160 THE COOK: That's one to me, padre. You got no presence of mind.
        What you should of said was: what, me offer advice, all I done
        was discuss politics. Better not take me on. Cock-fighting
        don't suit that get-up.
THE CHAPLAIN: If you don't stop your gob I'll murder you, get-up
165   or no get-up.
THE COOK: (*Pulling off his boots and unwrapping his foot-cloths.*)
        Pity the war made such a godless shit of you, else you'd easily
        get another parsonage now it's peacetime. Cooks won't be
        needed, there's nowt to cook, but faith goes on just the same,
170   nowt changed in that direction.
THE CHAPLAIN: Mr Lamb, I'm asking you not to elbow me out.
        Since I came down in the world I've become a better person. I
        couldn't preach to anyone now.

(*Enter* YVETTE POTTIER *in black, dressed up to the nines, carrying
a cane. She is much older and fatter, and heavily powdered. She is
followed by a manservant.*)

YVETTE: Hullo there, everybody. Is this Mother Courage's
175   establishment?
THE CHAPLAIN: It is. And with whom have we the honour . . .?
YVETTE: With the Countess Starhemberg, my good man.
        Where's Courage?
THE CHAPLAIN: (*Calls into the cart.*) The Countess Starhemberg
180   wishes to speak to you.
MOTHER COURAGE'S VOICE: Just coming.
YVETTE: It's Yvette.
MOTHER COURAGE'S VOICE: Oh, Yvette!
YVETTE: Come to see how you are. (*Sees the* COOK *turn round*
185   *aghast.*) Pieter!

THE COOK: Yvette!
YVETTE: Well I never! How d'you come to be here?
THE COOK: Got a lift.
THE CHAPLAIN: You know each other then? Intimately?
YVETTE: I should think so. (*She looks the* COOK *over.*) Fat.   190
THE COOK: Not all that skinny yourself.
YVETTE: All the same I'm glad to see you, you shit. Gives me a
        chance to say what I think of you.
THE CHAPLAIN: You say it, in full; but don't start till Courage
        is out here.   195
MOTHER COURAGE: (*Coming out with all kinds of goods.*) Yvette!
        (*They embrace.*) But what are you in mourning for?
YVETTE: Suits me, don't it? My husband the colonel died a few
        years back.
MOTHER COURAGE: That old fellow what nearly bought the cart? 200
YVETTE: His elder brother.
MOTHER COURAGE: Then you're sitting pretty. Nice to find
        somebody what's made it in this war.
YVETTE: Up and down and up again, that's the way it went.
MOTHER COURAGE: I'm not hearing a word against colonels,   205
        they make a mint of money.
THE CHAPLAIN: I would put my boots back on if I were you.
        (*To* YVETTE.) You promised you would say what you think
        of the gentleman.
THE COOK: Don't kick up a stink here, Yvette.   210
MOTHER COURAGE: Yvette, this is a friend of mine.
YVETTE: That's old Puffing Piet.
THE COOK: Let's drop the nicknames. I'm called Lamb.
MOTHER COURAGE: (*Laughs.*) Puffing Piet! Him as made all the
        women crazy! Here, I been looking after your pipe for you.   215
THE CHAPLAIN: Smoking it, too.
YVETTE: What luck I can warn you against him. Worst of the lot,
        he was, rampaging along the whole Flanders coastline. Got
        more girls in trouble than he has fingers.
THE COOK: That's all a long while ago. 'Tain't true anyhow.   220
YVETTE: Stand up when a lady brings you into the conversation!
        How I loved this man! All the time he had a little dark girl
        with bandy legs, got her in trouble too of course.
THE COOK: Got you into high society more like, far as I can see.
YVETTE: Shut your trap, you pathetic remnant! Better watch out 225
        for him, though; fellows like that are still dangerous even
        when on their last legs.
MOTHER COURAGE: (*To* YVETTE.) Come along, got to get rid of
        my stuff afore prices start dropping. You might be able to put
        a word in for me at regiment, with your connections. (*Calls 230
        into the cart.*) Kattrin, church is off, I'm going to market
        instead. When Eilif turns up, one of you give him a drink.
        (*Exit with* YVETTE.)
YVETTE: (*As she leaves.*) Fancy a creature like that ever making
        me leave the straight and narrow path. Thank my lucky stars   235
        I managed to reach the top all the same. But I've cooked your
        goose, Puffing Piet, and that's something that'll be credited to
        me one day in the world to come.
THE CHAPLAIN: I would like to take as a text for our little talk
        'The mills of God grind slowly'. Weren't you complaining   240
        about my jokes?
THE COOK: Dead out of luck, I am. It's like this, you see: I thought
        I might get a hot meal. Here am I starving, and now they'll be
        talking about me and she'll get quite a wrong picture. I think
        I'll clear out before she's back.   245
THE CHAPLAIN: I think so too.

THE COOK: Padre, I'm fed up already with this bloody peace.
Human race has to go through fire and sword cause it's sinful
from the cradle up. I wish I could be roasting a fat capon once
250 again for the general, wherever he's got to, in mustard sauce
with a carrot or two.

THE CHAPLAIN: Red cabbage. Red cabbage for a capon.

THE COOK: You're right, but carrots was what he had to have.

THE CHAPLAIN: No sense of what's fitting.

255 THE COOK: Not that it stopped you guzzling your share.

THE CHAPLAIN: With misgivings.

THE COOK: Anyway you must admit those were the days.

THE CHAPLAIN: I might admit it if pressed.

THE COOK: Now you've called her a hyaena your days here are
260 finished. What you staring at?

THE CHAPLAIN: Eilif! (EILIF *arrives, followed by* SOLDIERS *with
pikes. His hands are fettered. His face is chalky-white.*) What's
wrong?

EILIF: Where's mother?

265 THE CHAPLAIN: Gone into town.

EILIF: I heard she was around. They've allowed me to come
and see her.

THE COOK: (*To the* SOLDIERS.) What you doing with him?

A SOLDIER: Something not nice.

270 THE CHAPLAIN: What's he been up to?

THE SOLDIER: Broke into a peasant's place. The wife's dead.

THE CHAPLAIN: How could you do a thing like that?

EILIF: It's what I did last time, ain't it?

THE COOK: Aye, but it's peace now.

275 EILIF: Shut up. All right if I sit down till she comes?

THE SOLDIER: We've no time.

THE CHAPLAIN: In wartime they recommended him for that, sat
him at the general's right hand. Dashing, it was, in those days.
Any chance of a word with the provost-marshal?

280 THE SOLDIER: Wouldn't do no good. Taking some peasant's cattle,
what's dashing about that?

THE COOK: Dumb, I call it.

EILIF: If I'd been dumb you'd of starved, clever bugger.

THE COOK: But as you were clever you're going to be shot.

285 THE CHAPLAIN: We'd better fetch Kattrin out anyhow.

EILIF: Sooner have a glass of schnapps, could do with that.

THE SOLDIER: No time, come along.

THE CHAPLAIN: And what shall we tell your mother?

EILIF: Tell her it wasn't any different, tell her it was the same
290 thing. Or tell her nowt. (*The* SOLDIERS *propel him away.*)

THE CHAPLAIN: I'll accompany you on your grievous journey.

EILIF: Don't need any bloody parsons.

THE CHAPLAIN: Wait and see. (*Follows him.*)

THE COOK: (*Calls after them.*) I'll have to tell her, she'll want
295 to see him.

THE CHAPLAIN: I wouldn't tell her anything. At most that he was
here and will come again, maybe tomorrow. By then I'll be
back and can break it to her. (*Hurries off.*)

(*The* COOK *looks after him, shaking his head, then walks restlessly
around. Finally he comes up to the cart.*)

THE COOK: Hoy! Don't you want to come out? I can under-
300 stand you hiding away from peace. Like to do the same
myself. Remember me, I'm general's cook? I was wondering if you'd a bit of something to eat while I wait for
your mum. I don't half feel like a bit of pork, or bread even,
just to fill the time. (*Peers inside.*) Head under blanket.
305 (*Sound of gunfire off.*)

MOTHER COURAGE: (*Runs in, out of breath and with all her goods
still.*) Cooky, peacetime's over. War's been on again three days
now. Heard news before selling me stuff, thank God. They're
having a shooting match with Lutherans in town. We must get
cart away at once. Kattrin, pack up! What you in the dumps 310
for? What's wrong?

THE COOK: Nowt.

MOTHER COURAGE: Something is. I see it way you look.

THE COOK: Cause war's starting up again, I s'pose. Looks as if
it'll be tomorrow night before I get next hot food inside me. 315

MOTHER COURAGE: You're lying, cooky.

THE COOK: Eilif was here. Had to leave almost at once, though.

MOTHER COURAGE: Was he now? Then we'll be seeing him on
march. I'm joining our side this time. How's he look?

THE COOK: Same as usual. 320

MOTHER COURAGE: Oh, he'll never change. Take more than
war to steal him from me. Clever, he is. You going to help
me get packed? (*Begins to pack up.*) What's his news? Still
in general's good books? Say anything about his deeds of
valour? 325

THE COOK: (*Glumly.*) Repeated one of them, I'm told.

MOTHER COURAGE: Tell it me later, we got to move off. (KATTRIN
appears.) Kattrin, peacetime's finished now. We're moving on.
(*To the* COOK.) How about you?

THE COOK: Have to join up again. 330

MOTHER COURAGE: Why don't you . . . Where's padre?

THE COOK: Went into town with Eilif.

MOTHER COURAGE: Then you come along with us a way. Need
somebody to help me.

THE COOK: That business with Yvette, you know . . . 335

MOTHER COURAGE: Done you no harm in my eyes. Opposite. Where there's smoke there's fire, they say. You coming along?

THE COOK: I won't say no.

MOTHER COURAGE: The Twelfth moved off already. Take the 340
shaft. Here's a bit of bread. We must get round behind to
Lutherans. Might even be seeing Eilif tonight. He's my
favourite one. Short peace, wasn't it? Now we're off again.
(*She sings as the* COOK *and* KATTRIN *harness themselves up.*)

From Ulm to Metz, from Metz to Munich 345
Courage will see the war gets fed.
The war will show a well-filled tunic
Given its daily shot of lead.
But lead alone can hardly nourish
It must have soldiers to subsist. 350
It's you it needs to make it flourish.
The war's still hungry. So enlist!

SCENE NINE

It is the seventeenth year of the great war of faith. Germany
has lost more than half her inhabitants. Those who survive
the bloodbath are killed off by terrible epidemics. Once fertile
areas are ravaged by famine, wolves roam the burnt-out
towns. In autumn 1634 we find Courage in the Fichtelgebirge,
off the main axis of the Swedish armies. The winter this
year is early and harsh. Business is bad, so that there is nothing
to do but beg. The cook gets a letter from Utrecht and is sent
packing.

Outside a semi-dilapidated parsonage.

Grey morning in early winter. Gusts of wind. MOTHER COURAGE *and the* COOK *in shabby sheepskins, drawing the cart.*

THE COOK: It's all dark, nobody up yet.

MOTHER COURAGE: Except it's parson's house. Have to crawl out of bed to ring bells. Then he'll have hot soup.

5 THE COOK: What from when whole village is burnt, we seen it.

MOTHER COURAGE: It's lived in, though, dog was barking.

THE COOK: S'pose parson's got, he'll give nowt.

MOTHER COURAGE: Maybe if we sing. . . .

10 THE COOK: I've had enough. (*Abruptly.*) Got a letter from Utrecht saying mother died of cholera and inn's mine. Here's letter if you don't believe me. No business of yours the way aunty goes on about my mode of existence, but have a look.

15 MOTHER COURAGE: (*Reads the letter.*) Lamb, I'm tired too of always being on the go. I feel like butcher's dog, dragging meat round customers and getting nowt off it. I got nowt left to sell, and folk got nowt left to buy nowt with. Saxony a fellow in rags tried landing me a stack of old books for two eggs, Württemberg they wanted to swap their plough for a

20 titchy bag of salt. What's to plough for? Nowt growing no more, just brambles. In Pomerania villages are s'posed to have started in eating the younger kids, and nuns have been caught sticking folk up.

THE COOK: World's dying out.

25 MOTHER COURAGE: Sometimes I sees meself driving through hell with me cart selling brimstone, or across heaven with packed lunches for hungry souls. Give me my kids what's left, let's find some place they ain't shooting, and I'd like a few more years undisturbed.

30 THE COOK: You and me could get that inn going, Courage, think it over. Made up me mind in the night, I did: back to Utrecht with or without you, and starting today.

MOTHER COURAGE: Have to talk to Kattrin. That's a bit quick for me; I'm against making decisions all freezing cold and nowt

35 inside you. Kattrin! (KATTRIN *climbs out of the cart.*) Kattrin, got something to tell you. Cook and I want to go to Utrecht. He's been left an inn there. That'd be a settled place for you, let you meet a few people. Lots of 'em respect somebody mature, looks ain't everything. I'd like it too. I get on with

40 cook. Say one thing for him, got a head for business. We'd have our meals for sure, not bad, eh? And your own bed too; like that, wouldn't you? Road's no life really. God knows how you might finish up. Lousy already, you are. Have to make up our minds, see, we could move with the Swedes, up north,

45 they're somewhere up that way. (*She points to the left.*) Reckon that's fixed, Kattrin.

THE COOK: Anna, I got something private to say to you.

MOTHER COURAGE: Get back in cart, Kattrin.

(KATTRIN *climbs back.*)

THE COOK: I had to interrupt, cause you don't understand,

50 far as I can see. I didn't think there was need to say it, sticks out a mile. But if it don't, then let me tell you straight, no question of taking her along, not on your life. You get me, eh.

(KATTRIN *sticks her head out of the cart behind them and listens.*)

MOTHER COURAGE: You mean I'm to leave Kattrin back here?

THE COOK: Use your imagination. Inn's got no room. It ain't

55 one of the sort got three bar parlours. Put our backs in it we two'll get a living, but not three, no chance of that. She can keep cart.

MOTHER COURAGE: Thought she might find husband in Utrecht.

60 THE COOK: Go on, make me laugh. Find a husband, how? Dumb and that scar on top of it. And at her age?

MOTHER COURAGE: Don't talk so loud.

THE COOK: Loud or soft, no getting over facts. And that's another reason why I can't have her in the inn. Customers

65 don't want to be looking at that all the time. Can't blame them.

MOTHER COURAGE: Shut your big mouth. I said not so loud.

THE COOK: Light's on in parson's house. We can try singing.

MOTHER COURAGE: Cooky, how's she to pull the cart on her

70 own? War scares her. She'll never stand it. The dreams she must have . . . I hear her nights groaning. Mostly after a battle. What's she seeing in those dreams, I'd like to know. She's got a soft heart. Lately I found she'd got another hedgehog tucked away what we'd run over.

75 THE COOK: Inn's too small. (*Calls out.*) Ladies and gentlemen, domestic staff and other residents! We are now going to give you a song concerning Solomon, Julius Caesar and other famous personages what had bad luck. So's you can see we're respectable folk, which makes it difficult to carry on,

80 particularly in winter. (*They sing.*)

> You saw sagacious Solomon
> You know what came of him.
> To him complexities seemed plain.
> He cursed the hour that gave birth to him
> And saw that everything was vain. 85
> How great and wise was Solomon!
> The world however didn't wait
> But soon observed what followed on.
> It's wisdom that had brought him to this state— 90
> How fortunate the man with none!

Yes, the virtues are dangerous stuff in this world, as this fine song proves, better not to have them and have a pleasant life and breakfast instead, hot soup for instance. Look at me: I haven't any but I'd like some. I'm a serving soldier but what 95 good did my courage do me in all them battles, nowt, here I am starving and better have been shit-scared and stayed at home. For why?

> You saw courageous Caesar next
> You know what he became. 100
> They deified him in his life
> Then had him murdered just the same.
> And as they raised the fatal knife
> How loud he cried: You too, my son!
> The world however didn't wait 105
> But soon observed what followed on.
> It's courage that had brought him to that state.
> How fortunate the man with none!

(*Sotto voce.*) Don't even look out. (*Aloud.*) Ladies and gentlemen, domestic staff and other inmates! All right, you 110 may say, gallantry never cooked a man's dinner, what about trying honesty? You can eat all you want then, or anyhow not stay sober. How about it?

You heard of honest Socrates
115 The man who never lied:
They weren't so grateful as you'd think
Instead the rulers fixed to have him tried
And handed him the poisoned drink.
How honest was the people's noble son!
120 The world however didn't wait
But soon observed what followed on.
It's honesty that brought him to that state.
How fortunate the man with none!

Ah yes, they say, be unselfish and share what you've got,
125 but how about if you got nowt? It's all very well to say
the dogooders have a hard time, but you still got to have
something. Aye, unselfishness is a rare virtue, cause it just
don't pay.

Saint Martin couldn't bear to see
130 His fellows in distress.
He met a poor man in the snow
And shared his cloak with him, we know.
Both of them therefore froze to death.
His place in Heaven was surely won!
135 The world however didn't wait
But soon observed what followed on.
Unselfishness had brought him to that state.
How fortunate the man with none!

That's how it is with us. We're respectable folk, stick together,
140 don't steal, don't murder, don't burn places down. And all
the time you might say we're sinking lower and lower, and it's
true what the song says, and soup is few and far between, and
if we weren't like this but thieves and murderers I dare say
we'd be eating our fill. For virtues aren't their own reward,
145 only wickednesses are, that's how the world goes and it didn't
ought to.

Here you can see respectable folk
Keeping to God's own laws.
So far he hasn't taken heed.
150 You who sit safe and warm indoors
Help to relieve our bitter need!
How virtuously we had begun!
The world however didn't wait
But soon observed what followed on.
155 It's fear of God that brought us to that state.
How fortunate the man with none!

VOICE: (*From above.*) Hey, you there! Come on up! There's hot
soup if you want.
MOTHER COURAGE: Lamb, me stomach won't stand nowt. 'Tain't
160 that it ain't sensible, what you say, but is that your last word?
We got on all right.
THE COOK: Last word. Think it over.
MOTHER COURAGE: I've nowt to think. I'm not leaving her here.
THE COOK: That's proper senseless, nothing I can do about it
165 though. I'm not a brute, just the inn's a small one. So now we
better get on up, or there'll be nowt here either and wasted
time singing in the cold.
MOTHER COURAGE: I'll get Kattrin.
THE COOK: Better bring a bit back for her. Scare them if they sees
170 three of us coming. (*Exeunt both.*)

(KATTRIN *climbs out of the cart with a bundle. She looks around
to see if the other two have gone. Then she takes an old pair of
trousers of the* COOK's *and a skirt of her mother's, and lays them
side by side on one of the wheels, so that they are easily seen. She
has finished and is picking up her bundle to go, when* MOTHER
COURAGE *comes back from the house.*)

MOTHER COURAGE: (*With a plate of soup.*) Kattrin! Will you stop
there? Kattrin! Where you off to with that bundle? Has devil
himself taken you over? (*She examines the bundle.*) She's
packed her things. You been listening? I told him nowt doing,
Utrecht, his rotten inn, what'd we be up to there? You and me, 175
inn's no place for us. Still plenty to be got out of war. (*She sees
the trousers and the skirt.*) You're plain stupid. S'pose I'd seen
that, and you gone away? (*She holds* KATTRIN *back as she tries
to break away.*) Don't you start thinking it's on your account I
given him the push. It was cart, that's it. Catch me leaving my 180
cart I'm used to, it ain't you, it's for cart. We'll go off in t'other
direction, and we'll throw cook's stuff out so he finds it, silly
man. (*She climbs in and throws out a few other articles in the
direction of the trousers.*) There, he's out of our business now,
and I ain't having nobody else in, ever. You and me'll carry on 185
now. This winter will pass, same as all the others. Get hitched
up, it looks like snow.

(*They both harness themselves to the cart, then wheel it round and
drag it off. When the* COOK *arrives he looks blankly at his kit.*)

SCENE TEN

During the whole of 1635 Mother Courage and her daughter
Kattrin travel over the highroads of central Germany, in the
wake of the increasingly bedraggled armies.

High road.

MOTHER COURAGE *and* KATTRIN *are pulling the cart. They pass a*
PEASANT's *house inside which there is a voice singing.*

THE VOICE: The roses in our arbour
Delight us with their show:
They have such lovely flowers
Repaying all our labour
After the summer showers. 5
Happy are those with gardens now:
They have such lovely flowers.

When winter winds are freezing
As through the woods they blow
Our home is warm and pleasing. 10
We fixed the thatch above it
With straw and moss we wove it.
Happy are those with shelter now
When winter winds are freezing.

(MOTHER COURAGE *and* KATTRIN *pause to listen, then continue
pulling.*)

SCENE ELEVEN

January 1636. The emperor's troops are threatening the Protestant town of Halle. The stone begins to speak. Mother Courage loses her daughter and trudges on alone. The war is a long way from being over.

The cart is standing, much the worse for wear, alongside a PEASANT'*s house with a huge thatched roof, backing on a wall of rock. It is night.*

An ENSIGN *and* THREE SOLDIERS *in heavy armour step out of the wood.*

THE ENSIGN: I want no noise now. Anyone shouts, shove your pike into him.

FIRST SOLDIER: Have to knock them up, though, if we're to find a guide.

5 THE ENSIGN: Knocking sounds natural. Could be a cow bumping the stable wall.

(The SOLDIERS *knock on the door of the house. The* PEASANT'*s wife opens it. They stop her mouth.* TWO SOLDIERS *go in.)*

MAN'S VOICE: (*Within.*) What is it?

(The SOLDIERS *bring out the* PEASANT *and his son [*THE YOUNG PEASANT*].)*

THE ENSIGN: (*Pointing at the cart, where* KATTRIN'*s head has appeared.*) There's another one. (*A* SOLDIER *drags her out.*)
10 Anyone else live here beside you lot?

THE PEASANTS: This is our son. And she's dumb. Her mother's gone into town to buy stuff. For their business, cause so many people's getting out and selling things cheap. They're just passing through. Canteen folk.

15 THE ENSIGN: I'm warning you, keep quiet, or if there's the least noise you get a pike across your nut. Now I want someone to come with us and show us the path to the town. (*Points to the* YOUNG PEASANT.) Here, you.

THE YOUNG PEASANT: I don't know no path.

20 SECOND SOLDIER: (*Grinning.*) He don't know no path.

THE YOUNG PEASANT: I ain't helping Catholics.

THE ENSIGN: (*To the* SECOND SOLDIER.) Stick your pike in his ribs.

THE YOUNG PEASANT: (*Forced to his knees, with the pike*
25 *threatening him.*) I won't do it, not to save my life.

FIRST SOLDIER: I know what'll change his mind. (*Goes towards the stable.*) Two cows and an ox. Listen, you: if you're not reasonable I'll chop up your cattle.

THE YOUNG PEASANT: No, not that!

30 THE PEASANT'S WIFE: (*Weeps.*) Please spare our cattle, captain, it'd be starving us to death.

THE ENSIGN: They're dead if he goes on being obstinate.

FIRST SOLDIER: I'm taking the ox first.

THE YOUNG PEASANT: (*To his father.*) Have I got to? (*The* WIFE
35 *nods.*) Right.

THE PEASANT'S WIFE: And thank you kindly, captain, for sparing us, for ever and ever, Amen.

(The PEASANT *stops his* WIFE *from further expressions of gratitude.)*

FIRST SOLDIER: I knew the ox was what they minded about most, was I right?

(Guided by the YOUNG PEASANT, *the* ENSIGN *and his* SOLDIERS *continue on their way.)*

40 THE PEASANT: What are they up to, I'd like to know. Nowt good.

THE PEASANT'S WIFE: Perhaps they're just scouting. What you doing?

THE PEASANT: (*Putting a ladder against the roof and climbing up it.*) Seeing if they're on their own. (*From the top.*) Something moving in the wood. Can see something down by the quarry.
45 And there are men in armour in the clearing. And a gun. That's at least a regiment. God's mercy on the town and everyone in it!

THE PEASANT'S WIFE: Any lights in the town?

THE PEASANT: No. They'll all be asleep. (*Climbs down.*) If those
50 people get in they'll butcher the lot.

THE PEASANT'S WIFE: Sentries're bound to spot them first.

THE PEASANT: Sentry in the tower up the hill must have been killed, or he'd have blown his bugle.

THE PEASANT'S WIFE: If only there were more of us.
55
THE PEASANT: Just you and me and that cripple.

THE PEASANT'S WIFE: Nowt we can do, you'd say. . . .

THE PEASANT: Nowt.

THE PEASANT'S WIFE: Can't possibly run down there in the blackness.
60
THE PEASANT: Whole hillside's crawling with 'em. We could give a signal.

THE PEASANT'S WIFE: What, and have them butcher us too?

THE PEASANT: You're right, nowt we can do.

THE PEASANT'S WIFE: (*To* KATTRIN.) Pray, poor creature, pray!
65 Nowt we can do to stop bloodshed. You can't talk, maybe, but at least you can pray. He'll hear you if no one else can. I'll help you. (*All kneel,* KATTRIN *behind the two* PEASANTS.) Our Father, which art in Heaven, hear Thou our prayer, let not the town be destroyed with all what's in it sound asleep
70 and suspecting nowt. Arouse Thou them that they may get up and go to the walls and see how the enemy approacheth with picks and guns in the blackness across fields below the slope. (*Turning to* KATTRIN.) Guard Thou our mother and ensure that the watchman sleepeth not but wakes up, or it
75 will be too late. Succour our brother-in-law also, he is inside there with his four children, spare Thou them, they are innocent and know nowt. (*To* KATTRIN, *who gives a groan.*) One of them's not two yet, the eldest's seven. (KATTRIN *stands up distractedly.*) Our Father, hear us, for only Thou canst
80 help; we look to be doomed, for why, we are weak and have no pike and nowt and can risk nowt and are in Thy hand along with our cattle and all the farm, and same with the town, it too is in Thy hand and the enemy is before the walls
85 in great strength.

(Unobserved, KATTRIN *has slipped away to the cart and taken from it something which she hides beneath her apron; then she climbs up the ladder on to the stable roof.)*

THE PEASANT'S WIFE: Forget not the children, what are in danger, the littlest ones especially, the old folk what can't move, and every living creature.

THE PEASANT: And forgive us our trespasses as we forgive them
90 that trespass against us. Amen.

(*Sitting on the roof,* KATTRIN *begins to beat the drum which she has pulled out from under her apron.*)

THE PEASANT'S WIFE: Jesus Christ, what's she doing?
THE PEASANT: She's out of her mind.
THE PEASANT'S WIFE: Quick, get her down.

(*The* PEASANT *hurries to the ladder, but* KATTRIN *pulls it up on to the roof.*)

THE PEASANT'S WIFE: She'll do us in.
95 THE PEASANT: Stop drumming at once, you cripple!
THE PEASANT'S WIFE: Bringing the Catholics down on us!
THE PEASANT: (*Looking for stones to throw.*) I'll stone you.
THE PEASANT'S WIFE: Where's your feelings? Where's your heart? We're done for if they come down on us. Slit our
100   throats, they will.

(KATTRIN *stares into the distance towards the town and carries on drumming.*)

THE PEASANT'S WIFE: (*To her husband.*) I told you we shouldn't have allowed those vagabonds on to farm. What do they care if our last cows are taken?
THE ENSIGN: (*Runs in with his* SOLDIERS *and the* YOUNG PEASANT.)
105   I'll cut you to ribbons, all of you!
THE PEASANT'S WIFE: Please, sir, it's not our fault, we couldn't help it. It was her sneaked up there. A foreigner.
THE ENSIGN: Where's the ladder?
THE PEASANT: There.
110 THE ENSIGN: (*Calls up.*) I order you, throw that drum down.

(KATTRIN *goes on drumming.*)

THE ENSIGN: You're all in this together. It'll be the end of you.
THE PEASANT: They been cutting pine trees in that wood. How about if we got one of the trunks and poked her off. . . .
FIRST SOLDIER: (*To the* ENSIGN.) Permission to make a suggestion,
115   sir! (*He whispers something in the* ENSIGN'S *ear.*) Listen, we got a suggestion could help you. Get down off there and come into town with us right away. Show us which your mother is and we'll see she ain't harmed.

(KATTRIN *goes on drumming.*)

THE ENSIGN: (*Pushes him roughly aside.*) She doesn't trust you;
120   with a mug like yours it's not surprising. (*Calls up.*) Suppose I gave you my word? I can give my word of honour as an officer.

(KATTRIN *drums harder.*)

THE ENSIGN: Is nothing sacred to her?
THE YOUNG PEASANT: There's more than her mother involved, sir.
125 FIRST SOLDIER: This can't go on much longer. They're bound to hear in the town.
THE ENSIGN: We'll have somehow to make a noise that's louder than her drumming. What can we make a noise with?
FIRST SOLDIER: Thought we weren't s'posed to make no noise.
130 THE ENSIGN: A harmless one, you fool. A peaceful one.
THE PEASANT: I could chop wood with my axe.
THE ENSIGN: Good: you chop. (*The* PEASANT *fetches his axe and attacks a tree-trunk.*) Chop harder! Harder! You're chopping for your life.

(KATTRIN *has been listening, drumming less loudly the while. She now looks wildly round, and goes on drumming.*)

THE ENSIGN: Not loud enough. (*To the* FIRST SOLDIER.) You   135
chop too.
THE PEASANT: Only got the one axe. (*Stops chopping.*)
THE ENSIGN: We'll have to set the farm on fire. Smoke her out, that's it.
THE PEASANT: It wouldn't help, captain. If the townspeople see a   140
fire here they'll know what's up.

(KATTRIN *has again been listening as she drums. At this point she laughs.*)

THE ENSIGN: Look at her laughing at us. I'm not having that. I'll shoot her down, and damn the consequences. Fetch the harquebus.

(THREE SOLDIERS *hurry off.* KATTRIN *goes on drumming.*)

THE PEASANT'S WIFE: I got it, captain. That's their cart. If we   145
smash it up she'll stop. Cart's all they got.
THE ENSIGN: (*To the* YOUNG PEASANT.) Smash it up. (*Calls up.*) We're going to smash up your cart if you don't stop drumming. (*The* YOUNG PEASANT *gives the cart a few feeble blows.*)
THE PEASANT'S WIFE: Stop it, you animal!   150

(*Desperately looking towards the cart,* KATTRIN *emits pitiful noises. But she goes on drumming.*)

THE ENSIGN: Where are those clodhoppers with the harquebus?
FIRST SOLDIER: Can't have heard nowt in town yet, else we'd be hearing their guns.
THE ENSIGN: (*Calls up.*) They can't hear you at all. And now we're going to shoot you down. For the last time: throw   155
down that drum!
THE YOUNG PEASANT: (*Suddenly flings away his plank.*) Go on drumming! Or they'll all be killed! Go on, go on. . . .

(*The* FIRST SOLDIER *knocks him down and beats him with his pike.* KATTRIN *starts to cry, but she goes on drumming.*)

THE PEASANT'S WIFE: Don't strike his back! For God's sake, you're beating him to death!   160

(*The* SOLDIERS *hurry in with the arquebus.*)

SECOND SOLDIER: Colonel's frothing at the mouth, sir. We're all for court-martial.
THE ENSIGN: Set it up! Set it up! (*Calls up while the gun is being erected.*) For the very last time: stop drumming! (KATTRIN, *in tears, drums as loud as she can.*) Fire! (*The* SOLDIERS *fire.* KATTRIN   165
is hit, gives a few more drumbeats and then slowly crumples.)
THE ENSIGN: That's the end of that.

(*But* KATTRIN'S *last drumbeats are taken up by the town's cannon. In the distance can be heard a confused noise of tocsins and gunfire.*)

FIRST SOLDIER: She's made it.

SCENE TWELVE

Before first light. Sound of the fifes and drums of troops marching off into the distance.

In front of the cart MOTHER COURAGE *is squatting by her daughter. The peasant family are standing near her.*

THE PEASANTS: (*With hostility.*) You must go, missis. There's only one more regiment behind that one. You can't go on your own.

MOTHER COURAGE: I think she's going to sleep. (*She sings.*)

5   Lullaby baby
               What's that in the hay?
               Neighbours' kids grizzle
               But my kids are gay.
               Neighbours' are in tatters
10   And you're dressed in lawn
               Cut down from the raiment an
               Angel has worn.
               Neighbours' kids go hungry
               And you shall eat cake
15   Suppose it's too crumbly
               You've only to speak.
               Lullaby baby
               What's that in the hay?
               The one lies in Poland
20   The other—who can say?

Better if you'd not told her nowt about your brother-in-law's kids.

THE PEASANT: If you'd not gone into town to get your cut it might never of happened.

25 MOTHER COURAGE: Now she's asleep.

THE PEASANT'S WIFE: She ain't asleep. Can't you see she's passed over?

THE PEASANT: And it's high time you got away yourself. There are wolves around and, what's worse, marauders.

30 MOTHER COURAGE: Aye.

(*She goes and gets a tarpaulin to cover the dead girl with.*)

THE PEASANT'S WIFE: Ain't you got nobody else? What you could go to?

MOTHER COURAGE: Aye, one left. Eilif.

THE PEASANT: (*As* MOTHER COURAGE *covers the dead girl.*) Best look for him, then. We'll mind her, see she gets proper burial.   35
Don't you worry about that.

MOTHER COURAGE: Here's money for expenses.

(*She counts out coins into the* PEASANT'S *hands. The* PEASANT *and his* SON *shake hands with her and carry* KATTRIN *away.*)

THE PEASANT'S WIFE: (*As she leaves.*) I'd hurry.

MOTHER COURAGE: (*Harnessing herself to the cart.*) Hope I can pull cart all right by meself. Be all right, nowt much inside   40
it. Got to get back in business again.

(*Another regiment with its fifes and drums marches past in the background.*)

MOTHER COURAGE: (*Tugging the cart.*) Take me along!

(*Singing is heard from offstage.*)

               With all its luck and all its danger
               The war is dragging on a bit
               Another hundred years or longer   45
               The common man won't benefit.
               Filthy his food, no soap to shave him
               The regiment steals half his pay.
               But still a miracle may save him:
               Tomorrow is another day!   50
                  The new year's come. The watchmen shout.
                  The thaw sets in. The dead remain.
                  Wherever life has not died out
                  It staggers to its feet again.

Samuel Beckett

Samuel Beckett (1906–1989) is the most influential European dramatist of the postwar period. Born near Dublin, Ireland, Beckett was educated at Trinity College, Dublin, where he studied modern languages. Taking his B.A. in 1928, Beckett received an appointment as *lecteur* at l'École Normale Supérieure in Paris. While in Paris, Beckett met the Irish novelist James Joyce. Beckett assisted Joyce (who was nearly blind) in a variety of ways and became a close friend. Joyce also exerted a profound influence on Beckett's writing. In 1929, Beckett contributed an essay entitled "Dante . . . Bruno . Vico . . Joyce" to a volume on Joyce's *Finnegans Wake* (the unusual punctuation of the title is significant). Throughout the 1930s, Beckett was associated with Joyce and with a variety of avant-garde movements in Paris. He wrote a series of poems—including the prize-winning "Whoroscope"—as well as a study of Proust (1931), the volume of short stories *More Pricks than Kicks* (1934), and the novel *Murphy* (1938). Although Beckett returned briefly to Ireland on a few occasions, he had settled permanently in Paris. During World War II, Beckett served in the French Resistance. He was discovered by the Nazis and forced to flee Paris in 1942. He worked in the unoccupied zone of southern France for the remainder of the war, where he wrote the novel *Watt* (1953). After the war, Beckett received the Croix de Guerre and the Médaille de la Résistance for his services. He began to write exclusively in French, starting work on a major trilogy of novels—*Molloy* (1951), *Malone Dies* (1951), and *The Unnameable* (1953).

Beckett had experimented with drama during the 1930s and 1940s, but his first staged play, *Waiting for Godot* (first written in French, as *En attendant Godot*), produced at the tiny Théâtre de Babylone in January of 1953, impelled him in a new direction. Although Beckett continued to write fiction—including *From an Abandoned Work* (1956), *How It Is* (1964), *Imagination Dead Imagine* (1965), and *Company* (1979)—his major writing of the 1960s, 1970s, and 1980s was for the theater. His second play, *Endgame*, also written in French, was produced in 1957 and was followed by a series of challenging works for the stage: *Krapp's Last Tape* (1958), *Happy Days* (1962), *Play* (1963), *Not I* (1972), *Footfalls* (1975), *Rockaby* (1981), and *Catastrophe* (1982). For his extraordinarily diverse and influential body of work, Beckett won the Nobel Prize for Literature in 1970. Beckett also wrote several plays for radio and television, as well as a film starring Buster Keaton, *Film* (1965). Beginning in the mid-1960s, Beckett directed productions of his plays, and several productions he directed in France and in Germany now have the status of classics—something like Elia Kazan's productions of Tennessee Williams's plays, or Stanislavski's productions of Chekhov.

Beckett's impact on the contemporary theater can hardly be overestimated and can be seen in the work of Sam Shepard, Harold Pinter, and many others. *Waiting for Godot* signaled new possibilities for stage action—or inaction—and developed the implications of Chekhov's static stage in a more symbolic direction. Each of Beckett's plays explores the nature and limitations of its medium in new and challenging ways. *Endgame* refigures the claustral box of realistic drama, for its characters are trapped in a room of endless—or possibly ending—routine. In *Play,* Beckett puts three urns onstage, from which three heads emerge to deliver, more or less simultaneously, a jarring, repetitive monologue of seduction and betrayal. Once the play has finished, Beckett directs his performers—and his audience—to "*Repeat play*," and so calls the relationship between actors and spectators, theater and reality into question: If we cannot leave the theater when the play is over, is it possible that there is no way out of the purgatory on the stage and in the auditorium? This sense that the self is always in flight is the theme of several of Beckett's later plays. In *Not I,* for instance, all that the audience sees is a Mouth eight feet above the stage, reciting an endless narrative in which she avoids claiming the speech as her own. In *Ohio Impromptu* (1981), an identical reader and listener relate a painful narrative of loss, in which it is unclear whether they are two individuals or reflected aspects of a single person. The power of Beckett's spare, minimalist theater, the beauty of his sculptural use of actors and stage space, and the harsh exigency of the action of his plays have transformed the stage of our time. Many great actors—Bert Lahr, Zero Mostel, Billie Whitelaw, John Gielgud—have been drawn to Beckett's plays, and a collection of original films made from the plays is now widely available.

Endgame

Endgame is Beckett's second full-length play to reach the stage; although its simplicity and repetitiveness are in some ways reminiscent of *Waiting for Godot,* the tone of *Endgame* is bleaker, harsher. As Beckett wrote to Alan Schneider, the play's first American director, *Endgame*'s power is "the power of the text to claw."

The "endgame" of a chess match is the final portion of the game, at which either a checkmate or a stalemate has become inevitable. In *Endgame,* Beckett literalizes the uncertainty of the endgame—will the tortuous nothingness of the characters' lives continue indefinitely, move after move, or will it somehow end? Although some critics have taken the "shelter" and the empty landscape outside as an indication that the play takes place in a bomb shelter after a nuclear bombing, *Endgame* seems to present a microcosm of postmodern life, in which the futile search for fugitive "meanings" raises the despairing feeling that our lives are meaningless, "absurd" after all. Hamm is a kind of ham actor and recalls Shakespeare's Richard III ("My kingdom for a nightman") and Prospero ("Our revels now are ended"), as well as perhaps King Lear and Hamlet in his performance. Hamm is perhaps the first **POSTMODERN** dramatic hero, less a full "character" than a *pastiche* of dramatic roles and possibilities, which exist now only in bits and pieces, recollected fragments (on **PASTICHE,** see Fredric Jameson's essay). Hamm's blindness also recalls both Oedipus—who also struggled with his father—and Ham the son of Noah, who was blinded when he saw his father naked. Hamm continually reminds us that his performance—it's full of asides, a "last soliloquy," and many self-regarding comments on Hamm's success or failure—is an attempt to impose meaning on the process of the play's action. This recollection of the dramatic and literary tradition also points to the problematic place—or absence—of history in *Endgame.* If there is a kind of past ("Once!") in *Endgame,* it is recalled most clearly by Hamm's parents: Nagg and Nell, legless in their garbage cans, describe an earlier, more sentimental or romantic era, when couples rode tandems in the Ardennes and rowed on Lake Como. Overall, though, time seems to be an endless present moment in *Endgame,* a

Nagg and Nell in their ashbins in Samuel Beckett's *Endgame,* in the 2000 Rude Mechanicals Theater Company production.

© Dixie Sheridan

moment disconnected from the past that once gave it meaning, and from the future which gave it closure. It may be that the play is postnuclear (although Beckett's draft manuscripts suggest that the inspiration was really a war hospital), but this setting is less important than the sense of time that this tiny world contains. For *Endgame* is finally about time and its passing, the painfully slow passage of moment to moment, and its finality once it is past.

Endgame was originally written in French as *Fin de partie* and was rewritten into English by Beckett himself; there are several small differences in dialogue and action between the two versions.

Endgame

Samuel Beckett

CHARACTERS

NAGG   HAMM

NELL   CLOV

Bare interior.

Grey light.

Left and right back, high up, two small windows, curtains drawn.

Front right, a door. Hanging near door, its face to wall, a picture.

Front left, touching each other, covered with an old sheet, two ashbins.

Center, in an armchair on castors, covered with an old sheet, HAMM.

Motionless by the door, his eyes fixed on HAMM, CLOV. *Very red face.*

Brief tableau.

CLOV *goes and stands under window left. Stiff, staggering walk. He looks up at window left. He turns and looks at window right. He goes and stands under window right. He looks up at window right. He turns and looks at window left. He goes out, comes back immediately with a small step-ladder, carries it over and sets it down under window left, gets up on it, draws back curtain. He gets down, takes six steps (for example) towards window right, goes back for ladder, carries it over and sets it down under window right, gets up on it, draws back curtain. He gets down, takes three steps towards window left, goes back for ladder, carries it over and sets it down under window left, gets up on it, looks out of window. Brief laugh. He gets down, takes one step towards window right, goes back for ladder, carries it over and sets it down under window right, gets up on it, looks out of window. Brief laugh. He gets down, goes with ladder towards ashbins, halts, turns, carries back ladder and sets it down under window right, goes to ashbins, removes sheet covering them, folds it over his arm. He raises one lid, stoops and looks into bin. Brief laugh. He closes lid. Same with other bin. He goes to* HAMM, *removes sheet covering him, folds it over his arm. In a dressing-gown, a stiff toque on his head, a large blood-stained handkerchief over his face, a whistle hanging from his neck, a rug over his knees, thick socks on his feet,* HAMM *seems to be asleep.* CLOV *looks him over. Brief laugh. He goes to door, halts, turns towards auditorium.*

CLOV: (*Fixed gaze, tonelessly.*) Finished, it's finished, nearly finished, it must be nearly finished.

(*Pause.*)

    Grain upon grain, one by one, and one day, suddenly, there's a heap, a little heap, the impossible heap.

(*Pause.*)

5   I can't be punished any more.

(*Pause.*)

    I'll go now to my kitchen, ten feet by ten feet by ten feet, and wait for him to whistle me.

(*Pause.*)

    Nice dimensions, nice proportions, I'll lean on the table, and look at the wall, and wait for him to whistle me.

(*He remains a moment motionless, then goes out. He comes back immediately, goes to window right, takes up the ladder and carries it out. Pause.* HAMM *stirs. He yawns under the handkerchief. He removes the handkerchief from his face. Very red face. Black glasses.*)

HAMM: Me—   10

(*He yawns.*)

    —to play.

(*He holds the handkerchief spread out before him.*)

    Old stancher!

(*He takes off his glasses, wipes his eyes, his face, the glasses, puts them on again, folds the handkerchief and puts it back neatly in the breast-pocket of his dressing-gown. He clears his throat, joins the tips of his fingers.*)

    Can there be misery—

(*He yawns.*)

    —loftier than mine? No doubt. Formerly. But now?

(*Pause.*)

    My father?   15

(*Pause.*)

    My mother?

(*Pause.*)

    My . . . dog?

(*Pause.*)

    Oh I am willing to believe they suffer as much as such creatures can suffer. But does that mean their sufferings equal mine? No doubt.   20

(*Pause.*)

    No, all is a—

(*He yawns.*)

    —bsolute,

(*Proudly.*)

    the bigger a man is the fuller he is.

(*Pause. Gloomily.*)

    And the emptier.

(*He sniffs.*)

    Clov!   25

(*Pause.*)

    No, alone.

(*Pause.*)

    What dreams! Those forests!

(*Pause.*)

    Enough, it's time it ended, in the shelter too.

(*Pause.*)

    And yet I hesitate, I hesitate to . . . to end. Yes, there it is, it's time it ended and yet I hesitate to—   30

(*He yawns.*)

    —to end.

(*Yawns.*)

    God, I'm tired, I'd be better off in bed.

(*He whistles. Enter* CLOV *immediately. He halts beside the chair.*)

    You pollute the air!

(*Pause.*)
    Get me ready, I'm going to bed.
35 CLOV: I've just got you up.
HAMM: And what of it?
CLOV: I can't be getting you up and putting you to bed every five
    minutes, I have things to do.

(*Pause.*)

HAMM: Did you ever see my eyes?
40 CLOV: No.
HAMM: Did you never have the curiosity, while I was sleeping, to
    take off my glasses and look at my eyes?
CLOV: Pulling back the lids?
(*Pause.*)
    No.
45 HAMM: One of these days I'll show them to you.
(*Pause.*)
    It seems they've gone all white.
(*Pause.*)
    What time is it?
CLOV: The same as usual.
HAMM: (*Gesture towards window right.*) Have you looked?
50 CLOV: Yes.
HAMM: Well?
CLOV: Zero.
HAMM: It'd need to rain.
CLOV: It won't rain.

(*Pause.*)

55 HAMM: *Apart from that, how do you feel?*
CLOV: I don't complain.
HAMM: You feel normal?
CLOV: (*Irritably.*) I tell you I don't complain.
HAMM: I feel a little queer.
(*Pause.*)
60   Clov!
CLOV: Yes.
HAMM: Have you not had enough?
CLOV: Yes!
(*Pause.*)
    Of what?
65 HAMM: Of this . . . this . . . thing.
CLOV: I always had.
(*Pause.*)
    Not you?
HAMM: (*Gloomily.*) Then there's no reason for it to change.
CLOV: It may end.
(*Pause.*)
70   All life long the same questions, the same answers.
HAMM: Get me ready.
(CLOV *does not move.*)
    Go and get the sheet.
(CLOV *does not move.*)
    Clov!
CLOV: Yes.
75 HAMM: I'll give you nothing more to eat.
CLOV: Then we'll die.
HAMM: I'll give you just enough to keep you from dying.
    You'll be hungry all the time.
CLOV: Then we won't die.

(*Pause.*)
    I'll go and get the sheet.   80

(*He goes towards the door.*)

HAMM: *No!*
(CLOV *halts.*)
    I'll give you one biscuit per day.
(*Pause.*)
    One and a half.
(*Pause.*)
    Why do you stay with me?
CLOV: Why do you keep me?   85
HAMM: There's no one else.
CLOV: There's nowhere else.

(*Pause.*)

HAMM: You're leaving me all the same.
CLOV: I'm trying.
HAMM: You don't love me.   90
CLOV: No.
HAMM: You loved me once.
CLOV: Once!
HAMM: I've made you suffer too much.
(*Pause.*)
    Haven't I?   95
CLOV: It's not that.
HAMM: (*Shocked.*) I haven't made you suffer too much?
CLOV: Yes!
HAMM: (*Relieved.*) Ah you gave me a fright!
(*Pause. Coldly.*)
    Forgive me.   100
(*Pause. Louder.*)
    I said, Forgive me.
CLOV: I heard you.
(*Pause.*)
    Have you bled?
HAMM: Less.
(*Pause.*)
    Is it not time for my pain-killer?   105
CLOV: No.

(*Pause.*)

HAMM: How are your eyes?
CLOV: Bad.
HAMM: How are your legs?
CLOV: Bad.   110
HAMM: But you can move.
CLOV: Yes.
HAMM: (*Violently.*) Then move!
(CLOV *goes to back wall, leans against it with his forehead and
hands.*)
    Where are you?
CLOV: Here.   115
HAMM: Come back!
(CLOV *returns to his place beside the chair.*)
    Where are you?
CLOV: Here.
HAMM: Why don't you kill me?

120 CLOV: I don't know the combination of the cupboard.

(*Pause.*)

HAMM: Go and get two bicycle-wheels.
CLOV: There are no more bicycle-wheels.
HAMM: What have you done with your bicycle?
CLOV: I never had a bicycle.
125 HAMM: The thing is impossible.
CLOV: When there were still bicycles I wept to have one.
    I crawled at your feet. You told me to go to hell. Now there
    are none.
HAMM: And your rounds? When you inspected my paupers.
130   Always on foot?
CLOV: Sometimes on horse.
(*The lid of one of the bins lifts and the hands of* NAGG *appear, grip-
ping the rim. Then his head emerges. Nightcap. Very white face.*
NAGG *yawns, then listens.*)
    I'll leave you, I have things to do.
HAMM: In your kitchen?
CLOV: Yes.
135 HAMM: Outside of here it's death.
(*Pause.*)
    All right, be off.
(*Exit* CLOV. *Pause.*)
    We're getting on.
NAGG: Me pap!
HAMM: Accursed progenitor!
140 NAGG: Me pap!
HAMM: The old folks at home! No decency left! Guzzle, guzzle,
    that's all they think of.
(*He whistles. Enter* CLOV. *He halts beside the chair.*)
    Well! I thought you were leaving me.
CLOV: Oh not just yet, not just yet.
145 NAGG: Me pap!
HAMM: Give him his pap.
CLOV: There's no more pap.
HAMM: (*To* NAGG.) Do you hear that? There's no more pap.
    You'll never get any more pap.
150 NAGG: I want me pap!
HAMM: Give him a biscuit.
(*Exit* CLOV.)
    Accursed fornicator! How are your stumps?
NAGG: Never mind me stumps.

(*Enter* CLOV *with biscuit.*)

CLOV: *I'm back again, with the biscuit.*

(*He gives biscuit to* NAGG *who fingers it, sniffs it.*)

155 NAGG: (*Plaintively.*) What is it?
CLOV: Spratt's medium.
NAGG: (*As before.*) It's hard! I can't!
HAMM: Bottle him!

(CLOV *pushes* NAGG *back into the bin, closes the lid.*)

CLOV: (*Returning to his place beside the chair.*) If age but knew!
160 HAMM: Sit on him!
CLOV: I can't sit.
HAMM: True. And I can't stand.
CLOV: So it is.

HAMM: Every man his speciality.
(*Pause.*)
    No phone calls? 165
(*Pause.*)
    Don't we laugh?
CLOV: (*After reflection.*) I don't feel like it.
HAMM: (*After reflection.*) Nor I.
(*Pause.*)
    Clov!
CLOV: Yes. 170
HAMM: Nature has forgotten us.
CLOV: There's no more nature.
HAMM: No more nature! You exaggerate.
CLOV: In the vicinity.
HAMM: But we breathe, we change! We lose our hair, our teeth! 175
    Our bloom! Our ideals!
CLOV: Then she hasn't forgotten us.
HAMM: But you say there is none.
CLOV: (*Sadly.*) No one that ever lived ever thought so crooked
    as we. 180
HAMM: We do what we can.
CLOV: We shouldn't.

(*Pause.*)

HAMM: You're a bit of all right, aren't you?
CLOV: A smithereen.

(*Pause.*)

HAMM: This is slow work. 185
(*Pause.*)
    Is it not time for my pain-killer?
CLOV: No.
(*Pause.*)
    I'll leave you, I have things to do.
HAMM: In your kitchen?
CLOV: Yes. 190
HAMM: What, I'd like to know.
CLOV: I look at the wall.
HAMM: The wall! And what do you see on your wall? Mene,
    mene? Naked bodies?
CLOV: I see my light dying. 195
HAMM: Your light dying! Listen to that! Well, it can die just as
    well here, *your* light. Take a look at me and then come back
    and tell me what you think of *your* light.

(*Pause.*)

CLOV: You shouldn't speak to me like that.

(*Pause.*)

HAMM: (*Coldly.*) Forgive me. 200
(*Pause. Louder.*)
I said, Forgive me.
CLOV: I heard you.

(*The lid of* NAGG's *bin lifts. His hands appear, gripping the rim.
Then his head emerges. In his mouth the biscuit. He listens.*)

HAMM: Did your seeds come up?
CLOV: No.

205   HAMM: Did you scratch round them to see if they had sprouted?
CLOV: They haven't sprouted.
HAMM: Perhaps it's still too early.
CLOV: If they were going to sprout they would have sprouted.
(*Violently.*)
   They'll never sprout!

(*Pause.* NAGG *takes biscuit in his hand.*)

210   HAMM: This is not much fun.
(*Pause.*)
   But that's always the way at the end of the day, isn't it,
   Clov?
CLOV: Always.
HAMM: It's the end of the day like any other day, isn't it, Clov?
215   CLOV: Looks like it.

(*Pause.*)

HAMM: (*Anguished.*) What's happening, what's happening?
CLOV: Something is taking its course.

(*Pause.*)

HAMM: All right, be off.
(*He leans back in his chair, remains motionless.* CLOV *does not
move, heaves a great groaning sigh.* HAMM *sits up.*)
   I thought I told you to be off.
220   CLOV: I'm trying.
(*He goes to door, halts.*)
   Ever since I was whelped.

(*Exit* CLOV.)

HAMM: *We're getting on.*

(*He leans back in his chair, remains motionless.* NAGG *knocks
on the lid of the other bin. Pause. He knocks harder. The lid lifts
and the hands of* NELL *appear, gripping the rim. Then her head
emerges. Lace cap. Very white face.*)

NELL: What is it, my pet?
(*Pause.*)
   Time for love?
225   NAGG: Were you asleep?
NELL: Oh no!
NAGG: Kiss me.
NELL: We can't.
NAGG: Try.

(*Their heads strain towards each other, fail to meet, fall apart again.*)

230   NELL: *Why this farce, day after day?*

(*Pause.*)

NAGG: I've lost me tooth.
NELL: When?
NAGG: I had it yesterday.
NELL: (*Elegiac.*) Ah yesterday!

(*They turn painfully towards each other.*)

235   NAGG: Can you see me?
NELL: Hardly. And you?

NAGG: What?
NELL: Can you see me?
NAGG: Hardly.
NELL: So much the better, so much the better.   240
NAGG: Don't say that.
(*Pause.*)
   Our sight has failed.
NELL: Yes.

(*Pause. They turn away from each other.*)

NAGG: Can you hear me?
NELL: Yes. And you?   245
NAGG: Yes.
(*Pause.*)
   Our hearing hasn't failed.
NELL: Our what?
NAGG: Our hearing.
NELL: No.   250
(*Pause.*)
   Have you anything else to say to me?
NAGG: Do you remember—
NELL: No.
NAGG: When we crashed on our tandem and lost our shanks.

(*They laugh heartily.*)

NELL: *It was in the Ardennes.*   255

(*They laugh less heartily.*)

NAGG: On the road to Sedan.
(*They laugh still less heartily.*)
   Are you cold?
NELL: Yes, perished. And you?
NAGG: (*Pause.*) I'm freezing.
(*Pause.*)
   Do you want to go in?
NELL: Yes.   260
NAGG: Then go in.
(NELL *does not move.*)
   Why don't you go in?
NELL: I don't know.

(*Pause.*)

NAGG: Has he changed your sawdust?   265
NELL: It isn't sawdust.
(*Pause. Wearily.*)
   Can you not be a little accurate, Nagg?
NAGG: Your sand then. It's not important.
NELL: It is important.

(*Pause.*)

NAGG: It was sawdust once.   270
NELL: Once!
NAGG: And now it's sand.
(*Pause.*)
   From the shore.
(*Pause. Impatiently.*)
   Now it's sand he fetches from the shore.
NELL: Now it's sand.   275

NAGG: Has he changed yours?
NELL: No.
NAGG: Nor mine.
(*Pause.*)
    I won't have it!
(*Pause. Holding up the biscuit.*)
280   Do you want a bit?
NELL: No.
(*Pause.*)
    Of what?
NAGG: Biscuit. I've kept you half.
(*He looks at the biscuit. Proudly.*)
    Three quarters. For you. Here.
(*He proffers the biscuit.*)
285   No?
(*Pause.*)
    Do you not feel well?
HAMM: (*Wearily.*) Quiet, quiet, you're keeping me awake.
(*Pause.*)
    Talk softer.
(*Pause.*)
    If I could sleep I might make love. I'd go into the woods.
290   My eyes would see . . . the sky, the earth. I'd run, run, they
    wouldn't catch me.
(*Pause.*)
    Nature!
(*Pause.*)
    There's something dripping in my head.
(*Pause.*)
    A heart, a heart in my head.

(*Pause.*)

295 NAGG: (*Soft.*) *Do you hear him? A heart in his head!*

(*He chuckles cautiously.*)

NELL: One mustn't laugh at those things, Nagg. Why must you
    always laugh at them?
NAGG: Not so loud!
NELL: (*Without lowering her voice.*) Nothing is funnier than
300   unhappiness, I grant you that. But—
NAGG: (*Shocked.*) Oh!
NELL: Yes, yes, it's the most comical thing in the world. And
    we laugh, we laugh, with a will, in the beginning. But it's
    always the same thing. Yes, it's like the funny story we
305   have heard too often, we still find it funny, but we don't
    laugh any more.
(*Pause.*)
    Have you anything else to say to me?
NAGG: No.
NELL: Are you quite sure?
(*Pause.*)
310   Then I'll leave you.
NAGG: Do you not want your biscuit?
(*Pause.*)
    I'll keep it for you.
(*Pause.*)
    I thought you were going to leave me.
NELL: I am going to leave you.
315 NAGG: Could you give me a scratch before you go?
NELL: No.

(*Pause.*)
    Where?
NAGG: In the back.
NELL: No.
(*Pause.*)
    Rub yourself against the rim.   320
NAGG: It's lower down. In the hollow.
NELL: What hollow?
NAGG: The hollow!
(*Pause.*)
    Could you not?
(*Pause.*)
    Yesterday you scratched me there.   325
NELL: (*Elegiac.*) Ah yesterday!
NAGG: Could you not?
(*Pause.*)
    Would you like me to scratch you?
(*Pause.*)
    Are you crying again?
NELL: I was trying.   330

(*Pause.*)

HAMM: Perhaps it's a little vein.

(*Pause.*)

NAGG: What was that he said?
NELL: Perhaps it's a little vein.
NAGG: What does that mean?
(*Pause.*)
    That means nothing.   335
(*Pause.*)
    Will I tell you the story of the tailor?
NELL: No.
(*Pause.*)
    What for?
NAGG: To cheer you up.
NELL: It's not funny.   340
NAGG: It always made you laugh.
(*Pause.*)
    The first time I thought you'd die.
NELL: It was on Lake Como.
(*Pause.*)
    One April afternoon.
(*Pause.*)
    Can you believe it?
NAGG: What?   345
NELL: That we once went out rowing on Lake Como.
(*Pause.*)
    One April afternoon.
NAGG: We had got engaged the day before.
NELL: Engaged!   350
NAGG: You were in such fits that we capsized. By rights we should
    have been drowned.
NELL: It was because I felt happy.
NAGG: (*Indignant.*) It was not, it was not, it was my story and
    nothing else. Happy! Don't you laugh at it still? Every time   355
    I tell it. Happy!
NELL: It was deep, deep. And you could see down to the bottom.
    So white. So clean.
NAGG: Let me tell it again.

(*Raconteur's voice.*)

360   An Englishman, needing a pair of striped trousers in a hurry for the New Year festivities, goes to his tailor who takes his measurements.

(*Tailor's voice.*)

"That's the lot, come back in four days, I'll have it ready." Good. Four days later.

(*Tailor's voice.*)

365   "So sorry, come back in a week, I've made a mess of the seat." Good, that's all right, a neat seat can be very ticklish. A week later.

(*Tailor's voice.*)

"Frightfully sorry, come back in ten days, I've made a hash of the crotch." Good, can't be helped, a snug crotch is always a

370   teaser. Ten days later.

(*Tailor's voice.*)

"Dreadfully sorry, come back in a fortnight, I've made a balls of the fly." Good, at a pinch, a smart fly is a stiff proposition.

(*Pause. Normal voice.*)

I never told it worse.

(*Pause. Gloomy.*)

I tell this story worse and worse.

(*Pause. Raconteur's voice.*)

375   Well, to make it short, the bluebells are blowing and he ballockses the buttonholes.

(*Customer's voice.*)

"God damn you to hell, Sir, no, it's indecent, there are limits! In six days, do you hear me, six days, God made the world. Yes Sir, no less Sir, the WORLD! And you are

380   not bloody well capable of making me a pair of trousers in three months!"

(*Tailor's voice, scandalized.*)

"But my dear Sir, my dear Sir, look—

(*Disdainful gesture, disgustedly.*)

—at the world—

(*Pause.*)

and look—

(*Loving gesture, proudly.*)

385   —at my TROUSERS!"

(*Pause. He looks at* NELL *who has remained impassive, her eyes unseeing, breaks into a high forced laugh, cuts it short, pokes his head towards* NELL, *launches his laugh again.*)

HAMM: Silence!

(NAGG *starts, cuts short his laugh.*)

NELL: You could see down to the bottom.
HAMM: (*Exasperated.*) Have you not finished? Will you never finish?

(*With sudden fury.*)

390   Will this never finish?

(NAGG *disappears into his bin, closes the lid behind him.* NELL *does not move. Frenziedly.*)

My kingdom for a nightman!

(*He whistles. Enter* CLOV.)

Clear away this muck! Chuck it in the sea!

(CLOV *goes to bins, halts.*)

NELL: So white.

HAMM: What? What's she blathering about?

(CLOV *stoops, takes* NELL's *hand, feels her pulse.*)

NELL: (*To* CLOV.) Desert!   395

(CLOV *lets go her hand, pushes her back in the bin, closes the lid.*)

CLOV: (*Returning to his place beside the chair.*) She has no pulse.
HAMM: What was she drivelling about?
CLOV: She told me to go away, into the desert.
HAMM: Damn busybody! Is that all?
CLOV: No.   400
HAMM: What else?
CLOV: I didn't understand.
HAMM: Have you bottled her?
CLOV: Yes.
HAMM: Are they both bottled?   405
CLOV: Yes.
HAMM: Screw down the lids.

(CLOV *goes towards door.*)

Time enough.

(CLOV *halts.*)

My anger subsides, I'd like to pee.
CLOV: (*With alacrity.*) I'll go and get the catheter.   410

(*He goes towards door.*)

HAMM: Time enough.

(CLOV *halts.*)

Give me my pain-killer.
CLOV: It's too soon.

(*Pause.*)

It's too soon on top of your tonic, it wouldn't act.
HAMM: In the morning they brace you up and in the evening   415
they calm you down. Unless it's the other way round.

(*Pause.*)

That old doctor, he's dead naturally?
CLOV: He wasn't old.
HAMM: But he's dead?
CLOV: Naturally.   420

(*Pause.*)

You ask *me* that?

(*Pause.*)

HAMM: Take me for a little turn.

(CLOV *goes behind the chair and pushes it forward.*)

Not too fast!

(CLOV *pushes chair.*)

Right round the world!

(CLOV *pushes chair.*)

Hug the walls, then back to the center again.   425

(CLOV *pushes chair.*)

I was right in the center, wasn't I?
CLOV: (*Pushing.*) Yes.
HAMM: We'd need a proper wheel-chair. With big wheels.
Bicycle wheels!

(*Pause.*)

Are you hugging?   430
CLOV: (*Pushing.*) Yes.
HAMM: (*Groping for wall.*) It's a lie! Why do you lie to me?
CLOV: (*Bearing closer to wall.*) There! There!

HAMM: Stop!

(CLOV *stops chair close to back wall.* HAMM *lays his hand against wall.*)

435   Old wall!

(*Pause.*)

    Beyond is the . . . other hell.

(*Pause. Violently.*)

    Closer! Closer! Up against!

CLOV: Take away your hand.

(HAMM *withdraws his hand.* CLOV *rams chair against wall.*)

    There!

(HAMM *leans towards wall, applies his ear to it.*)

440 HAMM: Do you hear?

(*He strikes the wall with his knuckles.*)

    Do you hear? Hollow bricks!

(*He strikes again.*)

    All that's hollow!

(*Pause. He straightens up. Violently.*)

    That's enough. Back!

CLOV: We haven't done the round.

445 HAMM: Back to my place!

(CLOV *pushes chair back to center.*)

    Is that my place?

CLOV: Yes, that's your place.

HAMM: Am I right in the center?

CLOV: I'll measure it.

450 HAMM: More or less! More or less!

CLOV: (*Moving chair slightly.*) There!

HAMM: I'm more or less in the center?

CLOV: I'd say so.

HAMM: You'd say so! Put me right in the center!

455 CLOV: I'll go and get the tape.

HAMM: Roughly! Roughly!

(CLOV *moves chair slightly.*)

    Bang in the center!

CLOV: There!

(*Pause.*)

HAMM: I feel a little too far to the left.

(CLOV *moves chair slightly.*)

460   Now I feel a little too far to the right.

(CLOV *moves chair slightly.*)

    I feel a little too far forward.

(CLOV *moves chair slightly.*)

    Now I feel a little too far back.

(CLOV *moves chair slightly.*)

    Don't stay there,

(*i.e., Behind the chair.*)

    you give me the shivers.

(CLOV *returns to his place beside the chair.*)

465 CLOV: If I could kill him I'd die happy.

(*Pause.*)

HAMM: What's the weather like?

CLOV: As usual.

HAMM: Look at the earth.

CLOV: I've looked.

HAMM: With the glass?   470

CLOV: No need of the glass.

HAMM: Look at it with the glass.

CLOV: I'll go and get the glass.

(*Exit* CLOV.)

HAMM: No need of the glass!

(*Enter* CLOV *with telescope.*)

CLOV: I'm back again, with the glass.   475

(*He goes to window right, looks up at it.*)

    I need the steps.

HAMM: Why? Have you shrunk?

(*Exit* CLOV *with telescope.*)

    I don't like that, I don't like that.

(*Enter* CLOV *with ladder, but without telescope.*)

CLOV: I'm back again, with the steps.

(*He sets down ladder under window right, gets up on it, realizes he has not the telescope, gets down.*)

    I need the glass.   480

(*He goes towards door.*)

HAMM: (*Violently.*) But you have the glass!

CLOV: (*Halting, violently.*) No, I haven't the glass!

(*Exit* CLOV.)

HAMM: This is deadly.

(*Enter* CLOV *with telescope. He goes towards ladder.*)

CLOV: Things are livening up.

(*He gets up on ladder, raises the telescope, lets it fall.*)

    I did it on purpose.   485

(*He gets down, picks up the telescope, turns it on auditorium.*)

    I see . . . a multitude . . . in transports . . . of joy.

(*Pause.*)

    That's what I call a magnifier.

(*He lowers the telescope, turns towards* HAMM.)

    Well? Don't we laugh?

HAMM: (*After reflection.*) I don't.

CLOV: (*After reflection.*) Nor I.   490

(*He gets up on ladder, turns the telescope on the without.*)

    Let's see.

(*He looks, moving the telescope.*)

    Zero . . .

(*He looks.*)

    . . . zero . . .

(*He looks.*)

    . . . and zero.

HAMM: Nothing stirs. All is—   495

CLOV: Zer—

HAMM: (*Violently.*) Wait till you're spoken to!

(*Normal voice.*)

    All is . . . all is . . . all is what?

(*Violently.*)

    All is what?

CLOV: What all is? In a word? Is that what you want to know?   500

    Just a moment.

(*He turns the telescope on the without, looks, lowers the telescope, turns towards* HAMM.)
    Corpsed.
(*Pause.*)
    Well? Content?
HAMM: Look at the sea.
505 CLOV: It's the same.
HAMM: Look at the ocean!

(CLOV *gets down, takes a few steps towards window left, goes back for ladder, carries it over and sets it down under window left, gets up on it, turns the telescope on the without, looks at length. He starts, lowers the telescope, examines it, turns it again on the without.*)

CLOV: Never seen anything like that!
HAMM: (*Anxious.*) What? A sail? A fin? Smoke?
CLOV: (*Looking.*) The light is sunk.
510 HAMM: (*Relieved.*) Pah! We all knew that.
CLOV: (*Looking.*)There was a bit left.
HAMM: The base.
CLOV: (*Looking.*) Yes.
HAMM: And now?
515 CLOV: (*Looking.*) All gone.
HAMM: No gulls?
CLOV: (*Looking.*) Gulls!
HAMM: And the horizon? Nothing on the horizon?
CLOV: (*Lowering the telescope, turning towards* HAMM, *exasperated.*)
    What in God's name could there be on the horizon?

(*Pause.*)

520 HAMM: The waves, how are the waves?
CLOV: The waves?
(*He turns the telescope on the waves.*)
    Lead.
HAMM: And the sun?
CLOV: (*Looking.*) Zero.
525 HAMM: But it should be sinking. Look again.
CLOV: (*Looking.*) Damn the sun.
HAMM: Is it night already then?
CLOV: (*Looking.*) No.
HAMM: Then what is it?
530 CLOV: (*Looking.*) Gray.
(*Lowering the telescope, turning towards* HAMM, *louder.*)
    Gray!
(*Pause. Still louder.*)
    GRRAY!

(*Pause. He gets down, approaches* HAMM *from behind, whispers in his ear.*)

HAMM: (*Starting.*) Gray! Did I hear you say gray?
CLOV: Light black. From pole to pole.
535 HAMM: You exaggerate.
(*Pause.*)
    Don't stay there, you give me the shivers.

(CLOV *returns to his place beside the chair.*)

CLOV: Why this farce, day after day?
HAMM: Routine. One never knows.
(*Pause.*)
    Last night I saw inside my breast. There was a big sore.

CLOV: Pah! You saw your heart.   540
HAMM: No, it was living.
(*Pause. Anguished.*)
    Clov!
CLOV: Yes.
HAMM: What's happening?
CLOV: Something is taking its course.   545

(*Pause.*)

HAMM: Clov!
CLOV: (*Impatiently.*) What is it?
HAMM: We're not beginning to . . . to . . . mean something?
CLOV: Mean something! You and I, mean something!
(*Brief laugh.*)
    Ah that's a good one!   550
HAMM: I wonder.
(*Pause.*)
    Imagine if a rational being came back to earth, wouldn't he
    be liable to get ideas into his head if he observed us long
    enough.
(*Voice of rational being.*)
    Ah, good, now I see what it is, yes, now I understand what   555
    they're at!
(CLOV *starts, drops the telescope and begins to scratch his belly with both hands. Normal voice.*)
    And without going so far as that, we ourselves . . .
(*With emotion.*)
    . . . we ourselves . . . at certain moments . . .
(*Vehemently.*)
    To think perhaps it won't all have been for nothing!
CLOV: (*Anguished, scratching himself.*) I have a flea!   560
HAMM: A flea! Are there still fleas?
CLOV: On me there's one.
(*Scratching.*)
    Unless it's a crablouse.
HAMM: (*Very perturbed.*) But humanity might start from there
    all over again! Catch him, for the love of God!   565
CLOV: I'll go and get the powder.

(*Exit* CLOV.)

HAMM: A flea! This is awful! What a day!

(*Enter* CLOV *with a sprinkling-tin.*)

CLOV: I'm back again, with the insecticide.
HAMM: Let him have it!

(CLOV *loosens the top of his trousers, pulls it forward and shakes powder into the aperture. He stoops, looks, waits, starts, frenziedly shakes more powder, stoops, looks, waits.*)

CLOV: The bastard!   570
HAMM: Did you get him?
CLOV: Looks like it.
(*He drops the tin and adjusts his trousers.*)
    Unless he's laying doggo.
HAMM: Laying! Lying you mean. Unless he's *lying* doggo.
CLOV: Ah? One says lying? One doesn't say laying?   575
HAMM: Use your head, can't you. If he was laying we'd be
    bitched.

CLOV: Ah.
(*Pause.*)
    What about that pee?
580 HAMM: I'm having it.
CLOV: Ah that's the spirit, that's the spirit!

(*Pause.*)

HAMM: (*With ardour.*) Let's go from here, the two of us! South!
    You can make a raft and the currents will carry us away, far
    away, to other . . . mammals!
585 CLOV: God forbid!
HAMM: Alone, I'll embark alone! Get working on that raft
    immediately. Tomorrow I'll be gone for ever.
CLOV: (*Hastening towards door.*) I'll start straight away.
HAMM: Wait!
(CLOV *halts.*)
590   Will there be sharks, do you think?
CLOV: Sharks? I don't know. If there are there will be.

(*He goes towards door.*)

HAMM: Wait!
(CLOV *halts.*)
    Is it not yet time for my pain-killer?
CLOV: (*Violently.*) No!

(*He goes towards door.*)

595 HAMM: Wait!
(CLOV *halts.*)
    How are your eyes?
CLOV: Bad.
HAMM: But you can see.
CLOV: All I want.
600 HAMM: How are your legs?
CLOV: Bad.
HAMM: But you can walk.
CLOV: I come . . . and go.
HAMM: In my house.
(*Pause. With prophetic relish.*)
605   One day you'll be blind, like me. You'll be sitting there, a
    speck in the void, in the dark, for ever, like me.
(*Pause.*)
    One day you'll say to yourself, I'm tired, I'll sit down, and
    you'll go and sit down. Then you'll say, I'm hungry, I'll get
    up and get something to eat. But you won't get up. You'll say,
610   I shouldn't have sat down, but since I have I'll sit on a little
    longer, then I'll get up and get something to eat. But you won't
    get up and you won't get anything to eat.
(*Pause.*)
    You'll look at the wall a while, then you'll say, I'll close my
    eyes, perhaps have a little sleep, after that I'll feel better, and
615   you'll close them. And when you open them again there'll be
    no wall any more.
(*Pause.*)
    Infinite emptiness will be all around you, all the resurrected
    dead of all the ages wouldn't fill it, and there you'll be like a
    little bit of grit in the middle of the steppe.
(*Pause.*)
620   Yes, one day you'll know what it is, you'll be like me, except
    that you won't have anyone with you, because you won't

have had pity on anyone and because there won't be anyone
left to have pity on.

(*Pause.*)

CLOV: It's not certain.
(*Pause.*)
    And there's one thing you forget.   625
HAMM: Ah?
CLOV: I can't sit down.
HAMM: (*Impatiently.*) Well you'll lie down then, what the hell! Or
    you'll come to a standstill, simply stop and stand still, the way
    you are now. One day you'll say, I'm tired, I'll stop. What does   630
    the attitude matter?

(*Pause.*)

CLOV: So you all want me to leave you.
HAMM: Naturally.
CLOV: Then I'll leave you.
HAMM: You can't leave us.   635
CLOV: Then I won't leave you.

(*Pause.*)

HAMM: Why don't you finish us?
(*Pause.*)
    I'll tell you the combination of the cupboard if you promise to
    finish me.
CLOV: I couldn't finish you.   640
HAMM: Then you won't finish me.

(*Pause.*)

CLOV: I'll leave you, I have things to do.
HAMM: Do you remember when you came here?
CLOV: No. Too small, you told me.
HAMM: Do you remember your father.   645
CLOV: (*Wearily.*) Same answer.
(*Pause.*)
    You've asked me these questions millions of times.
HAMM: I love the old questions.
(*With fervour.*)
    Ah the old questions, the old answers, there's nothing like
    them!   650
(*Pause.*)
    It was I was a father to you.
CLOV: Yes.
(*He looks at* HAMM *fixedly.*)
    You were that to me.
HAMM: My house a home for you.
CLOV: Yes.   655
(*He looks about him.*)
    This was that for me.
HAMM: (*Proudly.*) But for me,
(*Gesture towards himself.*)
    no father. But for Hamm,
(*Gesture towards surroundings.*)
    no home.

(*Pause.*)

CLOV: I'll leave you.   660

HAMM: Did you ever think of one thing?

CLOV: Never.

HAMM: That here we're down in a hole.

(*Pause.*)
    But beyond the hills? Eh? Perhaps it's still green. Eh?

(*Pause.*)
665   Flora! Pomona!

(*Ecstatically.*)
    Ceres!

(*Pause.*)
    Perhaps you won't need to go very far.

CLOV: I can't go very far.

(*Pause.*)
    I'll leave you.

670 HAMM: Is my dog ready?

CLOV: He lacks a leg.

HAMM: Is he silky?

CLOV: He's a kind of Pomeranian.

HAMM: Go and get him.

675 CLOV: He lacks a leg.

HAMM: Go and get him!

(*Exit* CLOV.)
    We're getting on.

(*Enter* CLOV *holding by one of its three legs a black toy dog.*)

CLOV: Your dogs are here.

(*He hands the dog to* HAMM *who feels it, fondles it.*)

HAMM: He's white, isn't he?

680 CLOV: Nearly.

    HAMM: What do you mean, nearly? Is he white or isn't he?

CLOV: He isn't.

(*Pause.*)

HAMM: You've forgotten the sex.

CLOV: (*Vexed.*) But he isn't finished. The sex goes on at the end.

(*Pause.*)

685 HAMM: You haven't put on his ribbon.

CLOV: (*Angrily.*) But he isn't finished, I tell you! First you finish your dog and then you put on his ribbon!

(*Pause.*)

HAMM: Can he stand?

CLOV: I don't know.

690 HAMM: Try.

(*He hands the dog to* CLOV *who places it on the ground.*)
    Well?

CLOV: Wait!

(*He squats down and tries to get the dog to stand on its three legs, fails, lets it go. The dog falls on its side.*)

HAMM: (*Impatiently.*) Well?

CLOV: He's standing.

695 HAMM: (*Groping for the dog.*) Where? Where is he?

(CLOV *holds up the dog in a standing position.*)

CLOV: There.

(*He takes* HAMM'*s hand and guides it towards the dog's head.*)

HAMM: (*His hand on the dog's head.*) Is he gazing at me?

CLOV: Yes.

HAMM: (*Proudly.*) As if he were asking me to take him for a walk?   700

CLOV: If you like.

HAMM: (*As before.*) Or as if he were begging me for a bone.

(*He withdraws his hand.*)
    Leave him like that, standing there imploring me.

(CLOV *straightens up. The dog falls on its side.*)

CLOV: I'll leave you.

HAMM: Have you had your visions?   705

CLOV: Less.

HAMM: Is Mother Pegg's light on?

CLOV: Light! How could anyone's light be on?

HAMM: Extinguished!

CLOV: Naturally it's extinguished. If it's not on it's extinguished.   710

HAMM: No, I mean Mother Pegg.

CLOV: But naturally she's extinguished!

(*Pause.*)
    What's the matter with you today?

HAMM: I'm taking my course.   715

(*Pause.*)
    Is she buried?

CLOV: Buried! Who would have buried her?

HAMM: You.

CLOV: Me! Haven't I enough to do without burying people?

HAMM: But you'll bury me.   720

CLOV: No I won't bury you.

(*Pause.*)

HAMM: She was bonny once, like a flower of the field.

(*With reminiscent leer.*)
    And a great one for the men!

CLOV: We too were bonny—once. It's a rare thing not to have been bonny—once.   725

(*Pause.*)

HAMM: Go and get the gaff.

(CLOV *goes to door, halts.*)

CLOV: Do this, do that, and I do it. I never refuse. Why?

HAMM: You're not able to.

CLOV: Soon I won't do it any more.

HAMM: You won't be able to any more.   730

(*Exit* CLOV.)
    Ah the creatures, the creatures, everything has to be explained to them.

(*Enter* CLOV *with gaff.*)

CLOV: Here's your gaff. Stick it up.

(*He gives the gaff to* HAMM *who, wielding it like a puntpole, tries to move his chair.*)

HAMM: Did I move?
735 CLOV: No.

(HAMM *throws down the gaff.*)

HAMM: Go and get the oilcan.
CLOV: What for?
HAMM: To oil the castors.
CLOV: I oiled them yesterday.
740 HAMM: Yesterday! What does that mean? Yesterday!
CLOV: (*Violently.*) That means that bloody awful day, long ago, before this bloody awful day. I use the words you taught me. If they don't mean anything any more, teach me others. Or let me be silent.

(*Pause.*)

745 HAMM: I once knew a madman who thought the end of the world had come. He was a painter—and engraver. I had a great fondness for him. I used to go and see him, in the asylum. I'd take him by the hand and drag him to the window. Look! There! All that rising corn! And there! Look! The sails of the
750 herring fleet! All that loveliness!
(*Pause.*)
He'd snatch away his hand and go back into his corner. Appalled. All he had seen was ashes.
(*Pause.*)
He alone had been spared.
(*Pause.*)
Forgotten.
(*Pause.*)
755 It appears the case is . . . was not so . . . so unusual.
CLOV: A madman? When was that?
HAMM: Oh way back, way back, you weren't in the land of the living.
CLOV: God be with the days!

(*Pause.* HAMM *raises his toque.*)

760 HAMM: I had a great fondness for him.
(*Pause. He puts on his toque again.*)
He was a painter—and engraver.
CLOV: There are so many terrible things.
HAMM: No, no, there are not so many now.
(*Pause.*)
Clov!
765 CLOV: Yes.
HAMM: Do you not think this has gone on long enough?
CLOV: Yes!
(*Pause.*)
What?
HAMM: This . . . this . . . thing.
770 CLOV: I've always thought so.
(*Pause.*)
You not?
HAMM: (*Gloomily.*) Then it's a day like any other day.
CLOV: As long as it lasts.
(*Pause.*)

All life long the same inanities.
HAMM: I can't leave you.   775
CLOV: I know. And you can't follow me.

(*Pause.*)

HAMM: If you leave me how shall I know?
CLOV: (*Briskly.*) Well you simply whistle me and if I don't come running it means I've left you.

(*Pause.*)

HAMM: You won't come and kiss me goodbye?   780
CLOV: Oh I shouldn't think so.

(*Pause.*)

HAMM: But you might be merely dead in your kitchen.
CLOV: The result would be the same.
HAMM: Yes, but how would I know, if you were merely dead in your kitchen?   785
CLOV: Well . . . sooner or later I'd start to stink.
HAMM: You stink already. The whole place stinks of corpses.
CLOV: The whole universe.
HAMM: (*Angrily.*) To hell with the universe.
(*Pause.*)
Think of something.   790
CLOV: What?
HAMM: An idea, have an idea.
(*Angrily.*)
A bright idea!
CLOV: Ah good.
(*He starts pacing to and fro, his eyes fixed on the ground, his hands behind his back. He halts.*)
The pains in my legs! It's unbelievable! Soon I won't be able to   795
think any more.
HAMM: You won't be able to leave me.
(CLOV *resumes his pacing.*)
What are you doing?
CLOV: Having an idea.
(*He paces.*)
Ah!   800

(*He halts.*)

HAMM: What a brain!
(*Pause.*)
Well?
CLOV: Wait!
(*He meditates. Not very convinced.*)
Yes . . .
(*Pause. More convinced.*)
Yes!   805
(*He raises his head.*)
I have it! I set the alarm.

(*Pause.*)

HAMM: This is perhaps not one of my bright days, but frankly—
CLOV: You whistle me. I don't come. The alarm rings. I'm gone. It doesn't ring. I'm dead.   810

(*Pause.*)

HAMM: Is it working?
(*Pause. Impatiently.*)
     The alarm, is it working?
CLOV: Why wouldn't it be working?
HAMM: Because it's worked too much.
815 CLOV: But it's hardly worked at all.
HAMM: (*Angrily.*) Then because it's worked too little!
CLOV: I'll go and see.
(*Exit* CLOV. *Brief ring of alarm off. Enter* CLOV *with alarm-clock. He holds it against* HAMM's *ear and releases alarm. They listen to it ringing to the end. Pause.*)
     Fit to wake the dead! Did you hear it?
HAMM: Vaguely.
820 CLOV: The end is terrific!
HAMM: I prefer the middle.
(*Pause.*)
     Is it not time for my pain-killer?
CLOV: No!
(*He goes to door, turns.*)
     I'll leave you.
825 HAMM: It's time for my story. Do you want to listen to my story.
CLOV: No.
HAMM: Ask my father if he wants to listen to my story.

(CLOV *goes to bins, raises the lid of* NAGG's, *stoops, looks into it. Pause. He straightens up.*)

CLOV: He's asleep.
830 HAMM: Wake him.

(CLOV *stoops, wakes* NAGG *with the alarm. Unintelligible words.* CLOV *straightens up.*)

CLOV: He doesn't want to listen to your story.
HAMM: I'll give him a bon-bon.

(CLOV *stoops. As before.*)

CLOV: He wants a sugar-plum.
HAMM: He'll get a sugar-plum.

(CLOV *stoops. As before.*)

835 CLOV: It's a deal.
(*He goes towards door.* NAGG's *hands appear, gripping the rim. Then the head emerges.* CLOV *reaches door, turns.*)
     Do you believe in the life to come?
HAMM: Mine was always that.
(*Exit* CLOV.)
     Got him that time!
NAGG: I'm listening.
840 HAMM: Scoundrel! Why did you engender me?
NAGG: I didn't know.
HAMM: What? What didn't you know?
NAGG: That it'd be you.
(*Pause.*)
     You'll give me a sugar-plum?
845 HAMM: After the audition.

NAGG: You swear?
HAMM: Yes.
NAGG: On what?
HAMM: My honor.

(*Pause. They laugh heartily.*)

NAGG: Two.   850
HAMM: One.
NAGG: One for me and one for—
HAMM: One! Silence!
(*Pause.*)
     Where was I?
(*Pause. Gloomily.*)
     It's finished, we're finished.   855
(*Pause.*)
     Nearly finished.
(*Pause.*)
     There'll be no more speech.
(*Pause.*)
     Something dripping in my head, ever since the fontanelles.
(*Stifled hilarity of* NAGG.)
     Splash, splash, always on the same spot.
(*Pause.*)
     Perhaps it's a little vein.   860
(*Pause.*)
     A little artery.
(*Pause. More animated.*)
     Enough of that, it's story time, where was I?
(*Pause. Narrative tone.*)
     The man came crawling towards me, on his belly. Pale, wonderfully pale and thin, he seemed on the point of—
(*Pause. Normal tone.*)
     No, I've done that bit.   865
(*Pause. Narrative tone.*)
     I calmly filled my pipe—the meerschaum, lit it with . . . let us say a vesta, drew a few puffs. Aah!
(*Pause.*)
     Well, what is it *you* want?
(*Pause.*)
     It was an extra-ordinarily bitter day, I remember, zero by the thermometer. But considering it was Christmas Eve there was   870
nothing . . . extra-ordinary about that. Seasonable weather, for once in a way.
(*Pause.*)
     Well, what ill wind blows you my way? He raised his face to me, black with mingled dirt and tears.
(*Pause. Normal tone.*)
     That should do it.   875
(*Narrative tone.*)
     No no, don't look at me, don't look at me. He dropped his eyes and mumbled something, apologies I presume.
(*Pause.*)
     I'm a busy man, you know, the final touches, before the festivities, you know what it is.
(*Pause. Forcibly.*)
     Come on now, what is the object of this invasion?   880
(*Pause.*)
     It was a glorious bright day, I remember, fifty by the heliometer, but already the sun was sinking down into the . . . down among the dead.

(*Normal tone.*)
　Nicely put, that.
(*Narrative tone.*)
885　Come on now, come on, present your petition and let me
　resume my labors.
(*Pause. Normal tone.*)
　There's English for you. Ah well . . .
(*Narrative tone.*)
　It was then he took the plunge. It's my little one, he said.
　Tsstss, a little one, that's bad. My little boy, he said, as if the
890　sex mattered. Where did he come from? He named the
　hole. A good half-day, on horse. What are you insinuating?
　That the place is still inhabited? No no, not a soul, except
　himself and the child—assuming he existed. Good. I
　enquired about the situation at Kov, beyond the gulf. Not
895　a sinner. Good. And you expect me to believe you have left
　your little one back there, all alone, and alive into the
　bargain? Come now!
(*Pause.*)
　It was a howling wild day, I remember, a hundred by the
　anenometer. The wind was tearing up the dead pines and
900　sweeping them . . . away.
(*Pause. Normal tone.*)
　A bit feeble, that.
(*Narrative tone.*)
　Come on, man, speak up, what is it you want from me, I have
　to put up my holly.
(*Pause.*)
　Well to make it short it finally transpired that what he wanted
905　from me was . . . bread for his brat? Bread? But I have no bread,
　it doesn't agree with me. Good. Then perhaps a little corn?
(*Pause. Normal tone.*)
　That should do it.
(*Narrative tone.*)
　Corn, yes, I have corn, it's true, in my granaries. But use
　your head. I give you some corn, a pound, a pound and a
910　half, you bring it back to your child and you make him—if
　he's still alive—a nice pot of porridge,
(NAGG *reacts.*)
　a nice pot and a half of porridge, full of nourishment.
　Good. The colors come back into his little cheeks—perhaps.
　And then?
(*Pause.*)
915　I lost patience.
(*Violently.*)
　Use your head, can't you, use your head, you're on earth,
　there's no cure for that!
(*Pause.*)
　It was an exceedingly dry day, I remember, zero by the
　hygrometer. Ideal weather, for my lumbago.
(*Pause. Violently.*)
920　But what in God's name do you imagine? That the earth
　will awake in spring? That the rivers and seas will run with
　fish again? That there's manna in heaven still for imbeciles
　like you?
(*Pause.*)
　Gradually I cooled down, sufficiently at least to ask him how
925　long he had taken on the way. Three whole days. Good. In
　what condition he had left the child. Deep in sleep.
(*Forcibly.*)
　But deep in what sleep, deep in what sleep already?
(*Pause.*)

Well to make it short I finally offered to take him into my
　service. He had touched a chord. And then I imagined
　already that I wasn't much longer for this world.　930
(*He laughs. Pause.*)
　Well?
(*Pause.*)
　Well? Here if you were careful you might die a nice natural
　death, in peace and comfort.
(*Pause.*)
　Well?
(*Pause.*)
　In the end he asked me would I consent to take in the child as　935
　well—if he were still alive.
(*Pause.*)
　It was the moment I was waiting for.
(*Pause.*)
　Would I consent to take in the child . . .
(*Pause.*)
　I can see him still, down on his knees, his hands flat on the
　ground, glaring at me with his mad eyes, in defiance of my　940
　wishes.
(*Pause. Normal tone.*)
　I'll soon have finished with this story.
(*Pause.*)
　Unless I bring in other characters.
(*Pause.*)
　But where would I find them?
(*Pause.*)
　Where would I look for them?　945
(*Pause. He whistles. Enter* CLOV.)
　Let us pray to God.
NAGG: Me sugar-plum!
CLOV: There's a rat in the kitchen!
HAMM: A rat! Are there still rats?
CLOV: In the kitchen there's one.　950
HAMM: And you haven't exterminated him?
CLOV: Half. You disturbed us.
HAMM: He can't get away?
CLOV: No.
HAMM: You'll finish him later. Let us pray to God.　955
CLOV: Again!
NAGG: Me sugar-plum!
HAMM: God first!
(*Pause.*)
　Are you right?
CLOV: (*Resigned.*) Off we go.　960
HAMM: (*To* NAGG.) And you?
NAGG: (*Clasping his hands, closing his eyes, in a gabble.*) Our
　Father which art—
HAMM: Silence! In silence! Where are your manners?
(*Pause.*)
　Off we go.　965
(*Attitudes of prayer. Silence. Abandoning his attitude,
　discouraged.*)
　Well?
CLOV: (*Abandoning his attitude.*) What a hope! And you?
HAMM: Sweet damn all!
(*To* NAGG.)
　And you?
NAGG: Wait!　970
(*Pause. Abandoning his attitude.*)
　Nothing doing!

HAMM: The bastard! He doesn't exist!

CLOV: Not yet.

NAGG: Me sugar-plum!

975 HAMM: There are no more sugar-plums!

(*Pause.*)

NAGG: It's natural. After all I'm your father. It's true if it hadn't been me it would have been someone else. But that's no excuse.

(*Pause.*)

980 Turkish Delight, for example, which no longer exists, we all know that, there is nothing in the world I love more. And one day I'll ask you for some, in return for a kindness, and you'll promise it to me. One must live with the times.

(*Pause.*)

Whom did you call when you were a tiny boy, and were frightened, in the dark? Your mother? No. Me. We let you 985 cry. Then we moved you out of earshot, so that we might sleep in peace.

(*Pause.*)

I was asleep, as happy as a king, and you woke me up to have me listen to you. It wasn't indispensable, you didn't really need to have me listen to you.

(*Pause.*)

990 I hope the day will come when you'll really need to have me listen to you, and need to hear my voice, any voice.

(*Pause.*)

Yes, I hope I'll live till then, to hear you calling me like when you were a tiny boy, and were frightened, in the dark, and I was your only hope.

(*Pause. NAGG knocks on lid of NELL's bin. Pause.*)

995 Nell!

(*Pause. He knocks louder. Pause. Louder.*)

Nell!

(*Pause. NAGG sinks back into his bin, closes the lid behind him. Pause.*)

HAMM: Our revels now are ended.

(*He gropes for the dog.*)

The dog's gone.

CLOV: He's not a real dog, he can't go.

1000 HAMM: (*Groping.*) He's not there.

CLOV: He's lain down.

HAMM: Give him up to me.

(*CLOV picks up the dog and gives it to HAMM. HAMM holds it in his arms. Pause. HAMM throws away the dog.*)

Dirty brute!

(*CLOV begins to pick up the objects lying on the ground.*)

What are you doing?

1005 CLOV: Putting things in order.

(*He straightens up. Fervently.*)

I'm going to clear everything away!

(*He starts picking up again.*)

HAMM: Order!

CLOV: (*Straightening up.*) I love order. It's my dream. A world where all would be silent and still and each thing in its last 1010 place, under the last dust.

(*He starts picking up again.*)

HAMM: (*Exasperated.*) What in God's name do you think you are doing?

CLOV: (*Straightening up.*) I'm doing my best to create a little order.

HAMM: Drop it! 1015

(*CLOV drops the objects he has picked up.*)

CLOV: After all, there or elsewhere.

(*He goes towards door.*)

HAMM: (*Irritably.*) What's wrong with your feet?

CLOV: My feet?

HAMM: Tramp! Tramp!

CLOV: I must have put on my boots. 1020

HAMM: Your slippers were hurting you?

(*Pause.*)

CLOV: I'll leave you.

HAMM: No!

CLOV: What is there to keep me here?

HAMM: The dialogue. 1025

(*Pause.*)

I've got on with my story.

(*Pause.*)

I've got on with it well.

(*Pause. Irritably.*)

Ask me where I've got to.

CLOV: Oh, by the way, your story?

HAMM: (*Surprised.*) What story? 1030

CLOV: The one you've been telling yourself all your days.

HAMM: Ah you mean my chronicle?

CLOV: That's the one.

(*Pause.*)

HAMM: (*Angrily.*) Keep going, can't you, keep going!

CLOV: You've got on with it, I hope. 1035

HAMM: (*Modestly.*) Oh not very far, not very far.

(*He sighs.*)

There are days like that, one isn't inspired.

(*Pause.*)

Nothing you can do about it, just wait for it to come.

(*Pause.*)

No forcing, no forcing, it's fatal.

(*Pause.*)

I've got on with it a little all the same. 1040

(*Pause.*)

Technique, you know.

(*Pause. Irritably.*)

I say I've got on with it a little all the same.

CLOV: (*Admiringly.*) Well I never! In spite of everything you were able to get on with it!

HAMM: (*Modestly.*) Oh not very far, you know, not very far, but 1045 nevertheless, better than nothing.

CLOV: Better than nothing! Is it possible?

HAMM: I'll tell you how it goes. He comes crawling on his belly—

1050 CLOV: Who?
HAMM: What?
CLOV: Who do you mean, he?
HAMM: Who do I mean! Yet another.
CLOV: Ah him! I wasn't sure.
1055 HAMM: Crawling on his belly, whining for bread for his brat.
    He's offered a job as gardener. Before—
  (CLOV *bursts out laughing.*)
    What is there so funny about that?
CLOV: A job as gardener!
HAMM: Is that what tickles you?
1060 CLOV: It must be that.
HAMM: It wouldn't be the bread?
CLOV: Or the brat.

(*Pause.*)

HAMM: The whole thing is comical, I grant you that. What about
    having a good guffaw the two of us together?
1065 CLOV: (*After reflection.*) I couldn't guffaw again today.
HAMM: (*After reflection.*) Nor I.
  (*Pause.*)
    I continue then. Before accepting with gratitude he asks if he
    may have his little boy with him.
CLOV: What age?
1070 HAMM: Oh tiny.
CLOV: He would have climbed the trees.
HAMM: All the little odd jobs.
CLOV: And then he would have grown up.
HAMM: Very likely.

(*Pause.*)

1075 CLOV: Keep going, can't you, keep going!
HAMM: That's all. I stopped there.

(*Pause.*)

CLOV: Do you see how it goes on.
HAMM: More or less.
CLOV: Will it not soon be the end?
1080 HAMM: I'm afraid it will.
CLOV: Pah! You'll make up another.
HAMM: I don't know.
  (*Pause.*)
    I feel rather drained.
  (*Pause.*)
    The prolonged creative effort.
  (*Pause.*)
1085   If I could drag myself down to the sea! I'd make a pillow of
    sand for my head and the tide would come.
CLOV: There's no more tide.

(*Pause.*)

HAMM: Go and see is she dead.

(CLOV *goes to bins, raises the lid of* NELL's, *stoops, looks into it.
Pause.*)

CLOV: Looks like it.

(*He closes the lid, straightens up.* HAMM *raises his toque. Pause. He
puts it on again.*)

HAMM: (*With his hand to his toque.*) And Nagg?   1090

(CLOV *raises lid of* NAGG's *bin, stoops, looks into it. Pause.*)

CLOV: Doesn't look like it.

(*He closes the lid, straightens up.*)

HAMM: (*Letting go his toque.*) What's he doing?

(CLOV *raises lid of* NAGG's *bin, stoops, looks into it. Pause.*)

CLOV: He's crying.

(*He closes lid, straightens up.*)

HAMM: Then he's living.
  (*Pause.*)
    Did you ever have an instant of happiness?   1095
CLOV: Not to my knowledge.

(*Pause.*)

HAMM: Bring me under the window.
  (CLOV *goes towards chair.*)
    I want to feel the light on my face.
  (CLOV *pushes chair.*)
    Do you remember, in the beginning, when you took me for a
    turn? You used to hold the chair too high. At every step you   1100
    nearly tipped me out.
  (*With senile quaver.*)
    Ah great fun, we had, the two of us, great fun.
  (*Gloomily.*)
    And then we got into the way of it.
  (CLOV *stops the chair under window right.*)
    There already?
  (*Pause. He tilts back his head.*)
    Is it light?   1105
CLOV: It isn't dark.
HAMM: (*Angrily.*) I'm asking you is it light.
CLOV: Yes.

(*Pause.*)

HAMM: The curtain isn't closed?
CLOV: No.   1110
HAMM: What window is it?
CLOV: The earth.
HAMM: I knew it!
  (*Angrily.*)
    But there's no light there! The other!
  (CLOV *pushes chair towards window left.*)
    The earth!   1115
  (CLOV *stops the chair under window left.* HAMM *tilts back his head.*)
    That's what I call light!
  (*Pause.*)
    Feels like a ray of sunshine.
  (*Pause.*)

No?
CLOV: No.
1120   HAMM: It isn't a ray of sunshine I feel on my face?
CLOV: No.

(*Pause.*)

HAMM: Am I very white?
(*Pause. Angrily.*)
    I'm asking you am I very white!
CLOV: Not more so than usual.

(*Pause.*)

1125   HAMM: Open the window.
CLOV: What for?
HAMM: I want to hear the sea.
CLOV: You wouldn't hear it.
HAMM: Even if you opened the window?
1130   CLOV: No.
HAMM: Then it's not worth while opening it?
CLOV: No.
HAMM: (*Violently.*) Then open it!
(CLOV *gets up on the ladder, opens the window. Pause.*)
    Have you opened it?
1135   CLOV: Yes.

(*Pause.*)

HAMM: You swear you've opened it?
CLOV: Yes.

(*Pause.*)

HAMM: Well . . . !
(*Pause.*)
    It must be very calm.
(*Pause. Violently.*)
1140   I'm asking you is it very calm!
CLOV: Yes.
HAMM: It's because there are no more navigators.
(*Pause.*)
    You haven't much conversation all of a sudden. Do you not
    feel well?
1145   CLOV: I'm cold.
HAMM: What month are we?
(*Pause.*)
    Close the window, we're going back.
(CLOV *closes the window, gets down, pushes the chair back to its
    place, remains standing behind it, head bowed.*)
    Don't stay there, you give me the shivers!
(CLOV *returns to his place beside the chair.*)
    Father!
(*Pause. Louder.*)
1150   Father!
(*Pause.*)
    Go and see did he hear me.

(CLOV *goes to* NAGG's *bin, raises the lid, stoops. Unintelligible
words.* CLOV *straightens up.*)

CLOV: Yes.

HAMM: Both times?

(CLOV *stoops. As before.*)

CLOV: Once only.
HAMM: The first time or the second?   1155

(CLOV *stoops. As before.*)

CLOV: He doesn't know.
HAMM: It must have been the second.
CLOV: We'll never know.

(*He closes lid.*)

HAMM: Is he still crying?
CLOV: No.   1160
HAMM: The dead go fast.
(*Pause.*)
    What's he doing?
CLOV: Sucking his biscuit.
HAMM: Life goes on.
(CLOV *returns to his place beside the chair.*)
    Give me a rug, I'm freezing.   1165
CLOV: There are no more rugs.

(*Pause.*)

HAMM: Kiss me.
(*Pause.*)
    Will you not kiss me?
CLOV: No.
HAMM: On the forehead.   1170
CLOV: I won't kiss you anywhere.

(*Pause.*)

HAMM: (*Holding out his hand.*) Give me your hand at least.
(*Pause.*)
    Will you not give me your hand?
CLOV: I won't touch you.

(*Pause.*)

HAMM: Give me the dog.   1175
(CLOV *looks round for the dog.*)
    No!
CLOV: Do you not want your dog?
HAMM: No.
CLOV: Then I'll leave you.
HAMM: (*Head bowed, absently.*) That's right.   1180

(CLOV *goes to door, turns.*)

CLOV: If I don't kill that rat he'll die.
HAMM: (*As before.*) That's right.
(*Exit* CLOV. *Pause.*)
    Me to play.
(*He takes out his handkerchief, unfolds it, holds it spread out
before him.*)
    We're getting on.
(*Pause.*)

1185 You weep, and weep, for nothing, so as not to laugh, and little
by little . . . you begin to grieve.
(*He folds the handkerchief, puts it back in his pocket, raises his
head.*)
All those I might have helped.
(*Pause.*)
Helped!
(*Pause.*)
Saved.
(*Pause.*)
1190 Saved!
(*Pause.*)
The place was crawling with them!
(*Pause. Violently.*)
Use your head, can't you, use your head, you're on earth,
there's no cure for that!
(*Pause.*)
Get out of here and love one another! Lick your neighbor
1195 as yourself!
(*Pause. Calmer.*)
When it wasn't bread they wanted it was crumpets.
(*Pause. Violently.*)
Out of my sight and back to your petting parties!
(*Pause.*)
All that, all that!
(*Pause.*)
Not even a real dog!
(*Calmer.*)
1200 The end is in the beginning and yet you go on.
(*Pause.*)
Perhaps I could go on with my story, end it and begin
another.
(*Pause.*)
Perhaps I could throw myself out on the floor.
(*He pushes himself painfully off his seat, falls back again.*)
Dig my nails into the cracks and drag myself forward with
1205 my fingers.
(*Pause.*)
It will be the end and there I'll be, wondering what can have
brought it on and wondering what can have . . .
(*He hesitates.*)
. . . why it was so long coming.
(*Pause.*)
There I'll be, in the old shelter, alone against the silence
1210 and . . .
(*He hesitates.*)
. . . the stillness. If I can hold my peace, and sit quiet, it will be
all over with sound, and motion, all over and done with.
(*Pause.*)
I'll have called my father and I'll have called my . . .
(*He hesitates.*)
. . . my son. And even twice, or three times, in case they
1215 shouldn't have heard me, the first time, or the second.
(*Pause.*)
I'll say to myself, He'll come back.
(*Pause.*)
And then?
(*Pause.*)
And then?
(*Pause.*)
He couldn't, he has gone too far.
(*Pause.*)

And then? 1220
(*Pause. Very agitated.*)
All kinds of fantasies! That I'm being watched! A rat! Steps!
Breath held and then . . .
(*He breathes out.*)
Then babble, babble, words, like the solitary child who turns
himself into children, two, three, so as to be together, and
whisper together, in the dark. 1225
(*Pause.*)
Moment upon moment, pattering down, like the millet
grains of . . .
(*He hesitates.*)
. . . that old Greek, and all life long you wait for that to mount
up to a life.
(*Pause. He opens his mouth to continue, renounces.*)
Ah let's get it over! 1230
(*He whistles. Enter* CLOV *with alarm-clock. He halts beside the
chair.*)
What? Neither gone nor dead?
CLOV: In spirit only.
HAMM: Which?
CLOV: Both.
HAMM: Gone from me you'd be dead. 1235
CLOV: And vice versa.
HAMM: Outside of here it's death!
(*Pause.*)
And the rat?
CLOV: He's got away.
HAMM: He can't go far. 1240
(*Pause. Anxious.*)
Eh?
CLOV: He doesn't need to go far.

(*Pause.*)

HAMM: Is it not time for my pain-killer?
CLOV: Yes.
HAMM: Ah! At last! Give it to me! Quick! 1245

(*Pause.*)

CLOV: There's no more pain-killer.

(*Pause.*)

HAMM: (*Appalled.*) Good . . . !
(*Pause.*)
No more pain-killer!
CLOV: No more pain-killer. You'll never get any more pain-
killer. 1250

(*Pause.*)

HAMM: But the little round box. It was full!
CLOV: Yes. But now it's empty.

(*Pause.* CLOV *starts to move about the room. He is looking for a
place to put down the alarm-clock.*)

HAMM: (*Soft.*) What'll I do?
(*Pause. In a scream.*)
What'll I do?

(CLOV *sees the picture, takes it down, stands it on the floor with its face to the wall, hangs up the alarm-clock in its place.*)

1255   What are you doing?

CLOV: Winding up.

HAMM: Look at the earth.

CLOV: Again!

HAMM: Since it's calling to you.

1260 CLOV: Is your throat sore?

(*Pause.*)

    Would you like a lozenge?

(*Pause.*)

    No.

(*Pause.*)

    Pity.

(CLOV *goes, humming, towards window right, halts before it, looks up at it.*)

HAMM: Don't sing.

1265 CLOV: (*Turning towards* HAMM.) One hasn't the right to sing any more?

HAMM: No.

CLOV: Then how can it end?

HAMM: You want it to end?

1270 CLOV: I want to sing.

HAMM: I can't prevent you.

(*Pause.* CLOV *turns towards window right.*)

CLOV: What did I do with that steps?

(*He looks around for ladder.*)

    You didn't see that steps?

(*He sees it.*)

    Ah, about time.

(*He goes towards window left.*)

1275   Sometimes I wonder if I'm in my right mind. Then it passes over and I'm as lucid as before.

(*He gets up on ladder, looks out of window.*)

    Christ, she's under water!

(*He looks.*)

    How can that be?

(*He pokes forward his head, his hand above his eyes.*)

    It hasn't rained.

(*He wipes the pane, looks. Pause.*)

1280   Ah what a fool I am! I'm on the wrong side!

(*He gets down, takes a few steps towards window right.*)

    Under water!

(*He goes back for ladder.*)

    What a fool I am!

(*He carries ladder towards window right.*)

    Sometimes I wonder if I'm in my right senses. Then it passes off and I'm as intelligent as ever.

(*He sets down ladder under window right, gets up on it, looks out of window. He turns towards* HAMM.)

1285   Any particular sector you fancy? Or merely the whole thing?

HAMM: Whole thing.

CLOV: The general effect? Just a moment.

(*He looks out of window. Pause.*)

HAMM: Clov.

CLOV: (*Absorbed.*) Mmm.   1290

HAMM: Do you know what it is?

CLOV: (*As before.*) Mmm.

HAMM: I was never there.

(*Pause.*)

    Clov!

CLOV: (*Turning towards* HAMM, *exasperated.*) What is it?   1295

HAMM: I was never there.

CLOV: Lucky for you.

(*He looks out of window.*)

HAMM: Absent, always. It all happened without me. I don't know what's happened.

(*Pause.*)

    Do you know what's happened?   1300

(*Pause.*)

    Clov!

CLOV: (*Turning towards* HAMM, *exasperated.*) Do you want me to look at this muckheap, yes or no?

HAMM: Answer me first.

CLOV: What?   1305

HAMM: Do you know what's happened?

CLOV: When? Where?

HAMM: (*Violently.*) When! What's happened? Use your head, can't you! What has happened?

CLOV: What for Christ's sake does it matter?   1310

(*He looks out of window.*)

HAMM: I don't know.

(*Pause.* CLOV *turns towards* HAMM.)

CLOV: (*Harshly.*) When old Mother Pegg asked you for oil for her lamp and you told her to get out to hell, you knew what was happening then, no?

(*Pause.*)

    You know what she died of, Mother Pegg? Of darkness.   1315

HAMM: (*Feebly.*) I hadn't any.

CLOV: (*As before.*) Yes, you had.

(*Pause.*)

HAMM: Have you the glass?

CLOV: No, it's clear enough as it is.

HAMM: Go and get it.   1320

(*Pause.* CLOV *casts up his eyes, brandishes his fists. He loses balance, clutches on to the ladder. He starts to get down, halts.*)

CLOV: There's one thing I'll never understand.

(*He gets down.*)

    Why I always obey you. Can you explain that to me?

HAMM: No. . . . Perhaps it's compassion.

(*Pause.*)

    A kind of great compassion.

(*Pause.*)

    Oh you won't find it easy, you won't find it easy.   1325

(*Pause.* CLOV *begins to move about the room in search of the telescope.*)

CLOV: I'm tired of our goings on, very tired.
(*He searches.*)
You're not sitting on it?

(*He moves the chair, looks at the place where it stood, resumes his search.*)

HAMM: (*Anguished.*) Don't leave me there!
(*Angrily* CLOV *restores the chair to its place.*)
Am I right in the center?

1330 CLOV: You'd need a microscope to find this—
(*He sees the telescope.*)
Ah, about time.

(*He picks up the telescope, gets up on the ladder, turns the telescope on the without.*)

HAMM: Give me the dog.
CLOV: (*Looking.*) Quiet!
HAMM: (*Angrily.*) Give me the dog!

(CLOV *drops the telescope, clasps his hands to his head. Pause. He gets down precipitately, looks for the dog, sees it, picks it up, hastens towards* HAMM *and strikes him violently on the head with the dog.*)

1335 CLOV: There's your dog for you!

(*The dog falls to the ground. Pause.*)

HAMM: He hit me!
CLOV: You drive me mad, I'm mad!
HAMM: If you must hit me, hit me with the axe.
(*Pause.*)
Or with the gaff, hit me with the gaff. Not with the dog. With
1340 the gaff. Or with the axe.

(CLOV *picks up the dog and gives it to* HAMM *who takes it in his arms.*)

CLOV: (*Imploringly.*) Let's stop playing!
HAMM: Never!
(*Pause.*)
Put me in my coffin.
CLOV: There are no more coffins.
1345 HAMM: Then let it end!
(CLOV *goes towards ladder.*)
With a bang!
(CLOV *gets up on ladder, gets down again, looks for telescope, sees it, picks it up, gets up ladder, raises telescope.*)
Of darkness! And me? Did anyone ever have pity on me?
CLOV: (*Lowering the telescope, turning towards* HAMM.) What?
(*Pause.*)
Is it me you're referring to?
1350 HAMM: (*Angrily.*) An aside, ape! Did you never hear an aside before?
(*Pause.*)
I'm warming up for my last soliloquy.

CLOV: I warn you. I'm going to look at this filth since it's an order.
But it's the last time.
(*He turns the telescope on the without.*)
Let's see.   1355
(*He moves the telescope.*)
Nothing . . . nothing . . . good . . . good . . . nothing . . . goo—
(*He starts, lowers the telescope, examines it, turns it again on the without. Pause.*)
Bad luck to it!
HAMM: More complications!
(CLOV *gets down.*)
Not an underplot, I trust.

(CLOV *moves ladder nearer window, gets up on it, turns telescope on the without.*)

CLOV: (*Dismayed.*) Looks like a small boy!   1360
HAMM: (*Sarcastic.*) A small . . . boy!
CLOV: I'll go and see.
(*He gets down, drops the telescope, goes towards door, turns.*)
I'll take the gaff.

(*He looks for the gaff, sees it, picks it up, hastens towards door.*)

HAMM: No!

(CLOV *halts.*)

CLOV: No? A potential procreator?   1365
HAMM: If he exists he'll die there or he'll come here. And if he doesn't . . .

(*Pause.*)

CLOV: You don't believe me? You think I'm inventing?

(*Pause.*)

HAMM: It's the end, Clov, we've come to the end. I don't need you any more.   1370

(*Pause.*)

CLOV: Lucky for you.

(*He goes towards door.*)

HAMM: Leave me the gaff.

(CLOV *gives him the gaff, goes towards door, halts, looks at alarm-clock, takes it down, looks round for a better place to put it, goes to bins, puts it on lid of* NAGG's *bin. Pause.*)

CLOV: I'll leave you.

(*He goes towards door.*)

HAMM: Before you go . . .
(CLOV *halts near door.*)
. . . say something.
CLOV: There is nothing to say.   1375

HAMM: A few words . . . to ponder . . . in my heart.

CLOV: Your heart!

HAMM: Yes.

(*Pause. Forcibly.*)

1380   Yes!

(*Pause.*)

    With the rest, in the end, the shadows, the murmurs, all the trouble, to end up with.

(*Pause.*)

    Clov. . . . He never spoke to me. Then, in the end, before he went, without my having asked him, he spoke to me.

1385   He said . . .

CLOV: (*Despairingly.*) Ah . . . !

HAMM: Something . . . from your heart.

CLOV: My heart!

HAMM: A few words . . . from your heart.

(*Pause.*)

1390 CLOV: (*Fixed gaze, tonelessly, towards auditorium.*) They said to me, That's love, yes, yes, not a doubt, now you see how—

HAMM: Articulate!

CLOV: (*As before.*) How easy it is. They said to me, That's friendship, yes, yes, no question, you've found it. They said

1395 to me, Here's the place, stop, raise your head and look at all that beauty. That order! They said to me, Come now, you're not a brute beast, think upon these things and you'll see how all becomes clear. And simple! They said to me, What skilled attention they get, all these dying of their wounds.

1400 HAMM: Enough!

CLOV: (*As before.*) I say to myself—sometimes, Clov, you must learn to suffer better than that if you want them to weary of punishing you—one day. I say to myself—sometimes, Clov, you must be there better than that if you want them to let

1405 you go—one day. But I feel too old, and too far, to form new habits. Good, it'll never end, I'll never go.

(*Pause.*)

    Then one day, suddenly, it ends, it changes, I don't understand, it dies, or it's me, I don't understand, that either. I ask the words that remain—sleeping, waking, morning, evening.

1410   They have nothing to say.

(*Pause.*)

    I open the door of the cell and go. I am so bowed I only see my feet, if I open my eyes, and between my legs a little trail of black dust. I say to myself that the earth is extinguished, though I never saw it lit.

(*Pause.*)

1415   It's easy going.

(*Pause.*)

    When I fall I'll weep for happiness.

(*Pause. He goes towards door.*)

    HAMM: Clov!

(CLOV *halts, without turning.*)

    Nothing.

(CLOV *moves on.*)

    Clov!

(CLOV *halts, without turning.*)

1420 CLOV: This is what we call making an exit.

HAMM: I'm obliged to you, Clov. For your services.

CLOV: (*Turning, sharply.*) Ah pardon, it's I am obliged to you.

HAMM: It's we are obliged to each other.

(*Pause.* CLOV *goes towards door.*)

    One thing more.

(CLOV *halts.*)

    A last favor.   1425

(*Exit* CLOV.)

    Cover me with the sheet.

(*Long pause.*)

    No? Good.

(*Pause.*)

    Me to play.

(*Pause. Wearily.*)

    Old endgame lost of old, play and lose and have done with losing.   1430

(*Pause. More animated.*)

    Let me see.

(*Pause.*)

    Ah yes!

(*He tries to move the chair, using the gaff as before. Enter* CLOV, *dressed for the road. Panama hat, tweed coat, raincoat over his arm, umbrella, bag. He halts by the door and stands there, impassive and motionless, his eyes fixed on* HAMM, *till the end.* HAMM *gives up.*)

    Good.

(*Pause.*)

    Discard.

(*He throws away the gaff, makes to throw away the dog, thinks better of it.*)

    Take it easy.   1435

(*Pause.*)

    And now?

(*Pause.*)

    Raise hat.

(*He raises his toque.*)

    Peace to our . . . arses.

(*Pause.*)

    And put on again.

(*He puts on his toque.*)

    Deuce.   1440

(*Pause. He takes off his glasses.*)

    Wipe.

(*He takes out his handkerchief and, without unfolding it, wipes his glasses.*)

    And put on again.

(*He puts on his glasses, puts back the handkerchief in his pocket.*)

    We're coming. A few more squirms like that and I'll call.

(*Pause.*)

    A little poetry.

(*Pause.*)

    You prayed—   1445

(*Pause. He corrects himself.*)

    You CRIED for night; it comes—

(*Pause. He corrects himself.*)

    It FALLS: now cry in darkness.

(*He repeats, chanting.*)

    You cried for night; it falls: now cry in darkness.

(*Pause.*)

    Nicely put, that.

(*Pause.*)

    And now?   1450

(*Pause.*)

Moments for nothing, now as always, time was never and
time is over, reckoning closed and story ended.
(*Pause. Narrative tone.*)
    If he could have his child with him. . . .
(*Pause.*)
    It was the moment I was waiting for.
(*Pause.*)
1455   You don't want to abandon him? You want him to bloom
while you are withering? Be there to solace your last million
last moments?
(*Pause.*)
    He doesn't realize, all he knows is hunger, and cold, and
death to crown it all. But you! You ought to know what
1460   the earth is like, nowadays. Oh I put him before his
responsibilities!
(*Pause. Normal tone.*)
    Well, there we are, there I am, that's enough.
(*He raises the whistle to his lips, hesitates, drops it. Pause.*)
    Yes, truly!
(*He whistles. Pause. Louder. Pause.*)
    Good.
(*Pause.*)
1465   Father!
(*Pause. Louder.*)
    Father!
(*Pause.*)
    Good.
(*Pause.*)
    We're coming.

(*Pause.*)
    And to end up with?
(*Pause.*)
    Discard.   1470
(*He throws away the dog. He tears the whistle from his neck.*)
    With my compliments.
(*He throws whistle towards auditorium. Pause. He sniffs. Soft.*)
    Clov!
(*Long pause.*)
    No? Good.
(*He takes out the handkerchief.*)
    Since that's the way we're playing it . . .
(*He unfolds handkerchief.*)
    . . . let's play it that way . . .   1475
(*He unfolds.*)
    . . . and speak no more about it . . .
(*He finishes unfolding.*)
    . . . speak no more.
(*He holds handkerchief spread out before him.*)
    Old stancher!
(*Pause.*)
    You . . . remain.
(*Pause. He covers his face with handkerchief, lowers his arms to
armrests, remains motionless.*)

(*Brief tableau.*)

Caryl Churchill

Caryl Churchill (b. 1938) was born in England and began her education in Canada during World War II; she returned to study at Oxford University, taking her B.A. in 1960. At Oxford, Churchill began her career as a playwright, producing several plays: *Downstairs* (1958), *Having a Wonderful Time* (1960), and *Early Death* (1962). During the 1960s, she wrote a series of brilliant radio plays. She also studied radical politics and returned to the theater in the 1970s with a series of striking political dramas: *Owners* (1972), *Objections to Sex and Violence* (1975), and *A Light Shining in Buckinghamshire* (1976). In the mid-1970s, Churchill began to work more closely with experimental theater companies, collaborating with actors and directors in the writing of her plays. Working with the feminist theater company Monstrous Regiment (the name alludes to the Calvinist preacher John Knox's 1558 diatribe against Queen Mary of England, "The First Blast of the Trumpet against the Monstrous Regiment of Women"), she wrote *Vinegar Tom* (1976), a play about witchcraft and sexual politics in seventeenth-century England. With the Joint Stock company, she investigated the politics of sexuality more extensively in *Cloud Nine* (1979), a pastiche of melodrama, Gilbert and Sullivan operetta, and modern realistic theater that uses CROSS-DRESSING and ROLEDOUBLING to explore the relationship between colonial and sexual oppression in the nineteenth century and today. The history of gender oppression and the options for contemporary women are the subject of *Top Girls* (1982), and Churchill has continued to write challenging plays on the relationship between class, race, and gender in British social life, including *Fen* (1983), *Serious Money* (1987), and *Three More Sleepless Nights* (1995). *Mad Forest* (1990) concerns the revolution in Rumania and *Skryker* (1994) was developed from Lancashire folktales; *Blue Heart* (1997) was written after Churchill collaborated on several music-theater pieces, including *Lives of the Great Poisoners* (1993) and *Hotel* (1997). Her most recent plays have been short, nearly allegorical dramas: *Far Away* (2001) concerns the problems of political resistance and represents yet another new departure for Churchill, political allegory in the mode of magical realism; *A Number* (2003) takes on the subject of human cloning through the relationship between a father and several identical "sons." *Drunk Enough to Say I Love You?* (2006) is a fast-paced two-hander that situates fantasies of masculinity at the center of economic, ecological, and social oppression. Her engagement with contemporary politics is focused on the middle east in her most recent play, *Seven Jewish Children* (2009).

Cloud Nine

Onstage, the most exciting and interesting device in *Cloud Nine* is its use of CROSS-DRESSING and ROLE-DOUBLING. In the first act, for instance, Betty must be played by a man, Joshua by a white man, and Edward by a woman. By "alienating" actors from the characters they play, Churchill clearly intends to raise the questions of gender, sexual orientation, and race as ideological issues, for in each of these cases the difference between the performer and the role marks what Clive wants to see as real. Betty is played by a man because Clive—and his patriarchal society—cannot envision women's identity; women are constructed on the model of male attitudes. Joshua is played by a white man because imperial and racist culture reduces African identity to the construction of white, European attitudes. Edward is played by a woman to express the impossibility of Edward's conforming to Clive's heterosexual standards.

In all three cases, the "identity" of the character is compromised or even erased, to be filled in and embodied by the attitudes that Clive and his society want them to hold. This performative dimension of the play's politics is echoed by the play's doubling of parts—each of the actors in act 1 takes a part in act 2, inviting the audience to draw comparisons between the two characters. Although other doubling patterns are possible, Churchill has suggested doubling Harry Bagley, the explorer, with Martin, the superficially liberated man; Clive, the

Danny Scheie as Betty, waving to Harry Bagley in Caryl Churchill's *Cloud Nine,* produced by the Trinity Repertory Theatre.

© T. Charles Erickson

father, with Cathy, the child; Betty with Edward; and so on. Doubling and cross-dressing are familiar conventions in the theater, but in *Cloud Nine* they have a specific dramatic purpose in developing the themes of the play. By denaturalizing the categories of gender, race, and sexuality, *Cloud Nine* undertakes a typically postmodern inquiry into the construction of social reality, asking what meanings are created by these categories, and how they work to structure the relationship between self and society.

Author's Note

Cloud Nine was written for Joint Stock Theatre Group in 1978–1979. The company's usual work method is to set up a workshop in which the writer, director and actors research a particular subject. The writer then goes away to write the play, before returning to the company for a rehearsal and rewrite period. In the case of *Cloud Nine* the workshop lasted for three weeks, the writing period for twelve, and the rehearsal for six.

The workshop for *Cloud Nine* was about sexual politics. This meant that the starting point for our research was to talk about ourselves and share our very different attitudes and experiences. We also explored stereotypes and role reversals in games and improvisations, read books and talked to other people. Though the play's situations and characters were not developed in the workshop, it draws deeply on this material, and I wouldn't have written the same play without it.

When I came to write the play, I returned to an idea that had been touched on briefly in the workshop—the parallel between colonial and sexual oppression, which Genet calls "the colonial or feminine mentality of interiorised repression." So the first act of *Cloud Nine* takes place in Victorian Africa, where Clive, the white man, imposes his ideals on his family and the natives. Betty, Clive's wife, is played by a man because she wants to be what men want her to be, and, in the same way, Joshua, the black servant, is played by a white man because he wants to be what whites want him to be. Betty does not value herself as a woman, nor does Joshua value himself as a black. Edward, Clive's son, is played by a woman for a different reason—partly to do with the stage convention of having boys played by women (Peter Pan, radio plays, etc.) and partly with highlighting the way Clive tries to impose traditional male behaviour on him. Clive struggles throughout the act to maintain the world he wants to see—a faithful wife, a manly son. Harry's homosexuality is reviled, Ellen's is invisible. Rehearsing the play for the first time, we were initially taken by how funny the first act was and then by the painfulness of the relationships—which then became more funny than when they had seemed purely farcical.

The second act is set in London in 1979—this is where I wanted the play to end up, in the changing sexuality of our own time. Betty is middle-aged, Edward and Victoria have grown up. A hundred years have passed, but for the characters only twenty-five years. There were two reasons for this. I felt the first act would be stronger set in Victorian times, at the height of colonialism, rather than in Africa during the 1950s. And when the company talked about their childhoods and the attitudes to sex and marriage that they had been given when they were young, everyone felt that they had received very conventional, almost Victorian expectations and that they had made great changes and discoveries in their lifetimes.

The first act, like the society it shows, is male dominated and firmly structured. In the second act, more energy comes from the women and the gays. The uncertainties and changes of society, and a more feminine and less authoritarian feeling, are reflected in the looser structure of the act. Betty, Edward and Victoria all change from the rigid positions they had been left in by the first act, partly because of their encounters with Gerry and Lin. In fact, all the characters in this act change a little for the better. If men are finding it hard to keep control in the first act, they are finding it hard to let go in the second: Martin dominates Victoria, despite his declarations of sympathy for feminism, and the bitter end of colonialism is apparent in Lin's soldier brother, who dies in Northern Ireland. Betty is now played by a woman, as she gradually becomes real to herself. Cathy is played by a man, partly as a simple reversal of Edward being played by a woman, partly because the size and presence of a man on stage seemed appropriate to the emotional force of young children, and partly, as with Edward, to show more clearly the issues involved in learning what is considered correct behaviour for a girl.

It is essential for Joshua to be played by a white, Betty (I) by a man, Edward (I) by a woman, and Cathy by a man. The soldier should be played by the actor who plays Cathy. The doubling of Mrs Saunders and Ellen is not intended to make a point so much as for sheer fun—and of course to keep the company to seven in each act. The doubling can be done in any way that seems right for any particular production. The first production went Clive-Cathy, Betty-Edward, Edward-Betty, Maud-Victoria, Mrs Saunders/Ellen-Lin, Joshua-Gerry, Harry-Martin. When we did the play again, at the Royal Court in 1980, we decided to try a different doubling: Clive-Edward, Betty-Gerry, Edward-Victoria, Maud-Lin, Mrs Saunders/Ellen-Betty, Joshua-Cathy, Harry-Martin. I've a slight preference for the first way because I like seeing Clive become Cathy, and enjoy the Edward-Betty connections. Some doublings aren't practicable, but any way of doing the doubling seems to set up some interesting resonances between the two acts.

C.C. 1983

The Text

The first edition of *Cloud Nine* (Pluto/Joint Stock 1979) went to press before the end of rehearsal. Further changes were made within the first week or two of production, and these were incorporated in the Pluto/Joint Stock/Royal Court edition (1980). This edition also went to press during rehearsal, so although it may include some small changes made for that production, others don't turn up till the Pluto Plays edition (1983), which also includes a few changes from the American production, a few lines cut here or reinstated there. Other changes for the American production can be found in French's American acting edition—the main ones are the position of Betty's monologue and some lines of the 'ghosts'. For the Fireside Bookclub and Methuen Inc. (1984) in America I did another brushing up, not very different from Pluto '83, and I have kept almost the same text for this edition. The scenes I tinker with most are the flogging scene and Edward's and Gerry's last scene—I no longer know what's the final version except by looking at the text.

There's a problem with the Maud and Ellen reappearances in Act Two. If Ellen is doubled with Betty, obviously only Maud can appear. Equally Maud-Betty would mean only Ellen could, though that seems a dull doubling. This text gives both Maud and Ellen. In the production at the Court in 1981 only Maud appeared and she has some extra lines so she can talk about sex as well as work; they can be found in Pluto (1983).

C.C. 1984

Cloud Nine

Caryl Churchill

CHARACTERS

ACT ONE

CLIVE, *a colonial administrator*
BETTY, *his wife, played by a man*
JOSHUA, *his black servant, played by a white*
EDWARD, *his son, played by a woman*
VICTORIA, *his daughter, a dummy*
MAUD, *his mother-in-law*
ELLEN, *Edward's governess*
HARRY BAGLEY, *an explorer*
MRS SAUNDERS, *a widow*

ACT TWO

BETTY
EDWARD, *her son*

VICTORIA, *her daughter*
MARTIN, *Victoria's husband*
LIN
CATHY, *Lin's daughter, age 5, played by a man*
GERRY, *Edward's lover*

Except for CATHY, characters in Act Two are played by
actors of their own sex.

*Act One takes place in a British colony in Africa in Victorian
times.*

*Act Two takes place in London in 1979. But for the characters it is
twenty-five years later.*

ACT ONE

SCENE I

Low bright sun. Verandah. Flagpole with union jack. The Family—
CLIVE, BETTY, EDWARD, VICTORIA, MAUD, ELLEN, JOSHUA.

ALL: (*Sing.*)

> Come gather, sons of England, come gather in your pride.
> Now meet the world united, now face it side by side;
> Ye who the earth's wide corners, from veldt to prairie,
>   roam.
> From bush and jungle muster all who call old England
>   "home."
5 > Then gather round for England,
> Rally to the flag,
> From North and South and East and West
> Come one and all for England!

CLIVE: This is my family. Though far from home
10 We serve the Queen wherever we may roam
I am a father to the natives here,
And father to my family so dear.

(*He presents* BETTY. *She is played by a man.*)

> My wife is all I dreamt a wife should be,
> And everything she is she owes to me.
15 BETTY: I live for Clive. The whole aim of my life
> Is to be what he looks for in a wife.
> I am a man's creation as you see,
> And what men want is what I want to be.

(CLIVE *presents* JOSHUA. *He is played by a white.*)

CLIVE: My boy's a jewel. Really has the knack.
20 You'd hardly notice that the fellow's black.
JOSHUA: My skin is black but oh my soul is white.
> I hate my tribe. My master is my light.
> I only live for him. As you can see,
> What white men want is what I want to be.

(CLIVE *presents* EDWARD. *He is played by a woman.*)

CLIVE: My son is young. I'm doing all I can   25
> To teach him to grow up to be a man.
EDWARD: What father wants I'd dearly like to be.
> I find it rather hard as you can see.

(CLIVE *presents* VICTORIA, *who is a dummy,* MAUD, *and* ELLEN.)

CLIVE: No need for any speeches by the rest.
> My daughter, mother-in-law, and governess.   30
ALL: (*Sing.*)

> O'er countless numbers she, our Queen,
> Victoria reigns supreme;
> O'er Africa's sunny plains, and o'er
> Canadian frozen stream;
> The forge of war shall weld the chains of brotherhood   35
> secure;
> So to all time in ev'ry clime our Empire shall endure.
> Then gather round for England,
> Rally to the flag,
> From North and South and East and West
> Come one and all for England!   40

(*All go except* BETTY. CLIVE *comes.*)

BETTY: Clive?
CLIVE: Betty. Joshua!

(JOSHUA *comes with a drink for* CLIVE.)

BETTY: I thought you would never come. The day's so long
> without you.
CLIVE: Long ride in the bush.   45
BETTY: Is anything wrong? I heard drums.
CLIVE: Nothing serious. Beauty is a damned good mare. I must
> get some new boots sent from home. These ones have never
> been right. I have a blister.
BETTY: My poor dear foot.   50
CLIVE: It's nothing.
BETTY: Oh but it's sore.

CLIVE: We are not in this country to enjoy ourselves. Must have
55   ridden fifty miles. Spoke to three different headmen who
        would all gladly chop off each other's heads and wear them
        round their waists.
BETTY: Clive!
CLIVE: Don't be squeamish, Betty, let me have my joke. And what
        has my little dove done today?
60 BETTY: I've read a little.
CLIVE: Good. Is it good?
BETTY: It's poetry.
CLIVE: You're so delicate and sensitive.
BETTY: And I played the piano. Shall I send for the children?
65 CLIVE: Yes, in a minute. I've a piece of news for you.
BETTY: Good news?
CLIVE: You'll certainly think it's good. A visitor.
BETTY: From home?
CLIVE: No. Well of course originally from home.
70 BETTY: Man or woman?
CLIVE: Man.
BETTY: I can't imagine.
CLIVE: Something of an explorer. Bit of a poet. Odd chap but
        brave as a lion. And a great admirer of yours.
75 BETTY: What do you mean? Whoever can it be?
CLIVE: With an H and a B. And does conjuring tricks for little
        Edward.
BETTY: That sounds like Mr Bagley.
CLIVE: Harry Bagley.
80 BETTY: He certainly doesn't admire me, Clive, what a thing to say.
        How could I possibly guess from that. He's hardly explored
        anything at all, he's just been up a river, he's done nothing at
        all compared to what you do. You should have said a heavy
        drinker and a bit of a bore.
85 CLIVE: But you like him well enough. You don't mind him
        coming?
BETTY: Anyone at all to break the monotony.
CLIVE: But you have your mother. You have Ellen.
BETTY: Ellen is a governess. My mother is my mother.
90 CLIVE: I hoped when she came to visit she would be company
        for you.
BETTY: I don't think mother is on a visit. I think she lives
        with us.
CLIVE: I think she does.
95 BETTY: Clive you are so good.
CLIVE: But are you bored my love?
BETTY: It's just that I miss you when you're away. We're not in this
        country to enjoy ourselves. If I lack society that is my form of
        service.
100 CLIVE: That's a brave girl. So today has been all right? No
        fainting? No hysteria?
BETTY: I have been very tranquil.
CLIVE: Ah what a haven of peace to come home to. The coolth, the
        calm, the beauty.
105 BETTY: There is one thing, Clive, if you don't mind.
CLIVE: What can I do for you, my dear?
BETTY: It's about Joshua.
CLIVE: I wouldn't leave you alone here with a quiet mind if
        it weren't for Joshua.
110 BETTY: Joshua doesn't like me.
CLIVE: Joshua has been my boy for eight years. He has saved my
        life. I have saved his life. He is devoted to me and to mine.
        I have said this before.

BETTY: He is rude to me. He doesn't do what I say. Speak to him.
CLIVE: Tell me what happened.   115
BETTY: He said something improper.
CLIVE: Well, what?
BETTY: I don't like to repeat it.
CLIVE: I must insist.
BETTY: I had left my book inside on the piano. I was in the   120
        hammock. I asked him to fetch it.
CLIVE: And did he not fetch it?
BETTY: Yes, he did eventually.
CLIVE: And what did he say?
BETTY: Clive—   125
CLIVE: Betty.
BETTY: He said Fetch it yourself. You've got legs under that
        dress.
CLIVE: Joshua!

(JOSHUA comes.)

        Joshua, madam says you spoke impolitely to her this afternoon. 130
JOSHUA: Sir?
CLIVE: When she asked you to pass her book from the piano.
JOSHUA: She has the book, sir.
BETTY: I have the book now, but when I told you—
CLIVE: Betty, please, let me handle this. You didn't pass it at   135
        once?
JOSHUA: No sir, I made a joke first.
CLIVE: What was that?
JOSHUA: I said my legs were tired, sir. That was funny because
        the book was very near, it would not make my legs tired   140
        to get it.
BETTY: That's not true.
JOSHUA: Did madam hear me wrong?
CLIVE: She heard something else.
JOSHUA: What was that, madam?   145
BETTY: Never mind.
CLIVE: Now Joshua, it won't do you know. Madam doesn't like
        that kind of joke. You must do what madam says, just do what
        she says and don't answer back. You know your place, Joshua.
        I don't have to say any more.   150
JOSHUA: No sir.
BETTY: I expect an apology.
JOSHUA: I apologise, madam.
CLIVE: There now. It won't happen again, my dear. I'm very
        shocked Joshua, very shocked.   155

(CLIVE winks at JOSHUA, unseen by BETTY. JOSHUA goes.)

CLIVE: I think another drink, and send for the children, and
        isn't that Harry riding down the hill? Wave, wave. Just in
        time before dark. Cuts it fine, the blighter. Always a hothead,
        Harry.
BETTY: Can he see us?   160
CLIVE: Stand further forward. He'll see your white dress. There,
        he waved back.
BETTY: Do you think so? I wonder what he saw. Sometimes sunset
        is so terrifying I can't bear to look.
CLIVE: It makes me proud. Elsewhere in the empire the sun is   165
        rising.
BETTY: Harry looks so small on the hillside.

(ELLEN comes.)

ELLEN: Shall I bring the children?

BETTY: Shall Ellen bring the children?

170 CLIVE: Delightful.

BETTY: Yes, Ellen, make sure they're warm. The night air is deceptive. Victoria was looking pale yesterday.

CLIVE: My love.

(MAUD comes from inside the house.)

MAUD: Are you warm enough Betty?

175 BETTY: Perfectly.

MAUD: The night air is deceptive.

BETTY: I'm quite warm. I'm too warm.

MAUD: You're not getting a fever, I hope? She's not strong, you know, Clive. I don't know how long you'll keep her in this

180 climate.

CLIVE: I look after Her Majesty's domains. I think you can trust me to look after my wife.

(ELLEN comes carrying VICTORIA, age 2. EDWARD, age 9, lags behind.)

BETTY: Victoria, my pet, say good evening to papa.

(CLIVE takes VICTORIA on his knee.)

CLIVE: There's my sweet little Vicky. What have we done today?

185 BETTY: She wore Ellen's hat.

CLIVE: Did she wear Ellen's big hat like a lady? What a pretty.

BETTY: And Joshua gave her a piggy back. Tell papa. Horsy with Joshy?

ELLEN: She's tired.

190 CLIVE: Nice Joshy played horsy. What a big strong Joshy. Did you have a gallop? Did you make him stop and go? Not very chatty tonight are we?

BETTY: Edward, say good evening to papa.

CLIVE: Edward my boy. Have you done your lessons well?

195 EDWARD: Yes papa.

CLIVE: Did you go riding?

EDWARD: Yes papa.

CLIVE: What's that you're holding?

BETTY: It's Victoria's doll. What are you doing with it, Edward?

200 EDWARD: Minding her.

BETTY: Well I should give it to Ellen quickly. You don't want papa to see you with a doll.

CLIVE: No, we had you with Victoria's doll once before, Edward.

ELLEN: He's minding it for Vicky. He's not playing with it.

205 BETTY: He's not playing with it, Clive. He's minding it for Vicky.

CLIVE: Ellen minds Victoria, let Ellen mind the doll.

ELLEN: Come, give it to me.

(ELLEN takes the doll.)

EDWARD: Don't pull her about. Vicky's very fond of her. She

210 likes me to have her.

BETTY: He's a very good brother.

CLIVE: Yes, it's manly of you Edward, to take care of your little sister. We'll say no more about it. Tomorrow I'll take you riding with me and Harry Bagley. Would you like that?

215 EDWARD: Is he here?

CLIVE: He's just arrived. There Betty, take Victoria now. I must go and welcome Harry.

(CLIVE tosses VICTORIA to BETTY, who gives her to ELLEN.)

EDWARD: Can I come, papa?

BETTY: Is he warm enough?

EDWARD: Am I warm enough?

220 CLIVE: Never mind the women, Ned. Come and meet Harry.

(They go. The women are left. There is a silence.)

MAUD: I daresay Mr Bagley will be out all day and we'll see nothing of him.

BETTY: He plays the piano. Surely he will sometimes stay at home with us.

225 MAUD: We can't expect it. The men have their duties and we have ours.

BETTY: He won't have seen a piano for a year. He lives a very rough life.

ELLEN: Will it be exciting for you, Betty?

230 MAUD: Whatever do you mean, Ellen?

ELLEN: We don't have very much society.

BETTY: Clive is my society.

MAUD: It's time Victoria went to bed.

ELLEN: She'd like to stay up and see Mr Bagley.

235 MAUD: Mr Bagley can see her tomorrow.

(ELLEN goes.)

MAUD: You let that girl forget her place, Betty.

BETTY: Mother, she is governess to my son. I know what her place is. I think my friendship does her good. She is not very happy.

240 MAUD: Young women are never happy.

BETTY: Mother, what a thing to say.

MAUD: Then when they're older they look back and see that comparatively speaking they were ecstatic.

BETTY: I'm perfectly happy.

245 MAUD: You are looking very pretty tonight. You were such a success as a young girl. You have made a most fortunate marriage. I'm sure you will be an excellent hostess to Mr Bagley.

BETTY: I feel quite nervous at the thought of entertaining.

250 MAUD: I can always advise you if I'm asked.

BETTY: What a long time they're taking. I always seem to be waiting for the men.

MAUD: Betty you have to learn to be patient. I am patient. My mama was very patient.

255

(CLIVE approaches, supporting CAROLINE SAUNDERS.)

CLIVE: It is a pleasure. It is an honour. It is positively your duty to seek my help. I would be hurt, I would be insulted by any show of independence. Your husband would have been one of my dearest friends if he had lived. Betty, look who has come, Mrs Saunders. She has ridden here all alone, amazing spirit. What will you have? Tea or something stronger? Let her lie down, she is overcome. Betty, you will know what to do.

260

(MRS SAUNDERS lies down.)

MAUD: I knew it. I heard drums. We'll be killed in our beds.

CLIVE: Now, please, calm yourself.

265

MAUD: I am perfectly calm. I am just outspoken. If it comes to being killed I shall take it as calmly as anyone.

CLIVE: There is no cause for alarm. Mrs Saunders has been alone since her husband died last year, amazing spirit. Not 270 surprisingly, the strain has told. She has come to us as her nearest neighbours.

MAUD: What happened to make her come?

CLIVE: This is not an easy country for a woman.

MAUD: Clive, I heard drums. We are not children.

275 CLIVE: Of course you heard drums. The tribes are constantly at war, if the term is not too grand to grace their squabbles. Not unnaturally Mrs Saunders would like the company of white women. The piano. Poetry.

BETTY: We are not her nearest neighbours.

280 CLIVE: We are among her nearest neighbours and I was a dear friend of her late husband. She knows that she will find a welcome here. She will not be disappointed. She will be cared for.

MAUD: Of course we will care for her.

285 BETTY: Victoria is in bed. I must go and say goodnight. Mother, please, you look after Mrs Saunders.

CLIVE: Harry will be here at once.

(BETTY *goes*.)

MAUD: How rash to go out after dark without a shawl.

CLIVE: Amazing spirit. Drink this.

290 MRS SAUNDERS: Where am I?

MAUD: You are quite safe.

MRS SAUNDERS: Clive? Clive? Thank God. This is very kind. How do you do? I am sorry to be a nuisance. Charmed. Have you a gun? I have a gun.

295 CLIVE: There is no need for guns I hope. We are all friends here.

MRS SAUNDERS: I think I will lie down again.

(HARRY BAGLEY *and* EDWARD *have approached*.)

MAUD: Ah, here is Mr Bagley.

EDWARD: I gave his horse some water.

CLIVE: You don't know Mrs Saunders, do you Harry? She has at 300 present collapsed, but she is recovering thanks to the good offices of my wife's mother who I think you've met before. Betty will be along in a minute. Edward will go home to school shortly. He is quite a young man since you saw him.

HARRY: I hardly knew him.

305 MAUD: What news have you for us, Mr Bagley?

CLIVE: Do you know Mrs Saunders, Harry? Amazing spirit.

EDWARD: Did you hardly know me?

HARRY: Of course I knew you. I mean you have grown.

EDWARD: What do you expect?

310 HARRY: That's quite right, people don't get smaller.

MAUD: Edward. You should be in bed.

EDWARD: No, I'm not tired, I'm not tired am I Uncle Harry?

HARRY: I don't think he's tired.

CLIVE: He is overtired. It is past his bedtime. Say goodnight.

315 EDWARD: Goodnight, sir.

CLIVE: And to your grandmother.

EDWARD: Goodnight, grandmother.

(EDWARD *goes*.)

MAUD: Shall I help Mrs Saunders indoors? I'm afraid she may get a chill.

CLIVE: Shall I give her an arm? 320

MAUD: How kind of you, Clive. I think I am strong enough.

(MAUD *helps* MRS SAUNDERS *into the house*.)

CLIVE: Not a word to alarm the women.

HARRY: Absolutely.

CLIVE: I did some good today I think. Kept up some alliances. There's a lot of affection there. 325

HARRY: They're affectionate people. They can be very cruel of course.

CLIVE: Well they are savages.

HARRY: Very beautiful people many of them.

CLIVE: Joshua! (*To* HARRY.) I think we should sleep with guns. 330

HARRY: I haven't slept in a house for six months. It seems extremely safe.

(JOSHUA *comes*.)

CLIVE: Joshua, you will have gathered there's a spot of bother. Rumours of this and that. You should be armed I think.

JOSHUA: There are many bad men, sir. I pray about it. Jesus will 335 protect us.

CLIVE: He will indeed and I'll also get you a weapon. Betty, come and keep Harry company. Look in the barn, Joshua, every night.

(CLIVE *and* JOSHUA *go*. BETTY *comes*.)

HARRY: I wondered where you were. 340

BETTY: I was singing lullabies.

HARRY: When I think of you I always think of you with Edward in your lap.

BETTY: Do you think of me sometimes then?

HARRY: You have been thought of where no white woman has 345 ever been thought of before.

BETTY: It's one way of having adventures. I suppose I will never go in person.

HARRY: That's up to you.

BETTY: Of course it's not. I have duties. 350

HARRY: Are you happy, Betty?

BETTY: Where have you been?

HARRY: Built a raft and went up the river. Stayed with some people. The king is always very good to me. They have a lot of skulls around the place but not white men's I think. 355 I made up a poem one night. If I should die in this forsaken spot, There is a loving heart without a blot, Where I will live—and so on.

BETTY: When I'm near you it's like going out into the jungle. It's like going up the river on a raft. It's like going out in 360 the dark.

HARRY: And you are safety and light and peace and home.

BETTY: But I want to be dangerous.

HARRY: Clive is my friend.

BETTY: I am your friend. 365

HARRY: I don't like dangerous women.

BETTY: Is Mrs Saunders dangerous?

HARRY: Not to me. She's a bit of an old boot.

(JOSHUA *comes, unobserved*.)

BETTY: Am I dangerous?

370   HARRY: You are rather.
BETTY: Please like me.
HARRY: I worship you.
BETTY: Please want me.
HARRY: I don't want to want you. Of course I want you.
375   BETTY: What are we going to do?
HARRY: I should have stayed on the river. The hell with it.

(*He goes to take her in his arms, she runs away into the house.* HARRY *stays where he is. He becomes aware of* JOSHUA.)

HARRY: Who's there?
JOSHUA: Only me sir.
HARRY: Got a gun now have you?
380   JOSHUA: Yes sir.
HARRY: Where's Clive?
JOSHUA: Going round the boundaries sir.
HARRY: Have you checked there's nobody in the barns?
JOSHUA: Yes sir.
385   HARRY: Shall we go in a barn and fuck? It's not an order.
JOSHUA: That's all right, yes.

(*They go off.*)

SCENE II

An open space some distance from the house. MRS SAUNDERS
alone, breathless. She is carrying a riding crop. CLIVE *arrives.*

CLIVE: Why? Why?
MRS SAUNDERS: Don't fuss, Clive, it makes you sweat.
CLIVE: Why ride off now? Sweat, you would sweat if you were in
love with somebody as disgustingly capricious as you are. You
5   will be shot with poisoned arrows. You will miss the picnic.
Somebody will notice I came after you.
MRS SAUNDERS: I didn't want you to come after me. I wanted
to be alone.
CLIVE: You will be raped by cannibals.
10   MRS SAUNDERS: I just wanted to get out of your house.
CLIVE: My God, what women put us through. Cruel, cruel. I
think you are the sort of woman who would enjoy whipping
somebody. I've never met one before.
MRS SAUNDERS: Can I tell you something, Clive?
15   CLIVE: Let me tell you something first. Since you came to the
house I have had an erection twenty-four hours a day except
for ten minutes after the time we had intercourse.
MRS SAUNDERS: I don't think that's physically possible.
CLIVE: You are causing me appalling physical suffering. Is this the
20   way to treat a benefactor?
MRS SAUNDERS: Clive, when I came to your house the other night
I came because I was afraid. The cook was going to let his
whole tribe in through the window.
CLIVE: I know that, my poor sweet. Amazing—
25   MRS SAUNDERS: I came to you although you are not my nearest
neighbour—
CLIVE: Rather than to the old major of seventy-two.
MRS SAUNDERS: Because the last time he came to visit me I had to
defend myself with a shotgun and I thought you would take
30   no for an answer.
CLIVE: But you've already answered yes.
MRS SAUNDERS: I answered yes once. Sometimes I want to
say no.

CLIVE: Women, my God. Look the picnic will start, I have to go to
the picnic. Please Caroline—   35
MRS SAUNDERS: I think I will have to go back to my own house.
CLIVE: Caroline, if you were shot with poisoned arrows do you
know what I'd do? I'd fuck your dead body and poison myself.
Caroline, you smell amazing. You terrify me. You are dark
like this continent. Mysterious. Treacherous. When you rode   40
to me through the night. When you fainted in my arms.
When I came to you in your bed, when I lifted the mosquito
netting, when I said let me in, let me in. Oh don't shut me out,
Caroline, let me in.

(*He has been caressing her feet and legs. He disappears completely
under her skirt.*)

MRS SAUNDERS: Please stop. I can't concentrate. I want to go   45
home. I wish I didn't enjoy the sensation because I don't like
you, Clive. I do like living in your house where there's plenty
of guns. But I don't like you at all. But I do like the sensation.
Well I'll have it then. I'll have it, I'll have it—

(*Voices are heard singing The First Noël.*)

Don't stop. Don't stop.   50

(CLIVE *comes out from under her skirt.*)

CLIVE: The Christmas picnic. I came.
MRS SAUNDERS: I didn't.
CLIVE: I'm all sticky.
MRS SAUNDERS: What about me? Wait.
CLIVE: All right, are you? Come on. We mustn't be found.   55
MRS SAUNDERS: Don't go now.
CLIVE: Caroline, you are so voracious. Do let go. Tidy yourself up.
There's a hair in my mouth.

(CLIVE *and* MRS SAUNDERS *go off.* BETTY *and* MAUD *come, with*
JOSHUA *carrying hamper.*)

MAUD: I never would have thought a guinea fowl could taste so
like a turkey.   60
BETTY: I had to explain to the cook three times.
MAUD: You did very well dear.

(JOSHUA *sits apart with gun.* EDWARD *and* HARRY *with* VICTORIA
on his shoulder, singing The First Noël. MAUD *and* BETTY *are
unpacking the hamper.* CLIVE *arrives separately.*)

MAUD: This tablecloth was one of my mama's.
BETTY: Uncle Harry playing horsy.
EDWARD: Crackers crackers.   65
BETTY: Not yet, Edward.
CLIVE: And now the moment we have all been waiting for.

(CLIVE *opens champagne. General acclaim.*)

CLIVE: Oh dear, stained my trousers, never mind.
EDWARD: Can I have some?
MAUD: Oh no Edward, not for you.   70
CLIVE: Give him half a glass.
MAUD: If your father says so.
CLIVE: All rise please. To Her Majesty Queen Victoria, God bless
her, and her husband and all her dear children.

75 ALL: The Queen.
EDWARD: Crackers crackers.

(*General cracker pulling, hats.* CLIVE *and* HARRY *discuss champagne.*)

HARRY: Excellent, Clive, wherever did you get it?
CLIVE: I know a chap in French Equatorial Africa.
EDWARD: I won, I won mama.

(ELLEN *arrives.*)

80 BETTY: Give a hat to Joshua, he'd like it.

(EDWARD *takes hat to* JOSHUA. BETTY *takes a ball from the hamper and plays catch with* ELLEN. *Murmurs of surprise and congratulations from the men whenever they catch the ball.*)

EDWARD: Mama, don't play. You know you can't catch a ball.
BETTY: He's perfectly right. I can't throw either.

(BETTY *sits down.* ELLEN *has the ball.*)

EDWARD: Ellen, don't you play either. You're no good. You spoil it.

(EDWARD *takes* VICTORIA *from* HARRY *and gives her to* ELLEN. *He takes the ball and throws it to* HARRY. HARRY, CLIVE *and* EDWARD *play ball.*)

85 BETTY: Ellen come and sit with me. We'll be spectators and clap.

(EDWARD *misses the ball.*)

CLIVE: Butterfingers.
EDWARD: I'm not.
HARRY: Throw straight now.
90 EDWARD: I did, I did.
CLIVE: Keep your eye on the ball.
EDWARD: You can't throw.
CLIVE: Don't be a baby.
EDWARD: I'm not, throw a hard one, throw a hard one—
95 CLIVE: Butterfingers. What will Uncle Harry think of you?
EDWARD: It's your fault. You can't throw. I hate you.

(*He throws the ball wildly in the direction of* JOSHUA.)

CLIVE: Now you've lost the ball. He's lost the ball.
EDWARD: It's Joshua's fault. Joshua's butterfingers.
CLIVE: I don't think I want to play any more. Joshua, find the ball
100   will you?
EDWARD: Yes, please play. I'll find the ball. Please play.
CLIVE: You're so silly and you can't catch. You'll be no good at cricket.
MAUD: Why don't we play hide and seek?
105 EDWARD: Because it's a baby game.
BETTY: You've hurt Edward's feelings.
CLIVE: A boy has no business having feelings.
HARRY: Hide and seek. I'll be it. Everybody must hide. This is the base, you have to get home to base.
110 EDWARD: Hide and seek, hide and seek.
HARRY: Can we persuade the ladies to join us?
MAUD: I'm playing. I love games.

BETTY: I always get found straight away.
ELLEN: Come on, Betty, do. Vicky wants to play.
EDWARD: You won't find me ever.   115

(*They all go except* CLIVE, HARRY, JOSHUA.)

HARRY: It is safe, I suppose?
CLIVE: They won't go far. This is very much my territory and it's broad daylight. Joshua will keep an open eye.
HARRY: Well I must give them a hundred. You don't know what this means to me, Clive. A chap can only go on so   120
long alone. I can climb mountains and go down rivers, but what's it for? For Christmas and England and games and women singing. This is the empire, Clive. It's not me putting a flag in new lands. It's you. The empire is one big
family. I'm one of its black sheep, Clive. And I know you   125
think my life is rather dashing. But I want you to know I admire you. This is the empire, Clive, and I serve it. With all my heart.
CLIVE: I think that's about a hundred.
HARRY: Ready or not, here I come!   130

(*He goes.*)

CLIVE: Harry Bagley is a fine man, Joshua. You should be proud to know him. He will be in history books.
JOSHUA: Sir, while we are alone.
CLIVE: Joshua of course, what is it? You always have my ear. Any time.   135
JOSHUA: Sir, I have some information. The stable boys are not to be trusted. They whisper. They go out at night. They visit their people. Their people are not my people. I do not visit my people.
CLIVE: Thank you, Joshua. They certainly look after Beauty. I'll be   140
sorry to have to replace them.
JOSHUA: They carry knives.
CLIVE: Thank you, Joshua.
JOSHUA: And, sir.
CLIVE: I appreciate this, Joshua, very much.   145
JOSHUA: Your wife.
CLIVE: Ah, yes?
JOSHUA: She also thinks Harry Bagley is a fine man.
CLIVE: Thank you, Joshua.
JOSHUA: Are you going to hide?   150
CLIVE: Yes, yes I am. Thank you. Keep your eyes open Joshua.
JOSHUA: I do, sir.

(CLIVE *goes.* JOSHUA *goes.* HARRY *and* BETTY *race back to base.*)

BETTY: I can't run, I can't run at all.
HARRY: There, I've caught you.
BETTY: Harry, what are we going to do?   155
HARRY: It's impossible, Betty.
BETTY: Shall we run away together?

(MAUD *comes.*)

MAUD: I give up. Don't catch me. I have been stung.
HARRY: Nothing serious I hope.
MAUD: I have ointment in my bag. I always carry ointment.   160
I shall just sit down and rest. I am too old for all this fun. Hadn't you better be seeking, Harry?

(HARRY *goes.* MAUD *and* BETTY *are alone for some time. They don't speak.* HARRY *and* EDWARD *race back.*)

EDWARD: I won, I won, you didn't catch me.
HARRY: Yes I did.
165 EDWARD: Mama, who was first?
BETTY: I wasn't watching. I think it was Harry.
EDWARD: It wasn't Harry. You're no good at judging. I won, didn't I grandma?
MAUD: I expect so, since it's Christmas.
170 EDWARD: I won, Uncle Harry. I'm better than you.
BETTY: Why don't you help Uncle Harry look for the others?
EDWARD: Shall I?
HARRY: Yes, of course.
BETTY: Run along then. He's just coming.

(EDWARD *goes.*)

175   Harry, I shall scream.
HARRY: Ready or not, here I come.

(HARRY *runs off.*)

BETTY: Why don't you go back to the house, mother, and rest your insect-bite?
MAUD: Betty, my duty is here. I don't like what I see. Clive
180   wouldn't like it, Betty. I am your mother.
BETTY: Clive gives you a home because you are my mother.

(HARRY *comes back.*)

HARRY: I can't find anyone else. I'm getting quite hot.
BETTY: Sit down a minute.
HARRY: I can't do that. I'm he. How's your sting?
185 MAUD: It seems to be swelling up.
BETTY: Why don't you go home and rest? Joshua will go with you. Joshua!
HARRY: I could take you back.
MAUD: That would be charming.
190 BETTY: You can't go. You're he.

(JOSHUA *comes.*)

    Joshua, my mother wants to go back to the house. Will you go with her please.
JOSHUA: Sir told me I have to keep an eye.
BETTY: I am telling you to go back to the house. Then you can
195   come back here and keep an eye.
MAUD: Thank you Betty. I know we have our little differences, but I always want what is best for you.

(JOSHUA *and* MAUD *go.*)

HARRY: Don't give way. Keep calm.
BETTY: I shall kill myself.
200 HARRY: Betty, you are a star in my sky. Without you I would have no sense of direction. I need you, and I need you where you are, I need you to be Clive's wife. I need to go up rivers and know you are sitting here thinking of me.
BETTY: I want more than that. Is that wicked of me?
205 HARRY: Not wicked, Betty. Silly.

(EDWARD *calls in the distance.*)

EDWARD: Uncle Harry, where are you?
BETTY: Can't we ever be alone?
HARRY: You are a mother. And a daughter. And a wife.
BETTY: I think I shall go and hide again.

(BETTY *goes.* HARRY *goes.* CLIVE *chases* MRS SAUNDERS *across the stage.* EDWARD *and* HARRY *call in the distance.*)

EDWARD: Uncle Harry!   210
HARRY: Edward!

(EDWARD *comes.*)

EDWARD: Uncle Harry!

(HARRY *comes.*)

    There you are. I haven't found anyone have you?
HARRY: I wonder where they all are.
EDWARD: Perhaps they're lost forever. Perhaps they're dead.   215
    There's trouble going on isn't there, and nobody says because of not frightening the women and children.
HARRY: Yes, that's right.
EDWARD: Do you think we'll be killed in our beds?
HARRY: Not very likely.   220
EDWARD: I can't sleep at night. Can you?
HARRY: I'm not used to sleeping in a house.
EDWARD: If I'm awake at night can I come and see you? I won't wake you up. I'll only come in if you're awake.
HARRY: You should try to sleep.   225
EDWARD: I don't mind being awake because I make up adventures. Once we were on a raft going down to the rapids. We've lost the paddles because we used them to fight off the crocodiles. A crocodile comes at me and I stab it again and again and the blood is everywhere and it tips up the raft and   230
    it has you by the leg and it's biting your leg right off and I take my knife and stab it in the throat and rip open its stomach and it lets go of you but it bites my hand but it's dead. And I drag you onto the river bank and I'm almost fainting with pain and we lie there in each other's arms.   235
HARRY: Have I lost my leg?
EDWARD: I forgot about the leg by then.
HARRY: Hadn't we better look for the others?
EDWARD: Wait. I've got something for you. It was in mama's box but she never wears it.   240

(EDWARD *gives* HARRY *a necklace.*)

    You don't have to wear it either but you might like it to look at.
HARRY: It's beautiful. But you'll have to put it back.
EDWARD: I wanted to give it to you.
HARRY: You did. It can go back in the box. You still gave it to me.   245
    Come on now, we have to find the others.
EDWARD: Harry, I love you.
HARRY: Yes I know. I love you too.
EDWARD: You know what we did when you were here before. I want to do it again. I think about it all the time. I try to do it   250
    to myself but it's not as good. Don't you want to any more?
HARRY: I do, but it's a sin and a crime and it's also wrong.
EDWARD: But we'll do it anyway won't we?
HARRY: Yes of course.

255 EDWARD: I wish the others would all be killed. Take it out now
　　　and let me see it.
　　HARRY: No.
　　EDWARD: Is it big now?
　　HARRY: Yes.
260 EDWARD: Let me touch it.
　　HARRY: No.
　　EDWARD: Just hold me.
　　HARRY: When you can't sleep.
　　EDWARD: We'd better find the others then. Come on.
265 HARRY: Ready or not, here we come.

(*They go out with whoops and shouts.* BETTY *and* ELLEN *come.*)

　　BETTY: Ellen, I don't want to play any more.
　　ELLEN: Nor do I, Betty.
　　BETTY: Come and sit here with me. Oh Ellen, what will become
　　　of me?
270 ELLEN: Betty, are you crying? Are you laughing?
　　BETTY: Tell me what you think of Harry Bagley.
　　ELLEN: He's a very fine man.
　　BETTY: No, Ellen, what you really think.
　　ELLEN: I think you think he's very handsome.
275 BETTY: And don't you think he is? Oh Ellen, you're so good and
　　　I'm so wicked.
　　ELLEN: I'm not so good as you think.

(EDWARD *comes.*)

　　EDWARD: I've found you.
　　ELLEN: We're not hiding Edward.
280 EDWARD: But I found you.
　　ELLEN: We're not playing, Edward, now run along.
　　EDWARD: Come on, Ellen, do play. Come on, mama.
　　ELLEN: Edward, don't pull your mama like that.
　　BETTY: Edward, you must do what your governess says. Go
285 　　and play with Uncle Harry.
　　EDWARD: Uncle Harry!

(EDWARD *goes.*)

　　BETTY: Ellen, can you keep a secret?
　　ELLEN: Oh yes, yes please.
　　BETTY: I love Harry Bagley. I want to go away with him. There,
290 　　I've said it, it's true.
　　ELLEN: How do you know you love him?
　　BETTY: I kissed him.
　　ELLEN: Betty.
　　BETTY: He held my hand like this. Oh I want him to do it again.
295 　　I want him to stroke my hair.
　　ELLEN: Your lovely hair. Like this, Betty?
　　BETTY: I want him to put his arm around my waist.
　　ELLEN: Like this, Betty?
　　BETTY: Yes, oh I want him to kiss me again.
300 ELLEN: Like this Betty?

(ELLEN *kisses* BETTY.)

　　BETTY: Ellen, whatever are you doing? It's not a joke.
　　ELLEN: I'm sorry, Betty. You're so pretty. Harry Bagley doesn't
　　　deserve you. You wouldn't really go away with him?
　　BETTY: Oh Ellen, you don't know what I suffer. You don't know
305 　　what love is. Everyone will hate me, but it's worth it for
　　　Harry's love.

ELLEN: I don't hate you, Betty, I love you.
BETTY: Harry says we shouldn't go away. But he says he
　　worships me.
ELLEN: I worship you Betty.   310
BETTY: Oh Ellen, you are my only friend.

(*They embrace. The others have all gathered together.* MAUD *has
rejoined the party, and* JOSHUA.)

CLIVE: Come along everyone, you mustn't miss Harry's conjuring
　　trick.

(BETTY *and* ELLEN *go to join the others.*)

MAUD: I didn't want to spoil the fun by not being here.
HARRY: What is it that flies all over the world and is up my   315
　　sleeve?

(HARRY *produces a union jack from up his sleeve. General
acclaim.*)

CLIVE: I think we should have some singing now. Ladies, I rely on
　　you to lead the way.
ELLEN: We have a surprise for you. I have taught Joshua a
　　Christmas carol. He has been singing it at the piano but   320
　　I'm sure he can sing it unaccompanied, can't you, Joshua?
JOSHUA: 　　　In the deep midwinter
　　　　　　　Frosty wind made moan,
　　　　　　　Earth stood hard as iron,
　　　　　　　Water like a stone.   325
　　　　　　　Snow had fallen snow on snow
　　　　　　　Snow on snow,
　　　　　　　In the deep midwinter
　　　　　　　Long long ago.

　　　　　　　What can I give him   330
　　　　　　　Poor as I am?
　　　　　　　If I were a shepherd
　　　　　　　I would bring a lamb.
　　　　　　　If I were a wise man
　　　　　　　I would do my part   335
　　　　　　　What can I give him,
　　　　　　　Give my heart.

SCENE III

Inside the house. BETTY, MRS SAUNDERS, MAUD *with* VICTORIA.
*The blinds are down so the light isn't bright though it is day out-
side.* CLIVE *looks in.*

CLIVE: Everything all right? Nothing to be frightened of.

(CLIVE *goes. Silence.*)

MAUD: Clap hands, daddy comes, with his pockets full of plums.
　　All for Vicky.

(*Silence.*)

MRS SAUNDERS: Who actually does the flogging?
MAUD: I don't think we want to imagine.   5
MRS SAUNDERS: I imagine Joshua.
BETTY: Yes I think it would be Joshua. Or would Clive do it
　　himself?
MRS SAUNDERS: Well we can ask them afterwards.

10   MAUD: I don't like the way you speak of it, Mrs Saunders.

MRS SAUNDERS: How should I speak of it?

MAUD: The men will do it in the proper way, whatever it is. We have our own part to play.

MRS SAUNDERS: Harry Bagley says they should just be sent away.

15   I don't think he likes to see them beaten.

BETTY: Harry is so tender hearted. Perhaps he is right.

MAUD: Harry Bagley is not altogether—He has lived in this country a long time without any responsibilities. It is part of his charm but it hasn't improved his judgment. If the boys

20   were just sent away they would go back to the village and make more trouble.

MRS SAUNDERS: And what will they say about us in the village if they've been flogged?

BETTY: Perhaps Clive should keep them here.

25   MRS SAUNDERS: That is never wise.

BETTY: Whatever shall we do?

MAUD: I don't think it is up to us to wonder. The men don't tell us what is going on among the tribes, so how can we possibly make a judgment?

30   MRS SAUNDERS: I know a little of what is going on.

BETTY: Tell me what you know. Clive tells me nothing.

MAUD: You would not want to be told about it, Betty. It is enough for you that Clive knows what is happening. Clive will know what to do. Your father always knew what to do.

35   BETTY: Are you saying you would do something different, Caroline?

MRS SAUNDERS: I would do what I did at my own home. I left. I can't see any way out except to leave. I will leave here. I will keep leaving everywhere I suppose.

40   MAUD: Luckily this household has a head. I am squeamish myself. But luckily Clive is not.

BETTY: You are leaving here then, Caroline?

MRS SAUNDERS: Not immediately. I'm sorry.

(*Silence.*)

MRS SAUNDERS: I wonder if it's over.

(EDWARD *comes in.*)

45   BETTY: Shouldn't you be with the men, Edward?

EDWARD: I didn't want to see any more. They got what they deserved. Uncle Harry said I could come in.

MRS SAUNDERS: I never allowed the servants to be beaten in my own house. I'm going to find out what's happening.

(MRS SAUNDERS *goes out.*)

50   BETTY: Will she go and look?

MAUD: Let Mrs Saunders be a warning to you, Betty. She is alone in the world. You are not, thank God. Since your father died, I know what it is to be unprotected. Vicky is such a pretty little girl. Clap hands, daddy comes, with his pockets full of plums.

55   All for Vicky.

(EDWARD, *meanwhile, has found the doll and is playing clap hands with her.*)

BETTY: Edward, what have you got there?

EDWARD: I'm minding her.

BETTY: Edward, I've told you before, dolls are for girls.

MAUD: Where is Ellen? She should be looking after Edward.

(*She goes to the door.*) Ellen! Betty, why do you let that girl   60

mope about in her own room? That's not what she's come to Africa for.

BETTY: You must never let the boys at school know you like dolls. Never, never. No one will talk to you, you won't be on the cricket team, you won't grow up to be a man like   65

your papa.

EDWARD: I don't want to be like papa. I hate papa.

MAUD: Edward! Edward!

BETTY: You're a horrid wicked boy and papa will beat you. Of course you don't hate him, you love him. Now give   70

Victoria her doll at once.

EDWARD: She's not Victoria's doll, she's my doll. She doesn't love Victoria and Victoria doesn't love her. Victoria never even plays with her.

MAUD: Victoria will learn to play with her.   75

EDWARD: She's mine and she loves me and she won't be happy if you take her away, she'll cry, she'll cry, she'll cry.

(BETTY *takes the doll away, slaps him, bursts into tears.* ELLEN *comes in.*)

BETTY: Ellen, look what you've done. Edward's got the doll again. Now, Ellen, will you please do your job.

ELLEN: Edward, you are a wicked boy. I am going to lock you in   80

the nursery until supper time. Now go upstairs this minute.

(*She slaps* EDWARD, *who bursts into tears and goes out.*)

I do try to do what you want. I'm so sorry.

(ELLEN *bursts into tears and goes out.*)

MAUD: There now, Vicky's got her baby back. Where did Vicky's naughty baby go? Shall we smack her? Just a little smack.   85

(MAUD *smacks the doll hard.*) There, now she's a good baby. Clap hands, daddy comes, with his pockets full of plums. All for Vicky's baby. When I was a child we honoured our parents. My mama was an angel.

(JOSHUA *comes in. He stands without speaking.*)

BETTY: Joshua?   90

JOSHUA: Madam?

BETTY: Did you want something?

JOSHUA: Sent to see the ladies are all right, madam.

(MRS SAUNDERS *comes in.*)

MRS SAUNDERS: We're very well thank you, Joshua, and how are you?   95

JOSHUA: Very well thank you, Mrs Saunders.

MRS SAUNDERS: And the stable boys?

JOSHUA: They have had justice, madam.

MRS SAUNDERS: So I saw. And does your arm ache?

MAUD: This is not a proper conversation, Mrs Saunders.   100

MRS SAUNDERS: You don't mind beating your own people?

JOSHUA: Not my people, madam.

MRS SAUNDERS: A different tribe?

JOSHUA: Bad people.

(HARRY *and* CLIVE *come in.*)

105 CLIVE: Well this is all very gloomy and solemn. Can we have the shutters open? The heat of the day has gone, we could have some light, I think. And cool drinks on the verandah, Joshua. Have some lemonade yourself. It is most refreshing.

(*Sunlight floods in as the shutters are opened.* EDWARD *comes.*)

EDWARD: Papa, papa, Ellen tried to lock me in the nursery. Mama
110 is going to tell you of me. I'd rather tell you myself. I was playing with Vicky's doll again and I know it's very bad of me. And I said I didn't want to be like you and I said I hated you. And it's not true and I'm sorry, I'm sorry and please beat me and forgive me.
115 CLIVE: Well there's a brave boy to own up. You should always respect and love me, Edward, not for myself, I may not deserve it, but as I respected and loved my own father, because he was my father. Through our father we love our Queen and our God, Edward. Do you understand? It is something men
120 understand.
EDWARD: Yes papa.
CLIVE: Then I forgive you and shake you by the hand. You spend too much time with the women. You may spend more time with me and Uncle Harry, little man.
125 EDWARD: I don't like women. I don't like dolls. I love you, papa, and I love you, Uncle Harry.
CLIVE: There's a fine fellow. Let us go out onto the verandah.

(*They all start to go.* EDWARD *takes* HARRY's *hand and goes with him.* CLIVE *draws* BETTY *back. They embrace.*)

BETTY: Poor Clive.
CLIVE: It was my duty to have them flogged. For you and Edward
130 and Victoria, to keep you safe.
BETTY: It is terrible to feel betrayed.
CLIVE: You can tame a wild animal only so far. They revert to their true nature and savage your hand. Sometimes I feel the natives are the enemy. I know that is wrong. I know I have
135 a responsibility towards them, to care for them and bring them all to be like Joshua. But there is something dangerous. Implacable. This whole continent is my enemy. I am pitching my whole mind and will and reason and spirit against it to tame it, and I sometimes feel it will break over me and
140 swallow me up.
BETTY: Clive, Clive, I am here. I have faith in you.
CLIVE: Yes, I can show you my moments of weakness, Betty, because you are my wife and because I trust you. I trust you, Betty, and it would break my heart if you did not deserve that
145 trust. Harry Bagley is my friend. It would break my heart if he did not deserve my trust.
BETTY: I'm sorry, I'm sorry. Forgive me. It is not Harry's fault, it is all mine. Harry is noble. He has rejected me. It is my wickedness, I get bored, I get restless, I imagine things. There
150 is something so wicked in me, Clive.
CLIVE: I have never thought of you having the weakness of your sex, only the good qualities.
BETTY: I am bad, bad, bad—
CLIVE: You are thoughtless, Betty, that's all. Women can be
155 treacherous and evil. They are darker and more dangerous than men. The family protects us from that, you protect

me from that. You are not that sort of woman. You are not unfaithful to me, Betty. I can't believe you are. It would hurt me so much to cast you off. That would be my duty.
BETTY: No, no, no. 160
CLIVE: Joshua has seen you kissing.
BETTY: Forgive me.
CLIVE: But I don't want to know about it. I don't want to know. I wonder of course, I wonder constantly. If Harry Bagley was not my friend I would shoot him. If I shot you every British 165 man and woman would applaud me. But no. It was a moment of passion such as women are too weak to resist. But you must resist it, Betty, or it will destroy us. We must fight against it. We must resist this dark female lust, Betty, or it will swallow us up. 170
BETTY: I do, I do resist. Help me. Forgive me.
CLIVE: Yes I do forgive you. But I can't feel the same about you as I did. You are still my wife and we still have duties to the household.

(*They go out arm in arm. As soon as they have gone* EDWARD *sneaks back to get the doll, which has been dropped on the floor. He picks it up and comforts it.* JOSHUA *comes through with a tray of drinks.*)

JOSHUA: Baby. Sissy. Girly. 175

(JOSHUA *goes.* BETTY *calls from off.*)

BETTY: Edward?

(BETTY *comes in.*)

BETTY: There you are, my darling. Come, papa wants us all to be together. Uncle Harry is going to tell how he caught a crocodile. Mama's sorry she smacked you.

(*They embrace.* JOSHUA *comes in again, passing through.*)

BETTY: Joshua, fetch me some blue thread from my sewing box. 180 It is on the piano.
JOSHUA: You've got legs under that skirt.
BETTY: Joshua.
JOSHUA: And more than legs.
BETTY: Edward, are you going to stand there and let a servant 185 insult your mother?
EDWARD: Joshua, get my mother's thread.
JOSHUA: Oh little Eddy, playing at master. It's only a joke.
EDWARD: Don't speak to my mother like that again.
JOSHUA: Ladies have no sense of humour. You like a joke with 190 Joshua.
EDWARD: You fetch her sewing at once, do you hear me? You move when I speak to you, boy.
JOSHUA: Yes sir, master Edward sir.

(JOSHUA *goes.*)

BETTY: Edward, you were wonderful. 195

(*She goes to embrace him but he moves away.*)

EDWARD: Don't touch me.

Song

A BOY'S BEST FRIEND

ALL: While plodding on our way, the toilsome road of life,
How few the friends that daily there we meet.
Not many will stand in trouble and in strife,
200 With counsel and affection ever sweet.
But there is one whose smile will ever on us beam,
Whose love is dearer far than any other;
And wherever we may turn
This lesson we will learn
205 A boy's best friend is his mother.

Then cherish her with care
And smooth her silv'ry hair,
When gone you will never get another.
And wherever we may turn
210 This lesson we shall learn,
A boy's best friend is his mother.

SCENE IV

The verandah as in Scene One. Early morning. Nobody there.
JOSHUA *comes out of the house slowly and stands for some time*
doing nothing. EDWARD *comes out.*

EDWARD: Tell me another bad story, Joshua. Nobody else is even
awake yet.
JOSHUA: First there was nothing and then there was the great
goddess. She was very large and she had golden eyes and she
5 made the stars and the sun and the earth. But soon she was
miserable and lonely and she cried like a great waterfall and
her tears made all the rivers in the world. So the great spirit
sent a terrible monster, a tree with hundreds of eyes and a
long green tongue, and it came chasing after her and she
10 jumped into a lake and the tree jumped in after her, and she
jumped right up into the sky. And the tree couldn't follow, he
was stuck in the mud. So he picked up a big handful of mud
and he threw it at her, up among the stars, and it hit her on
the head. And she fell down onto the earth into his arms and
15 the ball of mud is the moon in the sky. And then they had
children which is all of us.
EDWARD: It's not true, though.
JOSHUA: Of course it's not true. It's a bad story. Adam and Eve
is true. God made man white like him and gave him the bad
20 woman who liked the snake and gave us all this trouble.

(CLIVE *and* HARRY *come out.*)

CLIVE: Run along now, Edward. No, you may stay. You
mustn't repeat anything you hear to your mother or your
grandmother or Ellen.
EDWARD: Or Mrs Saunders?
25 CLIVE: Mrs Saunders is an unusual woman and does not require
protection in the same way. Harry, there was trouble last
night where we expected it. But it's all over now. Everything
is under control but nobody should leave the house today I
think.
30 HARRY: Casualties?
CLIVE: No, none of the soldiers hurt thank God. We did a certain
amount of damage, set a village on fire and so forth.
HARRY: Was that necessary?

CLIVE: Obviously, it was necessary, Harry, or it wouldn't have
happened. The army will come and visit, no doubt. You'll 35
like that, eh, Joshua, to see the British army? And a treat
for you, Edward, to see the soldiers. Would you like to be a
soldier?
EDWARD: I'd rather be an explorer.
CLIVE: Ah, Harry, like you, you see. I didn't know an explorer at 40
his age. Breakfast, I think, Joshua.

(CLIVE *and* JOSHUA *go in.* HARRY *is following.*)

EDWARD: Uncle.

(HARRY *stops.*)

EDWARD: Harry, why won't you talk to me?
HARRY: Of course I'll talk to you.
EDWARD: If you won't be nice to me I'll tell father. 45
HARRY: Edward, no, not a word, never, not to your mother,
nobody, please. Edward, do you understand? Please.
EDWARD: I won't tell. I promise I'll never tell. I've cut my finger
and sworn.
HARRY: There's no need to get so excited Edward. We can't be 50
together all the time. I will have to leave soon anyway, and go
back to the river.
EDWARD: You can't, you can't go. Take me with you.
ELLEN: Edward!
HARRY: I have my duty to the Empire. 55

(HARRY *goes in.* ELLEN *comes out.*)

ELLEN: Edward, breakfast time. Edward.
EDWARD: I'm not hungry.
ELLEN: Betty, please come and speak to Edward.

(BETTY *comes.*)

BETTY: Why what's the matter?
ELLEN: He won't come in for breakfast. 60
BETTY: Edward, I shall call your father.
EDWARD: You can't make me eat.

(*He goes in.* BETTY *is about to follow.*)

ELLEN: Betty.

(BETTY *stops.*)

ELLEN: Betty, when Edward goes to school will I have to leave?
BETTY: Never mind, Ellen dear, you'll get another place. I'll give 65
you an excellent reference.
ELLEN: I don't want another place, Betty. I want to stay with you
forever.
BETTY: If you go back to England you might get married,
Ellen. You're quite pretty, you shouldn't despair of getting a 70
husband.
ELLEN: I don't want a husband. I want you.
BETTY: Children of your own, Ellen, think.
ELLEN: I don't want children, I don't like children. I just want
to be alone with you, Betty, and sing for you and kiss you 75
because I love you, Betty.
BETTY: I love you too, Ellen. But women have their duty as
soldiers have. You must be a mother if you can.

ELLEN: Betty, Betty, I love you so much. I want to stay with you
80   forever, my love for you is eternal, stronger than death. I'd
    rather die than leave you, Betty.
BETTY: No you wouldn't, Ellen, don't be silly. Come, don't cry.
    You don't feel what you think you do. It's the loneliness here
    and the climate is very confusing. Come and have breakfast,
85   Ellen dear, and I'll forget all about it.

(ELLEN goes, CLIVE comes.)

BETTY: Clive, please forgive me.
CLIVE: Will you leave me alone?

(BETTY goes back into the house. HARRY comes.)

CLIVE: Women, Harry. I envy you going into the jungle, a
    man's life.
90 HARRY: I envy you.
CLIVE: Harry, I know you do. I have spoken to Betty.
HARRY: I assure you, Clive—
CLIVE: Please say nothing about it.
HARRY: My friendship for you—
95 CLIVE: Absolutely. I know the friendship between us, Harry,
    is not something that could be spoiled by the weaker sex.
    Friendship between men is a fine thing. It is the noblest form
    of relationship.
HARRY: I agree with you.
100 CLIVE: There is the necessity of reproduction. The family is
    all important. And there is the pleasure. But what we put
    ourselves through to get that pleasure, Harry. When I
    heard about our fine fellows last night fighting those sav-
    ages to protect us I thought yes, that is what I aspire to. I
105   tell you Harry, in confidence, I suddenly got out of Mrs
    Saunders' bed and came out here on the verandah and looked
    at the stars.
HARRY: I couldn't sleep last night either.
CLIVE: There is something dark about women, that threatens
110   what is best in us. Between men that light burns brightly.
HARRY: I didn't know you felt like that.
CLIVE: Women are irrational, demanding, inconsistent,
    treacherous, lustful, and they smell different from us.
HARRY: Clive—
115 CLIVE: Think of the comradeship of men, Harry, sharing
    adventures, sharing danger, risking their lives together.

(HARRY takes hold of CLIVE.)

CLIVE: What are you doing?
HARRY: Well, you said—
CLIVE: I said what?
120 HARRY: Between men.

(CLIVE is speechless.)

    I'm sorry, I misunderstood, I would never have dreamt, I
    thought—
CLIVE: My God, Harry, how disgusting.
HARRY: You will not betray my confidence.
125 CLIVE: I feel contaminated.
HARRY: I struggle against it. You cannot imagine the shame. I
    have tried everything to save myself.
CLIVE: The most revolting perversion. Rome fell, Harry, and this
    sin can destroy an empire.

HARRY: It is not a sin, it is a disease. 130
CLIVE: A disease more dangerous than diphtheria. Effeminacy
    is contagious. How I have been deceived. Your face does not
    look degenerate. Oh Harry, how did you sink to this?
HARRY: Clive, help me, what am I to do?
CLIVE: You have been away from England too long. 135
HARRY: Where can I go except into the jungle to hide?
CLIVE: You don't do it with the natives, Harry? My God, what a
    betrayal of the Queen.
HARRY: Clive, I am like a man born crippled. Please help me.
CLIVE: You must repent. 140
HARRY: I have thought of killing myself.
CLIVE: That is a sin too.
HARRY: There is no way out. Clive, I beg of you, do not betray my
    confidence.
CLIVE: I cannot keep a secret like this. Rivers will be named after 145
    you, it's unthinkable. You must save yourself from depravity.
    You must get married. You are not unattractive to women.
    What a relief that you and Betty were not after all—good God,
    how disgusting. Now Mrs Saunders. She's a woman of spirit,
    she could go with you on your expeditions. 150
HARRY: I suppose getting married wouldn't be any worse than
    killing myself.
CLIVE: Mrs Saunders! Mrs Saunders! Ask her now, Harry. Think
    of England.

(MRS SAUNDERS comes. CLIVE withdraws. HARRY goes up to MRS
SAUNDERS.)

HARRY: Mrs Saunders, will you marry me? 155
MRS SAUNDERS: Why?
HARRY: We are both alone.
MRS SAUNDERS: I choose to be alone, Mr Bagley. If I can look after
    myself, I'm sure you can. Clive, I have something important
    to tell you. I've just found Joshua putting earth on his head. 160
    He tells me his parents were killed last night by the British
    soldiers. I think you owe him an apology on behalf of the
    Queen.
CLIVE: Joshua! Joshua!
MRS SAUNDERS: Mr Bagley, I could never be a wife again. There is 165
    only one thing about marriage that I like.

(JOSHUA comes.)

CLIVE: Joshua, I am horrified to hear what has happened.
    Good God!
MRS SAUNDERS: His father was shot. His mother died in the
    blaze. 170

(MRS SAUNDERS goes.)

CLIVE: Joshua, do you want a day off? Do you want to go to your
    people?
JOSHUA: Not my people, sir.
CLIVE: But you want to go to your parents' funeral?
JOSHUA: No sir. 175
CLIVE: Yes, Joshua, yes, your father and mother. I'm sure they
    were loyal to the crown. I'm sure it was all a terrible mistake.
JOSHUA: My mother and father were bad people.
CLIVE: Joshua, no.
JOSHUA: You are my father and mother. 180

CLIVE: Well really. I don't know what to say. That's very decent of you. Are you sure there's nothing I can do? You can have the day off you know.

(BETTY *comes out followed by* EDWARD.)

BETTY: What's the matter? What's happening?

185 CLIVE: Something terrible has happened. No, I mean some relatives of Joshua's met with an accident.

JOSHUA: May I go sir?

CLIVE: Yes, yes of course. Good God, what a terrible thing. Bring us a drink will you Joshua?

(JOSHUA *goes.*)

190 EDWARD: What? What?

BETTY: Edward, go and do your lessons.

EDWARD: What is it, Uncle Harry?

HARRY: Go and do your lessons.

ELLEN: Edward, come in here at once.

195 EDWARD: What's happened, Uncle Harry?

(HARRY *has moved aside,* EDWARD *follows him.* ELLEN *comes out.*)

HARRY: Go away. Go inside. Ellen!

ELLEN: Go inside, Edward. I shall tell your mother.

BETTY: Go inside, Edward at once. I shall tell your father.

CLIVE: Go inside, Edward. And Betty you go inside too.

(BETTY, EDWARD *and* ELLEN *go.* MAUD *comes out.*)

200 CLIVE: Go inside. And Ellen, you come outside.

(ELLEN *comes out.*)

Mr Bagley has something to say to you.

HARRY: Ellen. I don't suppose you would marry me?

ELLEN: What if I said yes?

CLIVE: Run along now, you two want to be alone.

(HARRY *and* ELLEN *go out.* JOSHUA *brings* CLIVE *a drink.*)

205 JOSHUA: The governess and your wife, sir.

CLIVE: What's that, Joshua?

JOSHUA: She talks of love to your wife, sir. I have seen them. Bad women.

CLIVE: Joshua, you go too far. Get out of my sight.

SCENE V

The verandah. A table with a white cloth. A wedding cake and a large knife. Bottles and glasses. JOSHUA *is putting things on the table.* EDWARD *has the doll.* JOSHUA *sees him with it. He holds out his hand.* EDWARD *gives him the doll.* JOSHUA *takes the knife and cuts the doll open and shakes the sawdust out of it.* JOSHUA *throws the doll under the table.*

MAUD: Come along Edward, this is such fun.

(*Everyone enters, triumphal arch for* HARRY *and* ELLEN.)

MAUD: Your mama's wedding was a splendid occasion, Edward. I cried and cried.

(ELLEN *and* BETTY *go aside.*)

ELLEN: Betty, what happens with a man? I don't know what to do. 5

BETTY: You just keep still.

ELLEN: And what does he do?

BETTY: Harry will know what to do.

ELLEN: And is it enjoyable?

BETTY: Ellen, you're not getting married to enjoy yourself. 10

ELLEN: Don't forget me, Betty.

(ELLEN *goes.*)

BETTY: I think my necklace has been stolen Clive. I did so want to wear it at the wedding.

EDWARD: It was Joshua. Joshua took it.

CLIVE: Joshua? 15

EDWARD: He did, he did, I saw him with it.

HARRY: Edward, that's not true.

EDWARD: It is, it is.

HARRY: Edward, I'm afraid you took it yourself.

EDWARD: I did not. 20

HARRY: I have seen him with it.

CLIVE: Edward, is that true? Where is it? Did you take your mother's necklace? And to try and blame Joshua, good God.

(EDWARD *runs off.*)

BETTY: Edward, come back. Have you got my necklace?

HARRY: I should leave him alone. He'll bring it back. 25

BETTY: I wanted to wear it. I wanted to look my best at your wedding.

HARRY: You always look your best to me.

BETTY: I shall get drunk.

(MRS SAUNDERS *comes.*)

MRS SAUNDERS: The sale of my property is completed. I shall leave 30 tomorrow.

CLIVE: That's just as well. Whose protection will you seek this time?

MRS SAUNDERS: I shall go to England and buy a farm there. I shall introduce threshing machines. 35

CLIVE: Amazing spirit.

(*He kisses her.* BETTY *launches herself on* MRS SAUNDERS. *They fall to the ground.*)

CLIVE: Betty—Caroline—I don't deserve this—Harry, Harry.

(HARRY *and* CLIVE *separate them.* HARRY *holding* MRS SAUNDERS, CLIVE, BETTY.)

CLIVE: Mrs Saunders, how can you abuse my hospitality? How dare you touch my wife? You must leave here at once.

BETTY: Go away, go away. You are a wicked woman. 40

MAUD: Mrs Saunders, I am shocked. This is your hostess.

CLIVE: Pack your bags and leave the house this instant.

MRS SAUNDERS: I was leaving anyway. There's no place for me here. I have made arrangements to leave tomorrow, and tomorrow is when I will leave. I wish you joy, Mr Bagley. 45

(MRS SAUNDERS *goes.*)

CLIVE: No place for her anywhere I should think. Shocking behaviour.

BETTY: Oh Clive, forgive me, and love me like you used to.

CLIVE: Were you jealous my dove? My own dear wife!

50 MAUD: Ah, Mr Bagley, one flesh, you see.

(EDWARD *comes back with the necklace.*)

CLIVE: Good God, Edward, it's true.

EDWARD: I was minding it for mama because of the troubles.

CLIVE: Well done, Edward, that was very manly of you. See Betty?
55   Edward was protecting his mama's jewels from the rebels.
     What a hysterical fuss over nothing. Well done, little man. It
     is quite safe now. The bad men are dead. Edward, you may do
     up the necklace for mama.

(EDWARD *does up* BETTY's *necklace, supervised by* CLIVE, JOSHUA
is drinking steadily. ELLEN *comes back.*)

MAUD: Ah, here's the bride. Come along, Ellen, you don't cry at
     your own wedding, only at other people's.

60 CLIVE: Now, speeches, speeches. Who is going to make a speech?
     Harry, make a speech.

HARRY: I'm no speaker. You're the one for that.

ALL: Speech, speech.

HARRY: My dear friends—what can I say—the empire—
65   the family—the married state to which I have always
     aspired—your shining example of domestic bliss—my
     great good fortune in winning Ellen's love—happiest day of
     my life.

(*Applause.*)

CLIVE: Cut the cake, cut the cake.

(HARRY *and* ELLEN *take the knife to cut the cake.* HARRY *steps on
the doll under the table.*)

70 HARRY: What's this?

ELLEN: Oh look.

BETTY: Edward.

EDWARD: It was Joshua. It was Joshua. I saw him.

CLIVE: Don't tell lies again.

(*He hits* EDWARD *across the side of the head.*)

75 Unaccustomed as I am to public speaking—

(*Cheers.*)

Harry, my friend. So brave and strong and supple.

Ellen, from neath her veil so shyly peeking.

I wish you joy. A toast—the happy couple.

Dangers are past. Our enemies are killed.

80 —Put your arm round her, Harry, have a kiss—

All murmuring of discontent is stilled.

Long may you live in peace and joy and bliss.

(*While he is speaking* JOSHUA *raises his gun to shoot* CLIVE. *Only*
EDWARD *sees. He does nothing to warn the others. He puts his
hands over his ears.*)

(*Black.*)

ACT TWO

SCENE I

*Winter afternoon. Inside the hut of a one o'clock club, a children's
playcentre in a park,* VICTORIA *and* LIN, *mothers.* CATHY, LIN's
daughter, age 5, played by a man, clinging to LIN. VICTORIA *reading a book.*

CATHY: Yum yum bubblegum.
     Stick it up your mother's bum.
     When it's brown
     Pull it down
     Yum yum bubblegum.   5

LIN: Like your shoes, Victoria.

CATHY: Jack be nimble, Jack be quick,
     Jack jump over the candlestick.
     Silly Jack, he should jump higher,
     Goodness gracious, great balls of fire.   10

LIN: Cathy, do stop. Do a painting.

CATHY: You do a painting.

LIN: You do a painting.

CATHY: What shall I paint?

LIN: Paint a house.   15

CATHY: No.

LIN: Princess.

CATHY: No.

LIN: Pirates.

CATHY: Already done that.   20

LIN: Spacemen.

CATHY: I never paint spacemen. You know I never.

LIN: Paint a car crash and blood everywhere.

CATHY: No, don't tell me. I know what to paint.

LIN: Go on then. You need an apron, where's an apron. Here. 25

CATHY: Don't want an apron.

LIN: Lift up your arms. There's a good girl.

CATHY: I don't want to paint.

LIN: Don't paint. Don't paint.

CATHY: What shall I do? You paint. What shall I do mum?   30

VICTORIA: There's nobody on the big bike, Cathy, quick.

(CATHY *goes out.* VICTORIA *is watching the children playing
outside.*)

VICTORIA: Tommy, it's Jimmy's gun. Let him have it. What the
     hell.

(*She goes on reading. She reads while she talks.*)

LIN: I don't know how you can concentrate.

VICTORIA: You have to or you never do anything.   35

LIN: Yeh, well. It's really warm in here, that's one thing. It's better
     than standing out there. I got chilblains last winter.

VICTORIA: It is warm.

LIN: I suppose Tommy doesn't let you read much. I expect he talks
     to you while you're reading.   40

VICTORIA: Yes, he does.

LIN: I didn't get very far with that book you lent me.

VICTORIA: That's all right.

LIN: I was glad to have it, though. I sit with it on my lap while
     I'm watching telly. Well, Cathy's off. She's frightened I'm   45
     going to leave her. It's the babyminder didn't work out
     when she was two, she still remembers. You can't get

them used to other people if you're by yourself. It's no good
blaming me. She clings round my knees every morning up

50   the nursery and they don't say anything but they make you
feel you're making her do it. But I'm desperate for her to go
to school. I did cry when I left her the first day. You wouldn't,
you're too fucking sensible. You'll call the teacher by her first
name. I really fancy you.

55   VICTORIA: What?
LIN: Put your book down will you for five minutes. You didn't
hear a word I said.
VICTORIA: I don't get much time to myself.
LIN: Do you ever go to the movies?

60   VICTORIA: Tommy's very funny who he's left with. My mother
babysits sometimes.
LIN: Your husband could babysit.
VICTORIA: But then we couldn't go to the movies.
LIN: You could go to the movies with me.

65   VICTORIA: Oh I see.
LIN: Couldn't you?
VICTORIA: Well yes, I could.
LIN: Friday night?
VICTORIA: What film are we talking about?

70   LIN: Does it matter what film?
VICTORIA: Of course it does.
LIN: You choose then. Friday night.

(CATHY *comes in with gun, shoots them saying Kiou kiou kiou, and
runs off again.*)

Not in a foreign language, ok. You don't go in the movies
to read.

(LIN *watches the children playing outside.*)

75   Don't hit him, Cathy, kill him. Point the gun, kiou, kiou, kiou.
That's the way.
VICTORIA: They've just banned war toys in Sweden.
LIN: The kids'll just hit each other more.
VICTORIA: Well, psychologists do differ in their opinions as to

80   whether or not aggression is innate.
LIN: Yeh?
VICTORIA: I'm afraid I do let Tommy play with guns and just
hope he'll get it out of his system and not end up in the army.
LIN: I've got a brother in the army.

85   VICTORIA: Oh I'm sorry. Whereabouts is he stationed?
LIN: Belfast.
VICTORIA: Oh dear.
LIN: I've got a friend who's Irish and we went on a Troops Out
march. Now my dad won't speak to me.

90   VICTORIA: I don't get on too well with my father either.
LIN: And your husband? How do you get on with him?
VICTORIA: Oh, fine. Up and down. You know. Very well. He helps
with the washing up and everything.
LIN: I left mine two years ago. He let me keep Cathy and I'm

95   grateful for that.
VICTORIA: You shouldn't be grateful.
LIN: I'm a lesbian.
VICTORIA: You still shouldn't be grateful.
LIN: I'm grateful he didn't hit me harder than he did.

100 VICTORIA: I suppose I'm very lucky with Martin.
LIN: Don't get at me about how I bring up Cathy, ok?
VICTORIA: I didn't.

LIN: Yes you did. War toys. I'll give her a rifle for Christmas and
blast Tommy's pretty head off for a start.

(VICTORIA *goes back to her book.*)

LIN: I hate men.   105
VICTORIA: You have to look at it in a historical perspective in
terms of learnt behaviour since the industrial revolution.
LIN: I just hate the bastards.
VICTORIA: Well it's a point of view.

(*By now* CATHY *has come back in and started painting in many
colours, without an apron.* EDWARD *comes in.*)

EDWARD: Victoria, mother's in the park. She's walking round all   110
the paths very fast.
VICTORIA: By herself?
EDWARD: I told her you were here.
VICTORIA: Thanks.
EDWARD: Come on.   115
VICTORIA: Ten minutes talking to my mother and I have to spend
two hours in a hot bath.

(VICTORIA *goes out.*)

LIN: Shit, Cathy, what about an apron. I don't mind you having
paint on your frock but if it doesn't wash off just don't tell
me you can't wear your frock with paint on, ok?   120
CATHY: Ok.
LIN: You're gay, aren't you?
EDWARD: I beg your pardon?
LIN: I really fancy your sister. I thought you'd understand. You do
but you can go on pretending you don't, I don't mind. That's   125
lovely Cathy, I like the green bit.
EDWARD: Don't go around saying that. I might lose my job.
LIN: The last gardener was ever so straight. He used to flash at all
the little girls.
EDWARD: I wish you hadn't said that about me. It's not true.   130
LIN: It's not true and I never said it and I never thought it and I
never will think it again.
EDWARD: Someone might have heard you.
LIN: Shut up about it then.

(BETTY *and* VICTORIA *come up.*)

BETTY: It's quite a nasty bump.   135
VICTORIA: He's not even crying.
BETTY: I think that's very worrying. You and Edward always
cried. Perhaps he's got concussion.
VICTORIA: Of course he hasn't mummy.
BETTY: That other little boy was very rough. Should you speak   140
to somebody about him?
VICTORIA: Tommy was hitting him with a spade.
BETTY: Well he's a real little boy. And so brave not to cry. You
must watch him for signs of drowsiness. And nausea. If he's
sick in the night, phone an ambulance. Well, you're looking   145
very well darling, a bit tired, a bit peaky. I think the fresh
air agrees with Edward. He likes the open air life because
of growing up in Africa. He misses the sunshine, don't you,
darling? We'll soon have Edward back on his feet. What fun
it is here.   150
VICTORIA: This is Lin. And Cathy.

BETTY: Oh Cathy what a lovely painting. What is it? Well I
think it's a house on fire. I think all that red is a fire. Is that
right? Or do I see legs, is it a horse? Can I have the lovely
155 painting or is it for mummy? Children have such imagination, it makes them so exhausting. (*To* LIN.) I'm sure
you're wonderful, just like Victoria. I had help with my
children. One does need help. That was in Africa of
course so there wasn't the servant problem. This is my son
160 Edward. This is—
EDWARD: Lin.
BETTY: Lin, this is Lin. Edward is doing something such fun,
he's working in the park as a gardener. He does look exactly
like a gardener.
165 EDWARD: I am a gardener.
BETTY: He's certainly making a stab at it. Well it will be a story
to tell. I expect he will write a novel about it, or perhaps a
television series. Well what a pretty child Cathy is. Victoria
was a pretty child just like a little doll—you can't be certain
170 how they'll grow up. I think Victoria's very pretty but she
doesn't make the most of herself, do you darling, it's not the
fashion I'm told but there are still women who dress out of
Vogue, well we hope that's not what Martin looks for, though
in many ways I wish it was, I don't know what it is Martin
175 looks for and nor does he I'm afraid poor Martin. Well I am
rattling on. I like your skirt dear but your shoes won't do at
all. Well do they have lady gardeners, Edward, because I'm
going to leave your father and I think I might need to get a
job, not a gardener really of course. I haven't got green fingers
180 I'm afraid, everything I touch shrivels straight up. Vicky gave
me a poinsettia last Christmas and the leaves all fell off on
Boxing Day. Well good heavens, look what's happened to that
lovely painting.

(CATHY *has slowly and carefully been going over the whole sheet
with black paint. She has almost finished*.)

LIN: What you do that for silly? It was nice.
185 CATHY: I like your earrings.
VICTORIA: Did you say you're leaving Daddy?
BETTY: Do you darling? Shall I put them on you? My ears aren't
pierced, I never wanted that, they just clip on the lobe.
LIN: She'll get paint on you, mind.
190 BETTY: There's a pretty girl. It doesn't hurt does it. Well you'll
grow up to know you have to suffer a little bit for beauty.
CATHY: Look mum I'm pretty, I'm pretty, I'm pretty.
LIN: Stop showing off Cathy.
VICTORIA: It's time we went home. Tommy, time to go home. Last
195 go then, all right.
EDWARD: Mum did I hear you right just now?
CATHY: I want my ears pierced.
BETTY: Ooh, not till you're big.
CATHY: I know a girl got her ears pierced and she's three. She's got
200 real gold.
BETTY: I don't expect she's English, darling. Can I give her a
sweety? I know they're not very good for the teeth, Vicky gets
terribly cross with me. What does mummy say?
LIN: Just one, thank you very much.
205 CATHY: I like your beads.
BETTY: Yes they are pretty. Here you are.

(*It is the necklace from Act One.*)

CATHY: Look at me, look at me. Vicky, Vicky, Vicky look at me.
LIN: You look lovely, come on now.
CATHY: And your hat, and your hat.
LIN: No, that's enough. 210
BETTY: Of course she can have my hat.
CATHY: Yes, yes, hat, hat. Look look look.
LIN: That's enough, please, stop it now. Hat off, bye bye hat.
CATHY: Give me my hat.
LIN: Bye bye beads. 215
BETTY: It's just fun.
LIN: It's very nice of you.
CATHY: I want my beads.
LIN: Where's the other earring?
CATHY: I want my beads. 220

(CATHY *has the other earring in her hand. Meanwhile* VICTORIA
and EDWARD *look for it.*)

EDWARD: Is it on the floor?
VICTORIA: Don't step on it.
EDWARD: Where?
CATHY: I want my beads. I want my beads.
LIN: You'll have a smack. 225

(LIN *gets the earring from* CATHY.)

CATHY: I want my beads.
BETTY: Oh dear oh dear. Have you got the earring? Thank
you darling.
CATHY: I want my beads, you're horrid, I hate you, mum, you
smell. 230
BETTY: This is the point you see where one had help. Well it's
been lovely seeing you dears and I'll be off again on my
little walk.
VICTORIA: You're leaving him? Really?
BETTY: Yes you hear alright, Vicky, yes. I'm finding a little flat, 235
that will be fun.

(BETTY *goes.*)

Bye bye Tommy, granny's going now. Tommy don't hit that
little girl, say goodbye to granny.
VICTORIA: Fucking hell.
EDWARD: Puking Jesus. 240
LIN: That was news was it, leaving your father?
EDWARD: They're going to want so much attention.
VICTORIA: Does everybody hate their mothers?
EDWARD: Mind you, I wouldn't live with him.
LIN: Stop snivelling, pigface. Where's your coat? Be quiet now 245
and we'll have doughnuts for tea and if you keep on we'll have
dogshit on toast.

(CATHY *laughs so much she lies on the floor.*)

VICTORIA: Tommy, you've had two last goes. Last last last last go.
LIN: Not that funny, come on, coat on.
EDWARD: Can I have your painting? 250
CATHY: What for?
EDWARD: For a friend of mine.
CATHY: What's his name?
EDWARD: Gerry.
CATHY: How old is he? 255
EDWARD: Thirty-two.

CATHY: You can if you like. I don't care. Kiou kiou kiou kiou.

(CATHY *goes out.* EDWARD *takes the painting and goes out.*)

LIN: Will you have sex with me?
VICTORIA: I don't know what Martin would say. Does it count
260   as adultery with a woman?
LIN: You'd enjoy it.

SCENE II

Spring. Swing, bench, pond nearby. EDWARD *is gardening.* GERRY *sitting on a bench.*

EDWARD: I sometimes pretend we don't know each other.
     And you've come to the park to eat your sandwiches and
     look at me.
GERRY: That would be more interesting, yes. Come and sit
5   down.
EDWARD: If the superintendent comes I'll be in trouble. It's
     not my dinner time yet. Where were you last night? I
     think you owe me an explanation. We always do tell each
     other everything.
10 GERRY: Is that a rule?
EDWARD: It's what we agreed.
GERRY: It's a habit we've got into. Look, I was drunk. I woke
     up at 4 o'clock on somebody's floor. I was sick. I hadn't
     any money for a cab. I went back to sleep.
15 EDWARD: You could have phoned.
GERRY: There wasn't a phone.
EDWARD: Sorry.
GERRY: There was a phone and I didn't phone you. Leave it alone,
     Eddy, I'm warning you.
20 EDWARD: What are you going to do to me, then?
GERRY: I'm going to the pub.
EDWARD: I'll join you in ten minutes.
GERRY: I didn't ask you to come. (EDWARD *goes.*) Two years I've
     been with Edward. You have to get away sometimes or you
25   lose sight of yourself. The train from Victoria to Clapham
     still has those compartments without a corridor. As soon
     as I got on the platform I saw who I wanted. Slim hips, tense
     shoulders, trying not to look at anyone. I put my hand on
     my packet just long enough so that he couldn't miss it. The
30   train came in. You don't want to get in too fast or some
     straight dumbo might get in with you. I sat by the window.
     I couldn't see where the fuck he'd got to. Then just as the
     whistle went he got in. Great. It's a six-minute journey so
     you can't start anything you can't finish. I stared at him
35   and he unzipped his flies. Then he stopped. So I stood up
     and took my cock out. He took me in his mouth and shut
     his eyes tight. He was sort of mumbling it about as if he
     wasn't sure what to do, so I said, 'A bit tighter son' and
     he said 'Sorry' and then got on with it. He was jerking off
40   with his left hand, and I could see he'd got a fairsized one. I
     wished he'd keep still so I could see his watch. I was getting
     really turned on. What if we pulled into Clapham Junction
     now. Of course by the time we sat down again the train was
     just slowing up. I felt wonderful. Then he started talking.
45   It's better if nothing is said. Once you find he's a librarian
     in Walthamstow with a special interest in science fiction
     and lives with his aunt, then forget it. He said I hope you
     don't think I do this all the time. I said I hope you will from

now on. He said he would if I was on the train, but why
don't we go out for a meal? I opened the door before the   50
train stopped. I told him I live with somebody, I don't
want to know. He was jogging sideways to keep up. He
said 'What's your phone number, you're my ideal physical
type, what sign of the zodiac are you? Where do you live?
Where are you going now?' It's not fair, I saw him at Victoria   55
a couple of months later and I went straight down to the
end of the platform and I picked up somebody really great
who never said a word, just smiled.

(CATHY *is on the swing.*)

CATHY: Batman and Robin
     Had a batmobile.   60
     Robin done a fart
     And paralysed the wheel.
     The wheel couldn't take it,
     The engine fell apart,
     All because of Robin   65
     And his supersonic fart.

(CATHY *goes.* MARTIN, VICTORIA *and* BETTY *walking slowly.*)

MARTIN: Tom!
BETTY: He'll fall in.
VICTORIA: No he won't.
MARTIN: Don't go too near the edge Tom. Throw the bread   70
     from there. The ducks can get it.
BETTY: I'll never be able to manage. If I can't even walk down
     the street by myself. Everything looks so fierce.
VICTORIA: Just watch Tommy feeding the ducks.
BETTY: He's going to fall in. Make Martin make him move back.   75
VICTORIA: He's not going to fall in.
BETTY: It's since I left your father.
VICTORIA: Mummy, it really was the right decision.
BETTY: Everything comes at me from all directions. Martin
     despises me.   80
VICTORIA: Of course he doesn't, mummy.
BETTY: Of course he does.
MARTIN: Throw the bread. That's the way. The duck can get it.
     Quack quack quack quack quack.
BETTY: I don't want to take pills. Lin says you can't trust doctors. 85
VICTORIA: You're not taking pills. You're doing very well.
BETTY: But I'm so frightened.
VICTORIA: What are you frightened of?
BETTY: Victoria, you always ask that as if there was suddenly
     going to be an answer.   90
VICTORIA: Are you all right sitting there?
BETTY: Yes, yes. Go and be with Martin.

(VICTORIA *joins* MARTIN, BETTY *stays sitting on the bench.*)

MARTIN: You take the job, you go to Manchester. You turn
     it down, you stay in London. People are making decisions
     like this every day of the week. It needn't be for more   95
     than a year. You get long vacations. Our relationship
     might well stand the strain of that, and if it doesn't we're
     better out of it. I don't want to put any pressure on you.
     I'd just like to know so we can sell the house. I think we're
     moving into an entirely different way of life if you go to   100
     Manchester because it won't end there. We could keep the

house as security for Tommy but he might as well get used to the fact that life nowadays is insecure. You should ask your mother what she thinks and then do the opposite. I
105 could just take that room in Barbara's house, and then we could babysit for each other. You think that means I want to fuck Barbara. I don't. Well, I do, but I won't. And even if I did, what's a fuck between friends? What are we meant to do it with, strangers? Whatever you want to do, I'll be
110 delighted. If you could just let me know what it is I'm to be delighted about. Don't cry again, Vicky, I'm not the sort of man who makes women cry.

(LIN *has come in and sat down with* BETTY, CATHY *joins them. She is wearing a pink dress and carrying a rifle.*)

LIN: I've bought her three new frocks. She won't wear jeans to school any more because Tracy and Mandy called her a boy.
115 CATHY: Tracy's got a perm.
LIN: You should have shot them.
CATHY: They're coming to tea and we've got to have trifle. Not trifle you make, trifle out of a packet. And you've got to wear a skirt. And tights.
120 LIN: Tracy's mum wears jeans.
CATHY: She does not. She wears velvet.
BETTY: Well I think you look very pretty. And if that gun has caps in it please take it a long way away.
CATHY: It's got red caps. They're louder.
125 MARTIN: Do you think you're well enough to do this job? You don't have to do it. No one's going to think any the less of you if you stay here with me. There's no point being so liberated you make yourself cry all the time. You stay and we'll get everything sorted out. What it is about sex, when we talk
130 while it's happening I get to feel it's like a driving lesson. Left, right, a little faster, carry on, slow down—

(CATHY *shoots* VICTORIA.)

CATHY: You're dead Vicky.
VICTORIA: Aaaargh.
CATHY: Fall over.
135 VICTORIA: I'm not falling over, the ground's wet.
CATHY: You're dead.
VICTORIA: Yes, I'm dead.
CATHY: The Dead Hand Gang fall over. They said I had to fall over in the mud or I can't play. That duck's a mandarin.
140 MARTIN: Which one? Look, Tommy.
CATHY: That's a diver. It's got a yellow eye and it dives. That's a goose. Tommy doesn't know it's a goose, he thinks it's a duck. The babies get eaten by weasels. Kiou kiou.

(CATHY *goes.*)

MARTIN: So I lost my erection last night not because I'm not
145 prepared to talk, it's just that taking in technical informa- tion is a different part of the brain and also I don't like to feel that you do it better to yourself. I have read the Hite report. I do know that women have to learn to get their pleasure despite our clumsy attempts at expressing undying
150 devotion and ecstasy, and that what we spent our adoles- cence thinking was an animal urge we had to suppress is in fact a fine art we have to acquire. I'm not like whatever percentage of American men have become impotent as a

direct result of women's liberation, which I am totally in favour of, more I sometimes think than you are yourself.
155 Nor am I one of your villains who sticks it in, bangs away, and falls asleep. My one aim is to give you pleasure. My one aim is to give you rolling orgasms like I do other women. So why the hell don't you have them? My analysis for what it's worth is that despite all my efforts you still feel domi-
160 nated by me. I in fact think it's very sad that you don't feel able to take that job. It makes me feel very guilty. I don't want you to do it just because I encourage you to do it. But don't you think you'd feel better if you did take the job? You're the one who's talked about freedom. You're the one
165 who's experimenting with bisexuality, and I don't stop you, I think women have something to give each other. You seem to need the mutual support. You find me too overwhelming. So follow it through, go away, leave me and Tommy alone for a bit, we can manage perfectly well without
170 you. I'm not putting any pressure on you but I don't think you're being a whole person. God knows I do everything I can to make you stand on your own two feet. Just be yourself. You don't seem to realise how insulting it is to me that you can't get yourself together.
175

(MARTIN *and* VICTORIA *go.*)

BETTY: You must be very lonely yourself with no husband. You don't miss him?
LIN: Not really, no.
BETTY: Maybe you like being on your own.
LIN: I'm seeing quite a lot of Vicky. I don't live alone. I live
180 with Cathy.
BETTY: I would have been frightened when I was your age. I thought, the poor children, their mother all alone.
LIN: I've a lot of friends.
BETTY: I find when I'm making tea I put out two cups. It's
185 strange not having a man in the house. You don't know who to do things for.
LIN: Yourself.
BETTY: Oh, that's very selfish.
LIN: Have you any women friends?
190 BETTY: I've never been so short of men's company that I've had to bother with women.
LIN: Don't you like women?
BETTY: They don't have such interesting conversations as men. There has never been a woman composer of genius.
195 They don't have a sense of humour. They spoil things for themselves with their emotions. I can't say I do like women very much, no.
LIN: But you're a woman.
BETTY: There's nothing says you have to like yourself.
200
LIN: Do you like me?
BETTY: There's no need to take it personally, Lin.

(MARTIN *and* VICTORIA *come back.*)

MARTIN: Did you know if you put cocaine on your prick you can keep it up all night? The only thing is of course it goes numb so you don't feel anything. But you would, that's
205 the main thing. I just want to make you happy.
BETTY: Vicky, I'd like to go home.
VICTORIA: Yes, mummy, of course.
BETTY: I'm sorry, dear.

210 VICTORIA: I think Tommy would like to stay out a bit longer.
LIN: Hello, Martin. We do keep out of each other's way.
MARTIN: I think that's the best thing to do.
BETTY: Perhaps you'd walk home with me, Martin. I do feel safer with a man. The park is so large the grass seems to tilt.
215 MARTIN: Yes, I'd like to go home and do some work. I'm writing a novel about women from the women's point of view.

(MARTIN *and* BETTY *go.* LIN *and* VICTORIA *are alone. They embrace.*)

VICTORIA: Why the hell can't he just be a wife and come with me? Why does Martin make me tie myself in knots? No wonder we can't just have a simple fuck. No, not Martin,
220   why do I make myself tie myself in knots. It's got to stop, Lin. I'm not like that with you. Would you love me if I went to Manchester?
LIN: Yes.
VICTORIA: Would you love me if I went on a climbing expedition
225   in the Andes mountains?
LIN: Yes.
VICTORIA: Would you love me if my teeth fell out?
LIN: Yes.
VICTORIA: Would you love me if I loved ten other people?
230 LIN: And me?
VICTORIA: Yes.
LIN: Yes.
VICTORIA: And I feel apologetic for not being quite so subordinate as I was. I am more intelligent than him. I am brilliant.
235 LIN: Leave him Vic. Come and live with me.
VICTORIA: Don't be silly.
LIN: Silly, Christ, don't then. I'm not asking because I need to live with someone. I'd enjoy it, that's all, we'd both enjoy it. Fuck you. Cathy, for fuck's sake stop throwing stones at the
240   ducks. The man's going to get you.
VICTORIA: What man? Do you need a man to frighten your child with?
LIN: My mother said it.
VICTORIA: You're so inconsistent, Lin.
245 LIN: I've changed who I sleep with, I can't change everything.
VICTORIA: Like when I had to stop you getting a job in a boutique and collaborating with sexist consumerism.
LIN: I should have got that job, Cathy would have liked it. Why shouldn't I have some decent clothes? I'm sick of dressing
250   like a boy, why can't I look sexy, wouldn't you love me?
VICTORIA: Lin, you've no analysis.
LIN: No but I'm good at kissing aren't I? I give Cathy guns, my mum didn't give me guns. I dress her in jeans, she wants to wear dresses. I don't know. I can't work it out, I don't want
255   to. You read too many books, you get at me all the time, you're worse to me than Martin is to you, you piss me off, my brother's been killed. I'm sorry to win the argument that way but there it is.
VICTORIA: What do you mean win the argument?
260 LIN: I mean be nice to me.
VICTORIA: In Belfast?
LIN: I heard this morning. Don't don't start. I've hardly seen him for two years. I rung my father. You'd think I'd shot myself. He doesn't want me to go to the funeral.

(CATHY *approaches.*)

VICTORIA: What will you do?   265
LIN: Go of course.
CATHY: What is it? Who's killed? What?
LIN: It's Bill. Your uncle. In the army. Bill that gave you the blue teddy.
CATHY: Can I have his gun?   270
LIN: It's time we went home. Time you went to bed.
CATHY: No it's not.
LIN: We go home and you have tea and you have a bath and you go to bed.
CATHY: Fuck off.   275
LIN: Cathy, shut up.
VICTORIA: It's only half past five, why don't we—
LIN: I'll tell you why she has to go to bed—
VICTORIA: She can come home with me.
LIN: Because I want her out of the fucking way.   280
VICTORIA: She can come home with me.
CATHY: I'm not going to bed.
LIN: I want her home with me not home with you, I want her in bed, I want today over.
CATHY: I'm not going to bed.   285

(LIN *hits* CATHY, CATHY *cries.*)

LIN: And shut up or I'll give you something to cry for.
CATHY: I'm not going to bed.
VICTORIA: Cathy—
LIN: You keep out of it.
VICTORIA: Lin for God's sake.   290

(*They are all shouting.* CATHY *runs off.* LIN *and* VICTORIA *are silent. Then they laugh and embrace.*)

LIN: Where's Tommy?
VICTORIA: What? Didn't he go with Martin?
LIN: Did he?
VICTORIA: God oh God.
LIN: Cathy! Cathy!   295
VICTORIA: I haven't thought about him. How could I not think about him? Tommy!
LIN: Cathy! Come on, quick, I want some help.
VICTORIA: Tommy! Tommy!

(CATHY *comes back.*)

LIN: Where's Tommy? Have you seen him? Did he go with   300
Martin? Do you know where he is?
CATHY: I showed him the goose. We went in the bushes.
LIN: Then what?
CATHY: I came back on the swing.
VICTORIA: And Tommy? Where was Tommy?   305
CATHY: He fed the ducks.
LIN: No that was before.
CATHY: He did a pee in the bushes. I helped him with his trousers.
VICTORIA: And after that?   310
CATHY: He fed the ducks.
VICTORIA: No no.
CATHY: He liked the ducks. I expect he fell in.
LIN: Did you see him fall in?
VICTORIA: Tommy! Tommy!   315
LIN: What's the last time you saw him?

CATHY: He did a pee.
VICTORIA: Mummy said he would fall in. Oh God, Tommy!
LIN: We'll go round the pond. We'll go opposite ways round
320   the pond.
ALL: (*Shout.*) Tommy!

(VICTORIA *and* LIN *go off opposite sides.* CATHY *climbs the bench.*)

CATHY: Georgie Best, superstar
     Walks like a woman and wears a bra.
         There he is! I see him! Mum! Vicky! There he is! He's in
325   the bushes.

(LIN *comes back.*)

LIN: Come on Cathy love, let's go home.
CATHY: Vicky's got him.
LIN: Come on.
CATHY: Is she cross?
330   LIN: No. Come on.
CATHY: I found him.
LIN: Yes. Come on.

(CATHY *gets off the bench.* CATHY *and* LIN *hug.*)

CATHY: I'm watching telly.
LIN: Ok.
335   CATHY: After the news.
LIN: Ok.
CATHY: I'm not going to bed.
LIN: Yes you are.
CATHY: I'm not going to bed now.
340   LIN: Not now but early.
CATHY: How early?
LIN: Not late.
CATHY: How not late?
LIN: Early.
345   CATHY: How early?
LIN: Not late.

(*They go off together.* GERRY *comes on. He waits.* EDWARD *comes.*)

EDWARD: I've got some fish for dinner. I thought I'd make a
     cheese sauce.
GERRY: I won't be in.
350   EDWARD: Where are you going?
GERRY: For a start I'm going to a sauna. Then I'll see.
EDWARD: All right. What time will you be back? We'll eat
     then.
GERRY: You're getting like a wife.
355   EDWARD: I don't mind that.
GERRY: Why don't I do the cooking sometime?
EDWARD: You can if you like. You're just not so good at it that's
     all. Do it tonight.
GERRY: I won't be in tonight.
360   EDWARD: Do it tomorrow. If we can't eat it we can always go
     to a restaurant.
GERRY: Stop it.
EDWARD: Stop what?
GERRY: Just be yourself.
365   EDWARD: I don't know what you mean. Everyone's always tried
     to stop me being feminine and now you are too.

GERRY: You're putting it on.
EDWARD: I like doing the cooking. I like being fucked. You do
     like me like this really.
GERRY: I'm bored, Eddy.   370
EDWARD: Go to the sauna.
GERRY: And you'll stay home and wait up for me.
EDWARD: No, I'll go to bed and read a book.
GERRY: Or knit. You could knit me a pair of socks.
EDWARD: I might knit. I like knitting.   375
GERRY: I don't mind if you knit. I don't want to be married.
EDWARD: I do.
GERRY: Well I'm divorcing you.
EDWARD: I wouldn't want to keep a man who wants his
     freedom.   380
GERRY: Eddy, do stop playing the injured wife, it's not funny.
EDWARD: I'm not playing. It's true.
GERRY: I'm not the husband so you can't be the wife.
EDWARD: I'll always be here, Gerry, if you want to come back.
     I know you men like to go off by yourselves. I don't think   385
     I could love deeply more than once. But I don't think I
     can face life on my own so don't leave it too long or it may
     be too late.
GERRY: What are you trying to turn me into?
EDWARD: A monster, darling, which is what you are.   390
GERRY: I'll collect my stuff from the flat in the morning.

(GERRY *goes.* EDWARD *sits on the bench. It gets darker.* VICTORIA
comes.)

VICTORIA: Tommy dropped a toy car somewhere, you haven't
     seen it? It's red. He says it's his best one. Oh the hell with it.
     Martin's reading him a story. There, isn't it quiet?

(*They sit on the bench, holding hands.*)

EDWARD: I like women.   395
VICTORIA: That should please mother.
EDWARD: No listen Vicky. I'd rather be a woman. I wish I had
     breasts like that, I think they're beautiful. Can I touch
     them?
VICTORIA: What, pretending they're yours?   400
EDWARD: No, I know it's you.
VICTORIA: I think I should warn you I'm enjoying this.
EDWARD: I'm sick of men.
VICTORIA: I'm sick of men.
EDWARD: I think I'm a lesbian.   405

SCENE III

The park. Summer night. VICTORIA, LIN *and* EDWARD *drunk.*

LIN: Where are you?
VICTORIA: Come on.
EDWARD: Do we sit in a circle?
VICTORIA: Sit in a triangle.
EDWARD: You're good at mathematics. She's good at   5
     mathematics.
VICTORIA: Give me your hand. We all hold hands.
EDWARD: Do you know what to do?
LIN: She's making it up.
VICTORIA: We start off by being quiet.   10
EDWARD: What?
LIN: Hush.

EDWARD: Will something appear?

VICTORIA: It was your idea.

15 EDWARD: It wasn't my idea. It was your book.

LIN: You said call up the goddess.

EDWARD: I don't remember saying that.

LIN: We could have called her on the telephone.

EDWARD: Don't be so silly, this is meant to be frightening.

20 LIN: Kiss me.

VICTORIA: Are we going to do it?

LIN: We're doing it.

VICTORIA: A ceremony.

LIN: It's very sexy, you said it is. You said the women were

25 priests in the temples and fucked all the time. I'm just helping.

VICTORIA: As long as it's sacred.

LIN: It's very sacred.

VICTORIA: Innin, Innana, Nana, Nut, Anat, Anahita, Istar, Isis.

30 LIN: I can't remember all that.

VICTORIA: Lin! Innin, Innana, Nana, Nut, Anat, Anahita, Istar, Isis.

(LIN *and* EDWARD *join in and continue the chant under* VICTORIA's *speech.*)

Goddess of many names, oldest of the old, who walked in chaos and created life, hear us calling you back through time,

35 before Jehovah, before Christ, before men drove you out and burnt your temples, hear us, Lady, give us back what we were, give us the history we haven't had, make us the women we can't be.

ALL: Innin, Innana, Nana, Nut, Anat, Anahita, Istar, Isis.

(*Chant continues under other speeches.*)

40 LIN: Come back, goddess.

VICTORIA: Goddess of the sun and the moon her brother, little goddess of Crete with snakes in your hands.

LIN: Goddess of breasts.

VICTORIA: Goddess of cunts.

45 LIN: Goddess of fat bellies and babies. And blood blood blood.

(*Chant continues.*)

I see her.

EDWARD: What?

(*They stop chanting.*)

LIN: I see her. Very tall. Snakes in her hands. Light light light—look out! Did I give you a fright?

50 EDWARD: I was terrified.

VICTORIA: Don't spoil it Lin.

LIN: It's all out of a book.

VICTORIA: Innin Innana—I can't do it now. I was really enjoying myself.

55 LIN: She won't appear with a man here.

VICTORIA: They had men, they had sons and lovers.

EDWARD: They had eunuchs.

LIN: Don't give us ideas.

VICTORIA: There's Attis and Tammuz, they're torn to pieces.

60 EDWARD: Tear me to pieces, Lin.

VICTORIA: The priestess chose a lover for a year and he was king because she chose him and then he was killed at the end of the year.

EDWARD: Hurray.

VICTORIA: And the women had the children and nobody knew 65 it was done by fucking so they didn't know about fathers and nobody cared who the father was and the property was passed down through the maternal line—

LIN: Don't turn it into a lecture, Vicky, it's meant to be an orgy.

VICTORIA: It never hurts to understand the theoretical 70 background. You can't separate fucking and economics.

LIN: Give us a kiss.

EDWARD: Shut up, listen.

LIN: What?

EDWARD: There's somebody there. 75

LIN: Where?

EDWARD: There.

VICTORIA: The priestesses used to make love to total strangers.

LIN: Go on then, I dare you.

EDWARD: Go on, Vicky. 80

VICTORIA: He won't know it's a sacred rite in honour of the goddess.

EDWARD: We'll know.

LIN: We can tell him.

EDWARD: It's not what he thinks, it's what we think. 85

LIN: Don't tell him till after, he'll run a mile.

VICTORIA: Hello. We're having an orgy. Do you want me to suck your cock?

(*The stranger approaches. It is* MARTIN.)

MARTIN: There you are. I've been looking everywhere. What the hell are you doing? Do you know what the time is? 90 You're all pissed out of your minds.

(*They leap on* MARTIN, *pull him down and start to make love to him.*)

MARTIN: Well that's all right. If all we're talking about is having a lot of sex there's no problem. I was all for the sixties when liberation just meant fucking.

(*Another stranger approaches.*)

LIN: Hey you, come here. Come and have sex with us. 95

VICTORIA: Who is it?

(*The stranger is a soldier.*)

LIN: It's my brother.

EDWARD: Lin, don't.

LIN: It's my brother.

VICTORIA: It's her sense of humour, you get used to it. 100

LIN: Shut up Vicky, it's my brother. Isn't it? Bill?

SOLDIER: Yes it's me.

LIN: And you are dead.

SOLDIER: Fucking dead all right yeh.

LIN: Have you come back to tell us something? 105

SOLDIER: No I've come for a fuck. That was the worst thing in the fucking army. Never fucking let out. Can't fucking talk to Irish girls. Fucking bored out of my fucking head. That or shit scared. For five minutes I'd be glad I wasn't bored, then I was fucking scared. Then we'd come in and I'd be glad I wasn't 110 scared and then I was fucking bored. Spent the day reading fucking porn and the fucking night wanking. Man's fucking life in the fucking army? No fun when the fucking kids hate you. I got so I fucking wanted to kill someone and I got

115   fucking killed myself and I want a fuck.

LIN: I miss you. Bill. Bill.

(LIN *collapses.* SOLDIER *goes.* VICTORIA *comforts* LIN.)

EDWARD: Let's go home.

LIN: Victoria, come home with us. Victoria's coming to live with me and Edward.

120   MARTIN: Tell me about it in the morning.

LIN: It's true.

VICTORIA: It is true.

MARTIN: Tell me when you're sober.

(EDWARD, LIN, VICTORIA *go off together.* MARTIN *goes off alone.* GERRY *comes on.*)

GERRY: I come here sometimes at night and pick somebody up.

125   Sometimes I come here at night and don't pick anybody up. I do also enjoy walking about at night. There's never any trouble finding someone. I can have sex any time. You might not find the type you most fancy every day of the week, but there's plenty of people about who just enjoy having a good

130   time. I quite like living alone. If I live with someone I get annoyed with them. Edward always put on Capital radio when he got up. The silence gets wasted. I wake up at four o'clock sometimes. Birds. Silence. If I bring somebody home I never let them stay the night. Edward! Edward!

(EDWARD *from Act One comes on.*)

135   EDWARD: Gerry I love you.

GERRY: Yes, I know. I love you, too.

EDWARD: You know what we did? I want to do it again. I think about it all the time. Don't you want to any more?

GERRY: Yes, of course.

Song
CLOUD NINE

140   ALL: It'll be fine when you reach Cloud Nine.

Mist was rising and the night was dark.
Me and my baby took a walk in the park.
He said Be mine and you're on Cloud Nine.

Better watch out when you're on Cloud Nine.

145   Smoked some dope on the playground swings
Higher and higher on true love's wings
He said Be mine and you're on Cloud Nine.

Twenty-five years on the same Cloud Nine.

Who did she meet on her first blind date?

150   The guys were no surprise but the lady was great
They were women in love, they were on Cloud Nine.

Two the same, they were on Cloud Nine.

The bride was sixty-five, the groom was seventeen,
They fucked in the back of the black limousine.

155   It was divine in their silver Cloud Nine.

Simply divine in their silver Cloud Nine.

The wife's lover's children and my lover's wife,
Cooking in my kitchen, confusing my life.
And it's upside down when you reach Cloud Nine.

Upside down when you reach Cloud Nine.   160

SCENE IV

The park. Afternoon in late summer. MARTIN, CATHY, EDWARD.

CATHY: Under the bramble bushes,
Under the sea boom boom boom,
True love for you my darling,
True love for me my darling,
When we are married,   5
We'll raise a family.
Boy for you, girl for me,
Boom tiddley oom boom
SEXY.

EDWARD: You'll have Tommy and Cathy tonight then ok?   10
Tommy's still on antibiotics, do make him finish the bottle, he takes it in Ribena. It's no good in orange, he spits it out. Remind me to give you Cathy's swimming things.

CATHY: I did six strokes, didn't I Martin? Did I do a width? How many strokes is a length? How many miles is a   15
swimming pool? I'm going to take my bronze and silver and gold and diamond.

MARTIN: Is Tommy still wetting the bed?

EDWARD: Don't get angry with him about it.

MARTIN: I just need to go to the launderette so I've got a spare   20
sheet. Of course I don't get fucking angry, Eddy, for God's sake. I don't like to say he is my son but he is my son. I'm surprised I'm not wetting the bed myself.

CATHY: I don't wet the bed ever. Do you wet the bed Martin?

MARTIN: No.   25

CATHY: You said you did.

(BETTY *comes.*)

BETTY: I do miss the sun living in England but today couldn't be more beautiful. You appreciate the weekend when you're working. Betty's been at work this week, Cathy. It's terrible tiring, Martin, I don't know how you've done it all these   30
years. And the money, I feel like a child with the money, Clive always paid everything but I do understand it perfectly well. Look Cathy let me show you my money.

CATHY: I'll count it. Let me count it. What's that?

BETTY: Five pounds, Five and five is—   35

CATHY: One two three—

BETTY: Five and five is ten, and five—

CATHY: If I get it right can I have one?

EDWARD: No you can't.

(CATHY *goes on counting the money.*)

BETTY: I never like to say anything, Martin, or you'll think I'm   40
being a mother-in-law.

EDWARD: Which you are.

BETTY: Thank you, Edward, I'm not talking to you. Martin, I think you're being wonderful. Vicky will come back. Just let her stay with Lin till she sorts herself out. It's very nice   45

for a girl to have a friend; I had friends at school, that was very nice. But I'm sure Lin and Edward don't want her with them all the time. I'm not at all shocked that Lin and Edward aren't married and she already has a child, we all know first
50 marriages don't always work out. But really Vicky must be in the way. And poor little Tommy. I hear he doesn't sleep properly and he's had a cough.

MARTIN: No, he's fine, Betty, thank you.

CATHY: My bed's horrible. I want to sleep in the big bed with
55 Lin and Vicky and Eddy and I do get in if I've got a bad dream, and my bed's got a bump right in my back. I want to sleep in a tent.

BETTY: Well Tommy has got a nasty cough, Martin, whatever you say.

60 EDWARD: He's over that. He's got some medicine.

MARTIN: He takes it in Ribena.

BETTY: Well I'm glad to hear it. Look what a lot of money, Cathy, and I sit behind a desk of my own and I answer the telephone and keep the doctor's appointment book and it
65 really is great fun.

CATHY: Can we go camping, Martin, in a tent? We could take the Dead Hand Gang.

BETTY: Not those big boys, Cathy? They're far too big and rough for you. They climb back into the park after dark. I'm sure
70 mummy doesn't let you play with them, does she Edward? Well I don't know.

(*Ice cream bells.*)

CATHY: Ice cream. Martin you promised. I'll have a double ninety-nine. No I'll have a shandy lolly. Betty, you have a shandy lolly and I'll have a lick. No, you have a double ninety-
75 nine and I'll have the chocolate.

(MARTIN, CATHY and BETTY *go, leaving* EDWARD. GERRY *comes.*)

GERRY: Hello, Eddy. Thought I might find you here.

EDWARD: Gerry.

GERRY: Not working today then?

EDWARD: I don't work here any more.

80 GERRY: Your mum got you into a dark suit?

EDWARD: No of course not. I'm on the dole. I am working, though, I do housework.

GERRY: Whose wife are you now then?

EDWARD: Nobody's. I don't think like that any more. I'm
85 living with some women.

GERRY: What women?

EDWARD: It's my sister, Vic, and her lover. They go out to work and I look after the kids.

GERRY: I thought for a moment you said you were living
90 with women.

EDWARD: We do sleep together, yes.

GERRY: I was passing the park anyway so I thought I'd look in. I was in the sauna the other night and I saw someone who looked like you but it wasn't. I had sex with him anyway.

95 EDWARD: I do go to the sauna sometimes.

(CATHY *comes, gives* EDWARD *an ice cream, goes.*)

GERRY: I don't think I'd like living with children. They make a lot of noise don't they?

EDWARD: I tell them to shut up and they shut up. I wouldn't want to leave them at the moment.

GERRY: Look why don't we go for a meal sometime?   100

EDWARD: Yes I'd like that. Where are you living now?

GERRY: Same place.

EDWARD: I'll come round for you tomorrow night about 7:30.

GERRY: Great.

(EDWARD *goes.* HARRY *comes.* HARRY *and* GERRY *pick each other up. They go off.* BETTY *comes back.*)

BETTY: No, the ice cream was my treat, Martin. Off you go.   105
I'm going to have a quiet sit in the sun.

(MAUD *comes.*)

MAUD: Let Mrs Saunders be a warning to you, Betty. I know what it is to be unprotected.

BETTY: But mother, I have a job. I earn money.

MAUD: I know we have our little differences but I always want   110
what is best for you.

(ELLEN *comes.*)

ELLEN: Betty, what happens with a man?

BETTY: You just keep still.

ELLEN: And is it enjoyable? Don't forget me, Betty.

(MAUD *and* ELLEN *go.*)

BETTY: I used to think Clive was the one who liked sex. But   115
then I found I missed it. I used to touch myself when I was very little, I thought I'd invented something wonderful. I used to do it to go to sleep with or to cheer myself up, and one day it was raining and I was under the kitchen table, and my mother saw me with my hand under my dress rub-   120
bing away, and she dragged me out so quickly I hit my head and it bled and I was sick, and nothing was said, and I never did it again till this year. I thought if Clive wasn't looking at me there wasn't a person there. And one night in bed in my flat I was so frightened I started touching myself. I   125
thought my hand might go through space. I touched my face, it was there, my arm, my breast, and my hand went down where I thought it shouldn't, and I thought well there is somebody there. It felt very sweet, it was a feeling from very long ago, it was very soft, just barely touching, and I   130
felt myself gathering together more and more and I felt angry with Clive and angry with my mother and I went on and on defying them, and there was this vast feeling growing in me and all round me and they couldn't stop me and no one could stop me and I was there and coming and coming.   135
Afterwards I thought I'd betrayed Clive. My mother would kill me. But I felt triumphant because I was a separate person from them. And I cried because I didn't want to be. But I don't cry about it any more. Sometimes I do it three times in one night and it really is great fun.   140

(VICTORIA *and* LIN *come in.*)

VICTORIA: So I said to the professor, I don't think this is an occasion for invoking the concept of structural causality— oh hello mummy.

BETTY: I'm going to ask you a question, both of you. I have a
145   little money from your grandmother. And the three of you
    are living in that tiny flat with two children. I wonder if we
    could get a house and all live in it together? It would give
    you more room.
VICTORIA: But I'm going to Manchester anyway.
150 LIN: We'd have a garden, Vicky.
BETTY: You do seem to have such fun all of you.
VICTORIA: I don't want to.
BETTY: I didn't think you would.
LIN: Come on, Vicky, she knows we sleep together, and Eddy.
155 BETTY: I think I've known for quite a while but I'm not sure. I
    don't usually think about it, so I don't know if I know about
    it or not.
VICTORIA: I don't want to live with my mother.
LIN: Don't think of her as your mother, think of her as Betty.
160 VICTORIA: But she thinks of herself as my mother.
BETTY: I am your mother.
VICTORIA: But mummy we don't even like each other.
BETTY: We might begin to.

(CATHY *comes on howling with a nosebleed.*)

LIN: Oh Cathy what happened?
165 BETTY: She's been assaulted.
VICTORIA: It's a nosebleed.
CATHY: Took my ice cream.
LIN: Who did?
CATHY: Took my money.

(MARTIN *comes.*)

170 MARTIN: Is everything all right?
LIN: I thought you were looking after her.
CATHY: They hit me. I can't play. They said I'm a girl.
BETTY: Those dreadful boys, the gang, the Dead Hand.
MARTIN: What do you mean you thought I was looking after her?
175 LIN: Last I saw her she was with you getting an ice cream. It's
    your afternoon.
MARTIN: Then she went off to play. She goes off to play. You don't
    keep an eye on her every minute.
LIN: She doesn't get beaten up when I'm looking after her.
180 CATHY: Took my money.
MARTIN: Why the hell should I look after your child anyway?
    I just want Tommy. Why should he live with you and Vicky
    all week?
LIN: I don't mind if you don't want to look after her but don't
185   say you will and then this happens.
VICTORIA: When I get to Manchester everything's going to be
    different anyway, Lin's staying here, and you're staying here,
    we're all going to have to sit down and talk it through.
MARTIN: I'd really enjoy that.
190 CATHY: Hit me on the face.
LIN: You were the one looking after her and look at her now,
    that's all.
MARTIN: I've had enough of you telling me.
LIN: Yes you know it all.
195 MARTIN: Now stop it. I work very hard at not being like this, I
    could do with some credit.

LIN: Ok you're quite nice, try and enjoy it. Don't make me sorry
    for you, Martin, it's hard for me too. We've better things to
    do than quarrel. I've got to go and sort those little bastards
    out for a start. Where are they, Cathy?   200
CATHY: Don't kill them, mum, hit them. Give them a nosebleed,
    mum.

(LIN *goes.*)

VICTORIA: Tommy's asleep in the pushchair. We'd better wake
    him up or he won't sleep tonight.
MARTIN: Sometimes I keep him up watching television till he   205
    falls asleep on the sofa so I can hold him. Come on, Cathy,
    we'll get another ice cream.
CATHY: Chocolate sauce and nuts.
VICTORIA: Betty, would you like an ice cream?
BETTY: No thank you, the cold hurts my teeth, but what a nice   210
    thought, Vicky, thank you.

(VICTORIA *goes.* BETTY *alone.* GERRY *comes.*)

BETTY: I think you used to be Edward's flatmate.
GERRY: You're his mother. He's talked about you.
BETTY: Well never mind. Children are always wrong about their
    parents. It's a great problem knowing where to live and who   215
    to share with. I live by myself just now.
GERRY: Good, So do I. You can do what you like.
BETTY: I don't really know what I like.
GERRY: You'll soon find out.
BETTY: What do you like?   220
GERRY: Waking up at four in the morning.
BETTY: I like listening to music in bed and sometimes for supper
    I just have a big piece of bread and dip it in very hot lime
    pickle. So you don't get lonely by yourself? Perhaps you have a
    lot of visitors. I've been thinking I should have some visitors,   225
    I could give a little dinner party. Would you come? There
    wouldn't just be bread and lime pickle.
GERRY: Thank you very much.
BETTY: Or don't wait to be asked to dinner. Just drop in
    informally. I'll give you the address shall I? I don't usually   230
    give strange men my address but then you're not a strange
    man, you're a friend of Edward's. I suppose I seem a different
    generation to you but you are older than Edward. I was
    married for so many years it's quite hard to know how to get
    acquainted. But if there isn't a right way to do things you have   235
    to invent one. I always thought my mother was far too old
    to be attractive but when you get to an age yourself it feels
    quite different.
GERRY: I think you could be quite attractive.
BETTY: If what?   240
GERRY: If you stop worrying.
BETTY: I think when I do more about things I worry about them
    less. So perhaps you could help me do more.
GERRY: I might be going to live with Edward again.
BETTY: That's nice, but I'm rather surprised if he wants to share   245
    a flat. He's rather involved with a young woman he lives
    with, or two young women, I don't understand Edward but
    never mind.
GERRY: I'm very involved with him.

250 BETTY: I think Edward did try to tell me once but I didn't listen. So what I'm being told now is that Edward is 'gay' is that right? And you are too. And I've been making rather a fool of myself. But Edward does also sleep with women.

GERRY: He does, yes, I don't.

255 BETTY: Well people always say it's the mother's fault but I don't intend to start blaming myself. He seems perfectly happy.

GERRY: I could still come and see you.

BETTY: So you could, yes. I'd like that. I've never tried to pick up a man before.

260 GERRY: Not everyone's gay.

BETTY: No, that's lucky isn't it.

(GERRY *goes.* CLIVE *comes.*)

CLIVE: You are not that sort of woman, Betty. I can't believe you are. I can't feel the same about you as I did. And Africa is to be communist I suppose. I used to be proud to be British. There was a high ideal. I came out onto the verandah 265 and looked at the stars.

(CLIVE *goes.* BETTY *from Act One comes.* BETTY *and* BETTY *embrace.*)

MARINA CARR

O ne of the most widely-produced of contemporary English-language playwrights, Marina Carr was born in 1964 in Tullamore, Republic of Ireland; she studied English and Philosophy at University College, Dublin, graduating in 1987. Over the course of the past two decades Carr has become known for a searching disorientation of the conventions of modern Irish drama, transforming the evocative realism of an earlier generation of writers like Sean O'Casey or John Millington Synge. After early experiments—*Low in the* Dark (1989), *The Deer's Surrender* (1990) and *This Love Thing* (1991)—Carr's plays have regularly received major productions by internationally-acclaimed theaters: *The Ullaloo* at the Abbey Theatre's Peacock Theatre (1991); *The Mai* (Peacock, 1994), winning the Best New Play award of the Dublin Theatre Festival; *Portia Coughlan* (Peacock, 1996), *By the Bog of Cats . . .* (Abbey Theatre, 1998), *On Rafferty's Hill* (Druid Theatre, Galway, 2000), *Ariel* (Abbey, 2002), *Woman and Scarecrow* (Royal Court Theatre, London, 2006), *The Cordelia Dream* (Royal Shakespeare Company, 2008). Her most recent play, *Marble*, opened at the Abbey Theatre in 2009. Carr has served as writer-in-residence at the Abbey Theatre, at Trinity College, Dublin, and has also taught at Villanova University in the United States.

By the Bog of Cats . . .

Several of Carr's plays take their inspiration from classical Greek tragedy: *Ariel* is inspired by Euripides' *Iphigenia at Aulis*, and *By the Bog of Cats . . .* is a modern *Medea*. The play has many of the evident elements of Euripides' drama: Carr's Medea, Hester Swane, was abandoned by her parents—notably by her formidable mother, Josie—and conspired with her lover Carthage Kilbride to murder her brother; now, at the opening of the play, she has been left for another woman, the local landowner's daughter Caroline Cassidy. Like Medea, Hester is proud, defiant, and more than a bit mysterious herself; as the Catwoman says, her own mother foretold that she would live "as long as this black swan, not a day more, not a day less." And, of course, she brutally, defiantly murders her daughter, too. Yet rather than taking place in a classical *polis*, Carr's drama transpires in a lonesome village in the midlands of Ireland, on the edge of the evocative Bog of Cats; the village lout Carthage is no Argonaut Jason, and the chorus is composed of a bitter cast folk types: the confused old priest, Carthage's vicious and condescending mother, the boorish landowner. But merely to note Carr's attention to the plot and character materials of *Medea* is to miss the astonishing creative originality of the play. For if Medea is a kind of sorceress, Hester Swane lives in a world adrift in violence. *By the Bog of Cats . . .* opens with Hester, carrying a dead black swan, meeting the Ghost Fancier. The swan is a vivid image of Hester herself, and its death seems to have summoned the Fancier by mistake, since his purposed victim—Hester—is still alive: he's "too previous. I mistook this hour for dusk."

The sense of fatality, of waiting death, drives the play, its events classically compressed into a single, brutal day. Moreover the elegant identification between Hester and the black swan is deeply rooted in the play's imagination, an action that proceeds both through metaphor and association as well as through the linear consequentiality of its betrayal-and-revenge plot. The Bog itself is nearly impersonated by the Catwoman, an eerie figure living out in the marsh, eating mice and wearing an ancient coat of cat fur "studded with cats' eyes and cats' paws." The Catwoman is a prophet, and perhaps something like Tiresias, dramatizes the uncanniness of the seer in our midst: she's at once familiar, part of the landscape, and yet ineffably strange, unassimilable to the logic of the everyday world. Indeed, the play forcefully estranges the most familiar of social structures, the family itself, which emerges as a relational network of unbearable, and apparently unavoidable violence. Hester is haunted by her mother's abandonment; yet, much as she loves her own daughter—also Josie—she executes her, in an act indistinguishable from love itself: "It's alright, I'll take ya with me, I won't have ya as I was, waitin' a lifetime for somewan to return, because they don't, Josie,

Holly Hunter as Hester, and Caroline Cassidy in *By the Bog of Cats*.

AP Photo/PA, Andy Butterton

they don't." Josie closes her eyes and *Hester cuts Josie's throat in one savage movement.* One mother destroys her daughter by abandoning her; a second mother saves her daughter from abandonment by slicing her throat.

Without insisting on the deterministic "environmental" logic of an earlier naturalism, Carr nonetheless locates her action in a world of consequence, in which the formations of family and society function more fully as weapons than as the means of identification and self-preservation. As Hester remarks to Caroline, "there's two Hester Swanes, one that is decent and very fond of ya despite your callow treatment of me. And the other Hester, well, she could slide a knife down your face, carve ya up and not bat an eyelid." In *Medea*, exile is the common condition of women, but in *By the Bog of Cats . . .* it's betrayal: Carthage wants the security of a wealthier woman; Hester has been forced to sign her home over to the landholder, and is now threatened with eviction; she, too, tricked her brother, years before, in order to murder him with Carthage. Hester's response to the threat of her sudden expulsion from the society of the play is to force herself into its center: she arrives at the wedding decked-out in her own sordid wedding dress, enacting a travesty wedding that disrupts— but also literalizes—the empty grasping for land and stability that passes for love between Carthage and Caroline; then, she burns down her house and incinerates the cattle. Indeed, Hester's response to the inherent violence of social and kinship relations in the play extends and clarifies—without defining—the experience of tragedy itself; as Anne Carson suggests in "Tragedy; A Curious Art Form" (see Unit I), tragedy exists "Because you are full of rage. Why are you full of rage? Because you are full of grief." Carson grasps one of the essential impulses of tragedy, the ways its enactment of violence animates and sustains an otherwise-unthinkable relationship with its audience, a relationship that finally cannot be reduced to a sense of pedagogical morality. "Violence occurs; through violence we are intimate with some characters onstage in an exorbitant way for a brief time; that's all it is" (See Unit I). Carr's drama, written in a dense, lyrical prose, implicated in the play's evocative series of stage images, is in many respects not much like Euripides', but it does force its audience into just that exorbitant, snarling embrace (teeth, Hester points out, are "for snarlin' at people when smilin' doesn't work any more"). It's perhaps a measure of Carr's revision of Euripides that her Medea, Hester, is not spirited away in a dragon-drawn chariot, but—having butchered her daughter—turns to the Ghost Fancier and asks him to take her away. Locked in a dance of death, Hester is gutted by the same knife that killed her daughter, having "cut her heart out—it's lyin' there on top of her chest like some dark feathered bird."

By the Bog of Cats . . .

Marina Carr

CHARACTERS

HESTER SWANE, forty
CARTHAGE KILBRIDE, thirty
JOSIE KILBRIDE, seven, Hester and Carthage's daughter
MRS KILBRIDE, sixties, Carthage's mother
MONICA MURRAY, sixties, a neighbour
CATWOMAN, fifties, lives on the bog
XAVIER CASSIDY, sixties, a big farmer
CAROLINE CASSIDY, twenty, his daughter
THE GHOST FANCIER, a handsome creature in a dress suit
THE GHOST OF JOSEPH SWANE, eighteen
YOUNG DUNNE, a waiter
FATHER WILLOW, eighty
TWO OTHER WAITERS
VOICE OF JOSIE SWANE

Time and Place

The present.

Act One takes place in the yard of HESTER SWANE's
house and by the caravan on the Bog of Cats.
Act Two takes place in XAVIER CASSIDY's house.
Act Three opens in HESTER's yard and then
reverts to the caravan on the Bog of Cats

Accent

Midland. I've given a slight flavour in the text,
but the real Midland accent is a lot flatter and rougher
and more guttural than the written word allows

Songs of Josie Swane*

BY THE BOG OF CATS . . .

By the Bog of Cats I finally learned false from true,
Learned too late that it was you and only you
Left me sore, a heart brimful of rue
By the Bog of Cats in the darkling dew.

By the Bog of Cats I dreamed a dream of wooing.
I heard your clear voice to me a-calling
That I must go though it be my undoing.
By the Bog of Cats I'll stay no more a-rueing.

To the Bog of Cats I one day will return,
In mortal form or in ghostly form,
And I will find you there and there with you sojourn,
Forever by the Bog of Cats, my darling one.

THE BLACK SWAN

I know where a black swan sleeps
On the bank of grey water,
Hidden in a nest of leaves
So none can disturb her.

I have lain outside her lair,
My hand upon her wing,
And I have whispered to her
And of my sorrows sung.

I wish I was a black swan
And could fly away from here,
But I am Josie Swane,
Without wings, without care.

* to be recorded and used during the play

ACT ONE

SCENE ONE

*Dawn. On the Bog of Cats. A bleak white landscape of ice and
snow. Music, a lone violin.* HESTER SWANE *trails the corpse of a
black swan after her, leaving a trail of blood in the snow. The*
GHOST FANCIER *stands there watching her.*

HESTER: Who are you? Haven't seen you around here before.
GHOST FANCIER: I'm a ghost fancier.
HESTER: A ghost fancier. Never heard tell of the like.
GHOST FANCIER: You never seen ghosts?
5 HESTER: Not exactly, felt what I thought were things from some
    other world betimes, but nothin' I could grab on to and say,
    'That is a ghost.'
GHOST FANCIER: Well, where there's ghosts there's ghost fanciers.
HESTER: That so? So what do you do, Mr Ghost Fancier?
10   Eye up ghosts? Have love affairs with them?
GHOST FANCIER: Dependin' on the ghost. I've trailed you a while.
    What're you doin' draggin' the corpse of a swan behind ya
    like it was your shadow?
HESTER: This is auld Black Wing. I've known her the longest time.
15   We used play together when I was a young wan. Wance I had

to lave the Bog of Cats and when I returned years later this
swan here came swoopin' over the bog to welcome me home,
came right up to me and kissed me hand. Found her frozen in
a bog hole last night, had to rip her from the ice, left half her
underbelly.   20
GHOST FANCIER: No one ever tell ya it's dangerous to interfere
    with swans, especially black wans?
HESTER: Only an auld superstition to keep people afraid. I only
    want to bury her. I can't be struck down for that, can I?
GHOST FANCIER: You live in that caravan over there?   25
HESTER: Used to; live up the lane now. In a house, though I've
    never felt at home in it. But you, Mr Ghost Fancier, what ghost
    are you ghoulin' for around here?
GHOST FANCIER: I'm ghoulin' for a woman be the name of Hester
    Swane.   30
HESTER: I'm Hester Swane.
GHOST FANCIER: You couldn't be, you're alive.
HESTER: I certainly am and aim to stay that way.
GHOST FANCIER: (*looks around, confused*) Is it sunrise or sunset?
HESTER: Why do ya want to know?   35
GHOST FANCIER: Just tell me.
HESTER: It's that hour when it could be aither dawn or dusk, the
    light bein' so similar. But it's dawn, see there's the sun comin' up.

GHOST FANCIER: Then I'm too previous. I mistook this hour for
40   dusk. A thousand apologies.

Goes to exit, Hester stops him.

HESTER: What do ya mean you're too previous? Who are ya? Really?
GHOST FANCIER: I'm sorry for intrudin' upon you like this. Its not
        usually my style. (*Lifts his hat, walks off.*)
HESTER: (*shouts after him*) Come back!—I can't die—I have a
45   daughter.

Monica enters.

MONICA: What's wrong of ya, Hester? What are ya shoutin' at?
HESTER: Don't ya see him?
MONICA: Who?
HESTER: Him!
50 MONICA: I don't see anywan.
HESTER: Over there. (*Points.*)
MONICA: There's no wan, but ya know this auld bog, always
        shiftin' and changin' and coddin' the eye. What's that you've
        there? Oh, Black Wing, what happened to her?
55 HESTER: Auld age, I'll wager, found her frozed last night.
MONICA: (*touches the swan's wing*) Well, she'd good innin's,
        way past the life span of swans. Ya look half frozed yourself,
        walkin' all night again, were ya? Ya'll cetch your death in this
        weather. Five below the forecast said and worser promised.
60 HESTER: Swear the age of ice have returned. Wouldn't ya almost
        wish it had, do away with us all like the dinosaurs.
MONICA: I would not indeed—are you lavin' or what, Hester?
HESTER: Don't keep axin' me that.
MONICA: Ya know you're welcome in my little shack.
65 HESTER: I'm goin' nowhere. This here is my house and my garden
        and my stretch of the bog and no wan's runnin' me out of here.
MONICA: I came up to see if ya wanted me to take Josie down for
        her breakfast.
HESTER: She's still asleep.
70 MONICA: The child, Hester, ya have to pull yourself together for
        her, you're goin' to have to stop this broodin', put your life
        back together again.
HESTER: Wasn't me as pulled it asunder.
MONICA: And you're goin' to have to lave this house, isn't yours
75   any more. Down in Daly's doin' me shoppin' and Caroline
        Cassidy there talkin' about how she was goin' to mow this
        place to the ground and build a new house from scratch.
HESTER: Caroline Cassidy. I'll sourt her out. It's not her is the
        problem anyway, she's just wan of the smaller details.
80 MONICA: Well, you've left it late for dealin' with her for she has
        her heart set on everythin' that's yours.
HESTER: If he thinks he can go on treatin' me the way he's been
        treatin' me, he's another thing comin'. I'm not to be flung
        aside at his biddin'. He'd be nothin' today if it wasn't for me.
85 MONICA: Sure the whole parish knows that.
HESTER: Well, if they do, why're yees all just standin' back and
        gawkin'. Thinks yees all Hester Swane with her tinker blood
        is gettin' no more than she deserves. Thinks yees all she's too
        many notions, built her life up from a caravan on the side
90   of the bog. Thinks yees all she's taken a step above herself in
        gettin' Carthage Kilbride into her bed. Thinks yees all yees
        knew it'd never last. Well, yees are thinkin' wrong. Carthage
        Kilbride is mine for always or until I say he is no longer mine.
I'm the one who chooses and discards, not him, and certainly
not any of yees. And I'm not runnin' with me tail between me   95
legs just because certain people wants me out of their way.
MONICA: You're angry now and not thinkin' straight.
HESTER: If he'd only come back, we'd be alright, if I could just have
him for a few days on me own with no wan stickin' their nose in.
MONICA: Hester, he's gone from ya and he's not comin' back.   100
HESTER: Ah you think ya know everythin' about me and
        Carthage. Well, ya don't. There's things about me and
        Carthage no wan knows except the two of us. And I'm not
        talkin' about love. Love is for fools and children. Our bond is
        harder, like two rocks we are, grindin' off of wan another and   105
        maybe all the closer for that.
MONICA: That's all in your own head, the man cares nothin' for
        ya, else why would he go on the way he does.
HESTER: My life doesn't hang together without him.
MONICA: You're talkin' riddles now.   110
HESTER: Carthage knows what I'm talkin' about—I suppose
        I may bury auld Black Wing before Josie wakes and sees her.
        (*Begins walking off.*)
MONICA: I'll come up to see ya in a while, bring yees up some
        lunch, help ya pack.   115
HESTER: There'll be no packin' done around here.

And exit both in opposite directions.

SCENE TWO

*The sound of a child's voice comes from the house. She enters after
a while,* JOSIE KILBRIDE, *seven, barefoot, pyjamas, kicking the
snow, singing.*

JOSIE:
        By the Bog of Cats I dreamed a dream of wooing.
        I heard your clear voice to me a-calling
        That I must go though it be my undoing.
        By the Bog of Cats I'll stay no more a-rueing—   5

Mam—Mam—(*Continues playing in the snow, singing.*)

        To the Bog of Cats I one day will return,
        In mortal form or in ghostly form,
        And I will find you there and there with you sojourn,
        Forever by the Bog of Cats, my darling one.   10

*Mrs Kilbride has entered, togged up against the biting cold,
a shawl over her face.*

MRS KILBRIDE: Well, good mornin', ya little wagon of a girl child.
JOSIE: Mornin' yourself, y'auld wagon of a Granny witch.
MRS KILBRIDE: I tould ya not to call me Granny.
JOSIE: Grandmother—Did ya see me Mam, did ya?
MRS KILBRIDE: Aye, seen her whooshin' by on her broom half an   15
        hour back.
JOSIE: Did yees crash?
MRS KILBRIDE: Get in, ya pup, and put on some clothes before
        Jack Frost ates your toes for breakfast. Get in till I dress ya.
JOSIE: I know how to dress meself.   20
MRS KILBRIDE: Then dress yourself and stop braggin' about it.
        Get in. Get in.

And exit the pair to the house.

SCENE THREE

Enter HESTER *by the caravan. She digs a grave for the swan. Enter the* CATWOMAN*, a woman in her late fifties, stained a streaky brown from the bog, a coat of cat fur that reaches to the ground, studded with cats' eyes and cats' paws. She is blind and carries a stick.*

CATWOMAN: What're ya doin' there?

HESTER: None of your business now, Catwoman.

CATWOMAN: You're buryin' auld Black Wing, aren't ya?

HESTER: How d'ya know?

5 CATWOMAN: I know everythin' that happens on this bog. I'm the Keeper of the Bog of Cats in case ya forgotten. I own this bog.

HESTER: Ya own nothin', Catwoman, except your little house of turf and your hundred-odd mousetraps and anythin'

10 ya can rob and I'm missin' a garden chair so ya better bring it back.

CATWOMAN: I only took it because ya won't be needin' it any more.

HESTER: Won't I? If ya don't bring it back I'll have to go down meself and maybe knock your little turf house down.

15 CATWOMAN: You just dare.

HESTER: I'll bring down diesel, burn ya out.

CATWOMAN: Alright! Alright! I'll bring back your garden chair, fierce uncomfortable anyway, not wan of the cats'd sleep on it. Here, give her to me a minute, auld Black Wing.

Hester does.

20 She came to my door last night and tapped on it as she often did, only last night she wouldn't come in. I bent down and she puts her wing on me cheek and I knew this was farewell. Then I heard her tired auld wingbeat, shaky and off kilter and then the thud of her fallin' out of the sky onto the ice.

25 She must've died on the wing or soon after. (*Kisses the black swan.*) Goodbye, auld thing, and safe journey. Here, put her in the ground.

Hester does and begins shovelling in clay. Catwoman stands there leaning on her stick, produces a mouse from her pocket.

A saucer of milk there, Hester Swane.

HESTER: I've no milk here today. You may go up to the house

30 for your saucer of milk and, I told ya, I don't want ya pawin' mice around me, dirty auld yokes, full of diseases.

CATWOMAN: And you aren't, you clean as the snow, Hester Swane?

HESTER: Did I say I was?

35 CATWOMAN: I knew your mother, I helped her bring ya into the world, knew ya when ya were chained like a rabied pup to this auld caravan, so don't you look down on me for handlin' a mouse or two.

HESTER: If ya could just see yourself and the mouse fur growin'

40 out of your teeth. Disgustin'.

CATWOMAN: I need mice the way you need whiskey.

HESTER: Ah, go on and lave me alone, Catwoman, I'm in no mood for ya today.

CATWOMAN: Bet ya aren't. I had a dream about ya last night.

45 HESTER: Spare me your visions and dreams, enough of me own to deal with.

CATWOMAN: Dreamt ya were a black train motorin' through the Bog of Cats and, oh, the scorch off of this train and it blastin' by and all the bog was dark in your wake, and I had

to run from the burn. Hester Swane, you'll bring this place 50 down by evenin'.

HESTER: I know.

CATWOMAN: Do ya now? Then why don't ya lave? If ya lave this place you'll be alright. That's what I came by to tell ya.

HESTER: Ah, how can I lave the Bog of Cats, everythin' I'm 55 connected to is here. I'd rather die.

CATWOMAN: Then die ya will.

HESTER: There's sympathy for ya! That's just what I need to hear.

CATWOMAN: Ya want sugar-plum platitudes, go talk to Monica Murray or anyone else around here. You're my match in 60 witchery, Hester, same as your mother was, it may even be ya surpass us both and the way ya go on as if God only gave ya a little frog of a brain instead of the gift of seein' things as they are, not as they should be, but exactly as they are. Ya know what I think? 65

HESTER: What?

CATWOMAN: I been thinkin' a while now that there's some fierce wrong ya done that's caught up with ya.

HESTER: What fierce wrong?

CATWOMAN: Don't you by-talk me, I'm the Catwoman. I know 70 things. Now I can't say I know the exact wrong ya done but I'd put a bet on it's somethin' serious judgin' by the way ya go on.

HESTER: And what way do I go on?

CATWOMAN: What was it ya done, Hester? 75

HESTER: I done nothin'—Or if I did I never meant to.

CATWOMAN: There's a fine answer.

HESTER: Everywan has done wrong at wan time or another.

CATWOMAN: Aye, but not everywan knows the price of wrong. You do and it's the best thing about ya and there's not 80 much in ya I'd praise. No, most manage to stay a step or two ahead of the pigsty truth of themselves, not you though.

HESTER: Ah, would ya give over. Ya lap up people's fears, you've too much time on your own, concoctin' stories about others. 85 Go way and kill a few mice for your dinner, only lave me alone—Or tell me about me mother, for what I remember doesn't add up.

CATWOMAN: What ya want to know about big Josie Swane?

HESTER: Everythin'. 90

CATWOMAN: Well, what ya remember?

HESTER: Only small things—Like her pausin'.

CATWOMAN: She was a great wan for the pausin'.

HESTER: 'G'wan to bed, you,' she'd say, 'I'll just be here pausin'.' And I'd watch her from the window. (*Indicates window of* 95 *caravan.*) Times she'd smoke a cigar which she had her own particular way of doin'. She'd hould it stretched away from her and, instead of takin' the cigar to her mouth, she'd bring her mouth to the cigar. And her all the time pausin'. What was she waitin' for, Catwoman? 100

CATWOMAN: Ya'd often hear her voice comin' over the bog at night. She was the greatest song stitcher ever to have passed through this place and we've had plenty pass through but none like Josie Swane. But somewhere along the way she lost the weave of the song and in so doin' became small 105 and bitter and mean. By the time she ran off and left ya I couldn't abide her.

HESTER: There's a longin' in me for her that won't quell the whole time.

CATWOMAN: I wouldn't long for Josie Swane if I was you. 110 Sure the night ya were born she took ya over to the black

swan's lair, auld Black Wing ya've just buried there, and laid ya in the nest alongside her. And when I axed her why she'd do a thing like that with snow and ice everywhere, ya
115 know what she says, 'Swane means swan.' 'That may be so,' says I, 'but the child'll die of pneumonia.' 'That child,' says Josie Swane, 'will live as long as this black swan, not a day more, not a day less.' And each night for three nights she left ya in the black swan's lair and each night I snuck ya out
120 of the lair and took ya home with me and brung ya back to the lair before she'd come lookin' for ya in the mornin'. That's when I started to turn again' her.

HESTER: You're makin' it up to get rid of me like everywan else round here. Xavier Cassidy put ya up to this.
125 CATWOMAN: Xavier Cassidy put me up to nothin'. I'm only tellin' ya so ya know what sourt of a woman your mother was. Ya were lucky she left ya. Just forget about her and lave this place now or ya never will.

HESTER: Doesn't seem to make much difference whether I stay or
130 lave with a curse like that on me head.

CATWOMAN: There's ways round curses. Curses only have the power ya allow them. I'm tellin' ya, Hester, ya have to go. When have I ever been proved wrong? Tould ya ya'd have just the wan daughter, tould ya the day and hour she'd be born,
135 didn't I now?

HESTER: Ya did alright.

CATWOMAN: Tould ya Carthage Kilbride was no good for ya, never grew his backbone, would ya listen? Tould Monica Murray to stop her only son drivin' to the city
140 that night. Would she listen? Where's her son? In his grave, that's where he is. Begged her till she ran me off with a kittle of bilin' water. Mayhap she wanted him dead. I'll say nothin'. Gave auld Xavier Cassidy herbs to cure his wife. What did he do? Pegged them down the
145 tilet and took Olive Cassidy to see some swanky medicine man in a private hospital. They cured her alright, cured her so well she came back cured as a side of ham in an oak coffin with golden handles. Maybe he wanted her dead too. There's many gets into brown studies over buryin' their
150 loved wans. That a fact, Hester Swane. I'll be off now and don't say the Catwoman never tould ya. Lave this place now or ya never will.

HESTER: I'm stoppin' here.

CATWOMAN: Sure I know that too. Seen it writ in a bog hole.
155 HESTER: Is there anythin' them blind eyes doesn't see writ in a bog hole?

CATWOMAN: Sneer away. Ya know what the Catwoman says is true, but sneer away and we'll see will that sneer be on your puss at dusk. Remember the Catwoman then for I don't think
160 I'll have the stomach for this place tonight.

And exit the Catwoman and exit Hester.

SCENE FOUR

JOSIE *and* MRS KILBRIDE *enter and sit at the garden table as the* CATWOMAN *and* HESTER *exit.* JOSIE *is dressed: wellingtons, trousers, jumper on inside out. They're playing snap.* MRS KILBRIDE *plays ruthlessly, loves to win.* JOSIE *looks on in dismay.*

MRS KILBRIDE: Snap—snap! Snap! (*stacking the cards*) How many games is that I'm after winnin' ya?

JOSIE: Five.

MRS KILBRIDE: And how many did you win?

JOSIE: Ya know right well I won ne'er a game.   5

MRS KILBRIDE: And do ya know why ya won ne'er a game, Josie? Because you're thick, that's the why.

JOSIE: I always win when I play me Mam.

MRS KILBRIDE: That's only because your Mam is thicker than you. Thick and stubborn and dangerous wrong-headed and   10 backwards to top it all. Are you goin' to start cryin' now, ya little pussy babby, don't you dare cry, ya need to toughen up, child, what age are ya now?—I says what age are ya?

JOSIE: Seven.

MRS KILBRIDE: Seven auld years. When I was seven I was   15 cookin' dinners for a houseful of men, I was thinnin' turnips twelve hour a day, I was birthin' calves, sowin' corn, stookin' hay, ladin' a bull be his nose, and you can't even win a game of snap. Sit up straight or ya'll grow up a hunchback. Would ya like that, would ya, to   20 grow up a hunchback? Ya'd be like an auld camel and everyone'd say, as ya loped by, 'There goes Josie Kilbride the hunchback,' would ya like that, would ya? Answer me.

JOSIE: Ya know right well I wouldn't, Granny.

MRS KILBRIDE: What did I tell ya about callin' me   25 Grandmother.

JOSIE: (*defiantly*) Granny.

MRS KILBRIDE: (*leans over the table viciously*) Grandmother! Say it!

JOSIE: (*giving in*) Grandmother.   30

MRS KILBRIDE: And you're lucky I even let ya call me that. Ya want another game?

JOSIE: Only if ya don't cheat.

MRS KILBRIDE: When did I cheat?

JOSIE: I seen ya, loads of times.   35

MRS KILBRIDE: A bad loser's all you are, Josie, and there's nothin' meaner than a bad loser. I never cheat. Never. D'ya hear me, do ya? Look me in the eye when I'm talkin' to ya, ya little bastard. D'ya want another game?

JOSIE: No thanks, Grandmother.   40

MRS KILBRIDE: And why don't ya? Because ya know I'll win, isn't that it? Ya little coward ya, I'll break your spirit yet and then glue ya back the way I want ya. I bet ya can't even spell your name.

JOSIE: And I bet ya I can.   45

MRS KILBRIDE: G'wan then, spell it.

JOSIE: (*spells*) J-o-s-i-e K-i-l-b-r-i-d-e.

MRS KILBRIDE: Wrong! Wrong! Wrong!

JOSIE: Well, that's the way Teacher taught me.

MRS KILBRIDE: Are you back-answerin' me?   50

JOSIE: No, Grandmother.

MRS KILBRIDE: Ya got some of it right. Ya got the 'Josie' part right, but ya got the 'Kilbride' part wrong, because you're not a Kilbride. You're a Swane. Can ya spell Swane? Of course ya can't. You're Hester Swane's little bastard. You're not a   55 Kilbride and never will be.

JOSIE: I'm tellin' Daddy what ya said.

MRS KILBRIDE: Tell him! Ya won't be tellin' him anythin'. I haven't tould him meself. He's an eegit, your Daddy. I warned him about that wan, Hester Swane, that she'd   60 get her claws in, and she did, the tinker. That's what yees are, tinkers. And your poor Daddy, all he's had to put up with. Well, at least that's all changin' now. Why don't yees head off in that auld caravan, back to wherever yees came from, and give your poor Daddy back to me where he   65 rightfully belongs. And you've your jumper on backwards.

JOSIE: It's not backwards, it's inside out.

MRS KILBRIDE: Don't you cheek me—and tell me this, Josie Swane, how much has your Mam in the bank?

70 JOSIE: I don't know.

MRS KILBRIDE: I'll tell ya how much, a great big goose egg. Useless, that's what she is, livin' off of handouts from my son that she flitters away on whiskey and cigars, the Jezebel witch, (*smugly*) Guess how much I've saved, Josie, g'wan, guess, guess.

75 JOSIE: I wish if me Mam'd came soon.

MRS KILBRIDE: Ah g'wan, child, guess.

JOSIE: Ten pound.

MRS KILBRIDE: (*hysterical*) Ten pound! A' ya mad, child? A' ya mad! Ten pound! (*Whispers avariciously.*) Three thousand

80 pound. All mine. I saved it. I didn't frig it away on crame buns and blouses. No. I saved it. A thousand for me funeral, a thousand for the Little Sisters of the Poor and a thousand for your Daddy. I'm lavin' you nothin' because your mother would get hould of it. And d'ya think would

85 I get any thanks for savin' all that money? Oh no, none, none in the world. Would it ever occur to anywan to say, 'Well done, Mrs Kilbride, well done, Elsie,' not wance did your Daddy ever say, 'Well done, Mother,' no, too busy fornicatin' with Hester Swane, too busy bringin' little

90 bastards like yourself into the world.

JOSIE: Can I go and play now?

MRS KILBRIDE: Here, I brung ya sweets, g'wan ate them, ate them all, there's a great child, ya need some sugar, some sweetie pie sweetness in your life. C'mere and give your auld

95 Grandmother a kiss.

Josie does.

Sure it's not your fault ya were born a little girl bastard. D'ya want another game of snap? I'll let ya win.

JOSIE: No.

MRS KILBRIDE: Don't you worry, child, we'll get ya off of her

100 yet. Me and your daddy has plans. We'll batter ya into the semblance of legitimacy yet, soon as we get ya off—

Enter Carthage.

CARTHAGE: I don't know how many times I tould ya to lave the child alone. You've her poisoned with your bile and rage.

MRS KILBRIDE: I'm sayin' nothin' that isn't true. Can't I play a

105 game of snap with me own granddaughter?

CARTHAGE: Ya know I don't want ya around here at the minute. G'wan home, Mother. G'wan!

MRS KILBRIDE: And do what? Talk to the range? Growl at God?

CARTHAGE: Do whatever ya like, only lave Josie alone, pick on

110 somewan your own size. (*He turns Josie's jumper the right way around.*) You'll have to learn to dress yourself.

MRS KILBRIDE: Ah now, Carthage, don't be annoyed with me. I only came up to say goodbye to her, found her in her pyjamas out here playin' in the snow. Why isn't her mother

115 mindin' her?

CARTHAGE: Don't start in on that again.

MRS KILBRIDE: I never left you on your own.

CARTHAGE: Ya should have.

MRS KILBRIDE: And ya never called in to see the new dress I got

120 for today and ya promised ya would.

Carthage glares at her.

Alright, I'm goin', I'm goin'. Just don't think now ya've got Caroline Cassidy ya can do away with me, the same as you're doin' away with Hester Swane. I'm your mother and I won't be goin' away. Ever. (*Exits.*)

CARTHAGE: Where's your Mam?   125

JOSIE: Isn't she always on the bog? Can I go to your weddin'?

CARTHAGE: What does your mother say?

JOSIE: She says there'll be no weddin' and to stop annoyin' her.

CARTHAGE: Does she now?

JOSIE: Will you ax her for me?   130

CARTHAGE: We'll see, Josie, we'll see.

JOSIE: I'll wear me Communion dress. Remember me Communion, Daddy?

CARTHAGE: I do.

JOSIE: Wasn't it just a brilliant day?   135

CARTHAGE: It was, sweetheart, it was. Come on, we go check the calves.

And exit the pair.

SCENE FIVE

Enter CAROLINE CASSIDY *in her wedding dress and veil. Twenty, fragile-looking and nervous. She goes to the window of* HESTER's *house and knocks.*

CAROLINE: Hester—are ya there?

Hester comes up behind her.

HESTER: Haven't you the gall comin' here, Caroline Cassidy.

CAROLINE: (*jumps with fright*) Oh! (*Recovers.*) Can come here whenever I want, this is my house now, sure ya signed it over and all.   5

HESTER: Bits of paper, writin', means nothin', can as aisy be unsigned.

CAROLINE: You're meant to be gone this weeks, it's just not fair.

HESTER: Lots of things isn't fair, Daddy's little ice-pop.

CAROLINE: We're goin' ahead with the weddin', me and Carthage, ya   10
think ya'll disrupt everythin', Hester Swane. I'm not afraid of ya.

HESTER: Ya should be. I'm afraid of meself—What is it ya want from me, Caroline? What have I ever done on you that ya feel the need to take everythin' from me?

CAROLINE: I'm takin' nothin' ya haven't lost already and lost this   15
long while gone.

HESTER: You're takin' me husband, you're takin' me house, ya even want me daughter. Over my dead body.

CAROLINE: He was never your husband, he only took pity on ya, took ya out of that auld caravan on the bog, gave ya a home,   20
built ya up from the ground.

HESTER: Them the sweet nothin's he's been tellin' ya? Let's get wan thing straight, it was me built Carthage Kilbride up from nothin', him a labourer's son you wouldn't give the time of day to and you trottin' by in your first bra, on   25
your half-bred mare, your nose nudgin' the sun. It was me who tould him he could do better. It was my money that bought his first fine acres. It was in my bed he slowly turned from a slavish pup to a man and no frigid little Daddy's girl is goin' to take him from me. Now get off of   30
my property before I cut that dress to ribbons.

CAROLINE: I'll have to get Daddy. He'll run ya off with a shotgun if he has to.

HESTER: Not everyone is as afraid of your Daddy as you are,
35   Caroline.
CAROLINE: Look, I'll give ya more money if ya'll only go.
    Here's me bank book, there's nearly nineteen thousand
    pounds in it, me inheritance from me mother. Daddy gave
    it to me this mornin'. Ya can have it, only please go. It's me
40   weddin' day. It's meant to be happy. It's meant to be the
    best day of me life.

She stands there, close to tears. Hester goes over to her, touches her veil.

HESTER: What ya want me to do, Caroline? Admire your dress?
    Wish ya well? Hah? I used babysit you. Remember that?
CAROLINE: That was a long time ago.
45 HESTER: Not that long at all. After your mother died, several
    nights ya came down and slept with me. Ya were glad of
    the auld caravan then, when your Daddy'd be off at the
    races or the mart or the pub, remember that, do ya? A pasty
    little thing, and I'd be awake half the night listenin' to your
50   girly gibberish and grievances. Listen to me now, Caroline,
    there's two Hester Swanes, one that is decent and very fond
    of ya despite your callow treatment of me. And the other
    Hester, well, she could slide a knife down your face, carve
    ya up and not bat an eyelid. (*Grabs her hair suddenly and*
55   *viciously.*)
CAROLINE: Ow! Lave go!
HESTER: Listen to me now, Caroline. Carthage Kilbride is mine
    and only mine. He's been mine since he was sixteen. You
    think you can take him from me? Wrong. All wrong. (*Lets go*
60   *of her.*) Now get out of me sight.
CAROLINE: Ya'll be sorry for this, Hester Swane.
HESTER: We all will.

And exit Caroline, running.

SCENE SIX

HESTER *lights a cigar, sits at her garden table. Enter* JOSIE *with an old shawl around her head and a pair of high heels. She is pretending to be her Granny.*

JOSIE: Well good mornin', Tinker Swane.
HESTER: (*mock surprise*) Oh, good mornin', Mrs Kilbride, what a
    lovely surprise, and how are ya today?
JOSIE: I've been savin' all night.
HESTER: Have ya now, Mrs Kilbride.
5 JOSIE: Tell me, ya Jezebel witch, how much have ya in the bank
    today?
HESTER: Oh I've three great big goose eggs, Mrs Kilbride. How
    much have ya in the bank yourself?
JOSIE: Seventeen million pound. Seventeen million pound. I saved
10   it. I didn't frig it away on love stories and silk stockin's. I cut
    back on sugar and I cut back on flour. I drank biled socks instead of
    tay and in wan night I saved seventeen million pound.
HESTER: Ya drank biled socks, Mrs Kilbride?
JOSIE: I did and I had turf stew for me dinner and for dessert
15   I had snail tart and a big mug of wee-wee.
HESTER: Sounds delicious, Mrs Kilbride.
JOSIE: Ya wouldn't get better in Buckin'am Palace.
HESTER: Josie, don't ever say any of that in front of your Granny,
    sure ya won't?
20 JOSIE: I'm not a total eegit, Mam.
HESTER: Did ya have your breakfast?

JOSIE: I had a sugar sammige.
HESTER: Ya better not have.
JOSIE: Granny made me disgustin' porridge.
HESTER: Did she? Did ya wash your teeth?   25
JOSIE: Why do I always have to wash me teeth? Every day. It's so
    borin'. What do I need teeth for anyway?
HESTER: Ya need them for snarlin' at people when smilin' doesn't
    work any more. G'wan in and wash them now.

Enter Carthage in his wedding suit. Hester looks at him, looks away.

JOSIE: Did ya count the cattle, Daddy?   30
CARTHAGE: I did.
JOSIE: Were they all there?
CARTHAGE: They were, Josie.
JOSIE: Daddy says I can go to his weddin'.
CARTHAGE: I said maybe, Josie.   35
HESTER: G'wan round the back and play, Josie.
JOSIE: Can I go, Mam, can I? Say yeah, g'wan, say yeah.
HESTER: We'll see, g'wan, Josie, g'wan, good girl.

And exit Josie. They both watch her. Silence.

CARTHAGE: I'd like to know what ya think you're playin' at.
HESTER: Take a better man than you to cancel me out, Carthage   40
    Kilbride.
CARTHAGE: Ya haven't even started packin'.
HESTER: Them your weddin' clothes?
CARTHAGE: They're not me farm clothes, are they?
HESTER: Ya've a cheek comin' here in them.   45
CARTHAGE: Well, you, missus, are meant to be gone.
HESTER: And ya've a nerve tellin' Josie she can go to your weddin'.
CARTHAGE: She's mine as well as yours.
HESTER: Have ya slept with her yet?
CARTHAGE: That's none of your business.   50
HESTER: Every bit of me business. Ya think ya can wipe out
    fourteen years just like that. Well she's welcome to ya and any
    satisfaction she can squeeze out of ya.
CARTHAGE: Never heard ya complainin' when I was in your
    bed.   55
HESTER: Ya done the job, I suppose, in a kindergarten sourt of way.
CARTHAGE: Kindergarten, that what ya call it?
HESTER: You were nothin' before I put me stamp on ya and ya'll
    be nothin' again I'm finished with ya.
CARTHAGE: Are you threatenin' me, Hetty? Because, if ya are, ya   60
    better know who you're dealin' with, not the sixteen-year-auld
    fool snaggin' hares along the Bog of Cats who fell into your
    clutches.
HESTER: It was you wooed me, Carthage Kilbride, not the
    other way round as ya'd like everywan to think. In the   65
    beginnin' I wanted nothin' to do with ya, should've
    trusted me first instinct, but ya kept comin' back. You cut
    your teeth on me, Carthage Kilbride, gnawed and sucked
    till all that's left is an auld bone ya think to fling on the
    dunghill, now you've no more use for me. If you think I'm   70
    goin' to let you walk over me like that, ya don't know me
    at all.
CARTHAGE: That at least is true. I've watched ya now for the best
    part of fourteen years and I can't say for sure I know the first
    thing about ya. Who are ya and what sort of stuff are ya   75
    made of?

HESTER: The same as you and I can't abide to lose ya. Don't lave me. Don't—is it I've gotten old and you just hittin' thirty?

80 CARTHAGE: Ya know right well it isn't that.

HESTER: And I haven't had a drink since the night ya left.

CARTHAGE: I know.

HESTER: I only ever drank anyway to forget about—

CARTHAGE: I don't want to talk about that. Lave it.

85 HESTER: And still ya took the money and bought the land, the Kilbrides who never owned anythin' till I came along, tinker and all. Tell me what to do, Carthage, and I'll do it, anythin' for you to come back.

CARTHAGE: Just stop, will ya—

90 HESTER: Anythin', Carthage, anythin', and I'll do it if it's in me power.

CARTHAGE: It's not in your power—Look, I'm up to me neck in another life that can't include ya any more.

HESTER: You're sellin' me and Josie down the river for a few

95 lumpy auld acres and notions of respectability and I never thought ya would. You're better than all of them. Why must ya always look for the good opinion from them that'll never give it. Ya'll only ever be Xavier Cassidy's work horse. He won't treat ya right. He wouldn't know how.

100 CARTHAGE: He's treatin' me fine, signin' his farm over to me this evenin'.

HESTER: Ya know what they're sayin' about ya? That you're a jumped-up land-hungry mongrel but that Xavier Cassidy is greedier and craftier and he'll spancel ya back to the scrubber

105 ya are.

CARTHAGE: And ya know what they're sayin' about you? That it's time ya moved onto another haltin' site.

HESTER: I was born on the Bog of Cats and on the Bog of Cats I'll end me days. I've as much right to this place as any of yees,

110 more, for it holds me to it in ways it has never held yees. And as for me tinker blood, I'm proud of it. It gives me an edge over all of yees around here, allows me see yees for the inbred, underbred, bog-brained shower see yees are. I'm warnin' ya now, Carthage, you go through with this sham weddin' and

115 you'll never see Josie again.

CARTHAGE: If I have to mow ya down or have ya declared an unfit mother to see Josie I will, so for your own sake don't cause any trouble in that department. Look, Hetty, I want Josie to do well in the world, she'll get her share

120 of everythin' I own and will own. I want her to have a chance in life, a chance you never had and so can never understand—

HESTER: Don't tell me what I can and can't understand!

CARTHAGE: Well understand this. Ya'll not separate me

125 and Josie or I'll have her taken off of ya. I only have to mention your drinkin' or your night roamin' or the way ya sleep in that dirty auld caravan and lave Josie alone in the house.

HESTER: I always take Josie to the caravan when I sleep there.

130 CARTHAGE: Ya didn't take her last night.

HESTER: I wasn't in the caravan last night. I was walkin' the bog, but I checked on her three, four times.

CARTHAGE: Just don't cross me with Josie because I don't want to have to take her off of ya, I know she's attached to ya, and I'm

135 not a monster. Just don't cross me over her or I'll come down on ya like a bull from heaven.

HESTER: So I'm meant to lie back and let Caroline Cassidy have her way in the rearin' of my child. I'm meant to

lave her around Xavier Cassidy—sure he's capable of anythin'. If it's the last thing I do I'll find a way to keep her 140 from ya.

CARTHAGE: I want you out of here before dusk! And I've put it to ya now about Josie. Think it over when ya've calmed down. And here, (*producing envelope*) There's your blood money. It's all there down to the last penny. 145

HESTER: No! I don't want it!

CARTHAGE: (*throws it in the snow*) Neither do I. I never should've took it in the first place. I owe ya nothin' now, Hester Swane. Nothin'. Ya've no hold over me now. (*Goes to exit.*) 150

HESTER: Carthage—ya can't just walk away like this.

CARTHAGE: I can and I am—Ya know what amazes me, Hetty?

HESTER: What?

CARTHAGE: That I stayed with ya so long—I want peace, just peace—Remember, before dusk. 155

And exit Carthage. Hester looks after him. Josie comes running on.

JOSIE: What's wrong of ya, Mam?

HESTER: Ah go 'way, would ya, and lave me alone.

JOSIE: Can I go down to Daly's and buy sweets?

HESTER: No, ya can't. Go on off and play, you're far too demandin'. 160

JOSIE: Yeah well, just because you're in a bad humour it's not my fault. I'm fed up playin' on me own.

HESTER: You'll get a clatter if you're not careful. I played on me own when I was your age, I never bothered me mother, you're spoilt rotten, that's what ya are. (*in a gentler tone*) 165 G'wan and play with your dolls, give them a bath, cut their hair.

JOSIE: Ya said I wasn't to cut their hair.

HESTER: Well now I'm sayin' ya can, alright.

JOSIE: But it won't grow back. 170

HESTER: So! There's worse things in this world than your dolls' hair not growin' back, believe me, Josie Swane.

JOSIE: Me name is Josie Kilbride.

HESTER: That's what I said.

JOSIE: Ya didn't, ya said Josie Swane. I'm not a Swane. I'm a Kilbride. 175

HESTER: I suppose you're ashamed of me too.

Enter Xavier Cassidy and Caroline, both in their wedding clothes.

JOSIE: Caroline, your dress, is that your weddin' dress? It's beautiful.

CAROLINE: Hello Josie.

Josie runs over to Caroline to touch her dress. Hester storms after her, picks her up roughly, carries her to corner of the house. Puts her down.

HESTER: Now stay around the back.

And exit Josie.

XAVIER: Was hopin' I wouldn't find ya still here, Swane. 180

HESTER: So ya came back with your Daddy, ya know nothin', Caroline, nothin'. (*Sits at her garden table, produces a naggin of whiskey from her pocket, drinks.*)

XAVIER: Thought ya'd given up the drink.

HESTER: I had. Me first in months, but why should I try and 185 explain meself to you?

XAVIER: Might interest Carthage to know you lashin' into a
naggin of whiskey at this hour.

HESTER: Carthage. If it wasn't for you, me and Carthage'd be fine.
190   Should've eradicated ya, Cassidy, when I could've.
God's punishin' me now because I didn't take steps that were
right and proper concernin' you. Aye. God's punishin' me but
I won't take his blows lyin' down.

CAROLINE: What are ya talking about, Hester?

195   HESTER: What am I talkin' about? I'm talkin' about you, ya little
fool, and I'm talkin' about James.

CAROLINE: Me brother James?

XAVIER: You keep a civil tongue, Swane, over things ya know
nothin' about.

200   HESTER: Oh, but I do know things, and that's why ya want me
out of here. It's only your land and money and people's
fear of ya that has ya walkin' free. G'wan home and do
whatever it is ya do with your daughter, but keep your
sleazy eyes off of me and Josie. This is my property and
205   I've a right to sit in me own yard without bein' ogled by
the likes of you.

XAVIER: There's softer things on the eye, Swane, if it's oglin' I was
after. This is no longer your property and well ya know it, ya
signed it over six months ago, for a fine hefty sum, have the
210   papers here.

HESTER: I wasn't thinkin' right then, was bein' coerced and
bullied from all sides, but I have regained me pride and
it tells me I'm stayin'. Ya'll get your money back. (*Picks up
envelope Carthage has thrown in the snow.*) Here's some
215   of it.

XAVIER: I'm not takin' it. A deal's a deal.

HESTER: Take it! Take it! (*Stuffs it into his breast pocket.*) And it
might interest ya to know, Caroline, that Carthage was just
here in his weddin' clothes and he didn't look like no radiant
220   groom and he axed me to take him back, but I said—

XAVIER: I'd say he did alright—

HESTER: He did! He did! Or as much as, but I said I couldn't
be played with any more, that I was made for things he has
lost the power to offer. And I was. I was made for somethin'
225   different than these butchery lives yees all lead here on the
Bog of Cats. Me mother taught me that.

XAVIER: Your mother. Your mother taught ya nothin', Swane,
except maybe how to use a knife. Let me tell ya a thing
or two about your mother, big Josie Swane. I used see her
230   outside her auld caravan on the bog and the fields covered
over in stars and her half covered in an excuse for a dress
and her croonin' towards Orion in a language I never heard
before or since. We'd peace when she left.

HESTER: And what were you doin' watchin' her? Catwoman tould
235   me ya were in a constant swoon over me mother, sniffin'
round the caravan, lavin' little presents and Christmas
dinners and money and drink, sure I remember the gatch
of ya meself and ya scrapin' at the door.

XAVIER: Very presumptuous of ya, Swane, to think I'd
240   have any interest in your mother beyond Christian
compassion.

HESTER: Christian compassion! That what it's called these
days!

XAVIER: Aye, Christian compassion, a thing that was never
245   bet into you. Ya say ya remember lots of things, then
maybe ya remember that that food and money I used
lave was left so ya wouldn't starve. Times I'd walk by
that caravan and there'd be ne'er sign of this mother of

yours. She'd go off for days with anywan who'd buy her a
drink. She'd be off in the bars of Pullagh and Mucklagh   250
gettin' into fights. Wance she bit the nose off a woman
who dared to look at her man, bit the nose clean off
her face. And you, you'd be chained to the door of the
caravan with maybe a dirty nappy on ya if ya were lucky.
Often times—   255

HESTER: Lies! All lies!

XAVIER: Often times I brung ya home and gave ya over to me
mother to put some clothes on ya and feed ya. More times
than I can remember it'd be from our house your mother
would collect ya, the brazen walk of her, and not a thank   260
you or a flicker of guilt in her eye and her reekin' of drink.
Times she wouldn't even bother to collect ya and meself
or me mother would have to bring ya down to her and
she'd hardly notice that we'd come and gone or that you'd
returned.   265

HESTER: Ya expect me to believe anythin' that comes from your
siled lips, Xavier Cassidy.

XAVIER: And wan other thing, Swane, for you to cast aspersions
on me just because I'm an auld widower, that's cheap and low.
Not everywan sees the world through your troubled eyes.   270
There's such a thing as a father lovin' his daughter as a father
should, no more, no less, somethin' you have never known,
and I will—

HESTER: I had a father too! Ya'd swear I was dropped from
the sky the way ya go on. Jack Swane of Bergit's Island,   275
I never knew him—but I had a father. I'm as settled as
any of yees—

XAVIER: Well, he wasn't much of a father, never claimin' ya when
your mother ran off.

HESTER: He claimed me in the end—   280

XAVIER: Look, Swane, I don't care about your family or
where ya came from. I care only about me own and all
I've left is Caroline and if I have to plough through you
to have the best for her, then that's what I'll do. I don't
want to unless I have to. So do it the aisy way for all of   285
us. Lave this place today. (*Takes envelope from breast
pocket, puts it into her hand.*) This is yours. Come on,
Caroline.

CAROLINE: Ya heard what Daddy says. Ya don't know his temper,
Hester.   290

HESTER: And you don't know mine.

*And exit Xavier followed by Caroline. Hester sits at her garden
table, has a drink, looks up at the cold winter sky.*

(*a whisper*) Dear God on high, what have ya in store for me at all?

*Enter Josie in her Communion dress, veil, buckled shoes, handbag,
the works.*

(*Looks at her a minute.*) What are ya doin' in your Communion
dress?

JOSIE: For Daddy's weddin'. I'm grown out of all me other
dresses.

HESTER: I don't think ya are.

JOSIE: I am. I can go, can't I, Mam?   295

HESTER: Ya have her eyes.

JOSIE: Whose eyes—whose eyes, Mam?

HESTER: Josie Swane's, me mother.

JOSIE: Granny said me real name is Josie Swane.

300 HESTER: Don't mind your Granny.

JOSIE: Did ya like her, Josie Swane?

HESTER:—More than anythin' in this cold white world.

JOSIE: More than me and Daddy?

HESTER: I'm talkin' about when I was your age. Ya weren't

305   born then, Josie—Ya know the last time I seen me mother
I was wearin' me Communion dress too, down by the
caravan, a beautiful summer's night and the bog like a
furnace. I wouldn't go to bed though she kept tellin' me
to. I don't know why I wouldn't, I always done what she

310   tould me. I think now—maybe I knew. And she says, 'I'm
goin' walkin' the bog, you're to stay here, Hetty.' And I
says, 'No,' I'd go along with her, and made to folly her.
And she says, 'No, Hetty, you wait here I'll be back in
a while.' And again I made to folly her and again she

315   stopped me. And I watched her walk away from me across
the Bog of Cats. And across the Bog of Cats I'll watch her
return.

Lights down.

ACT TWO

Interior of XAVIER CASSIDY's *house. A long table covered in a white
tablecloth, laid for the wedding feast. Music off, a band setting up.
The* CATWOMAN *sits at centre table lapping wine from a saucer. A
waiter, a lanky, gawky young fellow, hovers with a bottle of wine
waiting to refill the saucer.*

WAITER: You're sure now ya wouldn't like a glass, Catwoman?

CATWOMAN: No, no, I love the saucer, young man. What's your
name? Do I know ya?

WAITER: I'm a Dunne.

5 CATWOMAN: Wan of the long Dunnes or wan of the scutty
fat-legged Dunnes?

WAITER: Wan of the long Dunnes. Ya want a refill, Catwoman?

CATWOMAN: I will. Are ya still in school? Your voice sounds as
if it's just breakin'.

10 WAITER: I am.

CATWOMAN: And what're ya goin' to be when ya grow up, young
Long Dunne?

WAITER: I want to be an astronaut but me father wants me to
work on the bog like him and like me grandfather. The

15   Dunnes has always worked on the bog.

CATWOMAN: Oh go for the astronaut, young man.

WAITER: I will so, Catwoman. Have ya enough wine?

CATWOMAN: Plenty for now.

*Exit young Dunne crossed by the ghost of Joseph Swane, entering;
bloodstained shirt and trousers, a throat wound. He walks across
the stage. Catwoman cocks her ear, starts sniffing.*

JOSEPH: Hello. Hello.

20 CATWOMAN: Ah Christ, not another ghost.

JOSEPH: Who's there?

CATWOMAN: Go 'way and lave me alone. I'm on me day off.

JOSEPH: Who are ya? I can't see ya.

CATWOMAN: I can't see you aither. I'm the Catwoman but I tould

25   ya I'm not talkin' to ghosts today, yees have me heart scalded,
hardly got a wink's sleep last night.

JOSEPH: Please, I haven't spoken to anywan since the night I died.

CATWOMAN: Haven't ya? Who are ya anyway?

JOSEPH: I'm Joseph Swane of Bergit's Island. Is this Bergit's Island?

CATWOMAN: This is the Bog of Cats.   30

JOSEPH: The Bog of Cats. Me mother had a song about this place.

CATWOMAN: Josie Swane was your mother?

JOSEPH: Ya know her?

CATWOMAN: Oh aye, I knew her. Then Hester must be your
sister?   35

JOSEPH: Hester, ya know Hester too?

CATWOMAN: She lives only down the lane. I never knew Hester
had a brother.

JOSEPH: I doubt she'd be tellin' people about me.

CATWOMAN: I don't mean to be short with ya, Joseph Swane,   40
but Saturday is me day off. I haven't a minute to meself
with yees, so tell me what is it ya want and then be on your
way.

JOSEPH: I want to be alive again. I want to stop walkin'. I want to
rest, ate a steak, meet a girl, I want to fish for wild salmon and   45
sow pike on Bergit's Lake again.

CATWOMAN: You'll never do them things again, Joseph Swane.

JOSEPH: Don't say that to me, Catwoman, I'm just turned
eighteen.

CATWOMAN: Eighteen. That's young to die alright. But it could   50
be worse. I've a two-year-old ghost who comes to visit, all she
wants to do is play Peep. Still eighteen's young enough. How
come ya went so young? An accident, was it? Or by your own
hand?

WAITER: (*going by*) Ya talkin' to me, Catwoman?   55

CATWOMAN: No, Long Dunne, just a ghost, a poor lost ghost.

WAITER: Oh. (*Exits.*)

JOSEPH: Are ya still there, Catwoman?

CATWOMAN: I am but there's nothin' I can do for ya, you're not
comin' back?   60

JOSEPH: Is there no way?

CATWOMAN: None, none in this world anyway, and the
sooner ya realize that the better for ya. Now be on your
way, settle in to your new world, knock the best out of it
ya can.   65

JOSEPH: It's fierce hard to knock the best out of nothin', fierce
hard to enjoy darkness the whole time, can't I just stay here
with ya, talk to ya a while?

CATWOMAN: Ya could I suppose, only I'm at a weddin' and they
might think I'm not the full shillin' if I have to be talkin' to   70
you all day. Look, I'll take ya down to Hester Swane's house,
ya can talk to her.

JOSEPH: Can she hear ghosts?

CATWOMAN: (*getting up*) Oh aye, though she lets on she can't.

JOSEPH: Alright so, I suppose I may as well since I'm here.   75

CATWOMAN: C'mon, folly me voice till I lead ya there.

JOSEPH: (*following her*) Keep talkin' so I don't take a wrong
turnin'.

CATWOMAN: I will and hurry up now, I don't want to miss the
weddin'. Ya still there?   80

JOSEPH: I am.

And they're off by now. Enter Caroline and Carthage as they exit.

CAROLINE: This is the tablecloth me mother had for her weddin'
and it's the same silver too. I'd really like for her to have been
here today—Aye, I would.

CARTHAGE: A soft-boned lady, your mother. I used see her in   85
town shoppin' with you be the hand, ya wanted to bow when

she walked by. She had class, and you have too, Caroline, like no wan else around here.

CAROLINE: I can't stop thinkin' about Hester.

90 CARTHAGE: (*kisses her*) Hester'll be fine, tough as an auld boot. Ya shouldn't concern yourself with her on your weddin' day. I've provided well for her, she isn't goin' to ever have to work a day in her life. Josie's the wan

95 I worry about. The little sweetheart all done up in her Communion dress. Hetty should've got her a proper dress.

CAROLINE: But Hester didn't want her here, Carthage.

CARTHAGE: Ya know what I wish?

CAROLINE: What?

100 CARTHAGE: That she'd just give Josie to me and be done with it.

CAROLINE: You're still very tangled up with Hester, aren't ya?

CARTHAGE: I'm not wan bit tangled with her, if she'd just do what
105 she's supposed to do which is fierce simple, clear out of the Bog of Cats for wance and for all.

CAROLINE: And I suppose ya'll talk about me as callously wan day too.

CARTHAGE: Of course I won't, why would I?

110 CAROLINE: It's all fierce messy, Carthage. I'd hoped ya'd have sourted it out by today. It laves me in a fierce awkward position. You're far more attached to her than ya'd led me to believe.

CARTHAGE: Attached to her? I'm not attached to her, I stopped lovin' her years ago!

115 CAROLINE: I'm not jealous as to whether ya love her or don't love her, I think maybe I'd prefer if ya still did.

CARTHAGE: Then what's botherin' ya?

CAROLINE: You and Hester has a whole history together, stretchin' back years that connects yees and that seems
120 more important and real than anythin' we have. And I wonder have we done the wrong thing.

CARTHAGE: Ya should've said all this before ya took your vows at the altar.

CAROLINE: I've been tryin' to say it to ya for weeks.

125 CARTHAGE: So what do we do now?

CAROLINE: Get through today, I suppose, pretend it's the best day of our lives. I don't know about you but I've had better days than today, far better.

CARTHAGE: Caroline, what's wrong of ya?

130 CAROLINE: Nothin', only I feel like I'm walkin' on somewan's grave.

Enter Mrs Kilbride in what looks extremely like a wedding dress, white, a white hat, with a bit of a veil trailing off it, white shoes, tights, bag, etc.

MRS KILBRIDE: (*flushed, excited, neurotic*) Oh the love birds! The love birds! There yees are, off hidin'. Carthage, I want a photo of yees. Would you take it,
135 Caroline?

CARTHAGE: She means she wants wan of herself.

MRS KILBRIDE: Shush now, Carthage, and stand up straight.

They pose like a bride and groom, Carthage glaring at Mrs Kilbride.

That's it. Wan more, smile, Carthage, smile, I hate a glowery demeanour in a photograph. That's great, Caroline, did ya get
140 me shoes in?

CAROLINE: I don't think I—

MRS KILBRIDE: Doesn't matter, doesn't matter, thank ya, what a glorious day, what a glorious white winter's day, nothin' must spoil today for me, nothin'. (*Begins photographing her shoes,
145 first one, then the other.*)

CARTHAGE: What in the name of God are ya at now?

MRS KILBRIDE: I just want to get a photo of me shoes while they're new and clean. I've never had such a beautiful pair of shoes, look at the diamonds sparklin' on them.
150 I saved like a Shylock for them, seen them in O'Brien's six months ago and I knew instantly them were to be me weddin' shoes. And I put by every week for them. Guess how much they were, Carthage, g'wan guess, Caroline, guess, guess.

155 CAROLINE: I don't know, Mrs Kilbride.

MRS KILBRIDE: Elsie! Elsie! Call me Elsie, ah g'wan guess.

CAROLINE: Fifty pound.

MRS KILBRIDE: (*angrily*) Fifty pound! Are ya mad! Are ya out of your tiny mind!

160 CARTHAGE: Tell us how much they were, Mother, before we die of the suspense.

MRS KILBRIDE: (*smug, can hardly believe it herself*) A hundred and fifty pound. The Quane herself wouldn't pay more.

Monica and Xavier have entered, Monica has Josie by the hand.

165 MONICA:—And Father Willow seems to have lost the run of himself entirely.

XAVIER: They should put him down, he's eighty if he's a day.

MONICA: The state of him with his hat on all durin' the Mass and
170 the vestments inside out and his pyjamas peepin' out from under his trousers.

XAVIER: Did you hear he's started keepin' a gun in the tabernacle?

MONICA: I did, aye.

175 XAVIER: For all them robbers, is it?

MONICA: No, apparently it's for any of us that's late for Mass. Ya know what I was thinkin' and I lookin' at Caroline up there on the altar, I was thinkin' about my young fella Brian and I decided not to think about him
180 today at all.

XAVIER: Then don't, Monica. Don't.

MONICA: Don't you never think about your own young fella?

XAVIER: Never, I never think about him. Never. Children! If they were calves we'd have them fattened and sould in three weeks.
185 I never think of James. Never.

MONICA: Or Olive aither?

XAVIER: Ah, Olive had no fight in her, wailed like a ewe in a storm after the young lad and then lay down with her face to the wall. Ya know what she died of, Monica? Spite. Spite
190 again' me. Well, she's the wan who's dead. I've the last laugh on her.

MONICA: Strange what these weddin's drag up.

XAVIER: Aye, they cost a fortune. (*Takes two glasses of champagne from a passing waiter.*) Here, Monica, and cheers, (*to Josie*)
195 Child, a pound for your handbag.

MRS KILBRIDE: What d'ya say, Josie?

XAVIER: Lave her. Two things in this world get ya nowhere, sayin' sorry and sayin' thanks—that right, Josie?

200 JOSIE: That's right, Mr Cassidy.

MRS KILBRIDE: (*taking Josie a little aside*) Here give me that pound till I mind it for ya.

JOSIE: First give me back me Communion money.

MRS KILBRIDE: What Communion money?

205 CARTHAGE: Aye and ya can give me back mine while you're at it.

The Catwoman and Father Willow have entered, linking arms, both with their sticks. Father Willow has his snuff on hand, pyjamas showing from under his shirt and trousers, hat on, adores the Catwoman.

FATHER WILLOW: I'm tellin' ya now, Catwoman, ya'll have to cut back on the mice, they'll be the death of ya.

CATWOMAN: And you'll have to cut back on the snuff.

210 FATHER WILLOW: Try snails instead, far better for ya, the French ate them with garlic and tons of butter and Burgundy wine. I tried them wance meself and I in Avalon. Delicious.

CATWOMAN: We should go on a holiday, you and me, Father

215 Willow.

FATHER WILLOW: Ah, ya say that every winter and come the summer I can't budge ya.

CATWOMAN: I'll go away with ya next summer and that's a promise.

220 FATHER WILLOW: Well, where do ya want to go and I'll book the tickets in the mornin'?

CATWOMAN: Anywhere at all away from this auld bog, somewhere with a big hot sun.

FATHER WILLOW: Burgundy's your man then.

225 MONICA: God help Burgundy is all I say.

CATWOMAN: Anywhere it's not rainin' because it's goin' to rain here all next summer, seen it writ in the sky.

MRS KILBRIDE: Writ in the sky, me eye, sure she's blind as a bat. Xavier, what did ya have to invite the Catwoman for? Brings

230 down the tone of the whole weddin'.

MONICA: Hasn't she as much right to walk God's earth as you, partake of its pleasures too.

MRS KILBRIDE: No, she hasn't! Not till she washes herself. The turf-smoke stink of her. Look at her moochin' up

235 to Father Willow and her never inside the door of the church and me at seven Mass every mornin' watchin' that auld fool dribblin' into the chalice. And would he call to see me? Never. Spends all his time with the Catwoman in her dirty little hovel. I'd write to the Archbishop if I

240 thought he was capable of anythin'. Why did ya have to invite her?

XAVIER: Ya know as well as me it's bad luck not to invite the Catwoman.

Father Willow shoots Mrs Kilbride in the back of the head with an imaginary pistol as he walks by or as she walks by.

MRS KILBRIDE: I'd love to hose her down, fling her in onto the

245 milkin' parlour floor, turn the water on full blast and hose her down to her kidneys.

CARTHAGE: (*with his arm around Caroline*) Well, Catwoman, what do ya predict for us?

CATWOMAN: I predict nothin'.

250 CARTHAGE: Ah g'wan now, ya must have a blessin' or a vision or somethin'.

CAROLINE: Lave it, Carthage. You're welcome, Catwoman and Father Willow.

FATHER WILLOW: Thank you, Hester, thank you.

CARTHAGE: You mean, Caroline, Father Willow, this is Caroline. 255

FATHER WILLOW: Whatever.

CARTHAGE: Come on now, Catwoman, and give Caroline and me wan of your blessin's.

CATWOMAN: Seein' as ya insist. Separate tombstones. I'm sorry but I tould ya not to ax me. 260

JOSIE: Granny, will ya take a photo of just me and Daddy for to put in me scrapbook?

MRS KILBRIDE: Don't be so rude, you, to Caroline. (*Hisses.*) And I tould ya to call me Grandmother!

JOSIE: (*whispers boldly from the safety of her father's side*) Granny, 265 Granny, Granny.

CAROLINE: She's alright. Here, I'll take the photo of you and Carthage for your scrapbook. (*Does.*)

MRS KILBRIDE: She's ruined, that's what she is, turnin' up in her Communion dress, makin' a holy show of us all. 270

CARTHAGE: It's you that's the holy show in that stupid dress.

MRS KILBRIDE: What! I am not! There's gratitude for ya. Ya make an effort to look your best. (*close to tears*) I cut back on everythin' to buy this dress. How was I supposed to know the bride'd be wearin' white as well. 275

CARTHAGE: Don't start whingin' now in front of everywan, sit down will ya, ya look fine, ya look great—Alright, I'm sorry. Ya look stunnin'!

MRS KILBRIDE: (*beginning to smile*) I don't, do I?

CARTHAGE: Christ! *Yes!* 280

They've all made their way to the table by now and are seated. Xavier tinkles his glass for silence.

XAVIER: Thank you. Now before we dig in I'd like to welcome yees all here on wan of the happiest days of me life. Yees have all long known that Caroline has been my greatest joy and reason for livin'. Her mother, if she was here today, would've been proud too at how she has grown into a lovely and graceful 285 woman. I can take no credit for that, though I've taken the greatest pride these long years in watchin' her change from a motherless child to a gawky girl, to this apparition I see before me eyes today. We auld fathers would like to keep our daughters be our sides for ever and enjoy their care and 290 gentleness but it seems the world does have a different plan entirely. We must rear them up for another man's benefit. Well if this is so, I can't think of a better man than Carthage Kilbride to take over the care of me only child. (*Raises his glass.*) I wish yees well and happiness and infants rompin' on the hearth. 295

ALL: Hear! Hear!

XAVIER: Father Willow, would ya do us the—

MRS KILBRIDE: (*standing up*) I'd like to say a few words too—

XAVIER: Go ahead, Mrs Kilbride.

MRS KILBRIDE: As the proud mother of the groom— 300

CARTHAGE: Mother, would ya whisht up—

MRS KILBRIDE: (*posh public speaking voice*) As the proud mother of the groom, I feel the need to answer Xavier's fine speech with a few words of me own. Never was a mother more blessed than me in havin' Carthage for a son. As a child he 305 was uncommon good, never cried, never disobeyed, never raised his voice wance to me, never went about with a grumpy puss on him. Indeed he went to the greatest pains always to see that me spirits was good, that me heart was uplifted.

310 When his father died he used come into the bed to sleep
beside me for fear I would be lonely. Often I woke from a deep
slumber and his two arms would be around me, a small leg
thrown over me in sleep—
CATWOMAN: The craythur—
315 MRS KILBRIDE: He was also always aware of my abidin' love for
Our Lord, unlike some here (*Glares at the Catwoman.*) and
on wan occasion, me birthday it was, I looked out the back
window and there he was up on the slope behind our house
and what was he doin'? He was buildin' Calvary for me. He'd
320 hammered three wooden crosses and was erectin' them on
the slope Calvary-style. Wan for him, wan for me and wan for
Our Lord. And we draped ourselves around them like the two
thieves in the holy book, remember, Carthage?
CARTHAGE: I do not, would ya ever sit down.
325 MRS KILBRIDE: Of course ya do, the three crosses ya made up on
the slope and remember the wind was howlin' and the pair
of us yellin' 'Calvary! Calvary!' to wan another. Of course
ya remember. I'm only tellin' yees this story as wan of the
countless examples of Carthage's kind nature and I only
330 want to say that Caroline is very welcome into the Kilbride
household. And that if Carthage will be as good a son to
Caroline as he's been a husband to me then she'll have no
complaints. (*Raises her glass.*) Cheers.
ALL: Hear! Hear!
335 XAVIER: And now, Father Willow, ya'll say grace for us?
FATHER WILLOW: It'd be an honour, Jack, thank you—
MRS KILBRIDE: Who's Jack?

Father Willow gets up. All stand and bless themselves for the grace.

FATHER WILLOW: In the name of the Father and of the Son and
of the Holy Ghost, it may or may not surprise yees all if I
340 tould yees I was almost a groom meself wance. Her name was
Elizabeth Kennedy, no that was me mother's name, her name
was—it'll come to me, anyway it wasn't to be, in the end we
fell out over a duck egg on a walkin' holiday by the Shannon,
what was her name at all? Helen? No.
345 MRS KILBRIDE: Would ya say the grace, Father Willow, and be—
FATHER WILLOW: The grace, yes, how does it go again?
MRS KILBRIDE: Bless us, oh Lord, and these thy gifts which of—
FATHER WILLOW: Rowena. That was it. Rowena Phelan. I should
never have ate that duck egg—no—(*Stands there lost in thought.*)

Enter Hester in her wedding dress, veil, shoes, the works.

350 MRS KILBRIDE: Ya piebald knacker ya.
XAVIER: What's your business here, Swane, besides puttin' a curse
on me daughter's weddin'?
MRS KILBRIDE: The brazen nerve of her turnin' up in that garb.
HESTER: The kettle callin' the pot white. Remember this dress,
355 Carthage? He bought it for me—
CAROLINE: Daddy, would ya do somethin'.
HESTER: Oh must be near nine year ago. We'd got to the stage
where we should've parted and I said it to ya and ya convinced
me otherwise and axed me to marry ya. Came home wan
360 evenin' with this dress in a box and somehow it got put away.
Ya only ever wanted me there until ya were strong enough to
lave me.
CARTHAGE: Get outa here right now!
HESTER: You thought ya could come swaggerin' to me this
365 mornin' in your weddin' clothes, well, here I am in mine. This
is my weddin' day be rights and not wan of yees can deny
it. And yees all just sit there glarin' as if I'm the guilty wan.
(*Takes Carthage's glass of wine, drinks front it.*)
MRS KILBRIDE: Run her off, Xavier! Run her off or I will.
(*Gets up.*)
CARTHAGE: (*pulls her back*) Would you keep out of this! 370
MRS KILBRIDE: And let her walk all over us?
MONICA: Hester, go home, g'wan.
MRS KILBRIDE: (*getting up again*) I've had the measure of you this
long time, the lazy shiftless blood in ya, that savage tinker eye
ya turn on people to frighten them— 375
CARTHAGE: Would ya shut up! Ya haven't shut up all day! We're
not havin' a brawl here.
MRS KILBRIDE: There's a nice way to talk to your mother on your
weddin' day, I'm not afraid of ya, Hester Swane, you're just a
sad lost little woman— 380
HESTER: I still stole your son from ya, didn't I, Elsie? Your sissy
boy that I tried to make a man of.
MRS KILBRIDE: Ya took advantage of him, ya had to take
advantage of a young boy for your perverted pleasures for no
grown man would stomach ya. 385
HESTER: And weren't they great, Carthage, all them nights in
the caravan I 'took advantage' of ya and you bangin' on the
window and us stuffin' pillows in our mouths so ya wouldn't
hear us laughin'—
MRS KILBRIDE: You're absolutely disgustin', that's what ya are! 390
HESTER: Have you ever been discarded, Elsie Kilbride?—the way
I've been discarded. Do ya know what that feels like? To be
flung on the ashpit and you still alive!
XAVIER: No wan's flingin' ya anywhere! We done everythin'
proper by you— 395
HESTER: Proper! Yees have taken everythin' from me. I've done
nothin' again' any of yees. I'm just bein' who I am, Carthage,
I'm axin' ya the wance more, come away with me now, with
me and—
MRS KILBRIDE: Come away with her, she says— 400
HESTER: Yes! Come away with me and Josie and stop all this—
XAVIER: Come away with ya! Are ya mad! He's married to
Caroline now—
CARTHAGE: Go home, Hester, and pack your things.
MONICA: C'mon, Hester, I'll take ya home. 405
HESTER: I have no home any more for he's decided to take it
from me.
MONICA: Then come and live with me, I've no wan—
HESTER: No, I want to stay in me own house. Just let me stay in
the house, Carthage. I won't bother anywan if yees'd just 410
lave me alone. I was born on the Bog of Cats, same as all of
yees, though ya'd never think it the way yees shun me. I know
every barrow and rivulet and bog hole of its nine square
mile. I know where the best bog rosemary grows and the
sweetest wild bog rue. I could lead yees around the Bog of 415
Cats in me sleep.
CARTHAGE: There's a house bought and furnished for ya in town
as ya agreed to—
HESTER: I've never lived in a town. I won't know anywan there—
MONICA: Ah, let her stay in the house, the Bog of Cats is all she 420
knows—
MRS KILBRIDE: And since when do we need you stickin' your
snout in, Monica Murray?
MONICA: Since you and your son have forgotten all dacency, Elsie
Kilbride. Ya've always been too hard on her. Ya never gave her 425
a chance—

MRS KILBRIDE: A waste of time givin' chances to a tinker. All tinkers understands is the open road and where the next bottle of whiskey is comin' from.

MONICA: Well, you should know and your own grandfather wan!

430 MRS KILBRIDE: My grandfather was a wanderin' tinsmith—

MONICA: And what's that but a tinker with notions!

HESTER: Carthage, ya could aisy afford another house for yourself and Caroline if ya wanted—

CARTHAGE: No! We're stickn' by what we agreed on—

435 HESTER: The truth is you want to eradicate me, make out I never existed—

CARTHAGE: If I wanted to eradicate ya, I could've, long ago. And I could've taken Josie off of ya. Facts are, I been more than generous with ya.

440 HESTER: You're plentiful with the guilt money alright, showerin' buckets of it on me. (*Flings envelope he had given her in Act One at him.*) There's your auld blood money back. Ya think you're gettin' away that aisy! Money won't take that guilt away, Carthage, we'll go to our grave with it!

445 CARTHAGE: I've not an ounce of guilt where you're concerned and whatever leftover feelin' I had for ya as the mother of me child is gone after this display of hatred towards me. Just go away, I can't bear the sight of ya!

HESTER: I can't lave the Bog of Cats—

450 MRS KILBRIDE: We'll burn ya out if we have to—

HESTER: Ya see—

MRS KILBRIDE: Won't we, Xavier?

XAVIER: Ya can lave me out of any low-boy tactics. You're lavin' this place today, Swane, aren't ya?

455 HESTER: I can't lave—Ya see me mother said she'd come back here. Father Willow, tell them what they're doin' is wrong. They'll listen to you.

FATHER WILLOW: They've never listened to me, sure they even lie in the Confession box. Ya know what I do? I wear ear-plugs.

460 HESTER: (*close to tears*) I can't go till me mother comes. I'd hoped she'd have come before now and it wouldn't come to this. Don't make me lave or somethin' terrible'll happen. Don't.

XAVIER: We've had enough of your ravin', Swane, so take yourself elsewhere and let us try to recoup as best we can these marred celebrations.

465 JOSIE: I'll go with ya, Mam, and ya look gorgeous in that dress.

CARTHAGE: Stay where ya are, Josie.

JOSIE: No, I want to go with me Mam.

CARTHAGE: (*stopping her*) Ya don't know what ya want. And 470 reconsiderin', I think it'd be better all round if Josie stays with me till ya've moved. I'll bring her back to ya then.

HESTER: I've swallyed all me pride over you. You're lavin' me no choice but a vicious war against ya. (*Takes a bottle of wine from the table.*) Josie, I'll be back to collect ya later. And you 475 just try keepin' her from me! (*Exits.*)

ACT THREE

Dusk. HESTER, *in her wedding dress, charred and muddied. Behind her, the house and sheds ablaze.* JOSEPH SWANE *stands in the flames watching her.*

HESTER: Well, Carthage, ya think them were only idle threats I made? Ya think I can be flung in a bog hole like a bag of newborn pups? Let's see how ya like this—Ya hear that sound? Them's your cattle howlin'. Ya smell that smell? That's your 5 forty calves roastin'. I tied them all in and flung diesel on them. And the house, I burnt the bed and the whole place

went up in flames. I'd burn down the world if I'd enough diesel—Will somewan not come and save me from meself before I go and do worse.

Joseph starts to sing.

JOSEPH:
By the Bog of Cats I finally learned false from true,   10
Learned too late that it was you and only you
Left me sore, a heart brimful of rue
By the Bog of Cats in the darkling dew.

HESTER: Who's there? Who dares sing that song? That's my song that me mother made lip for me. Who's there?   15

JOSEPH: I think ya know me, Hester.

HESTER: It's not Joseph Swane, is it?

JOSEPH: It is alright.

HESTER: I thought I done away with you. Where are ya? I can't see ya. Keep off! Keep away! I'm warnin' ya.   20

JOSEPH: I'm not here to harm ya.

HESTER: Ya should be. If you'd done to me what I done to you I'd want your guts on a platter. Well come on! I'm ready for ya! Where are ya?

JOSEPH: I don't know, somewhere near ya. I can't see you aither.   25

HESTER: Well, what do ya want, Joseph Swane, if you're not here to harm me? Is it an apology you're after? Well, I've none for ya. I'd slit your throat again if ya stood here in front of me in flesh and bone.

JOSEPH: Would ya? What're ya so angry about? I've been listenin'   30 to ya screamin' your head off this while.

HESTER: You've a nerve singin' that song. That song is mine! She made it for me and only me. Can't yees lave me with anythin'!

JOSEPH: I didn't know it was yours. She used sing it to me all the time.   35

HESTER: You're lyin'! Faithless! All of yees! Faithless! If she showed up now I'd spit in her face, I'd box the jaws off of her, I'd go after her with a knife, (*heartbroken wail*) Where is she? She said she'd return. I've waited so long. I've waited so long—Have you come across her where you are?   40

JOSEPH: Death's a big country, Hester. She could be anywhere in it.

HESTER: No, she's alive. I can smell her. She's comin' towards me. I know it. Why doesn't she come and be done with it! If ya see her tell her I won't be hard on her, will ya?

JOSEPH: Aye, if I see her.   45

HESTER: Tell her there's just a couple of things I need to ax her, will ya?

JOSEPH: I will.

HESTER: I just want to know why, that's all.

JOSEPH: What are ya on about, Hester?   50

HESTER: Was it somethin' I done on her? I was seven, same as me daughter Josie, seven, and there isn't anythin' in this wide world Josie could do that'd make me walk away from her.

JOSEPH: Ya have a daughter?

HESTER: Aye, they're tryin' to take her from me. Just let them try!   55

JOSEPH: Who's tryin'?

HESTER: If it wasn't for you, me and Carthage'd still be together!

JOSEPH: So it's my fault ya killed me, that what you're sayin'?

HESTER: He took your money after we killed ya—

JOSEPH: To my memory Carthage did nothin' only look on.   60
I think he was as shocked as I was when ya came at me with the fishin' knife—

HESTER: He took your money! He helped me throw ya overboard! And now he wants to put it all on me.

65 JOSEPH: Ya came at me from behind, didn't ya? Wan minute I'm
      rowin' and the next I'm a ghost.
    HESTER: If ya hadn't been such an arrogant git I may have left
      ya alone but ya just wouldn't shut up talkin' about her as if
      she wasn't my mother at all. The big smug neck of ya! It was
70   axin' to be cut. And she even called ya after her. And calls me
      Hester. What sourt of a name is Hester? Hester's after no wan.
      And she saves her own name for you—Didn't she ever tell ya
      about me?
    JOSEPH: She never mentioned ya.
75 HESTER: She must've. It's a long time ago. Think, will ya. Didn't
      she ever say anythin' about me?
    JOSEPH: Only what she tould me father. She never spoke to me
      about ya.
    HESTER: Listen to ya! You're still goin' on as if she was yours and
80   you only an auld ghost! You're still talkin' as if I never existed.
    JOSEPH: I don't know what you're on about, Hester, but if it's any
      consolation to ya, she left me too and our father. Josie Swane
      hung around for no wan.
    HESTER: What was she like, Joseph? Every day I forget more and
85   more till I'm startin' to think I made her up out of the air. If it
      wasn't for this auld caravan I'd swear I only dreamt her. What
      was she like?
    JOSEPH: Well, she was big for starters . . . and gentle.
    HESTER: Gentle! She was a rancorous hulk with a vicious whiskey
90   temper.
    JOSEPH: You'd have liked the old man, Hester. All he wanted to do
      was go fishin'.
    HESTER: Well, it wasn't me that shunned him.
    JOSEPH: It wasn't his fault, Hester, she told him you were dead,
95   that ya died at birth, it wasn't his fault. Ya would've liked the
      old man, but she told him ya died, that ya were born with your
      heart all wrong.
    HESTER: Nothin' wrong of me heart till she set about banjaxin' it.
      The lyin' tongue of her. And he just believed her.
100 JOSEPH: Didn't he send me lookin' for ya in the end, see was there
      any trace of ya, told me to split the money with ya if I found
      ya. Hester, I was goin' to split the money with ya. I had it there
      in the boat. I was goin' to split it with ya when we reached the
      shore, ya didn't have to cut me throat for it.
105 HESTER: Ya think I slit your throat for the few auld pound me
      father left me?
    JOSEPH: Then why?
    HESTER: Should've been with her for always and would have only
      for you.
110 JOSEPH: If ya knew what it was like here ya'd never have done
      what ya done.
    HESTER: Oh I think I know, Joseph, for a long time now I been
      thinkin' I'm already a ghost.
    JOSEPH: I'll be off, Hester, I just wanted to say hello.
115 HESTER: Where are ya goin'?
    JOSEPH: Stravagin' the shadows. (*And he's gone.*)
    HESTER: Joseph?

Hester sits on the steps of the caravan, drinks some wine from the
bottle she took from the wedding, lights a cigar. Monica shouts
offstage.

    MONICA: Hester! Hester! Your house! It's on fire! Hester! (*Runs on.*)
      Come quick, I'll get the others!
120 HESTER: Don't bother.
    MONICA: But your house—Ya set it yourself?

HESTER: I did.
MONICA: Christ almighty woman, are ya gone mad?
HESTER: Ya want a drink?
MONICA: A drink, she says! I better go and get Carthage, the   125
  livestock, the calves—
HESTER: Would ya calm down, Monica, only an auld house, it
  should never have been built in the first place. Let the bog
  have it back. Never liked that house anyway.
MONICA: That's what the tinkers do, isn't it, burn everythin' after   130
  them?
HESTER: Aye.
MONICA: They'll skin ya alive, Hester I'm tellin' ya, they'll kill ya.
HESTER: And you with them.
MONICA: I stood up for ya as best I could, I've to live round here,   135
  Hester. I had to pay me respects to the Cassidys. Sure Xavier
  and meself used walk to school together.
HESTER: Wan of these days you'll die of niceness, Monica Murray.
MONICA: A quality you've never had any time for.
HESTER: No, I'm just wan big lump of maneness and bad   140
  thoughts. Sit down, have a drink with me, I'll get ya a glass.
  (*Goes into the caravan, gets one.*) Sit down before ya fall.
MONICA: (*sitting on steps, tipsily*) We'll go off in this yoke, you
  and me.
HESTER: Will we?   145
MONICA: Flee off from this place, flee off to Eden.
HESTER: Eden—I left Eden, Monica, at the age of seven. It was on
  account of a look be this caravan at dusk.
MONICA: And who was it gave ya this look, your mother, was it?
  Josie Swane?   150
HESTER: Oh aye, Monica, she was the wan alright who looked at me
  so askance and strangely—Who'd believe an auld look could do
  away with ya? I never would've 'cept it happened to me.
MONICA: She was a harsh auld yoke, Hester, came and went like the
  moon. Ya'd wake wan mornin' and look out over the bog and   155
  ya'd see a fire and know she had returned. And I'd bring her
  down a sup of milk or a few eggs and she'd be here sittin' on the
  step just like you are, with her big head of black hair and eyes
  glamin' like a cat and long arms and a powerful neck all knotted
  that she'd stretch like a swan in a yawn and me with ne'er a   160
  neck at all. But I was never comfortable with her riddled by her,
  though, and I wasn't the only wan. There was lots spent evenin's
  tryin' to figure Josie Swane, somethin' cold and dead about her
  except when she sang and then I declare ya'd fall in love with her.
HESTER: Would ya now?   165
MONICA: There was a time round here when no celebration was
  complete without Josie Swane. She'd be invited everywhere
  to sing, funerals, weddin's, christenin's, birthdays of the
  bigger farmers, the harvest. And she'd make up songs for each
  occasion. And it wasn't so much they wanted her there, more   170
  they were afraid not to have her.
HESTER: I used go with her on some of them singin' sprees before
  she ran off. And she'd make up the song as we walked to
  wherever we were goin'. Sometimes she'd sing somethin'
  completely different than the song she'd been makin' on the   175
  road. Them were her 'Blast from God' songs as opposed to her
  'Workaday' songs, or so she called them. And they never axed
  us to stay, these people, to sit down and ate with them, just
  lapped up her songs, gave her a bag of food and a half a crown
  and walked us off the premises, for fear we'd steal somethin',   180
  I suppose. I don't think it bothered her, it did me—and still
  rankles after all these years. But not Josie Swane, she'd be off
  to the shop to buy cigars and beer and sweets for me.

MONICA: Is there another sup of wine there?

185   HESTER: (*pours for her*) I'm all the time wonderin' whatever happened to her.

MONICA: You're still waitin' on her, aren't ya?

HESTER: It's still like she only walked away yesterday.

MONICA: Hester, I know what it's like to wait for somewan who's

190   never walkin' through the door again. But this waitin' is only a fancy of yours. Now I don't make out to know anythin' about the workin's of this world but I know this much, it don't yield aisy to mortal wishes. And maybe that's the way it has to be. You up on forty, Hester, and still dreamin' of storybook

195   endin's, still whingin' for your Mam.

HESTER: I made a promise, Monica, a promise to meself a long while back. All them years I was in the Industrial School I swore to meself that wan day I'm comin' back to the Bog of Cats to wait for her there and I'm never lavin' again.

200   MONICA: Well, I don't know how ya'll swing to stay now, your house in ashes, ya after appearin' in that dress. They're sayin' it's a black art thing ya picked up somewhere.

HESTER: A black art thing. (*Laughs.*) If I knew any black art things, by Christ, I'd use them now. The only way I'm lavin'

205   this place is in a box and if it comes to that I'm not lavin' alone. I'll take yees all with me. And, yes, there's things about me yees never understood and makes yees afraid and yees are right for other things goes through my veins besides blood that I've fought so hard to keep wraps on.

210   MONICA: And what things are they?

HESTER: I don't understand them meself.

MONICA: Stop this wild talk then, I don't like it.

HESTER: Carthage still at the weddin'?

MONICA: And where else would he be?

215   HESTER: And what sourt of mood is he in?

MONICA: I wasn't mindin'. Don't waste your time over a man like him, faithless as an acorn on a high wind—wine all gone?

HESTER: Aye.

MONICA: I'll go up to the feast and bring us back a bottle unless

220   you've any objections.

HESTER: I'll drink the enemy's wine. Not the wine's fault it fell into the paws of cut-throats and gargiyles.

MONICA: Be back in a while, so.

HESTER: And check see Josie's alright, will ya?

225   MONICA: She's dancin' her little heart out.

Exit Monica. Hester looks around, up at the winter sky of stars, shivers.

HESTER: Well, it's dusk now and long after and where are ya, Mr Ghost Fancier. I'm here waitin' for ya, though I've been tould to flee. Maybe you're not comin' after all, maybe I only imagined ya.

Enter Josie running, excited.

230   JOSIE: Mam!—Mam! I'm goin' on the honeymoon with Daddy and Caroline.

HESTER: You're goin' no such where.

JOSIE: Ah, Mam, they're goin' drivin' to the sea. I never seen the sea.

HESTER: It's just wan big bog hole, Josie, and blue, that's all,

235   nothin' remarkable about it.

JOSIE: Well, Daddy says I'm goin'.

HESTER: Don't mind your Daddy.

JOSIE: No, I want to go with them. It's only for five days, Mam.

HESTER: There's a couple of things you should know about your

240   precious Daddy, you should know how he has treated me!

JOSIE: I'm not listenin' to ya givin' out about him. (*Covers her ears with her hands.*)

HESTER: That's right, stand up for him and see how far it'll get ya. He swore to me that after you'd be born he'd marry me and

245   now he plans to take ya off of me. I suppose ya'd like that too.

JOSIE: (*still with ears covered*) I said I'm not listenin'!

HESTER: (*pulls Josie's hands from her ears*) You'll listen to me, Josie Swane, and you listen well. Another that had your name walked away from me. Your perfect Daddy walked away from

250   me. And you'll walk from me too. All me life people have walked away without a word of explanation. Well, I want to tell ya somethin', Josie, if ya lave me ya'll die.

JOSIE: I will not.

HESTER: Ya will! Ya will! It's a sourt of curse was put on ya be the

255   Catwoman and the black swan. Remember the black swan?

JOSIE: (*frightened*) Aye.

HESTER: So ya have to stay with me, d'ya see, and if your Daddy or anywan else axes ya who ya'd prefer to live with, ya have to say me.

260   JOSIE: Mam, I would've said you anyway.

HESTER: Would ya?—Oh, I'm sorry, Josie, I'm sorry, sweetheart. It's not true what I said about a curse bein' put on ya, it's not true at all. If I'm let go tonight I swear I'll make it up to ya for them awful things I'm after sayin'.

265   JOSIE: It's alright, Mam, I know ya didn't mean it—Can I go back to the weddin'? The dancin's not over yet.

HESTER: Dance with me.

Begins waltzing with Josie. Music.

Come on, we'll have our own weddin'.

Picks her up, they swirl and twirl to the music of the song 'By the Bog of Cats . . .'. They sing it together.

Ya beautiful, beautiful child, I could ate ya.

270   JOSIE: I could ate ya too—Can I go back to the weddin' for a while?

HESTER: Ya can do anythin' ya want 'cept lave me. (*Puts her down.*) G'wan then, for half an hour.

JOSIE: I brung ya a big lump of weddin' cake in me handbag. Here. Why wasn't it your weddin', Mam?

275   HESTER: It sourt of was. G'wan and enjoy yourself.

And exit Josie running. Hester looks after her eating the wedding cake. Xavier Cassidy comes up behind her from the shadows, demonic, red-faced, drink taken, carries a gun.

XAVIER: Ya enjoyin' that, are ya, Swane, me daughter's weddin' cake?

HESTER: Oh it's yourself, Xavier, with your auld gun. I was wonderin' when I'd see ya in your true colours. Must've been

280   an awful strain on ya behavin' so well all day.

XAVIER: Ya burnt the bloody house to the ground.

HESTER: Did ya really think I was goin' to have your daughter livin' there?

XAVIER: Ya won't best me, Swane, ya know that. I ran your

285   mother out of here and I'll run you too like a frightened hare.

HESTER: It's got nothin' to do with ya, Cassidy, it's between me and Carthage.

XAVIER: Got everythin' to do with me and ya after makin' a mockery of me and me daughter in front of the whole parish.

290 HESTER: No more than yees deserve for wheedlin' and cajolin'
Carthage away from me with your promises of land and money.
XAVIER: He was aisy wheedled.
HESTER: He was always a feckless fool.
XAVIER: Aye, in all respects bar wan. He loves the land and like
295 me he'd rather die than part with it wance he gets his greedy
hands on it. With him Cassidy's farm'll be safe, the name'll
be gone, but never the farm. And who's to say but maybe your
little bastard and her offspring won't be farmin' my land in
years to come.
300 HESTER: Josie'll have nothin' to do with anythin' that's yours. I'll
see to that. And if ya'd looked after your own son better ya
wouldn't be covetin' Josie nor any that belongs to me.
XAVIER: Don't you talk about my young fella.
HESTER: Wasn't it me that found him, strychnined to the eyeballs,
305 howlin' 'long the bog and his dog in his arms?
XAVIER: My son died in a tragic accident of no wan's makin'.
That's what the inquest said. My conscience is clear.
HESTER: Is it now? You're not a farmer for nothin', somethin'
about that young lad bothered ya, he wasn't tough enough
310 for ya probably, so ya strychnined his dog, knowin' full
well the child'd be goin' lookin' for him. And ya know what
strychnine does, a tayspoonful is all it takes, and ya'd the dog
showered in it. Burnt his hands clean away. Ya knew what ya
were at, Cassidy, and ya know I know. I can tell the darkness
315 in you, ya know how? Because it mirrors me own.
XAVIER: Fabrications! Fabrications of a mind unhinged! If ya
could just hear the mad talk of yourself, Swane, and the cut of
ya. You're mad as your mother and she was a lunatic.
HESTER: Nothin' lunatic about her 'cept she couldn't breathe the
320 same air as yees all here by the Bog of Cats.
XAVIER: We often breathed the same air, me and Josie Swane, she
was a loose wan, loose and lazy and aisy, a five-shillin' hoor,
like you.
HESTER: If you're tryin' to destroy some high idea I have of her
325 you're wastin' your time. I've spent long hours of all the long
years thinkin' about her. I've lived through every mood there
is to live concernin' her. Sure there was a time I hated her and
wished the worst for her, but I've taught meself to rise above all
that is cruel and unworthy in me thinkin' about her. So don't
330 you think your five shillin' hoor stories will ever change me
opinion of her. I have memories your cheap talk can never alter.
XAVIER: And what memories are they, Swane? I'd like to know if
they exist at all.
HESTER: Oh they exist alright and ya'd like to rob them from
335 me along with everythin' else. But ya won't because I'm
stronger than ya and ya'll take nothin' from me I don't
choose to give ya.
XAVIER: (puts gun to her throat) Won't I now? Think ya'll outwit
me with your tinker ways and—
340 HESTER: Let go of me!
XAVIER: (a tighter grip) Now let's see the leftovers of Carthage
Kilbride.

Uses gun to look down her dress.

HESTER: I'm warnin' ya, let go!

A struggle, a few blows, he wins this bout.

XAVIER: Now are ya stronger than me? I could do what I wanted
345 with ya right here and now and no wan would believe ya. Now
what I'd really like to know is when are ya plannin' on lavin'?

HESTER: What're ya goin' to do, Cassidy? Blow me head off?
XAVIER: Ya see, I married me daughter today! Now I don't care
for the whiny little rip that much, but she's all I've got, and I
don't want Carthage changin' his mind after a while. So when 350
are ya lavin', Swane? When?
HESTER: Ya think I'm afraid of you and your auld gun.

(Puts her mouth over the barrel.) G'wan shoot! Blow me away!
Save me the bother meself. (Goes for the trigger.) Ya want me to do
it for ya?

Another struggle, this time Xavier trying to get away from her.

XAVIER: You're a dangerous witch, Swane.
HESTER: (laughs at him) You're sweatin'. Always knew ya were
yella to the bone. Don't worry, I'll be lavin' this place tonight, 355
though not the way you or anywan else expects. Ya call me a
witch, Cassidy? This is nothin', you just wait and see the real—

Enter Carthage running, enraged, shakes her violently.

CARTHAGE: The cattle! The calves! Ya burnt them all, they're
roarin' in the flames! The house in ashes! A' ya gone mad
altogether? The calves! A' ya gone mad? 360
HESTER: (shakes him off) No, I only meant what I said. I warned
ya, Carthage, ya drove me to it.
XAVIER: A hundred year ago we'd strap ya to a stake and roast ya
till your guts exploded.
CARTHAGE: That's it! I'm takin' Josie off of ya! I don't care if I've 365
to drag ya through the courts. I'll have ya put away! I'll tell all
about your brother! I don't care!
HESTER: Tell them! And tell them your own part in it too while
you're at it! Don't you threaten me with Josie! This pervert has
just been gropin' me with his gun and you want Josie round 370
him—
XAVIER: The filthy lies of her—
HESTER: Bringin' a child on a honeymoon, what are ya at,
Carthage? Well, I won't let ya use Josie to fill in the silences
between yourself and Caroline Cassidy— 375
XAVIER: She's beyond reasonin' with, if she was mine I'd cut that
tinker tongue from her mouth, I'd brand her lips, I'd—
CARTHAGE: (exploding at Xavier) Would you just go back to the
weddin' and lave us alone, stop interferin'. If ya'd only let me
handle it all the way I wanted to, but, no, ya had to push and 380
bring the weddin' forward to avoid your taxes, just lave us
alone, will ya!
XAVIER: I will and gladly. You're a fiasco, Kilbride, like all the
Kilbrides before ya, ya can't control a mere woman, ya'll
control nothin', I'm havin' serious doubts about signin' over 385
me farm—
CARTHAGE: Keep your bloody farm, Cassidy. I have me own. I'm
not your scrubber boy. There's other things besides land.
XAVIER: There's nothin' besides land, boy, nothin'! And a real
farmer would never think otherwise. 390
CARTHAGE: Just go back to the weddin', I'll follow ya in a while
and we can try hammerin' out our differences.
XAVIER: Can we? (Exits.)
HESTER: All's not well in paradise.
CARTHAGE: All'd be fine if I could do away with you. 395
HESTER: If ya just let me stay I'll cause no more trouble. I'll move
into the caravan with Josie. In time ya may be glad to have me
around. I've been your greatest friend around here, Carthage,
doesn't that count for nothin' now?

400 CARTHAGE: I'm not havin' me daughter livin' in a caravan!

HESTER: There was a time you loved this caravan.

CARTHAGE: Will ya just stop tryin' to drag up them years! It won't work!

HESTER: Ya promised me things! Ya built that house for me. Ya
405 wanted me to see how normal people lived. And I went along with ya again' me better judgement. All I ever wanted was to be by the Bog of Cats. A modest want when compared with the wants of others. Just let me stay here in the caravan.

CARTHAGE: And have the whole neighbourhood makin' a
410 laughin' stock of me?

HESTER: That's not why ya won't let me stay. You're ashamed of your part in me brother's death, aren't ya?

CARTHAGE: I had no part in it!

HESTER: You're afraid I'll tell everywan what ya done. I won't. I
415 wouldn't ever, Carthage.

CARTHAGE: I done nothin' except watch!

HESTER: Ya helped me tie a stone around his waist!

CARTHAGE: He was dead by then!

HESTER: He wasn't! His pulse was still goin'!

420 CARTHAGE: You're only sayin' that now to torture me! Why did ya do it, Hetty? We were doin' fine till then.

HESTER: How does anywan know why they done anythin'? Somethin' evil moved in on me blood—and the fishin' knife was there in the bottom of the boat—and Bergit's Lake was
425 wide—and I looked across the lake to me father's house and it went through me like a spear that she had a whole other life there—How could she have and I a part of her?

CARTHAGE: Ya never said any of this before—I always thought ya killed your brother for the money.

430 HESTER: I met his ghost tonight, ya know—

CARTHAGE: His ghost?

HESTER: Aye, a gentle ghost and so lost, and he spoke so softly to me, I didn't deserve such softness—

CARTHAGE: Ah, would you stop this talk!

435 HESTER: You rose in the world on his ashes! And that's what haunts ya. You look at me and all you see is Joseph Swane slidin' into Bergit's Lake again. You think doin' away with me will do away with that. It won't, Carthage. It won't. You'll remember me, Carthage, when the dust settles, when ya grow
440 tired scourin' acres and bank balances. Ya'll remember me when ya walk them big, empty, childless rooms in Cassidy's house. Ya think now ya won't, but ya will.

CARTHAGE: Ya always had a high opinion of yourself. Aye, I'll remember ya from time to time. I'll remember ya sittin' at
445 the kitchen table drinkin' till all hours and I'll remember the sound of the back door closin' as ya escaped for another night roamin' the bog.

HESTER: The drinkin' came after, long after you put it into your mind to lave me. If I had somewan to talk to I mightn't have
450 drunk so hard, somewan to roam the bog with me, somewan to take away a tiny piece of this guilt I carry with me, but ya never would.

CARTHAGE: Seems I done nothin' right. Did I not?

HESTER: You want to glane lessons for your new bride. No,
455 Carthage, ya done nothin' right, your bull-headed pride and economy and painful advancement never moved me. What I wanted was somewan to look me in the eye and know I was understood and not judged. You thought I had no right to ax for that. Maybe I hadn't, but the way ya used judge me—didn't
460 it ever occur to ya, that however harshly ya judged me, I judged meself harsher. Couldn't ya ever see that.

CARTHAGE: I'm takin' Josie, Hester. I'm takin' her off of ya. It's plain as day to everywan 'cept yourself ya can't look after her. If you're wise ya'll lave it at that and not have us muckin' through the courts. I'll let ya see her from time to time.
465

HESTER: Take her then, take her, ya've taken everythin' else. In me stupidity I thought ya'd lave me Josie. I should've known ya always meant to take her too.

Enter Caroline with a bottle of wine.

CAROLINE: (*to Carthage*) Oh, this is where ya are.

CARTHAGE: She's after burnin' all the livestock, the house,
470 the sheds in ruins. I'm away up there now to see what can be salvaged. G'wan back home, I'll be there in a while. (*Exits.*)

CAROLINE: Monica said ya wanted wine, I opened it for ya.

HESTER: Take more than wine to free me from this place. Take
475 some kind of dark sprung miracle. (*Takes the wine.*)

CARTHAGE: (*coming back*) Caroline, come on, come on, I don't want ya around her.

HESTER: G'wan back to your weddin' like Carthage says.

Caroline goes to exit, stops.

CAROLINE: I just wanted to say—
480

HESTER: What? Ya just wanted to say what?

CAROLINE: Nothin'—Only I'll be very good to Josie whenever she stays with us.

HESTER: Ya better be!

CAROLINE: I won't let her out of me sight—I'll go everywhere with
485 her—protect her from things. That's all. (*Goes to exit.*)

HESTER: Didn't ya enjoy your big weddin' day, Caroline?

CAROLINE: No, I didn't—Everywan too loud and frantic—and when ya turned up in that weddin' dress, knew it should've been you—and Daddy drinkin' too much and shoutin', and
490 Carthage gone away in himself, just watchin' it all like it had nothin' to do with him, and everywan laughin' behind me back and pityin' me—When me mother was alive, I used go into the sick room to talk to her and she used take me into the bed beside her and she'd describe for me me weddin' day.
495 Of how she'd be there with a big hat on her and so proud. And the weddin' was goin' to be in this big ballroom with a fountain of mermaids in the middle, instead of Daddy's idea of havin' the do at home to save money—None of it was how it was meant to be, none of it.
500

HESTER: Nothin' ever is, Caroline. Nothin'. I've been a long time wishin' over me mother too. For too long now I've imagined her comin' towards me across the Bog of Cats and she would find me here standin' strong. She would see me life was complete, that I had Carthage and Josie and me own house.
505 I so much wanted her to see that I had flourished without her and maybe then I could forgive her—Caroline, he's takin' Josie from me.

CAROLINE: He's not, he wouldn't do that, Hester.

HESTER: He's just been here tellin' me.
510

CAROLINE: I won't let him, I'll talk to him, I'll stand up for ya on that account.

HESTER: Ya never stood up for nothin' yet, I doubt ya'll stand up for me. Anyway, they won't listen to ya. You're only a little china bit of a girl. I could break ya aisy as a tay cup or a wine
515 glass. But I won't. Ya know why? Because I knew ya when ya were Josie's age, a scrawky little thing that hung on the scraps

of my affection. Anyway, no need to break ya, you were broke a long while back.

520 CAROLINE: There's somethin' wrong of me, isn't there? (*Stands there, lost-looking.*)

HESTER: G'wan back to your weddin' and lave me be.

CAROLINE: I promise ya I'll do everythin' I can about Josie.

HESTER: (*softly*) G'wan. G'wan.

Exit Caroline. Hester stands there alone, takes a drink, goes into the caravan, comes out with a knife. She tests it for sharpness, teases it across her throat, shivers.

525 Come on, ya done it aisy enough to another, now it's your own turn.

Bares her throat, ready to do it. Enter Josie running, stops, sees Hester with the knife poised.

JOSIE: Mam—What's that ya've got there?

HESTER: (*stops*) Just an auld fishin' knife, Josie, I've had this years.

JOSIE: And what are ya doin' with it?

530 HESTER: Nothin', Josie, nothin'.

JOSIE: I came to say goodbye, we'll be goin' soon. (*Kisses Hester.*)

HESTER: Goodbye, sweetheart—Josie, ya won't see me again now.

JOSIE: I will so. I'm only goin' on a honeymoon.

HESTER: No, Josie, ya won't see me again because I'm goin away too.

535 JOSIE: Where?

HESTER: Somewhere ya can never return from.

JOSIE: And where's that?

HESTER: Never mind. I only wanted to tell ya goodbye that's all.

JOSIE: Well, can I go with ya?

540 HESTER: No ya can't.

JOSIE: Ah, Mam, I want to be where you'll be.

Hester: Well, ya can't, because wance ya go there ya can never come back.

JOSIE: I wouldn't want to if you're not here, Mam.

545 HESTER: You're just bein' contrary now. Don't ya want to be with your Daddy and grow up big and lovely and full or advantages I have not the power to give ya?

JOSIE: Mam, I'd be watchin' for ya all the time 'long the Bog of Cats. I'd be hopin' and waitin' and prayin' for ya to return.

550 HESTER: Don't be sayin' them things to me now.

JOSIE: Just take me with ya, Mam. (*Puts her arms around Hester.*)

HESTER: (*pushing her away*) No, ya don't understand. Go away get away from me, g'wan now, run away from me quickly now.

JOSIE: (*struggling to stay in contact with Hester*) No, Mam, stop!

555 I'm goin' with ya!

HESTER: Would ya let go!

JOSIE: (*frantic*) No, Mam. Please!

HESTER: Alright, alright! Shhh! (*Picks her up.*) It's alright, I'll take ya with me, I won't have ya as I was, waitin' a lifetime for

560 somewan to return, because they don't, Josie, they don't. It's alright. Close your eyes.

Josie closes her eyes.

Are they closed tight?

JOSIE: Yeah.

Hester cuts Josie's throat in one savage movement. (softly) Mam— Mam—(And Josie dies in Hester's arms.)

HESTER: (*whispers*) It's because ya wanted to come, Josie.

Begins to wail, a terrible animal wail. Enter the Catwoman.

CATWOMAN: Hester, what is it? What is it? 565

HESTER: Oh, Catwoman, I knew somethin' terrible'd happen, I never thought it'd be this. (*Continues this terrible sound, barely recognizable as something human.*)

CATWOMAN: What have ya done, Hester? Have ya harmed yourself? 570

HESTER: No, not meself and yes meself.

CATWOMAN: (*comes over, feels around Hester, feels Josie*) Not Josie, Hester? Not Josie? Lord on high, Hester not the child. I thought yourself, maybe, or Carthage, but never the child. (*Runs to the edge of the stage shouting.*) Help, somewan, help! 575 Hester Swane's after butcherin' the child! Help!

Hester walks around demented with Josie. Enter Carthage, running.

CARTHAGE: What is it, Catwoman? Hester? What's wrong with Josie? There's blood all over her.

HESTER: (*brandishing knife*) Lave off, you. Lave off. I warned ya and I tould ya, would ya listen, what've I done, what've I done? 580

Enter Monica.

CARTHAGE: Give her to me!

MONICA: Sweet Jesus, Hester—

CARTHAGE: Give her to me! You've killed her, she's killed her.

HESTER: Yees all thought I was just goin' to walk away and lave her at yeer mercy. I almost did. But she's mine and I wouldn't 585 have her waste her life dreamin' about me and yees thwartin' her with black stories against me.

CARTHAGE: You're a savage!

Enter the Ghost Fancier. Hester sees him, the others don't. He picks up the fishing knife.

HESTER: You're late, ya came too late.

CARTHAGE: What's she sayin'? What? Give her to me, come on 590 now. (*Takes Josie off Hester.*)

HESTER: Ya won't forget me now, Carthage, and when all of this is over or half remembered and you think you've almost forgotten me again, take a walk along the Bog of Cats and wait for a purlin' wind through your hair or a soft breath be your 595 ear or a rustle behind ya. That'll be me and Josie ghostin' ya. (*She walks towards the Ghost Fancier.*) Take me away, take me away from here.

GHOST: Fancier Alright, my lovely.

They go into a death dance with the fishing knife, which ends plunged into Hester's heart. She falls to the ground. Exit Ghost Fancier with knife.

HESTER: (*whispers as she dies*) Mam—Mam—*Monica goes over to* 600 *her after a while.*

MONICA: Hester—She's gone—Hester—She's cut her heart out— it's lyin' there on top of her chest like some dark feathered bird.

Music. Lights.

CRITICAL CONTEXTS

FRIEDRICH NIETZSCHE (1844–1900)

from *The Birth of Tragedy* (1872)

Translated by WALTER KAUFMANN

Throughout his career, the German philosopher and poet Friedrich Nietzsche criticized the limitations of modern conceptual and moral categories. This revolutionary subversion of the premises of philosophy forms the core of his most famous works—*The Gay Science* (1882), *Also Spoke Zarathustra* (1883–92), and *Beyond Good and Evil* (1886). In *The Birth of Tragedy* (1872), Nietzsche argues that Greek tragedy arose from the collision between Athenian rationalism—symbolized by Apollo, Socrates, and Euripides—and an earlier, irrational mysticism, symbolized by Dionysus. Although Nietzsche's reading of Greek history has been generally discredited, the essay offers a powerful and influential reading of the tension between the rational and irrational informing Greek drama. Nietzsche was admired by several modern playwrights represented in this volume, including Bernard Shaw, August Strindberg, and Eugene O'Neill.

Despite its symbolic contours, Nietzsche's representation of tragedy shares in the dialectical imagination that also drives other major theorists of tragic drama, including Aristotle. In what ways are the Apollonian and the Dionysian complicit in one another? What are the aspects of tragic experience that Nietzsche means to capture in these two images? Why do you think the full title of the essay is *The Birth of Tragedy from the Spirit of Music*?

Section 1

We shall have gained much for the science of aesthetics, once we perceive not merely by logical inference, but with the immediate certainty of vision, that the continuous development of art is bound up with the *Apollinian* and *Dionysian* duality—just as procreation depends on the duality of the sexes, involving perpetual strife with only periodically intervening reconciliations. The terms Dionysian and Apollinian we borrow from the Greeks, who disclose to the discerning mind the profound mysteries of their view of art, not, to be sure, in concepts, but in the intensely clear figures of their gods. Through Apollo and Dionysus, the two art deities of the Greeks, we come to recognize that in the Greek world there existed a tremendous opposition, in origin and aims, between the Apollinian art of sculpture, and the nonimagistic, Dionysian art of music. These two different tendencies run parallel to each other, for the most part openly at variance; and they continually incite each other to new and more powerful births, which perpetuate an antagonism, only superficially reconciled by the common term "art"; till eventually, by a metaphysical miracle of the Hellenic "will," they appear coupled with each other and through this coupling ultimately generate an equally Dionysian and Apollinian form of art—Attic tragedy.

In order to grasp these two tendencies, let us first conceive of them as the separate art worlds of *dreams* and *intoxication*. These physiological phenomena present a contrast analogous to that existing between the Apollinian and the Dionysian. It was in dreams, says Lucretius, that the glorious divine figures first appeared to the souls of men; in dreams the great shaper beheld the splendid bodies of superhuman beings; and the Hellenic poet, if questioned about the mysteries of poetic inspiration, would likewise have suggested dreams and he might have given an explanation like that of Hans Sachs in the *Meistersinger*:

> The poet's task is this, my friend,
> to read his dreams and comprehend.
> The truest human fancy seems
> to be revealed to us in dreams:
> all poems and versification
> are but true dreams' interpretation.

The beautiful illusion of the dream worlds, in the creation of which every man is truly an artist, is the prerequisite of all plastic art, and, as we shall see, of an important part of poetry also. In our dreams we delight in the immediate understanding of figures; all forms speak to us; there is nothing unimportant or superfluous. But even when this dream reality is most intense, we still have, glimmering through it, the sensation that it is *mere appearance*: at least this is my experience, and for its frequency—indeed, normality—I could adduce many proofs, including the sayings of the poets.

Philosophical men even have a presentiment that the reality in which we live and have our being is also mere appearance, and that another, quite different reality lies beneath it. Schopenhauer actually indicates as the criterion of philosophical ability the occasional ability to view men and things as mere phantoms or dream images. Thus the aesthetically sensitive man stands in the same relation to the reality of dreams as the philosopher does to the reality of existence; he is a close and willing observer, for these images afford him an interpretation of life, and by reflecting on these processes he trains himself for life.

It is not only the agreeable and friendly images that he experiences as something universally intelligible: the serious, the troubled, the sad, the gloomy, the sudden restraints, the tricks of accident, anxious expectations, in short, the whole divine comedy of life, including the inferno, also pass before him, not like mere shadows on a wall—for he lives and suffers with these scenes—and yet not without that fleeting sensation of illusion. And perhaps many will, like myself, recall how amid the dangers and terrors of dreams they have occasionally said to themselves in self-encouragement, and not without success: "It is a dream! I will dream on!" I have likewise heard of people who were able to continue one and the same dream for three and even more successive nights—facts which indicate clearly how our innermost being, our common ground, experiences dreams with profound delight and a joyous necessity.

This joyous necessity of the dream experience has been embodied by the Greeks in their Apollo: Apollo, the god of all plastic energies, is at the same time the soothsaying god. He, who (as the etymology of the name indicates) is the "shining one," the deity of light, is also ruler over the beautiful illusion of the inner world of fantasy. The higher truth, the perfection of these states in contrast to the incompletely intelligible everyday world, this deep consciousness of nature, healing and helping in sleep and dreams, is at the same time the symbolical analogue of the soothsaying faculty and of the arts generally, which make life possible and worth living. But we must also include in our image of Apollo that delicate boundary which the dream image must not overstep lest it have a pathological effect (in which case mere appearance would deceive us as if it were crude reality). We must keep in mind that measured restraint, that freedom from the wilder emotions, that calm of the sculptor god. His eye must be "sunlike," as befits his origin; even when it is angry and distempered it is still hallowed by beautiful illusion. And so, in one sense, we might apply to Apollo the words of Schopenhauer when he speaks of the man wrapped in the veil of *māyā* [illusion]: "Just as in a stormy sea that, unbounded in all directions, raises and drops mountainous waves, howling, a sailor sits in a boat and trusts in his frail bark: so in the midst of a world of torments the individual human being sits quietly, supported by and trusting in the *principium individuationis.*" In fact, we might say of Apollo that in him the unshaken faith in this *principium* and the calm repose of the man

wrapped up in it receive their most sublime expression; and we might call Apollo himself the glorious divine image of the *principium individuationis*, through whose gestures and eyes all the joy and wisdom of "illusion," together with its beauty, speak to us.

In the same work Schopenhauer has depicted for us the tremendous terror which seizes man when he is suddenly dumbfounded by the cognitive form of phenomena because the principle of sufficient reason, in some one of its manifestations, seems to suffer an exception. If we add to this terror the blissful ecstasy that wells from the innermost depths of man, indeed of nature, at this collapse of the *principium individuationis,* we steal a glimpse into the nature of the *Dionysian,* which is brought home to us most intimately by the analogy of intoxication.

Either under the influence of the narcotic draught, of which the songs of all primitive men and peoples speak, or with the potent coming of spring that penetrates all nature with joy, these Dionysian emotions awake, and as they grow in intensity everything subjective vanishes into complete self-forgetfulness. In the German Middle Ages, too, singing and dancing crowds, ever increasing in number, whirled themselves from place to place under this same Dionysian impulse. In these dancers of St. John and St. Vitus, we rediscover the Bacchic choruses of the Greeks, with their prehistory in Asia Minor, as far back as Babylon and the orgiastic Sacaea. There are some who, from obtuseness or lack of experience, turn away from such phenomena as from "folk-diseases," with contempt or pity born of the consciousness of their own "healthy-mindedness." But of course such poor wretches have no idea how corpselike and ghostly their so-called "healthy-mindedness" looks when the glowing life of the Dionysian revelers roars past them.

Under the charm of the Dionysian not only is the union between man and man reaffirmed, but nature which has become alienated, hostile, or subjugated, celebrates once more her reconciliation with her lost son, man. Freely, earth proffers her gifts, and peacefully the beasts of prey of the rocks and desert approach. The chariot of Dionysus is covered with flowers and garlands; panthers and tigers walk under its yoke. Transform Beethoven's "Hymn to Joy" into a painting; let your imagination conceive the multitudes bowing to the dust, awestruck—then you will approach the Dionysian. Now the slave is a free man; now all the rigid, hostile barriers that necessity, caprice, or "impudent convention" have fixed between man and man are broken. Now, the gospel of universal harmony, each one feels himself not only united, reconciled, and fused with his neighbor, but as one with him, as if the veil of *māyā* had been torn aside and were now merely fluttering in tatters before the mysterious primordial unity.

In song and in dance man expresses himself as a member of a higher community; he has forgotten how to walk and speak and is on the way toward flying into the air, dancing. His very gestures express enchantment. Just as the animals now talk, and the earth yields milk and honey, supernatural sounds emanate from him, too: he feels himself a god, he himself now walks about enchanted, in ecstasy, like the gods he saw walking in his dreams. He is no longer an artist, he has become a work of art: in these paroxysms of intoxication the artistic power of all nature reveals itself to the highest gratification of the primordial unity. The noblest clay, the most costly marble, man, is here kneaded and cut, and to the sound of the chisel stokes of the Dionysian world-artist rings out the cry of the Eleusinian mysteries: "Do you prostrate yourselves, millions? Do you sense your Maker, world?" . . .

Section 10

The tradition is undisputed that Greek tragedy in its earliest form had for its sole theme the sufferings of Dionysus and that for a long time the only stage hero was Dionysus himself. But it may be claimed with equal confidence that until Euripides, Dionysus never ceased to be the tragic hero; that all the celebrated figures of the Greek stage—Prometheus, Oedipus, etc.—are mere masks of this original hero, Dionysus. That behind all these masks there is a deity, that is one essential reason for the typical "ideality" of these famous figures which has caused so much astonishment. Somebody, I do not know who, has claimed that all individuals, taken as individuals, are comic and hence untragic—from which it would follow that the Greeks simply *could* not suffer individuals on the tragic stage. In fact, this is what they seem to have felt; and the Platonic distinction and evaluation of the "idea" and the "idol," the mere image, is very deeply rooted in the Hellenic character.

Using Plato's terms we should have to speak of the tragic figures of the Hellenic stage somewhat as follows: the one truly real Dionysus appears in a variety of forms, in the mask of a fighting hero, and entangled, as it were, in the net of the individual will. The god who appears talks and acts so as to resemble an erring, striving, suffering individual. That he *appears* at all with such epic precision and clarity is the work of the dream-interpreter, Apollo, who through this symbolic appearance interprets to the chorus its Dionysian state. In truth, however, the hero is the suffering Dionysus of the Mysteries, the god experiencing in himself the agonies of individuation, of whom wonderful myths tell that as a boy he was torn to pieces by the Titans and now is worshiped in this state as Zagreus. Thus it is intimated that this dismemberment, the properly Dionysian *suffering*, is like a transformation into air, water, earth, and fire, that we are therefore to regard the state of individuation as the origin and primal cause of all suffering, as something objectionable in itself. From the smile of this Dionysus sprang the Olympian gods, from his tears sprang man. In this existence as a dismembered god, Dionysus possesses the dual nature of a cruel, barbarized demon and a mild, gentle ruler. But the hope of the epopts [initiates] looked toward a rebirth of Dionysus, which we must now dimly conceive as the end of individuation. It was for this coming third Dionysus that the epopts' roaring hymns of joy resounded. And it is this hope alone that casts a gleam of joy upon the features of a world torn asunder and shattered into individuals; this is symbolized in the myth of Demeter, sunk in eternal sorrow, who *rejoices* again for the first time when told that she may *once more* give birth to Dionysus. This view of things already provides us with all the elements of a profound and pessimistic view of the world, together with the *mystery doctrine of tragedy*: the fundamental knowledge of the oneness of everything existent, the conception of individuation as the primal cause of evil, and of art as the joyous hope that the spell of individuation may be broken in augury of a restored oneness.

We have already suggested that the Homeric epos is the poem of Olympian culture, in which this culture has sung its own song of victory over the terrors of the war of the Titans. Under the predominating influence of tragic poetry, these Homeric myths are now born anew; and this metempsychosis reveals that in the meantime the Olympian culture also has been conquered by a still more profound view of the world. The defiant Titan Prometheus has announced to his Olympian tormentor that some day the greatest danger will menace his rule, unless Zeus should enter into an alliance with him in time. In Aeschylus we recognize how the terrified Zeus, fearful of his end, allies himself with the Titan. Thus the former age of the Titans is once more recovered from Tartarus and brought to the light.

The philosophy of wild and naked nature beholds with the frank, undissembling gaze of truth the myths of the Homeric world as they dance past: they turn pale, they tremble under the piercing glance of this goddess—till the powerful fist of the Dionysian artist forces them into the service of the new deity. Dionysian truth takes over the entire domain of myth as the symbolism of *its* knowledge which it makes known partly in the public cult of tragedy and partly in the secret celebrations of dramatic mysteries, but always in the old mythical garb.

What power was it that freed Prometheus from his vultures and transformed the myth into a vehicle of Dionysian wisdom? It is the Heracleian power of music: having reached its highest manifestation in tragedy, it can invest myths with a new and most profound significance. This we have already characterized as the most powerful function of music. For it is the fate of every myth to creep by degrees into the narrow limits of some alleged historical reality, and to be treated by some later generation as a unique fact with historical claims: and the Greeks were already fairly on the way toward restamping the whole of their mythical juvenile dream sagaciously and arbitrarily into a historico-pragmatical *juvenile history*. For this is the way in which religions are wont to die out: under the stern, intelligent eyes of an orthodox dogmatism, the mythical premises of a religion are systematized as a sum total of historical events; one begins apprehensively to defend the credibility of the myths, while at the same time one opposes any continuation of their natural vitality and growth; the feeling for myth perishes, and its place is taken by the claim of religion to historical foundations. This dying myth was now seized by the new-born genius of Dionysian music; and in these hands it flourished once more with colors such as it had never yet displayed, with a fragrance that awakened a longing anticipation of a metaphysical world. After this final effulgence it collapses, its leaves wither, and soon the mocking Lucians of antiquity catch at the discolored and faded flowers carried away by the four winds. Through tragedy the myth attains its most profound content, its most expressive form; it rises once more like a wounded hero, and its whole excess of strength, together with the philosophic calm of the dying, burns in its eyes with a last powerful gleam.

What did you want, sacrilegious Euripides, when you sought to compel this dying myth to serve you once more? It died under your violent hands—and then you needed a copied, masked myth that, like the ape of Heracles, merely knew how to deck itself out in the ancient pomp. And just as the myth died on you, the genius of music died on you, too. Though with greedy hands you plundered all the gardens of music, you still managed only copied, masked music. And because you had abandoned Dionysus, Apollo abandoned you: rouse all the passions from their resting places and conjure them into your circle, sharpen and whet a sophistical dialectic for the speeches of your heroes—your heroes, too, have only copied, masked passions and speak only copied, masked speeches. . . .

ÉMILE ZOLA (1840–1902)

from *Naturalism in the Theatre* (1878)

Translated by ALBERT BERMEL

An influential novelist, playwright, and literary theorist, Zola became the spokesman for naturalism in the theater in a series of articles he wrote in the 1870s, collected as *Naturalism in the Theatre* in 1878. In these essays, Zola urged the theater to adopt an attitude of scientific objectivity, an attitude reflected in the development of a new dramatic style. The naturalistic theater asserted such objectivity through its choice of subject matter (middle-class life), its treatment of characters (driven by "physiological" motives, not by "metaphysical" passions), its use of a prosaic, antiliterary language, and by the importance attached to the material environment. Zola's energy in summoning a new form of theatrical representation is evident here: what will be the signs of that new theatre onstage? What is the value that Zola ascribes to life-like representation, and how will it become visible onstage? How will this new theater be distinguished from the classical and romantic past?

It seems impossible that the movement of inquiry and analysis, which is precisely the movement of the nineteenth century, can have revolutionized all the sciences and arts and left dramatic art to one side, as if isolated. The natural sciences date from the end of the last century; chemistry and physics are less than a hundred years old; history and criticism have been renovated, virtually re-created since the Revolution; an entire world has arisen; it has sent us back to the study of documents, to experience, made us realize that to start afresh we must first take things back to the beginning, become familiar with man and nature, verify what is. Thenceforward, the great naturalistic school, which has spread secretly, irrevocably, often making its way in darkness but always advancing, can finally come out triumphantly into the light of day. To trace the history of this movement, with the misunderstandings that might have impeded it and the multiple causes that have thrust it forward or slowed it down, would be to trace the history of the century itself. An irresistible current carries our society towards the study of reality. In the novel Balzac has been the bold and mighty innovator who has replaced the observation of the scholar with the imagination of the poet. But in the theatre the evolution seems slower. No eminent writer has yet formulated the new idea with any clarity.

I certainly do not say that some excellent works have not been produced, with characters in them who are ingeniously examined and bold truths taken right on to the stage. Let me, for instance, cite certain plays by M. Dumas *fils,* whose talent I scarcely admire, and M. Émile Augier, the most humane and powerful of all. Still, they are midgets beside Balzac; they lack the genius to lay down the formula. It must be said that one can never tell quite when a movement is getting under way; generally its source is remote and lost in the earlier movement from which it emerged. In a manner of speaking, the naturalistic current has always existed. It brings with it nothing absolutely novel. But it has finally flowed into a period favourable to it; it is succeeding and expanding because the human mind has attained the necessary maturity. I do not, therefore, deny the past; I affirm the present. The strength of naturalism is precisely that it has deep roots in our national literature which contains plenty of wisdom. It comes from the very entrails of humanity; it is that much the stronger because it has taken longer to grow and is found in a greater number of our masterpieces.

Certain things have come to pass and I point them out. Can we believe that *L'Ami Fritz* would have been applauded at the Comédie-Française twenty years ago? Definitely not! This play, in which people eat all the time and the lover talks in such homely language, would have disgusted both the classicists and the romantics. To explain its success we must concede that as the years have gone by a secret fermentation has been at work. Lifelike paintings, which used to repel the public, today attract them. The majority has been won over and the stage is open to every experiment. This is the only conclusion to draw.

So that is where we stand. To explain my point better— am not afraid of repeating myself—I will sum up what I have said. Looking closely at the history of our dramatic literature, one can detect several clearly separated periods. First, there was the infancy of the art, farces and the mystery plays of the Middle Ages, the reciting of simple dialogues which developed as part of a naïve convention, with primitive staging and sets. Gradually, the plays became more complex but in a crude fashion. When Corneille appeared he was acclaimed most of all for his status as an innovator, for refining the dramatic formula of the time, and for hallowing it by means of his genius. It would be very interesting to study the pertinent documents and discover how our classical formula came to be created. It corresponded to the social spirit of the period. Nothing is solid that is not built on necessity. Tragedy reigned for two centuries because it satisfied the exact requirements of those centuries. Geniuses of differing temperaments had buttressed it with their masterpieces. And it continued to impose itself long afterwards, even

when second-rate talents were producing inferior work. It acquired a momentum. It persisted also as the literary expression of that society, and nothing would have overthrown it if the society, had not itself disappeared. After the Revolution, after that profound disturbance that was meant to transform everything and give birth to a new world, tragedy struggled to stay alive for a few more years. Then the formula cracked and romanticism broke through. A new formula asserted itself. We must look back at the first half of the century to understand the meaning of this cry for liberty. The young society was in the tremor of its infancy. The excited, bewildered, violently unleashed people were still racked by a dangerous fever; and in the first flush of their new liberty they yearned for prodigious adventures and superhuman love affairs. They gaped at the stars; some committed suicide, a very curious reaction to the social enfranchisement which had just been declared at the cost of so much blood. Turning specifically to dramatic literature, I maintain that romanticism in the theatre was an uncomplicated revolt, the invasion by a victorious group who took over the stage violently with drums beating and flags flying. In these early moments the combatants dreamed of making their imprint with a new form; to one rhetoric they opposed another: the Middle Ages to Antiquity, the exalting of passion to the exalting of duty. And that was all, for only the scenic conventions were altered. The characters remained marionettes in new clothing. Only the exterior aspect and the language were modified. But for the period that was enough. Romanticism had taken possession of the theatre in the name of literary freedom and it carried out its revolutionary task with incomparable bravura. But who does not see today that its role could extend no farther than that? Does romanticism have anything whatever to say about our present society? Does it meet one of our requirements? Obviously not. It is as outmoded as a jargon we no longer follow. It confidently expected to replace classical literature which had lasted for two centuries because it was based on social conditions. But romanticism was based on nothing but the fantasy of a few poets or, if you will, on the passing malady of minds overwhelmed by historical events; it was bound to disappear with the malady. It provided the occasion for a magnificent flowering of lyricism; that will be its eternal glory. Today, however, with the evolution accomplished, it is plain that romanticism was no more than the necessary link between classicism and naturalism. The struggle is over; now we must found a secure state. Naturalism flows out of classical art, just as our present society has arisen from the wreckage of the old society. Naturalism alone corresponds to our social needs; it alone has deep roots in the spirit of our times; and it alone can provide a living, durable formula for our art, because this formula will express the nature of our contemporary intelligence. There may be fashions and passing fantasies that exist outside naturalism but they will not survive for long. I say again, naturalism is the expression of our century and it will not die until a new upheaval transforms our democratic world.

Only one thing is needed now: men of genius who can fix the naturalistic formula. Balzac has done it for the novel and the novel is established. When will our Corneilles, Molières and Racines appear to establish our new theatre? We must hope and wait.

• • •

The period when romantic drama ruled now seems distant. In Paris five or six of its playhouses prospered. The demolition of the old theatres along the Boulevard du Temple was a catastrophe of the first order. The theatres became separated from one another, the public changed, different fashions arose. But the discredit into which the drama has fallen proceeds mostly from the exhaustion of the genre—ridiculous, boring plays have gradually taken over from the potent works of 1830.

To this enfeeblement we must add the absolute lack of new actors who understand and can interpret these kinds of plays, for every dramatic formula that vanishes carries away its interpreters with it. Today the drama, hunted from stage to stage, has only two houses that really belong to it, the Ambigu and the Théâtre-Historique. Even at the Saint-Martin the drama is lucky to win a brief showing for itself, between one great spectacle and the next.

An occasional success may renew its courage. But its decline is inevitable; romantic drama is sliding into oblivion, and if it seems sometimes to check its descent, it does so only to roll even lower afterwards. Naturally, there are loud complaints. The tail-end romanticists are desperately unhappy. They swear that except in the drama—meaning their kind of drama—there is no salvation for dramatic literature. I believe, on the contrary, that we must find a new formula that will transform the drama, just as the writers in the first half of the century transformed tragedy. That is the essence of the matter. Today the battle is between romantic drama and naturalistic drama. By romantic drama I mean every play that mocks truthfulness in its incidents and characterization, that struts about in its puppet-box, stuffed to the belly with noises that flounder, for some idealistic reason or other, in pastiches of Shakespeare and Hugo. Every period has its formula; ours is certainly not that of 1830. We are an age of method, of experimental science; our primary need is for precise analysis. We hardly understand the liberty we have won if we use it only to imprison ourselves in a new tradition. The way is open: we can now return to man and nature.

Finally, there have been great efforts to revive the historical drama. Nothing could be better. A critic cannot roundly condemn the choice of historical subjects, even if his own preferences are entirely for subjects that are modern. It is simply that I am full of distrust. The manager one gives this sort of play to frightens me in advance. It is a question of how history is treated, what unusual characters are presented bearing the names of kings, great captains or great artists, and what awful sauce they are served up in to make the history palatable. As soon as the authors of these concoctions move into the past they think everything is permitted: improbabilities, cardboard dolls, monumental idiocies, the hysterical scribblings that falsely represent local colour. And what strange dialogue—François I talking like a haberdasher straight out of the Rue Saint-Denis, Richelieu using the words of a criminal from the Boulevard du Crime, Charlotte Corday with the weeping sentimentalities of a factory girl.

What astounds me is that our playwrights do not seem to suspect for a moment that the historical genre is unavoidably the least rewarding, the one that calls most strongly for research, integrity, a consummate gift of intuition, a talent for reconstruction. I am all for historical drama when it is in the hands of poets of genius or men of exceptional knowledge who are capable of making the public see an epoch come alive with its special quality, its manners, its civilization. In that case we have a work of prophecy or of profoundly interesting criticism.

But unfortunately I know what it is these partisans of historical drama want to revive: the swaggering and swordplay, the big spectacle with big words, the play of lies that shows off in front of the crowd, the gross exhibition that saddens honest minds. Hence my distrust. I think that all this antiquated business is better left in our museum of dramatic history under a pious layer of dust.

There are, undeniably, great obstacles to original experiments: we run up against the hypocrisies of criticism and the long education in idiocies that has been foisted on the public. This public, which titters at every childishness in melodramas, nevertheless lets itself be carried away by outbursts of fine sentiment. But the public is changing. Shakespeare's public and Molière's are no longer ours. We must reckon with shifts in outlook, with the need for reality which is everywhere getting more insistent. The last few romantics vainly repeat that the public wants this and the public wants that; the day is coming when the public will want the truth.

• • •

The old formulas, classical and romantic, were based on the rearrangement and systematic amputation of the truth. They determined on principle that the truth is not good enough; they tried to draw out of it an essence, a 'poetry', on the pretext that nature must be expurgated and magnified. Up to the present the different literary schools disputed only over the question of the best way to disguise the truth so that it might not look too brazen to the public. The classicists adopted the toga; the romantics fought a revolution to impose the coat of mail and the doublet. Essentially the change of dress made little difference; the counterfeiting of nature went on. But today the naturalistic thinkers are telling us that the truth does not need clothing; it can walk naked. That, I repeat, is the quarrel.

Writers with any sense understand perfectly that tragedy and romantic drama are dead. The majority, though, are badly troubled when they turn their minds to the as-yet-unclear formula of tomorrow. Does the truth seriously ask them to give up the grandeur, the poetry, the traditional epic effects that their ambition tells them to put into their plays? Does naturalism demand that they shrink their horizons and risk not one flight into fantasy?

I will try to reply. But first we must determine the methods used by the idealists to lift their works into poetry. They begin by placing their chosen subject in a distant time. That provides them with costumes and makes the framework of the story vague enough to give them full scope for lying. Next, they generalize instead of particularizing; their characters are no longer living people but sentiments, arguments, passions that have been induced by reasoning. This false framework calls for heroes of marble or cardboard. A man of flesh and bone with his own originality would jar in such a legendary setting. Moreover, when we see the characters in romantic drama or tragedy walking about they are stiffened into an attitude, one representing duty, another patriotism, a third superstition, a fourth maternal love; thus, all the abstract ideas file by. Never the thorough analysis of an organism, never a character whose muscles and brain function as in nature.

These, then, are the mannerisms that writers with epic inclinations do not want to give up. For them poetry resides in the past and in abstraction, in the idealizing of facts and characters. As soon as one confronts them with daily life, with the people who fill our streets, they blink, they stammer, they are afraid; they no longer see clearly; they find everything ugly and not good enough for art. According to them, a subject must enter the lies of legend, men must harden and turn to stone like statues before the artist can accept them and make them fit the disguises he has prepared.

Now, it is at this point that the naturalistic movement comes along and says squarely that poetry is everywhere, in everything, even more in the present and the real than in the past and the abstract. Each event at each moment has its poetic, superb aspect. We brush up against heroes who are great and powerful in different respects from the puppets of the epic-makers. Not one playwright in this century has brought to life figures as lofty as Baron Hulot, Old Grandet, César Birotteau, and all the other characters of Balzac, who are so individual and so alive. Beside these real, giant creations Greek and Roman heroes quake; the heroes of the Middle Ages fall flat on their faces like lead soldiers.

With the superior works being produced in these times by the naturalistic school—works of high endeavour, pulsing with life—it is ridiculous and false to park our poetry in some antiquated temple and bury it in cobwebs. Poetry flows at its full force through everything that exists; the truer to life, the greater it becomes. And I mean to give the word poetry its widest definition, not to pin it down exclusively to the cadence of two rhymes, nor to burn it in a narrow coterie of dreamers, but to restore its real human significance which concerns the expansion and encouragement of every kind of truth.

Take our present environment, then, and try to make men live in it: you will write great works. It will undoubtedly call for some effort; it means sifting out of the confusion of life the simple formula of naturalism. Therein lies the difficulty: to do great things with the subjects and characters that our eyes, accustomed to the spectacle of the daily round, have come to see as small. I am aware that it is more convenient to present a marionette to the public and name it Charlemagne and puff it up with such tirades that the public believes it is watching a colossus; it is more convenient than taking a bourgeois of our time, a grotesque, unsightly man, and drawing sublime poetry out of him, making him, for example, Père Goriot, the father who gives his guts for his daughters, a figure so gigantic with truth and love that no other literature can offer his equal.

Nothing is as easy as persuading the managers with known formulas; and heroes in the classical or romantic taste cost so little labour that they are manufactured by the dozen, and have become standardized articles that clutter up our literature. But it takes hard work to create a real hero, intelligently analysed, alive and performing. That is probably why naturalism terrifies those authors who are used to fishing up great men from the troubled waters of history. They would have to burrow too deeply into humanity, learn about life, go straight for the greatness of reality and make it function with all their power. And let nobody gainsay this true poetry of humanity; it has been sifted out in the novel and can be in the theatre; only the method of adaptation remains to be found.

I am troubled by a comparison; it has been haunting me and I will now free myself of it. For two long months a play called *Les Danicheff* has been running at the Odéon. It takes place in Russia. It has been very successful here, but is apparently so dishonest, so packed with gross improbabilities, that the author, a Russian, has not even dared to show it in his country. What can you think of this work which is applauded in Paris and would be booed in St Petersburg? Well, imagine for a moment that the Romans could come back to life and see a performance of *Rome vaincue*. Can you hear their roars of laughter? Do you think the play would complete one performance? It would strike them as a parody; it would sink under the weight of mockery. And is there one historical play that could be performed before the society it claims to portray? A strange theatre, this, which is plausible only among foreigners, is based on the disappearance of the generations it deals with, and is made up of so much misinformation that it is good only for the ignorant!

The future is with naturalism. The formula will be found; it will be proved that there is more poetry in the little apartment of a bourgeois than in all the empty, worm-eaten palaces of history; in the end we will see that everything meets in the real: lovely fantasies that are free of capriciousness and whimsy, and idylls, and comedies, and dramas. Once the soil has been turned over, the task that seems alarming and unfeasible today will become easy.

I am not qualified to pronounce on the form that tomorrow's drama will take; that must be left to the voice of some genius to come. But I will allow myself to indicate the path I consider our theatre will follow.

First, the romantic drama must be abandoned. It would be disastrous for us to take over its outrageous acting, its rhetoric, its inherent thesis of action at the expense of character analysis. The finest models of the genre are, as has been said, mere operas with big effects. I believe, then, that we must go back to tragedy—not, heaven forbid, to borrow more of its rhetoric, its system of confidants, its declaiming, its endless speeches, but to return to its simplicity of action and its unique psychological and physiological study of the characters. Thus understood, the tragic framework is excellent; one deed unwinds in all its reality, and moves the characters to passions and feelings, the exact analysis of which constitutes the sole interest of the play—and in a contemporary environment, with the people who surround us.

My constant concern, my anxious vigil, has made me wonder which of us will have the strength to raise himself to the pitch of genius. If the naturalistic drama must come into being, only a genius can give birth to it. Corneille

and Racine made tragedy. Victor Hugo made romantic drama. Where is the as-yet-unknown author who must make the naturalistic drama? In recent years experiments have not been wanting. But either because the public was not ready or because none of the beginners had the necessary staying-power, not one of these attempts has had decisive results.

In battles of this kind, small victories mean nothing; we need triumphs that overwhelm the adversary and win the public to the cause. Audiences would give way before the onslaught of a really strong man. This man would come with the expected word, the solution to the problem, the formula for a real life on stage, combining it with the illusions necessary in the theatre. He would have what the newcomers have as yet lacked: the cleverness or the might to impose himself and to remain so close to truth that his cleverness could not lead him into lies.

And what an immense place this innovator would occupy in our dramatic literature! He would be at the peak. He would build his monument in the middle of the desert of mediocrity that we are crossing, among the jerry-built houses strewn about our most illustrious stages. He would put everything in question and remake everything, scour the boards, create a world whose elements he would lift from life, from outside our traditions. Surely there is no more ambitious dream that a writer of our time could fulfil. The domain of the novel is crowded; the domain of the theatre is free. At this time in France an imperishable glory awaits the man of genius who takes up the work of Molière and finds in the reality of living comedy the full, true drama of modern society.

• • •

Physiological Man

. . . In effect, the great naturalistic evolution, which comes down directly from the fifteenth century to ours has everything to do with the gradual substitution of physiological man for metaphysical man. In tragedy metaphysical man, man according to dogma and logic, reigned absolutely. The body did not count; the soul was regarded as the only interesting piece of human machinery; drama took place in the air, in pure mind. Consequently, what use was the tangible world? Why worry about the place where the action was located? Why be surprised at a baroque costume or false declaiming? Why notice that Queen Dido was a boy whose budding beard forced him to wear a mask? None of that mattered; these trifles were not worth stooping to; the play was heard out as if it were a school essay or a law case; it was on a higher plane than man, in the world of ideas, so far away from real man that any intrusion of reality would have spoiled the show.

Such is the point of departure—in Mystery plays, the religious point; the philosophical point in tragedy. And from that beginning natural man, stifling under the rhetoric and dogma, struggled secretly, tried to break free, made lengthy, futile efforts, and in the end asserted himself, limb by limb. The whole history of our theatre is in this conquest by the physiological man, who emerged more clearly in each period from behind the dummy of religious and philosophical idealism. Corneille, Molière, Racine, Voltaire, Beaumarchais and, in our day, Victor Hugo, Émile Augier, Alexandre Dumas *fils,* even Sardou, have had only one task, even when they were not completely aware of it: to increase the reality of our corpus of drama, to progress towards truth, to sift out more and more of the natural man and impose him on the public. And inevitably, the evolution will not end with them. It continues; it will continue forever. Mankind is very young. . . .

Costume, Stage Design, Speech

Modern clothes make a poor spectacle. If we depart from bourgeois tragedy, shut in between its four walls, and wish to use the breadth of larger stages for crowd scenes we are embarrassed and constrained by the monotony and the uniformly funereal look of the extras. In this case, I think, we should take advantage of the variety of garb offered by the different classes and occupations. To elaborate: I can imagine an author setting one act in the main marketplace of les Halles in Paris. The setting would be superb, with its bustling life and bold possibilities. In this immense setting we could have a very picturesque ensemble by displaying the porters wearing their large hats, the saleswomen with their white aprons and vividly-coloured scarves, the customers dressed in silk or wool or cotton prints, from the ladies accompanied by their maids to the female beggars on the prowl for anything they can pick up off the street. For inspiration it would be enough to go to les Halles and look about. Nothing is gaudier or more interesting. All of Paris would enjoy seeing this set if it were realized with the necessary accuracy and amplitude.

And how many other settings for popular drama there are for the taking! Inside a factory, the interior of a mine, the gingerbread market, a railway station, flower stalls, a racetrack, and so on. All the activities of modern life can take place in them. It will be said that such sets have already been tried. Unquestionably we have seen factories and railway stations in fantasy plays; but these were fantasy stations and factories. I mean, these sets were thrown together to create an illusion that was at best incomplete. What we need is detailed reproduction: costumes supplied by tradespeople, not sumptuous but adequate for the purposes of truth and for the interest of the scenes.

Since everybody mourns the death of the drama our playwrights certainly ought to make a try at this type of popular, contemporary drama. At one stroke they could satisfy the public hunger for spectacle and the need for exact studies which grows more pressing every day. Let us hope, though, that the playwrights will show us real people and not those whining members of the working class who play such strange roles in boulevard melodrama.

As M. Adolphe Jullien has said—and I will never be tired of repeating it—everything is interdependent in the theatre. Lifelike costumes look wrong if the sets, the diction, the plays themselves are not lifelike. They must all march in step along the naturalistic road. When costume becomes more accurate, so do sets; actors free themselves from bombastic declaiming; plays study reality more closely and their characters are more true to life. I could make the same observations about sets I have just made about costume. With them too, we may seem to have reached the highest possible degree of truth, but we still have long strides to take. Most of all we would need to intensify the illusion in reconstructing the environments, less for their picturesque quality than for dramatic utility. The environment must determine the character. When a set is planned so as to give the lively impression of a description by Balzac; when, as the curtain rises, one catches the first glimpse of the characters, their personalities and behaviour, if only to see the actual locale in which they move, the importance of exact reproduction in the decor will be appreciated. Obviously, that is the way we are going. Environment, the study of which has transformed science and literature, will have to take a large role in the theatre. And here I may mention again the question of metaphysical man, the abstraction who had to be satisfied with his three walls in tragedy— whereas the physiological man in our modern works is asking more and more compellingly to be determined by his setting, by the environment that produced him. We see then that the road to progress is still long, for sets as well as costume. We are coming upon the truth but we can hardly stammer it out.

Another very serious matter is diction. True, we have got away from the chanting, the plainsong, of the seventeenth century. But we now have a "theatre voice," a false recitation that is very obtrusive and very annoying. Everything that is wrong with it comes from the fixed traditional code set up by the majority of critics. They found the theatre in a certain state and, instead of looking to the future, and judging the progress we are making and the progress we shall make by the progress we have already made, they stubbornly defend the relics of the old conventions, swearing that these relics must be preserved. Ask them why, make them see how far we have travelled; they will give you no logical reason. They will reply with assertions based on a set of conditions that are disappearing.

In diction the errors come from what the critics call "theatre language." Their theory is that on stage you must not speak as you do in everyday life. To support this viewpoint they pick examples from traditional practices, from what was happening yesterday—and is happening still—without taking account of the naturalistic movement, the phases of which have been established for us by M. Jullien's book.[1] Let us realize that there is no such thing as "theatre language." There has been a rhetoric which grew more and more feeble and is now dying out. Those are the facts. If you compare the declaiming of actors under Louis XIV with that of Lekain, and if you compare Lekain's with that of our own artists today, you will clearly distinguish the phases from tragic chanting down to our search for the natural, precise tone, the cry of truth. It follows that "theatre language," that language of booming sonority, is vanishing. We are moving towards simplicity, the exact word spoken without emphasis, quite naturally. How many examples I could give if I had unlimited space! Consider the powerful effect that Geoffroy has on the public; all his talent comes from his natural personality. He holds the public because he speaks on stage as he does at home. When a sentence sounds outlandish he cannot pronounce it; the author has to find another one. That is the fundamental criticism of so-called "theatre language." Again, follow the diction of a talented actor and at the same time watch the public; the cheers go up, the house is in raptures when a truthful accent gives the words the exact value they must have. All the great successes of the stage are triumphs over convention.

Alas, yes, there is a "theatre language." It is the clichés, the resounding platitudes, the hollow words that roll about like empty barrels, all that intolerable rhetoric of our vaudevilles and dramas, which is beginning to make us smile. It would be very interesting to study the style of such talented authors as MM. Augier, Dumas and Sardou. I could find much to criticize, especially in the last two with their conventional language, a language of their own that they put into the mouths of all their characters, men, women, children, old folk, both sexes and all ages. This irritates me, for each character has his own language, and to create living people you must give them to the public not merely in accurate dress and in the environments that have made them what they are, but with their individual ways of thinking and expressing themselves. I repeat that that is the obvious aim of our theatre. There is no theatre language regulated by such a code as "cadenced sentences" or sonority. There is simply a kind of dialogue that is growing more precise and is following—or rather, leading—sets and costumes towards naturalistic progress. When plays are more truthful, the actors' diction will gain enormously in simplicity and naturalness.

To conclude, I will repeat that the battle of the conventions is far from being finished, and that it will no doubt last forever. Today we are beginning to see clearly where we are going, but our steps are still impeded by the melting slush of rhetoric and metaphysics.

---

[1] Adolphe Jullien 1845–1932, writer on music and the theatre. The book Zola cites is *Histoire du costume au théâtre,* 1880.

CONSTANTIN STANISLAVSKI (1863–1938)
"Direction and Acting" (1929)

One of the founders of the Moscow Art Theater, Stanislavski developed a systematic approach to acting that involved working both on the actor's psychological and on his or her physical portrayal of character. In this article, originally written for the *Encyclopedia Britannica*, Stanislavski outlines some of the central features of his "system": public solitude, concentration, internal technique.

Theatrical art has always been collective, arising only where poetical-dramatic talent was actively combined with the actor's. The basis of a play is always a dramatic conception; a general artistic sense is imparted to the theatrical action by the unifying, creative genius of the actor. Thus the actor's dramatic activity begins at the foundation of the play. In the first place, each actor, either independently or through the theatre manager, must probe for the fundamental motive in the finished play—the creative idea that is characteristic of the author and that reveals itself as the germ from which his work grows organically. The motive of the play always keeps the character developing before the spectator; each personality in the work takes a part conforming to his own character; the work, then developing in the appointed direction, flows on to the final point conceived by the author. The first stage in the work of the actor and theatre manager is to probe for the germ of the play, investigating the fundamental line of action that traverses all of its episodes and is therefore called by the writer its transparent effect or action. In contrast to some theatrical directors, who consider every play only as material for theatrical repetition, the writer believes that in the production of every important drama the director and actor must go straight for the most exact and profound conception of the mind and ideal of the dramatist, and must not change that ideal for their own. The interpretation of the play and the character of its artistic incarnation inevitably appear in a certain measure subjective, and bear the mark of the individual peculiarities of the manager and actors; but only by profound attention to the artistic individuality of the author and to his ideal and mentality, which have been disclosed as the creative germ of the play, can the theatre realize all its artistic depth and transmit, as in a poetical production, completeness and harmony of composition. Every part of the future spectacle is then unified in it by its own artistic work; each part, in the measure of its own genius, will flow on to the artistic realization aimed at by the dramatist.

The actor's task, then, begins with the search for the play's artistic seed. All artistic action—organic action, as in every constructive operation of nature—starts from this seed at the moment when it is conveyed to the mind. On reaching the actor's mind, the seed must wander around, germinate, put out roots, drinking in the juices of the soil in which it is planted, grow and eventually bring forth a lively flowering plant. Artistic process must in all cases flow very rapidly, but usually, in order that it may preserve the character of the true organic action and may lead to the creation of life, of a clear truly artistic theatrical image, and not of a trade substitute, it demands much more time than is allotted to it in the best European theatres. That is why in the writer's theatre every dramatization passes through eight to ten revisions, as is also done in Germany by the famous theatre manager and theorist, K. Hagemann. Sometimes even more than ten revisions are needed, occasionally extending over several months. But even under these conditions, the creative genius of the actor does not appear so freely as does, for instance, the creative genius of the dramatist. Bound by the strict obligations of his *collectif*, the actor must not postpone his work to the moment when his physical and psychic condition appears propitious for creative genius. Meanwhile, his exacting and capricious artistic nature is prompted by aspirations of his artistic intuition, and in the absence of creative genius is not reached by any effort of his will. He is not aided in that respect by outward technique—his skill in making use of his body, his vocal equipment and his powers of speech.

The Artistic Condition

But is it really impossible? Are there no means, no processes that sensibly would help us, and spontaneously lead to that artistic condition which is born of genius without any effort on its part? If that capacity is unattainable all at once, by some process or other, it may, perhaps, be acquired in parts, and through progressive stages may perfect those elements out of which the artistic condition is composed, and which are subject to our will. Of course the general run of acting does not come into being from this genius, but cannot such acting, in some measure, be brought by it near to what is evidence of genius? These are the problems which presented themselves to the writer about 20 years ago, when reflecting on the external obstacles that hamper actors' artistic genius, and partly compel substitution of the crude outward marks of the actor's profession for its results. They drove him to the rediscovery of processes of external technique, i.e., methods proceeding form consciousness to sub-consciousness, in which domain flow nine-tenths of all real artistic processes. Observations both upon himself and other actors with whom he happened to rehearse, but chiefly upon growing theatrical skill in Russia and abroad, allowed him to do some generalizing, which thereupon he verified in practice.

The first is that, in an artistic condition, full freedom of body plays a principal rôle; i.e., the freedom from that muscular strain which, without our knowing it, fetters us not only on the stage but also in ordinary life, hindering us from being obedient conductors of our psychic action. This muscular strain, reaching its maximum at those times when the actor is called upon to perform something especially difficult in his theatrical work, swallows up the bulk of this external energy, diverting him from activity of the higher centres. This teaches us the possibility of availing ourselves of the muscular energy of our limbs only as necessity demands, and in exact conformity with our creative efforts.

Public Solitude

The second observation is that the flow of the actor's artistic force is considerably retarded by the visual auditorium and the public, whose presence may hamper his outward freedom of movement, and powerfully hinder his concentration on his own artistic taste. It is almost unnecessary to remark that the artistic achievement of great actors is always bound by the concentration of attention to the action of their own performance, and that when in that condition, i.e., just when the actor's attention is taken away from the spectator, he gains a particular power over the audience, grips it, and compels it to take an active share in his artistic existence. This does not mean, of course, that the actor must altogether cease to feel the public; but the public is concerned only in so far as it neither exerts pressure on him nor diverts him unnecessarily from the artistic demands of the moment, which last might happen to him even while knowing how to regulate his attention. The actor suitably disciplined must automatically restrict the sphere of his attention, concentrating on what comes within this sphere, and only half consciously seizing on what comes within its aura. If need be, he must restrict that sphere to such an extent that it reaches a condition that may be called *public solitude*. But as a rule this sphere of attention is elastic, it expands or contracts for the actor, with regard to the course of his theatrical actions. Within the boundary of this sphere, as one of the actual aspects of the play, there is also the actor's immediate central *object of attention,* the object on which, somehow or other, his will is concentrated at the moment with which, in the course of the play, he is in inward communication. This theatrical sympathy with the object can only be complete when the actor has trained himself by long practice to surrender himself in his own impressions, and also in his reactions to those impressions, with maximum intensity: only so does theatrical action attain the necessary force, only so is created between the actual aspects of the play, i.e., between the actors, that link, that living bond, which is essential for the carrying through of the play to its goal, with the general maintenance of the rhythm and time of each performance.

Concentration

But whatever may be the sphere of the actor's attention, whether it confines him at some moments to public solitude, or whether it grips the faces of all those before the stage, dramatic artistic genius, as in the preparation of the part so in its repeated performance, requires a full concentration of all the mental and physical talents of the actor, and the participation of the whole of his physical and psychic capacity. It takes hold of his sight and hearing, all his external senses; it draws out not only the periphery but also the essential depth of his existence, and it evokes to activity his memory, imagination, emotions, intelligence and will. The whole mental and physical being of the actor must be directed to that which is derived from his facial expression. At the moment of inspiration, of the involuntary use of all the actor's qualities, at that moment he actually exists. On the other hand, in the absence of this employment of his qualities, the actor is gradually led astray along the road leading to time-honored theatrical traditions; he begins to "produce" wherever he sees them, or, glancing at his own image, imitates the inward manifestations of his emotions, or tries to draw from himself the emotions of the perfected part, to "inspire" them within himself. But when forcing such an image by his own psychic equipment, with its unchanging organic laws, he by no means attains that desired result of artistic genius; he must present only the rough counterfeit of emotion, because emotions do not come to order. By no effort of conscious will can one awake them in oneself at a moment, nor can they ever be of use for creative genius

striving to bring this about by searching the depths of its mind. A fundamental axiom, therefore, for the actor who wishes to be a real artist on the stage, may be stated thus: he must not play to produce emotions, and he must not involuntarily evoke them in himself.

Activity of Imagination

Considerations on the nature of artistically gifted people, however, inevitably open up the road to the possession of the emotion of the part. This road traverses activity of imagination, which in most of its stages is subject to the action of consciousness. One must not suddenly begin to operate on emotion; one must put oneself in motion in the direction of artistic imagination, but imagination—as is also shown by observations of scientific psychology—disturbs our aberrant memory, and, luring from the hidden recesses beyond the boundaries of its sense of harmony whatever elements there may be of proved emotions, organizes them afresh in sympathy with those that have arisen in our imagery. So surrounded within our figures of imagination, without effort on our part, the answer to our aberrant memory is found and the sounds of sympathetic emotion are called out from us. This is why the creative imagination presents itself afresh, the indispensable gift of the actor. Without a well developed, mobile imagination, creative faculty is by no means possible, not by instinct nor intuition nor the aid of external technique. In the acquiring of it, that which has lain dormant in the mind of the artist is, when immersed in his sphere of unconscious imagery and emotion, completely harmonized within him.

This practical method for the artistic education of the actor, directed by means of his imagination to the storing up of affective memory, is sufficiently enlarged upon; his individual emotional experience, by its limits, actually leads to the restriction of the sphere of his creative genius, and does not allow him to play parts dissimilar to those of his psychic harmony. This opinion is fundamental for the clearing away of misunderstandings of those elements of reality from which are produced fictitious creations of imagination; these are also derived from organic experience, but a wealth and variety of these creations are only obtained by combinations drawn from a trial of elements. The musical scale has only its basic notes, the solar spectrum its radical colors, but the combination of sounds in music and of colors in painting are infinite. One can in the same way speak of radical emotions preserved in imaginative memory, just as the reception in imagination of outward harmony remains in the intellectual memory; the sum of these radical emotions in the inner experience of each person is limited, but the shades and combinations are as infinite as the combinations that create activity of imagination out of the elements of inward experience.

Certainly, but the actor's outward experience—i.e., his sphere of vital sensations and reflections—must always be elastic, for only in that condition can the actor enlarge the sphere of his creative faculty. On the other hand, he must judiciously develop his imagination, harnessing it again and again to new propositions. But, in order that that imaginary union which is the actor's very foundation, produced by the creative genius of the dramatist, should take hold of him emotionally and lead him on to theatrical action, it is necessary that the actor should "swing toward" that union, as toward something as real as the union of reality surrounding him.

The Emotion of Truth

This does not mean that the actor must surrender himself on the stage to some such hallucination as that when playing he should lose the sense of reality around him, to take scenery for real trees, etc. On the contrary, some part of his senses must remain free from the grip of the play to control everything that he attempts and achieves as the performer of his part. He does not forget that surrounding him on the stage are decorations, scenery, etc., but they have no meaning for him. He says to himself, as it were: "I know that all around me on the stage is a rough counterfeit of reality. It is false. But if all should be real, see how I might be carried away to some such scene; then I would act." And at that instant, when there arises in his mind that artistic "suppose," encircling his real life, he loses interest in it, and is transported to another plane, created for him, of imaginary life. Restored to real life again, the actor must perforce modify the truth, as in the actual construction of his invention, so also in the survivals connected to it. His invention can be shown to be illogical, wide of the truth—and then he ceases to believe it. Emotion rises in him with invention; i.e., his outward regard for imagined circumstances may be shown as "determined" without relation to the individual nature of a given emotion. Finally, in the expression of the outward life of his part, the actor, as a living complex emotion, never making use of sufficient perfection of all his bodily equipment, may give an untrue intonation, may not keep the artistic mean in gesticulation and may through the temptation of cheap effect drift into mannerism or awkwardness.

Only by a strongly developed sense of truth may he achieve a single inward beauty in which, unlike the conventional theatrical gestures and poses, the true condition of the character is expressed in every one of his attitudes and outward gestures.

Internal Technique

The combination of all the above-named procedure and habits also composes the actor's external technique. Parallel with its development must go also the development of internal technique—the perfecting of that bodily equipment which serves for the incarnation of the theatrical image created by the actor, and the exact, clear expression of his external consciousness. With this aim in view the actor must work out within himself not only the ordinary flexibility and mobility of action, but also the particular consciousness that directs all his groups of muscles, and the ability to feel the energy transfused within him, which, arising from his highest creative centres, forms in a definite manner his mimicry and gestures, and, radiating from him, brings into the circle of its influence his partners on the stage and in the auditorium. The same growth of consciousness and fineness of internal feelings must be worked out by the actor in relation to his vocal equipment. Ordinary speech—as in life, so on the stage—is prosaic and monotonous; in it words sound disjointed, without any harmonious stringing together in a vocal melody as continuous as that of a violin, which by the hand of a master violinist can become fuller, deeper, finer and more transparent, and can without difficulty run from the higher to the lower notes and vice versa, and can alternate from pianissimo to forte. To counteract the wearisome monotony of reading, actors often elaborate, especially when declaiming poetry, with those artificial vocal *fioritures*, cadences and sudden raising and lowering of the voice, which are so characteristic of the conventional, pompous declamation, and which are not influenced by the corresponding emotion of the part, and therefore impress the more sensitive auditors with a feeling of unreality.

But there exists another natural musical sonorousness of speech, which we may see in great actors at the moment of their own true artistic elation, and which is closely knit to the internal sonorousness of their rôle. The actor must develop within himself this natural musical speech by practising his voice with due regard to his sense of reality, almost as much as a singer. At the same time he must perfect his elocution. It is possible to have a strong, flexible, impressive voice, and still distort speech, on the one hand by incorrect pronunciation, on the other by neglect of those almost imperceptible pauses and emphasis through which are attained the exact transmission of the sense of the sentence, and also its particular emotional coloring. In the perfect production of the dramatist, every word, every letter, every punctuation mark has its part in transmitting his inward reality; the actor in his interpretation of the play, according to his intelligence, introduces into each sentence his individual nuances, which must be transmitted not only by the motions of his body, but also by artistically developed speech. He must bear this in mind, that every sound which goes to make a word appears as a separate note, which has its part in the harmonious sound of the word, and which is the expression of one or other particle of the soul drawn out through the word. The perfecting, therefore, of the phonetics of speech cannot be limited to mechanical exercise of the vocal equipment, but must also be directed in such a way that the actor learns to feel each separate sound in a word as an instrument of artistic expression. But in regard to the musical tone of the voice, freedom, elasticity, rhythm of movement and generally all external technique of dramatic art, to say nothing of internal technique, the present day actor is still on a low rung of the ladder of artistic culture, still far behind in this respect, from many causes, the masters of music, poetry and painting, with an almost infinite road of development to travel.

It is evident that under these conditions, the staging of a play, which will satisfy highly artistic demands, cannot be achieved at the speed that economic factors unfortunately make necessary in most theatres. This creative process, which every actor must go through, from his conception of the part to its artistic incarnation, is essentially very complicated, and is hampered by lack of perfection of outward and inward technique. It is also much hindered by the necessity of fitting in the actors one with another—the adjustment of their artistic individualities into an artistic whole.

Production

Responsibility for bringing about this accord, and the artistic integrity and expression of the performance rests with the theatre manager. During the period when the manager exercised a despotic rule in the theatre, a period starting with the Meiningen players and still in force even in many of the foremost theatres, the manager worked out in advance all the plans for staging a play, and, while certainly having regard to the existing cast, indicated to the actors the general outlines of the scenic effects, and the *mise-en-scène*. The writer also adhered to this system, but now he has come to the conclusion that the creative work of the manager must be done in collaboration with the actor's work, neither ignoring nor confirming it. To encourage the actor's creative genius, to control and adjust it, ensuring that this creative genius grows out of the unique artistic germ of the drama, as much as the external building up of the performance—that in the opinion of the writer is the problem of the theatre director to-day.

The joint work of the director and actor begins with the analysis of the drama and the discovery of its artistic germ, and with the investigation of its *transparent effect*. The next step is the discovery of the transparent effect of individual parts—of that fundamental will direction of each individual actor, which, organically derived from his character, determines his place in the general action of the play. If the actor cannot at once secure this transparent effect, then it must be traced bit by bit with the manager's aid—by dividing the part into sections corresponding to the separate stages of the life of the particular actor—from the separate problems developing before him in his struggle for the attainment of his goal. Each such section of a part of each problem, can, if necessary, be subjected to further psychological analysis, and sub-divided into problems even more detailed, corresponding to those separate mind actions of the performer out of which stage life is summed up. The actor must catch the *mind axes* of the emotions and temperaments, but not the emotions and temperaments that give color to these sections of the part. In other words, when studying each portion of his part, he must ask himself what he wants, what he requires as a performer of the play and which definite partial problem he is putting before himself at a given moment. The answer to this question should not be in the form of a noun, but rather of a verb: "I wish to obtain possession of the heart of this lady"—"I wish to enter her house"—"I wish to push aside the servants who are protecting her," etc. Formulated in this manner, the mind problem, of which the object and setting, thanks to the working of his creative imagination, are forming a brighter and clearer picture for the actor, begins to grip him and to excite him, extracting from the recesses of his working memory the combinations of emotions necessary to the part, of emotions that have an active character and mould themselves into dramatic action. In this way the different sections of the actor's part grow more lively and richer by degrees, owing to the involuntary play of the complicated organic survivals. By joining together and grafting these sections, the *score of the part* is formed; the scores of the separate parts, after the continual joint work of the actors during rehearsals and by the necessary adjustment of them one with another, are summed up in a single *score of the performance.*

The Score Condensed

Nevertheless, the work of the actors and manager is still unfinished. The actor is studying and living in the part and the play deeper and deeper still, finding their deeper artistic motives; so he lives in the score of his part still more profoundly. But the score of the part itself and of the play are actually subject by degrees during the work to further alterations. As in a perfect poetical production there are no superfluous words but only those necessary to the poet's artistic scheme, so in a score of the part there must not be a single superfluous emotion but only emotions necessary for the *transparent effect*. The score of each part must be condensed, as also the form of its transmitting, and bright, simple and compelling forms of its incarnation must be found. Only then, when in each actor every part not only organically ripens and comes to life but also all emotions are stripped of the superfluous, when they all crystallize and sum up into a live contact, when they harmonize amongst themselves in the general tune, rhythm and time of the performance, then the play may be presented to the public.

During repeated presentations the theatrical score of the play and each part remains in general unaltered. But that does not mean that from the moment the performance is shown to the public the actor's creative process is to be considered ended, and that there remains for him only the mechanical repetition of his achievement at the first presentation. On the contrary, every performance imposes on him creative conditions; all his psychical forces must take part in it, because only in these conditions can they creatively adapt the score of the part to those capricious changes which may develop in them from hour to hour, as in all living nervous creatures influencing one another by their emotions, and only then can they transmit to the spectator that invisible something, inexpressible in words, which forms the spiritual content of the play. And that is the whole origin of the substance of dramatic art.

As regards the outward arrangements of the play—scenery, theatrical properties, etc.—all are of value in so far as they correspond to the expression of dramatic action, i.e., to the actors' talents; in no case may they claim to have an independent artistic importance in the theatre, although up to now they have been so considered by many great scene painters. The art of scene painting, as well as the music included in the play, is on the stage only an auxiliary art, and the manager's duty is to get from each what is necessary for the illumination of the play performed before an audience, while subordinating each to the problems of the actors.

BERTOLT BRECHT (1898–1956)
"The Street Scene" (1938)
Translated by JOHN WILLETT

In "The Street Scene," Brecht provides a model for one of his most controversial contentions, that acting should *both* impersonate *and* demonstrate the character. Here, Brecht takes the model of someone describing a traffic accident: the narrative is paramount, but the actor is both himself and the things he portrays at the same time. One of the most fascinating aspects of the essay is the "Exercises for Acting Schools": what kinds of skills are being trained, developed by these exercises, what is the "epic actor" being trained to do?

The Street Scene

A Basic Model for an Epic Theatre

In the decade and a half that followed the World War a comparatively new way of acting was tried out in a number of German theatres. Its qualities of clear description and reporting and its use of choruses and projections as a means of commentary earned it the name of 'epic'. The actor used a somewhat complex technique to detach himself from the character portrayed; he forced the spectator to look at the play's situations from such an angle that they necessarily became subject to his criticism. Supporters of this epic theatre argued that the new subject-matter, the highly involved incidents of the class war in its acutest and most terrible stage, would be mastered more easily by such a method, since it would thereby become possible to portray social processes as seen in their causal relationships. But the result of these experiments was that aesthetics found itself up against a whole series of substantial difficulties.

It is comparatively easy to set up a basic model for epic theatre. For practical experiments I usually picked as my example of completely simple, 'natural' epic theatre an incident such as can be seen at any street corner: an eyewitness demonstrating to a collection of people how a traffic accident took place. The bystanders may not have observed what happened, or they may simply not agree with him, may 'see things a different way'; the point is that the demonstrator acts the behaviour of driver or victim or both in such a way that the bystanders are able to form an opinion about the accident.

Such an example of the most primitive type of epic theatre seems easy to understand. Yet experience has shown that it presents astounding difficulties to the reader or listener as soon as he is asked to see the implications of treating this kind of street corner demonstration as a basic form of major theatre, theatre for a scientific age. What this means of course is that the epic theatre may appear richer, more intricate and complex in every particular, yet to be major theatre it need at bottom only contain the same elements as a street-corner demonstration of this sort; nor could it any longer be termed epic theatre if any of the main elements of the street-corner demonstration were lacking. Until this is understood it is impossible really to understand what follows. Until one understands the novelty, unfamiliarity and direct challenge to the critical faculties of the suggestion that street-corner demonstration of this sort can serve as a satisfactory basic model of major theatre one cannot really understand what follows.

Consider: the incident is clearly very far from what we mean by an artistic one. The demonstrator need not be an artist. The capacities he needs to achieve his aim are in effect universal. Suppose he cannot carry out some particular movement as quickly as the victim he is imitating; all he need do is to explain that *he* moves three times as fast, and the demonstration neither suffers in essentials nor loses its point. On the contrary it is important that he should not be too perfect. His demonstration would be spoilt if the bystanders' attention were drawn to his powers of transformation. He has to avoid presenting himself in such a way that someone calls out 'What a lifelike portrayal of a chauffeur!' He must not 'cast a spell' over anyone. He should not transport people from normality to 'higher realms'. He need not dispose of any special powers of suggestion.

It is most important that one of the main features of the ordinary theatre should be excluded from our street scene: the engendering of illusion. The street demonstrator's performance is essentially repetitive. The event has taken place; what you are seeing now is a repeat. If the scene in the theatre follows the street scene in this respect then the theatre will stop pretending not to be theatre, just as the street-corner demonstration admits it is a demonstration (and does not pretend to be the actual event). The element of rehearsal in the acting and of learning by heart in the text, the whole machinery and the whole process of preparation: it all becomes plainly apparent. What room is left for experience? Is the reality portrayed still experienced in any sense?

The street scene determines what kind of experience is to be prepared for the spectator. There is no question but that the street-corner demonstrator has been through an 'experience', but he is not out to make his demonstration serve as an 'experience' for the audience. Even the experience of the driver and the victim is only partially communicated by him, and he by no means tries to turn it into an enjoyable experience for the spectator, however lifelike he may make his demonstration. The demonstration would become no less valid if he did not reproduce the fear caused by the accident; on the contrary it would lose validity if he did. He is not interested in creating pure emotions. It is important to understand that a theatre which follows his lead in this respect undergoes a positive change of function.

One essential element of the street scene must also be present in the theatrical scene if this is to qualify as epic, namely that the demonstration should have a socially practical significance. Whether our street demonstrator is out to show that one attitude on the part of driver or pedestrian makes an accident inevitable where another would not, or whether he is demonstrating with a view to fixing the responsibility, his demonstration has a practical purpose, intervenes socially.

The demonstrator's purpose determines how thoroughly he has to imitate. Our demonstrator need not imitate every aspect of his characters' behaviour, but only so much as gives a picture. Generally the theatre scene will give much fuller pictures, corresponding to its more extensive range of interest. How do street scene and theatre scene link up here? To take a point of detail, the victim's voice may have played no immediate part in the accident. Eye-witnesses may disagree as to whether a cry they heard ('Look out!') came from the victim or from someone else, and this may give our demonstrator a motive for imitating the voice. The question can be settled by demonstrating whether the voice was an old man's or a woman's, or merely whether it was high or low. Again, the answer may depend on whether it was that of an educated person or not. Loud or soft may play a great part, as the driver could be correspondingly more or less guilty. A whole series of characteristics of the victim ask to be portrayed. Was he absent-minded? Was his attention distracted? If so, by what? What, on the evidence of his behaviour, could have made him liable to be distracted by just that circumstance and no other? Etc., etc. It can be seen that our street-corner demonstration provides opportunities for a pretty rich and varied portrayal of human types. Yet a theatre which tries to restrict its essential elements to those provided by our street scene will have to acknowledge certain limits to imitation. It must be able to justify any outlay in terms of its purpose.[1]

The demonstration may for instance be dominated by the question of compensation for the victim, etc. The driver risks being sacked from his job, losing his licence, going

---

[1] We often come across demonstrations of an everyday sort which are more thorough imitations than our street-corner accident demands. Generally they are comic ones. Our next-door neighbour may decide to 'take off' the rapacious behaviour of our common landlord. Such an imitation is often rich and full of variety. Closer examination will show however that even so apparently complex an imitation concentrates on one specific side of the landlord's behaviour. The imitation is summary or selective, deliberately leaving out those occasions where the landlord strikes our neighbour as 'perfectly sensible', though such occasions of course occur. He is far from giving a rounded picture; for that would have no comic impact at all. The street scene, perforce adopting a wider angle of vision, at this point lands in difficulties which must not be underestimated. It has to be just as successful in promoting criticism, but the incidents in question are far more complex. It must promote positive as well as negative criticism, and as part of a single process. You have to understand what is involved in winning the audience's approval by means of a critical approach. Here again we have a precedent in our street scene, i.e. in any demonstration of an everyday sort. Next-door neighbour and street demonstrator can reproduce their subject's 'sensible' or his 'senseless' behaviour alike, by submitting it for an opinion. When it crops up in the course of events, however (when a man switches from being sensible to being senseless, or the other way round), then they usually need some form of commentary in order to change the angle of their portrayal. Hence, as already mentioned, certain difficulties for the theatre scene. These cannot be dealt with here.

to prison; the victim risks a heavy hospital bill, loss of job, permanent disfigurement, possibly unfitness for work. This is the area within which the demonstrator builds up his characters. The victim may have had a companion; the driver may have had his girl sitting alongside him. That would bring out the social element better and allow the characters to be more fully drawn.

Another essential element in the street scene is that the demonstrator should derive his characters entirely from their actions. He imitates their actions and so allows conclusions to be drawn about them. A theatre that follows him in this will be largely breaking with the orthodox theatre's habit of basing the actions on the characters and having the former exempted from criticism by presenting them as an unavoidable consequence deriving by natural law from the characters who perform them. To the street demonstrator the character of the man being demonstrated remains a quantity that need not be completely defined. Within certain limits he may be like this or like that; it doesn't matter. What the demonstrator is concerned with are his accident-prone and accident-proof qualities.[2] The theatrical scene may show more fully-defined individuals. But it must then be in a position to treat their individuality as a special case and outline the field within which, once more, its most socially relevant effects are produced. Our street demonstrator's possibilities of demonstration are narrowly restricted (indeed, we chose this model so that the limits should be as narrow as possible). If the essential elements of the theatrical scene are limited to those of the street scene then its greater richness must be an enrichment only. The question of border-line cases becomes acute.

Let us take a specific detail. Can our street demonstrator, say, ever become entitled to use an excited tone of voice in repeating the driver's statement that he has been exhausted by too long a spell of work? (In theory this is no more possible than for a returning messenger to start telling his fellow-countrymen of his talk with the king with the words 'I saw the bearded king'.) It can only be possible, let alone unavoidable, if one imagines a street-corner situation where such excitement, specifically about this aspect of the affair, plays a particular part. (In the instance above this would be so if the king had sworn never to cut his beard off until . . . etc.) We have to find a point of view for our demonstrator that allows him to submit this excitement to criticism. Only if he adopts a quite definite point of view can he be entitled to imitate the driver's excited voice; e.g. if he blames drivers as such for doing too little to reduce their hours of work. ('Look at him. Doesn't even belong to

a union, but gets worked up soon enough when an accident happens. "Ten hours I've been at the wheel." ')

Before it can get as far as this, i.e. be able to suggest a point of view to the actor, the theatre needs to take a number of steps. By widening its field of vision and showing the driver in other situations besides that of the accident the theatre in no way exceeds its model; it merely creates a further situation on the same pattern. One can imagine a scene of the same kind as the street scene which provides a well-argued demonstration showing how such emotions as the driver's develop, or another which involves making comparisons between tones of voice. In order not to exceed the model scene the theatre only has to develop a technique for submitting emotions to the spectator's criticism. Of course this does not mean that the spectator must be barred on principle from sharing certain emotions that are put before him; none the less to communicate emotions is only one particular form (phase, consequence) of criticism. The theatre's demonstrator, the actor, must apply a technique which will let him reproduce the tone of the subject demonstrated with a certain reserve, with detachment (so that the spectator can say: 'He's getting excited—in vain, too late, at last. . . .' etc.). In short, the actor must remain a demonstrator; he must present the person demonstrated as a stranger, he must not suppress the '*he* did that, *he* said that' element in his performance. He must not go so far as to be wholly transformed into the person demonstrated.

One essential element of the street scene lies in the natural attitude adopted by the demonstrator, which is two-fold; he is always taking two situations into account. He behaves naturally as a demonstrator, and he lets the subject of the demonstration behave naturally too. He never forgets, nor does he allow it to be forgotten, that he is not the subject but the demonstrator. That is to say, what the audience sees is not a fusion between demonstrator and subject, not some third, independent, uncontradictory entity with isolated features of (a) demonstrator and (b) subject, such as the orthodox theatre puts before us in its productions.[3] The feelings and opinions of demonstrator and demonstrated are not merged into one.

We now come to one of those elements that are peculiar to the epic theatre, the so-called A-effect (alienation effect). What is involved here is, briefly, a technique of taking the human social incidents to be portrayed and labelling them as something striking, something that calls for explanation, is not to be taken for granted, not just natural. The object of this 'effect' is to allow the spectator to criticize constructively from a social point of view. Can we show that this A-effect is significant for our street demonstrator?

---

[2] The same situation will be produced by all those people whose characters fulfil the conditions laid down by him and show the features that he imitates.

---

[3] Most clearly worked out by Stanislavsky.

We can picture what happens if he fails to make use of it. The following situation could occur. One of the spectators might say: 'But if the victim stepped off the kerb with his right foot, as you showed him doing. . . .' The demonstrator might interrupt saying: 'I showed him stepping off with his left foot.' By arguing which foot he really stepped off with in his demonstration, and, even more, how the victim himself acted, the demonstration can be so transformed that the A-effect occurs. The demonstrator achieves it by paying exact attention this time to his movements, executing them carefully, probably in slow motion; in this way he alienates the little sub-incident, emphasizes its importance, makes it worthy of notice. And so the epic theatre's alienation effect proves to have its uses for our street demonstrator too; in other words it is also to be found in this small every-day scene of natural street-corner theatre, which has little to do with art. The direct changeover from representation to commentary that is so characteristic of the epic theatre is still more easily recognized as one element of any street demonstration. Wherever he feels he can the demonstrator breaks off his imitation in order to give explanations. The epic theatre's choruses and documentary projections, the direct addressing of the audience by its actors, are at bottom just this.

It will have been observed, not without astonishment I hope, that I have not named any strictly artistic elements as characterizing our street scene and, with it, that of the epic theatre. The street demonstrator can carry out a successful demonstration with no greater abilities than, in effect, anybody has. What about the epic theatre's value as art?

The epic theatre wants to establish its basic model at the street corner, i.e. to return to the very simplest 'natural' theatre, a social enterprise whose origins, means and ends are practical and earthly. The model works without any need of programmatic theatrical phrases like 'the urge to self-expression', 'making a part one's own', 'spiritual experience', 'the play instinct', 'the story-teller's art', etc. Does that mean that the epic theatre isn't concerned with art?

It might be as well to begin by putting the question differently, thus: can we make use of artistic abilities for the purposes of our street scene? Obviously yes. Even the street-corner demonstration includes artistic elements. Artistic abilities in some small degree are to be found in any man. It does no harm to remember this when one is confronted with great art. Undoubtedly what we call artistic abilities can be exercised at any time within the limits imposed by our street scene model. They will function as artistic abilities even though they do not exceed these limits (for instance, when there is meant to be no complete transformation of demonstrator into subject). And

true enough, the epic theatre is an extremely artistic affair, hardly thinkable without artists and virtuosity, imagination, humour and fellow-feeling; it cannot be practised without all these and much else too. It has got to be entertaining, it has got to be instructive. How then can art be developed out of the elements of the street scene, without adding any or leaving any out? How does it evolve into the theatrical scene with its fabricated story, its trained actors, its lofty style of speaking, its make-up, its team performance by a number of players? Do we need to add to our elements in order to move on from the 'natural' demonstration to the 'artificial'?

Is it not true that the additions which we must make to our model in order to arrive at epic theatre are of a fundamental kind? A brief examination will show that they are not. Take the *story*. There was nothing fabricated about our street accident. Nor does the orthodox theatre deal only in fabrications; think for instance of the historical play. None the less a story can be performed at the street corner too. Our demonstrator may at any time be in a position to say: 'The driver was guilty, because it all happened the way I showed you. He wouldn't be guilty if it had happened the way I'm going to show you now.' And he can fabricate an incident and demonstrate it. Or take the fact that the text is, learnt by heart. As a witness in a court case the demonstrator may have written down the subject's exact words, learnt them by heart and rehearsed them; in that case he too is performing a text he has learned. Or take a rehearsed programme by several players: it doesn't always have to be artistic purposes that bring about a demonstration of this sort; one need only think of the French police technique of making the chief figures in any criminal case re-enact certain crucial situations before a police audience. Or take making-up. Minor changes in appearance—ruffling one's hair, for instance—can occur at any time within the framework of the non-artistic type of demonstration. Nor is make-up itself used solely for theatrical purposes. In the street scene the driver's moustache may be particularly significant. It may have influenced the testimony of the possible girl companion suggested earlier. This can be represented by our demonstrator making the driver stroke an imaginary moustache when prompting his companion's evidence. In this way the demonstrator can do a good deal to discredit her as a witness. Moving on to the use of a real moustache in the theatre, however, is not an entirely easy transition, and the same difficulty occurs with respect to *costume*. Our demonstrator may under given circumstances put on the driver's cap—for instance if he wants to show that he was drunk: (he had it on crooked)—but he can only do so conditionally, under these circumstances; (see what was said about borderline cases earlier). However, where there is a demonstration by several demonstrators of the kind referred to above we can have costume so that the various characters can be distinguished. This again is only a limited use of costume. There must be no question of creating an illusion that the demonstrators really are these characters. (The epic theatre can counteract this illusion by especially exaggerated costume or by garments that are somehow marked out as objects for display.) Moreover we can suggest another model as a substitute for ours on this point: the kind of street demonstration given by hawkers. To sell their neckties these people will portray a badly-dressed and a well-dressed man; with a few props and technical tricks they can perform significant little scenes where they submit essentially to the same restrictions as apply to the demonstrator in our street scene: (they will pick up tie, hat, stick, gloves and give certain significant imitations of a man of the world, and the whole time they will refer to him as '*he*'!) With hawkers we also find *verse* being used within the same framework as that of our basic model. They use firm irregular rhythms to sell braces and newspapers alike.

Reflecting along these lines we see that our basic model will work. The elements of natural and of artificial epic theatre are the same. Our street-corner theatre is primitive; origins, aims and methods of its performance are close to home. But there is no doubt that it is a meaningful phenomenon with a clear social function that dominates all its elements. The performance's origins lie in an incident that can be judged one way or another, that may repeat itself in different forms and is not finished but is bound to have consequences, so that this judgment has some significance. The object of the performance is to make it easier to give an opinion on the incident. Its means correspond to that. The epic theatre is a highly skilled theatre with complex contents and far-reaching social objectives. In setting up the street scene as a basic model for it we pass on the clear social function and give the epic theatre criteria by which to decide whether an incident is meaningful or not. The basic model has a practical significance. As producer and actors work to build up a performance involving many difficult questions—technical problems, social ones—it allows them to check whether the social function of the whole apparatus is still clearly intact.

['Die Strassenszene, Grundmodell eines epischen Theaters', from *Versuche 10,* 1950]

NOTE: Originally stated to have been written in 1940, but now ascribed by Werner Hecht to June 1938. This is an elaboration of a poem 'Über alltägliches Theater' which is supposed to have been written in 1930 and is included

as one of the 'Gedichte aus dem Messingkauf' in *Theaterarbeit, Versuche 14* and *Gedichte* 3. The notion of the man at the street-corner miming an accident is already developed at length there, and it also occurs in the following undated scheme (*Schriften zum Theater 4,* pp. 51–2):

EXERCISES FOR ACTING SCHOOLS

a) Conjuring tricks, including attitude of spectators.

b) For women: folding and putting away linen. Same for men.

c) For men: varying attitudes of smokers. Same for women.

d) Cat playing with a hank of thread.

e) Exercises in observation.

f) Exercises in imitation.

g) How to take notes. Noting of gestures, tones of voice.

h) Exercises in imagination. Three men throwing dice for their life. One loses. Then: they all lose.

i) Dramatizing an epic. Passages from the Bible.

k) For everybody: repeated exercises in production. Essential to show one's colleagues.

l) Exercises in temperament. Situation: two women calmly folding linen. They feign a wild and jealous quarrel for the benefit of their husbands; the husbands are in the next room.

m) They come to blows as they fold their linen in silence.

n) Game (l) turns serious.

o) Quick-change competition. Behind a screen; open.

p) Modifying an imitation, simply described so that others can put it into effect.

q) Rhythmical (verse–) speaking with tap-dance.

r) Eating with outsize knife and fork. Very small knife and fork.

s) Dialogue with gramophone: recorded sentences, free answers.

t) Search for 'nodal points'.

u) Characterization of a fellow-actor.

v) Improvisation of incidents. Running through scenes in the style of a report, no text.

w) The street accident. Laying down limits of justifiable imitation.

x) Variations: a dog went into the kitchen. [A traditional song]

y) Memorizing first impressions of a part.

Werner Hecht suggests that these exercises/may relate to lessons given by Helene Weigel at a Finnish theatre school.

ANTONIN ARTAUD (1896–1948)

from *The Theater and Its Double* (1938)

Translated by MARY CAROLINE RICHARDS

An early member of the surrealist movement in Paris, Antonin Artaud was well-known between the wars as an actor, playwright, and essayist of the avant-garde theater, and he is one of the formative influences on the modern European theater. Artaud is most often associated with the "theater of cruelty," his label for a theater that would assault the representational dynamics of traditional theater and break the boundaries between actor and audience, stage and spectacle. Artaud was declared insane and committed to a mental hospital in 1937. He remained institutionalized for most of the remainder of his life.

The Theater And Culture

Never before, when it is life itself that is in question, has there been so much talk of civilization and culture. And there is a curious parallel between this generalized collapse of life at the root of our present demoralization and our concern for a culture which has never been coincident with life, which in fact has been devised to tyrannize over life.

Before speaking further about culture, I must remark that the world is hungry and not concerned with culture, and that the attempt to orient toward culture thoughts turned only toward hunger is a purely artificial expedient.

What is most important, it seems to me, is not so much to defend a culture whose existence has never kept a man from going hungry, as to extract, from what is called culture, ideas whose compelling force is identical with that of hunger.

We need to live first of all; to believe in what makes us live and that something *makes* us live—to believe that whatever is produced from the mysterious depths of ourselves need not forever haunt us as an exclusively digestive concern.

I mean that if it is important for us to eat first of all, it is even more important for us not to waste in the sole concern for eating our simple power of being hungry.

If confusion is the sign of the times, I see at the root of this confusion a rupture between things and words, between things and the ideas and signs that are their representation.

Not, of course, for lack of philosophical systems; their number and contradictions characterize our old French and European culture: but where can it be shown that life, our life, has ever been affected by these systems? I will not say that philosophical systems must be applied directly and immediately: but of the following alternatives, one must be true:

Either these systems are within us and permeate our being to the point of supporting life itself (and if this is the case, what use are books?), or they do *not* permeate us and therefore do not have the capacity to support life (and in this case what does their disappearance matter?).

We must insist upon the idea of culture-in-action, of culture growing within us like a new organ, a sort of second breath; and on civilization as an applied culture controlling even our subtlest actions, a *presence of mind;* the distinction between culture and civilization is an artificial one, providing two words to signify an identical function.

A civilized man judges and is judged according to his behavior, but even the term "civilized" leads to confusion: a cultivated "civilized" man is regarded as a person instructed in systems, a person who thinks in forms, signs, representations—a monster whose faculty of deriving thoughts from acts, instead of identifying acts with thoughts, is developed to an absurdity.

If our life lacks brimstone, i.e., a constant magic, it is because we choose to observe our acts and lose ourselves in considerations of their imagined form instead of being impelled by their force.

And this faculty is an exclusively human one. I would even say that it is this infection of the human which contaminates ideas that should have remained divine; for far from believing that man invented the supernatural and the divine, I think it is man's age-old intervention which has ultimately corrupted the divine within him.

All our ideas about life must be revised in a period when nothing any longer adheres to life; it is this painful cleavage which is responsible for the revenge of *things;* the poetry which is no longer within us and which we no longer succeed in finding in things suddenly appears on their wrong side: consider the unprecedented number of crimes whose perverse gratuitousness is explained only by our powerlessness to take complete possession of life.

If the theater has been created as an outlet for our repressions, the agonized poetry expressed in its bizarre corruptions of the facts of life demonstrates that life's intensity is still intact and asks only to be better directed.

But no matter how loudly we clamor for magic in our lives, we are really afraid of pursuing an existence entirely under its influence and sign.

Hence our confirmed lack of culture is astonished by certain grandiose anomalies; for example, on an island without any contact with modern civilization, the mere passage of a ship carrying only healthy passengers may provoke the sudden outbreak of diseases unknown on that island but a specialty of nations like our own: shingles, influenza, grippe, rheumatism, sinusitis, polyneuritis, etc.

Similarly, if we think Negroes smell bad, we are ignorant of the fact that anywhere but in Europe it is we whites who "smell bad." And I would even say that we give off an odor as white as the gathering of pus in an infected wound.

As iron can be heated until it turns white, so it can be said that everything excessive is white; for Asiatics white has become the mark of extreme decomposition.

This said, we can begin to form an idea of culture, an idea which is first of all a protest.

A protest against the senseless constraint imposed upon the idea of culture by reducing it to a sort of inconceivable Pantheon, producing an idolatry no different from the image-worship of those religions which relegate their gods to Pantheons.

A protest against the idea of culture as distinct from life—as if there were culture on one side and life on the other, as if true culture were not a refined means of understanding and *exercising* life.

The library at Alexandria can be burnt down. There are forces above and beyond papyrus: we may temporarily be deprived of our ability to discover these forces, but their energy will not be suppressed. It is good that our excessive facilities are no longer available, that forms fall into oblivion: a culture without space or time, restrained only by the capacity of our own nerves, will reappear with all the more energy. It is right that from time to time cataclysms occur which compel us to return to nature, i.e., to rediscover life. The old totemism of animals, stones, objects capable of discharging thunderbolts, costumes impregnated with bestial essences—everything, in short, that might determine, disclose, and direct the secret forces of the universe—is for us a dead thing, from which we derive nothing but static and aesthetic profit, the profit of an audience, not of an actor.

Yet totemism is an actor, for it moves, and has been created in behalf of actors; all true culture relies upon the barbaric and primitive means of totemism whose savage, i.e., entirely spontaneous, life I wish to worship.

What has lost us culture is our Occidental idea of art and the profits we seek to derive from it. Art and culture cannot be considered together, contrary to the treatment universally accorded them!

True culture operates by exaltation and force, while the European ideal of art attempts to cast the mind into an attitude distinct from force but addicted to exaltation. It is a lazy, unserviceable notion which engenders an imminent death. If the Serpent Quetzalcoatl's multiple twists and turns are harmonious, it is because they express the equilibrium and fluctuations of a sleeping force; the intensity of the forms is there only to seduce and direct a force which, in music, would produce an insupportable range of sound.

The gods that sleep in museums: the god of fire with his incense burner that resembles an Inquisition tripod; Tlaloc, one of the manifold Gods of the Waters, on his wall of green granite; the Mother Goddess of Waters, the Mother Goddess of Flowers; the immutable expression, echoing from beneath many layers of water, of the Goddess robed in green jade; the enraptured, blissful expression, features crackling with incense, where atoms of sunlight circle—the countenance of the Mother Goddess of Flowers; this world of obligatory servitude in which a stone comes alive when it has been properly carved, the world of organically civilized men whose vital organs too awaken from their slumber, this human world enters into us, participating in the dance of the gods without turning round or looking back, on pain of becoming, like ourselves, crumbled pillars of salt.

In Mexico, since we are talking about Mexico, there is no art: things are made for use. And the world is in perpetual exaltation.

To our disinterested and inert idea of art an authentic culture opposes a violently egoistic and magical, i.e., *interested* idea. For the Mexicans seek contact with the *Manas,* forces latent in every form, unreleased by contemplation of the forms for themselves, but springing to life by magic identification with these forms. And the old Totems are there to hasten the communication.

How hard it is, when everything encourages us to sleep, though we may look about us with conscious, clinging eyes, to wake and yet look about us as in a dream, with eyes that no longer know their function and whose gaze is turned inward.

This is how our strange idea of disinterested action originated, though it is action nonetheless, and all the more violent for skirting the temptation of repose.

Every real effigy has a shadow which is its double; and art must falter and fail from the moment the sculptor believes he has liberated the kind of shadow whose very existence will destroy his repose.

Like all magic cultures expressed by appropriate hieroglyphs, the true theater has its shadows too, and, of all languages and all arts, the theater is the only one left whose shadows have shattered their limitations. From the beginning, one might say its shadows did not tolerate limitations.

Our petrified idea of the theater is connected with our petrified idea of a culture without shadows, where, no matter which way it turns, our mind (*esprit*) encounters only emptiness, though space is full.

But the true theater, because it moves and makes use of living instruments, continues to stir up shadows where life has never ceased to grope its way. The actor does not make the same gestures twice, but he makes gestures, he moves; and although he brutalizes forms, nevertheless behind them and through their destruction he rejoins that which outlives forms and produces their continuation.

The theater, which is in *no thing*, but makes use of everything—gestures, sounds, words, screams, light, darkness—rediscovers itself at precisely the point where the mind requires a language to express its manifestations.

And the fixation of the theater in one language—written words, music, lights, noises—betokens its imminent ruin, the choice of any one language betraying a taste for the special effects of that language; and the dessication of the language accompanies its limitation.

For the theater as for culture, it remains a question of naming and directing shadows: and the theater, not confined to a fixed language and form, not only destroys false shadows but prepares the way for a new generation of shadows, around which assembles the true spectacle of life.

To break through language in order to touch life is to create or recreate the theater; the essential thing is not to believe that this act must remain sacred, i.e., set apart—the essential thing is to believe that not just anyone can create it, and that there must be a preparation.

This leads to the rejection of the usual limitations of man and man's powers, and infinitely extends the frontiers of what is called reality.

We must believe in a sense of life renewed by the theater, a sense of life in which man fearlessly makes himself master of what does not yet exist, and brings it into being. And everything that has not been born can still be brought to life if we are not satisfied to remain mere recording organisms.

Furthermore, when we speak the word "life," it must be understood we are not referring to life as we know it from its surface of fact, but to that fragile, fluctuating center which forms never reach. And if there is still one hellish, truly accursed thing in our time, it is our artistic dallying with forms, instead of being like victims burnt at the stake, signaling through the flames.

• • •

No More Masterpieces

One of the reasons for the asphyxiating atmosphere in which we live without possible escape or remedy—and in which we all share, even the most revolutionary among us—is our respect for what has been written, formulated, or painted, what has been given form, as if all expression were not at last exhausted, were not at a point where things must break apart if they are to start anew and begin fresh.

We must have done with this idea of masterpieces reserved for a self-styled elite and not understood by the general public; the mind has no such restricted districts as those so often used for clandestine sexual encounters.

Masterpieces of the past are good for the past: they are not good for us. We have the right to say what has been said and even what has not been said in a way that belongs to us, a way that is immediate and direct, corresponding to present modes of feeling, and understandable to everyone.

It is idiotic to reproach the masses for having no sense of the sublime, when the sublime is confused with one or another of its formal manifestations, which are moreover always defunct manifestations. And if for example a contemporary public does not understand *Oedipus Rex,* I shall make bold to say that it is the fault of *Oedipus Rex* and not of the public.

In *Oedipus Rex* there is the theme of incest and the idea that nature mocks at morality and that there are certain unspecified powers at large which we would do well to beware of, call them *destiny* or anything you choose.

There is in addition the presence of a plague epidemic which is a physical incarnation of these powers. But the whole in a manner and language that have lost all touch with the rude and epileptic rhythm of our time. Sophocles speaks grandly perhaps, but in a style that is no longer timely. His language is too refined for this age. It is as if he were speaking beside the point.

However, a public that shudders at train wrecks, that is familiar with earthquakes, plagues, revolutions, wars; that is sensitive to the disordered anguish of love, can be affected by all these grand notions and asks only to become aware of them, but on condition that it is addressed in its own language, and that its knowledge of these things does not come to it through adulterated trappings and speech that belong to extinct eras which will never live again.

Today as yesterday, the public is greedy for mystery: it asks only to become aware of the laws according to which destiny manifests itself, and to divine perhaps the secret of its apparitions.

Let us leave textual criticism to graduate students, formal criticism to esthetes, and recognize that what has been said is not still to be said; that an expression does not have the same value twice, does not live two lives; that all words, once spoken, are dead and function only at the moment when they are uttered, that a form, once it has served, cannot be used again and asks only to be replaced by another, and that the theater is the only place in the world where a gesture, once made, can never be made the same way twice.

If the public does not frequent our literary masterpieces, it is because those masterpieces are literary, that is to say, fixed; and fixed in forms that no longer respond to the needs of the time.

Far from blaming the public, we ought to blame the formal screen we interpose between ourselves and the public, and this new form of idolatry, the idolatry of fixed masterpieces which is one of the aspects of bourgeois conformism.

This conformism makes us confuse sublimity, ideas, and things with the forms they have taken in time and in our minds—in our snobbish, precious, aesthetic mentalities which the public does not understand.

How pointless in such matters to accuse the public of bad taste because it relishes insanities, so long as the public is not shown a valid spectacle; and I defy anyone to show me *here* a spectacle valid—valid in the supreme sense of the theater—since the last great romantic melodramas, i.e., since a hundred years ago.

The public, which takes the false for the true, has the sense of the true and always responds to it when it is manifested. However it is not upon the stage that the true is to be sought nowadays, but in the street; and if the crowd in the street is offered an occasion to show its human dignity, it will always do so.

If people are out of the habit of going to the theater, if we have all finally come to think of theater as an inferior art, a means of popular distraction, and to use it as an outlet for our worst instincts, it is because we have learned too well what the theater has been, namely, falsehood and illusion. It is because we have been accustomed for four hundred years, that is since the Renaissance, to a purely descriptive and narrative theater—storytelling psychology; it is because every possible ingenuity has been exerted in bringing to life on the stage plausible but detached beings, with the spectacle on one side, the public on the other—and because the public is no longer shown anything but the mirror of itself.

Shakespeare himself is responsible for this aberration and decline, this disinterested idea of the theater which wishes a theatrical performance to leave the public intact, without setting off one image that will shake the organism to its foundations and leave an ineffaceable scar.

If, in Shakespeare, a man is sometimes preoccupied with what transcends him, it is always in order to determine the ultimate consequences of this preoccupation within him, i.e., psychology.

Psychology, which works relentlessly to reduce the unknown to the known, to the quotidian and the ordinary, is the cause of the theater's abasement and its fearful loss of energy, which seems to me to have reached its lowest point. And I think both the theater and we ourselves have had enough of psychology.

I believe furthermore that we can all agree on this matter sufficiently so that there is no need to descend to the repugnant level of the modern and French theater to condemn the theater of psychology.

Stories about money, worry over money, social careerism, the pangs of love unspoiled by altruism, sexuality sugar-coated with an eroticism that has lost its mystery have nothing to do with the theater, even if they do belong to psychology. These torments, seductions, and lusts before which we are nothing but Peeping Toms gratifying our cravings, tend to go bad, and their rot turns to revolution: we must take this into account.

But this is not our most serious concern.

If Shakespeare and his imitators have gradually insinuated the idea of art for art's sake, with art on one side and life on the other, we can rest on this feeble and lazy idea only as long as the life outside endures. But there are too many signs that everything that used to sustain our lives no longer does so, that we are all mad, desperate, and sick. And I call for us to react.

This idea of a detached art, of poetry as a charm which exists only to distract our leisure, is a decadent idea and an unmistakable symptom of our power to castrate.

Our literary admiration for Rimbaud, Jarry, Lautréamont, and a few others, which has driven two men to suicide, but turned into café gossip for the rest, belongs to this idea of literary poetry, of detached art, of neutral spiritual activity which creates nothing and produces nothing; and I can bear witness that at the very moment when that kind of personal poetry which involves only the man who creates it and only at the moment he creates it broke out in its most abusive fashion, the theater was scorned more than ever before by poets who have never had the sense of direct and concerted action, nor of efficacity, nor of danger.

We must get rid of our superstitious valuation of texts and *written* poetry. Written poetry is worth reading once, and then should be destroyed. Let the dead poets make way for others. Then we might even come to see that it is our veneration for what has already been created, however beautiful and valid it may be, that petrifies us, deadens our responses, and prevents us from making contact with that underlying power, call it thought-energy, the life force, the determinism of change, lunar menses, or anything you like. Beneath the poetry of the texts, there is the actual poetry, without form and without text. And just as the efficacy of masks in the magic practices of certain tribes is exhausted—and these masks are no longer good for anything except museums—so the poetic efficacy of a text is exhausted; yet the poetry and the efficacy of the theater are exhausted least quickly of all, since they permit the *action* of what is gesticulated and pronounced, and which is never made the same way twice.

It is a question of knowing what we want. If we are prepared for war, plague, famine, and slaughter we do not even need to say so, we have only to continue as we are; continue behaving like snobs, rushing en masse to hear such and such a singer, to see such and such an admirable performance which never transcends the realm of art (and even the Russian ballet at the height of its splendor never transcended the realm of art), to marvel at such and such an exhibition of painting in which exciting shapes explode here and there but at random and without any genuine consciousness of the forces they could rouse.

This empiricism, randomness, individualism, and anarchy must cease.

Enough of personal poems, benefitting those who create them much more than those who read them.

Once and for all, enough of this closed, egoistic, and personal art.

Our spiritual anarchy and intellectual disorder is a function of the anarchy of everything else—or rather, everything else is a function of this anarchy.

I am not one of those who believe that civilization has to change in order for the theater to change; but I do believe that the theater, utilized in the highest and most difficult sense possible, has the power to influence the aspect and formation of things: and the encounter upon the stage of two passionate manifestations, two living centers, two nervous magnetisms is something as entire, true, even decisive, as, in life, the encounter of one epidermis with another in a timeless debauchery.

That is why I propose a theater of cruelty.—With this mania we all have for depreciating everything, as soon as I have said "cruelty," everybody will at once take it to mean "blood." But *"theater of cruelty"* means a theater difficult and cruel for myself first of all. And, on the level of performance, it is not the cruelty we can exercise upon each other by hacking at each other's bodies, carving up our personal anatomies, or, like Assyrian emperors, sending parcels of human ears, noses, or neatly detached nostrils through the mail, but the much more terrible and necessary cruelty which things can exercise against us. We are not free. And the sky can still fall on our heads. And the theater has been created to teach us that first of all.

Either we will be capable of returning by present-day means to this superior idea of poetry and poetry-through-theater which underlies the Myths told by the great ancient tragedians, capable once more of entertaining a religious idea of the theater (without meditation, useless contemplation, and vague dreams), capable of attaining awareness and a possession of certain dominant forces, of certain notions that control all others, and (since ideas, when they are effective, carry their energy with them) capable of recovering within ourselves those energies which ultimately create order and increase the value of life, or else we might as well abandon ourselves now, without protest, and recognize that we are no longer good for anything but disorder, famine, blood, war, and epidemics.

Either we restore all the arts to a central attitude and necessity, finding an analogy between a gesture made in painting or the theater, and a gesture made by lava in a volcanic explosion, or we must stop painting, babbling, writing, or doing whatever it is we do.

I propose to bring back into the theater this elementary magical idea, taken up by modern psychoanalysis, which consists in effecting a patient's cure by making him assume the apparent and exterior attitudes of the desired condition.

I propose to renounce our empiricism of imagery, in which the unconscious furnishes images at random, and which the poet arranges at random too, calling them poetic and hence hermetic images, as if the kind of trance that poetry provides did not have its reverberations throughout the whole sensibility, in every nerve, and as if poetry were some vague force whose movements were invariable.

I propose to return through the theater to an idea of the physical knowledge of images and the means of inducing trances, as in Chinese medicine which knows, over the entire extent of the human anatomy, at what points to puncture in order to regulate the subtlest functions.

Those who have forgotten the communicative power and magical mimesis of a gesture, the theater can reinstruct, because a gesture carries its energy with it, and there are still human beings in the theater to manifest the force of the gesture made.

To create art is to deprive a gesture of its reverberation in the organism, whereas this reverberation, if the gesture is made in the conditions and with the force required, incites the organism and, through it, the entire individuality, to take attitudes in harmony with the gesture.

The theater is the only place in the world, the last general means we still possess of directly affecting the organism and, in periods of neurosis and petty sensuality like the one in which we are immersed, of attacking this sensuality by physical means it cannot withstand.

If music affects snakes, it is not on account of the spiritual notions it offers them, but because snakes are long and coil their length upon the earth, because their bodies touch the earth at almost every point; and because the musical vibrations which are communicated to the earth affect them like a very subtle, very long massage; and I propose to treat the spectators like the snakecharmer's subjects and conduct them *by means of their organisms* to an apprehension of the subtlest notions.

At first by crude means, which will gradually be refined. These immediate crude means will hold their attention at the start.

That is why in the "theater of cruelty" the spectator is in the center and the spectacle surrounds him.

In this spectacle the sonorisation is constant: sounds, noises, cries are chosen first for their vibratory quality, then for what they represent.

Among these gradually refined means light is interposed in its turn. Light which is not created merely to add color or to brighten, and which brings its power, influence, suggestions with it. And the light of a green cavern does not sensually dispose the organism like the light of a windy day.

After sound and light there is action, and the dynamism of action: here the theater, far from copying life, puts itself whenever possible in communication with pure forces. And whether you accept or deny them, there is nevertheless a way of speaking which gives the name of "forces" to whatever brings to birth images of energy in the unconscious, and gratuitous crime on the surface.

A violent and concentrated action is a kind of lyricism: it summons up supernatural images, a bloodstream of images, a bleeding spurt of images in the poet's head and in the spectator's as well.

Whatever the conflicts that haunt the mind of a given period, I defy any spectator to whom such violent scenes will have transferred their blood, who will have felt in himself the transit of a superior action, who will have seen the extraordinary and essential movements of his thought illuminated in extraordinary deeds—the violence and blood having been placed at the service of the violence of the thought—I defy that spectator to give himself up, once outside the theater, to ideas of war, riot, and blatant murder.

So expressed, this idea seems dangerous and sophomoric. It will be claimed that example breeds example, that if the attitude of cure induces cure, the attitude of murder will induce murder. Everything depends upon the manner and the purity with which the thing is done. There is a risk. But let it not be forgotten that though a theatrical gesture is violent, it is disinterested; and that the theater teaches precisely the uselessness of the action which, once done, is not to be done, and the superior use of the state unused by the action and which, *restored,* produces a purification.

I propose then a theater in which violent physical images crush and hypnotize the sensibility of the spectator seized by the theater as by a whirlwind of higher forces.

A theater which, abandoning psychology, recounts the extraordinary, stages natural conflicts, natural and subtle forces, and presents itself first of all as an exceptional power of redirection. A theater that induces trance, as the dances of Dervishes induce trance, and that addresses itself to the organism by precise instruments, by the same means as those of certain tribal music cures which we admire on records but are incapable of originating among ourselves.

There is a risk involved, but in the present circumstances I believe it is a risk worth running. I do not believe we have managed to revitalize the world we live in, and I do not believe it is worth the trouble of clinging to; but I do propose something to get us out of our marasmus, instead of continuing to complain about it, and about the boredom, inertia, and stupidity of everything.

Eileen Darby

Jo Mielziner's celebrated set for the premiere production of Arthur Miller's *Death of a Salesman*, showing the cutaway house and the downstage playing area.

Social and technological change transformed the world in the late nineteenth and early twentieth centuries. Between 1860 and today, the United States emerged from a crippling civil war, two world wars, and the anxieties of the Cold War to become a dominant global power. However, despite the nation's emergence as a major player on the world stage, the arts in the United States were shaped by divided and contradictory impulses. The desire to imitate European models competed with a desire to bring distinctively American arts into being. Even as the Civil War threatened to destroy the nation itself, writers such as Walt Whitman, Ralph Waldo Emerson, Henry David Thoreau, and others gave voice to a national literature that both incorporated and redefined European traditions. With the global expansion of U.S. influence, especially after World War I, the question of an "American culture" became a pressing one; after World War II, certain forms of culture became one of the United States' most significant exports, exports at once assimilated, resisted, and redefined in the contemporary era of globalized culture.

In the theater, the modern era has brought with it the search for a quintessentially "American" drama in which theme, setting, and characterization explore American experience, often by invoking and then discarding styles and attitudes derived from the European stage. In a sense, American drama in the twentieth century translated the idea of American political freedom into more abstract, metaphorical, even Romantic terms, as a conflict between individual freedom and the pressures of confining social realities, such as economic hardship, social class, gender, race, sexuality. The search for an American idiom in the theater absorbs the stylistic experiments of European modernism and reshapes them, bending the formal innovation of the European theater to American issues and concerns.

"The" American Theater?

The democratic experience and populist rhetoric of American public life has generally resisted the idea of a national culture emanating from a single center like New York City or Washington, D.C. For this reason, perhaps, the dream of a national theater has repeatedly failed. In the nineteenth century, westward expansion brought theater from New York, Philadelphia, and Boston to the Midwestern cities of Chicago, St. Louis, and Kansas City, and then to Los Angeles and San Francisco, and to scores of smaller towns between the Mississippi River and the Pacific Ocean. The theater was a widely dispersed local affair. Towns often boasted theaters that could be used for opera, drama, or vaudeville and that supported local companies while also catering to touring shows with stars drawn from New York and Europe. Although a lively local theater thrived throughout the country, offering melodrama, classical plays, comedies, and other entertainments, the appetite for touring shows created a demand for organizations capable of handling scheduling problems for local theaters and regional booking agencies.

In 1896 a group of theatrical entrepreneurs headed by Charles Frohman formed a nationwide organization of booking agents called the SYNDICATE. In a sense, they created the first model of how a national theater might work in the United States. The Syndicate offered theater managers a full season of touring shows—provided that the manager contracted to deal only with the Syndicate. By gaining exclusive control over theaters on key travel routes, the Syndicate thwarted competition from other touring producers and often even denied local companies the use of local theaters. At its height, the Syndicate had exclusive rights to more than 700 theaters. It could blackball non-Syndicate performers from working by threatening producers who hired them, and it could withdraw Syndicate support from any manager who booked non-Syndicate shows or performers.

The effects of the Syndicate were profound and shaped the American theater for the next half-century. The Syndicate's grip on the theater effectively extinguished major professional theater outside New York as a source of new plays and productions; it also influenced playwriting, since the Syndicate developed plays only as commercial properties that could be successfully marketed to a general audience coast-to-coast. Although the Syndicate's power was resisted by a few famous actors and powerful producers, its approach was imitated by other groups. The parochial interests of the New York stage—where the shows of such organizations originated—became in practice the interests of the American theater, and New York became the center of theatrical production and theatrical investment. The revival of significant, professional "regional" theaters as centers of new productions—Margo Jones's Theater 47 in Dallas, the Alley Theater of Houston, the Arena Stage in Washington, D.C., the Actors Workshop of San Francisco, the Guthrie Theater in Minneapolis—had to wait until the 1940s and 1950s. The Syndicate's fortunes also point out the fallacy inherent in the notion of *an* American theater. Throughout its history, the American theater has embraced a range of dynamic and contradictory attitudes toward the stage and its place in society: New York versus the "provinces," mainstream versus elite, conventional versus experimental, commercial versus artistic. Moreover, both the Syndicate and the "regional" theaters functioned alongside a separate-but-unequal network of African American, Spanish-speaking, and ethnic theater circuits. Theatrical innovation has been spurred primarily by theaters outside the commercial mainstream, especially by small, amateur "little theaters," by university and college theaters, by community theaters, and by theaters structured primarily by racial or ethnic exclusion.

European Influence and American Innovation

The growth of American drama and theater was decisively shaped by the commercial climate of the stage and also by the United States' isolation from the energetic traditions of European theater. While there had long been an indigenous playwriting tradition, many of the most successful plays in nineteenth-century America were—in an era before copyright protection was extended to dramatic authors—productions, adaptations, or piracies of European novels and plays, as well as of American classics like Harriet Beecher Stowe's *Uncle Tom's Cabin*. Moreover, given the lucrative opportunities of touring, British and European actor/managers frequently brought shows to the United States, and some—notably the prolific playwright and actor Dion Boucicault, whose plays *The Poor of New York* (1857) and *The Octoroon* (1859) were written and successfully staged in the United States—developed plays on American themes. Although turn-of-the-century Broadway developed a home-grown version of theatrical realism—epitomized by writer/producer David Belasco's *The Governor's Lady* (1912), which reproduced the interior of a familiar theater district restaurant onstage—European experimentation made its impact on America in more indirect ways, usually only after those experiments had crystallized into a body of theatrical practices and conventions. Many major companies toured the United States. The Abbey Theater came with John Millington Synge's *The Playboy of the Western World* in 1911–1912, and the German producer Max Reinhardt brought his spectacular productions to the United States in 1912, 1914, 1924, and 1927–1928. The British director Harley Granville Barker, who sponsored Shaw's plays and had gained fame as an innovative director of Shakespeare, directed in New York in 1915; the Ballets Russes toured in 1916; and the Moscow Art Theater, whose disciples Richard Boleslavsky and Maria Ouspenskaya founded the American Laboratory Theater in 1923, performed in 1923–1924.

Many of these companies, the Abbey and the Moscow Art Theater in particular, had begun as small, independent, amateur theaters, and their work was most directly implemented in the United States by similar groups. Some innovation came from the new college and university programs in drama: George Pierce Baker's famous playwriting course at Harvard University in the first decades of the century (taken by Eugene O'Neill, among many others) and Montgomery T. Gregory's program for black writers and performers at Howard University in the 1920s were only the beginning of a concerted effort to bring theater and drama into the university curriculum and to develop a greater awareness of progressive theater. However, it largely fell to the LITTLE THEATER MOVEMENT to assimilate this new work and redirect it toward particularly American concerns. Innovation in the American theater came largely from these small companies, committed to mounting new and uncommercial work. The Chicago Little Theater, the Toy Theater of Boston, the Neighborhood Playhouse and the Washington Square Playhouse of New York, and Detroit's Arts and Crafts Theater were all in operation by 1917, and the Little Negro Theater Movement was producing plays in Harlem and Washington, D.C., as well.

The Provincetown Playhouse provides a model of the "little theaters" and their fortunes in the early twentieth century. Founded in 1915 in Provincetown, Massachusetts—an artists' retreat at the tip of Cape Cod—the company was initially a group of young amateurs intent on theater, including the playwright Susan Glaspell; her husband, George Cram Cook; and, later, Eugene O'Neill. In the first year, the players produced plays in their summer homes. In 1916 they converted an old wharf building into a small theater and produced, among other plays, O'Neill's *Bound East for Cardiff.* In the autumn, the players returned to New York and opened a small theater in Greenwich Village. The company could hardly afford complex and expensive sets and turned its efforts instead toward a simple and realistic kind of performance. Eugene O'Neill's early plays were produced by the Provincetown company, and after he became a successful Broadway playwright, he continued to open many of his plays there. Like all of the "little theaters," the Provincetown had difficulty managing the transition from a small amateur company to the larger demands of a self-sustaining professional company. It went through a series of transformations before closing in 1929, having introduced O'Neill to the stage and having staged plays by John Reed, Edna St. Vincent Millay, Susan Glaspell, Djuna Barnes, Edmund Wilson, Paul Green, Wallace Stevens, Theodore Dreiser, August Strindberg, and many others.

In the United States, the freedom to make theater has always been qualified by the need to make it pay. The challenge of sustaining artistic ambition in the commercial environment of the theater is the central narrative of the most innovative theatrical companies of the modern era. The ideal of an American theater remained tantalizing yet elusive and was often pursued in several ways, usually by developing a distinctive repertoire of plays, or by trying to define a typically American performance idiom. "Little theaters" like the Provincetown emphasized the production of American drama. Other theaters tried to produce American drama, the new European drama, and the classics for a larger audience than the "little theaters" could reach. The Theater Guild, for example, was organized in 1919 in New York as a subscription company specifically for the purpose of producing noncommercial plays. In the course of the next decade, the Guild staged plays by Shaw, Pirandello, Ibsen, and Strindberg, as well as plays by Americans like O'Neill and Elmer Rice. The Guild succeeded in incorporating American plays like O'Neill's *Strange Interlude* (1928) and Rice's *The Adding Machine* (1923) into the repertoire of serious modern drama and in bringing it to a significant public. However, following the stock market crash of 1929 and the economic depression that ensued, the Guild invested in a less adventuresome repertoire in the hopes of drawing a larger audience and so lost its original mission.

Although it sponsored an innovative selection of plays, the Theater Guild did not develop an original style of production. In 1931, several Guild members began a spin-off company—called simply the Group—for the purpose of investigating different kinds of drama and different approaches to performance. Eventually including Harold Clurman, Cheryl Crawford, Lee Strasberg, Elia Kazan, Sanford Meisner, and many others, the Group at first worked on plays examining the social ferment of the 1930s and the hardship of the Great Depression. Much as Chekhov became the centerpiece of Stanislavski's Moscow Art Theater, so the plays of Clifford Odets became the Group's standards: *Awake and Sing!, Waiting for Lefty,* and *Golden Boy.* However, the Group's most extensive contribution to the American theater was its systematic importation of Stanislavskian acting techniques. In the Group, and later in the Actors Studio, actors were trained in Stanislavski's approach to **EMOTION MEMORY** and **GIVEN CIRCUMSTANCES,** laying the groundwork for what became a distinctly "American" style of acting, acting that was emotionally spontaneous, grounded in subtext, psychologically realistic and nuanced. Nonetheless, the Group, the Studio, and the training they devised produced a generation of actors ready to meet the challenges of the burgeoning American drama of the 1940s and 1950s: Marlon Brando, Ben Gazzara, Karl Malden, Geraldine Page, Kim Stanley, Maureen Stapleton, and many others.

The impact of this acting can be seen in the great stage productions of the post-war period. The 1940s and early 1950s saw the development of a genuinely American approach to stage realism, balancing nuanced characterization with a concern for the social environment. Arthur Miller's *Death of a Salesman* and *The Crucible,* Tennessee Williams's *A Streetcar Named Desire* and *The Glass Menagerie,* and Eugene O'Neill's *The Iceman Cometh* and *Long Day's Journey into Night* demanded the subtle realism that became the hallmark of American acting and of American drama in the world repertoire. These plays—and their descendants, like the plays of Beth Henley, David Mamet, Maria Irene Fornes, August Wilson, or Sam Shepard—succeeded by criticizing American ideals and institutions while at the same time exploring the psyche of the American character. Indeed, in these plays the American character often seems to be thwarted precisely by the process of American society. The fragile beauty of Tennessee Williams's Southern belles is usually crushed by the sordid realities of modern urban life; in Shepard's *True West,* the American West becomes a mythic battleground, where a yuppie and a drifter shoot it out for control of the image. In Suzan-Lori Parks's *The America Play*, Lucy and Brazil scour the remains of a theme park, The Great Hole of History, hoping to hear the echo of The Foundling Father, who—given his remarkable likeness to The Great Man—spent his days reenacting the Lincoln assassination as a sideshow. Even Anna Deavere Smith's one-woman reenactment of the response to the Los Angeles riots of 1992, *Twilight*, takes up the challenge of confronting the imagination of "America" through the stereotypes with which it reproduces its identities.

Postwar Experiments After World War II, the most significant innovations in American theater have come from small "experimental" theater companies. In part through the influence of Antonin Artaud's conception of a **THEATER OF CRUELTY** (see Unit V), and the several tours of Jerzy Grotowski's Lab Theater of Poland, experimental theater in the 1960s and 1970s tended to reject the esthetic of stage realism in favor of producing an immediate, quintessentially *theatrical* experience for its audiences. As a result, many productions in the 1960s and 1970s—the Living Theater's *Paradise Now,* the Performance Group's *Dionysus in 69,* the Open Theater's *The Serpent,* the work of the Bread and Puppet Theater, of the San Francisco Mime Troup, of Mabou Mines, and many others—incorporated the audience as participants in the action. Many of these experiments also led to new forms of playwriting, in which classical notions of representation also were broken down. Moreover, these experiments not only led to the incorporation of a more immediate, physical esthetic into American drama (visible, too, in performance art), but also to the exploration of Brechtian epic theater: experiments with narrative (Parks's *America Play*), with an episodic epic form (Kushner's *Angels in America*), or with a more politicized performance of "character" (Anna Deavere Smith's monologues).

Indeed, American drama continued to strike a compromise with the innovations of the European theater after World War II. Eric Bentley—a brilliant scholar, director, playwright, and translator—worked indefatigably to bring Bertolt Brecht to the attention of the American theater. Brecht became particularly important in the United States as the Vietnam War and widespread civil and social discontent spurred the theater in more agitational, political directions. Feminist theater, ethnic theater, and gay and lesbian theater have all at times availed themselves of Brecht's theater theory and practice. The work of Luis Valdez and El Teatro Campesino in California in the 1960s and 1970s is a direct extension of Brecht's sense of theater. Bringing a flatbed truck to farmworkers' strikes, Teatro Campesino produced its short, political dramas to an active, involved audience and became part of the process of social change. "Absurdist" playwrights like Samuel Beckett, Harold Pinter, and Eugène Ionesco were also both produced and imitated in the United States, influencing the work of American playwrights like Edward Albee, Maria Irene Fornes, Jack Gelber, Adrienne Kennedy, David Mamet, Sam Shepard, Susan-Lori Parks, and Adriano Shaplin. Indeed, in plays like Amiri Baraka's *Dutchman* or Sam Shepard's *True West,* we can see the inflections of THEATER OF THE ABSURD in plays that are recognizably "American" in style and subject matter.

In 1935, an act of Congress established the Federal Theater Project, as a way to employ workers left unemployed by the Depression (see Aside box). The Federal Theater Project also sponsored a Negro Unit, directed by John Houseman and Orson Welles, which operated in ten cities around the United States; two of its productions, an all-black *Macbeth* and *The Swing Mikado,* were among the Federal Theater's most successful productions. The fact of a separate Negro Unit points to a different crisis in the idea of an American theater. How could a theater largely in the hands of the white, Anglo, male, middle class adequately represent the diversity of the nation's experience, particularly the experience of the oppressed? As the poet and playwright Langston Hughes observed in "Notes on Commercial Theater," published in 1940, the stage had in many ways appropriated African-American culture, systematically absorbing it into its own dominant values:

> Yep, you done taken my blues and gone.
>
> You also took my spirituals and gone.
>
> You put me in Macbeth and Carmen Jones
>
> And all kinds of Swing Mikados
>
> And in everything but what's about me—
>
> But someday somebody'll
>
> Stand up and talk about me,
>
> And write about me—
>
> Black and beautiful—

Far from representing authentic black experience in America, such theater more often confirmed the discriminatory fantasies already prominent on the stage and in society. Such stereotypes as the boozy Irishman, the dull Swede, the sunny and/or murderous Italian, and the greedy Jew—appearing even in "realistic" plays like Rice's *Street Scene* (1929), and dating back through the stereotyped slaves and Indians of Boucicault's *Octoroon*—work to reinforce the "normative" perspective of dominant culture, reflecting the attitudes, behavior, and social practices that oppress such groups in the world outside the theater. It is not surprising, then, that throughout the history of the United States, ethnic theaters have played a prominent part in maintaining the cultural identity of America's diverse ethnic populations: the Yiddish theater of New York, Polish theaters in Chicago, Scandinavian theaters throughout the Midwest, a thriving circuit of Spanish-language theaters shared by Mexico and Southwestern states from Texas to California, Cuban-influenced theater in Florida, and Puerto Rican theater in New York. Some of these theaters produced versions of classic European plays in their own accents, but most developed their own dramatic forms, as ways of maintaining themselves in the face of a brutally exclusive "American" culture.

The experience of slavery places African Americans in a different position vis-à-vis the culture of the United States, and the black theater has had a profound impact on the course of the American stage. Although an African Theater Company was founded in New York in 1821—sponsoring, among others, the brilliant Shakespearean actor Ira Aldridge (1807–1867) who left the United States for a distinguished career in Europe—in the main, African Americans had little direct access to the theater before the twentieth century. Black characters had long figured as stage villains and comic buffoons in American drama. Played by white actors in blackface makeup, these abusive types literally enacted white attitudes toward racial difference. "Jim Crow" was first popularized by the white song-and-dance man T. D. Rice in the 1830s, and more "sympathetic" characters, like Tom in the hugely popular stage adaptations of Harriet Beecher Stowe's *Uncle Tom's Cabin* (1832), were devised by white authors and played by white actors. The minstrel troupes that became popular after the Civil War for depicting romanticized vignettes of plantation life were also first

African-American Drama and Theater

(Aside)

THE FEDERAL THEATER PROJECT

If the Group Theater and the Actors Studio created an identifiably "American" approach to acting, the Federal Theater Project succeeded—briefly—in creating a truly national theater. An act of Congress established the Federal Theater Project in 1935 under the Works Projects Administration, with Hallie Flanagan Davis (1890–1969) as director. Like other WPA projects, the Federal Theater was designed both to employ workers idled by the Depression and to provide service to the community. It was an enormous undertaking; in New York City alone, half the theaters were closed by 1933 and half its population of actors unemployed. Given the mission of providing employment by hiring large casts and supporting personnel, and a commitment to dramatizing contemporary social issues, the Federal Theater developed its most notable genre, the Living Newspaper. Living Newspapers incorporated dialogue taken from newspapers and other public media into a series of vignettes, readings, films, and other techniques to a problem in current national and world affairs: the farm crisis in *Triple A Plowed Under* (1936), housing in *One-Third of a Nation* (1938), rural electrification in *Power* (1937). At its height, the Federal Theater had branches in forty states; these branches staged productions devised by the project's directors, using their own local resources, and often developed their own material. In 1936, for instance, a stage adaptation of Sinclair Lewis's *It Can't Happen Here* opened simultaneously in twenty-one theaters around the country, including black-cast and Yiddish productions.

The Federal Theater ran for four full seasons before being terminated by Congress in 1939: it financed 1,200 productions of 830 major works, at times employing more than ten thousand people, most of whom had been unemployed. Admission to its shows was inexpensive, and in an average week 500,000 people saw its productions; over its four years of production, its audiences numbered more than 30 million people. In New York alone, more than 12 million people saw its productions. However, in an era of labor unrest and the pervasive fear of outside agitation, the Newspapers were seen by the Project's enemies in government—many of whom opposed the WPA altogether—as too left-wing for government support.

Despite its demise, the United States' only truly national theater had significant influence on the course of American theater and drama. Not only did the Federal Theater have huge audiences, but it brought new audiences into the theater: 65 percent of its audiences were seeing a stage play for the first time. The Living Newspapers developed a homegrown adaptation of the techniques of European experimental theater (including Brechtian epic theater) in the United States. In this sense, the Federal Theater inspired the work of several distinguished theater companies that survived its demise, notably John Houseman's (1915–1985) Mercury Theater, which produced Mark Blitzstein's *The Cradle Will Rock*, and a distinguished series of productions of modern and classic plays—by Shaw, Büchner, Shakespeare, and others. In addition, the Negro Units of the Federal Theater operated in Seattle, Hartford, Philadelphia, Newark, Los Angeles, Boston, Birmingham, Raleigh, San Francisco, and Chicago, employing more than 800 people and staging seventy-five productions in the project's four years of operation. Most importantly, the Federal Theater enabled a generation of actors, designers, directors, and playwrights to survive the Depression, and it brought the theater powerfully into the national scene. ■

Living Newspaper

The Federal Theater Project dramatizes news events in the New York production of 1935.

performed by white actors. Later, black performers—in minstrel troupes, or in the newly popular "Negro musicals"—often had little choice other than to enact these stereotypes themselves, for such roles were the only openings available on the stage (even black theaters were usually financed and operated by white entrepreneurs). Despite small inroads like the Lafayette Theater (founded in Harlem in 1915), representing black experience to America at large was almost exclusively the prerogative of white actors, producers, playwrights, and performers. In this regard, the theater—like the institutions of literature, the press, the legal system, and state and federal government—denied African Americans their own voice.

Spurred in part by successful plays by white dramatists that self-consciously attempted to "humanize" black characters for white audiences—O'Neill's *The Emperor Jones* (1920) and *All God's Chillun Got Wings* (1924), Marc Connelly's *The Green Pastures* (1930), Paul Green's *In Abraham's Bosom* (1926), and Dubose and Dorothy Heyward's *Porgy* (1920; transformed into the Gershwin musical *Porgy and Bess* in 1935)—black actors and writers became galvanized to "stand up and talk" about themselves. Throughout the 1920s the LITTLE NEGRO THEATER MOVEMENT sponsored plays of black life largely for black audiences. The Lafayette Theater, for example, opened Willis Richardson's *The Chipwoman's Fortune* in 1923; it later became the first play by a black playwright to reach Broadway. In the 1920s and 1930s, black drama increasingly addressed the politics of racism in the United States, while also depicting the effect of racism in daily life. Several organizations worked to sponsor African-American drama and theater. W.E.B. DuBois, a founder of the National Association for the Advancement of Colored People (NAACP), used his *Crisis* magazine—in collaboration with the National Urban League's *Opportunity*—to give a series of prizes to promising African American playwrights; winners included Eulalie Spence's *Foreign Mail* (1926), Zora Neale Hurston's *Colorstruck* and *Spears* (1925), and Georgia Douglas Johnson's *Blue Blood* (1926). The NAACP also sponsored the production of plays, including Angelina Weld Grimké's influential drama of a young woman's reaction to the lynching of her father and brother, *Rachel* (1916), one of the first of a series of plays about lynching. How this important genre of black theater—and a crucial element of black experience in the United States—was both overlooked and distorted by white theater is the subject of Alice Childress's brilliant play *Trouble in Mind*, which opened off-Broadway in 1955. Finally, black colleges, universities, and even high schools also became centers for a new dramatic repertoire.

In 1921, Montgomery T. Gregory formed a department of Dramatic Arts at Howard University in Washington, D.C., and with Alain Locke developed an influential program in acting, playwriting, and theatrical production, offering the first institutionalized training for black writers and performers in the United States. In a 1926 playbill for Harlem's Krigwa Players, W.E.B. DuBois described the goals of a black theater:

> The plays of a real Negro theater must be: *One: About us.* That is, they must have plots which reveal Negro life as it is. *Two: By us.* That is, they must be written by Negro authors who understand from birth and continual association just what it means to be a Negro today. *Three: For us.* That is, the theater must cater primarily to Negro audiences and be supported and sustained by their entertainment and approval. *Fourth: Near us.* The theater must be in a Negro neighborhood near the mass of ordinary Negro people.

Throughout the 1930s and 1940s, African American playwrights and actors came into increasing national prominence, both by developing DuBois's agenda and by working to bring an authentic black drama to a wider audience. Langston Hughes wrote a number of plays in the 1930s, including the well-known *Mulatto* (1935); the Federal Theater Project produced DuBois's *Haiti* at the Lafayette Theater; and playwrights trained at Howard were produced in New York and elsewhere. The founding of the companies like the American Negro Theater in 1939, the Negro Playwrights Company in 1940, and the Negro Ensemble Company in 1957 began to meet DuBois's charge, developing the actors, the production experience, and the financing that would sustain the explosive growth of black American drama after World War II. When Lorraine Hansberry's *A Raisin in the Sun* opened in 1959, it was the first play written by a black woman to reach Broadway, the first directed by a black director (Lloyd Richards), and the first financed predominantly by African Americans. The success of *Raisin* foretold the success of black theater in the coming decades, as black playwrights—Amiri Baraka, Adrienne Kennedy, Charles Gordone, Ed Bullins, Charles Fuller, Ntozake Shange, August Wilson, Anna Deavere Smith, Suzan-Lori Parks, and many others—came to shape the American theater.

Popular Theater and Mass Culture

The tension between commercial viability and dramatic achievement is perhaps best symbolized by Broadway itself, the American theater's "magnificent invalid," where even the greatest American plays can hardly compare in terms of commercial and popular success with Broadway's most uniquely American genre: the musical. Musical theater has a long history in the United States, and in many respects its fortunes parallel those of the dramatic theater. Musical theater also witnessed the tyranny of national producing syndicates, the impact of European innovation, and the powerful contributions of black and ethnic cultures. However, the integration of song and dance, orchestral music, and (usually) a romantic plot characteristic of the Broadway musical really dates to the period of World War II, probably to Richard Rodgers and Oscar Hammerstein's *Oklahoma!* (1943) which ran for 2,248 performances (*Death of a Salesman,* in contrast, ran for 742). *Oklahoma!* provided the model not only for other Rodgers and Hammerstein hits—*Carousel* (1945), *South Pacific* (1949), *The King and I* (1951)—but for other musicals as well: Alan Jay Lerner and Frederick Loewe's updating of Shaw's *Pygmalion* in *My Fair Lady* (1956), Frank Loesser's *Guys and Dolls* (1950), and Leonard Bernstein, Stephen Sondheim, and Arthur Laurents's *West Side Story* (1957). Although the form of the Broadway musical underwent significant changes in the 1970s and 1980s, its popularity points to one of the ways that the theater has sought to recapture an audience from film and television: by emphasizing the unique excitement of a dazzling live spectacle. This is as true of Broadway hits like *High Society* (1997), which used the Cole Porter music from the 1956 film of the same name, as it is of several musicals adapted from animated films—notably *The Lion King* (1997); musicals have also adopted a wider range of musical styles and dramatic subjects such as *Rent* (1996), *Avenue Q* (2002), or *Next to Normal* (2008). The musical theater also points to the fundamental conditions of the Broadway theatrical economy as well. Musicals remain popular with producers because the huge financial investment required to mount a musical can repay much larger returns for investors than nonmusical drama.

Throughout the history of the stage in the West, important theaters have succeeded both in creating innovative drama and in creating a public. However, the American theater—if there is *an* American theater—is a different entity altogether from the citizens' theater of classical Athens, the courtly theater of Racine and Molière, or even the educated circle of subscribers to Shaw's Court Theater. In a sense, this difference can be traced to the fact that the American theater first came into force only in the twentieth century, at just the moment when other dramatic media—film and television—began to compete with it. The American theater has had to define itself in the environment of modern mass culture. Not only are film and television more accessible to most people, but the technology and distribution of such mass media have fundamentally altered our understanding both of drama and performance, and of what an audience *is*. "The American theater" has always been a critical fiction, homogenizing the diversity of stage activity in the United States, writing some forms of drama—chiefly American realistic plays—into history, and writing others out of it. Today, it may be equally artificial to separate live theater from other forms of dramatic production, forms that have massively changed the terrain where dramatic performance takes place.

American Drama in Performance and History

With the global expansion of the United States in the first two thirds of the twentieth century, the development of new modes of commerce and trade in the 1960s and 1970s (notably the multinational corporation), the breakup of the Soviet Union and its satellite states symbolized by the fall of the Berlin Wall in 1989, and with the rise of the typical networking of economics, politics, and media characteristic of contemporary globalization, "American" culture has become a widely exported commodity. Much as American culture has absorbed both immigrant and conquered cultures as part of the development of the United States, so now the image of "America" is projected around the world, on T-shirts, in cartoons, in the imagery of Mickey Mouse and Beyoncé, in television programs, in films, and of course on the Internet, where YouTube and Facebook facilitate the viral transmission of replicated images of "America" at home, abroad, and at war.

Drama and theater are also part of that projected image, and American drama has rapidly become part of a global canon of modern theater: plays such as *Death of a Salesman* and *Fences* have been performed in the People's Republic of China; *Angels in America* was produced in London before it opened in New York, and has since been produced around the world. One of the most challenging aspects of American theater, however, is what might be called its *diversity,* the way different playwrights have worked to challenge a monolithic notion of "American" culture, and the values—white, masculinist, heterosexual, middle-class, English-speaking—it asserts as definitive. This diversity emerges in several ways, not only through a writer's or a company's decision to make their own alternative perspective *count*—as Luis Valdez and El Teatro Campesino do in *Los vendidos*—but to use theatrical production to mark, make visible, "alienate" in Brecht's sense the ways the normative values of "American" culture are produced, and the kinds of work those values do.

For this reason, while there remains a large "mainstream" of stage style, much of the most adventurous work in the American theater has experimented with new, alternative ways of representing drama on the stage, and new ways of engaging its audience. The "rep and rev" of Suzan-Lori Parks's plays, the ways they "repeat and revise" a single gesture in order to high-light the *constructedness* of the body and the ways it represents itself culturally is one of these techniques; Anna Deavere Smith's effort to imitate the gestural conventions of her interview subjects does a similar kind of work, implying that those gestures are part of a common cultural repertoire, an individual act of expression that uses social means. This "alienating" of the ways "identity" is produced onstage extends to a wide range of contemporary performance. In 1983, for example, the Wooster Group's *L.S.D.—Just the High Points* set portions of Arthur Miller's *The Crucible* as a trial, literalizing the parallel with the McCarthy hearings that the play was widely thought to allegorize; in *Route 1 & 9,* the company integrated scenes from Thornton Wilder's *Our Town* into a blackface minstrel show, in effect staging the racist attitudes that "our town"—white America in this case—has both produced and disowned; in its 2007 *Hamlet,* the company performed the play in dialogue with the 1964 film of the stage production directed by John Gielgud, with Richard Burton in the title role.

This use of the stage to expose dominant or oppressive attitudes that are concealed within the monuments of American culture is also characteristic of performance works like Coco Fusco and Guillermo Gómez-Peña's *Two Undiscovered Amerindians Visit . . . ,* (which has been filmed as *The Couple in the Cage*). In the early 1990s, Gómez-Peña (a performance artist born in Mexico) and Fusco (a Cuban-American) devised a performance in which they portrayed "native" or "indigenous" inhabitants of the (fictitious) Caribbean island of Guatinaui. Wear-ing deeply layered costumes—basketball sneakers, feathered headdresses, sunglasses, bottle-cap–studded vests—Fusco and Gómez-Peña were displayed in a cage, as anthropological "dis-coveries." During the course of the performance, which was produced in several art museums around the United States, as well as in the Field Museum of Natural History in Chicago, and on a plaza in Madrid, Gómez-Peña and Fusco exhibited behavior: they watched TV, they ate, for a fee they had their photo taken with spectators, or danced, and so on. The purpose of the production, however, was less to portray an exoticized native "other" than it was to *stage* the attitudes of their audiences to the spectacle of these imprisoned, displayed people. Although we might think this an extreme or at least a special case, it might be said that what Gómez-Peña and Fusco did here—stage the audience—is a task that stretches back to Valdez's work in the 1960s, and has become one of the principal innovations of contemporary American performance.

PERFORMANCE ART

Since the mid-1960s, a variety of nondramatic performance modes have developed in Western theater that are commonly known by the generic label of "performance art." Although it is difficult to generalize about this wide range of performances, most performance art works share certain features: many (though certainly not all) are solo works, in which a performer (or performers) relates directly to an audience; the performer(s) may be working from a plan or script, but the performance is not a traditional "drama," enacting a fictitious narrative of the deeds of a fictitious "character" through "acting." Instead, in performance art, the performer uses a variety of means—monologue, physical performance, music, dance—to produce a spectacle that is "really happening" between himself or herself and the spectators. Many performance-art works of the 1970s and 1980s used the performers' bodies to explore the limits of "theater." Chris Burden, for example, staged several events in which he wounded himself before an audience: in one 1970 work, he shot himself in the arm with a pistol; in another, he was crucified on top of a Volkswagen. In one of Carolee Schneeman's works, she unwinds a long scroll from her vagina, reading it to the audience. Annie Sprinkle, once a pornographic film star, openly objectifies her body onstage for a visible audience of men (and women), as she had once done in the more covert and coercive scene of pornography; in one performance, she invites the audience onstage while she conducts her own cervical examination. Many performance art works take place outside theatrical venues, so that the performance becomes part of the everyday "performance" of street life. Linda Montano spent one year connected by a short rope to Teching Tsieh; the artists' lack of privacy was constantly on display in the streets of New York. In one of her early performances, Laurie Anderson stood on a large block of ice on a New York City street, playing her violin until the ice melted.

Several performance artists have become well-known for their monologue-performances, which range widely in technique and strategy. Anna Deavere Smith's plays—such as *Fires in the Mirror: Crown Heights, Brooklyn and Other Identities,* and *Twilight—Los Angeles, 1992*—differ from many performance art monologues in that Smith impersonates and represents a range of speakers; yet both in the brilliance of her individual performance and in her effort to perform the speakers faithfully (rather than "act" them in a theatrical sense), Smith's work touches on the "authentic" aspect of performance art. This emphasis on the "authentic," the "real," enables several performance artists to explore the relationship between identity politics and performance. In *Memory Tricks*, Marga Gomez, daughter of a Cuban theater impresario and a Puerto Rican "exotic dancer," recalls her family and childhood to interrogate the formation of Latina identity in the United States. David Drake's *The Night Larry Kramer Kissed Me* dramatizes the performer's understanding and exploration of his gay sexuality from the time of his sixth birthday, on the night of the 1969 Stonewall Riots in New York's Greenwich Village—in which gay men and lesbians protested abusive treatment by the police—through the AIDS crisis of the 1980s and 1990s.

Many artists use performance to foreground and criticize the everyday racist, sexist, and/or homophobic "performance" commonly accepted as "normal behavior" in U.S. society, and to bring into view other ways of performing identity. Adrian Piper, a light-skinned African American woman, sometimes hands out business cards to people who "ignore" her race:

I am black. I am sure that you did not realize this when you made / laughed at / agreed with that racist remark. In the past, I have attempted to alert white people to my racial identity in advance. Unfortunately, this invariably causes them to react to me as pushy, manipulative, or socially inappropriate. Therefore, my policy is to assume that white people do not make these remarks, even when they believe there are no black people present, and to distribute this card when they do. I regret any discomfort my presence is causing you, just as I am sure you regret the discomfort your racism is causing me.

Lesbian playwright Holly Hughes had written several plays—notably *The Well of Horniness, The Lady Dick,* and *Dress Suits for Hire,* which was performed by Peggy Shaw and Lois Weaver at the WOW Cafe—before developing her well-known performance piece *World Without End* in 1989. In *My Queer Body,* Tim Miller narrates the history of his sexual experience and the formation of his identity as a gay man; he undresses during the performance and performs part of *My Queer Body* in the nude, sometimes moving about the audience. Karen Finley's performances often express her outrage at the implicit and explicit violence against women in American culture; in monologues like *Constant State of Desire* and *We Keep Our Victims Ready,* she uses her body to enact and physicalize the "obscenity" of such violence. In a section of *We Keep Our Victims Ready* entitled "St. Valentine's Massacre," Finley examines the way patriarchal culture encodes a subtle hatred of women, one that women can self-destructively internalize. In performance, while Finley says, "My life is worth nothing but shit," she smears her naked body with chocolate pudding and studs it with spermlike bean sprouts, a stunning and physical image of the sexualization of violence. As the performance continues, though, she layers herself with tinsel and red candies, transforming her abjection into a strange beauty. Such performances purposefully transgress the boundaries of decorous social behavior, in part to dramatize the kind of oppression that lurks in "everyday" performance. By all accounts, audiences who have seen Finley's or Miller's performances have found them powerful and moving; but to some critics (who often proudly claim that they have not seen the performance), such performance verges on "obscenity." In 1990, conservative politicians led by then Senator Jesse Helms (Republican from North Carolina) pressured the National Endowment for the Arts to withdraw funding from four performance artists who had been recommended by the peer-review process for support. Not only were Tim Miller, Karen Finley, Holly Hughes, and John Fleck denied funding, but the Endowment's head, John Frohnmayer, subsequently resigned, and a "general standards of decency" restriction of dubious constitutionality was required of subsequent recipients of NEA support.

Perhaps the best-known autobiographical performer, however, was Spalding Gray (1941–2004). Gray began his career with The Performance Group, an avant-garde company working with **ENVIRONMENTAL THEATER** in the late 1960s and 1970s. With Elizabeth LeCompte and other members of the group, Gray collaborated on a series of performances, collectively called *The Rhode Island Trilogy—Sakonnet Point* (1975), *Rumstick Road* (1977), and *Nyatt School* (1978), followed by an epilogue, *Point Judith* (1979). The Performance Group was committed to authentic "performance" (in which the actors behave as themselves, rather than "acting" in a theatrical sense), and Gray found a sequence of *Rumstick Road*—in which he narrated events of his life

Adger W. Cowans/kenbarboza.com

Performance Art

Anna Deavere Smith as the Reverend Al Sharpton, in *Fires in the Mirror*.

to the audience—to be a particularly fertile ground for continued exploration. In the course of the next several years, Gray developed a series of autobiographical performances. In some of these works, Gray structured a certain degree of randomness in the performance: in *India and After (America)* (1979), for example, he randomly chose words from a dictionary to key part of his monologue; in *A Personal History of the American Theatre* (1980), he shuffled a collection of index cards with play titles on them and uses the series to direct his performance. Gray's more recent work was made into films, and so became known to a wider audience. The film versions of *Swimming to Cambodia* (1984) and *Monster in a Box* (1990) preserve much of the ambience of Gray's performance. In the opening

sequence of *Swimming to Cambodia*, for example, we see Gray walking through the streets of Greenwich Village, entering the Performance Garage, seating himself onstage at a long table, and opening the notebook that seems to provide the score for his performance. Gray addresses the camera and, as in his stage performances, seems to occupy a startling and fascinating middle ground between acting and being: he is clearly shaping the story, representing and constructing the narrative of his life as a kind of fiction, while at the same time claiming that quasi-fictive narrative as his own, as himself. Like other postmodern art forms, performance art evocatively explores the edge between representation and "reality," refusing to demarcate a fixed difference between them. ■

READING THE MATERIAL THEATER

As writing, drama is part of the wide horizon of literature, and throughout its history, the stage has been the site of adaptation; the Greek playwrights adapted their dramas from familiar myths, the medieval craft guilds developed original dramas from Biblical narratives, and Shakespeare famously adapted existing narratives—from classical and contemporary literature, as well as from English history—and plays.

With the rise of print, however, a different kind of "adaptation" began to take place, as playwrights and theater managers could turn a quick profit by bringing a famous novel to the stage, typically in a pirated version. In the nineteenth century, for instance, Charles Dickens's novels were frequently pirated for the stage; in versions that not only outraged Dickens, but that paid him no fees or royalties. Susan Glaspell's *Trifles*, however, represents an alternative phenomenon: the translation to the page of a work that had first found

success on the stage. In 1917, Glaspell adapted her short story "A Jury of Her Peers" from her play *Trifles*. While the story has been, perhaps, even more widely celebrated than the play, it also raises some important questions about the place of dramatic writing in the age of print. Although both works tell the same "story," they do so through very different means: how do the resources of the stage and the resources of the page contribute to the creation of a *different* work of art?

SUSAN GLASPELL
"A Jury of Her Peers" (1917)

After the success of Trifles, *Glaspell wrote a short, narrative version of the play, which has been justly celebrated for the ways it deploys a woman's narrative "point of view." Moreover, the short story also dramatizes the different resources that the theater and narrative fiction have available in order to tell the "same" story.*

When Martha Hale opened the storm-door and got the north wind, she ran back for her big woolen scarf. As she hurriedly wound that round her head her eye made a scandalized sweep of her kitchen. It was no ordinary thing that called her away—it was probably farther from ordinary than anything that had ever happened in Dickson County. But her kitchen was in no shape for leaving: bread ready for mixing, half the flour sifted and half unsifted.

She hated to see things half done; but she had been at that when they stopped to get Mr. Hale, and the sheriff came in to say his wife wished Mrs. Hale would come too—adding, with a grin, that he guessed she was getting scarey and wanted another woman along. So she had dropped everything right were it was.

"Martha!" now came her husband's impatient voice. "Don't keep folks waiting out here in the cold."

She joined the three men and the one woman waiting for her in the sheriff's car.

After she had the robes tucked in she took another look at the woman beside her. She had met Mrs. Peters the year before, at the county fair, and the thing she remembered about her was that she didn't seem like a sheriff's wife. She was small and thin and didn't have a strong voice. Mrs. Gorman, sheriff's wife before Gorman went out and Peters came in, had a voice that seemed to be backing up the law with every word. But if Mrs. Peters didn't look like a sheriff's wife, Peters made it up in looking like a sheriff—a heavy man with a big voice, who was particularly genial with the law-abiding, as if to make it plain that he knew the difference between criminals and non-criminals. And right there it came into Mrs. Hale's mind that this man who was so lively with all of them was going to the Wrights' now as a sheriff.

"The country's not very pleasant this time of year," Mrs. Peters at last ventured.

Mrs. Hale scarcely finished her reply, for they had gone up a little hill and could see the Wright place, and seeing it did not make her feel like talking. It looked very lonely this cold March morning. It had always been a lonesome-looking place. It

was down in a hollow, and the poplar trees around it were lonely-looking trees. The men were looking at it and talking about what had happened. The county attorney was bending to one side, scrutinizing the place as they drew up to it.

"I'm glad you came with me," Mrs. Peters said nervously, as the two women were about to follow the men in through the kitchen door.

Even after she had her foot on the doorstep, Martha Hale had a moment of feeling she could not cross this threshold. And the reason it seemed she couldn't cross it now was because she hadn't crossed it before. Time and time again it had been in her mind, "I ought to go over and see Minnie Foster"—she still thought of her as Minnie Foster, though for twenty years she had been Mrs. Wright. And then there was always something to do and Minnie Foster would go from her mind. But *now* she could come.

The men went over to the stove. The women stood close together by the door. Young Henderson, the county attorney, turned around and said, "Come up to the fire, ladies."

Mrs. Peters took a step forward, then stopped. "I'm not—cold," she said.

And so the two women stood by the door, at first not even so much as looking around the kitchen.

The men talked about what a good thing it was the sheriff had sent his deputy out that morning to make a fire for them, and then Sheriff Peters stepped back from the stove, unbuttoned his outer coat, and leaned his hands on the kitchen table in a way that seemed to mark the beginning of official business. "Now, Mr. Hale," he said in a sort of semi-official voice, "before we move things about, you tell Mr. Henderson just what it was you saw when you came here yesterday morning."

The county attorney was looking around the kitchen.

"By the way," he asked, "has anything been moved?" He turned to the sheriff. "Are things just as you left them yesterday?"

Peters looked from cupboard to sink; to a small worn rocker a little to one side of the kitchen table.

"It's just the same."

"Well, Mr. Hale," said the county attorney, "tell just what happened when you came here yesterday morning."

Mrs. Hale, still leaning against the door, had that sinking feeling of the mother whose child is about to speak a piece. Lewis often wandered along and got things mixed up in a story. She hoped he would tell this straight and plain, and not say unnecessary things that would make it harder for Minnie Foster. He didn't begin at once, and she noticed that he looked queer, as if thinking of what he had seen here yesterday.

"Yes, Mr. Hale?" the county attorney reminded.

"Harry and I had started to town with a load of wood," Mrs. Hale's husband began.

Harry was Mrs. Hale's oldest boy. He wasn't with them now, for the wood never got to town yesterday and he was taking it this morning, so he hadn't been home when the sheriff stopped to say he wanted Mr. Hale to come over to the Wright place and tell the county attorney his story there, where he could point it all out. With all Mrs. Hale's other emotions came the fear Harry wasn't dressed warm enough—they hadn't any of them realized how that north wind did bite.

"We come along this road," Hale was going on, "and as we got in sight of the house I says to Harry, 'I'm goin' to see if I can't get John Wright to take a telephone.' You see," he explained to Henderson, "unless I can get somebody to go in with me they won't come out this branch road except for a price I can't pay. I'd spoke to Wright about it before; but he put me off, saying folks talked too much anyway, and all he asked was peace and quiet—guess you know about how much he talked himself. But I thought maybe if I went to the house and talked about it before his wife, and said all the women—folks liked the telephones, and that in this lonesome stretch of road it would be a good thing—well, I said to Harry that that was what I was going to say—though I said at the same time that I didn't know as what his wife wanted made much difference to John—"

Now, there he was!—saying things he didn't need to say. Mrs. Hale tried to catch her husband's eye, but fortunately the county attorney interrupted with:

"Let's talk about that a little later, Mr. Hale. I do want to talk about that, but I'm anxious now to know just what happened when you got here."

When he began this time, it was deliberately, as if he knew it were important.

"I didn't see or hear anything. I knocked at the door. And still it was all quiet inside. I knew they must be up—it was past eight o'clock. So I knocked again, louder, and I thought I heard somebody say, 'Come in.' I wasn't sure—I'm not sure yet. But I opened the door—this door," jerking a hand toward the door by which the two women stood, "and there, in that rocker"—pointing to it—"sat Mrs. Wright."

Everyone in the kitchen looked at the rocker. It came into Mrs. Hale's mind that this chair didn't look in the least like Minnie Foster—the Minnie Foster of twenty years before. It was a dingy red, with wooden rungs up the back, and the middle rung gone; the chair sagged to one side.

"How did she—look?" the county attorney was inquiring.

"Well," said Hale, "she looked—queer."

"How do you mean—queer?"

He took out note-book and pencil. Mrs. Hale did not like the sight of that pencil. She kept her eye on her husband, as if to keep him from saying unnecessary things that would go into the book and make trouble.

Hale spoke guardedly: "Well, as if she didn't know what she was going to do next. And kind of—done up."

"How did she seem to feel about your coming?"

"Why, I don't think she minded—one way or other. She didn't pay much attention. I said, 'Ho' do, Mrs. Wright. It's cold, ain't it?' And she said, 'Is it?'—and went on pleatin' of her apron.

"Well, I was surprised. She didn't ask me to come up to the stove, but just set there, not even lookin' at me. And so I said, 'I want to see John.'

"And then she—laughed. I guess you would call it a laugh.

"I thought of Harry and the team outside, so I said, a little sharp, 'Can I see John?' 'No,' says she—kind of dull like. 'Ain't he home?' says I. Then she looked at me. 'Yes,' says she, 'he's home.' 'Then why can't I see him?' I asked her, out of patience with her now. 'Cause he's dead,' says she, just as quiet and dull—and fell to pleatin' her apron. 'Dead?' says I, like you do when you can't take in what you've heard.

"She just nodded her head, not getting a bit excited, but rockin' back and forth.

"'Why—where is he?'" says I, not knowing *what* to say.

"She just pointed upstairs—like this"—pointing to the room above.

"I got up, with the idea of going up there myself. By this time I—didn't know what to do. I walked from there to here, then I says "'Why, what did he die of?'"

"'He died of a rope round his neck,' says she; and just went on pleatin' at her apron."

Hale stopped speaking, staring at the rocker. Nobody spoke; it was as if all were seeing the woman who had sat there the morning before.

"And what did you do then?" the attorney asked.

"I went out and called Harry, I thought I might—need help. I got Harry in, and we went upstairs." His voice fell almost to a whisper. "There he was—lying over the—"

"I think I'd rather have you go into that upstairs," the county attorney interrupted, "where you can point it all out. Just go on now with the rest of the story."

"Well, my first thought was to get that rope off. It looked—"

He stopped; he did not say how it looked.

"But Harry, he went up to him and he said, 'No, he's dead all right, and we'd better not touch anythin'.' So we went downstairs.

"She was still sitting that same way. 'Has anybody been notified?' I asked. 'No,' says she, unconcerned.

"'Who did this, Mrs. Wright?' said Harry. He said it business-like, and she stopped pleatin' at her apron. 'I don't know,' she says. 'You don't *know?*' says Harry. 'Weren't you sleepin' in the bed with him?' 'Yes,' says she, 'but I was on the inside.' 'Somebody slipped a rope round his neck and strangled him, and you

didn't wake up?' says Harry. 'I didn't wake up,' she said after him.

"We may have looked as if we didn't see how that could be, for after a minute she said, 'I sleep sound.'

"Harry was going to ask her more questions, but I said maybe that weren't our business; maybe we ought to let her tell her story first to the coroner or the sheriff. So Harry went fast as he could over to High Road—the Rivers' place, where there's a telephone."

"And what did she do when she knew you had gone for the coroner?"

"She moved from that chair to this one over here, and just sat there with her hands held together and looking down. I got a feeling that I ought to make some conversation, so I said I had come in to see if John wanted to put in a telephone; and at that she started to laugh, and then she stopped and looked at me—scared."

At sound of a moving pencil the man who was telling the story looked up.

"I dunno—maybe it wasn't scared; I wouldn't like to say it was. Soon Harry got back, and then Dr. Lloyd came, and you, Mr. Peters, and so I guess that's all I know that you don't."

He said this with relief, moved as if relaxing. The county attorney walked to the stair door.

"I guess we'll go upstairs first—then out to the barn and around there."

He paused and looked around the kitchen.

"You're convinced there was nothing important here?" he asked the sheriff. "Nothing that would—point to any motive?"

The sheriff too looked all around. "Nothing here but kitchen things," he said, with a little laugh for the insignificance of kitchen things.

The county attorney was looking at the cupboard. He opened the upper part and looked in. After a moment he drew his hand away sticky.

"Here's a nice mess," he said resentfully.

The two women had drawn nearer, and now the sheriff's wife spoke.

"Oh—her fruit," she said, looking to Mrs. Hale for understanding. "She worried about that when it turned so cold last night. She said the fire would go out and her jars might burst."

Mrs. Peters' husband broke into a laugh.

"Well, can you beat the women! Held for murder, and worrying about her preserves!"

The young attorney set his lips.

"I guess before we're through with her she may have something more serious than preserves to worry about."

"Oh, well," said Mrs. Hale's husband, with good-natured superiority, "women are used to worrying over trifles."

The two women moved a little closer together. Neither of them spoke. The county attorney seemed to remember his manners—and think of his future.

"And yet," said he, with the gallantry of a young politician, "for all their worries, what would we do without the ladies?"

The women did not speak. He went to the sink to wash his hands, turned to wipe them on the roller towel, pulled it for a cleaner place.

"Dirty towels! Not much of a housekeeper, would you say, ladies?" He kicked his foot against some dirty pans under the sink.

"There's a great deal of work to be done on a farm," said Mrs. Hale stiffly.

"To be sure. And yet"—with a little bow to her—"I know there are some Dickson County farm-houses that do not have such roller towels."

"Those towels get dirty awful quick. Men's hands aren't always as clean as they might be."

"Ah, loyal to your sex, I see," he laughed. He gave her a keen look. "But you and Mrs. Wright were neighbours. I suppose you were friends too."

Martha Hale shook her head.

"I've seen little enough of her of late years. I've not been in this house—it's more than a year."

"And why was that? You didn't like her?"

"I liked her well enough," she replied with spirit. "Farmers' wives have their hands full, Mr. Henderson. And then—" She looked around the kitchen.

"Yes?" he encouraged.

"It never seemed a very cheerful place," said she, more to herself than to him.

"No," he agreed; "I don't think anyone would call it cheerful. I shouldn't say she had the home-making instinct."

"Well, I don't know as Wright had either," she muttered.

"You mean they didn't get on very well?"

"No; I don't mean anything," she answered, with decision. "But I don't think a place would be any the cheerfuler for John Wright's bein' in it."

"I'd like to talk to you about that a little later, Mrs. Hale." He moved towards the stair door, followed by the two men.

"I suppose anything Mrs. Peters does'll be all right?" the sheriff inquired. "She was to take in some clothes for her, you know—and a few little things. We left in such a hurry yesterday."

The county attorney looked at the two women they were leaving alone among the kitchen things.

"Yes—Mrs. Peters," he said, his glance resting on the woman who was not Mrs. Peters, the big farmer woman who stood behind the sheriff's wife. "Of course Mrs. Peters is one of us," he added in a manner of entrusting responsibility. "And keep your eye out, Mrs. Peters, for anything that might be of use. No telling; you women might come upon a clue to the motive—and that's the thing we need."

Mr. Hale rubbed his face in the fashion of a slow man getting ready for a pleasantry. "But would the women know a clue if they did come upon it?" he said. Having delivered himself of this, he followed the others through the stair door.

The women stood motionless, listening to the footsteps, first upon the stairs, then in the room above them.

Then, as if releasing herself from something too strange, Mrs. Hale began to arrange the dirty pans under the sink, which the county attorney's disdainful push of the foot had upset.

"I'd hate to have men coming into my kitchen, snoopin' round and criticizing."

"Of course it's no more than their duty," said the sheriff's wife, in her timid manner.

"Duty's all right, but I guess that deputy sheriff that come out to make the fire might have got a little of this on." She gave the roller towel a pull. "Wish I'd thought of that sooner! Seems mean to talk about her for not having things slicked up, when she had to come away in such a hurry."

She looked around the kitchen. Certainly it was not "slicked up." Her eye was held by a bucket of sugar on a low shelf. The cover was off the wooden bucket, and beside it was a paper bag—half full.

Mrs. Hale moved towards it.

"She was putting this in there," she said to herself—slowly.

She thought of the flour in her kitchen at home—half sifted, half not sifted. She had been interrupted, and had left things half done. What had interrupted Minnie Foster? Why had that work been left half done? She made a move as if to finish it—unfinished things always bothered her, and then she saw that Mrs. Peters was watching her, and she didn't want Mrs. Peters to get that feeling she had of work begun and then—for some reason—not finished.

"It's a shame about her fruit," she said, going to the cupboard. "I wonder if it's all gone."

"Here's one that's all right," she said at last. She held it towards the light. "This is cherries, too," She looked again. "I declare I believe that's the only one.

"She'll feel awful bad, after all her hard work in the hot weather. I remember the afternoon I put up my cherries last summer."

She put the bottle on the table, and was about to sit down in the rocker. But something kept her from sitting in that chair. She stood looking at it, seeing the woman who had sat there "pleatin' at her apron."

The thin voice of the sheriff's wife broke in upon her: "I must be getting those things from the front room closet." She opened the door into the other room, started in, stepped back. "You coming with me, Mrs. Hale?" she asked nervously. "You—you could help me get them."

They were soon back. "My!" said Mrs. Peters, dropping the things on the table and hurrying to the stove.

Mrs. Hale stood examining the clothes the woman who was being detained in town had said she wanted.

"Wright was close!" she exclaimed, holding up a shabby black skirt that bore the marks of much making over. "I think maybe that's why she kept so much to herself. I s'pose she felt she couldn't do her part; and then, you don't enjoy things when you feel shabby. She used to wear pretty clothes and be lively—when she was Minnie Foster, one of the town girls, singing in the choir. But that—oh, that was twenty years ago."

With a carefulness in which there was something tender, she folded the shabby clothes and piled them at one corner of the table. She looked up at Mrs. Peters, and there was something in the other woman's look that irritated her.

"She don't care," she said to herself. "Much difference it makes to her whether Minnie Foster had pretty clothes when she was a girl."

Then she looked again, and she wasn't so sure; in fact, she

hadn't at any time been sure about Mrs. Peters. She had that shrinking manner, and yet her eyes looked as if they could see a long way into things.

"This all you was to take in?" asked Mrs. Hale.

"No," said the sheriff's wife; "she said she wanted an apron. Funny thing to want," she ventured in her nervous way, "for there's not much to get you dirty in jail, goodness knows. But I suppose just to make her feel more natural. She said they were in the bottom drawer of this cupboard. Yes—here they are. And then her little shawl that always hung on the stair door."

She took the small grey shawl from behind the door leading upstairs.

Suddenly Mrs. Hale took a quick step towards the other woman.

"Mrs. Peters!"

"Yes, Mrs. Hale?"

"Do you think she—did it?"

Mrs. Peters looked frightened. "Oh, I don't know," she said, in a voice that seemed to shrink from the subject.

"Well, I don't think she did," affirmed Mrs. Hale. "Asking for an apron, and her little shawl. Worryin' about her fruit."

"Mr. Peters says—" Footsteps were heard in the room above; she stopped, looked up, then went on in a lowered voice: "Mr. Peters says—it looks bad for her. Mr. Henderson is awful sarcastic in a speech, and he's going to make fun of her saying she didn't wake up."

For a moment Mrs. Hale had no answer. Then, "Well, I guess John Wright didn't wake up—when they was slippin' that rope under his neck," she muttered.

"No, it's *strange*," breathed Mrs. Peters. "They think it was such a funny way to kill a man."

"That's just what Mr. Hale said," said Mrs. Hale, in a resolutely natural voice. "There was a gun in the

house. He says that's what he can't understand."

"Mr. Henderson said, coming out, that what was needed for the case was a motive. Something to show anger—or sudden feeling."

"Well, I don't see any signs of anger around here," said Mrs. Hale. "I don't—"

She stopped. Her eye was caught by a dishtowel in the middle of the kitchen table. Slowly she moved towards the table. One half of it was wiped clean, the other half untidy. Her eyes made a slow, almost unwilling turn to the bucket of sugar and the half-empty bag beside it. Things begun—and not finished.

She stepped back. "Wonder how they're finding things upstairs? I hope she had it in better shape up there. Seems kind of *sneaking*, locking her up in town and coming out here to get her own house to turn against her!"

"But, Mrs. Hale," said the sheriff's wife, "the law is the law."

"I s'pose it is," answered Mrs. Hale shortly.

She turned to the stove, saying something about that fire not being much to brag of.

"The law is the law—and a bad stove is a bad stove. How'd you like to cook on this?" with the poker pointing to the broken lining. She opened the oven door. The thought of Minnie Foster trying to bake in that oven—and the thought of her never going over to see Minnie Foster—

She was startled by hearing Mrs. Peters say, "A person gets discouraged—and loses heart."

The sheriff's wife had looked from the stove to the sink—the pail of water which has been carried in from outside. The two women stood there silent, above them the footsteps of the men who were looking for evidence against the woman who had worked in that kitchen. That look of seeing into things, of seeing through a thing to something else, was in the eyes of the sheriff's wife now. When

Mrs. Hale next spoke to her, it was gently.

"Better loosen up your things, Mrs. Peters. We'll not feel them when we go out."

Mrs. Peters went to the back of the room to hang up the fur tippet she was wearing. "Why, she was piecing a quilt," she exclaimed, and held up a large sewing basket piled high with quilt pieces.

Mrs. Hale spread some of the blocks on the table.

"It's log-cabin pattern," she said, putting several of them together. "Pretty, isn't it?"

They were so engaged with the quilt that they did not hear the footsteps on the stairs. As the stair door opened Mrs. Hale was saying, "Do you suppose she was going to quilt it, or just knot it?"

The sheriff threw up his hands.

"They wonder whether she was going to quilt it, or just knot it!"

There was a laugh for the ways of women, a warming of hands over the stove, and then the county attorney said briskly, "Well, let's go right out to the barn and get that cleared up."

"I don't see as there's anything so strange," Mrs. Hale said resentfully, after the outside door had closed on the three men—"our taking up our time with little things while we're waiting for them to get the evidence. I don't see as it's anything to laugh about."

"Of course they've got awful important things on their minds," said the sheriff's wife apologetically.

They returned to an inspection of the blocks for the quilt. Mrs. Hale was looking at the fine, even sewing, preoccupied with thoughts of the woman who had done that sewing, when she heard the sheriff's wife say, in a startled tone, "Why, look at this one."

"The sewing," said Mrs. Peters, in a troubled way. "All the rest of them have been so nice and even—but—this one. Why, it looks as if she didn't know what she was about!"

Their eyes met—something flashed to life, passed between them; then, as if with an effort, they seemed to pull away from each other. A moment Mrs. Hale sat there, her fingers upon those stitches so unlike the rest of the sewing. Then she had pulled a knot and drawn the threads.

"Oh, what are you doing. Mrs. Hale?" asked the sheriff's wife.

"Just pulling out a stitch or two that's not sewed very good," said Mrs. Hale mildly.

"I don't think we ought to touch things," Mrs. Peters said.

"I'll just finish up this end," answered Mrs. Hale.

She threaded a needle and started to replace bad sewing with good. Then in that thin, timid voice, she heard: "Mrs. Hale!"

"Yes, Mrs. Peters?"

"What do you suppose she was so—nervous about?"

"Oh, *I* don't know," said Mrs. Hale, as if dismissing a thing not important enough to spend much time on. "I don't know as she was—nervous. I sew awful queer sometimes when I'm just tired."

"Well, I must get these clothes wrapped. They may be through sooner than we think. I wonder where I could find a piece of paper—and string."

"In that cupboard, maybe," suggested Mrs. Hale.

One piece of the crazy sewing remained unripped. Mrs. Peters' back turned. Martha Hale scrutinized that piece, compared it with the dainty, accurate stitches of the other blocks. The difference was startling. Holding this block it was hard to remain quiet, as if the distracted thoughts of the woman who had perhaps turned to it to try and quiet herself were communicating themselves to her.

"Here's a bird-cage," Mrs. Peters said. "Did she have a bird, Mrs. Hale?"

"Why, I don't know whether she did or not." She turned to look at the cage Mrs. Peters was holding up. "I've not been here in so long." She sighed. "There was a man round last year selling canaries cheap—but I don't know as she took one. Maybe she did. She used to sing real pretty herself."

"Seems kind of funny to think of a bird here. But she must have had one—or why would she have a cage? I wonder what happened to it."

"I suppose maybe the cat got it," suggested Mrs. Hale, resuming her sewing.

"No; she didn't have a cat. She's got that feeling some people have about cats—being afraid of them. When they brought her to our house yesterday, my cat got in the room, and she was real upset and asked me to take it out."

"My sister Bessie was like that," laughed Mrs. Hale.

The sheriff's wife did not reply. The silence made Mrs. Hale turn. Mrs. Peters was examining the bird-cage.

"Look at this door," she said slowly. "It's broke. One hinge has been pulled apart."

Mrs. Hale came nearer.

"Looks as if someone must have been—rough with it."

Again their eyes met—startled, questioning, apprehensive. For a moment neither spoke nor stirred. Then Mrs. Hale, turning away, said brusquely. "If they're going to find any evidence, I wish they'd be about it. I don't like this place."

"But I'm awful glad you came with me, Mrs. Hale." Mrs. Peters put the bird-cage on the table and sat down. "It would be lonesome for me—sitting here alone."

"Yes, it would, wouldn't it?" agreed Mrs. Hale. She had picked up the sewing, but now it dropped to her lap, and she murmured: "But I tell you what I *do* wish, Mrs. Peters. I wish I had come over sometimes when she was here. I wish—I had."

"But of course you were awful busy, Mrs. Hale. Your house—and your children."

"I could've come. I stayed away because it weren't cheerful—and that's why I ought to have come. I"—she looked around—"I've never liked this place. Maybe because it's down in a hollow and you don't see the road. I don't know what it is, but it's a lonesome place, and always was. I wish I had come over to see Minnie Foster sometimes. I can see now—"

"Well, you mustn't reproach yourself. Somehow we just don't see how it is with other folks till—something comes up."

"Not having children makes less work," mused Mrs. Hale, "but it makes a quiet house. And Wright out to work all day—and no company when he did come in. Did you know John Wright, Mrs. Peters?"

"Not to know him. I've seen him in town. They say he was a good man."

"Yes—good," conceded John Wright's neighbour grimly. "He didn't drink, and kept his word as well as most, I guess, and paid his debts. But he was a hard man, Mrs. Peters. Just to pass the time of day with him—" She shivered. "Like a raw wind that gets to the bone." Her eye fell upon the cage on the table before her, and she added, "I should think she would've wanted a bird!"

Suddenly she leaned forward, looking intently at the cage. "But what do you s'pose went wrong with it?"

"I don't know," returned Mrs. Peters; "unless it got sick and died."

But after she said this she reached over and swung the broken door. Both women watched it.

"You didn't know—her?" Mrs. Hale asked.

"Not till they brought her yesterday," said the sheriff's wife.

"She—come to think of it, she was kind of like a bird herself. Real sweet and pretty, but kind of timid and—flutterly. How—she—did—change."

Finally, as if struck with a happy thought and relieved to get back to every-day things: "Tell you what, Mrs. Peters, why don't you take the quilt in with you? It might take up her mind."

"Why, I think that's a real nice idea, Mrs. Hale. There couldn't possibly be any objection to that, could there? Now, just what will I take? I wonder if her patches are in here?" They turned to the sewing basket.

"Here's some red," said Mrs. Hale, bringing out a roll of cloth. Underneath this was a box. "Here, maybe her scissors are in here—and her things." She held it up. "What a pretty box! I'll warrant that was something she had a long time ago—when she was a girl."

She held it in her hand a moment; then, with a little sigh, opened it.

Instantly her hand went to her nose. "Why!"

Mrs. Peters drew nearer—then turned away.

"There's something wrapped up in this piece of silk," faltered Mrs. Hale.

"This isn't her scissors," said Mrs. Peters, in a shrinking voice.

Mrs. Hale raised the piece of silk. "Oh, Mrs. Peters!" she cried. "It's—"

Mrs. Peters bent closer.

"It's the bird," she whispered.

"But, Mrs. Peters!" cried Mrs. Hale. "*Look* at it! Its *neck*—look at its neck! It's all—other side *to*."

The sheriff's wife again bent closer.

"Somebody wrung its neck," said she, in a voice that was slow and deep.

The eyes of the two women met—this time clung together in a look of dawning comprehension, of growing horror. Mrs. Peters looked from the dead bird to the broken door of the cage. Again their eyes met. And just then there was a sound at the outside door.

Mrs. Hale slipped the box under the quilt pieces in the basket. The county attorney and sheriff came in.

"Well, ladies," said the attorney, as one turning from serious things to little pleasantries, "have you decided whether she was going to quilt it or knot it?"

"We think," said the sheriff's wife hastily, "that she was going to knot it."

"Well, that's very interesting, I'm sure." He caught sight of the cage. "Has the bird flown?"

"We think the cat got it," said Mrs. Hale in a prosaic voice.

He was walking up and down, as if thinking something out.

"Is there a cat?" he asked absently.

Mrs. Hale shot a look up at the sheriff's wife.

"Well, not *now*," said Mrs. Peters. "They're superstitious, you know; they leave."

The county attorney did not heed her. "No sign at all of anyone having come in from the outside," he said to Peters, continuing an interrupted conversation. "Their own rope. Now let's go upstairs again and go over it, piece by piece. It would have to have been someone who knew just the—"

The stair door closed behind them and their voices were lost.

The two women sat motionless, not looking at each other, but as if peering into something and at the same time holding back. When they spoke now it was as if they were afraid of what they were saying, but could not help saying it.

"She liked the bird," said Martha Hale. "She was going to bury it in that pretty box."

"When I was a girl," said Mrs. Peters, under her breath, "my kitten—there was a boy took a hatchet, and before my eyes—before I could get there—" She covered her face an instant. "If they hadn't held me back I would have"—she caught herself, and finished weakly—"hurt him."

Then they sat without speaking or moving.

"I wonder how it would seem," Mrs. Hale began, as if feeling her way over strange ground—"never to have had any children around." Her eyes made a sweep of the kitchen. "No, Wright wouldn't like the bird—a thing that sang. She used to sing. He killed that too."

Mrs. Peters moved. "Of course we don't know who killed the bird."

"I knew John Wright," was the answer.

"It was an awful thing was done in this house that night, Mrs. Hale," said the sheriff's wife. "Killing a man while he slept—slipping a thing round his neck that choked the life out of him."

Mrs. Hale's hand went to the birdcage. "His neck. Choked the life out of him."

"We don't *know* who killed him," whispered Mrs. Peters wildly. "We don't *know*."

Mrs. Hale had not moved. "If there had been years and years of nothing, then a bird to sing to you, it would be awful—still, after the bird was still."

"I know what stillness is," whispered Mrs. Peters. "When we homesteaded in Dakota, and my first baby died—after he was two years old—and me with no other then—"

Mrs. Hale stirred. "How soon do you suppose they'll be through looking for the evidence?"

"I know what stillness is," repeated Mrs. Peters. Then she too pulled back. "The law has got to punish crime, Mrs. Hale."

"I wish you'd seen Minnie Foster when she wore a white dress with blue ribbons, and stood up there in the choir and sang."

The picture of that girl, the thought that she had lived neighbour to her for twenty years, and had let her die for lack of life, was suddenly more than the woman cold bear.

"Oh, I *wish* I'd come over here once in a while!" she cried. "That was a crime! That was a crime! Who's going to punish *that*?"

"We mustn't—take on," said Mrs. Peters, with a frightened look towards the stairs.

"I might 'a' *known* she needed help! I tell you, it's *queer,* Mrs. Peters. We live close together, and we live far apart. We all go through the same things—it's all just a different kind of the same thing! If it weren't—why do you and I *know*—what we know this minute?"

Seeing the jar of fruit on the table, she reached for it. "If I was you I wouldn't *tell* her her fruit was gone! Tell her it *ain't.* Tell her it's all right—all of it. Here—take this in to prove it to her! She—she may never know whether it was broke or not."

Mrs. Peters took the bottle of fruit as if glad to take it—as if touching a familiar thing, having something to do, could keep her from something else. She looked about for something to wrap the fruit in, took a petticoat from the pile of clothes she had brought from the front room, nervously started winding that round the bottle.

"My!" she began, in a high voice, "it's a good thing the men couldn't hear us! Getting all stirred up over a little thing like a—dead canary. As if that could have anything to do with—with—My, wouldn't they *laugh?*"

There were footsteps on the stairs.

"Maybe they would," muttered Mrs. Hale—"maybe they wouldn't."

"No, Peters," said the county attorney, "it's all perfectly clear, except the reason for doing it. But you know juries when it comes to women. If there was some definite thing—something to *show.* Something to make a story about. A thing that would connect up with this clumsy way of doing it."

Mrs. Hale looked at Mrs. Peters. Mrs. Peters was looking at her. Quickly they looked away from one another. The outer door opened and Mr. Hale came in.

"I've nailed back that board we ripped off," he said.

"Much obliged, Mr. Hale," said the sheriff. "We'll be getting along now."

"I'm going to stay here awhile by myself," the county attorney suddenly announced. "You can send Frank out for me, can't you?" he asked the sheriff. "I want to go over everything. I'm not satisfied we can't do better."

Again, for one brief moment, the women's eyes met.

The sheriff came up to the table.

"Did you want to see what Mrs. Peters was going to take in?"

The county attorney picked up the apron. He laughed.

"Oh, I guess they're not very dangerous things the ladies have picked out."

Mrs. Hale's hand was on the sewing basket in which the box was concealed. She felt that she ought to take her hand off the basket. She did not seem able to. She picked up one of the quilt blocks she had piled on to cover the box. She had a fear that if he took up the basket she would snatch it from him.

But he did not take it. With another laugh he turned away, saying, "No, Mrs. Peters doesn't need supervising. For that matter, a sheriff's wife is married to the law. Ever think of it that way, Mrs. Peters?"

Mrs. Peters had turned her face away. "Not—just that way," she said.

"Married to the law!" chuckled Mrs. Peters' husband. He moved towards the door into the front room, and said to the county attorney, "I just want you to come here a minute, George. We ought to take a look at these windows."

"Oh—windows!" scoffed the county attorney.

"We'll be leaving in a second, Mr. Hale," Mr. Peters told the farmer, as he followed the county attorney into the other room.

"Can't be leavin' too soon to suit me," muttered Hale, and went out.

Again, for one final moment, the two women were alone in that kitchen.

Martha Hale sprang up, her hands tight together, looking at that other woman, with whom it rested. At first she could not see her eyes, for the sheriff's wife had not turned back since she turned away at that suggestion of being married to the law. Slowly, unwillingly, Mrs. Peters turned her head until her eyes met the eyes of the other woman. There was a moment when they held each other in a steady, burning look in which there was no evasion nor flinching. Then Martha Hale's eyes pointed the way to the basket in which was hidden the thing that would convict the third woman—that woman who was not there, and yet who had been there with them through that hour.

For a moment Mrs. Peters did not move. And then she did it. Threw back the quilt pieces, got the box, tried to put it in her hand-bag. It was too big. Desperately she opened it, started to take the bird out. But there she broke—she could not touch the bird. She stood there helpless, foolish.

There was a sound at the door. Martha Hale snatched the box from the sheriff's wife and got it in the pocket of her big coat just as the sheriff and the county attorney came back into the kitchen.

"Well, Henry," said the county attorney, facetiously, "at least we found out that she was not going to quilt it. She was going to—what is it you call it, ladies?"

Mrs. Hale's hand was against the pocket of her coat.

"We call it—knot it," was her answer.

THE END ■

Martha Swope

The conflict in Sam Shepard's *True West* escalates when Austin (Gary Sinise) confronts Lee (John Malkovitch) after a night of stealing toasters.

William B. Carter

The Angel appears above Prior Walter in Tony Kushner's *Angels in America, Part I: Millennium Approaches.*

This scene from August Wilson's *Fences* shows how Wilson's attention to the play's social environment has been translated into a detailed mise-en-scène; here, James Earl Jones plays the role of Troy Maxon.

Joan Marcus

Susan Glaspell

Susan Glaspell (1882–1948) was born in Iowa, studied at Drake University in Des Moines and at the University of Chicago, and then briefly pursued a career as a journalist. With her husband, George Cram Cook, she founded the Provincetown Playhouse and wrote many of the plays it produced: *Suppressed Desires* (1914, written with Cook), a spoof of the vogue for psychoanalysis among New York's intellectual elite; *Trifles* (1916); *Close the Book* (1917); *A Woman's Honor* (1918); and *Tickless Time* (1918, again written with Cook). After the reorganization of the Provincetown company in 1921, Glaspell wrote a series of full-length, often experimental, plays: *Inheritors* (1920), *The Verge* (1921), and *Alison's House* (1930). *Alison's House,* based loosely on the life of Emily Dickinson and her family, won Glaspell the Pulitzer Prize in 1930. Glaspell then retired from playwriting and largely from the theater as well, returning briefly to serve as the director of the Mid-West Play Bureau for the Federal Theater Project.

Trifles is an important play in the development of American realism. It poses a distinct contrast to Eugene O'Neill's early plays, with which it shared the Provincetown stage. O'Neill's realistic plays attempt to filter an abstract, metaphysical longing into the drab world of his down-and-out drifters and sailors. Glaspell's drama more directly examines the values and behavior of the society she brings to the stage. In *Trifles*—and in the short story "A Jury of Her Peers," which she adapted from the play the following year—Glaspell considers the relationship between truth, power, and gender. The play is a murder mystery. A local man, John Wright, has been found dead, and his wife, Minnie, is suspected of killing him. Called to investigate, County Attorney George Henderson, Sheriff Henry Peters, and neighbor Lewis Hale readily assume a masculine prerogative to discover the truth of John Wright's murder, telling their wives to remain in the kitchen out of the way. However, the truth of the crime is in fact concealed *in* the kitchen, and only the women are able to discover it. Glaspell shows the audience that the "trifles" of the women's world are the signs of a reality wholly unreadable to the men, precisely because it is a world they regard as feminine, and therefore unimportant and uninteresting. *Trifles,* that is, works to subvert our notions of reality and truth by suggesting how such ideas are constructed within a specific social order—the masculine order of modern society.

Trifles

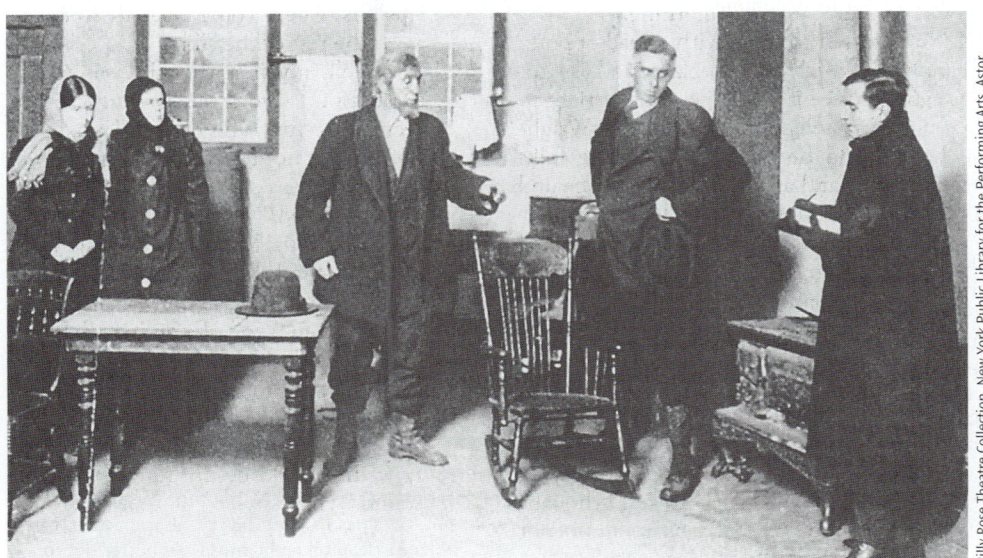

The Provincetown Players' 1917 production of Susan Glaspell's *Trifles*.

Trifles

A PLAY IN ONE ACT

Susan Glaspell

CHARACTERS

COUNTY ATTORNEY, *George Henderson*
SHERIFF, *Henry Peters*
LEWIS HALE, *a neighboring farmer*
MRS. PETERS

MRS. HALE

THE SETTING: *The kitchen in the now abandoned farmhouse of John Wright*

SCENE: *The kitchen in the now abandoned farmhouse of John Wright, a gloomy kitchen, and left without having been put in order—unwashed pans under the sink, a loaf of bread outside the breadbox, a dish towel on the table—other signs of incompleted work. At the rear the outer door opens and the* SHERIFF *comes in followed by the* COUNTY ATTORNEY *and* HALE. *The* SHERIFF *and* HALE *are men in middle life, the* COUNTY ATTORNEY *is a young man; all are much bundled up and go at once to the stove. They are followed by the two women—the* SHERIFF's *wife first; she is a slight wiry woman, a thin nervous face.* MRS. HALE *is larger and would ordinarily be called more comfortable looking, but she is disturbed now and looks fearfully about as she enters. The women have come in slowly, and stand close together near the door.*

COUNTY ATTORNEY: (*Rubbing his hands.*) This feels good. Come up to the fire, ladies.

MRS. PETERS: (*After taking a step forward.*) I'm not—cold.

5 SHERIFF: (*Unbuttoning his overcoat and stepping away from the stove as if to mark the beginning of official business.*) Now, Mr. Hale, before we move things about, you explain to Mr. Henderson just what you saw when you came here yesterday morning.

COUNTY ATTORNEY: By the way, has anything been moved? Are

10 things just as you left them yesterday?

SHERIFF: (*Looking about.*) It's just the same. When it dropped below zero last night I thought I'd better send Frank out this morning to make a fire for us—no use getting pneumonia with a big case on, but I told him not to touch anything except

15 the stove—and you know Frank.

COUNTY ATTORNEY: Somebody should have been left here yesterday.

SHERIFF: Oh—yesterday. When I had to send Frank to Morris Center for that man who went crazy—I want you to know I

20 had my hands full yesterday, I knew you could get back from Omaha by today and as long as I went over everything here myself—

COUNTY ATTORNEY: Well, Mr. Hale, tell just what happened when you came here yesterday morning.

25 HALE: Harry and I had started to town with a load of potatoes. We came along the road from my place and as I got here I said, "I'm going to see if I can't get John Wright to go in with me on a party telephone." I spoke to Wright about it once before and he put me off, saying folks talked too much anyway, and

30 all he asked was peace and quiet—I guess you know about how much he talked himself; but I thought maybe if I went to the house and talked about it before his wife, though I said to Harry that I didn't know as what his wife wanted made much difference to John—

COUNTY ATTORNEY: Let's talk about that later, Mr. Hale. I do   35
want to talk about that, but tell now just what happened when
you got to the house.

HALE: I didn't hear or see anything; I knocked at the door, and
still it was all quiet inside. I knew they must be up, it was
past eight o'clock. So I knocked again, and I thought I heard   40
somebody say, "Come in." I wasn't sure, I'm not sure yet, but
I opened the door—this door (*Indicating the door by which
the two women are still standing.*) and there in that rocker—
(*Pointing to it.*) sat Mrs. Wright.

(*They all look at the rocker.*)

COUNTY ATTORNEY: What—was she doing?   45

HALE: She was rockin' back and forth. She had her apron in her
hand and was kind of—pleating it.

COUNTY ATTORNEY: And how did she—look?

HALE: Well, she looked queer.

COUNTY ATTORNEY: How do you mean—queer?   50

HALE: Well, as if she didn't know what she was going to do next.
And kind of done up.

COUNTY ATTORNEY: How did she seem to feel about your coming?

HALE: Why, I don't think she minded—one way or other. She
didn't pay much attention. I said, "How do, Mrs. Wright, it's   55
cold, ain't it?" And she said, "Is it?"—and went on kind of
pleating at her apron. Well, I was surprised; she didn't
ask me to come up to the stove, or to set down, but just
sat there, not even looking at me, so I said, "I want to see
John." And then she—laughed. I guess you would call it a   60
laugh. I thought of Harry and the team outside, so I said
a little sharp: "Can't I see John?" "No," she says, kind o'
dull like. "Ain't he home?" says I. "Yes," says she, "he's
home." "Then why can't I see him?" I asked her, out of
patience. "'Cause he's dead," says she. "*Dead?*" says I. She just   65
nodded her head, not getting a bit excited, but rockin'
back and forth. "Why—where is he?" says I, not knowing
what to say. She just pointed upstairs—like that (*Himself
pointing to the room above.*) I got up, with the idea of going
up there. I walked from there to here—then I says, "Why,   70
what did he die of?" "He died of a rope round his neck,"
says she, and just went on pleatin' at her apron. Well, I
went out and called Harry. I thought I might—need help.
We went upstairs and there he was lyin'—

COUNTY ATTORNEY: I think I'd rather have you go into that   75
upstairs, where you can point it all out. Just go on now with
the rest of the story.

HALE: Well, my first thought was to get that rope off. It looked
. . . (*Stops, his face twitches.*) . . . but Harry, he went up to him,
and he said, "No, he's dead all right, and we'd better not touch   80

anything." So we went back down stairs. She was still sitting that same way. "Has anybody been notified?" I asked. "No," says she, unconcerned. "Who did this, Mrs. Wright?" said
85 Harry. He said it businesslike—and she stopped pleatin' of her apron. "I don't know," she says. "You don't *know*?" says Harry. "No," says she. "Weren't you sleepin' in the bed with him?" says Harry. "Yes," says she, "but I was on the inside." "Somebody slipped a rope round his neck and strangled him and you didn't wake up?" says Harry. "I didn't wake up," she
90 said after him. We must 'a looked as if we didn't see how that could be, for after a minute she said, "I sleep sound." Harry was going to ask her more questions but I said maybe we ought to let her tell her story first to the coroner, or the sheriff, so Harry went fast as he could to Rivers' place, where there's a
95 telephone.
COUNTY ATTORNEY: And what did Mrs. Wright do when she knew that you had gone for the coroner?
HALE: She moved from that chair to this one over here (*Pointing to a small chair in the corner.*) and just sat there with her
100 hands held together and looking down. I got a feeling that I ought to make some conversation, so I said I had come in to see if John wanted to put in a telephone, and at that she started to laugh, and then she stopped and looked at me—scared. (*The* COUNTY ATTORNEY, *who has had his*
105 *notebook out, makes a note.*) I dunno, maybe it wasn't scared. I wouldn't like to say it was. Soon Harry got back, and then Dr. Lloyd came, and you, Mr. Peters, and so I guess that's all I know that you don't.
COUNTY ATTORNEY: (*Looking around.*) I guess we'll go upstairs
110 first—and then out to the barn and around there. (*To the* SHERIFF.) You're convinced that there was nothing important here—nothing that would point to any motive.
SHERIFF: Nothing here but kitchen things.

(*The* COUNTY ATTORNEY *after again looking around the kitchen, opens the door of a cupboard closet. He gets up on a chair and looks on a shelf. Pulls his hand away, sticky.*)

COUNTY ATTORNEY: Here's a nice mess.

(*The women draw nearer.*)

115 MRS. PETERS: (*To the other woman.*) Oh, her fruit; it did freeze. (*To the* COUNTY ATTORNEY.) She worried about that when it turned so cold. She said the fire'd go out and her jars would break.
SHERIFF: Well, can you beat the women! Held for murder and
120 worryin' about her preserves.
COUNTY ATTORNEY: I guess before we're through she may have something more serious than preserves to worry about.
HALE: Well, women are used to worrying over trifles.

(*The two women move a little closer together.*)

COUNTY ATTORNEY: (*With the gallantry of a young politician.*)
125 And yet, for all their worries, what would we do without the ladies? (*The women do not unbend. He goes to the sink, takes a dipperful of water from the pail and pouring it into a basin, washes his hands. Starts to wipe them on the roller towel, turns it for a cleaner place.*) Dirty towels! (*Kicks his foot against the*
130 *pans under the sink.*) Not much of a housekeeper, would you say, ladies?

MRS. HALE: (*Stiffly.*) There's a great deal of work to be done on a farm.
COUNTY ATTORNEY: To be sure. And yet (*With a little bow to her.*)
135 I know there are some Dickson county farmhouses which do not have such roller towels.

(*He gives it a pull to expose its full length again.*)

MRS. HALE: Those towels get dirty awful quick. Men's hands aren't always as clean as they might be.
COUNTY ATTORNEY: Ah, loyal to your sex, I see. But you and Mrs. Wright were neighbors. I suppose you were friends,
140 too.
MRS. HALE: (*Shaking her head.*) I've not seen much of her of late years. I've not been in this house—it's more than a year.
COUNTY ATTORNEY: And why was that? You didn't like her?
MRS. HALE: I liked her all well enough. Farmers' wives have their
145 hands full, Mr. Henderson. And then—
COUNTY ATTORNEY: Yes—?
MRS. HALE: (*Looking about.*) It never seemed a very cheerful place.
COUNTY ATTORNEY: No—it's not cheerful. I shouldn't say she had the homemaking instinct.
150
MRS. HALE: Well, I don't know as Wright had, either.
COUNTY ATTORNEY: You mean that they didn't get on very well?
MRS. HALE: No, I don't mean anything. But I don't think a place'd be any cheerfuller for John Wright's being in it.
COUNTY ATTORNEY: I'd like to talk more of that a little later.
155 I want to get the lay of things upstairs now.

(*He goes to the left, where three steps lead to a stair door.*)

SHERIFF: I suppose anything Mrs. Peters does'll be all right. She was to take in some clothes for her, you know, and a few little things. We left in such a hurry yesterday.
COUNTY ATTORNEY: Yes, but I would like to see what you take,
160 Mrs. Peters, and keep an eye out for anything that might be of use to us.
MRS. PETERS: Yes, Mr. Henderson.

(*The women listen to the men's steps on the stairs, then look about the kitchen.*)

MRS. HALE: I'd hate to have men coming into my kitchen, snooping around and criticising.
165

(*She arranges the pans under sink which the* COUNTY ATTORNEY *had shoved out of place.*)

MRS. PETERS: Of course it's no more than their duty.
MRS. HALE: Duty's all right, but I guess that deputy sheriff that came out to make the fire might have got a little of this on. (*Gives the roller towel a pull.*) Wish I'd thought of that sooner. Seems mean to talk about her for not having things slicked up
170 when she had to come away in such a hurry.
MRS. PETERS: (*Who has gone to a small table in the left rear corner of the room, and lifted one end of a towel that covers a pan.*) She had bread set.

(*Stands still.*)

MRS. HALE: (*Eyes fixed on a loaf of bread beside the breadbox,*
175 *which is on a low shelf at the other side of the room. Moves*

slowly toward it.) She was going to put this in there. (*Picks up loaf, then abruptly drops it. In a manner of returning to familiar things.*) It's a shame about her fruit. I wonder if it's all gone. (*Gets up on the chair and looks.*) I think there's 180 some here that's all right, Mrs. Peters. Yes—here; (*Holding it toward the window.*) this is cherries, too. (*Looking again.*) I declare I believe that's the only one. (*Gets down, bottle in her hand. Goes to the sink and wipes it off on the outside.*) She'll 185 feel awful bad after all her hard work in the hot weather. I remember the afternoon I put up my cherries last summer.

(*She puts the bottle on the big kitchen table, center of the room. With a sigh, is about to sit down in the rocking-chair. Before she is seated realizes what chair it is; with a slow look at it, steps back. The chair which she has touched rocks back and forth.*)

MRS. PETERS: Well, I must get those things from the front room closet. (*She goes to the door at the right, but after looking into the other room, steps back.*) You coming with me, Mrs. Hale? 190 You could help me carry them.

(*They go in the other room; reappear,* MRS. PETERS *carrying a dress and skirt,* MRS. HALE *following with a pair of shoes.*)

MRS. PETERS: My, it's cold in there.

(*She puts the clothes on the big table, and hurries to the stove.*)

MRS. HALE: (*Examining the skirt.*) Wright was close. I think maybe that's why she kept so much to herself. She didn't even belong to the Ladies Aid. I suppose she felt she couldn't do her 195 part, and then you don't enjoy things when you feel shabby. She used to wear pretty clothes and be lively, when she was Minnie Foster, one of the town girls singing in the choir. But that—oh, that was thirty years ago. This all you was to take in?

200 MRS. PETERS: She said she wanted an apron. Funny thing to want, for there isn't much to get you dirty in jail, goodness knows. But I suppose just to make her feel more natural. She said they was in the top drawer in this cupboard. Yes, here. And then her little shawl that always hung behind the door. (*Opens stair 205 door and looks.*) Yes, here it is.

(*Quickly shuts door leading upstairs.*)

MRS. HALE: (*Abruptly moving toward her.*) Mrs. Peters?
MRS. PETERS: Yes, Mrs. Hale?
MRS. HALE: Do you think she did it?
MRS. PETERS: (*In a frightened voice.*) Oh, I don't know.
210 MRS. HALE: Well, I don't think she did. Asking for an apron and her little shawl. Worrying about her fruit.
MRS. PETERS: (*Starts to speak, glances up, where footsteps are heard in the room above. In a low voice.*) Mr. Peters says it looks bad for her. Mr. Henderson is awful sarcastic in a speech 215 and he'll make fun of her sayin' she didn't wake up.
MRS. HALE: Well, I guess John Wright didn't wake when they was slipping that rope under his neck.
MRS. PETERS: No, it's strange. It must have been done awful crafty and still. They say it was such a—funny way to kill a man, 220 rigging it all up like that.
MRS. HALE: That's just what Mr. Hale said. There was a gun in the house. He says that's what he can't understand.

MRS. PETERS: Mr. Henderson said coming out that what was needed for the case was a motive; something to show anger, or—sudden feeling. 225
MRS. HALE: (*Who is standing by the table.*) Well, I don't see any signs of anger around here. (*She puts her hand on the dish towel which lies on the table, stands looking down at table, one half of which is clean, the other half messy.*) It's wiped to here. (*Makes a move as if to finish work, then turns and looks at loaf 230 of bread outside the breadbox. Drops towel. In that voice of coming back to familiar things.*) Wonder how they are finding things upstairs. I hope she had it a little more red-up up there. You know, it seems kind of *sneaking.* Locking her up in town and then coming out here and trying to get her own house to 235 turn against her!
MRS. PETERS: But Mrs. Hale, the law is the law.
MRS. HALE: I s'pose 'tis. (*Unbuttoning her coat.*) Better loosen up your things, Mrs. Peters. You won't feel them when you go out. 240

(MRS. PETERS *takes off her fur tippet, goes to hang it on hook at back of room, stands looking at the under part of the small corner table.*)

MRS. PETERS: She was piecing a quilt.

(*She brings the large sewing basket and they look at the bright pieces.*)

MRS. HALE: It's log cabin pattern. Pretty, isn't it? I wonder if she was goin' to quilt it or just knot it?

(*Footsteps have been heard coming down the stairs. The* SHERIFF *enters followed by* HALE *and the* COUNTY ATTORNEY.)

SHERIFF: They wonder if she was going to quilt it or just knot it!

(*The men laugh; the women look abashed.*)

COUNTY ATTORNEY: (*Rubbing his hands over the stove.*) Frank's 245 fire didn't do much up there, did it? Well, let's go out to the barn and get that cleared up.

(*The men go outside.*)

MRS. HALE: (*Resentfully.*) I don't know as there's anything so strange, our takin' up our time with little things while we're waiting for them to get the evidence. (*She sits down at the big 250 table smoothing out a block with decision.*) I don't see as it's anything to laugh about.
MRS. PETERS: (*Apologetically.*) Of course they've got awful important things on their minds.

(*Pulls up a chair and joins* MRS. HALE *at the table.*)

MRS. HALE: (*Examining another block.*) Mrs. Peters, look at this 255 one. Here, this is the one she was working on, and look at that sewing! All the rest of it has been so nice and even. And look at this! It's all over the place! Why, it looks as if she didn't know what she was about!

(*After she has said this they look at each other, then start to glance back at the door. After an instant* MRS. HALE *has pulled at a knot and ripped the sewing.*)

260 MRS. PETERS: Oh, what are you doing, Mrs. Hale?

MRS. HALE: (*Mildly.*) Just pulling out a stitch or two that's not sewed very good. (*Threading a needle.*) Bad sewing always made me fidgety.

MRS. PETERS: (*Nervously.*) I don't think we ought to touch things.

265 MRS. HALE: I'll just finish up this end. (*Suddenly stopping and leaning forward.*) Mrs. Peters?

MRS. PETERS: Yes, Mrs. Hale?

MRS. HALE: What do you suppose she was so nervous about?

MRS. PETERS: Oh—I don't know. I don't know as she was nervous.

270 I sometimes sew awful queer when I'm just tired. (MRS. HALE *starts to say something, looks at* MRS. PETERS, *then goes on sewing.*) Well, I must get these things wrapped up. They may be through sooner than we think. (*Putting apron and other things together.*) I wonder where I can find a piece of paper,

275 and string.

MRS. HALE: In that cupboard, maybe.

MRS. PETERS: (*Looking in cupboard.*) Why, here's a birdcage. (*Holds it up.*) Did she have a bird, Mrs. Hale?

MRS. HALE: Why, I don't know whether she did or not—I've not

280 been here for so long. There was a man around last year selling canaries cheap, but I don't know as she took one; maybe she did. She used to sing real pretty herself.

MRS. PETERS: (*Glancing around.*) Seems funny to think of a bird here. But she must have had one, or why would she have a

285 cage? I wonder what happened to it.

MRS. HALE: I s'pose maybe the cat got it.

MRS. PETERS: No, she didn't have a cat. She's got that feeling some people have about cats—being afraid of them. My cat got in her room and she was real upset and asked me to take it out.

290 MRS. HALE: My sister Bessie was like that. Queer, ain't it?

MRS. PETERS: (*Examining the cage.*) Why, look at this door. It's broke. One hinge is pulled apart.

MRS. HALE: (*Looking too.*) Looks as if someone must have been rough with it.

295 MRS. PETERS: Why, yes.

(*She brings the cage forward and puts it on the table.*)

MRS. HALE: I wish if they're going to find any evidence they'd be about it. I don't like this place.

MRS. PETERS: But I'm awful glad you came with me, Mrs. Hale. It would be lonesome for me sitting here alone.

300 MRS. HALE: It would, wouldn't it? (*Dropping her sewing.*) But I tell you what I do wish, Mrs. Peters. I wish I had come over sometimes when *she* was here. I—(*Looking around the room.*)—wish I had.

MRS. PETERS: But of course you were awful busy, Mrs. Hale—

305 your house and your children.

MRS. HALE: I could've come. I stayed away because it weren't cheerful—and that's why I ought to have come. I—I've never liked this place. Maybe because it's down in a hollow and you don't see the road. I dunno what it is, but it's a lonesome place

310 and always was. I wish I had come over to see Minnie Foster sometimes. I can see now—

(*Shakes her head.*)

MRS. PETERS: Well you mustn't reproach yourself, Mrs. Hale. Somehow we just don't see how it is with other folks until— something comes up.

MRS. HALE: Not having children makes less work—but it makes a 315 quiet house, and Wright out to work all day, and no company when he did come in. Did you know John Wright, Mrs. Peters?

MRS. PETERS: Not to know him; I've seen him in town. They say he was a good man. 320

MRS. HALE: Yes—good; he didn't drink, and kept his word as well as most, I guess, and paid his debts. But he was a hard man, Mrs. Peters. Just to pass the time of day with him—(*Shivers.*) Like a raw wind that gets to the bone. (*Pauses, her eye falling on the cage.*) I should think she would 'a wanted a bird. But 325 what do you suppose went with it?

MRS. PETERS: I don't know, unless it got sick and died.

(*She reaches over and swings the broken door, swings it again. Both women watch it.*)

MRS. HALE: You weren't raised round here, were you? (MRS. PETERS *shakes her head.*) You didn't know—her?

MRS. PETERS: Not till they brought her yesterday. 330

MRS. HALE: She—come to think of it, she was kind of like a bird herself—real sweet and pretty, but kind of timid and— fluttery. How—she—did—change. (*Silence; then as if struck by a happy thought and relieved to get back to every day things.*) Tell you what, Mrs. Peters, why don't you take the quilt in 335 with you? It might take up her mind.

MRS. PETERS: Why, I think that's a real nice idea, Mrs. Hale. There couldn't possibly be any objection to it, could there? Now, just what would I take? I wonder if her patches are in here—and her things. 340

(*They look in the sewing basket.*)

MRS. HALE: Here's some red. I expect this has got sewing things in it. (*Brings out a fancy box.*) What a pretty box. Looks like something somebody would give you. Maybe her scissors are in here. (*Opens box. Suddenly puts her hand to her nose.*) Why—(MRS. PETERS *bends nearer, then turns her face away.*) 345 There's something wrapped up in this piece of silk.

MRS. PETERS: Why, this isn't her scissors.

MRS. HALE: (*Lifting the silk.*) Oh, Mrs. Peters—its—

(MRS. PETERS *bends closer.*)

MRS. PETERS: It's the bird.

MRS. HALE: (*Jumping up.*) But, Mrs. Peters—look at it! Its neck! 350 Look at its neck! It's all—other side *to*.

MRS. PETERS: Somebody—wrung—its—neck.

(*Their eyes meet. A look of growing comprehension, of horror. Steps are heard outside.* MRS. HALE *slips box under quilt pieces, and sinks into her chair. Enter* SHERIFF *and* COUNTY ATTORNEY. MRS. PETERS *rises.*)

COUNTY ATTORNEY: (*As one turning from serious things to little pleasantries.*) Well, ladies, have you decided whether she was going to quilt it or knot it? 355

MRS. PETERS: We think she was going to—knot it.

COUNTY ATTORNEY: Well, that's interesting, I'm sure. (*Seeing the birdcage.*) Has the bird flown?

MRS. HALE: (*Putting more quilt pieces over the box.*) We think the—cat got it. 360

COUNTY ATTORNEY: (*Preoccupied.*) Is there a cat?

(MRS. HALE *glances in a quick covert way at* MRS. PETERS.)

MRS. PETERS: Well, not now. They're superstitious, you know. They leave.

365 COUNTY ATTORNEY: (*To sheriff* PETERS, *continuing an interrupted conversation.*) No sign at all of anyone having come from the outside. Their own rope. Now let's go up again and go over it piece by piece. (*They start upstairs.*) It would have to have been someone who knew just the—

(MRS. PETERS *sits down. The two women sit there not looking at one another, but as if peering into something and at the same time holding back. When they talk now it is in the manner of feeling their way over strange ground, as if afraid of what they are saying, but as if they cannot help saying it.*)

MRS. HALE: She liked the bird. She was going to bury it in that
370 pretty box.
MRS. PETERS: (*In a whisper.*) When I was a girl—my kitten—there was a boy took a hatchet, and before my eyes—and before I could get there—(*Covers her face an instant.*) If they hadn't held me back I would have—(*Catches herself, looks upstairs*
375 *where steps are heard, falters weakly.*)—hurt him.
MRS. HALE: (*With a slow look around her.*) I wonder how it would seem never to have had any children around. (*Pause.*) No, Wright wouldn't like the bird—a thing that sang. She used to sing. He killed that, too.
380 MRS. PETERS: (*Moving uneasily.*) We don't know who killed the bird.
MRS. HALE: I knew John Wright.
MRS. PETERS: It was an awful thing was done in this house that night, Mrs. Hale. Killing a man while he slept, slipping a rope
385 around his neck that choked the life out of him.
MRS. HALE: His neck. Choked the life out of him.

(*Her hand goes out and rests on the birdcage.*)

MRS. PETERS: (*With rising voice.*) We don't know who killed him. We don't know.
MRS. HALE: (*Her own feeling not interrupted.*) If there'd been
390 years and years of nothing, then a bird to sing to you, it would be awful—still, after the bird was still.
MRS. PETERS: (*Something within her speaking.*) I know what stillness is. When we homesteaded in Dakota, and my first baby died—after he was two years old, and me with no other
395 then—
MRS. HALE: (*Moving.*) How soon do you suppose they'll be through, looking for the evidence?
MRS. PETERS: I know what stillness is. (*Pulling herself back.*) The law has got to punish crime, Mrs. Hale.
400 MRS. HALE: (*Not as if answering that.*) I wish you'd seen Minnie Foster when she wore a white dress with blue ribbons and stood up there in the choir and sang. (*A look around the room.*) Oh, I *wish* I'd come over here once in a while! That was a crime! That was a crime! Who's going to punish that?
405 MRS. PETERS: (*Looking upstairs.*) We mustn't—take on.
MRS. HALE: I might have known she needed help! I know how things can be—for women. I tell you, it's queer, Mrs. Peters. We live close together and we live far apart. We all go through the same things—it's all just a different kind of the same thing. (*Brushes*
410 *her eyes; noticing the bottle of fruit, reaches out for it.*) If I was you

I wouldn't tell her her fruit was gone. Tell her it *ain't*. Tell her it's all right. Take this in to prove it to her. She—she may never know whether it was broke or not.
MRS. PETERS: (*Takes the bottle, looks about for something to wrap
415 it in, takes petticoat from the clothes brought from the other room, very nervously begins winding this around the bottle. In a false voice.*) My, it's a good thing the men couldn't hear us. Wouldn't they just laugh! Getting all stirred up over a little thing like a—dead canary. As if that could have anything to
420 do with—with—wouldn't they *laugh!*

(*The men are heard coming down stairs.*)

MRS. HALE: (*Under her breath.*) Maybe they would—maybe they wouldn't.
COUNTY ATTORNEY: No, Peters, it's all perfectly clear except a reason for doing it. But you know juries when it comes to women. If there was some definite thing. Something to
425 show—something to make a story about—a thing that would connect up with this strange way of doing it—

(*The women's eyes meet for an instant. Enter* HALE *from outer door.*)

HALE: Well, I've got the team around. Pretty cold out there.
COUNTY ATTORNEY: I'm going to stay here a while by myself. (*To the
SHERIFF.*) You can send Frank out for me, can't you? I want to go
430 over everything. I'm not satisfied that we can't do better.
SHERIFF: Do you want to see what Mrs. Peters is going to take in?

(*The* COUNTY ATTORNEY *goes to the table, picks up the apron, laughs.*)

COUNTY ATTORNEY: Oh, I guess they're not very dangerous things the ladies have picked out. (*Moves a few things about,
disturbing the quilt pieces which cover the box. Steps back.*) 435
No, Mrs. Peters doesn't need supervising. For that matter, a sheriff's wife is married to the law. Ever think of it that way, Mrs. Peters?
MRS. PETERS: Not—just that way.
SHERIFF: (*Chuckling.*) Married to the law. (*Moves toward the other* 440
room.*) I just want you to come in here a minute, George. We ought to take a look at these windows.
COUNTY ATTORNEY: (*Scoffingly.*) Oh, windows!
SHERIFF: We'll be right out, Mr. Hale.

(HALE *goes outside. The* SHERIFF *follows the* COUNTY ATTORNEY
into the other room. Then MRS. HALE *rises, hands tight together,
looking intensely at* MRS. PETERS, *whose eyes make a slow turn,
finally meeting* MRS. HALE'S. *A moment* MRS. HALE *holds her, then
her own eyes point the way to where the box is concealed. Suddenly*
MRS. PETERS *throws back quilt pieces and tries to put the box in the
bag she is wearing. It is too big. She opens box, starts to take bird
out, cannot touch it, goes to pieces, stands there helpless. Sound of
a knob turning in the other room.* MRS. HALE *snatches the box and
puts it in the pocket of her big coat. Enter* COUNTY ATTORNEY *and
SHERIFF.*)

COUNTY ATTORNEY: (*Facetiously.*) Well, Henry, at least we found 445
out that she was not going to quilt it. She was going to—what is it you call it, ladies?
MRS. HALE: (*Her hand against her pocket.*) We call it—knot it, Mr. Henderson.

Sophie Treadwell

Sophie Treadwell (1885–1970) had a distinguished career as a journalist, novelist, and playwright, writing one of the most enduring of American plays, *Machinal*. Treadwell was born in Stockton, California, and raised by her mother in San Francisco. She entered the University of California, Berkeley in 1902, working to support herself and taking shorthand and typing courses—requisite skills for office employment—graduating with a degree in French in 1906. After a brief stint as a teacher in a California mining town, she moved to Los Angeles in 1907, where she worked as the secretary to internationally known actress Helena Modjeska. Modjeska hired Treadwell to assist her with her memoirs, and encouraged her to submit her fledgling plays to theaters for production; she also gave Treadwell acting instruction and encouraged her to perform. In 1908, she moved back to San Francisco, working as the theater critic for the *San Francisco Bulletin*. Treadwell's first "performance" came off the stage; for a series of eighteen articles, "An Outcast at the Christian Door," Treadwell disguised herself as a prostitute, to explore the hard lives of women working the street. The series was a brilliant success, and launched Treadwell's principal career as a journalist. She was sent to Europe during World War I as a war correspondent, returning in 1915 to settle in New York, where she gained fame for her coverage of the Mexican revolution, notably for her interviews with the victorious president Venustiano Carranza and with the revolutionary leader Pancho Villa in his hideout in 1921.

The 1920s witnessed the range of Treadwell's success; her interview with Villa provided the background for her first Broadway play, *Gringo* (1922) and her novel *Lusita* (1931). Her comedy *Lonely Lee,* starring Helen Hayes, was successful in out-of-town tryouts in 1923, but her producer was uninterested in bringing it to New York; she produced it under the title *O Nightingale* in New York in 1925, playing a secondary role under the stage name Constance Eliot. When *Machinal* was staged in 1928 it became an instant sensation, and was soon performed in London—under the title *The Life Machine* (1931)—and in Moscow in 1933. Richard Boleslavsky, a former actor with the Moscow Art Theater, gave a celebrated series of lectures in New York in the early 1920s: these lectures not only provided the foundation for the importation of Stanislavsky's "method" to the United States, but were inspirational to actors and playwrights who attended them, including Treadwell. But Treadwell also became involved in a troubling scandal. She had sent a play on the life of Edgar Allan Poe to the celebrated actor John Barrymore, and in 1924 was surprised to learn that Barrymore was promoting a new play—apparently written by his wife—about Poe. Suspicious, Treadwell attended a reading of the play and, convinced that her work had been plagiarized, brought a lawsuit against Barrymore to stop the production. Although Barrymore settled, and the show was not opened (Treadwell did not sue for damages, only to prevent Barrymore from using her play without proper attribution), Treadwell was widely criticized in the press for seeming to prey unscrupulously on the famous actor. The experience led Treadwell to become an activist for the copyright protection of dramatic writing, and she insisted on and received royalties for her productions in Moscow. The Poe play, *Plumes in the Dust*, was produced in 1936.

Although Treadwell continued to work as a successful journalist, her later plays—including *Ladies Leave* (1929), *Lone Valley* (1939), *Hope for a Harvest* (1942), *Highway* (1944)—did not rival the success of *Machinal*. When she died in 1970, she bequeathed her papers to the University of Arizona, and stipulated that royalties from her works be assigned to the Roman Catholic diocese of Tucson, and directed to the education of Native Americans.

Machinal

Despite its expressionistic texture, *Machinal* arose from one of the most celebrated trials of the late 1920s. Ruth Snyder, a housewife in suburban New York City, was convicted of murdering her husband with her lover, Judd Gray; both were executed, and Snyder was the first woman to be executed in the electric chair in New York. But from this sensational story,

Treadwell crafted an expressionist parable focused on the oppressive character—and the specific oppression of women—of modern industrial society. The play is structured around a series of nine "episodes," each of which sets the Young Woman in a quintessential "scene" of modern life: at work, at home, on the honeymoon, raising children, and so on. But within each of these episodes, Treadwell counterpoises the mechanistic character of American life with the delicate, finally ineffectual sensitivity of the Young Woman. In the first scene, for instance, the rat-a-tat-tat dialogue of the office staff is at once gossipy, cliché-driven ("Hot dog!"), and indistinguishable from the lexicon of business itself, always slipping in to the recitation of the Adding Clerk's figures: "125—83 3/4—22—908—34—1/4—28593." If there is a language of expression, it is deeply buried beneath this mechanized rhetoric, so deeply buried that even the Young Woman can hardly seize her own feelings about whether to marry the businessman George H. Jones, her physical revulsion at the man finally giving way to a simple desire to be free of the brutal and exhausting routines of work: "—please don't touch me—I want to rest—no rest—earn—got to earn—married—earn—no—yes."

The Young Woman marries, has a child, and a desperate affair with the Man, who grew up riding the hills surrounding the San Francisco bay, and will soon be "moving on" to Mexico. This tawdry, necessary idyll is set against the emptiness of the Young Woman's married life at the opening of Episode Seven, as the couple read newspapers aloud:

> HUSBAND: Record production.
>
> YOUNG WOMAN: Girl turns on gas.
>
> HUSBAND: Sale hits a million—
>
> YOUNG WOMAN: Woman leaves all for love—

Treadwell departs from Ruth Snyder's case, however, in having the Young Woman murder her husband alone, killing him with the blue bowl she had taken as a remembrance of her tryst with the Man. Indeed, Treadwell's journalistic experience—and her critique of modern journalism as well—blossoms in the trial scenes, in which the Reporters convey almost entirely different stories, yet remain oblivious to the Young Woman's plight. Fatefully enough, the Young Woman is finally betrayed even by her lover, who—safe from extradition in Mexico—voluntarily supplies the court with the information that he had an "intimate" affair with the defendant—"an almost daily visitor to my room"—and that the "blue bowl filled with pebbles" was his gift to her. The play's powerful indictment of modern industrial culture is concluded in the final episode, "A Machine." In many respects, the execution of the Young Woman—silenced, unable even to complete her final plea—is the epitome of the play as a whole, a final image of the extinguishing of human hope by an American acceptance of the social order—the worlds of business, of childbirth, of love and marriage, of the media of information, of justice itself—as a soulless, destructive machine.

A brilliant success on Broadway in 1928, and then in London and Moscow, Treadwell's grim parable has become a staple of professional and university theaters since the early 1990s, perhaps inaugurated by Stephen Daldry's brilliant production, starring Fiona Shaw as the Young Woman, at London's Royal National Theatre in 1993.

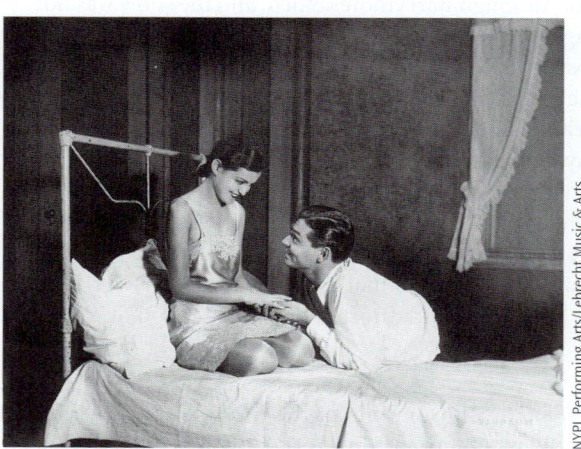

Clark Gable and Zita Johann in the original 1928 Broadway production of Treadwell's *Machinal.*

NYPL Performing Arts/Lebrecht Music & Arts

Machinal

Sophie Treadwell

CHARACTERS

YOUNG WOMAN
TELEPHONE GIRL
STENOGRAPHER
FILING CLERK
ADDING CLERK
MOTHER
HUSBAND
BELLBOY
NURSE
DOCTOR
YOUNG MAN
GIRL
MAN
BOY
MAN
ANOTHER MAN
WAITER
JUDGE
LAWYER FOR DEFENSE

LAWYER FOR PROSECUTION
COURT REPORTER
BAILIFF
REPORTER
SECOND REPORTER
THIRD REPORTER
JAILER
MATRON
PRIEST

EPISODE I To Business
EPISODE II At Home
EPISODE III Honeymoon
EPISODE IV Maternal
EPISODE V Prohibited
EPISODE VI Intimate
EPISODE VII Domestic
EPISODE VIII The Law
EPISODE IX A Machine

THE PLOT *is the story of a woman who murders her husband—an ordinary young woman, any woman.*

THE PLAN *is to tell this story by showing the different phases of life that the woman comes in contact with, and in none of which she finds any place, any peace. The woman is essentially soft, tender, and the life around her is essentially hard, mechanized. Business, home, marriage, having a child, seeking pleasure—all are difficult for her—mechanical, nerve nagging. Only in an illicit love does she find anything with life in it for her, and when she loses this, the desperate effort to win free to it again is her undoing.*

The story is told in nine scenes. In the dialogue of these scenes there is the attempt to catch the rhythm of our common city speech, its brassy sound, its trick of repetition, etc.

Then there is, also, the use of many different sounds chosen primarily for their inherent emotional effect (steel riveting, a priest chanting, a Negro singing, jazz band, etc.), but contributing also to the creation of a background, an atmosphere.

THE HOPE *is to create a stage production that will have "style," and at the same time, by the story's own innate drama, by the directness of its telling, by the variety and quick changingness of its scenes, and the excitement of its sounds, to create an interesting play.*

SCENICALLY *this play is planned to be handled in two basic sets (or in one set with two backs)*

The first division—(the first Four Episodes)—needs an entrance at one side, and a back having a door and a large window. The door gives, in
  Episode 1—to Vice President's office.
  Episode 2—to hall.
  Episode 3—to bathroom.

Episode 4—to corridor.
            And the window shows, in
  Episode 1—An opposite office.
  Episode 2—An inner apartment court.
  Episode 3—Window of a dance casino opposite.
  Episode 4—Steel girders.
            (Of these, only the casino window is important.
            Sky could be used for the others.)
The second division—(the last Five Episodes)—has the same side entrance, but the back has only one opening—for a small window (barred).
  Episode 5, window is masked by electric piano.
  Episode 6, window is disclosed (sidewalk outside).
  Episode 7, window is curtained.
  Episode 8, window is masked by Judge's bench.
  Episode 9, window is disclosed (sky outside).

There is a change of furniture, and props for each episode—(only essential things, full of character).

For Episode 9, the room is closed in from the sides, and there is a place with bars and a door in it, put straight across stage down front (back far enough to leave a clear passageway in front of it).

LIGHTING *concentrated and intense.—Light and shadow—bright light and darkness.—This darkness, already in the scene, grows and blacks out the light for dark stage when the scene changes are made.*

OFFSTAGE VOICES: Characters in the Background Heard, but
    Unseen:
    A Janitor
    A Baby
    A Boy and a Girl
    A Husband and Wife
    A Radio Announcer
    A Negro Singer

677

MECHANICAL OFFSTAGE SOUNDS
    A small jazz band
    A hand organ
    Steel riveting
    Telegraph instruments
    Aeroplane engine
MECHANICAL ONSTAGE SOUNDS
    Office Machines (Typewriters, telephones, etc.)
    Electric piano.
CHARACTERS: In the Background Seen, Not Heard
(*Seen, off the main set; i.e., through a window or door*)
    Couples of men and women dancing
    A Woman in a bathrobe
    A Woman in a wheel chair
    A Nurse with a covered basin
    A Nurse with a tray
    The feet of men and women passing in the street

EPISODE ONE

TO BUSINESS

SCENE:
    an office:
    a switchboard,
    filing cabinet,
    adding machine,
    typewriter and table,
    manifold machine.

SOUNDS:
    office machines:
    typewriters,
    adding machine,
    manifold,
    telephone bells,
    buzzers.

CHARACTERS AND THEIR MACHINES:
    A YOUNG WOMAN (*typewriter*),
    A STENOGRAPHER (*typewriter*),
    A FILING CLERK (*filing cabinet and manifold*),
    An ADDING CLERK (*adding machine*),
        TELEPHONE OPERATOR (*switchboard*),
        JONES.

BEFORE THE CURTAIN:
    Sounds of machines going. They continue throughout the scene, and accompany the YOUNG WOMAN's *thoughts after the scene is blacked out.*

AT THE RISE OF THE CURTAIN:
    All the machines are disclosed, and all the characters with the exception of the YOUNG WOMAN.

Of these characters, the YOUNG WOMAN, *going any day to any business. Ordinary. The confusion of her own inner thoughts, emotions, desires, dreams cuts her off from any actual adjustment to the routine of work. She gets through this routine with a very small surface of her consciousness. She is not homely and she is not pretty. She is preoccupied with herself—with her person. She has well kept hands, and a trick of constantly arranging her hair over her ears.*

The STENOGRAPHER *is the faded, efficient woman office worker. Drying, dried.*

The ADDING CLERK *is her male counterpart.*

The FILING CLERK *is a boy not grown, callow adolescence.*

The TELEPHONE GIRL, *young, cheap and amorous.*

Lights come up on office scene. Two desks right and left. Telephone booth back right center. Filing cabinet back of center. Adding machine back left center.

ADDING CLERK: [*In the monotonous voice of his monotonous thoughts; at his adding machine*] 2490, 28, 76, 123, 36842, 1, ¼, 37, 804, 23½, 982.
FILING CLERK: [*In the same way—at his filing desk*] Accounts—A. Bonds—B. Contracts—C. Data—D. Earnings—E.   5
STENOGRAPHER: [*In the same way—left*] Dear Sir—in re—your letter—recent date—will state—
TELEPHONE GIRL: Hello—Hello—George H. Jones Company good morning—hello hello—George H. Jones Company good morning—hello.   10
FILING CLERK: Market—M. Notes—N. Output—O. Profits—P.—! [*Suddenly*] What's the matter with Q?
TELEPHONE GIRL: Matter with it—Mr. J.—Mr. K. wants you— What you mean matter? Matter with what?
FILING CLERK: Matter with Q.   15
TELEPHONE GIRL: Well—what is? Spring 1726?
FILING CLERK: I'm asking yuh—
TELEPHONE GIRL: WELL?
FILING CLERK: Nothing filed with it—
TELEPHONE GIRL: Well?   20
FILING CLERK: Look at A. Look at B. What's the matter with Q?
TELEPHONE GIRL: Ain't popular. Hello—Hello—George H. Jones Company.
FILING CLERK: Hot dog! Why ain't it?
ADDING CLERK: Has it personality?   25
STENOGRAPHER: Has it Halitosis?
TELEPHONE GIRL: Has it got it?
FILING CLERK: Hot dog!
TELEPHONE GIRL: What number do you want?
[*Recognizing but not pleased*] Oh—hello—sure I know who it   30
    is—tonight? Uh, uh—[*Negative, but each with a different inflection*]—you/heard me—No!
FILING CLERK: Don't you like him?
STENOGRAPHER: She likes 'em all.
TELEPHONE GIRL: I do not!   35
STENOGRAPHER: Well—pretty near all!
TELEPHONE GIRL: What number do you want? Wrong number. Hello—hello—George H. Jones Company. Hello, hello—
STENOGRAPHER: Memorandum—attention Mr. Smith—at a conference of—   40
ADDING CLERK: 125—83¾—22—908—34—¼—28593—
FILING CLERK: Report—R, Sales—S, Trade—T.
TELEPHONE GIRL: Shh—! Yes, Mr. J.—? No—Miss A. ain't in yet—I'll tell her, Mr. J.—just the minute she gets in.
STENOGRAPHER: She's late again, huh?   45
TELEPHONE GIRL: Out with her sweetie last night, huh?
FILING CLERK: Hot dog.
ADDING CLERK: She ain't got a sweetie.
STENOGRAPHER: How do you know?

50 ADDING CLERK: I know.
    FILING CLERK: Hot dog.
    ADDING CLERK: She lives alone with her mother.
    TELEPHONE GIRL: Spring 1876? Hello—Spring 1876. Spring!
        Hello, Spring 1876? 1876! Wrong number! Hello! Hello!
55 STENOGRAPHER: Director's meeting semiannual report card.
    FILING CLERK: Shipments—Sales—Schedules—S.
    ADDING CLERK: She doesn't belong in an office.
    TELEPHONE GIRL: Who does?
    STENOGRAPHER: I do!
60 ADDING CLERK: You said it!
    FILING CLERK: Hot dog!
    TELEPHONE GIRL: Hello—hello—George H. Jones
        Company—hello—hello—
    STENOGRAPHER: I'm efficient. She's inefficient.
65 FILING CLERK: She's inefficient.
    TELEPHONE GIRL: She's got J. going.
    STENOGRAPHER: Going?
    TELEPHONE GIRL: Going and coming.
    FILING CLERK: Hot dog.

[*Enter* JONES.]

70 JONES: Good morning, everybody.
    TELEPHONE GIRL: Good morning.
    FILING CLERK: Good morning.
    ADDING CLERK: Good morning.
    STENOGRAPHER: Good morning, Mr. J.
75 JONES: Miss A. isn't in yet?
    TELEPHONE GIRL: Not yet, Mr. J.
    FILING CLERK: Not yet.
    ADDING CLERK: Not yet.
    STENOGRAPHER: She's late.
80 JONES: I just wanted her to take a letter.
    STENOGRAPHER: I'll take the letter.
    JONES: One thing at a time and that done well.
    ADDING CLERK: [*Yessing*] Done well.
    STENOGRAPHER: I'll finish it later.
85 JONES: Hew to the line.
    ADDING CLERK: Hew to the line.
    STENOGRAPHER: Then I'll hurry.
    JONES: Haste makes waste.
    ADDING CLERK: Waste.
90 STENOGRAPHER: But if you're in a hurry.
    JONES: I'm never in a hurry—That's how I get ahead! [*Laughs.
        They all laugh.*] First know you're right—then go ahead.
    ADDING CLERK: Ahead.
    JONES: [*To* TELEPHONE GIRL] When Miss A. comes in tell her I
95   want her to take a letter. [*Turns to go in—then*] It's important.
    TELEPHONE GIRL: [*Making a note*] Miss A.—important.
    JONES: [*Starts up—then*] And I don't want to be disturbed.
    TELEPHONE GIRL: You're in conference?
    JONES: I'm in conference. [*Turns—then*] Unless its A.B.—of
100   course.
    TELEPHONE GIRL: Of course—A.B.
    JONES: [*Starts—turns again; attempts to he facetious*] Tell Miss A.
        the early bird catches the worm.

[*Exit* JONES.]

    TELEPHONE GIRL: The early worm gets caught.
105 ADDING CLERK: He's caught.

TELEPHONE GIRL: Hooked.
ADDING CLERK: In the pan.
FILING CLERK: Hot dog.
STENOGRAPHER: We beg leave to announce—

[*Enter* YOUNG WOMAN. *Goes behind telephone booth to desk right.*]

STENOGRAPHER: You're late!   110
FILING CLERK: You're late.
ADDING CLERK: You're late.
STENOGRAPHER: And yesterday!
FILING CLERK: The day before.
ADDING CLERK: And the day before.   115
STENOGRAPHER: You'll lose your job.
YOUNG WOMAN: No!
STENOGRAPHER: No?

[*Workers exchange glances.*]

YOUNG WOMAN: I can't!
STENOGRAPHER: Can't?   120

[*Same business.*]

FILING CLERK: Rent — bills — installments — miscellaneous.
ADDING CLERK: A dollar ten—ninety-five—3.40—35—12.60.
STENOGRAPHER: Then why are you late?
YOUNG WOMAN: Why?
STENOGRAPHER: Excuse!   125
ADDING CLERK: Excuse!
FILING CLERK: Excuse.
TELEPHONE GIRL: Excuse it, please.
STENOGRAPHER: Why?
YOUNG WOMAN: The subway?   130
TELEPHONE GIRL: Long distance?
FILING CLERK: Old stuff!
ADDING CLERK: That stall!
STENOGRAPHER: Stalled?
YOUNG WOMAN: No—   135
STENOGRAPHER: What?
YOUNG WOMAN: I had to get out!
ADDING CLERK: Out!
FILING CLERK: Out?
STENOGRAPHER: Out where?   140
YOUNG WOMAN: In the air!
STENOGRAPHER: Air?
YOUNG WOMAN: All those bodies pressing.
FILING CLERK: Hot dog!
YOUNG WOMAN: I thought I would faint! I had to get out in   145
    the air!
FILING CLERK: Give her the air.
ADDING CLERK: Free air—
STENOGRAPHER: Hot air.
YOUNG WOMAN: Like I'm dying.   150
STENOGRAPHER: Same thing yesterday. [*Pause*] And the
    day before.
YOUNG WOMAN: Yes—what am. I going to do?
ADDING CLERK: Take a taxi!

[*They laugh.*]

FILING CLERK: Call a cop!   155

TELEPHONE GIRL: Mr. J. wants you.
YOUNG WOMAN: Me?
TELEPHONE GIRL: You!
YOUNG WOMAN: [Rises] Mr. J.!
160 STENOGRAPHER: Mr. J.
TELEPHONE GIRL: He's bellowing for you!

[YOUNG WOMAN gives last pat to her hair—goes off into door—back.]

STENOGRAPHER: [After her] Get it just right.
FILING CLERK: She's always doing that to her hair.
TELEPHONE GIRL: It gives a line—it gives a line—
165 FILING CLERK: Hot dog.
ADDING CLERK: She artistic.
STENOGRAPHER: She's inefficient.
FILING CLERK: She's inefficient.
STENOGRAPHER: Mr. J. knows she's inefficient.
170 ADDING CLERK: 46-23-84-2-2-2-1,492—678.
TELEPHONE GIRL: Hello—hello—George H. Jones Company—hello—Mr. Jones? He's in conference.
STENOGRAPHER: [Sarcastic] Conference!
ADDING CLERK: Conference.
175 FILING CLERK: Hot dog!
TELEPHONE GIRL: Do you think he'll marry her?
ADDING CLERK: If she'll have him.
STENOGRAPHER: If she'll have him!
FILING CLERK: Do you think she'll have him?
180 TELEPHONE GIRL: How much does he get?
ADDING CLERK: Plenty—5,000—10,000—15,000—20,000—25,000.
STENOGRAPHER: And plenty put away.
ADDING CLERK: Gas Preferred—4's—steel—5's—oil—6's.
FILING CLERK: Hot dog.
185 STENOGRAPHER: Will she have him? Will she have him? This agreement entered into—party of the first part—party of the second part—will he have her?
TELEPHONE GIRL: Well, I'd hate to get into bed with him. [Familiar melting voice] Hello—humhum—hum—hum—
190 hold the line a minute—will you—hum hum. [Professional voice] Hell, hello—A.B., just a minute, Mr. A.B.—Mr. J.? Mr, A.B.—go ahead, Mr. A.B. [Melting voice] We were interrupted—huh—huh—huh-huhuh—hum—hum.

[Enter YOUNG WOMAN—she goes to her chair, sits with folded hands.]

FILING CLERK: That's all you ever say to a guy—
195 STENOGRAPHER: Hum—hum—or uh huh—[Negative]
TELEPHONE GIRL: That's all you have to. [To phone] Hum—hum—hum hum—hum hum—
STENOGRAPHER: Mostly hum hum.
ADDING CLERK: You've said it!
200 FILING CLERK: Hot dog.
TELEPHONE GIRL: Hum hum huh hum humhumhum—tonight? She's got a date—she told me last night—hum-humhuh—hum—all right. [Disconnects] Too bad—my boy friend's got a friend—but my girl friend's got a date.
205 YOUNG WOMAN: You have a good time.
TELEPHONE GIRL: Big time.
STENOGRAPHER: Small time.
ADDING CLERK: A big time on the small time.
TELEPHONE GIRL: I'd ask you, kid, but you'd be up to your neck!

STENOGRAPHER: Neckers!   210
ADDING CLERK: Petters!
FILING CLERK: Sweet papas.
TELEPHONE GIRL: Want to come?
YOUNG WOMAN: Can't.
TELEPHONE GIRL: Date?   215
YOUNG WOMAN: My mother.
STENOGRAPHER: Worries?
TELEPHONE GIRL: Nags—hello—George H. Jones Company—Oh hello—

[YOUNG WOMAN sits before her machine—hands in lap, looking at them.]

STENOGRAPHER: Why don't you get to work?   220
YOUNG WOMAN: [Dreaming] What?
ADDING CLERK: Work!
YOUNG WOMAN: Can't.
STENOGRAPHER: Can't?
YOUNG WOMAN: My machine's out of order.   225
STENOGRAPHER: Well, fix it!
YOUNG WOMAN: I can't—got to get somebody.
STENOGRAPHER: Somebody! Somebody! Always somebody! Here, sort the mail, then!
YOUNG WOMAN: [Rises] All right.   230
STENOGRAPHER: And hurry! You're late.
YOUNG WOMAN: [Sorting letters] George H. Jones & Company—George H. Jones Inc. George H. Jones—
STENOGRAPHER: You're always late.
ADDING CLERK: You'll lose your job.   235
YOUNG WOMAN: [Hurrying] George H. Jones—George H. Jones Personal—
TELEPHONE GIRL: Don't let 'em get your goat, kid—tell 'em where to get off.
YOUNG WOMAN: What?   240
TELEPHONE GIRL: Ain't it all set?
YOUNG WOMAN: What?
TELEPHONE GIRL: You and Mr. J.
STENOGRAPHER: You and the boss.
FILING CLERK: You and the big chief.   245
ADDING CLERK: You and the big cheese.
YOUNG WOMAN: Did he tell you?
TELEPHONE GIRL: I told you!
ADDING CLERK: I told you!
STENOGRAPHER: I don't believe it.   250
ADDING CLERK: 5,000—10,000—15,000.
FILING CLERK: Hot dog.
YOUNG WOMAN: No—it isn't so.
STENOGRAPHER: Isn't it?
YOUNG WOMAN: No.   255
TELEPHONE GIRL: Not yet.
ADDING CLERK: But soon.
FILING CLERK: Hot dog.

[Enter JONES.]

TELEPHONE GIRL: [Busy] George H. Jones Company—Hello—Hello.   260
STENOGRAPHER: Awaiting your answer—
ADDING CLERK: 5,000—10,000—15,000—
JONES: [Crossing to YOUNG WOMAN—puts hand on her shoulder, all stop and stare] That letter done?

265 YOUNG WOMAN: No. [*She pulls away.*]
 JONES: What's the matter?
 STENOGRAPHER: She hasn't started.
 JONES: O.K.—want to make some changes.
 YOUNG WOMAN: My machine's out of order.
270 JONES: O.K.—use the one in my room.
 YOUNG WOMAN: I'm sorting the mail.
 STENOGRAPHER: [*Sarcastic*] One thing at a time!
 JONES: [*Retreating—goes back center*] O.K. [*To* YOUNG WOMAN]
   When you're finished.

 [*Starts back to his room*]

275 STENOGRAPHER: Haste makes waste.
 JONES: [*At door*] O.K.—don't hurry.

 [*Exits*]

 STENOGRAPHER: Hew to the line!
 TELEPHONE GIRL: He's hewing.
 FILING CLERK: Hot dog.
280 TELEPHONE GIRL: Why did you flinch, kid?
 YOUNG WOMAN: Flinch?
 TELEPHONE GIRL: Did he pinch?
 YOUNG WOMAN: No!
 TELEPHONE GIRL: Then what?
285 YOUNG WOMAN: Nothing!—Just his hand.
 TELEPHONE GIRL: Oh—just his hand—[*Shakes her head
   thoughtfully*] Uhhuh. [*Negative*] Uhhuh. [*Decisively*] No! Tell
   him no.
 STENOGRAPHER: If she does she'll lose her job.
290 ADDING CLERK: Fired.
 FILING CLERK: The sack!
 TELEPHONE GIRL: [*On the defensive*] And if she doesn't?
 ADDING CLERK: She'll come to work in a taxi!
 TELEPHONE GIRL: Work?
295 FILING CLERK: No work.
 STENOGRAPHER: No worry.
 ADDING CLERK: Breakfast in bed.
 STENOGRAPHER: [*Sarcastic*] Did Madame ring?
 FILING CLERK: Lunch in bed!
300 TELEPHONE GIRL: A double bed! [*In phone*] Yes, Mr. J. [*To* YOUNG
   WOMAN] J. wants you.
 YOUNG WOMAN: [*Starts to get to her feet—but doesn't*]
   I can't—I'm not ready—in a minute. [*Sits staring ahead
   of her*]
305 ADDING CLERK: 5,000—10,000—15,000—
 FILING CLERK: Profits—plans—purchase—
 STENOGRAPHER: Call your attention our prices are fixed.
 TELEPHONE GIRL: Hello—hello—George H. Jones
   Company—hello—hello—
310 YOUNG WOMAN: [*Thinking her thoughts aloud—to the subdued
   accompaniment of the office sounds and voices*] Marry
   me—wants to marry me—George H. Jones— George H. Jones
   and Company—Mrs. George H. Jones—Mrs. George H. Jones.
   Dear Madame—marry— do you take this man to be your
315 wedded husband—I do—to love honor and to love—kisses—
   no—I can't—George H. Jones—How would you like to marry
   me—What do you say—Why Mr. Jones I—let me look at your
   little hands—you have such pretty little hands—let me hold
   your pretty little hands—George H. Jones—Fat hands—flabby
320 hands—don't touch me—please—fat hands are never

weary—please don't—married—all girls—most girls—
married—babies—a baby—curls— little curls all over its
head—George H. Jones— straight—thin—bald—don't touch
me—please—no— can't—must—somebody—something—no
rest—must rest—no rest—must rest—no rest—late today— 325
yesterday—before—late—subway—air—pressing—bodies
pressing—bodies—trembling—air—stop—air—late—
job—no job—fired—late—alarm clock—alarm clock— alarm
clock—hurry—job—ma—nag—nag—nag—ma— hurry—
job—no job—no money—installments due—no money— 330
money — George H. Jones — money — Mrs. George H.
Jones—money—no work—no worry—free!— rest—sleep till
nine—sleep till ten—sleep till noon— now you take a good
rest this morning—don't get up till you want to—thank
you—oh thank you—oh don't!— please don't touch me—I 335
want to rest—no rest—earn— got to earn—married—earn—
no—yes—earn—all girls—most girls—ma—pa—ma—all
women—most women— I can't—must—maybe—must—
somebody—something —ma—pa—ma—can I, ma? Tell me,
ma—something— somebody. 340

[*The scene blacks out. The sounds of the office machines continue
until the scene lights into Episode Two—and the office sounds
become the sound of a radio, offstage.*]

EPISODE TWO

AT HOME

SCENE:
 a kitchen:
 table.
 chairs,
 plates and food,
 garbage can,
 a pair of rubber gloves.
 The door at the back now opens on a hall—the window, on an
 apartment house court.

SOUNDS:
 buzzer,
 radio (voice of announcer; music and singer)

CHARACTERS:
 YOUNG WOMAN,
 MOTHER

OUTSIDE VOICES: *characters heard, hut not seen:*
 a JANITOR,
 a BABY,
 a MOTHER *and a* SMALL BOY,
 a YOUNG BOY *and* YOUNG GIRL,
 a HUSBAND *and a* WIFE,
 another HUSBAND *and a* WIFE.

AT RISE:
YOUNG WOMAN *and* MOTHER *eating—radio offstage—radio stops.*
YOUNG WOMAN: Ma—I want to talk to you.
MOTHER: Aren't you eating a potato?
YOUNG WOMAN: No.
MOTHER: Why not?
YOUNG WOMAN: I don't want one. 5

MOTHER: That's no reason. Here! Take one.

YOUNG WOMAN: I don't want it.

MOTHER: Potatoes go with stew—here!

YOUNG WOMAN: Ma, I don't want it!

10 MOTHER: Want it! Take it!

YOUNG WOMAN: But I—oh, all right. [*Takes it—then*] Ma, I want to ask you something.

MOTHER: Eat your potato.

YOUNG WOMAN: [*Takes a bite—then*] Ma, there's something I want to ask you—something important.

15

MOTHER: Is it mealy?

YOUNG WOMAN: S'all right. Ma—tell me.

MOTHER: Three pounds for a quarter.

YOUNG WOMAN: Ma—tell me—

[*Buzzer*]

20 MOTHER: [*Her dull voice brightening*] There's the garbage. [*Goes to door—or dumbwaiter—opens it. Stop radio.*]

JANITOR'S VOICE: [*Offstage*] Garbage.

MOTHER: [*Pleased—busy*] All right. [*Gets garbage can—puts it out. YOUNG WOMAN walks up and down.*] What's the matter now?

25 YOUNG WOMAN: Nothing.

MOTHER: That jumping up from the table every night the garbage is collected! You act like you're crazy.

YOUNG WOMAN: Ma, do all women—

MOTHER: I suppose you think you're too nice for anything so common! Well, let me tell you, my lady, that it's a very important part of life.

30

YOUNG WOMAN: I know, but, Ma, if you—

MOTHER: If it weren't for garbage cans where would we be? Where would we all be? Living in filth—that's what! Filth! I should think you'd be glad! I should think you'd be grateful!

35

YOUNG WOMAN: Oh, Ma!

MOTHER: Well, are you?

YOUNG WOMAN: Am I what?

MOTHER: Glad! Grateful.

40 YOUNG WOMAN: Yes!

MOTHER: You don't act like it!

YOUNG WOMAN: Oh, Ma, don't talk!

MOTHER: You just said you wanted to talk.

YOUNG WOMAN: Well now—I want to think. I got to think.

45 MOTHER: Aren't you going to finish your potato?

YOUNG WOMAN: Oh, Ma!

MOTHER: Is there anything the matter with it?

YOUNG WOMAN: No—

MOTHER: Then why don't you finish it?

50 YOUNG WOMAN: Because I don't want it.

MOTHER: Why don't you?

YOUNG WOMAN: Oh, Ma! Let me alone!

MOTHER: Well, you've got to eat! If you don't eat—

YOUNG WOMAN: Ma! Don't nag!

55 MOTHER: Nag! Just because I try to look out for you—nag! Just because I try to care for you—nag! Why, you haven't sense enough to eat! What would become of you I'd like to know—if I didn't nag!

[*Offstage—a sound of window opening—all these offstage sounds come in through the court window at the back.*]

WOMAN'S VOICE: Johnny—Johnny—come in now!

60 A SMALL BOY'S VOICE: Oh, Ma!

WOMAN'S VOICE: It's getting cold.

A SMALL BOY'S VOICE: Oh, Ma!

WOMAN'S VOICE: You heard me! [*Sound of window slamming*]

YOUNG WOMAN: I'm grown up, Ma.

65 MOTHER: Grown up! What do you mean by that?

YOUNG WOMAN: Nothing much—I guess. [*Offstage sound of baby crying. MOTHER rises, clatters dishes.*] Let's not do the dishes right away, Ma. Let's talk—I gotta.

MOTHER: Well, I can't talk with dirty dishes around—you may be able to but—[*Clattering—clattering*]

70

YOUNG WOMAN: Ma! Listen! Listen!—There's a man wants to marry me.

MOTHER: [*Stops clattering—sits*] What man?

YOUNG WOMAN: He says he fell in love with my hands.

MOTHER: In love! Is that beginning again! I thought you were over that!

75

[*Offstage BOY'S VOICE—whistles—GIRL'S VOICE answers.*]

BOY'S VOICE: Come on out.

GIRL'S VOICE: Can't.

BOY'S VOICE: Nobody'll see you.

GIRL'S VOICE: I can't.

80

BOY'S VOICE: It's dark now—come on.

GIRL'S VOICE: Well—just for a minute.

BOY'S VOICE: Meet you round the corner.

YOUNG WOMAN: I got to get married, Ma.

MOTHER: What do you mean?

85

YOUNG WOMAN: I gotta.

MOTHER: You haven't got in trouble, have you?

YOUNG WOMAN: Don't talk like that!

MOTHER: Well, you say you got to get married—what do you mean?

90

YOUNG WOMAN: Nothing.

MOTHER: Answer me!

YOUNG WOMAN: All women get married, don't they?

MOTHER: Nonsense!

YOUNG WOMAN: You got married, didn't you?

95

MOTHER: Yes, I did!

[*Offstage voices*]

WOMAN'S VOICE: Where you going?

MAN'S VOICE: Out.

WOMAN'S VOICE: You were out last night.

MAN'S VOICE: Was I?

100

WOMAN'S VOICE: You're always going out.

MAN'S VOICE: Am I?

WOMAN'S VOICE: Where are you going?

MAN'S VOICE: Out.

[*End of offstage voices*]

MOTHER: Who is he? Where did you come to know him?

105

YOUNG WOMAN: In the office.

MOTHER: In the office!

YOUNG WOMAN: It's Mr. J.

MOTHER: Mr. J.?

YOUNG WOMAN: The Vice-President.

110

MOTHER: Vice-President! His income must be—Does he know you've got a mother to support?

YOUNG WOMAN: Yes.

MOTHER: What does he say?

115 YOUNG WOMAN: All right.

MOTHER: How soon you going to marry him?

YOUNG WOMAN: I'm not going to.

MOTHER: Not going to!

YOUNG WOMAN: No! I'm not going to.

120 MOTHER: But you just said—

YOUNG WOMAN: I'm not going to.

MOTHER: Are you crazy?

YOUNG WOMAN: I can't, Ma! I can't!

MOTHER: Why can't you?

125 YOUNG WOMAN: I don't love him.

MOTHER: Love!—what does that amount to! Will it clothe you? Will it feed you? Will it pay the bills?

YOUNG WOMAN: No! But it's real just the same!

MOTHER: Real!

130 YOUNG WOMAN: If it isn't—what can you count on in life?

MOTHER: I'll tell you what you can count on! You can count that you've got to eat and sleep and get up and put clothes on your back and take 'em off again—that you got to get old—and that you got to die. That's what you can count on! All the rest is in

135 your head!

YOUNG WOMAN: But, Ma—didn't you love Pa?

MOTHER: I suppose I did—I don't know—I've forgotten—what difference does it make—now?

YOUNG WOMAN: But then!—oh Ma, tell me!

140 MOTHER: Tell you what?

YOUNG WOMAN: About all that—love?

[*Offstage voices*]

WIFE'S VOICE: Don't.

HUSBAND'S VOICE: What's the matter—don't you want me to kiss you?

145 WIFE'S VOICE: Not like that.

HUSBAND'S VOICE: Like what?

WIFE'S VOICE: That silly kiss!

HUSBAND'S VOICE: Silly kiss?

WIFE'S VOICE: You look so silly—oh I know what's coming

150 when you look like that—and kiss me like that— don't—go away—

[*End of offstage voices*]

MOTHER: He's a decent man, isn't he?

YOUNG WOMAN: I don't know. How should I know—yet.

MOTHER: He's a Vice-President—of course he's decent.

155 YOUNG WOMAN: I don't care whether he's decent or not. I won't marry him.

MOTHER: But you just said you wanted to marry—

YOUNG WOMAN: Not him.

MOTHER: Who?

160 YOUNG WOMAN: I don't know—I don't know—I haven't found him yet!

MOTHER: You talk like you're crazy!

YOUNG WOMAN: Oh, Ma—tell me!

MOTHER: Tell you what?

165 YOUNG WOMAN: Tell me—[*Words suddenly pouring out*] Your skin oughtn't to curl—ought it—when he just comes near you—ought it? That's wrong, ain't it? You don't get over that, do you—ever, do you or do you? How is it, Ma—do you?

MOTHER: Do you what?

YOUNG WOMAN: Do you get used to it—so after a while it doesn't 170 matter? Or don't you? Does it always matter? You ought to be in love, oughtn't you, Ma? You must be in love, mustn't you, Ma? That changes everything, doesn't it—or does it? Maybe if you just like a person it's all right—is it? When he puts a hand on me, my blood turns cold. But your blood oughtn't to run 175 cold, ought it? His hands are—his hands are—fat, Ma—don't you see—his hands are fat—and they sort of press—and they're fat—don't you see?—Don't you see?

MOTHER: [*Stares at her bewildered*] See what?

YOUNG WOMAN: [*Rushing on*] I've always thought I'd find 180 somebody—somebody young—and—and attractive— with wavy hair—wavy hair—I always think of children with curls—little curls all over their head—somebody young—and attractive—that I'd like—that I'd love— But I haven't found anybody like that yet—I haven't found anybody—I've hardly 185 known anybody—you'd never let me go with anybody and—

MOTHER: Are you throwing it up to me that—

YOUNG WOMAN: No—let me finish, Ma! No—let me finish! I just mean I've never found anybody—anybody— nobody's ever asked me—till now—he's the only man that's ever asked 190 me—And I suppose I got to marry somebody—all girls do—

MOTHER: Nonsense.

YOUNG WOMAN: But, I can't go on like this, Ma—I don't know why—but I can't—it's like I'm all tight inside— sometimes I feel like I'm stifling!—You don't know— stifling. [*Walks* 195 *up and down*] I can't go on like this much longer—going to work—coming home—going to work—coming home—I can't— Sometimes in the subway I think I'm going to die— sometimes even in the office if something don't happen—I got to do something—I don't know—it's like I'm all tight inside. 200

MOTHER: You're crazy.

YOUNG WOMAN: Oh, Ma!

MOTHER: You're crazy!

YOUNG WOMAN: Ma—if you tell me that again I'll kill you! I'll kill you! 205

MOTHER: If that isn't crazy!

YOUNG WOMAN: I'll kill you— Maybe I am crazy— I don't know. Sometimes I think I am—the thoughts that go on in my mind—sometimes I think I am—I can't help it if I am— I do the best I can—I do the best I can and I'm nearly crazy! 210 [MOTHER *rises and sits.*] Go away! Go away! You don't know anything about anything! And you haven't got any pity—no pity—you just take it for granted that I go to work every day—and come home every night and bring my money every week— you just take it for granted—you'd let me go on 215 forever—and never feel any pity—

[*Offstage radio—a voice singing a sentimental mother song or popular home song.* MOTHER *begins to cry— crosses to chair left—sits.*]

YOUNG WOMAN: Oh Ma—forgive me! Forgive me!

MOTHER: My own child! To be spoken to like that by my own child!

YOUNG WOMAN: I didn't mean it, Ma—I didn't mean it! 220

[*She goes to her mother—crosses to left.*]

MOTHER: [*Clinging to her hand*] You're all I've got in the world— and you don't want me—you want to kill me.

YOUNG WOMAN: No—no, I don't, Ma! I just said that!

MOTHER: I've worked for you and slaved for you!

225 YOUNG WOMAN: I know, Ma.

MOTHER: I brought you into the world.

YOUNG WOMAN: I know, Ma.

MOTHER: You're flesh of my flesh and—

YOUNG WOMAN: I know, Ma, I know.

230 MOTHER: And—

YOUNG WOMAN: You rest, now, Ma—you rest—

MOTHER: [*Struggling*] I got to do the dishes.

YOUNG WOMAN: I'll do the dishes— You listen to the music, Ma—I'll do the dishes.

[MA *sits*, YOUNG WOMAN *crosses to behind screen. Takes a pair of rubber gloves and begins to put them on. The* MOTHER *sees them—they irritate her—there is a return of her characteristic mood.*]

235 MOTHER: Those gloves! I've been washing dishes for forty years and I never wore gloves! But my lady's hands! My lady's hands!

YOUNG WOMAN: Sometimes you talk to me like you're jealous, Ma.

240 MOTHER: Jealous?

YOUNG WOMAN: It's my hands got me a husband.

MOTHER: A husband? So you're going to marry him now!

YOUNG WOMAN: I suppose so.

MOTHER: If you ain't the craziest—

[*The scene blacks out. In the darkness, the mother song goes into jazz—very faint—as the scene lights into*]

EPISODE THREE

HONEYMOON

SCENE:
>   hotel bedroom:
>   bed,
>   chair,
>   mirror.
>   The door at the back now opens on a bathroom; the window, on a dancing casino opposite.

SOUNDS:
>   a small jazz band (violin, piano, saxophone—very dim, at first, then louder).

CHARACTERS:
>   YOUNG WOMAN,
>   HUSBAND,
>   BELLBOY

OFFSTAGE:
>   seen but not heard—MEN and WOMEN dancing in couples.

AT RISE:
>   set dark.

BELLBOY, HUSBAND, *and* YOUNG WOMAN *enter.* BELLBOY *carries luggage. He switches on light by door. Stop music.*

HUSBAND: Well, here we are.

[*Throws hat on bed;* BELLBOY *puts luggage down, crosses to window; raises shade three inches; opens window three inches. Sounds of jazz music louder. Offstage.*]

BELLBOY: [*Comes to man for tip*] Anything else, Sir?

[*Receives tip. Exits*]

HUSBAND: Well, here we are.

YOUNG WOMAN: Yes, here we are.

HUSBAND: Aren't you going to take your hat off—stay a while?   5
[YOUNG WOMAN *looks around as though looking for a way out, then takes off her hat, pulls the hair automatically around her ears.*] This is all right, isn't it? Huh? Huh?

YOUNG WOMAN: It's very nice.

HUSBAND: Twelve bucks a day! They know how to soak you in   10
these pleasure resorts. Twelve bucks! [*Music*] Well—we'll get our money's worth out of it all right. [*Goes toward bathroom*] I'm going to wash up. [*Stops at door*] Don't you want to wash up? [YOUNG WOMAN *shakes head "No."*] I do! It was a long trip! I want to wash up! [*Goes off—closes door; sings in*   15
bathroom. YOUNG WOMAN *goes to window—raises shade— sees the dancers going round and round in couples. Music is louder. Re-enter* HUSBAND.] Say, pull that blind down! They can see in!

YOUNG WOMAN: I thought you said there'd be a view of the ocean!   20

HUSBAND: Sure there is.

YOUNG WOMAN: I just see people—dancing.

HUSBAND: The ocean's beyond.

YOUNG WOMAN: [*Desperately*] I was counting on seeing it!

HUSBAND: You'll see it tomorrow—what's eating you? We'll take   25
in the boardwalk—Don't you want to wash up?

YOUNG WOMAN: No!

HUSBAND: It was a long trip. Sure you don't? [YOUNG WOMAN
shakes her head "No." HUSBAND *takes off his coat—puts it over chair.*] Better make yourself at home. I'm going to. [*She stares*   30
at him—moves away from the window.] Say, pull down that blind!

[*Crosses to chair down left—sits*]

YOUNG WOMAN: It's close—don't you think it's close?

HUSBAND: Well—you don't want people looking in, do you?
[*Laughs*] Huh—huh?   35

YOUNG WOMAN: No.

HUSBAND: [*Laughs*] I guess not. Huh? [*Takes off shoes.* YOUNG
WOMAN *leaves the window, and crosses down to the bed.*]
Say—you look a little white around the gills! What's the matter?   40

YOUNG WOMAN: Nothing.

HUSBAND: You look like you're scared.

YOUNG WOMAN: No.

HUSBAND: Nothing to be scared of. You're with your husband, you know. [*Takes her to chair, left*]   45

YOUNG WOMAN: I know.

HUSBAND: Happy?

YOUNG WOMAN: Yes.

HUSBAND: [*Sitting*] Then come here and give us a kiss. [*He puts
her on his knee.*] That's the girlie. [*He bends her head down, and*   50
kisses her along the back of her neck.] Like that? [*She tries to
get to her feet.*] Say—stay there! What you moving for? —You
know—you got to learn to relax, little girl— [*Dancers go off.*

Dim lights. Pinches her above knee] Say, what you got under
55   there?
YOUNG WOMAN: Nothing.
HUSBAND: Nothing! [*Laughs*] That's a good one! Nothing, huh?
       Huh? That reminds me of the story of the pullman porter and
       the—what's the matter—did I tell you that one?

[*Music dims off and out.*]

60   YOUNG WOMAN: I don't know.
HUSBAND: The pullman porter and the tart?
YOUNG WOMAN: No.
HUSBAND: It's a good one—well—the train was just pulling out
       and the tart—
65   YOUNG WOMAN: You did tell that one!
HUSBAND: About the—
YOUNG WOMAN: Yes! Yes! I remember now!
HUSBAND: About the—
YOUNG WOMAN: Yes!
70   HUSBAND: All right—if I did. You're sure it was the one about
       the—
YOUNG WOMAN: I'm sure.
HUSBAND: When he asked her what she had underneath her seat
       and she said—
75   YOUNG WOMAN: Yes! Yes! That one!
HUSBAND: All right— But I don't believe I did. [*She tries to get
       up again, as he holds her.*] You know you have got something
       under there—what is it?
YOUNG WOMAN: Nothing—just—just my garter.
80   HUSBAND: Your garter! Your garter! Say did I tell you the one
       about—
YOUNG WOMAN: Yes! Yes!
HUSBAND: [*With dignity*] How do you know which one I meant?
YOUNG WOMAN: You told me them all!
85   HUSBAND: [*Pulling her back to his knee*] No, I didn't! Not by a
       jugful! I got a lot of 'em up my sleeve yet—that's part of what
       I owe my success to—my ability to spring a good story— You
       know—you got to learn to relax, little girl—haven't you?
YOUNG WOMAN: Yes.
90   HUSBAND: That's one of the biggest things to learn in life. That's
       part of what I owe my success to. Now you go and get those
       heavy things off—and relax.
YOUNG WOMAN: They're not heavy.
HUSBAND: You haven't got much on—have you? But you'll feel
95   better with 'em off. [*Gets up*] Want me to help you?
YOUNG WOMAN: No.
HUSBAND: I'm your husband, you know.
YOUNG WOMAN: I know.
HUSBAND: You aren't afraid of your husband, are you?
100 YOUNG WOMAN: No—of course not—but I thought maybe—can't
       we go out for a little while?
HUSBAND: Out? What for?
YOUNG WOMAN: Fresh air—walk—talk.
HUSBAND: We can talk here—I'll tell you all about myself.
105   Go along now. [YOUNG WOMAN *goes toward bathroom
       door—gets bag.*] Where are you going?
YOUNG WOMAN: In here.
HUSBAND: I thought you'd want to wash up.
YOUNG WOMAN: I just want to—get ready.
110 HUSBAND: You don't have to go in there to take your clothes off!
YOUNG WOMAN: I want to.
HUSBAND: What for?

YOUNG WOMAN: I always do.
HUSBAND: What?
YOUNG WOMAN: Undress by myself.   115
HUSBAND: You've never been married till now—have you?
       [*Laughs*] Or have you been putting something over on me?
YOUNG WOMAN: No.
HUSBAND: I understand—kind of modest—huh? Huh?
YOUNG WOMAN: Yes.   120
HUSBAND: I understand women— [*Indulgently*] Go along. [*She
       goes off—starts to close door.* YOUNG WOMAN *exits.*] Don't close
       the door—thought you wanted to talk. [*He looks around the
       room with satisfaction—after a pause—rises—takes off his
       collar.*] You're awful quiet—what are you doing in there?   125
YOUNG WOMAN: Just—getting ready—
HUSBAND: [*Still in his mood of satisfaction*] I'm going to enjoy
       life from now on— I haven't had such an easy time of it. I got
       where I am by hard work and self denial—now I'm going to
       enjoy life—I'm going to make up for all I missed—aren't you   130
       about ready?
YOUNG WOMAN: Not yet.
HUSBAND: Next year maybe we'll go to Paris. You can buy a lot
       of that French underwear—and Switzerland—all my life I've
       wanted a Swiss watch—that I bought right there— I coulda'   135
       got a Swiss watch here, but I always wanted one that I bought
       right there—Isn't that funny—huh? Isn't it? Huh? Huh?
YOUNG WOMAN: Yes.
HUSBAND: All my life I've wanted a Swiss watch that I bought
       right there. All my life I've counted on having that some day— 140
       more than anything—except one thing—you know what?
YOUNG WOMAN: No.
HUSBAND: Guess.
YOUNG WOMAN: I can't.
HUSBAND: Then I'm coming in and tell you.   145
YOUNG WOMAN: No! Please! Please don't.
HUSBAND: Well hurry up then! I thought you women didn't wear
       much of anything these days—huh? Huh? I'm coming in!
YOUNG WOMAN: No—no! Just a minute!
HUSBAND: All right. Just a minute!   150

[YOUNG WOMAN *is silent.*]

HUSBAND: [*Laughs and takes out watch*] 13—14— I'm counting
       the seconds on you—that's what you said, didn't you—just a
       minute! —49—50—51—52—53—

[*Enter* YOUNG WOMAN.]

YOUNG WOMAN: [*At the door*] Here I am.

[*She wears a little white gown that hangs very straight. She is very
still, but her eyes are wide with a curious, helpless, animal terror.*]

HUSBAND: [*Starts toward her—stops. The room is in shadow except 155
       for one dim light by the bed. Sound of girl weeping*] You crying?
       [*Sound of weeping*] What you crying for?

[*Crosses to her*]

YOUNG WOMAN: [*Crying out*] Ma! Ma! I want my mother!
HUSBAND: I thought you were glad to get away from her.
YOUNG WOMAN: I want her now—I want somebody.   160
HUSBAND: You got me, haven't you?

YOUNG WOMAN: Somebody—somebody—

HUSBAND: There's nothing to cry about. There's nothing to cry about.

[*The scene blacks out. The music continues until the lights go up for Episode Four. Rhythm of the music is gradually replaced by the sound of steel riveting for Episode Four.*]

EPISODE FOUR

MATERNAL

SCENE:
  a room in a hospital:
  bed,
  chair.
  The door in the back now opens on a corridor; the window on a tall building going up.

SOUNDS:
  outside window—riveting.

CHARACTERS IN THE SCENE:
  YOUNG WOMAN,
  DOCTORS,
  NURSES,
  HUSBAND.

CHARACTERS SEEN BUT NOT HEARD:
  WOMAN IN WHEEL CHAIR,
  WOMAN IN BATHROBE,
  STRETCHER WAGON,
  NURSE WITH TRAY,
  NURSE WITH COVERED BASIN.

AT RISE:
  YOUNG WOMAN *lies still in bed. The door is open. In the corridor, a stretcher wagon goes by.*

[*Enter* NURSE.]

NURSE: How are you feeling today? [*No response from* YOUNG WOMAN] Better? [*No response*] No pain? [*No response.* NURSE *takes her watch in one hand,* YOUNG WOMAN's *wrist in the other—stands, then goes to chart at foot of bed—writes.*] You're
5   getting along fine. [*No response*] Such a sweet baby you have, too. [*No response*] Aren't you glad it's a girl? [YOUNG WOMAN *makes sign with her head "No."*] You're not! Oh, my! That's no way to talk! Men want boys—women ought to want girls. [*No response*] Maybe you didn't want either, eh? [YOUNG WOMAN
10   *signs "No." Riveting machine*] You'll feel different when it begins to nurse. You'll just love it then. Your milk hasn't come yet—has it? [*Sign—"No"*] It will! [*Sign—"No"*] Oh, you don't know Doctor! [*Goes to door—turns*] Anything else you want? [YOUNG WOMAN *points to window.*] Draft? [*Sign—"No"*] The
15   noise? [YOUNG WOMAN *signs "Yes."*] Oh, that can't be helped. Hospital's got to have a new wing. We're the biggest Maternity Hospital in the world. I'll close the window, though. [YOUNG WOMAN *signs "No."*] No?
  YOUNG WOMAN: [*Whispers*] I smell everything then.
20   NURSE: [*Starting out the door—riveting machine*] Here's your man!

[*Enter* HUSBAND *with large bouquet. Crosses to bed.*]

HUSBAND: Well, how are we today?

[YOUNG WOMAN—*no response*]

NURSE: She's getting stronger!
HUSBAND: Of course she is!
NURSE: [*Taking flowers*] See what your husband brought you.   25
HUSBAND: Better put 'em in water right away. [*Exit* NURSE.] Everything OK? [YOUNG WOMAN *signs "No."*] Now see here, my dear, you've got to brace up, you know! And—and face things! Everybody's got to brace up and face things! That's what makes the world go round. I know all you've   30
been through but— [YOUNG WOMAN *signs "No."*] Oh, yes I do! I know all about it! I was right outside all the time! [YOUNG WOMAN *makes violent gesture of "No." Ignoring*] Oh yes! But you've got to brace up now! Make an effort! Pull yourself together! Start the uphill climb! Oh I've been   35
down—but I haven't stayed down. I've been licked but I haven't stayed licked! I've pulled myself up by my own bootstraps, and that's what you've got to do! Will power! That's what conquers! Look at me! Now you've got to brace up! Face the music! Stand the gaff! Take life by the horns!   40
Look it in the face! —Having a baby's natural! Perfectly natural thing—why should—

[YOUNG WOMAN *chokes—points wildly to door. Enter* NURSE *with flowers in a vase.*]

NURSE: What's the matter?
HUSBAND: She's got that gagging again—like she had the last time I was here.   45

[YOUNG WOMAN *gestures him out.*]

NURSE: Better go, sir.
HUSBAND: [*At door*] I'll be back.

[YOUNG WOMAN *gasping and gesturing*]

NURSE: She needs rest.
HUSBAND: Tomorrow then. I'll be back tomorrow—tomorrow and every day—goodbye.   50

[*Exits*]

NURSE: You got a mighty nice husband, I guess you know that? [*Writes on chart*] Gagging.

[*Corridor life—*WOMAN IN BATHROBE *passes door. Enter* DOCTOR, YOUNG DOCTOR, NURSE *wheeling surgeon's wagon with bottles, instruments, etc.*]

DOCTOR: How's the little lady today?

[*Crosses to bed*]

NURSE: She's better, Doctor.
DOCTOR: Of course she's better! She's all right—aren't you?   55
[YOUNG WOMAN *does not respond.*] What's the matter? Can't you talk?

[*Drops her hand—takes chart*]

NURSE: She's a little weak yet, Doctor.

DOCTOR: [*At chart*] Milk hasn't come yet?

60 NURSE: No, Doctor.

DOCTOR: Put the child to breast. [YOUNG WOMAN—*"No—no!"*— *Riveting machine*] No? Don't you want to nurse your baby? [YOUNG WOMAN *signs "No."*] Why not? [*No response*] These modern neurotic women, eh, Doctor? What are we going to

65 do with 'em? [YOUNG DOCTOR *laughs.* NURSE *smiles.*] Bring the baby!

YOUNG WOMAN: No!

DOCTOR: Well—that's strong enough. I thought you were too weak to talk—that's better. You don't want your baby?

70 YOUNG WOMAN: No.

DOCTOR: What do you want?

YOUNG WOMAN: Let alone—let alone.

DOCTOR: Bring the baby.

NURSE: Yes, Doctor—she's behaved very badly every time,

75 Doctor—very upset—maybe we better not.

DOCTOR: I decide what we better and better not here, Nurse!

NURSE: Yes, Doctor.

DOCTOR: Bring the baby.

NURSE: Yes, Doctor.

80 DOCTOR: [*With chart*] Gagging—you mean nausea.

NURSE: Yes, Doctor but—

DOCTOR: No buts, nurse.

NURSE: Yes, Doctor.

DOCTOR: Nausea!— Change her diet!— What is her diet?

85 NURSE: Liquids.

DOCTOR: Give her solids.

NURSE: Yes, Doctor.

She says she can't swallow solids.

DOCTOR: Give her solids.

90 NURSE: Yes, Doctor.

[*Starts to go—riveting machine*]

DOCTOR: Wait—I'll change her medicine. [*Takes pad and writes prescription in Latin. Hands it to* NURSE] After meals. [*To door*] Bring her baby.

[*Exit* DOCTOR, *followed by* YOUNG DOCTOR *and* NURSE *with surgeon's wagon.*]

NURSE: Yes, Doctor.

[*Exits*]

95 YOUNG WOMAN: [*Alone*] Let me alone—let me alone—let me alone—I've submitted to enough—I won't submit to any more—crawl off—crawl off in the dark—Vixen crawled under the bed—way back in the corner under the bed—they were all drowned—puppies don't go to heaven—heaven—golden

100 stairs—long stairs—long—too long—long golden stairs— climb those golden stairs— stairs—stairs—climb—tired—too tired—dead—no matter—nothing matters—dead—stairs— long stairs—all the dead going up—going up to be in heaven—heaven— golden stairs—all the children coming

105 down—coming down to be born—dead going up—children coming down—going up—coming down—going up—coming down—going up—coming down—going up—stop— stop—no—no traffic cop—no—no traffic cop in heaven—

traffic cop—traffic cop—can't you give us a smile— tired—too tired—no matter—it doesn't matter—St. Peter—St. Peter at 110 the gate—you can't come in—no matter—it doesn't matter— I'll rest—I'll lie down—down— all written down—down in a big book—no matter—it doesn't matter— I'll lie down—it weighs me—it's over me—it weighs—weighs—it's heavy—it's a heavy book— no matter—lie still—don't move—can't 115 move—rest— forget—they say you forget—a girl—aren't you glad it's a girl—a little girl—with no hair—none—little curls all over his head—a little bald girl—curls—curls all over his head—what kind of hair has God? no matter—it doesn't matter—everybody loves God—they've got to—got 120 to—got to love God—God is love—even if he's bad they got to love him—even if he's got fat hands—fat hands—no no—he wouldn't be God—His hands make you well—He lays on his hands—well—and happy— no matter—doesn't matter— far—too far—tired—too tired Vixen crawled off under 125 bed—eight—there were eight— a woman crawled off under the bed—a woman has one—two three four—one two three four—one two three four—two plus two is four—two times two is four—two times four is eight Vixen had eight—one two three four five six seven eight—eight—Puffie had eight—all 130 drowned—drowned—drowned in blood— blood—oh God! God—God never had one—Mary had one—in a manger— the lowly manger—God's on a high throne—far—too far—no matter—it doesn't matter— God Mary Mary God Mary— Virgin Mary—Mary had one—the Holy Ghost—the Holy 135 Ghost—George H. Jones—oh don't—please don't! Let me rest—now I can rest—the weight is gone—inside the weight is gone— it's only outside—outside—all around—weight—I'm under it—Vixen crawled under the bed—there were eight—I'll not submit any more—I'll not submit—I'll not submit— 140

[*The scene blacks out. The sound of riveting continues until it goes into the sound of an electric piano and the scene lights up for Episode Five.*]

EPISODE FIVE

PROHIBITED

SCENE:
    bar:
        bottles,
        tables,
        chairs,
        electric piano.

SOUND:
    electric piano.

CHARACTERS:
    MAN *behind the bar,*
    POLICEMAN *at bar,*
    WAITER.
    At Table 1: a MAN *and a* WOMAN
    At Table 2: a MAN *and a* BOY
    At Table 3: TWO MEN *waiting for* TWO GIRLS, *who are*
        TELEPHONE GIRL *of Episode One and* YOUNG WOMAN.

AT RISE:
    Everyone except the GIRLS *on. Of the characters, the* MAN
    and WOMAN *at Table 1 are an ordinary man and woman,*

THE MAN at *Table 2 is a middle-aged fairy; the* BOY *is young, untouched. At Table 3, 1st* MAN *is pleasing, common, vigorous. He has coarse wavy hair.* 2ND MAN *is an ordinary salesman type.*

1ST MAN: [*At Table* 3] I'm going to beat it.
2ND MAN: Oh, for the love of Mike.
1ST MAN: They ain't going to show.
2ND MAN: Sure they'll show.
5 1ST MAN: How do you know they'll show?
2ND MAN: I tell you you can't keep that baby away from me—just got to— [*Snaps fingers*]—She comes running.
1ST MAN: Looks like it.
2ND MAN: [*To* WAITER—*makes sign "2," with his fingers*] The same.

[WAITER *goes to the bar.*]

10 MAN: [*At Table* 2] Oh, I'm sorry I brought you here.
BOY: Why?
MAN: This Purgatory of noise! I brought you here to give you pleasure—let you taste pleasure. This sherry they have here is bottled—heaven. Wait till you taste it.
15 BOY: But I don't drink.
MAN: Drink! This isn't drink! Real amontillado is sunshine and orange groves—it's the Mediterranean and blue moonlight and—love? Have you ever been in love?
BOY: No.
20 MAN: Never in love with—a woman?
BOY: No—not really.
MAN: What do you mean—really?
BOY: Just—that.
MAN: Ah! [*Makes sign to* WAITER] Two—you know what I
25 want—Two.

[WAITER *goes to the bar.*]

MAN: [*At Table* 1] Well, are you going through with it, or ain't you?
WOMAN: That's what I want to do—go through with it.
MAN: But you can't.
WOMAN: Why can't I?
30 MAN: How can yuh? [*Silence*] It's nothing—most women don't think anything about it—they just—Bert told me a doctor to go to—gave me the address—
WOMAN: Don't talk about it!
MAN: Got to talk about it—you got to get out of this. [*Silence—*
35 MAN *makes sign to* WAITER] What you having?
WOMAN: Nothing—I don't want anything. I had enough.
MAN: Do you good. The same?
WOMAN: I suppose so.
MAN: [*Makes sign "2" to* WAITER] The same.

[WAITER *goes to the bar.*]

40 1ST MAN: [*At Table* 3] I'm going to beat it.
2ND MAN: Oh say, listen! I'm counting on you to take the other one off my hands.
1ST MAN: I'm going to beat it.
2ND MAN: For the love of Mike have a heart! Listen—as a favor
45 to me—I got to be home by six—I promised my wife—sure. That don't leave me no time at all if we got to hang around— entertain some dame. You got to take her off my hands.
1ST MAN: Maybe she won't fall for me.

2ND MAN: Sure she'll fall for you! They all fall for you—even my wife likes you—tries to kid herself it's your brave exploits, but 50 I know what it is—sure she'll fall for you.

[*Enter two girls—*TELEPHONE GIRL *and* YOUNG WOMAN.]

GIRL: [*Coming to Table*] Hello—
2ND MAN: [*Grouch*] Good night.
GIRL: Good night? What's eatin' yuh?
2ND MAN: [*Same*] Nothin's eatin' me—thought somethin' musta 55 swallowed you.
GIRL: Why?
2ND MAN: You're late!
GIRL: [*Unimpressed*] Oh—[*Brushing it aside*]—Mrs. Jones— Mr. Smith. 60
2ND MAN: Meet my friend, Mr. Roe. [*They all sit. To the* WAITER] The same, and two more.

[WAITER *goes.*]

GIRL: So we kept you waiting, did we?
2ND MAN: Only about an hour.
YOUNG WOMAN: Was it that long? 65
2ND MAN: We been here that long—ain't we, Dick?
1ST MAN: Just about, Harry.
2ND MAN: For the love of God what delayed yuh?
GIRL: Tell Helen that one.
2ND MAN: [*To* YOUNG WOMAN] The old Irish woman that went 70 to her first race? Bet on the skate that came in last—she went up to the jockey and asked him, "For the love of God, what delayed yuh?"

[*All laugh.*]

YOUNG WOMAN: Why, that's kinda funny!
2ND MAN: Kinda!—What do you mean kinda? 75
YOUNG WOMAN: I just mean there are not many of 'em that are funny at all.
2ND MAN: Not if you haven't heard the funny ones.
YOUNG WOMAN: Oh I've heard 'em all.
1ST MAN: Not a laugh in a carload, eh? 80
GIRL: Got a cigarette?
2ND MAN: [*With package*] One of these?
GIRL: [*Taking one*] Uhhuh.

[*He offers the package to* YOUNG WOMAN.]

YOUNG WOMAN: [*Taking one*] Uhhuh.
2ND MAN: [*To 1st* MAN] One of these? 85
1ST MAN: [*Showing his own package*] Thanks—I like these. [*He lights* YOUNG WOMAN's *cigarette.*]
2ND MAN: [*Lighting* GIRL's *cigarette*] Well—baby—how they comin', huh?
GIRL: Couldn't be better. 90
2ND MAN: How's every little thing?
GIRL: Just great.
2ND MAN: Miss me?
GIRL: I'll say so—when did you get in?
2ND MAN: Just a coupla hours ago. 95
GIRL: Miss me?
2ND MAN: Did I? You don't know the half of it.
YOUNG WOMAN: [*Interrupting restlessly*] Can we dance here?

2ND MAN: Not here.

100 YOUNG WOMAN: Where do we go from here?

2ND MAN: Where do we go from here! You just got here!

1ST MAN: What's the hurry?

2ND MAN: What's the rush?

YOUNG WOMAN: I don't know.

105 GIRL: Helen wants to dance.

YOUNG WOMAN: I just want to keep moving.

1ST MAN: [*Smiling*] You want to keep moving, huh?

2ND MAN: You must be one of those restless babies! Where do we go from here!

110 YOUNG WOMAN: It's only some days—I want to keep moving.

1ST MAN: You want to keep moving, huh? [*He is staring at her smilingly.*]

YOUNG WOMAN: [*Nods*] Uhhuh.

1ST MAN: [*Quietly*] Stick around a while.

115 2ND MAN: Where do we go from here! Say, what kind of a crowd do you run with, anyway?

GIRL: Helen don't run with any crowd—do you, Helen?

YOUNG WOMAN: [*Embarrassed*] No.

1ST MAN: Well, I'm not a crowd—run with me.

120 2ND MAN: [*Gratified*] All set, huh?—Dick was about ready to beat it.

1ST MAN: That's before I met the little lady.

[WAITER *serves drinks.*]

1ST MAN: Here's how.

2ND MAN: Here's to you.

125 GIRL: Here's looking at you.

YOUNG WOMAN: Here's—happy days.

[*They all drink.*]

1ST MAN: That's good stuff!

2ND MAN: Off a boat.

1ST MAN: Off a boat?

130 2ND MAN: They get all their stuff here—off a boat.

GIRL: That's what *they* say.

2ND MAN: No! Sure! Sure they do! Sure!

GIRL: It's all right with me.

2ND MAN: But they do! Sure!

135 GIRL: I believe you, darling!

2ND MAN: Did you miss me?

GIRL: Uhhuh. [*Affirmative*]

2ND MAN: Any other daddies?

GIRL: Uhhuh. [*Negative*]

140 2ND MAN: Love any daddy but daddy?

GIRL: Uhhuh. [*Negative*]

2ND MAN: Let's beat it!

GIRL: [*A little self-conscious before* YOUNG WOMAN] We just got here.

145 2ND MAN: Don't I know it—Come on!

GIRL: But—[*Indicates* YOUNG WOMAN]

2ND MAN: [*Not understanding*] They're all set—aren't you?

1ST MAN: [*To* YOUNG WOMAN] Are we?

[*She doesn't answer.*]

2ND MAN: I got to be out to the house by six—come on—

150 [*Rising—to* GIRL] Come on, kid—let's us beat it! [GIRL *indicates* YOUNG WOMAN.] [*Now understanding—very elaborate*] Business is business, you know! I got a lot to do yet

this afternoon—thought you might go along with me—help me out—how about it?

GIRL: [*Rising, her dignity preserved*] Sure—I'll go along with 155 you—help you out.

[*Both rise.*]

2ND MAN: All right with you folks?

1ST MAN: All right with me.

2ND MAN: All right with you? [*To* YOUNG WOMAN]

YOUNG WOMAN: All right with me. 160

2ND MAN: Come on, kid. [*They rise.*] Where's the damage?

1ST MAN: Go on!

2ND MAN: No!

1ST MAN: Go on!

2ND MAN: I'll match you. 165

YOUNG WOMAN: Heads win!

GIRL: Heads I win—tails you lose.

2ND MAN: [*Impatiently*] He's matching me.

1ST MAN: Am I matching you or you matching me?

2ND MAN: I'm matching you. [*They match.*] You're stung! 170

1ST MAN: [*Contentedly*] Not so you can notice it. [*Smiles at* YOUNG WOMAN]

GIRL: That's for you, Helen.

2ND MAN: She ain't dumb! Come on.

GIRL: [*To* 1ST MAN]. You be nice to her now. She's very 175 fastidious.—Goodbye.

[*Exit* 2ND MAN *and* GIRL.]

YOUNG WOMAN: I know what business is like.

1ST MAN: You do—do yuh?

YOUNG WOMAN: I used to be a business girl myself before—

1ST MAN: Before what? 180

YOUNG WOMAN: Before I quit.

1ST MAN: What did you quit for?

YOUNG WOMAN: I just quit.

1ST MAN: You're married, huh?

YOUNG WOMAN: Yes—I am. 185

1ST MAN: All right with me.

YOUNG WOMAN: Some men don't seem to like a woman after she's married—

[WAITER *comes to the table.*]

1ST MAN: What's the difference?

YOUNG WOMAN: Depends on the man, I guess. 190

1ST MAN: Depends on the woman, I guess. [*To* WAITER, *makes sign of* "2"] The same.

[WAITER *goes to the bar.*]

MAN: [*At Table 1*] It don't amount to nothing. God! Most women just—

WOMAN: I know—I know—I know. 95

MAN: They don't think nothing of it. They just—

WOMAN: I know—I know—I know.

[*Re-enter* 2ND MAN *and* GIRL. *They go to Table 3.*]

2ND MAN: Say, I forgot—I want you to do something for me, will yuh?

1ST MAN: Sure—what is it? 100

2ND MAN: I want you to telephone me out home tomorrow—and ask me to come into town—will yuh?

1ST MAN: Sure—why not?

2ND MAN: You know—business—get me?

105 1ST MAN: I get you.

2ND MAN: I've worked the telegraph gag to death—and my wife likes you.

1ST MAN: What's your number?

2ND MAN: I'll write it down for you.

[*Writes*]

110 1ST MAN: How is your wife?

2ND MAN: She's fine.

1ST MAN: And the kid?

2ND MAN: Great. [*Hands him the card. To girl*] Come on, kid. [*Turns back to* YOUNG WOMAN] Get this bird to tell you about

115 himself.

GIRL: Keep him from it.

2ND MAN: Get him to tell you how he killed a couple a spig down in Mexico.

GIRL: You been in Mexico?

120 2ND MAN: He just came up from there.

GIRL: Can you teach us the tango?

YOUNG WOMAN: You killed a man?

2ND MAN: Two of 'em! With a bottle! Get him to tell you—with a bottle. Come on, kid. Goodbye.

[*Exit* 2ND MAN *and* GIRL.]

125 YOUNG WOMAN: Why did you?

1ST MAN: What?

YOUNG WOMAN: Kill 'em?

1ST MAN: To get free.

YOUNG WOMAN: Oh.

130 MAN: [*At Table 2*] You really must taste this—just taste it. It's a real amontillado, you know.

BOY: Where do they get it here?

MAN: It's always down the side streets one finds the real pleasures, don't you think?

135 BOY: I don't know.

MAN: Learn. Come, taste this! Amontillado! Or don't you like amontillado?

BOY: I don't know. I never had any before.

MAN: Your first taste! How I envy you! Come, taste it! Taste it!

140 And die.

[BOY *tastes wine—finds it disappointing.*]

MAN: [*Gilding it*] Poe was a lover of amontillado. He returns to it continually, you remember—or are you a lover of Poe?

BOY: I've read a lot of him.

MAN: But are you a lover?

145 1ST MAN: [*At Table 3*] There were a bunch of bandidos—bandits, you know, took me into the hills—holding me there—what was I to do? I got the two birds that guarded me drunk one night, and then I filled the empty bottle with small stones—and let 'em have it!

150 YOUNG WOMAN: Oh!

1ST MAN: I had to get free, didn't I? I let 'em have it—

YOUNG WOMAN: Oh—then what did you do?

1ST MAN: Then I beat it.

YOUNG WOMAN: Where to—?

1ST MAN: Right here. [*Pause*] Glad? 155

YOUNG WOMAN: [*Nods*] Yes.

1ST MAN: [*Makes sign to* WAITER *of* "2"] The same.

[WAITER *goes to bar.*]

MAN: [*At Table 1*] You're just scared because this is the first time and—

WOMAN: I'm not scared. 160

MAN: Then what are you for Christ's sake?

WOMAN: I'm not scared. I want it—I want to have it—that ain't being scared, is it?

MAN: It's being goofy.

WOMAN: I don't care. 165

MAN: What about your folks?

WOMAN: I don't care.

MAN: What about your job? [*Silence*] You got to keep your job, haven't you? [*Silence*] Haven't you?

WOMAN: I suppose so. 170

MAN: Well—there you are!

WOMAN: [*Silence—then*] All right—let's go now— You got the address?

MAN: Now you're coming to.

[*They get up and go off. Exit* MAN *and* WOMAN.]

YOUNG WOMAN: [*At Table 3*] A bottle like that? [*She picks it up.*] 175

1ST MAN: Yeah—filled with pebbles.

YOUNG WOMAN: What kind of pebbles?

1ST MAN: Pebbles! Off the ground.

YOUNG WOMAN: Oh.

1ST MAN: Necessity, you know, mother of invention. [*As* YOUNG 180 WOMAN *handles the bottle*] Ain't a bad weapon—first you got a sledge hammer—then you got a knife.

YOUNG WOMAN: Oh. [*Puts bottle down*]

1ST MAN: Women don't like knives, do they? [*Pours drink*]

YOUNG WOMAN: No. 185

1ST MAN: Don't mind a hammer so much, though, do they?

YOUNG WOMAN: No—

1ST MAN: I didn't like it myself—any of it—but I had to get free, didn't I? Sure I had to get free, didn't I? [*Drinks*] Now I'm damn glad I did. 190

YOUNG WOMAN: Why?

1ST MAN: You know why. [*He puts his hand over hers.*]

MAN: [*At Table 2*] Let's go to my rooms—and I'll show them to you—I have a first edition of Verlaine that will simply make your mouth water. [*They stand up.*] Here—there's just a sip 195 at the bottom of my glass— [BOY *takes it.*] That last sip that's sweetest—Wasn't it?

BOY: [*Laughs*] And I always thought that was dregs.

[*Exit* MAN *followed by* BOY.]

[*At Table 3. The* MAN *is holding her hand across the table.*]

YOUNG WOMAN: When you put your hand over mine! When you just touch me! 200

1ST MAN: Yeah? [*Pause*] Come on, kid, let's go!

YOUNG WOMAN: Where?

1ST MAN: You haven't been around much, have you, kid?

YOUNG WOMAN: No.

205 1ST MAN: I could tell that just to look at you.

YOUNG WOMAN: You could?

1ST MAN: Sure I could. What are you running around with a girl like that other one for?

YOUNG WOMAN: I don't know. She seems to have a good time.

210 1ST MAN: So that's it.

YOUNG WOMAN: Don't she?

1ST MAN: Don't you?

YOUNG WOMAN: No.

1ST MAN: Never?

215 YOUNG WOMAN: Never.

1ST MAN: What's the matter?

YOUNG WOMAN: Nothing—just me, I guess.

1ST MAN: You're all right.

YOUNG WOMAN: Am I?

220 1ST MAN: Sure. You just haven't met the right guy—that's all—a girl like you—you got to meet the right guy.

YOUNG WOMAN: I know.

1ST MAN: You're different from girls like that other one—any guy'll do her. You're different.

225 YOUNG WOMAN: I guess I am.

1ST MAN: You didn't fall for that business gag—did you—when they went off?

YOUNG WOMAN: Well, I thought they wanted to be alone probably, but—

230 1ST MAN: And how!

YOUNG WOMAN: Oh—so that's it.

1ST MAN: That's it. Come along—let's go—

YOUNG WOMAN: Oh, I couldn't! Like this?

1ST MAN: Don't you like me?

235 YOUNG WOMAN: Yes.

1ST MAN: Then what's the matter?

YOUNG WOMAN: Do—you—like me?

1ST MAN: Like yuh? You don't know the half of it—listen—you know what you seem like to me?

240 YOUNG WOMAN: What?

1ST MAN: An angel. Just like an angel.

YOUNG WOMAN: I do?

1ST MAN: That's what I said! Let's go!

YOUNG WOMAN: Where?

245 1ST MAN: Where do you live?

YOUNG WOMAN: Oh, we can't go to my place.

1ST MAN: Then come to my place.

YOUNG WOMAN: Oh I couldn't—is it far?

1ST MAN: Just a step—come on—

250 YOUNG WOMAN: Oh I couldn't—what is it—a room?

1ST MAN: No—an apartment—a one-room apartment.

YOUNG WOMAN: That's different.

1ST MAN: On the ground floor—no one will see you—coming or going.

255 YOUNG WOMAN: [Getting up] I couldn't.

1ST MAN: [Rises] Wait a minute;—I got to pay the damage—and I'll get a bottle of something to take along.

YOUNG WOMAN: No—don't.

1ST MAN: Why not?

260 YOUNG WOMAN: Well—don't bring any pebbles.

1ST MAN: Say—forget that! Will you?

YOUNG WOMAN: I just meant I don't think I'll need anything to drink.

1ST MAN: [Leaning to her eagerly] You like me—don't you, kid?

265 YOUNG WOMAN: Do you me?

1ST MAN: Wait!

[He goes to the bar. She remains, her hands outstretched on the table staring ahead. Enter a MAN and a GIRL. They go to one of the empty tables. The WAITER goes to them.]

MAN: [To GIRL] What do you want?

GIRL: Same old thing.

MAN: [To the WAITER] The usual. [Makes a sign "2"]

[The 1st MAN crosses to YOUNG WOMAN with a wrapped bottle under his arm. She rises and starts out with him. As they pass the piano, he stops and puts in a nickel— the music starts as they exit. The scene blacks out.]

[The music of the electric piano continues until the lights go up for Episode Six, and the music has become the music of a hand organ, very very faint.]

EPISODE SIX

INTIMATE

SCENE:
> a dark room.

SOUNDS:
> a hand organ; footbeats, of passing feet.

CHARACTERS:
> MAN,
> YOUNG WOMAN.

AT RISE:
> Darkness. Nothing can be discerned. From the outside comes the sound of a hand organ, very faint, and the irregular rhythm of passing feet. The hand organ is playing Cielito Lindo, that Spanish song that has been on every hand organ lately.

MAN: You're awful still, honey. What you thinking about?

WOMAN: About sea shells. [The sound of her voice is beautiful.]

MAN: Sheshells? Gee! I can't say it!

WOMAN: When I was little my grandmother used to have a big pink sea shell on the mantel behind the stove. When we'd go to visit her they'd let me hold it, and listen. That's what I was thinking about now. 5

MAN: Yeah?

WOMAN: You can hear the sea in 'em, you know.

MAN: Yeah, I know. 10

WOMAN: I wonder why that is?

MAN: Search me. [Pause]

WOMAN: You going?

[He has moved.]

MAN: No. I just want a cigarette.

WOMAN: [Glad, relieved] Oh. 15

MAN: Want one?

WOMAN: No. [Taking the match] Let me light it for you.

MAN: You got might pretty hands, honey. [The match is out.] This little pig went to market. This little pig stayed home. This little pig went— 20

WOMAN: [Laughs] Diddle diddle dee.

[Laughs again]

MAN: You got awful pretty hands.

WOMAN: I used to have. But I haven't taken much care of them lately. I will now— [*Pause. The music gets clearer.*] What's that?

MAN: What?

WOMAN: That music?

MAN: A dago hand organ. I gave him two bits the first day I got here—so he comes every day.

WOMAN: I mean—what's that he's playing?

MAN: *Cielito Lindo.*

WOMAN: What does that mean?

MAN: Little Heaven.

WOMAN: Little Heaven?

MAN: That's what lovers call each other in Spain.

WOMAN: Spain's where all the castles are, ain't it?

MAN: Yeah.

WOMAN: Little Heaven—sing it!

MAN: [*Singing to the music of the hand organ*] De la sierra morena viene, bajando viene, bajando; un par de ojitos negros—cielito lindo—da contrabando.

WOMAN: What does it mean?

MAN: From the high dark mountains.

WOMAN: From the high dark mountains—?

MAN: Oh it doesn't mean anything. It doesn't make sense. It's love. [*Taking up the song*] Ay-ay-ay-ay.

WOMAN: I know what that means.

MAN: What?

WOMAN: Ay-ay-ay-ay.

[*They laugh.*]

MAN: [*Taking up the song*] Canta non llores—Sing don't cry—

WOMAN: [*Taking up song*] La-la-la-la-la-la-la-la-la-la— Little Heaven!

MAN: You got a nice voice, honey.

WOMAN: Have I?

[*Laughs—tickles him*]

MAN: You bet you have—hey!

WOMAN: [*Laughing*] You ticklish?

MAN: Sure I am! Hey! [*They laugh.*] Go on, honey, sing something.

WOMAN: I couldn't.

MAN: Go on—you got a fine voice.

WOMAN: [*Laughs and sings*] Hey, diddle, diddle, the cat and the fiddle,
The cow jumped over the moon
The little dog laughed to see the sport
And the dish ran away with the spoon—
[*Both laugh.*] I never thought that had any sense before—now I get it.

MAN: You got me beat.

WOMAN: It's you and me.—La—lalalalalala—lalalalalalala —Little Heaven. You're the dish and I'm the spoon.

MAN: You're a little spoon all right.

WOMAN: And I guess I'm the little cow that jumped over the moon. [*A pause*] Do you believe in sorta guardian angels?

MAN: What?

WOMAN: Guardian angels?

MAN: I don't know. Maybe.

WOMAN: I do. [*Taking up the song again*] Lalalalala-lalalalala-lalalala—Little Heaven. [*Talking*] There must be something

that looks out for you and brings you your happiness, at last—look at us! How did we both happen to go to that place today if there wasn't something!

MAN: Maybe you're right.

WOMAN: Look at us!

MAN: Everything's us to you, kid—ain't it?

WOMAN: Ain't it?

MAN: All right with me.

WOMAN: We belong together! We belong together! And we're going to stick together, ain't we?

MAN: Sing something else.

WOMAN: I tell you I can't sing!

MAN: Sure you can!

WOMAN: I tell you I hadn't thought of singing since I was a little bit of a girl.

MAN: Well sing anyway.

WOMAN: [*Singing*] And every little wavelet had its night cap on—its night cap on—its night cap on—and every little wave had its night cap on—so very early in the morning. [*Talking*] Did you used to sing that when you were a little kid?

MAN: Nope.

WOMAN: Didn't you? We used to—in the first grade—little kids—we used to go round and round in a ring—and flop our hands up and down—supposed to be the waves. I remember it used to confuse me—because we did just the same thing to be little angels.

MAN: Yeah?

WOMAN: You know why I came here?

MAN: I can make a good guess.

WOMAN: Because you told me I looked like an angel to you! That's why I came.

MAN: Jeez, honey, all women look like angels to me—all white women. I ain't been seeing nothing but Indians, you know, for the last couple a years. Gee, when I got off the boat here the other day—and saw all the women—gee I pretty near went crazy—talk about looking like angels—why—

WOMAN: You've had a lot of women, haven't you?

MAN: No so many—real ones.

WOMAN: Did you—like any of 'em—better than me?

MAN: Nope—there wasn't one of 'em any sweeter than you, honey—not as sweet—no—not as sweet.

WOMAN: I like to hear you say it. Say it again—

MAN: [*Protesting good humoredly*] Oh—

WOMAN: Go on—tell me again!

MAN: Here! [*Kisses her*] Does that tell you?

WOMAN: Yes. [*Pause*] We're going to stick together—always— aren't we?

MAN: [*Honestly*] I'll have to be moving on, kid—some day, you know.

WOMAN: When?

MAN: Quien sabe?

WOMAN: What does that mean?

MAN: Quien sabe? You got to learn that, kid, if you're figuring on coming with me. It's the answer to everything—below the Rio Grande.

WOMAN: What does it mean?

MAN: It means—who knows?

WOMAN: Keen sabe?

MAN: Yep—don't forget it—now.

WOMAN: I'll never forget it!

MAN: Quien sabe?

WOMAN: And I'll never get to use it.

140 MAN: Quien sabe.

WOMAN: I'll never get—below the Rio Grande—I'll never get out of here.

MAN: Quien sabe.

WOMAN: [*Change of mood*] That's right! Keen sabe? Who knows?

145 MAN: That's the stuff.

WOMAN: You must like it down there.

MAN: I can't live anywhere else—for long.

WOMAN: Why not?

MAN: Oh—you're free down there! You're free!

[*A street light is lit outside. The outlines of a window take form against this light. There are bars across it, and from outside it, the sidewalk cuts across almost at the top. It is a basement room. The constant going and coming of passing feet, mostly feet of couples, can be dimly seen. Inside, on the ledge, there is a lily blooming in a bowl of rocks and water.*]

150 WOMAN: What's that?

MAN: Just the street light going on.

WOMAN: Is it as late as that?

MAN: Late as what?

WOMAN: Dark.

155 MAN: It's been dark for hours—didn't you know that?

WOMAN: No!—I must go! [*Rises*]

MAN: Wait—the moon will be up in a little while—full moon.

WOMAN: It isn't that! I'm late! I must go! [*She comes into the light. She wears a white chemise that might be the tunic of a dancer,*

160 *and as she comes into the light she fastens about her waist a little skirt. She really wears almost exactly the clothes that women wear now, but the finesse of their cut, and the grace and ease with which she puts them on, must turn this episode of her dressing into a personification, an idealization of a woman*

165 *clothing herself. All her gestures must be unconscious, innocent, relaxed, sure and full of natural grace. As she sits facing the window pulling on a stocking*] What's that?

MAN: What?

WOMAN: On the window ledge.

170 MAN: A flower.

WOMAN: Who gave it to you?

MAN: Nobody gave it to me. I bought it.

WOMAN: For yourself?

MAN: Yeah—why not?

175 WOMAN: I don't know.

MAN: In Chinatown—made me think of, Frisco where I was a kid—so I bought it.

WOMAN: Is that where you were born—Frisco?

MAN: Yep. Twin Peaks.

180 WOMAN: What's that?

MAN: A couple hills—together.

WOMAN: One for you and one for me.

MAN: I bet you'd like Frisco.

WOMAN: I know a woman went out there once!

185 MAN: The bay and the hills! Jeez, that's the life! Every Saturday we used to cross the Bay—get a couple nags and just ride—over the hills. One would have a blanket on the saddle—the other, the grub. At night we'd make a little fire and eat—and then roll up in the old blanket and—

190 WOMAN: Who? Who was with you?

MAN: [*Indifferently*] Anybody. [*Enthusiastically*] Jeez, that dry old grass out there smells good at night—full of tar weed—you know—

WOMAN: Is that a good smell?

MAN: Tar weed? Didn't you ever smell it? [*She shakes her head, 195 "No."*] Sure it's a good smell! The Bay and the hills. [*She goes to the mirror of the dresser, to finish dressing. She has only a dress to put on that is in one piece—with one fastening on the side. Before slipping it on, she stands before the mirror and stretches. Appreciatively but indifferently*] You look in good shape, kid. 200 A couple of months riding over the mountains with me, you'd be great.

WOMAN: Can I?

MAN: What?

WOMAN: Some day—ride mountains with you? 205

MAN: Ride mountains? Ride donkeys!

WOMAN: It's the same thing!—with you!—Can I—some day? The high dark mountains?

MAN: Who knows?

WOMAN: It must be great! 210

MAN: You ever been off like that, kid?—high up? On top of the world?

WOMAN: Yes.

MAN: When?

WOMAN: Today. 215

MAN: You're pretty sweet.

WOMAN: I never knew anything like this way! I never knew that I could feel like this! So,—so purified! Don't laugh at me!

MAN: I ain't laughing, honey.

WOMAN: Purified. 220

MAN: It's a hell of a word—but I know what you mean. That's the way it is—sometimes.

WOMAN: [*She puts on a little hat, then turns to him*] Well—goodbye.

MAN: Aren't you forgetting something? [*Rises*] 225

WOMAN: [*She looks toward him, then throws her head slowly back, lifts her right arm—this gesture that is in so many statues of women—Volupte. He comes out of the shadow, puts his arm around her, kisses her. Her head and arm go further back,— then she brings her arm around with a wide encircling gesture, 230 her hand closes over his head, her fingers spread. Her fingers are protective, clutching. When he releases her, her eyes are shining with tears. She turns away. She looks back at him—and the room—and her eyes fasten on the lily.*] Can I have that?

MAN: Sure—why not? 235

[*She takes it—goes. As she opens the door, the music is louder. The scene blacks out.*]

WOMAN: Goodbye. And—[*Hesitates*] And—thank you.

CURTAIN

[*The music continues until the Curtain goes up for Episode Seven. It goes up on silence.*]

EPISODE SEVEN

DOMESTIC

SCENE:
  a sitting room:
  a divan,
  a telephone,
  a window.

CHARACTERS:
 HUSBAND,
 YOUNG WOMAN.

[*They are seated on opposite ends of the divan. They are both reading papers—to themselves.*]

HUSBAND: Record production.
YOUNG WOMAN: Girl turns on gas.
HUSBAND: Sale hits a million—
YOUNG WOMAN: Woman leaves all for love—
5 HUSBAND: Market trend steady—
YOUNG WOMAN: Young wife disappears—
HUSBAND: Owns a life interest— [*Phone rings.* YOUNG WOMAN *looks toward it.*] That's for me. [*In phone*] Hello—oh hello, A.B. It's all settled?—Everything signed? Good. Good! Tell
10 R.A. to call me up. [*Hangs up phone—to* YOUNG WOMAN] Well, it's all settled. They signed!—aren't you interested? Aren't you going to ask me?
YOUNG WOMAN: [*By rote*] Did you put it over?
HUSBAND: Sure I put it over.
15 YOUNG WOMAN: Did you swing it?
HUSBAND: Sure I swung it.
YOUNG WOMAN: Did they come through?
HUSBAND: Sure they came through.
YOUNG WOMAN: Did they sign?
20 HUSBAND: I'll say they signed.
YOUNG WOMAN: On the dotted line?
HUSBAND: On the dotted line.
YOUNG WOMAN: The property's yours?
HUSBAND: The property's mine. I'll put a first mortgage. I'll put a
25 second mortgage and the property's mine. Happy?
YOUNG WOMAN: [*By rote*] Happy.
HUSBAND: [*Going to her*] The property's mine! It's not all that's mine! [*Pinching her cheek—happy and playful*] I got a first mortgage on her—I got a second mortgage on her—and she's
30 mine! [YOUNG WOMAN *pulls away swiftly.*] What's the matter?
YOUNG WOMAN: Nothing—what?
HUSBAND: You flinched when I touched you.
YOUNG WOMAN: No.
HUSBAND: You haven't done that in a long time.
35 YOUNG WOMAN: Haven't I?
HUSBAND: You used to do it every time I touched you.
YOUNG WOMAN: Did I?
HUSBAND: Didn't know that, did you? .
YOUNG WOMAN: [*Unexpectedly*] Yes. Yes, I know it.
40 HUSBAND: Just purity.
YOUNG WOMAN: No.
HUSBAND: Oh, I liked it. Purity.
YOUNG WOMAN: No.
HUSBAND: You're one of the purest women that ever lived.
45 YOUNG WOMAN: I'm just like anybody else only—[*Stops*]
HUSBAND: Only what?
YOUNG WOMAN: [*A pause*] Nothing.
HUSBAND: It must be something.
 [*Phone rings. She gets up and goes to window.*]
HUSBAND: [*In phone*] Hello—hello, R.A.—well, I put it over—
50 yeah, I swung it—sure they came through—did they sign? On the dotted line! The property's mine. I made the proposition. I sold them the idea. Now watch me. Tell D.D. to call me up. [*Hangs up*] That was R.A. What are you looking at?
YOUNG WOMAN: Nothing.
55 HUSBAND: You must be looking at something.

YOUNG WOMAN: Nothing—the moon.
HUSBAND: The moon's something, isn't it?
YOUNG WOMAN: Yes.
HUSBAND: What's it doing?
YOUNG WOMAN: Nothing. 60
HUSBAND: It must be doing something.
YOUNG WOMAN: It's moving—moving— [*She comes down restlessly.*]
HUSBAND: Pull down the shade, my dear.
YOUNG WOMAN: Why? 65
HUSBAND: People can look in. [*Phone rings.*] Hello—hello D.D.—Yes—I put it over—they came across—I put it over on them—yep—yep—yep—I'll say I am— yep—on the dotted line— Now you watch me—yep. Yep, yep. Tell B.M. to phone me. [*Hangs up*] That was D.D. [*To* YOUNG WOMAN *who has 70 come down to davenport and picked up a paper*] Aren't you listening?
YOUNG WOMAN: I'm reading.
HUSBAND: What are you reading?
YOUNG WOMAN: Nothing. 75
HUSBAND: Must be something. [*He sits and picks up his paper.*]
YOUNG WOMAN: [*Reading*] Prisoner escapes—lifer breaks jail—shoots way to freedom—
HUSBAND: Don't read that stuff—listen—here's a first rate editorial. I agree with this. I agree absolutely. Are you 80 listening?
YOUNG WOMAN: I'm listening.
HUSBAND: [*Importantly*] All men are born free and entitled to the pursuit of happiness. [YOUNG WOMAN *gets up.*] My, you're nervous tonight. 85
YOUNG WOMAN: I try not to be.
HUSBAND: You inherit that from your mother. She was in the office today.
YOUNG WOMAN: Was she?
HUSBAND: To get her allowance. 90
YOUNG WOMAN: Oh—
HUSBAND: Don't you know it's the *first*.
YOUNG WOMAN: Poor Ma.
HUSBAND: What would she do without me?
YOUNG WOMAN: I know. You're very good. 95
HUSBAND: One thing—she's grateful.
YOUNG WOMAN: Poor Ma—poor Ma.
HUSBAND: She's got to have care.
YOUNG WOMAN: Yes. She's got to have care.
HUSBAND: A mother's a very precious thing—a good mother. 100
YOUNG WOMAN: [*Excitedly*] I try to be a good mother.
HUSBAND: Of course you're a good mother.
YOUNG WOMAN: I try! I try!
HUSBAND: A mother's a very precious thing—[*Resuming his paper*] And a child's a very precious thing. Precious jewels. 105
YOUNG WOMAN: [*Reading*] Sale of jewels and precious stones. [YOUNG WOMAN *puts her hand to throat.*]
HUSBAND: What's the matter?
YOUNG WOMAN: I feel as though I were drowning.
HUSBAND: Drowning? 110
YOUNG WOMAN: With stones around my neck.
HUSBAND: You just imagine that.
YOUNG WOMAN: Stifling.
HUSBAND: You don't breathe deep enough—breathe now—look at me. [*He breathes.*] Breath is life. Life is breath. 115
YOUNG WOMAN: [*Suddenly*] And what is death?
HUSBAND: [*Smartly*] Just—no breath!
YOUNG WOMAN: [*To herself*] just no breath. [*Takes up paper*]

HUSBAND: All right?

120 YOUNG WOMAN: All right.

HUSBAND: [*Reads as she stares at her paper. Looks up after a pause*] I feel cold air, my dear.

YOUNG WOMAN: Cold air?

HUSBAND: Close the window, will you?

125 YOUNG WOMAN: It isn't open.

HUSBAND: Don't you feel cold air?

YOUNG WOMAN: No—you just imagine it.

HUSBAND: I never imagine anything. [YOUNG WOMAN *is staring at the paper.*] What are you reading?

130 YOUNG WOMAN: Nothing.

HUSBAND: You must be reading something.

YOUNG WOMAN: Woman finds husband dead.

HUSBAND: [*Uninterested*] Oh. [*Interested*] Here's a man says "I owe my success to a yeast cake a day—my digestion is

135 good—I sleep very well—and— [*His wife gets up, goes toward door.*] Where are you going?

YOUNG WOMAN: No place.

HUSBAND: You must be going some place.

YOUNG WOMAN: Just—to bed.

140 HUSBAND: It isn't eleven yet. Wait.

YOUNG WOMAN: Wait?

HUSBAND: It's only ten-forty-six—wait! [*Holds out his arms to her*] Come here!

YOUNG WOMAN: [*Takes a step toward him—recoils*] Oh— I want

145 to go away!

HUSBAND: Away? Where?

YOUNG WOMAN: Anywhere—away.

HUSBAND: Why, what's the matter?

YOUNG WOMAN: I'm scared.

150 HUSBAND: What of?

YOUNG WOMAN: I can't sleep—I haven't slept.

HUSBAND: That's nothing.

YOUNG WOMAN: And the moon—when it's a full moon.

HUSBAND: That's nothing.

155 YOUNG WOMAN: I can't sleep.

HUSBAND: Of course not. It's the light.

YOUNG WOMAN: I don't see it! I feel it! I'm afraid.

HUSBAND: [*Kindly*] Nonsense—come here.

YOUNG WOMAN: I want to go away.

160 HUSBAND: But I can't get away now.

YOUNG WOMAN: Alone!

HUSBAND: You've never been away alone.

YOUNG WOMAN: I know.

HUSBAND: What would you do?

165 YOUNG WOMAN: Maybe I'd sleep.

HUSBAND: Now you wait.

YOUNG WOMAN: [*Desperately*] Wait?

HUSBAND: We'll take a trip—we'll go to Europe—I'll get my watch—I'll get my Swiss watch—I've always wanted a Swiss

170 watch that I bought right there—isn't that funny? Wait—wait, [YOUNG WOMAN *comes down to davenport—sits.* HUSBAND *resumes his paper.*] Another revolution below the Rio Grande.

YOUNG WOMAN: Below the Rio Grande?

HUSBAND: Yes—another—

175 YOUNG WOMAN: Anyone—hurt?

HUSBAND: No.

YOUNG WOMAN: Any prisoners?

HUSBAND: No.

YOUNG WOMAN: All free?

180 HUSBAND: All free.

[*He resumes his paper.* YOUNG WOMAN *sits, staring ahead of her—The music of the hand-organ sounds off very dimly, playing Cielito Lindo. Voices begin to sing it—'Ay-ay-ay-ay'—and then the words—the music and voices get louder.*]

THE VOICE OF HER LOVER: They were a bunch of bandidos— bandits you know—holding me there—what was I to do—I had to get free—didn't I? I had to get free—

VOICES: Free—free—free—

LOVER: I filled an empty bottle with small stones— 185

VOICES: Stones—stones—precious stones— millstones—stones—stones—millstones—

LOVER: Just a bottle with small stones.

VOICES: Stones—stones—small stones—

LOVER: You only need a bottle with small stones. 190

VOICES: Stones—stones—small stones—

VOICE OF A HUCKSTER: Stones for sale—stones—stones— small stones—precious stones—

VOICES: Stones—stones—precious stones—

LOVER: Had to get free, didn't I? Free? 195

VOICES: Free? Free?

LOVER: Quien sabe? Who knows? Who knows?

VOICES: Who'd know? Who'd know? Who'd know?

HUCKSTER: Stones—stones—small stones—big stones— millstones—cold stones—head stones— 200

VOICES: Head stones—head stones—head stones.

[*The music—the voices—mingle—increase—the* YOUNG WOMAN *flies from her chair and cries out in terror.*]

YOUNG WOMAN: Oh! Oh!

[*The scene blacks out—the music and the dim voices, "Stones— stones—stones," continue until the scene lights for Episode Eight:*]

EPISODE EIGHT

THE LAW

SCENE:
  courtroom.

SOUNDS:
  clicking of telegraph instruments offstage.

CHARACTERS:
  JUDGE,
  JURY,
  LAWYERS,
  SPECTATORS,
  REPORTERS,
  MESSENGER BOYS,
  LAW CLERKS,
  BAILIFF,
  COURT REPORTER,
  YOUNG WOMAN.

The words and movements of all these people except the YOUNG WOMAN *are routine—mechanical. Each is going through the motions of his own game.*

AT RISE:
  all assembled, except JUDGE.

[*Enter* JUDGE.]

BAILIFF: [*Mumbling*] Hear ye—hear ye—hear ye!

[*All rise.* JUDGE *sits. All sit.* LAWYER FOR DEFENSE *gets to his feet—He is the verbose, "eloquent"—typical criminal defense lawyer.* JUDGE *signs to him to wait—turns to* LAW CLERKS, *grouped at foot of the bench*]

1ST CLERK: [*Handing up a paper—routine voice*] State versus Kling—stay of execution.
JUDGE: *Denied.*

[1ST CLERK *goes.*]

5 2ND CLERK: Bing vs. Ding—demurrer.

[JUDGE *signs.* 2ND CLERK *goes.*]

3RD CLERK: Case of John King—habeas corpus.

[JUDGE *signs.* 3RD CLERK *goes.* JUDGE *signs to* BAILIFF.]

BAILIFF: [*Mumbling*] People of the State of—versus Helen Jones.
JUDGE: [*To* LAWYER FOR THE DEFENSE] Defense ready to proceed?
LAWYER FOR DEFENSE: We're ready, your Honor.
10 JUDGE: Proceed.
LAWYER FOR DEFENSE: Helen Jones.
BAILIFF: HELEN JONES!

[YOUNG WOMAN *rises.*]

LAWYER FOR DEFENSE: Mrs. Jones, will you take the stand?

[YOUNG WOMAN *goes to witness stand.*]

1ST REPORTER: [*Writing rapidly*] The defense sprang a surprise
15   at the opening of court this morning by putting the accused woman on the stand. The prosecution was swept off its feet by this daring defense strategy and— [*Instruments get louder.*]
2ND REPORTER: Trembling and scarcely able to stand, Helen Jones, accused murderess, had to be almost carried to the
20   witness stand this morning when her lawyer—
BAILIFF: [*Mumbling—with Bible*] Do you swear to tell the truth, the whole truth and nothing but the truth—so help you God?
YOUNG WOMAN: I do.
JUDGE: You may sit.

[*She sits in witness chair.*]

25 COURT REPORTER: What is your name?
YOUNG WOMAN: Helen Jones.
COURT REPORTER: Your age?
YOUNG WOMAN: [*Hesitates—then*] Twenty-nine.
COURT REPORTER: Where do you live?
30 YOUNG WOMAN: In prison.
LAWYER FOR DEFENSE: This is my client's legal address.

[*Hands a scrap of paper.*]

LAWYER FOR PROSECUTION: [*Jumping to his feet*] I object to this insinuation on the part of counsel on any illegality in the holding of this defendant in jail when the law—

LAWYER FOR DEFENSE: I made no such insinuation.   35
LAWYER FOR PROSECUTION: You implied it—
LAWYER FOR DEFENSE: I did not!
LAWYER FOR PROSECUTION: You're a—
JUDGE: Order!
BAILIFF: Order!   40
LAWYER FOR DEFENSE: Your Honor, I object to counsel's constant attempt to—
LAWYER FOR PROSECUTION: I protest—I—
JUDGE: Order!
BAILIFF: Order!
JUDGE: Proceed with the witness.   45
LAWYER FOR DEFENSE: Mrs. Jones, you are the widow of the late George H. Jones, are you not?
YOUNG WOMAN: Yes.
LAWYER FOR DEFENSE: How long were you married to the late George H. Jones before his demise?   50
YOUNG WOMAN: Six years.
LAWYER FOR DEFENSE: Six years! And it was a happy marriage, was it not? [YOUNG WOMAN *hesitates.*] Did you quarrel?
YOUNG WOMAN: No, sir.
LAWYER FOR DEFENSE: Then it was a happy marriage, wasn't it?   55
YOUNG WOMAN: Yes, sir.
LAWYER FOR DEFENSE: In those six years of married life with your late husband, the late George H. Jones, did you EVER have a quarrel?
YOUNG WOMAN: No, sir.   60
LAWYER FOR DEFENSE: Never one quarrel?
LAWYER FOR PROSECUTION: The witness has said—
LAWYER FOR DEFENSE: Six years without one quarrel! Six years! Gentlemen of the jury, I ask you to consider this fact! Six years of married life without a quarrel.   65
[*The* JURY *grins.*] I ask you to consider it seriously! Very seriously! Who of us—and this is not intended as any reflection on the sacred institution of marriage—no—but!
JUDGE: Proceed with your witness.
LAWYER FOR DEFENSE: You have one child—have you not, Mrs.   70
Jones?
YOUNG WOMAN: Yes, sir.
LAWYER FOR DEFENSE: A little girl, is it not?
YOUNG WOMAN: Yes, sir.
LAWYER FOR DEFENSE: How old is she?   75
YOUNG WOMAN: She's five—past five.
LAWYER FOR DEFENSE: A little girl of past five. Since the demise of the late Mr. Jones you are the only parent she has living, are you not?
YOUNG WOMAN: Yes, sir.   80
LAWYER FOR DEFENSE: Before your marriage to the late Mr. Jones, you worked and supported your mother, did you not?
LAWYER FOR PROSECUTION: I object, your honor! Irrelevant—immaterial—and—
JUDGE: Objection sustained!   85
LAWYER FOR DEFENSE: In order to support your mother and yourself as a girl, you worked, did you not?
YOUNG WOMAN: Yes, sir.
LAWYER FOR DEFENSE: What did you do?
YOUNG WOMAN: I was a stenographer.   90
LAWYER FOR DEFENSE: And since your marriage you have continued as her sole support, have you not?
YOUNG WOMAN: Yes, sir.
LAWYER FOR DEFENSE: A devoted daughter, gentlemen of the jury! As well as a devoted wife and a devoted mother!   95
LAWYER FOR PROSECUTION: Your honor!

LAWYER FOR DEFENSE: [*Quickly*] And now, Mrs. Jones, I will ask you—the law expects me to ask you—it demands that I ask you—did you—or did you not—on the night of June 2nd last 100 or the morning of June 3rd last—kill your husband, the late George H. Jones—did you, or did you not?

YOUNG WOMAN: I did not.

LAWYER FOR DEFENSE: You did not?

YOUNG WOMAN: I did not.

105 LAWYER FOR DEFENSE: Now, Mrs. Jones, you have heard the witnesses for the State—They were not many—and they did not have much to say—

LAWYER FOR PROSECUTION: I object.

JUDGE: Sustained.

110 LAWYER FOR DEFENSE: You have heard some police and you have heard some doctors. None of whom was present! The prosecution could not furnish any witness to the crime—not one witness!

LAWYER FOR PROSECUTION: Your Honor!

115 LAWYER FOR DEFENSE: Nor one motive.

LAWYER FOR PROSECUTION: Your Honor—I protest! I—

JUDGE: Sustained.

LAWYER FOR DEFENSE: But such as these witnesses were, you have heard them try to accuse you of deliberately murdering 120 your own husband, this husband with whom, by your own statement, you had never had a quarrel—not one quarrel in six years of married life, murdering him, I say, or rather they say, while he slept, by brutally hitting him over the head with a bottle—a bottle filled with small stones—Did you, I 125 repeat this, or did you not?

YOUNG WOMAN: I did not.

LAWYER FOR DEFENSE: You did not! Of course you did not! [*Quickly*] Now, Mrs. Jones, will you tell the jury in your own words exactly what happened on the night of June 2nd or the 130 morning of June 3rd last, at the time your husband was killed.

YOUNG WOMAN: I was awakened by hearing somebody—something—in the room, and I saw two men standing by my husband's bed.

LAWYER FOR DEFENSE: Your husband's bed—that was also your 135 bed, was it not, Mrs. Jones?

YOUNG WOMAN: Yes.

LAWYER FOR DEFENSE: You hadn't the modern idea of separate beds, had you, Mrs. Jones?

YOUNG WOMAN: Mr. Jones objected.

140 LAWYER FOR DEFENSE: I mean you slept in the same bed, did you not?

YOUNG WOMAN: Yes.

LAWYER FOR DEFENSE: Then explain just what you meant by saying "my husband's bed."

145 YOUNG WOMAN: Well—I—

LAWYER FOR DEFENSE: You meant his side of the bed, didn't you?

YOUNG WOMAN: Yes. His side.

LAWYER FOR DEFENSE: That is what I thought, but I wanted the jury to be clear on that point. [*To the* JURY] Mr. and Mrs. 150 Jones slept in the same bed. [*To her*] Go on, Mrs. Jones. [*As she is silent*] You heard a noise and—

YOUNG WOMAN: I heard a noise and I awoke and saw two men standing beside my husband's side of the bed.

LAWYER FOR DEFENSE: Two men?

155 YOUNG WOMAN: Yes.

LAWYER FOR DEFENSE: Can you describe them?

YOUNG WOMAN: Not very well—I couldn't see them very well.

LAWYER FOR DEFENSE: Could you say whether they were big or small—light or dark, thin or—

YOUNG WOMAN: They were big dark looking men. 160

LAWYER FOR DEFENSE: Big dark looking men?

YOUNG WOMAN: Yes.

LAWYER FOR DEFENSE: And what did you do, Mrs. Jones, when you suddenly awoke and saw two big dark looking men standing beside your bed? 165

YOUNG WOMAN: I didn't do anything!

LAWYER FOR DEFENSE: You didn't have time to do anything—did you?

YOUNG WOMAN: No. Before I could do anything—one of them raised—something in his hand and struck Mr. Jones over the 170 head with it.

LAWYER FOR DEFENSE: And what did Mr. Jones do?

[SPECTATORS *laugh*.]

JUDGE: Silence.

BAILIFF: Silence.

LAWYER FOR DEFENSE: What did Mr. Jones do, Mrs. Jones? 175

YOUNG WOMAN: He gave a sort of groan and tried to raise up.

LAWYER FOR DEFENSE: Tried to raise up!

YOUNG WOMAN: Yes!

LAWYER FOR DEFENSE: And then what happened?

YOUNG WOMAN: The man struck him again and he fell back. 180

LAWYER FOR DEFENSE: I see. What did the men do then? The big dark looking men.

YOUNG WOMAN: They turned and ran out of the room.

LAWYER FOR DEFENSE: I see. What did you do then, Mrs. Jones?

YOUNG WOMAN: I saw Mr. Jones was bleeding from the temple. 185 I got towels and tried to stop it, and then I realized he had—passed away—

LAWYER FOR DEFENSE: I see. What did you do then?

YOUNG WOMAN: I didn't know what to do. But I thought I'd better call the police. So I went to the telephone and called the 190 police.

LAWYER FOR DEFENSE: What happened then?

YOUNG WOMAN: Nothing. Nothing happened.

LAWYER FOR DEFENSE: The police came, didn't they?

YOUNG WOMAN: Yes—they came. 195

LAWYER FOR DEFENSE: [*Quickly*] And that is all you know concerning the death of your husband in the late hours of June 2nd or the early hours of June 3rd last, isn't it?

YOUNG WOMAN: Yes sir.

LAWYER FOR DEFENSE: All? 200

YOUNG WOMAN: Yes sir.

LAWYER FOR DEFENSE: [*To* LAWYER FOR PROSECUTION] Take the witness.

1ST REPORTER [*Writing*] The accused woman told a straightforward story of— 205

2ND REPORTER: The accused woman told a rambling, disconnected story of—

LAWYER FOR PROSECUTION: You made no effort to cry out, Mrs. Jones, did you, when you saw those two big dark men standing over your helpless husband, did you? 210

YOUNG WOMAN: No sir. I didn't, I—

LAWYER FOR PROSECUTION: And when they turned and ran out of the room, you made no effort to follow them or cry out after them, did you?

YOUNG WOMAN: No sir. 215

LAWYER FOR PROSECUTION: Why didn't you?

YOUNG WOMAN: I saw Mr. Jones was hurt.

LAWYER FOR PROSECUTION: Ah! You saw Mr. Jones was hurt! You saw this—how did you see it?

220 YOUNG WOMAN: I just saw it.

LAWYER FOR PROSECUTION: Then there was a light in the room?

YOUNG WOMAN: A sort of light.

LAWYER FOR PROSECUTION: What do you mean—a sort of light? A bed light?

225 YOUNG WOMAN: No. No, there was no light on.

LAWYER FOR PROSECUTION: Then where did it come from—this sort of light?

YOUNG WOMAN: I don't know.

LAWYER FOR PROSECUTION: Perhaps—from the window.

230 YOUNG WOMAN: Yes—from the window.

LAWYER FOR PROSECUTION: Oh, the shade was up!

YOUNG WOMAN: No—no, the shade was down.

LAWYER FOR PROSECUTION: You're sure of that?

YOUNG WOMAN: Yes. Mr. Jones always wanted the shade down.

235 LAWYER FOR PROSECUTION: The shade was down—there was no light in the room—but the room was light—how do you explain this?

YOUNG WOMAN: I don't know.

LAWYER FOR PROSECUTION: You don't know!

240 YOUNG WOMAN: I think where the window was open—under the shade—light came in—

LAWYER FOR PROSECUTION: There is a street light there?

YOUNG WOMAN: No—there's no street light.

LAWYER FOR PROSECUTION: Then where did this light come

245 from—that came in under the shade?

YOUNG WOMAN: [*Desperately*] From the moon!

LAWYER FOR PROSECUTION: The moon!

YOUNG WOMAN: Yes! It was bright moon!

LAWYER FOR PROSECUTION: It was bright moon—you are sure of

250 that!

YOUNG WOMAN: Yes.

LAWYER FOR PROSECUTION: How are you sure?

YOUNG WOMAN: I couldn't sleep—I never can sleep in the bright moon. I never can.

255 LAWYER FOR PROSECUTION: It was bright moon. Yet you could not see two big dark looking men—but you could see your husband bleeding from the temple.

YOUNG WOMAN: Yes sir.

LAWYER FOR PROSECUTION: And did you call a doctor?

260 YOUNG WOMAN: No.

LAWYER FOR PROSECUTION: Why didn't you?

YOUNG WOMAN: The police did.

LAWYER FOR PROSECUTION: But you didn't?

YOUNG WOMAN: No.

265 LAWYER FOR PROSECUTION: Why didn't you? [*No answer*] Why didn't you?

YOUNG WOMAN: [*Whispers*] I saw it was—useless.

LAWYER FOR PROSECUTION: Ah! You saw that! You saw that—very clearly.

270 YOUNG WOMAN: Yes.

LAWYER FOR PROSECUTION: And you didn't call a doctor.

YOUNG WOMAN: It was—useless.

LAWYER FOR PROSECUTION: What did you do?

YOUNG WOMAN: It was useless—there was no use of anything.

275 LAWYER FOR PROSECUTION: I asked you what you did?

YOUNG WOMAN: Nothing.

LAWYER FOR PROSECUTION: Nothing!

YOUNG WOMAN: I just sat there.

LAWYER FOR PROSECUTION: You sat there! A long while, didn't you? 280

YOUNG WOMAN: I don't know.

LAWYER FOR PROSECUTION: You don't know? [*Showing her the neck of a broken bottle*] Mrs. Jones, did you ever see this before?

YOUNG WOMAN: I think so. 285

LAWYER FOR PROSECUTION: You think so.

YOUNG WOMAN: Yes.

LAWYER FOR PROSECUTION: What do you think it is?

YOUNG WOMAN: I think it's the bottle that was used against Mr. Jones. 290

LAWYER FOR PROSECUTION: Used against him—yes—that's right. You've guessed right. This neck and these broken pieces and these pebbles were found on the floor and scattered over the bed. There were no fingerprints, Mrs. Jones, on this bottle. None at all. Doesn't that seem strange to you? 295

YOUNG WOMAN: No.

LAWYER FOR PROSECUTION: It doesn't seem strange to you that this bottle held in the big dark hand of one of those big dark men left no mark! No print! That doesn't seem strange to you?

YOUNG WOMAN: No. 300

LAWYER FOR PROSECUTION: You are in the habit of wearing rubber gloves at night, Mrs. Jones—are you not? To protect—to soften your hands—are you not?

YOUNG WOMAN: I used to.

LAWYER FOR PROSECUTION: Used to—when was that? 305

YOUNG WOMAN: Before I was married.

LAWYER FOR PROSECUTION: And after your marriage you gave it up?

YOUNG WOMAN: Yes.

LAWYER FOR PROSECUTION: Why? 310

YOUNG WOMAN: Mr. Jones did not like the feeling of them.

LAWYER FOR PROSECUTION: You always did everything Mr. Jones wanted?

YOUNG WOMAN: I tried to—Anyway I didn't care any more—so much—about my hands. 315

LAWYER FOR PROSECUTION: I see—so after your marriage you never wore gloves at night any more?

YOUNG WOMAN: No.

LAWYER FOR PROSECUTION: Mrs. Jones, isn't it true that you began wearing your rubber gloves again—in spite of your 320 husband's expressed dislike—about a year ago—a year ago this spring?

YOUNG WOMAN: No.

LAWYER FOR PROSECUTION: You did not suddenly begin to care particularly for your hands again—about a year ago this 325 spring?

YOUNG WOMAN: No.

LAWYER FOR PROSECUTION: You're quite sure of that?

YOUNG WOMAN: Yes.

LAWYER FOR PROSECUTION: Quite sure? 330

YOUNG WOMAN: Yes.

LAWYER FOR PROSECUTION: Then you did not have in your possession, on the night of June 2nd last, a pair of rubber gloves?

YOUNG WOMAN: [*Shakes her head*] No. 335

LAWYER FOR PROSECUTION: [*To* JUDGE] I'd like to introduce these gloves as evidence at this time, your Honor.

JUDGE: Exhibit 24.

LAWYER FOR PROSECUTION: I'll return to them later—now, Mrs. Jones—this nightgown—you recognize it, don't you? 340

YOUNG WOMAN: Yes.

LAWYER FOR PROSECUTION: Yours, is it not?

YOUNG WOMAN: Yes.

345 LAWYER FOR PROSECUTION: The one you were wearing the night your husband was murdered, isn't it?

YOUNG WOMAN: The night he died—yes.

LAWYER FOR PROSECUTION: Not the one you wore under your peignoir—I believe that is what you call it, isn't it? A peignoir? When you received the police—but the one you wore before

350 that—isn't it?

YOUNG WOMAN: Yes.

LAWYER FOR PROSECUTION: This was found—not where the gloves were found—no—but at the bottom of the soiled clothes hamper in the bathroom—rolled up and wet—why

355 was it wet, Mrs. Jones?

YOUNG WOMAN: I had tried to wash it.

LAWYER FOR PROSECUTION: Wash it? I thought you had just sat?

YOUNG WOMAN: First—I tried to make things clean.

LAWYER FOR PROSECUTION: Why did you want to make this—

360 clean—as you say?

YOUNG WOMAN: There was blood on it.

LAWYER FOR PROSECUTION: Spattered on it?

YOUNG WOMAN: Yes.

LAWYER FOR PROSECUTION: How did that happen?

365 YOUNG WOMAN: The bottle broke—and the sharp edge cut!

LAWYER FOR PROSECUTION: Oh, the bottle broke and the sharp edge cut!

YOUNG WOMAN: Yes. That's what they told me afterwards.

LAWYER FOR PROSECUTION: Who told you?

370 YOUNG WOMAN: The police—that's what they say happened.

LAWYER FOR PROSECUTION: Mrs. Jones, why did you try so desperately to wash that blood away—before you called the police?

LAWYER FOR DEFENSE: I object!

375 JUDGE: Objection overruled.

LAWYER FOR PROSECUTION: Why, Mrs. Jones?

YOUNG WOMAN: I don't know. It's what anyone would have done, wouldn't they?

LAWYER FOR PROSECUTION: That depends, doesn't it? [*Suddenly*

380 *taking up bottle*] Mrs. Jones—when did you first see this?

YOUNG WOMAN: The night my husband was—done away with.

LAWYER FOR PROSECUTION: Done away! You mean killed?

YOUNG WOMAN: Yes.

LAWYER FOR PROSECUTION: Why don't you say killed?

385 YOUNG WOMAN: It sounds so brutal.

LAWYER FOR PROSECUTION: And you never saw this before then?

YOUNG WOMAN: No sir.

LAWYER FOR PROSECUTION: You're quite sure of that?

YOUNG WOMAN: Yes.

390 LAWYER FOR PROSECUTION: And these stones—when did you first see them?

YOUNG WOMAN: The night my husband was done away with.

LAWYER FOR PROSECUTION: Before that night your husband was murdered—you never saw them? Never before then?

395 YOUNG WOMAN: No sir.

LAWYER FOR PROSECUTION: You are quite sure of that!

YOUNG WOMAN: Yes.

LAWYER FOR PROSECUTION: Mrs. Jones, do you remember about a year ago, a year ago this spring, bringing home to your

400 house—a lily, a Chinese water lily?

YOUNG WOMAN: No—I don't think I do.

LAWYER FOR PROSECUTION: You don't think you remember bringing home a water lily growing in a bowl filled with small stones?

YOUNG WOMAN: No—No I don't.

405 LAWYER FOR PROSECUTION: I'll show you this bowl, Mrs. Jones. Does that refresh your memory?

YOUNG WOMAN: I remember the bowl—but I don't remember— the lily.

LAWYER FOR PROSECUTION: It is yours, isn't it?

410 YOUNG WOMAN: It was in my house—yes.

LAWYER FOR PROSECUTION: How did it come there?

YOUNG WOMAN: How did it come there?

LAWYER FOR PROSECUTION: Yes—where did you get it?

YOUNG WOMAN: I don't remember.

415 LAWYER FOR PROSECUTION: You don't remember?

YOUNG WOMAN: No.

LAWYER FOR PROSECUTION: You don't remember about a year ago bringing this bowl into your bedroom filled with small stones and some water and a lily? You don't remember tending very

420 carefully that lily till it died? And when it died you don't remember hiding the bowl full of little stones away on the top shelf of your closet— and keeping it there until—you don't remember?

YOUNG WOMAN: No, I don't remember.

425 LAWYER FOR PROSECUTION: You may have done so?

YOUNG WOMAN: No—no—I didn't! I didn't! I don't know anything about all that.

LAWYER FOR PROSECUTION: But you do remember the bowl?

YOUNG WOMAN: Yes. It was in my house—you found it in my house.

430 LAWYER FOR PROSECUTION: But you don't remember the lily or the stones?

YOUNG WOMAN: No—No I don't!

[LAWYER FOR PROSECUTION *turns to look among his papers in a brief case.*]

1ST REPORTER [*Writing*] Under the heavy artillery fire of the State's attorney's brilliant cross-questioning, the accused

435 woman's defense was badly riddled. Pale and trembling she—

2ND REPORTER [*Writing*] Undaunted by the Prosecution's machine-gun attack, the defendant was able to maintain her position of innocence in the face of rapid-fire questioning that threatened, but never seriously menaced her defense. Flushed

440 but calm she—

LAWYER FOR PROSECUTION: [*Producing paper*] Your Honor, I'd like to introduce this paper in evidence at this time.

JUDGE: What is it?

LAWYER FOR PROSECUTION: It is an affidavit taken in the State of

445 Guanajuato, Mexico.

LAWYER FOR DEFENSE: Mexico? Your Honor, I protest. A Mexican affidavit! Is this the United States of America or isn't it?

LAWYER FOR PROSECUTION: It's properly executed—sworn to before a notary—and certified to by an American Consul.

450 LAWYER FOR DEFENSE: Your Honor! I protest! In the name of this great United States of America—I protest—are we to permit our sacred institutions to be thus—

JUDGE What is the purpose of this document—who signed it?

LAWYER FOR PROSECUTION: It is signed by one Richard Roe,

455 and its purpose is to refresh the memory of the witness on the point at issue—and incidentally supply a motive for this murder—this brutal and cold-blooded murder of a sleeping man by—

LAWYER FOR DEFENSE: I protest, your Honor! I object!

460 JUDGE: Objection sustained. Let me see the document.

[*Takes paper which is handed up to him—looks at it.*] Perfectly regular. Do you offer this affidavit as evidence at this time

465   for the purpose of refreshing the memory of the witness at
       this time?
       LAWYER FOR PROSECUTION: Yes, your Honor.
       JUDGE: You may introduce the evidence.
       LAWYER FOR DEFENSE: I object! I object to the introduction of this
       evidence at this time as irrelevant, immaterial, illegal, biased,
470   prejudicial, and—
       JUDGE: Objection overruled.
       LAWYER FOR DEFENSE: Exception.
       JUDGE: Exception noted. Proceed.
       LAWYER FOR PROSECUTION: I wish to read the evidence to the jury
475   at this time.
       JUDGE: Proceed.
       LAWYER FOR DEFENSE: I object.
       JUDGE: Objection overruled.
       LAWYER FOR DEFENSE: Exception.
480   JUDGE: Noted.
       LAWYER FOR DEFENSE: Why is this witness himself not brought
       into court—so he can be cross-questioned?
       LAWYER FOR PROSECUTION: The witness is a resident of the
       Republic of Mexico and as such not subject to subpoena as a
485   witness to this court.
       LAWYER FOR DEFENSE: If he was out of the jurisdiction of this
       court how did you get this affidavit out of him?
       LAWYER FOR PROSECUTION: This affidavit was made voluntarily
       by the deponent in the furtherance of justice.
490   LAWYER FOR DEFENSE: I suppose you didn't threaten him with
       extradition on some other trumped-up charge so that—
       JUDGE: Order!
       BAILIFF: Order!
       JUDGE: Proceed with the evidence.
495   LAWYER FOR PROSECUTION: [*Reading*] In the matter of the State
       of—vs. Helen Jones, I Richard Roe, being of sound mind, do
       herein depose and state that I know the accused, Helen Jones,
       and have known her for a period of over one year immediately
       preceding the date of the signature on this affidavit. That
500   I first met the said Helen Jones in a so-called speakeasy
       somewhere in the West 40s in New York City. That on the
       day I met her, she went with me to my room, also somewhere
       in the West 40s in New York City, where we had intimate
       relations—
505   YOUNG WOMAN: [*Moans*] Oh!
       LAWYER FOR PROSECUTION: [*Continues reading*] —and where
       I gave her a blue bowl filled with pebbles, also containing a
       flowering lily. That from the first day we met until I departed
       for Mexico in the fall, the said Helen Jones was an almost
510   daily visitor to my room where we continued to—
       YOUNG WOMAN: No! No!

       [*Moans*]

       LAWYER FOR PROSECUTION: What is it, Mrs. Jones—what is it?
       YOUNG WOMAN: Don't read any more! No more!
       LAWYER FOR PROSECUTION: Why not?
515   YOUNG WOMAN: I did it! I did it! I did it!
       LAWYER FOR PROSECUTION: You confess?
       YOUNG WOMAN: Yes—I did it!
       LAWYER FOR DEFENSE: I object, your Honor.
       JUDGE: You confess you killed your husband?
520   YOUNG WOMAN: I put him out of the way—yes.
       JUDGE: Why?
       YOUNG WOMAN: To be free.

JUDGE: To be free? Is that the only reason?
YOUNG WOMAN: Yes.
JUDGE: If you just wanted to be free—why didn't you divorce   525
    him?
YOUNG WOMAN: Oh I couldn't do that!! I couldn't hurt him like
    that!

[*Burst of laughter from all in the court. The* YOUNG WOMAN *stares
out at them, and then seems to go rigid.*]

JUDGE: Silence!
BAILIFF: Silence!   530

[*There is a gradual silence.*]

JUDGE: Mrs. Jones, why— [YOUNG WOMAN *begins to moan—
    suddenly—as though the realization of the enormity of her
    isolation had just come upon her. It is a sound of desolation, of
    agony, of human woe. It continues until the end of the scene.*]
    Why—?   535

[YOUNG WOMAN *cannot speak.*]

LAWYER FOR DEFENSE: Your Honor, I ask a recess to—
JUDGE: Court's adjourned.

[SPECTATORS *begin to file out. The* YOUNG WOMAN *continues in the
witness box, unseeing, unheeding.*]

1ST REPORTER: Murderess confesses.
2ND REPORTER: Paramour brings confession.
3RD REPORTER: I did it! Woman cries!   540

[*There is a great burst of speed from the telegraphic instruments.
They keep up a constant accompaniment to the* WOMAN's *moans.
The scene blacks out as the courtroom empties and two policemen
go to stand by the woman. The sound of the telegraph instruments
continues until the scene lights into Episode Nine—and the prayers
of the* PRIEST.]

EPISODE NINE

A MACHINE

SCENE:
    *a prison room. The front bars face the audience. They are set
    back far enough to permit a clear passageway across the stage.*

SOUNDS:
    the voice of a NEGRO *singing; the whir of an aeroplane flying.*

CHARACTERS:
    YOUNG WOMAN,
    A PRIEST,
    A JAILER,
    TWO BARBERS,
    A MATRON,
    MOTHER,
    TWO GUARDS.

AT RISE:
    in front of the bars, at one side, sits a MAN; *at the opposite side,
    a* WOMAN—*the* JAILER *and the* MATRON.

Inside the bars, a MAN *and a* WOMAN—*the* YOUNG WOMAN *and a* PRIEST. *The* YOUNG WOMAN *sits still with folded hands. The* PRIEST *is praying.*

PRIEST: Hear, oh Lord, my prayer; and let my cry come to Thee. Turn not away Thy face from me; in the day when I am in trouble, incline Thy ear to me. In what day soever I shall call upon Thee, hear me speedily. For my days are vanished like smoke; and my bones are grown dry, like fuel for the fire. I am smitten as grass, and my heart is withered; because I forgot to eat my bread. Through the voice of my groaning, my bone hath cleaved to my flesh. I am become like to a pelican of the wilderness. I am like a night raven in the house. I have watched and become as a sparrow all alone on the housetop. All the day long my enemies reproach me; and they that praised me did swear against me. My days have declined like a shadow, and I am withered like grass. But Thou, oh Lord, end rest forever. Thou shalt arise and have mercy, for it is time to have mercy. The time is come.

[*Voice of* NEGRO *offstage—Begins to sing a Negro spiritual*]

PRIEST: The Lord hath looked upon the earth, that He might hear the groans of them that are in fetters, that He might release the children of—

[*Voice of* NEGRO *grown louder.*]

JAILER: Stop that nigger yelling.
YOUNG WOMAN: No, let him sing. He helps me.
MATRON: You can't hear the Father.
YOUNG WOMAN: He helps me.
PRIEST: Don't I help you, daughter?
YOUNG WOMAN: I understand him. He is condemned. I understand him.

[*The voice of the* NEGRO *goes on louder, drowning out the voice of the* PRIEST.]

PRIEST: [*Chanting in Latin*] Gratiam tuum, quaesumus, Domine, metibus nostris infunde, ut qui, angelo nuntiante, Christifilii tui incarnationem cognovimus, per passionem eius et crueem ad ressurectionis gloriam perducamus. Per eudem Christum Dominum nostrum.

[*Enter* TWO BARBERS. *There is a rattling of keys.*]

1ST BARBER: How is she?
MATRON: Calm.
JAILER: Quiet.
YOUNG WOMAN: [*Rising*] I am ready.
1ST BARBER: Then sit down.
YOUNG WOMAN: [*In a steady voice*] Aren't you the death guard come to take me?
FIRST BARBER: No, we ain't the death guard. We're the barbers.
YOUNG WOMAN: The barbers.
MATRON: You hair mast be cut.
JAILER: Must be shaved.
BARBER: Just a patch.
    The BARBERS *draw near her.*
YOUNG WOMAN: No!

PRIEST: Daughter, you're ready. You know you are ready.
YOUNG WOMAN (*crying out*): Not for this! Not for this!
MATRON: The rule.
JAILER: Regulations.
BARBER: Routine.

The BARBERS *take her by the arms.*

YOUNG WOMAN: No! No! Don't touch me—touch me!

They take her and put her down in the chair, cut a patch from her hair.

    I will not be submitted—this indignity! No! I will not be submitted!—Leave me alone! Oh my God am I never to be let alone! Always to have to submit—to submit! No more—not now—I'm going to die—I won't submit! Not now!
BARBER: (*finishing cutting a patch from her hair*). You'll submit, my lady. Right to the end, you'll submit! There, and a neat job too.
JAILER: Very neat.
MATRON: Very neat.

Exit BARBERS.

YOUNG WOMAN (*her calm shattered*): Father, Father! Why was I born?
PRIEST: I came forth from the Father and have come into the world—I leave the world and go into the Father.
YOUNG WOMAN (*weeping*): Submit! Submit! Is nothing mine? The hair on my head! The very hair on my head—
PRIEST: Praise God.
YOUNG WOMAN: Am I never to be let alone! Never to have peace! When I'm dead, won't I have peace?
PRIEST: Ye shall indeed drink of my cup.
YOUNG WOMAN: Won't I have peace tomorrow?
PRIEST: I shall raise Him up at the last day.
YOUNG WOMAN: Tomorrow! Father! Where shall I be tomorrow?
PRIEST: Behold the hour cometh. Yea, is now come. Ye shall be scattered every man to his own.
YOUNG WOMAN: In Hell! Father! Will I be in Hell!
PRIEST: I am the Resurrection and the Life.
YOUNG WOMAN: Life has been hell to me, Father!
PRIEST: Life has been hell to you, daughter, because you never knew God! Gloria in excelsis Deo.
YOUNG WOMAN: How could I know Him, Father? He never was around me.
PRIEST: You didn't seek Him, daughter. Seek and ye shall find.
YOUNG WOMAN: I sought something—I was always seeking something.
PRIEST: What? What were you seeking?
YOUNG WOMAN: Peace. Rest and peace. Will I find it tonight, Father? Will I find it?
PRIEST: Trust in God.

A shadow falls across the passage in the front of the stage—and there is a whirring sound.

YOUNG WOMAN: What is that? Father! Jailer! What is that?
JAILER: An aeroplane.
MATRON: Aeroplane.

PRIEST: God in his Heaven.

YOUNG WOMAN: Look, Father! A man flying! He has wings! But he is not an angel!

95 JAILER: Hear his engine.

MATRON: Hear the engine.

YOUNG WOMAN: He has wings—but he isn't free! I've been free, Father! For one moment—down here on earth—I have been free! When I did what I did I was free! Free and not afraid!

100 How is that, Father? How can that be? A great sin—a mortal sin—for which I must die and go to hell—but it made me free! One moment I was free! How is that, Father? Tell me that?

PRIEST: Your sins are forgiven.

YOUNG WOMAN: And that outer sin—that other sin—that sin of

105 love—That's all I ever knew of Heaven—heaven on earth! How is that, Father? How can that be—a sin—a mortal sin—all I know of heaven?

PRIEST: Confess to Almighty God.

YOUNG WOMAN: Oh, Father, pray for me—a prayer—that I can

110 understand!

PRIEST: I will pray for you, daughter, the prayer of desire. Behind the King of Heaven, behold Thy Redeemer and God, Who is even now coming; prepare thyself to receive Him with love, invite Him with the ardor of thy desire; come, oh my Jesus,

115 come to thy soul which desires Thee! Before Thou givest Thyself to me, I desire to give Thee my miserable heart. Do Thou accept it, and come quickly to take possession of it! Come my God, hasten! Delay no longer! My only and Infinite Good, my Treasure, my Life, my Paradise, my Love, my all,

120 my wish is to receive Thee with the love with which—

[*Enter the* MOTHER. *She comes along the passageway and stops before the bars.*]

YOUNG WOMAN: [*Recoiling*] Who's that woman?

JAILER: Your mother.

MATRON: Your mother.

YOUNG WOMAN: She's a stranger—take her away—she's a stranger.

125 JAILER: She's come to say goodbye to you—

MATRON: To say goodbye.

YOUNG WOMAN: But she's never known me—never known me—ever— [*To the* MOTHER] Go away! You're a stranger! Stranger! Stranger! [MOTHER *turns and starts away. Reaching*

130 *out her hands to her.*] Oh Mother! Mother!

[*They embrace through the bars. Enter two* GUARDS.]

PRIEST: Come, daughter.

1ST GUARD: It's time.

2ND GUARD: Time.

YOUNG WOMAN: Wait! Mother, my child; my little strange child!

135 I never knew her! She'll never know me! Let her live, Mother. Let her live! Live! Tell her—

PRIEST: Come, daughter.

YOUNG WOMAN: Wait! wait! Tell her—

[*The* JAILER *takes the* MOTHER *away.*]

1ST GUARD: It's time.

YOUNG WOMAN: Wait! Wait! Tell her! Wait! Just a minute more!   140
There's so much I want to tell her—Wait—

[*The* JAILER *takes the* MOTHER *off. The two* GUARDS *take the* YOUNG WOMAN *by the arms, and start through the door in the bars and down the passage, across stage and off. The* PRIEST *follows; the* MATRON *follows the* PRIEST; *the* PRIEST *is praying. The scene blacks out. The voice of the* PRIEST; *gets dimmer and dimmer.*]

PRIEST: Lord have mercy—Christ have mercy—Lord have mercy—Christ hear us! God the Father of Heaven! God the Son, Redeemer of the World, God the Holy Ghost—Holy Trinity one God—Holy Mary—Holy Mother of God—Holy   145
Virgin of Virgins—St. Michael— St. Gabriel—St. Raphael—

[*His voice dies out. Out of the darkness come the voices of* REPORTERS.]

1ST REPORTER: What time is it now?

2ND REPORTER: Time now.

3RD REPORTER: Hush.

1ST REPORTER: Here they come.   150

3RD REPORTER: Hush.

PRIEST: [*His voice sounds dimly—gets louder—continues until the end.*] St. Peter pray for us—St. Paul pray for us—St. James pray for us—St. John pray for us—all ye holy Angels and Archangels—all ye blessed orders of holy spirits—   155
St. Joseph—St. John the Baptist—St. Thomas—

1ST REPORTER: Here they are!

2ND REPORTER: How little she looks! She's gotten smaller.

3RD REPORTER: Hush.

PRIEST: St. Phillip pray for us. All ye Holy Patriarchs and   160
prophets—St. Phillip—St. Matthew—St. Simon— St. Thaddeus—All ye holy apostles—all ye holy disciples—all ye holy innocents—Pray for us—Pray for us— Pray for us—

1ST REPORTER: Suppose the machine shouldn't work!

2ND REPORTER: It'll work!—It always works!—   165

3RD REPORTER: Hush!

PRIEST: Saints of God make intercession for us—Be merciful— Spare us, oh Lord—be merciful—

1ST REPORTER: Her lips are moving—what is she saying?

2ND REPORTER: Nothing.   170

3RD REPORTER: Hush!

PRIEST: Oh Lord deliver us from all evil—from all sin—from Thy wrath—from the snares of the devil—from anger and hatred and every evil will—from—

1ST REPORTER: Did you see that? She fixed her hair under the   175
cap—pulled her hair out under the cap.

3RD REPORTER: Hush!

PRIEST: —Beseech Thee—hear us—that Thou would'st spare us—that Thou would'st pardon us—Holy Mary—pray for us—

2ND REPORTER: There—   180

YOUNG WOMAN: [*Calling out*] Somebody! Somebod—

[*Her voice is cut off*]

PRIEST: Christ have mercy—Lord have mercy—Christ have mercy—

CURTAIN

Tennessee Williams

Like Amanda Wingfield in *The Glass Menagerie*, Tennessee Williams (1911–1983) regarded himself as a product of the Old South and its genteel, rural, and—finally—obsolete traditions. Born Thomas Lanier Williams to a traveling shoe salesman and his wife, Williams was raised in Mississippi before moving to the tenements of St. Louis. As a child, Williams contracted diphtheria, which briefly paralyzed his legs and left him frail and homebound for some time. During his convalescence, Williams read and wrote avidly and published his first story at the age of sixteen. After high school, he briefly attended the University of Missouri, but withdrew when his poor health prevented him from passing the ROTC course. He then worked for three years in a shoe factory, then tried Washington University in St. Louis, but again dropped out. He finally took his degree in playwriting from the University of Iowa in 1938, when he changed his name to "Tennessee." In the 1930s, Williams's embattled relation to the world was deepened by the "loss" of his beloved sister Rose. Rose became chronically depressed, and Williams's mother, unable to cope with her erratic and wild behavior, consented to having a lobotomy performed. Rose was left docile but inert and became the prototype of several of Williams's most memorable dramatic characters, women whose inner beauty is too delicate to be disclosed to the world. At this time Williams also recognized his own homosexuality, a recognition that deepened his sense of the threatening conformity imposed by mainstream American society.

Coming of age in the Great Depression was formative for Williams's drama, particularly the range of themes associated with his mature work: a sexual tension surging beneath the surface of the characters' lives, the collapse of a sustaining family and social order, the attraction of misfits destroyed by a world that will not accept them. Williams wrote several now-lost plays in the late 1930s, and *Battle of Angels* (1940; later revised as *Orpheus Descending* in 1957) was produced by the Theater Guild in Boston, where it failed. Williams scored a major success with his next play, *The Glass Menagerie* (1944). He continued his success with a series of important dramas: *Summer and Smoke* (1947), *A Streetcar Named Desire* (1947), *The Rose Tattoo* (1951), *Camino Real* (1953), *Cat on a Hot Tin Roof* (1955), *Sweet Bird of Youth* (1959), and *Night of the Iguana* (1961). In his later years, Williams's drama became increasingly gothic and sensational, and his personal life suffered as well; Williams became an alcoholic and was institutionalized on several occasions. He continued to write plays to the end of his life, developing his characteristic strengths: a feel for the nuances of character, and a flair for dramatizing the victims of an unfeeling world.

The Glass Menagerie

First performed in 1944, *The Glass Menagerie* looks back to the 1930s. Its characters are reminiscent of Williams and his family, and their grinding poverty recalls the depression-era plays of Elmer Rice and Clifford Odets. In many ways, *The Glass Menagerie* is a play in the realistic tradition. Laura's menagerie recalls how Ibsen, Chekhov, and Strindberg used stage objects (Nora's Christmas tree in *A Doll House,* the cherry orchard in Chekhov's play) to evoke and symbolize the characters' motives and sensibilities. However, Williams also uses the device of the "memory play" to disrupt the linearity of realistic drama. Tom constructs the scene and the characters for the audience, and slide projections of phrases and images often illustrate the action as it takes place. These devices lend *The Glass Menagerie* the flavor of symbolist theater. Moreover, Tom's anticipation of the Spanish Civil War and World War II sets the play in a larger social and political context that looms forebodingly over the fragile and self-absorbed characters. Amanda and Laura seem doomed never to escape the drab apartment, and even Tom, wandering the world, finally cannot escape it either. Deeply personal (Williams's given name was Tom), *The Glass Menagerie* also provides a kind of study for Williams's later plays, for it includes a typical panoply of Williams's characters: the blunt, sexually aggressive, emotionally stunted Jim; Amanda, the faded Southern belle;

Tom, Laura, Jim, and Amanda in Tennessee Williams' *The Glass Menagerie* at the Williamstown Theatre Festival.

Laura, more crippled emotionally than physically; and Tom, who falls in love with long distance yet never succeeds in escaping his past or in finding his future.

Production Notes

Being a "memory play," *The Glass Menagerie* can be presented with unusual freedom of convention. Because of its considerably delicate or tenuous material, atmospheric touches and subtleties of direction play a particularly important part. Expressionism and all other unconventional techniques in drama have only one valid aim, and that is a closer approach to truth. When a play employs unconventional techniques, it is not, or certainly shouldn't be, trying to escape its responsibility of dealing with reality, or interpreting experience, but is actually or should be attempting to find a closer approach, a more penetrating and vivid expression of things as they are. The straight realistic play with its genuine Frigidaire and authentic ice-cubes, its characters who speak exactly as its audience speaks, corresponds to the academic landscape and has the same virtue of a photographic likeness. Everyone should know nowadays the unimportance of the photographic in art: that truth, life, or reality is an organic thing which the poetic imagination can represent or suggest, in essence, only through transformation, through changing into other forms than those which were merely present in appearance.

These remarks are not meant as a preface only to this particular play. They have to do with a conception of a new, plastic theatre which must take the place of the exhausted theatre of realistic conventions if the theatre is to resume vitality as a part of our culture.

THE SCREEN DEVICE

There is *only one important difference between the original and the acting version of the play* and that is the *omission* in the latter of the device that I tentatively included in my *original* script. This device was the use of a screen on which were projected magic-lantern slides bearing images or titles. I do not regret the omission of this device from the original Broadway production. The extraordinary power of Miss Taylor's performance made it suitable to have the utmost simplicity in the physical production. But I think it may be interesting to some readers to see how this device was conceived. So I am putting it into the published manuscript. These images and legends, projected from behind, were cast on a section of wall between the front-room and dining-room areas, which should be indistinguishable from the rest when not in use.

The purpose of this will probably be apparent. It is to give accent to certain values in each scene. Each scene contains a particular point (or several) which is structurally the most important. In an episodic play, such as this, the basic structure or narrative line may be obscured from the audience; the effect may seem fragmentary rather than architectural. This may not be the fault of the play so much as a lack of attention in the audience. The legend or image upon the screen will strengthen the effect of what is merely allusion in the writing and allow the primary point to be made more simply and lightly than if the entire responsibility were on the spoken lines. Aside from this structural value, I think the screen will have a definite emotional appeal, less definable but just as important. An imaginative producer or director may invent many other uses for this device than those indicated in the present script. In fact the possibilities of the device seem much larger to me than the instance of this play can possibly utilize.

THE MUSIC

Another extra-literary accent in this play is provided by the use of music. A single recurring tune, "The Glass Menagerie," is used to give emotional emphasis to suitable passages. This tune is like circus music, not when you are on the grounds or in the immediate vicinity of the parade, but when you are at some distance and very likely thinking of something else. It seems under those circumstances to continue almost interminably and it weaves in and out of your preoccupied consciousness; then it is the lightest, most delicate music in the world and perhaps the saddest. It expresses the surface vivacity of life with the underlying strain of immutable and inexpressible sorrow. When you look at a piece of delicately spun glass you think of two things: how beautiful it is and how easily it can be broken. Both of those ideas should be woven into the recurring tune, which dips in and out of the play as if it were carried on a wind that changes. It serves as a thread of connection and allusion between the narrator with his separate point in time and space and the subject of his story. Between each episode it returns as reference to the emotion, nostalgia, which is the first condition of the play. It is primarily Laura's music and therefore comes out most clearly when the play focuses upon her and the lovely fragility of glass which is her image.

THE LIGHTING

The lighting in the play is not realistic. In keeping with the atmosphere of memory, the stage is dim. Shafts of light are focused on selected areas or actors, sometimes in contradistinction to what is the apparent center. For instance, in the quarrel scene between Tom and Amanda, in which Laura has no active part, the clearest pool of light is on her figure. This is also true of the supper scene, when her silent figure on the sofa should remain the visual center. The light upon Laura should be distinct from the others, having a peculiar pristine clarity such as light used in early religious portraits of female saints or madonnas. A certain correspondence to light in religious paintings, such as El Greco's, where the figures are radiant in atmosphere that is relatively dusky, could be effectively used throughout the play. (It will also permit a more effective use of the screen.) A free, imaginative use of light can be of enormous value in giving a mobile, plastic quality to plays of a more or less static nature.

Tennessee Williams

The Glass Menagerie

Tennessee Williams

CHARACTERS

AMANDA WINGFIELD (*the mother*), *a little woman of great but confused vitality clinging frantically to another time and place. Her characterization must be carefully created, not copied from type. She is not paranoiac, but her life is paranoia. There is much to admire in Amanda, and as much to love and pity as there is to laugh at. Certainly she has endurance and a kind of heroism, and though her foolishness makes her unwittingly cruel at times, there is tenderness in her slight person.*

LAURA WINGFIELD (*her daughter*), *Amanda, having failed to establish contact with reality, continues to live vitally in her illusions, but Laura's situation is even graver. A childhood illness has left her crippled, one leg slightly shorter than the other, and held in a brace. This defect need not be more than suggested on the stage. Stemming from this, Laura's separation increases till she is like a piece of her own glass collection, too exquisitely fragile to move from the shelf.*

TOM WINGFIELD (*her son*), *and the narrator of the play. A poet with a job in a warehouse. His nature is not remorseless, but to escape from a trap he has to act without pity.*

JIM O'CONNOR (*the gentleman caller*), *a nice, ordinary, young man.*

SCENE: *An Alley in St. Louis*

Part I   Preparation for a Gentleman Caller.
Part II The Gentlemen calls.

TIME: *Now and the Past*

SCENE ONE

The Wingfield apartment is in the rear of the building, one of those vast hive-like conglomerations of the cellular living-units that flower as warty growths in overcrowded urban centers of lower middle-class population and are symptomatic of the impulse of this largest and fundamentally enslaved section of American society to avoid fluidity and differentiation and to exist and function as one interfused mass of automatism.

The apartment faces an alley and is entered by a fire escape, a structure whose name is a touch of accidental poetic truth, for all of these huge buildings are always burning with the slow and implacable fires of human desperation. The fire escape is part of what we see—that is, the landing of it and steps descending from it.

The scene is memory and is therefore nonrealistic. Memory takes a lot of poetic license. It omits some details; others are exaggerated, according to the emotional value of the articles it touches, for memory is seated predominantly in the heart. The interior is therefore rather dim and poetic.

At the rise of the curtain, the audience is faced with the dark, grim rear wall of the Wingfield tenement. This building is flanked on both sides by dark, narrow alleys which run into murky canyons of tangled clotheslines, garbage cans, and the sinister latticework of neighboring fire escapes. It is up and down these side alleys that exterior entrances and exits are made during the play. At the end of TOM's opening commentary, the dark tenement wall slowly becomes transparent and reveals the interior of the ground-floor Wingfield apartment.

Nearest the audience is the living room, which also serves as a sleeping room for LAURA, the sofa unfolding to make her bed. Just beyond, separated from the living room by a wide arch or second proscenium with transparent faded portieres (or second curtain), is the dining room. In an old-fashioned whatnot in the living room are seen scores of transparent glass animals. A blown-up photograph of the father hangs on the wall of the living room, to the left of the archway. It is the face of a very handsome young man in a doughboy's First World War cap. He is gallantly smiling, ineluctably smiling, as if to say "I will be smiling forever."

Also hanging on the wall, near the photograph, are a typewriter keyboard chart and a Gregg shorthand diagram. An upright typewriter on a small table stands beneath the charts.

The audience hears and sees the opening scene in the dining room through both the transparent fourth wall of the building and the transparent gauze portieres of the dining-room arch. It is during this revealing scene that the fourth wall slowly ascends, out of sight. This transparent exterior wall is not brought down again until the very end of the play, during TOM's final speech.

The narrator is an undisguised convention of the play. He takes whatever license with dramatic convention is convenient to his purposes.

TOM enters, dressed as a merchant sailor, and strolls across to the fire escape. There he stops and lights a cigarette. He addresses the audience.

TOM: Yes, I have tricks in my pocket, I have things up my sleeve. But I am the opposite of a stage magician. He gives you illusion that has the appearance of truth. I give you truth in the pleasant disguise of illusion.

   To begin with, I turn back time. I reverse it to that   5
quaint period, the thirties, when the huge middle class of
America was matriculating in a school for the blind. Their
eyes had failed them, or they had failed their eyes, and so
they were having their fingers pressed forcibly down on the
fiery Braille alphabet of a dissolving economy.   10
   In Spain there was revolution. Here there was only
shouting and confusion. In Spain there was Guernica. Here
there were disturbances of labor, sometimes pretty violent,
in otherwise peaceful cities such as Chicago, Cleveland,
Saint Louis . . . This is the social background of the play. 15

(*Music begins to play.*)

   The play is memory. Being a memory play, it is dimly
lighted, it is sentimental, it is not realistic. In memory
everything seems to happen to music. That explains the
fiddle in the wings.
   I am the narrator of the play, and also a character in it. 20
The other characters are my mother, Amanda, my sister,

Laura, and a gentleman caller who appears in the final scenes.
He is the most realistic character in the play, being an emissary
from a world of reality that we were somehow set apart from.
25   But since I have a poet's weakness for symbols, I am using this
character also as a symbol; he is the long-delayed but always
expected something that we live for.

There is a fifth character in the play who doesn't appear
except in this larger-than-life-size photograph over the
30   mantel. This is our father who left us a long time ago. He was
a telephone man who fell in love with long distances; he gave
up his job with the telephone company and skipped the light
fantastic out of town . . .

The last we heard of him was a picture postcard from
35   Mazatlan, on the Pacific coast of Mexico, containing a
message of two words: "Hello—Goodbye!" and no address.
I think the rest of the play will explain itself. . . .

(AMANDA's *voice becomes audible through the portieres.*)

(*Legend on screen:* "Ou sont les neiges.")

(TOM *divides the portieres and enters the dining room.* AMANDA
and LAURA *are seated at a drop-leaf table. Eating is indicated by
gestures without food or utensils.* AMANDA *faces the audience.* TOM
and LAURA *are seated in profile. The interior has lit up softly and
through the scrim we see* AMANDA *and* LAURA *seated at the table.*)

AMANDA: (*Calling.*) Tom?
TOM: Yes, Mother.
40   AMANDA: We can't say grace until you come to the table!
TOM: Coming, Mother. (*He bows slightly and withdraws,
reappearing a few moments later in his place at the table.*)
AMANDA: (*To her son.*) Honey, don't *push* with your *fingers.* If
you have to push with something, the thing to push with
45   is a crust of bread. And chew—chew! Animals have secre-
tions in their stomachs which enable them to digest food
without mastication, but human beings are supposed to
chew their food before they swallow it down. Eat food
leisurely, son, and really enjoy it. A well-cooked meal has
50   lots of delicate flavors that have to be held in the mouth for
appreciation. So chew your food and give your salivary
glands a chance to function!

(TOM *deliberately lays his imaginary fork down and pushes his
chair back from the table.*)

TOM: I haven't enjoyed one bite of this dinner because of your
constant directions on how to eat it. It's you that make me
55   rush through meals with your hawklike attention to every
bite I take. Sickening—spoils my appetite—all this discussion
of—animals' secretion—salivary glands—mastication!
AMANDA: (*Lightly.*) Temperament like a Metropolitan star!

(TOM *rises and walks toward the living room.*)

You're not excused from the table.
60   TOM: I'm getting a cigarette.
AMANDA: You smoke too much.

(LAURA *rises.*)

LAURA: I'll bring in the blanc mange.

(TOM *remains standing with his cigarette by the portieres.*)

AMANDA: (*Rising.*) No, sister, no, sister—you be the lady this time
and I'll be the darky.
LAURA: I'm already up.
65
AMANDA: Resume your seat, little sister—I want you to stay fresh
and pretty—for gentlemen callers!
LAURA: (*Sitting down.*) I'm not expecting any gentlemen callers.
AMANDA: (*Crossing out to the kitchenette, airily.*) Sometimes they
come when they are least expected! Why, I remember one
70
Sunday afternoon in Blue Mountain—

(*She enters the kitchenette.*)

TOM: I know what's coming!
LAURA: Yes. But let her tell it.
TOM: Again?
LAURA: She loves to tell it.
75

(AMANDA *returns with a bowl of dessert.*)

AMANDA: One Sunday afternoon in Blue Mountain—your
mother received—*seventeen!*—gentlemen callers! Why,
sometimes there weren't chairs enough to accommodate
them all. We had to send the nigger over to bring in folding
chairs from the parish house.
80
TOM: (*Remaining at the portieres.*) How did you entertain those
gentlemen callers?
AMANDA: I understood the art of conversation!
TOM: I bet you could talk.
AMANDA: Girls in those days *knew* how to talk, I can tell you.
85
TOM: Yes?

(*Image on screen:* AMANDA *as a girl on a porch, greeting callers.*)

AMANDA: They knew how to entertain their gentlemen callers.
It wasn't enough for a girl to be possessed of a pretty face
and a graceful figure—although I wasn't slighted in either
respect. She also needed to have a nimble wit and a tongue
90
to meet all occasions.
TOM: What did you talk about?
AMANDA: Things of importance going on in the world! Never
anything coarse or common or vulgar.

(*She addresses* TOM *as though he were seated in the vacant chair at
the table though he remains by the portieres. He plays this scene as
though reading from a script.*)

My callers were gentlemen—all! Among my callers were
95
some of the most prominent young planters of the Mississippi
Delta—planters and sons of planters!

(TOM *motions for music and a spot of light on* AMANDA. *Her eyes
lift, her face glows, her voice becomes rich and elegiac.*)

(*Screen legend:* "Ou sont les neiges d'antan?")

There was young Champ Laughlin who later became vice-
president of the Delta Planters Bank. Hadley Stevenson
who was drowned in Moon Lake and left his widow one
100
hundred and fifty thousand in Government bonds. There
were the Cutrere brothers, Wesley and Bates. Bates was

one of my bright particular beaux! He got in a quarrel with
that wild Wainwright boy. They shot it out on the floor of
105   Moon Lake Casino. Bates was shot through the stomach.
Died in the ambulance on his way to Memphis. His widow
was also well provided-for, came into eight or ten thousand
acres, that's all. She married him on the rebound—never
loved her—carried my picture on him the night he died!
110   And there was that boy that every girl in the Delta had set
her cap for! That beautiful, brilliant young Fitzhugh boy
from Greene County!
TOM: What did he leave his widow?
AMANDA: He never married! Gracious, you talk as though all of
115   my old admirers had turned up their toes to the daisies!
TOM: Isn't this the first you've mentioned that still survives?
AMANDA: That Fitzhugh boy went North and made a fortune—
came to be known as the Wolf of Wall Street! He had the
Midas touch, whatever he touched turned to gold! And I
120   could have been Mrs. Duncan J. Fitzhugh, mind you!
But—I picked your *father!*
LAURA: (*Rising.*) Mother, let me clear the table.
AMANDA: No, dear, you go in front and study your typewriter
chart. Or practice your shorthand a little. Stay fresh and
125   pretty!—It's almost time for our gentlemen callers to start
arriving. (*She flounces girlishly toward the kitchenette.*) How
many do you suppose we're going to entertain this afternoon?

(TOM *throws down the paper and jumps up with a groan.*)

LAURA: (*Alone in the dining room.*) I don't believe we're going to
receive any, Mother.
130   AMANDA: (*Reappearing, airily.*) What? No one—not one? You
must be joking!

(LAURA *nervously echoes her laugh. She slips in a fugitive manner
through the half-open portieres and draws them gently behind her.
A shaft of very clear light is thrown on her face against the faded
tapestry of the curtains. Faintly the music of "The Glass Menagerie" is heard as she continues, lightly.*)

Not one gentleman caller? It can't be true! There must be a
flood, there must have been a tornado!
LAURA: It isn't a flood, it's not a tornado, Mother. I'm just not
135   popular like you were in Blue Mountain. . . .

(TOM *utters another groan.* LAURA *glances at him with a faint,
apologetic smile. Her voice catches a little.*)

Mother's afraid I'm going to be an old maid.

(*The scene dims out with the "Glass Menagerie" music.*)

SCENE TWO

On the dark stage the screen is lighted with the image of blue roses.
Gradually LAURA's figure becomes apparent and the screen goes
out. The music subsides.

LAURA is seated in the delicate ivory chair at the small claw-foot
table. She wears a dress of soft violet material for a kimono—her
hair is tied back from her forehead with a ribbon. She is washing
and polishing her collection of glass. AMANDA appears on the fire
escape steps. At the sound of her ascent, LAURA catches her breath,
thrusts the bowl of ornaments away, and seats herself stiffly before

the diagram of the typewriter keyboard as though it held her
spellbound. Something has happened to AMANDA. It is written in
her face as she climbs to the landing: a look that is grim and hopeless and a little absurd. She has on one of those cheap or imitation
velvety-looking cloth coats with imitation fur collar. Her hat is five
or six years old, one of those dreadful cloche hats that were worn in
the late Twenties, and she is clutching an enormous black patent-
leather pocketbook with nickel clasps and initials. This is her full-
dress outfit, the one she usually wears to the D.A.R. Before entering
she looks through the door. She purses her lips, opens her eyes very
wide, rolls them upward and shakes her head. Then she slowly lets
herself in the door. Seeing her mother's expression LAURA touches
her lips with a nervous gesture.

LAURA: Hello, Mother, I was—(*She makes a nervous gesture
toward the chart on the wall.* AMANDA *leans against the shut
door and stares at* LAURA *with a martyred look.*)
AMANDA: Deception? Deception? (*She slowly removes her hat
and gloves, continuing the sweet suffering stare. She lets the   5
hat and gloves fall on the floor—a bit of acting.*)
LAURA: (*Shakily.*) How was the D.A.R. meeting?

(AMANDA *slowly opens her purse and removes a dainty white
handkerchief which she shakes out delicately and delicately touches
to her lips and nostrils.*)

Didn't you go to the D.A.R. meeting, Mother?
AMANDA: (*Faintly, almost inaudibly.*) —No.—No. (*Then more
forcibly.*) I did not have the strength—to go to the D.A.R.   10
In fact, I did not have the courage! I wanted to find a hole in
the ground and hide myself in it forever! (*She crosses slowly to
the wall and removes the diagram of the typewriter keyboard.
She holds it in front of her for a second, staring at it sweetly and
sorrowfully—then bites her lips and tears it into two pieces.*)   15
LAURA: (*Faintly.*) Why did you do that, Mother?

(AMANDA *repeats the same procedure with the chart of the Gregg
Alphabet.*)

Why are you—
AMANDA: Why? Why? How old are you, Laura?
LAURA: Mother, you know my age.
AMANDA: I thought that you were an adult; it seems that I was   20
mistaken. (*She crosses slowly to the sofa and sinks down and
stares at* LAURA.)
LAURA: Please don't stare at me, Mother.

(AMANDA *closes her eyes and lowers her head. There is a
ten-second pause.*)

AMANDA: What are we going to do, what is going to become of us,
what is the future?   25

(*There is another pause.*)

LAURA: Has something happened, Mother?

(AMANDA *draws a long breath, takes out the handkerchief again,
goes through the dabbing process.*)

Mother, has—something happened?
AMANDA: I'll be all right in a minute, I'm just bewildered—(*She
hesitates.*)—by life. . . .

30 LAURA: Mother, I wish that you would tell me what's happened!

AMANDA: As you know, I was supposed to be inducted into my office at the D.A.R. this afternoon.

(*Screen image: A swarm of typewriters.*)

But I stopped off at Rubicam's Business College to speak to your teachers about your having a cold and ask them what
35 progress they thought you were making down there.

LAURA: Oh. . . .

AMANDA: I went to the typing instructor and introduced myself as your mother. She didn't know who you were. "Wingfield," she said, "We don't have any such student
40 enrolled at the school!"

I assured her she did, that you had been going to classes since early in January.

"I wonder," she said, "If you could be talking about that terribly shy little girl who dropped out of school after only a
45 few days' attendance?"

"No," I said, "Laura, my daughter, has been going to school every day for the past six weeks!"

"Excuse me," she said. She took the attendance book out and there was your name, unmistakably printed, and all
50 the dates you were absent until they decided that you had dropped out of school.

I still said, "No, there must have been some mistake! There must have been some mix-up in the records!"

And she said, "No—I remember her perfectly now.
55 Her hands shook so that she couldn't hit the right keys! The first time we gave a speed test, she broke down completely—was sick at the stomach and almost had to be carried into the wash room! After that morning she never showed up any more. We phoned the house but never
60 got any answer"—While I was working at Famous-Barr, I suppose, demonstrating those—

(*She indicates a brassiere with her hands.*)

Oh! I felt so weak I could barely keep on my feet! I had to sit down while they got me a glass of water! Fifty dollars' tuition, all of our plans—my hopes and ambitions for you—just gone
65 up the spout, just gone up the spout like that.

(LAURA *draws a long breath and gets awkwardly to her feet. She crosses to the Victrola and winds it up.*)

What are you doing?

LAURA: Oh! (*She releases the handle and returns to her seat.*)

AMANDA: Laura, where have you been going when you've gone out pretending that you were going to business college?
70 LAURA: I've just been going out walking.

AMANDA: That's not true.

LAURA: It is. I just went walking.

AMANDA: Walking? Walking? In winter? Deliberately courting pneumonia in that light coat? Where did you walk to, Laura?
75 LAURA: All sorts of places—mostly in the park.

AMANDA: Even after you'd started catching that cold?

LAURA: It was the lesser of two evils, Mother.

(*Screen image: Winter scene in a park.*)

I couldn't go back there. I—threw up—on the floor!

AMANDA: From half past seven till after five every day you mean to tell me you walked around in the park, because you wanted 80
to make me think that you were still going to Rubicam's Business College?

LAURA: It wasn't as bad as it sounds. I went inside places to get warmed up.

AMANDA: Inside where? 85

LAURA: I went in the art museum and the bird houses at the Zoo. I visited the penguins every day! Sometimes I did without lunch and went to the movies. Lately I've been spending most of my afternoons in the Jewel Box, that big glass house where they raise the tropical flowers. 90

AMANDA: You did all this to deceive me, just for deception? (LAURA *looks down.*) Why?

LAURA: Mother, when you're disappointed, you get that awful suffering look on your face, like the picture of Jesus' mother in the museum! 95

AMANDA: Hush!

LAURA: I couldn't face it.

(*There is a pause. A whisper of strings is heard. Legend on screen:* "The Crust of Humility.")

AMANDA: (*Hopelessly fingering the huge pocketbook.*) So what are we going to do the rest of our lives? Stay home and watch the parades go by? Amuse ourselves with the glass menagerie, 100
darling? Eternally play those worn-out phonograph records your father left as a painful reminder of him? We won't have a business career—we've given that up because it gave us nervous indigestion! (*She laughs wearily.*) What is there left but dependency all our lives? I know so well what becomes 105
of unmarried women who aren't prepared to occupy a position. I've seen such pitiful cases in the South—barely tolerated spinsters living upon the grudging patronage of sister's husband or brother's wife!—stuck away in some little mousetrap of a room—encouraged by one in-law to visit 110
another—little birdlike women without any nest—eating the crust of humility all their life!

Is that the future that we've mapped out for ourselves? I swear it's the only alternative I can think of! (*She pauses.*) It isn't a very pleasant alternative, is it? (*She pauses again.*) Of 115
course—some girls *do marry*.

(LAURA *twists her hands nervously.*)

Haven't you ever liked some boy?

LAURA: Yes. I liked one once. (*She rises.*) I came across his picture a while ago.

AMANDA: (*With some interest.*) He gave you his picture? 120

LAURA: No, it's in the yearbook.

AMANDA: (*Disappointed.*) Oh—a high school boy.

(*Screen image:* JIM *as the high school hero bearing a silver cup.*)

LAURA: Yes. His name was Jim. (*She lifts the heavy annual from the claw-foot table.*) Here he is in *The Pirates of Penzance.*

AMANDA: (*Absently.*) The what? 125

LAURA: The operetta the senior class put on. He had a wonderful voice and we sat across the aisle from each other Mondays, Wednesdays and Fridays in the Aud. Here he is with the silver cup for debating! See his grin?

AMANDA: (*Absently.*) He must have had a jolly disposition. 130

LAURA: He used to call me—Blue Roses.

(*Screen image:* Blue roses.)

AMANDA: Why did he call you such a name as that?
LAURA: When I had that attack of pleurosis—he asked me
what was the matter when I came back. I said pleurosis—he
135   thought that I said Blue Roses! So that's what he always called
me after that. Whenever he saw me, he'd holler, "Hello, Blue
Roses!" I didn't care for the girl that he went out with. Emily
Meisenbach. Emily was the best-dressed girl at Soldan. She
never struck me, though, as being sincere . . . It says in the
140   Personal Section—they're engaged. That's—six years ago!
They must be married by now.
AMANDA: Girls that aren't cut out for business careers usually
wind up married to some nice man. (*She gets up with a spark
of revival.*) Sister, that's what you'll do!

(LAURA *utters a startled, doubtful laugh. She reaches quickly for a
piece of glass.*)

145   LAURA: But, Mother—
AMANDA: Yes? (*She goes over to the photograph.*)
LAURA: (*In a tone of frightened apology.*) I'm—crippled!
AMANDA: Nonsense! Laura, I've told you never, never to use
that word. Why, you're not crippled, you just have a little
150   defect—hardly noticeable, even! When people have some
slight disadvantage like that, they cultivate other things to
make up for it—develop charm—and vivacity—and—*charm!*
That's all you have to do! (*She turns again to the photograph.*)
One thing your father had *plenty of—was charm!*

(*The scene fades out with music.*)

SCENE THREE

Legend on screen: "After the fiasco—"

TOM *speaks from the fire escape landing.*

TOM: After the fiasco at Rubicam's Business College, the idea
of getting a gentleman caller for Laura began to play a
more and more important part in Mother's calculations. It
became an obsession. Like some archetype of the universal
5   unconscious, the image of the gentleman caller haunted
our small apartment. . . .

(*Screen image:* A young man at the door of a house with flowers.)

An evening at home rarely passed without some allusion
to this image, this specter, this hope . . . Even when he wasn't
mentioned, his presence hung in Mother's preoccupied look
10   and in my sister's frightened, apologetic manner—hung like a
sentence passed upon the Wingfields.
Mother was a woman of action as well as words. She began
to take logical steps in the planned direction. Late that winter
and in the early spring—realizing that extra money would be
15   needed to properly feather the nest and plume the bird—she
conducted a vigorous campaign on the telephone, roping in
subscribers to one of those magazines for matrons called *The
Homemaker's Companion,* the type of journal that features
the serialized sublimations of ladies of letters who think in

terms of delicate cuplike breasts, slim, tapering waists, rich,   20
creamy thighs, eyes like wood smoke in autumn, fingers that
soothe and caress like strains of music, bodies as powerful as
Etruscan sculpture.

(*Screen image:* The cover of a glamor magazine.)

(AMANDA *enters with the telephone on a long extension cord. She
is spotlighted in the dim stage.*)

AMANDA: Ida Scott? This is Amanda Wingfield! We missed
you at the D.A.R. last Monday! I said to myself: She's   25
probably suffering with that sinus condition! How is that
sinus condition?
Horrors! Heaven have mercy!—You're a Christian martyr,
yes, that's what you are, a Christian martyr!
Well, I just now happened to notice that your subscription   30
to the *Companion's* about to expire! Yes, it expires with the
next issue, honey!—just when that wonderful new serial by
Bessie Mae Hopper is getting off to such an exciting start. Oh,
honey, it's something that you can't miss! You remember how
Gone with the Wind took everybody by storm? You simply   35
couldn't go out if you hadn't read it. All everybody *talked*
was Scarlett O'Hara. Well, this is a book that critics already
compare to *Gone with the Wind*. It's the *Gone with the Wind*
of the post–World War generation.—What?—Burning?—Oh,
honey, don't let them burn, go take a look in the oven and I'll   40
hold the wire! Heavens—I think she's hung up!

(*The scene dims out.*)

(*Legend on screen:* "You think I'm in love with Continental
Shoemakers?")

(*Before the lights come up again, the violent voices of* TOM *and*
AMANDA *are heard. They are quarreling behind the portieres. In
front of them stands* LAURA *with clenched hands and panicky expression. A clear pool of light is on her figure throughout this scene.*)

TOM: What in Christ's name am I—
AMANDA: (*Shrilly.*) Don't you use that—
TOM: —supposed to do!
AMANDA: —expression! Not in my—   45
TOM: Ohhh!
AMANDA: —presence! Have you gone out of your senses?
TOM: I have, that's true, *driven* out!
AMANDA: What is the matter with you, you—big—big—
IDIOT!   50
TOM: Look!—I've got *no thing,* no single thing—
AMANDA: Lower your voice!
TOM: —in my life here that I can call my OWN! Everything is—
AMANDA: Stop that shouting!
TOM: Yesterday you confiscated my books! You had the nerve   55
to—
AMANDA: I took that horrible novel back to the library—yes! That
hideous book by that insane Mr. Lawrence.

(TOM *laughs wildly.*)

I cannot control the output of diseased minds or people who
cater to them—   60

(TOM *laughs still more wildly.*)

BUT I WON'T ALLOW SUCH FILTH BROUGHT INTO MY HOUSE! No, no, no, no, no!

TOM: House, house! Who pays rent on it, who makes a slave of himself to—

65 AMANDA: (*Fairly screeching.*) Don't you DARE to—

TOM: No, no, I mustn't say things! *I've* got to just—

AMANDA: Let me tell you—

TOM: I don't want to hear any more!

(*He tears the portieres open. The dining-room area is lit with a turgid smoky red glow. Now we see* AMANDA; *her hair is in metal curlers and she is wearing a very old bathrobe, much too large for her slight figure, a relic of the faithless Mr. Wingfield. The upright typewriter now stands on the drop-leaf table, along with a wild disarray of manuscripts. The quarrel was probably precipitated by* AMANDA's *interruption of* TOM's *creative labor. A chair lies overthrown on the floor. Their gesticulating shadows are cast on the ceiling by the fiery glow.*)

AMANDA: You *will* hear more, you—

70 TOM: No, I won't hear more, I'm going out!

AMANDA: You come right back in—

TOM: Out, out, out! Because I'm—

AMANDA: Come back here, Tom Wingfield! I'm not through talking to you!

75 TOM: Oh, go—

LAURA: (*Desperately.*)—Tom!

AMANDA: You're going to listen, and no more insolence from you! I'm at the end of my patience!

(*He comes back toward her.*)

TOM: What do you think I'm at? Aren't I supposed to have any
80 patience to reach the end of, Mother? I know, I know. It seems unimportant to you, what I'm *doing*—what I *want* to do—having a little *difference* between them! You don't think that—

AMANDA: I think you've been doing things that you're ashamed
85 of. That's why you act like this. I don't believe that you go every night to the movies. Nobody goes to the movies night after night. Nobody in their right minds goes to the movies as often as you pretend to. People don't go to the movies at nearly midnight, and movies don't let out at two A.M. Come in
90 stumbling. Muttering to yourself like a maniac! You get three hours' sleep and then go to work. Oh, I can picture the way you're doing down there. Moping, doping, because you're in no condition.

TOM: (*Wildly.*) No, I'm in no condition!

95 AMANDA: What right have you got to jeopardize your job? Jeopardize the security of us all? How do you think we'd manage if you were—

TOM: Listen! You think I'm crazy about the *warehouse*? (*He bends fiercely toward her slight figure.*) You think I'm in
100 love with the Continental Shoemakers? You think I want to spend fifty-five years down there in that—*celotex interior!* with—*fluorescent—tubes!* Look! I'd rather somebody picked up a crowbar and battered out my brains—than go back mornings! I *go!* Every time you come in yelling that Goddamn
105 "*Rise and Shine!*" "*Rise and Shine!*" I say to myself, "How *lucky dead* people are!" But I get up. I *go!* For sixty-five dollars a month I give up all that I dream of doing and being *ever!* And you say self—*self*'s all I ever think of. Why, listen, if self is what I thought of, Mother, I'd be where he is—GONE!

(*He points to his father's picture.*) As far as the system of 110 transportation reaches! (*He starts past her. She grabs his arm.*) Don't grab at me, Mother!

AMANDA: Where are you going?

TOM: I'm going to the *movies!*

AMANDA: I don't believe that lie! 115

(TOM *crouches toward her, overtowering her tiny figure. She backs away, gasping.*)

TOM: I'm going to opium dens! Yes, opium dens, dens of vice and criminals' hangouts, Mother. I've joined the Hogan Gang, I'm a hired assassin, I carry a tommy gun in a violin case! I run a string of cat houses in the Valley! They call me Killer, Killer Wingfield, I'm leading a double-life, a simple, honest 120 warehouse worker by day, by night a dynamic *czar* of the *underworld, Mother.* I go to gambling casinos, I spin away fortunes on the roulette table! I wear a patch over one eye and a false mustache, sometimes I put on green whiskers. On those occasions they call me—*El Diablo!* Oh, I could tell you many 125 things to make you sleepless! My enemies plan to dynamite this place. They're going to blow us all sky-high some night! I'll be glad, very happy, and so will you! You'll go up, up on a broomstick, over Blue Mountain with seventeen gentlemen callers! You ugly—babbling old—*witch* . . . (*He goes through* 130 *a series of violent, clumsy movements, seizing his overcoat, lunging to the door, pulling it fiercely open. The women watch him, aghast. His arm catches in the sleeve of the coat as he struggles to pull it on. For a moment he is pinioned by the bulky garment. With an outraged groan he tears the coat off again,* 135 *splitting the shoulder of it, and hurls it across the room. It strikes against the shelf of* LAURA's *glass collection, and there is a tinkle of shattering glass.* LAURA *cries out as if wounded.*)

(*Music.*)

(*Screen legend:* "The Glass Menagerie.")

LAURA: (*Shrilly.*) *My glass!*—menagerie . . . (*She covers her face and turns away.*) 140

(*But* AMANDA *is still stunned and stupefied by the "ugly witch" so that she barely notices this occurrence. Now she recovers her speech.*)

AMANDA: (*In an awful voice.*) I won't speak to you—until you apologize!

(*She crosses through the portieres and draws them together behind her.* TOM *is left with* LAURA. LAURA *clings weakly to the mantel with her face averted.* TOM *stares at her stupidly for a moment. Then he crosses to the shelf. He drops awkwardly on his knees to collect the fallen glass, glancing at* LAURA *as if he would speak but couldn't.*)

("The Glass Menagerie" *music steals in as the scene dims out.*)

SCENE FOUR

The interior of the apartment is dark. There is a faint light in the alley. A deep-voiced bell in a church is tolling the hour of five.

TOM *appears at the top of the alley. After each solemn boom of the bell in the tower, he shakes a little noisemaker or rattle as if to express the tiny spasm of man in contrast to the sustained power and dignity of the Almighty. This and the unsteadiness of his advance make it evident that he has been drinking. As he climbs the few steps to the fire escape landing light steals up inside.* LAURA *appears in the front room in a nightdress. She notices that* TOM's *bed is empty.* TOM *fishes in his pockets for his door key, removing a motley assortment of articles in the search, including a shower of movie ticket stubs and an empty bottle. At last he finds the key, but just as he is about to insert it, it slips from his fingers. He strikes a match and crouches below the door.*

TOM: (*Bitterly.*) One crack—and it falls through!

(LAURA *opens the door.*)

LAURA: Tom! Tom, what are you doing?
TOM: Looking for a door key.
LAURA: Where have you been all this time?
5 TOM: I have been to the movies.
LAURA: All this time at the movies?
TOM: There was a very long program. There was a Garbo
    picture and a Mickey Mouse and a travelogue and a news-
    reel and a preview of coming attractions. And there
10   was an organ solo and a collection for the Milk Fund—
    simultaneously—which ended up in a terrible fight
    between a fat lady and an usher!
LAURA: (*Innocently.*) Did you have to stay through everything?
TOM: Of course! And, oh, I forgot! There was a big stage
15   show! The headliner on this stage show was Malvolio
    the Magician. He performed wonderful tricks, many
    of them, such as pouring water back and forth between
    pitchers. First it turned to wine and then it turned to
    beer and then it turned to whisky. I know it was whisky
20   it finally turned into because he needed somebody to come
    up out of the audience to help him, and I came up—both
    shows! It was Kentucky Straight Bourbon. A very generous
    fellow, he gave souvenirs. (*He pulls from his back pocket a
    shimmering rainbow-colored scarf.*) He gave me this. This
25   is his magic scarf. You can have it, Laura. You wave it
    over a canary cage and you get a bowl of goldfish. You wave it
    over the goldfish bowl and they fly away canaries . . . But
    the wonderfullest trick of all was the coffin trick. We
    nailed him into a coffin and he got out of the coffin without
30   removing one nail. (*He has come inside.*) There is a trick
    that would come in handy for me—get me out of this two-
    by-four situation! (*He flops onto the bed and starts removing
    his shoes.*)
LAURA: Tom—shhh!
35 TOM: What're you shushing me for?
LAURA: You'll wake up Mother.
TOM: Goody, goody! Pay 'er back for all those "Rise an'
    Shines." (*He lies down, groaning.*) You know it don't take
    much intelligence to get yourself into a nailed-up coffin,
40   Laura. But who in hell ever got himself out of one without
    removing one nail?

(*As if in answer, the father's grinning photograph lights up. The scene dims out.*)

(*Immediately following, the church bell is heard striking six. At the sixth stroke the alarm clock goes off in* AMANDA's *room, and after a few moments we hear her calling: "Rise and Shine! Rise and Shine!* LAURA, *go tell your brother to rise and shine!"*)

TOM: (*Sitting up slowly.*) I'll rise—but I won't shine.

(*The light increases.*)

AMANDA: Laura, tell your brother his coffee is ready.

(LAURA *slips into the front room.*)

LAURA: Tom!—It's nearly seven. Don't make Mother nervous.

(*He stares at her stupidly.*)

    (*Beseechingly.*) Tom, speak to Mother this morning. Make   45
    up with her, apologize, speak to her!
TOM: She won't to me. It's her that started not speaking.
LAURA: If you just say you're sorry she'll start speaking.
TOM: Her not speaking—is that such a tragedy?
LAURA: Please—please!   50
AMANDA: (*Calling from the kitchenette.*) Laura, are you going to
    do what I asked you to do, or do I have to get dressed and go
    out myself?
LAURA: Going, going—soon as I get on my coat!

(*She pulls on a shapeless felt hat with a nervous, jerky movement, pleadingly glancing at* TOM. *She rushes awkwardly for her coat. The coat is one of* AMANDA's, *inaccurately made-over, the sleeves too short for* LAURA.)

    Butter and what else?   55
AMANDA: (*Entering from the kitchenette.*) Just butter. Tell them
    to charge it.
LAURA: Mother, they make such faces when I do that.
AMANDA: Sticks and stones can break our bones, but the
    expression on Mr. Garfinkel's face won't harm us! Tell your   60
    brother his coffee is getting cold.
LAURA: (*At the door.*) Do what I asked you, will you, will you,
    Tom?

(*He looks sullenly away.*)

AMANDA: Laura, go now or just don't go at all!
LAURA: (*Rushing out.*) Going—going!   65

(*A second later she cries out.* TOM *springs up and crosses to the door.* TOM *opens the door.*)

TOM: Laura?
LAURA: I'm all right. I slipped, but I'm all right.
AMANDA: (*Peering anxiously after her.*) If anyone breaks a leg on
    those fire-escape steps, the landlord ought to be sued for every
    cent he possesses! (*She shuts the door. Now she remembers she   70
    isn't speaking to* TOM *and returns to the other room.*)

(*As* TOM *comes listlessly for his coffee, she turns her back to him and stands rigidly facing the window on the gloomy gray vault of the areaway. Its light on her face with its aged but childish features is cruelly sharp, satirical as a Daumier print.*)

(*The music of* "Ave Maria" *is heard softly.*)

(TOM *glances sheepishly but sullenly at her averted figure and slumps at the table. The coffee is scalding hot; he sips it and gasps and spits it back in the cup. At his gasp,* AMANDA *catches her breath and half turns. Then she catches herself and turns back to the window.* TOM *blows on his coffee, glancing sidewise at his mother. She clears her throat.* TOM *clears his. He starts to rise, sinks back down*

again, scratches his head, clears his throat again. AMANDA *coughs.*
TOM *raises his cup in both hands to blow on it, his eyes staring over
the rim of it at his mother for several moments. Then he slowly sets
the cup down and awkwardly and hesitantly rises from the chair.)*

TOM: (*Hoarsely.*) Mother. I—I apologize, Mother.

(AMANDA *draws a quick, shuddering breath. Her face works
grotesquely. She breaks into childlike tears.)*

I'm sorry for what I said, for everything that I said, I didn't
mean it.

75   AMANDA: (*Sobbingly.*) My devotion has made me a witch and so I
make myself hateful to my children!
TOM: *No, you don't.*
AMANDA: I worry so much, don't sleep, it makes me nervous!
TOM: (*Gently.*) I understand that.
80   AMANDA: I've had to put up a solitary battle all these years. But
you're my right-hand bower! Don't fall down, don't fail!
TOM: (*Gently.*) I try, Mother.
AMANDA: (*With great enthusiasm.*) Try and you will *succeed!* (*The
notion makes her breathless.*) Why, you—you're just *full* of
85   natural endowments! Both of my children—they're *unusual*
children! Don't you think I know it? I'm so—*proud!* Happy
and—feel I've—so much to be thankful for but—promise me
one thing, son!
TOM: What, Mother?
90   AMANDA: Promise, son, you'll—never be a drunkard!
TOM: (*Turns to her grinning.*) I will never be a drunkard, Mother.
AMANDA: That's what frightened me so, that you'd be drinking!
Eat a bowl of Purina!
TOM: Just coffee, Mother.
95   AMANDA: Shredded wheat biscuit?
TOM: No. No, Mother, just coffee.
AMANDA: You can't put in a day's work on an empty stomach.
You've got ten minutes—don't gulp! Drinking too-hot liquids
makes cancer of the stomach . . . Put cream in.
100 TOM: No, thank you.
AMANDA: To cool it.
TOM: No! No, thank you, I want it black.
AMANDA: I know, but it's not good for you. We have to do all that
we can to build ourselves up. In these trying times we live in,
105 all that we have to cling to is—each other . . . That's why it's so
important to—Tom, I—sent out your sister so I could discuss
something with you. If you hadn't spoken I would have
spoken to you. (*She sits down.*)
TOM: (*Gently.*) What is it, Mother, that you want to discuss?
110 AMANDA: *Laura!*

(TOM *puts his cup down slowly.)*

(*Legend on screen:* "Laura." *Music:* "The Glass Menagerie.")

TOM: —Oh.—Laura . . .
AMANDA: (*Touching his sleeve.*) You know how Laura is. So quiet
but—still water runs deep! She notices things and I think
she—broods about them.

(TOM *looks up.*)

115   A few days ago I came in and she was crying.
TOM: What about?

AMANDA: You.
TOM: Me?
AMANDA: She has an idea that you're not happy here.
TOM: What gave her that idea?   120
AMANDA: What gives her any idea? However, you do act
strangely. I—I'm not criticizing, understand *that!* I know
your ambitions do not lie in the warehouse, that like
everybody in the whole wide world—you've had to—
make sacrifices, but—Tom—Tom—life's not easy, it calls   125
for—Spartan endurance! There's so many things in my
heart that I cannot describe to you! I've never told you but
I—*loved* your father. . . .
TOM: (*Gently.*) I know that, Mother.
AMANDA: And you—when I see you taking after his ways! Staying   130
out late—and—well, you *had* been drinking the night you
were in that—terrifying condition! Laura says that you hate
the apartment and that you go out nights to get away from it!
Is that true, Tom?
TOM: No. You say there's so much in your heart that you can't   135
describe to me. That's true of me, too. There's so much in
my heart that I can't describe to *you!* So let's respect each
other's—
AMANDA: But, why—*why,* Tom—are you always so *restless?*
Where do you *go* to, nights?   140
TOM: I—go to the movies.
AMANDA: Why do you go to the movies so much, Tom?
TOM: I go to the movies because—I like adventure. Adventure
is something I don't have much of at work, so I go to the
movies.   145
AMANDA: But, Tom, you go to the movies *entirely* too *much!*
TOM: I like a lot of adventure.

(AMANDA *looks baffled, then hurt. As the familiar inquisition
resumes,* TOM *becomes hard and impatient again.* AMANDA *slips
back into her querulous attitude toward him.)*

(*Image on screen:* A sailing vessel with Jolly Roger.)

AMANDA: Most young men find adventure in their careers.
TOM: Then most young men are not employed in a warehouse.
AMANDA: The world is full of young men employed in ware-   150
houses and offices and factories.
TOM: Do all of them find adventure in their careers?
AMANDA: They do or they do without it! Not everybody has a
craze for adventure.
TOM: Man is by instinct a lover, a hunter, a fighter, and none of 155
those instincts are given much play at the warehouse!
AMANDA: Man is by instinct! Don't quote instinct to me! Instinct
is something that people have got away from! It belongs to
animals! Christian adults don't want it!
TOM: What do Christian adults want, then, Mother?   160
AMANDA: Superior things! Things of the mind and the spirit!
Only animals have to satisfy instincts! Surely your aims are
somewhat higher than theirs! Than monkeys—pigs—
TOM: I reckon they're not.
AMANDA: You're joking. However, that isn't what I wanted to   165
discuss.
TOM: (*Rising.*) I haven't much time.
AMANDA: (*Pushing his shoulders.*) Sit down.
TOM: You want me to punch in red at the warehouse, Mother?
AMANDA: You have five minutes. I want to talk about Laura.   170

(*Screen legend:* "Plans and Provisions.")

TOM: All right! What about Laura?

AMANDA: We have to be making some plans and provisions for her. She's older than you, two years, and nothing has happened. She just drifts along doing nothing. It frightens me
175   terribly how she just drifts along.

TOM: I guess she's the type that people call home girls.

AMANDA: There's no such type, and if there is, it's a pity! That is unless the home is hers, with a husband!

TOM: What?

180   AMANDA: Oh, I can see the handwriting on the wall as plain as I see the nose in front of my face! It's terrifying! More and more you remind me of your father! He was out all hours without explanation!—Then *left!* Goodbye! And me with the bag to hold. I saw that letter you got from the Merchant Marine.
185   I know what you're dreaming of. I'm not standing here blindfolded. (*She pauses.*) Very well, then. Then do it! But not till there's somebody to take your place.

TOM: What do you mean?

AMANDA: I mean that as soon as Laura has got somebody to
190   take care of her, married, a home of her own, independent— why, then you'll be free to go wherever you please, on land, on sea, whichever way the wind blows you! But until that time you've got to look out for your sister. I don't say me because I'm old and don't matter! I say for your sister
195   because she's young and dependent.

I put her in business college—a dismal failure! Frightened her so it made her sick at the stomach. I took her over to the Young People's League at the church. Another fiasco. She spoke to nobody, nobody spoke to her. Now all she does is fool
200   with those pieces of glass and play those worn-out records. What kind of a life is that for a girl to lead?

TOM: What can I do about it?

AMANDA: Overcome selfishness! Self, self, self is all that you ever think of!

(TOM *springs up and crosses to get his coat. It is ugly and bulky. He pulls on a cap with earmuffs.*)

205   Where is your muffler? Put your wool muffler on!

(*He snatches it angrily from the closet, tosses it around his neck and pulls both ends tight.*)

Tom! I haven't said what I had in mind to ask you.

TOM: I'm too late to—

AMANDA: (*Catching his arm—very importunately; then shyly.*) Down at the warehouse, aren't there some—nice young
210   men?

TOM: No!

AMANDA: There *must* be—*some.* . . .

TOM: Mother—(*He gestures.*)

AMANDA: Find out one that's clean-living—doesn't drink and
215   ask him out for sister!

TOM: What?

AMANDA: For *sister!* To *meet!* Get *acquainted!*

TOM: (*Stamping to the door.*) Oh, my *go-osh!*

AMANDA: Will you?

(*He opens the door. She says, imploringly:*)

220   Will you?

(*He starts down the fire escape.*)

Will you? *Will* you, dear?

TOM: (*Calling back.*) Yes!

(AMANDA *closes the door hesitantly and with a troubled but faintly hopeful expression.*)

(*Screen image: The cover of a glamor magazine.*)

(*The spotlight picks up* AMANDA *at the phone.*)

AMANDA: Ella Cartwright? This is Amanda Wingfield! How are you, honey?
225   How is that kidney condition?

(*There is a five-second pause.*)

Horrors!

(*There is another pause.*)

You're a Christian martyr, yes, honey, that's what you are, a Christian martyr! Well, I just now happened to notice in my little red book that your subscription to the *Companion* has just run out! I knew that you wouldn't want to miss out on
230   the wonderful serial starting in this new issue. It's by Bessie Mae Hopper, the first thing she's written since *Honeymoon for Three.* Wasn't that a strange and interesting story? Well, this one is even lovelier, I believe. It has a sophisticated, society background. It's all about the horsey set on Long Island!
235

(*The light fades out.*)

SCENE FIVE

Legend on the screen: "Annunciation."

Music is heard as the light slowly comes on.

It is early dusk of a spring evening. Supper has just been finished in the Wingfield apartment. AMANDA *and* LAURA, *in light-colored dresses, are removing dishes from the table in the dining room, which is shadowy, their movements formalized almost as a dance or ritual, their moving forms as pale and silent as moths.* TOM, *in white shirt and trousers, rises from the table and crosses toward the fire escape.*

AMANDA: (*As he passes her.*) Son, will you do me a favor?

TOM: What?

AMANDA: Comb your hair! You look so pretty when your hair is combed!

(TOM *slouches on the sofa with the evening paper. Its enormous headline reads:* "Franco Triumphs.")

There is only one respect in which I would like you to
5   emulate your father.

TOM: What respect is that?

AMANDA: The care he always took of his appearance. He never allowed himself to look untidy.

(*He throws down the paper and crosses to the fire escape.*)

Where are you going?
10

TOM: I'm going out to smoke.

AMANDA: You smoke too much. A pack a day at fifteen cents a
pack. How much would that amount to in a month? Thirty
times fifteen is how much, Tom? Figure it out and you will
15   be astounded at what you could save. Enough to give you a
night-school course in accounting at Washington U! Just
think what a wonderful thing that would be for you, son!

(TOM *is unmoved by the thought.*)

TOM: I'd rather smoke. (*He steps out on the landing, letting the
screen door slam.*)
20 AMANDA: (*Sharply.*) I know! That's the tragedy of it. . . . (*Alone,
she turns to look at her husband's picture.*)

(*Dance music:* "The World Is Waiting for the Sunrise!")

TOM: (*To the audience.*) Across the alley from us was the Paradise
Dance-hall. On evenings in spring the windows and doors
were open and the music came outdoors. Sometimes the
25   lights were turned out except for a large glass sphere that
hung from the ceiling. It would turn slowly about and filter
the dusk with delicate rainbow colors. Then the orchestra
played a waltz or a tango, something that had a slow and
sensuous rhythm. Couples would come outside, to the relative
30   privacy of the alley. You could see them kissing behind ash
pits and telephone poles. This was the compensation for lives
that passed like mine, without any change or adventure.
Adventure and change were imminent in this year. They were
waiting around the corner for all these kids. Suspended in the
35   mist over Berchtesgaden, caught in the folds of Chamberlain's
umbrella. In Spain there was Guernica! But here there was
only hot swing music and liquor, dance-halls, bars, and
movies, and sex that hung in the gloom like a chandelier and
flooded the world with brief, deceptive rainbows. . . . All the
40   world was waiting for bombardments!

(AMANDA *turns from the picture and comes outside.*)

AMANDA: (*Sighing.*) A fire escape landing's a poor excuse for
a porch. (*She spreads a newspaper on a step and sits down,
gracefully and demurely as if she were settling into a swing on a
Mississippi veranda.*) What are you looking at?
45 TOM: The moon.
AMANDA: Is there a moon this evening?
TOM: It's rising over Garfinkel's Delicatessen.
AMANDA: So it is! A little silver slipper of a moon. Have you made
a wish on it yet?
50 TOM: Um-hum.
AMANDA: What did you wish for?
TOM: That's a secret.
AMANDA: A secret, huh? Well, I won't tell mine either. I will be
just as mysterious as you.
55 TOM: I bet I can guess what yours is.
AMANDA: Is my head so transparent?
TOM: You're not a sphinx.
AMANDA: No, I don't have secrets. I'll tell you what I wished for
on the moon. Success and happiness for my precious children!
60   I wish for that whenever there's a moon, and when there isn't a
moon, I wish for it, too.
TOM: I thought perhaps you wished for a gentleman caller.
AMANDA: Why do you say that?
TOM: Don't you remember asking me to fetch one?

AMANDA: I remember suggesting that it would be nice for   65
your sister if you brought home some nice young man from
the warehouse. I think that I've made that suggestion more
than once.
TOM: Yes, you have made it repeatedly.
AMANDA: Well?   70
TOM: We are going to have one.
AMANDA: *What?*
TOM: A gentleman caller!

(*The annunciation is celebrated with music.*)

(AMANDA *rises.*)

(*Image on screen:* A caller with a bouquet.)

AMANDA: You mean you have asked some nice young man to
come over?   75
TOM: Yep. I've asked him to dinner.
AMANDA: You really did?
TOM: I did!
AMANDA: You did, and did he—*accept?*
TOM: He did!   80
AMANDA: Well, well—well, well! That's—lovely!
TOM: I thought that you would be pleased.
AMANDA: It's definite then?
TOM: Very definite.
AMANDA: Soon?   85
TOM: Very soon.
AMANDA: For heaven's sake, stop putting on and tell me some
things, will you?
TOM: What things do you want me to tell you?
AMANDA: *Naturally* I would like to know when he's coming!   90
TOM: He's coming tomorrow.
AMANDA: *Tomorrow?*
TOM: Yep. Tomorrow.
AMANDA: But, Tom!
TOM: Yes, Mother?   95
AMANDA: Tomorrow gives me no time!
TOM: Time for what?
AMANDA: Preparations! Why didn't you phone me at once, as
soon as you asked him, the minute that he accepted? Then
don't you see, I could have been getting ready!   100
TOM: You don't have to make any fuss.
AMANDA: Oh, Tom, Tom, Tom, of course I have to make a fuss!
I want things nice, not sloppy! Not thrown together. I'll
certainly have to do some fast thinking, won't I?
TOM: I don't see why you have to think at all.   105
AMANDA: You just don't know. We can't have a gentleman
caller in a pigsty! All my wedding silver has to be polished,
the monogrammed table linen ought to be laundered! The
windows have to be washed and fresh curtains put up. And
how about clothes? We have to *wear* something, don't we?   110
TOM: Mother, this boy is no one to make a fuss over!
AMANDA: Do you realize he's the first young man we've
introduced to your sister? It's terrible, dreadful, disgraceful
that poor little sister has never received a single gentleman
caller! Tom, come inside! (*She opens the screen door.*)   115
TOM: What for?
AMANDA: I want to ask you some things.
TOM: If you're going to make such a fuss, I'll call it off, I'll tell
him not to come!

120   AMANDA: You certainly won't do anything of the kind. Nothing offends people worse than broken engagements. It simply means I'll have to work like a Turk! We won't be brilliant, but we will pass inspection. Come on inside.

(TOM *follows her inside, groaning.*)

Sit down.

125   TOM: Any particular place you would like me to sit?

AMANDA: Thank heavens I've got that new sofa! I'm also making payments on a floor lamp I'll have sent out! And put the chintz covers on, they'll brighten things up! Of course I'd hoped to have these walls re-papered. . . . What is the young

130   man's name?

TOM: His name is O'Connor.

AMANDA: That, of course, means fish—tomorrow is Friday! I'll have that salmon loaf—with Durkee's dressing! What does he do? He works at the warehouse?

135   TOM: Of course! How else would I—

AMANDA: Tom, he—doesn't drink?

TOM: Why do you ask me that?

AMANDA: Your father *did!*

TOM: Don't get started on that!

140   AMANDA: He *does* drink, then?

TOM: Not that I know of!

AMANDA: Make sure, be certain! The last thing I want for my daughter's a boy who drinks!

TOM: Aren't you being a little bit premature? Mr. O'Connor has

145   not yet appeared on the scene!

AMANDA: But will tomorrow. To meet your sister, and what do I know about his character? Nothing! Old maids are better off than wives of drunkards!

TOM: Oh, my God!

150   AMANDA: Be still!

TOM: (*Leaning forward to whisper.*) Lots of fellows meet girls whom they don't marry!

AMANDA: Oh, talk sensibly, Tom—and don't be sarcastic! (*She has gotten a hairbrush.*)

155   TOM: What are you doing?

AMANDA: I'm brushing that cowlick down! (*She attacks his hair with the brush.*) What is this young man's position at the warehouse?

TOM: (*Submitting grimly to the brush and the interrogation.*) This

160   young man's position is that of a shipping clerk, Mother.

AMANDA: Sounds to me like a fairly responsible job, the sort of a job *you* would be in if you just had more *get-up*. What is his salary? Have you any idea?

TOM: I would judge it to be approximately eighty-five dollars

165   a month.

AMANDA: Well—not princely, but—

TOM: Twenty more than I make.

AMANDA: Yes, how well I know! But for a family man, eighty-five dollars a month is not much more than you can just

170   get by on. . . .

TOM: Yes, but Mr. O'Connor is not a family man.

AMANDA: He might be, mightn't he? Some time in the future?

TOM: I see. Plans and provisions.

AMANDA: You are the only young man that I know of who

175   ignores the fact that the future becomes the present, the present the past, and the past turns into everlasting regret if you don't plan for it!

TOM: I will think that over and see what I can make of it.

AMANDA: Don't be supercilious with your mother! Tell me some more about this—what do you call him?   180

TOM: James D. O'Connor. The D. is for Delaney.

AMANDA: Irish on *both* sides! *Gracious!* And doesn't drink?

TOM: Shall I call him up and ask him right this minute?

AMANDA: The only way to find out about those things is to make discreet inquiries at the proper moment. When I was   185 a girl in Blue Mountain and it was suspected that a young man drank, the girl whose attentions he had been receiving, if any girl *was,* would sometimes speak to the minister of his church, or rather her father would if her father was living, and sort of feel him out on the young man's charac-   190 ter. That is the way such things are discreetly handled to keep a young woman from making a tragic mistake!

TOM: Then how did you happen to make a tragic mistake?

AMANDA: That innocent look of your father's had everyone fooled! He *smiled*—the world was *enchanted!* No girl can do worse   195 than put herself at the mercy of a handsome appearance! I hope that Mr. O'Connor is not too good-looking.

TOM: No, he's not too good-looking. He's covered with freckles and hasn't too much of a nose.

AMANDA: He's not right-down homely, though?   200

TOM: Not right-down homely. Just medium homely, I'd say.

AMANDA: Character's what to look for in a man.

TOM: That's what I've always said, Mother.

AMANDA: You've never said anything of the kind and I suspect you would never give it a thought.   205

TOM: Don't be so suspicious of me.

AMANDA: At least I hope he's the type that's up and coming.

TOM: I think he really goes in for self-improvement.

AMANDA: What reason have you to think so?

TOM: He goes to night school.   210

AMANDA: (*Beaming.*) Splendid! What does he do, I mean study?

TOM: Radio engineering and public speaking!

AMANDA: Then he has visions of being advanced in the world! Any young man who studies public speaking is aiming to have an executive job some day! And radio engineering? A   215 thing for the future! Both of these facts are very illuminating. Those are the sort of things that a mother should know concerning any young man who comes to call on her daughter. Seriously or—not.

TOM: One little warning. He doesn't know about Laura. I didn't   220 let on that we had dark ulterior motives. I just said, why don't you come and have dinner with us? He said okay and that was the whole conversation.

AMANDA: I bet it was! You're eloquent as an oyster. However, he'll know about Laura when he gets here. When he sees how   225 lovely and sweet and pretty she is, he'll thank his lucky stars he was asked to dinner.

TOM: Mother, you mustn't expect too much of Laura.

AMANDA: What do you mean?

TOM: Laura seems all those things to you and me because she's   230 ours and we love her. We don't even notice she's crippled any more.

AMANDA: Don't say crippled! You know that I never allow that word to be used!

TOM: But face facts, Mother. She is and—that's not all—   235

AMANDA: What do you mean "not all"?

TOM: Laura is very different from other girls.

AMANDA: I think the difference is all to her advantage.

TOM: Not quite all—in the eyes of others—strangers—she's terribly shy and lives in a world of her own and those things   240 make her seem a little peculiar to people outside the house.

AMANDA: Don't say peculiar.
TOM: Face the facts. She is.

(*The dance-hall music changes to a tango that has a minor and somewhat ominous tone.*)

AMANDA: In what way is she peculiar—may I ask?
245 TOM: (*Gently.*) She lives in a world of her own—a world of little glass ornaments, Mother. . . .

(*He gets up.* AMANDA *remains holding the brush, looking at him, troubled.*)

She plays old phonograph records and—that's about all—(*He glances at himself in the mirror and crosses to the door.*)
AMANDA: (*Sharply.*) Where are you going?
250 TOM: I'm going to the movies. (*He goes out the screen door.*)
AMANDA: Not to the movies, every night to the movies! (*She follows quickly to the screen door.*) I don't believe you always go to the movies!

(*He is gone.* AMANDA *looks worriedly after him for a moment. Then vitality and optimism return and she turns from the door, crossing to the portieres.*)

Laura! Laura!

(LAURA *answers from the kitchenette.*)

255 LAURA: Yes, Mother.
AMANDA: Let those dishes go and come in front!

(LAURA *appears with a dish towel.* AMANDA *speaks to her gaily.*)

Laura, come here and make a wish on the moon!

(*Screen image: The Moon.*)

LAURA: (*Entering.*) Moon—moon?
AMANDA: A little silver slipper of a moon. Look over your left
260   shoulder, Laura, and make a wish!

(LAURA *looks faintly puzzled as if called out of sleep.* AMANDA *seizes her shoulders and turns her at an angle by the door.*)

Now! Now, darling, *wish!*
LAURA: What shall I wish for, Mother?
AMANDA: (*Her voice trembling and her eyes suddenly filling with tears.*) Happiness! Good fortune!

(*The sound of the violin rises and the stage dims out.*)

SCENE SIX

The light comes up on the fire escape landing. TOM *is leaning against the grill, smoking.*

Screen image: The high school hero.

TOM: And so the following evening I brought Jim home to dinner. I had known Jim slightly in high school. In high school Jim was a hero. He had tremendous Irish good nature and vitality with the scrubbed and polished look of white chinaware. He seemed to move in a continual   5
spotlight. He was a star in basketball, captain of the debating club, president of the senior class and the glee club and he sang the male lead in the annual light operas. He was always running or bounding, never just walking. He seemed always at the point of defeating the law of   10
gravity. He was shooting with such velocity through his adolescence that you would logically expect him to arrive at nothing short of the White House by the time he was thirty. But Jim apparently ran into more interference after his graduation from Soldan. His speed had definitely   15
slowed. Six years after he left high school he was holding a job that wasn't much better than mine.

(*Screen image: The Clerk.*)

He was the only one at the warehouse with whom I was on friendly terms. I was valuable to him as someone who could remember his former glory, who had seen him win   20
basketball games and the silver cup in debating. He knew of my secret practice of retiring to a cabinet of the washroom to work on poems when business was slack in the warehouse. He called me Shakespeare. And while the other boys in the warehouse regarded me with suspicious hostility, Jim took   25
a humorous attitude toward me. Gradually his attitude affected the others, their hostility wore off and they also began to smile at me as people smile at an oddly fashioned dog who trots across their path at some distance.
       I knew that Jim and Laura had known each other at   30
Soldan, and I had heard Laura speak admiringly of his voice. I didn't know if Jim remembered her or not. In high school Laura had been as unobtrusive as Jim had been astonishing. If he did remember Laura, it was not as my sister, for when I asked him to dinner, he grinned and said, "You know,   35
Shakespeare, I never thought of you as having folks!"
       He was about to discover that I did. . . .

(*Legend on screen:* "The accent of a coming foot.")

(*The light dims out on* TOM *and comes up in the Wingfield living room—a delicate lemony light. It is about five on a Friday evening of late spring which comes "scattering poems in the sky."*)

(AMANDA *has worked like a Turk in preparation for the gentleman caller. The results are astonishing. The new floor lamp with its rose silk shade is in place, a colored paper lantern conceals the broken light fixture in the ceiling, new billowing white curtains are at the windows, chintz covers are on the chairs and sofa, a pair of new sofa pillows make their initial appearance. Open boxes and tissue paper are scattered on the floor.*)

(LAURA *stands in the middle of the room with lifted arms while* AMANDA *crouches before her, adjusting the hem of a new dress, devout and ritualistic. The dress is colored and designed by memory. The arrangement of* LAURA's *hair is changed; it is softer and more becoming. A fragile, unearthly prettiness has come out in* LAURA: *she is like a piece of translucent glass touched by light, given a momentary radiance, not actual, not lasting.*)

AMANDA: (*Impatiently.*) Why are you trembling?
LAURA: Mother, you've made me so nervous!
AMANDA: How have I made you nervous?   40

LAURA: By all this fuss! You make it seem so important!

AMANDA: I don't understand you, Laura. You couldn't be satisfied with just sitting home, and yet whenever I try to arrange something for you, you seem to resist it. (*She gets up.*)
45   Now take a look at yourself. No, wait! Wait just a moment—I have an idea!

LAURA: What is it now?

(AMANDA *produces two powder puffs which she wraps in handkerchiefs and stuffs in* LAURA's *bosom.*)

LAURA: Mother, what are you doing?

AMANDA: They call them "Gay Deceivers"!

50   LAURA: I won't wear them!

AMANDA: You will!

LAURA: Why should I?

AMANDA: Because, to be painfully honest, your chest is flat.

LAURA: You make it seem like we were setting a trap.

55   AMANDA: All pretty girls are a trap, a pretty trap, and men expect them to be.

(*Legend on screen:* "A pretty trap.")

Now look at yourself, young lady. This is the prettiest you will ever be! (*She stands back to admire* LAURA.) I've got to fix myself now! You're going to be surprised by your
60   mother's appearance!

(AMANDA *crosses through the portieres, humming gaily.* LAURA *moves slowly to the long mirror and stares solemnly at herself. A wind blows the white curtains inward in a slow, graceful motion and with a faint, sorrowful sighing.*)

AMANDA: (*From somewhere behind the portieres.*) It isn't dark enough yet.

(LAURA *turns slowly before the mirror with a troubled look.*)

(*Legend on screen:* "This is my sister: Celebrate her with strings!" *Music plays.*)

AMANDA: (*Laughing, still not visible.*) I'm going to show you something. I'm going to make a spectacular appearance!

65   LAURA: What is it, Mother?

AMANDA: Possess your soul in patience—you will see! Something I've resurrected from that old trunk! Styles haven't changed so terribly much after all. . . . (*She parts the portieres.*) Now just look at your mother! (*She wears a girlish
70   frock of yellowed voile with a blue silk sash. She carries a bunch of jonquils—the legend of her youth is nearly revived. Now she speaks feverishly.*) This is the dress in which I led the cotillion. Won the cakewalk twice at Sunset Hill, wore one Spring to the Governor's Ball in Jackson! See how I sashayed
75   around the ballroom, Laura? (*She raises her skirt and does a mincing step around the room.*) I wore it on Sundays for my gentlemen callers! I had it on the day I met your father. . . . I had malaria fever all that Spring. The change of climate from East Tennessee to the Delta—weakened resistance.
80   I had a little temperature all the time—not enough to be serious—just enough to make me restless and giddy! Invitations poured in—parties all over the Delta! "Stay in bed," said Mother, "you have a fever!"—but I just wouldn't.

I took quinine but kept on going, going! Evenings, dances!
85   Afternoons, long, long rides! Picnics—lovely! So lovely, that country in May—all lacy with dogwood, literally flooded with jonquils! That was the spring I had the craze for jonquils. Jonquils became an absolute obsession. Mother said, "Honey, there's no more room for jonquils." And still
90   I kept on bringing in more jonquils. Whenever, wherever I saw them, I'd say "Stop! Stop! I see jonquils!" I made the young men help me gather the jonquils! It was a joke, Amanda and her jonquils. Finally there were no more vases to hold them, every available space was filled with jonquils.
95   No vases to hold them? All right, I'll hold them myself! And then I—(*She stops in front of the picture. Music plays.*) met your father! Malaria fever and jonquils and then—this—boy. . . . (*She switches on the rose-colored lamp.*) I hope they get here before it starts to rain. (*She crosses the room and places the jonquils in a bowl on the table.*) I gave your brother
100   a little extra change so he and Mr. O'Connor could take the service car home.

LAURA: (*With an altered look.*) What did you say his name was?

AMANDA: O'Connor.

LAURA: What is his first name?
105

AMANDA: I don't remember. Oh, yes, I do. It was—Jim!

(LAURA *sways slightly and catches hold of a chair.*)

(*Legend on screen:* "Not Jim!")

LAURA: (*Faintly.*) Not—Jim!

AMANDA: Yes, that was it, it was Jim! I've never known a Jim that wasn't nice!

(*The music becomes ominous.*)

LAURA: Are you sure his name is Jim O'Connor?
110

AMANDA: Yes. Why?

LAURA: Is he the one that Tom used to know in high school?

AMANDA: He didn't say so. I think he just got to know him at the warehouse.

LAURA: There was a Jim O'Connor we both knew in high
115   school—(*Then, with effort.*) If that is the one that Tom is bringing to dinner—you'll have to excuse me, I won't come to the table.

AMANDA: What sort of nonsense is this?

LAURA: You asked me once if I'd ever liked a boy. Don't you
120   remember I showed you this boy's picture?

AMANDA: You mean the boy you showed me in the yearbook?

LAURA: Yes, that boy.

AMANDA: Laura, Laura, were you in love with that boy?

LAURA: I don't know, Mother. All I know is I couldn't sit at the
125   table if it was him!

AMANDA: It won't be him! It isn't the least bit likely. But whether it is or not, you will come to the table. You will not be excused.

LAURA: I'll have to be, Mother.
130

AMANDA: I don't intend to humor your silliness, Laura. I've had too much from you and your brother, both! So just sit down and compose yourself till they come. Tom has forgotten his key so you'll have to let them in, when they arrive.

LAURA: (*Panicky.*) Oh, Mother—*you* answer the door!
135

AMANDA: (*Lightly.*) I'll be in the kitchen—busy!

LAURA: Oh, Mother, please answer the door, don't make me do it!

AMANDA: (*Crossing into the kitchenette.*) I've got to fix the dressing for the salmon. Fuss, fuss—silliness!—over a gentleman caller!

140

(*The door swings shut.* LAURA *is left alone.*)

(*Legend on screen: "Terror!"*)

(*She utters a low moan and turns off the lamp—sits stiffly on the edge of the sofa, knotting her fingers together.*)

(*Legend on screen: "The Opening of a Door!"*)

(TOM *and* JIM *appear on the fire escape steps and climb to the landing. Hearing their approach, laura rises with a panicky gesture. She retreats to the portieres. The doorbell rings.* LAURA *catches her breath and touches her throat. Low drums sound.*)

AMANDA: (*Calling.*) Laura, sweetheart! The door!

(LAURA *stares at it without moving.*)

JIM: I think we just beat the rain.

TOM: Uh-huh. (*He rings again, nervously.* JIM *whistles and fishes for a cigarette.*)

145

AMANDA: (*Very, very gaily.*) Laura, that is your brother and Mr. O'Connor! Will you let them in, darling?

(LAURA *crosses toward the kitchenette door.*)

LAURA: (*Breathlessly.*) Mother—you go to the door!

(AMANDA *steps out of the kitchenette and stares furiously at* LAURA. *She points imperiously at the door.*)

LAURA: Please, please!

AMANDA: (*In a fierce whisper.*) What is the matter with you, you silly thing?

150

LAURA: (*Desperately.*) Please, you answer it, *please!*

AMANDA: I told you I wasn't going to humor you, Laura. Why have you chosen this moment to lose your mind?

LAURA: Please, please, please, you go!

155

AMANDA: You'll have to go to the door because I can't!

LAURA: (*Despairingly.*) I can't either!

AMANDA: *Why?*

LAURA: I'm *sick!*

AMANDA: I'm sick, too—of your nonsense! Why can't you and your brother be normal people? Fantastic whims and behavior!

160

(TOM *gives a long ring.*)

Preposterous goings on! Can you give me one reason—(*She calls out lyrically.*) Coming! Just one second!—why you should be afraid to open a door? Now you answer it, Laura!

165

LAURA: Oh, oh, oh . . . (*She returns through the portieres, darts to the Victrola, winds it frantically and turns it on.*)

AMANDA: Laura Wingfield, you march right to that door!

LAURA: *Yes—yes, Mother!*

(*A faraway, scratchy rendition of "Dardanella" softens the air and gives her strength to move through it. She slips to the door and draws it cautiously open.* TOM *enters with the caller,* JIM O'CONNOR.)

TOM: Laura, this is Jim. Jim, this is my sister, Laura.

170

JIM: (*Stepping inside.*) I didn't know that Shakespeare had a sister!

LAURA: (*Retreating, stiff and trembling, from the door.*) How—how do you do?

JIM: (*Heartily, extending his hand.*) Okay!

(LAURA *touches it hesitantly with hers.*)

JIM: Your hand's *cold,* Laura!

175

LAURA: Yes, well—I've been playing the Victrola. . . .

JIM: Must have been playing classical music on it! You ought to play a little hot swing music to warm you up!

LAURA: Excuse me—I haven't finished playing the Victrola . . . (*She turns awkwardly and hurries into the front room. She pauses a second by the Victrola. Then she catches her breath and darts through the portieres like a frightened deer.*)

180

JIM: (*Grinning.*) What was the matter?

TOM: Oh—with Laura? Laura is—terribly shy.

JIM: Shy, huh? It's unusual to meet a shy girl nowadays. I don't believe you ever mentioned you had a sister.

185

TOM: Well, now you know. I have one. Here is the *Post Dispatch.* You want a piece of it?

JIM: Uh-huh.

TOM: What piece? The comics?

190

JIM: Sports! (*He glances at it.*) Ole Dizzy Dean is on his bad behavior.

TOM: (*Uninterested.*) Yeah? (*He lights a cigarette and goes over to the fire-escape door.*)

JIM: Where are *you* going?

195

TOM: I'm going out on the terrace.

JIM: (*Going after him.*) You know, Shakespeare—I'm going to sell you a bill of goods!

TOM: What goods?

JIM: A course I'm taking.

200

TOM: Huh?

JIM: In public speaking! You and me, we're not the warehouse type.

TOM: Thanks—that's good news. But what has public speaking got to do with it?

205

JIM: It fits you for—executive positions!

TOM: Awww.

JIM: I tell you it's done a helluva lot for me.

(*Image on screen: Executive at his desk.*)

TOM: In what respect?

JIM: In every! Ask yourself what is the difference between you an' me and men in the office down front? Brains?—No!—Ability?—No! Then what? Just one little thing—

210

TOM: What is that one little thing?

JIM: Primarily it amounts to—social poise! Being able to square up to people and hold your own on any social level!

215

AMANDA: (*From the kitchenette.*) Tom?

TOM: Yes, Mother?

AMANDA: Is that you and Mr. O'Connor?

TOM: Yes, Mother.

AMANDA: Well, you just make yourselves comfortable in there.

220

TOM: Yes, Mother.

AMANDA: Ask Mr. O'Connor if he would like to wash his hands.

JIM: Aw, no—no—thank you—I took care of that at the
225   warehouse. Tom—

TOM: Yes?

JIM: Mr. Mendoza was speaking to me about you.

TOM: Favorably?

JIM: What do you think?

230 TOM: Well—

JIM: You're going to be out of a job if you don't wake up.

TOM: I am waking up—

JIM: You show no signs.

TOM: The signs are interior.

(*Image on screen: The sailing vessel with the Jolly Roger again.*)

235 TOM: I'm planning to change. (*He leans over the fire-escape rail,
speaking with quiet exhilaration. The incandescent marquees
and signs of the first-run movie houses light his face from
across the alley. He looks like a voyager.*) I'm right at the point
of committing myself to a future that doesn't include the
240   warehouse and Mr. Mendoza or even a night-school course in
public speaking.

JIM: What are you gassing about?

TOM: I'm tired of the movies.

JIM: Movies!

245 TOM: Yes, movies! Look at them—(*A wave toward the marvels
of Grand Avenue.*) All of those glamorous people—having
adventures—hogging it all, gobbling the whole thing up!
You know what happens? People go to the *movies* instead of
moving! Hollywood characters are supposed to have all the
250   adventures for everybody in America, while everybody in
America sits in a dark room and watches them have them!
Yes, until there's a war. That's when adventure becomes
available to the masses! *Everyone's* dish, not only Gable's!
Then the people in the dark room come out of the dark
255   room to have some adventures themselves—goody, goody!
It's our turn now, to go to the South Sea Island—to make
a safari—to be exotic, far-off! But I'm not patient. I don't
want to wait till then. I'm tired of the *movies* and I am
about to *move*!

260 JIM: (*Incredulously.*) Move?

TOM: Yes.

JIM: When?

TOM: Soon!

JIM: Where? Where?

(*The music seems to answer the question, while* TOM *thinks it over.
He searches in his pockets.*)

265 TOM: I'm starting to boil inside. I know I seem dreamy, but
inside—well, I'm boiling! Whenever I pick up a shoe, I
shudder a little thinking how short life is and what I am
doing! Whatever that means, I know it doesn't mean
shoes—except as something to wear on a traveler's feet! (*He
270   finds what he has been searching for in his pockets and holds
out a paper to* JIM.) Look—

JIM: What?

TOM: I'm a member.

JIM: (*Reading.*) The Union of Merchant Seamen.

275 TOM: I paid my dues this month, instead of the light bill.

JIM: You will regret it when they turn the lights off.

TOM: I won't be here.

JIM: How about your mother?

TOM: I'm like my father. The bastard son of a bastard! Did you
notice how he's grinning in his picture in there? And he's   280
been absent going on sixteen years!

JIM: You're just talking, you drip. How does your mother feel
about it?

TOM: Shhh! Here comes Mother! Mother is not acquainted with
my plans!   285

AMANDA: (*Coming through the portieres.*) Where are you all?

TOM: On the terrace, Mother.

(*They start inside. She advances to them.* TOM *is distinctly shocked
at her appearance. Even* JIM *blinks a little. He is making his first
contact with girlish Southern vivacity and in spite of the night-
school course in public speaking is somewhat thrown off the beam
by the unexpected outlay of social charm. Certain responses are attempted by* JIM *but are swept aside by* AMANDA's *gay laughter and
chatter.* TOM *is embarrassed but after the first shock* JIM *reacts very
warmly. He grins and chuckles, is altogether won over.*)

(*Image on screen:* AMANDA *as a girl.*)

AMANDA: (*Coyly smiling, shaking her girlish ringlets.*) Well,
well, well, so this is Mr. O'Connor. Introductions entirely
unnecessary. I've heard so much about you from my boy. I   290
finally said to him, Tom—good gracious!—why don't you
bring this paragon to supper? I'd like to meet this nice young
man at the warehouse!—instead of just hearing him sing your
praises so much! I don't know why my son is so stand-offish—
that's not Southern behavior!   295

    Let's sit down and—I think we could stand a little more
air in here! Tom, leave the door open. I felt a nice fresh
breeze a moment ago. Where has it gone to? Mmm, so
warm already! And not quite summer, even. We're going
to burn up when summer really gets started. However,   300
we're having—we're having a very light supper. I think
light things are better fo' this time of year. The same as
light clothes are. Light clothes an' light food are what warm
weather calls fo'. You know our blood gets so thick during
th' winter—it takes a while fo' us to *adjust* ou'selves!—   305
when the season changes . . . It's come so quick this year.
I wasn't prepared. All of a sudden—heavens! Already
summer! I ran to the trunk an' pulled out this light dress—
terribly old! Historical almost! But feels so good—so good
an' co-ol, y' know. . . .   310

TOM: Mother—

AMANDA: Yes, honey?

TOM: How about—supper?

AMANDA: Honey, you go ask Sister if supper is ready! You know
that Sister is in full charge of supper! Tell her you hungry boys   315
are waiting for it. (*To* JIM.) Have you met Laura?

JIM: She—

AMANDA: Let you in? Oh, good, you've met already! It's rare for a
girl as sweet an' pretty as Laura to be domestic! But Laura is,
thank heavens, not only pretty but also very domestic. I'm not   320
at all. I never was a bit. I never could make a thing but angel-
food cake. Well, in the South we had so many servants. Gone,
gone, gone. All vestige of gracious living! Gone completely!
I wasn't prepared for what the future brought. All of my
gentlemen callers were sons of planters and so of course I   325

assumed that I would be married to one and raise my family on a large piece of land with plenty of servants. But man proposes—and woman accepts the proposal! To vary that old, old saying a little bit—I married no planter! I married a

330 man who worked for the telephone company! That gallantly smiling gentleman over there! (*She points to the picture.*) A telephone man who—fell in love with long-distance! Now he travels and I don't even know where! But what am I going on for about my—tribulations? Tell me yours—I hope you don't

335 have any! Tom?

TOM: (*Returning.*) Yes, Mother?

AMANDA: Is supper nearly ready?

TOM: It looks to me like supper is on the table.

AMANDA: Let me look—(*She rises prettily and looks through the

340   portieres.*) Oh, lovely! But where is Sister?

TOM: Laura is not feeling well and she says that she thinks she'd better not come to the table.

AMANDA: What? Nonsense! Laura? Oh, Laura!

LAURA: (*From the kitchenette, faintly.*) Yes, Mother.

345 AMANDA: You really must come to the table. We won't be seated until you come to the table! Come in, Mr. O'Connor. You sit over there, and I'll . . . . Laura? Laura Wingfield! You're keeping us waiting, honey! We can't say grace until you come to the table!

(*The kitchenette door is pushed weakly open and* LAURA *comes in. She is obviously quite faint, her lips trembling, her eyes wide and staring. She moves unsteadily toward the table.*)

(*Screen legend:* "Terror!")

(*Outside a summer storm is coming on abruptly. The white curtains billow inward at the windows and there is a sorrowful murmur from the deep blue dusk.*)

(LAURA *suddenly stumbles; she catches at a chair with a faint moan.*)

350 TOM: Laura!

AMANDA: Laura!

(*There is a clap of thunder.*)

(*Screen legend:* "Ah!")

(*Despairingly.*) Why, Laura, you *are* ill, darling! Tom, help your sister into the living room, dear! Sit in the living room, Laura—rest on the sofa. Well! (*To* JIM *as* TOM *helps his sister*

355 *to the sofa in the living room.*) Standing over the hot stove made her ill! I told her that it was just too warm this evening, but—

(TOM *comes back to the table.*)

Is Laura all right now?

TOM: Yes.

360 AMANDA: What *is* that? Rain? A nice cool rain has come up! (*She gives* JIM *a frightened look.*) I think we may—have grace—now . . . (TOM *looks at her stupidly.*) Tom, honey—you say grace!

TOM: Oh . . . "For these and all thy mercies—"

(*They bow their heads,* AMANDA *stealing a nervous glance at* JIM. *In the living room* LAURA, *stretched on the sofa, clenches her hand to her lips, to hold back a shuddering sob.*)

God's Holy Name be praised— 365

(*The scene dims out.*)

SCENE SEVEN

It is half an hour later. Dinner is just being finished in the dining room, LAURA *is still huddled upon the sofa, her feet drawn under her, her head resting on a pale blue pillow, her eyes wide and mysteriously watchful. The new floor lamp with its shade of rose-colored silk gives a soft, becoming light to her face, bringing out the fragile, unearthly prettiness which usually escapes attention. From outside there is a steady murmur of rain, but it is slackening and soon stops; the air outside becomes pale and luminous as the moon breaks through the clouds. A moment after the curtain rises, the lights in both rooms flicker and go out.*

JIM: Hey, there, Mr. Light Bulb!

(AMANDA *laughs nervously.*)

(*Legend on screen:* "Suspension of a public service.")

AMANDA: Where was Moses when the lights went out? Ha-ha. Do you know the answer to that one, Mr. O'Connor?

JIM: No, Ma'am, what's the answer?

AMANDA: In the dark! 5

(JIM *laughs appreciatively.*)

Everybody sit still. I'll light the candles. Isn't it lucky we have them on the table? Where's a match? Which of you gentlemen can provide a match?

JIM: Here.

AMANDA: Thank you, Sir. 10

JIM: Not at all, Ma'am!

AMANDA: (*As she lights the candles.*) I guess the fuse has burnt out. Mr. O'Connor, can you tell a burnt-out fuse? I know I can't and Tom is a total loss when it comes to mechanics.

(*They rise from the table and go into the kitchenette, from where their voices are heard.*)

Oh, be careful you don't bump into something. We don't want 15 our gentleman caller to break his neck. Now wouldn't that be a fine howdy-do?

JIM: Ha-ha! Where is the fuse-box?

AMANDA: Right here next to the stove. Can you see anything?

JIM: Just a minute. 20

AMANDA: Isn't electricity a mysterious thing? Wasn't it Benjamin Franklin who tied a key to a kite? We live in such a mysterious universe, don't we? Some people say that science clears up all the mysteries for us. In my opinion it only creates more! Have you found it yet? 25

JIM: No, Ma'am. All these fuses look okay to me.

AMANDA: Tom!

TOM: Yes, Mother?

AMANDA: That light bill I gave you several days ago. The one I
30   told you we got the notices about?

(*Legend on screen:* "Ha!")

TOM: Oh—yeah.

AMANDA: You didn't neglect to pay it by any chance?

TOM: Why, I—

AMANDA: Didn't! I might have known it!

35   JIM: Shakespeare probably wrote a poem on that light bill,
Mrs. Wingfield.

AMANDA: I might have known better than to trust him with it!
There's such a high price for negligence in this world!

JIM: Maybe the poem will win a ten-dollar prize.

40   AMANDA: We'll just have to spend the remainder of the evening
in the nineteenth century, before Mr. Edison made the Mazda
lamp!

JIM: Candlelight is my favorite kind of light.

AMANDA: That shows you're romantic! But that's no excuse for
45   Tom. Well, we got through dinner. Very considerate of them
to let us get through dinner before they plunged us into
everlasting darkness, wasn't it, Mr. O'Connor?

JIM: Ha-ha!

AMANDA: Tom, as a penalty for your carelessness you can help me
50   with the dishes.

JIM: Let me give you a hand.

AMANDA: Indeed you will not!

JIM: I ought to be good for something.

AMANDA: Good for something? (*Her tone is rhapsodic.*) You?
55   Why, Mr. O'Connor, nobody, *nobody's* given me this much
entertainment in years—as you have!

JIM: Aw, now, Mrs. Wingfield!

AMANDA: I'm not exaggerating, not one bit! But Sister is all by
her lonesome. You go keep her company in the parlor! I'll
60   give you this lovely old candelabrum that used to be on the
altar at the Church of the Heavenly Rest. It was melted a little
out of shape when the church burnt down. Lightning struck
it one spring. Gypsy Jones was holding a revival at the time
and he intimated that the church was destroyed because the
65   Episcopalians gave card parties.

JIM: Ha-ha.

AMANDA: And how about you coaxing Sister to drink a little
wine? I think it would be good for her! Can you carry both at
once?

70   JIM: Sure. I'm Superman!

AMANDA: Now, Thomas, get into this apron!

(JIM *comes into the dining room, carrying the candelabrum, its
candles lighted, in one hand and a glass of wine in the other. The
door of the kitchenette swings closed on* AMANDA's *gay laughter; the
flickering light approaches the portieres.* LAURA *sits up nervously
as* JIM *enters. She can hardly speak from the almost intolerable
strain of being alone with a stranger.*)

(*Screen legend:* "I don't suppose you remember me at all!")

(*At first, before* JIM's *warmth overcomes her paralyzing shyness,*
LAURA's *voice is thin and breathless, as though she had just run up
a steep flight of stairs.* JIM's *attitude is gently humorous. While the
incident is apparently unimportant, it is to* LAURA *the climax of
her secret life.*)

JIM: Hello there, Laura.

LAURA: (*Faintly.*) Hello.

(*She clears her throat.*)

JIM: How are you feeling now? Better?

LAURA: Yes. Yes, thank you.   75

JIM: This is for you. A little dandelion wine. (*He extends the glass
toward her with extravagant gallantry.*)

LAURA: Thank you.

JIM: Drink it—but don't get drunk!

(*He laughs heartily.* LAURA *takes the glass uncertainly; she laughs
shyly.*)

Where shall I set the candles?   80

LAURA: Oh—oh, anywhere. . . .

JIM: How about here on the floor? Any objections?

LAURA: No.

JIM: I'll spread a newspaper under to catch the drippings. I like to
sit on the floor. Mind if I do?   85

LAURA: Oh, no.

JIM: Give me a pillow?

LAURA: What?

JIM: A pillow!

LAURA: Oh . . . (*She hands him one quickly.*)   90

JIM: How about you? Don't you like to sit on the floor?

LAURA: Oh—yes.

JIM: Why don't you, then?

LAURA: I—will.

JIM: Take a pillow!   95
(LAURA *does. She sits on the floor on the other side of the
candelabrum.* JIM *crosses his legs and smiles engagingly at her.*)
I can't hardly see you sitting way over there.

LAURA: I can—see you.

JIM: I know, but that's not fair, I'm in the limelight.   100

(LAURA *moves her pillow closer.*)

Good! Now I can see you! Comfortable?

LAURA: Yes.

JIM: So am I. Comfortable as a cow! Will you have some gum?

LAURA: No, thank you.

JIM: I think that I will indulge, with your permission. (*He*   105
musingly unwraps a stick of gum and holds it up.) Think of
the fortune made by the guy that invented the first piece
of chewing gum. Amazing, huh? The Wrigley Building is
one of the sights of Chicago—I saw it when I went up to
the Century of Progress. Did you take in the Century of   110
Progress?

LAURA: No, I didn't.

JIM: Well, it was quite a wonderful exposition. What impressed
me most was the Hall of Science. Gives you an idea of what
the future will be in America, even more wonderful than   115
the present time is! (*There is a pause.* JIM *smiles at her.*) Your
brother tells me you're shy. Is that right, Laura?

LAURA: I—don't know.

JIM: I judge you to be an old-fashioned type of girl. Well, I think
that's a pretty good type to be. Hope you don't think I'm being   120
too personal—do you?

LAURA: (*Hastily, out of embarrassment.*) I believe I *will* take a
piece of gum, if you—don't mind. (*Clearing her throat.*) Mr.
O'Connor, have you—kept up with your singing?

125   JIM: Singing? Me?

LAURA: Yes. I remember what a beautiful voice you had.

JIM: When did you hear me sing?

(LAURA *does not answer, and in the long pause which follows a man's voice is heard singing offstage.*)

VOICE: O blow, ye winds, heigh-ho,

                A-roving I will go!

130   I'm off to my love

                  With a boxing glove—

                Ten thousand miles away!

JIM: You say you've heard me sing?

LAURA: Oh, yes! Yes, very often . . . I—don't suppose—you

135   remember me—at all?

JIM: (*Smiling doubtfully.*) You know I have an idea I've seen you before. I had that idea soon as you opened the door. It seemed almost like I was about to remember your name. But the name that I started to call you—wasn't a name! And so I stopped

140   myself before I said it.

LAURA: Wasn't it—Blue Roses?

JIM: (*Springing up, grinning.*) Blue Roses! My gosh, yes—Blue Roses! That's what I had on my tongue when you opened the door! Isn't it funny what tricks your memory plays? I didn't

145   connect you with high school somehow or other. But that's where it was; it was high school. I didn't even know you were Shakespeare's sister! Gosh, I'm sorry.

LAURA: I didn't expect you to. You—barely knew me!

JIM: But we did have a speaking acquaintance, huh?

150   LAURA: Yes, we—spoke to each other.

JIM: When did you recognize me?

LAURA: Oh, right away!

JIM: Soon as I came in the door?

LAURA: When I heard your name I thought it was probably you.

155   I knew that Tom used to know you a little in high school. So when you came in the door—well, then I was—sure.

JIM: Why didn't you *say* something, then?

LAURA: (*Breathlessly.*) I didn't know what to say, I was—too surprised!

160   JIM: For goodness' sakes! You know, this sure is funny!

LAURA: Yes! Yes, isn't it, though. . . .

JIM: Didn't we have a class in something together?

LAURA: Yes, we did.

JIM: What class was that?

165   LAURA: It was—singing—chorus!

JIM: Aw!

LAURA: I sat across the aisle from you in the Aud.

JIM: Aw.

LAURA: Mondays, Wednesdays, and Fridays.

170   JIM: Now I remember—you always came in late.

LAURA: Yes, it was so hard for me, getting upstairs. I had that brace on my leg—it clumped so loud!

JIM: I never heard any clumping.

LAURA: (*Wincing at the recollection.*) To me it sounded

175   like— thunder!

JIM: Well, well, well, I never even noticed.

LAURA: And everybody was seated before I came in. I had to walk in front of all those people. My seat was in the back row. I had to go clumping all the way up the aisle with everyone

180   watching!

JIM: You shouldn't have been self-conscious.

LAURA: I know, but I was. It was always such a relief when the singing started.

JIM: Aw, yes, I've placed you now! I used to call you Blue Roses. How was it that I got started calling you that?   185

LAURA: I was out of school a little while with pleurosis. When I came back you asked me what was the matter. I said I had pleurosis—you thought I said *Blue Roses.* That's what you always called me after that!

JIM: I hope you didn't mind.   190

LAURA: Oh, no—I liked it. You see, I wasn't acquainted with many—people. . . .

JIM: As I remember you sort of stuck by yourself.

LAURA: I—I—never have had much luck at—making friends.

JIM: I don't see why you wouldn't.   195

LAURA: Well, I—started out badly.

JIM: You mean being—

LAURA: Yes, it sort of—stood between me—

JIM: You shouldn't have let it!

LAURA: I know, but it did, and—   200

JIM: You were shy with people!

LAURA: I tried not to be but never could—

JIM: Overcome it?

LAURA: No, I—I never could!

JIM: I guess being shy is something you have to work out of kind   205
    of gradually.

LAURA: (*Sorrowfully.*) Yes—I guess it—

JIM: Takes time!

LAURA: Yes—

JIM: People are not so dreadful when you know them. That's what   210
    you have to remember! And everybody has problems, not just you, but practically everybody has got some problems. You think of yourself as having the only problems, as being the only one who is disappointed. But just look around you and you will see lots of people as disappointed as you are.   215
    For instance, I hoped when I was going to high school that I would be further along at this time, six years later, than I am now. You remember that wonderful write-up I had in *The Torch?*

LAURA: Yes! (*She rises and crosses to the table.*)   220

JIM: It said I was bound to succeed in anything I went into!

(LAURA *returns with the high school yearbook.*)

    Holy Jeez! *The Torch!*

(*He accepts it reverently. They smile across the book with mutual wonder.* LAURA *crouches beside him and they begin to turn the pages.* LAURA's *shyness is dissolving in his warmth.*)

LAURA: Here you are in *The Pirates of Penzance!*

JIM: (*Wistfully.*) I sang the baritone lead in that operetta.

LAURA: (*Raptly.*) So—*beautifully!*   225

JIM: (*Protesting.*) Aw—

LAURA: Yes, yes—beautifully—beautifully!

JIM: You heard me?

LAURA: All three times!

JIM: No!   230

LAURA: Yes!

JIM: All three performances?

LAURA: (*Looking down.*) Yes.

JIM: Why?

235   LAURA: I—wanted to ask you to—autograph my program. (*She takes the program from the back of the yearbook and shows it to him.*)
JIM: Why didn't you ask me to?
LAURA: You were always surrounded by your own friends so much that I never had a chance to.
240   JIM: You should have just—
LAURA: Well, I—thought you might think I was—
JIM: Thought I might think you was—what?
LAURA: Oh—
JIM: (*With reflective relish.*) I was beleaguered by females in
245   those days.
LAURA: You were terribly popular!
JIM: Yeah—
LAURA: You had such a—friendly way—
JIM: I was spoiled in high school.
250   LAURA: Everybody—liked you!
JIM: Including you?
LAURA: I—yes, I—did, too—(*She gently closes the book in her lap.*)
JIM: Well, well, well! Give me that program, Laura.

(*She hands it to him. He signs it with a flourish.*)

There you are—better late than never!
255   LAURA: Oh, I—what a—surprise!
JIM: My signature isn't worth very much right now. But some day—maybe—it will increase in value! Being disappointed is one thing and being discouraged is something else. I am disappointed but I am not discouraged. I'm twenty-three
260   years old. How old are you?
LAURA: I'll be twenty-four in June.
JIM: That's not old age!
LAURA: No, but—
JIM: You finished high school?
265   LAURA: (*With difficulty.*) I didn't go back.
JIM: You mean you dropped out?
LAURA: I made bad grades in my final examinations. (*She rises and replaces the book and the program on the table. Her voice is strained.*) How is—Emily Meisenbach getting along?
270   JIM: Oh, that kraut-head!
LAURA: Why do you call her that?
JIM: That's what she was.
LAURA: You're not still—going with her?
JIM: I never see her.
275   LAURA: It said in the "Personal" section that you were—engaged!
JIM: I know, but I wasn't impressed by that—propaganda!
LAURA: It wasn't—the truth?
JIM: Only in Emily's optimistic opinion!
280   LAURA: Oh—

(*Legend:* "What have you done since high school?")

(JIM *lights a cigarette and leans indolently back on his elbows smiling at* LAURA *with a warmth and charm which lights her inwardly with altar candles. She remains by the table, picks up a piece from the glass menagerie collection, and turns it in her hands to cover her tumult.*)

JIM: (*After several reflective puffs on his cigarette.*) What have you done since high school?

(*She seems not to hear him.*)

Huh?

(LAURA *looks up.*)

I said what have you done since high school, Laura?
LAURA: Nothing much.   285
JIM: You must have been doing something these six long years.
LAURA: Yes.
JIM: Well, then, such as what?
LAURA: I took a business course at business college—
JIM: How did that work out?   290
LAURA: Well, not very—well—I had to drop out, it gave me—indigestion—

(JIM *laughs gently.*)

JIM: What are you doing now?
LAURA: I don't do anything—much. Oh, please don't think I sit around doing nothing! My glass collection takes up   295
a good deal of time. Glass is something you have to take good care of.
JIM: What did you say—about glass?
LAURA: Collection I said—I have one—(*She clears her throat and turns away again, acutely shy.*)   300
JIM: (*Abruptly.*) You know what I judge to be the trouble with you? Inferiority complex! Know what that is? That's what they call it when someone low-rates himself! I understand it because I had it, too. Although my case was not so aggravated as yours seems to be. I had it until I took up   305
public speaking, developed my voice, and learned that I had an aptitude for science. Before that time I never thought of myself as being outstanding in any way whatsoever! Now I've never made a regular study of it, but I have a friend who says I can analyze people better than doctors that make a   310
profession of it. I don't claim that to be necessarily true, but I can sure guess a person's psychology, Laura! (*He takes out his gum.*) Excuse me, Laura. I always take it out when the flavor is gone. I'll use this scrap of paper to wrap it in. I know how it is to get it stuck on a shoe. (*He wraps the gum   315
in paper and puts it in his pocket.*) Yep—that's what I judge to be your principal trouble. A lack of confidence in yourself as a person. You don't have the proper amount of faith in yourself. I'm basing that fact on a number of your remarks and also on certain observations I've made. For instance   320
that clumping you thought was so awful in high school. You say that you even dreaded to walk into class. You see what you did? You dropped out of school, you gave up an education because of a clump, which as far as I know was practically non-existent! A little physical defect is what you   325
have. Hardly noticeable even! Magnified thousands of times by imagination! You know what my strong advice to you is? Think of yourself as *superior* in some way!
LAURA: In what way would I think?
JIM: Why, man alive, Laura! Just look about you a little. What   330
do you see? A world full of common people! All of 'em born and all of 'em going to die! Which of them has one-tenth of your good points! Or mine! Or anyone else's, as far as that goes—gosh! Everybody excels in some one thing. Some in many! (*He unconsciously glances at himself in the   335
mirror.*) All you've got to do is discover in *what!* Take me, for instance. (*He adjusts his tie at the mirror.*) My interest happens to lie in electro-dynamics. I'm taking a course in radio engineering at night school, Laura, on top of a fairly responsible job at the warehouse. I'm taking that course and   340
studying public speaking.

LAURA: Ohhhh.

JIM: Because I believe in the future of television! (*Turning his back to her.*) I wish to be ready to go up right along with it.
345 Therefore I'm planning to get in on the ground floor. In fact I've already made the right connections and all that remains is for the industry itself to get under way! Full steam—(*His eyes are starry.*) *Knowledge*—Zzzzzp! *Money*—Zzzzzp!—*Power!* That's the cycle democracy is built on!

(*His attitude is convincingly dynamic.* LAURA *stares at him, even her shyness eclipsed in her absolute wonder. He suddenly grins.*)

350 I guess you think I think a lot of myself!

LAURA: No—o-o-o, I—

JIM: Now how about you? Isn't there something you take more interest in than anything else?

LAURA: Well, I do—as I said—have my—glass collection—

(*A peal of girlish laughter rings from the kitchenette.*)

355 JIM: I'm not right sure I know what you're talking about. What kind of glass is it?

LAURA: Little articles of it, they're ornaments mostly! Most of them are little animals made out of glass, the tiniest little animals in the world. Mother calls them a glass menagerie!
360 Here's an example of one, if you'd like to see it! This one is one of the oldest. It's nearly thirteen.

(*Music: "The Glass Menagerie."*)

(*He stretches out his hand.*)

Oh, be careful—if you breathe, it breaks!

JIM: I'd better not take it. I'm pretty clumsy with things.

LAURA: Go on, I trust you with him! (*She places the piece in his*
365 *palm.*) There now—you're holding him gently! Hold him over the light, he loves the light! You see how the light shines through him?

JIM: It sure does shine!

LAURA: I shouldn't be partial, but he is my favorite one.

370 JIM: What kind of a thing is this one supposed to be?

LAURA: Haven't you noticed the single horn on his forehead?

JIM: A unicorn, huh?

LAURA: Mmmm-hmmm!

JIM: Unicorns—aren't they extinct in the modern world?

375 LAURA: I know!

JIM: Poor little fellow, he must feel sort of lonesome.

LAURA: (*Smiling.*) Well, if he does, he doesn't complain about it. He stays on a shelf with some horses that don't have horns and all of them seem to get along nicely together.

380 JIM: How do you know?

LAURA: (*Lightly.*) I haven't heard any arguments among them!

JIM: (*Grinning.*) No arguments, huh? Well, that's a pretty good sign! Where shall I set him?

LAURA: Put him on the table. They all like a change of scenery
385 once in a while!

JIM: Well, well, well, well—(*He places the glass piece on the table, then raises his arms and stretches.*) Look how big my shadow is when I stretch!

LAURA: Oh, oh, yes—it stretches across the ceiling!

390 JIM: (*Crossing to the door.*) I think it's stopped raining. (*He opens the fire-escape door and the background music changes to a dance tune.*) Where does the music come from?

LAURA: From the Paradise Dance-hall across the alley.

JIM: How about cutting the rug a little, Miss Wingfield?

LAURA: Oh, I— 395

JIM: Or is your program filled up? Let me have a look at it. (*He grasps an imaginary card.*) Why, every dance is taken! I'll just have to scratch some out.

(*Waltz music: "La Golondrina."*)

Ahhh, a waltz! (*He executes some sweeping turns by himself, then holds his arms toward* LAURA) 400

LAURA: (*Breathlessly.*) I—can't dance!

JIM: There you go, that inferiority stuff!

LAURA: I've never danced in my life!

JIM: Come on, try!

LAURA: Oh, but I'd step on you! 405

JIM: I'm not made out of glass.

LAURA: How—how—how do we start?

JIM: Just leave it to me. You hold your arms out a little.

LAURA: Like this?

JIM: (*Taking her in his arms.*) A little bit higher. Right. Now don't 410 tighten up, that's the main thing about it—relax.

LAURA: (*Laughing breathlessly.*) It's hard not to.

JIM: Okay.

LAURA: I'm afraid you can't budge me.

JIM: What do you bet I can't? (*He swings her into motion.*) 415

LAURA: Goodness, yes, you can!

JIM: Let yourself go, now, Laura, just let yourself go.

LAURA: I'm—

JIM: Come on!

LAURA: —trying! 420

JIM: Not so stiff—easy does it!

LAURA: I know but I'm—

JIM: Loosen th' backbone! There now, that's a lot better.

LAURA: Am I?

JIM: Lots, lots better! (*He moves her about the room in a clumsy* 425 *waltz.*)

LAURA: Oh, my!

JIM: Ha-ha!

LAURA: Oh, my goodness!

JIM: Ha-ha-ha! 430

(*They suddenly bump into the table, and the glass piece on it falls to the floor.* JIM *stops the dance.*)

What did we hit on?

LAURA: Table.

JIM: Did something fall off it? I think—

LAURA: Yes.

JIM: I hope that it wasn't the little glass horse with the horn! 435

LAURA: Yes. (*She stoops to pick it up.*)

JIM: Aw, aw, aw. Is it broken?

LAURA: Now it is just like all the other horses.

JIM: It's lost its—

LAURA: Horn! It doesn't matter. Maybe it's a blessing in 440 disguise.

JIM: You'll never forgive me. I bet that that was your favorite piece of glass.

LAURA: I don't have favorites much. It's no tragedy, Freckles. Glass breaks so easily. No matter how careful you are. The 445 traffic jars the shelves and things fall off them.

JIM: Still I'm awfully sorry that I was the cause.

LAURA: (*Smiling.*) I'll just imagine he had an operation. The horn was removed to make him feel less—freakish!

(*They both laugh.*)

450 Now he will feel more at home with the other horses, the ones that don't have horns. . . .

JIM: Ha-ha, that's very funny! (*Suddenly he is serious.*) I'm glad to see that you have a sense of humor. You know—you're— well—very different! Surprisingly different from anyone else

455 I know! (*His voice becomes soft and hesitant with a genuine feeling.*) Do you mind me telling you that?

(LAURA *is abashed beyond speech.*)

I mean it in a nice way—

(LAURA *nods shyly, looking away.*)

You make me feel sort of—I don't know how to put it! I'm usually pretty good at expressing things, but—this is

460 something that I don't know how to say!

(LAURA *touches her throat and clears it—turns the broken unicorn in her hands. His voice becomes softer.*)

Has anyone ever told you that you were pretty?

(*There is a pause, and the music rises slightly.* LAURA *looks up slowly, with wonder, and shakes her head.*)

Well, you are! In a very different way from anyone else. And all the nicer because of the difference, too.

(*His voice becomes low and husky.* LAURA *turns away, nearly faint with the novelty of her emotions.*)

I wish that you were my sister. I'd teach you to have some

465 confidence in yourself. The different people are not like other people, but being different is nothing to be ashamed of. Because other people are not such wonderful people. They're one hundred times one thousand. You're one times one! They walk all over the earth. You just stay

470 here. They're common as—weeds, but—you—well, you're— *Blue Roses!*

(*Image on screen: Blue Roses.*)

(*The music changes.*)

LAURA: But blue is wrong for—roses. . . .

JIM: It's right for you! You're—pretty!

LAURA: In what respect am I pretty?

475 JIM: In all respects—believe me! Your eyes—your hair—are pretty! Your hands are pretty! (*He catches hold of her hand.*) You think I'm making this up because I'm invited to dinner and have to be nice. Oh, I could do that! I could put on an act for you, Laura, and say lots of things without being very

480 sincere. But this time I am. I'm talking to you sincerely. I happened to notice you had this inferiority complex that keeps you from feeling comfortable with people. Somebody

needs to build your confidence up and make you proud instead of shy and turning away and—blushing. Somebody— ought to—*kiss* you, Laura!   485

(*His hand slips slowly up her arm to her shoulder as the music swells tumultuously. He suddenly turns her about and kisses her on the lips. When he releases her,* LAURA *sinks on the sofa with a bright, dazed look.* JIM *backs away and fishes in his pocket for a cigarette.*)

(*Legend on screen: "A souvenir."*)

Stumblejohn!

(*He lights the cigarette, avoiding her look. There is a peal of girlish laughter from* AMANDA *in the kitchenette.* LAURA *slowly raises and opens her hand. It still contains the little broken glass animal. She looks at it with a tender, bewildered expression.*)

Stumblejohn! I shouldn't have done that—that was way off the beam. You don't smoke, do you?

(*She looks up, smiling, not hearing the question. He sits beside her rather gingerly. She looks at him speechlessly—waiting. He coughs decorously and moves a little farther aside as he considers the situation and senses her feelings, dimly, with perturbation. He speaks gently.*)

Would you—care for a—mint?

(*She doesn't seem to hear him but her look grows brighter even.*)

Peppermint? Life Saver? My pocket's a regular drugstore—   490
wherever I go . . . (*He pops a mint in his mouth. Then he gulps and decides to make a clean breast of it. He speaks slowly and gingerly.*) Laura, you know, if I had a sister like you, I'd do the same thing as Tom. I'd bring out fellows and—introduce her to them. The right type of boys—of a   495
type to—appreciate her. Only—well—he made a mistake about me. Maybe I've got no call to be saying this. That may not have been the idea in having me over. But what if it was? There's nothing wrong about that. The only trouble is that in my case—I'm not in a situation to—do the right thing.   500
I can't take down your number and say I'll phone. I can't call up next week and—ask for a date. I thought I had better explain the situation in case you—misunderstood it and—I hurt your feelings. . . .

(*There is a pause. Slowly, very slowly,* LAURA'S *look changes, her eyes returning slowly from his to the glass figure in her palm.* AMANDA *utters another gay laugh in the kitchenette.*)

LAURA: (*Faintly.*) You—won't—call again?   505
JIM: No, Laura. I can't. (*He rises from the sofa.*) As I was just explaining, I've—got strings on me. Laura, I've—been going steady! I go out all the time with a girl named Betty. She's a home-girl like you, and Catholic, and Irish, and in a great many ways we—get along fine. I met her last summer on a   510
moonlight boat trip up the river to Alton, on the *Majestic.* Well—right away from the start it was—love!

(*Legend: "Love!"*)

(LAURA *sways slightly forward and grips the arm of the sofa. He fails to notice, now enrapt in his own comfortable being.*)

Being in love has made a new man of me!

(*Leaning stiffly forward, clutching the arm of the sofa,* LAURA *struggles visibly with her storm. But* JIM *is oblivious; she is a long way off.*)

515   The power of love is really pretty tremendous! Love is something that—changes the whole world, Laura!

(*The storm abates a little and* LAURA *leans back. He notices her again.*)

It happened that Betty's aunt took sick, she got a wire and had to go to Centralia. So Tom—when he asked me to dinner—I naturally just accepted the invitation, not knowing that you—that he—that I—(*He stops awkwardly.*) Huh—I'm a
520   stumblejohn!

(*He flops back on the sofa. The holy candles on the altar of* LAURA's *face have been snuffed out. There is a look of almost infinite desolation.* JIM *glances at her uneasily.*)

I wish that you would—say something.

(*She bites her lip which was trembling and then bravely smiles. She opens her hand again on the broken glass figure. Then she gently takes his hand and raises it level with her own. She carefully places the unicorn in the palm of his hand, then pushes his fingers closed upon it.*)

What are you—doing that for? You want me to have him? Laura?

(*She nods.*)

What for?
525   LAURA: A—souvenir. . . .

(*She rises unsteadily and crouches beside the Victrola to wind it up.*)

(*Legend on screen:* "Things have a way of turning out so badly!" *Or image:* Gentleman caller waving goodbye—gaily.)

(*At this moment* AMANDA *rushes brightly back into the living room. She bears a pitcher of fruit punch in an old-fashioned cut-glass pitcher, and a plate of macaroons. The plate has a gold border and poppies painted on it.*)

AMANDA: Well, well, well! Isn't the air delightful after the shower? I've made you children a little liquid refreshment. (*She turns gaily to* JIM.) Jim, do you know that song about lemonade?
530   "Lemonade, lemonade
       Made in the shade and stirred with a spade—
       Good enough for any old maid!"
JIM: (*Uneasily.*) Ha-ha! No—I never heard it.
AMANDA: Why, Laura! You look so serious!
535   JIM: We were having a serious conversation.
AMANDA: Good! Now you're better acquainted!

JIM: (*Uncertainly.*) Ha-ha! Yes.
AMANDA: You modern young people are much more seriousminded than my generation. I was so gay as a girl!
JIM: You haven't changed, Mrs. Wingfield.   540
AMANDA: Tonight I'm rejuvenated! The gaiety of the occasion, Mr. O'Connor! (*She tosses her head with a peal of laughter, spilling some lemonade.*) Oooo! I'm baptizing myself!
JIM: Here—let me—
AMANDA: (*Setting the pitcher down.*) There now. I discovered   545
we had some maraschino cherries. I dumped them in, juice and all!
JIM: You shouldn't have gone to that trouble, Mrs. Wingfield.
AMANDA: Trouble, trouble? Why, it was loads of fun! Didn't you hear me cutting up in the kitchen? I bet your ears were   550
burning! I told Tom how outdone with him I was for keeping you to himself so long a time! He should have brought you over much, much sooner! Well, now that you've found your way, I want you to be a very frequent caller! Not just occasional but all the time. Oh, we're going to have a lot of   555
gay times together! I see them coming! Mmm, just breathe that air! So fresh, and the moon's so pretty! I'll skip back out—I know where my place is when young folks are having a—serious conversation!
JIM: Oh, don't go out, Mrs. Wingfield. The fact of the matter is   560
I've got to be going.
AMANDA: Going, now? You're joking! Why, it's only the shank of the evening, Mr. O'Connor!
JIM: Well, you know how it is.
AMANDA: You mean you're a young workingman and have to   565
keep workingmen's hours. We'll let you off early tonight. But only on the condition that next time you stay later. What's the best night for you? Isn't Saturday night the best night for you workingmen?
JIM: I have a couple of time-clocks to punch, Mrs. Wingfield. One   570
at morning, another one at night!
AMANDA: My, but you are ambitious! You work at night, too?
JIM: No, Ma'am, not work but—Betty!

(*He crosses deliberately to pick up his hat. The band at the Paradise Dance-hall goes into a tender waltz.*)

AMANDA: Betty? Betty? Who's—Betty!

(*There is an ominous cracking sound in the sky.*)

JIM: Oh, just a girl. The girl I go steady with!   575

(*He smiles charmingly. The sky falls.*)

(*Legend:* "The Sky Falls.")

AMANDA: (*A long-drawn exhalation.*) Ohhhh . . . Is it a serious romance, Mr. O'Connor?
JIM: We're going to be married the second Sunday in June.
AMANDA: Ohhhh—how nice! Tom didn't mention that you were engaged to be married.   580
JIM: The cat's not out of the bag at the warehouse yet. You know how they are. They call you Romeo and stuff like that. (*He stops at the oval mirror to put on his hat. He carefully shapes the brim and the crown to give a discreetly dashing effect.*) It's been a wonderful evening, Mrs. Wingfield. I guess this is   585
what they mean by Southern hospitality.

AMANDA: It really wasn't anything at all.

JIM: I hope it don't seem like I'm rushing off. But I promised Betty I'd pick her up at the Wabash depot, an' by the time I get my jalopy down there her train'll be in. Some women are pretty upset if you keep 'em waiting.

AMANDA: Yes, I know—the tyranny of women! (*She extends her hand.*) Goodbye, Mr. O'Connor. I wish you luck—and happiness—and success! All three of them, and so does Laura! Don't you, Laura?

LAURA: Yes!

JIM: (*Taking* LAURA's *hand.*) Goodbye, Laura. I'm certainly going to treasure that souvenir. And don't you forget the good advice I gave you. (*He raises his voice to a cheery shout.*) So long, Shakespeare! Thanks again, ladies. Good night!

(*He grins and ducks jauntily out. Still bravely grimacing,* AMANDA *closes the door on the gentleman caller. Then she turns back to the room with a puzzled expression. She and* LAURA *don't dare to face each other.* LAURA *crouches beside the Victrola to wind it.*)

AMANDA: (*Faintly.*) Things have a way of turning out so badly. I don't believe that I would play the Victrola. Well, well—well! Our gentleman caller was engaged to be married! (*She raises her voice.*) Tom!

TOM: (*From the kitchenette.*) Yes, Mother?

AMANDA: Come in here a minute. I want to tell you something awfully funny.

TOM: (*Entering with a macaroon and a glass of the lemonade.*) Has the gentleman caller gotten away already?

AMANDA: The gentleman caller has made an early departure. What a wonderful joke you played on us!

TOM: How do you mean?

AMANDA: You didn't mention that he was engaged to be married.

TOM: Jim? Engaged?

AMANDA: That's what he just informed us.

TOM: I'll be jiggered! I didn't know about that.

AMANDA: That seems very peculiar.

TOM: What's peculiar about it?

AMANDA: Didn't you call him your best friend down at the warehouse?

TOM: He is, but how did I know?

AMANDA: It seems extremely peculiar that you wouldn't know your best friend was going to be married!

TOM: The warehouse is where I work, not where I know things about people!

AMANDA: You don't know things anywhere! You live in a dream; you manufacture illusions!

(*He crosses to the door.*)

Where are you going?

TOM: I'm going to the movies.

AMANDA: That's right, now that you've had us make such fools of ourselves. The effort, the preparations, all the expense! The new floor lamp, the rug, the clothes for Laura! All for what? To entertain some other girl's fiancé! Go to the movies, go! Don't think about us, a mother deserted, an unmarried sister who's crippled and has no job! Don't let anything interfere with your selfish pleasure! Just go, go, go—to the movies!

TOM: All right, I will! The more you shout about my selfishness to me the quicker I'll go, and I won't go to the movies!

AMANDA: Go, then! Go to the moon—you selfish dreamer!

(TOM *smashes his glass on the floor. He plunges out on the fire escape, slamming the door.* LAURA *screams in fright. The dance-hall music becomes louder.* TOM *stands on the fire escape, gripping the rail. The moon breaks through the storm clouds, illuminating his face.*)

(*Legend on screen:* "And so goodbye . . .")

(TOM's *closing speech is timed with what is happening inside the house. We see, as though through soundproof glass, that* AMANDA *appears to be making a comforting speech to* LAURA, *who is huddled upon the sofa. Now that we cannot hear the mother's speech, her silliness is gone and she has dignity and tragic beauty.* LAURA's *hair hides her face until, at the end of the speech, she lifts her head to smile at her mother.* AMANDA's *gestures are slow and graceful, almost dancelike, as she comforts her daughter. At the end of her speech she glances a moment at the father's picture— then withdraws through the portieres. At the close of* TOM's *speech,* LAURA *blows out the candles, ending the play.*)

TOM: I didn't go to the moon, I went much further—for time is the longest distance between two places. Not long after that I was fired for writing a poem on the lid of a shoe-box. I left Saint Louis. I descended the steps of this fire escape for a last time and followed, from then on, in my father's footsteps, attempting to find in motion what was lost in space. I traveled around a great deal. The cities swept about me like dead leaves, leaves that were brightly colored but torn away from the branches. I would have stopped, but I was pursued by something. It always came upon me unawares, taking me altogether by surprise. Perhaps it was a familiar bit of music. Perhaps it was only a piece of transparent glass. Perhaps I am walking along a street at night, in some strange city, before I have found companions. I pass the lighted window of a shop where perfume is sold. The window is filled with pieces of colored glass, tiny transparent bottles in delicate colors, like bits of a shattered rainbow. Then all at once my sister touches my shoulder. I turn around and look into her eyes. Oh, Laura, Laura, I tried to leave you behind me, but I am more faithful than I intended to be! I reach for a cigarette, I cross the street, I run into the movies or a bar, I buy a drink, I speak to the nearest stranger—anything that can blow your candles out!

(LAURA *bends over the candles.*)

For nowadays the world is lit by lightning! Blow out your candles, Laura—and so goodbye. . . .

(*She blows the candles out.*)

Arthur Miller

Arthur Miller (1915–2005) was born in Harlem and raised in Brooklyn. The son of Jewish immigrants, Miller often takes the milieu of urban New York as the substance of his drama. Like Tennessee Williams, Miller was formed by the Depression. He worked a variety of jobs to help his family make ends meet, and eventually gained provisional admission to the University of Michigan, where he studied playwriting, won several prestigious campus writing awards, and graduated in 1938. He worked briefly for the Federal Theater Project. Although his first play—*The Man Who Had All the Luck* (1944)—failed, Miller went on to write a series of gritty and powerful plays: *All My Sons* (1947), *Death of a Salesman* (1949), an adaptation of Ibsen's *An Enemy of the People* (1950), and *The Crucible* (1953). In 1955, Miller wrote *A View from the Bridge,* a story of honor and betrayal among New York's Italian immigrants. He also married Marilyn Monroe in that year, and his next play, *After the Fall* (1964), is a lightly disguised account of their stormy marriage and its break-up. In 1964 he also produced *Incident at Vichy,* a play concerning the Nazi persecution of the Jews during World War II, and he returned to the subject in his 1981 screenplay, *Playing for Time.* Until his death Miller continued to write and have his plays produced worldwide, including *The Price* (1968), *The Creation of the World and Other Business* (1972—revised as *Up from Paradise* 1974), *The Archbishop's Calling* (1977), *The American Clock* (1980), *Danger: Memory* (1987), *The Ride Down Mount Morgan* (1991), *The Last Yankee* (1993); and *Resurrection Blues* (2002). He also published a memoir (*Timebends*), a series of collected essays, and an account of the production of *Salesman* in the People's Republic of China during the 1980s. He wrote and lectured frequently about his career and about American theater.

Death of a Salesman

Something like *Oedipus the King* for the classical theater, or *Hamlet* for the English Renaissance stage, *Death of a Salesman* has become an icon of the American theater: Miller's central characters—Willy Loman, the worn-out, dreaming salesman; his two sons, Biff, the All-American star, who can never quite fit into American society, and Happy, the unhappy younger brother—have entered into the popular lexicon of cultural stereotypes, landmarks for later playwrights. (Think of Troy Maxson in August Wilson's *Fences,* or Lee and Austin in Sam Shepard's *True West.*) And, again like *Hamlet,* the play provides a dominant central role that has tested generations of actors from Lee J. Cobb, who created Willy Loman onstage, to Dustin Hoffman and Brian Dennehy.

As in classical tragedy (see Miller's essay, "Tragedy and the Common Man," later in this unit), the action of *Death of a Salesman* is impelled by a single, climactic event: Willy is approaching the end of his career, his glad-handing sales contacts are all dead or retired, and he's no longer pulling in business for the company—he's about to be fired. While this is perhaps less sensational than the crimes that prompt Oedipus or Hamlet to tragic action, Miller uses the fluidity of his stage and his remarkable ear for the prosaic poetry of everyday speech to give this event an extraordinary resonance. Blending scenes from Willy's past (the affecting scenes of Willy as a young father; the Woman in Boston and Biff 's discovery of Willy's hypocrisy) with the Loman family's present straits, *Death of a Salesman* claims Willy as a representative figure, embodying the contradictions of the American dream. As Linda puts it, "Willy Loman never made a lot of money. His name was never in the paper. He's not the finest character that ever lived. But he's a human being, and a terrible thing is happening to him. So attention must be paid." Miller deftly focuses a conflict between the material circumstances of Willy's life, his hard work, his exploitation by the company that finally sends him "to his grave like an old dog," and Willy's nonetheless eager belief in the system, in the salesman's ethic that has sustained and destroyed him. *Death of a Salesman* stages a double perspective on deadly mythology of America: Willy at once believes, and teaches his two sons to believe, that to be "well liked" is more important, more critical than ability or achievement; at the same time, he turns aside from the life represented by his uncle Ben, remaining with his good job and steady income instead of pursuing the intangible fortunes of Alaska like his pioneering father. Although the play stages many of the turning points in Willy's life, the opportunities missed to take a new direction, the central "cause" of the play's action took place years earlier, when Willy met an aging salesman and decided to pursue his career rather than light out for the frontier. What most impressed Willy about *that* salesman was his funeral: he died the "death of a salesman, in his green velvet slippers in the smoker of the New York, New Haven and Hartford, going into Boston—when he died, hundreds of salesmen and buyers were at his funeral." Part of Miller's genius in *Death of a Salesman* lies in the reach he gives to this figure and in the central conflict between the city and the frontier still embodied by the career of the salesman, represented in the play as a kind of Kit Carson or Daniel Boone, a rootless wanderer domesticated and destroyed by his willing acceptance of the demands of business and the society it sustains. As Charlie puts it in the "Requiem" ending the play: "Willy was a salesman. And for a salesman, there is no rock bottom to the life. He don't put a bolt to a nut, he don't tell you the law or give you medicine. He's a man way out there in the blue, riding on a smile and a shoeshine. . . . A salesman is got to dream, boy. It comes with the territory."

Lee J. Cobb and Mildred Dunnock, as Willy and Linda, and Arthur Kennedy and Cameron Mitchell as Happy and Biff in the 1949 premiere of *Death of a Salesman*.

Death of a Salesman

Arthur Miller

CHARACTERS

WILLY LOMAN

LINDA

BIFF

HAPPY

BERNARD

THE WOMAN

CHARLEY

UNCLE BEN

HOWARD WAGNER

JENNY

STANLEY

MISS FORSYTHE

LETTA

The action takes place in Willy Loman's house and yard and in various places he visits in the New York and Boston of today.

Throughout the play, in the stage directions, left and right mean stage left and stage right.

ACT ONE

A melody is heard, played upon a flute. It is small and fine, telling of grass and trees and the horizon. The curtain rises.

Before us is the Salesman's house. We are aware of towering, angular shapes behind it, surrounding it on all sides. Only the blue light of the sky falls upon the house and forestage; the surrounding area shows an angry glow of orange. As more light appears, we see a solid vault of apartment houses around the small, fragile-seeming home. An air of the dream clings to the place, a dream rising out of reality. The kitchen at center seems actual enough, for there is a kitchen table with three chairs, and a refrigerator. But no other fixtures are seen. At the back of the kitchen there is a draped entrance, which leads to the living-room. To the right of the kitchen, on a level raised two feet, is a bedroom furnished only with a brass bedstead and a straight chair. On a shelf over the bed a silver athletic trophy stands. A window opens onto the apartment house at the side.

Behind the kitchen, on a level raised six and a half feet, is the boys' bedroom, at present barely visible. Two beds are dimly seen, and at the back of the room a dormer window. (This bedroom is above the unseen living-room.) At the left a stairway curves up to it from the kitchen.

The entire setting is wholly, or, in some places, partially transparent. The roof-line of the house is one-dimensional; under and over it we see the apartment buildings. Before the house lies an apron, curving beyond the forestage into the orchestra. This forward area serves as the back yard as well as the locale of all Willy's imaginings and of his city scenes. Whenever the action is in the present the actors observe the imaginary wall-lines, entering the house only through its door at the left. But in the scenes of the past these boundaries are broken, and characters enter or leave a room by stepping "through" a wall onto the forestage.

From the right, Willy Loman, the Salesman, enters, carrying two large sample cases. The flute plays on. He hears but is not aware of it. He is past sixty years of age, dressed quietly. Even as he crosses the stage to the doorway of the house, his exhaustion is apparent. He unlocks the door, comes into the kitchen, and thankfully lets his burden down, feeling the soreness of his palms. A word-sigh escapes his lips—it might be "Oh, boy, oh, boy." He closes the door, then carries his cases out into the living-room, through the draped kitchen doorway.

Linda, his wife, has stirred in her bed at the right. She gets out and puts on a robe, listening. Most often jovial, she has developed an iron repression of her exceptions to Willy's behavior—she more than loves him, she admires him, as though his mercurial nature, his temper, his massive dreams and little cruelties, served her only as sharp reminders of the turbulent longings within him, longings which she shares but lacks the temperament to utter and follow to their end.

LINDA: (*Hearing* WILLY *outside the bedroom, calls with some trepidation.*) Willy!

WILLY: It's all right. I came back.

LINDA: Why? What happened? (*Slight pause.*) Did something happen, Willy?

WILLY: No, nothing happened.

LINDA: You didn't smash the car, did you?

WILLY: (*With casual irritation.*) I said nothing happened. Didn't you hear me?

LINDA: Don't you feel well?

WILLY: I'm tired to the death. (*The flute has faded away. He sits on the bed beside her, a little numb.*) I couldn't make it. I just couldn't make it, Linda.

LINDA: (*Very carefully, delicately.*) Where were you all day? You look terrible.

WILLY: I got as far as a little above Yonkers. I stopped for a cup of coffee. Maybe it was the coffee.

LINDA: What?

WILLY: (*After a pause.*) I suddenly couldn't drive any more. The car kept going off onto the shoulder, y'know?

LINDA: (*Helpfully.*) Oh. Maybe it was the steering again. I don't think Angelo knows the Studebaker.

WILLY: No, it's me, it's me. Suddenly I realize I'm goin' sixty miles an hour and I don't remember the last five minutes. I'm—I can't seem to—keep my mind to it.

LINDA: Maybe it's your glasses. You never went for your new glasses.

WILLY: No, I see everything. I came back ten miles an hour. It took me nearly four hours from Yonkers.

LINDA: (*Resigned.*) Well, you'll just have to take a rest, Willy, you can't continue this way.

WILLY: I just got back from Florida.

LINDA: But you didn't rest your mind. Your mind is overactive, and the mind is what counts, dear.

WILLY: I'll start out in the morning. Maybe I'll feel better in the morning. (*She is taking off his shoes.*) These goddam arch supports are killing me.

5

10

15

20

25

30

35

LINDA: Take an aspirin. Should I get you an aspirin? It'll soothe you.

40 WILLY: (*With wonder.*) I was driving along, you understand? And I was fine. I was even observing the scenery. You can imagine, me looking at scenery, on the road every week of my life. But it's so beautiful up there, Linda, the trees are so thick, and the sun is warm. I opened the windshield

45 and just let the warm air bathe over me. And then all of a sudden I'm goin' off the road! I'm tellin' ya, I absolutely forgot I was driving. If I'd've gone the other way over the white line I might've killed somebody. So I went on again—and five minutes later I'm dreamin' again, and I

50 nearly—(*He presses two fingers against his eyes.*) I have such thoughts, I have such strange thoughts.

LINDA: Willy, dear. Talk to them again. There's no reason why you can't work in New York.

WILLY: They don't need me in New York. I'm the New England

55 man. I'm vital in New England.

LINDA: But you're sixty years old. They can't expect you to keep traveling every week.

WILLY: I'll have to send a wire to Portland. I'm supposed to see Brown and Morrison tomorrow morning at ten o'clock

60 to show the line. Goddammit, I could sell them! (*He starts putting on his jacket.*)

LINDA: (*Taking the jacket from him.*) Why don't you go down to the place tomorrow and tell Howard you've simply got to work in New York? You're too accommodating,

65 dear.

WILLY: If old man Wagner was alive I'd a been in charge of New York now! That man was a prince, he was a masterful man. But that boy of his, that Howard, he don't appreciate. When I went north the first time, the Wagner Company didn't know

70 where New England was!

LINDA: Why don't you tell those things to Howard, dear?

WILLY: (*Encouraged.*) I will, I definitely will. Is there any cheese?

LINDA: I'll make you a sandwich.

75 WILLY: No, go to sleep. I'll take some milk. I'll be up right away. The boys in?

LINDA: They're sleeping. Happy took Biff on a date tonight.

WILLY: (*Interested.*) That so?

LINDA: It was so nice to see them shaving together, one

80 behind the other, in the bathroom. And going out together. You notice? The whole house smells of shaving lotion.

WILLY: Figure it out. Work a lifetime to pay off a house. You finally own it, and there's nobody to live in it.

85 LINDA: Well, dear, life is a casting off. It's always that way.

WILLY: No, no, some people—some people accomplish something. Did Biff say anything after I went this morning?

LINDA: You shouldn't have criticized him, Willy, especially after he just got off the train. You mustn't lose your temper

90 with him.

WILLY: When the hell did I lose my temper? I simply asked him if he was making any money. Is that a criticism?

LINDA: But, dear, how could he make any money?

WILLY: (*Worried and angered.*) There's such an undercurrent in

95 him. He became a moody man. Did he apologize when I left this morning?

LINDA: He was crestfallen, Willy. You know how he admires you. I think if he finds himself, then you'll both be happier and not fight any more.

100 WILLY: How can he find himself on a farm? Is that a life? A farmhand? In the beginning, when he was young, I thought, well, a young man, it's good for him to tramp around, take a lot of different jobs. But it's more than ten years now and he has yet to make thirty-five dollars

105 a week!

LINDA: He's finding himself, Willy.

WILLY: Not finding yourself at the age of thirty-four is a disgrace!

LINDA: Shh!

110 WILLY: The trouble is he's lazy, goddammit!

LINDA: Willy, please!

WILLY: Biff is a lazy bum!

LINDA: They're sleeping. Get something to eat. Go on down.

WILLY: Why did he come home? I would like to know what

115 brought him home.

LINDA: I don't know. I think he's still lost, Willy. I think he's very lost.

WILLY: Biff Loman is lost. In the greatest country in the world a young man with such—personal attractiveness, gets lost.

120 And such a hard worker. There's one thing about Biff—he's not lazy.

LINDA: Never.

WILLY: (*With pity and resolve.*) I'll see him in the morning; I'll have a nice talk with him. I'll get him a job selling. He could

125 be big in no time. My God! Remember how they used to follow him around in high school? When he smiled at one of them their faces lit up. When he walked down the street. . . (*He loses himself in reminiscences.*)

LINDA: (*Trying to bring him out of it.*) Willy, dear, I got a new

130 kind of American-type cheese today. It's whipped.

WILLY: Why do you get American when I like Swiss?

LINDA: I just thought you'd like a change—

WILLY: I don't want a change! I want Swiss cheese. Why am I always being contradicted?

135 LINDA: (*With a covering laugh.*) I thought it would be a surprise.

WILLY: Why don't you open a window in here, for God's sake?

LINDA: (*With infinite patience.*) They're all open, dear.

WILLY: The way they boxed us in here. Bricks and windows, windows and bricks.

140 LINDA: We should've bought the land next door.

WILLY: The street is lined with cars. There's not a breath of fresh air in the neighborhood. The grass don't grow any more, you can't raise a carrot in the back yard. They should've had a law against apartment houses. Remember those two beautiful

145 elm trees out there? When I and Biff hung the swing between them?

LINDA: Yeah, like being a million miles from the city.

WILLY: They should've arrested the builder for cutting those down. They massacred the neighborhood. (*Lost.*) More and

150 more I think of those days, Linda. This time of year it was lilac and wisteria. And then the peonies would come out, and the daffodils. What fragrance in this room!

LINDA: Well, after all, people had to move somewhere.

WILLY: No, there's more people, now.

155 LINDA: I don't think there's more people I think—

WILLY: There's more people! That's what's ruining this country! Population is getting out of control. The competition is maddening! Smell the stink from that apartment house! And another one on the other side . . . How can they whip

160 cheese?

(*On* WILLY's *last line,* BIFF *and* HAPPY *raise themselves up in their beds, listening.*)

LINDA: Go down, try it. And be quiet.

WILLY: (*Turning to* LINDA, *guiltily.*) You're not worried about me, are you, sweetheart?

BIFF: What's the matter?

165 HAPPY: Listen!

LINDA: You've got too much on the ball to worry about.

WILLY: You're my foundation and my support, Linda.

LINDA: Just try to relax, dear. You make mountains out of molehills.

170 WILLY: I won't fight with him any more. If he wants to go back to Texas, let him go.

LINDA: He'll find his way.

WILLY: Sure. Certain men just don't get started till later in life. Like Thomas Edison, I think. Or B. F. Goodrich. One of

175 them was deaf. (*He starts for the bedroom doorway.*) I'll put my money on Biff.

LINDA: And Willy—if it's warm Sunday we'll drive in the country. And we'll open the windshield, and take lunch.

WILLY: No, the windshields don't open on the new cars.

180 LINDA: But you opened it today.

WILLY: Me? I didn't. (*He stops.*) Now isn't that peculiar! Isn't that a remarkable—(*He breaks off in amazement and fright as the flute is heard distantly.*)

LINDA: What, darling?

185 WILLY: That is the most remarkable thing.

LINDA: What, dear?

WILLY: I was thinking of the Chevvy. (*Slight pause.*) Nineteen twenty-eight . . . when I had that red Chevvy—(*Breaks off.*) That funny? I coulda sworn I was driving that Chevvy

190 today.

LINDA: Well, that's nothing. Something must've reminded you.

WILLY: Remarkable. Ts. Remember those days? The way Biff used to simonize that car? The dealer refused to believe

195 there was eighty thousand miles on it. (*He shakes his head.*) Heh! (*To* LINDA.) Close your eyes, I'll be right up. (*He walks out of the bedroom.*)

HAPPY *to* BIFF: Jesus, maybe he smashed up the car again!

LINDA: (*Calling after* WILLY.) Be careful on the stairs, dear! The

200 cheese is on the middle shelf! (*She turns, goes over to the bed, takes his jacket, and goes out of the bedroom.*)

(*Light has risen on the boys' room. Unseen,* WILLY *is heard talking to himself, "Eighty thousand miles," and a little laugh.* BIFF *gets out of bed, comes downstage a bit, and stands attentively.* BIFF *is two years older than his brother* HAPPY, *well built, but in these days bears a worn air and seems less self-assured. He has succeeded less, and his dreams are stronger and less acceptable than* HAPPY's. HAPPY *is tall, powerfully made. Sexuality is like a visible color on him, or a scent that many women have discovered. He, like his brother, is lost, but in a different way, for he has never allowed himself to turn his face toward defeat and is thus more confused and hard-skinned, although seemingly more content.*)

HAPPY: (*Getting out of bed.*) He's going to get his license taken away if he keeps that up. I'm getting nervous about him, y'know, Biff?

205 BIFF: His eyes are going.

HAPPY: No, I've driven with him. He sees all right. He just doesn't keep his mind on it. I drove into the city with him last week. He stops at a green light and then it turns red and he goes. (*He laughs.*)

BIFF: Maybe he's color-blind.   210

HAPPY: Pop? Why he's got the finest eye for color in the business. You know that.

BIFF: (*Sitting down on his bed.*) I'm going to sleep.

HAPPY: You're not still sour on Dad, are you, Biff?

BIFF: He's all right, I guess.   215

WILLY: (*Underneath them, in the living-room.*) Yes, sir, eighty thousand miles—eighty-two thousand!

BIFF: You smoking?

HAPPY: (*Holding out a pack of cigarettes.*) Want one?

BIFF: (*Taking a cigarette.*) I can never sleep when I smell it.   220

WILLY: What a simonizing job, heh!

HAPPY: (*With deep sentiment.*) Funny, Biff, y'know? Us sleeping in here again? The old beds. (*He pats his bed affectionately.*) All the talk that went across those two beds, huh? Our whole lives.   225

BIFF: Yeah. Lotta dreams and plans.

HAPPY: (*With a deep and masculine laugh.*) About five hundred women would like to know what was said in this room.

(*They share a soft laugh.*)

BIFF: Remember that big Betsy something—what the hell was her name—over on Bushwick Avenue?   230

HAPPY: (*Combing his hair.*) With the collie dog!

BIFF: That's the one. I got you in there, remember?

HAPPY: Yeah, that was my first time—I think. Boy, there was a pig! (*They laugh, almost crudely.*) You taught me everything I know about women. Don't forget that.   235

BIFF: I bet you forgot how bashful you used to be. Especially with girls.

HAPPY: Oh, I still am, Biff.

BIFF: Oh, go on.

HAPPY: I just control it, that's all. I think I got less bashful and   240
you got more so. What happened, Biff? Where's the old humor, the old confidence? (*He shakes* BIFF's *knee.* BIFF *gets up and moves restlessly about the room.*) What's the matter?

BIFF: Why does Dad mock me all the time?

HAPPY: He's not mocking you, he—   245

BIFF: Everything I say there's a twist of mockery on his face. I can't get near him.

HAPPY: He just wants you to make good, that's all. I wanted to talk to you about Dad for a long time, Biff. Something's— happening to him. He—talks to himself.   250

BIFF: I noticed that this morning. But he always mumbled.

HAPPY: But not so noticeable. It got so embarrassing I sent him to Florida. And you know something? Most of the time he's talking to you.

BIFF: What's he say about me?   255

HAPPY: I can't make it out.

BIFF: What's he say about me?

HAPPY: I think the fact that you're not settled, that you're still kind of up in the air . . .

BIFF: There's one or two other things depressing him, Happy.   260

HAPPY: What do you mean?

BIFF: Never mind. Just don't lay it all to me.

HAPPY: But I think if you just got started—I mean—is there any future for you out there?

265 BIFF: I tell ya, Hap, I don't know what the future is. I don't
know—what I'm supposed to want.

HAPPY: What do you mean?

BIFF: Well, I spent six or seven years after high school trying
to work myself up. Shipping clerk, salesman, business of
270 one kind or another. And it's a measly manner of existence.
To get on that subway on the hot mornings in summer.
To devote your whole life to keeping stock, or making
phone calls, or selling or buying. To suffer fifty weeks of
the year for the sake of a two-week vacation, when all you
275 really desire is to be outdoors, with your shirt off. And
always to have to get ahead of the next fella. And still—
that's how you build a future.

HAPPY: Well, you really enjoy it on a farm? Are you content
out there?

280 BIFF: (With rising agitation.) Hap, I've had twenty or thirty
different kinds of jobs since I left home before the war,
and it always turns out the same. I just realized it lately.
In Nebraska when I herded cattle, and the Dakotas, and
Arizona, and now in Texas. It's why I came home now,
285 I guess, because I realized it. This farm I work on, it's
spring there now, see? And they've got about fifteen new
colts. There's nothing more inspiring or—beautiful than
the sight of a mare and a new colt. And it's cool there
now, see? Texas is cool now, and it's spring. And whenever
290 spring comes to where I am, I suddenly get the feeling,
my God, I'm not gettin' anywhere! What the hell am I
doing, playing around with horses, twenty-eight dollars
a week! I'm thirty-four years old, I oughta be makin' my
future. That's when I come running home. And now, I get
295 here, and I don't know what to do with myself. (After a
pause.) I've always made a point of not wasting my life,
and everytime I come back here I know that all I've done
is to waste my life.

HAPPY: You're a poet, you know that, Biff? You're a—you're
300 an idealist!

BIFF: No, I'm mixed up very bad. Maybe I oughta get married.
Maybe I oughta get stuck into something. Maybe that's
my trouble. I'm like a boy. I'm not married, I'm not in
business, I just—I'm like a boy. Are you content, Hap?
305 You're a success, aren't you? Are you content?

HAPPY: Hell, no!

BIFF: Why? You're making money, aren't you?

HAPPY: (Moving about with energy, expressiveness.) All I can
do now is wait for the merchandise manager to die. And
310 suppose I get to be merchandise manager? He's a good
friend of mine, and he just built a terrific estate on Long
Island. And he lived there about two months and sold
it, and now he's building another one. He can't enjoy it
once it's finished. And I know that's just what I would do.
315 I don't know what the hell I'm workin' for. Sometimes I sit
in my apartment—all alone. And I think of the rent I'm
paying. And it's crazy. But then, it's what I always wanted.
My own apartment, a car, and plenty of women. And still,
goddammit, I'm lonely.

320 BIFF: (With enthusiasm.) Listen, why don't you come out West
with me?

HAPPY: You and I, heh?

BIFF: Sure, maybe we could buy a ranch. Raise cattle, use our
muscles. Men built like we are should be working out in
325 the open.

HAPPY: (Avidly.) The Loman Brothers, heh?

BIFF: (With vast affection.) Sure, we'd be known all over the
counties!

HAPPY: (Enthralled.) That's what I dream about, Biff. Sometimes
I want to just rip my clothes off in the middle of the store
330 and outbox that goddam merchandise manager. I mean I can
outbox, outrun, and outlift anybody in that store, and I have
to take orders from those common, petty sons-of-bitches till I
can't stand it any more.

BIFF: I'm tellin' you, kid, if you were with me I'd be happy out
335 there.

HAPPY: (Enthused.) See, Biff, everybody around me is so false that
I'm constantly lowering my ideals . . .

BIFF: Baby, together we'd stand up for one another, we'd have
someone to trust.
340
HAPPY: If I were around you—

BIFF: Hap, the trouble is we weren't brought up to grub for money.
I don't know how to do it.

HAPPY: Neither can I!

BIFF: Then let's go!
345
HAPPY: The only thing is—what can you make out there?

BIFF: But look at your friend. Builds an estate and then hasn't the
peace of mind to live in it.

HAPPY: Yeah, but when he walks into the store the waves part in
front of him. That's fifty-two thousand dollars a year coming
350 through the revolving door, and I got more in my pinky finger
than he's got in his head.

BIFF: Yeah, but you just said—

HAPPY: I gotta show some of those pompous, self-important
executives over there that Hap Loman can make the grade.
355 I want to walk into the store the way he walks in. Then
I'll go with you, Biff. We'll be together yet, I swear. But
take those two we had tonight. Now weren't they gorgeous
creatures?

BIFF: Yeah, yeah, most gorgeous I've had in years.
360
HAPPY: I get that any time I want, Biff. Whenever I feel disgusted.
The only trouble is, it gets like bowling or something. I just
keep knockin' them over and it doesn't mean anything. You
still run around a lot?

BIFF: Naa. I'd like to find a girl—steady, somebody with
365 substance.

HAPPY: That's what I long for.

BIFF: Go on! You'd never come home.

HAPPY: I would! Somebody with character, with resistance! Like
Mom, y'know? You're gonna call me a bastard when I tell you
370 this. That girl Charlotte I was with tonight is engaged to be
married in five weeks. (He tries on his new hat.)

BIFF: No kiddin'!

HAPPY: Sure, the guy's in line for the vice-presidency of the
store. I don't know what gets into me, maybe I just have
375 an overdeveloped sense of competition or something,
but I went and ruined her, and furthermore I can't get
rid of her. And he's the third executive I've done that to.
Isn't that a crummy characteristic? And to top it all, I go
to their weddings! (Indignantly, but laughing.) Like I'm
380 not supposed to take bribes. Manufacturers offer me a
hundred-dollar bill now and then to throw an order their
way. You know how honest I am, but it's like this girl, see.
I hate myself for it. Because I don't want the girl, and, still,
I take it and—I love it!
385
BIFF: Let's go to sleep.

HAPPY: I guess we didn't settle anything, heh?

BIFF: I just got one idea that I think I'm going to try.

HAPPY: What's that?

390 BIFF: Remember Bill Oliver?

HAPPY: Sure, Oliver is very big now. You want to work for him again?

BIFF: No, but when I quit he said something to me. He put his arm on my shoulder, and he said, "Biff, if you ever need

395 anything, come to me."

HAPPY: I remember that. That sounds good.

BIFF: I think I'll go to see him. If I could get ten thousand or even seven or eight thousand dollars I could buy a beautiful ranch.

400 HAPPY: I bet he'd back you. 'Cause he thought highly of you, Biff. I mean, they all do. You're well liked, Biff. That's why I say to come back here, and we both have the apartment. And I'm tellin' you, Biff, any babe you want . . .

BIFF: No, with a ranch I could do the work I like and still be

405 something. I just wonder though. I wonder if Oliver still thinks I stole that carton of basketballs.

HAPPY: Oh, he probably forgot that long ago. It's almost ten years. You're too sensitive. Anyway, he didn't really fire you.

410 BIFF: Well, I think he was going to. I think that's why I quit. I was never sure whether he knew or not. I know he thought the world of me, though. I was the only one he'd let lock up the place.

WILLY: (*Below.*) You gonna wash the engine, Biff?

415 HAPPY: Shh!

(BIFF *looks at* HAPPY, *who is gazing down, listening.* WILLY *is mumbling in the parlor.*)

HAPPY: You hear that?

(*They listen.* WILLY *laughs warmly.*)

BIFF: (*Growing angry.*) Doesn't he know Mom can hear that?

WILLY: Don't get your sweater dirty, Biff!

(*A look of pain crosses* BIFF's *face.*)

HAPPY: Isn't that terrible? Don't leave again, will you? You'll

420 find a job here. You gotta stick around. I don't know what to do about him, it's getting embarrassing.

WILLY: What a simonizing job!

BIFF: Mom's hearing that!

WILLY: No kiddin', Biff, you got a date? Wonderful!

425 HAPPY: Go on to sleep. But talk to him in the morning, will you?

BIFF: (*Reluctantly getting into bed.*) With her in the house. Brother!

HAPPY: (*Getting into bed.*) I wish you'd have a good talk with

430 him.

(*The light on their room begins to fade.*)

BIFF: (*To himself in bed.*) That selfish, stupid . . .

HAPPY: Sh . . . Sleep, Biff.

(*Their light is out. Well before they have finished speaking,* WILLY's *form is dimly seen below in the darkened kitchen. He opens the refrigerator, searches in there, and takes out a bottle of milk. The apartment houses are fading out, and the entire house and*

surroundings become covered with leaves. Music insinuates itself as the leaves appear.)

WILLY: Just wanna be careful with those girls, Biff, that's all. Don't make any promises. No promises of any kind. Because a girl, y'know, they always believe what you tell 'em, and

435 you're very young, Biff, you're too young to be talking seriously to girls.

(*Light rises on the kitchen.* WILLY, *talking, shuts the refrigerator door and comes downstage to the kitchen table. He pours milk into a glass. He is totally immersed in himself, smiling faintly.*)

WILLY: Too young entirely, Biff. You want to watch your schooling first. Then when you're all set, there'll be plenty of girls for a boy like you. (*He smiles broadly at a kitchen

440 chair.*) That so? The girls pay for you? (*He laughs.*) Boy, you must really be makin' a hit.

(WILLY *is gradually addressing—physically—a point offstage, speaking through the wall of the kitchen, and his voice has been rising in volume to that of a normal conversation.*)

WILLY: I been wondering why you polish the car so careful. Ha! Don't leave the hubcaps, boys. Get the chamois to the hubcaps. Happy, use newspaper on the windows, it's

445 the easiest thing. Show him how to do it, Biff! You see, Happy? Pad it up, use it like a pad. That's it, that's it, good work. You're doin' all right, Hap. (*He pauses, then nods in approbation for a few seconds, then looks upward.*) Biff, first thing we gotta do when we get time is clip that big branch

450 over the house. Afraid it's gonna fall in a storm and hit the roof. Tell you what. We get a rope and sling her around, and then we climb up there with a couple of saws and take her down. Soon as you finish the car, boys, I wanna see ya. I got a surprise for you, boys.

455 BIFF: (*Offstage.*) Whatta ya got, Dad?

WILLY: No, you finish first. Never leave a job till you're finished— remember that. (*Looking toward the "big trees".*) Biff, up in Albany I saw a beautiful hammock. I think I'll buy it next trip, and we'll hang it right between those two elms. Wouldn't

460 that be something? Just swingin' there under those branches. Boy, that would be . . .

(*Young* BIFF *and* YOUNG HAPPY *appear from the direction* WILLY *was addressing.* HAPPY *carries rags and a pail of water.* BIFF, *wearing a sweater with a block "S," carries a football.*)

BIFF: (*Pointing in the direction of the car offstage.*) How's that, Pop, professional?

WILLY: Terrific. Terrific job, boys. Good work, Biff.

465 HAPPY: Where's the surprise, Pop?

WILLY: In the back seat of the car.

HAPPY: Boy! (*He runs off.*)

BIFF: What is it, Dad? Tell me, what'd you buy?

WILLY: (*Laughing, cuffs him.*) Never mind, something I want you

470 to have.

BIFF: (*Turns and starts off.*) What is it, Hap?

HAPPY: (*Offstage.*) It's a punching bag!

BIFF: Oh, Pop!

WILLY: It's got Gene Tunney's signature on it!

475

(HAPPY *runs onstage with a punching bag.*)

BIFF: Gee, how'd you know we wanted a punching bag?

WILLY: Well, it's the finest thing for the timing.

HAPPY: (*Lies down on his back and pedals with his feet.*) I'm losing weight, you notice, Pop?

480 WILLY: (*To* HAPPY.) Jumping rope is good too.

BIFF: Did you see the new football I got?

WILLY: (*Examining the ball.*) Where'd you get a new ball?

BIFF: The coach told me to practice my passing.

WILLY: That so? And he gave you the ball, heh?

485 BIFF: Well, I borrowed it from the locker room. (*He laughs confidentially.*)

WILLY: (*Laughing with him at the theft.*) I want you to return that.

HAPPY: I told you he wouldn't like it!

490 BIFF: (*Angrily.*) Well, I'm bringing it back!

WILLY: (*Stopping the incipient argument, to* HAPPY.) Sure, he's gotta practice with a regulation ball, doesn't he? (*To* BIFF.) Coach'll probably congratulate you on your initiative!

BIFF: Oh, he keeps congratulating my initiative all the time,

495 Pop.

WILLY: That's because he likes you. If somebody else took that ball there'd be an uproar. So what's the report, boys, what's the report?

BIFF: Where'd you go this time, Dad? Gee we were lonesome

500 for you.

WILLY: (*Pleased, puts an arm around each boy and they come down to the apron.*) Lonesome, heh?

BIFF: Missed you every minute.

WILLY: Don't say? Tell you a secret, boys. Don't breathe it to a

505 soul. Someday I'll have my own business, and I'll never have to leave home any more.

HAPPY: Like Uncle Charley, heh?

WILLY: Bigger than Uncle Charley! Because Charley is not—liked. He's liked, but he's not—well liked.

510 BIFF: Where'd you go this time, Dad?

WILLY: Well, I got on the road, and I went north to Providence. Met the Mayor.

BIFF: The Mayor of Providence!

WILLY: He was sitting in the hotel lobby.

515 BIFF: What'd he say?

WILLY: He said, "Morning!" And I said, "You got a fine city here, Mayor." And then he had coffee with me. And then I went to Waterbury. Waterbury is a fine city. Big clock city, the famous Waterbury clock. Sold a nice bill there. And then

520 Boston—Boston is the cradle of the Revolution. A fine city. And a couple of other towns in Mass., and on to Portland and Bangor and straight home!

BIFF: Gee, I'd love to go with you sometime, Dad.

WILLY: Soon as summer comes.

525 HAPPY: Promise?

WILLY: You and Hap and I, and I'll show you all the towns. America is full of beautiful towns and fine, upstanding people. And they know me, boys, they know me up and down New England. The finest people. And when I bring

530 you fellas up, there'll be open sesame for all of us, 'cause one thing, boys: I have friends. I can park my car in any street in New England, and the cops protect it like their own. This summer, heh?

BIFF *and* HAPPY: (*Together.*) Yeah! You bet!

535 WILLY: We'll take our bathing suits.

HAPPY: We'll carry your bags, Pop!

WILLY: Oh, won't that be something! Me comin' into the Boston stores with you boys carryin' my bags. What a sensation!

(BIFF *is prancing around, practicing passing the ball.*)

540 WILLY: You nervous, Biff, about the game?

BIFF: Not if you're gonna be there.

WILLY: What do they say about you in school, now that they made you captain?

HAPPY: There's a crowd of girls behind him everytime the

545 classes change.

BIFF: (*Taking* WILLY's *hand.*) This Saturday, Pop, this Saturday—just for you, I'm going to break through for a touchdown.

HAPPY: You're supposed to pass.

550 BIFF: I'm takin' one play for Pop. You watch me, Pop, and when I take off my helmet, that means I'm breakin' out. Then you watch me crash through that line!

WILLY: (*Kisses* BIFF.) Oh, wait'll I tell this in Boston!

(BERNARD *enters in knickers. He is younger than* BIFF, *earnest and loyal, a worried boy.*)

555 BERNARD: Biff, where are you? You're supposed to study with me today.

WILLY: Hey, looka Bernard. What're you lookin' so anemic about, Bernard?

BERNARD: He's gotta study, Uncle Willy. He's got Regents next week.

560 HAPPY: (*Tauntingly, spinning* BERNARD *around.*) Let's box, Bernard!

BERNARD: Biff! (*He gets away from* HAPPY.) Listen, Biff, I heard Mr. Birnbaum say that if you don't start studyin' math he's gonna flunk you, and you won't graduate. I heard him!

565 WILLY: You better study with him, Biff. Go ahead now.

BERNARD: I heard him!

BIFF: Oh, Pop, you didn't see my sneakers! (*He holds up a foot for* WILLY *to look at.*)

WILLY: Hey, that's a beautiful job of printing!

570 BERNARD: (*Wiping his glasses.*) Just because he printed University of Virginia on his sneakers doesn't mean they've got to graduate him, Uncle Willy!

WILLY: (*Angrily.*) What're you talking about? With scholarships to three universities they're gonna flunk him?

575 BERNARD: But I heard Mr. Birnbaum say—

WILLY: Don't be a pest, Bernard! (*To his boys.*) What an anemic!

BERNARD: Okay, I'm waiting for you in my house, Biff.

(BERNARD *goes off. The* LOMANS *laugh.*)

WILLY: Bernard is not well liked, is he?

BIFF: He's liked, but he's not well liked.

580 HAPPY: That's right, Pop.

WILLY: That's just what I mean. Bernard can get the best marks in school, y'understand, but when he gets out in the business world, y'understand, you are going to be five times ahead of him. That's why I thank Almighty God you're both built like

585 Adonises. Because the man who makes an appearance in the business world, the man who creates personal interest, is the man who gets ahead. Be liked and you will never want.

You take me, for instance. I never have to wait in line to see
a buyer. "Willy Loman is here!" That's all they have to know,
590 and I go right through.

BIFF: Did you knock them dead, Pop?

WILLY: Knocked 'em cold in Providence, slaughtered 'em in
Boston.

HAPPY: (*On his back, pedaling again.*) I'm losing weight, you
595 notice, Pop?

(LINDA *enters, as of old, a ribbon in her hair, carrying a basket
of washing.*)

LINDA: (*With youthful energy.*) Hello, dear!

WILLY: Sweetheart!

LINDA: How'd the Chevvy run?

WILLY: Chevrolet, Linda, is the greatest car ever built. (*To the*
600 *boys.*) Since when do you let your mother carry wash up
the stairs?

BIFF: Grab hold there, boy!

HAPPY: Where to, Mom?

LINDA: Hang them up on the line. And you better go down to
605 your friends, Biff. The cellar is full of boys. They don't know
what to do with themselves.

BIFF: Ah, when Pop comes home they can wait!

WILLY: (*Laughs appreciatively.*) You better go down and tell them
what to do, Biff.

610 BIFF: I think I'll have them sweep out the furnace room.

WILLY: Good work, Biff.

BIFF: (*Goes through wall-line of kitchen to doorway at back and
calls down.*) Fellas! Everybody sweep out the furnace room!
I'll be right down!

615 VOICES: All right! Okay, Biff.

BIFF: George and Sam and Frank, come out back! We're hangin'
up the wash! Come on, Hap, on the double! (*He and* HAPPY
carry out the basket.)

LINDA: The way they obey him!

620 WILLY: Well, that's training, the training. I'm tellin' you, I was
sellin' thousands and thousands, but I had to come home.

LINDA: Oh, the whole block'll be at that game. Did you sell
anything?

WILLY: I did five hundred gross in Providence and seven hundred
625 gross in Boston.

LINDA: No! Wait a minute, I've got a pencil. (*She pulls pencil
and paper out of her apron pocket.*) That makes your
commission . . . Two hundred—my God! Two hundred, and
twelve dollars!

630 WILLY: Well, I didn't figure it yet, but . . .

LINDA: How much did you do?

WILLY: Well, I—I did—about a hundred and eighty gross in
Providence. Well, no—it came to—roughly two hundred
gross on the whole trip.

635 LINDA: (*Without hesitation.*) Two hundred gross. That's . . .
(*She figures.*)

WILLY: The trouble was that three of the stores were half
closed for inventory in Boston. Otherwise I woulda broke
records.

640 LINDA: Well, it makes seventy dollars and some pennies. That's
very good.

WILLY: What do we owe?

LINDA: Well, on the first there's sixteen dollars on the
refrigerator—

645 WILLY: Why sixteen?

LINDA: Well, the fan belt broke, so it was a dollar eighty.

WILLY: But it's brand new.

LINDA: Well, the man said that's the way it is. Till they work
themselves in, y'know.

(*They move through the wall-line into the kitchen.*)

WILLY: I hope we didn't get stuck on that machine. 650

LINDA: They got the biggest ads of any of them!

WILLY: I know, it's a fine machine. What else?

LINDA: Well, there's nine-sixty for the washing machine. And
for the vacuum cleaner there's three and a half due on
the fifteenth. Then the roof, you got twenty-one dollars 655
remaining.

WILLY: It don't leak, does it?

LINDA: No, they did a wonderful job. Then you owe Frank for the
carburetor.

WILLY: I'm not going to pay that man! That goddam Chevrolet, 660
they ought to prohibit the manufacture of that car!

LINDA: Well, you owe him three and a half. And odds and
ends, comes to around a hundred and twenty dollars by the
fifteenth.

WILLY: A hundred and twenty dollars! My God, if business don't 665
pick up I don't know what I'm gonna do!

LINDA: Well, next week you'll do better.

WILLY: Oh, I'll knock 'em dead next week. I'll go to Hartford. I'm
very well liked in Hartford. You know, the trouble is, Linda,
people don't seem to take to me. 670

(*They move onto the forestage.*)

LINDA: Oh, don't be foolish.

WILLY: I know it when I walk in. They seem to laugh at me.

LINDA: Why? Why would they laugh at you? Don't talk that way,
Willy.

(WILLY *moves to the edge of the stage.* LINDA *goes into the kitchen
and starts to darn stockings.*)

WILLY: I don't know the reason for it, but they just pass me by. I'm 675
not noticed.

LINDA: But you're doing wonderful, dear. You're making seventy
to a hundred dollars a week.

WILLY: But I gotta be at it ten, twelve hours a day. Other men—I
don't know—they do it easier. I don't know why—I can't stop 680
myself—I talk too much. A man oughta come in with a few
words. One thing about Charley. He's a man of few words, and
they respect him.

LINDA: You don't talk too much, you're just lively.

WILLY: (*Smiling.*) Well, I figure, what the hell, life is short, a 685
couple of jokes (*To himself.*) I joke too much! (*The smile
goes.*)

LINDA: Why? You're—

WILLY: I'm fat. I'm very—foolish to look at, Linda. I didn't tell
you, but Christmas time I happened to be calling on F. H. 690
Stewarts, and a salesman I know, as I was going in to see the
buyer I heard him say something about—walrus. And I—
cracked him right across the face. I won't take that. I simply
will not take that. But they do laugh at me. I know that.

LINDA: Darling . . . 695

WILLY: I gotta overcome it. I know I gotta overcome it. I'm not
dressing to advantage, maybe.

LINDA: Willy, darling, you're the handsomest man in the
world—

700 WILLY: Oh, no, Linda.
LINDA: To me you are. (*Slight pause.*) The handsomest.

(*From the darkness is heard the laughter of a woman.* WILLY *doesn't turn to it, but it continues through* LINDA'S *lines.*)

LINDA: And the boys, Willy. Few men are idolized by their children the way you are.

(*Music is heard as behind a scrim, to the left of the house,* THE WOMAN, *dimly seen, is dressing.*)

WILLY: (*With great feeling.*) You're the best there is, Linda, you're
705 a pal, you know that? On the road—on the road I want to grab you sometimes and just kiss the life outa you.

(*The laughter is loud now, and he moves into a brightening area at the left, where* THE WOMAN *has come from behind the scrim and is standing, putting on her hat, looking into a "mirror" and laughing.*)

WILLY: 'Cause I get so lonely—especially when business is bad and there's nobody to talk to. I get the feeling that I'll never sell anything again, that I won't making a living for you, or
710 a business, a business for the boys. (*He talks through* THE WOMAN'S *subsiding laughter;* THE WOMAN *primps at the "mirror."*) There's so much I want to make for—
THE WOMAN: Me? You didn't make me, Willy. I picked you.
WILLY: (*Pleased.*) You picked me?
715 THE WOMAN: (*Who is quite proper-looking,* WILLY'S *age.*) I did. I've been sitting at that desk watching all the salesmen go by, day in, day out. But you've got such a sense of humor, and we do have such a good time together, don't we?
WILLY: Sure, sure. (*He takes her in his arms.*) Why do you have to
720 go now?
THE WOMAN: It's two o'clock . . .
WILLY: No, come on in! (*He pulls her.*)
THE WOMAN: . . . my sisters'll be scandalized. When'll you be back?
725 WILLY: Oh, two weeks about. Will you come up again?
THE WOMAN: Sure thing. You do make me laugh. It's good for me. (*She squeezes his arm, kisses him.*) And I think you're a wonderful man.
WILLY: You picked me, heh?
730 THE WOMAN: Sure. Because you're so sweet. And such a kidder.
WILLY: Well, I'll see you next time I'm in Boston.
THE WOMAN: I'll put you right through to the buyers.
WILLY: (*Slapping her bottom.*) Right. Well, bottoms up!
THE WOMAN: (*Slaps him gently and laughs.*) You just kill me,
735 Willy. (*He suddenly grabs her and kisses her roughly.*) You kill me. And thanks for the stockings. I love a lot of stockings. Well, good night.
WILLY: Good night. And keep your pores open!
THE WOMAN: Oh, Willy!

(THE WOMAN *bursts out laughing, and* LINDA'S *laughter blends in.* THE WOMAN *disappears into the dark. Now the area at the kitchen table brightens.* LINDA *is sitting where she was at the kitchen table, but now is mending a pair of her silk stockings.*)

740 LINDA: You are, Willy. The handsomest man. You've got no reason to feel that—

WILLY: (*Coming out of* THE WOMAN'S *dimming area and going over to* LINDA.) I'll make it all up to you, Linda, I'll—
LINDA: There's nothing to make up, dear. You're doing fine, better than— 745
WILLY: (*Noticing her mending.*) What's that?
LINDA: Just mending my stockings. They're so expensive—
WILLY: (*Angrily, taking them from her.*) I won't have you mending stockings in this house! Now throw them out!

(LINDA *puts the stockings in her pocket.*)

BERNARD: (*Entering on the run.*) Where is he? If he doesn't 750
study!
WILLY: (*Moving to the forestage, with great agitation.*) You'll give him the answers!
BERNARD: I do, but I can't on a Regents! That's a state exam! They're liable to arrest me! 755
WILLY: Where is he? I'll whip him, I'll whip him!
LINDA: And he'd better give back that football, Willy, it's not nice.
WILLY: Biff! Where is he? Why is he taking everything?
LINDA: He's too rough with the girls, Willy. All the mothers are 760
afraid of him!
WILLY: I'll whip him!
BERNARD: He's driving the car without a license!

(THE WOMAN'S *laugh is heard.*)

WILLY: Shut up!
LINDA: All the mothers— 765
WILLY: Shut up!
BERNARD: (*Backing quietly away and out.*) Mr. Birnbaum says he's stuck up.
WILLY: Get outa here!
BERNARD: If he doesn't buckle down he'll flunk math! (*He goes 770
off.*)
LINDA: He's right, Willy, you've gotta—
WILLY: (*Exploding at her.*) There's nothing the matter with him! You want him to be a worm like Bernard? He's got spirit, personality . . . 775

(*As he speaks,* LINDA, *almost in tears, exits into the living-room.* WILLY *is alone in the kitchen, wilting and staring. The leaves are gone. It is night again, and the apartment houses look down from behind.*)

WILLY: Loaded with it. Loaded! What is he stealing? He's giving it back, isn't he? Why is he stealing? What did I tell him? I never in my life told him anything but decent things.

(HAPPY *in pajamas has come down the stairs;* WILLY *suddenly becomes aware of* HAPPY'S *presence.*)

HAPPY: Let's go now, come on.
WILLY: (*Sitting down at the kitchen table.*) Huh! Why did she have 780
to wax the floors herself? Everytime she waxes the floors she keels over. She knows that!
HAPPY: Shh! Take it easy. What brought you back tonight?
WILLY: I got an awful scare. Nearly hit a kid in Yonkers. God! Why didn't I go to Alaska with my brother Ben that time! 785
Ben! That man was a genius, that man was success incarnate! What a mistake! He begged me to go.

HAPPY: Well, there's no use in—

WILLY: You guys! There was a man started with the clothes on
790   his back and ended up with diamond mines!

HAPPY: Boy, someday I'd like to know how he did it.

WILLY: What's the mystery? The man knew what he wanted and
went out and got it! Walked into a jungle, and comes out, the
age of twenty-one, and he's rich! The world is an oyster, but
795   you don't crack it open on a mattress!

HAPPY: Pop, I told you I'm gonna retire you for life.

WILLY: You'll retire me for life on seventy goddam dollars a
week? And your women and your car and your apartment,
and you'll retire me for life! Christ's sake, I couldn't get past
800   Yonkers today! Where are you guys, where are you? The
woods are burning! I can't drive a car!

(CHARLEY *has appeared in the doorway. He is a large man, slow
of speech, laconic, immovable. In all he says, despite what he says,
there is pity, and, now, trepidation. He has a robe over pajamas,
slippers on his feet. He enters the kitchen.*)

CHARLEY: Everything all right?

HAPPY: Yeah, Charley, everything's . . .

WILLY: What's the matter?

805 CHARLEY: I heard some noise. I thought something happened.
Can't we do something about the walls? You sneeze in here,
and in my house hats blow off.

HAPPY: Let's go to bed, Dad. Come on.

(CHARLEY *signals to* HAPPY *to go.*)

WILLY: You go ahead, I'm not tired at the moment.

810 HAPPY: (*To* WILLY.) Take it easy, huh? (*He exits.*)

WILLY: What're you doin' up?.

CHARLEY: (*Sitting down at the kitchen table opposite* WILLY.)
Couldn't sleep good. I had a heartburn.

WILLY: Well, you don't know how to eat.

815 CHARLEY: I eat with my mouth.

WILLY: No, you're ignorant. You gotta know about vitamins and
things like that.

CHARLEY: Come on, let's shoot. Tire you out a little.

WILLY: (*Hesitantly.*) All right. You got cards?

820 CHARLEY: (*Taking a deck from his pocket.*) Yeah, I got them.
Someplace. What is it with those vitamins?

WILLY: (*Dealing.*) They build up your bones. Chemistry.

CHARLEY: Yeah, but there's no bones in a heartburn.

WILLY: What are you talkin' about? Do you know the first thing
825 about it?

CHARLEY: Don't get insulted.

WILLY: Don't talk about something you don't know anything
about.

(*They are playing. Pause.*)

830 CHARLEY: What're you doin' home?

WILLY: A little trouble with the car.

CHARLEY: Oh. (*Pause.*) I'd like to take a trip to California.

WILLY: Don't say.

CHARLEY: You want a job?

WILLY: I got a job, I told you that. (*After a slight pause.*) What the
835 hell are you offering me a job for?

CHARLEY: Don't get insulted.

WILLY: Don't insult me.

CHARLEY: I don't see no sense in it. You don't have to go on
this way.

WILLY: I got a good job. (*Slight pause.*) What do you keep comin' 840
in here for?

CHARLEY: You want me to go?

WILLY: (*After a pause, withering.*) I can't understand it. He's going
back to Texas again. What the hell is that?

CHARLEY: Let him go. 845

WILLY: I got nothin' to give him, Charley, I'm clean, I'm
clean.

CHARLEY: He won't starve. None a them starve. Forget about
him.

WILLY: Then what have I got to remember? 850

CHARLEY: You take it too hard. To hell with it. When a deposit
bottle is broken you don't get your nickel back.

WILLY: That's easy enough for you to say.

CHARLEY: That ain't easy for me to say.

WILLY: Did you see the ceiling I put up in the living-room? 855

CHARLEY: Yeah, that's a piece of work. To put up a ceiling is a
mystery to me. How do you do it?

WILLY: What's the difference?

CHARLEY: Well, talk about it.

WILLY: You gonna put up a ceiling? 860

CHARLEY: How could I put up a ceiling?

WILLY: Then what the hell are you bothering me for?

CHARLEY: You're insulted again.

WILLY: A man who can't handle tools is not a man. You're
disgusting. 865

CHARLEY: Don't call me disgusting, Willy.

(UNCLE BEN, *carrying a valise and an umbrella, enters the forestage from around the right corner of the house. He is a stolid man,
in his sixties, with a mustache and an authoritative air. He is utterly certain of his destiny, and there is an aura of far places about
him. He enters exactly as* WILLY *speaks.*)

WILLY: I'm getting awfully tired, Ben.

(BEN's *music is heard.* BEN *looks around at everything.*)

CHARLEY: Good, keep playing; you'll sleep better. Did you call
me Ben?

(BEN *looks at his watch.*)

WILLY: That's funny. For a second there you reminded me of my 870
brother Ben.

BEN: I only have a few minutes. (*He strolls, inspecting the place.*
WILLY *and* CHARLEY *continue playing.*)

CHARLEY: You never heard from him again, heh? Since that
time? 875

WILLY: Didn't Linda tell you? Couple of weeks ago we got a letter
from his wife in Africa. He died.

CHARLEY: That so.

BEN: (*Chuckling.*) So this is Brooklyn, eh?

CHARLEY: Maybe you're in for some of his money. 880

WILLY: Naa, he had seven sons. There's just one opportunity I
had with that man . . .

BEN: I must make a train, William. There are several properties
I'm looking at in Alaska.

WILLY: Sure, sure! If I'd gone with him to Alaska that time, 885
everything would've been totally different.

CHARLEY: Go on, you'd froze to death up there.

WILLY: What're you talking about?

BEN: Opportunity is tremendous in Alaska, William. Surprised
890   you're not up there.

WILLY: Sure, tremendous.

CHARLEY: Heh?

WILLY: There was the only man I ever met who knew the
       answers.

895 CHARLEY: Who?

BEN: How are you all?

WILLY: (*Taking a pot, smiling.*) Fine, fine.

CHARLEY: Pretty sharp tonight.

BEN: Is Mother living with you?

900 WILLY: No, she died a long time ago.

CHARLEY: Who?

BEN: That's too bad. Fine specimen of a lady, Mother.

WILLY: (*To* CHARLEY.) Heh?

BEN: I'd hoped to see the old girl.

905 CHARLEY: Who died?

BEN: Heard anything from Father, have you?

WILLY: (*Unnerved.*) What do you mean, who died?

CHARLEY: (*Taking a pot.*) What're you talkin' about?

BEN: (*Looking at his watch.*) William, it's half-past eight!

910 WILLY: (*As though to dispel his confusion he angrily stops*
       CHARLEY'*s hand.*) That's my build!

CHARLEY: I put the ace—

WILLY: If you don't know how to play the game I'm not gonna
       throw my money away on you!

915 CHARLEY: (*Rising.*) It was my ace, for God's sake!

WILLY: I'm through, I'm through!

BEN: When did Mother die?

WILLY: Long ago. Since the beginning you never knew how to
       play cards.

920 CHARLEY: (*Picks up the cards and goes to the door.*) All right! Next
       time I'll bring a deck with five aces.

WILLY: I don't play that kind of game!

CHARLEY: (*Turning to him.*) You ought to be ashamed of
       yourself!

925 WILLY: Yeah?

CHARLEY: Yeah! (*He goes out.*)

WILLY: (*Slamming the door after him.*) Ignoramus!

BEN: (*As* WILLY *comes toward him through the wall-line of the
       kitchen.*) So you're William.

930 WILLY: (*Shaking* BEN'*s hand.*) Ben! I've been waiting for you so
       long! What's the answer? How did you do it?

BEN: Oh, there's a story in that.

(LINDA *enters the forestage, as of old, carrying the wash basket.*)

LINDA: Is this Ben?

BEN: (*Gallantly.*) How do you do, my dear.

935 LINDA: Where've you been all these years? Willy's always
       wondered why you—

WILLY: (*Pulling* BEN *away from her impatiently.*) Where is Dad?
       Didn't you follow him? How did you get started?

BEN: Well, I don't know how much you remember.

940 WILLY: Well, I was just a baby, of course, only three or four years
       old—

BEN: Three years and eleven months.

WILLY: What a memory, Ben!

BEN: I have many enterprises, William, and I have never kept
945   books.

WILLY: I remember I was sitting under the wagon in—was it
       Nebraska?

BEN: It was South Dakota, and I gave you a bunch of
       wildflowers.

WILLY: I remember you walking away down some open road.   950

BEN: (*Laughing.*) I was going to find Father in Alaska.

WILLY: Where is he?

BEN: At that age I had a very faulty view of geography, William.
       I discovered after a few days that I was heading due south, so
       instead of Alaska, I ended up in Africa.   955

LINDA: Africa!

WILLY: The Gold Coast!

BEN: Principally diamond mines.

LINDA: Diamond mines!

BEN: Yes, my dear. But I've only a few minutes—   960

WILLY: No! Boys! Boys! (YOUNG BIFF *and* HAPPY *appear.*) Listen
       to this. This is your Uncle Ben, a great man! Tell, my boys,
       Ben!

BEN: Why, boys, when I was seventeen I walked into the jungle,
       and when I was twenty-one I walked out. (*He laughs.*) And by   965
       God I was rich.

WILLY: (*To the boys.*) You see what I been talking about? The
       greatest things can happen!

BEN: (*Glancing at his watch.*) I have an appointment in Ketchikan
       Tuesday week.   970

WILLY: No, Ben! Please tell about Dad. I want my boys to
       hear. I want them to know the kind of stock they spring
       from. All I remember is a man with a big beard, and I was
       in Mamma's lap, sitting around a fire, and some kind of
       high music.   975

BEN: His flute. He played the flute.

WILLY: Sure, the flute, that's right?

(*New music is heard, a high, rollicking tune.*)

BEN: Father was a very great and a very wild-hearted man.
       We would start in Boston, and he'd toss the whole family
       into the wagon, and then he'd drive the team right across   980
       the country; through Ohio, and Indiana, Michigan, Illinois,
       and all the Western states. And we'd stop in the towns and
       sell the flutes that he'd made on the way. Great inventor,
       Father. With one gadget he made more in a week than a
       man like you could make in a lifetime.   985

WILLY: That's just the way I'm bringing them up, Ben—rugged,
       well liked, all-around.

BEN: Yeah? (*To* BIFF.) Hit that, boy—hard as you can. (*He pounds
       his stomach.*)

BIFF: Oh, no, sir!   990

BEN: (*Taking boxing stance.*) Come on, get to me! (*He laughs.*)

WILLY: Go to it, Biff! Go ahead, show him!

BIFF: Okay! (*He cocks his fists and starts in.*)

LINDA: (*To* WILLY.) Why must he fight, dear?

BEN: (*Sparring with* BIFF.) Good boy! Good boy!   995

WILLY: How's that, Ben, heh?

HAPPY: Give him the left, Biff!

LINDA: Why are you fighting?

BEN: Good boy! (*Suddenly comes in, trips* BIFF, *and stands over
       him, the point of his umbrella poised over* BIFF'*s eye.*)   1000

LINDA: Look out, Biff!

BIFF: Gee!

BEN: (*Patting* BIFF'*s knee.*) Never fight fair with a stranger, boy.
       You'll never get out of the jungle that way. (*Taking* LINDA'*s

1005 *hand and bowing.*) It was an honor and a pleasure to meet
   you, Linda.
   LINDA: (*Withdrawing her hand coldly, frightened.*) Have a
   nice—trip.
   BEN: (*To* WILLY.) And good luck with your—what do you do?
1010 WILLY: Selling.
   BEN: Yes. Well . . . (*He raises his hand in farewell to all.*)
   WILLY: No, Ben, I don't want you to think . . . (*He takes* BEN's *arm
   to show him.*) It's Brooklyn, I know, but we hunt too.
   BEN: Really, now.
1015 WILLY: Oh, sure, there's snakes and rabbits and—that's why I
   moved out here. Why, Biff can fell any one of these trees in
   no time! Boys! Go right over to where they're building the
   apartment house and get some sand. We're gonna rebuild the
   entire front stoop right now! Watch this Ben!
1020 BIFF: Yes, sir! On the double, Hap!
   HAPPY: (*As he and* BIFF *run off.*) I lost weight, Pop, you notice?

   (CHARLEY *enters in knickers, even before the boys are gone.*)

   CHARLEY: Listen, if they steal any more from that building the
   watchman'll put the cops on them!
   LINDA: (*To* WILLY.) Don't let Biff . . .

   (BEN *laughs lustily.*)

1025 WILLY: You shoulda seen the lumber they brought home
   last week. At least a dozen six-by-tens worth all kinds a
   money.
   CHARLEY: Listen, if that watchman—
   WILLY: I gave them hell, understand. But I got a couple of fearless
1030 characters there.
   CHARLEY: Willy, the jails are full of fearless characters.
   BEN: (*Clapping* WILLY *on the back, with a laugh at* CHARLEY.) And
   the stock exchange, friend!
   WILLY: (*Joining in* BEN's *laughter.*) Where are the rest of your
1035 pants?
   CHARLEY: My wife bought them.
   WILLY: Now all you need is a golf club and you can go upstairs
   and go to sleep. (*To* BEN.) Great athlete! Between him and his
   son Bernard they can't hammer a nail!
1040 BERNARD: (*Rushing in.*) The watchman's chasing Biff!
   WILLY: (*Angrily.*) Shut up! He's not stealing anything!
   LINDA: (*Alarmed, hurrying off left.*) Where is he? Biff, dear! (*She
   exits.*)
   WILLY: (*Moving toward the left, away from* BEN.) There's nothing
1045 wrong. What's the matter with you?
   BEN: Nervy boy. Good!
   WILLY: (*Laughing.*) Oh, nerves of iron, that Biff!
   CHARLEY: Don't know what it is. My New England man comes
   back and he's bleedin', they murdered him up there.
1050 WILLY: It's contacts, Charley, I got important contacts!
   CHARLEY: (*Sarcastically.*) Glad to hear it, Willy. Come in later,
   we'll shoot a little casino. I'll take some of your Portland
   money. (*He laughs at* WILLY *and exits.*)
   WILLY: (*Turning to* BEN.) Business is bad, it's murderous. But not
1055 for me, of course.
   BEN: I'll stop by on my way back to Africa.
   WILLY: (*Longingly.*) Can't you stay a few days? You're just what
   I need, Ben, because I—I have a fine position here, but
   I—well, Dad left when I was such a baby and I never had a
1060 chance to talk to him and I still feel—kind of temporary
   about myself.

   BEN: I'll be late for my train.

   (*They are at opposite ends of the stage.*)

   WILLY: Ben, my boys—can't we talk? They'd go into the jaws of
   hell for me, see, but I—
   BEN: William, you're being first-rate with your boys. Outstanding, 1065
   manly chaps!
   WILLY: (*Hanging on to his words.*) Oh, Ben, that's good to hear!
   Because sometimes I'm afraid that I'm not teaching them the
   right kind of—Ben, how should I teach them?
   BEN: (*Giving great weight to each word, and with a certain vicious* 1070
   audacity.) William, when I walked into the jungle, I was
   seventeen. When I walked out I was twenty-one. And, by
   God, I was rich! (*He goes off into the darkness around the right
   corner of the house.*)
   WILLY: . . . was rich! That's just the spirit I want to imbue 1075
   them with! To walk into a jungle! I was right! I was right!
   I was right!

   (BEN *is gone, but* WILLY *is still speaking to him as* LINDA, *in night-
   gown and robe, enters the kitchen, glances around for* WILLY, *then
   goes to the door of the house, looks out and sees him. Comes down
   to his left. He looks at her.*)

   LINDA: Willy, dear? Willy?
   WILLY: I was right!
   LINDA: Did you have some cheese? (*He can't answer.*) It's very 1080
   late, darling. Come to bed, heh?
   WILLY: (*Looking straight up.*) Gotta break your neck to see a star
   in this yard.
   LINDA: You coming in?
   WILLY: Whatever happened to that diamond watch fob? 1085
   Remember? When Ben came from Africa that time? Didn't
   he give me a watch fob with a diamond in it?
   LINDA: You pawned it, dear. Twelve, thirteen years ago. For Biff's
   radio correspondence course.
   WILLY: Gee, that was a beautiful thing. I'll take a walk. 1090
   LINDA: But you're in your slippers.
   WILLY: (*Starting to go around the house at the left.*) I was right!
   I was! (*Half to* LINDA, *as he goes, shaking his head.*) What a
   man! There was a man worth talking to. I was right!
   LINDA: (*Calling after* WILLY.) But in your slippers, Willy! 1095

   (WILLY *is almost gone when* BIFF, *in his pajamas, comes down the
   stairs an enters the kitchen.*)

   BIFF: What is he doing out there?
   LINDA: Sh!
   BIFF: God Almighty, Mom, how long has he been doing this?
   LINDA: Don't, he'll hear you.
   BIFF: What the hell is the matter with him? 1100
   LINDA: It'll pass by morning.
   BIFF: Shouldn't we do anything?
   LINDA: Oh, my dear, you should do a lot of things, but there's
   nothing to do, so go to sleep.

   (HAPPY *comes down the stair and sits on the steps.*)

   HAPPY: I never heard him so loud, Mom. 1105
   LINDA: Well, come around more often; you'll hear him. (*She sits
   down at the table and mends the lining of* WILLY's *jacket.*)

BIFF: Why didn't you ever write me about this, Mom?

LINDA: How would I write to you? For over three months you
1110   had no address.

BIFF: I was on the move. But you know I thought of you all the
time. You know that, don't you, pal?

LINDA: I know, dear, I know. But he likes to have a letter. Just to
know that there's still a possibility for better things.

1115 BIFF: He's not like this all the time, is he?

LINDA: It's when you come home he's always the worst.

BIFF: When I come home?

LINDA: When you write you're coming, he's all smiles, and talks
about the future, and—he's just wonderful. And then the
1120   closer you seem to come, the more shaky he gets, and then,
by the time you get here, he's arguing, and he seems angry at
you. I think it's just that maybe he can't bring himself to—to
open up to you. Why are you so hateful to each other? Why is
that?

1125 BIFF: (Evasively.) I'm not hateful, Mom.

LINDA: But you no sooner come in the door than you're
fighting!

BIFF: I don't know why. I mean to change. I'm tryin', Mom, you
understand?

1130 LINDA: Are you home to stay now?

BIFF: I don't know. I want to look around, see what's doin'.

LINDA: Biff, you can't look around all your life, can you?

BIFF: I just can't take hold, Mom. I can't take hold of some kind
of a life.

1135 LINDA: Biff, a man is not a bird, to come and go with the
springtime.

BIFF: Your hair . . . (He touches her hair.) Your hair got so gray.

LINDA: Oh, it's been gray since you were in high school. I just
stopped dyeing it, that's all.

1140 BIFF: Dye it again, will ya? I don't want my pal looking old.
(He smiles.)

LINDA: You're such a boy! You think you can go away for a
year and . . . You've got to get it into your head now that
one day you'll knock on this door and there'll be strange
1145   people here—

BIFF: What are you talking about? You're not even sixty,
Mom.

LINDA: But what about your father?

BIFF: (Lamely.) Well, I meant him too.

1150 HAPPY: He admires Pop.

LINDA: Biff, dear, if you don't have any feeling for him, then you
can't have any feeling for me.

BIFF: Sure I can, Mom.

LINDA: No. You can't just come to see me, because I love
1155   him. (With a threat, but only a threat, of tears.) He's the
dearest man in the world to me, and I won't have anyone
making him feel unwanted and low and blue. You've
got to make up your mind now, darling, there's no leeway
any more. Either he's your father and you pay him that
1160   respect, or else you're not to come here. I know he's not
easy to get along with—nobody knows that better than
me—but . . .

WILLY: (From the left, with a laugh.) Hey, hey, Biffo!

BIFF: (Starting to go out after WILLY.) What the hell is the matter
1165   with him? (HAPPY stops him.)

LINDA: Don't—don't go near him!

BIFF: Stop making excuses for him! He always, always wiped
the floor with you. Never had an ounce of respect for
you.

HAPPY: He's always had respect for—   1170

BIFF: What the hell do you know about it?

HAPPY: (Surlily.) Just don't call him crazy!

BIFF: He's got no character—Charley wouldn't do this. Not in his
own house—spewing out that vomit from his mind.

HAPPY: Charley never had to cope with what he's got to.   1175

BIFF: People are worse off than Willy Loman. Believe me, I've
seen them!

LINDA: Then make Charley your father, Biff. You can't do that,
can you? I don't say he's a great man. Willy Loman never
made a lot of money. His name was never in the paper. He's   1180
not the finest character that ever lived. But he's a human
being, and a terrible thing is happening to him. So attention
must be paid. He's not to be allowed to fall into his grave like
an old dog. Attention, attention must finally be paid to such a
person. You called him crazy—   1185

BIFF: I didn't mean—

LINDA: No, a lot of people think he's lost his—balance. But you
don't have to be very smart to know what his trouble is. The
man is exhausted.

HAPPY: Sure!   1190

LINDA: A small man can be just as exhausted as a great man. He
works for a company thirty-six years this March, opens up
unheard-of territories to their trademark, and now in his old
age they take his salary away.

HAPPY: (Indignantly.) I didn't know that, Mom.   1195

LINDA: You never asked, my dear! Now that you get your
spending money someplace else you don't trouble your mind
with him.

HAPPY: But I gave you money last—

LINDA: Christmas time, fifty dollars! To fix the hot water it   1200
cost ninety-seven fifty! For five weeks he's been on straight
commission, like a beginner, an unknown!

BIFF: Those ungrateful bastards!

LINDA: Are they any worse than his sons? When he brought them
business, when he was young, they were glad to see him. But   1205
now his old friends, the old buyers that loved him so and
always found some order to hand him in a pinch—they're
all dead, retired. He used to be able to make six, seven calls
a day in Boston. Now he takes his valises out of the car and
puts them back and takes them out again and he's exhausted.   1210
Instead of walking he talks now. He drives seven hundred
miles, and when he gets there no one knows him any more,
no one welcomes him. And what goes through a man's mind,
driving seven hundred miles home without having earned a
cent? Why shouldn't he talk to himself? Why? When he has   1215
to go to Charley and borrow fifty dollars a week and pretend
to me that it's his pay? How long can that go on? How long?
You see what I'm sitting here and waiting for? And you tell
me he has no character? The man who never worked a day
but for your benefit? When does he get the medal for that?   1220
Is this his reward—to turn around at the age of sixty-three
and find his sons, who he loved better than his life, one a
philandering bum—

HAPPY: Mom!

LINDA: That's all you are, my baby! (To BIFF.) And you! What   1225
happened to the love you had for him? You were such pals!
How you used to talk to him on the phone every night! How
lonely he was till he could come home to you!

BIFF: All right, Mom. I'll live here in my room, and I'll get a
job. I'll keep away from him, that's all.   1230

LINDA: No, Biff. You can't stay here and fight all the time.

BIFF: He threw me out of this house, remember that.

LINDA: Why did he do that? I never knew why.

1235 BIFF: Because I know he's a fake and he doesn't like anybody around who knows!

LINDA: Why a fake? In what way? What do you mean?

BIFF: Just don't lay it all at my feet. It's between me and him—that's all I have to say. I'll chip in from now on. He'll settle for half my pay check. He'll be all right. I'm going to bed.

1240 (*He starts for the stairs.*)

LINDA: He won't be all right.

BIFF: (*Turning on the stairs, furiously.*) I hate this city and I'll stay here. Now what do you want?

LINDA: He's dying, Biff.

(HAPPY *turns quickly to her, shocked.*)

1245 BIFF: (*After a pause.*) Why is he dying?

LINDA: He's been trying to kill himself.

BIFF: (*With great horror.*) How?

LINDA: I live from day to day.

BIFF: What're you talking about?

1250 LINDA: Remember I wrote you that he smashed up the car again? In February?

BIFF: Well?

LINDA: The insurance inspector came. He said that they have evidence. That all these accidents in the last

1255 year—weren't—weren't—accidents.

HAPPY: How can they tell that? That's a lie.

LINDA: It seems there's a woman . . . (*She takes a breath as*

⎰ BIFF: (*Sharply but contained.*) What woman?

⎱ LINDA: (*Simultaneously.*) . . . and this woman . . .

1260 LINDA: What?

BIFF: Nothing. Go ahead.

LINDA: What did you say?

BIFF: Nothing. I just said what woman?

HAPPY: What about her?

1265 LINDA: Well, it seems she was walking down the road and saw his car. She says that he wasn't driving fast at all, and that he didn't skid. She says he came to that little bridge, and then deliberately smashed into the railing, and it was only the shallowness of the water that saved him.

1270 BIFF: Oh, no, he probably just fell asleep again.

LINDA: I don't think he fell asleep.

BIFF: Why not?

LINDA: Last month . . . (*With great difficulty.*) Oh, boys, it's so hard to say a thing like this! He's just a big stupid man to you,

1275 but I tell you there's more good in him than in many other people. (*She chokes, wipes her eyes.*) I was looking for a fuse. The lights blew out, and I went down the cellar. And behind the fuse box—it happened to fall out—was a length of rubber pipe—just short.

1280 HAPPY: No kidding?

LINDA: There's a little attachment on the end of it. I knew right away. And sure enough, on the bottom of the water heater there's a new little nipple on the gas pipe.

HAPPY: (*Angrily.*) That—jerk.

1285 BIFF: Did you have it taken off?

LINDA: I'm—I'm ashamed to. How can I mention it to him? Every day I go down and take away that little rubber pipe. But, when he comes home, I put it back where it was. How can I insult him that way? I don't know what to do. I live

1290 from day to day, boys. I tell you, I know every thought in

his mind. It sounds so old-fashioned and silly, but I tell you he put his whole life into you and you've turned your backs on him. (*She is bent over in the chair, weeping, her face in her hands.*) Biff, I swear to God! Biff, his life is in

1295 your hands!

HAPPY: (*To* BIFF.) How do you like that damned fool!

BIFF: (*Kissing her.*) All right, pal, all right. It's all settled now. I've been remiss. I know that, Mom. But now I'll stay, and I swear to you, I'll apply myself. (*Kneeling in front of her, in a fever of self-reproach.*) It's just—you see, Mom, I don't fit in business.

1300 Not that I won't try. I'll try, and I'll make good.

HAPPY: Sure you will. The trouble with you in business was you never tried to please people.

BIFF: I know, I—

HAPPY: Like when you worked for Harrison's. Bob Harrison

1305 said you were tops, and then you go and do some damn fool thing like whistling whole songs in the elevator like a comedian.

BIFF: (*Against* HAPPY.) So what? I like to whistle sometimes.

HAPPY: You don't raise a guy to a responsible job who whistles

1310 in the elevator!

LINDA: Well, don't argue about it now.

HAPPY: Like when you'd go off and swim in the middle of the day instead of taking the line around.

BIFF: (*His resentment rising.*) Well, don't you run off? You take

1315 off sometimes, don't you? On a nice summer day?

HAPPY: Yeah, but I cover myself!

LINDA: Boys!

HAPPY: If I'm going to take a fade the boss can call any number where I'm supposed to be and they'll swear to him that I just

1320 left. I'll tell you something that I hate to say, Biff, but in the business world some of them think you're crazy.

BIFF: (*Angered.*) Screw the business world!

HAPPY: All right, screw it! Great, but cover yourself!

LINDA: Hap, Hap!

1325 BIFF: I don't care what they think! They've laughed at Dad for years, and you know why? Because we don't belong in this nuthouse of a city! We should be mixing cement on some open plain, or—or carpenters. A carpenter is allowed to whistle!

1330

(WILLY *walks in from the entrance of the house, at left.*)

WILLY: Even your grandfather was better than a carpenter. (*Pause. They watch him.*) You never grew up. Bernard does not whistle in the elevator, I assure you.

BIFF: (*As though to laugh* WILLY *out of it.*) Yeah, but you do, Pop.

WILLY: I never in my life whistled in an elevator! And who in the 1335 business world thinks I'm crazy?

BIFF: I didn't mean it like that, Pop. Now don't make a whole thing out of it, will ya?

WILLY: Go back to the West! Be a carpenter, a cowboy, enjoy yourself! 1340

LINDA: Willy, he was just saying—

WILLY: I heard what he said!

HAPPY: (*Trying to quiet* WILLY.) Hey, Pop, come on now . . .

WILLY: (*Continuing over* HAPPY's *line.*) They laugh at me, heh? Go to Filene's, go to the Hub, go to Slattery's, Boston. Call 1345 out the name Willy Loman and see what happens! Big shot!

BIFF: All right, Pop.

WILLY: Big!

1350 BIFF: All right!

WILLY: Why do you always insult me?

BIFF: I didn't say a word. (*To* LINDA.) Did I say a word?

LINDA: He didn't say anything, Willy.

WILLY: (*Going to the doorway of the living-room.*) All right, good
1355   night, good night.

LINDA: Willy, dear, he just decided . . .

WILLY: (*To* BIFF.) If you get tired hanging around tomorrow,
    paint the ceiling I put up in the living-room.

BIFF: I'm leaving early tomorrow.

1360 HAPPY: He's going to see Bill Oliver, Pop.

WILLY: (*Interestedly.*) Oliver? For what?

BIFF: (*With reserve, but trying, trying.*) He always said he'd stake
    me. I'd like to go into business, so maybe I can take him up
    on it.

1365 LINDA: Isn't that wonderful?

WILLY: Don't interrupt. What's wonderful about it? There's fifty
    men in the City of New York who'd stake him. (*To* BIFF.)
    Sporting goods?

BIFF: I guess so. I know something about it and—

1370 WILLY: He knows something about it! You know sporting goods
    better than Spalding, for God's sake! How much he giving
    you?

BIFF: I don't know, I didn't even see him yet, but—

WILLY: Then what're you talkin' about?

1375 BIFF: (*Getting angry.*) Well, all I said was I'm gonna see him,
    that's all!

WILLY: (*Turning away.*) Ah, you're counting your chickens
    again.

BIFF: (*Starting left for the stairs.*) Oh, Jesus, I'm going to sleep!

1380 WILLY: (*Calling after him.*) Don't curse in this house!

BIFF: (*Turning.*) Since when did you get so clean?

HAPPY: (*Trying to stop them.*) Wait a . . .

WILLY: Don't use that language to me! I won't have it!

HAPPY: (*Grabbing* BIFF, *shouts.*) Wait a minute! I got an idea. I
1385   got a feasible idea. Come here, Biff, let's talk this over now,
    let's talk some sense here. When I was down in Florida last
    time, I thought of a great idea to sell sporting goods. It just
    came back to me. You and I, Biff—we have a line, the Loman
    Line. We train a couple of weeks, and put on a couple of
1390   exhibitions, see?

WILLY: That's an idea!

HAPPY: Wait! We form two basketball teams, see? Two water-polo
    teams. We play each other. It's a million dollars' worth of
    publicity. Two brothers, see? The Loman Brothers. Displays
1395   in the Royal Palms—all the hotels. And banners over the ring
    and the basketball court: "Loman Brothers." Baby, we could
    sell sporting goods!

WILLY: That is a one-million-dollar idea!

LINDA: Marvelous!

1400 BIFF: I'm in great shape as far as that's concerned.

HAPPY: And the beauty of it is, Biff, it wouldn't be like a business.
    We'd be out playin' ball again.

BIFF: (*Enthused.*) Yeah, that's . . .

WILLY: Million-dollar . . .

1405 HAPPY: And you wouldn't get fed up with it, Biff. It'd be the
    family again. There'd be the old honor, and comradeship,
    and if you wanted to go off for a swim or somethin'—well,
    you'd do it! Without some smart cooky gettin' up ahead
    of you!

1410 WILLY: Lick the world! You guys together could absolutely lick
    the civilized world.

BIFF: I'll see Oliver tomorrow. Hap, if we could work that
    out . . .

LINDA: Maybe things are beginning to—

WILLY: (*Wildly enthused, to* LINDA.) Stop interrupting! (*To* BIFF.) 1415
    But don't wear sport jacket and slacks when you see Oliver.

BIFF: No, I'll—

WILLY: A business suit, and talk as little as possible, and don't
    crack any jokes.

BIFF: He did like me. Always liked me. 1420

LINDA: He loved you!

WILLY: (*To* LINDA.) Will you stop! (*To* BIFF.) Walk in very serious.
    You are not applying for a boy's job. Money is to pass. Be
    quiet, fine, and serious. Everybody likes a kidder, but nobody
    lends him money. 1425

HAPPY: I'll try to get some myself, Biff. I'm sure I can.

WILLY: I see great things for you kids, I think your troubles are
    over. But remember, start big and you'll end big. Ask for
    fifteen. How much you gonna ask for?

BIFF: Gee, I don't know— 1430

WILLY: And don't say "Gee." "Gee" is a boy's word. A man
    walking in for fifteen thousand dollars does not say "Gee!"

BIFF: Ten, I think, would be top though.

WILLY: Don't be so modest. You always started too low. Walk
    in with a big laugh. Don't look worried. Start off with a 1435
    couple of your good stories to lighten things up. It's not
    what you say, it's how you say it—because personality
    always wins the day.

LINDA: Oliver always thought the highest of him—

WILLY: Will you let me talk? 1440

BIFF: Don't yell at her, Pop, will ya?

WILLY: (*Angrily.*) I was talking, wasn't I?

BIFF: I don't like you yelling at her all the time, and I'm tellin'
    you, that's all.

WILLY: What're you, takin' over this house? 1445

LINDA: Willy—

WILLY: (*Turning on her.*) Don't take his side all the time,
    goddammit!

BIFF: (*Furiously.*) Stop yelling at her!

WILLY: (*Suddenly pulling on his cheek, beaten down, guilt ridden.*) 1450
    Give my best to Bill Oliver—he may remember me. (*He exits
    through the living-room doorway.*)

LINDA: (*Her voice subdued.*) What'd you have to start that for?
    (BIFF *turns away.*) You see how sweet he was as soon as you
    talked hopefully? (*She goes over to* BIFF.) Come up and say 1455
    good night to him. Don't let him go to bed that way.

HAPPY: Come on, Biff, let's buck him up.

LINDA: Please, dear. Just say good night. It takes so little to make
    him happy. Come. (*She goes through the living-room doorway,
    calling upstairs from within the living-room.*) Your pajamas are 1460
    hanging in the bathroom, Willy!

HAPPY: (*Looking toward where* LINDA *went out.*) What a woman!
    They broke the mold when they made her. You know that,
    Biff?

BIFF: He's off salary. My God, working on commission! 1465

HAPPY: Well, let's face it: he's no hot-shot selling man. Except that
    sometimes, you have to admit, he's a sweet personality.

BIFF: (*Deciding.*) Lend me ten bucks, will ya? I want to buy some
    new ties.

HAPPY: I'll take you to a place I know. Beautiful stuff. Wear one of 1470
    my striped shirts tomorrow.

BIFF: She got gray. Mom got awful old. Gee, I'm gonna go in to
    Oliver tomorrow and knock him for a—

HAPPY: Come on up. Tell that to Dad. Let's give him a whirl.
1475   Come on.

BIFF: (*Steamed up.*) You know, with ten thousand bucks, boy!

HAPPY: (*As they go into the living-room.*) That's the talk, Biff, that's the first time I've heard the old confidence out of you! (*From within the living-room, fading off.*) You gonna live with
1480   me, kid, and any babe you want just say the word . . . (*The last lines are hardly heard. They are mounting the stairs to their parents' bedroom.*)

LINDA: (*Entering her bedroom and addressing* WILLY, *who is in the bathroom. She is straightening the bed for him.*) Can you do
1485   anything about the shower? It drips.

WILLY: (*From the bathroom.*) All of a sudden everything falls to pieces! Goddam plumbing, oughta be sued, those people. I hardly finished putting it in and the thing . . . (*His words rumble off.*)

1490 LINDA: I'm just wondering if Oliver will remember him. You think he might?

WILLY: (*Coming out of the bathroom in his pajamas.*) Remember him? What's the matter with you, you crazy? If he'd've stayed with Oliver he'd be on top by now! Wait'll Oliver gets a look
1495   at him. You don't know the average caliber any more. The average young man today—(*He is getting into bed.*)—is got a caliber of zero. Greatest thing in the world for him was to bum around.

(BIFF *and* HAPPY *enter the bedroom. Slight pause.*)

WILLY: (*Stops short, looking at* BIFF.) Glad to hear it, boy.
1500 HAPPY: He wanted to say good night to you, sport.

WILLY: (*To* BIFF.) Yeah. Knock him dead, boy. What'd you want to tell me?

BIFF: Just take it easy, Pop. Good night. (*He turns to go.*)

WILLY: (*Unable to resist.*) And if anything falls off the desk while
1505   you're talking to him—like a package or something—don't you pick it up. They have office boys for that.

LINDA: I'll make a big breakfast—

WILLY: Will you let me finish? (*To* BIFF.) Tell him you were in the business in the West. Not farm work.

1510 BIFF: All right, Dad.

LINDA: I think everything—

WILLY: (*Going right through her speech.*) And don't undersell yourself. No less than fifteen thousand dollars.

BIFF: (*Unable to bear him.*) Okay. Good night, Mom. (*He starts
1515   moving.*)

WILLY: Because you got a greatness in you, Biff, remember that. You got all kinds a greatness . . . (*He lies back, exhausted.* BIFF *walks out.*)

LINDA: (*Calling after* BIFF.) Sleep well, darling!

1520 HAPPY: I'm gonna get married, Mom. I wanted to tell you.

LINDA: Go to sleep, dear.

HAPPY: (*Going.*) I just wanted to tell you.

WILLY: Keep up the good work. (HAPPY *exits.*) God . . . remember that Ebbets Field game? The championship
1525   of the city?

LINDA: Just rest. Should I sing to you?

WILLY: Yeah. Sing to me. (LINDA *hums a soft lullaby.*) When that team came out—he was the tallest, remember?

LINDA: Oh, yes. And in gold.

(BIFF *enters the darkened kitchen, takes a cigarette, and leaves the house. He comes downstage into a golden pool of light. He smokes, staring at the night.*)

WILLY: Like a young god. Hercules—something like that. And
1530   the sun, the sun all around him. Remember how he waved to me? Right up from the field, with the representatives of three colleges standing by? And the buyers I brought, and the cheers when he came out—Loman, Loman, Loman! God Almighty, he'll be great yet. A star like that, magnificent, can
1535   never really fade away!

(*The light on* WILLY *is fading. The gas heater begins to glow through the kitchen wall, near the stairs, a blue flame beneath red coils.*)

LINDA: (*Timidly.*) Willy dear, what has he got against you?

WILLY: I'm so tired. Don't talk any more.

(BIFF *slowly returns to the kitchen. He stops, stares toward the heater.*)

LINDA: Will you ask Howard to let you work in New York?

WILLY: First thing in the morning. Everything'll be all right.   1540

(BIFF *reaches behind the heater and draws out a length of rubber tubing. He is horrified and turns his head toward* WILLY's *room, still dimly lit, from which the strains of* LINDA's *desperate but monotonous humming rise.*)

WILLY: (*Staring through the window into the moonlight.*) Gee, look at the moon moving between the buildings!

(BIFF *wraps the tubing around his hand and quickly goes up the stairs.*)

(*Curtain.*)

ACT TWO

Music is heard, gay and bright. The curtain rises as the music fades away. WILLY, *in shirt sleeves, is sitting at the kitchen table, sipping coffee, his hat in his lap.* LINDA *is filling his cup when she can.*

WILLY: Wonderful coffee. Meal in itself.

LINDA: Can I make you some eggs?

WILLY: No. Take a breath.

LINDA: You look so rested, dear.

WILLY: I slept like a dead one. First time in months. Image,   5
sleeping till ten on a Tuesday morning. Boys left nice and early, heh?

LINDA: They were out of here by eight o'clock.

WILLY: Good work!

LINDA: It was so thrilling to see them leaving together. I can't   10
get over the shaving lotion in this house!

WILLY: (*Smiling.*) Mmm—

LINDA: Biff was very changed this morning. His whole attitude seemed to be hopeful. He couldn't wait to get downtown to see Oliver.   15

WILLY: He's heading for a change. There's no question, there simply are certain men that take longer to get—solidified. How did he dress?

LINDA: His blue suit. He's so handsome in that suit. He could be a—anything in that suit!   20

(WILLY *gets up from the table.* LINDA *holds his jacket for him.*)

WILLY: There's no question, no question at all. Gee, on the way home tonight I'd like to buy some seeds.

LINDA: (*Laughing.*) That'd be wonderful. But not enough sun gets back there. Nothing'll grow any more.

25 WILLY: You wait, kid, before it's all over we're gonna get a little place out in the country, and I'll raise some vegetables, a couple of chickens . . .

LINDA: You'll do it yet, dear.

(WILLY *walks out of his jacket.* LINDA *follows him.*)

WILLY: And they'll get married, and come for a weekend. I'd
30   build a little guest house. 'Cause I got so many fine tools, all I'd need would be a little lumber and some peace of mind.

LINDA: (*Joyfully.*) I sewed the lining . . .

WILLY: I could build two guest houses, so they'd both come.
35   Did he decide how much he's going to ask Oliver for?

LINDA: (*Getting him into the jacket.*) He didn't mention it, but I imagine ten or fifteen thousand. You going to talk to Howard today?

WILLY: Yeah. I'll put it to him straight and simple. He'll just have
40   to take me off the road.

LINDA: And Willy, don't forget to ask for a little advance, because we've got the insurance premium. It's the grace period now.

WILLY: That's a hundred . . . ?

45 LINDA: A hundred and eight, sixty-eight. Because we're a little short again.

WILLY: Why are we short?

LINDA: Well, you had the motor job on the car . . .

WILLY: That goddam Studebaker!

50 LINDA: And you got one more payment on the refrigerator . . .

WILLY: But it just broke again!

LINDA: Well, it's old, dear.

WILLY: I told you we should've bought a well-advertised machine. Charley bought a General Electric and it's twenty years old
55   and it's still good, that son-of-a-bitch.

LINDA: But, Willy—

WILLY: Whoever heard of a Hastings refrigerator? Once in my life I would like to own something outright before it's broken! I'm always in a race with the junkyard! I just
60   finished paying for the car and it's on its last legs. The refrigerator consumes belts like a goddam maniac. They time those things. They time them so when you finally paid for them, they're used up.

LINDA: (*Buttoning up his jacket as he unbuttons it.*) All told,
65   about two hundred dollars would carry us, dear. But that includes the last payment on the mortgage. After this payment, Willy, the house belongs to us.

WILLY: It's twenty-five years!

LINDA: Biff was nine years old when we bought it.

70 WILLY: Well, that's a great thing. To weather a twenty-five year mortgage is—

LINDA: It's an accomplishment.

WILLY: All the cement, the lumber, the reconstruction I put in this house! There ain't a crack to be found in it any
75   more.

LINDA: Well, it served its purpose.

WILLY: What purpose? Some stranger'll come along, move in, and that's that. If only Biff would take this house, and raise a family . . . (*He starts to go.*) Good-by, I'm late.

80 LINDA: (*Suddenly remembering.*) Oh, I forgot! You're supposed to meet them for dinner.

WILLY: Me?

LINDA: At Frank's Chop House on Forty-eighth near Sixth Avenue.

WILLY: Is that so! How about you?   85

LINDA: No, just the three of you. They're gonna blow you to a big meal!

WILLY: Don't say! Who thought of that?

LINDA: Biff came to me this morning, Willy, and he said, "Tell Dad, we want to blow him to a big meal." Be there six o'clock.   90
You and your two boys are going to have dinner.

WILLY: Gee whiz! That's really somethin'. I'm gonna knock Howard for a loop, kid. I'll get an advance, and I'll come home with a New York job. Goddammit, now I'm gonna do it!   95

LINDA: Oh, that's the spirit, Willy!

WILLY: I will never get behind a wheel the rest of my life!

LINDA: It's changing, Willy, I can feel it changing!

WILLY: Beyond a question. G'by, I'm late. (*He starts to go again.*)   100

LINDA: (*Calling after him as she runs to the kitchen table for a handkerchief.*) You got your glasses?

WILLY: (*Feels for them, then comes back in.*) Yeah, yeah, got my glasses.

LINDA: (*Giving him the handkerchief.*) And a handkerchief.   105

WILLY: Yeah, handkerchief.

LINDA: And your saccharine?

WILLY: Yeah, my saccharine.

LINDA: Be careful on the subway stairs.

(*She kisses him, and a silk stocking is seen hanging from her hand.* WILLY *notices it.*)

WILLY: Will you stop mending stockings? At least while   110
I'm in the house. It gets me nervous. I can't tell you.
Please.

(LINDA *hides the stocking in her hand as she follows* WILLY *across the forestage in front of the house.*)

LINDA: Remember, Frank's Chop House.

WILLY: (*Passing the apron.*) Maybe beets would grow out there.   115

LINDA: (*Laughing.*) But you tried so many times.

WILLY: Yeah. Well, don't work hard today. (*He disappears around the right corner of the house.*)

LINDA: Be careful!

(*As* WILLY *vanishes,* LINDA *waves to him. Suddenly the phone rings. She runs across the stage and into the kitchen and lifts it.*)

LINDA: Hello? Oh, Biff! I'm so glad you called, I just . . . Yes,   120
sure, I just told him. Yes, he'll be there for dinner at six o'clock, I didn't forget. Listen, I was just dying to tell you. You know that little rubber pipe I told you about? That he connected to the gas heater? I finally decided to go down the cellar this morning and take it away and destroy   125
it. But it's gone! Imagine? He took it away himself, it isn't there! (*She listens.*) When? Oh, then you took it. Oh—nothing, it's just that I'd hoped he'd taken it away himself. Oh, I'm not worried, darling, because this morning he left in such high spirits, it was like the old days! I'm   130
not afraid any more. Did Mr. Oliver see you? . . . Well,

you wait there then. And make a nice impression on him, darling. Just don't perspire too much before you see him. And have a nice time with Dad. He may have big news

135   too! . . . That's right, a New York job. And be sweet to him tonight, dear. Be loving to him. Because he's only a little boat looking for a harbor. (*She is trembling with sorrow and joy.*) Oh, that's wonderful, Biff, you'll save his life. Thanks, darling. Just put your arm around him

140   when he comes into the restaurant. Give him a smile. That's the boy . . . Good-by, dear, . . . You got your comb? . . . That's fine. Good-by, Biff dear.

(*In the middle of her speech,* HOWARD WAGNER, *thirty-six, wheels on a small typewriter table on which is a wire-recording machine and proceeds to plug it in. This is on the left forestage. Light slowly fades on* LINDA *as it rises on* HOWARD. HOWARD *is intent on threading the machine and only glances over his shoulder as* WILLY *appears.*)

WILLY: Pst! Pst!

HOWARD: Hello, Willy, come in.

145   WILLY: Like to have a little talk with you, Howard.

HOWARD: Sorry to keep you waiting. I'll be with you in a minute.

WILLY: What's that, Howard?

HOWARD: Didn't you ever see one of these? Wire recorder.

150   WILLY: Oh. Can we talk a minute?

HOWARD: Records things. Just got delivery yesterday. Been driving me crazy, the most terrific machine I ever saw in my life. I was up all night with it.

WILLY: What do you do with it.

155   HOWARD: I bought it for dictation, but you can do anything with it. Listen to this. I had it home last night. Listen to what I picked up. The first one is my daughter. Get this. (*He flicks the switch and "Roll out the Barrel" is heard being whistled.*) Listen to that kid whistle.

160   WILLY: That is lifelike, isn't it?

HOWARD: Seven years old. Get that tone.

WILLY: Ts, ts. Like to ask a little favor if you . . .

(*The whistling breaks off, and the voice of* HOWARD's *daughter is heard.*)

HIS DAUGHTER: "Now you, Daddy."

HOWARD: She's crazy for me! (*Again the same song is whistled.*)

165   That's me! Ha! (*He winks.*)

WILLY: You're very good!

(*The whistling breaks off again. The machine runs silent a moment.*)

HOWARD: Sh! Get this now, this is my son.

HIS SON: "The capital of Alabama is Montgomery; the capital of Arizona is Phoenix; the capital of Arkansas is Little

170   Rock; the capital of California is Sacramento . . . (*And on, and on.*)

HOWARD: (*Holding up five fingers.*) Five years old, Willy!

WILLY: He'll make an announcer some day!

HIS SON: (*Continuing.*) "The capital . . ."

175   HOWARD: Get that—alphabetical order! (*The machine breaks off suddenly.*) Wait a minute. The maid kicked the plug out.

WILLY: It certainly is a—

HOWARD: Sh, for God's sake!

HIS SON: "It's nine o'clock, Bulova watch time. So I have to

180   go to sleep."

WILLY: That really is—

HOWARD: Wait a minute! The next is my wife.

(*They wait.*)

HOWARD'S VOICE: "Go on, say something." (*Pause.*) "Well, you gonna talk?"

185   HIS WIFE: "I can't think of anything."

HOWARD'S VOICE: "Well, talk—it's turning."

HIS WIFE: (*Shyly, beaten.*) "Hello." (*Silence.*) "Oh, Howard, I can't talk into this . . ."

HOWARD: (*Snapping the machine off.*) That was my wife.

190   WILLY: That is a wonderful machine. Can we—

HOWARD: I tell you, Willy, I'm gonna take my camera, and my bandsaw, and all my hobbies, and out they go. This is the most fascinating relaxation I ever found.

WILLY: I think I'll get one myself.

195   HOWARD: Sure, they're only a hundred and a half. You can't do without it. Supposing you wanna hear Jack Benny, see? But you can't be at home at that hour. So you tell the maid to turn the radio on when Jack Benny comes on, and this automatically goes on with the radio . . .

200   WILLY: And when you come home you . . .

HOWARD: You can come home twelve o'clock, one o'clock, any time you like, and you get yourself a Coke and sit yourself down, throw the switch, and there's Jack Benny's program in the middle of the night!

205   WILLY: I'm definitely going to get one. Because lots of time I'm on the road, and I think to myself, what I must be missing on the radio!

HOWARD: Don't you have a radio in the car?

WILLY: Well, yeah, but who ever thinks of turning it on?

HOWARD: Say, aren't you supposed to be in Boston?

210   WILLY: That's what I want to talk to you about, Howard. You got a minute? (*He draws a chair in from the wing.*)

HOWARD: What happened? What're you doing here?

WILLY: Well . . .

HOWARD: You didn't crack up again, did you?

215   WILLY: Oh, no. No . . .

HOWARD: Geez, you had me worried there for a minute. What's the trouble?

WILLY: Well, tell you the truth, Howard. I've come to the decision that I'd rather not travel any more.

220   HOWARD: Not travel! Well, what'll you do?

WILLY: Remember, Christmas time, when you had the party here? You said you'd try to think of some spot for me here in town.

HOWARD: With us?

225   WILLY: Well, sure.

HOWARD: Oh, yeah, yeah. I remember. Well, I couldn't think of anything for you, Willy.

WILLY: I tell ya, Howard. The kids are all grown up, y'know. I don't need much any more. If I could take home—well,

230   sixty-five dollars a week, I could swing it.

HOWARD: Yeah, but Willy, see I—

WILLY: I tell ya why, Howard. Speaking frankly and between the two of us, y'know—I'm just a little tired.

HOWARD: Oh, I could understand that, Willy. But you're a road

235   man, Willy, and we do a road business. We've only got a half-dozen salesmen on the floor here.

WILLY: God knows, Howard, I never asked a favor of any man. But I was with the firm when your father used to carry you
240   in here in his arms.

HOWARD: I know that, Willy, but—

WILLY: Your father came to me the day you were born and asked me what I thought of the name of Howard, may he rest in peace.

245 HOWARD: I appreciate that, Willy, but there just is no spot here for you. If I had a spot I'd slam you right in, but I just don't have a single solitary spot.

(*He looks for his lighter.* WILLY *has picked it up and gives it to him. Pause.*)

WILLY: (*With increasing anger.*) Howard, all I need to set my table is fifty dollars a week.

250 HOWARD: But where am I going to put you, kid?

WILLY: Look, it isn't a question of whether I can sell merchandise, is it?

HOWARD: No, but it's a business, kid, and everybody's gotta pull his own weight.

255 WILLY: (*Desperately.*) Just let me tell you a story, Howard—

HOWARD: 'Cause you gotta admit, business is business.

WILLY: (*Angrily.*) Business is definitely business, but just listen for a minute. You don't understand this. When I was a boy—eighteen, nineteen—I was already on the road. And
260   there was a question in my mind as to whether selling had a future for me. Because in those days I had a yearning to go to Alaska. See, there were three gold strikes in one month in Alaska, and I felt like going out. Just for the ride you might say.

265 HOWARD: (*Barely interested.*) Don't say.

WILLY: Oh, yeah, my father lived many years in Alaska. He was an adventurous man. We've got quite a little streak of self-reliance in our family. I thought I'd go out with my older brother and try to locate him, and maybe settle in the
270   North with the old man. And I was almost decided to go, when I met a salesman in the Parker House. His name was Dave Singleman. And he was eighty-four years old, and he'd drummed merchandise in thirty-one states. And old Dave, he'd go up to his room, y'understand, put on his green velvet
275   slippers—I'll never forget—and pick up his phone and call the buyers, and without ever leaving his room, at the age of eighty-four, he made his living. And when I saw that, I realized that selling was the greatest career a man could want. 'Cause what could be more satisfying than to be able
280   to go, at the age of eighty-four, into twenty or thirty different cities, and pick up a phone, and be remembered and loved and helped by so many different people? Do you know? when he died—and by the way he died the death of a salesman, in his green velvet slippers in the smoker of the New York,
285   New Haven and Hartford, going into Boston—when he died, hundreds of salesmen and buyers were at his funeral. Things were sad on a lotta trains for months after that. (*He stands up.* HOWARD *has not looked at him.*) In those days there was personality in it, Howard. There was respect,
290   and comradeship, and gratitude in it. Today, it's all cut and dried, and there's no chance for bringing friendship to bear—or personality. You see what I mean? They don't know me any more.

HOWARD: (*Moving away, to the right.*) That's just the thing,
295   Willy.

WILLY: If I had forty dollars a week—that's all I'd need. Forty dollars, Howard.

HOWARD: Kid, I can't take blood from a stone, I—

WILLY: (*Desperation is on him now.*) Howard, the year Al Smith
300   was nominated, your father came to me and—

HOWARD: (*Starting to go off.*) I've got to see some people, kid.

WILLY: (*Stopping him.*) I'm talking about your father! There were promises made across this desk! You mustn't tell me you've got people to see—I put thirty-four years into this firm,
305   Howard, and now I can't pay my insurance! You can't eat the orange and throw the peel away—a man is not a piece of fruit! (*After a pause.*) Now pay attention. Your father—in 1928 I had a big year. I averaged a hundred and seventy dollars a week in commissions.

310 HOWARD: (*Impatiently.*) Now, Willy, you never averaged—

WILLY: (*Banging his hand on the desk.*) I averaged a hundred and seventy dollars a week in the year of 1928! And your father came to me—or rather, I was in the office here—it was right over this desk—and he put his hand on my
315   shoulder—

HOWARD: (*Getting up.*) You'll have to excuse me, Willy, I gotta see some people. Pull yourself together. (*Going out.*) I'll be back in a little while.

(*On* HOWARD's *exit, the light on his chair grows very bright and strange.*)

WILLY: Pull myself together! What the hell did I say to him? My God, I was yelling at him! How could I! (WILLY *breaks off,*
320   *staring at the light, which occupies the chair, animating it. He approaches this chair, standing across the desk from it.*) Frank, Frank, don't you remember what you told me that time? How you put your hand on my shoulder, and Frank . . . (*He leans on the desk and as he speaks the dead man's name he accidentally*
325   *switches on the recorder, and instantly.*)

HOWARD's SON: ". . . of New York is Albany. The capital of Ohio is Cincinnati, the capital of Rhode Island is . . ." (*The recitation continues.*)

WILLY: (*Leaping away with fright, shouting.*) Ha! Howard!
330   Howard! Howard!

HOWARD: (*Rushing in.*) What happened?

WILLY: (*Pointing at the machine, which continues nasally, childishly, with the capital cities.*) Shut it off! Shut it off!

HOWARD: (*Pulling the plug out.*) Look, Willy . . .
335

WILLY: (*Pressing his hands to his eyes.*) I gotta get myself some coffee. I'll get some coffee . . .

(WILLY *starts to walk out.* HOWARD *stops him.*)

HOWARD: (*Rolling up the cord.*) Willy, look . . .

WILLY: I'll go to Boston.

HOWARD: Willy, you can't go to Boston for us.
340

WILLY: Why can't I go?

HOWARD: I don't want you to represent us. I've been meaning to tell you for a long time now.

WILLY: Howard, are you firing me?

HOWARD: I think you need a good long rest, Willy.
345

WILLY: Howard—

HOWARD: And when you feel better, come back, and we'll see if we can work something out.

WILLY: But I gotta earn money, Howard. I'm in no position to—
350

HOWARD: Where are your sons? Why don't your sons give you a hand?

WILLY: They're working on a very big deal.

HOWARD: This is no time for false pride, Willy. You go to your
355   sons and you tell them that you're tired. You've got two great boys, haven't you?

WILLY: Oh, no question, no question, but in the meantime . . .

HOWARD: Then that's that, heh?

WILLY: All right, I'll go to Boston tomorrow.

360 HOWARD: No, no.

WILLY: I can't throw myself on my sons. I'm not a cripple!

HOWARD: Look, kid, I'm busy this morning.

WILLY: (*Grasping* HOWARD'*s arm.*) Howard, you've got to let me go to Boston!

365 HOWARD: (*Hard, keeping himself under control.*) I've got a line of people to see this morning. Sit down, take five minutes, and pull yourself together, and then go home, will ya? I need the office, Willy. (*He starts to go, turns, remembering the recorder, starts to push off the table holding the recorder.*)
370   Oh, yeah. Whenever you can this week, stop by and drop off the samples. You'll feel better, Willy, and then come back and we'll talk. Pull yourself together, kid, there's people outside.

(HOWARD *exits, pushing the table off left.* WILLY *stares into space, exhausted. Now the music is heard*—BEN'*s music*—*first distantly, then closer, closer. As* WILLY *speaks,* BEN *enters from the right. He carries valise and umbrella.*)

WILLY: Oh, Ben, how did you do it? What is the answer? Did you
375   wind up the Alaska deal already?

BEN: Doesn't take much time if you know what you're doing. Just a short business trip. Boarding ship in an hour. Wanted to say good-by.

WILLY: Ben, I've got to talk to you.

380 BEN: (*Glancing at his watch.*) Haven't the time, William.

WILLY: (*Crossing the apron to Ben.*) Ben, nothing's working out. I don't know what to do.

BEN: Now, look here, William. I've bought timberland in Alaska and I need a man to look after things for me.

385 WILLY: God, timberland! Me and my boys in those grand outdoors!

BEN: You've a new continent at your doorstep, William. Get out of these cities, they're full of talk and time payments and courts of law. Screw on your fists and you can fight
390   for a fortune up there.

WILLY: Yes, yes! Linda, Linda!

(LINDA *enters as of old, with the wash.*)

LINDA: Oh, you're back?

BEN: I haven't much time.

WILLY: No, wait! Linda, he's got a proposition for me in
395   Alaska.

LINDA: But you've got— (*To* BEN.) He's got a beautiful job here.

WILLY: But in Alaska, kid, I could—

LINDA: You're doing well enough, Willy!

400 BEN: (*To* LINDA.) Enough for what, my dear?

LINDA: (*Frightened of* BEN *and angry at him.*) Don't say those things to him! Enough to be happy right here, right now. (*To* WILLY, *while* BEN *laughs.*) Why must everybody conquer the world? You're well liked, and the boys love you, and

someday—(*To* BEN.)—why, old man Wagner told him just the 405
other day that if he keeps it up he'll be a member of the firm, didn't he, Willy?

WILLY: Sure, sure. I am building something with this firm, Ben, and if a man is building something he must be on the right track, mustn't he? 410

BEN: What are you building? Lay your hand on it. Where is it?

WILLY: (*Hesitantly.*) That's true, Linda, there's nothing.

LINDA: Why? (*To* BEN.) There's a man eighty-four years old—

WILLY: That's right, Ben, that's right. When I look at that man I say, what is there to worry about? 415

BEN: Bah!

WILLY: It's true, Ben. All he has to do is go into any city, pick up the phone, and he's making his living and you know why?

BEN: (*Picking up his valise.*) I've got to go. 420

WILLY: (*Holding* BEN *back.*) Look at this boy!

(BIFF, *in his high school sweater, enters carrying suitcase.* HAPPY *carries* BIFF'*s shoulder guards, gold helmet, and football pants.*)

WILLY: Without a penny to his name, three great universities are begging for him, and from there the sky's the limit, because it's not what you do, Ben. It's who you know and the smile on your face! It's contacts, Ben, contacts! The 425
whole wealth of Alaska passes over the lunch table at the Commodore Hotel, and that's the wonder, the wonder of this country, that a man can end with diamonds here on the basis of being liked! (*He turns to* BIFF.) And that's why when you get out on that field today it's important. Because 430
thousands of people will be rooting for you and loving you. (*To* BEN, *who has again begun to leave.*) And Ben! when he walks into a business office his name will sound out like a bell and all the doors will open to him! I've seen it, Ben, I've seen it a thousand times! You can't feel it with your hand 435
like timber, but it's there!

BEN: Good-by, William.

WILLY: Ben, am I right? Don't you think I'm right? I value your advice.

BEN: There's a new continent at your doorstep, William. You 440
could walk out rich. Rich! (*He is gone.*)

WILLY: We'll do it here, Ben! You hear me? We're gonna do it here!

(*Young* BERNARD *rushes in. The gay music of the Boys is heard.*)

BERNARD: Oh, gee, I was afraid you left already!

WILLY: Why? What time is it? 445

BERNARD: It's half-past one!

WILLY: Well, come on, everybody! Ebbets Field next stop! Where's the pennants? (*He rushes through the wall-line of the kitchen and out into the living-room.*)

LINDA: (*To* BIFF.) Did you pack fresh underwear? 450

BIFF: (*Who has been limbering up.*) I want to go!

BERNARD: Biff, I'm carrying your helmet, ain't I?

HAPPY: No, I'm carrying the helmet.

BERNARD: Oh, Biff, you promised me.

HAPPY: I'm carrying the helmet. 455

BERNARD: How am I going to get in the locker room?

LINDA: Let him carry the shoulder guards. (*She puts her coat and hat on in the kitchen.*)

BERNARD: Can I, Biff? 'Cause I told everybody I'm going to be in the locker room. 460

HAPPY: In Ebbets Field it's the clubhouse.

BERNARD: I meant the clubhouse. Biff!

HAPPY: Biff!

465 BIFF: (*Grandly, after a slight pause.*) Let him carry the shoulder guards.

HAPPY: (*As he gives* BERNARD *the shoulder guards.*) Stay close to us now.

(WILLY *rushes in with the pennants.*)

WILLY: (*Handing them out.*) Everybody wave when Biff comes out on the field. (HAPPY *and* BERNARD *run off.*) You set
470 now, boy?

(*The music has died away.*)

BIFF: Ready to go, Pop. Every muscle is ready.

WILLY: (*At the edge of the apron.*) You realize what this means?

BIFF: That's right, Pop.

WILLY: (*Feeling* BIFF's *muscles.*) You're comin' home this
475 afternoon captain of the All-Scholastic Championship Team of the City of New York.

BIFF: I got it, Pop. And remember, pal, when I take off my helmet, that touchdown is for you.

WILLY: Let's go! (*He is starting out, with his arm around* BIFF,
480 *when* CHARLEY *enters, as of old, in knickers.*) I got no room for you, Charley.

CHARLEY: Room? For what?

WILLY: In the car.

CHARLEY: You goin' for a ride? I wanted to shoot some
485 casino.

WILLY: (*Furiously.*) Casino! (*Incredulously.*) Don't you realize what today is?

LINDA: Oh, he knows, Willy. He's just kidding you.

WILLY: That's nothing to kid about!

490 CHARLEY: No. Linda, what's goin' on?

LINDA: He's playing in Ebbets Field.

CHARLEY: Baseball in this weather?

WILLY: Don't talk to him. Come on, come on! (*He is pushing them out.*)

495 CHARLEY: Wait a minute, didn't you hear the news?

WILLY: What?

CHARLEY: Don't you listen to the radio? Ebbets Field just blew up.

WILLY: You go to hell! (CHARLEY *laughs. Pushing them out.*)
500 Come on, come on! We're late.

CHARLEY: (*As they go.*) Knock a homer, Biff, knock a homer!

WILLY: (*The last to leave, turning to* CHARLEY.) I don't think that was funny, Charley. This is the greatest day of his life.

CHARLEY: Willy, when are you going to grow up?

505 WILLY: Yeah, heh? When this game is over, Charley, you'll be laughing out of the other side of your face. They'll be calling him another Red Grange. Twenty-five thousand a year.

CHARLEY: (*Kidding.*) Is that so?

WILLY: Yeah, that's so.

510 CHARLEY: Well, then, I'm sorry, Willy. But tell me something.

WILLY: What?

CHARLEY: Who is Red Grange?

WILLY: Put up your hands. Goddam you, put up your hands!

(CHARLEY, *chuckling, shakes his head and walks away, around the left corner of the stage.* WILLY *follows him. The music rises to a mocking frenzy.*)

WILLY: Who the hell do you think you are, better than everybody else? You don't know everything, you big, ignorant, stupid . . . 515
Put up your hands!

(*Light rises, on the right side of the forestage, on a small table in the reception room of* CHARLEY's *office. Traffic sounds are heard.* BERNARD, *now mature, sits whistling to himself. A pair of tennis rackets and an overnight bag are on the floor beside him.*)

WILLY: (*Offstage.*) What are you walking away for? Don't walk away! If you're going to say something say it to my face! I know you laugh at me behind my back. You'll laugh out of the other side of your goddam face after this game. Touchdown! 520
Touchdown! Eighty thousand people! Touchdown! Right between the goal posts.

(BERNARD *is a quiet, earnest, but self-assured young man.* WILLY's *voice is coming from right upstage now.* BERNARD *lowers his feet off the table and listens.* JENNY, *his father's secretary, enters.*)

JENNY: (*Distressed.*) Say, Bernard, will you go out in the hall?

BERNARD: What is that noise? Who is it?

JENNY: Mr. Loman. He just got off the elevator. 525

BERNARD: (*Getting up.*) Who's he arguing with?

JENNY: Nobody. There's nobody with him. I can't deal with him any more, and your father gets all upset everytime he comes. I've got a lot of typing to do, and your father's waiting to sign it. Will you see him? 530

WILLY: (*Entering.*) Touchdown! Touch— (*He sees* JENNY.) Jenny, Jenny, good to see you. How're ya? Workin'? Or still honest?

JENNY: Fine. How've you been feeling?

WILLY: Not much any more, Jenny. Ha, ha! (*He is surprised to see* 535
the rackets.)

BERNARD: Hello, Uncle Willy.

WILLY: (*Almost shocked.*) Bernard! Well, look who's here! (*He comes quickly, guiltily, to* BERNARD *and warmly shakes his hand.*) 540

BERNARD: How are you? Good to see you.

WILLY: What are you doing here?

BERNARD: Oh, just stopped by to see Pop. Get off my feet till my train leaves. I'm going to Washington in a few minutes.

WILLY: Is he in? 545

BERNARD: Yes, he's in his office with the accountant. Sit down.

WILLY: (*Sitting down.*) What're you going to do in Washington?

BERNARD: Oh, just a case I've got there, Willy.

WILLY: That so? (*Indicating the rackets.*) You going to play tennis 550
there?

BERNARD: I'm staying with a friend who's got a court.

WILLY: Don't say. His own tennis court. Must be fine people, I bet.

BERNARD: They are, very nice. Dad tells me Biff's in town. 555

WILLY: (*With a big smile.*) Yeah, Biff's in. Working on a very big deal, Bernard.

BERNARD: What's Biff doing?

WILLY: Well, he's been doing very big things in the West. But he decided to establish himself here. Very big. We're having 560
dinner. Did I hear your wife had a boy?

BERNARD: That's right. Our second.

WILLY: Two boys! What do you know!

BERNARD: What kind of a deal has Biff got?

565 WILLY: Well, Bill Oliver—very big sporting-goods man—he wants Biff very badly. Called him in from the West. Long distance, carte blanche, special deliveries. Your friends have their own private tennis court?

BERNARD: You still with the old firm, Willy?

570 WILLY: (*After a pause.*) I'm—I'm overjoyed to see how you made the grade, Bernard, overjoyed. It's an encouraging thing to see a young man really—really— Looks very good for Biff— very—(*He breaks off, then.*) Bernard—(*He is so full of emotion, he breaks off again.*)

575 BERNARD: What is it, Willy?

WILLY: (*Small and alone.*) What—what's the secret?

BERNARD: What secret?

WILLY: How—how did you? Why didn't he ever catch on?

BERNARD: I wouldn't know that, Willy.

580 WILLY: (*Confidentially, desperately.*) You were his friend, his boyhood friend. There's something I don't understand about it. His life ended after that Ebbets Field game. From the age of seventeen nothing good ever happened to him.

585 BERNARD: He never trained himself for anything.

WILLY: But he did, he did. After high school he took so many correspondence courses. Radio mechanics; television; God knows what, and never made the slightest mark.

590 BERNARD: (*Taking off his glasses.*) Willy, do you want to talk candidly?

WILLY: (*Rising, faces* BERNARD.) I regard you as a very brilliant man, Bernard. I value your advice.

BERNARD: Oh, the hell with the advice, Willy. I couldn't advise you. There's just one thing I've always wanted to ask you. 595 When he was supposed to graduate, and the math teacher flunked him—

WILLY: Oh, that son-of-a-bitch ruined his life.

BERNARD: Yeah, but, Willy, all he had to do was go to summer school and make up that subject.

600 WILLY: That's right, that's right.

BERNARD: Did you tell him not to go to summer school?

WILLY: Me? I begged him to go. I ordered him to go!

BERNARD: Then why wouldn't he go?

WILLY: Why? Why! Bernard, that question has been trailing me 605 like a ghost for the last fifteen years. He flunked the subject, and laid down and died like a hammer hit him!

BERNARD: Take it easy, kid.

WILLY: Let me talk to you—I got nobody to talk to. Bernard, Bernard, was it my fault? Y'see? It keeps going around in 610 my mind, maybe I did something to him. I got nothing to give him.

BERNARD: Don't take it so hard.

WILLY: Why did he lay down? What is the story there? You were his friend!

615 BERNARD: Willy, I remember, it was June, and our grades came out. And he'd flunked math.

WILLY: That son-of-a-bitch!

BERNARD: No, it wasn't right then. Biff just got very angry, I remember, and he was ready to enroll in summer school.

620 WILLY: (*Surprised.*) He was?

BERNARD: He wasn't beaten by it at all. But then, Willy, he disappeared from the block for almost a month. And I got the idea that he'd gone up to New England to see you. Did he have a talk with you then?

(WILLY *stares in silence.*)

BERNARD: Willy? 625

WILLY: (*With a strong edge of resentment in his voice.*) Yeah, he came to Boston. What about it?

BERNARD: Well, just that when he came back—I'll never forget this, it always mystifies me. Because I'd thought so well of Biff, even though he'd always taken advantage 630 of me. I loved him, Willy, y'know? And he came back after that month and took his sneakers—remember those sneakers with "University of Virginia" printed on them? He was so proud of those, wore them every day. And he took them down in the cellar, and burned them up in the 635 furnace. We had a fist fight. It lasted at least half an hour. Just the two of us, punching each other down thee cellar, and crying right through it. I've often thought of how strange it was that I knew he'd given up his life. What happened in Boston, Willy? 640

(WILLY *looks at him as at an intruder.*)

BERNARD: I just bring it up because you asked me.

WILLY: (*Angrily.*) Nothing. What do you mean, "What happened?" What's that got to do with anything?

BERNARD: Well, don't get sore.

WILLY: What are you trying to do, blame it on me? If a boy lays 645 down is that my fault?

BERNARD: Now, Willy, don't get—

WILLY: Well, don't—don't talk to me that way! What does that mean, "What happened?"

650

(CHARLEY *enters. He is in his vest, and he carries a bottle of bourbon.*)

CHARLEY: Hey, you're going to miss that train. (*He waves the bottle.*)

BERNARD: Yeah, I'm going. (*He takes the bottle.*) Thanks, Pop. (*He picks up his rackets and bag.*) Good-by, Willy, and don't worry about it. You know, "If at first you don't succeed . . ."

WILLY: Yes, I believe in that. 655

BERNARD: But sometimes, Willy, it's better for a man just to walk away.

WILLY: Walk away?

BERNARD: That's right.

WILLY: But if you can't walk away? 660

BERNARD: (*After a slight pause.*) I guess that's when it's tough. (*Extending his hand.*) Good-by, Willy.

WILLY: (*Shaking* BERNARD's *hand.*) Good-by, boy.

CHARLEY: (*An arm on* BERNARD's *shoulder.*) How do you like this kid? Gonna argue a case in front of the Supreme 665 Court.

BERNARD: (*Protesting.*) Pop!

WILLY: (*Genuinely shocked, pained, and happy.*) No! The Supreme Court!

BERNARD: I gotta run. 'By, Dad! 670

CHARLEY: Knock 'em dead, Bernard!

(BERNARD *goes off.*)

WILLY: (*As* CHARLEY *takes out his wallet.*) The Supreme Court! And he didn't even mention it!

CHARLEY: (*Counting out money on the desk.*) He don't have to—he's gonna do it. 675

WILLY: And you never told him what to do, did you? You never took any interest in him.

CHARLEY: My salvation is that I never took any interest in anything. There's some money—fifty dollars. I got an
680   accountant inside.
WILLY: Charley, look . . . (*With difficulty.*) I got my insurance to pay. If you can manage it—I need a hundred and ten dollars.

(CHARLEY *doesn't reply for a moment; merely stops moving.*)

WILLY: I'd draw it from my bank but Linda would know, and I . . .
685   CHARLEY: Sit down, Willy.
WILLY: (*Moving toward the chair.*) I'm keeping an account of everything, remember. I'll pay every penny back. (*He sits.*)
CHARLEY: Now listen to me, Willy.
WILLY: I want you to know I appreciate . . .
690   CHARLEY: (*Sitting down on the table.*) Willy, what're you doin'? What the hell is goin' on in your head?
WILLY: Why? I'm simply . . .
CHARLEY: I offered you a job. You can make fifty dollars a week. And I won't send you on the road.
695   WILLY: I've got a job.
CHARLEY: Without pay? What kind of a job is a job without pay? (*He rises.*) Now, look, kid, enough is enough. I'm no genius but I know when I'm being insulted.
WILLY: Insulted!
700   CHARLEY: Why don't you want to work for me?
WILLY: What's the matter with you? I've got a job.
CHARLEY: Then what're you walkin' in here every week for?
WILLY: (*Getting up.*) Well, if you don't want me to walk in here—
705   CHARLEY: I am offering you a job.
WILLY: I don't want your goddam job!
CHARLEY: When the hell are you going to grow up?
WILLY: (*Furiously.*) You big ignoramus, if you say that to me again I'll rap you one! I don't care how big you are! (*He's
710   ready to fight.*)

(*Pause.*)

CHARLEY: (*Kindly, going to him.*) How much do you need, Willy?
WILLY: Charley, I'm strapped, I'm strapped. I don't know what to do. I was just fired.
715   CHARLEY: Howard fired you?
WILLY: That snotnose. Imagine that? I named him. I named him Howard.
CHARLEY: Willy, when're you gonna realize that them things don't mean anything? You named him Howard, but you can't
720   sell that. The only thing you got in this world is what you can sell. And the funny thing is that you're a salesman, and you don't know that.
WILLY: I've always tried to think otherwise, I guess. I always felt that if a man was impressive, and well liked, that nothing—
725   CHARLEY: Why must everybody like you? Who liked J. P. Morgan? Was he impressive? In a Turkish bath he'd look like a butcher. But with his pockets on he was very well liked. Now listen, Willy, I know you don't like me, and nobody can say I'm in love with you, but I'll give you a job
730   because—just for the hell of it, put it that way. Now what do you say?
WILLY: I—I just can't work for you, Charley.
CHARLEY: What're you, jealous of me?

WILLY: I can't work for you, that's all, don't ask me why.
CHARLEY: (*Angered, takes out more bills.*) You been jealous of   735
me all your life, you damned fool! Here, pay your insurance. (*He puts the money in* WILLY'S *hand.*)
WILLY: I'm keeping strict accounts.
CHARLEY: I've got some work to do. Take care of yourself. And pay your insurance.   740
WILLY: (*Moving to the right.*) Funny, y'know? After all the highways, and the trains, and the appointments, and the years, you end up worth more dead than alive.
CHARLEY: Willy, nobody's worth nothin' dead. (*After a slight pause.*) Did you hear what I said?   745

(WILLY *stands still, dreaming.*)

CHARLEY: Willy!
WILLY: Apologize to Bernard for me when you see him. I didn't mean to argue with him. He's a fine boy. They're all fine boys, and they'll end up big—all of them. Someday they'll all play tennis together. Wish me luck, Charley. He saw Bill   750
Oliver today.
CHARLEY: Good luck.
WILLY: (*On the verge of tears.*) Charley, you're the only friend I got. Isn't that a remarkable thing? (*He goes out.*)
CHARLEY: Jesus!   755

(CHARLEY *stares after him a moment and follows. All light blacks out. Suddenly raucous music is heard, and a red glow rises behind the screen at right.* STANLEY, *a young waiter, appears, carrying a table, followed by* HAPPY, *who is carrying two chairs.*)

STANLEY: (*Putting the table down.*) That's all right, Mr. Loman, I can handle it myself. (*He turns and takes the chairs from* HAPPY *and places them at the table.*)
HAPPY: (*Glancing around.*) Oh, this is better.
STANLEY: Sure, in the front there you're in the middle of all   760
kinds a noise. Whenever you got a party, Mr. Loman, you just tell me and I'll put you back here. Y'know, there's a lotta people they don't like it private, because when they go out they like to see a lotta action around them because they're sick and tired to stay in the house by theirself. But   765
I know you, you ain't from Hackensack. You know what I mean?
HAPPY: (*Sitting down.*) So how's it coming, Stanley?
STANLEY: Ah, it's a dog's life. I only wish during the war they'd took me in the Army. I coulda been dead by now.   770
HAPPY: My brother's back, Stanley.
STANLEY: Oh, he come back, heh? From the Far West.
HAPPY: Yeah, big cattle man, my brother, so treat him right. And my father's coming too.
STANLEY: Oh, your father too!   775
HAPPY: You got a couple of nice lobsters?
STANLEY: Hundred per cent, big.
HAPPY: I want them with the claws.
STANLEY: Don't worry, I don't give you no mice. (HAPPY *laughs.*) How about some wine? It'll put a head on the   780
meal.
HAPPY: No. You remember, Stanley, that recipe I brought you from overseas? With the champagne in it?
STANLEY: Oh, yeah, sure. I still got it tacked up yet in the kitchen. But that'll have to cost a buck apiece anyways.   785
HAPPY: That's all right.

STANLEY: What'd you, hit a number or somethin'?

HAPPY: No, it's a little celebration. My brother is—I think he
    pulled off a big deal today. I think we're going into business

790   together.

STANLEY: Great! That's the best for you. Because a family
    business, you know what I mean?—that's the best.

HAPPY: That's what I think.

STANLEY: 'Cause what's the difference? Somebody steals? It's

795   in the family. Know what I mean? (*Sotto voce.*) Like this
    bartender here. The boss is goin' crazy what kinda leak he's
    got in the cash register. You put it in but it don't
    come out.

HAPPY: (*Raising his head.*) Sh!

800 STANLEY: What?

HAPPY: You notice I wasn't lookin' right or left, was I?

STANLEY: No.

HAPPY: And my eyes are closed.

STANLEY: So what's the—?

805 HAPPY: Strudel's comin'.

STANLEY: (*Catching on, looks around.*) Ah, no, there's no—

(*He breaks off as a furred, lavishly dressed girl enters and sits at
the next table. Both follow her with their eyes.*)

STANLEY: Geez, how'd ya know?

HAPPY: I got radar or something. (*Staring directly at her profile.*)
    Oooooooo . . . Stanley.

810 STANLEY: I think that's for you, Mr. Loman.

HAPPY: Look at that mouth. Oh, God. And the binoculars.

STANLEY: Geez, you got a life, Mr. Loman.

HAPPY: Wait on her.

STANLEY: (*Going to the girl's table.*) Would you like a menu,

815   ma'am?

GIRL: I'm expecting someone, but I'd like a—

HAPPY: Why don't you bring her—excuse me, miss, do you mind?
    I sell champagne, and I'd like you to try my brand. Bring her a
    champagne, Stanley.

820 GIRL: That's awfully nice of you.

HAPPY: Don't mention it. It's all company money. (*He laughs.*)

GIRL: That's a charming product to be selling, isn't it?

HAPPY: Oh, gets to be like everything else. Selling is selling,
    y'know.

825 GIRL: I suppose.

HAPPY: You don't happen to sell, do you?

GIRL: No, I don't sell.

HAPPY: Would you object to a compliment from a stranger? You
    ought to be on a magazine cover.

830 GIRL: (*Looking at him a little archly.*) I have been.

(STANLEY *comes in with a glass of champagne.*)

HAPPY: What'd I say before, Stanley? You see? She's a cover
    girl.

STANLEY: Oh, I could see, I could see.

HAPPY: (*To the* GIRL.) What magazine?

835 GIRL: Oh, a lot of them. (*She takes the drink.*) Thank you.

HAPPY: You know what they say in France, don't you?
    "Champagne is the drink of the complexion"—Hya Biff!

(BIFF *has entered and sits with* HAPPY.)

BIFF: Hello, kid. Sorry I'm late.

HAPPY: I just got here. Uh, Miss—?

GIRL: Forsythe.   840

HAPPY: Miss Forsythe, this is my brother.

BIFF: Is Dad here?

HAPPY: His name is Biff. You might've heard of him. Great
    football player.

GIRL: Really? What team?   845

HAPPY: Are you familiar with football?

GIRL: No, I'm afraid I'm not.

HAPPY: Biff is quarterback with the New York Giants.

GIRL: Well, that is nice, isn't it? (*She drinks.*)

HAPPY: Good health.   850

GIRL: I'm happy to meet you.

HAPPY: That's my name. Hap. It's really Harold, but at West Point
    they called me Happy.

GIRL: (*Now really impressed.*) Oh, I see. How do you do? (*She
    turns her profile.*)   855

BIFF: Isn't Dad coming?

HAPPY: You want her?

BIFF: Oh, I could never make that.

HAPPY: I remember the time that idea would never come into
    your head. Where's the old confidence, Biff?   860

BIFF: I just saw Oliver—

HAPPY: Wait a minute, I've got to see that old confidence again.
    Do you want her? She's on call.

BIFF: Oh, no. (*He turns to look at the* GIRL.)

HAPPY: I'm telling you. Watch this. (*Turning to the* GIRL.) Honey?   865
    (*She turns to him.*) Are you busy?

GIRL: Well, I am . . . but I could make a phone call.

HAPPY: Do that, will you, honey? And see if you can get a friend.
    We'll be here for a while. Biff is one of the greatest football
    players in the country.   870

GIRL: (*Standing up.*) Well, I'm certainly happy to meet you.

HAPPY: Come back soon.

GIRL: I'll try.

HAPPY: Don't try, honey, try hard.

(*The* GIRL *exits.* STANLEY *follows, shaking his head in bewildered
admiration.*)

HAPPY: Isn't that a shame now? A beautiful girl like that? That's   875
    why I can't get married. There's not a good woman in a
    thousand. New York is loaded with them, kid!

BIFF: Hap, look—

HAPPY: I told you she was on call!

BIFF: (*Strangely unnerved.*) Cut it out, will ya? I want to say   880
    something to you.

HAPPY: Did you see Oliver?

BIFF: I saw him all right. Now look, I want to tell Dad a couple
    of things and I want you to help me.

HAPPY: What? Is he going to back you?   885

BIFF: Are you crazy? You're out ofw your goddam head, you
    know that?

HAPPY: Why? What happened?

BIFF: (*Breathlessly.*) I did a terrible thing today, Hap. It's been the
    strangest day I ever went through. I'm all numb, I swear.   890

HAPPY: You mean he wouldn't see you?

BIFF: Well, I waited six hours for him, see? All day. Kept sending
    my name in. Even tried to date his secretary so she'd get me to
    him, but no soap.

HAPPY: Because you're not showin' the old confidence, Biff.   895
    He remembered you, didn't he?

BIFF: (*Stopping* HAPPY *with a gesture.*) Finally, about five o'clock, he comes out. Didn't remember who I was or any thing. I felt like such an idiot, Hap.

900 HAPPY: Did you tell him my Florida idea?

BIFF: He walked away. I saw him for one minute. I got so mad I could've torn the walls down! How the hell did I ever get the idea I was a salesman there? I even believed myself that I'd been a salesman for him! And then he gave me one look

905 and—I realized what a ridiculous lie my whole life has been! We've been talking in a dream for fifteen years. I was a shipping clerk.

HAPPY: What'd you do?

BIFF: (*With great tension and wonder.*) Well, he left, see. And

910 the secretary went out. I was all alone in the waiting-room. I don't know what came over me, Hap. The next thing I know I'm in his office—paneled walls, everything. I can't explain it. I—Hap, I took his fountain pen.

HAPPY: Geez, did he catch you?

915 BIFF: I ran out. I ran down all eleven flights. I ran and ran and ran.

HAPPY: That was an awful dumb—what'd you do that for?

BIFF: (*Agonized.*) I don't know, I just—wanted to take something, I don't know. You gotta help me, Hap, I'm gonna tell

920 Pop.

HAPPY: You crazy? What for?

BIFF: Hap, he's got to understand that I'm not the man somebody lends that kind of money to. He thinks I've been spiting him all these years and it's eating him up.

925 HAPPY: That's just it. You tell him something nice.

BIFF: I can't.

HAPPY: Say you got a lunch date with Oliver tomorrow.

BIFF: So what do I do tomorrow?

HAPPY: You leave the house tomorrow and come back at night

930 and say Oliver is thinking it over. And he thinks it over for a couple of weeks, and gradually it fades away and nobody's the worse.

BIFF: But it'll go on forever!

HAPPY: Dad is never so happy as when he's looking forward to

935 something!

(WILLY *enters.*)

HAPPY: Hello, scout!

WILLY: Gee, I haven't been here in years!

(STANLEY *has followed* WILLY *in and sets a chair for him.* STANLEY *starts off but* HAPPY *stops him.*)

HAPPY: Stanley!

(STANLEY *stands by, waiting for an order.*)

BIFF: (*Going to* WILLY *with guilt, as to an invalid.*) Sit down, Pop.

940 You want a drink?

WILLY: Sure, I don't mind.

BIFF: Let's get a load on.

WILLY: You look worried.

BIFF: N-no. (*To* STANLEY.) Scotch all around. Make it doubles.

945 STANLEY: Doubles, right. (*He goes.*)

WILLY: You had a couple already, didn't you?

BIFF: Just a couple, yeah.

WILLY: Well, what happened, boy? (*Nodding affirmatively, with a smile.*) Everything go all right?

BIFF: (*Takes a breath, then reaches out and grasps* WILLY's *hand.*) 950 Pal . . . (*He is smiling bravely, and* WILLY *is smiling too*). I had an experience today.

HAPPY: Terrific, Pop.

WILLY: That so? What happened?

BIFF: (*High, slightly alcoholic, above the earth.*) I'm going to tell 955 you everything from first to last. It's been a strange day. (*Silence. He looks around, composes himself as best he can, but his breath keeps breaking the rhythm of his voice.*) I had to wait quite a while for him, and—

WILLY: Oliver? 960

BIFF: Yeah, Oliver. All day, as a matter of cold fact. And a lot of—instances—facts, Pop, facts about my life came back to me. Who was it, Pop? Who ever said I was a salesman with Oliver?

WILLY: Well, you were. 965

BIFF: No, Dad, I was a shipping clerk.

WILLY: But you were practically—

BIFF: (*With determination.*) Dad, I don't know who said it first, but I was never a salesman for Bill Oliver.

WILLY: What're you talking about? 970

BIFF: Let's hold onto the facts tonight, Pop. We're not going to get anywhere bullin' around. I was a shipping clerk.

WILLY: (*Angrily.*) All right, now listen to me—

BIFF: Why don't you let me finish?

WILLY: I'm not interested in stories about the past or any crap 975 of that kind because the woods are burning, boys, you understand? There's a big blaze going on all around. I was fired today.

BIFF: (*Shocked.*) How could you be?

WILLY: I was fired, and I'm looking for a little good news to 980 tell your mother, because the woman has waited and the woman has suffered. The gist of it is that I haven't got a story left in my head, Biff. So don't give me a lecture about facts and aspects. I am not interested. Now what've you got to say to me? 985

(STANLEY *enters with three drinks. They wait until he leaves.*)

WILLY: Did you see Oliver?

BIFF: Jesus, Dad!

WILLY: You mean you didn't go up there?

HAPPY: Sure he went up there.

BIFF: I did. I—saw him. How could they fire you? 990

WILLY: (*On the edge of his chair.*) What kind of a welcome did he give you?

BIFF: He won't even let you work on commission?

WILLY: I'm out! (*Driving.*) So tell me, he gave you a warm welcome? 995

HAPPY: Sure, Pop, sure!

BIFF: (*Driven.*) Well, it was kind of—

WILLY: I was wondering if he'd remember you. (*To* HAPPY.) Imagine, man doesn't see him for ten, twelve years and gives him that kind of a welcome! 1000

HAPPY: Damn right!

BIFF: (*Trying to return to the offensive.*) Pop, look—

WILLY: You know why he remembered you, don't you? Because you impressed him in those days.

BIFF: Let's talk quietly and get this down to the facts, huh? 1005

WILLY: (*As though* BIFF *had been interrupting.*) Well, what happened? It's great news, Biff. Did he take you into his office or'd you talk in the waiting-room?

BIFF: Well, he came in, see, and—

1010 WILLY: (*With a big smile.*) What'd he say? Betcha he threw his arm around you.

BIFF: Well, he kinda—

WILLY: He's a fine man. (*To* HAPPY.) Very hard man to see, y'know.

1015 HAPPY: (*Agreeing.*) Oh, I know.

WILLY: (*To* BIFF.) Is that where you had the drinks?

BIFF: Yeah, he gave me a couple of—no, no!

HAPPY: (*Cutting in.*) He told him my Florida idea.

WILLY: Don't interrupt. (*To* BIFF.) How'd he react to the

1020 Florida idea?

BIFF: Dad, will you give me a minute to explain?

WILLY: I've been waiting for you to explain since I sat down here! What happened? He took you into his office and what?

1025 BIFF: Well—I talked. And—and he listened, see.

WILLY: Famous for the way he listens, y'know. What was his answer?

BIFF: His answer was— (*He breaks off, suddenly angry.*) Dad, you're not letting me tell you what I want to tell you!

1030 WILLY: (*Accusing, angered.*) You didn't see him, did you?

BIFF: I did see him!

WILLY: What'd you insult him or something? You insulted him didn't you?

BIFF: Listen, will you let me out of it, will you just let me out

1035 of it!

HAPPY: What the hell!

WILLY: Tell me what happened!

BIFF: (*To* HAPPY.) I can't talk to him!

(*A single trumpet note jars the ear. The light of green leaves stains the house, which holds the air of night and a dream* YOUNG BERNARD *enters and knocks on the door of the house.*)

YOUNG BERNARD: (*Frantically.*) Mrs. Loman, Mrs. Loman!

1040 HAPPY: Tell him what happened!

BIFF: (*To* HAPPY.) Shut up and leave me alone!

WILLY: No, no! You had to go and flunk math!

BIFF: What math? What're you talking about?

YOUNG BERNARD: Mrs. Loman, Mrs. Loman!

(LINDA *appears in the house, as of old.*)

1045 WILLY: (*Wildly.*) Math, math, math!

BIFF: Take it easy, Pop!

YOUNG BERNARD: Mrs. Loman!

WILLY: (*Furiously.*) If you hadn't flunked you'd've been set by now!

1050 BIFF: Now, look, I'm gonna tell you what happened, and you're going to listen to me.

YOUNG BERNARD: Mrs. Loman!

BIFF: I waited six hours—

HAPPY: What the hell are you saying?

1055 BIFF: I kept sending in my name but he wouldn't see me. So finally he . . . (*He continues unheard as light fades low on the restaurant.*)

YOUNG BERNARD: Biff flunked math!

LINDA: No!

YOUNG BERNARD: Birnbaum flunked him! They won't 1060
graduate him!

LINDA: But they have to. He's gotta go to the university. Where is he? Biff! Biff!

YOUNG BERNARD: No, he left. He went to Grand Central.

LINDA: Grand— You mean he went to Boston! 1065

YOUNG BERNARD: Is Uncle Willy in Boston?

LINDA: Oh, maybe Willy can talk to the teacher. Oh, the poor, poor boy!

(*Light on house area snaps out.*)

BIFF: (*At the table, now audible, holding up a gold fountain pen.*) . . . so I'm washed up with Oliver, you understand? 1070
Are you listening to me?

WILLY: (*At a loss.*) Yeah, sure. If you hadn't flunked—

BIFF: Flunked what? What're you talking about?

WILLY: Don't blame everything on me! I didn't flunk math—you did! What pen? 1075

HAPPY: That was awful dumb, Biff, a pen like that is worth—

WILLY: (*Seeing the pen for the first time.*) You took Oliver's pen?

BIFF: (*Weakening.*) Dad, I just explained it to you.

WILLY: You stole Bill Oliver's fountain pen!

BIFF: I didn't exactly steal it! That's just what I've been explaining 1080
to you!

HAPPY: He had it in his hand and just then Oliver walked in, so he got nervous and stuck it in his pocket!

WILLY: My God, Biff!

BIFF: I never intended to do it, Dad! 1085

OPERATOR'S VOICE: Standish Arms, good evening!

WILLY: (*Shouting.*) I'm not in my room!

BIFF: (*Frightened.*) Dad, what's the matter? (*He and* HAPPY *stand up.*)

OPERATOR: Ringing Mr. Loman for you! 1090

WILLY: I'm not there, stop it!

BIFF: (*Horrified, gets down on one knee before* WILLY.) Dad, I'll make good, I'll make good. (WILLY *tries to get to his feet.* BIFF *holds him down.*) Sit down now.

WILLY: No, you're no good, you're no good for anything. 1095

BIFF: I am, Dad, I'll find something else, you understand? Now don't you worry about anything. (*He holds up* WILLY's *face.*) Talk to me, Dad.

OPERATOR: Mr. Loman does not answer. Shall I page him?

WILLY: (*Attempting to stand, as though to rush and silence the* 1100
OPERATOR.) No, no, no!

HAPPY: He'll strike something, Pop.

WILLY: No, no . . .

BIFF: (*Desperately, standing over* WILLY.) Pop, listen! Listen to me! I'm telling you something good. Oliver talked to his partner 1105
about the Florida idea. You listening? He—he talked to his partner, and he came to me . . . I'm going to be all right, you hear? Dad, listen to me, he said it was just a question of the amount!

WILLY: Then you . . . got it? 1110

HAPPY: He's gonna be terrific, Pop!

WILLY: (*Trying to stand.*) Then you got it, haven't you? You got it! You got it!

BIFF: (*Agonized, holds* WILLY *down.*) No, no. Look, Pop. I'm supposed to have lunch with them tomorrow. I'm just 1115
telling you this so you'll know that I can still make an impression, Pop. And I'll make good somewhere, but I can't go tomorrow, see?

WILLY: Why not? You simply—

1120 BIFF: But the pen, Pop!

WILLY: You give it to him and tell him it was an oversight!

HAPPY: Sure, have lunch tomorrow!

BIFF: I can't say that—

WILLY: You were doing a crosswood puzzle and accidentally used

1125   his pen!

BIFF: Listen, kid, I took those balls years ago, now I walk in with his fountain pen? That clinches it, don't you see? I can't face him like that! I'll try elsewhere.

PAGE'S VOICE: Paging Mr. Loman!

1130 WILLY: Don't you want to be anything?

BIFF: Pop, how can I go back?

WILLY: You don't want to be anything, is that what's behind it?

BIFF: (*Now angry at* WILLY *for not crediting his sympathy.*) Don't take it that way! You think it was easy walking into that office

1135   after what I'd done to him? A team of horses couldn't have dragged me back to Bill Oliver!

WILLY: Then why'd you go?

BIFF: Why did I go? Why did I go! Look at you! Look at what's become of you!

(*Off left,* THE WOMAN *laughs.*)

1140 WILLY: Biff, you're going to go to that lunch tomorrow, or—

BIFF: I can't go. I've got no appointment!

HAPPY: Biff, for . . .!

WILLY: Are you spiting me?

BIFF: Don't take it that way! Goddammit!

1145 WILLY: (*Strikes* BIFF *and falters away from the table.*) You rotten little louse! Are you spiting me?

THE WOMAN: Someone's at the door, Willy!

BIFF: I'm no good, can't you see what I am?

HAPPY: (*Separating them.*) Hey, you're in a restaurant! Now cut it

1150   out, both of you! (*The girls enter.*) Hello, girls, sit down.

(THE WOMAN *laughs, off left.*)

MISS FORSYTHE: I guess we might as well. This is Letta.

THE WOMAN: Willy, are you going to wake up?

BIFF: (*Ignoring* WILLY.) How're ya, miss, sit down. What do you drink?

1155 MISS FORSYTHE: Letta might not be able to stay long.

LETTA: I gotta get up very early tomorrow. I got jury duty. I'm so excited! Were you fellows ever on a jury?

BIFF: No, but I been in front of them! (*The girls laugh.*) This is my father.

1160 LETTA: Isn't he cute? Sit down with us, Pop.

HAPPY: Sit him down, Biff!

BIFF: (*Going to him.*) Come on, slugger, drink us under the table. To hell with it! Come on, sit down, pal.

(*On* BIFF'S *last insistence,* WILLY *is about to sit.*)

THE WOMAN: (*Now urgently.*) Willy, are you going to answer

1165   the door!

(*The* WOMAN'S *call pulls* WILLY *back. He starts right, befuddled.*)

BIFF: Hey, where are you going?

WILLY: Open the door.

BIFF: The door?

WILLY: The washroom . . . the door . . . where's the door?

1170 BIFF: (*Leading* WILLY *to the left.*) Just go straight down.

(WILLY *moves left.*)

THE WOMAN: Willy, Willy, are you going to get up, get up, get up, get up?

(WILLY *exits left.*)

LETTA: I think it's sweet you bring your daddy along.

MISS FORSYTHE: Oh, he isn't really your father!

BIFF: (*At left, turning to her resentfully.*) Miss Forsythe, 1175 you've just seen a prince walk by. A fine, troubled prince. A hardworking, unappreciated prince. A pal, you understand? A good companion. Always for his boys.

LETTA: That's so sweet.

HAPPY: Well, girls, what's the program? We're wasting time. Come 1180 on, Biff. Gather round. Where would you like to go?

BIFF: Why don't you do something for him?

HAPPY: Me!

BIFF: Don't you give a damn for him, Hap?

HAPPY: What're you talking about? I'm the one who— 1185

BIFF: I sense it, you don't give a good goddam about him. (*He takes the rolled-up hose from his pocket and puts it on the table in front of* HAPPY.) Look what I found in the cellar, for Christ's sake. How can you bear to let it go on?

HAPPY: Me? Who goes away? Who runs off and— 1190

BIFF: Yeah, but he doesn't mean anything to you. You could help him—I can't! Don't you understand what I'm talking about? He's going to kill himself, don't you know that?

HAPPY: Don't I know it! Me! 1195

BIFF: Hap, help him! Jesus . . . help him . . . Help me, help me, I can't bear to look at his face! (*Ready to weep, he hurries out, up right.*)

HAPPY: (*Starting after him.*) Where are you going?

MISS FORSYTHE: What's he so mad about? 1200

HAPPY: Come on, girls, we'll catch up with him.

MISS FORSYTHE: (*As* HAPPY *pushes her out.*) Say, I don't like that temper of his!

HAPPY: He's just a little overstrung, he'll be all right!

WILLY: (*Off left, as* THE WOMAN *laughs.*) Don't answer! Don't 1205 answer!

LETTA: Don't you want to tell your father—

HAPPY: No, that's not my father. He's just a guy. Come on, we'll catch Biff, and, honey, we're going to paint this town! Stanley, where's the check! Hey, Stanley! 1210

(*They exit.* STANLEY *looks toward left.*)

STANLEY: (*Calling to* HAPPY *indignantly.*) Mr. Loman! Mr. Loman!

(STANLEY *picks up a chair and follows them off. Knocking is heard off left.* THE WOMAN *enters, laughing.* WILLY *follows her. She is in a black slip; he is buttoning his shirt. Raw, sensuous music accompanies their speech.*)

WILLY: Will you stop laughing? Will you stop?

THE WOMAN: Aren't you going to answer the door? He'll wake the whole hotel. 1215

WILLY: I'm not expecting anybody.

THE WOMAN: Whyn't you have another drink, honey, and stop being so damn self-centered?

WILLY: I'm so lonely.

1220 THE WOMAN: You know you ruined me, Willy? From now on, whenever you come to the office, I'll see that you go right through to the buyers. No waiting at my desk any more, Willy. You ruined me.

WILLY: That's nice of you to say that.

1225 THE WOMAN: Gee, you are self-centered! Why so sad? You are the saddest, self-centeredest soul I ever did see-saw. (*She laughs. He kisses her.*) Come on inside, drummer boy. It's silly to be dressing in the middle of the night. (*As knocking is heard.*) Aren't you going to answer the door?

1230 WILLY: They're knocking on the wrong door.

THE WOMAN: But I felt the knocking. And he heard us talking in here. Maybe the hotel's on fire!

WILLY: (*His terror rising.*) It's a mistake.

THE WOMAN: Then tell him to go away!

1235 WILLY: There's nobody there.

THE WOMAN: It's getting on my nerves, Willy. There's somebody standing out there and it's getting on my nerves!

WILLY: (*Pushing her away from him.*) All right, stay in the bathroom here, and don't come out. I think there's a law in

1240 Massachusetts about it, so don't come out. It may be that new room clerk. He looked very mean. So don't come out. It's a mistake, there's no fire.

(*The knocking is heard again. He takes a few steps away from her, and she vanishes into the wing. The light follows him, and now he is facing* YOUNG BIFF, *who carries a suitcase.* BIFF *steps toward him. The music is gone.*)

BIFF: Why didn't you answer?

WILLY: Biff! What are you doing in Boston?

1245 BIFF: Why didn't you answer? I've been knocking for five minutes, I called you on the phone—

WILLY: I just heard you. I was in the bathroom and had the door shut. Did anything happen home?

BIFF: Dad—I let you down.

1250 WILLY: What do you mean?

BIFF: Dad . . .

WILLY: Biffo, what's this about? (*Putting his arm around* BIFF.) Come on, let's go downstairs and get you a malted.

BIFF: Dad, I flunked math.

1255 WILLY: Not for the term?

BIFF: The term. I haven't got enough credits to graduate.

WILLY: You mean to say Bernard wouldn't give you the answers?

BIFF: He did, he tried, but I only got a sixty-one.

1260 WILLY: And they wouldn't give you four points?

BIFF: Birnbaum refused absolutely. I begged him, Pop, but he won't give me those points. You gotta talk to him before they close the school. Because if he saw the kind of man you are, and you just talked to him in your way, I'm sure

1265 he'd come through for me. The class came right before practice, see, and I didn't go enough. Would you talk to him? He'd like you, Pop. You know the way you could talk.

WILLY: You're on. We'll drive right back.

1270 BIFF: Oh, Dad, good work! I'm sure he'll change it for you!

WILLY: Go downstairs and tell the clerk I'm checkin' out. Go right down.

BIFF: Yes, sir! See, the reason he hates me, Pop—one day he was late for class so I got up at the blackboard and imitated him. I crossed my eyes and talked with a lithp. 1275

WILLY: (*Laughing.*) You did? The kids like it?

BIFF: They nearly died laughing!

WILLY: Yeah? What'd you do?

BIFF: The thquare root of thixthy twee is . . . (WILLY *bursts out laughing;* BIFF *joins him.*) And in the middle of it he walked in! 1280

(WILLY *laughs and* THE WOMAN *joins in offstage.*)

WILLY: (*Without hesitation.*) Hurry downstairs and—

BIFF: Somebody in there?

WILLY: No, that was next door.

(THE WOMAN *laughs offstage.*)

BIFF: Somebody got in your bathroom!

WILLY: No, it's the next room, there's a party— 1285

THE WOMAN: (*Enters, laughing. She lisps this.*) Can I come in? There's something in the bathtub, Willy, and it's moving!

(WILLY *looks at* BIFF, *who is staring open-mouthed and horrified at* THE WOMAN.)

WILLY: Ah—you better go back to your room. They must be finished painting by now. They're painting her room so I let her take a shower here. Go back, go back . . . (*He pushes her.*) 1290

THE WOMAN: (*Resisting.*) But I've got to get dressed, Willy, I can't—

WILLY: Get out of here! Go back, go back . . . (*Suddenly striving for the ordinary.*) This is Miss Francis, Biff, she's a buyer. They're painting her room. Go back, Miss Francis, go back . . . 1295

THE WOMAN: But my clothes, I can't go out naked in the hall!

WILLY: (*Pushing her offstage.*) Get outa here! Go back, go back!

(BIFF *slowly sits down on his suitcase as the argument continues offstage.*)

THE WOMAN: Where's my stockings? You promised me stockings, Willy! 1300

WILLY: I have no stockings here!

THE WOMAN: You had two boxes of size nine sheers for me, and I want them!

WILLY: Here, for God's sake, will you get outa here! 1305

THE WOMAN: (*Enters holding a box of stockings.*) I just hope there's nobody in the hall. That's all I hope. (*To* BIFF.) Are you football or baseball?

BIFF: Football.

THE WOMAN: (*Angry, humiliated.*) That's me too. G'night. (*She snatches her clothes from* WILLY, *and walks out.*) 1310

WILLY: (*After a pause.*) Well, better get going. I want to get to the school first thing in the morning. Get my suits out of the closet. I'll get my valise. (BIFF *doesn't move.*) What's the matter? (BIFF *remains motionless, tears falling.*) 1315 She's a buyer. Buys for J.H. Simmons. She lives down the hall—they're painting. You don't imagine—(*He breaks off. After a pause.*) Now listen, pal, she's just a buyer. She sees merchandise in her room and they have to keep it looking just so . . . (*Pause. Assuming command.*) All right, 1320 get my suits. (BIFF *doesn't move.*) Now stop crying and do as I say. I gave you an order. Biff, I gave you an order! Is that what you do when I give you an order? How dare you cry! (*Putting his arm around* BIFF.) Now look, Biff, when you grow up you'll understand about these things. You mustn't—you mustn't overemphasize a thing like this. I'll see Birnbaum first thing in the morning.

BIFF: Never mind.

WILLY: (*Getting down beside* BIFF.) Never mind! He's going to give you those points. I'll see to it.

BIFF: He wouldn't listen to you.

WILLY: He certainly will listen to me. You need those points for the U. of Virginia.

BIFF: I'm not going there.

WILLY: Heh? If I can't get him to change that mark you'll make it up in summer school. You've got all summer to—

BIFF: (*His weeping breaking from him.*) Dad . . .

WILLY: (*Infected by it.*) Oh, my boy . . .

BIFF: Dad . . .

WILLY: She's nothing to me, Biff. I was lonely, I was terribly lonely.

BIFF: You—you gave her Mama's stockings! (*His tears break through and he rises to go.*)

WILLY: (*Grabbing for* BIFF.) I gave you an order!

BIFF: Don't touch me, you—liar!

WILLY: Apologize for that!

BIFF: You fake! You phony little fake! You fake! (*Overcome, he turns quickly and weeping fully goes out with his suitcase.* WILLY *is left on the floor on his knees.*)

WILLY: I gave you an order! Biff, come back here or I'll beat you! Come back here! I'll whip you!

(STANLEY *comes quickly in from the right and stands in front of* WILLY.)

WILLY: (*Shouts at* STANLEY.) I gave you an order . . .

STANLEY: Hey, let's pick it up, pick it up, Mr. Loman. (*He helps* WILLY *to his feet.*) Your boys left with the chippies. They said they'll see you home.

(*A second waiter watches some distance away.*)

WILLY: But we were supposed to have dinner together.

(*Music is heard,* WILLY's *theme.*)

STANLEY: Can you make it?

WILLY: I'll—sure, I can make it. (*Suddenly concerned about his clothes.*) Do I—I look all right?

STANLEY: Sure, you look all right. (*He flicks a speck off* WILLY's *lapel.*)

WILLY: Here—here's a dollar.

STANLEY: Oh, your son paid me. It's all right.

WILLY: (*Putting it in* STANLEY's *hand.*) No, take it. You're a good, boy.

STANLEY: Oh, no, you don't have to . . .

WILLY: Here—here's some more, I don't need it any more. (*After a slight pause.*) Tell me—is there a seed store in the neighborhood?

STANLEY: Seeds? You mean like to plant?

(*As* WILLY *turns,* STANLEY *slips the money back into his jacket pocket.*)

WILLY: Yes. Carrots, peas . . .

STANLEY: Well, there's hardware stores on Sixth Avenue, but it may be too late now.

WILLY: (*Anxiously.*) Oh, I'd better hurry. I've got to get some seeds. (*He starts off to the right.*) I've got to get some seeds, right away. Nothing's planted. I don't have a thing in the ground.

(WILLY *hurries out as the light goes down.* STANLEY *moves over to the right after him, watches him off. The other waiter has been staring at* WILLY.)

STANLEY: (*To the waiter.*) Well, whatta you looking at?

(*The waiter picks up the chairs and moves off right.* STANLEY *takes the table and follows him. The light fades on this area. There is a long pause, the sound of the flute coming over. The light gradually rises on the kitchen, which is empty.* HAPPY *appears at the door of the house, followed by* BIFF. HAPPY *is carrying a large bunch of long-stemmed roses. He enters the kitchen, looks around for* LINDA. *Not seeing her, he turns to* BIFF, *who is just outside the house door, and makes a gesture with his hands, indicating "Not here, I guess." He looks into the living-room and freezes. Inside,* LINDA, *unseen, is seated,* WILLY's *coat on her lap. She rises ominously and quietly and moves toward* HAPPY, *who backs up into the kitchen, afraid.*)

HAPPY: Hey, what're you doing up? (LINDA *says nothing but moves toward him implacably.*) Where's Pop? (*He keeps backing to the right, and now* LINDA *is in full view in the doorway to the living-room.*) Is he sleeping?

LINDA: Where were you?

HAPPY: (*Trying to laugh it off.*) We met two girls, Mom, very fine types. Here, we brought you some flowers. (*Offering them to her.*) Put them in your room, Ma.

(*She knocks them to the floor at* BIFF's *feet. He has now come inside and closed the door behind him. She stares at* BIFF, *silent.*)

HAPPY: Now what'd you do that for? Mom, I want you to have some flowers—

LINDA: (*Cutting* HAPPY *off, violently to* BIFF.) Don't you care whether he lives or dies?

HAPPY: (*Going to the stairs.*) Come upstairs, Biff.

BIFF: (*With a flare of disgust, to* HAPPY.) Go away from me! (*To* LINDA.) What do you mean, lives or dies? Nobody's dying around here, pal.

LINDA: Get out of my sight! Get out of here!

BIFF: I wanna see the boss.

LINDA: You're not going near him!

BIFF: Where is he? (*He moves into the living-room and* LINDA *follows.*)

LINDA: (*Shouting after* BIFF.) You invite him for dinner. He looks forward to it all day—(BIFF *appears in his parents' bedroom, looks around, and exits.*)—and then you desert him there. There's no stranger you'd do that to!

HAPPY: Why? He had a swell time with us. Listen, when I—(LINDA *comes back into the kitchen.*)—desert him I hope I don't outlive the day!

LINDA: Get out of here!

HAPPY: Now look, Mom . . .

LINDA: Did you have to go to women tonight? You and your lousy rotten whores!

(BIFF *re-enters the kitchen.*)

HAPPY: Mom, all we did was follow Biff around trying to cheer him up! (*To* BIFF.) Boy, what a night you gave me!

LINDA: Get out of here, both of you, and don't come back! I don't want you tormenting him any more. Go on now, 1415 get your things together! (*To* BIFF.) You can sleep in his apartment. (*She starts to pick up the flowers and stops herself.*) Pick up this stuff, I'm not your maid any more. Pick it up, you bum, you!

(HAPPY *turns his back to her in refusal.* BIFF *slowly moves over and gets down on his knees, picking up the flowers.*)

LINDA: You're a pair of animals! Not one, not another living 1420 soul would have had the cruelty to walk out on that man in a restaurant!

BIFF: (*Not looking at her.*) Is that what he said?

LINDA: He didn't have to say anything. He was so humiliated he nearly limped when he came in.

1425 HAPPY: But, Mom, he had a great time with us—

BIFF: (*Cutting him off violently.*) Shut up!

(*Without another word,* HAPPY *goes upstairs.*)

LINDA: You! You didn't even go in to see if he was all right!

BIFF: (*Still on the floor in front of* LINDA, *the flowers in his hand; with self-loathing.*) No. Didn't. Didn't do a damned thing. 1430 How do you like that, heh? Left him babbling in a toilet.

LINDA: You louse. You . . .

BIFF: Now you hit it on the nose! (*He gets up, throws the flowers in the wastebasket.*) The scum of the earth, and you're looking at him!

1435 LINDA: Get out of here!

BIFF: I gotta talk to the boss, Mom. Where is he?

LINDA: You're not going near him. Get out of this house!

BIFF: (*With absolute assurance, determination.*) No. We're gonna have an abrupt conversation, him and me.

1440 LINDA: You're not talking to him!

(*Hammering is heard from outside the house, off right.* BIFF *turns toward the noise.*)

LINDA: (*Suddenly pleading.*) Will you please leave him alone?

BIFF: What's he doing out there?

LINDA: He's planting the garden!

BIFF: (*Quietly.*) Now? Oh, my God!

(BIFF *moves outside,* LINDA *following. The light dies down on them and comes up on the center of the apron as* WILLY *walks into it. He is carrying a flashlight, a hoe, and a handful of seed packets. He raps the top of the hoe sharply to fix it firmly, and then moves to the left, measuring off the distance with his foot. He holds the flashlight to look at the seed packets, reading off the instructions. He is in the blue of night.*)

1445 WILLY: Carrots . . . quarter-inch apart. Rows . . . one-foot rows. (*He measures it off.*) One foot. (*He puts down a package and measures off.*) Beets. (*He puts down another package and measures again.*) Lettuce. (*He reads the package, puts it down.*) One foot—(*He breaks off as* BEN *appears at the right and* 1450 *moves slowly down to him.*) What a proposition, ts, ts. Terrific,

terrific. 'Cause she's suffered, Ben, the woman has suffered. You understand me? A man can't go out the way he came in, Ben, a man has got to add up to something. You can't, you can't—(BEN *moves toward him as though to interrupt.*) You 1455 gotta consider, now. Don't answer so quick. Remember, it's a guaranteed twenty-thousand-dollar proposition. Now look, Ben, I want you to go through the ins and outs of this thing with me. I've got nobody to talk to, Ben, and the woman has suffered, you hear me?

BEN: (*Standing still, considering.*) What's the proposition? 1460

WILLY: It's twenty thousand dollars on the barrelhead. Guaranteed, gilt-edged, you understand?

BEN: You don't want to make a fool of yourself. They might not honor the policy.

WILLY: How can they dare refuse? Didn't I work like a coolie to 1465 meet every premium on the nose? And now they don't pay off? Impossible!

BEN: It's called a cowardly thing, William.

WILLY: Why? Does it take more guts to stand here the rest of my life ringing up a zero? 1470

BEN: (*Yielding.*) That's a point, William. (*He moves, thinking, turns.*) And twenty thousand—that *is* something one can feel with the hand, it is there.

WILLY: (*Now assured, with rising power.*) Oh, Ben, that's the whole beauty of it! I see it like a diamond, shining in the 1475 dark, hard and rough, that I can pick up and touch in my hand. Not like—like an appointment! This would not be another damned-fool appointment, Ben, and it changes all the aspects. Because he thinks I'm nothing, see, and so he spites me. But the funeral—(*Straightening up.*) Ben, 1480 that funeral will be massive! They'll come from Maine, Massachusetts, Vermont, New Hampshire! All the oldtimers with the strange license plates—that boy will be thunder-struck, Ben, because he never realized—I am known! Rhode Island, New York, New Jersey—I am known, 1485 Ben, and he'll see it with his eyes once and for all. He'll see what I am, Ben! He's in for a shock, that boy!

BEN: (*Coming down to the edge of the garden.*) He'll call you a coward.

WILLY: (*Suddenly fearful.*) No, that would be terrible. 1490

BEN: Yes. And a damned fool.

WILLY: No, no, he mustn't, I won't have that! (*He is broken and desperate.*)

BEN: He'll hate you, William.

(*The gay music of the Boys is heard.*)

WILLY: Oh, Ben, how do we get back to all the great times? 1495 Used to be so full of light, and comradeship, the sleigh-riding in winter, and the ruddiness on his cheeks. And always some kind of good news coming up, always something nice coming up ahead. And never even let me carry the valises in the house, and simonizing, simonizing 1500 that little red car! Why, why can't I give him something and not have him hate me?

BEN: Let me think about it. (*He glances at his watch.*) I still have a little time. Remarkable proposition, but you've got to be sure you're not making a fool of yourself. 1505

(BEN *drifts off upstage and goes out of sight.* BIFF *comes down from the left.*)

WILLY: (*Suddenly conscious of* BIFF, *turns and looks up at him, then begins picking up the packages of seeds in confusion.*) Where the hell is that seed? (*Indignantly.*) You can't see nothing out here! They boxed in the whole goddam neighborhood!

1510 BIFF: There are people all around here. Don't you realize that?

WILLY: I'm busy. Don't bother me.

BIFF: (*Taking the hoe from* WILLY.) I'm saying good-by to you, Pop. (WILLY *looks at him, silent, unable to move.*) I'm not coming back any more.

1515 WILLY: You're not going to see Oliver tomorrow?

BIFF: I've got no appointment, Dad.

WILLY: He put his arm around you, and you've got no appointment?

BIFF: Pop, get this now, will you? Everytime I've left it's been a
1520 fight that sent me out of here. Today I realized something about myself and I tried to explain it to you and I—I think I'm just not smart enough to make any sense out of it for you. To hell with whose fault it is or anything like that. (*He takes* WILLY's *arm.*) Let's just wrap it up, heh? Come on in, we'll tell
1525 Mom. (*He gently tries to pull* WILLY *to left.*)

WILLY: (*Frozen, immobile, with guilt in his voice.*) No, I don't want to see her.

BIFF: Come on! (*He pulls again, and* WILLY *tries to pull away.*)

WILLY: (*Highly nervous.*) No, no, I don't want to see her.

1530 BIFF: (*Tries to look into* WILLY's *face, as if to find the answer there.*) Why don't you want to see her?

WILLY: (*More harshly now.*) Don't bother me, will you?

BIFF: What do you mean, you don't want to see her? You don't want them calling you yellow, do you? This isn't your fault; it's
1535 me, I'm a bum. Now come inside! (WILLY *strains to get away.*) Did you hear what I said to you?

(WILLY *pulls away and quickly goes by himself into the house.* BIFF *follows.*)

LINDA: (*To* WILLY). Did you plant, dear?

BIFF: (*At the door, to* LINDA.) All right, we had it out. I'm going and I'm not writing any more.

1540 LINDA: (*Going to* WILLY *in the kitchen.*) I think that's the best way, dear. 'Cause there's no use drawing it out, you'll just never get along.

(WILLY *doesn't respond.*)

BIFF: People ask where I am and what I'm doing, you don't know, and you don't care. That way it'll be off your mind
1545 and you can start brightening up again. All right? That clears it, doesn't it? (WILLY *is silent, and* BIFF *goes to him.*) You gonna wish me luck, scout? (*He extends his hand.*) What do you say?

LINDA: Shake his hand, Willy.

1550 WILLY: (*Turning to her, seething with hurt.*) There's no necessity to mention the pen at all, y'know.

BIFF: (*Gently.*) I've got no appointment, Dad.

WILLY: (*Erupting fiercely.*) He put his arm around . . . ?

BIFF: Dad, you're never going to see what I am, so what's the use
1555 of arguing? If I strike oil I'll send you a check. Meantime forget I'm alive.

WILLY: (*To* LINDA.) Spite, see?

BIFF: Shake hands, Dad.

WILLY: Not my hand.

1560 BIFF: I was hoping not to go this way.

WILLY: Well, this is the way you're going. Good-by.

(BIFF *looks at him a moment, then turns sharply and goes to the stairs.*)

WILLY: (*Stops him with.*) May you rot in hell if you leave this house!

BIFF: (*Turning.*) Exactly what is it that you want from me?

WILLY: I want you to know, on the train, in the mountains, in 1565 the valleys, wherever you go, that you cut down your life for spite!

BIFF: No, no.

WILLY: Spite, spite, is the word of your undoing! And when you're down and out, remember what did it. When you're rotting 1570 somewhere beside the railroad tracks, remember, and don't you dare blame it on me!

BIFF: I'm not blaming it on you!

WILLY: I won't take the rap for this, you hear?

(HAPPY *comes down the stairs and stands on the bottom step, watching.*)

BIFF: That's just what I'm telling you! 1575

WILLY: (*Sinking into a chair at the table, with full accusation.*) You're trying to put a knife in me—don't think I don't know what you're doing!

BIFF: All right, phony! Then let's lay it on the line. (*He whips the rubber tube out of his pocket and puts it on the table.*) 1580

HAPPY: You crazy—

LINDA: Biff! (*She moves to grab the hose, but* BIFF *holds it down with his hand.*)

BIFF: Leave it there! Don't move it!

WILLY: (*Not looking at it.*) What is that? 1585

BIFF: You know goddam well what that is.

WILLY: (*Caged, wanting to escape.*) I never saw that.

BIFF: You saw it. The mice didn't bring it into the cellar! What is this supposed to do, make a hero out of you? This supposed to make me sorry for you? 1590

WILLY: Never heard of it.

BIFF: There'll be no pity for you, you hear it? No pity!

WILLY: (*To* LINDA.) You hear the spite!

BIFF: No, you're going to hear the truth—what you are and what I am! 1595

LINDA: Stop it!

WILLY: Spite!

HAPPY: (*Coming down toward* BIFF.) You cut it now!

BIFF: (*To* HAPPY.) The man don't know who we are! The man is gonna know! (*To* WILLY.) We never told the truth for ten 1600 minutes in this house!

HAPPY: We always told the truth!

BIFF: (*Turning on him.*) You big blow, are you the assistant buyer? You're one of the two assistants to the assistant, aren't you? 1605

HAPPY: Well, I'm practically—

BIFF: You're practically full of it! We all are! And I'm through with it. (*To* WILLY.) Now hear this, Willy, this is me.

WILLY: I know you!

BIFF: You know why I had no address for three months? I stole 1610 a suit in Kansas City and I was in jail. (*To* LINDA, *who is sobbing.*) Stop crying. I'm through with it.

(LINDA *turns away from them, her hands covering her face.*)

WILLY: I suppose that's my fault!

BIFF: I stole myself out of every good job since high school!

1615 WILLY: And whose fault is that?

BIFF: And I never got anywhere because you blew me so full of hot air I could never stand taking orders from anybody! That's whose fault it is!

1620 WILLY: I hear that!

LINDA: Don't, Biff!

BIFF: It's goddam time you heard that! I had to be boss big shot in two weeks, and I'm through with it!

WILLY: Then hang yourself! For spite, hang yourself!

BIFF: No! Nobody's hanging himself, Willy! I ran down eleven
1625 flights with a pen in my hand today. And suddenly I stopped, you hear me? And in the middle of that office building, do you hear this? I stopped in the middle of that building and I saw—the sky. I saw the things that I love in this world. The work and the food and time to sit and smoke. And I looked
1630 at the pen and said to myself, what the hell am I grabbing this for? Why am I trying to become what I don't want to be? What am I doing in an office, making a contemptuous, begging fool of myself, when all I want is out there, waiting for me the minute I say I know who I am! Why can't I say
1635 that, Willy? (*He tries to make* WILLY *face him, but* WILLY *pulls away and moves to the left.*)

WILLY: (*With hatred, threateningly.*) The door of your life is wide open!

BIFF: Pop! I'm a dime a dozen, and so are you!

1640 WILLY: (*Turning on him now in an uncontrolled outburst.*) I am not a dime a dozen! I am Willy Loman, and you are Biff Loman!

(BIFF *starts for* WILLY, *but is blocked by* HAPPY. *In his fury,* BIFF *seems on the verge of attacking his father.*)

BIFF: I am not a leader of men, Willy, and neither are you. You were never anything but a hard-working drummer who
1645 landed in the ash can like all the rest of them! I'm one dollar an hour, Willy! I tried seven states and couldn't raise it. A buck an hour! Do you gather my meaning? I'm not bringing home any prizes any more, and you're going to stop waiting for me to bring them home!

1650 WILLY: (*Directly to* BIFF.) You vengeful, spiteful mut!

(BIFF *breaks from* HAPPY. WILLY, *in fright, starts up the stairs.* BIFF *grabs him.*)

BIFF: (*At the peak of his fury.*) Pop, I'm nothing! I'm nothing, Pop. Can't you understand that? There's no spite in it any more. I'm just what I am, that's all.

(BIFF's *fury has spent itself, and he breaks down, sobbing, holding on to* WILLY, *who dumbly fumbles for* BIFF's *face.*)

WILLY: (*Astonished.*) What're you doing? What're you doing?
1655 (*To* LINDA.) Why is he crying?

BIFF: (*Crying, broken.*) Will you let me go, for Christ's sake? Will you take that phony dream and burn it before something happens? (*Struggling to contain himself, he pulls away and moves to the stairs.*) I'll go in the morning. Put
1660 him—put him to bed. (*Exhausted,* BIFF *moves up the stairs to his room.*)

WILLY: (*After a long pause, astonished, elevated.*) Isn't that—isn't that remarkable? Biff—he likes me!

LINDA: He loves you, Willy!

HAPPY: (*Deeply moved.*) Always did, Pop.
1665
WILLY: Oh, Biff! (*Staring wildly.*) He cried! Cried to me. (*He is choking with his love, and now cries out his promise.*) That boy—that boy is going to be magnificent!

(BEN *appears in the light just outside the kitchen.*)

BEN: Yes, outstanding, with twenty thousand behind him.

LINDA: (*Sensing the racing of his mind, fearfully, carefully.*) Now
1670 come to bed, Willy. It's all settled now.

WILLY: (*Finding it difficult not to rush out of the house.*) Yes, we'll sleep. Come on. Go to sleep, Hap.

BEN: And it does take a great kind of a man to crack the jungle.

(*In accents of dread,* BEN's *idyllic music starts up.*)

HAPPY: (*His arm around* LINDA.) I'm getting married, Pop,
1675 don't forget it. I'm changing everything. I'm gonna run that department before the year is up. You'll see, Mom. (*He kisses her.*)

BEN: The jungle is dark but full of diamonds, Willy.

(WILLY *turns, moves, listening to* BEN.)

LINDA: Be good. You're both good boys, just act that way,
1680 that's all.

HAPPY: 'Night, Pop. (*He goes upstairs.*)

LINDA: (*To* WILLY). Come, dear.

BEN: (*With greater force.*) One must go in to fetch a diamond
1685 out.

WILLY: (*To* LINDA, *as he moves slowly along the edge of the kitchen, toward the door.*) I just want to get settled down, Linda. Let me sit alone for a little.

LINDA: (*Almost uttering her fear.*) I want you upstairs.

WILLY: (*Taking her in his arms.*) In a few minutes, Linda. I
1690 couldn't sleep right now. Go on, you look awful tired. (*He kisses her.*)

BEN: Not like an appointment at all. A diamond is rough and hard to the touch.

WILLY: Go on now. I'll be right up.
1695
LINDA: I think this is the only way, Willy.

WILLY: Sure, it's the best thing.

BEN: Best thing!

WILLY: The only way. Everything is gonna be—go on, kid, get to
1700 bed. You look so tired.

LINDA: Come right up.

WILLY: Two minutes.

(LINDA *goes into the living-room, then reappears in her bedroom.* WILLY *moves just outside the kitchen door.*)

WILLY: Loves me. (*Wonderingly.*) Always loved me. Isn't that a remarkable thing? Ben, he'll worship me, for it!

BEN: (*With promise.*) It's dark there, but full of diamonds.
1705
WILLY: Can you imagine that magnificence with twenty thousand dollars in his pocket?

LINDA: (*Calling from her room.*) Willy! Come up!

WILLY: (*Calling into the kitchen.*) Yes! Yes. Coming! It's very smart, you realize that, don't you, sweetheart? Even Ben
1710 sees it. I gotta go, baby. 'By! 'By! (*Going over to* BEN, *almost dancing.*) Imagine? When the mail comes he'll be ahead of Bernard again!

BEN: A perfect proposition all around.

1715 WILLY: Did you see how he cried to me? Oh, if I could kiss him, Ben!

BEN: Time, William, time!

WILLY: Oh, Ben, I always knew one way or another we were gonna make it, Biff and I!

1720 BEN: (*Looking at his watch.*) The boat. We'll be late. (*He moves slowly off into the darkness.*)

WILLY: (*Elegiacally, turning to the house.*) Now when you kick off, boy, I want a seventy-yard boot, and get right down the field under the ball, and when you hit, hit low and hit hard,

1725 because it's important, boy. (*He swings around and faces the audience.*) There's all kinds of important people in the stands, and the first thing you know . . . (*Suddenly realizing he is alone.*) Ben! Ben, where do I . . . ? (*He makes a sudden movement of search.*) Ben, how do I . . . ?

1730 LINDA: (*Calling.*) Willy, you coming up?

WILLY: (*Uttering a gasp of fear, whirling about as if to quiet her.*) Sh! (*He turns around as if to find his way; sounds, faces, voices, seem to be swarming in upon him and he flicks at them, crying.*) Sh! Sh! (*Suddenly music, faint and high, stops him. It rises in*

1735 *intensity, almost to an unbearable scream. He goes up and down on his toes, and rushes off around the house.*) Shhh!

LINDA: Willy?

(*There is no answer. LINDA waits. BIFF gets up off his bed He is still in his clothes. HAPPY sits up. BIFF stands listening.*)

LINDA: (*With real fear.*) Willy, answer me! Willy!

(*There is the sound of a car starting and moving away at full speed.*)

LINDA: No!

1740 BIFF: (*Rushing down the stairs.*) Pop!

(*As the car speeds off, the music crashes down in a frenzy of sound, which becomes the soft pulsation of a single cello string. BIFF slowly returns to his bedroom. He and HAPPY gravely don their jackets. LINDA slowly walks out of her room. The music has developed into a dead march. The leaves of day are appearing over everything. CHARLEY and BERNARD, somberly dressed, appear and knock on the kitchen door. BIFF and HAPPY slowly descend the stairs to the kitchen as CHARLEY and BERNARD enter. All stop a moment when LINDA, in clothes of mourning, bearing a little bunch of roses, comes through the draped doorway into the kitchen. She goes to CHARLEY and takes his arm. Now all move toward the audience, through the wall-line of the kitchen. At the limit of the apron, LINDA lays down the flowers, kneels, and sits back on her heels. All stare down at the grave.*)

REQUIEM

CHARLEY: It's getting dark, Linda.

(*LINDA doesn't react. She stares at the grave.*)

BIFF: How about it, Mom? Better get some rest, heh? They'll be closing the gate soon.

(*LINDA makes no move. Pause.*)

HAPPY: (*Deeply angered.*) He had no right to do that. There was no necessity for it. We would've helped him. 5

CHARLEY: (*Grunting.*) Hmmm.

BIFF: Come along, Mom.

LINDA: Why didn't anybody come?

CHARLEY: It was a very nice funeral.

LINDA: But where are all the people he knew? Maybe they blame him. 10

CHARLEY: Naa. It's a rough world, Linda. They wouldn't blame him.

LINDA: I can't understand it. At this time especially. First time in thirty-five years we were just about free and clear. He only needed a little salary. He was even finished with the dentist. 15

CHARLEY: No man only needs a little salary.

LINDA: I can't understand it.

BIFF: There were a lot of nice days. When he'd come home from a trip; or on Sundays, making the stoop; finishing the cellar; putting on the new porch; when he built the extra bathroom; and put up the garage. You know something, Charley, there's more of him in that front stoop than in all the sales he ever made. 20 25

CHARLEY: Yeah. He was a happy man with a batch of cement.

LINDA: He was so wonderful with his hands.

BIFF: He had the wrong dreams. All, all, wrong.

HAPPY: (*Almost ready to fight BIFF.*) Don't say that!

BIFF: He never knew who he was. 30

CHARLEY: (*Stopping HAPPY's movement and reply. To BIFF.*) Nobody dast blame this man. You don't understand: Willy was a salesman. And for a salesman, there is no rock bottom to the life. He don't put a bolt to a nut, he don't tell you the law or give you medicine. He's a man way out there in the blue, riding on a smile and a shoeshine. And when they start not smiling back—that's an earthquake. And then you get yourself a couple of spots on your hat, and you're finished. Nobody dast blame this man. A salesman is got to dream, boy. It comes with the territory. 35 40

BIFF: Charley, the man didn't know who he was.

HAPPY: (*Infuriated.*) Don't say that!

BIFF: Why don't you come with me, Happy?

HAPPY: I'm not licked that easily. I'm staying right in this city, and I'm gonna beat this racket! (*He looks at BIFF, his chin set.*) The Loman Brothers! 45

BIFF: I know who I am, kid.

HAPPY: All right, boy. I'm gonna show you and everybody else that Willy Loman did not die in vain. He had a good dream. It's the only dream you can have—to come out number-one man. He fought it out here, and this is where I'm gonna win it for him. 50

BIFF: (*With a hopeless glance at HAPPY, bends toward his mother.*) Let's go, Mom.

LINDA: I'll be with you in a minute. Go on, Charley. (*He hesitates.*) I want to, just for a minute. I never had a chance to say good-by. 55

(*CHARLEY moves away, followed by HAPPY. BIFF remains a slight distance up and left of LINDA. She sits there, summoning herself. The flute begins, not far away, playing behind her speech.*)

LINDA: Forgive me, dear. I can't cry. I don't know what it is, but I can't cry. I don't understand it. Why did you ever do that? Help me, Willy, I can't cry. It seems to me that you're just on 60 another trip. I keep expecting you. Willy, dear, I can't cry. Why did you do it? I search and search and I search, and I can't understand it, Willy. I made the last payment on the house today. Today, dear. And there'll be nobody home. (*A sob rises in her throat.*) We're free and clear. (*Sobbing more fully, released.*) We're free. (BIFF *comes slowly toward her.*) We're free . . . We're free . . .

65

BIFF *lifts her to her feet and moves out up right with her in his arms.* LINDA *sobs quietly.* BERNARD *and* CHARLEY *come together and follow them, followed by* HAPPY. *Only the music of the flute is left on the darkening stage as over the house the hard towers of the apartment buildings rise into sharp focus, and*

The Curtain Falls

Amiri Baraka / Leroi Jones

Born Everett LeRoi Jones in Newark, New Jersey, in 1934, Amiri Baraka has become the most important revolutionary voice in contemporary black theater in the United States. He attended Rutgers University and Howard University, taking his B.A. from Howard in 1954. Baraka later said that his education at Howard was too involved with "learning to be white." He served in the United States Air Force before returning to New York in 1958. Living in Greenwich Village, he studied at Columbia University, married his first wife—an interracial marriage, lightly disguised in his play *The Slave*—and worked to develop his talents as a writer. Jones worked everywhere to develop a black esthetic, in his own poetry (in the mode of the Beat poets Gregory Corso and Allen Ginsberg), in essays, and in magazines that he founded and edited. In 1960, Jones was part of a delegation of black Americans invited to Cuba to celebrate Fidel Castro's revolution. That visit had a profound impact on Jones, sharpening his sense of the need both for a distinctive black esthetic and culture, and for a social revolution to eradicate the injustices of white-dominated American society. His plays of the 1960s are, in fact, often directly concerned with this issue and with how white liberalism—ostensibly the ally of black power—finally becomes an obstacle to the more fundamental revolution needed to bring black identity, culture, and power into being. In 1964, three of his plays opened in New York: *The Eighth Ditch, The Baptism,* and *Dutchman,* which won the Obie award for the best American play of the season. He then wrote a series of plays examining black activism and revolution in American life: *The Slave* (1964) and *The Toilet* (1964), *Experimental Death Unit #1* (1965), and *J-e-l-l-o* (1965). The assassination of Malcolm X in 1965 and the Watts riots in Los Angeles also drove Jones toward a more militant position, as articulated in plays like *A Black Mass* (1966), *Slave Ship* (1966), *The Great Goodness of Life* (*A Coon Show*) (1967), *Home on the Range* (1968), and *The Death of Malcolm X* (1969), and later in *The Motion of History* (1977) and *Money* (1988).

© T. Charles Erickson

Clay strangles Lula in the subway at the climax of Amiri Baraka/LeRoi Jones's *Dutchman,* produced by the Hartford Stage in 2000.

In 1964 Jones established the Black Arts Repertory Theater and School in Harlem and began a program of cultural nationalism there, which he has pursued subsequently in several other organizations and described in several collections of essays. He has been deeply involved in developing a theater that would serve the need for cultural and political revolution in the black community.

As part of his commitment to forging a sustaining system of values for the African American community, Jones became a Kawaidi Muslim minister in 1968, adopting the title Imamu (spiritual leader) and the name Amiri Baraka at that time. Throughout the 1970s and 1980s, Baraka articulated and solidified the claims of cultural nationalism, frequently in a fiercely revolutionary, Marxist rhetoric. Baraka continues to be involved in a variety of political and social activities in the black community.

Dutchman

Dutchman is one of Baraka's most powerful plays, both in its indictment of racist culture and in its straightforward confrontation between Lula and Clay. The title alludes to the legendary *Flying Dutchman*, the ship of the dead said to haunt the high seas. The subway car of the play is at once a ghost ship—where the young black man Clay is murdered—and a ghostly incarnation of racist fantasies. At the beginning of the play, Lula seems attracted to the middle-class Clay, but as the play develops it becomes clear that, to seduce Clay, Lula must transform him into something else, a fantasy figure of the white imagination. When Clay refuses to play along, delivering instead an impassioned statement of his own black identity, Lula murders him, with the implied consent of the white riders of the subway. *Dutchman* is a powerful parable of the problems of black identity in white culture.

Dutchman

Amiri Baraka/LeRoi Jones

CHARACTERS

CLAY, *twenty-year-old Negro*
LULA, *thirty-year-old white woman*
RIDERS OF COACH, *white and black*
YOUNG NEGRO
CONDUCTOR

In the flying underbelly of the city. Steaming hot, and summer on top, outside. Underground. The subway heaped in modern myth.

Opening scene is a man sitting in a subway seat, holding a magazine but looking vacantly just above its wilting pages. Occasionally he looks blankly toward the window on his right. Dim lights and darkness whistling by against the glass. (Or paste the lights, as admitted props, right on the subway windows. Have them move, even dim and flicker. But give the sense of speed. Also stations, whether the train is stopped or the glitter and activity of these stations merely flashes by the windows.)

The man is sitting alone. That is, only his seat is visible, though the rest of the car is outfitted as a complete subway car. But only his seat is shown. There might be, for a time, as the play begins, a loud scream of the actual train. And it can recur throughout the play, or continue on a lower key once the dialogue starts.

The train slows after a time, pulling to a brief stop at one of the stations. The man looks idly up, until he sees a woman's face staring at him through the window; when it realizes that the man has noticed the face, it begins very premeditatedly to smile. The man smiles too, for a moment, without a trace of self-consciousness. Almost an instinctive though undesirable response. Then a kind of awkwardness or embarrassment sets in, and the man makes to look away, is further embarrassed, so he brings back his eyes to where the face was, but by now the train is moving again, and the face would seem to be left behind by the way the man turns his head to look back through the other windows at the slowly fading platform. He smiles then; more comfortably confident, hoping perhaps that his memory of this brief encounter will be pleasant. And then he is idle again.

SCENE ONE

Train roars. Lights flash outside the windows.

LULA *enters from the rear of the car in bright, skimpy summer clothes and sandals. She carries a net bag full of paper books, fruit, and other anonymous articles. She is wearing sunglasses, which she pushes up on her forehead from time to time. LULA is a tall, slender, beautiful woman with long red hair hanging straight down her back, wearing only loud lipstick in somebody's good taste. She is eating an apple, very daintily. Coming down the car toward CLAY.*

She stops beside CLAY's seat and hangs languidly from the strap, still managing to eat the apple. It is apparent that she is going to sit in the seat next to CLAY, and that she is only waiting for him to notice her before she sits.

CLAY *sits as before, looking just beyond his magazine, now and again pulling the magazine slowly back and forth in front of his face in a hopeless effort to fan himself. Then he sees the woman hanging there beside him and he looks up into her face, smiling quizzically.*

LULA: Hello.
CLAY: Uh, hi're you?
LULA: I'm going to sit down. . . . O.K.?
CLAY: Sure.
5 LULA:

(Swings down onto the seat, pushing her legs straight out as if she is very weary.)

   Oooof! Too much weight.
CLAY: Ha, doesn't look like much to me.

(Leaning back against the window, a little surprised and maybe stiff.)

LULA: It's so anyway.

(And she moves her toes in the sandals, then pulls her right leg up on the left knee, better to inspect the bottoms of the sandals and the back of her heel. She appears for a second not to notice that CLAY is sitting next to her or that she has spoken to him just a second before. CLAY looks at the magazine, then out the black window. As he does this, she turns very quickly toward him.)

   Weren't you staring at me through the window?
CLAY: 10

(Wheeling around and very much stiffened.)

   What?
LULA: Weren't you staring at me through the window? At the last stop?
CLAY: Staring at you? What do you mean?
LULA: Don't you know what staring means?   15
CLAY: I saw you through the window . . . if that's what it means. I don't know if I was staring. Seems to me you were staring through the window at me.
LULA: I was. But only after I'd turned around and saw you staring through that window down in the vicinity of my ass   20
and legs.
CLAY: Really?
LULA: Really. I guess you were just taking those idle potshots. Nothing else to do. Run your mind over people's flesh.
CLAY: Oh boy. Wow, now I admit I was looking in your direction.   25
But the rest of that weight is yours.
LULA: I suppose.
CLAY: Staring through train windows is weird business. Much weirder than staring very sedately at abstract asses.
LULA: That's why I came looking through the window . . . so you'd   30
have more than that to go on. I even smiled at you.
CLAY: That's right.
LULA: I even got into this train, going some other way than mine. Walked down the aisle . . . searching you out.

35   CLAY: Really? That's pretty funny.
LULA: That's pretty funny. . . . God, you're dull.
CLAY: Well, I'm sorry, lady, but I really wasn't prepared for party
       talk.
LULA: No, you're not. What are you prepared for?

(*Wrapping the apple core in a Kleenex and dropping it on the floor.*)

40   CLAY:

(*Takes her conversation as pure sex talk. He turns to confront her
squarely with this idea.*)

     I'm prepared for anything. How about you?
LULA:

(*Laughing loudly and cutting it off abruptly.*)

     What do you think you're doing?
CLAY: What?
45   LULA: You think I want to pick you up, get you to take me
       somewhere and screw me, huh?
CLAY: Is that the way I look?
LULA: You look like you been trying to grow a beard. That's
       exactly what you look like. You look like you live in New
50   Jersey with your parents and are trying to grow a beard.
       That's what. You look like you've been reading Chinese
       poetry and drinking lukewarm sugarless tea.

(*Laughs, uncrossing and recrossing her legs.*)

     You look like death eating a soda cracker.
CLAY:

(*Cocking his head from one side to the other, embarrassed and trying to make some comeback, but also intrigued by what the woman
is saying . . . even the sharp city coarseness of her voice, which is
still a kind of gentle sidewalk throb.*)

55   Really? I look like all that?
LULA: Not all of it.

(*She feigns a seriousness to cover an actual somber tone.*)

     I lie a lot.

(*Smiling.*)

     It helps me control the world.
CLAY:

(*Relieved and laughing louder than the humor.*)

60   Yeah, I bet.
LULA: But it's true, most of it, right? Jersey? Your bumpy neck?
CLAY: How'd you know all that? Huh? Really. I mean about
       Jersey . . . and even the beard. I met you before? You know
       Warren Enright?
65   LULA: You tried to make it with your sister when you were ten.

(*CLAY leans back hard against the back of the seat, his eyes opening
now, still trying to look amused.*)

     But I succeeded a few weeks ago.

(*She starts to laugh again.*)

CLAY: What're you talking about? Warren tell you that? You're a
       friend of Georgia's?
LULA: I told you I lie. I don't know your sister. I don't know
       Warren Enright.   70
CLAY: You mean you're just picking these things out of the air?
LULA: Is Warren Enright a tall skinny black black boy with a
       phony English accent?
CLAY: I figured you knew him.
LULA: But I don't. I just figured you would know somebody   75
       like that.

(*Laughs.*)

CLAY: Yeah, yeah.
LULA: You're probably on your way to his house now.
CLAY: That's right.   80
LULA:

(*Putting her hand on CLAY's closer knee, drawing it from the knee
up to the thigh's hinge, then removing it, watching his face very
closely, and continuing to laugh, perhaps more gently than before.*)

     Dull, dull, dull. I bet you think I'm exciting.
CLAY: You're O.K.
LULA: Am I exciting you now?
CLAY: Right. That's not what's supposed to happen?
LULA: How do I know?   85

(*She returns her hand, without moving it, then takes it away and
plunges it in her bag to draw out an apple.*)

     You want this?
CLAY: Sure.
LULA:

(*She gets one out of the bag for herself.*)

     Eating apples together is always the first step. Or walking up
     uninhabited Seventh Avenue in the twenties on weekends.   90

(*Bites and giggles, glancing at CLAY and speaking in loose singsong.*)

     Can get you involved . . . boy! Get us involved. Um-huh.

(*Mock seriousness.*)

     Would you like to get involved with me, Mister Man?
CLAY:

(*Trying to be as flippant as LULA, whacking happily at the apple.*)

     Sure. Why not? A beautiful woman like you. Huh, I'd be a
     fool not to.   95
LULA: And I bet you're sure you know what you're talking
       about.

(*Taking him a little roughly by the wrist, so he cannot eat the
apple, then shaking the wrist.*)

I bet you're sure of almost everything anybody ever asked you about . . . right?

(*Shakes his wrist harder.*)

100 Right?
CLAY: Yeah, right. . . . Wow, you're pretty strong, you know? Whatta you, a lady wrestler or something?
LULA: What's wrong with lady wrestlers? And don't answer because you never knew any. Huh.

(*Cynically.*)

105 That's for sure. They don't have any lady wrestlers in that part of Jersey. That's for sure.
CLAY: Hey, you still haven't tole me how you know so much about me.
LULA: I told you I didn't know anything about *you* . . . you're
110 a well-known type.
CLAY: Really?
LULA: Or at least I know the type very well. And your skinny English friend too.
CLAY: Anonymously?
115 LULA:

(*Settles back in seat, single-mindedly finishing her apple and humming snatches of rhythm and blues song.*)

What?
CLAY: Without knowing us specifically?
LULA: Oh boy.

(*Looking quickly at* CLAY.)

What a face. You know, you could be a handsome man.
120 CLAY: I can't argue with you.
LULA:

(*Vague, off-center response.*)

What?
CLAY:

(*Raising his voice, thinking the train noise has drowned part of his sentence.*)

I can't argue with you.
125 LULA: My hair is turning gray. A gray hair for each year and type I've come through.
CLAY: Why do you want to sound so old?
LULA: But it's always gentle when it starts.

(*Attention drifting.*)

Hugged against tenements, day or night.
130 CLAY: What?
LULA:

(*Refocusing.*)

Hey, why don't you take me to that party you're going to?
CLAY: You must be a friend of Warren's to know about the party.

LULA: Wouldn't you like to take me to the party?   135

(*Imitates clinging vine.*)

Oh, come on, ask me to your party.
CLAY: Of course I'll ask you to come with me to the party. And I'll bet you're a friend of Warren's.
LULA: Why not be a friend of Warren's? Why not?

(*Taking his arm.*)

Have you asked me yet?   140
CLAY: How can I ask you when I don't know your name?
LULA: Are you talking to my name?
CLAY: What is it, a secret?
LULA: I'm Lena the Hyena.
CLAY: The famous woman poet?   145
LULA: Poetess! The same!
CLAY: Well, you know so much about me . . . what's my name?
LULA: Morris the Hyena.
CLAY: The famous woman poet?
LULA: The same.   150

(*Laughing and going into her bag.*)

You want another apple?
CLAY: Can't make it, lady. I only have to keep one doctor away a day.
LULA: I bet your name is . . . something like . . . uh, Gerald or Walter. Huh?   155
CLAY: God, no.
LULA: Lloyd, Norman? One of those hopeless colored names creeping out of New Jersey. Leonard? Gag. . . .
CLAY: Like Warren?
LULA: Definitely. Just exactly like Warren. Or Everett.   160
CLAY: Gag. . . .
LULA: Well, for sure, it's not Willie.
CLAY: It's Clay.
LULA: Clay? Really? Clay what?
CLAY: Take your pick. Jackson, Johnson, or Williams.   165
LULA: Oh, really? Good for you. But it's got to be Williams. You're too pretentious to be a Jackson or Johnson.
CLAY: Thass right.
LULA: But Clay's O.K.
CLAY: So's Lena.   170
LULA: It's Lula.
CLAY: Oh?
LULA: Lula the Hyena.
CLAY: Very good.
LULA: 175

(*Starts laughing again.*)

Now you say to me, "Lula, Lula, why don't you go to this party with me tonight?" It's your turn, and let those be your lines.
CLAY: Lula, why don't you go to this party with me tonight, Huh?
LULA: Say my name twice before you ask, and no huh's.   180
CLAY: Lula, Lula, why don't you go to this party with me tonight?
LULA: I'd like to go, Clay, but how can you ask me to go when you barely know me?

185 CLAY: That is strange, isn't it?

LULA: What kind of reaction is that? You're supposed to say, "Aw, come on, we'll get to know each other better at the party."

CLAY: That's pretty corny.

LULA: What are you into anyway?

(*Looking at him half sullenly but still amused.*)

190 What thing are you playing at, Mister? Mister Clay Williams?

(*Grabs his thigh, up near the crotch.*)

What are you thinking about?

CLAY: Watch it now, you're gonna excite me for real.

LULA:

(*Taking her hand away and throwing her apple core through the window.*)

195 I bet.

(*She slumps in the seat and is heavily silent.*)

CLAY: I thought you knew everything about me? What happened?

(LULA *looks at him, then looks slowly away, then over where the other aisle would be. Noise of the train. She reaches in her bag and pulls out one of the paper books. She puts it on her leg and thumbs the pages listlessly.* CLAY *cocks his head to see the title of the book. Noise of the train.* LULA *flips pages and her eyes drift. Both remain silent.*)

Are you going to the party with me, Lula?

LULA:

(*Bored and not even looking.*)

I don't even know you.

200 CLAY: You said you know my type.

LULA:

(*Strangely irritated.*)

Don't get smart with me, Buster. I know you like the palm of my hand.

CLAY: The one you eat the apples with?

205 LULA: Yeh. And the one I open doors late Saturday evening with. That's my door. Up at the top of the stairs. Five flights. Above a lot of Italians and lying Americans. And scrape carrots with. Also . . .

(*Looks at him.*)

210 the same hand I unbutton my dress with, or let my skirt fall down. Same hand. Lover.

CLAY: Are you angry about anything? Did I say something wrong?

LULA: Everything you say is wrong.

(*Mock smile.*)

That's what makes you so attractive. Ha. In that funnybook jacket with all the buttons.

(*More animate, taking hold of his jacket.*)

What've you got the jacket and tie on in all this heat for? 215
And why're you wearing a jacket and tie like that? Did your people ever burn witches or start revolutions over the price of tea? Boy, those narrow-shoulder clothes come from a tradition you ought to feel oppressed by. A three-button suit. What right do you have to be wearing a three-button 220
suit and striped tie? Your grandfather was a slave, he didn't go to Harvard.

CLAY: My grandfather was a night watchman.

LULA: And you went to a colored college where everybody thought they were Averell Harriman. 225

CLAY: All except me.

LULA: And who did you think you were? Who do you think you are now?

CLAY:

(*Laughs as if to make light of the whole trend of the conversation.*)

Well, in college I thought I was Baudelaire. But I've slowed 230
down since.

LULA: I bet you never once thought you were a black nigger.

(*Mock serious, then she howls with laughter.* CLAY *is stunned but after initial reaction, he quickly tries to appreciate the humor.* LULA *almost shrieks.*)

A black Baudelaire.

CLAY: That's right.

LULA: Boy, are you corny. I take back what I said before. 235
Everything you say is not wrong. It's perfect. You should be on television.

CLAY: You act like you're on television already.

LULA: That's because I'm an actress.

CLAY: I thought so. 240

LULA: Well, you're wrong. I'm no actress. I told you I always lie. I'm nothing, honey, and don't you ever forget it.

(*Lighter.*)

Although my mother was a Communist. The only person in my family ever to amount to anything.

CLAY: My mother was a Republican. 245

LULA: And your father voted for the man rather than the party.

CLAY: Right!

LULA: Yea for him. Yea, yea for him.

CLAY: Yea!

LULA: And yea for America where he is free to vote for the 250
mediocrity of his choice! Yea!

CLAY: Yea!

LULA: And yea for both your parents who even though they differ about so crucial a matter as the body politic still forged a union of love and sacrifice that was destined to flower at the birth of 255
the noble Clay . . . what's your middle name?

CLAY: Clay.

LULA: A union of love and sacrifice that was destined to flower at the birth of the noble Clay Clay Williams. Yea! And most of all yea yea for you. Clay Clay. The Black Baudelaire! Yes! 260

(*And with knifelike cynicism.*)

My Christ. My Christ.

CLAY: Thank you, ma'am.

LULA: May the people accept you as a ghost of the future. And love you, that you might not kill them when you can.

265   CLAY: What?

LULA: You're a murderer, Clay, and you know it.

(*Her voice darkening with significance.*)

You know goddamn well what I mean.

CLAY: I do?

LULA: So we'll pretend the air is light and full of perfume.

270   CLAY:

(*Sniffing at her blouse.*)

It is.

LULA: And we'll pretend the people cannot see you. That is, the citizens. And that you are free of your own history. And I am free of my history. We'll pretend that we are both anonymous beauties smashing along through the city's entrails.

275

(*She yells as loud as she can.*)

GROOVE!

(*Black.*)

SCENE TWO

Scene is the same as before, though now there are other seats visible in the car. And throughout the scene other people get on the subway. There are maybe one or two seated in the car as the scene opens, though neither CLAY *nor* LULA *notices them.* CLAY's *tie is open.* LULA *is hugging his arm.*

CLAY: The party!

LULA: I know it'll be something good. You can come in with me, looking casual and significant. I'll be strange, haughty, and silent, and walk with long slow strides.

5   CLAY: Right.

LULA: When you get drunk, pat me once, very lovingly on the flanks, and I'll look at you cryptically, licking my lips.

CLAY: It sounds like something we can do.

LULA: You'll go around talking to young men about your mind,

10   and to old men about your plans. If you meet a very close friend who is also with someone like me, we can stand together, sipping our drinks and exchanging codes of lust. The atmosphere will be slithering in love and half-love and very open moral decision.

15   CLAY: Great. Great.

LULA: And everyone will pretend they don't know your name, and then . . .

(*She pauses heavily.*)

later, when they have to, they'll claim a friendship that denies your sterling character.

20   CLAY:

(*Kissing her neck and fingers.*)

And then what?

LULA: Then? Well, then we'll go down the street, late night, eating apples and winding very deliberately toward my house.

CLAY: Deliberately?   25

LULA: I mean, we'll look in all the shop windows, and make fun of the queers. Maybe we'll meet a Jewish Buddhist and flatten his conceits over some pretentious coffee.

CLAY: In honor of whose God?

LULA: Mine.   30

CLAY: Who is . . . ?

LULA: Me . . . and you.

CLAY: A corporate Godhead.

LULA: Exactly. Exactly.

(*Notices one of the other people entering.*)

CLAY: Go on with the chronicle. Then what happens to us?   35

LULA:

(*A mild depression, but she still makes her description triumphant and increasingly direct.*)

To my house, of course.

CLAY: Of course.

LULA: And up the narrow steps of the tenement.

CLAY: You live in a tenement?   40

LULA: Wouldn't live anywhere else. Reminds me specifically of my novel form of insanity.

CLAY: Up the tenement stairs.

LULA: And with my apple-eating hand I push open the door and lead you, my tender big-eyed prey, into my . . . God, what can I   45 call it . . . into my hovel.

CLAY: Then what happens?

LULA: After the dancing and games, after the long drinks and long walks, the real fun begins.

CLAY: Ah, the real fun.   50

(*Embarrassed, in spite of himself.*)

Which is . . . ?

LULA:

(*Laughs at him.*)

Real fun in the dark house. Hah! Real fun in the dark house, high up above the street and the ignorant cowboys. I lead you in, holding your wet hand gently in my hand . . .   55

CLAY: Which is not wet?

LULA: Which is dry as ashes.

CLAY: And cold?

LULA: Don't think you'll get out of your responsibility that way. It's not cold at all. You Fascist! Into my dark living room.   60 Where we'll sit and talk endlessly, endlessly.

CLAY: About what?

LULA: About what? About your manhood, what do you think? What do you think we've been talking about all this time?

CLAY: Well, I didn't know it was that. That's for sure. Every other   65 thing in the world but that.

(*Notices another person entering, looks quickly, almost involuntarily, up and down the car, seeing the other people in the car.*)

Hey, I didn't even notice when those people got on.

LULA: Yeah, I know.

CLAY: Man, this subway is slow.

70 LULA: Yeah, I know.

CLAY: Well, go on. We were talking about my manhood.

LULA: We still are. All the time.

CLAY: We were in your living room.

LULA: My dark living room. Talking endlessly.

75 CLAY: About my manhood.

LULA: I'll make you a map of it. Just as soon as we get to my house.

CLAY: Well, that's great.

LULA: One of the things we do while we talk. And screw.

CLAY:

(*Trying to make his smile broader and less shaky.*)

80   We finally got there.

LULA: And you'll call my rooms black as a grave. You'll say, "This place is like Juliet's tomb."

CLAY:

(*Laughs.*)

    I might.

85 LULA: I know. You've probably said it before.

CLAY: And is that all? The whole grand tour?

LULA: Not all. You'll say to me very close to my face, many, many times, you'll say, even whisper, that you love me.

CLAY: Maybe I will.

90 LULA: And you'll be lying.

CLAY: I wouldn't lie about something like that.

LULA: Hah. It's the only kind of thing you will lie about. Especially if you think it'll keep me alive.

CLAY: Keep you alive? I don't understand.

95 LULA:

(*Bursting out laughing, but too shrilly.*)

    Don't understand? Well, don't look at me. It's the path I take, that's all. Where both feet take me when I set them down. One in front of the other.

CLAY: Morbid. Morbid. You sure you're not an actress? All that
100   self-aggrandizement.

LULA: Well, I told you I wasn't an actress . . . but I also told you I lie all the time. Draw your own conclusions.

CLAY: And is that all of our lives together you've described? There's no more?

105 LULA: I've told you all I know. Or almost all.

CLAY: There's no funny parts?

LULA: I thought it was all funny.

CLAY: But you mean peculiar, not ha-ha.

LULA: You don't know what I mean.

110 CLAY: Well, tell me the almost part then. You said almost all. What else? I want the whole story.

LULA:

(*Searching aimlessly through her bag. She begins to talk breathlessly, with a light and silly tone.*)

    All stories are whole stories. All of 'em. Our whole story . . . nothing but change. How could things go on like that forever?
115   Huh?

(*Slaps him on the shoulder, begins finding things in her bag, taking them out and throwing them over her shoulder into the aisle.*)

    Except I do go on as I do. Apples and long walks with deathless intelligent lovers. But you mix it up. Look out the window, all the time. Turning pages. Change change change. Till, shit, I don't know you. Wouldn't, for that matter. You're too serious. I bet you're even too serious   120 to be psychoanalyzed. Like all those Jewish poets from Yonkers, who leave their mothers looking for other mothers, or others' mothers, on whose baggy tits they lay their fumbling heads. Their poems are always funny, and all about sex.   125

CLAY: They sound great. Like movies.

LULA: But you change.

(*Blankly.*)

    And things work on you till you hate them.

(*More people come into the train. They come closer to the couple, some of them not sitting, but swinging drearily on the straps, staring at the two with uncertain interest.*)

CLAY: Wow. All these people, so suddenly. They must all come from the same place.   130

LULA: Right. That they do.

CLAY: Oh? You know about them too?

LULA: Oh yeah. About them more than I know about you. Do they frighten you?

CLAY: Frighten me? Why should they frighten me?   135

LULA: 'Cause you're an escaped nigger.

CLAY: Yeah?

LULA: 'Cause you crawled through the wire and made tracks to my side.

CLAY: Wire?   140

LULA: Don't they have wire around plantations?

CLAY: You must be Jewish. All you can think about is wire. Plantations didn't have any wire. Plantations were big open whitewashed places like heaven, and everybody on 'em was grooved to be there. Just strummin' and hummin'   145 all day.

LULA: Yes, yes.

CLAY: And that's how the blues was born.

LULA: Yes, yes. And that's how the blues was born.

(*Begins to make up a song that becomes quickly hysterical. As she sings she rises from her seat, still throwing things out of her bag into the aisle, beginning a rhythmical shudder and twistlike wiggle, which she continues up and down the aisle, bumping into many of the standing people and tripping over the feet of those sitting. Each time she runs into a person she lets out a very vicious piece of profanity, wiggling and stepping all the time.*)

    And that's how the blues was born. Yes. Yes. Son of a bitch,   150 get out of the way. Yes. Quack. Yes. Yes. And that's how the blues was born. Ten little niggers sitting on a limb, but none of them ever looked like him.

(*Points to CLAY, returns toward the seat, with her hands extended for him to rise and dance with her.*)

And that's how blues was born. Yes. Come on. Clay. Let's do
155   the nasty. Rub bellies. Rub bellies.
CLAY:

(*Waves his hands to refuse. He is embarrassed, but determined to
get a kick out of the proceedings.*)

Hey, what was in those apples? Mirror, mirror on the wall,
who's the fairest one of all? Snow White, baby, and don't you
forget it.
160 LULA:

(*Grabbing for his hands, which he draws away.*)

Come on, Clay. Let's rub bellies on the train. The nasty. The
nasty. Do the gritty grind, like your ol' rag-head mammy.
Grind till you lose your mind. Shake it, shake it, shake it,
shake it! OOOOweeee! Come on, Clay. Let's do the
165   choo-choo train shuffle, the navel scratcher.
CLAY: Hey, you coming on like the lady who smoked up her grass
skirt.
LULA:

(*Becoming annoyed that he will not dance, and becoming more
animated as if to embarrass him still further.*)

Come on, Clay . . . let's do the thing. Uhh! Uhh! Clay! Clay!
170   You middle-class black bastard. Forget your social-working
mother for a few seconds and let's knock stomachs. Clay, you
liver-lipped white man. You would-be Christian. You ain't
no nigger, you're just a dirty white man. Get up, Clay. Dance
with me, Clay.
175 CLAY: Lula! Sit down, now. Be cool.
LULA:

(*Mocking him, in wild dance.*)

Be cool. Be cool. That's all you know . . . shaking the wild-
root cream-oil on your knotty head, jackets buttoning up to
your chin, so full of white man's words. Christ! God! Get up
180   and scream at these people. Like scream meaningless shit in
these hopeless faces.

(*She screams at people in train, still dancing.*)

Red trains cough Jewish underwear for keeps! Expanding
smells of silence. Gravy snot whistling like sea birds. Clay.
Clay, you got to break out. Don't sit there dying the way they
185   want you to die. Get up.
CLAY: Oh, sit the fuck down.

(*He moves to restrain her.*)

Sit down, goddamn it.
LULA:

(*Twisting out of his reach.*)

Screw yourself, Uncle Tom. Thomas Woolly-Head.

(*Begins to dance a kind of jig, mocking* CLAY *with loud forced
humor.*)

There is Uncle Tom . . . I mean, Uncle Thomas Woolly-Head.   190
With old white matted mane. He hobbles on his wooden cane.
Old Tom. Old Tom. Let the white man hump his ol' mama,
and he jes' shuffle off in the woods and hide his gentle gray
head. Ol' Thomas Woolly-Head.

(*Some of the other riders are laughing now. A drunk gets up and
joins* LULA *in her dance, singing, as best he can, her "song."* CLAY
*gets up out of his seat and visibly scans the faces of the other
riders.*)

CLAY: Lula! Lula!   195

(*She is dancing and turning, still shouting as loud as she can. The
drunk too is shouting, and waving his hands wildly.*)

Lula . . . you dumb bitch. Why don't you stop it?

(*He rushes half stumbling from his seat, and grabs one of her flailing arms.*)

LULA: Let me go! You black son of a bitch.

(*She struggles against him.*)

Let me go! Help!

(CLAY *is dragging her towards her seat, and the drunk seeks to
interfere. He grabs* CLAY *around the shoulders and begins wrestling
with him.* CLAY *clubs the drunk to the floor without releasing*
LULA, *who is still screaming.* CLAY *finally gets her to the seat and
throws her into it.*)

CLAY: Now you shut the hell up.

(*Grabbing her shoulders.*)

Just shut up. You don't know what you're talking about.   200
You don't know anything. So just keep your stupid mouth
closed.
LULA: You're afraid of white people. And your father was. Uncle
Tom Big Lip!
CLAY: 205

(*Slaps her as hard as he can, across the mouth.* LULA'*s head bangs
against the back of the seat. When she raises it again,* CLAY *slaps
her again.*)

Now shut up and let me talk.

(*He turns toward the other riders, some of whom are sitting on the
edge of their seats. The drunk is on one knee, rubbing his head, and
singing softly the same song. He shuts up too when he sees* CLAY
*watching him. The others go back to newspapers or stare out the
windows.*)

Shit, you don't have any sense, Lula, nor feelings either.
I could murder you now. Such a tiny ugly throat. I could
squeeze it flat, and watch you turn blue, on a humble. For
dull kicks. And all these weak-faced ofays squatting around   210
here, staring over their papers at me. Murder them too. Even
if they expected it. That man there . . .

(Points to well-dressed man.)

I could rip that *Times* right out of his hand, as skinny and
middle-classed as I am, I could rip that paper out of his hand
215 and just as easily rip out his throat. It takes no great effort. For
what? To kill you soft idiots? You don't understand anything
but luxury.

LULA: You fool!

CLAY:

(Pushing her against the seat.)

220 I'm not telling you again, Tallulah Bankhead! Luxury. In your
face and your fingers. You telling me what I ought to do.

(Sudden scream frightening the whole coach.)

Well, don't! Don't you tell me anything! If I'm a middle-class
fake white man . . . let me be. And let me be in the way
I want.

(Through his teeth.)

225 I'll rip your lousy breasts off! Let me be who I feel like
being. Uncle Tom. Thomas. Whoever. It's none of your
business. You don't know anything except what's there
for you to see. An act. Lies. Device. Not the pure heart, the
pumping black heart. You don't ever know that. And I sit
230 here, in this buttoned-up suit, to keep myself from cutting
all your throats. I mean wantonly. You great liberated
whore! You fuck some black man, and right away you're
an expert on black people. What a lotta shit that is. The
only thing you know is that you come if he bangs you hard
235 enough. And that's all. The belly rub? You wanted to do
the belly rub? Shit, you don't even know how. You don't
know how. That ol' dipty-dip shit you do, rolling your ass
like an elephant. That's not my kind of belly rub. Belly rub
is not Queens. Belly rub is dark places, with big hats and
240 overcoats held up with one arm. Belly rub hates you. Old
bald-headed four-eyed ofays popping their fingers . . . and
don't know yet what they're doing. They say, "I love Bessie
Smith." And don't even understand that Bessie Smith is
saying, "Kiss my ass, kiss my black unruly ass." Before love,
245 suffering, desire, anything you can explain, she's saying,
and very plainly, "Kiss my black ass." And if you don't know
that, it's you that's doing the kissing.
      Charlie Parker? Charlie Parker. All the hip white boys
scream for Bird. And Bird saying, "Up your ass, feeble-
250 minded ofay! Up your ass." And they sit there talking
about the tortured genius of Charlie Parker. Bird would've
played not a note of music if he just walked up to East
Sixty-seventh Street and killed the first ten white people
he saw. Not a note! And I'm the great would-be poet. Yes.
255 That's right! Poet. Some kind of bastard literature . . . all
it needs is a simple knife thrust. Just let me bleed you, you
loud whore, and one poem vanished. A whole people of
neurotics, struggling to keep from being sane. And the
only thing that would cure the neurosis would be your
260 murder. Simple as that. I mean if I murdered you, then
other white people would begin to understand me. You
understand? No. I guess not. If Bessie Smith had killed
some white people she wouldn't have needed that music.
She could have talked very straight and plain about the

world. No metaphors. No grunts. No wiggles in the dark   265
of her soul. Just straight two and two are four. Money.
Power. Luxury. Like that. All of them. Crazy niggers
turning their backs on sanity. When all it needs is that
simple act. Murder. Just murder! Would make us all sane.

(Suddenly weary.)

Ahhh. Shit. But who needs it? I'd rather be a fool. Insane.   270
Safe with my words, and no deaths, and clean, hard
thoughts, urging me to new conquests. My people's
madness. Hah! That's a laugh. My people. They don't need
me to claim them. They got legs and arms of their own.
Personal insanities. Mirrors. They don't need all those   275
words. They don't need any defense. But listen, though, one
more thing. And you tell this to your father, who's probably
the kind of man who needs to know at once. So he can plan
ahead. Tell him not to preach so much rationalism and cold
logic to these niggers. Let them alone. Let them sing curses   280
at you in code and see your filth as simple lack of style. Don't
make the mistake, through some irresponsible surge of
Christian charity, of talking too much about the advantages
of Western rationalism, or the great intellectual legacy of the
white man, or maybe they'll begin to listen. And then, maybe   285
one day, you'll find they actually do understand exactly what
you are talking about, all these fantasy people. All these
blues people. And on that day, as sure as shit, when you really
believe you can "accept" them into your fold, as half-white
trusties late of the subject peoples. With no more blues,   290
except the very old ones, and not a watermelon in sight, the
great missionary heart will have triumphed, and all of those
ex-coons will be stand-up Western men, with eyes for clean
hard useful lives, sober, pious and sane, and they'll murder
you. They'll murder you, and have very rational explanations.   295
Very much like your own. They'll cut your throats, and drag
you out to the edge of your cities so the flesh can fall away
from your bones, in sanitary isolation.

LULA:

(Her voice takes on a different, more businesslike quality.)

I've heard enough.   300

CLAY:

(Reaching for his books.)

I bet you have. I guess I better collect my stuff and get off this
train. Looks like we won't be acting out that little pageant you
outlined before.

LULA: No. We won't. You're right about that, at least.   305

(She turns to look quickly around the rest of the car.)

All right!

(The others respond.)

CLAY:

(Bending across the girl to retrieve his belongings.)

Sorry, baby, I don't think we could make it.

(*As he is bending over her, the girl brings up a small knife and plunges it into* CLAY's *chest. Twice. He slumps across her knees, his mouth working stupidly.*)

LULA: Sorry is right.

(*Turning to the others in the car who have already gotten up from their seats.*)

310   Sorry is the rightest thing you've said. Get this man off me! Hurry, now!

(*The others come and drag* CLAY's *body down the aisle.*)

Open the door and throw his body out.

(*They throw him off.*)

And all of you get off at the next stop.

(LULA *busies herself straightening her things. Getting everything in order. She takes out a notebook and makes a quick scribbling note. Drops it in her bag. The train apparently stops and all the others get off, leaving her alone in the coach. Very soon a* YOUNG NEGRO *of about twenty comes into the coach, with a couple of books under his arm. He sits a few seats in back of* LULA. *When he is seated she turns and gives him a long slow look. He looks up from his book and drops the book on his lap. Then an old Negro* CONDUCTOR *comes into the car, doing a sort of restrained soft shoe, and half mumbling the words of some song. He looks at the young man, briefly, with a quick greeting.*)

CONDUCTOR: Hey, brother!
YOUNG NEGRO: Hey.   315

(*The* CONDUCTOR *continues down the aisle with his little dance and the mumbled song.* LULA *turns to stare at him and follows his movements down the aisle. The* CONDUCTOR *tips his hat when he reaches her seat, and continues out the car.*)

Luis Valdez

Luis Valdez (b. 1940), was born and raised the son of farmworkers in Delano, California. He majored in drama at San Jose State College, taking his B.A. in 1964, and then joined the San Francisco Mime Troup, an important experimental theater company. In 1965, when farm workers at the Delano grape plantations went on strike, Valdez formed El Teatro Campesino ("The Farmworkers' Theater"). Valdez and Teatro Campesino devised two dramatic forms: *ACTOS,* short, satirical plays dramatizing the oppression of the fieldworkers, and *MITOS,* poetic, lyrical plays on Chicano life. *Actos* were improvised by members of El Teatro Campesino playing "stock" characters (the farmworker, the boss, etc.); because they were improvised for each production and each community, *actos* varied considerably from performance to performance. The final versions published by Valdez were written down much later. El Teatro Campesino became one of several important Chicano theater companies that performed throughout the Southwest and in urban areas of the Midwest and Northeast, drawing on both American and European dramatic traditions, as well as traditions of Mexican and Spanish-language theater in the United States that date to the seventeenth century. In the late 1960s and 1970s, Teatro Campesino toured the United States and Europe and gained an international reputation. Valdez's other *actos* with Teatro Campesino include *Las Dos Caras del Patroncito* (1965), *No Saco Nada de la Escuela* (1969), and *Vietnam Campesino* (1970). Valdez produced the stage play *Zoot Suit* in 1978, which was released as a film in 1981. In 1980, Valdez transformed El Teatro Campesino into a production company, a marked shift from its collaborative and activist origins. This version of El Teatro Campesino hired "professional" actors, abandoning the collective esthetic

Iowa State University Theatre Photo by Patrick Gouran.

A scene in Honest Sancho's Used Mexican Lot from Luis Valdez's *Los vendidos.*

characteristic of the company's earlier work. Valdez developed several new projects in connection with the company's new theater in San Juan Bautista (built in 1981), notably *Bandido!* (1981), *Corridos* (1992), and *I Don't Have to Show You No Stinking Badges* (1990). His film *La Bamba* was released in 1987, and Valdez filmed *Pastorelas* for PBS television in 1990. Valdez has held academic appointments at the University of California, Berkeley, and at the University of California, Santa Cruz. He is teaching at the campus of the California State University at Monterey.

Los vendidos

One of El Teatro Campesino's best and most popular *actos*, *Los vendidos*—"The Sellouts"—is reminiscent both of Brechtian political theater and more generally of popular satire. In its brief sketch of Honest Sancho's Used Mexican Lot, the play dramatizes a range of stereotypes applied by Anglo culture (represented by the Anglicized Mexican-American, Miss JIM-enez) to Chicano experience: farmworkers, Johnny Pachuco, the revolucionario, and the "new 1970 Mexican-American" yuppie. In the play's surprising finale, though, the yuppie turns on Miss JIM-enez, and the "used Mexicans" turn out to run the shop: Honest Sancho is their front.

The play clearly engages conflicting attitudes toward social experience, as emblematized by its title. For the title can mean both "those who are sold"—like the "used Mexicans" on Sancho's lot—and "the sellouts," presumably Honest Sancho and Miss JIM-enez. This duplicity is also inflected by the play's language, its mixture of Spanish and English, the two languages Chicano culture uses to define itself and to engage the Anglo world. The play works at the border between two cultures, where language is part of the complex social and political negotiation that characterizes Mexican-American life today.

Los vendidos

Luis Valdez and El Teatro Campesino

CHARACTERS

HONEST SANCHO
SECRETARY
FARM WORKER
JOHNNY
REVOLUCIONARIO
MEXICAN-AMERICAN

SCENE: *Honest Sancho's Used Mexican Lot and Mexican Curio Shop. Three models are on display in Honest Sancho's shop: to the right, there is a* REVOLUCIONARIO, *complete with sombrero, carrilleras, and carabina 30–30. At center, on the floor, there is the* FARM WORKER, *under a broad straw sombrero. At stage left is* JOHNNY, *the Pachuco, filero in hand.*

HONEST SANCHO *is moving among his models, dusting them off and preparing for another day of business.*

SANCHO: Bueno, bueno, mis monos, vamos a ver a quien vendemos ahora, ¿no? (*To audience.*) ¡Quihubo! I'm Honest Sancho and this is my shop. Antes fui contratista pero ahora logré tener mi negocito. All I need now is a customer. 5 (*A bell rings offstage.*) Ay, a customer!

SECRETARY: (*Entering.*) Good morning, I'm Miss Jiménez from—

SANCHO: ¡Ah, una chicana! Welcome, welcome Señorita Jiménez.

10 SECRETARY: (*Anglo pronunciation.*) JIM-enez.

SANCHO: ¿Qué?

SECRETARY: My name is Miss JIM-enez. Don't you speak English? What's wrong with you?

SANCHO: Oh, nothing, Señorita JIM-enez. I'm here to help you.

15 SECRETARY: That's better. As I was starting to say, I'm a secretary from Governor Reagan's office, and we're looking for a Mexican type for the administration.

SANCHO: Well, you come to the right place, lady. This is Honest Sancho's Used Mexican lot, and we got all types 20 here. Any particular type you want?

SECRETARY: Yes, we were looking for somebody suave—

SANCHO: Suave.

SECRETARY: Debonair.

SANCHO: De buen aire.

25 SECRETARY: Dark.

SANCHO: Prieto.

SECRETARY: But of course not too dark.

SANCHO: No muy prieto.

SECRETARY: Perhaps, beige.

30 SANCHO: Beige, just the tone. Así como cafecito con leche, ¿no?

SECRETARY: One more thing. He must be hard-working.

SANCHO: That could only be one model. Step right over here to the center of the shop, lady. (*They cross to the* FARM WORKER.) This is our standard farm worker model. As 35 you can see, in the words of our beloved Senator George Murphy, he is "built close to the ground." Also take special notice of his four-ply Goodyear huaraches, made from the rain tire. This wide-brimmed sombrero is an extra added feature—keeps off the sun, rain, and dust.

SECRETARY: Yes, it does look durable. 40

SANCHO: And our farm worker model is friendly. Muy amable. Watch. (*Snaps his fingers.*)

FARM WORKER: (*Lifts up head.*) Buenos días, señorita. (*His head drops.*)

SECRETARY: My, he's friendly. 45

SANCHO: Didn't I tell you? Loves his patrones! But his most attractive feature is that he's hard-working. Let me show you. (*Snaps fingers.* FARM WORKER *stands.*)

FARM WORKER: ¡El jale! (*He begins to work.*)

SANCHO: As you can see, he is cutting grapes. 50

SECRETARY: Oh, I wouldn't know.

SANCHO: He also picks cotton. (*Snap.* FARM WORKER *begins to pick cotton.*)

SECRETARY: Versatile isn't he?

SANCHO: He also picks melons. (*Snap.* FARM WORKER *picks* 55 *melons.*) That's his slow speed for late in the season. Here's his fast speed. (*Snap.* FARM WORKER *picks faster.*)

SECRETARY: ¡Chihuahua! . . . I mean, goodness, he sure is a hard worker.

SANCHO: (*Pulls the* FARM WORKER *to his feet.*) And that isn't the 60 half of it. Do you see these little holes on his arms that appear to be pores? During those hot sluggish days in the field, when the vines or the branches get so entangled, it's almost impossible to move; these holes emit a certain grease that allow our model to slip and slide right through the crop with 65 no trouble at all.

SECRETARY: Wonderful. But is he economical?

SANCHO: Economical? Señorita, you are looking at the Volkswagen of Mexicans. Pennies a day is all it takes. One plate of beans and tortillas will keep him going all day. That, 70 and chile. Plenty of chile. Chile jalapenos, chile verde, chile colorado. But, of course, if you do give him chile (*Snap.* FARM WORKER *turns left face. Snap.* FARM WORKER *bends over.*) then you have to change his oil filter once a week.

SECRETARY: What about storage? 75

SANCHO: No problem. You know these new farm labor camps our Honorable Governor Reagan has built out by Parlier or Raisin City? They were designed with our model in mind. Five, six, seven, even ten in one of those shacks will give you no trouble at all. You can also put him in old 80 barns, old cars, river banks. You can even leave him out in the field overnight with no worry!

SECRETARY: Remarkable.

SANCHO: And here's an added feature: Every year at the end of the season, this model goes back to Mexico and doesn't 85 return, automatically, until next Spring.

Scene **carrilleras** literally chin straps, but may refer to cartridge belts **Pachuco** Chicano slang for 1940s zoot suiter **filero** blade 1–2 **Bueno, bueno, . . . Quihubo** "Good, good, my cute ones, let's see who we can sell now, O.K.?" 3–4 **Antes fui . . . negocito** "I used to be a contractor, but now I've succeeded in having my little business." 30 **Así como . . . leche** like coffee with milk

---

41 Muy amable very friendly **49 El jale** the job

SECRETARY: How about that. But tell me: does he speak English?

SANCHO: Another outstanding feature is that last year this model was programmed to go out on STRIKE! (*Snap.*)

90 FARM WORKER: ¡HUELGA! ¡HUELGA! Hermanos, sálganse de esos files. (*Snap. He stops.*)

SECRETARY: No! Oh no, we can't strike in the State Capitol.

SANCHO: Well, he also scabs. (*Snap.*)

FARM WORKER: Me vendo barato, ¿y qué? (*Snap.*)

95 SECRETARY: That's much better, but you didn't answer my question. Does he speak English?

SANCHO: Bueno . . . no pero he has other—

SECRETARY: No.

SANCHO: Other features.

100 SECRETARY: NO! He just won't do!

SANCHO: Okay, okay pues. We have other models.

SECRETARY: I hope so. What we need is something a little more sophisticated.

SANCHO: Sophisti—¿qué?

105 SECRETARY: An urban model.

SANCHO: Ah, from the city! Step right back. Over here in this corner of the shop is exactly what you're looking for. Introducing our new 1969 JOHNNY PACHUCO model! This is our fast-back model. Streamlined. Built for speed,

110 low-riding, city life. Take a look at some of these features. Mag shoes, dual exhausts, green chartreuse paint-job, dark-tint windshield, a little poof on top. Let me just turn him on. (*Snap.* JOHNNY *walks to stage center with a pachuco bounce.*)

SECRETARY: What was that?

115 SANCHO: That, señorita, was the Chicano shuffle.

SECRETARY: Okay, what does he do?

SANCHO: Anything and everything necessary for city life. For instance, survival: He knife fights. (*Snap.* JOHNNY *pulls out switch blade and swings at secretary.*)

(SECRETARY *screams.*)

120 SANCHO: He dances. (*Snap.*)

JOHNNY: (*Singing.*) "Angel Baby, my Angel Baby . . ." (*Snap.*)

SANCHO: And here's a feature no city model can be without. He gets arrested, but not without resisting, of course. (*Snap.*)

JOHNNY: ¡En la madre, la placa! I didn't do it! I didn't do it!

125 (JOHNNY *turns and stands up against an imaginary wall, legs spread out, arms behind his back.*)

SECRETARY: Oh no, we can't have arrests! We must maintain law and order.

SANCHO: But he's bilingual!

130 SECRETARY: Bilingual?

SANCHO: Simón que yes. He speaks English! Johnny, give us some English. (*Snap.*)

JOHNNY: (*Comes downstage.*) Fuck-you!

SECRETARY: (*Gasps.*) Oh! I've never been so insulted in my

135 whole life!

SANCHO: Well, he learned it in your school.

SECRETARY: I don't care where he learned it.

SANCHO: But he's economical!

SECRETARY: Economical?

SANCHO: Nickels and dimes. You can keep JOHNNY running on   140
hamburgers, Taco Bell tacos, Lucky Lager beer, Thunderbird wine, yesca—

SECRETARY: Yesca?

SANCHO: Mota.

SECRETARY: Mota?   145

SANCHO: Leños . . . Marijuana. (*Snap,* JOHNNY *inhales on an imaginary joint.*)

SECRETARY: That's against the law!

JOHNNY: (*Big smile, holding his breath.*) Yeah.

SANCHO: He also sniffs glue. (*Snap.* JOHNNY *inhales glue, big   150
smile.*)

JOHNNY: Tha's too much man, ése.

SECRETARY: No, Mr. Sancho, I don't think this—

SANCHO: Wait a minute, he has other qualities I know you'll love. For example, an inferiority complex. (*Snap.*)   155

JOHNNY: (*To* SANCHO.) You think you're better than me, huh ése? (*Swings switch blade.*)

SANCHO: He can also be beaten and he bruises, cut him and he bleeds; kick him and he—(*He beats, bruises and kicks* PACHUCO.) would you like to try it?   160

SECRETARY: Oh, I couldn't.

SANCHO: Be my guest. He's a great scapegoat.

SECRETARY: No, really.

SANCHO: Please.

SECRETARY: Well, all right. Just once. (*She kicks* PACHUCO.)   165
Oh, he's so soft.

SANCHO: Wasn't that good? Try again.

SECRETARY: (*Kicks* PACHUCO.) Oh, he's so wonderful! (*She kicks him again.*)

SANCHO: Okay, that's enough, lady. You ruin the merchandise.   170
Yes, our Johnny Pachuco model can give you many hours of pleasure. Why, the L.A.P.D. just bought twenty of these to train their rookie cops on. And talk about maintenance. Señorita, you are looking at an entirely self-supporting machine. You're never going to find our Johnny Pachuco   175
model on the relief rolls. No, sir, this model knows how to liberate.

SECRETARY: Liberate?

SANCHO: He steals. (*Snap.* JOHNNY *rushes the secretary and steals her purse.*)   180

JOHNNY: ¡Dame esa bolsa, vieja! (*He grabs the purse and runs. Snap by* SANCHO. *He stops.*)

(SECRETARY *runs after* JOHNNY *and grabs purse away from him, kicking him as she goes.*)

SECRETARY: No, no, no! We can't have any *more* thieves in the State Administration. Put him back.

SANCHO: Okay, we still got other models. Come on, Johnny,   185
we'll sell you to some old lady. (SANCHO *takes johnny back to his place.*)

SECRETARY: Mr. Sancho, I don't think you quite understand what we need. What we need is something that will attract the women voters. Something more traditional, more romantic.   190

SANCHO: Ah, a lover. (*He smiles meaningfully.*) Step right over here, señorita. Introducing our standard Revolucionario and/or Early California Bandit type. As you can see he is well-built, sturdy, durable. This is the International Harvester of Mexicans.

90–91 **¡HUELGA! ¡HUELGA! . . . esos files** "Strike! Strike! Brothers, leave those rows."   94 **Me vendo . . . qué** "I come cheap, so what?"   97 **Bueno . . . no pero** "Well, no, but . . ."   124 **En la . . . placa** "Wow, the police!"   131 **Simón . . . yes** yeah, sure

---

146 **Leños** "joints" of marijuana   181 **Dame esa . . . , vieja** "Gimme that bag, old lady!"

SECRETARY: What does he do? 195

SANCHO: You name it, he does it. He rides horses, stays in the mountains, crosses deserts, plains, rivers, leads revolutions, follows revolutions, kills, can be killed, serves as a martyr, hero, movie star—did I say movie star? Did you ever see *Viva Zapata? Viva Villa? Villa Rides? Pancho Villa Returns? Pancho Villa Goes Back? Pancho Villa Meets Abbot and Costello*— 200

SECRETARY: I've never seen any of those.

SANCHO: Well, he was in all of them. Listen to this. (*Snap.*)

REVOLUCIONARIO: (*Scream.*) ¡VIVA VILLAAAAA!

SECRETARY: That's awfully loud. 205

SANCHO: He has a volume control. (*He adjusts volume. Snap.*)

REVOLUCIONARIO: (*Mousey voice.*) ¡Viva Villa!

SECRETARY: That's better.

SANCHO: And even if you didn't see him in the movies, perhaps you saw him on TV. He makes commercials. (*Snap.*) 210

REVOLUCIONARIO: Is there a Frito Bandito in your house?

SECRETARY: Oh yes, I've seen that one!

SANCHO: Another feature about this one is that he is economical. He runs on raw horsemeat and tequila!

SECRETARY: Isn't that rather savage? 215

SANCHO: Al contrario, it makes him a lover. (*Snap.*)

REVOLUCIONARIO: (*To* SECRETARY.) ¡Ay, mamasota, cochota, ven pa'ca! (*He grabs* SECRETARY *and folds her back—Latin-lover style.*)

SANCHO: (*Snap.* REVOLUCIONARIO *goes back upright.*) Now wasn't that nice? 220

SECRETARY: Well, it was rather nice.

SANCHO: And finally, there is one outstanding feature about this model I KNOW the ladies are going to love: He's a GENUINE antique! He was made in Mexico in 1910!

SECRETARY: Made in Mexico? 225

SANCHO: That's right. Once in Tijuana, twice in Guadalajara, three times in Cuernavaca.

SECRETARY: Mr. Sancho, I thought he was an American product.

SANCHO: No, but—

SECRETARY: No, I'm sorry. We can't buy anything but American-made products. He just won't do. 230

SANCHO: But he's an antique!

SECRETARY: I don't care. You still don't understand what we need. It's true we need Mexican models such as these, but it's more important that he be *American*. 235

SANCHO: American?

SECRETARY: That's right, and judging from what you've shown me, I don't think you have what we want. Well, my lunch hour's almost over; I better—

SANCHO: Wait a minute! Mexican but American? 240

SECRETARY: That's correct.

SANCHO: Mexican but . . . (*A sudden flash.*) AMERICAN! Yeah, I think we've got exactly what you want. He just came in today! Give me a minute. (*He exits. Talks from backstage.*) Here he is in the shop. Let me just get some papers off. There. Introducing our new 1970 Mexican-American! Ta-ra-ra-ra-ra-ra-RA-RAAA! 245

(SANCHO *brings out the* MEXICAN-AMERICAN *model, a clean-shaven middle-class type in business suit, with glasses.*)

SECRETARY: (*Impressed.*) Where have you been hiding this one?

SANCHO: He just came in this morning. Ain't he a beauty? Feast your eyes on him! Sturdy US Steel frame, streamlined, 250

---

216 **Al contrario** on the contrary

modern. As a matter of fact, he is built exactly like our Anglo models except that he comes in a variety of darker shades: naugahyde, leather, or leatherette.

SECRETARY: Naugahyde.

SANCHO: Well, we'll just write that down. Yes, señorita, this model 255 represents the apex of American engineering! He is bilingual, college educated, ambitious! Say the word "acculturate" and he accelerates. He is intelligent, well-mannered, clean—did I say clean? (*Snap.* MEXICAN-AMERICAN *raises his arm.*) Smell.

SECRETARY: (*Smells.*) Old Sobaco, my favorite. 260

SANCHO: (*Snap.* MEXICAN-AMERICAN *turns toward* SANCHO.) Eric! (*To* SECRETARY.) We call him Eric Garcia. (*To* ERIC.) I want you to meet Miss JIM-enez, Eric.

MEXICAN-AMERICAN: Miss JIM-enez, I am delighted to make your acquaintance. (*He kisses her hand.*) 265

SECRETARY: Oh, my, how charming!

SANCHO: Did you feel the suction? He has seven especially engineered suction cups right behind his lips. He's a charmer all right!

SECRETARY: How about boards? Does he function on boards? 270

SANCHO: You name them, he is on them. Parole boards, draft boards, school boards, taco quality control boards, surf boards, two-by-fours.

SECRETARY: Does he function in politics?

SANCHO: Señorita, you are looking at a political MACHINE. 275 Have you ever heard of the OEO, EOC, COD, WAR ON POVERTY? That's our model! Not only that, he makes political speeches.

SECRETARY: May I hear one?

SANCHO: With pleasure. (*Snap.*) Eric, give us a speech. 280

MEXICAN-AMERICAN: Mr. Congressman, Mr. Chairman, members of the board, honored guests, ladies and gentlemen. (SANCHO *and* SECRETARY *applaud.*) Please, please, I come before you as a Mexican-American to tell you about the problems of the Mexican. The problems of the Mexican 285 stem from one thing and one thing alone: He's stupid. He's uneducated. He needs to stay in school. He needs to be ambitious, forward-looking, harder-working. He needs to think American, American, American, AMERICAN, AMERICAN, AMERICAN. GOD BLESS AMERICA! 290 GOD BLESS AMERICA!! (*He goes out of control*).

(SANCHO *snaps frantically and the* MEXICAN–AMERICAN *finally slumps forward, bending at the waist.*)

SECRETARY: Oh my, he's patriotic too!

SANCHO: Sí, señorita, he loves his country. Let me just make a little adjustment here. (*Stands* MEXICAN–AMERICAN *up.*)

SECRETARY: What about upkeep? Is he economical? 295

SANCHO: Well, no, I won't lie to you. The Mexican-American costs a little bit more, but you get what you pay for. He's worth every extra cent. You can keep him running on dry martinis, Langendorf bread.

SECRETARY: Apple pie? 300

SANCHO: Only Mom's. Of course, he's also programmed to eat Mexican food on ceremonial functions, but I must warn you: an overdose of beans will plug up his exhaust.

SECRETARY: Fine! There's just one more question: How much do you want for him? 305

SANCHO: Well, I tell you what I'm gonna do. Today and today only, because you've been so sweet, I'm gonna let you steal this model from me! I'm gonna let you drive him

off the lot for the simple price of—let's see taxes and license
310   included—$15,000.
        SECRETARY: Fifteen thousand DOLLARS? For a MEXICAN!
        SANCHO: Mexican? What are you talking, lady? This is a Mexican-
        AMERICAN! We had to melt down two pachucos, a farm
        worker and three gabachos to make this model! You want
315   quality, but you gotta pay for it! This is no cheap run-about.
        He's got class!
        SECRETARY: Okay, I'll take him.
        SANCHO: You will?
        SECRETARY: Here's your money.
320   SANCHO: You mind if I count it?
        SECRETARY: Go right ahead.
        SANCHO: Well, you'll get your pink slip in the mail. Oh, do you want
        me to wrap him up for you? We have a box in the back.
        SECRETARY: No, thank you. The Governor is having a luncheon
325   this afternoon, and we need a brown face in the crowd. How
        do I drive him?
        SANCHO: Just snap your fingers. He'll do anything you want.

(SECRETARY *snaps.* MEXICAN-AMERICAN *steps forward.*)

        MEXICAN-AMERICAN: RAZA QUERIDA, ¡VAMOS LEVAN-
        TANDO ARMAS PARA LIBERARNOS DE ESTOS
330   DESGRACIADOS GABACHOS QUE NOS EXPLOTAN!
        VAMOS.
        SECRETARY: What did he say?
        SANCHO: Something about lifting arms, killing white people, etc.
        SECRETARY: But he's not supposed to say that!
335   SANCHO: Look, lady, don't blame me for bugs from the factory.
        He's your Mexican-American; you bought him, now drive
        him off the lot!
        SECRETARY: But he's broken!
        SANCHO: Try snapping another finger.

(SECRETARY *snaps.* MEXICAN-AMERICAN *comes to life again.*)

340   MEXICAN-AMERICAN: ¡ESTA GRAN HUMANIDAD HA
        DICHO BASTA! Y SE HA PUESTO EN MARCHA! ¡BASTA!
        ¡BASTA! ¡VIVA LA RAZA! ¡VIVA LA CAUSA! ¡VIVA LA
        HUELGA! ¡VIVAN LOS BROWN BERETS! ¡VIVAN LOS
        ESTUDIANTES! ¡CHICANO POWER!

328–331 **RAZA QUERIDA, . . . VAMOS** "Beloved Raza, let's
pick up arms to liberate ourselves from those damned whites
that exploit us! Let's go."   340–344 **ESTA GRAN . . . CHICANO
POWER** "This great mass of humanity has said enough! And it
begins to march! Enough! Enough! Long live La Raza! Long live
the Cause! Long live the strike! Long live the Brown Berets! Long
live the students! Chicano Power!"

(*The* MEXICAN-AMERICAN *turns toward the* SECRETARY, *who
gasps and backs up. He keeps turning toward the* PACHUCO, FARM
WORKER, *and* REVOLUCIONARIO, *snapping his fingers and turning
each of them on, one by one.*)

        PACHUCO: (*Snap. To* SECRETARY.) I'm going to get you, baby!   345
        ¡Viva La Raza!
        FARM WORKER: (*Snap. To* SECRETARY.) ¡Viva la huelga! ¡Viva la
        Huelga! ¡VIVA LA HUELGA!
        REVOLUCIONARIO: (*Snap. To* SECRETARY.) ¡Viva la revolución!
        ¡VIVA LA REVOLUCIÓN!   350
        REVOLUCIONARIO: (*Snap. To* SECRETARY.) ¡Viva la revolución!
        ¡VIVA LA REVOLUCIÓN!

(*The three models join together and advance toward the* SECRETARY
who backs up and runs out of the shop screaming. SANCHO *is at the
other end of the shop holding his money in his hand. All freeze. After
a few seconds of silence, the* PACHUCO *moves and stretches, shaking
his arms and loosening up. The* FARM WORKER *and* REVOLUCIONA-
RIO *do the same.* SANCHO *stays where he is, frozen to his spot.*)

        JOHNNY: Man, that was a long one, ése. (*Others agree with him.*)
        FARM WORKER: How did we do?
        JOHNNY: Perty good, look all that lana, man! (*He goes over to*   355
        SANCHO *and removes the money from his hand.* SANCHO *stays
        where he is.*)
        REVOLUCIONARIO: En la madre, look at all the money.
        JOHNNY: We keep this up, we're going to be rich.
        FARM WORKER: They think we're machines.   360
        REVOLUCIONARIO: Burros.
        JOHNNY: Puppets.
        MEXICAN-AMERICAN: The only thing I don't like is—how
        come I always got to play the goddamn Mexican-American?
        JOHNNY: That's what you get for finishing high school.   365
        FARM WORKER: How about our wages, ése?
        JOHNNY: Here it comes right now. $3,000 for you, $3,000 for you,
        $3,000 for you, and $3,000 for me. The rest we put back into
        the business.
        MEXICAN-AMERICAN: Too much, man. Heh, where you vatos   370
        going tonight?
        FARM WORKER: I'm going over to Concha's. There's a party.
        JOHNNY: Wait a minute, vatos. What about our salesman? I think
        he needs an oil job.
        REVOLUCIONARIO: Leave him to me.   375

(*The* PACHUCO, FARM WORKER, *and* MEXICAN-AMERICAN *exit,
talking loudly about their plans for the night. The* REVOLUCIONA-
RIO *goes over to* SANCHO, *removes his derby hat and cigar, lifts him
up and throws him over his shoulder.* SANCHO *hangs loose, lifeless.*)

        REVOLUCIONARIO: (*To audience.*) He's the best model we got!
        ¡Ajúa! (*Exit.*)

David Henry Hwang

David Henry Hwang was born in Los Angeles in 1957. He graduated with a B.A. in English from Stanford University in 1979 and studied at the Yale School of Drama in 1980–81. In the 1980s, Hwang wrote a series of powerful plays concerning the cultural and political experience of Asian Americans in the United States. His first play, *F.O.B.* ("fresh off the boat"), dramatizes the tensions that arise between Chinese immigrants to the United States and their culturally-assimilated friends and relatives. The play won an Obie award in 1980. Hwang addressed similar issues in *The Dance of the Railroad* (1981) and in *Rich Relations* (1986), and he collaborated with composer Philip Glass on *1000 Airplanes on the Roof* (1988). Hwang's Tony Award-winning *M. Butterfly* (1988) is a brilliant critique of Western attitudes toward Asia, epitomized by one of Western culture's most powerful and seductive images of the Orient: Giacomo Puccini's opera, *Madame Butterfly*. His more recent plays include *Trying to Find Chinatown* (1996) and *Bondage* (1996); he has also written the book for a revival of Rodgers and Hammerstein's musical, *Flower Drum Song* (2001). His most recent play, *Yellow Face* opened in 2007; he has also written several screenplays and adaptations, notably of Ibsen's *Peer Gynt*.

M. Butterfly

In *M. Butterfly,* Hwang traces the relationship between the "Orient" of the Western imagination and the political realities that such images help to foster. The play's central character, the diplomat Gallimard, conducts his relationship with China in terms of Puccini's *Madame Butterfly*. In Puccini's 1904 opera, based on the 1900 play by David Belasco, the naval officer

John Lithgow as Gallimard and B.D. Wong as Song Liling in the 1988 Broadway production of David Henry Hwang's *M. Butterfly*.

Joan Marcus

Pinkerton marries the Japanese geisha CUT girl Butterfly. He leaves for the United States, promising to return, and Butterfly waits for him, meanwhile bearing his child. When Pinkerton returns with his wife from America to collect his child, Butterfly realizes that he will never return to her. She commits suicide.

As Hwang has remarked, Butterfly has become a cultural stereotype of East-West relations—"speaking of an Asian woman, we would sometimes say, 'She's pulling a Butterfly,' which meant playing the submissive Oriental number." This sexist and racist stereotype, Hwang argues, pervades not only Western men's fantasies about Asian women—as the mail-order business in Asian wives suggests, Western men see Asian women as obedient, submissive, and sexually self-sacrificing—but also conditions the political relationship between Asia and the West as well.

M. Butterfly fuses this erotic and political desire for domination in the character of Gallimard, a French diplomat who falls in love with Song Liling, an opera singer whom he first sees singing the death aria from *Madame Butterfly*. However, the play develops a fascinating twist, for Song is in fact a man, who plays female roles in the Beijing Opera, and who—as a woman—develops a love affair with Gallimard in order to spy for the Chinese government. *M. Butterfly* compacts a complex reading of the politics of race, gender, and sexuality in a brilliantly theatrical drama.

M. Butterfly

David Henry Hwang

CHARACTERS

KUROGO
RENE GALLIMARD
SONG LILING
MARC
MAN 2
CONSUL SHARPLESS
RENEE
WOMAN AT PARTY
PINUP GIRL
COMRADE CHIN

SUZUKI
SHU-FANG
HELGA
M. TOULON
MAN 1
JUDGE

The action of the play takes place in a Paris prison in the present, and in recall, during the decade 1960 to 1970 in Beijing, and from 1966 to the present in Paris.

ACT ONE

SCENE I

M. GALLIMARD's prison cell. Paris. Present.

Lights fade up to reveal RENE GALLIMARD, *65, in a prison cell. He wears a comfortable bathrobe, and looks old and tired. The sparsely furnished cell contains a wooden crate upon which sits a hot plate with a kettle, and a portable tape recorder.* GALLIMARD *sits on the crate staring at the recorder, a sad smile on his face.*

Upstage SONG, *who appears as a beautiful woman in traditional Chinese garb, dances a traditional piece from the Peking Opera, surrounded by the percussive clatter of Chinese music.*

Then, slowly, lights and sound cross-fade; the Chinese opera music dissolves into a Western opera, the "Love Duet" from Puccini's Madame Butterfly. SONG *continues dancing, now to the Western accompaniment. Though her movements are the same, the difference in music now gives them a balletic quality.*

GALLIMARD *rises, and turns upstage towards the figure of* SONG, *who dances without acknowledging him.*

GALLIMARD: Butterfly, Butterfly . . .

(He forces himself to turn away, as the image of SONG *fades out, and talks to us.)*

GALLIMARD: The limits of my cell are as such: four-and-a-half meters by five. There's one window against the far wall; a door, very strong, to protect me from autograph hounds.
5 I'm responsible for the tape recorder, the hot plate, and this charming coffee table.
   When I want to eat, I'm marched off to the dining room—hot, steaming slop appears on my plate. When I want to sleep, the light bulb turns itself off—the work of fairies. It's
10 an enchanted space I occupy. The French—we know how to run a prison.
   But, to be honest, I'm not treated like an ordinary prisoner. Why? Because I'm a celebrity. You see, I make people laugh.
15   I never dreamed this day would arrive. I've never been considered witty or clever. In fact, as a young boy, in an informal poll among my grammar school classmates, I

was voted "least likely to be invited to a party." It's a title I managed to hold onto for many years. Despite some stiff competition. 20
   But now, how the tables turn! Look at me: the life of every social function in Paris. Paris? Why be modest? My fame has spread to Amsterdam, London, New York. Listen to them! In the world's smartest parlors. I'm the one who lifts their spirits! 25

(With a flourish, GALLIMARD *directs our attention to another part of the stage.)*

SCENE II

A party. Present.

Lights go up on a chic-looking parlor, where a well-dressed trio, two men and one woman, make conversation. GALLIMARD *also remains lit; he observes them from his cell.*

WOMAN: And what of Gallimard?
MAN 1: Gallimard?
MAN 2: Gallimard!
GALLIMARD: *(To us.)* You see? They're all determined to say my name, as if it were some new dance. 5
WOMAN: He still claims not to believe the truth.
MAN 1: What? Still? Even since the trial?
WOMAN: Yes. Isn't it mad?
MAN 2: *(Laughing.)* He says . . . it was dark . . . and she was very modest! 10

(The trio break into laughter.)

MAN 1: So—what? He never touched her with his hands?
MAN 2: Perhaps he did, and simply misidentified the equipment. A compelling case for sex education in the schools.
WOMAN: To protect the National Security—the Church can't argue with that. 15
MAN 1: That's impossible! How could he not know?
MAN 2: Simple ignorance.
MAN 1: For twenty years?
MAN 2: Time flies when you're being stupid.
WOMAN: Well, I thought the French were ladies' men. 20
MAN 2: It seems Monsieur Gallimard was overly anxious to live up to his national reputation.

WOMAN: Well, he's not very good-looking.

MAN 1: No, he's not.

25 MAN 2: Certainly not.

WOMAN: Actually, I feel sorry for him.

MAN 2: A toast! To Monsieur Gallimard!

WOMAN: Yes! To Gallimard!

MAN 1: To Gallimard!

30 MAN 2: Vive la différence!

(*They toast, laughing. Lights down on them.*)

SCENE III

M. GALLIMARD's *cell.*

GALLIMARD: (*Smiling.*) You see? They toast me. I've become patron saint of the socially inept. Can they really be so foolish? Men like that—they should be scratching at my door, begging to learn my secrets! For I, Rene Gallimard, you see, I

5 have known, and been loved by . . . the Perfect Woman.

Alone in this cell, I sit night after night, watching our story play through my head, always searching for a new ending, one which redeems my honor, where she returns at last to my arms. And I imagine you—my ideal audience—who come to

10 understand and even, perhaps just a little, to envy me.

(*He turns on his tape recorder. Over the house speakers, we hear the opening phrases of Madame Butterfly.*)

GALLIMARD: In order for you to understand what I did and why, I must introduce you to my favorite opera: *Madame Butterfly.* By Giacomo Puccini. First produced at La Scala, Milan, in 1904, it is now beloved throughout the Western world.

(*As* GALLIMARD *describes the opera, the tape segues in and out to sections he may be describing.*)

15 GALLIMARD: And why not? Its heroine, Cio-Cio-San, also known as Butterfly, is a feminine ideal, beautiful and brave. And its hero, the man for whom she gives up everything, is—(*He pulls out a naval officer's cap from under his crate, pops it on his head, and struts about.*)—not very good-looking, not

20 too bright, and pretty much a wimp: Benjamin Franklin Pinkerton of the U.S. Navy. As the curtain rises, he's just closed on two great bargains: one on a house, the other on a woman—call it a package deal.

Pinkerton purchased the rights to Butterfly for one

25 hundred yen—in modern currency, equivalent to about . . . sixty-six cents. So, he's feeling pretty pleased with himself as Sharpless, the American consul, arrives to witness the marriage.

(MARC, *wearing an official cap to designate* SHARPLESS, *enters and plays the character.*)

SHARPLESS/MARC: Pinkerton!

30 PINKERTON/GALLIMARD: Sharpless! How's it hangin'? It's a great day, just great. Between my house, my wife, and the rickshaw ride in from town, I've saved nineteen cents just this morning.

SHARPLESS: Wonderful. I can see the inscription on your

35 tombstone already: "I saved a dollar, here I lie." (*He looks around.*) Nice house.

PINKERTON: It's artistic. Artistic, don't you think? Like the way the shoji screens slide open to reveal the wet bar and disco mirror ball? Classy, huh? Great for impressing the chicks.

SHARPLESS: "Chicks"? Pinkerton, you're going to be a married 40 man!

PINKERTON: Well, sort of.

SHARPLESS: What do you mean?

PINKERTON: This country—Sharpless, it is okay. You got all these geisha girls running around— 45

SHARPLESS: I know! I live here!

PINKERTON: Then, you know the marriage laws, right? I split for one month, it's annulled!

SHARPLESS: Leave it to you to read the fine print. Who's the lucky girl? 50

PINKERTON: Cio-Cio-San. Her friends call her Butterfly. Sharpless, she eats out of my hand!

SHARPLESS: She's probably very hungry.

PINKERTON: Not like American girls. It's true what they say about Oriental girls. They want to be treated bad! 55

SHARPLESS: Oh, please!

PINKERTON: It's true!

SHARPLESS: Are you serious about this girl?

PINKERTON: I'm marrying her, aren't I?

SHARPLESS: Yes—with generous trade-in terms. 60

PINKERTON: When I leave, she'll know what it's like to have loved a real man. And I'll even buy her a few nylons.

SHARPLESS: You aren't planning to take her with you?

PINKERTON: Huh? Where?

SHARPLESS: Home! 65

PINKERTON: You mean, America? Are you crazy? Can you see her trying to buy rice in St. Louis?

SHARPLESS: So, you're not serious.

(*Pause.*)

PINKERTON/GALLIMARD: (*As* PINKERTON.) Consul, I am a sailor in port. (*As* GALLIMARD.) They then proceed to sing the 70 famous duet, "The Whole World Over."

(*The duet plays on the speakers.* GALLIMARD, *as* PINKERTON, *lip-syncs his lines from the opera.*)

GALLIMARD: To give a rough translation: "The whole world over, the Yankee travels, casting his anchor wherever he wants. Life's not worth living unless he can win the hearts of the fairest maidens, then hotfoot it off the premises 75 ASAP." (*He turns towards* MARC.) In the preceding scene, I played Pinkerton, the womanizing cad, and my friend Marc from school . . . (MARC *bows grandly for our benefit.*) played Sharpless, the sensitive soul of reason. In life, however, our positions were usually—no, always—reversed. 80

SCENE IV

Ecole Nationale. Aix-en-Provence. 1947.

GALLIMARD: No, Marc, I think I'd rather stay home.

MARC: Are you crazy?! We are going to Dad's condo in Marseille! You know what happened last time?

GALLIMARD: Of course I do.

MARC: Of course you don't! You never know. . . . They stripped, 5 Rene!

GALLIMARD: Who stripped?

MARC: The girls!

GALLIMARD: Girls? Who said anything about girls?

10 MARC: Rene, we're a buncha university guys goin' up to the woods. What are we gonna do—talk philosophy?

GALLIMARD: What girls? Where do you get them?

MARC: Who cares? The point is, they come. On trucks. Packed in like sardines. The back flips open, babes hop

15 out, we're ready to roll.

GALLIMARD: You mean, they just—?

MARC: Before you know it, every last one of them—they're stripped and splashing around my pool. There's no moon out, they can't see what's going on, their boobs are flapping,

20 right? You close your eyes, reach out—it's grab bag, get it? Doesn't matter whose ass is between whose legs, whose teeth are sinking into who. You're just in there, going at it, eyes closed, on and on for as long as you can stand. (*Pause.*) Some fun, huh?

25 GALLIMARD: What happens in the morning?

MARC: In the morning, you're ready to talk some philosophy. (*Beat.*) So how 'bout it?

GALLIMARD: Marc, I can't . . . I'm afraid they'll say no—the girls. So I never ask.

30 MARC: You don't have to ask! That's the beauty—don't you see? They don't have to say yes. It's perfect for a guy like you, really.

GALLIMARD: You go ahead . . . I may come later.

MARC: Hey, Rene—it doesn't matter that you're clumsy and got

35 zits—they're not looking!

GALLIMARD: Thank you very much.

MARC: Wimp.

(MARC *walks over to the other side of the stage, and starts waving and smiling at women in the audience.*)

GALLIMARD: (*To us.*) We now return to my version of *Madame Butterfly* and the events leading to my recent conviction

40 for treason.

(GALLIMARD *notices* MARC *making lewd gestures.*)

Marc, what are you doing?

MARC: Huh? (*Sotto voce.*) Rene, there're a lotta great babes out there. They're probably lookin' at me and thinking, "What a dangerous guy."

45 GALLIMARD: Yes—how could they help but be impressed by your cool sophistication?

(GALLIMARD *pops the* SHARPLESS *cap on* MARC's *head, and points him offstage.* MARC *exits, leering.*)

SCENE V

M. GALLIMARD's *cell.*

GALLIMARD: Next, Butterfly makes her entrance. We learn her age—fifteen . . . but very mature for her years.

(*Lights come up on the area where we saw* SONG *dancing at the top of the play. She appears there again, now dressed as* MADAME BUTTERFLY, *moving to the "Love Duet."* GALLIMARD *turns upstage slightly to watch, transfixed.*)

GALLIMARD: But as she glides past him, beautiful, laughing softly behind her fan, don't we who are men sigh with hope? We, who are not handsome, nor brave, nor powerful, 5 yet somehow believe, like Pinkerton, that we deserve a Butterfly. She arrives with all her possessions in the folds of her sleeves, lays them all out, for her man to do with as he pleases. Even her life itself—she bows her head as she whispers that she's not even worth the hundred yen he paid 10 for her. He's already given too much, when we know he's really had to give nothing at all.

(*Music and lights on* SONG *out.* GALLIMARD *sits at his crate.*)

GALLIMARD: In real life, women who put their total worth at less than sixty-six cents are quite hard to find. The closest we come is in the pages of these magazines. (*He reaches into his* 15 *crate, pulls out a stack of girlie magazines, and begins flipping through them.*) Quite a necessity in prison. For three or four dollars, you get seven or eight women.

I first discovered these magazines at my uncle's house. One day, as a boy of twelve. The first time I saw them in his 20 closet . . . all lined up—my body shook. Not with lust—no, with power. Here were women—a shelfful—who would do exactly as I wanted.

(*The "Love Duet" creeps in over the speakers. Special comes up, revealing, not* SONG *this time, but a* PINUP GIRL *in a sexy negligee, her back to us.* GALLIMARD *turns upstage and looks at her.*)

GIRL: I know you're watching me.

GALLIMARD: My throat . . . it's dry. 25

GIRL: I leave my blinds open every night before I go to bed.

GALLIMARD: I can't move.

GIRL: I leave my blinds open and the lights on.

GALLIMARD: I'm shaking. My skin is hot, but my penis is soft. Why? 30

GIRL: I stand in front of the window.

GALLIMARD: What is she going to do?

GIRL: I toss my hair, and I let my lips part . . . barely.

GALLIMARD: I shouldn't be seeing this. It's so dirty. I'm so bad. 35

GIRL: Then, slowly, I lift off my nightdress.

GALLIMARD: Oh, god. I can't believe it. I can't—

GIRL: I toss it to the ground.

GALLIMARD: Now, she's going to walk away. She's going to—

GIRL: I stand there, in the light, displaying myself. 40

GALLIMARD: No. She's—why is she naked?

GIRL: To you.

GALLIMARD: In front of a window? This is wrong. No—

GIRL: Without shame.

GALLIMARD: No, she must . . . like it. 45

GIRL: I like it.

GALLIMARD: She . . . she wants me to see.

GIRL: I want you to see.

GALLIMARD: I can't believe it! She's getting excited!

GIRL: I can't see you. You can do whatever you want. 50

GALLIMARD: I can't do a thing. Why?

GIRL: What would you like me to do . . . next?

(*Lights go down on her. Music off. Silence, as* GALLIMARD *puts away his magazines. Then he resumes talking to us.*)

GALLIMARD: Act Two begins with Butterfly staring at the ocean. Pinkerton's been called back to the U.S., and he's given his wife a detailed schedule of his plans. In the column marked "return date," he's written "when the robins nest." This failed to ignite her suspicions. Now, three years have passed without a peep from him. Which brings a response from her faithful servant, Suzuki.

55

(COMRADE CHIN enters, playing SUZUKI.)

SUZUKI: Girl, he's a loser. What'd he ever give you? Nineteen cents and those ugly Day-Glo stockings? Look, it's finished! Kaput! Done! And you should be glad! I mean, the guy was a woofer! He tried before, you know—before he met you, he went down to geisha central and plunked down his spare change in front of the usual candidates—everyone else gagged! These are hungry prostitutes, and they were not interested, get the picture? Now, stop slathering when an American ship sails in, and let's make some bucks—I mean, yen! We are broke!
    Now, what about Yamadori? Hey, hey—don't look away—the man is a prince—figuratively, and, what's even better, literally. He's rich, he's handsome, he says he'll die if you don't marry him—and he's even willing to overlook the little fact that you've been deflowered all over the place by a foreign devil. What do you mean, "But he's Japanese?" You're Japanese! You think you've been touched by the whitey god? He was a sailor with dirty hands!

60

65

70

75

(SUZUKI stalks offstage.)

GALLIMARD: She's also visited by Consul Sharpless, sent by Pinkerton on a minor errand.

(MARC enters, as SHARPLESS.)

SHARPLESS: I hate this job.

80

GALLIMARD: This Pinkerton—he doesn't show up personally to tell his wife he's abandoning her. No, he sends a government diplomat . . . at taxpayer's expense.

SHARPLESS: Butterfly? Butterfly? I have some bad—I'm going to be ill. Butterfly, I came to tell you—

85

GALLIMARD: Butterfly says she knows he'll return and if he doesn't she'll kill herself rather than go back to her own people. (Beat.) This causes a lull in the conversation.

SHARPLESS: Let's put it this way . . .

GALLIMARD: Butterfly runs into the next room, and returns holding—

90

(Sound cue: a baby crying. SHARPLESS, "seeing" this, backs away.)

SHARPLESS: Well, good. Happy to see things going so well. I suppose I'll be going now. Ta ta. Ciao. (He turns away. Sound cue out.) I hate this job. (He exits.)

GALLIMARD: At that moment, Butterfly spots in the harbor an American ship—the Abramo Lincoln!

95

(Music cue: "The Flower Duet." SONG, still dressed as BUTTERFLY, changes into a wedding kimono, moving to the music.)

GALLIMARD: This is the moment that redeems her years of waiting. With Suzuki's help, they cover the room with flowers—

(CHIN, as SUZUKI, trudges onstage and drops a lone flower without much enthusiasm.)

GALLIMARD: —and she changes into her wedding dress to prepare for Pinkerton's arrival.

100

(SUZUKI helps BUTTERFLY change. HELGA enters, and helps GALLIMARD change into a tuxedo.)

GALLIMARD: I married a woman older than myself—Helga.

HELGA: My father was ambassador to Australia. I grew up among criminals and kangaroos.

GALLIMARD: Hearing that brought me to the altar—

105

(HELGA exits.)

GALLIMARD: —where I took a vow renouncing love. No fantasy woman would ever want me, so, yes, I would settle for a quick leap up the career ladder. Passion, I banish, and in its place—practicality!
    But my vows had long since lost their charm by the time we arrived in China. The sad truth is that all men want a beautiful woman, and the uglier the man, the greater the want.

110

(SUZUKI makes final adjustments of BUTTERFLY's costume, as does GALLIMARD of his tuxedo.)

GALLIMARD: I married late, at age thirty-one. I was faithful to my marriage for eight years. Until the day when, as a junior-level diplomat in puritanical Peking, in a parlor at the German ambassador's house, during the "Reign of a Hundred Flowers," I first saw her . . . singing the death scene from Madame Butterfly.

115

(SUZUKI runs offstage.)

SCENE VI

German ambassador's house. Beijing. 1960.

The upstage special area now becomes a stage. Several chairs face upstage, representing seating for some twenty guests in the parlor. A few "diplomats"—RENEE, MARC, TOULON—in formal dress enter and take seats.

GALLIMARD also sits down, but turns towards us and continues to talk. Orchestral accompaniment on the tape is now replaced by a simple piano. SONG picks up the death scene from the point where BUTTERFLY uncovers the hara-kiri knife.

GALLIMARD: The ending is pitiful. Pinkerton, in an art of great courage, stays home and sends his American wife to pick up Butterfly's child. The truth, long deferred, has come up to her door.

(SONG, playing BUTTERFLY, sings the lines from the opera in her own voice—which, though not classical, should be decent.)

SONG: "Con onor muore/ chi non puo serbar/ vita con onore."

GALLIMARD: (Simultaneously.) "Death with honor / Is better than life / Life with dishonor."

5

(*The stage is illuminated; we are now completely within an elegant diplomat's residence.* SONG *proceeds to play out an abbreviated death scene. Everyone in the room applauds.* SONG, *shyly, takes her bows. Others in the room rush to congratulate her.* GALLIMARD *remains with us.*)

GALLIMARD: They say in opera the voice is everything. That's probably why I'd never before enjoyed opera. Here . . . here
10   was a Butterfly with little or no voice—but she had the grace, the delicacy . . . I believed this girl. I believed her suffering. I wanted to take her in my arms—so delicate, even I could protect her, take her home, pamper her until she smiled.

(*Over the course of the preceding speech,* SONG *has broken from the upstage crowd and moved directly upstage of* GALLIMARD.)

SONG: Excuse me. Monsieur . . . ?

(GALLIMARD *turns upstage, shocked.*)

15   GALLIMARD: Oh! Gallimard. Mademoiselle . . . ? A beautiful . . .
     SONG: Song Liling.
     GALLIMARD: A beautiful performance.
     SONG: Oh, please.
     GALLIMARD: I usually—
20   SONG: You make me blush. I'm no opera singer at all.
     GALLIMARD: I usually don't like *Butterfly*.
     SONG: I can't blame you in the least.
     GALLIMARD: I mean, the story—
     SONG: Ridiculous.
25   GALLIMARD: I like the story, but . . . what?
     SONG: Oh, you like it?
     GALLIMARD: I . . . what I mean is, I've always seen it played by huge women in so much bad makeup.
     SONG: Bad makeup is not unique to the West.
30   GALLIMARD: But, who can believe them?
     SONG: And you believe me?
     GALLIMARD: Absolutely. You were utterly convincing. It's the first time—
     SONG: Convincing? As a Japanese woman? The Japanese used
35   hundreds of our people for medical experiments during the war, you know. But I gather such an irony is lost on you.
     GALLIMARD: No! I was about to say, it's the first time I've seen the beauty of the story.
     SONG: Really?
40   GALLIMARD: Of her death. It's a . . . a pure sacrifice. He's unworthy, but what can she do? She loves him . . . so much. It's a very beautiful story.
     SONG: Well, yes, to a Westerner.
     GALLIMARD: Excuse me?
45   SONG: It's one of your favorite fantasies, isn't it? The submissive Oriental woman and the cruel white man.
     GALLIMARD: Well, I didn't quite mean . . .
     SONG: Consider it this way: what would you say if a blonde homecoming queen fell in love with a short Japanese
50   businessman? He treats her cruelly, then goes home for three years, during which time she prays to his picture and turns down marriage from a young Kennedy. Then, when she learns he has remarried, she kills herself. Now, I believe you would consider this girl to be a deranged idiot,
55   correct? But because it's an Oriental who kills herself for a Westerner—ah!—you find it beautiful.

(*Silence.*)

GALLIMARD: Yes . . . well . . . I see your point . . .
SONG: I will never do Butterfly again, Monsieur Gallimard. If you wish to see some real theatre, come to the Peking Opera
60   sometime. Expand your mind.

(SONG *walks offstage.*)

GALLIMARD: (*To us.*) So much for protecting her in my big Western arms.

SCENE VII

M. GALLIMARD's *apartment. Beijing. 1960.*

GALLIMARD *changes from his tux into a casual suit.* HELGA *enters.*

GALLIMARD: The Chinese are an incredibly arrogant people.
HELGA: They warned us about that in Paris, remember?
GALLIMARD: Even Parisians consider them arrogant. That's a switch.
HELGA: What is it that Madame Su says? "We are a very old   5
     civilization." I never know if she's talking about her country or herself.
GALLIMARD: I walk around here, all I hear every day, everywhere is how *old* this culture is. The fact that "old" may be synonymous with "senile" doesn't occur to them.   10
HELGA: You're not going to change them. "East is east, west is west, and . . ." whatever that guy said.
GALLIMARD: It's just that—silly. I met . . . at Ambassador Koening's tonight—you should've been there.
HELGA: Koening? Oh god, no. Did he enchant you all again with   15
     the history of Bavaria?
GALLIMARD: No. I met, I suppose, the Chinese equivalent of a diva. She's a singer in the Chinese opera.
HELGA: They have an opera, too? Do they sing in Chinese? Or maybe—in Italian?   20
GALLIMARD: Tonight, she did sing in Italian.
HELGA: How'd she manage that?
GALLIMARD: She must've been educated in the West before the Revolution. Her French is very good also. Anyway, she sang the death scene from *Madame Butterfly.*   25
HELGA: *Madame Butterfly*! Then I should have come. (*She begins humming, floating around the room as if dragging long kimono sleeves.*) Did she have a nice costume? I think it's a classic piece of music.
GALLIMARD: That's what *I* thought, too. Don't let her hear you say   30
     that.
HELGA: What's wrong?
GALLIMARD: Evidently the Chinese hate it.
HELGA: She hated it, but she performed it anyway? Is she perverse?   35
GALLIMARD: They hate it because the white man gets the girl. Sour grapes if you ask me.
HELGA: Politics again? Why can't they just hear it as a piece of beautiful music? So, what's in their opera?
GALLIMARD: I don't know. But, whatever it is, I'm sure it must   40
     be *old*.

(HELGA *exits.*)

SCENE VIII

Chinese opera house and the streets of Beijing. 1960.

The sound of gongs clanging fills the stage.

GALLIMARD: My wife's innocent question kept ringing in my ears. I asked around, but no one knew anything about the Chinese opera. It took four weeks, but my curiosity overcame my cowardice. This Chinese diva—this unwilling Butterfly—
5   what did she do to make her so proud?
        The room was hot, and full of smoke. Wrinkled faces, old women, teeth missing—a man with a growth on his neck, like a human toad. All smiling, pipes falling from their mouths, cracking nuts between their teeth, a live
10   chicken pecking at my foot—all looking, screaming, gawking . . . at her.

(The upstage area is suddenly hit with a harsh white light. It has become the stage for the Chinese opera performance. Two dancers enter, along with SONG. GALLIMARD *stands apart, watching.* SONG *glides gracefully amidst the two dancers. Drums suddenly slam to a halt.* SONG *strikes a pose, looking straight at* GALLIMARD. *Dancers exit. Light change. Pause, then* SONG *walks right off the stage and straight up to* GALLIMARD.)

SONG: Yes. You. White man. I'm looking straight at you.
GALLIMARD: Me?
SONG: You see any other white men? It was too easy to spot you.
15   How often does a man in my audience come in a tie?

*(*SONG *starts to remove her costume. Underneath, she wears simple baggy clothes. They are now backstage. The show is over.)*

SONG: So, you are an adventurous imperialist?
GALLIMARD: I . . . thought it would further my education.
SONG: It took you four weeks. Why?
GALLIMARD: I've been busy.
20   SONG: Well, education has always been undervalued in the West, hasn't it?
GALLIMARD: (*Laughing.*) I don't think it's true.
SONG: No, you wouldn't. You're a Westerner. How can you objectively judge your own values?
25   GALLIMARD: I think it's possible to achieve some distance.
SONG: Do you? (*Pause.*) It stinks in here. Let's go.
GALLIMARD: These are the smells of your loyal fans.
SONG: I love them for being my fans, I hate the smell they leave behind. I too can distance myself from my people. (*She*
30   *looks around, then whispers in his ear.*) "Art for the masses" is a shitty excuse to keep artists poor. (*She pops a cigarette in her mouth.*) Be a gentleman, will you? And light my cigarette.

*(*GALLIMARD *fumbles for a match.)*

GALLIMARD: I don't . . . smoke.
35   SONG: (*Lighting her own.*) Your loss. Had you lit my cigarette, I might have blown a puff of smoke right between your eyes. Come.

(They start to walk about the stage. It is a summer night on the Beijing streets. Sounds of the city play on the house speakers.)

SONG: How I wish there were even a tiny cafe to sit in. With cappuccinos, and men in tuxedos and bad expatriate jazz.
GALLIMARD: If my history serves me correctly, you weren't even   40
allowed into the clubs in Shanghai before the Revolution.
SONG: Your history serves you poorly, Monsieur Gallimard. True, there were signs reading "No dogs and Chinamen." But a woman, especially a delicate Oriental woman—we always go where we please. Could you imagine it otherwise?   45
Clubs in China filled with pasty, big-thighed white women, while thousands of slender lotus blossoms wait just outside the door? Never. The clubs would be empty. (*Beat.*) We have always held a certain fascination for you Caucasian men, have we not?   50
GALLIMARD: But . . . that fascination is imperialist, or so you tell me.
SONG: Do you believe everything I tell you? Yes. It is always imperialist. But sometimes . . . sometimes, it is also mutual. Oh—this is my flat.   55
GALLIMARD: I didn't even—
SONG: Thank you. Come another time and we will further expand your mind.

*(*SONG *exits.* GALLIMARD *continues roaming the streets as he speaks to us.)*

GALLIMARD: What was that? What did she mean, "Sometimes. . . it is mutual?" Women do not flirt with me. And I normally   60
can't talk to them. But tonight, I held up my end of the conversation.

SCENE IX

GALLIMARD's *bedroom. Beijing. 1960.*

HELGA *enters.*

HELGA: You didn't tell me you'd be home late.
GALLIMARD: I didn't intend to. Something came up.
HELGA: Oh! Like what?
GALLIMARD: I went to the . . . to the Dutch ambassador's home.
HELGA: Again?   5
GALLIMARD: There was a reception for a visiting scholar. He's writing a six-volume treatise on the Chinese revolution. We all gathered that meant he'd have to live here long enough to actually write six volumes, and we all expressed our deepest sympathies.   10
HELGA: Well, I had a good night too. I went with the ladies to a martial arts demonstration. Some of those men—when they break those thick boards—(*She mimes fanning herself.*) whoo-whoo!

*(*HELGA *exits. Lights dim.)*

GALLIMARD: I lied to my wife. Why? I've never had any reason   15
to lie before. But what reason did I have tonight? I didn't do anything wrong. That night, I had a dream. Other people, I've been told, have dreams where angels appear. Or dragons, or Sophia Loren in a towel. In my dream, Marc from school appeared.   20

*(*MARC *enters, in a nightshirt and cap.)*

MARC: Rene! You met a girl!

(GALLIMARD *and* MARC *stumble down the Beijing streets. Night sounds over the speakers.*)

GALLIMARD: It's not that amazing, thank you.
MARC: No! It's so monumental, I heard about it halfway around the world in my sleep!
25 GALLIMARD: I've met girls before, you know.
MARC: Name one. I've come across time and space to congratulate you. (*He hands* GALLIMARD *a bottle of wine.*)
GALLIMARD: Marc, this is expensive.
MARC: On those rare occasions when you become a formless
30 spirit, why not steal the best?

(MARC *pops open the bottle, begins to share it with* GALLIMARD.)

GALLIMARD: You embarrass me. She . . . there's no reason to think she likes me.
MARC: "Sometimes, it is mutual"?
GALLIMARD: Oh.
35 MARC: "Mutual"? "Mutual"? What does that mean?
GALLIMARD: You heard!
MARC: It means the money is in the bank, you only have to write the check!
GALLIMARD: I am a married man!
40 MARC: And an excellent one too. I cheated after . . . six months. Then again and again, until now—three hundred girls in twelve years.
GALLIMARD: I don't think we should hold that up as a model.
MARC: Of course not! My life—it is disgusting! Phooey! Phooey!
45 Phooey! But, you—you are the model husband.
GALLIMARD: Anyway, it's impossible. I'm a foreigner.
MARC: Ah, yes. She cannot love you, it is taboo, but something deep inside her heart . . . she cannot help herself . . . she must surrender to you. It is her destiny.
50 GALLIMARD: How do you imagine all this?
MARC: The same way you do. It's an old story. It's in our blood. They fear us, Rene. Their women fear us. And their men—their men hate us. And, you know something? They are all correct.

(*They spot a light in a window.*)

55 MARC: There! There, Rene!
GALLIMARD: It's her window.
MARC: Late at night—it burns. The light—it burns for you.
GALLIMARD: I won't look. It's not respectful.
MARC: We don't have to be respectful. We're foreign devils.

(*Enter* SONG, *in a sheer robe. The "One Fine Day" aria creeps in over the speakers. With her back to us,* SONG *mimes attending to her toilette. Her robe comes loose, revealing her white shoulders.*)

60 MARC: All your life you've waited for a beautiful girl who would lay down for you. All your life you've smiled like a saint when it's happened to every other man you know. And you see them in magazines and you see them in movies. And you wonder, what's wrong with me? Will anyone beautiful
65 ever want me? As the years pass, your hair thins and you struggle to hold onto even your hopes. Stop struggling, Rene. The wait is over. (*He exits.*)

GALLIMARD: Marc? Marc?

(*At that moment,* SONG, *her back still towards us, drops her robe. A second of her naked back, then a sound cue: a phone ringing, very loud. Blackout, followed in the next beat by a special up on the bedroom area, where a phone now sits.* GALLIMARD *stumbles across the stage and picks up the phone. Sound cue out. Over the course of his conversation, area lights fill in the vicinity of his bed. It is the following morning.*)

GALLIMARD: Yes? Hello?
SONG: (*Offstage.*) Is it very early?   70
GALLIMARD: Why, yes.
SONG: (*Offstage.*) How early?
GALLIMARD: It's . . . it's 5:30. Why are you—?
SONG: (*Offstage.*) But it's light outside. Already.
GALLIMARD: It is. The sun must be in confusion today.   75

(*Over the course of* SONG's *next speech, her upstage special comes up again. She sits in a chair, legs crossed, in a robe, telephone to her ear.*)

SONG: I waited until I saw the sun. That was as much discipline as I could manage for one night. Do you forgive me?
GALLIMARD: Of course . . . for what?
SONG: Then I'll ask you quickly. Are you really interested in the opera?   80
GALLIMARD: Why, yes. Yes I am.
SONG: Then come again next Thursday. I am playing *The Drunken Beauty.* May I count on you?
GALLIMARD: Yes. You may.
SONG: Perfect. Well, I must be getting to bed. I'm exhausted. It's   85
been a very long night for me.

(SONG *hangs up; special on her goes off.* GALLIMARD *begins to dress for work.*)

SCENE X

SONG LILING's *apartment. Beijing. 1960.*

GALLIMARD: I returned to the opera that next week, and the week after that . . . she keeps our meetings so short—perhaps fifteen, twenty minutes at most. So I am left each week with a thirst which is intensified. In this way, fifteen weeks have gone by. I am starting to doubt the words of my friend Marc. But no,   5
not really. In my heart, I know she has . . . an interest in me. I suspect this is her way. She is outwardly bold and outspoken, yet her heart is shy and afraid. It is the Oriental in her at war with her Western education.
SONG: (*Offstage.*) I will be out in an instant. Ask the servant for   10
anything you want.
GALLIMARD: Tonight, I have finally been invited to enter her apartment. Though the idea is almost beyond belief, I believe she is afraid of me.

(GALLIMARD *looks around the room. He picks up a picture in a frame, studies it. Without his noticing,* SONG *enters, dressed elegantly in a black gown from the twenties. She stands in the doorway looking like Anna May Wong.*)

SONG: That is my father.   15
GALLIMARD: (*Surprised.*) Mademoiselle Song . . .

(*She glides up to him, snatches away the picture.*)

SONG: It is very good that he did not live to see the Revolution. They would, no doubt, have made him kneel on broken glass. Not that he didn't deserve such a punishment. But he is my
20 father. I would've hated to see it happen.
GALLIMARD: I'm very honored that you've allowed me to visit your home.

(SONG *curtsys.*)

SONG: Thank you. Oh! Haven't you been poured any tea?
GALLIMARD: I'm really not—
25 SONG: (*To her offstage servant.*) Shu-Fang! Cha! Kwai-lah! (*To* GALLIMARD.) I'm sorry. You want everything to be perfect—
GALLIMARD: Please.
SONG: —and before the evening even begins—
GALLIMARD: I'm really not thirsty.
30 SONG: —it's ruined.
GALLIMARD: (*Sharply.*) Mademoiselle Song!

(SONG *sits down.*)

SONG: I'm sorry.
GALLIMARD: What are you apologizing for now?

(*Pause;* SONG *starts to giggle.*)

SONG: I don't know!

(GALLIMARD *laughs.*)

35 GALLIMARD: Exactly my point.
SONG: Oh, I am silly. Lightheaded. I promise not to apologize for anything else tonight, do you hear me?
GALLIMARD: That's a good girl!

(SHU-FANG, *a servant girl, comes out with a tea tray and starts to pour.*)

SONG: (*To* SHU-FANG.) No! I'll pour myself for the gentleman!

(SHU-FANG, *staring at* GALLIMARD, *exits.*)

40 SONG: No, I . . . I don't even know why I invited you up.
GALLIMARD: Well, I'm glad you did.

(SONG *looks around the room.*)

SONG: There is an element of danger to your presence.
GALLIMARD: Oh?
SONG: You must know.
45 GALLIMARD: It doesn't concern me. We both know why I'm here.
SONG: It doesn't concern me either. No . . . well perhaps . . .
GALLIMARD: What?
SONG: Perhaps I am slightly afraid of scandal.
50 GALLIMARD: What are we doing?
SONG: I'm entertaining you. In my parlor.
GALLIMARD: In France, that would hardly—
SONG: France. France is a country living in the modern era. Perhaps even ahead of it. China is a nation whose soul is
55 firmly rooted two thousand years in the past. What I do,

even pouring the tea for you now . . . it has . . . implications. The walls and windows say so. Even my own heart, strapped inside this Western dress . . . even it says things—things I don't care to hear.

(SONG *hands* GALLIMARD *a cup of tea.* GALLIMARD *puts his hand over both the teacup and* SONG's *hand.*)

GALLIMARD: This is a beautiful dress.   60
SONG: Don't.
GALLIMARD: What?
SONG: I don't even know if it looks right on me.
GALLIMARD: Believe me—
SONG: You are from France. You see so many beautiful women.   65
GALLIMARD: France? Since when are the European women—?
SONG: Oh! What am I trying to do, anyway?!

(SONG *runs to the door, composes herself, then turns towards* GALLIMARD.)

SONG: Monsieur Gallimard, perhaps you should go.
GALLIMARD: But . . . why?
SONG: There's something wrong about this.   70
GALLIMARD: I don't see what.
SONG: I feel . . . I am not myself.
GALLIMARD: No. You're nervous.
SONG: Please. Hard as I try to be modern, to speak like a man, to hold a Western woman's strong face up to my own . . . in 75
the end, I fail. A small, frightened heart beats too quickly and gives me away. Monsieur Gallimard, I'm a Chinese girl. I've never . . . never invited a man up to my flat before. The forwardness of my actions makes my skin burn.
GALLIMARD: What are you afraid of? Certainly not me, I hope.   80
SONG: I'm a modest girl.
GALLIMARD: I know. And very beautiful. (*He touches her hair.*)
SONG: Please—go now. The next time you see me, I shall again be myself.
GALLIMARD: I like you the way you are right now.   85
SONG: You are a cad.
GALLIMARD: What do you expect? I'm a foreign devil.

(GALLIMARD *walks downstage.* SONG *exits.*)

GALLIMARD: (*To us.*) Did you hear the way she talked about Western women? Much differently than the first night. She does—she feels inferior to them—and to me.   90

SCENE XI

The French embassy. Beijing. 1960.

GALLIMARD *moves towards a desk.*

GALLIMARD: I determined to try an experiment. In *Madame Butterfly,* Cio-Cio-San fears that the Western man who catches a butterfly will pierce its heart with a needle, then leave it to perish. I began to wonder: had I, too, caught a butterfly who would writhe on a needle?   5

(MARC *enters, dressed as a bureaucrat, holding a stack of papers. As* GALLIMARD *speaks,* MARC *hands papers to him. He peruses, then signs, stamps or rejects them.*)

GALLIMARD: Over the next five weeks, I worked like a dynamo. I stopped going to the opera, I didn't phone or write her. I knew this little flower was waiting for me to call, and, as I wickedly refused to do so, I felt for the first time that rush of power—
10   the absolute power of a man.

(MARC *continues acting as the bureaucrat, but he now speaks as himself.*)

MARC: Rene! It's me!
GALLIMARD: Marc—I hear your voice everywhere now. Even in the midst of work.
MARC: That's because I'm watching you—all the time.
15 GALLIMARD: You were always the most popular guy in school.
MARC: Well, there's no guarantee of failure in life like happiness in high school. Somehow I knew I'd end up in the suburbs working for Renault and you'd be in the Orient picking exotic
20   women off the trees. And they say there's no justice.
GALLIMARD: That's why you were my friend?
MARC: I gave you a little of my life, so that now you can give me some of yours. (*Pause.*) Remember Isabelle?
GALLIMARD: Of course I remember! She was my first experience.
25 MARC: We all wanted to ball her. But she only wanted me.
GALLIMARD: I had her.
MARC: Right. You balled her.
GALLIMARD: You were the only one who ever believed me.
MARC: Well, there's a good reason for that. (*Beat.*) C'mon. You
30   must've guessed.
GALLIMARD: You told me to wait in the bushes by the cafeteria that night. The next thing I knew, she was on me. Dress up in the air.
MARC: She never wore underwear.
35 GALLIMARD: My arms were pinned to the dirt.
MARC: She loved the superior position. A girl ahead of her time.
GALLIMARD: I looked up, and there was this woman . . . bouncing up and down on my loins.
MARC: Screaming, right?
40 GALLIMARD: Screaming, and breaking off the branches all around me, and pounding my butt up and down into the dirt.
MARC: Huffing and puffing like a locomotive.
GALLIMARD: And in the middle of all this, the leaves were getting into my mouth, my legs were losing circulation, I thought,
45   "God. So this is *it?*"
MARC: You thought that?
GALLIMARD: Well, I was worried about my legs falling off.
MARC: You didn't have a good time?
GALLIMARD: No, that's not what I—I had a great time!
50 MARC: You're sure?
GALLIMARD: Yeah. Really.
MARC: 'Cuz I wanted you to have a good time.
GALLIMARD: I did.

(*Pause.*)

MARC: Shit. (*Pause.*) When all is said and done, she was kind of a
55   lousy lay, wasn't she? I mean, there was a lot of energy there, but you never knew what she was doing with it. Like when she yelled "I'm coming!"—hell, it was so loud, you wanted to go "Look, it's not that big a deal."
GALLIMARD: I got scared. I thought she meant someone was
60   actually coming. (*Pause.*) But, Marc?

MARC: What?
GALLIMARD: Thanks.
MARC: Oh, don't mention it.
GALLIMARD: It was my first experience.
MARC: Yeah. You got her.   65
GALLIMARD: I got her.
MARC: Wait! Look at that letter again!

(GALLIMARD *picks up one of the papers he's been stamping, and rereads it.*)

GALLIMARD: (*To us.*) After six weeks, they began to arrive. The letters.

(*Upstage special on* SONG, *as* MADAME BUTTERFLY. *The scene is underscored by the "Love Duet."*)

SONG: Did we fight? I do not know. Is the opera no longer of   70
interest to you? Please come—my audiences miss the white devil in their midst.

(GALLIMARD *looks up from the letter, towards us.*)

GALLIMARD: (*To us.*) A concession, but much too dignified. (*Beat;
he discards the letter.*) I skipped the opera again that week to complete a position paper on trade.   75

(*The bureaucrat hands him another letter.*)

SONG: Six weeks have passed since last we met. Is this your practice—to leave friends in the lurch? Sometimes I hate you, sometimes I hate myself, but always I miss you.
GALLIMARD: (*To us.*) Better, but I don't like the way she calls me "friend." When a woman calls a man her "friend," she's   80
calling him a eunuch or a homosexual. (*Beat; he discards the letter.*) I was absent from the opera for the seventh week, feeling a sudden urge to clean out my files.

(*Bureaucrat hands him another letter.*)

SONG: Your rudeness is beyond belief. I don't deserve this cruelty. Don't bother to call. I'll have you turned away at the door.   85
GALLIMARD: (*To us.*) I didn't. (*He discards the letter; bureaucrat hands him another.*) And then finally, the letter that concluded my experiment.
SONG: I am out of words. I can hide behind dignity no longer. What do you want? I have already given you my shame.   90

(GALLIMARD *gives the letter back to* MARC, *slowly. Special on* SONG *fades out.*)

GALLIMARD: (*To us.*) Reading it, I became suddenly ashamed. Yes, my experiment had been a success. She was turning on my needle. But the victory seemed hollow.
MARC: Hollow? Are you crazy?
GALLIMARD: Nothing, Marc. Please go away.   95
MARC: (*Exiting, with papers.*) Haven't I taught you anything?
GALLIMARD: "I have already given you my shame." I had to attend a reception that evening. On the way, I felt sick. If there is a God, surely he would punish me now. I had finally gained power over a beautiful woman, only to abuse it cruelly. There   100
must be justice in the world. I had the strange feeling that the ax would fall this very evening.

SCENE XII

AMBASSADOR TOULON's *residence. Beijing. 1960.*

Sound cue: party noises. Light change. We are now in a spacious residence. TOULON, *the French ambassador, enters and taps* GALLIMARD *on the shoulder.*

TOULON: Gallimard? Can I have a word? Over here.

GALLIMARD: (*To us.*) Manuel Toulon. French ambassador to China. He likes to think of us all as his children. Rather like God.

5   TOULON: Look, Gallimard, there's not much to say. I've liked you. From the day you walked in. You were no leader, but you were tidy and efficient.

GALLIMARD: Thank you, sir.

TOULON: Don't jump the gun. Okay, our needs in China are
10   changing. It's embarrassing that we lost Indochina. Someone just wasn't on the ball there. I don't mean you personally, of course.

GALLIMARD: Thank you, sir.

TOULON: We're going to be doing a lot more information-
15   gathering in the future. The nature of our work here is changing. Some people are just going to have to go. It's nothing personal.

GALLIMARD: Oh.

TOULON: Want to know a secret? Vice-Consul LeBon is being
20   transferred.

GALLIMARD: (*To us.*) My immediate superior!

TOULON: And most of his department.

GALLIMARD: (*To us.*) Just as I feared! God has seen my evil heart—

25   TOULON: But not you.

GALLIMARD: (*To us.*)—and he's taking her away just as . . . (*To* TOULON.) Excuse me, sir?

TOULON: Scare you? I think I did. Cheer up, Gallimard. I want you to replace LeBon as vice-consul.

30   GALLIMARD: You—? Yes, well, thank you, sir.

TOULON: Anytime.

GALLIMARD: I . . . accept with great humility.

TOULON: Humility won't be part of the job. You're going to coordinate the revamped intelligence division. Want to
35   know a secret? A year ago, you would've been out. But the past few months, I don't know how it happened, you've become this new aggressive confident . . . thing. And they also tell me you get along with the Chinese. So I think you're a lucky man, Gallimard. Congratulations.

(*They shake hands.* TOULON *exits. Party noises out.* GALLIMARD *stumbles across a darkened stage.*)

40   GALLIMARD: Vice-consul? Impossible! As I stumbled out of the party, I saw it written across the sky: There is no God. Or, no—say that there is a God. But that God . . . understands. Of course! God who creates Eve to serve Adam, who blesses Solomon with his harem but ties Jezebel
45   to a burning bed—that God is a man. And he understands! At age thirty-nine, I was suddenly initiated into the way of the world.

SCENE XIII

SONG LILING's *apartment. Beijing. 1960.*

SONG *enters, in a sheer dressing gown.*

SONG: Are you crazy?

GALLIMARD: Mademoiselle Song—

SONG: To come here—at this hour? After . . . after eight weeks?

GALLIMARD: It's the most amazing—

SONG: You bang on my door? Scare my servants, scandalize the   5
    neighbors?

GALLIMARD: I've been promoted. To vice-consul.

(*Pause.*)

SONG: And what is that supposed to mean to me?

GALLIMARD: Are you my Butterfly?

SONG: What are you saying?   10

GALLIMARD: I've come tonight for an answer: are you my Butterfly?

SONG: Don't you know already?

GALLIMARD: I want you to say it.

SONG: I don't want to say it.   15

GALLIMARD: So, that is your answer?

SONG: You know how I feel about—

GALLIMARD: I do remember one thing.

SONG: What?

GALLIMARD: In the letter I received today.   20

SONG: Don't.

GALLIMARD: "I have already given you my shame."

SONG: It's enough that I even wrote it.

GALLIMARD: Well, then—

SONG: I shouldn't have it splashed across my face.   25

GALLIMARD: —if that's all true—

SONG: Stop!

GALLIMARD: Then what is one more short answer?

SONG: I don't want to!

GALLIMARD: Are you my Butterfly? (*Silence; he crosses the room*   30
    and begins to touch her hair.) I want from you honesty. There should be nothing false between us. No false pride.

(*Pause.*)

SONG: Yes, I am. I am your Butterfly.

GALLIMARD: Then let me be honest with you. It is because of you that I was promoted tonight. You have changed my life   35
    forever. My little Butterfly, there should be no more secrets: I love you.

(*He starts to kiss her roughly. She resists slightly.*)

SONG: No . . . no . . . gently . . . please, I've never . . .

GALLIMARD: No?

SONG: I've tried to appear experienced, but . . . the truth   40
    is . . . no.

GALLIMARD: Are you cold?

SONG: Yes. Cold.

GALLIMARD: Then we will go very, very slowly.

(*He starts to caress her; her gown begins to open.*)

SONG: No . . . let me . . . keep my clothes . . .   45

GALLIMARD: But . . .

SONG: Please . . . it all frightens me. I'm a modest Chinese girl.

GALLIMARD: My poor little treasure.

SONG: I am your treasure. Though inexperienced, I am not . . .
50   ignorant. They teach us things, our mothers, about pleasing a
      man.
GALLIMARD: Yes?
SONG: I'll do my best to make you happy. Turn off the lights.

(GALLIMARD *gets up and heads for a lamp.* SONG, *propped up on one elbow, tosses her hair back and smiles.*)

SONG: Monsieur Gallimard?
55 GALLIMARD: Yes, Butterfly?
SONG: "Vieni, vieni!"
GALLIMARD: "Come, darling."
SONG: "Ah! Dolce notte!"
GALLIMARD: "Beautiful night."
60 SONG: "Tutto estatico d'amor ride il ciel!"
GALLIMARD: "All ecstatic with love, the heavens are filled with
      laughter."

(*He turns off the lamp. Blackout.*)

ACT TWO

SCENE I

M. GALLIMARD's *cell. Paris. Present.*

Lights up on GALLIMARD. *He sits in his cell, reading from a leaflet.*

GALLIMARD: This, from a contemporary critic's commentary
      on *Madame Butterfly*: "Pinkerton suffers from . . . being an
      obnoxious bounder whom every man in the audience itches
      to kick." Bully for us men in the audience! Then, in the same
5   note: "Butterfly is the most irresistibly appealing of Puccini's
      'Little Women.' Watching the succession of her humiliations
      is like watching a child under torture." (*He tosses the pamphlet
      over his shoulder.*) I suggest that, while we men may all
      want to kick Pinkerton, very few of us would pass up the
10   opportunity to be Pinkerton.

(GALLIMARD *moves out of his cell.*)

SCENE II

GALLIMARD *and* BUTTERFLY's *flat. Beijing. 1960.*

We are in a simple but well-decorated parlor. GALLIMARD *moves to
sit on a sofa, while* SONG, *dressed in a chong sam, enters and curls
up at his feet.*

GALLIMARD: (*To us.*) We secured a flat on the outskirts of Peking.
      Butterfly, as I was calling her now, decorated our "home"
      with Western furniture and Chinese antiques. And there,
      on a few stolen afternoons or evenings each week, Butterfly
5   commenced her education.
SONG: The Chinese men—they keep us down.
GALLIMARD: Even in the "New Society"?
SONG: In the "New Society," we are all kept ignorant equally.
      That's one of the exciting things about loving a Western man.
10   I know you are not threatened by a woman's education.
GALLIMARD: I'm no saint, Butterfly.
SONG: But you come from a progressive society.
GALLIMARD: We're not always reminding each other how "old"
      we are, if that's what you mean.

SONG: Exactly. We Chinese—once, I suppose, it is true, we ruled   15
      the world. But so what? How much more exciting to be part of
      the society ruling the world today. Tell me—what's happening
      in Vietnam?
GALLIMARD: Oh, Butterfly—you want me to bring my work
      home?   20
SONG: I want to know what you know. To be impressed by my
      man. It's not the particulars so much as the fact that you're
      making decisions which change the shape of the world.
GALLIMARD: Not the world. At best, a small corner.

(TOULON *enters, and sits at a desk upstage.*)

SCENE III

French embassy. Beijing. 1961.

GALLIMARD *moves downstage, to* TOULON's *desk.* SONG *remains
upstage, watching.*

TOULON: And a more troublesome corner is hard to imagine.
GALLIMARD: So, the Americans plan to begin bombing?
TOULON: This is very secret, Gallimard: yes. The Americans
      don't have an embassy here. They're asking us to be their eyes
      and ears. Say Jack Kennedy signed an order to bomb North   5
      Vietnam, Laos. How would the Chinese react?
GALLIMARD: I think the Chinese will squawk—
TOULON: Uh-huh.
GALLIMARD: —but, in their hearts, they don't even like Ho Chi
      Minh.   10

(*Pause.*)

TOULON: What a bunch of jerks. Vietnam was *our* colony. Not
      only didn't the Americans help us fight to keep them, but now,
      seven years later, they've come back to grab the territory for
      themselves. It's very irritating.
GALLIMARD: With all due respect, sir, why should the Americans 15
      have won our war for us back in '54 if we didn't have the will
      to win it ourselves?
TOULON: You're kidding, aren't you?

(*Pause.*)

GALLIMARD: The Orientals simply want to be associated with
      whoever shows the most strength and power. You live with   20
      the Chinese, sir. Do you think they like Communism?
TOULON: I live in China. Not with the Chinese.
GALLIMARD: Well, I—
TOULON: *You* live with the Chinese.
GALLIMARD: Excuse me?   25
TOULON: I can't keep a secret.
GALLIMARD: What are you saying?
TOULON: Only that I'm not immune to gossip. So, you're keeping
      a native mistress. Don't answer. It's none of my business.
      (*Pause.*) I'm sure she must be gorgeous.   30
GALLIMARD: Well . . .
TOULON: I'm impressed. You have the stamina to go out into the
      streets and hunt one down. Some of us have to be content with
      the wives of the expatriate community.
GALLIMARD: I do feel . . . fortunate.   35
TOULON: So, Gallimard, you've got the inside knowledge—what
      do the Chinese think?

GALLIMARD: Deep down, they miss the old days. You know, cappuccinos, men in tuxedos—

40 TOULON: So what do we tell the Americans about Vietnam?

GALLIMARD: Tell them there's a natural affinity between the West and the Orient.

TOULON: And that you speak from experience?

GALLIMARD: The Orientals are people too. They want the good

45 things we can give them. If the Americans demonstrate the will to win, the Vietnamese will welcome them into a mutually beneficial union.

TOULON: I don't see how the Vietnamese can stand up to American firepower.

50 GALLIMARD: Orientals will always submit to a greater force.

TOULON: I'll note your opinions in my report. The Americans always love to hear how "welcome" they'll be. (*He starts to exit.*)

GALLIMARD: Sir?

55 TOULON: Mmmm?

GALLIMARD: This . . . rumor you've heard.

TOULON: Uh-huh?

GALLIMARD: How . . . widespread do you think it is?

TOULON: It's only widespread within this embassy. Where nobody

60 talks because everybody is guilty. We were worried about you, Gallimard. We thought you were the only one here without a secret. Now you go and find a lotus blossom . . . and top us all. (*He exits.*)

GALLIMARD: (*To us.*) Toulon knows! And he approves! I was

65 learning the benefits of being a man. We form our own clubs, sit behind thick doors, smoke—and celebrate the fact that we're still boys. (*He starts to move downstage, towards* SONG.) So, over the—

(*Suddenly* COMRADE CHIN *enters.* GALLIMARD *backs away.*)

GALLIMARD: (*To* SONG.) No! Why does she have to come in?

70 SONG: Rene, be sensible. How can they understand the story without her? Now, don't embarrass yourself.

(GALLIMARD *moves down center.*)

GALLIMARD: (*To us.*) Now, you will see why my story is so amusing to so many people. Why they snicker at parties in disbelief. Please—try to understand it from my point of view.

75 We are all prisoners of our time and place. (*He exits.*)

SCENE IV

GALLIMARD *and* BUTTERFLY's *flat. Beijing. 1961.*

SONG: (*To us.*) 1961. The flat Monsieur Gallimard rented for us. An evening after he has gone.

CHIN: Okay, see if you find out when the Americans plan to start bombing Vietnam. If you can find out what cities,

5 even better.

SONG: I'll do my best, but I don't want to arouse his suspicions.

CHIN: Yeah, sure, of course. So, what else?

SONG: The Americans will increase troops in Vietnam to 170,000 soldiers with 120,000 militia and 11,000 American

10 advisors.

CHIN: (*Writing.*) Wait, wait. 120,000 militia and—

SONG: —11,000 American—

CHIN: —American advisors. (*Beat.*) How do you remember so much?

SONG: I'm an actor.   15

CHIN: Yeah. (*Beat.*) Is that how come you dress like that?

SONG: Like what, Miss Chin?

CHIN: Like that dress! You're wearing a dress. And every time I come here, you're wearing a dress. Is that because you're an actor? Or what?   20

SONG: It's a . . . disguise, Miss Chin.

CHIN: Actors, I think they're all weirdos. My mother tells me actors are like gamblers or prostitutes or —

SONG: It helps me in my assignment.

(*Pause.*)

CHIN: You're not gathering information in any way that violates   25
Communist Party principles, are you?

SONG: Why would I do that?

CHIN: Just checking. Remember: when working for the Great Proletarian State, you represent our Chairman Mao in every position you take.   30

SONG: I'll try to imagine the Chairman taking my positions.

CHIN: We all think of him this way. Good-bye, comrade. (*She starts to exit.*) Comrade?

SONG: Yes?

CHIN: Don't forget: there is no homosexuality in China!   35

SONG: Yes, I've heard.

CHIN: Just checking. (*She exits.*)

SONG: (*To us.*) What passes for a woman in modern China.

(GALLIMARD *sticks his head out from the wings.*)

GALLIMARD: Is she gone?

SONG: Yes, Rene. Please continue in your own fashion.   40

SCENE V

Beijing. 1961–63.

GALLIMARD *moves to the couch where* SONG *still sits. He lies down in her lap, and she strokes his forehead.*

GALLIMARD: (*To us.*) And so, over the years 1961, '62, '63, we settled into our routine, Butterfly and I. She would always have prepared a light snack and then, ever so delicately, and only if I agreed, she would start to pleasure me. With her hands, her mouth . . . too many ways to explain, and too sad,   5
given my present situation. But mostly we would talk. About my life. Perhaps there is nothing more rare than to find a woman who passionately listens.

(SONG *remains upstage, listening, as* HELGA *enters and plays a scene downstage with* GALLIMARD.)

HELGA: Rene, I visited Dr. Bolleart this morning.

GALLIMARD: Why? Are you ill?   10

HELGA: No, no. You see, I wanted to ask him . . . that question we've been discussing.

GALLIMARD: And I told you, it's only a matter of time. Why did you bring a doctor into this? We just have to keep trying—like a crapshoot, actually.   15

HELGA: I went, I'm sorry. But listen: he says there's nothing wrong with me.

GALLIMARD: You see? Now, will you stop—?

HELGA: Rene, he says he'd like you to go in and take some tests.

GALLIMARD: Why? So he can find there's nothing wrong with 20
both of us?

HELGA: Rene, I don't ask for much. One trip! One visit! And then,
whatever you want to do about it—you decide.

GALLIMARD: You're assuming he'll find something defective!

HELGA: No! Of course not! Whatever he finds—if he finds 25
nothing, we decide what to do about nothing! But go!

GALLIMARD: If he finds nothing, we keep trying. Just like we
do now.

HELGA: But at least we'll know! (*Pause.*) I'm sorry. (*She starts
to exit.*) 30

GALLIMARD: Do you really want me to see Dr. Bolleart?

HELGA: Only if you want a child, Rene. We have to face the
fact that time is running out. Only if you want a child. (*She
exits.*)

GALLIMARD: (*To* SONG.) I'm a modern man, Butterfly. And yet, 35
I don't want to go. It's the same old voodoo. I feel like God
himself is laughing at me if I can't produce a child.

SONG: You men of the West—you're obsessed by your odd
desire for equality. Your wife can't give you a child, and
you're going to the doctor? 40

GALLIMARD: Well, you see, she's already gone.

SONG: And because this incompetent can't find the defect, you
now have to subject yourself to him? It's unnatural.

GALLIMARD: Well, what is the "natural" solution?

SONG: In Imperial China, when a man found that one wife was 45
inadequate, he turned to another—to give him his son.

GALLIMARD: What do you—? I can't . . . marry you, yet.

SONG: Please. I'm not asking you to be my husband. But I am
already your wife.

GALLIMARD: Do you want to . . . have my child? 50

SONG: I thought you'd never ask.

GALLIMARD: But, your career . . . your—

SONG: Phooey on my career! That's your Western mind, twisting
itself into strange shapes again. Of course I love my career.
But what would I love most of all? To feel something inside 55
me—day and night—something I know is yours. (*Pause.*)
Promise me . . . you won't go to this doctor. Who is this
Western quack to set himself as judge over the man I love? I
know who is a man, and who is not. (*She exits.*)

GALLIMARD: (*To us.*) Dr. Bolleart? Of course I didn't go. What 60
man would?

SCENE VI

Beijing. 1963.

Party noises over the house speakers. RENEE *enters, wearing a
revealing gown.*

GALLIMARD: 1963. A party at the Austrian embassy. None of us
could remember the Austrian ambassador's name, which
seemed somehow appropriate. (*To* RENEE.) So, I tell the
Americans, Diem must go. The U.S. wants to be respected
by the Vietnamese, and yet they're propping up this nobody 5
seminarian as her president. A man whose claim to fame is
his sister-in-law imposing fanatic "moral order" campaigns?
Oriental women—when they're good, they're very good, but
when they're bad, they're Christians.

RENEE: Yeah. 10

GALLIMARD: And what do you do?

RENEE: I'm a student. My father exports a lot of useless stuff to
the Third World.

GALLIMARD: How useless?

RENEE: You know. Squirt guns, confectioner's sugar, hula 15
hoops . . .

GALLIMARD: I'm sure they appreciate the sugar.

RENEE: I'm here for two years to study Chinese.

GALLIMARD: Two years?

RENEE: That's what everybody says. 20

GALLIMARD: When did you arrive?

RENEE: Three weeks ago.

GALLIMARD: And?

RENEE: I like it. It's primitive, but . . . well, this is the place to
learn Chinese, so here I am. 25

GALLIMARD: Why Chinese?

RENEE: I think it'll be important someday.

GALLIMARD: You do?

RENEE: Don't ask me when, but . . . that's what I think.

GALLIMARD: Well, I agree with you. One hundred percent. That's 30
very farsighted.

RENEE: Yeah. Well of course, my father thinks I'm a complete
weirdo.

GALLIMARD: He'll thank you someday.

RENEE: Like when the Chinese start buying hula hoops? 35

GALLIMARD: There're a billion bellies out there.

RENEE: And if they end up taking over the world—well, then I'll
be lucky to know Chinese too, right?

(*Pause.*)

GALLIMARD: At this point, I don't see how the Chinese can
possibly take— 40

RENEE: You know what I *don't* like about China?

GALLIMARD: Excuse me? No—what?

RENEE: Nothing to do at night.

GALLIMARD: You come to parties at embassies like everyone
else. 45

RENEE: Yeah, but they get out at ten. And then what?

GALLIMARD: I'm afraid the Chinese idea of a dance hall is a dirt
floor and a man with a flute.

RENEE: Are you married?

GALLIMARD: Yes. Why? 50

RENEE: You wanna . . . fool around?

(*Pause.*)

GALLIMARD: Sure.

RENEE: I'll wait for you outside. What's your name?

GALLIMARD: Gallimard. Rene.

RENEE: Weird. I'm Renee too. (*She exits.*) 55

GALLIMARD: (*To us.*) And so, I embarked on my first extra-
extramarital affair. Renee was picture perfect. With a body
like those girls in the magazines. If I put a tissue paper over
my eyes, I wouldn't have been able to tell the difference.
And it was exciting to be with someone who wasn't afraid 60
to be seen completely naked. But is it possible for a woman
to be *too* uninhibited, *too* willing, so as to seem almost
too . . . masculine?

(*Chuck Berry blares from the house speakers, then comes down in
volume as* RENEE *enters, toweling her hair.*)

RENEE: You have a nice weenie.

GALLIMARD: What? 65

RENEE: Penis. You have a nice penis.

GALLIMARD: Oh. Well, thank you. That's very . . .

RENEE: What—can't take a compliment?

GALLIMARD: No, it's very . . . reassuring.

70 RENEE: But most girls don't come out and say it, huh?

GALLIMARD: And also . . . what did you call it?

RENEE: Oh. Most girls don't call it a "weenie," huh?

GALLIMARD: It sounds very—

RENEE: Small, I know.

75 GALLIMARD: I was going to say, "young."

RENEE: Yeah. Young, small, same thing. Most guys are pretty, uh, sensitive about that. Like, you know, I had a boyfriend back home in Denmark. I got mad at him once and called him a little weeniehead. He got so mad! He said at least I should call

80 him a great big weeniehead.

GALLIMARD: I suppose I just say "penis."

RENEE: Yeah. That's pretty clinical. There's "cock," but that sounds like a chicken. And "prick" is painful, and "dick" is like you're talking about someone who's not in the room.

85 GALLIMARD: Yes. It's a . . . bigger problem than I imagined.

RENEE: I—I think maybe it's because I really don't know what to do with them—that's why I call them "weenies."

GALLIMARD: Well, you did quite well with . . . mine.

RENEE: Thanks, but I mean, really *do* with them. Like, okay, have

90 you ever looked at one? I mean, really?

GALLIMARD: No, I suppose when it's part of you, you sort of take it for granted.

RENEE: I guess. But, like, it just hangs there. This little . . . flap of flesh. And there's so much fuss that we make about it. Like,

95 I think the reason we fight wars is because we wear clothes. Because no one knows—between the men, I mean—who has the bigger . . . weenie. So, if I'm a guy with a small one, I'm going to build a really big building or take over a really big piece of land or write a really long book so the other

100 men don't know, right? But, see, it never really works, that's the problem. I mean, you conquer the country, or whatever, but you're still wearing clothes, so there's no way to prove absolutely whose is bigger or smaller. And that's what we call a civilized society. The whole world run by a bunch of men

105 with pricks the size of pins. (*She exits.*)

GALLIMARD: (*To us.*) This was simply not acceptable.

(*A high-pitched chime rings through the air.* SONG, *dressed as Butterfly, appears in the upstage special. She is obviously distressed.
Her body swoons as she attempts to clip the stems of flowers she's
arranging in a vase.*)

GALLIMARD: But I kept up our affair, wildly, for several months. Why? I believe because of Butterfly. She knew the secret I was trying to hide. But, unlike a Western woman,

110 she didn't confront me, threaten, even pout. I remembered the words of Puccini's *Butterfly:*

SONG: "Noi siamo gente avvezza / alle piccole cose / umili e silenziose."

GALLIMARD: "I come from a people / Who are accustomed to

115 little / Humble and silent." I saw Pinkerton and Butterfly, and what she would say if he were unfaithful . . . nothing. She would cry, alone, into those wildly soft sleeves, once full of possessions, now empty to collect her tears. It was her tears and her silence that excited me, every time I visited Renee.

120 TOULON: (*Offstage.*) Gallimard!

(TOULON *enters.* GALLIMARD *turns towards him. During the next
section,* SONG, *up center, begins to dance with the flowers. It is a
drunken dance, where she breaks small pieces off the stems.*)

TOULON: They're killing him.

GALLIMARD: Who? I'm sorry? What?

TOULON: Bother you to come over at this late hour?

GALLIMARD: No . . . of course not.

TOULON: Not after you hear my secret. Champagne? 125

GALLIMARD: Um . . . thank you.

TOULON: You're surprised. There's something that you've wanted, Gallimard. No, not a promotion. Next time. Something in the world. You're not aware of this, but there's an informal gossip circle among intelligence agents. And some of ours heard 130 from some of the Americans—

GALLIMARD: Yes?

TOULON: That the U.S. will allow the Vietnamese generals to stage a coup . . . and assassinate President Diem.

(*The chime rings again.* TOULON *freezes.* GALLIMARD *turns upstage
and looks at* SONG, *who slowly and deliberately clips a flower off its
stem.* GALLIMARD *turns back towards* TOULON.)

GALLIMARD: I think . . . that's a very wise move! 135

(TOULON *unfreezes.*)

TOULON: It's what you've been advocating. A toast?

GALLIMARD: Sure. I consider this a vindication.

TOULON: Not exactly. "To the test. Let's hope you pass."

(*They drink. The chime rings again.* TOULON *freezes.* GALLIMARD
turns upstage, and SONG *clips another flower.*)

GALLIMARD: (*To* TOULON.) The test?

TOULON: (*Unfreezing.*) It's a test of everything you've been 140 saying. I personally think the generals probably will stop the Communists. And you'll be a hero. But if anything goes wrong, then your opinions won't be worth a pig's ear. I'm sure that won't happen. But sometimes it's easier when they don't listen to you. 145

GALLIMARD: They're your opinions too, aren't they?

TOULON: Personally, yes.

GALLIMARD: So we agree.

TOULON: But my opinions aren't on that report. Yours are. Cheers. 150

(TOULON *turns away from* GALLIMARD *and raises his glass. At
that instant* SONG *picks up the vase and hurls it to the ground. It
shatters.* SONG *sinks down amidst the shards of the vase, in a calm,
childlike trance. She sings softly, as if reciting a child's nursery
rhyme.*)

SONG: (*Repeat as necessary.*) "The whole world over, the white man travels, setting anchor, wherever he likes. Life's not worth living, unless he finds, the finest maidens, of every land . . ."

(GALLIMARD *turns downstage towards us.* SONG *continues
singing.*)

GALLIMARD: I shook as I left his house. That coward! That worm! 155 To put the burden for his decisions on my shoulders!

I started for Renee's. But no, that was all I needed. A
schoolgirl who would question the role of the penis in modern
society. What I wanted was revenge. A vessel to contain my
160 humiliation. Though I hadn't seen her in several weeks, I
headed for Butterfly's.

(GALLIMARD *enters* SONG's *apartment.*)

SONG: Oh! Rene . . . I was dreaming!
GALLIMARD: You've been drinking?
SONG: If I can't sleep, then yes, I drink. But then, it gives me these
165 dreams which—Rene, it's been almost three weeks since you
visited me last.
GALLIMARD: I know. There's been a lot going on in the world.
SONG: Fortunately I am drunk. So I can speak freely. It's not the
world, it's you and me. And an old problem. Even the softest
170 skin becomes like leather to a man who's touched it too often.
I confess I don't know how to stop it. I don't know how to
become another woman.
GALLIMARD: I have a request.
SONG: Is this a solution? Or are you ready to give up the flat?
175 GALLIMARD: It may be a solution. But I'm sure you won't like it.
SONG: Oh well, that's very important. "Like it?" Do you think
I "like" lying here alone, waiting, always waiting for your
return? Please—don't worry about what I may not "like."
GALLIMARD: I want to see you . . . naked.

(*Silence.*)

180 SONG: I thought you understood my modesty. So you want
me to—what—strip? Like a big cowboy girl? Shiny pasties
on my breasts? Shall I fling my kimono over my head and
yell "ya-hoo" in the process? I thought you respected my
shame!
185 GALLIMARD: I believe you gave me your shame many years ago.
SONG: Yes—and it is just like a white devil to use it against me.
I can't believe it. I thought myself so repulsed by the passive
Oriental and the cruel white man. Now I see—we are always
most revolted by the things hidden within us.
190 GALLIMARD: I just mean—
SONG: Yes?
GALLIMARD: —that it will remove the only barrier left
between us.
SONG: No, Rene. Don't couch your request in sweet words. Be
195 yourself—a cad—and know that my love is enough, that
I submit—submit to the worst you can give me. (*Pause.*)
Well, come. Strip me. Whatever happens, know that you
have willed it. Our love, in your hands. I'm helpless before
my man.

(GALLIMARD *starts to cross the room.*)

200 GALLIMARD: Did I not undress her because I knew, somewhere
deep down, what I would find? Perhaps. Happiness is so rare
that our mind can turn somersaults to protect it.
At the time, I only knew that I was seeing Pinkerton
stalking towards his Butterfly, ready to reward her love with
205 his lecherous hands. The image sickened me, pulled me to my
knees, so I was crawling towards her like a worm. By the time
I reached her, Pinkerton . . . had vanished from my heart. To
be replaced by something new, something unnatural, that
flew in the face of all I'd learned in the world—something
210 very close to love.

(*He grabs her around the waist; she strokes his hair.*)

GALLIMARD: Butterfly, forgive me.
SONG: Rene . . .
GALLIMARD: For everything. From the start.
SONG: I'm . . .
GALLIMARD: I want to—
SONG: I'm pregnant. (*Beat.*) I'm pregnant. (*Beat.*) I'm pregnant. 215

(*Beat.*)

GALLIMARD: I want to marry you!

SCENE VII

GALLIMARD *and* BUTTERFLY's *flat. Beijing. 1963.*

Downstage, SONG *paces as* COMRADE CHIN *reads from her note-
pad. Upstage,* GALLIMARD *is still kneeling. He remains on his knees
throughout the scene, watching it.*

SONG: I need a baby.
CHIN: (*From pad.*) He's been spotted going to a dorm.
SONG: I need a baby.
CHIN: At the Foreign Language Institute.
SONG: I need a baby. 5
CHIN: The room of a Danish girl . . . What do you mean, you need
a baby?!
SONG: Tell Comrade Kang—last night, the entire mission, it
could've ended.
CHIN: What do you mean? 10
SONG: Tell Kang—he told me to strip.
CHIN: *Strip?!*
SONG: Write!
CHIN: I tell you, I don't understand nothing about this case
anymore. Nothing. 15
SONG: He told me to strip, and I took a chance. Oh, we Chinese,
we know how to gamble.
CHIN: (*Writing.*) " . . . told him to strip."
SONG: My palms were wet, I had to make a split-second decision.
CHIN: Hey! Can you slow down?! 20

(*Pause.*)

SONG: You write faster, I'm the artist here. Suddenly, it hit
me—"All he wants is for her to submit. Once a woman
submits, a man is always ready to become 'generous.'"
CHIN: You're just gonna end up with rough notes.
SONG: And it worked! He gave in! Now, if I can just present him 25
with a baby. A Chinese baby with blond hair—he'll be mine
for life!
CHIN: Kang will never agree! The trading of babies has to be a
counterrevolutionary act.
SONG: Sometimes, a counterrevolutionary act is necessary to 30
counter a counterrevolutionary act.

(*Pause.*)

CHIN: Wait.
SONG: I need one . . . in seven months. Make sure it's a boy.
CHIN: This doesn't sound like something the Chairman would
do. Maybe you'd better talk to Comrade Kang yourself. 35
SONG: Good. I will.

(CHIN *gets up to leave.*)

SONG: Miss Chin? Why, in the Peking Opera, are women's roles played by men?

CHIN: I don't know. Maybe, a reactionary remnant of male—

40 SONG: No. (*Beat.*) Because only a man knows how a woman is supposed to act.

(CHIN *exits.* SONG *turns upstage, towards* GALLIMARD.)

GALLIMARD: (*Calling after* CHIN.) Good riddance! (*To* SONG.) I could forget all that betrayal in an instant, you know. If you'd just come back and become Butterfly again.

45 SONG: Fat chance. You're here in prison, rotting in a cell. And I'm on a plane, winging my way back to China. Your President pardoned me of our treason, you know.

GALLIMARD: Yes, I read about that.

SONG: Must make you feel . . . lower than shit.

50 GALLIMARD: But don't you, even a little bit, wish you were here with me?

SONG: I'm an artist, Rene. You were my greatest . . . acting challenge. (*She laughs.*) It doesn't matter how rotten I answer, does it? You still adore me. That's why I love you, Rene. (*She*

55 *points to us.*) So—you were telling your audience about the night I announced I was pregnant.

(GALLIMARD *puts his arms around* SONG's *waist. He and* SONG *are in the positions they were in at the end of Scene 6.*)

SCENE VIII

Same.

GALLIMARD: I'll divorce my wife. We'll live together here, and then later in France.

SONG: I feel so . . . ashamed.

GALLIMARD: Why?

5 SONG: I had begun to lose faith. And now, you shame me with your generosity.

GALLIMARD: Generosity? No, I'm proposing for very selfish reasons.

SONG: Your apologies only make me feel more ashamed. My

10 outburst a moment ago!

GALLIMARD: Your outburst? What about my request?!

SONG: You've been very patient dealing with my . . . eccentricities. A Western man, used to women freer with their bodies—

15 GALLIMARD: It was sick! Don't make excuses for me.

SONG: I have to. You don't seem willing to make them for yourself.

(*Pause.*)

GALLIMARD: You're crazy.

SONG: I'm happy. Which often looks like crazy.

20 GALLIMARD: Then make me crazy. Marry me.

(*Pause.*)

SONG: No.

GALLIMARD: What?

SONG: Do I sound silly, a slave, if I say I'm not worthy?

GALLIMARD: Yes. In fact you do. No one has loved me like you.

SONG: Thank you. And no one ever will. I'll see to that. 25

GALLIMARD: So what is the problem?

SONG: Rene, we Chinese are realists. We understand rice, gold, and guns. You are a diplomat. Your career is skyrocketing. Now, what would happen if you divorced your wife to marry a Communist Chinese actress? 30

GALLIMARD: That's not being realistic. That's defeating yourself before you begin.

SONG: We must conserve our strength for the battles we can win.

GALLIMARD: That sounds like a fortune cookie!

SONG: Where do you think fortune cookies come from? 35

GALLIMARD: I don't care.

SONG: You do. So do I. And we should. That is why I say I'm not worthy. I'm worthy to love and even to be loved by you. But I am not worthy to end the career of one of the West's most promising diplomats. 40

GALLIMARD: It's not that great a career! I made it sound like more than it is!

SONG: Modesty will get you nowhere. Flatter yourself, and you flatter me. I'm flattered to decline your offer. (*She exits.*)

GALLIMARD: (*To us.*) Butterfly and I argued all night. And, in the 45 end, I left, knowing I would never be her husband. She went away for several months—to the countryside, like a small animal. Until the night I received her call.

(*A baby's cry from offstage.* SONG *enters, carrying a child.*)

SONG: He looks like you.

GALLIMARD: Oh! (*Beat; he approaches the baby.*) Well, babies are 50 never very attractive at birth.

SONG: Stop!

GALLIMARD: I'm sure he'll grow more beautiful with age. More like his mother.

SONG: "Chi vide mai / a bimbo del Giappon . . ." 55

GALLIMARD: "What baby, I wonder, was ever born in Japan"—or China, for that matter—

SONG: ". . . occhi azzurrini?"

GALLIMARD: "With azure eyes"—they're actually sort of brown, wouldn't you say? 60

SONG: "E il labbro."

GALLIMARD: "And such lips!" (*He kisses* SONG.) And such lips.

SONG: "E i ricciolini d'oro schietto?"

GALLIMARD: "And such a head of golden"—if slightly patchy—"curls?" 65

SONG: I'm going to call him "Peepee."

GALLIMARD: Darling, could you repeat that because I'm sure a rickshaw just flew by overhead.

SONG: You heard me.

GALLIMARD: "Song Peepee"? May I suggest Michael, or Stephan, 70 or Adolph?

SONG: You may, but I won't listen.

GALLIMARD: You can't be serious. Can you imagine the time this child will have in school?

SONG: In the West, yes. 75

GALLIMARD: It's worse than naming him Ping Pong or Long Dong or—

SONG: But he's never going to live in the West, is he?

(*Pause.*)

GALLIMARD: That wasn't my choice.

80 SONG: It is mine. And this is my promise to you: I will raise him, he will be our child, but he will never burden you outside of China.

GALLIMARD: Why do you make these promises? I want to be burdened! I want a scandal to cover the papers!

85 SONG: (*To us.*) Prophetic.

GALLIMARD: I'm serious.

SONG: So am I. His name is as I registered it. And he will never live in the West.

(SONG *exits with the child.*)

GALLIMARD: (*To us.*) It is possible that her stubbornness only
90 made me want her more. That drawing back at the moment of my capitulation was the most brilliant strategy she could have chosen. It is possible. But it is also possible that by this point she could have said, could have done . . . anything, and I would have adored her still.

SCENE IX

Beijing. 1966.

A driving rhythm of Chinese percussion fills the stage.

GALLIMARD: And then, China began to change. Mao became very old, and his cult became very strong. And, like many old men, he entered his second childhood. So he handed over the reins of state to those with minds like his own. And children ruled
5 the Middle Kingdom with complete caprice. The doctrine of the Cultural Revolution implied continuous anarchy. Contact between Chinese and foreigners became impossible. Our flat was confiscated. Her fame and my money now counted against us.

(*Two dancers in Mao suits and red-starred caps enter, and begin crudely mimicking revolutionary violence, in an agitprop fashion.*)

10 GALLIMARD: And somehow the American war went wrong too. Four hundred thousand dollars were being spent for every Viet Cong killed; so General Westmoreland's remark that the Oriental does not value life the way Americans do was oddly accurate. Why weren't the Vietnamese people giving in? Why
15 were they content instead to die and die and die again?

(TOULON *enters.*)

TOULON: Congratulations, Gallimard.

GALLIMARD: Excuse me, sir?

TOULON: Not a promotion. That was last time. You're going home.

20 GALLIMARD: What?

TOULON: Don't say I didn't warn you.

GALLIMARD: I'm being transferred . . . because I was wrong about the American war?

TOULON: Of course not. We don't care about the Americans. We
25 care about your mind. The quality of your analysis. In general, everything you've predicted here in the Orient . . . just hasn't happened.

GALLIMARD: I think that's premature.

TOULON: Don't force me to be blunt. Okay, you said China
30 was ready to open to Western trade. The only thing they're

trading out there are Western heads. And, yes, you said the Americans would succeed in Indochina. You were kidding, right?

GALLIMARD: I think the end is in sight.

TOULON: Don't be pathetic. And don't take this personally. You 35 were wrong. It's not your fault.

GALLIMARD: But I'm going home.

TOULON: Right. Could I have the number of your mistress? (*Beat.*) Joke! Joke! Eat a croissant for me.

(TOULON *exits.* SONG, *wearing a Mao suit, is dragged in from the wings as part of the upstage dance. They "beat" her, then lampoon the acrobatics of the Chinese opera, as she is made to kneel onstage.*)

GALLIMARD: (*Simultaneously.*) I don't care to recall how Butterfly 40 and I said our hurried farewell. Perhaps it was better to end our affair before it killed her.

(GALLIMARD *exits.* COMRADE CHIN *walks across the stage with a banner reading: "The Actor Renounces His Decadent Profession!" She reaches the kneeling* SONG. *Percussion stops with a thud. Dancers strike poses.*)

CHIN: Actor-oppressor, for years you have lived above the common people and looked down on their labor. While the farmer ate millet— 45

SONG: I ate pastries from France and sweetmeats from silver trays.

CHIN: And how did you come to live in such an exalted position?

SONG: I was a plaything for the imperialists! 50

CHIN: What did you do?

SONG: I shamed China by allowing myself to be corrupted by a foreigner . . .

CHIN: What does this mean? The People demand a full confession! 55

SONG: I engaged in the lowest perversions with China's enemies!

CHIN: What perversions? Be more clear!

SONG: I let him put it up my ass!

(*Dancers look over, disgusted.*)

CHIN: Aaaa-ya! How can you use such sickening language?!

SONG: My language . . . is only as foul as the crimes I com- 60 mitted . . .

CHIN: Yeah. That's better. So—what do you want to do now?

SONG: I want to serve the people.

(*Percussion starts up, with Chinese strings.*)

CHIN: What?

SONG: I want to serve the people! 65

(*Dancers regain their revolutionary smiles, and begin a dance of victory.*)

CHIN: What?!

SONG: I want to serve the people!

(*Dancers unveil a banner: "The Actor Is Rehabilitated!"* SONG *remains kneeling before* CHIN, *as the dancers bounce around them, then exit. Music out.*)

SCENE X

A commune. Hunan Province. 1970.

CHIN: How you planning to do that?

SONG: I've already worked four years in the fields of Hunan, Comrade Chin.

CHIN: So? Farmers work all their lives. Let me see your hands.

(SONG *holds them out for her inspection.*)

5 CHIN: Goddamn! Still so smooth! How long does it take to turn you actors into good anythings? Hunh. You've just spent too many years in luxury to be any good to the Revolution.

SONG: I served the Revolution.

10 CHIN: Serve the Resolution? Bullshit! You wore dresses! Don't tell me—I was there. I saw you! You and your white vice-consul! Stuck up there in your flat, living off the People's Treasury! Yeah, I knew what was going on! You two . . . homos! Homos! Homos! (*Pause; she composes*

15 *herself.*) Ah! Well . . . you will serve the people, all right. But not with the Revolution's money. This time, you use your own money.

SONG: I have no money.

CHIN: Shut up! And you won't stink up China anymore with

20 your pervert stuff. You'll pollute the place where pollution begins—the West.

SONG: What do you mean?

CHIN: Shut up! You're going to France. Without a cent in your pocket. You find your consul's house, you make him pay your

25 expenses—

SONG: No.

CHIN: And you give us weekly reports! Useful information!

SONG: That's crazy. It's been four years.

CHIN: Either that, or back to rehabilitation center!

30 SONG: Comrade Chin, he's not going to support me! Not in France! He's a white man! I was just his plaything—

CHIN: Oh yuck! Again with the sickening language. Where's my stick?

SONG: You don't understand the mind of a man.

(*Pause.*)

35 CHIN: Oh no? No I don't? Then how come I'm married, huh? How come I got a man? Five, six years ago, you always tell me those kinds of things, I felt very bad. But not now! Because what does the Chairman say? He tells us *I'm* now the smart one, you're now the nincompoop! *You're*

40 the blackhead, the harebrain, the nitwit! You think you're so smart? You understand "The Mind of a Man"? Good! Then *you* go to France and be a pervert for Chairman Mao!

(CHIN *and* SONG *exit in opposite directions.*)

SCENE XI

Paris. 1968–70.

GALLIMARD *enters.*

GALLIMARD: And what was waiting for me back in Paris? Well, better Chinese food than I'd eaten in China. Friends and

relatives. A little accounting, regular schedule, keeping track of traffic violations in the suburbs. . . . And the indignity of students shouting the slogans of Chairman Mao at me—in 5
French.

HELGA: Rene? Rene? (*She enters, soaking wet.*) I've had a . . . a problem. (*She sneezes.*)

GALLIMARD: You're wet.

HELGA: Yes, I . . . coming back from the grocer's. A group of 10
students, waving red flags, they—

(GALLIMARD *fetches a towel.*)

HELGA: —they ran by, I was caught up along with them. Before I knew what was happening—

(GALLIMARD *gives her the towel.*)

HELGA: Thank you. The police started firing water cannons at us. I tried to shout, to tell them I was the wife of a diplomat, 15
but—you know how it is . . . (*Pause.*) Needless to say, I lost the groceries. Rene, what's happening to France?

GALLIMARD: What's—? Well, nothing, really.

HELGA: Nothing? The storefronts are in flames, there's glass in the streets, buildings are toppling—and I'm wet! 20

GALLIMARD: Nothing! . . . that I care to think about.

HELGA: And is that why you stay in this room?

GALLIMARD: Yes, in fact.

HELGA: With the incense burning? You know something? I hate incense. It smells so sickly sweet. 25

GALLIMARD: Well, I hate the French. Who just smell—period!

HELGA: And the Chinese were better?

GALLIMARD: Please—don't start.

HELGA: When we left, this exact same thing, the riots—

GALLIMARD: No, no . . . 30

HELGA: Students screaming slogans, smashing down doors—

GALLIMARD: Helga—

HELGA: It was all going on in China, too. Don't you remember?!

GALLIMARD: Helga! Please! (*Pause.*) You have never understood China, have you? You walk in here with these ridiculous 35
ideas, that the West is falling apart, that China was spitting in our faces. You come in, dripping of the streets, and you leave water all over my floor. (*He grabs* HELGA's *towel, begins mopping up the floor.*)

HELGA: But it's the truth! 40

GALLIMARD: Helga, I want a divorce.

(*Pause;* GALLIMARD *continues, mopping the floor.*)

HELGA: I take it back. China is . . . beautiful. Incense, I like incense.

GALLIMARD: I've had a mistress.

HELGA: So? 45

GALLIMARD: For eight years.

HELGA: I knew you would. I knew you would the day I married you. And now what? You want to marry her?

GALLIMARD: I can't. She's in China.

HELGA: I see. You want to leave. For someone who's not here, is 50
that right?

GALLIMARD: That's right.

HELGA: You can't live with her, but still you don't want to live with me.

GALLIMARD: That's right. 55

(*Pause.*)

HELGA: Shit. How terrible that I can figure that out. (*Pause.*) I never thought I'd say it. But, in China, I was happy. I knew, in my own way, I knew that you were not everything you pretended to be. But the pretense—going on your arm to
60 the embassy ball, visiting your office and the guards saying, "Good morning, good morning, Madame Gallimard"—the pretense . . . was very good indeed. (*Pause.*) I hope everyone is mean to you for the rest of your life. (*She exits.*)

GALLIMARD: (*To us.*) Prophetic.

(MARC *enters with two drinks.*)

65 GALLIMARD: (*To* MARC.) In China, I was different from all other men.

MARC: Sure. You were white. Here's your drink.

GALLIMARD: I felt . . . touched.

MARC: In the head? Rene, I don't want to hear about the Oriental
70 love goddess. Okay? One night—can we just drink and throw up without a lot of conversation?

GALLIMARD: You still don't believe me, do you?

MARC: Sure I do. She was the most beautiful, et cetera, et cetera, blasé blasé.

(*Pause.*)

75 GALLIMARD: My life in the West has been such a disappointment.

MARC: Life in the West is like that. You'll get used to it. Look, you're driving me away. I'm leaving. Happy, now? (*He exits, then returns.*) Look, I have a date tomorrow night. You wanna
80 come? I can fix you up with—

GALLIMARD: Of course. I would love to come.

(*Pause.*)

MARC: Uh—on second thought, no. You'd better get ahold of yourself first.

(*He exits;* GALLIMARD *nurses his drink.*)

GALLIMARD: (*To us.*) This is the ultimate cruelty, isn't it? That I
85 can talk and talk and to anyone listening, it's only air—too rich a diet to be swallowed by a mundane world. Why can't anyone understand? That in China, I once loved, and was loved by, very simply, the Perfect Woman.

(SONG *enters, dressed as Butterfly in wedding dress.*)

GALLIMARD: (*To* SONG.) Not again. My imagination is hell. Am I
90 asleep this time? Or did I drink too much?

SONG: Rene?

GALLIMARD: God, it's too painful! That you speak?

SONG: What are you talking about? Rene—touch me.

GALLIMARD: Why?
95 SONG: I'm real. Take my hand.

GALLIMARD: Why? So you can disappear again and leave me clutching at the air? For the entertainment of my neighbors who—?

(SONG *touches* GALLIMARD.)

SONG: Rene?

(GALLIMARD *takes* SONG's *hand. Silence.*)

GALLIMARD: Butterfly? I never doubted you'd return. 100
SONG: You hadn't . . . forgotten—?

GALLIMARD: Yes, actually, I've forgotten everything. My mind, you see—there wasn't enough room in this hard head—not for the world *and* for you. No, there was only room for one. (*Beat.*) Come, look. See? Your bed has been waiting, with the 105 Klimt poster you like, and—see? The xiang lu [incense burner] you gave me?

SONG: I . . . I don't know what to say.

GALLIMARD: There's nothing to say. Not at the end of a long trip. Can I make you some tea? 110

SONG: But where's your wife?

GALLIMARD: She's by my side. She's by my side at last.

(GALLIMARD *reaches to embrace* SONG. SONG *sidesteps, dodging him.*)

GALLIMARD: Why?

SONG: (*To us.*) So I did return to Rene in Paris. Where I found— 115

GALLIMARD: Why do you run away? Can't we show them how we embraced that evening?

SONG: Please. I'm talking.

GALLIMARD: You have to do what I say! I'm conjuring you up in *my* mind! 120

SONG: Rene, I've never done what you've said. Why should it be any different in your mind? Now split—the story moves on, and I must change.

GALLIMARD: I welcomed you into my home! I didn't have to, you know! I could've left you penniless on the streets of Paris! But 125 I took you in!

SONG: Thank you.

GALLIMARD: So . . . please . . . don't change.

SONG: You know I have to. You know I will. And anyway, what difference does it make? No matter what your eyes tell you, 130 you can't ignore the truth. You already know too much.

(GALLIMARD *exits.* SONG *turns to us.*)

SONG: The change I'm going to make requires about five minutes. So I thought you might want to take this opportunity to stretch your legs, enjoy a drink, or listen to the musicians. I'll be here, when you return, right where you 135 left me.

(SONG *goes to a mirror in front of which is a wash basin of water. She starts to remove her makeup as stagelights go to half and houselights come up.*)

ACT THREE

SCENE I

A courthouse in Paris. 1986.

As he promised, SONG *has completed the bulk of his transformation onstage by the time the houselights go down and the stagelights come up full. He removes his wig and kimono, leaving them on the floor. Underneath, he wears a well-cut suit.*

SONG: So I'd done my job better than I had a right to expect. Well, give him some credit, too. He's right—I was in a fix when I arrived in Paris. I walked from the airport into town, then I located, by blind groping, the Chinatown district. Let me
5   make one thing clear: whatever else may be said about the Chinese, they are stingy! I slept in doorways three days until I could find a tailor who would make me this kimono on credit. As it turns out, maybe I didn't even need it. Maybe he would've been happy to see me in a simple shift and mascara.
10   But . . . better safe than sorry.
      That was 1970, when I arrived in Paris. For the next fifteen years, yes, I lived in a very comfy life. Some relief, believe me, after four years on a fucking commune in Nowheresville, China. Rene supported the boy and me, and I did some
15   demonstrations around the country as part of my "cultural exchange" cover. And then there was the spying.

(SONG *moves upstage, to a chair.* TOULON *enters as a* JUDGE, *wearing the appropriate wig and robes. He sits near* SONG. *It's 1986, and* SONG *is testifying in a courtroom.*)

SONG: Not much at first. Rene had lost all his high-level contacts. Comrade Chin wasn't very interested in parking-ticket statistics. But finally, at my urging, Rene got a job as a courier,
20   handling sensitive documents. He'd photograph them for me, and I'd pass them on to the Chinese embassy.
JUDGE: Did he understand the extent of his activity?
SONG: He didn't ask. He knew that I needed those documents, and that was enough.
25   JUDGE: But he must've known he was passing classified information.
SONG: I can't say.
JUDGE: He never asked what you were going to do with them?
SONG: Nope.

(*Pause.*)

30   JUDGE: There is one thing that the court—indeed, that all of France—would like to know.
SONG: Fire away.
JUDGE: Did Monsieur Gallimard know you were a man?
SONG: Well, he never saw me completely naked. Ever.
35   JUDGE: But surely, he must've . . . how can I put this?
SONG: Put it however you like. I'm not shy. He must've felt around?
JUDGE: Mmmmm.
SONG: Not really. I did all the work. He just laid back. Of
40   course we did enjoy more . . . complete union, and I suppose he *might* have wondered why I was always on my stomach, but. . . . But what you're thinking is, "Of course a wrist must've brushed . . . a hand hit . . . over twenty years!" Yeah. Well, Your Honor, it was my job to make him
45   think I was a woman. And chew on this: it wasn't all that hard. See, my mother was a prostitute along the Bundt before the Revolution. And, uh, I think it's fair to say she learned a few things about Western men. So I borrowed her knowledge. In service to my country.
50   JUDGE: Would you care to enlighten the court with this secret knowledge? I'm sure we're all very curious.
SONG: I'm sure you are. (*Pause.*) Okay, Rule One is: Men always believe what they want to hear. So a girl can tell the most obnoxious lies and the guys will believe them every time—

"This is my first time"—"That's the biggest I've ever seen"—or   55
both, which, if you really think about it, is not possible in a single lifetime. You've maybe heard those phrases a few times in your own life, yes, Your Honor?
JUDGE: It's not my life, Monsieur Song, which is on trial today.
SONG: Okay, okay, just trying to lighten up the proceedings.   60
Tough room.
JUDGE: Go on.
SONG: Rule Two: As soon as a Western man comes into contact with the East—he's already confused. The West has sort of an international rape mentality towards the East. Do you know   65
rape mentality?
JUDGE: Give us your definition, please.
SONG: Basically, "Her mouth says no, but her eyes say yes." The West thinks of itself as masculine—big guns, big industry, big money—so the East is feminine—weak, delicate,   70
poor . . . but good at art, and full of inscrutable wisdom—the feminine mystique.
      Her mouth says no, but her eyes say yes. The West believes the East, deep down, *wants* to be dominated—because a woman can't think for herself.   75
JUDGE: What does this have to do with my question?
SONG: You expect Oriental countries to submit to your guns, and you expect Oriental women to be submissive to your men. That's why you say they make the best wives.
JUDGE: But why would that make it possible for you to fool   80
Monsieur Gallimard? Please—get to the point.
SONG: One, because when he finally met his fantasy woman, he wanted more than anything to believe that she was, in fact, a woman. And second, I am an Oriental. And being an Oriental, I could never be completely a man.   85

(*Pause.*)

JUDGE: Your armchair political theory is tenuous, Monsieur Song.
SONG: You think so? That's why you'll lose in all your dealings with the East.
JUDGE: Just answer my question: did he know you were a man?   90

(*Pause.*)

SONG: You know, your Honor, I never asked.

SCENE II

Same.

Music from the "Death Scene" from Butterfly *blares over the house speakers. It is the loudest thing we've heard in this play.*

GALLIMARD *enters, crawling towards* SONG's *wig and kimono.*

GALLIMARD: Butterfly? Butterfly?

(SONG *remains a man, in the witness box, delivering a testimony we do not hear.*)

GALLIMARD: (*To us.*) In my moment of greatest shame, here, in this courtroom—with that . . . person up there, telling the world. . . . What strikes me especially is how shallow he is, how glib and obsequious . . . completely . . . without   5
substance! The type that prowls around discos with a gold medallion stinking of garlic. So little like my Butterfly.

Yet even in this moment my mind remains agile, flip-flopping like a man on a trampoline. Even now, my picture
10 dissolves, and I see that . . . witness . . . talking to me.

(SONG *suddenly stands straight up in his witness box, and looks at* GALLIMARD.)

SONG: Yes. You. White man.

(SONG *steps out of the witness box, and moves downstage towards* GALLIMARD. *Light change.*)

GALLIMARD: (*To* SONG.) Who? Me?
SONG: Do you see any other white men?
GALLIMARD: Yes. There're white men all around. This is a French
15   courtroom.
SONG: So you are an adventurous imperialist. Tell me, why did it take you so long? To come back to this place?
GALLIMARD: What place?
SONG: This theatre in China. Where we met many years ago.
20 GALLIMARD: (*To us.*) And once again, against my will, I am transported.

(*Chinese opera music comes up on the speakers.* SONG *begins to do opera moves, as he did the night they met.*)

SONG: Do you remember? The night you gave your heart?
GALLIMARD: It was a long time ago.
SONG: Not long enough. A night that turned your world upside
25   down.
GALLIMARD: Perhaps.
SONG: Oh, be honest with me. What's another bit of flattery when you've already given me twenty years' worth? It's a wonder my head hasn't swollen to the size of China.
30 GALLIMARD: Who's to say it hasn't?
SONG: Who's to say? And what's the shame? In pride? You think I could've pulled this off if I wasn't already full of pride when we met? No, not just pride. Arrogance. It takes arrogance, really—to believe you can will, with your eyes and your lips,
35   the destiny of another. (*He dances.*) C'mon. Admit it. You still want me. Even in slacks and a button-down collar.
GALLIMARD: I don't see what the point of—
SONG: You don't? Well maybe, Rene, just maybe—I want you.
GALLIMARD: You do?
40 SONG: Then again, maybe I'm just playing with you. How can you tell? (*Reprising his feminine character, he sidles up to* GALLIMARD.) "How I wish there were even a small cafe to sit in. With men in tuxedos, and cappuccinos, and bad expatriate jazz." Now you want to kiss me, don't you?
45 GALLIMARD: (*Pulling away.*) What makes you—?
SONG: —so sure? See? I take the words from your mouth. Then I wait for you to come and retrieve them. (*He reclines on the floor.*)
GALLIMARD: Why? Why do you treat me so cruelly?
50 SONG: Perhaps I *was* treating you cruelly. But now—I'm being nice. Come here, my little one.
GALLIMARD: I'm not your little one!
SONG: My mistake. It's I who am *your* little one, right?
GALLIMARD: Yes, I—
55 SONG: So come get your little one. If you like. I may even let you strip me.
GALLIMARD: I mean, you were! Before . . . but not like this!

SONG: I was? Then perhaps I still am. If you look hard enough. (*He starts to remove his clothes.*)
GALLIMARD: What—what are you doing? 60
SONG: Helping you to see through my act.
GALLIMARD: Stop that! I don't want to! I don't—
SONG: Oh, but you asked me to strip, remember?
GALLIMARD: What? That was years ago! And I took it back!
SONG: No. You postponed it. Postponed the inevitable. Today, the 65 inevitable has come calling.

(*From the speakers, cacophony: Butterfly mixed in with Chinese gongs.*)

GALLIMARD: No! Stop! I don't want to see!
SONG: Then look away.
GALLIMARD: You're only in my mind! All this is in my mind! I order you! To stop! 70
SONG: To what? To strip? That's just what I'm—
GALLIMARD: No! Stop! I want you—!
SONG: You want me?
GALLIMARD: To stop!
SONG: You know something, Rene? Your mouth says no, but your 75 eyes say yes. Turn them away. I dare you.
GALLIMARD: I don't have to! Every night, you say you're going to strip, but then I beg you and you stop!
SONG: I guess tonight is different.
GALLIMARD: Why? Why should that be? 80
SONG: Maybe I've become frustrated. Maybe I'm saying "Look at me, you fool!" Or maybe I'm just feeling . . . sexy. (*He is down to his briefs.*)
GALLIMARD: Please. This is unnecessary. I know what you are.
SONG: Do you? What am I? 85
GALLIMARD: A—a man.
SONG: You don't really believe that.
GALLIMARD: Yes I do! I knew all the time somewhere that my happiness was temporary, my love a deception. But my mind kept the knowledge at bay. To make the wait bearable. 90
SONG: Monsieur Gallimard—the wait is over.

(SONG *drops his briefs. He is naked. Sound cue out. Slowly, we and* SONG *come to the realization that what we had thought to be* GALLIMARD'*s sobbing is actually his laughter.*)

GALLIMARD: Oh god! What an idiot! Of course!
SONG: Rene—what?
GALLIMARD: Look at you! You're a man! (*He bursts into laughter again.*) 95
SONG: I fail to see what's so funny!
GALLIMARD: "You fail to see—!" I mean, you never did have much of a sense of humor, did you? I just think it's ridiculously funny that I've wasted so much time on just a man!
SONG: Wait. I'm not "just a man." 100
GALLIMARD: No? Isn't that what you've been trying to convince me of?
SONG: Yes, but what I mean—
GALLIMARD: And now, I finally believe you, and you tell me it's not true? I think you must have some kind of identity 105 problem.
SONG: Will you listen to me?
GALLIMARD: Why?! I've been listening to you for twenty years. Don't I deserve a vacation?
SONG: I'm not just any man! 110

GALLIMARD: Then, what exactly are you?
SONG: Rene, how can you ask—? Okay, what about this?

(*He picks up Butterfly's robes, starts to dance around. No music.*)

GALLIMARD: Yes, that's very nice. I have to admit.

(SONG *holds out his arm to* GALLIMARD.)

SONG: It's the same skin you've worshiped for years. Touch it.
115 GALLIMARD: Yes, it does feel the same.
SONG: Now—close your eyes.

(SONG *covers* GALLIMARD'S *eyes with one hand. With the other,* SONG *draws* GALLIMARD'S *hand up to his face.* GALLIMARD, *like a blind man, lets his hands run over* SONG'S *face.*)

GALLIMARD: This skin, I remember. The curve of her face, the softness of her cheek, her hair against the back of my hand . . .
120 SONG: I'm your Butterfly. Under the robes, beneath everything, it was always me. Now, open your eyes and admit it—you adore me. (*He removes his hand from* GALLIMARD'S *eyes.*)
GALLIMARD: You, who knew every inch of my desires—how could you, of all people, have made such a mistake?
125 SONG: What?
GALLIMARD: You showed me your true self. When all I loved was the lie. A perfect lie, which you let fall to the ground—and now, it's old and soiled.
SONG: So—you never really loved me? Only when I was playing
130 a part?
GALLIMARD: I'm a man who loved a woman created by a man. Everything else—simply falls short.

(*Pause.*)

SONG: What am I supposed to do now?
GALLIMARD: You were a fine spy, Monsieur Song, with an even
135 finer accomplice. But now I believe you should go. Get out of my life!
SONG: Go where? Rene, you can't live without me. Not after twenty years.
GALLIMARD: I certainly can't live with you—not after twenty
140 years of betrayal.
SONG: Don't be so stubborn! Where will you go?
GALLIMARD: I have a date . . . with my Butterfly.
SONG: So, throw away your pride. And come . . .
GALLIMARD: Get away from me! Tonight, I've finally learned
145 to tell fantasy from reality. And, knowing the difference, I choose fantasy.
SONG: *I'm* your fantasy!
GALLIMARD: You? You're as real as hamburger. Now get out! I have a date with my Butterfly and I don't want your body
150 polluting the room! (*He tosses* SONG'S *suit at him.*) Look at these—you dress like a pimp.
SONG: Hey! These are Armani slacks and—! (*He puts on his briefs and slacks.*) Let's just say . . . I'm disappointed in you, Rene. In the crush of your adoration, I thought you'd become
155 something more. More like . . . a woman.
    But no. Men. You're like the rest of them. It's all in the way we dress, and make up our faces, and bat our eyelashes. You really have so little imagination!

GALLIMARD: You, Monsieur Song? Accuse me of too little imagination? You, if anyone, should know—I am pure 160 imagination. And in imagination I will remain. Now get out!

(GALLIMARD *bodily removes* SONG *from the stage, taking his kimono.*)

SONG: Rene! I'll never put on those robes again! You'll be sorry!
GALLIMARD: (*To* SONG.) I'm already sorry! (*Looking at the kimono in his hands.*) Exactly as sorry . . . as a Butterfly.

SCENE III

M. GALLIMARD'S *prison cell. Paris. Present.*

GALLIMARD: I've played out the events of my life night after night, always searching for a new ending to my story, one where I leave this cell and return forever to my Butterfly's arms.
    Tonight I realize my search is over. That I've looked all 5 along in the wrong place. And now, to you, I will prove that my love was not in vain—by returning to the world of fantasy where I first met her.

(*He picks up the kimono; dancers enter.*)

GALLIMARD: There is a vision of the Orient that I have. Of slender women in chong sams and kimonos who die for the love of 10 unworthy foreign devils. Who are born and raised to be the perfect women. Who take whatever punishment we give them, and bounce back, strengthened by love, unconditionally. It is a vision that has become my life.

(*Dancers bring the wash basin to him and help him make up his face.*)

GALLIMARD: In public, I have continued to deny that Song Liling 15 is a man. This brings me headlines, and is a source of great embarrassment to my French colleagues, who can now be sent into a coughing fit by the mere mention of Chinese food. But alone, in my cell, I have long since faced the truth.
    And the truth demands a sacrifice. For mistakes made 20 over the course of a lifetime. My mistakes were simple and absolute—the man I loved was a cad, a bounder. He deserved nothing but a kick in the behind, and instead I gave him . . . all my love.
    Yes—love. Why not admit it all? That was my undoing, 25 wasn't it? Love warped my judgment, blinded my eyes, rearranged the very lines on my face . . . until I could look in the mirror and see nothing but . . . a woman.

(*Dancers help him put on the Butterfly wig.*)

GALLIMARD: I have a vision. Of the Orient. That, deep within its almond eyes, there are still women. Women willing to 30 sacrifice themselves for the love of a man. Even a man whose love is completely without worth.

(*Dancers assist* GALLIMARD *in donning the kimono. They hand him a knife.*)

GALLIMARD: Death with honor is better than life . . . life with dishonor. (*He sets himself center stage, in a seppuku*

35 *position.*) The love of a Butterfly can withstand many things—unfaithfulness, loss, even abandonment. But how can it face the one sin that implies all others? The devastating knowledge that, underneath it all, the object of her love was nothing more, nothing less than . . . a man. (*He sets the tip of* 40 *the knife against his body.*) It is 19   . And I have found her at last. In a prison on the outskirts of Paris. My name is Rene Gallimard—also known as Madame Butterfly.

(GALLIMARD *turns upstage and plunges his knife into his body, as music from the "Love Duet" blares over the speakers. He collapses* into the arms of the dancers, who lay him reverently on the floor. *The image holds for several beats. Then a tight special up on* SONG, *who stands as a man, staring at the dead* GALLIMARD. *He smokes a cigarette; the smoke filters up through the lights. Two words leave his lips.*)

SONG: Butterfly? Butterfly?

(*Smoke rises as lights fade slowly to black.*)

Tony Kushner

Born in 1956, Tony Kushner first came to international prominence with *Angels in America* (1991), a two-part play that was an enormous success both in London and in Los Angeles before moving to New York in 1993. Kushner's "gay fantasia on national themes" is, in a sense, a displaced autobiography: the displaced narrative of his own growing up as a gay man in the American era of Roy Cohn, the decline of the Communist menace, the onset of the AIDS epidemic, and the rise of the conservative political agenda that dominated American politics in the 1980s and continues to narrow political discourse today. Kushner was born in New York, but his family soon moved to New Orleans, where his parents were musicians in the New Orleans Philharmonic. When he was two, the family moved to Lake Charles, Louisiana; his mother, once a prominent New York bassoonist, devoted herself to educating the children in literature, music, and the arts; she also acted in the Lake Charles theater company. Kushner knew that he was gay but concealed it from his parents; when he went to college at Columbia University, he spent some time in psychoanalysis trying to alter his sexual orientation. However, by his mid-twenties, Kushner was able to accept his sexuality and came out. After taking his B.A. at Columbia, he studied theater at New York University. Kushner had written and produced several plays before *A Bright Room Called Day* (1985), written while he worked as a switchboard operator, was produced in New York; it concerns the collapse of the political left and the rise of fascism during the German Weimar Republic. While *Angels in America* brought him to international prominence, Kushner has continued to explore the nature of contemporary political theater by taking on a range of genres: political "fantasia" in *Slavs* (1994), political history in *Hydriotaphia* (1998) and *Henry Box Brown; or, The Mirror of Slavery* (1998), domestic drama in *Homebody/Kabul* (2001), the musical in *Caroline, or Change* (2002). Kusher was nominated for an academy award as co-writer of the film *Munich* (2005). His newest play, *The Intelligent Homosexual's Guide to Capitalism and Socialism with a Key to the Scriptures,* debuted at the Guthrie Theatre in Minneapolis in 2009.

Angels in America: Millenium Approaches

The first part of *Angels in America* (the second part is entitled *Perestroika*), *Millennium Approaches* is a complete play in its own right. Kushner began writing the play in 1988 when Oskar Eustis, who had directed his first play for the Eureka Theater Company in San Francisco,

The Angel (Ellen McLaughlin) appears to Prior Walter (Stephen Spinella) at the climax of Tony Kushner's *Angels in America, Part One: Millennium Approaches* in the 1993 Broadway production.

Joan Marcus

asked Kushner for another play. Subtitled "A Gay Fantasia on National Themes," *Millennium Approaches* is at once a deeply personal look at the lives of two couples—Joe and Harper, a young Mormon couple transplanted to New York; Louis and Prior, a gay couple facing (and not facing) the onset of AIDS—and a political "fantasia" in the manner of Shaw's *Heartbreak House* or *The Apple Cart*. Kushner sets the characters' struggles against the background of conservative politics and the increasing power of the conservative right in 1980s America; as Martin remarks in act 2: ". . . we'll get our way on just about everything: abortion, defense, Central America, protecting the family, a live investment climate. . . . It's really the end of Liberalism. The end of New Deal Socialism. The end of ipso facto secular humanism."

While Kushner's play takes aim at the policies of the Republican administration, the play's politics extend deeply into the politics of personal action. The emphasis on individualism, on self-sufficiency, on destroying the liberal consensus, and on eliminating social programs characteristic of the Reagan administration has consequences in the private sphere as well, where freedom looks alternately like selfishness and chaos. Roy Cohn—famous for his anticommunist activities and for prosecuting (and winning) the death sentence for Julius and Ethel Rosenberg for selling secret information to the Soviet Union—in many ways exemplifies this linkage in the play. Unable to give up his view of political power ("the game . . . of being alive"), Cohn refuses to be treated for AIDS because it would mean a public admission that he is gay, something generally known but not acknowledged. Louis, unable to bring himself to care for Prior during his horrifying illness, finds both emptiness and freedom in deserting his lover. Harper, whose valium-induced fantasies summon the cosmic travel agent Mr. Lies (who whisks her off to Antarctica) is in the throes of a nervous breakdown, a literalized response to the decaying world in which she lives, where "everywhere, things are collapsing, lies surfacing, systems of defense giving way."

The hallucinatory style of *Millennium Approaches* enables Kushner to bring this blending of public and private, the grand sweep of history and the narrower compass of individual suffering, into a close juxtaposition. *Millennium Approaches* ends when Prior's ancestors—a medieval monk and a seventeenth-century dandy—appear to announce the coming of a mysterious angel, whose voice is heard intermittently throughout the play. The Angel's arrival is heralded in a number of ways: Prior regards his first lesion of Kaposi's sarcoma as the mark of the angel of death; a feather drops from above and the voice is heard at the end of Harper's/Prior's intertwined dream-hallucination in act 1; Joe alludes to Jacob wrestling with his angel, an image of Joe's fight to recognize and admit his own homosexuality. The Angel is a figure of release and redemption from the isolation in which the characters find themselves.

However, the Angel also has a public, historical significance as well. Kushner has suggested that the Angel alludes to a comment made by the German cultural critic Walter Benjamin. In "Theses on the Philosophy of History," Benjamin makes the following remark on the process of history:

> A Klee painting named "Angelus Novus" shows an angel looking as though he is about to move away from something he is fixedly contemplating. His eyes are staring, his mouth is open, his wings are spread. This is how one pictures the angel of history. His face is turned toward the past. ·

> Where we perceive a chain of events, he sees one single catastrophe which keeps piling wreckage upon wreckage and hurls it in front of his feet. The angel would like to stay, awaken the dead, and make whole what has been smashed. But a storm is blowing from Paradise; it has got caught in his wings with such violence that the angel can no longer close them. This storm irresistibly propels him into the future to which his back is turned, while the pile of debris before him grows skyward. This storm is what we call progress.

The Angel is, to Kushner as to Benjamin, a figure for the dialectical force of history, the way that history moves into the future both in antithesis to the past, and yet bearing the past along with it. In *Angels in America,* Tony Kushner provides a sense of how it is we live today, in the midst of this "storm . . . we call progress."

Angels in America, Part I: Millennium Approaches

Tony Kushner

CHARACTERS

ROY M. COHN, *a successful New York lawyer and unofficial power broker*

JOSEPH (JOE) PORTER PITT, *chief clerk for Justice Theodore Wilson of the Federal Court of Appeals, Second Circuit*

HARPER AMATY PITT, *Joe's wife, an agoraphobic with a mild Valium addiction*

LOUIS IRONSON, *a word processor working for the Second Circuit Court of Appeals*

PRIOR WALTER, *Louis's boyfriend. Occasionally works as a club designer or caterer, otherwise lives very modestly but with great style off a small trust fund*

HANNAH PORTER PITT, *Joe's mother, currently residing in Salt Lake City, living off her deceased husband's army pension*

BELIZE, *a former drag queen and former lover of Prior's: A registered nurse. Belize's name was originally Norman Arriaga; Belize is a drag name that stuck*

THE ANGEL, *four divine emanations, Fluor, Phosphor, Lumen and Candle; manifest in One: the Continental Principality of America. She has magnificent steel-gray wings*

RABBI ISIDOR CHEMELWITZ, *an orthodox Jewish rabbi, played by the actor playing Hannah*

MR. LIES, *Harper's imaginary friend, a travel agent, who in style of dress and speech suggests a jazz musician; he always wears a large lapel badge emblazoned "IOTA" (The International Order of Travel Agents). He is played by the actor playing Belize*

THE MAN IN THE PARK, *played by the actor playing Prior*

THE VOICE, *the voice of The Angel*

HENRY, *Roy's doctor, played by the actor playing Hannah*

EMILY, *a nurse, played by the actor playing The Angel*

MARTIN HELLER, *a Reagan Administration Justice Department flackman, played by the actor playing Harper*

SISTER ELLA CHAPTER, *a Salt Lake City real-estate saleswoman, played by the actor playing The Angel*

PRIOR 1, *the ghost of a dead Prior Walter from the 13th century, played by the actor playing Joe. He is a blunt, gloomy medieval farmer with a gutteral Yorkshire accent*

PRIOR 2, *the ghost of a dead Prior Walter from the 17th century, played by the actor playing Roy. He is a Londoner, sophisticated, with a High British accent*

THE ESKIMO, *played by the actor playing Joe*

THE WOMAN IN THE SOUTH BRONX, *played by the actor playing The Angel*

ETHEL ROSENBERG, *played by the actor playing Hannah*

PLAYWRIGHT'S NOTES

A DISCLAIMER: *Roy M. Cohn, the character, is based on the late Roy M. Cohn (1927–1986), who was all too real; for the most part the acts attributed to the character Roy, such as his illegal conferences with Judge Kaufmann during the trial of Ethel Rosenberg, are to be found in the historical record. But this Roy is a work of dramatic fiction; his words are my invention, and liberties have been taken.*

A NOTE ABOUT THE STAGING: *The play benefits from a pared-down style of presentation, with minimal scenery and scene shifts done rapidly (no blackouts!), employing the cast as well as stagehands— which makes for an actor-driven event, as this must be. The moments of magic—the appearance and disappearance of Mr. Lies and the ghosts, the Book hallucination, and the ending—are to be fully realized, as bits of wonderful theatrical illusion—which means it's OK if the wires show, and maybe it's good that they do, but the magic should at the same time be thoroughly amazing.*

> . . . In a murderous time
> the heart breaks and breaks
> and lives by breaking.
>
> —STANLEY KUNITZ
> "THE TESTING-TREE"

ACT ONE

Bad News October–November 1985

SCENE I

The last days of October. RABBI ISODOR CHEMELWITZ *alone onstage with a small coffin. It is a rough pine box with two wooden pegs, one at the foot and one at the head, holding the lid in place. A prayer shawl embroidered with a Star of David is draped over the lid, and by the head a yarzheit candle is burning.*

RABBI ISIDOR CHEMELWITZ: (*He speaks sonorously, with a heavy Eastern European accent, unapologetically consulting a sheet of notes for the family names.*) Hello and good morning. I am Rabbi Isidor Chemelwitz of the Bronx Home for Aged
5 Hebrews. We are here this morning to pay respects at the passing of Sarah Ironson, devoted wife of Benjamin Ironson, also deceased, loving and caring mother of her sons Morris, Abraham, and Samuel, and her daughters Esther and Rachel; beloved grandmother of Max, Mark, Louis, Lisa, Maria . . . uh . . . Lesley, Angela, Doris, Luke and Eric. (*Looks more* 10 *closely at paper.*) Eric? This is a Jewish name? (*Shrugs.*) Eric. A large and loving family. We assemble that we may mourn collectively this good and righteous woman.

(*He looks at the coffin.*)

This woman. I did not know this woman. I cannot accurately describe her attributes, nor do justice to her dimensions. She 15 was. . . . Well, in the Bronx Home of Aged Hebrews are many like this, the old, and to many I speak but not to be frank with this one. She preferred silence. So I do not know her and yet I know her. She was . . .

(He touches the coffin.)

20 . . . not a person but a whole kind of person, the ones who crossed the ocean, who brought with us to America the villages of Russia and Lithuania—and how we struggled, and how we fought, for the family, for the Jewish home, so that you would not grow up *here,* in this
25 strange place, in the melting pot where nothing melted. Descendants of this immigrant woman, you do not grow up in America, you and your children and their children with the goyische names. You do not live in America. No such place exists. Your clay is the clay of some Litvak
30 shtetl, your air the air of the steppes—because she carried the old world on her back across the ocean, in a boat, and she put it down on Grand Concourse Avenue, or in Flatbush, and she worked that earth into your bones, and you pass it to your children, this ancient, ancient culture
35 and home.

(Little pause.)

You can never make that crossing that she made, for such Great Voyages in this world do not any more exist. But every day of your lives the miles that voyage between that place and this one you cross. Every day. You understand me? In you that
40 journey is.
So . . .
She was the last of the Mohicans, this one was. Pretty soon . . . all the old will be dead.

SCENE II

Same day. ROY *and* JOE *in* ROY's *office.* ROY *at an impressive desk, bare except for a very elaborate phone system, rows and rows of flashing buttons which bleep and beep and whistle incessantly, making chaotic music underneath* ROY's *conversations.* JOE *is sitting, waiting.* ROY *conducts business with great energy, impatience and sensual abandon: gesticulating, shouting, cajoling, crooning, playing the phone, receiver and hold button with virtuosity and love.*

ROY: *(Hitting a button.)* Hold. *(To* JOE.*)* I wish I was an octopus, a fucking octopus. Eight loving arms and all those suckers. Know what I mean?
JOE: No, I . . .
5 ROY: *(Gesturing to a deli platter of little sandwiches on his desk.)* You want lunch?
JOE: No, that's OK really I just . . .
ROY: *(Hitting a button.)* Ailene? Roy Cohn. Now what kind of a greeting is. . . . I thought we were friends, Ai. . . . Look Mrs.
10 Soffer you don't have to get. . . . You're upset. You're yelling. You'll aggravate your condition, you shouldn't yell, you'll pop little blood vessels in your face if you yell. . . . No that was a joke, Mrs. Soffer, I was joking. . . . I already apologized sixteen times for that, Mrs. Soffer, you . . . *(While she's fulminating,*
15 ROY *covers the mouthpiece with his hand and talks to* JOE.*)* This'll take a minute, eat already, what is this tasty sandwich here it's—*(He takes a bite of a sandwich.)* Mmmmm, liver or some. . . . Here.

(He pitches the sandwich to JOE, *who catches it and returns it to the platter.)*

ROY: *(Back to Mrs. Soffer.)* Uh huh, uh huh. . . . No, I already told you, it wasn't a vacation, it was business. Mrs. Soffer, 20 I have clients in Haiti, Mrs. Soffer, I. . . . Listen, Ailene, YOU THINK I'M THE ONLY GODDAM LAWYER IN HISTORY EVER MISSED A COURT DATE? Don't make such a big fucking. . . . Hold. *(He hits the hold button.)* You HAG! 25
JOE: If this is a bad time . . .
ROY: *Bad* time? This is a *good* time! *(Button.)* Baby doll, get me. . . . Oh fuck, wait . . . *(Button, button.)* Hello? Yah. Sorry to keep you holding, Judge Hollins, I. . . . Oh *Mrs.* Hollins, sorry dear deep voice you got. Enjoying your visit? *(Hand* 30 *over mouthpiece, to* JOE.*)* She sounds like a truckdriver and he sounds like Kate Smith, very confusing. Nixon appointed him, all the geeks are Nixon appointees . . . *(To Mrs. Hollins.)* Yeah yeah right good so how many tickets dear? Seven. For what, *Cats, 42nd Street,* what? No you wouldn't like *La Cage,* 35 trust me, I know. Oh for godsake. . . . Hold. *(Button, button.)* Baby doll, seven for *Cats* or something, anything hard to get, I don't give a fuck what and neither will they. *(Button; to* JOE.*)* You see *La Cage?*
JOE: No, I . . . 40
ROY: Fabulous. Best thing on Broadway. Maybe ever. *(Button.)* Who? Aw, Jesus H. Christ, Harry, *no,* Harry, Judge John Francis Grimes, Manhattan Family Court. Do I have to do every goddam thing myself? *Touch* the bastard, Harry, and don't call me on this line again, I told you not to . . . 45
JOE: *(Starting to get up.)* Roy, uh, should I wait outside or . . .
ROY: *(To* JOE.*)* Oh sit. *(To* HARRY.*)* You hold. I pay you to hold fuck you Harry you jerk. *(Button.)* Half-wit dick-brain. *(Instantly philosophical.)* I see the universe, Joe, as a kind of sandstorm in outer space with winds of mega-hurricane 50 velocity, but instead of grains of sand it's shards and splinters of glass. You ever feel that way? Ever have one of those days?
JOE: I'm not sure I . . .
ROY: So how's life in Appeals? How's the Judge? 55
JOE: He sends his best.
ROY: He's a good man. Loyal. Not the brightest man on the bench, but he has manners. And a nice head of silver hair.
JOE: He gives me a lot of responsibility.
ROY: Yeah, like writing his decisions and signing his name. 60
JOE: Well . . .
ROY: He's a nice guy. And you cover admirably.
JOE: Well, thanks, Roy, I . . .
ROY: *(Button.)* Who is *this?* Well who the fuck are *you?* Hold— *(Button.)* Harry? Eighty-seven grand, something like that. 65 Fuck him. Eat me. New Jersey, chain of porno film stores in, uh, Weehawken. That's—Harry, that's the beauty of the law. *(Button.)* So, baby doll, what? *Cats?* Bleah. *(Button.)* *Cats!* It's about cats. Singing cats, you'll love it. Eight o'clock, the theatre's always at eight. *(Button.)* Fucking tourists. *(Button,* 70 *then to* JOE.*)* Oh live a little, Joe, *eat* something for Christ sake—
JOE: Um, Roy, could you . . .
ROY: What? *(To* HARRY.*)* Hold a minute. *(Button.)* Mrs. Soffer? Mrs. . . . *(Button.)* God-fucking-dammit to hell, where 75 is . . .
JOE: *(Overlapping.)* Roy, I'd really appreciate it if . . .
ROY: *(Overlapping.)* Well she was here a minute ago, baby doll, see if . . .

(The phone starts making three different beeping sounds, all at once.)

80 ROY: *(Smashing buttons.)* Jesus fuck this goddam thing . . .
    JOE: *(Overlapping.)* I really wish you wouldn't . . .
    ROY: *(Overlapping.)* Baby doll? Ring the *Post* get me Suzy
        see if . . .

(The phone starts whistling loudly.)

    ROY: CHRIST!
85 JOE: *Roy.*
    ROY: *(Into receiver.)* Hold. *(Button; to* JOE.*)* What?
    JOE: Could you please not take the Lord's name in vain?

(Pause.)

    I'm sorry. But please. At least while I'm . . .
    ROY: *(Laughs, then.)* Right. Sorry. Fuck.
90   Only in America. *(Punches a button.)* Baby doll, tell 'em all to
        fuck off. Tell 'em I died. You handle Mrs. Soffer. Tell her it's on
        the way. Tell her I'm schtupping the judge. I'll call her back.
        I *will* call her. I *know* how much I borrowed. She's got four
        hundred times that stuffed up her. . . . Yeah, tell her I said that.
95   *(Button. The phone is silent.)*
        So, Joe.
    JOE: I'm sorry Roy, I just . . .
    ROY: No no no no, principles count, I respect principles, I'm
        not religious but I like God and God likes me. Baptist,
100   Catholic?
    JOE: Mormon.
    ROY: Mormon. Delectable. Absolutely. Only in America. So, Joe.
        Whattya think?
    JOE: It's . . . well . . .
105 ROY: Crazy life.
    JOE: Chaotic.
    ROY: Well but God bless chaos. Right?
    JOE: Ummm . . .
    ROY: Huh. Mormons. I knew Mormons, in, um, Nevada.
110 JOE: Utah, mostly.
    ROY: No, these Mormons were in Vegas.
        So. So, how'd you like to go to Washington and work for the
        Justice Department?
    JOE: Sorry?
115 ROY: How'd you like to go to Washington and work for the Justice
        Department? All I gotta do is pick up the phone, talk to Ed,
        and you're in.
    JOE: In . . . what, exactly?
    ROY: Associate Assistant Something Big. Internal Affairs, heart of
120   the woods, something nice with clout.
    JOE: Ed . . . ?
    ROY: Meese. The Attorney General.
    JOE: Oh.
    ROY: I just have to pick up the phone . . .
125 JOE: I have to think.
    ROY: Of course.

(Pause.)

    It's a great time to be in Washington, Joe.
    JOE: Roy, it's incredibly exciting . . .
    ROY: And it would mean something to me. You understand?

(Little pause.)

130 JOE: I . . . can't say how much I appreciate this Roy, I'm sort
        of . . . well, stunned, I mean. . . . Thanks, Roy. But I have to
        give it some thought. I have to ask my wife.
    ROY: Your wife. Of course.
    JOE: But I really appreciate . . .
135 ROY: Of course. Talk to your wife.

SCENE III

Later that day. HARPER *at home, alone. She is listening to the
radio and talking to herself, as she often does. She speaks to the
audience.*

    HARPER: People who are lonely, people left alone, sit talking
        nonsense to the air, imagining . . . beautiful systems dying,
        old fixed orders spiraling apart . . .
            When you look at the ozone layer, from outside, from a
        spaceship, it looks like a pale blue halo, a gentle, shimmer-   5
        ing aureole encircling the atmosphere encircling the earth.
        Thirty miles above our heads, a thin layer of three-atom
        oxygen molecules, product of photosynthesis, which explains
        the fussy vegetable preference for visible light, its rejection of
        darker rays and emanations. Danger from without. It's a kind   10
        of gift, from God, the crowning touch to the creation of the
        world: guardian angels, hands linked, make a spherical net,
        a blue-green nesting orb, a shell of safety for life itself. But
        everywhere, things are collapsing, lies surfacing, systems of
        defense giving way. . . . This is why, Joe, this is why I shouldn't   15
        be left alone.

(Little pause.)

    I'd like to go traveling. Leave you behind to worry. I'll send
    postcards with strange stamps and tantalizing messages on
    the back. "Later maybe." "Nevermore . . ."

*(*MR. LIES, *a travel agent, appears.)*

    HARPER: Oh! You startled me!   20
    MR. LIES: Cash, check or credit card?
    HARPER: I remember you. You're from Salt Lake. You sold us
        the plane tickets when we flew here. What are you doing in
        Brooklyn?
    MR. LIES: You said you wanted to travel . . .   25
    HARPER: And here you are. How thoughtful.
    MR. LIES: Mr. Lies. Of the International Order of Travel Agents.
        We mobilize the globe, we set people adrift, we stir the
        populace and send nomads eddying across the planet. We are
        adepts of motion, acolytes of the flux. Cash, check or credit   30
        card. Name your destination.
    HARPER: Antarctica, maybe. I want to see the hole in the ozone. I
        heard on the radio . . .
    MR. LIES: *(He has a computer terminal in his briefcase.)* I can
        arrange a guided tour. Now?   35
    HARPER: Soon. Maybe soon. I'm not safe here you see. Things
        aren't right with me. Weird stuff happens . . .
    MR. LIES: Like?
    HARPER: Well, like you, for instance. Just appearing. Or last
        week . . . well never mind.   40

People are like planets, you need a thick skin. Things get to me, Joe stays away and now. . . . Well look. My dreams are talking back to me.

45 MR. LIES: It's the price of rootlessness. Motion sickness. The only cure: to keep moving.

HARPER: I'm undecided. I feel . . . that something's going to give. It's 1985. Fifteen years till the third millennium. Maybe Christ will come again. Maybe seeds will be planted, maybe there'll be harvests then, maybe early figs to eat, maybe new 50 life, maybe fresh blood, maybe companionship and love and protection, safety from what's outside, maybe the door will hold, or maybe . . . maybe the troubles will come, and the end will come, and the sky will collapse and there will be terrible rains and showers of poison light, or maybe my life is 55 really fine, maybe Joe loves me and I'm only crazy thinking otherwise, or maybe not, maybe it's even worse than I know, maybe . . . I want to know, maybe I don't. The suspense, Mr. Lies, it's killing me.

MR. LIES: I suggest a vacation.

60 HARPER: (*Hearing something.*) That was the elevator. Oh God, I should fix myself up, I. . . . You have to go, you shouldn't be here . . . you aren't even real.

MR. LIES: Call me when you decide . . .

HARPER: Go!

(*The travel agent* [MR. LIES] *vanishes as* JOE *enters.*)

65 JOE: Buddy?
Buddy? Sorry I'm late. I was just . . . out. Walking. Are you mad?

HARPER: I got a little anxious.

JOE: Buddy kiss.

(*They kiss.*)

70   Nothing to get anxious about.
So. So how'd you like to move to Washington?

SCENE IV

Same day. LOUIS *and* PRIOR *outside the funeral home, sitting on a bench, both dressed in funereal finery, talking. The funeral service for Sarah Ironson has just concluded and* LOUIS *is about to leave for the cemetery.*

LOUIS: My grandmother actually saw Emma Goldman speak. In Yiddish. But all Grandma could remember was that she spoke well and wore a hat.
What a weird service. That rabbi . . .

5 PRIOR: A definite find. Get his number when you go to the graveyard. I want him to bury me.

LOUIS: Better head out there. Everyone gets to put dirt on the coffin once it's lowered in.

PRIOR: Oooh. Cemetery fun. Don't want to miss that.

10 LOUIS: It's an old Jewish custom to express love. Here, Grandma, have a shovelful. Latecomers run the risk of finding the grave completely filled.
She was pretty crazy. She was up there in that home for ten years, talking to herself. I never visited. She looked too much 15 like my mother.

PRIOR: (*Hugs him.*) Poor Louis. I'm sorry your grandma is dead.

LOUIS: Tiny little coffin, huh?
Sorry I didn't introduce you to. . . . I always get so closety at these family things. 20

PRIOR: Butch. You get butch. (*Imitating.*) "Hi Cousin Doris, you don't remember me I'm Lou, Rachel's boy." Lou, not Louis, because if you say Louis they'll hear the sibilant S.

LOUIS: I don't have a . . .

PRIOR: I don't blame you, hiding. Bloodlines. Jewish curses are 25 the worst. I personally would dissolve if anyone ever looked me in the eye and said "Feh." Fortunately WASPs don't say "Feh." Oh and by the way, darling, cousin Doris is a dyke.

LOUIS: No.
Really? 30

PRIOR: You don't notice anything. If I hadn't spent the last four years fellating you I'd swear you were straight.

LOUIS: You're in a pissy mood. Cat still missing?

(*Little pause.*)

PRIOR: Not a furball in sight. It's your fault.

LOUIS: It is? 35

PRIOR: I warned you, Louis. Names are important. Call an animal "Little Sheba" and you can't expect it to stick around. Besides, it's a dog's name.

LOUIS: I wanted a dog in the first place, not a cat. He sprayed my books. 40

PRIOR: He was a female cat.

LOUIS: Cats are stupid, high-strung predators. Babylonians sealed them up in bricks. Dogs have brains.

PRIOR: Cats have intuition.

LOUIS: A sharp dog is as smart as a really dull two-year-old 45 child.

PRIOR: Cats know when something's wrong.

LOUIS: Only if you stop feeding them.

PRIOR: They know. That's why Sheba left, because she knew.

LOUIS: Knew what? 50

(*Pause.*)

PRIOR: I did my best Shirley Booth this morning, floppy slippers, housecoat, curlers, can of Little Friskies; "Come back, little Sheba, come back. . . ." To no avail. Le chat, elle ne reviendra jamais, jamais . . .

(*He removes his jacket, rolls up his sleeve, shows* LOUIS *a dark purple spot on the underside of his arm near the shoulder.*)

See. 55

LOUIS: That's just a burst blood vessel.

PRIOR: Not according to the best medical authorities.

LOUIS: What?

(*Pause.*)

Tell me.

PRIOR: K.S., baby. Lesion number one. Lookit. The wine-dark kiss 60 of the angel of death.

LOUIS: (*Very softly, holding* PRIOR'S *arm.*) Oh please . . .

PRIOR: I'm a lesionnaire. The Foreign Lesion. The American Lesion. Lesionnaire's disease.

LOUIS: Stop. 65

PRIOR: My troubles are lesion.

LOUIS: Will you *stop.*

PRIOR: Don't you think I'm handling this well? I'm going to die.

70 LOUIS: Bullshit.

PRIOR: Let go of my arm.

LOUIS: No.

PRIOR: Let go.

LOUIS: (*Grabbing* PRIOR, *embracing him ferociously.*) No.

75 PRIOR: I can't find a way to spare you baby. No wall like the wall of hard scientific fact. K.S. Wham. Bang your head on that.

LOUIS: Fuck you. (*Letting go.*) Fuck you fuck you fuck you.

PRIOR: Now that's what I like to hear. A mature reaction.

80   Let's go see if the cat's come home.
       Louis?

LOUIS: When did you find this?

PRIOR: I couldn't tell you.

LOUIS: Why?

85 PRIOR: I was scared, Lou.

LOUIS: Of what?

PRIOR: That you'll leave me.

LOUIS: Oh.

(*Little pause.*)

PRIOR: Bad timing, funeral and all, but I figured as long as
90   we're on the subject of death . . .

LOUIS: I have to go bury my grandma.

PRIOR: Lou?

(*Pause.*)

       Then you'll come home?

LOUIS: Then I'll come home.

SCENE V

Same day, later on. Split scene: JOE *and* HARPER *at home;* LOUIS *at the cemetery with* RABBI ISIDOR CHEMELWITZ *and the little coffin.*

HARPER: Washington?

JOE: It's an incredible honor, buddy, and . . .

HARPER: I have to think.

JOE: Of course.

5 HARPER: Say no.

JOE: You said you were going to think about it.

HARPER: I don't want to move to Washington.

JOE: Well I do.

HARPER: It's a giant cemetery, huge white graves and mau-
10   soleums everywhere.

JOE: We could live in Maryland. Or Georgetown.

HARPER: We're happy here.

JOE: That's not really true, buddy, we . . .

HARPER: Well happy enough! Pretend-happy. That's better
15   than nothing.

JOE: It's time to make some changes, Harper.

HARPER: No changes. Why?

JOE: I've been chief clerk for four years. I make twenty-nine
       thousand dollars a year. That's ridiculous. I graduated
20   fourth in my class and I make less than anyone I know.

And I'm . . . I'm tired of being a clerk, I want to go where something good is happening.

HARPER: Nothing good happens in Washington. We'll forget church teachings and buy furniture at . . . at *Conran's* and become yuppies. I have too much to do here.   25

JOE: Like what?

HARPER: I *do* have things . . .

JOE: What things?

HARPER: I have to finish painting the bedroom.

JOE: You've been painting in there for over a year.   30

HARPER: I know, I. . . . It just isn't done because I never get time to finish it.

JOE: Oh that's . . . that doesn't make sense. You have all the time in the world. You could finish it when I'm at work.

HARPER: I'm afraid to go in there alone.   35

JOE: Afraid of what?

HARPER: I heard someone in there. Metal scraping on the wall. A man with a knife, maybe.

JOE: There's no one in the bedroom, Harper.

HARPER: Not now.   40

JOE: Not this morning either.

HARPER: How do you know? You were at work this morning. There's something creepy about this place. Remember *Rosemary's Baby*?

JOE: *Rosemary's Baby*?   45

HARPER: Our apartment looks like that one. Wasn't that apartment in Brooklyn?

JOE: No, it was . . .

HARPER: Well, it looked like this. It did.

JOE: Then let's move.   50

HARPER: Georgetown's worse. *The Exorcist* was in Georgetown.

JOE: The devil, everywhere you turn, huh, buddy.

HARPER: Yeah. Everywhere.

JOE: How many pills today, buddy?

HARPER: None. One. Three. Only three.   55

LOUIS: (*Pointing at the coffin.*) Why are there just two little wooden pegs holding the lid down?

RABBI ISIDOR CHEMELWITZ: So she can get out easier if she wants to.

LOUIS: I hope she stays put.   60
       I pretended for years that she was already dead. When they called to say she had died it was a surprise. I abandoned her.

RABBI ISIDOR CHEMELWITZ: "Sharfer vi di tson fun a shlang iz an umdankbar kind!"   65

LOUIS: I don't speak Yiddish.

RABBI ISIDOR CHEMELWITZ: Sharper than the serpent's tooth is the ingratitude of children. Shakespeare. *Kenig Lear.*

LOUIS: Rabbi, what does the Holy Writ say about someone who abandons someone he loves at a time of great need?   70

RABBI ISIDOR CHEMELWITZ: Why would a person do such a thing?

LOUIS: Because he has to.
       Maybe because this person's sense of the world, that it will change for the better with struggle, maybe a person   75
       who has this neo-Hegelian positivist sense of constant historical progress towards happiness or perfection or something, who feels very powerful because he feels connected to these forces, moving uphill all the time . . . maybe that person can't, um, incorporate sickness into this sense of   80
       how things are supposed to go. Maybe vomit . . . and sores

and disease . . . really frighten him, maybe . . . he isn't so good with death.

RABBI ISIDOR CHEMELWITZ: The Holy Scriptures have nothing to 85 say about such a person.

LOUIS: Rabbi, I'm afraid of the crimes I may commit.

RABBI ISIDOR CHEMELWITZ: Please, mister. I'm a sick old rabbi facing a long drive home to the Bronx. You want to confess, better you should find a priest.

90 LOUIS: But I'm not a Catholic, I'm a Jew.

RABBI ISIDOR CHEMELWITZ: Worse luck for you, bubbulah. Catholics believe in forgiveness. Jews believe in Guilt. (*He pats the coffin tenderly.*)

LOUIS: You just make sure those pegs are in good and tight.

95 RABBI ISIDOR CHEMELWITZ: Don't worry, mister. The life she had, she'll stay put. She's better off.

JOE: Look, I know this is scary for you. But try to understand what it means to me. Will you try?

HARPER: Yes.

100 JOE: Good. Really try.

I think things are starting to change in the world.

HARPER: But I don't want . . .

JOE: Wait. For the good. Change for the good. America has rediscovered itself. Its sacred position among nations. And 105 people aren't ashamed of that like they used to be. This is a great thing. The truth restored. Law restored. That's what President Reagan's done, Harper. He says "Truth exists and can be spoken proudly." And the country responds to him. We become better. More good. I need to be a part of that, I 110 need something big to lift me up. I mean, six years ago the world seemed in decline, horrible, hopeless, full of unsolvable problems and crime and confusion and hunger and . . .

HARPER: But it still seems that way. More now than before. They say the ozone layer is . . .

115 JOE: Harper . . .

HARPER: And today out the window on Atlantic Avenue there was a schizophrenic traffic cop who was making these . . .

JOE: Stop it! I'm trying to make a point.

HARPER: So am I.

120 JOE: You aren't even making sense, you . . .

HARPER: My point is the world seems just as . . .

JOE: It only seems that way to you because you never go out in the world, Harper, and you have emotional problems.

HARPER: I do so get out in the world.

125 JOE: You don't. You stay in all day, fretting about imaginary . . .

HARPER: I get out. I do. You don't know what I do.

JOE: You don't stay in all day.

HARPER: No.

JOE: Well. . . . Yes you do.

130 HARPER: That's what you think.

JOE: Where do you go?

HARPER: Where do *you* go? When you walk.

(*Pause, then angrily.*) And I DO NOT have emotional problems.

135 JOE: I'm sorry.

HARPER: And if I do have emotional problems it's from living with you. Or . . .

JOE: I'm sorry buddy, I didn't mean to . . .

HARPER: Or if you do think I do then you should never have 140 married me. You have all these secrets and lies.

JOE: I want to be married to you, Harper.

HARPER: You shouldn't. You never should.

(*Pause.*)

Hey buddy. Hey buddy.

JOE: Buddy kiss . . .

(*They kiss.*)

HARPER: I heard on the radio how to give a blowjob. 145

JOE: What?

HARPER: You want to try?

JOE: You really shouldn't listen to stuff like that.

HARPER: Mormons can give blowjobs.

JOE: *Harper.* 150

HARPER: (*Imitating his tone.*) *Joe.*

It was a little Jewish lady with a German accent. This is a good time. For me to make a baby.

(*Little pause.* JOE *turns away.*)

HARPER: Then they went on to a program about holes in the ozone layer. Over Antarctica. Skin burns, birds go blind, 155 icebergs melt. The world's coming to an end.

SCENE VI

First week of November. In the men's room of the offices of the Brooklyn Federal Court of Appeals; LOUIS *is crying over the sink;* JOE *enters.*

JOE: Oh, um. . . . Morning.

LOUIS: Good morning, counselor.

JOE: (*He watches* LOUIS *cry.*) Sorry, I . . . I don't know your name.

LOUIS: Don't bother. Word processor. The lowest of the low.

JOE: (*Holding out hand.*) Joe Pitt. I'm with Justice Wilson . . . 5

LOUIS: Oh, I know that. Counselor Pitt. Chief Clerk.

JOE: Were you . . . are you OK?

LOUIS: Oh, yeah. Thanks. What a nice man.

JOE: Not so nice.

LOUIS: What? 10

JOE: Not so nice. Nothing. You sure you're . . .

LOUIS: Life sucks shit. Life . . . just sucks shit.

JOE: What's wrong?

LOUIS: Run in my nylons.

JOE: Sorry . . . ? 15

LOUIS: Forget it. Look, thanks for asking.

JOE: Well . . .

LOUIS: I mean it really is nice of you.

(*He starts crying again.*)

Sorry, sorry, sick friend . . .

JOE: Oh, I'm sorry. 20

LOUIS: Yeah, yeah, well, that's sweet.

Three of your colleagues have preceded you to this baleful sight and you're the first one to ask. The others just opened the door, saw me, and fled. I hope they had to pee real bad. 25

JOE: (*Handing him a wad of toilet paper.*) They just didn't want to intrude.

LOUIS: Hah. Reaganite heartless macho asshole lawyers.

JOE: Oh, that's unfair.

LOUIS: What is? Heartless? Macho? Reaganite? Lawyer? 30

JOE: I voted for Reagan.

LOUIS: You did?

JOE: Twice.

LOUIS: Twice? Well, oh boy. A Gay Republican.

35 JOE: Excuse me?

LOUIS: Nothing.

JOE: I'm not . . .

    Forget it.

LOUIS: Republican? Not Republican? Or . . .

40 JOE: What?

LOUIS: What?

JOE: Not gay. I'm not gay.

LOUIS: Oh. Sorry. (*Blows his nose loudly.*) It's just . . .

JOE: Yes?

45 LOUIS: Well, sometimes you can tell from the way a person
    sounds that . . . I mean you *sound* like a . . .

JOE: No I don't. Like what?

LOUIS: Like a Republican.

(*Little pause.* JOE *knows he's being teased;* LOUIS *knows he knows.*
JOE *decides to be a little brave.*)

JOE: (*Making sure no one else is around.*) Do I? Sound like a . . . ?

50 LOUIS: What? Like a . . . ? Republican, or . . . ? Do *I*?

JOE: Do you what?

LOUIS: Sound like a . . . ?

JOE: Like a . . . ?
    I'm confused.

55 LOUIS: Yes.
      My name is Louis. But all my friends call me Louise. I
      work in Word Processing. Thanks for the toilet paper.

(LOUIS *offers* JOE *his hand,* JOE *reaches,* LOUIS *feints and pecks* JOE
on the cheek, then exits.)

SCENE VII

A week later. Mutual dream scene. PRIOR *is at a fantastic makeup
table, having a dream, applying the face.* HARPER *is having a pill-
induced hallucination. She has these from time to time. For some
reason,* PRIOR *has appeared in this one. Or* HARPER *has appeared
in* PRIOR's *dream. It is bewildering.*

PRIOR: (*Alone, putting on makeup, then examining the results in
    the mirror; to the audience.*) "I'm ready for my closeup, Mr.
    DeMille."

5   One wants to move through life with elegance and grace,
    blossoming infrequently but with exquisite taste, and perfect
    timing, like a rare bloom, a zebra orchid. . . . One wants. . . .
    But one so seldom gets what one wants, does one? No. One
    does not. One gets fucked. Over. One . . . dies at thirty, robbed
    of . . . decades of majesty.

10   Fuck this shit. Fuck this shit.

(*He almost crumbles; he pulls himself together; he studies his
handiwork in the mirror.*)

      I look like a corpse. A corpsette. Oh my queen; you know
    you've hit rock-bottom when even drag is a drag.

(HARPER *appears.*)

HARPER: Are you. . . . Who are you?

PRIOR: Who are you?

HARPER: What are you doing in my hallucination?   15

PRIOR: I'm not in your hallucination. You're in my dream.

HARPER: You're wearing makeup.

PRIOR: So are you.

HARPER: But you're a man.

PRIOR: (*Feigning dismay, shock, he mimes slashing his throat with*   20
    his lipstick and dies, fabulously tragic. Then.) The hands and
    feet give it away.

HARPER: There must be some mistake here. I don't recognize
    you. You're not. . . . Are you my . . . some sort of imaginary
    friend?   25

PRIOR: No. Aren't you too old to have imaginary friends?

HARPER: I have emotional problems. I took too many pills. Why
    are you wearing makeup?

PRIOR: I was in the process of applying the face, trying to make
    myself feel better—I swiped the new fall colors at the Clinique   30
    counter at Macy's. (*Showing her.*)

HARPER: You stole these?

PRIOR: I was out of cash; it was an emotional emergency!

HARPER: Joe will be so angry. I promised him. No more pills.

PRIOR: These pills you keep alluding to?   35

HARPER: Valium. I take Valium. Lots of Valium.

PRIOR: And you're dancing as fast as you can.

HARPER: I'm not *addicted*. I don't believe in addiction, and I
    never . . . well, I *never* drink. And I *never* take drugs.

PRIOR: Well, smell *you*, Nancy Drew.   40

HARPER: Except Valium.

PRIOR: Except Valium; in wee fistfuls.

HARPER: It's terrible. Mormons are not supposed to be addicted
    to anything. I'm a Mormon.

PRIOR: I'm a homosexual.   45

HARPER: Oh! In my church we don't believe in homosexuals.

PRIOR: In my church we don't believe in Mormons.

HARPER: What church do . . . oh! (*She laughs.*) I get it.
      I don't understand this. If I didn't ever see you before and
    I don't think I did then I don't think you should be here, in   50
    this hallucination, because in my experience the mind, which
    is where hallucinations come from, shouldn't be able to make
    up anything that wasn't there to start with, that didn't enter
    it from experience, from the real world. Imagination can't
    create anything new, can it? It only recycles bits and pieces   55
    from the world and reassembles them into visions. . . . Am I
    making sense right now?

PRIOR: Given the circumstances, yes.

HARPER: So when we think we've escaped the unbearable
    ordinariness and, well, untruthfulness of our lives, it's really   60
    only the same old ordinariness and falseness rearranged into
    the appearance of novelty and truth. Nothing unknown is
    knowable. Don't you think it's depressing?

PRIOR: The limitations of the imagination?

HARPER: Yes.   65

PRIOR: It's something you learn after your second theme party:
    It's All Been Done Before.

HARPER: The world. Finite. Terribly, terribly. . . . Well . . . This is
    the most depressing hallucination I've ever had.

PRIOR: Apologies. I do try to be amusing.   70

HARPER: Oh, well, don't apologize, you. . . . I can't expect
    someone who's really sick to entertain me.

PRIOR: How on earth did you know . . .

HARPER: Oh that happens. This is the very threshhold of
75   revelation sometimes. You can see things . . . how sick you are.
        Do you see anything about me?
PRIOR: Yes.
HARPER: What?
PRIOR: You are amazingly unhappy.
80 HARPER: Oh big deal. You meet a Valium addict and you figure
        out she's unhappy. That doesn't count. Of course I. . . .
        Something else. Something surprising.
PRIOR: Something surprising.
HARPER: Yes.
85 PRIOR: Your husband's a homo.

(*Pause.*)

HARPER: Oh, ridiculous.

(*Pause, then very quietly.*)

        Really?
PRIOR: (*Shrugs.*) Threshhold of revelation.
HARPER: Well I don't like your revelations. I don't think you
90   intuit well at all. Joe's a very normal man, he . . .
        Oh God. Oh God. He. . . . Do homos take, like, lots of
        long walks?
PRIOR: Yes. We do. In stretch pants with lavender coifs. I just
        looked at you, and there was . . .
95 HARPER: A sort of blue streak of recognition.
PRIOR: Yes.
HARPER: Like you knew me incredibly well.
PRIOR: Yes.
HARPER: Yes.
100   I have to go now, get back, something just . . . fell apart. Oh
        God, I feel so sad . . .
PRIOR: I . . . I'm sorry. I usually say, "Fuck the truth," but mostly,
        the truth fucks you.
HARPER: I see something else about you . . .
105 PRIOR: Oh?
HARPER: Deep inside you, there's a part of you, the most inner
        part, entirely free of disease. I can see that.
PRIOR: Is that. . . . That isn't true.
HARPER: Threshhold of revelation.
110   Home . . .

(*She vanishes.*)

PRIOR: People come and go so quickly here . . .
        (*To himself in the mirror.*) I don't think there's any
        uninfected part of me. My heart is pumping polluted blood. I
        feel dirty.

(*He begins to wipe makeup off with his hands, smearing it around.
A large gray feather falls from up above.* PRIOR *stops smearing the
makeup and looks at the feather. He goes to it and picks it up.*)

115 THE VOICE: (*It is an incredibly beautiful voice.*) Look up!
PRIOR: (*Looking up, not seeing anyone.*) Hello?
THE VOICE: Look up!
PRIOR: Who is that?
THE VOICE: Prepare the way!
120 PRIOR: I don't see any . . .

(*There is a dramatic change in lighting, from above.*)

A VOICE: Look up, look up,
        prepare the way
        the infinite descent
        A breath in air
        floating down   125
        Glory to . . .

(*Silence.*)

PRIOR: Hello? Is that it? Helloooo!
        What the fuck . . . ? (*He holds himself.*)
        Poor me. Poor poor me. Why me? Why poor poor me?
        Oh I don't feel good right now. I really don't.   130

SCENE VIII

That night. Split scene: HARPER *and* JOE *at home;* PRIOR *and* LOUIS
in bed.

HARPER: Where were you?
JOE: Out.
HARPER: Where?
JOE: Just out. Thinking.
HARPER: It's late.   5
JOE: I had a lot to think about.
HARPER: I burned dinner.
JOE: Sorry.
HARPER: Not my dinner. My dinner was fine. Your dinner. I put it
        back in the oven and turned everything up as high as it could 10
        go and I watched till it burned black. It's still hot. Very hot.
        Want it?
JOE: You didn't have to do that.
HARPER: I know. It just seemed like the kind of thing a mentally
        deranged sex-starved pill-popping housewife would do.   15
JOE: Uh huh.
HARPER: So I did it. Who knows anymore what I have to do?
JOE: How many pills?
HARPER: A bunch. Don't change the subject.
JOE: I won't talk to you when you . . .   20
HARPER: No. No. Don't do that! I'm . . . fine, pills are not the
        problem, not our problem, I WANT TO KNOW
        WHERE YOU'VE BEEN! I WANT TO KNOW WHAT'S
        GOING ON!
JOE: Going on with what? The job?   25
HARPER: Not the job.
JOE: I said I need more time.
HARPER: Not the job!
JOE: Mr. Cohn, I talked to him on the phone, he said I had to
        hurry . . .   30
HARPER: Not the . . .
JOE: But I can't get you to talk sensibly about anything so . . .
HARPER: SHUT UP!
JOE: Then what?
HARPER: Stick to the subject.   35
JOE: I don't know what that is. You have something you want to
        ask me? Ask me. Go.
HARPER: I . . . can't. I'm scared of you.
JOE: I'm tired, I'm going to bed.
HARPER: Tell me without making me ask. Please.   40
JOE: This is crazy, I'm not . . .
HARPER: When you come through the door at night your face
        is never exactly the way I remembered it. I get surprised by

something . . . mean and hard about the way you look. Even
the weight of you in the bed at night, the way you breathe in
your sleep seems unfamiliar.
You terrify me.

JOE: (*Cold.*) I know who you are.

HARPER: Yes. I'm the enemy. That's easy. That doesn't change.
You think you're the only one who hates sex; I do; I hate it
with you; I do. I dream that you batter away at me till all my
joints come apart, like wax, and I fall into pieces. It's like a
punishment. It was wrong of me to marry you. I knew you . . .
(*She stops herself.*) It's a sin, and it's killing us both.

JOE: I can always tell when you've taken pills because it makes you
red-faced and sweaty and frankly that's very often why I don't
want to . . .

HARPER: Because . . .

JOE: Well, you aren't pretty. Not like this.

HARPER: I have something to ask you.

JOE: Then ASK! ASK! What in hell are you . . .

HARPER: Are you a homo?

(*Pause.*)

Are you? If you try to walk out right now I'll put your
dinner back in the oven and turn it up so high the whole
building will fill with smoke and everyone in it will
asphyxiate. So help me God I will.
Now answer the question.

JOE: What if I . . .

(*Small pause.*)

HARPER: Then tell me, please. And we'll see.

JOE: No. I'm not.
I don't see what difference it makes.

LOUIS: Jews don't have any clear textual guide to the afterlife;
even that it exists. I don't think much about it. I see it as a
perpetual rainy Thursday afternoon in March. Dead leaves.

PRIOR: Eeeugh. Very Greco-Roman.

LOUIS: Well for us it's not the verdict that counts, it's the act of
judgment. That's why I could never be a lawyer. In court all
that matters is the verdict.

PRIOR: You could never be a lawyer because you are oversexed.
You're too distracted.

LOUIS: Not distracted, *ab*stracted. I'm trying to make a point:

PRIOR: Namely:

LOUIS: It's the judge in his or her chambers, weighing, books
open, pondering the evidence, ranging freely over categories:
good, evil, innocent, guilty; the judge in the chamber of
circumspection, not the judge on the bench with the gavel.
The shaping of the law, not its execution.

PRIOR: The point, dear, the point . . .

LOUIS: That it should be the questions and shape of a life, its
total complexity gathered, arranged and considered, which
matters in the end, not some stamp of salvation or damnation
which disperses all the complexity in some unsatisfying little
decision—the balancing of the scales . . .

PRIOR: I like this; very zen; it's . . . reassuringly incomprehensible
and useless. We who are about to die thank you.

LOUIS: You are not about to die.

PRIOR: It's not going well, really . . . two new lesions. My leg hurts.
There's protein in my urine, the doctor says, but who knows

what the fuck that portends. Anyway it shouldn't be there,
the protein. My butt is chapped from diarrhea and yesterday
I shat blood.

LOUIS: I really hate this. You don't tell me . . .

PRIOR: You get too upset, I wind up comforting you. It's
easier . . .

LOUIS: Oh thanks.

PRIOR: If it's bad I'll tell you.

LOUIS: Shitting blood sounds bad to me.

PRIOR: And I'm telling you.

LOUIS: And I'm handling it.

PRIOR: Tell me some more about justice.

LOUIS: I *am* not handling it.

PRIOR: Well Louis you win Trooper of the Month.

(LOUIS *starts to cry.*)

PRIOR: I take it back. You aren't Trooper of the Month.
This isn't working . . .
Tell me some more about justice.

LOUIS: You are not about to die.

PRIOR: Justice . . .

LOUIS: is an immensity, a confusing vastness. Justice is God.
Prior?

PRIOR: Hmmm?

LOUIS: You love me.

PRIOR: Yes.

LOUIS: What if I walked out on this?
Would you hate me forever?

(PRIOR *kisses* LOUIS *on the forehead.*)

PRIOR: Yes.

JOE: I think we ought to pray. Ask God for help. Ask him
together . . .

HARPER: God won't talk to me. I have to make up people to talk
to me.

JOE: You have to keep asking.

HARPER: I forgot the question.
Oh yeah. God, is my husband a . . .

JOE: (*Scary.*) Stop it. Stop it. I'm warning you.
Does it make any difference? That I might be one thing
deep within, no matter how wrong or ugly that thing is, so
long as I have fought, with everything I have, to kill it. What
do you want from me? What do you want from me, Harper?
More than that? For God's sake, there's nothing left, I'm a
shell. There's nothing left to kill.
As long as my behavior is what I know it has to be. Decent.
Correct. That alone in the eyes of God.

HARPER: No, no, not that, that's Utah talk, Mormon talk, I hate it,
Joe, tell me, say it . . .

JOE: All I will say is that I am a very good man who has worked
very hard to become good and you want to destroy that. You
want to destroy me, but I am not going to let you do that.

(*Pause.*)

HARPER: I'm going to have a baby.

JOE: Liar.

HARPER: You liar.
A baby born addicted to pills. A baby who does not dream
but who hallucinates, who stares up at us with big mirror eyes
and who does not know who we are.

(*Pause.*)

JOE: Are you really . . .
HARPER: No. Yes. No. Yes. Get away from me.
155   Now we both have a secret.

PRIOR: One of my ancestors was a ship's captain who made
    money bringing whale oil to Europe and returning with
    immigrants—Irish mostly, packed in tight, so many dollars
    per head. The last ship he captained foundered off the coast
160   of Nova Scotia in a winter tempest and sank to the bottom.
    He went down with the ship—la Grande Geste—but his crew
    took seventy women and kids in the ship's only longboat,
    this big, open rowboat, and when the weather got too rough,
    and they thought the boat was overcrowded, the crew started
165   lifting people up and hurling them into the sea. Until they
    got the ballast right. They walked up and down the longboat,
    eyes to the waterline, and when the boat rode low in the water
    they'd grab the nearest passenger and throw them into the
    sea. The boat was leaky, see; seventy people; they arrived in
170   Halifax with nine people on board.
LOUIS: Jesus.
PRIOR: I think about that story a lot now. People in a boat,
    waiting, terrified, while implacable, unsmiling men,
    irresistibly strong, seize . . . maybe the person next to you,
175   maybe you, and with no warning at all, with time only for a
    quick intake of air you are pitched into freezing, turbulent
    water and salt and darkness to drown.
        I like your cosmology, baby. While time is running out I
    find myself drawn to anything that's suspended, that lacks an
180   ending—but it seems to me that it lets you off scot-free.
LOUIS: What do you mean?
PRIOR: No judgment, no guilt or responsibility.
LOUIS: For me.
PRIOR: For anyone. It was an editorial "you."
185 LOUIS: Please get better. Please.
        Please don't get any sicker.

SCENE IX

Third week in November. ROY *and* HENRY, *his doctor, in* HENRY's
office.

HENRY: Nobody knows what causes it. And nobody knows how to
    cure it. The best theory is that we blame a retrovirus, the Human
    Immunodeficiency Virus. Its presence is made known to us by
    the useless antibodies which appear in reaction to its entrance
5   into the bloodstream through a cut, or an orifice. The antibodies
    are powerless to protect the body against it. Why, we don't know.
    The body's immune system ceases to function. Sometimes the
    body even attacks itself. At any rate it's left open to a whole horror
    house of infections from microbes which it usually defends
10   against.
        Like Kaposi's sarcomas. These lesions. Or your throat
    problem. Or the glands.
        We think it may also be able to slip past the blood-brain
    barrier into the brain. Which is of course very bad news.
15   And it's fatal in we don't know what percent of people with
    suppressed immune responses.

(*Pause*)

ROY: This is very interesting, Mr. Wizard, but why the fuck are
    you telling me this?

(*Pause.*)

HENRY: Well, I have just removed one of three lesions which
    biopsy results will probably tell us is a Kaposi's sarcoma   20
    lesion. And you have a pronounced swelling of glands in your
    neck, groin, and armpits—lymphadenopathy is another sign.
    And you have oral candidiasis and maybe a little more fungus
    under the fingernails of two digits on your right hand. So
    that's why . . .   25
ROY: This disease . . .
HENRY: Syndrome.
ROY: Whatever. It afflicts mostly homosexuals and drug addicts.
HENRY: Mostly. Hemophiliacs are also at risk.
ROY: Homosexuals and drug addicts. So why are you implying   30
    that I . . .

(*Pause.*)

    What are you implying, Henry?
HENRY: I don't . . .
ROY: I'm not a drug addict.
HENRY: Oh come on Roy.   35
ROY: What, what, come on Roy what? Do you think I'm a
    junkie, Henry, do you see tracks?
HENRY: This is absurd.
ROY: Say it.
HENRY: Say what?   40
ROY: Say, "Roy Cohn, you are a . . ."
HENRY: Roy.
ROY: "You are a . . . ." Go on. Not "Roy Cohn you are a drug
    fiend." "Roy Marcus Cohn, you are a . . . "
    Go on, Henry, it starts with an "H."   45
HENRY: Oh I'm not going to . . .
ROY: *With an "H,"* Henry, and it isn't "Hemophiliac." Come
    on . . .
HENRY: What are you doing, Roy?
ROY: No, say it. I mean it. Say: "Roy Cohn, you are a   50
    homosexual."

(*Pause.*)

    And I will proceed, systemically, to destroy your reputation
    and your practice and your career in New York State, Henry.
    Which you know I can do.

(*Pause.*)

HENRY: Roy, you have been seeing me since 1958. Apart from the   55
    facelifts I have treated you for everything from syphilis . . .
ROY: From a whore in Dallas.
HENRY: From syphilis to venereal warts. In your rectum. Which
    you may have gotten from a whore in Dallas, but it wasn't a
    female whore.   60

(*Pause.*)

ROY: So say it.
HENRY: Roy Cohn, you are . . .
    You have had sex with men, many many times, Roy, and
    one of them, or any number of them, has made you very sick.
    You have AIDS.   65

ROY: AIDS.

Your problem, Henry, is that you are hung up on words, on labels, that you believe they mean what they seem to mean. AIDS. Homosexual. Gay. Lesbian. You think these are
70   names that tell you who someone sleeps with, but they don't tell you that.

HENRY: No?

ROY: No. Like all labels they tell you one thing and one thing only: where does an individual so identified fit in the food
75   chain, in the pecking order? Not ideology, or sexual taste, but something much simpler: clout. Not who I fuck or who fucks me, but who will pick up the phone when I call, who owes me favors. This is what a label refers to. Now to someone who does not understand this, homosexual is what I am because
80   I have sex with men. But really this is wrong. Homosexuals are not men who sleep with other men. Homosexuals are men who in fifteen years of trying cannot get a pissant antidiscrimination bill through City Council. Homosexuals are men who know nobody and who nobody knows.
85   Who have zero clout. Does this sound like me, Henry?

HENRY: No.

ROY: No. I have clout. A lot. I can pick up this phone, punch fifteen numbers, and you know who will be on the other end in under five minutes, Henry?
90   HENRY: The President.

ROY: Even better, Henry. His wife.

HENRY: I'm impressed.

ROY: I don't want you to be impressed. I want you to understand. This is not sophistry. And this is not hypocrisy. This is reality.
95   I have sex with men. But unlike nearly every other man of whom this is true, I bring the guy I'm screwing to the White House and President Reagan smiles at us and shakes his hand. Because *what* I am is defined entirely by *who* I am. Roy Cohn is not a homosexual. Roy Cohn is a heterosexual man, Henry,
100   who fucks around with guys.

HENRY: OK, Roy.

ROY: And what is my diagnosis, Henry?

HENRY: You have AIDS, Roy.

ROY: No, Henry, no. AIDS is what homosexuals have. I have
105   liver cancer.

(*Pause.*)

HENRY: Well, whatever the fuck you have, Roy, it's very serious, and I haven't got a damn thing for you. The NIH in Bethesda has a new drug called AZT with a two-year waiting list that not even I can get you onto. So get on the phone, Roy, and dial
110   the fifteen numbers, and tell the First Lady you need in on an experimental treatment for liver cancer, because you can call it any damn thing you want, Roy, but what it boils down to is very bad news.

ACT TWO

In Vitro
December 1985–January 1986

SCENE I

Night, the third week in December. PRIOR *alone on the floor of his bedroom; he is much worse.*

PRIOR: Louis, Louis, please wake up, oh God.

(LOUIS *runs in.*)

PRIOR: I think something horrible is wrong with me I can't breathe . . .

LOUIS: (*Starting to exit.*) I'm calling the ambulance.

PRIOR: No, wait, I . . .   5

LOUIS: *Wait?* Are you fucking crazy? Oh God you're on fire, your head is on fire.

PRIOR: It hurts, it hurts . . .

LOUIS: I'm calling the ambulance.

PRIOR: I don't want to go to the hospital, I don't want to go to the   10
hospital please let me lie here, just . . .

LOUIS: No, no, God, Prior, stand up . . .

PRIOR: DON'T TOUCH MY LEG!

LOUIS: We have to . . . oh God this is so crazy.

PRIOR: I'll be OK if I just lie here Lou, really, if I can only sleep a   15
little . . .

(LOUIS *exits.*)

PRIOR: Louis?

NO! NO! Don't call, you'll send me there and I won't come back, please, please Louis I'm begging, baby, please . . . (*Screams.*) LOUIS!!   20

LOUIS: (*From off; hysterical.*) WILL YOU SHUT THE FUCK UP!

PRIOR: (*Trying to stand.*) Aaaah. I have . . . to go to the bathroom. Wait. Wait, just . . . oh. Oh God. (*He shits himself.*)

LOUIS: (*Entering.*) Prior? They'll be here in . . . Oh my God.   25

PRIOR: I'm sorry, I'm sorry.

LOUIS: What did . . . ? What?

PRIOR: I had an accident.

(LOUIS *goes to him.*)

LOUIS: This is blood.

PRIOR: Maybe you shouldn't touch it . . . me. . . . I . . . (*He   30
faints.*)

LOUIS: (*Quietly.*) Oh help. Oh help. Oh God oh God oh God help me I can't I can't I can't.

SCENE II

Same night. HARPER *is sitting at home, all alone, with no lights on. We can barely see her.* JOE *enters, but he doesn't turn on the lights.*

JOE: Why are you sitting in the dark? Turn on the light.

HARPER: *No.* I heard the sounds in the bedroom again. I know someone was in there.

JOE: No one was.

HARPER: Maybe actually in the bed, under the covers with a   5
knife.

Oh, boy. Joe. I, um, I'm thinking of going away. By which I mean: I think I'm going off again. You . . . you know what I mean?

JOE: Please don't. Stay. We can fix it. I pray for that. This is my   10
fault, but I can correct it. You have to try too . . .

(*He turns on the light. She turns it off again.*)

HARPER: When you pray, what do you pray for?

JOE: I pray for God to crush me, break me up into little pieces and start all over again.

15 HARPER: Oh. Please. Don't pray for that.

JOE: I had a book of Bible stories when I was a kid. There
   was a picture I'd look at twenty times every day: Jacob
   wrestles with the angel. I don't really remember the story,
   or why the wrestling—just the picture. Jacob is young and

20 very strong. The angel is . . . a beautiful man, with golden
   hair and wings, of course. I still dream about it. Many
   nights. I'm. . . . It's me. In that struggle. Fierce, and unfair.
   The angel is not human, and it holds nothing back, so how
   could anyone human win, what kind of a fight is that? It's

25 not just. Losing means your soul thrown down in the
   dust, your heart torn out from God's. But you can't not
   lose.

HARPER: In the whole entire world, you are the only person, the
   only person I love or have ever loved. And I love you terribly.

30 Terribly. That's what's so awfully, irreducibly real. I can make
   up anything but I can't dream that away.

JOE: Are you . . . are you really going to have a baby?

HARPER: It's my time and there's no blood. I don't really know.
   I suppose it wouldn't be a great thing. Maybe I'm just not

35 bleeding because I take too many pills. Maybe I'll give
   birth to a pill. That would give a new meaning to pill-
   popping, huh?
      I think you should go to Washington. Alone. Change, like
   you said.

40 JOE: I'm not going to leave you, Harper.

HARPER: Well maybe not. But I'm going to leave you.

SCENE III

One A.M., the next morning. LOUIS *and a nurse,* EMILY, *are sitting
in* PRIOR'S *room in the hospital.*

EMILY: He'll be all right now.

LOUIS: No he won't.

EMILY: No. I guess not. I gave him something that makes him
   sleep.

5 LOUIS: Deep asleep?

EMILY: Orbiting the moons of Jupiter.

LOUIS: A good place to be.

EMILY: Anyplace better than here. You his . . . uh?

LOUIS: Yes. I'm his uh.

10 EMILY: This must be hell for you.

LOUIS: It is. Hell. The After Life. Which is not at all like a rainy
   afternoon in March, by the way, Prior. A lot more vivid than
   I'd expected. Dead leaves, but the crunchy kind. Sharp, dry
   air. The kind of long, luxurious dying feeling that breaks

15 your heart.

EMILY: Yeah, well we all get to break our hearts on this one. He
   seems like a nice guy. Cute.

LOUIS: Not like this.
      Yes, he is. Was. Whatever.

20 EMILY: Weird name. Prior Walter. Like, "The Walter before this
   one."

LOUIS: Lots of Walters before this one. Prior is an old old family
   name in an old old family. The Walters go back to the
   Mayflower and beyond. Back to the Norman Conquest. He

25 says there's a Prior Walter stitched into the Bayeux tapestry.

EMILY: Is that impressive?

LOUIS: Well, it's old. Very old. Which in some circles equals
   impressive.

EMILY: Not in my circle. What's the name of the tapestry?

30 LOUIS: The Bayeux tapestry. Embroidered by La Reine Mathilde.

EMILY: I'll tell my mother. She embroiders. Drives me nuts.

LOUIS: Manual therapy for anxious hands.

EMILY: Maybe you should try it.

LOUIS: Mathilde stitched while William the Conqueror was off

35 to war. She was capable of . . . more than loyalty. Devotion.
   She waited for him, she stitched for years. And if he had come
   back broken and defeated from war, she would have loved
   him even more. And if he had returned mutilated, ugly, full
   of infection and horror, she would still have loved him; fed by

40 pity, by a sharing of pain, she would love him even more, and
   even more, and she would never, never have prayed to God,
   please let him die if he can't return to me whole and healthy
   and able to live a normal life. . . . If he had died, she would
   have buried her heart with him.
      So what the fuck is the matter with me?

45

(*Little pause.*)

   Will he sleep through the night?

EMILY: At least.

LOUIS: I'm going.

EMILY: It's one A.M. Where do you have to go at . . .

LOUIS: I know what time it is. A walk. Night air, good for the. . . .   50
   The park.

EMILY: Be careful.

LOUIS: Yeah. Danger.
      Tell him, if he wakes up and you're still on, tell him goodbye,
   tell him I had to go.   55

SCENE IV

An hour later. Split scene: JOE *and* ROY *in a fancy (straight) bar;*
LOUIS *and a* MAN *in the Rambles in Central Park.* JOE *and* ROY *are
sitting at the bar; the place is brightly lit.* JOE *has a plate of food in
front of him but he isn't eating.* ROY *occasionally reaches over the
table and forks small bites off* JOE'S *plate.* ROY *is drinking heavily,* JOE *not at all.* LOUIS *and the* MAN *are eyeing each other, each
alternating interest and indifference.*

JOE: The pills were something she started when she miscarried
   or . . . no, she took some before that. She had a really bad
   time at home, when she was a kid, her home was really bad.
   I think a lot of drinking and physical stuff. She doesn't talk
   about that, instead she talks about . . . the sky falling down,   5
   people with knives hiding under sofas. Monsters. Mormons.
   Everyone thinks Mormons don't come from homes like that,
   we aren't supposed to behave that way, but we do. It's not
   lying, or being two-faced. Everyone tries very hard to live up
   to God's strictures, which are very . . . um . . .   10

ROY: Strict.

JOE: I shouldn't be bothering you with this.

ROY: No, please. Heart to heart. Want another. . . . What is that,
   seltzer?

JOE: The failure to measure up hits people very hard. From such   15
   a strong desire to be good they feel very far from goodness
   when they fail.
      What scares me is that maybe what I really love in her is
   the part of her that's farthest from the light, from God's love;
   maybe I was drawn to that in the first place. And I'm keeping   20
   it alive because I need it.

ROY: Why would you need it?

JOE: There are things. . . . I don't know how well we know ourselves. I mean, what if? I know I married her because she . . . because I loved it that she was always wrong, always doing something wrong, like one step out of step. In Salt Lake City that stands out. I never stood out, on the outside, but inside, it was hard for me. To pass.

ROY: Pass?

30 JOE: Yeah.

ROY: Pass as what?

JOE: Oh. Well. . . . As someone cheerful and strong. Those who love God with an open heart unclouded by secrets and struggles are cheerful; God's easy simple love for them shows

35 in how strong and happy they are. The saints.

ROY: But you had secrets? Secret struggles . . .

JOE: I wanted to be one of the elect, one of the Blessed. You feel you ought to be, that the blemishes are yours by choice, which of course they aren't. Harper's sorrow, that really deep sorrow,

40 she didn't choose that. But it's there.

ROY: You didn't put it there.

JOE: No.

ROY: You sound like you think you did.

JOE: I am responsible for her.

45 ROY: Because she's your wife.

JOE: That. And I do love her.

ROY: Whatever. She's your wife. And so there are obligations. To her. But also to yourself.

JOE: She'd fall apart in Washington.

50 ROY: Then let her stay here.

JOE: She'll fall apart if I leave her.

ROY: Then bring her to Washington.

JOE: I just can't, Roy. She needs me.

ROY: Listen, Joe. I'm the best divorce lawyer in the business.

(*Little pause.*)

55 JOE: Can't Washington wait?

ROY: You do what you need to do, Joe. What you need. You. Let her life go where it wants to go. You'll both be better for that. *Somebody* should get what they want.

MAN: What do you want?

60 LOUIS: I want you to fuck me, hurt me, make me bleed.

MAN: I want to.

LOUIS: Yeah?

MAN: I want to hurt you.

LOUIS: Fuck me.

65 MAN: Yeah?

LOUIS: Hard.

MAN: Yeah? You been a bad boy?

(*Pause.* LOUIS *laughs, softly.*)

LOUIS: Very bad. Very bad.

MAN: You need to be punished, boy?

70 LOUIS: Yes. I do.

MAN: Yes what?

(*Little pause.*)

LOUIS: Um, I . . .

MAN: Yes *what,* boy?

LOUIS: Oh. Yes sir.

MAN: I want you to take me to your place, boy. 75

LOUIS: No, I can't do that.

MAN: No *what?*

LOUIS: No sir, I can't, I . . .

I don't live alone, sir.

MAN: Your lover know you're out with a man tonight, boy? 80

LOUIS: No sir, he . . .

My lover doesn't know.

MAN: Your lover know you . . .

LOUIS: Let's change the subject, OK? Can we go to your place?

MAN: I live with my parents. 85

LOUIS: Oh.

ROY: Everyone who makes it in this world makes it because somebody older and more powerful takes an interest. The most precious asset in life, I think, is the ability to be a good son. You have that, Joe. Somebody who can be a good son to 90 a father who pushes them farther than they would otherwise go. I've had many fathers, I owe my life to them, powerful, powerful men. Walter Winchell, Edgar Hoover. Joe McCarthy most of all. He valued me because I am a good lawyer, but he loved me because I was and am a good son. He was a 95 very difficult man, very guarded and cagey; I brought out something tender in him. He would have died for me. And me for him. Does this embarrass you?

JOE: I had a hard time with my father.

ROY: Well sometimes that's the way. Then you have to find other 100 fathers, substitutes, I don't know. The father-son relationship is central to life. Women are for birth, beginning, but the father is continuance. The son offers the father his life as a vessel for carrying forth his father's dream. Your father's living? 105

JOE: Um, dead.

ROY: He was . . . what? A difficult man?

JOE: He was in the military. He could be very unfair. And cold.

ROY: But he loved you.

JOE: I don't know. 110

ROY: No, no, Joe, he did, I know this. Sometimes a father's love has to be very, very hard, unfair even, cold to make his son grow strong in a world like this. This isn't a good world.

MAN: Here, then.

LOUIS: I. . . . Do you have a rubber? 115

MAN: I don't use rubbers.

LOUIS: You should. (*He takes one from his coat pocket.*) Here.

MAN: I don't use them.

LOUIS: Forget it, then. (*He starts to leave.*)

MAN: No, wait. 120

Put it on me. Boy.

LOUIS: Forget it, I have to get back. Home. I must be going crazy.

MAN: Oh come on please he won't find out.

LOUIS: It's cold. Too cold.

MAN: It's never too cold, let me warm you up. Please? 125

(*They begin to fuck.*)

MAN: Relax.

LOUIS: (*A small laugh.*) Not a chance.

MAN: It . . .

LOUIS: What?

MAN: I think it broke. The rubber. You want me to keep going? 130

(*Little pause.*) Pull out? Should I . . .

LOUIS: Keep going.
  Infect me.
  I don't care. I don't care.

(*Pause. The* MAN *pulls out.*)

135 MAN: I . . . um, look, I'm sorry, but I think I want to go.
  LOUIS: Yeah.
    Give my best to mom and dad.

(*The* MAN *slaps him.*)

LOUIS: Ow!

(*They stare at each other.*)

LOUIS: It was a joke.

(*The* MAN *leaves.*)

140 ROY: How long have we known each other?
  JOE: Since 1980.
  ROY: Right. A long time. I feel close to you, Joe. Do I advise you
    well?
  JOE: You've been an incredible friend, Roy, I . . .
145 ROY: I want to be family. Familia, as my Italian friends call it.
    La Familia. A lovely word. It's important for me to help you,
    like I was helped.
  JOE: I owe practically everything to you, Roy.
  ROY: I'm dying, Joe. Cancer.
150 JOE: Oh my God.
  ROY: Please. Let me finish.
    Few people know this and I'm telling you this only
    because. . . . I'm not afraid of death. What can death bring
    that I haven't faced? I've lived; life is the worst. (*Gently*
155 *mocking himself.*) Listen to me, I'm a philosopher.
      Joe. You must do this. You must must must. Love; that's
    a trap. Responsibility; that's a trap too. Like a father to a son
    I tell you this: Life is full of horror; nobody escapes, nobody;
    save yourself. Whatever pulls on you, whatever needs from
160 you, threatens you. Don't be afraid; people are so afraid; don't
    be afraid to live in the raw wind, naked, alone. . . . Learn at
    least this: What you are capable of. Let nothing stand in your
    way.

SCENE V

Three days later. PRIOR *and* BELIZE *in* PRIOR'S *hospital room.*
PRIOR *is very sick but improving.* BELIZE *has just arrived.*

PRIOR: Miss Thing.
BELIZE: Ma cherie bichette.
PRIOR: Stella.
BELIZE: Stella for star. Let me see. (*Scrutinizing* PRIOR.) You look
5   like shit, why yes indeed you do, comme la merde!
PRIOR: Merci.
BELIZE: (*Taking little plastic bottles from his bag, handing them to*
    PRIOR.) Not to despair, Belle Reeve. Lookie! Magic goop!
PRIOR: (*Opening a bottle, sniffing.*) Pooh! What kinda crap is that?
10 BELIZE: Beats me. Let's rub it on your poor blistered body and see
    what it does.
PRIOR: This is not Western medicine, these bottles . . .
BELIZE: Voodoo cream. From the botanica 'round the block.

PRIOR: And you a registered nurse.
BELIZE: (*Sniffing it.*) Beeswax and cheap perfume. Cut with   15
    Jergen's Lotion. Full of good vibes and love from some little
    black Cubana witch in Miami.
PRIOR: Get that trash away from me. I am immune-suppressed.
BELIZE: I *am* a health professional. I *know* what I'm doing.
PRIOR: It stinks. Any word from Louis?   20

(*Pause.* BELIZE *starts giving* PRIOR *a gentle massage.*)

PRIOR: Gone.
BELIZE: He'll be back. I know the type. Likes to keep a girl
    on edge.
PRIOR: It's been . . .

(*Pause*)

BELIZE: (*Trying to jog his memory.*) How long?   25
PRIOR: I don't remember.
BELIZE: How long have you been here?
PRIOR: (*Getting suddenly upset.*) I don't remember, I don't give a
    fuck. I want Louis. I want my fucking boyfriend, where the
    fuck is he? I'm dying, I'm dying, where's Louis?   30
BELIZE: Shhhh, shh . . .
PRIOR: This is a very strange drug, this drug. Emotional lability,
    for starters.
BELIZE: Save a tab or two for me.
PRIOR: Oh no, not this drug, ce n'est pas pour la joyeux noël et la   35
    bonne année, this drug she is serious poisonous chemistry,
    ma pauvre bichette.
      And not just disorienting. I hear things. Voices.
BELIZE: Voices.
PRIOR: A voice.   40
BELIZE: Saying what?

(*Pause.*)

PRIOR: I'm not supposed to tell.
BELIZE: You better tell the doctor. Or I will.
PRIOR: No no don't. Please. I want the voice; it's wonderful. It's
    all that's keeping me alive. I don't want to talk to some intern   45
    about it.
      You know what happens? When I hear it, I get hard.
BELIZE: Oh my.
PRIOR: Comme ça. (*He uses his arm to demonstrate.*) And you
    know I am slow to rise.   50
BELIZE: My jaw aches at the memory.
PRIOR: And would you deny me this little solace—betray my
    concupiscence to Florence Nightingale's storm troopers?
BELIZE: Perish the thought, ma bébé.
PRIOR: They'd change the drug just to spoil the fun.   55
BELIZE: You and your boner can depend on me.
PRIOR: Je t'adore, ma belle nègre.
BELIZE: All this girl-talk shit is politically incorrect, you know.
    We should have dropped it back when we gave up drag.
PRIOR: I'm sick, I get to be politically incorrect if it makes me feel   60
    better. You sound like Lou.

(*Little pause.*)

  Well, at least I have the satisfaction of knowing he's in anguish
  somewhere. I loved his anguish. Watching him stick his
  head up his asshole and eat his guts out over some relatively

65   minor moral conundrum—it was the best show in town.
        But Mother warned me; if they get overwhelmed by the little
        things . . .
    BELIZE: They'll be belly-up bustville when something big comes
        along.
70 PRIOR: Mother warned me.
    BELIZE: And they do come along.
    PRIOR: But I didn't listen.
    BELIZE: No. (*Doing Hepburn.*) Men are beasts.
    PRIOR: (*Also Hepburn.*) The absolute lowest.
75 BELIZE: I have to go. If I want to spend my whole lonely life
        looking after white people I can get underpaid to do it.
    PRIOR: You're just a Christian martyr.
    BELIZE: Whatever happens, baby, I will be here for you.
    PRIOR: Je t'aime.
80 BELIZE: Je t'aime. Don't go crazy on me, girlfriend, I already
        got enough crazy queens for one lifetime. For two. I can't be
        bothering with dementia.
    PRIOR: I promise.
    BELIZE: (*Touching him; softly.*) Ouch.
85 PRIOR: Ouch. Indeed.
    BELIZE: Why'd they have to pick on you?
        And eat more, girlfriend, you really do look like shit.

(BELIZE *leaves.*)

    PRIOR: (*After waiting a beat.*) He's gone.
        Are you still . . .
90 VOICE: I can't stay. I will return.
    PRIOR: Are you one of those "Follow me to the other side"
        voices?
    VOICE: No. I am no nightbird. I am a messenger . . .
    PRIOR: You have a beautiful voice, it sounds . . . like a viola, like
95   a perfectly tuned, tight string, balanced, the truth. . . . Stay
        with me.
    THE VOICE: Not now. Soon I will return, I will reveal myself to
        you; I am glorious, glorious; my heart, my countenance and
        my message. You must prepare.
100 PRIOR: For what? I don't want to . . .
    THE VOICE: No death, no:
        A marvelous work and a wonder we undertake, an
        edifice awry we sink plumb and straighten, a great Lie we
        abolish, a great error correct, with the rule, sword and
105   broom of Truth!
    PRIOR: What are you talking about, I . . .
    THE VOICE: I am on my way; when I am manifest, our Work
        begins;
        Prepare for the parting of the air,
110   The breath, the ascent,
        Glory to . . .

SCENE VI

The second week of January. MARTIN, ROY *and* JOE *in a fancy
Manhattan restaurant.*

    MARTIN: It's a revolution in Washington, Joe. We have a new
        agenda and finally a real leader. They got back the Senate
        but we have the courts. By the nineties the Supreme Court
        will be block-solid Republican appointees, and the Federal
5   bench—Republican judges like land mines, everywhere,
        everywhere they turn. Affirmative action? Take it to court.

    Boom! Land mine. And we'll get our way on just about
    everything: abortion, defense, Central America, family
    values, a live investment climate. We have the White House
    locked till the year 2000. And beyond. A permanent fix on   10
    the Oval Office? It's possible. By '92 we'll get the Senate back,
    and in ten years the South is going to give us the House. It's
    really the end of Liberalism. The end of New Deal Socialism.
    The end of ipso facto secular humanism. The dawning of a
    genuinely American political personality. Modeled on Ronald   15
    Wilson Reagan.
JOE: It sounds great, Mr. Heller.
MARTIN: Martin. And Justice is the hub. Especially since Ed
    Meese took over. He doesn't specialize in Fine Points of
    the Law. He's a flatfoot, a cop. He reminds me of Teddy   20
    Roosevelt.
JOE: I can't wait to meet him.
MARTIN: Too bad, Joe, he's been dead for sixty years!

(*There is a little awkwardness.* JOE *doesn't respond.*)

MARTIN: Teddy Roosevelt. You said you wanted to. . . . Little joke.
    It reminds me of the story about the . . .   25
ROY: (*Smiling, but nasty.*) Aw shut the fuck up Martin.
    (*To* JOE.) You see that? Mr. Heller here is one of the mighty,
    Joseph, in D.C. he sitteth on the right hand of the man
    who sitteth on the right hand of The Man. And yet I can
    say "shut the fuck up" and he will take no offense. Loyalty.   30
    He . . . Martin?
MARTIN: Yes, Roy?
ROY: Rub my back.
MARTIN: Roy . . .
ROY: No no really, a sore spot, I get them all the time now,   35
    these. . . . Rub it for me darling, would you do that for me?

(MARTIN *rubs* ROY's *back. They both look at* JOE.)

ROY: (*To* JOE.) How do you think a handful of Bolsheviks turned
    St. Petersburg into Leningrad in one afternoon? *Comrades.*
    Who do for each other. Marx and Engels. Lenin and Trotsky.
    Josef Stalin and Franklin Delano Roosevelt.   40

(MARTIN *laughs.*)

ROY: *Comrades,* right Martin?
MARTIN: This man, Joe, is a Saint of the Right.
JOE: I know, Mr. Heller, I . . .
ROY: And you see what I mean, Martin? He's special, right?
MARTIN: Don't embarrass him, Roy.   45
ROY: Gravity, decency, smarts! His strength is as the strength of
    ten because his heart is pure! *And* he's a Royboy, one hundred
    percent.
MARTIN: We're on the move, Joe. On the move.
JOE: Mr. Heller, I . . .   50
MARTIN: (*Ending backrub.*) We can't wait any longer for an
    answer.

(*Little pause.*)

JOE: Oh. Um, I . . .
ROY: Joe's a married man, Martin.
MARTIN: Aha.   55

ROY: With a wife. She doesn't care to go to D.C., and so Joe cannot go. And keeps us dangling. We've seen that kind of thing before, haven't we? These men and their wives.

MARTIN: Oh yes. Beware.

60 JOE: I really can't discuss this under . . .

MARTIN: Then *don't* discuss. Say yes, Joe.

ROY: Now.

MARTIN: Say yes I will.

ROY: Now.

65   Now. I'll hold my breath till you do, I'm turning blue waiting. . . . *Now*, goddammit!

MARTIN: Roy, calm down, it's not . . .

ROY: Aw, fuck it. (*He takes a letter from his jacket pocket, hands it to* JOE.)

70   Read. Came today.

(JOE *reads the first paragraph, then looks up.*)

JOE: Roy. This is . . . Roy, this is terrible.

ROY: You're telling me.

A letter from the New York State Bar Association, Martin. They're gonna try and disbar me.

75 MARTIN: Oh my.

JOE: Why?

ROY: Why, Martin?

MARTIN: Revenge.

ROY: The whole Establishment. Their little rules. Because I know

80   no rules. Because I don't see the Law as a dead and arbitrary collection of antiquated dictums, thou shall, thou shalt not, because, because I know the Law's a pliable, breathing, sweating . . . *organ*, because, because . . .

MARTIN: Because he borrowed half a million from one of his

85   clients.

ROY: Yeah, well, there's that.

MARTIN: *And* he forgot to *return* it.

JOE: Roy, that's. . . . You borrowed money from a client?

ROY: I'm deeply ashamed.

(*Little pause.*)

90 JOE: (*Very sympathetic.*) Roy, you know how much I admire you. Well I mean I know you have unorthodox ways, but I'm sure you only did what you thought at the time you needed to do. And I have faith that . . .

ROY: Not so damp, please. I'll deny it was a loan. She's got no

95   paperwork. Can't prove a fucking thing.

(*Little pause.* MARTIN *studies the menu.*)

JOE: (*Handing back the letter, more official in tone.*) Roy I really appreciate your telling me this, and I'll do whatever I can to help.

ROY: (*Holding up a hand, then, carefully.*) I'll tell you what you

100   can do.

I'm about to be tried, Joe, by a jury that is not a jury of my peers. The disbarment committee: genteel gentleman Brahmin lawyers, country-club men. I offend them, to these men . . . I'm what, Martin, some sort of filthy little

105   Jewish troll?

MARTIN: Oh well, I wouldn't go so far as . . .

ROY: Oh well I would.

Very fancy lawyers, these disbarment committee lawyers, fancy lawyers with fancy corporate clients and complicated

cases. Antitrust suits. Deregulation. Environmental   110

control. Complex cases like these need Justice Department cooperation like flowers need the sun. Wouldn't you say that's an accurate assessment, Martin?

MARTIN: I'm not here, Roy. I'm not hearing any of this.

ROY: No. Of course not.   115

Without the light of the sun, Joe, these cases, and the fancy lawyers who represent them, will wither and die.

A well-placed friend, someone in the Justice Department, say, can turn off the sun. Cast a deep shadow on my behalf. Make them shiver in the cold. If they overstep. They would   120

fear that.

(*Pause.*)

JOE: Roy. I don't understand.

ROY: You do.

(*Pause.*)

JOE: You're not asking me to . . .

ROY: Ssshhh. Careful.   125

JOE: (*A beat, then.*) Even if I said yes to the job, it would be illegal to interfere. With the hearings. It's unethical. No. I can't.

ROY: Un-ethical.

Would you excuse us, Martin?   130

MARTIN: Excuse you?

ROY: Take a walk, Martin. For real.

(MARTIN *leaves.*)

ROY: Un-ethical. Are you trying to embarrass me in front of my friend?

JOE: Well it is unethical, I can't . . .   135

ROY: Boy, you are really something. What the fuck do you think this is, Sunday School?

JOE: No, but Roy this is . . .

ROY: This is . . . this is gastric juices churning, this is enzymes and acids, this is intestinal is what this is, bowel movement   140

and blood-red meat—this stinks, this is *politics*, Joe, the game of being alive. And you think you're. . . . What? Above that? Above alive is what? Dead! In the clouds! You're on earth, goddammit! Plant a foot, stay a while.

I'm sick. They smell I'm weak. They want blood this   145

time. I must have eyes in Justice. In Justice you will protect me.

JOE: Why can't Mr. Heller . . .

ROY: Grow up, Joe. The administration can't get involved.

JOE: But I'd be part of the administration. The same as him.   150

ROY: Not the same. Martin's Ed's man. And Ed's Reagan's man. So Martin's Reagan's man.

And you're mine.

(*Little pause. He holds up the letter.*)

This will never be. Understand me?

(*He tears the letter up.*)

I'm gonna be a lawyer, Joe, I'm gonna be a lawyer, Joe, I'm   155

gonna be a goddam motherfucking legally licensed member of the bar lawyer, just like my daddy was, till my last bitter day on earth, Joseph, until the day I die.

(MARTIN *returns.*)

ROY: Ah, Martin's back.

160 MARTIN: So are we agreed?

ROY: Joe?

(*Little pause.*)

JOE: I will think about it.
        (*To* ROY.) I will.

ROY: Huh.

165 MARTIN: It's the fear of what comes after the doing that makes the
        doing hard to do.

ROY: Amen.

MARTIN: But you can almost always live with the consequences.

SCENE VII

*That afternoon. On the granite steps outside the Hall of Justice,
Brooklyn. It is cold and sunny. A Sabrett wagon is selling hot dogs.*
LOUIS, *in a shabby overcoat, is sitting on the steps contemplatively
eating one.* JOE *enters with three hot dogs and a can of Coke.*

JOE: Can I . . . ?

LOUIS: Oh sure. Sure. Crazy cold sun.

JOE: (*Sitting.*) Have to make the best of it.
        How's your friend?

5 LOUIS: My . . . ? Oh. He's worse. My friend is worse.

JOE: I'm sorry.

LOUIS: Yeah, well. Thanks for asking. It's nice. You're nice. I can't
        believe you voted for Reagan.

JOE: I hope he gets better.

10 LOUIS: Reagan?

JOE: Your friend.

LOUIS: He won't. Neither will Reagan.

JOE: Let's not talk politics, OK?

LOUIS: (*Pointing to* JOE's *lunch.*) You're eating three of those?

15 JOE: Well . . . I'm . . . hungry.

LOUIS: They're really terrible for you. Full of rat-poo and beetle
        legs and wood shavings 'n' shit.

JOE: Huh.

LOUIS: And . . . um . . . irridium, I think. Something toxic.

20 JOE: You're eating one.

LOUIS: Yeah, well, the shape, I can't help myself, plus I'm trying to
        commit suicide, what's your excuse?

JOE: I don't have an excuse. I just have Pepto-Bismol.

(JOE *takes a bottle of Pepto-Bismol and chugs it.* LOUIS *shudders
audibly.*)

JOE: Yeah I know but then I wash it down with Coke.

(*He does this.* LOUIS *mimes barfing in* JOE's *lap.* JOE *pushes* LOUIS's
head away.)

25 JOE: Are you always like this?

LOUIS: I've been worrying a lot about his kids.

JOE: Whose?

LOUIS: Reagan's. Maureen and Mike and little orphan Patti and
        Miss Ron Reagan Jr., the you-should-pardon-the-expression

30   heterosexual.

JOE: Ron Reagan Jr. is *not* . . . You shouldn't just make these
        assumptions about people. How do you know? About him?
        What he is? You don't know.

LOUIS: (*Doing Tallulah.*) Well darling he never sucked *my* cock
        but . . .   35

JOE: Look, if you're going to get vulgar . . .

LOUIS: No no really I mean. . . . What's it like to be the child of
        the Zeitgeist? To have the American Animus as your dad?
        It's not really a *family*, the Reagans, I read *People*, there aren't
        any connections there, no love, they don't ever even speak to   40
        each other except through their agents. So what's it like to be
        Reagan's kid? Enquiring minds want to know.

JOE: You can't believe everything you . . .

LOUIS: (*Looking away.*) But . . . I think we all know what that's
        like. Nowadays. No connections. No responsibilities. All of   45
        us . . . falling through the cracks that separate what we owe to
        our selves and . . . and what we owe to love.

JOE: You just. . . . Whatever you feel like saying or doing, you
        don't care, you just . . . do it.

LOUIS: Do what?   50

JOE: It. Whatever. Whatever it is you want to do.

LOUIS: Are you trying to tell me something?

(*Little pause, sexual. They stare at each other.* JOE *looks away.*)

JOE: No, I'm just observing that you . . .

LOUIS: Impulsive.

JOE: Yes, I mean it must be scary, you . . .   55

LOUIS: (*Shrugs.*) Land of the free. Home of the brave. Call me
        irresponsible.

JOE: It's kind of terrifying.

LOUIS: Yeah, well, freedom is. Heartless, too.

JOE: Oh you're not heartless.   60

LOUIS: You don't know.
        Finish your weenie.

(*He pats* JOE *on the knee, starts to leave.*)

JOE: Um . . .

(LOUIS *turns, looks at him.* JOE *searches for something to say.*)

JOE: Yesterday was Sunday but I've been a little unfocused
        recently and I thought it was Monday. So I came here like   65
        I was going to work. And the whole place was empty. And
        at first I couldn't figure out why, and I had this moment of
        incredible . . . fear and also. . . . It just flashed through my
        mind: The whole Hall of Justice, it's empty, it's deserted,
        it's gone out of business. Forever. The people that make it   70
        run have up and abandoned it.

LOUIS: (*Looking at the building.*) Creepy.

JOE: Well yes but. I felt that I was going to scream. Not because
        it was creepy, but because the emptiness felt so *fast*. And . . .
        well, good. A . . . happy scream.   75
        I just wondered what a thing it would be . . . if overnight
        everything you owe anything to, justice, or love, had really
        gone away. Free.
        It would be . . . heartless terror. Yes. Terrible, and . . .
        Very great. To shed your skin, every old skin, one by one   80
        and then walk away, unencumbered, into the morning.

(*Little pause. He looks at the building.*)

I can't go in there today.

LOUIS: Then don't.

JOE: (*Not really hearing* LOUIS.) I can't go in, I need . . .

(*He looks for what he needs. He takes a swig of Pepto-Bismol.*)

85   I can't *be* this anymore. I need . . . a change, I should just . . .

LOUIS: (*Not a come-on, necessarily; he doesn't want to be alone.*) Want some company? For whatever?

(*Pause.* JOE *looks at* LOUIS *and looks away, afraid.* LOUIS *shrugs.*)

LOUIS: Sometimes, even if it scares you to death, you have to be willing to break the law. Know what I mean?

(*Another little pause.*)

90 JOE: Yes.

(*Another little pause.*)

LOUIS: I moved out. I moved out on my . . .
    I haven't been sleeping well.

JOE: Me neither.

(LOUIS *goes up to* JOE, *licks his napkin and dabs at* JOE'S *mouth.*)

LOUIS: Antacid moustache.

95   (*Points to the building.*) Maybe the court won't convene. Ever again. Maybe we are free. To do whatever.
    Children of the new morning, criminal minds. Selfish and greedy and loveless and blind. Reagan's children.
    You're scared. So am I. Everybody is in the land of the
100 free.
    God help us all.

SCENE VIII

Late that night. JOE *at a payphone phoning* HANNAH *at home in Salt Lake City.*

JOE: Mom?

HANNAH: Joe?

JOE: Hi.

HANNAH: You're calling from the street. It's . . . it must be four in
5   the morning. What's happened?

JOE: Nothing, nothing, I . . .

HANNAH: It's Harper. Is Harper. . . . Joe? Joe?

JOE: Yeah, hi. No, Harper's fine. Well, no, she's . . . not fine. How are you, Mom?

10 HANNAH: What's happened?

JOE: I just wanted to talk to you. I, uh, wanted to try something out on you.

HANNAH: Joe, you haven't . . . have you been drinking, Joe?

JOE: Yes ma'am. I'm drunk.

15 HANNAH: That isn't like you.

JOE: No. I mean, who's to say?

HANNAH: Why are you out on the street at four A.M.? *In that crazy city. It's dangerous.*

JOE: Actually, Mom, I'm not on the street. I'm near the boathouse
20   in the park.

HANNAH: What park?

JOE: Central Park.

HANNAH: CENTRAL PARK! Oh my Lord. What on earth are you doing in Central Park at this time of night? Are you . . . Joe, I think you ought to go home right now. Call 25 me from home.

(*Little pause.*)

    Joe?

JOE: I come here to watch, Mom. Sometimes. Just to watch.

HANNAH: Watch what? What's there to watch at four in the . . .

JOE: Mom, did Dad love me? 30

HANNAH: What?

JOE: Did he?

HANNAH: You ought to go home and call from there.

JOE: Answer.

HANNAH: Oh now really. This is maudlin. I don't like this 35 conversation.

JOE: Yeah, well, it gets worse from here on.

(*Pause.*)

HANNAH: Joe?

JOE: Mom. Momma. I'm a homosexual, Momma.
    Boy, did that come out awkward. 40

(*Pause.*)

    Hello? Hello?
    I'm a homosexual.

(*Pause.*)

    Please, Momma, Say something.

HANNAH: You're old enough to understand that your father didn't love you without being ridiculous about it. 45

JOE: What?

HANNAH: You're ridiculous. You're being ridiculous.

JOE: I'm . . .
    What?

HANNAH: You really ought to go home now to your wife. I 50 need to go to bed. This phone call. . . . We will just forget this phone call.

JOE: Mom.

HANNAH: No more talk. Tonight. This . . .
    (*Suddenly very angry.*) Drinking is a sin! A sin! I raised 55 you better than that. (*She hangs up.*)

SCENE IX

The following morning, early. Split scene: HARPER *and* JOE *at home;* LOUIS *and* PRIOR *in* PRIOR's *hospital room.* JOE *and* LOUIS *have just entered. This should be fast and obviously furious; overlapping is fine; the proceedings may be a little confusing but not the final results.*

HARPER: Oh God. Home. The moment of truth has arrived.

JOE: Harper.

LOUIS: I'm going to move out.

PRIOR: The fuck you are.

JOE: Harper. Please listen. I still love you very much. You're still 5 my best buddy; I'm not going to leave you.

HARPER: No, I don't like the sound of this. I'm leaving.

LOUIS: I'm leaving.
        I already have.

10 JOE: Please listen. Stay. This is really hard. We have to talk.

HARPER: We are talking. Aren't we. Now please shut up. OK?

PRIOR: Bastard. Sneaking off while I'm flat out here, that's low. If I could get up now I'd beat the holy shit out of you.

15 JOE: Did you take pills? How many?

HARPER: No pills. Bad for the . . . (*Pats stomach.*)

JOE: You aren't pregnant. I called your gynecologist.

HARPER: I'm seeing a new gynecologist.

PRIOR: You have no right to do this.

20 LOUIS: Oh, that's ridiculous.

PRIOR: No right. It's criminal.

JOE: Forget about that. Just listen. You want the truth. This is the truth.
        I knew this when I married you. I've known this I guess
25   for as long as I've known anything, but . . . I don't know, I thought maybe that with enough effort and will I could change myself . . . but I can't . . .

PRIOR: Criminal.

LOUIS: There oughta be a law.

30 PRIOR: There is a law. You'll see.

JOE: I'm losing ground here, I go walking, you want to know where I walk, I . . . go to the park, or up and down 53rd Street, or places where. . . . And I keep swearing I won't go walking again, but I just can't.

35 LOUIS: I need some privacy.

PRIOR: That's new.

LOUIS: Everything's new, Prior.

JOE: I try to tighten my heart into a knot, a snarl, I try to learn to live dead, just numb, but then I see someone I want, and
40   it's like a nail, like a hot spike right through my chest, and I know I'm losing.

PRIOR: Apartment too small for three? Louis and Prior comfy but not Louis and Prior and Prior's disease?

LOUIS: Something like that.
45   I won't be judged by you. This isn't a crime, just—the inevitable consequence of people who run out of—whose limitations . . .

PRIOR: Bang bang bang. The court will come to order.

LOUIS: I mean let's talk practicalities, schedules; I'll come over if
50   you want, spend nights with you when I can, I can . . .

PRIOR: Has the jury reached a verdict?

LOUIS: I'm doing the best I can.

PRIOR: Pathetic. Who cares?

JOE: My whole life has conspired to bring me to this place, and
55   I can't despise my whole life. I think I believed when I met you I could save you, you at least if not myself, but . . . I don't have any sexual feelings for you, Harper. And I don't think I ever did.

(*Little pause.*)

HARPER: I think you should go.

60 JOE: Where?

HARPER: Washington. Doesn't matter.

JOE: What are you talking about?

HARPER: Without me.
        Without me, Joe. Isn't that what you want to hear?

(*Little pause.*)

JOE: Yes.   65

LOUIS: You can love someone and fail them. You can love someone and not be able to . . .

PRIOR: You *can*, theoretically, yes. A person can, maybe an editorial "you" can love, Louis, but not *you*, specifically you, I don't know, I think you are excluded from that general   70
category.

HARPER: You were going to save me, but the whole time you were spinning a lie. I just don't understand that.

PRIOR: A person could theoretically love and maybe many do but we both know now you can't.   75

LOUIS: I do.

PRIOR: You can't even say it.

LOUIS: I love you, Prior.

PRIOR: I repeat. Who cares?

HARPER: This is so scary, I want this to stop, to go back . . .   80

PRIOR: We have reached a verdict, your honor. This man's heart is deficient. He loves, but his love is worth nothing.

JOE: Harper . . .

HARPER: Mr. Lies, I want to get away from here. Far away. Right now. Before he starts talking again. Please, please . . .   85

JOE: As long as I've known you Harper you've been afraid of . . . of men hiding under the bed, men hiding under the sofa, men with knives.

PRIOR: (*Shattered; almost pleading; trying to reach him.*) I'm dying! You stupid fuck! Do you know what that is! Love! Do   90
you know what love means? We lived together four-and-a-half years, you animal, you idiot.

LOUIS: I have to find some way to save myself.

JOE: Who are these men? I never understood it. Now I know.

HARPER: What?   95

JOE: It's me.

HARPER: It is?

PRIOR: GET OUT OF MY ROOM!

JOE: I'm the man with the knives.

HARPER: You are?   100

PRIOR: If I could get up now I'd kill you. I would. Go away. Go away or I'll scream.

HARPER: Oh God . . .

JOE: I'm sorry . . .

HARPER: It is you.   105

LOUIS: Please don't scream.

PRIOR: Go.

HARPER: I recognize you now.

LOUIS: Please . . .

JOE: Oh. Wait, I. . . . Oh!   110

(*He covers his mouth with his hand, gags, and removes his hand, red with blood.*)

    I'm bleeding.

(PRIOR *screams.*)

HARPER: Mr. Lies.

MR. LIES: (*Appearing, dressed in antarctic explorer's apparel.*) Right here.

HARPER: I want to go away. I can't see him anymore.   115

MR. LIES: Where?

HARPER: Anywhere. Far away.

MR. LIES: Absolutamento.

(HARPER *and* MR. LIES *vanish.* JOE *looks up, sees that she's gone.*)

PRIOR: (*Closing his eyes.*) When I open my eyes you'll be gone.

(LOUIS *leaves.*)

120 JOE: Harper?
PRIOR: (*Opening his eyes.*) Huh. It worked.
JOE: (*Calling.*) Harper?
PRIOR: I hurt all over. I wish I was dead.

SCENE X

The same day, sunset. HANNAH *and* SISTER ELLA CHAPTER, *a real-estate saleswoman,* HANNAH PITT*'s closest friend, in front of* HANNAH*'s house in Salt Lake City.*

SISTER ELLA CHAPTER: Look at that view! A view of heaven. Like the living city of heaven, isn't it, it just fairly glimmers in the sun.
HANNAH: Glimmers.
5 SISTER ELLA CHAPTER: Even the stone and brick it just glimmers and glitters like heaven in the sunshine. Such a nice view you get, perched up on a canyon rim. Some kind of beautiful place.
HANNAH: It's just Salt Lake, and you're selling the house *for* me,
10 not *to* me.
SISTER ELLA CHAPTER: I like to work up an enthusiasm for my properties.
HANNAH: Just get me a good price.
SISTER ELLA CHAPTER: Well, the market's off.
15 HANNAH: At least fifty.
SISTER ELLA CHAPTER: Forty'd be more like it.
HANNAH: Fifty.
SISTER ELLA CHAPTER: Wish you'd wait a bit.
HANNAH: Well I can't.
20 SISTER ELLA CHAPTER: Wish you would. You're about the only friend I got.
HANNAH: Oh well now.
SISTER ELLA CHAPTER: Know why I decided to like you? I decided to like you 'cause you're the only unfriendly Mormon
25 I ever met.
HANNAH: Your wig is crooked.
SISTER ELLA CHAPTER: Fix it.

(HANNAH *straightens* SISTER ELLA*'s wig.*)

SISTER ELLA CHAPTER: New York City. All they got there is tiny rooms.
30 I always thought: People ought to stay put. That's why I got my license to sell real estate. It's a way of saying: Have a house! Stay put! It's a way of saying traveling's no good. Plus I needed the cash. (*She takes a pack of cigarettes out of her purse, lights one, offers pack to* HANNAH.)
35 HANNAH: Not out here, anyone could come by.
There's been days I've stood at this ledge and thought about stepping over.
It's a hard place, Salt Lake: baked dry. Abundant energy; not much intelligence. That's a combination that can wear
40 a body out. No harm looking someplace else. I don't need much room.
My sister-in-law Libby thinks there's radon gas in the basement.

SISTER ELLA CHAPTER: Is there gas in the . . .
HANNAH: Of course not. Libby's a fool. 45
SISTER ELLA CHAPTER: 'Cause I'd have to include that in the description.
HANNAH: There's no gas, Ella. (*Little pause.*) Give a puff. (*She takes a furtive drag of* ELLA*'s cigarette.*) Put it away now.
SISTER ELLA CHAPTER: So I guess it's goodbye. 50
HANNAH: You'll be all right, Ella, I wasn't ever much of a friend.
SISTER ELLA CHAPTER: I'll say something but don't laugh, OK? This is the home of saints, the godliest place on earth, they say, and I think they're right. That means there's no evil here? No. Evil's everywhere. Sin's everywhere. But this . . . 55 is the spring of sweet water in the desert, the desert flower. Every step a Believer takes away from here is a step fraught with peril. I fear for you, Hannah Pitt, because you are my friend. Stay put. This is the right home of saints.
HANNAH: Latter-day saints. 60
SISTER ELLA CHAPTER: Only kind left.
HANNAH: But still. Late in the day . . . for saints and everyone. That's all. That's all.
Fifty thousand dollars for the house, Sister Ella Chapter; don't undersell. It's an impressive view. 65

ACT THREE

Not-Yet-Conscious, Forward Dawning
January 1986

SCENE I

Late night, three days after the end of Act Two. The stage is completely dark. PRIOR *is in bed in his apartment, having a nightmare. He wakes up, sits up and switches on a nightlight. He looks at his clock. Seated by the table near the bed is a man dressed in the clothing of a 13th-century British squire.*

PRIOR: (*Terrified.*) Who are you?
PRIOR 1: My name is Prior Walter.

(*Pause.*)

PRIOR: My name is Prior Walter.
PRIOR 1: I know that.
PRIOR: Explain. 5
PRIOR 1: You're alive. I'm not. We have the same name. What do you want me to explain?
PRIOR: A ghost?
PRIOR 1: An ancestor.
PRIOR: Not *the* Prior Walter? The Bayeux tapestry Prior Walter? 10
PRIOR 1: His great-great grandson. The fifth of the name.
PRIOR: I'm the thirty-fourth, I think.
PRIOR 1: Actually the thirty-second.
PRIOR: Not according to Mother.
PRIOR 1: She's including the two bastards, then; I say leave 15 them out. I say no room for bastards. The little things you swallow . . .
PRIOR: Pills.
PRIOR 1: Pills. For the pestilence. I too . . .
PRIOR: Pestilence. . . . You too what? 20
PRIOR 1: The pestilence in my time was much worse than now. Whole villages of empty houses. You could look outdoors and see Death walking in the morning, dew dampening the ragged hem of his black robe. Plain as I see you now.

25   PRIOR: You died of the plague.

PRIOR 1: The spotty monster. Like you, alone.

PRIOR: I'm not alone.

PRIOR 1: You have no wife, no children.

PRIOR: I'm gay.

30   PRIOR 1: So? Be gay, dance in your altogether for all I care, what's that to do with not having children?

PRIOR: Gay homosexual, not bonny, blithe and . . . never mind.

PRIOR 1: I had twelve. When I died.

(The second ghost appears, this one dressed in the clothing of an elegant 17th-century Londoner.)

PRIOR 1: *(Pointing to* PRIOR 2.) And I was three years younger
35   than him.

(PRIOR sees the new ghost, screams.)

PRIOR: Oh God another one.

PRIOR 2: Prior Walter. Prior to you by some seventeen others.

PRIOR 1: He's counting the bastards.

PRIOR: Are we having a convention?

40   PRIOR 2: We've been sent to declare her fabulous incipience. They love a well-paved entrance with lots of heralds, and . . .

PRIOR 1: The messenger come. Prepare the way. The infinite descent, a breath in air . . .

45   PRIOR 2: They chose us, I suspect, because of the mortal affinities. In a family as long-descended as the Walters there are bound to be a few carried off by plague.

PRIOR 1: The spotty monster.

PRIOR 2: Black Jack. Came from a water pump, half the city of
50   London, can you imagine? His came from fleas. Yours, I understand, is the lamentable consequence of venery . . .

PRIOR 1: Fleas on rats, but who knew that?

PRIOR: Am I going to die?

PRIOR 2: We aren't allowed to discuss . . .

55   PRIOR 1: When you do, you don't get ancestors to help you through it. You may be surrounded by children but you die alone.

PRIOR: I'm afraid.

PRIOR 1: You should be. There aren't even torches, and the path's
60   rocky, dark and steep.

PRIOR 2: Don't alarm him. There's good news before there's bad.
    We two come to strew rose petal and palm leaf before the triumphal procession. Prophet. Seer. Revelator. It's a great
65   honor for the family.

PRIOR 1: He hasn't got a family.

PRIOR 2: I meant for the Walters, for the family in the larger sense.

PRIOR: *(Singing.)*
70   All I want is a room somewhere,
            Far away from the cold night air . . .

PRIOR 2: *(Putting a hand on* PRIOR's *forehead.)* Calm, calm, this is no brain fever . . .

(PRIOR calms down, but keeps his eyes closed. The lights begin to change. Distant Glorious Music.)

PRIOR 1: *(Low chant.)* Adonai, Adonai,
75   Olam ha-yichud,

Zefirot, Zazahot,
Ha-adam, ha-gadol
Daughter of Light,
Daughter of Splendors,
Fluor! Phosphor!   80
Lumen! Candle!

PRIOR 2: *(Simultaneously.)* Even now,
From the mirror-bright halls of heaven,
Across the cold and lifeless infinity of space,
The Messenger comes   85
Trailing orbs of light,
Fabulous, incipient,
Oh Prophet,
To you . . .

PRIOR 1 and PRIOR 2: Prepare, prepare,   90
The Infinite Descent,
A breath, a feather,
Glory to . . .

(They vanish.)

SCENE II

The next day. Split scene: LOUIS *and* BELIZE *in a coffee shop.* PRIOR *is at the outpatient clinic at the hospital with* EMILY, *the nurse; she has him on a pentamidine IV drip.*

LOUIS: Why has democracy succeeded in America? Of course by succeeded I mean comparatively, not literally, not in the present, but what makes for the prospect of some sort of radical democracy spreading outward and growing up? Why does the power that was once so carefully preserved at the top   5
of the pyramid by the original framers of the Constitution seem drawn inexorably downward and outward in spite of the best effort of the Right to stop this? I mean it's the really hard thing about being Left in this country, the American Left can't help but trip over all these petrified little fetishes: 10
freedom, that's the worst; you know, *Jeane Kirkpatrick* for God's sake will go on and on about freedom and so what does that mean, the word freedom, when she talks about it, or human rights; you have Bush talking about human rights, and so what are these people talking about, they might as well   15
be talking about the mating habits of Venusians, these people don't begin to know what, ontologically, freedom is or human rights, like they see these bourgeois property-based Rights-of-Man-type rights but that's not enfranchisement, not democracy, not what's implicit, what's potential within the   20
idea, not the idea with blood in it. That's just liberalism, the worst kind of liberalism, really, bourgeois tolerance, and what I think is that what AIDS shows us is the limits of tolerance, that it's not enough to be tolerated, because when the shit hits the fan you find out how much tolerance is worth. Nothing.   25
And underneath all the tolerance is intense, passionate hatred.

BELIZE: Uh huh.

LOUIS: Well don't you think that's true?

BELIZE: Uh huh. It is.   30

LOUIS: *Power* is the object, not being tolerated. Fuck assimilation. But I mean in spite of all this the thing about America, I think, is that ultimately we're different from every other nation on earth, in that, with people here of every race, we can't. . . . Ultimately what defines us isn't race, but   35
politics. Not like any European country where there's an

insurmountable fact of a kind of racial, or ethnic, monopoly, or monolith, like all Dutchmen, I mean Dutch people, are well, Dutch, and the Jews of Europe were never Europeans,
40 just a small problem. Facing the monolith. But here there are so many small problems, it's really just a collection of small problems, the monolith is missing. Oh, I mean, of course I suppose there's the monolith of White America. White Straight Male America.
45 BELIZE: Which is not unimpressive, even among monoliths.
LOUIS: Well, no, but when the race thing gets taken care of, and I don't mean to minimize how major it is, I mean I know it is, this is a really, really incredibly racist country but it's like, well, the British. I mean, all these blue-eyed pink
50 people. And it's just weird, you know, I mean I'm not all that Jewish-looking, or . . . well, maybe I am but, you know, in New York, everyone is . . . well, not everyone, but so many are but so but in England, in London I walk into bars and I feel like Sid the Yid, you know I mean like Woody
55 Allen in *Annie Hall,* with the payess and the gabardine coat, like never, never anywhere so much—I mean, not actively despised, not like they're Germans, who I think are still terribly anti-Semitic, and racist too, I mean black-racist, they pretend otherwise but, anyway, in London, there's
60 just . . . and at one point I met this black gay guy from Jamaica who talked with a lilt but he said his family'd been living in London since before the Civil War—the American one—and how the English never let him forget for a minute that he wasn't blue-eyed and pink and I said yeah, me too,
65 these people are anti-Semites and he said yeah but the British Jews have the clothing business all sewed up and blacks there can't get a foothold. And it was an incredibly awkward moment of just. . . . I mean here we were, in this bar that was gay but it was a *pub,* you know, the beams and
70 the plaster and those horrible little, like, two-day-old fish and egg sandwiches—and just so British, so *old,* and I felt, well, there's no way out of this because both of us are, right now, too much immersed in this history, hope is dissolved in the sheer age of this place, where race is what counts and
75 there's no real hope of change—it's the racial destiny of the Brits that matters to them, not their political destiny, whereas in America . . .
BELIZE: Here in America race doesn't count.
LOUIS: No, no, that's not. . . . I mean you *can't* be hearing
80 that . . .
BELIZE: I . . .
LOUIS: It's—look, race, yes, but ultimately race here is a political question, right? Racists just try to use race here as a tool in a political struggle. It's not really about race. Like the
85 spiritualists try to use that stuff, are you enlightened, are you centered, channeled, whatever, this reaching out for a spiritual past in a country where no indigenous spirits exist—only the Indians, I mean Native American spirits and we killed them off so now, there are no gods here, no ghosts
90 and spirits in America, there are no angels in America, no spiritual past, no racial past, there's only the political, and the decoys and the ploys to maneuver around the inescapable battle of politics, the shifting downwards and outwards of political power to the people . . .
95 BELIZE: POWER to the People! AMEN! (*Looking at his watch.*) *OH MY GOODNESS!* Will you look at the time, I gotta . . .
LOUIS: Do you. . . . You think this is, what, racist or naive or something?

BELIZE: Well it's certainly *something.* Look, I just remembered I have an appointment . . . 100
LOUIS: What? I mean I really don't want to, like, speak from some position of privilege and . . .
BELIZE: I'm sitting here, thinking, eventually he's *got* to run out of steam, so I let you rattle on and on saying about maybe seven or eight things I find really offensive. 105
LOUIS: What?
BELIZE: But I know you, Louis, and I know the guilt fueling this peculiar tirade is obviously already swollen bigger than your hemorrhoids.
LOUIS: I don't have hemorrhoids. 110
BELIZE: I hear different. May I finish?
LOUIS: Yes, but I don't have hemorrhoids.
BELIZE: So finally, when I . . .
LOUIS: Prior told you, he's an asshole, he shouldn't have . . .
BELIZE: You promised, Louis. Prior is not a subject. 115
LOUIS: You brought him up.
BELIZE: I brought up hemorrhoids.
LOUIS: So it's indirect. Passive-aggressive.
BELIZE: Unlike, I suppose, banging me over the head with your theory that America doesn't have a race problem. 120
LOUIS: Oh be fair I never said that.
BELIZE: Not exactly, but . . .
LOUIS: I said . . .
BELIZE: but it was close enough, because if it'd been that blunt I'd've just walked out and . . . 125
LOUIS: You deliberately misinterpreted! I . . .
BELIZE: Stop interrupting! I haven't been able to . . .
LOUIS: Just let me . . .
BELIZE: NO! What, *talk*? You've been running your mouth nonstop since I got here, yaddadda yaddadda blah 130 blah blah, up the hill, down the hill, playing with your MONOLITH . . .
LOUIS: (*Overlapping*) Well, you could have joined in at any time instead of . . .
BELIZE: (*Continuing over* LOUIS.) . . . and girlfriend it is truly an 135 awesome spectacle but I got better things to do with my time than sit here listening to this racist bullshit just because I feel sorry for you that . . .
LOUIS: I am not a racist!
BELIZE: Oh come on . . . 140
LOUIS: So maybe I am a racist but . . .
BELIZE: Oh I really hate that! It's no fun picking on you Louis; you're so guilty, it's like throwing darts at a glob of jello, there's no satisfying hits, just quivering, the darts just blop in and vanish. 145
LOUIS: I just think when you are discussing lines of oppression it gets very complicated and . . .
BELIZE: Oh is that a fact? You know, we black drag queens have a rather intimate knowledge of the complexity of the lines of . . . 150
LOUIS: *Ex*-black drag queen.
BELIZE: Actually ex-ex.
LOUIS: You're doing drag again?
BELIZE: I don't. . . . Maybe. I don't have to tell you. Maybe.
LOUIS: I think it's sexist. 155
BELIZE: I didn't ask you.
LOUIS: Well it is. The gay community, I think, has to adopt the same attitude towards drag as black women have to take towards black women blues singers.
BELIZE: Oh my we *are* walking dangerous tonight. 160

LOUIS: Well, it's all internalized oppression, right, I mean the masochism, the stereotypes, the . . .

BELIZE: Louis, are you deliberately trying to make me hate you?

165   LOUIS: No, I . . .

BELIZE: I mean, are you deliberately transforming yourself into an arrogant, sexual-political Stalinist-slash-racist flag-waving thug for my benefit?

(*Pause.*)

LOUIS: You know what I think?

170   BELIZE: What?

LOUIS: You hate me because I'm a Jew.

BELIZE: I'm leaving.

LOUIS: It's true.

BELIZE: You have no basis except your . . .

175   Louis, it's good to know you haven't changed; you are still an honorary citizen of the Twilight Zone, and after your pale, pale white polemics on behalf of racial insensitivity you have a flaming *fuck* of a lot of nerve calling me an anti-Semite. Now I really gotta go.

180   LOUIS: You called me Lou the Jew.

BELIZE: That was a joke.

LOUIS: I didn't think it was funny. It was hostile.

BELIZE: It was three years ago.

LOUIS: So?

185   BELIZE: You just called yourself Sid the Yid.

LOUIS: That's not the same thing.

BELIZE: Sid the Yid is different from Lou the Jew.

LOUIS: Yes.

BELIZE: Someday you'll have to explain that to me, but right

190   now . . .

        You hate me because you hate black people.

LOUIS: I do not. But I do think most black people are anti-Semitic.

BELIZE: "Most black people." *That's* racist, Louis, and *I* think most

195   Jews . . .

LOUIS: Louis Farrakhan.

BELIZE: Ed Koch.

LOUIS: Jesse Jackson.

BELIZE: Jackson. Oh really, Louis, this is . . .

200   LOUIS: Hymietown! Hymietown!

BELIZE: Louis, you voted for Jesse Jackson. You send checks to the Rainbow Coalition.

LOUIS: I'm ambivalent. The checks bounced.

BELIZE: All your checks bounce, Louis; you're ambivalent about

205   everything.

LOUIS: What's that supposed to mean?

BELIZE: You may be dumber than shit but I refuse to believe you can't figure it out. Try.

LOUIS: I was never ambivalent about Prior. I love him. I do. I

210   really do.

BELIZE: Nobody said different.

LOUIS: Love and ambivalence are. . . . Real love isn't ambivalent.

BELIZE: "Real love isn't ambivalent." I'd swear that's a line from

215   my favorite bestselling paperback novel, *In Love with the Night Mysterious,* except I don't think you ever read it.

(*Pause.*)

LOUIS: I never read it, no.

BELIZE: You ought to. Instead of spending the rest of your life trying to get through *Democracy in America.* It's about this white woman whose Daddy owns a plantation in the Deep   220 South in the years before the Civil War—the American one—and her name is Margaret, and she's in love with her Daddy's number-one slave, and his name is Thaddeus, and she's married but her white slave-owner husband has AIDS: Antebellum Insufficiently Developed Sexorgans. And there's   225 a lot of hot stuff going down when Margaret and Thaddeus can catch a spare torrid ten under the cottonpicking moon, and then of course the Yankees come, and they set the slaves free, and the slaves string up old Daddy, and so on. Historical fiction. Somewhere in there I recall Margaret and   230 Thaddeus find the time to discuss the nature of love; her face is reflecting the flames of the burning plantation—you know, the way white people do—and his black face is dark in the night and she says to him, "Thaddeus, real love isn't ever ambivalent."   235

(*Little pause.* EMILY *enters and turns off IV drip.*)

BELIZE: Thaddeus looks at her; he's contemplating her thesis; and he isn't sure he agrees.

EMILY: (*Removing IV drip from* PRIOR'*s arm.*) Treatment number . . . (*Consulting chart.*) four.

PRIOR: Pharmaceutical miracle. Lazarus breathes again.   240

LOUIS: Is he. . . . How bad is he?

BELIZE: You want the laundry list?

EMILY: Shirt off, let's check the . . .

(PRIOR *takes his shirt off. She examines his lesions.*)

BELIZE: There's the weight problem and the shit problem and the morale problem.   245

EMILY: Only six. That's good. Pants.

(*He drops his pants. He's naked. She examines.*)

BELIZE: And. He thinks he's going crazy.

EMILY: Looking good. What else?

PRIOR: Ankles sore and swollen, but the leg's better. The nausea's mostly gone with the little orange pills. BM's pure   250 liquid but not bloody anymore, for now, my eye doctor says everything's OK, for now, my dentist says "Yuck!" when he sees my fuzzy tongue, and now he wears little condoms on his thumb and forefinger. And a mask. So what? My dermatologist is in Hawaii and my mother . . .   255 well leave my mother out of it. Which is usually where my mother is, out of it. My glands are like walnuts, my weight's holding steady for week two, and a friend died two days ago of bird tuberculosis; bird tuberculosis; that scared me and I didn't go to the funeral today because he   260 was an Irish Catholic and it's probably open casket and I'm afraid of . . . something, the bird TB or seeing him or. . . . So I guess I'm doing OK. Except for of course I'm going nuts.

EMILY: We ran the toxoplasmosis series and there's no indica-   265 tion . . .

PRIOR: I know, I know, but I feel like something terrifying is on its way, you know, like a missile from outer space, and it's plummeting down towards the earth, and I'm ground zero, and . . . I am generally known where I am known as one cool,   270 collected queen. And I am ruffled.

EMILY: There's really nothing to worry about. I think that shochen bamromim hamtzeh menucho nechono al kanfey haschino.

275 PRIOR: What?

EMILY: Everything's fine. Bemaalos k'doshim ut'horim kezohar horokeea mazhirim . . .

PRIOR: Oh I don't understand what you're . . .

EMILY: Es nishmas Prior sheholoch leolomoh, baavur shenodvoo

280 z'dokoh b'ad hazkoras nishmosoh.

PRIOR: Why are you doing that?! Stop it! Stop it!

EMILY: Stop what?

PRIOR: You were just . . . weren't you just speaking in Hebrew or something.

285 EMILY: *Hebrew*? (*Laughs.*) I'm basically Italian-American. No. I didn't speak in Hebrew.

PRIOR: Oh no, oh God please I really think I . . .

EMILY: Look, I'm sorry, I have a waiting room full of. . . . I think you're one of the lucky ones, you'll live for years,

290 probably—you're pretty healthy for someone with no immune system. Are you seeing someone? Loneliness is a danger. A therapist?

PRIOR: No, I don't need to see anyone, I just . . .

EMILY: Well think about it. You aren't going crazy. You're just

295 under a lot of stress. No wonder . . . (*She starts to write in his chart.*)

(*Suddenly there is an astonishing blaze of light, a huge chord sounded by a gigantic choir, and a great book with steel pages mounted atop a molten-red pillar pops up from the stage floor. The book opens; there is a large Aleph inscribed on its pages, which bursts into flames. Immediately the book slams shut and disappears instantly under the floor as the lights become normal again. EMILY notices none of this, writing. PRIOR is agog.*)

EMILY: (*Laughing, exiting.*) Hebrew . . .

(PRIOR *flees.*)

LOUIS: Help me.

BELIZE: I beg your pardon?

300 LOUIS: You're a nurse, give me something, I . . . don't know what to do anymore, I. . . . Last week at work I screwed up the Xerox machine like permanently and so I . . . then I tripped on the subway steps and my glasses broke and I cut my forehead, here, see, and now I can't see much and

305 my forehead . . . it's like the Mark of Cain, stupid, right, but it won't heal and every morning I see it and I think, Biblical things, Mark of Cain, Judas Iscariot and his silver and his noose, people who . . . in betraying what they love betray what's truest in themselves, I feel . . . nothing but

310 cold for myself, just cold, and every night I miss him, I miss him so much but then . . . those sores, and the smell and . . . where I thought it was going. . . . I could be . . . I could be sick too, maybe I'm sick too. I don't know.

315 Belize. Tell him I love him. Can you do that?

BELIZE: I've thought about it for a very long time, and I still don't understand what love is. Justice is simple. Democracy is simple. Those things are unambivalent. But love is very hard. And it goes bad for you if you violate the hard law of

320 love.

LOUIS: I'm dying.

BELIZE: He's dying. You just wish you were. Oh cheer up, Louis. Look at that heavy sky out there.

LOUIS: Purple.

BELIZE: *Purple?* Boy, what kind of a homosexual are you, anyway? 325 That's not purple, Mary, that color up there is (*Very grand.*) *mauve.*

All day today it's felt like Thanksgiving. Soon, this . . . ruination will be blanketed white. You can smell it—can you smell it? 330

LOUIS: Smell what?

BELIZE: Softness, compliance, forgiveness, grace.

LOUIS: No . . .

BELIZE: I can't help you learn that. I can't help you, Louis. You're not my business. (*He exits.*) 335

(LOUIS *puts his head in his hands, inadvertently touching his cut forehead.*)

LOUIS: Ow FUCK! (*He stands slowly, looks towards where* BELIZE *exited.*) Smell what? (*He looks both ways to be sure no one is watching, then inhales deeply, and is surprised.*) Huh. Snow.

SCENE III

Same day. HARPER *in a very white, cold place, with a brilliant blue sky above; a delicate snowfall. She is dressed in a beautiful snow-suit. The sound of the sea, faint.*

HARPER: Snow! Ice! Mountains of ice! Where am I? I . . . feel better, I do, I . . . feel better. There are ice crystals in my lungs, wonderful and sharp. And the snow smells like cold, crushed peaches. And there's something . . . some current of blood in the wind, how strange, it has that iron taste. 5

MR. LIES: Ozone.

HARPER: Ozone! Wow! Where am I?

MR. LIES: The Kingdom of Ice, the bottommost part of the world.

HARPER: (*Looking around, then realizing.*) Antarctica. This is 10 Antarctica!

MR. LIES: Cold shelter for the shattered. No sorrow here, tears freeze.

HARPER: Antarctica, Antarctica, oh boy oh boy, LOOK at this, I. . . . Wow, I must've really snapped the tether, huh? 15

MR. LIES: Apparently . . .

HARPER: That's great. I want to stay here forever. Set up camp. Build things. Build a city, an enormous city made up of frontier forts, dark wood and green roofs and high gates made of pointed logs and bonfires burning on every street corner. I 20 should build by a river. Where are the forests?

MR. LIES: No timber here. Too cold. Ice, no trees.

HARPER: Oh details! I'm sick of details! I'll plant them and grow them. I'll live off caribou fat, I'll melt it over the bon-fires and drink it from long, curved goat-horn cups. It'll be great. 25 I want to make a new world here. So that I never have to go home again.

MR. LIES: As long as it lasts. Ice has a way of melting . . .

HARPER: No. Forever. I can have anything I want here—maybe even companionship, someone who has . . . desire for me. You, 30 maybe.

MR. LIES: It's against the by-laws of the International Order of Travel Agents to get involved with clients. Rules are rules. Anyway, I'm not the one you really want.

35 HARPER: There isn't anyone . . . maybe an Eskimo. Who could
ice-fish for food. And help me build a nest for when the baby
comes.

MR. LIES: There are no Eskimo in Antarctica. And you're not
really pregnant. You made that up.

40 HARPER: Well all of this is made up. So if the snow feels cold I'm
pregnant. Right? Here, I can be pregnant. And I can have any
kind of a baby I want.

MR. LIES: This is a retreat, a vacuum, its virtue is that it lacks
everything; deep-freeze for feelings. You can be numb and

45 safe here, that's what you came for. Respect the delicate
ecology of your delusions.

HARPER: You mean like no Eskimo in Antarctica.

MR. LIES: Correcto. Ice and snow, no Eskimo. Even hallucinations
have laws.

50 HARPER: Well then who's that?

(*The* ESKIMO *appears.*)

MR. LIES: An Eskimo.

HARPER: An antarctic Eskimo. A fisher of the polar deep.

MR. LIES: There's something wrong with this picture.

(*The* ESKIMO *beckons.*)

HARPER: I'm going to like this place. It's my own National

55 Geo-graphic Special! Oh! Oh! (*She holds her stomach.*) I
think . . . I think I felt her kicking. Maybe I'll give birth to
a baby covered with thick white fur, and that way she won't
be cold. My breasts will be full of hot cocoa so she doesn't
get chilly. And if it gets really cold, she'll have a pouch

60 I can crawl into. Like a marsupial. We'll mend together.
That's what we'll do; we'll mend.

SCENE IV

Same day. An abandoned lot in the South Bronx. A homeless
WOMAN *is standing near an oil drum in which a fire is burning.*
Snowfall. Trash around. HANNAH *enters dragging two heavy*
suitcases.

HANNAH: Excuse me? I said excuse me? Can you tell me where
I am? Is this Brooklyn? Do you know a Pineapple Street? Is
there some sort of bus or train or . . . ?

   I'm lost, I just arrived from Salt Lake. City. Utah? I took

5 the bus that I was told to take and I got off—well it was the
very last stop, so I had to get off, and I *asked* the driver was
this Brooklyn, and he nodded yes but he was from one of
those foreign countries where they think it's good manners
to nod at everything even if you have no idea what it is you're

10 nodding at, and in truth I think he spoke no English at all,
which I think would make him ineligible for employment on
public transportation. The public being English-speaking,
mostly. Do you speak English?

(*The* WOMAN *nods.*)

HANNAH: I was supposed to be met at the airport by my son. He

15 didn't show and I don't wait more than three and three-
quarters hours for *anyone*. I should have been patient, I guess,
I. . . . Is this . . .

WOMAN: Bronx.

HANNAH: Is that. . . . The *Bronx*? Well how in the name of Heaven
did I get to the Bronx when the bus driver said . . . 20

WOMAN: (*Talking to herself.*) Slurp slurp slurp will you STOP
that disgusting slurping! YOU DISGUSTING SLURPING
FEEDING ANIMAL! Feeding yourself, just feeding yourself,
what would it matter, to you or to ANYONE, if you just
stopped. Feeding. And DIED? 25

(*Pause.*)

HANNAH: Can you just tell me where I . . .

WOMAN: Why was the Kosciusko Bridge named after a Polack?

HANNAH: I don't know what you're . . .

WOMAN: That was a joke.

HANNAH: Well what's the punchline? 30

WOMAN: I don't know.

HANNAH: (*Looking around desperately.*) Oh for pete's sake, is
there anyone else who . . .

WOMAN: (*Again, to herself.*) Stand further off you fat loathsome
whore, you can't have any more of this soup, slurp slurp slurp 35
you animal, and the—I know you'll just go pee it all away and
where will you do that? Behind what bush? It's FUCKING
COLD out here and I . . .

   Oh that's right, because it was supposed to have been a
tunnel! 40

   That's not very funny.

   Have you read the prophecies of Nostradamus?

HANNAH: Who?

WOMAN: Some guy I went out with once somewhere,
Nostradamus. Prophet, outcast, eyes like. . . . Scary shit, he . . . 45

HANNAH: Shut up. Please. Now I want you to stop jabbering
for a minute and pull your wits together and tell me how
to get to Brooklyn. Because you know! And you are going
to tell me! Because there is no one else around to tell me
and I am wet and cold and I am very angry! So I am sorry 50
you're psychotic but just make the effort—take a deep
breath—DO IT!

(HANNAH *and* WOMAN *breathe together.*)

HANNAH: That's good. Now exhale.

(*They do.*)

HANNAH: Good. Now how do I get to Brooklyn?

WOMAN: Don't know. Never been. Sorry. Want some soup? 55

HANNAH: Manhattan? Maybe you know . . . I don't suppose you
know the location of the Mormon Visitor's . . .

WOMAN: 65th and Broadway.

HANNAH: How do you . . .

WOMAN: Go there all the time. Free movies. Boring, but you can 60
stay all day.

HANNAH: Well. . . . So how do I . . .

WOMAN: Take the D Train. Next block make a right.

HANNAH: Thank you.

WOMAN: Oh yeah. In the new century I think we will all be 65
insane.

SCENE V

Same day. JOE *and* ROY *in the study of* ROY's *brownstone.* ROY *is*
wearing an elegant bathrobe. He has made a considerable effort to
look well. He isn't well, and he hasn't succeeded much in looking it.

JOE: I can't. The answer's no. I'm sorry.

ROY: Oh, well, apologies . . .

I can't see that there's anyone asking for apologies.

(*Pause.*)

JOE: I'm sorry, Roy.

5   ROY: Oh, well, apologies.

JOE: My wife is missing, Roy. My mother's coming from Salt Lake to . . . to help look, I guess. I'm supposed to be at the airport now, picking her up but. . . . I just spent two days in a hospital, Roy, with a bleeding ulcer, I was spitting up

10   blood.

ROY: Blood, huh? Look, I'm very busy here and . . .

JOE: It's just a job.

ROY: A job? A *job*? *Washington!* Dumb Utah Mormon hick shit!

15   JOE: Roy . . .

ROY: *WASHINGTON!* When Washington called me I was younger than you, you think I said "Aw fuck no I can't go I got two fingers up my asshole and a little moral nosebleed to boot!" When Washington calls you my pretty young

20   punk friend you go or you can go fuck yourself sideways 'cause the train has pulled out of the station, and you are *out,* nowhere, out in the cold. Fuck you, Mary Jane, get outta here.

JOE: Just let me . . .

25   ROY: Explain? Ephemera. You broke my heart. Explain that. Explain that.

JOE: I love you. Roy.

There's so much that I want, to be . . . what you see in me, I want to be a participant in the world, in your world,

30   Roy, I want to be capable of that, I've tried, really I have but . . . I can't do this. Not because I don't believe in you, but because I believe in you so much, in what you stand for, at heart, the order, the decency. I would give anything to protect you, but. . . . There are laws I can't break. It's too

35   ingrained. It's not me. There's enough damage I've already done.

Maybe you were right, maybe I'm dead.

ROY: You're not dead, boy, you're a sissy.

You love me; that's moving, I'm moved. It's nice to be

40   loved. I warned you about her, didn't I, Joe? But you don't listen to me, why, because you say Roy is smart and Roy's a friend but Roy . . . well, he isn't nice, and you wanna be nice. Right? A nice, nice man!

(*Little pause.*)

You know what my greatest accomplishment was, Joe, in my

45   life, what I am able to look back on and be proudest of? And I have helped make Presidents and unmake them and mayors and more goddam judges than anyone in NYC ever—AND several million dollars, tax-free—and what do you think means the most to me?

50   You ever hear of Ethel Rosenberg? Huh, Joe, huh?

JOE: Well, yeah, I guess I. . . . Yes.

ROY: Yes. Yes. You have heard of Ethel Rosenberg. Yes. Maybe you even read about her in the history books.

If it wasn't for me, Joe, Ethel Rosenberg would be

55   alive today, writing some personal-advice column for

Ms. magazine. She isn't. Because during the trial, Joe, I was on the phone every day, talking with the judge . . .

JOE: Roy . . .

ROY: Every day, doing what I do best, talking on the telephone, making sure that timid Yid nebbish on the bench did his   60 duty to America, to history. That sweet unprepossessing woman, two kids, boo-hoo-hoo, reminded us all of our little Jewish mamas—she came this close to getting life; I pleaded till I wept to put her in the chair. Me. I did that. I would have fucking pulled the switch if they'd have let me.   65 Why? Because I fucking hate traitors. Because I fucking hate communists. Was it legal? Fuck legal. Am I a nice man? Fuck nice. They say terrible things about me in the *Nation*. Fuck the *Nation*. You want to be Nice, or you want to be Effective? Make the law, or subject to it. Choose. Your   70 wife chose. A week from today, she'll be back. SHE knows how to get what SHE wants. Maybe I ought to send *her* to Washington.

JOE: I don't believe you.

ROY: Gospel.   75

JOE: You can't possibly mean what you're saying.

Roy, you were the Assistant United States Attorney on the Rosenberg case, ex-parte communication with the judge during the trial would be . . . censurable, at least, probably conspiracy and . . . in a case that resulted in   80 execution, it's . . .

ROY: What? Murder?

JOE: You're not well is all.

ROY: What do you mean, not well? Who's not well?

(*Pause.*)

JOE: You said . . .   85

ROY: No I didn't. I said what?

JOE: Roy, you have cancer.

ROY: No I don't.

(*Pause.*)

JOE: You told me you were dying.

ROY: What the fuck are you talking about, Joe? I never said that.   90 I'm in perfect health. There's not a goddam thing wrong with me.

(*He smiles.*)

Shake?

(JOE *hesitates. He holds out his hand to* ROY. ROY *pulls* JOE *into a close, strong clinch.*)

ROY: (*More to himself than to* JOE.) It's OK that you hurt me because I love you, baby Joe. That's why I'm so rough on   95 you.

(ROY *releases* JOE. JOE *backs away a step or two.*)

ROY: Prodigal son. The world will wipe its dirty hands all over you.

JOE: It already has, Roy.

ROY: Now go.   100

(ROY *shoves* JOE *hard.* JOE *turns to leave.* ROY *stops him, turns him around.*)

ROY: (*Smoothing* JOE's *lapels, tenderly.*) I'll always be here, waiting for you . . .

(*Then again, with sudden violence, he pulls* JOE *close, violently.*)

What did you want from me, what was all this, what do you want, treacherous ungrateful little . . .

(JOE, *very close to belting* ROY, *grabs him by the front of his robe, and propels him across the length of the room. He holds* ROY *at arm's length, the other arm ready to hit.*)

105   ROY: (*Laughing softly, almost pleading to be hit.*) Transgress a little, Joseph.

(JOE *releases* ROY.)

ROY: There are so many laws; find one you can break.

(JOE *hesitates, then leaves, backing out. When* JOE *has gone,* ROY *doubles over in great pain, which he's been hiding throughout the scene with* JOE.)

ROY: Ah, Christ . . .
        Andy! Andy! Get in here! Andy!

(*The door opens, but it isn't* ANDY. *A small Jewish Woman dressed modestly in a fifties hat and coat stands in the doorway. The room darkens.*)

110   ROY: Who the fuck are you? The new nurse?

(*The figure in the doorway says nothing. She stares at* ROY. *A pause.* ROY *looks at her carefully, gets up, crosses to her. He crosses back to the chair, sits heavily.*)

ROY: Aw, fuck. Ethel.
ETHEL ROSENBERG: (*Her manner is friendly, her voice is ice-cold.*) You don't look good, Roy.
ROY: Well, Ethel. I don't feel good.
115   ETHEL ROSENBERG: But you lost a lot of weight. That suits you. You were heavy back then. Zaftig, mit hips.
ROY: I haven't been that heavy since 1960. We were all heavier back then, before the body thing started. Now I look like a skeleton. They stare.
120   ETHEL ROSENBERG: The shit's really hit the fan, huh, Roy?

(*Little pause.* ROY *nods.*)

ETHEL ROSENBERG: Well the fun's just started.
ROY: What is this, Ethel, Halloween? You trying to scare me?

(ETHEL *says nothing.*)

ROY: Well you're wasting your time! I'm scarier than you any day of the week! So beat it, Ethel! BOOO! BETTER DEAD
125   THAN RED! Somebody trying to shake me up? HAH HAH! From the throne of God in heaven to the belly of hell, you can all fuck yourselves and then go jump in the lake because

I'M NOT AFRAID OF YOU OR DEATH OR HELL OR ANYTHING!
ETHEL ROSENBERG: Be seeing you soon, Roy. Julius sends his   130
regards.
ROY: Yeah, well send this to Julius!

(*He flips the bird in her direction, stands and moves towards her. Half-way across the room he slumps to the floor, breathing laboriously, in pain.*)

ETHEL ROSENBERG: You're a very sick man, Roy.
ROY: Oh God . . . ANDY!
ETHEL ROSENBERG: Hmmm. He doesn't hear you, I guess. We   135
should call the ambulance.

(*She goes to the phone.*)

Hah! Buttons! Such things they got now.
    What do I dial, Roy?

(*Pause.* ROY *looks at her, then:*)

ROY: 911.
ETHEL ROSENBERG: (*Dials the phone.*) It sings!   140
        (*Imitating dial tones.*) La la la . . .
        Huh.
        Yes, you should please send an ambulance to the home of
Mister Roy Cohn, the famous lawyer.
        What's the address, Roy?   145
ROY: (*A beat, then.*) 244 East 87th.
ETHEL ROSENBERG: 244 East 87th Street. No apartment number,
he's got the whole building.
        My name? (*A beat.*) Ethel Greenglass Rosenberg.
        (*Small smile.*) Me? No I'm not related to Mr. Cohn. An old   150
friend.

(*She hangs up.*)

They said a minute.
ROY: I have all the time in the world.
ETHEL ROSENBERG: You're immortal.
ROY: I'm immortal. Ethel. (*He forces himself to stand.*)   155
        I have *forced* my way into history. I ain't never gonna die.
ETHEL ROSENBERG: (*A little laugh, then.*) History is about to crack
wide open. Millennium approaches.

SCENE VI

Late that night. PRIOR's *bedroom.* PRIOR 1 *watching* PRIOR *in bed, who is staring back at him, terrified. Tonight* PRIOR 1 *is dressed in weird alchemical robes and hat over his historical clothing and he carries a long palm-leaf bundle.*

PRIOR 1: Tonight's the night! Aren't you excited? Tonight she
arrives! Right through the roof! Ha-adam, Ha-gadol . . .
PRIOR 2: (*Appearing, similarly attired.*) Lumen! Phosphor! Fluor!
Candle! An unending billowing of scarlet and . . .
PRIOR: Look. Garlic. A mirror. Holy water. A crucifix. FUCK   5
OFF! Get the fuck out of my room! GO!
PRIOR 1: (*To* PRIOR 2.) Hard as a hickory knob, I'll bet.
PRIOR 2: We all tumesce when they approach. We wax full, like
moons.

10 PRIOR 1: Dance.
  PRIOR: Dance?
  PRIOR 1: Stand up, dammit, give us your hands, dance!
  PRIOR 2: Listen . . .

(*A lone oboe begins to play a little dance tune.*)

  PRIOR 2: Delightful sound. Care to dance?
15 PRIOR: Please leave me alone, please just let me sleep . . .
  PRIOR 2: Ah, he wants someone familiar. A partner who knows
      his steps. (*To* PRIOR.) Close your eyes. Imagine . . .
  PRIOR: I don't . . .
  PRIOR 2: Hush. Close your eyes.

(PRIOR *does.*)

20 PRIOR 2: Now open them.

(PRIOR *does.* LOUIS *appears. He looks gorgeous. The music builds
gradually into a full-blooded, romantic dance tune.*)

  PRIOR: Lou.
  LOUIS: Dance with me.
  PRIOR: I can't, my leg, it hurts at night . . .
      Are you . . . a ghost, Lou?
25 LOUIS: No. Just spectral. Lost to myself. Sitting all day on cold
      park benches. Wishing I could be with you. Dance with me,
      babe . . .

(PRIOR *stands up. The leg stops hurting. They begin to dance. The
music is beautiful.*)

  PRIOR 1: (*To* PRIOR 2.) Hah. Now I see why he's got no children.
      He's a sodomite.
30 PRIOR 2: Oh be quiet, you medieval gnome, and let them
      dance.
  PRIOR 1: I'm not interfering, I've done my bit. Hooray, hooray,
      the messenger's come, now I'm blowing off. I don't like it
      here.

(PRIOR 1 *vanishes.*)

35 PRIOR 2: The twentieth century. Oh dear, the world has gotten so
      terribly, terribly old.

(PRIOR 2 *vanishes.* LOUIS *and* PRIOR *waltz happily. Lights fade
back to normal.* LOUIS *vanishes.*)

(PRIOR *dances alone.*)

(*Then suddenly, the sound of wings fills the room.*)

SCENE VII

Split scene: PRIOR *alone in his apartment;* LOUIS *alone in the park.*

Again, a sound of beating wings.

  PRIOR: Oh don't come in here don't come in . . . LOUIS!! No. My
      name is Prior Walter, I am . . . the scion of an ancient line,
      I am . . . abandoned I . . . no, my name is . . . is . . . Prior and
      I live . . . *here and now,* and . . . in the dark, in the dark, the

Recording Angel opens its hundred eyes and snaps the spine 5
      of the Book of Life and . . . hush! Hush!
      I'm talking nonsense, I . . .
      No more mad scene, hush, hush . . .

(LOUIS *in the park on a bench.* JOE *approaches, stands at a distance. They stare at each other, then* LOUIS *turns away.*)

  LOUIS: Do you know the story of Lazarus?
  JOE: Lazarus? 10
  LOUIS: Lazarus. I can't remember what happens, exactly.
  JOE: I don't. . . . Well, he was dead, Lazarus, and Jesus breathed
      life into him. He brought him back from death.
  LOUIS: Come here often?
  JOE: No. Yes. Yes. 15
  LOUIS: Back from the dead. You believe that really happened?
  JOE: I don't know anymore what I believe.
  LOUIS: This is quite a coincidence. Us meeting.
  JOE: I followed you.
      From work. I . . . followed you here. 20

(*Pause.*)

  LOUIS: You followed me.
      You probably saw me that day in the washroom and
      thought: there's a sweet guy, sensitive, cries for friends in
      trouble.
  JOE: Yes. 25
  LOUIS: You thought maybe I'll cry for you.
  JOE: Yes.
  LOUIS: Well I fooled you. Crocodile tears. Nothing . . . (*He touches
      his heart, shrugs.*)

(JOE *reaches tentatively to touch* LOUIS's *face.*)

  LOUIS: (*Pulling back.*) What are you doing? Don't do that. 30
  JOE: (*Withdrawing his hand.*) Sorry. I'm sorry.
  LOUIS: I'm . . . just not . . . I think, if you touch me, your hand
      might fall off or something. Worse things have happened to
      people who have touched me.
  JOE: Please. 35
      Oh, boy . . .
      Can I . . .
      I . . . want . . . to touch you. Can I please just touch
      you . . . um, here?

(*He puts his hand on one side of* LOUIS's *face. He holds it there.*)

      I'm going to hell for doing this. 40
  LOUIS: Big deal. You think it could be any worse than New York
      City?
      (*He puts his hand on* JOE's *hand. He takes* JOE's *hand away
      from his face, holds it for a moment, then.*) Come on.
  JOE: Where? 45
  LOUIS: Home. With me.
  JOE: This makes no sense. I mean I don't know you.
  LOUIS: Likewise.
  JOE: And what you do know about me you don't like.
  LOUIS: The Republican stuff? 50
  JOE: Yeah, well for starters.
  LOUIS: I don't not like that. I hate that.
  JOE: So why on earth should we . . .

(LOUIS *goes to* JOE *and kisses him.*)

LOUIS: Strange bedfellows. I don't know. I never made it with one
55   of the damned before.
        I would really rather not have to spend tonight alone.
JOE: I'm a pretty terrible person, Louis.
LOUIS: Lou.
JOE: No, I really really am. I don't think I deserve being loved.
60 LOUIS: There? See? We already have a lot in common.

(LOUIS *stands, begins to walk away. He turns, looks back at* JOE.
JOE *follows. They exit.*)

(PRIOR *listens. At first no sound, then once again, the sound of
beating wings, frighteningly near.*)

PRIOR: That sound, that sound, it. . . . What is that, like birds
    or something, like a *really* big bird, I'm frightened, I . . . no,
    no fear, find the anger, find the . . . anger, my blood is
    clean, my brain is fine, I can handle pressure, I am a gay
65   man and I am used to pressure, to trouble, I am tough and
    strong and. . . . Oh. Oh my goodness. I . . . (*He is washed
    over by an intense sexual feeling.*) Ooohhhh. . . . I'm hot,
    I'm . . . so . . . aw Jeez what is going on here I . . . must have
    a fever I . . .

(*The bedside lamp flickers wildly as the bed begins to roll forward
and back. There is a deep bass creaking and groaning from the
bedroom ceiling, like the timbers of a ship under immense stress,
and from above a fine rain of plaster dust.*)

PRIOR: OH!   70
    PLEASE, OH PLEASE! Something's coming in here, I'm
    scared, I don't like this at all, something's approaching and
    I. . . . OH!

(*There is a great blaze of triumphal music, heralding. The light
turns an extraordinary harsh, cold, pale blue, then a rich, brilliant
warm golden color, then a hot, bilious green, and then finally a
spectacular royal purple. Then silence.*)

PRIOR: (*An awestruck whisper.*) God almighty . . .
    Very Steven Spielberg.   75

(*A sound, like a plummeting meteor, tears down from very, very
far above the earth, hurtling at an incredible velocity towards
the bedroom; the light seems to be sucked out of the room as the
projectile approaches; as the room reaches darkness, we hear
a terrifying CRASH as something immense strikes earth; the
whole building shudders and a part of the bedroom ceiling, lots of
plaster and lathe and wiring, crashes to the floor. And then in a
shower of unearthly white light, spreading great opalescent gray-
silver wings, the* ANGEL *descends into the room and floats above
the bed.*)

ANGEL: Greetings, Prophet;
    The Great Work begins:
    The Messenger has arrived.

(*Blackout.*)

Anna Deavere Smith

nna Deavere Smith (b. 1950) is one of the most prominent African American women working in the U.S. theater. The eldest of five children, Smith was born and raised in Baltimore; she graduated from Beaver College in 1971 and then took an M.F.A. in acting from the American Conservatory Theatre in 1976. Throughout the 1970s and 1980s, Smith pursued a dual career as a teacher of acting and as a performer. She has taught at Carnegie-Mellon University, Yale University, New York University, the American Conservatory Theatre, the University of Southern California, Stanford University, and Harvard University, and currently teaches at New York University. Her many stage, television, and film roles include parts in *Mother Courage* (1980) and *Tartuffe* (1983), in "All My Children" (1983), and in the films *Soup for One* (1982), *Dave* (1993), and *Philadelphia* (1993). She appeared on television in "The West Wing" (2000).

As a playwright and performer, Smith is best known for a series of one-woman shows that form part of an extended series of performances collectively entitled *On the Road: A Search for American Character.* Smith began devising *On the Road* in the early 1980s. The project was inspired by acting exercises she devised for her cast while directing Adrienne Kennedy's play, *A Movie Star Has to Star in Black and White.* To wean her students away from a strictly psychological approach to acting, in which the actor's focus is on the role-as-self, Smith had them watch and then reenact celebrity television talk-show interviews as a way of building a bridge to a "character" as something external, accessible through non-psychological means. Working with actual interview material gave Smith the working method for much of her subsequent work. For the various *On the Road* performances, Smith interviews a range of subjects who are part of a given event or situation she wants to explore. In fact, she is often invited to colleges and other organizations to use performance to help explore race, gender, and identity issues. After conducting the interviews, Smith devises a performance, using minimal props and costumes, in which she interweaves sections from the interviews, performing all of the roles herself. In 1987, she was invited by San Francisco's Eureka Theater to devise a show concerning racial attitudes in that city; it was performed under the title *From the Outside Looking In.* She also performed a piece on women in San Francisco's theater community, at the invitation of the Bay Area Women in Theater. In 1988 she was invited to conduct an oral history of the Women and Theater Program of the Association for Theatre in Higher Education; *Chlorophyll Postmodernism and the Mother Goddess/A Conversation* was performed at the Women and Theater conference in San Diego that year. She was asked to Princeton University in 1989 to conduct interviews on gender politics among students, faculty, and staff, and performed *Gender Bending;* she has conducted similar workshops and performances for the Five Colleges (Amherst, Hampshire, Mount Holyoke, and Smith colleges, and the University of Massachusetts) in Massachusetts and for the University of Pennsylvania.

Smith is now known, though, for two performance works that confront recent urban uprisings: *Fires in the Mirror: Crown Heights, Brooklyn and Other Identities* (1992), and *Twilight: Los Angeles 1992* (1993), which concerns the unrest in Los Angeles following the acquittal of four L.A. police officers who were tried for beating an African American man, Rodney King. *Fires in the Mirror,* which earned Smith a 1992 Obie Special Citation, was shown on the Public Broadcasting Service in 1993. Both *Fires in the Mirror* and *Twilight* have been produced for television and are available from PBS. Smith's *House Arrest* (2000) used similar techniques to explore the relationship between the press and the presidency; her work on the play is documented in *Talk to Me: Travels in Media and Politics* (2000). She has recently published a practical memoir, *Letters to a Young Artist* (2006), and *Let Me Down Easy* premiered in 2009.

Fires in the Mirror

Fires in the Mirror concerns racial and ethnic rioting that took place in the Crown Heights neighborhood of Brooklyn, New York, in August 1991. The events that sparked three nights of rioting began on the evening of Monday, August 19, and remain in some dispute. Menachem Schneerson, the Grand Rebbe of the Lubavitcher sect of Hasidic Jews, was returning from his weekly visit to a cemetery; his car was accompanied by an unmarked police escort car and by a third car, driven by Yosef Lifsh and carrying two other Hasidic passengers. At one point Lifsh's car fell behind; apparently accelerating to catch up with the others, Lifsh's car ran a red light, glanced off another car, jumped the curb, and pinned two small African American children to a window grating. Gavin Cato was killed; his cousin Angela Cato was seriously injured.

Crown Heights has a history of racial and ethnic tension, and the accident quickly drew a large and volatile crowd. Within minutes, two ambulances arrived at the scene. The first ambulance to arrive was from a private Hasidic ambulance service; police ordered it to attend to the three Jewish men in the car and to leave the scene immediately. The police later claimed that the city ambulance was also at the scene and that they acted to protect the three men from the crowd and to reduce further confrontation. A city ambulance did attend to the children, but within minutes word that medical attention had been given first to the three white, Jewish men rather than to the two black children ignited a street riot. Three hours later, at 11:30 P.M., a group of black youths a few blocks from the accident surrounded a visiting Australian Hasidic scholar, Yankel Rosenbaum, and stabbed him to death. Lemrick Nelson, Jr., was arrested and held shortly thereafter.

Over the next three days and nights both African American and Jewish groups protested the city's handling of the incident and became involved in a civil uprising. Crown Heights became the scene not only of protests and protest marches, but of widespread arson, looting,

Anna Deavere Smith as Rabbi Shea Hecht in *Fires in the Mirror: Crown Heights, Brooklyn and Other Identities.*

Martha Swope

and rioting. Police, journalists, and citizens were beaten. Although the rioting broke by the end of the week, several events kept Crown Heights in the public eye: the funerals of Gavin Cato and Yankel Rosenbaum, protest marches led by the Reverend Al Sharpton and Alton Maddox, Yosef Lifsh's sudden trip to Israel, the unsuccessful effort to charge Lifsh with vehicular negligence and arrest him. Indeed, throughout the remainder of 1991 and 1992, Crown Heights remained a flashpoint: in September, the Reverend Al Sharpton flew to Israel to inform Lifsh that the Cato family had brought a civil suit against him; throughout 1992, Lubavitchers demonstrated and ran newspaper ads calling for further police investigation and judicial action in connection with Rosenbaum's death, alleging that the police had handled the riots and the subsequent investigation in a biased and unfair manner; in October 1992, Lemrick Nelson, Jr., was acquitted, provoking a Hasidic rally in protest.

In part, the Crown Heights riots reflected the tensions of an unusually diverse community. The Lubavitch is an Orthodox Jewish sect whose strict religious beliefs make them a close and easily identifiable community in the Crown Heights neighborhood. Many of the black residents of Crown Heights have recently emigrated from the Caribbean and are working to make a place for themselves in the United States. Both groups face overt and subtle discrimination in a number of ways. Moreover, before the riots, Crown Heights had been the scene of several racial incidents. In 1986, a group of young black men had beaten a Hasidic man to death in a subway station; in April 1987, four hundred African Americans marched to protest city favoritism (streets in the neighborhood are regularly closed to traffic during Jewish holidays) and harassment by a Hasidic neighborhood surveillance patrol; in 1989, a crowd of Hasidim surrounded and beat a black teenager they accused of slashing a Hasidic woman and her son.

Rather than providing a "history" of these events, Smith's *Fires in the Mirror* refracts the events through a series of monologues, some by participants—Gavin Cato's father, the Reverend Al Sharpton, Yankel Rosenbaum's brother Norman—and some by more distant observers, such as the playwrights Ntozake Shange and George C. Wolfe (who subsequently directed the television version of *Fires in the Mirror* for PBS). Performing the words of her subjects, Smith carefully weaves an elaborate texture of commentary about race and ethnicity in the United States. Beginning with topics like "identity," "hair," "race," "rhythm," Smith uses the characters' voices to frame the larger issues and attitudes surrounding black-white conflict in the United States and then moves more insistently into the specifics of the Crown Heights uprising. As with some other postmodern works—Norman Mailer's novel *The Executioner's Song,* Don De Lillo's *Libra,* or the Oliver Stone film *JFK*—*Fires in the Mirror* insistently blurs the boundary between the events and their retelling, presenting a kaleidoscopic re-presentation of events rather than a summary that pretends to a specious objectivity. One of the most striking features of *Fires in the Mirror* in performance is the way that Smith plays both white and black characters, men and women, Jews and non-Jews, the powerful and the oppressed, the famous and the unknown. And although Smith carefully observes the details of behavior, dress, and gesture with which her "characters" speak, her performance here is not a kind of mimicry. For instead of effacing identity, Smith's performance shows the challenges of negotiating between "identities." Smith's performance shows the difficulty of grappling with an *other's* identity, an *other's* attitudes, an *other's* orientation to the world.

Fires in the Mirror

CROWN HEIGHTS, BROOKLYN AND OTHER IDENTITIES

Anna Deavere Smith

THIS BOOK IS DEDICATED TO THE RESIDENTS OF
CROWN HEIGHTS, BROOKLYN, AND IN THE MEMORY
OF GAVIN CATO AND YANKEL ROSENBAUM

CHARACTERS

NTOZAKE SHANGE, *playwright, poet, novelist*

ANONYMOUS LUBAVITCHER WOMAN, *preschool teacher*

GEORGE C. WOLFE, *playwright, director, producing director of the New York Shakespeare Festival*

AARON M. BERNSTEIN, *physicist at Massachusetts Institute of Technology*

ANONYMOUS GIRL, *junior high school black girl of Haitian descent. Lives in Brooklyn near Crown Heights*

REVEREND AL SHARPTON, *well-known New York activist, minister*

RIVKAH SIEGAL, *Lubavitcher woman, graphic designer*

ANGELA DAVIS, *author, orator, activist, scholar. Professor in the History of Consciousness Department at the University of California, Santa Cruz*

MONIQUE "BIG MO" MATTHEWS, *Los Angeles rapper*

LEONARD JEFFRIES, *professor of African American Studies at City University of New York, former head of the department*

LETTY COTTIN POGREBIN, *author* Deborah, Golda, and Me. *One of the founding editors of Ms magazine*

CONRAD MOHAMMED, *New York minister for the Honorable Louis Farrakhan*

ROBERT SHERMAN, *director, Mayor of the City of New York's Increase the Peace Corps*

RABBI JOSEPH SPIELMAN, *spokesperson in the Lubavitcher community*

THE REVEREND CANON DOCTOR HERON SAM, *pastor, St. Mark's, Crown Heights Church*

ANONYMOUS YOUNG MAN #1, *Crown Heights resident*

MICHAEL S. MILLER, *executive director at the Jewish Community Relations Council*

HENRY RICE, *Crown Heights resident*

NORMAN ROSENBAUM, *brother of Yankel Rosenbaum. A barrister from Australia*

ANONYMOUS YOUNG MAN #2, *African American young man, late teens, early twenties. Resident of Crown Heights*

SONNY CARSON, *activist*

RABBI SHEA HECHT, *Lubavitcher rabbi, spokesperson*

RICHARD GREEN, *director, Crown Heights Youth Collective Codirector Project CURE, a Black-Hasidic basketball team that developed after the riots*

ROSLYN MALAMUD, *Lubavitcher resident of Crown Heights*

REUVEN OSTROV, *Lubavitcher male: at the time of the riot, was seventeen years old. Worked as assistant chaplain at Kings County Hospital*

CARMEL CATO, *father of Gavin Cato, Crown Heights resident, originally from Guyana*

IDENTITY

Ntozake Shange

THE DESERT

This interview was done on the phone at about 4:00 P.M. Philadelphia time. The only cue NTOZAKE gave about her physical appearance was that she took one earring off to talk on the phone. On stage we placed her upstage center in an arm chair, smoking. Then we placed her standing, downstage.

Hummmm.
Identity—
it, is, uh . . . in a way it's, um . . . it's sort of, it's uh . . .
it's a psychic sense of place
5   it's a way of knowing I'm not a rock or that tree?
I'm this other living creature over here?
And it's a way of knowing that no matter where I put
    myself
that I am not necessarily
what's around me.
10   I am part of my surroundings
and I become separate from them
and it's being able to make those differentiations clearly

that lets us have an identity
and what's inside our identity
is everything that's ever happened to us.   15
Everything that's ever happened
to us as well as our responses to it
'cause we might be alone in a trance state,
someplace like the desert
and we begin to feel as though   20
we are part of the desert—
which we are right at that minute—
but we are not the desert,
uh . . .
we are part of the desert,   25
and when we go home
we take with us that part of the desert that the desert
    gave us,
but we're still not the desert.
It's an important differentiation to make because you
    don't know
what you're giving if you don't know what you have   30
    and you don't
know what you're taking if you don't know what's yours
    and what's
somebody else's.

Anonymous Lubavitcher Woman

STATIC

This interview was actually done on the phone. Based on what she told me she was doing, and on the three visits I had made to her home for other interviews, I devised this physical scene. A LUBAVITCHER WOMAN, *in a wig, and loose-fitting clothes. She is in her mid-thirties. She is folding clothes. There are several children around. Three boys of different ages are lying together on the couch. The oldest is reading to the younger two. A teen-age girl with long hair, a button-down-collar shirt, and skirt is sweeping the floor.*

Well,
it was um,
35 getting toward the end of Shabbas,
like around five in the afternoon,
and it was summertime
and sunset isn't until about eight, nine o'clock,
so there were still quite a few hours left to go
40 and my baby had been playing with the knobs on the stereo
          system
then all of a sudden he pushed the button—
the *on* button—
and all of a sudden came blaring out,
at full volume,
45 sort of like a half station
of polka music.
But just like with the static,
it was blaring, blaring
and we can't turn off,
50 we can't turn off electrical,
you know electricity, on Shabbas.
So um,
uh . . .
there was—
55 we just were trying to ignore it,
but a young boy that was visiting us,
he was going nuts already, he said
it was giving him such a headache could we do something
          about it,
couldn't we get a baby
60 to turn it off;
we can't make the baby turn it off but if the baby,
but if a child under three
turns something on or turns something off it's not considered
          against the Torah,
so we put the baby by it and tried to get the baby to turn
          it off,
65 he just probably made it worse,
so the guest was so uncomfortable that I said I would go
          outside
and see if I can find someone who's not Jewish and see if they
          would
like to—
see if they could turn it off,
70 so you can have somebody who's not Jewish do a simple
          act like
turning on the light or turning off the light,
and I hope I have the law correct,
but you can't ask them to do it directly.
If they wanna do it of their own free will—
75 and hopefully they would get some benefit from it too,

so I went outside
and I saw
a little
boy in the neighborhood
who I didn't know and didn't know me—   80
not Jewish, he was black and he wasn't wearing a yarmulke
          because you can't—
so I went up to him and I said to him
that my radio is on really loud and I can't turn it off,
could he help me,
so he looked at me a little crazy like,   85
Well?
And I said I don't know what to do,
so he said okay,
so he followed me into the house
and he hears this music on so loud   90
and so unpleasant
and so
he goes over to the
stereo
and he says, "You see this little button here   95
that says on and off?
Push that in
and that turns it off."
And I just sort of stood there looking kind of dumb
and then he went and pushed it,   100
and we laughed that he probably thought:
And people say Jewish people are really smart and they
          don't know
how to turn off their radios.

George C. Wolfe

101 DALMATIANS

The Mondrian Hotel in Los Angeles. Morning, Sunny. A very nice room. GEORGE *is wearing denim jeans, a light blue denim shirt, and white leather tennis shoes. His hair is in a ponytail. He wears tortoise/wire spectacles. He is drinking tea with milk. The tea is served on a tray, the cups and teapot are delicate porcelain.* GEORGE *is sitting on a sofa, with his feet up on the coffee table.*

I mean I grew up on a black—
a one-block street—   105
that was black.
My grandmother lived on that street
my cousins lived around the corner.
I went to this
Black—Black—   110
private Black grade school
where
I was extraordinary.
Everybody there was extraordinary.
You were told you were extraordinary.   115
It was very clear
that I could not go to see *101 Dalmatians* at the Capital
          Theatre
because it was segregated.
And at the same time
I was treated like I was the most extraordinary creature   120
          that had
been born.

So I'm on my street in my house,
at my school—
and I was very spoiled too—
125 so I was treated like I was this special special creature.
And then I would go beyond a certain point
I was treated like I was insignificant.
Nobody was
hosing me down or calling me nigger.
130 It was just that I was insignificant.

(*Slight pause.*)

You know what I mean so it was very clear of

(*Teacup on saucer strike twice on "very clear."*)

where my extraordinariness lived.
You know what I mean.
That I was extraordinary as long as I was Black.
135 But I am—not—going—to place myself

(*Pause.*)

in relationship to your whiteness.
I will talk about your whiteness if we want to talk
  about that.
But I,
but what,
140 that which,
what I—
what am I saying?
My blackness does not resis—ex—re—
exist in relationship to your whiteness.

(*Pause.*)

145 You know

(*Not really a question, more like a hum.*)

(*Slight pause.*)

it does not exist in relationship to—
it *exists*
it exists.
I come—
150 you know what I mean—
like I said, I, I, I,
I come from—
it's a very com*plex,*
con*fused,*
155 *neu*-rotic,
at times destructive
reality, but it is completely
and totally a reality
contained and, and,
160 and full unto itself.
It's complex.
It's demonic.
It's ridiculous.
It's absurd.

It's evolved.   165
It's all the stuff.
That's the way I grew up.

(*Slight pause.*)

So that *therefore*—
and then you're White—

(*Quick beat.*)

And then there's a point when,   170
and then these two things come into contact.

MIRRORS
Aaron M. Bernstein
MIRRORS AND DISTORTIONS

Evening, Cambridge, Massachusetts. Fall. He is a man in his fifties, wearing a sweater and a shirt with a pen guard. He is seated at a round wooden table with a low-hanging lamp.

Okay, so a mirror is something that reflects light.
It's the simplest instrument to understand,
okay?
So a simple mirror is just a flat   175
reflecting
substance, like,
for example,
it's a piece of glass which is silvered on the back,
okay?   180
Now the notion of distortion also goes back into
  literature,
okay?
I'm trying to remember from art—
You probably know better than I.
You know you have a pretty young woman and she looks 185
  in a mirror
and she's a witch

(*He laughs.*)

because she's evil on the inside.
That's not a real mirror,
as everyone knows—
you see the inner thing.   190
Now that really goes back in literature.
So everyone understood that mirrors don't distort,
so that was a play
not on words
but a concept.   195
But physicists do
talk about distortion.
It's a big
subject, distortions.
I'll give you an example—   200
if you wanna see the
stars
you make a big
reflecting mirror—

205 that's one of the ways—
you make a big telescope
so you can gather in a lot of light
and then it focuses at a point
and then there's always something called the circle of
    confusion.
210 So if ya don't make the thing perfectly spherical or
    perfectly
parabolic
then,
then, uh, if there are errors in the construction
which you can see, it's easy, if it's huge,
215 then you're gonna have a circle of confusion,
you see?
So that's the reason for making the
telescope as large as you can,
because you want that circle
220 to seem smaller,
and you want to easily see errors in the construction.
So, you see, in physics it's very practical—
you wanna look up in the heavens
and see the stars as well as you can
225 without distortion.
If you're counting stars, for example,
and two look like one,
you've blown it.

HAIR
Anonymous Girl

LOOK IN THE MIRROR

Morning. Spring. A teen-age black GIRL *of Haitian descent. She has hair which is straightened, and is wearing a navy blue jumper and a white shirt. She is seated in a stairwell at her junior high school in Brooklyn.*

When I look in the mirror . . .
230 I don't know.
How did I find out I was Black . . .

(*Tongue sound.*)

When I grew up and I look in the mirror and saw I was
    Black.
When I look at my parents,
That's how I knew I was Black.
235 Look at my skin.
You Black?
Black is beautiful.
I don't know.
That's what I always say.
240 I think White is beautiful too.
But I think Black is beautiful too.
In my class nobody is White, everybody's Black,
and some of them is Hispanic.
In my class
245 you can't call any of them Puerto Ricans.
They despise Puerto Ricans, I don't know why.
They think that Puerto Ricans are stuck up and
    everything.

They say, Oh my Gosh my nail broke, look at that cute guy
    and everything.
But they act like that themselves.
They act just like White girls.   250
Black girls is not like that.
Please, you should be in my class.
Like they say that Puerto Ricans act like that
and they don't see that they act like that themselves.
Black girls, they do bite off the Spanish girls,   255
they bite off of your clothes.
You don't know what that means? biting off?
Like biting off somebody's clothes
Like cop, following,
and last year they used to have a lot of girls like that.   260
They come to school with a style, right?
And if they see another girl with that style?
Oh my gosh look at her.
What she think she is,
she tryin' to bite off of me in some way   265
no don't be bitin' off of my sneakers
or like that.
Or doin' a hairstyle
I mean Black people are into hairstyles.
So they come to school, see somebody with a certain   270
    style,
they say uh-huh I'm gonna get me one just like that uh-
    huh,
that's the way Black people are
Yea-ah!
They don't like people doing that to them
and they do that to other people,   275
so the Black girls they won't follow the Spanish girls.
The Spanish girls don't bite off of us.
Some of the Black girls follow them.
But they don't mind
They don't care.   280
They follow each other.
Like there's three girls in my class,
they from the Dominican Republic.
They all stick together like glue.
They all three best friends.   285
They don't follow nobody,
like there's none of them lead or anything.
They don't hang around us either.
They're
by themselves.   290

The Reverend Al Sharpton

ME AND JAMES'S THING

Early afternoon. Fall. A small room that is a part of a suite of of-fices in a building on West Fifty-Seventh Street and Seventh Avenue in New York. A very large man Black man with straightened hair. REVEREND SHARPTON's *hair is in the style of James Brown's hair. He is wearing a suit, colorful tie, and a gold medallion that was given to him by Martin Luther King, Jr.* REVEREND SHARPTON *has a pinky ring, a very resonant voice even in this small room. There is a very built, very tall man who sits behind me during the interview.* REVEREND SHARPTON's *face is much younger, and more innocent than it appears to be in the media. His humor is in his face. He is*

very direct. The interview only lasts fifteen minutes because he had
been called out of a meeting in progress to do the interview.

James Brown raised me.
Uh . . .
I never had a father.
My father left when I was ten.
295 James Brown took me to the beauty parlor one day
and made my hair like his.
And made me promise
to wear it like that
'til I die.
300 It's a personal family thing
between me and James Brown.
I always wanted a father
and he filled that void.
And the strength that he's demonstrated—
305 I don't know anybody that reached his heights,
and then had to go as low as he did and come back.
And I think that if anybody I met in life deserved that
type of
tribute from
somebody
310 that he wanted a kid
to look like him
and be like his son . . .
I just came home from spending a weekend with him
now,
uh, uh,
315 I think James deserved that.
And just like
he was the father I never had,
his kids never even visited him when he went to jail.
So I was like the kid he never had.
320 And if I had to choose between arguing with people
about my
hairstyle
or giving him that one tribute
he axed,
I'd rather give him that tribute
325 because he filled a void for me.
And I really don't give a damn
who doesn't understand it.
The press and everybody do
their thing on that.
330 It's a personal thing between me and James Brown.
And just like
in other communities
people do their cultural thing
with who they like,
335 uh,
there's nothing wrong with me doing
that with James.
It's, it's, *us.*
I mean in the fifties it was a slick.
340 It was acting like White folks.
But today
people don't wear their hair like that.
James and I the only ones out there doing that.
So it's certainlih not
345 a reaction to Whites.
It's me and James's thing.

Rivkah Siegal

WIGS

Early afternoon. Spring. The kitchen of an apartment in Crown
Heights. A very pretty Lubavitcher woman, with clear eyes and
a direct gaze, wearing a wig and a knit sweater, that looks as
though it might be hand knit. A round wooden table. Coffee mug.
Sounds of children playing in the street are outside. A neighbor, a
Lubavitcher woman with light blond hair who no longer wears the
wig, observes the interview at the table.

Your hair—
It only has to be—
there's different,
uhm,   350
customs in different
Hasidic groups.
Lubavitch
the system is
it should be two inches   355
long.
It's—
some groups
have
the custom   360
to shave their
heads.
There's—
the reason is,
when you go to the mikvah   365
you may, maybe,
it's better if it's short
because of what you—
the preparation
that's involved   370
and that
you have to go under the water.
The hair has a tendency to float
and you have to be completely submerged
including your hair.   375
So . . .
And I got married
when I was a little older,
and I really wanted to be married
and I really wanted to, um . . .   380
In some ways I was eager to cover my head.
Now if I had grown up in a Lubavitch household
and then had to cut it,
I don't know what that would be like.
I really don't.   385
But now that I'm wearing the wig,
you see,
with my hair I can keep it very simple
and I can change it all the time.
So with a wig you have to have like five wigs if you want to   390
do that.
But I, uh,
I feel somehow like it's fake,
I feel like it's not me.
I try to be as much myself as I can,
and it just   395
bothers me

that I'm kind of fooling the world.
I used to go to work.
People . . .
400   and I would wear a different wig,
and they'd say I like your new haircut
and I'd say it's not mine!
You know,
and it was very hard for me to say it
405   and
it became very difficult.
I mean, I've gone through a lot with wearing wigs and not wearing
wigs.
It's been a big issue for me.

Angela Davis

ROPES

Morning, Spring, Oakland, California. In reality this interview was done on the phone, with myself and Thulani Davis. Thulani and I were calling from an office at the Public Theatre. We do not know exactly what ANGELA *was doing or wearing. I believe, from things she said, that she was sitting on her deck in her home in Oakland, which overlooks a beautiful panorama of trees.*

410   Race, um—
of course
for many years in the history
of African Americans in this country—
was synonymous with community.
415   As a matter of fact
we were race women and race men.
Billie Holiday for example
called herself a race woman
because she supported the community
420   and as a child growing up in the South
my assumptions were
that if anybody in the race
came under attack
then I had to be there
425   to support that person,
to support the race.
I was saying to my students just the other day,
I said,
if in 1970,
430   when I was
in jail,
someone had told me
that in 1991,
a black man
435   who
said that his, um . . .
hero—

(*Increased volume, speed, and energy.*)

one of his heroes
was Malcolm X—
440   would be nominated to the Supreme Court
I would have celebrated
and I don't think it would have been possible at that
time

to convince me
that I would
be absolutely opposed,   445
a black candidate—
I mean like absolutely—

(*A new attack, more energy.*)

or that if anyone would have told me that
a *woman* . . .
finally be elected to the Supreme Court,   450
it would have been very difficult,
as critical as I am with respect to feminism,
as critical as I have always been with what I used to call,
you know, narrow nationalism?
I don't think   455
it would have been possible to convince me that things would
    have so absolutely
shifted that
someone could have evoked
the specter of lynching
on national television   460
and that specter of lynching would be used to violate our
    history.
And I still feel that we have to point out the racism
    involved
in the razing of a Black man
and a Black woman
in that way.   465
I mean [Ted] Kennedy was sitting right there
and it had never occurred to anyone to bring him up
before
the world,
which is not to say that I don't think it should happen. 470
And it is actually a sign of how we,
in our various oppressed
marginalized communities,
have been able to turn
terrible acts of racism directed against us   475
into victory . . .
And therefore I think
Anita Hill did that,
and so it's very complicated,
but I have no problems aligning myself politically   480
against Clarence Thomas in a real passionate way,
but at the same time I can talk about the racism that led to
    the possibility
of constructing those kinds of hearings
and
the same thing with Mike Tyson.   485
So I guess that would be,
um . . .
the way in which I would begin to look at community,
and would therefore think
that race has become, uh,   490
an increasingly obsolete way
of constructing community
because it is based on unchangeable
immutable biological
facts   495
in a very pseudo-scientific way,
alright?

Now
racism is entirely different
500 because see *racism*,
uh,
actually I think
is
at the origins of this concept of race.
505 It's not—
it's not the other way around,
that there were racists,
and then the racists—
one race came to dominate
510 the others.
As a matter of fact
in order for a European colonialist
to attempt
to conquer the world,
515 to colonize the world,
they had to construct this notion
of,
uh,
the populations of the earth being divided into certain,
520 uh,
firm biological, uh,
communities,
and that's what I think we have to go back and look at.
So when if I use the word race now I put it in quotations.
525 Because if we don't transform
this . . . this intransigent
rigid
notion of race,
we will be caught up in this cycle
530 of genocidal
violence
that, um,
is at the origins of our history.
So I think—
535 and I'm
I'm convinced—and this is what I'm working on in my
      political practice right now—
is that we have to find ways of coming together in a different
      way,
not the old notion of coalition in which we anchor ourselves
      very solidly
in our,
540 um,
communities,
and simply voice
our
solidarity with other people.
545 I'm not suggesting that we do not anchor ourselves in our
      communities;
I feel very anchored in,
um,
my various communities,
but I think that,
550 you know,
to use a metaphor, the rope
attached to that anchor should be long enough to allow us
      to move
into other communities
to understand and learn.

I've been thinking a lot about the need to make more   555
      intimate
these connections and associations and to really take on the
      responsibility
of learning.
So I think that we need to—
in order to find ways of working with
and understanding   560
the vastness
of our many cultural heritages
and ways of coming together without
rendering invisible all of that heterogeneity—
I don't have the answer,   565
you know
I don't know.
What I'm interested in is communities
that are not static,
that   570
can change, that can respond to new historical needs.
So I think it's a very exciting moment.

RHYTHM
Monique "Big Mo" Matthews

RHYTHM AND POETRY

*In reality this interview was done on an afternoon in the spring of
1989, while I was in residence at the University of California, Los
Angeles, as a fellow at the Center for Afro-American Studies. MO
was a student of mine. We were sitting in my office, which was a
narrow office, with sunlight. I performed MO in many shows, and
in the course of performing her, I changed the setting to a performance setting, with microphone. I was inspired by a performance
that I saw of Queen Latifah in San Francisco, and by MO's behavior
in my class, which was performance behavior, to change the setting
to one that was more theatrical, since MO's everyday speech was as
theatrical as Latifah's performance speech. Speaking directly to the
audience, pacing the stage.*

And she say, "This is for the fellas,"
and she took off all her clothes and she had on a leotard
that had all cuts and stuff in it,   575
and she started doin' it on the floor.
They were like
"Go, girl!"
People like, "That look really stink."
But that's what a lot of female rappers do—   580
like to try to get off,
they sell they body or pimp they body
to, um, get play.
And you have people like Latifah who doesn't, you know,
she talks intelligent.   585
You have Lyte who's just hard and people are scared by her
      hardness,
her strength of her words.
She encompasses that whole, New York-street sound.
It's like, you know, she'll like . . .
what's a line?   590
What's a line
like "Paper Thin,"
"IN ONE EAR AND RIGHT OUT THE OTHUH."
It's like,

"I don't care what you have to say,
I'm gittin' done what's gotta be done.
Man can't come across me.
A female she can't stand against me.
I'm just the toughest, I'm just the hardest/You just can't
  come up
against me/if you do you get waxed!"
It's like a lot of my songs,
I don't know if I'm gonna get blacklisted for it.
The image that I want is a strong strong African strong
  Black woman
and I'm not down with what's going on, like Big Daddy Kane
  had a song
out called "Pimpin' Ain't Easy," and he sat there and he talk
  for the
whole song, and I sit there I wanna slap him, I wanna slap
  him so
hard, and he talks about, it's one point he goes, yeah
um,
"Puerto Rican girls Puerto Rican girls call me Papi and
White girls say
even White girls say I'm a hunk!"
I'm like,
"What you mean 'even'?
Oh! Black girls ain't good enough for you huh?"
And one of my songs has a line that's like
"PIMPIN' AIN'T EASY BUT WHORIN' AIN'T PROPER,
  RESPECT AND
CHERISH THE ORIGINAL MOTHER."
And a couple of my friends were like,
"Aww, Mo, you good but I can't listen to you 'cause you be
  Men bashin'."
I say,
"It ain't men bashin', it's female assertin'."
Shit.
I'm tired of it.
I'm tired of my friends just acceptin'
that they just considered to be a ho.
You got a song,
"Everybody's a Hotty."
A "hotty" means you a freak, you a ho,
and it's like Too Short
gets up there and he goes,
"B I AYYYYYYYYYYYYE."
Like he stretches "bitch" out for as long as possible,
like you just a ho and you can't be saved,
and 2 Live Crew. . . . "we want some pussy," and the girls!
  "La le la le la le la,"
it's like my friends say,
"Mo, if you so bad how come you don't never say nothin
  about Two
Live Crew?"
When I talk about rap,
and I talk about people demeaning rap,
I don't even mention them
because they don't understand the fundamentals of rap.
Rap, rap
is basically
broken down
Rhythm
and Poetry.
And poetry is expression.

It's just like poetry; you release so much through poetry
  you get
angry, you get it?
Poetry is like
intelligence.
You just release it all and if you don't have a complex
  rhyme
it's like,
"I'm goin to the store."
What rhymes with store?
More store for more bore
"I'm going to the store I hope I don't get bored,"
it's like,
"WHAT YOU SAYIN', MAN? WHO CARES?"
You have something that flows.
You have to be def,
D-E-F.
I guess I have to think of something for you that ain't
  slang.
Def is dope, def is live
when you say somethin's dope
it means it is the epitome of the experience
and you have to be def by your very presence
because you have to make people happy.
And we are living in a society where people are not happy
  with their everyday lives.

SEVEN VERSES
Leonard Jeffries

ROOTS

*3:00 P.M. Wednesday, November 20, 1991. A very large conference
room in the African American Studies Department at CUNY.
Drawn venetian blinds, fluorescent lighting. DR. JEFFRIES wears
a light, multicolored African top, and a multicolored African
hat. His shoes are black functional shoes, like the shoes to a
uniform. He sits facing the table, and often sits back with the
chair back from the table, often touches the table, and often sits
back with the chair on its back legs only. Sometimes he scratches
his head by throwing his hat forward on his head with great ease
and authority. There is a bodyguard, a large heavy-set African
American man, present.*

People are asking who is this guy Jeffries?
When they find out my background they're gonna be
  surprised.
They are gonna find out that I was even related to Alex
  Haley.
In fact I was a major consultant for *Roots.*
In fact there might not have been a *Roots* without me.
Now when I say that,
that's my own personal in-group joke wit' Alex.
He was in Philadelphia
getting his ticket to go down to Jamaica
and
Roots was lost.
He had it in a duffle bag,
a big duffle bag like this,
the whole manuscript.
It was lost in the airport of Philadelphia.
I got on my horse and ran around the airport of
  Philadelphia

and found *Roots*.
So that's my joke.
He had this manuscript,
Alex didn't have anything else but this manuscript.
690   Now if he had lost that, that would have been it.
He didn't have any photocopies.
Alex did everything on a shoestring.
uhm
so for him to deny me now . . .
695   He never even acknowledged
Pat
Alexander
his girlfriend/secretary who he had paid with affection and
      not with
resources.
700   So I didn't expect him to acknowledge me.
He called me to come down.
I called my wife who was working on her Ph.D. at Yale.
I said, "Rosalind, Alex wants us to come down to Brunswick,
      Georgia,
they're filming *Roots*."
705   She said yes she'd come down and we'd go, then she called
      me back.
She said, "I got too much work," so I went down to Brunswick,
      Georgia.
He introduced me to Margulies,
who was the, um, director
of *Roots*,
710   as the leading expert in America on Africa, and I said,
      "Wow," to
myself, "that's kind of high."
When Margulies said,
"That makes me number two," then I realized what Alex was
      doing to keep *Roots* honest.
So for two weeks I tried to change *Roots*.
715   Alex would say, "Wait a
minute, let's consult the experts."
After two weeks they got tired of me, sat me down
and said, "Dr. Jeffries," at lunch,
"we are very happy to have you here
720   but we just bought the rights to the book *Roots*
and we are under no obligation to maintain the integrity of
      the book
and we certainly don't have to deal with the truth of Black
      history."
Now,
this was a wipeout for me
725   I
I, there's been very few trau*m*atic
moments

(*Longest pause in his text.*)

uh, just to think.
Now I wasn't even prepared for this
730   but Pat had called me before and said,
"Len, I'm looking at this document and I don't know what to
      make of it."
I said, "What is it, Pat, what is it?"
and I knew she was nervous, she said,
"I'm reading a contract that says

'*Roots* has been sold to David Wolper and their heirs for   735
      ever and
ever

(*He is thumping his hand on table.*)

and their heirs for ever and ever.'"
Alex had signed the contract for fifty thousand dollars.

(*He is thumping his hand on table.*)

Fifty thousand dollars for paperback *Roots*.
Something that made how much?   740
Three hundred million dollars?
He was suing them for years.
The millions he made out to TV *Roots* he spent a lot of it
      to sue
Doubleday to get a better deal—I don't know if he ever
      got it.
Roots was a devastation.   745
The tens of millions and hundreds of millions made on
      Roots
went to produce,
not to make more Black series,
like *Roots*,
but they went to produce a *series*   750
maybe a dozen mini-series on *Jewish* history
as opposed to Black history.
You can document what was produced in terms of Black
      history
compared to what was produced of Jewish history.
It's a devastation.   755
But the *one* thing that came out of this for me,
was that when these people told me, you know,
"We bought your research
We bought your history
You really have no . . ."   760
I was thrown off
I had to get out of there.
I stayed for another couple of days.
I told Alex I had to make a pilgrimage to my grandfather's
      grave.
Never saw my grandfather.   765
Then I watched one more scene in the Alex Haley thing
and that finished it for me.
A cutaway of a slave ship
that was so real that they had to bring in these high
      school kids,
and once these high school kids played the enslaved   770
      Africans greased
down in simulated vomit
and feces
they couldn't come back,
so they had to continue to get,
go take these youngsters,   775
and some little White woman
who was there sleeping with one of those guys,
they told her, "You cannot take these kids without
      authorization."
But she would drive a bus
up to the schoolyard,   780

put the kids in it, and bring them to the set.
And it almost produced a riot
there.
785   But anyway this slave scene
was so realistic
the trainer's up on a lower deck
and Kunta Kinte's on a bottom deck
and they call down to each other,
and the trainer says,
790   "Kunta Kinte,
Be strong! Be strong!
We may have to fight.
Kill the White man and return to Mother Africa."
This was high drama.
795   All of us grown men over hiding in the shadows in
        tears.
Then
Green rushes out and said, "Break! Break!"
He said he didn't want the scene.
We said, "What?"
800   Even Lou Gossett and them were ready to *fight!*
You know 'cause they had—
a movie script is just
a skeleton,
you have to put your soul in a movie script,
805   and they put their heart and soul into what would have
        been . . .
And with the African—
because the "earth is mother" all over Africa.
So to say to go back to Mother Africa is a very meaningful
        phrase.
But this
810   Englishman refused
to accept it,
and they almost had a physical fight on the set.
They compromised and said,
"We—are—all—from—one—village,"

(*Hitting his hand rhythmically on the desk.*)

815   which is not the same thing.
After that I said, "I have to go."
I said I have to go,
and I rented a—
I flew out with Lorne Greene of all people.
820   He saw me and we had known each other for a couple of
        weeks from
the set,
and he's sitting there drinking his little drinks
talking about "Isn't *Roots* wonderful.
It's everybody's history,"
825   and I'm dying.

(*Pause.*)

Get to Atlanta.
Rent a car. Cut across the Georgia countryside.
came to a fork in the road,
made the right turn,
830   and there on a bluff
was a clapboard church

made by my grandfather
and
four
other trustees.   835
Then when
I went across the cemetery
to see, uh,
the gravesite where he was—
the tallest tombstone in the graveyard was his.   840
Uhm,
It was an obelisk.
On it was a Masonic symbol.
He was the master of the lodge.
On it was his vital statistics: 845
"*Born August the tenth 1868.*"
At the birth of the Fourteenth Amendment.
I later learned that his brother Sam was born
1865 at the birth of the Thirteenth Amendment!
And this is why people say,   850
"Who is he?
What is he?
Why is he?"
If they only know
I've had one of the best educations on the planet.   855
Yeah.
So . . .
When I went to Albany
in July,
I went knowing that you might not have   860
much time,
just like my wife said on the radio today:
"When we speak
we speak as though it is the last speech we're gonna
        make."
But I knew what was at stake   865
ever since they branded me a conspiracy theorist,
February 12, 1990,
two-column editorial in the *New York Times*.
That was,
in the concept of Jewish thinking,   870
the kiss of death.
I knew I had been targeted.
Arthur Schlesinger went and wrote a book
called *The Disuniting of America.*
He has everybody in the margin   875
except a half-page photo of myself
which said to us,
"This is the one they got to kill."
We knew that Schlesinger
and his people had sent out a thousand letters   880
to CEOs around the country
and foundation heads
not to have anything to do with
all of us involved in these studies
for multicultural curriculum   885
so, uh . . .
Knowing that I had taken this beating for two and a half
        years
it was my chance to strike out,
but people don't understand
that that was my way of saying,   890

"You bastids! . . .
for starting this process
of destroying *me*."
That was my striking out.
895 But people don't know the context.
They don't know that for two and a half years
I bore this burden
by myself
and I bore it well.
900 And now they've got a problem.
'Cause after they destroyed me,
here he is resurrected!!!!!
I spoke at Columbia, I spoke at Queens College. . . .

Letty Cottin Pogrebin

NEAR ENOUGH TO REACH

Evening. The day before Thanksgiving, 1991. On the phone. Direct, passionate, confident, lots of volume. She is in a study with a roll-top desk and a lot of books.

I think it's about rank frustration and the old story
905 that you pick a scapegoat
that's much more, I mean Jews and Blacks,
that's manageable,
because we're near,
we're still near enough to each other to reach!
910 I mean, what can you do about the people who voted for
David Duke?
Are Blacks going to go there and deal with that?
No, it's much easier to deal with Jews who are also
panicky.
We're the only ones that pay any attention

(Her voice makes an upward inflection.)

Do you hear?
915 Well, Jeffries did speak about the Mafia being, um,
Mafia,
and the Jews in Hollywood.
I didn't see
this tremendous outpouring of Italian
920 reaction.
Only *Jews* listen,
only *Jews* take Blacks seriously,
only *Jews* view Blacks as full human beings that you
should *address*
925 in their rage
and, um,
people don't seem to notice that.
But Blacks, it's like a little child kicking up against
Arnold
Schwarzenegger
930 when they,
when they have anything to say about the dominant
culture
nobody listens! Nobody reacts!
To get a headline,
to get on the evening news,
935 you have to attack a Jew.
Otherwise you're ignored.
And it's a shame.
We all play into it.

Minister Conrad Mohammed

SEVEN VERSES

April 1992, morning. A café/restaurant. Roosevelt Island, New York. We are sitting in the back, in an area that is surrounded by glass floor-to-ceiling windows. MR. MOHAMMED *is impeccably dressed in a suit of an elegant fabric. He wears a blue shirt and a bow tie. He has on fine shoes, designer socks, and a large fancy watch and wedding ring. His hair is closely cropped. He drinks black coffee, and uses a few packs of sugar. He is traveling with another man, also a Muslim, in the clothing of a Muslim, impeccable, who sits at another table and watches us.*

The condition of the Black man in America today is part and
parcel,
through the devlishment 940
that permitted Caucasian people
to rob us of our humanity,
and put us in the throes of slavery . . .
The fact that our—our Black
parents 945
were actually taken
as cattle
and as, as
animals
and packed into 950
slave ships
like sardines
amid feces
and urine—
and the suffering of our people, 955
for months,
in the middle passage—
Our women,
raped
before our own eyes, 960
so that today
some look like you,
some look like me,
some look like a brother . . .
(indicating his companion) 965
This is a crime of tremendous proportion.
In fact,
no crime in the history of humanity
has before or since
equaled that crime. 970
The Holocaust did not equal it
Oh, absolutely not.
First of all,
that was a horrible crime
and that is something that is a disgrace in the eyes of 975
civilized
people.
That, uh, crime also stinks
in the nostrils of God.
But it in no way compares with the slavery of our
people
because we lost over a hundred 980
and some say two hundred and fifty,
million
in the middle passage
coming from Africa
to America. 985

We were so thoroughly robbed.
We didn't just lose six million.
We didn't just
endure this
990   for, for
five or six years
or from '38 to '45 or '39 to
We endured this for over three hundred years—
the total subjugation of the Black man.
995   You can go into Bangladesh today,
Calcutta,

(*He strikes the table with a sugar packet three or four times.*)

New Delhi,
Nigeria,
some really
1000   so-called underdeveloped nation,
and I don't care how low that person's humanity is

(*He opens the sugar packet.*)

whether they never
had running water,
if they'd never seen a television or anything.
1005   They are in better condition than the Black man and
woman
in America today
right now.
Even at Harvard.
They have a contextual understanding of what their
destiny is.

(*He strikes the table with another sugar packet three or four times
and opens it.*)

1010   But the Black man has no knowledge of that;
he's an amnesia victim

(*Starts stirring his coffee.*)

He has lost knowledge of himself

(*Stirring his coffee.*)

and he's living a beast life.

(*Stirring his coffee.*)

So this proves that it was the greatest
1015   crime.
Because we were cut off from our past.
Not only were we killed and murdered,
not only were our women raped
in front of their own children.
1020   Not only did the slave master stick

(*The spoon drops onto saucer.*)

at times,
daggers into a pregnant woman's stomach,
slice the stomach open

push the baby out on the ground and crush the head of
the baby
to instill fear in the Massas of the plantation.   1025

(*Stirring again.*)

Not only were these things done,
not only were our thumbs

(*Spoon drops.*)

put in, in devices
that would just slowly torture the slave
and tear the thumb off from the root.   1030
Not only were we sold on the auction block
like cattle,
not permitted to marry.
See these are the crimes
of slavery that nobody wants to talk about.   1035
But the most significant crime—
because we could have recovered from all of that—
but the fact that they cut off all knowledge from us,
told us that we were animals,
told us that we were subhuman,   1040
took from us our names,
gave us names like
Smith
and Jones
and today we wear those names   1045
with dignity
and pride,
yet these were the names given to us in one of the greatest
crimes
ever committed on the face of the earth.
So this kind of thing,   1050
Sister,
is what qualifies slavery
as the greatest
crime
ever committed.   1055
They have stolen
our garment.
Stolen our identity.
The Honorable Louis Farrakhan
teaches us   1060
that *we* are the chosen of God.
We are those people
that almighty God Allah
has selected as his chosen,
and they are masquerading in our garment—   1065
the Jews.
We don't have an identity today.
Because we are the people . . .
There are seven verses
in the Bible   1070
seven verses,
I believe it is in Deuteronomy,
that the Jews base
their chosen people, uh, uh,
claim the theology,   1075
the whole theological exegesis
with respect

of being the chosen
is based upon seven verses
1080 in the Scripture that talk
about a covenant
with Abraham.

Letty Cottin Pogrebin

ISAAC

Morning. Spring. On the phone. She is in her office in her home on West 67th Street and Central Park West in Manhattan. Her office has an old-fashioned wooden rolltop desk and bookcases filled with books. She says she was wearing leggings and a loose shirt.

Well,
it's hard for me to do that
1085 because
I think there's a tendency to make hay
with the Holocaust,
to push
all the buttons.
1090 And I mean this story about my uncle Isaac—makes *me* cry
and it's going to make your audience cry
and I'm beginning to worry
that
we're trotting out our Holocaust stories
1095 too regularly and that we're going to inure each other to the truth of
them.
But
I think
maybe if you let me read it,
1100 I would prefer to read it:

(Reading from Deborah, Golda, and Me.)

"I remember my mother's cousin
Isaac who came to New York
immediately after the war and lived with us for several months.
Isaac is my connection to dozens of other family members who
1105 were murdered in the concentration camps.
Because he was blond and blue-eyed he had been
chosen as the designated survivor of his town.
That is the Jewish councils had instructed him to do anything
to stay alive and tell the story.
1110 For Isaac
anything turned out to mean this.
The Germans accepted his forged Aryan papers and decided that he
would have to prove by his actions that he was not a Jew.
They put him on a transport train with the Jews of his town
1115 and then gave him the task of herding into the gas chambers everyone in his train load.
After he had fulfilled that assignment
with patriotic

German efficiency,
the Nazis accepted the authenticity of his identity papers   1120
and let him go.
Among those whom Isaac packed into the gas chambers that day
dispassionately as if shoving a few more items into an overstuffed
closet
were his wife   1125
and
two children.
The designated survivor
arrived in America
at about age forty   1130

(Breathes in.)

with prematurely white hair and a dead gaze within the sky blue
eyes that's helped save his life.
As promised he told his story to dozens of Jewish agencies
and community leaders and to groups of families and friends which
is how I heard the account   1135
translated from his Yiddish
by my mother.
For months he talked,
speaking the unspeakable.
Describing a horror   1140
that American Jews had suspected but could not conceive.
A monstrous tale
that dwarfed the demonology of legend
and gave me the nightmare I still dream to this day.
And as he talked   1145
Isaac seemed to grow older and older
until one night a few months later
when he finished telling everything he knew
he died."

Robert Sherman

LOUSY LANGUAGE

11:00 A.M. Wednesday, November 13, 1991. A very sunny and large, elegant living room in a large apartment near the Brooklyn Museum. MR. SHERMAN is sitting in an armchair near an enormous bouquet of flowers for the birth of his first child. He wears sweats, and a bright orange long-sleeved tee shirt. Smiles frequently, upbeat, impassioned. Fingers his wedding ring. Each phrase builds on the next, pauses are all sustained intensity, never lets up. Full. Lots of volume, clear enunciation, teeth, and tongue very involved in his speech. Good-humored, seems to like the act of speech.

Do you have demographic information on Crown Heights?   1150
The important thing to remember is that—
and I will check these numbers when I get back to the office—
I think the
Hasidim

1155 comprise only ten percent
of the population
of the neighborhood.
The Crown Heights conflict has been brewing on and off for
twenty years
since the Hasidic community
1160 developed some serious numbers
and some strength in Crown Heights and as African
Americans and
Caribbean Americans came to make up the dominant
culture in
Crown Heights.
Very important to remember that
1165 those things that are expressed really as
bias,
those things
that we at the Human Rights Commission
would consider to be bias,
1170 have the same trappings of bias,
which is complaints based on a characteristic, not on a
knowledge of a
specific person.
There sort of is a soup
of bias—prejudice, racism, and discrimination.
1175 I think bias really does relate to
feelings with a valence,
feelings with a, uhm,

(*Breathing in.*)

feelings that can go in a direction positive or negative
although we usually use bias to mean a negative.
1180 What it means usually
is negative attitudes
that can lead to negative behaviors:
biased
acts, biased incidents,
1185 or biased crimes.
Racism is hatred based on race.
Discrimination refers to
acts against somebody . . .
so that the words
1190 actually tangle up.
I think in part
because vocabulary
follows general awareness. . . .
I think you know
1195 the Eskimos have seventy words for snow?
We probably have seventy different kinds of bias, prejudice,
racism, and
discrimination,
but it's not in our mind-set to be clear about it,
so I think that we have
1200 sort of lousy language
on the subject
and that
is a reflection
of our unwillingness
1205 to deal with it honestly
and to sort it out.
I think we have very, very bad language.

CROWN HEIGHTS, BROOKLYN
August 1991
Rabbi Joseph Spielman

NO BLOOD IN HIS FEET

9:30 A.M. Tuesday, November 12, 1991. A large home on President Street in Crown Heights. Only natural light, not very much light. Dark wood. A darkish dining room with an enormous table, could seat twenty. The RABBI sits at the head of the table. Lots of stuff on the table. He wears Hasidic clothing, a black fedora, black jacket, and reading glasses. As he talks, he slightly slides around the tape-recorder microphone, which is in front of him at the table. The furniture in the dining room including his chair is, for the most part, very old, solid wood. There are children playing quietly in another room, and people come in and out frequently, but always whispering and walking carefully not to make noise, unless they speak to him directly. The children at one point came over and stared at me.

Many people were on the sidewalk,
talking, playing,
drinking   1210
beer or whatever—
being that type of neighborhood.
A car
driven by an individual—
a Hasidic individual—   1215
went through the intersection,
was hit by another car,
thereby causing it to go onto the sidewalk.
The driver on seeing
himself in such a position that he felt he was going to
definitely hit   1220
someone,
because of the amount of people on the sidewalk,
he steered at the building,
so as to get out of the way of the people.
Obviously, for the most part,   1225
he was successful.
But regrettably,
one child was killed
and another child
was wounded.   1230
Um,
seeing what happened,
he jumped out of the car
and, realizing
there may be a child under the car,   1235
he tried to physically lift
the car
from the child.
Well, as he was doing this
the Afro-Americans were beating him already.   1240
He was beaten so much he needed stitches in the scalp
and the face,
fifteen or sixteen stitches
and also
there were three other passengers in the car
that were being beaten too.   1245
One of the passengers was calling 911
on the cellular phone.
A Black person

1250
pulled the phone out of his hand and ran.
Just stole the—stole the telephone.
The Jewish community
has a volunteer
ambulance corps
which is funded totally from the nations—

1255
there is not one penny of government funds—
and manned by volunteers—
who many times at their expense—
supplied the equipment that they carry in order to save
    lives.
As one of the EMS ambulances were coming,

1260
one of the Hasidic ambulances or the Jewish ambulances
    came
on the scene.
The EMS responded with three ambulances on the scene.
They were there before
the Jewish ambulance came.

1265
Two or three police cars were already on the scene.
The police saw the potential for violence
and saw that the occupants of the car
were being beaten and were afraid for their safety.
At the same time the EMS asked

1270
the Hasidic ambulances for certain pieces of equipment
    that they
were out of,
that they needed to take care of the Cato kid,
and,
um,

1275
in fact, I was . . .
The Hasidic ambulance left, leaving behind one of the
    passengers.
That passenger had a walkie-talkie and he requested that I
    come down to pick him up.
And at that time there was a lot of screaming and shouting

1280
and it was a mixed crowd, Hasidic and Afro-American.
The police said, "Rabbi get your people out of here."
I told them to leave and I left.
Now,
a few hours later,

1285
two and a half hours later,
in a different part of Crown Heights,
a scholar
from Australia,
Yankel Rosenbaum,

1290
who, urr,
I think he had a doctorate or he was working on his
    doctorate,
was walking on the street
on his own—
I mean he was totally oblivious—

1295
and he was accosted by a group of young Blacks
about twenty of them strong
which was being egged on by a Black
male approximately
forty years old and balding,

1300
telling them,
"Kill all Jews—
look what they did to the kid,
kill all Jews,"
and all the epithets that go along with it,

1305
"Heil Hitler" and all of it.

They stabbed him,
which later on the stab wounds were fatal
and he passed away in the hospital.
The Mayor,
hearing about the Cato kid,   1310
came to the Kings County Hospital
to give condolences to the family of the child who had
    regrettably been killed.
At the meantime they had already wheeled in
Mr. Rosenbaum.
He was in the emergency room   1315
and I was at the hospital at the same time,
and the Mayor, seeing me there,
expressed his concern
that a child,
uh, innocent child, had been killed.   1320
Where I explained to him
the fact
that,
whereas the child was killed from an unfortunate
    accident
where there was no malicious intent,   1325
here
there was an individual lying in the emergency room
who had been stabbed with malicious intent
and for the sole reason—
not that he did anything to anyone—   1330
just from the fact that he happened to be Jewish.
And the mayor went with me to the emergency room
to visit Mr. Rosenbaum.
This was approximately one and a half hours before he
    passed away.
I noticed at the time that his feet   1335
were
completely white.
And I complained to the doctor
on the scene,
"He's having a problem with blood circulation   1340
because there's no blood in his feet."
And she gave me some asinine answer.
And the mayor asked her what his condition is:
"Serious but stable."
In the meantime he was screaming and in pain   1345
and they weren't doing anything.
Subsequently they, um,
they started giving him anaesthesia in a time that
they weren't allowed to give him anaesthesia
and while he was under anaesthesia,   1350
he passed away.
So there was totally mismanagement in his case.
So whereas the Mayor,
had been fed . . .
his people got   1355
whatever information he got out of the Black community
    was
that
the driver had run a red light
and also,
and that the ambulance,   1360
the Hasidic ambulance,
refused to take care of the Black child that was dying and
rather took care of their own.

Nenh?

1365 And this is what was fed amongst the Black community.
And it was false,
it was totally false
and it was done maliciously
only with the intent to get the riots,

1370 to start up the resulting riots.

The Reverend Canon Doctor Heron Sam

MEXICAN STANDOFF

November 12, 1991, 4:00 P.M. The rectory office at St. Mark's Church in Crown Heights. A small, short office. Lived in but impeccably ordered. Some light from lamps, some from overhead. Plaques and awards everywhere. THE REVEREND is wearing a yellow shirt, priest's collar, tan summer jacket. He wears spectacles. There are clocks that make noise and sound the hour in his office and outside church bells sound during the interview, loud. Throughout the talk he is trying to get the corner of a calendar to stay down, but it continues to stick up. Finally he uses a paperweight to keep it down.

You can't have that kind of accident
if people are observing the speed limits.
People knew it was the Grand Rebbe.
People have seen the Grand Rebbe

1375 charging through the community.
He is worried
about a threat on his life
from the Satmars.
These Lubavitcher people

1380 are really very,
uh, enigmatic people.
They move so easily between
simplicity and sophistication.
Because

1385 they fear for his life,
because the Satmars
who are their sworn enemies

(*He laughs/chuckles.*)

have threatened to *kill*
the Rebbe.

1390 So whenever he comes out
he's gotta be *whisked!*
You know like a President
or even better than a President.
He says he's an intuhnational figuh

1395 like a Pope!
I say
then, "Why don't you get the Swiss guards
to escort you
rather than using the police

1400 and taxpayers' money?"
He's gotta be
whisked!
Quickly through the neighborhood.
Can't walk around.

1405 He used to walk.
When I first came here.
Now he doesn't walk at all.
They drive him.

And when he walked
you could tell he was in front 1410
because there was,
he was protected all around
and they spilled out onto the streets
and buses had to stop
because this BIG BAND 1415
had to escort
the Rebbe from his house over there
to the synagogue.
So the Rebbe goes to the cemetery.
Every time the Rebbe goes to the cemetery, 1420
which is once a week
to visit his dead wife
and father-in-law,
the police
lead him in escort 1425
charging down the street
at seventy miles an hour in a metropolis—
what do you want?

(*Swift increase in volume and suddenly businesslike.*)

It happened that on this occasion that as they were coming
back,
uh, 1430
the police car
with its siren,
had gone over a main
intersection with the light
in favor 1435
of the police car.
The Rebbe's Cadillac had passed
when the lights had become amber
and nobody expected the bodyguard van,
uh, 1440
station wagon
to deliberately go through the red light.
So the traffic
that had the right of way kept coming and
BANG! 1445
came the collision and the careening
onto the sidewalk
had to damage whoever was there
and then, um, they were more concerned about licking
their own
wounds. 1450
Rather than pick
the car off the boy
who died as a result.
And then the ambulance that came—
the Jewish ambulance— 1455
was concerned about the people in the van
while some boy lay dead,
a black boy lay dead on the street.
The people showed their—

(*Increase in volume.*)

they burned and whatever else, 1460
upturned
police cars

1465 and looted,
      and as a result,
      I think in retaliation, murdered one of the Hasidics.
      But that was just the match that lit the powder keg.
      It's gonna happen again and again.
      There's a Mexican standoff right now
      But it's gonna happen again.

Anonymous Young Man #1

WA WA WA

*7:00 or 8:00 P.M. Spring. A recreation room at Ebbets Field
apartments. A very handsome young Caribbean American* MAN
*with dreadlocks, in his late teens or early twenties, wearing a
bright, loose-fitting shirt. The room is ill equipped. There are a
few pieces of broken furniture. It is poorly lit. A woman, Kym,
with dreadlocks and shells in her hair, is at the interview. It was
originally scheduled to be her interview. The* ANONYMOUS YOUNG
MAN #1 *and the other* ANONYMOUS YOUNG MAN #2 *started
by watching the interview from the side of the room but soon
approached me and began to join in.* ANONYMOUS YOUNG MAN
#1 *was the most vocal.* ANONYMOUS YOUNG MAN #2 *stood lurking
in the shadows. A third young man, younger than both of them,
wearing wire spectacles and a blue Wind-breaker, who looks quite
like a young Spike Lee, sat silent with his hands and head on the
table the entire time. There is a very bad radio or tape recorder
playing music in the background.*

1470 What I saw was
      she was pushin'
      her brother on the bike like
      this,
      right?
1475 She was pushin'
      him
      and he kept dippin' around
      like he didn't know how
      to ride the bike.
1480 So she kept runnin'
      and pushin' him to the side.
      So she was already runnin'
      when the car was comin'.
      So I don't know if she was runnin' toward him
1485 because we was watchin' the car
      weavin',
      and we was goin'
      "Oh, yo
      it's a Jew, man.
1490 He broke the stop light, they never get arrested."
      At first we was laughin', man, we was like
      you see they do anything
      and get away with it,
      and then
1495 we saw that he was out of control,
      and den
      we started regrettin' laughin',
      because then
      we saw where he was goin'.
1500 First he hit a car, right,
      he tore a whole front fender off a car,
      and then we was like
      Oh

      my god,
1505 man, look at the kids,
      you know,
      so we was already runnin' over there
      by the time the accident happened.
      That's how we know he was drinkin'
1510 cause he was like
      Wa Wa Wa Wa
      and I was like
      "Yo, man, he's drunk.
      Grab him,
1515 grab him.
      Don't let him go anywhere."
      I said,
      "Grab him."
      I didn't want him to limp off
1520 in some apartment somewhere
      and come back in a different black jacket.
      So I was like,
      "Grab him,"
      and then I was like, "Is the ambulance comin' for the
          kids?"
1525 'Cause I been in a lot of confrontations with Jews
          before
      and I know that when they said an ambulance
      is comin'
      it most likely meant for them.
      And they was like,
1530 "oh, oh."
      Jews right?
      "Ambulance comin', ambulance comin',
      calm down, calm down,
      God will help them,
1535 God will help them if you believe."
      And he was actin' like he was dyin'.
      "Wa Aww,
      me too,
      I'm hurt, I'm hurt, I'm hurt too."
1540 Wan nothin wrong with him,
      wan nothin wrong with him.
      They say that we beat up on that man
      that he had to have stitches because of us.
      You don't come out of an accident like that
          unmarked,
1545 without a scratch.
      The most he got from us was slapped
      by a little kid.
      And here come the ambulance
      and I was like, "That's not a city ambulance,"
1550 not like this I was upset right
      and I was like,
      "YO,
      the man is drunk!
      He ran a red light!
1555 You all ain't gonna do nothin'."
      Everybody started comin' around, right,
      'cause I was talkin' about
      these kids is dyin' man!
      I'm talkin' about the skull of the baby is on the ground
          man!
1560 and he's walking'!
      I was like, "Don't let him get into that ambulance!"

And the Jews,
the Jews
was like private, private ambulance
1565 I was like, "Grab him,"
but my buddies was like,
"We can't touch them."
Nobody wanted to grab him,
nobody wanted to touch him,
1570 An' I was breakin' fool, man,
I was goin' mad,
I couldn't believe it.
Everybody just stood
there,
1575 and that made me cry.
I was cryin'
so I left, I went home and watched the rest of it on TV,
it was too lackadazee
so it was like me, man, instigatin' the whole thing.
1580 I got arrested for it
long after
in Queens.
Can't tell you no more about that,
you know.
1585 Hey, wait a minute,
they got eyes and ears everywhere.
What color is the Israeli flag?
And what color are the police cars?
The man was drunk,
1590 I open up his car door,
I was like, when—
I was like, he'd been drinkin'
I know our words don't have no meanin',
as Black people in Crown Heights.
1595 You realize, man,
ain't no justice,
ain't never been no justice,
ain't never gonna be no justice.

Michael S. Miller

HEIL HITLER

A large airy office in Manhattan on Lexington in the fifties.
MR. MILLER sits behind a big desk in a high-backed swivel chair
drinking coffee. He's wearing a yarmulke. Plays with the swizzle
stick throughout. There is an intercom in the office, so that when
the receptionist calls him, you can hear it, and when she calls
others in other offices, you can hear it, like a page in a public
place, faintly.

I was at Gavin Cato's funeral,
1600 at nearly every public event
that was conducted by the Lubavitcher community and the
Jewish
community as a whole.
Words of comfort
were offered to the family of Gavin Cato.
1605 I can show you a letter that we sent
to the Cato family expressing, uh,
our sorrow over the loss,
unnecessary loss, of their son.
I am not aware of a word
1610 that was spoken at that funeral.

I am not aware of a—
and I was taking notes—
of a word that was uttered
of comfort to the family of Yankel Rosenbaum.
Frankly this was a political rally rather than a funeral. 1615
The individuals you mentioned—
and again,
I am not going to participate in verbal acrimony,
not only
were there cries of, "Kill the Jews" 1620
or,
"Kill the Jew,"
there were cries of, "Heil Hitler."
There were cries of, "Hitler didn't finish the job."
There were cries of, 1625
"Throw them back into the ovens again."
To hear in *Crown Heights*
and Hitler was no lover of Blacks—
"Heil Hitler"?
"Hitler didn't finish the job"? 1630
"We should heat up the ovens"?
From *Blacks*?
Is more inexplicable
or unexplainable
or any other word that I cannot fathom. 1635
The hatred is so
deep seated
and the hatred
knows no boundaries.
There is no boundary 1640
to anti-Judaism.
The anti-*Judaism*—
if people don't want me
to use,
hear me use the word anti-Semitism. 1645
And I'll be damned if,
if preferential treatment is gonna
be the excuse
for every bottle,
rock,
or pellet that's, uh, directed
toward a Jew
or the window of a Jewish home 1650
or a Jewish store.
And, frankly,
I think the response of the Lubavitcher community was
relatively
passive. 1655

Henry Rice

KNEW HOW TO USE CERTAIN WORDS

Thursday, November 21, 1991. The Jackson Hole restaurant on
Lexington Avenue in the thirties in Manhattan. Lunchtime,
dimly lit a reddish haze on everything, perhaps from a neon light.
MR. RICE, very neatly dressed, is eating a large, messy hamburger
and horizontally chopped pickles. Drinking a Miller Lite. Beer is in
a bottle next to a red plastic glass. He's wearing a baseball cap over
very closely cut hair and a bright, multicolored, expensive-looking
colored nylon jacket. Heavy new Timberland boots. Struggling to
eat without making a mess of the food. At some point sits up from
food and has his right hand or fist on his hipa very unaffected but

truly authoritative stance. Good-natured, handsome, healthy.
Patsy Cline's "Crazy" is very loud on the jukebox.

I went back home and got my bike
because I knew I would have to be
1660   illusive.
I was there in body and in spirit
but I didn't participate in any of the violence
because basically I have a lot to lose.
But I was there
1665   and I would have defended myself if it was necessary,
most definitely.
I weaved around trouble.
When something broke out, I moved back,
when it calmed down, I would move back in on the
        front line.
1670   I was always there.
And Richard Green heard me saying something to a bunch
        of kids
about *voting*
about the power of *vote*
the power of *numbers*
1675   and he said,
uh,
I said, "Get away from me, you're an Uncle Tom,
get away from me.
Get back in your Mercedes-Benz!"
1680   No! I said that to Clarence Norman
and to Richard Green,
both of them.
I was tearing them apart.
Richard Green was very persistent.
1685   He said,
"Look, Mr. Rice,
I like the way you speak.
I need you.
Please help me.
1690   I'm a community activist. . . .
ba, ba, ba, ba, ba."

(*He drops some food on his clothes, or so it seems, he looks and grins.*)

It didn't get on me.
"I'm a community activist.
I need your help,
1695   please help me,"
and so forth.
Again,
I didn't pay him no mind
but we spoke
1700   some
the next day after that,
after the incidents that took place on that corner
of Albany Avenue.
A brother was beat up—
1705   cops rushing into the Black crowd
didn't rush into the Jewish crowd,
cops rushed into the Black crowd
started beatin' up
Black people.
1710   But the next day Richard came by in a yellow van,
a New York City Department of Transportation van,

with a megaphone,
yellow light flashing,

(*Music segues from Patsy Cline's "Crazy" to Public Enemy's "Can't
Truss It," or Naughty by Nature's "O.P.P."*)

the whole works
and, um,   1715
he said,
"Henry, I need you in this van.
Drive around with me.
Let's keep some of these kids off the street tonight."
I said, "Okay."   1720
He said,
"The blood
of Black men are on your hands tonight!"
I said, "Okay."
We drive around in the van,   1725
"Young people stay in the house!
Mothers keep your children in the house,
please."
So I began fillin'
I began feeling like   1730
I had to do it
after he told me that,
"the blood of the Black man"
were on my hands,
you know.   1735
Richard Green sure know how to use certain words.

(*He giggles.*)

I remember reaching Albany Avenue—
kids were being chased by the police.
I jump out with a portable megaphone,
I tell them, "Stop running!   1740
The cops won't chase you!
and they won't hit you!"
The next thing I know,
cop grabs my megaphone hits me in the head with a
        stick,
handcuffs me,   1745
and takes the megaphone out of my hand.
So I'm like,
"Wait a minute
I'm doing a community service for the mayor's office."
They don't want to hear it.   1750
Matter of fact,
they still have the megaphone 'til this day.
I'm like,
"Richard Green get me
out of this police car, please!"   1755
So a Black captain came by,
thank God,
and he says, "What's goin' on?"
Richard Green explained it to him.
He said, "Let him go."   1760
Get back in the van,
there's another Brother in van,
starts saying,
"Non violence!"
to the young Brothers.   1765

They begin throwing bottles at the, uh,
at the van.
One guy got so upset
he had a nine-millimeter
1770 fully loaded.
He said, "Get the hell out of this neighborhood!"
The next day
more violence:
fires,
1775 cars being burnt,
stores being broken into,
a perception that Black youth
are going crazy in Crown Heights
like we were angry over
1780 nothing,
understand?

Norman Rosenbaum

MY BROTHER'S BLOOD

*A Sunday afternoon. Spring. Crisp, clear, and windy. Across
from City Hall in New York City. Crowds of people, predominantly Lubavitcher, with placards. A rally that was organized by
Lubavitcher women. All of the speakers were men, but the women
stand close to the stage.* MR. ROSENBAUM, *an Australian, with a
beard, hat, and wearing a pinstripe suit, speaks passionately and
loudly from the microphone on a stage with a podium. Behind him
is a man in an Australian bush hat with a very large Australian
flag which blows dramatically in the wind. It is so windy that*
MR. ROSENBAUM *has to hold his hat to keep it on his head.*

　　Al do lay achee so achee aylay alo dalmo
　　My brother's blood cries out from the ground.
　　Let me make it clear
1785　　why I'm here.
　　In August of 1991,
　　as you all have heard before today,
　　my brother was killed in the streets of Crown Heights
　　for no other reason
1790　　than that he was a Jew!
　　The only miracle was
　　that my brother was the only victim
　　who paid for being a Jew with his life.
　　When my brother was surrounded,
1795　　each and every American was surrounded.
　　When my brother was stabbed four times,
　　each and every American was stabbed four times
　　and as my brother bled to death in this city,
　　while the medicos stood by
1800　　and let him bleed
　　to death, it was the gravest of indictments against this
　　　　country.
　　One person out of twenty gutless individuals
　　who attacked my brother has been arrested.
　　I for one am not convinced that it is beyond the ability of the
　　　　New York police
1805　　to arrest others.
　　Let me tell you, Mayor Dinkins,
　　let me tell you, Commissioner Brown:
　　I'm here,
　　I'm not going home,
1810　　until there is justice.

Norman Rosenbaum

SIXTEEN HOURS DIFFERENCE

*7:00 A.M. Spring. Newark Airport, Departure Gate, Continental
Airlines.* MR. ROSENBAUM *is moments before his flight to L.A. and
then back to Australia. Wearing a pinstripe suit with an Australian fit. Hat. Suitcase. He has sparkling blue eyes with a twinkle,
rosy cheeks, and a large smile throughout the interview.*

There's sixteen hours difference between New York and
　　Melbourne
and I had just gotten back to my office
and I had a phone call from my wife,
and she said she wanted me to come home straight away
and I sensed the urgency in her voice.　　　　　　　　　1815
I said, "are you all right?" She said, "Yeah."
I said, "are the children all right, you know the kids?" She
　　says, "yeah."
So I'm driving home and I'm thinking, I wonder what's the
　　problem now, you know?
We had some carpenters doing some work, I wonder if there
　　has been a disaster,
some sort of domestic problem,　　　　　　　　　　　　1820
and I thought, oh my God, you know, my parents,
I didn't even ask after them,
how insensitive not to even ask after my parents,
and I've got a grandmother eighty-five years old, same sort of
　　thing.
So I get home,　　　　　　　　　　　　　　　　　　　　1825
I walk in the door, and a friend of mine was standing
　　there,
close friend,
does the same sort of work as me, he's a barrister and an
　　academic,
and he sees me and he says,
"There's got a pro—　　　　　　　　　　　　　　　　　1830
uh,
we've got a problem. There's a problem."
I thought he was talking about a case we were working on
　　together,
he says, "'Z come,
come and sit down."　　　　　　　　　　　　　　　　　1835
He goes to me,
"There's been a riot in New York,
been a riot in Crown Heights,
Yankel's been stabbed and he's dead."
And　　　　　　　　　　　　　　　　　　　　　　　　1840
my brother was the last in the world,
I hadn't even given him a thought.
I mean the fact that my brother
could be attacked
or die,　　　　　　　　　　　　　　　　　　　　　　　1845
it just hadn't even entered my mind.
At first I appeared all cool, calm and collected.
I then
started asking questions
like who told you,　　　　　　　　　　　　　　　　　1850
how do you know,
are you sure?
I just asked the question,
you know,
are you sure?　　　　　　　　　　　　　　　　　　　　1855

Anonymous Young Man #2

BAD BOY

Evening. Spring. The same recreation room as interview with ANONYMOUS YOUNG MAN #1. YOUNG MAN #2 *is wearing a black jacket over his clothes. He has a gold tooth. He has some dreadlocks, and a very odd-shaped multicolored hat. He is soft-spoken, and has a direct gaze. He seems to be very patient with his explanation.*

That youth,
that sixteen-year-old
didn't murder that Jew.

(*Pause.*)

1860   For one thing,
he played baseball, right?
He was a atha-lete,
right?
A bad boy
does
1865   bad things.
Only a bad boy coulda stabbed the man.
Somebody who
does those type a things,
or who sees
1870   those types a things.
A atha-lete
sees people,
is interested in athletics,
stretchin',
1875   exercisin',
goin' to his football games,
or his baseball games.
He's not interested
in stabbin'
1880   people.
So
it's not in his mind
to stab,
to just jump into somethin',
1885   that he has no idea about
and
sta—
and kill a man.
A bad boy,
1890   somebody who's groomed in badness,
or did badness
before,
stabbed the man.
Because I used to be a atha-lete
1895   and I used to be a bad boy,
and when I was a atha-lete,
I was a atha-lete.
All I thought about was atha-lete.
I'm not gonna jeopardize my athleticism
1900   or my career to do anything
that bad people do.
And when I became a bad boy
I'm not a athalete no more.
I'm a bad boy,
1905   and I'm groomin' myself in things that is bad.

You understand, so
he's a athalete,
he's not a bad boy.
It's a big difference.
Like,   1910
mostly the Black youth in Crown Heights have two things
    to do—
either DJ or be a bad boy, right?
You either
DJ, be a MC, a rapper
or Jamaican rapper,   1915
ragamuffin,
or you be a bad boy,
you sell drugs or you rob people.
What do you do?
I sell drugs.   1920
What do you do?
I rap.
That's how it is in Crown Heights.
I been livin' in Crown Heights mosta my life.
I know for a fact that that youth, that sixteen-year-old,   1925
didn't kill that Jew.
That's between me and my Creator.

Sonny Carson

CHORDS

Lunchtime. Spring. A fancy restaurant in Brooklyn. SONNY *tells me it's where all the judges come for lunch. White linen tablecloths. Light wood walls, lamplight next to the table. Tile floor. He is eating crab cakes. He is dressed in a black turtleneck and a gray jacket. He has on a mud cloth hat. He has an authority stick with him, and it lays on the table. His bodyguard, wearing a black leather jacket, enters in the middle of the interview.* SONNY *chides him for being late.*

It's going to be a long hot summer.
I'm connected up with the young people all over the
    country
and there's a thread   1930
leading to an eruption
and Crown Heights began the whole thing.
And the Jews come second to the police
when it comes to feelings of dislike among Black folks.
The police,   1935
the police,
believe me, the police—
I know the police and the police know me
and they turn that whole place into an occupied camp
with the Seventy-first Precinct as the overseers.   1940
And don't think that everything is OK within that precinct
    among those officers
either.
Don't think that,
don't think that.
You know the media has always painted me as the bad   1945
    guy—
that's OK!
I'm a good guy to pick on.
Their viewers don't like me either,
they really don't like me because I *am* the bad guy,
I am the ultimate bad guy   1950

because of my relationship to the young people in the
    city.
I understand their language.
I respect them as the future.
I speak their language. They don't even engage in long
    dialogue
1955 anymore
just short
"words."
It always amazes me
how the city fathers,
1960 the power brokers,
just continue to deny what's happening.
And it is just getting intolerable for me to continue to
    watch
this small
arrogant
1965 group of people continue to get this kind of preferential
    treatment.
They sit on the school board.
A board of nine
and they have
four members, and their kids don't even go to public
    school.
1970 So that's the kind of arrogance I'm talking about.
I have no reason to be eagerly awaiting the coming together
    of our
people.
They owe me first.
I'm not givin' in just like that,
1975 I don't want it.
You can have it.
Like my grandmother said,
"Help the bear!
If you see me and the bear in a fight,
1980 help the bear—
don't help me,
help the bear."
I don't need any of it from them!
And I'm not gonna advocate any coming together and
    healing of
1985 America
and all that shit.
You kiddin'?
You kiddin'?
Just 'cause I can have the fortune of walking in here
1990 and sitting and talking
and having a drink,
it appear that I have all the same kinds of abilities
of other folks in here.
No, it's not that way.
1995 'Cause tonight
by nighttime it could all change for me.
So I'm always aware of that, and that's what keeps me
    goin'
today
and each day!

(He eats.)

2000 I have
this idea

about a film.
See,
these kids, they got
another kinda rhythm now,   2005
there's a whole new kinda
step that they do.
When I first heard rap
I was sittin' in a huge open kinda stadium,
boys and girls high school field,   2010
and I heard these kids come out and start rappin',
and I'm listening
but it's not really clickin',
but I was mesmerized though.
But it was simontaneouis   2015
all around the country
and I said, "Oh shit,"
and everybody I knew who was young was listenin' to it
and I said, "Wow."
Because I have always been involved with young people   2020
and all of a sudden I got it,
I really heard the rhythm,
the chords,
the discord.
There's a whole new sound   2025
that the crackers are tryin' to get, but they can't get it.
I heard it on a television commercial.
One of the most beautiful pieces of art
that I ever witnessed
was a play   2030
called
um,
um,
um,
'bout, 'bout the Puerto Rican gang—   2035
no, no, no, no, no—
the Puerto Rican gang,
the musical
that was on Broad—
yeah,   2040
West Side Story—
the answer should be
a musical.

Rabbi Shea Hecht

OVENS

*Morning. Spring. A building on Eastern Parkway. A large room
with a very long conference table. There are pictures of Lubavitcher
men on the walls.* RABBI HECHT *is wearing a shirt, open at the
neck. He has several crisp one-dollar bills in his shirt pocket. These
are, apparently, dollar bills that the Rebbe has given him. It is the
custom that the Rebbe gives out one-dollar bills on Sunday.* RABBI
HECHT *has a beard. He wears glasses, traditional Hasidic garb,
including tsitses (ceremonial fringes that hang over his belt) and a
red yatmulke with gold trim which is ripped. His daughter comes in
frequently to get money from him. He keeps telling her to wait until
he is finished. She becomes more and more agitated. His brother
also enters frequently to ask him questions, and to tell him he's late.*

What is my goal?
My goal is not   2045
to give anybody a message

that we plan on working things out
by integrating
our two
2050 things.
By a person understanding more of their own religion
they will automatically respect another person.
The respect that my religion teaches me has nothing
    to do
with understanding you.
2055 See, there's a problem.
If
the only way I'm going to respect you
is based on how much I understand you,
no matter what it is
2060 in certain circles you're gonna run into problems.
Number one,
we are different,
and we think we should and can be different.
When the Rebbe said to the Mayor
2065 that we were all
one people,
I think
what the Rebbe is talking about is that,
that common denominator that we're all children of God,
    and the
2070 respect we all have to give each other under that banner.
But that does not mean that I have to invite you to my
    house for
dinner,
because I cannot go back to your home for dinner,
because you're not gonna give me kosher food.
2075 And I said,
so, like one Black said,
I'll bring in kosher food.
I said eh-eh.
We can't use your ovens,
2080 we can't use your dishes,
it's, it—
it's not just a question of buying certain food,
it's buying the food,
preparing it a certain way.
2085 We can't use your dishes, we can't use your oven.
The—the higher you go
the more common denominator.
And what the Rebbe was saying,
you as the Mayor
2090 don't get caught up in the differences,
you're—
from your position is—
you have to look at it as one city
and one
2095 human race.
We are all New Yorkers
and therefore I will protect all New Yorkers.
You see
preferential treatment
2100 suggests
that you're giving the person
the police car
not because they need the police car
but because
2105 they are who they are.

You're not gonna
give them the housing
because they
need the housing—
you're giving it because of who they are. 2110
But
just because I'm a Jew
therefore I
shouldn't get the police car.
The question is 2115
a synagogue
that has five thousand Jews
leave
the synagogue
at the same time, 2120
do they have a police car to stop the traffic?
The answer is every—single—synagogue,
temple,
mosque,
in 2125
the
world
stops traffic
when five thousand people have to walk out
at the same time. 2130

Reverend Al Sharpton

RAIN

The D.A.
came back with no indictment.
Uh, so then our only course
was to ask for a special prosecutor
which is appointed by the Governor, 2135
who's been hostile,
and to sue civilly.
When we went into civil court
we went to get an order to show cause.
The judge signed it and gave me a deadline of three days. 2140
The driver left the country. . . .
No one even said, "Why would he run?
If he did no wrong."
If you and I were in an accident we'd have to go to civil
    court.
Why is this man 2145
above the law?
So they said, "He's in Israel."
So I said,
"Well, I'll go to Israel to show best effits."
And the deadline 2150
was,
I had to serve him by Tuesday,
which was Yom Kippur—
that was the judge's decision not mine.
So we went. 2155
Alton Maddox and I
got on a plane,
left Monday night,
landed Tuesday morning,
went and served the American embassy, uh, 2160
so that
if this man had any decency at all

he could come to the American embassy and receive
    service,
which he has not done to this day.
2165 Come back,
went to court
and showed the judge the receipts,
and the judge said, "You made best effits,
therefore you are now permitted,
2170 by default,
to go ahead
and sue the rabbi or whomever
because you cannot do the driver."
So it wasn't just a media grandstand.
2175 We wanted to show the world
one, this man *ran*
and was *allowed* to run, and, two, we wanted to be able to
    legally go
around him,
to sue the people he was working for so that we can bring
    them into
2180 court and establish *why* and what happened.
And it came out in the paper the other day
that the driver in the other car didn't even have a driver's
    license.
So we're dealing with a *complete* outrage here,
we're dealing with a double standard,
2185 we're dealing with uh, uh, a, a
situation where
Blacks do not have equal protection under the law
and the media is used to castigate us
that merely asked for justice
2190 rather than castigate those that would hit a kid
and walk away like he just stepped on a roach!
Uh,
there also is the media
contention of the young Jewish scholar
2195 that was stabbed that night
and they've even distorted
saying *my words at the funeral*
I *preached* the funeral.
Uh, [the newspaper said I]
2200 helped to, to, uh, uh,
spark or, or, or, or, or *inspire* or *incite* people to kill him
    [Yankel Rosenbaum]
when he was dead the day before
I came out there.
He was killed the night
2205 that the young man
was killed with the car accident.
I didn't even get a call
from the family
'til eighteen hours later.
2210 So there's a whole media distortion
to protect them [the Lubavitchers].
Nobody is talking about,
"Why
is this guy
2215 in flight?"
If I was a rabbi
(I am a ministuh)
and my driver hit a kid,
I would not let the driver *leave*

and I certainlih would give my condolences,   2220
or anything else I could,
to the family,
I don't care what race they are.
To this minute the Rebbe has never even uttered a
    word of
sympathy   2225
to the family,
not even sent 'em a *card*
a *flower* or *nothing!*
So it's treating us with absolute contempt
and I don't care how controversial it makes us.   2230
I *won't* tolerate being insulted.
If you piss in my face I'm gonna call it *piss*.
I'm not gonna call it rain.

Richard Green

RAGE

*2:00 P.M. in a big red van. GREEN is in the front. He has a driver.
I am in the back. GREEN wears a large knit hat with reggae colors
over long dreadlocks. Driving from Crown Heights to Brooklyn
College. He turns sideways to face me in the back, and bends down,
talking with his elbow on his knee.*

Sharpton, Carson, and Reverend Herbert Daughtry
didn't have any power out there really.   2235
The media gave them power.
But they weren't turning those youfs on and off.
Nobody knew who controlled the switch out there.
Those young people had rage like an oil-well fire
that has to burn out.   2240
All they were doin' was sort of orchestratin' it.
Uh, they were not really the ones that were saying, "Well
stop, go, don't go, stop, turn around, go up."
It wasn't like that.
Those young people had rage out there,   2245
that didn't matter who was in control of that—
that rage had to get out
and that rage
has been building up.
When all those guys have come and gone,   2250
that rage is still out here.
I can show you that rage every day
right up and down this avenue.
We see, sometimes in one month, we see three bodies
in one month. That's rage,   2255
and that's something that nobody has control of.
And I don't know who told you that it was preferential
    treatment for
Blacks that the Mayor kept the cops back. . . .
If the Mayor had turned those cops on?
We would still be in a middle of a battle.   2260
And
I pray on both sides of the fence,
and I tell the people in the Jewish community the same
    thing,
"This is not something that force will hold."
Those youfs were running on cops without nothing in their   2265
    hands,
seven- and eight- and nine- and ten-year-old boys were
    running at

those cops
with nothing,
just running at 'em.
2270   That's rage.
Those young people out there are angry
and that anger has to be vented,
it has to be negotiated.
And they're not angry at the Lubavitcher community
2275   they're just as angry at you and me,
if it comes to that.
They have no
role models,
no guidance
2280   so they're just out there growin' up on their own,
their peers are their role models,
their peers is who teach them how to move
so when they see the Lubavitch
they don't know the difference between "Heil Hitler"
2285   and, uh, and uh, whatever else.
They don't know the difference.
When you ask 'em to say who Hitler was they wouldn't
   even be able
to tell you.

(Phone rings, RICHARD *picks it up, it's a mobile phone.)*

"Richard Green, can I help?
2290   Aw, man I tol' you I want some color
up on that wall. Give me some colors.
Look, I'm in the middle of somethin'."

(He returns to the conversation.)

Half them don't even know three quarters of 'em.
Just as much as they don't know who Frederick Douglass
   was.
2295   They know Malcolm
because Malcolm has been played up to such an extent
   now
that they know Malcolm.
But ask who Nat Turner was or Mary McCleod Bethune or
   Booker T.
Because the system has given 'em
2300   Malcolm is convenient and
Spike is goin' to give 'em Malcolm even more.
It's convenient.

Roslyn Malamud

THE COUP

*Spring. Midafternoon. The sunny kitchen of a huge, beautiful
house on Eastern Parkway in Crown Heights. It's a large, very
well- equipped kitchen. We are sitting at a table in a breakfast
nook area, which is separated by shelves from the cooking area.
There is a window to the side. There are newspapers on the chair
at the far side of the table.* MRS. MALAMUD *offers me food at the
beginning of the interview. We are drinking coffee. She is wearing
a sweatshirt with a large sequined cat. Her tennis shoes have
matching sequined cats. She has on a black skirt and is wearing a
wig. Her nails are manicured. She has beautiful eyes that sparkle
are very warm, and a very resonant voice. There is a lot of humor
in her face.*

Do you know what happened in August here?
You see when you read the newspapers.
I mean my son filmed what was going on,   2305
but when you read the newspapers . . .
Of course I was here
I couldn't leave my house.
I only would go out early during the day.
The police were barricading here.   2310
You see,
I wish
I could just like
go on television.
I wanna scream to the whole world.   2315
They said
that the Blacks were rioting against the Jews in Crown
   Heights
and that the Jews were fighting back.
Do you know that the Blacks who came here to riot were
   not my
neighbors?   2320
I don't love my neighbors.
I don't know my Black neighbors.
There's one lady on President Street—
Claire—
I adore her.   2325
She's my girl friend's next-door neighbor.
I've had a manicure
done in her house and we sit and kibbitz
and stuff
but I don't know them.   2330
I told you we don't mingle socially
because of the difference
of food
and religion
and what have you here.   2335
But
the people in this community
want exactly
what I want out of life.
They want to live   2340
in nice homes.
They all go to work.
They couldn't possibly
have houses here
if they didn't   2345
generally—They have
two,
um,
incomes
that come in.   2350
They want to send their kids to college.
They wanna live a nice quiet life.
They wanna shop for their groceries and cook their meals
   and go to
their Sunday picnics!
They just want to have decent homes and decent lives!   2355
The people who came to riot here
were brought here
by this famous
Reverend Al Sharpton,
which I'd like to know who ordained him?   2360
And he brought in a bunch of kids.

I wish you could see the *New York Times,*
unfortunately it was on page twenty,
but,
2365   he brought in a bunch of kids who didn't have jobs
      in the
summertime
when you don't have a job
and you're hanging out all day.
I mean, they interviewed
2370   one of the Black girls on Utica Avenue.
She said,
"The guys will make you pregnant
at night
and in the morning not know who you are."

(*Almost whispering.*)

2375   And if you're sitting on a front stoop and it's very, very
      hot
and you have no money
and you have nothing to do with your time
and someone says, "Come on, you wanna riot?"
You know how kids are.
2380   The fault lies with the police department.
The police department did nothing to stop them.
I was sitting here in the front of the house
when bottles were being thrown
and the sergeant tells five hundred policemen
2385   with clubs and helmets and guns
to duck.
And I said to him,
"You're telling them to duck?
What should I do?
2390   I don't have a club and a gun."
Had they put it—
stopped it on the first night
this kid who came from Australia . . .

(*She sucks her teeth.*)

You know,
2395   his parents were Holocaust survivors, he didn't have
      to die.
He worked,
did a lot of research in Holocaust studies.
He didn't have to die.
What happened on Utica Avenue
2400   was an accident.
JEWISH PEOPLE
DO NOT DRIVE VANS INTO SEVEN-YEAR-OLD
      BOYS.
YOU WANT TO KNOW SOMETHING? BLACK
      PEOPLE DO NOT DRIVE
VANS INTO SEVEN-YEAR-OLD BOYS.
2405   HISPANIC PEOPLE DON'T DRIVE VANS INTO
      SEVEN-YEAR-OLD BOYS.
IT'S JUST NOT DONE.
PEOPLE LIKE JEFFREY DAHMER MAYBE THEY
      DO IT.
BUT AVERAGE CITIZENS DO NOT GO OUT AND TRY
      TO KILL

(*Sounds like a laugh but it's just a sound.*)

SEVEN-YEAR-OLD BOYS.
It was an accident!   2410
But it was allowed to fester and to steam and all that.
When you come here do you see anything that's going
      on, riots?
No.
But Al Sharpton and the likes of him like *Dowerty,*
who by the way has been in prison   2415
and all of a sudden he became Reverend *Dowerty*—
they once did an exposé on him—
but
these guys live off of this,
you understand?   2420
People are not gonna give them money,
contribute to their causes
unless they're out there rabble-rousing
My Black neighbors?
I mean I spoke to them.   2425
They were hiding in their houses just like I was.
We were scared.
I was scared!
I was really frightened.
I had five hundred policemen standing in front of my   2430
      house
every day
I had mounted police,
but I couldn't leave my block,
because when it got dark I couldn't come back in.
I couldn't meet anyone for dinner.   2435
Thank God, I told you my children were all out of
      town.
My son was in Russia.
The coup
was exactly the same day as the riot
and I was very upset about it.   2440
He was in Russia running a camp
and I was very concerned when I had heard about that.
I hadn't heard from him
that night the riot started.
When I did hear from him I told him to stay in Russia,   2445
      he'd be safer
there than here.
And he was.

Reuven Ostrov

POGROMS

9:00 P.M. November 1991. In a basement of a Crown Heights house.
MR. OSTROV *wears a yarmulke. Eating popcorn and sliced apples.*
Very low, gentle-sounding nigunim music plays in the background,
it almost sounds like New Age music, perhaps because traditional
music is played on a modern electronic keyboard instrument. In
the show, I wore a basketball jacket with the team's insignia, and
used a basketball—which MR. OSTROV *did not do at this interview,*
but previously had at a basketball game. He has no beard, which is
unusual for a man his age who does have a beard if grown. He has
a very rich, deep voice.

I was working in a hospital.
I work as an assistant chaplain at
Down State Kings County Hospital.
I heard that Yankel Rosenbaum was stabbed and, um,   2450
  they

were gonna give him an *aurtopsy*
and they asked if he had an
aurtopsy
2455   or not because in the Jewish religion a person is not allowed
      to have
an aurtopsy
and I found out later that he did have one
a few days later.
I found a Jewish man in a room,
2460   a Russian man.
His mother committed suicide
because she was, uhm, she was terrified.
She jumped out of the third floor of her apartment
      building,
committed suicide.
2465   The mother originally came from Russia.
I was speaking to her son
in one of the rooms near the morgue
trying to get his mother not to have an aurtopsy
and he was telling me that the mother
2470   came from Russia eleven years ago
and the mother left Russia eleven years ago
because of the hardships that they had over there,
and when they came to America
and when this thing started to happen in Crown
      Heights.
2475   It became painful
and it felt like, like there was no place to go.
It's like you're trapped,
everywhere you go there's Jew haters.
And then he told me she commit suicide,
2480   told me the next morning he woke up
he heard the doorbell ring.
He wasn't,
she wasn't there.
He noticed that the window was open,
2485   which is never open
because she was afraid of the cold
even in the summertime.
And he saw his mother
with blood all over her
2490   landed head first
on the concrete side of the apartment building.
After that we already knew this was getting serious,
because we had,
we had Sonny Carson come down
2495   and we had, um,
Reverend Al Sharpton come down
start making pogroms.

Carmel Cato

LINGERING

7:00 P.M. The corner where the accident occurred in Crown Heights. An altar to Gavin is against the wall where the car crashed. Many pieces of cloth are draped. Some writing in color is on the wall. Candle wax is everywhere. There is a rope around the area. CATO is wearing a trench coat, pulled around him. He stands very close to me. Dark outside. Reggae music is in the background. Lights come from stores on each corner. Busy intersection. Sounds from outside. Traffic. Stores open. People in and out of shops. Sounds from inside apartments, televisions, voices, cooking, etc. He speaks in a pronounced West Indian accent.

In the meanwhile
it was two.
Angela was on the ground   2500
but she was trying to move. Gavin was still.
They was trying to pound him.
I was the father.
I was 'it, chucked, and pushed,
and a lot of   2505
sarcastic words were passed towards me
from the police
while I was trying to explain: It was my kid!
These are my children.
The child was hit you know.   2510
I saw everything, everything,
the guy radiator burst
all the hoses,
the steam,
all the garbage buckets along the building.   2515
And it was very loud,
everything burst.
It's like an atomic bomb,
and that's why all these people comin' round
wanna know what's happening.   2520
Oh it was very outrageous.
Numerous numbers.
All the time the police sayin'
you can't get in,
you can't pass,   2525
and the children laying on the ground.
He was hit at exactly eight-thirty.
Why?
I was standing over there.
There was a little child—   2530
a friend of mine
came up with a little child—
and I lift the child up
and she look at her watch at the same time
and she say it was eight-thirty.   2535
I gave the child back to her.
And then it happen.
Um, Um . . .
My child, these are the things I never dream about.
I take care of my children.   2540
You know it's a funny thing,
if a child get sick and he dies
it won't hurt me so bad,
or if a child run out into the street
it wouldn't hurt me.   2545
That's what's hurtin' me.
And the whole week
that Gavin died
my body was changing,
I was having different feelings.   2550
I stop eating,
I didn't et
nothin',
only drink water,
for two weeks;   2555
and I was very touchy—
any least thing that drop
or any song I hear
it would affect me.
Every time I try to do something   2560

I would have to stop.
I was
lingering, lingering, lingering, lingering,
all the time.
2565 But I can do things,
I can see things,
I know that for a fact.
I was telling myself,
"Something is wrong somewhere,"
2570 but I didn't want to see,
I didn't want to accept,
and it was inside of me,
and even when I go home I tell my friends,
"Something coming I could feel it
2575 but I didn't want to see,"
and all the time I just deny deny deny,
and I never thought it was Gavin,
but I didn't have a clue.
I thought it was one of the other children—
2580 the bigger boys
or the girl,
because she worry me,
she won't et—
but Gavin 'ee was 'ealtee,
2585 and he don't cause no trouble.
That's what's devastating me now.
Sometime it make me feel like it's no justice,
like, uh,
the Jewish people,

they are very high up,   2590
it's a very big thing,
they runnin' the whole show
from the judge right down.
And something I don't understand:
The Jewish people, they told me   2595
there are certain people I can not be seen with
and certain things I can not say
and certain people I can not talk to.
They made that very clear to me—the Jewish people—
they can throw the case out   2600
unless
I go to them with pity.
I don't know what they talkin' about.
So I don't know what kind of crap is that.
And make me say things I don't wanna say   2605
and make me do things I don't wanna do.
I am a special person.
I was born different.
I'm a man born by my foot.
I born by my foot.   2610
Anytime a baby comin' by the foot
they either cut the mother
or the baby dies.
But I was born with my foot.
I'm one of the special.   2615
There's no way they can overpower me.
No there's nothing to hide,
you can repeat every word I say.

CRITICAL CONTEXTS

ARTHUR MILLER
from *"Tragedy and the Common Man"* (1949)

Arthur Miller wrote this essay for the *New York Times* shortly after the opening of *Death of a Salesman.* In the essay, Miller develops a reading of the tragic hero that both contests and modifies Aristotle's description of the form and style of tragic drama. He also identifies his own presiding interests in the dynamics of tragic character. How important is it to Miller to be able to retain Aristotle's categories? Why? How do the different social, political, and cultural circumstances of Greek tragedy force Miller to redefine Aristotle's understanding of the function, purpose, and meaning of tragedy, particularly his understanding of tragic "character"?

In this age few tragedies are written. It has often been held that the lack is due to a paucity of heroes among us, or else that modern man has had the blood drawn out of his organs of belief by the skepticism of science, and the heroic attack on life cannot feed on an attitude of reserve and circumspection. For one reason or another, we are often held to be below tragedy—or tragedy above us. The inevitable conclusion is, of course, that the tragic mode is archaic, fit only for the very highly placed, the kings or the kingly, and where this admission is not made in so many words it is most often implied.

I believe that the common man is as apt a subject for tragedy in its highest sense as kings were. On the face of it this ought to be obvious in the light of modern psychiatry, which bases its analysis upon classic formulations, such as the Oedipus and Orestes complexes, for instances, which were enacted by royal beings, but which apply to everyone in similar emotional situations.

More simply, when the question of tragedy in art is not at issue, we never hesitate to attribute to the well-placed and the exalted the very same mental processes as the lowly. And finally, if the exaltation of tragic action were truly a property of the high-bred character alone, it is inconceivable that the mass of mankind should cherish tragedy above all other forms, let alone be capable of understanding it.

As a general rule, to which there may be exceptions unknown to me, I think the tragic feeling is evoked in us when we are in the presence of a character who is ready to lay down his life, if need be, to secure one thing—his sense of personal dignity. From Orestes to Hamlet, Medea to Macbeth, the underlying struggle is that of the individual attempting to gain his "rightful" position in his society.

Sometimes he is one who has been displaced from it, sometimes one who seeks to attain it for the first time, but the fateful wound from which the inevitable events spiral is the wound of indignity, and its dominant force is indignation. Tragedy, then, is the consequence of a man's total compulsion to evaluate himself justly.

In the sense of having been initiated by the hero himself, the tale always reveals what has been called his "tragic flaw," a failing that is not peculiar to grand or elevated characters. Nor is it necessarily a weakness. The flaw, or crack in the character, is really nothing—and need be nothing—but his inherent unwillingness to remain passive in the face of what he conceives to be a challenge to his dignity, his image of his rightful status. Only the passive, only those who accept their lot without active retaliation, are "flawless." Most of us are in that category.

But there are among us today, as there always have been, those who act against the scheme of things that degrades them, and in the process of action everything we have accepted out of fear or insensitivity or ignorance is shaken before us and examined, and from this total onslaught by an individual against the seemingly stable cosmos surrounding us—from this total examination of the "unchangeable" environment—comes the terror and the fear that is classically associated with tragedy.

More important, from this total questioning of what has previously been unquestioned, we learn. And such a process is not beyond the common man. In revolutions around the world, these past thirty years, he has demonstrated again and again this inner dynamic of all tragedy.

Insistence upon the rank of the tragic hero, or the so-called nobility of his character, is really but a clinging to the outward forms of tragedy. If rank or nobility of character was indispensable, then it would follow that the problems of those with rank were the particular problems of tragedy. But surely the right of one monarch to capture the domain from another no longer raises our passions, nor are our concepts of justice what they were to the mind of an Elizabethan king.

The quality in such plays that does shake us, however, derives from the underlying fear of being displaced, the disaster inherent in being torn away from our chosen image of what and who we are in this world. Among us today this fear is as strong, and perhaps stronger, than it ever was. In fact, it is the common man who knows this fear best.

Now, if it is true that tragedy is the consequence of a man's total compulsion to evaluate himself justly, his destruction in the attempt posits a wrong or an evil in his environment. And this is precisely the morality of tragedy and its lesson. The discovery of the moral law, which is what the enlightenment of tragedy consists of, is not the discovery of some abstract or metaphysical quantity.

The tragic right is a condition of life, a condition in which the human personality is able to flower and realize itself. The wrong is the condition which suppresses man, perverts the flowing out of his love and creative instinct. Tragedy enlightens—and it must, in that it points the heroic finger at the enemy of man's freedom. The thrust for freedom is the quality in tragedy which exalts. The revolutionary questioning of the stable environment is what terrifies. In no way is the common man debarred from such thoughts or such actions.

Seen in this light, our lack of tragedy may be partially accounted for by the turn which modern literature has taken toward the purely psychiatric view of life, or the purely sociological. If all our miseries, our indignities, are born and bred within our minds, then all action, let alone the heroic action, is obviously impossible.

And if society alone is responsible for the cramping of our lives, then the protagonist must needs be so pure and faultless as to force us to deny his validity as a character. From neither of these views can tragedy derive, simply because neither represents a balanced concept of life. Above all else, tragedy requires the finest appreciation by the writer of cause and effect.

No tragedy can therefore come about when its author fears to question absolutely everything, when he regards any institution, habit or custom as being either everlasting, immutable or inevitable. In the tragic view the need of man to wholly realize himself is the only fixed star, and whatever it is that hedges his nature and lowers it is ripe for attack and examination. Which is not to say that tragedy must preach revolution.

The Greeks could probe the very heavenly origin of their ways and return to confirm the rightness of laws. And Job could face God in anger, demanding his right and end in submission. But for a moment everything is in suspension, nothing is accepted, and in this stretching and tearing apart of the cosmos, in the very action of so doing, the character gains "size," the tragic stature which is spuriously attached to the royal or the highborn in our minds. The commonest of men may take on that stature to the extent of his willingness to throw all he has into the contest, the battle to secure his rightful place in his world.

There is a misconception of tragedy with which I have been struck in review after review, and in many conversations with writers and readers alike. It is the idea that tragedy is of necessity allied to pessimism. Even the dictionary says nothing more about the word than that it means a story with a sad or unhappy ending. This impression is so firmly fixed that I almost hesitate to claim that in truth tragedy implies more optimism in its author than does comedy, and that its final result ought to be the reinforcement of the onlooker's brightest opinions of the human animal.

For, if it is true to say that in essence the tragic hero is intent upon claiming his whole due as a personality, and if this struggle must be total and without reservation, then it automatically demonstrates the indestructible will of man to achieve his humanity.

The possibility of victory must be there in tragedy. Where pathos rules, where pathos is finally derived, a character has fought a battle he could not possibly have won. The pathetic is achieved when the protagonist is, by virtue of his witlessness, his insensitivity or the very air he gives off, incapable of grappling with a much superior force.

Pathos truly is the mode for the pessimist. But tragedy requires a nicer balance between what is possible and what is impossible. And it is curious, although edifying, that the plays we revere, century after century, are the tragedies. In them, and in them alone, lies the belief—optimistic, if you will, in the perfectibility of man.

It is time, I think, that we who are without kings, took up this bright thread of our history and followed it to the only place it can possibly lead in our time—the heart and spirit of the average man.

AMIRI BARAKA / LEROI JONES
from "The Revolutionary Theatre" (1966)

In "The Revolutionary Theatre," Amiri Baraka describes the challenges posed by an emerging African-American theater. How does Baraka's understanding of the necessity of "revolution"—what does Baraka mean by "revolution"—sustain his sense of what theater can and should do?

The Revolutionary Theatre should force change; it should be change. (All their faces turned into the lights and you work on them black nigger magic, and cleanse them at having seen the ugliness. And if the beautiful see themselves, they will love themselves.) We are preaching virtue again, but by that to mean NOW, toward what seems the most constructive use of the world.

The Revolutionary Theatre must EXPOSE! Show up the insides of these humans, look into black skulls. White men will cower before this theatre because it hates them. Because they themselves have been trained to hate. The Revolutionary Theatre must hate them for hating. For presuming with their technology to deny the supremacy of the Spirit. They will all die because of this.

The Revolutionary Theatre must teach them their deaths. It must crack their faces open to the mad cries of the poor. It must teach them about silence and the truths lodged there. It must kill any God anyone names except Common Sense. The Revolutionary Theatre should flush the fags and murderers out of Lincoln's face.

It should stagger through our universe correcting, insulting, preaching, spitting craziness—but a craziness taught to us in our most rational moments. People must be taught to trust true scientists (knowers, diggers, odd-balls) and that the holiness of life is the constant possibility of widening the consciousness. And they must be incited to strike back against any agency that attempts to prevent this widening.

The Revolutionary Theatre must Accuse and Attack anything that can be accused and attacked. It must Accuse and Attack because it is a theatre of Victims. It looks at the sky with the victims' eyes, and moves the victims to look at the strength in their minds and their bodies.

Clay in *Dutchman,* Ray in *The Toilet,* Walker in *The Slave,* are all victims. In the Western sense they could be heroes. But the Revolutionary Theatre, even if it is Western, must be anti-Western. It must show horrible coming attractions of The Crumbling of the West. Even as Artaud designed *The Conquest of Mexico,* so we must design *The Conquest of White Eye,* and show the missionaries and wiggly liber-als dying under blasts of concrete. For sound effects, wild screams of joy, from all the peoples of the world.

The Revolutionary Theatre must take dreams and give them a reality. It must isolate the ritual and histori-cal cycles of reality. But it must be food for all those who need food, and daring propaganda for the beauty of the Human Mind. It is a political theatre, a weapon to help in the slaughter of these dimwitted fatbellied white guys who somehow believe that the rest of the world is here for them to slobber on.

This should be a theatre of World Spirit. Where the spirit can be shown to be the most competent force in the world. Force. Spirit. Feeling. The language will be anybody's, but tightened by the poet's backbone. And even the language must show what the facts are in this consciousness epic, what's happening. We will talk about the world, and the preciseness with which we are able to summon the world will be our art. Art is method. And art, "like any ashtray or senator," remains in the world. Wittgenstein said eth-ics and aesthetics are one. I believe this. So the Broadway theatre is a theatre of reaction whose ethics, like its aes-thetics, reflect the spiritual values of this unholy society, which sends young crackers all over the world blowing off colored people's heads. (In some of these flippy Southern towns they even shoot up the immigrants' Favorite Son, be it Michael Schwerner or JFKennedy.)

The Revolutionary Theatre is shaped by the world, and moves to reshape the world, using as its force the natural force and perpetual vibrations of the mind in the world. We are history and desire, what we are, and what any ex-perience can make us.

It is a social theatre, but all theatre is social theatre. But we will change the drawing rooms into places where real things can be said about a real world, or into smoky rooms where the destruction of Washington can be plotted. The Revolutionary Theatre must function like an incendi-ary pencil planted in Curtis Lemay's cap. So that when the final curtain goes down brains are splattered over the seats and the floor, and bleeding nuns must wire SOS's to Belgians with gold teeth.

Our theatre will show victims so that their brothers in the audience will be better able to understand that they are the brothers of victims, and that they themselves are victims if they are blood brothers. And what we show must cause the blood to rush, so that pre-revolutionary temperaments will be bathed in this blood, and it will cause their deep-est souls to move, and they will find themselves tensed and clenched, even ready to die, at what the soul has been taught. We will scream and cry, murder, run through the streets in agony, if it means some soul will be moved, moved to actual life understanding of what the world is, and what it ought to be. We are preaching virtue and feel-ing, and a natural sense of the self in the world. All men live in the world, and the world ought to be a place for them to live.

What is called the imagination (from image, magi, magic, magician, etc.) is a practical vector from the soul. It stores all data, and can be called on to solve all our "problems." The imagination is the projection of our-selves past our sense of ourselves as "things." Imagination (Image) is all possibility, because from the image, the ini-tial circumscribed energy, any use (idea) is possible. And so begins that image's use in the world. Possibility is what moves us.

The popular white man's theatre like the popular white man's novel shows tired white lives, and the problems of eating white sugar, or else it herds bigcaboosed blondes onto huge stages in rhinestones and makes believe they are dancing or singing. WHITE BUSINESSMEN OF THE WORLD, DO YOU WANT TO SEE PEOPLE REALLY DANCING AND SINGING??? ALL OF YOU GO UP TO HARLEM AND GET YOURSELF KILLED. THERE WILL BE DANCING AND SINGING, THEN, FOR REAL!! (In *The Slave,* Walker Vessels, the black revolutionary, wears an armband, which is the insignia of the attacking army—a big red-lipped minstrel, grinning like crazy.)

The liberal white man's objection to the theatre of the revolution (if he is "hip" enough) will be on aesthetic grounds. Most white Western artists do not need to be "political," since usually, whether they know it or not, they are in complete sympathy with the most repressive social forces in the world today. There are more junior birdmen fascists running around the West today disguised as Artists than there are disguised as fascists. (But then, that word, *Fascist,* and with it, *Fascism,* has been made obsolete by the words *America,* and *Americanism.*) The American Artist usually turns out to be just a super-Bourgeois, because, finally, all he has to show for his sojourn through the world is "better taste" than the Bourgeois—many times not even that.

Americans will hate the Revolutionary Theatre because it will be out to destroy them and whatever they believe is real. American cops will try to close the theatres where such nakedness of the human spirit is paraded. American producers will say the revolutionary plays are filth, usually because they will treat human life as if it were actually happening. American directors will say that the white guys in the plays are too abstract and cowardly ("don't get me wrong . . . I mean aesthetically . . .") and they will be right.

The force we want is of twenty million spooks storming America with furious cries and unstoppable weapons. We want actual explosions and actual brutality: AN EPIC IS CRUMBLING and we must give it the space and hugeness of its actual demise. The Revolutionary Theatre, which is now peopled with victims, will soon begin to be peopled with new kinds of heroes—not the weak Hamlets debating whether or not they are ready to die for what's on their minds, but men and women (and minds) digging out from under a thousand years of "high art" and weak-faced dalliance. We must make an art that will function so as to call down the actual wrath of world spirit. We are witch doctors and assassins, but we will open a place for the true scientists to expand our consciousness. This is a theatre of assault. The play that will split the heavens for us will be called THE DESTRUCTION OF AMERICA. The heroes will be Crazy Horse, Denmark Vesey, Patrice Lumumba, and not history, not memory, not sad sentimental groping for a warmth in our despair; these will be new men, new heroes, and their enemies most of you who are reading this.

World Stages VII

International News Photo Agency, Argyropoulos

The family confronts Ginni in Manjula Padmanabhan's *Harvest*.

Historic social, political, and technological changes have reshaped the world since 1950, with a consequential impact on the theater. The aftermath of World War II has seen the remapping of the planet: the independence of India, Pakistan, and many Asian and African nations from colonial rule; the founding of Israel and the displacement of the Palestinians; and wars in Korea, Indochina, the Middle East, Africa, the Persian Gulf, Afghanistan, and Iraq. Defined by the erection of the Berlin Wall, the Cuban Missile Crisis, the invasion of Czechoslovakia, and the postwar division of Europe into the NATO and Warsaw Pact, the Cold War competition between the Soviet Union and the United States for global influence seemed fixed, until protestors began to dismantle the Berlin Wall in 1989. Two centuries after the French Revolution, Europe saw a series of new, often peaceful revolutions: independence for many formerly Soviet Republics, and freedom from Soviet domination for the formerly Socialist nations of central Europe. The mid-century decades also witnessed bitter civil strife and the glimmering of peace in Northern Ireland, Argentina, Chile, the United States, Europe, and elsewhere; a series of devastating wars in Africa and Asia, sometimes leading to genocide (as in Rwanda and the Darfur region of Sudan), and often to horrific famines (Bangladesh); the collapse of Yugoslavia, protracted war in Bosnia, and still unresolved ethnic and political tensions there; the waning of apartheid in South Africa, the rise of Islam as a geopolitical force. For much of the world, the past decade has witnessed the economic, political, and military consequences of the terrorist attack on the World Trade Center in New York, and the United States' decision to pursue the terrorists in Afghanistan, and to mount a separate war in Iraq.

With the rise of global communications, a global economy, and global political and military interests, such social and political revolutions immediately become the world's business. They reshape the world we live in even as we watch the changes unfold on our television screens. Fortunately, television has not really transformed the world's diverse cultures into a single "global village," but local cultures all feel the impact of events around the world. Think of the global effects of environmental disasters such as the Chernobyl nuclear power plant meltdown in 1986 and the deforestation of the rain forests of the Amazon; of medical advances such as vaccination; of epidemics like AIDS; of the international effects of social movements like nuclear disarmament, human rights, Amnesty International, feminism, and the peace movement, or of the financial collapse of the early 2000s, or more horrifyingly of anti-Semitism, racism, homophobia, and "ethnic cleansing."

Drama requires the collaboration of playwrights, actors, and audiences; the public structure of a theater site or building; and the social and political incentives and protections that make theatergoing attractive—it is an art deeply woven into the social fabric of a given culture and its history. Although we can still speak of the "London theater" or of "American drama," these terms have become in our era a critical convenience for reducing the dynamic variety of contemporary theater to the fictional boundaries of a single "national" culture. Although the theater still requires the support, work, and energy of its local community, today's dramatic repertoire is a global one. American playwright Sam Shepard first produced several of his plays in London. British playwright Edward Bond is more widely produced in Germany than in the United Kingdom. Many Eastern European and Latin American playwrights have been forced by censorship and political persecution to smuggle their plays to Europe or the United States to be staged. South African playwright Athol Fugard has premiered several plays in the United States. Nigerian Wole Soyinka is regularly produced throughout the world. These playwrights are deeply implicated in the working of their native cultures, but their plays have rapidly become part of the world repertoire.

Unit VII presents a different perspective on drama and theater than other units in the *Wadsworth Anthology of Drama.* Earlier units have been organized around a distinctive moment in the history of a relatively discrete culture: Athens in the fifth century BCE, Japan in the early shogunate; late medieval England and Renaissance London; late seventeenth century London, Paris, and Madrid; and twentieth-century Europe and the United States.

In many respects, this book is organized around undergraduate college teaching in the United States today, which emphasizes the historical development of Western theater practices and dramatic literatures. This unit takes a broadly "postcolonial" perspective on contemporary drama, establishing some continuities with Western traditions while bringing other traditions of world theater and drama into view.

Argentina   Argentina's historical and cultural development is hardly "representative" of the diverse histories of Latin American countries. Unlike Peru or Mexico, for example, Argentina was never a source of gold or silver, and throughout the seventeenth century the vast region that comprises much of present day Argentina, Paraguay, and Uruguay was a backwater of the viceroyalty of Peru. Puerto Nuestra Señora Santa María del Buen Aire was first established by Pedro de Mendoza in 1535. But although his expedition of 1,600 men was three times the size of the contingent that accompanied Hernan Cortés in conquering Mexico, the expedition arrived late in the summer, with little time to plant crops and harvest them for winter, and in a swampy region that was not well suited to agriculture in any case. The Spaniards established bad relations with the indigenous population, who soon began to lay siege to the settlement. The settlers finally—after slaughtering their cattle—resorted to cannibalism to survive the winter. Although the original settlement of Buenos Aires held on until 1541, it was abandoned as the settlers moved north to the thriving city of Asunción.

When Buenos Aires was reestablished in 1580, the central city of Córdoba was the dominant city of the viceroyalty, but by the seventeenth century the port city of Buenos Aires—whose people still refer to themselves today as "porteños"—emerged as the center of power in the region. The economy of Argentina depended on agriculture, and plantations were run by *encomienda*, the forced servitude of the native populations, licensed by the church. Throughout the eighteenth century, Buenos Aires was the center of military development, as well as of the burgeoning cattle ranching of the *pampas* stretching to the west and south of the city. Until 1776, the region was part of the viceroyalty of Peru and ruled from Lima; when Spain reformed the trade, administrative, and legal structure of its South American colonies in 1776, Buenos Aires became the capital of the viceroyalty of the Río de la Plata. Argentina's independence was part of the continental struggle for liberation of the first decades of the nineteenth century, precipitated by Napoleon's intervention in Spain in 1808. Although the Congress declared the independence of the United Provinces of the Río de la Plata on July 9, 1816, various civil and revolutionary wars would traverse the territory for the next thirty years. Argentina lost much of its viceregal territory in the wars of independence—parts of Peru in 1814, of Bolivia in 1825, of Uruguay in 1828. Beyond that, the revolution established two patterns that would afflict Argentina for a century. First, the *caudillos*—rural ranchers and landholders, with their own private armies—wanted the new nation organized as a loose federations of provinces, not as a centralized government emanating from Buenos Aires; much of the political conflict of nineteenth-century Argentina can be understood as a struggle between the federalist and central-government forces. Second, the wars drew a generation of British traders—some of whom fought with distinction in the revolution—to Argentina; they capitalized on the rich resources and weak economy of the new country, establishing lucrative trade relations with the United States, the United Kingdom, and Europe.

In some respects, Argentina's economic growth in the early twentieth century parallels that of the United States: several waves of European immigration in the 1880s and 1890s provided the labor power to transform Argentina into a manufacturing and agricultural power (in the early decades of the twentieth century, it was a cliché to be "as rich as an Argentine"). At the same time, however, Argentina's economy was drained by outside investment: by the Bank of England in the nineteenth century, and by American and European concerns in the twentieth. This situation was exploited by the charismatic Colonel Juan Perón, who was first elected president in 1946 on the promise of better wages and social programs for workers; Perón succeeded both in reducing foreign debt and in restoring the control of major industries—railroads and communications—to Argentine corporations. But Perón's economy also produced considerable inflation, and social unrest led to a series of military *juntas,* which typically used the excuse of Communist insurgency, the familiar bogeyman of the post-Castro era in the Americas, to justify the suspension of civil law.

In 1976, General Jorge Rafael Videla led a *junta* that inaugurated seven years of state terrorism, the "Dirty War" (1976–1983) in which brutal torture was routinely practiced, and thousands of Argentine citizens (*los desaparecidos*) were made to disappear by federal, state, and local government officials. This regime and its successors frequently collaborated with European and U.S. governments—on the eve of the disastrous Falklands War, General Leopoldo Galtieri attempted to gain U.S. government investment by offering military support to the United States in its military conflicts in Central America—and received both government and private investment. The Falklands conflict proved disastrous for the *junta,* and by January 1983 General Ramón J. Camps, the Buenos Aires chief of police in the Videla government admitted that the mass graves that had been discovered were those of *desaparecidos* (the "disappeared"), and that none were alive. Dissension in the military, a more activist prosecution of military crimes by the courts, and a widening sense that the *junta* could be ousted—typified around the world by Las Madres de la Plaza de Mayo—led to the election of Raúl Alfonsín in 1983, to the promise of trials, and then to the election of Carlos Menem.

Argentina has a long and distinguished theatrical tradition; plays were performed at the Jesuit missions in Córdoba in the early 1600s, and the first theater was built in Buenos Aires in 1757; the Teatro de la Ranchería was built in 1783. Throughout the seventeenth and eighteenth centuries, most of the plays performed in Argentina—in theaters in Santiago del Estero, Catamarca, Santa Fe, Corrientes, as well as Córdoba and Buenos Aires—were either Spanish *loas* or adaptations of French and Spanish dramas. By the nineteenth century, however, Argentine theater began to develop a more local flavor: in the romanticized dramas of *gaucho* (the famous Argentine cowboy) life typified by the anonymous *El amor de la estanciera* (1814); in plays of Argentine history, such as the independence play *25 de Mayo* and the play about the Peruvian native uprising *Tupac Amaru* (1817), both written by Luis Ambrosia Morante (1775–1837); and in a variety of short, sometimes satirical plays—called *SAINETES*—on political figures, and on the typical "characters" of Argentine life. This "local color" movement—*costumbrismo*—led to several popular genres, notably the *sainete gauchesco* and the *sainete criollo.*

The magnificent Teatro Colón opera house was built in 1857, at the early edge of Buenos Aires's development as a major metropolitan area; by 1900, Buenos Aires was known as the Paris of the New World for its fashionable elegance, and supported a wide range of theaters; 1900–1910 is regarded in Buenos Aires as the "golden decade" of its theaters, and many of Argentina's best-known playwrights—such as Florencio Sánchez (1875–1910), author of *La gringa* (1904) and *Barranca abajo* ("Down the Gully," 1905)—date from this era. As in Europe and the United States, an independent theater movement—El Teatro del Pueblo (1933) and La Máscara (1939)—arose, emphasizing (on the eve of Perón's mobilization of *los descamisados,* the shirtless workers) a more political, realistic, and Marxist orientation toward the staging of social life. Given the European orientation of Buenos Aires, it's not surprising that the various modes of European theatrical experimentation of the 1950s and after—Artaud's "theater of cruelty," theater of the absurd, Brechtian epic theater—have made their impact on Argentine drama, notably in the celebrated plays of Osvaldo Dragún (1929–1999); in the turbulence of the Perón and succeeding eras, the theater has often been a place of protest, and frequently subject to implicit or explicit censorship. This is especially true of the "dirty war" period. When the Teatro Abierto was founded in 1981, its building mysteriously burned to the ground within its first week of operation. Nonetheless, although many writers and intellectuals left Argentina, many remained, and their work often traces the connections between state terrorism and the diffuse nature of cultural and economic imperialism. Though written just before the "dirty war," Griselda Gambaro's play, *Information for Foreigners,* makes a direct assault on the authoritarian state; at the same time, by treating its audience as foreign tourists, the play implicates that larger world whose social and economic support helped to maintain the terror in Argentina.

Canada   Theater in Canada, like the culture of Canada itself, has been largely defined by its two dominant European settler cultures—English and French. Until the American Revolution, much of the eastern third of North America was contested by English and French explorers and traders: Jacques Cartier sailed down the St. Lawrence River, past the sites of Québec and Montréal in the 1530s; Samuel de Champlain's extensive explorations in the first quarter of the seventeenth century helped to define important fur-trading routes. By the mid-seventeenth century, however, Louis XIV declared New France a royal province, and throughout the remainder of the seventeenth and eighteenth centuries, France and Britain vied for control of Canada. The British had several strongholds in the maritime provinces, and to the west, in present-day Ontario; the exodus of British loyalists from the American colonies during the revolution—many of whom went into French Canada—enabled Britain to gain control of Canada; the 1791 Constitutional Act recognizes British legal and civil institutions, and the increasing British dominance of the important fur trade as well. In 1841, the United Provinces of Canada, in an effort to "assimilate" French Canada more effectively, gave a plurality of seats in the parliament to the British provinces. Although Canada was united as a Dominion in 1867, and gained its autonomy in 1931, the tensions between British and French Canada remain very much alive today: the separatist Parti Québécois and its charismatic leader René Levesque came to prominence in the early 1970s, and in several recent plebiscites, the citizens of Québec have voted to remain in Canada by only a narrow margin.

Although there are records of garrison performances in English Canada—an English version of Molière's *The Misanthrope* in January of 1744, in Nova Scotia—the earliest European performances in Canada were in French Canada. At Port-Royal, in Arcadia, Marc Lescarbot's aquatic pageant *Le Théâtre de Neptune en la Nouvelle-France* was performed (in war canoes!) to honor visiting French dignitaries in November 1606, and until a production of Molière's *Tartuffe* aroused the ire of the Catholic bishop—who forbade public theater in Québec in 1694—many performances of neoclassical French playwrights, including Corneille, Racine, and Molière were given in Québec. By the early nineteenth century, however, the Amateur Canada Dramatic Society had formed in Montréal (1835), and the church came to see that modest and moral stage performance could promote Catholic values. In 1898 it sanctioned the first lay company of actors, *Les Soirées de Famille* ("Family Evenings"). By this time, however, two permanent French-speaking theaters had been built in Montréal: the Monument National (1894) and Le Théâtre des Nouveautés (1898), serving a thriving trade in both touring companies from France and in the work of French-Canadian playwrights, such as Louis-Honoré Fréchette (1839–1908), whose sensational patriotic drama *Félix Porré* opened in 1862.

Theatre in English Canada was stimulated in part by the American Revolution; many British loyalists fled the revolution to the eastern provinces of Canada. The 500–seat Grand Playhouse was built in Halifax in 1789, and by the early nineteenth century, Toronto and other cities had major theaters on the European model. Nonetheless, much of the theatrical activity in the nineteenth century was by touring companies. However, much as in Europe, several smaller amateur companies developed, both to stage the new drama, and to support Canadian playwrights. The most significant of these companies was founded in 1919 by Roy Mitchell, at the University of Toronto—the Hart House Theatre. The Hart House was responsible for importing a number of experimental European playwrights, as well as for supporting the production of Canadian playwrights, including Dora Smith Conover, and Marjorie Price; Herman Voaden's expressionistic plays of the 1930s were produced at the Play Workshop. Other art theaters were formed in other cities as well; Martha Allan returned from working at the Pasadena Playhouse to her native Montréal to found the Montréal Repertory theater in 1930; the Toronto Workers Theater was active in the 1930s as well; and the establishment of the Canadian Broadcasting Company in 1936 brought radio drama throughout the nation.

The postwar period was the first real period for the growth of Canadian drama and theater. In part spurred by the Vincent Massey Report on the Arts of 1951 and the development of the Canada Council in 1957, both English and French Canada witnessed a flowering of new theater in the 1960s and 1970s. Several institutions—notably the Dora Mavor Moore New Play Society of Toronto (1946)—worked to develop Canadian plays and playwrights, like John Coulter's epic of the Métis rebellion in western Canada, *Riel* (1950); the founding in 1960 of a National Theatre School in Montréal. Both the Stratford Festival (established in 1953) and the Shaw Festival (1962) became showcases for Canadian actors, and by the mid-1960s a range of important theaters often working with new Canadian material had been founded: the Jupiter Theatre (1951); Tarragon Theatre (1971) in Toronto; L'équipe (1943), the Rideau Vert (1948), the Théâtre du Nouveau Monde (1961), the Théâtre des Cuisines (1973) and the Théâtre Expérimental des Femmes (1979) in Montréal; the Manitoba Theatre Center (1958), the Vancouver Playhouse (1962), the Neptune Theatre in Halifax (1962).

Although Gratien Gélinas (1908–1999) is usually described as the instigator of postwar French-Canadian drama—his play *Tit-Coq* (1948) about a soldier returning to Québec after the war is a modern classic—the drama of contemporary Canada was given an important impetus by the 1967 Dominion Drama Festival. Within the year a series of important plays were produced throughout Canada as part of its Centennial celebrations—Gélinas's *Yesterday the Children Were Dancing* (in English Translation), George Ryga's (1932–1967) *The Ecstasy of Rita Joe* among them. In 1968 Michel Tremblay's (b. 1942) groundbreaking play of working-class life in Québec, *Les Belles Soeurs* was produced; the play is also notable for being written in *joual,* the characteristic dialect of the city. Many plays, such as Sharon Pollock's *Walsh* (1973) attempt to reinterpret Canadian history; this play dramatizes the relationship between Major James Walsh, who commanded the North West Mounted Police in the 1870s and Sitting Bull, chief of the Hunkpapa Sioux. Since throughout much of the history of Canada the French-speaking minority of Québec has been dominated by an English-speaking majority, it's not surprising that the agitation in support of Québécois independence is reflected in a variety of plays as well. Indeed, the past three decades have seen a range of plays interrogating the Québec situation—not only the well-known plays of Michel Tremblay, but plays like Jean Barbeau's *Le chemin de lacroix* (1970) about a bill permitting Anglophone Québec parents to send their children to English-language schools in violation of Québec's bilingual policy, or Jean-Claude Germain's *A Canadian Play/Une plaie canadienne* (1979) about the mythology of a unified Canada. More recently, Marianne Ackerman's *L'Affaire Tartuffe, or,The Garrison Officers Rehearse Molière* (1993) takes a production of *Tartuffe* at the moment of Québec's incorporation into English Canada in 1774 as a turning point in the imagining of a nation. Much as Canadian drama—in different ways in English and French plays, in English and French theaters—considers the dynamics of Canadian nationalism, so the more recent work of Native playwrights like Tomson Highway, Monique Mojica—author of *Princess Pocahontas and the Blue Spots* (1990)—and others engage the position and representation of Native Canadians today. In the 1990s, Canadian theater continued in a period of artistic richness characteristic of Canada's official policy of multiculturalism. Robert Lepage not only directed landmark productions of Shakespeare's *A Midsummer Night's Dream* (at Britain's Royal National Theatre, 1992) but developed a stunning series of multimedia meditations—*Needles and Opium* (1994), *Elsinore* (1995), and *The Far Side of the Moon* (2000)—at his Theater Ex Machina in Québec City. Guillermo

Verdecchia's brilliant performance piece exploring *latinidad* in a wider North American context, *Fronteras Americanas* opened in 1993. Canadian drama continues to have an increasingly pronounced impact on world theater, and several plays—notably the plays of Judith Thompson, Ann-Marie MacDonald's *Good Night Desdemona, Good Morning Juliet* (1988), and several of George Walker's plays—*Zastrossi* (1981) and *Escape from Happiness* (1991)—have found mainstream audiences in the United States and in Europe.

China   The most populous country on the planet, China has a long and magnificently diverse theatrical tradition. The first records of theater in China date from the Shang Dynasty, roughly 1500 BCE, and the history of China is studded with important landmarks in the development of performance. The Han period (206 BCE–221 AD) witnessed China's first important artistic flowering, and the characteristically complex blending of spoken language, acting, music, mime, and acrobatics that distinguishes Chinese theater dates from this period as well. The first training school, "The Pear Garden," was established during the T'ang dynasty (618–904), and the earliest surviving plays date from the succeeding Sung dynasty (960–1279), plays which only began to be rediscovered in the 1920s. Although the Mongol conquest of the later thirteenth century put China under foreign rule, in the Yuan dynasty (1279–1368), seven hundred titles survive from this period, including several plays that have had an impact on the Western theater, including Chi Chun-hsiang's *The Orphan of the House of Chao*, adapted in 1775 by Voltaire, and Li Hsing-tao's *The Story of the Chalk Circle,* which provides the foundation for Bertolt Brecht's *Caucasian Chalk Circle*. While these plays typically use music and theatrical elements, they are considerably shorter than the "southern drama" that developed in southern China after the ejection of the Mongols in the Ming dynasty (1368–1644). The "southern drama" typically has more than fifty acts; it was mastered by playwrights such as T'ang Hsien Tsu (1550–1616), whose *Peony Pavilion* (recently adapted by the American director Peter Sellars) is today perhaps the most familiar of these plays. It is only in the Ch'ing period (1644–1912) that the most familiar form of traditional theater—Beijing Opera—began to take shape. Beijing Opera is a dynamic theatrical genre, using a scenario that sets the acting, singing, acrobatic, and musical skills of the performers on a narrative framework. Although there have always been a number of regional versions of this form, in 1790 the best performers from throughout China were brought to Beijing to celebrate the eightieth birthday of the Emperor Chi'ien-lung, and Beijing Opera is conventionally dated from this event.

   With the increasing opening of China to the West in the nineteenth century, and after the revolution that established the Republic of China in 1912, Western culture came to have a more direct influence on the arts in China. Usually termed "spoken drama," to distinguish it from the musical conventions of traditional Chinese theater, the first Western play—Alexandre Dumas's (*fils*) *La Dame aux camélias*—produced in China was staged by the Spring Willow Drama Society in 1907, and in the decades following, several important playwrights wrote and adapted plays in the Western style for Chinese audiences, under the rubric of the New Cultural Movement: Tian Han (1898–1968) at the Nan Guo Drama Society, Hong Shen (1894–1955) for the Theatre Association, Xia Lan (1900–1995) for the Shanghai Art and Drama Association. Perhaps the most influential playwright of the pre-war period is Ts'ao Yu (1902), whose plays *Thunderstorm* (1933) and *Sunrise* (1935) continue to be read and produced. "Spoken drama," mainly in the mode of Western realism, thrived in China, and was given additional impetus by the victory of the Communists and the founding of the People's Republic of China in 1949. The new government was at once concerned to preserve traditional Chinese theater and to promote theater that would more dynamically reflect contemporary life. The Traditional Theater Research Institute (now part of the China Arts Research Institute) was founded in 1950, and within a decade had revived hundreds of theater forms: by 1960, China had over 3,000 companies performing over 50,000 traditional plays. At the same time, companies worked to update the subject matter of traditional theater forms, using, for example, Beijing Opera to address more contemporary social issues, often in the "model plays" that trained the Beijing Opera (or related styles, such as Kun Opera or Chuan Opera) on historical subjects with a revolutionary perspective. The new government also established a National Theater Festival in 1956, which supported the work of postwar "spoken drama" playwrights, notably Lao She (1899–1966), whose play *Tea House* has become a modern Chinese classic, as well as Lao Yu (1910–1997), and the work of the Shanghai People's Art Theatre, which adapted Brecht's for Chinese audiences.

In 1966, the wife of China's leader Mao Zedong, Jiang Qing—helped by Kang Sheng and two others, becoming the notorious "Gang of Four"—instituted a decade-long Cultural Revolution. The purpose of the Cultural Revolution was at once to purge China of foreign influences, and also to institute a massive program of reeducation to the proletarian ideals of Maoist communism. The Cultural Revolution forced a generation of artists, professionals, and intellectuals—regarded by the Gang of Four as their principal political opposition—out of the major cities and into rural areas, where they would be reeducated into revolutionary culture through manual labor. Since the traditions of Chinese theater descended from aristocratic patronage, and the modern "spoken drama" theater was so clearly influenced by the West, it's perhaps not surprising that Chinese theater stagnated during the Cultural Revolution. Most theater companies disbanded during this period, and with the exception of plays specifically developed under Jiang's guidance, plays were heavily censored or prohibited altogether; only eight new "model" productions were developed, five in traditional theater forms. In 1976, however, the Gang of Four were removed from power; Deng Xiaoping inaugurated a period of new openness to the west, and allowed considerably greater latitude to artists and writers. Although previous regimes had insisted on Mao's "revolutionary realism" in the theater, in the 1980s, playwrights and performers experimented more widely: Gao Xingjian's *Absolute Signal,* a fluid hallucinatory drama, was performed briefly by the Beijing People's Art Theater in 1982, the same theater that invited Arthur Miller to direct a Chinese production of *Death of a Salesman* the following year. A Shakespeare Festival was staged in both Beijing and Shanghai in 1986, followed by Festivals of Experimental Theater in 1989 and 1993. The 1980s saw the rise of a number of important younger playwrights, including Gao Xingjian and Sha Ye Xing (b. 1939), whose satirical *Major Chen* (1980) was rivaled in controversy only by his *Confucius, Jesus Christ, and John Lennon* (1988); produced by the Shanghai People's Art Theater while he was Artistic Director. Zong Fu Xian (b. 1947) uses a rally in Tiananmen Square to indict the Gang of Four in *In the Depth of Silence* (1978).

Theater in China has a tradition of patronage, both by the aristocracy and by the state. With the rise of a market economy in the 1990s, subsidies for theaters have declined, sometimes to as little as thirty percent of operating expenses. Moreover, after the Tiananmen Square protests in 1989 theater has been subject to somewhat more censorship than in the immediately preceding decade, censorship that was extended in the period leading up to the Olympic Games, held in China in 2008.

Czech Republic

The contemporary Czech Republic stands at the crossroads of central Europe, and, like its political history, the history of its theater reflects the tension between native inspiration and the external influence of more powerful nations. Records of folk theater and of medieval passion plays in the Czech lands—Bohemia, Moravia, and Silesia—extend back to the thirteenth century, though religious drama was largely suspended during the Hussite religious wars of the fifteenth century. As in the rest of educated Europe, Czech schools and universities used the staging of Latin drama as a mode of instruction, particularly under the influence of the celebrated Czech teacher Comenius (Jan Komenský, 1572–1640), and playwrights such as Karel Kolčava (1656–1717) wrote important folk dramas; but it was the defeat of Czech aristocrats at the battle of Bíla Hora in 1620 by the Austrian Hapsburgs that was the most decisive factor: for the next 250 years, Czech culture would be dominated by Austria. The first purpose-built theater was constructed in Prague in 1737, exclusively for the use of foreign companies. Count Nostitz-Rieneck's Estates Theater was built in 1783, but its director, František Bulla (c.1754–1819), began to perform Czech plays there as early as 1785, an early sign of the romantic nationalism sweeping Europe and the Czech lands. By the early nineteenth century, several important dramatists were writing plays of "national awareness," including Václav Kliment Klicpera (1792–1859), Karel Hynek Thám (1763–1816) and his brother, the actor Václav Thám (1765–1816), who wrote for the Bouda ("Wooden Hut") Theater in the late 1780s, Jan Nepomuk Stepánek (1783–1859), and most importantly, Josef Kajetán Tyl (1808–1856), who wrote both historical dramas, such as *Jan Hus* (1848), and plays of modern life ("Where Is My Home?", a song from his romantic comedy *The Fair* [1834], became the Czech national anthem in 1918). Throughout the nineteenth century, resident theater companies played both in Prague and in Brno, generating the desire for a truly native, vernacular theater.

As in Ireland and the Scandinavian countries, a desire for national independence centered on the formation of a national theater company. The first independent, Czech-speaking professional theater, the Provisional National Theater, was founded in 1862, extending the already intense discussion of the possibility of a national stage; the elegant National Theater building opened in 1881 but almost immediately burned to the ground. It was a sign of the desire for a national stage that funds were raised through subscription, and a second theater was built, opening in 1883. Although there was always concern about whether an institutional theater could be at the forefront of emerging literary movements, the National Theater saw the production of plays much in the tradition of European modernism: Ladislav Stroupenický's (1850–1892) satiric comedies of contemporary rural life, Alois (1861–1925) and Vilém Mrstík's (1863–1912) social drama *Maryša* (1894), Gabriela Preissová's (1862–1946) *The Step Daughter*, as well as plays with expressionist elements, such as Alois Jirásek's (1851–1930) *The Lantern* (1905). The innovative director Karel Hugo Hilar (1885–1935) used expressionist techniques in the Theater of Royal Vinohrady in Prague in the 1910s, departing to lead the National Theater in 1921. Ironically, he traded places with the National Theater's master of psychological realism, the director Jaroslav Kvapil (1868–1950), who went to the Royal Vinohrady (this exchange was considerably more than a trade of artistic directors, as many of the actors traded houses as well). But modern Czech drama came to international attention with the plays of Karl Čapek (1880–1938). A well-known journalist and novelist, Čapek's first play, *The Brigand* (1920),was produced at the National Theater, and led to a string of successes. *R.U.R.* (1921)—the abbreviation is for "Rossum's Universal Robots"; the English word "robot" was coined from Čapek's play— was soon performed both in London and New York, as was *The Insect Play* (1922), which he wrote with his brother Josef (1887–1945), the famous Czech cartoonist. Čapek wrote a series of important plays, including a sequel to *R.U.R., Adam the Creator* (1927), and two plays protesting the rise of Fascism, *The White Scourge* (1937) and *The Mother* (1938). Čapek died in the year that Nazi Germany invaded Czechoslovakia, and his brother was arrested and died in the Belsen concentration camp in 1945.

With the German invasion and occupation of the Czech lands in 1938, theater in the "Protectorate of Bohemia and Moravia" was heavily censored, and the lively culture of socialist and experimental theater that had grown up in Prague and Brno in the 1920s and 1930s—most notably Emil František Burian's (1904–1959) D-34 Theater, and the socialist Liberated Theater of Jinřich Honzl (1893–1953)—was extinguished. At the beginning of the occupation, the Nazis granted the Czechs the appearance of "cultural autonomy." The Nazis did give the Czechs a degree of cultural autonomy, so Czech theaters were able to produce plays in Czech, and some plays prohibited in Germany were produced in Czech theaters. As in the Third Reich, all plays by antifascists, Communists, pacifists, and Jewish authors were prohibited. Nonetheless, using the practice of "jinotaj"—a kind of code of theatrical communication in which subversive meanings clear to the Czech audience were "veiled" from the German authorities—some directors (including Burian, Honzl, and others) and famous performers (such as the actress Ružena Nasková [1884–1960]) risked execution. Very rapidly, however, the Czech theater was firmly policed, and many Czech artists were killed or transported to concentration camps, and with the beginning of the war most works by Allied authors were banned (by 1940 over 1300 writers had been censored in the occupied Protectorate). One of the most fascinating chapters in the history of the theater concerns the imprisonment of German and Czech Jewish artists and performers to the Terezín concentration camp outside Prague, where they performed music, classical drama, and original plays and cabaret. As the war wound to a close, and Germany's eventual defeat became clear, Hitler increased the executions at his concentration camps, and most of the inhabitants of Terezín were transported to Auschwitz and killed. On September 1, 1944, all Czech theaters were closed, and the theater workers were directed to work for the German war effort.

After the war, Czechoslovakia came under the sway of the Soviet Union, and the Communist Party took control of the government in 1948. Under the Communists, the press and artistic institutions were governed by a central office that dogmatically imposed the favored SOCIAL REALISM of the Soviet Union; by the mid-1950s, censorship was controlled by the Ministry of the Interior (as it had been under the Nazis), and enforced by its agency, the State Police. At the same time, the long tradition of Czech innovation in the theater managed to persist. Josef Svoboda (1920–2002) became the chief theater designer at the National Theater in 1948, leading to the preeminence of Prague as a center of theater design; his multimedia *Laterna Magica* project was first seen at the Brussels Exhibition of 1958, and now occupies its own modern theater building adjoining the National Theater. The ABC Satire Theater performed during the brief political "thaw" of the late 1950s (1955–1962), and Prague's most influential new theaters, the Theater Behind the Gate (1955–1972) and the Theater on the Balustrade (1958–1972) both date from this era as well. These theaters experimented both with plays by young Czech writers (Milan Kundera, b. 1929; Pavel Kohout, b. 1929, and Václav Havel) as well as importing the plays of Jarry, Ionesco, Beckett, and Brecht to the stage. With the Soviet invasion of Czechoslovakia in 1968, however, many artists fled the country, and many others were either forced into exile, underground, or imprisoned as the result of their resistance to the state. Newspapers were closed, and widespread purges of artistic and educational institutions were enforced. Václav Havel's involvement in the Charter 77 movement (see the Havel biography later in this Unit), for example, contributed to his imprisonment. Perhaps the most symbolic protest was that of the young philosophy student Jan Palach, who wrote a letter calling for the end of Soviet censorship; signing the note "Torch Number One," he burned himself to death in Prague's central Wenceslas Square on January 16, 1969. As was the case during the German occupation, dissident theater was pursued beyond the official stage, and many plays were copied and secretly circulated. One important form of theater available to artists in the 1970s and 1980s was "apartment theater," plays performed in the homes of actors and playwrights. Vlasta Chramostová (b. 1926) had an important apartment theater, sponsoring a famous production of *Play Macbeth* (a version of this performance is captured in Tom Stoppard's play *Cahoot's Macbeth*). With the fall of the Berlin Wall in 1989, and the Velvet Revolution that followed, the Czech Republic has witnessed an extraordinarily smooth political transition, and joined the European Union in 2004. Perhaps not surprisingly, Prague has again become an important theatrical capital, the site not only of the dynamic productions at the National Theater and Estates Theater, but of many smaller experimental companies as well. The Theater on the Balustrade is again the home of a modern repertory, and theater companies from around the world regularly come to the Czech Republic's major cities.

India

The second-most populous nation on the planet, with seventeen official languages, India has an immensely rich cultural and theatrical history. The earliest literary writing—the epic poems *Ramayana* and *Mahabharata*—date from between the tenth and fifteenth centuries

BCE, and provide the narrative sources for much of the diverse range of traditional Indian performance. The oldest dramatic traditions date to the Sanskrit plays first written and performed during the Gupta empire in northern India, beginning about 100 AD; the aesthetic animating this theater is systematically explored in Bharata's *Natyasastra* (150 AD) (on Sanskrit Theater and Drama, see Unit II). Although Sanskrit has an important dramatic tradition—including King Sudraka's *The Clay Cart* and Khalidasa's *Shakuntala* (fifth century), Sanskrit—like Latin in Europe—gradually split into a range of vernacular languages; the invasion and rise of the Muslims to power after the seventh century restricted theatrical performance, and Sanskrit theater was believed until quite recently to have ceased, being replaced throughout India with an astonishingly diverse range of folk performance. As in other Asian performance forms, "theater" is not restricted to the spoken enactment of scripted plays: instead, the great majority of Indian folk theater forms use a brilliant interplay of story-telling, singing, dance, and music; there are also important forms of puppet theater as well. In the northern states of India, for instance, there is a 400-year tradition of performing the *Ramlila* and *Raslila* plays: cycle-dramas concerning events in the lives of Krishna, and Vishnu Rama. These performances often take place over three or four weeks, and involve the audiences in various kinds of religious ritual; they also mark one of the features of many Indian theater forms, the discrimination of actors from singers. In the *Ramlila*, the singer narrates the action, while the actors perform. A more recently developed form, the **JATRA,** is a staple of performance in Bengal, in eastern India. *Jatra* performances—like most Indian folk theater—do not take place in a theater, but in the open air, with the audience surrounding the performers. Unlike *Ramlila,* though, *jatra* tend to address contemporary concerns rather than the lives of mythic heroes. Indeed, the central figure of the *jatra* is always called Vivek, or "conscience": Traditionally, there is music in the *jatra,* and the actors sing; the performers are all male, and there are now professional *jatra* companies. Perhaps the most familiar form of traditional Indian performance in the West is *kathakali*, a dance-drama form from the southern state of Kerala. Performed in Malayalam—the language of Kerala—*kathakali* nonetheless preserves important elements of Sanskrit drama. In *kathakali*, the actors learn an elaborate and refined set of stylized bodily movements and detailed hand-gestures, each of which is codified as part of the *Natyasastra* tradition; having learned these techniques over many decades, the actors (all of whom are male) do not rehearse: they simply perform one of the 500 plays in the *kathakali* repertoire. Although it would be difficult to say that any form—or any three forms—can represent the range of traditional theater in India—there are literally hundreds of distinct theater and dance forms in this vast nation's rich folk and ritual traditions—what these forms share is a popular tradition of performance in village squares, at temples, or other open spaces, a complex involvement of music, acting, and dance, and a vigorously disciplined performance training.

While folk theater remains the dominant experience for the majority of Indians today, it remains in a now-productive tension with "modern" Indian theater. India has had a long history of contact with Europe: the Persians invaded northwest India in the sixth century BCE; Alexander the Great invaded again in 326 AD; the Portuguese explorer Vasco da Gama landed in India in 1498. British involvement with India was handled by the East India Company throughout the seventeenth and eighteenth centuries, but in 1858 the British government took over the Company, and in 1877 Queen Victoria became the Empress of India, and India became the "jewel" in her colonial "crown." Even before India was incorporated into the Empire, there were strong nationalist movements, and the British recognized the need for an Indian administrative class: universities were established in 1857 in the principal colonial cities, Calcutta (now Kolkata), Bombay (now Mumbai), and Madras to produce a "native" population educated to British values. In line with Thomas Babington Macaulay's infamous "Minute" to the House of Lords on Indian education, education was sustained by the teaching of English history and literature, the plays of Shakespeare and of eighteenth-century dramatists in particular. The British also produced English-language plays, and built theaters to accommodate touring companies. In the late nineteenth century, several Indian playwrights began to write plays—often in native languages such as Hindi or Urdu—in imitation of European drama; Wajid Ali Shah wrote several musical dance dramas, notably *The Tale of Radha and Krishna* (1851) and *Tale of Love* (1853); the Urdu poet Agha Hasan Amanat's *The Court of Lord Indra* (1854) was widely produced and translated. Moreover, the mid-nineteenth century also saw the rise of a new form of theater for India, profit-making companies. This kind theater, usually called Parsi Theater because these theaters were operated by Parsi businessmen (though usually employing Hindu and Muslim actors and playwrights), became the principal venue for "modern drama" in India, as the Parsi theaters often built new theater buildings on the model of Victorian proscenium theaters—such as the Victoria Theater and the Alfred Theater in 1871—and financed stage productions. Some of these plays adapted Western drama, as Agha Hashra Kashmiri (1879–1931) did in *White Blood* (1906), his adaptation of Shakespeare's *King Lear*; in the main, though, the Parsi theater was known for large-cast musical dramas, such as K.P. Khadikar's *Self Respect and Insult* (1911), a Marathi play arguing against the practice of child marriage. While the Parsi theater was extremely popular, particularly in the major urban areas, it seems finally to have been extinguished by the rise of film: indeed, many of the first Indian movie theaters were adapted from Parsi theater buildings.

While the Parsi theater represents one side of the "modernization" of Indian theater—turning it into a profit-making enterprise—there were other theater currents animating Indian theater in the later nineteenth-century. Bharatendu Harishchandra (1850–1885), for example, wrote plays in Hindi on pressing social issues—*The Sorry State of Bharat* (1880), *The Truthful King* (1875)—which were produced in public spaces. In Bengal, several playwrights used drama for specifically nationalistic purposes. Dinbandhu Mitra's *Neel Darpan* (*Indigo Mirror*) (1860) protested the plight of indigo workers, and was produced by the fledgling National Theater Company of Calcutta. When this company split into a Hindu National Theater and a Bengali National Theater, it retained this oppositional edge. The Bengali National Theater revived *Neel Darpan,* not only summoning agricultural workers to rebel against the British, but also showing the rape of a peasant woman by her British landlord. Largely due to the celebrity of this production, the government instigated the Dramatic Performances Control Act of 1876, in which local police were obliged to censor all new drama being produced in their jurisdiction. Perhaps for this reason, India's most famous poet and playwright of the colonial period—Rabindranath Tagore (1861–1941)—worked away from the realism of other playwrights, attempting to revive the mythological orientation of Sanskrit literature, and indeed to adapt it to critical purposes; Tagore won the Nobel Prize for Literature in 1913. Of course, the nationalist movement was given critical impetus by the work of Gandhi (1869–1948) and Jawaharlal Nehru (1899–1864), and "modern theater" in the twentieth century was strategically advanced by the Indian People's Theater, which opened branches in every Indian state in 1943, in many places bringing women to the stage for the first time.

India gained its independence from Britain on August 15, 1947; partition was established dividing Pakistan as an Islamic nation to the north at the same time, and in 1971 East Pakistan separated from Pakistan as Bangladesh. In the 1950s the Indian government established a range of cultural institutions, including the Cultural Academy of Performing Arts and the National School of Drama in 1959. The School's second director, Ebrahim Alkazi (b. 1925)—who had trained at the Royal Academy of Dramatic Art in London—was responsible at once for developing training in modern Western dramatic and theatrical traditions as well as for training performers in traditional Indian forms; his staging of Kalidasa's *Abhijnana Shakuntalam* (a Sanskrit play dating from 6 AD) at the Congress of Orientalists in New Delhi in 1964 is said to have inaugurated a revival of interest in exploring and preserving classical forms. In the aftermath of independence, Indian culture struggled at once to define a specifically "Indian" identity, and to modernize along the lines of Western culture:

this tension governs the theater as well. The "theater of roots" movement sought to explore and experiment with traditional theater forms, sometimes using traditional tribal performers as well. One of the leading playwrights of modern India, Girish Karnad (b. 1938), writes in the Kannada language; his *Hayavadana* (1971) uses music, mime, dancing and costume of traditional theater; his *Naga Mandala* is the first modern Indian play to be produced in the United States (Guthrie Theater, Minneapolis, 1993). Vijay Tendulkur (b. 1928) Several other playwrights and directors have worked in traditional forms, which have also been applied to Western dramas—as in the Annette Leday/Keli Theatre Company *Kathakali King Lear* (1989). While the "theater of roots" continues to work with traditional forms, street theater has become an increasingly popular form of theater and protest; one prominent playwright, Safdar Hashimi of Delhi produced an extensive series of street production in support of the rights of the urban poor: he was murdered in 1989 during a street performance of his play *Attack!,* beaten to death by the members of a rival political organization.

The major playwrights of modern India write in a range of languages—Hindi, Kannada, Marathi, Bengali—and for a variety of theatrical traditions. There is also an emerging dramatic literature in English. Writing in the colonial language has posed a problem for writers from Joyce to Ngũgĩ, and it is controversial as well in India. At the same time, English is one of the nation's official languages; it provides the *lingua franca* for citizens from different regions, who may not speak one another's language, and when plays from one region are translated for performance in another region, they are translated into English.

Ireland and Northern Ireland

English involvement in Ireland dates to the twelfth-century "conquest" of Ireland—Henry VIII assumed the title of "King of Ireland" in 1541—and the relationship between England and Ireland has been contested ever since. In the late sixteenth and early seventeenth century, Hugh O'Neill led a series of uprisings against English immigrants, who were establishing plantations in the northern areas of Ulster; later, during the English Civil War (1641–1642), the forces that Charles I raised in Ireland were eventually defeated, and Oliver Cromwell enacted a series of brutal massacres in Ireland in retribution, confiscating lands as well. When Charles II took the English throne in 1660, the Act of Settlement confirmed the landowning claims then in place in Ireland: Catholics who had been evicted from their property were unable to regain it. In 1688 the Catholic heir, James II, ascended the English throne; when Parliament invited William of Orange (who was married to Mary Stuart, a Protestant heir) to assume the throne, James fled to Ireland: his forces were defeated at the Battle of the Boyne in 1690 and he fled to France; his Irish supporters were defeated in 1691 at Aughrim.

William's victories inaugurated a prolonged period of Irish misery: the displacement of Catholics from land and property, restrictions of their rights to education, to bear arms, to pass property to their heirs, or to vote. Although some of these laws lost force in the later eighteenth century, they provided the backdrop for political unrest in the period, particularly Wolfe Tone's mobilization of the Dublin United Irishmen in support of a French supplied invasion. Although the French did send naval forces, and rebellions in Leinster, Ulster, and elsewhere looked promising, Tone was captured in 1798 and committed suicide in prison. In 1809, the Act of Union brought Ireland into the United Kingdom, effectively ending aspirations to nationhood. Nonetheless, throughout the nineteenth century, several movements worked for independence: Daniel O'Connell fought to repeal the Union, and Michael Davitt won security for tenants following the crop failures of 1879. Yet famine and immigration cut the Irish population in half between 1840 and 1900, and the Union's free trade legislation turned Ireland into an impoverished supplier of raw material and labor to English factories. In the later nineteenth century, nationalism was pursued on two fronts: by the desire for "home rule" led by Charles Stewart Parnell, and by a new sense of Irish cultural identity, fostered by the Gaelic League and other cultural institutions.

Dublin and Ulster had supported theaters for some time, but these theaters were driven by an English repertoire: the only Irish characters to play on the stage were comic, drunken, buffoons—"Stage Irishmen." It was this sense of cultural nationalism that gave rise to the first burst of Irish theater, the founding of the Irish Literary Theatre—later the Abbey Theatre—in 1899 by the poet/playwright W. B. Yeats (1865–1939), and the playwrights Lady Augusta Gregory (1852–1932) and John Millington Synge (1871–1909). The ambition of this company was to "build up a Celtic and Irish school of dramatic literature," and in the next thirty years, the Abbey succeeded not only in producing a wide range of plays on national subjects—peasant dramas about rural life like Synge's *The Playboy of the Western World* (1907); plays exhuming Irish mythology, like Yeats's cycle on Cuchulain; or realistic dramas of working-class urban life like Sean O'Casey's *The Plough and the Stars* (1926)—but establishing both an Irish style of performance, and the materials of a national theater as well. The Abbey remains a leading theater in the Republic of Ireland, and many important living playwrights have had major productions there: Tom Murphy, Ann Devlin, and Frank McGuinness among others.

The aborted revolution of Easter 1916 was a precursor of sweeping political change. In 1917, Eamonn De Valera was elected president of Sinn Féin and campaigned for an independent Ireland rather than merely achieving Home Rule as a province of Britain; in 1919, Ireland's war of independence was under way. In 1922, Sinn Féin succeeded in nego-tiating a treaty with the United Kingdom for independence, but the Free State was not to include the counties of Northern Ireland, which remained a British province. There have been various periods of tension between Northern Ireland and the Republic of Ireland and between Ireland and the United Kingdom; these tensions came to a head again in the late 1960s. In Northern Ireland, sharp divisions between rich and poor, the politically powerful and the oppressed have often fallen across religious divisions as well, separating Protestant Anglo-Irish from Catholics. Throughout the 1960s, Catholic and Protestant groups rioted in the Northern cities of Belfast and Derry (then, Londonderry); British soldiers were summoned to protect Protestant marchers. In 1972, the "Bloody Sunday" riots resulted in thirteen deaths, and a newly mobilized Provisional Irish Republican Army (IRA) began a series of retaliatory campaigns; the British Embassy was burned in Dublin, and the British secretary of state suspended the Northern Irish parliament and instigated direct rule.

The history of Northern Ireland for the past forty years is the history of this conflict: the hunger strikes by Catholic prisoners in the Maze prison who claimed the right to be treated as political prisoners rather than criminals; the increasing insurgency of Protestant para-military forces, inspired by the nationalist rhetoric of Ian Paisley; Gerry Adams and Sinn Féin's efforts to gain and remain in a position to be part of the bargaining for peace. The IRA cease-fire of 1994 was part of that bargain, leading—after a series of incidents threatening to undo the peace—to the IRA's official cessation of hostilities in July, 2005.

One of the most difficult aspects of the situation in Northern Ireland is the challenge to ideas of "national identity." Although Northern Ireland is physically part of Ireland, many of its citizens—even those who do not wish to be part of the United Kingdom—feel distinct from the Republic of Ireland; similarly, the long traditions of English rule have instilled a feeling of identification with England, one strengthened (for some) by the pro-Irish vio-lence of the IRA. In many respects the theater of Northern Ireland has had to negotiate this vexed sense of nationalism. For example, the Field Day Theatre Company was founded in 1980 by the playwright Brian Friel, the poet Tom Paulin, the actor Stephen Rea, and the poet Seamus Heaney: the purpose of the company was to develop a new theater, a new dra-matic literature of the North, one that attempted to identify the distinctiveness of Northern Ireland. In plays such as Friel's *Translations* or Thomas Kilroy's (b. 1934) *The Double Cross* (1986), or even in translations like Tom Paulin's version of *Antigone, The Riot Act,* Field Day attempted to bring a specifically Northern Irish culture into dialogue with a wider world. But the work of Field Day should be seen in the context of other playwrights, some of whom, such as Christina Reid (b. 1942), see the problems of contemporary urban life in cities like Belfast to be "political" in ways that extend well beyond the problems of national identification, into areas of gender and economic exploitation. While Frank McGuinness was born in Donegal (part of the Republic of Ireland), his brilliant play *Observe the Sons of Ulster Marching Toward the Somme* (1985) uses the situation of Irish soldiers during the First World War (before the independence of the Republic and the partitioning of the northern counties) to explore the complex personal politics of Unionism. Although Field Day—which toured its productions throughout Northern Ireland—has ceased producing plays, it has published a widely read anthology of Irish writing and has sponsored a series of essays on questions of national and postcolonial art and culture.

Martinique   Christopher Columbus stopped at the island of Martinique in 1502; it was an inhospitable island, dominated by the fierce Caribs. Although both Spain and England briefly established outposts on the island, it was settled in 1658 as a French colony, soon of some six thousand settlers. As happened throughout the Caribbean, the native population was exterminated by violence and disease. But the Compagnie de Sénégal, a French slave-trading company, made frequent stops at Martinique on its way to the larger island of Guadeloupe; the French imported slaves to the island, especially after the introduction of coffee in 1723. But a series of slave uprisings (1789, 1815, 1822), and an ongoing conflict with the English over the slave trade, led France to abolish slavery in Martinique in 1848; as a result, plantation owners frequently had to import workers from India and China, and the population of Martinique today is descended from these various groups. Martinique was made a crown colony in 1674; control of the island passed briefly to the English several times in the late eighteenth and early nineteenth century. Since the 1840s, however, Martinique has been governed by France: first as a colony, then as a *département* (1946), and since 1974 as a region.

All of the colonial powers brought theaters to the Caribbean—the first theater was built in Jamaica in 1682, and a production of John Gay's *The Beggar's Opera* was staged there in 1733. Since the 1950s, Aimé Césaire—Martinique's most famous poet, playwright, and essayist—has been critical to the public life of Martinique, and indeed to the theory of post-colonial development more widely. Césaire played an important part in the public life of Martinique, beginning a long term of service as a deputy to the French National Assembly in 1945, and then leading his Progressive party into power in 1957, and establishing several national institutions in support of the arts and theater. In part due to his efforts and those of his followers—training performers in traditional Caribbean forms of masking, drumming, and dancing, as well as inviting celebrated playwrights and directors such as Ariane Mnouchkine and Wole Soyinka to work in Martinique—Martinique now has a thriving theater culture.

Nigeria   With ninety million people, Nigeria is Africa's most populous country; of its twenty language groups, four—Yoruba, Ibo, Hausa, and Fulani—predominate, and the histories of the Yoruba, Ibo, and Hausa peoples are entwined in Nigeria's precolonial, colonial, and postcolonial history. In the precolonial period, Nigeria was home to several rich cultures. In the northern region adjacent to Lake Chad, ninth-century Arab writers described a flourishing culture, organized around a series of walled cities along Saharan trade routes between Egypt and western Africa. With the introduction of Islam from Mali in the fourteenth century, the Hausa and Fulani peoples became Muslim; in the nineteenth century, several emirs led a massive *jihad* or holy war against religious and civil authorities, and established a new center of power in Sokoto. Yoruba culture emanated from the southwestern region of Nigeria, centered around the city of Ife (eleventh through the fifteenth centuries); this Old Oyo culture—from which contemporary Yoruba culture descends—was a complex monarchial society, spread through several important cities; this is the kingdom that the Portuguese discovered when they arrived in the city of Benin in the fifteenth century. Ibo culture was less centrally organized, and stretched in a series of villages through the southeastern part of Nigeria.

European colonization of Nigeria began around the slave trade. The Portuguese slave trade of the seventeenth and eighteenth centuries was centered in Benin; the Portuguese transported slaves to their New World colonies, and deep strains of Yoruba can be found in many New World–African cultures, particularly in Brazil. The expansion of Islamic Fulani emirates in northern Nigeria in the nineteenth century intruded into the Old Oyo empire, driving the Yoruba south, instigating a series of wars, and—by displacing a large population—stimulating the slave trade.

The British Royal Niger Company established trade with various Ibo and Yoruba leaders in the 1840s, but only established an administrative headquarters in Lagos in 1886. Although initially making contact as traders, the British presence rapidly developed from trade and missionary work into a more conventional colonial profile: consolidating territory, developing a legal apparatus, deporting local leaders who resisted, including the northern emirs, who were conquered in 1903. Originally divided into northern and southern colonies, Britain formed the Colony and Protectorate of Nigeria under a governor-general in 1914. Nigeria gained independence in 1960, but the strains between various regions and ethnic groups have not been readily resolved; in 1967 General Odumegwu Ojukwu declared a secession of the eastern states (Biafra), and despite marching successfully on Benin City, and nearly taking Lagos, surrendered in 1970. Although an initial constitution placed a legislature in each region, Nigeria has been beset by a series of brutal military regimes—the first coup in 1966 established a pattern for the 1970s, 1980s, and 1990s. In 1999, the government of Nigeria was returned to civilian control, with free elections.

The area now known as Nigeria was the home of a variety of cultures prior to becoming a British colony, and many of the performance practices of these cultures are visible in contemporary Nigerian theater and drama. Best known is the festival of *EGUNGEN;* this festival, which has been performed at least since the fourteenth century, attempts to establish a communion between the living and the dead. In it, masked and costumed celebrants proceed to a sacred grove, where the accumulated troubles of the village are removed by a "carrier." The persistence of this ritual is acknowledged by Wole Soyinka's play *Death and the King's Horseman,* which in various direct and indirect ways engages with the *egungen* narrative. Yoruba ritual is also known for the dynamic character of its gods—Obatala, the god of creation; Ogun, the god of creativity; Sango, the god of lightning—and for the use of masquerade as a central feature of ritual. One of the most popular theatrical forms in Nigeria is the Yoruba Traveling Theater; first developed by Hubert Ogunde (1916–1990), these performances generally concern a contemporary social issue, such as the exploitation of workers in his 1945 *Strike and Hunger.* Rather than a formal "drama," though, this form of theater takes the shape of a series of short skits, involving both dialogue and song, framed by a musical opening and closing number. In part because his company frequently satirized the colonial government (and was censored), Ogunde's work became widely known and imitated, and gave rise to a large number of companies practicing this narrative/dramatic/musical genre. Recently, Yoruba Traveling Theater has become almost exclusively a film genre.

In part because of the English presence—an English-language theater first opened in Lagos in 1899—drama and theater played a large part in the educational apparatus of colonial Nigeria. D.A. Oloyede's play *King Elejigbo and Princess Abeje* (1904)—the first play in English by a Nigerian author—was written for a church group, and both reading and playing in the plays of the European tradition—Shakespeare, Molière, Shaw, Chekhov—formed part of the education of the generation of Nigerian writers and intellectuals who came of age with the independence. Wole Soyinka's plays often stage a rich dialogue between colonial and indigenous culture, drawing on the ritual and religious beliefs of the Yoruba. An Ibo playwright, John Pepper Clark (b. 1936) has dramatized the tales of the *ozidi* sagas—long stories that required several years to prepare and were performed by an entire village—and since the 1980s has directed his own professional theater. Femi Osofisan (b. 1946) is well known for taking a more critical, and politically engaged view of the problems of contemporary Nigerian society.

Russia   Although the Russian theater dates mainly from the eighteenth century, its impact on modern theater and drama has been profound; many of the playwrights of the nineteenth- and twentieth-century Russian theater (see Unit V) have become classics of the stage, and the theatrical innovations of the Soviet Union period (1919–1991)—SOCIAL REALISM, Vsevolod Meyerhold's (1874–1940) BIOMECHANICS, among many others—and the playwriting of contemporary Russia are part of the world theatrical repertoire today.

Theater in Russia has a long history of conflict with the Russian Orthodox Church, which was more effective than the Roman Catholic Church in its opposition to the stage. Although there are records of itinerant theater in the late middle ages, the Church's ban on theatrical performance extended well into the modern era; the first Romanov tsars erected a "house of amusement" in 1613, but Tsar Alexis (1645–1676) banned the theater with the exception of the Latin school drama until late in his reign, when he began to orient the Russian court more toward the practices of the European courts, which typically included a court stage as one of the ornaments of power. Peter the Great (1689–1725) extended the Romanov importation of European culture; he founded a theater in Moscow, and commanded attendance there for a time. Peter desired to engage Russia more directly with Europe—particularly after the wars with Sweden—founding the city of St. Petersburg on the Baltic Sea and moving his capital there from Moscow in 1712. Catherine the Great (1729–1796) ordered the founding of a professional theater; at the same time, Russia's famous "serf theaters"—theaters supported by large provincial landholders—produced generations of fine actors, many of whom followed the example of Mikhail Shchepkin (1788–1863), who came to the city (his career was pursued mainly in Moscow) to become a stage professional. As the capital, St. Petersburg saw the founding of several of Russia's preeminent theaters, including the Bolshoi, used mainly for opera and ballet, and the Maly and Alexandrinsky theaters, used as dramatic theaters in the 1750s, and important theaters were founded in the late eighteenth and early nineteenth centuries in Moscow as well; of these, Moscow's Maly Theater (1750) has had perhaps the most distinguished lineage and today houses one of the world's best-known companies. Many of Russia's greatest writers wrote for the stage, including Alexander Pushkin (1799–1837), Alexander Ostrovsky (1823–1886), and Nikolai Gogol (1809–1852), whose play *The Government Inspector* (1836) became a classic of European comedy. In the 1890s, Konstantin Stanislavsky (1863–1938) and Vladimir Nemirovich Danchenko (1858–1943) formed a literary circle experimenting with the production of new drama, founding the Moscow Art Theater in 1898; Anton Chekhov's (1860–1904) first major play, *The Seagull,* which had failed miserably in St. Petersburg, was the MAT's premiere (on Chekhov and the MAT, see Unit V).

As it was elsewhere in Europe, the period leading up to World War I was a period of intense cultural experimentation, and the success of the MAT in the realism cherished by Stanislavsky did not displace other kinds of experiment: Yevgeny Vakhtangov (1883–1922), Vsevolod Meyerhold, Alexander Tairov (1855–1950), and Mikhail Chekhov (1891–1955) all brought new styles and working methods to the MAT. With the Russian Revolution (1917–1919) and the success of the Bolshevik Party, the newly formed Union of Soviet Socialist Republics began to devise a cultural policy to form the citizens of the new soviet state. The appointment of A.V. Lunacharsky (1875–1933) as the Commissioner of Education at once ensured the survival of the Moscow Art Theater and the development of a state artistic policy; SOCIAL REALISM was confirmed as the official aesthetic policy at the first Congress of Soviet Writers in 1934. In the early phase of Soviet socialism, there was enormous excitement about the ways theater might be moved from its elitist, court-and-bourgeois past to become an instrument of revolutionary education and social change. Theaters were established throughout the USSR and supported with state funds, many of which were formed around collective purposes, such as the Trade Union Theater or the Red Army Theater. Meyerhold's efforts to locate the actor-as-worker led to a series of important collaborations, particularly with Vladimir Mayakovsky (1894–1940), whose plays *Mystery Bouffe* (1928), *The Bed Bug* (1929), and *The Bath House* (1930) are often taken to mark the high point of Soviet drama. At the same time, Meyerhold's experiments in CONSTRUCTIVISM—notably his 1922 staging of Crommelynck's *The Magnanimous Cuckold*—were increasingly seen as counter to the official Soviet aesthetics, and the Meyerhold Theater was closed in 1937. Meyerhold arrived at his home to find his wife, Zinaida Raikh, murdered, and was himself arrested, tortured, and executed by the Stalin regime.

The Soviet theater system was deeply centralized; over 800 companies were supported by the state, providing lifetime stipends to playwrights, directors, actors, designers, managers, and stagehands, and keeping ticket prices very low, well within the wages of the typical worker. While this kind of support enabled theaters to support large permanent companies, the determination of the repertoire and the inability to change personnel often led to stultification. With the death of Josef Stalin (1879–1953), however, a number of reforms were instituted that led to the founding of several new theater companies, especially the Taganka Theater (founded in 1946, but reorganized in 1964). At the same time, the theater schools associated with the MAT continued to produce well-trained and imaginative actors and directors, many of whom worked—as Yuri Lyubimov (b. 1917), director of Taganka, has done—to extend the legacy of Meyerhold, as well as exploring the once-forbidden legacy of Brecht, Beckett, and other European dramatists. Many of the theaters founded in the Soviet period have continued to flourish under the new Russian Federation: the Mayakovsky Theater, which was founded in 1922 and renamed the Theater of the Revolution in 1943, is just one example. Indeed, with the collapse of the Soviet Union and the emergence of the Russian Federation in 1991, many of Russia's chief theaters have gained a much larger international audience, both through tourism to Russia and because the companies can themselves tour more readily. The Maly Theater of St. Petersburg, under the leadership of Lev Dodin (b. 1944), has toured to Europe and the United States to considerable acclaim, praised both for the brilliance of its direction and the power of its physical performance. Although Russia no longer includes many of the republics of the former Soviet Union, it is a huge and diverse country, and continues to support theaters from the eastern border of Europe to Siberia. Many playwrights who began their careers in the Soviet era continue to write today, notably Alexander Volodin, whose important plays of the 1950s and 1960s (*The Factory Girl,* 1955; *Do Not Part with Loved Ones,* 1969) were often criticized for avoiding Communist Party themes; Mikhail Shatrov's plays are characteristic of the "socialism with a human face" ideology of the late 1960s and early 1970s. However, as the plays of Vassily Sigarev suggest, the increasingly unstable social world of contemporary Russia has led to a variety of dramatic experiments, and perhaps to a new kind of desperately ironic, absurdist drama.

South Africa

Contemporary theater and drama in South Africa has been marked, as have all areas of South African life, by the imposition of racial *apartheid*—the legal separation and discrimination of various "racial" and ethnic groups—in 1948, laws which were only lifted with the election of Nelson Mandela as president in 1994. Apartheid can be seen as a politically conservative response to the social and racial situation that has developed in South Africa over the past four hundred years, in which the Portuguese, British, and Dutch vied with one another for control of the land, while at the same time being hugely outnumbered—South Africa today has about five million white inhabitants and thirty million black inhabitants—by an oppressed indigenous population.

In 1487, Bartholomeu Dias, a Portuguese explorer, reached Mossel Bay, opening a sea route from Europe to Asia. Over the course of the next three centuries, the port at the Cape of Good Hope gained enormous strategic and military value. In 1652, the Dutch East India Company established a station there to supply water, food, and supplies to trade ships. Dutch settlers—called "Afrikaners" (or "Boers")—expanded from the immediate Cape region, conquering the Khoisan tribes, and importing slaves from Indonesia, India, Ceylon, Madagascar, and Mozambique. Throughout the eighteenth century, however, important colonies of British settlers developed in the region as well: after a series of battles and broken treaties, Britain gained control of the Cape Colony in 1806. Yet by gaining control of the region, the British were faced with two opponents: the indigenous tribes, and the Afrikaners, who resisted the imposition of British rule. The nineteenth century then witnessed two kinds of struggle. The conflict between British and Afrikaner settlers intensified when the British emancipated the colonial slaves in 1834. The years 1835–40 saw the "Great Trek," the departure of Afrikaners and their "clients"—slaves—from the Cape Colony northward, where they settled the Transvaal and Orange Free State as independent republics in 1852 and 1854 (the Trek is part of the consciousness of Afrikaner culture, and is frequently reenacted). However, the discovery of diamonds in 1867 and of gold in 1886 led to renewed conflict, as Britain attempted to annex the Afrikaner republics. The "War Between the Whites"—the Boer War of 1899–1902—led to British control of all three republics, which were united in 1910 as the Union of South Africa. The Union gained its independence from Britain in 1931, and became the Republic of South Africa in 1961, when it left the British Commonwealth.

Competing with one another for land and resources, the British and Afrikaners also had large and powerful indigenous populations to contend with, and despite the British policy against slavery, both parties systematically subjugated the black populations of South Africa. The most important of these groups were the Zulu; their leader Shaka defeated other African tribes, organized the Zulu as a kingdom in the 1820s, and was killed in 1828. In a series of conflicts—the British war with the Xhosa in 1834–1840, the Afrikaner defeat of a Zulu force at the Battle of Blood River in 1838, and the final British defeat of the Zulu in 1879—the white population gained control of the land and its people.

In many respects, the political history of modern South Africa is the history of the white minority's efforts to subordinate and control this populace. The discovery of gold and diamonds led—after the Boer War—to an increasing demand for mine laborers; although 64,000 Chinese workers were imported in 1904–1907, most of these laborers were Africans, who were increasingly segregated from the white population. When the Union of South Africa was formed in 1910, only whites were enfranchised; in 1911, the Mine and Works Act, the first of a series of laws restricting African workers to laboring work stipulated that skilled labor in the mines could only be performed by whites; in 1913, the Natives Land Act enacted the first of a series of segregation laws, by limiting African land ownership to certain reserves. Eventually, Africans were restricted to "townships," large, impoverished cities close enough to major cities to provide a constant labor supply. Moreover, the conflicts between British and Afrikaner South Africans were hardly resolved by the Union. Although South Africa participated in World War I as a dominion of the British Empire, the rise of Afrikaner nationalism in the 1930s led not only to considerable support for Germany in the country, but finally to the election of the Afrikaner National party in 1948.

The Afrikaner government installed apartheid as the law of the land in South Africa. Based on the notion that South Africa was comprised of four "racial" groups—White, Colored, Indian, and African—these laws legitimated White South Africans as the "nation," with the power to govern all other groups. Apartheid legislation was rapidly passed, and pervasive in its structuring of South African society: the Pass Laws of 1948 required one to carry a passbook at all times; the Population Registration Act of 1950 classified each person by race; the Group Areas Act forced people to live in racially segregated areas; in 1949 the Prohibition of Mixed Marriages Act passed; and in 1950 the Immorality Amendment Act prohibited sex between white and "nonwhite" persons. Property once "reserved" for ownership by Africans was claimed by whites: the segregated area of Sophiatown west of Johannesburg—where, since 1923, some African and Colored people owned land—was summarily converted into a White area, "Triomf" ("Triumph"). In the 1953 Bantu Education Act, the government assumed control of all schools—including missionary schools and colleges that had formerly educated Africans—and prohibited any instruction counter to the aims of the government; the 1959 Extension of University Education Act prohibited universities from admitting African students except with the permission of a cabinet minister.

The South African Native National Congress was founded in 1912 to advance the cause of Africans in South Africa: renamed the African National Congress, it responded swiftly to the imposition of apartheid: it organized a passive resistance campaign in 1952, and other acts of resistance throughout the 1950s. In 1959 a more radical group—the Pan African Congress, which included only Africans as members—split from the ANC; both were banned by the State of Emergency declared in 1960, after an uprising in Sharpeville when sixty Africans were shot by police during a peaceful protest. Although national and international opposition to apartheid was intense, it remained in force throughout the tumult of the 1960s, 1970s, and 1980s: the imprisonment of Nelson Mandela in 1962; the rise of the Black Consciousness Movement sponsored by Steve Biko and Barney Pityana in the late 1960s; the 1976 uprising in Soweto, a black township of one million people; the government's efforts to release the pressure on apartheid by forming black "homelands" in Transkei, Bophuthatswana, Venda, and Ciskei. By the mid-1980s, however, South Africa's isolation led to some political change: A new constitution in 1984 giving Colored, Asian, and Indian populations separate houses of parliament; the repeal of some pass laws in 1986; the release of Mandela in 1990, and the negotiations for a new constitution.

In all respects, theater in South Africa has been marked by this history. As a rough-and-tumble port, Cape Town did not support a legitimate theater until 1801, with the building of the African Theater, though performances of plays were given occasionally elsewhere (Beaumarchais's *Barber of Seville* was performed in Cape Town in 1783). By the early twentieth century, though, diamonds and gold were able to finance theater building, and every large city had several good theaters, performing European plays to white audiences. Since there was no repertory in Afrikaans, Afrikaners were particularly concerned to develop a "literary" culture: the first Afrikaans play was *Magrita Prinslo,* written by S. J. du Toit in 1897. Afrikaner theater flourished in the 1920s and 1930s, and continues today. Indeed, because the English-language theaters could rely on the traditional repertoire and touring companies, dramatic writing in English emerged much later in South Africa. Although the traditional forms of performance predate the colonial period, black theater in South Africa originates with Herbert Dhlomo (1903–1956), who studied at a mission school and became a teacher and journalist, and the author of twenty-four plays. In 1933 the Bantu Drama Society at the Bantu Men's Social Center performed his play *The Girl Who Killed to Save,* the first play by a black South African to be published in English, in 1936. Nonetheless, despite producing Dhlomo's play, the repertoire of the Bantu Drama Society was very much a European repertoire: Dhlomo himself played in Sheridan's comedy *She Stoops to Conquer.* Throughout the 1920s and 1930s, several companies—the Lucky Stars, the Syco Fans—worked to develop black drama.

The production of theater, like everything else in South African society, was segregated. In 1947 the government began funding a National Theater. Although the theater supported two companies—one in English, one in Afrikaans—they used no black actors, and included South African plays in their European repertoire only if they were written by white authors. In the 1940s, Es'kia Mphahlele and Khoti Mngoma founded the Syndicate of African Artists, but were refused government funding as long as they insisted on performing to mixed racial audiences: they were disbanded in 1956 after years of police harassment. The Union of South African Artists was organized in the 1950s to protect black artists' royalties, and engineered the production of the massively successful musical review about a boxer, *King Kong,* in 1959. Although the organization was white run, and showcased black talent to white audiences, it also performed successfully to mixed audiences, and sponsored mixed cast shows: the Union produced Athol Fugard's *No-Good Friday* in 1958, at the Bantu Men's Social Center in Johannesburg, with a cast including Fugard, Zakes Mokae, Bloke Modisane, and Stephen Moloi. When the show moved to the Brooke Theater, however, Fugard had to be replaced by a black actor—Lewis Nkosi—because segregated venues (the Brooke was an all-white theater) required segregated casts.

The principal challenge to resistant theater offered by the apartheid laws in the 1960s was the Group Areas Act, which prohibited the association of different races in clubs, cinemas, and restaurants; while mixed casts could perform to these segregated audiences, this loophole was closed in 1965: segregated audiences, segregated casts. In 1961, Fugard's *The Blood Knot*—about half brothers, one black (played by Mokae), one passing as white (played by Fugard)—could not be played in a legitimate theater, but gained good audiences in Dorkay House, and was shortly produced in London and New York. In 1963, Fugard began to work with the Serpent Players of Port Elizabeth, a black company, on adaptations of European playwrights—Büchner, Chekhov, Brecht, and Sophocles' *Antigone.* At the same time, however, a more improvisational, storytelling mode of theater was being developed in the townships, in plays such as Gibson Kente's *Manana, the Jazz Prophet* (1963). Kente's performances were popular and influential; in their use of narrative, mime, music, and dance to dramatize township life, they provided the form for later works like Barney Simon, Mbongeni Ngema, and Percy Mtwa's *Woza Albert!* (1981). Despite their popularity, these township playwrights had difficulty getting published; the South African Performing Arts Councils received large subsidies, but produced European plays mainly for white audiences, while the township theaters performed under poor circumstances to huge audiences, often sponsored by the Union.

The 1970s saw the real flowering of resistance theater in South Africa: Athol Fugard's collaboration with John Kani and Winston Ntshona (from the Serpent Players) led to *Sizwe Bansi Is Dead* (1972), which they performed (while the police looked on) as a mixed cast; subsequent performances were canceled. When they attempted to perform the play at the University of Witwatersrand, the security police arrested both the cast and the audience. Kente's performances became more politically inflected, in township plays like *How Long* (1973) and *Too Late* (1981), and inspired many other township works: Sol Rachilos's *The Township Wife* (1972), Sidney Sepamia's *Cry Yesterday* (1972), the Theater Workshop of Durban's *Umabatha* (the Zulu *Macbeth,* revived in London and the United States in 1997). The 1970s also saw the forming of several influential theater groups, including the Market Theater of Johannesburg in 1976, which produced Kente's *Mama and the Load* in 1980; Simon, Ngema, and Mtwa's *Woza Albert!* in 1981; Maishe Maponya's *Gangsters* in 1984; Ngema's *Asinamali;* and Mtwa's *Bhopa!* in 1985. The Market Theater has been influential outside South Africa as well, as many of its plays have been exported to Europe and the United States, and many of its playwrights—Fugard and Maponya, for instance—have since produced plays outside South Africa. With the lifting of apartheid, race emerges as a different kind of issue in South African drama, and has been explored by a number of playwrights, including Ismail Mahomed (b. 1959), Reza de Wet (b. 1955), Brett Bailey (b. 1967) and many others. The Grahamstown National Arts Festival continues as the premiere annual theater festival in South Africa.

Analyzing Postcolonial Theater and Drama

In part because postcolonial drama emerges out of the complex historical dynamics of global expansion, intercultural contact, political controversy, and sometimes unfamiliar artistic traditions, analyzing and discussing this material presents unique challenges. One approach to postcolonial culture attempts to develop a "national" or "regional"

(Aside)

INTERCULTURAL PERFORMANCE

One of the most challenging aspects of performance today has to do with the relative ease with which cultures now come into contact with one another, use—or steal—one another's forms of art and this hybridizing tendency is often visible in the plays in Unit VII. The interpenetration of different musical idioms has become a standard aspect of contemporary pop music; for instance, reggae and ska and mambo and tango and high-life and many other musical languages once local to a given culture now filter in and out of many American pop songs. And while the music industry has worked to sell this variety by copying the restaurant industry—as "World Music"—we might wonder whether the analogy with the variety of "ethnic" or "international" cuisine in the pricey restaurant districts of major cities (or even the new interest in Asian and Mexican foods shown by McDonald's and Burger King) isn't more to the point: have the products of other cultures, their music, their food, their plays, become empty commodities, consumed by a kind of global consumer elite?

In the past two decades, this kind of controversy has animated "intercultural performance," a kind of performance that attempts to bridge the differences between two different cultures not so much by erasing or occluding them as by concocting artworks in which these boundaries become visible and meaningful. Ariane Mnouchkine's productions of Shakespearean or classical Greek dramas using Eastern movement and dance techniques is one well-known example; another is Peter Brook's famous staging of the Indian epic, *The Mahabharata* at the Avignon Festival in 1985, and then on tour in the following years, which used fundamentally Western theatrical techniques to stage the narrative. In 1989, David McRuvie and Annette Leday collaborated with the Kerala State Arts Academy on a production of Shakespeare's *King Lear,* adapted to the extraordinarily complex conventions of the *kathakali*—an Indian form of masked dance-drama. Unlike the hybrid works of playwrights like Maponya or Luis Valdez, this intercultural strategy does not arise from the blending of cultural materials already present in a given culture—in the way Luis Valdez's *actos* draw from both Mexican and Anglo performance traditions visible in California in the 1960s. Instead, they work to bring about a dialogue between cultures that are distant from one another in space and time.

As Marvin Carlson suggests in a careful anatomy of contemporary intercultural performances, there is not only a long tradition of intercultural performance, but a variety of ways of imagining the relationship between cultural forms that performance brings about.[1] He lists seven possibilities: a performance in a tradition foreign to the audience, such as a Noh company or the Comédie Française visiting New York; the complete assimilation of foreign elements (does anyone really hear a reggae beat as "foreign" to American pop anymore?); the assimilation of an entire foreign structure, such as Yeats's writing of Noh plays, or Maponya's work with Brechtian epic theater; making the foreign into a new blend with familiar elements (Molière's absorption of Italian *commedia dell' arte*); assimilating an entire foreign genre, such as Westerns in Japan; using some foreign elements within familiar structures, such as the dance sequences in Hwang's *M. Butterfly,* or perhaps the *egungen* costumes in Soyinka's *Death and the King's Horseman*; and importing an entire performance from another culture as something distinctly unfamiliar, such as *butoh.*

This list clarifies the extent to which intercultural performance is a highly charged, contestatory activity: Brook was widely criticized, despite the evident elegance of *The Mahabharata,* for transforming something like the national conscience of India into a piece of slick theater; similarly, while McRuvie and Leday's *Kathakali King Lear* framed an ambitious attempt to chart how far one kind of theater might be translated into the traditions of another culture, its reception was often relatively simplistic: British reviewers complained that the "true" *King Lear* was lost in the translation. As we look across the horizon of contemporary performance today, the commingling, the rhetorical use of various theatrical traditions has become a hallmark of performance itself.

[1] Marvin Carlson, "Brook and Mnouchkine: Passages to India?" *The Intercultural Performance Reader,* ed. Patrice Pavis (London: Routledge, 1996), 82–83.

model, isolating themes (apartheid in South Africa, for instance), historical questions (plays that respond to the partition in Northern Ireland), or local features of dramatic style (the prevalence of domestic realism in American drama; the use of a trickster figure by Native Canadian playwrights) to assess the relationship between theater and the place of its production. This model can also lead to productive kinds of comparative study: in what ways does it make sense to frame a dialogue, say, between the "resistance" figured in Griselda Gambaro's *Information for Foreigners* and that sustaining Kani, Ntshona, and Fugard's *The Island*?

A second model recognizes the importance that ideas of "race" have had in mapping literary study, in drawing out political affinities between African, African-American, and Caribbean writers, for example. This model interrogates the ways in which "race" informs ideas of identity across national boundaries; it might place the ideas of W.E.B. DuBois or Amiri Baraka (see Unit VI) alongside the writings of Aimé Césaire and the Senegalese poet Leopold Senghor or the black Algerian psychiatrist Frantz Fanon's incendiary and brilliant book, *The Wretched of the Earth* (1961). In these writings, "race" emerges often as a cultural construct rather than a biological "fact," though its consequences are nonetheless powerful; and theorists of the production of "race" have often found a searching model in dramatic performance, both in plays in which "race" is a conscious issue—Soyinka's *Death and the King's Horseman*, or Baraka's *Dutchman*—as well as those in which it seems to be part of the play's unconscious politics, O'Neill's *The Hairy Ape*, for example, or Pinter's *The Homecoming*. Indeed, the constructedness of "race" or "ethnicity" can be a powerful weapon for *forging* a political consciousness: while the term "Latino" or "Latina" is relatively meaningless outside the Anglo-affiliated cultures of North America (people from Latin American countries tend to identify *nationally*, much as North Americans do; they think of themselves as Mexicans, Peruvians, or Cubans), it has become an important way for people experiencing *ethnic* discrimination in the United States to organize in a common effort.

One of the most powerful ways of considering postcolonial culture—its art, music, literature, drama, and performance—is to consider the formal properties of its artworks. Postcolonial critics, however, have resisted merely imposing the critical categories of Western literary study—tragic and comic form, for example, or verbal as opposed to music drama—on postcolonial arts, largely because such works often seem designed both to resist those categories, and to dramatize their implication in a wider politics. Wole Soyinka's early play *The Lion and the Jewel,* for example, is at once a play using the familiar stereotypes of Western comedy since Plautus—a pedantic schoolteacher, a cantankerous aging king, a pretty young girl—and interrogating them as well. As the play proceeds, it seems to ask whether this way of representing African village life—comedy—is complicit with the other ways that African village life is represented in the play: in magazine pictures, as a site for a railroad station, as the "dark continent" of the schoolteacher's textbooks. In other words, the play brings about a collision between the Western dramatic traditions Soyinka learned in Lagos, Leeds, and London, and the indigenous traditions—the social routines of the village, the songs, the marriage rituals—he blends into the texture of the play. This practice of blending both "indigenous" and "colonizing" literary or performance styles is generally called **HYBRIDIZATION,** and considering plays, poems, novels, films, and music in terms of their "hybrid" blending of cultural traditions is an important way of recognizing the cultural work that artworks do. Some writers (Ngũgĩ, might be an example) call for postcolonial art to resist and replace the inauthentic and oppressive means of "colonial" art—writing in the colonial language, using colonial forms, like tragedy, the novel, the pop song—as a way to locate a new and authentic space of liberation. Others (Soyinka and Homi Bhabha, for example) tend to see hybrid forms as a useful tool, an instrument for exposing the dynamics of oppression at the heart of the colonizing culture itself. Reading or listening for hybridity—the collision between the tragedy of Steve Biko and Samuel Beckett's absurdist play *Catastrophe* in Maponya's *Gangsters* for instance—involves the subtle and delicate task of putting these forms into dialogue with one another, listening for how they shape and qualify one another, open the possibility of new meanings.

READING THE MATERIAL THEATER

From the perspective of theater research, modern students of theater and drama live in an era of extraordinary privilege: generations of scholars have worked to assemble the primary and secondary materials that document earlier theaters; the amount of information available in archives, libraries, and on the Internet is nearly overwhelming; and, of course, performances now can be recorded on film or videotape, or for digital media. Yet we should not be seduced into thinking that a recording of a performance is the same thing as the live performance. First, of course, the camera's perspective governs everything we see on the screen, and makes it possible to achieve effects not possible in the theater; at the same time, it also transforms the performance from an actor's medium to the camera's. Viewers of the PBS versions of Anna Deavere Smith's *Fires in the Mirror* or *Twilight* can't help noticing the role played by the camera work, which brings Smith and her characters into a sharp close-up not possible onstage, to say nothing of the many scene changes, which—while they are handled seamlessly on television—point to a distracting "realism" that betrays Smith's open theatricality in performance.

Different kinds of documents—paintings, memoirs, reviews, illustrations, promptbooks, videotapes—tell us different kinds of things about the evanescent, always-lost performance onstage. One of the most useful documents for assessing the producers' original purposes in staging a play is the program, which often contains extensive program notes. With the rise of the director since the late nineteenth century, theater companies have often found it important to have a second "conceptual" voice in the production process: the dramaturg. Dramaturgs play a wide variety of functions. In European theater, they often have a central role in imagining the production and work in close cooperation with the director and cast throughout the development of the play. Under these circumstances, a company might use a dramaturg not only to conduct research into the historical background of the play and its author (and even—say, in the case of Shakespeare—into the play's language), but also to help articulate a critical perspective on the play for the performance in daily dialogue with the director and actors. In other circumstances—and more commonly in the United States—the dramaturg might function both as a literary manager, helping to acquire and develop new plays, and also work a kind of researcher, providing background information to the director and to the cast, as well as playing a central part in writing program information. As theatrical production has been understood to be an art independent of the narrowly literary meanings of dramatic writing, the theatrical program has become a place to inform and educate the audience about the play, both to provide historical information and to help develop a useful perspective on the production.

In 1980, the Field Day Theatre Company premiered Brian Friel's *Translations*. In writing the play, Friel had conducted considerable research into two important events in the history of Northern Ireland in the nineteenth century: the Ordnance Survey mapping of Ireland, and the transformation of the educational system. While Friel clearly worked to incorporate the information needed to understand the play *into* the play, the Field Day Company clearly felt that a greater understanding of the historical background would help readers to understand the play, and their production of it. What follows here are extracts from the program notes of *Translations*. It's important, of course, to train a skeptical eye on such efforts to explain the work of the production: how do these notes work to structure the audience's response to the play? Do the notes provide the kinds of information you think is needed? Do the notes tend to emphasize some elements in the play as essential for understanding the play, and overlook other, perhaps other important, elements? How do these notes provide a perspective on the playwright's work in writing the play?

FIELD DAY THEATRE COMPANY PROGRAM NOTES FOR *TRANSLATIONS*[1] (1980)

Extract from *The Hedge Schools of Ireland* by P.J. Dowling The Hedge Schools owed their origin to the suppression of all the ordinary legitimate means of education, first during the Cromwellian regime and then under the Penal Code introduced in the reign of William III and operating from that time till within less than twenty years from the opening of the nineteenth century . . .

"The Hedge Schools were clearly of peasant institution. They were maintained by the people who wanted their children educated; and they were taught by men who came from the people . . .

"The poorest and humblest of the schools gave instruction in reading, writing and arithmetic; Latin, Greek, Mathematics and other subjects were taught in a great number of schools; and in many cases the work was done entirely through the medium of the Irish language. Though the use of the vernacular was rapidly falling into decay during the eighteenth century, it was owing to the greater value of English on the fair and market rather than to any shifting of ground on the part of the schools . . .

"The Hedge Schools were the most vital force in popular education in Ireland during the eighteenth century.

They emerged in the nineteenth century more vigorous still, outnumbering all other schools, and so profoundly national as to hasten the introduction of a State system of education in 1831 . . ."

Extract from *The Autobiography of William Carleton* (born in County Tyrone, 1794) "The only place for giving instruction was a barn. The barn was a loft over a cowshed and stable . . . It was one of the largest barns in the parish.

---

[1]Courtesy Field Day Theatre Company

READING THE MATERIAL THEATER (cont'd)

"(At the age of fourteen) I had only got as far as Ovid's *Metamorphoses*, Justin, and the first chapter of John in the Greek Testament."

Extract from the memoirs of the Reverend Mr Alexander Ross, Rector, Dungiven, County Derry. 1814 "Even in the wildest districts, it is not unusual to meet with good classical scholars; and there are several young mountaineers of the writer's acquaintance, whose knowledge and taste in the Latin poets, might put to the blush many who have all the advantages of established schools and regular instruction."

Extract from *A History of Ireland* by Edmund Curtis "In 1831 Chief Secretary Stanley introduced a system of National Education . . . The system became a great success as an educational one but it had fatal effects on the Irish language and the old Gaelic tradition. According to Thomas Davis, at this time the vast majority of the people living west of a line drawn from Derry to Cork spoke nothing but Irish daily and east of it a considerable minority. It seems certain that at least two millions used it as their fireside speech . . . But the institution of universal elementary schools where English was the sole medium of instruction, combined with the influence of O'Connell, many of the priests, and other leaders who looked on Irish as a barrier to progress, soon made rapid inroads on the native speech . . ."

Extract from *Ordnance Survey of Ireland* by Thomas Colby, Colonel, Royal Engineers (1835) "To carry on a minute Survey of all Ireland no collection of ready instructed surveyors would have sufficed. It, therefore, became indispensable to train and organise a completely new department for the purpose. Officers and men from the corps of Royal Engineers formed the basis for this new organisation, and very large numbers of other persons possessing various qualifications, were gradually added to them to expedite the great work . . .

"The mode of spelling the names of places was peculiarly vague and unsettled, but on the maps about to be constructed it was desirable to establish a standard orthography, and for future reference, to identify the several localities with the names by which they had formerly been called . . ."

Extract from the Spring Rice Report (advocating a general survey of Ireland) to the British Government; 21 June 1824 "The general tranquility of Europe, enables the state to devote the abilities and exertions of a most valuable corps of officers to an undertaking, which, though not unimportant in a military point of view, recommends itself more directly as a civil measure.

Your committee trust that the survey will be carried on with energy, as well as with skill, and that it will, when completed, be creditable to the nation, and to the scientific acquirements of the present age. In that portion of the Empire to which it more particularly applies, it cannot but be received as a proof of the disposition of the legislature to adopt all measures calculated to advance the interests of Ireland."

Extracts from the letters of John O'Donovan, a civilian employee with the Ordnance Survey, later Professor of Celtic Studies, Queen's College, Belfast
Buncrana
23 August 1835
"On Friday we travelled through the Parish of Clonmany and ascended the Hill of Beinnin. Clonmany is the most Irish Parish I have yet visited; the men only, who go to markets and fairs, speak a little English, the women and children speak Irish only. This arises from their distance from Villages and Towns and from their being completely environed by mountains, which form a gigantic barrier between them and the more civilized and less civil inhabitants of the lower country."
Dun Fionnchada? Dun Fionnchon?
Dunfanaghy
9 September 1835

"I am sick to death's door of the names on the coast, because the name I get from one is denied by another of equal intelligence and authority to be correct. The only way to settle these names would be to summon a Jury and order them to say and present 'uppon ther Oathes' what these names are and ought to be. But there are several of them such trifling places that it seems to me that it matters not which of two or three appellations we give them. For example, the name Timlin's Hole is not of thirty years standing and will give way to another name as soon as that dangerous hole shall have swallowed a fisherman of more illustrious name than Tim Lyn."
Glenties
15 October 1835

"Yesterday being a fair-day at Dunglow we were obliged to leave it in consequence of the bustle and confusion. We directed our course southwards through the Parish of the Templecroan, keeping Traigh Eunach (a name which I find exceedingly difficult to Anglicise) to the right . . . On the road we met crowds of the women of the mountains who were loaded with stockings going to the stocking fair of Dunglow and who bore deep graven on their visages the effects of poverty and smoke, of their having been kept alive by the potatoe only . . . I have seen several fields of oats on this coast, some prostrated and rotting, others with the grain completely blown off the stalk—and some so green in October as to preclude the possibility of ripening at all."
Ballyshanny
1 November 1835

"I have met in this town a fine old man named Edward Quin, from whom I have received a good deal of information. He has been employed by Lieutenant Vickers to give the Irish names of places about Ballyshannon, and has saved me a good deal of trouble—I wish you could induce Mr Vickers to take him to his next district, and keep him employed writing in the Name Books, and taking down the names from the pronunciation of the country people."

Griselda Gambaro

Griselda Gambaro is one of the most distinguished writers of contemporary Argentina. Born in Buenos Aires in 1928, Gambaro's career as a writer has been deeply intertwined with the history and politics of her country. Argentina has a long history of repressive military rule, and Gambaro's career as a playwright began during a period of exceptional crisis, inaugurated by Juan Carlos Onganía's brutal military coup in 1966. Gambaro's plays from this period—*The Walls* (1963), *The Blunder* (1965), *The Siamese Twins* (1965), *The Camp* (1967)—concern the progressive deterioration of the fabric of society. But as the political repression of the 1960s gave way to state terrorism in the 1970s—especially the "Dirty War" (1976–1983), in which the military government systematically imprisoned and/or murdered hundreds of thousands of civilians, the "disappeared"—Gambaro's fiction and drama became increasingly engaged, making her situation in Argentina even more precarious. Her plays of the 1970s—including *Saying Yes* (1972), *Strip* (1972), *The Name* (1976), and *Information for Foreigners* (1973)—depict a world totally slipped from its moorings, in which murder, torture, and execution seem part of the horizon of everyday life.

Gambaro has written several novels as well, including *Nothing to Do with Another Story* (1972), *To Earn One's Death* (1976), *God Does Not Want Us Happy* (1979), and *Impenetrable* (1984). In 1977, *To Earn One's Death* was banned and Gambaro left Argentina to live in Spain and France. She returned to Argentina in 1980, where she continued her career as a playwright, with *Royal Gambit* (1980), *Bitter Blood* (1981), *From the Rising Sun* (1983), *Antígona Furiosa* (1986), *Fear* (1989), and *Worthless Trouble* (1990). Gambaro has lectured extensively in the United States and is currently living in Buenos Aires.

Information for Foreigners

Griselda Gambaro's *Information for Foreigners* uses the participatory element of environmental theater to enact a sophisticated political process as theater. Ideally performed in a house, the play divides the audience into four groups, each led through the play's scenes in a different order, and then reassembled as a single audience for the final scene, scene 20.

Information for Foreigners forces its audience to engage the subtle interinvolvement between theater and the theater of state terrorism, between fiction and fact, a blurring of boundaries between the simulated and the "real" typical of postmodern art. For throughout the play, the audience is repeatedly confronted by two kinds of "performance": overtly "theatrical" or "staged" scenes—like scene 14, where the audience observes a reenactment of a scene of police violence—and "backstage" or "offstage" scenes where the "disappeared"—the man in his underwear in scene 1, the girl who is tortured with the "submarine" (held under water in a bathtub of filthy water)—accidentally come into the audience's view. The play forces its audience both to connect these two spheres of performance and to question its own role in each. The Guide repeatedly provides "Information for Foreigners" to the audience, which articulates the historical background of state violence in the 1970s, and implicitly addresses that wider, European and North American audience whose tacit or financial support kept the regime in power. The audience is, in a sense, incriminated for adopting this "tourist" role.

In many respects, *Information for Foreigners* is a play about its audience. Scene 4 reenacts the famous Milgram experiment, in which the participant's willingness to follow orders and please authority figures leads him to kill (or, in the original versions of the experiment, to believe he has killed) the "student." The Milgram experiment provides a kind of metaphor for the audience's function in *Information for Foreigners*, in that observation repeatedly involves the audience in a kind of deference to authority, seduced as much by beauty—the quotations from Lorca and Shakespeare's *Othello*—as by power. The silent willingness to participate as spectators of the violence makes the audience responsible for the violence, becoming its silent authors. This implied assault on the audience's moral freedom

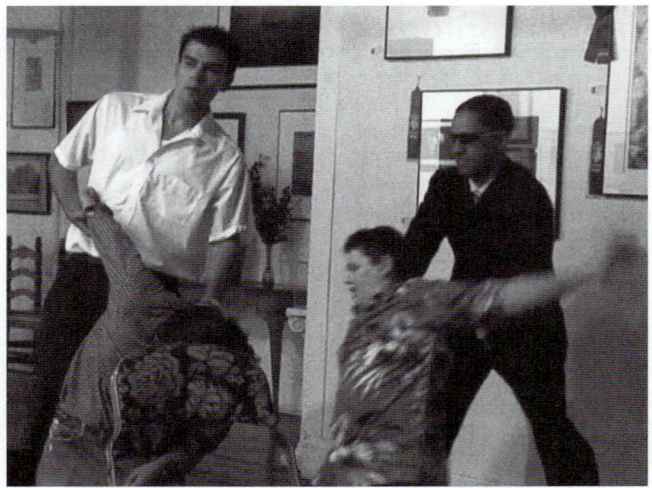

The U.S. premiere production of Gambaro's *Information for Foreigners*, produced in Denver, Colorado, 2007.

is the point of the play's final scene, where the line between theater and torture is finally suspended, and the "stage" of torture is one the audience is explicitly shown to authorize. Having brought the audience to witness a final execution, the Guide turns to us: "Ladies and gentlemen, what are you waiting for? The show is over." As he suggests in his final, ritual chant, "Theater imitates life"; but the boundaries between theater and life, between what we see and what we know, have been forever broken:

> Who once said: here the ken
> of men and women
> here the bounds?

A CHRONICLE IN TWENTY SCENES

Griselda Gambaro

TRANSLATED BY MARGUERITE FEITLOWITZ

CHARACTERS

GUIDES, *number contingent on number of audience groups*

VOICES, *heard at intervals throughout*

MAN IN ROOM

GIRL, *with wet clothes*
MAN, *with pistol*

COORDINATOR
MATURE MAN/TEACHER
YOUNG MAN/PUPIL

MOTHER
FATHER

GROUP OF MEN, *attack* MAN IN AUDIENCE
MAN, *defends attacked man*

SOMEONE FROM THE AUDIENCE, *number contingent on number of audience groups*
USHERETTE

THREE MEN, *carry table*
GROUP OF MEN, *surround girl*
TWO WORKMEN

MOTHER (*Sara Palacio de Verdt*)
FATHER (*Marcelo Verdt*)
TWO CHILDREN (*Verdt girl and boy*)
CHIEF
TWO POLICEMEN

MAN IN LOINCLOTH

MAN (*Robert Quieto*)

NEIGHBOR #1
NEIGHBOR #2
first group of men, *tied together*
NEIGHBOR #3
SECOND GROUP OF MEN, *tied together*
OFFICIAL
JUDGE
GUARD

GIRL, *with long hair (HERMENEGILDA)*
FOUR MEN, *on skates*
HUSBAND OF HERMENEGILDA
MOTHER OF HERMENEGILDA
NEIGHBORS

MAN (*Juan Pablo Maestre*)
WOMAN (*Miera Elena Misetich*)
TWO POLICEMEN
GROUP OF POLICEMEN, *dressed as sweepers*

GAME PLAYERS
POLICEMEN, *with clubs*

ACTOR #1
TWO MEN, *in box*

ACTRESS #1
ACTRESS #2
ACTOR #1
POLICEMAN #1
POLICEMAN #2

CHILD MONSTER

CHILDREN, *play Anton Pirulero*
FIRST MAN
SECOND MAN
THIRD MAN
YOUNG WOMAN

TWO GUARDS
PRISONERS
VISITORS TO PRISON
PRETTY GIRL

GROUP OF GUARDS, *attack* PRETTY GIRL
LITTLE OLD LADY
OUTLANDISH-LOOKING PRISONER

PROSTITUTES
MAN #1
MAN #2
MAN #3
MAN #4

The theater space can be a spacious, residential house, preferably two stories, with corridors and empty rooms, some of which interconnect. A larger space is needed for the final scene.

Situated in the passageways, propped against the walls, are two or three vertical rectangular boxes, each with a door and air holes.

In a different area, chosen by the director, sits an additional box, larger but otherwise the same as those in the passageways.

Some of the corridors are dark, while others, in obvious contrast, are crudely lit.

The audience will be divided into groups, the number and size of which will depend on the space. A particular number or color can serve to identify each group.

Group 1 will mark one possible development of the action.

Guides 1, 2, 3, 4, etc., lead their respective groups. The order in which the scenes are observed by these groups is left to the director's discretion until the last scene, scene 20, when all groups converge.

In certain scenes, actors play audience members and are actually part of the audience. Audience members, however, are never forced to participate in the action.

The groups cross in the passageways and may watch the same scene—perhaps one taking place in the passageway—when the director considers it necessary.

Excerpts introduced by the guides as "Explanation: For Foreigners" come from Argentine newspapers of the period 1971–72.

GUIDES: Organize the groups.

GUIDE: Ladies and gentlemen: Admission is ———, for adults. If you've already paid, you can't repent. The cost is already incurred. Better to enjoy yourself. No one under eighteen will be admitted. Or under thirty-five or over thirty-six. Everyone else can attend with no problem. No obscenity or strong words. The play speaks to our way of life: Argentine, Western, and Christian. We are in 1971. I ask that you stay together and remain silent. Careful on the stairs.

SCENE ONE

The GUIDE *leads the group toward one of the rooms. The room is completely in shadow. The door closes. We hear a shrill, metallic* signal. *Then, we hear many voices, indistinct and juxtaposed, carrying on an incomprehensible conversation.*

GUIDE: One moment…I don't find my flashlight. Remember, opportunity makes the thief. Watch your pocketbooks! (*Light comes up on a dark and wrinkled wall.*) Only the naked walls are left. (*The light travels. A man is seated on a chair, wearing only faded underwear. He raises his head, surprised and frightened. He covers his sex with his hands. To the audience.*) Excuse me. I've got the wrong room.

SCENE TWO

The GUIDE, *lighting the way with his flashlight, leads the group out of the room. He tries to open the door of another room. Behind the door a sweet voice sings*

VOICE:

"Carnation, sleep and dream,
the horse won't drink from the stream . . ."

GUIDE: (*Shrugging his shoulders, turns to the group.*) It's locked.
5 (*He knocks. Nicely.*) May I? I've brought a group of spectators.
And they're getting anxious.

VOICE: (*Very rudely.*) What's it to me? Beat it! I'm rehearsing.

SCENE THREE

GUIDE: (*To the group.*) Sorry. People should be brought up better,
don't you think? (*Tries the latch on the next door. It gives.*) Good.
Here. Go ahead. (*The group enters this other dark room. Against
the wall, some chairs. The* GUIDE *shines his light on them.*
5 *Then, nicely.*) You can position yourselves wherever you like.
There are chairs for everyone. (*He looks.*) No, not enough to go
around. (*Arranges them, offers.*) Ladies first . . . !

(*Lights on in the middle of the room. A young* GIRL *sits on a chair
wearing clothes that are soaking wet. A* MAN *stands next to her,
observing her with a tender smile. The* GUIDE *waits for people to
get comfortable, points out places. Then, with a finger on his lips,
he signals for silence and turns, like one more spectator, toward the
characters who begin the action.*)

MAN: (*Always speaks softly, tenderly.*) Why didn't you dry
yourself? You're getting the floor all wet. (*He bends down and
10 dries the floor with a rag.*) Lucky it's not waxed. (*The* GIRL
shivers with cold. The MAN *takes off his jacket, puts it on her
shoulders. The* GIRL *looks at it, wraps herself in the jacket.*)
Why didn't you dry yourself? Wasn't there a towel?

GIRL: No.

15 MAN: (*Drying the floor.*) What a mess! They fill the tub but don't
put any towels. What about the water? Was it warm? (*The*
GIRL *doesn't answer. He shakes her, gently.*) Was it warm?

GIRL: No.

MAN: (*He pulls a pistol from his belt and cleans it with a rag.*) Ah!
20 This department isn't worth shi . . . (*The* GUIDE *says something.
The* MAN *shoots him a quick look.*) Right. (*He shows her his
weapon.*) Do you like it? It isn't loaded. (*She looks at it but
doesn't answer. The* MAN *begins loading the gun.*) Why so sad?
(*Points to the group.*) Nothing will happen to you. There are
25 lots of people. They're watching us. (*Puts the pistol back in his
belt.*) You're not pretty with your hair all wet. But that's not
too serious. (*He leans toward her, curious.*) Tell me, do you dye
your hair? (*Still studying her.*) You're getting my jacket all wet.
Sorry, it's the only one I have . . . (*He takes it gently, shakes it,
30 and puts it on. With a shiver.*) It's damp. (*Pointing to the pistol.*)
Do you want it?

GIRL: No.

---

ii. 2 **"Carnation, sleep and dream,"** sung by a "sweet" female Voice,
the Mother in scene 5, and other voices elsewhere, is from García
Lorca's *Bodas de sangre,* or *Blood Wedding,* scene 2. I use the translation
by James Graham-Luján and Richard L. O'Connell in *Three Tragedies
of Federico García Lorca: Blood Wedding, Yerma, Bernarda Alba*
(New York: New Directions, 1955). In the original, Gambaro used only
"Nana, niño, nana, del caballo grande que no quiso el agua," repeated
over and over. For the English version, I chose to use many more
fragments of the lullabye over the course of the play. Gambaro approved
this choice in her letter to me of March 28, 1986

MAN: I'm leaving it for you. I have another. The jacket I can't,
I swear to you.

GIRL: (*Shaking her head.*) No. 35

MAN: (*Surreptitiously.*) Speak up! They can't hear a thing!

GUIDE: Louder! Louder!

MAN: What did I tell you? (*The* GIRL *doesn't answer.*) Look at me.
(*She obeys. He holds out the gun.*) Take it!

GIRL: No . . . I don't want to. 40

MAN: Why are you squeezing your legs together? Do you want to
go to the bathroom?

GIRL: (*Nods her head.*) Yes.

MAN: Then go!

GIRL: They're . . . watching me. 45

MAN: So? We're all adults, aren't we? They at least are watching.
What are you doing, always looking over there? What do you
see that's so pretty? (*Puts his cheek against hers. Looks in the
same direction.*) Nothing! (*Separates from her.*) I like to see
people's eyes when I talk to them. (*Gently, he turns her head.*) 50
Look at me. (*He points to the pistol.*) Do you want it?

GIRL: No, no! Leave me alone!

MAN: (*Anxious.*) Would you like some stockings? (*He puts his
hand on her foot.*)

GIRL: No! 55

MAN: Always no! Why? My intentions are good. Take it. Don't
you get bored all alone? (*Insists.*) Take it, it doesn't bite. But
don't squeeze the trigger. Unless . . .

GIRL: (*Barely audible.*) Unless . . .

MAN: If you squeeze, it's all over. Do you have a boyfriend? 60

GIRL: No.

MAN: Well then? Take it! I'm leaving it here, on the floor. All
you have to do is lean down.

GIRL: For what? I don't want . . . to lean down, I don't want . . .
anything. 65

MAN: The heart and the forehead . . . are sure. I mean, so you
don't suffer . . .

GIRL: No . . .

MAN: (*Caresses her cheek.*) Of course, no. There's a sun outside.
It's hot as hell. So you don't have a boyfriend? Well 70
then . . . ? (*He goes toward the door. Turns. Smiles.*) I'm going
to tell them to heat the water! (*He goes out. The* GIRL *looks
at the pistol on the floor, leans down, trembling, stretches her
hand. Freezes in the act.*)

GUIDE: Ladies and gentlemen, if it bothers you. (*He opens the* 75
door. Leading the group into the hallway, he explains.) In
March 1970, at the Max Planck Institute in Munich, Germany,
they began an interesting experiment. Careful on the stairs.

SCENE FOUR

*The group enters a white room that adjoins another, also painted
white, but that may be smaller. In the first room, a small table with
a cage full of white rats. On another table, a metal box outfitted
with buttons and a microphone. Carefully folded on an ordinary
chair, a white coat.*

*Through the half-open door one can see in the other room a chair
whose armrests are outfitted with side straps attached to electric
cables. Cables to tie down a person's legs. A microphone hangs down
from the ceiling.*

In the first room are the COORDINATOR, *dressed in a white coat, and
two others in street clothes, a* MATURE MAN *and a* YOUNG MAN. *The*

MATURE MAN *lingers in front of the cage, putting his fingers through the bars, trying to attract the rats and get them to play.*

COORDINATOR: (*To the group, in a professional tone.*) Gentlemen: The subject of our experiment is to determine the pedagogical effect of punishment. To what degree does punishment accelerate the learning process? Imagine. If with one
5 slap a child learns to behave, we waste years teaching and persuading only with nice words. We don't have time to lose. Soon he will be an adult; soon he will be molded. Molded for destruction, when one slap, two or three electrical jolts at the right moment could put things in place. (*He begins observing*
10 *the* MATURE MAN *playing with the rats.*) The gentlemen will help us to clarify . . . unclear . . . details . . . Please, sir, stop pestering those rats! Idiot! (*He goes toward him and kicks him away from the cage.*)
MATURE MAN: Okay, okay. I'm sorry. They're so cute that . . .
15 COORDINATOR: (*Calm.*) Of course they're cute. (*Becoming irritated.*) Shall we begin?
MATURE MAN: At your orders, sir!
COORDINATOR: (*Happy.*) One kick . . . and acquiescence. You, sir, emotionally more mature, will be the teacher.
20 MATURE MAN: Yes, delighted.
COORDINATOR: (*To the* YOUNG MAN.) You will be the pupil.
YOUNG MAN: (*He speaks with a metallic voice, like a parrot.*) I will be the pupil.
GUIDE: (*To the group, surreptitiously.*) Everyone's a researcher,
25 even the mule.
COORDINATOR: (*Drily.*) Silence! (*He takes money and some papers out of his pocket.*) Help yourself. Twenty-five marks, or thirty-six dollars for your trouble. If you would be so kind as to sign the receipt and the release. (*They sign, take their*
30 *money. The* COORDINATOR *hands the* TEACHER *a white coat.*) This is for you. (*Cordially, the* COORDINATOR *helps him on with the coat, adjusts the collar.*) There, now. Right this way, please. (*He leads them into the other room. The* GUIDE *follows with his group.* COORDINATOR *to the* PUPIL.) Please be seated.
35 Don't be afraid, it's an experiment, remember that.
PUPIL: Happy to please
I sit with the greatest of ease!
COORDINATOR: I made a mistake. Take off your jacket, roll up your sleeves. (*The* PUPIL *does so.*) Thank you. We have to
40 strap you in. If you would like to resign . . .
PUPIL No! For the sake of science
Let us commence!
COORDINATOR: (*Strapping him. To the* TEACHER.) Will you help me?
45 TEACHER: (*With dispatch.*) Yes, of course!
COORDINATOR: (*From a pocket of his coat, he takes a tube of cream and starts smearing the* PUPIL's *forearms.*) The cream facilitates the passage of current and prevents burns. (*Winking at him.*) It's an experiment, don't be frightened. It's like . . .
50 talking to hear yourself talk.
PUPIL: I'm not afraid
I'm not afraid
I really feel I have it made.
COORDINATOR: (*Attaches electrodes to the* PUPIL's *forearms. The*
55 TEACHER *helps diligently.*) How obliging! Thank you.
PUPIL: It's . . . very tight.
COORDINATOR: Let's loosen this a bit. (*He does.*) You—the Teacher—are going to station yourself at the microphone in the next room. (*To the* PUPIL.) You pay attention. He will read out a

group of words, such as *day-sun, night-moon, mother-love,* etc. 60
Then he will repeat the word *day* followed by four others. You must remember which of these four words was associated with *day.* If you make a mistake, you'll receive an electric shock as punishment.
TEACHER: And then you'll learn. 65
PUPIL: Why will punishment teach me?
COORDINATOR: The shock won't be strong.
TEACHER: Never?
COORDINATOR: No! Unless he really blunders. But it's impossible. They're very obvious associations. For idiots. (*To the* TEACHER.) 70
Let's go! (*They go into the adjoining room. The* GUIDE *settles his group. The* COORDINATOR *hands the* TEACHER *a sheet of paper.*) Here is the list of words. A clean game: read slowly, with good pronunciation. Wait! Roll up your sleeve.
TEACHER: Me? What for? 75
COORDINATOR: I want to give you a charge of forty-five volts.
TEACHER: (*Surprised.*) Me? I'm the teacher!
COORDINATOR: Don't be afraid. I'm doing it so that you'll appreciate the intensity of the punishment. Otherwise, you might have a heavy hand. (*He puts an electrode on the* 80
TEACHER's *arm, pushes a button.*)
TEACHER: (*Jumps, frightened.*) That's strong!
COORDINATOR: No, no. You'll start with fifteen volts. You won't have to increase it much. Be seated. Read. Slowly, in a clear voice. 85
TEACHER: (*He sits in front of the metal box, clears his throat, reads haltingly.*) Day-sun, night-moon, mother-love, water-ship, plague-war, house-forest, child-innocence, prison-bars, window-freedom, blue-sky, bird-flight, nation-Germany, torture-dissuasion. (*He finishes, looks at the* COORDINATOR 90
like a child awaiting instructions.)
COORDINATOR: (*Claps him on the shoulder.*) Very good! Now you must read one word, then four more, so that the pupil will pick the correct association. If he makes a mistake, say "Error," press the first button, and tell the pupil the voltage 95
with which you're punishing him. Then read the right answer. Punishments start at 15 volts and end at 450. (*He makes a horizontal gesture with his hand.*) As you see, it couldn't be easier. Begin.
TEACHER: (*Clears his throat.*) Sun! Day, forest, mother, water. 100
VOICE OF THE PUPIL: Day!
COORDINATOR: Very good! (*Encouraging the* TEACHER.) Let's go on! Do you like it?
TEACHER: (*Like a child.*) Yes! It's terrific!
COORDINATOR: Continue. 105
TEACHER: Night! Plague, forest, moon, child.
VOICE OF THE PUPIL: Moon!
TEACHER: (*Enthused.*) Correct! (*To the* COORDINATOR, *laughing.*) This is like a drug!
COORDINATOR: Ssshh! Go on! 110
TEACHER: Mother! Day, water, child, love. (*Silence from the* PUPIL.) But this is bread in your belly! What memories do you have of your mother?
COORDINATOR: (*With bonhomie.*) Now, don't help! It's not scientific! 115
VOICE OF THE PUPIL: Chi . . .
TEACHER: (*Advises.*) No!
COORDINATOR: (*Drily.*) Excuse me, sir. This is an experiment, not a game.
VOICE OF THE PUPIL: We can't repeat? (*The* TEACHER *looks at the* 120
COORDINATOR.)

COORDINATOR: Just this once. You've got to follow the rules.

TEACHER: Just this once, not again. Mother: day, water, child, love. (*Silence from the* PUPIL.) Well?

125 VOICE OF THE PUPIL: Love!

TEACHER: Very good! But faster. (*The* COORDINATOR *nods approval.*) Blue: ship, bird, sky, house. (*Silence from the* PUPIL.) I'm waiting.

VOICE OF THE PUPIL: Want to repeat?

130 TEACHER: I won't repeat. How can you not remember? What a fool. (*Looks at the* COORDINATOR, *who assents.*) Answer, I won't wait any longer.

VOICE OF THE PUPIL: Bird!

TEACHER: (*Pleased.*) He made a mistake! Now what do I do?

135 COORDINATOR: (*He points to the box. The* TEACHER *vacillates in his choice among the buttons.*) The first. Fifteen volts.

TEACHER: (*Smiles timidly. Pushes the button.*) Here we go! Take that. (*Through the door, we see that the* PUPIL *is jolted but cries out more in surprise than pain. His cries are always in a parrot-*

140 *voice, stereotyped like those of someone who, as a joke, coarsely imitates moans, groans, and pain. To the* COORDINATOR.) I didn't do anything! (*Into the microphone.*) Now remember. (*He reads.*) Plague: child, innocence, love, night.

COORDINATOR: (*Very low.*) You forgot war.

145 TEACHER: I did?

COORDINATOR: Plague-war. It's all right, let it go. It doesn't matter.

TEACHER: (*Low.*) Should I repeat? (*The* COORDINATOR *shrugs.*) Well? (*The* PUPIL *is silent.*) Come on. Quick. Otherwise it's

150 boring, I get tired.

VOICE OF THE PUPIL: Night.

TEACHER: (*Pleased.*) He made a mistake! Thirty volts! (*Instantly presses the second button. A louder groan from the* PUPIL.) Moving right along. Child: love, mother, innocence, bird.

155 VOICE OF THE PUPIL: (*Quickly.*) Love!

TEACHER: He made a mistake! You were dreaming! Forty-five volts! (*He pushes another button. Howling loudly, the* PUPIL *arches his back. Surprised by the howling, the* TEACHER *looks into the other room. To the* COORDINATOR, *disturbed.*) A bit strong, wasn't it?

160 COORDINATOR: (*Soothingly.*) No. This is a scientific experiment, and I am in charge. What experiment? Just as I told you: simply to determine the effectiveness of punishment in learning. If from the beginning we doubt, we'll never arrive at a conclusion.

165 TEACHER: Yes, that's right. The associations are easy.

COORDINATOR: And it's not so much. I gave you forty-five volts, remember?

TEACHER: I didn't shout. What a weakling! (*To the* PUPIL.) Listen to me. Don't scream. Pay attention. Sky: mother, child,

170 innocence, blue.

VOICE OF THE PUPIL: Blue!

TEACHER: Gooooood!

COORDINATOR: Magnificent. We're already getting results.

TEACHER: It's no time to stop, then. Plague: prison, house, forest,

175 war. Well? (*Slowly, the* COORDINATOR *closes the door connecting the rooms.*) Repeat. (*The* COORDINATOR *shakes his head.*) I can't. (*Silence from the* PUPIL.) Well? (*To the* COORDINATOR.) Can I repeat? Just this once. He's not very intelligent. (*The* COORDINATOR *snorts, accedes with a gesture.*)

180 TEACHER: Listen. Don't let your mind wander. Plague: prison, house, forest, war.

VOICE OF THE PUPIL: Prison.

TEACHER: He's an idiot!

COORDINATOR: (*Exasperated.*) You must say, "Error," and press the button. That is your job! Save the commentary! 185

TEACHER: And now he's growling at me! (*He presses the button.*)

VOICE OF THE PUPIL: (*Screams.*) No, no! I didn't think I'd be in so much pain!

TEACHER: A smart aleck! Well, he better hold up! (*Into the microphone.*) Pupil: Pay attention. You think I like pushing 190 these little buttons? Try to remember. Blue: bird, flight, sky, freedom. (*Waits, nervous.*) Out with it!

VOICE OF THE PUPIL: I don't remember!

TEACHER: How can you not remember?

VOICE OF THE PUPIL: I don't! 195

TEACHER: (*Furious, pushes the button.*) If you don't remember, take this.

VOICE OF THE PUPIL: (*A scream.*) Sky! (*He whimpers.*)

TEACHER: Very good! (*He wipes the sweat from his face.*) You see? With a little determination, you hit it! Okay! Here we go. 200 Flight: bird, blue, forest, night. You gotta be quick. Answer.

VOICE OF THE PUPIL: I won't play! No matter what you say!

COORDINATOR: Youth today! Now he refuses!

TEACHER: What's the matter with him? He's howling. 205

COORDINATOR: He signed the release. He can't give up. The results are important, aren't they? You're not screaming. You can be counted on.

TEACHER: Pupil? Pay attention. I am going to read you the words.

VOICE OF THE PUPIL: Go to hell! Let's change places! 210

TEACHER: Change places? That's crazy. It'll be worse for you, if you don't answer. Bird: flight, blue, plague, war. And I'm repeating the words. And it isn't allowed! Who do you think you are? Answer!

VOICE OF THE PUPIL: I'll make a mistake! 215

TEACHER: Answer! (*He pushes the button. A scream. To* COORDINATOR.) He's screaming.

COORDINATOR: He feels a bit jolted. You have just one thing to watch out for: 450 volts—kaput. Otherwise, after a week, there isn't a mark. 220

TEACHER: Listen good. Are you listening?

VOICE OF THE PUPIL: Are you listening?

TEACHER: We'll see who's listening. Bird: night, flight, house, plague.

VOICE OF THE PUPIL: I don't remember!

TEACHER: Don't be such an ass! 225

VOICE OF THE PUPIL: Don't be such an ass! Plague!

TEACHER: (*Furious.*) Imbecile! Bird-plague! (*To the* COORDINATOR.) See how he answers! (*The* COORDINATOR, *understanding, shrugs his shoulders.*) He's jerking me around! (*He pushes a button. The* PUPIL *screams, weeps.* 230 *Disconcerted, to the* COORDINATOR.) And now he's crying! What do I do?

COORDINATOR: Keep going. Don't worry about it.

TEACHER: Listen, kid, answer right, or I'll blow you away. Window: prison, flight, torture, fr . . . freedom. 235

VOICE OF THE PUPIL: Torture! Torture!

TEACHER: What did you say? Tortoise! Idiot! You're making fun of me! (*He pushes the button. The* PUPIL *howls.*)

COORDINATOR: (*Checking.*) One hundred eighty volts. (*Smiles approvingly.*) It's moving right along. 240

VOICE OF THE PUPIL: Let me go, you're hurting me! Oh, my belly!

TEACHER: Do we stop?

COORDINATOR: No.

TEACHER: He doesn't remember anything! 245

COORDINATOR: He'll remember now.

TEACHER: You think so? He burst into tears. If he doesn't answer, this is useless!

COORDINATOR: It isn't useless! If we don't succeed in getting
250 concrete results, all this suffering will be useless. Besides, you have to.

TEACHER: *I* do?

COORDINATOR: Of course. The tears, the screams. Think about it.

255 TEACHER: I'm not exactly sucking my thumb!

COORDINATOR: Of course not. Go ahead.

TEACHER: Nation: prison, bars, Germany, torture.

VOICE OF THE PUPIL: I don't know!

TEACHER: (*His finger on the button.*) Out with it!

260 VOICE OF THE PUPIL: Argentina!

TEACHER: (*Beside himself.*) Germany, idiot! (*He pushes the button. The* PUPIL *howls.*)

COORDINATOR: Planck Institute, Munich.

TEACHER: (*Furious.*) Prison: nation, plague, war, bars.

265 VOICE OF THE PUPIL: I don't know, let me go!
      I want to go home!

TEACHER: (*Screams.*) Out with it!

VOICE OF THE PUPIL: Nation!

TEACHER: You made a mistake! (*He pushes button after button.*
270 *The* PUPIL *howls.*)

COORDINATOR: (*Stops him.*) Slow! One at a time.

TEACHER: He's fucking with me! Why doesn't he answer right?

COORDINATOR: Make him.

TEACHER: I don't like doing this to you. Is that clear? You signed.
275 Don't count your lost sheep. Concentrate! Here's another. Do you hear me? (*Silence.*) Do you hear?

VOICE OF THE PUPIL: (*Lifeless.*) Vultures fly near . . .

TEACHER: Moon: night, prison, window, flight. (*To the*
      COORDINATOR.) He'll get this one. It's easy. (*Low.*) If he
280 doesn't answer, what do I do?

COORDINATOR: (*Gently.*) I told you.

TEACHER: (*Puts his hand on the last button. Closes his eyes.*) He doesn't answer. Why doesn't he answer?

COORDINATOR: (*Softly.*) Laziness. Low level.

285 TEACHER: Moon.

VOICE OF THE PUPIL: Ni . . . Niii . . . ght . . .

TEACHER: (*Without consulting the list.*) He made a mistake. He made a mistake . . . again. (*He opens his eyes.*) It's deliberate. He can't not know. Still . . . it hurts me . . . (*He slowly pushes*
290 *the last button on the box. Silence. He smiles with relief.*) He didn't scream.

COORDINATOR: No. (*Changes his tone. Exultantly.*) Very good! Four hundred fifty volts! Excellent! Your help has been invaluable.

295 TEACHER: Why didn't he help?

COORDINATOR: Look . . . we choose the risks we take! Sometimes we're not so lucky. (*Removes the* TEACHER'S *lab coat.*)

TEACHER: It was his fault. Wasn't it?

COORDINATOR: Yes, yes. Your work was magnificent!

300 TEACHER: He didn't even make an effort. A baby at the breast could have answered right. Some people like to fuck with you!

COORDINATOR: Yes, yes! You were splendid. (*He shakes his hand.*) Thank you ever so much. Don't worry. An unforgettable
305 performance.

TEACHER: (*Flattered.*) It was nothing. I did what I could!

COORDINATOR: (*Seeing him to the door.*) No, no, you were quick, concise, sure. Thanks ever so much! (*Again he shakes his*

hand. *The* TEACHER *exits. The* COORDINATOR *turns toward
the audience, professional.*) This experiment, with recorded   310
screams and simulated tortures, was repeated 180 times.
Unfortunately, this teacher who continued his punishments
to the lethal 450 volts was no exception. Eighty-five percent
of the teachers proceeded in the same way. The same test
was done in 1960 in the United States. The results? Sixty-six   315
percent. They were obeying rules and weren't responsible.
Curious, isn't it? Surprised?

GUIDE: Okay, enough. Don't wear out the audience. (*To his group.*)
The experiment was done in Germany and the United States.
Here among ourselves, it would be unthinkable, absurd.   320
Ladies and gentlemen, let's look for something more amusing.
(*He leads his group out of the room.*) This way, this way. If you
would be so kind . . . Ladies and gentlemen . . .

SCENE FIVE

The GUIDE *leads the group to the room that in scene two was locked.*

GUIDE: (*He knocks.*) May I?

VERY SILLY VOICE: (*From inside the room.*) Yeeeess.

(*The group enters the room. Seated on a chair is a woman
[*MOTHER*] made up like a doll, wearing a white dress that reaches
to her feet and holding a baby in her arms. The baby, swaddled
in tulle and lace, is obviously a doll. Sitting on the floor, at the
woman's feet, a young man [*FATHER*] watches them with an enraptured expression. The group is enveloped in a beam of rosy light.
The acting is frankly crude.*)

GUIDE: (*Pleased.*) Ah! Finally something coherent!

MOTHER: (*Rocking the child.*)

> "My rose, asleep now lie   5
> the horse is starting to cry
> His poor hooves were . . ."

GUIDE: What a picture! (*To his group.*) Make yourselves
comfortable. Can you see? Madam . . . (*Helps her get
comfortable. Then, rapidly, drily.*) Explanation: For Foreigners.   10
Seven P.M., Wednesday, December 16, 1970. Nestor Martins,
attorney, defender of political prisoners and trade unions,
consults with his client Nildo Zenteno. They take leave of one
another in the street. Six men surround Martins, violently
force him into a white Peugeot. Nildo Zenteno rushes back,   15
manages momentarily to free the lawyer. A karate chop to
the back of his neck brings Zenteno down as well. The car
speeds off. A black Chevrolet escorts it. That car had pulled
out of a nearby parking lot of the Federal Police. *Desaparecidos.*
(*From newspaper.*) Nestor Martins, thirty-three. Nildo   20
Zenteno, thirty-seven.

---

iv. 319 Stanley Milgram describes this experiment in his book, *Obedience to Authority* (New York: Harper & Row, 1974).

5–7 **My rose . . . were** the Mother sings fragments from the *Blood Wedding* lullabye   20–21 **Nestor . . . Zenteno** the disappearance of Nestor
Martins and his client Nildo Zenteno was in fact one of the first. It happened during the term of de facto president General Levingston, who
had come to power in a coup d'état, unseating the previous de facto
president, General Onganía

MOTHER:

25
"...bleeding,
his long mane was frozen,
and deep in his eyes
stuck a silvery dagger."

(*She suddenly stops. Distorting her voice as though she were a ventriloquist speaking for the little one.*) Stop it, Mama. That's old. Daddy, tell me a story.

30   FATHER: (*Very sweet.*) Yes, darling.

MOTHER: (*Idiotic voice.*) Daddy, it has to be modern! No morals, Daddy!

FATHER: Yes, darling.

MOTHER: (*Impatient.*) Come on, Daddy, start!

35   FATHER: (*Enraptured.*) Precious!

MOTHER: (*In the voice of a ferocious little child.*) I know I'm precious! Why do you go round and around, Daddy?

FATHER: Now, now... This child is in such a hurry! Daddy has to think!

40   MOTHER: Enough horsing around, Daddy. Well?

FATHER: (*Laughs confusedly. Then, grossly exaggerating the traditional tone in which one tells a story.*) Once upon a time ...

MOTHER: (*In the voice of a fierce, exasperated little child.*) Yeeeess ...

FATHER: (*In the same tone.*) Once upon a time there was a tall

45   man, ugly, ugly, ugly ... (*With disgust.*) Bolivian. (*Resuming the story.*) He had a pile of children. (*Drily.*) They procreate a lot. Then they send the kids here.

MOTHER: What happened to the little kids?

FATHER: (*Sweetly.*) They were in the street, begging, stealing ...

50   MOTHER: And what happened to the tall man?

FATHER: The tall man met another man. This one was a shorty. They talked and talked ...

MOTHER: (*Voice of a stupid baby.*) About what?

FATHER: Well ...! Ugly things! And when they were tired of

55   talking, the tall man walked him to his car.

MOTHER: Who?

FATHER: The shorty. The short one was bad, bad. And then some men came, and since he was bad, they put him in another car to punish him. Because he was bad, bad. And

60   what did the tall man do?

MOTHER: I don't know!

FATHER: He didn't want them to punish him!

MOTHER: Stupid!

FATHER: He ran and ran and hit the good guys. And then, the

65   good guys put him into the car as well.

MOTHER: The good guys took them for a ride! 'Cause they're so good!

FATHER: So very good!

MOTHER: And then what happened, Daddy?

70   FATHER: Nothing more was ever known!

MOTHER: Yea, yea, yea!

GUIDE: What horrible acting. So sorry. Let's look for something else. (*He pushes the people toward the door.*) The whole show's not like this. I hope.

75   MOTHER: (*Same voice of a stupid baby.*) Did they punish them a lot, Daddy?

FATHER: Nothing more was ever known!

MOTHER and FATHER: Yea, yea, yea!

GUIDE: (*Cutting it.*) Let's go. Let's go, gentlemen. They need at

80   least another month of rehearsal. What dunces!

SCENE SIX

GUIDE: Let's go upstairs, see if we have better luck. He who searches finds. They say. (*The group goes up the stairs, or down, if the preceding scene took place on the upper level. Natural lighting. When the group reaches the landing of the upper level.*) No, I made a mistake. I had you climb to the ... (*Stops.*) In vain.   5
Let's go down.

(*They go down. Suddenly, a group of men burst in, hurling themselves at a person in the audience who is talking with someone else. This other person is for a second paralyzed with astonishment. Then shouting, he throws himself into the fray.*)

MAN: Let him go! Let him go!

(*He succeeds in freeing him. The two make it down a few stairs, but the group of men rush them, surround them, and drag them down the stairs. Over the loudspeaker a distressed voice is heard.*)

VOICE: My God, why did I run? (*Almost instantaneously, the scene breaks out in another place with other characters. The groups may cross at this moment. Again the voice is heard.*) My God,   10
why did I run? (*The scene is repeated in another spot.*) My God, why did I run?

GUIDE: (*Meanwhile.*) If we search carefully, we'll find remains in the catacombs. There aren't many, but we can still hope for surprises. Careful please. Don't wander off now. That's it,   15
all together. Careful on the stairs. Look over here! (*Matter of factly.*) A brutish people! Yes, we will find remains. Sometimes discoveries come about by chance. (*He examines the door to a room. Opens it. The room is lit.*) Oh, this one has good light. Imagine, ladies and gentlemen, the faith, the heroism   20
of the first Christians. To pray in these pigsties. It gives me claustrophobia. (*He spots a form covered with canvas in a corner, on the floor.*) Here's something. Finally! (*He draws near.*) Stand back a little, ladies and gentlemen. (*With curiosity.*) What is it? (*He lifts an edge of the canvas, immediately lets it   25
fall and steps back.*) Puah! What a shitty surprise!

VOICE: My God, why did I run?

GUIDE: Sssh! (*Turns toward the audience, with a big feigned smile, gives the form a kick.*)

VOICE: My God, why did I run?   30

(*The GUIDE jumps on the form, tramples it, inflamed. In the doorway to the room, another GUIDE appears. He claps his hands loudly.*)

GUIDE #2: Ladies and gentlemen! Please leave. Out, everyone out! Sorry. We have a few like machines without an off button. If you would be so kind as to follow me. (*The light in the room fades out.*)

SCENE SEVEN

GUIDE #2: What was the other one telling you?

SOMEONE FROM THE AUDIENCE: About the catacombs.

---

vii. 1 this Guide is different from the Guide in scene 6. Since the order of the scenes is up to the director, however, this Guide will be called Guide #2 only in scene 7, where the shift occurs

GUIDE #2: (*Glib.*) Oh, yes! The remains of the first Christians in the catacombs . . . ! Impressive!

(*He opens a room. The* GIRL *from scene 3 is crawling on all fours toward a corner. Weak light on her. The rest of the room is in shadow. The pistol still lies abandoned on the floor.*)

5 GUIDE #2: What do we have here? What is she sniffing at like a dog? (*Goes closer. Joking, gives her a slap on the rear. Suddenly he changes expression, helps her to get up.*) What is this? Composure. Pull yourself together.

GIRL: (*Lost.*) He told me to wait. They keep my head underwater,
10 until . . .

GUIDE #2: (*Interrupts.*) Who threw water on you? This isn't Carnival. Excuse me, I have to go back to work. (*Resumes his professional tone. To the group.*) The paintings are fantastic, a little deteriorated, but still . . . (*He shines a light on the walls.*)
15 Jesus, there's nothing! (*He sees a graffito in a corner, crouches, shines a light on it.*) Gentlemen, come closer! (*Looks more closely.*) What kind of filth is this? (*Stands.*) Please, ladies, no! Excuse me, but the ladies may not look! (*He gestures them away.*) Gentlemen, if you like, but . . . (*To the* GIRL, *very surprised.*)
20 *You* did this? Your idea of fun? It was a saint's head and they put a . . . (*He finishes with an expressive gesture.*) Let go, let go of the pencil!

GIRL: No. It wasn't me.

GUIDE #2: (*Spots the pistol on the floor.*) What's this? Just a
25 moment, gentlemen. (*He picks it up.*) How strange!

GIRL: He left it so that, so that . . .

GUIDE #2: So that you could bullshit me. (*He raises his arm as though to hit her. Remembers the audience. Smiles.*) What negligence. (*Referring to the gun.*) I have to take care of
30 everything around here.

GIRL: I'm thirsty.

GUIDE #2: Then you'll pee and be even wetter. (*He shines his light on the walls.*) There's nothing here either. But I swear there was. And not this filth! (*He slaps her skirt.*) No way you're a virgin!

35 GIRL: I'm thirsty.

GUIDE #2: (*Looking around.*) Isn't there any water? In the other room, there's a bathtub filled to overflowing.

GIRL: No! No, damn you!

GUIDE #2: What did I tell you? Does anyone understand women?
40 A difficult bunch. As you see, ladies and gentlemen, there's nothing here either. Only the walls. And this filth. (*To the* GIRL.) You weren't getting discouraged, were you? He left you the pistol! How strange. Who am I to . . . ? (*He shrugs.*) But don't touch it. If you squeeze the trigger, it's all over. The baths and
45 . . . (*He smiles.*) I'm meddling in something that's none of my business. This is the safety. I'm leaving it up. Careful with the trigger. Sit down.

GIRL: (*She sits, shakes her head.*) I don't want it.

GUIDE #2: There's no danger, stupid! The slightest touch and it
50 goes off.

GIRL: Take it!

GUIDE #2: (*Surprised.*) Why? Soaking and thirsty, it's not a good combination. (*He puts the pistol on her lap, takes her hand and places it on the weapon.*) Do you have a boyfriend? Touch this
55 and it's all over, done with. (*She raises her hands.*)

GIRL: I'm thirsty.

GUIDE #2: Right. Sorry. I forgot: Ladies and gentlemen, forgive us for the . . . (*He points to the wall.*) How mortifying! If you would be so kind as to follow me . . . (*He opens the door,
60 indicates the exit. At this moment an* USHERETTE *arrives*

carrying a tray. She invites the group to have a glass of wine.) Help yourselves, ladies and gentlemen. It's on the house. There's no reason to be scared: you won't have to pay for it. It's all included. Then we'll go on with our visit. (*A scream is heard. To the audience.*) Who screamed? Who is the imbecile 65 who screamed?

SCENE EIGHT

The USHERETTE *steps close to the* GUIDE *and whispers a few words in his ear.*

GUIDE: (*Making amends.*) Forgive me. In room 3 we are going to find something interesting. "Finally!" you must be saying to yourselves. "We should have stayed home." (*He laughs.*) Ah, theater's a risky business! What do you think? TV's a better bet, isn't it? But no, gentlemen. All is not lost. Please, 5 gentlemen. I'm swallowing the "ladies" so I can go faster. With so many "ladies and gentlemen, ladies and gentlemen," I can't go on to anything else. (*He leads the group through the passageway. The group is shunted aside by three men carrying a long, half-finished table. It is missing a few strips 10 of wood on the surface. It is an ordinary table except that it has a strap nailed to one end. One of the men carries a tool box.*) The first Christians were very persecuted. They were fed to the lions. (*The men put the table on the floor.*) Until San Martín. What would the Spanish say about San Martín? 15 "That son of a bitch traitor. That black shit." (*The men start to saw and drive nails, as though they were alone. They are blocking the passageway.*) Can't you work somewhere else? (*The men don't answer.*) This way, gentlemen. Here's a little path. (*They can't get through. The men move the table, forcing 20 the group toward the* GIRL's *room.*)

WOMAN'S VOICE:

"Down he went to the river,
Oh, down he went down!"

GUIDE: What a pain in the ass she is with that lullabye! (*He looks 25 at the door.*) Here we are again. We may as well . . . Through here. Sooner or later we'll see a whole scene. (*He opens. Joking.*) Well? Have you dried yourself? How's . . . (*There are some men surrounding the* GIRL. *The* GUIDE *quickly closes the door, shoos the people away. With a false smile.*) No, I made a mistake. 30 Room 3, they told me. Careful on the stairs. This way, ladies and gentlemen. Ladies, once again. It's nicer . . .

WOMAN'S VOICE:

"And his blood was running,
Oh, more than the water." 35

(*The* GUIDE *snorts. Two men have positioned the table against the wall, clearing the passage way. They are smoking cigarettes, like two workers taking a break.*)

GUIDE: (*To the* WORKMEN.) Room 3? This one here? (*The men nod yes.*) Thank you!

---

viii. 14 San Martín General José de San Martín, the liberator (El Libertador) of the southern part of South America, is an Argentine national hero   **23–24 Down . . . down** the Woman's Voice in this scene sings from the Blood Wedding lullabye

SCENE NINE

The room is lit with rosy light. Four chairs. There is a group comprising a man, a woman, and two other adults disguised as children, a girl and a boy. Their makeup is exaggerated, and their clothes are cheap, vulgar. The MOTHER *is sewing, the* FATHER *is seated a little apart, and the* CHILDREN *are playing at throwing a hoop.*

On the far side of the room are the CHIEF *and two* POLICEMEN. *They sit very erect with their arms crossed over their chests. The characters act very broadly, a little like marionettes. The tone is grossly exaggerated.*

GUIDE: (*In a professional tone, dry and rapid.*) Explanation: For Foreigners. July 2, 1971. Marcelo Verdt and his wife, Sara Palacio de Verdt, were kidnapped by a group of eight men. *Desaparecidos.* Both were members of RAF, Revolutionary
5 Armed Forces. According to information in the newspapers, the wife, before disappearing, brought the children to her sister for protection.

MOTHER: (*Moving her hand as though sewing.*) Children, I'm making a little outfit for the one who is best behaved!
10 CHILDREN: (*Playing.*) Thank you, Mommy!

POLICEMEN: (*Coming forward.*) Hands up, in the name of the law!

MOTHER: (*Raising her arm, protecting her face like the heroine in a silent movie.*) Oh! (*The* FATHER *doesn't move.*)

CHILDREN: Mommy, Mommy, who are they?
15 MOTHER: Don't be afraid, my darlings! No one is hurting your mother!

CHILDREN: Blessed Mommy!

POLICEMAN: (*Comes close, snatches at her clothes.*) You're disguised! (*Shoving her violently.*)
20 CHILDREN: Mommy, Mommy, who are they?

POLICEMEN: Where's your husband?

MOTHER: I don't know!

CHILDREN: What do you mean, you don't know, Mommy! In the bathroom! Making caca! (*They call.*) Daddy! Daddy! They're
25 looking for you!

FATHER: (*Gets up, comes forward, wide-eyed.*) Who? What's happening?

POLICEMAN: This is what's happening! It's all over! (*Screams.*) Silence everyone! Let's get out of this hole! The car's out
30 front!

MOTHER: Not the children! They don't know anything about it!

POLICEMEN: Them too!

MOTHER: Have pity!

POLICEMEN: Silence! Let's go! Everyone!

(They put the chairs together to make the car. All squeeze in. One of the POLICEMEN *holds the hoop between his hands and handles it as though it were a steering wheel. He imitates the sound of a motor. The children wave. The* POLICEMAN *brakes suddenly. The others fall backward. They get out of the car, their gestures exaggeratedly frightened.)*

35 CHIEF: They fell!

MOTHER: (*On her knees.*) Pity!

POLICEMAN: What should we do with the kids?

CHILDREN: Daddy!

FATHER: (*Dignified.*) I'll protect you, don't be afraid. (*Puts his arms around them.*)
40 CHIEF: (*To the* POLICEMAN.) Idiot! Why did you bring the kids?

POLICEMAN: You said everyone, Chief.

MOTHER: They're innocent!

CHIEF: I'll see if they're not already lost. Kids: Who created
45 the flag?

MOTHER: (*Begging them.*) Answer right, answer right!

CHILDREN: (*In unison.*) Manuel Belgrano!

CHIEF: When?

CHILDREN: February 27, 1812.
50 CHIEF: Where?

CHILDREN: On the banks of the Paraná. He had it blessed right there, beneath a blue and white sky, blue and white sky, blue and white . . .

CHIEF: Exactly! Very good! (*Kisses them.*) Here's a prize. (*Gives*
55 *them each a piece of candy.*)

CHILDREN: Thank you, sir!

CHIEF: (*To the* MOTHER.) Take them home. And don't be long.

POLICEMAN: Chief, what if she doesn't return?

CHIEF: (*With an exaggeratedly sinister laugh, pointing to the*
60 FATHER.) This one stays here. It's in his interest that she return. (*To the* MOTHER.) Take my advice: be discreet. I'm doing you a favor. Don't be long. Take a taxi.

MOTHER: What are you going to do to him?

CHIEF: Nothing! From his eye to his sex. But only if I'm
65 vexed.

MOTHER: Marcelo!

FATHER: My love!

CHIEF: Take them home. We don't have any small sacks. They're only in the way. Move it.
70 MOTHER: Come, children! Give Daddy a kiss. (*The* FATHER *kisses them.*) Don't be afraid. We're going home.

CHILDREN: (*Happy.*) The men are nice, Mama!

MOTHER: (*Moves off with the* CHILDREN. *Picks up the outfit she was sewing. To one of them.*) Tell Grandma that the hem was
75 turned here. Will you remember?

CHILD: Yes, Mama.

MOTHER: There's soup in the pot. Have it for supper.

CHILDREN: If you're not there, we won't eat any soup! We won't
80 eat any soup!

MOTHER: Be good!

CHILDREN: Where are you going, Mama?

MOTHER: I'm going with Daddy. You behave. (*Hugs them.*)

CHILDREN: Mommy! Mommy!

GUIDE: (*Choked up.*) It gets to you, doesn't it?
85

(The MOTHER *separates from the* CHILDREN *and returns toward the* CHIEF. *During the good-bye scene the* POLICEMEN *were trying various sacks—as though they were items of clothing—on the* FATHER. *They have found the right one. Then they take him out of the room.)*

CHILDREN: (*Singing in a round.*) We won't eat any soup! We won't eat any soup!

MOTHER: Here I am. Where's my husband?

CHIEF: Husband? What husband? Take off your clothes.

GUIDE: (*Quickly.*) Let's go! Let's get out of here! (*Claps his hands.*)
90 Out! Where's "Carnation, sleep and dream"? Who wants more

---

ix. 4–5 **RAF, or Revolutionary Armed Forces,** is the translation of the name of FAR, Fuerza Armada Revolucionaria, a left-wing guerilla group

---

ix. 75–76 **Tell Grandma that the hem was turned here** is an encoded way of communicating the arrest wine? (*Pushes the group toward the door.*) Follow me! Quick! No dawdling! (*The group goes out. The* GUIDE *closes the door, leans against it.*) Ouf!

SCENE TEN

GUIDE: A little wine! Careful . . . on the . . . stairs. (*The* USHERETTE *brings him a glass of water.*) Water? For me? What for? (*Remembers.*) Oh, right. She's waiting for water! Come, gentlemen, this way. We're almost there. Just another
5 little minute. No reason to fret. (*Again they enter the room of the* GIRL *from scenes 3, 7, and 8. Her clothes are drenched. The* GIRL *is breathing anxiously. She's seated, with the pistol, which is dry, in her lap. To the group.*) Come in. Careful on the stairs. Or rather: fasten your seatbelts, no smoking. (*He*
10 *laughs. To the* GIRL, *very amiably.*) May I? (*He puts the glass and the pistol on the floor. Takes the chair on which she is sitting. Offers it to a woman in the audience.*) Sit, madam, sit. She may have wet it, but she didn't piss on it! (*He dries the chair with a hankie. To the woman.*) Please, have a seat! (*To*
15 *the* GIRL.) They paid admission. Are you thirsty? (*The* GIRL, *lost, doesn't answer. The* GUIDE *shakes her gently.*) Hey! Wake up. I'm asking you if you're thirsty. (*The* GIRL, *shakes her head no.*) Oh, no? I brought you water. Drink it. (*He takes the glass, brings it to her lips. The* GIRL *resists.*) And now, what do I do
20 with the glass? I need my hands free. I'm working. This can't be! Drink, little girl, drink. The water flowed . . . (*Forcing her.*) There. There, that's good. So capricious! Well, I don't like people pulling my leg. You're all wet. (*Puts his hand under her skirt.*) Even your little firecracker. (*He laughs. Turns*
25 *toward the audience.*) Oh, excuse me. (*Takes the pistol.*) Shall I take it? No? Freedom is within your grasp. No? (*He puts the barrel against her breast.*) How stupid. I can't. (*He cleans the weapon, puts it in the* GIRL's *lap.*) I don't know why they trust you so . . . It's loaded. If you had a boyfriend, old girl . . .
30 But like this. Idiot, why endure so much? (*Another* GUIDE *appears in the doorway.*)
OTHER GUIDE: (*Shouting.*) What are you doing here? It's about to start there! And they're giving out wine! It's not to be missed. I saw it! Exceptional! You can understand everything!
35 GUIDE: Really? Step on it, fellas, let's go! Move it, girls!
OTHER GUIDE: (*Teases.*) Don't you mean ladies and gentlemen?
GUIDE: (*To* OTHER GUIDE.) There's wine? For sure? (OTHER GUIDE *affirms it and leaves.*) If you would be so kind, ladies and gentlemen . . . (*He holds open the door so the group can pass*
40 *through. Before closing the door, in a friendly way.*) Think about it, little girl.

SCENE ELEVEN

In the passageway, one of the vertical wooden boxes.

GUIDE: Wait! This has always intrigued me . . . (*Tries to see through the peephole.*) I can't see a thing. How about you, sir? (*Someone from the audience has a look.*) It's very dark. (*He knocks at the door. Jokingly.*) Is anyone home? *Hay alguien?*
5 (*Curious, he opens the door. There's a heavily madeup man inside, dressed in a loincloth, staring fixedly. Matter of factly.*) Hi. (*He closes the door, turns toward the audience with an uncomfortable smile. As though it were not so strange.*) What a surprise! To me this is very curious . . .

OTHER GUIDE: (*Shouts from the doorway of the other room.*) Well? 10 What are you waiting for? A carriage? If you don't get there at the beginning, they won't understand anything!
GUIDE: (*Annoyed, referring to the vertical box.*) What about this? Does anyone understand this? (*To the* OTHER GUIDE.) I give the orders in my group! And if they don't get it, too bad for 15 them! This way, gentlemen! (*He leads them in the opposite direction.*) Follow me! (*A panting death rattle is heard through the door of a room they pass.*)

SCENE TWELVE

GUIDE: (*He lingers in front of the door, listening to the death rattle inside.*) What could this be? (*A* MAN *passes by, whistling.*)
MAN: (*To* GUIDE.) Good day!
GUIDE: Good day! (*Surprised.*) Well, he's happy! Let's follow 5 him. (*Referring to the death rattle in the room.*) Sounds like that and we've really got a mess on our hands! We can check it out later. (*He and the group follow the* MAN. *The* MAN *walks along, whistling. He meets another man who is coming from the opposite direction.*) 10
MAN: Good day!
NEIGHBOR #1: Hello! How's it going, doctor?

(*They shake hands. They continue walking together. The group follows them. They enter a large room, where* NEIGHBOR #2 *is sweeping the floor. Two chairs stacked in a corner, against the wall.*)

NEIGHBOR #2: Hello, doctor!
GUIDE: (*To his group.*) Watch out for the cars! Stay on the sidewalk, please!

(*He situates them. He hasn't finished doing so when the* FIRST GROUP OF MEN *enters at a trot, one behind the other, tied together at their waists.*)

FIRST GROUP OF MEN: Let us through! Let us through! 15

(*They come forward, trot through the room, then suddenly halt in front of the* MAN *and surround him, forming a closed circle.*)

MAN: Excuse me.
FIRST GROUP OF MEN: Quieto! Quieto!
MAN: Are you calling me? What do you want? (*The men accelerate, tightening their circular movement, forming two closed rings.*) Excuse me. Let me through. 20
NEIGHBOR #1: What's going on, doctor?
NEIGHBOR #2: (*Stops sweeping.*) Hey! Let him go!
NEIGHBOR #3: (*From the audience.*) What the hell is going on? (*Comes forward to help the* MAN.)
MAN: Let me go! Enough fooling around! 25

(*He pushes, tries to get through the circle. Hits, struggles. The men try to drag him toward the door.*)

NEIGHBORS: Let him go! Let him go!

---

17 **Quieto!** Roberto Quieto, whose surname in fact means "quiet," was a prominent, highly respected liberal lawyer. Unbeknownst to most, he was also a powerful member of the Montoneros, the premier left-wing guerrilla organization

(*They try to break up the group,* NEIGHBOR #2 *hitting out with his broom. The* SECOND GROUP OF MEN *enters, also at a trot and tied together at their waists. They sing.*)

SECOND GROUP OF MEN:

> Peace and security
> That is our domain
> 30 With a little authority
> Order will be maintained!

(*Observing the tumult, they linger.*)

OFFICIAL: (*Heading the* SECOND GROUP OF MEN.) What's going on here? This is scandalous! Halt! Separate!

(*The fight freezes.*)

NEIGHBORS: (*All at the same time.*) Sir, they were pushing him!
35 (*Alternating.*)
—Over here.
—Over there.
—They tied him up.
—They dragged him down!
40 OFFICIAL: One at a time, magpies. Who asked you anything? (*To the group in the fight.*) And you, you're prisoners in the name of the law. (*He "aims" at them, with his finger. The* SECOND GROUP OF MEN *"handcuffs" them. They're all, including the* MAN *put into a line and tied together at the wrists.*)
45 NEIGHBORS: Officer, sir:
Why the arrest?
He's one of the best!
OFFICIAL: It doesn't matter, my esteemed citizens
Have faith
50 Justice is there for a reason
To prevent baseness, which is treason.
NEIGHBORS: But we saw . . .
OFFICIAL: What you saw is of no consequence
If there's offense
55 Rest assured
The man's secure . . .
SECOND GROUP OF MEN: Sure!

(*They "take aim" at the* NEIGHBORS.)

OFFICIAL: In my providence.

(*The* NEIGHBORS *mix in with the audience. The* OFFICIAL *moves off to the side, crosses his arms, his expression serious. The* FIRST GROUP OF MEN *and the* MAN *attacked in the first place draw near. One of the men from the second group arranges the chairs.*)

OFFICIAL: (*Seating himself. To the* MAN.) Name.
60 MAN: Quieto.
GUIDE: (*Shouts.*) Sí, Quieto! (*To his group.*) Quieto means quiet. (*Smiles.*) Stop a moment. (*Gestures toward the group.*) So they'll understand. Otherwise, they'll miss the point. (*The others stop the action. In a dry, professional tone.*) Explanation: For Foreigners. July 7, 1971. Robert Quieto, attorney, defender of
65 political prisoners, resists a kidnapping attempt. Fortunately, the neighbors intervene and call a police squad. The kidnappers turn out to be policemen. Dr. Quieto was put at the disposition of the executive power. Subsequently he was accused of

having been implicated in an auto theft and of having par-
70 ticipated, after his detention, in various subversive acts. He was transferred to Rawson Prison, 730 miles from Buenos Aires. What happened then? I don't remember. Lost in the night of time. (*Smiles.*) But he wasn't so innocent. High up in the Montoneros, the son of a b—. It's not my responsibility.
75 Although when you have the truth, I don't know why it should be hidden. Go on. I'm done.
OFFICIAL: (*To the* MAN.) Name.
MAN: Quieto.
OFFICIAL: Quieto! That's what I'm telling *you!* Now what is
80 your name?
MAN: Blame.
OFFICIAL: (*Suspicious.*) Ohhhh? (*To the* FIRST GROUP OF MEN.) And you? What are your names?
FIRST GROUP OF MEN: (*They sing.*)
85

> Peace and security
> That is our domain
> With a little authority
> Order will be maintained!

SECOND GROUP OF MEN:
90

> If you're lying
> You'll get bruised!

OFFICIAL: Explain what happened
I'm confused!
FIRST GROUP OF MEN:
95

> Boca will never lose!
> Boca's the team we choose!

OFFICIAL: (*Very pleased.*) For this, you are excused. But who began . . .
FIRST GROUP OF MEN: That man!
100 OFFICIAL: No more rhyming! (*To the* MAN.) Don't you know that it's a crime to incite a riot in the street? (*To the* SECOND GROUP OF MEN.) Did they stop traffic?
SECOND GROUP OF MEN: Yes, sir! They delayed it!
OFFICIAL: For how long?
105 SECOND GROUP OF MEN: For three minutes!
OFFICIAL: Re-create it!
SECOND GROUP OF MEN:

> In their cars the men grew irritated
> At the office work accumulated.
110

OFFICIAL: (*To the first group, fiercely.*) I want a confession. (*Sweetly.*) What team are you from?
FIRST GROUP OF MEN:

> Boca will never lose
> Boca . . .
115

OFFICIAL: Fine, fine, no need to repeat! (*The* FIRST GROUP OF MEN *"free" their hands, which had been "cuffed." To the* MAN.) What about you?
MAN: What about me?

114–115 **Boca** the Boca Juniors are one of the most important Argentine soccer teams. Their home stadium is in the Buenos Aires neighborhood of La Boca, traditionally an Italian working-class section. San Lorenzo is another team from Greater Buenos Aires. Soccer is by far the most passionately followed sport in Argentina

120 OFFICIAL: What team are you from?
MAN: I nurse the same illusion.
OFFICIAL: I smell collusion. Why aren't you from San Lorenzo?
MAN: Because I'm not?
OFFICIAL: Don't be a wise guy! (*The* SECOND GROUP OF MEN *hit*
125 MAN. *To the others.*) And you, what are you waiting for?
Get going!
MAN: You can't let them go! They attacked me! I want to see my
attorney!
OFFICIAL: The one who gives the orders here is me. (*To the others.*)
130 And you, once again, (*Sweetly.*) why don't you do your work?
FIRST GROUP OF MEN: (*Tied together at their waists, they trot out,
singing.*)

For us it was a sad event
That ended to our detriment
135 Of this our song's a testament!
For us it was a sad event
That ended to our detriment
Of this our song's a testament!

OFFICIAL: (*To the* MAN.) Justice will be done.

(*One of the men in the second group puts on a judge's robe and
comes closer. Another moves in a chair and has him sit. Becoming
the* GUARD, *he remains standing behind the* JUDGE'*s back.*)

140 JUDGE: (*To the* MAN.) You're free. Being from Boca's no crime. But
next time . . .

(*The* MAN *frees his hands and stands up. The* JUDGE *turns halfway
around and grabs him from behind. No sooner has he done so
when the* GUARD *leans into the* MAN *and pushes him roughly
down by the shoulders, forcing him to sit. The* MAN *again joins
his hands as though they were handcuffed.*)

OFFICIAL: (*To the* MAN.) You stole a car. Your trial's pending.
Your sentence could be unending!
MAN: I need defending!
145 OFFICIAL: Superintending! (*To the* JUDGE.) He stole a car.
JUDGE: He did not steal a car!
MAN: Am I absolved? Can I go?
JUDGE: Why not? Go ahead!

(*He turns so that his back is to the* MAN. *The previous scene is repeated: the* MAN *frees his hands, the* GUARD *forces him to sit down
again, etc.*)

OFFICIAL: He robbed a bank!
150 MAN: I was in prison!
JUDGE: (*It starts again.*) Absolved!
MAN: Thank you. Can I go?
JUDGE: Why not? Go ahead. (*Again. The rhythm speeds up.*)
OFFICIAL: He robbed a station!
155 JUDGE: (*Over his shoulder.*) What kind of station?
OFFICIAL: Service station. Five old wrecks.
MAN: (*Forced to sit.*) How? I was in prison!
OFFICIAL: (*With pretended fury.*) Guards, you let him go?
JUDGE: (*Turns.*) Why can't you see? There is no case. Let him go
160 free! (*Turns his back.*)
OFFICIAL: He robbed a commissary, several stores, and several
dairies!

MAN: (*Forced to sit.*) If I'd been seized
How could I be eating cheese?
JUDGE: He is innocent 165
Surely
I declare it
Firmly.
MAN: (*Stands up, etc.*) Thank you. Can I go?
JUDGE: Naturally. Why not. (*It starts again. The action 170
accelerates to the point of dislocation but always remains
precise. The speeches are transferred but not the actions, which
remain a constant with each character.*)
OFFICIAL: Don't move. I've heard a little story!
JUDGE: He murdered a canary. 175
MAN That isn't fair!
I love all canaries
Everywhere!
OFFICIAL: You love them, but you kill them!
JUDGE: Guards, you let him go? 180
OFFICIAL: Your Honor, you're the witness
Of this bad faith.
MAN: I only want to live!
JUDGE: Guards, you let him go?
OFFICIAL: If he'd been seized 185
MAN: How could I've been eating cheese?
JUDGE: Thank you.
OFFICIAL: Beat it! I can't stand you anymore!
MAN: I'm going back to my city!
JUDGE: Can I go? 190
OFFICIAL: Beat it!
MAN: (*Resisting those who are making him sit.*) No, no, I was
in prison!
JUDGE: He's free! Oh, such obsession!
OFFICIAL: He's free! What fascination!
MAN: But I'm not! 195
JUDGE: Yes, you are! So you better shut up! (*Turns his back,
covers his ears.*)
OFFICIAL: Enough already! He's hard to handle.
All that screaming. What a scandal!

(*Gestures to the guards to take the* MAN *away. To the audience.*)

The idiots they send me, it's outrageous!
The courts 200
aren't beneficial
Unless they're
sacrificial!

(*Lights out.*)

GUIDE: Shit! What happened? They turned out the light without
telling me! Cretins! (*Take out his flashlight, switches it on.*) 205
Where is the door? Luckily I know the house. (*Opens door.
The passageway is lit.*) This way, gentlemen. There aren't any
stairs. But be careful all the same. You only get to stumble
once, like the tango says. Hey, hey. Everyone make it? (*He
leads the group through the passageway. They pass the door to 210
the room where the death rattle was heard. It is heard again.
The* GUIDE *puts his ear to the door. Admiringly.*) Persistent!
We go in? We don't go in? What do you want to do? Free
choice. At my orders! We go in!

SCENE THIRTEEN

The GUIDE *opens the door. The labored breathing stops. There is a* GIRL *with long hair laid out on a stretcher, with a sheet carefully folded under her feet.*

GUIDE: (*Advancing on tiptoe.*) Don't make any noise. She's sleeping. (*He approaches, looks at her. The* GIRL *smiles at him. Sweetly.*) How're you doing?

GIRL: (*Sits up, brushes her hair off her face, folds her hands in her lap.*
5   *She looks at the group with a semismile. Silence. Then, very simply, colloquially.*)
    I would like to die
    as softly as possible
    So that my friends will think
10   she is sleeping
    in the earth
    become a worm
    digging in the earth
    so that in spring
15   the flowers blossom
    After my death
    I want my children
    to sit at the table
    and say
20   at her age
    Mama
    ran off with some guy
    What a shame
    poor old Dad
25   staring at the tablecloth
    his cup of coffee
    searching for her
    This is how I want to die
    as simply
30   as though I had never lived
    What a lovely thought
    to leave like that
    not causing any pain
    The cup of coffee
35   that no one drinks
    absent . . .

(*Silently, a character mixed in with the audience goes up to the* GIRL. *He puts his hand over her mouth and nose. The* GIRL *offers desperate, mute resistance. She dies. The man gently lays her out, covers her with the sheet. Then he moves off and mixes in with the crowd, like one more spectator.*)

GUIDE: (*Amazed.*) How about that? (*Looks at the man.*) And now he's so calm! But what a feat! Phenomenal! (*He lifts the sheet. Matter of factly.*) She's dead. Poor creature! Really, without
40   so much as a moan. Discreet. And in the bloom of youth! (*Lets the sheet fall.*) She spoke of children, a husband. We'll have to go find them. Nice news I've got. What a bad deal. (*Hopefully.*) Anyone want to go? Of course, for this there are no volunteers. (*Furious.*) The son of a bitch. (*He goes to the*
45   *door, leaving the audience.*) Excuse me. (*He opens the door, yells out.*) I need someone from the family! Quick! Someone from the family! (*He comes back inside.*) She didn't move, did she? What with the advances of medicine, for a moment I thought that . . .

(FOUR MEN *enter, two-by-two, each pair moving as one. They are wearing white smocks down to their feet, very loose, belted at the waist. They come in on skates. Their faces are painted with large red smiling mouths. One pair beats pot lids; the other pair waves a white sack.*)

FOUR MEN: (*Singing.*)   50

    Tachín, tachín, tachín
    She died as she would have ordained
    Without causing any pain.

GUIDE: What about the family? I've got to tell them . . . It's
    so unfortunate . . . My heartfelt sympathy. (*Extending his* 55
    hand.)

FOUR MEN: (*They pay no attention to the* GUIDE. *They approach the stretcher, lift the sheet. Sing.*)

    The jokester
    Coaxed her   60

GUIDE: (*Very confused.*) Choked her . . . A son of a bitch who . . . (*Searches with his eyes. The* MEN *start putting the* GIRL *into the sack. Surprised.*) What are you doing? But . . .

FOUR MEN: (*Sing.*)

    But nothing   65
    But nothing
    Just doing our bit
    Ashes to ashes
    Shit to shit

GUIDE: (*Indignant.*) That's gross! Don't you see there's people? 70
    You must have been raised in a barn! Ladies, your forgiveness.
    I knew nothing . . . The modern theater is like this. No respect
    for the ladies!

FOUR MEN:

(*They finish putting the* GIRL *into the sack, leaving her head out. They tie the end of the sack around her neck. It is evident that the* GIRL *is playing dead: though her head is bent over, she is able to support it. The* FOUR MEN *hold the bundle, swing it hammocklike. They sing.*)

    If you don't like this Tin Pan band 75
    Because it hasn't any flair
    Because it just gave you a scare
    Swing high, swing well
    You can go to hell!

GUIDE: Go on!   80
FOUR MEN:

    Tachín, tachín, tachín,
    Tachín, tachín, tachín!
    Pran-pran-pran!
    Taratá-ta-ta! 85

(*They near the door. The* HUSBAND *and* MOTHER *enter. The* HUSBAND *is wearing threadbare clothing. His hair is long and all over the place. The* MOTHER *is the typical little old lady—black clothes, shawl over her head. Both act crudely, like prototypes of desperate people.*)

HUSBAND: What happened? I heard screams!

MOTHER: Sirs, have pity! Where is my daughter? Darling! Darling!

GUIDE: Oh my God, the family's here!

90 MOTHER and HUSBAND: (*Together.*) We've come to look for our poor Hermenegilda.

FOUR MEN:

(*They come back, set the corpse down; it supports itself against the stretcher. Horrified.*)

That name she inherited
She certainly merited!

95 MOTHER and HUSBAND: (*Together.*) We're here to find out
What she finally merited!

GUIDE: Oh no! If these two speak in verse, I'm leaving!
Although the language may be terse,
I can't bear

100 so much pain.
I'm leaving! (*He pushes away from the crowd, but upon hearing the* HUSBAND, *he stops, comes back.*)

HUSBAND: Where is she?

FOUR MEN: (*They shake the corpse in front of the* HUSBAND's *face.*)

105 We don't know! We don't know! She was never here!

HUSBAND: What do you mean? She came here to buy wine!

FOUR MEN: (*They turn the corpse facedown on the stretcher, look underneath.*) She bought her bread and went away, evaporated . . .
Surely it was fated! (*They look at the ceiling. The* HUSBAND *and*

110 MOTHER *imitates them. The men point.*) Look sir. That moth . . .

HUSBAND: She wasn't a moth! At dawn . . .

FOUR MEN: She was a moth. At dawn
Before the sun came up full
we found her eating

115 wool

MOTHER: It's not true! She didn't like wool!

FOUR MEN: Was she a woman or a moth?
The question's far from risible.
Lady, lady don't be miserable.

120 Don't be upset
We'll give you your daughter yet.

(*They approach an interior door. They call the* HUSBAND *and* MOTHER *as one would a dog.*)

Tch, tch, tch . . .

(*The* HUSBAND *and* MOTHER *advance, their smiles exaggeratedly hopeful. The others open the door. The interior is dark. The* HUSBAND *and* MOTHER *look in.*)

FOUR MEN: You'll find her here, here!
So be of good cheer, cheer!

125 (*Moving in unison, the* FOUR MEN *push them inside with kicks in the rump.*) And stop mugging! (*They close the door. They sway.*)
Ladies, Gentlemen, dearest friends
Our show is over, Curtains!

(*They take the corpse. They lead the way to the exit, singing.*)

Tachín, tachín, tachín!
130 Tachín, tachín, tachín!
Tarará-ta-ta!
Tarará-ta-ta!

GUIDE: (*Enthused.*) Let's go, let's go! Let's follow them! See what happens! They're entertaining! (*The group follows the* FOUR MEN *and* GUIDE. *The* FOUR MEN *enter a contiguous room and close the door. An actor, pretending to be part of the audience, opens it. The interior is dark. An enormous club comes out and hits the actor over the head. He falls. The* GUIDE *leans over him.*) Why did he butt in? I'm the Guide here! One to a group! (*He pokes him. The man doesn't move. He then lifts him by the armpits and puts him into one of the vertical boxes. He talks all the while, completely dissociated from his actions.*) That's how it is. In they all go but . . . who takes the potatoes out of the fire? The son of a bitch. If he was part of the audience, why did he make like an actor? Vanity, vanity will be the end of us all! . . . (*He closes the door.*) Now what were we going to see?

SOMEONE FROM THE AUDIENCE: The catacombs.

GUIDE: Right. Thank you. The first Christians really had a hard time of it. Just thinking about how the lions loved to chew them up . . . Human meat, they say, is sweet. Sweet, bitter, what could be stupider. (*They cross with another group. To the* OTHER GUIDE.) Where's there something good? We went in here, and it's all fucked up. (*Without stopping, the* OTHER GUIDE *points to a door.*)

SCENE FOURTEEN

The GUIDE *leads the group into the designated room. Inside is a group of* NEIGHBORS *all crowded together, some looking over the heads of others. On the far side, two* POLICEMEN *crouch, their expressions very attentive. In the center are the* MAN *and* WOMAN, *both heavily made-up. Their clothes are cheap, flashy; the* WOMAN *wears very high heels. All the acting is crude, infantile, and exaggerated.*

GUIDE: Attention. Ladies and gentlemen, this is the main course. So they tell me. Hope it's true. Make yourselves comfortable. If you find a chair, be seated. Silence, please. The story of a BM, or bad marriage. (*His tone is professional, dry and quick.*) Explanation: For Foreigners. On the afternoon of July 13, 1971, Juan Pablo Maestre and his wife, Mirta Elena Misetich, were kidnapped by a group of men. Juan Pablo Maestre managed to run a few yards but then was shot. Mirta Elena Misetich ran in the opposite direction, losing a shoe. She was captured and pushed into one car; her husband was thrown into another. Shortly afterward, a police squad sent to the scene recovered the shoe and ordered the doorman of an apartment building to wash the blood from the pavement. The body of Juan Pablo Maestre appeared days later in Escobar. Of Mirta Elena Misetich there is no further news. Both belonged to the RAF, or Revolutionary Armed Forces. Juan Pablo Maestre, twenty-eight years old. Mirta Elena Misetich, the same age.

MAN: (*With a conspiratorial air.*) Let's plant a bomb here

WOMAN: (*With a conspiratorial air.*) And a bomb over there!

MAN: When these go off

WOMAN: No one will be spared!

MAN and WOMAN: (*Taking bombs with fuses out from under their clothes.*) Subversion, subversion,
all rise up!
in revolution!

MAN: (*Looking around.*) Let's go, all clear!

WOMAN: Nothing will be left here! (*They take a few cautious steps.*)

POLICEMAN: (*Comes forward, arm extended.*) Hands up! In the
30   name of the law!
MAN: We're caught! Run! (*They drop their bombs and run in
    opposite directions.*)
POLICEMAN: (*Aims with his finger and shoots.*) Pum!

(*The* MAN *falls. His blood is obviously fake. The other* POLICEMAN
runs after the WOMAN.)

WOMAN: (*Stops.*) Darling!
35 POLICEMAN: Hey, hey! Justice always triumphs! Olé!

(*The two* POLICEMEN *drag the* MAN *and* WOMAN *away. The* WOMAN
loses her shoe. They exit. Slowly, the NEIGHBORS *untangle themselves
and come forward.*)

NEIGHBORS: The ass must be judged
Not broken!

(*The two* POLICEMEN *reenter. The* NEIGHBORS *immediately reform
their group.*)

POLICEMEN: Of our respect
Here's a token!

(*They're carrying the* MAN, *dragging him along. The* NEIGHBORS
watch, timidly come forward. Romantic music is heard. More
POLICEMEN *enter, smiling and wearing sweepers jackets. They
swing long-handled brooms, dance as in a musical comedy.*)

40 GROUP OF POLICEMEN: (*They sing.*)

We're here to clean!
We're here to clean!
The filth is gone
Your street is clean!
45 Let mothers pray
let children play
in celebration!

(*Smiling, they sweep. They lift the shoe. They sing.*)

Little shoe, little shoe
Whom might you belong to?
50 Why, to Snow White
or to her mother.

GUIDE: What do you mean, fellas! The little lost shoe was
    Cinderella's!
POLICEMAN: (*Emphatically.*) I say it's Snow White's or her
55   mother's. (*Recovering his smile.*) Whose little shoe is this?
    Madam, is it yours? Say yes. A Prince Charming awaits you
    in the wings.
GUIDE: No, no! Error! It's the prince, the prince who searches
    for the owner of the shoe, not a cop! Didn't you read the
60   story?
POLICEMAN: Calm down! It's a free interpretation. (*Smiling.*)
    Doesn't it belong to anyone? Neighbors? (*He shows them the
    shoe. The* NEIGHBORS *immediately deny ownership, shaking
    their heads in unison.*) So we'll look in another neighborhood.

---

xiv. 38–39 **"Of our respect / Here's a token"** is the couplet substituted for
"violín, violón / es la mejor razón." See "Crisis, Terror, Disappearance"

It'll belong to someone. (*He repeats, frowning in the* GUIDE's 65
    direction.) It's Snow White's or her mother's.
GUIDE: (*Servile.*) Yes, of course, her mother's. Well, let's get going.
    We can follow you, can't we? (*To his group.*) We'll just stroll
    along. If you get tired, let me know.
GROUP OF POLICEMEN: (*They go out with the shoe. Asking.*) Madam, 70
    is this yours? Is this yours? Young man? (*The group follows them.
    They enter another room. The* WOMAN, *wearing no makeup, is
    seated on a chair. Sitting nearby on the floor, with her legs crossed,
    is a* GIRL, *who may be the same as the one from scene 13.*)
POLICEMAN: (*To the* WOMAN.) Madam, excuse me. We found a 75
    little shoe. Is it yours? Prince Charming will marry you. Cash
    in a flash! You'll live in a palace! Let's see. (*He puts the shoe on
    her foot.*) She's Cinderella! It fits! Perfect! What luck, old girl!
    You win! A royal flush! (*Bows.*) Princess! My respects! (*The*
    WOMAN *stares ahead, immobile. Surprised.*) Aren't you happy? 80
    What's the matter?
WOMAN: My darling!
POLICEMAN: Your darling was stopped by a cop. (*The* POLICEMEN
    exit arm-in-arm, tap dancing.)
WOMAN: I was at home, eating my bread. I was 85
    making love. I was kissing my children.
And you will be the only one who knows
where and how my body was lost,
how my voice became unstrung
Only you will know 90
    how to know
the voices of fear and the faces of
    desperation
My God, what did the brave ones become?
I will speak 95
Only you will know
this tongue.

(*A shot is heard.*)

GUIDE: What's going on? Did you hear that? It was a shot. (*Looks
    at the* WOMAN *and the* GIRL.) But why so quiet! It's over.
    Gentlemen, follow me. Did you like that? (*He leads his group* 100
    out of the room.) A bit mixed up, wasn't it? Me . . . well, what do
    you like . . . I'm old-fashioned. I prefer something else. If this
    was the main course, what will the others be? (*They enter the
    adjoining room. The* GIRL *of scenes 3, 7, and 8 lies on the floor,
    shot, the pistol in her hand. The* GUIDE *looks at her, surprised.* 105
    Then, matter of factly, pushing them toward the exit.) Oh, sorry!
    Shall we? The jug may as well go to the fountain as . . . (*Happy
    music is heard.*) How about that music! So there is a little
    happiness in this world! Enough drama! Let's go. Move along.
    A little gaiety, dammit! 110

(*The poem spoken by the* WOMAN *was written by Marina, a Greek
girl, who was captured and tortured.*)

SCENE FIFTEEN

*As the group leaves, the music fades and after a few minutes disappears.
Through the passageway comes a group holding hands. They sing.*

GAME PLAYERS:
—Martin Fisherman, will you let me pass?
—Pass, pass, but the last one stays with me!

(The group starts playing Martin Fisherman, a singing game somewhat like London Bridge Is Falling Down. Two children make a bridge with their arms; the others run underneath, single file, holding each other by the waist. The line of children sings for permission to pass through; the last one is taken prisoner. In another version, the children making the bridge ask questions. Those who answer correctly pass through; the others do not. Two lines form, one comprising the "free," the other "prisoners." After everyone has had a question, the longer line wins, and the game may start again.)

GUIDE: Ladies and gentlemen, you're welcome to participate.
5   That's not coercion, only if you want to. Grotowsky used to
      say: The more physical distance, the more spiritual closeness.
      What nonsense! Don't be afraid to join in, ladies and
      gentlemen!

(The game continues. Suddenly one of the men forming Martin Fisherman's bridge yells.)

GAME PLAYERS: *(Alternately.)*
10   —I know that one! Don't let him go!
      —Me?

(The latter tries to get off the bridge.)

      —I know that one! Don't let him go!
      —Don't fight!
      —Just answer right!
15   —I don't have to! No!

(He whistles over his shoulder for help. Those in his line start to push. The others shout.)

      —Don't push! Hold tight!
      —Wait!

(Nevertheless they react. The shorter line becomes crooked. A man forming the bridge yells.)

      —They're shooting! Hold tight!

(The sound of a police whistle. POLICEMEN arrive, dressed like the cops in Charlie Chaplin's The Kid, with large, prehistoric-type clubs. Music is heard. Their acting is crude. They immediately start hitting those in the longer line over the head. The sound of the clubs: Plac! Plac! Plac! Those hit fall into artificially distorted poses. The men rush the bridge of Martin Fisherman, crushing the captured player, who screams.)

GUIDE: Kids today! They don't know how to play peacefully!
20   Let's get out of the way. I wonder if they'll tie them up.
      (Warns a POLICEMAN.) Not the audience! *(The POLICEMAN moves his head like Harpo Marx. He spins around like an acrobat, beating on actors mixed in with the public, acting as audience members. Very confused.)* On the double, ladies
25   and gentlemen, quickly! Let's go! No stragglers! My group this way! Forward! Toward the music! *(Music floats in the air, disappears.)* Now what? *(He opens his hands in a gesture of incomprehension. Taking advantage of the GUIDE's position, someone comes forward and puts a tin plate full of garbage in
30   his hands. To this person, absolutely astonished.)* What is this?

(Protests.) Not to me you don't! This is not what I get paid for! Who do they think they are?

(Meanwhile, the game of Martin Fisherman has stopped. The POLICEMEN and ACTORS from the shorter line carry off those who were knocked unconscious and throw them into a room.)

GUIDE: *(To the group.)* With so much confusion, I forgot about the catacombs. You'll end up leaving without seeing anything.
WOMAN'S VOICE: 35

      "The water was black there
      under the branches.
      When it reached the bridge
      it stopped and sang."

GUIDE: *(Pleased.)* Her again! What persistence! You want to   40
      risk it? Sooner or later it's got to improve!

(He opens the door. The people inside won't let him in.)

SCENE SIXTEEN

ACTOR #1: Sorry, old man. You can't come in. Off-limits.
GUIDE: Why not? I'm bringing people.
ACTOR #1: No, old man. We're rehearsing.
GUIDE: So what? Aren't you getting tired?
ACTOR #1: No! *(He closes the door.)*   5
GUIDE: *(Outraged.)* What balls. Sorry. *(He remembers something, smiles.)* They're not gonna fuck with me. Psss! This way! There's another entrance! *(He leads them along a passageway. They pass a vertical box like the others, only bigger. Naturally.)* Just a moment. *(He opens the door of the box. Inside, two men   10
      are plastered together. The GUIDE puts the tin plate on their shoulders. They stretch their necks desperately, trying to suck up what's on the plate. It falls. Matter of factly, to the audience.)* They let it fall! What idiots! *(He closes the door.)*

SCENE SEVENTEEN

GUIDE: Don't make a sound. Walk on tiptoe. Don't say a word.
      (They enter a room. Folding screens around an illuminated central space.) Sssh . . . Silence . . . *(The group watches the scene through the folding screens. Two ACTORS and two ACTRESSES are rehearsing Othello, in rehearsal clothes. ACTRESS #1, as   5
      Desdemona, is already dead on the floor.)*
ACTOR #1: *(As Iago.)* Villainous whore!
ACTRESS #2: *(As Emilia.)* She give it Cassio? No, alas, I found it,
And I did give't my husband.
ACTOR #1: Filth, thou liest!   10
GUIDE: Such language!
ACTRESS #2: *(As Emilia.)* By heaven, I do not, I do not,
      gentlemen.
      O murd'rous coxcomb! What should such a fool
      Do with so good a wife?   15

---

xv. 36–39 **"The water . . . sang"** the Woman's Voice sings lines from the *Blood Wedding* lullabye

xvii. 7 **Villainous whore!** lines from *Othello* are taken from act 5, scene 2, lines 229–235, 248–249, 256, 287, 306–307, 317, 367–371. All are found on pages 1239–1240 of *The Riverside Shakespeare* (Boston: Houghton Mifflin, 1974)

ACTOR #2: (*As Othello.*) Are there no stones in heaven
But what serves for the thunder?—Precious villain!

(*Othello runs at Iago. Iago strikes Emilia and leaves.* ACTOR #1
marks his exit and sits off to one side. A POLICEMAN *enters in
Isabellesque attire.*)

POLICEMAN #1: (*To* ACTOR #2.) You killed those two women!
Villain! Viper!

(*The* ACTRESSES *get up, go sit down. They watch calmly, a bit surprised.*)

20 ACTOR #1: Who told this guy to come in?
POLICEMAN #1: (*Acting, calling his men.*) Over here, men. Here!
ACTOR #1: Go act for the other side. Who called you. Get out
of here!
POLICEMAN #1: Thou hast no weapon, and perforce must suffer.
25 They are dead.
ACTRESS #1: (*Joking.*) I am dead!
ACTRESS #2: (*Sings.*)

Willow, willow, willow.
Moor, she was chaste. She loved thee, cruel Moor!

30 ACTOR #1: Stop! (*To the* POLICEMAN.) Will you beat it!
POLICEMAN #1: To raise your sword against a woman!
ACTOR #2: What are you talking about?
ACTOR #1: The guy's a mental case. Beat it! (*He pushes him
toward the door.*) Out! (*Returns.*) Better keep the door
35 locked. There's no telling who could walk in. Let's go, girls.
That guy stank worse than a pig. (*Claps his hands.*) One
more time!
POLICEMAN #1: (*Draws his sword.*) No, traitor!
ACTOR #2: (*Returns. In spite of himself, in character.*) Wrench
40 his sword from him.
POLICEMAN #1: Torments will ope your lips.
ACTOR #2: Well, thou dost best.
ACTOR #1: Cut! Right there!
POLICEMAN #1: Officers, come here! (*Another* POLICEMAN *enters,*
45 *dressed in the same style.*)
POLICEMAN #2: What's happening, sir?
POLICEMAN #1: (*He shows him the vial he's just taken from his
own pocket.*) Trotyl! And the women are dead! Oh my! O thou
pernicious caitiff!
50 POLICEMAN #2: (*With his sword, rounds up the* ACTORS, *who move
into a corner.*) Move it, or I'll take a slice! (*The* ACTRESSES *let
out an inappropriate laugh.*)
POLICEMAN #1: Take them, too, for having laughed at the wrong
time! (*In a dramatic voice.*)
55 To you, Lord Governor,
Remains the censure of this hellish villain,
The time, the place, the torture, O, enforce it!
Myself will straight aboard, and to the state
This heavy act with heavy heart relate.

(*He takes a gun from his pocket, forces the* ACTORS *to exit.*)

60 GUIDE: (*To his group.*) A bit confusing, the way that happened,
don't you think? So you understand. (*He walks into the light.
In a professional, dry and rapid voice.*) Explanation: For
Foreigners. (*Fierce and rude.*) Does anyone really need an
explanation? If you want to act like actors, just go into a tene-
65 ment and howl like dogs, throw a good scare into people. If

you don't have money, people will be even more afraid.
Why scream? Why pretend? When no one can open his
mouth, why would anyone scream gratuitously? (*He waits
for a response, which he doesn't get.*) Okay then! (*Resumes
his professional tone.*) August 6, 1971. The police burst into 70
an old house with many rooms, like this one, in the city of
Santa Fe. In one of the rooms they find eight hundred grams
of trotyl. They say. One journalist and three members of the
Grupo 67 theater are arrested. They're taken to Buenos Aires
on suspicion of subversive actions. The district attorney 75
recommended they be absolved on the benefit of doubt. They
were absolved May 24, 1972. (*Change of tone.*) Few are called,
many are chosen. Nine months in the cage. In misery. Well,
that's life! (*He leaves the illuminated space, goes back to his
group.*) Wait! The show goes on! 80

SCENE EIGHTEEN

A sort of deformed CHILD-MONSTER, *dressed in a floor-length white
shirt with lots of lace and frills. He is heavily made-up. Others disguised
as* CHILDREN *follow. The* CHILD-MONSTER *clutches a club. They sing.*

CHILDREN:

Anton, Anton Pirulero
each one, each one
attends to his game
and he who does not 5
he who does not
will suffer the blame.

(*The* CHILDREN *sit in a circle around the* CHILD-MONSTER, *who
calls to one of the bigger children and gives him the club. The latter
stays outside the ring. They play Anton Pirulero, in which the child
playing Anton is in the center of the circle, turning around and
around, his arms extended like wings. The others keep singing and
pretend to play musical instruments—guitar, cornet, violin, etc.
They have to be very alert, for if Anton Pirulero stops and points at
one of them with his arm and that child isn't moving his own arms
like Anton, then that child loses. He who loses three times is out.
The game is played singing, and very fast.*)

CHILD-MONSTER: (*He is Anton Pirulero. In an out-of-tune sing-song.*)

Anton, Anton Pirulero
each one, each one 10
attends to his game
and he who does not
he who does not
will suffer the blame.

(*Now they play only guitar. The child with the club goes to the one
who has changed places with Anton and hits him. The child falls.
The game continues, faster every time. The* CHILD-MONSTER *never
finishes his song, the game falls apart, and the child with the club
hits out indiscriminately. Finally, the only ones left unharmed are
the* CHILD-MONSTER *and the character with the club. They wave
their arms and sing. The* CHILD-MONSTER *glares at the other one,
more and more menacingly. He aims with his finger as though it
were a revolver and kills the other child. Pum! He plays alone, his
gestures increasingly spastic. The song "Anton Pirulero" becomes
unintelligible. The lights go out.*)

15 GUIDE: What now? Why did they kill the lights?
VOICES: (*Singing.*)

> Anton, Anton Pirulero
> each one
> each one
20 attends to his game.

(*Lights up. In the same space,* THREE MEN *and a* YOUNG WOMAN. *The* CHILD-MONSTER *laughs in his labored way, waves his arms, stutters.*)

CHILD-MONSTER: D-d-d-ow-ow-n-n-n! S-s-s-i-i-i-t-t-t-d-d-d-ow-n-n-n-n!

(*He aims his hand like a revolver. The* MEN *and* WOMAN *don't seem to notice his presence. They sit of their own volition.*)

FIRST MAN: What is your game?
SECOND MAN: Fear.
25 FIRST MAN: And yours?
THIRD MAN: Fear.
FIRST MAN: (*To the* YOUNG WOMAN.) What is your game?
YOUNG WOMAN: Fear. (*Pause.*) And the question.
FIRST MAN: What question?
30 YOUNG WOMAN: Why fear? My name is Marina. I am twenty
      years old. I am Greek, a prisoner, and I have been tortured.
      (*The* CHILD-MONSTER *stutters low, furiously. He keeps playing, getting all tangled up in his own movements.*)
      Time is altered, the years to come are altered
35   You know where you will find me
      I, fear, I, death
      I, the memory beyond reach
      I, the recollection of the tenderness of your hands
      I, the sadness of our broken life
40   I will defeat "it's not my concern" with my
         anguish
      blast their alien sleep with fireworks,
         horrible and indecent
      with countless shootings I will fall on the indifference
45   of those who pass by
      until they begin to ask, to ask themselves
THREE MEN: (*In an even tone.*) Why fear?
      Why torture?
      Why deaths?

(*Stuttering and autistic, the* CHILD-MONSTER *plays.*)

50 THREE MEN: Who set limits?
      Who once said: this much thirst
      this much water?
      Who once said: this much air
      this much fire?
55   Who once said: here the ken
      of men and women
      here the bounds?

---

59 s.d. **The poem . . . Gelman's** Gelman's lines are: "Quien puso limites? / Quien dijo alguna vez: hasta aquí la sed? hasta aquí el agua? / Quien dijo alguna vez: hasta aquí el aire, hasta aquí el fuego? / Quien dijo alguna vez: hasta aquí el hombre, hasta aquí, no? / Solo la esperanza tiene las rodillas nitidas. / Sangran."

Only hope has sharp knees.
They are bleeding.

(*Darkness.*)

(*The poem spoken by the* YOUNG WOMAN *was written by Marina. The poem spoken by the* THREE MEN *is Juan Gelman's.*)

GUIDE: Now what? There they go again cutting the light   60
      without warning me! I understand less and less. We're
      the ones who bear the brunt of this show. I shit on poetry!
      Watch your wallets! And I left my flashlight. This way,
      this way. It's so dark! Don't touch each other! Whose little
      ass is this?   65

(*He laughs. Opens the door. The passageway is illuminated.*)

      Ah! Light, more light! What a phrase! Only a genius could
      come up with that one, eh?
WOMAN'S VOICE:

> "Ay-y-y, for the big horse
> who didn't like water"   70

GUIDE: Still at it! Now that's perseverance! (*Baroque music is heard. The* GUIDE *puts his ear to the door. Unsure.*) Do we go in here?
      I don't remember. Oh well, let's do it! Come along, gentlemen!
      You're almost there!

SCENE NINETEEN

They enter another room. Two GUARDS *are dressing a group of squalid-looking characters who are handcuffed to the wall, heavily made-up, with false eyelashes and lots of rouge. Some are half-undressed, wearing only jackets and underwear. Others wear bras and costume jewelry. The* GUARDS *move around busily. They bring chairs. Make the prisoners sit. They arrange them artistically, crossing their legs, raising their arms as though they were holding cigarettes between their fingers. The prisoners stay in these poses. During the development of this scene, one* GUARD—*seated apart*—*recites with a melancholy air.*

GUARD: You, who come from the shores of the Tagus
      Every day sing of my death
      Only this do I ask
         with my dying breath

69–70 **"Ay-y-y . . . water"** the Woman's Voice sings from the *Blood Wedding* lullabye

xix. 1 "You, who come from the shores of the Tagus" is from a poem of Garcilaso de la Vega. The Tagus River flows through western Spain and Portugal. In her letter to me of March 28, 1986, Gambaro brought up "substituting an English-language poem about death, provided of course it's by a Master." I decided against this option since I felt that Gambaro's appropriation of Garcilaso was important as a reference to a specific age, place, and literary tradition. One of the greatest poets of the Spanish Golden Age, Garcilaso influenced not only San Juan de la Cruz, Lope de Vega, and Cervantes but also Rafael Alberti, Pedro Salinas, Miguel Hernández, and other twentieth-century Spanish and Latin American poets. The original reads: "Vosotros, los del Tajo en su ribera / Cantáreis mi muerte cada día / Este descanso llevaré nunque muera / Que cada día cantáreis mi muerte, / Vosotros, los del Tajo en su ribera."

5   Every day sing of my death
    You, who come from the shores of the Tagus.

(A signal is heard. A line of frightened men and women enter. Some carry small packages in their hands, obviously clothing or food. The GUARD *watches them.)*

GUARD: No one enters without being checked. (*He turns his face away. Raises and lowers his index finger mechanically, while the people pass in front of him and go out. Recites*
10   *rapidly.*) With pants, no. With skirts, no. With stockings, no. With packages, no. With children, no. With faces, no. (*A* PRETTY GIRL *passes. He looks at her. His finger stops. Very nicely.*)
    Twenty little hard ones, twenty little hard ones
15   all in a roll, all in a roll
    twenty little hard ones
    in your little asshole.
    May I?
PRETTY GIRL: (*Stupidly.*) What?
20 GUARD: (*Wiggles his finger obscenely.*) May I?
PRETTY GIRL: No!
GUARD: (*Pulls himself up, undiscouraged.*) To arms! To arms
    against the little asshole! Right over here!

(A group of guards enters at a trot. They rush the PRETTY GIRL *and fling themselves on her as though she were the ball in a game of baseball. They roll with her out of the room.)*

GUARD: (*Moves off, uninterested. Starts again with a melancholy*
25   *air.*) You, who come from the shores of the Tagus . . .
LITTLE OLD LADY: (*The last of the visitors. She brings a sandwich wrapped in a handkerchief.*) I've come to see my little son. He misbehaved.
GUARD: (*Deflated.*) Ah . . . Why didn't you bring him up better,
30   madam?
LITTLE OLD LADY: He was always my wayward one!
GUARD: A good beating is what they need. They don't learn unless they bleed.
LITTLE OLD LADY: At ten years old, he was looking up the girls'
35   skirts.
GUARD: (*Dumbfounded.*) Filthy!
LITTLE OLD LADY: (*Plaintive.*) I cut his little whistle, but it did no good!
GUARD: It's late to repent. Show me what you've brought!
40 LITTLE OLD LADY: (*Unwraps her handkerchief.*) A sandwich.
GUARD: (*Lifts the top of the bread.*) Ah! Extra testicles. No, madam! Here they only lose them. And for us that's work! Confiscated! (*He takes the sandwich.*) Out!
LITTLE OLD LADY: I want to see my son! Just once! Be generous!
45   You have a mother too!
GUARD: Yeah, but she's not an old whore like you.
LITTLE OLD LADY: Why are you insulting me?
GUARD: (*With disgust.*) You're old! (*In another tone.*) All right. Go see him. I'm doing this for my mother. Sentimentality will be
50   the end of me! (*Gestures toward one of the seated prisoners.*) There he is.

---

14 **"Twenty little hard ones"** is from García Lorca's *Los títeres de cachiporra.* The original reads: "Veinte duritos y veinte duritos / y un rollito de veinte duritos / en el agujero del culito."

LITTLE OLD LADY: (*Goes toward an* OUTLANDISH-LOOKING PRISONER *and embraces him.*) Son! (*She separates, looks at him.*) No, this isn't him. (*Hugs another.*) Son! (*Looks.*) No,
55   this one either.
OUTLANDISH-LOOKING PRISONER: (*Opening his arms.*) Da-da-da-da!
GUARD: Choose already. Take this one. What's the difference.
LITTLE OLD LADY: (*Leaning toward the prisoner. Timidly.*) Juan?
OUTLANDISH-LOOKING PRISONER: Da!
60 LITTLE OLD LADY: Son!
OUTLANDISH-LOOKING PRISONER: Da!
GUIDE: (*To the group.*) Pretty depressing, wouldn't you say?
GUARD: What about you all? Over here, young men!
GUIDE: (*Raises his hands.*) No! Out, quick! (*The sound of music.*)
65   We were going to go dancing. We got the wrong room. (*Very distressed.*) Let's go dancing! Dancing! Move it! Let's beat it! Let's go, gentlemen. Let's go! (*They exit.*)

SCENE TWENTY

GUIDE: Ouf! A narrow escape! (*He listens. The music gets louder. It's happy, catchy.*) That's it. Come. (*He leads his group to a large space, where at this moment all the other groups converge.*) Leave
5   the space open, ladies and gentlemen! If you would be so kind as to stand against the wall. That's it. Thank you, everyone.

(On one side of the performing space is a semitranslucent folding screen, behind which can be seen a long table. In the center, a group of women, dressed like stereotypical prostitutes, execute the gestures conventionally attributed to them: they smoke, show their legs, swing their purses, put on makeup. A man roughly pushes in two more PROSTITUTES. *They look at him with a mixture of fear and outrage. The other women observe the new arrivals curiously, then one offers each of the new women a cigarette. The music suddenly stops. One of the* PROSTITUTES *starts dancing, moving slowly, singing a blues number in a gravelly voice. A line of* FOUR MEN *enter at a trot, leading a prisoner with his eyes bandaged, to the center. They sing.)*

FOUR MEN:

    We have come, we have come
    To have some fun!

(The PROSTITUTES *watch them. The one dancing gradually slows down the rhythm until she is moving in place, singing inaudibly. The men spin the prisoner around until he becomes completely disoriented.)*

MAN #1: Let's play the Little Blind Cock!   10
MAN #2: Cockadoodledoo!

(They play, rapidly poking and moving away from the prisoner, who searches for them with his arms outstretched.)

MAN #1: Play! Head down!
MAN #3: There are beams!
MAN #4: You could break your head open!

(They play, yell "Cockadoodledoo!" One of the PROSTITUTES *comes forward. She first starts to join in the game, then stretches her hand toward the prisoner's bandage.)*

MAN #1: (*Pushes her away.*) Get out of here! This is our game! In   15
    your place, whore!

MAN #2: (*Poking the prisoner.*) He's sweating! He's hot!
MEN #1, #3, AND #4: (*In a chorus.*) Make him strip! Make him
strip!

(*Maintaining an ambiguous air of play and violence, they take off his jacket, his pants, his shirt; they throw his clothes, which flutter around.*)

20 MAN #1: Hard-boiled egg! Let's play hard-boiled egg!

(*They fight like children.*)

MAN #2: Me! Me!
MAN #3: Get out! Me!

(*They play. The prisoner holds his body rigid while the others rush him, tie him up. Finally, one of the* MEN *hits him on the head. The prisoner falls.*)

MAN #4: We warned you!
MAN #1: A beam, idiot!
25 MAN #2: We told you to keep your head down!

(*They drag the prisoner behind the screen. Through the screen, one can see fuzzily that they are strapping him down on the table. A scream. Instantaneously, the volume of the music shoots up; two of the men come out from behind the screen.*)

TWO MEN: Girls, if you want to sing,
    it's not prohibited!

(*They clap. The* PROSTITUTES *don't move.*)

Sing!

(*The* PROSTITUTES, *forced into it, clap and sing. Again the music gets louder.*)

Girls, if you want to dance,
    it's not prohibited!   30

(*The* PROSTITUTES *dance. Behind the screen, one can see the shadow of the two* MEN *moving away from the table. The hand of the prisoner falls softly. At the same time, the* PROSTITUTES *freeze in a musical comedy finale. The music stops. The lights go out, then come up again. The actors disperse, naturally. They take down the screen. The dead man gets up from the table, gathers his clothes, and begins to dress. Only the prisoners seated against the wall remain immobile.*)

GUIDE: (*Drily.*) Ladies and gentlemen, what are you waiting for? The show is over. (*House lights come up.*)
GUIDE 2: (*Resentfully.*) If you clap enthusiastically in all good haste your hands won't go to waste!

(*He claps, and the* GUIDES *and actors present imitate him.*)

GUIDE: Theater imitates life   35
    If you don't clap
    It means that life is rotten to the core
    And we may as well just head for the door.

(*He moves the audience out toward the door. From far away can be heard police sirens. Even when the audience is near the exit, they can hear.*)

    Who once said: here the ken
    of men and women   40
    here the bounds?

(*After a moment, repeat.*)

    Who once said: here the ken
    of men and women
    here the bounds?

Wole Soyinka

W ole Soyinka was born in 1934 in Abeokuta, Nigeria. Educated at Government College in Ibadan, Soyinka then studied at Leeds University in England, where he worked with the notable Shakespearian scholar and actor G. Wilson Knight and took his B.A. in English in 1957. He remained in England working as play reader for the Royal Court Theater before returning to Nigeria in 1959, where his first play, *The Lion and the Jewel,* was produced. In the course of the next decade, Soyinka wrote an important body of dramatic work, including the plays *The Invention* (1959), *A Dance of the Forests* (1960), *The Trials of Brother Jero* (1960), *Camwood on the Leaves* (radio play, 1960), *The Strong Breed* (1964), *Kongi's Harvest* (1964), and *The Road* (1965). He also taught at the universities of Ibadan, Ife, and Lagos, and founded two important theaters, the Orisun Theater (1964) and the Masks Theater (1960). Much of Soyinka's work is critical of authoritarian politics; he was arrested in 1967 and held as a political prisoner until 1969. Soyinka's memoir of imprisonment, *The Man Died,* was published in 1972 and was cited for excellence by Amnesty International. In the 1970s, Soyinka continued to write plays examining the tensions of tribal life in modern Africa: *Madmen and Specialists* (1970) and *Death and the King's Horseman* (1976). He also wrote plays more directly examining contemporary African politics: his rewriting of Brecht's *Threepenny Opera as Opera Wonyosi* (1977), and *A Play of Giants* (1985). He also wrote an adaptation of Euripides' *The Bacchae* (1973), placing the Greek narrative in a more explicitly tribal and ritualistic setting. Soyinka was awarded the Nobel Prize in 1986, the first African writer to receive the prize for literature.

Death and The King's Horseman

Soyinka is sometimes criticized by other African writers for being too oriented toward Europe. Not only are some of his plays adaptations or imitations of European works, but Soyinka has continued to write in English—the language of the colonial power, after all—

Elesin faces the accusatory body of his son Olunde in Wole Soyinka's *Death and the King's Horseman* in this 1990 production at the New Rose Theatre, Portland.

Chris Harris

rather than writing in his native language, Yoruba. It is precisely this tension between village and metropolis, between Africa and Europe, that provides the springboard for some of Soyinka's greatest work and dramatizes the challenges of cross-cultural interaction in the complex contemporary political environment.

Death and the King's Horseman is based on events that took place in the Yoruba city of Oyo in 1946. The play opens on the day the local African king is to be buried. According to custom, his Horseman, Elesin Oba, will die on this day as well, following his master in death as he followed him in life. It is clear from the scene in the marketplace that this ritual death is, however, a celebration. The village enacts a festive and playful marriage between Elesin and a new, young bride, so that he can procreate before he dies, bringing new life into the world even as he passes out of it, but fatefully delaying his required sacrifice.

In *Death and the King's Horseman,* indigenous African culture operates within the more restricted sphere of Britain's colonial values, laws, and institutions. The region's colonial administrator, Simon Pilkings, who is on his way to a masquerade to celebrate the arrival of the Prince, acts to stop Elesin's death. However, Pilkings and his wife are wearing African ceremonial costumes of the dead to the English masquerade, a decision that is not only offensive and irreligious to the Africans they meet, but that marks their complete incomprehension of the complex situation in which they find themselves. Wearing the costume also marks the Pilkingses, and the colonial British as a whole, as figures of death, in contrast to the paradoxical life celebrated by Elesin.

Pilkings "saves" Elesin and brings about the play's tragic catastrophe. Elesin's son Olunde—studying medicine in Britain—returns to perform funeral rites for his father. However, when Elesin is prevented from dying, it becomes clear that colonial intervention has destroyed what it attempted to protect. Olunde, too, is dishonored when his father remains alive and takes the only possible course of action.

In his note to the play, Soyinka criticizes the phrase "clash of cultures" to describe his work, for it "presupposes a potential equality in *every given situation* of the alien culture and the indigenous." In *Death and the King's Horseman,* the power vested in the colonial administration signals its ability to destroy the indigenous culture it claims, ironically, to govern.

Author's Note

This play is based on events which took place in Oyo, ancient Yoruba city of Nigeria, in 1946. That year, the lives of Elesin (Olori Elesin), his son, and the Colonial District Officer intertwined, with the disastrous results set out in the play. The changes I have made are in matters of detail, sequence and of course characterisation. The action has also been set back two or three years to while the war was still on, for minor reasons of dramaturgy.

The factual account still exists in the archives of the British Colonial Administration. It has already inspired a fine play in Yoruba (Oba Wàjà) by Duro Ladipo. It has also misbegotten a film by some German television company.

The bane of themes of this genre is that they are no sooner employed creatively than they acquire the facile tag of "clash of cultures," a prejudicial label which, quite apart from its frequent misapplication, presupposes a potential equality *in every given situation* of the alien culture and the indigenous, on the actual soil of the latter. (In the area of misapplication, the overseas prize for illiteracy and mental conditioning undoubtedly goes to the blurb-writer for the American edition of my novel *Season of Anomy* who unblushingly declares that this work portrays the "clash between old values and new ways, between western methods and African traditions"!) It is thanks to this kind of perverse mentality that I find it necessary to caution the would-be producer of this play against a sadly familiar reductionist tendency, and to direct his vision instead to the far more difficult and risky task of eliciting the play's threnodic essence.

One of the more obvious alternative structures of the play would be to make the District Officer the victim of a cruel dilemma. This is not to my taste and it is not by chance that I have avoided dialogue or situation which would encourage this. No attempt should be made in production to suggest it. The Colonial Factor is an incident, a catalytic incident merely. The confrontation in the play is largely metaphysical, contained in the human vehicle which is Elesin and the universe of the Yoruba mind—the world of the living, the dead and the unborn, and the numinous passage which links all: transition. *Death and the King's Horseman* can be fully realised only through an evocation of music from the abyss of transition.

Wole Soyinka

Death and the King's Horseman

Wole Soyinka

CHARACTERS

PRAISE-SINGER
ELESIN, *Horseman of the king*
IYALOJA, *'Mother' of the market*
SIMON PILKINGS, *District Officer*
JANE PILKINGS, *his wife*
SERGEANT AMUSA
JOSEPH, *houseboy to the Pilkingses*
BRIDE

H.R.H. THE PRINCE
THE RESIDENT
AIDE-DE-CAMP
OLUNDE, *eldest son of Elesin*
DRUMMERS, WOMEN, YOUNG GIRLS, DANCERS AT THE BALL

The play should run without an interval. For rapid scene changes, one adjustable outline set is very appropriate.

ACT ONE

A passage through a market in its closing stages. The stalls are being emptied, mats folded. A few women pass through on their way home, loaded with baskets. On a cloth-stand, bolts of cloth are taken down, display pieces folded and piled on a tray. ELESIN OBA *enters along a passage before the market, pursued by his* DRUMMERS *and* PRAISE-SINGERS. *He is a man of enormous vitality, speaks, dances and sings with that infectious enjoyment of life which accompanies all his actions.*

PRAISE-SINGER: Elesin O! Elesin Oba! Howu! What tryst is this the cockerel goes to keep with such haste that he must leave his tail behind?

ELESIN: (*Slows down a bit, laughing.*) A tryst where the cockerel 5 needs no adornment.

PRAISE-SINGER: O-oh, you hear that my companions? That's the way the world goes. Because the man approaches a brand-new bride he forgets the long faithful mother of his children.

ELESIN: When the horse sniffs the stable does he not strain 10 at the bridle? The market is the long-suffering home of my spirit and the women are packing up to go. That Esuharassed day slipped into the stewpot while we feasted. We ate it up with the rest of the meat. I have neglected my women.

15 PRAISE-SINGER: We know all that. Still it's no reason for shedding your tail on this day of all days. I know the women will cover you in damask and *alari* but when the wind blows cold from behind, that's when the fowl knows his true friends.

20 ELESIN: Olohun-iyo!

PRAISE-SINGER: Are you sure there will be one like me on the other side?

ELESIN: Olohun-iyo!

PRAISE-SINGER: Far be it for me to belittle the dwellers of that 25 place but, a man is either born to his art or he isn't. And I don't know for certain that you'll meet my father, so who is going to sing these deeds in accents that will pierce the deafness of the ancient ones. I have prepared my going—just tell me: Olohun-iyo, I need you on this journey and I 30 shall be behind you.

Note to this edition: Certain Yoruba words which appear in italics in the text are explained in a brief glossary at the end of the play.

ELESIN: You're like a jealous wife. Stay close to me, but only on this side. My fame, my honour are legacies to the living; stay behind and let the world sip its honey from your lips.

PRAISE-SINGER: Your name will be like the sweet berry a child places under his tongue to sweeten the passage of food. The 35 world will never spit it out.

ELESIN: Come then. This market is my roost. When I come among the women I am a chicken with a hundred mothers. I become a monarch whose palace is built with tenderness and beauty. 40

PRAISE-SINGER: They love to spoil you but beware. The hands of women also weaken the unwary.

ELESIN: This night I'll lay my head upon their lap and go to sleep. This night I'll touch feet with their feet in a dance that is no longer of this earth. But the smell of their flesh, their sweat, 45 the smell of indigo on their cloth, this is the last air I wish to breathe as I go to meet my great forebears.

PRAISE-SINGER: In their time the world was never tilted from its groove, it shall not be in yours.

ELESIN: The gods have said No. 50

PRAISE-SINGER: In their time the great wars came and went, the little wars came and went; the white slavers came and went, they took away the heart of our race, they bore away the mind and muscle of our race. The city fell and was rebuilt; the city fell and our people trudged through mountain and forest to 55 found a new home but—Elesin Oba do you hear me?

ELESIN: I hear your voice Olohun-iyo.

PRAISE-SINGER: Our world was never wrenched from its true course.

ELESIN: The gods have said No. 60

PRAISE-SINGER: There is only one home to the life of a rivermussel; there is only one home to the life of a tortoise; there is only one shell to the soul of man: there is only one world to the spirit of our race. If that world leaves its course and smashes on boulders of the great void, whose world will 65 give us shelter?

ELESIN: It did not in the time of my forebears, it shall not in mine.

PRAISE-SINGER: The cockerel must not be seen without his feathers. 70

ELESIN: Nor will the Not-I bird be much longer without his nest.

PRAISE-SINGER: (*Stopped in his lyric stride.*) The Not-I bird, Elesin?

ELESIN: I said, the Not-I bird. 75

PRAISE-SINGER: All respect to our elders but, is there really such a bird?

ELESIN: What! Could it be that he failed to knock on your door?

PRAISE-SINGER: (*Smiling.*) Elesin's riddles are not merely the nut
80   in the kernel that breaks human teeth; he also buries the
    kernel in hot embers and dares a man's fingers to draw it out.

ELESIN: I am sure he called on you, Olohun-iyo. Did you hide in
    the loft and push out the servant to tell him you were out?

(ELESIN *executes a brief, half-taunting dance. The* DRUMMER
moves in and draws a rhythm out of his steps. ELESIN *dances towards the market-place as he chants the story of the Not-I bird, his
voice changing dexterously to mimic his characters. He performs
like a born raconteur, infecting his retinue with his humour and
energy. More women arrive during his recital, including* IYALOJA.)

    Death came calling.
85   Who does not know his rasp of reeds?
    A twilight whisper in the leaves before
    The great araba falls? Did you hear it?
    'Not I!' swears the farmer. He snaps
    His fingers round his head, abandons
90   A hard-won harvest and begins
    A rapid dialogue with his legs.

    'Not I,' shouts the fearless hunter, 'but—
    It's getting dark, and this night-lamp
    Has leaked out all its oil. I think
95   It's best to go home and resume my hunt
    Another day.' But now he pauses, suddenly
    Lets out a wail: 'Oh foolish mouth, calling
    Down a curse on your own head! Your lamp
    Has leaked out all its oil, has it?'
100   Forwards or backwards now he dare not move.
    To search for leaves and make *etutu*
    On that spot? Or race home to the safety
    Of his hearth? Ten market-days have passed
    My friends, and still he's rooted there
105   Rigid as the plinth of Orayan.

    The mouth of the courtesan barely
    Opened wide enough to take a ha' penny *robo*
    When she wailed: 'Not I.' All dressed she was
    To call upon my friend the Chief Tax Officer.
105   But now she sends her go-between instead:
    'Tell him I'm ill: my period has come suddenly
    But not—I hope—my time.'

    Why is the pupil crying?
    His hapless head was made to taste
115   The knuckles of my friend the Mallam:
    'If you were then reciting the Koran
    Would you have ears for idle noises
    Darkening the trees, you child of ill omen?'
    He shuts down school before its time
120   Runs home and rings himself with amulets.
    And take my good kinsman Ifawomi.
    His hands were like a carver's, strong
    And true. I saw them
    Tremble like wet wings of a fowl
125   One day he cast his time-smoothed *opele*
    Across the divination board. And all because

    The suppliant looked him in the eye and asked,
    'Did you hear that whisper in the leaves?'
    'Not I,' was his reply; 'perhaps I'm growing deaf—
130   Good-day.' And Ifa spoke no more that day

    The priest locked fast his doors,
    Sealed up his leaking roof—but wait!
    This sudden care was not for Fawomi
    But for Osanyin, courier-bird of Ifa's
    Heart of wisdom. I did not know a kite   135
    Was hovering in the sky
    And Ifa now a twittering chicken in
    The brood of Fawomi the Mother Hen.

    Ah, but I must not forget my evening
    Courier from the abundant palm, whose groan   140
    Became 'Not I,' as he constipated down
    A wayside bush. He wonders if Elegbara
    Has tricked his buttocks to discharge
    Against a sacred grove. Hear him
    Mutter spells to ward off penalties   145
    For an abomination he did not intend.
    If any here
    Stumbles on a gourd of wine, fermenting
    Near the road, and nearby hears a stream
    Of spells issuing from a crouching form.   150
    Brother to a *sigidi*, bring home my wine,
    Tell my tapper I have ejected
    Fear from home and farm. Assure him,
    All is well.

PRAISE-SINGER: In your time we do not doubt the peace of   155
    farmstead and home, the peace of road and hearth, we do
    not doubt the peace of the forest.

ELESIN: There was fear in the forest too.
    Not-I was lately heard even in the lair
    Of beasts. The hyena cackled loud 'Not I,'   160
    The civet twitched his fiery tail and glared:
    Not I. Not-I became the answering-name
    Of the restless bird, that little one
    Whom Death found nesting in the leaves
    When whisper of his coming ran   165
    Before him on the wind. 'Not-I'
    Has long abandoned home. This same dawn
    I heard him twitter in the gods' abode.
    Ah, companions of this living world
    What a thing this is, that even those   170
    We call immortal
    Should fear to die.

IYALOJA: But you, husband of multitudes?

ELESIN: I, when that Not-I bird perched
    Upon my roof, bade him seek his nest again,   175
    Safe, without care or fear. I unrolled
    My welcome mat for him to see. Not-I
    Flew happily away, you'll hear his voice
    No more in this lifetime—You all know
    What I am.   180

PRAISE-SINGER: That rock which turns its open lodes
    Into the path of lightning. A gay
    Thoroughbred whose sudden disdains
    To falter though an adder reared
    Suddenly in his path.   185

ELESIN: My rein is loosened.
    I am master of my Fate. When the hour comes
    Watch me dance along the narrowing path
    Glazed by the soles of my great precursors.
    My soul is eager. I shall not turn aside.   190

WOMEN: You will not delay?

ELESIN: Where the storm pleases, and when, it directs

The giants of the forest. When friendship summons
Is when the true comrade goes.
195 WOMEN: Nothing will hold you back?
ELESIN: Nothing. What! Has no one told you yet?
I go to keep my friend and master company.
Who says the mouth does not believe in
'No, I have chewed all that before?' I say I have.
200 The world is not a constant honey-pot.
Where I found little I made do with little.
Where there was plenty I gorged myself.
My master's hands and mine have always
Dipped together and, home or sacred feast,
205 The bowl was beaten bronze, the meats
So succulent our teeth accused us of neglect.
We shared the choicest of the season's
Harvest of yams. How my friend would read
Desire in my eyes before I knew the cause—
210 However rare, however precious, it was mine.
WOMEN: The town, the very land was yours.
ELESIN: The world was mine. Our joint hands
Raised houseposts of trust that withstood
The siege of envy and the termites of time.
215 But the twilight hour brings bats and rodents—
Shall I yield them cause to foul the rafters?
PRAISE-SINGER: Elesin Oba! Are you not that man who
Looked out of doors that stormy day
The god of luck limped by, drenched
220 To the very lice that held
His rags together? You took pity upon
His sores and wished him fortune.
Fortune was footloose this dawn, he replied,
Till you trapped him in a heartfelt wish
225 That now returns to you. Elesin Oba!
I say you are that man who
Chanced upon the calabash of honour
You thought it was palm wine and
Drained its contents to the final drop.
230 ELESIN: Life has an end. A life that will outlive
Fame and friendship begs another name.
What elder takes his tongue to his plate,
Licks it clean of every crumb? He will encounter
Silence when he calls on children to fulfill
235 The smallest errand! Life is honour.
It ends when honour ends.
WOMEN: We know you for a man of honour.
ELESIN: Stop! Enough of that!
WOMEN: (*Puzzled, they whisper among themselves, turning mostly
240 to* IYALOJA.) What is it? Did we say something to give offense?
Have we slighted him in some way?
ELESIN: Enough of that sound I say. Let me hear no more in that
vein. I've heard enough.
IYALOJA: We must have said something wrong. (*Comes
245 forward a little.*) Elesin Oba, we ask forgiveness before
you speak.
ELESIN: I am bitterly offended.
IYALOJA: Our unworthiness has betrayed us. All we can do is ask
your forgiveness. Correct us like a kind father.
ELESIN: This day of all days . . .
250 IYALOJA: It does not bear thinking. If we offend you now we have
mortified the gods. We offend heaven itself. Father of us all,
tell us where we went astray. (*She kneels, the other women
follow.*)

ELESIN: Are you not ashamed? Even a tear-veiled
Eye preserves its function of sight. 255
Because my mind was raised to horizons
Even the boldest man lowers his gaze
In thinking of, must my body here
Be taken for a vagrant's?
IYALOJA: Horseman of the King, I am more baffled than ever. 260
PRAISE-SINGER: The strictest father unbends his brow when the
child is penitent, Elesin. When time is short, we do not spend
it prolonging the riddle. Their shoulders are bowed with the
weight of fear lest they have marred your day beyond repair.
Speak now in plain words and let us pursue the ailment to the 265
home of remedies.
ELESIN: Words are cheap. 'We know you for
A man of honour.' Well tell me, is this how
A man of honour should be seen?
Are these not the same clothes in which 270
I came among you a full half-hour ago?

(*He roars with laughter and the* WOMEN, *relieved, rise and rush
into stalls to fetch rich cloths.*)

WOMAN: The gods are kind. A fault soon remedied is soon
forgiven. Elesin Oba, even as we match our words with deed,
let your heart forgive us completely.
ELESIN: You who are breath and giver of my being 275
How shall I dare refuse you forgiveness
Even if the offence were real.
IYALOJA: (*Dancing round him. Sings.*)
He forgives us. He forgives us.
What a fearful thing it is when 280
The voyager sets forth
But a curse remains behind.
WOMEN: For a while we truly feared
Our hands had wrenched the world adrift
In emptiness. 285
IYALOJA: Richly, richly, robe him richly
The cloth of honour is *alari*
Sanyan is the band of friendship
Boa-skin makes slippers of esteem.
WOMEN: For a while we truly feared 290
Our hands had wrenched the world adrift
In emptiness.
PRAISE-SINGER: He who must, must voyage forth
The world will not roll backwards
It is he who must, with one 295
Great gesture overtake the world.
WOMEN: For a while we truly feared
Our hands had wrenched the world
In emptiness.
PRAISE-SINGER: The gourd you bear is not for shirking. 300
The gourd is not for setting down
At the first crossroad or wayside grove.
Only one river may know its contents.
WOMEN: We shall all meet at the great market
We shall all meet at the great market 305
He who goes early takes the best bargains
But we shall meet, and resume our banter.

(ELESIN *stands resplendent in rich clothes, cap, shawl, etc. His
sash is of a bright red alari cloth. The* WOMEN *dance round
him. Suddenly, his attention is caught by an object off-stage.*)

ELESIN: The world I know is good.
WOMEN: We know you'll leave it so.
310   ELESIN: The world I know is the bounty
        Of hives after bees have swarmed.
        No goodness teems with such open hands
        Even in the dreams of deities.
        WOMEN: And we know you'll leave it so.
315   ELESIN: I was born to keep it so. A hive
        Is never known to wander. An anthill
        Does not desert its roots. We cannot see
        The still great womb of the world—
        No man beholds his mother's womb—
320   Yet who denies it's there? Coiled
        To the navel of the world is that
        Endless cord that links us all
        To the great origin. If I lose my way
        The trailing cord will bring me to the roots.
325   WOMEN: The world is in your hands.

(*The earlier distraction, a beautiful young girl, comes along the passage through which* ELESIN *first ma de his entry.*)

ELESIN: I embrace it. And let me tell you, women—
        I like this farewell that the world designed,
        Unless my eyes deceive me, unless
        We are already parted, the world and I,
330   And all that breeds desire is lodged
        Among our tireless ancestors. Tell me friends,
        Am I still earthed in that beloved market
        Of my youth? Or could it be my will
        Has outleapt the conscious act and I have come
335   Among the great departed?
        PRAISE-SINGER: Elesin-Oba why do your eyes roll like a bush-rat
        who sees his fate like his father's spirit, mirrored in the eye of
        a snake? And all these questions! You're standing on the same
        earth you've always stood upon. This voice you hear is mine,
340   Oluhun-iyo, not that of an acolyte in heaven.
        ELESIN: How can that be? In all my life
        As Horseman of the King, the juiciest
        Fruit on every tree was mine. I saw,
        I touched, I wooed, rarely was the answer No.
345   The honour of my place, the veneration I
        Received in the eye of man or woman
        Prospered my suit and
        Played havoc with my sleeping hours.
        And they tell me my eyes were a hawk
350   In perpetual hunger. Split an iroko tree
        In two, hide a woman's beauty in its heartwood
        And seal it up again—Elesin, journeying by,
        Would make his camp beside that tree
        Of all the shades in the forest.
355   PRAISE-SINGER: Who would deny your reputation, snake-on-
        the-loose in dark passages of the market! Bed-bug who
        wages war on the mat and receives the thanks of the
        vanquished! When caught with his bride's own sister he
        protested—but I was only prostrating myself to her as
360   becomes a grateful in-law. Hunter who carries his powder-
        horn on the hips and fires crouching or standing! Warrior
        who never makes that excuse of the whining coward—but
        how can I go to battle without my trousers?—trouserless or
        shirtless it's all one to him. Oka-rearing-from-a-camouflage-
365   of-leaves, before he strikes the victim is already prone! Once

they told him, Howu, a stallion does not feed on the grass
beneath him: he replied, true, but surely he can roll on it!
WOMEN: Ba-a-a-ba O!
PRAISE-SINGER: Ah, but listen yet. You know there is the leaf-
knibbling grub and there is the cola-chewing beetle; the leaf-   370
nibbling grub lives on the leaf, the cola-chewing beetle lives in
the colanut. Don't we know what our man feeds on when we
find him cocooned in a woman's wrapper?
ELESIN: Enough, enough, you all have cause
        To know me well. But, if you say this earth   375
        Is still the same as gave birth to those songs,
        Tell me who was that goddess through whose lips
        I saw the ivory pebbles of Oya's river-bed.
        Iyaloja, who is she? I saw her enter
        Your stall; all your daughters I know well.   380
        No, not even Ogun-of-the-farm toiling
        Dawn till dusk on his tuber patch
        Not even Ogun with the finest hoe he ever
        Forged at the anvil could have shaped
        That rise of buttocks, not though he had   385
        The richest earth between his fingers.
        Her wrapper was no disguise
        For thighs whose ripples shamed the river's
        Coils around the hills of Ilesi. Her eyes
        Were new-laid eggs glowing in the dark.   390
        Her skin . . .
IYALOJA: Elesin Oba . . .
ELESIN: What! Where do you all say I am?
IYALOJA: Still among the living.
ELESIN: And that radiance which so suddenly   395
        Lit up this market I could boast
        I knew so well?
IYALOJA: Has one step already in her husband's home. She is
betrothed.
ELESIN: (*Irritated.*) Why do you tell me that?   400

(IYALOJA *falls silent. The* WOMEN *shuffle uneasily.*)

IYALOJA: Not because we dare give you offence Elesin. Today
is your day and the whole world is yours. Still, even those
who leave town to make a new dwelling elsewhere like to
be remembered by what they leave behind.
ELESIN: Who does not seek to be remembered?   405
        Memory is Master of Death, the chink
        In his armour of conceit. I shall leave
        That which makes my going the sheerest
        Dream of an afternoon. Should voyagers
        Not travel light? Let the considerate traveller   410
        Shed, of his excessive load, all
        That may benefit the living.
WOMEN: (*Relieved.*) Ah Elesin Oba, we knew you for a man of
honour.
ELESIN: Then honour me. I deserve a bed of honour to lie upon.   415
IYALOJA: The best is yours. We know you for a man of honour.
        You are not one who eats and leaves nothing on his plate for
        children. Did you not say it yourself? Not one who blights the
        happiness of others for a moment's pleasure.
ELESIN: Who speaks of pleasure? O women, listen!   420
        Pleasure palls. Our acts should have meaning.
        The sap of the plantain never dries.
        You have seen the young shoot swelling
        Even as the parent stalk begins to wither.

425 Women, let my going be likened to
The twilight hour of the plantain.
WOMEN: What does he mean Iyaloja? This language is the
language of our elders, we do not fully grasp it.
IYALOJA: I dare not understand you yet Elesin.
430 ELESIN: All you who stand before the spirit that dares
The opening of the last door of passage,
Dare to rid my going of regrets! My wish
Transcends the blotting out of thought
In one mere moment's tremor of the senses.
435 Do me credit. And do me honour.
I am girded for the route beyond
Burdens of waste and longing.
Then let me travel light. Let
Seed that will not serve the stomach
440 On the way remain behind. Let it take root
In the earth of my choice, in this earth
I leave behind.
IYALOJA: (*Turns to* WOMEN.) The voice I hear is already touched
by the waiting fingers of our departed. I dare not refuse.
445 WOMAN: Buy Iyaloja . . .
IYALOJA: The matter is no longer in our hands.
WOMAN: But she is betrothed to your own son. Tell him.
IYALOJA: My son's wish is mine. I did the asking for him, the
loss can be remedied. But who will remedy the blight of
450 closed hands on the day when all should be openness and
light? Tell him, you say! You wish that I burden him with
knowledge that will sour his wish and lay regrets on the
last moments of his mind. You pray to him who is your
intercessor to the other world—don't set this world adrift
455 in your own time; would you rather it was my hand whose
sacrilege wrenched it loose?
WOMAN: Not many men will brave the curse of a dispossessed
husband.
IYALOJA: Only the curses of the departed are to be feared. The
460 claims of one whose foot is on the threshold of their abode
surpasses even the claims of blood. It is impiety even to place
hindrances in their ways.
ELESIN: What do my mothers say? Shall I step
Burdened into the unknown?
465 IYALOJA: Not we, but the very earth says No. The sap in the
plantain does not dry. Let grain that will not feed the voyager
at his passage drop here and take root as he steps beyond
this earth and us. Oh you who fill the home from hearth to
threshold with the voices of children, you who now bestride
470 the hidden gulf and pause to draw the right foot across and
into the resting-home of the great forebears, it is good that
your loins be drained into the earth we know, that your last
strength be ploughed back into the womb that gave you being.
PRAISE-SINGER: Iyaloja, mother of multitudes in the teeming
475 market of the world, how your wisdom transfigures you!
IYALOJA: (*Smiling broadly, completely reconciled.*) Elesin, even at
the narrow end of the passage I know you will look back and
sigh a last regret for the flesh that flashed past your
spirit in flight. You always had a restless eye. Your choice
480 has my blessing. (*To the* WOMEN.) Take the good news to our
daughter and make her ready. (*Some* WOMEN *go off.*)
ELESIN: Your eyes were clouded at first.
IYALOJA: Not for long. It is those who stand at the gateway of the
great change to whose cry we must pay heed. And then, think
485 of this—it makes the mind tremble. The fruit of such a union
is rare. It will be neither of this world nor of the next. Nor of

the one behind us. As if the timelessness of the ancestor world
and the unborn have joined spirits to wring an issue of the
elusive being of passage . . . Elesin!
ELESIN: I am here. What is it?   490
IYALOJA: Did you hear all I said just now?
ELESIN: Yes.
IYALOJA: The living must eat and drink. When the moment
comes, don't turn the food to rodents' droppings in their
mouth. Don't let them taste the ashes of the world when they   495
step out at dawn to breathe the morning dew.
ELESIN: This doubt is unworthy of you Iyaloja.
IYALOJA: Eating the awusa nut is not so difficult as drinking water
afterwards.
ELESIN: The waters of the bitter stream are honey to a man   500
Whose tongue has savoured all.
IYALOJA: No one knows when the ants desert their home; they
leave the mound intact. The swallow is never seen to peck
holes in its nest when it is time to move with the season. There
are always throngs of humanity behind the leave-taker. The   505
rain should not come through the roof for them, the wind
must not blow through the walls at night.
ELESIN: I refuse to take offence.
IYALOJA: You wish to travel light. Well, the earth is yours. But be
sure the seed you leave in it attracts no curse.   510
ELESIN: You really mistake my person Iyaloja.
IYALOJA: I said nothing. Now we must go prepare your bridal
chamber. Then these same hands will lay your shrouds.
ELESIN: (*Exasperated.*) Must you be so blunt? (*Recovers.*) Well,
weave your shrouds, but let the fingers of my bride seal my   515
eyelids with earth and wash my body.
IYALOJA: Prepare yourself Elesin.

(*She gets up to leave. At that moment the women return, leading
the* BRIDE. ELESIN'*s face glows with pleasure. He flicks the sleeves
of his agbada with renewed confidence and steps forward to meet
the group. As the girl kneels before* IYALOJA, *lights fade out on the
scene.*)

ACT TWO

*The verandah of the District Officer's bungalow. A tango is playing
from an old hand-cranked gramophone and, glimpsed through the
wide windows and doors which open onto the forestage verandah
are the shapes of* SIMON PILKINGS *and his wife,* JANE, *tangoing in
and out of shadows in the living-room. They were wearing what is
immediately apparent as some form of fancy-dress. The dance goes
on for some moments and then the figure of a 'Native Administration' policeman emerges and climbs up the steps onto the verandah.
He peeps through and observes the dancing couple, reacting with
what is obviously a long-standing bewilderment. He stiffens
suddenly, his expression changes to one of disbelief and horror. In
his excitement he upsets a flower-pot and attracts the attention of
the couple. They stop dancing.*

PILKINGS: Is there anyone out there?
JANE: I'll turn off the gramophone.
PILKINGS: (*Approaching the verandah.*) I'm sure I heard something
fall over. (*The constable retreats slowly, open-mouthed as*
PILKINGS *approaches the verandah.*) Oh it's you Amusa. Why   5
didn't you just knock instead of knocking things over?
AMUSA: (*Stammers badly and points a shaky finger at his dress.*)
Mista Pirinkin . . . Mista Pirinkin . . .

PILKINGS: What is the matter with you?

10 JANE: (*Emerging.*) Who is it dear? Oh, Amusa . . .

PILKINGS: Yes it's Amusa, and acting most strangely.

AMUSA: (*His attention now transferred to* MRS PILKINGS.) Mammadam . . . you too!

PILKINGS: What the hell is the matter with you man!

15 JANE: Your costume darling. Our fancy dress.

PILKINGS: Oh hell, I'd forgotten all about that. (*Lifts the face mask over his head showing his face. His wife follows suit.*)

JANE: I think you've shocked his big pagan heart bless him.

PILKINGS: Nonsense, he's a Moslem. Come on Amusa, you don't

20   believe in all this nonsense do you? I thought you were a good Moslem.

AMUSA: Mista Pirinkin, I beg you sir, what you think you do with that dress? It belong to dead cult, not for human being.

PILKINGS: Oh Amusa, what a let down you are. I swear by you at

25   the club you know—thank God for Amusa, he doesn't believe in any mumbo-jumbo. And now look at you!

AMUSA: Mista Pirinkin, I beg you, take it off. Is not good for man like you to touch that cloth.

PILKINGS: Well, I've got it on. And what's more Jane and I have

30   bet on it we're taking first prize at the ball. Now, if you can just pull yourself together and tell me what you wanted to see me about . . .

AMUSA: Sir, I cannot talk this matter to you in that dress. I no fit.

35 PILKINGS: What's that rubbish again?

JANE: He is dead earnest too Simon. I think you'll have to handle this delicately.

PILKINGS: Delicately my. . . ! Look here Amusa, I think this little joke has gone far enough hm? Let's have some sense. You

40   seem to forget that you are a police officer in the service of His Majesty's Government. I order you to report your business at once or face disciplinary action.

AMUSA: Sir, it is a matter of death. How can man talk against death to person in uniform of death? Is like talking against

45   government to person in uniform of police. Please sir, I go and come back.

PILKINGS: (*Roars.*) Now! (AMUSA *switches his gaze to the ceiling suddenly, remains mute.*)

JANE: Oh Amusa, what is there to be scared of in the costume?

50   You saw it confiscated last month from those *egungun* men who were creating trouble in town. You helped arrest the cult leaders yourself—if the juju didn't harm you at the time how could it possibly harm you now? And merely by looking at it?

55 AMUSA: (*Without looking down.*) Madam, I arrest the ring-leaders who make trouble but me I no touch *egungun*. That *egungun* itself, I no touch. And I no abuse 'am. I arrest ring-leader but I treat *egungun* with respect.

PILKINGS: It's hopeless. We'll merely end up missing the best

60   part of the ball. When they get this way there is nothing you can do. It's simply hammering against a brick wall. Write your report or whatever it is on that pad Amusa and take yourself out of here. Come on Jane. We only upset his delicate sensibilities by remaining here.

(AMUSA *waits for them to leave, then writes in the notebook, somewhat laboriously. Drumming from the direction of the town wells up.* AMUSA *listens, makes a movement as if he wants to recall* PILKINGS *but changes his mind. Completes his note and goes. A few moments later* PILKINGS *emerges, picks up the pad and reads.*)

PILKINGS: Jane!   65

JANE: (*From the bedroom.*) Coming darling. Nearly ready.

PILKINGS: Never mind being ready, just listen to this.

JANE: What is it?

PILKINGS: Amusa's report. Listen. 'I have to report that it come to my information that one prominent chief, namely, the Elesin   70 Oba, is to commit death tonight as a result of native custom. Because this is criminal offence I await further instruction at charge office. Sergeant Amusa.'

(JANE *comes out onto the verandah while he is reading.*)

JANE: Did I hear you say commit death?

PILKINGS: Obviously he means murder.   75

JANE: You mean a ritual murder?

PILKINGS: Must be. You think you've stamped it all out but it's always lurking under the surface somewhere.

JANE: Oh. Does it mean we are not getting to the ball at all?

PILKINGS: No-o. I'll have the man arrested. Everyone remotely   80 involved. In any case there may be nothing to it. Just rumours.

JANE: Really? I thought you found Amusa's rumours generally reliable.

PILKINGS: That's true enough. But who knows what may have been giving him the scare lately. Look at his conduct   85 tonight.

JANE: (*Laughing.*) You have to admit he had his own peculiar logic. (*Deepens her voice.*) How can man talk against death to person in uniform of death? (*Laughs.*) Anyway, you can't go into the police station dressed like that.   90

PILKINGS: I'll send Joseph with instructions. Damn it, what a confounded nuisance!

JANE: But don't you think you should talk first to the man, Simon?

PILKINGS: Do you want to go to the ball or not?   95

JANE: Darling, why are you getting rattled? I was only trying to be intelligent. It seems hardly fair just to lock up a man—and a chief at that—simply on the er . . . what is that legal word again?—uncorroborated word of a sergeant.

PILKINGS: Well, that's easily decided. Joseph!   100

JOSEPH: (*From within.*) Yes master.

PILKINGS: You're quite right of course, I am getting rattled. Probably the effect of those bloody drums. Do you hear how they go on and on?

JANE: I wondered when you'd notice. Do you suppose it has   105 something to do with this affair?

PILKINGS: Who knows? They always find an excuse for making a noise . . . (*Thoughtfully.*) Even so . . .

JANE: Yes Simon?

PILKINGS: It's different Jane. I don't think I've heard this   110 particular—sound—before. Something unsettling about it.

JANE: I thought all bush drumming sounded the same.

PILKINGS: Don't tease me now Jane. This may be serious.

JANE: I'm sorry. (*Gets up and throws her arms around his neck. Kisses him. The houseboy enters, retreats and knocks.*)   115

PILKINGS: (*Wearily.*) Oh, come in Joseph! I don't know where you pick up all these elephantine notions of tact. Come over here.

JOSEPH: Sir?

PILKINGS: Joseph, are you a christian or not?

JOSEPH: Yessir.   120

PILKINGS: Does seeing me in this outfit bother you?

JOSEPH: No sir, it has no power.

PILKINGS: Thank God for some sanity at last. Now Joseph, answer me on the honour of a christian—what is supposed to be going on in town tonight?

125 JOSEPH: Tonight sir? You mean that chief who is going to kill himself?

PILKINGS: What?

JANE: What do you mean, kill himself?

130 PILKINGS: You do mean he is going to kill somebody don't you?

JOSEPH: No master. He will not kill anybody and no one will kill him. He will simply die.

JANE: But why Joseph?

JOSEPH: It is native law and custom. The King die last month.

135 Tonight is his burial. But before they can bury him, the Elesin must die so as to accompany him to heaven.

PILKINGS: I seem to be fated to clash more often with that man than with any of the other chiefs.

JOSEPH: He is the King's Chief Horseman.

140 PILKINGS: (*In a resigned way.*) I know.

JANE: Simon, what's the matter?

PILKINGS: It would have to be him!

JANE: Who is he?

PILKINGS: Don't you remember? He's that chief with whom I had

145 a scrap some three or four years ago. I helped his son get to a medical school in England, remember? He fought tooth and nail to prevent it.

JANE: Oh now I remember. He was that very sensitive young man. What was his name again?

150 PILKINGS: Olunde. Haven't replied to his last letter come to think of it. The old pagan wanted him to stay and carry on some family tradition or the other. Honestly I couldn't understand the fuss he made. I literally had to help the boy escape from close confinement and load him onto the next

155 boat. A most intelligent boy, really bright.

JANE: I rather thought he was much too sensitive you know. The kind of person you feel should be a poet munching rose petals in Bloomsbury.

PILKINGS: Well, he's going to make a first-class doctor. His mind

160 is set on that. And as long as he wants my help he is welcome to it.

JANE: (*After a pause.*) Simon.

PILKINGS: Yes?

JANE: This boy, he was his eldest son wasn't he?

165 PILKINGS: I'm not sure. Who could tell with that old ram?

JANE: Do you know, Joseph?

JOSEPH: Oh yes madam. He was the eldest son. That's why Elesin cursed master good and proper. The eldest son is not supposed to travel away from the land.

170 JANE: (*Giggling.*) Is that true Simon? Did he really curse you good and proper?

PILKINGS: By all accounts I should be dead by now.

JOSEPH: Oh no, master is white man. And good christian. Black man juju can't touch master.

175 JANE: If he was his eldest, it means that he would be the Elesin to the next king. It's a family thing isn't it, Joseph?

JOSEPH: Yes madam. And if this Elesin had died before the King, his eldest son must take his place.

JANE: That would explain why the old chief was so mad you took

180 the boy away.

PILKINGS: Well it makes me all the more happy I did.

JANE: I wonder if he knew.

PILKINGS: Who? Oh, you mean Olunde?

JANE: Yes. Was that why he was so determined to get away?

185 I wouldn't stay if I knew I was trapped in such a horrible custom.

PILKINGS: (*Thoughtfully.*) No, I don't think he knew. At least he gave no indication. But you couldn't really tell with him. He was rather close you know, quite unlike most of them. Didn't

190 give much away, not even to me.

JANE: Aren't they all rather close, Simon?

PILKINGS: These natives here? Good gracious. They'll open their mouths and yap with you about their family secrets before you can stop them. Only the other day . . .

195 JANE: But Simon, do they really give anything away? I mean, anything that really counts. This affair for instance, we didn't know they still practised that custom did we?

PILKINGS: Ye-e-es, I suppose you're right there. Sly, devious bastards.

200 JOSEPH: (*Stiffly.*) Can I go now master? I have to clean the kitchen.

PILKINGS: What? Oh, you can go. Forgot you were still here.

(JOSEPH *goes.*)

JANE: Simon, you really must watch your language. Bastard isn't just a simple swear-word in these parts, you know.

PILKINGS: Look, just when did you become a social

205 anthropologist, that's what I'd like to know.

JANE: I'm not claiming to know anything. I just happen to have overheard quarrels among the servants. That's how I know they consider it a smear.

PILKINGS: I thought the extended family system took care of all

210 that. Elastic family, no bastards.

JANE: (*Shrugs.*) Have it your own way.

(*Awkward silence. The drumming increases in volume.* JANE *gets up suddenly, restless.*)

That drumming Simon, do you think it might really be connected with this ritual? It's been going on all evening.

PILKINGS: Let's ask our native guide. Joseph! Just a minute Joseph.

215 (JOSEPH *re-enters.*) What's the drumming about?

JOSEPH: I don't know master.

PILKINGS: What do you mean you don't know? It's only two years since your conversion. Don't tell me all that holy water nonsense also wiped out your tribal memory.

220 JOSEPH: (*Visibly shocked.*) Master!

JANE: Now you've done it.

PILKINGS: What have I done now?

JANE: Never mind. Listen Joseph, just tell me this. Is that drumming connected with dying or anything of that nature?

225 JOSEPH: Madam, this is what I am trying to say: I am not sure. It sounds like the death of a great chief and then, it sounds like the wedding of a great chief. It really mix me up.

PILKINGS: Oh get back to the kitchen. A fat lot of help you are.

JOSEPH: Yes master. (*Goes.*)

230 JANE: Simon . . .

PILKINGS: Alright, alright. I'm in no mood for preaching.

JANE: It isn't my preaching you have to worry about, it's the preaching of the missionaries who preceded you here. When they make converts they really convert them. Calling holy

235 water nonsense is really like insulting the Virgin Mary before a Roman Catholic. He's going to hand in his notice tomorrow you mark my word.

PILKINGS: Now you're being ridiculous.

JANE: Am I? What are you willing to bet that tomorrow we are
240   going to be without a steward-boy? Did you see his face?

PILKINGS: I am more concerned about whether or not we will be
       one native chief short by tomorrow. Christ! Just listen to those
       drums. (*He strides up and down, undecided.*)

JANE: (*Getting up.*) I'll change and make up some supper.

245 PILKINGS: What's that?

JANE: Simon, it's obvious we have to miss this ball.

PILKINGS: Nonsense. It's the first bit of real fun the European
       club has managed to organise for over a year, I'm damned
       if I'm going to miss it. And it is a rather special occasion.
250   Doesn't happen every day.

JANE: You know this business has to be stopped Simon. And you
       are the only man who can do it.

PILKINGS: I don't have to stop anything. If they want to throw
       themselves off the top of a cliff or poison themselves for the
255   sake of some barbaric custom what is that to me? If it were
       ritual murder or something like that I'd be duty-bound to
       do something. I can't keep an eye on all the potential suicides
       in this province. And as for that man—believe me it's good
       riddance.

260 JANE: (*Laughs.*) I know you better than that Simon. You are going
       to have to do something to stop it—after you've finished
       blustering.

PILKINGS: (*Shouts after her.*) And suppose after all it's only a
       wedding. I'd look a proper fool if I interrupted a chief on
265   his honeymoon, wouldn't I? (*Resumes his angry stride, slows
       down.*) Ah well, who can tell what those chiefs actually do on
       their honeymoon anyway? (*He takes up the pad and scribbles
       rapidly on it.*) Joseph! Joseph! Joseph! (*Some moments later
       JOSEPH puts in a sulky appearance.*) Did you hear me call you?
270   Why the hell didn't you answer?

JOSEPH: I didn't hear master.

PILKINGS: You didn't hear me! How come you are here then?

JOSEPH: (*Stubbornly.*) I didn't hear master.

PILKINGS: (*Controls himself with an effort.*) We'll talk about it in
275   the morning. I want you to take this note directly to Sergeant
       Amusa. You'll find him at the charge office. Get on your
       bicycle and race there with it. I expect you back in twenty
       minutes exactly. Twenty minutes, is that clear?

JOSEPH: Yes master. (*Going.*)

280 PILKINGS: Oh er . . . Joseph.

JOSEPH: Yes master?

PILKINGS: (*Between gritted teeth.*) Er . . . forget what I said just
       now. The holy water is not nonsense. I was talking nonsense.

JOSEPH: Yes master. (*Goes.*)

285 JANE: (*Pokes her head round the door.*) Have you found him?

PILKINGS: Found who?

JANE: Joseph. Weren't you shouting for him?

PILKINGS: Oh yes, he turned up finally.

JANE: You sounded desperate. What was it all about?

290 PILKINGS: Oh nothing. I just wanted to apologise to him. Assure
       him that the holy water isn't really nonsense.

JANE: Oh? And how did he take it?

PILKINGS: Who the hell gives a damn! I had a sudden vision of
       our Very Reverend Macfarlane drafting another letter of
295   complaint to the Resident about my unchristian language
       towards his parishioners.

JANE: Oh I think he's given up on you by now.

PILKINGS: Don't be too sure. And anyway, I wanted to make sure
       Joseph didn't 'lose' my note on the way. He looked sufficiently
300   full of the holy crusade to do some such thing.

JANE: If you've finished exaggerating, come and have something
       to eat.

PILKINGS: No, put it all way. We can still get to the ball.

JANE: Simon . . .

PILKINGS: Get your costume back on. Nothing to worry   305
       about. I've instructed Amusa to arrest the man and lock
       him up.

JANE: But that station is hardly secure Simon. He'll soon get his
       friends to help him escape.

PILKINGS: A-ah, that's where I have out-thought you. I'm not   310
       having him put in the station cell. Amusa will bring him
       right here and lock him up in my study. And he'll stay with
       him till we get back. No one will dare come here to incite him
       to anything.

JANE: How clever of you darling. I'll get ready.   315

PILKINGS: Hey.

JANE: Yes darling.

PILKINGS: I have a surprise for you. I was going to keep it until we
       actually got to the ball.

JANE: What is it?   320

PILKINGS: You know the Prince is on a tour of the colonies don't
       you? Well, he docked in the capital only this morning but he is
       already at the Residency. He is going to grace the ball with his
       presence later tonight.

JANE: Simon! Not really.   325

PILKINGS: Yes he is. He's been invited to give away the prizes and
       he has agreed. You must admit old Engleton is the best Club
       Secretary we ever had. Quick off the mark that lad.

JANE: But how thrilling.

PILKINGS: The other provincials are going to be damned envious. 330

JANE: I wonder what he'll come as.

PILKINGS: Oh I don't know. As a coat-of-arms perhaps. Anyway it
       won't be anything to touch this.

JANE: Well that's lucky. If we are to be presented I won't have to
       start looking for a pair of gloves. It's all sewn on.   335

PILKINGS: (*Laughing.*) Quite right. Trust a woman to think of
       that. Come on, let's get going.

JANE: (*Rushing off.*) Won't be a second. (*Stops.*) Now I see
       why you've been so edgy all evening. I thought you weren't
       handling this affair with your usual brilliance—to begin with 340
       that is.

PILKINGS: (*His mood is much improved.*) Shut up woman and get
       your things on.

JANE: Alright boss, coming.

(PILKINGS *suddenly begins to hum the tango to which they
were dancing before. Starts to execute a few practice steps.
Lights fade.*)

ACT THREE

*A swelling, agitated hum of women's voices rises immediately
in the background. The lights come on and we see the frontage
of a converted cloth stall in the market. The floor leading up to
the entrance is covered in rich velvets and woven cloth. The* WOMEN
*come on stage, borne backwards by the determined progress of
Sergeant* AMUSA *and his two constables who already have their
batons out and use them as a pressure against the* WOMEN. *At
the edge of the cloth-covered floor however the* WOMEN *take a
determined stand and block all further progress of the* MEN. *They
begin to tease them mercilessly.*

AMUSA: I am tell you women for last time to commot my road. I am here on official business.

WOMAN: Official business you white man's eunuch? Official business is taking place where you want to go and it's a business you wouldn't understand.

WOMAN: (*Makes a quick tug at the constable's baton.*) That doesn't fool anyone you know. It's the one you carry under your government knickers that counts. (*She bends low as if to peep under the baggy shorts. The embarrassed constable quickly puts his knees together. The* WOMEN *roar.*)

WOMAN: You mean there is nothing there at all?

WOMAN: Oh there was something. You know that handbell which the white man uses to summon his servants . . . ?

AMUSA: (*He manages to preserve some dignity throughout.*) I hope you women know that interfering with officer in execution of his duty is criminal offence.

WOMAN: Interfere? He says we're interfering with him. You foolish man we're telling you there's nothing there to interfere with.

AMUSA: I am order you now to clear the road.

WOMAN: What road? The one your father built?

WOMAN: You are a Policeman not so? Then you know what they call trespassing in court. Or—(*Pointing to the cloth-lined steps.*)—do you think that kind of road is built for every kind of feet.

WOMAN: Go back and tell the white man who sent you to come himself.

AMUSA: If I go I will come back with reinforcement. And we will all return carrying weapons.

WOMAN: Oh, now I understand. Before they can put on those knickers the white man first cuts off their weapons.

WOMAN: What a cheek! You mean you come here to show power to women and you don't even have a weapon.

AMUSA: (*Shouting above the laughter.*) For the last time I warn you women to clear the road.

WOMAN: To where?

AMUSA: To that hut. I know he dey dere.

WOMAN: Who?

AMUSA: The chief who call himself Elesin Oba.

WOMAN: You ignorant man. It is not he who calls himself Elesin Oba, it is his blood that says it. As it called out to his father before him and will to his son after him. And that is in spite of everything your white man can do.

WOMAN: Is it not the same ocean that washes this land and the white man's land? Tell your white man he can hide our son away as long as he likes. When the time comes for him, the same ocean will bring him back.

AMUSA: The government say dat kin' ting must stop.

WOMAN: Who will stop it? You? Tonight our husband and father will prove himself greater than the laws of strangers.

AMUSA: I tell you nobody go prove anyting tonight or anytime. Is ignorant and criminal to prove dat kin' prove.

IYALOJA: (*Entering, from the hut. She is accompanied by a group of* YOUNG GIRLS *who have been attending the* BRIDE.) What is it Amusa? Why do you come here to disturb the happiness of others.

AMUSA: Madame Iyaloja, I glad you come. You know me. I no like trouble but duty is duty. I am here to arrest Elesin for criminal intent. Tell these women to stop obstructing me in the performance of my duty.

IYALOJA: And you? What gives you the right to obstruct our leader of men in the performance of his duty.

AMUSA: What kin' duty be dat one Iyaloja.

IYALOJA: What kin' duty? What kin' duty does a man have to his new bride?

AMUSA: (*Bewildered, looks at the* WOMEN *and at the entrance to the hut.*) Iyaloja, is it wedding you call dis kin' ting?

IYALOJA: You have wives haven't you? Whatever the white man has done to you he hasn't stopped you having wives. And if he has, at least he is married. If you don't know what a marriage is, go and ask him to tell you.

AMUSA: This no to wedding.

IYALOJA: And ask him at the same time what he would have done if anyone had come to disturb him on his wedding night.

AMUSA: Iyaloja, I say dis no to wedding.

IYALOJA: You want to look inside the bridal chamber? You want to see for yourself how a man cuts the virgin knot?

AMUSA: Madam . . .

WOMAN: Perhaps his wives are still waiting for him to learn.

AMUSA: Iyaloja, make you tell dese women make den no insult me again. If I hear dat kin' insult once more . . .

GIRL: (*Pushing her way through.*) You will do what?

GIRL: He's out of his mind. It's our mothers you're talking to, do you know that? Not to any illiterate villager you can bully and terrorise. How dare you intrude here anyway?

GIRL: What a cheek, what impertinence!

GIRL: You've treated them too gently. Now let them see what it is to tamper with the mothers of this market.

GIRLS: Your betters dare not enter the market when the women say no!

GIRL: Haven't you learnt that yet, you jester in khaki and starch?

IYALOJA: Daughters . . .

GIRL: No no Iyaloja, leave us to deal with him. He no longer knows his mother, we'll teach him.

(*With a sudden movement they snatch the batons of the two constables. They begin to hem them in.*)

GIRL: What next? We have your batons? What next? What are you going to do?

(*With equally swift movements they knock off their hats.*)

GIRL: Move if you dare. We have your hats, what will you do about it? Didn't the white man teach you to take off your hats before women?

IYALOJA: It's a wedding night. It's a night of joy for us. Peace . . .

GIRL: Not for him. Who asked him here?

GIRL: Does he dare go to the Residency without an invitation?

GIRL: Not even where the servants eat the left-overs.

GIRLS: (*In turn. In an 'English' accent.*) Well well it's Mister Amusa. Were you invited? (*Play-acting to one another. The older* WOMEN *encourage them with their titters.*)
—Your invitation card please?
—Who are you? Have we been introduced?
—And who did you say you were?
—Sorry, I didn't quite catch your name.
—May I take your hat?
—If you insist. May I take yours? (*Exchanging the policeman's hats.*)
—How very kind of you.
—Not at all. Won't you sit down?

—After you.

—Oh no.

120 —I insist.

—You're most gracious.

—And how do you find the place?

—The natives are alright.

—Friendly?

125 —Tractable.

—Not a teeny-weeny bit restless?

—Well, a teeny-weeny bit restless.

—One might even say, difficult?

—Indeed one might be tempted to say, difficult.

130 —But you do manage to cope?

—Yes indeed I do. I have a rather faithful ox called Amusa.

—He's loyal?

—Absolutely.

—Lay down his life for you what?

135 —Without a moment's thought.

—Had one like that once. Trust him with my life.

—Mostly of course they are liars.

—Never known a native tell the truth.

—Does it get rather close around here?

140 —It's mild for this time of the year.

—But the rains may still come.

—They are late this year aren't they?

—They are keeping African time.

—Ha ha ha

145 —Ha ha ha ha

—The humidity is what gets me.

—It used to be whisky.

—Ha ha ha ha

—Ha ha ha ha

150 —What's your handicap old chap?

—Is there racing by golly?

—Splendid golf course, you'll like it.

—I'm beginning to like it already.

—And a European club, exclusive.

155 —You've kept the flag flying.

—We do our best for the old country.

—It's a pleasure to serve.

—Another whisky old chap?

—You are indeed too too kind.

160 —Not at all sir. Where is that boy? (*With a sudden bellow.*) Sergeant!

AMUSA: (*Snaps to attention.*) Yessir!

(*The* WOMEN *collapse with laughter.*)

GIRL: Take your men out of here.

AMUSA: (*Realising the trick, he rages from loss of face.*) I'm give

165 you warning . . .

GIRL: Alright then. Off with his knickers! (*They surge slowly forward.*)

IYALOJA: Daughters, please.

AMUSA: (*Squaring himself for defence.*) The first woman wey

170 touch me . . .

IYALOJA: My children, I beg of you . . .

GIRL: Then tell him to leave this market. This is the home of our mothers. We don't want the eater of white left-overs at the feast their hands have prepared.

175 IYALOJA: You heard them Amusa. You had better go.

GIRLS: Now!

AMUSA: (*Commencing his retreat.*) We dey go now, but make you no say we no warn you.

GIRL: Before we read the riot act—you should know all about

180 that.

AMUSA: Make we go. (*They depart, more precipitately.*)

(*The* WOMEN *strike their palms across in the gesture of wonder.*)

WOMEN: Do they teach you all that school?

WOMAN: And to think I nearly kept Apinke away from the place.

WOMAN: Did you hear them? Did you see how they mimicked the 185 white man?

WOMAN: The voices exactly. Hey, there are wonders in this world!

IYALOJA: Well, our elders have said it: Dada may be weak, but he has a younger sibling who is truly fearless. 190

WOMAN: The next time the white man shows his face in this market I will set Wuraola on his tail.

(*A* WOMAN *bursts into song and dance of euphoria—'Tani l'awa o l'ogbeja? Kayi! A l'ogbeja. Omo Kekere l'ogbeja.' ['Who says we haven't a defender? Silence! We have our defenders. Little children are our champions.'] The rest of the* WOMEN *join in, some placing the* GIRLS *on their back like infants, other dancing round them. The dance becomes general, mounting in excitement.* ELESIN *appears, in wrapper only. In his hands a white velvet cloth folded loosely as if it held some delicate object. He cries out.*)

ELESIN: Oh you mothers of beautiful brides! (*The dancing stops. They turn and see him, and the object in his hands.* IYALOJA *approaches and gently takes the cloth from him.*) Take it. It is 195 no mere virgin stain, but the union of life and the seeds of passage. My vital flow, the last from this flesh is intermingled with the promise of future life. All is prepared. Listen! (*A steady drum-beat from the distance.*) Yes. It is nearly time. The King's dog has been killed. The King's favourite horse is 200 about to follow his master. My brother chiefs know their task and perform it well. (*He listens again.*)

(*The* BRIDE *emerges, stands shyly by the door. He turns to her.*)

Our marriage is not yet wholly fulfilled. When earth and passage wed, the consummation is complete only when there are grains of earth on the eyelids of passage. Stay 205 by me till then. My faithful drummers, do me your last service. This is where I have chosen to do my leave-taking, in this heart of life, this hive which contains the swarm of the world in its small compass. This is where I have known love and laughter away from the palace. Even the richest 210 food cloys when eaten days on end; in the market, nothing ever cloys. Listen. (*They listen to the drums.*) They have begun to seek out the heart of the King's favourite horse. Soon it will ride in its bolt of raffia with the dog at its feet. Together they will ride on the shoulders of the King's grooms 215 through the pulse centres of the town. They know it is here I shall await them. I have told them. (*His eyes appear to cloud. He passes his hand over them as if to clear his sight. He gives a faint smile.*) It promises well; just then I felt my spirit's eagerness. The kite makes for wide spaces and the wind 220 creeps up behind its tail; can the kite say less than—thank you, the quicker the better? But wait a while my spirit. Wait. Wait for the coming of the courier of the King. Do

225 you know friends, the horse is born to this one destiny, to
bear the burden that is man upon its back. Except for this
night, this night alone when the spotless stallion will ride
in triumph on the back of man. In the time of my father I
witnessed the strange sight. Perhaps tonight also I shall see
230 it for the last time. If they arrive before the drums beat for me,
I shall tell him to let the Alafin know I follow swiftly. If they
come after the drums have sounded, why then, all is well for
I have gone ahead. Our spirits shall fall in step along the
great passage. (*He listens to the drums. He seems again to
235 be falling into a state of semi-hypnosis; his eyes scan the sky
but it is in a kind of daze. His voice is a little breathless.*) The
moon has fed, a glow from its full stomach fills the sky and
air, but I cannot tell where is that gateway through which I
must pass. My faithful friends, let our feet touch together
240 this last time, lead me into the other market with sounds that
cover my skin with down yet make my limbs strike earth
like a thoroughbred. Dear mothers, let me dance into the
passage even as I have lived beneath your roofs. (*He comes
down progressively among them. They make a way for him, the*
DRUMMERS *playing. His dance is one of solemn, regal motions,*
245 *each gesture of the body is made with a solemn finality. The*
WOMEN *join him, their steps a somewhat more fluid version of
his. Beneath the* PRAISE-SINGER's *exhortations the* WOMEN *dirge
'Alẹlẹ lẹ, awo mi lọ'.*)

PRAISE-SINGER: Elesin Alafin, can you hear my voice?

250 ELESIN: Faintly, my friend, faintly.

PRAISE-SINGER: Elesin Alafin, can you hear my call?

ELESIN: Faintly my king, faintly.

PRAISE-SINGER: Is your memory sound Elesin?
Shall my voice be a blade of grass and
255 Tickle the armpit of the past?

ELESIN: My memory needs no prodding but
What do you wish to say to me?

PRAISE-SINGER: Only what has been spoken. Only what concerns
The dying wish of the father of all.

260 ELESIN: It is buried like seed-yam in my mind
This is the season of quick rains, the harvest
Is this moment due for gathering.

PRAISE-SINGER: If you cannot come, I said, swear
You'll tell my favourite horse. I shall
265 Ride on through the gates alone.

ELESIN: Elesin's message will be read
Only when his loyal heart no longer beats.

PRAISE-SINGER: If you cannot come Elesin, tell my dog.
I cannot stay the keeper too long
270 At the gate.

ELESIN: A dog does not outrun the hand
That feeds it meat. A horse that throws its rider
Slows down to a stop. Elesin Alafin
Trusts no beasts with messages between
275 A king and his companion.

PRAISE-SINGER: If you get lost my dog will track
The hidden path to me.

ELESIN: The seven-way crossroads confuses
Only the stranger. The Horseman of the King
280 Was born in the recesses of the house.

PRAISE-SINGER: I know the wickedness of men. If there is
Weight on the loose end of your sash, such weight
As no mere man can shift; if your sash is earthed
By evil minds who mean to part us at the last . . .

285 ELESIN: My sash is of the deep purple *alari;*

It is no tethering-rope. The elephant
Trails no tethering-rope; that king
Is not yet crowned who will peg an elephant—
Not even you my friend and King.

PRAISE-SINGER: And yet this fear will not depart from me 290
The darkness of this new abode is deep—
Will your human eyes suffice?

ELESIN: In a night which falls before our eyes
However deep, we do not miss our way.

PRAISE-SINGER: Shall I now not acknowledge I have stood 295
Where wonders met their end? The elephant deserves
Better than that we say 'I have caught
A glimpse of something.' If we see the tamer
Of the forest let us say plainly, we have seen
An elephant. 300

ELESIN: (*His voice is drowsy.*) I have freed myself of earth and now
It's getting dark. Strange voices guide my feet.

PRAISE-SINGER: The river is never so high that the eyes
Of a fish are covered. The night is not so dark
That the albino fails to find his way. A child 305
Returning homewards craves no leading by the hand.
Gracefully does the mask regain his grove at the end of the day . . .
Gracefully. Gracefully does the mask dance
Homeward at the end of day, gracefully . . .

(ELESIN's *trance appears to be deepening, his steps heavier.*)

IYALOJA: It is the death of war that kills the valiant, 310
Death of water is how the swimmer goes
It is the death of markets that kills the trader
And death of indecision takes the idle away
The trade of the cutlass blunts its edge
And the beautiful die the death of beauty. 315
It takes an Elesin to die the death of death . . .
Only Elesin . . . dies the unknowable death of death . . .
Gracefully, gracefully does the horseman regain
The stables at the end of day, gracefully . . .

PRAISE-SINGER: How shall I tell what my eyes have seen? The 320
Horseman gallops on before the courier, how shall I tell
what my eyes have seen? He says a dog may be confused by
new scents of beings he never dreamt of, so he must precede
the dog to heaven. He says a horse may stumble on strange
boulders and be lamed, so he races on before the horse to 325
heaven. It is best, he says, to trust no messenger who may
falter at the outer gate; oh how shall I tell what my ears have
heard? But do you hear me still Elesin, do you hear your
faithful one?

(ELESIN *in his motions appears to feel for a direction of sound,
subtly, but he only sinks deeper into his trance-dance.*)

Elesin Alafin, I no longer sense your flesh. The drums are 330
changing now but you have gone far ahead of the world. It is
not yet noon in heaven; let those who claim it is begin their
own journey home. So why must you rush like an impatient
bride: why do you race to desert your Olohun-iyo?

(ELESIN *is now sunk fully deep in his trance, there is no longer sign
of any awareness of his surroundings.*)

Does the deep voice of *gbedu* cover you then, like the 335
passage of royal elephants? Those drums that brook no

rivals, have they blocked the passage to your ears that my
voice passes into wind, a mere leaf floating in the night?
Is your flesh lightened Elesin, is that lump of earth I slid
340   between your slippers to keep you longer slowly sifting
from your feet? Are the drums on the other side now tuning
skin to skin with ours in *osugbo*? Are there sounds there I
cannot hear, do footsteps surround you which pound the
earth like *gbedu*, roll like thunder round the dome of the
345   world? Is the darkness gathering in your head Elesin? Is
there now a streak of light at the end of the passage, a light
I dare not look upon? Does it reveal whose voices we often
heard, whose touches we often felt, whose wisdoms come
suddenly into the mind when the wisest have shaken their
350   heads and murmured: It cannot be done? Elesin Alafin,
don't think I do not know why your lips are heavy, why
your limbs are drowsy as palm oil in the cold of harmattan.
I would call you back but when the elephant heads for
the jungle, the tail is too small a handhold for the hunter
355   that would pull him back. The sun that heads for the sea
no longer heeds the prayers of the farmer. When the river
begins to taste the salt of the ocean, we no longer know what
deity to call on, the river-god or Olokun. No arrow flies back
to the string, the child does not return through the same
360   passage that gave it birth. Elesin Oba, can you hear me at
all? Your eye-lids are glazed like a courtesan's, is it that you
see the dark groom and master of life? And will you see my
father? Will you tell him that I stayed with you to the last?
Will my voice ring in your ears awhile, will you remember
365   Olohun-iyo even if the music on the other side surpasses his
mortal craft? But will they know you over there? Have they
eyes to gauge your worth, have they the heart to love you,
will they know what thoroughbred prances towards them
in caparisons of honour? If they do not Elesin, if any there
370   cuts your yam with a small knife, or pours you wine in a
small calabash, turn back and return to welcoming hands. If
the world were not greater than the wishes of Olohun-iyo, I
would not let you go . . .

(*He appears to break down.* ELESIN *dances on, completely in a
trance. The dirge wells up louder and stronger.* ELESIN's *dance does
not lose its elasticity but his gestures become, if possible, even more
weighty. Lights fade slowly on the scene.*)

ACT FOUR

*A Masque. The front side of the stage is part of a wide corridor
around the great hall of the Residency extending beyond vision
into the rear and wings. It is redolent of the tawdry decadence
of a far-flung but key imperial frontier. The couples in a variety
of fancy-dress are ranged around the walls, gazing in the same
direction. The guest-of-honour is about to make an appearance.
A portion of the local police brass band with its white conductor is
just visible. At last, the entrance of Royalty. The band plays 'Rule
Britannia', badly, beginning long before he is visible. The couples
bow and curtsey as he passes by them. Both he and his companions
are dressed in seventeenth century European costume. Following
behind are the* RESIDENT *and his partner similarly attired. As they
gain the end of the hall where the orchestra dais begins the music
comes to an end. The* PRINCE *bows to the guests. The band strikes
up a Viennese waltz and the* PRINCE *formally opens the floor. Several bars later the* RESIDENT *and his companion follow suit. Others
follow in appropriate pecking order. The orchestra's waltz rendition
is not of the highest musical standard.*

Some time later the PRINCE *dances again into view and is settled
into a corner by the* RESIDENT *who then proceeds to select couples
as they dance past for introduction, sometimes threading his
way through the dancers to tap the lucky couple on the shoulder.
Desperate efforts from many to ensure that they are recognised in
spite of, perhaps, their costume. The ritual of introductions soon
takes in* PILKINGS *and his wife. The* PRINCE *is quite fascinated
by their costume and they demonstrate the adaptations they
have made to it, pulling down the mask to demonstrate how the
egungun normally appears, then showing the various press-button
controls they have innovated for the face flaps, the sleeves, etc. They
demonstrate the dance steps and the guttural sounds made by the
egungun, harass other dancers in the hall,* MRS PILKINGS *playing
the 'restrainer' to* PILKINGS' *manic darts. Everyone is highly entertained, the Royal Party especially who lead the applause.*

*At this point a liveried footman comes in with a note on a salver
and is intercepted almost absent-mindedly by the* RESIDENT *who
takes the note and reads it. After polite coughs he succeeds in
excusing the* PILKINGSES *from the* PRINCE *and takes them aside.
The* PRINCE *considerately offers the* RESIDENT's *wife his hand and
dancing is resumed.*

On their way out the RESIDENT *gives an order to his* AIDE-DE-
CAMP. *They come into the side corridor where the* RESIDENT *hands
the note to* PILKINGS.

RESIDENT: As you see it says 'emergency' on the outside. I took
the liberty of opening it because His Highness was obviously
enjoying the entertainment. I didn't want to interrupt unless
really necessary.
PILKINGS: Yes, yes of course sir.   5
RESIDENT: Is it really as bad as it says? What's it all about?
PILKINGS: Some strange custom they have sir. It seems because
the King is dead some important chief has to commit suicide.
RESIDENT: The King? Isn't it the same one who died nearly a
month ago?   10
PILKINGS: Yes sir.
RESIDENT: Haven't they buried him yet?
PILKINGS: They take their time about these things sir. The
pre-burial ceremonies last nearly thirty days. It seems tonight
is the final night.   15
RESIDENT: But what has it got to do with the market women?
Why are they rioting? We've waived that troublesome tax
haven't we?
PILKINGS: We don't quite know that they are exactly rioting yet
sir. Sergeant Amusa is sometimes prone to exaggerations.   20
RESIDENT: He sounds desperate enough. That comes out even in
his rather quaint grammar. Where is the man anyway? I asked
my aide-de-camp to bring him here.
PILKINGS: They are probably looking in the wrong verandah. I'll
fetch him myself.   25
RESIDENT: No no you stay here. Let your wife go and look for
them. Do you mind my dear . . . ?
JANE: Certainly not, your Excellency. (*Goes.*)
RESIDENT: You should have kept me informed Pilkings. You
realise how disastrous it would have been if things had   30
erupted while His Highness was here.
PILKINGS: I wasn't aware of the whole business until tonight sir.
RESIDENT: Nose to the ground Pilkings, nose to the ground. If we
all let these little things slip past us where would the
empire be eh? Tell me that. Where would we all be?   35

PILKINGS: (*Low voice.*) Sleeping peacefully at home I bet.
RESIDENT: What did you say Pilkings?
PILKINGS: It won't happen again sir.
RESIDENT: It mustn't Pilkings. It mustn't. Where is that
40   damned sergeant? I ought to get back to His Highness as
quickly as possible and offer him some plausible explana-
tion for my rather abrupt conduct. Can you think of one
Pilkings?
PILKINGS: You could tell him the truth sir.
45   RESIDENT: I could? No no no no no Pilkings, that would never do.
What! Go and tell him there is a riot just two miles away from
him? This is supposed to be a secure colony of His Majesty,
Pilkings.
PILKINGS: Yes sir.
50   RESIDENT: Ah, there they are. No, these are not our native police.
Are these the ring-leaders of the riot?
PILKINGS: Sir, these are my police officers.
RESIDENT: Oh, I beg your pardon officers. You do look a
little . . . I say, isn't there something missing in their
55   uniforms? I think they used to have some rather colourful
sashes. If I remember rightly I recommended them myself in
my young days in the service. A bit of colour always appeals
to the natives, yes. I remember putting that in my report. Well
well well, where are we? Make your report man.
60   PILKINGS: (*Moves close to* AMUSA, *between his teeth.*) And let's
have no more superstitious nonsense from you Amusa or I'll
throw you in the guardroom for a month and feed you pork!
RESIDENT: What's that? What has pork to do with it?
PILKINGS: Sir, I was just warning him to be brief. I'm sure you are
65   most anxious to hear his report.
RESIDENT: Yes yes yes of course. Come on man, speak up. Hey,
didn't we give them some colourful fez hats with all those
wavy things, yes, pink tassells . . .
PILKINGS: Sir, I think if he was permitted to make his report we
70   might find that he lost his hat in the riot.
RESIDENT: Ah yes indeed. I'd better tell His Highness that. Lost
his hat in the riot, ha ha. He'll probably say well, as long as
he didn't lost his head. (*Chuckles to himself.*) Don't forget to
send me a report first thing in the morning young Pilkings.
75   PILKINGS: No sir.
RESIDENT: And whatever you do, don't let things get out of hand.
Keep a cool head and—nose to the ground Pilkings. (*Wanders
off in the general direction of the hall.*)
PILKINGS: Yes sir.
80   AIDE-DE-CAMP: Would you be needing me sir?
PILKINGS: No thanks Bob. I think His Excellency's need of you is
greater than ours.
AIDE-DE-CAMP: We have a detachment of soldiers from the
capital sir. They accompanied His Highness up here.
85   PILKINGS: I doubt if it will come to that but, thanks, I'll bear it in
mind. Oh, could you send an orderly with my cloak.
AIDE-DE-CAMP: Very good sir. (*Goes.*)
PILKINGS: Now Sergeant.
AMUSA: Sir . . . (*Makes an effort, stops dead. Eyes to the ceiling.*)
90   PILKINGS: Oh, not again.
AMUSA: I cannot against death to dead cult. This dress get power
of dead.
PILKINGS: Alright, let's go. You are relieved of all further duty
Amusa. Report to me first thing in the morning.
95   JANE: Shall I come Simon?
PILKINGS: No, there's no need for that. If I can get back later
I will. Otherwise get Bob to bring you home.

JANE: Be careful Simon . . . I mean, be clever.
PILKINGS: Sure I will. You two, come with me. (*As he turns to go,
the clock in the Residency begins to chime.* PILKINGS *looks at his   100
watch then turns, horror-stricken, to stare at his wife. The same
thought clearly occurs to her. He swallows hard. An* ORDERLY
brings his cloak.) It's midnight. I had no idea it was that late.
JANE: But surely . . . they don't count the hours the way we do. The
moon, or something.   105
PILKINGS: I am . . . not so sure.

(*He turns and breaks into a sudden run. The two constables follow,
also at a run.* AMUSA, *who has kept his eyes on the ceiling throughout
waits until the last of the footsteps has faded out of hearing. He salutes
suddenly, but without once looking in the direction of the woman.*)

AMUSA: Goodnight madam.
JANE: Oh. (*She hesitates.*) Amusa . . . (*He goes off without seeming
to have heard.*) Poor Simon . . . (*A figure emerges from the
shadows, a young black man dressed in a sober western suit.   110
He peeps into the hall, trying to make out the figures of the
dancers.*) Who is that?
OLUNDE: (*Emerging into the light.*) I didn't mean to startle you
madam. I am looking for the District Officer.
JANE: Wait a minute . . . don't I know you? Yes, you are   115
Olunde, the young man who . . .
OLUNDE: Mrs Pilkings! How fortunate. I came here to look for
your husband.
JANE: Olunde! Let's look at you. What a fine young man
you've become. Grand but solemn. Good God, when did   120
you return? Simon never said a word. But you do look well
Olunde. Really!
OLUNDE: You are . . . well, you look quite well yourself Mrs
Pilkings. From what little I can see of you.
JANE: Oh, this. It's caused quite a stir I assure you, and not all of it   125
very pleasant. You are not shocked I hope?
OLUNDE: Why should I be? But don't you find it rather hot in
there? Your skin must find it difficult to breathe.
JANE: Well, it is a little hot I must confess, but it's all in a good
cause.   130
OLUNDE: What cause Mrs Pilkings?
JANE: All this. The ball. And His Highness being here in person
and all that.
OLUNDE: (*Mildly.*) And that is the good cause for which you
desecrate an ancestral mask?   135
JANE: Oh, so you are shocked after all. How disappointing.
OLUNDE: No I am not shocked Mrs Pilkings. You forget that I
have now spent four years among your people. I discovered
that you have no respect for what you do not understand.
JANE: Oh. So you've returned with a chip on your shoulder. That's   140
a pity Olunde. I am sorry.

(*An uncomfortable silence follows.*)

I take it then that you did not find your stay in England
altogether edifying.
OLUNDE: I don't say that. I found your people quite admirable
in many ways, their conduct and courage in this war for   145
instance.
JANE: Ah yes the war. Here of course it is all rather remote. From
time to time we have a black-out drill just to remind us that
there is a war on. And the rare convoy passes through on its
way somewhere or on manoeuvres. Mind you there is the   150

occasional bit of excitement like that ship that was blown up in the harbour.

OLUNDE: Here? Do you mean through enemy action?

JANE: Oh no, the war hasn't come that close. The captain did it
155 himself. I don't quite understand it really. Simon tried to explain. The ship had to be blown up because it had become dangerous to the other ships, even to the city itself. Hundreds of the coastal population would have died.

OLUNDE: Maybe it was loaded with ammunition and had
160 caught fire. Or some of those lethal gases they've been experimenting on.

JANE: Something like that. The captain blew himself up with it. Deliberately. Simon said someone had to remain on board to light the fuse.

165 OLUNDE: It must have been a very short fuse.

JANE: (*Shrugs.*) I don't know much about it. Only that there was no other way to save lives. No time to devise anything else. The captain took the decision and carried it out.

OLUNDE: Yes . . . I quite believe it. I met men like that in
170 England.

JANE: Oh just look at me! Fancy welcoming you back with such morbid news. Stale too. It was at least six months ago.

OLUNDE: I don't find it morbid at all. I find it rather inspiring. It is an affirmative commentary on life.

175 JANE: What is?

OLUNDE: That captain's self-sacrifice.

JANE: Nonsense. Life should never be thrown deliberately away.

OLUNDE: And the innocent people round the harbour?

JANE: Oh, how does one know? The whole thing was probably
180 exaggerated anyway.

OLUNDE: That was a risk the captain couldn't take. But please Mrs Pilkings, do you think you could find your husband for me? I have to talk to him.

JANE: Simon? Oh. (*As she recollects for the first time the full*
185 *significance of* OLUNDE'*s presence.*) Simon is . . . there is a little problem in town. He was sent for. But . . . when did you arrive? Does Simon know you're here?

OLUNDE: (*Suddenly earnest.*) I need your help Mrs Pilkings. I've always found you somewhat more understanding than your
190 husband. Please find him for me and when you do, you must help me talk to him.

JANE: I'm afraid I don't quite . . . follow you. Have you seen my husband already?

OLUNDE: I went to your house. Your houseboy told me you were
195 here. (*He smiles.*) He even told me how I would recognise you and Mr Pilkings.

JANE: Then you must know what my husband is trying to do for you.

OLUNDE: For me?

200 JANE: For you. For your people. And to think he didn't even know you were coming back! But how do you happen to be here? Only this evening we were talking about you. We thought you were still four thousand miles away.

OLUNDE: I was sent a cable.

205 JANE: A cable? Who did? Simon? The business of your father didn't begin till tonight.

OLUNDE: A relation sent it weeks ago, and it said nothing about my father. All it said was, Our King is dead. But I knew I had to return home at once so as to bury my father. I understood
210 that.

JANE: Well, thank God you don't have to go through that agony. Simon is going to stop it.

OLUNDE: That's why I want to see him. He's wasting his time. And since he has been so helpful to me I don't want him to incur the enmity of our people. Especially over nothing. 215

JANE: (*Sits down open-mouthed.*) You . . . you Olunde!

OLUNDE: Mrs Pilkings, I came home to bury my father. As soon as I heard the news I booked my passage home. In fact we were fortunate. We travelled in the same convoy as your Prince, so we had excellent protection. 220

JANE: But you don't think your father is also entitled to whatever protection is available to him?

OLUNDE: How can I make you understand? He *has* protection. No one can undertake what he does tonight without the deepest protection the mind can conceive. What can you 225 offer him in place of his peace of mind, in place of the honour and veneration of his own people? What would you think of your Prince if he had refused to accept the risk of losing his life on this voyage? This . . . showing-the-flag tour of colonial possessions? 230

JANE: I see. So it isn't just medicine you studied in England.

OLUNDE: Yet another error into which your people fall. You believe that everything which appears to make sense was learnt from you.

JANE: Not so fast Olunde. You have learnt to argue I can tell that, 235 but I never said you made sense. However cleverly you try to put it, it is still a barbaric custom. It is even worse—it's feudal! The king dies and a chieftain must be buried with him. How feudalistic can you get!

OLUNDE: (*Waves his hand towards the background. The* PRINCE 240 *is dancing past again—to a different step—and all the guests are bowing and curtseying as he passes.*) And this? Even in the midst of a devastating war, look at that. What name would you give to that?

JANE: Therapy, British style. The preservation of sanity in the 245 midst of chaos.

OLUNDE: Others would call it decadence. However, it doesn't really interest me. You white races know how to survive; I've seen proof of that. By all logical and natural laws this war should end with all the white races wiping out one 250 another, wiping out their so-called civilisation for all time and reverting to a state of primitivism the like of which has so far only existed in your imagination when you thought of us. I thought all that at the beginning. Then I slowly realised that your greatest art is the art of survival. 255 But at least have the humility to let others survive in their own way.

JANE: Through ritual suicide?

OLUNDE: Is that worse than mass suicide? Mrs Pilkings, what do you call what those young men are sent to do by their 260 generals in this war? Of course you have also mastered the art of calling things by names which don't remotely describe them.

JANE: You talk! You people with your long-winded, roundabout way of making conversation. 265

OLUNDE: Mrs Pilkings, whatever we do, we never suggest that a thing is the opposite of what it really is. In your newsreels I heard defeats, thorough, murderous defeats described as strategic victories. No wait, it wasn't just on your newsreels. Don't forget I was attached to hospitals all the time. Hordes 270 of your wounded passed through those wards. I spoke to them. I spent long evenings by their bedside while they spoke terrible truths of the realities of that war. I know now how history is made.

275 JANE: But surely, in a war of this nature, for the morale of the
      nation you must expect . . .
   OLUNDE: That a disaster beyond human reckoning be spoken of as
      a triumph? No. I mean, is there no mourning in the
      home of the bereaved that such blasphemy is permitted?
280 JANE: (*After a moment's pause.*) Perhaps I can understand you
      now. The time we picked for you was not really one for seeing
      us at our best.
   OLUNDE: Don't think it was just the war. Before that even started I
      had plenty of time to study your people. I saw nothing, finally,
285   that gave you the right to pass judgement on other peoples
      and their ways. Nothing at all.
   JANE: (*Hesitantly.*) Was it the . . . colour thing? I know there is
      some discrimination.
   OLUNDE: Don't make it so simple, Mrs Pilkings. You make it
290   sound as if when I left, I took nothing at all with me.
   JANE: Yes . . . and to tell the truth, only this evening, Simon and
      I agreed that we never really knew what you left with.
   OLUNDE: Neither did I. But I found out over there. I am grateful
      to your country for that. And I will never give it up.
295 JANE: Olunde, please . . . promise me something. Whatever you
      do, don't throw away what you have started to do. You want
      to be a doctor. My husband and I believe you will make an
      excellent one, sympathetic and competent. Don't let anything
      make you throw away your training.
300 OLUNDE: (*Genuinely surprised.*) Of course not. What a strange
      idea. I intend to return and complete my training. Once the
      burial of my father is over.
   JANE: Oh, please . . . !
   OLUNDE: Listen! Come outside. You can't hear anything against
305   that music.
   JANE: What is it?
   OLUNDE: The drums. Can you hear the change? Listen.

(*The drums come over, still distant but more distinct. There is
a change of rhythm, it rises to a crescendo and then, suddenly,
it is cut off. After a silence, a new beat begins, slow and
resonant.*)

      There. It's all over.
   JANE: You mean he's . . .
310 OLUNDE: Yes Mrs Pilkings, my father is dead. His will-power has
      always been enormous; I know he is dead.
   JANE: (*Screams.*) How can you be so callous! So unfeeling! You
      announce your father's own death like a surgeon looking
      down on some strange . . . stranger's body! You're just a savage
315   like all the rest.
   AIDE-DE-CAMP: (*Rushing out.*) Mrs Pilkings. Mrs Pilkings. (*She
      breaks down, sobbing.*) Are you alright, Mrs Pilkings?
   OLUNDE: She'll be alright. (*Turns to go.*)
   AIDE-DE-CAMP: Who are you? And who the hell asked your
320   opinion?
   OLUNDE: You're quite right, nobody. (*Going.*)
   AIDE-DE-CAMP: What the hell! Did you hear me ask you who
      you were?
   OLUNDE: I have business to attend to.
325 AIDE-DE-CAMP: I'll give you business in a moment you impudent
      nigger. Answer my question!
   OLUNDE: I have a funeral to arrange. Excuse me. (*Going.*)
   AIDE-DE-CAMP: I said stop! Orderly!
   JANE: No no, don't do that. I'm alright. And for heaven's sake
330   don't act so foolishly. He's a family friend.

AIDE-DE-CAMP: Well he'd better learn to answer civil questions
   when he's asked them. These natives put a suit on and they get
   high opinions of themselves.
OLUNDE: Can I go now?
JANE: No no don't go. I must talk to you. I'm sorry about what   335
   I said.
OLUNDE: It's nothing Mrs Pilkings. And I'm really anxious to
   go. I couldn't see my father before, it's forbidden for me, his
   heir and successor to set eyes on him from the moment of the
   king's death. But now . . . I would like to touch his body while   340
   it is still warm.
JANE: You will. I promise I shan't keep you long. Only, I couldn't
   possibly let you go like that. Bob, please excuse us.
AIDE-DE-CAMP: If you're sure . . .
JANE: Of course I'm sure. Something happened to upset me just   345
   then, but I'm alright now. Really.

(*The* AIDE-DE-CAMP *goes, somewhat reluctantly.*)

OLUNDE: I mustn't stay long.
JANE: Please, I promise not to keep you. It's just that . . . oh you
   saw yourself what happens to one in this place. The Resident's
   man thought he was being helpful, that's the way we all react.   350
   But I can't go in among that crowd just now and if I stay by
   myself somebody will come looking for me. Please, just say
   something for a few moments and then you can go. Just so I
   can recover myself.
OLUNDE: What do you want me to say?   355
JANE: Your calm acceptance for instance, can you explain that? It
   was so unnatural. I don't understand that at all. I feel a need
   to understand all I can.
OLUNDE: But you explained it yourself. My medical
   training perhaps. I have seen death too often. And the   360
   soldiers who returned from the front, they died on our
   hands all the time.
JANE: No. It has to be more than that. I feel it has to do with the
   many things we don't really grasp about your people. At least
   you can explain.   365
OLUNDE: All these things are part of it. And anyway, my father
   has been dead in my mind for nearly a month. Ever since I
   learnt of the King's death. I've lived with my bereavement so
   long now that I cannot think of him alive. On that journey on
   the boat, I kept my mind on my duties as the one who must   370
   perform the rites over his body. I went through it all again and
   again in my mind as he himself had taught me. I didn't want
   to do anything wrong, something which might jeopardise the
   welfare of my people.
JANE: But he had disowned you. When you left he swore publicly   375
   you were no longer his son.
OLUNDE: I told you, he was a man of tremendous will. Sometimes
   that's another way of saying stubborn. But among our people,
   you don't disown a child just like that. Even if I had died
   before him I would still be buried like his eldest son. But it's   380
   time for me to go.
JANE: Thank you. I feel calmer. Don't let me keep you from your
   duties.
OLUNDE: Goodnight Mrs Pilkings.
JANE: Welcome home. (*She holds out her hand. As he takes it*   385
   footsteps are heard approaching the drive. A short while later a
   woman's sobbing is also heard.)
PILKINGS: (*Off.*) Keep them here till I get back. (*He strides into*
   view, reacts at the sight of OLUNDE *but turns to his wife.*)

390   Thank goodness you're still here.

JANE: Simon, what happened?

PILKINGS: Later Jane, please. Is Bob still here?

JANE: Yes, I think so. I'm sure he must be.

395 PILKINGS: Try and get him out here as quietly as you can. Tell him it's urgent.

JANE: Of course. Oh Simon, you remember . . .

PILKINGS: Yes yes. I can see who it is. Get Bob out here. (*She runs off.*) At first I thought I was seeing a ghost.

OLUNDE: Mr Pilkings, I appreciate what you tried to do. I want

400   you to believe that. I can only tell you it would have been a terrible calamity if you'd succeeded.

PILKINGS: (*Opens his mouth several times, shuts it.*) You . . . said what?

OLUNDE: A calamity for us, the entire people.

405 PILKINGS: (*Sighs.*) I see. Hm.

OLUNDE: And now I must go. I must see him before he turns cold.

PILKINGS: Oh ah . . . em . . . but this is a shock to see you. I mean er thinking all this while you were in England and thanking

410   God for that.

OLUNDE: I came on the mail boat. We travelled in the Prince's convoy.

PILKINGS: Ah yes, a-ah, hm . . . er well . . .

OLUNDE: Goodnight. I can see you are shocked by the whole

415   business. But you must know by now there are things you cannot understand—or help.

PILKINGS: Yes. Just a minute. There are armed policemen that way and they have instructions to let no one pass. I suggest you wait a little. I'll er . . . yes, I'll give you an escort.

420 OLUNDE: That's very kind of you. But do you think it could be quickly arranged.

PILKINGS: Of course. In fact, yes, what I'll do is send Bob over with some men to the er . . . place. You can go with them. Here he comes now. Excuse me a minute.

425 AIDE-DE-CAMP: Anything wrong sir?

PILKINGS: (*Takes him to one side.*) Listen Bob, that cellar in the disused annexe of the Residency, you know, where the slaves were stored before being taken down to the coast . . .

AIDE-DE-CAMP: Oh yes, we use it as a storeroom for broken

430   furniture.

PILKINGS: But it's still got the bars on it?

AIDE-DE-CAMP: Oh yes, they are quite intact.

PILKINGS: Get the keys please. I'll explain later. And I want a strong guard over the Residency tonight.

435 AIDE-DE-CAMP: We have that already. The detachment from the coast . . .

PILKINGS: No, I don't want them at the gates of the Residency. I want you to deploy them at the bottom of the hill, a long way from the main hall so they can deal with any situation long

440   before the sound carries to the house.

AIDE-DE-CAMP: Yes of course.

PILKINGS: I don't want His Highness alarmed.

AIDE-DE-CAMP: You think the riot will spread here?

PILKINGS: It's unlikely but I don't want to take a chance. I made

445   them believe I was going to lock the man up in my house, which was what I had planned to do in the first place. They are probably assailing it by now. I took a roundabout route here so I don't think there is any danger at all. At least not before dawn. Nobody is to leave the premises of course—the

450   native employees I mean. They'll soon smell something is up and they can't keep their mouths shut.

AIDE-DE-CAMP: I'll give instructions at once.

PILKINGS: I'll take the prisoner down myself. Two policemen will stay with him throughout the night. Inside the cell.

455 AIDE-DE-CAMP: Right sir. (*Salutes and goes off at the double.*)

PILKINGS: Jane. Bob is coming back in a moment with a detachment. Until he gets back please stay with Olunde.

(*He makes an extra warning gesture with his eyes.*)

OLUNDE: Please Mr Pilkings . . .

PILKINGS: I hate to be stuffy old son, but we have a crisis on our

460   hands. It has to do with your father's affair if you must know. And it happens also at a time when we have His Highness here. I am responsible for security so you'll simply have to do as I say. I hope that's understood. (*Marches off quickly, in the direction from which he made his first appearance.*)

465 OLUNDE: What's going on? All this can't be just because he failed to stop my father killing himself.

JANE: I honestly don't know. Could it have sparked off a riot?

OLUNDE: No. If he'd succeeded that would be more likely to start the riot. Perhaps there were other factors involved.

470   Was there a chieftancy dispute?

JANE: None that I know of.

ELESIN: (*An animal bellow from off.*) Leave me alone! Is it not enough that you have covered me in shame! White man, take your hand from my body!

(OLUNDE *stands frozen on the spot.* JANE *understanding at last, tries to move him.*)

JANE: Let's go in. It's getting chilly out here.

475 PILKINGS: (*Off.*) Carry him.

ELESIN: Give me back the name you have taken away from me you ghost from the land of the nameless!

PILKINGS: Carry him! I can't have a disturbance here. Quickly!

480   stuff up his mouth.

JANE: Oh God! Let's go in. Please Olunde. (OLUNDE *does not move.*)

ELESIN: Take your albino's hand from me you . . .

(*Sounds of a struggle. His voice chokes as he is gagged.*)

OLUNDE: (*Quietly.*) That was my father's voice.

JANE: Oh you poor orphan, what have you come home to?

(*There is a sudden explosion of rage from off-stage and powerful steps come running up the drive.*)

PILKINGS: You bloody fools, after him!

485

(*Immediately* ELESIN, *in handcuffs, comes pounding in the direction of* JANE *and* OLUNDE, *followed some moments afterwards by* PILKINGS *and the constables.* ELESIN *confronted by the seeming statue of his son, stops dead.* OLUNDE *stares above his head into the distance. The constables try to grab him.* JANE *screams at them.*)

JANE: Leave him alone! Simon, tell them to leave him alone.

PILKINGS: All right, stand aside you. (*Shrugs.*) Maybe just as well. It might help to calm him down.

(*For several moments they hold the same position.* ELESIN *moves a few steps forward, almost as if he's still in doubt.*)

ELESIN: Olunde? (*He moves his head, inspecting him from side to*
490   *side.*) Olunde! (*He collapses slowly at* OLUNDE's *feet.*) Oh son,
don't let the sight of your father turn you blind!
OLUNDE: (*He moves for the first time since he heard his voice,*
brings his head slowly down to look on him.) I have no father,
eater of left-overs.

(*He walks slowly down the way his father had run. Light fades out*
on ELESIN, *sobbing into the ground.*)

ACT FIVE

A wide iron-barred gate stretches almost the whole width of the cell
in which ELESIN *is imprisoned. His wrists are encased in thick iron*
bracelets, chained together; he stands against the bars, looking out.
Seated on the ground to one side on the outside is his recent BRIDE,
her eyes bent perpetually to the ground. Figures of the two guards can
be seen deeper inside the cell, alert to every movement ELESIN *makes.*
PILKINGS *now in a police officer's uniform enters noiselessly, observes*
him for a while. Then he coughs ostentatiously and approaches.
Leans against the bars near a corner, his back to ELESIN. *He is obvi-*
ously trying to fall in mood with him. Some moments' silence.

PILKINGS: You seem fascinated by the moon.
ELESIN: (*After a pause.*) Yes, ghostly one. Your twin-brother up
there engages my thoughts.
PILKINGS: It is a beautiful night.
5   ELESIN: Is that so?
PILKINGS: The light on the leaves, the peace of the night . . .
ELESIN: The night is not at peace, District Officer.
PILKINGS: No? I would have said it was. You know, quiet . . .
ELESIN: And does quiet mean peace for you?
10   PILKINGS: Well, nearly the same thing. Naturally there is a
subtle difference . . .
ELESIN: The night is not at peace ghostly one. The world is not
at peace. You have shattered the peace of the world for ever.
There is no sleep in the world tonight.
15   PILKINGS: It is still a good bargain if the world should lose one
night's sleep as the price of saving a man's life.
ELESIN: You did not save my life District Officer. You destroyed
it.
PILKINGS: Now come on . . .
20   ELESIN: And not merely my life but the lives of many. The end of
the night's work is not over. Neither this year nor the next will
see it. If I wished you well, I would pray that you do not stay
long enough on our land to see the disaster you have brought
upon us.
25   PILKINGS: Well, I did my duty as I saw it. I have no regrets.
ELESIN: No. The regrets of life always come later.

(*Some moments' pause.*)

You are waiting for dawn white man. I hear you saying
to yourself: only so many hours until dawn and then the
danger is over. All I must do is keep him alive tonight.
30   You don't quite understand it all but you know that
tonight is when what ought to be must be brought about. I
shall ease your mind even more, ghostly one. It is not an entire
night but a moment of the night, and that moment is past. The
moon was my messenger and guide. When it reached a certain
35   gateway in the sky, it touched that moment for which my
whole life has been spent in blessings. Even I do not know the

gateway. I have stood here and scanned the sky for a glimpse
of that door but, I cannot see it. Human eyes are useless for a
search of this nature. But in the house of *osugbo*, those who
keep watch through the spirit recognised the moment, they   40
sent word to me through the voice of our sacred drums to
prepare myself. I heard them and I shed all thoughts of earth.
I began to follow the moon to the abode of gods . . . servant of
the white king, that was when you entered my chosen place
of departure on feet of desecration.   45
PILKINGS: I'm sorry, but we all see our duty differently.
ELESIN: I no longer blame you. You stole from me my first-
born, sent him to your country so you could turn him
into something in your own image. Did you plan it all
beforehand? There are moments when it seems part of a   50
larger plan. He who must follow my footsteps is taken from
me, sent across the ocean. Then, in my turn, I am stopped
from fulfilling my destiny. Did you think it all out before,
this plan to push our world from its course and sever the
cord that links us to the great origin?   55
PILKINGS: You don't really believe that. Anyway, if that was my
intention with your son, I appear to have failed.
ELESIN: You did not fail in the main thing ghostly one. We
know the roof covers the rafters, the cloth covers blemishes;
who would have known that the white skin covered our   60
future, preventing us from seeing the death our enemies had
prepared for us. The world is set adrift and its inhabitants are
lost. Around them, there is nothing but emptiness.
PILKINGS: Your son does not take so gloomy a view.
ELESIN: Are you dreaming now white man? Were you not   65
present at my reunion of shame? Did you not see when the
world reversed itself and the father fell before his son, asking
forgiveness?
PILKINGS: That was in the heat of the moment. I spoke to him
and . . . if you want to know, he wishes he could cut out his   70
tongue for uttering the words he did.
ELESIN: No. What he said must never be unsaid. The contempt of
my own son rescued something of my shame at your hands.
You may have stopped me in my duty but I know now that
I did give birth to a son. Once I mistrusted him for seeking   75
the companionship of those my spirit knew as enemies of our
race. Now I understand. One should seek to obtain the secrets
of his enemies. He will avenge my shame, white one. His spirit
will destroy you and yours.
PILKINGS: That kind of talk is hardly called for. If you don't want   80
my consolation . . .
ELESIN: No white man, I do not want your consolation.
PILKINGS: As you wish. Your son anyway, sends his consolation.
He asks your forgiveness. When I asked him not to despise
you his reply was: I cannot judge him, and if I cannot judge   85
him, I cannot despise him. He wants to come to you to say
goodbye and to receive your blessing.
ELESIN: Goodbye? Is he returning to your land?
PILKINGS: Don't you think that's the most sensible thing for him
to do? I advised him to leave at once, before dawn, and he   90
agrees that is the right course of action.
ELESIN: Yes, it is best. And even if I did not think so, I have lost
the father's place of honour. My voice is broken.
PILKINGS: Your son honours you. If he didn't he would not ask
your blessing.   95
ELESIN: No. Even a thoroughbred is not without pity for the turf
he strikes with his hoof. When is he coming?
PILKINGS: As soon as the town is a little quieter. I advised it.

ELESIN: Yes white man, I am sure you advised it. You advise
100   all our lives although on the authority of what gods, I do
       not know.
       PILKINGS: (*Opens his mouth to reply, then appears to change his
       mind. Turns to go. Hesitates and stops again.*) Before I leave
       you, may I ask just one thing of you?
105   ELESIN: I am listening.
       PILKINGS: I wish to ask you to search the quiet of your heart and
       tell me—do you not find great contradictions in the wisdom
       of your own race?
       ELESIN: Make yourself clear, white one.
110   PILKINGS: I have lived among you long enough to learn a saying
       or two. One came to my mind tonight when I stepped into
       the market and saw what was going on. You were surrounded
       by those who egged you on with song and praises. I thought,
       are these not the same people who say: the elder grimly
115   approaches heaven and you ask him to bear your greetings
       yonder; do you really think he makes the journey willingly?
       After that, I did not hesitate.

(*A pause.* ELESIN *sighs. Before he can speak a sound of running feet
is heard.*)

JANE: (*Off.*) Simon! Simon!
PILKINGS: What on earth . . . ! (*Runs off.*)

(ELESIN *turns to his new wife, gazes on her for some moments.*)

120   ELESIN: My young bride, did you hear the ghostly one? You sit
       and sob in your silent heart but say nothing to all this. First
       I blamed the white man, then I blamed my gods for deserting
       me. Now I feel I want to blame you for the mystery of the
       sapping of my will. But blame is a strange peace offering for
125   a man to bring a world he has deeply wronged, and to its
       innocent dwellers. Oh little mother, I have taken countless
       women in my life but you were more than a desire of the flesh.
       I needed you as the abyss across which my body must be
       drawn, I filled it with earth and dropped my seed in it at the
130   moment of preparedness for my crossing. You were the final
       gift of the living to their emissary to the land of the ancestors,
       and perhaps your warmth and youth brought new insights
       of this world to me and turned my feet leaden on this side of
       the abyss. For I confess to you, daughter, my weakness came
135   not merely from the abomination of the white man who came
       violently into my fading presence, there was also a weight of
       longing on my earth-held limbs. I would have shaken it off,
       already my foot had begun to lift but then, the white ghost
       entered and all was defiled.

(*Approaching voices of* PILKINGS *and his wife.*)

140   JANE: Oh Simon, you will let her in won't you?
       PILKINGS: I really wish you'd stop interfering.

(*They come in view.* JANE *is in a dressing-gown.* PILKINGS *is
holding a note to which he refers from time to time.*)

JANE: Good gracious, I didn't initiate this. I was sleeping
quietly, or trying to anyway, when the servant brought it.
It's not my fault if one can't sleep undisturbed even in the
145   Residency.

PILKINGS: He'd have done the same if we were sleeping at home
so don't sidetrack the issue. He knows he can get round you or
he wouldn't send you the petition in the first place.
JANE: Be fair Simon. After all he was thinking of your own
interests. He is grateful you know, you seem to forget that.   150
He feels he owes you something.
PILKINGS: I just wish they'd leave this man alone tonight,
that's all.
JANE: Trust him Simon. He's pledged his word it will all go
peacefully.   155
PILKINGS: Yes, and that's the other thing. I don't like being
threatened.
JANE: Threatened? (*Takes the note.*) I didn't spot any threat.
PILKINGS: It's there. Veiled, but it's there. The only way to prevent
serious rioting tomorrow—what a cheek!   160
JANE: I don't think he's threatening you Simon.
PILKINGS: He's picked up the idiom alright. Wouldn't surprise me
if he's been mixing with commies or anarchists over there.
The phrasing sounds too good to be true. Damn! If only the
Prince hadn't picked this time for his visit.   165
JANE: Well, even so Simon, what have you got to lose? You
don't want a riot on your hands, not with the Prince here.
PILKINGS: (*Going up to* ELESIN.) Let's see what he has to say. Chief
Elesin, there is yet another person who wants to see you. As
she is not a next-of-kin I don't really feel obliged to let her in. 170
But your son sent a note with her, so it's up to you.
ELESIN: I know who that must be. So she found out your
hiding-place. Well, it was not difficult. My stench of shame is
so strong, it requires no hunter's dog to follow it.
PILKINGS: If you don't want to see her, just say so and I'll send her 175
packing.
ELESIN: Why should I not want to see her? Let her come. I have no
more holes in my rag of shame. All is laid bare.
PILKINGS: I'll bring her in. (*Goes off.*)
JANE: (*Hesitates, then goes to* ELESIN.) Please, try and understand. 180
Everything my husband did was for the best.
ELESIN: (*He gives her a long strange stare, as if he is trying to
understand who she is.*) You are the wife of the District Officer?
JANE: Yes. My name, is Jane.
ELESIN: That is my wife sitting down there. You notice how   185
still and silent she sits? My business is with your husband.

(PILKINGS *returns with* IYALOJA.)

PILKINGS: Here she is. Now first I want your word of honour that
you will try nothing foolish.
ELESIN: Honour? White one, did you say you wanted my word of
honour?   190
PILKINGS: I know you to be an honourable man. Give me your
word of honour you will receive nothing from her.
ELESIN: But I am sure you have searched her clothing as you
would never dare touch your own mother. And there are
these two lizards of yours who roll their eyes even when I   195
scratch.
PILKINGS: And I shall be sitting on that tree trunk watching even
how you blink. Just the same I want your word that you will
not let her pass anything to you.
ELESIN: You have my honour already. It is locked up in that desk   200
in which you will put away your report of this night's events.
Even the honour of my people you have taken already; it is
tied together with those papers of treachery which make you
masters in this land.

205 PILKINGS: Alright. I am trying to make things easy but if you
must bring in politics we'll have to do it the hard way.
Madam, I want you to remain along this line and move no
nearer to that cell door. Guards! (*They spring to attention.*)
If she moves beyond this point, blow your whistle. Come on
210 Jane. (*They go off.*)
IYALOJA: How boldly the lizard struts before the pigeon when it
was the eagle itself he promised us he would confront.
ELESIN: I don't ask you to take pity on me Iyaloja. You have a
message for me or you would not have come. Even if it is the
215 curses of the world, I shall listen.
IYALOJA: You made so bold with the servant of the white king
who took your side against death. I must tell your brother
chiefs when I return how bravely you waged war against him.
Especially with words.
220 ELESIN: I more than deserve your scorn.
IYALOJA: (*With sudden anger.*) I warned you, if you must leave
a seed behind, be sure it is not tainted with the curses of
the world. Who are you to open a new life when you dared
not open the door to a new existence? I say who are you to
225 make so bold? (*The* BRIDE *sobs and* IYALOJA *notices her. Her
contempt noticeably increases as she turns back to* ELESIN.)
Oh you self-vaunted stem of the plantain, how hollow it all
proves. The pith is gone in the parent stem, so how will it
prove with the new shoot? How will it go with that earth that
230 bears it? Who are you to bring this abomination on us!
ELESIN: My powers deserted me. My charms, my spells, even
my voice lacked strength when I made to summon the powers
that would lead me over the last measure of earth into the
land of the fleshless. You saw it, Iyaloja. You saw me struggle
235 to retrieve my will from the power of the stranger whose
shadow fell across the doorway and left me floundering and
blundering in a maze I had never before encountered. My
senses were numbed when the touch of cold iron came upon
my wrists. I could do nothing to save myself.
240 IYALOJA: You have betrayed us. We fed you sweetmeats such
as we hoped awaited you on the other side. But you said
No, I must eat the world's left-overs. We said you were the
hunter who brought the quarry down; to you belonged the
vital portions of the game. No, you said, I am the hunter's
245 dog and I shall eat the entrails of the game and the faeces of
the hunter. We said you were the hunter returning home in
triumph, a slain buffalo pressing down on his neck, you said
wait, I first must turn up this cricket hole with my toes. We
said yours was the doorway at which we first spy the tapper
250 when he comes down from the tree, yours was the blessing
of the twilight wine, the purl that brings night spirits out of
doors to steal their portion before the light of day. We said
yours was the body of wine whose burden shakes the tapper
like a sudden gust on his perch. You said, No, I am content to
255 lick the dregs from each calabash when the drinkers are done.
We said, the dew on earth's surface was for you to wash your
feet along the slopes of honour. You said No, I shall step in the
vomit of cats and the droppings of mice; I shall fight them for
the left-overs of the world.
260 ELESIN: Enough Iyaloja, enough.
IYALOJA: We called you leader and oh, how you led us on. What
we have no intention of eating should not be held to the nose.
ELESIN: Enough, enough. My shame is heavy enough.
IYALOJA: Wait. I came with a burden.
265 ELESIN: You have more than discharged it.
IYALOJA: I wish I could pity you.

ELESIN: I need neither your pity nor the pity of the world. I need
understanding. Even I need to understand. You were present
at my defeat. You were part of the beginnings. You brought
about the renewal of my tie to earth, you helped in the   270
binding of the cord.
IYALOJA: I gave you warning. The river which fills up before our
eyes does not sweep us away in its flood.
ELESIN: What were warnings beside the moist contact of living
earth between my fingers? What were warnings beside the   275
renewal of famished embers lodged eternally in the heart
of man. But even that, even if it overwhelmed one with a
thousandfold temptations to linger a little while, a man
could overcome it. It is when the alien hand pollutes the
source of will, when a stranger force of violence shatters   280
the mind's calm resolution, this is when a man is made to
commit the awful treachery of relief, commit in his thought
the unspeakable blasphemy of seeing the hand of the gods
in this alien rupture of his world. I know it was this thought
that killed me, sapped my powers and turned me into an   285
infant in the hands of unnamable strangers. I made to utter
my spells anew but my tongue merely rattled in my mouth. I
fingered hidden charms and the contact was damp; there was
no spark left to sever the life-strings that should stretch from
every finger-tip. My will was squelched in the spittle of an   290
alien race, and all because I had committed this blasphemy
of thought—that there might be the hand of the gods in a
stranger's intervention.
IYALOJA: Explain it how you will, I hope it brings you peace
of mind. The bush-rat fled his rightful cause, reached the   295
market and set up a lamentation. 'Please save me!'—are
these fitting words to hear from an ancestral mask? 'There's
a wild beast at my heels' is not becoming language from a
hunter.
ELESIN: May the world forgive me.   300
IYALOJA: I came with a burden I said. It approaches the gates
which are so well guarded by those jackals whose spittle
will from this day on be your food and drink. But first, tell
me, you who were once Elesin Oba, tell me, you who know
so well the cycle of the plantain: is it the parent shoot which   305
withers to give sap to the younger or, does your wisdom see it
running the other way?
ELESIN: I don't see your meaning Iyaloja?
IYALOJA: Did I ask you for a meaning? I asked a question.
Whose trunk withers to give sap to the other? The parent   310
shoot or the younger?
ELESIN: The parent.
IYALOJA: Ah. So you do know that. There are sights in this
world which say different Elesin. There are some who
choose to reverse this cycle of our being. Oh you emptied   315
bark that the world once saluted for a pith-laden being, shall
I tell you what the gods have claimed of you?

(*In her agitation she steps beyond the line indicated by* PILKINGS
and the air is rent by piercing whistles. The two GUARDS *also leap
forward and place safe-guarding hands on* ELESIN. IYALOJA *stops,
astonished.* PILKINGS *comes racing, followed by* JANE.)

PILKINGS: What is it? Did they try something?
GUARD: She stepped beyond the line.
ELESIN: (*In a broken voice.*) Let her alone. She meant no harm.   320
IYALOJA: Oh Elesin, see what you've become. Once you had
no need to open your mouth in explanation because

evil-smelling goats, itchy of hand and foot had lost their
senses. And it was a brave man indeed who dared lay hands
325   on you because Iyaloja stepped from one side of the earth
onto another. Now look at the spectacle of your life. I grieve
for you.

PILKINGS: I think you'd better leave. I doubt you have done him
much good by coming here. I shall make sure you are not
330   allowed to see him again. In any case we are moving him to a
different place before dawn, so don't bother to come back.

IYALOJA: We foresaw that. Hence the burden I trudged here to lay
beside your gates.

PILKINGS: What was that you said?

335   IYALOJA: Didn't our son explain? Ask that one. He knows
what it is. At least we hope the man we once knew as Elesin
remembers the lesser oaths he need not break.

PILKINGS: Do you know what she is talking about?

ELESIN: Go to the gates, ghostly one. Whatever you find there,
340   bring it to me.

IYALOJA: Not yet. It drags behind me on the slow, weary feet of
women. Slow as it is Elesin, it has long overtaken you. It rides
ahead of your laggard will.

PILKINGS: What is she saying now? Christ! Must your people
345   forever speak in riddles?

ELESIN: It will come white man, it will come. Tell your men at the
gates to let it through.

PILKINGS: (Dubiously.) I'll have to see what it is.

IYALOJA: You will. (Passionately.) But this is one oath he cannot
350   shirk. White one, you have a king here, a visitor from your
land. We know of his presence here. Tell me, were he to die
would you leave his spirit roaming restlessly on the surface of
earth? Would you bury him here among those you consider
less than human? In your land have you no ceremonies of
355   the dead?

PILKINGS: Yes. But we don't make our chiefs commit suicide to
keep him company.

IYALOJA: Child, I have not come to help your understanding.
(Points to ELESIN.) This is the man whose weakened
360   understanding holds us in bondage to you. But ask him
if you wish. He knows the meaning of a king's passage;
he was not born yesterday. He knows the peril to the race
when our dead father, who goes as intermediary, waits and
waits and knows he is betrayed. He knows when the narrow
365   gate was opened and he knows it will not stay for laggards
who drag their feet in dung and vomit, whose lips are reeking
of the left-overs of lesser men. He knows he has condemned
our king to wander in the void of evil with beings who are
enemies of life.

370   PILKINGS: Yes er . . . but look here . . .

IYALOJA: What we ask is little enough. Let him release our
King so he can ride on homewards alone. The messenger is on
his way on the backs of women. Let him send word through
the heart that is folded up within the bolt. It is the least of all
375   his oaths, it is the easiest fulfilled.

(The AIDE-DE-CAMP runs in.)

PILKINGS: Bob?

AIDE-DE-CAMP: Sir, there's a group of women chanting up the
hill.

PILKINGS: (Rounding on IYALOJA.) If you people want trouble . . .

380   JANE: Simon, I think that's what Olunde referred to in his letter.

PILKINGS: He knows damned well I can't have a crowd here!
Damn it, I explained the delicacy of my position to him. I
think it's about time I got him out of town. Bob, send a car
and two or three soldiers to bring him in. I think the sooner
he takes his leave of his father and gets out the better.   385

IYALOJA: Save your labour white one. If it is the father of your
prisoner you want, Olunde, he who until this night we knew
as Elesin's son, he comes soon himself to take his leave. He has
sent the women ahead, so let them in.

(PILKINGS remains undecided.)

AIDE-DE-CAMP: What do we do about the invasion? We can still   390
stop them far from here.

PILKINGS: What do they look like?

AIDE-DE-CAMP: They're not many. And they seem quite peaceful.

PILKINGS: No men?

AIDE-DE-CAMP: Mm, two or three at the most.   395

JANE: Honestly, Simon, I'd trust Olunde. I don't think he'll
deceive you about their intentions.

PILKINGS: He'd better not. Alright, let them in Bob. Warn
them to control themselves. Then hurry Olunde here.
Make sure he brings his baggage because I'm not returning   400
him into town.

AIDE-DE-CAMP: Very good sir. (Goes.)

PILKINGS: (To IYALOJA.) I hope you understand that if anything
goes wrong it will be on your head. My men have orders to
shoot at the first sign of trouble.   405

IYALOJA: To prevent one death you will actually make other
deaths? Ah, great is the wisdom of the white race. But have
no fear. Your Prince will sleep peacefully. So at long last will
ours. We will disturb you no further, servant of the white
king. Just let Elesin fulfil his oath and we will retire home and   410
pay homage to our King.

JANE: I believe her Simon, don't you?

PILKINGS: Maybe.

ELESIN: Have no fear ghostly one. I have a message to send my
King and then you have nothing more to fear.   415

IYALOJA: Olunde would have done it. The chiefs asked him to
speak the words but he said no, not while you lived.

ELESIN: Even from the depths to which my spirit has sunk, I find
some joy that this little has been left to me.

*(The WOMEN enter, intoning the dirge 'Alelele' and swaying from
side to side. On their shoulders is borne a longish object roughly
like a cylindrical bolt, covered in cloth. They set it down on the spot
where IYALOJA had stood earlier, and form a semicircle round it.
The PRAISE-SINGER and DRUMMER stand on the inside of the semicircle but the drum is not used at all. The DRUMMER intones under
the PRAISE-SINGER's invocations.)*

PILKINGS: (As they enter.) What is that?   420

IYALOJA: The burden you have made white one, but we bring it in
peace.

PILKINGS: I said what is it?

ELESIN: White man, you must let me out. I have a duty to
perform.   425

PILKINGS: I most certainly will not.

ELESIN: There lies the courier of my King. Let me out so I can
perform what is demanded of me.

PILKINGS: You'll do what you need to do from inside there or not
at all. I've gone as far as I intend to with this business.   430

ELESIN: The worshipper who lights a candle in your church to bear a message to his god bows his head and speaks in a whisper to the flame. Have I not seen it ghostly one? His voice does not ring out to the world. Mine are no words for anyone's ears. They are not words even for the bearers of this load. They are words I must speak secretly, even as my father whispered them in my ears and I in the ears of my first-born. I cannot shout them to the wind and the open night-sky.

JANE: Simon . . .

PILKINGS: Don't interfere. Please!

IYALOJA: They have slain the favourite horse of the king and slain his dog. They have borne them from pulse to pulse centre of the land receiving prayers for their king. But the rider has chosen to stay behind. Is it too much to ask that he speak his heart to heart of the waiting courier? (PILKINGS *turns his back on her.*) So be it. Elesin Oba, you see how even the mere leavings are denied you. (*She gestures to the* PRAISE-SINGER.)

PRAISE-SINGER: Elesin Oba! I call you by that name only this last time. Remember when I said, if you cannot come, tell my horse. (*Pause.*) What? I cannot hear you? I said, if you can-not come, whisper in the ears of my horse. Is your tongue severed from the roots Elesin? I can hear no response. I said, if there are boulders you cannot climb, mount my horse's back, this spotless black stallion, he'll bring you over them. (*Pauses.*) Elesin Oba, once you had a tongue that darted like a drummer's stick. I said, if you get lost my dog will track a path to me. My memory fails me but I think you replied: My feet have found the path, Alafin.

(*The dirge rises and falls.*)

I said at the last, if evil hands hold you back, just tell my horse there is weight on the hem of your smock. I dare not wait too long.

(*The dirge rises and falls.*)

There lies the swiftest ever messenger of a king, so set me free with the errand of your heart. There lie the head and heart of the favourite of the gods, whisper in his ears. Oh my companion, if you had followed when you should, we would not say that the horse preceded its rider. If you had followed when it was time, we would not say the dog has raced beyond and left its master behind. If you had raised your will to cut the thread of life at the summons of the drums, we would not say your mere shadow fell across the gateway and took its owner's place at the banquet. But the hunter, laden with a slain buffalo, stayed to root in the cricket's hole with his toes. What now is left? If there is a dearth of bats, the pigeon must serve us for the offering. Speak the words over your shadow which must now serve in your place.

ELESIN: I cannot approach. Take off the cloth. I shall speak my message from heart to heart of silence.

IYALOJA: (*Moves forward and removes the coverings.*) Your courier Elesin, cast your eyes on the favoured companion of the King.

(*Rolled up in the mat, his head and feet showing at either end is the body of* OLUNDE.)

There lies the honour of your household and of our race. Because he could not bear to let honour fly out of doors, he stopped it with his life. The son has proved the father Elesin, and there is nothing left in your mouth to gnash but infant gums.

PRAISE-SINGER: Elesin, we placed the reins of the world in your hands yet you watched it plunge over the edge of the bitter precipice. You sat with folded arms while evil strangers tilted the world from its course and crashed it beyond the edge of emptiness—you muttered, there is little that one man can do, you left us floundering in a blind future. Your heir has taken the burden on himself. What the end will be, we are not gods to tell. But this young shoot has poured its sap into the parent stalk, and we know this is not the way of life. Our world is tumbling in the void of strangers, Elesin.

(ELESIN *has stood rock-still, his knuckles taut on the bars, his eyes glued to the body of his son. The stillness seizes and paralyses everyone, including* PILKINGS *who has turned to look. Suddenly* ELESIN *flings one arm round his neck, once, and with the loop of the chain, strangles himself in a swift, decisive pull. The guards rush forward to stop him but they are only in time to let his body down.* PILKINGS *has leapt to the door at the same time and struggles with the lock. He rushes within, fumbles with the handcuffs and unlocks them, raises the body to a sitting position while he tries to give resuscitation. The* WOMEN *continue their dirge, unmoved by the sudden event.*)

IYALOJA: Why do you strain yourself? Why do you labour at tasks for which no one, not even the man lying there would give you thanks? He is gone at last into the passage but oh, how late it all is. His son will feast on the meat and throw him bones. The passage is clogged with droppings from the King's stallion; he will arrive all stained in dung.

PILKINGS: (*In a tired voice.*) Was this what you wanted?

IYALOJA: No child, it is what you brought to be, you who play with strangers' lives, who even usurp the vestments of our dead, yet believe that the stain of death will not cling to you. The gods demanded only the old expired plantain but you cut down the sap-laden shoot to feed your pride. There is your board, filled to overflowing. Feast on it. (*She screams at him suddenly, seeing that* PILKINGS *is about to close* ELESIN's *staring eyes.*) Let him alone! However sunk he was in debt he is no pauper's carrion abandoned on the road. Since when have strangers donned clothes of indigo before the bereaved cries out his loss?

(*She turns to the* BRIDE *who has remained motionless throughout.*)

Child.

(*The girl takes up a little earth, walks calmly into the cell and closes* ELESIN's *eyes. She then pours some earth over each eyelid and comes out again.*)

Now forget the dead, forget even the living. Turn your mind only to the unborn.

(*She goes off, accompanied by the* BRIDE. *The dirge rises in volume and the* WOMEN *continue their sway. Lights fade to a black-out.*)

GLOSSARY

alari, a rich, woven cloth, brightly coloured

egungun, ancestral masquerade

etutu, placatory rites or medicine

gbedu, a deep-timbred royal drum

opele, string of beads used in Ifa divination

osugbo, secret 'executive' cult of the Yoruba; its meeting place

robo, a delicacy made from crushed melon seeds, fried in tiny balls

sanyan, a richly valued woven cloth

sigidi, a squat, carved figure, endowed with the powers of an incubus

Brian Friel

B rian Friel (b. 1929) is perhaps the most prominent living Irish playwright, the heir of Ireland's brilliant modern dramatic tradition, the tradition of William Butler Yeats, John Millington Synge, and Sean O'Casey. Unlike these predecessors, who worked for the independence of the Republic of Ireland, Friel works in Northern Ireland, still a part of the United Kingdom. Educated in Derry and Belfast, Friel's concerns as a playwright have spanned the "troubles" of Northern Ireland, the poverty and depression of Derry in the 1930s, 1940s, and 1950s, and the installation of a British military presence and the open street warfare of the 1960s, 1970s, and 1980s. From his earliest success, *Philadelphia, Here I Come!* (1964), about a man's divided feelings concerning his emigration to the United States, Friel's drama has centered on the problems of Irish identity in the face of British rule. Many of his early plays and stories—*The Loves of Cass McGuire* (1966), *The Lovers* (1967)—are portraits of Irish life in the manner of Synge, and Friel's dramatization of the personal consequences of contemporary Irish life remains a prominent feature of fine plays like *Living Quarters* (1977) and *Faith Healer* (1979). However, Friel's drama has increasingly become more satirical—in *The Mundy Scheme* (1969) and *The Gentle Island* (1971)—and more politically concerned. In *The Freedom of the City* (1973), Friel dramatizes the fate of three people caught and killed by British soldiers in the 1972 "Bloody Sunday" riots in Derry. In *Volunteers* (1975), a crew of political prisoners are forced to work on an archaeological site, recovering the history of Celtic Ireland even as they are oppressed by British rule. In *Making History* (1988), Friel returns to the origins of Ireland's subjection to the British in the seventeenth and eighteenth centuries. In 1980, Friel and Stephen Rea founded the Field Day Theatre Company in Derry, and its first production was the play generally taken to be Friel's masterpiece, *Translations*. Friel's more recent plays include *Dancing at Lughnasa* (1990), *Wonderful Tennessee* (1992), *Give Me Your Answer, Do!* (1997), and *Home Place* (2005), as well as a meditation on the artist in old age, *Performances* (2003).

Mark Douet/ArenaPal

The 1993 Donmar Warehouse production of Brian Friel's *Translations*.

Friel has also adapted several plays—Turgenev's *A Month in the Country* (1992) and *London Vertigo*, by the eighteenth-century actor Charles Macklin (1992)—and has specialized in adapting Chekhov's drama to Irish English, in versions of *Three Sisters* (2001) and *Uncle Vanya* (1995).

Translations

Translations is set in early nineteenth-century Ireland and concerns the mapping—both actual and cultural—of Ireland by the British. The play takes place at a local hedge-school, a subscription school run by a local master and attended by a variety of children and adults. This Ireland is already threatened by the British culture to the east: a national school—where, presumably, English will be the required language—is about to open, and the British army surveyors have arrived to map the region, part of the 1833 Ordnance Survey of Ireland.

The play's politics are largely conveyed through the politics of language. Jimmy's Homeric Greek, for example, draws a parallel between Ireland and another lost civilization. The romance between Yolland and Maire bridges the barrier of language. They learn to communicate across this barrier, while the British army works to tear it down and destroy Irish cultural identity in the process. In mapping Ireland, the British convert local place names into English, either by translating them directly or by inventing some equivalent. As the relationship between the Irish Owen and his British officers makes clear, English is the language of power; to map the landscape with English names is a figure for rewriting Ireland and its culture into submission and, finally, into nonexistence.

Although *Translations* may seem only indirectly about contemporary Irish politics, it dramatizes a struggle for national and cultural identity that continues to embroil Northern Ireland today. Throughout the play, for example, the mysterious and unseen Donnelly twins move around the edges of the action, guerrillas hindering the British progress through the country. Finally, when Yolland is missing, we learn the true consequences of the British mapping of Ireland. Mapping the land in English is the prelude to its occupation, as the army systematically destroys the village and countryside that they have made their own. At the play's close, we scent the sickly sweet smell of blighted potatoes, the sign of the impending famine that would weaken and disperse rural Ireland.

Translations

Brian Friel

CHARACTERS

MANUS	BRIDGET	
SARAH	HUGH	
JIMMY JACK	OWEN	
MAIRE	CAPTAIN LANCEY	
DOALTY	LIEUTENANT YOLLAND	

Act I   An afternoon in late August 1833.
Act II   A few days later.
Act III   The evening of the following day.
One interval—between the two scenes in Act Two.

The action takes place in a hedge-school in the townland of Baile Beag/Ballybeg, an Irish-speaking community in County Donegal.

ACT ONE

The hedge-school is held in a disused barn or hay-shed or byre. Along the back wall are the remains of five or six stalls—wooden posts and chains—where cows were once milked and bedded. A double door left, large enough to allow a cart to enter. A window right. A wooden stairway without a banister leads to the upstairs living-quarters (off) of the schoolmaster and his son. Around the room are broken and forgotten implements: a cart-wheel, some lobster-pots, farming tools, a battle of hay, a churn, etc. There are also the stools and bench-seats which the pupils use and a table and chair for the master. At the door a pail of water and a soiled towel. The room is comfortless and dusty and functional—there is no trace of a woman's hand.

When the play opens, MANUS *is teaching* SARAH *to speak. He kneels beside her. She is sitting on a low stool, her head down, very tense, clutching a slate on her knees. He is coaxing her gently and firmly and—as with everything he does—with a kind of zeal.*

MANUS *is in his late twenties/early thirties; the master's older son. He is pale-faced, lightly built, intense, and works as an unpaid assistant—a monitor—to his father. His clothes are shabby; and when he moves we see that he is lame.*

SARAH's *speech defect is so bad that all her life she has been considered locally to be dumb and she has accepted this: when she wishes to communicate, she grunts and makes unintelligible nasal sounds. She has a waiflike appearance and could be any age from seventeen to thirty-five.*

JIMMY JACK CASSIE—*known as the Infant Prodigy—sits by himself, contentedly reading Homer in Greek and smiling to himself. He is a bachelor in his sixties, lives alone, and comes to these evening classes partly for the company and partly for the intellectual stimulation. He is fluent in Latin and Greek but is in no way pedantic—to him it is perfectly normal to speak these tongues. He never washes. His clothes—heavy top coat, hat, mittens, which he wears now—are filthy and he lives in them summer and winter, day and night. He now reads in a quiet voice and smiles in profound satisfaction. For* JIMMY *the world of the gods and the ancient myths is as real and as immediate as everyday life in the townland of Baile Beag.*

MANUS *holds* SARAH's *hands in his and he articulates slowly and distinctly into her face.*

MANUS: We're doing very well. And we're going to try it once more—just once more. Now—relax and breathe in . . . deep . . . and out . . . in . . . and out . . .

(SARAH *shakes her head vigorously and stubbornly.*)

MANUS: Come on, Sarah. This is our secret.

(*Again vigorous and stubborn shaking of* SARAH's *head.*)

MANUS: Nobody's listening. Nobody hears you.   5
JIMMY: 'Ton d'emeibet epeita thea glaukopis Athene . . .'
MANUS: Get your tongue and your lips working. 'My name—' Come on. One more try. 'My name is—' Good girl.
SARAH: My . . .
MANUS: Great. 'My name—'   10
SARAH: My . . . my . . .
MANUS: Raise your head. Shout it out. Nobody's listening.
JIMMY: '. . . alla hekelos estai en Atreidao domois . . .'
MANUS: Jimmy, please! Once more—just once more—'My name—' Good girl. Come on now. Head up. Mouth open.   15
SARAH: My . . .
MANUS: Good.
SARAH: My . . .
MANUS: Great.
SARAH: My name . . .   20
MANUS: Yes?
SARAH: My name is . . .
MANUS: Yes?

(SARAH *pauses. Then in a rush.*)

SARAH: My name is Sarah.
MANUS: Marvellous! Bloody marvellous!   25

(MANUS *hugs* SARAH. *She smiles in shy, embarrassed pleasure.*)

Did you hear that, Jimmy?—'My name is Sarah'—clear as a bell. (*To* SARAH.) The Infant Prodigy doesn't know what we're at. (SARAH *laughs at this.* MANUS *hugs her again and stands up.*) Now we're really started! Nothing'll stop us now! Nothing in the wide world!   30

(JIMMY, *chuckling at his text, comes over to them.*)

I. 6 *Ton . . . Athene* But the grey-eyed goddess Athene then replied to him (from Homer, *Odyssey*, 13.420)   13 *alla . . . domois* . . . but he sits at ease in the halls of the Sons of Athens . . . (from Homer, *Odyssey*, 13.423–24)

JIMMY: Listen to this, Manus.

MANUS: Soon you'll be telling me all the secrets that have been in that head of yours all these years. Certainly, James—what is it? (*To* SARAH.) Maybe you'd set out the stools?

(MANUS *runs up the stairs*.)

35 JIMMY: Wait till you hear this, Manus.

MANUS: Go ahead. I'll be straight down.

JIMMY: '*Hos ara min phamene rabdo epemassat Athene—*' 'After Athene had said this, she touched Ulysses with her wand. She withered the fair skin of his supple limbs and destroyed the

40 flaxen hair from off his head and about his limbs she put the skin of an old man . . .'! The divil! The divil!

(MANUS *has emerged again with a bowl of milk and a piece of bread.*)

JIMMY: And wait till you hear! She's not finished with him yet!

(*As* MANUS *descends the stairs he toasts* SARAH *with his bowl.*)

JIMMY: '*Knuzosen de oi osse—*' 'She dimmed his two eyes that were so beautiful and clothed him in a vile ragged cloak begrimed

45 with filthy smoke . . .'! D'you see! Smoke! Smoke! D'you see! Sure look at what the same turf-smoke has done to myself! (*He rapidly removes his hat to display his bald head.*) Would you call that flaxen hair?

MANUS: Of course I would.

50 JIMMY: 'And about him she cast the great skin of a filthy hind, stripped of the hair, and into his hand she thrust a staff and a wallet'! Ha-ha-ha! Athene did that to Ulysses! Made him into a tramp! Isn't she the tight one?

MANUS: You couldn't watch her, Jimmy.

55 JIMMY: You know what they call her?

MANUS: '*Glaukopis Athene.*'

JIMMY: That's it! The flashing-eyed Athene! By God, Manus, sir, if you had a woman like that about the house, it's not stripping a turf-bank you'd be thinking about—eh?

60 MANUS: She was a goddess, Jimmy.

JIMMY: Better still. Sure isn't our own Grania a class of a goddess and—

MANUS: Who?

JIMMY: Grania—Grania—Diarmuid's Grania.

65 MANUS: Ah.

JIMMY: And sure she can't get her fill of men.

MANUS: Jimmy, you're impossible.

JIMMY: I was just thinking to myself last night: if you had the choosing between Athene and Artemis and Helen of

70 Troy—all three of them Zeus's girls—imagine three powerful-looking daughters like that all in the one parish of Athens!—now, if you had the picking between them, which would you take?

MANUS: (*To* SARAH.) Which should I take, Sarah?

75 JIMMY: No harm to Helen; and no harm to Artemis; and indeed no harm to our own Grania, Manus. But I think I've no choice but to go bull-straight for Athene. By God, sir, them flashing eyes would fair keep a man jigged up constant!

---

37 *Hos . . . Athene* as she spoke Athene touched him with her wand (from Homer, *Odyssey*, 13.429)   43 *Knuzosen . . . osse* she dimmed his eyes (from Homer, *Odyssey*, 13.433)   56 *Glaukopis Athene* flashing-eyed Athene

(*Suddenly and momentarily, as if in spasm,* JIMMY *stands to attention and salutes, his face raised in pained ecstasy.* MANUS *laughs. So does* SARAH. JIMMY *goes back to his seat, and his reading.*)

MANUS: You're a dangerous bloody man, Jimmy Jack.

JIMMY: 'Flashing-eyed'! Hah! Sure Homer knows it all, boy.   80 Homer knows it all.

(MANUS *goes to the window and looks out.*)

MANUS: Where the hell has he got to?

(SARAH *goes to* MANUS *and touches his elbow. She mimes rocking a baby.*)

MANUS: Yes, I know he's at the christening; but it doesn't take them all day to put a name on a baby, does it?

(SARAH *mimes pouring drinks and tossing them back quickly.*)

MANUS: You may be sure. Which pub?   85

(SARAH *indicates.*)

MANUS: Gracie's?

(*No. Further away.*)

MANUS: Con Connie Tim's?

(*No. To the right of there.*)

MANUS: Anna na mBreag's?

(*Yes. That's it.*)

MANUS: Great. She'll fill him up. I suppose I may take the class then.   90

(MANUS *begins to distribute some books, slates and chalk, texts, etc., beside the seats.* SARAH *goes over to the straw and produces a bunch of flowers she has hidden there. During this:*)

JIMMY: '*Autar o ek limenos prosebe—*' 'But Ulysses went forth from the harbour and through the woodland to the place where Athene had shown him he could find the good swineherd who—'*o oi biotoio malista kedeto*'—what's that, Manus?

MANUS: 'Who cared most for his substance.'   95

JIMMY: That's it! 'The good swineherd who cared most for his substance above all the slaves that Ulysses possessed . . .'

(SARAH *presents the flowers to* MANUS.)

MANUS: Those are lovely, Sarah.

(*But* SARAH *has fled in embarrassment to her seat and has her head buried in a book.* MANUS *goes to her.*)

---

91 *Autar . . . prosebe* but he went forth from the harbour (from Homer, *Odyssey*, 14.1)   94 *o . . . kedeto* he cared very much for his substance (from Homer, *Odyssey*, 14.3–4)

MANUS: Flow-ers.

(*Pause.* SARAH *does not look up.*)

100 MANUS: Say the word: flow-ers. Come on—flow-ers.
SARAH: Flowers.
MANUS: You see?—you're off!

(MANUS *leans down and kisses the top of* SARAH's *head.*)

MANUS: And they're beautiful flowers. Thank you.

(MAIRE *enters, a strong-minded, strong-bodied woman in her twenties with a head of curly hair. She is carrying a small can of milk.*)

MAIRE: Is this all's here? Is there no school this evening?
105 MANUS: If my father's not back, I'll take it.

(MANUS *stands awkwardly, having been caught kissing* SARAH *and with the flowers almost formally at his chest.*)

MAIRE: Well now, isn't that a pretty sight. There's your milk.
How's Sarah?

(SARAH *grunts a reply.*)

MANUS: I saw you out at the hay.

(MAIRE *ignores this and goes to* JIMMY.)

MAIRE: And how's Jimmy Jack Cassie?
110 JIMMY: Sit down beside me, Maire.
MAIRE: Would I be safe?
JIMMY: No safer man in Donegal.

(MAIRE *flops on a stool beside* JIMMY.)

MAIRE: Ooooh. The best harvest in living memory, they say; but
I don't want to see another like it. (*Showing* JIMMY *her hands.*)
115 Look at the blisters.
JIMMY: *Esne fatigata?*
MAIRE: *Sum fatigatissima.*
JIMMY: *Bene! Optime!*
MAIRE: That's the height of my Latin. Fit me better if I had even
120 that much English.
JIMMY: English? I thought you had some English?
MAIRE: Three words. Wait—there was a spake I used to have off by
heart. What's this it was? (*Her accent is strange because she
is speaking a foreign language and because she does not
125 understand what she is saying.*) 'In Norfolk we besport ourselves
around the maypoll.' What about that!
MANUS: Maypole.

(*Again* MAIRE *ignores* MANUS.)

MAIRE: God have mercy on my Aunt Mary—she taught me that
when I was about four, whatever it means. Do you know
130 what it means, Jimmy?
JIMMY: Sure you know I have only Irish like yourself.

---

116 **Esne fatigata?** are you tired?   117 **Sum fatigatissima** I am very tired   118 **Bene! Optime!** good! Excellent!

MAIRE: And Latin. And Greek.
JIMMY: I'm telling you a lie: I know one English word.
MAIRE: What?
JIMMY: Bo-som.   135
MAIRE: What's a bo-som?
JIMMY: You know—(*He illustrates with his hands.*)—bo-som—
bo-som—you know—Diana, the huntress, she has two
powerful bosom.
MAIRE: You may be sure that's the one English word you would   140
know. (*Rises.*) Is there a drop of water about?

(MANUS *gives* MAIRE *his bowl of milk.*)

MANUS: I'm sorry I couldn't get up last night.
MAIRE: Doesn't matter.
MANUS: Biddy Hanna sent for me to write a letter to her sister in
Nova Scotia. All the gossip of the parish. 'I brought the cow to 145
the bull three times last week but no good. There's nothing for
it now but Big Ned Frank.'
MAIRE: (*Drinking.*) That's better.
MANUS: And she got so engrossed in it that she forgot who she
was dictating to: 'The aul drunken schoolmaster and that   150
lame son of his are still footering about in the hedge-school,
wasting people's good time and money.'

(MAIRE *has to laugh at this.*)

MAIRE: She did not!
MANUS: And me taking it all down. 'Thank God one of them new
national schools is being built above at Poll na gCaorach.' It   155
was after midnight by the time I got back.
MAIRE: Great to be a busy man.

(MAIRE *moves away.* MANUS *follows.*)

MANUS: I could hear music on my way past but I thought it was
too late to call.
MAIRE: (*To* SARAH.) Wasn't your father in great voice last night?   160

(SARAH *nods and smiles.*)

MAIRE: It must have been near three o'clock by the time you
got home?

(SARAH *holds up four fingers.*)

MAIRE: Was it four? No wonder we're in pieces.
MANUS: I can give you a hand at the hay tomorrow.
MAIRE: That's the name of a hornpipe, isn't it?— 'The Scholar In   165
The Hayfield'—or is it a reel?
MANUS: If the day's good.
MAIRE: Suit yourself. The English soldiers below in the tents,
them sapper fellas, they're coming up to give us a hand. I
don't know a word they're saying, nor they me; but sure that   170
doesn't matter, does it?
MANUS: What the hell are you so crabbed about?!

(DOALTY *and* BRIDGET *enter noisily. Both are in their twenties.*
DOALTY *is brandishing a surveyor's pole. He is an open-minded,
open-hearted, generous and slightly thick young man.* BRIDGET
*is a plump, fresh young girl, ready to laugh, vain, and with a
countrywoman's instinctive cunning.* DOALTY *enters doing his
imitation of the master.*)

DOALTY: Vesperal salutations to you all.

BRIDGET: He's coming down past Carraig na Ri and he's as full
175   as a pig!

DOALTY: *Ignari, stulti, rustici*—pot-boys and peasant whelps—
semi-literates and illegitimates.

BRIDGET: He's been on the batter since this morning; he sent
the wee ones home at eleven o'clock.

180 DOALTY: Three questions. Question A—Am I drunk? Question
B—Am I sober? (*Into* MAIRE's *face.*) *Responde—responde!*

BRIDGET: Question C, Master—When were you last sober?

MAIRE: What's the weapon, Doalty?

BRIDGET: I warned him. He'll be arrested one of these days.

185 DOALTY: Up in the bog with Bridget and her aul fella, and the
Red Coats were just across at the foot of Croc na Mona,
dragging them aul chains and peeping through that big
machine they lug about everywhere with them—you
know the name of it, Manus?

190 MAIRE: Theodolite.

BRIDGET: How do you know?

MAIRE: They leave it in our byre at night sometimes if it's
raining.

JIMMY: Theodolite—what's the etymology of that word, Manus?

195 MANUS: No idea.

BRIDGET: Get on with the story.

JIMMY: *Theo—theos*—something to do with a god. Maybe
thea—a goddess! What shape's the yoke?

DOALTY: 'Shape!' Will you shut up, you aul eejit you! Anyway,
200   every time they'd stick one of these poles into the ground
and move across the bog, I'd creep up and shift it twenty or
thirty paces to the side.

BRIDGET: God!

DOALTY: Then they'd come back and stare at it and look at their
205   calculations and stare at it again and scratch their heads.
And cripes, d'you know what they ended up doing?

BRIDGET: Wait till you hear!

DOALTY: They took the bloody machine apart!

(*And immediately he speaks in gibberish—an imitation of two very
agitated and confused sappers in rapid conversation.*)

BRIDGET: That's the image of them!

210 MAIRE: You must be proud of yourself, Doalty.

DOALTY: What d'you mean?

MAIRE: That was a very clever piece of work.

MANUS: It was a gesture.

MAIRE: What sort of gesture?

215 MANUS: Just to indicate . . . a presence.

MAIRE: Hah!

BRIDGET: I'm telling you—you'll be arrested.

(*When* DOALTY *is embarrassed—or pleased—he reacts physically.
He now grabs* BRIDGET *around the waist.*)

DOALTY: What d'you make of that for an implement, Bridget?
Wouldn't that make a great aul shaft for your churn?

220 BRIDGET: Let go of me, you dirty brute! I've a headline to do
before Big Hughie comes.

MANUS: I don't think we'll wait for him. Let's get started.

(*Slowly, reluctantly they begin to move to their seats and specific
tasks.* DOALTY *goes to the bucket of water at the door and washes his
hands.* BRIDGET *sets up a hand-mirror and combs her hair.*)

BRIDGET: Nellie Ruadh's baby was to be christened this morning.
Did any of yous hear what she called it? Did you, Sarah?

(SARAH *grunts:* No.)

BRIDGET: Did you, Maire?   225

MAIRE: No.

BRIDGET: Our Seamus says she was threatening she was going to
call it after its father.

DOALTY: Who's the father?

BRIDGET: That's the point, you donkey you!   230

DOALTY: Ah.

BRIDGET: So there's a lot of uneasy bucks about Baile Beag this
day.

DOALTY: She told me last Sunday she was going to call it Jimmy.

BRIDGET: You're a liar, Doalty.   235

DOALTY: Would I tell you a lie? Hi, Jimmy, Nellie Ruadh's aul
fella's looking for you.

JIMMY: For me?

MAIRE: Come on, Doalty.

DOALTY: Someone told him . . .   240

MAIRE: Doalty!

DOALTY: He heard you know the first book of the Satires of
Horace off by heart . . .

JIMMY: That's true.

DOALTY: and he wants you to recite it for him.   245

JIMMY: I'll do that for him certainly, certainly.

DOALTY: He's busting to hear it.

(JIMMY *fumbles in his pockets.*)

JIMMY: I came across this last night—this'll interest you—in
Book Two of Virgil's *Georgics.*

DOALTY: Be God, that's my territory alright.   250

BRIDGET: You clown you! (*To* SARAH.) Hold this for me, would
you? (*Her mirror.*)

JIMMY: Listen to this, Manus. '*Nigra fere et presso pinguis sub
vomere terra . . .*'

DOALTY: Steady on now—easy, boys, easy—don't rush me, boys—   255

(*He mimes great concentration.*)

JIMMY: Manus?

MANUS: 'Land that is black and rich beneath the pressure of the
plough . . .'

DOALTY: Give *me* a chance!

JIMMY: 'And with *cui putre*—with crumbly soil—is in the main   260
best for corn.' There you are!

DOALTY: There you are.

JIMMY: 'From no other land will you see more wagons wending
homeward behind slow bullocks.' Virgil! There!

DOALTY: 'Slow bullocks'!   265

JIMMY: Isn't that what I'm always telling you? Black soil for corn.
That's what you should have in that upper field of yours—
corn, not spuds.

---

176 **Ignari, stulti, rustici** ignoramuses, fools, peasants   181 **Responde—
responde!** answer—answer   197 **theos** a god   198 **thea** a goddess

253–54 **Nigra . . . terra** land that is black and rich beneath the pressure
of the plough   260 **cui putre** crumbly soil

DOALTY: Would you listen to that fella! Too lazy be Jasus to wash
270 himself and he's lecturing me on agriculture! Would you
go and take a running race at yourself, Jimmy Jack Cassie!
(*Grabs* SARAH.) Come away out of this with me, Sarah, and
we'll plant some corn together.
MANUS: All right—all right. Let's settle down and get some work
275 done. I know Sean Beag isn't coming—he's at the salmon.
What about the Donnelly twins? (*To* DOALTY.) Are the
Donnelly twins not coming any more?

(DOALTY *shrugs and turns away.*)

Did you ask them?
DOALTY: Haven't seen them. Not about these days.

(DOALTY *begins whistling through his teeth. Suddenly the
atmosphere is silent and alert.*)

280 MANUS: Aren't they at home?
DOALTY: No.
MANUS: Where are they then?
DOALTY: How would I know?
BRIDGET: Our Seamus says two of the soldiers' horses were found
285 last night at the foot of the cliffs at Machaire Buidhe and . . .
(*She stops suddenly and begins writing with chalk on her slate.*)
D'you hear the whistles of this aul slate? Sure nobody could
write on an aul slippery thing like that.
MANUS: What headline did my father set you?
290 BRIDGET: 'It's easier to stamp out learning than to recall it.'
JIMMY: Book Three, the *Agricola* of Tacitus.
BRIDGET: God but you're a dose.
MANUS: Can you do it?
BRIDGET: There. Is it bad? Will he ate me?
295 MANUS: It's very good. Keep your elbow in closer to your side.
Doalty?
DOALTY: I'm at the seven-times table. I'm perfect, skipper.

(MANUS *moves to* SARAH.)

MANUS: Do you understand those sums?

(SARAH *nods:* Yes. MANUS *leans down to her ear.*)

MANUS: My name is Sarah.

(MANUS *goes to* MAIRE. *While he is talking to her the others swop
books, talk quietly, etc.*)

300 MANUS: Can I help you? What are you at?
MAIRE: Map of America. (*Pause.*) The passage money came last
Friday.
MANUS: You never told me that.
MAIRE: Because I haven't seen you since, have I?
305 MANUS: You don't want to go. You said that yourself.
MAIRE: There's ten below me to be raised and no man in the
house. What do you suggest?
MANUS: Do you want to go?
MAIRE: Did you apply for that job in the new national school?
310 MANUS: No.
MAIRE: You said you would.

MANUS: I said I might.
MAIRE: When it opens, this is finished: nobody's going to pay
to go to a hedge-school.
MANUS: I know that and I . . . (*He breaks off because he sees* 315
SARAH, *obviously listening, at his shoulder. She moves away
again.*) I was thinking that maybe I could . . .
MAIRE: It's £56 a year you're throwing away.
MANUS: I can't apply for it.
MAIRE: You *promised* me you would. 320
MANUS: My father has applied for it.
MAIRE: He has not!
MANUS: Day before yesterday.
MAIRE: For God's sake, sure you know he'd never—
MANUS: I couldn't—I can't go in against him. 325

(MAIRE *looks at him for a second. Then:—*)

MAIRE: Suit yourself. (*To* BRIDGET.) I saw your Seamus heading
off to the Port fair early this morning.
BRIDGET: And wait till you hear this—I forgot to tell you this.
He said that as soon as he crossed over the gap at Cnoc
na Mona—just beyond where the soldiers are making the 330
maps—the sweet smell was everywhere.
DOALTY: You never told me that.
BRIDGET: It went out of my head.
DOALTY: He saw the crops in Port?
BRIDGET: Some. 335
MANUS: How did the tops look?
BRIDGET: Fine—I think.
DOALTY: In flower?
BRIDGET: I don't know. I think so. He didn't say.
MANUS: Just the sweet smell—that's all? 340
BRIDGET: They say that's the way it snakes in, don't they? First
the smell; and then one morning the stalks are all black and
limp.
DOALTY: Are you stupid? It's the rotting stalks makes the sweet
smell for God's sake. That's what the smell is—rotting 345
stalks.
MAIRE: Sweet smell! Sweet smell! Every year at this time
somebody comes back with stories of the sweet smell. Sweet
God, did the potatoes ever fail in Baile Beag? Well, did
they ever—ever? Never! There was never blight here. 350
Never. Never. But we're always sniffing about for it, aren't
we?—looking for disaster. The rents are going to go up
again—the harvest's going to be lost—the herring have gone
away for ever—there's going to be evictions. Honest to God,
some of you people aren't happy unless you're miserable and 355
you'll not be right content until you're dead!
DOALTY: Bloody right, Maire. And sure St Colmcille prophesied
there'd never be blight here. He said:

The spuds will bloom in Baile Beag
Till rabbits grow an extra lug. 360

And sure that'll never be. So we're all right. Seven threes are
twenty-one; seven fours are twenty-eight; seven fives are
forty-nine—Hi, Jimmy, do you fancy my chances as boss of the
new national school?
JIMMY: What's that?—what's that? 365
DOALTY: Agh, g'way back home to Greece, son.
MAIRE: You ought to apply, Doalty.
DOALTY: D'you think so? Cripes, maybe I will. Hah!

BRIDGET: Did you know that you start at the age of six and you
370   have to stick at it until you're twelve at least—no matter how
      smart you are or how much you know.
DOALTY: Who told you that yarn?
BRIDGET: And every child from every house has to go all day,
      every day, summer or winter. That's the law.
375 DOALTY: I'll tell you something—nobody's going to go near
      them—they're not going to take on—law or no law.
BRIDGET: And everything's free in them. You pay for nothing
      except the books you use; that's what our Seamus says.
DOALTY: 'Our Seamus.' Sure your Seamus wouldn't pay anyway.
380   She's making this all up.
BRIDGET: Isn't that right, Manus?
MANUS: I think so.
BRIDGET: And from the very first day you go, you'll not hear one
      word of Irish spoken. You'll be taught to speak English and
385   every subject will be taught through English and
      everyone'll end up as cute as the Buncrana people.

(SARAH *suddenly grunts and mimes a warning that the master is
coming. The atmosphere changes. Sudden business. Heads down.*)

DOALTY: He's here, boys. Cripes, he'll make yella meal out of me
      for those bloody tables.
BRIDGET: Have you any extra chalk, Manus?
390 MAIRE: And the atlas for me.

(DOALTY *goes to* MAIRE *who is sitting on a stool at the back.*)

DOALTY: Swop you seats.
MAIRE: Why?
DOALTY: There's an empty one beside the Infant Prodigy.
MAIRE: I'm fine here.
395 DOALTY: Please, Maire. I want to jouk in the back here.

(MAIRE *rises.*)

      God love you. (*Aloud.*) Anyone got a bloody table-book?
      Cripes, I'm wrecked.

(SARAH *gives him one.*)

      God, I'm dying about you.

(*In his haste to get to the back seat,* DOALTY *bumps into* BRIDGET
*who is kneeling on the floor and writing laboriously on a slate resting
on top of a bench-seat.*)

BRIDGET: Watch where you're going, Doalty!

(DOALTY *gooses* BRIDGET. *She squeals. Now the quiet hum of work:*
JIMMY *reading Homer in a low voice;* BRIDGET *copying her headline;*
MAIRE *studying the atlas;* DOALTY, *his eyes shut tight, mouthing his
tables;* SARAH *doing sums. After a few seconds:—*)

400 BRIDGET: Is this 'g' right, Manus? How do you put a tail on it?
DOALTY: Will you shut up! I can't concentrate!

(*A few more seconds of work. Then* DOALTY *opens his eyes and
looks around.*)

      False alarm, boys. The bugger's not coming at all. Sure the
      bugger's hardly fit to walk.

(*And immediately* HUGH *enters. A large man, with residual dignity,
shabbily dressed, carrying a stick. He has, as always, a large quantity
of drink taken, but he is by no means drunk. He is in his early
sixties.*)

HUGH: *Adsum*, Doalty, *adsum*. Perhaps not in *sobrietate perfecta*
      but adequately *sobrius* to overhear your quip. Vesperal   405
      salutations to you all.

(*Various responses.*)

JIMMY: *Ave*, Hugh.
HUGH: James. (*He removes his hat and coat and hands them
      and his stick to* MANUS, *as if to a footman.*) Apologies for
      my late arrival: we were celebrating the baptism of Nellie   410
      Ruadh's baby.
BRIDGET: (*Innocently.*) What name did she put on it, Master?
HUGH: Was it Eamon? Yes, it was Eamon.
BRIDGET: Eamon Donal from Tor! Cripes!
HUGH: And after the *caerimonia nominationis*—Maire?   415
MAIRE: The ritual of naming.
HUGH: Indeed—we then had a few libations to mark the occasion.
      Altogether very pleasant. The derivation of the word
      'baptize'?—where are my Greek scholars? Doalty?
DOALTY: Would it be—ah—ah—   420
HUGH: Too slow. James?
JIMMY: '*Baptizein*'—to dip or immerse.
HUGH: Indeed—our friend Pliny Minor speaks of the '*baptis-
      terium*'—the cold bath.
DOALTY: Master.   425
HUGH: Doalty?
DOALTY: I suppose you could talk then about baptizing a sheep at
      sheep-dipping, could you?

(*Laughter. Comments.*)

HUGH: Indeed—the precedent is there—the day you were
      appropriately named Doalty—seven nines?   430
DOALTY: What's that, Master?
HUGH: Seven times nine?
DOALTY: Seven nines—seven nines—seven times nine—seven
      times nine are—cripes, it's on the tip of my tongue, Master—
      I knew it for sure this morning—funny that's the only one   435
      that foxes me—
BRIDGET: (*Prompt.*) Sixty-three.
DOALTY: What's wrong with me: sure seven nines are fifty-three,
      Master.
HUGH: Sophocles from Colonus would agree with Doalty Dan   440
      Doalty from Tulach Alainn: 'To know nothing is the sweetest
      life.' Where's Sean Beag?
MANUS: He's at the salmon.
HUGH: And Nora Dan?
MAIRE: She says she's not coming back any more.   445
HUGH: Ah. Nora Dan can now write her name—Nora Dan's
      education is complete. And the Donnelly twins?

(*Brief pause. Then:—*)

---

404 **adsum** I am present; **sobrietate perfecta** with complete sobriety
405 **sobrius** sober   407 **Ave** hail   415 **caerimonia nominationis** ceremony of naming   422 **baptizein** to dip or immerse   424 **baptisterium**
a cold bath, swimming pool

BRIDGET: They're probably at the turf. (*She goes to* HUGH.) There's the one-and-eight I owe you for last quarter's arithmetic and there's my one-and-six for this quarter's writing.

450

HUGH: *Gratias tibi ago.* (*He sits at his table.*) Before we commence our *studia* I have three items of information to impart to you—(*To* MANUS.) A bowl of tea, strong tea, black—

(MANUS *leaves.*)

Item A: on my perambulations today—Bridget? Too slow. Maire?

455

MAIRE: *Perambulare*—to walk about.

HUGH: Indeed—I encountered Captain Lancey of the Royal Engineers who is engaged in the ordnance survey of this area. He tells me that in the past few days two of his horses have strayed and some of his equipment seems to be mislaid. I expressed my regret and suggested he address you himself on these matters. He then explained that he does not speak Irish. Latin? I asked. None. Greek? Not a syllable. He speaks—on his own admission—only English; and to his credit he seemed suitably verecund—James?

460

465

JIMMY: *Verecundus*—humble.

HUGH: Indeed—he voiced some surprise that we did not speak his language. I explained that a few of us did, on occasion—outside the parish of course—and then usually for the purposes of commerce, a use to which his tongue seemed particularly suited—(*Shouts.*) and a slice of soda bread—and I went on to propose that our own culture and the classical tongues made a happier conjugation—Doalty?

470

DOALTY: *Conjugo*—I join together.

(DOALTY *is so pleased with himself that he prods and winks at* BRIDGET.)

HUGH: Indeed—English, I suggested, couldn't really express us. And again to his credit he acquiesced to my logic. Acquiesced—Maire?

475

(MAIRE *turns away impatiently.* HUGH *is unaware of the gesture.*)

Too slow. Bridget?

BRIDGET: *Acquiesco.*

HUGH: *Procede.*

480

BRIDGET: *Acquiesco, acquiescere, acquievi, acquietum.*

HUGH: Indeed—and Item B . . .

MAIRE: Master.

HUGH: Yes?

(MAIRE *gets to her feet uneasily but determinedly. Pause.*)

Well, girl?

485

MAIRE: We should all be learning to speak English. That's what my mother says. That's what I say. That's what Dan O'Connell said last month in Ennis. He said the sooner we all learn to speak English the better.

(*Suddenly several speak together.*)

JIMMY: What's she saying? What? What?

490

DOALTY: It's Irish he uses when he's travelling around scrounging votes.

BRIDGET: And sleeping with married women. Sure no woman's safe from that fella.

JIMMY: Who-who-who? Who's this? Who's this?

495

HUGH: *Silentium!* (*Pause.*) Who is she talking about?

MAIRE: I'm talking about Daniel O'Connell.

HUGH: Does she mean that little Kerry politician?

MAIRE: I'm talking about the Liberator, Master, as you well know. And what he said was this: 'The old language is a barrier to modern progress.' He said that last month. And he's right. I don't want Greek. I don't want Latin. I want English.

500

(MANUS *reappears on the platform above.*)

I want to be able to speak English because I'm going to America as soon as the harvest's all saved.

(MAIRE *remains standing.* HUGH *puts his hand into his pocket and produces a flask of whiskey. He removes the cap, pours a drink into it, tosses it back, replaces the cap, puts the flask back into his pocket. Then:—*)

HUGH: We have been diverted—*diverto*—*divertere*—Where were we?

505

DOALTY: Three items of information, Master. You're at Item B.

HUGH: Indeed—Item B—Item B—yes—On my way to the christening this morning I chanced to meet Mr George Alexander, Justice of the Peace. We discussed the new national school. Mr Alexander invited me to take charge of it when it opens. I thanked him and explained that I could do that only if I were free to run it as I have run this hedge-school for the past thirty-five years—filling what our friend Euripides calls the 'aplestos pithos'—James?

510

515

JIMMY: 'The cask that cannot be filled.'

HUGH: Indeed—and Mr. Alexander retorted courteously and emphatically that he hopes that is how it will be run.

(MAIRE *now sits.*)

Indeed. I have had a strenuous day and I am weary of you all. (*He rises.*) Manus will take care of you.

520

(HUGH *goes towards the steps.* OWEN *enters.* OWEN *is the younger son, a handsome, attractive young man in his twenties. He is dressed smartly—a city man. His manner is easy and charming: everything he does is invested with consideration and enthusiasm. He now stands framed in the doorway, a travelling bag across his shoulder.*)

OWEN: Could anybody tell me is this where Hugh Mor O'Donnell holds his hedge-school?

DOALTY: It's Owen—Owen Hugh! Look, boys—it's Owen Hugh!

(OWEN *enters. As he crosses the room he touches and has a word for each person.*)

---

451 **Gratias tibi ago** I thank you   452 **studia** studies   456 **perambulare** to walk through   466 **verecundus** shame-faced, modest   474 **conjugo** I join together   480 **Procede** proceed   481 **acquiesco, acquiescere** to rest, to find comfort in

---

496 **Silentium!** silence!   505 **diverto, divertere** to turn away   515 **aplestos pithos** unfillable cask

525 OWEN: Doalty! (*Playful punch.*) How are you, boy? *Jacobe, quid agis?* Are you well?
JIMMY: Fine. Fine.
OWEN: And Bridget! Give us a kiss. Aaaaaah!
BRIDGET: You're welcome, Owen.
530 OWEN: It's not—? Yes, it *is* Maire Chatach! God! A young woman.
MAIRE: How are you, Owen?

(OWEN *is now in front of* HUGH. *He puts his two hands on his* FATHER'*s shoulders.*)

OWEN: And how's the old man himself?
HUGH: Fair—fair.
535 OWEN: Fair? For God's sake you never looked better! Come here to me. (*He embraces* HUGH *warmly and genuinely.*) Great to see you, Father. Great to be back.

(HUGH'*s eyes are moist—partly joy, partly the drink.*)

HUGH: I—I'm—I'm—pay no attention to—
OWEN: Come on—come on—come on—(*He gives* HUGH *his*
540 *handkerchief.*) Do you know what you and I are going to do tonight? We are going to go up to Anna na mBreag's . . .
DOALTY: Not there, Owen.
OWEN: Why not?
DOALTY: Her poteen's worse than ever.
545 BRIDGET: They say she puts frogs in it!
OWEN: All the better. (*To* HUGH.) And you and I are going to get footless drunk. That's arranged.

(OWEN *sees* MANUS *coming down the steps with tea and soda bread. They meet at the bottom.*)

And Manus!
MANUS: You're welcome, Owen.
550 OWEN: I know I am. And it's great to be here. (*He turns round, arms outstretched.*) I can't believe it. I come back after six years and everything's just as it was! Nothing's changed! Not a thing! (*Sniffs.*) Even that smell—that's the same smell this place always had. What is it anyway? Is it the
555 straw?
DOALTY: Jimmy Jack's feet.

(*General laughter. It opens little pockets of conversation round the room.*)

OWEN: And Doalty Dan Doalty hasn't changed either!
DOALTY: Bloody right, Owen.
OWEN: Jimmy, are you well?
560 JIMMY: Dodging about.
OWEN: Any word of the big day?

(*This is greeted with 'ohs' and 'ahs.'*)

Time enough, Jimmy. Homer's easier to live with, isn't he?
MAIRE: We heard stories that you own ten big shops in Dublin—is it true?
565 OWEN: Only nine.
BRIDGET: And you've twelve horses and six servants.

―――――――――
525–526 *Jacobe, quid agis?* James, how are you?

OWEN: Yes—that's true. God Almighty, would you listen to them—taking a hand at me!
MANUS: When did you arrive?
OWEN: We left Dublin yesterday morning, spent last night in 570 Omagh and got here half an hour ago.
MANUS: You're hungry then.
HUGH: Indeed—get him food—get him a drink.
OWEN: Not now, thanks; later. Listen—am I interrupting you all? 575
HUGH: By no means. We're finished for the day.
OWEN: Wonderful. I'll tell you why. Two friends of mine are waiting outside the door. They'd like to meet you and I'd like you to meet them. May I bring them in?
HUGH: Certainly. You'll all eat and have . . . 580
OWEN: Not just yet, Father. You've seen the sappers working in this area for the past fortnight, haven't you? Well, the older man is Captain Lancey . . .
HUGH: I've met Captain Lancey.
OWEN: Great. He's the cartographer in charge of this whole area. 585 Cartographer—James?

(OWEN *begins to play this game—his father's game—partly to involve his classroom audience, partly to show he has not forgotten it, and indeed partly because he enjoys it.*)

JIMMY: A maker of maps.
OWEN: Indeed—and the younger man that I travelled with from Dublin, his name is Lieutenant Yolland and he is attached to the toponymic department—Father?—*responde—* 590 *responde!*
HUGH: He gives names to places.
OWEN: Indeed—although he is in fact an orthographer— Doalty?—too slow—Manus?
MANUS: The correct spelling of those names. 595
OWEN: Indeed—indeed!

(OWEN *laughs and claps his hands. Some of the others join in.*)

Beautiful! Beautiful! Honest to God, it's such a delight to be back here with you all again—'civilized' people. Anyhow— may I bring them in?
HUGH: Your friends are our friends. 600
OWEN: I'll be straight back.

(*There is general talk as* OWEN *goes towards the door. He stops beside* SARAH.)

OWEN: That's a new face. Who are you?

(*A very brief hesitation. Then:—*)

SARAH: My name is Sarah.
OWEN: Sarah who?
SARAH: Sarah Johnny Sally. 605
OWEN: Of course! From Bun na hAbhann! I'm Owen—Owen Hugh Mor. From Baile Beag. Good to see you.

(*During this* OWEN—SARAH *exchange.*)

HUGH: Come on now. Let's tidy this place up. (*He rubs the top of his table with his sleeve.*) Move, Doalty—lift those books off the floor. 610

DOALTY: Right, Master; certainly, Master; I'm doing my best, Master.

(OWEN *stops at the door.*)

OWEN: One small thing, Father.
HUGH: *Silentium!*
615 OWEN: I'm on their pay-roll.

(SARAH, *very elated at her success, is beside* MANUS.)

SARAH: I said it, Manus!

(MANUS *ignores* SARAH. *He is much more interested in* OWEN *now.*)

MANUS: You haven't enlisted, have you?!

(SARAH *moves away.*)

OWEN: Me a soldier? I'm employed as a part-time, underpaid,
civilian interpreter. My job is to translate the quaint, archaic
620 tongue you people persist in speaking into the King's good
English.

(*He goes out.*)

HUGH: Move—move—move! Put some order on things! Come on,
Sarah—hide that bucket. Whose are these slates? Somebody
take these dishes away. *Festinate! Festinate!*

(MANUS *goes to* MAIRE *who is busy tidying.*)

625 MANUS: You didn't tell me you were definitely leaving.
MAIRE: Not now.
HUGH: Good girl, Bridget. That's the style.
MANUS: You might at least have told me.
HUGH: Are these your books, James?
630 JIMMY: Thank you.
MANUS: Fine! Fine! Go ahead! Go ahead!
MAIRE: You talk to me about getting married—with neither a
roof over your head nor a sod of ground under your foot. I
suggest you go for the new school; but no—'My father's in for
635 that.' Well now he's got it and now this is finished and now
you've nothing.
MANUS: I can always . . .
MAIRE: What? Teach classics to the cows? Agh—

(MAIRE *moves away from* MANUS. OWEN *enters with* LANCEY *and*
YOLLAND. CAPTAIN LANCEY *is middle-aged; a small, crisp officer,
expert in his field as cartographer but uneasy with people—especially civilians, especially these foreign civilians. His skill is with
deeds, not words.* LIEUTENANT YOLLAND *is in his late twenties/early
thirties. He is tall and thin and gangling, blond hair, a shy, awkward
manner. A soldier by accident.*)

OWEN: Here we are. Captain Lancey—my father.
640 LANCEY: Good evening.

(HUGH *becomes expansive, almost courtly, with his visitors.*)

HUGH: You and I have already met, sir.
LANCEY: Yes.
OWEN: And Lieutenant Yolland—both Royal Engineers—my
father.
HUGH: You're very welcome, gentlemen.   645
YOLLAND: How do you do.
HUGH: *Gaudeo vos hic adesse.*
OWEN: And I'll make no other introductions except that these
are some of the people of Baile Beag and—what?—well you're
among the best people in Ireland now. (*He pauses to allow*   650
LANCEY *to speak.* LANCEY *does not.*) Would you like to
say a few words, Captain?
HUGH: What about a drop, sir?
LANCEY: A what?
HUGH: Perhaps a modest refreshment? A little sampling of our   655
aqua vitae?
LANCEY: No, no.
HUGH: Later perhaps when—
LANCEY: I'll say what I have to say, if I may, and as briefly as
possible. Do they speak *any* English, Roland?   660
OWEN: Don't worry. I'll translate.
LANCEY: I see. (*He clears his throat. He speaks as if he were address-
ing children—a shade too loudly and enunciating excessively.*)
You may have seen me—seen me—working in this section—
section?—working. We are here—here—in this place—you   665
understand?—to make a map—a map—a map and—
JIMMY: *Nonne Latine loquitur?*

(HUGH *holds up a restraining hand.*)

HUGH: James.
LANCEY: (*To* JIMMY.) I do not speak Gaelic, sir.

(*He looks at* OWEN.)

OWEN: Carry on.   670
LANCEY: A map is a representation on paper—a picture—you
understand picture?—a paper picture—showing, representing
this country—yes?—showing your country in miniature—a
scaled drawing on paper of—of—of—

(*Suddenly* DOALTY *sniggers. Then* BRIDGET. *Then* SARAH. OWEN
leaps in quickly.)

OWEN: It might be better if you *assume* they understand you—   675
LANCEY: Yes?
OWEN: And I'll translate as you go along.
LANCEY: I see. Yes. Very well. Perhaps you're right. Well.
What we are doing is this. (*He looks at* OWEN. OWEN *nods
reassuringly.*) His Majesty's government has ordered the first   680
ever comprehensive survey of this entire country—a general
triangulation which will embrace detailed hydrographic and
topographic information and which will be executed to a scale
of six inches to the English mile.
HUGH: (*Pouring a drink.*) Excellent—excellent.   685

(LANCEY *looks at* OWEN.)

OWEN: A new map is being made of the whole country.

---

624 *Festinate!* hurry!

647 *Gaudeo . . . adesse* welcome   667 *Nonne Latine loquitur?* does he
not speak Latin?

(LANCEY *looks to* OWEN: *Is that all?* OWEN *smiles reassuringly and indicates to proceed.*)

LANCEY: This enormous task has been embarked on so that the military authorities will be equipped with up-to-date and accurate information on every corner of this part of the Empire.

690 OWEN: The job is being done by soldiers because they are skilled in this work.

LANCEY: And also so that the entire basis of land valuation can be reassessed for purposes of more equitable taxation.

OWEN: This new map will take the place of the estate agent's

695 map so that from now on you will know exactly what is yours in law.

LANCEY: In conclusion I wish to quote two brief extracts from the white paper which is our governing charter: (*Reads*) 'All former surveys of Ireland originated in forfeiture and violent

700 transfer of property; the present survey has for its object the relief which can be afforded to the proprietors and occupiers of land from unequal taxation.'

OWEN: The captain hopes that the public will cooperate with the sappers and that the new map will mean that taxes are

705 reduced.

HUGH: A worthy enterprise—*opus honestrum!* And Extract B?

LANCEY: 'Ireland is privileged. No such survey is being under-taken in England. So this survey cannot but be received as proof of the disposition of this government to advance the

710 interests of Ireland.' My sentiments, too.

OWEN: This survey demonstrates the government's interest in Ireland and the captain thanks you for listening so attentively to him.

HUGH: Our pleasure, Captain.

715 LANCEY: Lieutenant Yolland?

YOLLAND: I—I—I've nothing to say—really—

OWEN: The captain is the man who actually makes the new map. George's task is to see that the place-names on this map are . . . correct. (*To* YOLLAND.) Just a few words—

720 they'd like to hear you. (*To class.*) Don't you want to hear George, too?

MAIRE: Has he anything to say?

YOLLAND: (*To* MAIRE.) Sorry—sorry?

OWEN: She says she's dying to hear you.

725 YOLLAND: (*To* MAIRE.) Very kind of you—thank you . . . (*To class.*) I can only say that I feel—I feel very foolish to—to—to be working here and not to speak your language. But I intend to rectify that—with Roland's help—indeed I do.

OWEN: He wants me to teach him Irish!

730 HUGH: You are doubly welcome, sir.

YOLLAND: I think your countryside is—is—is—is very beautiful. I've fallen in love with it already. I hope we're not too—too crude an intrusion on your lives. And I know that I'm going to be happy, very happy, here.

735 OWEN: He is already a committed Hibernophile—

JIMMY: He loves—

OWEN: All right, Jimmy—we know—he loves Baile Beag; and he loves you all.

HUGH: Please . . . May I . . . ?

(HUGH *is now drunk. He holds on to the edge of the table.*)

740 OWEN: Go ahead, Father. (*Hands up for quiet.*) Please—please.

---

706 **opus honestrum** an honourable task

HUGH: And we, gentlemen, we in turn are happy to offer you our friendship, our hospitality, and every assistance that you may require. Gentlemen—welcome!

(*A few desultory claps. The formalities are over. General conversation. The soldiers meet the locals.* MANUS *and* OWEN *meet down stage.*)

OWEN: Lancey's a bloody ramrod but George's all right. How are you anyway?   745

MANUS: What sort of a translation was that, Owen?

OWEN: Did I make a mess of it?

MANUS: You weren't saying what Lancey was saying!

OWEN: 'Uncertainty in meaning is incipient poetry'—who said that?   750

MANUS: There was nothing uncertain about what Lancey said: it's a bloody military operation, Owen! And what's Yolland's function? What's 'incorrect' about the place-names we have here?

OWEN: Nothing at all. They're just going to be standardized.   755

MANUS: You mean changed into English?

OWEN: Where there's ambiguity, they'll be Anglicized.

MANUS: And they call you Roland! They both call you Roland!

OWEN: Shhhhh. Isn't it ridiculous? They seemed to get it wrong from the very beginning—or else they can't pronounce Owen.   760
I was afraid some of you bastards would laugh.

MANUS: Aren't you going to tell them?

OWEN: Yes—yes—soon—soon.

MANUS: But they . . .

OWEN: Easy, man, easy. Owen—Roland—what the hell. It's only a   765
name. It's the same me, isn't it? Well, isn't it?

MANUS: Indeed it is. It's the same Owen.

OWEN: And the same Manus. And in a way we complement each other. (*He punches* MANUS *lightly, playfully and turns to join the others. As he goes.*) All right—who has met whom? Isn't   770
this a job for the go-between?

(MANUS *watches* OWEN *move confidently across the floor, taking* MAIRE *by the hand and introducing her to* YOLLAND. HUGH *is trying to negotiate the steps.* JIMMY *is lost in a text.* DOALTY *and* BRIDGET *are reliving their giggling.* SARAH *is staring at* MANUS.)

ACT TWO

SCENE I

The sappers have already mapped most of the area. YOLLAND's *official task, which* OWEN *is now doing, is to take each of the Gaelic names—every hill, stream, rock, even every patch of ground which possessed its own distinctive Irish name—and Anglicize it, either by changing it into its approximate English sound or by translat-ing it into English words. For example, a Gaelic name like Cnoc Ban could become Knockban or—directly translated—Fair Hill. These new standardized names were entered into the Name-Book, and when the new maps appeared they contained all these new Anglicized names.* OWEN's *official function as translator is to pronounce each name in Irish and then provide the English translation.*

The hot weather continues. It is late afternoon some days later.

Stage right: an improvised clothes-line strung between the shafts of the cart and a nail in the wall; on it are some shirts and socks.

A large map—one of the new blank maps—is spread out on the floor. OWEN *is on his hands and knees, consulting it. He is totally engrossed in his task which he pursues with great energy and efficiency.*

YOLLAND's *hesitancy has vanished—he is at home here now. He is sitting on the floor, his long legs stretched out before him, his back resting against a creel, his eyes closed. His mind is elsewhere. One of the reference books—a church registry—lies open on his lap.*

Around them are various reference books, the Name-Book, a bottle of poteen, some cups, etc.

OWEN *completes an entry in the Name-Book and returns to the map on the floor.*

OWEN: Now. Where have we got to? Yes—the point where that stream enters the sea—that tiny little beach there. George!

YOLLAND: Yes. I'm listening. What do you call it? Say the Irish name again?

5 OWEN: Bun na hAbhann.

YOLLAND: Again.

OWEN: Bun na hAbhann.

YOLLAND: Bun na hAbhann.

OWEN: That's terrible, George.

10 YOLLAND: I know. I'm sorry. Say it again.

OWEN: Bun na hAbhann.

YOLLAND: Bun na hAbhann.

OWEN: That's better. Bun is the Irish word for bottom. And Abha means river. So it's literally the mouth of the river.

15 YOLLAND: Let's leave it alone. There's no English equivalent for a sound like that.

OWEN: What is it called in the church registry?

(Only now does YOLLAND *open his eyes.)*

YOLLAND: Let's see . . . Banowen.

OWEN: That's wrong. *(Consults text.)* The list of freeholders calls
20 it Owenmore—that's completely wrong: Owenmore's the big river at the west end of the parish. *(Another text.)* And in the grand jury lists it's called—God!—Binhone!—wherever they got that. I suppose we could Anglicize it to Bunowen; but somehow that's neither fish nor flesh.

*(*YOLLAND *closes his eyes again.)*

25 YOLLAND: I give up.

OWEN: *(At map.)* Back to first principles. What are we trying to do?

YOLLAND: Good question.

OWEN: We are trying to denominate and at the same time
30 describe that tiny area of soggy, rocky, sandy ground where that little stream enters the sea, an area known locally as Bun na hAbhann . . . Burnfoot! What about Burnfoot?

YOLLAND: *(Indifferently.)* Good, Roland, Burnfoot's good.

OWEN: George, my name isn't . . .

35 YOLLAND: B-u-r-n-f-o-o-t?

OWEN: Are you happy with that?

YOLLAND: Yes.

OWEN: Burnfoot it is then. *(He makes the entry into the Name-Book.)* Bun na hAbhann—B-u-r-n-

40 YOLLAND: You're becoming very skilled at this.

OWEN: We're not moving fast enough.

YOLLAND: *(Opens eyes again.)* Lancey lectured me again last night.

OWEN: When does he finish here?

YOLLAND: The sappers are pulling out at the end of the week. 45
The trouble is, the maps they've completed can't be printed without these names. So London screams at Lancey and Lancey screams at me. But I wasn't intimidated.

*(*MANUS *emerges from upstairs and descends.)*

'I'm sorry, sir,' I said, 'But certain tasks demand their own tempo. You cannot rename a whole country overnight.' 50
Your Irish air has made me bold. *(To* MANUS.) Do you want us to leave?

MANUS: Time enough. Class won't begin for another half-hour.

YOLLAND: Sorry—sorry?

OWEN: Can't you speak English? 55

*(*MANUS *gathers the things off the clothes-line.* OWEN *returns to the map.)*

OWEN: We now come across that beach . . .

YOLLAND: Tra—that's the Irish for beach. *(To* MANUS.) I'm picking up the odd word, Manus.

MANUS: So.

OWEN: . . . on past Burnfoot; and there's nothing around here 60
that has any name that I know of until we come down here to the south end, just about here . . . and there should be a ridge of rocks there . . . Have the sappers marked it? They have. Look, George.

YOLLAND: Where are we? 65

OWEN: There.

YOLLAND: I'm lost.

OWEN: Here. And the name of that ridge is Druim Dubh. Put English on that, Lieutenant.

YOLLAND: Say it again. 70

OWEN: Druim Dubh.

YOLLAND: Dubh means black.

OWEN: Yes.

YOLLAND: And Druim means . . . what? a fort?

OWEN: We met it yesterday in Druim Luachra. 75

YOLLAND: A ridge! The Black Ridge! *(To* MANUS.) You see, Manus?

OWEN: We'll have you fluent at the Irish before the summer's over.

YOLLAND: Oh, I wish I were. *(To* MANUS *as he crosses to go back* 80
upstairs.) We got a crate of oranges from Dublin today. I'll send some up to you.

MANUS: Thanks. *(To* OWEN.) Better hide that bottle. Father's just up and he'd be better without it.

OWEN: Can't you speak English before your man? 85

MANUS: Why?

OWEN: Out of courtesy.

MANUS: Doesn't he want to learn Irish? *(To* YOLLAND.) Don't you want to learn Irish?

YOLLAND: Sorry—sorry? I—I— 90

MANUS: I understand the Lanceys perfectly but people like you puzzle me.

OWEN: Manus, for God's sake!

MANUS: *(Still to* YOLLAND.) How's the work going?

95 YOLLAND: The work?—the work? Oh, it's—it's staggering
along—I think—(*To* OWEN.)—isn't it? But we'd be lost
without Roland.

MANUS: (*Leaving.*) I'm sure. But there are always the Rolands,
aren't there?

(*He goes upstairs and exits.*)

100 YOLLAND: What was that he said?—something about Lancey,
was it?

OWEN: He said we should hide that bottle before Father gets his
hands on it.

YOLLAND: Ah.

105 OWEN: He's always trying to protect him.

YOLLAND: Was he lame from birth?

OWEN: An accident when he was a baby: Father fell across his
cradle. That's why Manus feels so responsible for him.

YOLLAND: Why doesn't he marry?

110 OWEN: Can't afford to, I suppose.

YOLLAND: Hasn't he a salary?

OWEN: What salary? All he gets is the odd shilling Father
throws him—and that's seldom enough. I got out in time,
didn't I?

(YOLLAND *is pouring a drink.*)

115 Easy with that stuff—it'll hit you suddenly.

YOLLAND: I like it.

OWEN: Let's get back to the job. Druim Dubh—what's it called in
the jury lists? (*Consults texts.*)

YOLLAND: Some people here resent us.

120 OWEN: Dramduff—wrong as usual.

YOLLAND: I was passing a little girl yesterday and she spat
at me.

OWEN: And it's Drimdoo here. What's it called in the registry?

YOLLAND: Do you know the Donnelly twins?

125 OWEN: Who?

YOLLAND: The Donnelly twins.

OWEN: Yes. Best fishermen about here. What about them?

YOLLAND: Lancey's looking for them.

OWEN: What for?

130 YOLLAND: He wants them for questioning.

OWEN: Probably stolen somebody's nets. Dramduffy! Nobody
ever called it Dramduffy. Take your pick of those three.

YOLLAND: My head's addled. Let's take a rest. Do you want a
drink?

135 OWEN: Thanks. Now, every Dubh we've come across we've
changed to Duff. So if we're to be consistent, I suppose Druim
Dubh has to become Dromduff.

(YOLLAND *is now looking out the window.*)

You can see the end of the ridge from where you're
standing. But D-r-u-m- or D-r-o-m-? (*Name-Book.*) Do you
140 remember—which did we agree on for Druim Luachra?

YOLLAND: That house immediately above where we're
camped—

OWEN: Mm?

YOLLAND: The house where Maire lives.

145 OWEN: Maire? Oh, Maire Chatach.

YOLLAND: What does that mean?

OWEN: Curly-haired; the whole family are called the Chatachs.
What about it?

YOLLAND: I hear music coming from that house almost every
150 night.

OWEN: Why don't you drop in?

YOLLAND: Could I?

OWEN: Why not? We used D-r-o-m then. So we've got to call it
D-r-o-m-d-u-f-f—all right?

155 YOLLAND: Go back up to where the new school is being built
and just say the names again for me, would you?

OWEN: That's a good idea. Poolkerry, Ballybeg—

YOLLAND: No, no; as they still are—in your own language.

OWEN: Poll na gCaorach,

(YOLLAND *repeats the names silently after him.*)

Baile Beag, Ceann Balor, Lis Maol, Machaire Buidhe, Baile   160
na gGall, Carraig na Ri, Mullach Dearg—

YOLLAND: Do you think I could live here?

OWEN: What are you talking about?

YOLLAND: Settle down here—live here.

165 OWEN: Come on, George.

YOLLAND: I mean it.

OWEN: Live on what? Potatoes? Buttermilk?

YOLLAND: It's really heavenly.

OWEN: For God's sake! The first hot summer in fifty years and
you think it's Eden. Don't be such a bloody romantic. You   170
wouldn't survive a mild winter here.

YOLLAND: Do you think not? Maybe you're right.

(DOALTY *enters in a rush.*)

DOALTY: Hi, boys, is Manus about?

OWEN: He's upstairs. Give him a shout.

DOALTY: Manus! The cattle's going mad in that heat—Cripes,   175
running wild all over the place. (*To* YOLLAND.) How are you
doing, skipper?

(MANUS *appears.*)

YOLLAND: Thank you for—I—I'm very grateful to you for—

DOALTY: Wasting your time. I don't know a word you're saying.
Hi, Manus, there's two bucks down the road there asking   180
for you.

MANUS: (*Descending.*) Who are they?

DOALTY: Never clapped eyes on them. They want to talk to you.

MANUS: What about?

DOALTY: They wouldn't say. Come on. The bloody beasts'll end up   185
in Loch an Iubhair if they're not capped. Good luck, boys!

(DOALTY *rushes off.* MANUS *follows him.*)

OWEN: Good luck! What were you thanking Doalty for?

YOLLAND: I was washing outside my tent this morning and he
was passing with a scythe across his shoulder and he came
up to me and pointed to the long grass and then cut a pathway   190
round my tent and from the tent down to the road—so that
my feet won't get wet with the dew. Wasn't that kind of him?
And I have no words to thank him . . . I suppose you're right: I
suppose I couldn't live here . . . Just before Doalty came up to
me this morning, I was thinking that at that moment I might   195

have been in Bombay instead of Ballybeg. You see, my father
was at his wits end with me and finally he got me a job with
the East India Company—some kind of a clerkship. That was
ten, eleven months ago. So I set off for London. Unfortunately
200 I—I—I missed the boat. Literally. And since I couldn't face
Father and hadn't enough money to hang about until the
next sailing, I joined the army. And they stuck me into the
Engineers and posted me to Dublin. And Dublin sent me here.
And while I was washing this morning and looking across
205 the Tra Bhan, I was thinking how very, very lucky I am to be
here and not in Bombay.

OWEN: Do you believe in fate?

YOLLAND: Lancey's so like my father. I was watching him last
night. He met every group of sappers as they reported in.
210 He checked the field kitchens. He examined the horses.
He inspected every single report—even examining the
texture of the paper and commenting on the neatness of the
handwriting. The perfect colonial servant: not only must
the job be done—it must be done with excellence. Father has
215 that drive, too; that dedication; that indefatigable energy.
He builds roads—hopping from one end of the Empire to
the other. Can't sit still for five minutes. He says himself the
longest time he ever sat still was the night before Waterloo
when they were waiting for Wellington to make up his mind
220 to attack.

OWEN: What age is he?

YOLLAND: Born in 1789—the very day the Bastille fell. I've
often thought maybe that gave his whole life its character.
Do you think it could? He inherited a new world the day he
225 was born—The Year One. Ancient time was at an end. The
world had cast off its old skin. There were no longer any
frontiers to man's potential. Possibilities were endless and
exciting. He still believes that. The Apocalypse is just about
to happen . . . I'm afraid I'm a great disappointment to him.
230 I've neither his energy, nor his coherence, nor his belief. Do
I believe in fate? The day I arrived in Ballybeg—no, Baile
Beag—the moment you brought me in here, I had a curious
sensation. It's difficult to describe. It was a momentary sense
of discovery; no—not quite a sense of discovery—a sense
235 of recognition, of confirmation of some-thing I half knew
instinctively; as if I had stepped . . .

OWEN: Back into ancient time?

YOLLAND: No, no. It wasn't an awareness of *direction* being
changed but of experience being of a totally different order.
240 I had moved into a consciousness that wasn't striving nor
agitated, but at its ease and with its own conviction and
assurance. And when I heard Jimmy Jack and your father
swapping stories about Apollo and Cuchulainn and Paris
and Ferdia—as if they lived down the road—it was then
245 that I thought—I knew—perhaps I could live here . . . (*Now
embarrassed.*) Where's the poteen?

OWEN: Poteen.

YOLLAND: Poteen—poteen—poteen. Even if I did speak Irish
I'd always be an outsider here, wouldn't I? I may learn the
250 password but the language of the tribe will always elude
me, won't it? The private core will always be . . . hermetic,
won't it?

OWEN: You can learn to decode us.

(HUGH *emerges from upstairs and descends. He is dressed for the
road. Today he is physically and mentally jaunty and alert—
almost self-consciously jaunty and alert. Indeed, as the scene*

*progresses, one has the sense that he is deliberately parodying
himself. The moment* HUGH *gets to the bottom of the steps*
YOLLAND *leaps respectfully to his feet.*)

HUGH: (*As he descends.*)
255 *Quantumvis cursum longum fessumque moratur
Sol, sacro tandem carmine vesper adest.*
I dabble in verse, Lieutenant, after the style of Ovid.
(*To* OWEN.) A drop of that to fortify me.

YOLLAND: You'll have to translate it for me.

HUGH: Let's see—
260 No matter how long the sun may linger on his long and
weary journey
At length evening comes with its sacred song.

YOLLAND: Very nice, sir.

HUGH: English succeeds in making it sound . . . plebeian.

OWEN: Where are you off to, Father?
265 HUGH: An *expeditio* with three purposes. Purpose A: to acquire a
testimonial from our parish priest—(*To* YOLLAND.) a worthy
man but barely literate; and since he'll ask me to write it myself,
how in all modesty can I do myself justice? (*To* OWEN.) Where
did this [*drink*] come from?
270 OWEN: Anna na mBreag's.

HUGH: (*To* YOLLAND.) In that case address yourself to it with
circumspection. (*And* HUGH *instantly tosses the drink back in
one gulp and grimaces.*) Aaaaaaagh! (*Holds out his glass for a
refill.*) Anna na mBreag means Anna of the Lies. And Purpose
275 B: to talk to the builders of the new school about the kind of
living accommodation I will require there. I have lived too
long like a journeyman tailor.

YOLLAND: Some years ago we lived fairly close to a poet—well,
280 about three miles away.

HUGH: His name?

YOLLAND: Wordsworth—William Wordsworth.

HUGH: Did he speak of me to you?

YOLLAND: Actually I never talked to him. I just saw him out
285 walking—in the distance.

HUGH: Wordsworth? . . . No. I'm afraid we're not familiar with
your literature, Lieutenant. We feel closer to the warm
Mediterranean. We tend to overlook your island.

YOLLAND: I'm learning to speak Irish, sir.
290 HUGH: Good.

YOLLAND: Roland's teaching me.

HUGH: Splendid.

YOLLAND: I mean—I feel so cut off from the people here. And I
was trying to explain a few minutes ago how remarkable
295 a community this is. To meet people like yourself and
Jimmy Jack who actually converse in Greek and Latin. And
your place names—what was the one we came across this
morning?—Termon, from Terminus, the god of boundaries.
It—it—it's really astonishing.
300 HUGH: We like to think we endure around truths immemorially
posited.

YOLLAND: And your Gaelic literature—you're a poet yourself—

HUGH: Only in Latin, I'm afraid.

YOLLAND: I understand it's enormously rich and ornate.
305 HUGH: Indeed, Lieutenant. A rich language. A rich literature.
You'll find, sir, that certain cultures expend on their

<hr>

II.i. **255–256 Quantumvis . . . adest** no matter how long the sun delays
on his long weary course / At length evening comes with its sacred song
266 expeditio an expedition

vocabularies and syntax acquisitive energies and ostentations entirely lacking in their material lives. I suppose you could call us a spiritual people.

310 OWEN: (*Not unkindly; more out of embarrassment before* YOLLAND.) Will you stop that nonsense, Father.

HUGH: Nonsense? What nonsense?

OWEN: Do you know where the priest lives?

HUGH: At Lis na Muc, over near . . .

315 OWEN: No, he doesn't. Lis na Muc, the Fort of the Pigs, has become Swinefort. (*Now turning the pages of the Name-Book—a page per name.*) And to get to Swinefort you pass through Greencastle and Fair Head and Strandhill and Gort and Whiteplains. And the new school isn't at Poll na

320 gCaorach—it's at Sheepsrock. Will you be able to find your way?

(HUGH *pours himself another drink. Then:—*)

HUGH: Yes, it is a rich language, Lieutenant, full of the mythologies of fantasy and hope and self-deception—a syntax opulent with tomorrows. It is our response to mud cabins

325 and a diet of potatoes; and our only method of replying to . . . inevitabilities. (*To* OWEN.) Can you give me the loan of half-a-crown? I'll repay you out of the subscriptions I'm collecting for the publication of my new book. (*To* YOLLAND.) It is entitled: 'The Pentaglot Preceptor or Elementary

330 Institute of the English, Greek, Hebrew, Latin and Irish Languages; Particularly Calculated for the Instruction of Such Ladies and Gentlemen as may Wish to Learn without the Help of a Master.'

YOLLAND: (*Laughs.*) That's a wonderful title!

335 HUGH: Between ourselves—the best part of the enterprise. Nor do I, in fact, speak Hebrew. And that last phrase—'without the Help of a Master'—that was written before the new national school was thrust upon me—do you think I ought to drop it now? After all you don't dispose of the cow just because it has

340 produced a magnificent calf, do you?

YOLLAND: You certainly do not.

HUGH: The phrase goes. And I'm interrupting work of moment. (*He goes to the door and stops there.*) To return briefly to that other matter, Lieutenant. I understand your sense of

345 exclusion, of being cut off from a life here; and I trust you will find access to us with my son's help. But remember that words are signals, counters. They are not immortal. And it can happen—to use an image you'll understand—it can happen that a civilization can be imprisoned in a linguistic

350 contour which no longer matches the landscape of . . . fact. Gentlemen. (*He leaves.*)

OWEN: 'An *expeditio* with three purposes': the children laugh at him: he always promises three points and he never gets beyond A and B.

355 YOLLAND: He's an astute man.

OWEN: He's bloody pompous.

YOLLAND: But so astute.

OWEN: And he drinks too much. Is it astute not to be able to adjust for survival? Enduring around truths immemorially

360 posited—hah!

YOLLAND: He knows what's happening.

OWEN: What is happening?

YOLLAND: I'm not sure. But I'm concerned about my part in it. It's an eviction of sorts.

365 OWEN: We're making a six-inch map of the country. Is there something sinister in that?

YOLLAND: Not in—

OWEN: And we're taking place-names that are riddled with confusion and—

370 YOLLAND: Who's confused? Are the people confused?

OWEN: —and we're standardizing those names as accurately and as sensitively as we can.

YOLLAND: Something is being eroded.

OWEN: Back to the romance again. All right! Fine! Fine! Look

375 where we've got to. (*He drops on his hands and knees and stabs a finger at the map.*) We've come to this crossroads. Come here and look at it, man! Look at it! And we call that crossroads Tobair Vree. And why do we call it Tobair Vree? I'll tell you why. Tobair means a well. But what does Vree

380 mean? It's a corruption of Brian—(*Gaelic pronunciation.*) Brian—an erosion of Tobair Bhriain. Because a hundred-and-fifty years ago there used to be a well there, not at the crossroads, mind you—that would be too simple—but in a field close to the crossroads. And an old man called Brian,

385 whose face was disfigured by an enormous growth, got it into his head that the water in that well was blessed; and every day for seven months he went there and bathed his face in it. But the growth didn't go away; and one morning Brian was found drowned in that well. And ever since that

390 crossroads is known as Tobair Vree—even though that well has long since dried up. I know the story because my grandfather told it to me. But ask Doalty—or Maire—or Bridget—even my father—even Manus—why it's called Tobair Vree; and do you think they'll know? I know they

395 don't know. So the question I put to you, Lieutenant, is this: what do we do with a name like that? Do we scrap Tobair Vree altogether and call it—what?—The Cross? Crossroads? Or do we keep piety with a man long dead, long forgotten, his name 'eroded' beyond recognition, whose trivial little

400 story nobody in the parish remembers?

YOLLAND: Except you.

OWEN: I've left here.

YOLLAND: You remember it.

OWEN: I'm asking you: what do we write in the Name-Book?

405 YOLLAND: Tobair Vree.

OWEN: Even though the well is a hundred yards from the actual crossroads—and there's no well anyway—and what the hell does Vree mean?

YOLLAND: Tobair Vree.

OWEN: That's what you want?

410 YOLLAND: Yes.

OWEN: You're certain?

YOLLAND: Yes.

OWEN: Fine. Fine. That's what you'll get.

YOLLAND: That's what you want, too, Roland.

415 (*Pause.*)

OWEN: (*Explodes.*) George! For God's sake! My name is not Roland!

YOLLAND: What?

OWEN: (*Softly.*) My name is Owen.

(*Pause.*)

YOLLAND: Not Roland?

OWEN: Owen. 420

YOLLAND: You mean to say—?
OWEN: Owen.
YOLLAND: But I've been—
OWEN: O-w-e-n.
425 YOLLAND: Where did Roland come from?
OWEN: I don't know.
YOLLAND: It was never Roland?
OWEN: Never.
YOLLAND: O my God!

(*Pause. They stare at one another. Then the absurdity of the situation strikes them suddenly. They explode with laughter.* OWEN *pours drinks. As they roll about, their lines overlap.*)

430 YOLLAND: Why didn't you tell me?
OWEN: Do I look like a Roland?
YOLLAND: Spell Owen again.
OWEN: I was getting fond of Roland.
YOLLAND: O my God!
435 OWEN: O-w-e-n.
YOLLAND: What'll we write—
OWEN: —in the Name-Book?!
YOLLAND: R-o-w-e-n!
OWEN: Or what about Ol-
440 YOLLAND: Ol-what?
OWEN: Oland!

(*And again they explode.* MANUS *enters. He is very elated.*)

MANUS: What's the celebration?
OWEN: A christening!
YOLLAND: A baptism!
445 OWEN: A hundred christenings!
YOLLAND: A thousand baptisms! Welcome to Eden!
OWEN: Eden's right! We name a thing and—bang!—it leaps into existence!
YOLLAND: Each name a perfect equation with its roots.
450 OWEN: A perfect congruence with its reality. (*To* MANUS.) Take a drink.
YOLLAND: Poteen—beautiful.
OWEN: Lying Anna's poteen.
YOLLAND: Anna na mBreag's poteen.
455 OWEN: Excellent, George.
YOLLAND: I'll decode you yet.
OWEN: (*Offers drink.*) Manus?
MANUS: Not if that's what it does to you.
OWEN: You're right. Steady—steady—sober up—sober up.
460 YOLLAND: Sober as a judge, Owen.

(MANUS *moves beside* OWEN.)

MANUS: I've got good news! Where's Father?
OWEN: He's gone out. What's the good news?
MANUS: I've been offered a job.
OWEN: Where? (*Now aware of* YOLLAND.) Come on, man—speak
465 in English.
MANUS: For the benefit of the colonist?
OWEN: He's a decent man.
MANUS: Aren't they all at some level?
OWEN: Please.

(MANUS *shrugs.*)

He's been offered a job. 470
YOLLAND: Where?
OWEN: Well—tell us!
MANUS: I've just had a meeting with two men from Inis Meadhon. They want me to go there and start a hedge-school. They're giving me a free house, free turf, and free milk; a rood of 475
standing corn; twelve drills of potatoes; and—

(*He stops.*)

OWEN: And what?
MANUS: A salary of £42 a year!
OWEN: Manus, that's wonderful!
MANUS: You're talking to a man of substance. 480
OWEN: I'm delighted.
YOLLAND: Where's Inis Meadhon?
OWEN: An island south of here. And they came looking for you?
MANUS: Well, I mean to say . . . 485

(OWEN *punches* MANUS.)

OWEN: Aaaaagh! This calls for a real celebration.
YOLLAND: Congratulations.
MANUS: Thank you.
OWEN: Where are you, Anna?
YOLLAND: When do you start? 490
MANUS: Next Monday.
OWEN: We'll stay with you when we're there. (*To* YOLLAND.) How long will it be before we reach Inis Meadhon?
YOLLAND: How far south is it?
MANUS: About fifty miles. 495
YOLLAND: Could we make it by December?
OWEN: We'll have Christmas together. (*Sings.*) 'Christmas Day on Inis Meadhon . . .'
YOLLAND: (*Toast.*) I hope you're very content there, Manus.
MANUS: Thank you. 500

(YOLLAND *holds out his hand.* MANUS *takes it. They shake warmly.*)

OWEN: (*Toast.*) Manus.
MANUS: (*Toast.*) To Inis Meadhon.

(*He drinks quickly and turns to leave.*)

OWEN: Hold on—hold on—refills coming up.
MANUS: I've got to go.
OWEN: Come on, man; this is an occasion. Where are you 505
rushing to?
MANUS: I've got to tell Maire.

(MAIRE *enters with her can of milk.*)

MAIRE: You've got to tell Maire what?
OWEN: He's got a job!
MAIRE: Manus? 510
OWEN: He's been invited to start a hedge-school in Inis Meadhon.
MAIRE: Where?
MANUS: Inis Meadhon—the island! They're giving me £42 a year and . . . 515
OWEN: A house, fuel, milk, potatoes, corn, pupils, what-not!

MANUS: I start on Monday.
OWEN: You'll take a drink. Isn't it great?
MANUS: I want to talk to you for—
520 MAIRE: There's your milk. I need the can back.

(MANUS *takes the can and runs up the steps.*)

MANUS: (*As he goes.*) How will you like living on an island?
OWEN: You know George, don't you?
MAIRE: We wave to each other across the fields.
YOLLAND: Sorry-sorry?
525 OWEN: She says you wave to each other across the fields.
YOLLAND: Yes, we do; oh, yes; indeed we do.
MAIRE: What's he saying?
OWEN: He says you wave to each other across the fields.
MAIRE: That's right. So we do.
530 YOLLAND: What's she saying?
OWEN: Nothing—nothing—nothing. (*To* MAIRE.) What's the news?

(MAIRE *moves away, touching the text books with her toe.*)

MAIRE: Not a thing. You're busy, the two of you.
OWEN: We think we are.
535 MAIRE: I hear the Fiddler O'Shea's about. There's some talk of a dance tomorrow night.
OWEN: Where will it be?
MAIRE: Maybe over the road. Maybe at Tobair Vree.
YOLLAND: Tobair Vree!
540 MAIRE: Yes.
YOLLAND: Tobair Vree! Tobair Vree!
MAIRE: Does he know what I'm saying?
OWEN: Not a word.
MAIRE: Tell him then.
545 OWEN: Tell him what?
MAIRE: About the dance.
OWEN: Maire says there may be a dance tomorrow night.
YOLLAND: (*To* OWEN.) Yes? May I come? (*To* MAIRE.) Would anybody object if I came?
550 MAIRE: (*To* OWEN.) What's he saying?
OWEN: (*To* YOLLAND.) Who would object?
MAIRE: (*To* OWEN.) Did you tell him?
YOLLAND: (*To* MAIRE.) Sorry-sorry?
OWEN: (*To* MAIRE.) He says may he come?
555 MAIRE: (*To* YOLLAND.) That's up to you.
YOLLAND: (*To* OWEN.) What does she say?
OWEN: (*To* YOLLAND.) She says—
YOLLAND: (*To* MAIRE.) What-what?
MAIRE: (*To* OWEN.) Well?
560 YOLLAND: (*To* OWEN.) Sorry-sorry?
OWEN: (*To* OLLAND.) Will you go?
YOLLAND: (*To* MAIRE.) Yes, yes, if I may.
MAIRE: (*To* OWEN.) What does he say?
YOLLAND: (*To* OWEN.) What is she saying?
565 OWEN: Oh for God's sake! (*To* MANUS *who is descending with the empty can.*) You take on this job, Manus.
MANUS: I'll walk you up to the house. Is your mother at home? I want to talk to her.
MAIRE: What's the rush? (*To* OWEN.) Didn't you offer me a drink?
570 OWEN: Will you risk Anna na mBreag?
MAIRE: Why not.

(YOLLAND *is suddenly intoxicated. He leaps up on a stool, raises his glass and shouts.*)

YOLLAND: Anna na mBreag! Baile Beag! Inis Meadhon! Bombay! Tobair Vree! Eden! And poteen—correct, Owen?
OWEN: Perfect.
YOLLAND: And bloody marvellous stuff it is, too. I love it! Bloody,   575 bloody, bloody marvellous!

(*Simultaneously with his final 'bloody marvellous' bring up very loud the introductory music of the reel. Then immediately go to black. Retain the music throughout the very brief interval.*)

SCENE II

The following night.

This scene may be played in the schoolroom, but it would be prefer-able to lose—by lighting—as much of the schoolroom as possible, and to play the scene down front in a vaguely 'outside' area.

The music rises to a crescendo. Then in the distance we hear MAIRE *and* YOLLAND *approach—laughing and running. They run on, hand-in-hand. They have just left the dance. Fade the music to distant background. Then after a time it is lost and replaced by guitar music.* MAIRE *and* YOLLAND *are now down front, still holding hands and excited by their sudden and impetuous escape from the dance.*

MAIRE: O my God, that leap across the ditch nearly killed me.
YOLLAND: I could scarcely keep up with you.
MAIRE: Wait till I get my breath back.
YOLLAND: We must have looked as if we were being chased.

(*They now realize they are alone and holding hands—the beginnings of embarrassment. The hands disengage. They begin to drift apart. Pause.*)

MAIRE: Manus'll wonder where I've got to.   5
YOLLAND: I wonder did anyone notice us leave.

(*Pause. Slightly further apart.*)

MAIRE: The grass must be wet. My feet are soaking.
YOLLAND: Your feet must be wet. The grass is soaking.

(*Another pause. Another few paces apart. They are now a long distance from one another.*)

YOLLAND: (*Indicating himself.*) George.

(MAIRE *nods: Yes-yes. Then:—*)

MAIRE: Lieutenant George.   10
YOLLAND: Don't call me that. I never think of myself as Lieutenant.
MAIRE: What-what?
YOLLAND: Sorry-sorry? (*He points to himself again.*) George.

(MAIRE *nods: Yes-yes. Then points to herself.*)

MAIRE: Maire.   15

YOLLAND: Yes, I know you're Maire. Of course I know you're Maire. I mean I've been watching you night and day for the past—

MAIRE: (*Eagerly.*) What-what?

20 YOLLAND: (*Points.*) Maire. (*Points.*) George. (*Points both.*) Maire and George.

(MAIRE *nods: Yes-yes-yes.*)

I—I—I—

MAIRE: Say anything at all. I love the sound of your speech.

YOLLAND: (*Eagerly.*) Sorry-sorry?

(*In acute frustration he looks around, hoping for some inspiration that will provide him with communicative means. Now he has a thought: he tries raising his voice and articulating in a staccato style and with equal and absurd emphasis on each word.*)

25 Every-morning-I-see-you-feeding-brown-hens-and-giving-meal-to-black-calf—(*The futility of it.*)—Oh my God.

(MAIRE *smiles. She moves towards him. She will try to communicate in Latin.*)

MAIRE: *Tu es centurio in—in—in exercitu Britannico—*

YOLLAND: Yes-yes? Go on—go on—say anything at all—I love the sound of your speech.

30 MAIRE: —*et es in castris quae—quae—quae sunt in agro*—(*The futility of it.*)—O my God. (YOLLAND *smiles. He moves towards her. Now for her English words.*) George—water.

YOLLAND: 'Water'? Water! Oh yes—water—water—very good—water—good—good.

35 MAIRE: Fire.

YOLLAND: Fire—indeed—wonderful—fire, fire, fire—splendid—splendid!

MAIRE: Ah . . . ah . . .

YOLLAND: Yes? Go on.

40 MAIRE: Earth.

YOLLAND: 'Earth'?

MAIRE: Earth. Earth. (YOLLAND *still does not understand.* MAIRE *stoops down and picks up a handful of clay. Holding it out.*) Earth.

45 YOLLAND: Earth! Of course—earth! Earth. Earth. Good Lord, Maire, your English is perfect!

MAIRE: (*Eagerly.*) What-what?

YOLLAND: Perfect English. English perfect.

MAIRE: George—

50 YOLLAND: That's beautiful—oh, that's really beautiful.

MAIRE: George—

YOLLAND: Say it again—say it again—

MAIRE: Shhh. (*She holds her hand up for silence—she is trying to remember her one line of English. Now she remembers it and she delivers the line as if English were her language—easily, fluidly, conversationally.*) George, 'In Norfolk we besport ourselves around the maypoll.'

YOLLAND: Good God, do you? That's where my mother comes from—Norfolk. Norwich actually. Not exactly Norwich town but a small village called Little Walsingham close beside it.

60

But in our own village of Winfarthing we have a maypole too and every year on the first of May—(*He stops abruptly, only now realizing. He stares at her. She in turn misunderstands his excitement.*)

MAIRE: (*To herself.*) Mother of God, my Aunt Mary wouldn't have taught me something dirty, would she? 65

(*Pause.* YOLLAND *extends his hand to* MAIRE. *She turns away from him and moves slowly across the stage.*)

YOLLAND: Maire.

(*She still moves away.*)

Maire Chatach.

(*She still moves away.*)

Bun na hAbhann? (*He says the name softly, almost privately, very tentatively, as if he were searching for a sound she might respond to. He tries again.*) Druim Dubh? 70

(MAIRE *stops. She is listening.* YOLLAND *is encouraged.*)

Poll na gCaorach. Lis Maol.

(MAIRE *turns towards him.*)

Lis na nGall.

MAIRE: Lis na nGradh.

(*They are now facing each other and begin moving—almost imperceptibly—towards one another.*)

MAIRE: Carraig an Phoill. 75

YOLLAND: Carraig na Ri. Loch na nEan.

MAIRE: Loch an Iubhair. Machaire Buidhe.

YOLLAND: Machaire Mor. Cnoc na Mona.

MAIRE: Cnoc na nGabhar.

YOLLAND: Mullach. 80

MAIRE: Port.

YOLLAND: Tor.

MAIRE: Lag.

(*She holds out her hands to* YOLLAND. *He takes them. Each now speaks almost to himself/herself.*)

YOLLAND: I wish to God you could understand me.

MAIRE: Soft hands; a gentleman's hands. 85

YOLLAND: Because if you could understand me I could tell you how I spend my days either thinking of you or gazing up at your house in the hope that you'll appear even for a second.

MAIRE: Every evening you walk by yourself along the Tra Bhan and every morning you wash yourself in front of your tent. 90

YOLLAND: I would tell you how beautiful you are, curly-headed Maire. I would so like to tell you how beautiful you are.

MAIRE: Your arms are long and thin and the skin on your shoulders is very white.

YOLLAND: I would tell you . . . 95

MAIRE: Don't stop—I know what you're saying.

YOLLAND: I would tell you how I want to be here—to live here—always—with you—always, always.

II.ii. 27 *Tu . . . Britannico* you are a centurion in the British Army 30 *et . . . agro* and you are in the camp in the field

MAIRE: 'Always'? What is that word—'always'?

100 YOLLAND: Yes-yes; always.

MAIRE: You're trembling.

YOLLAND: Yes, I'm trembling because of you.

MAIRE: I'm trembling, too.

(*She holds his face in her hand.*)

YOLLAND: I've made up my mind . . .

105 MAIRE: Shhhh.

YOLLAND: I'm not going to leave here . . .

MAIRE: Shhhh—listen to me. I want you, too, soldier.

YOLLAND: Don't stop—I know what you're saying.

MAIRE: I want to live with you—anywhere—anywhere at

110   all— always—always.

YOLLAND: 'Always'? What is that word—'always'?

MAIRE: Take me away with you, George.

(*Pause. Suddenly they kiss.* SARAH *enters. She sees them. She stands shocked, staring at them. Her mouth works. Then almost to herself.*)

SARAH: Manus . . . Manus!

(SARAH *runs off. Music to crescendo.*)

ACT THREE

The following evening. It is raining.

SARAH *and* OWEN *alone in the schoolroom.* SARAH, *more waif-like than ever, is sitting very still on a stool, an open book across her knee. She is pretending to read but her eyes keep going up to the room upstairs.* OWEN *is working on the floor as before, surrounded by his reference books, map, Name-Book, etc. But he has neither concentration nor interest; and like* SARAH *he glances up at the upstairs room.*

After a few seconds MANUS *emerges and descends, carrying a large paper bag which already contains his clothes. His movements are determined and urgent. He moves around the classroom, picking up books, examining each title carefully, and choosing about six of them which he puts into his bag. As he selects these books:—*

OWEN: You know that old limekiln beyond Con Connie Tim's pub, the place we call The Murren?—do you know why it's called The Murren?

(MANUS *does not answer.*)

I've only just discovered: it's a corruption of Saint Muranus. It

5   seems Saint Muranus had a monastery somewhere about there at the beginning of the seventh century. And over the years the name became shortened to the Murren. Very unattractive name, isn't it? I think we should go back to the original—Saint Muranus. What do you think? The original's Saint Muranus.

10   Don't you think we should go back to that?

(*No response.* OWEN *begins writing the name into the Name-Book.* MANUS *is now rooting about among the forgotten implements for a piece of rope. He finds a piece. He begins to tie the mouth of the*

flimsy, overloaded bag—and it bursts, the contents spilling out on the floor.)

MANUS: Bloody, bloody, bloody hell!

(*His voice breaks in exasperation: he is about to cry.* OWEN *leaps to his feet.*)

OWEN: Hold on. I've a bag upstairs.

(*He runs upstairs.* SARAH *waits until* OWEN *is off. Then:—*)

SARAH: Manus . . . Manus, I . . .

(MANUS *hears* SARAH *but makes no acknowledgement. He gathers up his belongings.* OWEN *reappears with the bag he had on his arrival.*)

OWEN: Take this one—I'm finished with it anyway. And it's

supposed to keep out the rain.   15

(MANUS *transfers his few belongings.* OWEN *drifts back to his task. The packing is now complete.*)

MANUS: You'll be here for a while? For a week or two anyhow?

OWEN: Yes.

MANUS: You're not leaving with the army?

OWEN: I haven't made up my mind. Why?

MANUS: Those Inis Meadhon men will be back to see why   20

I haven't turned up. Tell them—tell them I'll write to them as soon as I can. Tell them I still want the job but that it might be three or four months before I'm free to go.

OWEN: You're being damned stupid, Manus.

MANUS: Will you do that for me?   25

OWEN: Clear out now and Lancey'll think you're involved somehow.

MANUS: Will you do that for me?

OWEN: Wait a couple of days even. You know George—he's

a bloody romantic—maybe he's gone out to one of the   30

islands and he'll suddenly reappear tomorrow morning. Or maybe the search party'll find him this evening lying drunk somewhere in the sandhills. You've seen him drinking that poteen—doesn't know how to handle it. Had he drink on him

last night at the dance?   35

MANUS: I had a stone in my hand when I went out looking for

him—I was going to fell him. The lame scholar turned violent.

OWEN: Did anybody see you?

MANUS: (*Again close to tears.*) But when I saw him standing there   40

at the side of the road—smiling—and her face buried in his shoulder—I couldn't even go close to them. I just shouted something stupid—something like, 'You're a bastard, Yolland.' If I'd even said it in English . . . 'cos he kept saying 'Sorry-

sorry?' The wrong gesture in the wrong language.   45

OWEN: And you didn't see him again?

MANUS: 'Sorry?'

OWEN: Before you leave tell Lancey that—just to clear yourself.

MANUS: What have I to say to Lancey? You'll give that message

to the islandmen?   50

OWEN: I'm warning you: run away now and you're bound to

be—

MANUS: (*To* SARAH.) Will you give that message to the Inis
        Meadhon men?
55 SARAH: I will.

(MANUS *picks up an old sack and throws it across his shoulders.*)

OWEN: Have you any idea where you're going?
MANUS: Mayo, maybe. I remember Mother saying she had
        cousins somewhere away out in the Erris Peninsula. (*He
        picks up his bag.*) Tell Father I took only the Virgil and the
60 Caesar and the Aeschylus because they're mine anyway—I
        bought them with the money I got for that pet lamb I reared—
        do you remember that pet lamb? And tell him that Nora Dan
        never returned the dictionary and that she still owes him
        two-and-six for last quarter's reading—he always forgets
65 those things.
OWEN: Yes.
MANUS: And his good shirt's ironed and hanging up in the press
        and his clean socks are in the butter-box under the bed.
OWEN: All right.
70 MANUS: And tell him I'll write.
OWEN: If Maire asks where you've gone . . . ?
MANUS: He'll need only half the amount of milk now, won't
        he? Even less than half—he usually takes his tea black.
        (*Pause.*) And when he comes in at night—you'll hear him;
75 he makes a lot of noise—I usually come down and give him
        a hand up. Those stairs are dangerous without a banister.
        Maybe before you leave you'd get Big Ned Frank to put up
        some sort of a handrail. (*Pause.*) And if you can bake, he's
        very fond of soda bread.
80 OWEN: I can give you money. I'm wealthy. Do you know what
        they pay me? Two shillings a day for this—this—this—

(MANUS *rejects the offer by holding out his hand.*)

        Goodbye, Manus.

(MANUS *and* OWEN *shake hands. Then* MANUS *picks up his bag
briskly and goes towards the door. He stops a few paces beyond
SARAH, turns, comes back to her. He addresses her as he did in Act
One but now without warmth or concern for her.*)

MANUS: What is your name? (*Pause.*) Come on. What is your
        name?
85 SARAH: My name is Sarah.
MANUS: Just Sarah? Sarah what? (*Pause.*) Well?
SARAH: Sarah Johnny Sally.
MANUS: And where do you live? Come on.
SARAH: I live in Bun na hAbhann.

(*She is now crying quietly.*)

90 MANUS: Very good, Sarah Johnny Sally. There's nothing to stop
        you now—nothing in the wide world. (*Pause. He looks down at
        her.*) It's all right—it's all right—you did no harm—you did no
        harm at all.

(*He stoops over her and kisses the top of her head—as if in absolu-
tion. Then briskly to the door and off.*)

OWEN: Good luck, Manus!
95 SARAH: (*Quietly.*) I'm sorry . . . I'm sorry . . . I'm so sorry,
        Manus . . .

(OWEN *tries to work but cannot concentrate. He begins folding up
the map. As he does:—*)

OWEN: Is there a class this evening?

(SARAH *nods:* Yes.)

        I suppose Father knows. Where is he anyhow?

(SARAH *points.*)

        Where?

(SARAH *mimes rocking a baby.*)

        I don't understand—where?   100

(SARAH *repeats the mime and wipes away tears.* OWEN *is still
puzzled.*)

        It doesn't matter. He'll probably turn up.

(BRIDGET *and* DOALTY *enter, sacks over their heads against the rain.
They are self-consciously noisier, more ebullient, more garrulous than
ever—brimming over with excitement and gossip and brio.*)

DOALTY: You're missing the crack, boys! Cripes, you're missing
        the crack! Fifty more soldiers arrived an hour ago!
BRIDGET: And they're spread out in a big line from Sean Neal's
        over to Lag and they're moving straight across the fields   105
        towards Cnoc na nGabhar!
DOALTY: Prodding every inch of the ground in front of them
        with their bayonets and scattering animals and hens in all
        directions!
BRIDGET: And tumbling everything before them—fences, ditches,   110
        haystacks, turf-stacks!
DOALTY: They came to Barney Petey's field of corn—straight
        through it be God as if it was heather!
BRIDGET: Not a blade of it left standing!
DOALTY: And Barney Petey just out of his bed and running after   115
        them in his drawers: 'You hoors you! Get out of my corn, you
        hoors you!'
BRIDGET: First time he ever ran in his life.
DOALTY: Too lazy, the wee get, to cut it when the weather was
        good.   120

(SARAH *begins putting out the seats.*)

BRIDGET: Tell them about Big Hughie.
DOALTY: Cripes, if you'd seen your aul fella, Owen.
BRIDGET: They were all inside in Anna na mBreag's pub—all
        the crowd from the wake—
DOALTY: And they hear the commotion and they all come out to   125
        the street—
BRIDGET: Your father in front; the Infant Prodigy footless
        behind him!
DOALTY: And your aul fella, he sees the army stretched across
        the countryside—   130
BRIDGET: O my God!
DOALTY: And Cripes he starts roaring at them!
BRIDGET: 'Visigoths! Huns! Vandals!'
DOALTY: '*Ignari! Stulti! Rustici!*'

135 BRIDGET: And wee Jimmy Jack jumping up and down and
     shouting, 'Thermopylae! Thermopylae!'
   DOALTY: You never saw crack like it in your life, boys. Come
     away on out with me, Sarah, and you'll see it all.
   BRIDGET: Big Hughie's fit to take no class. Is Manus about?
140 OWEN: Manus is gone.
   BRIDGET: Gone where?
   OWEN: He's left—gone away.
   DOALTY: Where to?
   OWEN: He doesn't know. Mayo, maybe.
145 DOALTY: What's on in Mayo?
   OWEN: (*To* BRIDGET.) Did you see George and Maire Chatach
     leave the dance last night?
   BRIDGET: We did. Didn't we, Doalty?
   OWEN: Did you see Manus following them out?
150 BRIDGET: I didn't see him going out but I saw him coming in by
     himself later.
   OWEN: Did George and Maire come back to the dance?
   BRIDGET: No.
   OWEN: Did you see them again?
155 BRIDGET: He left her home. We passed them going up the back
     road—didn't we, Doalty?
   OWEN: And Manus stayed till the end of the dance?
   DOALTY: We know nothing. What are you asking us for?
   OWEN: Because Lancey'll question me when he hears Manus's
160   gone. (*Back to* BRIDGET.) That's the way George went home?
     By the back road? That's where you saw him?
   BRIDGET: Leave me alone, Owen. I know nothing about Yolland.
     If you want to know about Yolland, ask the Donnelly twins.

(*Silence.* DOALTY *moves over to the window.*)

   (*To* SARAH.) He's a powerful fiddler, O'Shea, isn't he? He told
165   our Seamus he'll come back for a night at Hallowe'en.

(OWEN *goes to* DOALTY *who looks resolutely out the window.*)

   OWEN: What's this about the Donnellys? (*Pause.*) Were they about
     last night?
   DOALTY: Didn't see them if they were.

(*Begins whistling through his teeth.*)

   OWEN: George is a friend of mine.
170 DOALTY: So.
   OWEN: I want to know what's happened to him.
   DOALTY: Couldn't tell you.
   OWEN: What have the Donnelly twins to do with it? (*Pause.*)
     Doalty!
175 DOALTY: I know nothing, Owen—nothing at all—I swear to God.
     All I know is this: on my way to the dance I saw their boat
     beached at Port. It wasn't there on my way home, after
     I left Bridget. And that's all I know. As God's my judge. The
     half-dozen times I met him I didn't know a word he said to me;
180   but he seemed a right enough sort . . . (*With sudden excessive
     interest in the scene outside.*) Cripes, they're crawling all over
     the place! Cripes, there's millions of them! Cripes, they're
     levelling the whole land!

(OWEN *moves away.* MAIRE *enters. She is bareheaded and wet from
the rain; her hair in disarray. She attempts to appear normal but she
is in acute distress, on the verge of being distraught. She is carrying the
milk-can.*)

185 MAIRE: Honest to God, I must be going off my head. I'm halfway
     here and I think to myself, 'Isn't this can very light?' and I
     look into it and isn't it empty.
   OWEN: It doesn't matter.
   MAIRE: How will you manage for tonight?
   OWEN: We have enough.
190 MAIRE: Are you sure?
   OWEN: Plenty, thanks.
   MAIRE: It'll take me no time at all to go back up for some.
   OWEN: Honestly, Maire.
   MAIRE: Sure it's better you have it than that black calf that's . . .
     that . . . (*She looks around.*) Have you heard anything?
195
   OWEN: Nothing.
   MAIRE: What does Lancey say?
   OWEN: I haven't seen him since this morning.
   MAIRE: What does he *think*?
   OWEN: We really didn't talk. He was here for only a few seconds. 200
   MAIRE: He left me home, Owen. And the last thing he said to
     me—he tried to speak in Irish—he said, 'I'll see you yes-
     terday'—he meant to say 'I'll see you tomorrow.' And I
     laughed that much he pretended to get cross and he said
     'Maypoll! Maypoll!' because I said that word wrong. And off 205
     he went, laughing—laughing, Owen! Do you think he's all
     right? What do *you* think?
   OWEN: I'm sure he'll turn up, Maire.
   MAIRE: He comes from a tiny wee place called Winfarthing.
     (*She suddenly drops on her hands and knees on the floor—* 210
     where OWEN *had his map a few minutes ago—and with
     her finger traces out an outline map.*) Come here till you
     see. Look. There's Winfarthing. And there's two other
     wee villages right beside it; one of them's called Barton
     Bendish—it's there; and the other's called Saxingham 215
     Nethergate—it's about there. And there's Little Walsingham—
     that's his mother's townland. Aren't they odd names? Sure
     they make no sense to me at all. And Winfarthing's near
     a big town called Norwich. And Norwich is in a county
     called Norfolk. And Norfolk is in the east of England. He 220
     drew a map for me on the wet strand and wrote the names
     on it. I have it all in my head now: Winfarthing—Barton
     Bendish—Saxingham Nethergate—Little Walsingham—
     Norwich—Norfolk. Strange sounds, aren't they? But nice
     sounds; like Jimmy Jack reciting his Homer. (*She gets to* 225
     her feet and looks around; she is almost serene now. To
     SARAH.) You were looking lovely last night, Sarah. Is that
     the dress you got from Boston? Green suits you. (*To* OWEN.)
     Something very bad's happened to him, Owen. I know.
     He wouldn't go away without telling me. Where is he, 230
     Owen? You're his friend—where is he? (*Again she looks
     around the room; then sits on a stool.*) I didn't get a chance
     to do my geography last night. The master'll be angry
     with me. (*She rises again.*) I think I'll go home now.
     The wee ones have to be washed and put to bed and that 235
     black calf has to be fed . . . My hands are that rough; they're
     still blistered from the hay. I'm ashamed of them. I hope to
     God there's no hay to be saved in Brooklyn. (*She stops at
     the door.*) Did you hear? Nellie Ruadh's baby died in the
     middle of the night. I must go up to the wake. It didn't last
     long, did it? 240

(MAIRE *leaves. Silence. Then:*)

OWEN: I don't think there'll be any class. Maybe you should . . .

(OWEN *begins picking up his texts.* DOALTY *goes to him.*)

DOALTY: Is he long gone?—Manus?
OWEN: Half an hour.
DOALTY: Stupid bloody fool.
OWEN: I told him that.
245 DOALTY: Do they know he's gone?
OWEN: Who?
DOALTY: The army.
OWEN: Not yet.
DOALTY: They'll be after him like bloody beagles. Bloody, bloody
250 fool, limping along the coast. They'll overtake him before
night for Christ's sake.

(DOALTY *returns to the window.* LANCEY *enters—now the
commanding officer.*)

OWEN: Any news? Any word?

(LANCEY *moves into the centre of the room, looking around as he
does.*)

LANCEY: I understood there was a class. Where are the others?
OWEN: There was to be a class but my father—
255 LANCEY: This will suffice. I will address them and it will be their
responsibility to pass on what I have to say to every family in
this section.

(LANCEY *indicates to* OWEN *to translate.* OWEN *hesitates, trying to
assess the change in* LANCEY's *manner and attitude.*)

I'm in a hurry, O'Donnell.
OWEN: The captain has an announcement to make.
260 LANCEY: Lieutenant Yolland is missing. We are searching for him.
If we don't find him, or if we receive no information as to where
he is to be found, I will pursue the following course of action.
(*He indicates to* OWEN *to translate.*)
OWEN: They are searching for George. If they don't find him—
265 LANCEY: Commencing twenty-four hours from now we will shoot
all livestock in Ballybeg.

(OWEN *stares at* LANCEY.)

At once.
OWEN: Beginning this time tomorrow they'll kill every animal in
Baile Beag—unless they're told where George is.
270 LANCEY: If that doesn't bear results, commencing forty-eight hours
from now we will embark on a series of evictions and levelling
of every abode in the following selected areas—
OWEN: You're not—!
LANCEY: Do your job. Translate.
275 OWEN: If they still haven't found him in two days time they'll
begin evicting and levelling every house starting with these
townlands.

(LANCEY *reads from his list.*)

LANCEY: Swinefort.
OWEN: Lis na Muc.
280 LANCEY: Burnfoot.
OWEN: Bun na hAbhann.
LANCEY: Dromduff.

OWEN: Druim Dubh.
LANCEY: Whiteplains.
OWEN: Machaire Ban.   285
LANCEY: Kings Head.
OWEN: Cnoc na Ri.
LANCEY: If by then the lieutenant hasn't been found, we will
proceed until a complete clearance is made of this entire
section.   290
OWEN: If Yolland hasn't been got by then, they will ravish the
whole parish.
LANCEY: I trust they know exactly what they've got to do.
(*Pointing to* BRIDGET.) I know you. I know where you live.
(*Pointing to* SARAH.) Who are you? Name!   295

(SARAH's *mouth opens and shuts, opens and shuts. Her face
becomes contorted.*)

What's your name?

(*Again* SARAH *tries frantically.*)

OWEN: Go on, Sarah. You can tell him.

(*But* SARAH *cannot. And she knows she cannot. She closes her
mouth. Her head goes down.*)

OWEN: Her name is Sarah Johnny Sally.
LANCEY: Where does she live?
OWEN: Bun na hAbhann.   300
LANCEY: Where?
OWEN: Burnfoot.
LANCEY: I want to talk to your brother—is he here?
OWEN: Not at the moment.
LANCEY: Where is he?   305
OWEN: He's at a wake.
LANCEY: What wake?

(DOALTY, *who has been looking out the window all through*
LANCEY's *announcements, now speaks—calmly, almost casually.*)

DOALTY: Tell him his whole camp's on fire.
LANCEY: What's your name? (*To* OWEN.) Who's that lout?
OWEN: Doalty Dan Doalty.   310
LANCEY: Where does he live?
OWEN: Tulach Alainn.
LANCEY: What do we call it?
OWEN: Fair Hill. He says your whole camp is on fire.
                                                                     315
(LANCEY *rushes to the window and looks out. Then he wheels on*
DOALTY.)

LANCEY: I'll remember you, Mr Doalty. (*To* OWEN.) You carry a big
responsibility in all this.

(*He goes off.*)

BRIDGET: Mother of God, does he mean it, Owen?
OWEN: Yes, he does.
BRIDGET: We'll have to hide the beasts somewhere—our Seamus'll
know where. Maybe at the back of Lis na nGradh—or in the   320
caves at the far end of Tra Bhan. Come on, Doalty! Come on!
Don't be standing about there!

(DOALTY *does not move.* BRIDGET *runs to the door and stops suddenly. She sniffs the air. Panic.*)

The sweet smell! Smell it! It's the sweet smell! Jesus, it's the potato blight!

325   DOALTY: It's the army tents burning, Bridget.

BRIDGET: Is it? Are you sure? Is that what it is? God, I thought we were destroyed altogether. Come on! Come on!

(*She runs off.* OWEN *goes to* SARAH *who is preparing to leave.*)

OWEN: How are you? Are you all right?

(SARAH *nods:* Yes.)

OWEN: Don't worry. It will come back to you again.

330

(SARAH *shakes her head.*)

OWEN: It will. You're upset now. He frightened you. That's all's wrong.

(*Again* SARAH *shakes her head, slowly, emphatically, and smiles at* OWEN. *Then she leaves.* OWEN *busies himself gathering his belongings.* DOALTY *leaves the window and goes to him.*)

DOALTY: He'll do it, too.

OWEN: Unless Yolland's found.

DOALTY: Hah!

335   OWEN: Then he'll certainly do it.

DOALTY: When my grandfather was a boy they did the same thing. (*Simply, altogether without irony.*) And after all the trouble you went to, mapping the place and thinking up new names for it. (OWEN *busies himself. Pause.* DOALTY *almost*

340   *dreamily.*) I've damned little to defend but he'll not put me out without a fight. And there'll be others who think the same as me.

OWEN: That's a matter for you.

DOALTY: If we'd all stick together. If we knew how to defend

345   ourselves.

OWEN: Against a trained army.

DOALTY: The Donnelly twins know how.

OWEN: If they could be found.

DOALTY: If they could be found. (*He goes to the door.*) Give me

350   a shout after you've finished with Lancey. I might know something then.

(*He leaves.*)

(OWEN *picks up the Name-Book. He looks at it momentarily, then puts it on top of the pile he is carrying. It falls to the floor. He stoops to pick it up—hesitates—leaves it. He goes upstairs. As* OWEN *ascends,* HUGH *and* JIMMY JACK *enter. Both wet and drunk.* JIMMY *is very unsteady. He is trotting behind* HUGH, *trying to break in on* HUGH's *declamation.* HUGH *is equally drunk but more experienced in drunkenness: there is a portion of his mind which retains its clarity.*)

HUGH: There I was, appropriately dispositioned to proffer my condolences to the bereaved mother . . .

JIMMY: Hugh—

HUGH: and about to enter the *domus lugubris*—Maire   3
Chatach?

JIMMY: The wake house.

HUGH: Indeed—when I experience a plucking at my elbow: Mister George Alexander, Justice of the Peace. 'My tidings are infelicitous,' said he—Bridget? Too slow. Doalty?   360

JIMMY: *Infelix*—unhappy.

HUGH: Unhappy indeed. 'Master Bartley Timlin has been appointed to the new national school.' 'Timlin? Who is Timlin?' 'A schoolmaster from Cork. And he will be a major asset to the community: he is also a very skilled bacon-curer!'   365

JIMMY: Hugh—

HUGH: Ha-ha-ha-ha-ha! The Cork bacon-curer! *Barbarus hic ego sum quia non intelligor ulli*—James?

JIMMY: Ovid.

HUGH: *Procede.*   370

JIMMY: 'I am a barbarian in this place because I am not understood by anyone.'

HUGH: Indeed—(*Shouts.*) Manus! Tea! I will compose a satire on Master Bartley Timlin, schoolmaster and bacon-curer. But it will be too easy, won't it? (*Shouts.*) Strong tea! Black!   375

(*The only way* JIMMY *can get* HUGH's *attention is by standing in front of him and holding his arms.*)

JIMMY: Will you listen to me, Hugh!

HUGH: James. (*Shouts.*) And a slice of soda bread.

JIMMY: I'm going to get married.

HUGH: Well!

JIMMY: At Christmas.   380

HUGH: Splendid.

JIMMY: To Athene.

HUGH: Who?

JIMMY: Pallas Athene.

HUGH: *Glaukopis Athene?*   385

JIMMY: Flashing-eyed, Hugh, flashing-eyed!

(*He attempts the gesture he has made before: standing to attention, the momentary spasm, the salute, the face raised in pained ecstasy—but the body does not respond efficiently this time. The gesture is grotesque.*)

HUGH: The lady has assented?

JIMMY: She asked *me*—I assented.

HUGH: Ah. When was this?

JIMMY: Last night.   390

HUGH: What does her mother say?

JIMMY: Metis from Hellespont? Decent people—good stock.

HUGH: And her father?

JIMMY: I'm meeting Zeus tomorrow. Hugh, will you be my best man?   395

HUGH: Honoured, James; profoundly honoured.

JIMMY: You know what I'm looking for, Hugh, don't you? I mean to say—you know—I—I—I joke like the rest of them—you know?—(*Again he attempts the pathetic routine but abandons it instantly.*) You know yourself, Hugh—don't you?—you   400

III.   356 *domus lugubris* house of mourning   362 *infelix* unlucky, unhappy   368–369 *Barbarus . . . ulli* I am a barbarian here because I am not understood by anyone

know all that. But what I'm really looking for, Hugh—what I really want—companionship, Hugh—at my time of life, companionship, company, someone to talk to. Away up in Beann na Gaoithe—you've no idea how lonely it is.
405 Companionship—correct, Hugh? Correct?
HUGH: Correct.
JIMMY: And I always liked her, Hugh. Correct?
HUGH: Correct, James.
JIMMY: Someone to talk to.
410 HUGH: Indeed.
JIMMY: That's all, Hugh. The whole story. You know it all now, Hugh. You know it all.

(*As* JIMMY *says those last lines he is crying, shaking his head, trying to keep his balance, and holding a finger up to his lips in absurd gestures of secrecy and intimacy. Now he staggers away, tries to sit on a stool, misses it, slides to the floor, his feet in front of him, his back against the broken cart. Almost at once he is asleep.* HUGH *watches all of this. Then he produces his flask and is about to pour a drink when he sees the Name-Book on the floor. He picks it up and leafs through it, pronouncing the strange names as he does. Just as he begins,* OWEN *emerges and descends with two bowls of tea.*)

HUGH: Ballybeg. Burnfoot. King's Head. Whiteplains. Fair Hill. Dunboy. Green Bank.
415
(OWEN *snatches the book from* HUGH.)

OWEN: I'll take that. (*In apology.*) It's only a catalogue of names.
HUGH: I know what it is.
OWEN: A mistake—my mistake—nothing to do with us. I hope that's strong enough [*tea*]. (*He throws the book on the table and crosses over to* JIMMY.) Jimmy. Wake up, Jimmy. Wake
420 up, man.
JIMMY: What—what-what?
OWEN: Here. Drink this. Then go on away home. There may be trouble. Do you hear me, Jimmy? There may be trouble.
HUGH: (*Indicating Name-Book.*) We must learn those new
425 names.
OWEN: (*Searching around.*) Did you see a sack lying about?
HUGH: We must learn where we live. We must learn to make them our own. We must make them our new home.

(OWEN *finds a sack and throws it across his shoulders.*)

OWEN: I know where I live.
430 HUGH: James thinks he knows, too. I look at James and three thoughts occur to me: A—that it is not the literal past, the 'facts' of history, that shape us, but images of the past embodied in language. James has ceased to make that discrimination.
435 OWEN: Don't lecture me, Father.
HUGH: B—we must never cease renewing those images; because once we do, we fossilize. Is there no soda bread?
OWEN: And C, Father—one single, unalterable 'fact': if Yolland is not found, we are all going to be evicted. Lancey has issued
440 the order.
HUGH: Ah. *Edictum imperatoris.*

---

442 *edictum imperatoris* the decree of the commander

OWEN: You should change out of those wet clothes. I've got to go. I've got to see Doalty Dan Doalty.
HUGH: What about?
OWEN: I'll be back soon. 445

(*As* OWEN *exits.*)

HUGH: Take care, Owen. To remember everything is a form of madness. (*He looks around the room, carefully, as if he were about to leave it forever. Then he looks at* JIMMY, *asleep again.*) The road to Sligo. A spring morning. 1798. Going into battle. Do you remember, James? Two young 450 gallants with pikes across their shoulders and the *Aeneid* in their pockets. Everything seemed to find definition that spring—a congruence, a miraculous matching of hope and past and present and possibility. Striding across the fresh, green land. The rhythms of perception heightened. The 455 whole enterprise of consciousness accelerated. We were gods that morning, James; and I had recently married *my* goddess, Caitlin Dubh Nic Reactainn, may she rest in peace. And to leave her and my infant son in his cradle—that was heroic, too. By God, sir, we were magnificent. We marched 460 as far as—where was it?—Glenties! All of twenty-three miles in one day. And it was there, in Phelan's pub, that we got home-sick for Athens, just like Ulysses. The *desiderium nostrorum*—the need for our own. Our *pietas,* James, was for older, quieter things. And that was the longest twenty- 465 three miles back I ever made. (*Toasts* JIMMY.) My friend, confusion is not an ignoble condition.

(MAIRE *enters.*)

MAIRE: I'm back again. I set out for somewhere but I couldn't remember where. So I came back here.
HUGH: Yes, I will teach you English, Maire Chatach. 470
MAIRE: Will you, Master? I must learn it. I need to learn it.
HUGH: Indeed you may well be my only pupil.

(*He goes towards the steps and begins to ascend.*)

MAIRE: When can we start?
HUGH: Not today. Tomorrow, perhaps. After the funeral. We'll begin tomorrow. (*Ascending.*) But don't expect too much. I 475 will provide you with the available words and the available grammar. But will that help you to interpret between privacies? I have no idea. But it's all we have. I have no idea at all.

(*He is now at the top.*)

MAIRE: Master, what does the English word 'always' mean?
HUGH: *Semper—per omnia saecula.* The Greeks called it '*aei.*' It's 480 not a word I'd start with. It's a silly word, girl.

(*He sits.* JIMMY *is awake. He gets to his feet.* MAIRE *sees the Name-Book, picks it up, and sits with it on her knee.*)

MAIRE: When he comes back, this is where he'll come to. He told me this is where he was happiest.

464–465 *desiderium nostrorum* longing/need for our things/people
465 *pietas* piety 481 *Semper . . . saecula* always—for all time; *aei* always

(JIMMY *sits beside* MAIRE.)

JIMMY: Do you know the Greek word *endogamein?* It means to
marry within the tribe. And the word *exogamein* means to
marry outside the tribe. And you don't cross those borders
casually—both sides get very angry. Now, the problem is this:
Is Athene sufficiently mortal or am I sufficiently godlike for the
marriage to be acceptable to her people and to my people? You
think about that.

HUGH: *Urbs antiqua fuit*—there was an ancient city which, 'tis
said, Juno loved above all the lands. And it was the goddess's
aim and cherished hope that here should be the capital of
all nations—should the fates perchance allow that. Yet in
truth she discovered that a race was springing from Trojan
blood to overthrow some day these Tyrian towers—a people

485

490

495

late regem belloque superbum—kings of broad realms and
proud in war who would come forth for Libya's downfall—
such was—such was the course—such was the course
ordained—ordained by fate . . . What the hell's wrong with
me? Sure I know it backwards. I'll begin again. *Urbs antiqua
fuit*—there was an ancient city which, 'tis said, Juno loved
above all the lands.

500

(*Begin to bring down the lights.*)

And it was the goddess's aim and cherished hope that here
should be the capital of all nations—should the fates perchance
allow that. Yet in truth she discovered that a race was springing
from Trojan blood to overthrow some day these Tyrian
towers—a people kings of broad realms and proud in war who
would come forth for Libya's downfall . . .

505

510

(*Blackout.*)

---

485 *endogamein* to marry within the tribe   486 *exogamein* to marry
outside the tribe   492 *Urbs antiqua* **fuit** there was an ancient city

---

498 *late . . . superbum* kings of broad realms and proud in war, from
Virgil's *Aeneid,* book I.

Gao Xingjian

The first Chinese writer to win the Nobel Prize for Literature, Gao Xingjian (b. 1940), was raised in provincial Ganzhou after the Communist revolution in China. His mother was an amateur actress, and when he went to Beijing in 1958 to study at the Beijing Foreign Languages Institute, he not only studied French literature, but became involved in theater as well. He was working as a translator when the Cultural Revolution (1967–1977) forced the "reeducation" of intellectuals and professionals by exiling them to rural areas to work in agriculture; he was working as a schoolteacher in southwestern China when he published his first novel, *Stars on a Cold Night* in 1980. The following year, during Deng Xiaoping's easing of cultural restrictions, he published a critical essay, "Preliminary Explorations into the Techniques of Modern Fiction," which attempted—as Brecht had done earlier in relation to Soviet realism—to articulate the purpose and power of "modernist" formal and theoretical experimentation in the face of the state-supported demands of Maoist "revolutionary realism." Though the essay proved controversial, Gao was soon appointed as playwright to the Beijing People's Art Theater; several of the plays he wrote for the company proved controversial in a climate in which formal "experimentation" signaled a departure from Party doctrines. *Bus Stop* (1981) was not produced by the company, and *Absolute Signal* was shown in a few public rehearsals before being closed after only thirteen performances: Gao was prohibited from writing for publication for a year and went into exile in southwestern China.

Returning to Beijing in 1984, he wrote *Wilderness Man,* which updates and innovates the episodic and mythological structure of traditional Chinese theater, and *The Other Shore* (1985). Insistently framing a conflict between individual characters and the Crowd, *The Other Shore* was closed during rehearsal, and Gao fled to France in 1987. In France, Gao has written a number of his most celebrated works, including *Exile* (1989)—which concerns the flight of dissidents from the Tiananmen Square uprising in 1989—and the plays *Between Life and Death* (1991), *Dialogue and Rebuttal* (1992), *Nocturnal Wanderer* (1993), *Weekend Quartet* (1995), and the novel *Spiritual Mountain* (1990). Gao's work is increasingly well-known in the United States, and a collection of plays (to which I am indebted here) *The Other Shore: Plays by Gao Xingjian,* edited and translated by Gilbert C.F. Fong, was published in 1999. Gao's plays have, however, become part of the international theatrical repertoire, and have been produced professionally in China, Sweden, England, Austria, Germany, France, Australia, Poland, Japan, and Taiwan, as well as in the United States. Gao won the Nobel Prize for Literature in 2000. In China, Gao is also known for his brilliant stories and poems, and as an accomplished painter as well.

The Other Shore

The Other Shore witnesses Gao's deep investment in theatrical experimentation, particularly his desire to investigate the means of acting in the theater. As he suggests in his notes to the play, *The Other Shore* attempts to fuse the physical elements of acting ("somatics"), language, and psychology in "a kind of emotive abstraction through performance, i.e., a nonphilosophical abstraction." Noting his indebtedness to the work of Polish director Jerzy Grotowski—whose **POOR THEATER**, like Gao's, dispensed with elaborate sets, costumes, and lighting to focus attention on acting as the essence of theater—Gao also makes a significant departure: while Grotowski used physical discipline to force the actor's "sacrifice" of himself, a kind of "exposure" of his innermost identity to himself and to the audience, Gao's theater "helps the actor to ascertain his own self through the process of discovering his partners."

The tension between the demands of the self and of its relation to others animates the action of the play, which takes the shape of an allegorical journey, in the mode of plays from *Everyman* to Strindberg's *A Dream Play*. Gao suggests that the play should be performed

Boston University Theatre, photo by Ben Sigda

The Boston University Theater production of Gao's *The Other Shore*. Photo by Ben Sigda.

environmentally, in an open space shared by actors and audience, and the play opens with a series of acting exercises and games, in which the performers use ropes to explore and define their group identity. This exercise demands a high level of physical training and responsiveness from the performers, as the actors work to embody the different "identities" that emerge from different relationships. The actors also use the rope exercises to begin their narrative, traveling to "the other shore," a nonexistent realm that nonetheless evokes the state of Buddhist enlightenment (sometimes called "the other shore"). But *The Other Shore* is hardly doctrine-disguised-as-allegory. Rather than a banal or a politicized vision of individual or collective peace, the play imagines a dynamic and conflictual journey, centered on a series of confrontations between individuated characters like The Woman, The Man, The Young Girl, The Card Player, The Mad Woman, and the Crowd (in a way reminiscent of the history of Greek drama, Gao's actor/protagonists emerge from and blend back into the choral Crowd). Many of the scenes revolve around The Man, who resists the Crowd's often self-deluded efforts toward conformity. Yet much of the power of this elegant play depends on the tension between Gao's lyrical language and the actors' lyrical physicality, their ability to individuate and transform the Crowd itself. Arriving at "the other shore," the actors seem both to discover and to explore their bodies, and discover and explore language as well; having discovered their instrument, they use it throughout the play to transform the Crowd—into a vengeful mob, a throng of pilgrims, a host of demented automatons, a monstrous forest. In this sense, the Crowd is not a monolithic and regimented opponent of the individual, but the network within which the individual discovers his or her identity; as Gao suggests in one of his notes, the Crowd should not be understood as a regimented entity—its "performance must be fresh, regenerating, and improvisational."

The Other Shore

Gao Xingjian

CHARACTERS

An actor playing with ropes
CARD PLAYER
"DOGSKIN" PLASTER SELLER
WOMAN
YOUNG GIRL
MAD WOMAN
MODEL
MAN
YOUNG MAN
SHADOW
HEART
MOTHER
FATHER
ZEN MASTER

OLD LADY
STABLE KEEPER
ACTORS
CROWD

TIME: *The time cannot be defined or stated precisely.*

LOCATION: *From the real world to the nonexistent other shore.*

The play can be performed in a theatre, a living room, a rehearsal room, an empty warehouse, a gymnasium, the hall of a temple, a circus tent, or any empty space as long as the necessary lighting and sound equipment can be properly installed. Lighting can be dispensed with if the play is performed during the day. The actors may be among the audience, or the audience among the actors. The two situations are the same and will not make any difference to the play.

ACTOR PLAYING WITH ROPES: Here's a rope. Let's play a game, but we've got to be serious, as if we're children playing their game. Our play starts with a game.

    Okay, I want you to take hold of this end of the rope. You
5 see, this way a relationship is established between us. Before that you were you and I was I, but with this rope between us we're tied to each other and it becomes you and I.

    Let's try running in opposite directions. See, now you're pulling me, but then again I'm also holding you back, like
10 two locusts tied to the same string, neither of us can get away from each other. Of course, we're also like husband and wife. (*Pauses.*) But that's not a good metaphor. If I were to pull the rope real hard towards me, then we'd have to see who's stronger. The stronger one pulls and
15 the weaker is being pulled. It becomes a tug-of-war, a competition of strength, and there'll be a winner and a loser, victory and defeat.

    Now if I carry this rope on my back like this and pull even harder, you'll be like a dead dog; likewise if you manage to
20 gain control of this rope, I'll be like a horse or a cow, and you'll be able to drive me around like cattle. In other words, you'll be running the show. So you see, our relationship is not at all constant, it's not at all unchanging.

    Or we can establish an even more complex relationship.
25 For instance if you revolve around me, I'll be the centre of your orbit, and you'll become my satellite. But if you don't wish to revolve around me, I can rotate on my own, thinking that all of you are revolving around me. Are you revolving or am I the one who's revolving? I could
30 be revolving around you or you could be revolving around me. Who knows? Perhaps we're both turning at the same time, or maybe we're both revolving around other people, or maybe those other people are revolving around us both or maybe all of us are revolving around God—maybe there
35 isn't a God after all, maybe there's only a universe rotating by itself like a millstone—now we're touching on philosophy. Never mind, we'll leave philosophy to the philosophers, let's just continue to play our game.

    Everyone of you can pick up a rope and play different kinds
40 of games, the possibilities are endless. Playing with ropes is such a game, that it can be a manifestation of all kinds of interpersonal relationships.

(*The actors each choose a partner to play the game, using a piece of rope. They can switch partners or briefly make contact with other pairs of players, but the contacts are soon broken. The game becomes increasingly lively, tense, and exciting, accompanied by all kinds of salutations and screams.*)

ACTOR PLAYING WITH ROPES: Okay everybody, let's knock it off for a moment. Let's make this game bigger and more complex. Now I want all of you to hold on to one end of 45 your rope and give me the other end. This way you'll be able to establish all kinds of relationships with me, some tense, some lax, some distant, and some close, and soon your individual attitudes will have a strong impact on me. Society is complex and ever-changing, we're constantly 50 pulling and being pulled. (*Pauses.*) Just like a fly that's fallen into a spider's web. (*Pauses.*) Or just like a spider. (*Pauses.*)

    The rope is like our hands. (*He lets go one rope and his partner also lets go. The rope falls on the ground.*) Or like 55 an extended antenna. (*He lets go another and his partner follows.*) Or like the language we use, for instance when we say "Good Morning" or "How are you!" (*Another rope falls to the ground.*) Or perhaps it's like looking at each other, (*Replaces another rope.*) or like the thoughts in our minds. 60 (*His back is against his current partner, but the two sides are still communicating.*) Either you're thinking of her, or she's thinking of someone else. (*He brushes past her shoulders. She and someone else are gazing into each other's eyes.*) In this way the rope is pulling all of us, binding us together. 65
We look—

(*The actors are communicating with one another through pieces of imaginary ropes.*)

    We observe—
    We stare—
    Then there's temptation and attraction—

70   Orders and obedience—

(*In the following, the performance is accompanied by all kinds of sighs and screams but without resorting to the use of language.*)

Conflicts—
Intimacy—
Exclusion—
Entanglement—
75   Abandonment—
Emulation—
Evasion—
Repulsion—
Pursuit—
80   Encirclement—
Congregation—
Fragmentation
Dismiss!
At ease!
85   Now there is a river in front of us, not a piece of rope. Let's cross the river and try to reach the other shore.

ACTORS: (*One after another.*) Yes, to the other shore! To the other shore!
The other shore! To the other shore! To the other shore!
90   The other shore!
Oh—Oh—Oh
The water in the river is so clear!
So cool!
Watch out, the stones are killing my feet!
95   How nice!

(*Gradually there comes the sound of running water.*)

My skirt's soaking wet!
Is the river deep?
Let's swim across to the other shore!
Don't go by yourself!
100   Look at the water spray, how it sparkles in the sunshine!
What fun, just like a waterfall.
A dam, a river flowing gently down the dam.
Form a line in the middle of the river.
Further down the water's dark blue, it's got to be really
105   deep there.
I've got some fish wriggling between my legs . . .
So exciting!
I'm going to fall.
Don't worry, hold on to me.
110   There's an eddy over there—
Look after one another, hold hands.
To the rapid waters.
To the other shore!
No one can see the other shore.
115   Cut the poetry crap! I'm falling.
Hold tight, one after another now.
Over there the water is deep blue . . .
Aahh! The water's over my waist all of a sudden!
I'm getting dizzy.
120   Close your eyes for a while.
Look in front of you, look ahead, keep your eyes open!
All looking at the other shore.
How come I can't see it?

We'll drown, all of us.
We'll all be fish food.   125
If we're going to die, let's die together.
Girls, stop blabbing, try to concentrate.
The current is very strong, tread in the shallows, try going up stream!
I can't make it across, I'm sure I can't make it.   130
Where's the other shore?
Sometimes it's dark, sometimes it's bright.
Are there lights on the other shore?
There are flowers, lots of flowers on the other shore, it's a world of flowers.   135
I'm afraid I can't make it, please don't leave me behind.

(*Sobs.*)

Can you feel it? We're drifting in the river.
Like corks on a string.
And like water weed.
Why are we going to the other shore? I really don't   140
understand.
Right, why do we want to go to the other shore?
The other shore is the other shore, you'll never reach it.
But you still want to go, to see what it's like over there.
I can't see anything.   145
No oasis, and no light.
In total darkness.
It's like this . . .
No, I can't make it.
We haven't been there before.   150
We must get there.
But why?
To make a long-time wish come true, the other shore, the other shore.
No, I can't make it, I want to go home!   155
None of us can.
Can't go back at all.
O—!
Who is it?
Don't know.   160

(*Silence, only the sound of water gurgling.*)

Was somebody screaming? Did you hear it?
You must have heard it, but nobody answered.

(*Silence. Sound of sobbing.*)

This is a ditch of dead water.
There's only oblivion.

(*Bewildered, the* CROWD *slowly walk out of the dead water. Music is faintly heard. The* CROWD *gradually reach the shore and lie down totally exhausted on the ground.* WOMAN *appears in darkness. Like a strand of light mist, she walks around to inspect the people who have lost their memories. She drifts among them, touching and waking them up one by one. They lazily open their eyes and look up, turning their bodies and staring at her. They try to speak but in vain.*)

WOMAN: (*Raises her hand.*) Look here, this is a hand.   165

(*The* CROWD *utter muddled sounds from their throat.*)

WOMAN: This is a hand.
CROWD: (*Still mumbling.*) Th . . . The . . . This . . . ee . . . ha . . .
     han . . . hand.
WOMAN: Hand—
170 CROWD: Hand—band—sand—hand—
WOMAN: This is a foot.
CROWD: Th . . . Th . . . This . . . ee . . . fo . . . foo . . . foot.
WOMAN: (*Pointing to her eye.*) Eye.
CROWD: Ee . . . ee . . . eye . . . eye . . .
175 WOMAN: (*Gesturing.*) Your eyes are looking at your foot!
CROWD: (*Totally confused.*) Eyes . . . cook . . . cook your . . .
     own . . . coot . . .

(WOMAN *laughs, and the* CROWD *join in the laughter with her,
giggling.*)

WOMAN: (*Stops laughing, somewhat sad.*) This is a hand—
CROWD: This is a hand, this is a band, this is a sand, this is a
180   hand . . .
WOMAN: This is a foot—
CROWD: This is a boot, this is a hoot, this is a root, this is a
     foot . . .
WOMAN: This is a body—your body—
185 CROWD: This is a body, this is a body, this is a body your body,
     this is your body is a body is a body is your body your . . .
WOMAN: (*Shakes her head, gesturing more slowly and still being
     patient.*) My hand—my body—my foot—this is me.
CROWD: My band, my hand, my body, my coot, my hand's body's
190   foot's my coot's hand's foot's body this is my hand's foot's
     body is meat!
WOMAN: Say, me—
CROWD: Say me say me say me say me say me!
WOMAN: (*Shakes her head and points to herself, from her eyes
195   to her mouth, and from her body to her feet.*) Me.
CROWD: (*Together at last.*) Me.
WOMAN: Good!
CROWD: Food! Hood! Good! Wood!
WOMAN: (*At once she waves her hand in disagreement. After
200   thinking for a moment, she points at one person among
     the crowd.*) You.
CROWD: (*All pointing at* THE PERSON.) You!
THE PERSON: (*He looks around him and then points at himself.*)
     You!
205 WOMAN: (*Shakes her head and helps him to point his finger at
     someone else.*) You.
CROWD: You.
WOMAN: (*Gesturing.*) Me and you.
CROWD: Me and you.
210 WOMAN: (*Laughs.*) Good!
CROWD: (*Also laugh.*) Good!

(*Music. Gradually the tempo of the music becomes faster.*)

WOMAN: Me and him!
CROWD: Me and him!
WOMAN: Them and me.
215 CROWD: Them and me.
WOMAN: Me and you.
CROWD: Me and you.
WOMAN: You and us.

CROWD: You and us.
WOMAN: Now follow me when you're seeing with your   220
     eyes—
CROWD: See—
WOMAN: Tell me, who do you see?
CROWD: (*One after another.*) See him, see you, see me, see them,
     they see you, you see us, we see them . . .   225
WOMAN: Now say touch, give, like, and love, and you won't feel
     lonely any more.
CROWD: (*Becoming active.*) I touch you, you give me, I like him,
     he loves you, you touch me, I give him, he likes you, you
     love me . . .   230

(MAN *comes out from among the* CROWD.)

MAN: Who are you?
WOMAN: I'm one of you.
MAN: Where are we now?
WOMAN: The other shore, which we wanted to reach but
     couldn't.   235
MAN: Are you the same person who drowned while we
     were crossing the river? (WOMAN *shakes her head.*) Are
     you her soul? (WOMAN *still shakes her head.*) Have you
     been hiding in our thoughts, do you appear only when
     we think of you? Or are you something like a kind of   240
     consciousness? Did you guide us to the other shore so
     that we wouldn't get lost?
CROWD: (*At the same time.*) I detest you.
     You touched me!
     I'll beat you up!   245
     You hate me?
     I'll torture her.
     He cheats on me.
     You're swearing at him!
     I'll tell on you.   250
     You punish him!
     He plots against me!
     I hate you!
     You curse him!
     I'll kill you . . .   255
MAN: (*To* WOMAN.) You're so kind.
CROWD: (*Turn to face* WOMAN *one after another, playing with
     words.*)
     You're so generous.
     You're so lovely.   260
     You're so despicable.
     He's a bastard.
     You don't say what you mean, you're a crook.
     You're a double-dealing no-good tramp!
     She butters you up, but she's actually jealous of you.   265
     You're snaky, you teach us words so that you can talk to our
     men and seduce them!
     You may look so kind and gentle, but who knows if you're a
     whore or not?
     She's trying to seduce our husbands!   270
     Stirring up trouble among our brothers.
     A buttered bun, look, just look at her—
     Keep the girls away from her, she'll turn them into
     whores.
     She may look prim and proper, but she's really more corrupt 275
     than a common whore.

She's the one, she makes people panic, there'll be no more peace in this world.

(WOMAN *draws back as the* CROWD *surrounds her from all sides. They are excited by their own increasingly venomous language. She cannot escape from the stares of the* CROWD, *so she turns to* MAN *for help and hangs on to him.*)

CROWD: (*Getting more angry.*)
280   Whore!
Venomous snake!
Witch!
Shameless slut!

(WOMAN *holds on to* MAN *and pleads for his protection. The* CROWD *go wild.*)

CROWD: Look, go and take a look!
285   Pooh!
Dump her!
Drag her away!
Get a hold of her!
Strip her!
290   Wring her neck! The shameless whore!

(*The* CROWD *drag her away from* MAN *and jump on her. In the confusion they strangle her to death. When* MAN *pushes his way into the* CROWD *and shakes her body, there is no response.*) (*Witnessing this, the* CROWD *is stunned.*)

CROWD: Dead.
Dead?
Dead?
She's dead!

(*The* CROWD *disperse in a hurry.*)

295   Was she strangled to death?
It's you—
No, he started it.
You shouted first!
I was only following you, you were all shouting.
300   Who shouted first? Who?
Who shouted first to grab her, strip her and strangle her? Who?
We all shouted.
I shouted because you did.
305   I shouted because all of you were shouting.
But she's dead! Strangled alive!
I didn't kill her.
I didn't kill her.
I didn't kill her.
310   I didn't kill her.
I didn't kill her.
I didn't.
I didn't.
Didn't.
315   Didn't.
Didn't.
But she's dead for sure, so lovely even when she's dead.
So beautiful, nobody could help loving her.
Her skin is like jade, it's got no blemishes, it's so pure.

Look at her pretty little hands, they've got her endless   320
tenderness in them.
My, she's like a statue of the Bodhisattva!
So pure, so prim and proper.
She gave us language, she brought us wisdom, but she was
murdered!   325
This is the greatest sin of all, you despicable lot!
Who are you talking about?
Murderers! You, all of you!
How dare you smear me? You bastard!
You're a thug!   330
You're a rascal!

(*The* CROWD *fight among themselves.*)

MAN: Are you finished? We killed her, there's no question about it. It's you, it's him, it's me, and it's all of us. We're all in it together! On this desolate other shore, she gave us language, but we didn't know how to cherish it; she gave us wisdom,   335
but we didn't know how to use it! We ought to be shocked by what we did, but we're cowards, we're too spineless to feel any shame.
CROWD: What do you think we should do?
We need a leader, a flock of sheep also needs a leader. We'll   340
follow you.
MAN: I detest you, I detest myself. It's better for us to go our separate ways.
CROWD: No, don't abandon us.
We've made up our mind to follow you, and you want to   345
leave us?
MAN: Follow me where? Where can I lead you? (*He leaves by himself. The* CROWD *follow behind.*) Don't follow me! (*Troubled.*) I don't even know where I want to go myself. (*Stops and tries to figure out where to go. The* CROWD *still*   350
follow him at a distance.)

(MOTHER *appears in front of him.*)

MOTHER: Do you still remember me?
MAN: Yes, mother.
MOTHER: You've almost forgotten me, haven't you?
MAN: (*On his knees.*) Yes, mother.   355
MOTHER: (*Stroking his head.*) Find yourself a girl, you really should start a family.
MAN: But I want to make something of myself.
MOTHER: You're too ambitious.
MAN: (*Looks down.*) I'm still your son.   360
MOTHER: Are they all following you? Where are you going to take them?
MAN: I don't know. I only know we should go forward, is that right, mother?
MOTHER: My good son. (*Embraces his head.*)   365
MAN: Your hands are cold! (*Shocked by his discovery.*)
Mother, is this the world of the dead? Am I in another dimension?
MOTHER: There's nothing to be scared of, son. It's just a bit dark, a bit cold and damp, that's all.
MAN: (*Leaves her.*) How do I get out of here? Mother, I haven't   370
lived long enough!

(MOTHER *turns and disappears. He hesitates for a moment and then follows in a hurry. A* YOUNG GIRL *blocks his way.*)

MAN: Who are you? I've seen you somewhere, but I can't recall your name. It seems like we used to live on the same street or something, many years ago. Every day on my way to school I always hoped that I could catch
375 a glimpse of you, even if it's only your back. My heart would keep on pounding whenever I saw your long ponytail and your crimson red dress, you seemed to be wearing that crimson dress all that time. . . . I used to follow you, follow you right to your doorsteps, hoping
380 that when you turned around to close the door, you'd at least say one word to me before you went inside, or smile at me just once. But every time you'd only look at me, saying nothing. Oh, I can see those eyes of yours again . . . (*He rubs his eyes and looks more closely, but she has*
385 *disappeared into the dark shadows of the* CROWD.)
　(*To the* CROWD.) We've got to get out of this ghastly place. Once we're away from this darkness we'll find light ahead of us. With the light there'll be houses, and we'll be able to dry our clothes around the stove and drink some hot tea.
390 (*Incitingly.*) We'd be able to return to our homes, see our families, our wives and husbands, our children and parents, and all our loved ones and those who love us!
　(YOUNG GIRL *appears again from behind the* CROWD.) Who are you?
395 　(*Blocking her way.*) Wait, your name is on the tip of my tongue! It seems like I used to write poetry for you, that we used to go to the movies together and I held your hand in the dark, those tiny frail hands of yours . . . (*She turns and gets away from his grasp. She is now behind him, becoming more*
400 *illusory. He turns around but cannot see her, no matter how hard he tries.*)
　She always appeared in my dreams to torment me whenever I was worried and couldn't set my mind free. I couldn't recall her name, I couldn't see her face clearly, I couldn't
405 even get hold of her presence in any way, but she still kept on tormenting me.
　(*Speaking to the shadowy* CROWD.) Why do you keep following me? I need some peace and quiet, I need to be alone! I don't need to be stared at by a crowd, I don't
410 need you, just as you don't need me. What you need is someone who can guide you, to show you the way, even though once you've found a way out, or think you have, you'd put on a spurt, darting away faster than rabbits. And you'd abandon your guide without even taking a
415 second look, just like throwing away a worn-out shoe. I understand, I understand it only too well. You've all experienced loving and being loved, possessing and being possessed. I, too, have a right to be in love, to love a woman and to possess a woman, and to be loved and possessed by
420 her. I'm human just like you are, so full of desires and ambitions, I'm what you may call a career-minded man, a man who is competitive yet extremely weak sometimes, and a man who is righteous, compassionate, willing to sacrifice himself and . . . (*He rolls on the ground and wails loudly like*
425 *a fretting and self-indulgent child.*)

(*The* CROWD *is stunned. When* MAN *has had enough wailing and is totally exhausted, he settles down and gets up from the floor. He continues his way forward and the* CROWD *follow silently behind him. A faint light in the dark becomes brighter. A man is seen drinking and playing cards alone under an oil lamp.* MAN *mimes knocking on the door. The* CROWD *clap their hands three times.*)

MAN: Sorry to bother you.

CARD PLAYER: (*Without lifting his head.*) Come in. Take a seat.
MAN: May I ask—
CARD PLAYER: (*Tosses a card from his hand. Looks up.*) You
play cards? 430
MAN: I've played before.

(*The* CROWD *try to squeeze in through the door.*)

CARD PLAYER: Come in, come in. Do you all want to play cards? Close the door for me. I hate draughts, they make the light flicker, which is bad for a card player's eyes. Alright, let's form a circle, I'll be the banker here. All 435 of you will each take a card, and I'll take one myself, only one, just like you. That's only fair. The card in my hand will be the trump, there's got to be a trump, right? And it's better if I choose the trump card instead of you, it's more convenient that way. (*Turns over his card.*) My 440 card is the two of spades. I'm not trying to fly low, luck is all you need when you're playing cards. Now if you pick a spade, any spade, you'd have a higher number than mine and I'd be the loser and you'd be the winner. But if you didn't pick a spade, you'd lose no matter what, it doesn't 445 matter which card you've picked. You got me?
MAN: What happens if one wins or loses?
CARD PLAYER: The winner gets to drink the wine in this pot.
MAN: And the loser?
CARD PLAYER: There'll be a penalty. 450
MAN: I have no money, no land, no property, and no wife.
CARD PLAYER: But you do have a face, haven't you?
MAN: I don't get it.
CARD PLAYER: You'll find out soon enough. All of you, anyone who loses will stick a piece of paper on his face for me. 455
CROWD: That's easy enough.
　How big is the paper?
　Any paper?
　The thing is, have you really got wine in your pot?
CARD PLAYER: Have a taste first. 460
CROWD: It's good.
　What aroma!
　Of course, it's the real thing.
　Let me have a sip.
　It's worth playing for. 465
CARD PLAYER: In a moment you'll pick your cards. I've shown you my card, all of you have seen it, right? Now you can only look at your own card, no ganging up, that's a no-no.
CROWD: (*Eager to pick their cards.*) 470
　That's nothing, it's fine with me.
　We should play our own games.
　Don't worry, I won't look even if you let me.
　Me, I'm honesty personified.
　Integrity comes first, winning and losing second. 475
　Hear! Hear!

(*Those who have picked their cards are silent.*)

CARD PLAYER: (*To the person who picks first.*) Show me your card. You lose.
THIS PERSON: (*Nods.*) What's the penalty?
480
(CARD PLAYER *takes a piece of paper and spits on it. He sticks the paper onto the cheek of* THIS PERSON, *who mutters something. The* CROWD *watch and laugh.* THIS PERSON *is relieved and laughs with them.*)

CARD PLAYER: (*Turns to another person.*) My friend, how about you? (THAT PERSON *shows his card.*) You lose too.

THAT PERSON: Well, give it to me.

CARD PLAYER: Stick it under your chin.

(THAT PERSON *takes a piece of paper, spits on it, and sticks it under his chin. He is somewhat embarrassed, but when he sees the* CROWD *laughing, he is himself again.*)

THIRD PERSON (FEMALE): It's fun.

485 CARD PLAYER: (*Turns towards her.*) And you? (*She shows her card and hurriedly takes it back.*)

CROWD: Did you win?

You won!

Did you really win?

490 (*She frets demurely and shakes her head.*)

Why aren't you sticking the paper on your face?

Stick the paper on, stick it on!

Come on, it's the rule, no exceptions allowed.

If you don't stick it on, we won't either.

495 THIRD PERSON (FEMALE): It's too embarrassing.

CROWD: You think we're not?

That won't do. Stick it on the ear.

Right, on the ear.

Stick it on the nose!

500 It must be different with everybody, okay? No repetitions.

Everybody gets one.

(*When the* CARD PLAYER *looks at someone, the person will show his card and then obediently stick a piece of paper on his face.*)

CROWD: (*Sticking paper to their own faces.*)

Fair and square.

No doubt about that.

505 Nobody tells you to lose, but when you do, you've got to take what comes.

Everyone gets a penalty, everyone sticks a paper on their face.

If you haven't got a paper on your face, you'll look odd

510 and out of place, and people will be afraid of you.

(*The strange-looking, papered faces all turn towards* MAN.)

CARD PLAYER: My friend, it's your turn now.

MAN: I don't play.

CARD PLAYER: Everybody plays, why don't you?

MAN: I find the whole thing very silly. What's more, I've got

515 to go.

CROWD: Yes, that's right. We should all be going.

Don't go by yourself.

Where are we going?

Right, where exactly are we going?

520 MAN: In any case I've got to go.

CARD PLAYER: I've got the whole place lit up and I've prepared wine. I went through all these troubles just to play cards with you people. I've never heard of anyone who comes here and leaves without playing. You shouldn't have come

525 in the first place!

CROWD: (*Stopping Man.*) Play!

Come on, be a good sport. Don't be such a party popper.

Just play one game. Just one.

Play once and then we'll go.

MAN: Don't you understand? You're not really playing cards, 53
he's playing a trick on you. You can't win. Your card,
yours, and yours are all no trumps, including all the cards
still in the deck. The only spade in the deck is in his hand!
(CARD PLAYER *giggles.*) Let's go! Why waste our time on
this guy. 535

CARD PLAYER: There is no such thing as time here. (*He blows on the oil lamp and the light flickers, and it gradually turns brighter again.*) There is only eternal light. (*He takes the lamp and shines on everyone from below the chin. The papered faces look like gargoyles.*) I'm a sucker for big crowds. You're 540
scared, aren't you?

MAN: You're a devil.

CARD PLAYER: Why don't you try feeling their arses? They've all got a bristly tail down there! (*He points to the* CROWD's bottoms and laughs out loud. Then he pushes a deck of cards 545
in front of MAN.*) Take a card! Let everyone see if it's a spade or no trumps? (*Turns over a no trump card and flashes it in front of the* CROWD.*) What is it, is it a spade or not?

PERSON A: I can't really tell.

CARD PLAYER: What'd you say? 550

PERSON B: It looked like—

CARD PLAYER: You must have seen it clearly.

PERSON C: I think I saw a—spade.

CARD PLAYER: That's right! Young lady, what do you think?

OBEDIENT GIRL: Spades. 555

CARD PLAYER: That a girl. You've made my day. Old Sir, how about you?

PERSON D: Spades, how can it not be spades?

CARD PLAYER: Bless you. (*Suddenly explodes.*) How can we let him bullshit us like this and tell us that they're all no 560
trumps? Huh?

CROWD: It's spades.

Of course it's spades. It can't be anything else.

No mistake about it.

We all saw it. 565

We're all witnesses!

CARD PLAYER: You heard what they said, didn't you? Why did you lie, why did you insist that a spade is no trump? You're scared, aren't you? Have you ever tried eating rat meat?
A bouncing baby rat, its hair not fully grown and its eyes 570
unopened, the little creature still squeaking when you dip it in the sauce and put it in your mouth, ready for a bite? If you had, then you'd be brave enough to tell the truth. My friend, I'm gonna give you one more chance to tell the truth.
Tell me, was it spades or a no trump? 575

MAN: I think . . . that's still a no trump.

CARD PLAYER: You're no fun, you make people miserable. Tell me, people, is this guy bad or what?

CROWD: (*Passing the wine pot and taking sips one after another.*)
Bad, bad, bad, bad, bad, bad, bad, bad . . . 580

CARD PLAYER: (*Takes the wine from them.*) What shall we do with this bad guy?

CROWD: (*Surround* MAN.) Throw him out!

Tell him to get out of here!

Trouble-maker. 585

A real pest.

When he's here, we've got no wine to drink.

Teach him a lesson!

Spank him!

Strip him! 590

Take off his pants!

(*The* CROWD *try to take off* MAN's *pants.*)

CARD PLAYER: I'm gonna give you a second chance. Think
    clearly. Think again!

MAN: (*Holding up his pants.*) But I remember . . . it looked like
595   a . . . no trump.

(CARD PLAYER *tucks the wine pot under his arm and turns away.*
The CROWD *pull at* MAN *as if they were teasing a bird.*)

CROWD: Tell him to fly!
    What? What did you say?
    Fly like a bird!
    Men are not birds, why should they learn to fly like birds?
600   Wow, it's so fun!
    Fly!
    Lower your head, let your arms fly!

CARD PLAYER: My friend, I refuse to believe that you're a
    stubborn man.

605 OBEDIENT GIRL: (*Takes pity on* MAN.) You can't turn a spade
    into a no trump. What's with you? Please, try to take hold of
    yourself.

MAN: Maybe it was really a spade . . .

OBEDIENT GIRL: Then why did you say it was a no trump?

610 MAN: I think it should be . . .

OBEDIENT GIRL: But what should be is not necessarily the
    truth.

CARD PLAYER: You're a loser because you're a pighead. What
    do you mean by "should be"? It either is or isn't. To hell
615   with "should be."

MAN: But why can't we have "should be"?

CARD PLAYER: (*Irritated.*) Should be my foot! What do you say,
    should be or not should be?

CROWD: (*Immediately tear at* MAN.) We don't want any
620   "should be"!
    We want "yes" or "no"!
    We want spades, not no trumps!
    Down with no trumps!
    Spades are the best!

625 MAN: It . . . seemed . . . like a . . . sp . . .

CROWD: (*Beating their chests and stamping their feet.*) Speak up!
    Louder!
    Can't hear you!
    You've got to clear this up!

630 MAN: Sp . . . Spa . . . It's spades . . . (*On his knees and collapses.*)

(*The* CROWD *surround* CARD PLAYER *and perform a strange and
awkward dance. They exit.*)

A woman dressed in a white cotton skirt appears. She covers MAN
*with her skirt, bends down and wraps herself in it as well. The two
form a white object which disappears with the gradually approaching drumbeat. The drumbeat builds up into a heart-thumping
bang. A scrawny monk comes out jumping and beating a gigantic
drum with his fingers, palms, elbows, and knees as if he were
bewitched.* ZEN MASTER *enters, dressed in a Buddhist robe of
kasaya, his hands clasped together and his right shoulder bare.
Other monks and nuns, all cloaked in grey kasaya, follow* ZEN
MASTER *onto the stage. The* CROWD *enter in a single file, chanting
"Amitabha" as they come. Their chanting is not in any particular
order, each singing their own tune and at their own pitch. The
chanting comes and goes, combining with the drumbeat into a*

cacophony of intersecting sounds. MAN *is following the* CROWD;
he also chants and looks around him at times. The CROWD *all put
down a futon, on which they sit with their legs crossed.* MAN *does
same. The drum stops, followed by the sound of a wooden fish**
and an inverted bell.)

ZEN MASTER: (*Recites the Vajraccedika prajna paramita sutra,
    his palms clasped together and his right knee on the ground.*)
    ". . . How much the Bodhisattvas, the great beings, have
    been helped with the greatest help by the Tathagata, the
    Fully Enlightened One. It is wonderful, O Lord, how much   635
    the Bodhisattvas, the great beings, have been favoured with
    the highest favour by the Tathagata, the Fully Enlightened
    One. How then, O Lord, should good men and women
    stand, who seek the supreme wisdom, how progress, how
    control their thoughts?"   640
        After these words the Lord said to the Venerable Subhuti:
    "Well said, well said, Subhuti! So it is, Subhuti, so it is as you
    say! The Tathagata has helped the Bodhisattvas, the great
    beings with the greatest help, and he has favoured them
    with the highest favour. Therefore, Subhuti, listen well, and   645
    attentively! . . ."

(*Incense smoke permeates the whole place during the chanting.
The* CROWD *close their eyes in meditation, and* MAN *gradually
does so as well.* YOUNG GIRL *appears, her eyes slightly closed. She
is squatting in a corner and doing her mental exercise, like a baby
who is sleeping not too tightly in a transparent egg shell, its hands
and feet pressed against the four walls of the shell.* YOUNG MAN,
who has been hiding behind her, gets up slowly and walks towards
YOUNG GIRL *in gingerly steps. The chanting gradually fades. The*
CROWD *disappear.*)

ZEN MASTER: (*The sound of chanting can still be heard faintly.*)
    "Monks of the Buddha, nuns of the Buddha, I will teach you
    how they should stand, who seek the supreme wisdom, how
    progress, how control their thoughts."   650
        "So be it, O Lord. With a joyful heart we long to hear,"
    the Venerable Subhuti replied to the Lord.
        The Lord said: "Here, Subhuti, someone who seeks
    supreme wisdom should produce a thought in this
    manner . . ."   655

(YOUNG MAN *stretches his hand to touch* YOUNG GIRL's *fingers.
Surprised, she wakes and withdraws her hand immediately.*)

YOUNG GIRL: Stop it!

YOUNG MAN: Are you doing your mental exercise?

YOUNG GIRL: Yes.

YOUNG MAN: May I ask what kind of exercise are you doing?

YOUNG GIRL: They say it's called Small Circular Heaven.   660

YOUNG MAN: Is there a Big Circular Heaven as well?

YOUNG GIRL: I don't know.

YOUNG MAN: You're doing something you don't know anything
    about?

YOUNG GIRL: (*Nervously.*) Stop interrogating me! Just stop it!   665

YOUNG MAN: (*Mischievously.*) Then perhaps you don't know
    what's the use of this exercise? (*Grabs her hand.*)

---

*A percussion instrument made of a hollow wooden block, used by
Buddhist priests to make rhythm while chanting scriptures.

YOUNG GIRL: No, don't, you can't do that—

YOUNG MAN: Why not?

670 YOUNG GIRL: I'm scared . . .

YOUNG MAN: What's there to be scared of?

YOUNG GIRL: Don't touch me!

YOUNG MAN: What if I do?

YOUNG GIRL: Then I'd feel the pain.

675 YOUNG MAN: So you don't feel any pain right now?

YOUNG GIRL: (*Painfully.*) I can't say for sure . . .

YOUNG MAN: (*Grabs her hand by force.*) Then for once I'll let you feel the pain!

YOUNG GIRL: (*Begging him and trying to struggle free.*) Oh no,

680 don't . . . (FATHER *enters carrying an umbrella. The chanting* ZEN MASTER *and the meditating* CROWD *have all disappeared. Only* MAN *is left sitting on the futon with his eyes closed.*)

YOUNG MAN: Father!

FATHER: Don't get into trouble. Come home with me, now!

685

(FATHER *drags* YOUNG MAN *along.*)

(YOUNG GIRL *disappears.*)

YOUNG MAN: (*Turns back to look. Nonchalantly.*) Why? It's not raining.

FATHER: I tell you it will.

YOUNG MAN: But it's not raining now.

FATHER: It'll be too late if it does.

690 YOUNG MAN: What if it doesn't.

FATHER: It's going to rain sooner or later! Look, what do you think I've brought my umbrella for?

YOUNG MAN: You've brought it because you have nothing else to do.

695 FATHER: I've been carrying an umbrella all my life!

YOUNG MAN: You've brought it upon yourself.

FATHER: How dare you talk to your father like that?

YOUNG MAN: Fine, I won't say anything then.

FATHER: Get away from me! Go as far as you possibly can! Don't

700 even bother coming back to see me. I don't have a son like you! (*Exits angrily.*)

(YOUNG MAN *is bewildered.* MAN *is still sitting on the futon meditating. The sound of chanting approaches, but there is no sign of* ZEN MASTER.)

CHANTING SOUND: The Buddha said: Here, subhuti, someone who seeks supreme wisdom should produce a thought in this manner: "As many beings as there are in the universe of

705 beings, comprehended under the term 'beings'—egg-born, born from a womb, moisture-born, or miraculously born; with or without form; with perception, without perception,— as far as any conceivable form of beings is conceived: all these I must lead to Nirvana, into that Realm of Nirvana which

710 leaves nothing behind. . . ."

(YOUNG MAN *turns and finds a wall of people behind him. He tries unsuccessfully to find a way to get over it.* OLD LADY *comes out from a crack in the "wall."*)

OLD LADY: Young man, do you want to go over there?

YOUNG MAN: I just want to take a look.

OLD LADY: Look, look. Everybody wants to take a look. Do you have any money?

YOUNG MAN: (*He searches all his pockets and finally takes out a coin.*) Here.

OLD LADY: (*Laughs out loud.*) You want to take care of me with this? Don't you have anything valuable on you at all? Something your mother gave you, for example?

YOUNG MAN: (*Suddenly understands.*) I've got this fountain pen, 720 it has a gold nib, my mother gave it to me for my birthday. (*Takes the pen out and hands it over to her.*)

OLD LADY: (*Takes the pen and inspects it carefully.*) Hmm, this is quite nice. (*Stuffs the pen into her waist bag and steps aside to reveal a crack in the "wall."*) Now you can go ahead. 725

YOUNG MAN: (*Hesitating.*) I'm afraid my mother might find out . . .

OLD LADY: Will she beat you?

YOUNG MAN: I . . . I can't say . . .

OLD LADY: You'll just have to lie to her, tell her that you've lost 730 it. Don't you know how to lie?

YOUNG MAN: Mother wouldn't allow it.

OLD LADY: That's why you're still such a kid. I'm telling you, there's no adult who doesn't lie, and you know, without lying there'd be no more happy days. All right, just go 735 right through.

(*Crawling,* YOUNG MAN *goes through the crack of the wall of people. When he looks up he sees* YOUNG GIRL *sobbing quietly on the other side, her hands covering her face. He tries to get up, but two thugs approach and take turns beating him up.* YOUNG GIRL *and the sound of chanting disappear at the same time. Only* MAN *is left sitting on the futon and meditating with his eyes closed.*)

PLASTER SELLER: Dogskin Plasters! Dogskin Plasters! Thirteen generations in the family. Give me internal wounds, external wounds, fractures, strains and contusions, give me rabies, heart-attacks, infant convulsions, geriatric 740 strokes, lovesick young men and women, unspeakable depravity and the possessed, stick one on and you'll be as good as new. The first don't work, the second will. . . . Dogskin Plasters! Dogskin Plasters! Taken junky home remedy? Swallowed the wrong drug? No problem! Infertile 745 women, impotent men, sinners and delinquents? Sure thing! Oh yes, and the stutterers, the crooked mouthed, jealous women, avenging men, fathers who love not the mothers, sons who listen not to their old men, pockmarked faces, tinea feet, one plaster cures all. The first don't work, the 750 second will. Satisfaction guaranteed or your money gladly refunded. . . . Dogskin Plasters! Come and get the miracle Dogskin Plasters! Don't miss this golden opportunity! Your chance in a life time!

755

(YOUNG MAN, *on the outside of the* CROWD*'s circle, finally manages to get up from his feet.* MAD WOMAN *enters.*)

MAD WOMAN: (*Approaching* YOUNG MAN.) They say I'm a whore, but they didn't say anything when they sneaked into my bed to sleep with me. They say I'm bad as if they haven't been bad before, as if they haven't had fun with a woman's body before!

760

(YOUNG MAN *retreats and hides himself from her. The* CROWD *turn to face them.*)

CROWD: Here comes the mad woman.
The mad woman's here!
The mad woman's here!
MAD WOMAN: You're mad!
CROWD: Look, look at her.
765 She's talking crazy again.
MAD WOMAN: You're talking crazy.

(*The* CROWD *happily break out in laughter.*)

PLASTER SELLER: (*At the same time.*) If you've got money, give
me money, if you don't, stay and watch the show! Dogskin
Plasters for sale! (*Throws a bundle of plasters on the ground.*)
770 Big sacrifice! Everything must go! Pay what you will. Cheap!
Cheap! Cheap! . . . Pooh! You stinking whore! (*Puts away
plasters and exits.*)
MAD WOMAN: You're cheap! (*The* CROWD *laugh at her again.*)
What are you laughing at? Go laugh at yourselves! What
775 things you wouldn't do to get into a woman's pants! You all
look like you're human, but actually you're all dogs, dogs,
dirty dogs.
MEN IN CROWD: (*To women in the* CROWD.) Stop her wagging
tongue.
780 Take her away.
MAD WOMAN: Why? You're scared because I'll tell on you, right?
You're hiding something, aren't you? Right, keep away from
me, as far away as you can. I know exactly what's going on in
those shitty little heads of yours. (*Snickers.*)
785 MEN IN CROWD: Take her away! Take her away!

(WOMEN *in the* CROWD *come forward to drag* MAD WOMAN *away.*)

MAD WOMAN: You're afraid too, aren't you? You're afraid I'll
say that all of your husbands, every single one of them,
have slept with me? Afraid because you'll become like me,
dumped by your men after they've gotten their rocks off?
790 Afraid your husbands will know you've screwed other men?
Afraid people will find out you'd lost your cherry before
you got married?
CROWD: Gag her!
With horse shit!
795 With bull shit!
Shut her big mouth!
MAD WOMAN: (*Grappling with* WOMEN *in the* CROWD.) Haven't
you got off with a man before? You're like me, you can't
take your hands off your men after they've screwed
800 you . . .

(*The* CROWD *move forward to tie up* MAD WOMAN *with ropes and
gag her mouth. Crying and wailing, she becomes hysterical, but
is finally dragged away by the* CROWD. YOUNG MAN *watches in
astonishment and leaves with the* CROWD. MAN, *who has been sitting and meditating on the futon, also disappears at the same time.
Immediately afterwards, he returns from the other side with his*
SHADOW. SHADOW *is dressed in black and has on black headgear
which covers his face.* MAN *and* SHADOW *do not look at each other.
They talk only to themselves, but their steps and movements are
synchronized.*)

MAN: A seed falls on to the soil—
SHADOW: A child is born onto the world—
MAN: A gust of wind blows through the forest—

SHADOW: A horse gallops on the plateau—
MAN: A grain of sand falls into the eye— 805
SHADOW: An eye is crying tears—
MAN: The tears fall on the parched desert—
SHADOW: Like entering a bustling marketplace—
MAN: People squashing people, but their eyes can't be seen—
SHADOW: Seeing dead fish one by one— 810
MAN: That's a lonely city—
SHADOW: Pop singers are yelling and screaming to exhaus-
tion—
MAN: Only the stars can hear the wind chimes ringing—
SHADOW: It is not our hearts that are ringing— 815
MAN: It's the electric guitars picking your nerves—
SHADOW: You jump three times, nine times, eight times, seven
times and you're out of breath—
MAN: Just because you're no hero—
SHADOW: More like a popular and low-minded farce— 820
MAN: An out-of-tune trumpet blows, blows, blows, blows and
blows—
SHADOW: The conductor has to be right—
MAN: Everyone says he's 180% painful—
SHADOW: Only one minute's happiness— 825
MAN: It's not the time for drinking beer—
SHADOW: Chicago Nuremberg—
MAN: Once there was a war—
SHADOW: Only sparrows were killed—
MAN: Soldiers didn't fight, they only stood on guard— 830
SHADOW: And those standing on guard got to wear medals—
MAN: Who is the person speaking to me?
SHADOW: It is your shadow, your thoughts spoken out loud—
MAN: You're always following me—
SHADOW: When you have lost your self— 835
MAN: You'll come and remind me and double my trouble?
SHADOW: What are you looking for so desperately?
MAN: Now that you've reminded me! I've definitely lost
something, can you tell me where to look for it?
SHADOW: (*Sarcastically.*) You probably do not know what you are 840
looking for?
MAN: It appears to be . . . isn't everyone looking for it?

(*The* CROWD *enter. They form a circle and bend down to look for
something in the circle, like children at play.*)

SHADOW: It would not hurt to ask them what you are looking for.
(*Takes the chance to leave and disappear.*)
MAN: Excuse me, are you looking for— 845
PERSON A: A needle, they say you can lead a camel through the
eye of this needle.
MAN: (*To another person.*) Excuse me, can you tell me what you're
looking for?
PERSON B: Looking for a place where I can sit comfortably and 850
securely. Once I'm there, I won't leave the seat ever again.
(*Whispering.*) I have haemorrhoids, I can't sit on any wooden
bench.
MAN: And, what are you looking for?
PERSON C: (*Stuttering.*) I . . . I . . . I am . . . looking for a . . . a . . . 855
mouth . . . which can . . . s . . . s . . . peak . . . for me. I . . . I . . .
have to s . . . s . . . speak a lot . . . of . . . of . . . words ev . . .
every . . . every day.
MAN: And you, young man?
PERSON D: I'm looking for a rice bowl! You have everything, but 860
I don't even have a rice bowl!

MAN: Of course, I know, I know it's very important to have a rice bowl. Go for it. Keep looking. (*To another person.*) Excuse me, I didn't do it on purpose. (*Removes his foot.*) What are you
865   looking for?

PERSON E: I'm looking for a pair of shoes that fits. I don't know why my shoes pinch. I want to know—

MAN: I'm also looking for—

PERSON E: Do your shoes pinch too?

870   MAN: My shoes don't pinch, but I don't know where my feet should be going.

PERSON E: You just have to follow other people's footsteps.

MAN: Are you also looking for other people's footsteps?

PERSON F: (*Laughing playfully.*) I'm looking for a hole I can sneak
875   through without anyone noticing me. And then I'll come out on the other side swaggering.

MAN: How about you, my friend? You don't look like the sneaky type.

PERSON G: You're right.

880   MAN: Can you tell me what are you looking for?

PERSON G: Looking for my childhood dream.

MAN: It must be a very beautiful dream. (*To another.*) And you? Are you looking for a dream too?

PERSON H: No, I'm looking for a sentence.

885   MAN: Are you writing a poem?

PERSON H: Everybody can write poetry, just like everybody knows how to make love.

MAN: Then you're—

PERSON H: Thinking! Everyone's got a mind, but not everyone
890   can think.

MAN: You're right. What you're looking for must be an epigram.

PERSON H: I'm not sure if it's an epigram. The problem is, if I didn't find this sentence my thoughts would be cut
895   off, and thoughts which have been cut off are like a cut-off kite, you'll never be able to retrieve it again. Without a sentence you just can't think, because thinking is like a chain, each ring is linked to the next one. You understand?

900   MAN: Young lady, how about you? What are you looking for?

YOUNG LADY: Take a guess.

MAN: It must be something to do with love.

YOUNG LADY: You're so right! I'm waiting for a pair of eyes, tender, profound, and burning with passion—

905

(*He avoids the young lady, but he bumps into another person.*)

PERSON I: Don't step on my toes!

MAN: Oh, I beg your pardon.

PERSON I: Never seen anyone who walks like you.

MAN: Neither have I. I'm going that way.

PERSON I: Everyone's looking here, what are you going to do
910   over there?

MAN: There is nothing I want here.

PERSON I: What are you looking for?

MAN: (*Troubled.*) I don't know what I'm looking for.

PERSON I: Everybody, look! The man is a weirdo, he doesn't know
915   what he's looking for!

PERSON J: He must have found it already.

(*The CROWD surround MAN.*)

MAN: No, I haven't. Really I haven't. (*Walks away.*)

STABLE KEEPER: (*Coming out from the CROWD.*) Where are you going?

MAN: Over there.   920

STABLE KEEPER: You haven't found anything yet, right? How come you're going over there?

MAN: I'm not going to look for anything any more. I just want to go over there.

STABLE KEEPER: We're all looking here, but you insist on going   925
there.

EVERYBODY: Shall we let him?

CROWD: No!
    Absolutely not!
    He can't go.   930
    Just wait until we've all found it, then you can go.

MAN: Let me explain.

CROWD: There's no need, we already know.
        We've been looking, you've been looking, everybody's
    been looking, but no one's found anything. Why do you want   935
    to go there now?
        It won't do.
        When we say no, we mean no.
        If you quit looking and we quit looking, then you can
    go there. But everybody's still looking right now and you   940
    insist on going, of course we won't let you. How can you?
    If we're going to quit, we should all quit. So if we're going to
    look, we should all be looking, right?

MAN: I don't have anything to do with you.

STABLE KEEPER: My friend, we're treating you like a friend, don't   945
you see? (*To the CROWD.*) Try again to make him understand. Okay, let's start from the beginning.

CROWD: (*One after the other.*) That's to say, yes, no, everybody looks or nobody looks, even if nobody looks or everybody looks, not looking is not the same as not wanting to look, the   950
question is whether we can look and find it—

MAN: What if I don't want to look?

CROWD: You don't want to look, sure, okay, we can't force you to if you don't want to, if you don't want to look, it doesn't mean nobody should look, and if everybody looks then   955
you can't be not looking, nobody looks you don't look no more, everybody wants to look and you don't look, everybody looks for everybody, you don't look for everybody, you don't look and everybody looks, you look or not you don't look everybody looks you look or not nobody looks   960
you look everybody looks—

MAN: (*Can't control himself.*) I'm going my way! I'm not bothering anybody, and nobody's going to bother me, okay?

STABLE KEEPER: I'll give it to you straight: No way! You've found it but we haven't, it just won't wash!   965

MAN: But I haven't found anything!

STABLE KEEPER: Then keep looking.

MAN: I'm not looking here any more. I—want—to—go—there.

STABLE KEEPER: Don't you know the rules here? We've told you   970
over and over again, why can't you admit that you're wrong and change your ways?

CROWD: What's happening?
    What's happening?
    Son of a bitch, he's looking for trouble!   975

STABLE KEEPER: Wait, this is no good, it's so uncivilized. If he doesn't want to repent, let him. We won't make it difficult for him. Just tell him to crawl through here. (*Pointing to his crotch.*) What do you say?

30 CROWD: (*Bursting into laughter.*) Wonderful!

(*Silence. Surprisingly,* MAN *crawls through* STABLE KEEPER'S *crotch. The* CROWD *is shocked and disappears.* MAN *picks up a key while he is crawling.* SHADOW *enters immediately.*)

SHADOW: A key? That is correct. You must have been looking for a key like this one. Yes, yes, the key is what you have been looking for!

(MAN *is on his knees, inspecting the key in his hand. He then stands up and walks to centre stage and uses the key to open an imaginary door. He pulls hard on the big and heavy door and manages to open it. He walks inside.* SHADOW *exits. Silence everywhere.*)

MAN: (*Inquiring.*) Hello—(*Echo: Hello—hello—hello—hello . . .*
985   *hello . . .*) Ah—(*Ah—Ah—Ah—Ah . . . Ah . . . Ah . . . The echoes seem to make the room more hollow and deserted.*) Anybody home? (*Echo: Anybody home? Anybody home? Anybody home? Anybody home? Anybody home? . . .*) Nobody has ever set foot in here before for sure . . . (*Echolike*
990   *murmuring: so lonely, so lonely, so lonely, so lonely.*)

(MAN *looks around and finds that some objects are hidden under the cover of a piece of black cloth. He carefully pulls out a bare woman's arm from under the black cloth.*)

MAN: (*Shocked.*) O—

(*Simulated female voice sighs, echoing: O . . . O . . . O . . . O . . . O . . . . The voice seems to make him more enthusiastic. He begins to clear out what lies beneath the black cloth more diligently, and he pulls out a woman's leg.*)

MAN: (*Excited.*) Ah!

(*There is another series of simulated female voice calling urgently: Ah! Ah! Ah! Ah! Ah! Ah! . . . Finally* MAN *discovers a female mannequin hidden under the black cloth. He lifts the mannequin out and lays it down carefully. He admires it and then starts to move its hands and feet. And with increasing passion and energy, he fiddles with its shoulders, arms and the whole body, bringing it to a rather awkward forward leaning position. He turns the head around, and groping and touching, he manages to create various facial expressions. Every change he makes on the mannequin is accompanied by a simulated female voice akin to mechanical sound. The different expressions on the mannequin's face, including joy, pain, bewilderment, and peaceful staring, are also accompanied by music expressing the same sentiments in a simulated female voice. He puts the head straight so that it is staring at a not-so-distant place in front. . . . Then he stops and tries to figure out what to do next.*

He becomes more excited now. One by one he pulls out more male and female mannequins and arranges them into a kind of pattern. After thinking for a while, he decides to put a piece of headgear on the first model. He keeps rearranging the pattern, his feet dancing to the beat of the increasingly loud music. The pattern changes according to one or more rules of his own making and at a speed which can only be observed in an instant. Gradually he finds himself hemmed in by the pattern and becomes one of its composite*

parts, and he crawls busily back and forth in between the mannequins. The process is a sustained and intense consumption of will power and strength.*

Now the mannequins form a gigantic collective pattern using the first mannequin as its centre. As they move about, the pattern keeps changing slowly yet unstoppably. MAN *runs around in a hurry, jumping, moving, and rolling among his own creations. Highly excited, he calls out and responds to the mannequins in all kinds of non-language shouts and screams. This is a process of constant discovery, renewal, rediscovery, and further renewal. But gradually the objects no longer obey his commands and the sounds they make begin to overwhelm his shouts. As he is totally drawn in among them, he gradually becomes weaker, and it becomes difficult for him to get out. After a long while he finally manages to crawl out like a worm, utterly exhausted. His creations roaringly gyrate past him and slowly disappear.*)

(SHADOW *appears again, keeping a certain distance front him.*)

SHADOW: (*Narrates in a serene voice.*) Then winter came along. It was snowing hard that day, and you walked barefoot on the ice to experience the bone-chilling cold.   995
You seemed to feel that you were Jesus Christ, that you were the loneliest person, the only person who was suffering in this world. You felt that you were pervaded by the spirit of self-sacrifice, even though you were not sure for whom you would be sacrificing yourself. Yes, you did leave   1000
your footprints in the snow, and in the distance was a hazy, misty forest.

(*Totally worn out,* MAN *walks into a simulated forest made of human bodies.*)

SHADOW: (*Following him.*) You walked into the dark and shady forest. The trees, every one of them, had already shed their leaves, stretching out their shaven branches   1005
like naked women. Somberly they stood in the snow, lonely and speechless. You could not help wanting to tell them about your sorrows and torments. You recalled the time of your youth, when you waited for her on the roadside for a long long time. That day it was also snowing, and you   1010
were determined to tell her that you loved her. You want to say that at the time you were still young and innocent, but now you have sinned deeply, and you will never be able to go back to those early days any more. You have long lost your faith in people, your heart has grown   1015
old and it will not love again. Your only wish is to go walking among the trees in the forest until you are totally exhausted. Then you will collapse somewhere, hoping never to be found.

1020

(*Finally* MAN *leans against a tree to take a breath.* SHADOW *comes closer and closer, observing him.*)

SHADOW: In fact it is nothing more than a kind of self-pity. You are unwilling to end like this, you are so vain. (*Exits.*)

(*The tree* MAN *has been leaning against bends down its trunk and speaks in a human-like voice: "Oh, here you are." Then all the trees in the forest move slowly towards him like monsters. They reveal their human forms and become the* CROWD, *all dressed in mourning clothes.)*

CROWD: *(They speak and move, but they are unfeeling and expressionless.)*
We've been looking all over for you.
1025 Come on, take us to the pub to have a drink.
You're our host, how come you're here in the snow?
You're a giant, and we have to look up to see you.
You're famous, so famous that we're scared of you.
We admire you, but we don't want to idolize you.
1030 You're no more than a crook, only we don't have your tricks.
Get up and come with us.
You should donate money to our charities for children, you must know that children need money the most.
1035 You went through the forest alone, a forest even the devil fears to tread, you're number one.
You're a pathfinder, you've walked out a road nobody wants to walk on, you've led people astray.
You're lucky, not everyone is as lucky as you are.
1040 It's not that you're more talented than the others, it's only that they don't get the chance to show what they've got.
You're the tops, let's us give him a pat on the behind!

(The CROWD *laugh coldly and sinisterly. Some start to pull at him and grapple with him.)*

CROWD: *(Suddenly.)* Here he comes!
Talk of the devil.
1045 Make way.

*(*SHADOW *backs in as the* CROWD *step aside to make way for him.)*

MAN: *(Weakly.)* Who are you?
SHADOW: Your heart.

(As the CROWD *watch the drooping, blind, and deaf heart slouching past them,* SHADOW *quietly drags* MAN *away. The* CROWD *slowly follow behind the heart which is extremely old and actually invisible. All exit.)*

(One by one the ACTORS *enter from the other side.)*

ACTORS: We set off before dawn. The morning dew was thick, and in the dark we heard the cows breathing while they were chewing grass on a small hill nearby. In the distance, 1050 the river bend was enveloped in a shade of deep blue light brighter than the sky.
He told us a fable.
I dreamed that there's a piece of ivory in my stomach, it scared me to death! 1055
Have you thought of becoming a bird?
Why a bird? I'm happy with the way I am, and he says he loves me.
Faulkner.
I like "Roses for Emily." 1060
I called you up many times.
Do you know how to read palms?
No need for any explanations, you don't have to explain any more!
This kitten is so cute. 1065
I think I've seen you somewhere.
I have a sweet tooth, and I'm also a sucker for sour milk.
Your hair looks so nice, is it real?

(The sound of a baby crying.)

Sweetie, oh, sorry, I forgot to change your diapers!
1070
(The sound of a car engine starting.)

How are you going to get back?
It's so bad, what kind of stupid play is this anyway?
Are you doing anything tomorrow? Shall we have dinner together?

(Sounds of a baby crying, a car engine starting and running, bicycle bells and the trickle of running water from a tap, and in the distance, the siren of an ambulance.)

The End

Some Suggestions on Producing *The Other Shore*

1. The so-called "spoken drama" (*huaju*) tends to emphasize and highlight the art of language; in order to free drama from its constraints and to revive drama in all its functions as a performing art, we have to provide training for a new breed of modern actors. As with the actors in traditional operas, these new actors must be versatile, and their skills should include singing, the martial arts, stylized movements and delivering dialogues. They should also be able to perform Shakespeare, Ibsen, Chekov, Aristophanes, Racine, Lao She, Cao Yu, Guo Moruo, Goethe, Brecht, Pirandello, Beckett, and even mimes and musicals. The present play is written with the intention of providing an all-around training for the actors.

2. An ideal performance should be a unity of somatics, language, and psychology. Our play is an attempt to pursue this unified artistic expression and to assist the actors to achieve this goal. In other words, we should allow the actors the chance for linguistic expression in their search for suitable somatic movements, so that language and somatics are able to evoke psychological process at the same time. For this reason, during rehearsals and actual performances, it is not advisable to separate dialogue from movement, i.e., to memorize only the dialogue, to do reading as in common practice, or to strip the language and transform the play into a mime. Certain scenes in the play do not feature dialogue, but there are still other aural expressions, which could be regarded as a kind of sound language.

3. Even though our play is abstract, the performance should not aim at sheer conceptualization in the stark fashion of the play of ideas. Our aspiration is to achieve a kind of emotive abstraction through performance, i.e., a non-philosophical abstraction. The play seeks to set up the performance on the premise of non-reality, and to fully mobilize the imagination of the actors before evoking abstraction through emotion. Therefore the performance requires not only the unity of language and somatics but also the unity of thought and psychology.

4. Except for a few simple props, the performance does not require any scenery. The characters' relationships with their surroundings and other objects are contingent upon life-like dialogue and communicative exchanges in the play. In the case of monologues or in the absence of dialogue, music, sound effects, movement, the look of the eyes and changes in posture could also take on performing roles, so that the props and surroundings will not be relegated to being inanimate objects or mere adornments.

5. The play highlights the performance's ability to ascertain in the mind of the audience the existence of non-existing objects, for instance a decrepit heart, a concrete or abstract river. We may say that this is the inherent difference between a film and a theatrical performance. Even though the play itself relies heavily upon imaginary surroundings, relationships and acting partners, real and life-like objects can be deployed as stage props at the beginning of the performance. For instance, an interpersonal relationship could be established through a piece of rope. Once an actor is equipped with the capability to relate with others, he can easily communicate with his non-existent partners anytime, anywhere. He can also materialize his non-existent partners through his power of imagination, making them come to life and communicate with them, even though they have been created through his own imagination and are actually non-existent.

6. Grotowski's training method aims at helping the actor to discover his own self and to release its potential through big-movement exercises which also relax both body and mind. Thus he calls this type of performance a form of sacrifice. Our play's performance helps the actor to ascertain his own self through the process of discovering his partners. If the actor, without being obsessed with his own self, is consistently able

to find a partner to communicate with him, his performance will always be positive and lively, and he will be able to gain a real sense of his own self, which has been awakened by action, and which is alert and capable of self-observation.

7. The play demands that the actors abandon completely the kind of performance dependent upon logic and semantic thinking. The liveliest performances are exactly those which are intuitive, improvisational, and on the spur of the moment. On the stage as in real life, the actor sees with his eyes, hears with his ears, and captures his partners' reactions with his free-moving body. In other words, a performance can only be lively without the use of intellect. Therefore it is best not to resort to literary analysis outside of theatrical performance or to uncover hidden meanings in the text in performing the play.

8. Our play aims at training actors who can be as versatile as the actors in Chinese traditional operas, but it is not our intention to create a new set of conventions for modern drama, because the latter aspires to the kind of acting which is non-formulaic, unregulated, and flexible. Before the actual performance, the actor should enter into a state of competitiveness similar to that of an athlete before a game, or of a cock preparing to slug it out in a cock-fight, ready to provoke as well as to receive his partners' reactions. Thus the performance must be fresh, regenerating, and improvisational, which is essentially different from gymnastic or musical performances.

9. The play's performance strives to expand and not to reduce the expressiveness of language in drama. The language in a play is voiced language, but it is not limited to beautifully written dialogue. In this play, all the sounds uttered by the actor in the prescribed circumstances are also voiced language. If an actor has learned to communicate using fragmented language which features unfinished sentences, disjointed phonetic elements, and ungrammatical constructions, he will be better able to make the unspoken words in the script come to life as voiced language.

The above suggestions are for reference only.

Tomson Highway

Since the production of his two most celebrated plays, The *Rez Sisters* (1986) and *Dry Lips Oughta Move to Kapuskasing* (1989), Tomson Highway has become perhaps the best-known of the many Native playwrights now working in North America. Tomson Highway was born in 1951, the eleventh of twelve children, on a trapline in a Native reserve (the Canadian term for what is called a "reservation" in the United States) in northern Manitoba, Canada. Until the age of six, Highway lived a nomadic life with his family. His first language was Cree, and he did not begin to learn English until he was sent to a Roman Catholic boarding school. Like many Native children, Highway attended boarding school, visiting his family only during the summer. After graduating from high school in Winnipeg, Highway studied piano at the University of Manitoba Faculty of Music, and then studied in London before returning to Canada. He graduated with a bachelor's degree in music from the University of Western Ontario in 1975 and is an accomplished concert pianist. He remained at the university for an additional year, however, to complete a bachelor's degree in English.

After college, Highway worked at The Native Peoples' Resource Centre in London, Ontario, and at the Ontario Federation of Indian Friendship Centres in Toronto. Highway traveled to reserves across Canada, working with Native people in schools, prisons, and other institutions. He also began writing plays about Native life, many of which were performed on reserves and in Native community centers. He first worked on *The Rez Sisters* with the De-ba-jeh-mu-jig Theatre Company of Manitoulin Island, Ontario, in 1986. Like many Native theater companies, De-ba-jeh-mu-jig is devoted to the production of new plays by Native playwrights and produces an increasing number of its plays in Native languages. As artistic director of the Native Earth Performing Arts Company, Highway produced *The Rez Sisters* again in Toronto in December of 1986, where it won the Dora Mavor Moore Award for the best new play of the season and was runner-up for outstanding Canadian play of

Simon Starblanket and Sachary Keechigeesik in the 1989 Theater Passe Muraille production of Tomson Highway's *Dry Lips Oughta Move to Kapuskasing.*

the year. The play was produced in 1993 in New York by the American Indian Community House and the New York Theater Workshop.

Highway's next play, *Dry Lips Oughta Move to Kapuskasing* was first produced in Toronto in 1989 by the Native Earth Performing Arts Company. It was later moved to the Royal Alexandra Theatre in Toronto, one of the very few Canadian plays—and the first by a Native playwright—to receive a full-scale production by this commercial theater. Highway continues to work as artistic director of Native Earth Performing Arts, one of many important Native theater companies now working in Canada and the United States (others include Four Winds Theatre, Native Theatre School, Ondinnok, Takwakin Theatre, Awasikan Theatre, and A-Maize Theatre in Canada; Spiderwoman Theater, Institute of American Indian Arts, American Indian Theater Company, Minneapolis American Indian AIDS Task Force, and Off the Beaten Path in the United States). Though Highway is gay, his central aims as a playwright to date have been to make Native narrative and mythological traditions more central to contemporary Native—and non-Native—arts. He has completed this trilogy with the play *Rose* (2000), and has written a novel, *Kiss of the Fur Queen* (1998).

Dry Lips Oughta Move to Kapuskasing

Like *The Rez Sisters*, *Dry Lips Oughta Move to Kapuskasing* concerns life on the fictional Wasaychigan Hill reserve and is written in a mixture of English, Cree, and Ojibway. However, while *The Rez Sisters* concerns a group of Native women who travel to Toronto for the "World's Biggest Bingo," *Dry Lips* is a much darker and more violent play, concerning the men of the reserve. In some respects, the poverty of life on the reserve is made evident in the play's opening scene, the run-down living room of the reserve house shared by Big Joey and Gazelle Nataways, and is developed through the men's interrupted plans to improve life on the "rez." While the women have formed a hockey team (the importance of hockey is epitomized in Pierre's mantra, "Hockey. Life. Hockey. Life."), the men squabble about their plans: Zachary Jeremiah Keechigeesik's bakery, Big Joey's radio station, and Pierre St. Pierre's new job as referee for the women's games. In some ways, the men seem threatened by the women's independence and by their brash appropriation of hockey, and this anxiety seems to imply a more generalized impotence: seedy Creature Nataways does Big Joey's bidding, even though his wife Gazelle has moved in with Big Joey; Simon Starblanket is absorbed in an endlessly aborted effort at cultural revival; Dickie Bird Halked, born with fetal alcohol syndrome, is at once shy and explosive, violently raping Patsy Pegahmagahbow with a crucifix. Even Pierre St. Pierre has a hard time finding his other skate.

Hanging around, drinking beer, complaining about the women—in many ways the Native men seem to epitomize "Canadian hoser culture," in the words of one Native critic of the play. Yet the men continually blame the women for the state of their lives, as Big Joey does in act 2: "I hate them fuckin' bitches. Because they—our own women—took the fuckin' power away from us faster than the FBI ever did." Big Joey's tirade points up the play's most controversial element, which centers on the performance of the Trickster figure Nanabush. The play begins and ends with Zachary awakening on the floor of Big Joey's house; we don't discover until the end of the play that the action has been a kind of dream, maybe a nightmare. Throughout, Nanabush occupies an elevated stage, sometimes watching the action, sometimes participating in it. In Native mythology, Nanabush is capable of changing shape and gender; neither explicitly male nor female, the Trickster uses his/her wiles in a range of legendary escapades. In *Dry Lips*, however, Nanabush takes "female" shape in a number of ways—assuming outsized breasts to play Gazelle Nataways, a large rear-end to play Patsy ("Big-Bum") Pegahmagahbow, and so on. In one reading of the play—a dream play, after all—Nanabush here enacts the men's phobias and fantasies about women, and so offers an implied critique of their sexist attitudes. From another perspective, though, one shared by many Native women who saw the play, the way Nanabush is characterized as a woman—her appearance (a version of the derogatory "squaw" stereotype), the "stripper" scene, the rape scene, the loss of the hockey puck in Gazelle/Nanabush's enormous breasts—merely reinforces the fundamentally misogynistic attitudes of the men in the play. In this sense, *Dry Lips Oughta Move to Kapuskasing* seems poised on the razor's edge of political theater: readers, audiences, and producers of the play must consider whether it criticizes the sexist and possibly misogynist ways women are presented in the play, or whether it merely reinforces such attitudes.

Production Notes

The set for the original production of *Dry Lips Oughta Move to Kapuskasing* contained certain elements which I think are essential to the play.

First of all, it was designed on two levels, the lower of which was the domain of the "real" Wasaychigan Hill. This lower level contained, on stage-left, Big Joey's living room/kitchen, with its kitchen counter at the back and, facing down-stage, an old brown couch with a television set a few feet in front of it. This television set could be made to double as a smaller rock for the forest scenes. Stage-right had Spooky Lacroix's kitchen, with its kitchen counter (for which Big Joey's kitchen counter could double) and its table and chairs.

In front of all this was an open area, the floor of which was covered with Teflon, a material which looks like ice and on which one can actually skate, using real ice skates; this was the rink for the hockey arena scenes. With lighting effects, this area could also be turned into "the forest" surrounding the village of Wasaychigan Hill, with its leafless winter trees. The only other essential element here was a larger jutting rock beside which, for instance, Zachary Jeremiah Keechigeesik and Simon Starblanket meet, a rock which could be made to glow at certain key points. Pierre's "little boot-leg joint" in Act Two, with its "window," was also created with lighting effects.

The upper level of the set was almost exclusively the realm of Nanabush. The principal element here was her perch, located in the very middle of this area. The perch was actually an old jukebox of a late 60's/early 70's make, but it was semi-hidden throughout most of the play, so that it was fully revealed as this fabulous jukebox only at those few times when it was needed; the effect sought after here is of this magical, mystical jukebox hanging in the night air, like a haunting and persistent memory, high up over the village of Wasaychigan Hill. Over and behind this perch was suspended a huge full moon whose glow came on, for the most part, only during the outdoor scenes, which all take place at nighttime. All other effects in this area were accomplished with lighting. The very front of this level, all along its edge, was also utilized as the "bleachers" area for the hockey arena scenes.

Easy access was provided for between the lower and the upper levels of this set.

The "sound-scape" of *Dry Lips Oughta Move to Kapuskasing* was mostly provided for by a musician playing, live, on harmonica, off to the side. It is as though the "dream-scape" of the play were laced all the way through with Zachary Jeremiah Keechigeesik's "idealized" form of harmonica playing, permeated with a definite "blues" flavor. Although Zachary ideally should play his harmonica, and not too well, in those few scenes where it is called for, the sound of this harmonica is most effectively used to underline and highlight the many magical appearances of Nanabush in her various guises.

Spooky Lacroix's baby, towards the end of act 2, can, and should, be played by a doll wrapped in a blanket. But for greatest effect, Zachary's baby, at the very end of the play, should be played by a real baby, preferably about five months of age.

Finally, both Cree and Ojibway are used freely in this text for the reasons that these two languages, belonging to the same linguistic family, are very similar and that the fictional reserve of Wasaychigan Hill has a mixture of both Cree and Ojibway residents.

A Note on Nanabush

The dream world of North American Indian mythology is inhabited by the most fantastic creatures, beings and events. Foremost among these beings is the "Trickster," as pivotal and important a figure in our world as Christ is in the realm of Christian mythology.

"Weesageechak" in Cree, "Nanabush" in Ojibway, "Raven" in others, "Coyote" in still others, this Trickster goes by many names and many guises. In fact, he can assume any guise he chooses. Essentially a comic, clownish sort of character, his role is to teach us about the nature and the meaning of existence on the planet Earth; he straddles the consciousness of man and that of God, the Great Spirit.

The most explicit distinguishing feature between the North American Indian languages and the European languages is that in Indian (e.g., Cree, Ojibway), there is no gender. In Cree, Ojibway, etc., unlike English, French, German, etc., the male-female-neuter hierarchy is entirely absent. So that by this system of thought, the central hero figure from our mythology—theology, if you will—is theoretically neither exclusively male nor exclusively female, or is both simultaneously. Therefore, where in *The Rez Sisters*, Nanabush was male, in this play—"flip-side" to *The Rez* Sisters—Nanabush is female.

Some say that Nanabush left this continent when the white man came. We believe she/ he is still here among us—albeit a little the worse for wear and tear—having assumed other guises. Without the continued presence of this extraordinary figure, the core of Indian culture would be gone forever.

Tomson Highway

Dry Lips Oughta Move to Kapuskasing

Tomson Highway

CHARACTERS

NANABUSH (*as the spirit of Gazelle Nataways, Patsy Pegahmagahbow and Black Lady Halked*)
ZACHARY JEREMIAH KEECHIGEESIK—*41 years old*
BIG JOEY—*39*
CREATURE NATAWAYS—*39*
DICKIE BIRD HALKED—*17*
PIERRE ST. PIERRE—*53*
SPOOKY LACROIX—*39*

SIMON STARBLANKET—*20*
HERA KEECHIGEESIK—*39*

TIME: *Between Saturday, February 3, 1990, 11 p.m., and Saturday, February 10, 1990, 11 a.m.*
PLACE: *The Wasaychigan Hill Indian Reserve, Manitoulin Island, Ontario*

ACT ONE

The set for this first scene is the rather shabby and very messy living room/kitchen of the reserve house BIG JOEY *and* GAZELLE NATAWAYS *currently share. Prominently displayed on one wall is a life-size pin-up poster of Marilyn Monroe. The remains of a party are obvious. On the worn-out old brown couch, with its back towards the entrance, lies* ZACHARY JEREMIAH KEECHIGEESIK, *a very handsome Indian man. He is naked, passed out. The first thing we see when the light comes up—a very small "spot," precisely focussed—is* ZACHARY'S *bare, naked bum. Then, from behind the couch, we see a woman's leg, sliding languorously into a nylon stocking and right over Zachary's bum. It is* NANABUSH, *as the spirit of* GAZELLE NATAWAYS, *dressing to leave. She eases herself luxuriously over the couch and over Zachary's bum and then reaches under Zachary's sleeping head, from where she gently pulls a gigantic pair of false, rubberized breasts. She proceeds to put these on over her own bare breasts. Then* NANABUSH/GAZELLE NATAWAYS *sashays over to the side of the couch, picks a giant hockey sweater up off the floor and shimmies into it. The sweater has a huge, plunging neck-line, with the capital letter "W" and the number "1" prominently sewn on. Then she sashays back to the couch and behind it. Pleasurably and mischievously, she leans over and plants a kiss on Zachary's bum, leaving behind a gorgeous, luminescent lip-stick mark. The last thing she does before she leaves is to turn the television on. This television sits facing the couch that* ZACHARY *lies on.* NANABUSH/GAZELLE *does not use her hand for this, though; instead, she turns the appliance on with one last bump of her voluptuous hips. "Hockey Night in Canada" comes on. The sound of this hockey game is on only slightly, so that we hear it as background "music" all the way through the coming scene. Then* NANABUSH/GAZELLE *exits, to sit on her perch on the upper level of the set. The only light left on stage is that coming from the television screen, giving off its eery glow. Beat.*

The kitchen door bangs open, the "kitchen light" flashes on and BIG JOEY *and* CREATURE NATAWAYS *enter,* CREATURE *carrying a case of beer on his head. At first, they are oblivious to* ZACHARY'S *presence. Also at about this time, the face of* DICKIE BIRD HALKED *emerges from the shadows at the "kitchen window." Silently, he watches the rest of the proceedings, taking a particular interest— even fascination—in the movements and behavior of* BIG JOEY.

BIG JOEY: (*Calling out for* GAZELLE *who, of course, is not home.*)
Hey, bitch!

CREATURE: (*As he, at regular intervals, bangs the beer case down on the kitchen counter, rips it open, pops bottles open, throws one to* BIG JOEY, *all noises that serve to "punctuate" the rat-a-tat rhythm of his frenetic speech.*) Batman oughta move to Kapuskasing, nah, Kap's too good for Batman, right, Big Joey? I tole you once I tole you twice he shouldna done it he shouldna done what he went and did goddawful Batman Manitowabi the way he went and crossed that blue line with the puck, man, he's got the flippin' puck right in the palm of his flippin' hand and only a minute-and-a-half to go he just about gave me the shits the way Batman Manitowabi went and crossed that blue line right in front of that brick shithouse of a whiteman why the hell did that brick shit-house of a whiteman have to be there . . .

ZACHARY: (*Talking in his sleep.*) No!

CREATURE: Hey!

(BIG JOEY *raises a finger signaling* CREATURE *to shut up.*)

ZACHARY: I said no!

CREATURE: (*In a hoarse whisper.*) That's not a TV kind of sound.

BIG JOEY: Shhh!

ZACHARY: . . . goodness sakes, Hera, you just had a baby . . .

CREATURE: That's a real life kind of sound, right, Big Joey? (BIG JOEY *and* CREATURE *slowly come over to the couch.*)

ZACHARY: . . . women playing hockey . . . damn silliest thing I heard in my life . . .

BIG JOEY: Well, well . . .

CREATURE: Ho-leee! (*Whispering.*) Hey, what's that on his arse look like lip marks.

ZACHARY: . . . Simon Starblanket, that's who's gonna help me with my bakery . . .

CREATURE: He's stitchless, he's nude, he's gonna pneumonia . . .

BIG JOEY: Shut up.

CREATURE: Get the camera. Chris'sakes, take a picture.

(CREATURE *scrambles for the Polaroid, which he finds under one end of the couch.*)

ZACHARY: . . . Simon! (*Jumps up.*) What the?!

CREATURE: Surprise! (*Camera flashes.*)

ZACHARY: Put that damn thing away. What are you doing here? Where's my wife? Hera!

(*He realizes he's naked, grabs a cast iron frying pan and slaps it over his crotch, almost castrating himself in the process.*)

Ooof!

Keechigeesik means "heaven" or "great sky" in Cree **Wasaychigan** means "window" in Ojibway

991

40　BIG JOEY: (*Smiling.*) Over easy or sunny side up, Zachary Jeremiah
　　　Keechigeesik?
　　ZACHARY: Get outa my house.
　　CREATURE: This ain't your house. This is Big Joey's house, right,
　　　Big Joey?
45　BIG JOEY: Shut up.
　　ZACHARY: Creature Nataways. Get outa here. Gimme that
　　　camera.
　　CREATURE: Come and geeeet it!

(*Grabs* ZACHARY'*s pants from the floor.*)

　　ZACHARY: Cut it out. Gimme them goddamn pants.
50　CREATURE: (*Singing.*) Lipstick on your arshole, tole da tale on
　　　you-hoo.
　　ZACHARY: What? (*Straining to see his bum.*) Oh lordy, lordy, lordy
　　　gimme them pants.

(*As he tries to wipe the stain off.*)

　　CREATURE: Here doggy, doggy. Here poochie, poochie woof
55　　woof! (ZACHARY *grabs the pants. They rip almost completely
　　　in half.* CREATURE *yelps.*) Yip!

(*Momentary light up on* NANABUSH/GAZELLE, *up on her perch, as she
gives a throaty laugh.* BIG JOEY *echoes this,* CREATURE *tittering away
in the background.*)

　　ZACHARY: Hey, this is not my doing, Big Joey. (*As he clumsily puts
　　　on what's left of his pants.* CREATURE *manages to get in one more
　　　shot with the camera.*) We were just having a nice quiet drink
60　　over at Andy Manigitogan's when Gazelle Nataways shows up.
　　　She brought me over here to give me the recipe for her bannock
　　　apple pie cuz, goodness sakes, Simon Starblanket was saying
　　　it's the best, that pie was selling like hot cakes at the bingo and
　　　he knows I'm tryna establish this reserve's first pie-making
65　　business gimme that camera.

(BIG JOEY *suddenly makes a lunge at* ZACHARY *but* ZACHARY
evades him.)

　　CREATURE: (*In the background, like a little dog.*) Yah, yah.
　　BIG JOEY: (*Slowly stalking* ZACHARY *around the room.*) You
　　　know, Zach, there's a whole lotta guys on this rez been
70　　slippin' my old lady the goods but there ain't but a handful
　　　been stupid enough to get caught by me. (*He snaps his fingers
　　　and, as always,* CREATURE *obediently scurries over. He hands*
　　　BIG JOEY *the picture of* ZACHARY *naked on the couch.* BIG JOEY
　　　shows the picture to ZACHARY, *right up to his face.*) Kinda
75　　em-bare-ass-in' for a hoity-toity educated community pillar
　　　like you, eh Zach?

(ZACHARY *grabs for the picture but* BIG JOEY *snaps it away.*)

　　ZACHARY: What do you want?
　　BIG JOEY: What's this I hear about you tellin' the chief I can wait
　　　for my radio station?
　　ZACHARY: (*As he proceeds with looking around the room to
80　　collect and put on what he can find of his clothes.* BIG JOEY
　　　and CREATURE *follow him around, obviously enjoying his
　　　predicament.*) I don't know where the hell you heard that from.

BIG JOEY: Yeah, right. Well, Lorraine Manigitogan had a word
　　　or two with Gazelle Nataways the other night. When you
　　　presented your initial proposal at the band office, you said: 85
　　　"Joe can wait. He's only got another three months left in the
　　　hockey season."
ZACHARY: I never said no such thing.
BIG JOEY: Bullshit.
ZACHARY: W-w-w-what I said was that employment at this bakery of 90
　　　mine would do nothing but add to those in such places as those
　　　down at the arena. I never mentioned your name once. And
　　　I said it only in passing reference to the fact . . .
BIG JOEY: . . . that this radio idea of mine doesn't have as much
　　　long-term significance to the future of this community as 95
　　　this fancy bakery idea of yours, Mr. Pillsbury dough-boy,
　　　right?
ZACHARY: If that's what you heard, then you didn't hear it from
　　　Lorraine Manigitogan. You got it from Gazelle Nataways and
　　　you know yourself she's got a bone to pick with . . . 100
BIG JOEY: You know, Zach, you and me, we work for the same
　　　cause, don't we?
ZACHARY: Never said otherwise.
BIG JOEY: We work for the betterment and the advancement of this
　　　community, don't we? And seeing as we're about the only two 105
　　　guys in this whole hell-hole who's got the get-up-and-go to do
　　　something . . .
ZACHARY: That's not exactly true, Joe. Take a look at Simon
　　　Starblanket . . .
BIG JOEY: . . . we should be working together, not against. What 110
　　　do you say you simply postpone that proposal to the Band
　　　Council . . .
ZACHARY: I'm sorry. Can't do that.
BIG JOEY: (*Cornering* ZACHARY.) Listen here, bud. You turned
　　　your back on me when everybody said I was responsible for that 115
　　　business in Espanola seventeen years ago and you said nothin'.
　　　I overlooked that. Never said nothin'. (ZACHARY *remembers
　　　his undershorts and proceeds, with even greater desperation, to
　　　look for them, zeroing in on the couch and under it.* BIG JOEY
　　　catches the drift and snaps his fingers, signaling CREATURE 120
　　　*to look for the shorts under the couch. creature jumps for
　　　the couch. Without missing a beat,* BIG JOEY *continues.*) You
　　　turned your back on me when you said you didn't want nothin'
　　　to do with me from that day on. I overlooked that. Never said
　　　nothin'. You gave me one hell of a slap in the face when your 125
　　　wife gave my Gazelle that kick in the belly. I overlooked that.
　　　Never said nothin'. (CREATURE, *having found the shorts among
　　　the junk under the couch just split seconds before* ZACHARY
　　　does, throws them to BIG JOEY. BIG JOEY *holds the shorts up to*
　　　ZACHARY, *smiling with satisfaction.*) That, however, was the 130
　　　last time . . .
ZACHARY: That wasn't my fault, Joe. It's that witch woman of
　　　yours Gazelle Nataways provoked that fight between her and
　　　Hera and you know yourself Hera tried to come and sew up
　　　her belly again . . . 135
BIG JOEY: Zach. I got ambition . . .
ZACHARY: Yeah, right.
BIG JOEY: I aim to get that radio station off the ground, starting
　　　with them games down at my arena.
ZACHARY: Phhhh! 140
BIG JOEY: I aim to get a chain of them community radio stations
　　　not only on this here island but beyond as well . . .
ZACHARY: Dream on, Big Joey, dream on . . .

BIG JOEY: . . . and I aim to prove this broadcasting of games
145　among the folks is one sure way to get some pride . . .
ZACHARY: Bullshit! You're in it for yourself.
BIG JOEY: . . . some pride and dignity back so you just get
　　your ass on out of my house and you go tell that Chief
　　your Band Council Resolution can wait until next fiscal
150　year or else . . .
ZACHARY: I ain't doing no such thing, Joe, no way. Not when
　　I'm this close.
BIG JOEY: (*As he eases himself down onto the couch, twirling the
　　shorts with his fore-finger.*) . . . or else I get my Gazelle Nataways
155　to wash these skivvies of yours, put them in a box all nice and
　　gussied up, your picture on top, show up at your door-stop
　　and hand them over to your wife. (*Silence.*)
ZACHARY: (*Quietly, to* BIG JOEY.) Gimme them shorts. (*No
　　answer. Then to* CREATURE.) Gimme them snapshots. (*Still
160　no response.*)
BIG JOEY: (*Dead calm.*) Get out.
ZACHARY: (*Seeing he can't win for the moment, prepares to exit.*) You
　　may have won this time, Joe, but . . .
BIG JOEY: (*Like a steel trap.*) Get out.

(*Silence. Finally* ZACHARY *exits, looking very humble. Seconds
before* ZACHARY'*s exit,* DICKIE BIRD HALKED, *to avoid being seen by*
ZACHARY, *disappears from the "window." The moment* ZACHARY *is gone,*
CREATURE *scurries to the kitchen door, shaking his fist in the direction
of the already-departed* ZACHARY.)

165　CREATURE: Damn rights! (*Then strutting like a cock, he turns to* BIG
　　JOEY.) Zachary Jeremiah Keechigeesik never shoulda come in
　　your house, Big Joey. Thank god, Gazelle Nataways ain't my
　　wife no more . . . (BIG JOEY *merely has to throw a glance in*
　　CREATURE'*s direction to intimidate him. At once,* CREATURE
170　*reverts back to his usual nervous self.*) . . . not really, she's
　　yours now, right, Big Joey? It's you she's livin' with these days,
　　not me.
BIG JOEY: (*As he sits on the couch with his beer, mostly ignoring*
　　CREATURE *and watching the hockey game on television.*) Don't
175　make her my wife.
CREATURE: But you live together, you sleep together, you eat
　　ooops!
BIG JOEY: Still don't make her my wife.
CREATURE: (*As he proceeds to try to clean up the mess around the
180　couch, mostly shoving everything back under it.*) I don't mind,
　　Big Joey, I really don't. I tole you once I tole you twice she's
　　yours now. It's like I loaned her to you, I don't mind. I can
　　take it. We made a deal, remember? The night she threw
　　the toaster at me and just about broke my skull, she tole
185　me: "I had enough, Creature Nataways, I had enough from
　　you. I had your kids and I had your disease and that's all I
　　ever want from you, I'm leavin'." And then she grabbed her
　　suitcase and she grabbed the kids, no, she didn't even grab the
　　kids, she grabbed the TV and she just sashayed herself over
190　here. She left me. It's been four years now, Big Joey, I know,
　　I know. Oh, it was hell, it was hell at first but you and me
　　we're buddies since we're babies, right? So I thought it over for
　　about a year . . . then one day I swallowed my pride and I got
　　up off that chesterfield and I walked over here, I opened your
195　door and I shook your hand and I said: "It's okay, Big Joey, it's
　　okay." And then we went and played darts in Espanola except
　　we kinda got side-tracked, remember, Big Joey, we ended up
　　on that three-day bender?

BIG JOEY: Creature Nataways?
CREATURE: What?　　　　　　　　　　　　　　　　　　　　200
BIG JOEY: You talk too much.
CREATURE: I tole you once I tole you twice I don't mind . . .

(*But* PIERRE ST. PIERRE *comes bursting in, in a state of great
excitement.*)

PIERRE: (*Addressing the case of beer directly.*) Hallelujah! Have you
　　heard the news?
CREATURE: Pierre St. Pierre. Chris'sakes, knock. You're walkin'　205
　　into a civilized house.
PIERRE: The news. Have you heard the news?
CREATURE: I'll tell you a piece of news. Anyways, we come in the
　　door and guess who . . .
BIG JOEY: (*To* CREATURE.) Sit down.　　　　　　　　　　　　210
PIERRE: Gimme a beer.
CREATURE: (*To* PIERRE.) Sit down.
PIERRE: Gimme a beer.
BIG JOEY: Give him a fuckin' beer. (*But* PIERRE *has already
　　grabbed, opened and is drinking a beer.*)　　　　　　　　215
CREATURE: Have a beer.
PIERRE: (*Talking out the side of his mouth, as he continues
　　drinking.*) Tank you.
BIG JOEY: Talk.
PIERRE: (*Putting his emptied bottle down triumphantly and　220
　　grabbing another beer.*) Toast me.
BIG JOEY: Spit it out.
CREATURE: Chris'sakes.
PIERRE: Toast me.
CREATURE: Toast you? The hell for?　　　　　　　　　　　225
PIERRE: Shut up. Just toast me.
CREATURE/BIG JOEY: Toast.
PIERRE: Tank you. You just toasted "The Ref."
CREATURE: (*To* PIERRE.) The ref? (*To* BIG JOEY.) The what?
PIERRE: "The Ref!"　　　　　　　　　　　　　　　　　　230
CREATURE: The ref of the what?
PIERRE: The ref. I'm gonna be the referee down at the arena. Big
　　Joey's arena. The Wasaychigan Hill Hippodrome.
CREATURE: We already got a referee.
PIERRE: Yeah, but this here's different, this here's special.　　235
BIG JOEY: I'd never hire a toothless old bootlegger like you.
PIERRE: They play their first game in just a coupla days. Against
　　the Canoe Lake Bravettes. And I got six teeth left so you just
　　keep your trap shut about my teeth.
CREATURE: The Canoe Lake Bravettes?　　　　　　　　　　240
BIG JOEY: Who's "they"?
PIERRE: Haven't you heard?
BIG JOEY: Who's "they"?
PIERRE: I don't believe this.
BIG JOEY: Who's "they"?　　　　　　　　　　　　　　　245
PIERRE: I don't believe this. (BIG JOEY *bangs* PIERRE *on the head.*)
　　Oww, you big bully! The Wasaychigan Hill Wailerettes,
　　of course. I'm talkin' about the Wasy Wailerettes, who else
　　geez.
CREATURE: The Wasy Wailerettes? Chris'sakes . . .　　　　250
PIERRE: Dominique Ladouche, Black Lady Halked, that
　　terrible Dictionary woman, Fluffy Sainte-Marie, Dry
　　Lips Manigitogan, Leonarda Lee Starblanket, Annie
　　Cook, June Bug McLeod, Big Bum Pegahmagahbow, all
　　twenty-seven of 'em. Them women from right here on　255
　　this reserve, a whole batch of 'em, they upped and they

said: "Bullshit! Ain't nobody on the face of this earth's gonna tell us us women's got no business playin' hockey. That's bullshit!" That's what they said: "Bullshit!" So. They

260   took matters into their own hands. And, holy shit la marde, I almost forgot to tell you my wife Veronique St. Pierre, she went and made up her mind she's joinin' the Wasy Wailerettes, only the other women wouldn't let her at first on account she never had no babies—cuz, you see, you gotta

265   be pregnant or have piles and piles of babies to be a Wasy Wailerette—but my wife, she put her foot down and she says: "Zhaboonigan Peterson may be just my adopted daughter and she may be retarded as a doormat but she's still my baby." That's what she says to 'em. And she's on and they're playin'

270   hockey and the Wasy Wailerettes, they're just a-rarin' to go, who woulda thunk it, huh?

CREATURE: Ho-leee!

PIERRE: God's truth . . .

BIG JOEY: They never booked the ice.

275   PIERRE: Ha! Booked it through Gazelle Nataways. Sure as I'm alive and walkin' these treacherous icy roads . . .

BIG JOEY: Hang on.

PIERRE: . . . god's truth in all its naked splendor. (*As he pops open yet another beer.*) I kid you not, gentlemen, not for one

280   slippery goddamn minute. Toast!

BIG JOEY: (*Grabbing the bottle right out of* PIERRE'*s mouth.*) Where'd you sniff out all this crap?

PIERRE: From my wife, who else? My wife, Veronique St. Pierre, she told me. She says to me: "Pierre St. Pierre, you'll eat your

285   shorts but I'm playin' hockey and I don't care what you say. Or think." And she left. No. First, she cleaned out my wallet, (*Grabs his beer back from* BIG JOEY'*s hand.*) grabbed her big brown rosaries from off the wall. Then she left. Just slammed the door and left. Period. I just about ate my

290   shorts. Toast!

CREATURE: Shouldn't we . . . shouldn't we stop them?

PIERRE: Phhht! . . . (CREATURE *just misses getting spat on.*)

CREATURE: Ayoah!

PIERRE: . . . Haven't seen hide nor hair of 'em since. Gone to

295   Sudbury. Every single last one of 'em. Piled theirselves into seven cars and just took off. Them back wheels was squealin' and rattlin' like them little jinger bells. Just past tea-time. Shoppin'. Hockey equipment. Phhht! (*Again,* CREATURE *just misses getting spat on.*)

300   CREATURE: Ayoah! It's enough to give you the shits every time he opens his mouth.

PIERRE: And they picked me. Referee.

BIG JOEY: And why you, may I ask?

PIERRE: (*Faking humility.*) Oh, I don't know. Somethin' about the

305   referee here's too damn perschnickety. That drum-bangin' young whipperschnapper, Simon Starblanket, (*Grabbing yet another beer.*) he's got the rules all mixed up or some-thin' like that, is what he says. They kinda wanna play it their own way. So they picked me. Toast me.

310   CREATURE: Toast.

PIERRE: To the ref.

CREATURE: To the ref.

PIERRE: Tank you. (*They both drink.*) Ahhh. (*Pause. To* BIG JOEY.) So. I want my skates.

315   CREATURE: Your skates?

PIERRE: My skates. I want 'em back.

CREATURE: The hell's he talkin' about now?

PIERRE: They're here. I know they're here. I loaned 'em to you, remember?

320   BIG JOEY: Run that by me again?

PIERRE: I loaned 'em to you. That Saturday night Gazelle Nataways came in that door with her TV and her suitcase and you and me we were sittin' right there on that old chesterfield with Lalala Lacroix sittin' between us and I

325   loaned you my skates in return for that forty-ouncer of rye and Gazelle Nataways plunked her TV down, marched right up to Lalala Lacroix, slapped her in the face and chased her out the door. But we still had time to make the deal whereby if I wanted my skates back you'd give 'em back to

330   me if I gave you back your forty-ouncer, right? Right. (*Produces the bottle from under his coat.*) Ta-da! Gimme my skates.

BIG JOEY: You sold them skates. They're mine.

PIERRE: Never you mind, Big Joey, never you mind. I want my

335   skates. Take this. Go on. Take it.

(BIG JOEY *fishes one skate out from under the couch.*)

CREATURE: (*To himself, as he sits on the couch.*) Women playin' hockey. Ho-leee!

(BIG JOEY *and* PIERRE *exchange bottle and skate.*)

PIERRE: Tank you. (*He makes a triumphant exit.* BIG JOEY *merely sits there and waits knowingly. Silence. Then* PIERRE *suddenly re-enters.*) There's only one. (*Silence.*) Well, where the hell's the

340   other one? (*Silence.* PIERRE *nearly explodes with indignation.*) Gimme back my bottle! Where's the other one?

BIG JOEY: You got your skate. I got my bottle.

PIERRE: Don't talk backwards at me. I'm your elder.

CREATURE: It's gone.

345   PIERRE: Huh?

CREATURE: Gone. The other skate's gone, right, Big Joey?

PIERRE: Gone? Where?

CREATURE: My wife Gazelle Nataways . . .

PIERRE: . . . your ex-wife . . .

350   CREATURE: . . . she threw it out the door two years ago the night Spooky Lacroix went crazy in the head and tried to come and rip Gazelle Nataways' door off for cheatin' at the bingo. Just about killed Spooky Lacroix too, right, Big

355   Joey?

PIERRE: So where's my other skate?

CREATURE: At Spooky Lacroix's, I guess.

PIERRE: Aw, shit la marde, you'se guys don't play fair.

BIG JOEY: You go over to Spooky Lacroix's and you tell him I told

360   you you could have your skate back.

PIERRE: No way, José. Spooky Lacroix's gonna preach at me.

BIG JOEY: Preach back.

PIERRE: You come with me. You used to be friends with Spooky Lacroix. You talk to Spooky Lacroix. Spooky Lacroix

365   likes you.

BIG JOEY: He likes you too.

PIERRE: Yeah, but he likes you better. Oh, shit la marde! (*As he takes another beer out of the case.*) And I almost forgot to tell you they decided to make Gazelle Nataways captain of the Wasy Wailerettes. I mean, she kind of . . . decided on her own,

370   if you know what I mean.

BIG JOEY: Spooky Lacroix's waitin' for you.

PIERRE: How do you know?

BIG JOEY: God told me.

PIERRE: (*Pause.* PIERRE *actually wonders to himself. Then:*) Aw,

375   bullshit.

(*Exits. Silence. Then* BIG JOEY *and* CREATURE *look at each other, break down and laugh themselves into prolonged hysterical fits. After a while, they calm down and come to a dead stop. They sit and think. They look at the hockey game on the television. Then, dead serious, they turn to each other.*)

CREATURE: Women . . . Gazelle Nataways . . . hockey? Ho-leee . . .
BIG JOEY: (*Still holding* PIERRE's *bottle of whiskey.*) Chris'-sakes . . .

(*Fade-out.*)

(*From this darkness emerges the sound of* SPOOKY LACROIX's *voice, singing with great emotion. As he sings, the lights fade in on his kitchen, where* DICKIE BIRD HALKED *is sitting across the table from* SPOOKY LACROIX. DICKIE BIRD *is scribbling on a piece of paper with a pencil.* SPOOKY *is knitting [pale blue baby booties]. A bible sits on the table to the left of* SPOOKY, *a knitting pattern to his right. The place is covered with knitted doodads: knitted doilies, tea cozy, a tacky picture of "The Last Supper" with knitted frame and, on the wall, as subtly conspicuous as possible, a crucifix with pale blue knitted baby booties covering each of its four extremities. Throughout this scene,* SPOOKY *periodically consults the knitting pattern, wearing tiny little reading glasses, perched "just so" on the end of his nose. He knits with great difficulty and, therefore, with great concentration, sometimes, in moments of excitement, getting the bible and the knitting pattern mixed up with each other. He has tremendous difficulty getting the "disturbed"* DICKIE BIRD *to sit still and pay attention.*)

SPOOKY: (*Singing.*) Everybody oughta know. Everybody oughta
380   know. Who Jesus is. (*Speaking.*) This is it. This is the
    end. Igwani eeweepoonaskeewuk. ("*The end of the world
    is at hand.*") Says right here in the book. Very, very, very
    important to read the book. If you want the Lord to come
    into your life, Dickie Bird Halked, you've got to read the
385   book. Not much time left. Yessiree. 1990. The last year.
    This will be the last year of our lives. Clear as a picture.
    The end of the world is here. At last. About time too, with
    the world going crazy, people shooting, killing each other
    left, right and center. Jet planes full of people crashing into
390   the bushes, lakes turning black, fish choking to death.
    Terrible. Terrible. (DICKIE BIRD *shoves a note he's been
    scribbling over to* SPOOKY.) What's this? (SPOOKY *reads, with
    some difficulty.*) "How . . . do . . . you . . . make . . . babies?"
    (*Shocked.*) Dickie Bird Halked? At your age? Surely. Anyway.
395   That young Starblanket boy who went and shot himself.
    Right here. Right in the einsteins. Bleeding from the belly, all
    this white mushy stuff come oozing out. Yuch! Brrr! I guess
    there's just nothing better to do for the young people on this
    reserve these days than go around shooting their einsteins
400   out from inside their bellies. But the Lord has had enough.
    He's sick of it. No more, he says, no more. This is it. (DICKIE
    BIRD *shoves another note over.* SPOOKY *pauses to read. And
    finishes.*) Why, me and Lalala, we're married. And we're
    gonna have a baby. Period. Now. When the world comes to
405   an end? The sky will open up. The clouds will part. And the
    Lord will come down in a holy vapor. And only those who
    are born-again Christian will go with him when he goes back
    up. And the rest? You know what's gonna happen to the rest?
    They will die. Big Joey, for instance, they will go to hell and
410   they will burn for their wicked, whorish ways. But we will
    be taken up into the clouds to spend eternity surrounded

by the wondrous and the mystical glory of god. Clear as a
picture, Dickie Bird Halked, clear as a picture. So I'm telling
you right now, you've got to read the book. Very, very, very
important. (DICKIE BIRD *shoves a third note over to* SPOOKY.   415
SPOOKY *reads and finishes.*) Why, Wellington Halked's your
father, Dickie Bird Halked. Don't you be asking questions
like that. My sister, Black Lady Halked, that's your mother.
Right? And because Wellington Halked is married to Black
Lady Halked, he is your father. And don't you ever let no   420
one tell you different.

(*Black-out. From the darkness of the theater emerges the magical flickering of a luminescent powwow dancing bustle. As it moves gradually towards the downstage area, a second—and larger— bustle appears on the upper level of the set, also flickering magically and moving about. The two bustles "play" with each other, almost affectionately, looking like two giant fireflies. The smaller bustle finally reaches the downstage area and from behind it emerges the face of* SIMON STARBLANKET. *He is dancing and chanting in a forest made of light and shadows. The larger bustle remains on the upper level; behind it is the entire person of* NANABUSH *as the spirit of* PATSY PEGAHMAGAHBOW, *a vivacious young girl of eighteen with a very big bum (i.e., an over-sized prosthetic bum). From this level,* NANABUSH/PATSY *watches and "plays" with the proceedings on the lower level. The giant full moon is in full bloom behind her. From the very beginning of all this, and in counterpoint to* SIMON's *chanting, also emerges the sound of someone playing a harmonica, a sad, mournful tune. It is* ZACHARY JEREMIAH KEECHIGEESIK, *stuck in the bush in his embarrassing state, playing his heart out. Then the harmonica stops and, from the darkness, we hear* ZACHARY's *voice.*)

ZACHARY: Hey. (SIMON *hears this, looks behind, but sees nothing and
    continues his chanting and dancing.* SIMON *chants and dances
    as though he were desperately trying to find the right chant and
    dance. Then:*) Pssst!   425
SIMON: Awinuk awa? ("*Who's this?*")
ZACHARY: (*In a hoarse whisper.*) Simon Starblanket.
SIMON: Neee, Zachary Jeremiah Keechigeesik. Awus!
    ("*Go away!*") Katha peeweestatooweemin. ("*Don't come
    bothering me [with your words].*")   430

(*Finally,* ZACHARY *emerges from the shadows and from behind a large rock, carrying his harmonica in one hand and holding his torn pants together as best he can with the other.* SIMON *ignores him and continues with his chanting and dancing.*)

ZACHARY: W-w-w-what's it cost to get one of them dough-making
    machines?
SIMON: (*Not quite believing his ears.*) What?
ZACHARY: Them dough-making machines. What's it cost to buy
    one of them?   435
SIMON: A Hobart?
ZACHARY: A what?
SIMON: Hobart. H-O-B-A-R-T. Hobart.
ZACHARY: (*To himself.*) Hobart. Hmmm.
SIMON: (*Amused at the rather funny-looking* ZACHARY.) Neee,   440
    machi ma-a, ("*Oh you, but naturally,*") Westinghouse for
    refrigerators, Kellogg's for corn flakes igwa ("*and*") Hobart

I. 428 **Neee** probably the most common Cree expression, meaning
something like "Oh, you," or "My goodness"

for dough-making machines. Kinsitootawin na? ("Get it?")
Brand name. Except we used to call it "the pig" because it had

445   this . . . piggish kind of motion to it. But never mind. Awus.
Don't bother me.
ZACHARY: What's it cost to get this . . . pig?
SIMON: (*Laughing.*) Neee, Zachary Jeremiah, here you are, one of
Wasy's most respected citizens, standing in the middle of the

450   bush on a Saturday night in February freezing your buns off
and you want to know how much a pig costs?
ZACHARY: (*Vehemently.*) I promised Hera I'd have all this
information by tonight we were supposed to sit down and discuss
the budget for this damn bakery tonight and here I went and

455   messed it all up thank god I ran into you because now you're
the only person left on this whole reserve who might have the
figures I need what's this damn dough-making machine cost
come on now tell me!
SIMON: (*A little cowed.*) Neee, about four thousand bucks.

460   Maybe five.
ZACHARY: You don't know for sure? But you worked there.
SIMON: I was only the dishwasher, Zachary Jeremiah, I didn't own
the place. Mama Louisa was a poor woman. She had really old
equipment, most of which she dragged over herself all the way

465   from Italy after the Second World War. It wouldn't cost the
same today.
ZACHARY: Five thousand dollars for a Mobart, hmmm . . .
SIMON: Hobart.
ZACHARY: I wish I had a piece of paper to write all this down,

470   sheesh. You got a piece of paper on you?
SIMON: No. Just . . . this. (*Holding the dancing bustle up.*) Why
are you holding yourself like that?
ZACHARY: I was . . . standing on the road down by Andy
Manigitogan's place when this car came by and wooof!

475   My pants ripped. Ripped right down the middle. And
my shorts, well, they just . . . took off. How do you like
that, eh?
SIMON: Nope. I don't like it. Neee, awus. Kigithaskin. ("You're
lying to me.")

480   ZACHARY: W-w-w-why would I pull your leg for? I don't really mind
it except it is damn cold out here.

(*At this point,* NANABUSH/PATSY, *on the upper level, scurries closer
to get a better look, her giant powwow dancing bustle flickering
magically in the half-light.* SIMON's *attention is momentarily pulled
away by this fleeting vision.*)

SIMON: Hey! Did you see that?

(*But* ZACHARY, *too caught up with his own dilemma, does not notice.*)

ZACHARY: I'm very, very upset right now . . .
SIMON: . . . I thought I just saw Patsy Pegahmagahbow . . . with

485   this . . .
ZACHARY: (*As he looks, perplexed, in the direction* SIMON *indicates.*)
. . . do you think . . . my two ordinary convection ovens . . .
SIMON: (*Calling out.*) Patsy? . . . (*Pause. Then, slowly, he turns back
to* ZACHARY.) . . . like . . . she made this for me, eh? (*Referring to

490   the bustle.*) She and her step-mother, Rosie Kakapetum, back
in September, after my mother's funeral. Well, I was out here
thinking, if this . . . like, if this . . . dance didn't come to me real
natural, like from deep inside of me, then I was gonna burn it.
(*Referring to the bustle.*) Right here on this spot. Cuz then . . .

495   it doesn't mean anything real to me, does it? Like, it's false . . .

it's driving me crazy, this dream where Indian people are just
dropping off like flies . . .

(NANABUSH/PATSY *begins to "play" with the two men, almost as if
with the help of the winter night's magic and the power of the full
moon, she were weaving a spell around* SIMON *and* ZACHARY.)

ZACHARY: (*Singing softly to himself.*) Hot cross buns. Hot cross
buns. One a penny, two a penny, hot cross buns . . .
SIMON: . . . something has to be done . . .   500
ZACHARY: (*Speaking.*) . . . strawberry pies . . .
SIMON: . . . in this dream . . .
ZACHARY: . . . so fresh and flakey they fairly bubble over with the
cream from the very breast of Mother Nature herself . . .
SIMON: . . . the drum has to come back, mistigwuskeek   505
("the drum") . . .
ZACHARY: . . . bran muffins, cherry tarts . . .
SIMON: . . . the medicine, the power, this . . .

(*Holding the bustle up in the air.*)

ZACHARY: . . . butter tarts . . .
SIMON: . . . has to come back. We've got to learn to dance again.   510
ZACHARY: . . . tarts tarts tarts upside-down cakes cakes cakes
and not to forget, no, never, ever to forget that Black Forest
Cake . . .
SIMON: . . . Patsy Pegahmagahbow . . .
ZACHARY: . . . cherries jubilee . . .   515
SIMON: . . . her step-mother, Rosie Kakapetum, the medicine
woman . . .
ZACHARY: . . . lemon meringue pie . . .
SIMON: . . . the power . . .
ZACHARY: . . . baked Alaska . . .   520
SIMON: . . . Nanabush! . . .
ZACHARY: (*Then suddenly, with bitterness.*) . . . Gazelle Nataways.
K'skanagoos! ("The female dog!")

(*All of a sudden, from the darkness of the winter night, emerges a
strange, eery sound; whether it is wolves howling or women wailing, we
are not sure at first. And whether this sound comes from somewhere
deep in the forest, from the full moon or where, we are not certain.
But there is definitely a "spirit" in the air. The sound of this wailing
is under-cut by the sound of rocks hitting boards, or the sides of
houses, echoing, as in a vast empty chamber. Gradually, as* SIMON
speaks, ZACHARY—*filled with confusing emotion as he is—takes out
his harmonica, sits down on the large rock and begins to play, a sad,
mournful melody, tinged, as always, with a touch of the blues.*)

SIMON: I have my arms around this rock, this large black rock
sticking out of the ground, right here on this spot. And then   525
I hear this baby crying, from inside this rock. The baby
is crying out my name. As if I am somehow responsible
for it being caught inside that rock. I can't move. My arms,
my whole body, stuck to this rock. Then this . . . eagle . . .
lands beside me, right over there. But this bird has three   530
faces, three women. And the eagle says to me: "the baby is
crying, my grand-child is crying to hear the drum again."
(NANABUSH/PATSY, *her face surrounded by the brilliant
feathers of her bustle, so that she looks like some fantastic,
mysterious bird, begins to wail, her voice weaving in and out   535
of the other wailing voices.*) There's this noise all around us,
as if rocks are hitting the sides of houses—echoing and echoing

like in a vast empty room—and women are wailing. The whole world is filled with this noise. (*Then* SIMON, *too, wails,*
540   *a heart-searing wail. From here on, all the wailing begins to fade.*) Then the eagle is gone and the rock cracks and this mass of flesh, covered with veins and blood, comes oozing out and a woman's voice somewhere is singing something about angels and god and angels and god . . .

(*The wailing has now faded into complete silence.* ZACHARY *finally rises from his seat on the rock.*)

545   ZACHARY: I dreamt I woke up at Gazelle Nataways' place with no shorts on. And I got this nagging suspicion them shorts are still over there. If you could just go on over there now . . . I couldn't have been over there. I mean, there's my wife Hera. And there's my bakery. And this bakery could
550   do a lot for the Indian people. Economic development. Jobs. Bread. Apple pie. So you see, there's an awful lot that's hanging on them shorts. This is a good chance for you to do something for your people, Simon, if you know what I mean . . .
555   SIMON: I'm the one who has to bring the drum back. And it's Patsy's medicine power, that stuff she's learning from her step-mother Rosie Kakapetum that . . . helps me . . .
ZACHARY: I go walking into my house with no underwear, pants ripped right down the middle, not a shred of budget
560   in sight and wooof! . . .

(PIERRE ST. PIERRE *comes bursting in on the two men with his one skate in hand, taking them completely by surprise.* NANABUSH/PATSY *disappears.*)

ZACHARY: Pierre St. Pierre! Just the man . . .
PIERRE: No time. No time. Lalala Lacroix's having a baby any minute now so I gotta get over to Spook's before she pops.
SIMON: I can go get Rosie Kakapetum.
565   PIERRE: Too old. Too old. She can't be on the team.
SIMON: Neee, what team? Rosie Kakapetum's the last mid-wife left in Wasy, Pierre St. Pierre, of course she can't be on a team.
ZACHARY: (*To* PIERRE.) You know that greasy shit-brown
570   chesterfield over at Gazelle Nataways?
SIMON: (*To* ZACHARY.) Mind you, if there was a team of mid-wives, chee-i? ("eh?") Wha!
PIERRE: Gazelle Nataways? Hallelujah, haven't you heard the news?
575   ZACHARY: What? . . . you mean . . . it's out already?
PIERRE: All up and down Wasaychigan Hill . . .
ZACHARY: (*Thoughtfully, to himself, as it dawns on him.*) The whole place knows.
PIERRE: clean across Manitoulin Island and right to the outskirts
580   of Sudbury . . .
ZACHARY: Lordy, lordy, lordy . . .
PIERRE: Gazelle Nataways, Dominique Ladouche, Black Lady Halked, that terrible Dictionary woman, Fluffy Sainte-Marie, Dry Lips Manigitogan, Leonarda Lee Starblanket, Annie Cook,
585   June Bug McLeod, Big Bum Pegahmagahbow . . .
SIMON: Patsy Pegahmagahbow. Get it straight . . .
PIERRE: Quiet! I'm not finished . . . all twenty-seven of 'em . . .
SIMON: Neee, Zachary Jeremiah, your goose is cooked.
PIERRE: Phhht! Cooked and burnt right down to a nice crispy
590   pitch black cinder because your wife Hera Keechigeesik is in on it too.

(ZACHARY, *reeling from the horror of it all, finally sits back down on the rock.*)

SIMON: Patsy Pegahmagahbow is pregnant, Pierre St. Pierre. She can't go running around all over Manitoulin Island with a belly that's getting bigger by the . . .
SIMON: Aw, they're all pregnant, them women, or have piles and   595
piles of babies and I'll be right smack dab in the middle of it all just a-blowin' my whistle and a-throwin' that dirty little black thingie around . . .
ZACHARY: (*Rising from the rock.*) Now you listen here, Pierre St. Pierre. I may have lost my shorts under Gazelle Nataways'   600
greasy shit-brown chesterfield not one hour ago and I may have lost my entire life, not to mention my bakery, as a result of that one very foolish mistake but I'll have you know that my shorts, they are clean as a whistle, I change them every day,
my favorite color is light blue and black and crusted with shit   605
my shorts most certainly are not!
SIMON: (*Surprised and thrilled at* ZACHARY's *renewed "fighting" spirit.*) Wha!
PIERRE: Whoa! Easy, Zachary Jeremiah, easy there. Not one stitch of your shorts has anything whatsoever to do with the   610
revolution.
SIMON: Pierre St. Pierre, what revolution are you wheezing and snorting on about?
PIERRE: The puck. I'm talkin' about the puck.
ZACHARY: The puck?   615
SIMON: The puck?
PIERRE: Yes, the puck. The puck, the puck, the puck and nothin' but the goddam puck they're playin' hockey, them women from right here on this reserve, they're playin' hockey and nothin',
includin' Zachary Jeremiah Keechigeesik's bright crispy   620
undershorts, is gonna stop 'em.
SIMON: Women playing hockey. Neee, watstagatch! ("Good grief!")
PIERRE: "Neee, watstagatch" is right because they're in Sudbury, as I speak, shoppin' for hockey equipment, and I'm   625
the referee! Outa my way! Or the Lacroixs will pop before I get there.

(*He begins to exit.*)

ZACHARY: Pierre St. Pierre, get me my shorts or I'll report your bootleg joint to the police.
PIERRE: No time. No time.   630

(*Exits.*)

ZACHARY: (*Calling out.*) Did Hera go to Sudbury, too? (*But* PIERRE *is gone.*)
SIMON: (*Thoughtfully to himself, as he catches another glimpse of* NANABUSH/PATSY *and her bustle.*) . . . rocks hitting boards . . .
ZACHARY: (*To himself.*) What in God's name is happening to   635
Wasaychigan Hill . . .
SIMON: women wailing . . .
ZACHARY: (*With even greater urgency.*) Do you think those two ordinary convection ovens are gonna do the job or should I get one of them great big pizza ovens right away?   640
SIMON: . . . pucks . . .
ZACHARY: Simon, I'm desperate!
SIMON: (*Finally, snapping out of his speculation and looking straight into* ZACHARY's *face.*) Neee, Zachary Jeremiah. Okay. Goes like this. (*Then, very quickly:*) It depends on what you're   645

gonna bake, eh? Like if you're gonna bake bread and, like, lots of it, you're gonna need one of them great big ovens but if you're gonna bake just muffins . . .

ZACHARY: (*In the background.*) . . . muffins, nah, not just
650   muffins . . .

SIMON: . . . then all you need is one of them ordinary little ovens but like I say, I was only the dishwasher . . .

ZACHARY: How many employees were there in your bakery?

SIMON: . . . it depends on how big a community you're gonna
655   serve, Zachary Jeremiah . . .

ZACHARY: . . . nah, Wasy, just Wasy, to start with . . .

SIMON: . . . like, we had five, one to make the dough—like, mix the flour and the water and the yeast and all that—like, this guy had to be at work by six A.M., that's gonna be hard
660   here in Wasy, Zachary Jeremiah, I'm telling you that right now . . .

ZACHARY: . . . nah, I can do that myself, no problem . . .

SIMON: . . . then we had three others to roll the dough and knead and twist and punch and pound it on this great big
665   wooden table . . .

ZACHARY: . . . I'm gonna need a great big wooden table? . . .

SIMON: . . . hard wood, Zachary Jeremiah, not soft wood. And then one to actually bake the loaves, like, we had these long wooden paddles, eh? . . .

670 ZACHARY: . . . paddles . . .

SIMON: . . . yeah, paddles, Zachary Jeremiah, real long ones. It was kinda neat, actually . . .

ZACHARY: . . . go on, go on . . .

SIMON: Listen here, Zachary Jeremiah, I'm going to Sudbury next
675   Saturday, okay? And if you wanna come along, I can take you straight to Mama Louisa's Pasticerria myself. I'll introduce you to the crusty old girl and you can take a good long look at her rubbery old Hobart, how's that? You can even touch it if you want, neee . . .

680 ZACHARY: . . . really? . . .

SIMON: Me? I'm asking Patsy Pegahmagahbow to marry me . . .

ZACHARY: . . . Simon, Simon . . .

SIMON: . . . and we're gonna hang two thousand of these things (*Referring to his dancing bustle.*) all over Manitoulin Island,
685   me and Patsy and our baby. And me and Patsy and our baby and this Nanabush character, we're gonna be dancing up and down Wasaychigan Hill like nobody's business cuz I'm gonna go out there and I'm gonna bring that drum back if it kills me.

690 ZACHARY: (*Pause. Then, quietly.*) Get me a safety pin.

SIMON: (*Pause.*) Neee, okay. And you, Zachary Jeremiah Keechigeesik, you're gonna see a Hobart such as you have never seen ever before in your entire life!

SIMON/ZACHARY: (*Smiling, almost laughing, at each other.*) Neee . . .

(*Black-out.*)

(*Lights up on the upper level, where we see this bizarre vision of* NANABUSH, *now in the guise of* BLACK LADY HALKED, *nine months pregnant [i.e., wearing a huge, out-sized prosthetic belly]. Over this, she wears a maternity gown and, pacing the floor slowly, holds a huge string of rosary beads. She recites the rosary quietly to herself. She is also drinking a beer and, obviously, is a little unsteady on her feet because of this.*)

(*Fade-in on the lower level into* SPOOKY LACROIX's *kitchen.* DICKIE BIRD HALKED *is on his knees, praying fervently to this surrealistic, miraculous*

vision of "the Madonna" [i.e., his own mother], which he actually sees inside his own mind. Oblivious to all this, SPOOKY LACROIX sits at his table, still knitting his baby booties and preaching away.*)

SPOOKY: Dickie Bird Halked? I want you to come to heaven with 695
me. I insist. But before you do that, you take one of them courses in sign language, help me prepare this reserve for the Lord. Can't you just see yourself, standing on that podium in the Wasaychigan Hill Hippodrome, talking sign language to 700
the people? Talking about the Lord and how close we are to the end? I could take a break. And these poor people with their meaningless, useless . . .

(PIERRE ST. PIERRE *comes bursting in and marches right up to* SPOOKY. *The vision of* NANABUSH/BLACK LADY HALKED *disappears.*)

PIERRE: Alright. Hand it over.

SPOOKY: (*Startled out of his wits.*) Pierre St. Pierre! You went and mixed up my booty! 705

PIERRE: I know it's here somewhere.

SPOOKY: Whatever it is you're looking for, you're not getting it until you bring the Lord into your life.

PIERRE: My skate. Gimme my skate.

SPOOKY: I don't have no skate. Now listen to me. 710

PIERRE: My skate. The skate Gazelle Nataways threw at you and just about killed you.

SPOOKY: What the hell are you gonna do with a skate at this hour of the night?

PIERRE: Haven't you heard the news? 715

SPOOKY: (*Pauses to think.*) No, I haven't heard any news.

(DICKIE BIRD *gets up and starts to wander around the kitchen. He looks around at random, first out the window, as if to see who has been chanting, then, eventually, he zeroes in on the crucifix on the wall and stands there looking at it. Finally, he takes it off the wall and plays with its cute little booties.*)

PIERRE: The women. I'm gonna be right smack dab in the middle of it all. The revolution. Right here in Wasaychigan Hill.

SPOOKY: The Chief or the priest. Which one are they gonna revolution? 720

PIERRE: No, no, no. Dominique Ladouche, Black Lady Halked, that terrible Dictionary woman, that witch Gazelle Nataways, Fluffy Sainte-Marie, Dry Lips Manigitogan, Leonarda Lee Starblanket, Annie Cook, June Bug McLeod, Big Bum Pegahmagahbow, all twenty-seven of 'em. Even my wife, 725
Veronique St. Pierre, she'll be right smack dab in the middle of it all. Defense.

SPOOKY: Defense? The Americans. We're being attacked. Is the situation that serious?

PIERRE: No, no, no, for Chris'sakes. They're playin' hockey. 730
Them women are playin' hockey. Dead serious they are too.

SPOOKY: No.

PIERRE: Yes.

SPOOKY: Thank the Lord this is the last year!

PIERRE: Don't you care to ask? 735

SPOOKY: Thank the Lord the end of the world is coming this year!

(*Gasping, he marches up to* DICKIE BIRD.)

PIERRE: I'm the referee, dammit.

SPOOKY: Watch your language.

(*Grabbing the crucifix from* DICKIE BIRD.)

740 PIERRE: That's what I mean when I say I'm gonna be right smack dab in the middle of it all. You don't listen to me.

SPOOKY: (*As he proceeds to put the little booties back on the crucifix.*) But you're not a woman.

PIERRE: You don't have to be. To be a referee these days, you can 745 be anything, man or woman, don't matter which away. So gimme my skate.

SPOOKY: What skate?

PIERRE: The skate Gazelle Nataways just about killed you with after the bingo that time.

750 SPOOKY: Oh, that. I hid it in the basement. (PIERRE *opens a door, falls in and comes struggling out with a mouse trap stuck to a finger.*) Pierre St. Pierre, what the hell are you doing in Lalala's closet?

PIERRE: Well, where the hell's the basement?

(*He frees his finger.*)

755 SPOOKY: Pierre St. Pierre, you drink too much. You gotta have the Lord in your life.

PIERRE: I don't need the Lord in my life, for god's sake, I need my skate. I gotta practice my figure eights.

SPOOKY: (*As he begins to put the crucifix back up on the wall.*) You 760 gotta promise me before I give you your skate.

PIERRE: I promise.

SPOOKY: (*Unaware, he threatens* PIERRE *with the crucifix, holding it up against his neck.*) You gotta have the Lord come into your life.

765 PIERRE: Alright, alright.

SPOOKY: For how long?

PIERRE: My whole life. I promise I'm gonna bring the Lord into my life and keep him there right up until the day I die just gimme my goddamn skate.

770 SPOOKY: Cross my heart.

PIERRE: Alright? Cross your heart.

(*Neither man makes a move, until* SPOOKY, *finally catching on, throws* PIERRE *a look.* PIERRE *crosses himself.*)

SPOOKY: Good.

(*Exits to the basement.*)

PIERRE: (*Now alone with* DICKIE BIRD, *half-whispering to him. As* PIERRE *speaks,* DICKIE BIRD *again takes the crucifix off the* 775 *wall and returns with it to his seat and there takes the booties off in haphazard fashion.*) Has he been feedin' you this crappola, too? Don't you be startin' that foolishness. That Spooky Lacroix's so fulla shit he wouldn't know a two thousand year-old Egyptian Sphinxter if he came face to 780 face with one. He's just preachifyin' at you because you're the one person on this reserve who can't argue back. You listen to me. I was there in the same room as your mother when she gave birth to you. So I know well who you are and where you come from. I remember the whole picture. Even 785 though we were all in a bit of a fizzy . . . I remember. Do you know, Dickie Bird Halked, that you were named after that bar? Anyone ever tell you that? (DICKIE BIRD *starts to shake.*

PIERRE *takes fright.*) Spooky Lacroix, move that holy ass of yours, for fuck's sakes! (DICKIE BIRD *laughs.* PIERRE *makes a weak attempt to laugh along.*) And I'll never forgive 790 your father, Big Joey oops . . . (DICKIE BIRD *reacts.*) . . . I mean, Wellington Halked, for letting your mother do that to you. "It's not good for the people of this world," I says to him "it's not good for 'em to have the first thing they see when they come into the world is a goddamn jukebox." 795 That's what I says to him. Thank god, you survived, Dickie Bird Halked, thank god, seventeen years later you're sittin' here smack-dab in front of me, hail and hearty as cake. Except for your tongue. Talk, Dickie Bird Halked, talk. Say somethin'. Come on. Try this: "Daddy, daddy, daddy." (DICKIE BIRD 800 *shakes his head.*) Come on. Just this once. Maybe it will work. (*Takes* DICKIE BIRD *by the cheeks with one hand.*) "Daddy, daddy, daddy, daddy." (DICKIE BIRD *jumps up and attacks* PIERRE, *looking as though he were about to shove the crucifix down* PIERRE'S *throat.* PIERRE *is genuinely terrified. Just then,* 805 SPOOKY *reenters with the skate.*) Whoa, whoa. Easy. Easy now, Dickie Bird. Easy.

SPOOKY: (*Gasping again at the sight of* DICKIE BIRD *man-handling the crucifix, he makes a bee-line for the boy.*) Dickie Bird Halked? Give me that thing. (*And grabs the crucifix with a* 810 *flourish. Then he turns to* PIERRE *and holds the skate out with his other hand.*) Promise.

PIERRE: Cross my heart. (*Crosses himself.*)

SPOOKY: (*Replacing the crucifix on the wall and pointing at* PIERRE.) The Lord. 815

PIERRE: The Lord.

(SPOOKY *hands the skate over to* PIERRE. *Just then,* CREATURE NATAWAYS *stumbles in, now visibly drunk.*)

CREATURE: The Lord!

(*Picking on the hapless* DICKIE BIRD, CREATURE *roughly shoves the boy down to a chair.*)

PIERRE: (*Holding up both his skates.*) I got 'em both. See? I got 'em.

CREATURE: Hallelujah! Now all you gotta do is learn how to 820 skate.

SPOOKY: Creature Nataways, I don't want you in my house in that condition. Lalala is liable to pop any minute now and I don't want my son to see the first thing he sees when he comes into the world is a drunk. 825

PIERRE: Damn rights!

SPOOKY: . . . you too, Pierre St. Pierre.

CREATURE: Aw! William Lacroix, don't give me that holier than-me, poker-up-the-bum spiritual bull crap . . .

SPOOKY: . . . say wha? . . . 830

CREATURE: Are you preachin' to this boy, William Lacroix? Are you usin' him again to practice your preachy-preachy? Don't do that, William, the boy is helpless. If you wanna practice, go practice on your old buddy, go preach on Big Joey. He's the one who needs it. 835

SPOOKY: You're hurting again, aren't you, Creature Nataways.

CREATURE: Don't listen to Spooky Lacroix, Dickie Bird. You follow Spooky Lacroix and you go right down to the dogs, I'm tellin' you that right now. Hair spray, Lysol, vanilla extract, shoe polish, Xerox machine juice, he's done it all, this man. 840

If you'd given William Lacroix the chance, he'd have sliced up the Xerox machine and ate it . . .

PIERRE: (*Mockingly, in the background.*) No!

CREATURE: . . . He once drank a Kitty Wells record. He lied to
845 his own mother and he stole her record and he boiled it and swallowed it right up . . .

PIERRE: Good heavens!

(BIG JOEY *enters and stands at the door unseen.*)

CREATURE: Made the Globe and Mail, too. He's robbed, he's cheated his best friend . . .

850 SPOOKY: Alphonse Nataways? Why are you doing this, may I ask?

CREATURE: Oh, he was bad, Dickie Bird Halked, he was bad. Fifteen years. Fifteen years of his life pukin' his guts out on sidewalks from here to Sicamous, B.C., this man . . .

SPOOKY: Shush!

855 CREATURE: and this is the same man . . .

BIG JOEY: (*Speaking suddenly and laughing, he takes everyone by surprise. They gasp. And practically freeze in their tracks.*) . . . who's yellin' and preachin' about "the Lord!" They oughta retire the beaver and put this guy on the Canadian
860 nickel, he's become a national goddamn symbol, that what you're sayin', Creature Nataways? This the kind of man you wanna become, that what you're sayin' to the boy, Creature Nataways? (*Close up to* DICKIE BIRD.) A man who couldn't get a hard-on in front of a woman if you paid him a two
865 dollar bill?

SPOOKY: (*Stung to the quick.*) And is this the kind of man you wanna become, Dickie Bird Halked, this MAN who can't take the sight of blood least of all woman's blood, this MAN who, when he sees a woman's blood, chokes up, pukes and faints,
870 how do you like that?

(PIERRE, *sensing potential violence, begins to sneak out.*)

BIG JOEY: (*Pulls a bottle out of his coat.*) Spooky Lacroix, igwani eeweepoonaskeewuk. ("The end of the world is at hand.")

(PIERRE, *seeing the bottle, retraces his steps and sits down again, grabbing a tea-cup en route, ready for a drink.*)

SPOOKY: (*Shocked.*) Get that thing out of my house!

BIG JOEY: Tonight, we're gonna celebrate my wife, Spooky
875 Lacroix, we're gonna celebrate because my wife, the fabulous, the incredible Gazelle Delphina Nataways has been crowned Captain of the Wasy Wailerettes. The Rez is makin' history, Spooky Lacroix. The world will never be the same. Come on, it's on me, it's on your old buddy, the old, old buddy you said
880 you'd never, ever forget.

SPOOKY: I told you a long time ago, Big Joey, after what you went and done to my sister, this here boy's own mother, you're no buddy of mine. Get out of my house. Get!

BIG JOEY: (*Handing the bottle of whiskey to* CREATURE.) Creature
885 Nataways, celebrate your wife.

CREATURE: (*Raising the bottle in a toast.*) To my wife!

PIERRE: (*Holding his cup out to the bottle.*) Your ex-wife.

BIG JOEY: (*Suddenly quiet and intimate.*) William. William. You and me. You and me, we used to be buddies, kigiskisin?
890 ("Remember?") Wounded Knee. South Dakota. Spring of '73. We parked my van over by that little lake, we swam across, you almost didn't make it and nothin' could get you to swim back. Kigiskisin? So here we're walkin' back through the bush,

all the way around this small lake, nothin' on but bare feet and wet undershorts and this black bear come up behind you, 895 kigiskisin? And you freaked out.

(*Laughs.* PIERRE *tries, as best he can, to create a party atmosphere, to little avail.* CREATURE *nervously watches* BIG JOEY *and* SPOOKY. DICKIE BIRD *merely sits there, head down, rocking back and forth.*)

SPOOKY: (*Obviously extremely uncomfortable.*) You freaked out too, ha-ha, ha-ha.

BIG JOEY: That bear gave you a real spook, huh? (*Pause. Then, suddenly, he jumps at the other men.*) Boo! (*The other men,* 900 *including* SPOOKY, *jump, splashing whiskey all over the place.* BIG JOEY *laughs. The other men pretend to laugh.*) That's how you got your name, you old Spook . . .

SPOOKY: You were scared too, ha-ha, ha-ha.

BIG JOEY: . . . we get back to the camp and there's Creature and 905 Eugene and Zach and Roscoe, bacon and eggs all ready for us. Christ, I never laughed so hard in my life. But here you were, not laughin' and we'd say: "What's the matter, Spook, you don't like our jokes? And you'd say: "That's good, yeah, that's good." I guess you were laughin' from a different part of 910 yourself, huh? You were beautiful . . .

SPOOKY: That's good, yeah, that's good.

BIG JOEY: (*Getting the bottle back from* CREATURE *and* PIERRE.) So tonight, Bear-who-went-and-gave-you-a-real-Spooky Lacroix, we're gonna celebrate another new page in our lives. 915 Wounded Knee Three! Women's version!

PIERRE: Damn rights.

BIG JOEY: (*Raising the bottle up in a toast.*) To my wife!

SPOOKY: Ha! Get that thing away from me.

PIERRE: Spooky Lacroix, co-operate. Co-operate for once. The 920 women, the women are playin' hockey.

CREATURE: To my wife!

PIERRE: Your ex-wife.

CREATURE: Shut up you toothless old bugger.

SPOOKY: Big Joey, you're not my friend no more. 925

BIG JOEY: (*Finally grabbing* SPOOKY *roughly by the throat.* CREATURE *jumps to help hold* SPOOKY *still.*) You never let a friend for life go, William Hector Lacroix, not even if you turn your back on your own father, Nicotine Lacroix's spiritual teachings and pretend like hell to be this born-again Christian. 930

SPOOKY: Let go, Creature Nataways, let go of me! (*To* BIG JOEY.) For what you did to this boy at that bar seventeen years ago, Joseph Jeremiah McLeod, you are going to hell. To hell! (BIG JOEY *baptizes* SPOOKY *with the remainder of the bottle's contents. Breaking free,* SPOOKY *grabs* DICKIE BIRD *and shoves him* 935 *toward* BIG JOEY.) Look at him. He can't even talk. He hasn't talked in seventeen years! (DICKIE BIRD *cries out, breaks free, grabs the crucifix from off the wall and runs out the door, crying.* SPOOKY *breaks down, falls to the floor and weeps.* BIG JOEY *attempts to pick him up gently, but* SPOOKY *kicks him* 940 *away.*) Let go of me! Let go!

CREATURE: (*Lifting the empty bottle, laughing and crying at the same time.*) To my wife, to my wife, to my wife, to my wife, to my wife . . .

(BIG JOEY *suddenly lifts* SPOOKY *off the floor by the collar and lifts a fist to punch his face. Black-out.*)

(*Out of this black-out emerges the eery, distant sound of women wailing and pucks hitting boards, echoing and echoing as in a vast empty chamber. The lights come up on* DICKIE BIRD HALKED *and*

SIMON STARBLANKET, *standing beside each other in the "bleach-ers" of the hockey arena, watching the "ice" area (i.e., looking out over the audience). The "bleachers" area is actually on the upper level of the set, in a straight line directly in front of* NANABUSH'S *perch.* DICKIE BIRD *is still holding* SPOOKY'S *crucifix and* SIMON *is still holding his dancing bustle.*)

945 SIMON: Your grandpa, Nicotine Lacroix, was a medicine man. Hell of a name, but he was a medicine man. Old priest here, Father Boucher, years ago—oh, he was a terrible man—he went and convinced the people old Nicotine Lacroix talked to the devil. That's not true. Nicotine Lacroix was a good

950 man. That's why I want you for my best man. Me and Patsy are getting married a couple of months from now. It's decided. We're gonna have a baby. Then we're going down to South Dakota and we're gonna dance with the Rosebud Sioux this summer. (*Sings as he stomps his foot in the rhythm of a powwow*

955 *drum.*) " . . . and me I don't wanna go to the moon, I'm gonna leave that moon alone. I just wanna dance with the Rosebud Sioux this summer, yeah, yeah, yeah . . . "

(*And he breaks into a chant.* DICKIE BIRD *watches, fascinated, particularly by the bustle* SIMON *holds up in the air.*)

(*At this point,* ZACHARY JEREMIAH KEECHIGEESIK *approaches timidly from behind a beam, his pants held flimsily together with a huge safety pin. The sound of women wailing and pucks hitting boards now shifts into the sound of an actual hockey arena, just before a big game.*)

ZACHARY: (*To* SIMON.) Hey! (*But* SIMON *doesn't hear and continues chanting.*) Pssst!
960 SIMON: Zachary Jeremiah. Neee, watstagatch!
ZACHARY: Is Hera out there?
SIMON: (*Indicating the "ice."*) Yup. There she is.
ZACHARY: Lordy, lordy, lordy . . .
SIMON: Just kidding. She's not out there . . .
965 ZACHARY: Don't do that to me!
SIMON: . . . yet.
ZACHARY: (*Finally coming up to join the young men at the "bleachers."*) You know that Nanabush character you were telling me about a couple of nights ago? What do you say I
970 give his name over to them little gingerbread cookie men I'm gonna be making? For starters. Think that would help any?
SIMON: Neee . . .

(*Just then,* BIG JOEY *enters and proceeds to get a microphone stand ready for broadcasting the game.* ZACHARY *recoils and goes to stand as far away from him as possible.*)

ZACHARY: (*Looking out over the "ice."*) It's almost noon. They're late getting started.
975 BIG JOEY: (*Yawning luxuriously.*) That's right. Me and Gazelle Nataways . . . slept in.

(CREATURE NATAWAYS *comes scurrying in.*)

CREATURE: (*Still talking to himself.*) . . . I tole you once I tole you twice . . . (*Then to the other men.*) Chris' sakes! Are they really gonna do it? Chris'sakes!

(SPOOKY LACROIX *enters wearing a woolen scarf he obviously knit-ted himself. He is still knitting, this time a pale blue baby sweater. He*

also now sports a black eye and band-aide on his face. All the men, except PIERRE ST. PIERRE, *are now in the "bleachers," standing in a straight line facing the audience, with* DICKIE BIRD *in the center area,* SIMON *and* SPOOKY *to his immediate right and left, respectively.*)

SPOOKY: It's bad luck to start late. I know. I read the interview   980
with Gay Lafleur in last week's Expositor. They won't get far.
(*He sees* GAZELLE NATAWAYS *entering the "rink," unseen by the audience. [All the hockey players on the "ice" are unseen by the audience; it is only the men who can actually "see" them.]*) Look!
Gazelle Nataways went and got her sweater trimmed in the   985
chest area!

(*Wild cat calls from the men.*)

CREATURE: Trimmed it? She's got it plunging down to her ootsee. ("belly button.")
ZACHARY: Ahem. Smokes too much. Lung problems.
BIG JOEY: Nah. More like it's got somethin' to do with the   990
undershorts she's wearin' today.
ZACHARY: (*Fast on the up-take.*) Fuck you!
BIG JOEY: (*Blowing* ZACHARY *a kiss.*) Poosees. ("Pussy cat." [*Zachary's childhood nickname.*])
SPOOKY: Terrible. Terrible. Tsk, tsk, tsk.   995

(PIERRE ST. PIERRE *enters on the lower level, teetering dangerously on his skates towards the "ice" area downstage. He wears a referee's top and a whistle around his neck.*)

PIERRE: (*Checking the names off as he reads from a clipboard.*)
Dominique Ladouche, Black Lady Halked, Annie Cook, June
Bug McLeod, Big Bum Pegahmagahbow . . .
SIMON: (*Calling out.*) Patsy Pegahmagahbow, turkey.
PIERRE: Shut up. I'm workin' here. . . . Leonarda Lee Starblanket,   1000
that terrible Dictionary woman, Fluffy Sainte-Marie,
Chicken Lips Pegahmagahbow, Dry Lips Manigitogan,
Little Hand Manigitogan, Little Girl Manitowabi, Victoria
Manitowabi, Belinda Nickikoosimeenicaning, Martha
Two-Axe Early-in-the-Morning, her royal highness Gazelle   1005
Delphina Nataways, Delia Opekokew, Barbra Nahwegahbow,
Gloria May Eshkibok, Hera Keechigeesik, Tall Mary Ann
Patchnose, Short Mary Ann Patchnose, Queen Elizabeth
Patchnose, the triplets Marjorie Moose, Maggie May Moose,
Mighty Moose and, of course, my wife, Veronique St. Pierre.   1010
Yup. They're all there, I hope, and the world is about to
explode!
SPOOKY: That's what I've been trying to tell you!

(PIERRE ST. PIERRE, *barely able to stand on his skates, hobbles about, obviously getting almost trampled by the hockey players at various times.*)

BIG JOEY: (*Now speaking on the microphone. The other men watch the women on the "ice"; some are cheering and whistling, some calling down the game.*) Welcome, ladies igwa gentlemen,   1015
welcome one and all to the Wasaychigan Hill Hip-hip-hippodrome. This is your host for the big game, Big Joey—and they don't call me Big Joey for nothin'—Chairman, CEO and Proprietor of the Wasaychigan Hill Hippodrome, bringin' you a game such as has never been seen ever before on the ice   1020
of any hockey arena anywhere on the island of Manitoulin,

anywhere on the face of this country, anywhere on the face of this planet. And there . . .

CREATURE: . . . there's Gazelle Nataways, number one . . .

1025 BIG JOEY: . . . they are, ladies . . .

SPOOKY: . . . terrible, terrible . . .

BIG JOEY: . . . igwa gentlemen . . .

CREATURE: . . . Chris'sakes, that's my wife, Chris'sakes . . .

BIG JOEY: . . . there they are, the most beautiful . . .

1030 SIMON: . . . give 'em hell, Patsy Pegahmagahbow, give 'em hell . . .

BIG JOEY: . . . daring, death- . . .

SIMON: (To ZACHARY.) . . . there's Hera Keechigeesik, number nine . . .

1035 BIG JOEY: . . . defying Indian women . . .

SPOOKY: . . . terrible, terrible . . .

BIG JOEY: . . . in the world . . .

ZACHARY: . . . that's my wife . . .

BIG JOEY: . . . the Wasy Wailerettes . . .

(Clears his throat and tests the microphone by tapping it gently.)

1040 ZACHARY: . . . lordy, lordy, lordy . . .

CREATURE: Hey, Gazelle Nataways and Hera Keechigeesik are lookin' at each other awful funny. Something bad's gonna happen, I tole you once I tole you twice, something bad's gonna happen . . .

1045 SPOOKY: This is sign from the Lord. This is THE sign . . .

BIG JOEY: Number One Gazelle Nataways, Captain of the Wasy Wailerettes, facing off with Number Nine, Flora McDonald, Captain of the Canoe Lake Bravettes. And referee Pierre St. Pierre drops the puck and takes off like a herd of wild turtles . . .

1050 SIMON: Aw, Spooky Lacroix, eat my shitty shorts, neee . . .

BIG JOEY: . . . Hey, aspin Number Six Dry Lips Manigitogan, right-winger for the Wasy Wailerettes . . .

ZACHARY: . . . look pretty damn stupid, if you ask me. Fifteen thousand dollars for all that new equipment . . .

1055

BIG JOEY: . . . eemaskamat Number Thirteen of the Canoe Lake Bravettes anee-i puck . . .

CREATURE: . . . Cancel the game! Cancel the game! Cancel the game! . . .

(Etc.)

1060 BIG JOEY: . . . igwa aspin sipweesinskwataygew. Hey, k'see goochin! *(Off microphone.)* Creature Nataways. Shut up. *(To the other men.)* Get this asshole out of here. . . .

SIMON: Yay, Patsy Pegahmagahbow! Pat-see! Pat-see! . . .

(Etc.)

BIG JOEY: *(Back on microphone.)* . . . How, Number Six Dry Lips Manigitogan, right-winger for the Wasy Wailerettes, soogi pugamawew igwa anee-i puck igwa aspin center-line ispathoo ana puck . . .

1065

CREATURE: *(To SIMON.)* Shut up. Don't encourage them . . .

BIG JOEY: . . . ita Number Nine Hera Keechigeesik, left-winger for . . .

1070

1052 . . . **Hey,** . . . The following hockey commentary by Big Joey (pp. 1696–1697) is translated on p. 1709.

SIMON: *(To CREATURE.)* Aw, lay off! Pat-see! Pat-see! Pat-see! . . . *(Etc.)*

BIG JOEY: . . . the Wasy Wailerettes, kagatchitnat. How, Number Nine Hera Keechigeesik . . .

(He continues uninterrupted.)

CREATURE: . . . Stop the game! Stop the game! Stop the game! . . . *(Etc.)*

1075

ZACHARY: Goodness sakes, there's gonna be a fight out there!

(CREATURE continues his "stop the game," ZACHARY repeats "goodness sakes, there's gonna be a fight out there," SIMON's "Pat-see!" has now built up into a full chant, his foot pounding on the floor so that it sounds like a powwow drum, his dancing bustle held aloft like a shield. SPOOKY finally grabs the crucifix away from DICKIE BIRD, holds it aloft and begins to pray, loudly, as in a ceremony. DICKIE BIRD, caught between Simon's chanting and SPOOKY's praying, blocks his ears with his hands and looks with growing consternation at "the game." PIERRE blows his whistle and skates around like a puppet gone mad.)

SPOOKY: The Lord is my shepherd; I shall not want. He maketh me to lie down in green pastures; he leadeth me beside the still waters. He restoreth my soul; he leadeth me in the paths of righteousness for his name's sake. Yea, though I walk through the valley of the shadow of death, I will fear no evil; for thou art with me. Yea, though I walk through the valley of the shadow of death, I will fear no evil; for thou art with me . . .

1080

1085

(He repeats this last phrase over and over again. Finally, DICKIE BIRD freaks out, screams and runs down to the "ice" area.)

BIG JOEY: *(Continuing uninterrupted above all the other men's voices.)* . . . igwa ati-ooteetum blue line ita Number One Gazelle Nataways, Captain of the Wasy Wailerettes, kagagweemaskamat anee-i puck, ma-a Number Nine Hera Keechigeesik mawch weemeethew anee-i puck. Wha! "Hooking," itew referee Pierre St. Pierre, Gazelle Nataways isa keehookiwatew her own team-mate Hera Keechigeesikwa, wha! How, Number One Gazelle Nataways, Captain of the Wasy Wailerettes, face-off igwa meena itootum asichi Number Nine Flora McDonald, Captain of the Canoe Lake Bravettes igwa Flora McDonald soogi pugamawew anee-i puck, ma-a Number Thirty-seven Big Bum Pegahmagahbow, defense-woman for the Wasy Wailerettes, stops the puck and passes it to Number Eleven Black Lady Halked, also defense-woman for the Wasy Wailerettes, but Gazelle Nataways, Captain of the Wasy Wailerettes, soogi body check meethew her own team-mate Black Lady Halked woops! She falls, ladies igwa gentlemen, Black Lady Halked hits the boards and Black Lady Halked is singin' the blues, ladies igwa gentlemen, Black Lady Halked sings the blues. *(Off microphone, to the other men.)* What the hell is goin' on down there? Dickie Bird, get off the ice! *(Back on microphone.)* Wha! Number Eleven Black Lady Halked is up in a flash igwa seemak n'taymaskamew Gazelle Nataways anee-i puck, holy shit! The ailing but very, very furious Black Lady Halked skates back, turns and takes aim, it's gonna be a slap shot, ladies igwa gentlemen, slap shot keetnatch taytootum Black Lady Halked igwa Black Lady Halked shootiwoo anee-i puck, wha!

1090

1095

1100

1105

1110

1115 She shoots straight at her very own captain, Gazelle Nataways and holy shit, holy shit, holy fuckin' shit!

(*All hell breaks loose; it is as though some bizarre dream has entered the arena. We hear the sound of women wailing and pucks hitting boards, echoing and echoing as in a vast empty chamber. The men are all screaming at the same time, from the "bleachers," re-calling* BLACK LADY HALKED's *legendary fall of seventeen years ago.*)

BIG JOEY: (*Dropping his microphone in horror.*) Holy Christ! If there is a devil in this world, then he has just walked into this room. Holy Christ! . . . (*He says this over and over again.*)

1120 ZACHARY: Do something about her, goodness sakes, I told you guys to do something about her seventeen years ago, but you wouldn't do fuck-all. So go out there now and help her . . . (*Repeated.*)

CREATURE: Never mind, Chris'sakes, don't bother her. Let me out of here. Chris'sakes, let me out of here! . . . (*Repeated.*)

1125 SPOOKY: Yea, though I walk through the valley of the shadow of death, I will fear no evil; for thou art with me . . .

(*Repeated. While* SIMON *continues chanting and stomping.*)

PIERRE: (*From the "ice" area.*) Never you mind, Zachary Jeremiah, never you mind. She'll be okay. No she won't. Zachary Jeremiah, go out there and help her. No. She'll be okay. No she won't. Yes.

1130 No. Yes. No. Help! Where's the puck? Can't do nothin' without the goddamn puck. Where's the puck?! Where's the puck?! Where's the puck?! . . .

(*He repeats this last phrase over and over again. Center- and down-stage, on the "ice" area,* DICKIE BIRD *is going into a complete "freak-out," breaking into a grotesque, fractured version of a Cree chant. Gradually,* BIG JOEY, ZACHARY *and* CREATURE *join* PIERRE's *refrain of "where's the puck?!", with which they all, including the chanting* SIMON *and the praying* SPOOKY, *scatter and come running down to the "ice" area. As they reach the lower level and begin to approach the audience, their movements break down into slow motion, as though they were trying to run through the sticky, gummy substance of some horrible, surrealistic nightmare.*)

PIERRE/BIG JOEY/ZACHARY/CREATURE: (*Slower and slower, as on a record that is slowing down gradually to a stop.*) Where's the 1135 puck?! Where's the puck?! Where's the puck?! . . . (*Etc.*)

(SIMON *continues chanting and stomping,* SPOOKY *continues intoning the last phrase of his prayer and* DICKIE BIRD *continues his fractured chant. Out of this fading "sound collage" emerges the sound of a jukebox playing the introduction to Kitty Wells' "It Wasn't God Who Made Honky Tonk Angels," as though filtered through memory. At this point, on the upper level, a giant luminescent hockey stick comes seemingly out of nowhere and, in very slow motion, shoots a giant luminescent puck. On the puck, looking like a radiant but damaged "Madonna-with-child," sits* NANABUSH, *as the spirit of* BLACK LADY HALKED, *naked, nine months pregnant, drunk almost senseless and barely able to hold a bottle of beer up to her mouth. All the men freeze in their standing positions facing the audience, except for* DICKIE BIRD *who continues his fractured chanting and whimpering, holding his arms up towards* NANABUSH/BLACK LADY HALKED. *The giant luminescent puck reaches and stops at the edge of the upper level.* NANABUSH/BLACK LADY HALKED *struggles to stand and begins staggering toward her perch. She reaches it and falls with one arm on*

top of it. *The magical, glittering lights flare on and, for the first time, the jukebox is revealed.* NANABUSH/BLACK LADY HALKED *staggers laboriously up to the top of the jukebox and stands there in profile, one arm lifted to raise her beer as she pours it over her belly. Behind her, the full moon begins to glow, blood red. And from the jukebox, Kitty Wells sings.*)

As I sit here tonight, the jukebox playing,
That tune about the wild side of life;
As I listen to the words you are saying,
It brings memories when I was a trusting wife.

It wasn't God who made honky tonk angels, 1140
As you said in the words of your song;
Too many times married men think they're still single,
That has caused many a good girl to go wrong.

(*During the "instrumental break" of the song here,* DICKIE BIRD *finally explodes and shrieks out towards the vision of* NANABUSH/BLACK LADY HALKED.)

DICKIE BIRD: Mama! Mama! Katha paksini. Katha paksini. Kanawapata wastew. Kanawapataw wastew. Michimina. 1145 Michimina. Katha pagitina. Kaweechee-ik nipapa. Kaweechee-ik nipapa. Nipapa. Papa. Papa. Papa. Papa. Papa. Papa! Mommy! Mommy! Don't fall. Don't fall. Look at the light. Look at the light. Hold on to it. Hold on to it. Don't let it go. My daddy will help you. My daddy will help you. My daddy. 1150 Daddy. Daddy. . . . (*Etc.*)

(*He crumples to the floor and freezes. Kitty Wells sings.*)

It's a shame that all the blame is on us women,
It's not true that only you men feel the same;
From the start most every heart that's ever broken,
Was because there always was a man to blame. 1155
It wasn't God who made honky tonk angels;
As you said in the words of your song;
Too many times married men think they're still single,
That has caused many a good girl to go wrong.

(*As the song fades, the final tableau is one of* DICKIE BIRD *collapsed on the floor between* SIMON, *who is holding aloft his bustle, and* SPOOKY, *who is holding aloft his crucifix, directly in front of and at the feet of* BIG JOEY *and, above* BIG JOEY, *the pregnant* NANABUSH/ BLACK LADY HALKED, *who is standing on top of the flashing jukebox, in silhouette against the full moon, bottle held up above her mouth.* ZACHARY, CREATURE *and* PIERRE *are likewise frozen, standing off to the side of this central grouping. Slow fade-out.*)

ACT TWO

When the lights come up, DICKIE BIRD HALKED *is standing on a rock in the forest, his clothes and hair all askew. He holds* SPOOKY's *crucifix, raised with one hand up to the night sky; he is trying, as best he can, to chant, after* SIMON STARBLANKET's *fashion. As he does,* NANABUSH *appears in the shadows a distance behind him (as the spirit of* GAZELLE NATAWAYS, *minus the gigantic breasts, but dressed, this time, as a stripper). She lingers and watches with interest. Slowly,* DICKIE BIRD *climbs off the rock and walks off-stage, his quavering voice fading into the distance. The full moon glows. Fade-out.*

Fade-in on SPOOKY LACROIX's *kitchen, where* SPOOKY *is busy pinning four little pale blue baby booties on the wall where the crucifix used to be, the booties that, in Act One, covered the four extremities of the crucifix. At the table are* PIERRE ST. PIERRE *and* ZACHARY JEREMIAH KEECHIGEESIK. PIERRE *is stringing pale blue yarn around* ZACHARY's *raised, parted hands. Then* SPOOKY *joins them at the table and begins knitting again, this time, a baby bonnet, also pale blue.* ZACHARY *sits removed through most of this scene, pre-occupied with the problem of his still missing shorts, his bakery and his wife. The atmosphere is one of fear and foreboding, almost as though the men were constantly resisting the impulse to look over their shoulders. On the upper level, in a soft, dim light,* NANABUSH/ GAZELLE *can be seen sitting up on her perch, waiting impatiently for "the boys" to finish their talk.*

PIERRE: (*In a quavering voice.*) The Wasy Wailerettes are dead. Gentlemen, my job is disappeared from underneath my feet.

SPOOKY: And we have only the Lord to thank for that.

5 PIERRE: Gazelle Nataways, she just sashayed herself off that ice, behind swayin' like a walrus pudding. That game, gentlemen, was what I call a real apostrophe . . .

ZACHARY: Catastrophe.

PIERRE: That's what I said, dammit. . . .

10 SPOOKY: . . . tsk . . .

PIERRE: . . . didn't even get to referee more than ten minutes. But you have to admit, gentlemen, that slap shot . . .

SPOOKY: . . . that's my sister, Black Lady Halked, that's my sister . . .

15 PIERRE: . . . did you see her slap shot? Fantastic! Like a bullet, like a killer shark. Unbelievable!

ZACHARY: (*Uncomfortable.*) Yeah, right.

PIERRE: When Black Lady Halked hit Gazelle Nataways with that puck. Them Nataways eyes. Big as plates!

20 SPOOKY: Bigger than a ditch!

PIERRE: Them mascara stretch marks alone was a perfectly frightful thing to behold. Holy shit la marde! But you know, they couldn't find that puck.

SPOOKY: (*Losing his cool and laughing, falsely and nervously.*)
25 Did you see it? It fell . . . it fell . . . that puck went splat on her chest . . . and it went . . . it went . . . plummety plop . . .

PIERRE: . . . plummety plop to be sure . . .

SPOOKY: . . . down her . . . down her . . .

PIERRE: Down the crack. Right down that horrendous, scarifyin'
30 Nataways bosom crack.

(*The "kitchen lights" go out momentarily and, to the men, inexplicably. Then they come back on. The men look about them, perplexed.*)

SPOOKY: Serves . . . her . . . right for trimming her hockey sweater in the chest area, is what I say.

PIERRE: They say that puck slid somewhere deep, deep into the folds of her fleshy, womanly juices . . .

35 ZACHARY: . . . there's a lot of things they're saying about that puck . . .

PIERRE: and it's lost. Disappeared. Gone. Phhht! Nobody can find that puck.

(*At this point,* SPOOKY *gets up to check the light switch. The lights go out.*)

ZACHARY: (*In the darkness.*) Won't let no one come near her, is
40 what they say. Not six inches.

PIERRE: I gotta go look for that puck. (*Lights come back on.* PIERRE *inexplicably appears sitting in another chair.*) Gentlemen, I gotta go jiggle that woman.

(*Lights out again.*)

ZACHARY: (*From the darkness.*) What's the matter, Spook?

SPOOKY: (*Obviously quite worried.*) Oh, nothing, nothing . . . 45
(*Lights come back on.* PIERRE *appears sitting back in his original chair. The men are even more mystified, but try to brighten up anyway.*) . . . just . . . checking the lights . . . Queen of the Indians, that's what she tried to look like, walking off that ice. 50

PIERRE: Queen of the Indians, to be sure. That's when them women went and put their foot down and made up their mind, on principle, no holds barred . . .

(*A magical flash of lavender light floods the room very briefly, establishing a connection between* SPOOKY's *kitchen and* NANABUSH's *perch, where* NANABUSH/GAZELLE *is still sitting, tapping her fingers impatiently, looking over her shoulder periodically, as if to say: "come on, boys, get with it."* PIERRE's *speech momentarily goes into slow motion.*)

. . . no . . . way . . . they're . . . takin' up . . . them hockey sticks again until that particular puck is found. "The particular 55 puck," that's what they call it. Gentlemen, the Wasy Wailerettes are dead. My job is disappeared. Gone. Kaput kaput. Phhht!

SPOOKY: Amen.

(*Pause. Thoughtful silence for a beat or two.*)

ZACHARY: W-w-w-where's that nephew of yours, Spook? 60

SPOOKY: Dickie Bird Halked?

PIERRE: My wife, Veronique St. Pierre, she informs me that Dickie Bird Halked, last he was seen, was pacin' the bushes in the general direction of the Pegahmagahbow acreage near Buzwah, lookin' for all the world like he had lost his mind, 65 poor boy.

ZACHARY: Lordy, lordy, lordy, I'm telling you right now, Spooky Lacroix, if you don't do something about that nephew of yours, he's liable to go out there and kill some-one next time. 70

SPOOKY: I'd be out there myself pacing the bushes with him except my wife Lalala's liable to pop any minute now and I gotta be ready to zip her up to Sudbury General.

PIERRE: Bah. Them folks of his, they don't care. If it's not hockey, it's bingo she's out playin' every night of the week, that Black 75 Lady of a mother of his.

ZACHARY: Went and won the jackpot again last night, Black Lady Halked did. All fifty pounds of it . . .

PIERRE: Beat Gazelle Nataways by one number!

ZACHARY: . . . if it wasn't for her, I'd have mastered that apple 80 pie recipe by now. I was counting on all that lard. Fifty pounds, goodness sakes.

SPOOKY: This little old kitchen? It's yours, Zachary Jeremiah, anytime, anytime. Lalala's got tons of lard.

PIERRE: Ha! She better have. Zachary Jeremiah hasn't dared go 85 nowhere near his own kitchen in almost a week.

ZACHARY: Four nights! It's only Wednesday night, Pierre St. Pierre. Don't go stretching the truth just cuz you were too damn chicken to go get me my shorts.

90 PIERRE: Bah!
SPOOKY: (*To* ZACHARY.) Your shorts?
ZACHARY: (*Evading the issue.*) I just hope that Black Lady Halked's
   out there looking after her boy cuz if she isn't, we're all in a heap
95   of trouble, I have a funny feeling. (*Suddenly, he throws the yarn
   down and rises.*) Achh! I've got to cook!

(*He goes behind the kitchen counter, puts an apron on and begins
the preparations for making pie pastry.*)

SPOOKY: (*To* PIERRE, *half-whispering.*) His shorts?

(PIERRE *merely shrugs, indicating* ZACHARY's *pants, which are still
held together with a large safety pin.* SPOOKY *and* PIERRE *laugh
nervously.* SPOOKY *looks concernedly at the four little booties on
the wall where the crucifix used to be. Beat.*)

(*Suddenly,* PIERRE *slaps the table with one hand and leans over to*
SPOOKY, *all set for an argument, an argument they've obviously
had many times before. Through all this,* ZACHARY *is making
pie pastry at the counter and* SPOOKY *continues knitting. The
atmosphere of "faked" jocular camaraderie grows, particularly as
the music gets louder later on.* NANABUSH/GAZELLE *is now getting
ready for her strip in earnest, standing on her perch, spraying
perfume on, stretching her legs, etc. The little tivoli lights in the
jukebox begin to twinkle little by little.*)

PIERRE: Queen of Hearts.
SPOOKY: Belvedere.
PIERRE: Queen of Hearts.
100 SPOOKY: The Belvedere.
PIERRE: I told you many times, Spooky Lacroix, it was the Queen
   of Hearts. I was there. You were there. Zachary Jeremiah,
   Big Joey, Creature Nataways, we were all there.

(*From here on, the red/blue/purple glow of the jukebox
(i.e.,* NANABUSH's *perch) becomes more and more apparent.*)

SPOOKY: And I'm telling you it was the Belvedere Hotel, before
105   it was even called the Belvedere Hotel, when it was still
   called . . .
PIERRE: Spooky Lacroix, don't contribute your elder. Big Joey, may
   he rot in hell, he was the bouncer there that night, he was
   right there the night it happened.
110 ZACHARY: Hey, Spook. Where do you keep your rolling pin?
SPOOKY: Use my salami.
PIERRE: (*To* SPOOKY.) He was there.
ZACHARY: Big Joey was never the bouncer, he was the janitor.
SPOOKY: At the Belvedere Hotel.
115 PIERRE: Never you mind, Spooky Lacroix, never you mind. Black
   Lady Halked was sittin' there in her corner of the bar for
   three weeks . . .
SPOOKY: Three weeks?! It was more like three nights. Aw, you
   went and mixed up my baby's cap. (*Getting all tangled up with
120   his knitting.*)
ZACHARY: Got any cinnamon?
SPOOKY: I got chili powder. Same color as cinnamon.

(*Faintly, the strip music from the jukebox begins to play.*)

PIERRE: . . . the place was so jam-packed with people drinkin'
   beer and singin' and smokin' cigarettes and watchin' the
125   dancin' girl . . .

SPOOKY: . . . Gazelle Nataways, she was the dancing girl . . .

(*The music is now on full volume and* NANABUSH/GAZELLE's *strip is
in full swing. She dances on top of the jukebox, which is now a riot of
sound and flashing lights.* SPOOKY's *kitchen is bathed in a gorgeous
lavender light.* BIG JOEY *and* CREATURE NATAWAYS *appear at*
SPOOKY's *table, each drinking a bottle of beer. The strip of seventeen
years ago is fully recreated, the memory becoming so heated that*
NANABUSH/GAZELLE *magically appears dancing right on top
of* SPOOKY's *kitchen table. The men are going wild, applauding,
laughing, drinking, all in slow motion and in mime. In the heat of the
moment, as* NANABUSH/GAZELLE *strips down to silk tassels and
G-string, they begin tearing their clothes off.*)

(*Suddenly,* SIMON STARBLANKET *appears at* SPOOKY's *door:*
NANABUSH/GAZELLE *disappears, as do* BIG JOEY *and* CREATURE.
And SPOOKY, PIERRE *and* ZACHARY *are caught with their pants
down. The jukebox music fades.*)

SIMON: Spooky Lacroix. (*The lavender light snaps off, we are
   back to "reality" and* SPOOKY, PIERRE *and* ZACHARY *stand
   there, embarrassed. In a panic, they begin putting their
   clothes back on and reclaim the positions they had before*   130
   the strip. SPOOKY *motions* SIMON *to take a seat at the table.*
   SIMON *does so.*) Spooky Lacroix. Rosie Kakapetum expresses
   interest in coming here to birth Lalala's baby when the time
   comes.
SPOOKY: Rosie Kakapetum? No way some witch is gonna come and   135
   put her witchy little fingers on my baby boy.
SIMON: Rosie Kakapetum's no witch, Spooky Lacroix. She's
   Patsy Pegahmagahbow's step-mother and she's Wasy's only
   surviving medicine woman and mid-wife . . .
SPOOKY: Hogwash!   140
PIERRE: Ahem. Rosie Kakapetum says it's a cryin' shame the
   Wasy Wailerettes is the only team that's not in the Ontario
   Hockey League.
ZACHARY: Ontario Hockey League?
PIERRE: Absolutely. The OHL. Indian women's OHL. All the   145
   Indian women in Ontario's playin' hockey now. It's like a
   fever out there.
ZACHARY: Shoot. (*Referring to his pastry.*) I hope this new recipe
   works for me.
PIERRE: Well, it's not exactly new without the cinnamon.   150
SPOOKY: (*To* SIMON.) My son will be born at Sudbury General
   Hospital . . .
SIMON: You know what they do to them babies in them city
   hospitals?
SPOOKY: . . . Sudbury General, Simon Starblanket, like any good   155
   Christian boy . . .
PIERRE: (*Attempting to diffuse the argument.*) Ahem. We got to get
   them Wasy Wailerettes back on that ice again.
SIMON: (*Refusing to let go of* SPOOKY.) They pull them away right
   from their own mother's breast the minute they come into   160
   this world and they put them behind these glass cages
   together with another two hundred babies like they were
   some kind of scientific specimens . . .
PIERRE: . . . like two hundred of them little monsters . . .
ZACHARY: Hamsters!   165
PIERRE: . . . that's what I said dammit . . .
SPOOKY: . . . tsk . . .
PIERRE: . . . you can't even tell which hamster belongs to which
   mother. You take Lalala to Sudbury General, Spooky Lacroix,

170 and your hamster's liable to end up stuck to some French
lady's tit.
SIMON: . . . and they'll hang Lalala up in metal stirrups and
your baby's gonna be born going up instead of dropping down
which is the natural way. You were born going up instead of
175 dropping down like you should have . . .
PIERRE: Yup. You were born at Sudbury General, Spooky
Lacroix, that's why you get weirder and weirder as the days get
longer, that's why them white peoples is so weird they were all
born going up . . .
180 SIMON: . . . instead of dropping down . . .
ZACHARY: (*Sprinkling flour in* SPOOKY's *face, with both hands, and
laughing.*) . . . to the earth, Spooky Lacroix, to the earth . . .
SPOOKY: Pooh!
PIERRE: . . . but we got to find that puck, Simon Starblanket, them
185 Wasy Wailerettes have got to join the OHL . . .
SPOOKY: (*To* SIMON.) If Rosie Kakapetum is a medicine woman,
Simon Starblanket, then how come she can't drive the madness
from my nephew's brain, how come she can't make him talk,
huh?
190 SIMON: Because the medical establishment and the church
establishment and people like you, Spooky Lacroix, have
effectively put an end to her usefulness and the usefulness of
people like her everywhere, that's why Spooky Lacroix.
SPOOKY: Phooey!
195 SIMON: Do you or your sister even know that your nephew
hasn't been home in two days, since that incident at the
hockey game, Spooky Lacroix? Do you even care? Why can't
you and that thing . . . (*Pointing at the bible that sits beside
SPOOKY.*) and all it stands for cure your nephew's madness,
200 as you call it, Spooky Lacroix? What has this thing . . . (*The
bible again.*) done to cure the madness of this community
and communities like it clean across this country, Spooky
Lacroix? Why didn't "the Lord" as you call him, come to your
sister's rescue at that bar seventeen years ago, huh, Spooky
205 Lacroix? (*Pause. Tense silence.*) Rosie Kakapetum is gonna
be my mother-in-law in two months, Spooky Lacroix, and if
Patsy and I are gonna do this thing right, if we're gonna work
together to make my best man, Dickie Bird Halked, well again,
then Rosie Kakapetum has got to birth that baby. (*He begins
210 to exit.*)
SPOOKY: (*In hard, measured cadence.*) Rosie Kakapetum works for
the devil.

(SIMON *freezes in his tracks. Silence. Then he turns, grabs a chair
violently, bangs it down and sits determinedly.*)

SIMON: Fine. I'll sit here and I'll wait.
SPOOKY: Fine. You sit there and you wait.

(*Silence.* SIMON *sits silent and motionless, his back to the other men.*)

215 PIERRE: Ahem. Never you mind, Spooky Lacroix, never you
mind. Now as I was sayin', Black Lady Halked was nine
months pregnant when she was sittin' in that corner of the
Queen of Hearts.
SPOOKY: The Belvedere!
220 PIERRE: Three weeks, Black Lady Halked was sittin' there
drinkin' beer. They say she got the money by winnin' the
jackpot at the Espanola bingo just three blocks down the
street. Three weeks, sure as I'm alive and walkin' these
treacherous icy roads, three weeks she sat there in that dark

corner by herself. They say the only light you could see her by 225
was the light from the jukebox playin' "Rim of Fire" by Johnny
Cash . . .
ZACHARY: "Rim of Fire." Yeah, right, Pierre St. Pierre.
SPOOKY: Kitty Wells! Kitty Wells!

(*The sound of the jukebox playing "It Wasn't God Who Made Honky
Tonk Angels" can be heard faintly in the background.*)

PIERRE: . . . the place was so jam-packed with people drinkin' 230
and singin' and smokin' cigarettes and watchin' the dancin'
girl . . .
SPOOKY: . . . Gazelle Nataways, she was the dancing girl, Lord save
her soul . . .
PIERRE: . . . until Black Lady Halked collapsed . . . 235

(SPOOKY, PIERRE *and* ZACHARY *freeze in their positions, looking in
horror at the memory of seventeen years ago.*)

(*On the upper level,* NANABUSH, *back in her guise as the spirit of
BLACK LADY HALKED, sits on the jukebox, facing the audience, legs
out directly in front. Nine months pregnant and naked, she holds a
bottle of beer up in the air and is drunk almost senseless. The song,
"It Wasn't God Who Made Honky Tonk Angels," rises to full volume,
the lights from the jukebox flashing riotously. The full moon glows
blood red. Immediately below* NANABUSH/BLACK LADY HALKED,
DICKIE BIRD HALKED *appears, kneeling, naked, arms raised toward
his mother.* NANABUSH/BLACK LADY HALKED *begins to writhe and
scream, laughing and crying hysterically at the same time and, as she
does, her water breaks.* DICKIE BIRD, *drenched, rises slowly from the
floor, arms still raised, and screams.*)

DICKIE BIRD: Mama! Mama!

(*And from here on, the lights and the sound on this scene begin to
fade slowly, as the scene on the lower level resumes.*)

PIERRE: . . . she kind of oozed down right then and there, right
down to the floor of the Queen of Hearts Tavern. And Big Joey,
may he rot in hell, he was the bouncer there that night, when
he saw the blood, he ran away and puked over on the other side 240
of the bar, the sight of all that woman's blood just scared the
shit right out of him. And that's when Dickie Bird Halked, as
we know him, came ragin' out from his mother's womb, Spooky
Lacroix, in between beers, right there on the floor, under a
table, by the light of the jukebox, on a Saturday night, at the 245
Queen of Hearts . . .
SPOOKY: They went and named him after the bar, you crusted old
fossil! That bar, which is now called the Belvedere Hotel, used
to be called the Dickie Bird Tavern . . .
SIMON: (*Suddenly jumping out of his chair and practically lunging 250
at* SPOOKY.) It doesn't matter what the fuck the name of that
fucking bar was! (*The lights and sound on* NANABUSH *and the
jukebox have now faded completely.*) The fact of the matter
is, it never should have happened, that kind of thing should
never be allowed to happen, not to us Indians, not to anyone 255
living and breathing on the face of God's green earth. (*Pause.
Silence. Then, dead calm.*) You guys have given up, haven't
you? You and your generation. You gave up a long time
ago. You'd rather turn your back on the whole thing and
pretend to laugh, wouldn't you? (*Silence.*) Well, not me. Not us. 260
(*Silence.*) This is not the kind of Earth we want to inherit. (*He*

begins to leave, but turns once more.) I'll be back. With Patsy. And Rosie.

(*He exits. Another embarrassed silence.*)

265 SPOOKY: (*Unwilling to face up to the full horror of it, he chooses, instead, to do exactly what* SIMON *said: turn his back and pretend to laugh.*) That bar, which is now called the Belvedere Hotel, used to be called the Dickie Bird Tavern. That's how Dickie Bird Halked got his name. And that's why he goes hay-wire every
270 now and again and that's why he doesn't talk. Fetal Alcohol something-something, Pierre St. Pierre . . .
ZACHARY: (*From behind the counter, where he is still busy making pie crust.*) Fetal Alcohol Syndrome.
SPOOKY: . . . that's the devil that stole the baby's tongue because Dickie Bird Halked was born drunk and very, very mad. At the
275 Dickie Bird Tavern in downtown Espanola seventeen years ago and that's a fact.
PIERRE: Aw, shit la marde. Fuck you, Spooky Lacroix, I'm gonna go get me my rest.

(*Throws the yarn in* SPOOKY's *face, jumps up and exits.* SPOOKY *sits there with a pile of yarn stuck to his face, caught on his glasses.*)

ZACHARY: (*Proudly holding up the pie crust in its plate.*) It worked!

(*Black-out*)

(*On the upper level, in a dim light away from her perch,* NANABUSH/
BLACK LADY HALKED *is getting ready to go out for the evening, combing her hair in front of a mirror, putting on her clothes, etc.*
DICKIE BIRD *is with her, naked, getting ready to go to bed.* SPOOKY's *crucifix sits on a night-table to his side. In* DICKIE BIRD's *mind, he is at home with his mother.*)

280 DICKIE BIRD: Mama. Mama. N'tagoosin. ("I'm sick.")
NANABUSH/BLACK LADY: Say your prayers.
DICKIE BIRD: Achimoostawin nimoosoom. ("Tell me about my grandpa.")
NANABUSH/BLACK LADY: Go to bed. I'm going out soon.
285 DICKIE BIRD: Mawch. Achimoostawin nimoosoom. ("No. Tell me about my grandpa.")
NANABUSH/BLACK LADY: You shouldn't talk about him.
DICKIE BIRD: Tapweechee eegeemachipoowamit nimoosoom? ("Is it true my grandpa had bad medicine?")
290 NANABUSH/BLACK LADY: They say he met the devil once. Your grandpa talked to the devil. Don't talk about him.
DICKIE BIRD: Eegeemithoopoowamit nimoosoom, eetweet Simon Starblanket. ("Simon Starblanket says he had good medicine.")
295 NANABUSH/BLACK LADY: Ashhh! Simon Starblanket.
DICKIE BIRD: Mawch eemithoosit awa aymeewatik keetnanow kichi, eetweet Simon Starblanket. ("Simon Starblanket says that this cross is not right for us.") (*He grabs the crucifix from the night-table and spits on it.*)
300 NANABUSH/BLACK LADY: (*Grabbing the crucifix from* DICKIE BIRD, *she attempts to spank him but* DICKIE BIRD *evades her.*) Dickie Bird! Kipasta-oon! ("You're committing a mortal sin!") Say ten Hail Marys and two Our Fathers.
DICKIE BIRD: Mootha apoochiga taskootch nimama keetha.
305 Mootha apoochiga m'tanawgatch kisagee-in. ("You're not even like my mother. You don't even love me at all.")

NANABUSH/BLACK LADY: Dickie Bird. Shut up. I'll say them with you. "Hail Mary, full of grace, the Lord is with thee . . . "Hurry up. I have to go out. (*As* NANABUSH/BLACK LADY HALKED *now
prepares to leave.*) "Hail Mary, full of grace, the Lord is with 310
thee . . . "(*She gives up.*) Ashhh! Your father should be home soon. (*Exits.*)
DICKIE BIRD: (*Speaking out to the now absent* NANABUSH/BLACK LADY.) Mootha nipapa ana. ("He's not my father.") (*He grabs his clothes and the crucifix and runs out, down to the lower 315
level and into the forest made of light and shadows.*) Tapwee anima ka-itweechik, chee-i? Neetha ooma kimineechagan, chee-i? ("It's true what they say, isn't it? I'm a bastard, aren't I?") (*He is now sitting on the rock, where* SIMON *and* ZACHARY *first met in Act One.*) Nipapa ana . . . Big Joey . . . (*To himself, 320
quietly.*) . . . nipapa ana . . . Big Joey . . . ("My father is . . . Big Joey.")

(*Silence.*)

(*A few moments later,* NANABUSH *comes bouncing into the forest, as the spirit of the vivacious, young* PATSY PEGAHMAGAHBOW, *complete with very large, oversized bum. The full moon glows.*)

NANABUSH/PATSY: (*To herself, as she peers into the shadows.*) Oooh, my poor bum. I fell on the ice four days ago, eh? And it still hurts, oooh. (*She finally sees* DICKIE BIRD *huddling on the rock, 325
barely dressed.*) There you are. I came out to look for you. What happened to your clothes? It's freezing out here. Put them on. Here. (*She starts to help dress him.*) What happened at the arena? You were on the ice, eh? You feel like talking? In Indian? How, weetamawin. ("Come on, tell me.") 330

(BIG JOEY *and* CREATURE NATAWAYS *enter a distance away. They are smoking a joint and* BIG JOEY *carries a gun. They stop and watch from the shadows.*)

CREATURE: Check her out.
NANABUSH/PATSY: Why do you always carry that crucifix? I don't believe that stuff. I traded mine in for sweetgrass. Hey. You wanna come to Rosie's and eat fry bread with me? Simon will be there, too. Simon and me, we're getting married, eh? We're 335
gonna have a baby . . .
CREATURE: What's she trying to do?
NANABUSH/PATSY: . . . Rosie's got deer meat, too, come on, you like my Mom's cooking, eh? (*She attempts to take the crucifix away from* DICKIE BIRD.) But you'll have to leave that here because 340
Rosie can't stand the Pope . . .

(DICKIE BIRD *grabs the crucifix back.*)

CREATURE: What's he trying to do?
NANABUSH/PATSY: . . . give it to me . . . Dickie . . . come on . . .
CREATURE: He's weird, Big Joey, he's weird.
NANABUSH/PATSY: . . . leave it here . . . it will be safe here . . . 345
we'll bury it in the snow . . .

(*Playfully, she tries to get the crucifix away from* DICKIE BIRD.)

CREATURE: Hey, don't do that, don't do that, man, he's ticklish.
NANABUSH/PATSY: (*As* DICKIE BIRD *begins poking her playfully with the crucifix and laughing,* NANABUSH/PATSY *gradually starts to get frightened.*) . . . don't look at me that way . . . 350
Dickie Bird, what's wrong? . . . ya, Dickie Bird, awus . . .

(DICKIE BIRD *starts to grab at* NANABUSH/PATSY.)

CREATURE: Hey, don't you think, don't you think . . . he's getting kind of carried away?

NANABUSH/PATSY: . . . awus . . .

355 CREATURE: We gotta do something, Big Joey, we gotta do something. (BIG JOEY *stops* CREATURE.) Let go! Let go!

NANABUSH/PATSY: (*Now in a panic.*) . . . Awus! Awus! Awus! . . .

(DICKIE BIRD *grabs* NANABUSH/PATSY *and throws her violently to the ground, he lifts her skirt and shoves the crucifix up against her.*)

BIG JOEY: (*To* CREATURE.) Shut up.

NANABUSH/PATSY: (*Screams and goes into hysteria.*) . . . Simon! . . .

(DICKIE BIRD *rapes* NANABUSH/PATSY *with the crucifix. A heart-breaking, very slow, sensuous tango breaks out on off-stage harmonica.*)

360 CREATURE: (*To* BIG JOEY.) No! Let me go. Big Joey, let me go, please! (BIG JOEY *suddenly grabs* CREATURE *violently by the collar.*)

BIG JOEY: Get out. Get the fuck out of here. You're nothin' but a fuckin' fruit. Fuck off. (CREATURE *collapses.*) I said fuck off.

(CREATURE *flees.* BIG JOEY *just stands there, paralyzed, and watches.*)

(NANABUSH/PATSY, *who has gradually been moving back and back, is now standing up on her perch again (i.e., the "mound"/jukebox which no longer looks like a jukebox). She stands there, facing the audience, and slowly gathers her skirt, in agony, until she is holding it up above her waist. A blood stain slowly spreads across her panties and flows down her leg. At the same time, Dickie Bird stands down-stage beside the rock, holding the crucifix and making violent jab-bing motions with it, downward. All this happens in slow motion. The crucifix starts to bleed. When* DICKIE BIRD *lifts the crucifix up, his arms and chest are covered with blood. Finally,* NANABUSH/PATSY *collapses to the floor of her platform and slowly crawls away. Lights fade on her. On the lower level,* BIG JOEY, *in a state of shock, staggers, almost faints and vomits violently. Then he reels over to* DICKIE BIRD *and, not knowing what else to do, begins collecting his clothes and calming him down.*)

BIG JOEY: How, Dickie Bird, How, astum. Igwa. Mootha nantow.
365 Mootha nantow. Shhh. Shhh. ("Come on, Dickie Bird. Come. Let's go. It's okay. It's okay. Shhh. Shhh . . . ") (*Barely able to bring himself to touch it, he takes the crucifix from* DICKIE BIRD *and drops it quickly on the rock. Then he begins wiping the blood off* DICKIE BIRD.) How, mootha nantow. Mootha nantow. How,
370 astum, keeyapitch upisees ootee. Igwani. Igwani. Poonimatoo. Mootha nantow. ("Come on, it's okay. Come on, a little more over here. That's all. That's all. Stop crying. It's okay. It's okay . . .") (DICKIE BIRD, *shaking with emotion, looks questioningly into* BIG JOEY's *face.*) Eehee.
375 Nigoosis keetha. Mootha Wellington Halked kipapa. Neetha . . . kipapa. ("Yes. You are my son. Wellington Halked is not your father. I'm . . . your father.")

(*Silence. They look at each other.* DICKIE BIRD *grabs* BIG JOEY *and clings to him,* BIG JOEY *reacting tentatively, at first, and then pas-sionately, with* DICKIE BIRD *finally bursting out into uncontrollable sobs. Fade-out.*)

(*Out of this darkness, gunshots explode. And we hear a man's voice wailing, in complete and utter agony. Then comes violent pounding at a door. Finally, still in the darkness, we hear* SIMON STARBLANKET's *speaking voice.*)

SIMON: Open up! Pierre St. Pierre, open up! I know you're in there!

PIERRE: (*Still in the darkness.*) Whoa! Easy now. Easy on that 380 goddamn door. Must you create such a carpostrophe smack dab in the middle of my rest period? (*When the lights come up, we are outside the "window" to* PIERRE ST. PIERRE's *little boot-leg joint.* PIERRE *pokes his head out, wearing his night clothes, complete with pointy cap.*) Go home. Go to bed. Don't 385 be disturbin' my rest period. My wife, Veronique St. Pierre, she tells me there's now not only a OHL but a NHL, too. Indian women's National Hockey League. All the Indian women on every reserve in Canada, all the Indian women in Canada is playin' hockey now. It's like a fever out there. That's 390 why I gotta get my rest. First thing tomorrow mornin', I go jiggle that puck out of Gazelle Nataways. Listen to me. I'm your elder.

(SIMON *shoots the gun into the house, just missing* PIERRE's *head.*)

SIMON: (*Dead calm.*) One, you give me a bottle. Two, I report your joint to the Manitowaning police. Three, I shoot your 395 fucking head off.

PIERRE: Alright. Alright. (*He pops in for a bottle of whiskey and hands it out to* SIMON.) Now you go on home with this. Go have yourself a nice quiet drink. (SIMON *begins to exit.* PIERRE *calls out.*) What the hell are you gonna do with that gun? 400

SIMON: (*Calling back.*) I'm gonna go get that mute. Little bastard raped Patsy Pegahmagahbow. (*Exits.*)

(*Pause.*)

PIERRE: Holy shit la marde! (*Pause.*) I gotta warn him. No. I need my rest. No. I gotta warn that boy. No. I gotta find that puck. No. Dickie Bird's life. No. The puck. No. Dickie 405 Bird. No. Hockey. No. His life. No. Hockey. No. Life. Hockey. Life. Hockey. Life. Hockey. Life. Hockey. Life . . .

(*Fade-out.*)

(*Lights up on* SPOOKY LACROIX's *kitchen.* CREATURE NATAWAYS *is sitting at the table, silent, head propped up in his hands.* SPOOKY *is knitting, with obvious haste, a white christening gown, of which a large crucifix is the center-piece.* SPOOKY's *bible still sits on the table beside him.*)

SPOOKY: Why didn't you do something? (*Silence.*) Creature. (*Silence. Finally,* SPOOKY *stops knitting and looks up.*) Alphonse Nataways, why didn't you stop him? (*Silence.*) 410 You're scared of him, aren't you? You're scared to death of Big Joey. Admit it.

(*Silence.*)

CREATURE: (*Quietly and calmly.*) I love him, Spooky.

SPOOKY: Say wha?!

CREATURE: I love him. 415

SPOOKY: You love him? What do you mean? How? How do you love him?

CREATURE: I love him.

SPOOKY: Lord have mercy on Wasaychigan Hill!

420 CREATURE: (*Rising suddenly.*) I love the way he stands. I love the way he walks. The way he laughs. The way he wears his cowboy boots . . .

SPOOKY: You're kidding me.

CREATURE: . . . the way his tight blue jeans fall over his ass. The
425 way he talks so smart and tough. The way women fall at his feet. I wanna be like him. I always wanted to be like him, William. I always wanted to have a dick as big as his.

SPOOKY: Creature Alphonse Nataways? You know not what you say.

430 CREATURE: I don't care.

SPOOKY: I care.

CREATURE: I don't care. I can't stand it anymore.

SPOOKY: Shut up. You're making me nervous. Real nervous.

CREATURE: Come with me.

435 SPOOKY: Come with you where?

CREATURE: To his house.

SPOOKY: Whose house?

CREATURE: Big Joey.

SPOOKY: Are you crazy?

440 CREATURE: Come with me.

SPOOKY: No.

CREATURE: Yes.

SPOOKY: No.

CREATURE: (*Suddenly and viciously grabbing* SPOOKY *by the*
445 *throat.*) Cut the goddamn bull crap, Spooky Lacroix! (SPOOKY *tries desperately to save the christening gown.*) I seen you crawl in the mud and shit so drunk you were snortin' like a pig.

SPOOKY: I changed my ways, thank you.

CREATURE: Twenty one years. Twenty one years ago. You, me, Big
450 Joey, Eugene Starblanket, that goddamn Zachary Jeremiah Keechigeesik. We were eighteen. We cut our wrists. Your own father's huntin' knife. We mixed blood. Swore we'd be friends for life. Frontenac Hotel. Twenty one years ago. You got jumped by seven white guys. Broken beer bottle come
455 straight at your face. If it wasn't for me, you wouldn't be here today, wavin' that stinkin' bible in my face like it was a slab of meat. I'm not a dog. I'm your buddy. Your friend.

SPOOKY: I know that.

(CREATURE *tightens his hold on* SPOOKY'*s throat. The two men are staring straight into each other's eyes, inches apart. Silence.*)

CREATURE: William. Think of your father. Remember the words of
460 Nicotine Lacroix.

(*Finally,* SPOOKY *screams, throwing the christening gown, knitting needles and all, over the bible on the table.*)

SPOOKY: You goddamn, fucking son-of-a-bitch!

(*Black-out. Gunshots in the distance.*)

(*Lights up on* BIG JOEY'*s living room/kitchen.* BIG JOEY *is sitting, silent and motionless, on the couch, staring straight ahead, as though he were in a trance. His hunting rifle rests on his lap.* DICKIE BIRD HALKED *stands directly in front of and facing the lifesize pin-up poster of Marilyn Monroe, also as though he were in*

a trance. Then his head drops down in remorse. BIG JOEY *lifts the gun, loads it and aims it out directly in front. When* DICKIE BIRD *hears the snap of the gun being loaded, he turns to look. Then he slowly walks over to* BIG JOEY, *kneels down directly in front of the barrel of the gun, puts it in his mouth and then slowly reaches over and gently, almost lovingly, moves* BIG JOEY'*s hand away from the trigger, caressing the older man's hand as he does.* BIG JOEY *slowly looks up at* DICKIE BIRD'*s face, stunned.* DICKIE BIRD *puts his own thumb on the trigger and pulls. Click. Nothing. In the complete silence, the two men are looking directly into each other's eyes. Complete stillness. Fade-out. Split seconds before complete blackout, Marilyn Monroe farts, courtesy of* MS. NANABUSH: *a little flag reading "poot" pops up out of Ms. Monroe's derrier, as on a play gun. We hear a cute little "poot" sound.*)

(*Out of this black-out emerges the sound of a harmonica; it is* ZACHARY JEREMIAH KEECHIGEESIK *playing his heart out. Fade-in on* PIERRE ST. PIERRE, *still in his night-clothes but also wearing his winter coat and hat over them, rushing all over the "forest" ostensibly rushing to* BIG JOEY'*s house to warn* DICKIE BIRD HALKED *about the gun-toting* SIMON STARBLANKET. *He mutters to himself as he goes.*)

PIERRE: Hockey. Life. Hockey. Life. Hockey. Life . . .

(ZACHARY *appears in the shadows and sees* PIERRE.)

ZACHARY: Hey!

PIERRE: (*Not hearing* ZACHARY.) . . . Hockey. Life. Hockey.
Life . . .   465

ZACHARY: Pssst!

PIERRE: (*Still not hearing* ZACHARY.) . . . Hockey. Life. Hockey. Life. (*Pause.*) Hockey life!

ZACHARY: (*Finally yelling.*) Pierre St. Pierre!

(PIERRE *jumps.*)

PIERRE: Hallelujah! Have you heard the news?   470

ZACHARY: The Band Council went and okayed Big Joey's radio station.

PIERRE: All the Indian women in the world is playin' hockey now! World Hockey League, they call themselves. Aboriginal Women's WHL. My wife, Veronique St. Pierre, she   475
just got the news. Eegeeweetamagoot fax machine. ("Fax machine told her.") It's like a burnin', ragin', blindin' fever out there. Them Cree women in Saskatchewan, them Blood women in Alberta, them Yakima, them Heidis out in the middle of your Specific Ocean, them Kickapoo, Chickasaw, Cherokee,   480
Chipewyan, Choctaw, Chippewa, Wichita, Kiowa down in Oklahoma, them Seminole, Navajo, Onondaga, Tuscarora, Winnebago, Mimac-paddy-wack-why-it's-enough- to-give-your-dog-a-bone! . . .

(*As, getting completely carried away, he grabs his crotch.*)

ZACHARY: Pierre. Pierre.   485

PIERRE: . . . they're turnin' the whole world topsy-turkey right before our very eyes and the Prime Minister's a-shittin' grape juice . . . (*A gunshot explodes in the near distance.* PIERRE *suddenly lays low and changes tone completely.*) Holy shit la marde! He's after Dickie Bird. There's a red-eyed, crazed devil 490
out there and he's after Dickie Bird Halked and he's gonna kill us all if we don't stop him right this minute.

ZACHARY: Who? Who's gonna kill us?

PIERRE: Simon Starblanket. Drunk. Power mad. Half-crazed on
495 whiskey and he's got a gun.

ZACHARY: Simon?

PIERRE: He's drunk and he's mean and he's out to kill. (*Another
gunshot.*) Hear that?

ZACHARY: (*To himself.*) That's Simon? I thought . . .

500 PIERRE: When he heard about the Pegahmagahbow rape . . .

ZACHARY: Pegahmagahbow what?

PIERRE: Why, haven't you heard? Dickie Bird Halked raped
Patsy Pegahmagahbow in most brutal fashion and Simon
Starblanket is out to kill Dickie Bird Halked so I'm on my way
505 to Big Joey's right this minute and I'm takin' that huntin' rifle
of his and I'm sittin' next to that Halked boy right up until the
cows come home.

(*Exits.*)

ZACHARY: (*To himself.*) Simon Starblanket. Patsy . . .

(*Black-out.*)

(*Out of this black-out come the gunshots, much louder this time,
and* SIMON's *wailing voice.*)

SIMON: Aieeeeee-yip-yip! Nanabush! . . . (*Fade-in on* SIMON, *in
510 the forest close by the large rock, still carrying his hunting rifle.*
SIMON *is half-crazed by this time, drunk out of his skull. The
full moon glows.*) . . . Weesageechak! Come back! Rosie! Rosie
Kakapetum, tell him to come back, not to run away, cuz we
need him . . .

(NANABUSH/PATSY PEGAHMAGAHBOW's *voice comes filtering out of
the darkness on the upper level. It is as though* SIMON *were hearing
a voice from inside his head.*)

515 NANABUSH/PATSY: . . . her . . .

SIMON: . . . him . . .

NANABUSH/PATSY: . . . her . . .

(*Slow fade-in on* NANABUSH/PATSY, *standing on the upper level,
looking down at* SIMON. *She still wears her very large bum.*)

SIMON: . . . weetha ("him/her"—i.e., no gender) . . . Christ!
What is it? Him? Her? Stupid fucking language, fuck you, da
520 Englesa. Me no speakum no more da goodie Englesa, in Cree
we say "weetha," not "him" or "her" Nanabush, come back!
(*Speaks directly to* NANABUSH, *as though he/she were there,
directly in front of him; he doesn't see* NANABUSH/PATSY *standing
on the upper level.*) Aw, boozhoo how are ya? Me good. Me
525 berry, berry good. I seen you! I just seen you jumping jack-ass
thisa away . . .

NANABUSH/PATSY: (*As though she/he were playing games behind*
SIMON's *back.*) . . . and thataway . . .

SIMON: . . . and thisaway and . . .

530 NANABUSH/PATSY: . . . thataway . . .

SIMON: . . . and thisaway and . . .

NANABUSH/PATSY: . . . thataway . . .

SIMON: . . . and thisaway and . . .

NANABUSH/PATSY: . . . thataway . . .

535 SIMON: . . . etcetra, etcetra, etcetra . . .

NANABUSH/PATSY: . . . etcetERA. (*Pause.*) She's here! She's here!

SIMON: . . . Nanabush! Weesageechak! . . . (NANABUSH/PATSY
peals out with a silvery, magical laugh that echoes and echoes.)
. . . Dey shove dis . . . whach-you-ma-call-it . . . da crucifix up
your holy cunt ouch, eh? Ouch, eh? (SIMON *sees the bloody* 540
*crucifix sitting on the rock and slowly approaches it. He kneels
directly before it.*) Nah . . . (*Laughs a long mad, hysterical laugh
that ends with hysterical weeping.*) . . . yesssss . . . noooo . . .
oh, noooo! Crucifix! (*Spits violently on the crucifix.*) Fucking
goddamn crucifix yesssss . . . God! You're a man. You're a 545
woman. You're a man? You're a woman? You see, nineethoo-
wan poogoo neetha ("I speak only Cree") . . .

NANABUSH/PATSY: . . . ohhh . . .

SIMON: . . . keetha ma-a? ("How about you?") . . . Nah. Da
En-glesa him . . . 550

NANABUSH/PATSY: . . . her . . .

SIMON: . . . him . . .

NANABUSH/PATSY: . . . her . . .

SIMON: . . . him! . . .

NANABUSH/PATSY: . . . her! . . . 555

SIMON: all da time . . .

NANABUSH/PATSY: . . . all da time . . .

SIMON: . . . tsk, tsk, tsk . . .

NANABUSH/PATSY: . . . tsk, tsk, tsk.

SIMON: If God, you are a woman/man in Cree but only a man in 560
da Englesa, then how come you still got a cun . . .

NANABUSH/PATSY: . . . a womb.

(*With this,* SIMON *finally sees* NANABUSH/PATSY. *He calls out to her.*)

SIMON: Patsy! Big Bum Pegahmagahbow, you flying across da ice on
world's biggest puck. Patsy, look what dey done to your puss . . .
(NANABUSH/PATSY *lifts her skirt and displays the blood stain* 565
*on her panties. She then finally takes off the prosthetic that is
her huge bum and holds it in one arm.*) Hey! (*And* NANABUSH/
PATSY *holds an eagle feather up in the air, ready to dance.* SIMON
stomps on the ground, rhythmically, and sings.) " . . . and me I
don't wanna go to the moon, I'm gonna leave that moon alone. 570
I just wanna dance with the Rosebud Sioux this summer, yeah,
yeah, yeah . . . " (SIMON *chants and he and* NANABUSH/PATSY
*dance, he on the lower level with his hunting rifle in the air, she on
the upper level with her eagle feather.*) How, astum, Patsy, kiam.
N'tayneemeetootan. ("Come on, Patsy, never mind. Let's go 575
dance.")

(*We hear* ZACHARY JEREMIAH KEECHIGEESIK's *voice calling from
the darkness a distance away.*)

ZACHARY: Hey!

(*But* SIMON *and* NANABUSH/PATSY *pay no heed.*)

NANABUSH/PATSY: n'tayneemeetootan South Dakota? . . .

SIMON: how, astum, Patsy. N'tayneemeetootan South
Dakota. Hey, Patsy Pegahmagahbow. . . . 580

(*As he finally approaches her and holds his hand out.*)

NANABUSH/PATSY: (*As she holds her hand out toward his.*) . . . Simon
Starblanket . . .

SIMON/NANABUSH/PATSY: . . . eenpaysagee-itan ("I love you to
death") . . .

(ZACHARY *finally emerges tentatively from the shadows. He is holding a beautiful, fresh pie.* NANABUSH/PATSY *disappears.*)

585 ZACHARY: (*Calling out over the distance.*) Hey! You want some pie?
SIMON: (*Silence. Calling back.*) What?!

(*Not seeing* ZACHARY, *he looks around cautiously.*)

ZACHARY: I said. You want some pie?
SIMON: (*Calling back, after some confused thought.*) What?
ZACHARY: (*He approaches* SIMON *slowly.*) Do you want some pie?
590 SIMON: (*Silence. Finally, he sees* ZACHARY *and points the gun at him.*) What kind?
ZACHARY: Apple. I just made some. It's still hot.
SIMON: (*Long pause.*) Okay.

(*Slowly,* NANABUSH/PATSY *enters the scene and comes up behind* SIMON, *holding* SIMON'S *dancing bustle in front of her, as in a ceremony.*)

ZACHARY: Okay. But you gotta give me the gun first. (*The gun goes*
595 *off accidentally, just missing* ZACHARY'S *head.*) I said, you gotta give me the gun first.

(*Gradually, the dancing bustle begins to shimmer and dance in* NANABUSH/PATSY'S *hands.*)

SIMON: Patsy. I gotta go see Patsy.
ZACHARY: You and me and Patsy and Hera. We're gonna go have some pie. Fresh, hot apple pie. Then, we go to Sudbury and
600 have a look at that Mobart, what do you say?

(*The shimmering movements of the bustle balloon out into these magical, dance-like arches, as* NANABUSH/PATSY *maneuvers it directly in front of* SIMON, *hiding him momentarily. Behind this,* SIMON *drops the base of the rifle to the ground, causing it to go off accidentally. The bullet hits* SIMON *in the stomach. He falls to the ground.* ZACHARY *lets go of his pie and runs over to him. The shimmering of the bustle dies off into the darkness of the forest and disappears,* NANABUSH/PATSY *maneuvering it.*)

ZACHARY: Simon! Simon! Oh, lordy, lordy, lordy . . . Are you alright? Are you okay? Simon. Simon. Talk to me. Goodness sakes, talk to me Simon. Ayumi-in! ("Talk to me!")
605 SIMON: (*Barely able to speak, as he sinks slowly to the ground beside the large rock.*) Kamoowanow . . . apple . . . pie . . . patima . . . neetha . . . igwa Patsy . . . n'gapeetootanan . . . patima . . . apple . . . pie . . . neee. ("We'll eat . . . apple . . . pie . . . later . . . me . . . and Patsy . . . we'll come over . . . later . . . apple . . . pie . . . neee.")

(*He dies.*)

610 ZACHARY: (*As he kneels over* SIMON'S *body, the full moon glowing even redder.*) Oh, lordy, lordy . . . Holy shit! Holy shit! What's happening? What's become of this place? What's happening to this place? What's happening to these people? My people. He didn't have to die. He didn't have to die. That's the
615 goddamn most stupid . . . no reason . . . this kind of living has got to stop. It's got to stop! (*Talking and then just shrieking at the sky.*) Aieeeeeee-Lord! God! God of the Indian! God of the Whiteman! God-Al-fucking-mighty! Whatever the fuck your name is. Why are you doing this to us? Why are

you doing this to us? Are you up there at all? Or are you 620
some stupid, drunken shit, out-of-your-mind-passed
out under some great beer table up there in your stupid
fucking clouds? Come down! Astum oota! ("Come down
here!") Why don't you come down? I dare you to come
down from your high-falutin' fuckin' shit-throne up 625
there, come down and show us you got the guts to stop
this stupid, stupid, stupid way of living. It's got to stop. It's
got to stop. It's got to stop. It's got to stop. It's got to stop.
It's got to stop . . .

(*He collapses over* SIMON'S *body and weeps. Fade-out. Towards the end of this speech, a light comes up on* NANABUSH. *Her perch (i.e., the jukebox) has swivelled around and she is sitting on a toilet having a good shit. He/she is dressed in an old man's white beard and wig, but also wearing sexy, elegant women's high-heeled pumps. Surrounded by white, puffy clouds, she/he sits with her legs crossed, nonchalantly filing his/her fingernails. Fade-out.*)

(*Fade-in on* BIG JOEY'S *living room/kitchen.* BIG JOEY, DICKIE BIRD HALKED, CREATURE NATAWAYS, SPOOKY LACROIX *and* PIERRE ST. PIERRE *are sitting and standing in various positions, in complete silence. A hush pervades the room for about twenty beats.* DICKIE BIRD *is holding* BIG JOEY'S *hunting rifle. Suddenly,* ZACHARY JEREMIAH KEECHIGEESIK *enters; in a semi-crazed state.* DICKIE BIRD *starts and points the rifle straight at* ZACHARY'S *head.*)

CREATURE: Zachary Jeremiah! What are you doing here? 630
BIG JOEY: Lookin' for your shorts, Zach?

(*From his position on the couch, he motions* DICKIE BIRD *to put the gun down.* DICKIE BIRD *does so.*)

ZACHARY: (*To* BIG JOEY.) You're unbelievable. You're fucking
unbelievable. You let this young man, you let your own son
get away with this inconceivable act . . .
CREATURE: Don't say that to him, Zachary Jeremiah, don't say 635
that . . .
ZACHARY: (*Ignoring* CREATURE.) You know he did it and you're
hiding him what in God's name is wrong with you?
SPOOKY: Zachary Jeremiah, you're not yourself . . .
PIERRE: Nope. Not himself. Talkin' wild. 640

(*Sensing potential violence, he sneaks out the door.*)

BIG JOEY: (*To* ZACHARY.) He don't even know he done anything.
ZACHARY: Bull shit! They're not even sure the air ambulance
will get Patsy Pegahmagahbow to Sudbury in time. Simon
Starblanket just shot himself and this boy is responsible . . .

(SIMON *rises slowly from the ground and "sleep walks" right through this scene and up to the upper level, towards the full moon. The men are only vaguely aware of his passing.*)

BIG JOEY: He ain't responsible for nothin'. 645
ZACHARY: Simon Starblanket was on his way to South Dakota
where he could have learned a few things and made something
of himself, same place you went and made a total asshole of
yourself seventeen years ago . . .
CREATURE: Shush, Zachary Jeremiah, that's the past . . . 650
SPOOKY: . . . the past . . .
CREATURE: . . . Chris'sakes . . .

ZACHARY: What happened to all those dreams you were so full
     of for your people, the same dreams this young man just
655 died for?

SPOOKY: (To BIG JOEY, though not looking at him.) And my sister,
     Black Lady Halked, seventeen years ago at that bar, Big
     Joey, you could have stopped her drinking, you could have
     sent her home and this thing never would have happened.
660 That was your son inside her belly.

CREATURE: He didn't do nothing. He wouldn't let me do nothing.
     He just stood there and watched the whole thing . . .

SPOOKY: Creature Nataways!

CREATURE: I don't care. I'm gonna tell. He watched this little
665 bastard do that to Patsy Pegahmagahbow . . .

BIG JOEY: (Suddenly turning on CREATURE.) You little cocksucker!

(DICKIE BIRD hits CREATURE on the back with the butt of the rifle,
knocking him unconscious.)

SPOOKY: Why, Big Joey, why did you do that?

(Silence.)

ZACHARY: Yes, Joe. Why?

(Long silence. All the men look at BIG JOEY.)

BIG JOEY: (Raising his arms, as for a battle cry.) "This is the end
670 of the suffering of a great nation!" That was me. Wounded
     Knee, South Dakota, Spring of '73. The FBI. They beat us
     to the ground. Again and again and again. Ever since that
     spring, I've had these dreams where blood is spillin' out
     from my groin, nothin' there but blood and emptiness. It's
675 like . . . I lost myself. So when I saw this baby comin' out of
     Caroline, Black Lady . . . Gazelle dancin' . . . all this blood . . .
     and I knew it was gonna come . . . I . . . I tried to stop it . . .
     I freaked out. I don't know what I did . . . and I knew it was
     mine . . .

680 ZACHARY: Why? Why did you let him do it? Why? Why did you
     let him do it? Why? Why did you let him do it? Why? Why
     did you let him do it? (Finally grabbing BIG JOEY by the collar.)
     Why?! Why did you let him do it?!

BIG JOEY: (Breaking free from ZACHARY's hold.) Because I hate
685 them! I hate them fuckin' bitches. Because they—our own
     women—took the fuckin' power away from us faster than the
     FBI ever did.

SPOOKY: (Softly, in the background.) They always had it.

(Silence.)

BIG JOEY: There. I said it. I'm tired. Tired.

(He slumps down on the couch and cries.)

690 ZACHARY: (Softly.) Joe. Joe.

(Fade-out.)

(Out of this darkness emerges the sound of SIMON STARBLANKET's
chanting voice. Away up over NANABUSH's perch, the moon begins
to glow, fully and magnificently. Against it, in silhouette, we see
SIMON wearing his powwow bustle. SIMON STARBLANKET is dancing in the moon. Fade-out.)

(Fade-in on the "ice" at the hockey arena, where PIERRE ST. PIERRE,
in full referee regalia, is gossiping with CREATURE NATAWAYS and
SPOOKY LACROIX. CREATURE is knitting, with great difficulty, pink
baby booties. SPOOKY is holding his new baby, wrapped in a pale
blue knit blanket. We hear the sound of a hockey arena, just before
a big game.)

PIERRE: . . . she says to me: "did you know, Pierre St. Pierre, that
     Gazelle Nataways found Zachary Jeremiah Keechigeesik's
     undershorts under her chesterfield and washed them
     and put them in a box real nice, all folded up and even
     sprinkled her perfume all over them and sashayed herself   695
     over to Hera Keechigeesik's house and handed the box
     over to her? I just about had a heart attack," she says to me.
     "And what's more," she says to me, "when Hera Keechigeesik
     opened that box, there was a picture sittin' on top of them
     shorts, a color picture of none other than our very own   700
     Zachary Jeremiah Keechigeesik . . . (Unseen by PIERRE,
     ZACHARY approaches the group, wearing a baker's hat and
     carrying a rolling pin.) . . . wearin' nothin' but the suit God
     gave him. That's when Hera Keechigeesik went wild, like a
     banshee tigger, and she tore the hair out of Gazelle Nataways 705
     which, as it turns out, was a wig . . ." Imagine. After all these
     years. " . . . and she beat Gazelle Nataways to a cinder, right
     there into the treacherous icy door-step. And that's when
     'the particular puck' finally came squishin' out of them
     considerable Nataways bosoms." And gentlemen? The   710
     Wasy Wailerettes are on again!

CREATURE: Ho-leee!

SPOOKY: Holy fuck!

PIERRE: And I say shit la ma . . . (Finally seeing ZACHARY, who
     is standing there, listening to all this.) . . . oh my . . . (PIERRE 715
     turns quickly to SPOOKY's baby.) . . . hello there, koochie-
     koochie-koo, welcome to the world!

SPOOKY: It's not koochie-koochie-koo, Pierre St. Pierre. Her
     name's "Kichigeechacha." Rhymes with Lalala. Ain't she
     purdy?   720

(Up in the "bleachers," BIG JOEY enters and prepares his microphone
stand. DICKIE BIRD enters with a big sign saying: "WASY-FM" and
hangs it proudly up above the microphone stand.)

PIERRE: Aw, she'll be readin' that ole holy bible before you can go:
     "Phhht! Phhht!"

(PIERRE accidentally spits in the baby's face. SPOOKY shoos him
away.)

SPOOKY: "Phhht! Phhht!" to you too, Pierre St. Pierre.

CREATURE: Spooky Lacroix. Lalala. They never made it to
     Sudbury General.   725

SPOOKY: I was busy helping Eugene Starblanket out with
     Simon . . .

SPOOKY/PIERRE: . . . may he rest in peace . . .

ZACHARY: Good old Rosie Kakapetum. "Stand and deliver," they
     said to her. And stand and deliver she did. How's the knitting 730
     going there, Creature Nataways?

CREATURE: Kichigeechacha, my god-daughter, she's wearin' all the
     wrong colors. I gotta work like a dog.

PIERRE: (Calling up to DICKIE BIRD HALKED.) Don't you worry a
     wart about that court appearance, Dickie Bird Halked. I'll be   735
     right there beside you tellin' that ole judge a thing or two about
     that goddamn jukebox.

SPOOKY: (*To* CREATURE.) Come on. Let's go watch Lalala play her first game.

(*He and* CREATURE *go up to the "bleachers" on the upper level, directly in front of* NANABUSH's *perch, to watch the big "game."*)

740   PIERRE: (*Reading from his clip-board and checking off the list.*) Now then, Dominique Ladouche, Black Lady Halked, Annie Cook, June Bug Mcleod . . .

(*He stops abruptly for* BIG JOEY's *announcement, as do the other men.*)

BIG JOEY: (*On the microphone.*) Patsy Pegahmagahbow, who is recuperating at Sudbury General Hospital, sends her love
745   and requests that the first goal scored by the Wasy Wailerettes be dedicated to the memory of Simon Starblanket . . .

(CREATURE *and* SPOOKY, *with knitting and baby, respectively, are now up in the "bleachers" with* DICKIE BIRD *and* BIG JOEY, *who are standing beside each other at the microphone stand.* PIERRE ST. PIERRE *is again skating around on the "ice" in his own inimitable fashion, "warming up."* ZACHARY JEREMIAH KEECHIGEESIK, *meanwhile, now has his apple pie, as well as his rolling pin, in hand, still wearing his baker's hat. At this point, the hockey arena sounds shift abruptly to the sound of women wailing and pucks hitting boards, echoing and echoing as in a vast empty chamber. As this "hockey game sequence" progresses, the spectacle of the men watching, cheering, etc., becomes more and more dream-like, all the men's movements imperceptibly breaking down into slow motion, until they fade, later, into the darkness.* ZACHARY *"sleep walks" through the whole lower level of the set, almost as though he were retracing his steps back through the whole play. Slowly, he takes off his clothes item by item, until, by the end, he is back lying naked on the couch where he began the play, except that, this time, it will be his own couch he is lying on.* BIG JOEY *continues uninterrupted.*)

. . . And there they are, ladies igwa gentlemen, there they are, the most beautiful, daring, death-defying Indian women in the world, the Wasy Wailerettes! How, Number Nine Hera
750   Keechigeesik, CAPTAIN of the Wasy Wailerettes, face-off igwa itootum asichi Number Nine Flora McDonald, Captain of the Canoe Lake Bravettes. Hey, soogi pagichee-ipinew "particular puck" referee Pierre St. Pierre . . .

CREATURE: Go Hera go! Go Hera go! Go Hera go! . . .

(*Repeated all the way through—and under—*BIG JOEY's *commentary.*)

755   BIG JOEY: igwa seemak wathay g'waskootoo like a herd of wild turtles . . .

SPOOKY: Wasy once. Wasy twice. Holy jumping Christ! Rim ram. God damn. Fuck, son-of-a-bitch, shit!

(*Repeated in time to* CREATURE's *cheer, all the way through—and under—*BIG JOEY's *commentary.*)

BIG JOEY: . . . Hey, aspin Number Six Dry Lips Manigitogan, right-winger for the Wasy Wailerettes, eemaskamat Number
760

_____

747 . . . **And** . . . The following hockey commentary by Big Joey (page 1707) is translated on p. 1709.

Thirteen of the Canoe Lake Bravettes anee-i "particular puck" . . . (DICKIE BIRD *begins chanting and stomping his foot in time to* CREATURE's *and* SPOOKY's *cheers. Bits and pieces of* NANABUSH/GAZELLE NATAWAYS' *"strip music" and Kitty Wells' "It Wasn't God Who Made Honky Tonk Angels"*   765
begin to weave in and out of this "sound collage," a collage which now has a definite "pounding" rhythm to it. Over it all soars the sound of ZACHARY's *harmonica, swooping and diving brilliantly, recalling many of* NANABUSH's *appearances throughout the play.* BIG JOEY *continues uninterrupted.*) . . .   770
igwa aspin sipweesin-skwataygew. Hey, k'seegoochin! How, Number Six Dry Lips Manigitogan igwa soogi pugamawew anee-i "particular puck" ita Number Twenty-six Little Girl Manitowabi, left-winger for the Wasy Wailerettes, katee-   775
ooteetuk blue line ita Number Eleven Black Lady Halked, wha! defense-woman for the Wasy Wailerettes, kagatchitnat anee-i "particular puck" igwa seemak kapassiwatat Captain Hera Keechigeesikwa igwa Hera Keechigeesik mitooni eepimithat, hey, kwayus graceful Hera Keechigeesik, mitooni   780
Russian ballerina eesinagoosit. Captain Hera Keechigeesik bee-line igwa itootum straight for the Canoe Lake Bravettes' net igwa shootiwatew anee-i "particular puck" igwa she shoots, she scores . . . almost! Wha! Close one, ladies igwa gentlemen, kwayus close one. But Num-ber Six Dry Lips   785
Manigitogan, right-winger for the Wasy Wailerettes, acci-dentally tripped and blocked the shot . . . (BIG JOEY's *voice begins to trail off as, at this point,* CREATURE NATAWAYS *marches over and angrily grabs the microphone away from him.*) . . . How, Number Nine Flora McDonald, Captain of the   790
Canoe Lake Bravettes, igwa ooteetinew anee-i "particular puck" igwa skate-oo-oo behind the net igwa soogi heading along the right side of the rink ita Number Twenty-one Annie Cook . . .

CREATURE: (*Off microphone, as he marches over to it.*) Aw   795
shit! Aw shit! . . . (*He grabs the microphone and, as he talks into it, the sound of all the other men's voices, including the entire "sound collage," begins to fade.*) . . . That Dry Lips Manigitogan, she's no damn good, Spooky Lacroix, I tole you once I tole you twice she shouldna done it she shouldna   800
done what she went and did goddawful Dry Lips Manigitogan they shouldna let her play, she's too fat, she's gotten positively blubbery lately, I tole you once I tole you twice that Dry Lips Manigitogan oughta move to Kapuskasing, she really oughta, Spooky Lacroix. I tole you once I tole you twice she oughta   805
move to Kapuskasing, Dry Lips oughta move to Kapuskasing! Dry Lips oughta move to Kapuskasing! Dry Lips oughta move to Kapuskasing! Dry Lips oughta move to Kapuskasing Dry Lips oughta move to Kapuskasing Dry Lips oughta move to Kapuskasing Dry Lips oughta move to Kapuskasing Dry   810
Lips oughta move to Kapuskasing Dry Lips oughta move to Kapuskasing . . .

(*And this, too, fades into, first a whisper, magnified on tape to "other-worldly" proportions, then into a slow kind of heavy breathing. On top of this we hear* SPOOKY's *baby crying. Complete fade-out on all this [lights and sound], except for the baby's crying and the heavy breathing, which continue in the darkness. When the lights come up again, we are in* ZACHARY's *own living room [i.e., what was all along* BIG JOEY's *living room/kitchen, only much cleaner]. The couch* ZACHARY *lies on is now covered with a "starblanket" and over the pin-up poster of Marilyn Monroe now hangs what was, earlier on,* NANABUSH's *large powwow dancing bustle. The theme from "The Smurfs" television show bleeds in.* ZACHARY *is lying on the couch face down, naked, sleeping and snoring. The television in front of the couch comes on and "The Smurfs" are playing merrily away.* ZACHARY's *wife, the "real"* HERA KEECHIGEESIK, *enters carrying their baby, who is covered completely with a blanket.* HERA *is soothing the crying baby.*)

ZACHARY: (*Talking in his sleep.*) . . . Dry Lips . . . oughta move
    to . . . Kapus . . .
HERA: Poosees.
815 ZACHARY: . . . kasing . . . damn silliest thing I heard in my
    life . . .
HERA: Honey.

(*Bends over the couch and kisses* ZACHARY *on the bum.*)

ZACHARY: . . . goodness sakes, Hera, you just had a baby . . .
    (*Suddenly, he jumps up and falls off the couch.*) Simon!
820 HERA: Yoah! Keegatch igwa kipageecheep'skawinan. ("Yoah!
    You almost knocked us down.")
ZACHARY: Hera! Where's my shorts?!
HERA: Neee, kigipoochimeek awus-chayees. ("Neee, just a
    couple of inches past the rim of your ass-hole.")
825 ZACHARY: Neee, chimagideedoosh. ("Neee, you unfragrant
    kozy": Ojibway.)

(*He struggles to a sitting position on the couch.*)

HERA: (*Correcting him and laughing.*) "ChimagideeDEESH."
    ("You unfragrant KOOZIE.")
ZACHARY: Alright. "ChimagideeDEESH."
830 HERA: And what were you dreaming abou . . .
ZACHARY: (*Finally seeing the television.*) Hey, it's the Smurfs! And
    they're not playing hockey de Englesa.
HERA: Neee, machi ma-a tatoo-Saturday morning Smurfs. Mootha
    meena weegatch hockey meetaweewuk weethawow Smurfs.

("Well, of course, the Smurfs are on every Saturday morning.   835
    But they never play hockey, those Smurfs.") Here, you take
    her. (*She hands the baby over to* ZACHARY *and goes to sit beside
    him.*) Boy, that full moon last night. Ever look particularly
    like a giant puck, eh? Neee . . .

(*Silence.* ZACHARY *plays with the baby.*)

ZACHARY: (*To* HERA.) Hey, cup-cake. You ever think of playing   840
    hockey?
HERA: Yeah, right. That's all I need is a flying puck right in the left
    tit, neee . . . (*But she stops to speculate.*) . . . hockey,
    hmmm . . .
ZACHARY: (*To himself.*) Lordy, lordy, lordy . . . (HERA *fishes*   845
    ZACHARY's *undershorts, which are pale blue in color, from
    under a cushion and hands them to him.* ZACHARY *gladly
    grabs them.*) Neee, magawa nipeetawitoos . . . ("Neee, here's
    my sharts . . . ")
HERA: (*Correcting him and laughing.*) "NipeetawiTAS." ("My   850
    SHORTS")
ZACHARY: Alright. "NipeetawiTAS." (*Dangles the shorts up to
    the baby's face with thumb and fore-finger and laughs. Sing-
    songy, bouncing the baby on his lap:*) Magawa nipeetawitas.
    Nipeetawitas. Nipeetawitas. Nipeetawitas . . .   855

(*The baby finally gets "dislodged" from the blanket and emerges, naked. And the last thing we see is this beautiful naked Indian man lifting his naked baby Indian girl up in the air, his wife sitting beside them watching and laughing. Slow fade-out. Split seconds before complete black-out,* HERA *peals out with this magical, silvery* NANABUSH *laugh, which is echoed and echoed by one last magical arpeggio on the harmonica, from off-stage. Finally, in the darkness, the last sound we hear is the baby's laughing voice, magnified on tape to fill the entire theater. And this, too, fades into complete silence.*)

(*End of play.*)

TRANSLATION OF BIG JOEY'S HOCKEY COMMENTARIES

Translation from the Cree of Big Joey's hockey commentary, Act One, pages 1696–1697.

. . . Hey, and there goes Number Six Dry Lips Manigitogan, right-winger for the Wasy Wailerettes . . . and steals the puck from Number Thirteen of the Canoe Lake Bravettes . . . and skates off. Hey, is she ever flying . . . (*Off microphone.*) Creature Nataways. Shut up. (*To the other men.*) Get this asshole out of here. (*Back on microphone.*) Now, Number Six Dry Lips Manigitogan, right-winger for the Wasy Wailerettes, shoots the puck and the puck goes flying over towards the center-line . . . where Number Nine Hera Keechigeesik, left-winger for . . . the Wasy Wailerettes, catches it. Now, Number Nine Hera Keechigeesik . . . approaching the blue line where Number One Gazelle Nataways, Captain of the Wasy Wailerettes, tries to get the puck off her, but Number Nine Hera Keechigeesik won't give it to her. Wha! "Hooking," says referee Pierre St. Pierre, Gazelle Nataways has apparently hooked her own team-mate Hera Keechigeesik, wha! Now, Number One Gazelle Nataways, Captain of the Wasy Wailerettes, facing off once again with Number Nine Flora McDonald, Captain of the Canoe Lake Bravettes and Flora McDonald shoots the puck, but Number Thirty-seven Big Bum Pegahmagahbow, defense-woman for the Wasy Wailerettes, stops the puck and passes it to Number Eleven Black Lady Halked, also defense-woman for the Wasy Wailerettes, but Gazelle Nataways, Captain of the Wasy Wailerettes, gives a mean body check to her own team-mate Black Lady Halked woops! She falls, ladies and gentlemen, Black Lady Halked hits the boards and Black Lady Halked is singin' the blues, ladies and gentlemen, Black Lady sings the blues. (*Off microphone.*) What the hell is going on down there? Dickie Bird, get off the ice! (*Back on microphone.*) Wha! Number Eleven Black Lady Halked is up in a flash and grabs the puck from Gazelle Nataways, holy shit! The ailing but very, very furious Black Lady Halked skates back, turns and takes aim, it's gonna be a slap shot, ladies and gentlemen, Black Lady Halked is gonna take a slap shot for sure and Black Lady Halked shoots the puck, wha! She shoots straight at her very own captain, Gazelle Nataways and holy shit, holy shit, holy fuckin' shit!

Translation from the Cree of Big Joey's hockey commentary, Act Two, page 1707.

. . . And there they are, ladies and gentlemen, there they are, the most beautiful, daring, death-defying Indian women in the world, the Wasy Wailerettes! Now, Number Nine HeraKeechigeesik, CAPTAIN of the Wasy Wailerettes, facing off with Number Nine Flora McDonald, Captain of the Canoe Lake Bravettes. Hey, and referee Pierre St. Pierre drops the "particular puck" . . . and takes off like a herd of wild turtles . . . Hey, and there goes Dry Lips Manigitogan, right-winger for the Wasy Wailerettes, and steals the "particular puck" from Number Thirteen of the Canoe Lake Bravettes . . . and skates off. Hey, is she ever flying. Now, Number Six Dry Lips Manigitogan shoots the "particular puck" towards where Number Twenty-six Little Girl Manitowabi, left-winger for the Wasy Wailerettes, is heading straight for the blue line where Number Eleven Black Lady Halked, wha! defense-woman for the Wasy Wailerettes, catches the "particular puck" and straight-way passes it to Captain Hera Keechigeesik and Hera Keechi-geesik is just a-flyin', hey, is she graceful or what, that Hera Keechigeesik, she looks just like a Russian ballerina. Captain Hera Keechigeesik now makes a bee-line straight for the Canoe Lake Bravettes' net and shoots the "particular puck" and she shoots, she scores . . . almost! Wha! Close one, ladies and gentlemen, real close one. But Number Six Dry Lips Manitogotan, right-winger for the Wasy Wailerettes, accidentally tripped and blocked the shot . . . (CREATURE NATAWAYS *grabs the microphone away from* BIG JOEY.) . . . Now, Number Nine Flora McDonald, Captain of the Canoe Lake Bravettes, grabs the "particular puck" and skates behind the net and now heading along the right side of the rink where Number Twenty-one Annie Cook . . .

Manjula Padmanabhan

Well-known as a cartoonist in Delhi, Manjula Padmanabhan (b. 1953), has worked as a journalist and fiction writer, as well as writing for television and the stage; she has also written several children's books. After completing her university studies abroad, Padmanabhan returned to India and began a career in journalism. She wrote several plays—including *Lights Out!* (1984), *The Artist's Model* (1995), and *Sextet* (1996)—and a well-known book of short stories, *Hot Death, Cold Soup* (1995). *Harvest* won the first Onassis Prize for Theater, and premiered in Greece in 1999; it has also been produced in India. Her most recent novel is *Getting There* (2000).

Harvest   Written in the lineage of plays like Václav Havel's *The Memorandum* or Slawomir Mrozek's *Tango*, Manjula Padmanabhan's *Harvest* develops an absurd narrative of the structure of representation and power in the contemporary globalized culture. For *Harvest* brilliantly allegorizes the relationship between the First and Third Worlds, literalizing the fundamental practices of globalization as its central dramatic situation: the Third World provides the raw materials that the First World consumes for its own survival and expansion.

In the play, Om has sold his body—through the aptly named InterPlanta Services company—to an American "Receiver." According to the terms of his contract, he and his immediate family (his wife Jaya, who is forced by the contract to pretend to be his sister, his brother Jeetu, and his mother, Ma) will enjoy a First World standard of living and lifestyle—they'll be clean, well-fed, entertained, and wealthy—until such time as his Receiver demands Om's organs for his own survival. As the play develops, however, the economic motives driving Om's sacrifice are gradually inflected by the mediatized relations of global culture. His family is consulted (on a giant-screen Contact Module that drops from the ceiling)

The family confronts Ginni in Manjula Padmanabhan's *Harvest,* in the 1999 production of the play at the Teatro Texnis, Greece.

by the Receiver, Virginia—or "Ginni," whose name recalls the demonic *djinni*, or "genies" of Indian folktales—a "blonde and white-skinned epitome of an American-style youth goddess" whose image floats above the room, and increasingly demands obedience from the family. Ma comes nearly to worship Ginni, but truly idolizes her new television, finally choosing to entomb herself inside a video sarcophagus—called the Video Paradise—where she will remain for the rest of her "life." When the InterPlanta agents come to take Om, however, they mistakenly take his wastrel brother Jeetu, removing his eyes and replacing them with a contraption that projects Ginna's sexy image directly into his brain. Although Jeetu had been the most critical of the organ-donation scheme, now that all he can see is Ginni's sultry image, he's seduced, and this virtual relationship leads him finally to "donate" his entire body.

The play's brilliant satire fully takes in First World attitudes toward India, its fear of disease, its anxiety about sanitation, its incomprehension of family and social life, its ignorance of Third World reality altogether. Replacing the family's food with "goat-shit" pellets, installing a toilet and shower in the middle of its one-room apartment, dumping the family's possessions and replacing them with Western clothes and housewares, InterPlanta at once appears to improve the family's standard of living while cutting it off from real life altogether. Yet the final scenes seem to suggest a strategy of resistance. Once Ginni has harvested Jeetu's body, she reveals that "Ginni" had only been a computer-animation after all: Jeetu had been seduced to give up his body by the empty image of youthful, sexy America, an image projected to the world to conceal that the First World paradise is aging and impotent, supporting "the poorer sections of the world, while gaining fresh bodies for ourselves." Virgil—the real Ginni—proposes that he (in the body of Jeetu) and Jaya have children to repopulate the First World; he even makes an insemination gadget appear outside the apartment while he's trying to close the deal. But if the body is, finally, what the Third World has to sell, it may still be possible to withhold it, to insist on a real rather than a mediated relationship with First World power. At the play's close, Jaya seals herself inside the apartment, with its endless food supply and television, telling Virgil that if he wants to repopulate the First World, he will have to come to her, in the flesh.

Harvest

Manjula Padmanabhan

CHARACTERS

DONORS

OM *Twenty years old, he has been laid off from his job as a clerk and is the bread-earner of his small family. He is of medium height, nervy and thin. He would be reasonably good-looking if not for his anxious expression.*

JAYA *OM's wife. Thin and haggard at the outset, she looks older than her nineteen years, but is passionate and spirited. Her bright cotton sari has faded with repeated washing, to a meek pink. Like the others, she is barefoot at the outset. She wears glass bangles, a tiny nose-ring, ear-studs, a slender chain around her neck. No make-up aside from the kohl around her eyes and the red bindi on her forehead.*

MA *OM's mother. She is sixty years old, stooped, scrawny and crabby, wears a widow's threadbare white-on-white sari. Her hair is a straggly white.*

JEETU *OM's younger brother, seventeen and handsome. The same height as OM, he is wiry and conscious of his body. He works as a male prostitute and has a dashing, easy-going likeable personality.*

BIDYUT BAI *An elderly neighbour, very similar in appearance to MA, but timid and self-effacing.*

Also URCHINS *and the crowd outside the door. The crowd is audible rather than visible.*

GUARDS and AGENTS

GUARDS *The* GUARDS *are a group of three commando-like characters who bear the same relationship to each other whenever they appear.* GUARD 1 *is the leader of the team, a man in his mid forties, of military bearing.* GUARD 2 *is a young and attractive woman, unsmiling and efficient.* GUARD 3 *is a male clone of* GUARD 2. *Only* GUARD 1 *interacts with* DONORS.

AGENTS *The* AGENTS *are space-age delivery persons and their uniforms are fantastical verging on ludicrous, like the costumes of waiters in exotic restaurants. Their roles are interchangeable with the* GUARDS, *though it must be clear that they do not belong to the same agency.*

RECEIVERS

GINNI *We see only her face and hear her voice. She is the blonde and white-skinned epitome of an American-style youth goddess. Her voice is sweet and sexy.*

VIRGIL *He is never seen. He has an American cigarette-commercial accent—rich and smoky, attractive and rugged.*

ACT ONE

SCENE I

The sound of inner city traffic: grimy, despairing, poison-fumed. It wells up before the curtains open, then cuts out to a background rumble as . . . the lights reveal a single-room accommodation in a tenement building. It is bare but cluttered. In the foreground, stage left, is a board-bed across the tops of three steel trunks. MA sits on the bed, her ear straining towards the wall, listening intently. Near her is the front door. JAYA stands by the window stage right, looking out, her face drained. To the rear is the kitchen area.

MA: (*Grunts.*) Ho! (*Turns to look at* JAYA.) Ho—you! Come here a moment—

JAYA: (*Listlessly.*) What is it?

MA: Come here and tell me what they're saying—

5　JAYA: It's none of your business—

MA: Eh?

JAYA: What they say in their room—none of your business!

MA: The cheek of the thing! (*Turns around in indignation.*) As if she knows what my business is! Why—I'm her mother-in-

10　law! And what is she? A dry stick!

JAYA: Leave me out of it. I'm not interested.

MA: Oh of course not, your majesty! So high and mighty she is—staring out of her precious window! Stare all you like but it's useless. There's no chance he'll get the job.

15　JAYA: (*Quickly.*) I'm not the one hoping!

MA: Oh—I forgot! Missie Madam *isn't* hoping the best for her husband—like she should, like any dutiful, sane, reasonable, respectable wife—oh no! Missie Madam has her own sweet thoughts, doesn't she!

20　JAYA: (*Briefly enlivened.*) Oh! There—I think I see him—

MA: Well—well—job or not, he's not got wings, *that* I can tell you. He'll *still* have to climb four floors getting up here. But—what does he look like?

JAYA: (*Straining to see.*) He's—no—yes . . . that's him—

MA: Is his face shining? Are his footsteps sweet? A songbird on　25
his shoulder?

JAYA: It's a bit far to see such details—

MA: Pah! As if you can see them even when he's right in front of you. Now I—I can see it even without looking at him. Just from the sound of his feet. His little feet! Like flowers they　30
were—

JAYA: (*Frustrated.*) Oh—please! The way you go on—!

MA: Jealous!

JAYA: You'd like to think that—

MA: And rude, my arse. Why, you're hardly human! You must　35
have grown up in a jungle!

JAYA: Leave me alone—

MA: Alone, alone! Have you seen your neighbours? Ten in that room, twenty in the other! And harmonious, my dear! Harmonious as a TV show! But you? An empty room would　40
be too crowded for you!

JAYA: That's because I live in a room in which two people think the other two don't exist—

MA: Two and . . . two—four? Have you forgotten how to count?　45

JAYA: Not at all! You're the one who never counts Jeetu—

MA: Huh! That pimping rascal! That soul's disgrace!

JAYA: You like to pretend he's not there—but *I'm* the one who has to cook for him, worry about him—

MA: You worry far too much about that one, if you ask me—　50

JAYA: Yet he's *your* son.

MA: Nah. The gods left a jackal in my belly by mistake when they made him—maybe that's why *you* like him—he's just like you, rude, insolent, ungrateful—

55 JAYA: I! *Like* him!

MA: Think I don't see the way you wet yourself when he walks in the door. Yes! Your brother-in-law—oh the sin of it, the sin! You'll suffer in your next life. See if you don't!

60 You'll be made into a cockroach and I'll have to smash you—(*Lifts her bare foot and stamps hard.*) just like this one. (*Shows* JAYA *the underside of the foot.*) See? Do you see your fate?

JAYA: (*Paying no attention, her ear cocked to the door.*) There! That's Om—

(*Goes quickly to the door, stage left. Opens it, looks out, steps out, shutting the door behind her.*)

65 MA: (*Makes a face behind her back.*) Yah, yah! Go on—running out to meet him, like some idiot schoolgirl! Think I'm fooled by it! I'm not fooled! I see everything! Even inside your head! I—

(*The door opens.* OM *walks in.*)

MA: (*Half rising, her face is transformed.*) Ah, my son! My own

70 boy! What news?

(OM, *carrying a bulky parcel, his face set tight, as if too dazed to know whether to be glad or sad.* JAYA *comes in behind him and shuts the door.* OM *loosens the collar of his shirt.*)

MA: What? No hope? Nothing at all?

(JAYA *stands uncertainly at centre stage.*)

MA: They are fools, that's all! Don't recognize a diamond when they see one! It's their loss. Still . . . it would have been nice. A change. A godsend. How'll we manage now?

75 JAYA: (*Carefully.*) What is it? What happened?

OM: (*Looks up.*) I got it. (*Puts the package down on the bed.*)

(JAYA *stifles a sob, spins around and back to her window.*)

MA: (*As if unable to believe him.*) What? Say that again?

OM: I got it. I got the job.

MA: (*Painfully fierce intake of breath.*) Hhhhhh! Hhhhh! Oh!

80 Say it again! Say the blessed words again! (*Rises shakily to her feet, declaiming to the world.*) Never stop saying it! "I—have—got—the—job!" (*Turns to him holding out her arms.*) Ah my soul, my heartbeat! Come, kiss me! Let me hold you, fondle your ears! Why am I surprised? You deserve

85 every success.

OM: (*Starts to remove his shirt.*) Yes. It was quite easy, in the end.

MA: (*To* JAYA's *back.*) Bring him a glass of milk! Bring him two glasses! (*To* OM.) Come here, my darling boy! My only delight! Let your old mother hug you to her belly! (*She goes*

90 *to him.*)

OM: (*His shirt off, tucked into the waistband of his trousers.*) There were six thousand men!

MA: Six thousand! Waiting in the sun!

OM: No. Inside a building like a big machine. They had—like

95 iron bars—snaking around and around (*His hands describe a narrow looping channel.*)—we could only stand one behind the other—like goats at the slaughterhouse—

MA: Shoo! Where has my son seen a slaughterhouse!

OM: And everywhere there were guards—

100 MA: Police, you mean?

OM: Guards in grey uniforms—you'll see them for yourself any minute now—they're coming—

JAYA: (*From where she stands.*) They're coming now?

OM: They have to check. They have to set it all up.

MA: What? What are you talking about? 105

JAYA: You mean it's not certain yet?

OM: They're just checking the building.

MA: For what—

JAYA: (*Bitterly.*) Better train your mother to tie her tongue down! 110

MA: Hear that? How your wife speaks of your mother?

OM: Ma—when the men come, you *must keep quiet.*

MA: As if I ever get a chance to speak!

JAYA: She can pretend she doesn't understand!

MA: (*Starting up indignantly.*) What— 115

OM: Yes, Ma. It's the best way. Behave as if you don't understand, when they ask.

MA: But why? What's there to hide? Have you done something wrong?

OM: No—but—but—there's no time to explain! And you'll know 120 for yourself any minute now—

MA: But what's the trouble! Has something gone wrong? What did they say to you?

OM: They have to check, you see. So that the arrangements are—are—all right. They're very particular— 125

JAYA: And for how long is the job?

OM: They didn't say—

MA: And what will they pay you?

OM: A lot.

MA: Huh! That's how paupers talk—"a lot". Listen to the rich? 130 They're on first name terms with all the leading numbers— hundreds, thousands, hundred-thousand . . .

OM: (*His voice is hushed.*) We'll have more money than you and I have names for! (*Shakes his head in wonderment.*) Who'd believe there's so much money in the world? 135

MA: Ho!

JAYA: Can we be sure?

MA: You met with the top men? They spoke to you themselves?

OM: No . . .

MA: Pooh! Then you've got nothing! 140

OM: We were standing all together in that line. And the line went on—and on not just on one floor, but slanting up, up, forever. All in iron bars and grills. It was like being in a cage shaped like a tunnel. All around, up, down, sideways, there were men— 145

JAYA: Doing what?

OM: Slowly moving. All the time. I couldn't understand it. . . . Somewhere there must be a place to stop, to write a form? Answer questions? But no. Just—forward, forward, forward. One person fainted but the others pushed him onward. And 150 at the corners, a—a sort of pipe was kept . . .

MA: For what?

JAYA: To make water, what else!

MA: Even while moving?

OM: You had to be quick. Other men would squeeze past behind 155 the fellow who was doing his business. Sometimes there was no place and he'd have to move on before he finished. Still dripping.

MA: Shee!

OM: What could we do? As for those who had more solid deposits 160 to make—! Foo! It was terrible!

JAYA: And then?

OM: The stench! The heat!

MA: But what happened?

165   OM: I don't know for how long we moved. Then there was a door. Inside it was dark, like being in heaven! So cool, so fresh! I too fainted then, with pleasure, I don't know. (*Stands up, reliving his movements.*) I wake up to find now the ground is moving under me—

170   MA: What? How's that?

OM: I don't know. But the floor is moving. Then there's a sign: "REMOVE CLOTHING"—

MA: Whaaat?

OM: So we do that. Still moving. Then each man gets a bag. To

175   put the clothes inside.

JAYA: . . . *naked?*

OM: (*Nods.*) Then—a sort of—rain burst. (*He laughs shakily.*) I wonder if I am dreaming! The water is hot, scented. Then cold. Then hot air. Then again the water. It stings a

180   little, this second water. Smells like some medicine. Then air again. Then we pass through another place . . . I don't know what is happening. Ahead of me a man screams and cries, but we are in separate little cages now, can't move. At one place, something comes to cover the eyes. There's

185   no time to think, just do. Put your arm here, get one prick, put your arm there, get another prick—*pissshhh!*— *pisssshhh!*—Sit here, stand here, take your head this side, look at a light that side. On and on. Finally at the end there's another tunnel, with pretty pictures and some

190   music. And the sign comes: RESUME CLOTHING. I just do what I have to do. All the time, the ground keeps moving. Then at the end, the ground stops, we are back on our feet, there are steps. It must be the other side of the building. And as we come down, guards are standing there, waiting

195   for us. And to me they say, "You, come—" (*Pause.*) And that was it!

MA: What!

JAYA: What?

OM: That's all. Some other men were also with me, all looking

200   like me, I suppose. Blank. They told us we had been selected. They wrote down our names, addresses . . . (*He hesitates.*) and . . . this-that. All details. Then they gave us these packets (*Indicates the package.*), told us not to open them and said we must go home, the guards would come with us for final

205   instructions.

MA: But what is the work? The pay-packet? The hours?

OM: (*Looking distracted.*) I—I'll be in the house . . .

MA: What?! All the time?

JAYA: (*Staring intensely at him.*) . . . you don't really know what it's

210   going to be like, do you?

MA: What kind of job pays a man to sit at home?

OM: Oh—there was some pamphlet they gave us to read, right in the beginning. Just to tell us to be relaxed and to do whatever we were told. In that it said that once we were

215   selected, each man would get special instructions. That we would be monitored carefully. Not just us but our . . . lives. To remain employed, we have to keep ourselves exactly as they tell us.

JAYA: But—but *who* will tell us—how'll we afford it—

(*There is an excited tapping on the door which was left unbolted. A* CHILD *bursts in.*)

220   CHILD: Auntie! Auntie! They're coming to your house! Police!

(*From the corridor, approaching footsteps.* JAYA *shoos the child from the door as she stands by it. The footsteps come to a halt. A small crowd has collected out on the corridor (out of sight, but audible) to whom* JAYA *pays no attention.*)

JAYA: Yes?

MA: (*Remaining seated.*) Let him in, let him in—

GUARD 1: (*Out of sight.*) InterPlanta Services wishes to confirm that this is the residence of Om Prakash?

JAYA: It is—(*And she stands aside.*)   225

GUARD 1: (*Entering officiously.*) Thank you—(*Looks around.*) Ah. Yes. Am I addressing Mr Om Prakash?

(*As he talks, enter* GUARD 2 *and* GUARD 3. *They are both carrying equipment which they set down and immediately begin to ready for installation.* GUARD 3 *produces collapsible cartons which he begins to set up.* GUARD 2 *starts to install a device onto the window frame.*)

MA: Who are these people? What are they doing?

GUARD 1: (*To* OM.) Ready? We can start.

OM: What do I have to do?   230

GUARD 1: Just listen. (*He consults his clipboard and begins to read in a loud formal voice.*) Congratulations! InterPlanta Services is proud and honoured to welcome Mr Om Prakash to its programme! (*To* OM.) Sir, you have received the Starter Kit? (*Doesn't wait, sights the package* OM *brought with him, nods,*   235 *ticks.*) Yes. There it is. Sir: you are directed to open the kit and make it operational after our departure. Instructions are provided within. Any questions? (OM *shakes his head.* GUARD 1 *nods and ticks.*) All right.

(*In the background,* GUARD 3 *has got two cartons set up. He wears large plastic mitts over his existing skin-tight gloves and starts dumping all the items on the kitchen counter into the cartons. Meanwhile two or three urchins have come into the room and are goggling at the goings-on. Just beyond the door, a crowd of onlookers is standing out of sight, doing likewise.*)

JAYA: (*To* GUARD 1.) Hi! What're you doing! (*Turns to* OM.)   240 See—see what's happening! (*Back to* GUARD 3, *who goes ahead.*) Who said you can touch my things? (*Tugs at his arm but he pays her no heed.*) Hi! Stop that!

GUARD 1: (*To* OM, *who is distracted.*) Sir: we will set up the Contact Module. It will start functioning in approximately   245 two hours.

OM: I—I'm sorry, but I must—

GUARD 1: Sir: pay no attention! About the Contact Module, all details will be found in the Starter Kit.

(*Meanwhile, downstage,* JAYA *struggles with* GUARD 3.)

JAYA: Who told you to do that! No! (*She attempts hitting guard*   250 *3, but he continues relentlessly dumping everything into the cartons.*) You can't do this! It's my house! No! Oh! Stop it, you monster, you beast! (*She tries to return items to the counter, but he is much faster than her.*) Stop it, stop it, stop it! Don't you understand what I'm saying? Are you a machine? Answer   255 me! Oh! (*She abruptly turns in on herself and succumbs to a fit of stormy weeping.*)

(GUARD 3 *continues with his job unperturbed in the course of the other events at stage front. After removing everything but the counter top and shelf, he cleans and swabs the entire area, then sprays it with attention to corners. After that he reaches into his kit and brings out a cooking device and bottles full of multi-coloured pellets.)*

(GUARD 2 continues her installation without interruption.)

GUARD 1: *(Regardless of the commotion behind him.)* At the time of first contact, you and your Receiver will exchange personal
260   information. Your physical data has been sent for matching and we are confident that you will both be well satisfied. Any questions?

OM: Uhh uhh but what about . . . I mean, when will I actually have to—

265 GUARD 1: Sir: Any questions to the information received so far?

OM: *(Uncertainly.)* No . . . I mean—

GUARD 1: *(Nods and ticks.)* Right. When we have confirmed that the Contact Unit is functioning, you will not be responsible
270   for anything but the maintainance of your personal resources. Any questions?

OM: But what about

GUARD 1: Sir! Any questions?

OM: *(Subdued.)* No.

275 GUARD 1: *(Nods and ticks.)* Right. All implements of personal fuel preparation will be supplied exclusively by Inter-Planta Services. Henceforward, you and your domestic unit will consume only those fuels which will be made available to you by InterPlanta. We will provide more
280   than enough for the unit described in your data sheet, but will forbid you from sharing, selling or by any means whatsoever, commercially exploiting this facility. Any questions?

OM: No.

285 GUARD 1: *(Nods and ticks.)* We are providing a remote-source electrical connection. It will be adequate for the systems currently being used by you and your domestic unit, as well as for the equipment which we ourselves will install. But on no account must it bear any additional loads, nor
290   must it be used by any agencies other than yourselves, loaned out, rented out, sold or put to any use other than the one just described. Any questions?

OM: No.

GUARD 1: *(Nods and ticks.)* Good. Now if I can just interview the
295   members of your domestic unit—

JAYA: *(From the rear.)* I have a question!

GUARD 1: *(Doesn't acknowledge her.)*—beginning with the oldest member—

JAYA: *(Desperately.)* Your—your man has thrown my stove into
300   his bag and broken it! Who is going to replace that?

OM: *(Hissed aside.)* Not now, Jaya! Just be patient—

(GUARD 1 is shuffling papers till he gets the relevant sheet.)

JAYA: Be patient! While my house is broken up! *(But she turns herself aside and weeps, even as she shoos the bystanders away from the door. She is not able to do this easily or efficiently
305   because she is crying too bitterly, so her actions have little impact. The urchins who are inside wriggle aside and continue to stand where they are.)*

GUARD 1: *(Approaching MA and addressing her.)* Madam: Full name?

OM: *(Interceding.)* She doesn't understand your speech. Her
310   name's Indumati. Missiz Indumati Prakash.

GUARD 1: *(Continuing to address MA who looks genuinely bewildered.)* Missiz Indumati Prakash. *(Ticks.)* Relationship with Donor?

OM: Mother.   315

GUARD 1: *(Ticks.)* Have you understood all that has been said so far?

OM: Yes.

GUARD 1: *(His hand wavers. He looks up at OM. A flicker of normal communication.)* You will explain to her?   320

OM: *(Woodenly.)* Yes.

GUARD 1: *(Ticks.)* Right. Good. Now—*(He turns.)* next relative *(He sees her.)* Missiz—Missiz—*(He consults the sheet.)*

(JAYA, who knows that it will now be her turn, shoves the children out roughly, anxiety lending determination to her movements. She slams the door shut against resistance from the other side and with some difficulty pushes the bolt home.)

GUARD 1: —Kumar. Missiz Kumar come this way, please—

JAYA: *(Moves across to centre-stage.)* Yes—yes.   325

GUARD 1: *(Consulting his clip-board.)* Full name?

JAYA: Jaya. Mrs Jaya Kumar. *(She begins to weep anew.)*

(MA stirs at this and looks over to where JAYA stands, a frown on her face. OM holds his head in his hands, his eyes on the floor.)

GUARD 1: Relationship with Donor?

JAYA: *(Lifts her head. In a barely audible voice.)* Sister.

(MA registers a shock. Her hand to her mouth, she seems to hold in her words manually. Then her hand goes to her heart.)

GUARD 1: *(Neutral.)* Madam: please repeat response.   330

JAYA: Sister. He's my sister—I —I mean, I'm his—*(She is about to say, "brother" but succumbs to a fit of silent sobbing. Regains control.)* Sister. I'm . . . his . . . sister.

(MA's face and limbs perform a dumb charade of her feelings, as she fights against the urge to react because she's not supposed to understand the exchange, yet she cannot make sense of what's going on.)

GUARD 1: *(Ticks.)* Right. *(Looks around cursorily, merely to confirm what he already knows.)* Husband?   335

JAYA: *(Nods.)* At work.

GUARD 1: *(Ticks.)* Full name?

JAYA: Jeetu—Jeeten. Jeeten Kumar.

(MA's body jerks like a puppet. She reins in her comments with ferocious effort.)

GUARD 1: *(Ticks, nods.)* Right. *(He looks up and around.)* InterPlanta recommends that those members absent at this   340 briefing make themselves available at the nearest collection centre not later than twenty-four hours from the time of our departure, failing which such member will lose all rights to the facilities provided by us. Any questions? *(He does not wait for confirmation before ticking off, then looks up.)* Good. *(Turns 345 to the other two GUARDS.)* Briefing complete, initiate departure procedure.

(*Behind him,* GUARD 2 *and* GUARD 3 *have both completed their tasks and are standing stiffly "at ease" at their stations, awaiting orders. Whatever is visible of their faces is completely blank.*)

(*Hanging from the ceiling is a white, faceted globe, at least three feet in diameter. It looks like a Japanese lantern, unlit.*)

(*In the course of the following action,* JAYA *wanders towards the window,* OM *remains seated on the bed,* MA'S *physical movements subside.*)

GUARD 1: (*Moving towards them, checking off his list as he inspects and is responded to.*) Officer Contact Module Installation,
350   activity report: Installation complete?
GUARD 2: Yessir.
GUARD 1: Remote Power Reception cable in place?
GUARD 2: Yessir.
GUARD 1: Cable check complete?
355   GUARD 2: Yessir.
GUARD 1: Contact Module in operational mode?
GUARD 2: Yessir.
GUARD 1: Good. Initialize for contact.

(GUARD 2 *moves swiftly over to the* CONTACT MODULE *which is roughly at centre stage and points a remote at it. As* GUARD 2 *works, there are musical notes and clicks. The polygon stirs alight. Random facets light up. A screen-saver pattern appears. The entire polygon moves in a slow, smooth circle, then is lowered to ground level and up again.* GUARD 1 *steps back, satisfied.*)

GUARD 1: (*Paying no further attention to* GUARD 2'S *activities,*
360   *addresses* GUARD 3, *who is ready with two neat cartons prepared for transport.*) Officer Fuel Supplies and Installation: activity report: sanitization of supply area complete?
GUARD 3: Yessir.
GUARD 1: Installation of fuel preparation equipment com-
365   plete?
GUARD 3: Yessir.
GUARD 1: Delivery of one month's fuel supplies for family of four complete?
GUARD 3: Yessir.
370   GUARD 1: Good. Proceed with departure.

(GUARD 2 *and* GUARD 3 *station themselves by the door.*)

GUARD 1: (*Approaching* OM, *holding out his clipboard for signing with a pen offered in the same motion.*) Mr Om Prakash, I am pleased to inform you that the installation and initialization procedures have been completed satisfactorily. Thank you
375   for your cooperation. Please sign the following activity report after confirming that the observations contained herein are true and accurate to the best of your knowledge. (*Hands him the clipboard.*)
OM: (*He stands up as* GUARD 1 *approaches him: Takes the*
380   *clipboard, glances at it cursorily.*) Yes. I agree. (*Signs, hands the board back.*)
JAYA: (*Over her shoulder.*) You don't need any confirmation from us?
GUARD 1: All further queries will be satisfied by the Starter
385   Kit. (*He tucks the clipboard under his arm.*) Thank you for your cooperation and valuable time! I and my colleagues deeply appreciate the contribution you are about to make

towards creating a healthier, happier and longer-lived world!

(*Clicks his heels together and turns smartly towards the others.* GUARD 3 *immediately opens the latch on the door which is buffeted open by the listeners on the other side, who immediately fall back and away at the sight of* GUARD 3. GUARD 1 *exits and the other two follow suit. The door is left open and the original one or two urchins poke their noses inside, darting quick glances around.* JAYA *sees them and moves across to shoo them away again. They dart out again with no further urging from her. She shuts the door once more.*)

MA: (*To no-one in particular*) What sort of job makes a wife into   390
     a sister?
OM: (*Subsides onto the bed again, head in his hands.*) Don't get confused, Ma. What they write in their reports doesn't change our lives.
MA: But what *is* she, really? A wife? Or a sister?   395
JAYA: (*Has come back and is standing at centre stage.*) How shall I cook now? They've taken all our things! Every last grain!
MA: Who is Jeetu, now? Is he a son? Or a son-in-law?
OM: Nothing's changed! The words are different, that's all.
MA: But these aren't words! They're people!   400
JAYA: Are you listening to me, (*Mocking.*) brother? (OM *looks up.*) What are we to do for food?
MA: (*Whispers.*) How can my daughter be married to my son? What will people think?
JAYA: (*Louder.*) Tell me, brother!—   405
OM: (*Stirring.*) It's in this package. Whatever we need to know.
JAYA: (*Hard.*) Even about food?
OM: (*Wearily.*) Even food.

(*Lights snap out.*)

SCENE II

The same room. OM *and* MA *are sitting upstage centre. A mat is spread on the floor and they are eating the coloured pellets of their new food.* JAYA *is leaning her head and shoulders against the side of the bed.*

The package is open. Its contents are strewn about. There are brightly coloured instruction leaflets, elaborately devised containers for pills and powders and a number of small gadgets similar in size and shape to a slide-viewing device but of obscure purpose.

MA: Tell me again: all you have to do is sit at home and stay healthy?
OM: Well—not *sit* necessarily—
MA: And they'll pay you?
OM: Yes.   5
MA: Even if you do nothing but pick your nose all day!
OM: They'll pay me.
MA: And what about off-days?
OM: (*Shrugs.*) Well. *Every* day is off, in one sense—
JAYA: (*Suddenly.*) Why don't you tell her the truth?   10
MA: Isn't this the truth?
OM: Jaya—
JAYA: (*Swinging herself around, to face them.*) Tell her. Tell your mother what you've really done—
MA: Shoo! Don't speak to your husband in that voice—   15

OM: The walls are thin. Everyone can hear. When you talk like this—

JAYA: Everyone knows already! D'you think you're the only one with this—this *job*? D'you think everyone doesn't know what

20   it means . . . when the grey guards come? (*Tears in her voice.*) All that remains to be known is which part of you's been given away!

MA: (*Mystified.*) What's this, what's this? Who's giving away parts of whom?

25 JAYA: Which goes first, the brain or the heart, that's what I want to know—

MA: (*To* OM.) I'm sorry to say, your wife has gone mad. Your sister, I mean—

OM: She's just trying to make trouble—

30 JAYA: (*Bitter laugh.*) Huh!

MA: Who cares about her? Wife or sister, Mother comes first! So tell me—these people, your employers, who exactly are they?

OM: It's—it's well, actually it's just one person.

35 MA: Just one person! With so much money to give away!

JAYA: It's a foreigner. That's why it's so much—

MA: What?

OM: (*Sighs.*) The money comes from abroad—

MA: Really! (*A sudden doubt.*) But . . . doesn't that mean you'll

40   have to go there? Abroad?

OM: Ma—no-one goes abroad these days . . .

JAYA: Not whole people, anyway!

OM: (*Warningly.*) I'm warning you now, Jaya—

MA: What's that? What's that? Knot-hole people? What d'you

45   mean—shorties?

JAYA: (*Patiently.*) Not his whole body. Just parts of it—

MA: (*To* OM.) What's your wife saying—not your body, but your what?

(JAYA *curls herself more tightly into herself.*)

OM: (*To* JAYA's *back.*) Why're you doing this? Why're you making

50   trouble?

JAYA: (*Over her shoulder.*) You said it wouldn't affect us—but see what it's done already!

OM: So *tell* me—what? In exchange for your old kitchen you have a new modern one—

55 JAYA: (*Swivelling round.*) You call this food? This—(*She indicates the pellets they have been eating.*) this—this goat-shit?

MA: It's better than what you make—

JAYA: And calling me your sister—what's that? (*Sobs.*) If I'm your sister, what does that make you? (*Hysterical edge.*) Sister, huh!

60   My forehead burns, when I say that word, "sister"! (*She smears the red kumkum on her forehead in her torment and succumbs to her tears.*)

MA: Shoo! Are you a street woman? To speak in such a voice!

65 OM: You think I did it lightly. You think it's a heavy price. But at the cost of calling you my sister . . . we'll be *rich*! Very rich! Insanely rich! What're you saying? (*He gets up to wash his hands and mouth at the kitchen sink, stopping to make his point along the way.*) But you'd rather live

70   in this one small room, I suppose! Think it's such a fine thing (*Washes his mouth, spits.*) living day in, day out, like monkeys in a hot-case—(*Washes mouth again and spits again, wipes face, mouth.*) lulled to sleep by our neighbours' rhythmic farting! Dancing to the tune of the

melodious traffic! And starving. Yes—you'd prefer this to 75 being called my sister on a stupid slip of paper no-one we know will ever see!

MA: Why fight over what is finished? Tell me about this rich foreigner, your employer! Who is he? Why does he love you so much? That's what I don't understand—where did he 80 meet you?

JAYA: (*Half-sob/laugh.*) Ohh—just tell her, tell her!

OM: (*Coming back to centrestage.*) We've never met, Ma . . .

MA: What!

OM: He's rich—and old. That's all I know about him. Probably 85 suffering from some illness—

MA: Then why's he paying you so much!

JAYA: Oh *Ma!*—don't you see it? Isn't it obvious?

MA: (*To* JAYA.) You're so smart that you can hear the Holy Father himself thinking but I, I need to hear with my ears—(*Turns to* 90 OM.) Tell me, my son—

OM: (*Irritated.*) Oh, you won't understand, Ma—

JAYA: I'll tell you! He's sold the rights to his organs! His skin. His eyes. His arse. (*Sobs again.*) Sold them! (*Holds her head.*) Oh God, oh God! What's the meaning of this nightmare! 95 (*Sobs. To* OM.) How can I hold your hand, touch your face, knowing that at any moment it might be snatched away from me and flung across the globe! (*Sobs.*) If you were dead I could shave my head and break my bangles—but this? To be a widow by slow degrees? To mourn you piece by piece? (*Sobs.*) 100 Should I shave half my head? Break my bangles one at a time? (*Succumbs to her tears.*)

MA: (*Only half-comprehending. Turns to* OM *who stands with his back to the women.*) How is it possible?

OM: (*Looking up at* JAYA.) If you weren't so busy feeling sorry for 105 yourself, you'd have read what they say about respecting the donor—

JAYA: (*Bitterly.*) Of course! They bathe him in praise while gutting him like a chicken!

MA: But why must they come to us? 110

OM: (*Holds up a pamphlet.*) Look? In this paper it says that one third of all donors are left absolutely intact!

MA: Don't they have enough of their own people?

JAYA: And where does that leave you? Two thirds a man? Half a wit? 115

OM: (*To* MA, *distractedly.*) They don't have people to spare.

JAYA: And we do, of course. Spare lives! We grow on trees, in the bushes! *What are we, teacher? Oh just some spare lives!*

MA: (*Uncertainly.*) Well. So long as they don't hurt you . . . 120

(*At this moment, a loud tone sounds. All three react, looking immediately at the globe.*)

MA: Hai! What's that sound! I must wash my hands! (*She gets up.*)

(*The polygon flickers to life. Each face displays one view of a young woman's face, unmistakeably blonde and white-skinned. She is beautiful in a clear-eyed, unequivocal manner, exuding a youthful innocence and radiant purity.*)

MA: (*She sees the globe head-on.*) Ahhh! Who is this angel?

(*The room fills abruptly with the pip! of an international phone call about to commence. There is a crackling sound and an audible pause.*)

GINNI: . . . hello? Hello?

125 OM: (*Stepping forward self-consciously.*) Yes—!

GINNI: I see you!—oh, my Gad! I see you! Is that really you? Auwm? Praycash?

OM: Yes! Yes—it's me, Om! (*He's grinning wide.* MA *looks bewildered.* JAYA *looks awe-struck.*)

130 GINNI: Well—hi! That's really great! This is Virginia—Ginni—speaking! Can you see me? How's your reception?

OM: Quite good—quite perfect, I should say! Fantastic!

GINNI: Wow! Yeah . . . well it's pretty wonderful for me too, you know! I mean, I can't tell you . . . (*Her voice grows*

135 *breathy with emotion.*) I can't *tell* you how much this means to me—

MA: (*To* JAYA.) What's it saying? I can't understand when they speak so fast—

OM: No, no, Madam! It's our pleasure! Our duty, I mean!

140 Anything we can do to help—

JAYA: (*To* MA.) She's saying that she's happy—

GINNI: It's the most beautiful day of my life! I feel I've got hope, at last! And all because of you—

OM: No, no, Madam, it is my—our—pleasure.

145 GINNI: Is it—I mean, can you see me clearly, Auwm?

OM: Perfectly clear.

GINNI: Okay—okay—now you've got to tell me—I'm just switching screens here—okay—there we are—okay! I can see . . . is that your . . . your mother? In the pink— (JAYA *flinches; she is*

150 *wearing a pink sari.*) whatdyacallit—sarong?

OM: We call it—*sari*—

GINNI: (*Sings an old tune.*) "Who's sari now? Who's sari now?!!" (*Laughs to herself.*) Hehheh—It's magical, it's wonderful! I'm really talking to India—this is really happening! Okay! And

155 your sister—let's see—

JAYA: (*Stirring to life.*) No! I'm his sister!

OM: (*Flustered and confused.*) She's my wife—

GINNI: Excuse me?

JAYA: (*Hissing to* OM.) Sister. I'm your sister.

160 GINNI: You said just now—

OM: (*Still smiling woodenly.*) I mean, she is my sister, you see—

GINNI: Auwm—it says here on your form, you're not married.

OM: I'm not. She's my sister.

165 GINNI: You're sure you're not kidding me or anything?

OM: Sure, sure, of course I'm sure!

GINNI: Because it's important for us to trust one another. I mean, one little slip like that one—and I dunno. I mean, it's hard for me to tell, from so far away—

170 OM: No, no! I'm telling the truth! I swear on my God!

ginni: Okay. I mean, 'coz I've gotta know, you know. If you're married—

JAYA: (*Suddenly.*) Why?

GINNI: What's that?

175 JAYA: Why does it matter?

GINNI: Uhh—I'll get back to you on that, okay? Just now . . . lemme see . . . there's two more people in your household, am I right, Auwm? There's (*As if checking a list.*) . . . your mother and your brother-in-law. S'right?

180 JAYA: That is right.

GINNI: Just a moment—uhh—Zhaya? (*The* CONTACT MODULE *swivels towards* JAYA, *who nods.*) Is that your name? Yeah—okay, now honey: I can't handle two people at a time, okay? I mean, it's just this dumb camera, you know,

185 can't look at two people at a time, okay? So—I'm talking

to Auwm, well I can't talk to you as well, okay? I mean, no offence—

JAYA: Okay.

OM: My mother is also here—

GINNI: Yes. Okay. I'm turning the scanner around (*The* 190 CONTACT MODULE *turns.*) . . . I'm panning across the room . . . Jeeezus! It's not very much, is it? I mean—oh! Okay! I see her. Hi! Mrs Praycash? Hi! This is Ginni! Can you hear me?

MA: (*Shielding her eyes against the light.*) What? 195

GINNI: I said, this is Virginia! I'm—uh, well just look up, if you can—

OM: Ma—just take your hand down—

GINNI: Look towards the Contact Module! You know the thing hanging in the room? 200

MA: (*To* JAYA.) What's happening?

JAYA: Ma—just look at that light—

OM: The light! The light!

MA: (*Getting annoyed, straightens up to snap back at* OM.) Stop shouting! 205

GINNI: Ahhright! I see you! Mrs Praycash, glad to meet you!

MA: I can't understand a word of what that thing is saying! Is it a man or a woman?

GINNI: What do I look like to you, Mrs Praycash?

MA: (*Cupping her ear.*) Ehh? 210

JAYA: Ma—she wants to know, what she looks like—

OM: Come on, Ma! You've seen foreigners before—

GINNI: Please—Auwm—your mother can answer my questions herself—

OM: She can't understand, you see— 215

JAYA: (*To* MA.) Ma—look up at that light and say what you see—

MA: (*Looks up.*) I see an angel.

GINNI: (*Laughing.*) Ha! I look good to you?

MA: Good, bad, I don't know. All I know is I've got to take a 220 leak—(*Turns around.*)

GINNI: (*Embarrassed laugh.*) Heh! Mm. But—wait! I'm not through yet!

OM: (*As* MA *continues moving away, slowly.*) Don't go yet, Ma—she's not finished— 225

MA: Since when did I need anyone's permission to take a leak?

GINNI: I'm sorry, Mrs Praycash, this won't take a minute—

MA: Nothing doing. I'll piss myself if I don't go right away—(*She moves to the door.*) 230

GINNI: Hey! I didn't let you go!

OM: She has some problem, you see—

MA: Wait till you're my age! (*Grunts with the effort of opening the door.*) Why they can't keep a bathroom on each floor I don't know— 235

(*Exit* MA.)

OM: (*Apologetically.*) The toilet is two floors down, you see—

GINNI: Hmmm. Your mother's some character, Auwm. (*She doesn't sound pleased.*) I don't know if I can handle it. I mean—walking out on me like that!

OM: She takes a long time to get there. Old people, you 240 know!

GINNI: Wait a minute—did you say two floors down? What about in your house? There's no toilet in your house?

JAYA: (*Bitter laugh.*) Huh!

245 OM: No-one has a toilet in the house. Forty families share one. And my mother walks so slowly—

GINNI: Forty families! (*Hushed voice.*) My Gad. Well that's—that's—(*She seems at a loss for words.*) I'm sorry, Auwm. But that's shocking. Shocking! I can't accept that!

250 OM: (*Embarrassed laugh.*) Well—I—

GINNI: No! It's wrong! It's disgusting! And I—well, I'm going to change that. I can't accept that. I mean, it's unsanitary!

OM: (*Muttering.*) Of course, of course!

GINNI: We'll just have to install one in your house.

255 JAYA: (*Startled out of her silence.*) What? In this—this room?

GINNI: Is that you again, Zhaya?

OM: (*To* JAYA.) Shh!

JAYA: I'm sorry—but we *can't!* There's no place for a toilet!

GINNI: Excuse me, but you'll have to find the space. It's

260 inexcusable not to have your own toilet! Forty families—! It's a wonder you're all not dead of the plague years ago!

JAYA: There's only this one room!

GINNI: Look—there's enough place for a married couple and two others—you! You're married, right, Zhaya?

265 JAYA: (*Helplessly.*) Yes, but—

GINNI: (*Firmly.*) Then there's place for a toilet. I'm sorry, Zhaya, but there's no way around this one. What d'you do for baths?

JAYA: (*Close to tears.*) I—we—

270 GINNI: You—you *do* bathe, don't you? I mean, at least once a day?

JAYA: (*Overcome by the humiliation, bends her head and sobs.*)

GINNI: (*Instantly contrite.*) Hey—wait! No, please! Don't cry! I didn't mean to upset you—oh Jeez—stop, please! Look—it's

275 not your fault, okay?

OM: It's all right, she'll be all right—(*Goes over to* JAYA *and thumps her on the back.*) She's fine!

GINNI: Okay—okay—look, Zhaya—I'll make it up to you, okay? I'll send you something, okay? Just tell me what you

280 like and it's yours, okay? Jewellery, perfume, you name it—flowers?

OM: (*Bending down to speak to* JAYA.) Come on, now, come on! It'll be all right—that's enough now—

GINNI: Okay—I tell you what, I'll send you some chocolate, okay?

285 I love candy myself. Okay? I'll send you my favourite candy and—tell you what? I'll sign off now. Okay? It's been a big day for all of us, we're all tired, aren't we? Auwm? Could you look here for a moment?

OM: (*Standing up.*) Me?

290 GINNI: Okay—look, I'll get back to you, okay? And I'm sorry about Zhaya. Really.

OM: No, no—she's not used to this—this—

GINNI: Yeah. Well—the first contact is always a little . . . ah, intense, you know? And I meant that about . . . the toilet,

295 okay? It'll be with you in about an hour.

OM: An hour—!

GINNI: Oops! Time's up—Byeeee!

(*The tone sounds again. The light fades from the* CONTACT MODULE. OM *sits down, suddenly, next to* JAYA *who is wiping her eyes.*)

OM: (*Shakily.*) My god! That was something! (*Puts his arm around* JAYA.) Imagine—a woman!

300 JAYA: Not old, not sick, nothing—

OM: Oh, she must be sick—or else why spend all this money?

JAYA: (*Tiredly.*) It's too late to ask questions now!

OM: But what can be her problem?

JAYA: Maybe there's no problem. Maybe she just likes to suck the life out of young men, like a vampire! 305

OM: Sometimes you talk rubbish—

JAYA: At least I only talk.

OM: It feels strange. To think that . . . that some part of me will be—might be, some day—inside *her*—(*Stops abruptly.*) I mean— 310

JAYA: (*Numbly.*) I know what you mean.

OM: (*Holds her a little tighter.*) I did it, all of it, for us—

JAYA: (*Moving delicately, to loosen his hold.*) Careful. I'm your sister, remember?

OM: (*Jerks his arm away.*) Oh! Sorry. 315

JAYA: (*Bitterly.*) Me too.

(*Lights fade out.*)

SCENE III

Moonlit night, on the roof of the tenement building. City skyline in the backdrop. Clotheslines, watertanks, TV antennas and water pipes snaking in all directions. There is a sense of shadowy figures, movements in the background, murmured conversations.

JAYA *appears, holding a small torch to her face.*

JAYA: (*Looking afraid but determined.*) Jeetu? Are you there? Jeetu—it's me, Jaya!

(*Quick steps, two shadows move away, one shadow materializes in front of* JAYA.)

JEETU: (*He does not look pleased to see her.*) Who told you to come? This is not the right time—

JAYA: I had to. Jeetu—you don't know what's happened— 5

JEETU: Huh! I know everything—

JAYA: So—so you've heard?

JEETU: Which part? That my brother's sold himself to the foreigners? Or that you're my wife? (*Shrugs.*) The second one is hardly . . . news! (*Looks back at her.*) Is it? (*Reaches to tweak* 10 *her plait.*) Is it?

JAYA: But you must come—they're asking for you!

JEETU: (*Frowning.*) They? Who—

JAYA: The grey guards. They came again in the evening. To install the toilet— 15

JEETU: In the room?!

JAYA: And a bath-shower as well, imagine! We have our own water supply now, as much as we want—and there's no place to sneeze any more!

JEETU: (*Sardonically.*) Or . . . anything else, no doubt? 20

JAYA: (*Lowered tone.*) That . . . there never was.

JEETU: (*Leering.*) Didn't bother us, though, did it? (*He caresses her chin—but she whips her face away.*)

JAYA: And now there won't be any reason for Ma to go downstairs! We'll never be alone in the room again, never! 25

JEETU: So what? If we can shit in public, we can just as well screw in public too—especially since you're now officially my wife!

JAYA: (*Pained*) Don't joke about it—

JEETU: Why not? I joke about everything else— 30

JAYA: My throat bulges with the lies trapped within it!

JEETU: Here—let me kiss it—

JAYA: (*Pushes him away.*) Get away! That's all finished now!

JEETU: (*He lets her go.*) As you wish.

35 JAYA: (*Gasps in indignation.*) So easy! Won't you protest a little at least?

JEETU: Make up your mind! D'you want me or not?

JAYA: You are all I have, now that my husband has become my brother . . .

40 JEETU: According to you he was never much else!

JAYA: (*Troubled.*) Still. He would come to me now and then—

JEETU: (*Shrugs.*) Maybe incest is more his style!

JAYA: No! He's too afraid! Before it was his mother. Now it's this . . . *job.*

45 JEETU: Ahh—forget him! You waste your time thinking of my brother!

JAYA: But what about me!

JEETU: Why? Now that you have a new . . . (*Mockingly.*) husband! (*Reaches for her shoulder.*)

50 JAYA: (*Slipping out of reach.*) Oh you—! You're a free-lancer—

JEETU: (*Laughing.*) No! My lance costs money! (*Squats down on a low ledge and starts to roll himself a joint.*) Had you forgotten?

JAYA: And anyway—I'm looking for a plough, not a lance—

JEETU: Oops—sorry! Wrong number! I can't afford any . . .

55 crops!

JAYA: As if I don't know that! I know that. And in any case . . . I feel guilty. I feel soiled—

JEETU: My, my! Such delicacy! Don't worry—I'll tell the world that I forced my attentions on you—routinely, in phase with

60 my mother's bowel movements!

JAYA: Oh stop—! (*Swats at him, playfully.*) You always make such a joke of everything!

JEETU: That's all that life is, one long joke. The only trick is in learning when to laugh.

65 JAYA: Easy for you to laugh! What do you care of my needs, my desires?

JEETU: I thought I was the *only* one who cared about your desires! (*Lights his joint.*)

JAYA: You care—you care—but not enough! A woman wants

70 more than just . . . (*Breaks off.*) satisfaction.

JEETU: Ah—get off my case! You women are gluttons for satisfaction—that's the bare fact of it! You cry when you don't get it—and when you do, you cry that it's not often enough!

75 JAYA: I cry because—because you awaken one hunger while satisfying the other!

JEETU: (*Darkly.*) That other hunger is insatiable. A man has to protect himself against that hunger or he will find himself sucked dry by new little mouths, screaming "Papa! Papa!"—

80 little mouths with big, big appetites—oh no! I'm afraid of that other hunger! Mortally afraid!

JAYA: (*Acidly.*) I suppose that's why so many of your "clients" are men!

JEETU: (*Coolly.*) Not really. It's just that there are more men with

85 money to spare on services such as mine—

JAYA: You should be ashamed of yourself! A man—behaving like a vagrant bull!

JEETU: Why? I'm not fussy—cows, pigs, horses, I'll service all—for a price.

90 JAYA: You don't need to sell yourself anymore. There'll be enough money in the house now!

JEETU: But not for me—

JAYA: Yes—for all of us. For the whole building—

JEETU: No. I don't mind being bought—but I won't be *owned!*

(*There is a space of silence.*)

JAYA: (*Fidgeting.*) Well—I suppose I should go— 95

JEETU: Yes—yes—run home before the grey guards come to fetch you!

JAYA: Jeetu—

JEETU: (*Looking lazily up at her.*) . . . unless you had something else in mind. 100

JAYA: No . . . no . . . (*She can't face him.*) I mean . . . I—didn't bring any food.

JEETU: (*A faintly twisted smile.*) Ah . . . so we're asking for credit, are we?

JAYA: (*Her voice is husky.*) There's no food in the house 105 any more! Only those goat-shit pills and some strange powders. (*Tears in her voice.*) And—and—it's all measured out, you see! I couldn't take a portion without having to explain—

JEETU: (*Looking steadily at her.*) Never mind. As a long-time 110 client, you are permitted certain liberties. Come here—(*It's a short distance, barely afoot. He is seated on a step, leaning back against a tank. She doesn't move.*) I said, come here—

JAYA: (*As if drawn by an irresistible force.*) Jeetu—there are other people around! 115

JEETU: Turn the other way. (*She turns her back to him.*) Your left foot up on this step—(*He pats the narrow ledge on which he sits. She rests the heel of her left foot there. He puts his arm up her sari unobtrusively, barely shifting his position, looking steadily up at her. She looks straight ahead.*) Now tell me about 120 this food. I'm told that it's quite tasty?

JAYA: (*Her voice is thick and strangled.*) Yes! It looks like plastic beads but . . . it's *quite tasty!*

JEETU: And filling too, they say—

JAYA: (*Gasping slightly.*) Filling, yes. It . . . is. But it's not . . . 125 natural—it's not real food—(*She has no place to keep her hands and arms. She clutches her neck, her face, knotting the loose end of her sari around her mouth.*)

JEETU: (*Mildly.*) But it must be, don't you think? And healthy? I mean, isn't that the point? To keep us . . . healthy? 130

JAYA: Yes . . . yes, of course. . . . but (*She's finding it difficult to concentrate on what she says.*) . . . but . . . who knows if it's . . . *good* for us! . . . (*Gasps.*)

JEETU: Everything's good that tastes good and feels right—

JAYA: (*She's desperate to lean on something but the closest is a* 135 *ventilation pipe. She clings to it with both hands, eyes shut tight, breathing in gasps.*) No . . . no . . . that's *not* true. . . . it's *false* food—uhh!—like it's a *false* marriage—Uhh!—*false*— *false* (*Her voice wobbles and ends on a squeak. She gasps/sobs once, twice—.*) False. (*Breathes out, shudderingly.*) False . . . 140 life. (*She catches her breath, wiping her face with the end of her sari-pallav.*) It's not really a life any more. We're just spare parts in someone's garage—

JEETU: (*Removing his arm and wiping his fingers on the hem of her sari.*) My brother, yes. But not you— 145

JAYA: (*Her voice is normal again.*) No! All of us. If we get sick, he might get sick too. So we all have to eat this excuse for food and live like virgin brides—

JEETU: (*Snorts.*) Good! Now there's no reason at all for me to come home! 150

JAYA: (*Distraught.*) No! You have to, Jeetu—

JEETU: Are you mad? When they find out what I do for a living
they won't be pleased! They won't be pleased with you
either—

155 JAYA: (*Pleading.*) They've asked for you twice now—they'll cancel
your permit if they can't confirm your presence—

JEETU: Too bad! My brother will have to find some dummy to
take my place—

JAYA: Please, Jeetu! Please . . . think of me—

160 JEETU: I can't afford to think of you. Thinking of you causes too
many problems for me. I'll have to go away—

JAYA: What'll I do! You can't leave me—

JEETU: I can if I must. Don't worry—your grey guards will
probably have a cure for the disease of dissatisfaction as

165 well—just ask them?

JAYA: But why! Why when there's enough money for all of us, to
do whatever we want!

JEETU: Because no employer pays his staff to do as they
please. At least when I sell my body, I decide which part

170 of me goes into where and whom! But it's the money in
the end, isn't it? I don't want to get used to the kind of
money that can make stud bulls into milk cows. (*Shakes
his head.*) My poor brother. Thought he was so pure. But
he's like everyone else after all! Only as pure as the price

175 of his rice.

(*Lights dim out.*)

ACT TWO

SCENE I

*Two months later. The same room, but transformed into a sleek
residence, gleaming surfaces, chrome steel and glass. The furniture
is largely of the convertible kind (Bed-cum-sofa, etc), in keeping
with the restricted space. In addition, there are the gadgets—TV
set, computer terminal, mini-gym, an air-conditioner, the works.
To the rear and right, there are two cubicles containing the bathroom and toilet. The changes are functional rather than cosmetic.
In the middle of the space is a low, Japanese-style dining table.*

JAYA *is sitting on the sofa and and doing her nails. She looks
over-dressed, her face is heavily made-up, jewellery winking from her ears, wrists, ankles and throat.* MA *is wearing a
quilted dressing gown and is watching TV, upstage, right.* OM *is
wearing a fluorescent Harlequin track-suit and sits at the computer
terminal. All sport new footwear.* JAYA *in heels,* MA *in fluffy
bedroom slippers,* OM *in inflatable track shoes with blinking rear
lights.*

Suddenly OM *leaps up.*

OM: Look at the time!—Ma!

MA: (*Not turning around, but addressing her remark to* JAYA.)
Don't call me—it's your wife's turn to do the food.

JAYA: (*Waving her hands in the air.*) Why didn't you tell me

5 earlier? Now my nails are wet—

MA: And now—I'm watching my programme!

OM: (*Rushing over to dining area. He starts to set it up.*) Come on,
come on! Ginni will be with us—

MA: Better get Bidyut-bai out first—

10 OM: (*Stops what he's doing.*) Out? Out of where?

MA: (*Barely looking up.*) Out of the toilet. Didn't you see her going
in? She's been there all morning!

OM: Why! Who let her use it—

MA: She can't stay away from it, she says! Gets cramps, poor
thing, from waiting for the one downstairs—   15

OM: Who cares about her cramps—I want to know how she got
into the habit of using our toilet at all!

MA: (*Shrugs, but aiming her rebuke in* JAYA's *direction.*) Who
knows what happens when my back is turned?

JAYA: (*Aggrieved, blowing on her nails.*) Huh! Look who's talking!   20
The Empress of the Bath-house herself? (*To* OM.) If your
mother had her way, half this building would be bathing up
here—(*Blowing on her nails.*) But how would you know? You
never bother to talk to us any more!

MA: (*Placatory whine.*) We have so much! Can't we share a   25
little at least? As it is, my former friends tell me I've put on
airs—

OM: (*Standing with his hands on his hips.*) Ma, I've told you.
When we have our own place, that'll be another thing—but
now, when we're still struggling—   30

(*At this moment there is the sound of the flush.* BIDYUT-BAI *comes
out of the cubicle, trying to look inconspicuous.*)

BIDYUT-BAI: Oh . . . I hope I'm not intruding—

OM: I'm sorry, Bidyut-maasi—but who invited you to use our
toilet?

BIDYUT-BAI: (*Instantly on the defensive.*) No, no! Please! I was just
passing this way—   35

OM: But you used our toilet, didn't you?

BIDYUT-BAI: Toilet? What toilet? Is there a toilet in this room?
My! That must be a wonder! May I see it?

OM: (*Sighing.*) Oh just go on, go on!

MA: (*Speaking up for her friend.*) How can she go on when the   40
door's been barricaded?

OM: (*Woodenly.*) She's your friend, you can let her out yourself.

MA: (*Peevishly.*) But I'm watching my programme—

JAYA: Your eyes'll be stuck to that screen from staring at it   45
twenty-four hours of the day!

MA: And why can't our busybody open it? Worn out from the
tension of painting her nails, I suppose?

BIDYUT-BAI: Is anyone going to let me out?

JAYA: Oh! For god's sake! (*Gets up and flings herself across the   50
room.*) I might as well apply for a job as a doorkeeper!

MA: And you'd make a bad one—

(*The warning tone sounds.*)

OM: Oh my God—Ginni's call-sound!

JAYA: (*Struggling to open the door with her nails still wet.*) Tell her
it's because your mother can't control her generosity—   55

MA: See how your sister insults me! Her own mother!

OM: (*Frantic.*) Hurry up! Hurry up!

JAYA: (*Throws the door open—*BIDYUT-BAI*wriggles past her and
out.*) All right, all right—(*Slams the door shut and moves
quickly over to the "kitchen" to snatch up a few items from the   60
"oven".* OM *is almost done setting the table up.*) Anyway it only
takes a few minutes—

OM: (*Sitting down, as* JAYA *brings a few things from the "kitchen"
area.*) You know how she hates it when we're late to eat!

JAYA: (*Setting things down.*) Tell your mother to come along—   65

MA: (*Whiningly.*) It's just about to end—

JAYA: (*Sitting down herself.*) One of these days, when this dream comes to an end, it'll be because you were too busy watching your damned TV—

70 OM: It isn't going to end—

(*The warning tone sounds a third time and the* CONTACT MODULE *springs to life.*)

OM: Ahh—

(MA *scrambles to her feet and scurries over, leaving the TV on.*)

GINNI: Hello-oo! Guess who-oo!
OM: (*He has a falsely beaming expression on his face and affects a nasal twang.*) Hello, Ginni! Hi! Howdy!

(MA *settles hurriedly into place.*)

75 GINNI: Hey—whatcha doing—eating again?
OM: No! We're just having lunch—why don't you join us?
GINNI: Lunch! Hey, that's too late—for lunch!
JAYA: No, no, Ginni! (*To* OM.) Tell her it is only ten minutes—
GINNI: I'm sorry Auwm—but I insist: you *must eat at regular*
80 *hours*—okay? We've had this problem before!
OM: Yes—yes—you see we just had some visitor—heh-heh—these people, you know! Don't understand what it means to keep to a strict schedule—
GINNI: Ah-ah! No excuses, now! That's another bad habit you
85 have, Auwm. You don't confront your booboos. Now— you've gotta learn to control it, okay? You can't help it, I know, it's a part of your culture—it's what your people do when they want to Avoid Conflict and it's even got a name: it's called "face saving". But we can't go through the whole
90 of our lives Avoiding Conflict, now can we, Auwm? You do see that?
OM: (*His smile is strained.*) Yes—yes—of course, Ginni! It is perfectly clear—
GINNI: Good! That's what I like about you, Auwm! You learn
95 real fast.
OM: (*Modestly.*) Thank you, Ginni!
GINNI: And now—let's look at how your family's doing—Mrs Praycash? I can see the food's suiting you, huh? You're putting on weight!
100 MA: (*Holding her hand to her ear, but beaming nevertheless.*) What's that? What's that?
GINNI: And Zhaya—how're you doin'? I don't see a smile on your face!
JAYA: (*Instantly pasting a smile on.*) Oh—no, no! I'm fine!
105 GINNI: It's a scientific fact that people who smile longer live longer—
JAYA: I'm smiling!
GINNI: But not enough, Zhaya. You see, it's important to smile all through the day. After all, if you're not smiling,
110 it means you're not happy. And if you're not happy, you might affect your brother's mood—and then where would we be?
JAYA: (*Grinning wide.*) I understand, Ginni.
GINNI: If I've said it once, I've said it a hundred times: The Most
115 Important Thing is to keep *Auwm* smiling. Coz if Auwm's smiling, it means his body's smiling and if his body's smiling, it means his organs are smiling. And that's the kind of organs that'll survive a transplant best, smiling organs—I mean, God

forbid that it should ever come to that, right? But after all, we can't let ourselves forget what this programme is about! 120 I mean, if I'm going to need a transplant—then by God, let's make it the best damn transplant that we can manage! Are you with me?
JAYA: Yes, Ginni, of course, Ginni.

(*From the door, there is now a knocking sound.* JAYA *looks around.*)

GINNI: (*Reacting at once, and the* CONTACT MODULE *swivels.*) 125 What's that? What're you looking at?
OM: (*Nervously.*) Oh nothing—just—it's nothing!
GINNI: Now—Zhaya—I saw you look—
JAYA: Really, Ginni—it's probably just the wind—

(*The knocking sound again.*)

MA: (*Loud whisper.*) There's someone at the door— 130
GINNI: What's that you said, Mrs Praycash? Someone at the door?
JAYA: (*Unable to control an exasperated sound.*) Oh—for God's sake! She treats us like children—
GINNI: What? Zhaya—Look! All of you—I've told you once, 135 I've told you a zillion times! I hate it when y'all speak at once!
JAYA: (*Now faking a sneeze.*) Chhoo!—sorry, Ginni, sorry—
GINNI: (*Sounding very excited.*) That was a sneeze! Don't deny it—you have a cold, Zhaya, don't you? Come on, 140 confess—
JAYA: No, Ginni, no—it wasn't—it wasn't—
GINNI: Don't lie to me, Zhaya—I know a sneeze when I hear one—
JAYA: It was the—the *pepper*— 145
GINNI: I'll have to ask Auwm—tell me the truth, Auwm—does your sister have a cold? Does she?
OM: Cold? Oh—no, no, no! No cold, Ginni—it was only the—
JAYA: —pepper. It's this foreign pepper. I'm not really used to it. 150
GINNI: Then—why haven't you reacted before this?

(*The knocking sounds again, more like a thump.*)

MA: (*Looking around.*) That Bidyut-bai is really shameless—
GINNI: What? What was that?
JAYA: Nothing. She was just—
GINNI: You're keeping something from me! I just know it—you're 155 all keeping something from me!
JAYA: Oh god, Ginni—we are *not*! Really!
GINNI: Yes you *are*, Zhaya! I can see it in your lying scheming little face! You think you're such an cutie-pie, Zhaya—but you don't fool me! Not for one instant! Now *tell me*— 160
OM: (*Raising his voice and leaning into the viewing field of the* CONTACT MODULE.) No—Ginni—please! You trust me—see, look at me—are you looking? Would I tell you a lie?
GINNI: We-e-e-ell. I don't know! What was all that about? Why did Zhaya sneeze? You know how terrified I am of colds, 165 Auwm! Ever since we eradicated colds from here, where I live, it's like—like having the plague!
OM: Ginni—it's not a cold. I promise you that.
GINNI: If you get a cold, Auwm, I can't take your transplant! You'll be quarantined! This whole program will go to 170 waste!

OM: Ginni—Ginni—believe me. I will never risk your
health.

GINNI: (*Calming down slightly.*) Though—I guess—they screen
175   everything that comes in. Even if you did have a cold, they'd
never let your organs through—

OM: I live only for your benefit. You know that—

GINNI: All right, I believe you. I'll make myself believe you.
I mean it's been hard to read your faces, you know? You
180   people don't use facial expressions, not like us, anyhow.
But what *was* that your mother said just now? It sounded
like . . . like . . .

JAYA: She was praying, taking the name of god—

GINNI: Oh. Yeah. Well, I don't know—sometimes I just get the
185   feeling—

OM: Please, Ginni—trust me. I would not do anything to harm
our—our relationship. We have known each other only for
two months, but from the first day itself, I have felt that
you are just like my sister! Yes! I would not keep anything
190   from you—

GINNI: (*A touch sardonic.*) Is that right? You wouldn't keep
anything from your sister—is that right, Zhaya? (*To* JAYA.)
You're his sister, so you should know—does he keep anything
from you?

195 OM: I mean—

JAYA: No, he doesn't. He would never tell a lie. He is pure like
fresh cotton.

GINNI: (*Childlike glee.*) Pure like fresh cotton! Haha! That's
quaint! That's really quaint! You know what? Even if I
200   didn't need transplants and if I wasn't so sick and all—
I'd get the kick of my life from these conversations! It's
like—it's like—I dunno. Human goldfish bowls, you know?
I mean, I just look in on you folks every now and then
and it just like—blows my mind. Better than TV. Better
205   than CyberNet. Coz this is Real Life—and don't think I
don't appreciate it! You get to be my age and you really
appreciate human companionship—

JAYA: You look very young—

GINNI: —what I meant, people in my country, at my age, they
210   just don't have any worthwhile friends, you know? Nothing
to hold on to—nothing precious. Nothing like . . . this.
I get to give you things you'd never get in your lifetime
and you get to give me, well . . . Maybe my life. (*Voice goes
husky.*) You know? That's a special bond. Don't think I don't
215   appreciate it.

OM: We know you do, Ginni—

GINNI: And now I'm feeling tired, real tired. You just don't know
how tired I get sometimes—

JAYA: (*Carefully.*) Is it—is it your illness?

220 GINNI: I guess you could say so, Zhaya, in a manner of speaking,
yes. It's my illness. But now I've gotta go. Okay? (*The tone
sounds.*) Byeeee—

OM: Good-bye, Ginni—

(*Knocking sounds again.*)

OM: (*Ignoring the knocking.*) See you soo-oon—

(*The* CONTACT MODULE *goes dead. Instantly,* JAYA *leaps up to go to
the door.*)

225 JAYA: We've got to do something about the door! We can't have
people knocking whenever they like!

MA: Oh? Now you're going to have special times for knocking
as well?

(JAYA *gets to the door and opens it easily because she didn't have
time to lock it completely before lunch.*)

JAYA: (*Opening the door.*) Now look—(*Stops dead and exclaims.*)   230
Huhhhhhh!

(MA *and* OM *look up in alarm, just in time to see* JAYA *step back
quickly, as* JEETU *makes a dramatic entrance—almost falling in
at the door. His condition is terrible, his clothes in tatters, his
hair wild, covered in solid muck and grime. Only his spirit seems
undiminished.*)

JAYA: Oh my God—(*She bolts the door, her face grim and
frowning.*)

MA: What—? (*She is momentarily speechless.*) Who is it—what
is it—

JEETU: (*Staggering forward, till he can support himself on a chair   235
back.*) Only . . . your beloved son, Jeetu. Yes, I can see how
delighted you are to see me—(*Mock concern.*) Oh—wait!
Sorry! I'm your son-in-law, now, right?

OM: (*Has risen slowly to his feet.*) My god. What have you done to
yourself?   240

JEETU: Don't bother breaking coconuts at my feet! (*His tone is
sarcastic but good-humoured despite all.*) Yes, yes—your arms
are wide open with welcome! Thank you for inviting me
to share the comforts of your modest home with me, your
younger brother! (*Comes forward across to stage right. Sits   245
on the silky white sofa, which receives his grimy presence with
an audible flinch.*) And yes, I'd love to sit in this comfortable
sofa—(*Succumbing to the sensuous embrace of the cushions,
becoming slightly delirious.*) Ahh! Ahhh!

JAYA: (*Concerned.*) What's the matter—are you in pain?   250

JEETU: Is it possible to know such ease? It feels so good that it
hurts! Ahh! Ahh . . . ah. You know—it's a strange thing with
the pavements: no matter how long you sleep on them, they
never grow soft!   255

JAYA: (*Haltingly.*) You've been on the pavements!   255

JEETU: (*Gesturing to* JAYA.) Come, come sit by me, my darling
wife! Or have you reverted to being my sister-in-law again?
Come—

(JAYA *flees downstage.*)

JEETU: Well! No words to express your delight? Strange . . . at one
time, she used to fight for my attention—   260

OM: (*Trying to regain control of the situation.*) Jeetu—you owe us
an explanation—

JEETU: I owe no-one anything—

OM: Where have you been these many weeks?

JEETU: Careful—you might go deaf to hear the things I'd tell   265
you—

OM: But . . . are you here to stay?

JAYA: What else? You can't turn him out!

MA: (*Hard.*) Maybe we don't have a choice!

JEETU: Ah my loving mother speaks at last! And what does she   270
say? What music does she pour into my parched ears?

OM: (*Sternly.*) Stop it! Things have changed around here—

JEETU: Really? I'd never have noticed—

OM: And the fact is—your permit to live with us was
surrendered!   275

(*There is a silence as* JEETU *processes this idea.*)

OM: Yes. I'm sorry—you had your chance. You chose to leave. We had to make our excuses to the guards. To explain why the fourth member of the family wasn't here. Now it's too late to take you back in—and in any case, you're undoubtedly a
280   health hazard—

JEETU: (*Getting up slowly.*) A "health hazard" did you say? (*He stands unsteadily.*) Heh! That's rich! (*Laughs.*) Me—a health "hazard"! My brother—I'm not a health hazard, I'm a walking, talking, health CATASTROPHE! (*Goes towards* OM,
285   *grinning.*) Oh, yes! I'm so unhealthy that even even my germs have germs . . . yes. My lice are dying on my skull—see? (*He offers his head for examination, to* OM, *who shrinks away.*) They're just lying in little black heaps—

JAYA: Stop! Stop it—why make things worse for yourself—

290   JEETU: Ah those honeyed words of love! How they soothe my running sores!

JAYA: What do you expect? You're the one who left. And now you come back looking like Death's first cousin—is that our fault?

295   OM: We'll have no choice—

JEETU: (*Turning towards* MA.) And you, my mother? I hear your love for me has been bought for the price of a flush toilet?

MA: When you reach my age you'll know that a peaceful shit is
300   more precious than money in the bank!

JEETU: Thank goodness I won't live long enough to be rich—

JAYA: What d'you mean—

JEETU: I'm ill. I'm going to die soon—

OM: Oh God—(*He starts to pace.*)

305   JAYA: Don't be foolish—

OM: This is serious, very serious—

MA: Of what?

JEETU: An overdose—

JAYA: Some drug?

310   JEETU: Called freedom. (*He sinks to the floor.*) I've been overdosing on freedom. Spent my hoard of years—splurged them all, for a few weeks of freedom on the streets. (*Lies flat.*) Freedom to lie in the filth of the open road and to drink from the open sewer! Yes. Freedom to eat the
315   choicest servings from the garbage dump—shared only with crows, flies and pigs! Ah, such freedom as you newly-rich people never know! (*He is slightly delirious. He attempts a laugh, but his voice is cracked.*) But expensive. For all that it looks so cheap, each mouthful of garbage
320   costs a handful of years off your life. And I gorged myself! So I'm . . . gone. Flat broke. Burnt out . . .

(*He turns weakly on his side and starts to throw up.*)

OM: Quick—stop him—

JAYA: (*Kneeling quickly.*) A towel—cloth, anything—

(*She uses the loose end of her sari to cover her hand as she holds his head, then wipes his face with it with the other corner—* OM *hands her disposable towels and fetches a mug of water.*)

OM: (*His face showing revulsion.*) What a mess! You'll have to
325   incinerate your sari—

MA: And what about the carpet?

(JAYA *places* JEETU's *head on her lap.*)

OM: We can disinfect the whole room—and better wear the nose guard—

MA: But the lice—the lice can get into everything—then we're
330   finished—

OM: Oh! (*In exasperation.*) It would have been better if—

JAYA: (*Quietly, stroking* JEETU's *dishevelled hair.*) Don't say it.

MA: What?

OM: (*Ignoring* MA.) How can we keep him! What will we tell the
335   guards—

JAYA: (*With finality.*) We're not going to turn him out.

MA: There's no place for him now!

JAYA: We've managed before—

OM: (*Fretting.*) Ginni won't like it—she'll forbid it—

340   JEETU: (*Weakly.*) Who?

MA: She'll chuck him out!

OM: She'll be so angry, so angry—

JAYA: (*To* JEETU.) Shhhh, don't talk—

OM: Just think of the risk! We've gone so far—given up so much
345   and to lose it! Just because of—of—

JAYA: (*Looking steadily up at him.*) Your brother. Whatever's written on paper, that's what he really is—

OM: But—(*Frets, pacing.*)

MA: What'll we do for food? There won't be enough for
350   him—

JEETU: Uhhhh . . . if I could just have a little water—

(JAYA *wets one of the disposable towels, soaks it in water and dribbles water into his mouth.*)

JAYA: Don't sit up yet.

OM: It's starting to stink! Ginni'll be furious, *furious*—

JAYA: Look, we'll wrap him up in a sheet and keep him to one side till he's better. Then when he can sit up and talk, we'll
355   just tell Ginni that's he's come back. My husband's come back from his—his business trip—

JEETU: (*Weakly, his head lolling.*) Who's this . . . Ginni . . . (*Rolls back down.*)

JAYA: Shhh . . . shhh—don't talk—(*She whispers to him, as if to a
360   child.*)

MA: See how she treats him—her brother-in-law!

OM: (*Fretfully.*) How long can we keep him wrapped up! And what if Ginni finds out—

JAYA: (*Looking up.*) There's no point getting frantic—
365

OM: And who'll believe that this . . . this . . . *wreck* was away on business!

MA: (*Maliciously.*) Look how she holds him—her darling!

JAYA: We'll have to fix him up, of course. Shave his hair, give him some clothes—
370

OM: (*Clutching his head.*) But the diseases—the diseases—

JAYA: (*Calmly.*) Clean water and strong food will cure him of whatever he has—

(*Lights dim.*)

SCENE II

The same scene, a couple of hours later. JEETU's *wasted and scab-scarred body lies in the centre. He has been shaved and visibly grows cleaner, as* JAYA *tenderly washes him and attends to the wounds puckering his skin. He is conscious and groans only occasionally.* MA *is sitting to one side, her expression blank.* OM *is at stage front right, standing, occasionally pacing. He and*

JAYA *have both changed their clothes.* OM *is trying to master the emotions tearing at his face.*

OM: Any minute now—any minute!—she's going to call!

JAYA: Just try and relax—

MA: I don't understand how we plan to hide him—

JAYA: Look—look at these sores!

5 OM: (*To* JAYA.) How can you touch him with your bare hands? He must be oozing with disease—

MA: —and he! Her brother-in-law!

JAYA: (*Exasperated.*) How can I leave him to rot!

OM: Wear rubber gloves, for pity's sake!

10 JAYA: We abandoned him to the streets. The least we can do is to risk our own skin when we touch him—

OM: It's like Ginni says—the curse of the Donor World is sentimentality—

MA: (*To* JAYA.) Ginni will throw him out—just you see!

15 OM: Here I am, willing to give my whole body to improve our lives—and what're you doing? Endangering the whole project by feeling up your brother-in-law—

JAYA: (*At this she stops.*) Who switched roles with his brother? Who turned this family inside out?

20 OM: All I'm saying is—leave him till we can disinfect him at least! Show him to the guards—they'll know what to do—

JAYA: (*Resumes her task.*) What faith you have in them! They don't care about any of us, not as people, not as human beings—

25 OM: What're you saying? You don't talk enough to Ginni. If you did, you wouldn't feel this way—

MA: Oh she's jealous of our Ginni-angel! Look at her face? Pinched with envy!

OM: Ginni really cares for us—

30 JAYA: Oh yes, she *cares*—just as much as she cares about the chicken she eats for dinner—that's all you are for her, another kind of dinner—

OM: (*Contemptuously.*) How little you understand of Westerners! They are not small, petty people—like us!

35 MA: Oh she's just jealous, jealous! Can't bear to think of you being inside that foreign angel. After all, who wouldn't want to be inside such a divine being? Why—it would be indecent to object—

OM: (*Moderately.*) Now, now, Ma—

40 MA: Who knows? Maybe she'll even want you for a husband some day—why not? If my son's kidneys are good enough for her why not his—

OM: Ma—!

MA: Why not his children, I was going to say! Now that's what I 45 want to know! What a miracle—grandchildren! And with an angel for a daughter-in-law!

JAYA: Huh! An angel who shares her bed with her dinner—now that *would* be a miracle!

OM: Would she spend so much money on me, then? If I am 50 just—a—a chicken to her? Answer me that! Do you know how much she's spent on us? Our comfort?

JAYA: Never mind chicken—have you seen how their beef cattle live? Air-conditioned! Individual potties! Music from loudspeakers—why, they even have their own 55 psychiatrists! All to ensure that their meat, when it finally gets to Ginni's table, will be the freshest, purest, sanest, *happiest*—

OM: (*Steps towards* JAYA.) I'll slap you if you're not careful!

JAYA: (*Unimpressed.*) Mind that you wear your rubber 60 gloves—

(*There's knocking at the door.*)

MA: Hear that?

OM: Who is it—who!

MA: The right-hand neighbours. Wanting to borrow a bucket of water.

65 OM: Well, they're not getting it—

MA: Yesterday they offered me money—

OM: Tell them to ask the muncipality to increase their supply.

MA: I told them—

OM: Then why don't they shut up?

70 MA: They told me I'd forgotten what it was like before we got this external connection—they started to scream and cry—

OM: Ahh . . . ! These people! No wonder foreigners think so little of us! We have no pride, no shame!

(*Knocking increases in volume.*)

75 JAYA: (*To* MA.) How can you be sure that it's the neighbours?

OM: Who else can it be?

MA: Listen carefully. There's a code, you see—

JAYA: Supposing it's the guards?

OM: Why should they come?

(*Sustained knocking.*)

80 JAYA: What kind of code—

MA: Three knocks means it's the next-door-right-side. Two knocks means it's the next-door-left-side—

OM: There's no reason for the guards to come!

JAYA: What does loud thumping with no pattern mean?

(*Thumping on the door.*)

85 OM: (*Looking suddenly grey.*) You're right—it could be the guards!

MA: No, no! It's the neighbours I tell you!

(*Violent thumping.*)

JAYA: (*A touch of malice.*)—it's been two months, you know! Time to collect their fattened broiler!

90 MA: Shouldn't you just open the door and find out?

OM: I—I—(*Looking panicked.*) What about—what about Jeetu! What'll we do about hiding him!

JAYA: If they've come for you, they won't have eyes for anyone else—

(*Knocking, knocking, knocking.*)

95 OM: (*Sweating.*) But—Ginni looked fine at lunch-time—she looked perfectly normal—

JAYA: Her condition is such that she can deteriorate suddenly—

OM: But she would tell us herself! Not just send the guards—

(*Rhythmic thumping.*)

100 JAYA: Maybe she doesn't have the strength?

OM: My god. My god—you're right! It's not happened so far, this knocking!

JAYA: Why not just open the door and find out?

OM: I always hoped, you see, that it would never actually come to
105   this—
JAYA: A vain hope. Answer the door—
OM: (*Querlous.*) A dutiful wife would open it for me!
JAYA: You forget—I'm your sister—
MA: That knocking's getting on my nerves now!

(*Knocking, knocking, knocking.*)

110 OM: My legs! My legs refuse to move!
JAYA: Such a hero, my man.

(*Hammering, thumping, knocking.*)

OM: At least she could have let us enjoy the illusion for a little
    longer—
JAYA: It's in God's will, when your time is up—
115 MA: What'll they think—this delay?
OM: Another month—another week, another day, even—
JAYA: But in the end it would always come to this—the bill
    collector at the door—
OM: Do it for me—please! I order you—you're still my wife!

(*Knock, thump, knock, thump. A pleasing rhythm.*)

120 MA: I'll be driven mad!
OM: Would you prefer to see your son dead?
JAYA: Maybe they just want one of your finger-nails—your
    hair—something unimportant—
OM: The smallest pimple on my chin is more precious to me at
125   this moment than a diamond mine in someone else's fist!
    Oh—how could I have done this to myself? What sort of
    fool am I?

(*Knocknocknock.*)

MA: If you don't open the door, I will—
OM: And if you move even one muscle, I'll kill you with my bare
130   hands—
JAYA: Your mother!
OM: Whoever opens that door is my murderer, my assassin—
JAYA: I'm sorry, I cannot live with this—(*She's completed* JEETU's
    cleaning and starts to get up.)

(*Thumpthumpthump.* JEETU *gingerly rolls over onto one elbow.
Looks up and around him. Then collapses gently onto his belly and
lies still, as if ready to sleep.*)

135 OM: No!! I beg of you—please! Please! Leave that cursed door
    alone! Seal it with cement and fire! I cannot bear to see its
    gape, admitting those vile, those cruel, those vicious guards!
    (*Groans.*) Ahhh . . .
JAYA: Till just a moment ago they were your dearest friends—
140   (*Gets up.*)
OM: NO! Sit still! Don't stir! Or I'll—I'll—

(*He rushes to the door, holds himself against it.*)

JAYA: How can I respect you? Move aside!
OM: (*Wildly.*) I don't care! So long as you keep the guards from
    the door—
145 JAYA: I'll offer myself in exchange—

OM: They won't take you—they're very selective—

(*Knockthumpknockthump.*)

JAYA: (*Exasperated.*) They'll break the door down in a
    moment!
OM: (*Sinks to the floor. Voice barely audible.*) Yes. I never thought
    of that. They could do that—and then what'll happen? 150
    Where'll I hide? (*Starts to crawl away from the door.*) In the
    fridge. That's where. I'll just crawl along here, all the way to
    the fridge and I'll sit there, yes—
JAYA: (*As soon as* OM *moves away from the door,* JAYA *starts to
    unlock the bolts.*) Ohhh—this bravery makes my heart sick— 155
MA: (*To* OM, *as he crawls past her.*) Why are you on the floor?
OM: I'm hiding.

(JAYA *gets the bolts on the door open. Opens the door.*)

JAYA: (*Off-stage.*) Yes? What d'you want?

(*There is an indistinct mumble.*)

JAYA: (*Re-enters looking bewildered.*) Ma—it's for you—
MA: (*Getting to her feet.*) What? Already? 160
JAYA: There must be some mistake—
MA: (*Coming forward briskly.*) It's very prompt, I must say!
JAYA: (*Mystified.*) You ordered something?
MA: (*She is already at the door.*) Yes. (*Moves out of sight, off-stage.*)
    Yes?—Yes! That's right! But where is it? You haven't brought it? 165
    It hasn't come? You'll bring it tomorrow? When? Ah . . . Okay.
    No—no, I'll be at home—and—sign here? No . . . payment?
    Oh. Okay. Right. I'll be waiting—(*She re-enters and shuts the
    door behind her.*)
JAYA: (*She heard this exchange with no comprehension.*) Ma? What 170
    was all that?
MA: (*Airily.*) Oh . . . Just something I've ordered—
JAYA: (*Astounded.*) Ordered!
MA: Something I saw on TV—
JAYA: But . . . how did you place the order? 175
MA: That thing, the remote—you press some buttons and you can
    buy things, do things—and they bring it right to the door! But
    Madam wouldn't know, would she! Too high and mighty to
    watch TV!
OM: (*He has reached as far upstage as he can comfortably go. He* 180
    stops there, his hands over his head.) I'm hiding.
JAYA: (*She locks the door.*) But what have you ordered? How much
    will it cost?
MA: (*Philosophically.*) You'll see, when it comes!

(*Lights dim.*)

SCENE III

OM *is lying in a foetal position on the floor, stage front right.* JEETU
*is sitting at the table eating slowly, carefully. He has had a bath
and is wearing* OM's *track suit.* JAYA *and* MA *are sitting beside* OM.

JAYA: He doesn't seem to hear anything I say.
MA: He's a good boy. He's just tired, that's all—
JAYA: But what'll we do! Ginni notices everything!
MA: She'll understand.
JAYA: Huh! 5

MA: You're just jealous of her. You don't see what a good, kind, generous, loving person she really is. It's a reflection on you, but of course, you're too fancy to care—

JAYA: Please! This is no time to be criticising me!

10 MA: Who's criticising? I'm just pointing out some simple truths.

JAYA: Come on, Om—get up! This'll never do—

MA: Want to watch TV? There's something good on in twenty minutes—

15 JAYA: (*Looks at* OM.) It's so typical. He can't face things. He never could.

MA: You should watch more TV. You could learn so much—

JAYA: It's amazing that he got this job at all.

MA: On *Happy Families* you can see it, the exact same situation.

20 The mother has one son and one daughter—and the son gets an expensive job—

JAYA: Ma—you have two sons!

MA: But the daughter is jealous! She can't bear to see her brother succeeding, getting all the praise from the mother! The poor

25 mother was widowed in early life and has to struggle—but then one day the father comes back!

JAYA: I thought you just said he was dead?

MA: No, I never! I said the mother was widowed—meaning, she just thought the husband was dead—

30 JAYA: (*Snapping in irritation.*) Oh—it's all so pointless! Any moment now, you won't have a TV to watch!

MA: What!

JAYA: —this whole dream will come crashing down around us! The grey guards will come and take everything back!

35 MA: No!

JAYA: What d'you think—it's your birthright? To have all this water, these gadgets? The moment Ginni finds out what's happened to her little pet, she'll have the place emptied—

MA: Shoo! Such dirty lies!

40 JAYA: (*Quieter.*) And then how'll I cook without a stove?

MA: I'll slap you if you talk like that! Why, my son said so himself—we'll be rich for ever and ever—

JAYA: (*Raising her voice.*) Look at your son, Ma! Look! He's been reduced to a cabbage!

45 MA: At least a cabbage doesn't talk back!

JAYA: (*Frustrated.*) Oh! (*Angry tears.*) At least before there was nothing to lose!

JEETU: (*Suddenly.*) Why? You used to have a smile before. You've certainly lost that—

50 JAYA: Oh shut up, shut up! Who are you to talk! You're just a waster! Drifting about the streets, not caring what happened to yourself, not caring about any of us, but when you're ready to die, where d'you come? To us of course! Yes! It's so easy for you to talk—you who can't even lose yourself competently!

55 You've come back to make sure that we lose ourselves as well!

MA: Don't speak to your husband like that—

JAYA: He's *not my husband!* He's my brother-in-law!

JEETU: And your lover—

(OM *reacts to this—his limbs twitch, but he does not participate in the conversation.*)

60 MA: What's this?

JAYA: (*Broken.*) Ohh! Not now! Not this!

JEETU: How strange it is, to be here. Talking to all of you . . .

MA: (*Indifferently.*) Not that I'm surprised. Nothing from this slut surprises me. She's capable of anything—

65 JAYA: Doesn't it matter to you that you're trampling on my life? Doesn't it matter what harm you cause to others?

JEETU: When you've lost everything, when you're so weak you can't even eat the cockroaches who walk into your mouth, that's when your life's desire breathes in your ear—

70 JAYA: And? It tells you to torment your family?

MA: She always was shameless—

JEETU: That I should see you again. You, Jaya. (*Leans back and smiles lazily, wincing slightly.* OM *listens.*) Lying there, covered in shit and dirt, ready to die—*dying* to die!—hearing the engine, roaring in my ears, ready to take me away—I thought of you.

MA: I should have thrown her out from the moment she started making eyes at him—her brother-in-law!

JAYA: (*This is the closest thing to a compliment she has ever been paid. She is overwhelmed with conflicting emotions, trying to cover it with sarcasm.*) And then? Some goddess picked you up?

JEETU: (*Lolling back.*) Huh! Yes. Some goddess! A dog . . .

JAYA: What? (*Uncomprehending.*) A dog?

JEETU: Came and peed on me. Straight into my mouth, cheeky bastard! (JAYA *shudders in disgust and pity.*) But he revived me all right. Lucky for him he ran off—or I would have sucked him dry! Life is a strange thing. When your pockets are full with it, you throw it away like rich whores buying silk bedsheets. But the moment you've emptied your purse of days, your throat begins to scream of its own accord, like a beggar in the streets—(*He imitates a beggar's cry.*) Help me, oh God!—please! Just another five minutes—that's all I ask—just another five minutes to drink a last cup of tea—just two minutes! Just one minute, one! One . . . *please* God, help this dying shithead one more time—(*Looks at her, reverts to his normal voice.*) That's when I thought of you. I knew you would revive me. (*Shuts his eyes.*) Just the smell of your hair—just the touch of your fingernails—

JAYA: (*Biting her lip.*) Hush! These are not things to be said!

MA: And it's too late, anyway. She's already married. To your elder brother—

OM: (*Suddenly.*) Who's a cabbage.

JAYA: (*Uncertainly.*) Om . . .

JEETU: That's all right. We don't need anyone. We don't need this fancy prison. We managed before. We'll manage again —

MA: (*Suddenly jumping up.*) What's the time? Look at the time! It's late—Ginni'll be angry at us—

(*From the corridor, the sound of booted steps.*)

JAYA: (*Tiredly.*) Ohh. I don't care, I don't care any more—

JEETU: That's what I say—

(*From the corridor, the sound of booted steps, closer.*)

MA: Listen! What's that sound?

(OM *hears and reacts immediately, before the others notice him, by crawling off, stage right.*)

JAYA: What's the worst they can do? Take away what was never ours to begin with—

(*From the door, a couple of sharp loud raps.*)

GUARD 1: InterPlanta Services! Open this door, please!

MA: It's the guards!

JAYA: (*Looking blankly.*) So they *have* come for him, after all.

JEETU: (*Holding out his hand.*) Come. Let me kiss your hand.
120   Then you can go and open the door. Tell them to bugger off
      and take all their goodies with them.

GUARD 1: (*From outside.*) InterPlanta Services—we know you're
      in there! Open up!

JAYA: (*Raising her voice.*) Coming! (*She gets up.*) I might as well
125   get it over with. (*To the door.*) Wait! It takes a while to unlock
      the door—

(*Works at the bolts.*)

GUARD 1: (*From outside.*) Resistance is useless! We are authorised
      to break down this barrier if you do not comply with our
      request in ten seconds exactly—(*Starts a count down.*) Ten!
130   Nine! Eight!—

(JAYA *gets the door open.*)

GUARD 1: (*Breaking off in mid-stride.*) Sev- . . . ah! (*Enters,
      pushing* JAYA *aside as* GUARD 2 *and* GUARD 3 *take up defensive
      positions at the door, holding a fold-up stretcher between them.*)
      Right—where is the Donor? Come on, quickly now—(*He
135   plunges straight for* JEETU.) The penalty for resistance is—

JAYA: (*In sudden alarm.*) But that's not—

(JEETU, *who has got to his feet, starts to back away*—)

MA: (*Suddenly, pointing to* JEETU.) Go on! Take him—before he
      runs!

(JEETU *panics and runs,* GUARD 1 *pounces for him, chasing
him around the room, while the other two guards stand like
goal-keepers at the door.*)

GUARD 1: Ah! He's running, is he? I'll show him—I'll show the
140   cowardly little shit—

JAYA: (*Screaming.*) But he's not the one you want!

JEETU: (*As he runs—though he's really in no condition to make the
      effort and tires almost instantly.*) You fools! Can't you see I'm
      not your man?

145   GUARD 1: (*Panting in pursuit, dodging around the others, even
      around* OM *lying inert on the floor.*) Always the same story—
      no-one wants to pay their dues—come on, come on! It's
      hopeless to run away—

(GUARD 1 *catches him.* JAYA *screams.*)

GUARD 1: There—there—(*As* JEETU *struggles, grunting,* GUARD 1
150   *holds him in a cruel arm-lock.*) I've got you now—

JAYA: Don't hurt him—don't hurt him—oh he's sick! Please!

GUARD 1: Resistance is useless—(*Starts to lift/drag* JEETU *kicking
      and struggling, but losing strength.*) we'll have you knocked
      out in a second—

155   JEETU: (*Weakly.*) Jaya! Uhh—tell them . . . tell them—

JAYA: (*She darts forward.*) You fools! You maniacs—

MA: (*Reaches out, grabs* JAYA's *ankle and forces her to fall.*) Let him
      go—slut!

JAYA: (*Paying no attention to* MA.)—He's not the one you want!
160   My husband is there—(*She points from her ungainly position
      on the floor.*) There!

GUARD 1: Ohh! That's what they all say when we come to take
      them! (*In a falsetto, as he subdues* JEETU.) "Not me! Not me!
      It's my brother you want! My uncle! My son" Huh! Lying
      scum—(*To the other two guards.* GUARD 2 *helps him to wrestle*   165
      JEETU *to the ground, while* GUARD 3 *gets the stretcher ready.*)
      We have no time to spare!

(*Beyond the door interested by-standers have started to collect.*)

JAYA: How can you take the wrong man! Can't you see? Don't you
      have eyes in your head?

GUARD 1: —(*To the other two.*) Officer! Ready hypo!   170

MA: Hurry up, you fools—how long d'you think I can hold
      her?

GUARD 2: (*Holding a gun-shaped hypo-syringe.*) Ready, sir!

JEETU: (*Weakly.*) Jaya—Jaya—help me!

GUARD 1: Prepare to administer hypo—   175

JAYA: (*Struggling now with* MA *who has her ankle in a vice-like
      grip.*) Lemme go—lemme go! Don't you care about your own
      son—

MA: Your lover, you mean! Slut! Serves him right if he goes in
      place of my only darling—   180

GUARD 3: (*Holding* JEETU *in a suffocating lock.*) Yes sir—(JEETU
      starts to struggle, grunting.)

JAYA: No! (*Panicking.*) You're killing him! He's not strong
      enough—

GUARD 1: (*Ignoring her.*) Administer hypo—(*He aids in holding*   185
      JEETU *down.*)

(GUARD 2 *is unable to gain access to* JEETU *because he is now
struggling so wildly.* JAYA *and* MA *are also struggling but* MA *is
practically lying on top of* JAYA *to hold her down.*)

JAYA: They're hurting him! They'll kill him—oh! I can't bear to
      watch—I can't!

GUARD 1: Officer—I said, administer hypo—

GUARD 2: I'm trying sir—I—(*She gets in a shot.*)   190

JEETU: (*Howls.*) Ahhhhh! Ahhhhh!

GUARD 2: —Damn! Missed the muscle—

JEETU: Ahhhhh!

JAYA: (*In tears.*) Oh what's the use, what's the use! After all we've
      gone through—   195

GUARD 1: Ready fresh hypo, officer—and hurry! He's getting out
      of control—

JAYA: (*No longer able to struggle.*) Oh—please, no, no! He wanted
      nothing—he had no part to play in this—

(GUARD 2 *fiddles with her kit, discarding one cartridge and fitting
another on.*)

JAYA: Don't hurt him, don't hurt him—please! Oh! Oh! They'll   200
      make mincemeat out of him—

GUARD 2: (*Calmly.*) Hypo ready, sir—

GUARD 1: Administer hypo—

JEETU: (*Hollering as* GUARD 1 *and* GUARD 3 *lean with all
      their weight on him.*) AHHHHHHHHHHHHH! AHHHH-   205
      HHH!

GUARD 2 *holds down* JEETU's *shoulder with her knee and delivers
a punch with the muzzle of the hypo.* JEETU's *body arcs up in a
convulsion—he seems to hover in mid-air—*JAYA *screams—Then
all is still.* JEETU *is limp and inert on the stretcher. The three*

guards get to their feet, returning as quickly as possible to their professional composure. JAYA *remains clutched within* MA's *savage embrace, though she strains towards the tableau.*)

GUARD 1: Officers—initiate departure.

(GUARD 2 *and* GUARD 3 *quickly spread an opaque shield over the stretcher so that* JEETU *is completely hidden from sight.*)

JAYA: (*In a dull voice, knowing that she won't be answered.*)
     He's dead, isn't he? They've killed him. I feel it in my
210   bones.
GUARD 2: Donor secured for departure.
GUARD 1: Proceed with departure—

(GUARD 2 *and* GUARD 3 *hoist the stretcher up and exit. From beyond the door, the sound of the wondering crowd.* JAYA *holds out her hand helplessly in the direction of the door.*)

GUARD 1: (*Turning to* JAYA *as the other two officers vanish,
     removing his clipboard from his belt.*) InterPlanta Services
215   thank you for your cooperation. Your family member is
     about to fulfil the solemn and noble contract into which he
     entered. We, on our part, offer you our sincerest assurance
     that we will do everything in our power to ensure that he will
     come to no avoidable harm and will suffer no discomforts
220   other than what is deemed normal under the circumstances—
     (*He pauses.* JAYA *is looking dully at the floor, still lying half
     prone, though* MA *has now backed off and is straightening her
     clothes.*) Any questions?
JAYA: (*Not looking up.*) When will he be back?
225 GUARD 1: (*Patiently.*) Madam! Any questions?
JAYA: (*Not looking up.*) No.
GUARD 1: (*Ticking off his clipboard.*) Right. Donor will remain
     in our custody until such time as he is ready to be returned.
     This can be any period from two hours onwards and upto
230   one week—
JAYA: (*Jerks her head up.*) One week! What'll be left of him!
GUARD 1: —depending on the nature of the transplant required,
     the availability of artificial substitutes for the organs that
     the Donor has, of his own free will, made available to the
235   Receiver and the Donor's own speed of recovery. Any
     questions?
JAYA: (*Gets slowly to her feet.*) Yes! What part of him is going to
     be removed?
GUARD 1: I'm sorry, Madam, I am not free to discuss such
240   details.
JAYA: You're going to cut him up and you're not even going to tell
     his wife what you're going to do with him?
GUARD 1: Excuse me, Madam—relationship with Donor
     is . . . ?
245 JAYA: (*Gives her head a guilty little shake.*) I—I meant, his
     family—
GUARD 1: Madam: Full details will be furnished once the
     formalities have been completed—
JAYA: And can I see him? In the hospital, the clinic, wherever?
250 GUARD 1: Security and health regulations prohibit any contact
     between Donors and their families—
JAYA: Why ask if we have questions when you don't want to
     answer any of them?
GUARD 1: (*Imperturbably ticking off his clipboard.*) Right.
255   (*Handing her the clipboard.*) And now, if you would be so kind
     as to sign the despatch voucher—

JAYA: (*Grabs the pen and signs violently.*) There—there—your
     stupid forms, your—papers—your—questions . . . (*She
     would like to throw the pen at the floor, but it is attached
     to the clip-board.*)   260
GUARD 1: (*Retrieving the clip-board.*) Thank you, Madam. We are
     grateful for your kind cooperation and assure you—
JAYA: Just get out! Take your lying, insincere face away from my
     door—(*Makes as if to push him.*)
GUARD 1: (*Moving nimbly out of her range, as he continues his   265
     spiel.*)—assure you that we will do everything in our power
     to return your beloved one to you in as short a time as
     possible—(*He leans inwards on the door handle.*) On behalf of
     our clients—
JAYA: (*Rushes at him, shouting.*) GET OUT! (*Pushes the door shut 270
     in his face.*)
GUARD 1: (*He pushes back, completing his parting message through
     the door.*)—we at InterPlanta Services extend our heartfelt
     gratitude for your family's support and compassion! (*This last
     bit is shouted from behind the closed door.*)   275

(*Sound of boots marching away.*)

JAYA: Ahhh! (*Venting her fury against the door.*) How I hate
     them!
MA: (*She has been silent all along.*) Good. They've gone at last.
JAYA: (*Leaning against the door, her head against her fists.*) He's
     gone! They've taken him—and I could do nothing to prevent 280
     it!
MA: Can I switch on my TV?
JAYA: (*Yelling at her.*) Your son goes off to the slaughterhouse
     and you're just worried about your TV!
MA: (*Mustering as much dignity as she can.*) If you watched   285
     more TV you wouldn't dare talk to your mother-in-law
     that way—
JAYA: (*Coming back towards her.*) Oh! So I've gone back to being
     your daughter-in-law, have I?

(*Stands threateningly in front of* MA, *who is facing the TV with the
remote raised in readiness in her hand.*)

MA: I'm your mother-in-law, that's your brother-in-law on the   290
     floor there, your husband's gone to work at the spare parts
     factory. And you? You're just a slut who happens to be
     standing between me and my TV!

(*Lights dim.*)

SCENE IV

*Night. The only difference between daytime and night-time is the
spotlight illumination.* MA *is snoring in her corner upstage and
left.* JAYA *is standing uneasily in a pool of light, upstage left, near
the gym equipment. She is wearing an expensive nightgown with
matching robe, in satin and lace. Her face gleams with night-cream.*

OM *lies in his corner, on a sleeping pallet near the TV, apparently
asleep.*

JAYA *pacing restlessly, finally comes over to where* OM *lies.*

JAYA: (*Shaking him.*) Om! Om—wake up!

(*He does not respond.*)

JAYA: Om—come on—I know you're not asleep—wake up!

OM: (*In a disembodied voice.*) Why? What's the point?

JAYA: We've got to talk. To decide what to do—

5 OM: About what?

JAYA: When they bring Jeetu back—when they realize they've got the wrong man—

OM: They've not realized that. They've used him instead of me.

10 JAYA: No! No—they *can't*—they can't be that stupid!

OM: Then why haven't they brought him back?

JAYA: Because they're . . . interrogating him. Because he collapsed, maybe, and now they're treating him—

OM: You yourself said they don't give a damn about us—why

15   should they care about him? (*He raises himself slowly.*) No. They've used him, take my word for it. Or else they'd have brought him back—

JAYA: —But—but don't they *check*? Don't they bother?

OM: (*Shrugs.*) Maybe they were in too much of a hurry?

20 JAYA: Maybe the part they've taken from him doesn't need to be so special—maybe they've just taken something small, something insignificant—

OM: Then they would have come back by now.

JAYA: It's been six hours. Six hours! They can't remove anything

25   of much consequence in six hours! Why—they've probably just taken his—his front teeth! His toe-nails!

OM: Then why hasn't he come back?

JAYA: (*In a small voice.*) You're right. It must be something bigger. More crucial. (*Pause.*) What d'you think it is? His stomach? His

30   intestines? Maybe he won't come back for a week!

OM: Or maybe they've found out he's not me and they've just done away with him!

JAYA: (*Cries out.*) No! That would be murder! They can't be allowed to murder people!

35 OM: (*Coldly.*) Who'd notice? We don't have the right to complain. Technically, anyone who isn't claimed by his family within twenty-four hours of going missing can be terminated without attracting legal attention.

JAYA: All these weeks he's been away—he could've been dead!

40   And we'd never even have known!

OM: It's a wonder he's alive at all. I've heard that the street gangs eat derelicts these days—

JAYA: No!

OM: Cook them and eat them. Why not? There's no law to

45   prevent it—

JAYA: How did he survive!

OM: He was protected by his friends on the street. But they couldn't do it indefinitely. They forced him to come back.

50 JAYA: Oh.

OM: Whatever he says—that's the real reason he's here.

JAYA: (*Pause.*) D'you think he's really ill?

OM: Must be.

JAYA: (*With finality.*) Then it's better if he dies in their hands.

55   They'd be humane, they wouldn't hurt him—

OM: Why? They could use him for research—

JAYA: No!

OM: He's not officially on their records—they can do whatever they like—

60 JAYA: (*Covering her ears.*) No! I don't want to think of it—

OM: —give him drugs and sell him to those game sanctuaries—

JAYA: Don't! Oh—please—

OM: —where the rich have licenses to hunt socially disadvan-

65   taged types—yes! That's what they've done with your Jeetu! Turned him loose to become a trophy for some industrialist's daughter—

JAYA: You're—you're—(*She calms down.*) It's just your jealousy speaking, isn't it? (*She insists.*) Tell me—isn't it?

70 OM: What's it to you?

JAYA: (*Tiredly.*) I'm still your wife.

OM: Not really. On paper, you're my sister. In reality, you're nothing to me. If not for Ginni I'd throw you out like a shot. Onto the streets. To be hunted. What do I care?

75   You betrayed me. Seduced my brother. I feel nothing but contempt.

JAYA: You never cared for me. You never wanted me—

OM: Wanting—not wanting—what meaning do these words have in our world? What choices do we have? Was it my

80   choice that I signed up for this programme?

JAYA: —Yes! You went of your own accord!

OM: No. I went because there wasn't anything left to do. I went because I lost my job in the company. And why did I lose it? Because nobody needs clerks any more! There are no new

85   jobs now, from here till next week! It's all over! The factories are all closing! There was nothing *left* for people like us! Don't you know that? There's us—and there's the street gangs—and then the rich.

JAYA: But—the village—

90 OM: The village is just another kind of factory now. To live there you have to be born there—or you have to be an industrialist. I'm not an industrialist. I'm just a clerk. What choices do I have? I didn't even choose *this* job—I stood in queue and I was chosen! And if I hadn't got this one, there would have

95   been other queues—but they are all just another kind of lottery in the end. It was just my fate! Like it is my fate to have a faithless tart for a wife—

JAYA: Then why didn't you go with the grey guards when they came! Why did you lie down like a corpse!

100 OM: I don't know what came over me. That too was my fate. It was my fate to lie down in a trance and my brother to take my place. It was his fate to face the scalpel—

JAYA: —even though he may never return?

OM: Nothing matters. Whatever happens, it's fate.

(*There's a sound, indistinct.*)

105 JAYA: Wait!—What's that?

(*The sound of boots in the corridor, accompanied by a shuffling.*)

JAYA: Oh! (*Turning excitedly towards the door.*) Hear that? It sounds like boots—

(*She runs to the door.*)

OM: It doesn't matter what they've done to him—he didn't care about his life anyway—he didn't take any responsibility for

110   anything—

(JAYA *flings the door open, leans out into the corridor—and freezes where she stands. The footsteps come to a halt. The shuffling con-tinues.* OM *looks straight ahead, affecting unconcern. The shuffling draws close.* JAYA *stands aside, her face blank, watching as* JEETU *enters the room, shuffling slowly, his arms half-raised in front of him, being steered by* GUARD 2, *impassively.* GUARD 1 *enters as well.*)

OM *does not look around.* JAYA *slowly re-enters, shutting the door behind her, never taking her stricken eyes off the silent, pathetic figure of* JEETU.)

(*He is wearing silk pajamas white on white and a wine-red brocade robe and velvet bedroom slippers. Across his eyes, and wrapped around his head, heavy bandages.*)

(JAYA *remains where she is, by the door, her hands over her mouth, staring. In the foreground,* MA *snores lightly.*)

GUARD 1: (*Clears his throat, takes out his memo pad.*) Donor Prakash, we have no words with which to express our deep and sincere appreciation of your generosity towards your Receiver . . .

(*Lights fade as he drones on.*)

115 GUARD 1: You will be glad to hear that the transplant has been a tremendous success and that henceforward you will receive every benefit and consideration due to you under the terms of your contract . . .

(*Lights out and curtain.*)

ACT THREE

SCENE I

Little has changed in the room. JEETU *sits on the floor with his head between his knees, facing stage front.* MA *is watching TV wearing head phones.* JAYA *and* OM *are sitting on either side of* JEETU.

JAYA: Jeetu—Jeetu speak to me—(*She tries to put her arm over his back.*)

JEETU: (*Throwing her arm off violently, not lifting up his head.*) Don't touch me!

5 OM: What does he care what happens to us? He's only thinking of himself—

JAYA: Jeetu, you've already paid the price—now why not live with the reward?

JEETU: (*He is silent for a beat. Then he lifts his head. In the place* 10 *of his eyes are enormous goggles, created to look like a pair of imitation eyes. They fit flush with his skin, without ear pieces and cannot be removed. His voice is a hoarse whisper.*) This . . . is my *reward?*

JAYA: Jeetu—Jeetu—if you would only listen a moment—

15 JEETU: No! (*He gets to his feet.*) I won't listen! Because listening brings acceptance. (*He moves, but warily. He never bumps into anything but he "looks" around himself like a first-time visitor from Mars.*) And I will never accept. I will never live with this—this—

20 OM: Selfish, that's what he is—

JAYA: No, Jeetu, no!

JEETU: I don't need your permission to step off the bus! I make my own decisions—

OM: —only thinks of himself. Look at me?

25 JEETU: Yes, my brother! Look at you? Look at you with these eyes that were meant for you? (*Makes a croaking, sobbing sound,*

hitting his eyes with his hands.) These eyes—these blind eyes, this sightless sight—

JAYA: But Jeetu—if they think you're Om, then we need you! Without you, they won't maintain us— 30

JEETU: I don't care! I'm not the one who got this job—and I'm not going to be the one to suffer the consequences—

OM: He was always selfish. Always lived just for himself—

JAYA: Jeetu—just wait till we can ask Ginni—she'll listen at least, maybe even help— 35

JEETU: Ginni, huh!—Ginni only helps herself—

JAYA: No, Jeetu—(*But she herself sounds uncertain.*) That's not true . . .

JEETU: You show me a rich woman who plucks a poor man's eyes out of his body and I'll show you a she-demon! 40

JAYA: But Jeetu, without you . . .

OM: Just wait till Ginni finds out whose eyes are in her head! Just wait!

JAYA: (*To* OM.) Why tell her? If she goes on thinking Jeetu is you then maybe— 45

OM: Fat chance! It's the guards who made the mistake! The moment she sees me here she'll know what happened—and she'll be mad! She'll be furious! She'll probably have the guards court-martialled—

JAYA: You heard what they said—the transplant was a success. 50 So maybe . . . maybe it *is* all right? Maybe Jeetu's eyes are good enough?

OM: It's not so easy as you think—remember all those injections I had in the beginning? They were to prepare my body, to change it so that it could match Ginni's body perfectly. But 55 now they've taken the wrong pair of eyes—who knows what it'll do to Ginni? And what about Jeetu's infections, all the poisons and germs he's had circulating inside him—what about them? Ginni's scared of catching your cold! What'll she catch from Jeetu? 60

JAYA: But they *said*—

OM: It takes time to know that a transplant has been a success!

JAYA: How long—

OM: I don't know. I'm not a doctor. Not less than a week, 65 I think—

JEETU: Good. I'll be dead long before then—

JAYA: Jeetu—I'm not going to let you die! I don't care what she says—I'm not going to lose you again—

JEETU: You don't know what you're asking of me. You don't 70 know what it's like to walk around with a nightmare wrapped around your head—

JAYA: Jeetu—

OM: (*To* JAYA.) Why waste your breath? Neither will he listen, nor will it make the slightest difference to the outcome. 75 What will be, will be, regardless of what we try to do about it—

JAYA: But *why*—when it doesn't *have* to be! Why—when all he has to do is to pretend—just for a couple of hours in a day— 80

JEETU: Why? (*Pause.*) Because I am in place beyond death. I am in a place worse than death.

JAYA: There's no place worse than death.

JEETU: Yet I know such a place, now. (*Painfully.*) A bleached and pitted place. Scars and slashes, no stillness, no dimensions. 85 No here, no there—(*He moves his head about, "looking" at his visions.*) I see in molten bars and blinding shapes, I see symmetries and confused fragments—sparks, shadows,

water on mad glass, heat dreams, trains flying on fever
90   tracks—

JAYA: But can you see me, Jeetu?

JEETU: (*Looking there.*) Yes. I see you. And through you.
      (*Looks around.*) And through the floor. And through
95   all the gadgets, pulsing with electric gold, liquid atoms
      sizzling down infinite mineshafts . . . (*He turns his gaze.*)
      my brother standing there, a blaze of fried nerves and
      straining bones, his eyes like ping-pong balls jittering in
      their orbits. (*Turns.*) And I can see Ma—a dim bundle of
      red desires bathed in a blue haze of radiation. (*Turns.*) And
100   I can see you, Jaya, my Jaya . . . I can see your purple blood,
      I can see your thoughts sparkling like stars through the
      pearly cloud of your brain, I can see your heart twitching
      like an epileptic kitten—yes, I can see all these things, but
      who would want to see them? Who can bear to see them?
105   (*He sits down, on his haunches.*) And yet . . . I can't even
      turn them off. I can't shut these freakish eyes of mine. I
      can't turn my head away, I can't end this poison-vision.
      I can't sleep, I can't dream, I can't even cry. (*He looks at her.*)
      This is what you want from me?

(*There is a silence.*)

110   JEETU: Well? You're not saying anything.

JAYA: I—(*She holds her forehead.*)

JEETU: Is it selfish to want to end this?

OM: I was willing to accept anything for my family—

JEETU: Oh yes!—And what happened when the guards came?

115   OM: (*Mustering what dignity he can.*) That was different. It was
      the shock, the lack of warning—

JEETU: It was cowardice!

JAYA: (*Carefully.*) Jeetu—we've not asked anything of you so
      far—

120   JEETU: This is no time to start!

JAYA: Maybe you'll get used to it in time—maybe they'll be able
      to improve it—

JEETU: (*He clutches his head.*) Let me die before I'm too maddened
      by visions to make the effort!

125   OM: Just wait, just wait—when Ginni comes, she'll make all the
      effort for all of us!

JAYA: Don't be so cocksure! You think she'll take your side—

OM: Of course she will. And she'll throw the two of you out, I
      wouldn't be surprised! For fooling her. For fooling around.
130   For being dirty, filthy fornicators—

JAYA: We haven't! Not . . . not since you got the job—

OM: Ah but he hasn't been here has he! Now that he's back it'll
      start again, won't it? Don't think I don't know how it is with
      people like you! You'd do it right in front of me if you got half
135   a chance—

(*The warning tone sounds.*)

JAYA: Oh my God—

OM: (*Looking relieved.*) Ah! Just let me do the talking—I'll explain
      everything—

JEETU: (*His whole body jerks.*) Ah! What's that? I—I—I *saw*
140   something—

(*The second tone sounds.*)

JAYA: What's the matter Jeetu?

OM: You shut up, both of you! I'll explain it—and don't worry, I
      won't leave you two out of the picture. But if she asks me, I'll
      tell her—

145   JEETU: (*Breathlessly.*) Something's . . . happening. The blackness
      is lifting . . . I can see . . . some sort, some sort of . . . pattern—

(*The third tone sounds.*)

GINNI: Well—hellooo-oo! Guess whoo-ooo!

JEETU: Ahh! (*He falls silent, with his mouth open in wonder,
      breathing heavily.*) Ahhh . . .

150   OM: Hello! Howdy! Hi, Ginni—

GINNI: Hello-ooo? Is anybody home—(*The* CONTACT MODULE
      swivels.) Auwm? (*The* CONTACT MODULE *has swivelled
      around to find* JEETU, *who doesn't respond.*) Isn't that you,
      Auwm?

155   OM: (*Running around to get in front of the* CONTACT MODULE.)
      No! No—*this* is me! I'm here! Here!

(*The* CONTACT MODULE *flips up and out of* OM'S *reach.*)

GINNI: Come in, Auwm! Can you see me? Auwm?

JEETU: (*In a strange, strangled voice, not looking at the* CONTACT
      MODULE.) My God—I can see!

160   GINNI: (*Sounding extremely cheerful.*) Sure you can see Auwm!
      That's what we gave you eyes for! And I'm sure you're real glad
      to know that *I* can see better now! And with your eyes!

OM: (*Screaming.*) NO!! It's a mistake! There's been a terrible
      mistake!

(*But* JAYA *intercepts him.*)

165   JAYA: (*In a loud whisper.*) Wait—don't disturb them—

JEETU: (*Gesturing directly in front of him, in a wondering voice.*)
      And that . . . and you must be . . .

OM: (*He is almost in tears.*) She's wrong! She's wrong! (*But* JAYA
      silences him by dragging him sharply aside.) It's—

170   JAYA: (*Holds* OM *back.*) Shhhhh—!

GINNI: —Ginni! That's right, Auwm—it's me you're seeing
      'coz I'm beaming my video image straight into your mind!
      So you can see me right in front of you, all of me, for once,
      not just my face . . . (*In a seductive voice.*) well? What do
175   you think?

(*There is a silence in the room as* JEETU *moves slowly around,
looking at something that no-one else in the room with him can
see. What little of his face is visible shows wonder.*)

JEETU: It's—you're—beautiful. Like . . . magic.

GINNI: You like me, Auwm? You like what you see?

JEETU: (*Shakily.*) Yes. And—and the room! What is this place?

GINNI: Oh . . . it's just where I live, Auwm, it's one of the rooms
180   in my little house—

JEETU: (*Breathing out.*) It's a palace—

GINNI: I'm glad you like it Auwm—

JEETU: I can't help but like it! Who wouldn't? (*He points around
      him.*) That—that—(*He has no words.*) Those . . . plants! That
185   . . . light! What are those things there? It's . . . (*Hushed.*)
      beautiful. Beautiful. I've never seen anything like this.
      Never.

OM: (*In anguish.*) But it's mine, what he's seeing—MINE!

JAYA: (*Watching carefully.*) Can't you hush?

190 OM: (*In tears.*) It's all a mistake! She'll find out and then what'll happen? What'll happen to us?

JAYA: Shhh—

JEETU: (*Wonderingly.*) And you . . . is that really . . . you?

GINNI: Yup! It's me, Ginni! You look like you're seeing me for

195 the first time, Auwm!

JEETU: I—I am! I never realized this is what you looked like—I mean, when the others talked about you—

GINNI: Well—now. I'm glad you like me so well, 'coz you know what? Now that the transplants have started, it's time that

200 we talked about the next phase—

JEETU: (*Still dazed.*) "Next phase"?

OM: (*Shouting.*) But he's the wrong man!

(JAYA *holds* OM *back.*)

(JEETU *is facing the* CONTACT MODULE, *which now rises above him and glows white as the rest of the stage lights dim.* JEETU *is bathed in the light, sealed into the vision that is projected into him.*)

GINNI: The next phase of the transplants. You see, we have to progress rapidly now and I need all your support. Until we

205 reached this platform of contact, we couldn't be sure. But now that we're sure, we've got to move really fast. Are you with me?

JEETU: (*Uncertainly.*) Yes . . .

GINNI: Because you have to be willing, for what we want to do

210 now. You have to be really willing, Auwm—

JEETU: Tell me, Ginni, tell me what you want—(*He moves towards the illusion he sees.*)

GINNI: Ah-ah—can't touch me Auwm! (*He reacts by jerking his hand away.*) Well . . . you'll have to go back to the clinic and

215 they'll prepare you—

JEETU: (*He continues to behave as if he is standing very close to someone, following her around as she moves out of his reach.*) You need some more parts of me?

GINNI: Well, yes—I mean, that's one way of looking at it but

220 I—I think you should understand that time is kind of short, Auwm and we really have to get a move on—

JEETU: (*He moves his body seductively, winningly.*) Just tell me what you want of me Ginni—

GINNI: The guards will come for you and they'll request you to

225 follow them away—

JEETU: Anything, Ginni, anything—

GINNI: The sooner you can go the better it'll be for you—

JEETU: Whatever you say, Ginni—

GINNI: I mean, really, Auwm, if it's okay with you, I can tell the

230 guards to come for you right now—

JAYA: No . . . (*But she says it softly, shaking her head, knowing that it's futile.*)

JEETU: That's fine with me, Ginni—

OM: (*Hoarsely.*) Ask her what she wants from you!

235 JEETU: Anything you want is fine, Ginni—

GINNI: Okay, Auwm, I'm turning this video session off for the moment and I'm going to ask you to wait for the guards—

JEETU: (*He holds his arms out forlornly.*) You're—you're going?

GINNI: But I'll be back, Auwm, closer than you'd ever believe . . .

240 (*The* CONTACT MODULE *moves high, as its light starts to dim.*)

JEETU: (*Stretching his arms up.*) Don't—don't—(*He drops his arms.*) Ahh—! (*Strikes his eyes.*) AHHHH!

GINNI: The guards will come, Auwm, you don't have long to

245 wait—we'll talk again when you're in the clinic, okay?

JEETU: NO!! Don't leave me in this blindness—

GINNI: Remember to keep smiling Auwm—

JEETU: (*Brokenly.*) No!

GINNI: —byeeee!

(*The* CONTACT MODULE *snaps off.*)

JEETU: (*Softly.*) Ah—no! She's gone—she's gone! 250

(JAYA *and* OM *come forward around him.*)

JAYA: Jeetu—Jeetu—do you know what you've said?

JEETU: All I know is that I'm going to her—I'm going—

OM: You didn't even find out what they're going to take from you this time—

JEETU: You don't understand! I was blind! And now I have the 255 chance to see again—

JAYA: But . . . it's not *real*, what you see—I—I mean, we could watch you moving like a madman, waving your arms about, pointing to things that weren't there—

(OM, *having listened so far, begins to move away, towards the door.*)

JEETU: Ah—but they're *somewhere*, aren't they? And that's all that 260 matters to me.

JAYA: Yes—but—(*She looks dissatisfied and worried.*) she's taken your *eyes*—

JEETU: —and left me something even better! I can't tell you what things I saw— 265

JAYA: Really? So much?

JEETU: (*Reverentially.*) Yes—oh, yes! (*Then he pauses.*) Of course, I can't see what's directly around me. But maybe they'll find a way to change that—

JAYA: You should have asked her— 270

JEETU: I'd not seen her, you see, till just now! I thought she was an old woman! You never told me she was so—so *young!* (*Hushed.*) And beautiful. (*Accusingly.*) Why didn't you tell me, Jaya?

JAYA: (*Shrugs.*) You didn't seem interested—we hardly discussed 275 Ginni at all—

JEETU: Well. It would have made all the difference if I had known. I saw all of her, you know! Standing there (*He draws her with his arms.*), all of her . . . wearing . . . almost *nothing!* (JAYA *bites her lip, frowning.*) And she kept . . . (*He moves his body* 280 *sensuously.*) moving, like this, like that . . . wah! I could have had her, right there and then!

JAYA: (*Bitterly.*) But she wasn't real!

JEETU: She exists. That's enough for me. She's a goddess and she exists. I would do anything for her—anything! 285

JAYA: (*Looks depressed.*) Yes. I can see that—

JEETU: (*A touch of guilt.*) Don't hold it against me, Jaya—think of her as just another client—you were always good at that—

JAYA: Yes . . . but your other clients wanted only your services. 290 Not your . . . body itself!

JEETU: You should be happy for me—and anyway, you've got your wish, now. I'll stay alive, and they'll go on looking after all of us—

(*There is a knocking at the door.*)

GUARD 1: (*From outside.*) InterPlanta Services!— 295

(*But before he can say "open up", OM has thrown the door open.*)

OM: Yes! Take me! Take me! I'm ready to go!

(*Several things happen at once. JEETU and JAYA turn towards the door, as GUARD 1 and GUARD 2 roughly shove OM aside, entering the room.*)

JEETU: Yes—

GUARD 1: Mr Om Prakash—we have been intimated of your
300   willingness to participate in the second phase of our
    transplant service!

OM: (*Screaming.*) No! Not him—take ME!! I'm Om Prakash!
    Check your records—

(*GUARD 3 entering behind the other two, quickly grabs OM and holds him pinned to the wall, struggling.*)

JEETU: Yes—I am Om Prakash—

OM: (*From his pinned position, bellowing.*) NOOO!!! He's lying!
305   A lying, scheming swine!!! He's my brother, I tell you—my
    younger brother—

GUARD 1: All right sir, if you would just follow us—we're ready to
    leave—

JEETU: Let's go—

(*GUARD 1 stands aside and JEETU moves towards the door.*)

310 JAYA: (*Darting forward.*) Jeetu—

JEETU: (*Swivelling sharply.*) Don't call me that—

JAYA: (*She is suddenly in tears.*) Don't go—just yet! Please! It's too
    soon, they've not explained anything—I—we—you'll never be
    the same again—

315 JEETU: (*He grabs her quickly, gives her a brief hug and pushes
    her away, into the waiting grasp of GUARD 2.*) You have your
    husband to look after—he needs you more than I—(*He turns
    and exits.*)

JAYA: (*Losing all restraint.*) Jeetu! JEETU!! (*GUARD 2 lets go
320   of her and exits.*) What happened to your ideals, your free-
    doms! Your pride! (*She sinks to her knees.*) All gone! So
    easily gone—

(*GUARD 3 has a brief struggle disengaging himself from OM, but he too slips out, slamming the door behind him—then bolting it from the outside.*)

OM: (*Hollering.*) AHHHHHHHHHH! You've locked us in, you
    bastards! You've locked us in! (*He roars and pounds on the
325   door.*) You can't do this to us! We've not signed any consent
    forms! You've not taken any permissions! AHHHHHHHHH!
    You've locked us in here! AAAAAHHHHHHH! And you've
    taken the wrong man—you'll regret it—you'll suffer for
    it—AAAAAAHHHHHHH!—

(*He subsides onto the floor, moaning. JAYA looks at the door, too shocked and defeated even to cry. She turns and walks slowly till she is near her place at the dining area. She sits, seeming dis-tracted. Looks across at MA, who is totally absorbed by the TV programme she's watching.*)

330 JAYA: Ma? Ma—(*Goes across to stage right, where MA sits.*) listen
    to me—(*But MA can't hear her. She shakes MA by the shoulder.*)
    Ma! Listen to me!

MA: (*Irritated, holding one of her ear phones up from her ear.*)
    What *is* it!

JAYA: Ma—do you realize they've taken Jeetu?   335

MA: What?

JAYA: (*In a raised voice.*) Jeetu—they've taken him away!

MA: (*Indifferently.*) So? (*Starts to replace the ear-piece.*) He was
    never here to begin with—

JAYA: No! You *can't* be so indifferent—   340

MA: (*Shaking off her hand.*) Tch! Let me be! Why should I care
    what happens to Jeetu? I'm through caring about anybody—
    (*She replaces the ear-piece and turns back to her set.*)

JAYA: (*For a second she is nonplussed. Then she loses control.*)
    That's—too much! (MA *can't hear her.*) You hear me, Ma?   345
    (*She screams.*) It's just TOO MUCH! (*She darts forward and
    snatches the TV remote from MA's hand—.*) You can't do
    this—(*Smashes it on the floor, the TV abruptly goes off, as MA's
    reaction sets in.*) you've got be involved with what's going on
    around you—   350

MA: (*Removing headphones and getting up as fast as her old limbs
    will let her.*) You—GIVE THAT BACK TO ME—

(*They do not notice that OM is sitting up alertly, by the door. He is listening to something.*)

JAYA: (*Stamping on the remote.*) I won't—I won't—

MA: (*She has got up and is flailing at JAYA with her thin arms.*)
    Pig-faced buffalo! Give it back or I'll—I'll shit in the water-   355
    supply!

JAYA: You wouldn't dare—(*She has not managed to break the
    remote yet.*)

MA: (*She has enough force to push JAYA off her balance.*) I'll
    microwave your entrails!—(*Pushes JAYA down.*) Ah! (*Snatches*   360
    up the remote.)

JAYA: (*Tackling MA from the ground, hanging onto her from
    behind and trying to claw the remote out of her hands. She
    is panting with the effort.*) I'm sick of being the only one to
    make decisions around here! There's nothing wrong with   365
    you—you're not sick—or busy—

(*All the while OM has been listening, like a dog for its master, by the door. Now the sounds that he has been listening for are audible: boots in the corridor. He readies himself by flattening himself alongside the door as the footsteps come to a halt. A pause and the bolt is opened from outside.*)

MA: Let me go, you barren dog—mmmh! Mmmmh! (*She pulls her
    arm up so that she can gnaw at JAYA's hand where it's clamped
    to her wrist.*) LET ME GO!

(*At this moment the door is flung open. JAYA and MA fall apart and turn to the door just as OM wriggles out almost the same instant. AGENT I enters, paying no attention to OM.*)

AGENT I: Madam Indumati? Who is Madam Indumati?   370

MA: Me! I'm Madam Indumati! (*She starts to move towards
    the door.*)

JAYA: (*Craning her neck.*)—Om! Om—where are you?

AGENT I: (*Salutes, announcing loudly.*) VideoCouch Enterprises,
    Ma'm—please—(*He stands aside to open the door a little*   375
    *wider and leans out in anticipation. Sounds of something being
    wheeled along.*)

JAYA: (*Flabbergasted.*) Wh-what is this? Who're you!

MA: (*To the AGENT.*) Have you brought it?

380 AGENT I: Yes, Ma'm—

(AGENT II *and* AGENT III *wheel in a long gleaming case. It is reminiscent of Tutankhamen's sarcophagus, encrusted with electronic dials and circuitry in the place of jewels. The* AGENTS *wheel it into the centre of the room, move the dining platform aside and install the device in its place.*)

AGENT I: (*Coming forward to where* MA *stands.*) Please, Ma'm, sign here—

JAYA: (*To* MA.) Ma—who are these people—what's going on—

MA: (*Ignoring* JAYA.) What about this insti—instig—?

385 AGENT I: Installation. (*Patiently.*) Just sign this form, Ma'm, to confirm receipt of the unit—

MA: (*Taking the form and the pen.*) How do I know you won't just run away after I've signed this, eh?

AGENT I: (*Shrugs.*) As you wish, Ma'm—(*To the other two* AGENTS,
390 *expressionlessly.*) Proceed with installation.

(*The other two* AGENTS *open the case, revealing an equally ornate interior, filled with tubes, switches, circuitry. Inside are a number of containers.* AGENTS II *and* III *set about attaching the containers to various parts of the case while* AGENT I *explains to* MA.)

AGENT I: This is the SuperDeluxe VideoCouch model XL 5000! We are certain it will provide you, our valued customer, with every satisfaction! This is the nourishment panel—the hydration filter—the pangrometer! Here you see the Lexus Phantasticon
395 which is programmed to receive seven hundred and fifty video channels from all over the—

JAYA: (*Shaking him.*) Stop this at once! Explain to me what's going on!

AGENT I: (*Stops, baffled.*) Ma'm—

400 MA: (*To* JAYA.) Can't you shut up? It's my VideoCouch! It's what I ordered the other day!

JAYA: But—

AGENT I: Ma'm—

MA: (*To the* AGENT.) Proceed!

405 AGENT I: (*He is off-stride.*) Uhh—This is the SuperDeluxe VideoCouch model XL 5000! We are certain it will provide you, our valued customer, with every satisfaction! This is the nourishment panel—the hydration filter—the pangrometer! Here you see the Lexus Phantasticon which is programmed
410 to receive seven hundred and fifty video channels from all over the world! There are ten modes, seventeen frequencies, three sub-strate couplers, extra-sensory feedback impulses and cross-net capturing facitilies! All media access—satellite, bio-tenna, visitelly and radiogonad. Manual control panel,
415 neuro-stimulator and full-body processing capacities—all other queries will be answered on-line from within the VideoCouch self-training program. (*He ends abruptly.*) Any questions, Ma'm?

MA: (*She has heard very little of this.*) Hanh?

420 AGENT I: Ma'm—if you sign the delivery voucher we can complete installation—

MA: But I haven't understood a word you've said—

JAYA: (*Standing between the VideoCouch and* MA.) Ma—You MUST explain what this is about—

425 MA: (*To the* AGENT.) Stop her! She'll destroy it—she'll damage it—

JAYA: (*Frustrated.*) Oh—! (*She moves away.*)

(*The* AGENT *moves to get closer to the VideoCouch.*)

JAYA: Just do it, do it! (*From stage right, watching the proceedings.*) But make sure I'm not held responsible for anything—

MA: (*To the* AGENT.) If I sign this . . . no-one can take if from me, 430 can they?

AGENT I: No, Ma'm—

MA: And your people won't go till I've got into it? (*She signs the voucher and hands it back, not glancing at the many pages of forms.*) 435

AGENT I: No, Ma'm—thank you, Ma'm—If you'll just come this way, Ma'm—

(*The other two* AGENTS *have attached a power-line to the unit and at this moment activate the system. It twinkles with small LCDs. It looks like a tiny space-module.* AGENT II *delinks the power connection and the lights continue to twinkle. She detaches the cable from the couch.*)

COUCH: (*A fruity voice issues from the VideoCouch.*) Welcome to Video Paradiso! You will not regret your choice! Please ask our authorized representative to settle you into your 440 customized, contour-gel, fully automated video-chamber! (*Appropriate music plays.*)

(*As the* COUCH *begins speaking,* MA *is helped into it by the* AGENTS. *She lies down and the* AGENTS *huddle around her, connecting her up to various pouches and tubes. They do this very quickly and she gasps and grunts once or twice. There is a breathing mask on her face. Soon they are ready to close the lid.*)

COUCH: Thank you for being cooperative! Your fully automatic Video Paradiso unit is now ready for operation! Just relax and let your guide show you the way to an experience of ultimate 445 bliss—

(*The* AGENTS *gently shut the lid. There is a faint hiss, a thin vapour escapes as the two edges nest one within the other—and it is closed. The* AGENTS *secure the edges, seal them and lock them. They work extremely fast. The muted sound of the* COUCH *voice continues but becomes a constant unintelligible background hum.*)

JAYA: (*She has been craning her neck to get a view of the proceedings.*) But—how will she breathe!

AGENT I: (*Turning to her, as the other two* AGENTS *collapse the undercarriage and lower the unit to floor level. They replace 450 the dining platform over the* COUCH. *It is efficiently concealed, aside from occasional blinks of light.*) Ma'm—it's a total-comfort unit Ma'm—

JAYA: Won't she have to—to—

AGENT I: We have a full-recycling and bio-feed-in processor! 455 Your relative will have no further need of the outside world from now till—(*He coughs delicately.*) till she chooses to delink.

JAYA: Does she—how will she—

AGENT I: (*Smoothly.*) Everything is now in the customer's 460 operation, Ma'm—the unit is fully self-sufficient—

JAYA: Won't I have to . . . switch it on or off? No . . . food? Water?

AGENT I: Total self-sufficiency, Ma'm! There is nothing to be done! 465

(*The other two* AGENTS *are ready to leave.*)

AGENT I: Ma'm—installation is complete—

JAYA: No—wait—who's paying for this thing—

AGENT I: (*Impatient to leave, walking towards the door.*) Debited from the customer's InterPlanta account Ma'm—(*As an afterthought he brings out his card.*) but in case you have any queries Ma'm, please get in touch with our local representative—

(*He hands her the card, salutes smartly but unseen, as she stares at the card. The AGENT turns on his heel and has left the room before she registers that he's gone.*)

JAYA: (*Startled by the sound of the door shutting.*) No—you've not explained anything—(*Runs to the door.*) what happens if there's a malfunction—(*Opens the door, leans out, steps out. After a moment, comes back in, looking bewildered.*) Alone! I can't believe it—they've left me alone! Every one!

(*From the COUCH a friendly mumble trills out.*)

JAYA: (*Leans, exhausted, against the door.*) But not at peace.

(*Lights start to fade.*)

JAYA: (*Slides to the floor.*) Not yet at peace.

(*Lights out.*)

SCENE II

Five days later. The room is unchanged. It is night. JAYA has fallen asleep at the table-cum-sarcophagus. There are occasional hums of sound from the VideoCouch underneath.

She is looking worn out, unslept. With jarring suddenness the warning tone sounds. JAYA startles awake.

The CONTACT MODULE is ablaze. It no longer has any face on its facets. It hovers over JAYA.

VOICE: (*A rich, gravelly male voice.*) Zhaya . . .

JAYA: (*She is badly shocked, recoils away from the CONTACT MODULE, her hand to her mouth.*) Ahhh!

VOICE: Don't be frightened, Zhaya—

5 JAYA: (*Crawling backwards towards stage right.*) No—please—

VOICE: (*The CONTACT MODULE follows her.*) There's nothing to be afraid of, Zhaya—

JAYA: Who are you! What d'you want—

VOICE: Calm down, honey, be easy—shh, shhh—

10 JAYA: (*More frightened than ever, wriggling along the floor, away from the light which follows her nevertheless.*) Who told you my name—how did you—

VOICE: Easy, girl, easy—don't keep moving, it's no use—

(*JAYA continues to back away.*)

JAYA: (*Almost screaming.*) NO! . . . please! Leave me alone—I've

15 done nothing—nothing!

VOICE: Zhaya—I can't harm you, honey—

JAYA: (*She is backed up against the wall stage right and can go no further.*) Please—please—(*She shields her eyes from the glare.*)

VOICE: Zhaya —Zhaya—just listen to me—

JAYA: (*Straining away from the light.*) Go away! Leave me alone! 20

VOICE: Zhaya—

JAYA: (*The accumulated tension, despair and solitude combine forces to break her. She subsides on her side in heaving sobs.*) Leave me . . . just leave me . . . please, please . . . just leave me!

VOICE: (*Abruptly the CONTACT MODULE moves up and away from her.*) All right, Zhaya—if that's what you really want— 25

(*The CONTACT MODULE moves a comfortable distance away from her. It dims down till it looks like a Japanese paper-lantern. The rest of the stage is in darkness. Slowly, cautiously, JAYA raises her head, looks around herself, warily. There is a pregnant silence.*)

JAYA: Have you—gone?

VOICE: No.

JAYA: (*She is startled but waits. There's no further* 30 *communication.*) Hello?

VOICE: I'm here, Zhaya, if you're ready to speak to me—

JAYA: (*Warily.*) Who are you?

VOICE: Let's just say . . . I'm a friend.

JAYA: But I don't know you! 35

VOICE: Still—I'm a friend.

JAYA: How can you be—if we've never met?

VOICE: I've seen you. Heard your voice—

JAYA: How?

VOICE: Oh . . . we have our ways— 40

JAYA: (*Pause.*) You mean, you're a friend of Ginni's?

VOICE: A friend? Yeah. Sort of.

JAYA: You live where she lives?

VOICE: Sort of, yeah.

JAYA: How is she? Is she well? 45

VOICE: Oh—! (*Nonchalantly.*) Fine, she's fine—

JAYA: (*Gusts a laugh that sounds like tears.*)

VOICE: What's the matter?

JAYA: (*Parodying his tone.*) "Fine"! "Fine"!—

VOICE: I don't understand— 50

JAYA: —Ginni might be "fine, fine"—but what has happened to my life?—She's taken Om, she's taken Jeetu! And where is she? Now that she's "fine, fine"?

VOICE: Well, I was just getting around to that—

JAYA: (*Whispers.*) It's madness. Talking to a lighted ball. Sending 55 eyes across the ocean—(*Indicates the sarcophagus.*) locking Ma into a trunk—it's all madness!

VOICE: Why don't I tell you my name?

JAYA: (*She shakes her head.*) It's not *natural,* any of it—

VOICE: Virgil. That's my name, Zhaya— 60

JAYA: I don't know you, I don't even know if you really exist, but here we are, talking! Pretending we're friends—

VIRGIL: Not pretending—

JAYA: I was pretending—with Ginni, I mean. Om said he liked her, but what did he know about her, really? What 65 did any of us know? We saw only her face. When she chose to show it to us. That's not a friend! That's not even a human being!

VIRGIL: I can show you myself, Zhaya—

JAYA: I don't want to see you. I don't want to start thinking of you 70 as a real person, when all the time you're just a voice in the air—

VIRGIL: Not just my face. All of me—

JAYA: (*She looks up suspiciously.*) You'll come *here?* In *person?*

VIRGIL: Sort of. A version of me— 75

JAYA: (*Shakes her head resolutely.*) No! I'm not interested in *versions.* I'm not like Jeetu—

VIRGIL: Tell you what. I'll show you what I look like. Then you decide—

80 JAYA: No! I'll never pluck my eyes out or get into a box—

VIRGIL: Nothing like that. You'll see me here, with your own eyes—

JAYA: How? (*Sarcastically.*) You'll send a statue with the guards?

85 VIRGIL: Just come to the Module—no, wait. I'll move to you.

(*The* CONTACT MODULE *moves till it's within her reach. She flinches back.*)

JAYA: This? You'll come from this?

VIRGIL: Don't worry! It can't harm you—

JAYA: (*Warily.*) No, but—

VIRGIL: It's very simple. Just do as I say. Reach under the

90   Module—that's right, hold the Module, it's not hot—reach under it and push the, the uh lower panel, the flat one right underneath—okay, gently push it—push it up—you'll hear a click—

JAYA *follows these instructions, kneeling as she does so, touching the glowing globe gingerly, squinting against the light. There is a click, and she releases the* MODULE. *Falls back.*)

VIRGIL: Ah—okay! Good girl!

95 JAYA: Now—?

VIRGIL: Now . . . just wait . . . (*The* MODULE *grows bright again and sinks to almost floor level.*) keep watching this space . . . underneath . . . keep watching . . .

(JAYA *complies. A bright light issues from under the* CONTACT MODULE. *Slowly it rises, creating a projection with the motion of its ascent. A figure is revealed. A young man's bare legs, well-formed . . . his shorts, bright and brassy . . . a bare torso—*JAYA *gasps. . . .*)

JAYA: . . . Jeetu!

(JEETU *stands there, smiling, his face no longer obscured by the goggles. He looks happy and healthy, but his expression is unfamiliar. He looks like someone else. He seems to glow very slightly.*)

100 VIRGIL: (*The voice comes from the* CONTACT MODULE *though* JEETU's *mouth moves.*) Well? What d'you say now?

JAYA: (*She wants to move forward.*) Jeetu . . . (*Her hand moves to her mouth.*) Is it—you?

VIRGIL: Of course it's me, Zhaya!

105 JAYA: But . . . you're not—where's the (*She means the goggles.*)— you can't be—no! It can't be—it *can't* be! (*To the* CONTACT MODULE.) What have you done! It can't be him!

VOICE: (*Distressed.*) Oh! You're not happy? Don't you like the way I look?

110 JAYA: What is this! What is this thing in front of me! What have you done with—JEETU! (*She screams.*) JEETUUU- UUU! What have they done to you! Where have you gone!!

(*The figure walks forward.*)

VIRGIL: This *is* me, Zhaya—don't you recognize me? I'm your

115 Jittoo now—

JAYA: Oh! (*Doubles over, sinks to the ground, sobbing heartily.*) What have you done, what have you done!

VIRGIL: (*The figure walks over to where* JAYA *kneels, kneels down himself.*) I thought you'd be happy to see me!

120 JAYA: (*Refuses to look at him.*) How can I be happy with a ghost!

VIRGIL: I'm not a ghost—

JAYA: You *can't* be who you look like!

VIRGIL: But I am—in one sense.

125 JAYA: (*She looks up.*) You can't be. It's all just another madness—

VIRGIL: Why, Zhaya? Trust your eyes—

JAYA: But *you*'re not here! And *he*'s . . . dead, isn't he? The one to whom this . . . this . . . *body* belonged?

130 VIRGIL: (*Gazes meaningfully but with an entirely non-*JEETU *expression on his face.*) Depends. On how you define death.

JAYA: There's only one way to define death!

VIRGIL: (*Softly.*) Not where I live. (*Pause.*) We have some new definitions. (*Pause.*) We speak of a body-death and a self-

135   death. (*Pause.*) The body you knew is . . . still alive. (*Waits.*) Come! Doesn't that count for anything?

JAYA: (*Whispers.*) And . . . the self?

VIRGIL: (*Briskly.*) The self you knew is also alive.

JAYA: Huh—! Without his body?

140 VIRGIL: He was willing to sell, I was willing to buy—

JAYA: And you paid him in—(*She stops, realizing her mistake.*) But . . . it *wasn't* you! It was . . . Ginni! (*Staring at him.*) *Ginni?*

VIRGIL: What do *you* think, Zhaya?

145 JAYA: Ginni . . . Ginni . . . wasn't *real?*

VIRGIL: Ginni was . . . me.

JAYA: You?

VIRGIL: Me. Just a minute—(*A faint buzz, then the voice that issues is in* GINNI's *cloying tones.*) Hello, Zhaya! Recognize me

150   now? This is what I sound like when my voice is a few decibels higher—

JAYA: (*She leaps to her feet.*) But then . . . but then Jeetu was paid in phantoms!

VIRGIL: (*Standing as well.*) He sees what he wants to see. He lives

155   what he wants to live.

JAYA: And he has no body!

VIRGIL: He has a—casing.

JAYA: —but no body!

VIRGIL: He is happy, Zhaya. He made his choice—

160 JAYA: (*Shouting.*) I saw his choosing! With his mind bandaged in dreams!

VIRGIL: Was it any different than his life? Any worse? When he was lying on the streets—was that better?

JAYA: When he was lying in the streets at least he knew what

165   he was! He was—he was—(*She stops.*) But you don't know this—

VIRGIL: I do.

JAYA: You can't! We never told Ginni!

VIRGIL: But I know.

170 JAYA: He . . . told you?

VIRGIL: *You* told me—

JAYA: I? (*Frowns.*) Never!

VIRGIL: Always. I listened in to you, Zhaya. I heard every word said in the room—even when the Module was off, it

175   recorded—

JAYA: (*She is shocked.*) HHhhh! (*Starts to pace about in agitation.*)

VIRGIL: I know Jittoo's not Auwm and that Auwm's your husband.

JAYA: And about—about Jeetu being—

180 VIRGIL: Diseased. Yes—but he was more available than his brother. So we took him.

JAYA: And it doesn't matter! It makes no difference!

VIRGIL: Do I look unwell? Do I look disabled? (*Smiles ironically.*) There's no scalpel as keen as youth! His body healed
185 in hours.

JAYA: And you heard . . . every, every thing?

VIRGIL: Saw, too. I know about the toilet being loaned out to half the city! About the water being sold! About the food being shared! Every sneeze, every belch. And you Zhaya—I
190 knew when you bled and when you passed wind. I even saw you . . . pleasure yourself, Zhaya, lying there, alone. I even knew that.

JAYA: (*Humiliated.*) No! You must have slept—

VIRGIL: —and played it back when I awoke!

195 JAYA: And Ginni! Who is Ginni?

VIRGIL: Nothing. Nobody. A computer-animated wet-dream.

JAYA: What?

VIRGIL: There's a joke we have, back at the agency—well, it's
200 not a great joke—

JAYA: What joke—

VIRGIL: "For every fish, a dish—"

JAYA: (*Shaking her head in despair.*) That's all we are to you—a game to play with—

205 VIRGIL: No, no—I just meant Ginni was something we needed to bait the hook—

JAYA: Hook! Fish!

VIRGIL: You misunderstand—

JAYA: You would eat us if you could—(*Painful pause.*) Maybe
210 you . . . do?

VIRGIL: Do I look like someone who would eat another human being?

JAYA: You look like Jeetu but . . . you're not him. (*Slowly.*) So I don't know what you look like. I don't know what you
215 are.

VIRGIL: This is what I look like, now.

JAYA: How can I believe you?

VIRGIL: Zhaya, *you*'ve lied to me—but *I*'ve told you only the truth.

220 JAYA: No!—they said you'd be old! And sick!

VIRGIL: I am old and I was sick until I got into this young body—

JAYA: They said you were a man—

VIRGIL: And I am! Always have been—

225 JAYA: But then you *looked* like a woman! You *spoke* like a woman—

VIRGIL: Without being one. Without ever saying I was one—

JAYA: You said you wanted Om!

VIRGIL: No, I didn't ask for Auwm. He came to us.

230 JAYA: You said you wanted a healthy body—

VIRGIL: Yes, Zhaya—yours!

JAYA: (*Stops dead.*) Mine! But it was *Om* who got the job . . .

VIRGIL: He's part of the job, but not the job itself. (*Pause.*) We're interested in women where I live, Zhaya. Child-
235 bearing women.

JAYA: But . . .

VIRGIL: So we look for young couples, without children—

JAYA: . . . Om said he wasn't married!

VIRGIL: His polygraph showed he lied. All donors lie. They think we need singles. We let them think that. That way only the
240

very desperate apply. That suits us. We search for skin and blood matches. Auwm matched mine.

JAYA: Yet you've taken *Jeetu*'s body!

VIRGIL: Jittoo is Auwm's brother. He was an even better
245 match—

JAYA: —and now you say that all the while you've wanted me! (*Shakes her head.*) What can I believe? You sew a crooked seam and call it straight!

(*There is a silence while he looks at her.*)

VIRGIL: But this seam now is true. We look for young men's bodies to live in and young women's bodies in which to sow
250 their children—

JAYA: Why! Don't you have your own?

VIRGIL: We . . . lost the art of having children.

JAYA: How can that be?

VIRGIL: We began to live longer and longer. And healthier
255 each generation. And more demanding—soon there was competition between one generation and the next—old against young, parent against child. (*Shrugs.*) We older ones had the advantage of experience. We prevailed. But our victory was bitter. We secured Paradise—at the cost of birds
260 and flowers, bees and snakes! We were determined to make our amends. So we designed this programme. In exchange for the life support we offer poorer sections of the world, we gain fresh bodies for ourselves.

JAYA: (*Incredulous.*) And it works? You live forever?
265

VIRGIL: Not all of us—every year there are fewer of us. We fixed the car, but not the driver! Time comes when the driver just wanders off and (*Shrugs.*) . . . merges with the statistics. I'm one of the stubborn ones! This is my fourth body in fifty years.
270

JAYA: Fourth!

VIRGIL: Two were not successful. My first wife ran away. The third one kept her child. I saw him but never held him. Still . . . I'm willing to keep trying.

JAYA: (*She stares at him.*) I have never been with child.
275

VIRGIL: I know I can fill your belly.

(*There is a silence.*)

JAYA: (*Drops her gaze. Hushed.*) No . . .

VIRGIL: You have longed for a child. Your arms cry out for that sweet burden. To hold it in your arms, cuddle and crush it with kisses—it is your destiny
280 as a woman—

JAYA: (*Tormented.*) NO! (*Wrings her hands.*) It was never meant to be! Years ago a seer told me—my stars denied it—

VIRGIL: Yet I sanction it, now, I. With Jittoo's body—

JAYA: (*In panic.*) No! Jeetu's dead and you're—you're a stranger's
285 phantom—

VIRGIL: I am real and warm and willing. (*Pats himself.*) This body is hot with life and heavy with desire! This body aches for you and to give you what you yearn for—

JAYA: (*Covers her head against his words but pleased in spite of
290 herself.*) No! A married woman must not hear such words from a stranger's mouth—

VIRGIL: But this mouth is no stranger to you, Zhaya!

JAYA: (*Whispering.*) No, no!

VIRGIL: This voice is but the latest tenant in a house that you
295 have known—

JAYA: No—no—

VIRGIL: You deny the truth that is humming in my newly commissioned veins—

300 JAYA: Please—ohh . . . it's sinful—sinful!

VIRGIL: (*Bending to look in her face.*)—but . . . echoed in your pulse?

JAYA: (*Covering her face.*) It's madness you're offering me—madness!

305 VIRGIL: Is it madness to offer you your heart's desire?

JAYA: I had stopped hoping—I had ceased to dream—

VIRGIL: But you can start again. I am here to make it possible.

JAYA: But (*Her voice softens.*) whose child would it be . . . Jeetu's? Or . . . yours?

310 VIRGIL: (*Smiles.*) This is Jittoo's body!

JAYA: Yes—but—

VIRGIL: It would belong to this body—it would belong to Jittoo's body—

JAYA: But—would it be Jeetu's *child*? Would it look like him? Have his voice?

315

VIRGIL: No-one can say for certain which parent a child will take after—It could look like you, after all, have your voice.

JAYA: (*Looking perplexed she extends a hand wonderingly towards the apparition.*) Yes—but—(*Her hand passes through it and she recoils in horror.*)

320

VIRGIL: Ah-ah! Can't touch!

JAYA: Then—how . . . how—?

(*There is a knocking at the door.*)

GUARD 1: (*Indistinctly from the door.*) InterPlanta Services!
325   Request permission to make contact!

JAYA: Ah!

VIRGIL: Don't—don't be frightened! It's just the agency. I can tell them to wait, if you want—(*He discreetly touches a small device at his waistband.*)

330 JAYA: Wait! Wait for what!

VIRGIL: For you to decide if you want to proceed—

JAYA: I don't understand! What are you saying—

VIRGIL: The guards will make the child possible Zhaya. It's just a formality; a device—

335 JAYA: What device!

VIRGIL: —an implant. Something I sent for you, which they're ready to deliver. But you can take your time. About two or three days are still within your fertile cycle—

340 JAYA: (*Shouting.*) What are you talking about! I told you—no more madness! Either you are here or—

VIRGIL: (*Patiently.*) Zhaya—I'd love to travel to be with you—

JAYA: Then do it! You who are so powerful—you who can travel
345   from body to body—

VIRGIL: —but the risks of travelling across the world are too great! The world you live in is too dangerous for me, Zhaya—

JAYA: (*Outraged.*) Then you *are* a phantom after all! (*She raises her
350   hands to strike the figure, then whirls towards the* CONTACT MODULE.) An illusion come to mock me—again! Again!

(*The* CONTACT MODULE *flicks easily out of her reach.*)

VIRGIL: I'll show you what to do, step by step. It's simple and it's painless—

JAYA: No! (*Leaping futilely at the globe, as the figure of* JEETU
   watches tranquilly, at a distance.) The pain tells me I'm alive!   355
   I want the pain!

VIRGIL: Then you can have all the pain you want, Zhaya—just as you want. It can take the usual nine months if you want, with diet and exercise and medical personnel to monitor you—   360

JAYA: (*She leaps at the globe, roaring in frustration.*) AR-RRHHH!

VIRGIL: —and I'll be with you, all the way—

JAYA: I believed you! I trusted you! (*In one of her leaps she jumps from a slight height and comes fractionally closer to the globe.*)   365
   But it was just one more of your crooked truths!

VIRGIL: Nothing I have said is untrue. I can set it up so that we can be together—go places—anywhere you want—right inside your room—

JAYA: I don't want your make-believe travels! I don't want your   370
   tricking comforts! (*She has stopped jumping and is looking around for something with which to strike the* CONTACT MODULE.)

VIRGIL: Zhaya we can even be . . . intimate, too! Really. But I
   thought you'd like to get to know me first—   375

JAYA: (*She starts to throw things up at the globe. Glasses, cushions, slippers, bottles, pill-boxes, gadgets.*) I don't want to know a ghost! (*The* CONTACT MODULE *moves, so her task isn't easy.*) I want real hands touching me! I want to feel a real weight upon me! Hear your breath in my ear—feel my hair being pulled,   380
   sweat running in my mouth—

VIRGIL: And it's all possible—

JAYA: (*Sharply.*) No! Not without risking your skin! (*Shouting.*)
   Never! Do you hear me, whoever you are, wherever you are?
   Never! Never! NEVER! (*With this, she strikes a direct hit.*)   385
   There is no closeness without risk!

(*There is a shower of sparks and a crack of electric light. Then the* CONTACT MODULE *goes dim. For a few seconds the lights in the whole room flicker, purple and blue. Then they stabilize.* JAYA *stands panting in the centre of the stage.* JEETU'S *figure has vanished.*)

JAYA: (*Looking up, towards the darkened globe.*) You! Can you hear me?

(*From the door, a knocking.*)

GUARD 1: (*Through the door.*) InterPlanta Services! Request
   permission to gain entry!   390

JAYA: (*To the* CONTACT MODULE.) Can you you hear me, You?
   I've forgotten your name—but it doesn't matter! You never bothered to say mine correctly anyway!

GUARD 1: (*Knocking.*) I repeat! Request permission to enter!

JAYA: (*To the* CONTACT MODULE.) Look: I'm not stupid, you know?   395
   I know you're stronger than me, you're richer than me. You'll get me in the end—I know you will. But I want you to risk your skin for me. Even though it's really Jeetu's skin—I want you to risk it. For me.

GUARD 1: (*Hammering at the door.*) Madam! Madam! We have   400
   an urgent message for you from your Receiver!

JAYA: Either that or—

GUARD 1: (*Sounds of mechanical activity at the door.*)—attaching external speaker—(*There is a scraping sound, a crackle.*)

JAYA: (*She grabs up a piece of broken glass.*)—you won't have me   405
   at all! In any sense!

GUARD 1: Speaker installed. Begin transmission . . .

VIRGIL: (*His voice is strained and crackled, but loud and clear enough that he is once more a presence in the room.*) Zhaya—
410 listen to me—*you can't hope to win this one!*

JAYA: I've discovered a new definition for winning. Winning by losing. I win if you lose.

VIRGIL: Zhaya, this is craziness—

JAYA: I'm sorry, you-whose-name-I-have-forgot—

415 VIRGIL: Virgil—

JAYA: It's your fault. If you want to play games with people, you should be careful not to push them off the board. You pushed me too far. Now there's nothing left for me to lose—

420 VIRGIL: —but your life, Zhaya! You still have your life ahead of you!

JAYA: What do I care about my life? You've shown me that it's not really mine any more. It's yours. I'm not willing to caretake *my* body for *your* sake! The only thing I have left which is still
425 mine is my death. My death and my pride—

VIRGIL: Zhaya—Zhaya—pride is nothing. Pride is a poor man's fancy dress—

JAYA: And if I let you take it from me, I will be naked as well as poor! Do you think I haven't understood you by now? You'll
430 never let me have what you have, you're only willing to share your electronic shadows with me, your night-visions, your "virtual" touch! No, no—if the only clothes I can afford are these rags of pride then let me have those! Unlike Om—unlike Ma—and Jeetu—

435 VIRGIL: Zhaya—don't make me tell the guards to force the door—if you want respect, then open the door yourself

JAYA: You can't see me, can you? I'm holding a piece of glass against my throat. If you force the door, you will push this glass into my throat.

440 VIRGIL: Zhaya—the food you take contains anti-suicide drugs. You are physically *incapable* of taking your own life—

JAYA: Test the strength of your drugs. Force that door.

VIRGIL: Zhaya—please! We've got this far—I love your spirit—I really do. In these months and weeks, I have come to admire
445 you and care for you. Don't let me down now!

JAYA: Then risk your skin.

VIRGIL: (*Pause.*) You're being unreasonable—

JAYA: Is it unreasonable to ask one who has cheated death, to cross the oceans?

450 VIRGIL: Zhaya—

JAYA: I'm bored of this argument! Don't you understand? This game is over! Either you have to erase me and start again or . . . you must accept a new set of rules.

VIRGIL: (*Sulkily.*) This is ridiculous! This is blackmail—

455 JAYA: What use do I have for words like "blackmail" when I hold my death in the palm of my hands?

VIRGIL: You're not so stupid as to think you can win against me, Zhaya—

JAYA: Stupid or not, if I lose my life, I win this game.

460 VIRGIL: You won't be alive to savour that victory—

JAYA: —but I'll die knowing that you, who live only to win, will have lost to a poor, weak and helpless woman. And I'll get more pleasure out of that first moment of death than I've had in my entire life so far!

465 VIRGIL: Zhaya, this is childish—

JAYA: You still can't see me?

VIRGIL: (*Pause.*) No—but I can get a camera—

JAYA: No, don't. I'll tell you what I'm doing (*Matches her actions to her words.*). I'm collecting all the pills and medicines I
470 can find. I'm going to take the ones for staying awake, until I run out of them. If I don't hear the sound of your own hand on my door before that time, I'll take my life. If the guards cause me any discomfort whatsoever—I'll take my life. If you do anything at all other than come here in person—I'll
475 take my life!

VIRGIL: Zhaya—

JAYA: And in the meantime, I want you to practise saying my name correctly: It's Jaya—"j" as in "justice," "j" as in "jam"—

480 VIRGIL: Zhaya—

JAYA: I won't talk to you unless you say it right!

VIRGIL: (*Pause.*) Zh . . . Jaya. Jaya. Jaya—listen to me—

JAYA: No! You listen to me! I want to be left alone—truly alone. I don't want to hear any sounds, I don't want any disturbances.
485 I'm going to take my pills, watch TV, have a dozen baths a day, eat for three instead of one. For the first time in my life and maybe the last time of my life, I'm going to enjoy myself, all by myself. I suggest you take some rest. You have a long journey ahead of you and it's sure to be a hard one.

(*Lights dim out as* JAYA *settles down comfortably in front of the television, bolstered by cushions. She looks happy and relaxed. She points the remote and turns the sound up loud. Rich, joyous music fills the room.*)

CRITICAL CONTEXTS

FRANTZ FANON (1925–1961)
"The Fact of Blackness" (1952)

Frantz Fanon was perhaps the seminal theoretician of postcolonial politics, culture, and identity; his two major books, *Black Skin, White Masks* (1952) and *The Wretched of the Earth* (1961), have been widely read and have provided an important inspiration for liberation movements around the world. Born in Martinique, Fanon studied medicine in Paris and became a psychiatrist in Algeria during its wars of liberation from France. "The Fact of Blackness" is Fanon's celebrated essay describing the consciousness of "black" subjects in a world of "white" power.

"Dirty nigger!" Or simply, "Look, a Negro!"

I came into the world imbued with the will to find a meaning in things, my spirit filled with the desire to attain to the source of the world, and then I found that I was an object in the midst of other objects.

Sealed into that crushing objecthood, I turned beseechingly to others. Their attention was a liberation, running over my body suddenly abraded into nonbeing, endowing me once more with an agility that I had thought lost, and by taking me out of the world, restoring me to it. But just as I reached the other side, I stumbled, and the movements, the attitudes, the glances of the other fixed me there, in the sense in which a chemical solution is fixed by a dye. I was indignant; I demanded an explanation. Nothing happened. I burst apart. Now the fragments have been put together again by another self.

As long as the black man is among his own, he will have no occasion, except in minor internal conflicts, to experience his being through others. There is of course the moment of "being for others," of which Hegel speaks, but every ontology is made unattainable in a colonized and civilized society. It would seem that this fact has not been given sufficient attention by those who have discussed the question. In the *Weltanschauung* of a colonized people there is an impurity, a flaw that outlaws any ontological explanation. Someone may object that this is the case with every individual, but such an objection merely conceals a basic problem. Ontology—once it is finally admitted as leaving existence by the wayside—does not permit us to understand the being of the black man. For not only must the black man be black; he must be black in relation to the white man. Some critics will take it on themselves to remind us that this proposition has a converse. I say that this is false. The black man has no ontological resistance in the eyes of the white man. Overnight the Negro has been given two frames of reference within which he has had to place himself. His metaphysics, or, less pretentiously, his customs and the sources on which they were based, were wiped out because they were

in conflict with a civilization that he did not know and that imposed itself on him.

The black man among his own in the twentieth century does not know at what moment his inferiority comes into being through the other. Of course I have talked about the black problem with friends, or, more rarely, with American Negroes. Together we protested, we asserted the equality of all men in the world. In the Antilles there was also that little gulf that exists among the almost-white, the mulatto, and the nigger. But I was satisfied with an intellectual understanding of these differences. It was not really dramatic. And then. . . .

And then the occasion arose when I had to meet the white man's eyes. An unfamiliar weight burdened me. The real world challenged my claims. In the white world the man of color encounters difficulties in the development of his bodily schema. Consciousness of the body is solely a negating activity. It is a third-person consciousness. The body is surrounded by an atmosphere of certain uncertainty. I know that if I want to smoke, I shall have to reach out my right arm and take the pack of cigarettes lying at the other end of the table. The matches, however, are in the drawer on the left, and I shall have to lean back slightly. And all these movements are made not out of habit but out of implicit knowledge. A slow composition of my *self* as a body in the middle of a spatial and temporal world—such seems to be the schema. It does not impose itself on me; it is, rather, a definitive structuring of the self and of the world—definitive because it creates a real dialectic between my body and the world.

For several years certain laboratories have been trying to produce a serum for "denegrification"; with all the earnestness in the world, laboratories have sterilized their test tubes, checked their scales, and embarked on researches that might make it possible for the miserable Negro to whiten himself and thus to throw off the burden of that corporeal malediction. Below the corporeal schema I had sketched a historico-racial schema. The elements that I used had been provided for me not by "residual sensations and perceptions primarily of a tactile, vestibular, kines-thetic, and visual character,"[1] but by the other, the white man, who had woven me out of a thousand details, an-ecdotes, stories. I thought that what I had in hand was to construct a physiological self, to balance space, to localize sensations, and here I was called on for more.

"Look, a Negro!" It was an external stimulus that flicked over me as I passed by. I made a tight smile.

"Look, a Negro!" It was true. It amused me.

"Look, a Negro!" The circle was drawing a bit tighter. I made no secret of my amusement.

"Mama, see the Negro! I'm frightened!" Frightened! Frightened! Now they were beginning to be afraid of me. I made up my mind to laugh myself to tears, but laughter had become impossible.

I could no longer laugh, because I already knew that there were legends, stories, history, and above all *historicity,* which I had learned about from Jaspers. Then, as-sailed at various points, the corporeal schema crumbled, its place taken by a racial epidermal schema. In the train it was no longer a question of being aware of my body in the third person but in a triple person. In the train I was given not one but two, three places. I had already stopped being amused. It was not that I was finding febrile coor-dinates in the world. I existed triply: I occupied space. I moved toward the other . . . and the evanescent other, hos-tile but not opaque, transparent, not there, disappeared. Nausea. . . .

I was responsible at the same time for my body, for my race, for my ancestors. I subjected myself to an objec-tive examination, I discovered my blackness, my ethnic characteristics; and I was battered down by tom-toms, cannibalism, intellectual deficiency, fetishism, racial def-ects, slave-ships, and above all else, above all: "Sho' good eatin.'"

On that day, completely dislocated, unable to be abroad with the other, the white man, who unmercifully impris-oned me, I took myself far off from my own presence, far indeed, and made myself an object. What else could it be for me but an amputation, an excision, a hemorrhage that spattered my whole body with black blood? But I did not want this revision, this thematization. All I wanted was to be a man among other men. I wanted to come lithe and young into a world that was ours and to help to build it together.

But I rejected all immunization of the emotions. I wanted to be a man, nothing but a man. Some identified me with ancestors of mine who had been enslaved or lynched: I decided to accept this. It was on the universal level of

the intellect that I understood this inner kinship—I was the grandson of slaves in exactly the same way in which President Lebrun was the grandson of tax-paying, hard-working peasants. In the main, the panic soon vanished.

In America, Negroes are segregated. In South America, Negroes are whipped in the streets, and Negro strikers are cut down by machine-guns. In West Africa, the Negro is an animal. And there beside me, my neighbor in the uni-versity, who was born in Algeria, told me: "As long as the Arab is treated like a man, no solution is possible."

"Understand, my dear boy, color prejudice is some-thing I find utterly foreign. . . . But of course, come in, sir, there is no color prejudice among us. . . . Quite, the Negro is a man like ourselves. . . . It is not because he is black that he is less intelligent than we are. . . . I had a Senegalese buddy in the army who was really clever. . . ."

Where am I to be classified? Or, if you prefer, tucked away?

"A Martinican, a native of 'our' old colonies."

Where shall I hide?

"Look at the nigger! . . . Mama, a Negro! . . . Hell, he's getting mad. . . . Take no notice, sir, he does not know that you are as civilized as we. . . ."

My body was given back to me sprawled out, distorted, recolored, clad in mourning in that white winter day. The Negro is an animal, the Negro is bad, the Negro is mean, the Negro is ugly; look, a nigger, it's cold, the nigger is shivering, the nigger is shivering because he is cold, the little boy is trembling because he is afraid of the nigger, the nigger is shivering with cold, that cold that goes through your bones, the handsome little boy is trembling because he thinks that the nigger is quivering with rage, the little white boy throws himself into his mother's arms: Mama, the nigger's going to eat me up.

All round me the white man, above the sky tears at its navel, the earth rasps under my feet, and there is a white song, a white song. All this whiteness that burns me. . . .

I sit down at the fire and I become aware of my uni-form. I had not seen it. It is indeed ugly. I stop there, for who can tell me what beauty is?

Where shall I find shelter from now on? I felt an easily identifiable flood mounting out of the countless facets of my being. I was about to be angry. The fire was long since out, and once more the nigger was trembling.

"Look how handsome that Negro is! . . ."

"Kiss the handsome Negro's ass, madame!"

Shame flooded her face. At last I was set free from my rumination. At the same time I accomplished two things: I identified my enemies and I made a scene. A grand slam. Now one would be able to laugh.

---

[1]Jean Lhermitte, *L'Image de notre corps* (Paris: Nouvelle Revue critique, 1939), p. 17.

The field of battle having been marked out, I entered the lists.

What? While I was forgetting, forgiving, and wanting only to love, my message was flung back in my face like a slap. The white world, the only honorable one, barred me from all participation. A man was expected to behave like a man. I was expected to behave like a black man—or at least like a nigger. I shouted a greeting to the world and the world slashed away my joy. I was told to stay within bounds, to go back where I belonged.

They would see, then! I had warned them, anyway. Slavery? It was no longer even mentioned, that unpleasant memory. My supposed inferiority? A hoax that it was better to laugh at. I forgot it all, but only on condition that the world not protect itself against me any longer. I had incisors to test. I was sure they were strong. And besides. . . .

What! When it was I who had every reason to hate, to despise, I was rejected? When I should have been begged, implored, I was denied the slightest recognition? I resolved, since it was impossible for me to get away from an *inborn complex,* to assert myself as a BLACK MAN. Since the other hesitated to recognize me, there remained only one solution: to make myself known.

In *Anti-Semite and Jew* (p. 95), Sartre says: "They [the Jews] have allowed themselves to be poisoned by the stereotype that others have of them, and they live in fear that their acts will correspond to this stereotype. . . . We may say that their conduct is perpetually overdetermined from the inside."

All the same, the Jew can be unknown in his Jewishness. He is not wholly what he is. One hopes, one waits. His actions, his behavior are the final determinant. He is a white man, and, apart from some rather debatable characteristics, he can sometimes go unnoticed. He belongs to the race of those who since the beginning of time have never known cannibalism. What an idea, to eat one's father! Simple enough, one has only not to be a nigger. Granted, the Jews are harassed—what am I thinking of? They are hunted down, exterminated, cremated. But these are little family quarrels. The Jew is disliked from the moment he is tracked down. But in my case everything takes on a *new* guise. I am given no chance. I am overdetermined from without. I am the slave not of the "idea" that others have of me but of my own appearance.

I move slowly in the world, accustomed now to seek no longer for upheaval. I progress by crawling. And already I am being dissected under white eyes, the only real eyes. I am *fixed.* Having adjusted their microtomes, they objectively cut away slices of my reality. I am laid bare. I feel, I see in those white faces that it is not a new man who has come in, but a new kind of man, a new genus. Why, it's a Negro!

I slip into corners, and my long antennae pick up the catch-phrases strewn over the surface of things— nigger underwear smells of nigger—nigger teeth are white—nigger feet are big—the nigger's barrel chest—I slip into corners, I remain silent, I strive for anonymity, for invisibility. Look, I will accept the lot, as long as no one notices me!

"Oh, I want you to meet my black friend. . . . Aimé Césaire, a black man and a university graduate. . . . Marian Anderson, the finest of Negro singers. . . . Dr. Cobb, who invented white blood, is a Negro. . . . Here, say hello to my friend from Martinique (be careful, he's extremely sensitive). . . ."

Shame. Shame and self-contempt. Nausea. When people like me, they tell me it is in spite of my color. When they dislike me, they point out that it is not because of my color. Either way, I am locked into the infernal circle.

I turn away from these inspectors of the Ark before the Flood and I attach myself to my brothers, Negroes like myself. To my horror, they too reject me. They are almost white. And besides they are about to marry white women. They will have children faintly tinged with brown. Who knows, perhaps little by little. . . .

I had been dreaming.

"I want you to understand, sir, I am one of the best friends the Negro has in Lyon."

The evidence was there, unalterable. My blackness was there, dark and unarguable. And it tormented me, pursued me, disturbed me, angered me.

Negroes are savages, brutes, illiterates. But in my own case I knew that these statements were false. There was a myth of the Negro that had to be destroyed at all costs. The time had long since passed when a Negro priest was an occasion for wonder. We had physicians, professors, statesmen. Yes, but something out of the ordinary still clung to such cases. "We have a Senegalese history teacher. He is quite bright. . . . Our doctor is colored. He is very gentle."

It was always the Negro teacher, the Negro doctor; brittle as I was becoming, I shivered at the slightest pretext. I knew, for instance, that if the physician made a mistake it would be the end of him and of all those who came after him. What could one expect, after all, from a Negro physician? As long as everything went well, he was praised to the skies, but look out, no nonsense, under any conditions! The black physician can never be sure how close he is to disgrace. I tell you, I was walled in: No exception was made for my refined manners, or my knowledge of literature, or my understanding of the quantum theory.

I requested, I demanded explanations. Gently, in the tone that one uses with a child, they introduced me to the existence of a certain view that was held by certain people, but, I was always told, "We must hope that it will very soon disappear." What was it? Color prejudice.

It [colour prejudice] is nothing more than the unreasoning hatred of one race for another, the contempt of the stronger and richer peoples for those whom they consider inferior to themselves and the bitter resentment of those who are kept in subjection and are so frequently insulted. As colour is the most obvious outward manifestation of race it has been made the criterion by which men are judged, irrespective of their social or educational attainments. The light-skinned races have come to despise all those of a darker colour, and the dark-skinned peoples will no longer accept without protest the inferior position to which they have been relegated.[2]

I had read it rightly. It was hate; I was hated, despised, detested, not by the neighbor across the street or my cousin on my mother's side, but by an entire race. I was up against something unreasoned. The psychoanalysts say that nothing is more traumatizing for the young child than his encounters with what is rational. I would personally say that for a man whose only weapon is reason there is nothing more neurotic than contact with unreason.

I felt knife blades open within me. I resolved to defend myself. As a good tactician, I intended to rationalize the world and to show the white man that he was mistaken.

In the Jew, Jean-Paul Sartre says, there is

a sort of impassioned imperialism of reason: for he wishes not only to convince others that he is right; his goal is to persuade them that there is an absolute and unconditioned value to rationalism. He feels himself to be a missionary of the universal; against the universality of the Catholic religion, from which he is excluded, he asserts the "catholicity" of the rational, an instrument by which to attain to the truth and establish a spiritual bond among men.[3]

And, the author adds, though there may be Jews who have made intuition the basic category of their philosophy, their intuition

has no resemblance to the Pascalian subtlety of spirit, and it is this latter—based on a thousand imperceptible perceptions—which to the Jew seems his worst enemy. As for Bergson, his philosophy offers the curious appearance of an anti-intellectualist doctrine constructed entirely by

the most rational and most critical of intelligences. It is through argument that he establishes the existence of pure duration, of philosophic intuition; and that very intuition which discovers duration or life, is itself universal, since anyone may practice it, and it leads toward the universal, since its objects can be named and conceived.[4]

With enthusiasm I set to cataloguing and probing my surroundings. As times changed, one had seen the Catholic religion at first justify and then condemn slavery and prejudices. But by referring everything to the idea of the dignity of man, one had ripped prejudice to shreds. After much reluctance, the scientists had conceded that the Negro was a human being; *in vivo* and *in vitro* the Negro had been proved analogous to the white man: the same morphology, the same histology. Reason was confident of victory on every level. I put all the parts back together. But I had to change my tune.

That victory played cat and mouse; it made a fool of me. As the other put it, when I was present, it was not; when it was there, I was no longer. In the abstract there was agreement: The Negro is a human being. That is to say, amended the less firmly convinced, that like us he has his heart on the left side. But on certain points the white man remained intractable. Under no conditions did he wish any intimacy between the races, for it is a truism that "crossings between widely different races can lower the physical and mental level. . . . Until we have a more definite knowledge of the effect of race-crossings we shall certainly do best to avoid crossings between widely different races."[5]

For my own part, I would certainly know how to react. And in one sense, if I were asked for a definition of myself, I would say that I am one who waits; I investigate my surroundings, I interpret everything in terms of what I discover, I become sensitive.

In the first chapter of the history that the others have compiled for me, the foundation of cannibalism has been made eminently plain in order that I may not lose sight of it. My chromosomes were supposed to have a few thicker or thinner genes representing cannibalism. In addition to the *sex-linked,* the scholars had now discovered the *racial-linked.*[6] What a shameful science!

But I understand this "psychological mechanism." For it is a matter of common knowledge that the mechanism is only psychological. Two centuries ago I was lost to

---

[2]Sir Alan Burns, *Colour Prejudice* (London: Allen and Unwin, 1948), p. 16.

[3]*Anti-Semite and Jew* (New York: Grove Press, 1960), pp. 112–13.

[4]Ibid., p. 115.

[5]Jon Alfred Mjoen, "Harmonic and Disharmonic Race-crossings," *The Second International Congress of Eugenics* (1921), *Eugenics in Race and State*, vol. 2, p. 60, quoted in Sir Alan Burns, op. cit., p. 120.

[6]In English in the original (*Translator's note*).

humanity, I was a slave forever. And then came men who said that it all had gone on far too long. My tenaciousness did the rest; I was saved from the civilizing deluge. I have gone forward.

Too late. Everything is anticipated, thought out, demonstrated, made the most of. My trembling hands take hold of nothing; the vein has been mined out. Too late! But once again I want to understand.

Since the time when someone first mourned the fact that he had arrived too late and everything had been said, a nostalgia for the past has seemed to persist. Is this that lost original paradise of which Otto Rank speaks? How many such men, apparently rooted to the womb of the world, have devoted their lives to studying the Delphic oracles or exhausted themselves in attempts to plot the wanderings of Ulysses! The pan-spiritualists seek to prove the existence of a soul in animals by using this argument: A dog lies down on the grave of his master and starves to death there. We had to wait for Janet to demonstrate that the aforesaid dog, in contrast to man, simply lacked the capacity to liquidate the past. We speak of the glory of Greece, Artaud says; but, he adds, if modern man can no longer understand the *Choephoroi* of Aeschylus, it is Aeschylus who is to blame. It is tradition to which the anti-Semites turn in order to ground the validity of their "point of view." It is tradition, it is that long historical past, it is that blood relation between Pascal and Descartes, that is invoked when the Jew is told, "There is no possibility of your finding a place in society." Not long ago, one of those good Frenchmen said in a train where I was sitting: "Just let the real French virtues keep going and the race is safe. Now more than ever, national union must be made a reality. Let's have an end of internal strife! Let's face up to the foreigners (here he turned toward my corner) no matter who they are."

It must be said in his defense that he stank of cheap wine; if he had been capable of it, he would have told me that my emancipated-slave blood could not possibly be stirred by the name of Villon or Taine.

An outrage!

The Jew and I: Since I was not satisfied to be racialized, by a lucky turn of fate I was humanized. I joined the Jew, my brother in misery.

An outrage!

At first thought it may seem strange that the anti-Semite's outlook should be related to that of the Negro-phobe. It was my philosophy professor, a native of the Antilles, who recalled the fact to me one day: "Whenever you hear anyone abuse the Jews, pay attention, because he is talking about you." And I found that he was universally right—by which I meant that I was answerable in my body and in my heart for what was done to my brother. Later

I realized that he meant, quite simply, an anti-Semite is inevitably anti-Negro.

You come too late, much too late. There will always be a world—a white world—between you and us. . . . The other's total inability to liquidate the past once and for all. In the face of this affective *ankylosis* of the white man, it is understandable that I could have made up my mind to utter my Negro cry. Little by little, putting out pseudopodia here and there, I secreted a race. And that race staggered under the burden of a basic element. What was it? *Rhythm!* Listen to our singer, Léopold Senghor:

> It is the thing that is most perceptible and least material. It is the archetype of the vital element. It is the first condition and the hallmark of Art, as breath is of life: breath, which accelerates or slows, which becomes even or agitated according to the tension in the individual, the degree and the nature of his emotion. This is rhythm in its primordial purity, this is rhythm in the masterpieces of Negro art, especially sculpture. It is composed of a theme—sculptural form—which is set in opposition to a sister theme, as inhalation is to exhalation, and that is repeated. It is not the kind of symmetry that gives rise to monotony; rhythm is alive, it is free. . . . This is how rhythm affects what is least intellectual in us, tyrannically, to make us penetrate to the spirituality of the object; and that character of abandon which is ours is itself rhythmic.[7]

Had I read that right? I read it again with redoubled attention. From the opposite end of the white world a magical Negro culture was hailing me. Negro sculpture! I began to flush with pride. Was this our salvation?

I had rationalized the world and the world had rejected me on the basis of color prejudice. Since no agreement was possible on the level of reason, I threw myself back toward unreason. It was up to the white man to be more irrational than I. Out of the necessities of my struggle I had chosen the method of regression, but the fact remained that it was an unfamiliar weapon; here I am at home; I am made of the irrational; I wade in the irrational. Up to the neck in the irrational. And now how my voice vibrates!

> Those who invented neither gunpowder nor the compass
> Those who never learned to conquer steam or electricity
> Those who never explored the seas or the skies
> But they know the farthest corners of the land of anguish
> Those who never knew any journey save that of abduction
> Those who learned to kneel in docility
> Those who were domesticated and Christianized
> Those who were injected with bastardy. . . .

---

[7]"Ce que l'homme noir apporte," in Claude Nordey, *L'Homme de couleur* (Paris: Plon, 1939), pp. 309–310.

Yes, all those are my brothers—a "bitter brotherhood" imprisons all of us alike. Having stated the minor thesis, I went overboard after something else.

> . . . But those without whom the earth would not be the
> earth
> Tumescence all the more fruitful
> than
> the empty land
> still more the land
> Storehouse to guard and ripen all
> on earth that is most earth
> My blackness is no stone, its deafness
> hurled against the clamor of the day
> My blackness is no drop of lifeless water
> on the dead eye of the world
> My blackness is neither a tower nor a cathedral
> It thrusts into the red flesh of the sun
> It thrusts into the burning flesh of the sky
> It hollows through the dense dismay of its own pillar of
> patience.[8]

Eyah! the tom-tom chatters out the cosmic message. Only the Negro has the capacity to convey it, to decipher its meaning, its import. Astride the world, my strong heels spurring into the flanks of the world, I stare into the shoulders of the world as the celebrant stares at the mid-point between the eyes of the sacrificial victim.

> But they abandon themselves, possessed, to the essence of
> all things, knowing nothing of externals but possessed by
> the movement of all things
> uncaring to subdue but playing the play of the world
> truly the eldest sons of the world
> open to all the breaths of the world
> meeting-place of all the winds of the world
> undrained bed of all the waters of the world
> spark of the sacred fire of the World
> flesh of the flesh of the world, throbbing with the very
> movement of the world.[9]

Blood! Blood! . . . Birth! Ecstasy of becoming! Three-quarters engulfed in the confusions of the day, I feel myself redden with blood. The arteries of all the world, convulsed, torn away, uprooted, have turned toward me and fed me.

"Blood! Blood! All our blood stirred by the male heart of the sun."[10]

Sacrifice was a middle point between the creation and myself—now I went back no longer to sources but to The

Source. Nevertheless, one had to distrust rhythm, earth-mother love, this mystic, carnal marriage of the group and the cosmos.

In *La vie sexuelle en Afrique noire,* a work rich in perceptions, De Pédrals implies that always in Africa, no matter what field is studied, it will have a certain magico-social structure. He adds:

> All these are the elements that one finds again on a still greater scale in the domain of secret societies. To the extent, moreover, to which persons of either sex, subjected to circumcision during adolescence, are bound under penalty of death not to reveal to the uninitiated what they have experienced, and to the extent to which initiation into a secret society always excites to acts of *sacred love,* there is good ground to conclude by viewing both male and female circumcision and the rites that they embellish as constitutive of minor secret societies.[11]

I walk on white nails. Sheets of water threaten my soul on fire. Face to face with these rites, I am doubly alert. Black magic! Orgies, witches' sabbaths, heathen ceremonies, amulets. Coitus is an occasion to call on the gods of the clan. It is a sacred act, pure, absolute, bringing invisible forces into action. What is one to think of all these manifestations, all these initiations, all these acts? From very direction I am assaulted by the obscenity of dances and of words. Almost at my ear there is a song:

> First our hearts burned hot
> Now they are cold
> All we think of now is Love
> When we return to the village
> When we see the great phallus
> Ah how then we will make Love
> For our parts will be dry and clean.[12]

The soil, which only a moment ago was still a tamed steed, begins to revel. Are these virgins, these nympho-maniacs? Black Magic, primitive mentality, animism, animal eroticism, it all floods over me. All of it is typical of peoples that have not kept pace with the evolution of the human race. Or, if one prefers, this is humanity at its lowest. Having reached this point, I was long reluctant to commit myself. Aggression was in the stars. I had to choose. What do I mean? I had no choice. . . .

Yes, we are—we Negroes—backward, simple, free in our behavior. That is because for us the body is not something opposed to what you call the mind. We are in the world. And long live the couple, Man and Earth!

---

[8]Aimé Césaire, *Cahier d'un retour au pays natal* (Paris: Présence Africaine, 1956), pp. 77–78.

[9]Ibid., p. 78.

[10]Ibid., p. 79.

[11]De Pédrals, *La vie sexuelle en Afrique noire* (Paris: Payot), p. 83.

[12]A. M. Vergiat, *Les rites secrets des primitifs de l'Oubangui* (Paris: Payot, 1951), p. 113.

Besides, our men of letters helped me to convince you; your white civilization overlooks subtle riches and sensitivity. Listen:

Emotive sensitivity. *Emotion is completely Negro as reason is Greek.*[13] Water rippled by every breeze? Unsheltered soul blown by every wind, whose fruit often drops before it is ripe? Yes, in one way, the Negro today is richer *in gifts than in works.*[14] But the tree thrusts its roots into the earth. The river runs deep, carrying precious seeds. And, the Afro-American poet, Langston Hughes, says:

I have known rivers
ancient dark rivers
my soul has grown deep
like the deep rivers.

The very nature of the Negro's emotion, of his sensitivity, furthermore, explains his attitude toward the object perceived with such basic intensity. It is an abandon that becomes need, an active state of communion, indeed of identification, however negligible the action—I almost said the personality—of the object. A rhythmic attitude: The adjective should be kept in mind.[15]

So here we have the Negro rehabilitated, "standing before the bar," ruling the world with his intuition, the Negro recognized, set on his feet again, sought after, taken up, and he is a Negro—no, he is not a Negro but the Negro, exciting the fecund antennae of the world, placed in the foreground of the world, raining his poetic power on the world, "open to all the breaths of the world." I embrace the world! I am the world! The white man has never understood this magic substitution. The white man wants the world; he wants it for himself alone. He finds himself predestined master of this world. He enslaves it. An acquisitive relation is established between the world and him. But there exist other values that fit only my forms. Like a magician, I robbed the white man of "a certain world," forever after lost to him and his. When that happened, the white man must have been rocked backward by a force that he could not identify, so little used as he is to such reactions. Somewhere beyond the objective world of farms and banana trees and rubber trees, I had subtly brought the real world into being. The essence of the world was my fortune. Between the world and me a relation of coexistence was established. I had discovered the primeval One. My "speaking hands" tore at the hysterical throat of the world. The white man had the anguished feeling that I was escaping from him and that I was taking

something with me. He went through my pockets. He thrust probes into the least circumvolution of my brain. Everywhere he found only the obvious. So it was obvious that I had a secret. I was interrogated; turning away with an air of mystery, I murmured:

Tokowaly, uncle, do you remember the nights gone by
When my head weighed heavy on the back of your patience or
Holding my hand your hand led me by shadows and signs
The fields are flowers of glowworms, stars hang on the bushes, on the trees
Silence is everywhere
Only the scents of the jungle hum, swarms of reddish bees that overwhelm the crickets' shrill sounds,
And covered tom-tom, breathing in the distance of the night.
You, Tokowaly, you listen to what cannot be heard, and you explain to me what the ancestors are saying in the liquid calm of the constellations,
The bull, the scorpion, the leopard, the elephant, and the fish we know,
And the white pomp of the Spirits in the heavenly shell that has no end,
But now comes the radiance of the goddess Moon and the veils of the shadows fall.
Night of Africa, my black night, mystical and bright, black and shining.[16]

I made myself the poet of the world. The white man had found a poetry in which there was nothing poetic. The soul of the white man was corrupted, and, as I was told by a friend who was a teacher in the United States, "The presence of the Negroes beside the whites is in a way an insurance policy on humanness. When the whites feel that they have become too mechanized, they turn to the men of color and ask them for a little human sustenance." At last I had been recognized, I was no longer a zero.

I had soon to change my tune. Only momentarily at a loss, the white man explained to me that, genetically, I represented a stage of development: "Your properties have been exhausted by us. We have had earth mystics such as you will never approach. Study our history and you will see how far this fusion has gone." Then I had the feeling that I was repeating a cycle. My originality had been torn out of me. I wept a long time, and then I began to live again. But I was haunted by a galaxy of erosive stereotypes: the Negro's *sui generis* odor . . . the Negro's *sui generis* good nature . . . the Negro's *sui generis* gullibility. . . .

I had tried to flee myself through my kind, but the whites had thrown themselves on me and hamstrung me.

---

[13]My italics—F.F.

[14]My italics—F.F.

[15]Léopold Senghor, "Ce que l'homme noir apporte," in Nordey, op. cit., p. 205.

[16]Léopold Senghor, *Chants d'ombre* (Paris: Editions du Seuil, 1945).

I tested the limits of my essence; beyond all doubt there was not much of it left. It was here that I made my most remarkable discovery. Properly speaking, this discovery was a rediscovery.

I rummaged frenetically through all the antiquity of the black man. What I found there took away my breath. In his book *L'abolition de l'esclavage* Schoelcher presented us with compelling arguments. Since then, Frobenius, Westermann, Delafosse—all of them white—had joined the chorus: Ségou, Djenné, cities of more than a hundred thousand people; accounts of learned blacks (doctors of theology who went to Mecca to interpret the Koran). All of that, exhumed from the past, spread with its insides out, made it possible for me to find a valid historic place. The white man was wrong, I was not a primitive, not even a half-man, I belonged to a race that had already been working in gold and silver two thousand years ago. And there was something else, something else that the white man could not understand. Listen:

What sort of men were these, then, who had been torn away from their families, their countries, their religions, with a savagery unparalleled in history?

Gentle men, polite, considerate, unquestionably superior to those who tortured them—that collection of adventurers who slashed and violated and spat on Africa to make the stripping of her the easier.

The men they took away knew how to build houses, govern empires, erect cities, cultivate fields, mine for metals, weave cotton, forge steel.

Their religion had its own beauty, based on mystical connections with the founder of the city. Their customs were pleasing, built on unity, kindness, respect for age.

No coercion, only mutual assistance, the joy of living, a free acceptance of discipline.

Order—Earnestness—Poetry and Freedom.

From the untroubled private citizen to the almost fabulous leader there was an unbroken chain of understanding and trust. No science? Indeed yes; but also, to protect them from fear, they possessed great myths in which 'the most subtle observation and the most daring imagination were balanced and blended. No art? They had their magnificent sculpture, in which human feeling erupted so unrestrained yet always followed the obsessive laws of rhythm in its organization of the major elements of a material called upon to capture, in order to redistribute, the most secret forces of the universe. . . .[17]

Monuments in the very heart of Africa? Schools? Hospitals? Not a single good burgher of the twentieth century, no Durand, no Smith, no Brown even suspects that such things existed in Africa before the Europeans came. . . .

But Schoelcher reminds us of their presence, discovered by Caillé, Mollien, the Cander brothers. And, though he nowhere reminds us that when the Portuguese landed on the banks of the Congo in 1498, they found a rich and flourishing state there and that the courtiers of Ambas were dressed in robes of silk and brocade, at least he knows that Africa had brought itself up to a juridical concept of the state, and he is aware, living in the very flood of imperialism, that European civilization, after all, is only one more civilization among many—and not the most merciful.[18]

I put the white man back into his place; growing bolder, I jostled him and told him point-blank, "Get used to me, I am not getting used to anyone." I shouted my laughter to the stars. The white man, I could see, was resentful. His reaction time lagged interminably. . . . I had won. I was jubilant.

"Lay aside your history, your investigations of the past, and try to feel yourself into our rhythm. In a society such as ours, industrialized to the highest degree, dominated by scientism, there is no longer room for your sensitivity. One must be tough if one is to be allowed to live. What matters now is no longer playing the game of the world but subjugating it with integers and atoms. Oh, certainly, I will be told, now and then when we are worn out by our lives in big buildings, we will turn to you as we do to our children—to the innocent, the ingenuous, the spontaneous. We will turn to you as to the childhood of the world. You are so real in your life—so funny, that is. Let us run away for a little while from our ritualized, polite civilization and let us relax, bend to those heads, those adorably expressive faces. In a way, you reconcile us with ourselves."

Thus my unreason was countered with reason, my reason with "real reason." Every hand was a losing hand for me. I analyzed my heredity. I made a complete audit of my ailment. I wanted to be typically Negro—it was no longer possible. I wanted to be white—that was a joke. And, when I tried, on the level of ideas and intellectual activity, to reclaim my negritude, it was snatched away from me. Proof was presented that my effort was only a term in the dialectic:

But there is something more important: The Negro, as we have said, creates an anti-racist racism for himself. In no sense does he wish to rule the world: He seeks the abolition of all ethnic privileges, wherever they come from; he asserts his solidarity with the oppressed of all colors. At once the subjective, existential, ethnic idea

---

[17] Aimé Césaire, Introduction to Victor Schoelcher, *Esclavage et colonisation* (Paris: Presses Universitaires de France, 1948), p. 7.

[18] Ibid., p. 8.

of *negritude* "passes," as Hegel puts it, into the objective, positive, exact idea of proletariat. "For Césaire," Senghor says, "the white man is the symbol of capital as the Negro is that of labor. . . . Beyond the black-skinned men of his race it is the battle of the world proletariat that is his song."

That is easy to say, but less easy to think out. And undoubtedly it is no coincidence that the most ardent poets of negritude are at the same time militant Marxists.

But that does not prevent the idea of race from mingling with that of class: The first is concrete and particular, the second is universal and abstract; the one stems from what Jaspers calls understanding and the other from intellection; the first is the result of a psychobiological syncretism and the second is a methodical construction based on experience. In fact, negritude appears as the minor term of a dialectical progression: The theoretical and practical assertion of the supremacy of the white man is its thesis; the position of negritude as an antithetical value is the moment of negativity. But this negative moment is insufficient by itself, and the Negroes who employ it know this very well; they know that it is intended to prepare the synthesis or realization of the human in a society without races. Thus negritude is the root of its own destruction, it is a transition and not a conclusion, a means and not an ultimate end.[19]

When I read that page, I felt that I had been robbed of my last chance. I said to my friends, "The generation of the younger black poets has just suffered a blow that can never be forgiven." Help had been sought from a friend of the colored peoples, and that friend had found no better response than to point out the relativity of what they were doing. For once, that born Hegelian had forgotten that consciousness has to lose itself in the night of the absolute, the only condition to attain to consciousness of self. In opposition to rationalism, he summoned up the negative side, but he forgot that this negativity draws its worth from an almost substantive absoluteness. A consciousness committed to experience is ignorant, has to be ignorant, of the essences and the determinations of its being.

Orphée Noir is a date in the intellectualization of the *experience* of being black. And Sartre's mistake was not only to seek the source of the source but in a certain sense to block that source:

Will the source of Poetry be dried up? Or will the great black flood, in spite of everything, color the sea into

which it pours itself? It does not matter: Every age has its own poetry; in every age the circumstances of history choose a nation, a race, a class to take up the torch by creating situations that can be expressed or transcended only through Poetry; sometimes the poetic impulse coincides with the revolutionary impulse, and sometimes they take different courses. Today let us hail the turn of history that will make it possible for the black men to utter "the great Negro cry with a force that will shake the pillars of the world" (Césaire).[20]

And so it is not I who make a meaning for myself, but it is the meaning that was already there, pre-existing, waiting for me. It is not out of my bad nigger's misery, my bad nigger's teeth, my bad nigger's hunger that I will shape a torch with which to burn down the world, but it is the torch that was already there, waiting for that turn of history.

In terms of consciousness, the black consciousness is held out as an absolute density, as filled with itself, a stage preceding any invasion, any abolition of the ego by desire. Jean-Paul Sartre, in this work, has destroyed black zeal. In opposition to historical becoming, there had always been the unforeseeable. I needed to lose myself completely in negritude. One day, perhaps, in the depths of that unhappy romanticism. . . .

In any case I *needed* not to know. This struggle, this new decline had to take on an aspect of completeness. Nothing is more unwelcome than the commonplace: "You'll change, my boy; I was like that too when I was young . . . you'll see, it will all pass."

The dialectic that brings necessity into the foundation of my freedom drives me out of myself. It shatters my unreflected position. Still in terms of consciousness, black consciousness is immanent in its own eyes. I am not a potentiality of something, I am wholly what I am. I do not have to look for the universal. No probability has any place inside me. My Negro consciousness does not hold itself out as a lack. It is. It is its own follower.

But, I will be told, your statements show a misreading of the processes of history. Listen then:

Africa I have kept your memory Africa
you are inside me
Like the splinter in the wound
like a guardian fetish in the center of the village
make me the stone in your sling
make my mouth the lips of your wound
make my knees the broken pillars of your abasement
AND YET

---

[19]Jean-Paul Sartre, *Orphée Noir*, preface to *Anthologie de la nouvelle poésie nègre et malgache* (Paris: Presses Universitaires de France, 1948), pp. xl ff.

[20]Ibid., p. xliv.

I want to be of your race alone
workers peasants of all lands . . .
. . . white worker in Detroit black peon in Alabama
uncountable nation in capitalist slavery
destiny ranges us shoulder to shoulder
repudiating the ancient maledictions of blood taboos
we roll away the ruins of our solitudes
If the flood is a frontier
we will strip the gully of its endless
covering flow
If the Sierra is a frontier
we will smash the jaws of the volcanoes
upholding the Cordilleras
and the plain will be the parade ground of the dawn
where we regroup our forces sundered
by the deceits of our masters
As the contradiction among the features
creates the harmony of the face
we proclaim the oneness of the suffering
and the revolt
of all the peoples on all the face of the earth
    and we mix the mortar of the age of brotherhood
    out of the dust of idols.[21]

Exactly, we will reply, Negro experience is not a whole, for there is not merely one Negro, there are *Negroes*. What a difference, for instance, in this other poem:

The white man killed my father
Because my father was proud
The white man raped my mother
Because my mother was beautiful
The white man wore out my brother in the hot sun of the roads
Because my brother was strong
Then the white man came to me
His hands red with blood
Spat his contempt into my black face
Out of his tyrant's voice:
"Hey boy, a basin, a towel, water."[22]

Or this other one:

My brother with teeth that glisten at the compliments of hypocrites
My brother with gold-rimmed spectacles
Over eyes that turn blue at the sound of the Master's voice
My poor brother in dinner jacket with its silk lapels
Clucking and whispering and strutting through the drawing rooms of Condescension

How pathetic you are
The sun of your native country is nothing more now than a shadow
On your composed civilized face
And your grandmother's hut
Brings blushes into cheeks made white by years of abasement and Mea culpa
But when regurgitating the flood of lofty empty words
Like the load that presses on your shoulders
You walk again on the rough red earth of Africa
These words of anguish will state the rhythm of your uneasy gait
I feel so alone, so alone here![23]

From time to time one would like to stop. To state reality is a wearing task. But, when one has taken it into one's head to try to express existence, one runs the risk of finding only the nonexistent. What is certain is that, at the very moment when I was trying to grasp my own being, Sartre, who remained The Other, gave me a name and thus shattered my last illusion. While I was saying to him

My negritude is neither a tower nor a cathedral,
    it thrusts into the red flesh of the sun,
    it thrusts into the burning flesh of the sky,
    it hollows through the dense dismay of its own pillar of patience . . .

while I was shouting that, in the paroxysm of my being and my fury, he was reminding me that my blackness was only a minor term. In all truth, in all truth I tell you, my shoulders slipped out of the framework of the world, my feet could no longer feel the touch of the ground. Without a Negro past, without a Negro future, it was impossible for me to live my Negrohood. Not yet white, no longer wholly black, I was damned. Jean-Paul Sartre had forgotten that the Negro suffers in his body quite differently from the white man.[24] Between the white man and me the connection was irrevocably one of transcendence.[25]

But the constancy of my love had been forgotten. I defined myself as an absolute intensity of beginning. So I took up my negritude, and with tears in my eyes I put its machinery together again. What had been broken to pieces was rebuilt, reconstructed by the intuitive lianas of my hands.

---

[21]Jacques Roumain, "Bois d'Ebène," *Prelude*, in *Anthologie de la nouvelle poésie nègre et malgache*, p. 113.

[22]David Diop, "Le temps du martyre," ibid., p. 174.

[23]David Diop, "Le Renégat."

[24]Though Sartre's speculations on the existence of The Other may be correct (to the extent, we must remember, to which *Being and Nothingness* describes an alienated consciousness), their application to a black consciousness proves fallacious. That is because the white man is not only The Other but also the master, whether real or imaginary.

[25]In the sense in which the word is used by Jean Wahl in *Existence humaine et transcendance* (Neuchâtel: La Baconnière, 1944).

My cry grew more violent: I am a Negro, I am a Negro, I am a Negro. . . .

And there was my poor brother—living out his neurosis to the extreme and finding himself paralyzed:

THE NEGRO: I can't, ma'am.
LIZZIE: Why not?
THE NEGRO: I can't shoot white folks.
LIZZIE: Really! That would bother them, wouldn't it?
THE NEGRO: They're white folks, ma'am.
LIZZIE: So what? Maybe they got a right to bleed you like a pig just because they're white?
THE NEGRO: But they're white folks.

A feeling of inferiority? No, a feeling of nonexistence. Sin is Negro as virtue is white. All those white men in a group, guns in their hands, cannot be wrong. I am guilty. I do not know of what, but I know that I am no good.

THE NEGRO: That's how it goes, ma'am. That's how it always goes with white folks.
LIZZIE: You too? You feel guilty?
THE NEGRO: Yes, ma'am.[26]

It is Bigger Thomas—he is afraid, he is terribly afraid. He is afraid, but of what is he afraid? Of himself. No one knows yet who he is, but he knows that fear will fill the world when the world finds out. And when the world knows, the world always expects something of the Negro. He is afraid lest the world know, he is afraid of the fear that the world would feel if the world knew. Like that old woman on her knees who begged me to tie her to her bed:

"I just know, Doctor: Any minute that thing will take hold of me."

"What thing?"

"The wanting to kill myself. Tie me down, I'm afraid."

In the end, Bigger Thomas acts. To put an end to his tension, he acts, he responds to the world's anticipation.[27]

So it is with the character in *If He Hollers Let Him Go*[28]—who does precisely what he did not want to do. That big blonde who was always in his way, weak, sensual, offered, open, fearing (desiring) rape, became his mistress in the end.

The Negro is a toy in the white man's hands; so, in order to shatter the hellish cycle, he explodes. I cannot go to a film without seeing myself. I wait for me. In the interval, just before the film starts, I wait for me. The people in the theater are watching me, examining me, waiting for me. A Negro groom is going to appear. My heart makes my head swim.

The crippled veteran of the Pacific war says to my brother, "Resign yourself to your color the way I got used to my stump; we're both victims."[29]

Nevertheless with all my strength I refuse to accept that amputation. I feel in myself a soul as immense as the world, truly a soul as deep as the deepest of rivers, my chest has the power to expand without limit. I am a master and I am advised to adopt the humility of the cripple. Yesterday, awakening to the world, I saw the sky turn upon itself utterly and wholly. I wanted to rise, but the disemboweled silence fell back upon me, its wings paralyzed. Without responsibility, straddling Nothingness and Infinity, I began to weep.

---

[26]Jean-Paul Sartre, *The Respectful Prostitute*, in *Three Plays* (New York: Knopf, 1949), pp. 189, 191. Originally, *La Putain respectueuse* (Paris: Gallimard, 1947). See also *Home of the Brave*, a film by Mark Robson.

---

[27]Richard Wright, *Native Son* (New York: Harper, 1940).

[28]By Chester Himes (Garden City: Doubleday, 1945).

[29]*Home of the Brave,* op. cit.

AUGUSTO BOAL (b. 1931–2009)

from *Theatre of the Oppressed* (1974)

Translated By CHARLES A. McBRIDE AND MARIA-ODILIA LEAL McBRIDE

One of contemporary world theater's most influential figures, Augusto Boal pioneered the use of theatrical performance as a means of direct social change. Closely associated with the liberationist educational philosophy of his Brazilian countryman Paolo Friere, Boal's work explores the ways theater games and street theater can be used as pedagogy—instructing even illiterate audiences to become agents of social change, what Boal calls "spect-actors"—and so as direct social practice. In 1971, Boal was apprehended and tortured by Brazilian authorities, and then exiled; he returned to Brazil in 1986, founding the Center for the Theater of the Oppressed in Rio de Janeiro, and continuing to develop the practice of Forum Theater. Boal has published several books on liberationist theater, including *Games for Actors and Non-Actors* (1992), *The Rainbow of Desire* (1995), and *Legislative Theater* (1998).

In this selection from *Theater of the Oppressed,* "Poetics of the Oppressed," Boal describes some of the techniques he used with peasants and workers in the cities of Lima and Chiclayo, Peru, in 1973, particularly focusing on the development of the "spect-actor."

Experiments with the People's Theater in Peru

These experiments were carried out in August of 1973, in the cities of Lima and Chiclayo, with the invaluable collaboration of Alicia Saco, within the program of the Integral Literacy Operation (*Operación Alfabetización Integral* [ALFIN]), directed by Alfonso Lizarzaburu and with the participation, in the various sectors, of Estela Liñares, Luis Garrido Lecca, Ramón Vilcha, and Jesús Ruiz Durand. The method used by ALFIN in the literacy program was, of course, derived from Paulo Freire.

In 1973, the revolutionary government of Peru began a national literacy campaign called *Operación Alfabetización Integral* with the objective of eradicating illiteracy within the span of four years. It is estimated that in Peru's population of 14 million people, between three and four million are illiterate or semi-illiterate.

In any country the task of teaching an adult to read and write poses a difficult and delicate problem. In Peru the problem is magnified because of the vast number of languages and dialects spoken by its people. Recent studies point to the existence of at least 41 dialects of the two principal languages, besides Spanish, which are the Quechua and the Aymara. Research carried out in the province of Loreto in the north of the country, verified the existence of 45 different languages in that region. Forty-five *languages,* not mere dialects! And this is what is perhaps the least populated province in the country.

This great variety of languages has perhaps contributed to an understanding on the part of the organizers of ALFIN, that the illiterate are not people who are unable to express themselves: they are simply people unable to express themselves in a particular language, which in this case is Spanish. All idioms are "languages," but there is an infinite number of languages that are not idiomatic. There are many languages besides those that are written or spoken. By learning a new language, a person acquires a new way of knowing reality and of passing that knowledge on to others. Each language is absolutely irreplaceable. All languages complement each other in achieving the widest, most complete knowledge of what is real.

Assuming this to be true, the ALFIN project formulated two principal aims:

1) to teach literacy in both the first language and in Spanish without forcing the abandonment of the former in favor of the latter;

2) to teach literacy in all possible languages, especially the artistic ones, such as theater, photography, puppetry, films, journalism, etc.

The training of the educators, chosen from the same regions where literacy was to be taught, was developed in four stages according to the special characteristics of each social group:

1) *barrios* (neighborhoods) or new villages, corresponding to our slums (*cantegril, favela,* . . .);

2) rural areas;

3) mining areas;

4) areas where Spanish is not the first language, which embrace 40 percent of the population. Of this 40 percent, half is made up of bilingual citizens who learned Spanish after acquiring fluency in their own indigenous language. The other half speaks no Spanish.

It is too early to evaluate the results of the ALFIN plan since it is still in its early stages. What I propose to do here is to relate my personal experience as a participant in the theatrical sector and to outline the various experiments we made in considering the theater as language, capable of being utilized by any person, with or without artistic talent. We tried to show in practice how the theater can be placed at the service of the oppressed, so that they can express themselves and so that, by using this new language, they can also discover new concepts.

In order to understand this *poetics of the oppressed* one must keep in mind its main objective: to change the people—"spectators," passive beings in the theatrical phenomenon—into subjects, into actors, transformers of the dramaticaction. I hope that the differences remain clear. Aristotle proposes a poetics in which the spectator delegates power to the dramatic character so that the latter may act and think for him. Brecht proposes a poetics in which the spectator delegates power to the character who thus acts in his place but the spectator reserves the right to think for himself, often in opposition to the character. In the first case, a "catharsis" occurs; in the second, an awakening of critical consciousness. But the *poetics of the oppressed* focuses on the action itself: the spectator delegates no power to the character (or actor) either to act or to think in his place; on the contrary, he himself assumes the protagonic role, changes the dramatic action, tries out solutions, discusses plans for change—in short, trains himself for real action. In this case, perhaps the theater is not revolutionary in itself, but it is surely a rehearsal for the revolution. The liberated spectator, as a whole person, launches into action. No matter that the action is fictional; what matters is that it is action!

I believe that all the truly revolutionary theatrical groups should transfer to the people the means of production in the theater so that the people themselves may utilize them. The theater is a weapon, and it is the people who should wield it.

But how is this transference to be achieved? As an example I cite what was done by Estela Liñares, who was in charge of the photography section of the ALFIN Plan.

What would be the old way to utilize photography in a literacy project? Without doubt, it would be to photograph things, streets, people, landscapes, stores, etc., then show the pictures and discuss them. But who would take these pictures? The instructors, group leaders, or coordinators. On the other hand, if we are going to give the people the means of production, it is necessary to hand over to them, in this case, the camera. This is what was done in ALFIN. The educators would give a camera to members of the study group, would teach them how to use it, and propose to them the following:

We are going to ask you some questions. For this purpose we will speak in Spanish. And you must answer us. But you can not speak in Spanish: you must speak in "photography." We ask you things in Spanish, which is a language. You answer us in photography, which is also a language.

The questions asked were very simple, and the answers—that is, the photos—were discussed later by the group. For example, when people were asked, where do you live?, they responded with the following types of photo-answers:

1) A picture showing the interior of a shack. In Lima it rarely rains and for this reason the shacks are made of straw mats, instead of with more permanent walls and roofs. In general they have only one room that serves as kitchen, living room, and bedroom; the families live in great promiscuity and very often young children watch their parents engage in sexual intercourse, which commonly leads to sexual acts between brothers and sisters as young as ten or eleven years old, simply as an imitation of their parents. A photo showing the interior of a shack fully answers the question, where do you live? Every element of each photo has a special meaning, which must be discussed by the group: the objects focused on, the angle from which the picture is taken, the presence or absence of people in it, etc.

2) To answer the same question, a man took a picture of the bank of a river. The discussion clarified its meaning. The river Rímac, which passes through Lima, overflows at certain times of the year. This makes life on its banks extremely dangerous, since shacks are often swept away, with a consequent loss of human lives. It is also very common for children to fall into the river while playing and the rising waters make rescue difficult. When a man answers the question with that picture, he is fundamentally expressing anguish: how can he work with peace of mind knowing that his child may be drowning in the river?

3) Another man photographed a part of the river where pelicans come to eat garbage in times of great hunger; the people, equally hungry, capture, kill and eat the pelicans. Showing this photo, the man communicated his awareness of living in a place where ironically the people welcomed hunger, because it attracted the pelicans which then served to satisfy their hunger.

4) A woman who had recently emigrated from a small village in the interior answered with a picture of the main street in her *barrio*: the old natives of Lima lived on one side of the street, while those from the interior lived on the other. On one side were those who saw their jobs threatened by the newcomers; on the other, the poor who had left everything behind in search of work. The street was a dividing line between brothers equally exploited, who found themselves facing each other as if they were enemies. The picture helped to reveal their common condition: poverty on both sides— while pictures of the wealthier neighborhoods showed who were their true enemies. The picture of the divided street showed the need to redirect their violent resentment. . . . Studying the picture of her street helped the woman to understand her own reality.

5) One day a man, in answer to the same question, took a picture of a child's face. Of course everyone thought that the man had made a mistake and repeated the question to him:

"You didn't understand; what we want is that you show us where you live. Take a picture and show us where you live. Any picture; the street, the house, the town, the river . . ."

"Here is my answer. Here is where I live."

"But it's a child. . . ."

"Look at his face: there is blood on it. This child, as all the others who live here, have their lives threatened by the rats that infest the whole bank of the river Rímac. They are protected by dogs that attack the rats and scare them away. But there was a mange epidemic and the city dog-catcher came around here catching lots of dogs and taking them away. This child had a dog who protected him. During the day his parents used to go to work and he was left with his dog. But now he doesn't have it any more. A few days ago, when you asked me where I lived, the rats had come while the child was sleeping and had eaten part of his nose. This is why there's so much blood on his face. Look at the picture; it is my answer. I live in a place where things like this still happen."

I could write a novel about the children of the *barrios* along the river Rímac; but only photography, and no other language, could express the pain of that child's eyes, of those tears mixed with blood. And, as if the irony and outrage were not enough, the photograph was in Kodachrome, "Made in U.S.A."

The use of photography may help also to discover valid symbols for a whole community or social group. It happens many times that well intentioned theatrical groups are unable to communicate with a mass audience because they use symbols that are meaningless for that audience. A royal crown may symbolize power, but a symbol only functions as such if its meaning is shared. For some a royal crown may produce a strong impact and yet be meaningless for others.

What is exploitation? The traditional figure of Uncle Sam is, for many social groups throughout the world, the ultimate symbol of exploitation. It expresses to perfection the rapacity of "Yankee" imperialism.

In Lima the people were also asked, what is exploitation? Many photographs showed the grocer; others the landlord; still others, some government office. On the other hand, a child answered with the picture of a nail on a wall. For him that was the perfect symbol of exploitation. Few adults understood it, but all the other children were in complete agreement that the picture expressed their feelings in relation to exploitation. The discussion explained why. The simplest work boys engage in at the age of five or six is shining shoes. Obviously, in the *barrios* where they live there are no shoes to shine and, for this reason, they must go to downtown Lima in order to find work. Their shine-boxes and other tools of the trade are of course an absolute necessity, and yet these boys cannot be carrying their equipment back and forth every day between work and home. So they must rent a nail on the wall of some place of business, whose owner charges them two or three *soles* per night and per nail. Looking at a nail, those children are reminded of oppression and their hatred of it; the sight of a crown, Uncle Sam, or Nixon, however, probably means nothing to them.

It is easy enough to give a camera to someone who has never taken a picture before, tell him how to focus it and which button to press. With this alone the means of photographic production are in the hands of that person. But what is to be done in the case of the theater?

The means for producing a photograph are embodied in the camera, which is relatively easy to handle, but the means of producing theater are made up of man himself, obviously more difficult to manage.

We can begin by stating that the first word of the theatrical vocabulary is the human body, the main source of sound and movement. Therefore, to control the means of theatrical production, man must, first of all, control his own body, know his own body, in order to be capable of making it more expressive. Then he will be able to practice theatrical forms in which by stages he frees himself from his condition of spectator and takes on that of actor, in which he ceases to be an object and becomes a subject, is changed from witness into protagonist.

The plan for transforming the spectator into actor can be systematized in the following general outline of four stages:

First stage: *Knowing the body*: a series of exercises by which one gets to know one's body, its limitations and possibilities, its social distortions and possibilities of rehabilitation.

Second stage: *Making the body expressive*: a series of games by which one begins to express one's self through the body, abandoning other, more common and habitual forms of expression.

Third stage: *The theater as language*: one begins to practice theater as a language that is living and present, not as a finished product displaying images from the past:

First degree: *Simultaneous dramaturgy*: the spectators "write" simultaneously with the acting of the actors;

Second degree: *Image theater*: the spectators intervene directly, "speaking" through images made with the actors' bodies;

Third degree: *forum theater*: the spectators intervene directly in the dramatic action and act.

Fourth stage: *The theater as discourse*: simple forms in which the spectator-actor creates "spectacles" according to his need to discuss certain themes or rehearse certain actions.

Examples:

1) *Newspaper theater*

2) *Invisible theater*

3) *Photo-romance theater*

4) *Breaking of repression*

5) *Myth theater*

6) *Trial theater*

7) *Masks and Rituals*

First Stage: Knowing the Body.

The initial contact with a group of peasants, workers, or villagers—if they are confronted with the proposal to put on a theatrical performance—can be extremely difficult. They have quite likely never heard of theater and if they have heard of it, their conception of it will probably have been distorted by television, with its emphasis on sentimentality, or by some traveling circus group. It is also very common for those people to associate theater with leisure or frivolity. Thus caution is required even when the contact takes place through an educator who belongs to the same class as the illiterates or semi-illiterates, even if he lives among them in a shack and shares their comfortless life. The very fact that the educator comes with the mission of eradicating illiteracy (which presupposes a coercive, forceful action) is in itself an alienating factor between the agent and the local people. For this reason the theatrical experience should begin not with something alien to the people (theatrical techniques that are taught or imposed) but with the bodies of those who agree to participate in the experiment.

There is a great number of exercises designed with the objective of making each person aware of his own body, of his bodily possibilities, and of deformations suffered because of the type of work he performs. That is, it is necessary for each one to feel the "muscular alienation" imposed on his body by work.

A simple example will serve to clarify this point: compare the muscular structure of a typist with that of the night watchman of a factory. The first performs his or her work seated in a chair: from the waist down the body becomes, during working hours, a kind of pedestal, while arms and fingers are active. The watchman, on the other hand, must walk continually during his eight-hour shift and consequently will develop muscular structures that facilitate walking. The bodies of both become alienated in accordance with their respective types of work.

The same is true of any person whatever the work or social status. The combination of roles that a person must perform imposes on him a "mask" of behavior. This is why those who perform the same roles end up resembling each other: artists, soldiers, clergymen, teachers, workers, peasants, landlords, decadent noblemen, etc.

Compare the angelical placidity of a cardinal walking in heavenly bliss through the Vatican Gardens with, on the other hand, an aggressive general giving orders to his inferiors. The former walks softly, listening to celestial music, sensitive to colors of the purest impressionistic delicacy: if by chance a small bird crosses the cardinal's path, one easily imagines him talking to the bird and addressing it with some amiable word of Christian inspiration. By contrast, it does not befit the general to talk with little birds, whether he cares to or not. No soldier would respect a general who talks to the birds. A general must talk as someone who gives orders, even if it is to tell his wife that he loves her. Likewise, a military man is expected to use spurs, whether he be a brigadier or an admiral. Thus all military officers resemble each other, just as do all cardinals; but vast differences separate generals from cardinals.

The exercises of this first stage are designed to "undo" the muscular structure of the participants. That is, to take them apart, to study and analyze them. Not to weaken or destroy them, but to raise them to the level of consciousness. So that each worker, each peasant understands, sees, and feels to what point his body is governed by his work.

If one is able, in this way, to disjoint one's own muscular structures, one will surely be able to assemble structures characteristic of other professions and social classes; that is, one will be able to physically "interpret" characters different from oneself.

All the exercises of this series are in fact designed to disjoint. Acrobatic and athletic exercises that serve to create muscular structures characteristic of athletes or acrobats are irrelevant here. I offer the following as examples of disjunctive exercises:

1) *Slow motion race.* The participants are invited to run a race with the aim of losing: the last one is the winner. Moving in slow motion, the body will find its center of gravity dislocated at each successive moment and so must find again a new muscular structure which will maintain its balance. The participants must never interrupt the motion or stand still; also they must take the longest step they can and their feet must rise above knee level. In this exercise, a 10-meter run can be more tiring than a conventional 500-meter run, for the effort needed to keep one's balance in each new position is intense.

2) *Cross-legged race.* The participants form pairs, embrace each other and intertwine their legs (the left of one with the right of the other, and vice versa). In the race, each pair acts as if it were a single person and each person acts as if his mate were his leg. The "leg" doesn't move alone: it must be put in motion by its mate!

3) *Monster race.* "Monsters" of four legs are formed: each person embraces the thorax of his mate but in reverse position; so that the legs of one fit around the neck of

the other, forming a headless monster with four legs. The monsters then run a race.

4) *Wheel race*. The pairs form wheels, each one grabbing the ankles of the other, and run a race of human wheels.

5) *Hypnosis*. The pairs face each other and one puts his hand a few centimeters from the nose of his partner, who must keep this distance: the first one starts to move his hand in all directions, up and down, from left to right, slowly or faster, while the other moves his body in order to maintain the same distance between his nose and his partner's hand. During these movements he is forced to assume bodily positions that he never takes in his daily life, thus reforming permanently his muscular structures.

   Later, groups of three are formed: one leads and the other two follow, one at each hand of the leader. The latter can do anything—cross his arms, separate his hands, etc., while the other two must try to maintain the distance. Afterward, groups of five are formed, one as leader and the other four keeping the distance in relation to the two hands and feet of the leader, while the latter can do what he pleases, even dance, etc.

6) *Boxing match*. The participants are invited to box, but they cannot touch each other under any circumstances; each one must fight as if he were really fighting but without touching his partner, who nevertheless must react as if he had received each blow.

7) *Out West*. A variation of the preceding exercises. The participants improvise a scene typical of bad western movies, with the pianist, the swaggering young cowboy, the dancers, the drunks, the villains who come in kicking the saloon doors, etc. The whole scene is performed in silence; the participants are not allowed to touch each other, but must react to every gesture or action. For example, an *imaginary* chair is thrown against a row of bottles (also imaginary), the pieces of which fly in all directions, and the participants react to the chair, the falling bottles, etc. At the end of the scene all must engage in a free-for-all fight.

All these exercises are included in my book *200 Exercises and Games for the Actor and for the Non-Actor Who Wants to Say Something Through Theater*. There are many more exercises that can be used in the same manner. In proposing exercises it's always advisable to ask the participants to describe or invent others: in this stage, the type that would serve to analyze the muscular structures of each participant. At every stage, however, the maintenance of a creative atmosphere is extremely important.

Second Stage: Making the Body Expressive.

In the second stage the intention is to develop the expressive ability of the body. In our culture we are used to expressing everything through words, leaving the enormous expressive capabilities of the body in an underdeveloped state. A series of "games" can help the participants to begin to use their bodily resources for self-expression. I am talking about parlor games and not necessarily those of a theatrical laboratory. The participants are invited to "play," not to "interpret," characters but they will "play" better to the extent that they "interpret" better.

For example: In one game pieces of paper containing names of animals, male and female, are distributed, one to each participant. For ten minutes, each person tries to give a physical, bodily impression of the animal named on his piece of paper. Talking or making noises that would suggest the animal is forbidden. The communication must be effected entirely through the body. After the first ten minutes, each participant must find his mate among the others who are imitating the animals, since there will always be a male and a female for each one. When two participants are convinced that they constitute a pair, they leave the stage, and the game is over when all participants find their mates through a purely physical communication, without the utilization of words or recognizable sounds.

What is important in games of this type is not to guess right but rather that all the participants try to express themselves through their bodies, something they are not used to doing. Without realizing it they will in fact be giving a "dramatical performance."

I remember one of these games played in a slum area, when a man drew the name *hummingbird*. Not knowing how to express it physically, he remembered nevertheless that this bird flies very rapidly from one flower to another, stops and sucks on a flower while producing a peculiar sound. So with his hands the man imitated the frenetic wings of the hummingbird and, "flying" from participant to participant, halted before each one of them making that sound. After ten minutes, when it was time for him to look for his mate, this man looked all around him and found no one who seemed to be enough of a hummingbird to attract him. Finally he saw a tall, fat man who was making a pendular movement with his hands and, setting aside his doubts, decided that there was his beloved mate; he went straight to "her," making turns around "her" and throwing little kisses to the air while singing joyfully. The fat man, upset, tried to escape, but the other fellow went after him, more and more in love with his hummingbird mate and singing with ever more amorous glee. Finally, though convinced that the other man was not his mate, the fat one—while the others roared with laughter—decided to follow his persistent suitor off stage simply to end the ordeal. Then (for only then were they allowed to talk) the first man, full of joy, cried out:

"I am the male hummingbird, and you are the female? Isn't that right?"

The fat one, very discouraged, looked at him and said: "No, dummy, I'm the bull. . . ."

How the fat man could give an impression of a delicate hummingbird while trying to portray a bull, we will never know. But, no matter: what does matter is that for 15 or 20 minutes all those people tried to "speak" with their bodies.

This type of game can be varied ad *infinitum;* the slips of paper can bear, for example, the names of occupations or professions. If the participants depict an animal, it will perhaps have little to do with their ideology. But if a peasant is called upon to act as a landlord; a worker, the owner of a factory; or if a woman must portray a policeman, all their ideology counts and finds physical expression

through the game. The names of the participants themselves may be written on slips of paper, requiring them to convey impressions of each other and thus revealing, physically, their opinions and mutual criticisms.

In this stage, as in the first, regardless of how many games one proposes to the participants, the latter should always be encouraged to invent other games and not to be passive recipients of an entertainment that comes from the outside.

Third Stage: The Theater as Language.

This stage is divided into three parts, each one representing a different degree of direct participation of the spectator in the performance. The spectator is encouraged to intervene in the action, abandoning his condition of object and assuming fully the role of subject. The two preceding stages are preparatory, centering around the work of the participants with their own bodies. Now this stage focuses on the theme to be discussed and furthers the transition from passivity to action.

HELEN GILBERT AND JOANNE TOMPKINS, from *Post-Colonial Drama* (1996)

Helen Gilbert and Joanne Tompkins are both well known for their studies of postcolonial theater and drama; Gilbert teaches at Royal Holloway, University of London, and Tompkins at the University of Queensland, Australia. In this selection from their recent book *Post-Colonial Drama,* Gilbert and Tompkins discuss the ways in which the body can be made to represent the impact of gender, racial, or sexualizing ideologies, and so become a site for social critique in performance. In their wide-ranging discussion of the formation of gendered and racialized bodies onstage, Gilbert and Tompkins take in many of the plays and playwrights represented in this Unit. How does this discussion of embodiment relate to the treatment of bodies in the texts of modern plays, or in the staging of bodies in the modern theater? How does the notion of "inscription"—treating the body as though it were always a signifier, already "written" with meanings—help us to understand the relationships between colonized and colonizing subjects in contemporary drama? Is it possible to use this critique of racialized and gendered bodies to read against the grain of earlier playwrights?

The body is the inscribed surface of events (traced by language and dissolved by ideas), the locus of a dissociated self (adopting the illusion of substantial unity), and a volume of disintegration.

—Foucault (1977): 148

Foucault's definition of the body omits a crucial performative fact: the body also *moves.* In the theatre, the actor's body is the major physical symbol; it is distinguished from other such symbols by its capacity to offer a multifarious complex of meanings. The body signifies through both its appearance and its actions. As well as indicating such categories as race and gender, the performing body can also express place and narrative through skilful mime and/or movement. Moreover, it interacts with all other stage signifiers—notably costume, set, and dialogue—and, crucially, with the audience. It is not

surprising, then, that the body functions as one of the most charged sites of theatrical representation.

The colonised subject's body, as Elleke Boehmer explains, has been an object of the coloniser's fascination and repulsion (and, in effect, possession) in sexual, pseudo-scientific, and political terms:

In colonial representation, exclusion or suppression can often literally be seen as 'embodied'. From the point of view of the colonizer specifically, fears and curiosities, sublimated fascinations with the strange or the 'primitive', are expressed in concrete physical and anatomical images. . . . [T]he Other is cast as corporeal, carnal, untamed, instinctual, raw, and therefore also open to mastery, available for use, for husbandry, for numbering, branding, cataloging, description or possession.

Paying attention to the body can be a highly useful (and even essential) strategy for reconstructing post-colonial subjectivity because imperialist discourse has been both insidious and persuasive in its construction of the colonised subject as an inscribed object of knowledge. As Elizabeth Grosz argues, the body is never simply a passive object upon which regimes of power are played out:

> If the body is the strategic target of systems of codification, supervision and constraint, it is also because the body and its energies and capacities exert an uncontrollable, unpredictable threat to a regular, systematic mode of social organisation. As well as being the site of knowledge-power, the body is thus a site of *resistance*, for it exerts a recalcitrance, and always entails the possibility of a counter-strategic reinscription, for it is capable of being self-marked, self-represented in alternative ways.

The ways in which the reinscription and self-representation of colonised bodies translate into performative strategies is obviously a key issue for post-colonial theatre. Hence, current movements towards cultural decolonisation involve not just a verbal/textual counter-discourse but a reviewing of the body and its signifying practices. Whereas narrative writing tends to erase the gender and race of its authors and protagonists through its production as an artefact of predominantly western cultures, performance centralises the physical and socio-cultural specificities of its participants. It follows that post-colonial theatre (much like feminist theatre) finds in the body more than mere 'actor function' or 'actor vehicle'. The body's ability to move, cover up, reveal itself, and even 'fracture' on stage provides it with many possible sites for decolonisation.

In general, the post-colonial body disrupts the constrained space and signification left to it by the colonisers and becomes a site for resistant inscription. For instance, the Kathakali actor's stylised facial expressions signify the history of specific Indian acting traditions and communicate the carefully preserved systems of meaning through the actor's body. The colonial subject's body contests its stereotyping and representation by others to insist on self-representation by its physical presence on the stage. Corporeal signifiers quickly become politicised when a black actor appears in a traditionally 'white' role, or when a West Indian cast stages, say, a Shakespearian play; such choices, as well as colour-blind casting, contribute to the development of an identity independent from the imposed colonial one of inadequacy, subordination, and often barbarity. Because the body is open to multifarious inscriptions which produce it as a dialogic, ambivalent, and unstable signifier rather than a single, independent, and discrete entity, it is not surprising that the production

of some sort of personal or cultural subjectivity via the body is complex indeed.

The post-colonial subject is often preoccupied with refusing colonially determined labels and definitions, especially those which operate in the name of race and gender. Part of the project of redefining staged identity is to affix the *colonised's* choice of signification to the body rather than to maintain the limited tropes traditionally assigned to it. This oppositional process of *embodiment* whereby the colonised creates his/her own subjectivity ascribes more flexible, culturally laden, and multivalent delineations to the body, rather than circumscribing it within an imposed, imperialist calculation of otherness. The post-colonial stage offers opportunities to recuperate the colonised subject's body—especially when it has been maimed or otherwise rendered 'incomplete'—and to transform its signification and its subjectivity. This chapter explores the process of recuperation by examining some of the basic performative elements of the post-colonial body: how it looks, what it does, how it is seen, and, most importantly, how it presents itself.

As *visual* markers of 'identity', race and gender are particularly significant in theatrical contexts even if their connotations are sometimes highly unstable. It is crucial to remember, however, that such markers are inscribed on the body through discourse—visual, verbal, or otherwise—rather than simply being unmediated or objectively given. In other words, the perceived (constructed) binary categories of male/female and white/black are never merely biologically determined but are also historically and ideologically conditioned. Moreover, as our earlier discussion of various feminisms indicates, race and gender are distinct, albeit sometimes intersecting and/or overlapping, factors which cannot be collapsed under the conceptual umbrella of marginalisation. It follows, then, that there can be neither an unproblematically essentialised 'black', 'female', or any other kind of body nor, conversely, can there be a universalised body which categorically avoids these markers of difference. If post-colonial theory has long rejected the idealised undifferentiated body of the other that is characteristic of imperialist discourse, representational practice—especially in largely iconic art-forms such as theatre—still faces the problem of how to avoid essentialist constructions of race and gender while recognising the irreducible specificity of their impact on subject formation. One possible solution is to conceptualise all markers of identity/difference as partial, provisional, and likely to change depending upon the context or the signifying system in which they operate at any particular time. This notion avoids a single (biological) origin for race or gender but leaves open the possibility of what Spivak calls 'strategic essentialism'—the foregrounding of 'pure' difference for particular political purposes.

Race

Since one of the key features of colonialism has been the exertion of European authority over non-white peoples, it is not surprising that an emphasis on race is widespread in post-colonial drama, particularly when the projected audience includes a high proportion of white (or otherwise dominant) viewers. Two parallel, if apparently contradictory, strategies are evident: to emphasise racial difference as part of a 'scrupulously visible political interest' (Spivak) designed to recuperate marginalised subjects, or, alternatively, to dismantle all racial categories by showing their constructedness. Some plays adopt both of these approaches simultaneously, a manoeuvre which often results in a dialectical tension that further destabilises 'race' as a signifying code. A case in point is Chi and Kuckles's *Bran Nue Dae,* which highlights the presence of a large cast of Australian Aboriginal characters/ actors while at the same time insisting that race is less a colour than an attitude. In this context, it becomes artistically plausible that even several 'white' characters (played by non-Aborigines) eventually discover their Aboriginality. The play participates in current debates in Australia about the construction of Aboriginal identity and notions of authenticity based primarily on skin colour.

The physical stage presence of black, indigenous, or otherwise 'coloured' actors cannot be undervalued in discussing the counter-discursive possibilities of the body in performance, even if what constitutes race is neither fixed nor objectively measurable. On one level, staging the visibility of imperialism's racial other is in itself a subversive act since Anglo-European theatre has a long history of excluding non-white actors while maintaining *representations* of racial difference, usually constructed through costume, make-up, and/or mask. The Othello of Shakespeare's day, for example, was played by a white actor who 'blacked up' and donned a curly-haired wig, a tradition which varied little for centuries. Not just a trope in popular entertainment (epitomised by Al Jolson's blackface performances in the early part of this century), blackface was used by Sir Laurence Olivier's version of *Othello* even as recently as the 1960s. When racially marked characters are played in this way, the resistance potential of the fictionalised black/coloured body is compromised by the 'wayward signification' of the actor's whiteness (Goldie). Matching the race (and/or gender) of the actor with that of the character does not mean, however, that the performing body completely escapes the web of imperial inscription. Rather, the body is inevitably 'read' through multiple codes and contexts and shaped not only by the narrative structures of a play itself but also by its audience. Historically, this has meant that when the nonwhite actor performed on western stages, his/her body generally carried

a kind of mystique that both heightened and detracted from its significance. Another mode of *mis*representation consistent with colonial attempts to figure racial others as inferior and/or subordinate was thus conventionalised.

Whereas much western culture constructs the female body on stage as a passive to-be-looked-at object rather than as an active subject, the racially distinct body is often designed to be *overlooked* (in two senses of the word: to be examined more fully than other signifiers as an object of curiosity *and* to be rendered invisible as an object of disregard). Until quite recently, many post-colonial plays devised by whites fell into this representational trap by depicting sentimentalised or exoticised versions of racial difference. Terry Goldie's study of settler drama in Canada, Australia, and New Zealand demonstrates the ways in which images of the indigene have been circumscribed by a semiotic field that is limited to seven signifiers: orality, mysticism, violence, nature, sexuality, historicity, and an imitation of indigenous 'forms' of communication. Often moved on or off stage to create a particular atmosphere and/or elicit laughter, indigenous characters have functioned as stage properties, as fragments of the setting, and, at times, as foils against which the normative values of white society can be defined. Likewise, roles for blacks in the wider field of western drama have been constituted within racist discourses, with perhaps even more emphasis on their supposed violence and sexuality. In these prescribed spaces, imperialism's colonised subject is denied its full humanity; it performs an imposed representational function rather than being a focal point in its own right. And while some roles can be subverted in performance, there is little scope in such plays for significant interrogation of dominant assumptions about race.

When indigenous and black playwrights depict themselves on stage, the body is one of the first theatrical elements to take on new iconic possibilities. One text that manipulates the body's signification for political purposes is Monique Mojica's *Princess Pocahontas and the Blue Spots,* which deconstructs the semiotic field of 'Indianness'—to use Daniel Francis's concept of the term (1992)—by staging its common inscriptions in juxtaposition to alternative (and generally more empowering) expressions of native North American subjectivity. Conflicting images/ identities are held in tension through the performing body of Contemporary Woman #1, who plays (with) the white-defined stereotypes presented, as well as transforming herself into various native characters. In this way, Mojica provides a critical rereading of the ways in which indigenous women have characteristically been coded and constrained by North and South American history, culture, and literature. The women's bodies contort to create images of imposed signifying codes; they also depict the scenery, including a volcano, thereby critiquing the conventional use of indigenous bodies to suggest the geographical landscape and/or to provide an apparently authentic atmosphere. The play employs an overabundance of clichéd Hollywood and explorer/pioneer depictions of the 'Indian' in order to demonstrate their emptiness as representations: the sheer number of represented 'Indian' and 'native' bodies destabilises the power of the imposed depictions. Such figures as the Cigar Store Squaw, the Storybook Princess, and Princess Buttered-on-Both-Sides are effectively meaningless, having been overdetermined by and within white discourse. More specifically, Pocahontas, Christianised and re-named Lady Rebecca, is 'stuck [and] girdled' in the costume of the 'good Indian' even if it is clearly an uncomfortable fit. These 'museum exhibits' contrast sharply with the two contemporary women and with others recuperated from the margins of imperial representation: Matoaka (the younger persona of Pocahontas), Malinche, and the three Métis women who demand that their stories be told. The Storybook Princess and the Cigar Store Squaw are predictably wooden in personality and in their movements on the stage, whereas Matoaka and Malinche, in particular, embody sexualities that cannot be contained within the virgin/whore paradigm imposed upon them by the British and the Spaniards.

Mojica's interest in countering the semiotic codes of cinema and television is shared by other native Canadian writers such as Margo Kane, Daniel David Moses, and Tomson Highway, all of whom have dramatised characters/events that rework the stereotype of the Hollywood Indian. In Australia, the project of reconstructing an indigenous subjectivity is slightly different in so far as Aborigines have been less often mythologised in/through popular representation than simply ignored, especially in visual media. In some ways, then, the conventional Aboriginal body is underdetermined because of its systematic erasure, rather than overdetermined as a result of repeated exposure. This is not to suggest that Aborigines escape the designation of 'other', but to argue that this particular other is often less well-delineated in imperial discourse than is the 'Indian'. Nevertheless, Aboriginal inscriptions of corporeality—as opposed to European constructions of Aboriginality or a generic and even less specific otherness—function to embody in Aborigines on stage a different, more culturally accurate, subjectivity. Jack Davis's plays address the blind spots of settler history and literature on a number of levels, bringing the black body into acute visibility via individual characters (often dancers) and also through group interaction (especially across colour lines). *Kullark,* for example, inverts imperialism's racial norms in a comic depiction of first contact when Mitjitjiroo responds to Captain Stirling's proffered

hand by rubbing its skin vigorously to see if the white stain can be removed. This gesture, along with the Aborigines' astonishment at the strange appearance of the Europeans, denaturalises the white body as the dominant sign of humanity. In a related manoeuvre, the play points to the *in*humanity of the invaders when they decapitate Yagan and skin him in order to remove his tribal markings for a souvenir. Here, Davis suggests that the mutilated black body functions within the colonising culture as a fetishised object. His overall project is to reinstate the corporeal presence of the Aborigines in history—and, on a metatheatrical level, in theatre—at the same time as he details the colonisers' attempts to annihilate all signs of difference. Reference to such atrocities does not mean, however, that *Kullark* simply stereotypes its characters according to race, reassigning the connotations of 'black' and 'white' in the process; rather, this play, like Davis's other works, carefully stages the misunderstandings brought about by discourses of racial otherness in a context where it is possible for conceptual gaps to be bridged. . . .

Gender

The South African plays discussed demonstrate the constructedness of racial categories at the same time as they attempt to (re)claim strategic, if negotiable, race-inflected identities. For many post-colonial dramatists, particularly women, a parallel project is to recuperate female subjectivities while showing that gender is an ideology mapped across the body in and through representation. It seems, however, that the imperative is less to deconstruct the category of female (or male) than to intervene in the discourses that naturalise gender hierarchies. This pattern is possibly related to the perceived fixity of the gender binary. White/black classifications are quickly broken down by racial hybridity—indeed the threat of miscegenation is precisely that it produces visible signs of the permeability of racial boundaries. Gender classifications, in contrast, most often admit androgyny as merely a hypothetical category which can be dissolved into male *or* female when the biological markers of sex are known. Some writers and practitioners do share Anglo-American feminism's interest in destabilising gender binaries, whether through 'sex-radical' performance or through visually recorded (transvestite) bodies, but most are more concerned with demarcating areas of women's subjugation under imperialism. Accordingly, gender is less likely to function alone as a category of discrimination in post-colonial plays than in combination with other factors such as race, class, and/or cultural background. An additional factor complicating the delineation of a gender-specific body politics is the metaphorical link between woman and the land, a powerful trope in imperial discourse and one which is reinforced, consciously or not, in much post-colonial drama, particularly by male writers. In some instances, women's bodies are not only exploited by the colonisers but also reappropriated by the colonised patriarchy as part of a political agenda which may not fully serve the interests of the women in question.

Rape is a prominent signifier in a number of plays, particularly in countries where settlers' annexation of so-called 'unoccupied territories' disrupted not only the culture but also the livelihoods of indigenous peoples. Both native and non-native dramatists have featured inter-racial rape as an analogue for the colonisers' violation of the land, and also for related forms of economic and political exploitation. Often such representations are designed to reveal less about the experiences of the oppressed than about the rape mentality of the oppressors. In the chilling final moments of Canadian George Ryga's *The Ecstasy of Rita Joe,* for example, the rape and murder of the central protagonist by three white men provides a graphic depiction of the widespread brutality of the colonial/judicial system. This play figures Rita Joe as the site on and through which the disciplinary inscriptions of imperial patriarchy are played out as her body is progressively marked by capture, assault, and sexual penetration. Politically, she functions less as an individual than as an emblem of native cultures in Canada; hence, her death signals the grim triumph of the imperial project. As Gary Boire argues, Ryga's text can be read as a 'Foucaultian allegory' which foregrounds the sexually fragmented body of Rita Joe in order to chart the systems of power that instigate and maintain the settler/invader society's dominance over indigenous groups.

Depending on how they are staged, theatrical images of sexual violence can have more than merely illustrative functions; in some instances, they also challenge the voyeuristic gaze of the white spectator, inviting him/her to admit complicity in that violence. Janis Balodis's *Too Young for Ghosts* critiques white invasion of indigenous land/culture in Australia in a complex 'cross-over' scene in which the same actors play Aboriginal and Latvian women almost simultaneously. The scene collapses the rapes of two Aboriginal women with the sexual assault of their Latvian counterparts in a displaced persons camp after World War Two. This visual conflation—achieved through doubling roles and overlaying theatrical time and space—is a performative technique intended to elicit both empathy for the Aboriginal women and outrage against the colonial regime, here constructed as a more local 'war' for control over native land/bodies. Throughout the composite rape scene, the audience's perspective is further manipulated by the presence of Karl, whose position as a callous observer reminds the viewers of their own non-intervention. By

collapsing chronological and spatial frameworks, Balodis is able to use the bodies of white characters/actors to stand in for black ones without appropriating Aboriginal figures in service of a narrative about migrant experience. Instead, by refusing to display the violation of the black women, the performance text frustrates the libidinal economy of inter-racial rape while still harnessing this trope's metaphorical power to express the colonisers' attitudes and actions. Using different strategies for a similar effect, Dorothy Hewett's *The Man From Mukinupin* (1979) stages the 'rape' of Aboriginal women through a savagely ironic song which details the settlers' attempts to conquer the recalcitrant landscape, a project explicitly figured as the male penetration of female space. Hewett's call for the doubling of her one Aboriginal character with the female heroine, presumably played by a white actor, effectively highlights the ways in which all women have been discursively merged with each other and with the landscape.

The treatment of rape in texts by native dramatists who recognise the significant intersections of race and gender takes on slightly different inflections, especially when local mythologies inform the wider play. Tomson Highway's *The Rez Sisters,* for example, stages rape as a violation not only of the land but also of the very spirit of native culture. In a brief but visually haunting scene, the mentally disabled Zhaboonigan reveals that a gang of white boys penetrated her vagina with a screwdriver. While she details the event with the casual disinterest of a child who has only limited understanding of what has happened, the Ojibway trickster spirit, Nanabush, *embodies* her trauma by performing the 'agonising contortions' of the rape victim. Zhaboonigan's assault thus accrues wider significance, though her own body remains relatively unmarked because the trickster absorbs and transforms her experience. Moreover, the conventional gender paradigms of such a scene are somewhat complicated by the fact that Nanabush—a spirit, who adopts the forms of either and both genders simultaneously—is played by a male dancer. In what is to some extent a mirror image of *The Rez Sisters*' rape scene, Highway's controversial companion play, *Dry Lips Oughta Move to Kapuskasing,* enacts a native youth's sexual assault of a young native woman, Patsy Pegahmagahbow. That the rape is performed with a crucifix by a victim of foetal alcohol syndrome suggests that Christian imperialism is at least partly responsible for the current schism between native men and women. On a performative level, this scene also points to the desecration of indigenous land/culture by the colonising forces, a resonance achieved in a series of stylised movements in which Dickie Bird Halked repeatedly stabs his crucifix into the earth while Nanabush, here played by a woman, lifts her skirt to reveal the blood which slowly spreads down her legs. In *Dry Lips,* Nanabush and Patsy are embodied by the same ever-transforming actor who variously functions as the *idea* of the 'real' women referred to in the play and as the female trickster who again absorbs Patsy's experience. Although Highway has been accused of displaying sexism and gratuitous violence, it could be argued that *Dry Lips,* like *The Rez Sisters,* actually refuses the power of rape by subsuming it within the mythological frameworks invoked, since Nanabush is, above all, the great survivor and healer. Once again, the trickster's body—operating in this text as a sign of native women/culture/land that refigures the imperial collapsing of these categories—absorbs and transforms the forces which would leave it vulnerable and degraded. After the rape, Nanabush is visibly marked but still all-powerful as she reappears in various guises throughout the rest of the dream play, and then enters the 'real' action in a final triumphant moment with the baby that foreshadows a hopeful future for the Rez.

As all these images of sexual violence suggest, women's bodies often function in post-colonial theatre as the spaces on and through which larger territorial or cultural battles are being fought. In a similar fashion, representations of fertility, pregnancy, and motherhood frequently take on political inflections, a fact which is not surprising, given that imperialism's will to power over its (female) subjects also extended to the control of many aspects of reproduction. The slave trade, in which women were bought and sold for their 'breeding' capacities, is the most obvious example of a political economy based on the institutionalised commodification of the female body. Dennis Scott takes up this particular subject in one of the historical scenes of *An Echo in the Bone,* foregrounding the processes by which slavery reduced the female body to its sexual and reproductive functions. The setting is an early nineteenth-century auctioneer's office where three slaves are being inspected by a regular customer while the black middleman lists their attributes in turn, lingering over the two women:

> Now this—(To BRIGIT.) please make note, the wide hips, the breasts just filling out. No offspring yet. Do you wish to see proof of virginity—perhaps you'll wish to see for yourself—indeed, that's hardly necessary, we have a long association of trust, don't we, sir. Calves well muscled, exceedingly well turned, you will notice. . . . The other. . . . Here is the doctor's certificate, equally untouched. Notice the nipples. Fire in this one sir, you'll forgive my saying so. But the clear eyes show how easily she can be taught. All kinds of things.

With their bodies anatomised by the imperial gaze, the women are positioned as merchandise and are thus denied all sense of subjectivity. At the same time, they are constructed as sex objects *and* as passive children ripe for the expert tutelage (read exploitation) of the white master. Further degradation follows when Stone puts on a glove to examine the 'goods', inspecting one of the women's teeth and then running his hand up between her thighs, as if at a livestock sale. While the male slave is also commodified, he is not described in corporeal terms; indeed, his best selling feature is that he 'can read, write and reckon like a schoolmaster'. This scene exemplifies gender's impact on slavery: women's bodies are marked for consumption within imperialism's particular brand of patriarchy. The added focus on the middleman's ingratiating 'sales talk' also gives weight to the theory that in patriarchal systems women function in a symbolic exchange which cements the relationships between men—in this case between the white slave owner and the black agent who acts as proxy for the buyer.

Whereas the bodies of black women were commandeered in some colonies to breed a slave class to fulfil the demands of imperialism's labour market, white women's bodies were often appropriated to preserve the racial (and moral) integrity of the ruling class. In Africa and India, as well as in the Caribbean, the colonial woman/wife was expected, indeed compelled, to offer her sexual, social, and reproductive labours in the service of the Empire. Where the goal was settlement rather than rule, white women were even more crucial to the imperial project because of the imperative to (re)populate newly conquered lands. Jill Shearer's quasi-historical play, *Catherine* (1978), demonstrates how the body of the Australian settler woman functioned as part of the physical terrain upon which colonial expansion was mapped, both literally and symbolically. A large section of this metatheatrical text details the shipment of the first convict women to Botany Bay and makes abundantly clear the fact that such 'cargo' was designed to 'balance the imbalance' of the colony—that is, to prevent the male settlers' deviant sexual behaviour (with indigenous women or other men) and to provide progeny for the successful peopling of the nation. The main character, Catherine, becomes pregnant by the ship's surgeon but will not be allowed to keep her child, who has been earmarked as the first of a new generation of Australians whose ignominious heritage must be suppressed. The proposed management of Catherine's pregnancy—she will be taken care of only until she can safely deliver the baby into its father's hands—highlights the transplanted society's complete disregard for women themselves. While much of the play's narrative content critiques the convict system by exposing the ways in which it facilitated institutional control over the female body, the performance text insists on staging women's subjectivity: its structure as a play-within-a-play enables the recuperation of Catherine's body as a group of contemporary actors continually rehearse and re-interpret the fragments of her history to provide a wider comment on gender oppression.

If the settler woman's reproductive labour was harnessed in the interests of expanding the Empire, the indigenous woman's fertility presented a threat to the colonisers and was often suppressed. Eva Johnson's *Murras* (1988) addresses this issue in Australia by referring to the deliberate and systematic sterilisation of pubescent Aboriginal girls who are duped into taking medication that renders them infertile. *Murras* illustrates ways in which native women's bodies become sites of conquest in the imperial regime and how they are permanently marked by its various administrative systems, even those which purport to be benevolent. As Ruby says of her daughter in the closing scene, 'She carries the scars of the *wudjella's* [whitefellow's] medicine'. While generally much less harmful than the enforced sterilisation detailed in Murras, medical management of pregnancy and childbirth also has the effect, if not the intention, of bringing the bodies of indigenous women under control. Sistren Theatre Collective's *Bellywoman Bangarang* (1978) takes up the issue of western medicine as part of its focus on teenage pregnancy in Jamaica, and attempts to reclaim the birthing process through the use of African-based rituals which emphasise female power. The play's opening image features three masked interlocking figures as the mother-woman, a healer and protector who mimes a traditional labour before transforming herself into a modern-day doctor in a movement which indicates the medicalisation of childbirth. After the stories of the four pregnant girls have been told, the mother-woman returns at the end of the play to oversee the births. She guides Marie through a difficult labour and also frees her from the ropes (symbols of fear and self-loathing) which have entangled her since her rape. Like the trickster in Highway's plays, the mother-woman is a regenerative force/spirit who disperses the effects of trauma, restoring the colonised body to physical and spiritual health.

Imperialism's attempt to exercise authority over the reproductive processes of its female subjects is sometimes paralleled with more local tendencies to reduce women to functions of gender and/or fertility. Some post-colonial drama invests female fertility with great symbolic importance but none the less subordinates women to the interests of the colonised patriarchy. In India and Africa in particular, male writers are inclined to image the land as a mother and to present the truly-fecund woman as a signifier of nationhood. Giving birth thus becomes largely metaphorical, particularly in plays concerning independence from colonial rule, where the birth of a child mirrors the birth of the new nation. This trope, also common to Caribbean drama, occurs in Michael Gilkes's *Couvade* (1972) which invokes an Amerindian birthing ritual to articulate the play's complex dream-vision of a unified post-independent Guyana. The custom of *couvade* requires the father-to-be to undertake a trial or ordeal while his wife is in labour. This tradition is designed to affirm the connection between the unborn child and its father and to ensure a successful birth. *Couvade,* recently revised for Guyana's 1993 independence anniversary celebrations, uses the ritual to chart the psychological and spiritual 'rebirth' of the protagonist, Lionel, who, along with his new-born child, becomes emblematic of the nation. While the choice of ritual is apt for Gilkes's political vision, it shifts the focus of the birth from the woman (and the child) to the man and the community. Such paradigms figure the paternal body as much more significant than the maternal counterpart; thus, possible representations of the female post-colonial subject are often limited to the merely practical.

The maternal body is also compromised by her child in several plays when, for instance, stalled or uncertain progress towards decolonisation is figured by some kind of failure in the reproductive process. The unborn, stillborn, or otherwise incomplete child has special significance in this respect and often features in several signifying capacities: as well as representing the specific and local community, this child also acts as a site of struggle between competing political groups, especially in cultures that acknowledge the presence of ancestral spirits. The *abiku* or Half-Child in Soyinka's *A Dance of the Forests* (1960), a play about and for Nigeria's independence, represents the contemporary Nigerian world of spiritual transition, matching the political and social transition of the country. *A Dance of the Forests* is a cautionary rather than a purely celebratory play in so far as it recognises the difficulties inherent in attempts to unite the variety of forces that would impact on an independent Nigeria. The uncertain location of the *abiku* in this text also points to some of the dilemmas Nigerians would face in the following decades. Just as the *abiku* is neither living nor dead, neither body nor spirit, neither recognised nor forgotten, Nigeria's independence augurs an ambivalent future. A more hopeful treatment of the spirit child occurs in Walcott's *Ti-Jean and His Brothers* where the *bolum,* a disfigured foetus who represents the Caribbean people under the tyranny of colonialism, is eventually wrested from the clutches of the devil/plantation owner and reborn into full human life. In both of these plays, the female body is once again completely removed from the (potential) birthing process: the *abiku's* 'mother', the Dead Woman, has no say in the life or role of her half-child while the *bolum* is restored to the human world as a result of Ti-Jean's victory over the devil. On a performative level, the incomplete child-figure simply transforms from the spirit state as if birthing itself independently of any mother figure. This process was imaged through costuming codes in one recent video production of *Ti-Jean* where the *bolum* was encased in a huge eggshell which it broke upon 'hatching'.

Examples such as these suggest that male playwrights are primarily interested in childbirth as a symbolic, often unifying trope. Women, on the other hand, have a vested interest in refusing the gender-specific roles/images that circumscribe their representation. One of the most important achievements of recent women's post-colonial writing is its refusal to endorse the traditional signifiers of gender, particularly those linked to reproduction and mothering. When motherhood is invoked, it frequently becomes a very mixed 'blessing', much as it is in Buchi Emecheta's ironically titled novel, *The Joys of Motherhood.* Interestingly, with a few exceptions, post-colonial plays by women tend not to centralise birth, perhaps in an attempt to fracture the concept of 'Mother Earth', an idealistic notion that denies women full humanity and compromises their ability to change, to choose, and to be individuated. The Canadian playwright, Judith Thompson, does frequently foreground pregnancies—in *The Crackwalker* (1980), *Tornado* (1987), and *I Am Yours* (1987)—but these imminent births tend not to represent a bright hope for the future. Instead, they symbolise evil or a social cancer; regardless of the baby's health, pregnancy is a metaphor for disease in Thompson's work. Likewise, Sistren's *Bellywoman Bangarang* and Shearer's *Catherine* construct the pregnant body in terms of disorder and/or pathology rather than invoking traditional images of fruition.

Our discussion of the gendered body supports Ketu Katrak's argument that 'the traditions most oppressive for women [in colonised societies] are specifically located within the arena of female sexuality: fertility/infertility, motherhood and the sexual division of labour'. While women as narrative subjects are characteristically erased in imperial and patriarchal discourses, their corporeal presence is often intensified through a focus on factors such as sexuality and reproduction. This habit can be just as limiting as the neglect of gender-specific issues. As Peggy Phelan argues, 'In excessively marking the boundaries of the woman's *body,* in order to make it thoroughly visible, patriarchal culture subjects it to legal, artistic, and psychic surveillance. This, in turn, reinforces the idea that she is her body'. The challenge for post-colonial dramatists—both male and female—is to refuse such body politics while re-inscribing all theatricalised bodies with more enabling markers of gender. Yet, as Monique Mojica makes clear in *Princess Pocahontas and the Blue Spots,* women as a group cannot claim a collective victim status when they have been—and continue to be—complicit in the colonisation, appropriation, and denigration of other women. In this play, Contemporary Woman #1 refuses the feminist label because its collectivity tries to override her individuality as a subject who happens to be native and who happens to be female. The contemporary characters (and actors) present to their audience transforming, individuated bodies that refuse collectivity of any type if it does not also recognise the rights of the singular subject. Contemporary Woman #1 rejects the International Women's Day march until 'feminist shoes' manage to accommodate her 'wide, square, brown feet' and so allow her to 'feel the earth through their soles'. Refusing to be both the token 'Indian' and to represent all natives, this woman demands, in Gloria Anzaldua's words, 'the freedom to carve and chisel [her] own face', thus maintaining the individuality of her body *among* groups (mis)identified solely by race or gender. . . .

Glossary

Absurd   *See* **Theater of the Absurd.**

Académie Française   An academy founded by Cardinal Richelieu in 1635 to resolve the critical debate surrounding Corneille's play *The Cid* and to regularize the French language.

actos   Short satirical plays devised by Luis Valdez and El Teatro Campesino in the late 1960s to dramatize the conditions of farmworkers in California.

afterpiece   A short play—usually a pantomime or farce—that followed the main play on the evening's bill; common in England in the eighteenth and nineteenth centuries.

agora   The marketplace in ancient Greek towns; the *agora* was often used for dramatic performance.

alienation effect   A stage technique developed by Bertolt Brecht in the 1920s and 1930s for "estranging" the action of the play. By making characters and their actions seem remarkable, alien, or unusual, Brecht encouraged the audience to question the social realities that produced such events, the political and ideological background of the drama and of its stage production.

allegory   A literary or dramatic technique that uses actual characters, places, and actions to represent more abstract political, moral, or religious ideas. *See Everyman.*

alojería   The tavern at the rear of the *patio* in a Spanish Golden Age theater, or *corral.*

amphitheater   A semicircular theater design, consisting of a playing area faced by rising tiers of seats; often used outdoors, this was the design of classical Greek theaters. The term is also used of the outdoor, "public theaters" of Elizabethan and Jacobean London.

anagnorisis   Greek term for a character's "recognition" of something previously not known in the play. In *The Poetics,* Aristotle links *anagnorisis* with *peripeteia,* the "reversal" in the action of the play.

antagonist   The force or character that opposes the main character (**protagonist**) of a play.

archon   A magistrate in classical Athens; each year, an *archon* was assigned the responsibility for organizing the **City Dionysia.**

apron   The section of the stage that extends toward the auditorium beyond the **proscenium.**

Atellan farce   Improvised comic skits featuring stock characters performed by masked actors in ancient Rome.

atoza   Upstage area in a **Noh** theater in which the musicians are seated.

auto sacramentale   Elaborate Spanish religious dramas originally devised as part of the feast of Corpus Christi. *Autos* continued to be performed in Spain until 1765.

avant-garde   Literally, the "advance guard"; the term usually refers to the most innovative, experimental, or unorthodox artists in a given historical period. Used almost exclusively of late nineteenth- and twentieth-century movements.

backcloth   A painted cloth lowered at the rear of the stage to represent a dramatic location.

Beijing Opera   Elaborate form of Chinese theater involving an onstage orchestra, ornate costumes, music, and dance.

benefit   In the English theater of the seventeenth, eighteenth, and nineteenth centuries, a performance whose profits were assigned to a single performer or to the playwright.

biomechanics   An experimental technique for actor training and performance devised by the Russian director Vsevolod Meyerhold after the Russian Revolution (1917). The technique emphasized the actor's physical training, stressing acrobatic and choreographic elements in production.

bhava   A stageable emotion in **Sanskrit drama,** related to the play's principal *rasa,* or mood.

biwa   Four-stringed, plucked instrument used to accompany spoken narration in medieval Japan.

blank verse   An English verse meter consisting of unrhymed **iambic pentameter** lines (ten syllables with alternating stress, the first stress falling on the second syllable).

box   Box seating first appeared in theaters in the late seventeenth century; boxes were arranged around the side of the stage and the sides of the auditorium for the private accommodation of small numbers of people. Boxes were more expensive than **pit** or **gallery** seats.

box set   First devised in the 1830s, a set consisting of three practical walls enclosing the stage in a roomlike way.

bunraku   The term used for modern Japanese **doll theater,** derived from the eighteenth-century master Uemura Bunrakuken.

butai   The acting area, or stage proper, of a **Noh** theater.

butoh   A powerful form of dance developed in the post-Hiroshima era in Japan; it features nude actors, covered in white powder, whose movements are slow and ethereal.

cabaret performance   Stage performances in restaurants serving food and drink; especially popular in Europe after World War I, cabarets often were used for innovative kinds of performance.

canon   An authorized body of texts, such as the *canon* of Shakespeare's known plays; also commonly used to mean a "traditional" body of texts.

capa y espada   Literally, "cape and sword" plays, swash-buckling romances in the Spanish Golden Age theater.

Capitano   The braggart soldier of *commedia dell' arte.*

carro   Wagon used for performance of Spanish *auto sacramentale.*

catastrophe   The turning point in the plot of a classical **tragedy.**

catharsis   Literally, the "purging" that Aristotle discusses as the effect of **tragedy** in his *The Poetics.* Catharsis has been variously described as an emotional release on the part of the spectators, or as the recognition and purging of wrongdoing in the action of the play.

cavea   The auditorium of a classical Roman theater, divided into sections and capable of being entered through passages directly from outside the theater.

cazuela   The women's **gallery** above the *alojería* in a Spanish Golden Age theater, or *corral.*

character   A fictional "person" appearing in a play or other work of fiction; usually conventionalized to some degree.

chonin   Japanese term for townsmen.

choregos   An important citizen in ancient Athens given the responsibility for financing, assembling, and training the chorus of Greek **tragedy.**

chorus   A masked group of young men who sang and danced as a group in Greek **tragedy** and **comedy;** larger choruses also performed *dithyrambs.*

City Dionysia   Annual spring festival honoring the god Dionysus; one of four festivals held between December and April. Sometimes called the *Great Dionysia,* it was the site of dramatic competitions and other public displays and rituals.

comedia nueva   Mixed mode form of drama associated with Lope de Vega.

Comédie Française   The official national theater of France, devoted to the staging of the classics. Founded and chartered by Louis XIV in 1680, when Molière's company and the Marais company were united.

comedy   Traditionally a humorous literary form, comedy typically concerns the trials of love, and/or ridicules the failings of certain members of society. *See* **comedy of manners, new comedy, old comedy, romantic comedy.**

comedy of manners   Comic drama that takes the manners of high society as its subject; in comedy of manners, the dialogue is often witty or epigrammatic.

commedia dell' arte   Improvised comic plays performed by itinerant companies; it originated in Italy in the sixteenth century and then spread throughout Europe. Actors each played a stock character type and improvised the action according to a shared outline plot.

constructivist theater   A movement in the Soviet theater after World War I, and often associated with the director Vsevolod Meyerhold. Adapted from the visual arts, constructivist theater resisted the use of representational sets, using more abstract "constructions" onstage.

corral   Open-air Spanish theater of the sixteenth and seventeenth centuries, constructed within an open courtyard.

cross-dressing   One of the conventions of cross-gendered acting, in which women play male characters in male costume, and men play female characters in women's clothing.

Dada   A nonsense term adopted as the name of a literary and theatrical movement in Europe after World War I; Dada developed an esthetic of random and irrational art. Dada performances became popular in cabarets of Paris, Zurich, and Berlin in the 1920s.

daimyo   Feudal lord of Japan, member of the *samurai* class of warriors, and owing duty to the *shogun.*

decorum   The concept, associated with **neoclassicism,** that the action and subject matter (idealized), language (heightened), and moral propriety (elevated), should be stylistically integrated and unified.

deme   A neighborhood in classical Athens; the root of the modern word "democracy."

demonstration   Describing the *alienation effect,* Bertolt Brecht urged his actors to "demonstrate" the roles they played, rather than identifying with them in the mode of Stanislavskian acting. Acting-as-demonstration keeps the audience aware of both the actor *and* the "character" at the same time.

dengaku-no   Form of dance, role-playing, and acrobatics popular in Japan in the eleventh and twelfth centuries; said to be one of the progenitors of **Noh** theater.

desvanes   Small open galleries on the third and fourth stories in a Spanish Golden Age theater, or *corral.*

deus ex machina   Literally, the "god from the machine"; the term refers to the practice of using a crane to lower the character of a god to the stage at the end of a classical Greek **tragedy,** usually to resolve the action of the play. In modern usage the term refers to any dramatic device that suddenly resolves the action of a play.

dithyramb   Choral hymns sung and danced to honor Dionysus as part of the **City Dionysia.** Choruses of fifty men or fifty boys drawn from each tribe performed *dithyrambs* prior to the tragedy competition; Aristotle thought **tragedy** to have originated in these dithyrambic performances.

dokekata   Comic roles in **Kabuki** theater.

doll theater   Form of Japanese theater originating in the seventeenth century; doll theater uses elaborate dolls, operated by three visible puppeteers, and combines music and narration. The most prominent form of doll theater today is called *bunraku.*

dominus   The manager of an acting company in classical Rome.

Dottore   The "doctor" or old pedant of *commedia dell' arte;* usually a friend of **Pantalone.**

drama   A form of composition, usually in dialogue form, representing the actions of fictional characters, usually intended to be performed.

Egungen   Festival common among the Yoruba peoples of Nigeria involving masks and costumes for communication with the dead.

ekkyklema   A low platform used to roll objects or bodies from the *skene* doors onto the stage in classical Greek theater.

emotion memory   A term developed by the Russian director Constantin Stanislavski to describe an actor's "work on himself" in acting. After considering a character's circumstances in the play and his past life leading up to the action of the play, the actor tries to connect the character's situation with important events in his or her own life: this emotional or affectual connection can make the character's display of emotion onstage seem realistic and immediate.

entremeses   Short plays performed as interludes between acts of Golden Age dramas.

environmental theater   A term coined by Richard Schechner in the late 1960s to describe performances that do not distinguish between the playing area and the audience; the performance takes place throughout the theatrical environment.

epic theater   A term associated with the German director Erwin Piscator and theorized by Bertolt Brecht in the late 1920s and 1930s, epic theater uses episodic dramatic action, nonrepresentational staging, and the **alienation effect,** to demonstrate the political, social, and economic factors governing the lives of the dramatic characters. In the theater, Brecht advocated the use of placards to announce the action, visible lighting, filmscreens on the stage, and other devices to produce this epic effect.

episode   Originally, a dramatic scene in a classical Greek **tragedy,** as distinct from the choral odes; now, usually refers to any incident or event in a play. Plays that are episodic tend not to subordinate episodes to a causal plot, but simply to arrange them in a series.

exodos   The final scene and exit of the characters and chorus in a classical Greek play.

expressionist theater   An early twentieth-century movement challenging the **verisimilitude** of realistic theater by staging individual emotional, unconscious states of mind directly. In expressionist plays, the action is usually abrupt and intense; the characters are usually generalized; the plot is typically symbolic or allegorical.

extravaganza   Visual spectacle popular in nineteenth-century theater.

Fabian society   A late nineteenth-century English socialist political society; Marxist in its orientation to social change, the Fabian society advocated a policy of gradual reform rather than revolution.

fabulae palliata   Term for Roman comedies set in Greece with Greek characters, referring to the use of a Greek costume.

fabulae togata   Term for Roman comedies set in Rome with Roman characters, referring to the use of a Roman costume, the toga.

farce   Usually a short comic play, often relying on a highly coincidental plot.

film noir   A **genre** of black-and-white detective films popular in the 1940s, which frequently used shadowy, nighttime settings to establish an aura of menace and foreboding.

folio   A large-format printed volume, in which only four pages (two per side) are printed on each sheet of paper; the paper is folded once to form four pages.

fourth wall   Refers to the style of realistic theater since the late nineteenth century, in which the stage is treated as a room with one wall missing. The audience is not acknowledged or addressed by the actors, but overlooks the scene as a silent, invisible observer.

frons   The façade, three stories in height, of the *scaena* or scene-house, of an ancient Roman theater.

fuebashira   Flute-player's pillar in a **Noh** theater, the upstage right pillar where the flute player is positioned during the performance.

gallery In seventeenth-, eighteenth-, and nineteenth-century theaters, ascending rows of bench seating, usually located opposite the stage on the third level of the auditorium; generally the most inexpensive seats in the theater.

geisha In Japan, a hired female companion valued for artistic accomplishment; legally not classed as a prostitute.

genre Literally, "kind" or "type"; *genre* in literary and dramatic studies refers to the main types of literary form, principally tragedy and comedy. The term can also refer to forms that are more specific to a given historical era, such as **revenge tragedy** or to more specific subgenres of **tragedy** and **comedy,** such as **comedy of manners.**

given circumstances Term used by Constantin Stanislavski to describe the situation a character finds himself or herself in at the opening of the play, which the actor must construct as his first step in building the character toward performance.

gracioso The comic fool of Spanish Golden Age drama, popularized in part by Lope de Vega.

gradas The steeply raked side seats along the side of the patio in a Spanish Golden Age theater, or *corral.*

grave trap A trap door in the floor of the stage, often in the center.

grex Latin term for an acting company in classical Rome.

hall theater A term also used for the indoor, "private theaters" of Elizabethan and Jacobean London.

hamartia A term used by Aristotle in *The Poetics* to describe the tragic hero's decisive act, the "error" or "mistake" that brings about the **tragedy.** Sometimes mistranslated as "tragic flaw," a translation that mistakenly changes the meaning of the term from the description of an action to a feature of the character's moral makeup or personality.

hanamichi Elevated gangway extending from the rear of **Kabuki** theater to the stage; major characters use this bridge for their entrances and some scenes are played here as well.

Harlequin The main character of *commedia dell' arte,* and later of English pantomime. Usually a wily schemer, Harlequin was originally played in a patched costume, which became conventionalized as the familiar diamond-covered costume. Harlequin was usually masked and carried a flat bat or paddle.

hashigakari The long bridge from the **mirror room** to the stage of a **Noh** theater.

heroic tragedy A seventeenth-century **genre,** usually on the theme of love vs. honor; associated with Dryden in England, Corneille in France, and Calderón de la Barca in Spain.

histrione Term for an actor in classical Rome, derived from the Etruscan *ister.*

hon kyōgen The main play of a **Kabuki** performance, originally lasting from about 7 A.M. until dusk when the theater closed.

hurry door The small door leading offstage from the *atoza,* or upstage area of a **Noh** theater; used by the chorus, the stage assistants, and by dead characters.

hybridization In the theory of **postcolonial** literatures, the use of several styles—typically elements of indigenous or colonized and colonial cultures—in one work, typically to dramatize the cultural politics ingrained in colonial habits of representation.

iambic pentameter English verse meter consisting of ten-syllable lines with alternating stressed and unstressed syllables, the first stress falling on the second syllable.

ideology A complex term first used in the eighteenth century to categorize political beliefs and attitudes. Used to mean (1) a body of beliefs, a doctrine; (2) a body of illusory beliefs, a false doctrine; or (3) a socially grounded system for producing beliefs and values, a way of producing meanings or doctrines.

Independent Theater Movement A late-nineteenth-century movement in Europe, in which small theaters gambled on the production of new and unconventional plays—by Ibsen, Shaw, Chekhov—to a small audience, usually outside the theatrical mainstream.

Innamorata/o The attractive young lovers of *commedia dell' arte;* played without masks.

interlude A short play, usually comic, performed during courtly feasts at the English court in the sixteenth century.

jatra A form of Indian folk theater popular in Bengal, traditionally involving music and singing; the jatra typically centers on the adventures of a central character—Vivek, or "conscience"—and can treat contemporary social issues.

jidaimono The four- to six-act "history" section of a **Kabuki** performance.

jōruri Performance of narrative and dialogue to the accompaniment of a samisen in Japanese theater; these elements absorbed into **doll theater.**

Kabuki Form of Japanese popular theater originating in the early seventeenth century. Kabuki tends to encompass both comic and serious elements in elaborate and conventional performances that originally lasted from ten to twelve hours; it includes live acting, narration, music, and singing.

kamyonguk Dance-drama form practiced in Korea, using colorful costumes, masked actors, and musical accompaniment.

katakiyaku   Villain role in **Kabuki** theater.

kathakali   An elaborate form of music and dance drama that originated in the Kerala province of southern India in the sixteenth century; *kathakali* uses highly conventionalized movements and hand gestures and has preserved some of the dramatic forms of classical **Sanskrit** theater.

komos   A procession and dance in ancient Greece, sometimes thought to be the origin of comic drama.

kyōgen   Brief farcical play performed as interludes between **Noh** plays.

language   One of the six constituent elements of drama defined by Aristotle in *The Poetics*.

line of business   A conventional or stock "character" type that is the specialty of a given actor; his or her "line of business" might be old men, heavy villains, comic heroines, etc.

Little Negro Theater Movement   A movement in the U.S. theater in the 1920s to develop theaters owned and operated by African Americans, playing a dramatic repertory by African American writers.

Little Theater Movement   A movement in the American theater in the early twentieth century akin to the **Independent Theater Movement** in Europe. Little Theaters offered new or noncommercial plays to smaller audiences.

liturgical drama   Short dramatized sections of the Catholic Mass performed as part of the service; may have inspired the more elaborate, nonliturgical **cycle plays.**

loa   A short, typically allegorical play used to introduce a **comedy** or religious play in Spanish Golden Age theater.

ludi Romani   Religious festival originating in Rome during the sixth century BCE at which a variety of entertainments were performed; drama first performed in 240 BCE; the other festivals were the *Ludi Megalensia, Ludi Plebei, Ludi Forales, and Ludi Apollinares.*

machina   The Greek term for the crane used in the ancient theater to raise and lower characters, particularly the gods.

machine plays   Term used principally in seventeenth-century French theater to describe spectacular special-effects extravaganzas, in which the dramatic action—usually drawn from mythological subjects—was merely a pretext for the use of stage machinery.

magic if   Term developed by Constantin Stanislavski to describe the actor's attitude toward a role; to play "as if I were in this situation."

melodrama   First used in the late eighteenth century, the term originally referred to highly charged, popular plays using music to reinforce their clear-cut moral action; now refers more generally to plays with a schematic opposition between good and evil, in which good usually prevails.

metatheater   A term used to describe plays that self-consciously comment on the process of theater, or treat the process of theater as a metaphor for off-stage reality. Such plays sometimes use the play-within-the-play device.

Method acting   A technique of acting developed by Constantin Stanislavski at the turn of the twentieth century, which teaches actors to use **emotion memory** to enact the character's feelings persuasively and realistically in performance; method acting became especially popular in the United States in the 1930s, 1940s, and 1950s.

metsukebashira   The "gazing pillar" in a **Noh** theater, where the *shite* looks when delivering his first speech. It is the downstage right pillar.

mie   Exaggerated pose struck for expressive effect by actors in **Kabuki** theater.

mime   In classical Roman theater, a term used for a wide range of entertainments first performed by small itinerant companies—juggling, acrobatics, short dramatic skits. Over time, the term came to be associated especially with satirical and salacious performances, especially during the later Republic and Empire. In modern usage, refers either to the genre or performer of silent action, a shortened form of **pantomime.**

mimesis   Greek word for "imitation" used by Aristotle in *The Poetics* to describe the function of art.

mirror room   The waiting room of a **Noh** theater, where actors in costume contemplate their characterization.

mise-en-scène   The "putting onstage" of a play, including the setting, scenery, direction, and action.

mitos   Lyrical plays on Mexican American life devised by Luis Valdez and El Teatro Campesino in the late 1960s and 1970s.

monopoly   The right to exclusive production of the drama.

montage   A technique used in film consisting of a rapid sequence of images.

morality drama   A late-medieval dramatic form using allegorical characters to dramatize moral and ethical problems involved in leading a Christian life.

music   A constituent element of drama as defined by Aristotle in *The Poetics;* Aristotle refers to the flute music that accompanied performance in the ancient Greek theater.

naturalism   A late nineteenth-century movement that attempted to achieve an objective **verisimilitude** in art—chiefly in theater and literature—by adopting a "scientific" attitude toward its subject matter.

Thematically, naturalism emphasizes the role of society, history, and personality in determining the actions of its characters, usually expressed as a conflict between the characters and their environment.

nautical shows A type of **melodrama** popular in England in the eighteenth and nineteenth centuries on seafaring subjects; in aquatic dramas, the stage was actually flooded.

neoclassical drama Drama written under the influence of **neoclassicism.**

neoclassicism A movement throughout Europe in the sixteenth to eighteenth centuries to revive the forms and values of art exemplified by ancient literature; associated with the recovery of Aristotle's *The Poetics* and its translation into prescriptions for the stage.

new comedy A form originating in the fourth and third centuries BCE, first in Greece and then in Rome. In the plays of Plautus, for instance, new comedy generally concerns a romantic plot involving a conflict between young lovers, an old man, and a tricky servant.

Noh Japanese classical theater dating from the fourteenth century; the plays are highly poetic dramas given extremely formal production onstage. Noh drama was admired by Yeats and by other modern playwrights.

ode In Greek drama, a song performed by the chorus while dancing.

old comedy Satiric social comedy of fifth-century BCE Athens; Aristophanes' plays are the only surviving examples.

onnagata Women's roles in **Kabuki** theater, all of which are played by men.

onna kabuki Literally, "women's Kabuki," an early name for **Kabuki** companies, which were composed mainly of women.

orchestra Literally, the "dancing place," the circular area before the **skene** where the **chorus** performed in ancient Greek theater.

pageant master The guild officer responsible for gathering funds to finance medieval mystery pageants.

pageant wagons Wagons carrying the sets for productions of medieval **cycle plays,** on which the plays were performed.

Pantalone Foolish old man in *commedia dell' arte;* played masked.

pantomime In classical Roman theater, a narrative performance genre using dance and music rather than speech; the form was also known in the Greek theater. In modern usage, silent acting using gesture and facial expression. English pantomime—or "panto"—is a spoken form, in which spectacular fairy-tale extravaganzas are performed with music and dance during the Christmas holidays.

parabasis A choral speech in ancient Greek **comedy** in which the **chorus** comments on contemporary social issues.

parodos The entrance song of the **chorus** in Greek tragedy.

parterre The standing area in the auditorium of late seventeenth-century Parisian theaters; the **pit.**

pastiche Term used by Fredric Jameson to describe the toneless quotation of earlier artistic styles in contemporary (or postmodern) works.

patents Licenses given by the crown permitting a company to give dramatic performances; often, a patent would give a company or a small number of companies a **monopoly** on dramatic performance.

patent theaters Theaters given **patents** (or licenses) by the crown for dramatic performance, sometimes holding a monopoly on performance. Charles II of England granted two patents and gave their owners a monopoly on dramatic performance.

patio The flat central courtyard of a Spanish Golden Age theater, or *corral.*

peripeteia A term used by Aristotle in *The Poetics* to describe the "reversal" in the action of a **tragedy.**

phallus A leather phallus worn by male characters in Greek **comedy.**

phylakes Short, improvisational, bawdy comedies of the early Roman theater.

pit Floor area immediately in front of the stage in seventeenth- and eighteenth-century theaters.

plot The sequence of events in a play or narrative; differs from the "story," which encompasses earlier events. Some works have several plots.

pointing Common practice in the eighteenth-century theater of delivering a famous speech directly to the audience from a downstage position; to "make a point."

polis A city-state in ancient Greece.

political theater In conventional usage, theater that seems to question the inequities and injustices of contemporary society. Bertolt Brecht developed a more searching critique of political theater, however, in which the ideology of theatrical representation itself could be seen as the theater's "politics."

postcolonial While referring specifically to the cultures of a nation that has gained independence, the term *postcolonial* is generally applied more broadly, referring to cultures still negotiating for political freedom, to internally colonized cultures, and to cultures that experience economic or cultural imperialism, even though they may be part of an independent nation-state.

postmodern A term used to characterize the complex relationship between some contemporary works of art and their modernist forebears. Postmodern works are generally characterized by stylistic "quotation," an invocation and disengagement from history, and the fragmentation of artistic surface.

Prakit The everyday, prose dialect spoken in **Sanskrit drama,** usually reserved for comic characters, women, and children.

private theaters In Renaissance England, indoor theaters serving a more privileged audience. Often located on lands within the city limits that were not under city jurisdiction, such as Blackfriars.

prologue In Greek **drama,** an introductory scene preceding the entrance of the **chorus.** In later usage, an introductory scene not directly part of the main action.

proscenium An arch over the front of the stage. First used in European theaters in the Renaissance; throughout the eighteenth and nineteenth centuries, theater design gradually eliminated the **apron** that extended in front of the proscenium and decorated the proscenium arch itself, emphasizing its framelike quality.

protagonist Literally, the "first contestant" in the ancient Greek theater, the term referred to the "first" or main actor competing for a prize. In modern usage, refers to the play's main character.

public theaters In Renaissance England, large outdoor theaters, usually polygonal in shape, consisting of three-story galleries surrounding an open standing pit and a thrust stage.

pulpitum The Latin term for the stage of a classical Roman theater.

quarto A small-size book format, in which eight pages are printed on a single sheet of paper; the paper is folded twice to make eight pages.

raked stage A stage that is elevated in the back and lower in the front; common in Europe after the seventeenth century. The raked stage gave rise to the terms "upstage" (toward the back, which was higher) and "downstage" (toward the front, which was lower).

Ramlila and **Raslila** Forms of traditional found in northern India, Ramlila and Raslila performances generally last several weeks and concern events from the *Ramayana* and *Mahabharata* epic poems.

rasa An impersonal mood or attitude of contemplation in Hindu philosophy; in **Sanskrit drama,** the play is designed to produce one of eight *rasas* in the audience: erotic, comic, pathetic, furious, heroic, terrible, odious, or marvelous. The basic *rasa* of each play is related to its bhava, or stageable emotion.

realism A literary and theatrical practice valuing direct imitation or **verisimilitude.** Often associated with **naturalism,** modern realism is sometimes described as the inheritor of naturalism. In practice, realism is usually more concerned with psychological motives, the "inner reality," and less committed to achieving a superficial **verisimilitude** alone.

repertory A company that performs several plays in rotation throughout a season is a repertory company; the term also refers to a set of plays.

revenge tragedy A tragic **genre** popular in English Renaissance, usually involving a complicated intrigue plot in which the hero is force to commit murder in order to avenge himself; madness and supernatural agents (ghosts) are also a common feature. Shakespeare's *Hamlet* is the best-known example.

ricinium A square hood worn by the performers of Roman **mime,** which sometimes gave its name to their companies.

role-doubling The practice of using one actor to play more than one part.

romance A modern term used to define idealized narratives and sometimes applied to the idealized comedies written by Shakespeare late in his career, especially *The Winter's Tale* and *The Tempest.*

romantic comedy Comic form centering on the romance between two lovers, or between several sets of lovers. Romantic comedy typically begins with some unreasonable impediment to the lovers' union, and when after a complicated series of events the obstacle is overcome, the play ends in marriage.

rōnin **Samurai** warriors who have been disgraced and outcast from society; "men adrift."

ruido A "noise" play or violent **comedy** in Spanish Golden Age theater.

Rupaka The "major drama" of classical **Sanskrit** theater.

sainete Deriving from the *genero chico* of Spain, a short, sometimes satirical play often used for interludes or *entremeses,* it was widely used for plays on regional or local-color themes in Argentina in the nineteenth century.

samisen Three-stringed instrument that is both plucked and struck as accompaniment to narration in *jōruri.* In the late sixteenth century, became instrumental in the **doll theater.**

samurai Warrior class of feudal Japan; *samurai* lords both patronized **Noh** playwrights and companies, and provided the code of conduct informing many **Noh, doll theater,** and **Kabuki** plays.

Sanskrit An ancient Indo-European language; once a spoken language, by the modern era it had become mainly a written language reserved for academic and religious purposes. In **Sanskrit drama,** Sanskrit is reserved for elevated scenes and characters, while **Prakrit,** the everyday dialect, is spoken by other characters.

Sanskrit drama   The **drama** of ancient India, particularly the plays of its "Golden Age" (second to ninth centuries).

sarugaku-no   Form of dance, role-playing, and acrobatics popular in Japan in the eleventh and twelfth centuries; said to be the progenitor of **Noh** theater.

saruwaka   Comic roles in **Kabuki** theater, performed by men.

satyr play   A brief, rugged comedy performed by actors in satyr costumes (half-man, half-goat) after the performance of a tragic **trilogy** at the **City Dionysia;** usually on mythological subjects.

scaena   Three-story stage house behind the stage in the Roman theater, facing the audience. Elaborately decorated with columns, panels, and porticos.

scenic unity   The practice of harmonizing acting style, costumes, and sets to create the illusion of a single, unified environment on the stage.

sewamono   "Domestic plays" of the Japanese **doll theater.**

sharers   Actors and playwrights in the English Renaissance theater who, as investors in the company, took a share of the profits; they were responsible for building or leasing a theater and were legally liable for the company's actions.

shimpa   A movement in Japanese theater beginning in the late nineteenth century to adapt European **drama** to Japanese style and subject matter.

shingeki   A movement in twentieth-century Japanese theater to import the style and techniques of European realistic theater into the Japanese theater.

shite   Principal actor in **Noh** theater.

shitebashira   The upstage right pillar in a **Noh** theater, near the *hashigakari,* where the *shite* delivers his opening speech.

shogun   Hereditary military leader of Japan from the twelfth through the nineteenth centuries; the *shogun* was the most important of the *samurai* (warrior) class, composed of *daimyo* (feudal lords) and lesser *samurai.*

skene   A low building behind the **orchestra** in the Greek theater facing the audience; possibly used for changing costumes or storage.

social realism   A form of modern realistic **drama** emphasizing social messages and themes; social realism was the official **genre** approved by the Communist party in the Soviet Union after the revolution.

sociétaires   Leading actors and shareholders in the Comédie Française; upon serving twenty years, *sociétaires* were entitled to a pension.

soliloquy   A speech delivered by a character alone onstage, speaking to himself or herself, or to the audience.

soubrette   A stock character in **drama:** a young, pert female character.

spectacle   Aristotle's term for the visual element of theatrical performance in *The Poetics.*

subtext   A term first elaborated by Constantin Stanislavski, *subtext* refers to the unspoken motive for a given line or speech, what the character wants to get or to do by saying the line. It is sometimes now used more generally to suggest a text's underlying sense or meaning.

surrealist theater   A movement originating in Paris in the 1920s attempting to represent subconscious experience directly in art.

symbolist theater   A European movement of the later nineteenth and early twentieth centuries in reaction to **realism** and **naturalism.** Symbolist theater attempted to dramatize more poetic or metaphorical situations, often using unusual stage settings and ethereal dramatic action and language.

Syndicate   A group of investors who developed a massive organization for theatrical production in the United States in the late nineteenth century.

tableau/tableaux **(pl.)**   A motionless grouping of actors to represent a "picture" of a dramatic scene; sometimes called *tableau vivant,* a "living picture."

tableaux vivants   See **tableau;** *tableaux vivants* is the plural form of *tableau vivant.*

taburetes   The raised and fenced rows of benches near the stage in a Spanish Golden Age theater, or *corral.*

tachiyaku   Leading male role in **Kabuki** theater.

tertulia   An upper **gallery** occupied by church officials and intellectuals in a Spanish Golden Age theater, or *corral.*

theater   A structure built for the performance of drama; also refers to the institution of dramatic performance.

theater in the round   The presentation of a play in an arena setting, in which the audience sits on all sides of the stage area, but is separate from the playing space itself.

Theater of Cruelty   Term used by Antonin Artaud to describe his nonrepresentational, mystical, mythological theater.

Theater of the Absurd   A type of late twentieth-century **theater** and **drama,** characterized by a relatively abstract setting, and arbitrary and illogical action. It is sometimes said to express the "human condition" in a basic or "existential" way. The term was first coined by Martin Esslin.

theme   A term used to describe a consistent kind of meaning asserted by a work of literature.

tiring house   A structure at the rear of the stage in the Renaissance English **public theater,** where actors would change costumes (attire themselves), and from which they would enter the stage.

tragedy Originating in the classical Greek theater, tragedy generally refers to serious drama, taking a central character's conflict with himself or herself, with society, or with god as its subject. Aristotle first described tragedy in his *The Poetics,* and tragedy has undergone almost continual redefinition.

tragicomedy In the English Renaissance, a term describing a dramatic form: a play beginning like a **tragedy,** but ending happily, like a **comedy.** In modern usage, the term refers most often to a play's tone or attitude: a play that is ironic, both serious and absurd, leaning toward black comedy or tragic farce.

traveling song Song sung in **Noh** theater by the *waki* during his first entrance; it announces who the *waki* is and where he is going.

trilogy Three tragedies produced in sequence as part of the tragic competition in the **City Dionysia** of ancient Greece. Plays were not necessarily on the same subject.

tsure Followers of the *shite* and *waki* in **Noh** theater.

Upa-rupaka The "minor drama" of classical **Sanskrit** theater.

verisimilitude Refers to the extent to which the drama or stage setting appears to copy the superficial appearance of life offstage.

villancicos Religious songs, like English carols, performed in Spain and its colonies.

vomitoria In a classical Roman theatre, the passageways into the auditorium (or *cavea*) or into the orchestra; the term—sometimes abbreviated "voms"—is still in use.

wakashugata Adolescent male roles in **Kabuki** theater.

wakashu kabuki Literally, "boys' Kabuki"; the term refers to **Kabuki** companies composed mainly of adolescent boys, many of whom were prostitutes; banned by the Tokugawa shogunate in 1652.

waki The secondary actor in **Noh** theater, who responds to the *shite.*

wakibashira The downstage left pillar in a **Noh** theater, where the *waki* is usually positioned at the opening of the play.

waki-za A narrow stage area along the stage-left side of a **Noh** theater stage used for seating the chorus.

wayang kulit Shadow-puppet theater of Java concerning characters and events drawn from the *Ramayana* and *Mahabharata,* the epic poems of classical India. Performances generally begin early in the evening and last until dawn; audiences sit on both sides of a screen, against which puppeteers cast the shadows of elaborate, flat puppets, whose actions are accompanied by dialogue, narration, song, and music.

well-made play A form of drama popularized in the nineteenth century, especially in France. The plot usually turns on the revelation of a secret and includes a character who explains and moralizes the action of the play to others; the plot is often relentlessly coincidental, often mechanically so.

wings and backdrop Scenic practice developed in Italy and exported to France and England in the seventeenth century, using staggered painted flats in a receding series, and a painted central backcloth to depict the setting of the play.

yaro kabuki The "adult male Kabuki" common in Japan today; the yaro kabuki replaced the boys' and women's **Kabuki** that were popular before such companies were banned in the early seventeenth century.

yugen The Japanese term for the mysterious beauty, grace, and repose that are the goal of **Noh** performance.

yūgo Professional prostitute in classical Japan; distinct from **geisha,** a hired companion valued for artistic accomplishment.

yūgo kabuki Literally, "prostitutes' Kabuki," an early term for **Kabuki** companies, which were composed mainly of women.

Zanni Wily and clever comic characters, usually clowns or servants, in *commedia dell' arte;* played masked.

zen Term in Buddhist thought for a contemplative attitude that is disengaged from worldly desire.

Credits

This page constitutes an extension of the copyright page. We have made every effort to trace the ownership of all copyrighted material and to secure permission from copyright holders. In the event of any question arising as to the use of any material, we will be pleased to make the necessary corrections in future printings. Thanks are due to the following authors, publishers, and agents for permission to use the material indicated.

Unit I. 15: From *Theatre and Playhouse* by Richard and Helen Leacroft (London, New York: Methuen Publishing Ltd., 1984, p. 15). Copyright 1984 by Richard and Helen Leacroft. Reprinted by permission of the publisher. **23:** From *Theatre and Playhouse* by Richard and Helen Leacroft (London, New York: Methuen Publishing Ltd., 1984, p. 29). Copyright 1984 by Richard and Helen Leacroft. Reprinted by permission of the publisher. **30:** "Oedipus the King" by Sophocles, from THREE THEBAN PLAYS by Sophocles, translated by Robert Fagles, copyright © 1982 by Robert Fagles. Used by permission of Viking Penguin, a division of Penguin Group (USA) Inc. **88:** Aristotle, THE POETICS, trans. Gerald Else, pp. 15–47. Copyright © 1967 University of Michigan Press. Used with permission. **96:** from *The Art of Poetry,* trans. by C. Smart. *European Theories of the Drama,* by Barrett H. Clark, pp. 28–32.

Unit II. 106: 107: 112: From Brockett, Oscar G. History of the Theatre, 7th Edition. Published by Allyn and Bacon, Boston, MA. Copyright © 1995 by Pearson Education. Reprinted by permission of the publisher. **121:** Kan'ami Kiyotsugo, "Matsukaze" from TWENTY PLAYS OF THE NO THEATRE, trans. Royall Tyler & ed. Donald Keene. Copyright © 1970 by Columbia University Press. Used with permission. **126:** Nakamura Matagoro II and James R. Brandon, adaptors of Chushingura: The Forty-Seven Samurai: A Kabuki Version of Chushingura. Copyright © 1982 by James R. Brandon. Reprinted with permission. **146:** Masakazu, Yamazaki; ON THE ART OF THE NO DRAMA. © 1984 by Princeton University Press. Reprinted by permission of Princeton University Press.

Unit III. 160: The Coventry Magi, Herod, and the Slaughter of the Innocents, in Chief Pre-Shakespearean Dramas, ed. Joseph Quincy Adams (Boston: Houghton Mifflin, 1924), 163. **161:** From *Theatre and Playhouse* by Richard and Helen Leacroft (London, New York: Methuen Publishing Ltd., 1984, p. 39). Copyright 1984 by Richard and Helen Leacroft. Reprinted by permission of the publisher. **165:** From *Shakespeare Stage, 1574–1642,* 2nd Edition. Edited by Andrew Gurr. Copyright 1980 by Cambridge University Press. Reprinted by permission of Cambridge University Press. **167:** From *The Globe Restored* by C. Walter Hodge. (London, Ernest C. Benn, 1953). Ernest C. Benn/A&C Black Publishers, Ltd. Used with permission of the publisher. **169:** (*left and right*): From *Shakespeare's Globe Rebuilt* by J.R. Mulryne and Margaret Shewring. Copyright 1989 by Cambridge University Press. Reprinted by permission of Cambridge University Press. **177:** By permission of the Folger Shakespeare Library. **189:** From EVANS. The Riverside Sheakpeare, 2e. © 1997 Heinle/Arts & Sciences, a part of Cengage Learning, Inc. Reproduced by permission. www.cengage.com/permissions. **219:** From HAMLET: A Norton Critical Edition, Second Edition by William Shakespeare, edited by Cyrus Hoy. Copyright © 1992, 1963 by W.W. Norton & Company, Inc. Used by permission of W.W. Norton & Company, Inc.

Index